Concise
Encyclopedia

RANDOM HOUSE

Concise
Encyclopedia

RANDOM HOUSE
NEW YORK

This edition has been completely updated and retypeset, based on a version originally published in Great Britain in different form by Helicon Publishing Ltd., Oxford, in 1994

Library of Congress Cataloging-in-Publication Data
Random House concise encyclopedia. - 1st. ed.
    p. cm.
  ISBN 0-679-76454-2 (alk. paper)
  AG5.R245 1995
  031-dc20   95-32728
                                     CIP

Printed in the United States of America

First US Edition

9 8 7 6 5 4 3 2 1

New York   Toronto   London   Sydney   Auckland

Editors

Managing Editor
Hilary McGlynn

Coordinating Editor
Avril Cridlan

Database and Text Editor
John Wright

Design
Terence Caven

Production
Tony Ballsdon

Contributors

Owen Adikibi PhD
Lesley and Roy Adkins
Christine Avery PhD
John Ayto MA
Paul Bahn
Bernard Balleine
Tia Cockerell LLB
Sue Cusworth
Nigel Davis MSc
Ian D Derbyshire PhD
J Denis Derbyshire PhD, FBIM
Col Michael Dewar
Dougal Dixon BSc, MSc
Nigel Dudley
George du Boulay FRCR, FRCP, Hon
    FACR
Ingrid von Essen
Eric Farge
Anna Farkas
Peter Fleming PhD
Kent Fedorowich BA, MA, PhD
Derek Gjertsen BA
Lawrence Garner BA
Wendy Grossman
Joseph Harrison BA, PhD
Michael Hitchcock PhD
Stuart Holroyd
Gerald M D Howat MA, MLitt, PhD,
    FRHistC
H G Jerrard PhD
Robin Kerrod FRAS
Charles Kidd
Stephen Kite B Arch, RIBA
Peter Lafferty MSc
Mike Lewis MBCS
Graham Ley MPhil
Carol Lister PhD, FSS

Graham Littler BSc, MSc, FSS
Robin Maconie MA
Morven MacKillop
Tom McArthur PhD
Isabel Miller BA PhD
Karin Mogg MSc PhD
Bob Moore PhD
David Munro PhD
Joanne O'Brien
Maureen O'Connor
Roger Owen MA, DPhil
Robert Paisley PhD
Martin Palmer
David Penfold PhD, MBCS
Paulette Pratt
Michael Pudlo MSc, PhD
Tim Pulleine
Chris Rhys
Ian Ridpath FRAS
Adrian Room MA
Simon Ross
Julian Rowe PhD
Paul Rowntree MA
Jack Schofield BA, MA
Emma Shackleton
Mark Slade MA
Steve Smyth
Jenrifer Speake MPhil
Joe Staines
Glyn Stone
Calum Storrie
Michael Thum
Norman Vance, PhD, Professor of
    English, Univ. of Sussex
Stephen Webster BSc, MPhil
Liz Whitelegg BSc

Preface

Arrangement of entries

Entries are ordered alphabetically, as if there were no spaces between words. Thus, entries for words beginning "federal" follow the order:

Federal Bureau of Investigation
federalism
Federalist

However, we have avoided a purely mechanical alphabetization in cases where a different order corresponds more with human logic. For example, sovereigns with the same name are grouped according to country before number, so that King Charles I of England is placed before Charles II of England, and not next to King Charles I of France. Words beginning "Mc" and "Mac" are treated as if they begin "Mac" and "St" and "Saint" are both treated as if they were spelt "Saint".

Foreign names and titles

Names of foreign sovereigns and places are usually shown in their English form, except where the foreign name is more familiar; thus, there are entries for Charles V of Spain, but Juan Carlos (not John Charles), and for Florence, not Firenze. Cross-references are provided in cases where confusion is possible.

Cross-references

Cross-references are shown by ◊ immediately preceding the reference. Cross-referencing is selective; a cross-reference is shown when another entry contains material directly relevant to the subject matter of an entry, in cases where the reader may not otherwise think of looking. Common alternative spellings, where there is no agreed consistent form, are also shown.

Units

SI (metric) units are used throughout for scientific entries. Commonly used measurements of distances, temperatures, sizes, and so on include both the US measurement and the metric equivalent.

Science and technology

Entries are generally placed under the better-known name, with the technical term given as a cross reference. To aid comprehension for the non-specialist, technical terms are frequently explained when used within the text of an entry, even though they may have their own entry elsewhere.

Chinese names

Pinyin, the preferred system for transcribing Chinese names of people and places, is generally used: thus, there is an entry at Mao Zedong, not Mao Tse-tung; an exception is made for a few names which are more familiar in their former (Wade-Giles) form, such as Sun Yat-sen and Chiang Kai-shek. Where confusion is likely, Wade-Giles forms are given as cross-references.

rain falling past window   rain falling past window
of stationary train   of moving train

direction in which   ★ true position
star seems to lie   of star

                                        starlight enters
                                        telescope

starlight reaches
eyepiece

◄───── movement of Earth

aberration of starlight *The aberration of starlight is an optical illusion caused by the motion of the Earth. Rain falling appears vertical when seen from the window of a stationary train; when seen from the window of a moving train, the rain appears to follow a sloping path. In the same way, light from a star "falling" down a telescope seems to follow a sloping path because the Earth is moving. This causes an apparent displacement, or aberration, in the position of the star.*

buried here; the Eisenhower Center, also here, includes a museum and library.

abiotic factor a nonorganic variable within the ecosystem, affecting the life of organisms. Examples include temperature, light, and soil structure. Abiotic factors can be harmful to the environment, as when sulfur dioxide emissions from power stations produce acid rain.

Abkhazia autonomous republic in Georgia, situated on the Black Sea *capital* Sukhumi *area* 3,320 sq mi/8,600 sq km *industries* tin, fruit, and tobacco *population* (1989) 526,000 *history* The region has been the scene of secessionist activity on the part of the minority Muslim Abkhazi community since 1989, culminating in the republic's declaration of independence 1992. Georgian troops invaded and took control Aug 1992, but secessionist guerrillas subsequently gained control of the northern half of the republic. In Oct 1993 they took the region's capital, Sukhumi, as well as much of the republic's remaining territory.

abolitionism in US and UK history, a movement culminating in the late 18th and early 19th centuries that aimed first to end the slave trade, and then to abolish the institution of ◊slavery and emancipate slaves.

aborigine any indigenous inhabitant of a region or country. The word often refers to the original peoples of areas colonized by Europeans, and especially to ◊Australian Aborigines.

abortion ending of a pregnancy before the fetus is developed sufficiently to survive outside the uterus. Loss of a fetus at a later gestational age is termed premature stillbirth. Abortion may be accidental (miscarriage) or deliberate (termination of pregnancy).

In the United States in 1989, a Supreme Court decision gave state legislatures the right to introduce some restrictions on the unconditional right, established by the Supreme Court in an earlier decision (Roe v Wade), for any woman to decide to have an abortion.

Abraham In the Old Testament, founder of the Jewish nation. In his early life he was called Abram. God promised him heirs and land for his people in Canaan (Israel), renamed him Abraham ("father of many nations"), and tested his faith by a command (later retracted) to sacrifice his son Isaac.

Abraham, Plains of plateau near Québec, Canada, where the British commander ◊Wolfe defeated the French under ◊Montcalm, Sept 13, 1759, during the French and Indian War (1754–63). The outcome of the battle established British supremacy in Canada.

Abrams v US US Supreme Court decision 1919 dealing with First Amendment rights in instances of sedition or espionage. Abrams, convicted of publishing pamphlets criticizing the US role in World War I and encouraging resistance to the war, appealed to the Supreme Court for protection under the right to free speech. The Court upheld the 1918 Sedition Law, ruling that Congress had the right to restrict speech that had a "tendency" toward harmful results. A famous dissent was filed by Justices Holmes and Brandeis.

abrasive substance used for cutting and polishing or for removing small amounts of the surface of hard materials. There are two types: natural and artificial abrasives, and their hardness is measured using the ◊Mohs' scale. Natural abrasives include quartz, sandstone, pumice, diamond, and corundum; artificial abrasives include rouge, whiting, and carborundum.

abscissa in ◊coordinate geometry, the *x*-coordinate of a point—that is, the horizontal distance of that point from the vertical or *y*-axis. For example, a point with the coordinates (4, 3) has an abscissa of 4. The *y*-coordinate of a point is known as the ordinate.

absolute (of a value) in computing, real and unchanging. For example, an *absolute address* is a location in memory and an *absolute cell reference* is a single fixed cell in a spreadsheet display. The opposite of absolute is relative.

absolute value or *modulus* in mathematics, the value, or magnitude, of a number irrespective of its sign. The absolute value of a number n is written $|n|$ (or sometimes as mod n), and is defined as the positive square root of n^2. For example, the numbers –5 and 5 have the same absolute value:

$$|5| = |-5| = 5$$

absolute zero lowest temperature theoretically possible, zero kelvin (0K), equivalent to −459.67°F/ −273.15°C/, at which molecules are motionless. Although the third law of ◊thermodynamics indicates the impossibility of reaching absolute zero exactly, a temperature of 7×10^{-6}K (seven millionths of a degree above absolute zero) was produced 1993 at Lancaster University, England. Near absolute zero, the physical properties of some materials change substantially (see

◊cryogenics); for example, some metals lose their electrical resistance and become superconductive.

absolutism or *absolute monarchy* system of government in which the ruler or rulers have unlimited power. The principle of an absolute monarch, given a right to rule by God (see ◊divine right of kings), was extensively used in Europe during the 17th and 18th centuries.

Absolute monarchy is contrasted with limited or constitutional monarchy, in which the sovereign's powers are defined or limited.

absorption in science, the taking up of one substance by another, such as a liquid by a solid (ink by blotting paper) or a gas by a liquid (ammonia by water). In biology, absorption describes the passing of nutrients or medication into and through tissues such as intestinal walls and blood vessels. In physics, absorption is the phenomenon by which a substance retains radiation of particular wavelengths; for example, a piece of blue glass absorbs all visible light except the wavelengths in the blue part of the spectrum; it also refers to the partial loss of energy resulting from light and other electromagnetic waves passing through a medium. In nuclear physics, absorption is the capture by elements, such as boron, of neutrons produced by fission in a reactor.

abstract art nonrepresentational art. Ornamental art without figurative representation occurs in most cultures. The modern abstract movement in sculpture and painting emerged in Europe and North America between 1910 and 1920. Two approaches produce different abstract styles: images that have been "abstracted" from nature to the point where they no longer reflect a conventional reality, and nonobjective, or "pure," art forms, without any reference to reality.

Abstract Expressionism US movement in abstract art that emphasized the act of painting, the expression inherent in the color and texture of the paint itself, and the interaction of artist, paint, and canvas. Abstract Expressionism emerged in New York in the early 1940s. Arshile Gorky, Franz Kline, Jackson Pollock, and Mark Rothko are associated with the movement.

Abu Dhabi sheikdom in SW Asia, on the Persian Gulf, capital of the ◊United Arab Emirates; area 26,000 sq mi/67,350 sq km; population (1982 est) 516,000. Formerly under British protection, it has been ruled since 1971 by Sheik Sultan Zayed bin al-Nahayan, who is also president of the Supreme Council of Rulers of the United Arab Emirates.

Abuja capital of Nigeria (formally designated as such 1982, although not officially recognized until 1992); population (1991) 378,700 (federal capital territory).

Shaped like a crescent, the city was designed by Japanese architect Kenzo Tange; it began construction 1976 as a replacement for Lagos.

abyssal zone dark ocean region 6,500–19,500 ft/2,000–6,000 m deep; temperature 39°F/4°C. Three-quarters of the area of the deep-ocean floor lies in the abyssal zone, which is too far from the surface for photosynthesis to take place. Some fish and crustaceans living there are blind or have their own light sources. The region above is the bathyal zone; the region below, the hadal zone.

Abyssinia former name of ◊Ethiopia.

abzyme in biotechnology, an artificially created antibody that can be used like an enzyme to accelerate reactions.

a/c abbreviation for *account*.

AC in physics, abbreviation for ◊*alternating current*.

acacia any of a large group of shrubs and trees of the genus *Acacia* of the legume family Leguminosae. Acacias include several North American species of the SW US and Mexico, the thorn trees of the African savanna, and the gum arabic tree *A. senegal* of N Africa. Acacias are found in warm regions of the world, particularly Australia.

Academy Award annual award in many categories, given since 1927 by the American Academy of Motion Picture Arts and Sciences (founded by Louis B Mayer of Metro-Goldwyn-Mayer 1927). Arguably the film community's most prestigious accolade, the award is a gold-plated statuette, which has been nicknamed "Oscar" since 1931.

acanthus any herbaceous plant of the genus *Acanthus* with handsome lobed leaves. Twenty species are found in the Mediterranean region and Old World tropics, including bear's breech *A. mollis*, whose leaves were used as a motif in classical architecture, especially on Corinthian columns.

Acapulco or *Acapulco de Juarez* port and vacation resort in S Mexico; population (1990) 592,200. There is deep-sea fishing, and tropical products are exported.

Acapulco was founded 1550 and was Mexico's major Pacific coast port until about 1815.

Sometimes called the Riviera of Mexico, it attracts many tourists to its beaches, luxury hotels, and gambling casinos.

acceleration rate of change of the velocity of a moving body. It is usually measured in feet per second per second (ft s^{-2}) or meters per second per second (m s^{-2}). Because velocity is a vector quantity (possessing both magnitude and direction) a body traveling at constant speed may be said to be accelerating if its direction of motion changes. According to Newton's second law of

---

Academy Awards: recent winners

1990	Best Picture: *Dances With Wolves*; Best Director: Kevin Costner *Dances With Wolves*; Best Actor: Jeremy Irons *Reversal of Fortune*; Best Actress: Kathy Bates *Misery*
1991	Best Picture: *The Silence of the Lambs*; Best Director: Jonathan Demme *The Silence of the Lambs*; Best Actor: Anthony Hopkins *The Silence of the Lambs*; Best Actress: Jodie Foster *The Silence of the Lambs*
1992	Best Picture: *Unforgiven*; Best Director: Clint Eastwood *Unforgiven*; Best Actor: Al Pacino *Scent of a Woman* ; Best Actress: Emma Thompson *Howard's End*
1993	Best Picture: *Schindler's List*; Best Director: Steven Spielberg *Schindler's List*; Best Actor: Tom Hanks *Philadelphia*; Best Actress: Holly Hunter *The Piano*
1994	Best Picture: *Forrest Gump;* Best Director: Robert Zemeckis *Forrest Gump;* Best Actor: Tom Hanks *Forrest Gump*; Best Actress: Jessica Lange *Blue Sky*

motion, a body will accelerate only if it is acted upon by an unbalanced, or resultant, ◊force.

accelerator in physics, a device to bring charged particles (such as protons and electrons) up to high speeds and energies, at which they can be of use in industry, medicine, and pure physics. At low energies, accelerated particles can be used to produce the image on a television screen and generate X-rays (by means of a ◊cathode-ray tube), destroy tumor cells, or kill bacteria. When high-energy particles collide with other particles, the fragments formed reveal the nature of the fundamental forces of nature.

accelerator board type of ◊expansion board that makes a computer run faster. It usually contains an additional ◊central processing unit.

access in computing, the way in which ◊file access is provided so that the data can be stored, retrieved, or updated by the computer.

access time or *reaction time* in computing, the time taken by a computer, after an instruction has been given, to read from or write to ◊memory.

accomplice in law, a person who acts with another in the commission or attempted commission of a crime, either as a principal or as an accessory.

accordion musical instrument of the free-reed organ type comprising left and right wind chests connected by flexible bellows. The right hand plays melody on a piano-style keyboard of 26 to 34 keys while the left hand has a system of push buttons for selecting single notes or chord harmonies.

accounting the principles and practice of systematically recording, presenting, and interpreting financial ◊accounts; financial record keeping and management of businesses and other organizations, from balance sheets to policy decisions, for tax or operating purposes. Forms of inflation accounting, such as CCA (current cost accounting) and CPP (current purchasing power) are aimed at providing valid financial comparisons over a period in which money values change.

Accra capital and port of Ghana; population (1984) 964,800. The port trades in cacao, gold, and timber. Industries include engineering, brewing, and food processing. Osu (Christiansborg) Castle is the presidential residence.

accumulator in electricity, a storage ◊battery—that is, a group of rechargeable secondary cells. A familiar example is the lead–acid automobile battery.

accumulator in computing, a special register, or memory location, in the ◊arithmetic and logic unit of the computer processor. It is used to hold the result of a calculation temporarily or to store data that is being transferred.

acetone common name for ◊propanone.

acetylene common name for ◊ethyne.

Achilles Greek hero of Homer's *Iliad*. He was the son of Peleus, king of the Myrmidons in Thessaly, and of the sea nymph Thetis, who rendered him invulnerable, except for the heel by which she held him, by dipping him in the river Styx. Achilles killed ◊Hector at the climax of the *Iliad*, and according to subsequent Greek legends was himself killed by Paris, who shot a poisoned arrow into Achilles' heel.

acid compound that, in solution in an ionizing solvent (usually water), gives rise to hydrogen ions (H^+ or protons). In modern chemistry, acids are defined as substances that are proton donors and accept electrons to form ◊ionic bonds. Acids react with ◊bases to form salts, and they act as solvents. Strong acids are corrosive; dilute acids have a sour or sharp taste, although in some organic acids this may be partially masked by other flavor characteristics.

acid rain acidic precipitation thought to be caused principally by the release into the atmosphere of sulfur dioxide (SO_2) and oxides of nitrogen. Sulfur dioxide is formed by the burning of fossil fuels, such as coal, that contain high quantities of sulfur; nitrogen oxides are contributed from various industrial activities and from automobile exhaust fumes.

aclinic line the magnetic equator, an imaginary line near the equator, where the compass needle balances horizontally, the attraction of the north and south magnetic poles being equal.

acne skin eruption, mainly occurring among adolescents and young adults, caused by inflammation of the sebaceous glands which secrete an oily substance (sebum), the natural lubricant of the skin. Sometimes the openings of the glands become blocked, causing the formation of pus-filled swellings. Teenage acne is seen mainly on the face, back, and chest.

Aconcagua extinct volcano in the Argentine Andes; the highest peak in the Americas, 22,834 ft/6,960 m. It was first climbed by Edward Fitzgerald's expedition 1897.

acorn fruit of the oak tree, a ◊nut growing in a shallow cup.

Acorn UK computer manufacturer. In the early 1980s, Acorn produced a series of home microcomputers, including the Electron and the Atom. Its most successful computer, BBC Microcomputer, was produced in conjunction with the BBC. Subsequent computers (the Master and the Archimedes) were less successful. Acorn was taken over by the Italian company Olivetti 1985.

acoustic coupler device that enables computer data to be transmitted and received through a normal telephone handset; the handset rests on the coupler to make the connection. A small speaker within the device is used to convert the computer's digital output

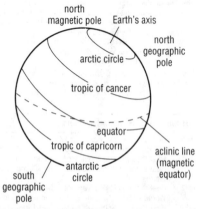

aclinic line *The magnetic equator, or the line at which the attraction of both magnetic poles is equal. Along the aclinic line, a compass needle swinging vertically will settle in a horizontal position.*

data into sound signals, which are then picked up by the handset and transmitted through the telephone system. At the receiving telephone, a second acoustic coupler or modem converts the sound signals back into digital data for input into a computer.

acoustics in general, the experimental and theoretical science of sound and its transmission; in particular, that branch of the science that has to do with the phenomena of sound in a particular space such as a room or theater. In architecture, the sound-reflecting character of a room.

acquired character feature of the body that develops during the lifetime of an individual, usually as a result of repeated use or disuse, such as the enlarged muscles of a weight-lifter.

acquired immune deficiency syndrome full name for the disease ◊AIDS.

acquittal in law, the setting free, after a trial, of someone charged with a crime.

It follows a verdict of "not guilty" and prevents retrial of a defendant on the same charges under the US Constitution.

acre traditional English land measure equal to 4,840 square yards (0.405 ha/4,047 sq m). Originally meaning a field, it was the size that a yoke of oxen could plow in a day.

Acrobat coding system developed by Adobe Systems for electronic publishing applications. Acrobat coding can be generated directly from ◊PostScript files.

acronym word formed from the initial letters and/or syllables of other words, intended as a pronounceable abbreviation; for example, NATO (*N*orth *A*tlantic *T*reaty *O*rganization), radar (*ra*dio *d*etecting *a*nd *r*anging), RAM (*r*andom-*a*ccess *m*emory) and FOR-TRAN (*for*mula *tran*slation).

acrostic a number of lines of writing, usually verse, whose initial letters (read downward) form a word, phrase, or sentence. A *single acrostic* is formed by the initial letters of lines only; a *double acrostic* is formed by the first and last letters.

acrylic fiber synthetic fiber often used as a substitute for wool. It was first developed 1947 but not produced in great volumes until the 1950s. Strong and warm, acrylic fiber is often used for casual and athletic wear, and as linings for boots and gloves.

acrylic paint any of a range of synthetic substitutes for ◊oil paint, mostly soluble in water. Acrylic paints are used in a variety of painting techniques, from wash to impasto. They dry quicker than oil paint, but lack the translucency of natural substances.

actinide any of a series of 15 radioactive metallic chemical elements with atomic numbers 89 (actinium) to 103 (lawrencium). Elements 89 to 95 occur in nature; the rest of the series are synthesized elements only. Actinides are grouped together because of their chemical similarities (for example, they are all bivalent), the properties differing only slightly with atomic number. The series is set out in a band in the ◊periodic table of the elements, as are the ◊lanthanides.

actinium white, radioactive, metallic element, the first of the actinide series, symbol Ac, atomic number 89, atomic weight 227; it is a weak emitter of high-energy alpha particles.

Actinium occurs with uranium and radium in ◊pitchblende and other ores, and can be synthesized by bombarding radium with neutrons. The longest-lived isotope, Ac-227, has a half-life of 21.8 years (all the other isotopes have very short half-lives). Actinium was discovered in 1899 by the French chemist André Debierne.

action in law, one of the proceedings whereby a person or agency seeks to enforce rights in a civil court.

Actions fall into three principal categories, namely civil (such as the enforcement of a debt), criminal (in which a government agency prosecutes a defendant accused of violation of a criminal law), and penal (violation of a law enacted to preserve public order).

action and reaction in physical mechanics, equal and opposite effects produced by a force acting on an object. For example, the pressure of expanding gases from the burning of fuel in a rocket engine (a force) produces an equal and opposite reaction, which causes the rocket to move.

action painting or *gesture painting* in abstract art, a form of Abstract Expressionism that emphasized the importance of the physical act of painting. Jackson ◊Pollock, the leading exponent, threw, dripped, and dribbled paint on to canvases fastened to the floor. Another principal exponent was Willem de Kooning.

Pollock was known to attack his canvas with knives and trowels and bicycle over it.

Actium, Battle of naval battle in which Octavian defeated the combined fleets of ◊Mark Antony and ◊Cleopatra 31 BC to become the undisputed ruler of the Roman world (as the emperor ◊Augustus). The site is at Akri, a promontory in W Greece.

acupuncture in alternative medicine, system of inserting long, thin metal needles into the body at predetermined points to relieve pain, as an anesthetic in surgery, and to assist healing. The needles are rotated manually or electrically. The method, developed in ancient China and increasingly popular in the West, is thought to work by somehow stimulating the brain's own painkillers, the ◊endorphins.

acute angle an angle between 0° and 90°; that is, an amount of turn that is less than a quarter of a circle.

AD in the Christian chronological system, abbreviation for *anno Domini*.

Ada high-level computer-programming language, developed and owned by the US Department of Defense, designed for use in situations in which a computer directly controls a process or machine, such as a military aircraft. The language took more than five years to specify, and became commercially available only in the late 1980s. It is named for English mathematician Ada Augusta Byron.

Adam family of Scottish architects and designers. *William Adam* (1689–1748) was the leading Scottish architect of his day, and his son *Robert Adam* (1728–1792) is considered one of the greatest British architects of the late 18th century, responsible for transforming the prevailing Palladian fashion in architecture to a Neo-Classical style.

Adam in the Old Testament, the first human. Formed by God from dust and given the breath of life, Adam was placed in the Garden of Eden, where ◊Eve was created from his rib and given to him as a companion. Because she tempted him, he tasted the forbidden fruit of the Tree of Knowledge of Good and Evil, for which trespass they were expelled from the Garden.

Adams Abigail Smith 1744–1818. First lady to US president John Adams and public figure. She married lawyer John Adams of Boston 1764; one of their children, John Quincy Adams, would become the sixth president. A strong supporter of the cause of American independence, she joined her husband on diplomatic missions to Paris and London after the Revolutionary War. As wife of the vice president 1789–97 and later president 1797–1801, she was widely respected.

Born in Weymouth, Massachusetts, she showed an early interest in public affairs. In detailed letters to her husband, she chronicled the events of her day and was an advocate of women's rights.

Adams Ansel 1902–1984. US photographer. He is known for his printed images of dramatic landscapes and organic forms of the American West. Light and texture were important elements in his photographs. He was associated with the zone system of exposure estimation and was a founder member of the "f/64" group which advocated precise definition.

Adams Charles Francis 1807–1886. US political leader, journalist, diplomat and son of John Quincy Adams. He was appointed US minister to England by Abraham Lincoln and unsuccessfully sought the 1872 Republican nomination for president.

Adams was born in Boston. After graduation from Harvard, he studied law with Daniel Webster. As a respected historian and abolitionist, he established the *Boston Whig* and accepted the vice-presidential nomination of the Free Soil party 1848. He later joined the Republican party and served in the US House of Representatives 1858–61.

Adams Gerry 1948– . Northern Ireland politician, president of Provisional Sinn Féin (the political wing of the Irish Republican Army) from 1978. He was elected member of Parliament for Belfast West 1983 but declined to take up his Westminster seat. He lost his seat in 1992. In August 1994 after initial doubts about his ability to influence the IRA, Adams announced a "complete cessation of military operations".

Adams Henry Brooks 1838–1918. US historian and novelist, a grandson of President John Quincy Adams. He published the acclaimed nine-volume *A History of the United States During the Administrations of Jefferson and Madison* 1889–91, a study of the evolution of democracy in the US.

Born in Boston, he graduated 1858 from Harvard University and later taught medieval history there 1870–77. He also was editor of the *North American Review* 1870–76.

Adams John 1735–1826. 2nd president of the US 1797–1801, and vice president 1789–97. He was a member of the Continental Congress 1774–78 and signed the Declaration of Independence. In 1779 he went to France and negotiated the treaty of 1783 that ended the American Revolution. In 1785 he became the first US ambassador in London.

He was born in Quincy, Massachusetts.

Adams John Quincy 1767–1848. 6th president of the US 1825–29. Eldest son of President John Adams, he was born in Quincy, Massachusetts, and became US minister in The Hague, Berlin, St Petersburg, and London. He negotiated the Treaty of Ghent to end the ◊War of 1812 on generous terms for the US. In 1817 he became ◊Monroe's secretary of state, formulated the ◊Monroe Doctrine 1823, and was elected president by the House of Representatives, despite receiving fewer votes than his main rival, Andrew ◊Jackson. As president, Adams was an advocate of strong federal government.

adaptation in biology, any change in the structure or function of an organism that allows it to survive and reproduce more effectively in its environment. In ◊evolution, adaptation is thought to occur as a result of random variation in the genetic makeup of organisms coupled with ◊natural selection. Species become extinct when they are no longer adapted to their environment—for instance, if the climate suddenly becomes colder.

ADC in electronics, abbreviation for ◊*analog-to-digital converter*.

adder European venomous snake, the common ◊viper *Vipera berus*. Growing to about 24 in/60 cm in length, it has a thick body, triangular head, a characteristic V-shaped mark on its head and, often, zigzag markings along the back. It feeds on small mammals and lizards. The *puff adder Bitis arietans* is a large, yellowish, thick-bodied viper up to 5 ft/1.6 m long, living in Africa and Arabia.

adder electronic circuit in a computer or calculator that carries out the process of adding two binary numbers. A separate adder is needed for each pair of binary ◊bits to be added. Such circuits are essential components of a computer's ◊arithmetic and logic unit (ALU).

addiction state of dependence caused by habitual use of drugs, alcohol, or other substances. It is characterized by uncontrolled craving, tolerance, and symptoms of

Adams, John Quincy John Quincy Adams, 6th president of the US, painted by Chapel. During his long second career in Congress (1831–48), "Old Man Eloquent", as he was called, won renewed respect throughout the North as an opponent of slavery. Although never an abolitionist, Adams fought the extension of slavery in the territories.

withdrawal when access is denied. Habitual use produces changes in body chemistry and treatment must be geared to a gradual reduction in dosage.

Addis Ababa or *Adis Abeba* capital of Ethiopia; population (1984) 1,413,000. It was founded 1887 by Menelik, chief of Shoa, who ascended the throne of Ethiopia 1889. His former residence, Menelik Palace, is now occupied by the government.

additive in food, any natural or artificial chemical added to prolong the shelf life of processed foods (salt or nitrates), alter the color or flavor of food, or improve its food value (vitamins or minerals). Many chemical additives are used and they are subject to regulation, since individuals may be affected by constant exposure even to traces of certain additives and may suffer side effects ranging from headaches and hyperactivity to cancer. Food companies in many countries are now required by law to list additives used in their products.

address in a computer memory, a number indicating a specific location. At each address, a single piece of data can be stored. For microcomputers, this normally amounts to one ◊byte (enough to represent a single character, such as a letter or digit).

address bus in computing, the electrical pathway or ◊bus used to select the route for any particular data item as it is moved from one part of a computer to another.

Addyston Pipe and Steel Co v US a US Supreme Court decision 1899 that granted the federal government certain regulatory powers over private businesses. The case resulted from a number of convictions of pipe-manufacturing firms for price fixing, a violation of the Sherman Antitrust Act. The pipe companies argued that manufacturing was not under federal regulation. The Court ruled that price fixing was a clear impingement on interstate commerce and was therefore under federal regulatory jurisdiction.

Adelaide capital and industrial city of South Australia; population (1990) 1,049,100. Industries include oil refining, shipbuilding, and the manufacture of electrical goods and automobiles. Grain, wool, fruit, and wine are exported. Founded 1836, Adelaide was named for William IV's queen.

Aden (Arabic *'Adan*) main port and commercial center of Yemen, on a rocky peninsula at the southwest corner of Arabia, commanding the entrance to the Red Sea; population (1984) 318,000. The city's economy is based on oil refining, fishing, and shipping. A British territory from 1839, Aden became part of independent South Yemen 1967; it was the capital of South Yemen until 1990.

history After annexation by Britain, Aden and its immediately surrounding area (47 sq mi/121 sq km) were developed as a ship-refueling station following the opening of the Suez Canal 1869. It was a colony 1937–63 and then, after a period of transitional violence among rival nationalist groups and British forces, was combined with the former Aden protectorate (112,000 sq mi/290,000 sq km) to create the Southern Yemen People's Republic 1967, which was renamed the People's Democratic Republic of Yemen 1970–90.

Adenauer Konrad 1876–1967. German Christian Democrat politician, chancellor of West Germany 1949–63. With the French president de Gaulle he achieved the postwar reconciliation of France and Germany and strongly supported all measures designed to strengthen the Western bloc in Europe.

adenoids masses of lymphoid tissue, similar to ◊tonsils, located in the upper part of the throat, behind the nose. They are part of a child's natural defenses against the entry of germs but usually shrink and disappear by the age of ten.

adhesive substance that sticks two surfaces together. Natural adhesives (glues) include gelatin in its crude industrial form (made from bones, hide fragments, and fish offal) and vegetable gums. Synthetic adhesives include thermoplastic and thermosetting resins, which are often stronger than the substances they join; mixtures of epoxy resin and hardener that set by chemical reaction; and elastomeric (stretching) adhesives for flexible joints. Superglues are fast-setting adhesives used in very small quantities.

adiabatic in physics, a process that occurs without loss or gain of heat, especially the expansion or contraction of a gas in which a change takes place in the pressure or volume, although no heat is allowed to enter or leave.

adjective grammatical ◊part of speech for words that describe nouns (for example, *new* and *beautiful*, as in "a new hat" and "a beautiful day"). Adjectives generally have three degrees (grades or levels for the description of relationships): the positive degree (*new*, *beautiful*), the comparative degree (*newer*, *more beautiful*), and the superlative degree (*newest*, *most beautiful*).

admiral any of several species of butterfly in the same family (Nymphalidae) as the tortoiseshells. The red admiral *Vanessa atalanta*, wingspan 2.5 in/6 cm, is found worldwide in the northern hemisphere. It migrates south each year from northern areas to subtropical zones.

adobe in architecture, a building method employing sun-dried earth bricks; also the individual bricks. The use of earth bricks and the construction of walls by enclosing earth within molds (*pisé de terre*) are the two principal methods of raw-earth building. The techniques are commonly found in the Southwest US, Spain, and Latin America.

adolescence in the human life cycle, the period between the beginning of puberty and adulthood.

Adonis in Greek mythology, a beautiful youth loved by the goddess ◊Aphrodite. He was killed while boarhunting but was allowed to return from the underworld for six months every year to rejoin her. The anemone sprang from his blood.

adoption permanent legal transfer of parental rights and duties in respect of a child from one person to another.

State laws determine processes for adoption, rights of adoptees (such as access to information about natural parents), and inheritance rights.

adrenal gland or *suprarenal gland* triangular gland situated on top of the kidney. The adrenals are soft and yellow, and consist of two parts: the cortex and medulla. The *cortex* (outer part) secretes various steroid hormones, controls salt and water metabolism, and regulates the use of carbohydrates, proteins, and fats. The *medulla* (inner part) secretes the hormones adrenaline and noradrenaline which, during times of stress, cause the heart to beat faster and harder, increase blood flow to the heart and muscle cells, and dilate airways in the lungs, thereby delivering more oxygen to cells throughout the body and in general preparing the body for "fight or flight".

adrenaline or *epinephrine* hormone secreted by the medulla of the ◊adrenal glands.

Adrian IV (Nicholas Breakspear) *c.* 1100–1159. Pope 1154–59, the only British pope. He secured the execution of Arnold of Brescia, crowned Frederick I Barbarossa as German emperor, refused Henry II's request that Ireland should be granted to the English crown in absolute ownership, and was at the height of a quarrel with the emperor when he died.

Adriatic Sea large arm of the Mediterranean Sea, lying NW to SE between the Italian and the Balkan peninsulas. The western shore is Italian; the eastern includes Croatia, Montenegro, and Albania, with a small strip of coastline owned by Slovenia. The sea is about 500 mi/805 km long, and its area is 52,220 sq mi/ 135,250 sq km.

adsorption taking up of a gas or liquid at the surface of another substance, usually a solid (for example, activated charcoal adsorbs gases). It involves molecular attraction at the surface, and should be distinguished from ◊absorption (in which a uniform solution results from a gas or liquid being incorporated into the bulk structure of a liquid or solid).

adultery voluntary sexual intercourse between a married person and someone other than his or her legal partner.

It is almost universally recognized as grounds for ◊divorce in the US, and is a punishable offense in some states. The legal definition of adultery varies: in some states both parties have to be married (to other people); in others it is adultery if the woman is married but not if only the man is married.

Adventist person who believes that Christ will return to make a second appearance on the Earth. Expectation of the Second Coming of Christ is found in New Testament writings generally. Adventist views are held in particular by the Seventh-Day Adventist church (with 1.5 million members in 200 countries), Christadelphians, the Jehovah's Witnesses, the Four Square Gospel Alliance, the Advent Christian church, and the Evangelical Adventist church.

adverb grammatical ◊part of speech for words that modify or describe verbs ("she ran *quickly*"), adjectives ("a *beautifully* clear day"), and adverbs ("they did it *really* well"). Most adverbs are formed from adjectives or past participles by adding *-ly* (*quick: quickly*) or *-ally* (*automatic: automatically*).

advertising any of various methods used by a company to increase the sales of its products or to promote a brand name.

Aegean Sea branch of the Mediterranean between Greece and Turkey; the Dardanelles connect it with the Sea of Marmara. The numerous islands in the Aegean Sea include Crete, the Cyclades, the Sporades, and the Dodecanese. There is political tension between Greece and Turkey over sea limits claimed by Greece around such islands as Lesvos, Chios, Samos, and Kos.

Aeneas in classical mythology, a Trojan prince who became the ancestral hero of the Romans. According to ◊Homer, he was the son of Anchises and the goddess Aphrodite. During the Trojan War he owed his life to the frequent intervention of the gods. The legend on which Virgil's epic poem the *Aeneid* is based describes his escape from Troy and his eventual settlement in Latium, on the Italian peninsula.

aerial or *antenna* in radio and television broadcasting, a conducting device that radiates or receives electromagnetic waves. The design of an aerial depends principally on the wavelength of the signal. Long waves (hundreds of meters in wavelength) may employ long wire aerials; short waves (several centimeters in wavelength) may employ rods and dipoles; microwaves may also use dipoles—often with reflectors arranged like a toast rack—or highly directional parabolic dish aerials. Because microwaves travel in straight lines, giving line-of-sight communication, microwave aerials are usually located at the tops of tall masts or towers.

aerobic in biology, descriptive of those living organisms that require oxygen (usually dissolved in water) for the efficient release of energy contained in food molecules, such as glucose. They include almost all living organisms (plants as well as animals) with the exception of certain bacteria, yeasts, and internal parasites.

aerobics (Greek "air" and "life") exercises to improve the performance of the heart and lungs. A strenuous application of movement to raise the heart rate to 120 beats per minute or more for sessions of 5–20 minutes' duration, 3–5 times per week.

aerodynamics branch of fluid physics that studies the forces exerted by air or other gases in motion—for example, the airflow around bodies (such as land vehicles, bullets, rockets, and aircraft) moving at speed through the atmosphere. For maximum efficiency, the aim is usually to design the shape of an object to produce a streamlined flow, with a minimum of turbulence in the moving air.

aeronautics science of travel through the Earth's atmosphere, including aerodynamics, aircraft structures, jet and rocket propulsion, and aerial navigation.

aerosol particles of liquid or solid suspended in a gas. Fog is a common natural example. Aerosol cans contain a substance such as scent or cleaner packed under pressure with a device for releasing it as a fine spray.

Most aerosol cans used chlorofluorocarbons (CFCs) as propellants until these were found to cause destruction of the ozone layer in the stratosphere.

Aeschylus *c.*525–*c.*456 BC. Athenian dramatist. He developed Greek tragedy by introducing the second actor, thus enabling true dialogue and dramatic action to occur independently of the chorus. Ranked with ◊Euripides and ◊Sophocles as one of the three great tragedians, Aeschylus composed some 90 plays between 500 and 456 BC, of which seven complete tragedies survive in his name: *Persians* 472 BC, *Seven Against Thebes* 467 BC, *Suppliants* 463 BC, the ◊*Oresteia* trilogy (*Agamemnon*, *Libation-Bearers*, and *Eumenides*) 458 BC, and *Prometheus Bound* (the last, although attributed to him, is of uncertain date and authorship).

Aesop by oral tradition, a writer of Greek fables. According to the historian Herodotus, he lived in the mid-6th century BC and was a slave.

The fables, which are ascribed to him, were collected at a later date and are anecdotal stories using animal characters to illustrate moral or satirical points.

Aesthetic Movement English artistic movement of the late 19th century, dedicated to the doctrine of "art for art's sake"—that is, art as a self-sufficient entity concerned solely with beauty and not with any moral or social purpose. Associated with the movement were the artists Aubrey Beardsley and James McNeill Whistler, the American, and the writers Walter Pater and Oscar Wilde.

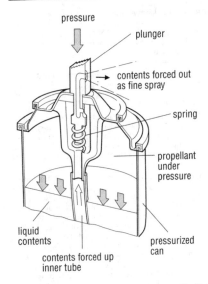

pressure

plunger

contents forced out as fine spray

spring

propellant under pressure

liquid contents

pressurized can

contents forced up inner tube

aerosol The aerosol can produces a fine spray of liquid particles, called an aerosol. When the top button is pressed, a valve is opened, allowing the pressurized propellant in the can to force out a spray of the liquid contents. As the liquid sprays from the can, the small amount of propellant dissolved in the liquid vaporizes, producing a fine spray of small droplets.

affidavit legal document, used in court applications and proceedings, in which a person swears that certain facts are true.

affinity in law, relationship by marriage not blood (for example, between a husband and his wife's blood relatives, a wife and her husband's blood relatives, or step-parent and stepchild), which may legally preclude their marriage. It is distinguished from consanguinity or blood relationship.

affinity in chemistry, the force of attraction (see ◊bond) between atoms that helps to keep them in combination in a molecule. The term is also applied to attraction between molecules, such as those of biochemical significance (for example, between ◊enzymes and substrate molecules). This is the basis for affinity ◊chromatography, by which biologically important compounds are separated.

affirmative action US government policy of positive discrimination that favors members of minority ethnic groups and women in such areas as employment and education, designed to counter the effects of long-term discrimination against them.

The policy has been controversial, and has prompted lawsuits by white males who have been denied jobs or education as a result. Positive discrimination in favor of ethnic-minority construction companies by local government was outlawed Jan 1989.

Afghanistan Republic of (*Jamhuria Afghanistan*) *area* 251,707 sq mi/652,090 sq km *capital* Kabul *towns and cities* Kandahar, Herat, Mazar-i-Sharif *physical* mountainous in center and NE, plains in N and SW *environment* an estimated 95% of the urban

population is without access to sanitation services *features* Hindu Kush mountain range (Khyber and Salang passes, Wakhan salient and Panjshir Valley), Amu Darya (Oxus) River, Helmand River, Lake Saberi *head of state* Burhanuddin Rabbani from 1992 *head of government* vacant *political system* emergent democracy *political parties* Hezb-i-Islami and Jámiat-i-Islami, Islamic fundamentalist mujaheddin; National Salvation Front, moderate mujaheddin *exports* dried fruit, natural gas, fresh fruits, carpets; small amounts of rare minerals, karakul lamb skins, and Afghan coats *currency* afgháni *population* (1993 est) 17,400,000 (more than 5 million became refugees after 1979); growth rate 0.6% p.a. *life expectancy* men 43, women 44 *languages* Pushtu, Dari (Persian) *media* no national daily newspaper; several radio stations, but in 1994 80% of adults listened regularly to the British Broadcasting Corporation (BBC) *religion* Muslim (80% Sunni, 20% Shiite) *literacy* men 44%, women 14% *GNP* $250 per head *chronology 1747* Afghanistan became an independent emirate. *1839–42 and 1878–80* Afghan Wars instigated by Britain to counter the threat to British India from expanding Russian influence in Afghanistan. *1919* Afghanistan recovered full independence following Third Afghan War. *1953* Lt Gen Daud Khan became prime minister and introduced reform program. *1963* Daud Khan forced to resign and constitutional monarchy established. *1973* Monarchy overthrown in coup by Daud Khan. *1978* Daud Khan ousted by Taraki and the PDPA. *1979* Taraki replaced by Hafizullah Amin; USSR entered country to prop up government; it installed Babrak Karmal in power. Amin executed. *1986* Replacement of Karmal as leader by Dr Najibullah Ahmadzai. Partial Soviet troop withdrawal. *1988* New non-Marxist constitution adopted. *1989* Complete withdrawal of Soviet troops; state of emergency imposed in response to intensification of civil war. *1991* US and Soviet military aid withdrawn. Mujaheddin began talks with Russians and Kabul government. *1992* April: Najibullah government overthrown. June: mujaheddin leader Burhanuddin Rabbani named interim head of state; Islamic law introduced. Sept: Hezb-i-Islami barred from government participation after shell attacks on Kabul. Dec: Rabbani elected president for two-year term. *1993* Jan: intensive fighting around Kabul; interim parliament appointed by

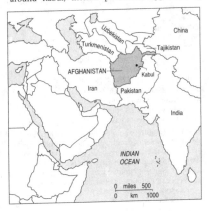

constituent assembly. March: peace agreement signed between Rabbani and dissident Hezb-i-Islami leader Gulbuddin Hekmatyar, under which Hekmatyar became prime minister. *1994* Jan: alliance of Hezb-i-Islami and other rebel forces renewed attacks on Kabul; Hekmatyar dismissed from premiership.

Africa second largest of the continents, three times the area of Europe *area* 11,620,451 sq mi/30,097,000 sq km *largest cities* (population over 1 million) Cairo, Algiers, Lagos, Kinshasa, Abidjan, Cape Town, Nairobi, Casablanca, El Gîza, Addis Ababa, Luanda, Dar-es Salaam, Ibadan, Douala, Mogadishu *features* Great Rift Valley, containing most of the great lakes of E Africa (except Lake Victoria); Atlas Mountains in the NW; Drakensberg mountain range in the SE; Sahara Desert (world's largest desert) in the N; Namib, Kalahari, and Great Karoo deserts in the S; Nile, Zaïre, Niger, Zambezi, Limpopo, Volta, and Orange rivers *physical* dominated by a uniform central plateau comprising a southern tableland with a mean altitude of 3,000 ft/1,070 m that falls northward to a lower elevated plain with a mean altitude of 1,300 ft/400 m. Although there are no great alpine regions or extensive coastal plains, Africa has a mean altitude of 2,000 ft/ 610 m, two times greater than Europe. The highest points are Mount Kilimanjaro 19,364 ft/5,900 m, and Mount Kenya 17,058 ft/5,200 m; the lowest point is Lac Assal in Djibouti –471 ft/–144 m. Compared with other continents, Africa has few broad estuaries or inlets and therefore has proportionately the shortest coastline (15,000 mi/24,000 km). The geographical extremities of the continental mainland are Cape Hafun in the E, Cape Almadies in the W, Ras Ben Sekka in the N, and Cape Agulhas in the S. The Sahel is a narrow belt of savanna and scrub forest which covers 1.7 billion acres/700 million hectares of W and central Africa; 75% of the continent lies within the tropics.

African National Congress (ANC) South African political party, founded 1912 as a multiracial nationalist organization with the aim of extending the franchise to the whole population and ending all racial discrimination. Its president from 1991 is Nelson ◊Mandela.

The ANC was banned by the government from 1960 to Jan 1990. During the early 1990s fighting between supporters of the ANC and the Zulu-based ◊Inkatha movement racked the townships, leaving thousands dead. Talks between the ANC and the South African government began Dec 1991, culminating in the adoption of a nonracial constitution 1993 and the ANC's agreement to participate in a power-sharing administration, as a prelude to full majority rule. In the country's first multiracial elections April 1994, the ANC won a sweeping victory, capturing 62% of the vote, and Mandela was elected president.

African violet herbaceous plant *Saintpaulia ionantha* from tropical central and E Africa, with velvety green leaves and scentless purple flowers. Different colors and double varieties have been bred.

Afrikaans language an official language (with English) of the Republic of South Africa and Namibia. Spoken mainly by the Afrikaners—descendants of Dutch and other 17th-century colonists—it is a variety of the Dutch language, modified by circumstance and the influence of German, French, and other immigrant as well as local languages. It became a standardized written language about 1875.

Afro-Asiatic language any of a family of languages spoken throughout the world. There are two main branches, the languages of N Africa and the languages originating in Syria, Mesopotamia, Palestine, and Arabia, but now found from Morocco in the west to the Persian Gulf in the east.

afterbirth in mammals, the placenta, umbilical cord and ruptured membranes, which become detached from the uterus and expelled soon after birth. In the natural world it is often eaten.

afterimage persistence of an image on the retina of the eye after the object producing it has been removed. This leads to persistence of vision, a necessary phenomenon for the illusion of continuous movement in films and television. The term is also used for the persistence of sensations other than vision.

Agamemnon in Greek mythology, a Greek hero of the Trojan wars, son of Atreus, king of Mycenae, and brother of Menelaus. He married Clytemnestra, and their children included Electra, Iphigenia, and Orestes. He sacrificed Iphigenia in order to secure favorable winds for the Greek expedition against Troy and after a ten years' siege sacked the city, receiving Priam's daughter Cassandra as a prize. On his return home, he and Cassandra were murdered by Clytemnestra and her lover, Aegisthus. His children Orestes and Electra later killed the guilty couple.

Agaña capital of Guam in the W Pacific; population (1980) 896. It is the administrative center of the island, bordered by residential Agana Heights and Apra Harbor.

agar jellylike carbohydrate, obtained from seaweeds. It is used mainly in microbiological experiments as a culture medium for growing bacteria and other microorganisms. The agar is resistant to breakdown by microorganisms, remaining a solid jelly throughout the course of the experiment.

It is also used as a laxative and in preserved foods.

agaric fungus of typical mushroom shape. Agarics include the field mushroom *Agaricus campestris* and the cultivated edible mushroom *A. brunnesiens*. Closely related is the often poisonous ◊*Amanita* genus, including the fly agaric *Amanita muscaria*.

Agassiz Jean Louis Rodolphe 1807–1873. Swiss-born US paleontologist and geologist. His interests were comparative zoology and Ice Age geology. In 1832 he accepted a professorship at the University of Neuchâtel; coming to the US 1846, he became a member of the faculty of Harvard. Agassiz, known as a conservative in his opposition to Darwin, conducted many expeditions to the American West. His massive *Contributions to the Natural History of the United States* was published 1857–62.

agate banded or cloudy type of ◊chalcedony, a silica, SiO_2, that forms in rock cavities. Agates are used as ornamental stones and for art objects.

agave any of several related plants with stiff sword-shaped spiny leaves arranged in a rosette. All species, of the genus *Agave* come from the warmer parts of the New World. They include *A. sisalina*, whose fibers are used for rope making, and the Mexican century plant *A. americana*. Alcoholic drinks such as ◊tequila and pulque are made from the sap of agave plants.

Agee James 1909–1955. US journalist, screenwriter, and author. He rose to national prominence as a result of his investigation of the plight of sharecroppers in the South during the Depression. In collaboration with photographer Walker Evans, he published the photo and text essay *Let Us Now Praise Famous Men* 1941. His screenwriting credits include *The African Queen* 1951 and *The Night of the Hunter* 1955. His novel *A Death in the Family* won a Pulitzer Prize 1958.

Born in Knoxville, Tennessee, Agee graduated from Harvard 1932 and embarked on a career as a magazine reporter and feature writer.

aggression in biology, behavior used to intimidate or injure another organism (of the same or of a different species), usually for the purposes of gaining a territory, a mate, or food. Aggression often involves an escalating series of threats aimed at intimidating an opponent without having to engage in potentially dangerous physical contact. Aggressive signals include roaring by elk, snarling by dogs, the fluffing up of feathers by birds, and the raising of fins by some species of fish.

Agincourt, Battle of battle of the Hundred Years' War in which Henry V of England defeated the French on Oct 25, 1415, mainly through the overwhelming superiority of the English longbow. The French lost more than 6,000 men to about 1,600 English casualties. As a result of the battle, Henry gained France and the French princess, Catherine of Valois, as his wife. The village of Agincourt (modern *Azincourt*) is south of Calais, in N France.

aging in common usage, the period of deterioration of the physical condition of a living organism that leads to death; in biological terms, the entire life process.

agnosticism belief that the existence of God cannot be proven; that in the nature of things the individual cannot know anything of what lies behind or beyond the world of natural phenomena. The term was coined 1869 by T H ◊Huxley.

agoraphobia ◊phobia involving fear of open spaces and public places. The anxiety produced can be so severe that some sufferers are unable to leave their homes for many years.

Agricola Gnaeus Julius AD 37–93. Roman general and politician. Born in Provence, he became consul AD 77, and then governor of Britain AD 78–85. He extended Roman rule to the Firth of Forth in Scotland and won the battle of Mons Graupius. His fleet sailed round the north of Scotland and proved Britain an island.

agriculture the practice of farming, including the cultivation of the soil (for raising crops) and the raising of domesticated animals. Crops are for human nourishment, animal fodder, or commodities such as cotton and sisal. Animals are raised for wool, milk, leather, dung (as fuel), or meat. The units for managing agricultural production vary from smallholdings and individually owned farms to corporate-run farms and collective farms run by entire communities.

agronomy study of crops and soils, a branch of agricultural science. Agronomy includes such topics as selective breeding (of plants and animals), irrigation, pest control, and soil analysis and modification.

Ahriman in ◊Zoroastrianism, the supreme evil spirit, lord of the darkness and death, waging war with his counterpart Ahura Mazda (Ormuzd) until a time when human beings choose to lead good lives and Ahriman is finally destroyed.

Ahura Mazda or *Ormuzd* in ◊Zoroastrianism, the spirit of supreme good. As god of life and light he will finally prevail over his enemy, Ahriman.

AI abbreviation for ◊*artificial intelligence*.

aid, foreign financial and other assistance given by richer, usually industrialized, countries to war-damaged or developing states.

AIDS (acronym for *acquired immune deficiency syndrome*) the gravest of the sexually transmitted diseases, or STDs. It is caused by the human immunodeficiency virus (HIV), now known to be a ◊retrovirus, an organism first identified 1983. HIV is transmitted in body fluids, mainly blood and genital secretions.

The AIDS virus is thought to have originated in Africa, where the disease is most widespread. In the United States, where there have been more than a quarter of a million AIDS cases by the beginning of 1994, there is a worrying link with tuberculosis, a disease undergoing a marked resurgence, particularly in inner city areas.

Aiken Conrad (Potter) 1899–1973. US poet, novelist, and short-story writer. His *Selected Poems* 1929 won the Pulitzer Prize. His works were influenced by early psychoanalytic theory and the use of the stream-of-consciousness technique. His verse, distinguished by its musicality, includes "A Letter from Li Po" 1955 and *A Seizure of Limericks* 1964. His novels include *Great Circle* 1933, and his collected short stories were published 1960.

Aiken Howard 1900– . US mathematician and computer pioneer. In 1939, in conjunction with engineers from ◊IBM, he started work on the design of an automatic calculator using standard business-machine components. In 1944 the team completed one of the first computers, the Automatic Sequence Controlled Calculator (known as the Mark 1), a programmable computer controlled by punched paper tape and using ◊punched cards.

ailanthus any tree or shrub of the genus *Ailanthus* of the quassia family. All have compound leaves made up of pointed leaflets and clusters of small greenish flowers with an unpleasant smell. The tree of heaven *Ailanthus altissima*, native to E Asia, is grown worldwide as an ornamental. It can grow to 100 ft/30 m in height and 3 ft/1 m in diameter.

air the earth's ◊atmosphere.

aircraft any aeronautical vehicle, which may be lighter than air (supported by buoyancy) or heavier than air (supported by the dynamic action of air on its surfaces). ◊Balloons and ◊airships are lighter-than-air craft. Heavier-than-air craft include the ◊airplane, glider, autogiro, and helicopter.

aircraft carrier oceangoing naval vessel with a broad, flat-topped deck for launching and landing military aircraft; an effort to provide a floating military base for warplanes too far from home for refueling, repairing, reconnaissance, escorting, and various attack and defense operations.

The USS *Enterprise* was the first nuclear-powered carrier 1961; it could go for almost 300,000 mi/480,000 km before refueling. Since aircraft are now capable of long-range flight, and with the possible use of sophisticated missiles, few carriers were built from the 1970s; their enormous cost, low speed, and vulnerability seem to preclude future construction.

air lock airtight chamber that allows people to pass between areas of different pressure; also an air bubble in a pipe that impedes fluid flow. An air lock may connect an environment at ordinary pressure and an environment that has high air pressure (such as a sub-

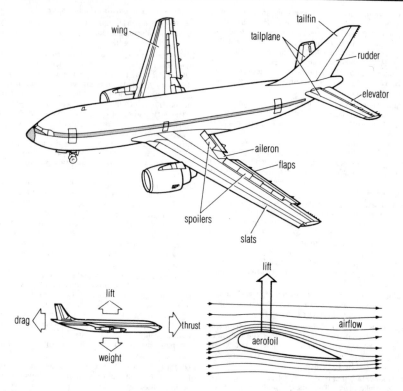

airplane In flight, the forces on an airplane are lift, weight, drag, and thrust. The lift is generated by the air flow over the wings, which have the shape of an airfoil. The drag results from the resistance of the air to the airplane's passage through it. Various moveable flaps on the wings and tail allow the airplane to be controlled. The rudder is moved to turn the airplane. The elevators allow the craft to climb or dive. The ailerons are used to bank the airplane while turning. The flaps, slats, and spoilers are used to reduce lift and speed during landing.

merged caisson used for tunneling or building dams or bridge foundations).

airplane powered heavier-than-air craft supported in flight by fixed wings. Airplanes can be propelled by the thrust of a jet engine, a rocket engine, or airscrew (propeller), as well as combinations of these. They must be designed aerodynamically, as streamlining ensures maximum flight efficiency. The shape of a plane depends on its use and operating speed—aircraft operating at well below the speed of sound need not be as streamlined as supersonic aircraft. The Wright brothers flew the first powered plane (a biplane) in Kitty Hawk, North Carolina, 1903. For the history of aircraft and aviation, see ◊flight.

air sac in birds, a thin-walled extension of the lungs. There are nine of these and they extend into the abdomen and bones, effectively increasing lung capacity. In mammals, it is another name for the alveoli in the lungs, and in some insects, for widenings of the trachea.

airship or *dirigible* any aircraft that is lighter than air and power-driven, consisting of an elliptical balloon that forms the streamlined envelope or hull and has below it the propulsion system (propellers), steering mechanism, and space for crew, passengers, and/or cargo. The balloon section is filled with lighter-than-air gas, either the nonflammable helium or, before helium was industrially available in large enough quantities, the easily ignited and flammable hydrogen. The envelope's form is maintained by internal pressure in the nonrigid (blimp) and semirigid (in which the nose and tail sections have a metal framework connected by a rigid keel) types. The rigid type (zeppelin) maintains its form using an internal metal framework. Airships have been used for luxury travel, polar exploration, warfare, and advertising.

Ajax Greek hero in Homer's *Iliad*. Son of Telamon, king of Salamis, he was second only to Achilles among the Greek heroes in the Trojan War. According to subsequent Greek legends, Ajax went mad with jealousy when ◊Agamemnon awarded the armor of the dead Achilles to ◊Odysseus. He later committed suicide in shame.

a.k.a. abbreviation for *also known as*.

Akbar Jalal ud-Din Mohammed 1542–1605. Mogul emperor of N India from 1556, when he succeeded his father. He gradually established his rule throughout N India. He is considered the greatest of the Mogul emperors, and the firmness and wisdom of his rule won him the title "Guardian of Mankind"; he was a patron of the arts.

Akhenaton another name for ◊Ikhnaton, pharaoh of Egypt.

Akihito 1933– . Emperor of Japan from 1989, succeeding his father Hirohito (Showa). His reign is called the Heisei ("achievement of universal peace") era.

Akkad northern Semitic people who conquered the Sumerians in 2350 BC and ruled Mesopotamia. The ancient city of Akkad in central Mesopotamia, founded by ◊Sargon I, was an imperial center in the late 3rd millennium BC ; the site is unidentified, but it was on the river Euphrates somewhere near Babylon.

Akron city in Ohio on the Cuyahoga River, 35 mi/56 km SE of Cleveland; population (1990) 660,000. Known as the "Rubber Capital of the World," it is home to the headquarters of several major tire and rubber companies, although production there had ended by 1982.

The city is also a major trucking center and the site of the University of Akron. Akron was first settled 1807. Dr B F Goodrich established a rubber factory 1870, and the industry grew immensely with the rising demand for tires from about 1910.

Aksum or *Axum* ancient Greek-influenced Semitic kingdom that flourished in the 1st–6th centuries AD and covered a large part of modern Ethiopia as well as the Sudan. The ruins of its capital, also called Aksum, lie NW of Aduwa, but the site has been developed as a modern city.

al- for Arabic names beginning *al-*, see rest of name; for example, for "al-Fatah", see ◊Fatah, al-.

Alabama state in southern US; nickname Heart of Dixie/Cotton State *area* 51,994 sq mi/134,700 sq km *capital* Montgomery *towns and cities* Birmingham, Mobile, Huntsville, Tuscaloosa *physical* the state comprises the Cumberland Plateau in the N; the Black Belt, or Canebrake, which is excellent cotton-growing country, in the center; and S of this, the coastal plain of Piny Woods. The Alabama River is the largest in the state *features* rivers: Alabama, Tennessee; Appalachian mountains; George Washington Carver Museum at the Tuskegee Institute (a college founded for African Americans by Booker T Washington); White House of the Confederacy at Montgomery; George C Marshall Space Flight Center at Huntsville; annual Mardi Gras celebration at Mobile; Helen Keller's birthplace at Tuscumbia *industries* cotton (still important though no longer prime crop); soy beans, peanuts, wood products, coal, livestock, poultry, iron, chemicals, textiles, paper *population* (1990) 4,040,600 *famous people* Hank Aaron, Tallulah Bankhead, Nat King Cole, W C Handy, Helen Keller, Joe Louis, Willie Mays, Jesse Owens, Leroy "Satchel" Paige, George C Wallace, Booker T Washington, Hank Williams, Tammy Wynette *history* first settled by the French in the early 18th century, it was ceded to Britain 1763, passed to the US 1783 and became a state 1819. It was one of the Confederate States, and Montgomery was the first capital of the Confederacy. Birmingham became the South's leading industrial center in the late 19th century. Alabama was in the forefront of the civil rights movement in the 1950s and 1960s: Martin Luther ◊King, Jr, led a successful boycott of segregated Montgomery buses in 1955; school integration began in the early 1960s despite the opposition of Governor George C Wallace; the 1965 Selma march resulted in federal voting-rights legislation.

alabaster naturally occurring fine-grained white or light-colored translucent form of gypsum, often streaked or mottled. A soft material, it is easily carved, but seldom used for outdoor sculpture.

Alamo, the mission fortress in San Antonio. It was besieged Feb 23–March 6, 1836 by ◊Santa Anna and 4,000 Mexicans; they killed the garrison of about 180, including Davy Crockett and Jim Bowie.

The struggle against such overwhelming odds made the battle of the Alamo a rallying point for the settlers in the Texas War of Independence from Mexico.

Alaric *c.*370–410. King of the Visigoths. In 396 he invaded Greece and retired with much booty to Illyria. In 400 and 408 he invaded Italy, and in 410 captured and sacked Rome, but died the same year on his way to invade Sicily.

Alaska largest state of the US, on the northwest extremity of North America, separated from the lower 48 states by British Columbia; nickname Last Frontier; territories include ◊Aleutian Islands *total area* 591,004 sq mi/1,530,700 sq km *land area* 570,833 sq mi/1,478,457 sq km *capital* Juneau *towns and cities* Anchorage, Fairbanks, Fort Yukon, Holy Cross, Nome *physical* much of Alaska is mountainous and includes Mount McKinley (Denali), 20,322 ft/6,194 m, the highest peak in North America, surrounded by Denali National Park. Caribou (descended from 2,000 reindeer imported from Siberia in early 1900s) thrive in the Arctic tundra, and elsewhere there are extensive forests *features* Yukon River; Rocky Mountains, including Mount McKinley and Mount Katmai, a volcano that erupted 1912 and formed the Valley of Ten Thousand Smokes (from which smoke and steam still escape and which is now a national monument); Arctic Wild Life Range, with the only large herd of indigenous North American caribou; Little Diomede Island, which is only 2.5 mi/4 km from Russian Big Diomede/ Ratmanov Island. The chief railroad line runs from Seward to Fairbanks, which is linked by highway (via Canada) with Seattle; near Fairbanks is the University of Alaska *products* oil, natural gas, coal, copper, iron, gold, tin, fur, salmon fisheries and canneries, lumber *population* (1990) 550,000; including 9% American Indians, Aleuts, and Inuits *history* various groups of Indians crossed the Bering land bridge 60,000–15,000 years ago; the Eskimo began to settle the Arctic coast from Siberia about 2000 BC ; the Aleuts settled the Aleutian archipelago about 1000 BC. The first European to visit Alaska was Vitus Bering 1741. Alaska was a Russian colony from 1744 until purchased by the US 1867 for $7,200,000; gold was discovered five years later. It became a state 1959. A Congressional act 1980 gave environmental protection to 104 million acres/42 million ha. Valuable mineral resources have been exploited from 1968, especially in the Prudhoe Bay area to the SE of Point Barrow. An oil pipeline (1977) runs from Prudhoe Bay to the port of Valdez. Oil spill from a tanker in Prince William Sound caused great environmental damage 1989. Under construction is an underground natural-gas pipeline to Chicago and San Francisco.

Albania Republic of (*Republika e Shqipërisë*) *area* 11,097 sq mi/28,748 sq km *capital* Tiranë *towns and cities*

Shkodër, Elbasan, Vlorë, chief port Durrës **physical** mainly mountainous, with rivers flowing E–W, and a narrow coastal plain **features** Dinaric Alps, with wild boar and wolves **head of state** Sali Berisha from 1992 **head of government** Alexandr Meksi from 1992 **political system** emergent democracy **political parties** Democratic Party of Albania (PSDS; formerly the Democratic Party: DP), moderate, market-oriented; Socialist Party of Albania (PSS), ex-communist; Human Rights Union (HMU), Greek minority party **exports** crude oil, bitumen, chrome, iron ore, nickel, coal, copper wire, tobacco, fruit, vegetables **currency** lek **population** (1993 est) 3,400,000; growth rate 1.9% p.a. **life expectancy** men 70, women 75 **languages** Albanian, Greek **religions** Muslim about 50%, Orthodox 18%, Roman Catholic 13% **literacy** 85% GNP $930 per head **chronology** *c.1468* Albania made part of the Ottoman Empire. *1912* Independence achieved from Turkey. *1925* Republic proclaimed. *1928–39* Monarchy of King Zog. *1939–44* Under Italian and then German rule. *1946* Communist republic proclaimed under the leadership of Enver Hoxha. *1949* Admitted into Comecon. *1961* Break with Khrushchev's USSR. *1967* Albania declared itself the "first atheist state in the world". *1978* Break with "revisionist" China. *1985* Death of Hoxha. *1987* Normal diplomatic relations restored with Canada, Greece, and West Germany. *1988* Attendance of conference of Balkan states for the first time since the 1930s. *1990* One-party system abandoned; first opposition party formed. *1991* Party of Labor of Albania (PLA) won first multiparty elections; Ramiz Alia reelected president; three successive governments formed. PLA renamed PSS. *1992* Presidential elections won by Democratic Party (DP); Sali Berisha elected president. Alia and other former communist officials charged with corruption and abuse of power; totalitarian and communist parties banned. *1993* DP renamed the Democratic Party of Albania (PSDS).

albatross large seabird, genus *Diomedea*, with long narrow wings adapted for gliding and a wingspan of up to 10 ft/3 m, mainly found in the southern hemisphere. It belongs to the order Procellariiformes, the same group as petrels and shearwaters.

Albert Prince Consort 1819–1861. Husband of British Queen ◊Victoria from 1840; a patron of the arts, science, and industry. Albert was the second son of the Duke of Saxe-Coburg-Gotha and first cousin to Queen Victoria, whose chief adviser he became. He planned the Great Exhibition of 1851; the profit was used to buy the sites in London of all the South Kensington museums and colleges and the Royal Albert Hall, built 1871. He died of typhoid.

Alberta province of W Canada **area** 255,223 sq mi/661,200 sq km **capital** Edmonton **towns and cities** Calgary, Lethbridge, Medicine Hat, Red Deer **physical** Rocky Mountains; dry, treeless prairie in the center and S; toward the N this merges into a zone of poplar, then mixed forest. The valley of the Peace River is the most northerly farming land in Canada (except for Inuit pastures), and there are good grazing lands in the foothills of the Rockies **features** Banff, Elk Island, Jasper, Waterton Lake, and Wood Buffalo national parks; annual Calgary stampede; extensive dinosaur finds near Drumheller **industries** coal; wheat, barley, oats, sugar beet in the S; more than a million head of cattle; oil and natural gas **population** (1991) 2,501,400 **history** in the 17th century much of its area was part of a grant to the ◊Hudson's Bay

Company for the fur trade, and the first trading posts were established in the late 18th century. The grant was bought by Canada 1869, and Alberta became a province 1905. After an oil strike in 1947, Alberta became a major oil and gas producer.

Alberti Leon Battista 1404–1472. Italian Renaissance architect and theorist. He set out the principles of Classical architecture, and their modification for Renaissance practice, in *De re aedificatoria/On Architecture* 1452. His designs for the churches of San Sebastiano, begun 1460, and San Andrea 1470 (both in Mantua)—the only two extant buildings entirely of his design—are bold in their use of Classical language but to a certain extent anticipate ◊Mannerism.

albinism rare hereditary condition in which the body has no tyrosinase, one of the enzymes that form the pigment melanin, normally found in the skin, hair, and eyes. As a result, the hair is white and the skin and eyes are pink. The skin and eyes are abnormally sensitive to light, and vision is often impaired. The condition occurs among all human and animal groups.

Albion ancient name for Britain used by the Greeks and Romans. It was mentioned by Pytheas of Massilia (4th century BC), and is probably of Celtic origin, but the Romans, having in mind the white cliffs of Dover, assumed it to be derived from *albus* (white).

albumin any of a group of sulfur-containing proteins. The best known is in the form of egg white; others occur in milk, and as a major component of serum. Many vegetables and fluids also contain albumins. They are soluble in water and dilute salt solutions, and are coagulated by heat.

alchemy supposed technique of transmuting base metals, such as lead and mercury, into silver and gold by the philosopher's stone, a hypothetical substance, to which was also attributed the power to give eternal life.

Alcibiades 450–404 BC. Athenian politician and general. He organized a confederation of Peloponnesian states against Sparta that collapsed after the battle of Mantinea 418 BC. Although accused of profaning the Eleusinian Mysteries, he was eventually accepted as the commander of the Athenian fleet. He achieved several victories such as Cyzicus 410 BC, before his forces were defeated at Notium 406. He was murdered in Phrygia by the Persians.

alcohol any member of a group of organic chemical compounds characterized by the presence of one or more aliphatic OH (hydroxyl) groups in the molecule, and which form ◊esters with acids. The main uses of alcohols are as solvents for gums, resins, lacquers, and varnishes; in the making of dyes; for essential oils in perfumery; and for medical substances in pharmacy. Alcohol (ethanol) is produced naturally in the ◊fermentation process and is consumed as part of alcoholic beverages.

alcoholic beverage any drink containing alcohol, often used for its intoxicating effects. ◊Ethanol (ethyl alcohol), a colorless liquid (C_2H_5OH) is the basis of all common intoxicants. Foods rich in sugars, such as grapes, produce this alcohol as a natural product of decay, called fermentation.

alcohol strength a measure of the amount of alcohol in an alcoholic beverage. Wine is measured as the percentage volume of alcohol at 68°F/20°C; liquors as a percentage of a mixture of alcohol and water containing by volume 50% ethyl alcohol at 60°F (called ◊proof spirit). Thus a whiskey labeled 100 proof contains 50% alcohol.

aldehyde any of a group of organic chemical compounds prepared by oxidation of primary alcohols, so that the OH (hydroxyl) group loses its hydrogen to give an oxygen joined by a double bond to a carbon atom (the aldehyde group, with the formula CHO).

The name is made up from *al*cohol *dehyd*rogenation—that is, alcohol from which hydrogen has been removed. Aldehydes are usually liquids and include methanal, ethanal, benzaldehyde, formaldehyde, and citral.

alder any tree or shrub of the genus *Alnus,* in the birch family Betulaceae, found mainly in cooler parts of the northern hemisphere and characterized by toothed leaves and catkins.

Sitka alder *A. sinuata* and red alder *A. rubra* are common to W North America.

Aleutian Islands volcanic island chain in the N Pacific, stretching 1,200 mi/1,900 km SW of Alaska, of which it forms part; population 6,000 Aleuts (most of whom belong to the Orthodox Church, plus a large US defense establishment). There are 14 large and more than 100 small islands running along the Aleutian Trench. The islands are mountainous, barren, and treeless; they are ice-free all year but are often foggy, with only about 25 days of sunshine recorded annually.

Alexander eight popes, including:

Alexander III (Orlando Barninelli) died 1181. Pope 1159–81. His authority was opposed by Frederick I Barbarossa, but Alexander eventually compelled him to render homage 1178. He supported Henry II of England in his invasion of Ireland, but imposed penance on him after the murder of Thomas à ◊Becket.

Alexander VI (Rodrigo Borgia) 1431–1503. Pope 1492–1503. Of Spanish origin, he bribed his way to the papacy, where he furthered the advancement of his illegitimate children, who included Cesare and Lucrezia ◊Borgia. When ◊Savonarola preached against his corrupt practices Alexander had him executed.

Alexander three czars of Russia:

Alexander I 1777–1825. Czar from 1801. Defeated by Napoleon at Austerlitz 1805, he made peace at Tilsit 1807, but economic crisis led to a break with Napoleon's Continental System and the opening of Russian ports to British trade; this led to Napoleon's ill-fated invasion of Russia 1812. After the Congress of Vienna 1815, Alexander hoped through the Holy Alliance with Austria and Prussia to establish a new Christian order in Europe.

After Napoleon's defeat Russia controlled the Congress Kingdom of Poland, for which a constitution was provided.

Alexander II 1818–1881. Czar from 1855. He embarked on reforms of the army, the government, and education, and is remembered as "the Liberator" for his emancipation of the serfs 1861, but he lacked the personnel to implement his reforms. However, the revolutionary element remained unsatisfied, and Alexander became increasingly autocratic and reactionary. He was assassinated by an anarchistic terrorist group, the ◊Nihilists.

Alexander III 1845–1894. Czar from 1881, when he succeeded his father, Alexander II. He pursued a

reactionary policy, promoting Russification and persecuting the Jews. He married Dagmar (1847–1928), daughter of Christian IX of Denmark and sister of Queen Alexandra of Britain, 1866.

Alexander three kings of Scotland:

Alexander I *c.*1078–1124. King of Scotland from 1107, known as *the Fierce.* He ruled to the north of the rivers Forth and Clyde while his brother and successor David ruled to the south. He assisted Henry I of England in his campaign against Wales 1114, but defended the independence of the church in Scotland. Several monasteries, including the abbeys of Inchcolm and Scone, were established by him.

Alexander II 1198–1249. King of Scotland from 1214, when he succeeded his father William the Lion. Alexander supported the English barons in their struggle with King John after ◊Magna Carta.

Alexander III 1241–1285. King of Scotland from 1249, son of Alexander II. In 1263, by military defeat of Norwegian forces, he extended his authority over the Western Isles, which had been dependent on Norway. He strengthened the power of the central Scottish government.

Alexander I Karageorgevich 1888–1934. Regent of Serbia 1912–21 and king of Yugoslavia 1921–34, as dictator from 1929. Second son of ◊Peter I, King of Serbia, he was declared regent for his father 1912 and on his father's death became king of the state of South Slavs—Yugoslavia—that had come into being 1918.

Alexander the Great 356–323 BC. King of Macedon from 336 BC and conqueror of the large Persian empire. As commander of the vast Macedonian army he conquered Greece 336, defeated the Persian king Darius in Asia Minor 333, then moved on to Egypt, where he founded Alexandria. He defeated the Persians again in Assyria 331, then advanced further east to reach the Indus. He conquered the Punjab before diminished troops forced his retreat.

Alexandria or *El Iskandariya* city, chief port, and second-largest city of Egypt, situated between the Mediterranean and Lake Maryut; population (1986) 5,000,000. It is linked by canal with the Nile and is an industrial city (oil refining, gas processing, and cotton and grain trading). Founded 331 BC by Alexander the Great, Alexandria was the capital of Egypt for over 1,000 years.

Alexandria, Library of library in Alexandria, Egypt, founded 330 BC by Ptolemy I and further expanded by ◊Ptolemy II.

It was the world's first state-funded scientific institution, and comprised a museum, teaching facilities, and a library that contained 700,000 scrolls, including much ancient Greek literature. It was burned down AD 640 at the time of the Arab conquest.

Alexandria, school of group of writers and scholars of Alexandria who made the city the chief center of culture in the Western world from about 331 BC to AD 642. They include the poets Callimachus, Apollonius Rhodius, and Theocritus; Euclid, pioneer of geometry; Eratosthenes, the geographer; Hipparchus, who developed a system of trigonometry; the astronomer Ptolemy, who gave his name to the Ptolemaic system of astronomy that endured for over 1,000 years; and the Jewish philosopher Philo. The Gnostics and Neoplatonists also flourished in Alexandria.

Alexeev Vasiliy 1942– . Soviet weight-lifter who broke 80 world records 1970–77, a record for any sport.

He was Olympic super-heavyweight champion twice, world champion seven times. He retired after the 1980 Olympics.

Alexius I (Comnenus) 1048–1118. Byzantine emperor 1081–1118. The Latin (W European) Crusaders helped him repel Norman and Turkish invasions, and he devoted great skill to buttressing the threatened empire. His daughter Anna Comnena chronicled his reign.

Alexius IV (Angelos) 1182–1204. Byzantine emperor from 1203, when, with the aid of the army of the Fourth Crusade, he deposed his uncle Alexius III. He soon lost the support of the Crusaders (by that time occupying Constantinople), and was overthrown and murdered by another Alexius, Alexius Mourtzouphlus (son-in-law of Alexius III) 1204, an act which the Crusaders used as a pretext to sack the city the same year.

alfalfa perennial tall herbaceous plant *Medicago sativa* of the pea family Leguminosae. It is native to Eurasia and bears spikes of small purple flowers in late summer. It is now a major fodder crop, generally processed into hay, meal, or silage. Alfalfa sprouts, the sprouted seeds, have become a popular salad ingredient.

Alfonso thirteen kings of León, Castile, and Spain, including:

Alfonso (X) el Sabio ("the Wise") 1221–1284. King of Castile from 1252. His reign was politically unsuccessful but he contributed to learning: he made Castilian the official language of the country and commissioned a history of Spain and an encyclopedia, as well as several translations from Arabic concerning, among other subjects, astronomy and games.

Alfonso XIII 1886–1941. King of Spain 1886–1931. He assumed power 1906 and married Princess Ena, granddaughter of Queen Victoria of the United Kingdom, in the same year. He abdicated 1931 soon after the fall of the Primo de Rivera dictatorship 1923–30 (which he supported), and Spain became a republic. His assassination was attempted several times.

Alfred the Great *c.*848–*c.*900. King of Wessex from 871. He defended England against Danish invasion, founded the first English navy, and put into operation a legal code. He encouraged the translation of works from Latin (some he translated himself), and promoted the development of the Anglo-Saxon Chronicle.

algae (singular *alga*) diverse group of plants (including those commonly called seaweeds) that shows great variety of form, ranging from single-celled forms to multicellular seaweeds of considerable size and complexity.

Marine algae help combat global warming by removing carbon dioxide from the atmosphere during photosynthesis.

Because of their diversity, botanists have established seven separate algae groupings or divisions, belonging to three different kingdoms: Cyanobacteria (blue-green algae) of the kingdom Monerans; Chrysophyta (golden algae diatoms), Englenophyta (plidosynthetic flagellates) and Pyrrophyta (dinoflagellates) of the kingdom Protists; and Rhodophyta (red algae), Phaeophyta (brown algae), and Chlorophyta (green algae) of the kingdom Plants.

algebra system of arithmetic applying to any set of nonnumerical symbols (usually letters), and the axioms and rules by which they are combined or operated upon; sometimes known as *generalized arithmetic*.

Alger Horatio 1832–1899. US writer of children's books. He wrote over 100 didactic moral tales in which the heroes rise from poverty to riches through hard work, luck, and good deeds, including the series "Ragged Dick" from 1867 and "Tattered Tom" from 1871.

Algeria Democratic and Popular Republic of (*al-Jumhuriya al-Jazairiya ad-Dimuqratiya ash-Shabiya*) *area* 919,352 sq mi/2,381,741 sq km *capital* Algiers (al-Jazair) *towns and cities* Constantine (Qacentina); ports are Oran (Ouahran), Annaba (Bône) *physical* coastal plains backed by mountains in N; Sahara desert in S *features* Atlas mountains, Barbary Coast, Chott Melrhir depression, Hoggar mountains *head of state* Liamine Zeroual from 1994 *head of government* Mokdad Sifi from 1994 *political system* military rule *political parties* National Liberation Front (FLN), nationalist socialist; Socialist Forces Front (FSS), Berber-based; Islamic Front for Salvation (FIS), Islamic fundamentalist (banned from 1992) *exports* oil, natural gas, iron, wine, olive oil *currency* dinar *population* (1993) 26,600,000 (83% Arab, 17% Berber); growth rate 3.0% p.a. *life expectancy* men 59, women 62 *languages* Arabic (official); Berber, French *media* journalists have been attacked and killed by Muslim fundamentalist guerrillas *religion* Sunni Muslim (state religion) *literacy* men 70%, women 45% *GNP* $2,090 per head (1991) *chronology* **1954** War for independence from France led by the FLN. **1962** Independence achieved from France. Republic declared. Ahmed Ben Bella elected prime minister. **1963** Ben Bella elected Algeria's first president. **1965** Ben Bella deposed by military, led by Colonel Houari Boumédienne. **1976** New constitution approved. **1978** Death of Boumédienne. **1979** Benjedid Chadli elected president. Ben Bella released from house arrest. FLN adopted new party structure. **1981** Algeria helped secure release of US prisoners in Iran. **1983** Chadli reelected. **1988** Riots in protest at government policies; 170 killed. Reform program introduced. Diplomatic relations with Egypt restored. **1989** Constitutional changes proposed, leading to limited political pluralism. **1990** Fundamentalist Islamic Front for Salvation (FIS) won Algerian municipal and provincial elections. **1991** Dec: FIS won first round of multiparty elections. **1992** Jan: Chadli resigned; military took control of government; Mohammed Boudiaf became president; FIS leaders detained. Feb: state of emergency declared. March: FIS ordered to disband. June: Boudiaf assassinated; Ali Kafi replaced him. **1993** Worsening civil strife; assassinations of politicians and other public figures; foreigners murdered. Government human-rights abuses reported. **1994** Jan: General Liamine Zeroual replaced Kafi as president. Fundamentalists stepped up campaign of violence. April: military regime began talks with fundamentalists. Sept: FIS leaders removed from prison and placed under house arrest. Oct: talks collapsed. **1995** Feb: Security forces quashed a revolt by militant Fundamentalist Muslims in the Serkadji prison. 96 prisoners were killed.

Algiers (Arabic *al-Jazair*; French *Alger*) capital of Algeria, situated on the narrow coastal plain between the Atlas Mountains and the Mediterranean; population (1984) 2,442,300.

ALGOL (acronym for *algorithmic language*) in computing, an early high-level programming language, developed in the 1950s and 1960s for scientific applications. A general-purpose language, ALGOL is best suited to mathematical work and has an algebraic style. Although no longer in common use, it has greatly influenced more recent languages, such as Ada and PASCAL.

algorithm procedure or series of steps that can be used to solve a problem.

In computer science, it describes the logical sequence of operations to be performed by a program. A ◊flow chart is a visual representation of an algorithm.

Ali c.598–660. 4th caliph of Islam. He was born in Mecca, the son of Abu Talib, uncle to the prophet Mohammed, who gave him his daughter Fatima in marriage. On Mohammed's death 632, Ali had a claim to succeed him, but this was not conceded until 656. After a stormy reign, he was assassinated. Around Ali's name the controversy has raged between the Sunni and the Shiites (see ◊Islam), the former denying his right to the caliphate and the latter supporting it.

Ali Mohammed. Adopted name of Cassius Marcellus Clay, Jr, 1942– . US boxer. Olympic light-heavyweight champion 1960, he went on to become world professional heavyweight champion 1964, and was the only man to regain the title twice. He was known for his fast footwork and extrovert nature.

CAREER HIGHLIGHTS
professional fights: 61
wins: 56 (37 knockouts)
draws: 0
defeats: 5
first professional fight: Oct 29, 1960 v. Tuna Hunsaker *(US)*
last professional fight: Dec 11, 1981 v. Trevor Berbick *(Canada)*

Alia Ramiz 1925– . Albanian communist politician, head of state 1982–92. He gradually relaxed the isolationist policies of his predecessor Enver Hoxha and following public unrest introduced political and economic reforms, including free elections 1991, when he was elected executive president. In 1994 Alia was convicted of abuse of power while in office and sentenced to nine years' imprisonment.

aliasing effect seen on computer screen or printer output, when smooth curves appear to made up of steps because the resolution is not high enough. ◊Antialiasing is a software technique that reduces this effect by using intermediate shades of color to create an apparently smoother curve.

alibi in law, a provable assertion that the accused was at some other place when a crime was committed.

alienation sense of isolation, powerlessness, and therefore frustration; a feeling of loss of control over one's life; a sense of estrangement from society or even from oneself. As a concept it was developed by the German philosophers ◊Hegel and ◊Marx; the latter used it as a description and criticism of the condition that developed among workers in capitalist society.

alimentary canal in animals, the tube through which food passes; it extends from the mouth to the anus. It is a complex organ, adapted for digestion. In human adults, it is about 30 ft/9 m long, consisting of the mouth cavity, pharynx, esophagus, stomach, and the small and large intestines.

aliphatic compound any organic chemical compound in which the carbon atoms are joined in straight chains, as in hexane (C_6H_{14}), or in branched chains, as in 2-methylpentane ($CH_3CH(CH_3)CH_2CH_2CH_3$).

alkali in chemistry, a compound classed as a ◊base that is soluble in water. Alkalis neutralize acids and are soapy to the touch.

The hydroxides of metals are alkalis: those of sodium (sodium hydroxide, NaOH) and of potassium (potassium hydroxide, KOH) being chemically powerful; both were derived from the ashes of plants.

alkali metal any of a group of six metallic elements with similar chemical bonding properties: lithium, sodium, potassium, rubidium, cesium, and francium. They form a linked group in the ◊periodic table of the elements. They are univalent (have a valence of one) and of very low density (lithium, sodium, and potassium float on water); in general they are reactive, soft, low-melting-point metals. Because of their reactivity they are only found as compounds in nature.

alkaline-earth metal any of a group of six metallic elements with similar bonding properties: beryllium, magnesium, calcium, strontium, barium, and radium. They form a linked group in the ◊periodic table of the elements. They are strongly basic, bivalent (have a valence of two), and occur in nature only in compounds.

alkaloid any of a number of physiologically active and frequently poisonous substances contained in some plants. They are usually organic bases and contain nitrogen. They form salts with acids and, when soluble, give alkaline solutions.

alkane member of a group of ◊hydrocarbons having the general formula C_nH_{2n+2}, commonly known as *paraffins*. Lighter alkanes, such as methane, ethane, propane, and butane, are colorless gases; heavier ones are liquids or solids. In nature they are found in natural gas and petroleum. As alkanes contain only single ◊covalent bonds, they are said to be saturated.

alkene member of the group of ◊hydrocarbons having the general formula C_nH_{2n}, formerly known as *olefins*. Lighter alkenes, such as ethene and propene, are gases, obtained from the cracking of oil fractions. Alkenes are unsaturated compounds, characterized by one or more double bonds between adjacent carbon atoms. They react by addition, and many useful compounds, such as poly(ethene) and bromoethane, are made from them.

alkyne member of the group of ◊hydrocarbons with the general formula C_nH_{2n-2}, formerly known as the *acetylenes*. They are unsaturated compounds, characterized by one or more triple bonds between adjacent carbon atoms. Lighter alkynes, such as ethyne, are gases; heavier ones are liquids or solids.

Allah Islamic name for God.

Allegheny Mountains range over 500 mi/800 km long extending from Pennsylvania to Virginia, rising to more than 4,900 ft/1,500 m and averaging 2,500 ft/ 750 m. The mountains are a major source of timber, coal, iron, and limestone. They initially hindered western migration, the first settlement to the west being Marietta 1788.

allele one of two or more alternative forms of a ◊gene at a given position (locus) on a chromosome, caused by a difference in the ◊DNA. Blue and brown eyes in humans are determined by different alleles of the gene for eye color.

Allen Woody. Adopted name of Allen Stewart Konigsberg 1935– . US film writer, director, and actor. He is known for his cynical, witty, often self-deprecating parody and offbeat humor. His film *Annie Hall* 1977 won him three Academy Awards.

His film career began with *What's New Pussycat?* 1965, which he wrote and in which he acted. Other films include *Take the Money and Run* 1969, *Bananas* 1971, *Play It Again, Sam* 1972, *Sleeper* 1973, *Love and Death* 1975, *Manhattan* 1979, *Midsummer Night's Sex Comedy* 1982, *Zelig* 1983, *Broadway Danny Rose* 1984, *Hannah and Her Sisters* 1986, *Radio Days* 1987, and *Husbands and Wives* 1992. His play *Don't Drink the Water* appeared on Broadway 1966. Allegations of child molestation and court battles followed his 1992 break with longtime companion Mia Farrow.

Allende Gossens Salvador 1908–1973. Chilean Marxist politician, president from 1970 until his death during a military coup in 1973.

allergy special sensitivity of the body that makes it react with an exaggerated response of the natural immune defense mechanism to the introduction of an otherwise harmless foreign substance (*allergen*).

Hay fever in summer is caused by an allergy to one or more kinds of pollen. Many asthmatics are allergic to certain kinds of dust or to microorganisms in animal fur or feathers. There are many different kinds of allergies, producing a range of effects. Some people experience skin reactions, such as dermatitis, from drugs, cosmetics or household cleaners; some suffer gastric upsets due to allergens in food. A severe allergic reaction may produce profound shock. Various drugs can be used to counteract allergic symptoms, including antihistamines and steroids.

Allies, the in World War I, the 23 countries allied against the Central Powers (Germany, Austria-Hungary, Turkey, and Bulgaria), including the US, the UK, France, Italy, Russia, and Australia and other Commonwealth nations; and in World War II, the 49 countries allied against the ◊Axis Powers (Germany, Italy, and Japan), including the US, the UK, the USSR, France, and Australia and other Commonwealth nations.

alligator reptile of the genus *Alligator*, related to the crocodile. There are two species: *A. mississipiensis*, the Mississippi alligator of the southern states of the US, and *A. sinensis* from the swamps of the lower Chang Jiang River in China. The former grows to about 12 ft/4 m, but the latter only to 5 ft/1.5 m. Alligators lay their eggs in sand; they swim well with lashing movements of the tail; they feed on fish and mammals but seldom attack people.

allopathy In ◊homeopathy a term used for orthodox medicine, using therapies designed to counteract the manifestations of the disease. In strict usage, allopathy is the opposite of homeopathy.

allotropy property whereby an element can exist in two or more forms (allotropes), each possessing different physical properties but the same state of matter (gas, liquid, or solid). The allotropes of carbon are diamond and graphite. Sulfur has several different forms (flowers of sulfur, plastic, rhombic, and monoclinic). These solids have different crystal structures, as do the white and gray forms of tin and the black, red, and white forms of phosphorus.

alloy metal blended with some other metallic or nonmetallic substance to give it special qualities, such as resistance to corrosion, greater hardness, or tensile strength. Useful alloys include bronze, brass, cupronickel, duralumin, German silver, gunmetal, pewter, solder, steel, and stainless steel.

alluvial deposit layer of broken rocky matter, or sediment, formed from material that has been carried in suspension by a river or stream and dropped as the velocity of the current changes. River plains and deltas are made entirely of alluvial deposits, but smaller pockets can be found in the beds of upland torrents.

Alma-Ata formerly (until 1921) *Vernyi* capital of Kazakhstan; population (1991) 1,151,300. Industries include engineering, printing, tobacco processing, textile manufacturing, and leather products.

Almohad Berber dynasty 1130–1269 founded by the Berber prophet Mohammed ibn Tumart (*c.*1080–1130). The Almohads ruled much of Morocco and Spain, which they took by defeating the ◊Almoravids; they later took the area that today forms Algeria and Tunis. Their policy of religious "purity" involved the forced conversion and massacre of the Jewish population of Spain. The Almohads were themselves defeated by the Christian kings of Spain 1212, and in Morocco 1269.

almond tree *Prunus amygdalus*, family Rosaceae, related to the peach and apricot. Dessert almonds are the kernels of the fruit of the sweet variety *P. amygdalus dulcis*, which is also the source of a low-cholesterol culinary oil. Oil of bitter almonds, from the variety *P. amygdalus amara*, is used in flavoring. Almond oil is also used for cosmetics, perfumes, and fine lubricants.

Almoravid Berber dynasty 1056–1147 founded by the prophet Abdullah ibn Tashfin, ruling much of Morocco and Spain in the 11th–12th centuries. The Almoravids came from the Sahara and in the 11th century began laying the foundations of an empire covering the whole of Morocco and parts of Algeria; their capital was the newly founded Marrakesh. In 1086 they defeated Alfonso VI of Castile to gain much of Spain. They were later overthrown by the ◊Almohads.

aloe plant of the genus *Aloe* of African plants, family Liliaceae, distinguished by their long, fleshy, spiny-edged leaves. The drug usually referred to as "bitter aloes" is a powerful cathartic prepared from the juice of the leaves of several of the species.

alpaca domesticated South American hoofed mammal *Lama pacos* of the camel family, found in Chile, Peru, and Bolivia, and herded at high elevations in the Andes. It is bred mainly for its long, fine, silky wool, and stands about 3 ft/1 m tall at the shoulder with neck and head another 2 ft/60 cm.

alpha in computing, a 64-bit RISC chip launched 1993 by Digital Equipment (DEC). It was seen as a rival to Intel's Pentium chip.

alphabet set of conventional symbols used for writing, based on a correlation between individual symbols and spoken sounds, so called from *alpha* (å) and *beta* (ƒ), the names of the first two letters of the classical Greek alphabet. The earliest known alphabet is from Palestine, about 1700 BC. Alphabetic writing now takes many forms—for example, the Hebrew *aleph-beth* and the Arabic script, both written from right to left; the Devanagari script of the Hindus, in which the symbols "hang" from a line common to all the symbols; and the Greek alphabet, with the first clearly delineated vowel symbols.

Alpha Centauri or *Rigil Kent* brightest star in the constellation Centaurus and the third brightest star in the sky. It is actually a triple star (see ◊binary star); the two brighter stars orbit each other every 80 years, and the third, Proxima Centauri, is the closest star to the Sun, 4.2 light-years away, 0.1 light-years closer than the other two.

alpha decay the spontaneous alteration of the nucleus of a radioactive atom, which transmutes the atom from one atomic number to another through the emission of a helium nucleus (known as an alpha particle).

As a result, the atomic number decreases by two and the atomic weight decreases by four.

alphanumeric data data made up of any of the letters of the alphabet and any digit from 0 to 9. The classification of data according to the type or types of character contained enables computer ◊validation systems to check the accuracy of data: a computer can be programmed to reject entries that contain the wrong type of character. For example, a person's name would be rejected if it contained any numeric data, and a bank-account number would be rejected if it contained any alphabetic data. An automobile's registration number, by comparison, would be expected to contain alphanumeric data but no punctuation marks.

alpha particle positively charged, high-energy particle emitted from the nucleus of a radioactive atom. It is one of the products of the spontaneous disintegration of radioactive elements (see ◊radioactivity) such as radium and thorium, and is identical with the nucleus of a helium atom—that is, it consists of two protons and two neutrons. The process of emission, *alpha decay*, transforms one element into another, decreasing the atomic (or proton) number by two and the atomic mass (or nucleon number) by four.

Alps mountain chain, the barrier between N Italy and France, Germany and Austria.

Peaks include *Mont Blanc*, the highest, 15,777 ft/ 4,809 m, first climbed by Jacques Balmat and Michel Paccard 1786; *Matterhorn* in the Pennine Alps, 14,694 ft/4,479 m, first climbed by Edward Whymper 1865 (four of the party of seven were killed when a rope broke during their descent); *Eiger* in the Bernese Alps/Oberland, 13,030 ft/3,970 m, with a near-vertical rock wall on the north face, first climbed 1858; *Jungfrau*, 13,673 ft/4,166 m; and *Finsteraarhorn* 14,027 ft/4,275 m.

Passes include *Brenner*, the lowest, Austria/Italy; *Great St Bernard*, one of the highest, 8,113 ft/2,472 m, Italy/Switzerland (by which Napoleon marched into Italy 1800); *Little St Bernard*, Italy/France (which Hannibal is thought to have used); and *St Gotthard*, S Switzerland, which Suvorov used when ordered by the czar to withdraw his troops from Italy. All have been superseded by all-weather road/rail tunnels. The Alps extend down the Adriatic coast into Slovenia, Croatia, Bosnia-Herzegovina, Yugoslavia, and N Albania with the Julian and Dinaric Alps.

Alsace region of France; area 3,204 sq mi/8,300 sq km; population (1986) 1,600,000. It consists of the *départements* of Bas-Rhin and Haut-Rhin, and its capital is Strasbourg.

Alsace-Lorraine area of NE France, lying west of the river Rhine. It forms the French regions of ◊Alsace and ◊Lorraine. The former iron and steel industries are being replaced by electronics, chemicals, and precision engineering. The German dialect spoken does not have equal rights with French, and there is autonomist sentiment.

alternating current (AC) electric current that flows for an interval of time in one direction and then in the opposite direction, that is, a current that flows in alternately reversed directions through or around a circuit. Electric energy is usually generated as alternating current in a power station, and alternating currents may be used for both power and lighting.

alternation of generations typical life cycle of terrestrial plants and some seaweeds, in which there are two distinct forms occurring alternately: *diploid* (having two sets of chromosomes) and *haploid* (one set of chromosomes). The diploid generation produces haploid spores by meiosis, and is called the sporophyte, while the haploid generation produces gametes (sex cells), and is called the gametophyte. The gametes fuse to form a diploid zygote which develops into a new sporophyte; thus the sporophyte and gametophyte alternate.

alternative energy energy from sources that are renewable and ecologically safe, as opposed to sources that are nonrenewable with toxic byproducts, such as coal, oil, or gas (fossil fuels), and uranium (for nuclear power). The most important alternative energy source is flowing water, harnessed as ◊hydroelectric power. Other sources include the oceans' tides and waves (see tidal power station and ◊wave power), wind (harnessed by windmills and wind turbines), the Sun (◊solar energy), and the heat trapped in the Earth's crust (◊geothermal energy).

alternative medicine see ◊medicine, alternative.

alternator electricity generator that produces an alternating current.

altimeter instrument used in aircraft that measures altitude, or height above sea level. The common type is a form of aneroid ◊barometer, which works by sensing the differences in air pressure at different altitudes. This must continually be recalibrated because of the change in air pressure with changing weather conditions. The ◊radar altimeter measures the height of the aircraft above the ground, measuring the time it takes for radio pulses emitted by the aircraft to be reflected. Radar altimeters are essential features of automatic and blind-landing systems.

Altiplano densely populated upland plateau of the Andes of South America, stretching from S Peru to NW Argentina. The height of the Altiplano is 10,000–13,000 ft/ 3,000–4,000 m.

alto voice or instrument between tenor and soprano. The traditional male alto voice of early opera, also known as *countertenor*, is trumpetlike and penetrating; the low-register female *contralto* ("contra-alto"), exemplified by English singer Kathleen Ferrier, is rich and mellow in tone. Alto is also the French name for the ◊viola.

altruism in biology, helping another individual of the same species to reproduce more effectively, as a direct result of which the altruist may leave fewer offspring itself. Female honey bees (workers) behave altruistically by rearing sisters in order to help their mother, the queen bee, reproduce, and forgo any possibility of reproducing themselves.

ALU abbreviation for ◊*arithmetic and logic unit*.

aluminum lightweight, silver-white, ductile and malleable, metallic element, symbol Al, atomic number 13, atomic weight 26.9815. It is the third most abundant element (and the most abundant metal) in the Earth's crust, of which it makes up about 8.1% by mass. It oxidizes rapidly, the layer of oxide on its surface making it highly resistant to tarnish, and is an excellent conductor of electricity. In its pure state aluminum is a weak metal, but when combined with elements such as copper, silicon, or magnesium it forms alloys of great strength. In nature it is found only in the combined state in many minerals, and is prepared commercially from the ore bauxite.

aluminum chloride $AlCl_3$ white solid made by direct combination of aluminum and chlorine.

$$2Al + 3Cl_2 \rightarrow 2AlCl_3$$

The anhydrous form is a typical covalent compound (see ◊covalent bond).

aluminum hydroxide or *alumina cream* $Al(OH)_3$ gelatinous precipitate formed when a small amount of alkali solution is added to a solution of an aluminum salt.

$$Al^{3+}_{(aq)} + 3OH^-_{(aq)} \rightarrow Al(OH)_{3(s)}$$

It is an amphoteric compound as it readily reacts with both acids and alkalis.

aluminum ore raw material from which aluminum is extracted. The main ore is bauxite, a mixture of minerals, found in economic quantities in Australia, Guinea, West Indies, and several other countries.

aluminum oxide or *alumina* Al_2O_3 white solid formed by heating aluminum hydroxide. It is an amphoteric oxide, since it reacts readily with both acids and alkalis, and it is used as a refractory (furnace lining) and in column ◊chromatography.

Alzheimer's disease common manifestation of ◊dementia, thought to afflict one in 20 people over 65. After heart disease, cancer, and strokes it is the most common cause of death in the Western world. Attacking the brain's "gray matter", it is a disease of mental processes rather than physical function, characterized by memory loss and progressive intellectual impairment.

AM in physics, abbreviation for *amplitude modulation*, one way in which radio waves are altered for the transmission of broadcasting signals. AM is constant in frequency, and varies the amplitude of the transmitting wave in accordance with the signal being broadcast.

Amal radical Lebanese ◊Shiite military force, established by Musa Sadr in the 1970s; its headquarters are in Borj al-Barajneh. The movement split into extremist and moderate groups 1982, but both sides agreed on the aim of increasing Shiite political representation in Lebanon.

amalgam any alloy of mercury with other metals. Most metals will form amalgams, except iron and platinum. Amalgam is used in dentistry for filling teeth, and usually contains copper, silver, and zinc as the main alloying ingredients. This amalgam is pliable when first mixed and then sets hard, but the mercury leaches out and may cause a type of heavy-metal poisoning.

Amanita genus of fungi (see ◊fungus), distinguished by a ring, or volva, round the stem, warty patches on the cap, and the clear white color of the gills. Many of the species are brightly colored and highly poisonous.

The fly agaric *A. muscaria* is a dangerous, poisonous toadstool with a white-spotted red cap, which grows under birch or pine. The buff-colored ◊death cap *A. phalloides* is deadly.

Amazon South American river, the world's second longest, 4,080 mi/6,570 km, and the largest in volume of water. Its main headstreams, the Marañón and the Ucayali, rise in central Peru and unite to flow E across Brazil for about 2,500 mi/4,000 km. It has 30,000 mi/48,280 km of navigable waterways, draining 2,750,000 sq mi/7,000,000 sq km, nearly half the South American landmass. It reaches the Atlantic on the equator, its estuary 50 mi/80 km wide, discharging a volume of water so immense that 40 mi/64 km out to sea, fresh water remains at the surface. The Amazon basin covers 3 million sq mi/7.5 million sq km, of which 2 million sq mi/5 million sq km is tropical forest containing 30% of all known plant and animal species (80,000 known species of trees, 3,000 known species of land vertebrates, 2,000 freshwater fish). It is the wettest region on Earth; average rainfall 8.3 ft/2.54 m a year.

Amazon in Greek mythology, a member of a group of female warriors living near the Black Sea, who cut off their right breasts to use the bow more easily. Their queen, Penthesilea, was killed by Achilles at the siege of Troy. The term Amazon has come to mean a large, strong woman.

Amazonia those regions of Brazil, Colombia, Ecuador, Peru, and Bolivia lying within the basin of the Amazon River.

amber fossilized resin from coniferous trees of the Middle Tertiary period. It is often washed ashore on the Baltic coast with plant and animal specimens preserved in it; many extinct species have been found preserved in this way. It ranges in color from red to yellow, and is used to make jewelry.

ameba any of a number of one-celled organisms, especially of the genus *Ameba*, that move and feed by extensions of their colorless gelatinous protoplasm. They reproduce by ◊binary fission. Some members of the genus *Entamoeba* are harmful parasites. See also ◊amebiasis.

amebiasis ongoing infection of the intestines, caused by the ameba *Entamoeba histolytica*, resulting in chronic dysentery and consequent weakness and dehydration. Endemic in the Third World, it is now occurring in North America and Europe.

Amenhotep III *c*.1400 BC King (pharaoh) of ancient Egypt who built great monuments at Thebes, including the temples at Luxor. Two portrait statues at his tomb were known to the Greeks as the colossi of Memnon; one was cracked, and when the temperature changed at dawn it gave out an eerie sound, then thought supernatural. His son *Amenhotep IV* changed his name to ◊Ikhnaton.

America western hemisphere of the Earth, containing the continents of ◊North America and ◊South America, with ◊Central America in between. This great landmass extends from the Arctic to the Antarctic, from beyond 75° N to past 55° S. The area is about 16 million sq mi/42 million sq km, and the estimated population is over 500 million. Politically, it consists of 36 nations and US, British, French, and Dutch dependencies.

American Expeditionary Force (AEF) US forces sent to fight in Europe after the US entered World War I April 1917. Although initially only a token force of one division went to France under General Pershing, by Nov 1918 the AEF comprised three armies each of three corps, a total of 1,338,000 combat troops.

American Indians: major tribes

area	tribe
North America	
Arctic	Inuit, Aleut
subarctic	Algonquin, Cree, Ottawa
NE woodlands	Huron, Iroquois, Mohican, Shawnee
SE woodlands	Cherokee, Choctaw, Creek, Hopewell, Natchez, Seminole
Great Plains	Blackfoot, Cheyenne, Comanche, Pawnee, Sioux
NW coast	Chinook, Tlingit, Tsimshian
Desert West	Apache, Navaho, Pueblo, Hopi, Mohave, Shoshone
Central America	Maya, Aztec, Olmec
South America	
eastern	Carib, Xingu
central	Guaraní, Miskito
western	Araucanian, Aymara, Chimú, Inca, Jivaro, Quechua

American Indian any of the aboriginal peoples of the Americas; the Arctic peoples (Inuit and Aleut) are often included, especially by the Bureau of Indian Affairs (BIA) of the Department of the Interior, responsible for overseeing policy on US Indian life, their reservations, education, and social welfare.

American Legion community organization in the US, originally for ex-servicemen of World War I, founded 1919. It has approximately 2.7 million members, and has admitted veterans of World War II, the Korean War, and the Vietnam War.

It was organized in Paris in 1919 at a meeting of representatives of all the divisions then in France and by the end of the year over a million members had enrolled, with no distinction made between officers and enlisted men. The organization has a strong national voice on issues concerning US veterans, and sponsors local welfare programs and essay contests.

American National Standards Institute (ANSI) US national standards body. It sets official procedures in (among other areas) computing and electronics. The ANSI ◊character set is the standard set of characters used by Windows-based computers.

American Revolution revolt 1775–83 of the British North American colonies that resulted in the establishment of the United States of America.

It was caused by colonial opposition to British economic exploitation and by the unwillingness of the colonists to pay for a standing army. It was also fueled by the colonists' antimonarchist sentiment and a desire to participate in the policies affecting them.

American Samoa see ◊Samoa, American.

americium radioactive metallic element of the ◊actinide series, symbol Am, atomic number 95, relative atomic mass 243.13; it was first synthesized 1944. It occurs in nature in minute quantities in ◊pitchblende and other uranium ores, where it is produced from the decay of neutron-bombarded plutonium, and is the element with the highest atomic number that occurs in nature. It is synthesized in quantity only in nuclear reactors by the bombardment of plutonium with neutrons. Its longest-lived isotope is Am-243, with a half-life of 7,650 years.

American Revolution: chronology

1773	A government tax on tea led Massachusetts citizens disguised as North American Indians to board British ships carrying tea and throw it into Boston harbor, the Boston Tea Party.
1774–75	The First Continental Congress was held in Philadelphia to call for civil disobedience in reply to British measures such as the Intolerable Acts, which closed the port of Boston and quartered British troops in private homes.
1775 April 19	Hostilities began at Lexington and Concord, Massachusetts. The first shots were fired when British troops, sent to seize illegal military stores and arrest rebel leaders John Hancock and Samuel Adams, were attacked by the local militia (minutemen).
May 10	Fort Ticonderoga, New York, was captured from the British.
June 17	The colonists were defeated in the first battle of the Revolution, the Battle of Bunker Hill (which actually took place on Breed's Hill, nearby); George Washington was appointed colonial commander in chief soon afterwards.
1776 July 4	The Second Continental Congress issued the Declaration of Independence, which specified some of the colonists' grievances and proclaimed an independent government.
Aug 27	Washington was defeated at Long Island and was forced to evacuate New York and retire to Pennsylvania.
Dec 26	Washington recrossed the Delaware River and defeated the British at Trenton, New Jersey.
1777 Jan 3	Washington defeated the British at Princeton, New Jersey.
Sept 11–Oct 4	British general William Howe defeated Washington at Brandywine and Germantown and occupied Philadelphia.
Oct 17	British general John Burgoyne surrendered at Saratoga, New York, and was therefore unable to link up with Howe.
1777–78	Washington wintered at Valley Forge, Pennsylvania, enduring harsh conditions and seeing many of his troops leave to return to their families.
1778	France, with the support of its ally Spain, entered the war on the US side (John Paul Jones led a French-sponsored naval unit).
1780 May 12	The British captured Charleston, South Carolina, one of a series of British victories in the South, but alienated support by enforcing conscription.
1781 Oct 19	British general Charles Cornwallis, besieged in Yorktown, Virginia, by Washington and the French fleet, surrendered.
1782	Peace negotiations opened.
1783 Sept 3	The Treaty of Paris recognized American independence.

amethyst variety of ◊quartz, SiO$_2$, colored violet by the presence of small quantities of impurities such as manganese or iron; used as a semiprecious stone. Amethysts are found chiefly in the Ural Mountains, India, the US, Uruguay, and Brazil.

amide any organic chemical derived from a fatty acid by the replacement of the hydroxyl group (–OH) by an amino group (–NH$_2$).

One of the simplest amides is acetamide (CH$_3$CONH$_2$), which has a strong mousy odor.

Amiga microcomputer produced by US company Commodore 1985 to succeed the Commodore C64 home computer. The original Amiga was based on the Motorola 68000 microprocessor and achieved significant success in the domestic market.

Amin (Dada) Idi 1926– . Ugandan politician, president 1971–79. He led the coup that deposed Milton Obote 1971, expelled the Asian community 1972, and exercised a reign of terror over his people. He fled to Libya when insurgent Ugandan and Tanzanian troops invaded the country 1979.

amine any of a class of organic chemical compounds in which one or more of the hydrogen atoms of ammonia (NH$_3$) have been replaced by other groups of atoms.

amino acid water-soluble organic ◊molecule, mainly composed of carbon, oxygen, hydrogen, and nitrogen, containing both a basic amino group (NH$_2$) and an acidic carboxyl (COOH) group. When two or more amino acids are joined together, they are known as ◊peptides; proteins are made up of interacting polypeptides (peptide chains consisting of more than three amino acids) and are folded or twisted in characteristic shapes.

Amis Kingsley 1922– . English novelist and poet. He was associated early on with the Angry Young Men group of writers. His sharply ironic works frequently debunk pretentious mediocrity; his first novel, the best-selling *Lucky Jim* 1954, is a comic portrayal of life in a provincial university. His later novels include *The Alteration* 1976, which imagines a 20th-century society dominated by the Catholic Church. He is the father of writer Martin Amis.

Amman capital and chief industrial center of Jordan; population (1986) 1,160,000. It is a major communications center, linking historic trade routes across the Middle East.

ammeter instrument that measures electric current, usually in ◊amperes.

Ammon in Egyptian mythology, the king of the gods, the equivalent of Zeus (Roman Jupiter). The name is also spelled Amen/Amun, as in the name of the pharaoh Tutankh*amen*. In art, he is represented as a ram, as a man with a ram's head, or as a man crowned with feathers. He had temples at Siwa oasis, Libya, and at Thebes, Egypt; his oracle at Siwa was patronized by the classical Greeks.

ammonia NH$_3$ colorless pungent-smelling gas, lighter than air and very soluble in water. It is made on an industrial scale by the ◊Haber process, and used mainly to produce nitrogenous fertilizers, some explosives, and nitric acid.

ammonite extinct marine ◊cephalopod mollusk of the order Ammonoidea, related to the modern nautilus. The shell was curled in a plane spiral and made up of numerous gas-filled chambers, the outermost containing the body of the animal. Many species flourished between 200 million and 65 million years ago, ranging in size from that of a small coin to 6 ft/2 m across.

amnesia loss or impairment of memory. As a clinical condition it may be caused by disease or injury to the brain, by some drugs, or by shock; in some cases it may be a symptom of an emotional disorder.

amnesty release of political prisoners under a general pardon, or a person or group of people from criminal liability for a particular action.

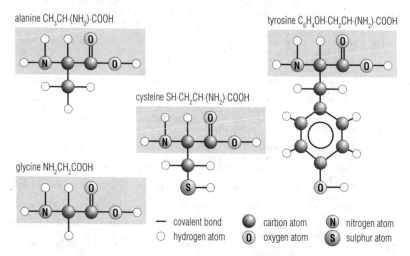

alanine CH$_3$CH·(NH$_2$)·COOH

tyrosine C$_6$H$_4$OH·CH$_2$CH·(NH$_2$)·COOH

cysteine SH·CH$_2$CH·(NH$_2$)·COOH

glycine NH$_2$CH$_2$COOH

— covalent bond
○ hydrogen atom
● carbon atom
Ⓞ oxygen atom
Ⓝ nitrogen atom
Ⓢ sulphur atom

amino acid Amino acids are natural organic compounds that make up proteins and can thus be considered the basic molecules of life. There are 20 different amino acids. They consist mainly of carbon, oxygen, hydrogen, and nitrogen. Each amino acid has a common core structure (consisting of two carbon atoms, two oxygen atoms, a nitrogen atom, and four hydrogen atoms) to which is attached a variable group, known as the R group. In glycine, the R group is a single hydrogen atom; in alanine, the R group consists of a carbon and three hydrogen atoms.

Amnesty International human-rights organization established in the UK 1961 to campaign for the release of prisoners of conscience worldwide; fair trials for all political prisoners; an end to the death penalty, torture, and other inhuman treatment of all prisoners; and the cessation of extrajudicial executions and "disappearances". It is politically and economically unaligned. Amnesty International has 1.1 million members, and section offices in 43 countries. The organization was awarded the Nobel Prize for Peace 1977.

amniocentesis sampling the amniotic fluid surrounding a fetus in the womb for diagnostic purposes. It is used to detect Down's syndrome and other genetic abnormalities.

ampere SI unit (abbreviation amp, symbol A) of electrical current. Electrical current is measured in a similar way to water current, in terms of an amount per unit time; one ampere represents a flow of about 6.28×10^{18} ◊electrons per second, or a rate of flow of charge of one coulomb per second.

amphetamine or *speed* powerful synthetic ◊stimulant. Benzedrine was the earliest amphetamine marketed, used as a "pep pill" in World War II to help soldiers overcome fatigue, and until the 1970s amphetamines were prescribed by doctors as an appetite suppressant for weight loss; as an antidepressant, to induce euphoria; and as a stimulant, to increase alertness.

Indications for its use today are very restricted because of severe side effects, including addiction. It is a sulfate or phosphate form of $C_9H_{13}N$.

amphibian member of the vertebrate class Amphibia, which generally spend their larval (tadpole) stage in fresh water, transferring to land at maturity (after ◊metamorphosis) and generally returning to water to breed. Like fish and reptiles, they continue to grow throughout life, and cannot maintain a temperature greatly differing from that of their environment. The class includes caecilians (wormlike in appearance), salamanders, frogs, and toads.

amplifier electronic device that magnifies the strength of a signal, such as a radio signal. The ratio of output signal strength to input signal strength is called the *gain* of the amplifier. As well as achieving high gain, an amplifier should be free from distortion and able to operate over a range of frequencies. Practical amplifiers are usually complex circuits, although simple amplifiers can be built from single transistors or valves.

amplitude maximum displacement of an oscillation from the equilibrium position. For a wave motion, it is the height of a crest (or the depth of a trough). With a sound wave, for example, amplitude corresponds to the intensity (loudness) of the sound. In AM (amplitude modulation) radio broadcasting, the required audio-frequency signal is made to modulate (vary slightly) the amplitude of a continuously transmitted radio carrier wave.

Amritsar industrial city in the Punjab, India; population (1981) 595,000. It is the holy city of ◊Sikhism, with the Guru Nanak University (named for the first Sikh guru) and the Golden Temple, from which armed demonstrators were evicted by the Indian army under General Dayal 1984, 325 being killed. Subsequently, Indian prime minister Indira Gandhi was assassinated in reprisal. In 1919 the city was the scene of the Amritsar Massacre.

Amsterdam capital of the Netherlands; population (1990) 695,100. Canals cut through the city link it with the North Sea and the Rhine, and as a Dutch port it is second only to Rotterdam. There is shipbuilding, printing, food processing, banking, and insurance.

Amu Darya formerly *Oxus* river in central Asia, flowing 1,578 mi/2,530 km from the ◊Pamirs to the ◊Aral Sea.

Amundsen Roald 1872–1928. Norwegian explorer who in 1903–06 became the first person to navigate the ◊Northwest Passage. Beaten to the North Pole by US explorer Robert Peary 1910, he reached the South Pole ahead of Captain Scott 1911.

Amur river in E Asia. Formed by the Argun and Shilka rivers, the Amur enters the Sea of Okhotsk. At its mouth at Nikolevsk it is 10 mi/16 km wide. For much of its course of over 2,730 mi/4,400 km it forms, together with its tributary, the Ussuri, the boundary between Russia and China.

amylase one of a group of ◊enzymes that break down starches into their component molecules (sugars) for use in the body. It occurs widely in both plants and animals. In humans, it is found in saliva and in pancreatic juices.

Anabaptist member of any of various 16th-century radical Protestant sects. They believed in adult rather than child baptism, and sought to establish utopian communities. Anabaptist groups spread rapidly in N Europe, particularly in Germany, and were widely persecuted.

anabolic steroid any ◊hormone of the ◊steroid group that stimulates tissue growth. Its use in medicine is limited to the treatment of some anemias and breast cancers; it may help to break up blood clots. Side effects include aggressive behavior, masculinization in women, and, in children, reduced height.

It is used in sports, such as weight lifting and track and field, to increase muscle bulk for greater strength and stamina but it is widely condemned because of dangerous side effects. In 1988 the Canadian sprinter Ben Johnson was stripped of an Olympic gold medal for having taken anabolic steroids.

anaconda South American snake *Eunectes murinus*, a member of the python and boa family, the Boidae. One of the largest snakes, growing to 30 ft/9 m or more, it is found in and near water, where it lies in wait for the birds and animals on which it feeds. The anaconda is not venomous, but kills its prey by coiling round it and squeezing until the creature suffocates.

anaerobic (of living organisms) not requiring oxygen for the release of energy from food molecules such as glucose. Anaerobic organisms include many bacteria, yeasts, and internal parasites.

In some bacteria, instead of oxygen, an inorganic compound, such as sulfate (SO_4), is the final acceptor of electrons stripped from food molecules during their breakdown.

In ◊fermentation (as practiced by yeasts) the final acceptor is an intermediate product of the glucose molecule being degraded.

analgesic agent for relieving pain. Opiates alter the perception or appreciation of pain and are effective in controlling "deep" visceral (internal) pain. Non-opiates, such as ◊aspirin, ◊paracetamol, and NSAIDs (nonsteroidal anti-inflammatory drugs), relieve musculoskeletal pain and reduce inflammation in soft tissues.

analog (of a quantity or device) changing continuously; by contrast a ◊digital quantity or device varies in series of distinct steps. For example, an analog clock measures time by means of a continuous movement of hands around a dial, whereas a digital clock measures time with a numerical display that changes in a series of discrete steps.

analog computer computer designed to receive and process continuously varying (analog) data. Analogue

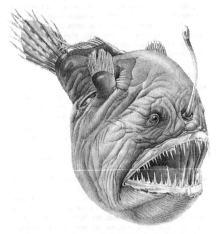

angler Angler fish entice their prey into their large mouths by means of a fishing rod—a modified dorsal ray with a fleshy lure at its tip. The female of this species (5 in/13 cm long) is very much larger than the male 1.75 in/ 4 cm long).

leaves in the embryo). They include the majority of flowers, herbs, grasses, and trees except conifers.

angle in mathematics, the amount of turn or rotation; it may be defined by a pair of rays (half-lines) that share a common endpoint but do not lie on the same line. Angles are measured in ◊degrees (°) or ◊radians (rads)—a complete turn or circle being 360° or 2π rads.

Angles are classified generally by their degree measures: *acute angles* are less than 90°; *right angles* are exactly 90° (a quarter turn); *obtuse angles* are greater than 90° but less than 180°; *reflex angles* are greater than 180° but less than 360°.

angler any of an order of fishes Lophiiformes, with flattened body and broad head and jaws. Many species have small, plantlike tufts on their skin. These act as camouflage for the fish as it waits, either floating among seaweed or lying on the sea bottom, twitching the enlarged tip of the threadlike first ray of its dorsal fin to entice prey.

Anglican Communion family of Christian churches including the Church of England, the US Episcopal Church, and those holding the same essential doctrines, that is the Lambeth Quadrilateral 1888 Holy Scripture as the basis of all doctrine, the Nicene and Apostles' Creeds, Holy Baptism and Holy Communion, and the historic episcopate.

angling fishing with rod and line. Competition angling exists and world championships take place for most branches of the sport. The oldest is the World Freshwater Championship, inaugurated 1957.

Anglo-Saxon one of the several Germanic invaders (Angles, Saxons, and Jutes) who conquered much of Britain between the 5th and 7th centuries. After the conquest kingdoms were set up, which are commonly referred to as the *Heptarchy*; these were united in the early 9th century under the overlordship of Wessex. The Norman invasion 1066 brought Anglo-Saxon rule to an end.

The Jutes probably came from the Rhineland and not, as was formerly believed, from Jutland. The Angles and Saxons came from Schleswig–Holstein, and may have united before invading. There was probably considerable intermarriage with the Romanized Celts of ancient Britain, although the latter's language and civilization almost disappeared. The English-speaking peoples of Britain, Canada, Australia, New Zealand, and the US are often referred to today as Anglo-Saxons, but the term is inaccurate, since the Welsh, Scots, and Irish are mainly of Celtic or Norse descent, and by the 1980s fewer than 15% of Americans were of British descent.

Angola People's Republic of (*República Popular de Angola*) *area* 481,226 sq mi/1,246,700 sq km *capital* and chief port Luanda *towns and cities* Lobito and Benguela, also ports; Huambo, Lubango *physical* narrow coastal plain rises to vast interior plateau with rainforest in NW; desert in S *features* Cuanza, Cuito, Cubango, and Cunene rivers; Cabinda enclave *head of state* José Eduardo dos Santos from 1979 *head of government* Marcolino José Carlos Moco from 1992 *political system* socialist republic *political parties* People's Movement for the Liberation of Angola–Workers' Party (MPLA–PT), Marxist-Leninist; National Union for the Total Independence of Angola (UNITA); National Front for the Liberation of Angola (FNLA) *exports* oil, coffee, diamonds, palm oil, sisal, iron ore, fish *currency* kwanza *population* (1993) 10,770,000 (largest ethnic group Ovimbundu); growth rate 2.5% p.a. *life expectancy* men 45, women 48 *languages* Portuguese (official); Bantu dialects *religions* Roman Catholic 68%, Protestant 20%, animist 12% *literacy* men 56%, women 29% *GNP* $620 per head *chronology 1575* Colonized by Portugal. *1926* Modern borders delineated. *1951* Angola became an overseas territory of Portugal. *1956* First independence movement formed, the People's Movement for the Liberation of Angola (MPLA). *1961* Unsuccessful independence rebellion. *1962* Second nationalist movement formed, FNLA. *1966* Third nationalist movement formed, UNITA. *1975* Independence achieved from Portugal. Transitional government formed representing MPLA, FNLA, UNITA, and Portuguese government. MPLA proclaimed People's Republic of Angola under the presidency of Dr Agostinho Neto. FNLA and UNITA proclaimed People's Democratic Republic of Angola. *1976* MPLA

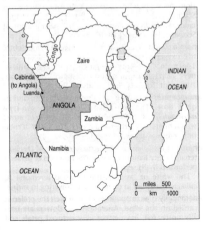

gained control of most of the country. South African troops withdrawn, but Cuban units remained. *1977* MPLA restructured to become MPLA–PT. *1979* Death of Neto, succeeded by José Eduardo dos Santos. *1980* UNITA guerrillas, aided by South Africa, continued raids against the Luanda government and bases of the South West Africa People's Organization (SWAPO) in Angola. *1984* South Africa promised to withdraw its forces if the Luanda government guaranteed that areas vacated would not by filled by Cuban or SWAPO units (the Lusaka Agreement). *1985* South African forces officially withdrawn. *1986* Further South African raids into Angola. UNITA continued to receive South African support. *1988* Peace treaty, providing for the withdrawal of all foreign troops, signed with South Africa and Cuba. *1989* Cease-fire agreed with UNITA broke down and guerrilla activity restarted. *1990* Peace offer by rebels. Return to multiparty politics promised. *1991* Peace agreement signed, civil war between MPLA–PT and UNITA officially ended. Amnesty for all political prisoners. *1992* MPLA–PT's general-election victory fiercely disputed by UNITA, plunging the country into renewed civil war. *1993* Fighting escalated. Dos Santos government recognized by US. United Nations sanctions imposed against UNITA. *1994* Agreement between government and UNITA to ensure fair presidential elections.

angstrom unit (symbol Å) of length equal to 10^{-10} meter or one-ten-millionth of a millimeter, used for atomic measurements and the wavelengths of electromagnetic radiation. It is named for the Swedish scientist A J Ångström.

Anguilla island in the E Caribbean *area* 62 sq mi/160 sq km *capital* The Valley *features* white coral-sand beaches; 80% of its coral reef has been lost through tourism (pollution and souvenir sales) *exports* lobster, salt *currency* Eastern Caribbean dollar *population* (1988) 7,000 *languages* English, Creole *government* from 1982, governor, executive council, and legislative house of assembly *history* a British colony from 1650, Anguilla was long associated with St Christopher–Nevis but revolted against alleged domination by the larger island and in 1969 declared itself a republic. A small British force restored order, and Anguilla retained a special position at its own request; since 1980 it has been a separate dependency of the UK.

Anhui or *Anhwei* province of E China, watered by the Chang Jiang (Yangtze River) *area* 54,000 sq mi/ 139,900 sq km *capital* Hefei *industries* cereals in the N; cotton, rice, tea in the S *population* (1990) 56,181,000.

anhydride chemical compound obtained by the removal of water from another compound; usually a dehydrated acid. For example, sulfur(VI) oxide (sulfur trioxide, SO_3) is the anhydride of sulfuric acid (H_2SO_4).

aniline $C_6H_5NH_2$ or *phenylamine* one of the simplest aromatic chemicals (a substance related to benzene, with its carbon atoms joined in a ring). When pure, it is a colorless oily liquid; it has a characteristic odor, and turns brown on contact with air. It occurs in coal tar, and is used in the rubber industry and to make drugs and dyes. It is highly poisonous.

animal or *metazoan* member of the ◊kingdom Animalia, one of the major categories of living things, the science of which is ◊zoology. Animals are all ◊heterotrophs (they obtain their energy from organic substances produced by other organisms); they have

eukaryotic cells (the genetic material is contained within a distinct nucleus) bounded by a thin cell membrane rather than the thick cell wall of plants. Most animals are capable of moving around for at least part of their life cycle.

animism in psychology and physiology, the view of human personality that attributes human life and behavior to a force distinct from matter.

In religious theory, the conception of a spiritual reality behind the material one: for example, beliefs in the soul as a shadowy duplicate of the body capable of independent activity, both in life and death. In anthropology, the concept of spirits residing in all natural phenomena and objects.

anion ion carrying a negative charge. During electrolysis, anions in the electrolyte move toward the anode (positive electrode).

Ankara (formerly *Angora*) capital of Turkey; population (1990) 2,559,500. Industries include cement, textiles, and leather products. It replaced Istanbul (then in Allied occupation) as capital 1923.

Annamese member of the majority ethnic group in Vietnam, comprising 90% of the population. The Annamese language is distinct from Vietnamese, though it has been influenced by Chinese and has loaned words from Khmer. Their religion combines elements of Buddhism, Confucianism, and Taoism, as well as ancestor worship.

Annapolis seaport and capital of Maryland; population (1984) 31,900. It was named for Princess (later Queen) Anne 1695.

The State House, built 1772–80, is the oldest US state capitol in continuous legislative use. It was in session here Nov 1783–Jun 1784 that ◊Congress received George ◊Washington's resignation as commander in chief 1783 and ratified the peace treaty that ended the Revolutionary War. The US Naval Academy is here, and John Paul Jones is buried in the chapel crypt.

Annapurna mountain 26,502 ft/8,075 m in the Himalayas, Nepal. The north face was first climbed by a French expedition (Maurice Herzog) 1950 and the south by a British team 1970.

Anne 1665–1714. Queen of Great Britain and Ireland 1702–14. She was the second daughter of James, Duke of York, who became James II, and Anne Hyde. She succeeded William III 1702. Events of her reign include the War of the Spanish Succession, Marlborough's victories at Blenheim, Ramillies, Oudenarde, and Malplaquet, and the union of the English and Scottish parliaments 1707. Anne was succeeded by George I.

Anne (full name Anne Elizabeth Alice Louise) 1950– . Princess of the UK, second child of Queen Elizabeth II, declared Princess Royal 1987. She is an excellent horsewoman, winning a gold medal at the 1976 Olympics, and is actively involved in global charity work, especially for children. She married Commander Timothy Lawrence Dec 1992.

annealing process of heating a material (usually glass or metal) for a given time at a given temperature, followed by slow cooling, to increase ductility and strength. It is a common form of ◊heat treatment.

annelid any segmented worm of the phylum Annelida. Annelids include earthworms, leeches, and marine worms such as lugworms.

Anne of Austria 1601–1666. Queen of France from 1615 and regent 1643–61. Daughter of Philip III of

Spain, she married Louis XIII of France (whose chief minister, Cardinal Richelieu, worked against her). On her husband's death she became regent for their son, Louis XIV, until his majority.

She chose her lover ◊Mazarin as her chief minister.

annual plant plant that completes its life cycle within one year, during which time it germinates, grows to maturity, bears flowers, produces seed, and then dies.

Examples include the field poppy *Papaver rheas* and golden ragwort *Senecio aureus vulgaris.* Among garden plants, some that are described as "annuals" are actually perennials, although usually cultivated as annuals because they cannot survive winter frosts. See also ◊ephemeral, ◊biennial.

anode the positive electrode toward which negative particles (anions, electrons) move within a device such as the cells of a battery, electrolytic cells, and diodes.

anodizing process that increases the resistance to ◊corrosion of a metal, such as aluminum, by building up a protective oxide layer on the surface. The natural corrosion resistance of aluminum is provided by a thin film of aluminum oxide; anodizing increases the thickness of this film and thus the corrosion protection.

anorexia lack of desire to eat, especially the pathological condition of *anorexia nervosa*, most often found in adolescent girls and young women, who may be obsessed with the desire to lose weight. Compulsive eating, or ◊bulimia, and distortions of body image often accompany anorexia.

anoxemia shortage of oxygen in the lungs and tissue. It may be due to breathing air deficient in oxygen (for instance, at high altitude or where there are noxious fumes), disease of the lungs, or some disorder where the oxygen-carrying capacity of the blood is impaired.

Anschluss the annexation of Austria with Germany, accomplished by the German chancellor Adolf Hitler March 12, 1938.

Austria was occupied jointly by the Allies until 1955, when it declared independence as a republic.

Anselm, St *c.*1033–1109. Medieval priest and philosopher. As abbot from 1078, he made the abbey of Bec in Normandy, France, a center of scholarship in Europe. He was appointed archbishop of Canterbury by William II of England 1093, but was later forced into exile. He holds an important place in the development of ◊scholasticism.

In his *Proslogion* he developed the ontological proof of theism, which proof God's existence from our capacity to conceive of a perfect being. His major work, *Cur deus homo?/Why did God become Man?*, treats the subject of the Atonement. He was canonized 1494.

ANSI abbreviation for ◊*American National Standards Institute*, a US national standards body.

ant insect belonging to the family Formicidae, and to the same order (Hymenoptera) as bees and wasps. Ants are characterized by a conspicuous "waist" and elbowed antennae. About 10,000 different species are known; all are social in habit, and all construct nests of various kinds. Ants are found in all parts of the world, except the polar regions. It is estimated that there are about 10 million billion ants.

Antananarivo formerly *Tananarive* capital of Madagascar, on the interior plateau, with a rail link to Tamatave; population (1986) 703,000. Industries include tobacco, food processing, leather goods, and clothing.

Antarctica continent surrounding the South Pole, arbitrarily defined as the region lying S of the Antarctic

Circle. Occupying 10% of the world's surface, Antarctica contains 90% of the world's ice and 70% of its fresh water *area* 5,400,000 sq mi/13,900,000 sq km *features* Mount Erebus on Ross Island is the world's southernmost active volcano; the Ross Ice Shelf is formed by several glaciers coalescing in the Ross Sea *physical* formed of two blocks of rock with an area of about 8 million sq mi/3 million sq km, Antarctica is covered by a cap of ice that flows slowly toward its 14,000 mi/22,400 km coastline, reaching the sea in high ice cliffs. The most southerly shores are near the 78th parallel in the Ross and Weddell seas. E Antarctica is a massive block of ancient rocks that surface in the Transantarctic Mountains of Victoria Land.

Separated by a deep channel, W Antarctica is characterized by the mountainous regions of Graham Land, the Antarctic Peninsula, Palmer Land, and Ellsworth Land; the highest peak is Vinson Massif (16,866 ft/ 5,139 m).

anteater mammal of the family Myrmecophagidae, order Edentata, native to Mexico, Central America, and tropical South America. An anteater lives almost entirely on ants and termites. It has toothless jaws, an extensile tongue, and claws for breaking into the nests of its prey.

anteater The anteater is a relative of the sloths, armadillos, and pangolins. There are four species, native to South and Central America. The giant anteater Myrmecophaga tridactyla is 6 ft/1.8 m long with an elongated face, hairy coat, and bushy tail. It lives in forests and savanna.

antelope any of numerous kinds of even-toed, hoofed mammals belonging to the cow family, Bovidae. Most antelopes are lightly built and good runners. They are grazers or browsers, and chew the cud. They range in size from the dik-diks and duikers, only 1 ft/30 cm high, to the eland, which can be 6 ft/1.8 m at the shoulder.

antenna in zoology, an appendage ("feeler") on the head. Insects, centipedes, and millipedes each have one pair of antennae but there are two pairs in crustaceans, such as shrimps. In insects, the antennae are involved with the senses of smell and touch; they are frequently complex structures with large surface areas that increase the ability to detect scents.

antenna in radio and television, another name for ◊aerial.

Anthony, St *c.*251–356. Also known as Anthony of Thebes. He was the founder of Christian monasticism. At the age of 20, he renounced all his possessions and began a hermetic life of study and prayer, later seeking further solitude in a cave in the desert.

anthracite hard, dense, shiny variety of ◊coal, containing over 90% carbon and a low percentage of ash and impurities, which causes it to burn without flame, smoke, or smell. Because of its purity, anthracite gives off relatively little sulfur dioxide when burned.

anthrax disease of livestock, occasionally transmitted to humans, usually via infected hides and fleeces. It may develop as black skin pustules or severe pneumonia. Treatment is with antibiotics. Vaccination is effective.

anthropology study of humankind, which developed following 19th-century evolutionary theory to investigate the human species, past and present, physically, socially, and culturally.

The four subdisciplines are physical anthropology, linguistics, cultural anthropology, and archeology.

antialiasing in computer graphics, a software technique for diminishing "jaggies"—steplike lines that should be smooth. Jaggies occur because the output device, the monitor or printer, does not have a high enough resolution to represent a smooth line. Antialiasing reduces the prominence of jaggies by surrounding the steps with intermediate shades of gray (for gray-scaling devices) or color (for color devices). Although this reduces the jagged appearance of the lines, it also makes them fuzzier.

antibiotic drug that kills or inhibits the growth of bacteria and fungi. It is derived from living organisms such as fungi or bacteria, which distinguishes it from synthetic antimicrobials.

antibody a protein molecule produced in the blood by B-lymphocytes (see ◊lymphocyte). Antibodies bind specific foreign agents that invade the body, tagging them for destruction by phagocytes (white blood cells that engulf and destroy invaders) or activating a chemical system that renders them harmless. Each antibody is specific for a particular ◊antigen (the molecular pattern unique to a foreign substance).

anticyclone area of high atmospheric pressure caused by descending air, which becomes warm and dry. Winds radiate from a calm center, taking a clockwise direction in the northern hemisphere and an counterclockwise direction in the southern hemisphere. Anticyclones are characterized by clear weather and the absence of rain and violent winds. In summer they bring hot, sunny days and in winter they bring fine, frosty spells. *Blocking anticyclones*, which prevent the normal air circulation of an area, can cause summer droughts and severe winters.

antidiarrheal any substance that controls diarrhea.

antiemetic any substance that counteracts nausea or vomiting.

antifreeze substance added to a water-cooling system (for example, that of an automobile) to prevent it freezing in cold weather.

The most common types of antifreeze contain the chemical ethylene glycol, or ($HOCH_2CH_2OH$), an organic alcohol with a freezing point of about 5°F/–15°C.

The addition of this chemical depresses the freezing point of water significantly. A solution containing 33.5% by volume of ethylene glycol will not freeze until about –4°F/–20°C. A 50% solution will not freeze until –31°F/–35°C.

antigen any substance that causes the production of ◊antibodies by the body's immune system. Common antigens include the proteins carried on the surface of bacteria, viruses, and pollen grains. The proteins of incompatible blood groups or tissues also act as antigens, which has to be taken into account in medical procedures such as blood transfusions and organ transplants.

Antigua and Barbuda State of *area* Antigua 108 sq mi/280 sq km, Barbuda 62 sq mi/161 sq km, plus Redonda 0.4 sq mi/1 sq km *capital* and chief port St John's *towns and cities* Codrington (on Barbuda) *physical* low-lying tropical islands of limestone and coral with some higher volcanic outcrops; no rivers and low rainfall result in frequent droughts and deforestation *features* Antigua is the largest of the Leeward Islands; Redonda is an uninhabited island of volcanic rock rising to 1,000 ft/305 m *head of state* Elizabeth II from 1981, represented by governor general James B Carlisle from 1993 *head of government* Lester Bird from 1993 *political system* liberal democracy *political parties* Antigua Labour Party (ALP), moderate, left of center; United Progressive Party (UPP), moderate, left of center *exports* sea-island cotton, rum, lobsters *currency* Eastern Caribbean dollar *population* (1993 est) 77,000; growth rate 1.3% p.a. *life expectancy* 70 years *language* English *media* no daily newspaper; weekly papers all owned by political parties *religion* Christian (mostly Anglican) *literacy* 96% *GNP* $4,770 per head (1991) *chronology* *1493* Antigua visited by Christopher Columbus. *1632* Antigua colonized by English settlers. *1667* Treaty of Breda formally ceded Antigua to Britain. *1871–1956* Antigua and Barbuda administered as part of the Leeward Islands federation. *1967* Antigua and Barbuda became an associated state within the Commonwealth, with full internal independence. *1971* PLM won the general election by defeating the ALP. *1976* PLM called for early independence, but ALP urged caution. ALP won the general election. *1981* Independence from Britain achieved. *1983* Assisted US invasion of Grenada. *1984* ALP won a decisive victory in the general election. *1985* ALP reelected. *1989* Another sweeping general election victory for the ALP under Vere Bird. *1991* Bird remained in power despite calls for his resignation. *1993* ALP reelected in general election; Lester Bird elected ALP leader. *1994* Lester Bird and ALP reelected.

antihistamine any substance that counteracts the effects of ◊histamine. Antihistamines may occur naturally or they may be synthesized.

Antilles group of West Indian islands, divided N–S into the *Greater Antilles* (Cuba, Jamaica, Haiti–Dominican Republic, Puerto Rico) and *Lesser Antilles*, subdivided into the Leeward Islands (Virgin Islands, St Christopher–Nevis, Antigua and Barbuda, Anguilla, Montserrat, and Guadeloupe) and the Windward Islands (Dominica, Martinique, St Lucia, St Vincent and the Grenadines, Barbados, and Grenada).

antimatter in physics, a form of matter in which most of the attributes (such as electrical charge, magnetic moment, and spin) of ◊elementary particles are reversed. Such particles (◊antiparticles) can be created in particle accelerators, such as those at Fermilab at Batavia, Illinois, and at ◊CERN in Geneva, Switzerland.

antimony silver-white, brittle, semimetallic element (a metalloid), symbol Sb (from Latin *stibium*), atomic number 51, atomic weight 121.75. It occurs chiefly as the ore stibnite, and is used to make alloys harder; it is also used in photosensitive substances in color photography, optical electronics, fireproofing, pigment, and medicine. It was employed by the ancient Egyptians in a mixture to protect the eyes from flies.

Antioch ancient capital of the Greek kingdom of Syria, founded 300 BC by ◊Seleucus I in memory of his father Antiochus, and famed for its splendor and luxury. Under the Romans it was an early center of Christianity. St Paul set off on his missionary journeys from here. It was captured by the Arabs 637. After a five-month siege 1098 Antioch was taken by the crusaders, who held it until 1268. The site is now occupied by the Turkish town of Antakya.

Antiochus thirteen kings of Syria of the Seleucid dynasty, including:

Antiochus (III) the Great *c.*241–187 BC. King of Syria from 223 BC, nephew of Antiochus II. He secured a loose control over Armenia and Parthia 209, overcame Bactria, received the homage of the Indian king of the Kabul valley, and returned by way of the Persian Gulf 204. He took possession of Palestine, entering Jerusalem 198. He crossed into NW Greece, but was decisively defeated by the Romans at Thermopylae 191 and at Magnesia 190. The Peace of Apamea 188 BC confined Seleucid rule to Asia.

Antiochus IV *c.*215–164 BC. King of Syria from 175 BC, known as Antiochus Epiphanes, the Illustrious, son of Antiochus III. He occupied Jerusalem about 170, seizing much of the Temple treasure, and instituted worship of the Greek type in the Temple in an attempt to eradicate Judaism. This produced the revolt of the Hebrews under the Maccabees; Antiochus died before he could suppress it.

Antiochus VII *c.*159–129 BC. King of Syria from 138 BC. The last strong ruler of the Seleucid dynasty, he took Jerusalem 134, reducing the Maccabees to subjection. He was defeated and killed in battle against the Parthians.

antioxidant any substance that prevents deterioration by oxidation in fats, oils, paints, plastics, and rubbers. When used as food ◊additives, antioxidants prevent fats and oils from becoming rancid when exposed to air, and thus extend their shelf life.

They are limited to 0.02% of the total content by FDA standards.

antiparticle in nuclear physics, a particle corresponding in mass and properties to a given ◊elementary particle but with the opposite electrical charge, magnetic properties, or coupling to other fundamental forces. For example, an electron carries a negative charge whereas its antiparticle, the positron, carries a positive one. When a particle and its antiparticle collide, they destroy each other, in the process called "annihilation", their total energy being converted to lighter particles and/or photons. A substance consisting entirely of antiparticles is known as ◊antimatter.

antipodes places at opposite points on the globe. The North Pole is antipodal to the South Pole.

antipope rival claimant to the elected pope for the leadership of the Roman Catholic Church, for instance in the Great Schism 1378–1417 when there were rival popes in Rome and Avignon.

antirrhinum or *snapdragon* any of several plants, genus *Antirrhinum*, in the figwort family Scrophulariaceae. Foxglove and toadflax are relatives. Antirrhinums are native to W North America and the Mediterranean region.

Antirrhinum majus is a common garden flower, native to the Mediterranean.

anti-Semitism literally, prejudice against Semitic people (see ◊Semite), but in practice it has meant prejudice or discrimination against, and persecution of, the Jews as an ethnic group. Historically this was practiced for almost 2,000 years by European Christians. Anti-Semitism was a tenet of Hitler's Germany, and in

the ◊Holocaust 1933–45 about 6 million Jews died in concentration camps and in local extermination ◊pogroms, such as the siege of the Warsaw ghetto. In eastern Europe, as well as in Islamic nations, anti-Semitism exists and is promulgated by neofascist groups. It is a form of ◊racism.

antiseptic any substance that kills or inhibits the growth of microorganisms. The use of antiseptics was pioneered by Joseph ◊Lister. He used carbolic acid (◊phenol), which is a weak antiseptic; antiseptics such as TCP are derived from this.

antler "horn" of a deer, often branched, and made of bone rather than horn. Antlers, unlike true horns, are shed and regrown each year. Reindeer of both sexes grow them, but in all other types of deer, only the males have antlers.

Antofagasta port of N Chile, capital of the region of Antofagasta; population (1990) 218,800. The area of the region is 48,366 sq mi/125,300 sq km; its population (1982) 341,000. Nitrates from the Atacama Desert are exported.

Antonioni Michelangelo 1912– . Italian film director. He is known for his subtle presentations of neuroses and personal relationships among the leisured classes. His elliptical approach to narrative is best seen in *L'Avventura* 1960.

Antrim county of Northern Ireland *area* 1,092 sq mi/2,830 sq km *towns and cities* Belfast (county town), Larne (port) *features* Giant's Causeway of natural hexagonal basalt columns on the N coast, which, according to legend, was built to enable the giants to cross between Ireland and Scotland; peat bogs; Antrim borders Lough Neagh, and is separated from Scotland by the North Channel, 30 km/20 mi wide *industries* potatoes, oats, linen, synthetic textiles, flax, shipbuilding. Manufacture of man-made fibers has largely replaced traditional linen production *population* (1981) 642,000.

Antwerp (Flemish *Antwerpen*, French *Anvers*) port in Belgium on the river Scheldt, capital of the province of Antwerp; population (1991) 467,500. One of the world's busiest ports, it has shipbuilding, oil-refining, petrochemical, textile, and diamond-cutting industries. The home of the artist Rubens is preserved, and many of his works are in the Gothic cathedral. The province of Antwerp has an area of 1,119 sq mi/2,900 sq km; population (1987) 1,588,000.

Anubis in Egyptian mythology, the jackal-headed god of the dead, son of Osiris. Anubis presided over the funeral cult, including embalming, and led the dead to judgment.

apartheid racial-segregation policy of the government of South Africa, which was legislated 1948, when the Afrikaner National Party gained power. Nonwhites—classified as Bantu (black), colored (mixed), or Indian—did not share full rights of citizenship with the 4.5 million whites (for example, the 23 million black people could not vote in parliamentary elections), and many public facilities and institutions were until 1990 restricted to the use of one race only; the establishment of ◊Black National States was another manifestation of apartheid. In 1991 President de Klerk repealed the key elements of apartheid legislation and by 1994 apartheid had ceased to exist.

apatosaurus large plant-eating dinosaur, formerly called *brontosaurus*, which flourished about 145 million years ago. Up to 69 ft/21 m long, it stood on four elephantlike legs and had a long tail, long neck, and small head. It probably snipped off low-growing vegetation with peglike front teeth, and swallowed it whole to be ground by pebbles in the stomach.

ape ◊primate of the family Pongidae, closely related to humans, including gibbon, orangutan, chimpanzee, and gorilla.

Apennines chain of mountains stretching the length of the Italian peninsula. A continuation of the Maritime Alps, from Genoa it swings across the peninsula to Ancona on the east coast, and then back to the west coast and into the "toe" of Italy. The system is continued over the Strait of Messina along the N Sicilian coast, then across the Mediterranean Sea in a series of islands to the Atlas Mountains of N Africa. The highest peak is Gran Sasso d'Italia at 9,560 ft/2,914 m.

aperture in photography, an opening in the camera that allows light to pass through the lens to strike the film. Controlled by shutter speed and the iris diaphragm, it can be set mechanically or electronically at various diameters.

aphid any of the family of small insects, Aphididae, in the order Homoptera, that live by sucking sap from plants. There are many species, often adapted to particular plants.

aphrodisiac any substance that arouses or increases sexual desire.

Sexual activity can be stimulated in humans and animals by drugs affecting the pituitary gland. Preparations commonly sold for the purpose can be dangerous (cantharidin) or useless (rhinoceros horn); alcohol and marijuana, popularly thought to be effective because they lessen inhibition, often have the opposite effect.

Aphrodite in Greek mythology, the goddess of love (Roman Venus, Phoenician Astarte, Babylonian Ishtar); said to be either a daughter of Zeus (in Homer) or sprung from the foam of the sea (in Hesiod). She was the unfaithful wife of Hephaestus, the god of fire, and the mother of Eros.

API abbreviation for ◊*Applications Program Interface*, a standard environment in which computer programs are written.

Apia capital and port of Western ◊Samoa, on the north coast of Upolu Island, in the W Pacific; population (1981) 33,000. It was the final home of the writer Robert Louis Stevenson 1888–94.

Apocrypha appendix to the Old Testament of the Bible, not included in the final Hebrew canon but recognized by Roman Catholics. There are also disputed New Testament texts known as Apocrypha.

Apollo in Greek and Roman mythology, the god of sun, music, poetry, prophecy, agriculture, and pastoral life, and leader of the Muses. He was the twin child (with ◊Artemis) of Zeus and Leto. Ancient statues show Apollo as the embodiment of the Greek ideal of male beauty. His chief cult centers were his supposed birthplace on the island of Delos, in the Cyclades, and Delphi.

Apollo project US space project to land a person on the Moon, achieved July 20, 1969, when Neil Armstrong was the first to set foot there. He was accompanied on the Moon's surface by Col Edwin E Aldrin, Jr; Michael Collins remained in the orbiting command module.

Apollo–Soyuz test project joint US–Soviet space mission in which an Apollo and a Soyuz craft docked while in orbit around the Earth on July 17, 1975. The craft remained attached for two days and crew members were able to move from one craft to the other through an air lock attached to the nose of the Apollo. The mission was designed to test rescue procedures as well as having political significance.

In the Apollo craft were Thomas Patten Stafford (commander), Vance DeVoe Brand, and Donald Kent Slayton; the Soyuz vehicle carried Alexei Archipovich Leonov (commander) and Valeri Nikolayevich Kubasov. The project began with the signing of an agreement May 1972 by US president Nixon and Soviet premier Kosygin.

Apo, Mount active volcano and highest peak in the Philippines, rising to 9,692 ft/2,954 m on the island of Mindanao.

apoplexy alternate name for ◊stroke.

apostle in the New Testament, any of the chosen 12 disciples sent out by Jesus after his resurrection to preach the Gospel.

In the earliest days of Christianity the term was extended to include some who had never known Jesus in the flesh, notably St Paul.

apostrophe mark (') used in written English and some other languages. In English it serves primarily to indicate either a missing letter (*mustn't* for *must not*) or number ('*47* for *1947*), or grammatical possession ("*John's* camera", "*women's* dresses"). It is often omitted in proper names (Publishers Association, Actors Studio, *Collins Dictionary*). Many people otherwise competent in writing have great difficulty with the apostrophe, which has never been stable at any point in its history.

Appalachians mountain system of E North America, stretching about 1,500 mi/2,400 km from Alabama to Québec, composed of ancient eroded rocks and rounded peaks. The chain separates the Mississippi–Missouri lowlands from the Atlantic coastal plain and includes the Allegheny, Catskill, White, and Blue Ridge mountains, the last having the highest peak, Mount Mitchell, 6,712 ft/2,045 m. The E edge has a fall line to the coastal plain where Philadelphia, Baltimore, and Washington stand. The Appalachians are heavily forested and have deposits of coal and other minerals.

appeal in law, an application for a rehearing of all or part of an issue that has already been dealt with by a lower court or tribunal.

The outcome can be a new decision on all or part of the points raised, or the previous decision may be upheld. In criminal cases, an appeal may be against conviction and either the prosecution or the defense may appeal against sentence.

appendicitis inflammation of the appendix, a small, blind extension of the bowel in the lower right abdomen. In an acute attack, the pus-filled appendix may burst, causing a potentially lethal spread of infection. Treatment is by removal (appendicectomy).

apple fruit of *Malus pumila*, a tree of the family Rosaceae.

There are several hundred varieties of cultivated apples, grown all over the world, which may be divided into eating, cooking, and cider apples. All are derived from the wild crab apple.

Apple US computer company, manufacturer of the ◊Macintosh range of computers.

Appleton layer band containing ionized gases in the Earth's upper atmosphere, above the E layer (formerly the Kennelly–Heaviside layer). It can act as a reflector of radio signals, although its ionic composition varies with the sunspot cycle. It is named after the English physicist Edward Appleton.

application in computing, a program or job designed for the benefit of the end user, such as a payroll system or a ◊word processor. The term is used to distinguish such programs from those that control the computer (◊systems programs) or assist the programmer, such as a ◊compiler.

applications package in computing, the set of programs and related documentation (such as instruction manuals) used in a particular application. For example, a typical payroll applications package would consist of separate programs for the entry of data, updating the master files, and printing the pay slips, plus documentation in the form of program details and instructions for use.

Applications Program Interface (API) in computing, standard environment, including tools, protocols, and other routines, in which programs can be written. An API ensures that all applications are consistent with the operating system and have a similar ◊user interface.

Appomattox village in Virginia, scene of the surrender April 9, 1865 of the Confederate army under Robert E Lee to the Union army under Ulysses S Grant, which ended the Civil War.

apricot fruit of *Prunus armeniaca*, a tree of the rose family Rosaceae, closely related to the almond, peach, plum, and cherry. It has yellow-fleshed fruit. Although native to the Far East, it has long been cultivated in Armenia, from where it was introduced into Europe and the US.

Apulia English form of Puglia, a region of Italy.

Aqaba, Gulf of gulf extending for 100 mi/160 km between the Negev and the Red Sea; its coastline is uninhabited except at its head, where the frontiers of Israel, Egypt, Jordan, and Saudi Arabia converge.

The two ports of Eilat (Israeli "Elath") and Aqaba, Jordan's only port, are situated here.

aquaculture the cultivation of fish and shellfish for human consumption; see ◊fish farming.

aqualung or *scuba* underwater breathing apparatus worn by divers, developed in the early 1940s by French diver Jacques Cousteau. Compressed-air cylinders strapped to the diver's back are regulated by a valve system and by a mouth tube to provide air to the diver at the same pressure as that of the surrounding water (which increases with the depth).

aquamarine blue variety of the mineral ◊beryl. A semiprecious gemstone, it is used in jewelry.

Aquarius zodiacal constellation a little south of the celestial equator near Pegasus. Aquarius is represented as a man pouring water from a jar. The Sun passes through Aquarius from late Feb to early March. In astrology, the dates for Aquarius are between about Jan 20 and Feb 18 (see ◊precession).

aquatint printmaking technique. When combined with ◊etching it produces areas of subtle tone as well as more precisely etched lines. Aquatint became common in the late 18th century.

aqueduct any artificial channel or conduit for water, often an elevated structure of stone, wood, or iron built for conducting water across a valley. The Greeks built a tunnel 4,200 ft/1,280 m long near Athens, 2,500 years ago. Many Roman aqueducts are still standing, for example the one at Nîmes in S France, built about AD 18 (which is 160 ft/48 m high).

aqueduct *Pont du Gard, Roman aqueduct near Nîmes, S France. Built 19 BC on the orders of Agrippa, it remains almost intact. The bridge across the Gardon Valley is the most spectacular section of an aqueduct almost 30 mi/48 km long. During the Roman occupation it carried 706,000 cu ft/20,000 cu m of water per day from the sources of the Eure and the Ayran down to Nîmes.*

aqueous humor watery fluid found in the space between the cornea and lens of the vertebrate eye. Similar to blood serum in composition, it is renewed every four hours.

aquifer any rock formation containing water. The rock of an aquifer must be porous and permeable (full of interconnected holes) so that it can absorb water. Aquifers are an important source of fresh water, for example, for drinking and irrigation, in many arid areas of the world and are exploited by the use of ◊artesian wells.

Aquinas St Thomas *c.*1226–1274. Neapolitan philosopher and theologian, the greatest figure of the school of ◊scholasticism. He was a Dominican monk, known as the "Angelic Doctor". In 1879 his works were recognized as the basis of Catholic theology. His *Summa contra Gentiles/Against the Errors of the Infidels* 1259–64 argues that reason and faith are compatible. He assimilated the philosophy of Aristotle into Christian doctrine.

Aquino (Maria) Corazon (born Cojuangco) 1933– . President of the Philippines 1986–92. She was instrumental in the nonviolent overthrow of President Ferdinand Marcos 1986. As president, she sought to rule in a conciliatory manner, but encountered opposition from left (communist guerrillas) and right (army coup attempts), and her land reforms were seen as inadequate.

Aquitaine region of SW France; capital Bordeaux; area 15,942 sq mi/41,300 sq km; population (1986) 2,718,000. It comprises the *départements* of Dordogne, Gironde, Landes, Lot-et-Garonne, and Pyrénées-Atlantiques. Red wines (Margaux, St Julien) are produced in the Médoc district, bordering the Gironde. Aquitaine was an English possession 1152–1452.

Arab any of a Semitic (see ◊Semite) people native to the Arabian peninsula, but now settled throughout North Africa and the nations of the Middle East.

Arab Emirates see ◊United Arab Emirates.

Arabia peninsula between the Persian Gulf and the Red Sea, in SW Asia; area 1,000,000 sq mi/2,600,000 sq km. The peninsula contains the world's richest oil and gas reserves. It comprises the states of Bahrain, Kuwait, Oman, Qatar, Saudi Arabia, the United Arab Emirates, and Yemen.

Arabian Sea northwestern branch of the ◊Indian Ocean.

Arabic language major Semitic language of the Hamito-Semitic family of W Asia and North Africa, originating among the Arabs of the Arabian peninsula. It is spoken today by about 120 million people in the Middle East and N Africa. Arabic script is written from right to left.

Arabic numerals or *Hindu-Arabic numerals* the symbols 0, 1, 2, 3, 4, 5, 6, 7, 8, 9, early forms of which were in use among the Arabs before being adopted by the peoples of Europe during the Middle Ages in place of ◊Roman numerals. The symbols appear to have originated in India and probably reached Europe by way of Spain.

Arab-Israeli Wars series of wars between Israel and various Arab states in the Middle East since the founding of the state of Israel 1948.

First Arab-Israeli War May 15, 1948–Jan 13/March 24, 1949. As soon as the independent state of Israel had been proclaimed by the Jews, it was invaded by combined Arab forces. The Israelis defeated them and

went on to annex territory until they controlled 75% of what had been Palestine under British mandate.

Second Arab-Israeli War Oct 29–Nov 4, 1956. After Egypt had taken control of the Suez Canal and blockaded the Straits of Tiran, Israel, with British and French support, invaded and captured Sinai and the Gaza Strip, from which it withdrew under heavy US pressure after the entry of a United Nations force.

Third Arab-Israeli War June 5–10, 1967, the *Six-Day War*. It resulted in the Israeli capture of the Golan Heights from Syria; the eastern half of Jerusalem and the West Bank from Jordan; and, in the south, the Gaza Strip and Sinai peninsula as far as the Suez Canal.

Fourth Arab-Israeli War Oct 6–24, 1973, the "October War" or *Yom Kippur War*, so called because the Israeli forces were taken by surprise on the Day of ◊Atonement, a Jewish holy day. It started with the recrossing of the Suez Canal by Egyptian forces who made initial gains, though there was some later loss of ground by the Syrians in the north. The war had 19,000 casualties.

Fifth Arab-Israeli War From 1978 the presence of Palestinian guerrillas in Lebanon led to Arab raids on Israel and Israeli retaliatory incursions, but on June 6, 1982, Israel launched a full-scale invasion. By June 14 Beirut was encircled, and ◊Palestine Liberation Organization (PLO) and Syrian forces were evacuated (mainly to Syria) Aug 21–31, but in Feb 1985 there was a unilateral Israeli withdrawal from the country without any gain or losses incurred. Israel maintains a "security zone" in S Lebanon and supports the South Lebanese Army militia as a buffer against Palestinian guerrilla incursions.

arachnid or *arachnoid* type of arthropod, including spiders, scorpions, and mites. They differ from insects in possessing only two main body regions, the cephalothorax and the abdomen, and in having eight legs.

Arafat Yassir 1929– . Palestinian nationalist politician, cofounder of al-◊Fatah 1957 and president of the ◊Palestine Liberation Organization (PLO) from 1969. His support for Saddam Hussein after Iraq's invasion of Kuwait 1990 weakened his international standing, but he was subsequently influential in the Middle East peace talks and in Sept 1993 reached a historic peace accord of mutual recognition with Israel, under which the Gaza Strip and Jericho were transferred to PLO control. In July 1994 he returned to the former occupied territories as head of an embryonic Palestinian state.

He was awarded the 1994 Nobel Prize for Peace jointly with Israeli president Yitzhak Rabin and foreign minister Shimon Peres.

Aragon autonomous region of NE Spain including the provinces of Huesca, Teruel, and Zaragoza; area 18,412 sq mi/47,700 sq km; population (1986) 1,215,000. Its capital is Zaragoza, and products include almonds, figs, grapes, and olives. Aragón was an independent kingdom 1035–1479.

Aral Sea inland sea divided between Kazakhstan and Uzbekistan, the world's fourth largest lake; former area 24,000 sq mi/62,000 sq km, but decreasing. Water from its tributaries, the Amu Darya and Syr Darya, has been diverted for irrigation and city use, and the sea is disappearing, with long-term consequences for the climate.

Aramaic language Semitic language of the Hamito-Semitic family of W Asia, the everyday language of

Palestine 2,000 years ago, during the Roman occupation and the time of Jesus.

Ararat, Mount double-peaked mountain in Turkey near the Iranian border; Great Ararat, at 16,854 ft/ 5,137 m, is the highest mountain in Turkey.

araucaria coniferous tree of the genus *Araucaria*, allied to the firs, with flat, scalelike needles. Once widespread, it is now native only to the southern hemisphere. Some grow to gigantic size. Araucarias include the monkey-puzzle tree *A. araucana*, the Australian bunya bunya pine *A. bidwillii*, and the Norfolk Island pine *A. heterophylla*.

Arawak member of an indigenous American people of the Caribbean and NE Amazon Basin. Arawaks lived mainly by shifting cultivation in tropical forests. They were driven out of many West Indian islands by another American Indian people, the Caribs, shortly before the arrival of the Spanish in the 16th century. Subsequently, their numbers on ◊Hispaniola declined from some 4 million in 1492 to a few thousand after their exploitation by the Spanish in their search for gold; the remaining few were eradicated by disease (smallpox was introduced 1518). Arawakan languages belong to the Andean-Equatorial group.

arbitrageur in finance, a person who buys securities (such as currency or commodities) in one country or market for immediate resale in another market, to take advantage of different prices.

arbitration submission of a dispute to a third, unbiased party for settlement. It may be personal litigation, a labor-union issue, or an international dispute.

arc in geometry, a section of a curved line or circle. A circle has three types of arc: a *semicircle*, which is exactly half of the circle; *minor arcs*, which are less than the semicircle; and *major arcs*, which are greater than the semicircle.

arch in masonry, a curved structure that supports the weight of material over an open space, as in a bridge or doorway. The first arches consisted of several wedge-shaped stones supported by their mutual pressure. The term is also applied to any curved structure that is an arch in form only, such as the Arc de Triomphe, Paris, 1806–36.

Archean or *Archeozoic* the earliest eon of geological time; the first part of the Precambrian, from the formation of Earth up to about 2,500 million years ago. It was a time when no life existed, and with every new discovery of ancient life its upper boundary is being pushed further back.

archaebacteria three groups of bacteria that are without a nucleus and whose DNA differs significantly from that of other bacteria (called the "eubacteria"). All are strict anaerobes, that is, they are killed by oxygen. This is thought to be a primitive condition and to indicate that the archaebacteria are related to the earliest life forms, which appeared about 4 trillion years ago, when there was little oxygen in the Earth's atmosphere.

archeopteryx extinct primitive bird, known from fossilized remains, about 160 million years old, found in limestone deposits in Bavaria, Germany. It is popularly known as "the first bird", although some earlier bird ancestors are now known. It was about the size of a crow and had feathers and wings, but in many respects its skeleton was reptilian (teeth and a long, bony tail) and very like some small meat-eating dinosaurs of the time.

archeology study of history (primarily but not exclusively the prehistoric and ancient periods), based on the examination of physical remains. Principal activities include preliminary field (or site) surveys, excavation (where necessary), and the classification, dating, and interpretation of finds. Since 1958 radiocarbon dating has been used to establish the age of archeological strata and associated materials.

archeozoology (or *zooarcheology*) branch of archeology involving the analysis of animal remains for information on physiology and ecology; for the interpretation of these remains in association with artifacts and people; and for data on subsistence, dietary and butchering patterns, animal domestication, and paleoenvironment.

archery use of the bow and arrow, originally in hunting and warfare, now as a competitive sport. The world governing body is the Fédération Internationale de Tir à l'Arc (FITA) founded 1931. In competitions, results are based on double FITA rounds; that is, 72 arrows at each of four targets at 90, 70, 50, and 30 meters (70, 60, 50, and 30 for women). The best possible score is 2,880.

Organizations in the US include the National Archery Association 1879 and, for actual hunting with the bow, the National Field Archery Association 1940.

Archie software for locating information on the ◊Internet. It can be difficult to locate a particular file because of the relatively unstructured nature of the Internet. Archie uses indexes of files and their locations on the Internet to find them quickly.

Archimedes *c.*287–212 BC. Greek mathematician who made major discoveries in geometry, hydrostatics, and mechanics. He formulated a law of fluid displacement (Archimedes' principle), and is credited with the invention of the Archimedes screw, a cylindrical device for raising water.

Archimedes' principle in physics, law stating that an object totally or partly submerged in a fluid displaces a volume of fluid that weighs the same as the apparent loss in weight of the object (which, in turn, equals the upward force, or upthrust, experienced by that object). It was discovered by the Greek mathematician Archimedes.

archipelago group of islands, or an area of sea containing a group of islands. The islands of an archipelago are usually volcanic in origin, and they sometimes represent the tops of peaks in areas around continental margins flooded by the sea.

architecture art of designing structures. The term covers the design of the visual appearance of structures; their internal arrangements of space; selection of external and internal building materials; design or selection of natural and artificial lighting systems, as well as mechanical, electrical, and plumbing systems; and design or selection of decorations and furnishings. Architectural style may emerge from evolution of techniques and styles particular to a culture in a given time period with or without identifiable individuals as architects, or may be attributed to specific individuals or groups of architects working together on a project.

arc lamp or *arc light* electric light that uses the illumination of an electric arc maintained between two electrodes. The British scientist Humphry Davy developed an arc lamp 1808, and its main use in recent years has been in movie projectors. The lamp consists of two carbon electrodes, between which a very high voltage is maintained. Electric current arcs (jumps) between the two, creating a brilliant light.

arc minute, arc second units for measuring small angles, used in geometry, surveying, map-making, and astronomy. An arc minute (symbol ') is one-sixtieth of a degree, and an arc second (symbol ") is one-sixtieth of an arc minute. Small distances in the sky, as between two close stars or the apparent width of a planet's disk, are expressed in minutes and seconds of arc.

Arctic, the that part of the northern hemisphere surrounding the North Pole; arbitrarily defined as the region lying N of the Arctic Circle (66° 32′N) or N of the tree line. There is no Arctic continent; the greater part of the region comprises the Arctic Ocean, which is the world's smallest ocean. Arctic climate, fauna, and flora extend over the islands and northern edges of continental land masses that surround the Arctic Ocean (Svalbard, Iceland, Greenland, Siberia, Scandinavia, Alaska, and Canada) *area* 14,000,000 sq mi/36,000,000 sq km *physical* pack-ice floating on the Arctic Ocean occupies almost the entire region between the North Pole and the coasts of North America and Eurasia, covering an area that ranges in diameter from 1,900 mi/3,000 km to 2,500 mi/4,000 km. The pack-ice reaches a maximum extent in Feb when its outer limit (influenced by the cold Labrador Current and the warm Gulf Stream) varies from 50°N along the coast of Labrador to 75°N in the Barents Sea N of Scandinavia. In spring the pack-ice begins to break up into ice floes which are carried by the south-flowing Greenland Current to the Atlantic Ocean. Arctic ice is at its minimum area in Aug. The greatest concentration of icebergs in Arctic regions is found in Baffin Bay. They are derived from the glaciers of W Greenland, then carried along Baffin Bay and down into the N Atlantic where they melt off Labrador and Newfoundland.

Arctic Ocean ocean surrounding the North Pole; area 5,400,000 sq mi/14,000,000 sq km. Because of the Siberian and North American rivers flowing into it, it has comparatively low salinity and freezes readily.

Arcturus or *Alpha Boötis* brightest star in the constellation Boötes and the fourth-brightest star in the sky. Arcturus is a red giant about 28 times larger than the Sun and 70 times more luminous, 36 light-years away from Earth.

Ardennes wooded plateau in NE France, SE Belgium, and N Luxembourg, cut through by the river Meuse; also a *département* of Champagne-Ardenne. There was heavy fighting here in World Wars I and II.

area the size of a surface. It is measured in square units, usually square inches (in^2), square yards (yd^2), or square miles (mi^2). Surface area is the area of the outer surface of a solid.

Arendt Hannah 1906–1975. German-born US scholar and political scientist. With the rise of the Nazis, she moved to Paris and emigrated to the US 1940. Her works include *The Origins of Modern Totalitarianism* 1951, *The Human Condition* 1958, *On Revolution* 1963, *Eichmann in Jerusalem* 1963, and *On Violence* 1972.

Arendt received her PhD from Heidelberg University 1928. During World War II she was research director for the Conference on Jewish Relations.

Ares in Greek mythology, the god of war, equivalent to the Roman ☿Mars. The son of Zeus and Hera, he was worshiped chiefly in Thrace.

Argentina Republic of (*República Argentina*) *area* 1,073,116 sq mi/2,780,092 sq km *capital* Buenos Aires (to move to Viedma) *towns and cities* Rosario, Córdoba, Tucumán, Mendoza, Santa Fé; ports are La Plata and Bahía Blanca *physical* mountains in W, forest and savanna in N, pampas (treeless plains) in E central area, Patagonian plateau in S; rivers Colorado, Salado, Paraná, Uruguay, Río de la Plata estuary *territories* part of Tierra del Fuego; disputed claims to S Atlantic islands and part of Antarctica *environment* an estimated 7,700 sq mi/20,000 sq km of land has been swamped with salt water *features* Andes mountains, with Aconcagua the highest peak in the W hemisphere; Iguaçú Falls *head of state and government* Carlos Menem from 1989 *political system* democratic federal republic *political parties* Radical Civic Union Party (UCR), moderate centrist; Justicialist Party (PJ), right-wing Peronist *exports* livestock products, cereals, wool, tannin, peanuts, linseed oil, minerals (coal, copper, molybdenum, gold, silver, lead, zinc, barium, uranium); the country has huge resources of oil, natural gas, hydroelectric power *currency* peso = 10,000 australs (which it replaced 1992) *population* (1993 est) 33,500,000 (mainly of Spanish or Italian origin, only about 30,000 American Indians surviving); growth rate 1.5% p.a. *life expectancy* men 68, women 75 *languages* Spanish (official); English, Italian, German, French *religion* Roman Catholic (state-supported) *literacy* men 96%, women 95% *GNP* $2,780 per head (1991) *chronology 1816* Independence achieved from Spain, followed by civil wars. *1946* Juan Perón elected president, supported by his wife "Evita". *1952* "Evita" Perón died. *1955* Perón overthrown and civilian administration restored. *1966* Coup brought back military rule. *1973* A Peronist party won the presidential and congressional elections. Perón returned from exile in Spain as president, with his third wife, Isabel, as vice president. *1974* Perón died, succeeded by Isabel. *1976* Coup resulted in rule by a military junta led by Lt Gen Jorge Videla. Congress dissolved, and hundreds of people, including Isabel Perón, detained. *1976–83* Ferocious campaign against left-wing elements, the "dirty war". *1978* Videla retired. Succeeded by General Roberto Viola, who promised a return to democracy. *1981* Viola died suddenly. Replaced by General Leopoldo Galtieri. *1982* With a deteriorating economy, Galtieri sought popular support by ordering an invasion of the British-held Falkland Islands. After losing the short war, Galtieri was removed and replaced by General Reynaldo Bignone. *1983* Amnesty law passed and democratic constitution of 1853 revived. General elections won by Raúl Alfonsín and the UCR. Armed forces under scrutiny. *1984* National Commission on the Disappearance of Persons (CONADEP) reported on over 8,000 people who had disappeared during the "dirty war" of 1976–83. *1985* A deteriorating economy forced Alfonsín to seek help from the International Monetary Fund and introduce an austerity program. *1986* Unsuccessful attempt on Alfonsín's life. *1988* Unsuccessful army coup. *1989* Carlos Menem, of the PJ, elected president. *1990* Full diplomatic relations with the UK restored. Menem elected PJ leader. Revolt by army officers thwarted. *1992* New currency introduced. *1993* Success for PJ in assembly elections. Menem's constitutional reforms approved, with clause allowing him to seek reelection. *1994* PJ won assembly elections but with reduced majority. Revised constitution adopted. *1995* Menem reelected outright.

argon colorless, odorless, nonmetallic, gaseous element, symbol Ar, atomic number 18, atomic weight 39.948. It is grouped with the ◊inert gases, since it was long believed not to react with other substances, but observations now indicate that it can be made to combine with boron fluoride to form compounds. It constitutes almost 1% of the Earth's atmosphere, and was discovered 1894 by British chemists John Rayleigh (1842–1919) and William ◊Ramsay after all oxygen and nitrogen had been removed chemically from a sample of air. It is used in electric discharge tubes and argon lasers.

Argonauts in Greek mythology, the band of heroes who accompanied ◊Jason when he set sail in the *Argo* to find the ◊Golden Fleece.

argument in computing, the value on which a ◊function operates. For example, if the argument 16 is operated on by the function "square root", the answer 4 is produced.

Argus in Greek mythology, a giant with 100 eyes. When he was killed by Hermes, Hera transplanted his eyes into the tail of her favorite bird, the peacock.

aria melodic solo song of reflective character, often with a contrasting middle section, expressing a moment of truth in the action of an opera or oratorio. Pioneered by Giacomo Carissimi, it became a set piece for virtuoso opera singers, for example Handel's aria "Where'er you walk" from the secular oratorio *Semele* 1744 to words by William Congreve. As an instrumental character piece, it is melodious and imitative of a vocal line.

Arianism a system of Christian theology that gave God the Father primacy over Christ. It was founded about 310 by Arius, and condemned as heretical at the Council of Nicaea 325.

Aries zodiacal constellation in the northern hemisphere between Pisces and Taurus, near Auriga, represented as the legendary ram whose golden fleece was sought by Jason and the Argonauts.

Its most distinctive feature is a curve of three stars of decreasing brightness. The brightest of these is Hamal or Alpha Arietis, 65 light years from Earth.

Ariosto Ludovico 1474–1533. Italian poet. He wrote Latin poems and comedies on Classical lines, including the poem *Orlando furioso* 1516, published 1532, an epic treatment of the ◊Roland story, the perfect poetic expression of the Italian Renaissance.

Aristarchus of Samos *c.*320–*c.*250 BC. Greek astronomer. The first to argue that the Earth moves around the Sun, he was ridiculed for his beliefs. He was also the first astronomer to estimate the sizes of the Sun and Moon and their distances from the Earth.

Aristide Jean-Bertrand 1953– . President of Haiti Dec 1990–Oct 1991 and from Oct 1994. A left-wing Catholic priest opposed to the right-wing regime of the Duvalier family, he campaigned for the National Front for Change and Democracy, representing a loose coalition of peasants, labor unionists, and clerics, and won 70% of the vote. He was deposed by the military Sept 1991 and took refuge in the United States. In Sept 1994, under an agreement brokered by former US president Jimmy Carter, US troops entered the island without resistance and the military stepped down. Aristide returned in Oct

Aristides *c.*530–468 BC. Athenian politician. He was one of the ten Athenian generals at the battle of ◊Marathon 490 BC and was elected chief archon, or magistrate. Later he came into conflict with the democratic leader Themistocles, and was exiled about 483 BC. He returned to fight against the Persians at Salamis 480 BC and in the following year commanded the Athenians at Plataea. As commander of the Athenian fleet he established the alliance of Ionian states known as the Delian League.

aristocracy social elite or system of political power associated with landed wealth, as in western Europe; with monetary wealth, as in Carthage and Venice; or with religious superiority, as with the Brahmins in India. The Prussian (Junker) aristocracy based its legitimacy not only on landed wealth but also on service to the state. Aristocracies are also usually associated with monarchy but have frequently been in conflict with the sovereign over their respective rights and privileges. In Europe, their economic base was undermined during the 19th century by inflation and falling agricultural prices, leading to their demise as a political force after 1914.

Aristophanes *c.*448–380 BC. Greek comedy dramatist. Of his 11 extant plays (of a total of over 40), the early comedies are remarkable for the violent satire with which he ridiculed the democratic war leaders. He also satirized contemporary issues such as the new learning of Socrates in *The Clouds* 423 BC and the power of women in *Lysistrata* 411. The chorus plays a prominent role, frequently giving the play its title, as in *The Wasps* 422, *The Birds* 414, and *The Frogs* 405.

Aristotle 384–322 BC. Greek philosopher who advocated reason and moderation. He maintained that sense experience is our only source of knowledge, and that by reasoning we can discover the essences of things, that is, their distinguishing qualities. In his works on ethics and politics, he suggested that human happiness consists in living in conformity with nature. He derived his political theory from the recognition that mutual aid is natural to humankind, and refused to set up any one constitution as universally ideal. Of Aristotle's works some 22 treatises survive, dealing with logic, metaphysics, physics, astronomy, meteorology, biology, psychology, ethics, politics, and literary criticism.

His works were lost to Europe after the decline of Rome, but they were reintroduced in the Middle Ages by Arab and Jewish scholars and became the basis of medieval ◊scholasticism.

arithmetic branch of mathematics concerned with the study of numbers and their properties. The fundamental operations of arithmetic are addition, subtraction, multiplication, and division. Raising to powers (for example, squaring or cubing a number), the extraction of roots (for example, square roots), percentages, fractions, and ratios are developed from these operations.

arithmetic and logic unit (ALU) in a computer, the part of the ◊central processing unit (CPU) that performs the basic arithmetic and logic operations on data.

arithmetic mean the average of a set of *n* numbers, obtained by adding the numbers and dividing by *n*. For example, the arithmetic mean of the set of 5 numbers 1, 3, 6, 8, and 12 is (1 + 3 + 6 + 8 + 12)/5 = 30/5 = 6.

arithmetic progression or *arithmetic sequence* sequence of numbers or terms that have a common difference between any one term and the next in the sequence. For example, 2, 7, 12, 17, 22, 27,... is an arithmetic sequence with a common difference of 5.

Arizona state in southwestern US; nickname Grand Canyon State *area* 113,500 sq mi/294,100 sq km *capital* Phoenix *towns and cities* Tucson, Scottsdale, Tempe, Mesa, Glendale, Flagstaff *physical* Colorado Plateau in the N and E, desert basins and mountains in the S and W, Colorado River, Grand Canyon *features* Grand Canyon National Park (the multicolored-rock gorge through which the Colorado River flows, 4–18 mi/6–29 km wide, up to 1.1 mi/1.7 km deep, and 217 mi/350 km/ long); Organ Pipe Cactus National Monument Park; deserts: Painted (including the Petrified Forest of fossil trees), Gila, Sonoran; dams: Roosevelt, Hoover; old London Bridge (transported 1971 to the tourist resort of Lake Havasu City) *industries* cotton under irrigation, livestock, copper, molybdenum, silver, electronics, aircraft *population* (1990) 3,665,000; including 4.5% American Indians (Navaho, Hopi, Apache), who by treaty own 25% of the state *famous people* Cochise, Wyatt Earp, Geronimo, Barry Goldwater, Zane Grey, Percival Lowell, Frank Lloyd Wright *history* part of New Spain 1752; part of Mexico 1824; passed to the US after the Mexican War 1848; territory 1863; statehood achieved 1912.

Arkansas state in S central US; nickname Wonder State/Land of Opportunity *area* 53,191 sq mi/137,800 sq km *capital* Little Rock *towns and cities* Fort Smith, Pine Bluff, Fayetteville *physical* Ozark Mountains and plateau in the W, lowlands in the E; Arkansas River; many lakes *features* Hot Springs National Park *industries* cotton, soy beans, rice, oil, natural gas, bauxite, timber, processed foods *population* (1990) 2,350,700 *famous people* Johnny Cash, Bill Clinton, J. William Fulbright, Douglas MacArthur, Winthrop Rockefeller *history* explored by Hernando de Soto 1541; European settlers 1648, who traded with local Indians; part of Louisiana Purchase 1803; statehood achieved 1836.

In 1957 President Eisenhower sent US troops to enforce a court order to desegregate Central High School in Little Rock after Governor Orval Faubus had called up the National Guard to block integration.

armadillo The horny bands and plates of the armadillo serve as armor. Many species can draw in their feet beneath the shell when attacked. The three-banded armadillo can roll itself into a ball.

Armada fleet sent by Philip II of Spain against England 1588. See ◊Spanish Armada.

armadillo mammal of the family Dasypodidae, with an armor of bony plates on its back. Some 20 species live between Texas and Patagonia and range in size from the fairy armadillo at 5 in/13 cm to the giant armadillo, 4.5 ft/1.5 m long. Armadillos feed on insects, snakes, fruit, and carrion. Some can roll into an armored ball if attacked; others rely on burrowing for protection.

Armageddon in the New Testament (Revelation 16), the site of the final battle between the nations that will end the world; it has been identified with Megiddo in Israel.

Armagh county of Northern Ireland *area* 483 sq mi/1,250 sq km *towns and cities* Armagh (county town), Lurgan, Portadown, Keady *features* smallest county of Northern Ireland; flat in the N, with many bogs; low hills in the S; the rivers Bann and Blackwater, flowing into Lough Neagh, and the Callan tributary of the Blackwater *industries* chiefly agricultural: apples, potatoes, flax, linen manufacture *population* (1981) 119,000.

armature in a motor or generator, the wire-wound coil that carries the current and rotates in a magnetic field. (In alternating-current machines, the armature is sometimes stationary.) The pole piece of a permanent magnet or electromagnet and the moving, iron part of a ◊solenoid, especially if the latter acts as a switch, may also be referred to as armatures.

Armenia Republic of *area* 11,500 sq mi/29,800 sq km *capital* Yerevan *towns and cities* Kumayri (formerly Leninakan) *physical* mainly mountainous (including Mount Ararat), wooded *features* State Academia Theatre of Opera and Ballet; Yerevan Film Studio *head of state* Levon Ter-Petrossian from 1990 *head of government* Gagik Arutyunyan from 1991 *political system* emergent democracy *political parties* Armenian Pan-National Movement (APM), left of center; Armenian Revolutionary Federation (ARF), centrist *products* copper, molybdenum, cereals, cotton, silk *currency* Russian ruble *population* (1993 est) 3,500,000 (90% Armenian, 5% Azeri, 2% Russian, 2% Kurd) *life expectancy* men 78, women 73 *language* Armenian *religion* traditionally Armenian Christian *GNP* $2,150 per head (1991) *chronology 1918* Became an independent republic. *1920* Occupied by the Red Army. *1936* Became a constituent republic of the USSR. *1988* Feb: demonstrations in Yerevan called for transfer of Nagorno-Karabakh from Azerbaijan to Armenian control. Dec: earthquake claimed around

25,000 lives. *1989* Jan–Nov: strife-torn Nagorno-Karabakh placed under direct rule from Moscow. Pro-autonomy APM founded. Nov: civil war erupted with Azerbaijan over Nagorno-Karabakh. *1990* March: USSR constitutional referendum boycotted. Aug: nationalists secured control of Armenian supreme soviet; former dissident Levon Ter-Petrossian indirectly elected president; independence declared. *1991* March: overwhelming support for independence in referendum. Dec: Armenia joined new Commonwealth of Independent States; granted diplomatic recognition by US; Nagorno-Karabakh declared its independence. *1992* Admitted into United Nations. Conflict over Nagorno-Karabakh worsened. *1993* July: Armenian forces gained control of more than one fifth of Azerbaijan, including much of Nagorno-Karabakh.

Armenian member of the largest ethnic group inhabiting Armenia. There are Armenian minorities in Azerbaijan (see ◊Nagorno-Karabakh), as well as in Turkey and Iran. Christianity was introduced to the ancient Armenian kingdom in the 3rd century. There are 4–5 million speakers of Armenian, which belongs to the Indo-European family of languages.

Armenian language one of the main divisions of the Indo-European language family. Old Armenian, the classic literary language, is still used in the liturgy of the Armenian Church. Armenian was not written down until the 5th century AD, when an alphabet of 36 (now 38) letters was evolved. Literature flourished in the 4th to 14th centuries, revived in the 18th, and continued throughout the 20th.

Contemporary Armenian, with modified grammar and enriched with words from other languages, is used by a group of 20th-century writers.

armistice cessation of hostilities while awaiting a peace settlement. "The Armistice" refers specifically to the end of World War I between Germany and the Allies Nov 11, 1918. On June 22, 1940, French representatives signed an armistice with Germany in the same railroad carriage at Compiègne as in 1918. No armistice was signed with either Germany or Japan 1945; both nations surrendered and there was no provision for the suspension of fighting. The Korean armistice, signed at Panmunjom July 27, 1953, terminated the Korean War 1950–53.

Armistice Day anniversary of the armistice signed Nov 11, 1918, ending World War I. In the US this holiday is now called Veterans Day.

armor body protection worn in battle. Body armor is depicted in Greek and Roman art. Chain mail was developed in the Middle Ages but the craft of the armorer in Europe reached its height in design in the 15th century, when knights, and to some extent, their horses, were encased in plate armor that still allowed freedom of movement.

Medieval Japanese armor was articulated, made of iron, gilded metal, leather, and silk. Contemporary bulletproof vests and riot gear are forms of armor. The term is used in a modern context to refer to a mechanized armored vehicle, such as a tank.

armored personnel carrier (APC) wheeled or tracked military vehicle designed to transport up to ten people. Armoured to withstand small-arms fire and shell splinters, it is used on battlefields.

arms control attempts to limit the arms race between the superpowers by reaching agreements to restrict the production of certain weapons; see ◊disarmament.

arms trade sale of weapons from a manufacturing country to another nation. Nearly 56% of the world's arms exports end up in Third World countries. Iraq, for instance, was armed in the years leading up to the 1991 Gulf War mainly by the USSR but also by France, Brazil, and South Africa.

Armstrong Louis ("Satchmo") 1901–1971. US jazz cornet and trumpet player and singer. His Chicago recordings in the 1920s with the Hot Five and Hot Seven brought him recognition for his warm and pure trumpet tone, his skill at improvisation, and his quirky, gravelly voice. From the 1930s he also appeared in films.

Armstrong Neil Alden 1930– . US astronaut. In 1969, he became the first person to set foot on the Moon, and said, "That's one small step for a man, one giant leap for mankind." The Moon landing was part of the ◊Apollo project.

Arnhem, Battle of in World War II, airborne operation by the Allies, Sept 17–26, 1944, to secure a bridgehead over the Rhine, thereby opening the way for a thrust toward the Ruhr and a possible early end to the war. It was only partially successful, with 7,600 casualties.

Arnold Benedict 1741–1801. US soldier and military strategist who, during the American Revolution, won the turning-point battle at Saratoga 1777 for the Americans. He is chiefly remembered as a traitor to the American side, having plotted to betray the strategic post at West Point to the British.

Since the plot failed, he was paid only a fraction of the money promised him.

Arnold General Henry "Hap" 1886–1950. US general and aviator; he was largely responsible for preparing the US aviation industry for World War II and the training program which allowed the air corps to expand. A firm believer in the ability of bombing to win wars, he favored attacking specific targets rather than bombing whole areas.

When the US Army Air Corps was disbanded upon the formation of the US Air Force 1947, he became the first five star commanding general of the Air Force.

Arnold Matthew 1822–1888. English poet and critic. His poems, characterized by their elegiac mood and pastoral themes, include *The Forsaken Merman* 1849, *Thyrsis* 1867 (commemorating his friend Arthur Hugh Clough), *Dover Beach* 1867, and *The Scholar Gypsy* 1853. Arnold's critical works include Essays in Criticism 1865 and 1888, and his highly influential *Culture and Anarchy* 1869, which attacks 19th-century philistinism.

aromatic compound organic chemical compound in which some of the bonding electrons are delocalized (shared among several atoms within the molecule and not localized in the vicinity of the atoms involved in bonding). The commonest aromatic compounds have ring structures, the atoms comprising the ring being either all carbon or containing one or more different atoms (usually nitrogen, sulfur, or oxygen). Typical examples are benzene (C_6H_6) and pyridine (C_6H_5N).

Arp Hans or Jean 1887–1966. French abstract painter and sculptor. He was one of the founders of the ◊Dada movement 1916, and was later associated with the Surrealists. Using chance and automatism, Arp developed an abstract sculpture whose sensuous form suggests organic shapes.

ARPANET (acronym for *Advanced Research Projects Agency Network*) early US network that forms the basis of the ◊Internet. It was set up 1969 by ARPA to provide services to US academic institutions and commercial organizations conducting computer science research. ARPANET pioneered many of today's networking techniques.

array in computer programming, a list of values that can all be referred to by a single variable name. Separate values are distinguished by using a *subscript* with each variable name.

Arrhenius Svante August 1859–1927. Swedish scientist, the founder of physical chemistry. Born near Uppsala, he became a professor at Stockholm in 1895, and made a special study of electrolysis. He wrote *Worlds in the Making* and *Destinies of the Stars*, and in 1903 received the Nobel Prize for Chemistry. In 1905 he predicted global warming as a result of carbon dioxide emission from burning fossil fuels.

arrowroot starchy substance derived from the roots and tubers of various tropical plants with thick, clumpy roots. The true arrowroot *Maranta arundinacea* was used by the Indians of South America as an antidote against the effects of poisoned arrows.

arsenic brittle, grayish-white, semimetallic element (a metalloid), symbol As, atomic number 33, atomic weight 74.92. It occurs in many ores and occasionally in its elemental state, and is widely distributed, being present in minute quantities in the soil, the sea, and the human body. In larger quantities, it is poisonous. The chief source of arsenic compounds is as a by-product from metallurgical processes. It is used in making semiconductors, alloys, and solders.

arson malicious and willful setting fire to property.

Often arson is a crime committed to claim insurance benefits fraudulently.

art in the broadest sense, all the processes and products of human skill, imagination, and invention; the opposite of nature. In contemporary usage, definitions of art usually reflect esthetic criteria, and the term may encompass literature, music, drama, painting, and sculpture. Popularly, the term is most commonly used to refer to the visual arts. In Western culture, esthetic criteria introduced by the ancient Greeks still influence our perceptions and judgments of art.

Art Deco style in the decorative arts which influenced design and architecture. It emerged in Europe in the 1920s and continued through the 1930s, becoming particularly popular in the US and France. A self-consciously modern style, originally called "Jazz Modern", it is characterized by angular, geometrical patterns and bright colors, and by the use of materials such as enamel, chrome, glass, and plastic. The graphic artist Erté was a fashionable exponent.

Artemis in Greek mythology, the goddess of chastity, the young of all creatures, the Moon, and the hunt (Roman Diana). She is the twin sister of ◊Apollo and was worshiped at cult centers throughout the Greek world, one of the largest of which was at Ephesus. Her great temple there, reconstructed several times in antiquity, was one of the ◊Seven Wonders of the World.

arteriosclerosis hardening of the arteries, with thickening and loss of elasticity. It is associated with smoking, aging, and a diet high in saturated fats. The term is used loosely as a synonym for ◊atherosclerosis.

artery vessel that carries blood from the heart to the rest of the body. It is built to withstand considerable pressure, having thick walls which contain smooth muscle fibers. During contraction of the heart muscle, arteries expand in diameter to allow for the sudden increase in pressure that occurs; the resulting ◊pulse or pressure wave can be felt at the wrist. Not all arteries carry oxygenated (oxygen-rich) blood; the pulmonary arteries convey deoxygenated (oxygen-poor) blood from the heart to the lungs.

artesian well well that is supplied with water rising from an underground water-saturated rock layer

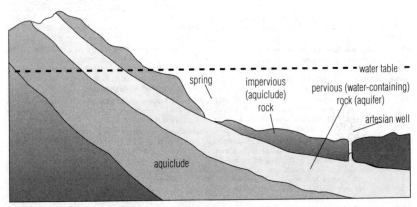

artesian well In an artesian well, water rises from an underground water-containing rock layer under its own pressure. Rain falls at one end of the water-bearing layer, or aquifer, and percolates through the layer. The layer fills with water up to the level of the water table. Water will flow from a well under its own pressure if the well head is below the level of the water table.

(◊aquifer). The water rises from the aquifer under its own pressure. Such a well may be drilled into an aquifer that is confined by impermeable rocks both above and below. If the water table (the top of the region of water saturation) in that aquifer is above the level of the well head, hydrostatic pressure will force the water to the surface.

The name comes from Artois (Latin *Artesium*), a historical region of N France, on the Strait of Dover, where the phenomenon was first observed.

arthritis inflammation of the joints, with pain, swelling, and restricted motion. Many conditions may cause arthritis, including gout, infection, and trauma to the joint. (See ◊rheumatoid arthritis.)

arthroplasty refashioning or replacement of a diseased joint. One of the most successful operations of this kind is total hip replacement.

arthropod member of the phylum Arthropoda; an invertebrate animal with jointed legs and a segmented body with a horny or chitinous casing (exoskeleton), which is shed periodically and replaced as the animal grows. Included are arachnids such as spiders and mites, as well as crustaceans, millipedes, centipedes, and insects.

Arthur Legendary British king and hero in stories of Camelot and the quest for the ◊Holy Grail. Arthur is said to have been born in Tintagel, Cornwall, and buried in Glastonbury, Somerset. He may have been a Romano-Celtic leader against pagan Saxon invaders.

artichoke either of two plants of the composite or sunflower family Compositae. The common or globe artichoke *Cynara scolymus* is native to the Mediterranean, and is a form of thistle. It is tall, with purplish blue flowers; the bracts of the unopened flower are eaten. The Jerusalem artichoke *Helianthus tuberosus* is a sunflower, native to North America. It has edible tubers, and its common name is a corruption of the Italian for sunflower, *girasole*.

article grammatical ◊part of speech. There are two articles in English: the *definite article the*, which serves to specify or identify a noun (as in "This is *the* book I need"), and the *indefinite article a* or (before vowels) *an*, which indicates a single unidentified noun ("They gave me *a* piece of paper and *an* envelope").

artifact any movable object that has been used, modified, or manufactured by humans, such as a tool, weapon or vessel.

artificial insemination (AI) introduction by instrument of semen from a sperm bank or donor into the female reproductive tract to bring about fertilization. Originally used by animal breeders to improve stock with sperm from high-quality males, in the 20th century it has been developed for use in humans, to help the infertile. See ◊in vitro fertilization.

The sperm for artificial insemination may come from the husband (AIH) or a donor (AID).

artificial intelligence (AI) branch of science concerned with creating computer programs that can perform actions comparable with those of an intelligent human. Current AI research covers such areas as planning (for robot behavior), language understanding, pattern recognition, and knowledge representation.

artificial respiration emergency procedure to restart breathing once it has stopped; in cases of electric shock or apparent drowning, for example, the first choice is the expired-air method, the **kiss of life** by mouth-to-mouth breathing until natural breathing is restored.

artificial selection in biology, selective breeding of individuals that exhibit particular characteristics that a plant or animal breeder wishes to develop. The development of particular breeds of cattle for improved meat production (such as the Aberdeen Angus) or milk production (such as Holsteins) are examples.

artillery collective term for military ◊firearms too heavy to be carried. Artillery can be mounted on tracks, wheels, ships or airplanes and includes cannons and rocket launchers.

Art Nouveau in the visual arts and architecture, a decorative style of about 1890–1910 which makes marked use of sinuous lines reminiscent of unfolding tendrils, stylized flowers and foliage, and flame shapes. In the US, it appears in the lamps and metalwork of Louis Comfort Tiffany; in England, it appears in the illustrations of Aubrey Beardsley; in Scotland, in the interior and exterior designs of Charles Rennie Mackintosh; in Spain, in the architecture of Antonio Gaudí; in France, in the architecture of Hector Guimard, the art glass of René Lalique, and the posters of Alphonse Mucha; and Belgium, in the houses and shops of Victor Horta. Art Nouveau took its name from a shop in Paris that opened 1895; it was also known as *Jugendstil* in Germany and *Stile Liberty* in Italy, after the fashionable London department store.

Aruba island in the Caribbean, the westernmost of the Lesser Antilles; an overseas part of the Netherlands *area* 75 sq mi/193 sq km *population* (1989) 62,400 *history* Aruba obtained separate status from the other Netherlands Antilles 1986 and has full internal autonomy.

arum any plant of the family Araceae, especially the Old World genus *Arum*. The arum called the trumpet lily *Zantedeschia aethiopica*, an ornamental plant, is a native of South Africa.

Jack-in-the-pulpit and skunk cabbage are North American arums belonging to related genera.

Arunachal Pradesh state of India, in the Himalayas on the borders of Tibet and Myanmar *area* 32,270 sq mi/83,600 sq km *capital* Itanagar *industries* rubber, coffee, spices, fruit, timber *population* (1991) 858,400 *language* 50 different dialects *history* formerly part of the state of Assam. It became a state of India 1987.

Aryan languages 19th-century name for the ◊Indo-European languages; the languages of the Aryan peoples of India. The name Aryan is no longer used by language scholars because of its association with the Nazi concept of white supremacy.

asa abbreviation for *Association of South East Asia* (1961–67), replaced by ASEAN, ◊*Association of Southeast Asian Nations*.

asbestos any of several related minerals of fibrous structure that offer great heat resistance because of their nonflammability and poor conductivity. Commercial asbestos is generally either made from serpentine ("white" asbestos) or from sodium iron silicate ("blue" asbestos). The fibers are woven together or bound by an inert material. Over time the fibers can work loose and, because they are small enough to float freely in the air or be inhaled, asbestos usage is now strictly controlled; exposure to its dust can cause cancer.

Ascension British island of volcanic origin in the S Atlantic, a dependency of St Helena since 1922;

population (1982) 1,625. The chief settlement is Georgetown.

ASCII (acronym for *American standard code for information interchange*) in computing, a coding system in which numbers are assigned to letters, digits, and punctuation symbols. Although computers work in ◊binary number code, ASCII numbers are usually quoted as decimal or ◊hexadecimal numbers. For example, the decimal number 45 (binary 0101101) represents a hyphen, and 65 (binary 1000001) a capital A. The first 32 codes are used for control functions, such as carriage return and backspace.

ascorbic acid $C_6H_8O_6$ or *vitamin C* a relatively simple organic acid found in citrus fruits and vegetables. It is soluble in water and destroyed by prolonged boiling, so soaking or overcooking of vegetables reduces their vitamin C content. Lack of ascorbic acid results in scurvy.

ASEAN acronym for ◊*Association of South East Asian Nations*.

asepsis practice of ensuring that bacteria are excluded from open sites during surgery, wound dressing, blood sampling, and other medical procedures. Aseptic technique is a first line of defense against infection.

asexual reproduction in biology, reproduction that does not involve the manufacture and fusion of sex cells, nor the necessity for two parents. The process carries a clear advantage in that there is no need to search for a mate nor to develop complex pollinating mechanisms; every asexual organism can reproduce on its own. Asexual reproduction can therefore lead to a rapid population buildup.

ash any tree of the worldwide genus *Fraxinus*, belonging to the olive family Oleaceae, with winged fruits. The ◊*mountain ash* or *rowan* belongs to the family Rosaceae.

Ashe Arthur Robert, Jr. 1943–1993. US tennis player and coach. He won the US national men's singles title at Forest Hills and the first US Open 1968. Known for his exceptionally strong serve, Ashe turned professional 1969. He won the Australian men's title 1970 and Wimbledon 1975. Cardiac problems ended his playing career 1979, but he continued his involvement with the sport as captain of the US Davis Cup team. In 1992 he launched a fund-raising campaign to combat AIDS, which he had contracted from a blood transfusion.

Ashgabat (formerly *Ashkhabad*) capital of Turkmenistan; population (1989) 402,000. The spelling was changed 1992 to reflect the Turkmen origin of the name. Industries include glass, carpets ("Bukhara" carpets are made here), cotton; the spectacular natural setting has been used by the film-making industry.

Ashkenazi (plural *Ashkenazim*) a Jew of German or E European descent, as opposed to a Sephardi, of Spanish, Portuguese, or N African descent.

Ashkhabad former name (to 1992) of ◊Ashgabat.

Ashley Laura (born Mountney) 1925–1985. Welsh designer. She established and gave her name to a Neo-Victorian country style in clothes and furnishings manufactured by her company from 1953. She founded a highly successful international chain of shops.

Ash Wednesday first day of Lent, the period in the Christian calendar leading up to Easter; in the Roman Catholic Church the foreheads of the congregation are marked with a cross in ash, as a sign of penitence.

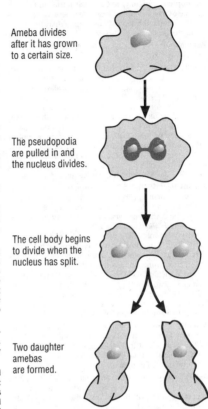

Ameba divides after it has grown to a certain size.

The pseudopodia are pulled in and the nucleus divides.

The cell body begins to divide when the nucleus has split.

Two daughter amebas are formed.

asexual reproduction Asexual reproduction is the simplest form of reproduction, occurring in many simple plants and animals. Binary fission, shown occurring in an ameba, is one of a number of asexual reproduction processes.

Asia largest of the continents, occupying one-third of the total land surface of the world *area* 17,000,000 sq mi/44,000,000 sq km *largest cities* (population over 5 million) Tokyo, Shanghai, Osaka, Beijing, Seoul, Calcutta, Bombay, Jakarta, Bangkok, Tehran, Hong Kong, Delhi, Tianjin, Karachi *features* Mount Everest, at 29,118 ft/8,872 m is the world's highest mountain; Dead Sea at –1,293 ft/–394 m is the world's lowest point below sea level; rivers (over 2,000 mi/3,200 km) include Chiang Jiang (Yangtze), Huang He (Yellow River), Ob-Irtysh, Amur, Lena, Mekong, Yenisei; lakes (over 7,000 sq mi/18,000 sq km/7,000) include Caspian Sea (the largest lake in the world), Aral Sea, Baikal (largest freshwater lake in Eurasia), Balkhash; deserts include the Gobi, Takla Makan, Syrian Desert, Arabian Desert, Negev *physical* lying in the eastern hemisphere, Asia extends from the Arctic Circle to just over 10° S of the equator. The Asian mainland, which forms the greater part of the Eurasian continent, lies entirely in the northern hemisphere and stretches from Cape Chelyubinsk at its northern extremity to Cape Piai at the southern tip of the Malay Peninsula. From Dezhneva Cape in the E, the mainland extends W over more than 165° longitude to Cape Baba in Turkey.

Asia Minor historical name for *Anatolia*, the Asian part of Turkey.

Asian native to or an inhabitant of the continent of Asia, which is the contiguous land mass east of the Ural Mountains, the traditional boundary between Europe and Asia. The region is culturally heterogenous with numerous distinctive ethnic and sociolinguistic groups, totaling over half the Earth's human population (including China, India, and Japan). Asians are of three main racial stocks: Mongoloid in the east; Caucasoid in the west; and Negroid in the Philippines and off-shore islands of the Indian Ocean. The Indians of the Americas were Asian migrants to the New World during the last Ice Age.

Asimov Isaac 1920–1992. Russian-born US author and editor of science fiction and nonfiction. He published more than 400 books including his science fiction *I, Robot* 1950 and the *Foundation* trilogy 1951–53, continued in *Foundation's Edge* 1983.

Asimov immigrated to the US as a child. He graduated from Columbia University with a PhD 1948. Trained as a biochemist, Asimov wrote numerous nonfiction works on scientific subjects.

These include *Building Blocks of the Universe* 1957; *Until the Sun Dies* 1977, about black holes; and *The Exploding Suns: The Secrets of the Supernovas* 1985. His science-fiction works include short stories, and he wrote two autobiographical volumes 1981, 1982.

Asmara or *Asmera* capital of Eritrea; 64 km/40 mi SW of Massawa on the Red Sea; population (1984) 275,385. Products include beer, clothes, and textiles. It has a naval school. In 1974 unrest here precipitated the end of the Ethiopian Empire.

Asoka Mauryan emperor of India *c.*268–232 BC, the greatest of the Mauryan rulers. He inherited an empire covering most of north and south-central India which, at its height, had a population of at least 30 million, with its capital at Pataliputra. A devout Buddhist, he renounced militarism and concentrated on establishing an efficient administration with a large standing army and a secret police.

asp any of several venomous snakes, including *Vipera aspis* of S Europe, allied to the adder, and the Egyptian cobra *Naja haje*, reputed to have been used by the Egyptian queen Cleopatra for her suicide.

asparagus any plant of the genus *Asparagus*, family Liliaceae, with small scalelike leaves and many needle-like branches. Native to Eurasia, *A. officinalis* is cultivated, and the young shoots are eaten as a vegetable.

aspartame noncarbohydrate sweetener used in foods under the trade-name Nutrasweet. It is about 200 times as sweet as sugar and, unlike saccharine, has no aftertaste.

aspen any of several species of ◊poplar tree, genus *Populus*. The European quaking aspen *P. tremula* has flattened leafstalks that cause the leaves to flutter with every breeze. The soft, light-colored wood is used for matches and paper pulp.

asphalt mineral mixture containing semisolid brown or black ◊bitumen, used in the construction industry. Asphalt is mixed with rock chips to form paving material, and the purer varieties are used for insulating material and for waterproofing masonry. It can be produced artificially by the distillation of ◊petroleum.

asphodel either of two related Old World genera (*Asphodeline* and *Asphodelus*) of plants of the lily family Liliaceae. *Asphodelus albus*, the white asphodel or king's spear, is found in Italy and Greece, sometimes covering large areas, and providing grazing for sheep. *Asphodeline lutea* is the yellow asphodel.

asphyxia suffocation; a lack of oxygen that produces a potentially lethal buildup of carbon dioxide waste in the tissues.

aspidistra Asiatic plant of the genus *Aspidistra* of the lily family Liliaceae. The Chinese *A. elatior* has broad, lanceolate leaves and, like all members of the genus, grows well in warm indoor conditions.

aspirin acetylsalicylic acid, a popular pain-relieving drug (◊analgesic) developed in the late 19th century as a household remedy for aches and pains. It relieves pain and reduces inflammation and fever. It is derived from the white willow tree *Salix alba*.

Aspirin may cause stomach bleeding, kidney damage, and hearing defects. It is no longer considered suitable for children under 12 because of a suspected link with a rare disease, Reye's syndrome. However, recent medical research suggests that an aspirin a day may be of value in preventing heart attack (myocardial infarction) and thrombosis.

Asquith Herbert Henry, 1st Earl of Oxford and Asquith 1852–1928. British Liberal politician, prime minister 1908–16. As chancellor of the Exchequer he introduced old-age pensions 1908. He limited the powers of the House of Lords and attempted to give Ireland Home Rule.

During World War I, his attitude of "wait and see" was not adapted to all-out war, and in Dec 1916 he was replaced by Lloyd George. In 1918 the Liberal election defeat led to the eclipse of the party.

ass any of several horselike, odd-toed, hoofed mammals of the genus *Equus*, family Equidae. Species include the African wild ass *E. asinus*, and the Asian wild ass *E. hemionus*. They differ from horses in their smaller size, larger ears, tufted tail, and characteristic bray. Donkeys and burros are domesticated asses.

Assad Hafez al 1930– . Syrian Ba'athist politician, president from 1971. He became prime minister after a bloodless military coup 1970, and the following year was the first president to be elected by popular vote. Having suppressed dissent, he was reelected 1978 and 1985. He is a Shia (Alawite) Muslim.

Assam state o˙ NE India *area* 30,262 sq mi/78,400 sq km *capital* Dispur *towns and cities* Guwahati *industries* half India's tea is grown and half its oil produced here; rice, jute, sugar, cotton, coal *population* (1991) 24,294,600, including 12 million Assamese (Hindus), 5 million Bengalis (chiefly Muslim immigrants from Bangladesh), Nepalis, and 2 million indigenous people (Christian and traditional religions) *language* Assamese *history* a thriving region from 1000 BC, Assam migrants came from China and Myanmar (Burma). After Burmese invasion 1826, Britain took control and made Assam a separate province 1874; it was included in the Dominion of India, except for most of the Muslim district of Silhet, which went to Pakistan 1947. Ethnic unrest started in the 1960s when Assamese was declared the official language. After protests, the Gara, Khasi, and Jainitia tribal hill districts became the state of Meghalaya 1971; the

Mizo hill district became the Union Territory of Mizoram 1972. There were massacres of Muslim Bengalis by Hindus 1983. In 1987 members of the Bodo ethnic group began fighting for a separate homeland. In the early 1990s the Marxist-militant United Liberation Front of Assam (ULFA), which had extorted payments from tea-exporting companies, spearheaded a campaign of separatist terrorist violence. In March 1991 it was reported that the ULFA, operating from the jungles of Myanmar, had been involved in 97 killings, mainly of Congress I politicians, since Nov 27, 1990.

assassination murder, usually of a political, royal, or public target. The term derives from the order of the Assassins, a Muslim sect that, in the 11th and 12th centuries, murdered officials to further its political ends.

assay in chemistry, the determination of the quantity of a given substance present in a sample. Usually it refers to determining the purity of precious metals.

assembler in computing, a program that translates a program written in an assembly language into a complete machine code program that can be executed by a computer. Each instruction in the assembly language is translated into only one machine-code instruction.

assembly language low-level computer-programming language closely related to a computer's internal codes. It consists chiefly of a set of short sequences of letters (mnemonics), which are translated, by a program called an assembler, into machine code for the computer's ◊central processing unit (CPU) to follow directly. In assembly language, for example, "JMP" means "jump" and "LDA" means "load accumulator". Assembly code is used by programmers who need to write very fast or efficient programs.

asset in accounting, anything owned by or owed to the company that is either cash or can be turned into cash. The term covers physical assets such as land or property of a company or individual, as well as financial assets such as cash, payments due from bills, and investments. Assets are divided into fixed assets and current assets. On a company's balance sheet, total assets must be equal to total liabilities (money and services owed).

asset stripping sale or exploitation by other means of the assets of a business, often one that has been taken over for that very purpose. The parts of the business may be potentially more valuable separately than together. Asset stripping is a major force for the more efficient use of assets.

assize in medieval Europe, the passing of laws, either by the king with the consent of nobles, as in the Constitutions of Clarendon 1164 by Henry II of England, or as a complete system, such as the *Assizes of Jerusalem*, a compilation of the law of the feudal kingdom of Jerusalem in the 13th century.

Association of South East Asian Nations (ASEAN) regional alliance formed in Bangkok 1967; it took over the nonmilitary role of the Southeast Asia Treaty Organization 1975. Its members are Indonesia, Malaysia, the Philippines, Singapore, Thailand, and (from 1984) Brunei; its headquarters are in Jakarta, Indonesia.

Assyria empire in the Middle East *c.*2500–612 BC, in N Mesopotamia (now Iraq); early capital Ashur, later Nineveh. It was initially subject to Sumer and intermittently to Babylon. The Assyrians adopted largely the Sumerian religion and structure of society. At its greatest extent the empire included Egypt and stretched from the E Mediterranean coast to the head of the Persian Gulf.

Astaire Fred. Adopted name of Frederick Austerlitz 1899–1987. US dancer, actor, singer, and choreographer. He starred in numerous films, including *Top Hat* 1935, *Easter Parade* 1948, and *Funny Face* 1957, many containing inventive sequences which he designed and choreographed himself. He made ten classic films with the most popular of his dancing partners, Ginger Rogers. He later played straight dramatic roles in such films as *On the Beach* 1959. He was the greatest popular dancer of his time.

astatine nonmetallic, radioactive element, symbol At, atomic number 85, atomic weight 210. It is a member of the ◊halogen group, and is very rare in nature. Astatine is highly unstable, with at least 19 isotopes; the longest lived has a half-life of about eight hours.

aster any plant of the large genus *Aster*, family Compositae, belonging to the same subfamily as the daisy. All asters have starlike flowers with yellow centers and outer rays (not petals) varying from blue and purple to white and the genus comprises a great variety of size. Many are cultivated as garden flowers, including the Michaelmas daisy *A. nova-belgii*.

The white wood aster *A. divaricatus* grows in open woods throughout most of the US.

asteroid or *minor planet* any of many thousands of small bodies, composed of rock and iron, that orbit the Sun. Most lie in a belt between the orbits of Mars and Jupiter, and are thought to be fragments left over from the formation of the ◊Solar System. About 100,000 may exist, but their total mass is only a few hundredths the mass of the Moon.

asthma chronic condition characterized by difficulty in breathing due to spasm of the bronchi (air passages) in the lungs. Attacks may be provoked by allergy, infection, and stress. The incidence of asthma may be increasing as a result of air pollution and occupational hazard. Treatment is with bronchodilators to relax the bronchial muscles and thereby ease the breathing, and in severe cases by inhaled ◊steroids that reduce inflammation of the bronchi.

astigmatism aberration occurring in the lens of the eye. It results when the curvature of the lens differs in two perpendicular planes, so that rays in one plane may be in focus while rays in the other are not. With astigmatic eyesight, the vertical and horizontal cannot be in focus at the same time; correction is by the use of a cylindrical lens that reduces the overall focal length of one plane so that both planes are seen in sharp focus.

Astor prominent US and British family. *John Jacob Astor* (1763–1848) was a US millionaire. His great-grandson *Waldorf Astor*, 2nd Viscount Astor (1879–1952), was a British politician, and served as Conservative Member of Parliament for Plymouth 1910–19, when he succeeded to the peerage. His US-born wife Nancy Witcher Langhorne (1879–1964), *Lady Astor*, was the first woman Member of Parliament to take a seat in the House of Commons 1919, when she succeeded her husband for the constituency of Plymouth.

Astor John Jacob 1763–1848. German-born US merchant who founded the monopolistic American Fur Company 1808. His subsidiary enterprise, the Pacific Fur Company, was created 1811 following the US government's Louisiana Purchase 1803 facilitating trade with the West. He founded Astoria, now in Oregon, as his trading post at the mouth of the Columbia River.

His estate endowed the Astor library, now a part of The New York Public Library.

astrology study of the relative position of the planets and stars in the belief that they influence events on Earth. The astrologer casts a horoscope based on the time and place of the subject's birth. Astrology has no proven scientific basis, but has been widespread since ancient times. Western astrology is based on the 12 signs of the zodiac; Chinese astrology is based on a 60-year cycle and lunar calendar.

In the US, horoscopes are syndicated in most newspapers and almost everyone, whether professing belief or not, knows his or her astrological sign.

astronomical unit unit (symbol AU) equal to the mean distance of the Earth from the Sun: 92,955,800 mi/149,597,870 km. It is used to describe planetary distances. Light travels this distance in approximately 8.3 minutes.

astronomy science of the celestial bodies: the Sun, the Moon, and the planets; the stars and galaxies; and all other objects in the universe. It is concerned with their positions, motions, distances, and physical conditions and with their origins and evolution. Astronomy thus divides into fields such as astrophysics, celestial mechanics, and cosmology. See also ◊gamma-ray astronomy and ◊radio astronomy.

astrophysics study of the physical nature of stars, galaxies, and the universe. It began with the development of spectroscopy in the 19th century, which allowed astronomers to analyze the composition of stars from their light. Astrophysicists view the universe as a vast natural laboratory in which they can study matter under conditions of temperature, pressure, and density that are unattainable on Earth.

Asunción capital and port of Paraguay, on the Paraguay River; population (1984) 729,000. It produces textiles, footwear, and food products. Founded 1537, it was the first Spanish settlement in the La Plata region.

Aswan winter resort in Upper Egypt; population (1985) 183,000. It is near the Aswan High Dam, built 1960–70, which keeps the level of the Nile constant throughout the year without flooding. It produces steel and textiles.

asylum, political in international law, refuge granted in another country to a person who, for political reasons, cannot return to his or her own country without putting himself or herself in danger. A person seeking asylum is a type of ◊refugee.

asymptote in ◊coordinate geometry, a straight line that a curve approaches more and more closely but never reaches. The x and y axes are asymptotes to the graph of xy = constant (a rectangular hyperbola).

asynchronous irregular or not synchronized. In computer communications, the term is usually applied to data transmitted irregularly rather than as a steady stream. Asynchronous communication uses start bits and stop bits to indicate the beginning and end of each piece of data.

Atacama Desert desert in N Chile; area about 31,000 sq mi/80,000 sq km. There are mountains inland, and the coastal area is rainless and barren.

The desert has silver and copper mines, and extensive nitrate deposits.

Atahualpa *c*.1502–1533. Last emperor of the Incas of Peru. He was taken prisoner 1532 when the Spaniards arrived and agreed to pay a substantial ransom, but he was accused of plotting against the conquistador Pizarro and was sentenced to be burned. On his consenting to Christian baptism, the sentence was commuted to strangulation.

Atatürk (Turkish "Father of the Turks") (Mustafa Kemal Atatürk) Name assumed 1934 by Mustafa Kemal Pasha 1881–1938. Turkish politician and general, first president of Turkey from 1923. After World War I he established a provisional rebel government and in 1921–22 the Turkish armies under his leadership expelled the Greeks who were occupying Turkey. He was the founder of the modern republic, which he ruled as virtual dictator, with a policy of consistent and radical westernization.

atavism (Latin *atavus* "ancestor") in genetics, the reappearance of a characteristic not apparent in the immediately preceding generations; in psychology, the manifestation of primitive forms of behavior.

atheism nonbelief in, or the positive denial of, the existence of a God or gods. A related concept is ◊agnosticism.

Athelstan *c*.895–939. King of the Mercians and West Saxons. Son of Edward the Elder and grandson of Alfred the Great, he was crowned king 925 at Kingston upon Thames. He subdued parts of Cornwall and Wales, and defeated the Welsh, Scots, and Danes at Brunanburh 937.

Athena in Greek mythology, the goddess of war, wisdom, and the arts and crafts (Roman Minerva), who was supposed to have sprung fully grown from the head of Zeus. In Homer's *Odyssey*, she is the protectress of ◊Odysseus and his son Telemachus. Her chief cult center was Athens, where the Parthenon was dedicated to her.

Athens (Greek *Athinai*) capital city of Greece and of ancient Attica; population (1981) 885,000, metropolitan area (1991) 3,096,800. Situated 5 mi/8 km NE of its port of Piraeus on the Gulf of Aegina, it is built around the rocky hills of the Acropolis 555 ft/169 m and the Areopagus 368 ft/112 m, and is overlooked from the NE by the hill of Lycabettus, 909 ft/277 m high. It lies in the S of the central plain of Attica, watered by the mountain streams of Cephissus and Ilissus. It has less green space than any other European capital (4%) and severe air and noise pollution.

atherosclerosis thickening and hardening of the walls of the arteries, associated with atheroma.

athletics collectively, all the sports, exercises, and contests that utilize and promote such physical skills as speed, agility, and stamina.

Atlanta capital and largest city of Georgia, US; population (1990) 394,000, metropolitan area 2,010,000. It was founded 1837 and was partly destroyed by General ◊Sherman 1864. There are Ford and Lockheed assembly plants, and it is the headquarters of Coca-Cola. In 1990 it was chosen as the host city for the 1996 summer Olympic Games.

Atlanta is also the financial, trade, and convention center for the SE US and has one of the busiest and most automated US airports. Educational institutions include Atlanta University, Emory University, the Georgia Institute of Technology, and Georgia State University. The city grew considerably in importance after 1900.

Atlantic City seaside resort in New Jersey; population (1990) 38,000. Formerly a family resort, Atlantic City has become a center for casino gambling, which was legalized 1978.

It is noted for its "boardwalk" and for being the basis of the Monopoly board game; the Miss America contest has been held here since 1921. It is also a convention center.

Atlantic Ocean ocean lying between Europe and Africa to the E and the Americas to the W, probably named for the legendary island continent of ◊Atlantis; area of basin 31,500,000 sq mi/81,500,000 sq km; including the Arctic Ocean and Antarctic seas, 41,000,000/106,200,000 sq km. The average depth is 2 mi/3 km; greatest depth the Milwaukee Depth in the Puerto Rico Trench 28,374 ft/8,648 m. The *Mid-Atlantic Ridge*, of which the Azores, Ascension, St Helena, and Tristan da Cunha form part, divides it from N to S. Lava welling up from this central area annually increases the distance between South America and Africa. The N Atlantic is the saltiest of the main oceans and has the largest tidal range.

Atlantis in Greek mythology, an island continent, said to have sunk following an earthquake. Although the Atlantic Ocean is probably named for it, the structure of the sea bottom rules out its ever having existed there. The Greek philosopher Plato created an imaginary early history for it and described it as a utopia.

Atlas in Greek mythology, one of the ◊Titans who revolted against the gods; as a punishment, he was compelled to support the heavens on his head and shoulders. Growing weary, he asked Perseus to turn him into stone, and he was transformed into Mount Atlas.

Atlas Mountains mountain system of NW Africa, stretching 1,500 mi/2,400 km from the Atlantic coast of Morocco to the Gulf of Gabes, Tunisia, and lying between the Mediterranean on the N and the Sahara on the S. The highest peak is Mount Toubkal 13,670 ft/4,167 m.

atmosphere mixture of gases that surrounds the Earth, prevented from escaping by the pull of the Earth's gravity. Atmospheric pressure decreases with height in the atmosphere. In its lowest layer, the atmosphere consists of nitrogen (78%) and oxygen (21%), both in molecular form (two atoms bonded together). The other 1% is largely argon, with very small quantities of other gases, including water vapor and carbon dioxide. The atmosphere plays a major part in the various cycles of nature (the water cycle, ◊carbon cycle, and ◊nitrogen cycle). It is the principal industrial source of nitrogen, oxygen, and argon, which are obtained by fractional distillation of liquid air.

atmosphere or *standard atmosphere* in physics, a unit (symbol atm) of pressure equal to 760 torr, 1013.25 millibars, or 1.01325×10^5 newtons per square meter. The actual pressure exerted by the atmosphere fluctuates around this value, which is assumed to be standard at sea level and 0°C, and is used when dealing with very high pressures.

atoll continuous or broken circle of ◊coral reef and low coral islands surrounding a lagoon.

atom smallest unit of matter that can take part in a chemical reaction, and which cannot be broken down chemically into anything simpler. An atom is made up of protons and neutrons in a central nucleus surrounded by electrons (see ◊atomic structure). The atoms of the various elements differ in atomic number,

atomic weight, and chemical behavior. There are 109 different types of atom, corresponding with the 109 known elements as listed in the ◊periodic table of the elements.

atomic bomb bomb deriving its explosive force from nuclear fission (see ◊nuclear energy) as a result of a neutron chain reaction, developed in the 1940s in the US into a usable weapon.

atomic clock timekeeping device regulated by various periodic processes occurring in atoms and molecules, such as atomic vibration or the frequency of absorbed or emitted radiation.

atomic energy former name for ◊nuclear energy.

atomic mass unit or *dalton unit* (symbol amu or u) unit of mass that is used to measure the relative mass of atoms and molecules. It is equal to one-twelfth of the mass of a carbon-12 atom, which is equivalent to the mass of a proton or 1.66×10^{-27} kg. The ◊atomic weight of an atom has no units; thus oxygen-16 has an atomic mass of 16 daltons, but an atomic weight of 16.

atomic number or *proton number* the number (symbol Z) of protons in the nucleus of an atom. It is equal to the positive charge on the nucleus. In a neutral atom, it is also equal to the number of electrons surrounding the nucleus. The 109 elements are arranged in the ◊periodic table of the elements according to their atomic number.

atomic radiation energy given out by disintegrating atoms during ◊radioactive decay, whether natural or synthesized. The energy may be in the form of fast-moving particles, known as ◊alpha particles and ◊beta particles, or in the form of high-energy electromagnetic waves known as ◊gamma radiation. Overlong exposure to atomic radiation can lead to ◊radiation sickness.

atomic structure internal structure of an ◊atom. The core of the atom is the *nucleus*, a dense body only one ten-thousandth the diameter of the atom itself. The simplest nucleus, that of hydrogen, comprises a single stable positively charged particle, the *proton*. Nuclei of other elements contain more protons and additional particles, called *neutrons*, of about the same mass as the proton but with no electrical charge. Each element has its own characteristic nucleus with a unique number of protons, the atomic number. The number of neutrons may vary. Where atoms of a single element have different numbers of neutrons, they are called ◊isotopes. Although some isotopes tend to be unstable and exhibit ◊radioactivity, they all have identical chemical properties.

High-energy physics research has discovered the existence of subatomic particles (see ◊particle physics) other than the proton, neutron, and electron. More than 300 kinds of particle are now known.

atomic weight or *atomic mass* the mass of an atom. It depends on the number of protons and neutrons in the atom, the electrons having negligible mass. It is calculated relative to one-twelfth the mass of an atom of carbon-12. If more than one ◊isotope of the element is present, the atomic weight is calculated by taking an average that takes account of the relative proportions of each isotope, resulting in values that are not whole numbers.

Atonement, Day of Jewish holy day (*Yom Kippur*) held on the tenth day of Tishri (Sept–Oct), the first

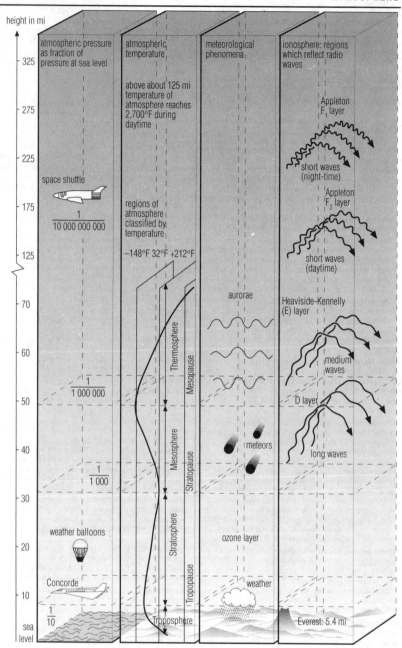

atmosphere *All but 1% of the Earth's atmosphere lies in a layer 19 mi/30 km above the ground. At a height of 18,000 ft/5,500 m, air pressure is half that at sea level. The temperature of the atmosphere varies greatly with height; this produces a series of layers, called the troposphere, stratosphere, mesosphere, and thermosphere.*

month of the Jewish year. It is a day of fasting, penitence, and cleansing from sin, ending the Ten Days of Penitence that follow *Rosh Hashanah*, the Jewish New Year.

ATP abbreviation for *adenosine triphosphate*, a nucleotide molecule found in all cells. It can yield large amounts of energy, and is used to drive the thousands of biological processes needed to sustain life, growth, movement, and reproduction. Green plants use light energy to manufacture ATP as part of the process of ◊photosynthesis. In animals, ATP is formed by the breakdown of glucose molecules, usually obtained from the carbohydrate component of a diet, in a series of reactions termed ◊respiration. It is the driving force behind muscle contraction and the synthesis of complex molecules needed by individual cells.

Attenborough Richard 1923– . English director, actor, and producer. He made his screen acting debut in *In Which We Serve* 1942, and later appeared in such films as *Brighton Rock* 1947 and *10 Rillington Place* 1970. He co-produced the socially-conscious *The Angry Silence* 1960, and directed *Oh! What a Lovely War* 1969. He subsequently concentrated on directing, including the epic biographies of *Gandhi* (which won eight Academy Awards) 1982, *Cry Freedom* 1987, and *Chaplin* 1992. He is the brother of naturalist David Attenborough.

Attica (Greek *Attiki*) region of Greece comprising Athens and the district around it; area 1,305 sq mi/3,381 sq km. It is renowned for its language, art, and philosophical thought in Classical times. It is a prefecture of modern Greece with Athens as its capital.

Attila *c.*406–453. King of the Huns in an area from the Alps to the Caspian Sea from 434, known to later Christian history as the "Scourge of God". He twice attacked the Eastern Roman Empire to increase the quantity of tribute paid to him, 441–443 and 447–449, and then attacked the Western Roman Empire 450–452.

Attlee Clement (Richard), 1st Earl 1883–1967. British Labour politician. In the coalition government during World War II he was Lord Privy Seal 1940–42, dominions secretary 1942–43, and Lord President of the Council 1943–45, as well as deputy prime minister from 1942. As prime minister 1945–51 he introduced a sweeping program of nationalization and a whole new system of social services.

Attorney General principal law officer. In the US, the principal officer of the federal government or of a state. Attorneys general act as chief officers for criminal and civil law and as chief legal representatives of their governments in government operations.

Auckland largest city in New Zealand, situated in N North Island; population (1991) 315,900. It fills the isthmus that separates its two harbors (Waitemata and Manukau), and its suburbs spread N across the Harbour Bridge. It is the country's chief port and leading industrial center, having iron and steel plants, engineering, automobile assembly, textiles, food processing, sugar refining, and brewing.

Auden W(ystan) H(ugh) 1907–1973. English-born US poet. He wrote some of his most original poetry, such as *Look, Stranger!* 1936, in the 1930s when he led the influential left-wing literary group that included Louis MacNeice, Stephen Spender, and Cecil Day Lewis. He moved to the US 1939, became a US citizen 1946, and

adopted a more conservative and Christian viewpoint, for example in *The Age of Anxiety* 1947.

audit official inspection of a company's accounts by a qualified accountant as required by law each year to ensure that the company balance sheet reflects the true state of its affairs.

audit trail record of computer operations, showing what has been done and, if available, who has done it. The term is taken from accounting, but audit trails are now widely used to check many aspects of computer security, in addition to use in accounts programs.

Augustine of Hippo, St 354–430. One of the early Christian leaders and writers known as the Fathers of the Church. He was converted to Christianity by Ambrose in Milan and became bishop of Hippo (modern Annaba, Algeria) 396. Among Augustine's many writings are his *Confessions*, a spiritual autobiography, and *De Civitate Dei/The City of God*, vindicating the Christian church and divine providence in 22 books.

Augustine, St ?–605. first archbishop of Canterbury, England. He was sent from Rome to convert England to Christianity by Pope Gregory I. He landed at Ebbsfleet in Kent 597 and soon after baptized Ethelbert, King of Kent, along with many of his subjects. He was consecrated bishop of the English at Arles in the same year, and appointed archbishop 601, establishing his see at Canterbury. Feast day May 26.

Augustus 63 BC – AD 14. Title of Octavian (Gaius Julius Caesar Octavianus), first of the Roman emperors. He joined forces with Mark Antony and Lepidus in the Second Triumvirate. Following Mark Antony's liaison with the Egyptian queen Cleopatra, Augustus defeated her troops at Actium 31 BC. As emperor (from 27 BC) he reformed the government of the empire, the army, and Rome's public services and was a patron of the arts. The period of his rule is known as the Augustan Age.

auk any member of the family Alcidae, consisting of marine diving birds including razorbills, puffins, murres, and guillemots. Confined to the northern hemisphere, they feed on fish and use their wings to "fly" underwater in pursuit.

Aung San 1916–1947. Burmese (Myanmar) politician. He was a founder and leader of the Anti-Fascist People's Freedom League, which led Burma's fight for independence from Great Britain. During World War II he collaborated first with Japan and then with the UK. In 1947 he became head of Burma's provisional government but was assassinated the same year by political opponents. His daughter ◊Suu Kyi (1961–) spearheaded a nonviolent prodemocracy movement in Myanmar from 1988.

Aurangzeb or *Aurungzebe* 1618–1707. Mogul emperor of N India from 1658. Third son of ◊Shah Jahan, he made himself master of the court by a palace revolution. His reign was the most brilliant period of the Mogul dynasty, but his despotic tendencies and Muslim fanaticism aroused much opposition.

Aurelian (Lucius Domitius Aurelianus) *c.*214– AD 275. Roman emperor from 270. A successful soldier, he was chosen emperor by his troops on the death of Claudius II. He defeated the Goths and Vandals, defeated and captured Zenobia of Palmyra, and was planning a campaign against Parthia when he was murdered. The *Aurelian Wall*, a fortification surrounding Rome, was built by Aurelian 271. It was made of concrete, and substantial ruins exist.

Aurelius Marcus Roman emperor; see ◊Marcus Aurelius Antoninus.

Auriga constellation of the northern hemisphere, represented as a man driving a chariot. Its brightest star is the first-magnitude ◊Capella, about 45 light-years from Earth; Epsilon Aurigae is an eclipsing binary star with a period of 27 years, the longest of its kind (last eclipse 1983).

aurochs (plural *aurochs*) extinct species of long-horned wild cattle *Bos primigenius* that formerly roamed Europe, SW Asia, and N Africa. It survived in Poland until 1627. Black to reddish or gray, it was up to 1.8 m/6 ft at the shoulder. It is depicted in many cave paintings, and is considered the ancestor of domestic cattle.

aurora colored light in the night sky near the Earth's magnetic poles, called *aurora borealis* ("northern lights") in the northern hemisphere and *aurora australis* in the southern hemisphere. Auroras are caused at heights of over 60 mi/100 km by a fast stream of charged particles from solar flares and low-density "holes" in the Sun's corona. These are guided by the Earth's magnetic field toward the north and south magnetic poles, where they enter the upper atmosphere and bombard the gases in the atmosphere, causing them to emit visible light.

Auschwitz (Polish *Oswiecim*) town near Kraków in Poland, the site of a notorious ◊concentration camp used by the Nazis in World War II to exterminate Jews and other political and social minorities, as part of the "final solution". Each of the four gas chambers could hold 6,000 people.

Austen Jane 1775–1817. English novelist. She described her raw material as "three or four families in a Country Village". *Sense and Sensibility* was published 1811, *Pride and Prejudice* 1813, *Mansfield Park* 1814, *Emma* 1816, *Northanger Abbey* and *Persuasion* 1818, all anonymously. She observed speech and manners with wit and precision, revealing her characters' absurdities in relation to high standards of integrity and appropriateness.

Austerlitz, Battle of battle on 2 Dec 1805, in which the French forces of Emperor Napoleon defeated those of Alexander I of Russia and Francis II of Austria at a small town in the Czech Republic (formerly in Austria), 12 mi/19 km E of Brno.

Austin Stephen Fuller 1793–1836. American pioneer and political leader. A settler in Texas 1821, he was a supporter of the colony's autonomy and was imprisoned 1833–35 for his opposition to Mexican rule. Released during the Texas revolution, he campaigned for US support. After the end of the war 1836, he was appointed secretary of state of the independent Republic of Texas but died shortly afterwards.
The state capital of Austin was named in his honor.

Australasia loosely applied geographical term, usually meaning Australia, New Zealand, and neighboring islands.

Australia Commonwealth of *area* 2,966,136 sq mi/ 7,682,300 sq km *capital* Canberra *towns and cities* Adelaide, Alice Springs, Brisbane, Darwin, Melbourne, Perth, Sydney, Hobart, Geelong, Newcastle, Townsville, Wollongong *physical* the world's smallest, flattest, and driest continent (40% lies in the tropics, 30% is desert, and 30% is marginal grazing); Great Sandy Desert; Gibson Desert; Great Victoria Desert; Simpson Desert; the Great Barrier Reef (largest coral

reef in the world, stretching 1,250 mi/2,000 km off E coast of Queensland); Great Dividing Range and Australian Alps in the E (Mount Kosciusko, 7,136 ft/ 2,229 m, Australia's highest peak).
The fertile SE region is watered by the Darling, Lachlan, Murrumbridgee, and Murray rivers; rivers in the interior are seasonal. Lake Eyre basin and Nullarbor Plain in the S *territories* Norfolk Island, Christmas Island, Cocos (Keeling) Islands, Ashmore and Cartier Islands, Coral Sea Islands, Heard Island and McDonald Islands, Australian Antarctic Territory *environment* an estimated 75% of Australia's northern tropical rain forest has been cleared for agriculture or urban development since Europeans first settled there in the early 19th century *features* Ayers Rock; Arnhem Land; Gulf of Carpentaria; Cape York Peninsula; Great Australian Bight; unique animal species include the kangaroo, koala, platypus, wombat, Tasmanian devil, and spiny anteater; of 800 species of bird, the budgerigar, cassowary, emu, kookaburra, lyre bird, and black swan are also unique as a result of Australia's long isolation from other continents *head of state* Elizabeth II from 1952, represented by governor general William George Hayden from 1989 *head of government* Paul Keating from 1991 *political system* federal constitutional monarchy *political parties* Australian Labor Party, moderate left of center; Liberal Party of Australia, moderate, liberal, free enterprise; National Party of Australia (formerly Country Party), centrist non-metropolitan *exports* world's largest exporter of sheep, wool, diamonds, alumina, coal, lead and refined zinc ores, and mineral sands; other exports include cereals, beef, veal, mutton, lamb, sugar, nickel (world's second largest producer), iron ore; principal trade partners are Japan, the US, and EC member states *currency* Australian dollar *population* (1993 est) 17,800,000; growth rate 1.5% p.a. *life expectancy* men 74, women 80 *languages* English, Aboriginal languages *religions* Anglican 26%, other Protestant 17%, Roman Catholic 26% *literacy* 99% *GNP* $16,590 per head (1991) *chronology 1901* Creation of Commonwealth of Australia. *1927* Seat of government moved to Canberra. *1942* Statute of Westminster Adoption Act gave Australia autonomy from UK in internal and external affairs. *1944* Liberal Party founded by Robert Menzies. *1951* Australia joined New Zealand and the US as a signatory to the ANZUS Pacific security treaty. *1966* Menzies resigned after being Liberal prime minister for 17 years, and was succeeded by Harold Holt. *1967* A referendum was passed giving Aborigines full

citizenship rights. *1968* John Gorton became prime minister after Holt's death. *1971* Gorton succeeded by William McMahon, heading a Liberal–Country Party coalition. *1972* Gough Whitlam became prime minister, leading a Labor government. *1975* Senate blocked the government's financial legislation; Whitlam dismissed by the governor-general, who invited Malcolm Fraser to form a Liberal–Country Party caretaker government. This action of the governor-general, John Kerr, was widely criticized. *1978* Northern Territory attained self-government. *1983* Labor Party, returned to power under Bob Hawke, convened meeting of employers and unions to seek consensus on economic policy to deal with growing unemployment. *1986* Australia Act passed by UK government, eliminating last vestiges of British legal authority in Australia. *1988* Labor foreign minister Bill Hayden appointed governor general designate. Free-trade agreement with New Zealand signed. *1990* Hawke won record fourth election victory, defeating Liberal Party by small majority. *1991* Paul Keating became new Labor Party leader and prime minister. *1992* Keating's popularity declined as economic problems continued. Oath of allegiance to British crown abandoned. *1993* Labor Party won surprise victory in general election, entering fifth term of office.

Australian Aborigine any of the 500 groups of indigenous inhabitants of the continent of Australia, who migrated to this region from S Asia about 40,000 years ago. They are dark-skinned Caucasoids, with fair hair in childhood and heavy dark beards and body hair in adult males. They were hunters and gatherers, living throughout the continent in small kin-based groups before European settlement. Several hundred different languages developed, including Aranda (Arunta), spoken in central Australia, and Murngin, spoken in Arnhem Land. In recent years a movement for the recognition of Aborigine rights has begun, with campaigns against racial discrimination in housing, education, wages, and medical facilities.

Aborigines make up about 1.5% of Australia's population of 16 million. They live in reserves as well as among the general population. They have an infant mortality four times the national average and an adult life expectancy 20 years below the average 76 years of other Australians.

Austria Republic of (*Republik österreich*) *area* 32,374 sq mi/83,500 sq km *capital* Vienna *towns and cities* Graz, Linz, Salzburg, Innsbruck *physical* landlocked mountainous state, with Alps in W and S and low relief in E where most of the population is concentrated *environment* Hainburg, the largest primeval forest left in Europe, under threat from a dam project (suspended 1990) *features* Austrian Alps (including Grossglockner and Brenner and Semmering passes); Lechtaler and Allgauer Alps N of river Inn; Carnic Alps on Italian border; river Danube *head of state* Thomas Klestil from 1992 *head of government* Franz Vranitzky from 1986 *political system* democratic federal republic *political parties* Socialist Party of Austria (SPÖ), democratic socialist; Austrian People's Party (ÖVP), progressive centrist; Freedom Party of Austria (FPÖ), moderate left of center; United Green Party of Austria (VGÖ), conservative ecological; Green Alternative Party (ALV), radical ecological *exports* lumber, textiles, clothing, iron and steel, paper, machinery and transport equipment, foodstuffs *currency* schilling *population* (1993 est) 7,900,000; growth rate 0.1% p.a. *life expectancy* men 72, women 79 *language*

German *religion* Roman Catholic 85%, Protestant 6% *literacy* 99% GNP $23,256 per head (1992) *chronology 1867* Emperor Franz Josef established dual monarchy of Austria–Hungary. *1914* Archduke Franz Ferdinand assassinated by a Serbian nationalist; Austria–Hungary invaded Serbia, precipitating World War I. *1918* Hapsburg empire ended; republic proclaimed. *1938* Austria incorporated into German Third Reich by Hitler (the *Anschluss*). *1945* Under Allied occupation, constitution of 1920 reinstated and coalition government formed by the SPÖ and the ÖVP. *1955* Allied occupation ended, and the independence of Austria formally recognized. *1966* ÖVP in power with Josef Klaus as chancellor. *1970* SPÖ formed a minority government, with Dr Bruno Kreisky as chancellor. *1983* Kreisky resigned and was replaced by Dr Fred Sinowatz, leading a coalition. *1986* Dr Kurt Waldheim elected president. Sinowatz resigned, succeeded by Franz Vranitzky, who formed a coalition of the SPÖ and the ÖVP, with ÖVP leader, Dr Alois Mock, as vice chancellor. *1990* Vranitzky reelected. *1992* Thomas Klestil elected president, replacing Waldheim. *1994* Referendum overwhelmingly supported European Union membership. Gains for right-wing parties in general election.

Austrian Succession, War of the war 1740–48 between Austria (supported by England and Holland) and Prussia (supported by France and Spain).

1740 The Holy Roman emperor Charles VI died and the succession of his daughter Maria Theresa was disputed by a number of European powers. Frederick the Great of Prussia seized Silesia from Austria.

1743 At Dettingen an army of British, Austrians, and Hanoverians under the command of George II was victorious over the French.

1745 An Austro-English army was defeated at Fontenoy but British naval superiority was confirmed, and there were gains in the Americas and India.

1748 The war was ended by the Treaty of Aix-la-Chapelle.

Austro-Hungarian Empire the Dual Monarchy established by the Hapsburg Franz Joseph 1867 between his empire of Austria and his kingdom of Hungary (including territory that became Czechoslovakia as well as parts of Poland, the Ukraine, Romania, Yugoslavia, and Italy). It collapsed autumn 1918 with the end of World War I. Only two king-emperors ruled: Franz Joseph 1867–1916 and Charles 1916–18.

authoritarianism rule of a country by a dominant elite who repress opponents and the press to maintain their own wealth and power. They are frequently indifferent to activities not affecting their security, and rival power centers, such as labor unions and political parties, are often allowed to exist, although under tight control. An extreme form is ◊totalitarianism.

autism, infantile rare disorder, generally present from birth, characterized by a withdrawn state and a failure to develop normally in language or social behavior. Although the autistic child may, rarely, show signs of high intelligence (in music or with numbers, for example) many have impaired intellect. The cause is unknown, but is thought to involve a number of factors, possibly including an inherent abnormality of the child's brain. Special education may bring about some improvement.

autochrome in photography, a single-plate additive color process devised by the ◊Lumière brothers 1903. It was the first commercially available process, in use 1907–35.

autocracy form of government in which one person holds absolute power. The autocrat has uncontrolled and undisputed authority. Russian government under the czars was an autocracy extending from the mid-16th century to the early 20th century. The title *Autocratix* (a female autocrat) was assumed by Catherine II of Russia in the 18th century.

autoexec.bat in computing, a file in the ◊MS-DOS operating system that is automatically run when the computer is ◊booted.

autogiro or *autogyro* heavier-than-air craft that supports itself in the air with a rotary wing, or rotor. The Spanish aviator Juan de la Cierva designed the first successful autogiro 1923. The autogiro's rotor provides only lift and not propulsion; it has been superseded by the helicopter, in which the rotor provides both. The autogiro is propelled by an orthodox propeller.

autoimmunity in medicine, condition where the body's immune responses are mobilized not against "foreign" matter, such as invading germs, but against the body itself. Diseases considered to be of autoimmune origin include myasthenia gravis, ◊rheumatoid arthritis, and lupus erythematosus.

automatic pilot control device that keeps an airplane flying automatically on a given course at a given height and speed. Devised by US business executive Lawrence Sperry 1912, the automatic pilot contains a set of gyroscopes that provide references for the plane's course. Sensors detect when the plane deviates from this course and send signals to the control surfaces—the ailerons, elevators, and rudder—to take the appropriate action. Autopilot is also used in missiles. Most airliners cruise on automatic pilot, also called autopilot and gyropilot, for much of the time.

automation widespread use of self-regulating machines in industry. Automation involves the addition of control devices, using electronic sensing and computing techniques, which often follow the pattern of human nervous and brain functions, to already mechanized physical processes of production and distribution; for example, steel processing, mining, chemical production, and road, rail, and air control.

automobile or *car* a small, driver-guided, passenger-carrying motor vehicle; originally the automated version of the horse-drawn carriage, meant to convey people and their goods over streets and roads. Most are four-wheeled and have water-cooled, piston-type internal-combustion engines fueled by gasoline or diesel. Variations have existed for decades that use ingenious and often nonpolluting power plants, but the automobile industry long ago settled on this general formula for the consumer market. Experimental and sports models are streamlined, energy-efficient, and hand-built.

automobile racing competitive racing of motor vehicles. It has forms as diverse as hill-climbing, stock-car racing, rallying, sports-automobile racing, and Formula One Grand Prix racing. The first organized race was from Paris to Rouen 1894.

autonomic nervous system in mammals, the part of the nervous system that controls those functions not controlled voluntarily, including the heart rate, activity of the intestines, and the production of sweat. There are two divisions of the autonomic nervous system. The *sympathetic* system responds to stress, when it speeds the heart rate, increases blood pressure and generally prepares the body for action. The *parasympathetic* system is more important when the body is at rest, since it slows the heart rate, decreases blood pressure, and stimulates the digestive system.

autonomy in politics, term used to describe political self-government of a state or, more commonly, a subdivision of a state. Autonomy may be based upon cultural or ethnic differences and often leads eventually to independence.

autopsy or *postmortem* examination of the internal organs and tissues of a dead body, performed to try to establish the cause of death.

autosuggestion conscious or unconscious acceptance of an idea as true, without demanding rational proof, but with potential subsequent effect for good or ill. Pioneered by the French psychotherapist Emile Coué (1857–1926) in healing, it is sometimes used in modern psychotherapy to conquer nervous habits and dependence on addictive substances such as tobacco and alcohol.

autotroph any living organism that synthesizes organic substances from inorganic molecules by using light or chemical energy. Autotrophs are the *primary producers* in all food chains since the materials they synthesize and store are the energy sources of all other organisms. All green plants and many planktonic organisms are autotrophs, using sunlight to convert carbon dioxide and water into sugars by ◊photosynthesis.

autumn crocus any member of the genus *Colchicum*, family Liliaceae. One species, the mauve *meadow saffron C. autumnale*, yields *colchicine*, which is used in treating gout and in plant breeding (it causes plants to double the numbers of their chromosomes, forming polyploids).

Auvergne ancient province of central France and modern region comprising the *départements* of Allier, Cantal, Haute-Loire, and Puy-de-Dôme *area* 10,036 sq mi/26,000 sq km *population* (1986) 1,334,000 *capital* Clermont-Ferrand *physical* mountainous, composed chiefly of volcanic rocks in several masses *industries* cattle, wheat, wine, and cheese *history* a Roman province, it was named for the ancient Gallic Avenni tribe whose leader, Vercingetorix, led a revolt against the Romans 52 BC. In the 14th century the Auvergne was divided into a duchy, dauphiny, and countship. The duchy and dauphiny were united by the dukes of Bourbon before being confiscated by Francis I 1527. The countship united with France 1615.

auxin plant ◊hormone that promotes stem and root growth in plants. Auxins influence many aspects of plant growth and development, including cell enlargement, inhibition of development of axillary buds, ◊tropisms, and the initiation of roots. *Synthetic auxins* are used in rooting powders for cuttings, and in some weedkillers, where high auxin concentrations cause such rapid growth that the plants die. They are also used to prevent premature fruitdrop in orchards. The most common naturally occurring auxin is known as indoleacetic acid, or IAA. It is produced in the shoot apex and transported to other parts of the plant.

avant-garde in the arts, those artists or works that are in the forefront of new developments in their media. The term was introduced (as was "reactionary") after the French Revolution, when it was used to describe any socialist political movement.

avatar in Hindu mythology, the descent of a deity to Earth in a visible form, for example the ten avatars of ◊Vishnu.

Avebury Europe's largest stone circle (diameter 1,252 ft/412 m), in Wiltshire, England. It was probably constructed in the Neolithic period 3,500 years ago, and is linked with nearby Silbury Hill.

Avedon Richard 1923– . US photographer born in New York City. A fashion photographer with *Harper's Bazaar* magazine in New York from the mid-1940s, he moved to *Vogue* 1965. He later became the highest-paid fashion and advertising photographer in the world. He became associated with the *New Yorker* 1993. Using large-format cameras, his work consists of intensely realistic images, chiefly portraits.

Many of his dramatic portraits were assembled in such books as *Observations* 1959 (text by Truman Capote) and *Nothing Personal* 1974 (text by James Baldwin).

average in statistics, a term used inexactly to indicate the typical member of a set of data. It usually refers to the ◊arithmetic mean. The term is also used to refer to the middle member of the set when it is sorted in ascending or descending order (the ◊median), and the most commonly occurring item of data (the mode), as in "the average family".

Averroës (Arabic *Ibn Rushd*) 1126–1198. Arabian philosopher who argued for the eternity of matter and against the immortality of the individual soul. His philosophical writings, including commentaries on Aristotle and on Plato's *Republic*, became known to the West through Latin translations. He influenced Christian and Jewish writers into the Renaissance, and reconciled Islamic and Greek thought in that philosophic truth comes through reason. St Thomas Aquinas opposed this position.

Avery Milton 1893–1965. US painter. His early work was inspired by ◊Matisse, portraying subjects in thin, flat, richly colored strokes. His later work although still figurative, shows the influence of Mark ◊Rothko and other experimental US artists.

Born in Altmar, New York, Avery received little formal training.

AVI (abbreviation for *Audio-Visual Interleave*) file format capable of storing moving images (such as video) with accompanying sound. AVI files can be replayed by any multimedia PC with ◊Windows 3.1 and a ◊soundcard. AVI files are frequently very large (around 50 Mbyte for a five-minute rock video, for example), so they are usually stored on ◊CD-ROM.

aviation see ◊flight for the history of aviation and airplanes.

Avicenna (Arabic *Ibn Sina*) 979–1037. Arabian philosopher and physician. He was the most renowned philosopher of medieval Islam. His *Canon Medicinae* was a standard work for many centuries. His philosophical writings were influenced by al-Farabi, Aristotle, and the neo-Platonists, and in turn influenced the scholastics of the 13th century.

Avignon city in Provence, France, capital of Vaucluse *département*, on the river Rhône NW of Marseilles; population (1990) 89,400. An important Gallic and Roman city, it has a 12th-century bridge (only half still standing), a 13th-century cathedral, 14th-century walls, and a palace built during the residence here of the popes, comprised of Le Palais Vieux (1334–42) to the North, and Le Palais Nouveau (1342–52) to the South. Avignon was papal property 1348–1791.

avocado tree *Persea americana* of the laurel family, native to Central America. Its dark-green, thick-skinned, pear-shaped fruit has buttery-textured flesh and is used in salads.

avocet wading bird, genus *Recurvirostra*, family Recurvirostridae, with a characteristic long, narrow, upturned bill used in sifting water as it feeds in the shallows. It is about 18 in/45 cm long, and has long legs, partly webbed feet, and black and white plumage. There are four species. Stilts belong to the same family.

Avogadro's hypothesis in chemistry, the law stating that equal volumes of all gases, when at the same temperature and pressure, have the same numbers of molecules. It was first propounded by Amedeo Avogadro.

avoirdupois system of weights based on the pound (0.45 kg), which consists of 16 ounces, each of 16 drams, with each dram equal to 27.34 grains (1.772 g).

Avon county of SW England, formed 1974 from the city and county of Bristol and parts of NE Somerset and SW Gloucestershire *area* 517 sq mi/1,340 sq km *towns and cities* Bristol (administrative headquarters), Bath, Weston-super-Mare, Avonmouth *features* low-lying basin bordered by Cotswold Hills in NE, Mendip Hills in S; river Avon flows west into Severn estuary *industries* aircraft and other engineering, tobacco, chemicals, printing, dairy products, food processing, financial services *population* (1991) 932,600 *famous people* John Cabot, Thomas Chatterton, W.G. Grace

Avon any of several rivers in England and Scotland. The Avon in Warwickshire is associated with Shakespeare.

axiom in mathematics, a statement that is assumed to be true and upon which theorems are proved by using logical deduction; for example, two straight lines cannot enclose a space. The Greek mathematician Euclid used a series of axioms that he considered could not be demonstrated in terms of simpler concepts to prove his geometrical theorems.

axis (plural *axes*) in geometry, one of the reference lines by which a point on a graph may be located. The horizontal axis is usually referred to as the *x*-axis, and the vertical axis as the *y*-axis. The term is also used to refer to the imaginary line about which an object may be said to be symmetrical (*axis of symmetry*)—for example, the diagonal of a square—or the line about which an object may revolve (*axis of rotation*).

Axis alliance of Nazi Germany and Fascist Italy before and during World War II. The *Rome–Berlin Axis* was formed 1936, when Italy was being threatened with sanctions because of its invasion of Ethiopia (Abyssinia). It became a full military and political alliance May 1939. A ten-year alliance between Germany, Italy, and Japan (*Rome–Berlin–Tokyo Axis*) was signed Sept 1940 and was subsequently joined by Hungary, Bulgaria, Romania, and the puppet states of Slovakia and Croatia. The Axis collapsed with the fall of Mussolini and the surrender of Italy 1943 and Germany and Japan 1945.

axolotl aquatic larval form ("tadpole") of any of several North American species of salamander, belonging to the family Ambystomatidae. Axolotls are remarkable because they can breed without changing to the adult form and will only metamorphose into adult salamanders in response to the drying-up of their ponds. The adults then migrate to another pond.

ayatollah honorific title awarded to Shiite Muslims in Iran by popular consent, as, for example, to Ayatollah Ruhollah ◊Khomeini.

aye-aye nocturnal tree-climbing prosimian *Daubentonia madagascariensis* of Madagascar, related to the lemurs. It is just over 3 ft/1 m long, including a tail 20 in/50 cm long.

Ayers Rock vast ovate mass of pinkish rock in Northern Territory, Australia; 1,110 ft/335 m high and 6 mi/ 9 km around. For the Aboriginals, whose paintings decorate its caves, it has magical significance.

Aymara member of an American Indian people of Bolivia and Peru, builders of a great culture, who were conquered first by the Incas and then by the Spaniards. Today 1.4 million Aymara farm and herd llamas and alpacas in the highlands; their language, belonging to the Andean-Equatorial language family, survives, and their Roman Catholicism incorporates elements of their old beliefs.

Ayurveda ancient Hindu system of medicine. The main principles are derived from the Vedas of the 1st century AD, and it is still practiced in India, using herbs, purgatives, and liniments, in Ayurvedic hospitals and dispensaries.

azalea any of various deciduous flowering shrubs, genus

aye-aye *The aye-aye is a nocturnal animal that lives in the dense forests of Madagascar. Closely related to the lemur, the aye-aye has large forward-looking eyes, powerful rodentlike teeth, large ears, and a particularly long middle finger which is used to dig insects out of tree trunks.*

Rhododendron, of the heath family Ericaceae. There are several species native to North American and Asia, and from these many cultivated varieties have been derived. Azaleas are closely related to the evergreen ◊rhododendrons of the same genus.

Azerbaijan Republic of *area* 33,400 sq mi/86,600 sq km *capital* Baku *towns and cities* Gyandzha (formerly Kirovabad), Sumgait *physical* Caspian Sea; the country ranges from semidesert to the Caucasus Mountains *head of state* Geidar Aliyev from 1993 *head of government* vacant *political system* emergent democracy *political parties* Republican Democratic Party, ex-communist-dominated; Popular Front, democratic nationalist; Islamic Party, fundamentalist *products* oil, iron, copper, fruit, vines, cotton, silk, carpets *currency* manat *population* (1993 est) 7,200,000 (83% Azeri, 6% Russian, 6% Armenian) *life expectancy* men 67, women 75 *language* Turkic *religion* traditionally Shiite Muslim *GNP* $1,670 per head (1991) *chronology* *1917–18* A member of the anti-Bolshevik Transcaucasian Federation. *1918* Became an independent republic. *1920* Occupied by the Red Army. *1922–36* Formed part of the Transcaucasian Federal Republic with Georgia and Armenia. *1936* Became a constituent republic of the USSR. *1988* Riots followed Nagorno-Karabakh's request for transfer to Armenia. *1989* Jan–Nov: Nagorno-Karabakh placed under direct rule from Moscow. Azerbaijan Popular Front established. Nov: civil war with Armenia. *1990* Jan: Soviet troops dispatched to Baku to restore order. Aug: communists won parliamentary elections. *1991* Aug: Azeri leadership supported attempted anti-Gorbachev coup; independence declared. Sept: former communist Ayaz Mutalibov elected president. Dec: joined new Commonwealth of Independent States; Nagorno-Karabakh declared independence. *1992* March: admitted into United Nations; accorded diplomatic recognition by the US; Mutalibov resigned. June: Albulfaz Elchibey, leader of the Popular Front, elected president; renewed campaign to capture Nagorno-Karabakh. *1993* June: President Elchibey fled military revolt, replaced by former Communist Party leader Geidar Aliyev. Rebel military leader Surat Huseynov appointed prime minister. July: Nagorno-Karabakh overtaken by Armenian forces. Oct: Aliyev elected president. *1994* Huseynov dismissed from premiership.

Azeri or *Azerbaijani* native of the Azerbaijan region of Iran (population 5,500,000) or of the Republic of Azerbaijan (formerly a Soviet republic) (population 7,145,600). Azeri is a Turkic language belonging to the Altaic family. Of the total population of Azeris, 70% are Shiite Muslims and 30% Sunni Muslims.

Azores group of nine islands in the N Atlantic, belonging to Portugal; area 867 sq mi/2,247 sq km; population (1987) 254,000. They are outlying peaks of the Mid-Atlantic Ridge and are volcanic in origin. The capital is Ponta Delgada on the main island, San Miguel.

AZT or *retrovir* or *zidovudine* trademark for azidothymidine, an antiviral drug used in the treatment of ◊AIDS.

Aztec member of a Mexican American Indian people that migrated south into the valley of Mexico in the 12th century, and in 1325 began reclaiming lake marshland to build their capital, Tenochtitlán, on the site of present-day Mexico City. Under Montezuma I (reigned from 1440), the Aztecs created a tribute empire in central Mexico. After the conquistador ◊Cortés landed 1519, ◊Montezuma II (reigned from 1502) was killed and Tenochtitlán subsequently destroyed. Nahuatl is the Aztec language; it belongs to the Uto-Aztecan family of languages.

BA in education, abbreviation for *Bachelor of Arts* degree.

Baader-Meinhof gang popular name for the West German left-wing guerrilla group the *Rote Armee Fraktion/Red Army Faction*, active from 1968 against what it perceived as US imperialism. The three main founding members were Andreas Baader (1943–1977), Gudrun Ensslin, and Ulrike Meinhof (1934–1976).

Baal divine title given to their chief male gods by the Phoenicians, or Canaanites. Their worship as fertility gods, often orgiastic and of a phallic character, was strongly denounced by the Hebrew prophets.

Babangida Ibrahim 1941– . Nigerian politician and soldier, president 1985–93. He became head of the Nigerian army 1983 and in 1985 led a coup against President Buhari, assuming the presidency himself. From 1992 he promised a return to civilian rule but resigned Aug 1993, his commitment to democracy increasingly in doubt.

babbler bird of the thrush family Muscicapidae with a loud babbling cry. Babblers, subfamily Timaliinae, are found in the Old World, and there are some 250 species in the group.

Babel Hebrew name for the city of ◊Babylon, chiefly associated with the *Tower of Babel* which, in the Genesis story in the Old Testament, was erected in the plain of Shinar by the descendants of Noah. It was a ziggurat, or staged temple, seven stories high (300 ft/ 100 m) and had a shrine of Marduk on the summit. It was built by Nabopolassar, father of Nebuchadnezzar, and was destroyed when Sennacherib sacked the city 689 BC.

Babi Yar ravine near Kiev, Ukraine, where more than 100,000 people (80,000 Jews; the others were Poles, Russians, and Ukrainians) were killed by the Nazis 1941. The site was ignored until the Soviet poet Yevtushenko wrote a poem called "Babi Yar" 1961 in protest at plans for a sports center on the site.

baboon large monkey of the genus *Papio*, with a long doglike muzzle and large canine teeth, spending much of its time on the ground in open country. Males, with head and body up to 3.5 ft/1.1 m long, are larger than females, and dominant males rule the "troops" in which baboons live. They inhabit Africa and SW Arabia.

Babur (Arabic "lion") (Zahir ud-Din Mohammed) 1483–1530. First Great Mogul of India from 1526. He was the great-grandson of the Mogul conqueror Tamerlane and, at the age of 11, succeeded his father, Omar Sheik Mirza, as ruler of Ferghana (Turkestan). In 1526 he defeated the emperor of Delhi at Panipat in the Punjab, captured Delhi and Agra (the site of the Taj Mahal), and established a dynasty that lasted until 1858.

Babylon capital of ancient Babylonia, on the bank of the lower Euphrates River. The site is now in Iraq, 55 mi/88 km S of Baghdad and 5 mi/8 km N of Hilla, which is built chiefly of bricks from the ruins of Babylon. The Hanging Gardens of Babylon, one of the ◊Seven Wonders of the World, were probably erected on a vaulted stone base, the only stone construction in the mud-brick city. They formed a series of terraces, irrigated by a hydraulic system.

Bacall Lauren. Adopted name of Betty Joan Perske 1924– . US actress. She became an overnight star when cast by Howard Hawks opposite Humphrey Bogart in *To Have and Have Not* 1944. She and Bogart married 1945 and starred together in *The Big Sleep* 1946. She returned to Hollywood after an eight-year absence with *Murder on the Orient Express* 1974 and two years later appeared in *The Shootist* 1976.

Bacchus in Greek and Roman mythology, the god of fertility (see ◊Dionysus) and of wine; his rites (the *Bacchanalia*) were orgiastic.

Bach Johann Sebastian 1685–1750. German composer. A master of ◊counterpoint, his music epitomizes the Baroque polyphonic style. His orchestral music includes the six *Brandenburg Concertos* 1721, other concertos for keyboard instrument and violin, four orchestral suites, sonatas for various instruments, six violin partitas, and six unaccompanied cello suites. Bach's keyboard music, for clavier and organ, his fugues, and his choral music are of equal importance. He also wrote chamber music and songs.

bacillus member of a group of rodlike ◊bacteria that occur everywhere in the soil and air. Some are responsible for diseases such as ◊anthrax or for causing food spoilage.

backgammon board game for two players, often used in gambling. It was known in Mesopotamia, Greece, and Rome and in medieval England.

baboon Hamadryas baboon of Ethiopia, Somalia, and southern Saudi Arabia. Like all baboons, this species has a doglike muzzle and a sloping back. They live in family groups consisting of an old male, several females, and their young, sleeping in trees or among rocks at night and wandering in search of food during the day.

background radiation radiation that is always present in the environment. By far the greater proportion (87%) of it is emitted from natural sources. Alpha and beta particles, and gamma radiation are radiated by the traces of radioactive minerals that occur naturally in the environment and even in the human body, and by radioactive gases such as radon and thoron, which are found in soil and may seep upward into buildings. Radiation from space (◊cosmic radiation) also contributes to the background level.

backing storage in computing, memory outside the ◊central processing unit used to store programs and data that are not in current use. Backing storage must be nonvolatile—that is, its contents must not be lost when the power supply to the computer system is disconnected.

backup in computing, a copy file that is transferred to another medium, usually a ◊floppy disk or tape. The purpose of this is to have available a copy of a file that can be restored in case of a fault in the system or the file itself. Backup files are also created by many applications (with the extension.BAC or.BAK); a version is therefore available of the original file before it was modified by the current application.

backup system in computing, a duplicate computer system that can take over the operation of a main computer system in the event of equipment failure. A large interactive system, such as an airline's ticket-booking system, cannot be out of action for even a few hours without causing considerable disruption. In such cases a complete duplicate computer system may be provided to take over and run the system should the main computer develop a fault or need maintenance.

Bacon Francis 1561–1626. English politician, philosopher, and essayist. He became Lord Chancellor 1618, and the same year confessed to bribe-taking, was fined £40,000 (which was later remitted by the king), and spent four days in the Tower of London. His works include *Essays* 1597, characterized by pith and brevity; *The Advancement of Learning* 1605, a seminal work discussing scientific method; the *Novum Organum* 1620, in which he redefined the task of natural science, seeing it as a means of empirical discovery and a method of increasing human power over nature; and *The New Atlantis* 1626, describing a utopian state in which scientific knowledge is systematically sought and exploited.

His writing helped to inspire the founding of the Royal Society.

Bacon Francis 1909–1992. Irish painter. Self-taught, he practiced abstract art, then developed a stark Expressionist style characterized by distorted, blurred figures enclosed in loosely defined space. One of his best-known works is *Study after Velázquez's Portrait of Pope Innocent X* 1953 (Museum of Modern Art, New York).

Bacon Roger 1214–1292. English philosopher, scientist, and a teacher at Oxford University. He was interested in alchemy, the biological and physical sciences, and magic. Many discoveries have been credited to him, including the magnifying lens. He foresaw the extensive use of gunpowder and mechanical automobiles, boats, and planes.

bacteria (singular *bacterium*) microscopic single-celled organisms lacking a nucleus. Bacteria are widespread, present in soil, air, and water, and as parasites on and in other living things. Some parasitic bacteria

badger The American badger is slightly smaller than its Eurasian cousin. Unlike the Eurasian badger, it is a solitary creature, and lives mainly on small rodents. It usually spends the day in its burrow or sett, emerging at night to hunt for mice, eggs, and reptiles. It is an excellent digger and can rapidly dig out burrowing rodents.

cause disease by producing toxins, but others are harmless and may even benefit their hosts. Bacteria usually reproduce by ◊binary fission (dividing into two equal parts), and since this may occur approximately every 20 minutes, a single bacterium is potentially capable of producing 16 million copies of itself in a day. It is thought that 1–10% of the world's bacteria have been identified.

bacteriophage virus that attacks ◊bacteria. Such viruses are now of use in genetic engineering.

Baden-Powell Robert Stephenson Smyth, 1st Baron Baden-Powell 1857–1941. British general, founder of the Scout Association. He fought in defense of Mafeking (now Mafikeng) during the Second South African War. After 1907 he devoted his time to developing the Scout movement, which rapidly spread throughout the world.

badger large mammal of the weasel family with molar teeth of a crushing type adapted to a partly vegetable diet, and short strong legs with long claws suitable for digging. The Eurasian *common badger* Meles meles is about 3 ft/1 m long, with long, coarse, grayish hair on the back, and a white face with a broad black stripe along each side. Mainly a woodland animal, it is harmless and nocturnal, and spends the day in a system of burrows called a "sett". It feeds on roots, a variety of fruits and nuts, insects, worms, mice, and young rabbits.

badminton racket game similar to lawn ◊tennis but played on a smaller court and with a shuttlecock (a half sphere of cork or plastic with a feather or nylon skirt) instead of a ball. The object of the game is to prevent the opponent from being able to return the shuttlecock.

Baffin Island island in the Northwest Territories, Canada *area* 195,875 sq mi/507,450 sq km *features* largest island in the Canadian Arctic; mountains rise above 6,000 ft/2,000 m, and there are several large lakes. The northernmost part of the strait separating Baffin Island from Greenland forms Baffin Bay, the southern end is Davis Strait.

It is named for English explorer William Baffin, who carried out research here 1614 during his search for the ◊Northwest Passage.

Baghdad historic city and capital of Iraq, on the river Tigris; population (1985) 4,649,000. Industries include oil refining, distilling, tanning, tobacco processing, and the manufacture of textiles and cement. Founded 762, it became Iraq's capital 1921. During the Gulf War 1991, the UN coalition forces bombed it in repeated air raids and destroyed much of the city.

bagpipes any of an ancient family of double-reed folk woodwind instruments employing a bladder or bellows as an air reservoir to a "chanter" or melody pipe, and optional "drones" providing a continuous accompanying harmony.

Bahadur Shah II 1775–1862. Last of the Mogul emperors of India. He reigned, though in name only, as king of Delhi 1837–57, when he was hailed by the mutineers of the Sepoy Rebellion as an independent emperor at Delhi. After the rebellion he was exiled to Burma with his family.

Baha'i religion founded in the 19th century from a Muslim splinter group, Babism, by the Persian Baha'ullah. His message in essence was that all great religious leaders are manifestations of the unknowable God and all scriptures are sacred. There is no priesthood: all Baha'is are expected to teach, and to work toward world unification. There are about 4.5 million Baha'is worldwide.

Bahamas Commonwealth of the *area* 5,352 sq mi/ 13,864 sq km *capital* Nassau on New Providence *towns and cities* Alice Town, Andros Town, Hope Town, Spanish Wells, Freeport, Moss Town, George Town *physical* comprises 700 tropical coral islands and about 1,000 cays *features* desert islands: only 30 are inhabited; Blue Holes of Andros, the world's longest and deepest submarine caves; the Exumas are a narrow spine of 365 islands *principal islands* Andros, Grand Bahama, Great Abaco, Eleuthera, New Providence, Berry Islands, Biminis, Great Inagua, Acklins, Exumas, Mayaguana, Crooked Island, Long Island, Cat Island, Rum Cay, Watling (San Salvador) Island *head of state* Elizabeth II from 1973, represented by governor general Cliffort Darling from 1992 *head of government* Hubert Ingraham from 1992 *political system* constitutional monarchy *political parties* Progressive Liberal Party (PLP), centrist; Free National Movement (FNM), center-left *exports* cement, pharmaceuticals, petroleum products, crawfish, salt, aragonite, rum, pulpwood; over half the islands' employment comes from tourism *currency* Bahamian dollar *population* (1993 est) 270,000; growth rate 1.8% p.a. *languages* English and some Creole *media* three independent daily newspapers *religions* 29% Baptist, 23% Anglican, 22% Roman Catholic *literacy* 99% *GNP* \$11,720 per head (1991) *chronology* *1964* Independence achieved from Britain. *1967* First national assembly elections; Lynden Pindling became prime minister. *1972* Constitutional conference to discuss full independence. *1973* Full independence achieved. *1983* Allegations of drug trafficking by government ministers. *1984* Deputy prime minister and two cabinet ministers resigned. Pindling denied any personal involvement and was endorsed as party leader. *1987* Pindling reelected despite claims of frauds. *1992* FNM led by Hubert Ingraham won absolute majority in assembly elections.

Bahrain State of (*Dawlat al Bahrayn*) *area* 266 sq mi/688 sq km *capital* Manama on the largest island (also called Bahrain) *towns and cities* Muharraq, Jidd Hafs, Isa Town; oil port Mina Sulman *physical* 35 islands, composed largely of sand-covered limestone; generally poor and infertile soil; flat and hot *environment* a wildlife park on Bahrain preserves the endangered oryx; most of the south of the island is preserved for the ruling family's falconry *features* causeway linking Bahrain to mainland Saudi Arabia; Sitra island is a communications center for the lower Persian Gulf and has a satellite-tracking station *head of state and government* Sheik Isa bin Sulman al-Khalifa from 1961 *political system* absolute emirate *political parties* none *exports* oil, natural gas, aluminum, fish *currency* Bahrain dinar *population* (1993) 538,000 (two-thirds are nationals); growth rate 4.4% p.a. *life expectancy* men 70, women 74 *languages* Arabic (official); Farsi, English, Urdu *religions* 85% Muslim (Shiite 60%, Sunni 40%) *literacy* men 82%, women 69% *GNP* \$6,910 per head (1991) *chronology* *1861* Became British protectorate. *1968* Britain announced its intention to withdraw its forces. Bahrain formed, with Qatar and the Trucial States, the Federation of Arab Emirates. *1971* Qatar and the Trucial States withdrew from the federation and Bahrain became an independent state. *1973* New constitution adopted, with an elected national assembly. *1975* Prime minister resigned and national assembly dissolved. Emir and his family assumed virtually absolute power. *1986* Gulf University established in Bahrain. A causeway was opened linking the island with Saudi Arabia. *1988* Bahrain recognized Afghan rebel government. *1991* Bahrain joined United Nations coalition that ousted Iraq from its occupation of Kuwait.

Baikal (Russian *Baykal Ozero*) freshwater lake in S Siberia, Russia, the largest in Asia, and the eighth largest in the world (area 12,150 sq mi/31,500 sq km); also the deepest in the world (up to 5,700 ft/1,640 m). Fed by more than 300 rivers, it is drained only by the Lower Angara. It has sturgeon fisheries and is rich in fauna.

bail a security, bonds, or money deposited with the court to obtain the temporary release of an arrested person, on the assurance that the person will obey the court, as by attending a legal proceeding at a stated time and place. If the person does not attend, the bail may be forfeited.

Baird John Logie 1888–1946. Scottish electrical engineer who pioneered television. In 1925 he gave the first public demonstration of television and in 1926 pioneered fiber optics, radar (in advance of Robert Watson-Watt), and "noctovision", a system for seeing at night by using infrared rays.

He also developed video recording on both wax records and magnetic steel disks (1926–27), color TV (1925–28), 3-D color TV (1925–46), and transatlantic TV (1928). In 1944 he developed facsimile television and demonstrated the world's first all-electronic color and 3-D color receiver (500 lines).

Bakelite first synthetic ◊plastic, created by Leo Baekeland in 1909. Bakelite is hard, tough, and heatproof, and is used as an electrical insulator. It is made by the reaction of phenol with formaldehyde, producing a powdery resin that sets solid when heated. Objects are made by subjecting the resin to compression molding (simultaneous heat and pressure in a mold).

Baker James (Addison), III 1930– . US Republican politician. Under President Reagan, he was White House chief of staff 1981–85 and Treasury secretary 1985–88. After managing George Bush's successful presidential campaign, Baker was appointed secretary of state 1989 and played a prominent role in the 1990–91 Gulf crisis and the subsequent search for a lasting Middle East peace settlement. In 1992 he left the State Department to become White House chief of staff and to oversee Bush's reelection campaign.

Baku capital city of the Republic of Azerbaijan, industrial port (oil refining) on the Caspian Sea; population (1987) 1,741,000. It is a major oil center and is linked by pipelines with Batumi on the Black Sea. In Jan 1990 there were violent clashes between the Azeri majority and the Armenian minority, and Soviet troops were sent to the region; over 13,000 Armenians subsequently fled from the city. In early March 1992, opposition political forces sponsored protests in the city that led to the resignation of President Mutalibov.

Balaclava, Battle of in the Crimean War, an engagement on Oct 25, 1854, near a town in Ukraine, 6 mi/10 km SE of Sevastopol. It was the scene of the ill-timed *Charge of the Light Brigade* of British cavalry against the Russian entrenched artillery. Of the 673 soldiers who took part, there were 272 casualties. *Balaclava helmets* were knitted hoods worn here by soldiers in the bitter weather.

balance apparatus for weighing or measuring mass. The various types include the *beam balance* consisting of a centrally pivoted lever with pans hanging from each end, and the *spring balance*, in which the object to be weighed stretches (or compresses) a vertical coil spring fitted with a pointer that indicates the weight on a scale. Kitchen and bathroom scales are balances.

balance of payments in economics, an account of a country's debit and credit transactions with other countries. Items are divided into the *current account*, which includes both visible trade (imports and exports of goods) and invisible trade (services such as transport, tourism, interest, and dividends), and the *capital account*, which includes investment in and out of the country, international grants, and loans. Deficits or surpluses on these accounts are brought into balance by buying and selling reserves of foreign currencies.

balance of power in politics, the theory that the best way of ensuring international order is to have power so distributed among states that no single state is able to achieve a dominant position. The term, which may also refer more simply to the actual distribution of power, is one of the most enduring concepts in international relations. Since the development of nuclear weapons, it has been asserted that the balance of power has been replaced by a *balance of terror*.

Balanchine George 1904–1983. Russian-born US choreographer. After leaving the USSR 1924, he worked with ◊Diaghilev in France. Moving to the US 1933, he became a major influence on dance, starting the New York City Ballet 1948. He was the most influential 20th-century choreographer of ballet in the US. He developed an "American Neo-Classic" dance style and made the New York City Ballet one of the world's great companies. His ballets are usually plotless and are performed in practice clothes to modern music. He also choreographed dances for five Hollywood films.

Balboa Vasco Núñez de 1475–1519. Spanish ◊conquistador. He founded a settlement at Darien (now Panama) 1511 and crossed the Isthmus in search of gold, reaching the Pacific Ocean (which he called the South Sea) on Sept 25, 1513, after a 25-day expedition. He was made admiral of the Pacific and governor of Panama but was removed by Spanish court intrigue, imprisoned, and executed.

bald cypress or *swamp cypress* tree of the genus *Taxodium*.

Baldwin James 1924–1987. US writer and civil-rights activist. He portrayed vividly the suffering and despair of African Americans in contemporary society. After his first novel, *Go Tell It On The Mountain* 1953, set in Harlem, and *Giovanni's Room* 1956, about a homosexual relationship in Paris, his writing became more politically indignant with *Another Country* 1962 and *The Fire Next Time* 1963, a collection of essays.

Baldwin Stanley, 1st Earl Baldwin of Bewdley 1867–1947. British Conservative politician, prime minister 1923–24, 1924–29, and 1935–37; he weathered the general strike 1926, secured complete adult suffrage 1928, and handled the abdication crisis of Edward VIII 1936, but failed to prepare Britain for World War II.

Balearic Islands (Spanish *Baleares*) group of Mediterranean islands forming an autonomous region of Spain; including ◊Majorca, ◊Minorca, ◊Ibiza, Cabrera, and Formentera *area* 1,930 sq mi/5,000 sq km *capital* Palma de Mallorca *industries* figs, olives, oranges, wine, brandy, coal, iron, slate; tourism is crucial *population* (1986) 755,000 *history* a Roman colony from 123 BC, the Balearic Islands were an independent Moorish kingdom 1009–1232; they were conquered by Aragón 1343.

Balfour Arthur James, 1st Earl of Balfour 1848–1930. British Conservative politician, prime minister 1902–05 and foreign secretary 1916–19, when he issued the Balfour Declaration 1917 supporting the establishment in Palestine of a national home for the Jewish people. He was involved in peace negotiations after World War I, signing the Treaty of Versailles.

Bali island of Indonesia, E of Java, one of the Sunda Islands *area* 2,240 sq mi/5,800 sq km *capital* Denpasar *physical* volcanic mountains *features* Balinese dancing, music, drama; 1 million tourists a year (1990) *industries* gold and silver work, woodcarving, weaving, copra, salt, coffee *population* (1989) 2,787,000 *history* Bali's Hindu culture goes back to the 7th century; the Dutch gained control of the island by 1908.

Baliol (or *Balliol*) John de c.1250–1314. King of Scotland 1292–96. As an heir to the Scottish throne on the death of Margaret, the Maid of Norway, his cause was supported by the English king, Edward I, against 12 other claimants. Having paid homage to Edward, Baliol was proclaimed king but soon rebelled and gave up the kingdom when English forces attacked Scotland.

Balkans peninsula of SE Europe, stretching into the Mediterranean Sea between the Adriatic and Aegean seas, comprising Albania, Bosnia-Herzegovina, Bulgaria, Croatia, Greece, Romania, Slovenia, the part of Turkey in Europe, and Yugoslavia. It is joined to the rest of Europe by an isthmus 750 mi/1,200 km wide between Rijeka on the W and the mouth of the Danube on the Black Sea to the E.

Balkan Wars two wars 1912–13 and 1913 (preceding World War I) which resulted in the expulsion by the Balkan states of Ottoman Turkey from Europe, except for a small area around Istanbul.

Ball John English priest, one of the leaders of the ◊Peasants' Revolt 1381, known as "the mad priest of Kent". A follower of John Wycliffe and a believer in social equality, he was imprisoned for disagreeing with the archbishop of Canterbury. During the revolt he was released from prison, and when in Blackheath, London, incited people against the ruling classes by preaching from the text "When Adam delved and Eve span, who was then the gentleman?" When the revolt collapsed he escaped but was captured near Coventry and executed.

Ball Lucille 1911–1989. US comedy actress. She began her film career as a bit player 1933, and appeared in dozens of movies over the next few years, including *Room Service* 1938 (with the Marx Brothers) and *Fancy Pants* 1950 (with Bob Hope). From 1951 to 1957 she starred with her husband, Cuban bandleader Desi Arnaz, in the television sitcom *I Love Lucy*, the first US television show filmed before an audience. It was followed by *The Lucy Show* 1962–68 and *Here's Lucy* 1968–74.

Her TV success limited her film output after 1950; her later films include *Mame* 1974. The television series are still transmitted in many countries.

ballad form of traditional narrative poetry, widespread in Europe and the US. Ballads are metrically simple, sometimes (as in Russia) unstrophic and unrhymed or (as in Denmark) dependent on assonance. Concerned with some strongly emotional event, the ballad is halfway between the lyric and the epic. Most English ballads date from the 15th century but may describe earlier events. Poets of the Romantic movement both in England and in Germany were greatly influenced by the ballad revival, as seen in, for example, the *Lyrical Ballads* 1798 of ◊Wordsworth and ◊Coleridge.

ballade in literature, a poetic form developed in France in the later Middle Ages from the ballad, generally consisting of one or more groups of three stanzas of seven or eight lines each, followed by a shorter stanza or envoy, the last line being repeated as a chorus. In music, a ballade is an instrumental piece based on a story; a form used in piano works by Chopin and Liszt.

Balladur Edouard 1929– . French Conservative politician, prime minister from 1993. During his first year of "co-habitation" with socialist president, François Mitterrand, he demonstrated the sureness of his political touch, retaining popular support despite active opposition to some of his more right-wing policies. He is a strong supporter of the European Union and of maintaining close relations between France and Germany.

Ballesteros Seve(riano) 1957– . Spanish golfer who came to prominence 1976 and has won several leading tournaments in the US, including the Masters Tournament 1980 and 1983. He has also won the British Open three times: in 1979, 1984, and 1988.

ballet theatrical representation in ◊dance form in which music also plays a major part in telling a story or conveying a mood. Some such form of entertainment existed in ancient Greece, but Western ballet as we know it today first appeared in Italy. From there it was brought by Catherine de' Medici to France in the form of a spectacle combining singing, dancing, and declamation. In the 20th century Russian ballet has had a vital influence on the classical tradition in the West, and ballet developed further in the US through the work of George Balanchine and the American Ballet Theater, and in the UK through the influence of Marie Rambert. ◊Modern dance is a separate development.

ballistics study of the motion and impact of projectiles such as bullets, bombs, and missiles. For projectiles from a gun, relevant exterior factors include temperature, barometric pressure, and wind strength; and for nuclear missiles these extend to such factors as the speed at which the Earth turns.

balloon lighter-than-air craft that consists of a gasbag filled with gas lighter than the surrounding air and an attached basket, or gondola, for carrying passengers and/or instruments. In 1783, the first successful human ascent was in Paris, in a hot-air balloon designed by the Montgolfier brothers Joseph Michel and Jacques Etienne.

ballot the process of voting in an election. In political elections in democracies ballots are usually secret: voters indicate their choice of candidate on a voting slip that is placed in a sealed ballot box or by pulling levers on a machine in a voting booth. *Ballot rigging* is a term used to describe elections that are fraudulent because of interference with the voting process or the counting of ◊votes.

ballroom dancing collective term for social dances such as the ◊foxtrot, quickstep, ◊tango, and ◊waltz.

balm, lemon garden herb, see ◊lemon balm.

balsam any of various garden plants of the genus *Impatiens* of the balsam family. They are usually annuals with spurred red or white flowers and pods that burst and scatter their seeds when ripe. In medicine and perfumery, balsam refers to various oily or gummy aromatic plant resins, such as balsam of Peru from the Central American tree *Myroxylon pereirae*.

Baltic Sea large shallow arm of the North Sea, extending NE from the narrow Skagerrak and Kattegat, between Sweden and Denmark, to the Gulf of Bothnia between Sweden and Finland. Its coastline is 5,000 mi/8,000 km long, and its area, including the gulfs of Riga, Finland, and Bothnia, is 163,000 sq mi/422,300 sq km.

Its shoreline is shared by Denmark, Germany, Poland, the Baltic States, Russia, Finland, and Sweden.

Baltic States collective name for the states of ◊Estonia, ◊Latvia, and ◊Lithuania, former constituent republics of the USSR (from 1940). They regained independence Sept 1991.

Baltimore industrial port and largest city in Maryland on the western shore of Chesapeake Bay, NE of Washington, DC; population (1990) 736,000. Industries include shipbuilding, oil refining, food processing, and the manufacture of steel, chemicals, and aerospace equipment.

It is the seat of Johns Hopkins University. It was named for the founder of Maryland, Lord Baltimore (1579–1632). The city of Baltimore dates from 1729 and was incorporated 1797. At Fort McHenry, Francis Scott Key wrote the poem, "The Star Spangled Banner". The writer Edgar Allan Poe and the baseball player Babe Ruth lived here.

Balzac Honoré de 1799–1850. French writer. He was one of the major novelists of the 19th century. His first success was *Les Chouans/The Chouans*, inspired by Walter Scott. This was the beginning of the long series of novels *La Comédie humaine/The Human Comedy* which includes *Eugénie Grandet* 1833, *Le Père Goriot* 1834, and *Cousine Bette* 1846. He also wrote the Rabelaisian *Contes drolatiques/Ribald Tales* 1833.

Bamako capital and port of Mali on the river Niger; population (1976) 400,000. It produces pharmaceuticals, chemicals, textiles, tobacco, and metal products.

bamboo any of numerous plants of the subgroup Bambuseae within the grass family Gramineae, mainly found in tropical and subtropical regions. Some species grow as tall as 120 ft/36 m. The stems are hollow and jointed and can be used in furniture, house, and boat construction. The young shoots are edible; paper is made from the stem.

banana any of several treelike tropical plants of the genus *Musa,* family Musaceae, which grow up to 25 ft/8 m high. The edible banana is the fruit of a sterile hybrid form.

Bandaranaike Sirimavo (born Ratwatte) 1916– . Sri Lankan politician who succeeded her husband Solomon Bandaranaike to become the world's first female prime minister, 1960–65 and 1970–77, but was expelled from parliament 1980 for abuse of her powers while in office.

Bandar Seri Begawan (formerly (until 1970) *Brunei Town*) capital and largest town of Brunei, 9 mi/14 km from the mouth of the Brunei River; population (1987 est) 56,300.

bandicoot small marsupial mammal inhabiting Australia and New Guinea. There are about 11 species, family Peramelidae, rat- or rabbit-sized and living in burrows. They have long snouts, eat insects, and are nocturnal. A related group, the rabbit bandicoots or bilbys, is reduced to a single species that is now endangered and protected by law.

bandwidth in computing and communications, the rate of data transmission, measured in bits per second (bps).

Bangkok capital and port of Thailand, on the river Chao Phraya; population (1990) 6,019,000. Products include paper, ceramics, cement, textiles, and aircraft. It is the headquarters of the Southeast Asia Treaty Organization (SEATO).

Bangladesh People's Republic of (*Gana Prajatantri Bangladesh*) (formerly *East Pakistan*) *area* 55,585 sq mi/144,000 sq km *capital* Dhaka (formerly Dacca) *towns and cities* ports Chittagong, Khulna *physical* flat delta of rivers Ganges (Padma) and Brahmaputra (Jamuna), the largest estuarine delta in the world; annual rainfall of 100 in/2,540 mm; some 75% of the land is less than 10 ft/3 m above sea level; hilly in extreme SE and NE *environment* deforestation on the slopes of the Himalayas increases the threat of flooding in the coastal lowlands of Bangladesh, which are also subject to devastating monsoon storms. The building of India's Farakka Barrage has reduced the flow of the Ganges in Bangladesh and permitted salt water to intrude further inland. Increased salinity has destroyed fisheries, contaminated drinking water, and damaged forests *head of state* Abdur Rahman Biswas from 1991 *head of government* Begum Khaleda Zia from 1991 *political system* emergent democratic republic *political parties* Bangladesh Nationalist Party (BNP), Islamic, right of center; Awami League (AL), secular, moderate socialist; Jatiya Dal (National Party), Islamic nationalist *exports* jute, tea, garments, fish products *currency* taka *population* (1993) 118,700,000; growth rate 2.17% p.a.; just over 1 million people live in small ethnic groups in the tropical Chittagong Hill Tracts, Mymensingh, and Sylhet districts *life expectancy* men 53, women 53 *language* Bangla (Bengali) *media* several daily newspapers but no circulation exceeds 150,000 (1994); state monopoly on newsprint; 80% of newspaper advertising is state financed (1994) and funding is withdrawn from papers that criticize the government. All radio and TV are state-owned *religions* Sunni Muslim 85%, Hindu 14% *literacy* men 47%, women 22% *GNP* \$220 per head (1991) *chronology 1947* Formed into eastern province of Pakistan on partition of British India. *1970* Half a million killed in flood. *1971* Bangladesh emerged as independent nation, under leadership of Sheik Mujibur Rahman, after civil war. *1974* Hundreds of thousands died in famine. *1975* Mujibur Rahman assassinated. Martial law imposed. *1976–77* Maj Gen Zia ur-Rahman assumed power. *1978–79* Elections held and civilian rule restored. *1981* Assassination of Maj. Gen. Zia. *1982* Lt Gen Ershad assumed power in army coup. Martial law reimposed. *1986* Elections held but disputed. Martial law ended. *1987* State of emergency declared in response to opposition demonstrations. *1988* Assembly elections boycotted by main opposition parties. State of emergency lifted. Islam made state religion. Monsoon floods left 30 million homeless and thousands dead. *1989* Power devolved to Chittagong Hill Tracts to end 14-year conflict between local people and army-protected settlers. *1990* Following mass antigovernment protests, President Ershad resigned; Shahabuddin Ahmad became interim president. *1991* Feb: elections resulted in coalition government with BNP dominant. April: cyclone killed around 139,000 and left up to 10 million homeless. Sept: parliamentary government restored; Abdur Rahman Biswas elected president.

Bangui capital and port of the Central African Republic, on the river Ubangi; population (1988) 597,000. Industries include beer, cigarettes, office machinery, and timber and metal products.

banjo resonant stringed musical instrument with a long fretted neck and circular drum-type sound box covered on the topside only by stretched skin (now usually plastic). It is played with a plectrum.

Banjul capital and chief port of Gambia, on an island at the mouth of the river Gambia; population (1983) 44,536. Established 1816 as a settlement for freed slaves, it was known as Bathurst until 1973.

bank financial institution that uses funds deposited with it to lend money to companies or individuals, and also provides financial services to its customers. The first banks opened in Italy and Catalonia around 1400.

A *central bank* (in the US, the Federal Reserve System) issues currency for the government, in order to provide cash for circulation and exchange. A *savings bank* serves personal accounts and is licensed by the state in which it and its branches may operate. A commercial bank may have branches throughout the nation, since it services businesses, and sometimes becomes an international institution. There are also various forms of both public and private savings and loan companies that are called banks.

bankruptcy process by which the property of a person (in legal terms, an individual or corporation) unable to pay debts is taken away under a court order and divided fairly among the person's creditors, after preferential payments such as taxes and wages. Proceedings may be instituted either by the debtor (voluntary bankruptcy) or by any creditor for a substantial sum (involuntary bankruptcy). Until "discharged", a bankrupt is severely restricted in financial activities.

Federal law distinguishes between complete bankruptcy and protection of the assets of a person for purposes of financial reorganization. This is commonly referred to as Chapter 11 bankruptcy, since it is provided for under Chapter 11 of the federal bankruptcy law, which allows businesses and individuals to continue to operate while reorganizing to pay debts.

Banks Nathaniel Prentiss 1816–1894. US politician and Civil War general. He was Speaker in the US House of Representatives 1854–57. At the outbreak of the war 1861, he was appointed major general in command of the Department of Annapolis. Defeated by Stonewall ◊Jackson in the Shenandoah Valley, he was sent to New Orleans 1863, taking command of the Department of the Gulf. He led the ill-fated Red River expedition 1864.

Bannister Roger Gilbert 1929– . English track and field athlete, the first person to run a mile in under four minutes. He achieved this feat at Oxford, England, on May 6, 1954, in a time of 3 min 59.4 sec.

Bannockburn, Battle of battle on June 24, 1314, in which ◊Robert (I) the Bruce of Scotland defeated the English under Edward II, who had come to relieve the besieged Stirling Castle. Named after the town of Bannockburn, S of Stirling, central Scotland.

Banting Frederick Grant 1891–1941. Canadian physician who discovered a technique for isolating the hormone insulin 1921 when, experimentally, he and his colleague Charles ◊Best tied off the ducts of the ◊pancreas to determine the function of the cells known as the islets of Langerhans. This allowed for the treatment of diabetes. Banting and John J R Macleod (1876–1935), his mentor, shared the 1923 Nobel Prize for Medicine, and Banting divided his prize with Best.

Bantu languages group of related languages belonging to the Niger-Congo family, spoken widely over the greater part of Africa south of the Sahara, including Swahili, Xhosa, and Zulu. Meaning "people" in Zulu, the word Bantu itself illustrates a characteristic use of prefixes: *mu-ntu* "man", *ba-ntu* "people".

banyan tropical Asian fig tree *Ficus benghalensis*, family Moraceae. It produces aerial roots that grow down from its spreading branches, forming supporting pillars that have the appearance of separate trunks.

baobab tree of the genus *Adansonia*, family Bombacaceae. It has rootlike branches, hence its nickname "upside-down tree", and a disproportionately thick girth, up to 30 ft/9 m in diameter. The pulp of its fruit is edible and is known as monkey bread.

Baobabs may live for 1,000 years and are found in Africa and Australia.

baptism immersion in or sprinkling with water as a religious rite of initiation. It was practiced long before the beginning of Christianity. In the Christian baptism ceremony, sponsors or godparents make vows on behalf of the child, which are renewed by the child at confirmation. It is one of the seven sacraments. The *amrit* ceremony in Sikhism is sometimes referred to as baptism.

Baptist member of any of several Protestant and evangelical Christian sects that practise baptism by immersion only upon profession of faith. Baptists seek their authority in the Bible. They originated among English Dissenters who took refuge in the Netherlands in the

early 17th century, and spread by emigration and, later, missionary activity. Of the world total of approximately 31 million, some 26.5 million are in the US and 265,000 in the UK.

The first Baptist church in America was organized in Rhode Island 1639. Baptism grew rapidly during the Great Awakening religious revival of the 18th century. After the American Revolution, Baptism spread into the South and among African Americans. The Southern Baptist Convention remains the largest Protestant denomination in the US.

Bara Theda. Adopted name of Theodosia Goodman 1890–1955. US silent-film actress. She became known as the "the vamp", and the first movie sex symbol, after appearing in *A Fool There Was* 1915, based on a poem by Rudyard Kipling, "The Vampire".

She was born in Cincinnati. As the most popular star of the Fox studios, Bara made more than 40 films during her relatively brief film career that extended from 1915 to 1920.

barb general name for fish of the genus *Barbus* and some related genera of the family Cyprinidae. As well as the barbel, barbs include many small tropical Old World species, some of which are familiar aquarium species. They are active egg-laying species, usually of "typical" fish shape and with barbels at the corner of the mouth.

Barbados area 166 sq mi/430 sq km *capital* Bridgetown *towns and cities* Speightstown, Holetown, Oistins *physical* most easterly island of the West Indies; surrounded by coral reefs; subject to hurricanes June–Nov *features* highest point Mount Hillaby 1,115 ft/340 m *head of state* Elizabeth II from 1966, represented by governor general Dame Nita Barrow from 1990 *head of government* Owen Arthur from 1994 *political system* constitutional monarchy *political parties* Barbados Labour Party (BLP), moderate, left of center; Democratic Labour Party (DLP), moderate, left of center; National Democratic Party (NDP), center *exports* sugar, rum, electronic components, clothing, cement *currency* Barbados dollar *population* (1993 est) 265,000; growth rate 0.5% p.a. *life expectancy* men 73, women 78 *language* English and Bajan (Barbadian English dialect) *media* two independent

baobab The Australian baobab, or gourd tree, grows in NW Australia. It has edible seeds, and the massive trunk is used as a source of water by animals and Aborigines.

daily newspapers *religions* 70% Anglican, 9% Methodist, 4% Roman Catholic *literacy* 99% *GNP* $6,630 per head (1991) *chronology 1627* Became British colony; developed as a sugar-plantation economy, initially on basis of slavery. *1834* Slaves freed. *1951* Universal adult suffrage introduced. BLP won general election. *1954* Ministerial government established. *1961* Independence achieved from Britain. DLP, led by Errol Barrow, in power. *1966* Barbados achieved full independence within Commonwealth. Barrow became the new nation's first prime minister. *1972* Diplomatic relations with Cuba established. *1976* BLP, led by Tom Adams, returned to power. *1983* Barbados supported US invasion of Grenada. *1985* Adams died; Bernard St John became prime minister. *1986* DLP, led by Barrow, returned to power. *1987* Barrow died; Erskine Lloyd Sandiford became prime minister. *1989* New NDP opposition formed. *1991* DLP, under Erskine Sandiford, won general election. *1994* BLP, led by Owen Arthur, returned to power.

Barbary ape tailless, yellowish-brown macaque monkey *Macaca sylvanus*, 20–30 in/55–75 cm long. Barbary apes are found in the mountains and wilds of Algeria and Morocco, especially in the forests of the Atlas mountains. They were introduced to Gibraltar, where legend has it that the British will leave if the ape colony dies out.

Barbary Coast North African coast of the Mediterranean Sea (named for the ◊Berbers) from which pirates operated against US and European shipping (taking hostages for ransom) from the 16th up to the 19th century.

President ◊Jefferson took action against them, sending in the US Navy with the Marines who landed on "the shores of Tripoli".

barberry any spiny shrub of the genus *Berberis* of the barberry family (Berberidaceae), having sour red berries and yellow flowers. These shrubs are often used as hedges.

The barberry family also includes plants such as the May apple *Podophyllum peltatum* of the E North American woodlands.

barbet small, tropical bird, often brightly colored. There are some 78 species of barbet in the family Capitonidae, about half living in Africa. Barbets eat insects and fruits and, being distant relations of woodpeckers, drill nest holes with their beaks. The name comes from the "little beard" of bristles at the base of the beak.

Barbey Daniel E 1889–1969. US rear admiral. Commissioned into the US Navy 1912, Barbey had a varied career, divided between sea service and administrative posts, and designed the DUKW amphibious truck 1941.

Promoted to rear admiral 1942, in 1943 he was given command of VII Amphibious Force of the 7th Fleet and took responsibility for all amphibious operations in the SW Pacific Area. In late 1945 he became commander of 7th Fleet before retiring 1951.

Barbie Klaus 1913–1991. German Nazi, a member of the ◊SS from 1936. During World War II he was involved in the deportation of Jews from the occupied Netherlands 1940–42 and in tracking down Jews and Resistance workers in France 1942–45. He was arrested 1983 and convicted of crimes against humanity in France 1987.

barbiturate hypnosedative drug, commonly known as a "sleeping pill", consisting of any salt or ester of

barbituric acid $C_4H_4O_3N_2$. It works by depressing brain activity. Most barbiturates, being highly addictive, are no longer prescribed and are listed as controlled substances.

Barbizon School French school of landscape painters of the mid-19th century, based at Barbizon in the forest of Fontainebleau. Members included Jean-François Millet, Diaz de la Peña (1807–1876), and Théodore Rousseau. They aimed to paint fresh, realistic scenes, sketching and painting their subjects in the open air.

Barbour Philip Pendleton 1783–1841. US jurist and political leader. He served as Speaker of the House in the US House of Representatives 1821–23. A strong supporter of states' rights, he was appointed federal district judge by President ◊Jackson 1830. He served on the US Supreme Court 1836–41, consistently ruling in favor of the prerogative of the states over federal authority.

Barbuda one of the islands that form the state of ◊Antigua and Barbuda.

Barcelona capital, industrial city (textiles, engineering, chemicals), and port of Catalonia, NE Spain; population (1991) 1,653,200. As the chief center of anarchism and Catalonian nationalism, it was prominent in the overthrow of the monarchy 1931 and was the last city of the republic to surrender to Franco 1939. In 1992 the city hosted the Summer Olympics.

bar code pattern of bars and spaces that can be read by a computer. Bar codes are widely used in retailing, industrial distribution, and public libraries. The code is read by a scanning device; the computer determines the code from the widths of the bars and spaces.

Bardeen John 1908–1991. US physicist who won a Nobel Prize 1956, with Walter Brattain and William Shockley, for the development of the transistor 1948. In 1972 he became the first double winner of a Nobel prize in the same subject (with Leon Cooper and John Schrieffer) for his work on superconductivity.

Bardot Brigitte 1934– . French film actress. A celebrated sex symbol of the 1960s, she did much to popularize French cinema internationally. Her films

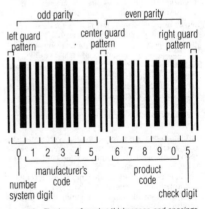

bar code *The bars of varying thicknesses and spacings represent two series of numbers, identifying the manufacturer and the product. Two longer, thinner bars mark the beginning and end of the manufacturer and product codes. The bar code is used on groceries, books, and most articles for sale in shops.*

include *Et Dieu créa la femme/And God Created Woman* 1950, *Viva Maria* 1965, and *Shalako* 1968.

Barebones Parliament English assembly called by Oliver ◊Cromwell to replace the "Rump Parliament" July 1653. It consisted of 140 members nominated by the army and derived its name from one of its members, Praise-God Barbon. Although they attempted to pass sensible legislation (civil marriage; registration of births, deaths, and marriages; custody of lunatics), its members' attempts to abolish tithes, patronage, and the court of chancery, and to codify the law, led to the resignation of the moderates and its dissolution Dec 1653.

baritone male voice pitched between bass and tenor, well suited to lieder (musical settings for poems). Dietrich Fischer-Dieskau (1925–) and Hermann Prey (1929–) are well-known German baritones.

barium soft, silver-white, metallic element, symbol Ba, atomic number 56, atomic weight 137.33. It is one of the alkaline-earth metals, found in nature as barium carbonate and barium sulfate. As the sulfate it is used in medicine: taken as a suspension (a "barium meal"), its progress is followed by using X-rays to reveal abnormalities of the alimentary canal. Barium is also used in alloys, pigments, and safety matches and, with strontium, forms the emissive surface in cathode-ray tubes. It was first discovered in barytes or heavy spar.

bark protective outer layer on the stems and roots of woody plants, composed mainly of dead cells. To allow for expansion of the stem, the bark is continually added to from within, and the outer surface often becomes cracked or is shed as scales. Trees deposit a variety of chemicals in their bark, including poisons. Many of these chemical substances have economic value because they can be used in the manufacture of drugs. Quinine, derived from the bark of the *Cinchona* tree, is used to fight malarial infections; curare, an anesthetic used in medicine, comes from the *Strychnus toxifera* tree in the Amazonian rainforest.

barley cereal belonging to the grass family (Gramineae). It resembles wheat but is more tolerant of cold and drafts. Cultivated barley *Hordeum vulgare* comprises three main varieties—six-rowed, four-rowed, and two-rowed.

bar mitzvah in Judaism, initiation of a boy, which takes place at the age of 13, into the adult Jewish community; less common is the *bat mitzvah* or *bat* for girls aged 12. The child reads a passage from the Torah in the synagogue on the Sabbath and is subsequently regarded as a full member of the congregation.

barnacle marine crustacean of the subclass Cirripedia. The larval form is free-swimming, but when mature, it fixes itself by the head to rock or floating wood. The animal then remains attached, enclosed in a shell through which the cirri (modified legs) protrude to sweep food into the mouth. Barnacles include the stalked *goose barnacle Lepas anatifera* found on ships' bottoms, and the *acorn barnacles*, such as *Balanus balanoides*, common on rocks.

Barnum P(hineas) T(aylor) 1810–1891. US showman. In 1871 he established the "Greatest Show on Earth", which included the midget "Tom Thumb", a circus, a menagerie, and an exhibition of "freaks", conveyed in 100 railroad carriages. In 1881, it merged with its chief competitor and has continued to this day as the Ringling Brothers and Barnum and Bailey Circus.

In 1850, in an attempt to change his image to that of an art promoter, Barnum managed the hugely successful US concert tour of Swedish soprano Jenny Lind, whom he dubbed "The Swedish Nightingale".

barometer instrument that measures atmospheric pressure as an indication of weather. Most often used are the *mercury barometer* and the *aneroid barometer*.

baron rank in the ◊peerage of the UK, above a baronet and below a viscount. Historically, any member of the higher nobility, a direct vassal (feudal servant) of the king, not bearing other titles such as duke or count. The term originally meant the vassal of a lord, but acquired its present meaning in the 12th century. Life peers are always of this rank.

Baroque in the visual arts, architecture, and music, a style flourishing in Europe 1600–1750, broadly characterized as expressive, flamboyant, and dynamic. Playing a central role in the crusading work of the Catholic Counter-Reformation, the Baroque used elaborate effects to appeal directly to the emotions. In some of its most characteristic works—such as Bernini's Cornaro Chapel containing his sculpture *The Ecstasy of St Theresa* 1645–52—painting, sculpture, decoration, and architecture were designed to create a single, dramatic effect. Many masterpieces of the Baroque emerged in churches and palaces in Rome, but the style soon spread throughout Europe, changing in character as it did so.

Baroque decorations were applied to building exteriors and interiors including furnishings.

barracuda large predatory fish *Sphyraena barracuda* found in the warmer seas of the world. It can grow over 6 ft/2 m long and has a superficial resemblance to a pike. Young fish shoal, but the older ones are solitary. The barracuda has very sharp shearing teeth and may attack people.

Barranquilla seaport in N Colombia, on the Magdalena River; population (1985) 1,120,900. Products include chemicals, tobacco, textiles, furniture, and footwear.

Barras Paul François Jean Nicolas, Count 1755–1829. French revolutionary. He was elected to the National Convention 1792 and helped to overthrow Robespierre 1794. In 1795 he became a member of the ruling Directory (see ◊French Revolution). In 1796 he brought about the marriage of his former mistress, Joséphine de Beauharnais, with Napoleon and assumed dictatorial powers. After Napoleon's coup d'état Nov 19, 1799, Barras fell into disgrace.

barrel a unit of liquid capacity, the value of which depends on the liquid being measured. It is used for petroleum, a barrel of which contains 42 gallons/159 liters; a barrel of alcohol contains 49.9 gallons/189 literᶜ.

Barrett Browning Elizabeth 1806–1861. English poet. In 1844 she published *Poems* (including "The Cry of the Children"), which led to her friendship with and secret marriage to Robert Browning 1846. The *Sonnets from the Portuguese* published 1847 were written during their courtship. Later works include *Casa Guidi Windows* 1851 and the poetic novel *Aurora Leigh* 1857. She was learned, fiery, and metrically experimental poet.

Barrie J(ames) M(atthew) 1860–1937. Scottish dramatist and novelist. His work includes *The Admirable Crichton* 1902 and the children's fantasy *Peter Pan* 1904.

Barrios de Chamorro Violeta. President of Nicaragua from 1990; see ◊Chamorro.

barrister in the UK, a lawyer qualified by study at the ◊Inns of Court to plead for a client in court. In Scotland such lawyers are called advocates. Barristers also undertake the writing of opinions on the prospects of a case before trial. They act for clients through the intermediary of lawyers. In the US an attorney may serve the functions of barrister and lawyer.

barrow burial mound, usually composed of earth but sometimes of stones, examples of which are found in many parts of the world. The two main types are *long*, dating from the New Stone Age, or Neolithic, and *round*, dating from the later Mesolithic peoples of the early Bronze Age.

Barrow northernmost town in the US, at Point Barrow, Alaska; the world's largest Eskimo settlement. Population (1990) 3,469. There is oil at nearby Prudhoe Bay, and the US Naval Research Laboratory is in the vicinity. Barrow developed as a whaling center about 1900.

Bartók Béla 1881–1945. Hungarian composer. His works combine folk elements with mathematical concepts of tonal and rhythmic proportion. His large output includes six string quartets, a *Divertimento* for string orchestra 1939, concertos for piano, violin, and viola, the *Concerto for Orchestra* 1942–45, a one-act opera *Duke Bluebeard's Castle* 1918, and graded teaching pieces for piano.

Bartolommeo Fra, also called *Baccio della Porta* c.1472–1517. Italian religious painter of the High Renaissance. He was active in Florence. He introduced Venetian artists to the Florentine High Renaissance style during a visit to Venice 1508, and took back with him to Florence a Venetian sense of color. *The Mystical Marriage of St Catherine* 1511 (Louvre, Paris) is one of his finest works.

Barton Clara 1821–1912. US health worker, founder of the American Red Cross 1881 and its president until 1904. A volunteer nurse, she tended the casualties of the Civil War 1861–65 and in 1864 General Benjamin Butler named her superintendent of nurses for his forces.

baryon in nuclear physics, a heavy subatomic particle made up of three indivisible elementary particles called quarks. The baryons form a subclass of the ◊hadrons and comprise the nucleons (protons and neutrons) and hyperons.

Baryshnikov Mikhail 1948– . Latvian-born dancer, now based in the US. He joined the Kirov Ballet 1967 and, after defecting from the Soviet Union 1974, joined the American Ballet Theater (ABT) as principal dancer, partnering Gelsey Kirkland. He left to join the New York City Ballet 1978–80, but rejoined ABT as director 1980–90. From 1990 he has danced for various companies including his own modern dance company, White Oak Project. His physical prowess and amazing aerial feats have combined with an impish sense of humor and dash to make him one of the most accessible of dancers.

Barzun Jacques Martin 1907– . French-born US historian and educator whose specialty was 19th-century European intellectual life. His book *The Modern Researcher* 1970 is recognized as a classic study of historical method. Among his many historical works is *Romanticism and the Modern Ego* 1943.

basal metabolic rate (BMR) minimum amount of energy needed by the body to maintain life. It is measured when the subject is awake but resting, and includes the energy required to keep the heart beating, sustain breathing, repair tissues, and keep the brain and nerves functioning. Measuring the subject's consumption of oxygen gives an accurate value for BMR, because oxygen is needed to release energy from food.

basalt commonest volcanic ◊igneous rock, and the principal rock type on the ocean floor; it is basic, that is, it contains relatively little silica: about 50%. It is usually dark gray but can also be green, brown, or black.

base in mathematics, the number of different single-digit symbols used in a particular number system. In our usual (decimal) counting system of numbers (with symbols 0, 1, 2, 3, 4, 5, 6, 7, 8, 9) the base is 10. In the ◊binary number system, which has only the symbols 1 and 0, the base is two. A base is also a number that, when raised to a particular power (that is, when multiplied by itself a particular number of times as in 10^2 = 10 x 10 = 100), has a ◊logarithm equal to the power. For example, the logarithm of 100 to the base ten is 2.

In geometry, the term is used to denote the line or area on which a polygon or solid stands.

base in chemistry, a substance that accepts protons, such as the hydroxide ion (OH$^-$) and ammonia (NH$_3$). Bases react with acids to give a salt. Those that dissolve in water are called ◊alkalis.

baseball a bat-and-ball game between two teams, played on a field called a diamond, because of the arrangement of the bases. Bats, balls, and gloves constitute the basic equipment. The game is divided into nine innings. During the "top" half of each inning the home team plays defense and the visiting team, offense. In the "bottom" half, the roles are reversed. There are nine defensive positions: the pitcher, who stands on a mound 60.5 ft/18.4 m from home plate; the catcher, who crouches behind home plate; the first, second, and third basemen, who stand at or near their respective bases (90 ft/27.4 m apart), which together with home plate form the diamond-shaped infield: the shortstop, who covers the infield between second and third bases; and the right, center, and left fielders, whose domain is the outfield, the dimensions of which vary from stadium to

baseball: recent World Series champions

1980	Philadelphia Phillies (NL*)
1981	Los Angeles Dodgers (NL)
1982	St Louis Cardinals (NL)
1983	Baltimore Orioles (AL**)
1984	Detroit Tigers (AL)
1985	Kansas City Royals (AL)
1986	New York Mets (NL)
1987	Minnesota Twins (AL)
1988	Los Angeles Dodgers (NL)
1989	Oakland Athletics (AL)
1990	Cincinnati Reds (NL)
1991	Minnesota Twins (AL)
1992	Toronto Blue Jays (AL)
1993	Toronto Blue Jays (AL)
1994	(Season cancelled)

*National League
**American League

stadium. In the US the highest-level professional teams are divided into the American League (AL) and the National League (NL). The league champions meet annually in the World Series.

Basel or *Basle* (French *Bâle*) financial, commercial, and industrial city (dyes, vitamins, agrochemicals, dietary products, genetic products) in Switzerland; population (1990) 171,000. Basel was a strong military station under the Romans. In 1501 it joined the Swiss confederation and later developed as a center for the Reformation.

base pair in biochemistry, the linkage of two base (purine or pyrimidine) molecules in ◊DNA. They are found in nucleotides, and form the basis of the genetic code.

Bashkir autonomous republic of Russia, with the Ural Mountains on the east *area* 55,430 sq mi/143,600 sq km *capital* Ufa *industries* minerals, oil, natural gas *population* (1982) 3,876,000 *languages* Russian, Bashkir (about 25%) *history* annexed by Russia 1557; became the first Soviet autonomous republic 1919. Since 1989 Bashkirs have demanded greater independence.

BASIC (acronym for *beginner's all-purpose symbolic instruction code*) high-level computer-programming language, developed 1964, originally designed to take advantage of ◊multiuser systems (which can be used by many people at the same time). The language is relatively easy to learn and is popular among microcomputer users.

Basie Count (William) 1904–1984. US jazz band leader and pianist. He developed the big-band sound and a simplified, swinging style of music. He led impressive groups of musicians in a career spanning more than 50 years. Basie's compositions include "One O'Clock Jump" and "Jumpin' at the Woodside".

basil or *sweet basil* plant *Ocimum basilicum* of the mint family Labiatae. A native of the tropics, it is cultivated as a culinary herb.

basil *Basil is a member of the mint family grown in many areas of the world as a cooking herb. The plant originated in India, where it is a perennial. In cooler climates, it is an annual or semiannual. It has white flowers and grows to a height of 18 in/45 cm.*

Basil II *c.*958–1025. Byzantine emperor from 976. His achievement as emperor was to contain, and later decisively defeat, the Bulgarians, earning for himself the title "Bulgar-Slayer" after a victory 1014. After the battle he blinded almost all 15,000 of the defeated, leaving only a few men with one eye to lead their fellows home. The Byzantine empire had reached its largest extent at the time of his death.

basilica Roman public building; a large roofed hall flanked by columns, generally with an aisle on each side, used for judicial or other public business. The earliest known basilica, at Pompeii, dates from the 2nd century BC. This architectural form was adopted by the early Christians for their churches.

basketball ball game between two teams of five players, played on both indoor and outdoor rectangular courts. Players move the ball by passing it or by dribbling it (bouncing it on the floor) while running. Basketball is played worldwide by both men and women and, with soccer, is one of the two most popular sports.

Basle alternative form of ◊Basel, a city in Switzerland.

Basque member of a people inhabiting the Basque Country of central N Spain and the extreme SW of France. The Basques are a pre-Indo-European people who largely maintained their independence until the 19th century. During the Spanish Civil War 1936–39, they were on the republican side defeated by Franco. Their language (*Euskara*) is unrelated to any other language. The Basque separatist movement ETA (*Euskadi ta Askatasuna*, "Basque Nation and Liberty") and the French organization Iparretarrak ("ETA fighters from the North Side") have engaged in guerrilla activity from 1968 in an attempt to secure a united Basque state.

Basra (Arabic *al-Basrah*) principal port in Iraq, in the Shatt-al-Arab delta, 60 mi/97 km from the Persian Gulf, founded in the 7th century; population (1977) 1.5 million (1991) 850,000. Exports include wool, oil, cereal, and dates. Aerial bombing during the 1991 Gulf War destroyed bridges, factories, power stations, water-treatment plants, sewage-treatment plants, and the port. A Shiite rebellion March 1991 was crushed by the Iraqi army, causing further death and destruction.

bas relief see ◊relief.

bass long-bodied scaly sea fish *Morone labrax* found in the N Atlantic and Mediterranean. They grow to 3 ft/ 1 m, and are often seen in shoals.

bass the lowest male voice. The best-known bass singers have been the Russians Fyodor Chaliapin and Boris Christoff.

The term also covers the bass instrument of a consort or family, for example bass clarinet, bass tuba, and bassoon, having a similar range. An instrument an octave lower than bass is a contrabass.

Bassein port in Myanmar (Burma), in the Irrawaddy delta, 125 km/78 mi from the sea; population (1983) 355,588. Bassein was founded in the 13th century.

Basse-Normandie or *Lower Normandy* coastal region of NW France lying between Haute-Normandie and Brittany (Bretagne). It includes the *départements* of Calvados, Manche, and Orne; area 6,794 sq mi/17,600 sq km; population (1986) 1,373,000. Its capital is Caen. Apart from stock farming, dairy farming, and textiles, the area produces Calvados (apple brandy).

Basseterre capital and port of St Christopher–Nevis, in the Leeward Islands; population (1980) 14,000.

Industries include data processing, rum, clothes, and electrical components.

bassoon double-reed woodwind instrument in B flat, the bass of the oboe family. It doubles back on itself in a tube about 7.5 ft/2.5 m long and has a rich and deep tone. The bassoon concert repertoire extends from the early Baroque via Vivaldi, Mozart, and Dukas to Stockhausen.

Bass Strait channel between Australia and Tasmania, named for British explorer George Bass; oil was discovered here in the 1960s.

Bastille castle of St Antoine, built about 1370 as part of the fortifications of Paris. It was made a state prison by Cardinal ◊Richelieu and was stormed by the mob that set the French Revolution in motion July 14, 1789. Only seven prisoners were found in the castle when it was stormed; the governor and most of the garrison were killed, and the Bastille was razed.

bat flying mammal in which the forelimbs are developed as wings capable of rapid and sustained flight. There are two main groups of bats: *megabats*, or *flying foxes*, which eat fruit, and *microbats*, which mainly eat insects. Although by no means blind, many microbats rely largely on echolocation for navigation and finding prey, sending out pulses of high-pitched sound and listening for the echo. Bats are nocturnal, and those native to temperate countries hibernate in winter. There are about 1,000 species of bats forming the order Chiroptera, making this the second-largest mammalian order; bats make up nearly one-quarter of the world's mammals. Although bats are widely distributed, bat populations have declined alarmingly and many species are now endangered.

Bataan peninsula in Luzon, the Philippines, which was defended against the Japanese in World War II by US and Filipino troops under General MacArthur Jan 1–April 9, 1942. MacArthur was evacuated, but some 67,000 Allied prisoners died on the *Bataan Death March* to camps in the interior.

batch processing in computing, a system for processing data with little or no operator intervention. Batches of data are prepared in advance to be processed during regular "runs" (for example, each night). This allows efficient use of the computer and is well suited to applications of a repetitive nature, such as a company payroll.

Bath historic city in Avon, England; population (1991) 78,700. Industries include printing, plastics, and engineering.

features Hot springs; the ruins of the baths after which it is named, as well as a great temple, are the finest Roman remains in Britain. Excavations 1979 revealed thousands of coins and "curses", offered at a place which was thought to be the link between the upper and lower worlds. The Gothic Bath Abbey has an unusually decorated west front and fan vaulting. There is much 18th-century architecture, notably the Royal Crescent by John Wood. The Assembly Rooms 1771 were destroyed in an air raid 1942 but reconstructed 1963. The Bath Festival Orchestra is based here.

history The Roman spa town of Aquae Sulis ("waters of Sul"—the British goddess of wisdom) was built in the first 20 years after the Roman invasion. In medieval times the hot springs were crown property, administered by the church, but the city was transformed in the 18th century to a fashionable spa, presided over by "Beau" Nash. At his home here the astronomer

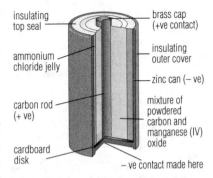

Labels: insulating top seal; brass cap (+ve contact); ammonium chloride jelly; insulating outer cover; zinc can (– ve); carbon rod (+ ve); mixture of powdered carbon and manganese (IV) oxide; cardboard disk; – ve contact made here

battery The common dry cell relies on chemical changes occurring between the electrodes—the central carbon rod and the outer zinc casing—and the ammonium chloride electrolyte to produce electricity. The mixture of carbon and manganese is used to increase the life of the cell.

William Herschel discovered Uranus 1781. Visitors included the novelists Tobias Smollett, Henry Fielding, and Jane Austen.

Batista Fulgencio 1901–1973. Cuban dictator 1933–44 and again 1952–59, after seizing power in a coup. His authoritarian methods enabled him to jail his opponents and amass a large personal fortune. He was overthrown by rebel forces led by Fidel ◊Castro 1959.

battery any energy-storage device allowing release of electricity on demand. It is made up of one or more electrical ◊cells. Primary-cell batteries are disposable; secondary-cell batteries, or ◊accumulators, are rechargeable. Primary-cell batteries are an extremely uneconomical form of energy, since they produce only 2% of the power used in their manufacture.

Battle Creek city in Michigan directly E of Kalamazoo; population (1990) 53,540. It became known as the cereal capital of the world after J H Kellogg, W K Kellogg, and C W Post established dry cereal and grain factories here. Battle Creek was also a station on the ◊Underground Railroad.

baud in computing, unit that measures the speed of data transmission. One baud represents a transmission rate of one bit per second.

Baudelaire Charles Pierre 1821–1867. French poet. His immensely influential work combined rhythmical and musical perfection with a morbid romanticism and eroticism, finding beauty in decadence and evil. His first and best-known book of verse was *Les Fleurs du mal/Flowers of Evil* 1857. Later volumes include *Les Paradis artificiels* 1860. He also published studies of Balzac and Flaubert, perceptive art criticism, and an autobiographical novel *La Fanfarlo* 1847. He was one of the major figures in the development of ◊Symbolism.

Baudouin 1930–1993. King of the Belgians 1951–93. In 1950 his father, ◊Leopold III, abdicated and Baudouin was known until his succession July 1951 as *Le Prince Royal*. During his reign he succeeded in holding together a country divided by religion and language, while presiding over the dismemberment of Belgium's imperial past. In 1960 he married Fabiola de Mora y Aragón (1928–), member of a Spanish noble family. He was succeeded by his brother, Alberto, 1993.

Bauhaus German school of architecture and design founded 1919 at Weimar in Germany by the architect Walter ◊Gropius in an attempt to fuse art, design, architecture, and crafts into a unified whole. Moved to Dessau under political pressure 1925 (where it was housed in a building designed by Gropius), the school was closed by the Nazis 1933. Among the artists associated with the Bauhaus were the painters Klee and Kandinsky and the architect Mies van der Rohe.

Baum L(yman) Frank 1856–1919. US writer. He was the author of the children's fantasy *The Wonderful Wizard of Oz* 1900 and its 13 sequels.

The series was continued by another author after his death. The film *The Wizard of Oz* 1939 with Judy Garland became a US classic.

bauxite principal ore of ◊aluminum, consisting of a mixture of hydrated aluminum oxides and hydroxides, generally contaminated with compounds of iron, which give it a red color. It is formed by the chemical weathering of rocks in tropical climates. Chief producers of bauxite are Australia, Guinea, Jamaica, Russia, Kazakhstan, Surinam, and Brazil.

Bavaria (German *Bayern*) administrative region (German *Land*) of Germany *area* 27,252 sq mi/70,600 sq km *capital* Munich *towns and cities* Nuremberg, Augsburg, Würzburg, Regensburg *features* largest of the German *Länder*; forms the Danube basin; festivals at Bayreuth and Oberammergau *industries* beer, electronics, electrical engineering, optics, automobiles, aerospace, chemicals, plastics, oil refining, textiles, glass, toys *population* (1988) 11,000,000 *famous people* Lucas Cranach, Adolf Hitler, Franz Josef Strauss, Richard Strauss *religions* 70% Roman Catholic, 26% Protestant *history* the last king, Ludwig III, abdicated 1918, and Bavaria declared itself a republic.

bay various species of ◊laurel, genus *Laurus*. The aromatic evergreen leaves are used for flavoring in cooking. There is also a golden-leaved variety.

Bayern German name for ◊Bavaria, a region of Germany.

Bay of Pigs inlet on the S coast of Cuba about 90 mi/145 km SW of Havana. It was the site of an unsuccessful invasion attempt by 1,500 US-sponsored Cuban exiles April 17–20, 1961; 1,173 were taken prisoner.

bayonet short sword attached to the muzzle of a firearm. The bayonet was placed inside the barrel of the muzzleloading muskets of the late 17th century. The *sock* or ring bayonet, invented 1700, allowed a weapon to be fired without interruption, leading to the demise of the pike.

BBC abbreviation for ◊*British Broadcasting Corporation.*

BC in the Christian calendar, abbreviation for *before Christ*; used with dates.

Beach Boys, the US pop group formed 1961. They began as exponents of vocal-harmony surf music with Chuck Berry guitar riffs (their hits include "Surfin' US" 1963 and "Help Me, Rhonda" 1965), but the compositions, arrangements, and production by Brian Wilson (1942–) became highly complex under the influence of psychedelic rock, as in "Good Vibrations" 1966. Wilson spent most of the next 20 years in retirement but returned with a solo album 1988.

beak horn-covered projecting jaws of a bird, or other horny jaws such as those of the tortoise or octopus. The beaks of birds are adapted by shape and size to specific diets.

Beaker people people thought to be of Iberian origin who spread out over Europe from the 3rd millennium BC. They were skilled in metalworking, and are identified by their use of distinctive earthenware beakers with various designs, of which the bell-beaker type was widely distributed throughout Europe. They favored inhumation (burial of the intact body), often round ◊barrows, or secondary burials in some form of chamber tomb. A beaker accompanied each burial, possibly to hold a drink for the deceased on their final journey.

bean any seed of numerous leguminous plants. Beans are rich in nitrogenous or protein matter and are grown both for human consumption and as food for cattle and horses. Varieties of bean are grown throughout Europe, the US, South America, China, Japan, SE Asia, and Australia.

bear large mammal with a heavily built body, short powerful limbs, and a very short tail. Bears breed once a year, producing one to four cubs. In northern regions they hibernate, and the young are born in the winter den. They are found mainly in North America and N Asia. The skin of the polar bear is black to conserve 80–90% of the solar energy trapped and channeled down the hollow hairs of its fur.

bear in business, a speculator who sells stocks or shares on the stock exchange expecting a fall in the price in order to buy them back at a profit, the opposite of a ◊bull. In a bear market, prices fall, and bears prosper.

Beard Charles Austin 1874–1948. US historian and a leader of the Progressive movement, active in promoting political and social reform. As a chief exponent of critical economic history, he published *An Economic Interpretation of the Constitution of the United States* 1913 and *The Economic Origins of Jeffersonian Democracy* 1915. With his wife, Mary, he wrote *A Basic History of the United States* 1944, long a standard textbook in the US.

Bear, Great and Little common names (and translations of the Latin) for the constellations ◊Ursa Major and ◊Ursa Minor respectively.

bearing device used in a machine to allow free movement between two parts, typically the rotation of a shaft in a housing. *Ball bearings* consist of two rings, one fixed to a housing, one to the rotating shaft. Between them are a set, or race, of steel balls. They are widely used to support shafts, as in the spindle in the hub of a bicycle wheel.

bearing the direction of a fixed point, or the path of a moving object, from a point of observation on the Earth's surface, expressed as an angle from the north. Bearings are taken by ◊compass and are measured in degrees (°), given as three-digit numbers increasing clockwise. For instance, north is 000°, northeast is 045°, south is 180°, and southwest is 225°.

Beat Generation or *Beat movement* US social and literary movement of the 1950s and early 1960s that sought personal liberation largely through Eastern mysticism, drugs, and music (particularly jazz). Members of the Beat Generation, called "beatniks," were usually in their teens and early twenties. The writers associated with the movement rejected traditional forms, favoring spontaneity and free forms. The most influential writers were Jack ◊Kerouac (who is credited with coining the term), Allen ◊Ginsberg, and William ◊Burroughs.

Beatles, the English pop group 1960–70. The members, all born in Liverpool, were John Lennon (1940–80, rhythm guitar, vocals), Paul McCartney (1942– , bass, vocals), George Harrison (1943– , lead guitar, vocals), and Ringo Starr (formerly Richard Starkey, 1940– , drums). Using songs written largely by Lennon and McCartney, the Beatles dominated rock music and pop culture in the 1960s.

In addition to experimenting with a wide range of musical styles, they greatly influenced subsequent bands, made films, and toured extensively. Their hit songs include "She Loves You" 1963, "Can't Buy Me Love" 1964, and "Yesterday" 1965. Their films include *A Hard Day's Night* 1964, *Help!* 1965, and the animated feature *Yellow Submarine* 1968, for which they provided the soundtrack. The Beatles continued to have an impact on the dress, hair, lifestyle, and thought of young people even after they pursued separate careers.

Beaton Cecil 1904–1980. English photographer. His elegant and sophisticated fashion pictures and society portraits often employed exotic props and settings. He adopted a more simple style for his wartime photographs of bomb-damaged London. He also worked as a stage and film designer, notably for the musicals *Gigi* 1959 and *My Fair Lady* 1965.

Beatrix 1938– . Queen of the Netherlands. The eldest daughter of Queen Juliana, she succeeded to the throne on her mother's abdication 1980. In 1966 she married West German diplomat Claus von Amsberg (1926–), who was created Prince of the Netherlands. Her heir is Prince Willem Alexander (1967–).

Beaufort scale system of recording wind velocity, devised by Francis Beaufort 1806. It is a numerical scale ranging from 0 to 17, calm being indicated by 0 and a hurricane by 12; 13–17 indicate degrees of hurricane force.

Beaumont city and port in Texas on the Neches River, NE of Houston; seat of Jefferson County; population (1990) 114,320. It is an oil-processing center for the surrounding oil fields and a shipping point via the Sabine–Neches canal to the Gulf of Mexico; other industries include shipbuilding and paper production.

In 1901, when a successful oil well was drilled in Spindletop Field, the modern oil industry began in the West.

Beauregard, Pierre Gustave Toutant *Remembered as the Confederate general who fired on Fort Sumter and so opened the American Civil War, Pierre Beauregard had a distinguished career, fighting at Bull Run, Shiloh, and Charleston.*

Beauregard Pierre Gustave Toutant 1818–1893. US military leader and Confederate general whose opening fire on ◊Fort Sumter, South Carolina, started the Civil War 1861. His military successes were clouded by his conflicts with Confederate president Jefferson Davis.

Beauregard was born in Louisiana and graduated from West Point in 1838. He distinguished himself during the Mexican War and then returned to

Beaufort scale

number and description	features	air speed (mi per hr)	(m per sec)
0 calm	smoke rises vertically; water smooth	less than 1	less than 0.3
1 light air	smoke shows wind direction; water ruffled	1–3	0.3–1.5
2 slight breeze	leaves rustle; wind felt on face	4–7	1.6–3.3
3 gentle breeze	loose paper blows around	8–12	3.4–5.4
4 moderate breeze	branches sway	13–18	5.5–7.9
5 fresh breeze	small trees sway, leaves blown off	19–24	8.0–10.7
6 strong breeze	whistling in telephone wires; sea spray from waves	25–31	10.8–13.8
7 moderate gale	large trees sway	32–38	13.9–17.1
8 fresh gale	twigs break from trees	39–46	17.2–20.7
9 strong gale	branches break from trees	47–54	20.8–24.4
10 whole gale	trees uprooted, weak buildings collapse	55–63	24.5–28.4
11 storm	widespread damage	64–72	28.5–32.6
12 hurricane	widespread structural damage	73–82	above 32.7
13		83–92	
14		93–103	
15		104–114	
16		115–125	
17		126–136	

Louisiana. In 1861 he was appointed superintendent of West Point, but resigned after four days to join the South.

At the outset of the Civil War, Beauregard achieved fame immediately for his attack on Fort Sumter. He played a leading role in the Confederate victory at the 1st Battle of Bull Run and prevented disaster at Shiloh (1862) through an orderly withdrawal. His disagreements with Davis, however, resulted in frequent changes in his commands. In 1865 he helped to delay the Union advance on Petersburg, Virginia. He spent his postwar years in New Orleans, where he was prominent in business and politics.

Beauvoir Simone de 1908–1986. French socialist, feminist, and writer who taught philosophy at the Sorbonne university in Paris 1931–43. Her book *Le Deuxième sexe/The Second Sex* 1949 became a seminal work for many feminists.

beaver aquatic rodent *Castor fiber* with webbed hind feet, a broad flat scaly tail, and thick waterproof fur. It has very large incisor teeth and fells trees to feed on the bark and to use the logs to construct the "lodge", in which the young are reared, food is stored, and much of the winter is spent.

Beaverbrook (William) Max(well) Aitken, 1st Baron Beaverbrook 1879–1964. British financier, newspaper proprietor, and politician, born in Canada. He bought a majority interest in the *Daily Express* 1919, founded the *Sunday Express* 1921, and bought the London *Evening Standard* 1929. He served in Lloyd George's World War I cabinet and Churchill's World War II cabinet.

bebop or *bop* hot jazz style, rhythmically complex, virtuosic, and highly improvisational. It was developed in New York in the 1940s and 1950s by Charlie Parker, Dizzy Gillespie, Thelonius Monk, and other African American musicians reacting against ◊swing music.

Becker Boris 1967– . German tennis player. In 1985, at the age of 17, he became the youngest winner of a singles title at Wimbledon. He has won the title three times and helped West Germany to win the Davis Cup 1988 and 1989. He also won the US Open 1989 and the Grand Prix Masters/ATP Tour World Championship 1992.

Becket St Thomas à 1118–1170. English priest and politician. He was chancellor to ◊Henry II 1155–62, when he was appointed archbishop of Canterbury. The interests of the church soon conflicted with those of the crown and Becket was assassinated; he was canonized 1172.

He resisted Henry's attempts to regulate relations between church and state, and was murdered by four knights before the altar of Canterbury cathedral.

Beckett Samuel 1906–1989. Irish novelist and dramatist. He wrote in both French and English. His play *En attendant Godot*—first performed in Paris 1952, and then in his own translation as *Waiting for Godot* 1955 in London, and New York 1956—is possibly the best-known example of Theatre of the Absurd, in which life is taken to be meaningless. This genre is taken to further extremes in *Fin de Partie/Endgame* 1957 and *Happy Days* 1961. Nobel Prize for Literature 1969.

becquerel SI unit (symbol Bq) of ◊radioactivity, equal to one radioactive disintegration (change in the nucleus of an atom when a particle or ray is given off) per second.

Becquerel (Antoine) Henri 1852–1908. French physicist who discovered penetrating radiation coming from uranium salts, the first indication of ◊radioactivity, and shared a Nobel Prize with Marie and Pierre ◊Curie 1903.

bed in geology, a single ◊sedimentary rock unit with a distinct set of physical characteristics or contained fossils, readily distinguishable from those of beds above and below. Well-defined partings called *bedding planes* separate successive beds or strata.

bedbug flattened wingless red-brown insect *Cimex lectularius* with piercing mouthparts. It hides by day in crevices or bedclothes and emerges at night to suck human blood.

Bede *c.*673–735. English theologian and historian, known as *the Venerable Bede*, active in Durham and Northumbria. He wrote many scientific, theological, and historical works. His *Historia Ecclesiastica Gentis Anglorum/Ecclesiastical History of the English People* 731 is a seminal source for early English history.

Bedell Smith Walter 1895–1961. US general; Eisenhower's staff officer for much of World War II. Among his many achievements was the negotiation of the Italian surrender 1943 and the surrender of German forces in NW Europe 1945.

A staff officer who had risen from the ranks, in 1941 he became secretary to the Joint Chiefs of Staff and US secretary of the Anglo-American Combined Chiefs of Staff. He became Chief of Staff to General ◊Eisenhower Sept 1942 and remained in this post until the end of the war.

Bedfordshire county of S central England *area* 479 sq mi/1,240 sq km *towns and cities* Bedford (administrative headquarters), Luton, Dunstable *features* low lying with Chiltern Hills in the SW; Whipsnade Zoo 1931, near Dunstable, a zoological park (500 acres/200 hectares) belonging to the London Zoological Society; Woburn Abbey, seat of the duke of Bedford *industries* cereals, vegetables, agricultural machinery, electrical goods, cement, clay, chalk, sand, gravel, motor vehicles. Agriculture is important, especially wheat and barley. It has one of the world's largest brickworks *population* (1991) 514,200 *famous people* John Bunyan, John Howard, Joseph Paxton.

Bedouin Arab of any of the nomadic peoples occupying the desert regions of Arabia and N Africa, now becoming increasingly settled. Their traditional trade was the rearing of horses and camels.

bee four-winged insect of the superfamily Apoidea in the order Hymenoptera, usually with a sting. There are over 12,000 species, of which fewer than 1 in 20 are social in habit. The *hive bee* or *honey bee Apis mellifera* establishes perennial colonies of about 80,000, the majority being infertile females (workers), with a few larger fertile males (drones), and a single very large fertile female (the queen). Worker bees live for no more than a few weeks, while a drone may live a few months, and a queen several years. Queen honey bees lay two kinds of eggs: fertilized, female eggs, which have two sets of chromosomes and develop into workers or queens, and unfertilized, male eggs, which have only one set of chromosomes and develop into drones.

beech genus of trees *Fagus*, of the family Fagaceae. Of the ten species in this genus only one is native to North America; others grow in Europe. The American beech *F. grandifolia* grows to 100 ft/30 m, with blue-gray bark; a broad, rounded crown; and leaves that are lanceolate, serrate, triangular, and edible.

Beecham Thomas 1879–1961. English conductor and impresario. He established the Royal Philharmonic

Orchestra 1946 and fostered the works of composers such as Delius, Sibelius, and Richard Strauss.

bee-eater bird *Merops apiaster* found in Africa, S Europe, and Asia. It feeds on a variety of insects, including bees, which it catches in its long narrow bill. Chestnut, yellow, and blue-green, it is gregarious, and generally nests in river banks and sandpits.

Beelzebub in the New Testament, the leader of the devils, sometimes identified with Satan and sometimes with his chief assistant (see ◊devil). In the Old Testament Beelzebub was a fertility god worshiped by the Philistines and other Semitic groups (Baal).

beer alcoholic drink made from water and malt (fermented barley or other grain), flavored with hops. Beer contains between 1% and 6% alcohol. One of the oldest alcoholic drinks, it was brewed in ancient China, Egypt, and Babylon.

The distinction between beer (containing hops) and ale (without hops) was made in medieval times. Beer is now a generic term including pilsner and lager. Stout is top fermented but is sweet and strongly flavored with roasted grain; lager (German "store") is a light beer, bottom fermented and matured over a longer period. Modern ales, like beer, are made with hops but are fermented more rapidly at relatively high temperatures. In the US, light (or lite) beers are made with more water, fewer calories, and less alcohol.

Beersheba industrial city in Israel; population (1987) 115,000. It is the chief center of the Negev Desert and has been a settlement from the Stone Age.

beet plant of the genus *Beta* of the goosefoot family Chenopodiaceae. The common beet *B. vulgaris* is used in one variety to produce sugar, and another, the mangelwurzel, is grown as cattle fodder. The beetroot, or red beet, *B. rubra* is a salad plant.

Beethoven Ludwig van 1770–1827. German composer and pianist. His mastery of musical expression in every genre made him the dominant influence on 19th-century music. Beethoven's repertoire includes concert overtures; the opera *Fidelio* 1805, revised 1814; five piano concertos and two for violin (one unfinished); 32 piano sonatas, including the *Moonlight* 1801 and *Appassionata* 1804–05; 17 string quartets; the Mass in D *Missa solemnis* 1824; and nine symphonies, as well as many youthful works. He usually played his own piano pieces and conducted his orchestral works until he was hampered by deafness 1801; nevertheless he continued to compose.

beetle common name of insects in the order Coleoptera (Greek "sheath-winged") with leathery forewings folding down in a protective sheath over the membranous hindwings, which are those used for flight. They pass through a complete metamorphosis. They include some of the largest and smallest of all insects: the largest is the **Hercules beetle** *Dynastes hercules* of the South American rainforests, 6 in/15 cm long; the smallest is only 0.02 in/0.05 cm long. Comprising more than 50% of the animal kingdom, beetles number some 370,000 named species, with many not yet described.

Begin Menachem 1913–1992. Israeli politician. He was leader of the extremist Irgun Zvai Leumi organization in Palestine from 1942 and prime minister of Israel 1977–83, as head of the right-wing Likud party. In 1978 Begin shared a Nobel Peace Prize with President Sadat of Egypt for work on the ◊Camp David Agreements for a Middle East peace settlement.

begonia any plant of the genus *Begonia* of the tropical and subtropical family Begoniaceae. Begonias have fleshy and succulent leaves, and some have large, brilliant flowers. There are numerous species native to the tropics, in particular South America and India.

Behan Brendan 1923–1964. Irish dramatist. His early experience of prison and knowledge of the workings of the ◊IRA (recounted in his autobiography *Borstal Boy* 1958) provided him with two recurrent themes in his plays. *The Quare Fellow* 1954 was followed by the tragicomedy *The Hostage* 1958, first written in Gaelic.

behaviorism school of psychology originating in the US, of which the leading exponent was John B Watson. Behaviorists maintain that all human activity can ultimately be explained in terms of conditioned reactions or reflexes and habits formed in consequence. Leading behaviorists include Ivan ◊Pavlov and B F ◊Skinner.

Behring Emil von 1854–1917. German physician who discovered that the body produces antitoxins, substances able to counteract poisons released by bacteria. Using this knowledge, he developed new treatments for diseases such as ◊diphtheria. He won the first Nobel Prize for Medicine, in 1901.

Beiderbecke Bix (Leon Bismarck) 1903–1931. US jazz cornetist, composer, and pianist. A romantic soloist with the bands of King Oliver, Louis Armstrong, and Paul Whiteman, Beiderbecke was the first acknowledged white jazz innovator. He was influenced by the classical composers Debussy, Ravel, and Stravinsky.

Beijing or *Peking* capital of China; part of its northeast border is formed by the Great Wall of China; population (1989) 6,800,000. The municipality of Beijing has an area of 6,871 sq mi/17,800 sq km and a population (1990) of 10,819,000. Industries include textiles, petrochemicals, steel, and engineering.

Beirut or *Beyrouth* capital and port of ◊Lebanon, devastated by civil war in the 1970s and 1980s, when it was occupied by armies of neighboring countries; population (1993) 1.2 million.

Belarus Republic of *area* 80,100 sq mi/207,600 sq km *capital* Minsk (Mensk) *towns and cities* Gomel, Vitebsk, Mogilev, Bobruisk, Grodno, Brest *physical* more than 25% forested; rivers W Dvina, Dnieper and its tributaries, including the Pripet and Beresina; the Pripet Marshes in the E; mild and damp climate *environment* large areas contaminated by fallout from Chernobyl *features* Belovezhskaya Pushcha (scenic forest reserve) *head of state* Alexandr Lukashenko from 1994 *head of government* Mikhail Chigir from 1994 *political system* emergent democracy *political parties* Byelorussian Popular Front (BPF; Adradzhenne), moderate nationalist; Byelorussian Social Democratic Group, moderate left of center; Christian Democratic Union of Belarus, centrist; Communist Party, left-wing *products* peat, agricultural machinery, fertilizers, glass, textiles, leather, salt, electrical goods, meat, dairy produce *currency* ruble and dukat *population* (1993 est) 10,440,000 (77% Byelorussian "Eastern Slavs", 13% Russian, 4% Polish, 1% Jewish) *life expectancy* men 64, women 75 *languages* Byelorussian, Russian *media* state control of major newspapers; restrictions on broadcasting. No official censorship but law banning publication of material that "insults human dignity" has been used to suppress criticism of individuals *religions* Roman Catholic, Russian Orthodox, with Baptist and Muslim minorities *chronology* **1918–19** Briefly independent from Russia. **1937–41** More than 100,000 people were shot in mass executions ordered by Stalin. *1941–44* Occupied by Nazi Germany. *1945* Became a founding member of the United Nations. *1986* April: fallout from the Chernobyl nuclear reactor in Ukraine contaminated a large area. *1989* Byelorussian Popular Front established as well as a more extreme nationalist organ-ization, the Tolaka group. *1990* Sept: Byelorussian established as state language and republi-can sovereignty declared. *1991* April: Minsk hit by gen-eral strike. Aug: declared independence; Communist Party suspended. Sept: reformist Shushkevich elected president. Dec: accorded diplomatic recognition by US; Commonwealth of Independent States formed in Minsk. *1993* Ratified START I; agreement to adhere to Nuclear Nonproliferation Treaty. Communist party reestablished. *1994* Merger of Russian and Belarusian economies agreed. President Shushkevich ousted. New constitution adopted. Alexandr Lukashenko elected president.

Belasco David 1859–1931. US dramatist and producer. His works include *Madame Butterfly* 1900 and *The Girl of the Golden West* 1905, both of which Puccini used as libretti for operas.

Belau, Republic of (formerly *Palau*) *area* 193 sq mi/ 508 sq km *capital* Koror (on Koror Island) *physical* more than 350 islands and atolls, mostly uninhabited; warm, humid climate, susceptible to typhoons *head of state and government* Kuniwo Nakamura from 1993 *political system* democratic republic *currency* US dol-lar *population* (1990) 15,100 *languages* Palauan and English *religion* Christianity, principally Roman Catholicism *chronology* *1899* Held by Germany, then known as Palau. *1921* Administered by Japan under League of Nations mandate. *1944* Occupied by US forces as a base for attack on the Philippines. *1947* Administered by US as part of the United Nations (UN) Trust Territory of the Pacific Islands. *1981* Acquired autonomy as the Republic of Belau. *1982* Implementation of Compact of Free Association with US delayed because of constitutional objections. *1985* President Haruo Remeliik assassinated; succeeded by Lazarus Salii. *1988* President Salii found dead; suc-ceeded by Ngiratkel Etpison. *1992* Kuniwo Nakamura elected president. Referendum approved constitutional amendment allowing implementation of Compact of Free Association with US. *1994* Idependence achieved. UN membership agreed.

Belfast city and industrial port in County Antrim and County Down, Northern Ireland, at the mouth of the river Lagan on Belfast Lough; the capital of Northern Ireland since 1920; population (1985) 300,000 (Protestants form the majority in E Belfast, Catholics in the W). It is the county town of County Antrim. Industries include shipbuilding, engineering, elec-tronics, aircraft, textiles, tobacco, linen, rope, and fer-tilizers. Since 1968 the city has been heavily damaged by civil disturbances.

Belgian Congo former name (1908–60) of ◊Zaire.

Belgium Kingdom of (French *Royaume de Belgique*, Flemish *Koninkrijk België*) *area* 11,784 sq mi/30,510 sq km *capital* Brussels *towns and cities* Ghent, Liège, Charleroi, Bruges, Mons, Namur, Leuven; ports are Antwerp, Ostend, Zeebrugge *physical* fertile coastal plain in NW, central rolling hills rise eastward, hills and forest in SE *environment* a 1989 government report judged the drinking water in Flanders to be "seriously substandard" and more than half the rivers and canals in that region to be in a "very bad" condi-tion *features* Ardennes Forest; rivers Scheldt and Meuse *head of state* King Albert from 1993 *head of*

government Jean-Luc Dehaene from 1992 *political system* federal constitutional monarchy *political par-ties* Flemish Christian Social Party (CVP), center-left; French Social Christian Party (PSC), center-left; Flemish Socialist Party (SP), left of center; French Socialist Party (PS), left of center; Flemish Liberal Party (PVV), moderate centrist; French Liberal Reform Party (PRL), moderate centrist; Flemish People's Party (VU), federalist; Flemish Green Party (Agalev); French Green Party (Ecolo) *exports* iron, steel, textiles, manufac-tured goods, petrochemicals, plastics, vehicles, dia-monds *currency* Belgian franc *population* (1993 est) 10,050,000 (comprising Flemings and Walloons); growth rate 0.1% p.a. *life expectancy* men 72, women 79 *languages* in the N (Flanders) Flemish (a Dutch dialect, known as *Vlaams*) 55%; in the S (Wallonia) Walloon (a French dialect) 32%; bilingual 11%; German (E border) 0.6%; all are official *religion* Roman Catholic 75% *literacy* 99% *GNP* $19,300 per head (1991) *chronology* *1830* Belgium became an independent kingdom. *1914* Invaded by Germany. *1940* Again invaded by Germany. *1948* Belgium became founding member of Benelux Customs Union. *1949* Belgium became founding member of Council of Europe and NATO. *1951* Leopold III abdi-cated in favor of his son Baudouin. *1952* Belgium became founding member of European Coal and Steel Community. *1957* Belgium became founding member of the European Economic Community. *1971* Steps toward regional autonomy taken. *1972* German-speaking members included in the cabinet for the first time. *1973* Linguistic parity achieved in government appointments. *1974* Leo Tindemans became prime minister. Separate regional councils and ministerial committees established. *1978* Wilfried Martens suc-ceeded Tindemans as prime minister. *1980* Open vio-lence over language divisions. Regional assemblies for Flanders and Wallonia and a three-member executive for Brussels created. *1981* Short-lived coalition led by Mark Eyskens was followed by the return of Martens. *1987* Martens head of caretaker government after breakup of coalition. *1988* Following a general elec-tion, Martens formed a new CVP–PS–SP–PSC–VU coalition. *1992* Martens-led coalition collapsed; Jean-Luc Dehaene formed a new CVP-led coalition. *1993* Federal system adopted, based on Flanders, Wallonia, and Brussels. King Baudouin died; succeeded by his brother, Prince Albert of Liege.

Belgrade (Serbo-Croatian *Beograd*) capital of Yugoslavia and Serbia, and Danube river port linked with the port of Bar on the Adriatic Sea; population (1991) 1,087,900. Industries include light engineering, food processing, textiles, pharmaceuticals, and electrical goods.

Belisarius *c.*505–565. Roman general under Emperor ◊Justinian I. He won major victories over the Persians in 530 and the Vandals in 533 when he sacked Carthage. Later he invaded Sicily and fought a series of campaigns against the Goths in Italy.

Belize (formerly *British Honduras*) *area* 8,864 sq mi/ 22,963 sq km *capital* Belmopan *towns and cities* ports Belize City, Dangriga, Punta Gorda; Orange Walk, Corozal *physical* tropical swampy coastal plain, Maya Mountains in S; over 90% forested *environment* since 1981 Belize has developed an extensive system of national parks and reserves to protect large areas of tropical forest, coastal mangrove, and offshore islands. Forestry has been replaced by agriculture and ecotourism, which are now the most important sectors of the economy; world's first jaguar reserve created 1986 in the Cockscomb Mountains *features* world's second longest barrier reef; Maya ruins *head of state* Elizabeth II from 1981, represented by governor general Colville Young from 1993 *head of government* Manuel Esquivel from 1993 *political system* constitutional monarchy *political parties* People's United Party (PUP), left of center; United Democratic Party (UDP), moderate conservative *exports* sugar, citrus fruits, rice, fish products, bananas *currency* Belize dollar *population* (1993) 230,000 (including Mayan minority in the interior); growth rate 2.5% p.a. *life expectancy* 60 years *languages* English (official); Spanish (widely spoken), native Creole dialects *media* no daily newspaper; several independent weekly tabloids *religions* Roman Catholic 60%, Protestant 35% *literacy* 95% *GNP* $2,050 per head (1991) *chronology* *1862* Belize became a British colony. *1954* Constitution adopted, providing for limited internal self-government. General election won by George Price. *1964* Self-government achieved from the UK (universal adult suffrage introduced). *1965* Two-chamber national assembly introduced, with Price as prime minister. *1970* Capital moved from Belize City to Belmopan. *1973* British Honduras became Belize. *1975* British troops sent to defend the disputed frontier with Guatemala. *1980* United Nations called for full independence. *1981* Full independence achieved. Price became prime minister. *1984* Price defeated in general election. Manuel Esquivel formed the government. The UK reaffirmed its undertaking to defend the frontier. *1989* Price and the PUP won the general election. *1991* Diplomatic relations with Guatemala established. *1993* UDP defeated PUP in general election; Esquivel returned as prime minister. Dec: British government announced its withdrawal of troops from the border.

Belize City chief port of Belize, and capital until 1970; population (1991) 46,000. After the city was destroyed by a hurricane 1961 it was decided to move the capital inland, to Belmopan.

Bell Alexander Graham 1847–1922. Scottish-born US scientist and inventor of the telephone. He patented his invention 1876, and later experimented with a type of phonograph and, in aeronautics, invented the tricycle undercarriage.

Born in Edinburgh, Bell was educated at the universities of Edinburgh and London and studied under his father, who developed a method for teaching the deaf to speak. In 1870 the family moved to Canada and

Bell came to the US, where he opened a school 1872 for teachers of the deaf in Boston. In 1873 he began teaching vocal physiology at Boston University. He became a US citizen 1882.

Bell also worked on converting seawater to drinking water and on air conditioning and sheep breeding.

belladonna or *deadly nightshade* poisonous plant *Atropa belladonna*, found in Europe and Asia. The dried powdered leaves contain ◊alkaloids from which the drugs atropine and hyoscine are extracted. Belladonna extract acts medicinally as an anticholinergic (blocking the passage of certain nerve impulses), and is highly toxic in large doses.

Bellamy Edward 1850–1898. US author and social critic. His utopian novel *Looking Backward: 2000–1887* 1888, was a huge bestseller and inspired wide public support for his political program of state socialism. He published a second utopian novel, *Equality* 1897.

bellflower general name for many plants of the family Campanulaceae, especially those of the genus *Campanula*. The white, pink, or blue flowers are bellshaped and showy. The varied leaf bluebell *C. rotundifolia* grows in northern North America and Europe.

Bellini family of Italian Renaissance painters. Jacopo and his sons Gentile and Giovanni were founders of the Venetian School in the 15th and early 16th centuries.

Bellow Saul 1915– . Canadian-born US novelist. From his first novel, *Dangling Man* 1944, Bellow has typically set his naturalistic narratives in Chicago and made his central character an anxious, Jewish-American intellectual. In *The Adventures of Augie March* 1953 and *Henderson the Rain King* 1959, he created confident and comic picaresque heroes, before

Bellow, Saul *The works of US novelist Saul Bellow combine cultural sophistication with the wisdom of the streets. Mainly set in Chicago and New York, they present characterizations of modern urban life and contain a sense of moral and social alarm. His many literary awards include the National Book Award 1965 and 1971, the Pulitzer Prize 1976, and the Nobel Prize 1976.*

Herzog 1964, which pitches a comic but distressed scholar into a world of darkening humanism. Later works, developing Bellow's depiction of an age of urban disorder and indifference, include the near-apocalyptic *Mr Sammler's Planet* 1970, *Humboldt's Gift* 1975, *The Dean's December* 1982, *More Die of Heartbreak* 1987, and the novella *A Theft* 1989. His finely styled works and skilled characterizations won him the Nobel Prize for Literature 1976. Later works include *Him with His Foot in His Mouth* 1984, and *More die of Heartbreak* 1987.

Bellows George Wesley 1882–1925. US painter. He is associated with the Ashcan School, and known for his vigorous portrayals of the drama of street life and sport. His most famous works, such as *Stag at Sharkey's* 1909, depict the violence and excitement of illegal boxing matches.

Belmont August 1816–1890. German-born US financier, who became the Rothschilds' exclusive representative in the US when he established a private bank in New York 1837. Belmont was a leading member of New York City society's most exclusive clique (the "400") and was instrumental in financing the costs of the Mexican War (1846–48).

Belmopan capital of ◊Belize from 1970; population (1991) 4,000. It replaced Belize City as the administrative center of the country.

Belo Horizonte industrial city (steel, engineering, textiles) in SE Brazil, capital of the fast-developing state of Minas Gerais; population (1991) 2,103,300. Built in the 1890s, it was Brazil's first planned modern city.

Beloit city in SE Wisconsin on the Rock River, SE of Madison; population (1990) 35,600. Industries include electrical machinery, shoes, generators, and diesel engines.

Belorussia see ◊Belarus.

Belshazzar in the Old Testament, the last king of Babylon, son of Nebuchadnezzar. During a feast (known as **Belshazzar's Feast**) he saw a message, interpreted by Daniel as prophesying the fall of Babylon and death of Belshazzar.

All of this is said to have happened on the same night that the city was invaded by the Medes and Persians (539 BC).

Ben Ali Zine el Abidine 1936– . Tunisian politician, president from 1987. After training in France and the US, he returned to Tunisia and became director-general of national security. He was made minister of the interior and then prime minister under the aging president for life, Habib ◊Bourguiba, whom he deposed 1987 in a bloodless coup with the aid of ministerial colleagues. He ended the personality cult established by Bourguiba and moved toward a pluralist political system. He was reelected 1994, with 99% of the popular vote.

Benares alternative transliteration of ◊Varanasi, a holy city in India.

Ben Bella Ahmed 1916– . Algerian politician. He was leader of the National Liberation Front (FLN) from 1952, the first prime minister of independent Algeria 1962–63, and its first president 1963–65. In 1965 Ben Bella was overthrown by Col Houari Boumédienne and detained until 1979. In 1985 he founded a new party, Mouvement pour la Démocratie en Algérie, and returned to Algeria 1990 after nine years in exile.

Benchley Robert 1889–1945. US humorist, actor, and drama critic. His books include *Of All Things* 1921 and *Benchley Beside Himself* 1943.

His film skit *How to Sleep* illustrates his ability to extract humor from everyday life.

Born in Massachusetts, he was associated with the writer Dorothy Parker, *The New Yorker* magazine, and the circle of wits at the Algonquin Round Table in New York. He was a master of gentle satire, left New York City for Hollywood, and wrote and appeared in several 1930s and 1940s films.

benchmark in computing, a measure of the performance of a piece of equipment or software, usually consisting of a standard program or suite of programs. Benchmarks can indicate whether a computer is powerful enough to perform a particular task, and so enable machines to be compared. However, they provide only a very rough guide to practical performance, and may lead manufacturers to design systems that get high scores with the artificial benchmark programs but do not necessarily perform well with day-to-day programs or data.

Benedictine order religious order of monks and nuns in the Roman Catholic Church, founded by St ◊Benedict at Subiaco, Italy, in the 6th century. It had a strong influence on medieval learning and reached the height of its prosperity early in the 14th century.

There are Benedictine monasteries in the US in Latrobe, Pennsylvania, and St Meinrad, Indiana. In 1985 there were 9,453 monks and 7,911 nuns living in Benedictine convents.

Benedict, St *c.*480–*c.*547. Founder of Christian monasticism in the West and of the ◊Benedictine order. He founded the monastery of Monte Cassino, Italy. Here he wrote out his rule for monastic life and was visited shortly before his death by the Ostrogothic king Totila, whom he converted to the Christian faith. His feast day is July 11.

Benelux (acronym for *Belgium, the Netherlands, and Luxembourg*) customs union agreed by Belgium, the Netherlands, and Luxembourg 1948, fully effective 1960. It was the precursor of the European Community (now the European Union).

Benes Eduard 1884–1948. Czechoslovak politician. He worked with Tomás ◊Masaryk toward Czechoslovak nationalism from 1918 and was foreign minister and representative at the League of Nations. He was president of the republic from 1935 until forced to resign by the Germans; he headed a government in exile in London during World War II. He returned home as president 1945 but resigned again after the Communist coup 1948.

Bengal former province of British India, divided 1947 into ◊West Bengal, a state of India, and East Bengal, from 1972 ◊Bangladesh. A famine in 1943, caused by a slump in demand for jute and a bad harvest, resulted in over 3 million deaths.

Bengal, Bay of part of the Indian Ocean lying between the east coast of India and the west coast of Myanmar (Burma) and the Malay Peninsula.

The Irrawaddy, Ganges, and Brahmaputra rivers flow into the bay. The principal islands are to be found in the Andaman and Nicobar groups.

Bengali person of Bengali culture from Bangladesh and India (W Bengal, Tripura). There are 80–150 million speakers of Bengali, an Indo-Iranian language belonging to the Indo-European family. It is the official language of Bangladesh and of the state of Bengal and is also used by emigrant Bangladeshi and Bengali communities in such countries as the US and the UK. Bengalis in Bangladesh are predominantly Muslim, whereas those in India are mainly Hindu.

Benghazi or *Banghazi* historic city and industrial port in N Libya on the Gulf of Sirte; population (1982) 650,000. It was controlled by Turkey between the 16th century and 1911, and by Italy 1911–42; it was a major naval supply base during World War II.

Ben-Gurion David. Adopted name of David Gruen 1886–1973. Israeli statesman and socialist politician, one of the founders of the state of Israel, the country's first prime minister 1948–53, and again 1955–63.

Benin People's Republic of (*République Populaire du Bénin*) *area* 43,472 sq mi/112,622 sq km *capital* Porto Novo (official), Cotonou (de facto) *towns and cities* Abomey, Natitingou, Parakou; chief port Cotonou *physical* flat to undulating terrain; hot and humid in S; semiarid in N *features* coastal lagoons with fishing villages on stilts; Niger River in NE *head of state and government* Nicéphore Soglo from 1991 *political system* socialist pluralist republic *political parties* Democratic Union of Progressive Forces (UDFP), left-wing, nationalist; Movement for Democratic and Social Progress (MDPS), left-wing; Union for Liberty and Development (ULD), left-wing; National Party for Democracy and Development (PNDD), left of center; Party of Democratic Renewal (PRD), left of center *exports* cocoa, peanuts, cotton, palm oil, petroleum, cement, sea products *currency* CFA franc *population* (1993) 5,010,000; growth rate 3% p.a. *life expectancy* men 46, women 50 *languages* French (official); Fon 47% and Yoruba 9% in south; six major tribal languages in north *religions* animist 65%, Christian 17%, Muslim 13% *literacy* men 32%, women 16% *GNP* $380 per head (1991) *chronology 1851* Under French control. *1958* Became self-governing dominion within the French Community. *1960* Independence achieved from France. *1960–72* Acute political instability, with switches from civilian to military rule. *1972* Military regime established by General Mathieu Kerekou. *1974* Kerekou announced that the country would follow a path of "scientific socialism". *1975* Name of country changed from Dahomey to Benin. *1977* Return to civilian rule under a new constitution. *1980* Kerekou formally elected president by the national revolutionary assembly. *1989* Marxist-Leninism dropped as official ideology. Strikes and protests against Kerekou's rule mounted; army deployed against protesters. *1990* Referendum support for multiparty politics. New constitution adopted. *1991* Multiparty elections held. President Kerekou replaced by Nicéphore Soglo.

Benioff zone seismically active zone dipping beneath a continent or continental margin behind a deep-sea trench. The zone is named for Hugo Benioff, a US seismologist who first described this feature. The zone is equivalent to what is called a subduction zone in plate tectonic theory, where one plate descends beneath another.

Benjamin Judah Philip 1811–1884. US Confederate official. Holding office in the US Senate 1852–61, he was a proponent of secession of the South and resigned from office at the outbreak of the Civil War. As one of the leaders of the Confederacy, he served as attorney general, secretary of war, and secretary of state.

Ben Nevis highest mountain in the British Isles (4,406 ft/1,343 m), in the Grampian Mountains, Scotland.

Benny Jack. Adopted name of Benjamin Kubelsky 1894–1974. US comedian notable for his perfect timing and lugubrious manner. Over the years, Benny appeared on the stage, in films, and on radio and television. His radio program, *The Jack Benny Show* from 1932, made him a national institution. Featuring his wife Mary Livingston, singer Dennis Day, announcer Don Wilson, and valet Eddie "Rochester" Anderson, it was produced for television in the 1950s. His film appearances, mostly in the 1930s and 1940s, included *To Be or Not to Be* 1942. He also played in *Charley's Aunt* 1941, *It's In the Bag* 1945, and *A Guide for the Married Man* 1967.

Born in Chicago, he began a musical career in local theater orchestras (playing the violin) and joined a vaudeville troupe. During the 1920s, he turned to comedy, taking the adopted name "Jack Benny" and developing his familiar miserly, yet harmless character.

bent or *bent grass* any grasses of the genus *Agrostis*. Creeping bent grass *A. stolonifera*, also known as fiorin, is common in N North America and Eurasia, including lowland Britain. It spreads by runners and bears large attractive panicles of yellow or purple flowers on thin stalks. It is often used on lawns and golf courses.

Bentham Jeremy 1748–1832. English philosopher, legal and social reformer, and founder of ◊utilitarianism. The essence of his moral philosophy is found in the pronouncement of his *Principles of Morals and Legislation* (written 1780, published 1789): that the object of all legislation should be "the greatest happiness for the greatest number".

Benton Thomas Hart 1782–1858. US political leader. He was elected to the US Senate 1820, where he served for the next 30 years. He distinguished himself as an

Benjamin, Judah Philip US lawyer and politician Judah Philip Benjamin was Confederate secretary of state during the American Civil War. Escaping to England at the end of the war, he became a lawyer and wrote a classic legal work, The Sale of Personal Property 1868.

outspoken opponent of the Bank of the United States and the extension of slavery as well as a strong supporter of westward expansion.

Moving to St Louis 1815, he opened a law practice and published the *Missouri Inquirer* 1818–20.

Benz Karl Friedrich 1844–1929. German automobile engineer who produced the world's first gasoline-driven motor vehicle. He built his first model engine 1878 and the gasoline-driven automobile 1885.

Benzedrine trade name for ◊amphetamine, a stimulant drug.

benzene C_6H_6 clear liquid hydrocarbon of characteristic odor, occurring in coal tar. It is used as a solvent and in the synthesis of many chemicals.

benzodiazepine any of a group of mood-altering drugs (tranquilizers), for example Librium and Valium. They are addictive and interfere with the process by which information is transmitted between brain cells, and various side effects arise from continued use. They were originally developed as muscle relaxants, and then excessively prescribed in the West as anxiety-relieving drugs.

benzoin resin obtained by making incisions in the bark of *Styrax benzoin*, a tree native to the East Indies. Benzoin is used in the preparation of cosmetics, perfumes, and incense.

The name is also used for several bushes of the genus *Lindera* of the laurel family, growing in E North America, especially the common spicebush *L. benzoin*.

Beograd Serbo-Croatian form of ◊Belgrade, the capital of Yugoslavia.

Beowulf Anglo-Saxon poem (composed *c*.700), the only complete surviving example of Germanic folk epic. It exists in a single manuscript copied in England about 1000 in the Cottonian collection of the British Museum.

Berber member of a non-Semitic Caucasoid people of North Africa who since prehistoric times inhabited Barbary, the Mediterranean coastlands from Egypt to the Atlantic. Their language, present-day Berber (a member of the Afro-Asiatic language family), is spoken by about one-third of Algerians and nearly two-thirds of Moroccans, 10 million people. Berbers are mainly agricultural, but some are still nomadic.

Bérégovoy Pierre 1925–1993. French socialist politician, prime minister 1992–93. A close ally of François ◊Mitterrand, he was named chief of staff 1981 after managing the successful presidential campaign. He was social affairs minister 1982–84 and finance minister 1984–86 and 1988–92. He resigned as premier following the Socialists' defeat in the March 1993 general election, and shortly afterwards committed suicide.

Berengaria of Navarre 1165–1230. Queen of England. The only English queen never to set foot in England, she was the daughter of King Sancho VI of Navarre. She married Richard I of England in Cyprus 1191, and accompanied him on his crusade to the Holy Land.

Berg Paul 1926– . US molecular biologist. In 1972, using gene-splicing techniques developed by others, Berg spliced and combined into a single hybrid the ◊DNA from an animal tumor virus (SV40) and the DNA from a bacterial virus. Berg's work aroused fears in other workers and excited continuing controversy. For his work on recombinant DNA, he shared the 1980 Nobel Prize for Chemistry with Walter Gilbert and Frederick ◊Sanger.

bergamot small, evergreen tree *Citrus bergamia* of the rue family Rutaceae. From the rind of its fruit a fragrant orange-scented essence used as a perfume is obtained. The sole source of supply is S Calabria, Italy, but the name comes from the town of Bergamo, in Lombardy.

Bergen industrial port (shipbuilding, engineering, fishing) in SW Norway; population (1991) 213,300. Founded 1070, Bergen was a member of the ◊Hanseatic League.

Bergman Ingmar 1918– . Swedish stage producer (from the 1930s) and film director (from the 1940s). He is regarded by many as one of the great masters of modern films. His work deals with complex moral, psychological, and metaphysical problems and is often strongly tinged with pessimism. His films include *Wild Strawberries* 1957, *The Seventh Seal* 1957, *Persona* 1966, *Autumn Sonata* 1978 and *Fanny and Alexander* 1982.

Bergman Ingrid 1917–1982. Swedish-born actress. She went to the US 1939 to appear in David Selznick's *Intermezzo* 1939 and later appeared in *Casablanca* 1942, *For Whom the Bell Tolls* 1943, and *Gaslight* 1944, for which she won an Academy Award. She projected a combination of radiance, refined beauty, and fortitude.

Her last film, *Autumn Sonata* 1978, was made by Ingmar Bergman. She also did stage plays and received an Emmy for the television film *A Woman Called Golda* 1982, portraying the Israeli prime minister.

Bergson Henri 1859–1941. French philosopher who believed that time, change, and development were the essence of reality. He thought that time was a continuous process in which one period merged imperceptibly into the next. In *Creative Evolution* 1907 he attempted to prove that all evolution and progress are due to the working of the *élan vital*, or life force. Nobel Prize for Literature 1928.

Beria Lavrenti 1899–1953. Soviet politician who in 1938 became minister of the interior and head of the Soviet police force that imprisoned, liquidated, and transported millions of Soviet citizens. On Stalin's death 1953, he attempted to seize power but was foiled and shot after a secret trial. Apologists for Stalin have blamed Beria for the atrocities committed by Soviet police during Stalin's dictatorship.

Bering Vitus 1681–1741. Danish explorer, the first European to sight Alaska. He died on Bering Island in the Bering Sea, both named after him, as is the Bering Strait, which separates Asia (Russia) from North America (Alaska).

Bering Sea section of the N Pacific between Alaska and Siberia, from the Aleutian Islands north to the Bering Strait.

Bering Strait strait between Alaska and Siberia, linking the N Pacific and Arctic oceans.

Berkeley city on San Francisco Bay in California; population (1990) 102,700. It is the site of an acclaimed branch of the University of California, noted for its nuclear research at the Lawrence Berkeley Laboratory. Berkeley was settled 1853.

Berkeley Busby. Adopted name of William Berkeley Enos 1895–1976. US choreographer and film director. He used ingenious and extravagant sets and teams of female dancers to create large-scale kaleidoscopic patterns through movement and costume when filmed from above, as in *Gold Diggers of 1933* and *Footlight*

Parade 1933. After Berkeley had choreographed more than 20 Broadway shows, producer Samuel Goldwyn engaged him for the musical film *Whoopee* 1930.

Berkeley William 1606–1677. British colonial administrator in North America, governor of the colony of Virginia 1641–77. Siding with the Royalists during the English Civil War, he was removed from the governorship by Oliver Cromwell 1652. He was reappointed 1660 by Charles II after the Restoration of the monarchy. However, growing opposition to him in the colony culminated in Bacon's Rebellion 1676 and in 1677 Berkeley was removed from office for his brutal repression of that uprising.

He was knighted by Charles I in 1639.

berkelium synthesized, radioactive, metallic element of the actinide series, symbol Bk, atomic number 97, atomic weight 247.

Berkshire or *Royal Berkshire* county of S central England *area* 486 sq mi/1,260 sq km *towns and cities* Reading (administrative headquarters), Eton, Slough, Maidenhead, Ascot, Bracknell, Newbury, Windsor, Wokingham *features* rivers Thames and Kennet; Inkpen Beacon, 975 ft/297 m; Bagshot Heath; Ridgeway Path, walkers' path (partly prehistoric) running from Wiltshire across the Berkshire Downs into Hertfordshire; Windsor Forest and Windsor Castle; Eton College; Royal Military Academy at Sandhurst; atomic-weapons research establishment at Aldermaston; the former main UK base for US cruise missiles at Greenham Common, Newbury.

Berlin industrial city (machine tools, electrical goods, paper, printing) and capital of the Federal Republic of Germany; population (1990) 3,102,500. After the division of Germany 1949, Bonn became the provisional capital of West Germany. The *Berlin Wall* divided the city from 1961 until it was dismantled 1989. Following reunification East and West Berlin were once more reunited as the 16th *Land* (state) of the Federal Republic.

Berlin Irving. Adopted name of Israel Baline 1888–1989. Russian-born US songwriter. His songs include such hits as "Alexander's Ragtime Band" 1911, "Always" 1925, "God Bless America" 1917 (published 1939), and "White Christmas" 1942, and the musicals *Top Hat* 1935, *Annie Get Your Gun* 1946, and *Call Me Madam* 1950. He also provided songs for films like *Blue Skies* 1946 and *Easter Parade* 1948.

The son of a poor Jewish cantor, Berlin learned music by ear. Many of his songs are "standards", the most popular and enduring of all time.

Berlin blockade the closing of entry to Berlin from the west by Soviet forces June 1948–May 1949. It was an attempt to prevent the other Allies (the US, France, and the UK) unifying the western part of Germany. The British and US forces responded by sending supplies to the city by air for over a year (the *Berlin airlift*). In May 1949 the blockade was lifted The blockade marked the formal division of the city into Eastern and Western sectors.

Berlin Wall dividing barrier between East and West Berlin 1961–89, erected by East Germany to prevent East Germans from leaving for West Germany. Escapers were shot on sight.

Berlioz (Louis) Hector 1803–1869. French Romantic composer. He is noted as the founder of modern orchestration. Much of his music was inspired by drama and literature and has a theatrical quality. He wrote symphonic works, such as *Symphonie fantastique*

1830–31 and *Roméo et Juliette* 1839; dramatic cantatas including *La Damnation de Faust* 1846 and *L'Enfance du Christ* 1854; sacred music; and three operas: *Benvenuto Cellini* 1838, *Les Troyens* 1856–58, and *Béatrice et Bénédict* 1862.

Berlusconi Silvio 1936– . Italian businessman and right-of-centre politician. After building a multi-million business empire, Fininvest, he turned his Milan-based pressure group, Forza Italia, into a political party to fight the 1994 general election. With the federalist Northern League and right-wing National Alliance, he won a clear parliamentary majority, but soon ran into difficulties over alleged conflict of interests. He resigned Dec 1994.

Bermuda British colony in the NW Atlantic Ocean *area* 21 sq mi/54 sq km *capital* and chief port Hamilton *features* consists of about 150 small islands, of which 20 are inhabited, linked by bridges and causeways; Britain's oldest colony *industries* Easter lilies, pharmaceuticals; tourism and banking are important *currency* Bermuda dollar *population* (1988) 58,160 *language* English *religion* Christian *government* under the constitution of 1968, Bermuda is a fully self-governing British colony, with a governor (Lord Waddington from 1992), senate, and elected House of Assembly (premier from 1982 John Swan, United Bermuda Party) *history* the islands were named for Juan de Bermudez, who visited them 1515, and were settled by British colonists 1609. Indian and African slaves were transported from 1616 and soon outnumbered the white settlers. Racial violence 1977 led to intervention, at the request of the government, by British troops.

Bern (French *Berne*) capital of Switzerland and of Bern canton, in W Switzerland on the Aare River; population (1990) 134,600; canton 945,600. It joined the Swiss confederation 1353 and became the capital 1848. Industries include textiles, chocolate, pharmaceuticals, light metal and electrical goods.

Bernard Claude 1813–1878. French physiologist and founder of experimental medicine. Bernard first demonstrated that digestion is not restricted to the stomach, but takes place throughout the small intestine. He discovered the digestive input of the pancreas, several functions of the liver, and the vasomotor nerves which dilate and contract the blood vessels and thus regulate body temperature.

Bernhardt Sarah. Adopted name of Rosine Bernard 1845–1923. French actress. She dominated the stage in her day, frequently performing at the Comédie-Française in Paris. She excelled in tragic roles, including Cordelia in Shakespeare's *King Lear*, the title role in Racine's *Phèdre*, and the male roles of Hamlet and of Napoleon's son in Edmond Rostand's *L'Aiglon*.

Bernini Gianlorenzo (Giovanni Lorenzo) 1598–1680. Italian sculptor, architect, and painter. He was a leading figure in the development of the Baroque style. His work in Rome includes the colonnaded piazza in front of St Peter's Basilica 1656, fountains (as in the Piazza Navona), and papal monuments. His sculpture includes *The Ecstasy of St Theresa* 1645–52 (Sta Maria della Vittoria, Rome) and numerous portrait busts.

Bernoulli's principle law stating that the speed of a fluid varies inversely with pressure, an increase in speed producing a decrease in pressure (such as a drop in hydraulic pressure as the fluid speeds up flowing through a constriction in a pipe) and vice versa. The principle also explains the pressure differences on each surface of an airfoil, which gives lift to the wing of an aircraft. The principle was named for Swiss mathematician and physicist Daniel Bernoulli.

Bernstein Leonard 1918–1990. US composer, conductor, and pianist. He was one of the most energetic and versatile of US musicians in the 20th century. His works, which established a vogue for realistic, contemporary themes, include symphonies such as *The Age of Anxiety* 1949, ballets such as *Fancy Free* 1944, and scores for musicals, including *Wonderful Town* 1953, *West Side Story* 1957, and *Mass* 1971 in memory of President John F Kennedy.

Born in Lawrence, Massachusetts, he was educated at Harvard University and the Curtis Institute of Music. From 1958 to 1970 he was musical director of the New York Philharmonic. Among his other works are *Jeremiah* 1944, *Facsimile* 1946, *Candide* 1956, and the *Chichester Psalms* 1965.

berry fleshy, many-seeded ◊fruit that does not split open to release the seeds. The outer layer of tissue, the exocarp, forms an outer sk¹n that is often brightly colored to attract birds to eat the fruit and thus disperse the seeds. Examples of berries are the tomato and the grape.

Berry Chuck (Charles) 1926– . US musician. He made his first recording, of the song "Maybellene", at Chess Records in Chicago 1955. Widely promoted by New York disk jockey Alan Freed, it became an early rock-and-roll classic. Recognized as one of the fathers of rock and roll, Berry enjoyed a revival of popularity in the 1970s and 1980s.

Berryman John 1914–1972. US poet. His emotionally intense, witty, and personal works often deal with sexual torments and are informed by a sense of suffering. After collections of short poems and sonnets, he wrote *Homage to Mistress Broadstreet* 1956, a romantic narrative featuring the first American poet, Anne Dudley (born 1612), and then introduced his guilt-ridden, antiheroic alter-ego, Henry, in *77 Dream Songs* 1964 (Pulitzer Prize) and *His Toy, His Dream, His Rest* 1968. Berryman, an alcoholic, committed suicide.

Bertolucci Bernardo 1940– . Italian film director. His work combines political and historical perspectives with an elegant and lyrical visual appeal. His films include *The Spider's Stratagem* 1970, *Last Tango in Paris* 1972, *1900* 1976, *The Last Emperor* 1987 (for which he received an Academy Award), and *The Sheltering Sky* 1990.

He is regarded as one of the most talented of the younger generation of Italian film directors. Among his other films are *The Conformist* 1970.

beryl mineral, beryllium aluminum silicate, $Be_3Al_2Si_6O_{18}$, which forms crystals chiefly in granite. It is the chief ore of beryllium. Two of its gem forms are aquamarine (light-blue crystals) and emerald (dark-green crystals).

Well-formed crystals of up to 200 tons have been found.

beryllium hard, light-weight, silver-white, metallic element, symbol Be, atomic number 4, atomic weight 9.012. It is one of the ◊alkaline-earth metals, with chemical properties similar to those of magnesium; in nature it is found only in combination with other elements. It is used to make sturdy, light alloys and to control the speed of neutrons in nuclear reactors. Beryllium oxide was discovered in 1798 by French

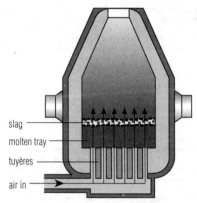

Bessemer process *In a Bessemer converter, a blast of high-pressure air oxidizes impurities in molten iron and converts it to steel.*

chemist Louis-Nicolas Vauquelin (1763–1829), but the element was not isolated until 1828, by Friedrich Wöhler and Antoine-Alexandre-Brutus Bussy independently. The name comes from Latin *beryllus*.

Berzelius Jöns Jakob 1779–1848. Swedish chemist who accurately determined more than 2,000 relative atomic and molecular masses. He devised (1813–14) the system of chemical symbols and formulae now in use and proposed oxygen as a reference standard for atomic masses. His discoveries include the elements cerium (1804), selenium (1817), and thorium (1828); he was the first to prepare silicon in its amorphous form and to isolate zirconium. The words *isomerism*, *allotropy*, and *protein* were coined by him.

Bessemer process the first cheap method of making ◊steel, invented by Henry Bessemer in England 1856. It has since been superseded by more efficient steel-making processes, such as the basic–oxygen process. In the Bessemer process compressed air is blown into the bottom of a converter, a furnace shaped like a cement mixer, containing molten pig iron. The excess carbon in the iron burns out, other impurities form a slag, and the furnace is emptied by tilting.

Best Charles Herbert 1899–1978. Canadian physiologist, one of the team of Canadian scientists including Frederick ◊Banting whose research resulted in 1922 in the discovery of insulin as a treatment for diabetes.

beta-blocker any of a class of drugs that block impulses that stimulate certain nerve endings (beta receptors) serving the heart muscle. This reduces the heart rate and the force of contraction, which in turn reduces the amount of oxygen (and therefore the blood supply) required by the heart. Beta-blockers may be useful in the treatment of angina, arrhythmia (abnormal heart rhythms), and raised blood pressure, and following heart attacks. They must be withdrawn from use gradually.

beta decay the spontaneous alteration of the nucleus of a radioactive atom, which transmutes the atom from one atomic number to another through the emission of either an electron (beta-minus decay) or a positron (beta-plus decay). In the more commonly occurring of the two, beta-minus decay, the atomic number increases by one (through the decay of a neutron, which converts to a proton emitting an electron and an antineutrino); in the less commonly occurring beta-plus decay, the atomic number decreases by one (the proton converts to a neutron, emitting a positron and a neutrino). The symbol used for the electron in beta-minus decay is $\int$; the symbol for the positron in beta-plus decay is $\int^+$.

beta particle electron ejected with great velocity from a radioactive atom that is undergoing spontaneous disintegration. Beta particles do not exist in the nucleus but are created on disintegration, beta decay, when a neutron converts to a proton to emit an electron.

beta version in computing, a pre-release version of ◊software or an ◊application program, usually distributed to a limited number of expert users (and often reviewers). Distribution of beta versions allows user testing and feedback to the developer, so that any necessary modifications can be made before release.

Betelgeuse or *Alpha Orionis* red supergiant star in the constellation of Orion and the tenth brightest star in the sky, although its brightness varies. It is 700 million mi/1,100 million km across, about 800 times larger than the Sun, roughly the same size as the orbit of Mars. It is over 10,000 times as luminous as the Sun, and lies 650 light-years from Earth.

betel nut fruit of the areca palm *Areca catechu,* used together with lime and betel pepper as a masticatory stimulant by peoples of the East and Papua New Guinea. Chewing it results in blackened teeth and a mouth stained deep red.

Bethlehem city in E Pennsylvania, population (1990) 71,428. Its former steel industry has been replaced by high technology.

Lehigh University is here. Bethlehem was founded 1741 by German immigrants.

Bethlehem (Hebrew *Beit-Lahm*) town on the west bank of the river Jordan, S of Jerusalem; population (1980) 14,000. It was occupied by Israel 1967. In the Bible it is mentioned as the birthplace of King David and Jesus.

Betjeman John 1906–1984. English poet and essayist. He was the originator of a peculiarly English light verse, nostalgic, and delighting in Victorian and Edwardian architecture. His *Collected Poems* appeared 1968 and a verse autobiography, *Summoned by Bells,* 1960. He became poet laureate 1972.

Bettelheim Bruno 1903–1990. Austrian-born US child psychologist. At the University of Chicago he founded a treatment center for emotionally disturbed children based on the principle of a supportive home environment. Among his most influential books are *Love Is Not Enough* 1950, *Truants from Life* 1954, and *Children of the Dream* 1962.

He received his PhD from the University of Vienna 1938. With the Nazi occupation of Austria, he was arrested and sent to the concentration camps at Dachau and Buchenwald, where he began a long-term study of the psychological effects of totalitarianism. He fled Europe 1939 and came to the US, where he joined the faculty of the University of Chicago.

beverage any liquid for drinking other than pure water. Beverages are made with plant products to impart pleasant flavors, nutrients, and stimulants to people's fluid intake. Examples include juices, tea, coffee, cocoa, cola drinks, and alcoholic beverages.

The juices of grapes and other fruits are fermented

to produce wines, while fermented cereals form the basis of beers and liquors. See also ◊alcoholic beverage.

Beverly Hills residential city and a part of greater Los Angeles, California, population (1990) 31,900. It is known as the home of Hollywood film stars.

Rodeo Drive is a popular shopping area for prestige goods.

Bhopal industrial city (textiles, chemicals, electrical goods, jewelry) and capital of Madhya Pradesh, central India; population (1981) 672,000. Nearby Bhimbetka Caves, discovered 1973, have the world's largest collection of prehistoric paintings, about 10,000 years old. In 1984 some 2,600 people died from an escape of the poisonous gas methyl isocyanate from a factory owned by US company Union Carbide; another 300,000 suffer from long-term health problems.

Bhumibol Adulyadej 1927– . King of Thailand from 1946. Born in the US and educated in Bangkok and Switzerland, he succeeded to the throne on the assassination of his brother. In 1973 he was active, with popular support, in overthrowing the military government of Marshal Thanom Kittikachorn and thus ended a sequence of army-dominated regimes in power from 1932.

Bhutan Kingdom of (*Druk-yul*) *area* 17,954 sq mi/ 46,500 sq km *capital* Thimbu (Thimphu) *towns and cities* Paro, Punakha, Mongar *physical* occupies southern slopes of the Himalayas; cut by valleys formed by tributaries of the Brahmaputra; thick forests in S *features* Gangkar Punsum (24,700 ft/ 7,529 m) is one of the world's highest unclimbed peaks *head of state and government* Jigme Singye Wangchuk from 1972 *political system* absolute monarchy *political parties* none officially; illegal Bhutan People's Party (BPP); Bhutan National Democratic Party (BNDP) *exports* timber, talc, fruit and vegetables, cement, distilled spirits, calcium carbide *currency* ngultrum; also Indian currency *population* (1993 est) 1,700,000; growth rate 2% p.a. (75% Ngalops and Sharchops, 25% Nepalese) *life expectancy* men 51, women 49 *languages* Dzongkha (official, a Tibetan dialect), Sharchop, Bumthap, Nepali, and English *media* one daily newspaper (*Kuensel*), published in Dzongkha, English, and Nepali editions; it gives the government's point of view *religions* 75% Lamaistic Buddhist (state religion), 25% Hindu *literacy* men 51%, women 25% *GNP* $468 per head (1990) *chronology 1865* Trade treaty with Britain signed. *1907* First hereditary monarch installed. *1910* Anglo-Bhutanese Treaty signed. *1949* Indo-Bhutan Treaty of Friendship signed. *1952* King Jigme Dorji Wangchuk installed. *1953* National assembly established. *1959* 4,000 Tibetan refugees given asylum. *1968* King established first cabinet. *1972* King died and was succeeded by his son Jigme Singye Wangchuk. *1979* Tibetan refugees told to take Bhutanese citizenship or leave; most stayed. *1983* Bhutan became a founding member of the South Asian Regional Association for Cooperation. *1988* King imposed "code of conduct" suppressing Nepalese customs. *1990* Hundreds of people allegedly killed during prodemocracy demonstrations.

Bhutto Benazir 1953– . Pakistani politician, leader of the Pakistan People's Party (PPP) from 1984 (in exile until 1986), prime minister of Pakistan 1988–90 (when the opposition maneuvered her from office and charged her with corruption) and again from 1993.

Bhutto Zulfikar Ali 1928–1979. Pakistani politician, president 1971–73; prime minister from 1973 until the 1977 military coup led by General Zia ul-Haq. In 1978 Bhutto was sentenced to death for conspiring to murder a political opponent and was hanged the following year. He was the father of Benazir Bhutto.

Biafra, Republic of African state proclaimed in 1967 when fears that Nigerian central government was increasingly in the hands of the rival Hausa tribe led the predominantly Ibo Eastern Region of Nigeria to secede under Lt Col Odumegwu Ojukwu. On the proclamation of Biafra, civil war ensued with the rest of the federation. In a bitterly fought campaign federal forces confined the Biafrans to a shrinking area of the interior by 1968, and by 1970 Biafra ceased to exist.

biathlon athletic competition that combines cross-country skiing with rifle marksmanship. Basic equipment consists of cross-country skis, poles, and boots, and bolt-action (nonautomatic) rifles. The biathlon began in Sweden as informal competition among hunters. The first modern biathlon event in the US was at Camp Hale, Colorado, 1956. In 1960, at the Winter Games in Squaw Valley, California, the sport became an Olympic event.

Bible the sacred book of the Jewish and Christian religions. The Hebrew Bible, recognized by both Jews and Christians, is called the ◊*Old Testament* by Christians. The ◊*New Testament* comprises books recognized by the Christian church from the 4th century as canonical. The Roman Catholic Bible also includes the ◊*Apocrypha*.

bicycle pedal-driven two-wheeled vehicle used in cycling. It consists of a metal frame mounted on two large wire-spoked wheels, with handlebars in front and a seat between the front and back wheels. The bicycle is an energy-efficient, nonpolluting form of transport, and it is estimated that 800 million bicycles are in use throughout the world—outnumbering automobiles three to one. China, India, Denmark, and the Netherlands are countries with a high use of bicycles.

Biddle Nicholas 1786–1844. US financier and public figure. An expert in international commerce, he was appointed a director of the Bank of the United States by President James Monroe 1819 and became president of the bank 1822. An extreme fiscal conservative, Biddle became the focus of Andrew ◊Jackson's campaigns against the power of the bank in 1828 and 1832. After the withdrawal of the bank's federal charter 1836, he remained its president under a state charter.

biennial plant plant that completes its life cycle in two years. During the first year it grows vegetatively and the surplus food produced is stored in its ◊perennating organ, usually the root. In the following year these food reserves are used for the production of leaves, flowers, and seeds, after which the plant dies. Many root vegetables are biennials, including the carrot *Daucus carota* and parsnip *Pastinaca sativa*. Some garden plants that are grown as biennials are actually perennials, for example, the wallflower *Cheiranthus cheiri*.

Bienville Jean Baptiste Le Moyne, Sieur de 1680–1768. French colonial administrator, governor of the North American colony of Louisiana 1706–13, 1717–23, and 1733–43. During his first term he founded the settlement at Mobile in Alabama and in his second term

established the Louisiana colonial capital at New Orleans. During his final term Bienville was drawn into a costly and ultimately unsuccessful war with the Indians of the lower Mississippi Valley.

Bierstadt Albert 1830–1902. German-born US landscape painter. His spectacular panoramas of the American wilderness fell out of favor after his death until interest in the ◊Hudson River School was rekindled in the late 20th century. A classic work is *Thunderstorm in the Rocky Mountains* 1859 (Museum of Fine Arts, Boston).

His *Discovery of the Hudson* hangs in the Capitol in Washington, DC.

big-band jazz ◊swing music created in the late 1930s and 1940s by bands of 13 or more players, such as those of Duke ◊Ellington and Benny Goodman. Big-band jazz relied on fixed arrangements, where there is more than one instrument to some of the parts, rather than improvisation. Big bands were mainly dance bands, and they ceased to be economically viable in the 1950s.

Big Bang in astronomy, the hypothetical "explosive" event that marked the origin of the universe as we know it. At the time of the Big Bang, the entire universe was squeezed into a hot, superdense state. The Big Bang explosion threw this compacted material outward, producing the expanding universe (see ◊red shift). The cause of the Big Bang is unknown; observations of the current rate of expansion of the universe suggest that it took place about 10–20 trillion years ago. The Big Bang theory began modern ◊cosmology.

Big Blue popular name for ◊IBM, derived from the company's size and its blue logo.

Big Dipper name for the seven brightest and most prominent stars in the constellation ◊Ursa Major, which in outline resemble a large dipper.

Bihari member of a N Indian people, also living in Bangladesh, Nepal, and Pakistan, and numbering over 40 million. The Bihari are mainly Muslim. The Bihari language is related to Hindi and has several widely varying dialects. It belongs to the Indic branch of the Indo-European family. Many Bihari were massacred during the formation of Bangladesh, which they opposed.

Bikini atoll in the ◊Marshall Islands, W Pacific, where the US carried out 23 atomic-and hydrogen-bomb tests (some underwater) 1946–58.

Bilbao industrial port (iron and steel, chemicals, cement, food) in N Spain, capital of Biscay province; population (1991) 372,200.

bilberry several species of shrubs of the genus *Vaccinium* of the heath family Ericaceae, closely related to North American blueberries.

bile brownish alkaline fluid produced by the liver. Bile is stored in the gall bladder and is intermittently released into the duodenum (small intestine) to aid digestion. Bile consists of bile salts, bile pigments, cholesterol, and lecithin. *Bile salts* assist in the breakdown and absorption of fats; *bile pigments* are the breakdown products of old red blood cells that are passed into the gut to be eliminated with the feces.

bilharzia or *schistosomiasis* disease that causes anemia, inflammation, formation of scar tissue, dysentery, enlargement of the spleen and liver, cancer of the bladder, and cirrhosis of the liver. It is contracted by bathing in water contaminated with human sewage.

Some 200 million people are thought to suffer from this disease in the tropics, and 750,000 people a year die.

billiards indoor game played, normally by two players, with tapered poles (called cues) and composition balls (one red, two white) on a rectangular table covered with a green, feltlike cloth (baize) without pockets. A variation popular in England is played on a table with six pockets, one at each corner and in each of the long sides at the middle. The game of pool is also called pocket billiards.

Billings city in S central Montana on the north shore of the Yellowstone River; seat of Yellowstone County; population (1990) 81,100. It is a center for transporting livestock and animal products and for vegetable and grain processing. Nearby, to the SE, is Big Horn Indian reservation where the Battle of Little Big Horn took place 1876.

bill of exchange or *bank draft* a written order in which a *drawer* orders a *drawee* to pay a specified sum to a *payee*. For example, a check is a bill of exchange drawn on a bank or banker. Once signed and endorsed, it becomes negotiable and can be discounted (sold for cash before the maturity date under face value) at current short-term interest rates.

bill of lading document giving proof of particular goods having been loaded on a ship. The person to whom the goods are being sent normally needs to show the bill of lading in order to obtain the release of the goods.

Bill of Rights in the US, the first ten amendments to the US ◊Constitution, incorporated 1791: *1* guarantees freedom of worship, of speech, of the press, of assembly, and to petition the government; *2* grants the right to keep and bear arms; *3* prohibits billeting of soldiers in private homes in peacetime; *4* forbids unreasonable search and seizure; *5* guarantees none be "deprived of life, liberty or property without due process of law" or compelled in any criminal case to be a witness against himself or herself; *6* grants the right to speedy trial, to call witnesses, and to have defense counsel; *7* grants the right to trial by jury of one's peers; *8* prevents the infliction of excessive bail or fines, or "cruel and unusual punishment"; *9, 10* provide a safeguard to the states and people for all rights not specifically delegated to the central government.

Bill of Rights in Britain, an act of Parliament 1689 which established it as the primary governing body of the country. The Bill of Rights embodied the Declarations of Rights which contained the conditions on which William and Mary were offered the throne. It made provisions limiting royal prerogative with respect to legislation, executive power, money levies, courts, and the army and stipulated Parliament's consent to many government functions.

Billy the Kid nickname of William H Bonney 1859–1881. US outlaw, a leader in the 1878 Lincoln County cattle war in New Mexico, who allegedly killed his first victim at 12 and was reputed to have killed 21 men by age 22, when he died.

Biloxi port in Mississippi, US; population (1990) 46,300. Chief occupations include tourism and seafood canning. Named after a local Indian people, Biloxi was founded 1719 by the French.

The city suffered heavy damage from Hurricane Camille 1969, but rebuilding was rapid.

binary fission in biology, a form of ◊asexual reproduction, whereby a single-celled organism, such as the ameba, divides into two smaller "daughter" cells. It can also occur in a few simple multicellular organisms, such as sea anemones, producing two smaller sea anemones of equal size.

binary number code code based on the binary number system, used to represent instructions and data in all modern digital computers—for example, in the ◊ASCII code system used by most microcomputers, the capital letter A is represented by the binary number 01000001.

binary number system number system to the base two, used in computing and electronics. All binary numbers are written using a combination of the digits 0 and 1.

binary search in computing, a rapid technique used to find any particular record in a list of records held in sequential order. The computer is programmed to compare the record sought with the record in the middle of the ordered list. This being done, the computer discards the half of the list in which the record does not appear, thereby reducing the number of records left to search by half. This process of selecting the middle record and discarding the unwanted half of the list is repeated until the required record is found.

binary star pair of stars moving in orbit around their common center of mass. Observations show that most stars are binary, or even multiple—for example, the nearest star system to the Sun, ◊Alpha Centauri.

binary weapon in chemical warfare, weapon consisting of two substances that in isolation are harmless but when mixed together form a poisonous nerve gas. They are loaded into the delivery system separately and combine after launch.

binding energy in physics, the amount of energy needed to break the nucleus of an atom into the neutrons and protons of which it is made.

binoculars optical instrument for viewing an object in magnification with both eyes; for example, field glasses and opera glasses. Binoculars consist of two telescopes containing lenses and prisms, which produce a stereoscopic effect as well as magnifying the image.

Use of prisms has the effect of "folding" the light path, allowing for a compact design.

binomial in mathematics, an expression consisting of two terms, such as $a + b$ or $a - b$.

binomial system of nomenclature in biology, the system in which all organisms are identified by a two-part Latinized name. Devised by the biologist ◊Linnaeus, it is also known as the Linnaean system. The first name is capitalized and identifies the ◊genus; the second identifies the ◊species within that genus.

biochemistry science concerned with the chemistry of living organisms: the structure and reactions of proteins (such as enzymes), nucleic acids, carbohydrates, and lipids.

biodegradable capable of being broken down by living organisms, principally bacteria and fungi. In biodegradable substances, such as food and sewage, the natural processes of decay lead to compaction and liquefaction, and to the release of nutrients that are then recycled by the ecosystem.

biodiversity (contraction of *biological diversity*) measure of the variety of the Earth's animal, plant, and

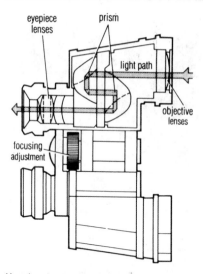

binoculars *An optical instrument that allows the user to focus both eyes on the magnified image at the same time. The essential components of binoculars are objective lenses, eye pieces, and a system of prisms to invert and reverse the image. A focusing system provides a sharp image by adjusting the relative positions of these components.*

microbial species; of genetic differences within species; and of the ecosystems that support those species. Its maintenance is important for ecological stability and as a resource for research into, for example, new drugs and crops. Research suggests that biodiversity is far greater than previously realized, especially among smaller organisms—for instance, it is thought that there are 30–40 million insects, of which only a million have so far been identified. Today, the most significant threat to biodiversity comes from the destruction of rainforests and other habitats in the southern hemisphere. In the 20th century, the destruction of habitats is believed to have resulted in the most severe and rapid loss of diversity in the history of the planet.

bioengineering the application of engineering to biology and medicine. Common applications include the design and use of artificial limbs, joints, and organs, including hip joints and heart valves.

biological warfare the use of living organisms, or of infectious material derived from them, to bring about death or disease in humans, animals, or plants. At least ten countries have this capability.

biology science of life. Biology includes all the life sciences—for example, anatomy and physiology (the study of the structure of living things), cytology (the study of cells), zoology (the study of animals) and botany (the study of plants), ecology (the study of habitats and the interaction of living species), animal behavior, embryology, and taxonomy, and plant breeding. Increasingly this century biologists have concentrated on molecular structures: biochemistry, biophysics, and genetics (the study of inheritance and variation). The pinnacle of this development

during the 1990s is the international ◊Human Genome Project, which will attempt to map the entire genetic code contained in the 23 pairs of human chromosomes.

bioluminescence production of light by living organisms. It is a feature of many deep-sea fishes, crustaceans, and other marine animals. On land, bioluminescence is seen in some nocturnal insects such as glow-worms and fireflies, and in certain bacteria and fungi. Light is usually produced by the oxidation of luciferin, a reaction catalyzed by the ◊enzyme luciferase. This reaction is unique, being the only known biological oxidation that does not produce heat. Animal luminescence is involved in communication, camouflage, or the luring of prey, but its function in other organisms is unclear.

biomass the total mass of living organisms present in a given area. It may be specified for a particular species (such as earthworm biomass) or for a general category (such as herbivore biomass). Estimates also exist for the entire global plant biomass. Measurements of biomass can be used to study interactions between organisms, the stability of those interactions, and variations in population numbers.

bionics design and development of electronic or mechanical artificial systems that imitate those of living things. The bionic arm, for example, is an artificial limb (◊prosthesis) that uses electronics to amplify minute electrical signals generated in body muscles to work electric motors, which operate the joints of the fingers and wrist.

biopsy removal of a living tissue sample from the body for diagnostic examination.

BIOS (acronym for *basic input/output system*) in computing, the part of the ◊operating system that handles input and output. The term is also used to describe the programs stored in ◊ROM (and called ROM BIOS), which are automatically run when a computer is switched on allowing it to ◊boot. BIOS is unaffected by upgrades to the operating system stored on disk.

biosphere the narrow zone that supports life on our planet. It is limited to the waters of the Earth, a fraction of its crust, and the lower regions of the atmosphere.

BioSphere 2 (BS2) ecological test project, a "planet in a bottle", in Arizona. Under a sealed glass dome, several different habitats are recreated, with representatives of nearly 4,000 species, including eight humans, to see how well air, water, and waste can be recycled in an enclosed environment and whether a stable ecosystem can be created.

biosynthesis synthesis of organic chemicals from simple inorganic ones by living cells—for example, the conversion of carbon dioxide and water to glucose by plants during ◊photosynthesis.

Other biosynthetic reactions produce cell constituents including proteins and fats.

biotechnology industrial use of living organisms to manufacture food, drugs, or other products. The brewing and baking industries have long relied on the yeast microorganism for ◊fermentation purposes, while the dairy industry employs a range of bacteria and fungi to convert milk into cheeses and yogurts. ◊Enzymes, whether extracted from cells or produced artificially, are central to most biotechnological applications.

birch any tree of the genus *Betula*, including about 40 species found in cool temperate parts of the northern

bird of paradise *The male blue bird of paradise displays to the female high up in the tree canopy. It swings upside down, exposing its bright blue plumage and tail streamers, at the same time uttering low mechanical-sounding cries.*

hemisphere. Birches grow rapidly, and their hard, beautiful wood is used for veneers and cabinet work.

Paper birch *B. papyrifera* is native to the N half of North America.

bird backboned animal of the class Aves, the biggest group of land vertebrates, characterized by warm blood, feathers, wings, breathing through lungs, and egg-laying by the female. There are nearly 8,500 species of birds.

bird of paradise one of 40 species of crowlike birds, family Paradiseidae, native to New Guinea and neighboring islands. Females are generally drably colored, but the males have bright and elaborate plumage used in courtship display. Hunted almost to extinction for their plumage, they are now subject to conservation.

Birendra Bir Bikram Shah Dev 1945– . King of Nepal from 1972, when he succeeded his father Mahendra; he was formally crowned 1975. King Birendra oversaw Nepal's return to multiparty politics and introduced a new constitution 1990.

Birmingham industrial city in the West Midlands, second largest city of the UK; population (1991) 961,000, metropolitan area 2,632,000. It is an important manufacturing and commercial center. Industries include engineering, motor vehicles, machine tools, aerospace control systems, plastics, chemicals, food, chocolates, jewelry, tires, glass, and guns.

Birmingham commercial and industrial city (iron, steel, chemicals, building materials, computers, cotton textiles) and largest city in Alabama, US; population (1990) 266,000.

Although the 55 ft/17 m statue of Vulcan (Roman god of the forge) still dominates the city from a nearby summit, US Steel shut down its works in what used to be the steelmaking center of the South. Settled 1813, Birmingham was notorious in the early 1960s for its enforcement of segregation, and the 1963 bombing of a church in which four African Americans were killed aroused international attention. In 1979 the city elected an African American mayor.

birth act of producing live young from within the body of female animals. Both viviparous and ovoviviparous

animals give birth to young. In viviparous animals, embryos obtain nourishment from the mother via a ◊placenta or other means.

In ovoviviparous animals, fertilized eggs develop and hatch in the oviduct of the mother and gain little or no nourishment from maternal tissues. See also ◊pregnancy.

birth control another name for ◊family planning; see also ◊contraceptive.

Biscay, Bay of bay of the Atlantic Ocean between N Spain and W France, known for rough seas and exceptionally high tides.

Bishkek (formerly *Pishpek* until 1926, and *Frunze* 1926–92) capital of Kyrgyzstan; population (1987) 632,000. It produces textiles, farm machinery, metal goods, and tobacco.

bishop priest next in rank to an archbishop in the Roman Catholic, Eastern Orthodox, Anglican or episcopal churches. A bishop has charge of a district called a *diocese*.

Bishops with more limited authority have the highest rank in certain Lutheran denominations and in the Methodist church.

Bismarck Otto Eduard Leopold, Prince von 1815–1898. German politician, prime minister of Prussia 1862–90 and chancellor of the German Empire 1871–90. He pursued an aggressively expansionist policy, waging wars against Denmark 1863–64, Austria 1866, and France 1870–71, which brought about the unification of Germany.

Bismarck Archipelago group of over 200 islands in the SW Pacific Ocean, part of ◊Papua New Guinea; area 19,200 sq mi/49,660 sq km/. The largest island is New Britain.

bismuth hard, brittle, pinkish-white, metallic element, symbol Bi, atomic number 83, atomic weight 208.98. It has the highest atomic number of all the stable elements (the elements from atomic number 84 up are radioactive). Bismuth occurs in ores and occasionally as a free metal (native metal). It is a poor conductor of heat and electricity, and is used in alloys of low melting point and in medical compounds to soothe gastric ulcers. The name comes from the Latin *besemutum*, from the earlier German *Wismut*.

bison large, hoofed mammal of the bovine family. There are two species, both brown. The *European bison* or *wisent Bison bonasus*, of which only a few protected herds survive, is about 7 ft/2 m high and weighs up to 2,500 lb/1,100 kg. The *North American bison* (often known as "buffalo") 'Bison bison' is slightly smaller, with a heavier mane and more sloping hindquarters. Formerly roaming the prairies in vast numbers, it was almost exterminated in the 19th century, but survives in protected areas. There were about 14,000 bison in North American reserves 1994.

Bissau capital and chief port of Guinea-Bissau, on an island at the mouth of the Geba River; population (1988) 125,000. Originally a fortified slave-trading center, Bissau became a free port 1869.

bit (contraction of *binary digit*) in computing, a single binary digit, either 0 or 1. A bit is the smallest unit of data stored in a computer; all other data must be coded into a pattern of individual bits. A ◊byte represents sufficient computer memory to store a single ◊character of data, and usually contains eight bits. For example, in the ◊ASCII code system used by most microcomputers the capital letter A would be stored in a single byte of memory as the bit pattern 01000001.

bit map in computing, a pattern of ◊bits used to describe the organization of data. Bit maps are used to store typefaces or graphic images (bit-mapped or ◊raster graphics), with 1 representing black (or a color) and 0 white.

bit pad computer input device; see ◊graphics tablet.

bittern any of several small herons, in particular the common bittern *Botaurus stellaris* of Europe and Asia where it is an inhabitant of marshy country. It is shy, stoutly built, has a streaked camouflage pattern and a loud, booming call.

bittersweet alternate name for the woody ◊nightshade plant.

bitumen impure mixture of hydrocarbons, including such deposits as petroleum, asphalt, and natural gas, although sometimes the term is restricted to a soft kind of pitch resembling asphalt.

bivalve marine or freshwater mollusk whose body is enclosed between two shells hinged together by a ligament on the dorsal side of the body.

Bizet Georges (Alexandre César Léopold) 1838–1875. French composer of operas. Among his works are *Les Pêcheurs de perles/The Pearl Fishers* 1863 and *La Jolie Fille de Perth/The Fair Maid of Perth* 1866. He also wrote the concert overture *Patrie* and incidental music to Alphonse Daudet's play *L'Arlésienne*. His operatic masterpiece *Carmen* was produced a few months before his death 1875.

Black Hugo LaFayette 1886–1971. US jurist. He was elected to the US Senate 1926 and despite his earlier association with the Ku Klux Klan, distinguished himself as a progressive populist. He was appointed to the US Supreme Court by Franklin D Roosevelt 1937, resigning shortly before his death.

Among his decisions concerning personal and civil rights were those rendered in *Board of Education* v *Barnette* 1943, *Korematsu* v *US* 1944, and *Gideon* v *Wainwright* 1963.

black beetle another name for ◊cockroach, although cockroaches belong to an entirely different order of insects (Dictyoptera) from the beetles (Coleoptera).

blackberry prickly shrub *Rubus fruticosus* of the rose family, closely allied to raspberries and dewberries, that is native to northern parts of Europe. It produces pink or white blossoms and edible, black, compound fruits.

The North American blackberry *R. allegheniensis* has white blossoms and grows wild in Canada and E US.

blackbird bird *Turdus merula* of the thrush family. The male is black with a yellow bill and eyelids, the female dark brown with a dark beak. About 10 in/25 cm long, it lays three to five blue-green eggs with brown spots. Its song is rich and flutelike.

black body in physics, a hypothetical object that completely absorbs all thermal (heat) radiation striking it. It is also a perfect emitter of thermal radiation.

blackcurrant variety of ◊currant.

Black Death great epidemic of bubonic ◊plague that ravaged Europe in the 14th century, killing between one-third and half of the population. The cause of the plague was the bacterium *Yersinia pestis*, transmitted by fleas borne by migrating Asian black rats. The name Black Death was first used in England in the early 19th century.

black economy see ◊underground economy.

blackfly plant-sucking insect, a type of ◊aphid. It is especially hungry for human blood in the NE of the US and attacks in May-July, during blackfly season.

Black Forest (German *Schwarzwald*) mountainous region of coniferous forest in Baden-Württemberg, W Germany. Bounded to the W and S by the Rhine, which separates it from the Vosges, it has an area of 1,800 sq mi/4,660 sq km and rises to 4,905 ft/1,493 m in the Feldberg. Parts of the forest have recently been affected by ◊acid rain.

black hole object in space whose gravity is so great that nothing can escape from it, not even light. Thought to form when massive stars shrink at the ends of their lives, a black hole sucks in more matter, including other stars, from the space around it. Matter that falls into a black hole is squeezed to infinite density at the center of the hole. Black holes can be detected because gas falling toward them becomes so hot that it emits X-rays.

blackmail criminal offense of extorting money with menaces or threats of detrimental action, such as exposure of some misconduct on the part of the victim.

Black Muslim member of a religious group founded 1929 in the US and led, from 1934, by Elijah Mohammed (then Elijah Poole) (1897–1975) after he had a vision of ◊Allah. Its growth from 1946 as a black separatist organization was due to ◊Malcolm X, the son of a Baptist minister who, in 1964, broke away and founded his own Organization for African-American Unity, preaching "active self-defense". Under the leadership of Louis Farrakhan, the movement underwent a recent revival.

black nationalism movement toward black separatism in the US during the 1960s; see ◊Black Power.

Black National State area in the Republic of South Africa set aside, from 1971, for development toward self-government by black Africans, in accordance with

◊apartheid. Before 1980 these areas were known as *black homelands* or *bantustans*. Making up less than 14% of the country, they tended to be situated in arid areas (though some had mineral wealth), often in scattered blocks. Those that achieved nominal independence were Transkei 1976, Bophuthatswana 1977, Venda 1979, and Ciskei 1981. They were not recognized outside South Africa because of their racial basis. Under the interim nonracial constitution, which came into effect April 1994, they became part of the republic's provincial structure, with guaranteed legislative and executive power.

Black Power movement toward black separatism in the US during the 1960s, embodied in the *Black Panther Party* founded 1966 by Huey Newton and Bobby Seale. Its declared aim was the creation of a separate black state in the US to be established by a black plebiscite under the aegis of the United Nations. Following a National Black Political Convention 1972, a National Black Assembly was established to exercise pressure on the Democratic and Republican parties.

Black Prince nickname of ◊Edward, Prince of Wales, eldest son of Edward III of England.

Black Sea (Russian *Chernoye More*) inland sea in SE Europe, linked with the seas of Azov and Marmara, and via the Dardanelles strait with the Mediterranean. Uranium deposits beneath it are among the world's largest. About 90% of the water is polluted, mainly by agricultural fertilizers.

Blackshirts term widely used to describe fascist paramilitary organizations. Originating with Mussolini's fascist Squadristi in the 1920s, it was also applied to the Nazi SS (*Schutzstaffel*).

blacksnake any of several species of snake. The blacksnake *Pseudechis porphyriacus* is a venomous snake of the cobra family found in damp forests and swamps in E Australia. The blacksnake, *Coluber constrictor* from eastern US, is a relative of the European grass snake, growing up to 4 ft/1.2 m long, and without venom.

blackthorn densely branched spiny European bush *Prunus spinosa*, family Rosaceae. It produces white blossom on black and leafless branches in early spring. Its sour, plumlike, blue-black fruit, the sloe, is used to make sloe gin.

Blackwell Elizabeth 1821–1910. English-born US physician, the first woman to qualify in medicine in the US 1849, and the first woman to be recognized as a qualified physician in the UK 1869.

Her example inspired many other aspiring female doctors.

black widow North American spider *Latrodectus mactans*. The male is small and harmless, but the female is 0.5 in/1.3 cm long with a red patch below the abdomen and a powerful venomous bite. The bite causes pain and fever in human victims, but they usually recover.

bladder hollow elastic-walled organ which stores the urine produced in the kidneys. It is present in the ◊urinary systems of some fishes, most amphibians, some reptiles, and all mammals. Urine enters the bladder through two ureters, one leading from each kidney, and leaves it through the urethra.

bladderwort any of a large genus *Utricularia* of carnivorous aquatic plants of the family Lentibulariaceae. They have leaves with bladders that entrap small aquatic animals.

Blair Tony (Anthony Charles Lynton) 1953– . British politician, leader of the Labour Party from 1994. A centrist in the manner of his predecessor John Smith, he became Labour's youngest leader by a large majority in the first fully democratic elections to the post July 1994.

Blake William 1757–1827. English poet, artist, engraver, and visionary. He was one of the most important figures of English Romanticism. His lyrics, as in *Songs of Innocence* 1789 and *Songs of Experience* 1794, express spiritual wisdom in radiant imagery and symbolism and are often written with a childlike simplicity. They include "London" and "The Tugger!". In prophetic books like *The Marriage of Heaven and Hell* 1790, *America* 1793, and *Milton* 1804, he created a vast personal mythology. He also created a new composite art form in engraving and hand-coloring his own works.

blank verse in literature, the unrhymed iambic pentameter or ten-syllable line of five stresses. First used by the Italian Gian Giorgio Trissino in his tragedy *Sofonisba* 1514–15, it was introduced to England about 1540 by the Earl of Surrey, who used it in his translation of Virgil's *Aeneid*. It was developed by Christopher Marlowe and Shakespeare, quickly becoming the distinctive verse form of Elizabethan and Jacobean drama. It was later used by Milton in *Paradise Lost* 1667 and by Wordsworth in *The Prelude* 1805. More recent exponents of blank verse in English include Thomas Hardy, T S Eliot, and Robert Frost.

Blarney small town in County Cork, Republic of Ireland, possessing, inset in the wall of the 15th-century castle, the *Blarney Stone*, reputed to give persuasive speech to those kissing it.

blasphemy written or spoken insult directed against religious belief or sacred things with deliberate intent to outrage believers.

There are numerous laws in the US against blasphemy, but they are rarely enforced.

blast furnace smelting furnace used to extract metals from their ores, chiefly pig iron from iron ore. The temperature is raised by the injection of an air blast.

bleaching decolorization of colored materials. The two main types of bleaching agent are the *oxidizing bleaches*, which bring about the ◊oxidation of pigments and include the ultraviolet rays in sunshine, hydrogen peroxide, and chlorine in household bleaches, and the *reducing bleaches*, which bring about ◊reduction and include sulfur dioxide.

blenny any fish of the family Blenniidae, mostly small fishes found near rocky shores, with elongated slimy bodies tapering from head to tail, no scales, and long pelvic fins set far forward.

Bligh William 1754–1817. English sailor who accompanied Captain James ◊Cook on his second voyage around the world 1772–74, and in 1787 commanded HMS *Bounty* on an expedition to the Pacific.

On the return voyage the crew mutinied 1789, and Bligh was cast adrift in a boat with 18 men. He was appointed governor of New South Wales 1805, where his discipline again provoked a mutiny 1808 (the Rum Rebellion). He returned to Britain, and was made an admiral 1811.

blindness complete absence or impairment of sight. It may be caused by heredity, accident, disease, or deterioration with age.

Aids under development include electronic devices

that convert print to recognizable mechanical speech; and sonic flashlights.

blind spot area where the optic nerve and blood vessels pass through the retina of the ◊eye. No visual image can be formed as there are no light-sensitive cells in this part of the retina.

Thus the organism is blind to objects that fall in this part of the visual field.

Blitzkrieg swift military campaign, as used by Germany at the beginning of World War II 1939–41. It was characterized by rapid movement by mechanized forces, supported by tactical air forces acting as "flying artillery" and is best exemplified by the campaigns in Poland 1939 and France 1940.

Bloch Ernest 1880–1959. Swiss-born US composer. Among his works are the lyrical drama *Macbeth* 1910, *Schelomo* for cello and orchestra 1916, five string quartets, and *Suite Hébraïque* for viola and orchestra 1953. He often used themes based on Jewish liturgical music and folk song.

Born in Geneva, Switzerland, he went to the US 1916 and became founder-director of the Cleveland Institute of Music 1920–25.

Bloch Felix 1905–1983. Swiss-US physicist who invented the analytical technique of nuclear magnetic resonance (NMR) ◊spectroscopy 1946. For this work he shared the Nobel Prize for Physics 1952 with US physicist Edward Purcell (1912–).

He was born in Zürich and was professor of physics at Stanford University, 1934–71.

block in computing, a group of records treated as a complete unit for transfer to or from ◊backing storage. For example, many disk drives transfer data in 512-byte blocks.

blood fluid circulating in the arteries, veins, and capillaries of vertebrate animals; the term also refers to the corresponding fluid in those invertebrates that possess a closed ◊circulatory system. Blood carries nutrients and oxygen to each body cell and removes waste products, such as carbon dioxide. It is also important in the immune response and, in many animals, in the distribution of heat throughout the body.

blood clotting complex series of events (known as the blood clotting cascade) that prevents excessive bleeding after injury. It is triggered by vitamin K. The result is the formation of a meshwork of protein fibers (fibrin) and trapped blood cells over the cut blood vessels.

blood group any of the types into which blood is classified according to the presence or otherwise of certain ◊antigens on the surface of its red cells. Red blood cells of one individual may carry molecules on their surface that act as antigens in another individual whose red blood cells lack these molecules. The two main antigens are designated A and B. These give rise to four blood groups: having A only (A), having B only (B), having both (AB), and having neither (O). Each of these groups may or may not contain the ◊rhesus factor. Correct typing of blood groups is vital in transfusion, since incompatible types of donor and recipient blood will result in coagulation, with possible death of the recipient.

blood pressure pressure, or tension, of the blood against the inner walls of blood vessels, especially of the arteries, due to the muscular pumping activity of the heart. Abnormally high blood pressure (◊hypertension) may be associated with various conditions or arise with no obvious cause; abnormally low blood

pressure (hypotension) occurs in ◊shock and after excessive fluid or blood loss from any cause.

blood test laboratory evaluation of a blood sample. There are numerous blood tests, from simple typing to establish the ◊blood group to sophisticated biochemical assays of substances, such as hormones, present in the blood only in minute quantities.

blood vessel tube that conducts blood either away from or toward the heart in multicellular animals. Freshly oxygenated blood is carried in the arteries—major vessels which give way to the arterioles (small arteries) and finally capillaries; deoxygenated blood is returned to the heart by way of capillaries, then venules (small veins) and veins.

Bloomington city in S central Indiana, southwest of Indianapolis; seat of Monroe County; population (1990) 60,600. It is an exporter of limestone from nearby quarries. It is also a center for the manufacture of electrical products and lifts. Indiana University 1820 is located here.

Bloomsbury Group intellectual circle of writers and artists based in Bloomsbury, London, which flourished in the 1920s. It centered on the house of publisher Leonard Woolf (1880–1969) and his wife, novelist Virginia ◊Woolf, and included the artists Duncan Grant and Vanessa Bell (1879–1961), the biographer Lytton ◊Strachey, art critics Roger Fry and Clive Bell (1881–1964), and the economist Maynard ◊Keynes. Typically modernist, their innovatory artistic contributions represented an important section of the English avant-garde. From their emphasis on close interpersonal relationships and their fastidious attitude toward contemporary culture arose many accusations of elitism.

blowfly any fly of the genus *Calliphora*, also known as bluebottle, or of the related genus *Lucilia*, when it is greenbottle. It lays its eggs in dead flesh, on which the maggots feed.

blueberry any of various North American acid-soil shrubs of the genus *Vaccinium* of the heath family. The genus also includes huckleberries, bilberries, deerberries, and cranberries, many of which resemble each other and are difficult to distinguish from blueberries. All have small, elliptical short-stalked leaves, slender green or reddish twigs, and whitish bell-like blossoms. Only true blueberries, however, have tiny granular speckles on their twigs. Blueberries have black or blue edible fruits, often covered with a white powder.

bluebird three species of a North American bird, genus *Sialia*, belonging to the thrush subfamily, Turdinae. The eastern bluebird *Sialia sialis* is regarded as the herald of spring. About 7 in/18 cm long, it has a reddish breast, the upper plumage being sky-blue, and a distinctive song.

blue chip in business and finance, a stock that is considered strong and reliable in terms of the dividend yield and capital value. Blue-chip companies are favored by stock-market investors more interested in security than risk taking.

bluegrass dense, spreading grass of the genus *Poa*, which is blue-tinted and grows in clumps. Various species are known from the northern hemisphere. Kentucky bluegrass *P. pratensis*, introduced to the US from Europe, provides pasture for horses.

blue-green algae or *cyanobacteria* single-celled, primitive organisms that resemble bacteria in their internal cell organization, sometimes joined together in colonies or filaments. Blue-green algae are among the oldest known living organisms and, with bacteria, belong to the kingdom Monera; remains have been found in rocks up to 3.5 trillion years old. They are widely distributed in aquatic habitats, on the damp surfaces of rocks and trees, and in the soil.

blue gum either of two Australian trees: Tasmanian blue gum *Eucalyptus globulus* of the myrtle family, with bluish bark, a chief source of eucalyptus oil; or Sydney blue gum *E. saligna*, a tall, straight tree. The former is cultivated extensively in California and has also been planted in South America, India, parts of Africa, and S Europe.

Blue Nile (Arabic *Bahr el Azraq*) river rising in the mountains of Ethiopia. Flowing W then N for 2,000 km/1,250 mi, it eventually meets the White Nile at Khartoum. The river is dammed at Roseires where a hydroelectric scheme produces 70% of Sudan's electricity.

Blue Ridge Mountains range extending from West Virginia to Georgia, and including Mount Mitchell 6,712 ft/ 2,045 m; part of the ◊Appalachians.

blues African-American music that originated in the work songs and spirituals of the rural American South in the late 19th century. It is characterized by a 12-bar, or occasionally 16-bar, construction and melancholy lyrics which relate tales of woe or unhappy love. The guitar has been the dominant instrument; harmonica and piano are also common. Blues guitar and vocal styles have played a vital part in the development of jazz, rock, and pop music in general.

blue shift in astronomy, a manifestation of the ◊Doppler effect in which an object appears bluer when it is moving toward the observer or the observer is moving toward it (blue light is of a higher frequency than other colors in the spectrum). The blue shift is the opposite of the ◊red shift.

boa any of various nonvenomous snakes of the family Boidae, found mainly in tropical and subtropical parts of the New World. Boas feed mainly on small mammals and birds. They catch these in their teeth or kill them by constriction (crushing the creature within their coils until it suffocates). The boa constrictor *Constrictor constrictor* can grow up to 18.5 ft/5.5 m long, but rarely reaches more than 12 ft/4 m. Other boas include the anaconda and the emerald tree boa *Boa canina*, about 6 ft/2 m long and bright green.

boa The emerald tree boa is the fastest-moving member of the boa family. It lives in trees, where it lies in wait for its prey—chiefly parrots, monkeys, and bats. It kills these with its teeth, not by constriction.

Boadicea alternative spelling of British queen ◊Boudicca.

boar wild member of the pig family, such as the Eurasian wild boar *Sus scrofa*, from which domestic pig breeds derive. The wild boar is sturdily built, being 4.5 ft/1.5 m long and 3 ft/1 m high, and possesses formidable tusks. Of gregarious nature and mainly woodland-dwelling, it feeds on roots, nuts, insects, and some carrion.

boat people illegal emigrants traveling by sea, especially those Vietnamese who left their country after the takeover of South Vietnam 1975 by North Vietnam. Some 160,000 Vietnamese fled to Hong Kong, many being attacked at sea by Thai pirates, and in 1989 50,000 remained there in cramped, squalid refugee camps. The UK government began forced repatriation 1990.

bobcat cat *Felis rufa* living in a variety of habitats from S Canada through to S Mexico. It is similar to the lynx, but only 2.5 ft/75 cm long, with reddish fur and less well-developed ear tufts.

bobsledding the sport of racing steel-bodied, steerable toboggans, crewed by two or four people, down mountain ice-chutes at speeds of up to 80 mph/130 kph. It was introduced as an Olympic event in 1924, and world championships have been held every year since 1931. Included among the major bobsledding events are the Olympic Championships (the four-crew event was introduced at the 1924 Winter Olympics and the two-crew in 1932); also the World Championships, the four-crew championship introduced in 1924 and the two-crew in 1931; in Olympic years winners automatically become world champions.

Boccaccio Giovanni 1313–1375. Italian writer and poet. He is chiefly known for the collection of tales called the *Decameron* 1348–53. Equally at home with tragic and comic narrative, he laid the foundations for the Humanism of the Renaissance and raised vernacular literature to the status enjoyed by the ancient classics.

Bodhidharma Indian Buddhist and teacher. He entered China from S India about 520 and was the founder of the Ch'an school. Ch'an focuses on contemplation leading to intuitive meditation, a direct pointing to and stilling of the human mind. In the 20th century, the Japanese variation, Zen, has attracted many followers in the West.

Boeing US military and commercial aircraft manufacturer. Among the models Boeing has produced are the B-17 Flying Fortress, 1935; the B-52 Stratofortress, 1952; the Chinook helicopter, 1961; the first jetliner, the Boeing 707, 1957; the ◊jumbo jet or Boeing 747, 1969; and the ◊jetfoil, 1975.

Boeotia ancient district of central Greece, of which ◊Thebes was the chief city. The *Boeotian League* (formed by ten city-states in the 6th century BC) superseded ◊Sparta in the leadership of Greece in the 4th century BC.

Boer Dutch settler or descendant of Dutch and Huguenot settlers in South Africa.

Boer War the second of the South African Wars 1899–1902, waged between Dutch settlers in South Africa and the British.

Boethius Anicius Manilus Severinus AD 480–524. Roman philosopher. While imprisoned on suspicion of treason by the emperor ◊Theodoric the Great, he wrote treatises on music and mathematics and *De*

Consolatione Philosophiae/The Consolation of Philosophy, a dialogue in prose. It was translated into European languages during the Middle Ages; English translations by Alfred the Great, Geoffrey Chaucer, and Queen Elizabeth I.

bog type of wetland where decomposition is slowed down and dead plant matter accumulates as ◊peat. Bogs develop under conditions of low temperature, high acidity, low nutrient supply, stagnant water, and oxygen deficiency. Typical bog plants are sphagnum moss, rushes, and cotton grass; insectivorous plants such as sundews and bladderworts are common in bogs (insect prey make up for the lack of nutrients).

Bogart Humphrey 1899–1957. US film actor. He achieved fame as the gangster in *The Petrified Forest* 1936. He became an international cult figure as the tough, romantic "loner" in such films as *The Maltese Falcon* 1941 and *Casablanca* 1942, a status resurrected in the 1960s and still celebrated today. He won an Academy Award for his role in *The African Queen* 1952.

Bogdanovich Peter 1939– . US film director, screenwriter, and producer. He was formerly a critic. *The Last Picture Show* 1971, a nostalgic look at a small Texas town in the 1950s, was followed by two films that attempted to capture the style of old Hollywood, *What's Up Doc?* 1972 and *Paper Moon* 1973.

Both made money but neither was a critical success. In 1990 he made *Texasville*, an unsuccessful follow-up to *The Last Picture Show*.

Bogotá capital of Colombia, South America; 8,660 ft/2,640 m above sea level on the edge of the plateau of the E Cordillera; population (1985) 4,185,000. It was founded 1538.

Bohemia area of Czech Republic, a fertile plateau drained by the Elbe and Vltava rivers. Rich in mineral resources, including uranium, coal, lignite, iron ore, silver, and graphite. The main cities are Prague and Plzen. The name Bohemia derives from the Celtic Boii, its earliest known inhabitants.

Bohr Niels Henrik David 1885–1962. Danish physicist. His theoretic work produced a new model of atomic structure, now called the Bohr model, and helped establish the validity of ◊quantum theory.

boiler any vessel that converts water into steam. Boilers are used in conventional power stations to generate steam to feed steam ◊turbines, which drive the electricity generators. They are also used in steamships, which are propelled by steam turbines, and in steam locomotives. Every boiler has a furnace in which fuel (coal, oil, or gas) is burned to produce hot gases, and a system of tubes in which heat is transferred from the gases to the water.

boiling point for any given liquid, the temperature at which the application of heat raises the temperature of the liquid no further, but converts it into vapor.

bolero Spanish dance in moderate triple time (3/4), invented in the late 18th century. It is performed by a solo dancer or a couple, usually with castanet accompaniment, and is still a contemporary form of dance in Caribbean countries. In music, Ravel's one-act ballet score *Boléro* 1928 is the most famous example, consisting of a theme which is constantly repeated and varied instrumentally, building to a powerful climax. The ballet was choreographed by Nijinsky for Ida Rubinstein 1928.

boletus genus of fleshy fungi belonging to the class Basidiomycetes, with thick stems and caps of various colors. The European *Boletus edulis* is edible, but some species are poisonous.

Boleyn Anne 1507–1536. Queen of England 1533–36. Henry VIII broke with the pope (see ◊Reformation) in order to divorce his first wife and marry Anne. She was married to him 1533 and gave birth to the future Queen Elizabeth I in the same year. Accused of adultery and incest with her half brother (a charge invented by Thomas ◊Cromwell), she was beheaded.

Bolingbroke title of Henry of Bolingbroke, Henry IV of England.

Bolívar Simón 1783–1830. South American nationalist, leader of revolutionary armies, known as *the Liberator*. He fought the Spanish colonial forces in several uprisings and eventually liberated his native Venezuela 1821, Colombia and Ecuador 1822, Peru 1824, and Bolivia (a new state named for him, formerly Upper Peru) 1825.

Bolivia Republic of (*República de Bolivia*) *area* 424,052 sq mi/1,098,581 sq km *capital* La Paz (seat of government), Sucre (legal capital and seat of judiciary) *towns and cities* Santa Cruz, Cochabamba, Oruro, Potosí *physical* high plateau (Altiplano) between mountain ridges (cordilleras); forest and lowlands (llano) in the E *features* Andes, lakes Titicaca (the world's highest navigable lake, 12,500 ft/3,800 m) and Poopó; La Paz is world's highest capital city (11,800 ft/3,600 m) *head of state and government* Gonzalo Sanchez de Lozada from 1993 *political system* emergent democratic republic *political parties* National Revolutionary Movement (MNR), center right; Movement of the Revolutionary Left (MIR), left of center; Nationalist Democratic Action (ADN), right of center *exports* tin, antimony (second largest world producer), other nonferrous metals, oil, gas (piped to Argentina), agricultural products, coffee, sugar, cotton *currency* boliviano *population* (1993 est) 8,010,000; (Quechua 25%, Aymara 17%, mestizo (mixed) 30%, European 14%); growth rate 2.7% p.a. *life expectancy* men 54, women 58 *languages* Spanish, Aymara, Quechua (all official) *religion* Roman Catholic 95% (state-recognized) *literacy* men 85%, women 71% *GNP* $650 per head (1991) *chronology* *1825* Liberated from Spanish rule by Simón Bolívar; independence achieved (formerly known as Upper Peru). *1952* Dr Víctor Paz Estenssoro elected president. *1956* Dr Hernán Siles Zuazo became president. *1960* Estenssoro returned to power. *1964* Army coup led by the vice president, General René Barrientos. *1966* Barrientos became president. *1967* Uprising, led by "Che" Guevara, put down with US help. *1969* Barrientos killed in plane crash, replaced by Vice President Siles Salinas. Army coup deposed him. *1970* Army coup put General Juan Torres González in power. *1971* Torres replaced by Col Hugo Banzer Suárez. *1973* Banzer promised a return to democratic government. *1974* Attempted coup prompted Banzer to postpone elections and ban political and labor-union activity. *1978* Elections declared invalid after allegations of fraud. *1980* More inconclusive elections followed by another coup, led by General Luis García. Allegations of corruption and drug trafficking led to cancellation of US and EC aid. *1981* García forced to resign. Replaced by General Celso Torrelio Villa. *1982* Torrelio resigned. Replaced by military junta led by General Guido Vildoso. Because of worsening economy, Vildoso asked congress to install a civilian administration. Dr Siles Zuazo chosen as president. *1983* Economic aid from US and Europe resumed. *1984* New coalition government formed by Siles. Abduction of president by right-wing officers. *1985* President Siles resigned. Election result inconclusive; Dr Paz Estenssoro chosen by congress as president. *1989* Jaime Paz Zamora (MIR), elected president in power-sharing arrangement with Banzer, pledged to maintain fiscal and monetary discipline and preserve free-market policies. *1993* MNR, under leadership of Gonzalo Sanchez de Lozada, won congressional and presidential elections.

Bolkiah Hassanal 1946– . Sultan of Brunei from 1967, following the abdication of his father, Omar Ali Saifuddin (1916–1986). As absolute ruler, Bolkiah also assumed the posts of prime minister and defense minister on independence 1984.

Böll Heinrich 1917–1985. German novelist. A radical Catholic and anti-Nazi, he attacked Germany's political past and the materialism of its contemporary society. His many publications include poems, short stories, and novels which satirized West German society, for example *Billard um Halbzehn/Billiards at Half-Past Nine* 1959 and *Gruppenbild mit Dame/Group Portrait with Lady* 1971. Nobel Prize for Literature 1972.

Bologna industrial city and capital of Emilia-Romagna, Italy, 50 mi/80 km N of Florence; population (1988) 427,000. It was the site of an Etruscan town, later of a Roman colony, and became a republic in the 12th century. It came under papal rule 1506 and was united with Italy 1860.

Bolshevik member of the majority of the Russian Social Democratic Party who split from the ◊Mensheviks 1903. The Bolsheviks, under ◊Lenin, advocated the destruction of capitalist political and economic institutions, and the setting-up of a socialist state with power in the hands of the workers. The Bolsheviks set the ◊Russian Revolution 1917 in motion.

They changed their name to the Russian Communist Party 1918.

They maintained power after the Civil War 1918–1921.

Boltzmann constant in physics, the constant (symbol *k*) that relates the kinetic energy (energy of motion) of a gas atom or molecule to temperature. Its value is 1.380662×10^{-23} joules per Kelvin. It is equal to the gas constant *R*, divided by Avogadro's number.

bomb container filled with explosive or chemical material and generally used in warfare. There are also ◊incendiary bombs and nuclear bombs and missiles (see ◊nuclear warfare). Any object designed to cause damage by explosion can be called a bomb (automobile bombs, letter bombs). Initially dropped from airplanes (from World War I), bombs were in World War II also launched by rocket (V1, V2). The 1960s saw the development of missiles that could be launched from aircraft, land sites, or submarines. In the 1970s laser guidance systems were developed to hit small targets with accuracy.

Bombay industrial port (textiles, engineering, pharmaceuticals, diamonds), commercial center, and capital of Maharashtra, W India; population (1981) 8,227,000. It is the center of the Hindi film industry.

Bonaparte Corsican family of Italian origin that gave rise to the Napoleonic dynasty: see ◊Napoleon I, ◊Napoleon II, and ◊Napoleon III. Others were the brothers and sister of Napoleon I: *Joseph* (1768–1844) whom Napoleon made king of Naples 1806 and Spain 1808; *Lucien* (1775–1840) whose handling of the Council of Five Hundred on 10 Nov 1799 ensured Napoleon's future; *Louis* (1778–1846) the father of

section through a long bone (the femur)

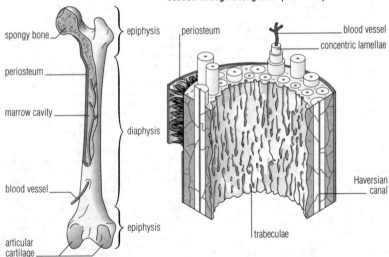

spongy bone — epiphysis — periosteum — blood vessel — concentric lamellae — periosteum — marrow cavity — diaphysis — blood vessel — epiphysis — Haversian canal — articular cartilage — trabeculae

bone *Bone is a network of fibrous material impregnated with mineral salts and as strong as reinforced concrete. The upper end of the thighbone or femur is made up of spongy bone, which has a fine lacework structure designed to transmit the weight of the body. The shaft of the femur consists of hard compact bone designed to resist bending. Fine channels carrying blood vessels, nerves, and lymphatics interweave even the densest bone.*

Napoleon III, who was made king of Holland 1806–10; *Caroline* (1782–1839) who married Joachim Murat 1800; *Jerome* (1784–1860) made king of Westphalia 1807.

bond in chemistry, the result of the forces of attraction that hold together atoms of an element or elements to form a molecule. The principal types of bonding are ◊ionic, ◊covalent, ◊metallic, and intermolecular (such as hydrogen bonding).

bond in commerce, a security issued by a government, local authority, company, bank, or other institution on fixed interest. Usually a long-term security, a bond may be irredeemable (with no date of redemption), secured (giving the investor a claim on the company's property or on a part of its assets), or unsecured (not protected by a lien). Property bonds are nonfixed securities with the yield fixed to property investment.

bone hard connective tissue comprising the ◊skeleton of most vertebrate animals. Bone is composed of a network of collagen fibers impregnated with mineral salts (largely calcium phosphate and calcium carbonate), a combination that gives it great density and strength, comparable in some cases with that of reinforced concrete. Enclosed within this solid matrix are bone cells, blood vessels, and nerves. The interior of the long bones of the limbs consists of a spongy matrix filled with a soft marrow that produces blood cells.

bone marrow substance found inside the cavity of bones. In early life it produces red blood cells but later on lipids (fat) accumulate and its color changes from red to yellow.

bonito any of various species of medium-sized tuna, predatory fish of the genus *Sarda*, in the mackerel family. The ocean bonito *Katsuwonus pelamis* grows to 3 ft/1 m and is common in tropical seas. The Atlantic bonito *Sarda sarda* is found in the Mediterranean and tropical Atlantic and grows to the same length but has a narrower body.

Bonn industrial city (chemicals, textiles, plastics, aluminum) in the Federal Republic of Germany, 15 m/18 km SSE of Cologne, on the left bank of the Rhine; population (1988) 292,000. It was the seat of government of West Germany 1949–90 and of the Federal Republic of Germany from 1990. A proposed move back to Berlin was shelved by the Bundesrat (upper chamber of parliament) 1991.

Bonnard Pierre 1867–1947. French painter, designer, and graphic artist. Influenced by Gauguin and Japanese prints, he specialized in intimate domestic scenes and landscapes, his paintings shimmering with color and light. With other members of *les Nabis*, he explored the decorative arts (posters, stained glass, furniture), but is most widely known for his series of nudes, for example, *Nude in the Bath* 1938 (Petit Palais, Paris).

Bonnie Prince Charlie Scottish name for ◊Charles Edward Stuart, pretender to the throne.

booby tropical seabird of the genus *Sula*, in the same family, Sulidae, as the northern ◊gannet. There are six species, including the circumtropical brown booby *S. leucogaster*. They inhabit coastal waters, and dive to catch fish. The name was given by sailors who saw the bird's tameness as stupidity.

bookkeeping process of recording commercial transactions in a systematic and established procedure. These records provide the basis for the preparation of accounts.

booklouse any of numerous species of tiny wingless insects of the order Psocoptera, especially *Atropus pulsatoria*, which lives in books and papers, feeding on starches and molds.

Boolean algebra set of algebraic rules, named for mathematician George Boole, in which TRUE and FALSE are equated to 0 and 1. Boolean algebra includes a series of operators (AND, OR, NOT, NAND (NOT AND), NOR, and XOR (exclusive OR)), which can be used to manipulate TRUE and FALSE values. It is the basis of computer logic because the truth values can be directly associated with ◊bits.

Boone Daniel 1734–1820. US pioneer who explored the Wilderness Road (East Virginia–Kentucky) 1775 and paved the way for the first westward migration of settlers.

Boone was born in Pennsylvania and spent most of his youth in North Carolina. During the American Revolution, he led militias against Indians allied with the British. He was captured by a Shawnee war party and so impressed the chief that he was adopted by the tribe. He left the Indians and continued to explore westward.

boot or *bootstrap* in computing, the process of starting up a computer. Most computers have a small, built-in boot program that starts automatically when the computer is switched on—its only task is to load a slightly larger program, usually from a hard disk, which in turn loads the main ◊operating system.

In microcomputers the operating system is often held in the permanent ◊ROM memory and the boot program simply triggers its operation.

Boötes constellation of the northern hemisphere represented by a herdsman driving a bear (Ursa Major) around the pole. Its brightest star is ◊Arcturus (or Alpha Bootis) about 36 light-years from Earth.

Booth John Wilkes 1839–1865. US actor and fanatical Confederate sympathizer who assassinated President Abraham ◊Lincoln April 14, 1865; he escaped with a broken leg and was later shot in a barn in Virginia when he refused to surrender.

He had earlier conceived a plan to kidnap Lincoln and decided to kill him in vengeance when the plan failed.

bootlegging illegal manufacture, distribution, or sale of a product. The term originated in the US, when the sale of alcohol to American Indians was illegal and bottles were hidden for sale in the legs of the jackboots of unscrupulous traders. The term was later used for all illegal liquor sales during the period of ◊Prohibition in the US 1920–33, and is often applied to unauthorized commercial tape recordings and the copying of computer software.

borage salad plant *Borago officinalis* native to S Europe and used in salads and medicinally. It has small blue flowers and hairy leaves.

Bordeaux port on the river Garonne, capital of Aquitaine, SW France, a center for the wine trade, oil refining, and aeronautics and space industries; population (1990) 213,300. Bordeaux was under the English crown for three centuries until 1453. In 1870, 1914, and 1940 the French government was moved here because of German invasion.

Borders region of Scotland *area* 1,815 sq mi/4,700 sq km *towns and cities* Newtown St Boswells (administrative headquarters), Hawick, Jedburgh *features* river Tweed; Lammermuir, Moorfoot, and Pentland hills; home of the novelist Walter Scott at Abbotsford; Dryburgh Abbey, burial place of Field Marshal Haig and Scott; ruins of 12th-century Melrose Abbey *industries* knitted goods, tweed, electronics, timber *population* (1991) 103,900 *famous people* Duns Scotus, James Murray, Mungo Park.

Borg Björn (Rune) 1956– . Swedish tennis player who won the men's singles title at Wimbledon five times 1976–80, a record since the abolition of the challenge system 1922. He also won six French Open singles titles 1974–75 and 1978–81 inclusive. In 1990 Borg announced plans to return to professional tennis, but he enjoyed little competitive success 1991–92.

Borges Jorge Luis 1899–1986. Argentine poet and short-story writer. He was an exponent of ◊magic realism. In 1961 he became director of the National Library, Buenos Aires, and was professor of English literature at the university there. He is known for his fantastic and paradoxical work *Ficciones/Fictions* 1944.

Borgia Cesare 1476–1507. Italian general, illegitimate son of Pope ◊Alexander VI. Made a cardinal at 17 by his father, he resigned to become captain-general of the papacy, campaigning successfully against the city republics of Italy. Ruthless and treacherous in war, he was an able ruler (the model for Machiavelli's *The Prince*), but his power crumbled on the death of his father. He was a patron of artists, including Leonardo da Vinci.

Borgia Lucrezia 1480–1519. Duchess of Ferrara from 1501. She was the illegitimate daughter of Pope ◊Alexander VI and sister of Cesare Borgia. She was married at 12 and again at 13 to further her father's ambitions, both marriages being annulled by him. At 18 she was married again, but her husband was murdered in 1500 on the order of her brother, with whom (as well as with her father) she was said to have committed incest. Her final marriage was to the Duke of Este, the son and heir of the Duke of Ferrara. She made the court a center of culture and was a patron of authors and artists such as Ariosto and Titian.

Born Max 1882–1970. German physicist who received a Nobel prize 1954 for fundamental work on the ◊quantum theory. He left Germany for the UK during the Nazi era.

Borneo third-largest island in the world, one of the Sunda Islands in the W Pacific; area 290,000 sq mi/754,000 sq km. It comprises the Malaysian territories of *Sabah* and ◊*Sarawak*; ◊*Brunei*; and, occupying by far the largest part, the Indonesian territory of *Kalimantan*. It is mountainous and densely forested. In coastal areas the people of Borneo are mainly of Malaysian origin, with a few Chinese, and the interior is inhabited by the indigenous Dyaks. It was formerly under both Dutch and British colonial influence until Sarawak was formed 1841.

boron nonmetallic element, symbol B, atomic number 5, relative atomic mass 10.811. In nature it is found only in compounds, as with sodium and oxygen in borax. It exists in two allotropic forms (see ◊allotropy): brown amorphous powder and very hard, brilliant crystals. Its compounds are used in the preparation of boric acid, water softeners, soaps, enamels, glass, and pottery glazes. In alloys it is used to harden steel. Because it absorbs slow neutrons, it is used to make boron carbide control rods for nuclear reactors. It is a necessary trace element in the human diet. The element was named by Humphry Davy, who isolated it 1808, from *borax* + -on, as in *carbon*.

Borromini Francesco 1599–1667. Swiss-born Italian Baroque architect. He was one of the two most important architects (with ◊Bernini, his main rival) in 17th-century Rome. Whereas Bernini designed in a florid, expansive style, his pupil Borromini developed a highly idiosyncratic and austere use of the Classical language of architecture. His genius may be seen in the cathedrals of San Carlo alle Quatro Fontane 1637–41, San Ivo della Sapienza 1643–60, and the Oratory of St Philip Neri 1638–50.

Bosch Hieronymus (Jerome) *c.*1450–1516. Early Dutch painter. His fantastic visions of weird and hellish creatures, as shown in *The Garden of Earthly Delights* about 1505–10 (Prado, Madrid), show astonishing imagination and a complex imagery. His religious subjects focused not on the holy figures but on the mass of ordinary witnesses, placing the religious event in a contemporary Dutch context and creating cruel caricatures of human sinfulness.

Bosnia-Herzegovina Republic of *area* 19,745 sq mi/51,129 sq km *capital* Sarajevo *towns and cities* Banja Luka, Mostar, Prijedor, Tuzla, Zenica *physical* barren, mountainous country *features* part of the Dinaric Alps, limestone gorges *head of state* Alija Izetbegovic from 1990 *head of government* Haris Silajdzic from 1993 *political system* emergent democracy *political parties* Party of Democratic Action (PDA), Muslim-oriented; Serbian Democratic Party (SDP), Serbian nationalist; Christian Democratic Union (CDU-BH), centrist; League of Communists (LC-BH), left-wing *products* citrus fruits and vegetables; iron, steel, textiles and leather goods; *population* (1993 est) 4,400,000 including 44% Muslims, 33% Serbs, 17% Croats; a complex patchwork of ethnically mixed communities *life expectancy* men 68, women 73 *language* Serbian variant of Serbo-Croatian *religions* Sunni Muslim, Serbian Orthodox, Roman Catholic *literacy* 86% *chronology* *1918* Incorporated in the future Yugoslavia. *1941* Occupied by Nazi Germany. *1945* Became republic within Yugoslav Socialist Federation. *1980* Upsurge in Islamic nationalism. *1990* Ethnic violence erupted between Muslims and Serbs. Communists defeated in multiparty elections;

coalition formed by Serb, Muslim, and Croatian parties. *1991* Aug: Serbia revealed plans to annex the SE part of the republic. Sept: Bosnian Serb enclaves established by force. Oct: "sovereignty" declared. Nov: plebiscite by Bosnian Serbs favored remaining within Yugoslavia; Bosnian Serbs and Croats established autonomous communities. *1992* Feb–March: Bosnian Muslims and Croats voted in favor of Bosnia-Herzegovina's independence; referendum boycotted by Bosnian Serbs. April: US and EC recognized Bosnian independence. Ethnic hostilities escalated, with Bosnian Serb forces occupying E and Bosnian Croat forces much of W; all-out civil war ensued. May: admitted into UN. June: UN forces drafted into Sarajevo to break three-month siege of city by Bosnian Serbs. Accusations of "ethnic cleansing" being practiced, particularly by Bosnian Serbs. Oct: UN ban on military flights over Bosnia-Herzegovina. First British troops deployed, under UN control. *1993* UN–EC peace plan failed. US began airdrops of food and medical supplies. Six UN "safe areas" created, intended as havens for Muslim civilians. Bosnian Croat-Serb partition plan rejected by Muslims. *1994* Feb: Bosnian Serb siege of Sarajevo lifted after UN–NATO ultimatum; Russian intervention accelerated Serb withdrawal. Bosnian Croat–Muslim federation formed after cease-fire in north. April: NATO bombed Bosnian Serb control positions around Gorazde (a UN-declared "safe area"). Bosnian Serbs later withdrew in response to UN ultimatum. Aug: Serbia imposed blockade against Bosnian Serbs. Hostilities renewed around Sarajevo and "safe area" of Bihac. Nov: US unilaterally lifted arms embargo against Bosnian Muslims. Dec: cease-fire negotiated by former US president Jimmy Carter. *1995* Jan–March: cease-fire broken intermittently. April: hostilities resumed. July: "safe area" of Srebenica overrun by Bosnian Serbs; mass exodus of Bosnian Muslim refugees to Tuzla.

boson in physics, an elementary particle whose spin can only take values that are whole numbers or zero. Bosons may be classified as ◊gauge bosons (carriers of the four fundamental forces) or ◊mesons. All elementary particles are either bosons or ◊fermions.

Bosporus (Turkish *Karadeniz Bogazi*) strait 17 mi/27 km long, joining the Black Sea with the Sea of Marmara and forming part of the water division between Europe and Asia; its name may be derived from the Greek legend of Io. Istanbul stands on its west side. The *Bosporus Bridge* 1973, 5,320 ft/1,621 m, links Istanbul and Anatolia (the Asian part of Turkey). In 1988 a second bridge across the straits was opened, linking Asia and Europe.

Boston industrial and commercial center, capital of Massachusetts; population (1990) 574,300; metropolitan area 4,171,600. It is a publishing center and industrial port on Massachusetts Bay, but the economy is dominated by financial and health services and government. Boston and Northeastern universities are here.

Harvard University and the Massachusetts Institute of Technology (MIT) are in neighboring Cambridge, across the Charles River. *features* Faneuil Hall, Old North Church, Paul Revere house, USS *Constitution* ("Old Ironsides"), New England Aquarium, Museum of Science, J F Kennedy National Historic Site *history* founded by Puritans 1630, Boston was a center of opposition to British trade restrictions, culminating in the Boston Tea Party 1773. After the first shots of the American Revolution in 1775 at nearby Lexington and Concord, the Battle of Bunker Hill was fought outside the city. The British withdrew from the city 1776. In the 19th century, Boston became the metropolis of New England. Urban redevelopment and the growth of service industries have compensated for the city's industrial decline.

Boston Tea Party protest 1773 by colonists in Massachusetts against the tea tax imposed on them by the British government before the ◊American Revolution.

Boswell James 1740–1795. Scottish biographer and diarist. He was a member of Samuel ◊Johnson's London Literary Club and the two men traveled to Scotland together 1773, as recorded in Boswell's *Journal of the Tour to the Hebrides* 1785. His *Life of Samuel Johnson* was published 1791. Boswell's ability to record Johnson's pithy conversation verbatim makes this a classic of English biography.

botanical garden place where a wide range of plants is grown, providing the opportunity to see a botanical diversity not likely to be encountered naturally. Among the earliest forms of botanical garden was the *physic garden*, devoted to the study and growth of medicinal plants; an example is the Chelsea Physic Garden in London, established 1673 and still in existence. Following increased botanical exploration, botanical gardens were used to test the commercial potential of new plants being sent back from all parts of the world.

In the US, there are both publicly and privately funded botanical gardens. Some botanical gardens and arboretums are devoted to local or New World plants while others preserve, protect, and propagate specialties, such as ornamentals. Most botanical gardens are open year round, with greenhouses and conservatories as well as extensive landscaped grounds and an exhibit hall that sells plants and offers an advisory service.

The New York Botanical Society runs the botanical garden at the Bronx Zoo in this way. Winterhur, the former du Pont estate, and Mount Vernon, the former home of George Washington, are now run as private historical sites and botanical gardens.

botany the study of ◊plants. It is subdivided into a number of specialized studies, such as the identification and classification of plants (taxonomy), their external formation (plant morphology), their internal arrangement (plant anatomy), their microscopic examination (plant histology), their functioning and life history (plant physiology), and their distribution over the Earth's surface in relation to their surroundings (plant ecology). Paleobotany concerns the study of fossil plants, while economic botany deals with the utility of plants. ◊Horticulture, ◊agriculture, and ◊forestry are branches of botany.

Botany Bay inlet on the east coast of Australia, 5 mi/8 km S of Sydney, New South Wales. Chosen 1787 as the site for a penal colony, it proved unsuitable. Sydney now stands on the site of the former settlement. The name Botany Bay continued to be popularly used for any convict settlement in Australia.

botfly any fly of the family Estridae. The larvae are parasites that feed on the skin (warblefly of cattle) or in the nasal cavity (nostrilflies of sheep and deer). The horse botfly belongs to another family, the

Gasterophilidae. It has a parasitic larva that feeds in the horse's stomach.

Bothwell James Hepburn, 4th Earl of Bothwell *c.*1536–1578. Scottish nobleman, third husband of ◊Mary Queen of Scots, 1567–70, alleged to have arranged the explosion that killed Darnley, her previous husband, 1567.

Tried and acquitted a few weeks after the assassination, he abducted Mary and married her on May 15th. A revolt ensued, and Bothwell fled. In 1570 Mary obtained a divorce, and Bothwell was confined in a castle in mainland Europe, where he died insane.

Botswana Republic of *area* 225,000 sq mi/582,000 sq km *capital* Gaborone *towns and cities* Mahalpye, Serowe, Tutume, Francistown *physical* desert in SW, plains in E, fertile lands and swamp in N *environment* the Okavango Swamp is threatened by plans to develop the area for mining and agriculture *features* Kalahari Desert in SW; Okavango Swamp in N, remarkable for its wildlife; Makgadikgadi salt pans in E; diamonds mined at Orapa and Jwaneng in partnership with De Beers of South Africa *head of state and government* Quett Ketumile Joni Masire from 1980 *political system* democratic republic *political parties* Botswana Democratic Party (BDP), moderate centrist; Botswana National Front (BNF), moderate, left of center *exports* diamonds (third largest producer in world), copper, nickel, meat products, textiles *currency* pula *population* (1993 est) 1,400,000 (Bamangwato 80%, Bangwaketse 20%); growth rate 3.5% p.a. *life expectancy* men 58, women 64 *languages* English (official), Setswana (national) *religions* Christian 50%, animist 50% *literacy* men 84%, women 65% *GNP* $2,590 per head (1991) *chronology* *1885* Became a British protectorate. *1960* New constitution created a legislative council. *1963* End of rule by High Commission. *1965* Capital transferred from Mafeking to Gaborone. Internal self-government achieved. Seretse Khama elected head of government. *1966* Independence achieved from Britain. New constitution came into effect; name changed from Bechuanaland to Botswana; Seretse Khama elected president. *1980* Seretse Khama died; succeeded by Vice President Quett Masire. *1984* Masire reelected. *1985* South African raid on Gaborone. *1987* Joint permanent commission with Mozambique established, to improve relations. *1989* BDP and Masire reelected. *1994* BDP and Masire reelected, but with reduced majority.

Botticelli Sandro 1445–1510. Florentine painter. He depicted religious and mythological subjects. He was patronized by the ruling ◊Medici family and deeply influenced by their Neoplatonic circle. It was for the Medicis that he painted *Primavera* 1478 and *The Birth of Venus* about 1482–84 (both in the Uffizi, Florence). From the 1490s he was influenced by the religious fanatic ◊Savonarola and developed a harshly expressive and emotional style, as seen in his *Mystic Nativity* 1500 (National Gallery, London).

Boudicca Queen of the Iceni (native Britons), often referred to by the Latin form *Boadicea*. Her husband, King Prasutagus, had been a tributary of the Romans, but on his death AD 60 the territory of the Iceni was violently annexed. Boudicca was scourged and her daughters raped. Boudicca raised the whole of SE England in revolt, and before the main Roman armies could return from campaigning in Wales she burned Londinium (London), Verulamium (St Albans), and Camulodunum (Colchester). Later the Romans under

governor Suetonius Paulinus defeated the British between London and Chester; they were virtually annihilated and Boudicca poisoned herself.

bougainvillea any plant of the genus of South American tropical vines *Bougainvillea*, of the four o'clock family Nyctaginaceae, now cultivated in warm countries throughout the world for the red and purple bracts that cover the flowers. They are named for the French navigator Louis Bougainville.

Boulanger Nadia (Juliette) 1887–1979. French music teacher and conductor. A pupil of Fauré, and admirer of Stravinsky, she included among her composition pupils at the American Conservatory in Fontainebleau, France, (from 1921) Aaron Copland, Roy Harris, Walter Piston, and Philip Glass.

She was the first woman to conduct the Royal Philharmonic, London, 1937, and the Boston Symphony, the New York Philharmonic, and the Philadelphia Orchestra 1938.

Boulder city in N central Colorado, northwest of Denver, in the eastern foothills of the Rocky Mountains; population (1990) 83,300. A center of scientific research, especially space research, it also has agriculture, mining, and tourism.

It is the site of the University of Colorado 1876.

Bourbon dynasty French royal house (succeeding that of Valois), beginning with Henry IV and ending with Louis XVI, with a brief revival under Louis XVIII, Charles X, and Louis Philippe. The Bourbons also ruled Spain almost uninterruptedly from Philip V to Alfonso XIII and were restored in 1975 (◊Juan Carlos); at one point they also ruled Naples and several Italian duchies. The Grand Duke of Luxembourg is also a Bourbon by male descent.

Bourdon gauge instrument for measuring pressure, patented by French watchmaker Eugène Bourdon 1849. The gauge contains a C-shaped tube, closed at one end. When the pressure inside the tube increases, the tube uncurls slightly causing a small movement at its closed end. A system of levers and gears magnifies this movement and turns a pointer, which indicates the pressure on a circular scale. Bourdon gauges are often fitted to cylinders of compressed gas used in industry and hospitals.

Bourgogne French name of ◊Burgundy, a region of E France.

Bourguiba Habib ben Ali 1903– . Tunisian politician, first president of Tunisia 1957–87. He became prime minister 1956, president (for life from 1974) and prime minister of the Tunisian republic 1957; he was overthrown in a bloodless coup 1987.

Bourke-White Margaret 1906–1971. US photographer. As an editor of *Fortune* magazine 1929–33, she traveled extensively in the USSR, publishing several collections of photographs. Later, with husband Erskine Caldwell, she also published photo collections of American and European subjects. She began working for *Life* magazine 1936, and covered combat in World War II and documented India's struggle for independence.

Born in New York and educated at Cornell Univeristy, Bourke-White began her career as a freelance industrial and architectural photographer.

Boutros-Ghali Boutros 1922– . Egyptian diplomat and politician, deputy prime minister 1991–92, secretary-general of the United Nations (UN) from 1992. He worked toward peace in the Middle East in the foreign ministry posts he held 1977–91. Since taking office at the UN he has encountered a succession of challenges regarding the organization's role in conflict areas such as Bosnia-Herzegovina, Somalia, Haiti, and Rwanda.

bovine somatotropin (BST) hormone that increases an injected cow's milk yield by 10–40%. It is a protein naturally occurring in milk and breaks down within the human digestive tract into harmless amino acids. However, doubts have arisen recently as to whether such a degree of protein addition could in the long term be guaranteed harmless either to cattle or to humans.

Bow Clara 1905–1965. US film actress. She was known as a "Jazz Baby" and the "It Girl" after her portrayal of a glamorous flapper in the silent film *It* 1927.

She made a smooth transition to sound with *The Wild Party* 1929. Other films include *Down to the Sea in Ships* 1925; *The Plastic Age, Kid Boots, Mantrap,* and *Dancing Mothers,* all 1926; *Rough House Rosie* 1927; *Red Hair* and *Three Weekends* both 1928; and *The Saturday Night Kid* 1929. She made her last film *Hoopla* 1933 and retired to her husband's ranch in Nevada.

bower bird New Guinean and N Australian bird of the family Ptilonorhynchidae, related to the ◊bird of paradise. The males are dull-colored, and build elaborate bowers of sticks and grass, decorated with shells, feathers, or flowers, and even painted with the juice of berries, to attract the females. There are 17 species.

bowling indoor sport in which a ball is rolled into a target of standing pins. There are many forms of the sport, but the term "bowling" usually refers to the most popular variety, tenpin. The ball used in tenpin bowling is sometimes plastic but more commonly hard rubber. An official ball (one allowed in league play) must weigh 10–16 lb/4.5–7.3 kg and may not exceed 8.6 in/21.8 cm in diameter. Finger holes are drilled into each ball. Methods of gripping differ from bowler to bowler but most common is the underhand three-finger grip (thumb, middle finger, and ring finger).

bowls a lawn bowling game played on a bowling green and indoors.

box any of several small evergreen trees and shrubs, genus *Buxus*, of the family Buxaceae, with small, leathery leaves. Some species are used as hedge plants and for shaping into garden ornaments.

boxing fighting with gloved fists, almost entirely a male sport. The sport dates from the 18th century, when fights were fought with bare knuckles and untimed rounds. Each round ended with a knock-down. Fighting with gloves became the accepted form in the latter part of the 19th century after the formulation of the Queensberry Rules 1867.

Boxing has school, amateur, semiprofessional, and professional matches.

Boyle's law law stating that the volume of a given mass of gas at a constant temperature is inversely proportional to its pressure. For example, if the pressure of a gas doubles, its volume will be reduced by a half, and vice versa. The law was discovered in 1662 by Irish physicist and chemist Robert Boyle.

Boyne, Battle of the battle fought July 1, 1690, in E Ireland, in which James II was defeated by William III and fled to France. It was the decisive battle of the War of English Succession, confirming a Protestant monarch. It took its name from the river Boyne which

rises in County Kildare and flows 69 mi/110 km NE to the Irish Sea.

BP abbreviation for ◊*British Petroleum*.

bps (abbreviation for *bits per second*) measure used in specifying data transmission rates.

brachiopod or *lamp shell* any member of the phylum Brachiopoda, marine invertebrates with two shells, resembling but totally unrelated to bivalves.

There are about 300 living species; they were much more numerous in past geological ages. They are suspension feeders, ingesting minute food particles from water. A single internal organ, the lophophore, handles feeding, aspiration, and excretion.

bracken large fern, especially *Pteridium aquilinum*, abundant in the northern hemisphere. A perennial rootstock throws up coarse fronds.

Bradford industrial city (engineering, chemicals, machine tools, electronics, printing) in West Yorkshire, England, 9 mi/14 km W of Leeds; population (1991) 457,300. It is the main city for wool textiles in the UK.

Bradley Omar Nelson 1893–1981. US general in World War II. In 1943 he commanded the 2nd US Corps in their victories in Tunisia and Sicily, leading to the surrender of 250,000 Axis troops, and in 1944 led the US troops in the invasion of France. His command, as the 12th Army Group, grew to 1.3 million troops, the largest US force ever assembled.

Born in Clark, Missouri, Bradley graduated from West Point 1915 and served in World War I. After World War II, he headed the Veterans Administration 1945–47, was chief of staff of the US Army 1948–49, and was the first chairman of the joint chiefs of staff 1949–53. He was appointed general of the army 1950 and retired from the army 1953. He wrote his memoirs in *A Soldier's Story* 1951.

Braganza the royal house of Portugal whose members reigned 1640–1910; another branch were emperors of Brazil 1822–89.

Bragg William Henry 1862–1942. British physicist. In 1915 he shared with his son **(William) Lawrence** *Bragg* (1890–1971) the Nobel Prize for Physics for their research work on X-rays and crystals.

Brahe Tycho 1546–1601. Danish astronomer who made accurate observations of the planets from which the German astronomer and mathematician Johann ◊Kepler proved that planets orbit the Sun in ellipses. His discovery and report of the 1572 supernova brought him recognition, and his observations of the comet of 1577 proved that it moved on an orbit among the planets, thus disproving the Greek view that comets were in the Earth's atmosphere.

Brahma in Hinduism, the creator of the cosmos, who forms with Vishnu and Siva the Trimurti, or three aspects of the absolute spirit.

Brahman in Hinduism, the supreme being, an abstract, impersonal world-soul into whom the *atman*, or individual soul, will eventually be absorbed when its cycle of rebirth is ended.

Brahmaputra river in Asia 1,800 mi/2,900 km long, a tributary of the Ganges.

Brahms Johannes 1833–1897. German composer, pianist, and conductor. Considered one of the greatest composers of symphonic music and of songs, his works include four symphonies, lieder (songs),

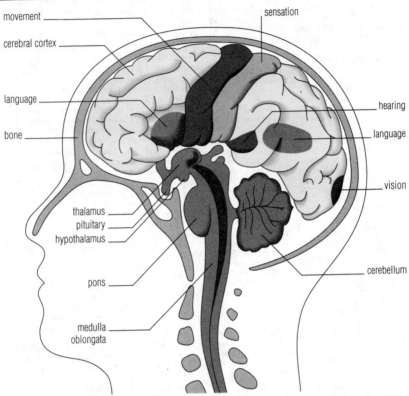

movement
cerebral cortex
language
bone
sensation
hearing
language
vision
thalamus
pituitary
hypothalamus
pons
medulla
oblongata
cerebellum

brain The structure of the human brain. At the back of the skull lies the cerebellum, which coordinates reflex actions that control muscular activity. The medulla controls respiration, heartbeat, and blood pressure. The hypothalamus is concerned with instinctive drives and emotions. The thalamus relays signals to and from various parts of the brain. The pituitary gland controls the body's hormones. Distinct areas of the large convoluted cerebral hemispheres that fill most of the skull are linked to sensations, such as hearing and sight, and voluntary activities, such as movement.

concertos for piano and for violin, chamber music, sonatas, and the choral *Ein Deutsches Requiem/A German Requiem* 1868. He performed and conducted his own works.

brain in higher animals, a mass of interconnected ◊nerve cells forming the anterior part of the ◊central nervous system, whose activities it coordinates and controls. In ◊vertebrates, the brain is contained by the skull. At the base of the brainstem, the *medulla oblongata* contains centers for the control of respiration, heartbeat rate and strength, and blood pressure. Overlying this is the *cerebellum*, which is concerned with coordinating complex muscular processes such as maintaining posture and moving limbs. The cerebral hemispheres (*cerebrum*) are paired outgrowths of the front end of the forebrain, in early vertebrates mainly concerned with the senses, but in higher vertebrates greatly developed and involved in the integration of all sensory input and motor output, and in thought, emotions, memory, and behavior.

brake device used to slow down or stop the movement of a moving body or vehicle. The mechanically applied caliper brake used on bicycles uses a scissor action to press hard rubber blocks against the wheel rim. The main braking system of an automobile works hydraulically: when the driver depresses the brake pedal, liquid pressure forces pistons to apply brakes on each wheel.

Bramante Donato *c*.1444–1514. Italian Renaissance architect and artist. Inspired by Classical designs and by the work of Leonardo da Vinci, he was employed by Pope Julius II in rebuilding part of the Vatican and St Peter's in Rome. The circular Tempietto of San Pietro in Montorio, Rome (commissioned 1502; built about 1510), is possibly his most important completed work. Though small in size, this circular colonaded building possesses much of the grandeur of ancient Roman buildings.

bramble any prickly bush of a genus *Rubus* belonging to the rose family Rosaceae. Examples are ◊blackberry, raspberry, and dewberry.

Brancusi Constantin 1876–1957. Romanian sculptor. He is a seminal figure in 20th-century art.

Active in Paris from 1904, he was a pioneer of abstract scultpure, developing increasingly simplified representations of natural, or organic, forms, for example the *Sleeping Muse* 1910 (Musée National d'Art Moderne, Paris), a sculpted head that gradually comes to resemble an egg.

Brandeis Louis Dembitz 1856–1941. US jurist. As a crusader for progressive causes, he helped draft social-welfare and labor legislation. In 1916, with his appointment to the US Supreme Court by President Wilson, he became the first Jewish justice and maintained his support of individual rights in his opposition to the 1917 Espionage Act and in his dissenting opinion in the first wiretap case, *Olmstead* v *US* 1928.

Born in Louisville, Kentucky, Brandeis was educated at Harvard and was admitted to the bar 1877. Brandeis University in Waltham, Massachusetts, is named in his honor.

Brandenburg administrative *Land* (state) of Germany *area* 10,000 sq mi/25,000 sq km *capital* Potsdam *towns and cities* Cottbus, Brandenburg, Frankfurt-on-Oder *industries* iron and steel, paper, pulp, metal products, semiconductors *population* (1990) 2,700,000 *history* The Hohenzollern rulers who took control of Brandenburg 1415 later acquired the powerful duchy of Prussia and became emperors of Germany. At the end of World War II, Brandenburg lost over 5,000 sq mi/12,950 sq km of territory when Poland advanced its frontier to the line of the Oder and Neisse rivers. The remainder, which became a region of East Germany, was divided 1952 into the districts of Frankfurt-on-Oder, Potsdam, and Cottbus. When Germany was reunited 1990, Brandenburg reappeared as a state of the Federal Republic.

Brando Marlon 1924–   . US actor. His powerful stage presence, mumbling speech, and use of Method acting earned him a place as a distinctive actor. He won best-actor Academy Awards for *On the Waterfront* 1954 and *The Godfather* 1972.

Brandt Willy. Adopted name of Karl Herbert Frahm 1913–1992. German socialist politician, federal chancellor (premier) of West Germany 1969–74. He played a key role in the remolding of the Social Democratic Party (SPD) as a moderate socialist force (leader 1964–87). As mayor of West Berlin 1957–66, Brandt became internationally known during the Berlin Wall crisis 1961. Nobel Peace Prize 1971.

He resigned from the chancellorship 1974 following the discovery that an aide had been an East German spy. Brandt continued to wield considerable influence in the SPD, in particular over the party's new radical left wing. He chaired the Brandt Commission on Third World problems 1977–83 and was a member of the European Parliament 1979–83.

Braque Georges 1882–1963. French painter. With Picasso, he founded the Cubist movement around 1907–10. His early work was influenced by Fauvism in its use of pure, bright color, but from 1907 he developed a geometric style and during the next few years he and Picasso worked very closely developing Cubism. It was during this period that he began to experiment with collage and invented the technique of gluing paper, wood, and other materials to canvas. His later work was more decorative but more restrained in its use of color.

Brasília capital of Brazil from 1960, 3,000 ft/1,000 m above sea level; population (1991) 1,841,000. It was designed by Lucio Costa (1902–1963), with Oscar Niemeyer as chief architect, as a completely new city to bring life to the interior.

brass metal ◊alloy of copper and zinc, with not more than 5% or 6% of other metals. The zinc content ranges from 20% to 45%, and the color of brass varies accordingly from coppery to whitish yellow. Brasses are characterized by the ease with which they may be shaped and machined; they are strong and ductile, resist many forms of corrosion, and are used for electrical fittings, ammunition cases, screws, household fittings, and ornaments.

Brassica any plant of the genus *Brassica,* family Cruciferae. The most familiar species is the common cabbage *Brassica oleracea,* with its varieties broccoli, cauliflower, kale, and brussels sprouts.

brass instrument any of a class of musical instruments made of brass or other metal, including trumpets, bugles, trombones, and horns. The function of a reed is served by the lips, shaped and tensed by the mouthpiece, acting as a valve releasing periodic pulses of pressurized air into the tube. Orchestral brass instruments are derived from signaling instruments that in their natural or valveless form produce a directionally focused range of tones from the harmonic series by overblowing to as high as the 16th harmonic. They are powerful and efficient generators, and produce tones of great depth and resonance.

Bratislava (German *Pressburg*) industrial port (engineering, chemicals, oil refining) and capital of the Slovak Republic, on the river Danube; population (1991) 441,500. It was the capital of Hungary 1526–1784 and capital of Slovakia (within Czechoslovakia) until 1993.

Brattain Walter Houser 1902–1987. US physicist. In 1956 he was awarded a Nobel Prize jointly with William Shockley and John Bardeen for their work on the development of the transistor, which replaced the comparatively costly and clumsy vacuum tube in electronics.

He was born in Amoy, China, the son of a teacher. From 1929 to 1967 he was on the staff of Bell Telephone Laboratories.

Braunschweig German form of ◊Brunswick, a city in Lower Saxony, Germany.

Brazil Federative Republic of (*República Federativa do Brasil*) *area* 3,285,618 sq mi/8,511,965 sq km *capital*

Brasília *towns and cities* São Paulo, Belo Horizonte, Curitiba, Manaus, Fortaleza; ports are Rio de Janeiro, Belém, Recife, Pôrto Alegre, Salvador *physical* the densely forested Amazon basin covers the northern half of the country with a network of rivers; the south is fertile; enormous energy resources, both hydroelectric (Itaipú dam on the Paraná, and Tucuruí on the Tocantins) and nuclear (uranium ores) *environment* Brazil has one-third of the world's tropical rainforest. It contains 55,000 species of flowering plants (the greatest variety in the world) and 20% of all the world's bird species. During the 1980s at least 7% of the Amazon rainforest was destroyed by settlers who cleared the land for cultivation and grazing *features* Mount Roraima, Xingu National Park; Amazon delta; Rio harbor *head of state and government* Fernando Henrique Cardoso from 1994 *political system* democratic federal republic *political parties* Social Democratic Party (PSDB), moderate, left of center; Brazilian Democratic Movement Party (PMDB), center-left; Liberal Front Party (PFL), moderate, left of center; Workers' Party (PDT), left of center; National Reconstruction Party (PRN), center-right *exports* coffee, sugar, soy beans, cotton, textiles, timber, motor vehicles, iron, chrome, manganese, tungsten, and other ores, as well as quartz crystals, industrial diamonds, gemstones; the world's sixth largest arms exporter *currency* real *population* (1993 est) 159,100,000 (including 200,000 Indians, survivors of 5 million, especially in Rondônia and Mato Grosso, mostly living on reservations); growth rate 2.2% p.a. *life expectancy* men 64, women 69 *languages* Portuguese (official); 120 Indian languages *religions* Roman Catholic 89%; Indian faiths *literacy* men 83%, women 80% *GNP* $2,680 per head (1987) *chronology* *1822* Independence achieved from Portugal; ruled by Dom Pedro, son of the refugee King John VI of Portugal. *1889* Monarchy abolished and republic established. *1891* Constitution for a federal state adopted. *1930* Dr Getúlio Vargas became president. *1945* Vargas deposed by the military. *1946* New constitution adopted. *1951* Vargas returned to office. *1954* Vargas committed suicide. *1956* Juscelino Kubitschek became president. *1960* Capital moved to Brasília. *1961* João Goulart became president. *1964* Bloodless coup made General Castelo Branco president; he assumed dictatorial powers, abolishing free political parties. *1967* New constitution adopted. Branco succeeded by Marshal da Costa e Silva. *1969* Da Costa e Silva resigned and a military junta took over. *1974* General Ernesto Geisel became president. *1978* General Baptista de Figueiredo became president. *1979* Political parties legalized again. *1984* Mass calls for a return to fully democratic government. *1985* Tancredo Neves became first civilian president in 21 years. Neves died and was succeeded by the vice president, José Sarney. *1988* New constitution approved, transferring power from the president to the congress. Measures announced to halt large-scale burning of Amazonian rainforest for cattle grazing. *1989* Fernando Collor (PRN) elected president, pledging free-market economic policies. *1990* Government won the general election offset by mass abstentions. *1992* Collor charged with corruption and replaced by Vice President Itamar Franco. Hosted Earth Summit. *1993* April: referendum rejected replacement of presidential system with parliamentary system or monarchy. Collor accused of "passive corruption". *1994* New currency introduced. Fernando Henrique Cardoso, of the PSDB, elected president.

Brazil nut gigantic South American tree *Bertholletia excelsa;* also its seed, which is rich in oil and highly nutritious. The seeds are enclosed in a hard outer casing, each fruit containing 10–20 seeds arranged like the segments of an orange. The timber of the tree is also valuable.

Brazzaville capital of the Congo, industrial port (foundries, railroad repairs, shipbuilding, shoes, soap, furniture, bricks) on the river Zaïre, opposite Kinshasa; population (1984) 595,000. There is a cathedral 1892 and the Pasteur Institute 1908. It stands on Pool Malebo (Stanley Pool).

breadfruit fruit of the tropical trees *Artocarpus communis* and *A. altilis* of the mulberry family Moraceae. It is highly nutritious and when baked is said to taste like bread. It is native to many South Pacific islands.

bream deep-bodied, flattened fish *Abramis brama* of the carp family, growing to about 1.6 ft/50 cm, typically found in lowland rivers across Europe.

The name bream is also applied to porgies, small-mouthed, deep-bodied marine fishes of the family Sparidae. The pinfish bream *Lagodon rhomboides* is found from Cape Cod S to the Gulf of Mexico. Several members of the North American sunfish family are also popularly referred to as bream.

breathing in terrestrial animals, the muscular movements whereby air is taken into the lungs and then expelled, a form of ◊gas exchange. Breathing is sometimes referred to as external respiration, for true respiration is a cellular (internal) process.

breath testing collecting a breath sample and analyzing it. Breath testing is useful in medicine to diagnose certain conditions. It is also used by the police to measure alcohol consumption.

Brecht Bertolt 1898–1956. German dramatist and poet. He was one of the most influential figures in 20th-century drama. A committed Marxist, he sought to develop an "epic theater" which aimed to destroy the "suspension of disbelief" usual in the theater and so encourage audiences to develop an active and critical attitude to a play's subject. He adapted John Gay's *The Beggar's Opera* as *Die Dreigroschenoper/The Threepenny Opera* 1928, set to music by Kurt Weill. Later plays include *Mutter Courage/Mother Courage* 1941, set during the Thirty Years' War, and *Der kaukasische Kreidekreis/The Caucasian Chalk Circle* 1949.

breeder reactor or *fast breeder* alternative names for ◊fast reactor, a type of nuclear reactor.

Bremen industrial port (iron, steel, oil refining, chemicals, aircraft, shipbuilding, automobiles) in Germany, on the river Weser 43 mi/69 km from the open sea; population (1988) 522,000.

Brennan William Joseph, Jr 1906– . US jurist and associate justice of the US Supreme Court 1956–90. He wrote many important Supreme Court majority decisions that assured the freedoms set forth in the First Amendment and established the rights of minority groups. He is especially noted for writing the majority opinion in *Baker v Carr* 1962, in which state voting reapportionment ensured "one person, one vote", and in *US v Eichman* 1990, which ruled that the law banning desecration of the flag was a violation of the right to free speech as provided for in the First Amendment.

Born in Newark, New Jersey, Brennan graduated from the University of Pennsylvania and Harvard Law

School. A New Jersey superior court 1949–52 and supreme court 1952–56 judge, he was appointed to the US Supreme Court by President Eisenhower. Considered a moderate liberal, his vote was usually cast with the majority during the years of the Court under Chief Justice Earl ◊Warren, but he became a key liberal influence when the court majority, under chief justices ◊Burger and ◊Rehnquist, shifted to the conservative side in the 1980s. He retired from the Court 1990, citing health reasons.

Brenner Pass lowest of the Alpine passes, 4,495 ft/ 1,370 m; it leads from Trentino–Alto Adige, Italy, to the Austrian Tirol, and is 12 mi/19 km long.

Brereton Lewis M 1890–1967. US general. He served as a fighter pilot in World War I and during World War II commanded various US air forces in the Far East, the Middle East, and latterly in Europe.

Brest naval base and industrial port (electronics, engineering, chemicals) on *Rade de Brest* (Brest Roads), a great bay at the western extremity of Brittany, France; population (1983) 201,000. Occupied as a U-boat base by the Germans 1940–44, the city was destroyed by Allied bombing and rebuilt.

Breton André 1896–1966. French writer and poet. He was among the leaders of the ◊Dada art movement. *Les Champs magnétiques/Magnetic Fields* 1921, an experiment in automatic writing, was one of the products of the movement. He was also a founder of ◊Surrealism, publishing *Le Manifeste de surréalisme/Surrealist Manifesto* 1924. Other works include *Najda* 1928, the story of his love affair with a medium.

Bretton Woods township in New Hampshire, US, where the United Nations Monetary and Financial Conference was held in 1944 to discuss postwar international payments problems. The agreements reached on financial assistance and measures to stabilize exchange rates led to the creation of the International Bank for Reconstruction and Development in 1945 and the International Monetary Fund (IMF).

There were 44 nations represented at the conference, which considered proposals by the US, UK, and Canadian governments. The IMF became a specialized agency of the UN 1947. The "Bretton Woods" system was based on a policy of fixed exchange rates, the elimination of exchange restrictions, currency convertibility, and a multilateral system of international payments.

Breuer Marcel 1902–1981. Hungarian-born architect and designer. He studied and taught at the ◊Bauhaus school in Germany. His tubular steel chair 1925 was the first of its kind. He moved to England, then to the US, where he was in partnership with Walter Gropius 1937–40. His buildings show an affinity with natural materials, as exemplified in the Bijenkorf, Rotterdam, the Netherlands (with Elzas) 1953.

brewing making of beer, ale, or other alcoholic beverage from ◊malt and ◊barley by steeping (mashing), boiling, and fermenting.

Mashing the barley releases its sugars. Yeast is then added, which contains the enzymes needed to convert the sugars into alcohol and carbon dioxide. Hops are added to give a bitter taste.

Brezhnev Leonid Ilyich 1906–1982. Soviet leader. A protégé of Stalin and Khrushchev, he came to power (after he and ◊Kosygin forced Khrushchev to resign) as general secretary of the Soviet Communist Party (CPSU) 1964–82 and was president 1977–82. Domestically he was conservative; abroad the USSR was established as a military and political superpower during the Brezhnev era, extending its influence in Africa and Asia.

Brian known as *Brian Boru* ("Brian of the Tribute") 926–1014. High king of Ireland from 976, who took Munster, Leinster, and Connacht to become ruler of all Ireland. He defeated the Norse at Clontarf, thus ending Norse control of Dublin, although he was himself killed. He was the last high king with jurisdiction over most of Scotland. His exploits were celebrated in several chronicles.

bribery corruptly receiving or agreeing to receive, giving or promising to give, any gift, loan, fee, reward, or advantage as an inducement or reward to persons in certain positions of trust. For example, it is an offense to improperly influence in this way judges or other judicial officers, members and officers of public bodies, or voters at public elections.

brick common building material, rectangular in shape, made of clay that has been fired in a kiln. Bricks are made by kneading a mixture of crushed clay and other materials into a stiff mud and extruding it into a ribbon. The ribbon is cut into individual bricks, which are fired at a temperature of up to about 1,800°F/1,000°C. Bricks may alternatively be pressed into shape in molds.

bridge structure that provides a continuous path or road over water, valleys, ravines, or above other roads. The basic designs and composites of these are based on the way they bear the weight of the structure and its load. *Beam*, or *girder*, bridges are supported at each end by the ground with the weight thrusting downward. *Cantilever* bridges are a complex form of girder. *Arch* bridges thrust outward but downward at their ends; they are in compression. *Suspension* bridges use cables under tension to pull inward against anchorages on either side of the span, so that the roadway hangs from the main cables by the network of vertical cables. The *cable-stayed* bridge relies on diagonal cables connected directly between the bridge deck and supporting towers at each end. Some bridges are too low to allow traffic to pass beneath easily, so they are designed with movable parts, like swing and draw bridges.

Today the longest spans are suspension bridges, with the measurement referring only to that part of the bridge actually suspended by cables.

bridge card game derived from whist. First played among members of the Indian Civil Service about 1900, bridge was taken to England in 1903. It is played in two forms: auction bridge and contract bridge.

bridge in computing, a device that connects two similar local area networks (LANs). Bridges transfer data in packets between the two networks, without making any changes or interpreting the data in any way. See also ◊brouter.

Bridgeport city in Connecticut on Long Island Sound; population (1990) 141,700. Industries include metal goods, electrical appliances, and aircraft, but many factories closed in the 1970s. The university was established 1927.

The P T Barnum Museum and Tom Thumb statues are here. Bridgeport was settled 1639.

Bridgetown port and capital of Barbados, founded 1628; population (1987) 8,000. Sugar is exported through the nearby deep-water port.

brigade military formation consisting of a minimum of two battalions, but more usually three or more, as well as supporting arms. There are typically about 5,000 soldiers in a brigade, which is commanded by a brigadier general. Two or more brigades form a division.

Brighton seaside resort on the E Sussex coast, England; population (1991) 143,600. It has Regency architecture and the Royal Pavilion 1782 in Oriental style. There are two piers and an aquarium.

brill flatfish *Scophthalmus laevis*, living in shallow water over sandy bottoms in the NE Atlantic and Mediterranean. It is a freckled sandy brown, and grows to 2 ft/60 cm.

Brinell hardness test test of the hardness of a substance according to the area of indentation made by a 0.4 in/10 mm hardened steel or sintered tungsten carbide ball under standard loading conditions in a test machine. The resulting Brinell number is equal to the load (kg) divided by the surface area (mm^2) and is named for its inventor, Swedish metallurgist Johann Brinell.

Brisbane industrial port (brewing, engineering, tanning, tobacco, shoes; oil pipeline from Moonie), capital of Queensland, E Australia, near the mouth of Brisbane River, dredged to carry oceangoing ships; population (1990) 1,301,700.

bristletail primitive wingless insect of the order Thysanura. Up to 0.8 in/2 cm long, bristletails have a body tapering from front to back, two long antennae, and three "tails" at the rear end. They include the *silverfish Lepisma saccharina* and the *firebrat Thermobia domestica*. Two-tailed bristletails constitute another insect order, the Diplura. They live under stones and fallen branches, feeding on decaying material.

Bristol industrial port (aircraft engines, engineering, microelectronics, tobacco, chemicals, paper, printing, soap, metal refining, chocolate), administrative headquarters of Avon, SW England; population (1991) 376,100. The old docks have been redeveloped for housing, industry, yachting facilities, and the National Lifeboat Museum. Further developments include a new city center, with Brunel's Temple Meads railroad station at its focus, and a weir across the Avon nearby to improve the waterside environment.

Britain island off the NW coast of Europe, one of the British Isles. It comprises England, Scotland, and Wales (together officially known as ◊Great Britain), and is part of the ◊United Kingdom. The name is derived from the Roman name Britannia, which in turn is derived from the ancient Celtic name of the inhabitants, *Bryttas*.

Britain, ancient period in the British Isles (excluding Ireland) extending through prehistory to the Roman occupation (1st century AD). Settled agricultural life evolved in Britain during the 3rd millennium BC. Neolithic society reached its peak in southern England, where it was capable of producing the great stone circles of Avebury and Stonehenge early in the 2nd millennium BC. It was succeeded in central southern Britain by the Early Bronze Age Wessex culture, with strong trade links across Europe. The Iron Age culture of the Celts was predominant in the last few centuries BC, and the Belgae (of mixed Germanic and Celtic stock) were partially Romanized in the century between the first Roman invasion of Britain under Julius Caesar (54 BC) and the Roman conquest (AD 43). For later history, see ◊England: history; ◊Scotland: history; ◊Wales: history; and ◊United Kingdom.

Britain, Battle of World War II air battle between German and British air forces over Britain lasting July 10–Oct 31, 1940.

British Broadcasting Corporation (BBC) the UK state-owned broadcasting network. It operates television and national and local radio stations, and is financed by the sale of television viewing licenses; it is not allowed to carry advertisements but it has an additional source of income through its publishing interests and the sales of its programs. Overseas radio broadcasts (World Service) have a government subsidy.

The BBC was converted from a private company (established 1922) to a public body 1927.

British Columbia province of Canada on the Pacific Ocean *area* 365,851 sq mi/947,800 sq km *capital* Victoria *towns and cities* Vancouver, Prince George, Kamloops, Kelowna *physical* Rocky Mountains and Coast Range; deeply indented coast; rivers include the Fraser and Columbia; over 80 lakes; more than half the land is forested *industries* fruit and vegetables; timber and wood products; fish; coal, copper, iron, lead; oil and natural gas; hydroelectricity *population* (1991) 3,185,900 *history* Captain Cook explored the coast 1778; a British colony was founded on Vancouver Island 1849, and the gold rush of 1858 extended settlement to the mainland; it became a province 1871. In 1885 the Canadian Pacific Railroad linking British Columbia to the east coast was completed.

British East India Company a commercial company 1600–1858 chartered by Queen Elizabeth I and given a monopoly of trade between England and the Far East. In the 18th century it became, in effect, the ruler of a large part of India, and a form of dual control by the company and a committee responsible to Parliament in London was introduced by Pitt's India Act 1784. The end of the monopoly of China trade came 1834, and after the Sepoy Rebellion 1857 the crown took complete control of the government of British India; the India Act 1858 abolished the company.

British Empire various territories all over the world conquered or colonized by Britain from about 1600, most now independent or ruled by other powers; the British Empire was at its largest at the end of World War I, with over 25% of the world's population and area. The ◊Commonwealth is composed of former and remaining territories of the British Empire.

The first successful British colony was Jamestown, Virginia, founded 1607.

British Honduras former name (to 1973) of ◊Belize.

British Indian Ocean Territory British colony in the Indian Ocean. It consists of the Chagos Archipelago some 1,200 mi/1,900 km NE of Mauritius *area* 23 sq mi/60 sq km *features* lagoons; US naval and air base on Diego Garcia *industries* copra, salt fish, tortoiseshell *population* (1982) 3,000 *history* purchased 1565 for $3 million by Britain from Mauritius to provide a joint US/UK base. The islands of Aldabra, Farquhar, and Desroches, some 300 mi/485 km N of Madagascar, originally formed part of the British Indian Ocean Territory but were returned to the administration of the Seychelles 1976.

British Isles group of islands off the northwest coast of Europe, consisting of Great Britain (England, Wales, and Scotland), Ireland, the Channel Islands, the Orkney and Shetland islands, the Isle of Man, and many other islands that are included in various counties, such as the Isle of Wight, Scilly Isles, Lundy Island, and the Inner and Outer Hebrides. The islands are divided from Europe by the North Sea, Strait of Dover, and the English Channel, and face the Atlantic to the W.

British Petroleum (BP) one of the world's largest oil concerns and Britain's largest company, with more than 128,000 employees in 70 countries. It was formed as the Anglo-Persian Oil Company 1909 and acquired the chemical interests of the Distillers Company 1967.

British Somaliland British protectorate comprising over 67,980 sq mi/176,000 sq km of territory on the Somali coast of E Africa from 1884 until the independence of Somalia 1960. British authorities were harassed by Somali nationalists under the leadership of Mohammed bin Abdullah Hassan.

British Virgin Islands part of the ◊Virgin Islands group in the West Indies.

Brittany (French *Bretagne*, Breton *Breiz*) region of NW France in the Breton peninsula between the Bay of Biscay and the English Channel; area 10,499 sq mi/27,200 sq km; capital Rennes; population (1987) 2,767,000. A farming region, it includes the *départements* of Côtes-du-Nord, Finistère, Ille-et-Vilaine, and Morbihan.

history Brittany was the Gallo-Roman province of Armourica after being conquered by Julius Caesar 56 BC. It was devastated by Norsemen after the Roman withdrawal. Established under the name of Brittany in the 5th century AD by Celts fleeing the Anglo-Saxon invasion of Britain, it became a strong, expansionist state that maintained its cultural and political independence, despite pressure from the Carolingians, Normans, and Capetians. In 1171, the duchy of Brittany was inherited by Geoffrey, son of Henry II of England, and remained in the Angevin dynasty's possession until 1203, when Geoffrey's son Arthur was murdered by King John, and the title passed to the Capetian Peter of Dreux. Under the Angevins, feudalism was introduced, and French influence increased under the Capetians. By 1547 it had been formally annexed by France, and the Breton language was banned in education. A separatist movement developed after World War II, and there has been guerrilla activity.

Britten (Edward) Benjamin 1913–1976. English composer. He often wrote for the individual voice; for example, the role in the opera *Peter Grimes* 1945, based on verses by George Crabbe, was created for his life companion Peter Pears. Among his many works are the *Young Person's Guide to the Orchestra* 1946; the chamber opera *The Rape of Lucretia* 1946; *Billy Budd* 1951; *A Midsummer Night's Dream* 1960; and *Death in Venice* 1973.

brittle-star any member of the echinoderm class Ophiuroidea. A brittle-star resembles a starfish, and has a small, central, rounded body and long, flexible, spiny arms used for walking. The small brittle-star *Amphipholis squamata* is grayish, about 2 in/4.5 cm across, and found on sea bottoms worldwide. It broods its young, and its arms can be luminous.

Brno industrial city (chemicals, arms, textiles, machinery) in the Czech Republic; population (1991) 388,000. Now the second largest city in the Czech Republic, Brno was formerly the capital of the Austrian crown land of Moravia.

broadbill primitive perching bird of the family Eurylaimidae, found in Africa and S Asia. Broadbills are forest birds and are often found near water. They are gregarious and noisy, have brilliant coloration and wide bills, and feed largely on insects.

broadcasting the transmission of sound and vision programs by ◊radio and ◊television. In the US, broadcasting licenses are issued to public organizations and competing commercial companies by the Federal Communications Commission.

broad-leaved tree another name for a tree belonging to the ◊angiosperms, such as ash, beech, oak, maple, or birch. The leaves are generally broad and flat, in contrast to the needlelike leaves of most ◊conifers. See also ◊deciduous tree.

broccoli variety of ◊cabbage.

Brodsky Joseph 1940– . Russian poet. He emigrated to the US 1972. His work, often dealing with themes of exile, is admired for its wit and economy of language, particularly in its use of understatement. Many of his poems, written in Russian, have been translated into English (*A Part of Speech* 1980). More recently he has also written in English. He was awarded the Nobel Prize for Literature in 1987 and became US poet laureate 1991.

Broglie Louis Victor de, 7th Duc de Broglie 1892–1987. French theoretical physicist. He established that all subatomic particles can be described either by particle equations or by wave equations, thus laying the foundations of wave mechanics. He was awarded the 1929 Nobel Prize for Physics.

brome grass any annual grasses of the genus *Bromus* of the temperate zone; some are used for forage, but many are weeds.

bromeliad any tropical or subtropical plant of the pineapple family Bromeliaceae, usually with stiff leathery leaves and bright flower spikes.

Many tropical species are epiphytes on rainforest trees. The pineapple plant *Ananas comosus* is widely cultivated for its fleshy collective fruit, resembling a pine cone, developed from a flower spike. Spanish moss *Tillandsia usneoides*, another bromeliad, grows in long strands from the branches of trees in the SE US and tropical America.

bromine dark, reddish brown, nonmetallic element, a volatile liquid at room temperature, symbol Br, atomic number 35, relative atomic mass 79.904. It is a member of the ◊halogen group, has an unpleasant odor, and is very irritating to mucous membranes. Its salts are known as bromides.

bronchitis inflammation of the bronchi (air passages) of the lungs, usually caused initially by a viral infection, such as a cold or flu. It is aggravated by environmental pollutants, especially smoking, and results in a persistent cough, irritated mucus-secreting glands, and large amounts of sputum.

Brontë three English novelists, daughters of a Yorkshire parson. *Charlotte* (1816–1855), notably with *Jane Eyre* 1847 and *Villette* 1853, reshaped autobiographical material into vivid narrative. *Emily* (1818–1848) in *Wuthering Heights* 1847 expressed the intensity and nature mysticism which also pervades her poetry

(*Poems* 1846). The more modest talent of *Anne* (1820–1849) produced *Agnes Grey* 1847 and *The Tenant of Wildfell Hall* 1848.

brontosaurus former name of a type of large, plant-eating dinosaur, now better known as ◊apatosaurus.

bronze alloy of copper and tin, yellow or brown in color. It is harder than pure copper, more suitable for casting, and also resists ◊corrosion. Bronze may contain as much as 25% tin, together with small amounts of other metals, mainly lead.

Bronze Age stage of prehistory and early history when copper and bronze became the first metals worked extensively and used for tools and weapons. It developed out of the ◊Stone Age, preceded the ◊Iron Age, and may be dated 5000–1200 BC in the Middle East and about 2000–500 BC in Europe. Recent discoveries in Thailand suggest that the Far East, rather than the Middle East, was the cradle of the Bronze Age.

broom any shrub of the family Leguminosae, especially species of the *Cytisus* and *Spartium,* often cultivated for their bright yellow flowers.

brouter device for connecting computer networks that incorporates the facilities of both a ◊bridge and a router. Brouters usually offer routing over a limited number of protocols, operating by routing where possible and bridging the remaining protocols.

Brown Capability (Lancelot) 1715–1783. English landscape gardener. He acquired his nickname because of his continual enthusiasm for the "capabilities" of natural landscapes.

Brown John 1800–1859. US slavery abolitionist. With 18 men, on the night of Oct 16, 1859, he seized the government arsenal at Harper's Ferry in W Virginia, apparently intending to distribute weapons to runaway slaves who would then defend a mountain stronghold, which Brown hoped would become a republic of former slaves. On Oct 18 the arsenal was stormed by US Marines under Col Robert E ◊Lee. Brown was tried and hanged on Dec 2, becoming a martyr and the hero of the popular song "John Brown's Body" about 1860.

brown dwarf hypothetical object less massive than a star, but heavier than a planet. Brown dwarfs would not have enough mass to ignite nuclear reactions at their centers, but would shine by heat released during their contraction from a gas cloud. Because of the difficulty of detection, no brown dwarfs have been spotted with certainty, but some astronomers believe that vast numbers of them may exist throughout the Galaxy.

Browning Robert 1812–1889. English poet. He was married to Elizabeth ◊Barrett Browning. His work is characterized by the use of dramatic monologue and an interest in obscure literary and historical figures. It includes the play *Pippa Passes* 1841 and the poems "The Pied Piper of Hamelin" 1842, "My Last Duchess" 1842, "Home Thoughts from Abroad" 1845, and "Rabbi Ben Ezra" 1864.

Brownshirts the SA (*Sturmabteilung*) or Storm Troops, the private army of the German Nazi party, who derived their name from the color of their uniform.

browser any computer program that allows the user to search for and view data. Browsers are usually limited to a particular type of data, so, for example, a graphics browser will display graphics files stored in many different file formats. Browsers do not permit the user to edit data, but are sometimes able to convert data

from one file format to another. Mosaic, a program that allows users to view documents on the ◊World-Wide Web, is an example of a browser.

Bruce one of the chief Scottish noble houses. ◊Robert (I) the Bruce and his son, David II, were both kings of Scotland descended from Robert de Bruis (died 1094), a Norman knight who arrived in England with William the Conqueror 1066.

Bruce Robert. King of Scotland; see ◊Robert (I) the Bruce.

Brüderhof Christian Protestant sect with beliefs similar to the ◊Mennonites. They live in groups of families (single persons are assigned to a family), marry only within the sect (divorce is not allowed), and retain a "modest" dress for women (cap or headscarf, and long skirts). In the US they are known as Hutterites.

They originated as an ◊Anabaptist sect in Moravia in 1529. Jacob Hutter, a Swiss minister, was their leader until martyred 1536. They survived relentless persecution in the 16th and 17th centuries.

Brueghel or *Bruegel* family of Flemish painters. *Pieter Brueghel the Elder* (*c*.1525–1569) was one of the greatest artists of his time. His pictures of peasant life helped to establish genre painting and he also popularized works illustrating proverbs, such as *The Blind leading the Blind* 1568 (Museo di Capodimonte, Naples). A contemporary taste for the macabre can be seen in *The Triumph of Death* 1562 (Prado, Madrid), which clearly shows the influence of Hieronymus Bosch. One of his best-known works is *Hunters in the Snow* 1565 (Kunsthistorisches Museum, Vienna).

Brown, John *Believing he was an instrument in the hands of God, the US abolitionist John Brown took direct action to liberate the slaves of the southern states. He organized the "underground railroad", a secret network that may have helped as many as 100,000 slaves to escape from southern states, and in 1859, believing he could lead an armed insurrection, he seized a government arsenal.*

Bruges (Flemish *Brugge*) historic city in NW Belgium; capital of W Flanders province, 10 mi/16 km from the North Sea, with which it is connected by canal; population (1991) 117,100. Bruges was the capital of medieval ◊Flanders and was the chief European wool manufacturing town as well as its chief market. The contemporary port handles coal, iron ore, oil, and fish; local industries include lace, textiles, paint, steel, beer, furniture, and motors.

Brugge Flemish form of ◊Bruges, a city in Belgium.

Brunei Islamic Sultanate of (*Negara Brunei Darussalam*) *area* 2,225 sq mi/5,765 sq km *capital* Bandar Seri Begawan *towns and cities* Tutong, Seria, Kuala Belait *physical* flat coastal plain with hilly lowland in W and mountains in E; 75% of the area is forested; the Limbang valley splits Brunei in two, and its cession to Sarawak 1890 is disputed by Brunei *features* Temburong, Tutong, and Belait rivers; Mount Pagon (6,070 ft/1,850 m) *head of state and government* HM Muda Hassanal Bolkiah Mu'izzaddin Waddaulah, Sultan of Brunei, from 1967 *political system* absolute monarchy *political party* Brunei National United Party (BNUP) *exports* liquefied natural gas (world's largest producer) and oil, both expected to be exhausted by the year 2000 *currency* Brunei dollar *population* (1993 est) 280,000 (65% Malay, 20% Chinese—few Chinese granted citizenship); growth rate 12% p.a. *life expectancy* 74 years *languages* Malay (official), Chinese (Hokkien), English *religion* 60% Muslim (official) *literacy* 86% *GNP* \$14,120 per head (1987) *chronology* 1888 Brunei became a British protectorate. *1941–45* Occupied by Japan. *1959* Written constitution made Britain responsible for defense and external affairs. *1962* Sultan began rule by decree. *1967* Sultan abdicated in favor of his son, Hassanal Bolkiah. *1971* Brunei given internal self-government. *1975* United Nations resolution called for independence for Brunei. *1984* Independence achieved from Britain, with Britain maintaining a small force to protect the oil and gas fields. *1985* A "loyal and reliable" political party, the Brunei National Democratic Party (BNDP), legalized. *1986* Death of former sultan, Sir Omar. Formation of multiethnic BNUP. *1988* BNDP banned.

Brunelleschi Filippo 1377–1446. Italian Renaissance architect. The first and one of the greatest of the Renaissance architects, he pioneered the scientific use of perspective. He was responsible for the construction of the dome of Florence Cathedral (completed 1436), a feat deemed impossible by many of his contemporaries.

His use of simple geometries and a modified Classical language lend his buildings a feeling of tranquility, to which many other early Renaissance architects aspired. His other works include the Ospedale degli Innocenti 1419 and the Pazzi Chapel 1429, both in Florence.

Brunswick (German *Braunschweig*) industrial city (chemical engineering, precision engineering, food processing) in Lower Saxony, Germany; population (1988) 248,000. It was one of the chief cities of N Germany in the Middle Ages and a member of the ◊Hanseatic League. It was capital of the duchy of Brunswick from 1671.

Brusa alternative form of ◊Bursa, a city in Turkey.

Brussels (Flemish *Brussel*, French *Bruxelles*) capital of Belgium, industrial city (lace, textiles, machinery, and chemicals); population (1987) 974,000 (80% French-speaking, the suburbs Flemish-speaking). It is the headquarters of the European Economic Community (EEC) and since 1967 of the international secretariat of ◊NATO. First settled in the 6th century, and a city from 1312, Brussels became the capital of the Spanish Netherlands 1530 and of Belgium 1830.

Brussels sprout one of the small edible buds along the stem of a variety (*Brassica oleracea* var. *gemmifera*) of ◊cabbage.

Brutus Marcus Junius *c.*78–42 BC. Roman senator and general, a supporter of ◊Pompey (against ◊Caesar) in the civil war. Pardoned by Caesar and raised to high office by him, he nevertheless plotted Caesar's assassination to restore the purity of the Republic. Brutus committed suicide when he was defeated (with ◊Cassius) by ◊Mark Antony, Caesar's lieutenant, at Philippi 42 BC.

Bryan William Jennings 1860–1925. US politician who campaigned unsuccessfully for the presidency three times: as the Populist and Democratic nominee 1896, as an anti-imperialist Democrat 1900, and as a Democratic tariff reformer 1908. He served as President Wilson's secretary of state 1913–15. In the early 1920s he was a leading fundamentalist and opponent of Clarence Darrow in the Scopes monkey trial.

He died shortly after from the strain.

bryophyte member of the Bryophyta, a division of the plant kingdom containing three classes: the Hepaticae (◊liverwort), Musci (◊moss), and Anthocerotae (◊hornwort). Bryophytes are generally small, low-growing, terrestrial plants with no vascular (water-conducting) system as in higher plants. Their life cycle shows a marked ◊alternation of generations. Bryophytes chiefly occur in damp habitats and require water for the dispersal of the male gametes (antherozoids).

bubble-jet printer in computing, an ◊ink-jet printer in which the ink is heated to boiling point so that it forms a bubble at the end of a nozzle. When the bubble bursts, the ink is transferred to the paper.

bubble memory in computing, a memory device based on the creation of small "bubbles" on a magnetic surface. Bubble memories typically store up to 4 megabits (4 million ◊bits) of information. They are not sensitive to shock and vibration, unlike other memory devices such as disk drives, yet, like magnetic disks, they are nonvolatile and do not lose their information when the computer is switched off.

bubble sort in computing, a technique for ◊sorting data. Adjacent items are continually exchanged until the data are in sequence.

bubonic plague epidemic disease of the Middle Ages; see ◊plague and ◊Black Death.

Bucaramanga industrial and commercial city (coffee, tobacco, cacao, cotton) in N central Colombia; population (1985) 493,929. It was founded by the Spanish 1622.

Bucharest (Romanian *Bucuresti*) capital and largest city of Romania; population (1985) 1,976,000, the conurbation of Bucharest district having an area of 587 sq mi/1,520 sq km and a population of 2,273,000. It was originally a citadel built by Vlad the Impaler (see ◊Dracula) to stop the advance of the Ottoman invasion in the 14th century. Bucharest became the capital of the princes of Wallachia 1698 and of

Romania 1861. Savage fighting took place in the city during Romania's 1989 revolution.

Buck Pearl S(ydenstricker) 1892–1973. US novelist. Daughter of missionaries to China, she spent much of her life there and wrote novels about Chinese life, such as *East Wind–West Wind* 1930 and *The Good Earth* 1931, for which she received a Pulitzer Prize 1932. She received the Nobel Prize for Literature 1938.
She wanted to make the East understandable to the West.

Buckinghamshire county of SE central England *area* 726 sq mi/1,880 sq km *towns and cities* Aylesbury (administrative headquarters), Buckingham, High Wycombe, Beaconsfield, Olney, Milton Keynes *features* Chiltern Hills; Chequers (country seat of the prime minister); Burnham Beeches and the church of the poet Gray's "Elegy" at Stoke Poges; Cliveden, a country house designed by Charles Barry (now a hotel, it was once the home of Nancy, Lady Astor); Bletchley Park, home of World War II code-breaking activities, now used as a training post for GCHQ (Britain's electronic surveillance center); Open University at Walton Hall; homes of the poets William Cowper at Olney and John Milton at Chalfont St Giles, and of the Tory prime minister Disraeli at Hughenden; Stowe gardens *products* furniture, chiefly beech; agricultural goods including barley, wheat, oats, sheep, cattle, poultry, pigs *population* (1991) 632,500 *famous people* John Hampden, Edmund Waller, William Herschel, George Gilbert Scott, Ben Nicholson.

buckminsterfullerene form of carbon, made up of molecules (buckyballs) consisting of 60 carbon atoms arranged in 12 pentagons and 20 hexagons to form a perfect sphere. It was named for the US architect and engineer Richard Buckminster Fuller because of its structural similarity to the geodesic dome that he designed. See ◊fullerene.

buckwheat any of several plants of the genus *Fagopyrum*, family Polygonaceae. The name usually refers to *F. esculentum*, which grows to about 3 ft/ 1 m and can grow on poor soil in a short summer. The highly nutritious black, triangular seeds (groats) are consumed by both animals and humans. They can be eaten either cooked whole or or as a cracked meal (kasha) or ground into flour, often made into pancakes.

buckyballs popular name for molecules of ◊buckminsterfullerene.

bud undeveloped shoot usually enclosed by protective scales; inside is a very short stem and numerous undeveloped leaves, or flower parts, or both. Terminal buds are found at the tips of shoots, while axillary buds develop in the axils of the leaves, often remaining dormant unless the terminal bud is removed or damaged. Adventitious buds may be produced anywhere on the plant, their formation sometimes stimulated by an injury, such as that caused by pruning.

Budapest capital of Hungary, industrial city (chemicals, textiles) on the river Danube; population (1989) 2,115,000. Buda, on the right bank of the Danube, became the Hungarian capital 1867 and was joined with Pest, on the left bank, 1872.

Buddha "enlightened one", title of Prince *Gautama Siddhartha c.*563–483 BC. Religious leader, founder of Buddhism, born at Lumbini in Nepal. At the age of 29 he left his wife and son and a life of luxury, to escape from the material burdens of existence. After six years

of austerity he realized that asceticism, like overindulgence, was futile, and chose the middle way of meditation. He became enlightened under a bo, or bodhi, tree near Buddh Gaya in Bihar, India. He began teaching at Varanasi, and founded the Sangha, or order of monks. He spent the rest of his life traveling around N India, and died at Kusinagara in Uttar Pradesh.

Buddhism one of the great world ◊religions, which originated in India about 500 BC. It derives from the teaching of the ◊Buddha, who is regarded as one of a series of such enlightened beings; there are no gods. The chief doctrine is that of ◊*karma*, good or evil deeds meeting an appropriate reward or punishment either in this life or (through ◊reincarnation) a long succession of lives. The main divisions in Buddhism are *Theravada* (or Hinayana) in SE Asia and *Mahayana* in N Asia; *Lamaism* in Tibet and *Zen* in Japan are among the many Mahayana sects. Its symbol is the lotus. There are over 247.5 million Buddhists worldwide.

buddleia any shrub or tree of the tropical genus *Buddleia*, family Buddleiaceae. The purple or white flower heads of the butterfly bush *B. davidii* attract large numbers of butterflies.

Budge Donald 1915– . US tennis player. He was the first to perform the Grand Slam when he won the Wimbledon, French, US, and Australian championships all in 1938.

CAREER HIGHLIGHTS

Wimbledon	
singles:	1937–38
doubles:	1937–38
mixed:	1937–38
US Open	
singles:	1937–38
doubles:	1936, 1938
mixed:	1937–38
French Open	
singles:	1938
Australian Open	
singles:	1938
He won 14 Grand Slam events.	

budgerigar small Australian parakeet *Melopsittacus undulatus* that feeds mainly on grass seeds. Normally it is bright green, but yellow, white, blue, and mauve varieties have been bred for the pet market.

Buenos Aires capital and industrial city of Argentina, on the south bank of the Río de la Plata; population (1991) 2,961,000, metropolitan area 7,950,400. It was founded 1536, and became the capital 1853.

buffalo The name commonly applied to the American ◊bison. It is also either of two species of wild cattle. The Asiatic water buffalo *Bubalis bubalis* is found domesticated throughout S Asia and wild in parts of India and Nepal. It likes moist conditions. Usually gray or black, up to 6 ft/1.8 m high, both sexes carry large horns. The African buffalo *Syncerus caffer* is found in Africa, south of the Sahara, where there is grass, water, and cover in which to retreat. There are a number of subspecies, the biggest up to 5 ft/1.6 m high, and black, with massive horns set close together over the head.

Buffalo industrial port in New York State at the east end of Lake Erie; population (1990) 328,100. It is linked with New York City by the New York State Barge Canal.

Grain from Buffalo's elevators is shipped overseas via the St Lawrence Seaway. An industrial city, Buffalo was hard hit by the closing of steel mills and auto factories in the late 1970s and early 1980s. The State University of New York at Buffalo and Canisius College are here. Settled in 1780, Buffalo was burned by the British during the War of 1812 but was soon rebuilt and flourished with the completion of the Erie Canal 1825.

buffer in computing, a part of the ◊memory used to store data temporarily while it is waiting to be used. For example, a program might store data in a printer buffer until the printer is ready to print it.

bug in computing, an error in a program. It can be an error in the logical structure of a program or a syntax error, such as a spelling mistake. Some bugs cause a program to fail immediately; others remain dormant, causing problems only when a particular combination of events occurs. The process of finding and removing errors from a program is called *debugging*.

bug in entomology, an insect belonging to the order Hemiptera. All these have two pairs of wings with forewings partly thickened.

They also have piercing mouthparts adapted for sucking the juices of plants or animals, the "beak" being tucked under the body when not in use.

Bugatti racing and sports-automobile company, founded by the Italian Ettore Bugatti (1881–1947). The first automobile was produced 1908, but it was not until 1924 that one of the great Bugattis, Type 35, was produced. Bugatti automobiles are credited with more race wins than any others. The company was taken over by Hispano Suiza after Bugatti's death 1947.

bugle compact valveless brass instrument with a shorter tube and less flared bell than the trumpet. Constructed of copper plated with brass, it has long been used as a military instrument for giving a range of signals based on the tones of a harmonic series. The bugle is conical whereas the trumpet is cylindrical.

Bujumbura capital of Burundi; population (1986) 272,600. Formerly called *Usumbura* (until 1962), it was founded 1899 by German colonists. The university was established 1960.

Bukhara or *Bokhara* central city in Uzbekistan; population (1987) 220,000. It is the capital of Bukhara region, which has given its name to carpets (made in Ashgabat). It is an Islamic center, with a Muslim theological training center. An ancient city in central Asia, it was formerly the capital of the independent emirate of Bukhara, annexed to Russia 1868.

Bukharest alternative form of ◊Bucharest, the capital of Romania.

Bukharin Nikolai Ivanovich 1888–1938. Soviet politician and theorist. A moderate, he was the chief Bolshevik thinker after Lenin. Executed on Stalin's orders for treason 1938, he was posthumously rehabilitated 1988.

Bulawayo industrial city and railroad junction in Zimbabwe; population (1982) 415,000. It lies at an altitude of 4,450 ft/1,355 m on the river Matsheumlope, a tributary of the Zambezi, and was founded on the site of the kraal (enclosed village), burned down 1893, of the Matabele chief, Lobenguela. It produces agricultural and electrical equipment. The former capital of Matabeleland, Bulawayo developed with the exploitation of gold mines in the neighborhood.

bulb underground bud with fleshy leaves containing a reserve food supply and with roots growing from its base. Bulbs function in vegetative reproduction and are characteristic of many monocotyledonous plants such as the daffodil, snowdrop, and onion. Bulbs are grown on a commercial scale in temperate countries.

bulbul small fruit-eating passerine bird of the family Pycnonotidae. There are about 120 species, mainly in the forests of the Old World tropics.

Bulfinch Charles 1763–1844. US architect. He became one of New England's leading architects after his design for the Massachusetts State House was accepted 1787. His designs include the Hollis Street Church, Harvard's University Hall, the Massachusetts General Hospital, and the Connecticut State House. In 1817 he was appointed architect of the US Capitol by President Monroe.

Involved in the municipal affairs of Boston, Bulfinch served on its board of selectmen 1791–1817.

Bulganin Nikolai 1895–1975. Soviet politician and military leader. His career began in 1918 when he joined the Cheka, the Soviet secret police. He helped to organize Moscow's defense in World War II, became a marshal of the USSR 1947, and was minister of defense 1947–49 and 1953–55. On the fall of Malenkov he became prime minister (chair of Council of Ministers) 1955–58 until ousted by Khrushchev.

Bulgaria Republic of (*Republika Bulgaria*) *area* 42,812 sq mi/110,912 sq km *capital* Sofia *towns and cities* Plovdiv, Ruse; Black Sea ports Burgas and Varna *physical* lowland plains in N and SE separated by mountains that cover three-quarters of the country *environment* pollution has virtually eliminated all species of fish once caught in the Black Sea. Vehicle-exhaust emissions in Sofia have led to dust concentrations more than twice the medically accepted level *features* key position on land route from Europe to Asia; Black Sea coast; Balkan and Rhodope mountains; Danube River in N *head of state* Zhelyu Zhelev from 1990 *head of government* (interim) Reneta Indjova from 1994 *political system* emergent democratic republic *political parties* Union of Democratic Forces (UDF), right of center; Bulgarian Socialist Party (BSP), left-wing, ex-communist; Movement for Rights and Freedoms (MRF), centrist; Civic Alliances for the Republic (CAR), left of center *exports* textiles, leather, chemicals, nonferrous metals, timber, machinery, tobacco, cigarettes (world's largest exporter) *currency* lev *population* (1993 est) 9,020,000 (including 900,000–1,500,000 ethnic Turks, concentrated in S and NE); growth rate 0.1% p.a. *life expectancy* men 70, women 76 *languages* Bulgarian, Turkish *media* official news agency state-controlled *religions* Eastern Orthodox Christian 90%, Sunni Muslim 10% *literacy* 93% *GNP* $1,840 per head (1991) *chronology* 1908 Bulgaria became a kingdom independent of Turkish rule. *1944* Soviet invasion of German-occupied Bulgaria. *1946* Monarchy abolished and communist-dominated people's republic proclaimed. *1947* Soviet-style constitution adopted. *1949* Death of Georgi Dimitrov, the communist government leader. *1954* Election of Todor Zhivkov as Communist Party general secretary; made nation a loyal satellite of USSR. *1971* Constitution modified; Zhivkov elected president. *1985–89* Large administrative and personnel changes made haphazardly under Soviet stimulus. *1987* New electoral law introduced multicandidate elections. *1989* Program of "Bulgarianization" resulted in mass exodus of Turks to Turkey. Nov:

Zhivkov ousted by Petar Mladenov. Dec: opposition parties allowed to form. *1990* April: BCP renamed Bulgarian Socialist Party (BSP). Aug: Dr Zhelyu Zhelev elected president. Nov: government headed by Andrei Lukanov resigned, replaced Dec by coalition led by Dimitur Popov. *1991* July: new constitution adopted. Oct: UDF beat BSP in general election by narrow margin; formation of first noncommunist, UDF-minority government under Filip Dimitrov. *1992* Zhelev became Bulgaria's first directly elected president. Dimitrov replaced by Lyuben Berov and nonparty government. *1993* Formal invitation to apply for European Community (now European Union) membership. *1994* Berov resigned due to ill-health. Parliament dissolved; Reneta Indjova appointed interim premier. General election won by BSP.

Bulgarian member of an ethnic group living mainly in Bulgaria. There are 8–8.5 million speakers of Bulgarian, a Slavic language belonging to the Indo-European family. The Bulgarians use the Cyrillic alphabet.

bulimia condition of continuous, uncontrolled overeating. Considered a manifestation of stress or depression, this eating disorder is found chiefly in young women. However, it may also arise as a result of brain damage or disease. When compensated for by forced vomiting or overdoses of laxatives, the condition is called *bulimia nervosa*. It is sometimes associated with ◊anorexia.

bull speculator who buys stocks or shares on the stock exchange expecting a rise in the price in order to sell them later at a profit, the opposite of a ◊bear. In a bull market, prices rise and bulls profit.

Bull John. Imaginary figure personifying England; see ◊John Bull.

bulletin board in computing, a center for the electronic storage of messages, usually accessed over the telephone network via ◊electronic mail and a ◊modem. Bulletin boards are usually dedicated to specific interest groups, and may carry messages, notices, and programs.

bullfighting the national sport of Spain (where there are more than 400 bullrings), which is also popular in Mexico, Portugal, and much of Latin America. It involves the ritualized taunting of a bull in a circular ring, until its eventual death at the hands of the matador. Originally popular in Greece and Rome, it was introduced into Spain by the Moors in the 11th century.

bullfinch Eurasian finch *Pyrrhula pyrrhula*, with a thick head and neck, and short heavy bill. It is small and blue-gray or black, the males being reddish and the females brown on the breast. Bullfinches are 6 in/15 cm long, and usually seen in pairs. They feed on tree buds as well as seeds and berries, and are usually seen in woodland. They also live in the Aleutians and on the Alaska mainland.

bullhead any of a North American family, Ictaluridae, of small freshwater catfish, for example, the black bullhead *Ictalurus melas*. Also, another name for the sculpin or other members of the family Cottidae.

Bull Run, Battles of in the Civil War, two victories for the Confederate army under General Robert E Lee at *Manassas* Junction, NE Virginia: *First Battle of Bull Run* July 21, 1861; *Second Battle of Bull Run* Aug 29–30, 1862. The Confederates called the engagements the first and second Battle of Manassas.

In the First Battle of Bull Run 34,000 Confederate troops routed 30,000 Union troops and challenged the North's complacent expectation of quick victory. In the Second Battle of Bull Run, Lee led 54,000 soldiers in a victory over Union forces, routing 63,000 Northern troops and opening an invasion route to the North.

Bülow Bernhard, Prince von 1849–1929. German diplomat and politician. He was chancellor of the German Empire 1900–09 under Kaiser Wilhelm II and, holding that self-interest was the only rule for any state, adopted attitudes to France and Russia that unintentionally reinforced the trend toward opposing European power groups: the ◊Triple Entente (Britain, France, Russia) and the ◊Triple Alliance (Germany, Austria–Hungary, Italy).

He resigned after losing the confidence of Emperor William II and the Reichstag.

bulrush any of a number of marsh plants (especially of the genus *Scirpus*) belonging to the ◊sedge family, having long, slender, solid stems tipped with brown spikelets of tiny flowers. Bulrushes are used in basket-making and thatching.

Bunker Hill, Battle of the first significant engagement in the ◊American Revolution, June 17, 1775, near a small hill in Charlestown (now part of Boston), Massachusetts; the battle actually took place on Breed's Hill. Although the colonists were defeated they were able to retreat to Boston and suffered fewer casualties than the British.

The failure to defeat the rebels soundly resulted in the replacement of General Thomas Gage as British commander.

Bunsen burner gas burner used in laboratories, consisting of a vertical metal tube through which a fine

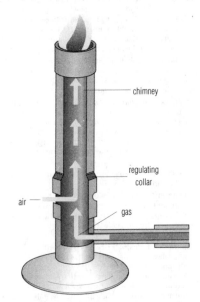

chimney

regulating collar

air

gas

Bunsen burner The Bunsen burner, used for heating laboratory equipment and chemicals. The flame can reach temperatures of 2,700 °F and is at its hottest when the collar is open.

jet of fuel gas is directed. Air is drawn in through air-holes near the base of the tube and the mixture is ignited and burns at the tube's upper opening.

bunting any of a number of sturdy, finchlike, passerine birds with short, thick bills, of the family Emberizidae, especially the genera *Passerim* and *Emberiza*. Most of these brightly colored birds are native to the New World.

Buñuel Luis 1900–1983. Spanish Surrealist film director (see ◊Surrealism). He collaborated with Salvador Dali on *Un chien andalou* 1928 and *L'Age d'or/The Golden Age* 1930, and established his solo career with *Los olvidados/The Young and the Damned* 1950. His works are often anticlerical, with black humor and erotic imagery.

Bunyan John 1628–1688. English author. A Baptist, he was imprisoned in Bedford 1660–72 for unlicensed preaching and wrote *Grace Abounding* 1666, which describes his early spiritual life. During a second jail sentence 1675 he started to write *The* ◊*Pilgrim's Progress*, the first part of which was published 1678. The fervor and imagination of this allegorical story of Christian's spiritual quest has ensured its continued popularity. Other works include *The Life and Death of Mr Badman* 1680, and *The Holy War* 1682.

bur or *burr* in botany, a type of "false fruit" or ◊pseudocarp, surrounded by numerous hooks; for instance, that of burdock *Arctium,* where the hooks are formed from bracts surrounding the flowerhead. Burs catch in the feathers or fur of passing animals, and thus may be dispersed over considerable distances.

The term is also used to include any type of fruit or seed with hooks, such as that of sandbur *Cenchrus,* a grass, and white avens *Geum canadese.*

burden of proof in court proceedings, the duty of a party to produce sufficient evidence to prove that his case is true.

In the US, the burden of proof is on the court, since the accused is presumed innocent; in many other countries, the accused is presumed guilty until cleared, thus putting the burden of proof on the defense.

burdock any of the bushy herbs belonging to the genus *Arctium* of the family Compositae, characterized by hairy leaves and ripe fruit enclosed in ◊burs with strong hooks.

bureaucracy organization whose structure and operations are governed to a high degree by written rules and a hierarchy of offices; in its broadest sense, all forms of administration, and in its narrowest, rule by officials.

Burger Warren Earl 1907– . US jurist and chief justice of the United States 1969–86. His term in the US Supreme Court was marked by a conservative turn in civil-rights matters. His majority decision in the Watergate tapes case *US v Nixon* 1974 was instrumental in bringing about Nixon's resignation.

Born in St Paul, Minnesota, Burger was educated at the University of Minnesota and was admitted to the bar 1931. President Eisenhower appointed him judge of the US Court of Appeals 1956. In 1969 Burger was named to the US Supreme Court, succeeding Chief Justice Earl Warren. Burger retired from the Court 1986 and was succeeded by William Rehnquist.

burgh former unit of Scottish local government, referring to a town enjoying a degree of self-government, abolished 1975; the terms *burgh* and *royal burgh*

once gave mercantile privilege but are now only an honorary distinction.

Burgundy ancient kingdom in the valleys of the rivers Rhône and Saône in E France and SW Germany, partly corresponding with modern-day Burgundy. Settled by the Teutonic Burgundi around AD 443, and brought under Frankish control 534, Burgundy played a central role in the medieval history of NW Europe.

Burgundy (French *Bourgogne*) modern region and former duchy of France that includes the *départements* of Côte-d'Or, Nièvre, Sâone-et-Loire, and Yonne; area 12,198 sq mi/31,600 sq km; population (1986) 1,607,000. Its capital is Dijon.

Burke Arleigh 1901– . US rear admiral. During World War II, he earned the nickname "31-knot Burke" from his aggressive patrolling policy in the South Pacific. His squadron covered the US landings at Bougainville 1944 and fought over 20 separate engagements with Japanese naval forces.

He later became Chief of Staff to Carrier Task Force 58, and was appointed to head the research and development department, in the Naval Bureau of Ordnance 1945.

Burke Edmund 1729–1797. British Whig politician and political theorist, born in Dublin, Ireland. In Parliament from 1765, he opposed the government's attempts to coerce the American colonists, for example in *Thoughts on the Present Discontents* 1770, and supported the emancipation of Ireland, but denounced the French Revolution, for example in *Reflections on the Revolution in France* 1790.

Burkina Faso The People's Democratic Republic of (formerly *Upper Volta*) *area* 105,811 sq mi/274,122 sq km *capital* Ouagadougou *towns and cities* Bobo-Dioulasso, Koudougou *physical* landlocked plateau with hills in W and SE; headwaters of the river Volta; semiarid in N, forest and farmland in S *environment* tropical savanna subject to overgrazing and deforestation *features* linked by rail to Abidjan in Ivory Coast, Burkina Faso's only outlet to the sea *head of state* Blaise Compaoré from 1987 *head of government* Roch Christian Kabore from 1994 *political system* transitional *political parties* Organization for Popular Democracy–Workers' Movement (ODP–MT), nationalist left-wing; National Convention of Progressive Patriots–Democratic Socialist Party (CNPP-PSD), left of center *exports* cotton, groundnuts, livestock, hides, skins, sesame, cereals *currency* CFA franc *population* (1993 est) 9,810,000; growth rate 2.4% p.a. *life expectancy* men 48, women 51 *languages* French (official); about 50 native Sudanic languages spoken by 90% of population *religions* animist 53%, Sunni Muslim 36%, Roman Catholic 11% *literacy* men 28%, women 9% *GNP* $350 per head (1991) *chronology 1958* Became a self-governing republic within the French Community. *1960* Independence from France, with Maurice Yaméogo as the first president. *1966* Military coup led by Col Lamizana. Constitution suspended, political activities banned, and a supreme council of the armed forces established. *1969* Ban on political activities lifted. *1970* Referendum approved a new constitution leading to a return to civilian rule. *1974* After experimenting with a mixture of military and civilian rule, Lamizana reassumed full power. *1977* Ban on political activities removed. Referendum approved a new constitution based on civilian rule. *1978* Lamizana elected president. *1980* Lamizana overthrown in bloodless coup led by Col Zerbo. *1982* Zerbo ousted in a coup by junior officers. Major

Ouédraogo became president and Thomas Sankara prime minister. *1983* Sankara seized complete power. *1984* Upper Volta renamed Burkina Faso, "land of upright men". *1987* Sankara killed in coup led by Blaise Compaoré. *1989* New government party ODP–MT formed by merger of other progovernment parties. Coup against Compaoré foiled. *1991* New constitution approved. Compaoré reelected president. *1992* Multiparty elections won by FP–Popular Front, renamed the CNPP–PSD. New government formed.

Burlington city in NW Vermont on the east shore of Lake Champlain; seat of Chittenden County; population (1990) 39,100. It is a port of entry to the US; industries include computer parts, steel, marble, lumber, dairy products, and tourism. It was a naval base during the War of 1812.

It is the site of the University of Vermont 1791.

Burlington Richard Boyle, 3rd Earl of Burlington 1694–1753. Anglo-Irish architectural patron and architect. He was one of the premier exponents of the Palladian style in Britain. His buildings are characterized by absolute adherence to the Classical rules.

Burma former name (to 1989) of ◊Myanmar.

Burman member of the largest ethnic group in Myanmar (formerly Burma). The Burmans, speakers of a Sino-Tibetan language, migrated from the hills of Tibet, settling in the areas around Mandalay by the 11th century AD.

burn in medicine, destruction of body tissue by extremes of temperature, corrosive chemicals, electricity, or radiation. *First-degree burns* may cause reddening; *second-degree burns* cause blistering and irritation but usually heal spontaneously; *third-degree burns* are disfiguring and may be life-threatening.

Burnham Forbes 1923–1985. Guyanese Marxist-Leninist politician. He was prime minister 1964–80, leading the country to independence 1966 and declaring it the world's first cooperative republic 1970. He was executive president 1980–85. Resistance to the US landing in Grenada 1983 was said to be due to his forewarning the Grenadans of the attack.

Burns Robert 1759–1796. Scottish poet. He used the Scots dialect at a time when it was not considered suitably "elevated" for literature. Burns's first volume, *Poems, Chiefly in the Scottish Dialect*, appeared 1786. In addition to his poetry, Burns wrote or adapted many songs, including "Auld Lang Syne".

Burr Raymond 1917–1993. Canadian actor. He graduated from playing assorted Hollywood villains to the heroes Perry Mason and Ironside in the long-running television series of the same names. He played the murderer in Alfred Hitchcock's *Rear Window* 1954.

His other films include *The Blue Gardenia* 1953 *The Adventures of Don Juan* 1948, and *Godzilla* (English-language version) 1956.

Burroughs Edgar Rice 1875–1950. US novelist. He wrote *Tarzan of the Apes* 1914, the story of an aristocratic child lost in the jungle and reared by apes, and followed it with over 20 more books about the Tarzan character. He also wrote a series of novels about life on Mars. He was born in Chicago.

Burroughs William S(eward) 1914– . US writer. One of the most culturally influential postwar writers, his work is noted for its experimental methods, black humor, explicit homo-eroticism, and apocalyptic vision. In 1944 he met Allen Ginsberg and Jack Kerouac, all three becoming leading members of the ◊Beat Generation. His first novel, *Junkie* 1953, documented his heroin addiction and expatriation to Mexico, where in 1951, he accidentally killed his common-law wife. He settled in Tangier 1954 and wrote his celebrated antinovel *Naked Lunch* 1959. In Paris, he developed collage-based techniques of writing, resulting in his "cut-up" science-fiction trilogy, *The Soft Machine* 1961, *The Ticket That Exploded* 1962, and *Nova Express* 1964.

He was born in St Louis, Missouri.

Bursa city in NW Turkey, with a port at Mudania; population (1990) 834,600. It was the capital of the Ottoman Empire 1326–1423.

Burton Richard Francis 1821–1890. British explorer and translator (he knew 35 oriental languages). He traveled mainly in the Middle East and NE Africa, often disguised as a Muslim; made two attempts to find the source of the Nile, 1855 and 1857–58 (on the second, with John Speke, he reached Lake Tanganyika); and wrote many travel books. He translated oriental erotica and the *Arabian Nights* 1885–88.

Burton Richard. Adopted name of Richard Jenkins 1925–1984. Welsh stage and screen actor. He had a rich, dramatic voice but his career was dogged by an often poor choice of roles. Films in which he appeared with his wife, Elizabeth ◊Taylor, include *Cleopatra* 1962 and *Who's Afraid of Virginia Woolf?* 1966. Among his later films are *Equus* 1977 and *Nineteen Eighty-Four* 1984.

Burundi Republic of (*Republika y'Uburundi*) *area* 10,744 sq mi/27,834 sq km *capital* Bujumbura *towns and cities* Gitega, Bururi, Ngozi, Muyinga *physical* landlocked grassy highland straddling watershed of Nile and Congo *features* Lake Tanganyika, Great Rift Valley *head of state* (interim) Sylvestre Ntibantunganya from 1994 *head of government* Anatole Kanyenkino from 1994 *political system* emergent democratic republic *political parties* Union for National Progress (UPRONA), nationalist socialist; Liberal Party (PL), centrist; People's Party (PP), centrist; Front for Democracy in Burundi (FRODEBU), centrist; Alliance for Rights and Development (ANDDE), left of center *exports* coffee, cotton, tea, nickel, hides, livestock, cigarettes, beer, soft drinks; there are 500 million metric tons of peat reserves in the basin of the Akanyaru River *currency* Burundi franc *population* (1993 est) 5,970,000 (of whom 15% are the Nilotic Tutsi, still holding most of the land and political power; 1% are Pygmy Twa, and the remainder Bantu Hutu); growth rate 2.8% p.a. *life expectancy* men 48, women 51 *languages* Kirundi (a

Bantu language) and French (both official), Kiswahili *religions* Roman Catholic 62%, Protestant 5%, Muslim 1%, animist 32% *literacy* men 61%, women 40% *GNP* $210 per head (1991) *chronology 1962* Separated from Ruanda-Urundi, as Burundi, and given independence as a monarchy under King Mwambutsa IV. *1966* King deposed by his son Charles, who became Ntare V; he was in turn deposed by his prime minister, Capt Michel Micombero, who declared Burundi a republic. *1972* Ntare V killed, allegedly by the Hutu ethnic group. Massacres of 150,000 Hutus by the rival Tutsi ethnic group, of which Micombero was a member. *1973* Micombero made president and prime minister. *1974* UPRONA declared the only legal political party, with the president as its secretary-general. *1976* Army coup deposed Micombero. Col Jean-Baptiste Bagaza appointed president by the Supreme Revolutionary Council. *1981* New constitution adopted, providing for a national assembly. *1984* Bagaza elected president as sole candidate. *1987* Bagaza deposed in coup. Maj Pierre Buyoya headed new Military Council for National Redemption. *1988* Some 24,000 majority Hutus killed by Tutsis. *1992* Abortive antigovernment coup; new multiparty constitution adopted. *1993* June: Melchior Ndadaye, a Hutu, elected president. Oct: Ndadye killed in military coup. Intertribal massacres followed. *1994* Jan: Cyprien Ntaryamira, a Hutu, elected president. April: Ntaryamira, with Rwandan president Juvenal Habyarimana, killed in airplane crash. Sylvestre Ntibantunganya became interim head of state. Power-sharing agreement between main political factions. *1995* Renewed ethnic violence following massacre of Hutu refugees by Tutsi militia.

bus in computing, the electrical pathway through which a computer processor communicates with some of its parts and/or peripherals. Physically, a bus is a set of parallel tracks that can carry digital signals; it may take the form of copper tracks laid down on the computer's ◊printed circuit boards (PCBs), or of an external cable or connection.

bus or *omnibus* vehicle that carries fare-paying passengers on a fixed route, with frequent stops where passengers can get on and off.

Bush George Herbert Walker 1924– . 41st president of the US 1989–93. A Republican, he was director of the Central Intelligence Agency (CIA) 1976–81 and US vice president 1981–89. In 1989, as president, he visited Eastern European countries undergoing reform, held a summit meeting at Malta with Soviet president Gorbachev, and sent US troops to Panama to oust that country's drug-trafficking president, Manuel Noriega. Bush led the UN coalition and sent US forces to Saudi Arabia to prepare for a military strike after Iraq annexed Kuwait 1990. In Jan 1991, he led the coalition war against Iraq that forced Saddam Hussein to remove his troops from Kuwait. He was instrumental in convincing Israel and several of its traditional Arab enemies to convene for a historic face-to-face meeting in Spain in Nov 1991. Domestic economic problems in 1991–92 were followed by his defeat in the 1992 presidential elections by Democrat Bill Clinton.

bushbuck antelope *Tragelaphus scriptus* found over most of Africa S of the Sahara. Up to 3 ft/1 m high, the males have keeled horns twisted into spirals, and are brown to blackish. The females are generally hornless, lighter, and redder. All have white markings, including stripes or vertical rows of dots down the sides. Rarely far from water, bushbuck live in woods and thick brush.

bushel dry measure used for grain and fruit, equal to four pecks or 32 qt/35.24 l.

bushmaster large snake *Lachesis muta*. It is a type of pit viper, and is related to the rattlesnakes. Up to 12 ft/4 m long, it is found in wooded areas of South and Central America, and is the largest venomous snake in the New World. When alarmed, it produces a noise by vibrating its tail among dry leaves.

business cycle period of time that includes a peak and trough of economic activity, as measured by a country's national income. In Keynesian economics, one of the main roles of the government is to smooth out the peaks and troughs of the business cycle by intervening in the economy, thus minimizing "overheating" and "stagnation".

bustard bird of the family Otididae, related to cranes but with a rounder body, a thicker neck, and a relatively short beak. Bustards are found on the ground on open plains and fields.

butane C_4H_{10} one of two gaseous alkanes (paraffin hydrocarbons) having the same formula but differing in structure. Normal butane is derived from natural gas; isobutane is a by-product of petroleum manufacture. Liquefied under pressure, it is used as a fuel for industrial and domestic purposes (for example, in portable cookers).

Buthelezi Chief Gatsha 1928– . South African Zulu leader and politician, president of the Zulu-based ◊Inkatha Freedom Party (IFP), which he founded as a paramilitary organization for attaining a nonracial democratic society in 1975. Buthelezi's threatened boycott of South Africa's first multiracial elections led to a dramatic escalation in factional violence, but he eventually agreed to register his party and in May 1994 was appointed home affairs minister in the country's first post-apartheid government.

Butte mining town in Montana in the Rocky Mountains; population (1990) 33,900. Butte was founded 1864 during a rush for gold, soon exhausted; copper was found some 20 years later on what was called "the richest hill on earth".

The last mine closed 1983. Butte is the seat of the Montana College of Mineral Science and Technology.

butter solid, edible yellowish fat made from whole milk. Making butter by hand, which is done by skimming off the cream and churning it, was traditionally a convenient means of preserving milk.

Salted butter has a longer shelf-life than sweet butter, salt being added as a preservative.

buttercup plant of the genus *Ranunculus* of the buttercup family with divided leaves and yellow flowers.

Species include the swamp buttercup *R. septentrionaiis* of the US.

butterfly insect belonging, like moths, to the order Lepidoptera, in which the wings are covered with tiny scales, often brightly colored. There are some 15,000 species of butterfly, many of which are under threat throughout the world due to the destruction of habitat.

butterfly fish any of several fishes, not all related. The freshwater butterfly fish *Pantodon buchholzi* of W Africa can leap from the water and glide for a short distance on its large winglike pectoral fins. Up to 4 in/ 10 cm in long, it lives in stagnant water. The tropical marine butterfly fishes, family Chaetodontidae, are brightly colored with laterally flattened bodies, often with long snouts which they poke into crevices in rocks and coral when feeding.

butterwort insectivorous plant, genus *Pinguicula*, of the bladderwort family, with purplish flowers and a rosette of flat leaves covered with a sticky secretion that traps insects.

buzzard any of a number of species of medium-sized hawks with broad wings, often seen soaring. The *common buzzard Buteo buteo* of Europe and Asia is about 1.8 ft/55 cm long with a wingspan of over 4 ft/ 1.2 m. It preys on a variety of small animals up to the size of a rabbit.

Byelorussia see ◊Belarus.

Byelorussian or *Belorussian* "White Russian" native of Belarus. Byelorussian, a Balto-Slavic language belonging to the Indo-European family, is spoken by about 10 million people, including some in Poland. It is written in the Cyrillic script. Byelorussian literature dates to the 11th century AD.

Byrd Richard Evelyn 1888–1957. US aviator and explorer. The first to fly over the North Pole (1926), he also flew over the South Pole (1929) and led five overland expeditions in Antarctica.

At the request of President Franklin D Roosevelt, he took command of the US Antarctic Service. Byrd maintained that new techniques could be used as supplements to traditional methods, rather than as replacements for them. In holding this view, he disagreed with Norwegian explorer Roald ◊Amundsen.

Byron George Gordon, 6th Baron Byron 1788–1824. English poet. He became the symbol of Romanticism and political liberalism throughout Europe in the 19th century. His reputation was established with the first two cantos of *Childe Harold* 1812. Later works include *The Prisoner of Chillon* 1816; *Beppo* 1818, *Mazeppa* 1819, and, most notably, the satirical *Don Juan* 1819–24. He left England 1816, spending most of his later life in Italy.

byte sufficient computer memory to store a single ◊character of data. The character is stored in the byte of memory as a pattern of ◊bits (binary digits), using a code such as ◊ASCII. A byte usually contains eight bits—for example, the capital letter F can be stored as the bit pattern 01000110.

Byzantine Empire the *Eastern Roman Empire* 395–1453, with its capital at Constantinople (formerly Byzantium, modern Istanbul).

Byzantine style style in the visual arts and architecture that originated in the 4th–5th centuries in Byzantium (the capital of the Eastern Roman Empire) and spread to Italy, throughout the Balkans, and to Russia, where it survived for many centuries. It is characterized by heavy stylization, strong linear emphasis, the use of rigid artistic stereotypes and rich colors such as gold. Byzantine artists excelled in mosaic work, manuscript painting, and religious ◊icon painting. In architecture, the dome supported on pendentives was in widespread use.

Byzantium (modern Istanbul) ancient Greek city on the Bosporus, founded as a colony of the Greek city of Megara on an important strategic site at the entrance to the Black Sea in about 660 BC. In AD 330 the capital of the Roman Empire was transferred there by Constantine the Great, who renamed it ◊Constantinople.

C high-level general-purpose computer-programming language popular on minicomputers and microcomputers. Developed in the early 1970s from an earlier language called BCPL, C was first used as the language of the operating system ◊Unix, though it has since become widespread beyond Unix. It is useful for writing fast and efficient systems programs, such as operating systems (which control the operations of the computer).

c. abbreviation for *circa* (Latin "about"); used with dates that are uncertain.

°C symbol for ◊Celsius (temperature scale), also called centigrade.

C++ in computing, a high-level programming language used in object-oriented applications. It is derived from the language C.

cabbage plant *Brassica oleracea* of the cress family Cruciferae, allied to the turnip and wild mustard, or charlock. It is a table vegetable, cultivated as early as 2000 BC, and the numerous commercial varieties include kale, Brussels sprouts, common cabbage, savoy, cauliflower, sprouting broccoli, and kohlrabi.

cabinet in government, a group of ministers that act as advisers to a country's executive. Cabinet members generally advise on, decide, or administer the government's policy. The US cabinet consists of the secretaries (heads) of the executive departments, appointed by the president and confirmed by the Senate. The secretaries are not members of Congress; they are advisers to the president. In the UK, the cabinet system originated under the Stuart monarchs; under William III it became customary for the king to select his ministers from the party with a parliamentary majority. The chief royal adviser was called the prime minister.

---

cabinet: US cabinet positions

Department of State
Department of the Treasury
Department of the Interior
Department of Agriculture
Department of Justice
Department of Commerce
Department of Labor
Department of Defense
Department of Housing and Urban Development
Department of Transportation
Department of Energy
Department of Education
Department of Health and Human Services
Department of Veteran Affairs

---

cable length unit of length, used on ships, originally the length of a ship's anchor cable or 120 fathoms (720 ft/219 m), but in British usage taken as one-tenth of a ◊nautical mile (608 ft/185 m).

cable television distribution of broadcast signals through cable relay systems.

Narrow-band systems were originally used to deliver services to areas with poor regular reception; systems with wider bands, using coaxial and fiberoptic cable, are increasingly used for distribution and development of home-based interactive services.

Caboto Giovanni or *John Cabot* 1450–1498. Italian navigator. Commissioned, with his three sons, by Henry VII of England to discover unknown lands, he arrived at Cape Breton Island on June 24, 1497, thus becoming the first European to reach the North American mainland (he thought he was in NE Asia). In 1498 he sailed again, touching Greenland, and probably died on the voyage.

cacao tropical American evergreen tree *Theobroma cacao* of the Sterculia family, now also cultivated in W Africa and Sri Lanka. Its seeds are cocoa beans, from which ◊cocoa and chocolate are prepared.

cacao beans see ◊cocoa and chocolate.

cache memory in computing, a reserved area of the immediate access memory used to increase the running speed of a computer program.

cactus (plural *cacti*) plant of the family Cactaceae, although the term is commonly applied to many different succulent and prickly plants. True cacti have a woody axis (central core) overlaid with an enlarged fleshy stem, which assumes various forms and is

cactus Cactus is the ancient Greek name for a prickly plant, now applied as a general term to many different succulent and prickly plants. They vary in shape and size and have no leaves, photosynthesis occurring in green stems. The lack of leaves is an adaptation for conserving water, as is the common spherical shape.

usually covered with spines (actually reduced leaves). They all have special adaptations to growing in dry areas.

CAD (acronym for *computer-aided design*) the use of computers in creating and editing design drawings. CAD also allows such things as automatic testing of designs and multiple or animated three-dimensional views of designs. CAD systems are widely used in architecture, electronics, and engineering, for example in the motor-vehicle industry, where automobiles designed with the assistance of computers are now commonplace.

A related development is ◊CAM (computer-assisted manufacturing).

caddis fly insect of the order Trichoptera. Adults are generally dull brown, mothlike, with wings covered in tiny hairs. Mouthparts are poorly developed, and many caddis flies do not feed as adults. They are usually found near water.

Cadiz Spanish city and naval base, capital and seaport of the province of Cadiz, standing on Cadiz Bay, an inlet of the Atlantic, 64 m/103 km S of Seville; population (1991) 156,600. After the discovery of the Americas 1492, Cadiz became one of Europe's most vital trade ports. The English adventurer Francis ◊Drake burned a Spanish fleet here 1587 to prevent the sailing of the ◊Armada.

cadmium soft, silver-white, ductile, and malleable metallic element, symbol Cd, atomic number 48, atomic weight 112.40. Cadmium occurs in nature as a sulfide or carbonate in zinc ores. It is a toxic metal that, because of industrial dumping, has become an environmental pollutant. It is used in batteries, electroplating, and as a constituent of alloys used for bearings with low coefficients of friction; it is also a constituent of an alloy with a very low melting point.

caecilian tropical amphibian of wormlike appearance. There are about 170 species known, forming the amphibian order Apoda (also known as Caecilia or Gymnophiona). Caecilians have a grooved skin that gives a "segmented" appearance; they have no trace of limbs, and mostly live below ground. Some species bear live young, others lay eggs.

Caedmon Earliest known English poet. According to the Northumbrian historian Bede, when Caedmon was a cowherd at the Christian monastery of Whitby, he was commanded to sing by a stranger in a dream, and on waking produced a hymn on the Creation. The poem is preserved in some manuscripts. Caedmon became a monk and may have composed other religious poems.

Caesar powerful family of ancient Rome, which included Gaius Julius Caesar, whose grand-nephew and adopted son ◊Augustus assumed the name of Caesar and passed it on to his adopted son ◊Tiberius. From then on, it was used by the successive emperors, becoming a title of the Roman rulers. The titles "czar" in Russia and "kaiser" in Germany were both derived from the name Caesar.

Caesar Gaius Julius 100–44 BC. Roman statesman and general. He formed with ◊Pompey and ◊Crassus the First Triumvirate 60 BC. He conquered Gaul 58–50 and invaded Britain 55 and 54. He fought against Pompey 49–48, defeating him at Pharsalus. After a period in Egypt Caesar returned to Rome as dictator from 46. He was assassinated by conspirators on the Ides of March 44.

Caesarean section surgical operation to deliver a baby by way of an incision in the mother's abdominal and uterine walls. It may be recommended for almost any obstetric complication implying a threat to mother or baby.

In 1992 22.6% of all deliveries in the US were by Caesarean section.

caffeine ◊alkaloid organic substance found in tea, coffee, and kola nuts; it stimulates the heart and central nervous system. When isolated, it is a bitter crystalline compound, $C_8H_{10}N_4O_2$. Too much caffeine (more than six average cups of tea or coffee a day) can be detrimental to health.

Cage John 1912–1992. US composer. His interest in Indian classical music led him to the view that the purpose of music was to change the way people listen. From 1948 he experimented with instruments, graphics, and methods of random selection in an effort to generate a music of pure incident. His ideas and collected writings, including *Silence* 1961 and *For the Birds* 1981, have profoundly influenced late 20th-century esthetics.

Cairo capital of Egypt, on the east bank of the river Nile 8 mi/13 km above the apex of the delta and 100 m/160 km from the Mediterranean; the largest city in Africa and in the Middle East; population (1985) 6,205,000; metropolitan area (1987) 13,300,000. An earthquake in a suburb of the city Oct 1992 left over 500 dead.

history El Fustat (Old Cairo) was founded by Arabs about AD 642, Al Qahira about 1000 by the ◊Fatimid ruler Gowhar. Cairo was the capital of the Ayyubid dynasty, one of whose sultans, Saladin, built the Citadel in the late 1100s.

CAL (acronym for *computer-assisted learning*) the use of computers in education and training: the computer displays instructional material to a student and asks questions about the information given; the student's answers determine the sequence of the lessons.

calamine $Zn_4Si_2O_7(OH)_2.H_2O$ native zinc silicate, an ore of zinc. The term also refers to a pink powder of zinc oxide mixed with 0.5% ferric oxide, used in lotions and ointments as a topical astringent.

Calamity Jane nickname of Martha Jane Burke *c*.1852–1903. US heroine of Deadwood, South Dakota. She worked as a teamster, transporting supplies to the mining camps, adopted male dress and, as an excellent shot, promised "calamity" to any aggressor. Many fictional accounts of the Wild West featured her exploits.

She was also known as Martha Jane Canary. During a smallpox epidemic 1878, she assisted in caring for the victims who had been abandoned by local citizens.

calceolaria plant of the *Calceolaria* figwort genus, family Scrophulariaceae, with brilliantly colored slipper-shaped flowers. Native to South America, calceolarias were introduced to Europe and the US in the 1830s.

calcite colorless, white, or light-colored common rock-forming mineral, calcium carbonate, $CaCO_3$. It is the main constituent of ◊limestone and marble and forms many types of invertebrate shell.

calcium soft, silvery-white metallic element, symbol Ca, atomic number 20, atomic weight 40.08. It is one of the ◊alkaline-earth metals. It is the fifth most abundant element (the third most abundant metal) in the Earth's crust. It is found mainly as its carbonate

$CaCO_3$, which occurs in a fairly pure condition as chalk and limestone (see ◊calcite). Calcium is an essential component of bones, teeth, shells, milk, and leaves, and it forms 1.5% of the human body by mass.

calcium carbonate $CaCO_3$ white solid, found in nature as limestone, marble, and chalk. It is a valuable resource, used in the making of iron, steel, cement, glass, slaked lime, bleaching powder, sodium carbonate and bicarbonate, and many other industrially useful substances.

calculator pocket-sized electronic computing device for performing numerical calculations. It can add, subtract, multiply, and divide; many calculators also compute squares and roots and have advanced trigonometric and statistical functions. Input is by a small keyboard and results are shown on a one-line computer screen, typically a ◊liquid-crystal display (LCD) or a light-emitting diode (LED). The first electronic calculator was manufactured by the Bell Punch Company in the US 1963.

calculus branch of mathematics that permits the manipulation of continuously varying quantities, used in practical problems involving such matters as changing speeds, problems of flight, varying stresses in the framework of a bridge, and alternating current theory. *Integral calculus* deals with the method of summation or adding together the effects of continuously varying quantities. *Differential calculus* deals in a similar way with rates of change. Many of its applications arose from the study of the gradients of the tangents to curves.

Calcutta largest city of India, on the river Hooghly, the westernmost mouth of the river Ganges, some 80 mi/130 km N of the Bay of Bengal.

It is the capital of West Bengal; population (1981) 9,166,000. It is chiefly a commercial and industrial center (engineering, shipbuilding, jute, and other textiles). Calcutta was the seat of government of British India 1773–1912. There is severe air pollution.

Calder Alexander 1898–1976. US abstract sculptor. He invented *mobiles*, suspended shapes that move in the lightest current of air. In the 1920s he began making wire sculptures and *stabiles* (static mobiles), colored abstract shapes attached by lines of wire. Huge versions adorn the Lincoln Center in New York City and UNESCO in Paris.

Calder was born in Philadelphia. An important early influence on him was the Ringling Brothers and Barnum and Bailey Circus, which inspired such works as his miniature *Circus* of wire marionettes. About 1930, his friendship with Joan ◊Miró and Piet ◊Mondrian influenced him to create abstract works. In 1943 the first retrospective of his work was exhibited at the Museum of Modern Art.

calendar division of the year into months, weeks, and days and the method of ordering the years. From year one, an assumed date of the birth of Jesus, dates are calculated backward (BC "before Christ" or BCE "before common era") and forward (AD, Latin *anno Domini* "in the year of the Lord", or CE "common era"). The *lunar month* (period between one new moon and the next) naturally averages 29.5 days, but the Western calendar uses for convenience a *calendar month* with a complete number of days, 30 or 31 (Feb has 28). For adjustments, since there are slightly fewer than six extra hours a year left over, they are added to Feb as a 29th day every fourth year (*leap year*), century years being excepted unless they are divisible by

400. For example, 1896 was a leap year; 1900 was not. 1996 is the next leap year.

Calgary city in Alberta, Canada, on the Bow River, in the foothills of the Rocky Mountains; at 3,440 ft/1,048 m it is one of the highest Canadian cities; population (1986) 671,000. It is the center of a large agricultural region and is the oil and financial center of Alberta and W Canada. The 1988 Winter Olympic Games were held here.

Cali city in SW Colombia, in the Cauca Valley 3,200 ft/975 m above sea level; population (1985) 1,398,276. Cali was founded 1536. It has textile, sugar, and engineering industries.

California Pacific-coast state of the US; nicknamed the Golden State (originally because of its gold mines, more recently because of its orange groves and sunshine) *area* 158,685 sq mi/411,100 sq km *capital* Sacramento *cities* Los Angeles, San Diego, San Francisco, San José, Fresno *physical* Sierra Nevada, including Yosemite and Sequoia national parks, Lake Tahoe, Mount Whitney (14,500 ft/4,418 m, the highest mountain in the lower 48 states); the Coast Range; Death Valley (282 ft/86 m below sea level, the lowest point in the Western hemisphere); Colorado and Mohave deserts; Monterey Peninsula; Salton Sea; the San Andreas fault; huge, offshore underwater volcanoes with tops 5 mi/8 km across *features* California Institute of Technology (Caltech); Lawrence Berkeley and Lawrence Livermore laboratories of the University of California, which share particle physics and nuclear weapons research with Los Alamos; Stanford University, which has the Hoover Institute and is the powerhouse of ◊Silicon Valley; Paul Getty art museum at Malibu, built in the style of a Roman villa; Hollywood *products* leading agricultural state with fruit (peaches, citrus, grapes in the valley of the San Joaquin and Sacramento rivers), nuts, wheat, vegetables, cotton, and rice, all mostly grown by irrigation, the water being carried by immense concrete-lined canals to the Central and Imperial valleys; beef cattle; timber; fish; oil; natural gas; aerospace technology; electronics (Silicon Valley); food processing; films and television programs; great reserves of energy (geothermal) in the hot water that lies beneath much of the state *population* (1990) 29,760,000, the most populous state of the US (69.9% white; 25.8% Hispanic; 9.6% Asian and Pacific islander, including many Vietnamese, 7.4% black; 0.8% American Indian) *famous people* Luther Burbank, Walt Disney, William Randolph Hearst, Jack London, Marilyn Monroe, Richard Nixon, Ronald Reagan, John Steinbeck *history* colonized by Spain 1769; ceded to the US after the Mexican War 1848; became a state 1850. The discovery of gold in the Sierra Nevada Jan 1848 was followed by the gold rush 1849–56.

The completion of the first transcontinental railroad 1869 fostered economic development. The Los Angeles area flourished with the growth of the film industry after 1910, oil discoveries in the early 1920s, and the development of aircraft plants and shipyards during World War II. Some 100,000 Californians of Japanese ancestry were interned during the war. California became the nation's most populous state in 1962. Northern California benefited from the growth of the electronics industry from the 1970s in what came to be called Silicon Valley. The state's economy suffered during the early 1990s as the defense industries declined. Devastating earthquakes occurred in the San Francisco Bay area 1989 and the San Fernando Valley–Los Angeles area 1993.

californium synthesized, radioactive, metallic element of the actinide series, symbol Cf, atomic number 98, atomic weight 251. It is produced in very small quantities and used in nuclear reactors as a neutron source. The longest-lived isotope, Cf-251, has a half-life of 800 years.

Caligula (Gaius Caesar) AD 12–41. Roman emperor, son of Germanicus and successor to Tiberius AD 37. Caligula was a cruel tyrant and was assassinated by an officer of his guard. He is believed to have been mentally unstable.

calipers instrument used for measuring the thickness or diameter of objects—for example, the internal and external diameter of pipes. Some calipers are made like a drawing compass, having two legs, often curved, pivoting about a screw at one end. The ends of the legs are placed in contact with the object to be measured, and the gap between the ends is then measured against a rule. The slide caliper looks like an adjustable wrench, and carries a scale for direct measuring, usually with a vernier scale for accuracy.

caliph title of civic and religious heads of the world of Islam. The first caliph was Abu Bakr. Nominally elective, the office became hereditary, held by the Umayyad dynasty 661–750 and then by the ◊Abbasid dynasty. After the death of the last Abbasid (1258), the title was claimed by a number of Muslim chieftains in Egypt, Turkey, and India. The most powerful of these were the Turkish sultans of the Ottoman Empire.

Callas Maria. Adopted name of Maria Kalogeropoulos 1923–1977. US lyric soprano. She was born in New York of Greek parents. With a voice of fine range and a gift for dramatic expression, she excelled in operas including *Norma, La Sonnambula, Madame Butterfly, Aïda, Tosca,* and *Medea.*

calligraphy art of handwriting, regarded in China and Japan as the greatest of the visual arts, and playing a large part in Islamic art because the depiction of the human and animal form is forbidden.

Printing and the typewriter reduced the need for calligraphy in the West until the 20th-century revival inspired by Edward Johnston (1872–1944).

calorie c.g.s. unit of heat, now replaced by the ◊joule (one calorie is approximately 4.2 joules). It is the heat required to raise the temperature of one gram of water by 1°C. In dietetics, the Calorie or kilocalorie is equal to 1,000 calories.

Calvin John (also known as *Cauvin* or *Chauvin*) 1509–1564. French-born Swiss Protestant church reformer and theologian. He was a leader of the Reformation in Geneva and set up a strict religious community there. His theological system is known as Calvinism, and his church government as ◊Presbyterianism. Calvin wrote (in Latin) *Institutes of the Christian Religion* 1536 and commentaries on the New Testament and much of the Old Testament.

Calvinism Christian doctrine as interpreted by John Calvin and adopted in Scotland, parts of Switzerland, and the Netherlands; by the ◊Puritans in England and New England, US; and by the subsequent Congregational and Presbyterian churches in the US. Its central doctrine is predestination, under which certain souls (the elect) are predestined by God through the sacrifice of Jesus to salvation, and the rest to damnation. Although Calvinism is rarely accepted today in its strictest interpretation, the 20th century has seen a Neo-Calvinist revival through the work of Karl Barth.

calypso West Indian satirical ballad with a syncopated beat. Calypso is a traditional song form of Trinidad, a feature of its annual carnival, with roots in W African praise singing. It was first popularized in the US by Harry Belafonte (1927–) in 1956. Mighty Sparrow (1935–) is Trinidad's best-known calypso singer.

calyx the collective term for the ◊sepals of a flower, forming the outermost whorl of the perianth. It surrounds the other flower parts and protects them while in bud. In some flowers, for example, the catchflies *Silene* of the pink family, the sepals are fused along their sides, forming a sticky tubular calyx.

cam part of a machine that converts circular motion to linear motion or vice versa. The *edge cam* in an automobile engine is in the form of a rounded projection on a shaft, the camshaft. When the camshaft turns, the cams press against linkages (plungers or followers) that open the valves in the cylinders.

CAM (acronym for *computer-aided manufacturing*) the use of computers to control production processes; in particular, the control of machine tools and ◊robots in factories. In some factories, the whole design and production system has been automated by linking ◊CAD (computer-aided design) to CAM.

cambium in botany, a layer of actively dividing cells (lateral meristem), found within stems and roots, that gives rise to secondary growth in perennial plants, causing an increase in girth. There are two main types of cambium: *vascular cambium*, which gives rise to secondary ◊xylem and ◊phloem tissues, and *cork cambium* (or phellogen), which gives rise to secondary cortex and cork tissues (see ◊bark).

Cambodia (formerly *Khmer Republic* 1970–76, *Democratic Kampuchea* 1976–79, and *People's Republic of Kampuchea* 1979–89) country in SE Asia, bounded N and NW by Thailand, N by Laos, E and SE by Vietnam, and SW by the Gulf of Thailand. *area* 69,880 sq mi/181,035 sq km *capital* Phnom Penh *towns and cities* Battambang, the seaport Kompong Som *physical* mostly flat forested plains with mountains in SW and N; Mekong River runs N–S *environment* infrastructure destroyed during the war, which

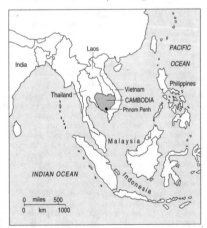

left 4–7 million land mines *features* ruins of ancient capital Angkor; Lake Tonle Sap *head of state* Prince Norodom Sihanouk from 1991 *head of government* Prince Norodom Ranariddh from 1993 *political system* limited constitutional monarchy *political parties* Cambodian People's Party (CPP), reform socialist (formerly the communist Kampuchean People's Revolutionary Party [KPRP]); Party of Democratic Kampuchea (Khmer Rouge), ultranationalist communist; Khmer People's National Liberation Front (KPNLF), anticommunist; United Front for an Independent, Neutral, Peaceful, and Cooperative Cambodia (FUNCINPEC), moderate, centrist *exports* rubber, rice, pepper, wood, cattle *currency* Cambodian riel *population* (1993) 12,000,000; growth rate 2.2% p.a. *life expectancy* men 50, women 52 *languages* Khmer (official), French *media* criticizing the king is prohibited *religion* Theravada Buddhist 95% *literacy* men 48%, women 22% *GNP* $200 per head (1991) *chronology 1863–1941* French protectorate. *1941–45* Occupied by Japan. *1946* Recaptured by France. *1953* Independence achieved from France. *1970* Prince Sihanouk overthrown by US-backed Lon Nol. *1975* Lon Nol overthrown by Khmer Rouge. *1976–78* Khmer Rouge introduced an extreme communist program, forcing urban groups into rural areas and bringing over 2.5 million deaths from famine, disease, and maltreatment. *1978–79* Vietnamese invasion and installation of Heng Samrin government. *1982* The three main anti-Vietnamese resistance groups formed an alliance under Prince Sihanouk. *1987* Vietnamese troop withdrawal began. *1989* Sept: completion of Vietnamese withdrawal. *1990* Nov: United Nations (UN) peace proposal rejected by Phnom Penh government. *1991* Oct: Peace agreement signed in Paris, providing for a UN Transitional Authority in Cambodia (UNTAC) to administer country in conjunction with all-party Supreme National Council; communism abandoned. Nov: Sihanouk returned. *1992* Political prisoners released; freedom of speech and party formation restored. Oct: Khmer Rouge refused to disarm in accordance with peace process. *1993* Free annual elections (boycotted by Khmer Rouge) resulted in surprise win by FUNCINPEC. New constitution adopted. Sihanouk reinstated as constitutional monarch. Prince Norodom Ranariddh, FUNCINPEC leader, appointed executive prime minister. Khmer Rouge continued fighting.

Cambrian period of geological time 570–510 million years ago; the first period of the Paleozoic era. All invertebrate animal life appeared, and marine algae were widespread. The earliest fossils with hard shells, such as trilobites, date from this period.

Cambridge city in England, on the river Cam (a river sometimes called by its earlier name, Granta), 50 mi/80 km N of London; population (1991) 91,900. It is the administrative headquarters of Cambridgeshire. The city is centered on Cambridge University (founded 12th century), some of whose outstanding buildings, including Kings College Chapel, back onto the river. Present-day industries include the manufacture of scientific instruments, radios, electronics, paper, flour milling, fertilizers, printing, and publishing.

Cambridgeshire county of E England *area* 1,316 sq mi/3,410 sq km *towns and cities* Cambridge (administrative headquarters), Ely, Huntingdon, Peterborough *features* fens; flat with very fertile, fenland soil; rivers: Ouse, Cam, Nene; Isle of Ely; Cambridge University; at Molesworth, a Royal Air Force base near Huntingdon, Britain's second cruise missile base was deactivated Jan 1989 *products* mainly agricultural, including cereals, fruit and vegetables; industries include electronics, food processing, and mechanical engineering *population* (1991) 645,100 *famous people* Oliver Cromwell, Octavia Hill, John Maynard Keynes.

camel large cud-chewing mammal of the even-toed hoofed order Artiodactyla. Unlike typical ruminants, it has a three-chambered stomach. It has two toes which have broad soft soles for walking on sand, and hooves resembling nails. There are two species, the single-humped *Arabian camel Camelus dromedarius* and the twin-humped *Bactrian camel C. bactrianus* from Asia. They carry a food reserve of fatty tissue in the hump, can go without drinking for long periods, can feed on salty vegetation, and withstand extremes of heat and cold, thus being well adapted to desert conditions.

camellia any oriental evergreen shrub with roselike flowers of the genus *Camellia*, tea family Theaceae. Numerous species, including *C. japonica* and *C. reticulata,* have been introduced into Europe, the US, and Australia.

camera apparatus used in ◊photography, consisting of a lens system set in a light-proof box inside of which a sensitized film or plate can be placed. The lens collects rays of light reflected from the subject and brings them together as a sharp image on the film; it has marked numbers known as ◊apertures, or f-stops, that reduce or increase the amount of light. Apertures also control depth of field. A shutter controls the amount of time light has to affect the film. There are small-, medium-, and large-format cameras; the format refers to the size of recorded image and the dimensions of the print obtained.

camera obscura darkened box with a tiny hole for projecting the inverted image of the scene outside on to a screen inside. For its development as a device for producing photographs, see ◊photography.

Cameroon Republic of (*République du Cameroun*) *area* 183,638 sq mi/475,440 sq km *capital* Yaoundé *towns and cities* chief port Douala; Nkongsamba, Garova *physical* desert in far north in the Lake Chad basin, mountains in W, dry savanna plateau in the intermediate area, and dense tropical rainforest in S *environment* the Korup National Park preserves 500 sq mi/1,300 sq km of Africa's fast-disappearing tropical rainforest. Scientists have identified nearly 100 potentially useful chemical substances produced naturally by the plants of this forest *features* Mount Cameroon 13,358 ft/4,070 m, an active volcano on the coast, W of the Adamawa Mountains *head of state* Paul Biya from 1982 *head of government* Simon Achidi Achu from 1992 *political system* emergent democratic republic *political parties* Democratic Assembly of the Cameroon People (RDPC), nationalist, left of center; National Union for Democracy and Progress (UNDP), center-left; Movement for the Defense of the Republic (MDR), left of center; Union of the Peoples of Cameroon (UPC), left of center *exports* cocoa, coffee, bananas, cotton, timber, rubber, groundnuts, gold, aluminum, crude oil *currency* CFA franc *population* (1993 est) 12,800,000; growth rate 2.7% p.a. *life expectancy* men 54, women 57 *languages* French and English in pidgin variations (official); there has been some discontent with the emphasis on French—there are 163 indigenous peoples with their own African languages *media* heavy government censorship *religions* Roman Catholic 35%, animist 25%, Muslim 22%, Protestant 18% *literacy* men 66%, women 43% *GNP* $940 per head (1991) *chronology 1884* Treaty signed establishing German rule. *1916* Captured by Allied forces in World War I. *1922* Divided between Britain and France. *1946* French Cameroon and British Cameroons made UN trust territories. *1960* French Cameroon became the independent Republic of Cameroon. Ahmadou Ahidjo elected president. *1961* Northern part of British Cameroon merged with Nigeria and southern part joined the Republic of Cameroon to become the Federal Republic of Cameroon. *1966* One-party regime introduced. *1972* New constitution made Cameroon a unitary state, the (United) Republic of Cameroon. *1973* New national assembly elected. *1982* Ahidjo resigned; succeeded by Paul Biya. *1983* Biya began to remove his predecessor's supporters; accused by Ahidjo of trying to create a police state. Ahidjo went into exile in France. *1984* Biya reelected; defeated a plot to overthrow him. Country's name changed to Republic of Cameroon. *1988* Biya reelected. *1990* Widespread public disorder. Biya granted amnesty to political prisoners. *1991* Constitutional changes made. *1992* Ruling RDPC won in first multiparty elections in 28 years. Biya's presidential victory challenged by opposition. *1993* Opposition leaders demanded constitutional reforms.

camouflage colors or structures that allow an animal to blend with its surroundings to avoid detection by other animals. Camouflage can take the form of matching the background color, of countershading (darker on top, lighter below, to counteract natural shadows), or of irregular patterns that break up the outline of the animal's body. More elaborate camouflage involves closely resembling a feature of the natural environment, as with the stick insect; this is closely akin to mimicry. Camouflage is also important as a military technique, disguising either equipment, troops, or a position in order to conceal them from an enemy.

campanile originally a bell tower erected near, or attached to, a church or town hall in Italy. The leaning tower of Pisa is an example; another is the great campanile of Florence, 90 m/275 ft high.

They were used as components of 19th-century American factory architecture in New England.

Camp David official country home of US presidents, situated in the Appalachian mountains, Maryland; it was originally named Shangri-la by Franklin D Roosevelt, but was renamed Camp David by Eisenhower (after his grandson).

It was briefly known (for security reasons) as Camp Number Four after the Kennedy assassination. It is guarded by Marines, and consists of a series of lodges, Aspen Lodge being the presidential residence. It was the site of talks held by President Carter to bring about an Egypt-Israel peace accord.

camphor $C_{10}H_{16}O$ volatile, aromatic ◊ketone substance obtained from the camphor tree *Cinnamomum camphora*. It is distilled from chips of the wood, and is used in insect repellents and medicinal inhalants and liniments, and in the manufacture of celluloid.

campion several plants of the genera *Lychnis* and *Silene*, belonging to the pink family (Caryophyllaceae), which include the garden campion *L. coronaria*, introduced from Europe, and the catchflies (genus *Silene*) of E North America.

Camus Albert 1913–1960. Algerian-born French writer. A journalist in France, he was active in the Resistance during World War II. His novels, which owe much to ◊existentialism, include *L'Etranger/The Outsider* 1942, *La Peste/The Plague* 1948, and *L'Homme révolté/The Rebel* 1952. Nobel Prize for Literature 1957.

Canaan ancient region between the Mediterranean and the Dead Sea, called in the Bible the "Promised Land" of the Israelites. It was occupied as early as the 3rd millennium BC by the Canaanites, a Semitic-speaking people who were known to the Greeks of the 1st millennium BC as Phoenicians. The capital was Ebla (now Tell Mardikh, Syria).

Canada area 3,849,674 sq mi/9,970,610 sq km *capital* Ottawa *towns and cities* Toronto, Monteral, Vancouver, Edmonton, Calgary, Winnipeg, Quebec, Hamilton, Saskatoon, Halifax *physical* mountains in W, with low-lying plains in interior and rolling hills in E. Climate varies from temperate in S to arctic in N *environment* sugar maples are dying in E Canada as a result of increasing soil acidification; nine rivers in Nova Scotia are now too acid to support salmon or trout reproduction *features* St Lawrence Seaway, Mackenzie River; Great Lakes; Arctic Archipelago; Rocky Mountains; Great Plains or Prairies; Canadian Shield; Niagara Falls; the world's second largest country *head of state* Elizabeth II from 1952, represented by governor general Ramon John Hnatyshyn from 1990 *head of government* Jean Chretien from 1993 *political system* federal constitutional monarchy *political parties* Progressive Conservative Party, free-enterprise, right of center; Liberal Party, nationalist, centrist; New Democratic Party (NDP), moderate left of center; Bloc Quebecois, Quebec-based, separatist *exports* wheat, timber, pulp, newsprint, fish (salmon), furs (ranched fox and mink exceed the value of wild furs), oil, natural gas, aluminum, asbestos (world's second largest producer), coal, copper, iron, zinc, nickel (world's largest producer), uranium (world's largest producer), motor vehicles and parts, industrial and agricultural machinery, fertilizers, chemicals *currency* Canadian dollar *population* (1993 est) 28,100,000—including 300,000 North American Indians, of whom 75% live on more than 2,000 reservations in Ontario and the four Western provinces; some 300,000 Métis

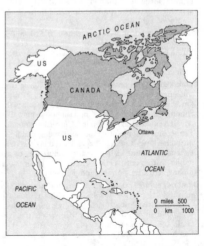

112

Canada: history

c. 35,000BC	People arrived in North America from Asia by way of Beringia.
c. 2000BC	Inuit (Eskimos) began settling Arctic coast from Siberia E to Greenland.
c.AD 1000	Vikings, including Leif Ericsson, landed in NE Canada, and started settlements that did not survive.
1497	John Cabot landed on Cape Breton Island.
1534	Jacques Cartier reached the Gulf of St. Lawrence.
1603	Samuel Champlain began his exploration of Canada.
1608	Champlain founded Québec.
1759	James Wolfe captured Québec.
1763	France ceded Canada to Britain under the Treaty of Paris.
1775–83	American Revolution caused Loyalist influx to New Brunswick and Ontario.
1791	Canada divided into English-speaking Upper Canada (much of modern Ontario) and French-speaking Lower Canada (much of modern Québec and mainland Newfoundland).
1793	Alexander Mackenzie reached the Pacific by land.
1812–14	War of 1812 between Britain and the US. US invasions repelled by both provinces.
1837	Rebellions led by William Lyon Mackenzie in Upper Canada and Louis Joseph Papineau in Lower Canada.
1840	Upper and Lower Canada united to form the Province of Canada.
1867	British North America Act created the Dominion of Canada (Ontario, Québec, Nova Scotia, and New Brunswick).
1869	Uprising, led by Louis Riel, against the Canadian government and the threat of a flood of white settlers into Rupert's Land.
1870	Manitoba created (from part of Rupert's Land) and joined confederation. North West (later Northwest) Territories created.
1871	British Columbia entered confederation.
1873	Prince Edward Island entered confederation.
1885	Northwest Rebellion crushed and leader Louis Riel hanged. Canadian Pacific Railroad completed.
1905	Alberta and Saskatchewan formed from the Northwest Territories and entered confederation.
1914–18	World War I—Canadian troops at 2nd Battle of Ypres, Vimy Ridge, Passchendaele, the Somme, and Cambrai.
1931	Canada became an independent nation. Norway renounced its claim to the Sverdrup Islands, confirming Canadian sovereignty in the entire Arctic Archipelago north of the Canadian mainland.
1939–45	World War II—Canadian participation in all theaters.
1949	Newfoundland joined the confederation.
1950–53	Korean War—Canada participated in United Nations force, and subsequently in almost all UN peacekeeping operations.

(people of mixed race) and 32,000 (1991) Inuit of whom 75% live in the Northwest Territories. Over half Canada's population lives in Ontario and Québec. Growth rate 1.1% p.a. *life expectancy* men 74, women 81 *languages* English, French (both official; about 70% speak English, 20% French, and the rest are bilingual); there are also North American Indian languages and the Inuit Inuktitut *religion* Roman Catholic 46%, Protestant 35% *literacy* 99% *GNP* $21,260 per head (1991) *chronology 1867* Dominion of Canada founded. *1949* Newfoundland joined Canada. *1957* Progressive Conservatives returned to power after 22 years in opposition. *1961* NDP formed. *1963* Liberals elected under Lester Pearson. *1968* Pearson succeeded by Pierre Trudeau. *1979* Joe Clark, leader of the Progressive Conservatives, formed a minority government; defeated on budget proposals. *1980* Liberals under Trudeau returned with a large majority. Québec referendum rejected demand for independence. *1982* Canada Act removed Britain's last legal control over Canadian affairs; "patriation" of Canada's constitution. *1983* Clark succeeded as leader of the Progressive Conservatives by Brian Mulroney. *1984* Trudeau retired and was succeeded as Liberal leader and prime minister by John Turner. Progressive Conservatives won the federal election with a large majority, and Mulroney became prime minister. *1988* Conservatives reelected with reduced majority on platform of free trade with the US. *1989* Free-trade agreement signed. Turner resigned as Liberal Party leader, and Ed Broadbent as NDP leader. *1990* Collapse of Meech Lake accord. Canada joined the coalition opposing Iraq's invasion of Kuwait. *1992* Gradual withdrawal of Canadian forces in Europe announced. Self-governing homeland for Inuit approved. Constitutional reform package, the Charlottetown Accord, rejected in national referendum. *1993* Feb: Mulroney resigned leadership of Conservative Party. June: Kim Campbell, the new party leader, became prime minister. Oct: Conservatives defeated in general election. Liberal leader Jean Chretien became prime minister. Dec: Kim Campbell resigned Conservative Party leadership.

canal artificial waterway constructed for drainage, irrigation, or navigation. *Irrigation canals* carry water for irrigation from rivers, reservoirs, or wells, and are designed to maintain an even flow of water over the whole length. *Navigation and ship canals* are constructed at one level between φlocks, and frequently link with rivers or sea inlets to form a waterway system. The Suez Canal 1869 and the Panama Canal 1914 eliminated long trips around continents and dramatically shortened shipping routes.

Irrigation canals, dug from ancient times, provided flood control as well as neolithic farming villages with an expanded area of rich alluvial soil, especially in the Tigris-Euphrates valley and along the Nile, where agricultural surpluses eventually allowed for the rise of civilizations. Navigation canals developed after irrigation and drainage canals; often they link two waterways and were at first level and shallow. Soon, those with inclined planes had towpaths along which men and animals towed vessels from one level to the next. Locks were invented to allow passage where great variations in level exist. By the 20th century mechanized tows and self-propelled barges were in use.

canary bird *Serinus canaria* of the finch family, found wild in the Canary Islands and Madeira. It is greenish with a yellow underside.

Canaries have been bred as cage birds in Europe since the 15th century, and many domestic varieties are yellow or orange.

Canary Islands (Spanish *Canarias*) group of volcanic islands 60 mi/100 km off the NW coast of Africa, forming the Spanish provinces of Las Palmas and Santa Cruz de Tenerife; area 2,818 sq mi/7,300 sq km; population (1986) 1,615,000. *features* The chief centers are Santa Cruz on Tenerife (which also has the highest peak in extracontinental Spain, Pico de Teide, 12,186 ft/3,713 m), and Las Palmas on Gran Canaria. The province of Santa Cruz comprises Tenerife, Palma, Gomera, and Hierro; the province of Las Palmas comprises Gran Canaria, Lanzarote, and Fuerteventura. There are also six uninhabited islets. The Northern Hemisphere Observatory (1981) is on the island of La Palma. Observation conditions are exceptionally good because there is no moisture, no artificial light pollution, and little natural airglow.

The Organization of African Unity (OAU) supports an independent Guanch Republic and revival of the Guanch language.

Canberra capital of Australia (since 1908), situated in the Australian Capital Territory, enclosed within New South Wales, on a tributary of the Murrumbidgee River; area (Australian Capital Territory including the port at Jervis Bay) 2,432 sq km/939 sq mi; population (1988) 297,300.

cancer group of diseases characterized by abnormal proliferation of cells.

Cancer (malignant) cells are usually degenerate, capable only of reproducing themselves (tumor formation). Malignant cells tend to spread from their site of origin by traveling through the bloodstream or lymphatic system.

Cancer faintest of the zodiacal constellations (its brightest stars are fourth magnitude). It lies in the Northern hemisphere, between Leo and Gemini, and is represented as a crab. Cancer's most distinctive feature is the star cluster Praesepe, popularly known as the Beehive. The Sun passes through the constellation during late July and early Aug. In astrology, the dates for Cancer are between about June 22 and July 22 (see ◊precession).

candela SI unit (symbol cd) of luminous intensity, which replaced the old units of candle and standard candle. It measures the brightness of a light itself rather than the amount of light falling on an object, which is called *illuminance* and measured in ◊lux.

candy confectionery made mainly from sucrose sugar. Other ingredients include glucose, milk, nuts, fat (animal and vegetable), and fruit. Boiled-sugar candy contains sugar, glucose, color, and flavoring, and is boiled, cooled, and shaped. *Chewing gum* consists of synthetic or vegetable gum with color, flavoring, and sometimes sweetener added. *Toffee* and *caramel* are made from sugar, glucose, animal fat, milk, and cream

or vegetable fat, heated and shaped. The US is the biggest producer of candy, though the UK has the highest consumption, with millions of pounds spent each year on advertising.

cane reedlike stem of various plants such as the sugar cane, bamboo, and, in particular, the group of palms called rattans, consisting of the genus *Calamus* and its allies. Their slender stems are dried and used for making walking sticks, baskets, and furniture.

Canetti Elias 1905–   . Bulgarian-born writer. He was exiled from Austria as a Jew 1938 and settled in England 1939. His books, written in German, include *Die Blendung/Auto da Fé* 1935. Nobel Prize for Literature 1981.

canning food preservation in hermetically sealed containers by the application of heat. Originated by Nicolas Appert in France 1809 with glass containers, it was developed by Peter Durand in England 1810 with cans made of sheet steel thinly coated with tin to delay corrosion. Cans for beer and soft drinks are now generally made of aluminum.

canoeing sport of propelling a lightweight, shallow boat, pointed at both ends, by paddles or sails. Currently, canoes are made from fiberglass, but original boats were of wooden construction covered in bark or skin. Canoeing was popularized as a sport in the 19th century.

canon law rules and regulations of the Christian church, especially the Greek Orthodox, Roman Catholic, and Anglican churches. Its origin is sought in the declarations of Jesus and the apostles. In 1983 Pope John Paul II issued a new canon law code reducing offenses carrying automatic excommunication, extending the grounds for annulment of marriage, removing the ban on marriage with non-Catholics, and banning labor union and political activity by priests.

Canopus or *Alpha Carinae* second brightest star in the sky (after Sirius), lying in the constellation Carina. It is a yellow-white supergiant about 120 light-years from Earth, and thousands of times more luminous than the Sun.

Canova Antonio 1757–1822. Italian Neo-Classical sculptor. He was based in Rome from 1781. He received commissions from popes, kings, and emperors for his highly finished marble portrait busts and groups of figures. He made several portraits of Napoleon.

Canova was born near Treviso. His reclining marble *Pauline Borghese as Venus* 1805–07 (Borghese Gallery, Rome) is a fine example of his cool, polished Classicism. He executed the tombs of popes Clement XIII, Pius VII, and Clement XIV. His marble sculptures include *Cupid and Psyche* 1793 (Louvre, Paris) and *The Three Graces* (Victoria and Albert Museum, London).

cantata in music, an extended work for voices, from the Italian, meaning "sung", as opposed to ◊sonata ("sounded") for instruments. A cantata can be sacred or secular, sometimes uses solo voices, and usually has orchestral accompaniment. The first printed collection of sacred cantata texts dates from 1670.

Canterbury historic cathedral city in Kent, England, on the river Stour, 62 mi/100 km SE of London; population (1981) 39,000. In 597 King Ethelbert welcomed ◊Augustine's mission to England here, and the city has since been the metropolis of the Anglican Communion and seat of the archbishop of

Canterbury. It is a tourist and shopping center.

Canterbury, archbishop of primate of all England, archbishop of the Church of England (Anglican), and first peer of the realm, ranking next to royalty. He crowns the sovereign, has a seat in the House of Lords, and is a member of the Privy Council. He is appointed by the prime minister.

cantilever beam or structure that is fixed at one end only, though it may be supported at some point along its length; for example, a diving board. The cantilever principle, widely used in construction engineering, eliminates the need for a second main support at the free end of the beam, allowing for more elegant structures and reducing the amount of materials required. Many large-span bridges have been built on the cantilever principle.

Canton alternative spelling of Kwangchow or ◊Guangzhou, a city in China.

Canute c. 995–1035. King of England from 1016, Denmark from 1018, and Norway from 1028. Having invaded England 1013 with his father, Sweyn, king of Denmark, he was acclaimed king on his father's death 1014 by his ◊Viking army. Canute defeated ◊Edmund (II) Ironside at Assandun, Essex, 1016, and became king of all England on Edmund's death. He succeeded his brother Harold as king of Denmark 1018, compelled King Malcolm to pay homage by invading Scotland about 1027, and conquered Norway 1028. He was succeeded by his illegitimate son Harold I.

capacitor or *condenser* device for storing electric charge, used in electronic circuits; it consists of two or more metal plates separated by an insulating layer called a dielectric.

Cape Canaveral promontory on the Atlantic coast of Florida 228 mi/367 km N of Miami, used as a rocket launch site by ◊NASA.

It was known 1963–73 as Cape Kennedy, to honor President John F Kennedy after his assassination. The ◊Kennedy Space Center is nearby.

Cape Cod hook-shaped peninsula in SE Massachusetts 60 mi/100 km long and 1–20 mi/1.6–32 km wide. Its beaches and woods make it a popular tourist area. It is separated from the rest of the state by the Cape Cod Canal. The islands of Martha's Vineyard and Nantucket are just S of the cape.

Cape Horn southernmost point of South America, in the Chilean part of the archipelago of ◊Tierra del Fuego; notorious for gales and heavy seas. It was named 1616 by Dutch explorer Willem Schouten (1580–1625) after his birthplace (Hoorn).

Capella or *Alpha Aurigae* brightest star in the constellation Auriga and the sixth brightest star in the sky. It consists of a pair of yellow giant stars 41 light-years from Earth, orbiting each other every 104 days.

Cape of Good Hope South African headland forming a peninsula between Table Bay and False Bay, Cape Town. The first European to sail around it was Bartholomew Diaz 1488. Formerly named Cape of Storms, it was given its present name by King John II of Portugal.

Capet Hugh 938–996. King of France from 987, when he claimed the throne on the death of Louis V. He founded the *Capetian dynasty*, of which various branches continued to reign until the French Revolution, for example, Valois and ◊Bourbon.

Cape Town (Afrikaans *Kaapstad*) port and oldest city (founded 1652) in South Africa, situated in the SW on

Table Bay; population (1985) 776,617. Industries include horticulture and trade in wool, wine, fruit, grain, and oil. It is the legislative capital of the Republic of South Africa and capital of Cape Province.

Cape Verde Republic of (*República de Cabo Verde*) *area* 1,557 sq mi/4,033 sq km *capital* Praia *towns and cities* Mindelo, Sal-Rei, Porto Novo *physical* archipelago of ten volcanic islands 350 mi/565 km W of Senegal; the windward (Barlavento) group includes Santo Antão, São Vicente, Santa Luzia, São Nicolau, Sal, and Boa Vista; the leeward (Sotovento) group comprises Maio, São Tiago, Fogo, and Brava; all but Santa Luzia are inhabited *features* strategic importance guaranteed by its domination of western shipping lanes; Sal, Boa Vista, and Maio lack water supplies but have fine beaches *head of state* Monteiro Mascarenhas from 1991 *head of government* Carlos Viega from 1991 *political system* socialist pluralist state *political parties* African Party for the Independence of Cape Verde (PAICV), African nationalist; Movement for Democracy (MPD) *exports* bananas, salt, fish *currency* Cape Verde escudo *population* (1993) 350,000 (including 100,000 Angolan refugees); growth rate 1.9% p.a. *life expectancy* men 67, women 69 *language* Creole dialect of Portuguese *religion* Roman Catholic 80% *literacy* 53% *GNP* $750 per head (1991) *chronology 15th century* First settled by Portuguese. *1951–74* Ruled as an overseas territory by Portugal. *1974* Moved toward independence through a transitional Portuguese–Cape Verde government. *1975* Independence achieved from Portugal. National people's assembly elected. Aristides Pereira became the first president. *1980* Constitution adopted providing for eventual union with Guinea-Bissau. *1981* Union with Guinea-Bissau abandoned and the constitution amended; became one-party state. *1990* Ruling PAICV's sole right to rule abolished. *1991* First multiparty elections held. New party, MPD, won majority in assembly. Pereira replaced by Monteiro Mascarenhas. *1992* New constitution adopted.

capital in architecture, a stone placed on the top of a column, pier, or pilaster, and usually wider on the upper surface than the diameter of the supporting shaft. A capital consists of three parts: the top member, called the *abacus*, a block that acts as the supporting surface to the superstructure; the middle portion, known as the bell or *echinus*; and the lower part, called the necking or *astragal*.

capital in economics, the stock of goods used in the production of other goods. *Financial capital* is accumulated or inherited wealth held in the form of assets, such as stocks and shares, property, and bank deposits.

capitalism economic system in which the principal means of production, distribution, and exchange are in private (individual or corporate) hands and competitively operated for profit. A *mixed economy* combines the private enterprise of capitalism and a degree of state monopoly, as in nationalized industries.

capital punishment punishment by death. Capital punishment is retained in 92 countries and territories (1990), including the US (37 states), China, and Islamic countries. It was abolished in the UK 1965 for all crimes except treason. Methods of execution include electrocution, lethal gas, hanging, shooting, lethal injection, garrotting, and decapitation.

In the US, the Supreme Court declared capital punishment unconstitutional 1972 (as a cruel and unusual punishment) but decided 1976 that this was

glucose molecules linked to form
the polysaccharide glycogen
(animal starch)

oxygen CH_2OH OH CH_2OH OH

O OH O OH

OH OH OH

OH carbon CH_2OH OH CH_2OH

hydrogen

carbohydrate *A molecule of the polysaccharide glycogen (animal starch) is formed from linked glucose ($C_6H_{12}O_6$) molecules. A typical glycogen molecule has 100–1,000 glucose units.*

not so in all circumstances. It was therefore reintroduced in some states, and in 1990 there were more than 2,000 prisoners on death row (awaiting execution) in the US. The first state to abolish capital punishment was Michigan 1847.

capitulum in botany, a flattened or rounded head (inflorescence) of numerous, small, stalkless flowers. The capitulum is surrounded by a circlet of petal-like bracts and has the appearance of a large, single flower.

It is characteristic of plants belonging to the daisy family Compositae, such as sunflowers *Helianthus*, goldenrods *Solidago*, and dandelions *Taraxacum*. The individual flowers are known as florets.

Capote Truman. Pen name of Truman Streckfus Persons 1924–1984. US novelist, journalist, and playwright. After achieving early success as a writer of sparkling prose in the stories of *Other Voices, Other Rooms* 1948 and the novel *Breakfast at Tiffany's* 1958, Capote's career flagged until the sensational "nonfiction novel" *In Cold Blood* 1965 made him a celebrity.

Capricornus zodiacal constellation in the southern hemisphere next to Sagittarius. It is represented as a fish-tailed goat, and its brightest stars are third magnitude. The Sun passes through it late Jan to mid-Feb In astrology, the dates for Capricornus (popularly known as Capricorn) are between about Dec 22 and Jan 19 (see ◊precession).

capsicum any pepper plant of the genus *Capsicum* of the nightshade family Solanaceae, native to Central and South America. The differing species produce green to red fruits that vary in size. The small ones are used whole to give the hot flavor of chili, or ground to produce cayenne pepper; the large pointed or squarish pods, known as sweet peppers, are mild-flavored and used as a vegetable.

capsule in botany, a dry, usually many-seeded fruit formed from an ovary composed of two or more fused ◊carpels, which splits open to release the seeds. The same term is used for the spore-containing structure of mosses and liverworts; this is borne at the top of a long stalk or seta.

capuchin monkey of the genus *Cebus* found in Central and South America, so called because the hairs on the head resemble the cowl of a Capuchin monk. Capuchins live in small groups, feed on fruit and insects, and have a long tail that is semiprehensile and can give support when climbing through the trees.

capybara world's largest rodent *Hydrochoerus hydrochaeris*, up to 4 ft/1.3 m long and 110 lb/50 kg in weight. It is found in South America, and belongs to the guinea-pig family. The capybara inhabits marshes and dense vegetation around water. It has thin, yellowish hair, swims well, and can rest underwater with just eyes, ears, and nose above the surface.

car popular name for ◊automobile.

carat unit for measuring the mass of precious stones, derived from the Arabic word *quirrat*, meaning "seed". Originally, 1 carat was the weight of a carob seed; it is now taken as 0.00705 oz/0.2 g, and is part of the troy system of weights. Also, an alternative spelling of ◊karat.

Caravaggio Michelangelo Merisi da 1573–1610. Italian early Baroque painter. He was active in Rome 1592–1606, then in Naples, and finally in Malta. He created a forceful style, using contrasts of light and shade, dramatic foreshortening, and a meticulous attention to detail. His life was as dramatic as his art (he had to leave Rome after killing a man in a brawl).

caraway herb *Carum carvi* of the carrot family Umbelliferae. Native to northern temperate Eurasian regions, it is grown for its spicy, aromatic seeds, which are used in cooking, medicine, and perfumery.

carbide compound of carbon and one other chemical element, usually a metal, silicon, or boron.

carbohydrate chemical compound composed of carbon, hydrogen, and oxygen, with the basic formula $C_m(H_2O)_n$, and related compounds with the same basic structure but modified functional groups. As sugar and starch, carbohydrates form a major energy-providing part of the human diet.

carbon nonmetallic element, symbol C, atomic number 6, relative atomic mass 12.011. It occurs on its own as diamond, graphite, and as fullerenes (the allotropes), as compounds in carbonaceous rocks such as chalk and limestone, as carbon dioxide in the atmosphere, as hydrocarbons in petroleum, coal, and natural gas, and as a constituent of all organic substances.

carbonate CO_3^{2-} ion formed when carbon dioxide dissolves in water; any salt formed by this ion and another chemical element, usually a metal.

carbon cycle sequence by which ◊carbon circulates and is recycled through the natural world. The carbon element from carbon dioxide, released into the

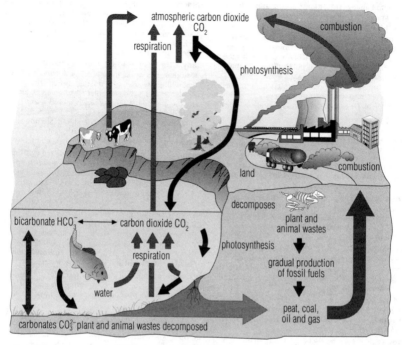

carbon cycle *The carbon cycle is necessary for the continuation of life. Since there is only a limited amount of carbon in the Earth and its atmosphere, carbon must be continuously recycled if life is to continue. Other chemicals necessary for life—nitrogen, sulfur, and phosphorus, for example—also circulate in natural cycles.*

atmosphere by living things as a result of ◊respiration, is taken up by plants during ◊photosynthesis and converted into carbohydrates; the oxygen component is released back into the atmosphere. Some of this carbon becomes locked up in coal and petroleum and other sediments. The simplest link in the carbon cycle occurs when an animal eats a plant and carbon is transferred from, say, a leaf cell to the animal body. The oceans absorb 25–40% of all carbon dioxide released into the atmosphere.

Today, the carbon cycle is in danger of being disrupted by the increased consumption and burning of fossil fuels, and the burning of large tracts of tropical forests, as a result of which levels of carbon dioxide are building up in the atmosphere and probably contributing to the ◊greenhouse effect.

carbon dating alternate name for ◊radiocarbon dating.

carbon dioxide CO_2 colorless, odorless gas, slightly soluble in water and denser than air. It is formed by the complete oxidation of carbon.

carbon fiber fine, black, silky filament of pure carbon produced by heat treatment from a special grade of Courtelle acrylic fiber, used for reinforcing plastics. The resulting composite is very stiff and, weight for weight, has four times the strength of high-tensile steel. It is used in the aerospace industry, automobiles, and electrical and sports equipment.

Carboniferous period of geological time 363–290 million years ago, the fifth period of the Paleozoic era. In the US it is divided into two periods: the Mississippian (lower) and the Pennsylvanian (upper).

Typical of the lower-Carboniferous rocks are shallow-water ◊limestones, while upper-Carboniferous rocks have ◊delta deposits with ◊coal (hence the name). Amphibians were abundant, and reptiles evolved during this period.

carbon monoxide CO colorless, odorless gas formed when carbon is oxidized in a limited supply of air. It is a poisonous constituent of automobile exhaust fumes, forming a stable compound with hemoglobin in the blood, thus preventing the hemoglobin from transporting oxygen to the body tissues.

carburetion any process involving chemical combination with carbon, especially the mixing or charging of a gas, such as air, with volatile compounds of carbon (gasoline, kerosene, or fuel oil) in order to increase potential heat energy during combustion. Carburetion applies to combustion in the cylinders of reciprocating gasoline engines of the types used in aircraft, road vehicles, or marine vessels. The device by which the liquid fuel is atomized and mixed with air is called a *carburetor*.

carcinogen any agent that increases the chance of a cell becoming cancerous (see ◊cancer), including various chemical compounds, some viruses, X-rays, and other forms of ionizing radiation. The term is often used more narrowly to mean chemical carcinogens only.

carcinoma malignant ◊tumor arising from the skin, the glandular tissues, or the mucous membranes that line the gut and lungs.

Cardano Girolamo 1501–1576. Italian physician, mathematician, philosopher, astrologer, and gambler. He is remembered for his theory of chance, his use of algebra, and many medical publications, notably the first clinical description of typhus fever.

Born in Pavia, he became professor of medicine there 1543, and wrote two works on physics and natural science, *De Subtilitate rerum* 1551 and *De Varietate rerum* 1557.

Cardiff (Welsh *Caerdydd*) seaport and capital of Wales (from 1955) and administrative headquarters of South and Mid Glamorgan, at the mouth of the Taff, Rhymney, and Ely rivers; population (1991) 270,100. Industries include automobile components, flour milling, ship repairs, electrical goods, paper, and cigars; there are also high-tech industries.

Cardin Pierre 1922– . French pioneering fashion designer. His clothes are bold and fantastic. He was the first to launch menswear (1960) and designer ready-to-wear collections (1963) and has given his name to a perfume.

cardinal in the Roman Catholic church, the highest rank next to the pope. Cardinals act as an advisory body to the pope and elect him. Their red hat is the badge of office. The number of cardinals has varied; there were 151 in 1989.

cardinal number in mathematics, one of the series of numbers 0, 1, 2, 3, 4,.... Cardinal numbers relate to quantity, whereas ordinal numbers (first, second, third, fourth,....) relate to order.

Carey George Leonard 1935– . 103rd archbishop of Canterbury from 1991. A product of a liberal evangelical background, he was appointed bishop of Bath and Wells 1987.

Caribbean Sea western part of the Atlantic Ocean between the southern coast of North America and the northern coasts of South America. Central America is to the W and the West Indies are the islands within the sea, which is about 1,700 mi/2,740 km long and 400–900 mi/650–1,500 km wide. It is from here that the ◊Gulf Stream turns toward Europe.

A number of continental American nations lie on its shores, and it contains the West Indies archipelago, which consists of independent island nations as well as dependencies of the US, France, the Netherlands, and the UK.

caribou the ◊reindeer of North America.

caricature in the arts or literature, an exaggerated portrayal of an individual or type, aiming to ridicule or otherwise expose the subject. Classical and medieval examples of pictorial caricatures survive. Artists of the 18th, 19th, and 20th centuries have often used caricature as a way of satirizing society and politics. Notable exponents include the French artist Honoré Daumier and the German George Grosz. In literature, caricatures have appeared since the comedies of Aristophanes in ancient Greece. Shakespeare and Dickens were adept at creating caricatures.

caries decay and disintegration, usually of the substance of teeth (cavity) or bone. It is caused by acids produced when the bacteria that live in the mouth break down sugars in the food. Fluoride, a low sugar intake, and regular brushing are all protective. Caries form mainly in the 45 minutes following consumption of sugary food.

Carlow county of the Republic of Ireland, in the province of Leinster; county town Carlow; area 347 sq mi/900 sq km; population (1991) 40,900. Mostly flat except for mountains in the S, the land is fertile, and well suited to dairy farming. Products include barley, wheat, and sugar beet.

Carlyle Thomas 1795–1881. Scottish essayist and social historian. His works include *Sartor Resartus* 1833–34, describing his loss of Christian belief; *The French Revolution* 1837; the pamphlet *Chartism* 1839, attacking the doctrine of *laissez-faire*, *Past and Present* 1843, the notable Letters and Speeches of Cromwell 1845, and the miniature life of his friend John Sterling 1851. His prose style was idiosyncratic, encompassing grand, thunderous rhetoric and deliberate obscurity.

carnation any of numerous double-flowered cultivated varieties of a plant *Dianthus caryophyllus* of the pink family. The flowers smell like cloves; they are divided into flake, bizarre, and picotees, according to whether the petals exhibit one or more colors on their white ground, have the color dispersed in strips, or have a colored border to the petals.

Carnegie Andrew 1835–1919. US industrialist and philanthropist, born in Scotland, who developed the Pittsburgh iron and steel industries, making the US the world's leading producer. He endowed public libraries, education, and various research trusts.

carnivore mammal of the order Carnivora. Although its name describes the flesh-eating ancestry of the order, it includes pandas, which are herbivorous, and civet cats that eat fruit.

The mammalian order Carnivora includes civet cats, raccoons, cats, dogs, and bears.

carob small Mediterranean tree *Ceratonia siliqua* of the legume family Leguminosae. Its pods, 8 in/20 cm long, are used as animal fodder; they are also the source of a chocolate substitute.

Carolines scattered archipelago in Micronesia, Pacific Ocean, consisting of over 500 coral islets; area 463 sq mi/1,200 sq km. The chief islands are Ponape, Kusai, and Truk in the eastern group, and Yap and Belau in the western group.

carp fish *Cyprinus carpio* found all over the world. It commonly grows to 1.8 ft/50 cm and 7 lb/3 kg, but may be even larger. It lives in lakes, ponds, and slow rivers. The wild form is drab, but cultivated forms may be golden, or may have few large scales (mirror carp) or be scaleless (leather carp). *Koi* carp are highly prized and can grow up to 3 ft/1 m long with a distinctive pink, red, white, or black coloring.

carpal tunnel syndrome compression of the median nerve at the wrist. It causes pain and numbness in the index and middle fingers and weakness in the thumb. It may require surgery.

It affected 223,000 workers in the US 1992.

Carpathian Mountains central European mountain system, forming a semicircle through Slovakia–Poland–Ukraine–Moldova–Romania, 900 mi/1,450 km long. The central *Tatra Mountains* on the Slovak–Polish frontier include the highest peak, Gerlachovka, 8,737 ft/2,663 m.

carpel female reproductive unit in flowering plants (◊angiosperms). It usually comprises an ◊ovary containing one or more ovules, the stalk or style, and a stigma at its top which receives the pollen. A flower may have one or more carpels, and they may be separate or fused together. Collectively the carpels of a flower are known as the gynoecium.

Carreras, José Spanish lyric tenor José Carreras made his mark playing opposite Montserrat Caballé. Favored for romantic roles including Flavio in Bellini's Norma and Ismaele in Verdi's Nabucco, he brings a distinctive intimacy to opera.

Carreras José 1947– . Spanish operatic tenor. His comprehensive repertoire includes Handel's *Samson* and whose recordings include *West Side Story* 1984 under Leonard Bernstein. His vocal presence, charmingly insinuating rather than forceful, is favored for Italian and French romantic roles.

carriage return (CR) in computing, a special code (◊ASCII value 13) that moves the screen cursor or a print head to the beginning of the current line. Most word processors and the ◊MS-DOS operating system use a combination of CR and line feed (LF—ASCII value 10) to represent a hard return. The ◊Unix system, however, uses only LF and therefore files transferred between MS-DOS and Unix require a conversion program.

carrier in medicine, anyone who harbors an infectious organism without ill effects but can pass the infection to others. The term is also applied to those who carry a recessive gene for a disease or defect without manifesting the condition.

Carroll Lewis. Pen name of Charles Lutwidge Dodgson 1832–1898. English author. He is best known for the children's classics *Alice's Adventures in Wonderland* 1865 and its sequel *Through the Looking-Glass* 1872. Among later works was the mock-heroic "nonsense" poem *The Hunting of the Snark* 1876. He was fascinated by the limits and paradoxes of language and thought, the exploration of which leads to the apparent nonsense of Alice's adventures. He was an Oxford don and also published mathematical works.

carrot hardy European biennial *Daucus carota* of the family Umbelliferae. Cultivated since the 16th century for its edible root, it has a high sugar content and also contains carotene, which is converted by the human liver to vitamin A.

Cartagena or *Cartagena de los Indes* port, industrial center, and capital of the department of Bolívar, NW Colombia; population (1985) 531,000. Plastics and chemicals are produced here.

cartel agreement among national or international firms to fix prices for their products. A cartel may restrict supply (output) to raise prices in order to increase member profits. It therefore represents a form of oligopoly. ◊OPEC, for example, is an oil cartel.

Carter Jimmy (James Earl) 1924– . 39th president of the US 1977–81, a Democrat. In 1976 he narrowly wrested the presidency from Gerald Ford. Features of his presidency were the return of the Panama Canal Zone to Panama, the Camp David Agreements for peace in the Middle East, and the Iranian seizure of US embassy hostages. He was defeated by Ronald Reagan 1980.

Born in Plains, Georgia; he served in the navy, studied nuclear physics, and after a spell as a peanut farmer entered politics 1953.

Cartesian coordinates in ◊coordinate geometry, components used to define the position of a point by its perpendicular distance from a set of two or more axes, or reference lines. For a two-dimensional area defined by two axes at right angles (a horizontal x-axis and a vertical y-axis), the coordinates of a point are given by its perpendicular distances from the y-axis and x-axis, written in the form (x,y). For example, a point P that lies three units from the y-axis and four units from the x-axis has Cartesian coordinates (3,4) (see ◊abscissa). In three-dimensional coordinate geometry, points are located with reference to a third, z-axis, mutually at right angles to the x and y axes.

Carthage ancient Phoenician port in N Africa founded by colonists from Tyre in the late 9th century BC ; it lay 10 mi/16 km N of Tunis, Tunisia. A leading trading center, it was in conflict with Greece from the 6th century BC, and then with Rome, and was destroyed by Roman forces 146 BC at the end of the ◊Punic Wars. About 45 BC, Roman colonists settled in Carthage, and it became the wealthy capital of the province of Africa. After its capture by the Vandals AD 439 it was little more than a pirate stronghold. From 533 it formed part of the Byzantine Empire until its final destruction by Arabs 698, during their conquest in the name of Islam.

Cartier Jacques 1491–1557. French navigator who, while seeking a north-west passage to China, was the first European to sail up the St Lawrence River 1534. He named the site of Montreal.

Cartier-Bresson Henri 1908– . French photographer. He is considered one of the greatest photographic artists. His documentary work was shot in black and white, using a small-format Leica camera. His work is remarkable for its tightly structured composition and his ability to capture the decisive moment. He was a founder member of the Magnum photographic agency.

cartilage flexible bluish white connective tissue made up of the protein collagen. In cartilaginous fish it forms the skeleton; in other vertebrates it forms the greater part of the embryonic skeleton, and is replaced by ◊bone in the course of development, except in areas of wear such as bone endings, and the disks between the backbones. It also forms structural tissue in the larynx, nose, and external ear of mammals.

cartography art and practice of drawing ◊maps.

cartoon humorous or satirical drawing or ◊caricature; a cartoon strip or comic strip; traditionally, the base design for a large fresco, mosaic, or tapestry, transferred to wall or canvas by tracing or pricking out the design on the cartoon and then dabbing with powdered charcoal to create a faint reproduction. Surviving examples include Leonardo da Vinci's *Virgin and St Anne* (National Gallery, London).

Cartwright Edmund 1743–1823. British inventor. He patented the power loom 1785, built a weaving mill 1787, and patented a wool-combing machine 1789.

Caruso Enrico 1873–1921. Italian operatic tenor. His voice was dark, with full-bodied tone and remarkable dynamic range. In 1902 he starred, with Nellie Melba, in Puccini's *La Bohème/Bohemian Life.* He was among the first opera singers to achieve lasting fame through phonograph recordings.

Carver George Washington 1864–1943. US agricultural chemist. Born a slave in Missouri, he was kidnapped and raised by his former owner, Moses Carver. He devoted his life to improving the economy of the US South and the condition of African Americans. He advocated the diversification of crops, promoted peanut production, and was a pioneer in the field of plastics.

Carver was honored as one of America's most influential and innovative agronomists.

Casablanca (Arabic *Dar el-Beida*) port, commercial and industrial center on the Atlantic coast of Morocco; population (1982) 2,139,000. It trades in fish, phosphates, and manganese. The Great Hassan II Mosque, completed 1989, is the world's largest; it is built on a platform (430,000 sq ft/40,000 sq m) jutting out over the Atlantic, with walls 200 ft/60 m high, topped by a hydraulic sliding roof, and a minaret 574 ft/175 m ft high.

Casals Pablo 1876–1973. Catalan cellist, composer, and conductor. He was largely self-taught. As a cellist, he was celebrated for his interpretations of J S Bach's unaccompanied suites. He wrote instrumental and choral works, including the Christmas oratorio *The Manger.*

He was an outspoken critic of fascism who openly defied Franco, and a tireless crusader for peace.

He married three times; his first wife was the Portuguese cellist Guilhermina Suggia (1888–1950).

Casanova de Seingalt Giovanni Jacopo 1725–1798. Italian adventurer, spy, violinist, librarian, and, according to his *Memoirs,* one of the world's great lovers. From 1774 he was a spy in the Venetian police service. In 1782 a libel got him into trouble, and after more wanderings he was in 1785 appointed librarian to Count Waldstein at his castle of Dûx in Bohemia. Here Casanova wrote his *Memoirs* (published 1826–38, although the complete text did not appear until 1960–61).

casein main protein of milk, from which it can be separated by the action of acid, the enzyme rennin, or bacteria (souring); it is also the main protein in cheese. Casein is used as a protein supplement in the treatment of malnutrition. It is used commercially in cosmetics, glues, and as a sizing for coating paper.

cash crop crop grown solely for sale rather than for the farmer's own use, for example, coffee, cotton, or sugar beet. Many Third World countries grow cash crops to meet their debt repayments rather than grow food for their own people. The price for these crops depends on financial interests, such as those of the multinational companies and the International Monetary Fund.

cashew tropical American tree *Anacardium occidentale,* family Anacardiaceae. Extensively cultivated in India and Africa, it produces poisonous kidney-shaped nuts that become edible after being roasted.

cash flow input of cash required to cover all expenses of a business, whether revenue or capital. Alternatively, the actual or prospective balance between the various outgoing and incoming movements which are designated in total. Cash flow is positive if receipts are greater than payments; negative if payments are greater than receipts.

Caspian Sea world's largest inland sea, divided between Iran, Azerbaijan, Russia, Kazakhstan, and Turkmenistan; area about 155,000 sq mi/400,000 sq km, with a maximum depth of 3,250 ft/1,000 m. The chief ports are Astrakhan and Baku. Drainage in the N and damming of the Volga and Ural rivers for hydroelectric power left the sea approximately 90 ft/28 m below sea level. In June 1991 opening of sluices in the dams caused the water level to rise dramatically, threatening towns and industrial areas.

Cassandra in Greek mythology, the daughter of Priam, King of Troy. Her prophecies (for example, of the fall of Troy) were never believed, because she had rejected the love of the god Apollo.

She was murdered with ◊Agamemnon by his wife Clytemnestra, having been awarded as a prize to the Greek hero on his sacking of Troy.

Cassatt Mary 1844–1926. US Impressionist painter and printmaker. She settled in Paris 1868. Her popular, colorful pictures of mothers and children show the influence of Japanese prints, for example *The Bath* 1892 (Art Institute, Chicago). She excelled in etching and pastel.

Born to a wealthy Philadephia family, in 1868 she settled in Paris and exhibited with the Impressionists 1879–81, 1886, the only American to do so. Her work, always respected in France, has gained recognition in the US in recent years; the largest collection is owned by the Philadelphia Art Museum.

cassava or *manioc* plant *Manihot utilissima,* belonging to the spurge family Euphorbiaceae. Native to South America, it is now widely grown throughout the tropics for its starch-containing roots, from which tapioca and bread are made.

Cassiopeia prominent constellation of the northern hemisphere, named for the mother of Andromeda. It has a distinctive W-shape, and contains one of the most powerful radio sources in the sky, Cassiopeia A, the remains of a ◊supernova (star explosion).

Cassius (Gaius Cassius Longinus) Roman soldier, one of the conspirators who killed Julius ◊Caesar 44 BC. He fought with Pompey against Caesar, and was pardoned after the battle of Pharsalus 48, but became a leader in the conspiracy of 44. After Caesar's death he joined Brutus, and committed suicide after their defeat at Philippi 42.

cassowary large flightless bird, genus *Casuarius,* found in New Guinea and N Australia, usually in forests. Related to the emu, the cassowary has a bare head with a horny casque, or helmet, on top, and brightly colored skin on the neck. Its loose plumage is black and its wings tiny, but it can run and leap well and defends itself by kicking. Cassowaries stand up to 5 ft/1.5 m tall.

caste stratification of Hindu society into four main groups: *Brahmans* (priests), *Kshatriyas* (nobles and warriors), *Vaisyas* (traders and farmers), and *Sudras* (servants); plus a fifth group, *Harijan* (untouchables). No upward or downward mobility exists, as in classed societies. The system dates from ancient times, and there are more than 3,000 subdivisions.

Castile kingdom founded in the 10th century, occupying the central plateau of Spain. Its union with

◊Aragon 1479, based on the marriage of Ferdinand and Isabella, effected the foundation of the Spanish state, which at the time was occupied and ruled by the ◊Moors. Castile comprised the two great basins separated by the Sierra de Gredos and the Sierra de Guadarrama, known traditionally as Old and New Castile. The area now forms the regions of Castilla–León and Castilla–La Mancha.

Castilian language member of the Romance branch of the Indo-European language family, originating in NW Spain, in the provinces of Old and New Castile. It is the basis of present-day standard Spanish (see ◊Spanish language) and is often seen as the same language, the terms *castellano* and *español* being used interchangeably in both Spain and the Spanish-speaking countries of the Americas.

cast iron cheap but invaluable constructional material, most commonly used for automobile engine blocks. Cast iron is partly refined pig (crude) ◊iron, which is very fluid when molten and highly suitable for shaping by casting; it contains too many impurities (for example, carbon) to be readily shaped in any other way. Solid cast iron is heavy and can absorb great shock but is very brittle.

castle fortified building or group of buildings, characteristic of medieval Europe. The castle underwent many changes, its size, design, and construction being largely determined by changes in siege tactics and the development of artillery. Outstanding examples are the 12th-century Krak des Chevaliers, Syria (built by crusaders); 13th-century Caernarvon Castle, Wales; and 15th-century Manzanares el Real, Spain.

Early castles (11th century) consisted of an earthen hill (motte) surrounded by wooden palisades enclosing a courtyard (bailey).

The motte supported a wooden keep. Later developments substituted stone for wood and utilized more elaborate defensive architectural detail. After introduction of gunpowder in the 14th century, castles became less defensible and increases in civil order led to their replacement by unfortified manor houses by the 16th century. Large stone fortifications became popular again in the 18th century, particularly those modeled after the principles of fortification introduced by the French architect Vauban, and were built as late as the first half of the 19th century. In the late 19th century, castlelike buildings were built as residences for the wealthy as part of the Romantic revival in Europe and America.

Castlereagh Robert Stewart, Viscount Castlereagh 1769–1822. British Tory politician. As chief secretary for Ireland 1797–1801, he suppressed the rebellion of 1798 and helped the younger Pitt secure the union of England, Scotland, and Ireland 1801. As foreign secretary 1812–22, he coordinated European opposition to Napoleon and represented Britain at the Congress of Vienna 1814–15.

castor-oil plant tall, tropical and subtropical shrub *Ricinus communis* of the spurge family Euphorbiaceae. The seeds, in North America called castor beans, yield the purgative castor oil and also ricin, one of the most powerful poisons known, which can be targeted to destroy cancer cells, while leaving normal cells untouched.

castration removal of the sex glands (either ovaries or testes). Male domestic animals may be castrated to prevent reproduction, to make them larger or more docile, or to eradicate disease.

Castro, Fidel The Cuban revolutionary leader Fidel Castro. After his overthrow of the right-wing Batista regime 1959, Castro maintained his leadership of Cuba despite the enmity of his powerful neighbor, the US. Since 1990 events in E Europe and the former USSR have left Castro increasingly isolated.

Male domestic animals, especially stallions and bovine bulls, are castrated to prevent undesirable sires from reproducing, to moderate their aggressive disposition and, for bulls, to improve their value as beef cattle (castrated bovines are called steer). Roosters are castrated (capons) to improve their flavor and increase their size. The effects of castration can also be achieved by chemical means, by administration of hormones, in humans and animals. If done in adulthood, sexual function may be retained (although infertile) as well as masculine features already established.

Castro (Ruz) Fidel 1927– . Cuban communist politician, prime minister 1959–76 and president from 1976. He led two unsuccessful coups against the right-wing Batista regime and led the revolution that overthrew the dictator 1959. He raised the standard of living for most Cubans but dealt harshly with dissenters. From 1990, deprived of the support of the USSR and experiencing the long-term effects of a US trade embargo, Castro faced increasing pressure for reform.

Castro built a strong military force and attempted to export his revolution to other Latin American countries.

cat small, domesticated, carnivorous mammal *Felis catus*, often kept as a pet or for catching small pests such as rodents. Found in many color variants, it may have short, long, or no hair, but the general shape and size is constant. All cats walk on the pads of their toes, and have retractile claws. They have strong limbs, large eyes, and acute hearing. The canine teeth are long and well-developed, as are the shearing teeth in the side of the mouth.

Catalan language member of the Romance branch of the Indo-European language family, an Iberian language closely related to Provençal in France.

It is spoken in Catalonia in NE Spain, the Balearic Islands, Andorra, and a corner of SW France.

Catalonia (Spanish *Cataluña*, Catalan *Catalunya*) autonomous region of NE Spain; area 12,313 sq mi/31,900 sq km; population (1986) 5,977,000. It includes Barcelona (the capital), Gerona, Lérida, and Tarragona. Industries include wool and cotton textiles; hydroelectric power is produced.

French Catalonia is the adjacent *département* of Pyrénées-Orientales.

catalyst substance that alters the speed of, or makes possible, a chemical or biochemical reaction but remains unchanged at the end of the reaction. ◊Enzymes are natural biochemical catalysts. In practice most catalysts are used to speed up reactions.

catalytic converter device fitted to the exhaust system of a motor vehicle in order to reduce toxic emissions from the engine. It converts harmful exhaust products to relatively harmless ones by passing the exhaust gases over a mixture of catalysts coated on a metal or ceramic honeycomb (a structure that increases the surface area and therefore the amount of active catalyst with which the exhaust gases will come into contact). *Oxidation catalysts* (small amounts of precious palladium and platinum metals) convert hydrocarbons (unburned fuel) and carbon monoxide into carbon dioxide and water, but do not affect nitrogen oxide emissions. *Three-way catalysts* (platinum and rhodium metals) convert nitrogen oxide gases into nitrogen and oxygen.

catamaran twin-hulled sailing vessel, based on the aboriginal craft of South America and the Indies, made of logs lashed together, with an outrigger. A similar vessel with three hulls is known as a trimaran. Automobile ferries with a wave-piercing catamaran design are also in use in parts of Europe and North America. They have a pointed main hull and two outriggers and travel at a speed of 35 knots (52.5 mph/84.5 kph).

cataract eye disease in which the crystalline lens or its capsule becomes cloudy, causing blindness. Fluid accumulates between the fibers of the lens and gives place to deposits of ◊albumin. These coalesce into rounded bodies, the lens fibers break down, and areas of the lens or the lens capsule become filled with opaque products of degeneration. The condition is estimated to have blinded more than 25 million people worldwide.

catechism teaching by question and answer on the Socratic method, but chiefly as a means of instructing children in the basics of the Christian creed. A person being instructed in this way in preparation for baptism or confirmation is called a *catechumen*.

A form of catechism was used for the catechumens in the early Christian church. Little books of catechism were written by Luther and Calvin at the Reformation.

category in philosophy, a fundamental concept applied to being that cannot be reduced to anything more elementary. Aristotle listed ten categories: substance, quantity, quality, relation, place, time, position, state, action, and passion.

caterpillar larval stage of a ◊butterfly or ◊moth. Wormlike in form, the body is segmented, may be hairy, and often has scent glands. The head has strong biting mandibles, silk glands, and a spinneret.

catfish fish belonging to the order Siluriformes, in which barbels (feelers) on the head are well-developed, so giving a resemblance to the whiskers of a cat. Catfishes are found worldwide, mainly in fresh water, and are farmed commercially in the US.

cathedral principal church of a bishop or archbishop, containing his throne which is usually situated on the south side of the choir. A cathedral is governed by a dean and chapter.

Formerly, cathedrals were distinguished as either monastic or secular, the clergy of the latter not being members of a regular monastic order. Because of their importance, cathedrals were for many centuries the main focus of artistic and architectural endeavor. Their artworks include stained glass, frescoes, mosaics, carvings in wood and stone, paintings (such as altarpieces), ironwork, and textiles. Most cathedrals were built during the Middle Ages and reflect the many styles of Romanesque and Gothic architecture. There are cathedrals in most of the important cities of the world.

Catherine (II) the Great 1729–1796. Empress of Russia from 1762, and daughter of the German prince of Anhalt-Zerbst. In 1745, she married the Russian grand duke Peter. Catherine was able to dominate him; six months after he became Czar Peter III in 1762, he was murdered in a coup and Catherine ruled alone. During her reign Russia extended its boundaries to include territory from wars with the Turks 1768–74, 1787–92, and from the partitions of Poland 1772, 1793, and 1795, as well as establishing hegemony over the Black Sea.

She admired and aided the French *Encyclopédistes*.

Catherine de' Medici 1519–1589. French queen consort of Henry II, whom she married 1533; daughter of Lorenzo de' Medici, Duke of Urbino; and mother of Francis II, Charles IX, and Henry III. At first outshone by Henry's mistress Diane de Poitiers (1490–1566), she became regent 1560–63 for Charles IX and remained in power until his death 1574.

Catherine of Aragon 1485–1536. First queen of Henry VIII of England, 1509–33, and mother of Mary I. Catherine had married Henry's elder brother Prince Arthur 1501 and on his death 1502 was betrothed to Henry, marrying him on his accession. She failed to produce a male heir and Henry divorced her without papal approval, thus creating the basis for the English ◊Reformation.

cathode in chemistry, the negative electrode of an electrolytic ◊cell, toward which positive particles (cations), usually in solution, are attracted. See ◊electrolysis.

cathode in electronics, the part of an electronic device in which electrons are generated. In a thermionic valve, electrons are produced by the heating effect of an applied current; in a photocell, they are produced by the interaction of light and a semiconducting material. The cathode is kept at a negative potential relative to the device's other electrodes (anodes) in order to ensure that the liberated electrons stream away from the cathode and toward the anodes.

cathode-ray tube vacuum tube in which a beam of electrons is produced and focused onto a fluorescent screen. It is an essential component of television receivers, computer visual display terminals, and oscilloscopes.

CAT scan or *CT scan* (acronym for *computerized axial tomography scan*) sophisticated method of X-ray imaging. Quick and noninvasive, CAT scanning is used in medicine as an aid to diagnosis, helping to pinpoint problem areas without the need for exploratory surgery. It is also used in archeology to investigate mummies.

Catskills US mountain range, mainly in SE New York State, west of the Hudson River; the highest point is Slide Mountain, 4,204 ft/1,281 m.

Long a vacation and resort center for New York City residents, the Catskills offer hiking, skiing, hunting and fishing, and the picturesque trails and scenes of woods, waterfalls, lakes, and streams that have attracted such painters as Frederic Church and Thomas Cole. It is the setting for *Rip Van Winkle*, one of Washington Irving's most popular tales.

cattle any large, ruminant, even-toed, hoofed mammal of the genus *Bos*, family Bovidae, including wild species such as the yak, gaur, gayal, banteng, and kouprey, as well as domestic breeds. Asiatic water buffaloes *Bubalus*, African buffaloes *Syncerus*, and American bison *Bison* are not considered true cattle. Cattle are bred for meat (beef cattle) or milk (dairy cattle).

Catullus Gaius Valerius *c*.84–54 BC. Roman lyric poet. He wrote in a variety of meters and forms, from short narratives and hymns to epigrams. Born in Verona, N Italy, he moved with ease through the literary and political society of late republican Rome. His love affair with the woman he called Lesbia provided the inspiration for many of his poems.

Caucasoid referring to one of the three major varieties (see ◊race) of humans, *Homo sapiens sapiens*, including the indigenous peoples of Europe, the Near East, North Africa, India, and Australia. Caucasoids exhibit the widest range of variation in physical traits, including straight to curly hair; fair to dark skin; blue, hazel, and brown eyes; blond, red, brown, and black hair; medium to heavy beard and body hair; small to high-bridged noses; medium to thin lips. The term was coined by the German anthropologist J F Blumenbach (1752–1840), who erroneously theorized that they originated in the Caucasus region. See also ◊Mongoloid, ◊Negroid.

Caucasus series of mountain ranges between the Caspian and Black seas, in the republics of Russia, Georgia, Armenia, and Azerbaijan; 750 mi/1,200 km long. The highest peak is Elbruz, 18,480 ft/5,633 m.

cauliflower variety of ◊cabbage *Brassica oleracea*, distinguished by its large, flattened head of fleshy, aborted flowers. It is similar to broccoli but less hardy.

cauterization in medicine, the use of special instruments to burn or fuse small areas of body tissue to destroy dead cells, prevent the spread of infection, or seal tiny blood vessels to minimize blood loss during surgery.

cavalier horseman of noble birth, but mainly used to describe a male supporter of Charles I in the English Civil War (Cavalier), typically with courtly dress and long hair (as distinct from a Roundhead); also a supporter of Charles II after the Restoration.

Cavan county of the Republic of Ireland, in the province of Ulster; county town Cavan; area 730 sq mi/1,890 sq km; population (1991) 52,800. The river Erne divides it into a narrow, mostly low-lying peninsula, 20 mi/30 km long, between Leitrim and Fermanagh, and an eastern section of wild and bare hill country. The soil is generally poor and the climate moist and cold. The chief towns are Cavan, population about 3,000; Kilmore, seat of Roman Catholic and Protestant bishoprics; and Virginia.

cave roofed-over cavity in the Earth's crust usually produced by the action of underground water or by waves on a seacoast. Caves of the former type commonly occur in areas underlain by limestone, such as Kentucky and many Balkan regions, where the rocks are soluble in water. A *pothole* is a vertical hole in rock caused by water descending a crack; it is thus open to the sky.

Cavendish Henry 1731–1810. English physicist. He discovered hydrogen (which he called "inflammable air") 1766, and determined the compositions of water and of nitric acid.

cavy short-tailed South American rodent, family Caviidae, of which the guinea-pig *Cavia porcellus* is an example. Wild cavies are grayish or brownish with rather coarse hair. They live in small groups in burrows, and have been kept for food since ancient times.

Caxton William *c*.1422–1491. The first English printer. He learned the art of printing in Cologne, Germany, 1471 and set up a press in Belgium where he produced the first book printed in English, his own version of a French romance, *Recuyell of the Historyes of Troye* 1474. Returning to England 1476, he established himself in London, where he produced the first book printed in England, *Dictes or Sayengis of the Philosophres* 1477.

A typeface is named for him.

Cayenne capital and chief port of French Guiana, on Cayenne Island, NE South America, at the mouth of the river Cayenne; population (1990) 41,700.

cayman or *caiman* large reptile, resembling the ◊crocodile.

Cayman Islands British island group in the West Indies *area* 100 sq mi/260 sq km/ *features* comprises three low-lying islands: Grand Cayman, Cayman Brac, and Little Cayman *government* governor, executive council, and legislative assembly *exports* seawhip coral, a source of ◊prostaglandins; shrimps; honey; jewelry *currency* CI dollar *population* (1988) 22,000 *language* English *history* discovered by Chrisopher Columbus 1503; acquired by Britain following the Treaty of Madrid 1670; became a dependency of Jamaica 1863. In 1962 the islands became a separate colony, although the inhabitants chose to remain British. From that date, changes in legislation attracted foreign banks and the Caymans are now an international financial center and tax haven as well as a tourist resort.

CCITT abbreviation for ◊*Comité Consultatif International Téléphonique et Télégraphique*, an organization that sets international communications standards.

CD abbreviation for ◊*compact disk; Corps Diplomatique* (French "Diplomatic Corps"); *certificate of deposit*.

CD-I (abbreviation for *compact disk-interactive*) compact disc developed by Philips for storing a combination of video, audio, text, and pictures. It is intended principally for the consumer market to be used in systems using a combination of computer and television. An alternative format is ◊DVI (digital video interactive).

CD-R (abbreviation for *compact disk-recordable*) compact disk on which data can be overwritten (compare ◊CD-ROM, compact disk read-only memory). The disk combines magnetic and optical technology: during the writing process, a laser melts the surface of the disk, thereby allowing the magnetic elements of the surface layer to be realigned.

CD-ROM (abbreviation for *compact-disk read-only memory*) computer storage device developed from the technology of the audio ◊compact disk. It consists of a plastic-coated metal disk, on which binary digital information is etched in the form of microscopic pits. This can then be read optically by passing a light beam over the disk. CD-ROMs typically hold about 550 ◊megabytes of data, and are used in distributing large amounts of text and graphics, such as encyclopedias, catalogs, and technical manuals.

CD-ROM XA (CD-ROM extended architecture) in computing, a set of standards for storing multimedia information on CD-ROM. Developed by Philips, Sony, and Microsoft, it is a partial development of the ◊CD-I standard. It interleaves data (as in CD-I) so that blocks of audio data are sandwiched between blocks of text, graphics, or video. This allows parallel streams of data to be handled, so that information can be seen and heard simultaneously. Unlike CD-I, CD-ROM XA disks are playable on any ◊CD-ROM drive with an appropriate interface.

CDTV (abbreviation for *Commodore Dynamic Total Vision*) multimedia computer system developed by Commodore. It is designed for the home and is a direct rival to ◊CD-I. It consists of a box about the size of a home video recorder, containing an Amiga 500 computer and a ◊CD-ROM drive. CDTV disks can store a combination of text, pictures, sound, and video. Like CD-I, CDTV plugs into a TV set and stereo system. CDTV cannot play CD-ROM or CD-I disks.

Ceausescu Nicolae 1918–1989. Romanian politician, leader of the Romanian Communist Party (RCP), in power 1965–89. He pursued a policy line independent of and critical of the USSR. He appointed family members, including his wife *Elena Ceausescu*, to senior state and party posts, and governed in an increasingly repressive manner, zealously implementing schemes that impoverished the nation. The Ceausescus were overthrown in a bloody revolutionary coup Dec 1989 and executed.

In Aug 1989 a report condemning Ceausescu for widespread human-rights violations was smuggled out of Romania and presented to a United Nations human-rights conference.

Cebu chief city and port of the island of Cebu in the Philippines; population (1990) 610,400; area of the island 1,964 sq mi/5,086 sq km. The oldest city of the Philippines, Cebu was founded as San Miguel 1565 and became the capital of the Spanish Philippines.

cecum in the ◊digestive system of animals, a blind-ending tube branching off from the first part of the large intestine, terminating in the appendix. It has no function in humans but is used for the digestion of cellulose by some grass-eating mammals.

cedar any of an Old World genus *Cedrus* of coniferous trees of the pine family Pinaceae. The *cedar of Lebanon* C. libani grows to great heights and age in the mountains of Syria and Asia Minor. Of the historic forests on Mount Lebanon itself, only a few stands of trees remain.

The name cedar is also applied to species of several genera of other coniferous trees in several families— for example, some ◊junipers, ◊cypresses, and ◊redwoods.

celandine two plants belonging to different families, and resembling each other only in their bright yellow flowers. The greater celandine *Chelidonium majus* belongs to the poppy family (Papaveraceae) and is a common introduced weed on wooded slopes in the US. The lesser celandine *Ranunculus ficaria* is a European member of the buttercup family.

Celebes English name for ◊Sulawesi, an island of Indonesia.

celery Old World plant *Apium graveolens* of the carrot family Umbelliferae. It grows wild in ditches and salt marshes and has a coarse texture and acrid taste. Cultivated varieties of celery are grown under cover to make them less bitter.

celestial sphere imaginary sphere surrounding the Earth, on which the celestial bodies seem to lie. The positions of bodies such as stars, planets, and galaxies are specified by their coordinates on the celestial sphere. The equivalents of latitude and longitude on the celestial sphere are called declination and right ascension (which is measured in hours from 0 to 24). The *celestial poles* lie directly above the Earth's poles, and the *celestial equator* lies over the Earth's equator. The celestial sphere appears to rotate once around the Earth each day, actually a result of the rotation of the Earth on its axis.

cell in biology, a discrete, membrane-bound portion of living matter, the smallest unit capable of an independent existence. All living organisms consist of one or more cells, with the exception of ◊viruses. Bacteria, protozoa, and many other microorganisms consist of single cells, whereas a human is made up of billions of cells. Essential features of a cell are the membrane, which encloses it and restricts the flow of substances in and out; the jellylike material within, the ◊cytoplasm; the ◊ribosomes, which carry out protein synthesis; and the ◊DNA, which forms the hereditary material.

cedar The true cedars are evergreen conifers growing from the Mediterranean to the Himalayas. They have tufts of small needles and cones of papery scales which carry the seeds. The name has long also been applied to trees with a similar type of wood, for example the Spanish cedar, whose wood is used in cigar boxes.

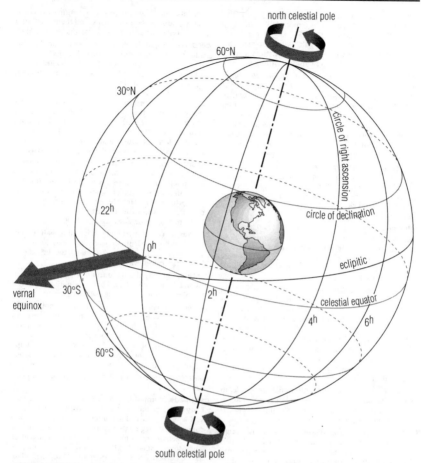

celestial sphere The main features of the celestial sphere. The equivalents of latitude and longitude on the celestial sphere are declination and right ascension. Declination runs from 0° at the celestial equator to 90° at the celestial poles. Right ascension is measured in hours eastward from the vernal equinox, one hour corresponding to 15° of longitude.

cell, electrical or *voltaic cell* or *galvanic cell* device in which chemical energy is converted into electrical energy; the popular name is ◊"battery", but this actually refers to a collection of cells in one unit. The reactive chemicals of a *primary cell* cannot be replenished, whereas *secondary cells*—such as storage batteries—are rechargeable: their chemical reactions can be reversed and the original condition restored by applying an electric current. It is dangerous to attempt to recharge a primary cell.

Each cell contains two conducting ◊electrodes immersed in an electrolyte, in a container. A spontaneous chemical reaction within the cell generates a negative charge (excess of electrons) on one electrode, and a positive charge (deficiency of electrons) on the other. The accumulation of these equal but opposite charges prevents the reaction from continuing unless

an outer connection (external circuit) is made between the electrodes allowing the charges to dissipate. When this occurs, electrons escape from the cell's negative terminal and are replaced at the positive, causing a current to flow. After prolonged use, the cell will become flat (cease to supply current). The first cell was made by Alessandro Volta in 1800.

Types of primary cells include the Daniell, Lalande, Leclanché, and so-called "dry" cells; secondary cells include Planté, Faure, and Edison. Newer types include the Mallory (mercury depolarizer), which has a very stable discharge curve and can be made in very small units (for example, for hearing aids), and the Venner battery, which can be made substantially solid for some purposes.

Cellini Benvenuto 1500–1571. Italian sculptor and goldsmith. He worked in the Mannerist style and wrote an arrogant but entertaining and informative autobiography (begun 1558). Among his works are a graceful bronze *Perseus* 1545–54 (Loggia dei Lanzi, Florence) and a celebrated gold salt cellar made for Francis I of France 1540–43 (Kunsthistorisches Museum, Vienna), topped by nude reclining figures.

cello common abbreviation for *violoncello*, tenor member of the ◊violin family and fourth member of the string quartet. Its solo potential was recognized by J S Bach, and a concerto repertoire extends from Haydn (who also gave the cello a leading role in his string quartets), and Boccherini to Dvořák, Elgar, Britten, Ligeti, and Lukas Foss. The *Bachianas Brasilieras 1* by Villa-Lobos is scored for eight cellos, and Boulez's *Messagesquisse* 1977 for seven cellos.

cellular phone or *cellphone* mobile radio telephone, one of a network connected to the telephone system by a computer-controlled communication system. Service areas are divided into small "cells", about 3 mi/5 km across, each with a separate low-power transmitter.

celluloid transparent or translucent, highly flammable, plastic material (a thermoplastic) made from cellulose nitrate and camphor. It was once used for toilet articles, novelties, and photographic film, but has now been replaced by the nonflammable substance ◊cellulose acetate.

cellulose complex ◊carbohydrate composed of long chains of glucose units. It is the principal constituent of the cell wall of higher plants, and a vital ingredient in the diet of many ◊herbivores. Molecules of cellulose are organized into long, unbranched microfibrils that give support to the cell wall. No mammal produces the enzyme cellulase, necessary for digesting cellulose; mammals such as rabbits and cows are only able to digest grass because the bacteria present in their gut can manufacture it.

Celsius scale of temperature, also called centigrade, in which the range from freezing to boiling of water is divided into 100 degrees, freezing point being 0 degrees and boiling point 100 degrees.

Celt member of an Indo-European people that originated in Alpine Europe and spread to the Iberian peninsula and beyond. They were ironworkers and farmers. In the 1st century BC they were defeated by the Roman Empire and by Germanic tribes and confined largely to Britain, Ireland, and N France.

Celtic languages branch of the Indo-European family, divided into two groups: the *Brythonic* or *P-Celtic* (Welsh, Cornish, Breton, and Gaulish) and the *Goidelic* or *Q-Celtic* (Irish, Scottish, and Manx Gaelic). Celtic languages once stretched from the Black Sea to Britain, but have been in decline for centuries, limited to the so-called "Celtic fringe" of western Europe.

cement any bonding agent used to unite particles in a single mass or to cause one surface to adhere to another. *Portland cement* is a powder obtained from burning together a mixture of lime (or chalk) and clay, and when mixed with water and sand or gravel, turns into mortar or concrete.

In geology, a chemically precipitated material such as carbonate that occupies the interstices of clastic rocks.

Cenozoic or *Caenozoic* era of geological time that began 65 million years ago and is still in process. It is divided into the Tertiary and Quaternary periods. The Cenozoic marks the emergence of mammals as a dominant group, including humans, and the formation of the mountain chains of the Himalayas and the Alps.

censorship suppression by authority of material considered immoral, heretical, subversive, libelous, damaging to state security, or otherwise offensive. It is generally more stringent under totalitarian or strongly religious regimes and in wartime.

Despite First Amendment protection of free speech, attempts at censorship are made by government agencies or groups; the question is often tested in the courts, especially with respect to sexually explicit material. Recently, efforts have been made to suppress certain pieces of music and works of art, on such grounds as racial harassment and social depravity.

census official count of the population of a country, originally for military call-up and taxation, later for assessment of social trends as other information regarding age, sex, and occupation of each individual was included. They may become unnecessary as computerized databanks are developed.

The first US census was taken in 1790.

centaur in Greek mythology, a creature half-human and half-horse. Centaurs were supposed to live in Thessaly, and be wild and lawless; the mentor of Heracles, Chiron, was an exception.

center of gravity the point in an object about which its weight is evenly balanced. In a uniform gravitational field, this is the same as the ◊center of mass.

center of mass or *center of gravity* the point in or near an object from which its total weight appears to originate and can be assumed to act. A symmetrical homogeneous object such as a sphere or cube has its center of mass at its physical center; a hollow shape (such as a cup) may have its center of mass in space inside the hollow.

centigrade alternate name for the ◊Celsius temperature scale.

centipede jointed-legged animal of the group Chilopoda, members of which have a distinct head and a single pair of long antennae. Their bodies are composed of segments (which may number nearly 200), each of similar form and bearing a single pair of legs. Most are small, but the tropical *Scolopendra gigantea* may reach 1 ft/30 cm in length. *Millipedes*, class Diplopoda, have fewer segments (up to 100), but have two pairs of legs on each.

Central African Republic (*République Centrafricaine*) *area* 240,260 sq mi/622,436 sq km *capital* Bangui *towns and cities* Berbérati, Bouar, Bossangoa *physical* landlocked flat plateau, with rivers flowing N and S, and hills in NE and SW; dry in N, rainforest in SW *environment* an estimated 87% of the urban population is without access to safe drinking water *features* Kotto and Mbali river falls; the Oubangui River rises 20 ft/6 m at Bangui during the wet season (June–Nov) *head of state* Ange-Felix Patasse from 1993 *head of government* Jean-Luc Mandaba from 1993 *political system* emergent democratic republic *political parties* Central African People's Liberation Party (MPLC), left of center; Central African Democratic Rally (RDC), nationalist *exports* diamonds, uranium, coffee, cotton, timber, tobacco *currency* CFA franc *population* (1993 est) 3,200,000 (more than 80 ethnic groups); growth rate 2.3% p.a. *life expectancy* men 48, women 53 *languages* Sangho (national), French (official), Arabic, Hunsa, and Swahili *religions* Protestant 25%, Roman Catholic 25%, Muslim 10%, animist 10%

literacy men 52%, women 25% *GNP* $390 per head (1991) *chronology 1960* Central African Republic achieved independence from France; David Dacko elected president. *1962* The republic made a one-party state. *1965* Dacko ousted in military coup led by Col. Bokassa. *1966* Constitution rescinded and national assembly dissolved. *1972* Bokassa declared himself president for life. *1977* Bokassa made himself emperor of the Central African Empire. *1979* Bokassa deposed by Dacko following violent repressive measures by the self-styled emperor, who went into exile. *1981* Dacko deposed in a bloodless coup, led by General André Kolingba, and an all-military government established. *1983* Clandestine opposition movement formed. *1984* Amnesty for all political party leaders announced. President Mitterrand of France paid a state visit. *1985* New constitution promised, with some civilians in the government. *1986* Bokassa returned from France, expecting to return to power; he was imprisoned and his trial started. General Kolingba reelected. New constitution approved by referendum. *1988* Bokassa found guilty and received death sentence, later commuted to life imprisonment. *1991* Opposition parties allowed to form. *1992* Abortive debate held on political reform; multiparty elections promised but then postponed. *1993* Sept: Kolingba released several thousand prisoners, including Bokassa. Ange-Felix Patasse elected president, ending twelve years of military dictatorship. Jean-Luc Mandaba appointed prime minister at head of coalition government. Nov: Bokassa stripped of his military rank.

Central America the part of the Americas that links Mexico with the Isthmus of Panama, comprising Belize, Costa Rica, El Salvador, Guatemala, Honduras, Nicaragua, and Panama.

It is also an isthmus, crossed by mountains that form part of the Cordilleras, rising to a maximum height of 13,845 ft/ 4,220 m. There are numerous active volcanoes. Central America is about 200,000 sq mi/523,000 sq km in area and has a population (1980) estimated at 22,700,000, mostly Indians or mestizos (of mixed white-Indian ancestry). Tropical agricultural products and other basic commodities and raw materials are exported.

Central Command military strike force consisting of units from the US army, navy, and air force, which operates in the Middle East and North Africa. Its headquarters are in Fort McDill, Florida. It was established 1979, following the Iranian hostage crisis and the Soviet invasion of Afghanistan, and was known as the Rapid Deployment Force until 1983. It commanded coalition forces in the Gulf War 1991.

Plagued by organizational problems, interservice rivalries, equipment shortages, and lack of access to bases in the Middle East, it was reorganized by President Reagan in 1983 as the US Central Command.

Central Intelligence Agency (CIA) US intelligence organization established 1947. It has actively intervened overseas, generally to undermine left-wing regimes or to protect US financial interests; for example, in the Congo (now Zaire) and Nicaragua. From 1980 all covert activity by the CIA had by law to be reported to Congress, preferably beforehand, and to be authorized by the president. Robert James Woolsey became CIA director 1993. In 1994 the CIA's estimated budget was around $3.1 billion; the total budget for the US intelligence agencies for 1994 was estimated at $28 billion.

The CIA belongs to the executive branch of government and acts on the president's orders. Historically, it runs both covert (secret) and overt (open) operations in the name of national security.

central nervous system (CNS) the brain and spinal cord, as distinct from other components of the ◊nervous system. The CNS integrates all nervous functions.

central processing unit (CPU) main component of a computer, the part that executes individual program instructions and controls the operation of other parts. It is sometimes called the central processor or, when contained on a single integrated circuit, a microprocessor.

centrifugal force useful concept in physics, based on an apparent (but not real) force. It may be regarded as a force that acts radially outward from a spinning or orbiting object, thus balancing the ◊centripetal force (which is real). For an object of mass m moving with a velocity v in a circle of radius r, the centrifugal force F equals mv^2/r (outward).

centripetal force force that acts radially inward on an object moving in a curved path. For example, with a weight whirled in a circle at the end of a length of string, the centripetal force is the tension in the string. For an object of mass m moving with a velocity v in a circle of radius r, the centripetal force F equals mv^2/r (inward). The reaction to this force is the centrifugal force.

Centronics interface standard type of computer ◊interface, used to connect computers to parallel devices, usually printers. (Centronics was an important printer manufacturer in the early days of microcomputing.)

cephalopod any predatory marine mollusk of the class Cephalopoda, with the mouth and head surrounded by tentacles. Cephalopods are the most intelligent, the fastest-moving, and the largest of all animals without backbones, and there are remarkable luminescent forms which swim or drift at great depths. They have the most highly developed nervous and sensory systems of all invertebrates, the eye in some closely paralleling that found in vertebrates. Examples include octopus, squid, and cuttlefish. Shells are rudimentary or absent in most cephalopods.

ceramics objects made from clay, hardened into a permanent form by baking (firing) at very high temperatures in a kiln. Ceramics are used for building construction and decoration (bricks, tiles), for specialist industrial uses (linings for furnaces used to manufacture steel, fuel elements in nuclear reactors, and so on), and for plates and vessels used in the home. Different types of clay and different methods and temperatures of firing create a variety of results. Ceramics may be cast in a mold or hand-built out of slabs of clay, coiled, or thrown on a wheel. Technically, the main categories are earthenware, stoneware, and hard-and softpaste porcelain (see under ◊pottery and porcelain).

cereal grass grown for its edible, nutrient-rich, starchy seeds. The term refers primarily to wheat, oats, rye, and barley, but may also refer to corn, millet, and rice. Cereals contain about 75% complex carbohydrates and 10% protein, plus fats and fiber (roughage). They store well. If all the world's cereal crop were consumed as whole-grain products directly by humans, everyone could obtain adequate protein and carbohydrate;

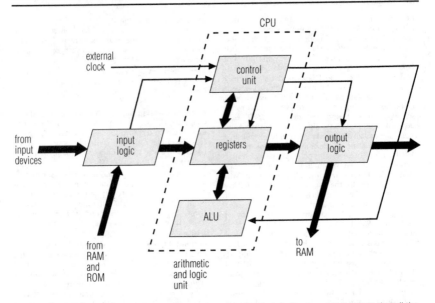

central processing unit, (CPU) *The central processing unit is the "brain" of a computer; it is here that all the computer's work is done. The arithmetic and logic unit (ALU) does the arithmetic, using the registers to store intermediate results, supervised by the control unit. Input and output circuits connect the ALU to external memory, input, and output devices.*

however, a large proportion of cereal production in affluent nations is used as animal feed to boost the production of meat, dairy products, and eggs.

cerebral hemorrhage or *apoplectic fit* in medicine, a ◊stroke in which a blood vessel bursts in the brain, caused by factors such as high blood pressure combined with hardening of the arteries, or chronic poisoning with lead or alcohol. It may cause death or damage parts of the brain, leading to paralysis or mental impairment. The effects are usually long-term and the condition may recur.

Ceres in Roman mythology, the goddess of agriculture, equivalent to the Greek ◊Demeter.

cerium malleable and ductile, gray, metallic element, symbol Ce, atomic number 58, atomic weight 140.12. It is the most abundant member of the lanthanide series, and is used in alloys, electronic components, nuclear fuels, and lighter flints. It was discovered 1804 by the Swedish chemists Jöns Berzelius and Wilhelm Hisinger (1766–1852), and, independently, by Martin Klaproth. The element was named for the then recently discovered asteroid Ceres.

CERN nuclear research organization founded 1954 as a cooperative enterprise among European governments. It has laboratories at Meyrin, near Geneva, Switzerland. It was originally known as the *Conseil Européen pour la Recherche Nucléaire* but subsequently renamed *Organisation Européenne pour la Recherche Nucléaire*, although still familiarly known as CERN. It houses the world's largest particle ◊accelerator, the Large Electron Positron Collider (LEP), with which notable advances have been made in ◊particle physics.

Cervantes Saavedra, Miguel de 1547–1616. Spanish novelist, playwright, and poet. His masterpiece *Don Quixote* (in full *El ingenioso hidalgo Don Quixote de la Mancha*) was published 1605. In 1613, his *Novelas ejemplares/Exemplary Novels* appeared, followed by *Viaje del Parnaso/The Voyage to Parnassus* 1614. A spurious second part of *Don Quixote* prompted Cervantes to bring out his own second part 1615, often considered superior to the first in construction and characterization.

cervical smear removal of a small sample of tissue from the cervix (neck of the womb) to screen for changes implying a likelihood of cancer. The procedure is also known as the *Pap test* after its originator, George Papanicolau.

cesium soft, silvery-white, ductile, metallic element, symbol Cs, atomic number 55, atomic weight 132.905. It is one of the ◊alkali metals, and is the most electropositive of all the elements. In air it ignites spontaneously, and it reacts vigorously with water. It is used in the manufacture of photocells.

Cetus constellation straddling the celestial equator (see ◊celestial sphere), represented as a sea monster. Cetus contains the long-period variable star ◊Mira, and Tau Ceti, one of the nearest stars visible with the naked eye.

Ceylon former name (to 1972) of ◊Sri Lanka.

Cézanne Paul 1839–1906. French Post-Impressionist painter. He was a leading figure in the development of modern art. He broke away from the Impressionists' concern with the ever-changing effects of light to develop a style that tried to capture the structure of natural forms, whether in landscapes, still lifes, or portraits. *Cardplayers* about 1890–95 (Louvre, Paris) is typical of his work.

CFC abbreviation for ◊*chlorofluorocarbon*.

CGA (abbreviation for *color graphics adapter*) in computing, first color display system for IBM PCs and compatible machines. It has been superseded by EGA, ◊VGA, SVGA, and ◊XGA.

c.g.s. system system of units based on the centimeter, gram, and second, as units of length, mass, and time respectively. It has been replaced for scientific work by the ◊SI units to avoid inconsistencies in definition of the thermal calorie and electrical quantities.

Chad Republic of (*République du Tchad*) *area* 495,624 sq mi/1,284,000 sq km *capital* Ndjamena (formerly Fort Lamy) *towns and cities* Sarh, Moundou, Abéché *physical* landlocked state with mountains and part of Sahara Desert in N; moist savanna in S; rivers in S flow NW to Lake Chad *head of state* Idriss Deby from 1990 *head of government* Delwa Kassire Koumakoye from 1993 *political system* emergent democratic republic *political parties* Alliance for Democracy and Progress (RDP), center-left; Union for Democracy and Progress (UPDT), center-left; Patriotic Movement of Salvation (MPS), center-left; Action for Unity and Socialism (ACTUS), center-left; Union for Democracy and the Republic (UDR), center-left *exports* cotton, meat, livestock, hides, skins *currency* CFA franc *population* (1993) 6,290,000; growth rate 2.3% p.a. Nomadic tribes move N–S seasonally in search of water *life expectancy* men 46, women 49 *languages* French, Arabic (both official), over 100 African languages spoken *religions* Muslim 44% (N), Christian 33%, animist 23% (S) *literacy* men 62%, women 18% *GNP* $267 per head (1992) *chronology 1960* Independence achieved from France, with François Tombalbaye as president. *1963* Violent opposition in the Muslim north, led by the Chadian National Liberation Front (Frolinat), backed by Libya. *1968* Revolt quelled with France's help. *1975* Tombalbaye killed in military coup led by Félix Malloum. Frolinat continued its resistance. *1978* Malloum tried to find a political solution by bringing the former Frolinat leader Hissène Habré into his government but they were unable to work together. *1979* Malloum forced to leave the country; an interim government was set up under General Goukouni. Habré continued his opposition with his Army of the North (FAN). *1981* Habré now in control of half the country. Goukouni fled and set up a "government in exile". *1983* Habré's regime recognized by the Organization for African Unity (OAU), but in the north Goukouni's supporters, with Libya's help, fought on. Eventually a cease-fire was agreed, with latitude 16°N dividing the country. *1984* Libya and France agreed to a withdrawal of forces. *1985* Fighting between Libyan-backed and French-backed forces intensified. *1987* Chad, France, and Libya agreed on cease-fire proposed by OAU. *1988* Full diplomatic relations with Libya restored. *1989* Libyan troop movements reported on border; Habré reelected, amended constitution. *1990* President Habré ousted in coup led by Idriss Deby. New constitution adopted, enshrining one-party system. *1991* Several antigovernment coups foiled. National charter providing for a transition to multi-party politics. *1992* Antigovernment coup foiled. Two new opposition parties approved. *1993* April: Fuidel Mounyar chosen as transitional prime minister pending multiparty elections. Nov: Mounyar replaced by Delwa Kassire Koumakoye.

Chad, Lake lake on the northeastern boundary of Nigeria. It once varied in extent between rainy and dry seasons from 20,000 sq mi/1,284,000 sq km to 7,000 sq mi/20,000 sq km, but a series of droughts 1979–89 reduced its area by 80%. The S Chad irrigation project used the lake waters to irrigate the surrounding desert, but the 2,500 mi/4,000 km of canals dug for the project are now permanently dry because of the shrinking size of the lake. The Lake Chad basin is being jointly developed for oil and natron by Cameroon, Chad, Niger, and Nigeria.

Chadwick James 1891–1974. British physicist. In 1932 he discovered the particle in the nucleus of an atom that became known as the neutron because it has no electric charge. He received the Nobel Prize for Physics 1935.

Chagall Marc 1887–1985. Russian-born French painter and designer. Much of his highly colored, fantastic imagery was inspired by the village life of his boyhood and by Jewish and Russian folk traditions. He designed stained glass, mosaics (for Israel's Knesset in the 1960s), the ceiling of the Paris Opera House 1964, tapestries, and stage sets. He was an original figure, often seen as a precursor of Surrealism, as in *I and the Village* 1911 (Museum of Modern Art, New York).

Chagas's disease disease common in Central and South America, infecting approximately 18 million people worldwide. It is caused by a trypanosome parasite, *Trypanosoma cruzi*, transmitted by several species of blood-sucking insect; it results in incurable damage to the heart, intestines, and brain. It is named for Brazilian doctor Carlos Chagas (1879–1934).

chain reaction in nuclear physics, a fission reaction that is maintained because neutrons released by the splitting of some atomic nuclei themselves go on to split others, releasing even more neutrons. Such a reaction can be controlled (as in a nuclear reactor) by using moderators to absorb excess neutrons. Uncontrolled, a chain reaction produces a nuclear explosion (as in an atomic bomb).

chalcedony form of quartz, SiO_2, in which the crystals are so fine-grained that they are impossible to distinguish with a microscope (cryptocrystalline). Agate, onyx, and carnelian are ◊gem varieties of chalcedony.

chalk soft, fine-grained, whitish rock composed of calcium carbonate, $CaCO_3$, extensively quarried for use in cement, lime, and mortar, and in the manufacture of cosmetics and toothpaste. *Blackboard chalk* in fact consists of gypsum (calcium sulfate, $CaSO_4.2H_2$).

Chamberlain (Arthur) Neville 1869–1940. British Conservative politician, son of Joseph Chamberlain. He was prime minister 1937–40; his policy of appeasement toward the fascist dictators Mussolini and Hitler (with whom he concluded the ◊Munich Agreement 1938) failed to prevent the outbreak of World War II. He resigned 1940 following the defeat of the British forces in Norway.

In 1938 Chamberlain went to Munich, Germany, and negotiated with Hitler on the Czechoslovak question. He was ecstatically received on his return and claimed that the Munich Agreement brought "peace in our time". However, Germany advanced against British allies and within a year Britain was at war.

Chamberlain (Joseph) Austen 1863–1937. British Conservative politician, elder son of Joseph Chamberlain; as foreign secretary 1924–29 he negotiated the Pact of Locarno, for which he won the Nobel Peace Prize 1925, and signed the Kellogg–Briand pact to outlaw war 1928.

Chamberlain Wilt (Wilton Norman) 1936– . US basketball player, nicknamed "Wilt the Stilt", who set a
record by averaging 50.4 points a game during the
1962 season, and was the only man to score 100
points in a game.

CAREER HIGHLIGHTS

total games:	1,045
points:	31,419 (average 30.1 per game)
records	
most points in a game:	100 (v. New York Knickerbockers 1962)
most points in a season:	4,029 (average 50.4 per game, 1962)
most seasons as NBA top scorer:	7 (1960–66)

He played professionally for the Philadelphia
Warriors, Philadelphia 76ers, Los Angeles Lakers, and
briefly for the Harlem Globetrotters. Playing against
the New York Knickerbockers 1962 he became the
only man to score 100 points in a National Basketball
Association (NBA) game. He was the only center to
lead the league in assists. He led the league in scoring
1960–66, was NBA Most Valuable Player 1960,
1966–68, and retired 1973 after a 13-year career.

chamber music music intended for performance in a
small room or chamber, rather than in the concert
hall, and usually written for instrumental combinations, played with one instrument to a part, as in the
string quartet.

chameleon any of some 80 or so species of lizard of the
family Chameleontidae. Some species have highly
developed color-changing abilities, which are caused
by changes in the intensity of light, of temperature,
and of emotion altering the dispersal of pigment gran-
ules in the layers of cells beneath the outer skin.

chamois goatlike mammal *Rupicapra rupicapra* found in
mountain ranges of S Europe and Asia Minor. It is
brown, with dark patches running through the eyes,
and can be up to 2.6 ft/80 cm high. Chamois are very
sure-footed, and live in herds of up to 30 members.

Chamorro Violeta Barrios de *c.*1939– . President of
Nicaragua from 1990. With strong US support, she
was elected to be the candidate for the National
Opposition Union (UNO) 1989, winning the presidency from David Ortega Saavedra Feb 1990 and thus
ending the period of ◊Sandinista rule.

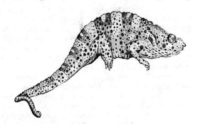

chameleon *Meller's chameleon of the savanna of
Tanzania and Malawi is the largest chameleon found
outside Madagascar, about 1.7 ft/55 cm long. It
feeds on small birds and insects, lying in wait on
branches to ambush them. Its coloration makes it
very hard to see among foliage.*

champagne sparkling white wine invented by Dom
Pérignon, a Benedictine monk, 1668. It is made from
a blend of grapes (*pinot noir* and *pinot chardonnay*)
grown in the Marne River region around Reims and
Epernay, in Champagne, NE France. After a first fermentation, sugar and yeast are added to the still wine,
which, when bottled, undergoes a second fermentation to produce the sparkle. Sugar syrup may be added
to make the wine sweet (*sec*) or dry (*brut*).

champignon any of a number of edible fungi of the
family Agaricaceae. The *fairy ring champignon
Marasmius oreades* is so called because its fruiting bodies (mushrooms) occur in rings around the outer edge
of the underground mycelium (threadlike tubes) of
the fungus.

Champlain Samuel de 1567–1635. French pioneer, soldier, and explorer in Canada. Having served in the
army of Henry IV and on an expedition to the West
Indies, he began his exploration of Canada 1603. In a
third expedition 1608 he founded and named
Québec, and was appointed lieutenant governor of
French Canada 1612.

Champlain, Lake lake in northeastern US (extending
some 6 mi/10 km into Canada) on the New
York–Vermont border; length 125 mi/201 km; area
430 sq mi/692 sq km. It is linked by canal to the St
Lawrence and Hudson rivers.

chancellor of the Exchequer in the UK, senior cabinet
minister responsible for the national economy. The
office, established under Henry III, originally entailed
keeping the Exchequer seal.

Chandler Raymond 1888–1959. US novelist. He turned
the pulp detective mystery form into a successful
genre of literature and created the quintessential private eye in the tough but chivalric loner, Philip
Marlowe. Marlowe is the narrator of such books as *The
Big Sleep* 1939 (filmed 1946), *Farewell My Lovely* 1940
(filmed 1944), *The Lady in the Lake* 1943 (filmed 1947),
and *The Long Goodbye* 1954 (filmed 1975). He also
wrote numerous screenplays, notably *Double
Indemnity* 1944, *Blue Dahlia* 1946, and *Strangers on a
Train* 1951.

Chandragupta Maurya ruler of N India *c.*325–*c.*297 BC,
founder of the Mauryan dynasty. He overthrew the
Nanda dynasty 325 and then conquered the Punjab
322 after the death of ◊Alexander the Great, expanding his empire west to Persia. He is credited with having united most of India.

Chanel Coco (Gabrielle) 1883–1971. French fashion
designer. She was renowned as a trendsetter and her
designs have been copied worldwide. She created the
"little black dress", the informal cardigan suit, costume jewelry, and perfumes.

Changchun industrial city and capital of Jilin province,
China; population (1989) 2,020,000. Machinery and
motor vehicles are manufactured. It is also the center
of an agricultural district.

Chang Jiang or *Yangtze Kiang* longest river of China,
flowing about 3,900 mi/6,300 km from Tibet to the
Yellow Sea. It is a main commercial waterway. The
Three Gorges Dam on the river was officially inaugurated Dec 1994.

Changsha port on the river Chang Jiang, capital of
Hunan province, China; population (1989) 1,300,000.
It trades in rice, tea, timber, and nonferrous metals;
works antimony, lead, and silver; and produces chemicals, electronics, porcelain, and embroideries.

Channel Islands group of islands in the English Channel, off the northwest coast of France; they are a possession of the British crown. They comprise the islands of Jersey, Guernsey, Alderney, Great and Little Sark, with the lesser Herm, Brechou, Jethou, and Lihou.

Channel Tunnel tunnel built beneath the English Channel, linking Britain with mainland Europe. It comprises twin rail tunnels, 31 mi/50 km long and 24 ft/7.3 m in diameter, located 130 ft/40 m beneath the seabed. Specially designed shuttle trains carrying automobiles and trucks run between terminals at Folkestone, Kent, and Sangatte, W of Calais, France. It was begun 1986, and the French and English sections were linked Dec 1990. It was officially opened May 6, 1994

chanson de geste epic poetry of the High Middle Ages in Europe. It probably developed from oral poetry recited in royal or princely courts, and takes as its subject the exploits of heroes, such as those associated with Charlemagne and the crusades. The best-known example is the *Chanson de Roland*.

chant singing of a formula, usually by a group, for confidence or spiritual improvement. Chants can be secular or religious, both Western and Eastern. Ambrosian and ◊Gregorian chants are forms of plainsong.

chaos theory or *chaology* branch of mathematics used to deal with chaotic systems—for example, an engineered structure, such as an oil platform, that is subjected to irregular, unpredictable wave stress.

chapel place of worship used by some Christian denominations; also, a part of a building used for Christian worship. A large church or cathedral may have several chapels.

Chaplin Charlie (Charles Spencer) 1889–1977. English film actor and director. He made his reputation as a tramp with a smudge moustache, bowler hat, and twirling cane in silent comedies from the mid-1910s, including *The Rink* 1916, *The Kid* 1920, and *The Gold Rush* 1925. His work often contrasts buffoonery with pathos, and his later films combine dialogue with mime and music, as in *The Great Dictator* 1940 and *Limelight* 1952. He was one of cinema's most popular and greatest stars.

Until sound films became common, he was the best known and most popular film star of his day. He was married four times, his third wife being actress Paulette Goddard, and his fourth, Oona, was the daughter of the dramatist Eugene O'Neill.

char or *charr* fish *Salvelinus alpinus* related to the trout, living in the Arctic coastal waters, and also in Europe and North America in some upland lakes.

characin freshwater fish belonging to the family Characidae. There are over 1,300 species, mostly in South and Central America, but also in Africa. Most are carnivores. In typical characins, unlike the somewhat similar carp family, the mouth is toothed, and there is a small dorsal adipose fin just in front of the tail.

character one of the symbols that can be represented in a computer. Characters include letters, numbers, spaces, punctuation marks, and special symbols.

character printer computer ◊printer that prints one character at a time.

character type check in computing, a ◊validation check to ensure that an input data item does not contain invalid characters. For example, an input name may be checked to ensure that it contains only letters of the alphabet or an input six-figure date may be checked to ensure it contains only numbers.

charcoal black, porous form of ◊carbon, produced by heating wood or other organic materials in the absence of air. It is used as a fuel in the smelting of metals such as copper and zinc, and by artists for making black line drawings. *Activated charcoal* has been powdered and dried so that it presents a much increased surface area for adsorption; it is used for filtering and purifying liquids and gases—for example, in drinking-water filters and gas masks.

Chardin Jean-Baptiste-Siméon 1699–1779. French painter. He took as his subjects naturalistic still lifes and quiet domestic scenes that recall the Dutch tradition. His work is a complete contrast to that of his contemporaries, the Rococo painters. He developed his own technique, using successive layers of paint to achieve depth of tone, and is generally considered one of the finest exponents of genre painting.

charge see ◊electric charge.

charge-coupled device (CCD) device for forming images electronically, using a layer of silicon that releases electrons when struck by incoming light. The electrons are stored in ◊pixels and read off into a computer at the end of the exposure. CCDs have now almost entirely replaced photographic film for applications such as astrophotography where extreme sensitivity to light is paramount.

charged particle beam high-energy beam of electrons or protons. Such beams are being developed as weapons.

Charge of the Light Brigade disastrous attack by the British Light Brigade of cavalry against the Russian entrenched artillery on Oct 25, 1854 during the Crimean War at the Battle of ◊Balaclava. Of the 673 soldiers who took part, there were 272 casualties.

chariot horse-drawn carriage with two wheels, used in ancient Egypt, Greece, and Rome, for fighting, processions, and races; it is thought to have originated in Asia. Typically, the fighting chariot contained a driver and a warrior, who would fight on foot, with the chariot providing rapid mobility.

Charlemagne (Charles [I] the Great) 742–814. King of the Franks from 768 and Holy Roman emperor from 800. By inheritance (his father was ◊Pepin the Short) and extensive campaigns of conquest, he united most of W Europe by 804, when after 30 years of war the Saxons came under his control. He reformed the legal, judicial, and military systems; established schools; and promoted Christianity, commerce, agriculture, arts, and literature. In his capital, Aachen, scholars gathered from all over Europe.

Charles (Mary) Eugenia 1919– . Dominican politician, prime minister from 1980; cofounder and first leader of the centrist Dominica Freedom Party (DFP). Two years after Dominica's independence the DFP won the 1980 general election and Charles became the Caribbean's first female prime minister. In 1993 she resigned the leadership of the DFP, but remained as prime minister pending the 1995 elections.

Charles Jacques Alexandre César 1746–1823. French physicist who studied gases and made the first ascent in a hydrogen-filled balloon 1783. His work on the expansion of gases led to the formulation of ◊Charles's law.

Charles I 1600–1649. King of Great Britain and Ireland from 1625, son of James I of England (James VI of Scotland). He accepted the petition of right 1628 but then dissolved Parliament and ruled without a parliament 1629–40. His advisers were Strafford and ◊Laud, who persecuted the Puritans and provoked the Scots to revolt. The ◊Short Parliament, summoned 1640, refused funds, and the ◊Long Parliament later that year rebelled. Charles declared war on Parliament 1642 but surrendered 1646 and was beheaded 1649. He was the father of Charles II.

Charles II 1630–1685. King of Great Britain and Ireland from 1660, when Parliament accepted the restoration of the monarchy after the collapse of Cromwell's Commonwealth; son of Charles I. His chief minister Clarendon, who arranged his marriage 1662 with Catherine of Braganza, was replaced 1667 with the Cabal of advisers. His plans to restore Catholicism in Britain led to war with the Netherlands 1672–74 in support of Louis XIV of France and a break with Parliament, which he dissolved 1681. He was succeeded by James II.

When Charles dissolved Parliament, the Whigs fled in terror. He now ruled without a Parliament, financed by Louis XIV. When the Whigs plotted a revolt, their leaders were executed.

Charles (full name Charles Philip Arthur George) 1948– . Prince of the UK, heir to the British throne, and Prince of Wales since 1958 (invested 1969). He is the first-born child of Queen Elizabeth II and the Duke of Edinburgh. He studied at Trinity College, Cambridge, 1967–70, before serving in the Royal Air Force and Royal Navy. He is the first royal heir since 1659 to have an English wife, Lady Diana Spencer, daughter of the 8th Earl Spencer. They have two sons and heirs, William (1982–) and Henry (1984–). Amid much publicity, Charles and Diana separated 1992.

Charles I king of France, better known as the Holy Roman emperor ◊Charlemagne.

Charles (II) the Bald king of France, see ◊Charles II, Holy Roman emperor.

Charles (V) the Wise 1337–1380. King of France from 1364. He was regent during the captivity of his father, John II, in England 1356–60, and became king on John's death. He reconquered nearly all France from England 1369–80.

Charles (VI) the Mad or *the Well-Beloved* 1368–1422. King of France from 1380, succeeding his father Charles V; he was under the regency of his uncles until 1388. He became mentally unstable 1392, and civil war broke out between the dukes of Orléans and Burgundy. Henry V of England invaded France 1415, conquering Normandy, and in 1420 forced Charles to sign the Treaty of Troyes, recognizing Henry as his successor.

Charles VII 1403–1461. King of France from 1429. Son of Charles VI, he was excluded from the succession by the Treaty of Troyes, but recognized by the south of France. In 1429 Joan of Arc raised the siege of Orléans and had him crowned at Reims. He organized France's first standing army and by 1453 had expelled the English from all of France except Calais.

Charles IX 1550–1574. King of France from 1560. Second son of Henry II and Catherine de' Medici, he succeeded his brother Francis II at the age of ten but remained under the domination of his mother's regency for ten years while France was torn by religious

wars. In 1570 he fell under the influence of the ◊Huguenot leader Gaspard de Coligny (1517–1572); alarmed by this, Catherine instigated his order for the Massacre of ◊St Bartholomew, which led to a new religious war.

Charles X 1757–1836. King of France from 1824. Grandson of Louis XV and brother of Louis XVI and Louis XVIII, he was known as the comte d'Artois before his accession. He fled to England at the beginning of the French Revolution, and when he came to the throne on the death of Louis XVIII, he attempted to reverse the achievements of the Revolution. A revolt ensued 1830, and he again fled to England.

Charles I Holy Roman emperor, better known as ◊Charlemagne.

Charles (II) the Bald 823–877. Holy Roman emperor from 875 and (as Charles II) king of France from 843. Younger son of Louis I (the Pious), he warred against his eldest brother, Emperor Lothair I. The Treaty of Verdun 843 made him king of the West Frankish Kingdom (now France and the Spanish Marches).

Charles (III) the Fat 839–888. Holy Roman emperor 881–87; he became king of the West Franks 885, thus uniting for the last time the whole of Charlemagne's dominions, but was deposed.

Charles IV 1316–1378. Holy Roman emperor from 1355 and king of Bohemia from 1346. Son of John of Luxembourg, king of Bohemia, he was elected king of Germany 1346 and ruled all Germany from 1347. He was the founder of the first German university in Prague 1348.

Charles V 1500–1558. Holy Roman emperor 1519–56. Son of Philip of Burgundy and Joanna of Castile, he inherited vast possessions, which led to rivalry from Francis I of France, whose alliance with the Ottoman Empire brought Vienna under siege 1529 and 1532. Charles was also in conflict with the Protestants in Germany until the Treaty of Passau 1552, which allowed the Lutherans religious liberty.

Charles VI 1685–1740. Holy Roman emperor from 1711, father of ◊Maria Theresa, whose succession to his Austrian dominions he tried to ensure, and himself claimant to the Spanish throne 1700, thus causing the War of the ◊Spanish Succession.

Charles (Karl Franz Josef) 1887–1922. Emperor of Austria and king of Hungary from 1916, the last of the Hapsburg emperors. He succeeded his great-uncle Franz Josef 1916 but was forced to withdraw to Switzerland 1918, although he refused to abdicate. In 1921 he attempted unsuccessfully to regain the crown of Hungary and was deported to Madeira, where he died.

Charles I 1500–1558. See ◊Charles V, Holy Roman emperor.

Charles II 1661–1700. King of Spain from 1665. The second son of Philip IV, he was the last of the Spanish Hapsburg kings. Mentally handicapped from birth, he bequeathed his dominions to Philip of Anjou, grandson of Louis XIV, which led to the War of the ◊Spanish Succession.

Charles III 1716–1788. King of Spain from 1759. Son of Philip V, he became duke of Parma 1732 and conquered Naples and Sicily 1734. On the death of his half brother Ferdinand VI (1713–1759), he became king of Spain, handing over Naples and Sicily to his son Ferdinand (1751–1825). At home, he reformed state finances, strengthened the armed forces, and expelled the Jesuits. During his reign, Spain was involved in the Seven Years' War with France against England. This led to the loss of Florida 1763, which was only regained when Spain and France supported the colonists during the American Revolution.

Charles IV 1748–1819. King of Spain from 1788, when he succeeded his father, Charles III; he left the government in the hands of his wife and her lover, the minister Manuel de Godoy (1767–1851). In 1808 Charles was induced to abdicate by Napoleon's machinations in favor of his son Ferdinand VII (1784–1833), who was subsequently deposed by Napoleon's brother Joseph. Charles was awarded a pension by Napoleon and died in Rome.

Charles XII 1682–1718. King of Sweden from 1697, when he succeeded his father, Charles XI. From 1700 he was involved in wars with Denmark, Poland, and Russia.

He won a succession of victories until, in 1709 while invading Russia, he was defeated at Poltava in the Ukraine, and forced to take refuge in Turkey until 1714. He was killed while besieging Fredrikshall, Norway, although it was not known whether he was murdered by his own side or by the enemy.

Charles XIV (Jean Baptiste Jules Bernadotte) 1763–1844. King of Sweden and Norway from 1818. A former marshal in the French army, in 1810 he was elected crown prince of Sweden under the name of Charles John (Carl Johan). Loyal to his adopted country, he brought Sweden into the alliance against Napoleon 1813, as a reward for which Sweden received Norway. He was the founder of the present dynasty.

Charles Edward Stuart the *Young Pretender* or *Bonnie Prince Charlie* 1720– . British prince, grandson of James II and son of James, the Old Pretender. In the Jacobite rebellion 1745 Charles won the support of the Scottish Highlanders; his army invaded England to claim the throne but was beaten back by the duke of Cumberland and routed at ◊Culloden 1746. Charles went into exile.

With a price of £30,000 on his head, Charles Edward fled to France, eventually settling in Italy 1766.

Charles Martel *c.*688–741. Frankish ruler (Mayor of the Palace) of the E Frankish kingdom from 717 and the whole kingdom from 731. His victory against the Moors at Moussais-la-Bataille near Tours 732 earned him his nickname of Martel, "the Hammer", because he halted the Islamic advance into ◊Moors into Europe.

Charles's law law stating that the volume of a given mass of gas at constant temperature is directly proportional to its absolute temperature (temperature in kelvin). It was discovered by French physicist Jacques Charles 1787, and independently by French chemist Joseph Gay-Lussac 1802.

Charles the Bold Duke of Burgundy 1433–1477. Son of Philip the Good, he inherited Burgundy and the Low Countries from him 1465. He waged wars attempting to free the duchy from dependence on France and restore it as a kingdom. He was killed in battle.

Charleston back-kicking dance of the 1920s that originated in Charleston, South Carolina, and became an American craze following the musical *Runnin' Wild* 1923.

Charleston main port and city of South Carolina; population (1990) 80,400. Industries include textiles,

clothing, and paper products. A nuclear-submarine naval base and an air-force base are nearby. The city dates from 1670. The Confederate shelling of Fort Sumter in Charleston harbor on April 12, 1861, initiated the Civil War.

Charleston is the setting for George Gershwin's folk opera *Porgy and Bess*. Spoleto Festival US, dating from 1977, attracts performing-arts groups. The world's first Medical Leech Museum opened in 1995.

Charlotte city in North Carolina, US, on the border with South Carolina; population (1990) 395,900. Industries include data processing, textiles, chemicals, machinery, and food products. It was the gold-mining center of the country until gold was discovered in California 1849.

Charlotte is the birthplace of James K Polk, 11th president of the US.

Charlotte Amalie capital, tourist resort, and free port of the US Virgin Islands, on the island of St Thomas; population (1980) 11,756. Boat building and rum distilling are among the economic activities. It was founded 1672 by the Danish West India Company.

Charon in Greek mythology, the boatman who ferried the dead over the rivers Acheron and Styx to ◊Hades, the underworld. A coin placed on the tongue of the dead paid for their passage.

Charybdis in Greek mythology, a whirlpool formed by a monster of the same name on one side of the narrow straits of Messina, Sicily, opposite the monster Scylla.

Chase William C 1895–1986. US general. He served with the US cavalry in World War I. In World War II, he served mainly in the Far East and Sept 1945 led the 1st Cavalry Division, the first US military force to enter Tokyo. After the war he became Chief of Staff 3rd Army, then went to Taiwan as military adviser to ◊Chiang Kai-shek until his retirement 1956.

From 1943, he commanded 1 Cavalry Brigade which recaptured the Admiralty Islands March 1944. He later took part in the invasion of the Philippines and led the first US troops into Manila Feb 3, 1945. He then took command of 38 Infantry Division and cleared the Japanese out of Bataan and supervised the airborne assault on Corregidor.

château country house or important residence in France. The term originally applied to a French medieval castle. The château was first used as a domestic building in the late 15th century. By the reign of Louis XIII (1610–43) fortifications such as moats and keeps were no longer used for defensive purposes, but merely as decorative features. The Loire valley contains some fine examples of châteaux.

Chateaubriand François René, vicomte de 1768–1848. French writer. He was a founder of Romanticism. In exile from the French Revolution 1794–99, he wrote *Atala* 1801 (based on his encounters with North American Indians) and the autobiographical *René*, which formed part of *Le Génie du Christianisme/The Genius of Christianity* 1802. He later wrote *Mémoires d'outre tombe/Memoirs from Beyond the Tomb* 1848–50.

Chatterton Thomas 1752–1770. English poet. His medieval-style poems and brief life were to inspire English Romanticism. Born in Bristol, he studied ancient documents he found in the Church of St Mary Redcliffe and composed poems he ascribed to a 15th-century monk, "Thomas Rowley", which were accepted as genuine. He committed suicide in London, after becoming destitute.

Chaucer Geoffrey *c.*1340–1400. English poet. *The Canterbury Tales*, a collection of stories told by a group of pilgrims on their way to Canterbury, reveals his knowledge of human nature and his stylistic variety, from urbane and ironic to simple and bawdy. Early allegorical poems, including *The Book of the Duchess*, were influenced by French poems like the *Roman de la Rose*. His *Troilus and Criseyde* is a substantial narrative poem about the tragic betrayal of an idealized courtly love.

Chavez Cesar (Estrada) 1927– . US labor organizer who founded the National Farm Workers Association 1962 and, with the support of the AFL-CIO and other major unions, embarked on a successful campaign to unionize California grape workers. He led boycotts of citrus fruits, lettuce, and grapes in the early 1970s, but disagreement and exploitation of migrant farm laborers continued despite his successes.

Born near Yuma, Arizona, to a family of migrant farm workers, Chavez was deeply influenced by the organizing efforts of Saul Alinsky among agricultural workers in California in the early 1950s. Chavez devoted himself to the cause of unionization and became director of the Community Service Organization 1958.

Chechnya mainly Muslim autonomous republic in S Russia, on the northern slopes of the Caucasus Mountains. *area* (including Ingushetia) 7,450 sq mi/19,300 km *capital* Grozny *industries* oil extraction (at one of the largest Russian oil fields); engineering, chemicals, building materials; timber *population* (1992) (including Ingushetia) 1,308,000 *history* After decades of resistance, the region was conquered by Russia 1859. It was an autonomous region of the USSR 1922–36 when it was joined to Ingushetia as the Autonomous Republic of Checheno-Ingush. In Nov 1991, following the seizure of power by General Dzhokhar Dudayev, the region declared its independence. After a brief, unsuccessful attempt to quell the rebellion, Moscow entered into negotiations over the republic's future. In 1992 Chechenya became an autonomous republic in its own right; later the same year fighting broke out between forces loyal to Dudayev and antiseparatist opposition forces, backed by Russia. Civil war developed Aug 1994 and in Dec 1994 Russian forces entered Chechenya, bombed the capital, and regained control of the region. By March 1995 an estimated 40,000 civilians had been killed and 250,000 were refugees. Chechnya's independence has not received international recognition.

checkers board game played on a ◊chess board. Each of the two players has 12 disk-shaped pieces, and attempts either to capture all the opponent's pieces or to block their movements.

checksum in computing, a control total of specific items of data. A checksum is used as a check that data have been input or transmitted correctly. It is used in communications and in accounts programs.

cheese food made from the *curds* (solids) of soured milk from cows, sheep, or goats, separated from the *whey* (liquid), then salted, put into molds, and pressed into firm blocks. Cheese is ripened with bacteria or surface fungi, and kept for a time to mature before eating.

cheetah large wild cat *Acinonyx jubatus* native to Africa, Arabia, and SW Asia, but now rare in some areas. Yellowish with black spots, it has a slim lithe build. It is up to 3 ft/1 m tall at the shoulder, and up to 5 ft/ 1.5 m. It can reach 70 mph/110 kph, but tires after about 400 yards. Cheetahs live in open country where they hunt small antelopes, hares, and birds.

Chekhov Anton (Pavlovich) 1860–1904. Russian dramatist and writer of short stories. His plays concentrate on the creation of atmosphere and delineation of internal development, rather than external action. His first play, *Ivanov* 1887, was a failure, as was *The Seagull* 1896 until revived by Stanislavsky 1898 at the Moscow Art Theatre, for which Chekhov went on to write his finest plays: *Uncle Vanya* 1897, *The Three Sisters* 1901, and *The Cherry Orchard* 1904.

chelate chemical compound whose molecules consist of one or more metal atoms or charged ions joined to chains of organic residues by coordinate (or dative covalent) chemical ◊bonds.

Chelyabinsk industrial city and capital of Chelyabinsk region, W Siberia, Russia; population (1987) 1,119,000. It has iron and engineering works and makes chemicals, motor vehicles, and aircraft.

chemical equation method of indicating the reactants and products of a chemical reaction by using chemical symbols and formulae. A chemical equation gives two basic pieces of information: (1) the reactants (on the left-hand side) and products (right-hand side); and (2) the reacting proportions (stoichiometry)— that is, how many units of each reactant and product are involved. The equation must balance; that is, the total number of atoms of a particular element on the left-hand side must be the same as the number of atoms of that element on the right-hand side.

chemical warfare use in war of gaseous, liquid, or solid substances intended to have a toxic effect on humans, animals, or plants. Together with ◊biological warfare, it was banned by the Geneva Protocol 1925 and the United Nations in 1989 also voted for a ban. The total US stockpile 1989 was estimated at 30,000 metric tons and the Soviet stockpile at 50,000 metric tons. In June 1990, the US and USSR agreed bilaterally to reduce their stockpile to 5,000 metric tons each by 2002. The US began replacing its stocks with new nerve-gas ◊binary weapons. In Jan 1993, over 120 nations, including the US and Russia, signed a treaty outlawing the manufacture, stockpiling, and use of chemical weapons.

chemisorption the attachment, by chemical means, of a single layer of molecules, atoms, or ions of gas to the surface of a solid or, less frequently, a liquid. It is the basis of catalysis (see ◊catalyst) and is of great industrial importance.

chemistry science concerned with the composition of matter (gas, liquid, or solid) and of the changes that take place in it under certain conditions.

chemosynthesis method of making ◊protoplasm (contents of a cell) using the energy from chemical reactions, in contrast to the use of light energy employed for the same purpose in ◊photosynthesis. The process is used by certain bacteria, which can synthesize organic compounds from carbon dioxide and water using the energy from special methods of ◊respiration.

chemotherapy any medical treatment with chemicals. It usually refers to treatment of cancer with cytotoxic and other drugs. The term was coined by the German bacteriologist Paul Ehrlich for the use of synthetic chemicals against infectious diseases.

Chengdu or *Chengtu* ancient city, capital of Sichuan province, China; population (1989) 2,780,000. It is a busy rail junction and has railroad workshops, and textile, electronics, and engineering industries. It has well-preserved temples.

Chennault Claire L 1890–1958. US pilot. He became famous during world War II as the leader of the "Flying Tigers", a volunteer force of 200 US pilots and engineers fighting alongside Chinese Nationalist forces.

Originally a pilot in the US Army Air Corps, Chennault was retired on medical grounds 1937 and then became an adviser and trainer on aviation for the Chinese Nationalist forces. He returned to duty with the US Army Air Force 1942 when the Flying Tigers were absorbed with the regular US air forces. An offensive against the Japanese 1943 was met with a strong counterattack which destroyed much of his force both in the air and on the ground. He resigned July 1945 after his advice on the future reorganization of the Chinese air force was rejected.

Cherenkov Pavel 1904–1990. Soviet physicist. In 1934 he discovered *Cherenkov radiation*; this occurs as a bluish light when charged atomic particles pass through water or other media at a speed in excess of that of light. He shared a Nobel Prize 1958 with his colleagues Ilya Frank and Igor Tamm for work resulting in a cosmic-ray counter.

Cherenkov discovered that this effect was independent of any medium and depended for its production on the passage of high velocity electrons. The phenomenon has also been claimed as the discovery of the French scientist Lucien Mallet.

Chernobyl town in central Ukraine; site of a nuclear power station. In April 1986 two huge explosions destroyed a central reactor, breaching the 1,000 tonne roof. In the immediate vicinity of Chernobyl, 31 people died (all firemen or workers at the plant) and 135,000 were permanently evacuated. It has been estimated that there will be an additional 20–40,000 deaths from cancer in the next 60 years.

cherry any of various trees of the genus *Prunus*, belonging to the rose family. Cherry trees are distinguished from plums and apricots by their fruits, which are spherical and smooth and not covered with a bloom. They are cultivated in temperate regions with warm summers and grow best in deep fertile soil.

Most cultivated cherries come from Europe. The common chokecherry *P. virginiana* is a widespread wild cherry tree of the US.

chervil any of several plants of the carrot family Umbelliferae. The garden chervil *Anthriscus cerefolium* has leaves with a sweetish odor, resembling parsley. It is used as a garnish and in soups. Chervil originated on the borders of Europe and Asia and was introduced to W Europe by the Romans.

Chesapeake Bay largest of the inlets on the Atlantic coast of the US, bordered by Maryland and Virginia. It is about 200 mi/320 km in length and 4–40 mi/6–64 km in width.

The Chesapeake Bay Bridge Tunnel connects both Virginia shores; farther north the Chesapeake Bay Bridge links the W Maryland shore near Annapolis to Kent Island.

Cheshire county of NW England *area* 896 sq mi/2,320 sq km *towns and cities* Chester (administrative headquarters), Warrington, Crewe, Widnes, Macclesfield, Congleton *features* chiefly a fertile plain, with the Pennines in the E; rivers: Mersey, Dee, Weaver; salt mines and geologically rich former copper workings

at Alderley Edge (in use from Roman times until the 1920s); Little Moreton Hall; discovery of Lindow Man, the first "bogman" to be found in mainland Britain, dating from around 500 BC ; Quarry Bank Mill at Styal is a cotton-industry museum *industries* textiles, chemicals, dairy products *famous people* the novelist Elizabeth Gaskell lived at Knutsford (the locale of *Cranford*); Charles Dodgson (Lewis Carroll) *population* (1991) 956,600.

chess board game originating as early as the 2nd century AD. Two players use 16 pieces each, on a board of 64 squares of alternating color, to try to force the opponent into a position where the main piece (the king) is threatened and cannot move to another position without remaining threatened.

chestnut tree of the genus *Castanea*, belonging to the beech family Fagaceae. The Spanish or sweet chestnut *C. sativa* produces edible nuts inside husks; its timber is also valuable. Horse chestnuts are quite distinct, belonging to the genus *Aesculus*, family Hippocastanaceae.

Horse chestnuts are also called buckeyes. The American chestnut *C. dentata* was a valued hardwood until it was virtually destroyed by an introduced fungus.

Chetnik member of a Serbian nationalist group that operated underground during the German occupation of Yugoslavia in World War II. Led by Col. Draza Mihailovic, the Chetniks initially received aid from the Allies, but this was later transferred to the communist partisans led by Tito. The term has also popularly been applied to Serb militia forces in the 1991–92 Yugoslav civil war.

Chiang Kai-shek (Pinyin *Jiang Jie Shi*) 1887–1975. Chinese nationalist ◊Guomindang (Kuomintang) general and politician, president of China 1928–31 and 1943–49, and of Taiwan from 1949, where he set up a US-supported right-wing government on his expulsion from the mainland by the communist forces.

Chicago financial and industrial city in Illinois on Lake Michigan. It is the third largest US city; population (1990) 2,783,700, metropolitan area 8,065,000. Industries include iron, steel, chemicals, electrical goods, machinery, meatpacking and food processing, publishing, and fabricated metals. The once famous stockyards are now closed.

chicken domestic fowl.

chickenpox or *varicella* common, usually mild disease, caused by a virus of the ◊herpes group and transmitted by airborne droplets. Chickenpox chiefly attacks children under the age of ten. The incubation period is two to three weeks. One attack normally gives immunity for life.

chickpea annual plant *Cicer arietinum*, family Leguminosae, which is grown for food in India and the Middle East. Its short, hairy pods contain edible pealike seeds.

chicory plant *Cichorium intybus*, family Compositae. Native to Europe and W Asia, it has large, usually blue, flowers. Its long taproot is used dried and roasted as a coffee substitute. As a garden vegetable, grown under cover, its blanched leaves are used in salads. It is related to ◊endive.

Chihuahua capital of Chihuahua state, Mexico, 800 mi/1,285 km NW of Mexico City; population (1984) 375,000. It was founded 1707. It is the center of a mining district and has textile mills.

Chile Republic of (*República de Chile*) *area* 292,257 sq mi/756,950 sq km *capital* Santiago *towns and cities* Concepción, Viña del Mar, Temuco; ports Valparaíso, Antofagasta, Arica, Iquique, Punta Arenas *physical* Andes mountains along E border, Atacama Desert in N, fertile central valley, grazing land and forest in S *territories* Easter Island, Juan Fernández Islands, part of Tierra del Fuego, claim to part of Antarctica *features* Atacama Desert is one of the driest regions in the world *head of state and government* Eduardo Frei from 1994 *political system* emergent democratic republic *political parties* Christian Democratic Party (PDC), moderate centrist; National Renewal Party (RN), right-wing *exports* copper (world's leading producer), iron, molybdenum (world's second largest producer), nitrate, pulp and paper, steel products, fishmeal, fruit *currency* peso *population* (1993) 13,440,000 (the majority are of European origin or are mestizos, of mixed American Indian and Spanish descent); growth rate 1.6% p.a. *life expectancy* men 69, women 76 *language* Spanish *religion* Roman Catholic 89% *literacy* men 94%, women 93% *GNP* $2,800 per head (1992) *chronology 1818* Achieved independence from Spain. *1964* PDC formed government under Eduardo Frei. *1970* Dr Salvador Allende became the first democratically elected Marxist president; he embarked on an extensive program of nationalization and social reform. *1973* Government overthrown by the CIA-backed military, led by General Augusto Pinochet. Allende killed. Policy of repression began during which all opposition was put down and political activity banned. *1981* New constitution, described as a "a transition to democracy", adopted. *1983* Growing opposition to the regime from all sides, with outbreaks of violence. *1988* Referendum on whether Pinochet should serve a further term resulted in a clear "No" vote. *1989* President Pinochet agreed to constitutional changes to allow pluralist politics. Patricio Aylwin (PDC) elected president; Pinochet remained as army commander in chief. *1990* Aylwin reached accord on end to military junta government. Pinochet censured by president. *1993* Ruling coalition successful in general election. *1994* PDC leader Eduardo Frei sworn in as president.

chili the pod, or powder made from the pod, of a variety of ◊capsicum, *Capsicum frutescens*, a hot, red pepper. It is widely used in cooking.

chimera or *chimaera* in Greek mythology, a fire-breathing animal with a lion's head, a goat's body, and a tail in the form of a snake; hence any apparent hybrid of two or more creatures. The chimera was killed by the hero ◊Bellerophon on the winged horse Pegasus.

chimpanzee highly intelligent African ape *Pan troglodytes* that lives mainly in rain forests but sometimes in wooded savanna. Chimpanzees are covered in thin but long black body hair, except for the face, hands, and feet, which may have pink or black skin. They normally walk on all fours, supporting the front of the body on the knuckles of the fingers, but can stand or walk upright for a short distance. They can grow to 4.5 ft/1.4 m tall, and weigh up to 110 lb/50 kg. They are strong and climb well, but spend time on the ground, living in loose social groups. The bulk of the diet is fruit, with some leaves, insects, and occasional meat. Chimpanzees can use "tools", fashioning twigs to extract termites from their nests.

China People's Republic of (*Zhonghua Renmin Gonghe Guo*) *area* 3,599,975 sq mi/9,596,960 sq km *capital* Beijing (Peking) *towns and cities* Chongqing (Chungking), Shenyang (Mukden), Wuhan, Nanjing (Nanking), Harbin; ports Tianjin (Tientsin), Shanghai, Qingdao (Tsingtao), Lüda (Lü-ta), Guangzhou (Canton) *physical* two-thirds of China is mountains or desert (N and W); the low-lying E is irrigated by rivers Huang He (Yellow River), Chang Jiang (Yangtze-Kiang), Xi Jiang (Si Kiang) *features* Great Wall of China; Gezhouba Dam; Ming Tombs; Terracotta Warriors (Xi'ain); Gobi Desert; world's most populous country *head of state* Jiang Zemin from 1993 *head of government* Li Peng from 1987 *political system* communist republic *political party* Chinese Communist Party (CCP), Marxist-Leninist-Maoist *exports* tea, livestock and animal products, silk, cotton, oil, minerals (China is the world's largest producer of tungsten and antimony), chemicals, light industrial goods *currency* yuan *population* (1993 est) 1,185,000,000 (the majority are Han or ethnic Chinese; the 67 million of other ethnic groups, including Tibetan, Uigur, and Zhuang, live in border

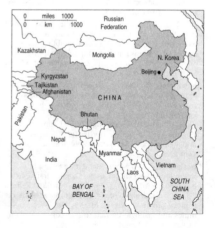

China: dynasties

dynasty	dates	major events
Hsia	1994–1523BC	agriculture, bronze, first writing
Shang or Yin	1523–1027	first major dynasty; first Chinese calendar
Chou	1027–255	developed society using money, iron, written laws; age of Confucius
Qin	255–206	unification after period of Warring States, building of Great Wall begun, roads built
Han	AD 206–220	first centralized and effectively administered empire; introduction of Buddhism
San Kuo	220–265	division into three parts, prolonged fighting (Three Kingdoms) and eventual victory of Wei over Chu and Wu; Confucianism superseded by Buddhism and Taoism
Tsin	265–420	beginning of Hun invasions in the north
Sui	581–618	reunification; barbarian invasions stopped; Great Wall refortified
T'ang	618–906	centralized government; empire greatly extended; period of excellence in sculpture, painting and poetry
Wu Tai (Five Dynasties)	907–960	economic depression and loss of territory in northern China, central Asia, and Korea; first use of paper money
Song	960–1279	period of calm and creativity; printing developed (movable type); central government restored; northern and western frontiers neglected and Mongol incursions begun
Yüan	1260–1368	beginning of Mongol rule in China, under Kublai Khan; Marco Polo visited China; dynasty brought to an end by widespread revolts, centered in Mongolia
Ming	1368–1644	Mongols driven out by native Chinese, Mongolia captured by 2nd Ming emperor; period of architectural development; Beijing flourished as new capital
Manchu	1644–1912	China once again under non-Chinese rule, the Qing conquered by nomads from Manchuria; trade with the West; culture flourished, but conservatism eventually led to the dynasty's overthrow by nationalistic revolutionaries led by Sun Yatsen

areas). The number of people of Chinese origin outside China, Taiwan, and Hong Kong is estimated at 15–24 million. Growth rate 1.2% p.a. *life expectancy* men 69, women 73 *languages* Chinese, including Mandarin (official), Cantonese, and other dialects *media* state control of broadcast media, recently undermined by spread of telecommunications equipment; TV satellite reception banned 1990 but several million dish aerials already in private hands; major newspapers Communist Party-owned *religions* officially atheist, but traditionally Taoist, Confucianist, and Buddhist; Muslim 13 million; Catholic 3–6 million (divided between the "patriotic" church established 1958 and the "loyal" church subject to Rome); Protestant 3 million *literacy* men 84%, women 62% *GNP* $370 per head (1991) *chronology* 1949 People's Republic of China proclaimed by Mao Zedong. *1954* Soviet-style constitution adopted. *1956–57* Hundred Flowers Movement encouraged criticism of the government. *1958–60* Great Leap Forward commune experiment to achieve "true communism". *1960* Withdrawal of Soviet technical advisers. *1962* Sino-Indian border war. *1962–65* Economic recovery program under Liu Shaoqi; Maoist "socialist education movement" rectification campaign. *1966–69* Great Proletarian Cultural Revolution; Liu Shaoqi overthrown. *1969* Ussuri River border clashes with USSR. *1970–76* Reconstruction under Mao and Zhou Enlai. *1971* Entry into United Nations. *1972* US president Nixon visited Beijing. *1975* New state constitution. Unveiling of Zhou's "Four Modernizations" program. *1976* Deaths of Zhou Enlai and Mao Zedong; appointment of Hua Guofeng as prime minister and Communist Party chair. Vice Premier Deng Xiaoping in hiding. Gang of Four arrested. *1977* Rehabilitation of Deng Xiaoping. *1979* Economic reforms introduced. Diplomatic relations opened with US. Punitive invasion of Vietnam. *1980* Zhao Ziyang appointed prime minister. *1981* Hu Yaobang succeeded Hua Guofeng as party chair. Imprisonment of Gang of Four. *1982* New state constitution adopted. *1984* "Enterprise management" reforms for industrial sector. *1986* Student prodemocracy demonstrations. *1987* Hu was replaced as party leader by Zhao, with Li Peng as prime minister. Deng left Politburo but remained influential. *1988* Yang Shangkun replaced Li Xiannian as state president. Economic reforms encountered increasing problems; inflation rocketed. *1989* Over 2,000 killed in prodemocracy student demonstrations in Tiananmen Square; international sanctions imposed. *1991* March: European Community (now European Union) and Japanese sanctions lifted. May: normal relations with USSR resumed. Nov: relations with Vietnam normalized. *1992* Historic visit by Japan's emperor. *1993* Jiang Zemin, Chinese Communist Party general secretary, replaced Yang Shangkun as president.

China Sea area of the Pacific Ocean bordered by China, Vietnam, Borneo, the Philippines, and Japan. Various groups of small islands and shoals, including the Paracels, 300 mi/500 km E of Vietnam, have been disputed by China and other powers because they lie in oil-rich areas.

chinchilla South American rodent *Chinchilla laniger* found in high, rather barren areas of the Andes in Bolivia and Chile. About the size of a small rabbit, it has long ears and a long bushy tail, and shelters in rock crevices. These gregarious animals have thick, soft, silver-gray fur, and were hunted almost to extinction for it. They are now farmed and protected in the wild.

Chinese native to or an inhabitant of China and Taiwan, or a person of Chinese descent. The Chinese comprise more than 25% of the world's population, and the Chinese language (Mandarin) is the largest member of the Sino-Tibetan family.

Although dialects vary considerably, there is a common written language, a non-phonetic script of characters representing concepts rather than sounds, similar to the way numbers represent quantities but may be pronounced differently in every language.

Chinese language language or group of languages of the Sino-Tibetan family, spoken in China, Taiwan, Hong Kong, Singapore, and Chinese communities throughout the world. Varieties of spoken Chinese differ greatly, but all share a written form using thousands of ideographic symbols—characters—which have changed little in 2,000 years. Nowadays, *putonghua* ("common speech"), based on the educated Beijing dialect known as Mandarin Chinese, is promoted throughout China as the national spoken and written language.

Chinese Revolution series of great political upheavals in China 1911–49 that eventually led to Communist Party rule and the establishment of the People's Republic of China. In 1912, a nationalist revolt overthrew the imperial Manchu dynasty. Led by Sun Yatsen 1923–25 and by Chiang Kai-shek 1925–49, the nationalists, or Guomindang, were increasing challenged by the growing communist movement. The 6,000 mi/10,000 km *Long March* to the NW by the communists 1934–35 to escape from attacks by the Guomindang forces resulted in ◊Mao Zedong's emergence as communist leader. During World War II 1939–45, the various Chinese political groups pooled military resources against the Japanese invaders. After World War II, the conflict reignited into open civil war 1946–49, until the Guomindang were defeated at Nanjing and forced to flee to Taiwan. Communist rule was established in the People's Republic of China under the leadership of Mao.

chip or *silicon chip* another name for an ◊integrated circuit, a complete electronic circuit on a slice of silicon (or other semiconductor) crystal only a few millimeters square.

chipmunk any of several species of small ground squirrel with characteristic stripes along its side. Chipmunks live in North America and E Asia, in a variety of habitats, usually wooded, and take shelter in burrows. They have pouches in their cheeks for carrying food.

They climb well but spend most of their time on or near the ground.

Chippendale Thomas *c.*1718–1779. English furniture designer. He set up his workshop in St Martin's Lane, London, 1753. His book *The Gentleman and Cabinet Maker's Director* 1754, was a significant contribution to furniture design. Although many of his most characteristic designs are Rococo, he also employed Louis XVI, Chinese, Gothic, and Neo-Classical styles. He worked mainly in mahogany.

Chirac Jacques 1932– . French conservative politician, prime minister 1974–76 and 1986–88 and president from 1995. He established the neo-Gaullist Rassemblement pour la République (RPR) 1976, and became mayor of Paris 1977.

chiropody care and treatment of feet. Originally, it referred to the treatment of hands as well as feet, but is now synonymous with podiatry.

chiropractic in alternative medicine, technique of manipulation of the spine and other parts of the body, based on the principle that disorders are attributable to aberrations in the functioning of the nervous system, which manipulation can correct.

Chisinau (Russian *Kishinev*) capital of Moldova, situated in a rich agricultural area; population (1989) 565,000. It is a commercial and cultural center; industries include cement, food processing, tobacco, and textiles.

Chissano Joaquim 1939– . Mozambique nationalist politician, president from 1986; foreign minister 1975–86. In Oct 1992 Chissano signed a peace accord with the leader of the rebel Mozambique National Resistance (MNR) party, bringing to an end 16 years of civil war, and in 1994 won the first free presidential elections.

chitin complex long-chain compound, or ◊polymer; a nitrogenous derivative of glucose. Chitin is widely found in invertebrates. It forms the exoskeleton of insects and other arthropods. It combines with protein to form a covering that can be hard and tough, as in beetles, or soft and flexible, as in caterpillars and other insect larvae. It is insoluble in water and resistant to acids, alkalis, and many organic solvents. In crustaceans such as crabs, it is impregnated with calcium carbonate for extra strength.

Chittagong city and port in Bangladesh, 10 mi/16 km from the mouth of the Karnaphuli River, on the Bay of Bengal; population (1981) 1,388,476. Industries include steel, engineering, chemicals, and textiles.

chive or *chives* bulbous perennial European plant *Allium schoenoprasum* of the lily family Liliaceae. It has long, tubular leaves and dense, round flower heads in blue or lilac, and is used as a garnish for salads.

chlamydia viruslike bacteria which live parasitically in animal cells, and cause disease in humans and birds. Chlamydiae are thought to be descendants of bacteria that have lost certain metabolic processes. In humans, a strain of chlamydia causes ◊trachoma, a disease found mainly in the tropics (a leading cause of blindness); venereally transmitted chlamydiae cause genital and urinary infections.

chloride Cl⁻ negative ion formed when hydrogen chloride dissolves in water, and any salt containing this ion, commonly formed by the action of hydrochloric acid (HCl) on various metals or by direct combination of a metal and chlorine. Sodium chloride (NaCl) is common table salt.

chlorine greenish-yellow, gaseous, nonmetallic element with a pungent odor, symbol Cl, atomic number 17, atomic weight 35.453. It is a member of the ◊halogen group and is widely distributed, in combination with the ◊alkali metals, as chlorates or chlorides.

chlorofluorocarbon (CFC) synthetic chemical that is odorless, nontoxic, nonflammable, and chemically inert. The first CFC was synthesized 1892, but no use was found for it until the 1920s. Since then their stability and apparently harmless properties have made CFCs popular as ◊aerosol cans, as refrigerants in refrigerators and air conditioners, and in the manufacture of foam packaging. They are partly responsible for the destruction of the ◊ozone layer. In June 1990 representatives of 93 nations, including the US, agreed to phase out production of CFCs and various other ozone-depleting chemicals by the end of the 20th century.

chloroform (technical name *trichloromethane*) CCl_3 clear, colorless, toxic, carcinogenic liquid with a characteristic pungent, sickly sweet smell and taste, formerly used as an anesthetic (now superseded by less harmful substances).

It is used as a solvent and in the synthesis of organic chemical compounds.

chlorophyll green pigment present in most plants; it is responsible for the absorption of light energy during ◊photosynthesis.

The pigment absorbs the red and blue-violet parts of sunlight but reflects the green, thus giving plants their characteristic color.

chocolate powder, syrup, confectionery, or beverage derived from cacao seeds. See ◊cocoa and chocolate.

choir body of singers, usually of sacred music, of more than one voice to a part, whose members are able to sight read music and hold a melody. A traditional cathedral choir of male voices is required to sing responses, hymns, and psalms appropriate to the church calendar.

cholera disease caused by infection with various strains of the bacillus *Vibrio cholerae*, transmitted in contaminated water and characterized by violent diarrhea and vomiting. It is prevalent in many tropical areas.

cholesterol white, crystalline sterol found throughout the body, especially in fats, blood, nerve tissue, and bile; it is also provided in the diet by foods such as eggs, meat, and butter. A high level of cholesterol in the blood is thought to contribute to atherosclerosis (hardening of the arteries).

Chomsky Noam 1928– . US professor of linguistics. He proposed a theory of transformational generative grammar, which attracted widespread interest because of the claims it made about the relationship between language and the mind and the universality of an underlying language structure. He has been a leading critic of the US government.

Chongqing or *Chungking*, also known as *Pahsien* city in Sichuan province, China, that stands at the confluence of the ◊Chang Jiang and Jialing Jiang rivers; population (1984) 2,733,700. Industries include iron, steel, chemicals, synthetic rubber, and textiles.

Chopin Frédéric (François) 1810–1849. Polish composer and pianist. He made his debut as a pianist at the age of eight. As a performer, Chopin revolutionized the technique of pianoforte-playing, turning the hands outward and favoring a light, responsive touch. His compositions for piano, which include two concertos and other works with orchestra, are characterized by great volatility of mood, and rhythmic fluidity.

He died Oct 17, 1849, and was buried in Père Lachaise cemetery in Paris.

chord in music, a group of three or more notes sounded together. The resulting combination of tones may be either harmonious or dissonant.

chordate animal belonging to the phylum Chordata, which includes vertebrates, sea squirts, amphioxi, and others. All these animals, at some stage of their lives, have a supporting rod of tissue (notochord or backbone) running down their bodies.

Chou En-lai alternative transliteration of ◊Zhou Enlai.

Chretien Jean 1934– . French-Canadian politician, prime minister from 1993. He won the leadership of the Liberal Party 1990 and defeated Kim Campbell in the Oct 1993 election. He has been a vigorous advocate of national unity and, although himself a Quebecois, has consistently opposed the province's separatist ambitions.

Christ the ◊Messiah as prophesied in the Hebrew Bible, or Old Testament.

Christian IV 1577–1648. King of Denmark and Norway from 1588. He sided with the Protestants in the Thirty Years' War (1618–48), and founded Christiania (now Oslo, capital of Norway). He was succeeded by Frederick II 1648.

Christianity world religion derived from the teaching of Jesus in the first third of the 1st century, with a present-day membership of about one trillion. It is divided into groups or denominations that differ in some areas of belief and practice. Its main divisions are the ◊Roman Catholic, ◊Eastern Orthodox, and ◊Protestant churches.

beliefs Christians believe in one God with three aspects: God the Father, God the Son (Jesus), and God the Holy Spirit, who is the power of God working in the world. God created everything that exists and showed his love for the world by coming to Earth as Jesus, and suffering and dying in order to be reconciled with humanity. Christians believe that three days after his death by crucifixion Jesus was raised to life by God's power, appearing many times in bodily form to his followers, and that he is now alive in the world through the Holy Spirit. Christians speak of the sufferings they may have to endure because of their faith, and the reward of everlasting life in God's presence, which is promised to those who have faith in Jesus Christ and who live according to his teaching.

Christian Science or *the Church of Christ, Scientist* sect established in the US by Mary Baker Eddy 1879. Christian Scientists believe that since God is good and is a spirit, matter and evil are not ultimately real. Consequently they refuse all medical treatment. The church has its own daily newspaper, the *Christian Science Monitor*.

Christie Agatha Mary Clarissa (born Miller) 1890–1976. English detective novelist. She created the characters Hercule Poirot and Miss Jane Marple. She wrote more than 70 novels, including *The Murder of Roger Ackroyd* 1926 and *Ten Little Indians* 1939. A number of her books have been filmed, for example *Murder on the Orient Express* 1975. Her play *The Mousetrap*, which opened in London 1952, is the longest continuously running show in the world.

Christmas Christian religious holiday, observed throughout the Western world on Dec 25 and traditionally marked by feasting and gift-giving. In the Christian church, it is the day on which the birth of Jesus is celebrated, although the actual birth date is unknown. Many of its customs have a non-Christian origin and were adapted from celebrations of the winter ◊solstice.

Christopher Warren 1925– . US Democrat politician, secretary of state from 1993. Trained as a lawyer, he was deputy attorney general under Jimmy Carter 1977–81 and led negotiations for the release of US hostages in Iran. In 1992 he masterminded the selection of Clinton's cabinet team. He is regarded as a skilled negotiator, unrestricted by strong political bias, and in Sept 1993 secured the signing of a historic Israeli-PLO accord in Washington.

In 1991 he headed an inquiry into a report released by the Los Angeles Police Department, alleging police brutality and racism prior to the Los Angeles Watts riots of 1965.

Christopher, St patron saint of travelers. His feast day, July 25, was dropped from the Roman Catholic liturgical calendar 1969.

chromatic scale musical scale proceeding by semitones. In theory the inclusion of all 12 notes makes it a neutral scale without the focus provided by the seven-tone diatonic major or minor scale; in practice however, owing to small deviations from equal temperament, it is possible for a trained ear to identify the starting point of a randomly chosen chromatic scale.

chromatography technique for separating or analyzing a mixture of gases, liquids, or dissolved substances. This is brought about by means of two immiscible substances, one of which (*the mobile phase*) transports the sample mixture through the other (*the stationary* *phase*). The mobile phase may be a gas or a liquid; the stationary phase may be a liquid or a solid, and may be in a column, on paper, or in a thin layer on a glass or plastic support. The components of the mixture are absorbed or impeded by the stationary phase to different extents and therefore become separated. The technique is used for both qualitative and quantitive analyses in biology and chemistry.

chromium hard, brittle, gray-white, metallic element, symbol Cr, atomic number 24, atomic weight 51.996. It takes a high polish, has a high melting point, and is very resistant to corrosion. It is used in chromium electroplating, in the manufacture of stainless steel and other alloys, and as a catalyst. Its compounds are used for tanning leather and for alums. In human nutrition it is a vital trace element. In nature, it occurs chiefly as chrome iron ore or chromite ($FeCr_2O_4$). Kazakhstan, Zimbabwe, and Brazil are sources.

chromosome structure in a cell nucleus that carries the ◊genes. Each chromosome consists of one very long strand of DNA, coiled and folded to produce a compact body. The point on a chromosome where a particular gene occurs is known as its locus. Most higher organisms have two copies of each chromosome (they are ◊diploid) but some have only one (they are ◊haploid). There are 46 chromosomes in a normal human cell.

chromosphere layer of mostly hydrogen gas about 6,000 mi/10,000 km deep above the visible surface of the Sun (the photosphere). It appears pinkish red during ◊eclipses of the Sun.

chronic fatigue syndrome medical condition characterized by long-term fatigue, irritability, confusion, and, often, inflammation of the brain. It is thought to be caused by a virus, an abnormality of the immune system, or a lack of hormones in the brain and endocrine system. It is called "Yuppie flu" because it is found most often in professional women—and sometimes men—in their thirties.

chronometer instrument for measuring time precisely, originally used at sea. It is designed to remain accurate through all conditions of temperature and pressure. The first accurate marine chronometer, capable of an accuracy of half a minute a year, was made 1761 by John Harrison in England.

The term is now applied to scientific timekeeping devices.

chrysanthemum any plant of the genus *Chrysanthemum* of the family Compositae, with about 200 species. There are hundreds of cultivated varieties, whose exact wild ancestry is uncertain. In the Far East the common chrysanthemum has been cultivated for more than 2,000 years and is the imperial emblem of Japan.

Chrysanthemums may be grown from seed, but are more usually propagated by cutting or division.

They were introduced into the West in 1789.

Chrysler Walter Percy 1875–1940. US industrialist. After World War I, he became president of the independent Maxwell Motor Company and went on to found the Chrysler Corporation 1925. By 1928 he had acquired Dodge and Plymouth, making Chrysler Corporation one of the largest US motor-vehicle manufacturers.

chub any of several large minnows of the carp family. Creek chub *Semotelus atromaculatus,* up to 12 in/ 30 cm, is found widely in North American streams.

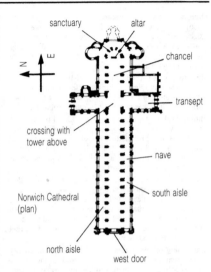

Norwich Cathedral (plan)

church The ground plan of a typical large cathedral church is in the shape of an elongated cross. The main altar is at the east end. A practical difficulty with this type of plan is that the clergy around the altar may be a long way from the worshipers in the nave.

Also, any of a number of small-mouthed marine fishes of the family Kyphosidae.

church building designed as a Christian place of worship. Churches were first built in the 3rd century, when persecution ceased under the Holy Roman emperor Constantine. The original church design was based on the Roman ◊basilica, with a central nave, aisles either side, and an apse at one end.

Churchill Randolph (Henry Spencer) 1849–1895. British Conservative politician, chancellor of the Exchequer and leader of the House of Commons 1886; father of Winston Churchill.

He married Jennie Jerome (1854–1921), daughter of a wealthy New Yorker, 1874.

Churchill Winston (Leonard Spencer) 1874–1965. British Conservative politician, prime minister 1940–45 and 1951–55. In Parliament from 1900, as a Liberal until 1923, he held a number of ministerial offices, including First Lord of the Admiralty 1911–15 and chancellor of the Exchequer 1924–29. Absent from the cabinet in the 1930s, he returned Sept 1939 to lead a coalition government 1940–45, negotiating with Allied leaders in World War II to achieve the unconditional surrender of Germany 1945; he led a Conservative government 1951–55. He received the Nobel Prize for Literature 1953.

Church of England established form of Christianity in England, a member of the Anglican Communion which includes the US Episcopal Church. It was dissociated from the Roman Catholic Church 1534. There were approximately 1,100,000 regular worshipers in 1988. In Nov 1992 the General Synod of the Church of England and the Anglican church in Australia voted in favor of the ordination of women.

CIA abbreviation for the US ◊*Central Intelligence Agency*.

cicada any of several insects of the family Cicadidae. Most species are tropical, but a few occur in Europe and North America. Young cicadas live underground, for up to 17 years in some species. The adults live on trees, whose juices they suck. The males produce a loud, almost continuous, chirping by vibrating membranes in resonating cavities in the abdomen.

Cicero Marcus Tullius 106–43 BC. Roman orator, writer, and politician. His speeches and philosophical and rhetorical works are models of Latin prose, and his letters provide a picture of contemporary Roman life. As consul 63 BC he exposed the Roman politician Catiline's conspiracy in four major orations.

cichlid any freshwater fish of the family Cichlidae. Cichlids are somewhat perchlike, but have a single nostril on each side instead of two. They are mostly predatory, and have deep, colorful bodies, flattened from side to side so that some are almost disk-shaped. Many are territorial in the breeding season and may show care of the young. There are more than 1,000 species found in South and Central America, Africa, and India.

Cid, El Rodrigo Díaz de Bivar 1040–1099. Spanish soldier, nicknamed *El Cid* ("the lord") by the ◊Moors. Born in Castile of a noble family, he fought against the king of Navarre and won his nickname *el Campeador* ("the Champion") by killing the Navarrese champion in single combat. Essentially a mercenary, fighting both with and against the Moors, he died while defending Valencia against them, and in subsequent romances became Spain's national hero.

cider juice pressed from apples as a beverage or for making vinegar. In the US, hard cider refers to fermented apple juice drunk as an alcoholic beverage. Alcoholic cider is produced in large quantities in the Americas, France, and England.

cigarette thin paper tube stuffed with shredded tobacco for smoking, now usually plugged with a filter. The first cigarettes were the *papelitos* smoked in South America about 1750. The habit spread to Spain and then throughout the world; today it is the most general form of tobacco smoking, although it is dangerous to the health of both smokers and nonsmokers who breathe in the smoke.

Since the 1960s warnings from the US Surgeon General have been added to packages and cartons, about the dangers of smoking and cancer, lung disease, heart disease, and the effects on the developing fetus.

Cimabue Giovanni (Cenni di Peppi) *c.*1240–1302. Italian painter. Active in Florence, he is traditionally styled the "father of Italian painting". His paintings retain the golden background of Byzantine art but the figures have a new naturalism. Among the works attributed to him are *Maestà* about 1280 (Uffizi, Florence), a huge Gothic image of the Virgin, with a novel softness and solidity that points forward to Giotto.

cinchona any shrub or tree of the tropical American genus *Chinchona* of the madder family Rubiaceae. ◊Quinine is produced from the bark of some species, and these are now cultivated in India, Sri Lanka, the Philippines, and Indonesia.

Cincinnati city and port in Ohio on the Ohio River; population (1990) 364,000. Chief industries include machinery, clothing, furniture making, wine,

chemicals, and meatpacking. Founded 1788, Cincinnati became a city 1819. It attracted large numbers of European immigrants, particularly Germans, during the 19th century.

Procter and Gamble, a household-products manufacturer, has its headquarters here. Xavier University and the University of Cincinnati are here, and it has a major symphony orchestra. William Howard Taft, 27th president of the US, was born in Cincinnati.

cinema 20th-century form of art and entertainment consisting of "moving pictures" in either black and white or color, projected onto a screen. Cinema borrows from the other arts, such as music, drama, and literature, but is entirely dependent for its origins on technological developments, including the technology of action photography, projection, sound reproduction, and film processing and printing (see ◊photography).

Throughout the 1980s cinema production was affected by the growth during the preceding decade of the video industry, which made films available for viewing on home television screens (see ◊videocassette recorder).

cinnabar mercuric sulfide, HgS, the only commercially useful ore of mercury. It is deposited in veins and impregnations near recent volcanic rocks and hot springs. The mineral itself is used as a red pigment, commonly known as *vermilion*.

Cinnabar is found in the US (California), Spain (Almadén), Peru, Italy, and Slovenia.

cinnamon dried inner bark of a tree *Cinnamomum zeylanicum* of the laurel family, grown in India and Sri Lanka. The bark is ground to make the spice used in curries and confectionery. Oil of cinnamon is obtained from waste bark and is used as flavoring in food and medicine.

cinquefoil any plant of the genus *Potentilla* of the rose family, usually with five-lobed leaves and brightly colored flowers. It is widespread in northern temperate regions.

Field cinquefoil *P. canadensis* is a low-growing perennial with yellow flowers native to E North America in dry grasslands and barrens.

circle perfectly round shape, the path of a point that moves so as to keep a constant distance from a fixed point (the center). Each circle has a *radius* (the distance from any point on the circle to the center), a *circumference* (the boundary of the circle), *diameters* (straight lines crossing the circle through the center), *chords* (lines joining two points on the circumference), *tangents* (lines that touch the circumference at one point only), *sectors* (regions inside the circle between two radii), and *segments* (regions between a chord and the circumference).

circuit in physics or electrical engineering, an arrangement of electrical components through which a current can flow. There are two basic circuits, series and parallel. In a series circuit, the components are connected end to end so that the current flows through all components one after the other. In a parallel circuit, components are connected side by side so that part of the current passes through each component. A circuit diagram shows in graphical form how components are connected together, using standard symbols for the components.

circulatory system system of vessels in an animal's body that transports essential substances (blood or other circulatory fluid) to and from the different parts

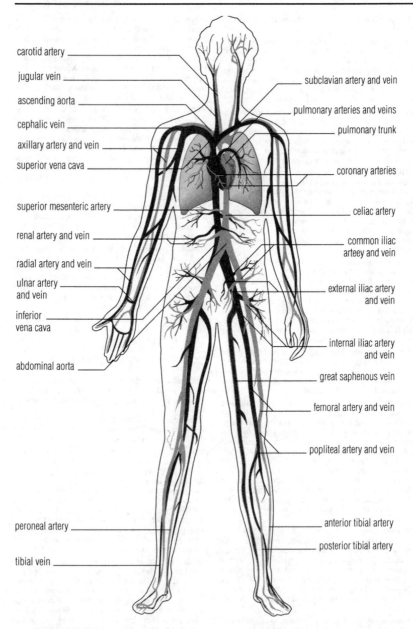

carotid artery
jugular vein
ascending aorta
cephalic vein
axillary artery and vein
superior vena cava
superior mesenteric artery
renal artery and vein
radial artery and vein
ulnar artery and vein
inferior vena cava
abdominal aorta
peroneal artery
tibial vein

subclavian artery and vein
pulmonary arteries and veins
pulmonary trunk
coronary arteries
celiac artery
common iliac arteey and vein
external iliac artery and vein
internal iliac artery and vein
great saphenous vein
femoral artery and vein
popliteal artery and vein
anterior tibial artery
posterior tibial artery

circulatory system Blood flows through 60,000 mi/96,500 km of arteries and veins, supplying oxygen and nutrients to organs and limbs. Oxygen-poor blood (blue) circulates from the heart to the lungs where oxygen is absorbed. Oxygen-rich blood (red) flows back to the heart and is then pumped round the body through the aorta, the largest artery, to smaller arteries and capillaries. Here oxygen and nutrients are exchanged with carbon dioxide and waste products and the blood returns to the heart via the veins. Waste products are filtered by the liver, spleen and kidneys and nutrients are absorbed from the stomach and small intestine.

of the body. Except for simple animals such as sponges and coelenterates (jellyfishes, sea anemones, corals), all animals have a circulatory system.

circumcision surgical removal of all or part of the fore-skin (prepuce) of the penis, usually performed on the newborn; it is traditionally practiced among Jews and Muslims. In some societies in Africa and the Middle East, female circumcision or clitoridectomy (removal of the labia minora and/or clitoris) is practiced on adolescents as well as babies; it is illegal in the West.

circumference in geometry, the curved line that encloses a curved plane figure, for example a ◊circle or an ellipse. Its length varies according to the nature of the curve, and may be ascertained by the appropriate formula. The circumference of a circle is πd or 2πr, where d is the diameter of the circle, r is its radius, and π is the constant pi, approximately equal to 3.1416.

cirrhosis any degenerative disease in an organ of the body, especially the liver, characterized by excessive development of connective tissue, causing scarring and painful swelling. Cirrhosis of the liver may be caused by an infection such as viral hepatitis, chronic obstruction of the common bile duct, chronic alcoholism or drug use, blood disorder, heart failure, or malnutrition. However, often no cause is apparent. If cirrhosis is diagnosed early, it can be arrested by treating the cause; otherwise it will progress to coma and death.

CIS abbreviation for ◊*Commonwealth of Independent States*, established 1992 by 11 former Soviet republics.

CISC (acronym for *complex instruction set computer*) in computing, a microprocessor (processor on a single chip) that can carry out a large number of machine code instructions—for example, the Intel 80386. The term was introduced to distinguish them from the more rapid RISC (reduced instruction set computer) processors, which handle only a smaller set of instructions.

citizens' band (CB) short-range radio communication facility (around 27 MHz) used by members of the public in the US and many European countries to talk to one another or call for emergency assistance.

citizenship status as a member of a state. In most countries citizenship may be acquired either by birth or by naturalization. The status confers rights such as voting and the protection of the law and also imposes responsibilities such as military service, in some countries.

citric acid HOOCCH₂C(OH)(COOH)CH₂COOH organic acid widely distributed in the plant kingdom; it is found in high concentrations in citrus fruits and has a sharp, sour taste. At one time it was commercially prepared from concentrated lemon juice, but now the main source is the fermentation of sugar with certain molds.

citrus any tree or shrub of the genus *Citrus*, family Rutaceae. Citruses are found in Asia and other warm parts of the world. They are evergreen and aromatic, and several species—the orange, lemon, lime, citron, and grapefruit—are cultivated for fruit.

city generally, a large and important town. In the Middle East and ancient Europe, and in the ancient civilizations of Mexico and Peru, cities were states in themselves. In the early Middle Ages, European cities were usually those towns that were episcopal sees (seats of bishops).

In the US, a city is an incorporated municipality whose boundaries and powers of self-government are defined by charter from the state in which it is located.

Ciudad Juárez city on the Rio Grande, in Chihuahua, N Mexico, on the US border; population (1990) 797,650. It is a center for cotton.

civet small to medium-sized carnivorous mammal found in Africa and Asia, belonging to the family Viverridae, which also includes ◊*mongooses* and ◊*genets*. Distant relations of cats, they generally have longer jaws and more teeth. All have a scent gland in the inguinal (groin) region. Extracts from this gland are taken from the *African civet Civettictis civetta* and used in perfumery.

civil aviation the operation of passenger and freight transport by air. With increasing traffic, control of air space is a major problem. The Federal Aviation Agency (FAA) is responsible for regulating development of aircraft, air navigation, traffic control, and communications in the US. The Civil Aeronautics Board is the US authority prescribing safety regulations and investigating accidents. The world's largest airline was the Soviet Union's government-owned Aeroflot (split between republics 1992), which operated 1,300 aircraft over 620,000 mi/1 million km of routes and carried over 110 million passengers a year.

civil defense or *civil protection* organized activities by the civilian population of a state to mitigate the effects of enemy attack.

civil engineering branch of engineering that is concerned with the construction of roads, bridges, aqueducts, waterworks, tunnels, canals, irrigation works, and harbors.

civil law legal system based on ◊Roman law. It is one of the two main European legal systems, ◊English (common) law being the other. Civil law may also mean the law relating to matters other than criminal law, such as ◊contract and tort.

civil-rights movement general term for efforts by African American people to improve their status in society after World War II. Following their significant contribution to the national effort in wartime, they began a sustained campaign for full civil rights which challenged racial discrimination. Despite favorable legislation such as the Civil Rights Act 1964 and the 1965 Voting Rights Act, growing discontent in northern states led to outbreaks of civil disorder, such as the Watts riots in Los Angeles, Aug 1965. Another riot in the city 1992, following the acquittal of policemen charged with beating an African American motorist, demonstrated continuing problems in American race relations. Other civil-rights movements have included women (see ◊women's movement) and homosexuals (see ◊homosexuality).

civil service the body of administrative staff appointed to carry out the policy of a government. In the US, federal employees are restricted in the role they may play in political activity, and they retain their posts (except at senior levels) when there is a change in administration.

Civil War also called in the South the *War Between the States* war 1861–65 between the Southern or Confederate States of America and the Northern or Union States. The former wished to maintain certain "states' rights", in particular the right to determine

Civil War, American, also called the War Between the States Union soldiers in trenches before a battle, Petersburg, Virginia, 1865. Petersburg, a port on the Appomattox River, was under siege for ten months. Its fall April 1865 helped to hasten the end of the war.

state law on the institution of slavery, and claimed the right to secede from the Union; the latter fought primarily to maintain the Union, with slave emancipation (proclaimed 1863) a secondary issue.

The issue of slavery had brought to a head long-standing social and economic differences between the two oldest sections of the country. A series of political crises was caused by the task of determining whether newly admitted states, such as California, should permit or prohibit slavery in their state constitutions. The political parties in the late 1850s came to represent only sectional interests—Democrats in the South, Republicans in the North. This breakdown of an underlying national political consensus (which had previously sustained national parties) led to the outbreak of hostilities, only a few weeks after the inauguration of the first Republican president, Abraham Lincoln.

Civil War, English the conflict between King Charles I and the Royalists (Cavaliers) on one side and the Parliamentarians (also called Roundheads) under Oliver ◊Cromwell on the other. Their differences centered on the king's unconstitutional acts but became a struggle over the relative powers of crown and Parliament. Hostilities began 1642 and a series of Royalist defeats (Marston Moor 1644, Naseby 1645) culminated in Charles's capture 1647 and execution 1649.

The war continued until the final defeat of Royalist forces at Worcester 1651. Cromwell became Protector (ruler) from 1651 until his death 1658.

Civil War, Spanish war 1936–39 precipitated by a military revolt led by General Franco against the Republican government. Inferior military capability led to the gradual defeat of the Republicans by 1939, and the establishment of Franco's dictatorship.

clam common name for a ◊bivalve mollusk. The giant clam *Tridacna gigas* of the Indopacific can grow to 3 ft/1 m across in 50 years and weigh, with the shell, 1,000 lb/500 kg.

A giant clam produces a trillion eggs in a single spawning.

clan social grouping based on ◊kinship. Some traditional societies are organized by clans, which are either matrilineal or patrilineal, and whose members must marry into another clan in order to avoid inbreeding.

Clapton Eric 1945– . English blues and rock guitarist, singer, and songwriter. Originally a blues purist, then one of the pioneers of heavy rock with Cream 1966–68, he returned to the blues after making the landmark album *Layla and Other Assorted Love Songs* 1970 by Derek and the Dominos. Solo albums include *Journeyman* 1989 and the acoustic *Unplugged* 1992, for which he received six Grammy awards 1993.

Clare county on the west coast of the Republic of Ireland, in the province of Munster; county town Ennis; area 1,231 sq mi/3,190 sq km; population (1991) 90,800.

clarinet any of a family of single-reed woodwind instruments of cylindrical bore. In their concertos for clarinet, Mozart and Weber exploited the instrument's range of tone from the dark low register rising to brilliance, and its capacity for sustained dynamic control. The ability of the clarinet both to blend and to contrast with other instruments make it popular for chamber music and as a solo instrument. It is also heard in military and concert bands and as a jazz instrument.

Clarke Arthur C(harles) 1917– . English science-fiction and nonfiction writer, who originated the plan

Civil War, American: chronology

1861 Feb	Having seceded from the Union, seven southern states (S Carolina, Mississippi, Florida, Alabama, Georgia, Louisiana, and Texas) sent representatives to Montgomery, Alabama, to form the rebel Confederate States of America under the presidency of Jefferson Davis. Their constitution legalized slavery.
April	Rebel forces attacked a Federal garrison at Fort Sumter, Charleston, S Carolina, capturing it April 14. President Lincoln proclaimed a blockade of southern ports.
April–May	Four more states seceded from the Union: Virginia (part remaining loyal, eventually becoming W Virginia), Arkansas, Tennessee, and N Carolina.
July	Battle of Bull Run was first major military engagement of the war, near Manassas Junction, Virginia; Confederate army under generals P.G.T. Bureaugard and Thomas "Stonewall" Jackson forced Union army to retreat to Washington, D.C.
1862 Feb	Union general Ulysses S. Grant captured strategically located forts Henry and Donelson in Tennessee.
April	Battle of Shiloh, the bloodiest Americans had yet fought, when at terrible cost Grant's army forced rebel troops to withdraw. Confederate government introduced conscription of male white citizens aged 18–35.
June–July	Seven Days' battles in Virginia between Union army under George B. McClellan and Confederate forces under generals Jackson and Robert E. Lee; McClellan withdrew, but continued to threaten the Confederate capital at Richmond, Virginia.
Aug	At second Battle of Bull Run, Lee's troops forced Union army to fall back again to Washington, D.C.
Sept	At Battle of Antietam, near Sharpsburg, Maryland, McClellan forced Lee to give up his offensive, but failed to pursue the enemy. Lincoln removed him from his command.
Dec	Lee inflicted heavy losses on Federal forces attackin his position at Battle of Fredericksburg, Virginia.
1863 Jan	Lincoln's Emancipation Proclamation came into effect, freeing slaves in the Confederate states (but not those in border states which had remained loyal to the Union). Some 200,000 African Americans eventually served in Union armies.
March	Federal government introduced conscription.
May	Battle of Chancellorsville, Virginia; Lee and Jackson routed Union forces.
July	Lee failed to break through Union lines at decisive Battle of Gettysburg, Pennsylvania, while Grant captured Vicksburg and the W and took control of the Mississippi, cutting the Confederacy in two.
Nov	Grant's victory at Chattanooga, Tennessee, led to his appointment as general in chief by Lincoln (March 1864). Lincoln's Gettysburg Address.
1864 May	Battle of the Wilderness, Virginia. Lee inflicted heavy casualties on Union forces, but Grant continued to move south through Virginia. They clashed again at Battle of Spotsylvania.
June	Battle of Cold Harbor claimed 12,000 casualties in a few hours. Grant wrote: "I propose to fight it out along this line if it takes all summer".
Sept	Union general William T. Sherman occupied Atlanta, Georgia, and marched through the state to the sea, cutting a wide swathe of destruction.
Nov	Lincoln reelected president.
Dec	Sherman marched into Savannah, Georgia, continuing over next three months into S and N Carolina.
1865 March	Lee failed to break through Union lines at Battle of Petersburg, Virginia.
April	Lee abandoned Confederate capital at Richmond, Virginia, and surrendered to Grant at Appomattox courthouse, Virginia. John Wilkes Booth assassinated President Lincoln at Ford's Theatre, Washington, D.C.
May	Last Confederate soldiers laid down their arms. The war had taken the lives of 359,528 Union troops and 258,000 Confederates, and cost $20 billion.

for a system of communications satellites in geostationary orbit 1945. His works include *Childhood's End* 1953, the short story "The Sentinel" 1968 (filmed by Stanley Kubrick as *2001: A Space Odyssey*), and *2010: Odyssey Two* 1982.

class in sociology, the main grouping of social stratification in industrial societies, based primarily on economic and occupational factors, but also referring to people's style of living or sense of group identity.

In the US, little acknowledgment is given to the notion of class. If asked, most Americans identify themselves as middle class, although social scientists use measurements of education level, income, and occupation to ascribe social strata.

class in biological classification, a group of related ◊orders. For example, all mammals belong to the class

Mammalia and all birds to the class Aves. Among plants, all class names end in "idae" (such as Asteridae) and among fungi in "mycetes"; there are no equivalent conventions among animals. Related classes are grouped together in a ◊phylum.

Classicism in art, music, and literature, a style that emphasizes the qualities traditionally considered characteristic of ancient Greek and Roman art, that is, reason, balance, objectivity, restraint, and strict adherence to form. The term Classicism (also ◊Neo-Classicism) is often used to characterize the culture of 18th-century Europe, and contrasted with 19th-century Romanticism.

classification in biology, the arrangement of organisms into a hierarchy of groups on the basis of their similarities in biochemical, anatomical, or physiological characters. The basic grouping is a ◊species, several of which may constitute a ◊genus, which in turn are grouped into families, and so on up through orders, classes, phyla (in plants, sometimes called divisions), to kingdoms.

Claude Lorrain (Claude Gelée) 1600–1682. French landscape painter. He was active in Rome from 1627. His distinctive, luminous, Classical style had a great impact on late 17th-and 18th-century taste. In his paintings, insignificant figures (mostly mythological or historical) are typically lost in great expanses of poetic scenery, as in *The Enchanted Castle* 1664 (National Gallery, London).

Claudius (Tiberius Claudius Drusus Nero Germanicus) 10 BC–AD 54. Nephew of ◊Tiberius, made Roman emperor by his troops AD 41, after the murder of his nephew ◊Caligula. Claudius was a scholar, historian, and able administrator. During his reign the Roman empire was considerably extended, and in 43 he took part in the invasion of Britain.

clausius in engineering, a unit of ◊entropy (the loss of energy as heat in any physical process). It is defined as the ratio of energy to temperature above absolute zero.

claustrophobia ◊phobia involving fear of enclosed spaces.

clavichord small domestic keyboard instrument of delicate tone developed in the 16th century on the principal of the monochord. Notes are sounded by a metal blade striking the string. The sound is clear and precise, and a form of vibrato (bebung) is possible by varying finger pressure on the key. It was superseded in the 18th century by the fortepiano.

clay very fine-grained ◊sedimentary deposit that has undergone a greater or lesser degree of consolidation. When moistened it is plastic, and it hardens on heating, which renders it impermeable. It may be white, gray, red, yellow, blue, or black, depending on its composition. Clay minerals consist largely of hydrous silicates of aluminum and magnesium together with iron, potassium, sodium, and organic substances. The crystals of clay minerals have a layered structure, capable of holding water, and are responsible for its plastic properties. According to international classification, in mechanical analysis of soil, clay has a grain size of less than 0.00008 in/0.002 mm.

Clay Cassius Marcellus, Jr, original name of boxer Mohammed ◊Ali.

Clay Henry 1777–1852. US politician. He stood unsuccessfully three times for the presidency: as a Democratic-Republican 1824, as a National Republican 1832, and as a Whig 1844. He supported the war of 1812 against Britain, and tried to hold the Union together on the slavery issue by the Missouri Compromise of 1820 and again in the compromise of 1850. He was secretary of state 1825–29 and devised an "American system" for the national economy.

A powerful orator, he was a strong leader of the House of Representatives. He fought a duel over the accusation that he had struck a corrupt deal with John Quincy ◊Adams to ensure the latter would be named president by the House in 1824.

clef in music, a symbol prefixed to a five-line stave indicating the pitch range to which the written notes apply. Introduced as a visual aid in plainchant notation, it is based on the letter G (treble clef), establishing middle C (C4) as a prime reference pitch, G4 a fifth higher for higher voices, and F3 a fifth lower for lower voices.

Cleisthenes Athenian statesman, the founder of Athenian democracy. He was exiled with his family, the Alcmaeonidae, and intrigued and campaigned against the Athenian tyrants, the Pisistratids. After their removal in 510 BC he developed a popular faction in favor of democracy, which was established by his reforms over the next decade.

clematis any temperate woody climbing plant of the genus *Clematis* with showy flowers. Clematis are a member of the buttercup family, Ranunculaceae.

Rock clematis *C. verticillaris* grows in woods and thickets in most of shady E North America.

Cleopatra c.68–30 BC. Queen of Egypt 51–48 and 47–30 BC. When the Roman general Julius Caesar arrived in Egypt, he restored her to the throne from which she had been ousted. Cleopatra and Caesar became lovers and she went with him to Rome. After Caesar's assassination 44 BC she returned to Alexandria and resumed her position as queen of Egypt. In 41 BC she was joined there by Mark Antony, one of Rome's rulers. In 31 BC Rome declared war on Egypt and scored a decisive victory in the naval Battle of Actium off the W coast of Greece. Cleopatra fled with her 60 ships to Egypt; Antony abandoned the struggle and followed her. Both he and Cleopatra committed suicide.

Cleveland (Stephen) Grover 1837–1908. 22nd and 24th president of the US, 1885–89 and 1893–97; the first Democratic president elected after the Civil War and the only president to hold office for two nonconsecutive terms. He attempted to check corruption in the civil service and reduce tariffs. These policies provoked political opposition, and he was defeated by Republican Benjamin Harrison 1888. He was returned to office 1892 and supported the Sherman Silver Purchase Act, which permitted free silver coinage and may have caused the economic panic of 1893.

He was a noninterventionist but in 1895 initiated arbitration that settled a boundary dispute between

Cleveland, (Stephen) Grover The 22nd and 24th president of the United States, Grover Cleveland, a Democrat. Cleveland is the only president to have served for two nonconsecutive terms of office.

Britain and Venezuela. An unswerving conservative, he refused to involve the government in economic affairs but used federal troops to end the Pullman strike 1894. Within a year of his taking office for the second time, 4 million were unemployed and the US was virtually bankrupt.

client-server architecture in computing, a system in which the mechanics of looking after data are separated from the programs that use the data. For example, the "server" might be a central database, typically located on a large computer that is reserved for this purpose. The "client" would be an ordinary program that requests data from the server as needed.

climate weather conditions at a particular place over a period of time. Climate encompasses all the meteorological elements and the factors that influence them. The primary factors that determine the variations of climate over the surface of the Earth are: (a) the effect of latitude and the tilt of the Earth's axis to the plane of the orbit about the Sun (66.5°); (b) the large-scale movements of different wind belts over the Earth's surface; (c) the temperature difference between land and sea; (d) contours of the ground; and (e) location of the area in relation to ocean currents. Catastrophic variations to climate may be caused by the impact of another planetary body, or by clouds resulting from volcanic activity. The most important local or global meteorological changes brought about by human activity are those linked with ◊ozone depleters and the ◊greenhouse effect.

clinical psychology discipline dealing with the understanding and treatment of health problems, particularly mental disorders. The main problems dealt with include anxiety, phobias, depression, obsessions, sexual and marital problems, drug and alcohol dependence, childhood behavioral problems, psychoses (such as schizophrenia), mental disability, and brain disease (such as dementia) and damage. Other areas of work include forensic psychology (concerned with criminal behavior) and health psychology.

Clinton Bill (William Jefferson) 1946– . 42nd president of the US 1993 - . A Democrat, he served as governor of Arkansas 1979–81 and 1983–93, establishing a liberal and progressive reputation. After winning the 1992 nomination for president, he chose Al Gore as his running mate. The 1992 campaign centered on the problems of the US economy, with Clinton successfully challenging the incumbent George Bush while weathering criticism of his avoidance of the military draft and other "character" issues. Clinton began his administration with ambitious plans for deficit reduction, military reforms and health care restructuring; all were met by strong opposition.

clipboard in computing, a temporary file or memory area where data can be stored before being copied into an application file. It is used, for example, in cut-and-paste operations.

Clive Robert, Baron Clive of Plassey 1725–1774. British soldier and administrator who established British rule in India by victories over French troops at Arcot 1751 and over the nawab of Bengal at Plassey 1757. He was governor of Bengal 1757–60 and 1765–66. On his return to Britain in 1766, his wealth led to allegations that he had abused his power. Although acquitted, he committed suicide.

clock rate the frequency of a computer's internal electronic clock. Every computer contains an electronic clock, which produces a sequence of regular electrical pulses used by the control unit to synchronize the components of the computer and regulate the fetch-execute cycle by which program instructions are processed.

clone an exact replica. In genetics, any one of a group of genetically identical cells or organisms. An identical ◊twin is a clone; so, too, are bacteria living in the same colony. The term clone has also been adopted by computer technology to describe a (nonexistent) device that mimics an actual one to enable certain software programs to run correctly.

closed shop a place of work, such as a factory or an office, where all workers within a section must belong to a single officially recognized labor union. Closed-shop agreements are negotiated between labor unions and management. Labor unions favor closed shops because 100% union membership gives them greater industrial power. Management can find it convenient because they can deal with workers as a group (collective bargaining) rather than having to negotiate with individual workers. In the US the closed shop was made illegal by the Taft-Hartley Act 1947, passed by Congress over Truman's veto. The closed shop was condemned by the European Court of Human Rights 1981.

clot-buster popular term for a small group of thrombolytic (clot-dissolving) drugs used in the treatment of heart attack.

clothes moth moth whose larvae feed on clothes, upholstery, and carpets. The adults are small golden or silvery moths. The natural habitat of the larvae is in the nests of animals, feeding on remains of hair and feathers, but they have adapted to human households and can cause considerable damage, for example, the common clothes moth *Tineola bisselliella*.

cloud water vapor condensed into minute water particles that float in masses in the atmosphere. Clouds, like fogs or mists, which occur at lower levels, are formed by the cooling of air containing water vapor, which generally condenses around tiny dust particles.

cloud chamber apparatus for tracking ionized particles. It consists of a vessel fitted with a piston and filled with air or other gas, saturated with water vapor. When the volume of the vessel is suddenly expanded by moving the piston outward, the vapor cools and a cloud of tiny droplets forms on any nuclei, dust, or ions present. As fast-moving ionizing particles collide with the air or gas molecules, they show as visible tracks.

clove dried, unopened flower bud of the clove tree *Eugenia caryophyllus*. A member of the myrtle family Myrtaceae, the clove tree is a native of the Maluku. Cloves are used for flavoring in cooking and confectionery. Oil of cloves, which has tonic and carminative qualities, is employed in medicine. The aromatic quality of cloves is shared to a large degree by the leaves, bark, and fruit of the tree.

clover any of an Old World genus *Trifolium* of low-growing leguminous plants, usually with compound leaves of three leaflets and small flowers in dense heads. Sweet clover refers to various species belonging to the related genus *Melilotus*.

Red clover *T. pratense* and white clover *T. repens* now grow widely in the US. The most common honey is made from clover and the most important source of fodder is red clover.

Clovis 465–511. Merovingian king of the Franks from 481. He succeeded his father Childeric as king of the

Salian (northern) Franks; defeated the Gallo-Romans (Romanized Gauls) near Soissons 486, ending their rule in France; and defeated the Alemanni, a confederation of Germanic tribes, near Cologne 496. He embraced Christianity and subsequently proved a powerful defender of orthodoxy against the Arian Visigoths, whom he defeated at Poitiers 507. He made Paris his capital.

club moss or *lycopod* any non-seed-bearing plant of the order Lycopodiales belonging to the Pteridophyta family. Club mosses are allied to the ferns and horsetails and, like them, reproduce by spores.

Lycopodium is the most common genus, with species mostly growing on forest floors.

clutch any device for disconnecting rotating shafts, used especially in an automobile's transmission system. In an automobile with a manual gearbox, the driver depresses the clutch when changing gear, thus disconnecting the engine from the gearbox.

Clwyd county of N Wales, created 1974 *area* 934 sq mi/2,420 sq km *towns and cities* Mold (administrative headquarters), Flint, Denbigh, Wrexham; seaside resorts: Colwyn Bay, Rhyl, Prestatyn *features* rivers: Dee, Clwyd; Clwydian range of mountains with Offa's Dyke along the main ridge; Chirk, Denbigh, Flint, and Rhuddlan castles; Greenfield Valley, NW of Flint, was in the forefront of the Industrial Revolution before the advent of steam and now has a museum of industrial archeology *products* dairy and meat products, optical glass, clothing, light engineering, paper, chemicals, limestone, microprocessors, plastics *population* (1991) 408,100 *famous people* George Jeffreys, Henry Morton Stanley *languages* English, 18% Welsh-speaking.

Clytemnestra in Greek mythology, the wife of ◊Agamemnon. With the help of her lover Aegisthus, she murdered her husband and his paramour Cassandra on his return from the Trojan War, and was in turn killed by her son Orestes.

cm symbol for *centimeter*.

coal black or blackish mineral substance formed from the compaction of ancient plant matter in tropical swamp conditions. It is used as a fuel and in the chemical industry. Coal is classified according to the proportion of carbon it contains. The main types are ◊*anthracite* (shiny, with about 90% carbon), **bituminous coal** (shiny and dull patches, about 75% carbon), and *lignite* (woody, grading into peat, about 50% carbon). Coal burning is one of the main causes of ◊acid rain.

coal gas gas produced when coal is destructively distilled or heated out of contact with the air. Its main constituents are methane, hydrogen, and carbon monoxide. Coal gas has been superseded by ◊natural gas for domestic purposes.

coalition association of political groups, usually for some limited or short-term purpose, such as fighting an election or forming a government when one party has failed to secure a majority in a legislature.

In 1990 a coalition of United Nations military forces was formed to free Kuwait from annexation by Iraq.

coastal erosion the erosion of the land by the constant battering of the sea's waves. This produces two effects. The first is a hydraulic effect, in which the force of the wave compresses air pockets in coastal rocks and cliffs, and the air then expands explosively. The second is the effect of corrasion, in which rocks and pebbles are flung against the cliffs, wearing them away. Frost shattering (or freeze-thaw), caused by the expansion of frozen seawater in cavities, and biological weathering, caused by the burrowing of rock-boring mollusks, also result in the breakdown of the rock.

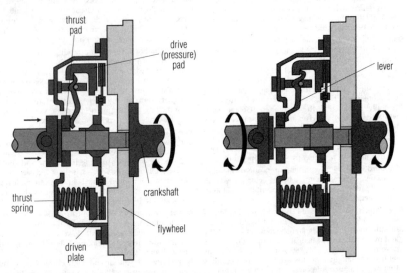

clutch The clutch consists of two main plates: a drive plate connected to the engine crankshaft and a driven plate connected to the wheels. When the clutch is disengaged, the drive plate does not press against the driven plate. When the clutch is engaged, the two plates are pressed into contact and the rotation of the crankshaft is transmitted to the wheels.

coast guard governmental organization whose members patrol a nation's seacoast to prevent smuggling, assist distressed vessels, watch for oil slicks, and so on.

The US Coast Guard 1915 has wide duties, including enforcing law and order on the high seas and navigable waters. During peacetime, it is administered under the Department of Transportation; in time of war, the Department of the Navy.

coati or *coatimundi* any of several species of carnivores of the genus *Nasua,* in the same family, Procyonidae, as the raccoons. A coati is a good climber and has long claws, a long tail, a good sense of smell, and a long, flexible piglike snout used for digging. Coatis live in packs in the forests of South and Central America.

coaxial cable electric cable that consists of a solid or stranded central conductor insulated from and surrounded by a solid or braided conducting tube or sheath. It can transmit the high-frequency signals used in television, telephone, and other telecommunications transmissions.

cobalt hard, lustrous, gray, metallic element, symbol Co, atomic number 27, atomic weight 58.933. It is found in various ores and occasionally as a free metal, sometimes in metallic meteorite fragments. It is used in the preparation of magnetic, wear-resistant, and high-strength alloys; its compounds are used in inks, paints, and varnishes.

Cobb Ty(rus Raymond), nicknamed "the Georgia Peach" 1886–1961. US baseball player, one of the greatest batters, home-run hitters, and base runners of all time. He played for Detroit and Philadelphia 1905–28, and won the American League batting average championship 12 times. He holds the record for runs scored (2,254) and lifetime batting average (.367). He had 4,191 hits in his career—a record that stood for almost 60 years.

COBOL (acronym for *common business-oriented language*) high-level computer-programming language, designed in the late 1950s for commercial data-processing problems; it has become the major language in this field. COBOL features powerful facilities for file handling and business arithmetic. Program instructions written in this language make extensive use of words and look very much like English sentences. This makes COBOL one of the easiest languages to learn and understand.

cobra any of several poisonous snakes, especially the genus *Naja,* of the family Elapidae, found in Africa and S Asia, species of which can grow from 3 ft/1 m to over 14 ft/4.3 m. The neck stretches into a hood when the snake is alarmed. Cobra venom contains nerve toxins powerful enough to kill humans.

coca South American shrub *Erythroxylon coca* of the coca family Erythroxylaceae, whose dried leaves are the source of cocaine.

It was used as a holy drug by the Andean Indians.

Coca-Cola trade name of a sweetened, carbonated drink, originally made with coca leaves and flavored with cola nuts, and containing caramel and caffeine. Invented in 1886, Coca-Cola was sold in every state of the US by 1895 and in 155 countries by 1987.

As a rule, Fanta, an orange-flavored soda made by Coca-Cola, preceded the cola-flavored soda in the Third World. With the increased presence of Americans in Third World nations, US imperialism became known as Coca-Colonialism.

cocaine alkaloid $C_{17}H_{21}NO_4$ extracted from the leaves of the coca tree. It has limited medical application, mainly as a local anesthetic agent that is readily absorbed by mucous membranes (lining tissues) of the nose and throat. It is both toxic and addictive. Its use as a stimulant is illegal. Crack is a derivative of cocaine.

cockatoo any of several crested parrots, especially of the genus *Cacatua.* They usually have light-colored plumage with tinges of red, yellow, or orange on the face, and an erectile crest on the head. They are native to Australia, New Guinea, and nearby islands.

cockchafer or *maybug* European beetle *Melolontha melolontha,* of the scarab family, up to 1.2 in/3 cm long, with clumsy, buzzing flight, seen on early summer evenings. Cockchafers damage trees by feeding on the foliage and flowers.

The larvae live underground for up to four years, feeding on grass and cereal roots.

Cockcroft John Douglas 1897–1967. British physicist. In 1932 he and the Irish physicist Ernest Walton succeeded in splitting the nucleus of an atom for the first time. In 1951 they were jointly awarded a Nobel Prize.

cockfighting the pitting of gamecocks against one another to make sport for onlookers and gamblers. In most countries it is illegal because of its cruelty.

The sport was extremely popular in feudal Europe. Cockfighting is still legal in many countries and continues surreptitiously in others. Fighting cocks are 1–2 years old when matched, and steel spurs are attached to their legs.

cockle any of over 200 species of bivalve mollusk with ribbed, heart-shaped shells. Some are edible and are sold in W European markets.

The Atlantic strawberry cockle *Americardia media,* about 1 in/2.5 cm across, is a common E North American species.

cockroach any of numerous insects of the family Blattidae, distantly related to mantises and grasshoppers. There are 3,500 species, mainly in the tropics. They have long antennae and biting mouthparts. They can fly, but rarely do so.

cocoa and chocolate food products made from the cacao (or cocoa) bean, fruit of a tropical tree *Theobroma cacao,* now cultivated mainly in Africa. Chocolate as a drink was introduced to Europe from the New World by the Spanish in the 16th century; eating-chocolate was first produced in the late 18th century. Cocoa and chocolate are widely used in

cobra The Indian cobra feeds on rodents, lizards, and frogs. As well as biting, the Indian cobra can defend itself by spitting venom through its fangs. The venom, reaching a distance of 6.5 ft/2 m, causes severe pain and damage if it enters the eyes of prey.

confectionery and drinks. More than 30 different pesticides are commonly used on cocoa crops, and traces of some have been detected in chocolate.

coconut fruit of the coconut palm *Cocos nucifera* of the family Arecaceae, which grows throughout the lowland tropics. The fruit has a large outer husk of fibers, which is split off and used for coconut matting and ropes. Inside this is the nut exported to temperate countries. Its hard shell contains white flesh and coconut milk, both of which are nourishing and palatable.

Cocteau Jean 1889–1963. French poet, dramatist, and film director. A leading figure in European Modernism, he worked with Picasso, Diaghilev, and Stravinsky. He produced many volumes of poetry, ballets such as *Le Boeuf sur le toit/The Ox on the Roof* 1920, plays, for example, *Orphée/Orpheus* 1926, and a mature novel of bourgeois French life, *Les Enfants terribles/Children of the Game* 1929, which he made into a film 1950.

cod any fish of the family Gadidae, especially the Atlantic cod, *Gadus morhua* found in the N Atlantic and Baltic. It is brown to gray with spots, white below, and can grow to 5 ft/1.5 m.

codeine opium derivative that provides ◊analgesia in mild to moderate pain. It also suppresses the cough center of the brain. It is an alkaloid, derived from morphine but less toxic and addictive.

Cody (William Frederick) *"Buffalo Bill"* 1846–1917. US scout and performer. From 1883 he toured the US and Europe with a Wild West show which featured the staging of Indian attacks and, for a time, the cast included Chief ◊Sitting Bull as well as Annie Oakley. His nickname derives from a time when he had a contract to supply buffalo carcasses to railroad laborers (over 4,000 in 18 months).

He was a heavy drinker and a trusting investor; he died in poverty after seeing his exploits recounted and exaggerated in novels of the West.

coeducation education of both boys and girls in one institution. In most countries coeducation has become favored over single-sex education, although there is some evidence to suggest that girls perform better in a single-sex institution, particularly in math and science.

In the US, 90% of schools and colleges are coeducational. In 1954, the USSR returned to its earlier coeducational system, which was partly abolished in 1944. In Islamic countries, coeducation is discouraged beyond the infant stage on religious principles.

coefficient the number part in front of an algebraic term, signifying multiplication. For example, in the expression $4x^2 + 2xy - x$, the coefficient of x^2 is 4 (because $4x^2$ means 4 x x^2), that of xy is 2, and that of x is -1 (because -1 x $x = -x$).

coelenterate any freshwater or marine organism of the phylum Coelenterata, having a body wall composed of two layers of cells. They also possess stinging cells. Examples are jellyfish, hydra, and coral.

coffee drink made from the roasted and ground bean-like seeds found inside the red berries of any of several species of shrubs of the genus *Coffea*, originally native to Ethiopia and now cultivated throughout the tropics. It contains a stimulant, ◊caffeine. The world's largest producers are Brazil, Colombia, and the Côte d'Ivoire; others include Indonesia (Java), Ethiopia, India, Hawaii, and Jamaica. *history* Coffee drinking began in Arab regions in the 14th century but did not

become common in Europe until 300 years later, when the first coffee houses were opened in Vienna, and soon after in Paris and London. In the American colonies, coffee became the substitute for tea when tea was taxed by the British.

cogito, ergo sum (Latin) "I think, therefore I am"; quotation from French philosopher René Descartes. The concept formed the basis of the philosophical doctrine of ◊dualism.

cognition in psychology, a general term covering the functions involved in synthesizing information—for example, perception (seeing, hearing, and so on), attention, memory, and reasoning.

Cohan George M(ichael) 1878–1942. US composer. His Broadway hit musical *Little Johnny Jones* 1904 included his songs "Give My Regards to Broadway" and "Yankee Doodle Boy". "You're a Grand Old Flag" 1906 further associated him with popular patriotism, as did his World War I song "Over There" 1917.

He was honored by Congress 1940.

cohesion in physics, a phenomenon in which interaction between two surfaces of the same material in contact makes them cling together (with two different materials the similar phenomenon is called adhesion). According to kinetic theory, cohesion is caused by attraction between particles at the atomic or molecular level. ◊Surface tension, which causes liquids to form spherical droplets, is caused by cohesion.

coil in medicine, another name for an ◊intrauterine device.

coke clean, light fuel produced when coal is strongly heated in an airtight oven. Coke contains 90% carbon and makes a useful domestic and industrial fuel (used, for example, in the iron and steel industries and in the production of town gas).

cola or *kola* any tropical tree of the genus *Cola*, especially *C. acuminata*, family Sterculiaceae. The nuts are chewed in W Africa for their high caffeine content, and in the West are used to flavor soft drinks.

cold, common minor disease of the upper respiratory tract, caused by a variety of viruses. Symptoms are headache, chill, nasal discharge, sore throat, and occasionally cough. Research indicates that the virulence of a cold depends on psychological factors and either a reduction or an increase of social or work activity, as a result of stress, in the previous six months.

coldblooded of animals, dependent on the surrounding temperature; see ◊*poikilothermy.*

cold fusion in nuclear physics, the fusion of atomic nuclei at room temperature. Were cold fusion to become possible it would provide a limitless, cheap, and pollution-free source of energy, and it has therefore been the subject of research around the world. In 1989, Martin Fleischmann (1927–) and Stanley Pons (1943–) of the University of Utah claimed that they had achieved cold fusion in the laboratory, but their results could not be substantiated.

Cold Harbor, Battle of Civil War engagement near Richmond, Virginia, June 1–12, 1864, in which the Confederate army under Robert E. ◊Lee repulsed Union attacks under Ulysses S. ◊Grant, inflicting as many as 6,000 casualties in an hour and forced Grant to adopt a siege of Petersburg. This demonstrated the tenacity of the Confederate forces late in the war and kept Grant's army largely stationary until April 1865.

Cold War ideological, political, and economic tensions 1945–90 between the USSR and Eastern Europe on the one hand and the US and Western Europe on the other. The Cold War was exacerbated by propaganda, covert activity by intelligence agencies, and economic sanctions; it intensified at times of conflict anywhere in the world. Arms-reduction agreements between the US and USSR in the late 1980s, and a diminution of Soviet influence in Eastern Europe, symbolized by the opening of the Berlin Wall 1989, led to a reassessment of positions, and the "war" officially ended 1990.

Coleridge Samuel Taylor 1772–1834. English poet. He was one of the founders of the Romantic movement. A friend of Southey and Wordsworth, he collaborated with the latter on *Lyrical Ballads* 1798. His poems include "The Rime of the Ancient Mariner", "Christabel", and "Kubla Khan"; critical works include *Biographia Literaria* 1817.

Colette Sidonie-Gabrielle 1873–1954. French writer. At 20 she married Henri Gauthier-Villars, a journalist known as "Willy", under whose name and direction her four "Claudine" novels, based on her own early life, were written. Divorced 1906, she worked as a striptease and mime artist for a while, but continued to write. Works from this later period include *Chéri* 1920, *La Fin de Chéri/The End of Chéri* 1926, and *Gigi* 1944.

colic spasmodic attack of pain in the abdomen, usually coming in waves. Colicky pains are caused by the painful muscular contraction and subsequent distension of a hollow organ; for example, the bowels, gall bladder (biliary colic), or ureter (renal colic).

colitis inflammation of the colon (large intestine) with diarrhea (often bloody). It is usually due to infection or some types of bacterial dysentery.

collage technique of pasting paper and other materials to a surface to create a picture. Picasso and Braque were the first to use collage, and the technique was frequently exploited by the Dadaists and Surrealists. Exponents include Hans Arp, Max Ernst, and Kurt Schwitters.

collagen protein that is the main constituent of connective tissue. Collagen is present in skin, cartilage, tendons, and ligaments. Bones are made up of collagen, with the mineral calcium phosphate providing increased rigidity.

collective security system for achieving international stability by an agreement among all states to unite against any aggressor. Such a commitment was embodied in the post–World War I League of Nations and also in the United Nations (UN), although the League was not able to live up to the ideals of its founders, nor has the UN been able to do so.

Collins J Lawton 1886–1963. US general. He first came to prominence on Guadalcanal 1942 leading the US 25th Infantry Division, which relieved the US Marines and completed the capture of the island. He then went to Europe and took part in ◊D-Day landings June 6, 1944 and the subsequent Allied drive through Europe.

colloid substance composed of extremely small particles of one material (the dispersed phase) evenly and stably distributed in another material (the continuous phase). The size of the dispersed particles (1–1,000 nanometers across) is less than that of particles in suspension but greater than that of molecules in true solution. Colloids involving gases include *aerosols* (dispersions of liquid or solid particles in a gas, as in fog or smoke) and *foams* (dispersions of gases in liquids).

Cologne (German *Köln*) industrial and commercial port in North Rhine–Westphalia, Germany, on the left bank of the Rhine, 22 mi/35 km from Düsseldorf; population (1988) 914,000. To the N is the Ruhr coalfield, on which many of Cologne's industries are based. They include motor vehicles, railroad wagons, chemicals, and machine tools. Cologne is an important transshipment center.

Colombia Republic of (*República de Colombia*) *area* 440,715 sq mi/1,141,748 sq km *capital* Santa Fé de Bogotá *towns and cities* Medellín, Cali, Bucaramanga; ports Barranquilla, Cartagena, Buenaventura *physical* the Andes mountains run N–S; flat coastland in W and plains (llanos) in E; Magdalena River runs N to Caribbean Sea; includes islands of Providencia, San Andrés, and Mapelo *features* Zipaquira salt mine and underground cathedral; Lake Guatavita, source of the legend of "El Dorado" *head of state and government* Ernesto Samper Pizano from 1994 *political system* democratic republic *political parties* Liberal Party (PL), centrist; April 19 Movement (ADM-19) left of center; National Salvation Movement (MSN), center-left; Conservative Party (PSC), right of center *exports* emeralds (world's largest producer), coffee (world's second largest producer), cocaine (country's largest export), bananas, cotton, meat, sugar, oil, skins, hides, tobacco *currency* peso *population* (1993 est) 34,900,800 (mestizo 68%, white 20%, American Indian 1%); growth rate 2.2% p.a. *life expectancy* men 66, women 72 *language* Spanish *media* TV satellite dishes must be registered *religion* Roman Catholic 95% *literacy* men 88%, women 86% *GNP* $1,280 per head (1991) *chronology 1886* Full independence achieved from Spain. Conservatives in power. *1930* Liberals in power. *1946* Conservatives in power. *1948* Left-wing mayor of Bogotá assassinated; widespread outcry. *1949* Start of civil war, "La Violencia", during which over 250,000 people died. *1957* Hoping to halt the violence, Conservatives and Liberals agreed to form a National Front, sharing the presidency. *1970* National Popular Alliance (ANAPO) formed as a left-wing opposition to the National Front. *1974* National Front accord temporarily ended. *1975* Civil unrest because of disillusionment with the government. *1978* Liberals, under Julio Turbay, revived the accord and began an intensive fight against drug dealers. *1982* Liberals maintained their control of congress but lost the presidency. The Conservative president,

US

Mexico

ATLANTIC OCEAN

Cuba

CARIBBEAN SEA

Panama

PACIFIC OCEAN

Bogotá

Venezuela

COLOMBIA

Ecuador

Brazil

0 miles 500
0 km 1000

Peru

Belisario Betancur, granted guerrillas an amnesty and freed political prisoners. *1984* Minister of justice assassinated by drug dealers; campaign against them stepped up. *1986* Virgilio Barco Vargas, Liberal, elected president by record margin. *1989* Drug cartel assassinated leading presidential candidate; Vargas declared antidrug war; bombing campaign by drug traffickers killed hundreds; police killed José Rodríguez Gacha, one of the most wanted cartel leaders. *1990* Cesar Gaviria Trujillo elected president. Liberals maintained control of congress. *1991* New constitution prohibited extradition of Colombians wanted*for trial in other countries; several leading drug traffickers arrested. Oct: Liberal Party won general election. *1992* Drug cartel leader Pablo Escobar escaped from prison. State of emergency declared. *1993* Escobar shot while attempting to avoid arrest. *1994* Ernesto Samper Pizano, Liberal, elected president.

Colombo capital and principal seaport of Sri Lanka, on the west coast near the mouth of the Kelani River; population (1990) 615,000, Greater Colombo about 1,000,000. It trades in tea, rubber, and cacao. It has iron-and steelworks and an oil refinery.

Colón second largest city in Panama, at the Caribbean end of the Panama Canal; population (1990) 140,900. It has a special economic zone (created 1948) used by foreign companies to avoid taxes on completed products in their home countries; $2 billion worth of goods passed through the zone in 1987, from dozens of countries and 600 companies. Unemployment in the city of Colón, outside the zone, was over 25% in 1991.

colonialism another name for *imperialism*.

color quality or wavelength of light emitted or reflected from an object. Visible white light consists of electromagnetic radiation of various wavelengths, and if a beam is refracted through a prism, it can be spread out into a spectrum, in which the various colors correspond to different wavelengths. From long to short wavelengths (from about 700 to 400 nanometers) the colors are red, orange, yellow, green, blue, indigo, and violet.

Colorado river in North America, rising in the Rocky Mountains and flowing 1,450 mi/2,333 km to the Gulf of California through Colorado, Utah, Arizona (including the Grand Canyon), and N Mexico. The many dams along its course, including Hoover and Glen Canyon, provide power and irrigation water, but have destroyed wildlife and scenery, and very little water now reaches the sea. To the W of the river in SE California is the *Colorado Desert*, an arid area of 2,000 sq mi/5,000 sq km. Its tributaries include the Gunnison, Green, Little Colorado, and Gila rivers. The Imperial Valley is irrigated by the Colorado River.

Colorado state in W central US; nickname Centennial State *area* 104,104 sq mi/269,700 sq km *capital* Denver *cities* Colorado Springs, Aurora, Lakewood, Fort Collins, Greeley, Pueblo *physical* Great Plains in the E; the main ranges of the Rocky Mountains (more than 14,000 ft/4,300 m); high plateaus of the Colorado Basin in the W *features* Rocky Mountain National Park; Pike's Peak; prehistoric cliff dwellings of the Mesa Verde National Park; Garden of the Gods (natural sandstone sculptures); Dinosaur and Great Sand Dunes national monuments; mining "ghost" towns; ski resorts, including Aspen, Vail, Steamboat Springs; US Air Force Academy *products* cereals, meat and dairy products, oil, coal, molybdenum, uranium,

iron, steel, machinery *population* (1990) 3,294,400 *famous people* Jack Dempsey, Douglas Fairbanks *history* first visited by Spanish explorers in the 16th century; claimed for Spain 1706; east portion passed to the US 1803 as part of the Louisiana Purchase, the rest in 1845 and 1848 as a result of the Mexican War. It attracted fur traders, and Denver was founded following the discovery of gold 1858. Colorado became a state 1876. Irrigated agriculture, ranching, tourism and outdoor sports, energy development, and the establishment of military bases fueled rapid growth after World War II.

coloratura in music, a rapid ornamental vocal passage with runs and trills. A *coloratura soprano* is a light, high voice suited to such music.

color blindness hereditary defect of vision that reduces the ability to discriminate certain colors, usually red and green. The condition is sex-linked, affecting men more than women.

coloring food ◊additive used to alter or improve the color of processed foods. Colorings include artificial colors, such as tartrazine and amaranth, which are made from petrochemicals, and the "natural" colors such as chlorophyll, caramel, and carotene. Some of the natural colors are actually synthetic copies of the naturally occurring substances, and some of these, notably the synthetically produced caramels, may be injurious to health.

color therapy in alternative medicine, application of light of appropriate wavelength to alleviate ailments or facilitate healing. Colored light affects not only psychological but also physiological states—for instance, long exposure to red light raises blood pressure and speeds up heartbeat and respiration rates, whereas exposure to blue has the reverse effect.

Colosseum amphitheater in ancient Rome, begun by the emperor Vespasian to replace the one destroyed by fire during the reign of Nero, and completed by his son Titus AD 80. It was 615 ft/187 m long and 160 ft/49 m high, and seated 50,000 people. Early Christians were martyred there by lions and gladiators. It could be flooded for mock sea battles.

Colt Samuel 1814–1862. US gunsmith who invented the revolver 1835 that bears his name.

Born in Hartford, Connecticut, Colt developed a gun that had an automatic revolving cylinder. When the US Army ordered a large number of guns during the Mexican War, he established his factory first near New Haven, Connecticut, and then at Hartford, where his business grew into an immense arms-manufacturing establishment.

Coltrane John (William) 1926–1967. US jazz saxophonist. He first came to prominence 1955 with the Miles ◊Davis quintet, later playing with Thelonious Monk 1957. He was a powerful and individual artist, whose performances featured much experimentation. His 1960s quartet was highly regarded for its innovations in melody and harmony.

Columba, St 521–597. Irish Christian abbot, missionary to Scotland. He was born in County Donegal of royal descent, and founded monasteries and churches in Ireland. In 563 he sailed with 12 companions to Iona, and built a monastery there that was to play a leading part in the conversion of Britain. Feast day June 9.

Columbia river in W North America, 1,215 mi/1,950 km length. It rises in British Columbia and flows through Washington to the Pacific below Astoria, after forming much of the boundary between Washington and Oregon. This fast-running river has enormous hydroelectric potential and is harnessed for irrigation and power by the Grand Coulee and other major dams. Although it is famous for salmon fishing, the catch is now much reduced. The mouth of the Columbia was discovered 1792.

columbine any plant of the genus *Aquilegia* of the buttercup family Ranunculaceae. All are perennial herbs with divided leaves and flowers with spurred petals.

Columbus capital of Ohio on the rivers Scioto and Olentangy; population (1990) 632,900. It has coalfield and natural gas resources nearby; its industries include the manufacture of automobiles, planes, missiles, and electrical goods.

Columbus Christopher (Spanish *Cristóbal Colón*) 1451–1506. Italian navigator and explorer who made four voyages to the New World: 1492 to San Salvador Island, Cuba, and Haiti; 1493–96 to Guadaloupe, Montserrat, Antigua, Puerto Rico, and Jamaica; 1498 to Trinidad and the mainland of South America; 1502–04 to Honduras and Nicaragua.

Believing that Asia could be reached by sailing westward, he eventually won the support of King Ferdinand and Queen Isabella of Spain and set off on his first voyage from Palos Aug 3, 1492 with three small ships, the *Niña*, the *Pinta*, and his flagship the *Santa Maria*. Land was sighted Oct 12, probably Watling Island (now San Salvador Island), and within a few weeks he reached Cuba and Haiti, returning to Spain March 1493.

Columbus Day (Oct 12), a public holiday, is named for him.

column in architecture, a structure, round or polygonal in plan, erected vertically as a support for some part of a building. Cretan paintings reveal the existence of wooden columns in Aegean architecture about 1500 BC. The Hittites, Assyrians, and Egyptians also used wooden columns, and they are a feature of the monumental architecture of China and Japan. In Classical architecture there are five principal types of column.

The Greeks and Romans used stone, as did later European, Asian, and American builders. Modern architects often design simple but elegant columns.

COM acronym for *computer output on microfilm/ microfiche*.

coma in medicine, a state of deep unconsciousness from which the subject cannot be roused. Possible causes include head injury, brain disease, liver failure, cerebral hemorrhage, and drug overdose.

Comaneci Nadia 1961– . Romanian gymnast. She won three gold medals at the 1976 Olympics at the age of 14, and was the first gymnast to record a perfect score of 10 in international competition. Upon retirement she became a coach of the Romanian team, but defected to Canada 1989.

CAREER HIGHLIGHTS

Olympic Games
1976: gold: beam, vault, floor exercise
1980: gold: beam, parallel bars

combine harvester or *combine* machine used for harvesting cereals and other crops, so called because it combines the actions of reaping (cutting the crop) and threshing (beating the ears so that the grain separates).

combustion burning, defined in chemical terms as the rapid combination of a substance with oxygen, accompanied by the evolution of heat and usually light. A slow-burning candle flame and the explosion of a mixture of gasoline vapor and air are extreme examples of combustion.

Comecon (acronym for *Council for Mutual Economic Assistance*, or *CMEA*) economic organization 1949–91, linking the USSR with Bulgaria, Czechoslovakia, Hungary, Poland, Romania, East Germany (1950–90), Mongolia (from 1962), Cuba (from 1972), and Vietnam (from 1978), with Yugoslavia as an associated member. Albania also belonged 1949–61. Its establishment was prompted by the ◊Marshall Plan. Comecon was formally disbanded June 1991.

comedy in the simplest terms, a literary work, usually dramatic, with a happy or amusing ending, as opposed to ◊tragedy. The comic tradition has undergone many changes since its Greek and Roman roots; although some comedies are timeless, such as those of Shakespeare and Molière, others are very representative of a particular era, relying upon topical allusion and current fashion.

comet small, icy body orbiting the Sun, usually on a highly elliptical path. A comet consists of a central nucleus a few miles across, and has been likened to a dirty snowball because it consists mostly of ice mixed with dust. As the comet approaches the Sun the nucleus heats up, releasing gas and dust which form a tenuous coma, up to 60,000 mi/100,000 km wide, around the nucleus. Gas and dust stream away from the coma to form one or more tails, which may extend for millions of miles.

comfrey any plant of the genus *Symphytum*, borage family Boraginaceae, with rough, hairy leaves and small bell-shaped flowers (blue, purple-pink, or white), found in Europe and W Asia.

Comintern acronym for *Communist International*.

Comité Consultatif International Téléphonique et Télégraphique (CCITT) international organization that determines international communications standards and protocols for data communications, including ◊fax.

command language in computing, a set of commands and the rules governing their use, by which users control a program. For example, an ◊operating system may have commands such as SAVE and DELETE, or a payroll program may have commands for adding and amending staff records.

commando member of a specially trained, highly mobile military unit. The term originated in South Africa in the 19th century, where it referred to Boer military reprisal raids against Africans and, in the South African Wars, against the British. Commando units have often carried out operations behind enemy lines.

commedia dell'arte popular form of Italian improvised comic drama in the 16th and 17th centuries, performed by trained troupes of actors and involving stock characters and situations. It exerted considerable influence on writers such as Molière and Carlo Goldoni, and on the genres of pantomime, harlequinade, and the Punch and Judy show. It laid the foundation for a tradition of mime, strong in France, that has continued with the modern mime of Jean-Louis Barrault and Marcel Marceau.

commensalism in biology, a relationship between two ◊species whereby one (the commensal) benefits from the association, whereas the other neither benefits nor suffers. For example, certain species of millipede and silverfish inhabit the nests of army ants and live by scavenging on the refuse of their hosts, but without affecting the ants.

commodity something produced for sale. Commodities may be consumer goods, such as radios, or producer goods, such as copper bars.

Commodity markets deal in raw or semiraw materials that are amenable to grading and that can be stored for considerable periods without deterioration.

common law that part of the English law not embodied in legislation. It consists of rules of law based on common custom and usage and on judicial decisions. English common law became the basis of law in the US and many other English-speaking countries.

Commons, House of the lower but more powerful of the two parts of the British and Canadian ◊parliaments.

commonwealth body politic founded on law for the common "weal" or good. Political philosophers of the 17th century, such as Thomas Hobbes and John Locke, used the term to mean an organized political community. In Britain it was specifically applied to the regime (*the Commonwealth*) of Oliver ◊Cromwell 1649–60.

Commonwealth of Independent States (CIS) successor body to the Union of Soviet Socialist Republics, initially formed as a new commonwealth of Slav republics on Dec 8, 1991, by the presidents of the Russian Federation, Belarus, and Ukraine. On Dec 21, eight of the nine remaining non-Slav republics—Moldova, Tajikistan, Armenia, Azerbaijan, Turkmenistan, Kazakhstan, Kyrgyzstan, and Uzbekistan—joined the CIS at a meeting held in Kazakhstan's capital, Alma Ata. The CIS formally came into existence Jan 1992 when President Gorbachev resigned and the Soviet government voted itself out of existence. It has no real, formal political institutions and its role is uncertain. Its headquarters are in Minsk (Mensk), Belarus. Georgia joined 1993.

Commonwealth, the (British) voluntary association of 51 countries and their dependencies that once formed part of the ◊British Empire and are now independent sovereign states. They are all regarded as "full members of the Commonwealth". Additionally, there are some 20 territories that are not completely sovereign and remain dependencies of the UK or another of the fully sovereign members, and are regarded as "Commonwealth countries". Heads of government meet every two years, apart from those of Nauru and Tuvalu. The Commonwealth has no charter or constitution, and is founded more on tradition and sentiment than on political or economic factors.

Commune, Paris two separate periods in the history of Paris 1789–94 and March–May 1871; see ◊Paris Commune.

communication in biology, the signaling of information by one organism to another, usually with the intention of altering the recipient's behavior. Signals used in communication may be *visual* (such as the human smile or the display of colorful plumage in birds), *auditory* (for example, the whines or barks of a dog), *olfactory* (such as the odors released by the scent glands of a deer), *electrical* (as in the pulses emitted by electric fish), or *tactile* (for example, the nuzzling of male and female elephants).

communications satellite relay station in space for sending telephone, television, telex, and other messages around the world. Messages are sent to and from the satellites via ground stations. Most communications satellites are in ◊geostationary orbit, appearing to hang fixed over one point on the Earth's surface.

Communion, Holy in the Christian church, another name for the ◊Eucharist.

communism revolutionary socialism based on the theories of the political philosophers Karl Marx and Friedrich Engels, emphasizing common ownership of the means of production and a planned economy. The principle held is that each should work according to his or her capacity and receive according to his or her needs. Politically, it seeks the overthrow of capitalism through a proletarian revolution. The first communist state was the USSR after the revolution of 1917. Revolutionary socialist parties and groups united to form communist parties in other countries during the interwar years. After World War II, communism was enforced in those countries that came under Soviet occupation.

China emerged after 1961 as a rival to the USSR in world communist leadership, and other countries attempted to adapt communism to their own needs. The late 1980s saw a movement for more individual freedoms in many communist countries, culminating in the abolition or overthrow of communist rule in Eastern European countries and Mongolia, and further state repression in China. The failed hard-line coup in the USSR against President Gorbachev 1991 resulted in the effective abandonment of communism there. Communism as the ideology of a nation state survives in only a handful of countries, notably China, Cuba, North Korea, Laos, and Vietnam, but even in these countries its survival into the next century is in doubt.

community in the social sciences, the sense of identity, purpose, and companionship that comes from belonging to a particular place, organization, or social group. The concept dominated sociological thinking in the first half of the 20th century, and inspired the academic discipline of *community studies*.

community service in the penal systems of the US and the UK, unpaid work in the service of the community (aiding children, the elderly, or the handicapped), performed by a convicted person by order of the court as an alternative to prison.

Comoros Federal Islamic Republic of (*Jumhuriyat al-Qumur al-Itthadiyah al-Islamiyah*) *area* 719 sq mi/ 1,862 sq km *capital* Moroni *towns and cities* Mutsamudu, Domoni, Fomboni *physical* comprises the volcanic islands of Njazídja, Nzwani, and Mwali (formerly Grande Comore, Anjouan, Moheli); at N end of Mozambique Channel *features* active volcano on Njazídja; poor tropical soil *head of state* Said Mohammed Djohar (interim administration) from 1989 *head of government* Mohammed Abdou Madi from 1994 *political system* emergent democracy *political parties* Comoran Union for Progress (Udzima), nationalist Islamic; National Union for Congolese Democracy (UNDC), left of center; Popular Democratic Movement (MDP), centrist *exports* copra, vanilla, cocoa, sisal, coffee, cloves, essential oils *currency* CFA franc *population* (1993 est) 510,000; growth rate 3.1% p.a. *life expectancy* men 56, women 57 *languages* Arabic (official), Comorian (Swahili and Arabic dialect), Makua, French *religions* Muslim (official) 86%, Roman Catholic 14% *literacy* 61% *GNP* $500 per head (1991) *chronology 1975* Independence achieved from France, but island of Mayotte remained part of France. Ahmed Abdallah elected president. The Comoros joined the United Nations. *1976* Abdallah overthrown by Ali Soilih. *1978* Soilih killed by mercenaries working for Abdallah. Islamic republic proclaimed and Abdallah elected president. *1979* The Comoros became a one-party state; powers of the federal government increased. *1985* Constitution amended to make Abdallah head of government as well as head of state. *1989* Abdallah killed by French mercenaries who took control of government; under French and South African pressure, mercenaries left Comoros, turning authority over to French administration and interim president Said Mohammad Djohar. *1990 and 1992* Antigovernment coups foiled. *1993* General election failed to provide any one party with overall assembly majority. Post of prime minister restored. *1994* Djohar's supporters won overall majority in assembly elections.

compact disk (or *CD*) disk for storing digital information, about 4.5 in/12 cm in across, mainly used for music, when it can have over an hour's playing time. The compact disk is made of aluminum with a transparent plastic coating; the metal disk underneath is etched by a ◊laser beam with microscopic pits that carry a digital code representing the sounds. During playback, a laser beam reads the code and produces signals that are changed into near-exact replicas of the original sounds.

company in the army, a subunit of a battalion. It consists of about 120 soldiers, and is commanded by a captain in the US Army. Four or five companies make a battalion.

compass any instrument for finding direction. The most commonly used is a magnetic compass, consisting of a thin piece of magnetic material with the north-seeking pole indicated, free to rotate on a pivot and mounted on a compass card on which the points of the compass are marked. When the compass is properly adjusted and used, the north-seeking pole will point to the magnetic north, from which true north can be found from tables of magnetic corrections.

A compass (or pair of compasses) is also an instrument used for drawing circles or taking measurements, consisting of a pair of pointed legs connected by a central pivot.

compiler computer program that translates programs written in a high-level language into machine code (the form in which they can be run by the computer). The compiler translates each high-level instruction into several machine-code instructions—in a process called *compilation*—and produces a complete independent program that can be run by the computer as often as required, without the original source program being present.

complementary number in number theory, the number obtained by subtracting a number from its base. For example, the complement of 7 in numbers to base 10 is 3. Complementary numbers are necessary in computing, as the only mathematical operation of which digital computers (including pocket calculators) are directly capable is addition. Two numbers can be subtracted by adding one number to the com-

plement of the other; two numbers can be divided by using successive subtraction (which, using complements, becomes successive addition); and multiplication can be performed by using successive addition.

The four main operations of arithmetic can thus all be reduced to various types of addition and made with the capability of a digital computer, using the binary number system.

complex in psychology, a group of ideas and feelings that have become repressed because they are distasteful to the person in whose mind they arose, but are still active in the depths of the person's unconscious mind, continuing to affect his or her life and actions, even though he or she is no longer fully aware of their existence. Typical examples include the ◊Oedipus complex and the inferiority complex.

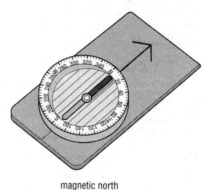

magnetic north

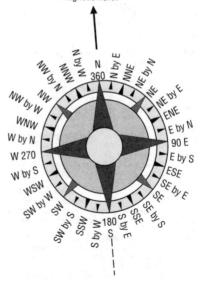

compass As early as 2500 BC, the Chinese were using pieces of magnetic rock, magnetite, as simple compasses. By the 12th century, European navigators were using compasses consisting of a needle-shaped magnet floating in a bowl of water.

complex number in mathematics, a number written in the form $a + ib$, where a and b are ◊real numbers and i is the square root of –1 (that is, $i^2 = -1$); i used to be known as the "imaginary" part of the complex number. Some equations in algebra, such as those of the form $x^2 + 5 = 0$, cannot be solved without recourse to complex numbers, because the real numbers do not include square roots of negative numbers.

Compositae daisy family, comprising dicotyledonous flowering plants characterized by flowers borne in composite heads (see ◊capitulum). It is the largest family of flowering plants, the majority being herbaceous. Birds seem to favor the family for use in nest "decoration", possibly because many species either repel or kill insects (see ◊pyrethrum). Species include the daisy and dandelion; food plants such as the artichoke, lettuce, and safflower; and the garden varieties of chrysanthemum, dahlia, and zinnia.

compost organic material decomposed by bacteria under controlled conditions to make a nutrient-rich natural fertilizer for use in gardening or farming. A well-made compost heap reaches a high temperature during the composting process, killing most weed seeds that might be present.

As the decomposers feed, they raise the temperature in the center of the compost as high as 150°F/66°C.

compound chemical substance made up of two or more ◊elements bonded together, so that they cannot be separated by physical means. Compounds are held together by ionic or covalent bonds.

compound interest interest calculated by computing the rate against the original capital plus reinvested interest each time the interest becomes due. When simple interest is calculated, only the interest on the original capital is added.

CompuServe large (US-based) public on-line data service. It is widely used for ◊electronic mail and ◊bulletin boards.

computer programmable electronic device that can input, store, process, and output data. Almost all modern computers are ◊digital computers, which

computer: chronology

1614	John Napier invented logarithms.
1615	William Oughtred invented the slide rule.
1623	Wilhelm Schickard (1592–1635) invented the mechanical calculating machine.
1645	Blaise Pascal produced a calculator.
1672–74	Gottfried Leibniz built his first calculator, the Stepped Reckoner.
1801	Joseph-Marie Jacquard developed an automatic loom controlled by punch cards.
1820	The first mass-produced calculator, the Arithometer, was developed by Charles Thomas de Colmar (1785–1870).
1822	Charles Babbage completed his first model for the difference engine.
1830s	Babbage created the first design for the analytical engine.
1890	Herman Hollerith developed the punched-card ruler for the US census.
1936	Alan Turing published the mathematical theory of computing.
1938	Konrad Zuse constructed the first binary calculator, using Boolean algebra.
1939	US mathematician and physicist J V Atanasoff (1903–) became the first to use electronic means for mechanizing arithmetical operations.
1943	The Colossus electronic code-breaker was developed at Bletchley Park, England. The Harvard University Mark I or Automatic Sequence Controlled Calculator (partly financed by IBM) became the first program-controlled calculator.
1946	ENIAC (acronym for electronic numerator, integrator, analyzer, and computer), the first general purpose, fully electronic digital computer, was completed at the University of Pennsylvania, US.
1948	Manchester University (England) Mark I, the first stored-program computer, was completed. William Shockley of Bell Laboratories invented the transistor.
1951	Launch of Ferranti Mark I, the first commercially produced computer. Whirlwind, the first real-time computer, was built for the US air-defense system. Grace Murray Hopper of Remington Rand invented the compiler computer program.
1952	EDVAC (acronym for electronic discrete variable
	computer) was completed at the Institute for Advanced Study, Princeton, US (by John Von Neumann and others).
1953	Magnetic core memory was developed.
1958	The first integrated circuit was constructed.
1963	The first minicomputer was built by Digital Equipment (DEC). The first electronic calculator was built by Bell Punch Company.
1964	Launch of IBM System/360, the first compatible family of computers. John Kemeny and Thomas Kurtz of Dartmouth College invented BASIC (Beginner's All-purpose Symbolic Instruction Code), a computer language similar to FORTRAN.
1965	The first supercomputer, the Control Data CD6600, was developed.
1971	The first microprocessor, the Intel 4004, was announced.
1974	CLIP-4, the first computer with a parallel architecture, was developed by John Backus at IBM.
1975	Altair 8800, the first personal computer (PC), or microcomputer, was launched.
1981	The Xerox Star system, the first WIMP system (acronym for windows, icons, menus, and pointing devices), was developed. IBM launched the IBM PC.
1984	Apple launched the Macintosh computer.
1985	The Inmos T414 transputer, the first "off-the-shelf" microprocessor for building parallel computers, was announced.
1988	The first optical microprocessor, which uses light instead of electricity, was developed.
1989	Wafer-scale silicon memory chips, able to store 200 million characters, were launched.
1990	Microsoft released Windows 3, a popular windowing environment for PCs.
1992	Philips launched the CD-I (Compact-Disc Interactive) player, based on CD audio technology, to provide interactive multimedia programs for the home user.
1993	Intel launched the Pentium chip containing 3.1 million transistors and capable of 100 MIPs (millions of instructions per second). The Personal Digital Assistant (PDA), which recognizes user's handwriting, went on sale.
1995	Intel releases details of the P6 microprocessor.

store and process data using ◊binary number codes. As a result of research and development, the size, speed, and capability of computers is always changing. A computer that, only a few years ago, might have been considered fast and powerful may today be considered obsolete; see ◊computer generation.

computer-aided design use of computers to create and modify design drawings; see ◊CAD.

computer art art produced with the help of a computer.

computer-assisted learning use of computers in education and training; see ◊CAL.

computer engineer job classification for computer personnel. A computer engineer repairs and maintains computer hardware.

computer game or *video game* any computer-controlled game in which the computer (sometimes) opposes the human player. Computer games typically employ fast, animated graphics on a ◊VDT (visual display terminal), and synthesized sound.

computer generation any of the five broad groups into which computers may be classified: *first generation* the earliest computers, developed in the 1940s and 1950s, made from valves and wire circuits; *second generation* from the early 1960s, based on transistors and printed circuits; *third generation* from the late 1960s, using integrated circuits and often sold as families of computers, such as the IBM 360 series; *fourth generation* using ◊microprocessors, large-scale integration (LSI), and sophisticated programming languages, still in use in the 1990s; and *fifth generation* based on parallel processing and very large-scale integration, currently under development.

computer graphics use of computers to display and manipulate information in pictorial form. Input may be achieved by scanning an image, by drawing with a mouse or stylus on a graphics tablet, or by drawing directly on the screen with a light pen.

computerized axial tomography medical technique, usually known as CAT scan, for noninvasive investigation of disease or injury.

computer operator job classification for computer personnel. Computer operators work directly with the computer, running the programs, changing disks and tapes, loading paper into printers, and ensuring all ◊data security procedures are followed.

computer program coded instructions for a computer; see ◊program.

computer simulation representation of a real-life situation in a computer program. For example, the program might simulate the flow of customers arriving at a bank. The user can alter variables, such as the number of cashiers on duty, and see the effect.

computer terminal the device whereby the operator communicates with the computer; see ◊terminal.

Comte Auguste 1798–1857. French philosopher regarded as the founder of sociology, a term he coined 1830. He sought to establish sociology as an intellectual discipline, using a scientific approach ("positivism") as the basis of a new science of social order and social development.

From 1816–18 he taught mathematics. He divided human knowledge into a hierarchy, with sociology at the top of the academic pyramid. Positivism offered a method of logical analysis and provided an ethical and moral basis for predicting and evaluating social progress.

Conakry capital and chief port of the Republic of Guinea; population (1983) 705,300. It is on the island of Tumbo, linked with the mainland by a causeway and by rail with Kankan, 300 mi/480 km to the NE. Bauxite and iron ore are mined nearby.

concave of a surface, curving inward, or away from the eye. For example, a bowl appears concave when viewed from above. In geometry, a concave polygon is one that has an interior angle greater than 180°. Concave is the opposite of ◊convex.

concentration camp prison camp for civilians in wartime or under totalitarian rule. The first concentration camps were devised by the British during the Second Boer War in South Africa 1899 for the detention of Afrikaner women and children (with the subsequent deaths of more than 20,000 people). A system of hundreds of concentration camps was developed by the Nazis in Germany and occupied Europe (1933–45) to imprison Jews and political and ideological opponents after Hitler became chancellor Jan 1933. The most infamous camps in World War II were the extermination camps of Auschwitz, Belsen, Dachau, Maidanek, Sobibor, and Treblinka. The total number of people who died at the camps exceeded 6 million, and some inmates were subjected to medical experimentation before being killed.

concerto composition, usually in three movements, for solo instrument (or instruments) and orchestra. It developed during the 18th century from the *concerto grosso* form for string orchestra, in which a group of solo instruments (concerto) is contrasted with a full orchestra (ripieno).

Concord town in Massachusetts, now a suburb of Boston; population (1990) 17,300. Concord was settled 1635 and was the site of the first battle of the American Revolution, April 19, 1775. The writers Ralph Waldo Emerson, Henry Thoreau, Nathaniel Hawthorne, and Louisa May Alcott lived here.

Although electronic equipment, metal products, and leather goods are manufactured, it is mainly a residential suburb of Boston, which lies 18 mi/29 km to the SW. The Minuteman National Historical Park is here.

concordance book containing an alphabetical list of the important words in a major work, with reference to the places in which they occur. The first concordance was one for the Latin Vulgate Bible compiled by a Dominican monk in the 13th century.

Alexander Cruden composed a concordance of the Bible in 1737, of which many editions have appeared. Concordances to Shakespeare, Milton, and other writers also appear in many editions.

Concorde the only supersonic airliner, which cruises at Mach 2, or twice the speed of sound, about 1,350 mph/2,170 kph. Concorde, the result of Anglo-French cooperation, made its first flight 1969 and entered commercial service seven years later. It is 202 ft/62 m long and has a wing span of nearly 84 ft/26 m. Dev·loping Concorde cost French and British taxpayers £2 billion.

concrete building material composed of cement, stone, sand, and water. It has been used since Egyptian and Roman times. Since the late 19th century, it has been increasingly employed as an economical alternative to materials such as brick and wood, and has been combined with steel to increase its tension capacity.

concussion temporary unconsciousness resulting from a blow to the head. It is often followed by amnesia for events immediately preceding the blow.

condensation conversion of a vapor to a liquid. This is frequently achieved by letting the vapor come into contact with a cold surface. It is an essential step in distillation processes, and is the process by which water vapor turns into fine water droplets to form ◊cloud.

conditioning in psychology, two major principles of behavior modification.

In *classical conditioning*, described by Ivan Pavlov, a new stimulus can evoke an automatic response by being repeatedly associated with a stimulus that naturally provokes that response. For example, the sound of a bell repeatedly associated with food will eventually trigger salivation, even if sounded without food being presented. In *operant conditioning*, described by US psychologists Edward Lee Thorndike (1874–1949) and B F Skinner, the frequency of a voluntary response can be increased by following it with a reinforcer or reward.

condom or *sheath* or *prophylactic* barrier contraceptive, made of rubber, which fits over an erect penis and holds in the sperm produced by ejaculation. It is an effective means of preventing pregnancy if used carefully, preferably with a ◊spermicide. A condom with spermicide is 97% effective; one without spermicide is 85% effective as a contraceptive. Condoms also give protection against sexually transmitted diseases, including AIDS.

condominium joint rule of a territory by two or more states, for example, Kanton and Enderbury islands in the South Pacific Phoenix group (under the joint control of Britain and the US for 50 years from 1939).

The term, often shortened to condo, has also come into use in North America to describe a type of joint property ownership of common areas of an apartment building or complex by each apartment owner.

condor large bird, a New World vulture *Vultur gryphus*, with wingspan up to 10 ft/3 m, weight up to 28 lbs/13 kg, and length up to 3.8 ft/1.2 m. It is black, with some white on the wings and a white frill at the base of the neck. It lives in the Andes and along the South American coast, and feeds on carrion. The Californian condor *Gymnogyps californianus* is a similar bird, on the verge of extinction.

conductance ability of a material to carry an electrical current, usually given the symbol G. For a direct current, it is the reciprocal of ◊resistance: a conductor of resistance R has a conductance of $1/R$. For an alternating current, conductance is the resistance R divided by the impedance Z: $G = R/Z$. Conductance was formerly expressed in reciprocal ohms (or mhos); the SI unit is the siemens (S).

conduction, electrical flow of charged particles through a material that gives rise to electric current. Conduction in metals involves the flow of negatively charged free ◊electrons. Conduction in gases and some liquids involves the flow of ◊ions that carry positive charges in one direction and negative charges in the other. Conduction in a semiconductor such as silicon involves the flow of electrons and positive holes.

conduction, heat flow of heat energy through a material without the movement of any part of the material itself (compare ◊conduction, electrical). Heat energy is present in all materials in the form of the kinetic energy of their vibrating molecules, and may be conducted from one molecule to the next in the form of this mechanical vibration. In the case of metals, which are particularly good conductors of heat, the free electrons within the material carry heat around very quickly.

conductor any material that conducts heat or electricity (as opposed to an insulator, or nonconductor). A good

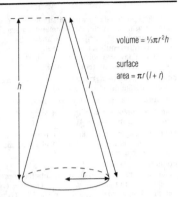

volume = $\frac{1}{3}\pi r^2 h$

surface area = $\pi r (l + r)$

cone *The volume and surface area of a cone are given by formulas involving a few simple dimensions.*

conductor has a high electrical or heat conductivity, and is generally a substance rich in free electrons such as a metal. A poor conductor (such as the nonmetals glass and porcelain) has few free electrons. Carbon is exceptional in being nonmetallic and yet (in some of its forms) a relatively good conductor of heat and electricity. Substances such as silicon and germanium, with intermediate conductivities that are improved by heat, light, or voltage, are known as ◊semiconductors.

cone in geometry, a solid or surface consisting of the set of all straight lines passing through a fixed point (the vertex) and the points of a circle or ellipse whose plane does not contain the vertex.

cone in botany, the reproductive structure of the conifers and cycads; also known as a strobilus. It consists of a central axis surrounded by numerous, overlapping, scalelike, modified leaves (sporophylls) that bear the reproductive organs. Usually there are separate male and female cones, the former bearing pollen sacs containing pollen grains, and the larger female cones bearing the ovules that contain the ova or egg cells. The pollen is carried from male to female cones by the wind (◊anemophily). The seeds develop within the female cone and are released as the scales open in dry atmospheric conditions, which favor seed dispersal.

Coney Island seaside resort on a peninsula in Brooklyn, in the SW of Long Island, New York. It has been popular for ocean bathing and its amusement parks since the 1840s.

Coney Island was named for the wild rabbits (coneys) that inhabited what was originally a small island.

Confederacy in US history, popular name for the *Confederate States of America*, the government established by 7 (later 11) Southern states in Feb 1861 when they seceded from the Union, precipitating the ◊Civil War. Montgomery, Alabama, was briefly the capital and then Richmond, Virginia, with Jefferson Davis the president. The states were Alabama, Arkansas, Florida, Georgia, Louisiana, Mississippi, North Carolina, South Carolina, Tennessee, Texas, and Virginia. The Confederacy fell after its army was defeated 1865 and General Robert E Lee surrendered.

Confederation, Articles of in US history, the initial means by which the 13 former British colonies created a form of national government. Ratified 1781, the articles established a unicameral legislature, Congress, with limited powers of raising revenue, regulating currency, and conducting foreign affairs. But because the individual states retained significant autonomy, the confederation was unmanageable. The articles were superseded by the US Constitution 1788.

confession in religion, the confession of sins practiced in Roman Catholic, Orthodox, and most Far Eastern Christian churches, and since the early 19th century revived in Anglican and Lutheran churches. The Lateran Council of 1215 made auricular confession (self-accusation by the penitent to a priest, who in Catholic doctrine is divinely invested with authority to give absolution) obligatory once a year.

confession in law, a criminal's admission of guilt. Since false confessions may be elicited by intimidation or ill treatment of the accused, the validity of confession in a court of law varies from one legal system to another. In the US a confession that is shown to be coerced does not void a conviction as long as it is supported by independent evidence.

configuration in computing, the way in which a system, whether it be ◊hardware and/or ◊software, is set up. A minimum configuration is often referred to for a particular application, and this will usually include a specification of processor, disk and memory size, and peripherals required.

confirmation rite practiced by a number of Christian denominations, including Roman Catholic, Anglican, and Orthodox, in which a previously baptized person is admitted to full membership in the church. In Reform Judaism there is often a confirmation service several years after the bar or bat mitzvah (initiation into the congregation).

Confucianism body of beliefs and practices based on the Chinese classics and supported by the authority of the philosopher Confucius. The origin of things is seen in the union of *yin* and *yang*, the passive and active principles. Human relationships follow the patriarchal pattern. For more than 2,000 years Chinese political government, social organization, and individual conduct was shaped by Confucian principles. In 1912, Confucian philosophy, as a basis for government, was dropped by the state.

Confucius (Latinized form of *Kong Zi*, "Kong the master") 551–479 BC. Chinese sage whose name is given to the ethical system of Confucianism. He placed emphasis on moral order and observance of the established patriarchal family and social relationships of authority, obedience, and mutual respect. His emphasis on tradition and ethics attracted a growing number of pupils during his lifetime. *The Analects of Confucius*, a compilation of his teachings, was published after his death.

conga Latin American dance, originally from Cuba, in which the participants form a winding line, take three steps forward or backward, and then kick.

conger any large marine eel of the family Congridae, especially the genus *Conger*. Conger eels live in shallow water, hiding in crevices during the day and active by night, feeding on fish and crabs. They are valued for food and angling.

The American conger *C. oceanicus* grows to 4.5 ft/ 1.4 m in length.

Congo Republic of (*République du Congo*) *area* 132,012 sq mi/342,000 sq km *capital* Brazzaville *towns and cities* chief port Pointe-Noire; N'Kayi, Loubomo *physical* narrow coastal plain rises to central plateau, then falls into northern basin; Zaïre (Congo) River on the border with Zaire; half the country is rainforest *environment* an estimated 93% of the rural population is

without access to safe drinking water *features* 70% of the population lives in Brazzaville, Pointe-Noire, or in towns along the railroad linking these two places *head of state* Pascal Lissouba from 1992 *head of government* Jacques-Joachim Yhombi-Opango from 1993 *political system* emergent democracy *political parties* Pan-African Union for Social Democracy (UPADS), moderate, left of center; Rally for Democracy and Development (RDD), center-left; Union for Democratic Renewal (URD), left-of-center, umbrella grouping, incorporating the Congolese Movement for Democracy and Integral Development (MCDDI) and the Congolese Labour Party (PCT), left-wing *exports* timber, petroleum, cocoa, sugar *currency* CFA franc *population* (1993 est) 2,700,000 (chiefly Bantu); growth rate 2.6% p.a. *life expectancy* men 52, women 57 *languages* French (official); many African languages *religions* animist 50%, Christian 48%, Muslim 2% *literacy* men 70%, women 44% *GNP* $1,120 per head (1991) *chronology 1910* Became part of French Equatorial Africa. *1960* Achieved independence from France, with Abbé Youlou as the first president. *1963* Youlou forced to resign. New constitution approved, with Alphonse Massamba-Débat as president. *1964* The Congo became a one-party state. *1968* Military coup, led by Capt. Marien Ngouabi, ousted Massamba-Débat. *1970* A Marxist state, the People's Republic of the Congo, was announced, with the PCT as the only legal party. *1977* Ngouabi assassinated. Col. Yhombi-Opango became president. *1979* Yhombi-Opango handed over the presidency to the PCT, who chose Col. Denis Sassou-Nguessou as his successor. *1984* Sassou-Nguessou elected for another five-year term. *1990* The PCT abandoned Marxist-Leninism and promised multiparty politics. *1991* 1979 constitution suspended. Country renamed the Republic of Congo. *1992* New constitution approved and multiparty elections held, giving UPADS-dominated coalition an assembly majority. Pascal Lissouba elected president. *1993* Ethnic conflicts intensified, and economy disintegrated. June and Oct elections declared void. *1994* International panel appointed to investigate results; UPADS-dominated coalition declared winner, with assembly majority.

Congregationalism form of church government adopted by those Protestant Christians known as Congregationalists, who let each congregation manage its own affairs, like the people of the Old Testament. The first Congregationalists established themselves in London and were called the Brownists after Robert Browne, who in 1581 defined the congregational principle. They opposed King James I and were supporters of Oliver ◊Cromwell. They became one of the most important forces in the founding of New England.

Congress national legislature of the US, consisting of the House of Representatives (435 members, apportioned to the states of the Union on the basis of population, and elected for two-year terms) and the Senate (100 senators, two for each state, elected for six years, one-third elected every two years). Both representatives and senators are elected by direct popular vote. Congress meets in Washington, DC, in the Capitol Building. An act of Congress is a bill passed by both houses.

Congreve William 1670–1729. English dramatist and poet. His first success was the comedy *The Old Bachelor* 1693, followed by *The Double Dealer* 1694, *Love for Love* 1695, the tragedy *The Mourning Bride* 1697, and *The Way of the World* 1700. His plays, which satirize the social affectations of the time, are characterized by elegant wit and wordplay, and complex plots.

conic section curve obtained when a conical surface is intersected by a plane. If the intersecting plane cuts both extensions of the cone, it yields a hyperbola; if it is parallel to the side of the cone, it produces a parabola. Other intersecting planes produce ◊circles or ◊ellipses.

conifer tree or shrub of the order Coniferales, in the gymnosperm or naked-seed-bearing group of plants. They are often pyramidal in form, with leaves that are either scaled or made up of needles; most are ever-green. Conifers include pines, spruces, firs, yews, junipers, and larches.

conjunction grammatical ◊part of speech that serves to connect words, phrases, and clauses. Coordinating conjunctions link parts of equal grammatical value; *and*, *but*, and *or* are the most common. Subordinating conjunctions link subordinate clauses to the main clause in a sentence; among the most common are *if*, *when*, and *though*.

conjunction in astronomy, the alignment of two celestial bodies as seen from Earth. A superior planet (or other object) is in conjunction when it lies behind the Sun. An ◊inferior planet (or other object) comes to *inferior conjunction* when it passes between the Earth and the Sun; it is at *superior conjunction* when it passes behind the Sun. *Planetary conjunction* takes place when a planet is closely aligned with another celestial object, such as the Moon, a star, or another planet.

conjunctivitis inflammation of the conjunctiva, the delicate membrane that lines the inside of the eyelids and covers the front of the eye. Symptoms include redness, swelling, and a watery or pus-filled discharge. It may be caused by infection, allergy, or other irritant.

Connacht province of the Republic of Ireland, comprising the counties of Galway, Leitrim, Mayo, Roscommon, and Sligo; area 6,612 sq mi/17,130 sq km/; population (1991) 422,900. The chief towns are Galway, Roscommon, Castlebar, Sligo, and Carrick-on-Shannon. Mainly lowland, it is agricultural and stock-raising country, with poor land in the W.

Connecticut state in NE US; nickname Constitution State/Nutmeg State *area* 5,018 sq mi /13,000 sq km *capital* Hartford *physical* highlands in the NW, Connecticut River *features* Yale University; Mystic Seaport (reconstruction of 19th-century village, with restored ships) *products* dairy, poultry, and market-garden products; tobacco, watches, clocks, silverware, helicopters, jet engines, nuclear submarines, hardware and locks, electrical and electronic equipment, guns and ammunition, optical instruments. Hartford is the center of the nation's insurance industry *population* (1990) 3,287,100 *famous people* Benedict Arnold, Phineas T. Barnum, Jonathan Edwards, Nathan Hale, Katharine Hepburn, Charles Ives, Edward H. Land, Eugene O'Neill, Wallace Stevens, Harriet Beecher Stowe, Mark Twain, Eli Whitney *history* Dutch navigator Adriaen Block was the first European to record the area 1614, and in 1633 Dutch colonists built a trading post near modern Hartford but it soon was settled by Puritan colonists from Massachusetts 1635. It was one of the original 13 colonies and became a state 1788. It prospered in the 19th century from shipbuilding, whaling, and growing industry. In the 20th century it became an important supplier of military equipment. Connecticut is second to Alaska among states in personal income per capita. Many of New York City's most affluent residential suburbs are in SW Connecticut.

Connery Sean 1930– . Scottish film actor. He was the first interpreter of James Bond in several films based on the novels of Ian Fleming. His films include *Dr No* 1962, *From Russia with Love* 1963, *Marnie* 1964, *Goldfinger* 1964, *Diamonds Are Forever* 1971, *A Bridge Too Far* 1977, *The Name of the Rose* 1986, and *The Untouchables* 1987 (Academy Award).

Connors Jimmy 1952– . US tennis player who won the Wimbledon title 1974 and 1982, and subsequently won ten Grand Slam events. He was one of the first players to popularize the two-handed backhand.

CAREER HIGHLIGHTS

Wimbledon	
singles:	1974, 1982
doubles:	1973
US Open	
singles:	1974, 1976, 1978, 1982–83
doubles:	1975
Australian Open	
singles:	1974
Grand Prix Masters	
1978	

conquistador any of the early Spanish explorers and adventurers in the Americas, such as Hernán Cortés (Mexico) and Francisco Pizarro (Peru).

Conrad Joseph. Pen name of Teodor Jozef Conrad Korzeniowski 1857–1924. English novelist, born in the Ukraine of Polish parents. He joined the French merchant marine at the age of 17 and first learned English at 21. His greatest works include the novels *Lord Jim* 1900, *Nostromo* 1904, *The Secret Agent* 1907, and *Under Western Eyes* 1911, the short novel *Heart of Darkness* 1902 and the short story "The Shadow Line" 1917. These combine a vivid sensuous evocation of various lands and seas with a rigorous, humane scrutiny of moral dilemmas, pitfalls, and desperation.

conscientious objector person refusing compulsory service, usually military, on moral, religious, or political grounds.

conscription legislation for all able-bodied male citizens (and female in some countries, such as Israel) to serve with the armed forces. It originated in France 1792, and in the 19th and 20th centuries became the established practice in almost all European states.

In the US conscription (the *draft*) was introduced during the Civil War—by the Confederates 1862 and by the Union side 1863. In World War I a Selective Service Act was passed 1917, then again 1940 in anticipation of US entry into World War II.

It remained in force (except for 15 months 1947–48) until after the US withdrawal from Vietnam 1973, although the system was changed to a lottery based on a registrant's birthday. This was done to rectify the inequities stemming from the deferment system that had allowed college students to delay their service. In 1980 Carter restored registration for a possible military draft for men at 18, but his proposal that it be extended to women was rejected by Congress. The US now has a policy based on all-volunteer armed forces.

consent, age of age at which consent may legally be given to sexual intercourse by a girl or boy.

In the US it varies according to state statutes.

conservation in the life sciences, action taken to protect and preserve the natural world, usually from pollution, overexploitation, and other harmful features of human activity. The late 1980s saw a great increase in public concern for the environment, with membership in conservation groups, such as ◊Friends of the Earth, the Sierra Club, and the Nature Conservancy rising sharply. Globally the most important issues include the depletion of atmospheric ozone by the action of chlorofluorocarbons (CFCs), the buildup of carbon dioxide in the atmosphere (thought to contribute to an intensification of the ◊greenhouse effect), and ◊deforestation.

conservatism approach to government favoring the maintenance of existing institutions and identified with a number of Western political parties, such as the US Republican, British Conservative, German Christian Democratic, and Australian Liberal parties. It tends to be explicitly nondoctrinaire and pragmatic but generally emphasizes free-enterprise capitalism, minimal government intervention in the economy, rigid law and order, and the importance of national traditions.

Conservative Party although there is a Conservative Party in the US, it is generally a minor element in national elections. The term is most often used in reference to the UK political party, one of the two historic British parties; the name replaced "Tory" in general use from 1830 onward. Traditionally the party of landed interests, it broadened its political base under Disraeli's leadership in the 19th century. The present Conservative Party's free-market capitalism is supported by the world of finance and the management of industry; its economic policies have increased the spending power of the majority, but also the gap between rich and poor; nationalized industries are sold off (see ◊privatization); military spending and close alliance with the US are favored.

console in computing, a combination of keyboard and screen (also described as a terminal). For a multiuser system, such as ◊Unix, there is only one system console from which the system can be administered, while there may be many user terminals.

Constable John 1776–1837. English artist. He was one of the greatest landscape painters of the 19th century. He painted scenes of his native Suffolk, including *The Haywain* 1821 (National Gallery, London), as well as castles, cathedrals, landscapes, and coastal scenes in other parts of Britain. Constable inherited the Dutch tradition of somber Realism, in particular the style of Jacob ◊Ruisdael. He aimed to capture the momentary changes of the weather as well as to create monumental images of British scenery, as in *The White Horse* 1819 (Frick Collection, New York) and *Salisbury Cathedral from the Bishop's Grounds* 1827 (Victoria and Albert Museum, London).

constant in mathematics, a fixed quantity or one that does not change its value in relation to ◊variables. For example, in the algebraic expression $y^2 = 5x - 3$, the numbers 3 and 5 are constants. In physics, certain quantities are regarded as universal constants, such as the speed of light in a vacuum.

Constantine II 1940– . King of the Hellenes (Greece). In 1964 he succeeded his father Paul I, went into exile 1967, and was formally deposed 1973.
He married Princess Anne-Marie of Denmark in 1964.

Constantine the Great c. AD 280–337. First Christian emperor of Rome and founder of Constantinople. He defeated Maxentius, joint emperor of Rome AD 312, and in 313 formally recognized Christianity. As sole emperor of the west of the empire, he defeated Licinius, emperor of the east, to become ruler of the Roman world 324. He presided over the church's first council at Nicaea 325. Constantine moved his capital to Byzantium on the Bosporus 330, renaming it Constantinople (now Istanbul).

Constantinople former name (330–1453) of Istanbul, Turkey. It was named for the Roman emperor Constantine the Great when he enlarged the Greek city of Byzantium 328 and declared it the capital of the ◊Byzantine Empire 330. Its elaborate fortifications enabled it to resist a succession of sieges, but it was captured by crusaders 1204, and was the seat of a Latin (Western European) kingdom until recaptured by the Greeks 1261. An attack by the Turks 1422 proved unsuccessful, but it was taken by another Turkish army May 29, 1453, after nearly a year's siege, and became the capital of the Ottoman Empire.

constellation one of the 88 areas into which the sky is divided for the purposes of identifying and naming celestial objects. The first constellations were simple, arbitrary patterns of stars in which early civilizations visualized gods, sacred beasts, and mythical heroes.

constitution body of fundamental laws of a state, laying down the system of government and defining the relations of the legislature, executive, and judiciary to each other and to the citizens. Since the French Revolution almost all countries (the UK is an exception) have adopted written constitutions; that of the US (1787) is the oldest.

Constructivism revolutionary movement in Russian art and architecture, founded in Moscow 1917 by Vladimir Tatlin, which drew its inspiration and materials from modern industry and technology. Initially confined to sculpture, its ideas were later adopted and expanded upon in architecture. Associated with the movement was the artist and architect El Lissitzky, the artists Naum Gabo and Antoine Pevsner, and the architects Vladimir Melnikov and Alexander (1883–1959), Leonid (1880–1933), and Viktor (1882–1950) Vesnin. By 1932 official Soviet disapproval had brought the movement effectively to a close, but its ideas had already spread to Europe, influencing the ◊Bauhaus and de ◊Stijl schools of architecture and design. Today, ◊Deconstructionism and much ◊High Tech architecture reflect its influence.

consul chief magistrate of ancient Rome after the expulsion of the last king 510 BC. The consuls were two annually elected magistrates, both of equal power; they jointly held full civil power in Rome and the chief military command in the field. After the establishment of the Roman Empire the office became purely honorary.

consumption in economics, the purchase of goods and services for final use, as opposed to spending by firms on capital goods, known as capital formation.
In national accounting, it means a country's total expenditure over a given period (usually a year) on goods and services, including expenditure on raw materials and defense.

contact lens lens, made of soft or hard plastic, that is worn in contact with the cornea and conjunctiva of the eye, beneath the eyelid, to correct defective vision. In special circumstances, contact lenses may be used as protective shells or for cosmetic purposes, such as changing eye color.

contempt of court behavior that shows lack of respect for the authority of a court of law, such as disobeying

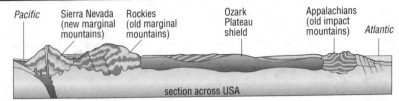

Pacific | Sierra Nevada (new marginal mountains) | Rockies (old marginal mountains) | Ozark Plateau shield | Appalachians (old impact mountains) | Atlantic

section across USA

continent *The North American continent is growing in the west as a result of collision with the Pacific plate. On the east of the wide area of the Ozark plateau shield lie the Appalachian mountains, showing where the continent once collided with another continent. The eastern coastal rifting formed when the continents broke apart. On the western edge, new impact mountains have formed.*

a court order, breach of an injunction, or improper use of legal documents. Behavior that disrupts, prejudices, or interferes with court proceedings either inside or outside the courtroom may also be contempt. The court may punish contempt with a fine or imprisonment.

continent any one of the seven large land masses of the Earth, as distinct from the oceans. They are Asia, Africa, North America, South America, Europe, Australia, and Antarctica. Continents are constantly moving and evolving (see ◊plate tectonics). A continent does not end at the coastline; its boundary is the edge of the shallow continental shelf, which may extend several hundred kilometers out to sea.

Continental Congress in US history, the federal legislature of the original 13 states, acting as a provisional revolutionary government during the ◊American Revolution. It convened in Philadelphia from 1774 until 1789, when the US Constitution was adopted. The Second Continental Congress, convened May 1775, was responsible for drawing up the ◊Declaration of Independence and, in 1777, the Articles of Confederation. The Congress authorized an army to resist the British and issued paper money to finance the war effort. It also oversaw the deliberations of the Constitutional Convention.

continental drift in geology, the theory that, about 250–200 million years ago, the Earth consisted of a single large continent (Pangaea), which subsequently broke apart to form the continents known today. The theory was proposed 1912 by German meteorologist Alfred Wegener, but such vast continental movements could not be satisfactorily explained until the study of ◊plate tectonics in the 1960s.

Contra member of a Central American right-wing guerrilla force attempting to overthrow the democratically elected Nicaraguan Sandinista government 1979–90. The Contras, many of them mercenaries or former members of the deposed dictator Somoza's guard, operated mainly from bases outside Nicaragua, mostly in Honduras, with covert US funding, as revealed by the ◊Irangate hearings 1986–87.

contraceptive any drug, device, or technique that prevents pregnancy. The contraceptive pill (the ◊Pill) contains female hormones that interfere with egg production or the first stage of pregnancy. The "morning-after" pill can be taken up to 72 hours after unprotected intercourse. Barrier contraceptives include ◊condoms (sheaths) and diaphragms, also called caps or Dutch caps; they prevent the sperm entering the cervix (neck of the womb).

◊Intrauterine devices, also known as IUDs or coils, cause a slight inflammation of the lining of the womb; this prevents the fertilized egg from becoming implanted. See also ◊family planning.

contract legal agreement between two or more parties, where each party agrees to do something. For example, a contract of employment is a legal agreement between an employer and an employee and lays out the conditions of employment. Contracts need not necessarily be written; they can be verbal contracts. In consumer law, for example, a contract is established when goods are sold.

In a contract each party mutually obliges himself or herself to the other for exchange of property or performance for a consideration.

contralto in music, a low-register female voice, also called an *◊alto*.

control unit the component of the ◊central processing unit that decodes, synchronizes, and executes program instructions.

convection heat energy transfer that involves the movement of a fluid (gas or liquid). According to ◊kinetic theory, molecules of fluid in contact with the source of heat expand and tend to rise within the bulk of the fluid. Less energetic, cooler molecules sink to take their place, setting up convection currents. This is the principle of natural convection in many domestic hot-water systems and space heaters.

convex of a surface, curving outward, or toward the eye. For example, the outer surface of a ball appears convex. In geometry, the term is used to describe any polygon possessing no interior angle greater than 180°. Convex is the opposite of ◊concave.

conveyancing administrative process involved in transferring title to land, usually on its sale or purchase.

convolvulus or *bindweed* any plant of the genus *Convolvulus* of the morning-glory family Convolvulaceae. They are characterized by their twining stems and by their petals, which are united into a funnel-shaped tube.

The hedge bindweed *C. sepium*, a trailing plant with spear-shaped leaves and large, pinkish-white flowers, is native to N Eurasia and North America.

convulsion series of violent contractions of the muscles over which the patient has no control. It may be associated with loss of consciousness. Convulsions may arise from any one of a number of causes, including brain disease (such as ◊epilepsy), injury, high fever, poisoning, and electrocution.

Cook James 1728–1779. British naval explorer. After surveying the St Lawrence 1759, he made three voyages: 1768–71 to Tahiti, New Zealand, and Australia; 1772–75 to the South Pacific; and 1776–79 to the

South and North Pacific, attempting to find the Northwest Passage and charting the Siberian coast. He was killed in Hawaii.

cooking heat treatment of food to make it more palatable, digestible, and safe. It breaks down connective tissue in meat, making it tender, and softens the cellulose in plant tissue. Some nutrients may be lost in the process, but this does not affect the overall nutritional value of a balanced diet.

Cook Islands group of six large and a number of smaller Polynesian islands 1,600 mi/2,600 km NE of Auckland, New Zealand; area 112 sq mi/290 sq km; population (1991) 19,000. Their main products include fruit, copra, and crafts. They became a self-governing overseas territory of New Zealand 1965.

Cook, Mount highest point, 12,353 ft/3,764 m, of the Southern Alps, a range of mountains running through New Zealand.

Coolidge (John) Calvin 1872–1933. 30th president of the US 1923–29, a Republican. As governor of Massachusetts 1919, he was responsible for crushing a Boston police strike. As Warren ◊Harding's vice president 1921–23, he succeeded to the presidency on Harding's death (Aug 2, 1923). He won the 1924 presidential election, and his period of office was marked by economic growth.

Coolidge, (John) Calvin *The Republican Calvin Coolidge, 30th president of the United States of America 1923–29. A taciturn man, he was widely admired and would in all probability have been reelected if he had run for a second term.*

Cooper Gary 1901–1962. US film actor. He epitomized the lean, true-hearted American, slow of speech but capable of outdoing the "bad guys". His films include *Lives of a Bengal Lancer* 1935, *Mr Deeds Goes to Town* 1936, *Sergeant York* 1940 (Academy Award), and *High Noon* 1952 (Academy Award).

Cooper James Fenimore 1789–1851. US writer, considered the first great US novelist. He wrote about 50 novels, mostly about the frontier, wilderness life, and the sea. He is best remembered for his Leatherstocking Tales, a series of five novels: *The Pioneers* 1823, *The Last of the Mohicans* 1826, *The Prairie* 1827, *The Pathfinder* 1840, and *The Deerslayer* 1841. All describe the adventures of the frontier hero Natty Bumppo before and after the American Revolution.

cooperative business organization with limited liability where each stockholder has only one vote however many shares they own. In a worker cooperative, it is the workers who are the stockholders and own the company. The workers decide on how the company is to be run. In a consumer cooperative, consumers control the company. Co-op shops and superstores are examples of consumer cooperatives. They are owned by regional cooperative retail groups.

cooperative movement the banding together of groups of people for mutual assistance in trade, manufacture, the supply of credit, housing, or other services. The original principles of the cooperative movement were laid down 1844 by the Rochdale Pioneers, under the influence of Robert Owen, and by Charles Fourier in France.

In the US, the period from 1915 to 1930 saw the greatest growth in the number of cooperative associations because they were recognized under statute laws rather than simply under common law. By the 1960s, agricultural cooperatives had declined dramatically because of mergers and more technically advanced marketing procedures.

The future for cooperative associations is seen in the areas of consumers' associations, workers' groups, and the housing market.

coordinate in geometry, a number that defines the position of a point relative to a point or axis (reference line). ◊Cartesian coordinates define a point by its perpendicular distances from two or more axes drawn through a fixed point mutually at right angles to each other. Polar coordinates define a point in a plane by its distance from a fixed point and direction from a fixed line.

coordinate geometry or *analytical geometry* system of geometry in which points, lines, shapes, and surfaces are represented by algebraic expressions. In plane (two-dimensional) coordinate geometry, the plane is usually defined by two axes at right angles to each other, the horizontal x-axis and the vertical y-axis, meeting at O, the origin. A point on the plane can be represented by a pair of ◊Cartesian coordinates, which define its position in terms of its distance along the x-axis and along the y-axis from O. These distances are respectively the x and y coordinates of the point.

coot any of various freshwater birds of the genus *Fulica* in the rail family. Coots are about 1.2 ft/38 cm long, and mainly black. They have a white bill, extending up the forehead in a plate, and big feet with lobed toes.

The American coot *F. americana* is found in North and South America and the Caribbean. It feeds on plants, insects, and small fish.

Copenhagen (Danish *København*) capital of Denmark, on the islands of Zealand and Amager; population (1990) 1,337,100 (including suburbs).

Copenhagen, Battle of naval victory April 2, 1801, by a British fleet under Sir Hyde Parker (1739–1807) and ◊Nelson over the Danish fleet. Nelson put his telescope to his blind eye and refused to see Parker's signal for withdrawal.

Copernicus Nicolaus 1473–1543. Polish astronomer who believed that the Sun, not the Earth, is at the center of the Solar System, thus defying the Christian church doctrine of the time. For 30 years he worked on the hypothesis that the rotation and the orbital motion of the Earth were responsible for the apparent movement of the heavenly bodies. His great work *De Revolutionibus Orbium Coelestium/About the Revolutions of the Heavenly Spheres* was not published until the year of his death.

Copland Aaron 1900–1990. US composer. His early works, such as his piano concerto 1926, were in the jazz idiom but he gradually developed a gentler style with a regional flavor drawn from American folk music. Among his works are the ballets *Billy the Kid* 1939, *Rodeo* 1942, and *Appalachian Spring* 1944 (based on a poem by Hart Crane), and *Inscape for Orchestra* 1967.

copper orange-pink, very malleable and ductile, metallic element, symbol Cu (from Latin *cuprum*), atomic number 29, atomic weight 63.546. It is used for its durability, pliability, high thermal and electrical conductivity, and resistance to corrosion.

Coppola Francis Ford 1939– . US film director and screenwriter. He directed *The Godfather* 1972, which became one of the biggest moneymaking films of all time, and its sequels *The Godfather Part II* 1974, which won seven Academy Awards, and *The Godfather Part III* 1990. His other films include *Apocalypse Now* 1979, *One from the Heart* 1982, *Rumblefish* 1983, *The Outsiders* 1983, and *Bram Stoker's Dracula* 1992.

copra dried meat from the kernel of the ◊coconut, used to make coconut oil.

Copt descendant of those ancient Egyptians who adopted Christianity in the 1st century and refused to convert to Islam after the Arab conquest. They now form a small minority (about 5%) of Egypt's population. *Coptic* is a member of the Hamito-Semitic language family. It is descended from the language of the ancient Egyptians and is the ritual language of the Coptic Christian church. It is written in the Greek alphabet with some additional characters derived from ◊demotic script.

copyright law applying to literary, musical, and artistic works (including plays, recordings, films, photographs, radio and television broadcasts, and, in the US and the UK, computer programs), which prevents the reproduction of the work, in whole or in part, without the author's consent.

In the US (since 1989) copyright lasts for a holder's lifetime plus 50 years, or a flat 75 years for a company copyright. It must be registered with the US Copyright Office of the Library of Congress to bring a court action. Works first federally copyrighted before 1978 must still be renewed in the 28th year to receive the second term of 47 years or it will fall into the public domain at the end of the 28th year. Various conditions apply to works published before 1989 and those between Jan 1, 1978, and March 1, 1989. For specific information, contact the Copyright Office, Library of Congress, Washington, DC. Copyright is internationally enforceable under the Berne Convention 1886 (ratified by the US March 1, 1989) and the Universal Copyright Convention 1952. Computer software is specifically covered in the US under the Copyright Act 1976 and the Computer Software Act 1980.

coral marine invertebrate of the class Anthozoa in the phylum Cnidaria, which also includes sea anemones and jellyfish. It has a skeleton of lime (calcium carbonate) extracted from the surrounding water. Corals exist in warm seas, at moderate depths with sufficient light. Some coral is valued for decoration or jewelry, for example, Mediterranean red coral *Corallum rubrum*.

Coral Sea or *Solomon Sea* part of the Pacific Ocean bounded by NE Australia, New Guinea, the Solomon Islands, Vanuatu, and New Caledonia. It contains numerous coral islands and reefs. The Coral Sea Islands are a territory of Australia; they comprise scattered reefs and islands over an area of about 386,000 sq mi/1,000,000 sq km. They are uninhabited except for a meteorological station on Willis Island. The ◊Great Barrier Reef lies along its western edge, just off the east coast of Australia.

In the World War II Battle of the Coral Sea, May 7–8, 1942, the US fleet prevented the Japanese from landing in SE New Guinea and thus threatening Australia. This was the first sea battle to be fought entirely by aircraft, launched from carriers, without any engagement between the actual warships themselves.

cor anglais or *English horn* alto ◊oboe in E flat with a distinctive tulip-shaped bell and warm nasal tone, heard to pastoral effect in Rossini's overture to *William Tell* 1829, and portraying a plaintive Sasha the duck in Prokofiev's *Peter and the Wolf* 1936.

Corbusier, Le French architect; see ◊Le Corbusier.

cordillera group of mountain ranges and their valleys, all running in a specific direction, formed by the continued convergence of two tectonic plates (see ◊plate tectonics) along a line.

The whole western section of North America, including the Rocky Mountains and the coastal ranges parallel to the contact between the North American and the Pacific plates, is called the Western Cordillera.

Córdoba city in central Argentina, on the Río Primero; population (1991) 1,179,000. It is the capital of Córdoba province. Main industries include cement, glass, textiles, and vehicles. Founded 1573, it has a university founded 1613, a military aviation college, an observatory, and a cathedral.

Córdoba capital of Córdoba province, Spain, on the river Guadalquivir; population (1991) 309,200. Paper, textiles, and copper products are manufactured here. It has many Moorish remains, including the mosque, now a cathedral, founded by 'Abd-ar-Rahman I 785, which is one of the largest Christian churches in the world. Córdoba was probably founded by the Carthaginians; it was held by the Moors 711–1236.

Corfu (Greek *Kérkyra*) northernmost and second largest of the Ionian islands of Greece, off the coast of Epirus in the Ionian Sea; area 414 sq mi/1,072 sq km; population (1981) 96,500. Its businesses include tourism, fruit, olive oil, and textiles. Its largest town is the port of Corfu (Kérkyra), population (1981) 33,560. Corfu was colonized by the Corinthians about 700 BC. Venice held it 1386–1797, Britain 1815–64.

coriander pungent fresh herb, the Eurasian plant *Coriandrum sativum*, a member of the parsley family Umbelliferae, also a spice: the dried ripe fruit. The spice is used commercially as a flavoring in meat products, bakery goods, tobacco, gin, liqueurs, chili, and curry powder. Both are much used in cooking in the Middle East, India, Mexico, and China.

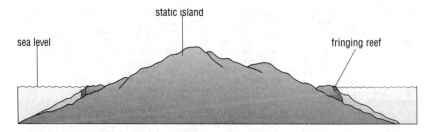

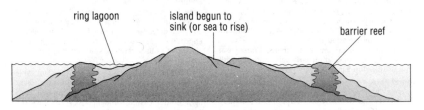

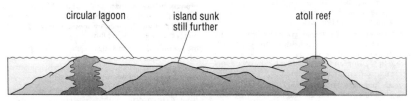

coral The formation of a coral atoll by the gradual sinking of a volcanic island. The reefs fringing the island build up as the island sinks, eventually producing a ring of coral around the spot where the island sank.

Corinth (Greek *Kórinthos*) port in Greece, on the isthmus connecting the Peloponnese with the mainland; population (1981) 22,650. The rocky isthmus is bisected by the 4 mi/6.5 km Corinth canal, opened 1893. The site of the ancient city-state of Corinth lies 4.5 mi/7 km SW of the port.

Coriolis effect the effect of the Earth's rotation on the atmosphere and on all objects on the Earth's surface. In the northern hemisphere it causes moving objects and currents to be deflected to the right; in the southern hemisphere it causes deflection to the left. The effect is named for its discoverer, French mathematician Gaspard Coriolis (1792–1843).

cork light, waterproof outer layers of the bark of the stems and roots of almost all trees and shrubs. The cork oak *Quercus suber*, a native of S Europe and N Africa, is cultivated in Spain and Portugal; the exceptionally thick outer layers of its bark provide the cork that is used commercially.

Cork largest county of the Republic of Ireland, in the province of Munster; county town Cork; area 2,880 sq mi/7,460 sq km; population (1991) 409,800. It is agricultural, but there is also some copper and manganese mining, marble quarrying, and river and sea fishing. Natural gas and oil fields are found off the S coast at Kinsale.

corm short, swollen, underground plant stem, surrounded by protective scale leaves, as seen in the genus *Crocus*. It stores food, provides a means of veg-

etative reproduction, and acts as a ◊perennnating organ.

cormorant any of various diving seabirds, mainly of the genus *Phalacrocorax*, about 3 ft/90 cm long, with webbed feet, long neck, hooked beak, and glossy black plumage. There are some 30 species of cormorant worldwide, including a flightless form *Nannopterum harrisi* in the Galápagos Islands. Cormorants generally feed on fish and shellfish. Some species breed on inland lakes and rivers.

corn cultivated New World plant *Zea mays* of the grass family, with the grain borne on cobs enclosed in husks. It is also called Indian corn. It was domesticated by 6,000 BC in Mesoamerica, where it grew wild. It became the staple crop for the ◊Neolithic farming villages and civilizations of Mexico and Peru; it was cultivated throughout most of the New World at the point of European contact. It was brought to Europe, Asia, and Africa by the colonizing powers, but its use is mainly for animal feed in those regions. In the US, a corn monoculture dominates the Midwest, where many hybrids have been developed for both human food and animal feed. Today it is grown extensively in all subtropical and warm temperate regions, and its range has been extended to colder zones by hardy varieties developed in the 1960s.

Corneille Pierre 1606–1684. French dramatist. His tragedies, such as *Horace* 1640, *Cinna* 1641, and *Oedipe*

1659, glorify the strength of will governed by reason, and established the French classical dramatic tradition. His first comedy, *Mélite*, was performed 1629, followed by others that gained him a brief period of favor with Cardinal Richelieu. His early masterpiece, *Le Cid* 1636, was attacked by the Academicians, although it received public acclaim, and was produced in the same year as *L'Illusion comique/The Comic Illusion*.

Cornell Katherine 1898–1974. German-born US actress. Her first major success came with an appearance on Broadway in *Nice People* 1921. This debut was followed by a long string of New York stage successes, several of which were directed by her husband, Guthrie McClintic. From 1930 she began to produce her own plays; the most famous of them, *The Barretts of Wimpole Street* 1931, was later taken on tour and produced for television 1956.

Born in Berlin of American parents, Cornell was attracted to the stage at an early age, appearing with the Washington Square Players 1916.

cornet three-valved brass band instrument, soprano member in B flat of a group of valved horns developed in Austria and Germany about 1820–50 for military band use. Of cylindrical bore, its compact shape and deeper conical bell allow greater speed and agility of intonation than the trumpet, at the expense of less tonal precision and brilliance.

cornflower plant *Centaurea cyanus* of the family Compositae. It is distinguished from the knapweeds by its deep azure-blue flowers. Formerly a common weed in N European wheat fields, it is now commonly grown in gardens as a herbaceous plant.

Cornish language extinct member of the ◊Celtic languages, a branch of the Indo-European language family, spoken in Cornwall, England, until 1777. Written Cornish first appeared in 10th-century documents; some religious plays were written in Cornish in the 15th and 16th centuries, but later literature is scanty, consisting mainly of folk tales and verses. In recent years the language has been revived in a somewhat reconstructed form by members of the Cornish nationalist movement.

Corn Laws in Britain until 1846, laws used to regulate the export or import of cereals in order to maintain an adequate supply for consumers and a secure price for producers. For centuries the Corn Laws formed an integral part of the mercantile system in England; they were repealed because they became an unwarranted tax on food and a hindrance to British exports.

cornstarch purified, fine, powdery starch made from corn, used as a thickener in cooking and to make corn syrup commercially.

cornucopia in Greek mythology, one of the horns of the goat Amaltheia, which was caused by Zeus to refill itself indefinitely with food and drink. In paintings, the cornucopia is depicted as a horn-shaped container spilling over with fruit and flowers.

Cornwall county in SW England including the Isles of ◊Scilly (Scillies) *area* (excluding Scillies) 1,370 sq mi/3,550 sq km *towns and cities* Truro (administrative headquarters), Camborne, Launceston; resorts of Bude, Falmouth, Newquay, Penzance, St Ives *features* Bodmin Moor (including Brown Willy 1,375 ft/ 419 m); Land's End peninsula; St Michael's Mount; rivers Tamar, Fowey, Fal, Camel; Poldhu, site of first transatlantic radio signal 1901; the Stannary or Tinners' Parliament has six members from each of the four Stannary towns: Losthwithiel, Launceston, Helston, and Truro *products* electronics, spring flowers, dairy farming, market gardening, tin (mined since the Bronze Age, some workings renewed 1960s, though the industry has all but disappeared—only one mine remaining, at South Crofty), kaolin (St Austell), fish *population* (1991) 469,300 *famous people* John Betjeman, Humphry Davy, Daphne Du Maurier, William Golding *history* the Stannary, established in the 11th century, ceased to meet 1752 but its powers were never rescinded at Westminster, and it was revived 1974 as a separatist movement. The flag of St Piran, a white St George's cross on a black ground, is used by separatists.

Cornwallis Charles, 1st Marquess 1738–1805. British general in the ◊American Revolution until 1781, when his defeat at Yorktown led to final surrender and ended the war. He then served twice as governor-general of India and once as viceroy of Ireland.

corona faint halo of hot (about 3,600,000°F/ 2,000,000°C) and tenuous gas around the Sun, which boils from the surface. It is visible at solar ◊eclipses or through a *coronagraph*, an instrument that blocks light from the Sun's brilliant disk. Gas flows away from the corona to form the ◊solar wind.

coronary artery disease condition in which the fatty deposits of ◊atherosclerosis form in the coronary arteries that supply the heart muscle, narrowing them and restricting the blood flow.

coroner official who investigates the deaths of persons who have died suddenly by acts of violence or under suspicious circumstances, by holding an inquest or ordering a postmortem examination (autopsy).

Corot Jean-Baptiste Camille 1796–1875. French painter. He created a distinctive landscape style using a soft focus and a low-key palette of browns, ochres, and greens. His early work, including Italian scenes of the 1820s, influenced the ◊Barbizon School of painters. Like them, Corot worked outdoors, but he also continued a conventional academic tradition with his romanticized paintings of women.

corporal punishment physical punishment of wrongdoers—for example, by whipping. It is still used as a punishment for criminals in many countries, especially under Islamic law. Corporal punishment of children by parents is illegal in some countries, including Sweden, Finland, Denmark, and Norway.

corporatism belief that the state in capitalist democracies should intervene to a large extent in the economy to ensure social harmony. In Austria, for example, corporatism results in political decisions often being taken after discussions between chambers of commerce, labor unions, and the government.

Correggio Antonio Allegri da c.1494–1534. Italian painter of the High Renaissance. His style followed the Classical grandeur of Leonardo da Vinci and Titian but anticipated the Baroque in its emphasis on movement, softer forms, and contrasts of light and shade.

correlation the degree of relationship between two sets of information. If one set of data increases at the same time as the other, the relationship is said to be positive or direct. If one set of data increases as the other decreases, the relationship is negative or inverse. Correlation can be shown by plotting a best-fit line on a scatter diagram.

corrosion the eating away and eventual destruction of metals and alloys by chemical attack. The rusting of ordinary iron and steel is the most common form of corrosion. Rusting takes place in moist air, when the iron combines with oxygen and water to form a brown-orange deposit of ◊rust (hydrated iron oxide). The rate of corrosion is increased where the atmosphere is polluted with sulfur dioxide. Salty road and air conditions accelerate the rusting of automobile bodies.

Corsica (French *Corse*) island region of France, in the Mediterranean off the west coast of Italy, N of Sardinia; it comprises the *départements* of Haute Corse and Corse du Sud *area* 3,358 sq mi/8,700 sq km *capital* Ajaccio (port) *physical* mountainous; ◊maquis vegetation *features* ◊maquis vegetation. Corsica's mountain bandits were eradicated 1931, but the tradition of the vendetta or blood feud lingers. The island is the main base of the Foreign Legion *government* its special status involves a 61-member regional parliament with the power to scrutinize French National Assembly bills applicable to the island and propose amendments *products* wine, olive oil *population* (1986) 249,000, including just under 50% native Corsicans. There are about 400,000 *émigrés*, mostly in Mexico and Central America, who return to retire *languages* French (official); the majority speak Corsican, an Italian dialect *famous people* Napoleon.

Cortés Hernán (Ferdinand) 1485–1547. Spanish conquistador. He conquered the Aztec empire 1519–21, and secured Mexico for Spain.

corticosteroid any of several steroid hormones secreted by the cortex of the ◊adrenal glands; also synthetic forms with similar properties. Corticosteroids have anti-inflammatory and immunosuppressive effects and may be used to treat a number of conditions, including rheumatoid arthritis, severe allergies, asthma, some skin diseases, and some cancers. Side effects can be serious, and therapy must be withdrawn very gradually.

cortisone natural corticosteroid produced by the ◊adrenal gland, now synthesized for its anti-inflammatory qualities and used in the treatment of rheumatoid arthritis.

Cortona Pietro da Italian Baroque painter; see ◊Pietro da Cortona.

corundum native aluminum oxide, Al_2O_3, the hardest naturally occurring mineral known apart from diamond (corundum rates 9 on the Mohs' scale of hardness); lack of cleavage also increases its durability. Its crystals are barrel-shaped prisms of the trigonal system. Varieties of gem-quality corundum are *ruby* (red) and *sapphire* (any color other than red, usually blue). Poorer-quality and synthetic corundum is used in industry, for example as an ◊abrasive.

cosine in trigonometry, a function of an angle in a right triangle found by dividing the length of the side adjacent to the angle by the length of the hypotenuse (the longest side). It is usually shortened to *cos*.

cosmic background radiation or *3° radiation* electromagnetic radiation left over from the original formation of the universe in the Big Bang around 15 trillion years ago. It corresponds to an overall background temperature of 3K (−454°F/−270°C), or 3°C above absolute zero. In 1992 the Cosmic Background Explorer satellite, COBE, detected slight "ripples" in the strength of the background radiation that are believed to mark the first stage in the formation of galaxies.

cosmic radiation streams of high-energy particles from outer space, consisting of protons, alpha particles, and light nuclei, which collide with atomic nuclei in the Earth's atmosphere, and produce secondary nuclear particles (chiefly ◊mesons, such as pions and muons) that shower the Earth.

cosmology study of the structure of the universe. Modern cosmology began in the 1920s with the discovery that the universe is expanding, which suggested that it began in an explosion, the ◊Big Bang. An alternative—now discarded—view, the ◊steady-state theory, claimed that the universe has no origin, but is expanding because new matter is being continually created.

Cossack people of S and SW Russia, Ukraine, and Poland, predominantly of Russian or Ukrainian origin, who took in escaped serfs and lived in independent communal settlements (military brotherhoods) from the 15th to the 19th century. Later they held land in return for military service in the cavalry under Russian and Polish rulers. After 1917, the various Cossack communities were incorporated into the Soviet administrative and collective system.

Costa Rica Republic of (*República de Costa Rica*) *area* 19,735 sq mi/51,100 sq km *capital* San José *towns and cities* ports Limón, Puntarenas *physical* high central plateau and tropical coasts; Costa Rica was once entirely forested, containing an estimated 5% of the Earth's flora and fauna *environment* by 1983 only 17% of the forest remained; half of the arable land had been cleared for cattle ranching, leading to landlessness, unemployment, and soil erosion; the massive environmental destruction also caused incalculable loss to the gene pool. It is now one of the leading centers of conservation in Latin America, with more than 10% of the country protected by national parks, and tree replanting proceeding at a rate of 60 sq mi/150 sq km per year *features* Poas Volcano; Guayabo pre-Colombian ceremonial site *head of state and government* Jose Maria Figueres Olsen from 1994

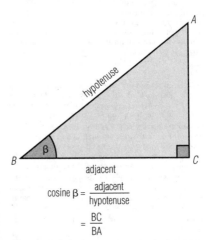

cosine The cotangent of angle β is equal to the ratio of the length of the adjacent side to the length of the hypotenuse (the longest side, opposite to the right angle).

political system liberal democracy **political parties** National Liberation Party (PLN), left of center; Christian Socialist Unity Party (PUSC), centrist coalition; ten minor parties **exports** coffee, bananas, cocoa, sugar, beef **currency** colón **population** (1993 est) 3,300,000 (including 1,200 Guaymi Indians); growth rate 2.6% p.a. **life expectancy** men 73, women 78 **language** Spanish (official) **religion** Roman Catholic 95% **literacy** men 93%, women 93% **GNP** $1,930 per head (1991) **chronology 1821** Independence achieved from Spain. **1949** New constitution adopted. National army abolished. José Figueres, cofounder of the PLN, elected president; he embarked on an ambitious socialist program. **1958–73** Mainly conservative administrations. **1974** PLN regained the presidency and returned to socialist policies. **1978** Rodrigo Carazo, conservative, elected president. Sharp deterioration in the state of the economy. **1982** Luis Alberto Monge (PLN) elected president. Harsh austerity program introduced to rebuild the economy. Pressure from the US to abandon neutral stance and condemn Sandinista regime in Nicaragua. **1983** Policy of neutrality reaffirmed. **1985** Following border clashes with Sandinista forces, a US-trained antiguerrilla guard formed. **1986** Oscar Arias Sánchez won the presidency on a neutralist platform. **1987** Arias won Nobel Prize for Peace for devising a Central American peace plan. **1990** Rafael Calderón (PUSC) elected president. **1994** Jose Maria Figueres Olsen (PLN) elected president.

Costner Kevin 1955– . US film actor. He emerged as a star in the late 1980s, with his role as law-enforcer Elliot Ness in *The Untouchables* 1987. Increasingly identified with the embodiment of idealism and high principle, Costner went on to direct and star in *Dances with Wolves* 1990, a Western sympathetic to the native American Indians, which won several Academy Awards. Subsequent films include *Robin Hood—Prince of Thieves* 1991, *JFK* 1991, *The Bodyguard* 1992, and *A Perfect World* 1993.

cotoneaster any shrub or tree of the Eurasian genus *Cotoneaster*, rose family Rosaceae, closely allied to the hawthorn and medlar. The fruits, though small and unpalatable, are usually bright red and conspicuous, often persisting through the winter. Some of the shrubs are cultivated for their attractive appearance.

Cotopaxi active volcano, situated to the S of Quito in Ecuador. It is 19,347 ft/5,897 m high and was first climbed 1872.

cotton tropical and subtropical herbaceous plant of the genus *Gossypium* of the mallow family Malvaceae. Fibers surround the seeds inside the ripened fruits, or bolls, and these are spun into yarn for cloth.

cotyledon structure in the embryo of a seed plant that may form a "leaf" after germination and is commonly known as a seed leaf. The number of cotyledons present in an embryo is an important character in the classification of flowering plants (◊angiosperms).

couch grass European grass *Agropyron repens* of the family Gramineae. It spreads rapidly by underground stems. It is considered a troublesome weed in North America, where it has been introduced.

cougar another name for the ◊puma, a large North American cat.

coulomb SI unit (symbol C) of electrical charge. One coulomb is the quantity of electricity conveyed by a current of one ◊ampere in one second.

Council of Europe body constituted May 1949 in Strasbourg, France (still its headquarters), to achieve greater unity between European countries, to facilitate their economic and social progress, and to uphold the principles of parliamentary democracy and respect for human rights. It has a **Committee** of foreign ministers, a **Parliamentary Assembly** (with members from national parliaments), and, to fulfill one of its main functions, a **European Commission on Human Rights**, which examines complaints about alleged human rights abuses. If the Commission is unable to achieve a friendly settlement after examining alleged violations, the case may be taken to the European Court of Human Rights for adjudication.

counterpoint in music, the art of combining different forms of an original melody with apparent freedom while preserving a harmonious effect. Giovanni Palestrina and J S Bach were masters of counterpoint.

Counter-Reformation movement initiated by the Catholic church at the Council of Trent 1545–63 to counter the spread of the ◊Reformation. Extending into the 17th century, its dominant forces included the rise of the Jesuits as an educating and missionary group and the deployment of the Spanish Inquisition in other countries.

countertenor the highest natural male voice, also called an ◊alto. It was favored by the Elizabethans for its heroic brilliance of tone.

country and western or *country music* popular music of the white US South and West; it evolved from the folk music of the English, Irish, and Scottish settlers and has a strong blues influence. Characteristic instruments are slide guitar, mandolin, and fiddle. Lyrics typically extol family values and traditional sex roles, and often have a strong narrative element. Country music encompasses a variety of regional styles, and ranges from mournful ballads to fast and intricate dance music.

The home of country and western is Nashville, Tennessee. It is played on radio stations throughout the US, and the 1980s saw its popularity spread even into Eastern urban centers like New York City, which had not been part of the country-and-western tradition.

county administrative unit of a country or state. In the US a county is a subdivision of a state; the power of counties differs widely between states. In the UK it is nowadays synonymous with "shire", although historically the two had different origins. Many of the English counties can be traced back to Saxon times. The republic of Ireland has 26 geographical and 27 administrative counties.

county palatine in medieval England, a county whose lord held particular rights, in lieu of the king, such as pardoning treasons and murders. Under William I there were four counties palatine: Chester, Durham, Kent, and Shropshire.

coup d'état or *coup* forcible takeover of the government of a country by elements from within that country, generally carried out by violent or illegal means. It differs from a revolution in typically being carried out by a small group (for example, of army officers or opposition politicians) to install its leader as head of government, rather than being a mass uprising by the people.

Courbet Gustave 1819–1877. French artist. He was a portrait, genre, and landscape painter. Reacting against academic trends, both Classicist and Romantic, he became a major exponent of ◊Realism, depicting contemporary life with an unflattering frankness. His *Burial at Ornans* 1850 (Musée d'Orsay,

Paris), showing ordinary working people gathered around a village grave, shocked the public and the critics with its "vulgarity".

Court Margaret (born Smith) 1942– . Australian tennis player. The most prolific winner in the women's game, she won a record 64 Grand Slam titles, including 25 at singles.

court martial court convened for the trial of persons subject to military discipline who are accused of violations of military laws.

The Uniform Code of Military Justice establishes military law and procedures for courts-martial in the US military.

Cousteau Jacques Yves 1910– . French oceanographer, known for his researches in command of the *Calypso* from 1951. He pioneered the invention of the aqualung 1943 and techniques in underwater filming. His film and television documentaries, and his many books helped establish him as a household name.

covalent bond chemical ◊bond produced when two atoms share one or more pairs of electrons (usually each atom contributes an electron). The bond is often represented by a single line drawn between the two atoms. Covalently bonded substances include hydrogen (H_2), water (H_2O), and most organic substances.

Covenanter in Scottish history, one of the Presbyterian Christians who swore to uphold their forms of worship in a National Covenant, signed Feb 28, 1638, when Charles I attempted to introduce a liturgy on the English model into Scotland.

Coventry industrial city in West Midlands, England; population (1991) 294,400. Manufacturing includes automobiles, electronic equipment, machine tools, agricultural machinery, man-made fibers, aerospace components, and telecommunications equipment.

Coward Noël 1899–1973. English dramatist, actor, revue-writer, director, and composer. He epitomized the witty and sophisticated man of the theater. From his first success with *The Young Idea* 1923, he wrote and appeared in plays and comedies on both sides of the Atlantic such as *Hay Fever* 1925, *Private Lives* 1930 with Gertrude Lawrence, *Design for Living* 1933, *Blithe Spirit* 1941, and *A Song at Twilight* 1966. His revues and musicals included *On With the Dance* 1925 and *Bitter Sweet* 1929.

cow parsley or *keck* tall perennial plant, *Anthriscus sylvestris*, of the carrot family. It grows in Europe, N Asia, and N Africa.

cowrie marine snail of the family Cypreidae, in which the interior spiral form is concealed by a double outer lip. The shells are hard, shiny, and often colored. Most cowries are shallow-water forms, and are found in many parts of the world, particularly the tropical Indo-Pacific. Cowries have been used as ornaments and fertility charms, and also as currency, for example the Pacific money cowrie *Cypraea moneta*.

Four species are found in the SE US and one in California.

coyote wild dog *Canis latrans*, in appearance like a small wolf, living from Alaska to Central America and east to New York. Its head and body are about 3 ft/90 cm long and brown, flecked with gray or black. Coyotes live in open country and can run at 40 mph/65 kph. Their main foods are rabbits and rodents. Although persecuted by humans for over a century, the species is very successful.

coypu another name for ◊nutria.

CP/M (abbreviation for *control program/monitor* or *control program for microcomputers*) one of the earliest ◊operating systems for microcomputers. It was written by Gary Kildall, who founded Digital Research, and became a standard for microcomputers based on the Intel 8080 and Zilog Z80 8-bit microprocessors. In the 1980s it was superseded by Microsoft's ◊MS-DOS, written for 16-bit microprocessors.

CPU in computing, abbreviation for ◊*central processing unit.*

crab any decapod (ten-legged) crustacean of the division Brachyura, with a broad, rather round, upper body shell (carapace) and a small ◊abdomen tucked beneath the body. Crabs are related to lobsters and crayfish. Mainly marine, some crabs live in fresh water or on land. They are alert carnivores and scavengers. They have a typical sideways walk, and strong pincers on the first pair of legs, the other four pairs being used for walking. Periodically, the outer shell is cast to allow for growth. The name "crab" is sometimes used for similar arthropods, such as the horseshoe crab, which is neither a true crab nor a crustacean.

There are many species of true crabs worldwide. The North American blue crab *Callinectes sapidus*, called the soft-shelled crab after molting, is about 6 in/15 cm wide. It is extensively fished along the Atlantic and Gulf coasts. Other true crabs include fiddler crabs (*Uca*), the males of which have one enlarged claw to wave at and attract females, and spider crabs, with small bodies and very long legs, including the Japanese spider crab *Macrocheira kaemperi* with a leg span of 11 ft/3.4 m. Hermit crabs (division Anomura) have a soft, spirally twisted abdomen and make their homes in empty shells of sea snails for protection.

Some tropical hermit crabs are found a considerable distance from the sea. The robber crab *Birgus latro* grows large enough to climb palm trees and feed on coconuts.

crab apple any of 25 species of wild ◊apple trees (genus *Malus*), native to temperate regions of the northern hemisphere. Numerous varieties of cultivated apples have been derived from *M. pumila*, the common native crab apple of SE Europe and central Asia. The fruit of native species is smaller and more bitter than that of cultivated varieties and is used in crab-apple jelly.

Crab nebula cloud of gas 6,000 light-years from Earth, in the constellation Taurus. It is the remains of a star that exploded as a ◊supernova (observed as a brilliant point of light on Earth 1054). At its center is a ◊pulsar that flashes 30 times a second. The name comes from its crablike shape.

Cracow alternative form of ◊Kraków, a Polish city.

Cranach Lucas 1472–1553. German painter, etcher, and woodcut artist. He was a leading figure in the German Renaissance. He painted many full-length nudes and precise and polished portraits, such as *Martin Luther* 1521 (Uffizi, Florence).

cranberry any of several trailing evergreen plants of the genus *Vaccinium* in the heath family Ericaceae, allied to bilberries and blueberries. They grow in marshy places and bear small, acid, crimson berries, high in vitamin C, used for making sauce and jelly.

crane in zoology, a large, wading bird of the family Gruidae, with long legs and neck, and powerful wings. Cranes are marsh-and plains-dwelling birds, feeding

crane The whooping crane *Grus americana* of N America is exceedingly rare in the wild. It breeds in Canada and migrates to the Texas coast in winter. Like all cranes, whooping cranes migrate in flocks, flying in V-formation or in lines, with necks forward and legs trailing.

on plants as well as insects and small animals. They fly well and are usually migratory. Their courtship includes frenzied, leaping dances. They are found in all parts of the world except South America.

crane fly or *daddy-longlegs* any fly of the family Tipulidae, with long, slender, fragile legs. They look like giant mosquitoes, but the adults are quite harmless. The larvae live in soil or water.

cranesbill any plant of the genus *Geranium,* which contains about 400 species. The plants are named for the beaklike protrusion attached to the seed vessels. When ripe, this splits into coiling spirals, which jerk the seeds out, assisting in their distribution.

Cranmer Thomas 1489–1556. English cleric, archbishop of Canterbury from 1533. A Protestant convert, he helped to shape the doctrines of the Church of England under Edward VI. He was responsible for the issue of the Prayer Books of 1549 and 1552, and supported the succession of Lady Jane Grey 1553.

Crassus Marcus Licinius *c.*108–53 BC. Roman general who crushed the ◊Spartacus uprising 71 BC. In 60 BC he joined with Caesar and Pompey in the First Triumvirate and obtained command in the east 55 BC. Invading Mesopotamia, he was defeated by the Parthians at the battle of Carrhae, captured, and put to death.

crater bowl-shaped depression, usually round and with steep sides. Craters are formed by explosive events such as the eruption of a volcano or by the impact of a meteorite. A caldera is a much larger feature.

Crawford Joan. Adopted name of Lucille Le Seur 1908–1977. US film actress. She became a star with her performance as a flapper (liberated young woman) in *Our Dancing Daughters* 1928. Later she appeared as a sultry, often suffering, mature woman. Her films include *Mildred Pierce* 1945 (for which she won an Academy Award), *Sudden Fear* 1952, and *Whatever Happened to Baby Jane?* 1962.

Beginning her career as a chorus girl 1924, Crawford

made her first film appearance 1925. In the 1930s she played in many Clark Gable films, and in *Grand Hotel* 1932. *Whatever Happened to Baby Jane?* was her last "great" film, before cameo appearances and *Trog* 1970.

Craxi Bettino 1934– . Italian socialist politician, leader of the Italian Socialist Party (PSI) 1976–93, prime minister 1983–87. In 1993, he was one of many politicians suspected of involvement in Italy's corruption network.

crayfish freshwater decapod (ten-limbed) crustacean belonging to several families structurally similar to, but smaller than, the lobster. Crayfish are brownish-green scavengers and are found in all parts of the world except Africa. They are edible, and some species are farmed.

The spiny lobster *Palinurus vulgaris,* is sometimes called crayfish; it is actually a marine lobster without pincers, and grows up to 20 in/50 cm in long.

Crécy, Battle of first major battle of the Hundred Years' War 1346. Philip VI of France was defeated by Edward III of England at the village of Crécy-en-Ponthieu, now in Somme *département,* France, 11 mi/18 km NE of Abbeville.

credit in economics, means by which goods or services are obtained without immediate payment, usually by agreeing to pay interest. The three main forms are *consumer credit* (usually extended to individuals by retailers), *bank credit* (such as overdrafts or personal loans), and *trade credit* (common in the commercial world both within countries and internationally).

Consumer credit is increasingly used to pay for goods. In the US 1992 it amounted to $792 billion, with about 18.5% of disposable income expended on installment buying and credit-card payments.

credit card card issued by a credit company, retail outlet, or bank, which enables the holder to obtain goods or services on credit (usually to a specified limit), payable on specified terms. The first credit card was introduced 1947 in the US.

Credit cards are usually made of or coated with plastic; using them may be called "paying with plastic."

creed in general, any system of belief; in the Christian church the verbal confessions of faith expressing the accepted doctrines of the church. The different forms are the Apostles' Creed, the ◊Nicene Creed, and the Athanasian Creed. The only creed recognized by the Orthodox Church is the Nicene Creed.

creeper any small, short-legged passerine bird of the family Certhidae. They spiral with a mouselike movement up tree trunks, searching for insects and larvae with their thin, down-curved beaks.

crème de la crème (French "the cream of the cream") the elite, the very best.

Creole in the West Indies and Spanish America, originally someone of European descent born in the New World; later someone of mixed European and African descent. In Louisiana and other states on the Gulf of Mexico, it applies either to someone of French or Spanish descent or (popularly) to someone of mixed French or Spanish and African descent.

Also, a patois or dialect based on French, Dutch, or English, as spoken in the West Indies.

creole language any ◊pidgin language that has ceased to be simply a trade jargon in ports and markets and has become the mother tongue of a particular community. Many creoles have developed into distinct languages with literatures of their own; for example,

Louisiana Creole, Jamaican Creole, Haitian Creole, Krio in Sierra Leone, and Tok Pisin, now the official language of Papua New Guinea.

cress any of several plants of the Cruciferae family, characterized by a pungent taste. The common European garden cress *Lepidium sativum* is cultivated worldwide.

Cretaceous period of geological time 146–65 million years ago. It is the last period of the Mesozoic era, during which angiosperm (seed-bearing) plants evolved, and dinosaurs reached a peak before their almost complete extinction at the end of the period. Chalk is a typical rock type of the second half of the period.

Crete (Greek *Kríti*) largest Greek island in the E Mediterranean Sea, 62 mi/100 km SE of mainland Greece *area* 3,234 sq mi/8,378 sq km *capital* Khaniá (Canea) *towns and cities* Iráklion (Heraklion), Rethymnon, Aghios Nikolaos *products* citrus fruit, olives, wine *population* (1991) 536,900 *language* Cretan dialect of Greek *history* it has remains of the Minoan civilization 3000–1400 BC (see ◊Knossos), and was successively under Roman, Byzantine, Venetian, and Turkish rule. The island was annexed by Greece 1913.

crib death death of an apparently healthy baby during sleep, also known as *sudden infant death syndrome* (SIDS). It is most common in the winter months, and strikes boys more than girls. The cause is not known.

Crick Francis 1916– . British molecular biologist. From 1949 he researched the molecular structure of DNA, and the means whereby characteristics are transmitted from one generation to another. For this work he was awarded a Nobel Prize (with Maurice ◊Wilkins and James ◊Watson) 1962.

cricket bat-and-ball game between two teams of 11 players each. It is played with a small solid ball and long flat-sided wooden bats, on a round or oval field, at the center of which is a finely mown pitch, 22 yd/20 m long. At each end of the pitch is a wicket made up of three upright wooden sticks (stumps), surmounted by two smaller sticks (bails). The object of the game is to score more runs than the opposing team. A run is normally scored by the batsman striking the ball and exchanging ends with his or her partner until the ball is returned by a fielder, or by hitting the ball to the boundary line for an automatic four or six runs.

A batsman stands at each wicket and is bowled a stipulated number of balls (usually six), after which another bowler bowls from the other wicket. A batsman can make an "out" in several ways. Games comprise either one or two innings per team. The exact origins are unknown. The first rules were drawn up in 1774 and modified following the formation of the Marylebone Cricket Club (MCC) in 1787.

cricket in zoology, an insect belonging to any of various families, especially the Grillidae, of the order Orthoptera. Crickets are related to grasshoppers. They have somewhat flattened bodies and long antennae. The males make a chirping noise by rubbing together special areas on the forewings. The females have a long needlelike egglaying organ (ovipositor). There are some 900 species known worldwide.

Crimea northern peninsula on the Black Sea, an autonomous republic of ◊Ukraine; formerly a region (1954–91) *area* 10,425 sq mi/27,000 sq km *capital* Simferopol *towns and cities* Sevastopol, Yalta *features* mainly steppe, but southern coast is a vacation resort;

home of the Black Sea fleet (ownership of which has been the source of a dispute between Russia and Ukraine) *products* iron, oil *population* 2.5 million (70% Russian, despite return of 150,000 Tatars since 1989) *history* Crimea was under Turkish rule 1475–1774; a subsequent brief independence was ended by Russian annexation 1783. Crimea was the republic of Taurida 1917–20 and the Crimean Autonomous Soviet Republic from 1920 until occupied by Germany 1942–1944. It was then reduced to a region, its Tatar people being deported to Uzbekistan for collaboration. Although they were exonerated 1967 and some were allowed to return, others were forcibly re-exiled 1979. A drift back to their former homeland began 1987 and a federal ruling 1988 confirmed their right to residency. Since 1991 the Crimea has sought to gain independence from the Ukraine; the latter has resisted all secessionist moves. A 1994 referendum in Crimea supported demands for greater autonomy and closer links with Russia.

Crimean War war 1853–56 between Russia and the allied powers of England, France, Turkey, and Sardinia. The war arose from British and French mistrust of Russia's ambitions in the Balkans. It began with an allied Anglo-French expedition to the Crimea to attack the Russian Black Sea city of Sevastopol. The battles of the river Alma, Balaclava (including the charge of the Light Brigade), and Inkerman 1854 led to a siege which, owing to military mismanagement, lasted for a year until Sept 1855. The war was ended by the Treaty of Paris 1856. The scandal surrounding French and British losses through disease led to the organization of proper military nursing services by Florence Nightingale.

criminal law body of law that defines the public wrongs (crimes) that are punishable by the state and establishes methods of prosecution and punishment. It is distinct from ◊civil law, which deals with legal relationships between individuals (including organizations), such as contract law.

Criminal offenses are either felonies or ◊misdemeanors. Felonies are more likely to require a formal charge, called an indictment, by a grand jury. Punishments include imprisonment, fines, suspended terms of imprisonment, probation, and ◊community service.

critical mass in nuclear physics, the minimum mass of fissile material that can undergo a continuous ◊chain reaction. Below this mass, too many ◊neutrons escape from the surface for a chain reaction to carry on; above the critical mass, the reaction may accelerate into a nuclear explosion.

Croatia Republic of *area* 21,824 sq mi/56,538 sq km *capital* Zagreb *towns and cities* chief port: Rijeka (Fiume); other ports: Zadar, Sibenik, Split, Dubrovnik *physical* Adriatic coastline with large islands; very mountainous, with part of the Karst region and the Julian and Styrian Alps; some marshland *features* popular sea resorts along the extensive Adriatic coastline *head of state* Franjo Tudjman from 1990 *head of government* Nikica Valentic from 1993 *political system* emergent democracy *political parties* Croatian Democratic Union (CDU), centrist; Croatian Social-Liberal Party (CSLP), left of center; Croatian Christian Democratic Party (CCDP), right-wing, nationalist *products* cereals, potatoes, tobacco, fruit, livestock, metal goods, textiles *currency* kuna *population* (1993 est) 4,850,000 including 75% Croats, 12% Serbs, and 1% Slovenes *life expectancy* men 67, women 74

language Croatian variant of Serbo-Croatian *media* no official censorship but no press or TV independent of government *religions* Roman Catholic (Croats); Orthodox Christian (Serbs) *literacy* 96% *GNP* $1,800 per head (1992) *chronology 1918* Became part of the kingdom that united the Serbs, Croats, and Slovenes. *1929* The kingdom of Croatia, Serbia, and Slovenia became Yugoslavia. Croatia continued its campaign for autonomy. *1941* Became a Nazi puppet state following German invasion. *1945* Became constituent republic of Yugoslavia. *1970s* Separatist demands resurfaced. Crackdown against anti-Serb separatist agitators. *1989* Formation of opposition parties permitted. *1990* April–May: Communists defeated by Tudjman-led Croatian Democratic Union (CDU) in first free election since 1938. Sept: "sovereignty" declared. Dec: new constitution adopted. *1991* March: Serb-dominated Krajina announced secession from Croatia. June: Croatia declared independence; military conflict with Serbia; internal civil war ensued. Oct: Croatia formally seceded from Yugoslavia. *1992* Jan: United Nations (UN) peace accord accepted; Croatia's independence recognized by European Community. March–April: UN peacekeeping force drafted into Croatia. April: independence recognized by US. May: became a member of the UN. Aug: Tudjman directly elected president; CDU won assembly elections. *1993* Jan: Croatian forces launched offensive to retake parts of Serb-held Krajina, violating 1992 UN peace accord. March: UN peacekeeping mandate extended. April: new government sworn in.

crocodile large aquatic carnivorous reptile of the family Crocodiliae, related to alligators and caymans, but distinguished from them by a more pointed snout and a notch in the upper jaw into which the fourth tooth in the lower jaw fits. Crocodiles can grow up to 20 ft/6 m, and have long, powerful tails that propel them when swimming. They can live up to 100 years.

crocus any plant of the genus *Crocus* of the iris family Iridaceae, native to Northern parts of the Old World, especially S Europe and Asia Minor. It has single yellow, purple, or white flowers and narrow, pointed leaves.

Croesus Last king of Lydia *c.*560–546 BC, famed for his wealth. Dominant over the Greek cities of the Asia Minor coast, he was defeated and captured by ◊Cyrus the Great and Lydia was absorbed into the Persian empire.

Cro-Magnon prehistoric human *Homo sapiens sapiens* believed to be ancestral to Europeans, the first skeletons of which were found 1868 in the Cro-Magnon cave near Les Eyzies, in the Dordogne region of France. They are thought to have superseded the Neanderthals in the Middle East, Africa, Europe, and Asia about 40,000 years ago. Although modern in skeletal form, they were more robust in build than some present-day humans. They hunted bison, reindeer, and horses, and are associated with Upper Paleolithic cultures, which produced fine flint and bone tools, jewelry, and naturalistic cave paintings.

Cromwell Oliver 1599–1658. English general and politician, Puritan leader of the Parliamentary side in the ◊Civil War. He raised cavalry forces (later called *Ironsides*) which aided the victories at Edgehill 1642 and ◊Marston Moor 1644, and organized the New Model Army, which he led (with General Fairfax) to victory at Naseby 1645. He declared Britain a republic ("the Commonwealth") 1649, following the execution of Charles I. As Lord Protector (ruler) from 1653, Cromwell established religious toleration and raised Britain's prestige in Europe on the basis of an alliance with France against Spain.

Cromwell was a critic of Charles I and became active in events leading to the Civil War. He signed the king's death warrant in 1648 and in the power struggle that followed sided with the army and the establishment of the Commonwealth. He expelled parliament and established the Protectorate. His foreign policy was dictated by religious and commercial considerations; he found no constitutional basis for his rule and refused the crown 1657.

Cromwell Thomas, Earl of Essex *c.*1485–1540. English politician who drafted the legislation making the Church of England independent of Rome. Originally in Lord Chancellor Wolsey's service, he became secretary to Henry VIII 1534 and the real director of government policy; he was executed for treason.

Cronus or *Cronus* in Greek mythology, ruler of the world and one of the ◊Titans. He was the father of Zeus, who overthrew him.

Crosby Bing (Harry Lillis) 1904–1977. US film actor and singer. He achieved world success with his distinctive style of crooning in such songs as "Pennies from

crocodile The estuarine or saltwater crocodile, of India, SE Asia, and Australasia, is one of the largest and most dangerous of its family. It has been known to develop a taste for human flesh. Hunted near to extinction for its leather, it is now protected by restrictions and the trade in skins is controlled.

Heaven" 1936 (featured in a film of the same name) and "White Christmas" 1942. He won an acting Oscar for *Going My Way* 1944, and made a series of "road" film comedies with Dorothy Lamour and Bob Hope, the last being *Road to Hong Kong* 1962.

croup inflammation of the larynx in small children, with harsh, difficult breathing and hoarse coughing. Croup is most often associated with viral infection of the respiratory tract.

crow any of 35 species of the genus *Corvus*, family Corvidae, which also includes jays and magpies. Ravens belong to the same genus as crows. Crows are usually about 1.5 ft/45 cm long, black, with a strong bill feathered at the base, and omnivorous with a bias toward animal food. They are considered to be very intelligent. It is estimated that there are only 11 birds of the species *Corvus hawaiiensis*, the wild Hawaiian crow, left in the wild.

crucifixion death by fastening to a cross, a form of capital punishment used by the ancient Romans, Persians, and Carthaginians, and abolished by the Roman emperor Constantine. Specifically, *the Crucifixion* refers to the execution by the Romans of ◊Jesus in this manner.

crusade European war against non-Christians and heretics, sanctioned by the pope; in particular, the Crusades, a series of wars 1096–1291 undertaken by European rulers to recover Palestine from the Muslims. Motivated by religious zeal, the desire for land, and the trading ambitions of the major Italian cities, the Crusades were varied in their aims and effects.

crustacean one of the class of arthropods that includes crabs, lobsters, shrimps, woodlice, and barnacles. The external skeleton is made of protein and chitin hardened with lime. Each segment bears a pair of appendages that may be modified as sensory feelers (antennae), as mouthparts, or as swimming, walking, or grasping structures.

cryogenics science of very low temperatures (approaching ◊absolute zero), including the production of very low temperatures and the exploitation of special properties associated with them, such as the disappearance of electrical resistance (◊superconductivity).

cryolite rare granular crystalline mineral (sodium aluminum fluoride), Na_3AlF_6, used in the electrolytic reduction of ◊bauxite to aluminum. It is chiefly found in Greenland.

Cryolite also occurs in Colorado at Pike's Peak.

crystal substance with an orderly three-dimensional arrangement of its atoms or molecules, thereby creating an external surface of clearly defined smooth faces having characteristic angles between them. Examples are table salt and quartz.

crystallography the scientific study of crystals. In 1912 it was found that the shape and size of the repeating atomic patterns (unit cells) in a crystal could be determined by passing X-rays through a sample. This method, known as ◊X-ray diffraction, opened up an entirely new way of "seeing" atoms. It has been found that many substances have a unit cell that exhibits all the symmetry of the whole crystal; in table salt (sodium chloride, NaCl), for instance, the unit cell is an exact cube.

Cuba Republic of (*República de Cuba*) *area* 42,820 sq mi/ 110,860 sq km *capital* Havana *towns and cities*

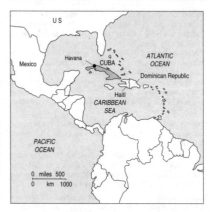

Santiago de Cuba, Camagüey *physical* comprises Cuba, the largest and westernmost of the West Indies, and smaller islands including Isle of Youth; low hills; Sierra Maestra mountains in SE *features* 2,100 mi/ 3,380 km of coastline, with deep bays, sandy beaches, coral islands and reefs; more than 1,600 islands surround the Cuban mainland *head of state and government* Fidel Castro Ruz from 1959 *political system* communist republic *political party* Communist Party of Cuba (PCC), Marxist-Leninist *exports* sugar, tobacco, coffee, nickel, fish *currency* Cuban peso *population* (1993 est) 11,000,000; 37% are white of Spanish descent, 51% mulatto, and 11% are of African origin; growth rate 0.6% p.a. *life expectancy* men 74, women 78 *language* Spanish *religion* Roman Catholic 85%; also Episcopalians and Methodists *literacy* men 95%, women 93% *GNP* $1,000 per head (1991) *chronology* 1492 Christopher Columbus landed in Cuba and claimed it for Spain. *1898* US defeated Spain in Spanish-American War; Spain gave up all claims to Cuba. *1901* Cuba achieved independence; Tomás Estrada Palma became first president of the Republic of Cuba. *1933* Fulgencia Batista seized power. *1944* Batista retired. *1952* Batista seized power again to begin an oppressive regime. *1953* Fidel Castro led an unsuccessful coup against Batista. *1956* Second unsuccessful coup by Castro. *1959* Batista overthrown by Castro. Constitution of 1940 replaced by a "Fundamental Law", making Castro prime minister, his brother Raúl Castro his deputy, and "Che" Guevara his number three. *1960* All US businesses in Cuba appropriated without compensation; US broke off diplomatic relations. *1961* US sponsored an unsuccessful invasion at the Bay of Pigs. Castro announced that Cuba had become a communist state, with a Marxist-Leninist program of economic development. *1962* Cuba expelled from the Organization of American States. Soviet nuclear missiles installed but subsequently removed from Cuba at US insistence. US trade embargo imposed. *1965* Cuba's sole political party renamed Cuban Communist Party (PCC). With Soviet help, Cuba began to make considerable economic and social progress. *1972* Cuba became a full member of the Moscow-based Council for Mutual Economic Assistance. *1976* New socialist constitution approved; Castro elected president. *1976–81* Castro became involved in extensive international commitments, sending troops as Soviet surrogates, particularly to Africa. *1982* Cuba joined other Latin

American countries in giving moral support to Argentina in its dispute with Britain over the Falklands. *1984* Castro tried to improve US-Cuban relations by discussing exchange of US prisoners in Cuba for Cuban "undesirables" in the US. *1988* Peace accord with South Africa signed, agreeing to withdrawal of Cuban troops from Angola. *1989* Reduction in Cuba's overseas military activities. *1991* Soviet troops withdrawn. *1992* Castro affirmed continuing support of communism. *1994* Economy deteriorated; refugee exodus.

cube in geometry, a regular solid figure whose faces are all squares. It has six equal-area faces and 12 equal-length edges.

cube to multiply a number by itself and then by itself again. For example, 5 cubed = 5^3 = 5 x 5 x 5 = 125. The term also refers to a number formed by cubing; for example, 1, 8, 27, 64 are the first four cubes.

Cubism revolutionary movement in early 20th-century painting, pioneering abstract forms. Its founders, Georges Braque and Pablo Picasso, were admirers of Paul Cézanne and were inspired by his attempt to create a highly structured visual language. In *analytical Cubism* (1907–12) three-dimensional objects were split into facets and analyzed before being "reassembled" as complex two-dimensional images. In *synthetic Cubism* (after 1912) the images became simpler, the colors brighter, and ◊collage was introduced. The movement attracted such artists as Juan Gris, Fernand Léger, and Pablo Delaunay, and the sculptor Jacques Lipchitz. Its message was that a work of art exists in its own right rather than as a representation of the real world.

Cuchulain Celtic hero, the chief figure in a cycle of Irish legends. He is associated with his uncle Conchobar, King of Ulster; his most famous exploits are described in *Taín Bó Cuailnge/The Cattle Raid of Cuchulain*.

cuckoo species of bird, any of about 200 members of the family Cuculidae, especially the Eurasian cuckoo *Cuculus canorus*, whose name derives from its characteristic call. Somewhat hawklike, it is about 1 ft/33 cm long, bluish gray and barred beneath (females sometimes reddish), and has a long, typically rounded tail. Cuckoos feed on insects, including hairy caterpillars that are distasteful to most birds. It is a "brood parasite", laying its eggs singly, at intervals of about 48 hours, in the nests of small insectivorous birds. As soon as the young cuckoo hatches, it ejects all other young birds or eggs from the nest and is tended by its "foster parents" until fledging. American species hatch and rear their own young.

cucumber trailing annual plant *Cucumis sativus* of the gourd family Cucurbitaceae, producing long, green-skinned fruit with crisp, translucent, edible flesh. Small cucumbers, called gherkins, usually the fruit of *C. anguria*, are often pickled.

Culloden, Battle of defeat 1746 of the ◊Jacobite rebel army of the British prince ◊Charles Edward Stuart by the Duke of Cumberland on a stretch of moorland in Inverness-shire, Scotland. This battle effectively ended the military challenge of the Jacobite rebellion.

Cultural Revolution Chinese mass movement 1966–69 begun by Communist Party chair Mao Zedong, directed against the upper middle class—bureaucrats, artists, and academics—who were killed, imprisoned, humiliated, or "resettled". Intended to "purify" Chinese communism, it was also an attempt by Mao

to renew his political and ideological pre-eminence inside China. Half a million people are estimated to have been killed.

culture in sociology and anthropology, the way of life of a particular society or group of people, including patterns of thought, beliefs, behavior, customs, traditions, rituals, dress, and language, as well as art, music, and literature. Sociologists and anthropologists use culture as a key concept in describing and analyzing human societies.

Cumbria county of NW England, created 1974 from Cumberland, Westmorland, and parts of NW Lancashire and NW Yorkshire *area* 2,629 sq mi/6,810 sq km *towns and cities* Carlisle (administrative headquarters), Barrow, Kendal, Whitehaven, Workington, Penrith *features* Lake District National Park, including Scafell Pike 3,210 ft/978 m, the highest mountain in England; Helvellyn 3,118 ft/950 m; Lake Windermere, the largest lake in England, 10.5 mi/17 km long, 1.6 km/1 mi wide; other lakes (Derwentwater, Ullswater); Grizedale Forest sculpture project; Furness peninsula; nuclear stations at Calder Hall (the world's first nuclear power station, 1956) and Sellafield (formerly Windscale) *products* the traditional coal, iron, and steel industries of the coast towns have been replaced by newer industries including chemicals, plastics, marine engineering, and electronics; in the N and E there is dairying, and West Cumberland Farmers is the country's largest agricultural cooperative *population* (1991) 483,100.

cumin seedlike fruit of the herb *Cuminum cyminum* of the carrot family Umbelliferae, with a bitter flavor. It is used as a spice in cooking.

cummings e e literary signature of Edward Estlin Cummings 1894–1962. US poet and novelist. He made his reputation with collections of poetry such as *Tulips and Chimneys* 1923. At first the poems gained notoriety for their idiosyncratic punctuation and typography (using only lowercase letters, for example), but their lyric power has gradually been recognized.

cuneiform ancient writing system formed of combinations of wedge-shaped strokes, usually impressed on clay. It was probably invented by the Sumerians, and was in use in Mesopotamia as early as the middle of the 4th millennium BC.

Cunningham Merce 1919– . US choreographer and dancer. He is recognized as the father of post-modernist, or experimental, dance. He liberated dance from its relationship with music, allowing it to obey its own dynamics.

Along with his friend and collaborator, composer John ◊Cage, he introduced chance into the creative process, such as tossing coins to determine options. Influenced by Martha ◊Graham, with whose company he was soloist 1939–45, he formed his own avant-garde dance company and school in New York 1953. His works include *The Seasons* 1947, *Antic Meet* 1958, *Squaregame* 1976, and *Arcade* 1985.

Cupid in Roman mythology, the god of love, identified with the Greek Eros.

cupronickel copper alloy (75% copper and 25% nickel), used in hardware products and for coinage.

US coins made with cupronickel include the dime, quarter, half-dollar, and dollar.

Curaçao island in the West Indies, one of the ◊Netherlands Antilles; area 171 sq mi/444 sq km; population (1988) 148,500. The principal industry, dating from 1918, is the refining of Venezuelan petroleum.

Curaçao was colonized by Spain 1527, annexed by the Dutch West India Company 1634, and gave its name from 1924 to the group of islands renamed the Netherlands Antilles 1948. Its capital is the port of Willemstad.

curare black, resinous poison extracted from the bark and juices of various South American trees and plants. Originally used on arrowheads by Amazonian hunters to paralyze prey, it blocks nerve stimulation of the muscles. Alkaloid derivatives (called curarines) are used in medicine as muscle relaxants during surgery.

Curie Marie (born Sklodovska) 1867–1934. Polish scientist. In 1898 she reported the possible existence of a new, powerfully radioactive element in pitchblende ores. Her husband, Pierre (1859–1906), abandoned his own researches to assist her, and in the same year they announced the existence of polonium and radium. They isolated the pure elements 1902. Both scientists refused to take out a patent on their discovery and were jointly awarded the Davy Medal 1903 and the Nobel Prize for Physics 1903, with Henri ◊Becquerel. Marie Curie wrote a Treatise on Radioactivity 1910, and was awarded the Nobel Prize for Chemistry 1911.

curium synthesized, radioactive, metallic element of the *actinide* series, symbol Cm, atomic number 96, relative atomic mass 247. It is produced by bombarding plutonium or americium with neutrons. Its longest-lived isotope has a half-life of 1.7×10^7 years.

Curium is used to generate heat and power in satellites or in remote places. Named in 1946 for Pierre and Marie Curie by Glenn Seaborg, it was first synthesized in 1944 by Seaborg at the University of California at Berkeley, by analogy with the corresponding ◊lanthanide, gadolinium (see ◊periodic table of the elements).

curlew wading bird of the genus *Numenius* of the sandpiper family, Scolopacidae. The curlew is between 14 in/36 cm and 1.8 ft/55 cm in length, and has mottled brown plumage, long legs, and a long, thin, downcurved bill. Several species live in N Europe, Asia, and North America. The name derives from its haunting flutelike call.

currant berry of a small seedless variety of cultivated grape *Vitis vinifera*. Currants are grown on a large scale in Greece and California and used dried in cooking and baking. Because of the similarity of the fruit, the name currant is also given to several species of shrubs in the genus *Ribes*, family Grossulariaceae.

The garden red currant *Ribes rubrum* is a native of S Europe and Asia, now also growing in North America. The European black currant *R. nigrum* is widely cultivated. The American black currant *R. americanum* is native to E North America, as is the skunk currant *R. glandulosum*.

current flow of a body of water or air, or of heat, moving in a definite direction. Ocean currents are fast-flowing currents of seawater generated by the wind or by variations in water density between two areas. They are partly responsible for transferring heat from the equator to the poles and thereby evening out the global heat imbalance. There are three basic types of ocean current: **drift currents** are broad and slow-moving; **stream currents** are narrow and swift-moving; and **upwelling currents** bring cold, nutrient-rich water from the ocean bottom.

curry traditional Indian mixture of spices used to flavor a dish of rice, meat, and/or vegetables. Spices include turmeric, fenugreek, cloves, chilis, cumin, cinnamon, ginger, black and cayenne pepper, coriander, and caraway.

cursor on a computer screen, the symbol that indicates the current entry position (where the next character will appear). It usually consists of a solid rectangle or underline character, flashing on and off.

Curtis Tony. Adopted name of Bernard Schwarz 1925– . US film actor who starred in the 1950s and 1960s in such films as *The Vikings* 1958 and *The Boston Strangler* 1968, as well as specializing in light comedies such as *Some Like It Hot* 1959, with Jack Lemmon and Marilyn Monroe.

custard apple any of numerous, primarily tropical trees and shrubs of the family Annonaceae. Several are cultivated for their large, edible, heart-shaped fruits. The pawpaw *Annona simina triloba* of the E US, and the pond-apple *A. glabra* of the West Indies are representatives.

Custer George A(rmstrong) 1839–1876. US Civil War general, the Union's youngest brigadier general as a result of a brilliant war record. He campaigned against the Sioux from 1874, and was killed with a detachment of his troops by the forces of Sioux chief Sitting Bull in the Battle of Little Bighorn, Montana: also called *Custer's last stand*, 25 June 1876.

Custer, George A(rmstrong) US general George A Custer during a Black Hills expedition 1874. Custer was now engaged on the campaign against the Sioux Indians that would lead to his famous "last stand" at the Battle of Little Big Horn 1876.

Customs and Excise government department responsible for taxes levied on imports (customs duty). Excise duties are levied on goods produced domestically or on licenses to carry on certain trades (such as sale of wines and spirits) or other activities (theatrical entertainments, betting, and so on) within a country.

In the US, excise duties are classed as Internal Revenue and customs are controlled by the Customs Bureau. Membership in the ◊European Union requires the progressive abolition of all internal tariffs between member states and adoption of a common external tariff by the end of 1992. In the UK, both come under the Board of Customs and Excise, which also administers VAT generally, although there are independent tax tribunals for appeal against the decisions of the commissioners.

cuttlefish any of a family, Sepiidae, of squidlike cephalopods with an internal calcareous shell (cuttlebone). The common cuttle *Sepia officinalis* of the Atlantic and Mediterranean is up to 1 ft/30 cm long. It swims actively by means of the fins into which the sides of its oval, flattened body are expanded, and jerks itself backward by shooting a jet of water from its "siphon".

cwt symbol for ◊*hundredweight*, a unit of weight equal to 100 lb (45.36 kg) in the US and 112 lb (50.8 kg) in the UK and Canada.

cyanide CN⁻ ion derived from hydrogen cyanide . (HCN), and any salt containing this ion (produced when hydrogen cyanide is neutralized by alkalis), such as potassium cyanide (KCN). The principal cyanides are potassium, sodium, calcium, mercury, gold, and copper. Certain cyanides are poisons.

cybernetics science concerned with how systems organize, regulate, and reproduce themselves, and also how they evolve and learn. In the laboratory, inanimate objects are created that behave like living systems. Applications range from the creation of electronic artificial limbs to the running of the fully automated factory where decision making machines operate up to managerial level.

cyberspace the imaginary, interactive "worlds" created by computers; often used interchangeably with "virtual world" or ◊"virtual reality". The invention of the word "cyberspace" is generally credited to US science-fiction writer William Gibson (1948–) and his first novel *Neuromancer* 1984.

cycad plant of the order Cycadales belonging to the gymnosperms. Some have a superficial resemblance to palms, others to ferns. Their large cones contain fleshy seeds. There are ten genera and about 80–100 species, native to tropical and subtropical countries. Cycads were widespread during the Mesozoic era.

cyclamen any plant of the genus *Cyclamen* of perennial plants of the primrose family Primulaceae, with heart-shaped leaves and petals that are twisted at the base and bent back. The flowers are usually white or pink, and several species are cultivated.

cyclone alternate name for a ◊depression, an area of low atmospheric pressure. A severe cyclone that forms in the tropics is called a tropical cyclone or ◊hurricane.

Cyclops in Greek mythology, one of a race of Sicilian giants, who had one eye in the middle of the forehead and lived as shepherds. ◊Odysseus blinded the Cyclops Polyphemus in Homer's *Odyssey*.

cylinder in geometry, a tubular solid figure with a circular base. In everyday use, the term applies to a *right cylinder*, the curved surface of which is at right angles to the base.

cymbal ancient percussion instrument of indefinite pitch, consisting of a shallow circular brass dish suspended at the center; either used in pairs clashed together or singly, struck with a beater. Smaller finger cymbals or *crotala*, used by Debussy and Stockhausen, are precise in pitch. Turkish or "buzz" cymbals incorporate loose rivets to extend the sound.

Cymbeline or *Cunobelin* King of the Catuvellauni AD 5–40, who fought unsuccessfully against the Roman invasion of Britain. His capital was at Colchester.

Cymru Welsh name for ◊Wales.

Cynic school of Greek philosophy (Cynicism), founded in Athens about 400 BC by Antisthenes, a disciple of Socrates, who advocated a stern and simple morality and a complete disregard of pleasure and comfort.

cypress any coniferous tree or shrub of the genera *Cupressus* and *Chamaecyparis*, family Cupressaceae. There are about 20 species, originating from temperate regions of the northern hemisphere. They have minute, scalelike leaves and cones made up of woody, wedge-shaped scales containing an aromatic resin.

All species of cypress native to the US occur in the west. Baldcypresses (genus *Taxodium*) belong to the redwood family and are found only in the S US and Mexico.

Cyprus Greek *Republic of Cyprus* (*Kypriakí Dimokratía*) in the south, and *Turkish Republic of Northern Cyprus* (*Kibris Cumhuriyeti*) in the north *area* 3,571 sq mi/9,251 sq km, 37% in Turkish hands *capital* Nicosia (divided between Greeks and Turks) *towns and cities* ports Limassol, Larnaca, Paphos (Greek); Morphou, and ports Kyrenia and Famagusta (Turkish) *physical* central plain between two E–W mountain ranges *features* archeological and historic sites; Mount Olympus 6,406 ft/1,953 m (highest peak); beaches *head of state and government* Glafkos Clerides (Greek) from 1993, Rauf Denktas (Turkish) from 1976 *political system* democratic divided republic *political parties* Democratic Front (DIKO), center-left; Progressive Party of the Working People (AKEL), socialist; Democratic Rally (DISY), centrist; Socialist Party (EDEK), socialist; *Turkish zone*: National Unity Party (NUP), Communal Liberation Party (CLP), Republican Turkish Party (RTP), New British Party (NBP) *exports* citrus, grapes, raisins, Cyprus sherry, potatoes, clothing, footwear *currency* Cyprus pound and Turkish lira *population* (1994) 725,000 (Greek Cypriot 78%, Turkish Cypriot 18%); growth rate 1.2% p.a. *life expectancy* men 74, women 79 *languages* Greek and Turkish (official), English *religions* Greek Orthodox 78%, Sunni Muslim 18% *literacy* 94% *GNP* $8,640 per head (1991) *chronology 1878* Came under British administration. *1955* Guerrilla campaign began against the British for enosis (union with Greece), led by Archbishop Makarios and General Grivas. *1956* Makarios and enosis leaders deported. *1959* Compromise agreed and Makarios returned to be elected president of an independent Greek-Turkish Cyprus. *1960* Independence achieved from Britain, with Britain retaining its military bases. *1963* Turks set up their own government in northern Cyprus. Fighting broke out between the two communities. *1964* United Nations peacekeeping force installed. *1971* Grivas returned to start a guerrilla war against the Makarios government. *1974* Grivas died. Military coup deposed Makarios, who fled to Britain. Nicos Sampson appointed president. Turkish army sent to northern Cyprus to confirm Turkish Cypriots' control; military regime in southern Cyprus collapsed; Makarios returned. Northern Cyprus declared itself the Turkish Federated State of Cyprus (TFSC), with Rauf Denktas as president. *1977* Makarios died; succeeded by Spyros Kyprianou. *1983* An independent Turkish Republic of Northern Cyprus proclaimed but recognized only by Turkey. *1984* United Nations (UN) peace proposals rejected. *1985* Summit meeting between Kyprianou and Denktas failed to reach agreement. *1988* Georgios Vassiliou elected Greek president. Talks with Denktas began under UN auspices. *1989* Peace talks abandoned. *1992* UN-sponsored peace talks collapsed. *1993* DISY leader Glafkos Clerides narrowly won presidential election to replace Vassiliou. *1994* European Court of Justice declared trade with northern Cyprus illegal.

Cyrano de Bergerac Savinien 1619–1655. French writer. He joined a corps of guards at 19 and performed heroic feats which brought him fame. He is the hero of a classic play by Edmond Rostand, in which his excessively long nose is used as a counterpoint to his chivalrous character.

Cyrenaic member of a school of Greek ◊hedonistic philosophy founded about 400 BC by Aristippus of Cyrene. He regarded pleasure as the only absolutely worthwhile thing in life but taught that self-control and intelligence were necessary to choose the best pleasures.

Cyrus the Great Founder of the Persian Empire. As king of Persia, he was originally subject to the Medes, whose empire he overthrew 550 BC. He captured ◊Croesus 546 BC, and conquered ◊Lydia, adding Babylonia (including Syria and Palestine) to his empire 539 BC, allowing exiled Jews to return to Jerusalem. He died fighting in Afghanistan.

cystic fibrosis hereditary disease involving defects of various tissues, including the sweat glands, the mucous glands of the bronchi (air passages), and the pancreas. The sufferer experiences repeated chest infections and digestive disorders and generally fails to thrive. In 1989 a gene for cystic fibrosis was identified by teams of researchers in Michigan and Toronto, Canada. This discovery enabled the development of a screening test for carriers; the disease can also be detected in the unborn child.

cystitis inflammation of the bladder, usually caused by bacterial infection, and resulting in frequent and painful urination. It is more common in women. Treatment is by antibiotics and copious fluids with vitamin C.

cytochrome one of a number of iron-containing, red proteins responsible for part of the process of ◊respiration by which food molecules are broken down in ◊aerobic organisms. Cytochromes are also used for the part of the process of ◊photosynthesis by which molecules of water are oxidized to oxygen gas. Cytochromes are part of the electron transport chain, by which energized electrons are passed along to release energy and to make ◊ATP.

cytoplasm the part of the cell outside the ◊nucleus. Strictly speaking, this includes all the organelles (mitochondria, chloroplasts, and so on), but often cytoplasm refers to the jellylike matter in which the organelles are embedded (correctly termed the cytosol).

czar alternative spelling of *tsar*, an emperor of Russia.

Czech Republic (*Ceská Republika*) *area* 30,461 sq mi/ 78,864 sq km *capital* Prague *towns and cities* Brno, Ostrava, Olomouc, Liberec, Plzen, Ustí nad Labem, Hradec Králové *physical* mountainous; rivers: Morava, Labe (Elbe), Vltava (Moldau) *environment* one of the most polluted areas of Europe; up to twenty times the permissible level of sulfur dioxide is released over Prague, where 75% of the drinking water fails to meet the country's health standards *features* summer and winter resort areas in Western Carpathian, Bohemian, and Sudetic mountain ranges *head of state* Václav Havel from 1993 *head of government* Václav Klaus

from 1993 *political system* emergent democracy *political parties* Civic Democratic Party (ODS), radical liberal; Christian Democratic Party (KDS), right of center; Christian Democratic Union–Czechoslovak People's Party (KDU–CSL), right of center; Czech Social Democratic Party (CSSD), left of center; Christian Social Union (KSU), left of center; Green Party (SZ), left of center, ecological; Agrarian Party (ZS), rural, left of center; Liberal National Social Party (LSNS), left-wing *exports* machinery, vehicles, coal, iron and steel, chemicals, glass, ceramics, clothing *currency* koruna (based on Czechoslovak koruna) *population* (1993) 10,330,000 (with German and other minorities); growth rate 0.4% p.a. *life expectancy* men 69, women 79 *language* Czech (official) *media* defamation of the republic or president is prohibited; defaming the government was made a crime 1993 *religions* Roman Catholic (75%), Protestant, Hussite, Orthodox *literacy* 99% *GDP* $26,600 million (1990); $2,562 per head *chronology 1526–1918* Under Hapsburg domination. *1918* Independence achieved from Austro-Hungarian Empire; Czechs joined Slovaks in forming Czechoslovakia as independent nation. *1948* Communists assumed power in Czechoslovakia. *1969* Czech Socialist Republic created under new federal constitution. *1989* Nov: prodemocracy demonstrations in Prague; new political parties formed and legalized, including Czech-based Civic Forum under Václav Havel; Communist Party stripped of powers. Dec: new "grand coalition" government formed; Havel appointed state president. Amnesty granted to 22,000 prisoners. *1990* July: Havel reelected president in multiparty elections. *1991* Civic Forum split into Civic Democratic Party (CDP) and Civic Movement (CM); evidence of increasing Czech and Slovak separatism. *1992* June: Václav Klaus, leader of the Czech-based CDP, became prime minister; Havel resigned following Slovak gains in assembly elections. Aug: creation of separate Czech and Slovak states agreed. *1993* Jan: Czech Republic became sovereign state, with Klaus as prime minister. Havel elected president. Admitted into United Nations. Major realignment of political parties. New currency introduced. Formal invitation to apply for European Community membership. *1994* Joined NATO's "partnership for peace" program.

dab small marine flatfish of the flounder family, especially the genus *Limanda*. Dabs live in the N Atlantic and around the coasts of Britain and Scandinavia.

Dacca alternate name for ◊Dhaka, the capital of Bangladesh.

Dachau site of a Nazi ◊concentration camp during World War II, in Bavaria, Germany. The first such camp to be set up, it opened early 1933 and functioned as a detention and forced labor camp until liberated 1945.

Dada or **Dadaism** artistic and literary movement founded 1915 in Zürich, Switzerland, by the Romanian poet Tristan Tzara (1896–1963) and others in a spirit of rebellion and disillusionment during World War I. Other Dadaist groups were soon formed by the artists Marcel ◊Duchamp and Man ◊Ray in New York, Francis Picabia in Barcelona, and Kurt Schwitters in Germany. The Dadaists produced deliberately antiesthetic images, often using photomontages with worded messages to express their political views, and directly scorned established art, as in Duchamp's *Mona Lisa* 1919, where a moustache and beard were added to Leonardo da Vinci's classic portrait.

daddy-longlegs popular name for a ◊crane fly.

Daedalus in Greek mythology, an Athenian artisan supposed to have constructed for King Minos of Crete the labyrinth in which the ◊Minotaur was imprisoned. When Minos became displeased with him, Daedalus fled from Crete with his son ◊Icarus using wings made by them from feathers fastened with wax.

daffodil any of several Old World species of the genus *Narcissus*, family Amaryllidaceae, distinguished by their trumpet-shaped flowers. The common daffodil of N Europe *N. pseudonarcissus* has large yellow flowers and grows from a large bulb. There are numerous cultivated forms.

Dagestan autonomous republic of S Russia, situated E of the ◊Caucasus, bordering the Caspian Sea; capital Makhachkala; area 19,421 sq mi/50,300 sq km/; population (1982) 1,700,000. It is mountainous, with deep valleys, and its numerous ethnic groups speak a variety of distinct languages. Annexed 1723 from Iran, which strongly resisted Russian conquest, it became an autonomous republic 1921.

Daguerre Louis Jacques Mande 1789–1851. French pioneer of photography. Together with Joseph Niépce, he is credited with the invention of photography (though others were reaching the same point simultaneously). In 1838 he invented the daguerreotype, a single image process superseded ten years later by Fox Talbot's negative/positive process.

dahlia any perennial plant of the genus *Dahlia*, family Compositae, comprising 20 species and many cultivated forms. Dahlias are stocky plants with showy flowers that come in a wide range of colors. They are native to Mexico and Central America.

Dahomey former name (until 1975) of the People's Republic of ◊Benin.

Daimler Gottlieb 1834–1900. German engineer who pioneered the modern automobile. In 1886 he produced his first motor vehicle and a motor-bicycle. He later joined forces with Karl ◊Benz and was one of the pioneers of the high-speed four-stroke gasoline engine.

daisy any of numerous species of perennial plants in the family Compositae, especially the field daisy of Europe and North America *Chrysanthemum leucanthemum* and the English common daisy *Bellis perennis*, with a single white or pink flower rising from a rosette of leaves.

daisywheel printing head in a computer printer or typewriter that consists of a small plastic or metal disk made up of many spokes (like the petals of a daisy). At the end of each spoke is a character in relief. The daisywheel is rotated until the spoke bearing the required character is facing an inked ribbon, then a hammer strikes the spoke against the ribbon, leaving the impression of the character on the paper beneath.

Dakar capital and chief port (with artificial harbor) of Senegal; population (1984) 1,000,000. It is an industrial center, and there is a university, established 1957.

Dalai Lama 14th incarnation 1935– . Spiritual and temporal head of the Tibetan state until 1959, when he went into exile in protest against Chinese annexation and oppression. His people have continued to demand his return.

Dali Salvador 1904–1989. Spanish painter and designer. In 1929 he joined the Surrealists and became notorious for his flamboyant eccentricity. Influenced by the psychoanalytic theories of Sigmund ◊Freud, he developed a repertoire of striking, hallucinatory images—distorted human figures, limp pocket watches, and burning giraffes—in superbly executed works, which he termed "hand-painted dream photographs". *The Persistence of Memory* 1931 (Museum of Modern Art, New York) is typical. By the late 1930s he had developed a more conventional style—this, and his apparent Fascist sympathies, led to his expulsion from the Surrealist movement 1938. It was in this more traditional though still highly inventive and idiosyncratic style that he painted such celebrated religious works as *The Crucifixion* 1951 (Glasgow Art School). He also painted portraits of his wife Gala.

Dallas commercial city in Texas; population (1990) 1,006,900, metropolitan area (with Fort Worth) 3,885,400. Industries include banking, insurance, oil, aviation, aerospace, and electronics.

Dallas–Fort Worth Regional Airport (opened 1973) is one of the world's largest. John F. ◊Kennedy was assassinated here 1963.

Dalmatia region divided between Croatia, Montenegro in Yugoslavia, and Bosnia-Herzegovina. The capital is Split. It lies along the eastern shore of the Adriatic Sea and includes a number of islands. The interior is mountainous. Important products are wine, olives, and fish. Notable towns in addition to the capital are Zadar, Sibenik, and Dubrovnik.

history Dalmatia became Austrian 1815 and by the treaty of Rapallo 1920 became part of the kingdom of the Serbs, Croats, and Slovenes (Yugoslavia from 1931), except for the town of Zadar (Zara) and the island of Lastovo (Lagosta), which, with neighboring islets, were given to Italy until transferred to Yugoslavia 1947.

Dalton John 1766–1844. English chemist who proposed the theory of atoms, which he considered to be the smallest parts of matter. He produced the first list of atomic weights in *Absorption of Gases* 1805 and put forward the law of partial pressures of gases (Dalton's law).

He was one of the first scientists to note and record color blindness (he was himself color blind).

dam structure built to hold back water in order to prevent flooding, to provide water for irrigation and storage, and to provide hydroelectric power. The biggest dams are of the earth-and rock-fill type, also called *embankment dams*. Broad valley sites usually have dams of puddled clay (clay which has been mixed with water to make it impermeable). Deep, narrow gorges dictate a *concrete dam*, where the strength of reinforced concrete can withstand the water pressures involved.

damages in law, compensation for a tort (such as personal injuries caused by negligence) or breach of contract.

In the case of breach of contract the complainant can claim all the financial loss he or she has suffered. Damages for personal injuries include compensation for loss of earnings, as well as for the injury itself. The court might reduce the damages if the claimant was partly to blame. In the majority of cases, the parties involved reach an out-of-court settlement (a compromise without going to court).

Damascus (Arabic *Dimashq*) capital of Syria, on the river Barada, SE of Beirut; population (1981) 1,251,000. It produces silk, wood products, and brass and copper ware. Said to be the oldest continuously inhabited city in the world, Damascus was an ancient city even in Old Testament times. Most notable of the old buildings is the Great Mosque, completed as a Christian church in the 5th century.

damson cultivated variety of plum tree *Prunus domestica* var. *institia*, distinguished by its small, oval, edible fruits, which are dark purple or blue to black in color.

dance rhythmic movement of the body, usually performed in time to music. Its primary purpose may be religious, magical, martial, social, or artistic—the last two being characteristic of nontraditional societies. The pre-Christian era had a strong tradition of ritual dance, and ancient Greek dance still exerts an influence on dance movement today. Although Western folk and social dances have a long history, the Eastern dance tradition long predates the Western. The European classical tradition dates from the 15th century in Italy, the first printed dance text from 16th-century France, and the first dance school in Paris from the 17th century. The 18th century saw the development of European classical ballet as we know it today, and the 19th century saw the rise of Romantic ballet. In the 20th century ◊modern dance firmly

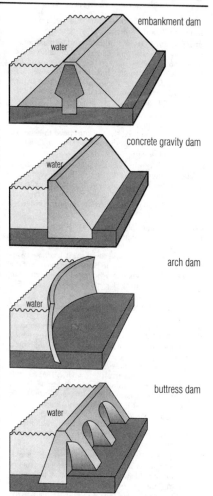

embankment dam

concrete gravity dam

arch dam

buttress dam

dam There are two basic types of dam: the gravity dam and the arch dam. The gravity dam relies upon the weight of its material to resist the forces imposed upon it; the arch dam uses an arch shape to take the forces in a horizontal direction into the sides of the river valley. Buttress dams are used to hold back very wide rivers or lakes.

established itself as a separate dance idiom, not based on classical ballet, and many divergent styles and ideas have grown from a willingness to explore a variety of techniques and amalgamate different traditions. .

dandelion plant *Taraxacum officinale* belonging to the Compositae family. The stalk rises from a rosette of leaves that are deeply indented like a lion's teeth, hence the name (from French *dent de lion*). The flower heads are bright yellow. The fruit is surmounted by the hairs of the calyx which constitute the familiar dandelion "clock".

Dandelions, introduced from Europe, now grow throughout North America.

Dane person of Danish culture from Denmark and N Germany. There are approximately 5 million speakers of Danish (including some in the US), a Germanic language belonging to the Indo-European family. The Danes are known for their seafaring culture, which dates back to the Viking age of expansion between the 8th and 10th centuries.

danegeld in English history, a tax imposed from 991 by Anglo-Saxon kings to pay tribute to the Vikings. After the Norman Conquest the tax continued to be levied until 1162, and the Normans used it to finance military operations.

Danelaw 11th-century name for the area of N and E England settled by the Vikings in the 9th century. It occupied about half of England, from the river Tees to the river Thames. Within its bounds, Danish law, customs, and language prevailed. Its linguistic influence is still apparent.

Danish language member of the North Germanic group of the Indo-European language family, spoken in Denmark and Greenland and related to Icelandic, Faeroese, Norwegian, and Swedish. It has had a particularly strong influence on Norwegian. As one of the languages of the Vikings, who invaded and settled in parts of Britain during the 9th to 11th centuries, Old Danish had a strong influence on English.

Dante Alighieri 1265–1321. Italian poet. His masterpiece *La divina commedia/The Divine Comedy* 1307–21 is an epic account in three parts of his journey through Hell, Purgatory, and Paradise, during which he is guided part of the way by the poet Virgil; on a metaphorical level, the journey is also one of Dante's own spiritual development. Other works include the philosophical prose treatise *Convivio/The Banquet* 1306–08, the first major work of its kind to be written in Italian rather than Latin; *Monarchia/On World Government* 1310–13, expounding his political theories; *De vulgari eloquentia/Concerning the Vulgar Tongue* 1304–06, an original Latin work on Italian, its dialects, and kindred languages; and *Canzoniere/Lyrics,* containing his scattered lyrics.

Danton Georges Jacques 1759–1794. French revolutionary. Originally a lawyer, during the early years of the Revolution he was one of the most influential people in Paris. He organized the uprising Aug 10, 1792, that overthrew Louis XVI and the monarchy, roused the country to expel the Prussian invaders, and in April 1793 formed the revolutionary tribunal and the *Committee of Public Safety,* of which he was the leader until July of that year.

Thereafter he lost power to the ◊Jacobins, and, when he attempted to recover it, was arrested and guillotined.

Danube (German *Donau*) second longest of European rivers, rising on the eastern slopes of the Black Forest, and flowing 1,776 mi/2,858 km across Europe to enter the Black Sea in Romania by a swampy delta.

Danzig German name for the Polish port of ◊Gdansk.

Daphne in Greek mythology, a ◊nymph who was changed into a laurel tree to escape from ◊Apollo's amorous pursuit.

Dardanelles (ancient name *Hellespont,* Turkish name *Canakkale Bogazi*) Turkish strait connecting the Sea of Marmara with the Aegean Sea; its shores are formed by the Gallipoli peninsula on the NW and the main-

land of Anatolia on the SE. It is 47 mi/75 km long and 3–4 mi/ 5–6 km wide.

Dare Virginia b. 1587. First English child born in America. She was the granddaughter of John White, the governor of Roanoke colony (now in North Carolina). White returned to England soon after her birth, leaving Dare in Roanoke with the rest of her settler family. English communication with Roanoke was cut off for nearly four years during the war with Spain 1585–88. In 1591 the crew of an English ship found the colony deserted.

The enigmatic inscription "Croatan" carved in a tree led to speculation that the settlers, fearful of hostile Indians, had perhaps taken refuge with the friendly Croatan.

Dar es Salaam chief seaport in Tanzania, on the Indian Ocean, and capital of Tanzania until its replacement by ◊Dodoma 1974; population (1985) 1,394,000.

dark matter hypothetical matter that, according to current theories of ◊cosmology, makes up 90–99% of the mass of the universe but so far remains undetected. Dark matter, if shown to exist, would explain many currently unexplained gravitational effects in the movement of galaxies.

Darnley Henry Stewart or Stuart, Lord Darnley 1545–1567. British aristocrat, second husband of Mary Queen of Scots from 1565, and father of James I of England (James VI of Scotland).

On the advice of her secretary, David Rizzio, Mary refused Darnley the crown matrimonial; in revenge, Darnley led a band of nobles who murdered Rizzio in Mary's presence. Darnley was assassinated 1567.

He was killed in an explosion (while ill in bed), probably by James ◊Bothwell, who became Mary's third husband. Mary's role in the plot remains controversial.

Darwin Charles Robert 1809–1882. English scientist who developed the modern theory of ◊evolution and proposed, with Alfred Russel Wallace, the principle of ◊natural selection. After research in South America and the Galápagos Islands as naturalist on HMS *Beagle* 1831–36, Darwin published *On the Origin of Species by Means of Natural Selection or the Preservation of Favoured Races in the Struggle for Life* 1859. This explained the evolutionary process through the principles of natural and sexual selection. It aroused bitter controversy because it disagreed with the literal interpretation of the Book of Genesis in the Bible.

dash punctuation mark (—) that can be used singly or in pairs (as a type of parenthesis, to mark off a clearly subordinate part of a sentence). A single dash is used to represent a sudden break or interruption in dialogue or an abrupt change of subject.

data facts, figures, and symbols, especially as stored in computers. The term is often used to mean raw, unprocessed facts, as distinct from information, to which a meaning or interpretation has been applied.

databases and record-keeping systems many computer applications involve some form of structured data storage, or database. For example, an accounting system might be built around a database containing details of customers and suppliers. In larger computers, the database is organized in such a way that it is available to any program that needs it, without the programs needing to be aware of how the data are actually stored. The term database is also sometimes used for simple record-keeping systems, such as mailing lists, in which there are facilities for searching, sorting, and producing records.

data bus in computing, the electrical pathway, or ◊bus, used to carry data between the components of the computer.

data compression in computing, techniques for reducing the amount of storage needed for a given amount of data. They include word tokenization (in which frequently used words are stored as shorter codes), variable bit lengths (in which common characters are represented by fewer ◊bits than less common ones), and run-length encoding (in which a repeated value is stored once along with a count).

data dictionary in computing, a file that holds data about data—for example, lists of files, number of records in each file, and types of fields. Data dictionaries are used by database software to enable access to the data; they are not normally accessible to the user.

data logging in computing, the process, usually automatic, of capturing and recording a sequence of values for later processing and analysis by computer. For example, the level in a water-storage tank might be automatically logged every hour over a seven-day period, so that a computer could produce an analysis of water use.

data processing (DP) use of computers for performing clerical tasks such as stock control, payroll, and dealing with orders. DP systems are typically ◊batch systems, running on mainframe computers. DP is sometimes called EDP (electronic data processing).

data security in computing, precautions taken to prevent the loss or misuse of data, whether accidental or deliberate. These include measures that ensure that only authorized personnel can gain entry to a computer system or file, and regular procedures for storing and "backing up" data, which enable files to be retrieved or recreated in the event of loss, theft, or damage.

A number of ◊verification and ◊validation techniques may also be used to prevent data from being lost or corrupted by misprocessing.

date palm tree of the genus *Phoenix*. The female tree produces the fruit, dates, in bunches weighing 20–25 lb/9–11 kg. Dates are an important source of food in the Middle East, being rich in sugar; they are dried for export. The tree also supplies timber, and materials for baskets, rope, and animal feed.

dating science of determining the age of geological structures, rocks, and fossils, and placing them in the context of geological time. The techniques are of two types: relative dating and absolute dating. *Relative dating* can be carried out by identifying fossils of creatures that lived only at certain times (marker fossils), and by looking at the physical relationships of rocks to other rocks of a known age. *Absolute dating* is achieved by measuring how much of a rock's radioactive elements have changed since the rock was formed, using the process of radiometric dating.

Datura genus of plants *Datura*, family Solanaceae, such as jimson weed, with handsome trumpet-shaped blooms. Species in this genus have narcotic properties.

dauphin title of the eldest son of the kings of France, derived from the personal name of a count, whose lands, known as the *Dauphiné*, traditionally passed to the heir to the throne from 1349 to 1830.

David *c.*1060–970 BC. Second king of Israel. According to the Old Testament he played the harp for King Saul to banish Saul's melancholy; he later slew the Philistine giant Goliath with a sling and stone. After Saul's death David was anointed king at Hebron, took Jerusalem, and made it his capital.

David sent Uriah (a soldier in his army) to his death in the front line of battle so that he might marry his widow, Bathsheba. David and Bathsheba's son Solomon became the third king.

David probably wrote a few of the psalms (of the Book of Psalms) and was celebrated as a secular poet. In both Jewish and Christian belief, the messiah would be a descendant of David; Christians hold this prophecy to have been fulfilled by Jesus Christ.

David Jacques-Louis 1748–1825. French Neo-Classical painter. He was an active supporter of, and unofficial painter to, the republic during the French Revolution, and was imprisoned 1794–95. In his *Death of Marat* 1793 (Musées Royaux, Brussels), he turned political murder into Classical tragedy. Later he devoted himself to the newly created Empire in paintings such as the vast, pompous *Coronation of Napoleon* 1805–07 (Louvre, Paris).

David I 1084–1153. King of Scotland from 1124. The youngest son of Malcolm III Canmore and St Margaret, he was brought up in the English court of Henry I, and in 1113 married Matilda, widow of the 1st earl of Northampton.

He invaded England 1138 in support of Queen Matilda, but was defeated at Northallerton in the Battle of the Standard, and again 1141.

David II 1324–1371. King of Scotland from 1329, son of ◊Robert (I) the Bruce. David was married at the age of four to Joanna, daughter of Edward II of England. In 1346 David invaded England, was captured at the battle of Neville's Cross, and imprisoned for 11 years.

David, St or *Dewi* Patron saint of Wales, Christian abbot and bishop. According to legend he was the son of a prince of Dyfed and uncle of King Arthur; he was responsible for the adoption of the leek as the national emblem of Wales, but his own emblem is a dove. Feast day March 1.

da Vinci see ◊Leonardo da Vinci, Italian Renaissance artist.

Davis Bette 1908–1989. US actress. She entered films 1930, and established a reputation as a forceful dramatic actress with *Of Human Bondage* 1934. Later films included *Dangerous* 1935 and *Jezebel* 1938, both winning her Academy Awards; *All About Eve* 1950; and *Whatever Happened to Baby Jane?* 1962. She continued to make films throughout the 1980s such as *The Whales of August* 1987, in which she co-starred with Lillian Gish.

Davis Jefferson 1808–1889. US politician, president of the short-lived Confederate States of America 1861–65. He was a leader of the Southern Democrats in the US Senate from 1857, and a defender of "humane" slavery; in 1860 he issued a declaration in favor of secession from the US. During the Civil War he assumed strong political leadership, but often disagreed with military policy. He was imprisoned for two years after the war, one of the few cases of judicial retribution against Confederate leaders.

Davis Miles (Dewey, Jr) 1926–1991. US jazz trumpeter, composer, and bandleader. He was one of the most influential and innovative figures in jazz. He pioneered bebop with Charlie Parker 1945, cool jazz in

Davis, Jefferson Jefferson Davis, who became
president of the American Confederacy 1861–65
during the Civil War.

the 1950s, and jazz-rock fusion from the late 1960s.
His albums include *Birth of the Cool* 1957 (recorded
1949 and 1950), *Sketches of Spain* 1959, *Bitches Brew*
1970, and *Tutu* 1985.

Davisson Clinton Joseph 1881–1958. US physicist.
With Lester Germer (1896–1971), he discovered that
electrons can undergo diffraction, so proving Louis de
Broglie's theory that electrons, and therefore all matter, can show wavelike structure. George ◊Thomson
carried through the same research independently, and
in 1937 the two men shared the Nobel Prize for
Physics.

Born in Illinois, Davisson worked under Owen
Richardson at Princeton before joining Bell Telephone
Labs in 1917.

Davy Humphry 1778–1829. English chemist. He discovered, by electrolysis, the metallic elements sodium
and potassium in 1807, and calcium, boron, magnesium, strontium, and barium in 1808. In addition, he
established that chlorine is an element and proposed
that hydrogen is present in all acids. He invented the
"safety lamp" for use in mines where methane was
present, enabling miners to work in previously unsafe
conditions.

As a laboratory assistant in Bristol in 1799, he discovered the respiratory effects of laughing gas (nitrous
oxide).

Dayan Moshe 1915–1981. Israeli general and politician.
As minister of defense 1967 and 1969–74, he was
largely responsible for the victory over neighboring
Arab states in the 1967 Six-Day War, but he was criti-
cized for Israel's alleged unpreparedness in the 1973
October War and resigned along with Prime Minister
Golda Meir.

Foreign minister from 1977, Dayan resigned 1979 in
protest over the refusal of the Begin government to
negotiate with the Palestinians.

Day-Lewis Cecil 1904–1972. Irish poet, British poet
laureate 1968–1972. With W H Auden and Stephen
Spender, he was one of the influential left-wing poets

of the 1930s. He also wrote detective novels under the
pseudonym *Nicholas Blake*.

Day-Lewis Daniel 1958– . English actor, noted for his
chameleonlike versatility. He first came to prominence in *My Beautiful Laundrette* and *A Room With a
View* both 1985. He won an Academy Award for his
performance as Christy Brown, the painter suffering
from cerebral palsy, in *My Left Foot* 1989. His other
films include *The Last of the Mohicans* 1992, *The Age of
Innocence*, and *In the Name of the Father* both 1993.

daylight saving time legal time for a given zone that is
one hour later than the standard time based on universal coordinated time (see ◊time). It is used to provide additional daylight during the summer at the
end of the usual working day.

Dayton city in Ohio; population (1990) 182,000. It produces precision machinery, household appliances,
and electrical equipment. It has an aeronautical
research center and a Roman Catholic university and
was the home of aviators Wilbur and Orville Wright.

The Aviation Hall of Fame is in the city, and Wright-
Patterson Air Force Base, which has an aviation
museum, is nearby. Dayton was settled in 1796.

dBASE family of microcomputer programs used for
manipulating large quantities of data; also, a related
◊fourth-generation language. The first version, dBASE
II, appeared in 1981; it has since become the basis for
a recognized standard for database applications,
known as Xbase.

D-day June 6, 1944, the day of the Allied invasion of
Normandy under the command of General
Eisenhower, with the aim of liberating Western Europe
from German occupation. The Anglo-American invasion fleet landed on the Normandy beaches on the
stretch of coast between the Orne River and St
Marcouf. Artificial harbors known as "Mulberries"
were constructed and towed across the Channel so
that equipment and armaments could be unloaded on
to the beaches. After overcoming fierce resistance the
allies broke through the German defenses; Paris was
liberated on Aug 25, and Brussels on Sept 2. D-day is
also a term now used for any crucial day.

DDT abbreviation for *dichloro-diphenyl-trichloroethane* ($ClC_6H_5)_2CHCHCl_2$) insecticide discovered
1939 by Swiss chemist Paul Müller. It is useful in the
control of insects that spread malaria, but resistant
strains develop. DDT is highly toxic and persists in
the environment and in living tissue. Its use is now
banned in most countries, but it continues to be used
on food plants in Latin America.

deadly nightshade another name for ◊belladonna, a
poisonous plant.

Dead Sea large lake, partly in Israel and partly in
Jordan, lying 1,293 ft/394 m below sea level; area 394
sq mi/1,020 sq km. The chief river entering it is the
Jordan; it has no outlet and the water is very salty.

Dead Sea Scrolls collection of ancient scrolls (rolls of
writing) and fragments of scrolls found 1947–56 in
caves on the W side of the Jordan, 7 mi/12 km S of
Jericho and 1 ml/2 km from the N end of the Dead
Sea, at Qumran. They include copies of Old Testament
books a thousand years older than those previously
known to be extant. The documents date mainly from
about 150 BC –AD 68, when the monastic community
that owned them, the Essenes, was destroyed by the
Romans because of its support for a revolt against
their rule.

Dean Dizzy (Jay Hanna) 1911–1974. US baseball player. He joined the St Louis Cardinals 1930 and made his major-league pitching debut 1932. Winning 30 games and leading the Cardinals to a World Series win, he was voted the National League's most valuable player 1934. Following an injury in the 1937 All-Star Game, his pitching suffered. He was traded to the Chicago Cubs, for whom he pitched until his retirement 1941.

Dean was elected to the Baseball Hall of Fame 1953.

Dean James (Byron) 1931–1955. US actor. Killed in an automobile accident after the public showing of his first film, *East of Eden* 1955, he posthumously became a cult hero with *Rebel Without a Cause* 1955 and *Giant* 1956.

He has become a symbol of teenage rebellion against American middle-class values.

Dean, James (Byron) American film star and cult hero James Dean, who personified the restless American youth of the 1950s. In just over a year, with only three films to his name, Dean became a screen icon. His posthumous growth in popularity reached legendary proportions, rivaling that of Rudolf Valentino.

death cessation of all life functions, so that the molecules and structures associated with living things become disorganized and indistinguishable from similar molecules found in non-living things. Living organisms expend large amounts of energy preventing their complex molecules from breaking up; cellular repair and replacement are vital processes in multicellular organisms. At death this energy is no longer available, and the processes of disorganization become inevitable. In medicine, death used to be pronounced with the permanent cessation of heartbeat. The advent of life-support equipment has made this point sometimes difficult to determine, and in controversial cases a person is now pronounced dead when the brain ceases to control the vital functions even if breathing and heartbeat are maintained (artificially).

death cap fungus ◊*Amanita phalloides*, the most poisonous mushroom known. The fruiting body has a scaly white cap and a collarlike structure near the base of the stalk.

death penalty another name for ◊capital punishment.

Death Valley depression 140 mi/225 km long and 4–16 mi/6–26 km wide in SE California, US. At 280 ft/85 m below sea level, it is the lowest point in North America. Bordering mountains rise to 10,000 ft/3,000 m. It is one of the world's hottest and driest places, with temperatures sometimes exceeding 125°F/51°C and an annual rainfall of less than 2 in/5.1 cm. Borax, iron ore, tungsten, gypsum, and salts are extracted.

deathwatch beetle any wood-boring beetle of the family Anobiidae, especially *Xestobium rufovillosum*. The larvae live in oaks and willows, and sometimes cause damage by boring in old furniture or structural timbers. To attract the female, the male beetle produces a ticking sound by striking his head on a wooden surface, and this is taken by the superstitious as a warning of approaching death.

Debrecen third largest city in Hungary, 120 mi/193 km E of Budapest, in the Great Plain (*Alföld*) region; population (1988) 217,000. It produces tobacco, agricultural machinery, and pharmaceuticals. Lajos ◊Kossuth declared Hungary independent of the ◊Hapsburgs here 1849. It is a commercial center and has a university founded 1912.

de Broglie see French physicists Maurice and Louis de ◊Broglie.

debt something that is owed by a person or organization, usually money, goods, or services, usually as a result of borrowing. Debt servicing is the payment of interest on a debt. The national debt of a country is the total money owed by the national government to private individuals, banks, and so on; international debt, the money owed by one country to another, began on a large scale with the investment in foreign countries by newly industrialized countries in the late 19th–early 20th centuries. International debt became a global problem as a result of the oil crisis of the 1970s.

debugging finding and removing errors, or ◊bugs, from a computer program or system.

Debussy (Achille-) Claude 1862–1918. French composer. He broke with German Romanticism and introduced new qualities of melody and harmony based on the whole-tone scale, evoking oriental music. His work includes *Prélude à l'après-midi d'un faune/Prelude to the Afternoon of a Faun* 1894, illustrating a poem by Mallarmé, and the opera *Pelléas et Mélisande* 1902.

DEC (abbreviation for *Digital Equipment Corporation*) US computer manufacturer. DEC was founded by US computer scientists Kenneth Olsen and Harlan Anderson, and was the first ◊minicomputer manufacturer. It became the world's second largest computer manufacturer, after ◊IBM, but made huge losses in the early 1990s. DEC's most successful computers were the PDP-11 and the VAX. The former was used in the creation of the ◊Unix operating system.

decathlon two-day athletic competition for men consisting of ten events: 100 meters, long jump, shot put, high jump, 400 meters (day one); 110 meters hurdles, discus, pole vault, javelin, 1,500 meters (day two). Points are awarded for performances, and the winner is the athlete with the greatest aggregate score. The decathlon is an Olympic event.

Decatur Stephen 1779–1820. US naval hero, who distinguished himself in the war with the Barbary pirates at Tripoli 1801–05 when he succeeded in boarding and burning the *Philadelphia*, a US frigate captured by the enemy. During the War of 1812, he commanded three vessels, captured the British frigate *Macedonian*, and was blockaded by the British. Then in Jan 1815, unaware that the war was over, he battled four British ships, taking one but surrendering to the three pursuers. In 1815 he was again sent to the Barbary Coast, where he forced the bey of Algiers to sign the treaty ending US tribute to Algeria.

decay, radioactive see ◊radioactive decay.

decibel unit (symbol dB) of measure used originally to compare sound intensities and subsequently electrical or electronic power outputs; now also used to compare voltages. An increase of 10 dB is equivalent to a 10-fold increase in intensity or power, and a 20-fold increase in voltage. A whisper has an intensity of 20 dB; 140 dB (a jet aircraft taking off nearby) is the threshold of pain.

deciduous of trees and shrubs, that shed their leaves at the end of the growing season or during a dry season to reduce ◊transpiration, the loss of water by evaporation. Examples of deciduous trees are oak and maple.

decimal fraction a ◊fraction in which the denominator is any higher power of 10. Thus $^3/_{10}$, $^3/_{100}$ and $^{23}/_{1000}$ are decimal fractions and are normally expressed as 0.3, 0.51, 0.023. The use of decimals greatly simplifies addition and multiplication of fractions, though not all fractions can be expressed exactly as decimal fractions.

decimal number system or *denary number system* the most commonly used number system, to the base ten. Decimal numbers do not necessarily contain a decimal point; 563, 5.63, and –563 are all decimal numbers. Other systems are mainly used in computing and include the ◊binary number system, octal number system, and ◊hexadecimal number system.

Declaration of Independence historic US document stating the theory of government on which the US was founded, based on the right "to life, liberty, and the pursuit of happiness". The statement was issued by the ◊Continental Congress July 4, 1776, renouncing all allegiance to the British crown and ending the political connection with Britain.

decoder in computing, an electronic circuit used to select one of several possible data pathways. Decoders are, for example, used to direct data to individual memory locations within a computer's immediate access memory.

decomposition process whereby a chemical compound is reduced to its component substances. In biology, it is the destruction of dead organisms either by chemical reduction or by the action of decomposers.

Deconstructionism in architecture, a style that fragments forms and space by taking the usual building elements of floors, walls, and ceilings and sliding them apart to create a sense of disorientation and movement.

Its proponents include Frank Gehry and Peter Eisenman in the US, Zaha Hadid in the UK, and Coop Himmelbau in Austria.

Dee river in Grampian Region, Scotland; length 87 mi/139 km. From its source in the Cairngorm Mountains, it flows E into the North Sea at Aberdeen (by an artificial channel). It is noted for salmon fishing.

deed legal document that passes an interest in property or binds a person to perform or abstain from some action. Deeds are of two kinds: indenture and deed poll. *Indentures* bind two or more parties in mutual obligations. A *deed poll* is made by one party only, such as when a person changes his or her name.

Bargain sale deeds convey title to property by contract but do not guarantee title unless they include a specific covenant to that effect; quitclaim deeds convey a grantor's interest but do not guarantee title; warranty deeds convey interest and guarantee title to the subject property.

deep-sea trench another term for ocean trench.

deer any of various ruminant, even-toed, hoofed mammals belonging to the family Cervidae. The male typically has a pair of antlers, shed and regrown each year. Most species of deer are forest-dwellers and are distributed throughout Eurasia and North America, but are absent from Australia and Africa S of the Sahara.

Native to North America are white-tailed deer *Odocoileus viginianus*, mule deer *O. hemionus*, wapiti or elk *Cervus canadensis*, moose *Alces alces*, and caribou or reindeer *Rangifer tarandus*. The last two also occur in Eurasia. Red deer *Cervus elaphus*, roe deer *Capreolus capreolus*, and fallow deer *Dama dama* are typical Eurasian species.

de Falla Manuel. Spanish composer; see ◊Falla, Manuel de.

Defender of the Faith one of the titles of the English sovereign, conferred on Henry VIII 1521 by Pope Leo X in recognition of the king's treatise against the Protestant Martin Luther. It appears on coins in the abbreviated form *F.D.* (Latin *Fidei Defensor*).

deflation in economics, a reduction in the level of economic activity, usually caused by an increase in interest rates and reduction in the money supply, increased taxation, or a decline in government expenditure.

Defoe Daniel 1660–1731. English writer. His *Robinson Crusoe* 1719, though purporting to be a factual account of shipwreck and solitary survival, was influential in the development of the novel. The fictional *Moll Flanders* 1722 and the partly factual *A Journal of the Plague Year* 1724 are still read for their concrete realism. A prolific journalist and pamphleteer, he was imprisoned 1702–04 for the ironic *The Shortest Way with Dissenters* 1702.

Defoe wrote numerous pamphlets and first achieved fame with the satire *The True-Born Englishman* 1701. His version of the contemporary short story "True Relation of the Apparition of one Mrs Veal" 1706 first revealed a gift for realistic narrative.

de Forest Lee 1873–1961. US inventor who held more than 300 patents, including the triode tube (which he called the audion) in 1906, precursor to the radio tube and one of the most influential inventions of the century. It generated, detected, and amplified radio waves. He also developed a movie-sound system and contributed to the phonograph, telephone, television, radar, and diathermy.

deforestation destruction of forest for timber, fuel, charcoal burning, and clearing for agriculture and extractive industries, such as mining, without planting new trees to replace those lost (reforestation) or working on a cycle that allows the natural forest to regenerate. Deforestation causes fertile soil to be blown away or washed into rivers, leading to ◊soil erosion, drought, flooding, and loss of wildlife. It may also increase the carbon dioxide content of the atmosphere and intensify the ◊greenhouse effect, because there are fewer trees absorbing carbon dioxide from the air for photosynthesis.

Degas (Hilaire Germain) Edgar 1834–1917. French Impressionist painter and sculptor. He devoted himself to lively, informal studies (often using pastels) of ballet, horse racing, and young women working. From the 1890s he turned increasingly to sculpture, modeling figures in wax in a fluent, naturalistic style.

de Gaulle Charles André Joseph Marie 1890–1970. French general and first president of the Fifth Republic 1958–69. He organized the Free French troops fighting the Nazis 1940–44, was head of the provisional French government 1944–46, and leader of his own Gaullist party. In 1958 the national assembly asked him to form a government during France's economic recovery and to solve the crisis in Algeria. He became president at the end of 1958, having changed the constitution to provide for a presidential system, and served until 1969.

Reelected president 1965, he violently quelled student demonstrations May 1968 when they were joined by workers. The Gaullist party, reorganized as Union des Democrats pour la Cinquième République, won an overwhelming majority in the elections of the same year. In 1969 he resigned after the defeat of the government in a referendum on constitutional reform. He retired to the village of Colombey-les-Deux-Eglises in NE France.

degree in mathematics, a unit (symbol °) of measurement of an angle or arc. A circle or complete rotation is divided into 360°. A degree may be subdivided into 60 minutes (symbol ′), and each minute may be subdivided in turn into 60 seconds (symbol ′).

Temperature is also measured in degrees, which are divided on a decimal scale. See also ◊Celsius, and ◊Fahrenheit.

De Havilland Geoffrey 1882–1965. British aircraft designer who designed and whose company produced the Moth biplane, the Mosquito fighter-bomber of World War II, and the postwar Comet, the world's first jet-driven airliner to enter commercial service.

Deirdre in Celtic mythology, the beautiful intended bride of Conchobar. She eloped with Noísi, and died of sorrow when Conchobar killed him and his brothers.

deism belief in a supreme being; but the term usually refers to a movement of religious thought in the 17th and 18th centuries, characterized by the belief in a rational "religion of nature" as opposed to the orthodox beliefs of Christianity.

Deists believed that God is the source of natural law but does not intervene directly in the affairs of the world, and that the only religious duty of humanity is to be virtuous.

de Klerk F(rederik) W(illem) 1936– . South African National Party politician, president 1989–94. He replaced P.W. Botha as party leader Feb 1989 and as state president Aug 1989. Projecting himself as a pragmatic conservative who sought gradual reform of the apartheid system, he won the Sept 1989 elections for his party, but with a reduced majority. In Feb 1990 he ended the ban on the ◊African National Congress (ANC) opposition movement and released its effective leader, Nelson Mandela, and by June 1991 he repealed all racially discriminating laws. He entered into negotiations with the ANC Dec 1991 and by Dec

1993 had gained parliament's approval of a new nonracial constitution. After a landslide victory for Mandela and the ANC in the first universal suffrage elections April 1994, De Klerk became second executive deputy president.

He was awarded the Nobel Prize for Peace jointly with Mandela 1993.

de Kooning Willem 1904– . Dutch-born US painter. He emigrated to the US 1926 and worked as a commercial artist. After World War II he became, together with Jackson Pollock, one of the leaders of the Abstract Expressionist movement, although he retained figural images, painted with quick, violent brushstrokes. His *Women* series, exhibited 1953, was criticized for its grotesque depictions of women.

De Kooning joined the faculty of the Yale Art School and became a member of the National Institute of Arts 1960 and received the Presidential Medal of Freedom 1964. His paintings were commissioned for numerous Work Projects Administration (WPA) projects, and he won praise for his mural in the Hall of Pharmacy at the 1939 New York World's Fair.

Delacroix Eugène 1798–1863. French Romantic painter. His prolific output included religious and historical subjects and portraits of friends, among them the musicians Paganini and Chopin. Antagonistic to the French academic tradition, he evolved a highly colored, fluid style, as in *The Death of Sardanapalus* 1829 (Louvre, Paris).

Delaware state in NE US; nickname First State/Diamond State *area* 5,300 sq km/2,046 sq mi *capital* Dover *cities* Wilmington, Newark *physical* two main divisions: (1) hilly and wooded; (2) gently undulating to the sea *features* one of the most industrialized states; headquarters of the Du Pont chemical firm; Rehoboth Beach; Winterthur Museum *industries* dairy, poultry, and market-garden produce; chemicals; motor vehicles; textiles *population* (1990) 666,200 *famous people* Du Pont family, J.P. Marquand *history* the first settlers were Dutch 1631 and Swedes 1638, but in 1664 the area was captured by the British and transferred to William Penn. A separate colony from 1704, it fought in the American Revolution as a state 1776, was one of the original 13 states, and was the first state to ratify the US Constitution, Dec 7, 1787. In 1802 the Du Pont gunpowder mill was established near Wilmington. Completion of the Philadelphia–Baltimore railroad line 1838, through Wilmington, fostered development. Delaware was famous as a chemical center by the early 1900s. Two auto-assembly plants and an oil refinery were built after World War II.

Delhi capital of India, comprising the walled city of *Old Delhi* (built 1639), situated on the west bank of the river Jumna, and *New Delhi* to the S, largely designed by English architect Edwin Lutyens and chosen to replace Calcutta as the seat of government 1912 (completed 1929; officially inaugurated 1931). Delhi is the administrative center of the Union Territory of Delhi and India's largest commercial and communications center; population (1991) 8,375,000.

delirium in medicine, a state of acute confusion in which the subject is incoherent, frenzied, and out of touch with reality. It is often accompanied by delusions or hallucinations.

Delius Frederick (Theodore Albert) 1862–1934. English composer. His haunting, richly harmonious works include the opera *A Village Romeo and Juliet* 1901; the choral pieces *Appalachia* 1903, *Sea Drift* 1904, *A Mass of Life* 1905; orchestral works such as *In a Summer Garden* 1908 and *A Song of the High Hills* 1911; chamber music; and songs.

His romantic style of writing was influenced by Grieg.

Delors Jacques 1925– . French socialist politician, finance minister 1981–84. As president of the European Commission 1984–94 he oversaw significant budgetary reform and the move toward a free European Community (now European Union) market, with increased powers residing in Brussels. Although criticized by some as being too federalist in outlook, he generally enjoyed a high-profile, successful presidency, including overseeing final ratification and implementation of the Maastricht Treaty on European union.

Delphi city of ancient Greece, situated in a rocky valley north of the gulf of Corinth, on the southern slopes of Mount Parnassus, site of a famous ◊oracle in the temple of Apollo. The site was supposed to be the center of the Earth and was marked by a conical stone, the *omphelos*. The oracle was interpreted by priests from the inspired utterances of the Pythian priestess until it was closed down by the Roman emperor Theodosius I AD 390.

delphinium any plant of the genus *Delphinium* belonging to the buttercup family Ranunculaceae. There are some 250 species, including the great flowered larkspur *D.grandiflorum*, an Asian form and one of the ancestors of the garden delphinium. Most species have blue, purple, or white flowers in a long spike.

del Sarto Andrea Italian Renaissance painter; see ◊Andrea del Sarto.

delta tract of land at a river's mouth, composed of silt deposited as the water slows on entering the sea. Familiar examples of large deltas are those of the Mississippi, Ganges and Brahmaputra, Rhône, Po, Danube, and Nile; the shape of the Nile delta is like the Greek letter *delta* Δ, and thus gave rise to the name.

de Maiziere Lothar 1940– . German politician, leader 1989–90 of the conservative Christian Democratic Union in East Germany. He became premier after East Germany's first democratic election April 1990 and negotiated the country's reunion with West Germany. In Dec 1990 he resigned from Chancellor Kohl's cabinet and as deputy leader of the CDU, following allegations that he had been an informer to the Stasi (East German secret police). In Sept 1991, he resigned from the legislature, effectively leaving active politics.

dementia mental deterioration as a result of physical changes in the brain. It may be due to degenerative change, circulatory disease, infection, injury, or chronic poisoning. *Senile dementia*, a progressive loss of mental faculties such as memory and orientation, is typically a disease process of old age, and can be accompanied by ◊depression.

Demeter in Greek mythology, the goddess of agriculture (Roman Ceres), daughter of Cronus and Rhea, and mother of Persephone by Zeus.

Demeter and Persephone were worshiped in a sanctuary at Eleusis, where one of the foremost ◊mystery religions of Greece was celebrated. She was later identified with the Egyptian goddess ◊Isis.

DeMille Agnes George 1905–1989. US choreographer. After becoming a member of the Ballet Theater, she choreographed a long string of Broadway hits, including *Oklahoma!* 1943, *Carousel* 1945, *Brigadoon* 1947, *Gentlemen Prefer Blondes* 1949, and *Paint Your Wagon* 1951. She founded the Agnes DeMille Dance Theater 1953.

democracy government by the people, usually through elected representatives. In the modern world, democracy has developed from the American and French revolutions.

Democratic Party one of the two main political parties of the US. It tends to be the party of the working person, as opposed to the Republicans, the party of big business, but the divisions between the two are not clear cut. Its stronghold since the Civil War has traditionally been industrial urban centers and the Southern states, but conservative Southern Democrats were largely supportive of Republican positions in the 1980s and helped elect President Reagan. Bill Clinton became the first Democrat president for 13 years in 1993.

demography study of the size, structure, dispersement, and development of human populations to establish reliable statistics on such factors as birth and death rates, marriages and divorces, life expectancy, and migration. Demography is used to calculate life tables, which give the life expectancy of members of the population by sex and age.

Demosthenes *c.*384–322 BC. Athenian politician, famed for his oratory. From 351 BC he led the party that advocated resistance to the growing power of ◊Philip of Macedon, and in his *Philippics*, a series of speeches, incited the Athenians to war. This policy resulted in the defeat of Chaeronea 338, and the establishment of Macedonian supremacy. After the death of Alexander he organized a revolt; when it failed, he took poison to avoid capture by the Macedonians.

Demotic Greek common or vernacular variety of the modern ◊Greek language.

demotic script cursive (joined) writing derived from Egyptian hieratic script, itself a cursive form of ◊hieroglyphic.

Demotic documents are known from the 6th century BC to about AD 470. It was written horizontally, from right to left.

Dempsey Jack (William Harrison) 1895–1983. US heavyweight boxing champion, nicknamed "the Manassa Mauler". He beat Jess Willard 1919 to win the title and held it until 1926, when he lost it to Gene Tunney. He engaged in the "Battle of the Long Count" with Tunney 1927.

Dene term used in Canada since the 1970s to describe the Native Americans (Athabaskan Indians) in the Northwest Territories. The official body representing them is called the Dene Nation.

Deneb or *Alpha Cygni* brightest star in the constellation Cygnus, and the 19th brightest star in the sky. It is one of the greatest supergiant stars known, with a true luminosity of about 60,000 times that of the Sun. Deneb is about 1,800 light-years from Earth.

Deng Xiaoping or *Teng Hsiao-ping* 1904– . Chinese political leader. A member of the Chinese Communist Party (CCP) from the 1920s, he took part in the Long March 1934–36. He was in the Politburo from 1955 until ousted in the Cultural Revolution 1966–69. Reinstated in the 1970s, he gradually took power and introduced a radical economic modernization program. He retired from the Politburo 1987 and from his last official position (as chair of State Military Commission) March 1990, but remained influential behind the scenes.

denier unit used in measuring the fineness of yarns, equal to the mass in grams of 9,000 meters of yarn. Thus 9,000 meters of 15 denier nylon, used in nylon stockings, weighs 0.5 oz/15 g, and in this case the thickness of thread would be 0.0017 in/0.00425 mm. The term is derived from the French silk industry; the *denier* was an old French silver coin.

In the US and Canada a unit called the drex, equal to the mass of 10,000 meters is used. The tex, equal to the mass of 1,000 meters, is the most common unit in the textile industry.

De Niro Robert 1943– . US actor of great magnetism and physical presence. He won Academy Awards for his performances in *The Godfather Part II* 1974 and *Raging Bull* 1980, for which role he put on weight in the interests of authenticity as the boxer gone to seed, Jake LaMotta. His other films include *Mean Streets* 1973, *Taxi Driver* 1976, *The Deer Hunter* 1978, *The Untouchables* 1987, *Midnight Run* 1988, and *Cape Fear* 1991. He showed his versatility in *The King of Comedy* 1982 and other Martin Scorsese films.

Denktas Rauf R 1924– . Turkish-Cypriot nationalist politician. In 1975 the Turkish Federated State of Cyprus (TFSC) was formed in the northern third of the island, with Denktas as its head, and in 1983 he became president of the breakaway Turkish Republic of Northern Cyprus (TRNC).

Denmark Kingdom of (*Kongeriget Danmark*) *area* 16,627 sq mi/43,075 sq km *capital* Copenhagen *towns and cities* Aarhus, Odense, Aalborg, Esbjerg, all ports *physical* comprises the Jutland peninsula and about 500 islands (100 inhabited) including Bornholm in the Baltic Sea; the land is flat and cultivated; sand dunes and lagoons on the W coast and long inlets (fjords) on the E; the main island is Sjælland (Zealand), where most of Copenhagen is located (the rest is on the island of Amager) *territories* the dependencies of Faeroe Islands and Greenland *features* Kronborg Castle in Helsingør (Elsinore); Tivoli Gardens (Copenhagen); Legoland Park in Sillund *head of state* Queen Margrethe II from 1972 *head of government* Poul Nyrup Rasmussen from 1993 *political system* liberal democracy *political parties* Social Democrats (SD), left of center; Conservative People's Party (KF), moderate center-right; Liberal Party (V), center-left; Socialist People's Party (SF),

moderate left-wing; Radical Liberals (RV), radical internationalist, left of center; Center Democrats (CD), moderate centrist; Progress Party (FP), radical antibureaucratic; Christian People's Party (KrF), interdenominational, family values *exports* bacon, dairy produce, eggs, fish, mink pelts, automobile and aircraft parts, electrical equipment, textiles, chemicals *currency* krone *population* (1993) 5,180,000; growth rate 0% p.a. *life expectancy* men 73, women 79 *languages* Danish (official); there is a German-speaking minority *religion* Lutheran 97% *literacy* 99% *GNP* \$23,660 per head (1991) *chronology 1940–45* Occupied by Germany. *1945* Iceland's independence recognized. *1947* Frederik IX succeeded Christian X. *1948* Home rule granted for Faeroe Islands. *1949* Became a founding member of NATO. *1960* Joined European Free Trade Association (EFTA). *1973* Left EFTA and joined European Economic Community (EEC). *1979* Home rule granted for Greenland. *1985* Strong non-nuclear movement in evidence. *1992* Rejection of Maastricht Treaty in national referendum. *1993* Schlüter resigned; replaced by Poul Nyrup Rasmussen at head of SD-led coalition government. Second referendum approved Maastricht Treaty after modifications. *1994* Left-wing gains in general election. Rasmussen-led coalition continued in power.

Denpasar capital town of Bali in the Lesser Sunda Islands of Indonesia; population (1980) 88,100. Industries include food processing, machinery, papermaking and printing, and handicrafts. There is a university (1962) and, housed in the temple and palace, a museum of Balinese art.

density measure of the compactness of a substance; it is equal to its mass per unit volume and is measured in kg per cubic meter/lb per cubic foot. Density is a scalar quantity. The density D of a mass m occupying a volume V is given by the formula: $D = m/V$ Relative density is the ratio of the density of a substance to that of water at 4°C.

dental formula way of showing what an animal's teeth are like. The dental formula consists of eight numbers separated by a line into two rows. The four above the line represent the teeth in one side of the upper jaw, starting at the front. If this reads 2 1 2 3 (as for humans) it means two incisors, one canine, two premolars, and three molars (see ◊tooth). The numbers below the line represent the lower jaw. The total number of teeth can be calculated by adding up all the numbers and multiplying by two.

dentistry care and treatment of the teeth and gums. *Orthodontics* deals with the straightening of the teeth for esthetic and clinical reasons, and *periodontics* with care of the supporting tissue (bone and gums).
The earliest dental school was opened in Baltimore, Maryland, 1839. An International Dental Federation was founded 1900.

dentition type and number of teeth in a species. Different kinds of teeth have different functions; a grass-eating animal will have large molars for grinding its food, whereas a meat-eater will need powerful canines for catching and killing its prey. The teeth that are less useful may be reduced in size or missing altogether. An animal's dentition is represented diagramatically by a ◊dental formula.

Denver city and capital of Colorado, on the South Platte River, near the foothills of the Rocky Mountains; population (1990) 467,600, Denver–Boulder metropolitan area 1,848,300. It is a processing

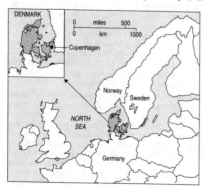

and distribution center for a large agricultural area and for natural resources (minerals, oil, gas).

deoxyribonucleic acid full name of ◊DNA.

Depardieu Gérard 1948– . French actor. He is renowned for his imposing physique and screen presence. His films include *Deux Hommes dans la ville* 1973, *Le Camion* 1977, *Mon Oncle d'Amérique* 1980, *The Moon in the Gutter* 1983, *Jean de Florette* 1985, and *Cyrano de Bergerac* 1990. His English-speaking films include the US romantic comedy *Green Card* 1990, *1492—Conquest of Paradise* 1992, and *My Father the Hero* 1994.

depreciation in economics, the decline of a currency's value in relation to other currencies. Depreciation also describes the fall in value of an asset (such as factory machinery) resulting from age, wear and tear, or other circumstances. It is an important factor in assessing company profits and tax liabilities.

depression in economics, a period of exceptionally low output and investment, with high unemployment. Specifically, the term describes two periods of crisis in world economy 1873–96 and 1929–39, also known as panics.

depression or *cyclone* or *low* in meteorology, a region of low atmospheric pressure. A depression forms as warm, moist air from the tropics mixes with cold, dry polar air, producing warm and cold boundaries (◊fronts) and unstable weather—low cloud and drizzle, showers, or fierce storms. The warm air, being less dense, rises above the cold air to produce the area of low pressure on the ground. Air spirals in toward the center of the depression in an counterclockwise direction in the northern hemisphere, clockwise in the southern hemisphere, generating winds up to gale force. Depressions tend to travel eastward and can remain active for several days.

A deep depression is one in which the pressure at the center is very much lower than that round about; it produces very strong winds, as opposed to a shallow depression in which the winds are comparatively light. A severe depression in the tropics is called a ◊hurricane, tropical cyclone, or typhoon, and is a great danger to shipping; a ◊tornado is a very intense, rapidly swirling depression, with a diameter of only a few hundred feet or so.

depression emotional state characterized by sadness, unhappy thoughts, apathy, and dejection. Sadness is a normal response to major losses such as bereavement or unemployment. After childbirth, postnatal depression is common. However, clinical depression, which is prolonged or unduly severe, often requires treatment, such as antidepressant medication, cognitive therapy, or, in very rare cases, electroconvulsive therapy (ECT), in which an electrical current is passed through the brain.

Depression costs the US around $12.4 billion each year in treatment. Another $23.8 billion is paid for by employers, arising from absenteeism and lost productivity.

De Quincey Thomas 1785–1859. English author. His works include *Confessions of an English Opium-Eater* 1821 and the essays "On the Knocking at the Gate in Macbeth" 1823 and "On Murder Considered as One of the Fine Arts" 1827. He was a friend of the poets Wordsworth and Coleridge.

Derby industrial city in Derbyshire, England; population (1991) 214,000. Products include rail locomotives, Rolls-Royce automobiles and airplane engines,

chemicals, paper, and electrical, mining, and engineering equipment.

Derby Edward (George Geoffrey Smith) Stanley, 14th Earl of Derby 1799–1869. British politician, prime minister 1852, 1858–59, and 1866–68.

Originally a Whig, he became secretary for the colonies 1830, and introduced the bill for the abolition of slavery. He joined the Tories 1834, and the split in the Tory Party over Robert Peel's free-trade policy gave Derby the leadership for 20 years.

Derbyshire county of N central England *area* 1,015 sq mi/2,630 sq km *towns and cities* Matlock (administrative headquarters), Derby, Chesterfield, Ilkeston *features* Peak District National Park (including Kinder Scout 2,088 ft/636 m); rivers: Derwent, Dove, Rother, Trent; Chatsworth House, Bakewell (seat of the Duke of Devonshire); Haddon Hall *industries* cereals; dairy and sheep farming; textiles; there have been pit and factory closures, but the area is being redeveloped, and there are large reserves of fluorite *population* (1991) 928,600 *famous people* Samuel Richardson, Thomas Cook, Marquess Curzon of Kedleston. *industries* cereals; dairy and sheep farming.

deregulation action to abolish or reduce government controls and supervision over private economic activities, as with the deregulation of the US airline industry 1978. Its purpose is to improve competition. Increased competition had the effect, in some areas, of driving smaller companies out of business. A tremendous increase in mergers, acquisitions, and bankruptcies followed deregulation as the stronger companies consumed the weaker. A wider array of services and lower prices in some industries also have resulted; see also ◊monetarism; ◊privatization.

De Roburt Hammer 1923–1992. President of Nauru 1968–76, 1978–83, and 1987–89. During the country's occupation 1942–45, he was deported to Japan. He became head chief of Nauru 1956 and was elected the country's first president 1968. He secured only a narrow majority in the 1987 elections and in 1989 was ousted on a no-confidence motion.

Derry county of Northern Ireland *area* 799 sq mi/2,070 sq km *towns and cities* Derry (county town, formerly Londonderry), Coleraine, Portstewart *features* rivers Foyle, Bann, and Roe; borders Lough Neagh *industries* mainly agricultural, but farming is hindered by the very heavy rainfall; flax, cattle, sheep, food processing, textiles, light engineering *population* (1981) 187,000 *famous people* Joyce Cary.

Derry (Gaelic *doire* "a place of oaks") historic city and port on the river Foyle, County Derry, Northern Ireland; population (1981) 89,100. It was known as Londonderry until 1984. Industries include textiles, chemicals, shirt manufacturing, and acetylene from naphtha. *features* the Protestant cathedral of St Columba (1633); the Guildhall (rebuilt 1912), containing stained glass windows presented by livery companies of the City of London.

Descartes René 1596–1650. French philosopher and mathematician. He believed that commonly accepted knowledge was doubtful because of the subjective nature of the senses, and attempted to rebuild human knowledge using as his foundation *cogito ergo sum* ("I think, therefore I am"). He also believed that the entire material universe could be explained in terms of mathematical physics, and founded coordinate geometry as a way of defining and manipulating geometrical shapes by means of algebraic expressions.

◊Cartesian coordinates, the means by which points are represented in this system, are named for him. Descartes also established the science of optics, and helped to shape contemporary theories of astronomy and animal behavior.

desert arid area without sufficient rainfall and, consequently, vegetation to support human life. The term includes the ice areas of the polar regions (known as cold deserts). Almost 33% of the Earth's land surface is desert, and this proportion is increasing.

De Sica Vittorio 1901–1974. Italian film director and actor. His *The Thief* 1949 is a landmark of Italian neorealism. Later films included *Umberto D* 1955, *Two Women* 1960, and *The Garden of the Finzi-Continis* 1971. His considerable acting credits include *The Earrings of Madame de...* 1953 and *The Millionaires* 1960. He was born in Sora, Caserta.

desktop publishing (DTP) use of microcomputers for small-scale typesetting and page makeup. DTP systems are capable of producing camera-ready pages (pages ready for photographing and printing), made up of text and graphics, with text set in different typefaces and sizes. The page can be previewed on the screen before final printing on a laser printer.

Des Moines capital city of Iowa, on the Des Moines River, a tributary of the Mississippi; population (1990) 193,200. It is a major road, railroad, and air center. Industries include printing, banking, insurance, and food processing.

Drake University is here. The Des Moines Art Center was designed by Eliel Saarinen. Incorporated 1851, Des Moines became the state capital 1857.

de Soto Hernando *c*.1496–1542. Spanish explorer who sailed with d'Avila (*c*.1400–1531) to Darien, Central America, 1519, explored the Yucatán Peninsula 1528, and traveled with Francisco Pizarro in Peru 1530–35. In 1538 he was made governor of Cuba and Florida. In his expedition of 1539, he explored Florida, Georgia, and the Mississippi River.

Emperor Charles V appointed de Soto governor of Florida in 1537. His expeditions may have penetrated Missouri and Louisiana. Upon his death on May 21, 1542, his companions buried his body in a river to preserve the local Indians' belief that de Soto had descended from heaven.

destroyer small, fast warship designed for antisubmarine work. Destroyers played a critical role in the convoy system in World War II.

Modern destroyers often carry guided missiles and displace 3,700–5,650 tons.

détente (French) reduction of political tension and the easing of strained relations between nations, for example, the ending of the Cold War 1989–90, although it was first used in the 1970s to describe the easing of East–West relations in the form of trade agreements and cultural exchanges.

detergent surface-active cleansing agent. The common detergents are made from ◊fats (hydrocarbons) and sulfuric acid, and their long-chain molecules have a type of structure similar to that of ◊soap molecules: a salt group at one end attached to a long hydrocarbon "tail". They have the advantage over soap in that they do not produce scum by forming insoluble salts with the calcium and magnesium ions present in hard water.

determinism in philosophy, the view that denies human freedom of action. Everything is strictly governed by the principle of cause and effect, and human action is no exception. It is the opposite of free will, and rules out moral choice and responsibility.

de   Tocqueville Alexis French politician; see ◊Tocqueville, Alexis de.

Detroit city in Michigan, situated on Detroit River; population (1990) 1,028,000, metropolitan area 4,665,200. It is an industrial center with the headquarters of Ford, Chrysler, and General Motors, hence its nickname, Motown (from "motor town"). Other manufactured products include metal products, machine tools, chemicals, office machines, and pharmaceuticals. During the 1960s and 1970s Detroit became associated with the "Motown Sound" of rock and soul music.

Detroit is a port on the St Lawrence Seaway and the home of Wayne State University and its Medical Center complex. The University of Detroit and the Detroit Institute of Arts are also here. A recent major development is the waterfront Renaissance Center complex.

deuterium naturally occurring heavy isotope of hydrogen, mass number 2 (one proton and one neutron), discovered by Harold Urey 1932. It is sometimes given the symbol D. In nature, about one in every 6,500 hydrogen atoms is deuterium. Combined with oxygen, it produces "heavy water" (D_2O), used in the nuclear industry.

de Valera Eámon 1882–1975. Irish nationalist politician, prime minister of the Irish Free State/Eire/Republic of Ireland 1932–48, 1951–54, and 1957–59, and president 1959–73. Repeatedly imprisoned, he participated in the Easter Rising 1916 and was leader of the nationalist ◊Sinn Féin party 1917–26, when he formed the republican ◊Fianna Fáil party; he directed negotiations with Britain 1921 but refused to accept the partition of Ireland until 1937.

devaluation in economics, the lowering of the official value of a currency against other currencies, so that exports become cheaper and imports more expensive. Used when a country is badly in deficit in its balance of trade, it results in the goods the country produces being cheaper abroad, so that the economy is stimulated by increased foreign demand.

developmental psychology study of development of cognition and behavior from birth to adulthood.

devil in Jewish, Christian, and Muslim theology, the supreme spirit of evil (*Beelzebub, Lucifer, Iblis*), or an evil spirit generally.

devilfish another name for ◊manta, a large fish.

Devon or *Devonshire* county of SW England *area* 2,594 sq mi/6,720 sq km *towns and cities* Exeter (administrative headquarters), Plymouth; resorts: Paignton, Torquay, Teignmouth, and Ilfracombe *features* rivers: Dart, Exe, Tamar; National Parks: Dartmoor, Exmoor; Lundy bird sanctuary and marine nature reserve in the Bristol Channel *industries* mainly agricultural, with sheep and dairy farming and beef cattle; cider and clotted cream; kaolin in the S; Honiton lace; Dartington glass *population* (1991) 1,010,000 *famous people* Francis Drake, John Hawkins, Charles Kingsley, Robert F Scott.

Devonian period of geological time 408–360 million years ago, the fourth period of the Paleozoic era. Many desert sandstones from North America and Europe date from this time. The first land plants flourished in the Devonian period, corals were abundant in the seas, amphibians evolved from air-breathing fish, and insects developed on land.

dew precipitation in the form of moisture that collects on the ground. It forms after the temperature of the ground has fallen below the ◊dew point of the air in contact with it. As the temperature falls during the night, the air and its water vapor become chilled, and condensation takes place on the cooled surfaces.

Dewar James 1842–1923. Scottish chemist and physicist who invented the vacuum flask (Thermos) 1872 during his research into the properties of matter at extremely low temperatures.

Dewey John 1859–1952. US philosopher who believed that the exigencies of a democratic and industrial society demanded new educational techniques. He expounded his ideas in numerous writings, including *School and Society* 1899, and founded a progressive school in Chicago. A pragmatist thinker, influenced by William James, Dewey maintained that there is only the reality of experience and made "inquiry" the essence of logic.

He was born in Vermont and from 1904 was professor of philosophy at Columbia University, New York.

Dewey Melvil 1851–1931. US librarian. In 1876, he devised the Dewey decimal system of classification for accessing, storing, and retrieving books, widely used in libraries. The system uses the numbers 000 to 999 to designate the major fields of knowledge, then breaks these down into more specific subjects by the use of decimals.

Dhaka or *Dacca* capital of Bangladesh from 1971, in Dhaka region, W of the river Meghna; population (1984) 3,600,000. It trades in jute, oilseed, sugar, and tea and produces textiles, chemicals, glass, and metal products.

Dhaulagiri mountain in the ◊Himalayas of W central Nepal, rising to 26,811 ft/8,172.

diabase igneous rock formed below the Earth's surface, a form of basalt, containing relatively little silica (basic in composition).

diabetes disease *diabetes mellitus* in which a disorder of the islets of Langerhans in the ◊pancreas prevents the body producing the hormone ◊insulin, so that sugars cannot be used properly.

Treatment is by strict dietary control and oral or injected insulin, depending on the type of diabetes. In 1989, it was estimated that 4% of the world's population had diabetes, and that there were 12 million sufferers in the US and Canada.

Diaghilev Sergei Pavlovich 1872–1929. Russian ballet impresario. In 1909 he founded the Ballets Russes/Russian Ballet (headquarters in Monaco), which he directed for 20 years. Through this company he brought Russian ballet to the West, introducing and encouraging a dazzling array of dancers, choreographers, composers, and artists, such as Anna Pavlova, Vaslav Nijinsky, Bronislava Nijinksa, Mikhail Fokine, Léonide Massine, George Balanchine, Igor Stravinsky, Sergey Prokofiev, Pablo Picasso, and Henri Matisse.

dialectic Greek term, originally associated with the philosopher Socrates' method of argument through dialogue and conversation. *Hegelian dialectic*, named for the German philosopher ◊Hegel, refers to an interpretive method in which the contradiction between a thesis and its antithesis is resolved through synthesis.

dialectical materialism political, philosophical, and economic theory of the 19th-century German thinkers Karl Marx and Friedrich Engels, also known as ◊Marxism.

dialysis Technique for removing waste products from the blood in chronic or acute kidney failure. There are two main methods, hemodialysis and peritoneal dialysis.

diamond generally colorless, transparent mineral, the hard crystalline form of carbon. It is regarded as a precious gemstone, and is the hardest substance known (10 on the ◊Mohs' scale). Industrial diamonds, which may be natural or synthetic, are used for cutting, grinding, and polishing.

Diana in Roman mythology, the goddess of chastity, hunting, and the Moon, daughter of Jupiter and twin of Apollo. Her Greek equivalent is the goddess ◊Artemis.

Diana Princess of Wales 1961– . The daughter of the 8th Earl Spencer, she married Prince Charles in St Paul's Cathedral, London 1981, the first English bride of a royal heir since 1659. She is descended from the only sovereigns from whom Prince Charles is not descended, Charles II and James II. She had two sons, William and Henry, before her separation from Charles 1992.

diaphragm thin muscular sheet separating the thorax from the abdomen in mammals. It is attached by way of the ribs at either side and the breastbone and backbone. Arching upward against the heart and lungs the diaphragm is important in the mechanics of breathing. It contracts at each inhalation, moving downward to increase the volume of the chest cavity, and relaxes at exhalation.

diarrhea excessive action of the bowels so that the feces are fluid or semifluid. It is caused by intestinal irritants (including some drugs and poisons), infection with harmful organisms (as in dysentery, salmonella, or cholera), or allergies.

diary informal record of day-to-day events, observations, or reflections, usually not intended for a general readership. One of the earliest diaries extant is that of a Japanese noblewoman, the *Kagero Nikki* 954–974, and the earliest known diary in English is that of Edward VI (ruled 1547–53). Notable diaries include those of Samuel Pepys and Anne Frank.

Diaspora dispersal of the Jews, initially from Palestine after the Babylonian conquest 586 BC, and then following the Roman sack of Jerusalem AD 70 and their crushing of the Jewish revolt of 135. The term has come to refer to all the Jews living outside Israel.

diatonic scale in music, a scale consisting of the seven notes of any major or minor key.

Diaz Bartolomeu *c.*1450–1500. Portuguese explorer, the first European to reach the Cape of Good Hope 1488, and to establish a route around Africa. He drowned during an expedition with Pedro Cabral.

dichloro-diphenyl-trichloroethane full name of the insecticide ◊DDT.

Dickens Charles 1812–1870. English novelist. He is enduringly popular for his memorable characters and his portrayal of the social evils of Victorian England. In 1836 he published the first number of the *Pickwick Papers*, followed by *Oliver Twist* 1838, the first of his "reforming" novels; *Nicholas Nickleby* 1839; *Barnaby Rudge* 1841; *The Old Curiosity Shop* 1841; and *David Copperfield* 1849. Among his later books are *A Tale of Two Cities* 1859 and *Great Expectations* 1861.

Dickinson Emily (Elizabeth) 1830–1886. US poet. She wrote most of her poetry between 1850 and the late 1860s and was particularly prolific during the Civil War years. She experimented with poetic rhythms, rhymes, and forms, as well as language and syntax. Her work is characterized by a wit and boldness that seem to contrast sharply with the reclusive life she led in Amherst, Massachusetts. Very few of her many short, mystical poems were published during her lifetime, and her work became well known only in the 20th century. The first collection of her poetry, *Poems by Emily Dickinson*, was published 1890.

Born in Amherst, she lived in near seclusion there after 1862.

dicotyledon major subdivision of the ◊angiosperms, containing the great majority of flowering plants. Dicotyledons are characterized by the presence of two seed leaves, or ◊cotyledons, in the embryo, which is usually surrounded by an endosperm. They generally have broad leaves with netlike veins.

Dicotyledons may be small plants such as the daisy and buttercup, shrubs such as the blueberry, or trees such as oak and birch. The other subdivision of the angiosperms is the monocotyledons.

dictatorship term or office of an absolute ruler, overriding the constitution. (In ancient Rome a dictator was a magistrate invested with emergency powers for six months.) Although dictatorships were common in Latin America during the 19th century, the only European example during this period was the rule of Napoleon III. The crises following World War I produced many dictatorships, including the regimes of Atatürk and Pilsudski (nationalist); Mussolini, Hitler, Primo de Rivera, Franco, and Salazar (all right-wing); and Stalin (Communist).

Diderot Denis 1713–1784. French philosopher. He is closely associated with the Enlightenment, the European intellectual movement for social and scientific progress, and was editor of the enormously influential *Encyclopédie* 1751–80.

Dido Phoenician princess. The legendary founder of Carthage, N Africa, she committed suicide to avoid marrying a local prince. In the Latin epic *Aeneid*, Virgil represents her death as the result of her desertion by the Trojan hero ◊Aeneas.

Diefenbaker John George 1895–1979. Canadian Progressive Conservative politician, prime minister 1957–63. In 1958, seeking to increase his majority in the House of Commons, Diefenbaker called for new elections; his party won the largest majority in Canadian history. In 1963, however, Diefenbaker refused to accept atomic warheads for missiles supplied by the US, and the Progressive Conservative Party was ousted after losing a no-confidence vote in parliament.

diesel engine ◊internal-combustion engine that burns a lightweight fuel oil. The diesel engine operates by compressing air until it becomes sufficiently hot to ignite the fuel. It is a piston-in-cylinder engine, like the ◊gasoline engine, but only air (rather than an air-and-fuel mixture) is taken into the cylinder on the first piston stroke (down). The piston moves up and compresses the air until it is at a very high temperature. The fuel oil is then injected into the hot air, where it burns, driving the piston down on its power stroke. For this reason the engine is called a compression-ignition engine.

diesel oil lightweight fuel oil used in diesel engines. Like gasoline, it is a petroleum product. When used in

vehicle engines, it is also known as *derv*—*d*iesel-*e*ngine *r*oad *v*ehicle.

diet the range of foods eaten by an animal, also a particular selection of food, or the overall intake and selection of food for a particular person or people. The basic components of a diet are a group of chemicals: proteins, carbohydrates, fats, vitamins, minerals, and water.

For humans, an adequate diet is one that fulfills the body's nutritional requirements and gives an energy intake proportional to the person's activity level (the average daily requirement is 2,400 calories for men, less for women, more for active children). In the Third World and in famine or poverty areas some 450 million people in the world subsist on fewer than 1,500 calories per day, whereas in the developed countries the average daily intake is 3,300 calories.

Dietrich Marlene (Maria Magdalene) 1904–1992. German-born US actress and singer. She appeared with Emil Jannings in both the German and American versions of the film *Der Blaue Engel/The Blue Angel* 1930, directed by Josef von Sternberg. She stayed in Hollywood, becoming a US citizen 1937. Her husky, sultry singing voice added to her appeal. Her other films include *Blonde Venus* 1932, *Destry Rides Again* 1939, and *Just a Gigolo* 1978.

diffraction the slight spreading of a light beam into a pattern of light and dark bands when it passes through a narrow slit or past the edge of an obstruction. A *diffraction grating* is a plate of glass or metal ruled with close, equidistant parallel lines used for separating a wave train such as a beam of incident light into its component frequencies (white light results in a spectrum).

diffusion spontaneous and random movement of molecules or particles in a fluid (gas or liquid) from a region in which they are at a high concentration to a region of lower concentration, until a uniform concentration is achieved throughout. No mechanical mixing or stirring is involved. For instance, if a drop of ink is added to water, its molecules will diffuse until their color becomes evenly distributed throughout.

digestive system mouth, stomach, intestine, and associated glands of animals, which are responsible for digesting food. The food is broken down by physical and chemical means in the ◊stomach; digestion is completed, and most nutrients are absorbed in the small intestine; what remains is stored and concentrated into feces in the large intestine. In birds, additional digestive organs are the crop and gizzard.

Digger or *True Leveller* member of an English 17th-century radical sect that attempted to seize and share out common land. The Diggers became prominent April 1649 when, headed by Gerrard Winstanley (*c*.1609–1660), they set up communal colonies near Cobham, Surrey, and elsewhere. These colonies were attacked by mobs and, being pacifists, the Diggers made no resistance. The support they attracted alarmed the government and they were dispersed 1650. Their ideas influenced the early ◊Quakers.

digit in mathematics, any of the numbers from 0 to 9 in the decimal system. Different bases have different ranges of digits. For example, the ◊hexadecimal system has digits 0 to 9 and A to F, whereas the binary system has two digits (or ◊bits), 0 and 1.

digital in electronics and computing, a term meaning "coded as numbers". A digital system uses two-state, either on/off or high/low voltage pulses, to encode,

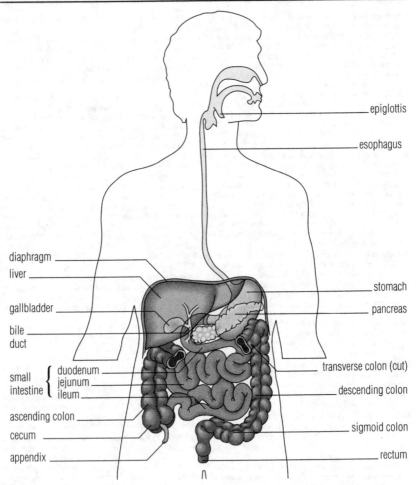

epiglottis

esophagus

diaphragm

liver

stomach

gallbladder

pancreas

bile
duct

small
intestine { duodenum
             jejunum
             ileum

transverse colon (cut)

descending colon

ascending colon

cecum

sigmoid colon

appendix

rectum

digestive system *The human digestive system. When food is swallowed, it is moved down the esophagus by the action of muscles (peristalsis) into the stomach. Digestion starts in the stomach as the food is mixed with enzymes and strong acid. After several hours, the food passes to the small intestine. Here more enzymes are added and digestion is completed. After all nutrients have been absorbed, the indigestible parts pass into the large intestine and thence to the rectum. The liver has many functions, such as storing minerals and vitamins and making bile, which is stored in the gall bladder until needed for the digestion of fats. The pancreas supplies enzymes. The appendix seems to have no function in human beings.*

digital audio tape (DAT) digitally recorded audio tape produced in cassettes that can carry two hours of sound on each side and are about half the size of standard cassettes. DAT players/recorders were developed 1987. Prerecorded cassettes are copy-protected. The first DAT for computer data was introduced 1988.

digital compact cassette (DCC) digitally recorded audio cassette that is roughly the same size as a standard cassette. It cannot be played on a normal tape recorder, though standard tapes can be played on a

DCC machine; this is known as "backward compatibility". The playing time is 90 minutes.

digital data transmission in computing, a way of sending data by converting all signals (whether pictures, sounds, or words) into numeric (normally binary) codes before transmission, then reconverting them on receipt. This virtually eliminates any distortion or degradation of the signal during transmission, storage, or processing.

digitalis plant of the genus *Digitalis* of the figwort family Scrophulariaceae, which includes the ◊foxgloves.

digital recording technique whereby the pressure of sound waves is sampled more than 30,000 times a second and the values converted by computer into precise numerical values. These are recorded and, during playback, are reconverted to sound waves.

digital video interactive powerful compression system used for storing video images on computer; see ◊DVI.

dik-dik any of several species of tiny antelope, genus *Madoqua*, found in Africa south of the Sahara in dry areas with scattered brush. Dik-diks are about 2 ft/60 cm long and 1.1 ft/35 cm tall, and are often seen in pairs. Males have short, pointed horns. The dik-dik is so named because of its alarm call.

dill herb *Anethum graveolens* of the carrot family Umbelliferae, whose bitter seeds and aromatic leaves are used for culinary and medicinal purposes.

Dillinger John 1903–1934. US bank robber and murderer. In 1923 he was convicted of armed robbery and spent the next ten years in state prison. Released in 1933, he led a gang on a robbery spree throughout the Midwest, staging daring raids on police stations to obtain guns. Named "Public Enemy Number One" by the Federal Bureau of Investigation (FBI), Dillinger led the authorities on a long chase. He was finally betrayed by his mistress, the mysterious "Lady in Red," and was killed by FBI agents in Chicago as he left a cinema.

Born in Indianapolis, Dillinger began a life of crime after deserting from the navy 1920.

dilution process of reducing the concentration of a solution by the addition of a solvent.

dimension in science, any directly measurable physical quantity such as mass (M), length (L), and time (T), and the derived units obtainable by multiplication or division from such quantities.

For example, acceleration (the rate of change of velocity) has dimensions (LT^{-2}), and is expressed in such units as km s^{-2}. A quantity that is a ratio, such as relative density or humidity, is dimensionless.

dimethyl sulfoxide (DMSO) $(CH_3)_2SO$ colorless liquid used as an industrial solvent and an antifreeze. It is obtained as a by-product of the processing of wood to paper.

dingo wild dog of Australia. Descended from domestic dogs brought from Asia by Aborigines thousands of years ago, it belongs to the same species *Canis familiaris* as other domestic dogs. It is reddish brown with a bushy tail, and often hunts at night. It cannot bark.

dinitrogen oxide alternate name for ◊nitrous oxide, or "laughing gas", one of the nitrogen oxides.

Dinkins David 1927– . Mayor of New York City 1990–93, a Democrat. He won a reputation as a moderate and consensual community politician and was Manhattan borough president before succeeding Edward I Koch to become New York's first black mayor. He lost his re-election bid 1993.

dinosaur any of a group (sometimes considered as two separate orders) of extinct reptiles living between 230 million and 65 million years ago. Their closest living relations are crocodiles and birds. Many species of dinosaur evolved during the millions of years they were the dominant large land animals. Most were large (up to 90 ft/27 m), but some were as small as chickens. They disappeared 65 million years ago for reasons not fully understood, although many theories exist.

Diocletian (Gaius Aurelius Valerius Diocletianus) AD 245–313. Roman emperor 284–305, when he abdicated in favor of Galerius. He reorganized and subdivided the empire, with two joint and two subordinate emperors, and in 303 initiated severe persecution of Christians.

diode combination of a cold anode and a heated cathode (or the semiconductor equivalent, which incorporates a *p–n* junction). Either device allows the passage of direct current in one direction only, and so is commonly used in a ◊rectifier to convert alternating current (AC) to direct current (DC).

Diogenes *c.*412–323 BC . Ascetic Greek philosopher of the ◊Cynic school.

He believed in freedom and self-sufficiency for the individual, and that the virtuous life was the simple life; he did not believe in social mores. His writings do not survive.

Dionysius two tyrants of the ancient Greek city of Syracuse in Sicily. *Dionysius the Elder* (432–367 BC) seized power 405 BC . His first two wars with Carthage further extended the power of Syracuse, but in a third (383–378 BC) he was defeated. He was a patron of ◊Plato. He was succeeded by his son, *Dionysius the Younger*, who was driven out of Syracuse by Dion 356; he was tyrant again 353, but in 343 returned to Corinth.

Dionysus in Greek mythology, the god of wine (son of Semele and Zeus), and also of orgiastic excess. He was attended by women called maenads who were believed to be capable of tearing animals to pieces with their bare hands when under his influence. He was identified with the Roman ◊Bacchus, whose rites were less savage.

Dior Christian 1905–1957. French couturier. He established his own Paris salon 1947 and made an impact with the "New Look"—long, cinch-waisted, and full-skirted—after wartime austerity.

Diouf Abdou 1935– . Senegalese left-wing politician, president from 1980. He became prime minister 1970 under President Leopold Senghor and, on his retirement, succeeded him, being reelected 1983, 1988, and 1993. His presidency has been characterized by authoritarianism.

diphtheria acute infectious disease in which a membrane forms in the throat (threatening death by ◊asphyxia), along with the production of a powerful toxin that damages the heart and nerves. The organism responsible is a bacterium (*Corynebacterium diphtheriae*). It is treated with antitoxin and antibiotics. Its incidence has been reduced greatly by immunization.

diplodocus plant-eating sauropod dinosaur that lived about 145 million years ago, the fossils of which have been found in the W US. Up to 88 ft/27 m long, most of which was neck and tail, it weighed about 11 metric tons. It walked on four elephantine legs, had nostrils on top of the skull, and peglike teeth at the front of the mouth.

diploid having two sets of ◊chromosomes in each cell. In sexually reproducing species, one set is derived from each parent, the ◊gametes, or sex cells, of each parent being ◊haploid (having only one set of chromosomes) due to meiosis (reduction cell division).

diplomacy process by which states attempt to settle their differences through peaceful means such as negotiation or ◊arbitration.

dipper any of various passerine birds of the family Cinclidae, found in hilly and mountainous regions across Eurasia and North America, where there are clear, fast-flowing streams. It can swim, dive, or walk along the bottom, using the pressure of water on its wings and tail to keep it down, while it searches for insect larvae and other small animals.

The American dipper *Cinclus mexicanus* of W North America, is about 8 in/20 cm long, sooty-gray overall, and resembles a wren.

Dirac Paul Adrien Maurice 1902–1984. British physicist who worked out a version of quantum mechanics consistent with special ◊relativity. The existence of the positron (positive electron) was one of its predictions. He shared the Nobel Prize for Physics 1933 with Austrian physicist Erwin Schrödinger (1887–1961).

direct access or *random access* type of ◊file access. A direct-access file contains records that can be accessed directly by the computer because each record has its own address on the storage disk.

direct current (DC) electric current that flows in one direction, and does not reverse its flow as ◊alternating current does. The electricity produced by a battery is direct current.

directory in computing, a list of file names, together with information that enables a computer to retrieve those files from ◊backing storage. The computer operating system will usually store and update a directory on the backing storage to which it refers. So, for example, on each ◊disk used by a computer a directory file will be created listing the disk's contents.

Dis in Roman mythology, the god of the underworld, also known as Orcus; he is equivalent to the Greek god ◊Pluto, ruler of Hades. Dis is also a synonym for the underworld itself.

disarmament reduction of a country's weapons of war. Most disarmament talks since World War II have been concerned with nuclear-arms verification and reduction, but biological, chemical, and conventional weapons have also come under discussion at the United Nations and in other forums. Attempts to limit the arms race (initially between the US and the USSR and since 1992 between the US and Russia) have included the ◊Strategic Arms Limitation Talks (SALT) of the 1970s and the ◊Strategic Arms Reduction Talks (START) of the 1980s–90s.

discrimination distinction made (social, economic, political, legal) between individuals or groups such that one has the power to treat the other unfavorably. *Negative discrimination*, often based on stereotype, includes anti-Semitism, apartheid, caste, racism, sexism, and slavery. *Positive discrimination*, or "affirmative action", is sometimes practiced in an attempt to counteract the effects of previous long-term discrimination. Minorities and, in some cases, majorities have been targets for discrimination.

National legislation in the US includes the Civil Rights Acts of 1964 and 1968, the Voting Rights Act 1965, and a movement to add an amendment to the Constitution mandating equal rights for women.

discus circular disk thrown by athletes who rotate the body to gain momentum from within a circle 8 ft/ 2.5 m in diameter. The men's discus weighs 4.4 lb/2 kg and the women's 2.2 lb/1 kg. Discus throwing was a competition in ancient Greece at gymnastic contests, such as those of the Olympic Games. It is an event in the modern Olympics and other athletics competitions.

disk in computing, a common medium for storing large volumes of data (an alternative to ◊magnetic tape.) A magnetic disk is rotated at high speed in a disk-drive unit as a read/write (playback or record) head passes over its surfaces to record or "read" the magnetic variations that encode the data. There are several types, including ◊floppy disks, ◊hard disks, and ◊CD-ROM.

disk drive mechanical device that reads data from and writes data to a magnetic ◊disk.

disk formatting in computing, preparing a blank magnetic disk so that data can be stored on it. Data are recorded on a disk's surface on circular tracks, each of which is divided into a number of sectors. In formatting a disk the computer's operating system adds control information such as track and sector numbers, which enables the data stored to be accessed correctly by the disk-drive unit.

Disney Walt (Walter Elias) 1901–1966. US filmmaker who became a pioneer of family entertainment. He and his brother established an animation studio in Hollywood in 1923, and his first Mickey Mouse animated cartoon (*Plane Crazy*) appeared in black and white 1928. *Steamboat Willie* 1928 was his first Mickey Mouse cartoon in color. He developed the "Silly Symphony," a type of cartoon based on the close association of music with the visual image, such as *Fantasia* 1940. His many feature-length cartoons include *Snow White and the Seven Dwarfs* 1938 (his first), *Pinocchio* 1939, *Dumbo* 1941, *Bambi* 1942, *Cinderella* 1950, *Alice in Wonderland* 1952, and *Peter Pan* 1953. In 1955, Disney opened his first theme park, Disneyland, in Anaheim, California.

dispersion in optics, the splitting of white light into a spectrum; for example, when it passes through a prism or a diffraction grating. It occurs because the prism (or grating) bends each component wavelength to a slightly different extent. The natural dispersion of light through raindrops creates a rainbow.

Disraeli Benjamin, Earl of Beaconsfield 1804–1881. British Conservative politician and novelist. Elected to Parliament 1837, he was chancellor of the Exchequer under Lord ◊Derby 1852, 1858–59, and 1866–68, and prime minister 1868 and 1874–80. His imperialist policies brought India directly under the crown, and he was personally responsible for purchasing control of the Suez Canal. The central Conservative Party organization is his creation. His popular, political novels reflect an interest in social reform and include *Coningsby* 1844 and *Sybil* 1845.

distemper any of several infectious diseases of animals characterized by catarrh, cough, and general weakness. Specifically, it refers to a virus disease in young dogs, also found in wild animals, which can now be prevented by vaccination. In 1988 an allied virus killed over 10,000 common seals in the Baltic and North seas.

District of Columbia seat of the federal government of the US, conterminous with the city of Washington, DC; area 69 sq mi/179 sq km. A rectangle along the Potomac River, donated by Maryland and Virginia, was selected as the federal seat of government 1791.

For many years the District of Columbia included other local entities besides Washington. At the request of its residents, the portion donated by Virginia was returned to the state 1846, thus confining the District of Columbia to the eastern shore of the Potomac

River. Residents elect a mayor and city council and a nonvoting delegate to the US Congress.

diuretic any drug that increases the output of urine by the kidneys. It may be used in the treatment of high blood pressure and to relieve ◊edema associated with heart, lung, kidney or liver disease, and some endocrine disorders.

dividend in business, the amount of money that company directors decide should be taken out of net profits for distribution to stockholders. It is usually declared as a percentage or fixed amount per share.

Most companies pay dividends quarterly; others once a year.

divine right of kings Christian political doctrine that hereditary monarchy is the system approved by God, hereditary right cannot be forfeited, monarchs are accountable to God alone for their actions, and rebellion against the lawful sovereign is therefore blasphemous.

Many of the latter group migrated to the American colonies to avoid persecution.

diving the sport of entering the water either from a springboard (3ft/1 m or 10 ft/3 m) above the water, or from a platform (33ft/10 m) above the water. Various differing starts are adopted, facing forward or backward, and somersaults, twists, and other positions or combinations thereof are performed in midair before entering the water. Pool depths of 20 ft/6 m are needed for high or platform diving, but 10 ft/3 m-deep pools may accommodate 1 or 3 meter diving. Points are awarded and the level of difficulty of each dive is used as a multiplying factor.

divorce legal dissolution of a lawful marriage. It is distinct from an annulment, which is a legal declaration that the marriage was invalid. The ease with which a divorce can be obtained in different countries varies considerably and is also affected by different religious practices.

Dixieland name given to a jazz style that originated in New Orleans in the early 20th century and worked its way up the Mississippi. It is characterized by improvisation and the playing back and forth of the cornet, trumpet, clarinet, and trombone. The steady background beat is supplied by the piano, bass, and percussion instrument players, who also have their turns to solo. It is usually played by bands of four to eight members.

Noted Dixieland musicians were King Oliver, Jelly Roll Morton, and Louis ◊Armstrong.

Djakarta variant spelling of Jakarta, the capital of Indonesia.

Djibouti chief port and capital of the Republic of Djibouti, on a peninsula 149mi/240 km SW of Aden and 351 mi/565 km NE of Addis Ababa; population (1988) 290,000.

Djibouti Republic of (*Jumhouriyya Djibouti*) *area* 8,955 sq mi/23,200 sq km *capital* (and chief port) Djibouti *towns and cities* Tadjoura, Obock, Dikhil *physical* mountains divide an inland plateau from a coastal plain; hot and arid *features* terminus of railroad link with Ethiopia; Lac Assal salt lake is the second lowest point on Earth (−471 ft/−144 m) *head of state* Hassan Gouled Aptidon from 1977 *head of government* Barkat Gourad Hamadou from 1988 *political system* authoritarian nationalism *political parties* People's Progress Assembly (RPP), nationalist; Democratic Renewal Party (PRD), moderate centrist *exports* acts mainly as a transit port for Ethiopia *currency* Djibouti

franc *population* (1993 est) 410,000 (Issa 47%, Afar 37%, European 8%, Arab 6%); growth rate 3.4% p.a. *life expectancy* men 47, women 51 *languages* French (official), Somali, Afar, Arabic *religion* Sunni Muslim *literacy* 19% *GNP* \$475 per head (1986) *chronology* *1884* Annexed by France as part of French Somaliland. *1967* French Somaliland became the French Territory of the Afars and the Issas. *1977* Independence achieved from France; Hassan Gouled was elected president. *1979* All political parties combined to form the People's Progress Assembly (RPP). *1981* New constitution made RPP the only legal party. Gouled reelected. Treaties of friendship signed with Ethiopia, Somalia, Kenya, and Sudan. *1984* Policy of neutrality reaffirmed. *1987* Gouled reelected. *1992* Constitution amended to provide for a multiparty system. *1993* Gouled reelected. *1994* Peace agreement reached with Afar militants, ending civil war.

DNA (abbreviation for *deoxyribonucleic acid*) complex giant molecule that contains, in chemically coded form, all the information needed to build, control, and maintain a living organism. DNA is a ladderlike double-stranded nucleic acid that forms the basis of genetic inheritance in all organisms, except for a few viruses that have only ◊RNA. In organisms other than bacteria it is organized into ◊chromosomes and contained in the cell nucleus.

Dnepropetrovsk city in Ukraine, on the right bank of the river Dnieper; population (1987) 1,182,000. It is the center of a major industrial region, with iron, steel, chemical, and engineering industries. It is linked with the Dnieper Dam, 31 mi/60 km downstream.

Dnieper or *Dnepr* river rising in the Smolensk region of Russia and flowing S through Belarus and Ukraine to enter the Black Sea E of Odessa; total length 1,400 mi/2,250 km.

dock or *sorrel* in botany, any of a number of plants of the genus *Rumex* of the buckwheat family Polygonaceae. They are tall, annual to perennial herbs, often with lance-shaped leaves and small, greenish flowers. Native to temperate regions, there are 30 North American and several British species.

Doctorow E(dgar) L(awrence) 1931– . US writer. He is noted for novels in which he weaves history and fiction together. His first novel, *The Book of Daniel* 1971, about the ◊Rosenbergs' trial and execution, won him instant fame. His other works include *Ragtime* 1975, *Loon Lake* 1980, *Lives of the Poet* 1984, *World's Fair* 1985, and *Billy Bathgate* 1989.

documentation in computing, the written information associated with a computer program or ◊applications package. Documentation is usually divided into two categories: program documentation and user documentation.

document image processing (DIP) scanning documents for storage on ◊CD-ROM. The scanned images are indexed electronically, which provides much faster access than is possible with either paper or ◊microform. See also ◊optical character recognition.

Dodge City city in SW Kansas, on the Arkansas River; population (1990) 21,100. It was a noted frontier cattle town in the days of the Wild West.

Founded 1872 with the arrival of the railroad, it became the terminus for cattle drives from the Santa Fe Trail. Wyatt Earp and Bat Masterson were law officials here, and Boot Hill Cemetery has been preserved. Farm and livestock-handling machinery are manufactured here.

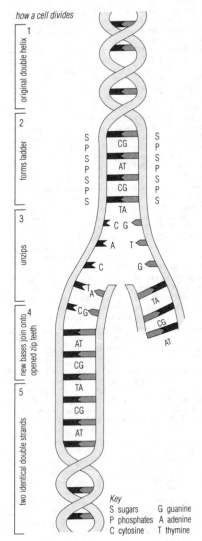

how a cell divides

1 — original double helix

2 — forms ladder

S P S P S P S

CG
AT
CG
TA

S P S P S P S

3 — unzips

C G
A   T
C   G

T A
C G

4 — new bases join onto opened zip teeth

TA
CG
AT

AT
CG
TA
CG
AT

5 — two identical double strands

Key
S sugars   G guanine
P phosphates   A adenine
C cytosine   T thymine

DNA *How the DNA molecule divides. The DNA molecule consists of two strands wrapped around each other in a spiral or helix. The main strands consist of alternate sugar (S) and phosphate (P) groups, and attached to each sugar is a nitrogenous base—adenine (A), cytosine (C), guanine (G), or thymine (T). The sequence of bases carries the genetic code which specifies the characteristics of offspring. The strands are held together by weak bonds between the bases, cytosine to guanine, and adenine to thymine. The weak bonds allow the strands to split apart, allowing new bases to attach, forming another double strand.*

dodo extinct bird *Raphus cucullatus* formerly found on the island of Mauritius, but exterminated before the end of the 17th century. Although related to the pigeons, it was larger than a turkey, with a bulky body and very short wings and tail. Flightless and trusting, it was easy prey to humans.

Dodoma capital (replacing Dar es Salaam 1974) of Tanzania; 3,713 ft/1,132 m above sea level; population (1985) 85,000. It is a center of communications, linked by rail with Dar es Salaam and Kigoma on Lake Tanganyika, and by road with Kenya to the N and Zambia and Malawi to the S.

Doe Samuel Kenyon 1950–1990. Liberian politician and soldier, head of state 1980–90. He seized power in a coup. In 1981 he made himself general and army commander in chief. In 1985 he was narrowly elected president, as leader of the newly formed National Democratic Party of Liberia. Having successfully put down an uprising April 1990, Doe was deposed and killed by rebel forces Sept 1990. His human-rights record was poor.

dog any carnivorous mammal of the family Canidae, including wild dogs, wolves, jackals, coyotes, and foxes. Specifically, the domestic dog *Canis familiaris*, the earliest animal descended from the wolf or jackal. Dogs were first domesticated over 10,000 years ago, and migrated with humans to all the continents. They have been selectively bred into many different varieties for use as working animals and pets.

In the US, the American Kennel Club sets standards for about 200 registered breeds.

dogbane any sometimes poisonous herbaceous North American plant of the genus *Apocynum*, with opposite leaves, small white or pink flowers, and milky juice.

The term also is used to designate any member of the dogbane family Apocynaceae, which includes various herbaceous plants, shrubs, and trees such as oleander and periwinkle.

doge chief magistrate in the ancient constitutions of Venice and Genoa. The first doge of Venice was appointed 697 with absolute power (modified 1297), and from his accession dates Venice's prominence in history. The last Venetian doge, Lodovico Manin, retired 1797 and the last Genoese doge 1804.

dogfish any of several small sharks found in the NE Atlantic, Pacific, and Mediterranean.

The spiny dogfish *Squalus acanthius* of the Pacific and Atlantic grows to about 4 ft/1.2 m long. It is a common subject for dissection in biology laboratories.

dogwood any of a genus *Cornus* of trees and shrubs of the dogwood family Cornaceae, native to temperate regions of North America and Eurasia. The flowering dogwood *Cornus florida* of the E US is often cultivated as an ornamental for its beautiful blooms consisting of clusters of small greenish flowers surrounded by four large white or pink petal-like bracts.

Doha (Arabic *Ad Dawhah*) capital and chief port of Qatar; population (1986) 217,000. Industries include oil refining, refrigeration plants, engineering, and food processing. It is the center of vocational training for all the Persian Gulf states.

doldrums area of low atmospheric pressure along the equator, in the intertropical convergence zone where the NE and SE trade winds converge. The doldrums are characterized by calm or very light winds, during which there may be sudden squalls and stormy weather. For this reason the areas are avoided as far as possible by sailing ships.

dollar monetary unit of several countries. In the US the dollar, which contains 100 cents, was adopted 1785 and is represented by the symbol "$." US dollars originally were issued as gold or silver coins; today both metal and paper dollars circulate, but paper predominates. Australia, Canada, and Hong Kong are among the other countries that use the dollar unit, but none of these dollars is equivalent in value to the US dollar.

dolomite white mineral with a rhombohedral structure, calcium magnesium carbonate (CaMg $(CO_3)_2$). The term also applies to a type of limestone rock where the calcite content is replaced by the mineral dolomite. Dolomite rock may be white, gray, brown, or reddish in color, commonly crystalline. It is used as a building material. The region of the Alps known as the Dolomites is a fine example of dolomite formation.

dolphin any of various highly intelligent aquatic mammals of the family Delphinidae, which also includes porpoises. There are about 60 species. The name "dolphin" is generally applied to species having a beaklike snout and slender body, whereas the name "porpoise" is reserved for the smaller species with a blunt snout and stocky body. Dolphins use sound (echolocation) to navigate, to find prey, and for communication. The common dolphin *Delphinus delphis* is found in all temperate and tropical seas. It is up to 8 ft/2.5 m long, and is dark above and white below, with bands of gray, white, and yellow on the sides. It has up to 100 teeth in its jaws. Dolphins feed on fish and squid.

dolphin The bottlenosed dolphin lives in groups of up to 15 individuals. There is extensive communication and cooperation between individuals. They can produce a range of clicks of various frequencies which they use for echolocation.

Domesday Book record of the survey of England carried out 1086 by officials of William the Conqueror in order to assess land tax and other dues, ascertain the value of the crown lands, and enable the king to estimate the power of his vassal barons. The name is derived from the belief that its judgment was as final as that of Doomsday.

dominant in music, the fifth note of the diatonic scale, for example, G in the C major scale. The chord of the dominant is related to the tonic chord by the dominant note, which corresponds to its third harmonic. Classical modulation involves a harmonic progression from the tonic to the dominant and back. The return may be a symmetrical journey, as in the binary form of a sonata by Scarlatti, or an abrupt resolution of dominant to tonic chords in a "perfect" cadence.

Domingo Placido 1937–   . Spanish lyric tenor. He specializes in Italian and French 19th-century operatic

roles to which he brings a finely-tuned dramatic temperament. As a youth in Mexico, he sang baritone roles in zarzuela (musical theater), moving up to tenor as a member of the Israel National Opera 1961–64. Since his New York debut 1965 he has established a world reputation as a sympathetic leading tenor, and has made many films including the 1988 version of Puccini's *Tosca* set in Rome, and the 1990 Zeffirelli production of Leoncavallo's *I Pagliacci/The Strolling Players*. A member of a musical family, he emigrated to Mexico in 1950. In 1986 he starred in the film version of *Otello*, and in 1991 sang his first Parsifal at the New York Met.

Dominica Commonwealth of *area* 290 sq mi/751 sq km *capital* Roseau, with a deepwater port *towns and cities* Portsmouth, Marigot *physical* second largest of the Windward Islands, mountainous central ridge with tropical rainforest features of great beauty, it has mountains of volcanic origin rising to 5,317 ft/ 1,620 m; Boiling Lake (an effect produced by escaping subterranean gas) *head of state* Clarence Seignoret from 1983 *head of government* Eugenia Charles from 1980 *political system* liberal democracy *political parties* Dominica Freedom Party (DFP), centrist; Labour Party of Dominica (LPD), left-of-center coalition; Dominica United Workers' Party (UWP), left-of-center *exports* bananas, coconuts, citrus, lime, bay oil *currency* Eastern Caribbean dollar; pound sterling; French franc *population* (1993 est) 88,000 (mainly black African in origin, but with a small Carib reserve of some 500); growth rate 1.3% p.a. *life expectancy* men 57, women 59 *languages* English (official), but the Dominican patois reflects earlier periods of French rule *media* one independent weekly newspaper *religion* Roman Catholic 80% *literacy* 97% *GNP* $2,440 per head (1991) *chronology 1763* Became British possession. *1978* Independence achieved from Britain. Patrick John, leader of Dominica Labour Party (DLP), elected prime minister. *1980* Dominica Freedom Party (DFP), led by Eugenia Charles, won convincing victory in general election. *1981* Patrick John implicated in plot to overthrow government. *1982* John tried and acquitted. *1985* John retried and found guilty. Regrouping of left-of-center parties resulted in new Labour Party of Dominica (LPD). DFP, led by Eugenia Charles, reelected. *1990* Charles elected to a third term. *1991* Windward Islands confederation proposed. *1993* Charles resigned DFP leadership, but continued as prime minister.

Dominican order Roman Catholic order of friars founded 1215 by St Dominic. The Dominicans are also known as Friars Preachers, Black Friars, or Jacobins. The order is worldwide and there is also an order of contemplative nuns; the habit is black and white.

The first house was established in Toulouse in 1215; in 1216 the order received papal recognition, and their rule was drawn up in 1220–21. They soon spread all over Europe. Dominicans have included Thomas Aquinas, Savonarola, and Las Casas.

Dominican Republic (*República Dominicana*) *area* 18,700 sq mi/48,442 sq km *capital* Santo Domingo *towns and cities* Santiago de los Caballeros, San Pedro de Macoris *physical* comprises eastern two-thirds of island of Hispaniola; central mountain range with fertile valleys *features* Pico Duarte 10,417 ft/3,174 m, highest point in Caribbean islands; Santo Domingo is the oldest European city in the western hemisphere *head of state and government* Joaquín Balaguer

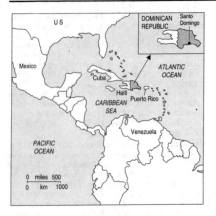

Ricardo from 1986 *political system* democratic republic *political parties* Dominican Revolutionary Party (PRD), moderate, left of center; Christian Social Reform Party (PRSC), independent socialist; Dominican Liberation Party (PLD), nationalist *exports* sugar, gold, silver, tobacco, coffee, nickel *currency* peso *population* (1993 est) 7,600,000; growth rate 2.3% p.a. *life expectancy* men 65, women 70 *language* Spanish (official) *religion* Roman Catholic 95% *literacy* men 85%, women 82% *GNP* $950 per head (1991) *chronology 1492* Visited by Christopher Columbus. *1844* Dominican Republic established. *1930* Military coup established dictatorship of Rafael Trujillo. *1937* Army massacred 19–20,000 Haitians living in the Dominican provinces adjoining the frontier. *1961* Trujillo assassinated. *1962* First democratic elections resulted in Juan Bosch, founder of the PRD, becoming president. *1963* Bosch overthrown in military coup. *1965* US Marines intervened to restore order and protect foreign nationals. *1966* New constitution adopted. Joaquín Balaguer, leader of PRSC, became president. *1978* PRD returned to power, with Silvestre Antonio Guzmán as president. *1982* PRD reelected, with Jorge Blanco as president. *1985* Blanco forced by International Monetary Fund to adopt austerity measures to save the economy. *1986* PRSC returned to power, with Balaguer re-elected president. *1990* Balaguer reelected by a small majority. *1994* Balaguer reelected; election results disputed by opposition but eventually declared valid.

domino theory idea popularized by US president Eisenhower in 1954 that if one country came under communist rule, adjacent countries were likely to fall to communism as well.

Initially used to justify US intervention in SE Asia, the domino theory has also been invoked in reference to Central America.

Don river in Russia, rising to the S of Moscow and entering the northeast extremity of the Sea of Azov; length 1,180 mi/1,900 km. In its lower reaches the Don is 1 mi/1.5 km wide, and for about four months of the year it is closed by ice. Its upper course is linked with the river Volga by a canal.

Donatello (Donato di Niccolo) *c.*1386–1466. Italian sculptor of the early Renaissance. He was instrumental in reviving the Classical style, as in his graceful bronze statue of the youthful *David* about 1433 (Bargello, Florence) and his equestrian statue of the

general *Gattamelata* 1447–50 (Piazza del Santo, Padua). The course of Florentine art in the 15th century was strongly influenced by his work.

Donau German name for the river ◊Danube.

Donegal mountainous county in Ulster province in the NW of the Republic of Ireland, surrounded on three sides by the Atlantic Ocean; area 1,864 sq mi/4,830 sq km; county town Lifford; population (1991) 127,900. The market town and port of Donegal is at the head of Donegal Bay in the SW. Commercial activities include sheep and cattle raising, tweed and linen manufacture, and some deep-sea fishing. The river Erne hydroelectric project (1952) involved the building of large power stations at Ballyshannon.

Donetsk city in Ukraine; capital of Donetsk region, situated in the Donets Basin, a major coal-mining area, 372 mi/600 km SE of Kiev; population (1987) 1,090,000. It has blast furnaces, rolling mills, and other heavy industries.

Donizetti Gaetano 1797–1848. Italian composer. He created more than 60 operas, including *Lucrezia Borgia* 1833, *Lucia di Lammermoor* 1835, *La Fille du régiment* 1840, *La Favorite* 1840, and *Don Pasquale* 1843. They show the influence of Rossini and Bellini, and are characterized by a flow of expressive melodies.

Don Juan character of Spanish legend, Don Juan Tenorio, supposed to have lived in the 14th century and notorious for his debauchery. Tirso de Molina, Molière, Mozart, Byron, and George Bernard Shaw have featured the legend in their works.

donkey another name for ◊ass.

Donne John 1571–1631. English metaphysical poet. His work consists of love poems, religious poems, verse satires, and sermons, most of which were first published after his death. His religious poems show the same passion and ingenuity as his love poetry. A Roman Catholic in his youth, he converted to the Church of England and finally became dean of St Paul's Cathedral, where he is buried.

doodlebug another name for ant lion.

Doomsday Book variant spelling of ◊Domesday Book, the English survey of 1086.

Doppler effect change in the observed frequency (or wavelength) of waves due to relative motion between the wave source and the observer. The Doppler effect is responsible for the perceived change in pitch of a

dromedary The dromedary is superbly adapted for life in hot, dry climates. It can go for long periods without drinking, and its body conserves moisture.

siren as it approaches and then recedes, and for the ◊red shift of light from distant stars. It is named for the Austrian physicist Christian Doppler (1803–1853).

Dorado constellation of the southern hemisphere, represented as a gold fish. It is easy to locate, since the Large ◊Magellanic Cloud marks its southern border.

Its brightest star is Alpha Doradus, just under 200 light-years from Earth.

Dordogne river in SW France, rising in Puy-de-Dôme *département* and flowing 300 mi/490 km to join the river Garonne 14 mi/23 km N of Bordeaux. It gives its name to a *département* and is a major source of hydro-electric power.

Doré Gustave 1832–1883. French artist. Chiefly known as a prolific illustrator, he was also active as a painter, etcher, and sculptor. He produced closely worked engravings of scenes from, for example, Rabelais, Dante, Cervantes, the Bible, Milton, and Edgar Allan Poe.

Dorian people of ancient Greece. They entered Greece from the N and took most of the Peloponnese from the Achaeans, perhaps destroying the ◊Mycenaean civilization; this invasion appears to have been completed before 1000 BC . Their chief cities were Sparta, Argos, and Corinth.

dormouse small rodent, of the family Gliridae, with a hairy tail. There are about ten species, living in Europe, Asia, and Africa. They are arboreal (live in trees) and nocturnal, and they hibernate during winter in cold regions.

The fat or edible dormouse *Glis glis* lives in continental Europe and is 12 in/30 cm long including its tail. It was a delicacy at Roman feasts.

Dorset county of SW England *area* 1,023 sq mi/2,650 sq km *towns and cities* Dorchester (administrative headquarters), Poole, Shaftesbury, Sherborne; resorts: Bournemouth, Lyme Regis, Weymouth *features* Chesil Bank, a shingle bank along the coast 11 mi/19 km long; Isle of Purbeck, a peninsula where china clay and Purbeck "marble" are quarried, and which includes Corfe Castle and the vacation resort of Swanage; Dorset Downs; Cranborne Chase; rivers Frome and Stour; Maiden Castle; Tank Museum at Royal Armoured Corps Center, Bovington, where the cottage of the soldier and writer T.E. ◊Lawrence is a museum; Canford Heath, the home of some of Britain's rarest breeding birds and reptiles (including the nightjar, Dartford warbler, sand lizard, and smooth snake) *industries* Wytch Farm is the largest onshore oil field in the UK; production at Wareham onshore oil field started 1991 *population* (1991) 645,200 *famous people* Anthony Ashley Cooper, Thomas Love Peacock, Thomas Hardy.

Dortmund industrial center in the ◊Ruhr, Germany, 36 mi/58 km NE of Düsseldorf; population (1988) 568,000. It is the largest mining town of the Westphalian coalfield and the southern terminus of the Dortmund–Ems Canal. The enlargement of the Wesel–Datteln Canal 1989, connecting Dortmund to the Rhine River, allows barges to travel between Dortmund and Rotterdam in the Netherlands. Industries include iron, steel, construction machinery, engineering, and brewing.

dory any of several marine fishes of the order Zeiformes. The American John Dory *Zenopsis ocellata*, to 2 ft/60 cm long, is deep-bodied with long spines on the dorsal and ventral fins. It lives in depths of 300 ft/90 m to 1,200 ft/365 m.

DOS (acronym for *disk operating system*) computer ◊operating system specifically designed for use with disk storage; also used as an alternate name for a particular operating system, ◊MS-DOS.

Dos Passos John (Roderigo) 1896–1970. US author. He made his reputation with the war novels *One Man's Initiation* 1919 and *Three Soldiers* 1921. His major work is the trilogy *U.S.A.* 1930–36. An epic, panoramic view of US life through three decades, and inspired by a communist and anarchist historical approach, it used such innovative structural devices as the "Newsreel", a collage of documentary information, and the "Camera Eye", the novelist's own stream-of-consciousness.

Born in Chicago, Dos Passos was a member of the post-World War I "lost generation", and his writing was shaped by his radical sympathies. He also wrote a second, less ambitious trilogy, *District of Columbia* 1939–49. Other works include *One Man's Initiation—1917* 1919 and *Midcentury* 1961.

Dostoevsky Fyodor Mihailovich 1821–1881. Russian novelist. Remarkable for their profound psychological insight, Dostoevsky's novels have greatly influenced Russian writers, and since the beginning of the 20th century have been increasingly influential abroad. In 1849 he was sentenced to four years' hard labor in Siberia, followed by army service, for printing socialist propaganda. *The House of the Dead* 1861 recalls his prison experiences, followed by his major works *Crime and Punishment* 1866, *The Idiot* 1868–69, and *The Brothers Karamazov* 1879–80.

dot matrix printer computer printer that produces each character individually by printing a pattern, or matrix, of very small dots. The printing head consists of a vertical line or block of either 9 or 24 printing pins. As the printing head is moved from side to side across the paper, the pins are pushed forward selectively to strike an inked ribbon and build up the dot pattern for each character on the paper beneath.

dotterel bird *Eudromias morinellus* of the plover family, nesting on high moors and tundra in Europe and Asia, and migrating south for the winter. About 9 in/23 cm long, it is clad in a pattern of black, brown, and white in summer, duller in winter, but always with white eyebrows and breastband. Females are larger than males, and the male incubates and rears the brood.

Douala or *Duala* chief port and industrial center (aluminum, chemicals, textiles, pulp) of Cameroon, on the Wouri river estuary; population (1981) 637,000. Known as Kamerunstadt until 1907, it was capital of German Cameroon 1885–1901.

double bass large bowed four-stringed (sometimes five-stringed) musical instrument, the bass of the violin family. It is descended from the bass viol or violone. Until 1950, after which it was increasingly superseded by the electric bass, it also provided bass support (plucked) for jazz and dance bands. Performers include Domenico Dragonetti, composer of eight concertos, the Russian-born US conductor Serge Koussevitsky (1874–1951), and the US virtuoso Gary Karr. The double bass features in the well-loved "Elephants" solo, No 5 of Saint-Saëns' *Carnival of the Animals* 1897.

Douglas capital of the Isle of Man in the Irish Sea; population (1986) 20,400. It is a vacation resort and terminus of shipping routes to and from Fleetwood and Liverpool; banking and financial services are important to the local economy.

Douglas Kirk. Adopted name of Issur Danielovitch Demsky 1916– . US film actor. Usually cast as a dynamic though often ill-fated hero, as in *Spartacus* 1960, he was a major star of the 1950s and 1960s in such films as *Ace in the Hole* 1951, *The Bad and the Beautiful* 1953, *Lust for Life* 1956, *The Vikings* 1958, *Seven Days in May* 1964, and *The War Wagon* 1967. He continues to act and produce. He is the father of actor Michael Douglas.

Douglas Michael 1944– . US film actor and producer. His acting range includes both romantic and heroic leads in films such as *Romancing the Stone* 1984 and *Jewel of the Nile* 1985, both of which he produced. He won an Academy Award for his portrayal of a ruthless businessman in *Wall Street* 1987. Among his other films are *Fatal Attraction* 1987 and *Basic Instinct* 1991.

Douglas fir any of some six species of coniferous evergreen tree of the family Pinaceae. The most common is *Pseudotsuga menziesii*, native to western North America and E Asia. It grows 200–300 ft/60–90 m, has long, flat, spirally-arranged needles and hanging cones, and produces hard, strong timber. *P. glauca* has shorter, bluish needles and grows to 100 ft/30 m in mountainous areas.

Douglas-Home Alec (Alexander Frederick), Baron Home of the Hirsel 1903– . British Conservative politician. He was foreign secretary 1960–63, and succeeded Harold Macmillan as prime minister 1963. He renounced his peerage (as 14th Earl of Home) to fight (and lose) the general election 1964, and resigned as party leader 1965. He was again foreign secretary 1970–74, when he received a life peerage. The playwright William Douglas-Home was his brother.

Doukhobor member of a Christian sect of Russian origin, now mainly found in Canada, also known as "Christians of the Universal Brotherhood".

They were long persecuted, mainly for refusing military service—the writer Tolstoy organized a relief fund for them—but in 1898 were permitted to emigrate and settled in Canada, where they number about 13,000, mainly in British Columbia and Saskatchewan. An extremist group, "the Sons of Freedom", staged demonstrations and guerrilla acts in the 1960s, leading to the imprisonment of about 100 of them. Some of the Doukhobor teachings resemble those of the Quakers.

Doulton Henry 1820–1897. English ceramicist. He developed special wares for the chemical, electrical, and building industries, and established the world's first stoneware-drainpipe factory 1846. From 1870 he created art pottery and domestic tablewares in Lambeth, S London, and Burslem, near Stoke-on-Trent.

Douro (Spanish *Duero*) river rising in N central Spain and flowing through N Portugal to the Atlantic at Porto; length 500 mi/800 km. Navigation at the river mouth is hindered by sand bars. There are hydroelectric installations. Vineyards (port and Mateus rosé) are irrigated with water from the river.

Dover, Strait of stretch of water separating England from France, and connecting the English Channel with the North Sea. It is about 22 mi/35 km long and 21 mi/34 km wide at its narrowest part. It is one of the world's busiest sea lanes.

Dow Jones Index (*Dow Jones Industrial 30 Share Index*) scale for measuring the average share price and percentage change of 30 major US industrial companies. It has been calculated and published since 1897 by the financial news publisher Dow Jones and Co.

Down county of SE Northern Ireland *area* 953 sq mi/2,470 sq km *towns and cities* Downpatrick (county town) *features* Mourne Mountains; Strangford sea lough *industries* agriculture *population* (1981) 339,200.

Downing Street street in Westminster, London, leading from Whitehall to St James's Park, named for Sir George Downing (died 1684), a diplomat under Cromwell and Charles II. *Number 10* is the official residence of the prime minister and *number 11* is the residence of the chancellor of the Exchequer.

Downing Street Declaration statement, issued jointly by UK prime minister John Major and Irish premier Albert Reynolds Dec 15 1993, setting out general principles for holding all-party talks on securing peace in Northern Ireland. The Declaration was warmly welcomed by mainstream politicians in the UK and the Republic of Ireland, but Northern Ireland parties were more guarded. However, after initial hesitation, Republican and Loyalist cease-fires were declared 1994 and an Ulster framework document to guide the peace negotiations issued by the UK and Irish governments Feb 1995.

download to retrieve a file from a ◊bulletin board using a ◊modem, or from another computer via a ◊network.

Down's syndrome condition caused by a chromosomal abnormality (the presence of an extra copy of chromosome 21), which in humans produces mental retardation; a flattened face; coarse, straight hair; and a fold of skin at the inner edge of the eye (hence the former name "mongolism"). The condition can be detected by prenatal testing.

Doyle Arthur Conan 1859–1930. Scottish writer. He created the detective Sherlock Holmes and his assistant Dr Watson, who first appeared in *A Study in Scarlet* 1887 and featured in a number of subsequent stories, including *The Hound of the Baskervilles* 1902. Conan Doyle also wrote historical romances (*Micah Clarke* 1889 and *The White Company* 1891) and the scientific romance *The Lost World* 1912.

D'Oyly Carte Richard 1844–1901. English producer of the Gilbert and Sullivan operas. They were performed at the Savoy Theatre, London, which he built. The D'Oyly Carte Opera Company, founded 1876, was disbanded 1982 following the ending of its monopoly on the Gilbert and Sullivan operas. The present company, founded 1988, moved to the Alexandra Theatre, Birmingham, 1991.

Dracula in the novel *Dracula* 1897 by Bram Stoker, the caped count who, as a vampire, drinks the blood of beautiful women. The original of Dracula is thought to have been Vlad Tepes, or Vlad the Impaler, ruler of medieval Wallachia, who used to impale his victims and then mock them.

dragon name popularly given to various sorts of lizard. These include the flying dragon *Draco volans* of SE Asia; the komodo dragon *Varanus komodoensis* of Indonesia, at over 10 ft/3 m the largest living lizard; and some Australian lizards with bizarre spines or frills.

dragonfly any of numerous insects of the order Odonata, including the damselfly. They all have long narrow bodies, two pairs of almost equal-sized, glassy wings with a network of veins; short, bristlelike antennae; powerful, "toothed" mouthparts; and very large compound eyes which may have up to 30,000 facets.

They hunt other insects by sight, both as adults and as aquatic nymphs.

Drake Francis c.1545–1596. English buccaneer and explorer. Having enriched himself as a pirate against Spanish interests in the Caribbean 1567–72, he was sponsored by Elizabeth I for an expedition to the Pacific, sailing round the world 1577–80 in the *Golden Hind*, robbing Spanish ships as he went. This was the second circumnavigation of the globe (the first was by the Portuguese explorer Ferdinand Magellan). Drake also helped to defeat the Spanish Armada 1588 as a vice admiral in the *Revenge*.

drama in theater, any play composed to be performed by actors for an audience. The term is also used collectively to group plays into historical or stylistic periods—for example, Greek drama, Restoration drama—as well as referring to the whole body of work written by a dramatist for performance. Drama is distinct from literature in that it is a performing art open to infinite interpretation, the product not merely of the dramatist but also of the collaboration of director, designer, actors, and technical staff. See also ◊comedy, ◊tragedy, mime, and pantomime.

dream series of events or images perceived through the mind during sleep. Their function is unknown, but Sigmund ◊Freud saw them as wish fulfillment (nightmares being failed dreams prompted by fears of "repressed" impulses). Dreams occur in periods of rapid eye movement (REM) by the sleeper, when the cortex of the brain is approximately as active as in waking hours. Dreams occupy about a fifth of sleeping time.

Dresden capital of the state of Saxony, Germany; population (1990) 520,000. Industries include chemicals, machinery, glassware, and musical instruments. It was one of the most beautiful German cities until its devastation by Allied fire-bombing 1945. Dresden county has an area of 1,602 sq mi/6,740 sq km and a population of 1,772,000.

Dreyfus Alfred 1859–1935. French army officer, victim of miscarriage of justice, anti-Semitism, and cover-up. Employed in the War Ministry, in 1894 he was accused of betraying military secrets to Germany, court-martialed, and sent to the penal colony on Devil's Island, French Guiana. When his innocence was discovered 1896 the military establishment tried to conceal it, and the implications of the Dreyfus affair were passionately discussed in the press until he was exonerated in 1906.

dromedary variety of Arabian ◊camel. The dromedary or one-humped camel has been domesticated since 400 BC . During a long period without water, it can lose up to one-quarter of its body weight without ill effects.

drug any of a range of substances, natural or synthetic, administered to humans and animals as therapeutic agents: to diagnose, prevent or treat disease or to assist recovery from injury. Traditionally many drugs were obtained from plants or animals; some minerals also had medicinal value. Today, increasing numbers of drugs are synthesized in the laboratory.

drug abuse the abuse of narcotic and hallucinogenic substances and stimulants.

Druidism religion of the Celtic peoples of the pre-Christian British Isles and Gaul. The word is derived from Greek *drus* "oak". The Druids regarded this tree as sacred; one of their chief rites was the cutting of mistletoe from it with a golden sickle. They taught the immortality of the soul and a reincarnation doctrine, and were expert in astronomy. The Druids are thought to have offered human sacrifices.

drum any of a class of percussion instruments including *slit drums* made of wood, *steel drums* fabricated from oil drums, and a majority group of *skin drums* consisting of a shell or vessel of wood, metal, or earthenware across one or both ends of which is stretched a membrane of hide or plastic.

Drums are among the oldest instruments known. Orchestral drums consist of timpani, tambourine, snare, side, and bass drums. Military bands of foot soldiers employ the snare and side drums, and among cavalry regiments a pair of kettledrums mounted on horseback are played on ceremonial occasions.

Recent innovations include the rotary tunable rototoms, electronic drums, and the drum machine, a percussion synthesizer.

drumlin geologic feature formed in formerly glaciated areas. It consists of long, streamlined hills formed from glacial till or unstratified glacial drift of clay, sand, boulders, and gravel. A drumlin's long axis is oriented in the direction of glacial flow, and its blunt nose points upstream, with the gentler slope trailing off downstream.

drupe fleshy ◊fruit containing one or more seeds which are surrounded by a hard, protective layer—for example cherry, almond, and plum. The wall of the fruit (◊pericarp) is differentiated into the outer skin (exocarp), the fleshy layer of tissues (mesocarp), and the hard layer surrounding the seed (endocarp).

Druse or *Druze* religious sect in the Middle East of some 500,000 people. They are monotheists, preaching that the Fatimid caliph al-Hakim (996–1021) is God; their scriptures are drawn from the Bible, the Koran, and Sufi allegories. Druse militia groups form one of the three main factions involved in the Lebanese civil war (the others are Amal Shiite Muslims and Christian Maronites).

The Druse military leader (from the time of his father's assassination 1977) is Walid Jumblatt.

dryad in Greek mythology, a forest ◊nymph or tree spirit.

Dryden John 1631–1700. English poet and dramatist. He is noted for his satirical verse and for his use of the heroic couplet. His poetry includes the verse satire *Absalom and Achitophel* 1681, *Annus Mirabilis* 1667, and "St Cecilia's Day" 1687. Plays include the heroic drama *The Conquest of Granada* 1670–71, the comedy *Marriage à la Mode* 1672, and *All for Love* 1678, a reworking of Shakespeare's *Antony and Cleopatra*.

dry ice solid carbon dioxide (CO_2), used as a refrigerant. At temperatures above –79°C/–110.2°F, it sublimes (turns into vapor without passing through a liquid stage) to gaseous carbon dioxide.

dry rot infection of timber in damp conditions by fungi, such as *Merulius lacrymans*, that form a thread-like surface. Whitish at first, the fungus later reddens as reproductive spores are formed. Fungoid tentacles also enter the fabric of the timber, rendering it dry-looking and brittle. Dry rot spreads rapidly through a building.

DTP abbreviation for ◊*desktop publishing*.

dualism in philosophy, the belief that reality is essentially dual in nature. The French philosopher René ◊Descartes, for example, referred to thinking and material substance. These entities interact but are fundamentally separate and distinct.

Dualism is contrasted with monism, the theory that reality is made up of only one substance.

Duarte José Napoleon 1925–1990. El Salvadorean politician, president 1980–82 and 1984–88. He was mayor of San Salvador 1964–70, and was elected president 1972, but exiled by the army 1982. On becoming president again 1984, he sought a negotiated settlement with the left-wing guerrillas 1986, but resigned on health grounds.

Dubai one of the ◊United Arab Emirates.

Dubcek Alexander 1921–1992. Czechoslovak politician, chair of the federal assembly 1989–92. He was a member of the Slovak ◊resistance movement during World War II, and became first secretary of the Communist Party 1967–69. He launched a liberalization campaign (called the Prague Spring) that was opposed by the USSR and led to the Soviet invasion of Czechoslovakia 1968. He was arrested by Soviet troops and expelled from the party 1970. In 1989 he gave speeches at prodemocracy rallies, and after the fall of the hard-line regime, he was elected speaker of the National Assembly in Prague, a position to which he was reelected 1990. He was fatally injured in an automobile crash Sept 1992.

Dublin county in the Republic of Ireland, in Leinster province, facing the Irish Sea; county town Dublin; area 355 sq mi/920 sq km; population (1986) 1,021,000. It is mostly level and low-lying, but rises in the S to 2,471 ft/753 m in Kippure, part of the Wicklow Mountains. The river Liffey enters Dublin Bay. Dublin, the capital of the Republic of Ireland, and Dún Laoghaire are the two major towns.

Dublin (Gaelic *Baile Atha Cliath*) capital and port on the east coast of the Republic of Ireland, at the mouth of the river Liffey, facing the Irish Sea; population (1991) 478,400, Greater Dublin, including Dún Laoghaire (1986 est) 921,000. It is the site of one of the world's largest breweries (Guinness); other industries include textiles, pharmaceuticals, electrical goods, whiskey distilling, glass, food processing, and machine tools.

Duchamp Marcel 1887–1968. French-born US artist. He achieved notoriety with his *Nude Descending a Staircase No 2* 1912 (Philadelphia Museum of Art), influenced by Cubism and Futurism. An active exponent of ◊Dada, he invented ready-mades, everyday items (for example, a bicycle wheel mounted on a kitchen stool) which he displayed as works of art.

duck any of several short-legged waterbirds with webbed feet and flattened bills, of the family Anatidae, which also includes the larger geese and swans. Ducks were domesticated for eggs, meat, and feathers by the ancient Chinese and the ancient Maya. Most ducks live in fresh water, feeding on worms and insects as well as vegetable matter. They are generally divided into dabbling ducks and diving ducks.

ductless gland alternate name for an ◊endocrine gland.

Dufourspitze second highest of the alpine peaks, 15,203 ft/4,634 m high. It is the highest peak in the Monte Rosa group of the Pennine Alps on the Swiss-Italian frontier.

Dufy Raoul 1877–1953. French painter and designer. Inspired by ◊Fauvism he developed a fluent, brightly colored style in watercolor and oils, painting scenes of gaiety and leisure, such as horse racing, yachting, and life on the beach. He also designed tapestries, textiles, and ceramics.

duiker any of several antelopes of the family Bovidae, common in Africa. Duikers are shy and nocturnal, and grow to 12–28 in/30–70 cm tall.

Duisburg river port and industrial city in North Rhine–Westphalia, Germany, at the confluence of the Rhine and Ruhr rivers; population (1987) 515,000. It is the largest inland river port in Europe. Heavy industries include oil refining and the production of steel, copper, zinc, plastics, and machinery.

dulcimer musical instrument, a form of ◊zither, consisting of a shallow open trapezoidal soundbox across which strings are stretched laterally; they are horizontally struck by lightweight hammers or beaters. It produces clearly-differentiated pitches of consistent quality and is more agile and wide-ranging in pitch than the harp or lyre. In Hungary the dulcimer, or cimbalon, is in current use.

Also an oval-shaped stringed instrument of the Appalachian Mountains that is played in the lap or on a surface by plucking the strings with a quill or plectrum.

Dulles John Foster 1888–1959. US lawyer and politician. Senior US adviser at the founding of the United Nations, he largely drafted the Japanese peace treaty of 1951. As secretary of state 1952–59 he was critical of Britain in the ◊Suez Crisis. He was the architect of US ◊Cold War foreign policy, securing SEATO and US intervention in support of South Vietnam following the expulsion of the French in 1954.

Duluth port in Minnesota on Lake Superior by the mouth of the St Louis River; population (1990) 85,500. It manufactures steel, flour, timber, and dairy products. The westernmost port on the St Lawrence Seaway, Duluth ships iron ore, grain, coal, oil, and timber. Permanent settlement on what had been a fur-trading post began 1852.

Dumas Alexandre 1802–1870. French author, known as Dumas *père* (the father). He is remembered for his historical romances, the reworked output of a "fiction-factory" of collaborators. They include *Les Trois Mousquetaires/The Three Musketeers* 1844 and its sequels. His play *Henri III et sa cour/Henry III and His Court* 1829 established French romantic historical drama. Dumas *fils* was his son.

Dumas Alexandre 1824–1895. French author, known as Dumas *fils* (the son of Dumas *père*). He is remembered for the play *La Dame aux camélias/The Lady of the Camellias* 1852, based on his own novel and the source of Verdi's opera *La Traviata*.

Du Maurier Daphne 1907–1989. English novelist. Her romantic fiction includes *Jamaica Inn* 1936, *Rebecca* 1938, and *My Cousin Rachel* 1951, and is set in Cornwall. Her work, though lacking in depth and original insights, is made compelling by her fine story-telling gift. *Jamaica Inn*, *Rebecca*, and her short story *The Birds* were made into films by the English director Alfred Hitchcock.

Dumfries and Galloway region of Scotland *area* 2,510 sq mi/6,500 sq km *towns and cities* Dumfries (administrative headquarters) *features* Solway Firth; Galloway Hills, setting of John Buchan's *The Thirty-*

Nine Steps; Glen Trool National Park; Ruthwell Cross, a runic cross dating from about 800 at the village of Ruthwell; Stranraer provides the shortest sea route to Ireland *industries* horses and cattle (for which the Galloway area was renowned), sheep, timber *population* (1991) 147,800 *famous people* Robert the Bruce, Robert Burns, Thomas Carlyle.

dump in computing, the process of rapidly transferring data to external memory or to a printer. It is usually done to help with debugging (see ◊bug) or as part of an error-recovery procedure designed to provide ◊data security. A ◊screen dump makes a printed copy of the current screen display.

dumping in international trade, when one country sells goods to another at below marginal cost or at a price below that in its own country. Countries dump to sell off surplus produce or to improve their competitive positions in the recipient country. The practice is deplored by ◊free trade advocates because of the artificial, unfair advantage it yields. Dumping is also used by protectionists to justify retaliatory measures.

Duncan Isadora 1877–1927. US dancer. A pioneer of modern dance, she adopted an emotionally expressive free form, dancing barefoot and wearing a loose tunic, inspired by the ideal of Hellenic beauty. She danced solos accompanied to music by Beethoven and other great composers, believing that the music should fit the grandeur of the dance.

Having made her base in Paris 1908, she toured extensively, often returning to Russia after her initial success there 1904.

Dundee city and fishing port, administrative headquarters of Tayside, Scotland, on the north side of the Firth of Tay; population (1991) 165,900. It is an important shipping and rail center. Industries include engineering, shipbuilding, textiles, electronics, printing, and food processing.

dune mound or ridge of wind-drifted sand. Loose sand is blown and bounced along by the wind, up the windward side of a dune. The sand particles then fall to rest on the lee side, while more are blown up from the windward side. In this way a dune moves gradually downwind.

Dunedin port on Otago harbor, South Island, New Zealand; population (1991) 116,500. It is a road, rail, and air center, with engineering and textile industries. The city was founded 1848 by members of the Free Church of Scotland. The university was established 1869.

Dunfermline industrial city near the Firth of Forth in Fife region, Scotland; population (1988 est) 42,700. It is the site of the naval base of Rosyth; industries include engineering, shipbuilding, electronics, and textiles. Many Scottish kings, including Robert the Bruce, are buried in Dunfermline Abbey. It is the birthplace of the industrialist Andrew Carnegie.

dunnock European bird *Prunella modularis* similar in size and coloring to the sparrow, but with a slate-gray head and breast, and more slender bill. It nests in bushes and hedges, and is often called the "hedge sparrow".

Durban principal port of Natal, South Africa, and second port of the republic; population (1985) 634,000, urban area 982,000. It exports coal, corn, and wool; imports heavy machinery and mining equipment; and is also a vacation resort.

Dürer Albrecht 1471–1528. German artist. He was the leading figure of the northern Renaissance. He was

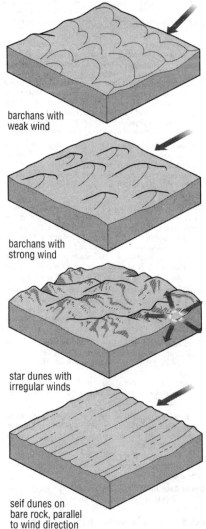

barchans with weak wind

barchans with strong wind

star dunes with irregular winds

seif dunes on bare rock, parallel to wind direction

dune *The shape of a dune indicates the prevailing wind pattern. Crescent-shaped dunes form in sandy deserts with winds from a constant direction. Seif dunes form on bare rocks, parallel to the wind direction. Irregular star dunes are formed by variable winds.*

born in Nuremberg and traveled widely in Europe. Highly skilled in drawing and a keen student of nature, he perfected the technique of woodcut and engraving, producing woodcut series such as the *Apocalypse* 1498 and copperplate engravings such as *The Knight, Death, and the Devil* 1513 and *Melancholia* 1514. His paintings include altarpieces and meticulously observed portraits, including many self-portraits.

Durham county of NE England *area* 942 sq mi/2,440 sq km *towns and cities* Durham (administrative headquarters), Darlington, Peterlee, Newton Aycliffe *features* Pennine Hills; rivers Wear and Tees; Beamish open-air industrial museum; one of Britain's richest coalfields (pits no longer functioning) *industries* sheep and dairy produce; clothing, chemicals. There are also iron and steel processing and light engineering industries *population* (1991) 593,400 *famous people* Elizabeth Barrett Browning, Anthony Eden.

Durkheim Emile 1858–1917. French sociologist, one of the founders of modern sociology, who also influenced social anthropology. He worked to establish sociology as a respectable and scientific discipline, capable of diagnosing social ills and recommending possible cures.

Durrell Lawrence (George) 1912–1990. English novelist and poet. Born in India, he joined the foreign service and lived mainly in the E Mediterranean, the setting of his novels, including the Alexandria Quartet: *Justine, Balthazar, Mountolive,* and *Clea* 1957–60; he also wrote travel books. His heady prose and bizarre characters reflect his exotic sources of inspiration. He was the brother of the naturalist Gerald Durrell.

Durrës chief port of Albania; population (1983) 72,000. It is a commercial and communications center, with flour mills, soap and cigarette factories, distilleries, and an electronics plant. It was the capital of Albania 1912–21.

Dushanbe formerly (1929–69) *Stalinabad* capital of Tajikistan, 100 mi/160 km N of the Afghan frontier; population (1987) 582,000. It is a road, rail, and air center.
    Industries include cotton mills, tanneries, meat-packing factories, and printing works. It is the seat of Tajik state university.

Düsseldorf industrial city of Germany, on the right bank of the river Rhine, 16 mi/26 km NW of Cologne, capital of North Rhine–Westphalia; population (1988) 561,000. It is a river port and the commercial and financial center of the Ruhr area, with food processing, brewing, agricultural machinery, textile, and chemical industries.

Dutch East India Company trading monopoly of the 17th and 18th centuries; see ◊East India Company (Dutch).

Dutch East Indies former Dutch colony, which in 1945 became independent as ◊Indonesia.

Dutch Guiana former Dutch colony, which in 1975 became independent as ◊Suriname.

Dutch language member of the Germanic branch of the Indo-European language family, often referred to by scholars as Netherlandic and taken to include the standard language and dialects of the Netherlands (excluding Frisian) as well as Flemish (in Belgium and N France) and, more remotely, its offshoot Afrikaans in South Africa.

Duvalier François 1907–1971. Right-wing president of Haiti 1957–71. Known as *Papa Doc*, he ruled as a dictator, organizing the Tontons Macoutes ("bogeymen") as a private security force to intimidate and assassi-

nate opponents of his regime. He rigged the 1961 elections in order to have his term of office extended until 1967, and in 1964 declared himself president for life. He was excommunicated by the Vatican for harassing the church, and was succeeded on his death by his son Jean-Claude Duvalier.

Duvalier Jean-Claude 1951– . Right-wing president of Haiti 1971–86. Known as *Baby Doc*, he succeeded his father François Duvalier, becoming, at the age of 19, the youngest president in the world. He continued to receive support from the US but was pressured into moderating some elements of his father's regime, yet still tolerated no opposition. In 1986, with Haiti's economy stagnating and with increasing civil disorder, Duvalier fled to France, taking much of the Haitian treasury with him.

DVI (abbreviation for *digital video interactive*) in computing, a powerful compression and decompression system for digital video and audio. DVI enables 72 minutes of full-screen, full-motion video and its audio track to be stored on a CD-ROM. Originally developed by the US firm RCA, DVI is now owned by Intel and has active support from IBM and Microsoft. It can be used on the hard disk of a PC as well as on a CD-ROM.

Dvořák Antonin (Leopold) 1841–1904. Czech composer. International recognition came with two sets of *Slavonic Dances* 1878 and 1886. He was director of the National Conservatory, New York, 1892–95. Works such as his *New World Symphony* 1893 reflect his interest in American folk themes, including black and native American. He wrote nine symphonies; tone poems; operas, including *Rusalka* 1900; large-scale choral works; the *Carnival* 1891–92 and other overtures; violin and cello concertos; chamber music; piano pieces; and songs. His Romantic music extends the Classical tradition of Beethoven and Brahms and displays the influence of Czech folk music.

Dvorak keyboard alternative keyboard layout to the normal typewriter keyboard layout (◊QWERTY). In the Dvorak layout the most commonly used keys are situated in the center, so that keying is faster.

dwarfism abnormally short stature. The most common form is *achondroplasia* an inherited disorder in which the limbs fail to reach a normal length. The achondroplastic dwarf has short limbs but a head and trunk of normal size. In pituitary dwarfism there is a deficiency of growth hormone; the pituitary dwarf is physically well proportioned but may be sexually underdeveloped. Intelligence is not affected.

Dyck Anthony van 1599–1641. Flemish painter. Born in Antwerp, van Dyck was an assistant to Rubens 1618–20, then briefly worked in England at the court of James I, and moved to Italy 1622. In 1626 he returned to Antwerp, where he continued to paint religious works and portraits. From 1632 he lived in England and produced numerous portraits of royalty and aristocrats, such as *Charles I on Horseback* about 1638 (National Gallery, London).

dye substance that, applied in solution to fabrics, imparts a color resistant to washing. *Direct dyes* combine with the material of the fabric, yielding a colored compound; *indirect dyes* require the presence of another substance (a mordant), with which the fabric must first be treated; *vat dyes* are colorless soluble substances that on exposure to air yield an insoluble colored compound.

Dyfed county of SW Wales, created 1974 *area* 2,227 sq mi/5,770 sq km *towns and cities* Carmarthen (administrative headquarters), Llanelli, Haverfordwest, Aberystwyth, Cardigan, Lampeter *features* Pembrokeshire Coast National Park; part of the Brecon Beacons National Park, including the Black Mountain; part of the Cambrian Mountains, including Plynlimon Fawr, 2,468 ft/752 m; the village of Laugharne, at the mouth of the river Tywi, which was the home of the writer Dylan Thomas; the Museum of the Woolen Industry at Dre-fach Felindre, and the Museum of Welsh religious life at Tre'rddôl *industries* anthracite (local mines produce about 50,000 metric tons a year); agricultural produce; oil from refinery at Milford Haven *population* (1991) 343,500 *languages* English; 44% Welsh-speaking *famous people* Giraldus Cambrensis, Dafydd ap Gwilym.

Dylan Bob. Adopted name of Robert Allen Zimmerman 1941– . US singer and songwriter. His lyrics provided catchphrases for a generation and influenced innumerable songwriters. He began in the folk-music tradition. His early songs, as on his albums *Freewheelin'* 1963 and *The Times They Are A-Changin'* 1964, were associated with the US civil-rights movement and antiwar protest. From 1965 he worked in an individualistic rock style, as on the albums *Highway 61 Revisited* 1965 and *Blonde on Blonde* 1966.

dynamics or *kinetics* in mechanics, the mathematical and physical study of the behavior of bodies under the action of forces that produce changes of motion in them.

dynamo former name for ◊generator.

dysentery infection of the large intestine causing abdominal cramps and painful ◊diarrhea with blood. There are two kinds of dysentery: *amebic* (caused by a protozoan), common in the tropics, which may lead to liver damage; and *bacterial*, the kind most often seen in the temperate zones.

dyslexia malfunction in the brain's synthesis and interpretation of written information, popularly known as "word blindness".

dysprosium silver-white, metallic element of the ◊lanthanide series, symbol Dy, atomic number 66, relative atomic mass 162.50. It is among the most magnetic of all known substances and has a great capacity to absorb neutrons.

E

eagle any of several genera of large birds of prey of the family Accipitridae, including the golden eagle *Aquila chrysaetos* of Eurasia and North America, which has a 2 ft/2 m wingspan and is dark brown.

In North America the golden eagle is found throughout most of the US, Canada, and N Mexico, with the exception of the SE. The larger spotted eagle *A. clanga* lives in Central Europe and Asia. The sea eagles *Haliaetus* include Steller's sea eagle *H. pelagicus*, mainly a carrion-feeder which breeds on sea cliffs.

eagle The bald eagle of N America lives along coasts, rivers, and lakes, where food is plentiful. During the mating season, couples indulge in spectacular courtship displays in which male and female birds lock talons in midair and somersault downward together.

Eakins Thomas 1844–1916. US painter. A trained observer of human anatomy and a devotee of photography, Eakins attempted to achieve a powerful visual Realism. His most memorable subjects are medical and sporting scenes, characterized by strong contrasts between light and shade, as in *The Gross Clinic* 1875 (Jefferson Medical College, Philadelphia), a group portrait of a surgeon, his assistants, and students.

His most memorable subjects were medical and sporting scenes. Among his larger-than-life-size sculptures commissioned for public monuments are the war memorials in Trenton, New Jersey, and Brooklyn, New York.

ear organ of hearing in animals. It responds to the vibrations that constitute sound, and these are translated into nerve signals and passed to the brain. A mammal's ear consists of three parts: outer ear, middle ear, and inner ear. The *outer ear* is a funnel that collects sound, directing it down a tube to the *ear drum* (tympanic membrane), which separates the outer and *middle ears*. Sounds vibrate this membrane, the mechanical movement of which is transferred to a smaller membrane leading to the *inner ear* by three small bones, the auditory ossicles. Vibrations of the inner ear membrane move fluid contained in the snail-shaped cochlea, which vibrates hair cells that stimulate the auditory nerve connected to the brain. Three fluid-filled canals of the inner ear detect changes of position; this mechanism, with other sensory inputs, is responsible for the sense of balance.

Earhart Amelia 1898–1937. US aviation pioneer and author, who in 1928 became the first woman to fly across the Atlantic. With copilot Frederick Noonan, she attempted a round-the-world flight 1937. Somewhere over the Pacific their plane disappeared.

Earth third planet from the Sun. It is almost spherical, flattened slightly at the poles, and is composed of three concentric layers: the core, the mantle, and the crust. About 70% of the surface (including the north and south polar icecaps) is covered with water. The Earth is surrounded by a life-supporting atmosphere and is the only planet on which life is known to exist. *mean distance from the Sun* 92,860,000 mi/149,500,000 km *equatorial diameter* 7,923 mi/12,756 km *circumference* 24,900 mi/40,070 km *rotation period* 23 hr 56 min 4.1 sec *year* (complete orbit, or sidereal period) 365 days 5 hr 48 min 46 sec. Earth's average speed around the Sun is 18.5 mps/ 30 kps; the plane of its orbit is inclined to its equatorial plane at an angle of 23.5°, the reason for the changing seasons. *atmosphere* nitrogen 78.09%; oxygen 20.95%; argon 0.93%; carbon dioxide 0.03%; and less than 0.0001% neon, helium, krypton, hydrogen, xenon, ozone, radon *surface* land surface 57,500,000 sq mi/150,000,000 sq km (greatest height above sea level 29,118 ft/8,872 m Mount Everest); water surface 139,400,000 sq mi/361,000,000 sq km (greatest depth 36,201 ft/11,034 m ◊Mariana Trench in the Pacific). The interior is thought to be an inner core about 1,600 mi/2,600 km in diameter, of solid iron and nickel; an outer core about 1,400 mi/2,250 km thick, of molten iron and nickel; and a mantle of mostly solid rock about 1,800 mi/2,900 km thick, separated by the Mohorovic discontinuity from the Earth's crust. The crust and the topmost layer of the mantle form about 12 major moving plates, some of which carry the continents. The plates are in constant, slow motion, called tectonic drift. *satellite* the ◊Moon *age* 4.6 trillion years. The Earth was formed with the rest of the ◊Solar System by consolidation of interstellar dust. Life began 3.5–4 trillion years ago.

earthquake shaking of the Earth's surface as a result of the sudden release of stresses built up in the Earth's crust. The study of earthquakes is called ◊seismology. Most earthquakes occur along ◊faults (fractures or

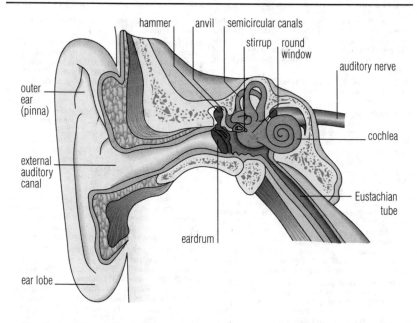

ear The structure of the ear. The three bones of the middle ear—hammer, anvil, and stirrup—vibrate in unison and magnify sounds about 20 times. The spiral-shaped cochlea is the organ of hearing. As sound waves pass down the spiral tube, they vibrate fine hairs lining the tube, which activate the auditory nerve connected to the brain. The semicircular canals are the organs of balance, detecting movements of the head.

breaks) in the crust. ◊Plate tectonic movements generate the major proportion: as two plates move past each other they can become jammed and deformed, and a series of shock waves (seismic waves) occur when they spring free. Their force (magnitude) is measured on the ◊Richter scale, and their effect (intensity) on the Mercalli scale. The point at which an earthquake originates is the *seismic focus*; the point on the Earth's surface directly above this is the *epicenter*.

Earth Summit (official name *United Nations Conference on Environment and Development*) international meeting in Rio de Janeiro, Brazil, June 1992, which drew up measures toward world environmental protection. Treaties were made to combat global warming and protect wildlife ("biodiversity") (the latter was not signed by the US).

earthworm ◊annelid worm of the class Oligochaeta. Earthworms are hermaphroditic and deposit their eggs in cocoons. They live by burrowing in the soil, feeding on the organic matter it contains. They are vital to the formation of humus, aerating the soil and leveling it by transferring earth from the deeper levels to the surface as castings.

Most North American earthworms belong to the genus *Lumbricus*. These are comparatively small, but some tropical forms reach over 3 ft/1 m in length. *Megascolides australis*, of Queensland, for instance, can be over 11 ft/3 m long.

earwig nocturnal insect of the order Dermaptera. The forewings are short and leathery and serve to protect the hindwings, which are large and are folded like a

earthquake: major 20th-century earthquakes

date	place	magnitude (Richter scale)	number of deaths
1906	San Francisco, US	8.3	450
1908	Messina, Italy	7.5	83,000
1915	Avezzano, Italy	7.5	29,980
1920	Gansu, China	8.6	100,000
1923	Tokyo, Japan	8.3	99,330
1927	Nan-Shan, China	8.3	200,000
1932	Gansu, China	7.6	70,000
1935	Quetta, India	7.5	30,000
1939	Erzincan, Turkey	7.9	30,000
1939	Chillán, Chile	8.3	28,000
1948	USSR	7.3	110,000
1970	N Peru	7.7	66,794
1976	Tangshan, China	8.2	242,000
1978	NE Iran	7.7	25,000
1980	El Asnam, Algeria	7.3	20,000
1985	Mexico	8.1	25,000
1988	Armenia, USSR	6.9	25,000
1989	San Francisco, US	7.1	300
1990	NW Iran	7.7	50,000
1993	Maharashtra, India	7.7	9,800
1995	Kobe, Japan	6.9–7	5,000

fan when at rest. Earwigs seldom fly. They have a pincerlike appendage in the rear. The male is distinguished by curved pincers; those of the female are straight. Earwigs are regarded as pests because they feed on flowers and fruit, but they also eat other insects, dead or alive. Eggs are laid beneath the soil, and the female cares for the young even after they have hatched. The male dies before the eggs have hatched. *Forficula* is the common genus in North America.

east one of the four cardinal points of the compass, indicating that part of the horizon where the Sun rises; when facing north, east is to the right.

East Anglia region of E England, formerly a Saxon kingdom, including Norfolk, Suffolk, and parts of Essex and Cambridgeshire. Norwich is the principal city of East Anglia. The Sainsbury Center for Visual Arts, opened 1978, at the University of East Anglia, has a collection of ethnographic art and sculpture. East Anglian ports such as Harwich and Felixstowe have greatly developed as trade with the rest of Europe has increased.

Easter spring feast of the Christian church, commemorating the Resurrection of Jesus. It is a moveable feast, falling on the first Sunday following the full moon after the vernal equinox (March 21), that is, between March 22 and April 25.

Dyed easter eggs, and pieces of candy shaped like eggs, young chickens, ducklings, lambs or rabbits—all symbolizing new life—are given to young children.

Easter Island or *Rapa Nui* Chilean island in the S Pacific Ocean, part of the Polynesian group, about 2,200 mi/3,500 km W of Chile; area about 64 sq mi/166 sq km; population (1985) 2,000. It was first reached by Europeans on Easter Sunday 1722.

On it stand over 800 huge carved statues (moai) and the remains of boat-shaped stone houses, the work of Neolithic peoples of unknown origin. The chief center is Hanga-Roa.

Eastern Orthodox Church see ◊Orthodox Church.

Easter Rising or *Easter Rebellion* in Irish history, a republican insurrection that began on Easter Monday, April 1916, in Dublin. It was inspired by the Irish Republican Brotherhood (IRB) in an unsuccessful attempt to overthrow British rule in Ireland. It was led by Patrick Pearse of the IRB and James Connolly of Sinn Féin.

East Germany see ◊Germany, East.

East India Company (British) commercial company 1600–1858 chartered by Queen Elizabeth I and given a monopoly of trade between England and the Far East. In the 18th century, the company became, in effect, the ruler of a large part of India, and a form of dual control by the company and a committee responsible to Parliament in London was introduced by Pitt's India Act 1784. The end of the monopoly of China trade came 1834, and after the Indian Mutiny 1857 the crown took complete control of the government of British India; the India Act 1858 abolished the company.

Eastman George 1854–1932. US entrepreneur and inventor who founded the Eastman Kodak photographic company 1892. He patented flexible film 1884, invented the Kodak box camera 1888, and introduced daylight-loading film 1892. By 1900 his company was selling a pocket camera for as little as one dollar. Eastman Kodak have long dominated the world photographic market.

The films first worked with chemicals fixed to a paper base 1884 and later on celluloid 1889. In 1928 he perfected a film process for color photography and development, an important service offered on fine

papers. He was known for his contributions to education and music.

East Sussex county of SE England, created 1974, formerly part of Sussex *area* 695 sq mi/1,800 sq km *towns and cities* Lewes (administrative headquarters), Newhaven (cross-channel port), Brighton, Eastbourne, Hastings, Bexhill, Winchelsea, Rye *features* Beachy Head, highest headland on the south coast at 590 ft/180 m, the east end of the South Downs; the Weald (including Ashdown Forest); Friston Forest; rivers: Ouse, Cuckmere, East Rother; Romney Marsh; the "Long Man" chalk hill figure at Wilmington, near Eastbourne; Herstmonceux, with a 15th-century castle (conference and exhibition center) and adjacent modern buildings, site of the Greenwich Royal Observatory 1958–90; other castles at Hastings, Lewes, Pevensey, and Bodiam; Battle Abbey and the site of the Battle of Hastings; Michelham Priory; Sheffield Park garden; University of Sussex at Falmer, near Brighton, founded 1961 *industries* electronics, gypsum, timber; light engineering; agricultural products, including cereals, hops, fruit, and vegetables *population* (1991) 690,400

East Timor disputed territory on the island of ◊Timor in the Malay Archipelago; prior to 1975, it was a Portuguese colony for almost 460 years. The people of East Timor are known as Maubere. *area* 5,706 sq mi/14,874 sq km *capital* Dili *industries* coffee *population* (1980) 555,000 *history* Following Portugal's withdrawal 1975, East Timor was left with a literacy rate of under 10% and no infrastructure. Civil war broke out and the left-wing Revolutionary Front of Independent East Timor (Fretilin) occupied the capital, calling for independence. In opposition, troops from neighboring Indonesia invaded the territory, declaring East Timor (*Loro Sae*) the 17th province of Indonesia July 1976. This claim is not recognized by the United Nations.

Eastwood Clint 1930– . US film actor and director. As the "Man with No Name" in *A Fistful of Dollars* 1964 and *The Good, the Bad, and the Ugly* 1966, he started the vogue for "spaghetti Westerns" (made in Italy or Spain). Later Westerns which he both starred in and directed include *High Plains Drifter* 1973, *The Outlaw Josey Wales* 1976, and *Unforgiven* 1992 (two Academy Awards). Other films include *In The Line of Fire* 1993.

ebony any of a group of hardwood trees of the ebony family Ebenaceae, especially some tropical persimmons of the genus *Diospyros*, native to Africa and Asia.

Their very heavy, hard, black timber polishes well and is used in cabinetmaking and inlaying; for piano keys and violin fingerboards, chin rests, and pegs; and for sculpture.

EC abbreviation for *European Community*, former name (to 1993) of the ◊European Union.

echidna or *spiny anteater* toothless, egg-laying, spiny mammal of the order Monotremata, found in Australia and New Guinea. There are two species: *Tachyglossus aculeatus*, the short-nosed echidna, and the rarer *Zaglossus bruijni*, the long-nosed echidna. They feed entirely upon ants and termites, which they dig out with their powerful claws and lick up with their prehensile tongues. When attacked, an echidna rolls itself into a ball, or tries to hide by burrowing in the earth.

echinoderm marine invertebrate of the phylum Echinodermata ("spiny-skinned"), characterized by a five-radial symmetry. Echinoderms have a water-vas-

echidna *The short-nosed echidna is found throughout Australia. Echidnas are egg-laying mammals (monotremes). They are nocturnal and live almost exclusively on ants and termites.*

cular system which transports substances around the body. They include starfishes (or sea stars), brittlestars, sea-lilies, sea-urchins, and sea-cucumbers. The skeleton is external, made of a series of limy plates, and echinoderms generally move by using tube-feet, small water-filled sacs that can be protruded or pulled back to the body.

echo repetition of a sound wave, or of a ◊radar or ◊sonar signal, by reflection from a surface. By accurately measuring the time taken for an echo to return to the transmitter, and by knowing the speed of a radar signal (the speed of light) or a sonar signal (the speed of sound in water), it is possible to calculate the range of the object causing the echo (◊echolocation).

A similar technique is used in echo sounders to estimate the depth of water under a ship's keel or the depth of a school of fish.

echolocation or *biosonar* method used by certain animals, notably bats, whales and dolphins, to detect the positions of objects by using sound. The animal emits a stream of high-pitched sounds, generally at ultrasonic frequencies (beyond the range of human hearing), and listens for the returning echoes reflected off objects to determine their exact location.

eclipse passage of an astronomical body through the shadow of another. The term is usually employed for solar and lunar eclipses, which may be either partial or total, but also, for example, for eclipses by Jupiter of its satellites. An eclipse of a star by a body in the Solar System is called an occultation.

Eco Umberto 1932– . Italian writer, semiologist, and literary critic. His works include *The Role of the Reader* 1979, the "philosophical thriller" *The Name of the Rose* 1983, and *Foucault's Pendulum* 1988.

ecology study of the relationship among organisms and the environments in which they live, including all living and nonliving components. The term was coined by the biologist Ernst Haeckel 1866.

economics social science devoted to studying the production, distribution, and consumption of wealth. It consists of the disciplines of *microeconomics*, the study of individual producers, consumers, or markets, and *macroeconomics*, the study of whole economies

or systems (in particular, areas such as taxation and public spending).

ectoparasite ◊parasite that lives on the outer surface of its host.

ECU abbreviation for *European Currency Unit*, the official monetary unit of the European Union. It is based on the value of the different currencies used in the ◊European Monetary System (EMS).

Ecuador country in South America, bounded N by Colombia, E and S by Peru, and W by the Pacific Ocean.

Ecuador Republic of (*República del Ecuador*) *area* 104,479 sq mi/270,670 sq km *capital* Quito *towns and cities* Cuenca; chief port Guayaquil *physical* coastal plain rises sharply to Andes Mountains, which are divided into a series of cultivated valleys; flat, low-lying rainforest in E *environment* about 25,000 species became extinct 1965–90 as a result of environmental destruction *features* Ecuador is crossed by the equator, from which it derives its name; Galápagos Islands; Cotopaxi is world's highest active volcano; rich wildlife in rainforest of Amazon basin *head of state and government* Sixto Duran Ballen from 1992 *political system* emergent democratic republic *political parties* Social Christian Party (PSC), right-wing; United Republican Party (PUR), right-of-center coalition; Ecuadorean Roldosist Party (PRE); Democratic Left (ID), left of center *exports* bananas, cocoa, coffee, sugar, rice, fruit, balsa wood, fish, petroleum *currency* sucre *population* (1993 est) 10,980,000; (mestizo 55%, Indian 25%, European 10%, black African 10%); growth rate 2.9% p.a. *life expectancy* men 65, women 69 *languages* Spanish (official), Quechua, Jivaro, and other Indian languages *religion* Roman Catholic 95% *literacy* men 88%, women 84% *GNP* $1,020 per head (1991) *chronology 1830* Independence achieved from Spain. *1925–48* Great political instability; no president completed his term of office. *1948–55* Liberals in power. *1956* First conservative president in 60 years. *1960* Liberals returned, with José Velasco as president. *1961* Velasco deposed and replaced by the vice president. *1962* Military junta installed. *1968* Velasco returned as president. *1972* A coup put the military back in power. *1978* New democratic constitution adopted. *1979* Liberals in power but opposed by right- and left-wing parties. *1982* Deteriorating economy provoked strikes, demonstrations, and a state of emergency. *1983* Austerity measures introduced. *1984–85* No party with a clear majority in the national congress; Febers Cordero narrowly won the presidency for the Conservatives. *1988* Rodrigo Borja Cevallos elected president for moderate left-wing coalition. *1992* PUR leader Sixto Duran Ballen elected president; PSC became largest party in congress.

ecumenical movement movement for reunification of the various branches of the Christian church. It began in the 19th century with the extension of missionary work to Africa and Asia, where the divisions created in Europe were incomprehensible; the movement gathered momentum from the need for unity in the face of growing secularism in Christian countries and of the challenge posed by such faiths as Islam. The *World Council of Churches* was founded 1948.

Edberg Stefan 1966– . Swedish tennis player. He won the junior Grand Slam 1983 and his first Grand Slam title, the Australian Open, 1985, repeated 1987. Other Grand Slam singles titles include Wimbledon 1988, 1990 and the US Open 1991 and 1992.

Eddy Mary Baker 1821–1910. US founder of the Christian Science movement.

Separated from her husband and in poor health, she discovered in 1862 the work of a faith healer named Phineas Quimby, who decisively influenced her belief in healing through divine grace, a belief enhanced by her own recovery.

edelweiss perennial alpine plant *Leontopodium alpinum*, family Compositae, with a white, woolly, star-shaped bloom, found in the high mountains of Eurasia.

edema any abnormal accumulation of fluid in tissues or cavities of the body; waterlogging of the tissues due to excessive loss of ◊plasma through the capillary walls. It may be generalized (the condition once known as dropsy) or confined to one area, such as the ankles.

Eden Anthony, 1st Earl of Avon 1897–1977. British Conservative politician, foreign secretary 1935–38, 1940–45, and 1951–55; prime minister 1955–57, when he resigned after the failure of the Anglo-French military intervention in the ◊Suez Crisis.

Edgar the Peaceful 944–975. King of all England from 959. He was the younger son of Edmund I, and strove successfully to unite English and Danes as fellow subjects.

EDI (abbreviation for *electronic dissemination of information* or *electronic data interchange*) the transfer of structured information in electronic form between computer systems in different organizations. EDI is principally used for exchange of information relating to business transactions and for electronic transfer of funds.

Edinburgh capital of Scotland and administrative center of the region of Lothian, near the southern shores of the Firth of Forth; population (1991) 418,900. Industries include printing, publishing, banking, insurance, chemical manufactures, distilling, brewing, and some shipbuilding. A cultural center, it holds a major annual festival of music and the arts. The university was established 1583.

Edinburgh, Duke of title of Prince ◊Philip of the UK.

Edison Thomas Alva 1847–1931. US scientist and inventor, with over 1,000 patents. In Menlo Park, New Jersey, 1876–87, he produced his most important inventions, including the electric light bulb 1879. He constructed a system of electric power distribution for consumers, the telephone transmitter, and the phonograph.

In 1869 he invented an automatic vote recorder and the improved stock ticker in 1871, which earned him enough to found his manufacturing plant in Newark, New Jersey. He moved to Menlo Park in 1876 and from there to West Orange, New Jersey, where he invented the movie camera, mimeograph, fluoroscope, and an improved battery. In 1889 he began the Edison Light Co., which became the General Electric Co.

Edmonton capital of Alberta, Canada, on the North Saskatchewan River; population (1986) 576,200. It is the center of an oil and mining area to the N and also an agricultural and dairying region. Petroleum pipelines link Edmonton with Superior, Wisconsin, and Vancouver, British Columbia.

Edmund (II) Ironside c.989–1016. King of England 1016, the son of Ethelred II the Unready. He led the resistance to ◊Canute's invasion 1015, and on

Ethelred's death 1016 was chosen king by the citizens of London, whereas the Witan (the king's council) elected Canute. In the struggle for the throne, Edmund was defeated by Canute at Assandun (Ashington), Essex, and they divided the kingdom between them; when Edmund died the same year, Canute ruled the whole kingdom.

Edo former name for ◊Tokyo until 1868.

EDP in computing, abbreviation for *electronic data processing*.

education process, beginning at birth, of developing intellectual capacity, manual skill, and social awareness, especially by instruction.

In its more restricted sense, the term refers to the process of imparting literacy, numeracy, and a generally accepted body of knowledge.

Edward (full name Edward Antony Richard Louis) 1964– . Prince of the UK, third son of Queen Elizabeth II. He is seventh in line to the throne after Charles, Charles's two sons, Andrew, and Andrew's two daughters.

Edward (called *the Black Prince*) 1330–1376. Prince of Wales, eldest son of Edward III of England. The epithet (probably posthumous) may refer to his black armor. During the Hundred Years' War he fought at the Battle of Crécy 1346 and captured the French king at Poitiers 1356. He ruled Aquitaine 1360–71; during the revolt that eventually ousted him, he caused the massacre of Limoges 1370.

Edward I 1239–1307. King of England from 1272, son of Henry III. Edward led the royal forces against Simon de Montfort in the Barons' War 1264–67, and was on a crusade when he succeeded to the throne. He established English rule over all Wales 1282–84, and secured recognition of his overlordship from the Scottish king, although the Scots (under Wallace and Bruce) fiercely resisted actual conquest. In his reign Parliament took its approximate modern form with the Model Parliament 1295. He was succeeded by his son Edward II.

Edward II 1284–1327. King of England from 1307, son of Edward I. Born at Caernarvon Castle, he was created the first Prince of Wales 1301. His invasion of Scotland 1314 to suppress revolt resulted in defeat at ◊Bannockburn. He was deposed 1327 by his wife Isabella (1292–1358), daughter of Philip IV of France, and her lover Roger de Mortimer, and murdered in Berkeley Castle, Gloucestershire. He was succeeded by his son Edward III.

In addition to military disasters, his reign was troubled by his extravagance and the unpopularity of his favorites.

Edward III 1312–1377. King of England from 1327, son of Edward II. He assumed the government 1330 from his mother, through whom in 1337 he laid claim to the French throne and thus began the ◊Hundred Years' War. He was succeeded by his grandson Richard II.

At 18 Edward imprisoned his mother Isabella of France and executed her lover Roger de Mortimer. In 1360 he surrendered his claim to the French throne, but the war resumed 1369, and his son John of Gaunt dominated the government in his later years.

Edward IV 1442–1483. King of England 1461–70 and from 1471. He was the son of Richard, Duke of York, and succeeded Henry VI in the Wars of the ◊Roses, temporarily losing the throne to Henry when Edward fell out with his adviser ◊Warwick, but regaining it at the

Battle of Barnet 1471. He was succeeded by his son Edward V.

Edward V 1470–1483. King of England 1483. Son of Edward IV, he was deposed three months after his accession in favor of his uncle (◊Richard III), and is traditionally believed to have been murdered (with his brother) in the Tower of London on Richard's orders.

Edward VI 1537–1553. King of England from 1547, son of Henry VIII and Jane Seymour. The government was entrusted to his uncle the Duke of Somerset (who fell from power 1549), and then to the Earl of Warwick, later created Duke of Northumberland. He was succeeded by his sister, Mary I.

Edward VII 1841–1910. King of Great Britain and Ireland from 1901. As Prince of Wales he was a prominent social figure, but his mother Queen Victoria considered him too frivolous to take part in political life. In 1860 he made the first tour of Canada and the US ever undertaken by a British prince.

He took a close interest in politics and was on good terms with party leaders. He succeeded to the throne 1901 and was crowned 1902. Although he overrated his political influence, he contributed to the Entente Cordiale 1904 with France and the Anglo-Russian agreement 1907.

Edward VIII 1894–1972. King of Great Britain and Northern Ireland Jan–Dec 1936, when he renounced the throne to marry Wallis Warfield Simpson. He was created Duke of Windsor and was governor of the Bahamas 1940–45, subsequently settling in France.

He succeeded his father George V on Jan 20, 1936, and on Dec 11 he abdicated. A divorcee, Mrs Simpson was not acceptable constitutionally as queen. They were married in France in May 1937.

Edward the Confessor *c.*1003–1066. King of England from 1042, the son of Ethelred II. He lived in Normandy until shortly before his accession. During his reign power was held by Earl Godwin and his son Harold, while the king devoted himself to religion, including the rebuilding of Westminster Abbey (consecrated 1065), where he is buried. His childlessness led ultimately to the Norman Conquest 1066. He was canonized 1161.

Edward the Elder *c.*870–924. King of the West Saxons. He succeeded his father ◊Alfred the Great 899. He reconquered SE England and the Midlands from the Danes, uniting Wessex and Mercia with the help of his sister, Athelflad. By the time Edward died, his kingdom was the most powerful in the British Isles. He was succeeded by his son ◊Athelstan.

Edward the Martyr *c.*963–978. King of England from 975. Son of King Edgar, he was murdered at Corfe Castle, Dorset, probably at his stepmother Aelfthryth's instigation (she wished to secure the crown for her son, Ethelred). He was canonized 1001.

EEC abbreviation for *European Economic Community*; see ◊European Union.

eel any fish of the order Anguilliformes. Eels are snake-like, with elongated dorsal and anal fins. They include the freshwater eels of Europe and North America (which breed in the Atlantic), the marine conger eels, and the morays of tropical coral reefs.

EFTA acronym for *European Free Trade Association*.

Egbert King of the West Saxons from 802, the son of Ealhmund, an under-king of Kent. By 829 he had united England for the first time under one king.

egg in animals, the ovum, or female ◊gamete (reproductive cell).

After fertilization by a sperm cell, it begins to divide to form an embryo. Eggs may be deposited by the female (ovipary) or they may develop within her body (vivipary and ◊ovovivipary). In the oviparous reptiles and birds, the egg is protected by a shell, and well supplied with nutrients in the form of yolk.

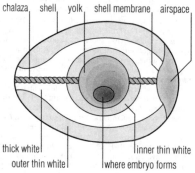

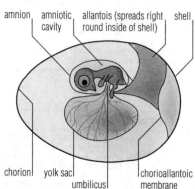

egg Section through a fertilized bird egg. Inside a bird's egg is a complex structure of liquids and membranes designed to meet the needs of the growing embryo. The yolk, which is rich in fat, is gradually absorbed by the embryo. The white of the egg provides protein and water. The chalaza is a twisted band of protein which holds the yolk in place and acts as a shock absorber. The airspace allows gases to be exchanged through the shell. The allantois contains many blood vessels which carry gases between the embryo and the outside.

eggplant perennial plant, *Solanum melongena*, a member of the nightshade family Solanaceae, originally native to tropical Asia. Its purple-skinned fruits are eaten as a vegetable.

ego in psychology, a general term for the processes concerned with the self and a person's conception of himself or herself, encompassing values and attitudes. In Freudian psychology, the term refers specifically to the element of the human mind that represents the conscious processes concerned with reality, in conflict with the ◊id (the instinctual element) and the ◊superego (the ethically aware element).

egret any of several herons with long feathers on the head or neck.

The snowy egret *Egretta thula* of North America, about 2 ft/60 cm long, was almost hunted to extinction for its graceful plumes before the practice was made illegal. The little egret *E. garzetta* 2 ft/60cm long, is found in Asia, Africa, S Europe, and Australia.

Egypt Arab Republic of (*Jumhuriyat Misr al-Arabiya*) *area* 1,001,450 sq km/386,990 sq mi *capital* Cairo *towns and cities* Gîza; ports Alexandria, Port Said, Suez, Damietta *physical* mostly desert; hills in E; fertile land along Nile valley and delta; cultivated and settled area is about 13,700 sq mi/35,500 sq km *environment* the Aswan Dam (opened 1970) on the Nile has caused widespread salinization and an increase in waterborne diseases in the area. A dramatic fall in the annual load of silt deposited downstream has reduced the fertility of cropland and led to coastal erosion *features* Aswan High Dam and Lake Nasser; Sinai; remains of ancient Egypt (pyramids, Sphinx, Luxor, Karnak, Abu Simbel, El Faiyum) *head of state* Mohammed Hosni Mubarak from 1981 *head of government* Atif Sidqi from 1981 *political system* democratic republic *political parties* National Democratic Party (NDP), moderate, left of center; Liberal Socialist Party, free enterprise; Socialist Labour Party, left of center; National Progressive Unionist Party, left-wing *exports* cotton and textiles, petroleum, fruit and vegetables *currency* Egyptian pound *population* (1993) 56,430,000; growth rate 2.4% p.a. *life expectancy* men 60, women 63 *languages* Arabic (official); ancient Egyptian survives to some extent in Coptic *media* state monopoly on radio and TV broadcasting;

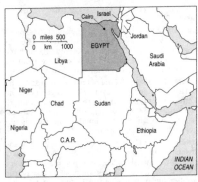

the largest publishing houses, newspapers, and magazines are owned and controlled by the state; both foreign and local press is censored on political and religious grounds, also films, plays, TV scripts; books may be banned. The theological institute El-Azhar vets all books and works of art that touch on Islam, as well as TV commercials and even public-health messages *religions* Sunni Muslim 95%, Coptic Christian 5% *literacy* men 63%, women 34% *GNP* $620 per head (1991) *chronology 1914* Egypt became a British protectorate. *1936* Independence achieved from Britain. King Fuad succeeded by his son Farouk. *1946* Withdrawal of British troops except from Suez Canal Zone. *1952* Farouk overthrown by army in bloodless coup. *1953* Egypt declared a republic, with General Neguib as president. *1956* Neguib replaced by Col. Gamal Nasser. Nasser announced nationalization of Suez Canal; Egypt attacked by Britain, France, and

---

Egypt, ancient: chronology

5000 BC	Egyptian culture already well established in the Nile Valley, with Neolithic farming villages.
3200	Menes united Lower Egypt (the delta) with his own kingdom of Upper Egypt.
2800	The architect Imhotep built the step pyramid at Sakkara.
c. 2600	**Old Kingdom** reached the height of its power and the kings of the 4th dynasty built the pyramids at El Gîza.
c. 2200–1800	**Middle Kingdom**, under which the unity lost toward the end of the Old Kingdom was restored.
1730	Invading Asian Hyksos people established their kingdom in the Nile Delta.
c. 1580	**New Kingdom** established by the 18th dynasty following the eviction of the Hyksos, with its capital at Thebes. The high point of ancient Egyptian civilization under the pharaohs Thothmes, Hatshepsut, Amenhotep, Ikhnaton (who moved the capital to Akhetaton), and Tutankhamen.
c. 1321	19th dynasty: Ramses I built a temple at Karnak, Ramses II the temple at Abu Simbel.
1191	Ramses III defeated the Indo-European Sea Peoples, but after him there was decline, and power within the country passed from the pharaohs to the priests of Ammon.
1090–663	**Late New Kingdom** during this period Egypt was often divided between two or more dynasties; the nobles became virtually independent.
8th–7th centuries	Brief interlude of rule by kings from Nubia.
666	The Assyrians under Ashurbanipal occupied Thebes.
663–609	Psammetichus I restored Egypt's independence and unity.
525	Egypt was conquered by Cambyses and became a Persian province.
c. 405–340	Period of independence.
332	Conquest by Alexander the Great. On the division of his empire, Egypt went to one of his generals, Ptolemy I, and his descendants, the Macedonian dynasty.
30	Death of Cleopatra, last of the Macedonians, and conquest by the Roman emperor Augustus; Egypt became a province of the Roman empire.
AD 641	Conquest by the Arabs; the Christianity of later Roman rule was for the most part replaced by Islam.

For later history, see ◊Egypt.

Israel. Cease-fire agreed because of US intervention. *1958* Short-lived merger of Egypt and Syria as United Arab Republic (UAR). Subsequent attempts to federate Egypt, Syria, and Iraq failed. *1967* Six-Day War with Israel ended in Egypt's defeat and Israeli occupation of Sinai and Gaza Strip. *1970* Nasser died suddenly; succeeded by Anwar Sadat. *1973* Attempt to regain territory lost to Israel led to defeat; cease-fire arranged by US secretary of state Henry Kissinger. *1977* Sadat's visit to Israel to address the Israeli parliament was criticized by Egypt's Arab neighbors. *1978–79* Camp David talks in the US resulted in a treaty between Egypt and Israel. Egypt expelled from the Arab League. *1981* Sadat assassinated, succeeded by Hosni Mubarak. *1983* Improved relations between Egypt and the Arab world; only Libya and Syria maintained a trade boycott. *1984* Mubarak's party victorious in the people's assembly elections. *1987* Mubarak reelected. Egypt readmitted to Arab League. *1988* Full diplomatic relations with Algeria restored. *1989* Improved relations with Libya; diplomatic relations with Syria restored. Mubarak proposed a peace plan. *1990* Gains for independents in general election. *1991* Participation in Gulf War on US-led side. Major force in convening Middle East peace conference in Spain. *1992* Outbreaks of violence between Muslims and Christians. *1993* Islamic militant campaign against government escalated. Mubarak sworn in for third term.

Ehrlich Paul 1854–1915. German bacteriologist and immunologist who produced the first cure for ◊syphilis. He developed the arsenic compounds, in particular Salvarsan, that were used in the treatment of syphilis prior to the discovery of antibiotics. He shared the 1908 Nobel Prize for Medicine with Ilya Mechnikov for his work on immunity.

eider large marine ◊duck, *Somateria mollissima*, highly valued for its soft down, which is used in quilts and cushions for warmth. The adult male has a black cap and belly and a green nape. The rest of the plumage is white with pink breast and throat while the female is a mottled brown. The bill is large and flattened. It is found on the northern coasts of the Atlantic and Pacific Oceans.

Eiffel (Alexandre) Gustave 1832–1923. French engineer who constructed the *Eiffel Tower* for the 1889 Paris Exhibition. The tower, made of iron, is 1,050 ft/320 m high, and stands in the Champ de Mars, Paris.
    Sightseers may ride to the top for a view.

Eigen Manfred 1927– . German chemist who worked on extremely rapid chemical reactions (those taking less than 1 millisecond). From 1954 he developed a technique by which very short bursts of energy could be applied to solutions, disrupting their equilibrium and enabling him to investigate momentary reactions, such as the formation and dissociation of water.
    For this work he shared the Nobel Prize in Chemistry 1967 with English chemists George Porter and Ronald Norrish.

Einstein Albert 1879–1955. German-born US physicist who formulated the theories of ◊relativity, and worked on radiation physics and thermodynamics. In 1905 he published the special theory of relativity, and in 1915 issued his general theory of relativity. He received the Nobel Prize for Physics 1921. His latest conception of the basic laws governing the universe was outlined in his ◊unified field theory, made public 1953.

Eisenhower, Dwight David ("Ike") US soldier and politician Dwight D Eisenhower. After commanding Allied forces in Europe during World War II, he became the 34th president of the US 1953.

einsteinium synthesized, radioactive, metallic element of the actinide series, symbol Es, atomic number 99, atomic weight 254.

Eire former name (1937–48) of Southern Ireland, now the Republic of ◊Ireland. In Gaelic the name Eire is also used to refer to the whole of Ireland.

Eisenhower Dwight David ("Ike") 1890–1969. 34th president of the US 1953–60, a Republican. A general in World War II, he commanded the Allied forces in Italy 1943, then the Allied invasion of Europe, and from Oct 1944 all the Allied armies in the West. As president he promoted business interests at home and conducted the ◊Cold War abroad. His vice president was Richard Nixon. He was well-liked and had a talent for administration.

EKG abbreviation for ◊*electrocardiogram*.

eland largest species of ◊antelope, *Taurotragus oryx*. Pale fawn in color, it is about 6 ft/2 m high, and both sexes have spiral horns about 18 in/45 cm long. It is found in central and southern Africa.

Elbe one of the principal rivers of Germany, 725 mi/ 1,166 km long, rising on the southern slopes of the Riesengebirge, Czech Republic, and flowing NW across the German plain to the North Sea.

Elbruz or *Elbrus* highest mountain (18,510 ft/5,642 m) on the continent of Europe, in the Caucasus, Georgia.

elder in botany, small tree or shrub of the genus *Sambucus*, of the honeysuckle family Caprifoliaceae, native to North America, Eurasia, and N Africa. Some are grown as ornamentals for their showy yellow, or white flower clusters and their colorful black or scarlet berries.

El Dorado fabled city of gold believed by the 16th-century Spanish and other Europeans to exist somewhere in the area of the Orinoco and Amazon rivers.

Eleanor of Aquitaine c.1122–1204. Queen of France 1137–51 as wife of Louis VII, and of England from 1154 as wife of Henry II. Henry imprisoned her 1174–89 for supporting their sons, the future Richard I and King John, in revolt against him.

Eleanor of Castile c.1245–1290. Queen of Edward I of England, the daughter of Ferdinand III of Castile. She married Prince Edward 1254, and accompanied him on his crusade 1270. She died at Harby, Nottinghamshire, and Edward erected stone crosses in towns where her body rested on the funeral journey to London. Several *Eleanor Crosses* are still standing, for example at Northampton.

election process of appointing a person to public office or a political party to government by voting. Elections were occasionally held in ancient Greek democracies; Roman tribunes were regularly elected.

electoral system see ◊vote and proportional representation.

electric charge property of some bodies that causes them to exert forces on each other. Two bodies both with positive or both with negative charges repel each other, whereas bodies with opposite or "unlike" charges attract each other, since each is in the ◊electric field of the other. In atoms, ◊electrons possess a negative charge, and ◊protons an equal positive charge. The ◊SI unit of electric charge is the coulomb (symbol C).

electric current the flow of electrically charged particles through a conducting circuit due to the presence of a ◊potential difference. The current at any point in a circuit is the amount of charge flowing per second; its SI unit is the ampere (coulomb per second).

electric field in physics, the electrically charged region of space surrounding an electrically charged body. In this region, an electric charge experiences a force owing to the presence of another electric charge.

electricity all phenomena caused by ◊electric charge, whether static or in motion. Electric charge is caused by an excess or deficit of electrons in the charged substance, and an electric current by the movement of electrons around a circuit. Substances may be electrical conductors, such as metals, which allow the passage of electricity through them, or insulators, such as rubber, which are extremely poor conductors. Substances with relatively poor conductivities that can be improved by the addition of heat or light are known as ◊semiconductors.

electrocardiogram (ECG) or (EKG) graphic recording of the electrical changes in the heart muscle, as detected by electrodes placed on the chest. Electrocardiography is used in the diagnosis of heart disease.

electroconvulsive therapy (ECT) or *electroshock therapy* treatment mainly for severe ◊depression, given under anesthesia and with a muscle relaxant. An electric current is passed through one or both sides of the brain to induce alterations in its electrical activity. The treatment can cause distress and loss of concentration and memory, and so there is much controversy about its use and effectiveness.

ECT is increasingly being seen in the US 1994 as the most effective treatment available for severe depression, when all other therapies have failed. The American Psychiatric Association maintain that it can help more than 80% of severely depressed patients.

electrocution death caused by electric current. It is used as a method of execution in some US states. The condemned person is strapped into a special chair and a shock of 1,800–2,000 volts is administered. See ◊capital punishment.

electrode any terminal by which an electric current passes in or out of a conducting substance; for example, the anode or cathode in a battery or the carbons in an arc lamp. The terminals that emit and collect the flow of electrons in thermionic ◊valves (electron tubes) are also called electrodes: for example, cathodes, plates, and grids.

electrolysis in chemistry, the production of chemical changes by passing an electric current through a solution or molten salt (the electrolyte), resulting in the migration of ions to the electrodes: positive ions (cations) to the negative electrode (cathode) and negative ions (anions) to the positive electrode (anode).

electromagnetic field in physics, the region in which a particle with an ◊electric charge experiences a force. If it does so only when moving, it is in a pure *magnetic field*; if it does so when stationary, it is in an *electric field*. Both can be present simultaneously.

electromagnetic force one of the four fundamental ◊forces of nature, the other three being gravity, the strong nuclear force, and the weak nuclear force. The ◊elementary particle that is the carrier for the electromagnetic (em) force is the photon.

electromagnetic waves oscillating electric and magnetic fields traveling together through space at a speed of nearly 186,000 mi/300,000 km per second. The (limitless) range of possible wavelengths or ◊frequencies of electromagnetic waves, which can be thought of as making up the *electromagnetic spectrum*, includes radio waves, infrared radiation, visible light, ultraviolet radiation, X-rays, and gamma rays.

electromotive force (emf) in physics, the greatest potential difference that can be generated by a source of current. This is always greater than the measured potential difference generated, due to the resistance of the wires and components, in the circuit.

electron stable, negatively charged ◊elementary particle; it is a constituent of all atoms, and a member of the class of particles known as ◊leptons. The electrons in each atom surround the nucleus in groupings called shells; in a neutral atom the number of electrons is equal to the number of protons in the nucleus. This electron structure is responsible for the chemical properties of the atom (see ◊atomic structure).

electronic mail or *e-mail* system that enables the users of a computer network to send messages to other users. The messages are usually placed in a reserved area of backing store on a central computer until they are retrieved by the receiving user. Passwords are frequently used to prevent unauthorized access to stored messages (see ◊data security).

electronic music term first applied 1954 to edited tape music composed primarily of electronically generated and modified tones, serially organized to objective scales of differentiation, to distinguish it from the more intuitive methodology of ◊concrete music. The term was subsequently extended to include prerecorded vocal and instrumental sounds organized in a similar way, as in Stockhausen's *Gesang der Jünglinge/Song of the Youths* 1955 and Berio's *Differences* for chamber ensemble and tape 1957. Other pioneers of electronic music are Milton Babbitt and Bruno Maderna.

electronics branch of science that deals with the emission of ◊electrons from conductors and ◊semiconductors, with the subsequent manipulation of these electrons, and with the construction of electronic devices. The first electronic device was the thermionic ◊valve, or vacuum tube, in which electrons moved in a vacuum, and led to such inventions as ◊radio, ◊television, ◊radar, and the digital ◊computer. Replacement of valves with the comparatively tiny and reliable transistor from 1948 revolutionized electronic development. Modern electronic devices are based on minute ◊integrated circuits (silicon chips), wafer-thin crystal slices holding tens of thousands of electronic components.

electron microscope instrument that produces a magnified image by using a beam of ◊electrons instead of light rays, as in an optical ◊microscope. An *electron lens* is an arrangement of electromagnetic coils that control and focus the beam. Electrons are not visible to the eye, so instead of an eyepiece there is a fluorescent screen or a photographic plate on which the electrons form an image. The wavelength of the electron beam is much shorter than that of light, so much greater magnification and resolution (ability to distinguish detail) can be achieved. The development of the electron microscope has made possible the observation of very minute organisms, viruses, and even large molecules.

element substance that cannot be split chemically into simpler substances. The atoms of a particular element all have the same number of protons in their nuclei (their atomic number). Elements are classified in the ◊periodic table of the elements. Of the 109 known elements, 95 are known to occur in nature (those with atomic numbers 1–95). Those from 96 to 109 do not occur in nature and are synthesized only, produced in particle accelerators. Eighty-one of the elements are stable; all the others, which include atomic numbers 43, 61, and from 84 up, are radioactive.

elementary particle or *fundamental particle* any of those particles that combine to form ◊atoms and all ◊matter, the most familiar being the electron, proton, and neutron. More than 200 particles have now been identified by physicists, categorized into several classes as characterized by their mass, electric charge, spin, magnetic moment, and interaction.

Although many particles were thought to be nondivisible and permanent, now most are known to be combinations of a small number of basic particles.

elephant mammal belonging to either of two surviving species of the order Proboscidea: the Asian elephant *Elephas maximus* and the African elephant *Loxodonta africana*. Elephants can grow to 13 ft/4 m and weigh up to 8 metric tons; they have a thick, gray, wrinkled skin, a large head, a long trunk used to obtain food and water, and upper incisors or tusks, which grow to a considerable length. The African elephant has very large ears and a flattened forehead, and the Asian species has smaller ears and a convex forehead. In India, Myanmar (Burma), and Thailand, Asiatic elephants are widely used for transport and logging.

elephantiasis in the human body, a condition of local enlargement and deformity, most often of a leg, though the scrotum, vulva, or breast may also be affected.

elevator any mechanical device for raising or lowering people or materials. It usually consists of a platform or boxlike structure suspended by motor-driven cables with safety ratchets along the sides of the shaft. US inventor Elisha Graves ◊Otis developed the first passenger safety elevator 1852, installed 1857. This invention permitted the development of skyscrapers from the 1880s. At first steam powered the movement, but hydraulic and then electric elevators were common from the early 1900s. Elevator operators worked controls and gates within the cab until the automatic, or self-starter, was introduced.

Elgar Edward (William) 1857–1934. English composer whose *Enigma Variations* 1899 brought him lasting fame. Although his celebrated oratorio *The Dream of Gerontius* 1900 (based on the written work by theologian John Henry Newman), was initially unpopular in Britain, it was well received at Düsseldorf 1902, leading to a surge of interest in his earlier works, including the *Pomp and Circumstance Marches* 1901.

Elijah In the Old Testament, a Hebrew prophet during the reigns of the Israelite kings Ahab and Ahaziah. He came from Gilead. He defeated the prophets of ◊Baal, and was said to have been carried up to heaven in a fiery chariot in a whirlwind. In Jewish belief, Elijah will return to Earth to herald the coming of the Messiah.

Eliot George. Pen name of Mary Ann Evans 1819–1880. English novelist. Her works include the pastoral *Adam Bede* 1859; *The Mill on the Floss* 1860, with its autobiographical elements; *Silas Marner* 1861, which contains elements of the folktale; and *Daniel Deronda* 1876. *Middlemarch*, published serially 1871–72, is considered her greatest novel for its confident handling of numerous characters and central social and moral issues. Her work is pervaded by a penetrating and compassionate intelligence.

Eliot T(homas) S(tearns) 1888–1965. US poet, playwright, and critic. He lived in London from 1915.

His first volume of poetry, *Prufrock and Other Observations* 1917, introduced new verse forms and rhythms; further collections include *The Waste Land* 1922, *The Hollow Men* 1925, and *Old Possum's Book of Practical Cats* 1939. His plays include *Murder in the Cathedral* 1935 and *The Cocktail Party* 1949. His critical works include *The Sacred Wood* 1920. Nobel Prize for Literature 1948.

Elisabethville former name of Lubumbashi, a town in Zaire.

Elizabeth the *Queen Mother* 1900– . Wife of King George VI of England. She was born Lady Elizabeth Angela Marguerite Bowes-Lyon, and on April 26, 1923 she married Albert, Duke of York, who became King George VI in 1936. Their children are Queen Elizabeth II and Princess Margaret.

Elizabeth I 1533–1603. Queen of England 1558–1603, the daughter of Henry VIII and Anne Boleyn. Through her Religious Settlement of 1559 she enforced the Protestant religion by law. She had ◊Mary Queen of Scots, executed 1587. Her conflict with Roman Catholic Spain led to the defeat of the ◊Spanish Armada 1588. The Elizabethan age was expansionist in commerce and geographical exploration, and arts and literature flourished. The rulers of many European states made unsuccessful bids to marry Elizabeth, and she used these bids to strengthen her power. She was succeeded by James I.

Elizabeth II 1926– . Queen of Great Britain and Northern Ireland from 1952, the elder daughter of George VI. She married her third cousin, Philip, the Duke of Edinburgh, 1947. They have four children: Charles, Anne, Andrew, and Edward.

elk or *wapiti* North American deer *Cervus canadensis*, closely related to the red ◊deer of Eurasia. Head and body length is about 8 ft/2.5 m, and shoulder height is about 5 ft/1.5 m. They are grayish-brown with a yellow rump patch. Males carry magnificent antlers up to 5.8 ft/1.8 m along the beam. In Europe, moose are called elk.

Ellesmere second largest island of the Canadian Arctic archipelago, Northwest Territories; area 82,097 sq mi/212,687 sq km. It is for the most part barren or glacier-covered.

Ellice Islands former name of ◊Tuvalu, a group of islands in the W Pacific Ocean.

Ellington Duke (Edward Kennedy) 1899–1974. US pianist. He had an outstanding career as a composer and arranger of jazz. He wrote numerous pieces for his own jazz orchestra, accentuating the strengths of individual virtuoso instrumentalists, and became one of the leading figures in jazz over a 55-year period. Some of his most popular compositions include "Mood Indigo", "Sophisticated Lady", "Solitude", and "Black and Tan Fantasy". He was one of the founders of big band jazz.

Ellison Ralph (Waldo) 1914–1994. US novelist. His *Invisible Man* 1952 portrays with humor and energy the plight of an African American whom postwar American society cannot acknowledge. It is regarded as one of the most impressive novels published in the US in the 1950s. He also wrote essays collected in *Shadow and Act* 1964.

The success of Ellison's work encouraged the development of black literature in the 1950s and 1960s.

elm any tree of the genus *Ulmus* of the family Ulmaceae, found in temperate regions of the N hemisphere and in mountainous parts of the tropics. All have doubly-toothed leaf margins and bear clusters of small flowers.

The American elm *U. americana* and slippery elm *U. rubra* are native to E North America.

elm The English elm has the typical elm leaf, oval, toothed, and distinctly lopsided. The seed is surrounded by a yellowish petal-like wing.

El Niño warm ocean surge of the ◊Peru Current, so called because it tends to occur at Christmas, recurring every 5–8 years or so in the E Pacific off South America. It involves a change in the direction of ocean currents, which prevents the upwelling of cold, nutrient-rich waters along the coast of Ecuador and Peru, killing fishes and plants. It is an important factor in global weather.

El Paso city in Texas, situated at the base of the Franklin Mountains, on the Rio Grande, opposite the Mexican city of Ciudad Juárez; population (1990) 515,300. It is the center of an agricultural and cattle-raising area, and there are electronics, food processing,packing, and leather industries, as well as oil refineries and industries based on local iron and copper mines. There are several military installations in the area.

El Salvador country in Central America, bounded N and E by Honduras, S and SW by the Pacific Ocean, and NW by Guatemala.

It was estimated that the civil war 1980–90 had claimed some 70,000 lives.

El Salvador Republic of (*República de El Salvador*) *area* 8,258 sq mi/21,393 sq km *capital* San Salvador *towns and cities* Santa Ana, San Miguel *physical* narrow coastal plain, rising to mountains in N with central plateau *features* smallest and most densely populated Central American country; Mayan archeological remains *head of state and government* Armando Calderón Sol from 1994 *political system* emergent democracy *political parties* Christian Democrats (PDC), anti-imperialist; National Republican Alliance (ARENA), right-wing; National Conciliation Party (PCN), right-wing; Farabundo Marti Liberation Front (FMLN), left-wing; Democratic Convergence (CD), right of center *exports* coffee, cotton, sugar *currency* colón *population* (1993 est) 5,580,000 (mainly of mixed Spanish and Indian ancestry; 10% Indian); growth rate 2.9% p.a. *life expectancy* men 64, women 69 *languages* Spanish, Nahuatl *religion* Roman Catholic 97% *literacy* men 76%, women 70% *GNP* $1,070 per head (1991) *chronology 1821* Independence achieved from Spain. *1931* Peasant unrest followed by a military coup. *1932* 30,000 peasants slaughtered following unrest, virtually eliminating native Salvadoreans. *1961* Following a coup, PCN established and in power. *1969* "Soccer" war with Honduras. *1972* Allegations of human-rights violations; growth of left-wing guerrilla activities. General Carlos Romero elected president. *1979* A coup replaced Romero with a military-civilian junta. *1980* Archbishop Oscar Romero assassinated; country on verge of civil war. José Duarte became first civilian president since 1931. *1981* Mexico and France recognized the guerrillas as a legitimate political force, but the US actively assisted the government in its battle against them. *1982* Assembly elections boycotted by left-wing parties and held amid considerable violence. *1986* Duarte sought a negotiated settlement with the guerrillas. *1988* Duarte resigned. *1989* Alfredo Cristiani (ARENA) became president in rigged elections; rebel attacks intensified. *1991* United Nations-sponsored peace accord signed by representatives of the government and the socialist guerrilla group, the FMLN. *1992* Peace accord validated; FMLN became political party. *1993* March: UN-sponsored commission published report on war atrocities. April: government amnesty cleared those implicated. July: top military leaders officially retired. *1994* Armando Calderón Sol (ARENA) elected president.

Elysium in Greek mythology, originally another name for the Islands of the Blessed, to which favored heroes were sent by the gods to enjoy a life after death. It was later a region in ◊Hades.

e-mail abbreviation for ◊*electronic mail.*

Emancipation Proclamation in US history, President Lincoln's Civil War announcement, Sept 22, 1862, stating that from the beginning of 1863 all black slaves in states still engaged in rebellion against the federal government would be emancipated. Slaves in border states still remaining loyal to the Union were excluded.

Lincoln had read a preliminary proclamation to his cabinet, who urged him to wait until a major Union victory before delivering it publicly.

embargo the legal prohibition by a government of trade with another country, forbidding foreign ships to leave or enter its ports. Trade embargoes may be imposed on a country seen to be violating international laws. A United Nations oil and arms embargo was imposed against the military regime in Haiti 1993–94.

They may be used as a tool of bilateral (political) policy, such as the embargo of sensitive technology that existed between the US and the USSR.

embryo early developmental stage of an animal or a plant following fertilization of an ovum (egg cell), or activation of an ovum by ◊parthenogenesis. In humans, the term embryo describes the fertilized egg during its first seven weeks of existence; from the eighth week onward it is referred to as a fetus.

emerald a clear, green gemstone variety of the mineral ◊beryl. It occurs naturally in Colombia, the Ural Mountains, in Russia, Zimbabwe, and Australia.

Emerson Ralph Waldo 1803–1882. US philosopher, essayist, and poet. He settled in Concord, Massachusetts, which he made a center of transcendentalism, and wrote *Nature* 1836, which states the movement's main principles emphasizing the value of self-reliance and the godlike nature of human souls. His two volumes of Essays (1841, 1844) made his reputation: Self-Reliance and Compensation in the earlier volume are among the best known.

emery grayish-black opaque metamorphic rock consisting of ◊corundum and magnetite, together with other minerals such as hematite. It is used as an ◊abrasive.

emf in physics, abbreviation for ◊*electromotive force.*

empiricism in philosophy, the belief that all knowledge is ultimately derived from sense experience. It is suspicious of metaphysical schemes based on a priori propositions, which are claimed to be true irrespective of experience. It is frequently contrasted with ◊rationalism.

employment agency agency for bringing together employers requiring labor and workers seeking employment. Employment agencies may be state run, as in state employment services, or private agencies paid either by client companies or by individuals seeking employment.

EMS abbreviation for ◊*European Monetary System.*

emu flightless bird *Dromaius novaehollandiae* native to Australia. It stands about 6 ft/1.8 m high and has coarse brown plumage, small rudimentary wings, short feathers on the head and neck, and powerful legs, well adapted for running and kicking.

The female has a curious bag or pouch in the wind-

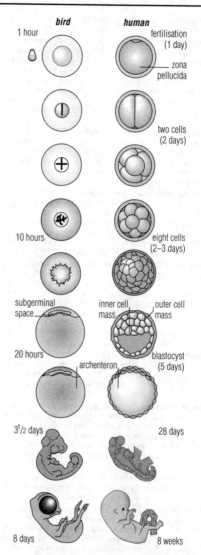

embryo The development of a bird and a human embryo. In the human, division of the fertilized egg, or ovum, begins within hours of conception. Within a week, a hollow, fluid-containing ball—a blastocyte—with a mass of cells at one end has developed. After the third week, the embryo has changed from a mass of cells into a recognizable shape. At four weeks, the embryo is 0.1 in/3 mm long, with a large bulge for the heart and small pits for the ears. At six weeks, the embryo is 0.6 in/1.5 cm with a pulsating heart and ear flaps. By the eighth week, the embryo (now technically a fetus) is 1 in/2.5 cm long and recognizably human, with eyelids, small fingers and toes.

pipe that enables her to emit the characteristic loud booming note.

emulator in computing, an item of software or firmware that allows one device to imitate the functioning of another. Emulator software is commonly used to allow one make of computer to run programs written for a different make of computer. This allows a user to select from a wider range of ◊applications programs, and perhaps to save money by running programs designed for an expensive computer on a cheaper model.

enamel vitrified (glasslike) coating of various colors used for decorative purposes on a metallic or porcelain surface. In *cloisonné* the various sections of the design are separated by thin metal wires or strips. In *champlevé* the enamel is poured into engraved cavities in the metal surface.

enclosure in Britain, appropriation of common land as private property, or the changing of open-field systems to enclosed fields (often used for sheep). This process began in the 14th century and became widespread in the 15th and 16th centuries. It caused poverty, homelessness, and rural depopulation, and resulted in revolts 1536, 1569, and 1607.

encyclopedia or *encyclopaedia* work of reference covering either all fields of knowledge or one specific subject. Although most encyclopedias are alphabetical, with cross-references, some are organized thematically with indexes, to keep related subjects together.

American encyclopedias include the *Encyclopedia Americana* and *Collier's Encyclopedia*, both prepared with attention to cultural and stylistic interpretations appropriate to the US.

endive cultivated annual plant *Cichorium endivia*, family Compositae, the leaves of which are used in salads and cooking. One variety has narrow, curled leaves; another has wide, smooth leaves. It is related to ◊chicory.

endocrine gland gland that secretes hormones into the bloodstream to regulate body processes. Endocrine glands are most highly developed in vertebrates, but are also found in other animals, notably insects. In humans the main endocrine glands are the pituitary, thyroid, parathyroid, adrenal, pancreas, ovary, and testis.

endometriosis common gynecological complaint in which patches of endometrium (the lining of the womb) are found outside the uterus.

endorphin natural substance (a polypeptide) that modifies the action of nerve cells. Endorphins are produced by the pituitary gland and hypothalamus of vertebrates. They lower the perception of pain by reducing the transmission of signals between nerve cells.

Endymion in Greek mythology, a beautiful young man loved by Selene, the Moon goddess. He was granted eternal sleep in order to remain forever young. Keats' poem *Endymion* 1818 is an allegory of searching for perfection.

energy capacity for doing ◊work. Potential energy (PE) is energy deriving from position; thus a stretched spring has elastic PE, and an object raised to a height above the Earth's surface, or the water in an elevated reservoir, has gravitational PE. A lump of coal and a tank of gasoline, together with the oxygen needed for their combustion, have chemical energy. Other sorts of energy include electrical and nuclear energy, and

light and sound. Moving bodies possess kinetic energy (KE). Energy can be converted from one form to another, but the total quantity stays the same (in accordance with the ◊conservation of energy principle). For example, as an apple falls, it loses gravitational PE but gains KE.

energy, alternative see ◊alternative energy

Engels Friedrich 1820–1895. German social and political philosopher, a friend of, and collaborator with, Karl ◊Marx on *The Communist Manifesto* 1848 and other key works. His later interpretations of Marxism, and his own philosophical and historical studies such as *Origins of the Family, Private Property, and the State* 1884 (which linked patriarchy with the development of private property), developed such concepts as historical materialism. His use of positivism and Darwinian ideas gave Marxism a scientific and deterministic flavor which was to influence Soviet thinking.

engine device for converting stored energy into useful work or movement. Most engines use a fuel as their energy store. The fuel is burned to produce heat energy—hence the name "heat engine"—which is then converted into movement. Heat engines can be classified according to the fuel they use (◊gasoline engine or ◊diesel engine), or according to whether the fuel is burned inside (◊internal combustion engine) or outside (◊steam engine) the engine, or according to whether they produce a reciprocating or rotary motion (◊turbine or ◊Wankel engine).

engineering the application of science to the design, construction, and maintenance of works, machinery, roads, railroads, bridges, harbor installations, engines,

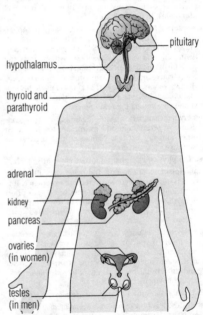

endocrine gland *The main human endocrine glands. These glands produce hormones—chemical messengers—which travel in the bloodstream to stimulate certain cells.*

ships, aircraft and airports, spacecraft and space stations, and the generation, transmission, and use of electrical power. The main divisions of engineering are aerospace, chemical, civil, electrical, electronic, gas, marine, materials, mechanical, mining, production, radio, and structural.

England largest division of the ◊United Kingdom. *area* 50,318 sq mi/130,357 sq km *capital* London *towns and cities* Birmingham, Cambridge, Coventry, Leeds, Leicester, Manchester, Newcastle-upon-Tyne, Nottingham, Oxford, Sheffield, York; ports Bristol, Dover, Felixstowe, Harwich, Liverpool, Portsmouth, Southampton *features* variability of climate and diversity of scenery; among European countries, only the Netherlands is more densely populated *exports* agricultural (cereals, rape, sugar beet, potatoes); meat and meat products; electronic (software) and telecommunications equipment (main centers Berkshire and Cambridge); scientific instruments; textiles and fashion goods; North Sea oil and gas, petrochemicals, pharmaceuticals, fertilizers; beer; china clay, pottery, porcelain, and glass; film and television programs, and sound recordings. Tourism is important. There are worldwide banking and insurance interests *currency* pound sterling *population* (1991) 47,055,200 *language* English, with more than 100 minority languages *religions* Christian, with the Church of England as the established church, 31,500,000; and various Protestant groups, of which the largest is the Methodist 1,400,000; Roman Catholic about 5,000,000; Muslim 900,000; Jewish 410,000; Sikh 175,000; Hindu 140,000. For *government* and *history*, see ◊Britain, ancient; ◊England: history; ◊United Kingdom.

English Channel stretch of water between England and France, leading in the W to the Atlantic Ocean, and in the E via the Strait of Dover to the North Sea; it is also known as *La Manche* (French "the sleeve") from its shape. The ◊Channel Tunnel, opened 1994, runs between Folkestone, Kent, and Sangatte, W of Calais.

English language member of the Germanic branch of the Indo-European language family. It is traditionally described as having passed through four major stages over about 1,500 years: *Old English* or *Anglo-Saxon* (c.500–1050), rooted in the dialects of invading settlers (Jutes, Saxons, Angles, and Frisians); *Middle English* (c.1050–1550), influenced by Norman French after the Conquest 1066 and by ecclesiastical Latin; *Early Modern English* (c.1550–1700), including a standardization of the diverse influences of Middle English; and *Late Modern English* (c.1700 onward), including in particular the development and spread of current Standard English. Through extensive exploration, colonization, and trade, English spread worldwide from the 17th century onward and remains the most important international language of trade and technology. It is used in many variations, for example, British, American, Canadian, West Indian, Indian, Singaporean, and Nigerian English, and many pidgins and creoles.

English law one of the major European legal systems, Roman law being the other. English law has spread to many other countries, including former English colonies such as the US, Canada, Australia, and New Zealand.

engraving art of creating a design by means of inscribing blocks of metal, wood, or some other hard material with a point. With *intaglio printing* the design is cut into the surface of a plate, usually metal. It is these cuts, often very fine, which hold the ink. In *relief printing*, by contrast, it is the areas left when the rest has been cut away which are inked for printing. See ◊printmaking.

enlightenment in Buddhism, the term used to translate the Sanskrit *bodhi*, awakening: perceiving the reality of the world, or the unreality of the self, and becoming liberated from suffering (Sanskrit *duhkha*). It is the gateway to nirvana.

Enlightenment European intellectual movement that reached its high point in the 18th century. Enlightenment thinkers were believers in social progress and in the liberating possibilities of rational and scientific knowledge. They were often critical of existing society and were hostile to religion, which they saw as keeping the human mind chained down by superstition.

Entebbe city in Uganda, on the northwest shore of Lake Victoria, 12 mi/20 km SW of Kampala, the capital; 1,136 m/3,728 ft above sea level; population (1983) 21,000. Founded 1893, it was the administrative center of Uganda 1894–1962.

enterprise zone special zone designated by government to encourage industrial and commercial activity, usually in economically depressed areas. Investment is attracted by means of tax reduction and other financial incentives.

In the US, the creation of enterprise zones was an important part of the early Reagan administration's plan to encourage private investment in inner-city and other economically depressed areas. It was also a step in the process of reducing government involvement in the economy. The plan called for the creation of up to 25 zones a year for a three-year period. Tax incentives would reduce by as much as 75% the corporate income taxes, and capital-gains taxes would be eliminated entirely for participating businesses.

entropy in ◊thermodynamics, a parameter representing the state of disorder of a system at the atomic, ionic, or molecular level; the greater the disorder, the higher the entropy. Thus the fast-moving disordered molecules of water vapor have higher entropy than those of more ordered liquid water, which in turn have more entropy than the molecules in solid crystalline ice.

Enver Pasha 1881–1922. Turkish politician and soldier. He led the military revolt 1908 that resulted in the Young Turks' revolution (see ◊Turkey). He was killed fighting the Bolsheviks in Turkestan.

environment in ecology, the sum of conditions affecting a particular organism, including physical surroundings, climate, and influences of other living organisms. See also ◊biosphere and ◊habitat.

environmental audit another name for ◊green audit, the inspection of a company to assess its environmental impact.

enzyme biological ◊catalyst produced in cells, and capable of speeding up the chemical reactions necessary for life by converti\ng one molecule (substrate) into another. Enzymes are not themselves destroyed by this process. They are large, complex ◊proteins, and are highly specific, each chemical reaction requiring its own particular enzyme. The enzyme fits into a "slot" (active site) in the substrate molecule, forming an enzyme–substrate complex that lasts until the substrate is altered or split, after which the enzyme can fall away. The substrate may therefore be compared to a lock, and the enzyme to the key required to open it.

Eocene second epoch of the Tertiary period of geological time, 56.5–35.5 million years ago. Originally considered the earliest division of the Tertiary, the name means "early recent", referring to the early forms of mammals evolving at the time, following the extinction of the dinosaurs.

eolian referring to sediments carried, formed, eroded, or deposited by the wind. Such sediments include desert sands and dunes as well as deposits of windblown silt, called loess, carried long distances from deserts and from stream sediments derived from the melting of glaciers.

ephemeral plant plant with a very short life cycle, sometimes as little as six or eight weeks. It may complete several generations in one growing season.

A number of common weeds are ephemerals—for example, many groundsels (ragworts and squawweeds) *Senecio* and many desert plants. The latter take advantage of short periods of rain to germinate and reproduce, passing the dry season as dormant seeds.

Ephesus ancient Greek seaport in Asia Minor, a center of the ◊Ionian Greeks, with a temple of Artemis destroyed by the Goths AD 262. Now in Turkey, it is one of the world's largest archeological sites. St Paul visited the city and addressed a letter (◊epistle) to the Christians there.

epic narrative poem or cycle of poems dealing with some great deed—often the founding of a nation or the forging of national unity—and often using religious or cosmological themes. The two major epic poems in the Western tradition are *The Iliad* and *The Odyssey*, attributed to ◊Homer, and which were probably intended to be chanted in sections at feasts.

epicenter the point on the Earth's surface immediately above the seismic focus of an ◊earthquake. Most damage usually takes place at an earthquake's epicenter. The term sometimes refers to a point directly above or below a nuclear explosion ("at ground zero").

Epicureanism system of philosophy that claims soundly based human happiness is the highest good, so that its rational pursuit should be adopted. It was named for the Greek philosopher Epicurus. The most distinguished Roman Epicurean was ◊Lucretius.

epidermis outermost layer of ◊cells on an organism's body. In plants and many invertebrates such as insects, it consists of a single layer of cells. In vertebrates, it consists of several layers of cells.

In vertebrates, such as reptiles, birds, and mammals, the outermost layer of cells is dead, forming a tough, waterproof layer, which is sloughed off continuously or shed periodically.

epilepsy medical disorder characterized by a tendency to develop fits, which are convulsions or abnormal feelings caused by abnormal electrical discharges in the cerebral hemispheres of the ◊brain. Epilepsy can be controlled with a number of anticonvulsant drugs.

Epiphany festival of the Christian church, held 6 Jan, celebrating the coming of the Magi (the three Wise Men) to Bethlehem with gifts for the infant Jesus, and symbolizing the manifestation of Jesus to the world. It is the 12th day after Christmas, and marks the end of the Christmas festivities.

epiphyte any plant that grows on another plant or object above the surface of the ground, and has no roots in the soil. An epiphyte does not parasitize the plant it grows on but merely uses it for support. Its nutrients are obtained from rainwater, organic debris such as leaf litter, or from the air.

episcopacy in the Christian church, a system of government in which administrative and spiritual power over a district (diocese) is held by a bishop.

The Roman Catholic, Eastern Orthodox, Anglican, and Episcopal churches are episcopalian; episcopacy also exists in the Lutheran Church of Scandinavia and of the US, where bishops are elected for districts called "synods", and in most branches of the American Methodist Church, where bishops are supervisory officials.

epistemology branch of philosophy that examines the nature of knowledge and attempts to determine the limits of human understanding. Central issues include how knowledge is derived and how it is to be validated and tested.

epistle in the New Testament, any of the 21 letters to individuals or to the members of various churches written by Christian leaders, including the 13 written by St ◊Paul. The term also describes a letter with a suggestion of pomposity and literary affectation, and a letter addressed to someone in the form of a poem, as in the epistles of ◊Horace and Alexander ◊Pope.

epoch subdivision of a geological period in the geological time scale. Epochs are sometimes given their own names (such as the Paleocene, Eocene, Oligocene, Miocene, and Pliocene epochs comprising the Tertiary period), or they are referred to as the late, early, or middle portions of a given period (as the Late Cretaceous or the Middle Triassic epoch).

Epsom salts $MgSO_4 \cdot 7H_2O$ hydrated magnesium sulfate, used as a relaxant and laxative and added to baths to soothe the skin. The name is derived from a bitter saline spring at Epsom, Surrey, England, which contains the salt in solution.

Epstein Jacob 1880–1959. American-born British sculptor. Initially influenced by Rodin, he turned to primitive forms after Brancusi and is chiefly known for his controversial muscular nude figures such as *Genesis* 1931 (Whitworth Art Gallery, Manchester). He was better appreciated as a portraitist (bust of Einstein, 1933), and in later years executed several monumental figures, notably the expressive bronze of *St Michael and the Devil* 1959 (Coventry Cathedral).

equator *terrestrial equator* or the great circle whose plane is perpendicular to the Earth's axis (the line joining the poles). Its length is 24,901.8 mi/40,092 km, divided into 360 degrees of longitude. The equator encircles the broadest part of the Earth, and represents 0° latitude. It divides the Earth into two halves, called the northern and the southern hemispheres.

Equatorial Guinea Republic of (*República de Guinea Ecuatorial*) *area* 10,828 sq mi/28,051 sq km *capital* Malabo (Bioko) *towns and cities* Bata, Mbini (Río Muni) *physical* comprises mainland Río Muni, plus the small islands of Corisco, Elobey Grande and Elobey Chico, and Bioko (formerly Fernando Po) together with Annobón (formerly Pagalu) *features* volcanic mountains on Bioko *head of state* Teodoro Obiang Nguema Mbasogo from 1979 *head of government* Silvestre Siale Bileka from 1993 *political system* emergent democratic republic *political parties* Democratic Party of Equatorial Guinea (PDGE), nationalist, right of center, militarily controlled; People's Social Democratic Convention (CSDP), left of center; Social Democratic Union (UDS), left of center; Liberal Party, left of center *exports* cocoa, coffee, timber *currency* ekuele; CFA franc *population* (1993 est) 390,000 (plus 110,000 estimated to live in exile abroad); growth rate 2.2% p.a. *life expectancy* men 46, women 50 *languages* Spanish (official); pidgin English is widely spoken, and on Annobón (whose people were formerly slaves of the Portuguese) a Portuguese dialect; Fang and other African dialects spoken on Río Muni *religions* nominally Christian, mainly Catholic, but in 1978 Roman Catholicism was banned *literacy* men 64%, women 37% *GNP* $330 per head (1991) *chronology* *1778* Fernando Po (Bioko Island) ceded to Spain. *1885* Mainland territory came under Spanish rule; colony known as Spanish Guinea. *1968* Independence achieved from Spain. Francisco Macias Nguema became first president, soon assuming dictatorial powers. *1979* Macias overthrown and replaced by his nephew, Teodoro Obiang Nguema Mbasogo, who established a military regime. Macias tried and executed. *1982* Obiang elected president unopposed for another seven years. New constitution adopted. *1989* Obiang reelected president. *1992* New constitution adopted; elections held, but president continued to nominate candidates for top government posts. *1993* PDGE won first multiparty elections on low turnout.

equestrianism skill in horse riding, as practiced under International Equestrian Federation rules. An Olympic sport, there are three main branches of equestrianism: showjumping, dressage, and three-day eventing.

equilateral of a geometrical figure, having all sides of equal length.

For example, a rhombus is an equilateral parallelogram. An equilateral triangle is also equiangular, which means that all three angles are equal as well.

equity system of law supplementing the ordinary rules of law where the application of these would operate harshly in a particular case; sometimes it is regarded as an attempt to achieve "natural justice". So understood, equity appears as an element in most legal systems, and in a number of legal codes judges are instructed to apply both the rules of strict law and the principles of equity in reaching their decisions.

equity a company's assets, less its liabilities, which are the property of the owner or stockholders. Popularly, equities are stocks and shares which do not pay interest at fixed rates but pay dividends based on the company's performance. The value of equities tends to rise over the long term, but in the short term they are a risk investment because prices can fall as well as rise.

Equity is also used to refer to the paid value of mortgaged real property, most commonly a house. With changes in US tax regulations, from the late 1980s, home-equity loans (second mortgages) have become a very popular financial tool, since the interest is, like mortgage interest, tax deductible.

era any of the major divisions of geological time, each including several periods, but smaller than an eon. The currently recognized eras all fall within the Phanerozoic eon—or the vast span of time, starting about 570 million years ago, when fossils are found to become abundant. The eras in ascending order are the Paleozoic, Mesozoic, and Cenozoic. We are living in the Recent epoch of the Quaternary period of the Cenozoic era.

Erasmus Desiderius *c.*1466–1536. Dutch scholar and leading humanist of the Renaissance era, who taught and studied all over Europe and was a prolific writer.

His pioneer translation of the Greek New Testament (with parallel Latin text) 1516 exposed the Vulgate as a second-hand document. Although opposed to dogmatism and abuse of church power, he remained impartial during Martin ◊Luther's conflict with the pope.

erbium soft, lustrous, grayish, metallic element of the ◊lanthanide series, symbol Er, atomic number 68, relative atomic mass 167.26. It occurs with the element yttrium or as a minute part of various minerals. It was discovered 1843 by Carl Mosander (1797–1858), and named for the town of Ytterby, Sweden, near which the lanthanides (rare-earth elements) were first found.

Erebus, Mount the world's southernmost active volcano, 12,452 ft/3,794 m high, on Ross Island, Antarctica.

Erfurt city in Germany on the river Gera, capital of the state of Thuringia; population (1990) 217,000. It is in a rich horticultural area, and its industries include textiles, typewriters, and electrical goods.

ergo (Latin) therefore; hence.

ergonomics study of the relationship between people and the furniture, tools, and machinery they use at work. The object is to improve work performance by removing sources of muscular stress and general fatigue: for example, by presenting data and control panels in easy-to-view form, making office furniture comfortable, and creating a generally pleasant environment.

ergot certain parasitic fungi (especially the genus *Claviceps*), whose brown or black grainlike masses replace the kernels of rye or other cereals. *C. purpurea* attacks the rye plant. Ergot poisoning is caused by eating infected bread, resulting in burning pains, gangrene, and convulsions.

Erhard Ludwig 1897–1977. West German Christian Democrat politician, chancellor of the Federal Republic 1963–66. The "economic miracle" of West Germany's recovery after World War II is largely attributed to Erhard's policy of social free enterprise which he initiated during his period as federal economics minister (1949–63).

erica in botany, any plant of the genus *Erica*, family Ericaceae, including the heathers. There are about 500 species, distributed mainly in South Africa with some in Europe.

Ericsson Leif Norse explorer, son of Eric the Red, who sailed west from Greenland *c.* 1000 to find a country first sighted by Norsemen 986. He visited Baffin Island then sailed along the Labrador coast to Newfoundland, which was named "Vinland" (Wine Land), because he discovered grape vines growing there.

Eric the Red *c.*950–1010. Allegedly the first European to find Greenland. According to a 13th-century saga, he was the son of a Norwegian chieftain, and was banished from Iceland about 982 for murder. He then sailed westward and discovered a land that he called Greenland.

Eridanus in astronomy, the sixth largest constellation, which meanders from the celestial equator deep into the southern hemisphere of the sky. Its brightest star is Achernar. Eridanus is represented as a river.

Erie, Lake fourth largest of the Great Lakes of North America, connected to Lake Ontario by the Niagara River and bypassed by the Welland Canal; area 9,930 sq mi/25,720 sq km.

Eritrea State of *area* 48,250 sq mi/125,000 sq km *capital* Asmara *towns and cities* Keren, Adigrat; ports: Asab, Massawa *physical* coastline along the Red Sea 620 mi/1,000 km; narrow coastal plain that rises to an inland plateau *features* Dahlak Islands *head of state and government* Issaias Afwerki from 1993 *political system* emergent democracy *political parties* People's Front for Democracy and Justice (PFDJ) (formerly Eritrean People's Liberation Front: EPLF), militant nationalist; Eritrean National Pact Alliance (ENPA), moderate, centrist *products* coffee, salt, citrus fruits, grains, cotton *currency* birr *population* (1993 est) 3,500,000 *languages* Amharic (official), Tigrinya (official), Arabic, Afar, Bilen, Hidareb, Kunama, Nara, Rashaida, Saho, and Tigre *media* one bi-weekly newspaper (*Hadas Eritra*), government-owned, published in Tigrinya and Arabic, circulation (1993) 30,000; three monthly newssheets, all owned by Christian churches and published in Tigrinya. The national radio station broadcasts in six languages *religions* Muslim, Coptic Christian *GNP* $77 per head (1991) *chronology 1962* Annexed by Ethiopia; secessionist movement began. *1974* Ethiopian emperor Haile Selassie deposed by military; Eritrean People's Liberation Front (EPLF) continued struggle for independence. *1990* Port of Massawa captured by Eritrean forces. *1991* Ethiopian president Mengistu Haile Mariam overthrown. EPLF secured whole of Eritrea. Ethiopian government acknowledged Eritrea's right to secede. Issaias Afwerki became secretary-general of provisional government. *1993* Independence approved in regional referendum and formally recognized by Ethiopia. Transitional government established for four-year period. Issaias Afwerki elected president; independence formally declared. *1994* EPLF renamed the PFDJ. New national assembly and state council created.

Erivan alternative transliteration of ◊Yerevan, the capital of Armenia.

ERM abbreviation for ◊*Exchange Rate Mechanism*.

ermine short-tailed weasel *Mustela erminea*, of the N hemisphere, whose winter coat becomes white. In N latitudes the coat becomes completely white, except for a black tip to the tail, but in warmer regions the back may remain brownish. The alternate Eurasian name "stoat" is used especially during the summer, when the coat is brown. The fur is used commercially.

Ernst Max 1891–1976. German Surrealist artist. He worked in France 1922–38 and in the US from 1941. He was an active Dadaist, experimenting with collage, photomontage, and surreal images, and helped found the Surrealist movement 1924.

erosion wearing away of the Earth's surface, caused by the breakdown and transportation of particles of rock or soil (by contrast, ◊weathering does not involve transportation). Agents of erosion include the sea, rivers, glaciers, and wind.

Water, consisting of sea waves and currents, rivers, and rain; ice, in the form of glaciers; and wind, hurling sand fragments against exposed rocks and moving dunes along, are the most potent forces of erosion. People also contribute to erosion by bad farming practices and the cutting down of forests, which can lead to the formation of dust bowls.

ESA abbreviation for ◊*European Space Agency*.

escape velocity in physics, minimum velocity with which an object must be projected for it to escape from the gravitational pull of a planetary body. In the case of the Earth, the escape velocity is 6.9 mps/

11.2 kps; the Moon 1.5 mps/2.4 kps; Mars 3.1 mps/ 5 kps; and Jupiter 37 mps/59.6 kps.

escrow in law, a document sealed and delivered to a third party and not released or coming into effect until some condition has been fulfilled or performed, whereupon the document takes full effect.

Money deposited with a neutral third party to be delivered when conditions of a contract are fulfilled, as in real estate transactions, is commonly referred to as escrow.

Eskimo member of a group of Asian, North American, and Greenland Arctic peoples who migrated east from Siberia about 2,000 years ago, exploiting the marine coastal environment and the tundra.

Eskimo *An Eskimo mother and child from Nome, Alaska, in about 1915. Despite their wide distribution over a vast area, the Eskimos, most of whom live in small, isolated family units, have preserved a remarkable degree of cultural and linguistic identity. They share a rich mythology and a way of life finely attuned to their harsh environment.*

esophagus the passage by which food travels from mouth to stomach. The human esophagus is about 9 in/23 cm long. Its upper end is at the bottom of the ◊pharynx, immediately behind the windpipe.

ESP abbreviation for ◊*extrasensory perception*.

esparto grass *Stipa tenacissima*, native to S Spain, S Portugal, and the Balearics, but now widely grown in dry, sandy locations throughout the world. The plant is just over 3 ft/1 m high, producing grayish-green leaves, which are used for making paper, ropes, baskets, mats, and cables.

A similar grass *Lygeum spartum* from the same area and used for the same purposes is also called esparto.

Esperanto language devised 1887 by Polish philologist Ludwig L Zamenhof (1859–1917) as an international auxiliary language. For its structure and vocabulary it draws on Latin, the Romance languages, English, and German.

essay short piece of nonfiction, often dealing with a particular subject from a personal point of view. The essay became a recognized genre with French writer Montaigne's Essais 1580 and in English with Francis Bacon's Essays 1597. Today the essay is a part of journalism: articles in the broadsheet newspapers are in the essay tradition.

Essen city in North Rhine–Westphalia, Germany; population (1988) 615,000. It is the administrative center of the Ruhr region, situated between the rivers Emscher and Ruhr, and has textile, chemical, and electrical industries. Its 9th–14th-century minster is one of the oldest churches in Germany.

Essequibo longest river in Guyana, South America, rising in the Guiana Highlands of S Guyana; length 630 mi/1,014 km. Part of the district of Essequibo, which lies to the W of the river, is claimed by Venezuela.

Essex county of SE England *area* 1,417 sq mi/3,670 sq km *towns and cities* Chelmsford (administrative headquarters), Colchester; ports: Harwich, Tilbury; resorts: Southend-on-Sea, Clacton *features* former royal hunting ground of Epping Forest (controlled from 1882 by the City of London); the marshy coastal headland of the Naze; since 1111 at Great Dunmow the Dunmow flitch (side of cured pork) can be claimed every four years by any couple proving to a jury they have not regretted their marriage within the year (winners are few); Stansted, London's third airport *industries* dairy products, cereals, fruit, sugar beet, oysters *population* (1991) 1,528,600.

Essex Robert Devereux, 2nd Earl of Essex 1566–1601. English soldier and politician. He became a favorite with Queen Elizabeth I from 1587, but was executed because of his policies in Ireland.

estate in law, the rights that a person has in relation to any property. *Real estate* is an interest in any land; *personal estate* is an interest in any other kind of property.

Estate property refers to the assets of a deceased person.

ester organic compound formed by the reaction between an alcohol and an acid, with the elimination of water. Unlike ◊salts, esters are covalent compounds.

estheticism in the arts, the doctrine that holds art is an end in itself and does not need to have any moral, religious, political, or educational purpose. The writer Théophile Gautier popularized the doctrine "*l'art pour l'art*" ("art for art's sake") 1832, and it was taken up in mid-19th-century France by the Symbolist poets and painters. It flourished in the English ◊Esthetic Movement of the late 19th century. An emphasis on form rather than content in art remained influential in the West well into the 20th century.

esthetics branch of philosophy that deals with the nature of beauty, especially in art. It emerged as a distinct branch of inquiry in the mid-18th century.

estivation in zoology, a state of inactivity and reduced metabolic activity, similar to ◊hibernation, that occurs during the dry season in species such as lungfishes and snails. In botany, the term is used to describe the way in which flower petals and sepals are folded in the buds. It is an important feature in ◊plant classification.

Estonia Republic of *area* 17,000 sq mi/45,000 sq km *capital* Tallinn *towns and cities* Tartu, Narva, Kohtla-Järve, Pärnu *physical* lakes and marshes in a partly forested plain; 481 mi/774 km of coastline; mild climate *environment* former Soviet army bases are contaminated by toxic chemicals, radioactive waste, and oil;

cleanup cost of billions of dollars *features* Lake Peipus and Narva River forming boundary with Russian Federation; Baltic islands, the largest of which is Saaremaa Island *head of state* Lennart Meri from 1992 *head of government* Andres Tarand from 1994 *political system* emergent democracy *political parties* Estonian Popular Front (EPF) (Rahvarinne), nationalist; Association for a Free Estonia, nationalist; Fatherland Group (Isamaa), right-wing; International Movement, ethnic Russian; Estonian Green Party, environmentalist *products* oil and gas (from shale), wood products, flax, dairy and pig products *currency* kroon *population* (1993 est) 1,620,000 (Estonian 62%, Russian 30%, Ukrainian 3%, Byelorussian 2%) *life expectancy* men 66, women 75 *language* Estonian, allied to Finnish *religion* traditionally Lutheran *GNP* $3,380 per head (1991) *chronology 1918* Estonia declared its independence. March: Soviet forces, who had tried to regain control from occupying German forces during World War I, were overthrown by German troops. Nov: Soviet troops took control after German withdrawal. *1919* Soviet rule overthrown with help of British navy; Estonia declared a democratic republic. *1934* Fascist coup replaced government. *1940* Estonia incorporated into USSR. *1941–44* German occupation during World War II. *1944* USSR regained control. *1980* Beginnings of nationalist dissent. *1988* Adopted own constitution, with power of veto on all centralized Soviet legislation. Popular Front established to campaign for democracy. Estonia's state assembly voted to declare the republic autonomous in all matters except military and foreign affairs; rejected by USSR as unconstitutional. *1989* Estonian replaced Russian as main language. *1990* Feb: Communist Party monopoly of power abolished; multiparty system established. March: pro-independence candidates secured majority after republic elections; coalition government formed with Popular Front leader Edgar Savisaar as prime minister; Arnold Rüütel became president. May: prewar constitution partially restored. *1991* March: independence approved by national vote. Aug: full independence declared after abortive anti-Gorbachev coup; Communist Party outlawed. Sept: independence recognized. *1992* Jan: Savisaar resigned over food and energy shortages; new government formed by Tiit Vahl. June: new constitution adopted. Sept: presidential and parliamentary elections inconclusive. Oct: Fatherland Group leader Lennart Meri chosen by parliament to replace Rüütel; Mart Laar became prime minister. *1994* Russian troops withdrawn. Sept: Laar resigned after losing vote of confidence. Oct: Andres Tarand became prime minister.

Estonian member of the largest ethnic group in Estonia. There are 1 million speakers of the Estonian language, a member of the Finno-Ugric branch of the Ural·c family. Most live in Estonia.

estrogen any of a group of hormones produced by the ◊ovaries of vertebrates; the term is also used for various synthetic hormones that mimic their effects. (Some estrogens are also secreted by the cortex of the ◊adrenal glands.) The principal estrogen in mammals is estradiol. Estrogens promote the development of female secondary sexual characteristics; stimulate egg production; and, in mammals, prepare the lining of the uterus for pregnancy.

estrus in mammals, the period during a female's reproductive cycle (also known as the estrous cycle) when mating is most likely to occur. It usually coincides with ovulation.

estuary river mouth widening into the sea, where fresh water mixes with salt water and tidal effects are felt.

Estuaries are extremely rich in life forms and are breeding grounds for thousands of species. Water pollution threatens these ecosystems.

etching printmaking technique in which a metal plate (usually copper or zinc) is covered with a waxy overlayer (ground) and then drawn on with an etching needle. The exposed areas are then "etched", or bitten into, by a corrosive agent (acid), so that they will hold ink for printing.

ethanol common name *ethyl alcohol* C_2H_5OH alcohol found in beer, wine, cider, spirits, and other alcoholic drinks. When pure, it is a colorless liquid with a pleasant odor, miscible with water or ether; it burns in air with a pale blue flame. The vapor forms an explosive mixture with air and may be used in high-compression internal combustion engines. It is produced naturally by the fermentation of carbohydrates by yeast cells.

Industrially, it can be made by absorption of ethene and subsequent reaction with water, or by the reduction of ethanal in the presence of a catalyst, and is widely used as a solvent.

Ethelbert *c.*552–616. King of Kent 560–616. He was defeated by the West Saxons 568 but later became ruler of England S of the river Humber. Ethelbert received the Christian missionary Augustine 597 and later converted to become the first Christian ruler of Anglo-Saxon England. He issued the first written code of laws known in England.

Ethelred (II) the Unready *c.* 968–1016. King of England from 978. He tried to buy off the Danish raiders by paying Danegeld. In 1002, he ordered the massacre of the Danish settlers, provoking an invasion by Sweyn I of Denmark. War with Sweyn and Sweyn's son, Canute, occupied the rest of Ethelred's reign. He was nicknamed the "Unready" because of his apparent lack of foresight.

ether in chemistry, any of a series of organic chemical compounds having an oxygen atom linking the carbon atoms of two hydrocarbon radical groups (general formula R-O-R'); also the common name for ethoxyethane $C_2H_5OC_2H_5$ (also called diethyl ether).

This is used as an anesthetic and as an external cleansing agent before surgical operations. It is also used as a solvent, and in the extraction of oils, fats, waxes, resins, and alkaloids.

ethics area of ◊philosophy concerned with human values, which studies the meanings of moral terms and theories of conduct and goodness; also called *moral philosophy*. It is one of the three main branches of contemporary philosophy.

Ethiopia People's Democratic Republic of (*Hebretesebawit Ityopia*, formerly known as *Abyssinia*) *area* 423,403 sq mi/1,096,900 sq km *capital* Addis Ababa *towns and cities* Jimma, Dire Dawa, Harar *physical* a high plateau with central mountain range divided by Rift Valley; plains in E; source of Blue Nile River *environment* more than 90% of the forests of the Ethiopian highlands have been destroyed since 1900 *features* Danakil and Ogaden deserts; ancient remains (in Aksum, Gondar, Lalibela, among others); only African country to retain its independence during the colonial period *head of state* Meles Zenawi from 1991 *head of government* Tamirat Layne from 1991 *political system* transition to democratic socialist republic *political parties* Ethiopian People's

Revolutionary Democratic Front (EPRDF), nationalist, left of center; Tigré People's Liberation Front (TPLF); Ethiopian People's Democratic Movement (EPDM); Oromo People's Democratic Organization (OPDO) *exports* coffee, pulses, oilseeds, hides, skins *currency* birr *population* (1993) 51,980,000 (Oromo 40%, Amhara 25%, Tigré 12%, Sidamo 9%); growth rate 2.5% p.a. *life expectancy* men 45, women 49 *languages* Amharic (official), Tigrinya, Orominga, Arabic *media* both state-owned and independent newspapers exist, but journalists are often jailed *religions* Sunni Muslim 45%, Christian (Ethiopian Orthodox Church, which has had its own patriarch since 1976) 40% *literacy* 66% *GNP* $120 per head (1991). The country's debt-service payments 1993–95 will be $2 billion *chronology 1889* Abyssinia reunited by Menelik II. *1930* Haile Selassie became emperor. *1962* Eritrea annexed by Haile Selassie; resistance movement began. *1973–74* Severe famine in N Ethiopia. *1974* Haile Selassie deposed and replaced by a military government led by General Teferi Benti. Ethiopia declared a socialist state. *1977* Teferi Benti killed and replaced by Col. Mengistu Haile Mariam. *1977–79* "Red Terror" period in which Mengistu's regime killed thousands of innocent people. *1981–85* Ethiopia spent at least $2 billion on arms. *1984* Workers' Party of Ethiopia (WPE) declared the only legal political party. *1985* Worst famine in more than a decade; Western aid sent and forcible internal resettlement programs undertaken. *1987* New constitution adopted, Mengistu Mariam elected president. New famine; food aid hindered by guerrillas. *1988* Mengistu agreed to adjust his economic policies in order to secure IMF assistance. Influx of refugees from Sudan. *1989* Coup attempt against Mengistu foiled. Peace talks with Eritrean rebels mediated by former US president Carter reported some progress. *1990* Rebels captured port of Massawa. *1991* Mengistu overthrown; transitional government set up by EPRDF. EPLF secured Eritrea; Eritrea's right to secede recognized. Meles Zenawi elected Ethiopia's new head of state and government. *1993* Eritrean independence recognized after referendum. *1994* Assembly elections won by ruling EPLF.

ethnic cleansing the forced expulsion of one ethnic group by another, particularly of Muslims by Serbs in ◊Bosnia-Herzegovina from 1992. As part of a policy of creating a Greater Serbia, Bosnian-Serb forces compelled thousands of non-Serbs to abandon their homes, allowing Serb families from other parts of the former Yugoslavia to occupy them. The practice, reminiscent of the Nazi purge of the Jews in Germany, created nearly 700,000 refugees and was widely condemned by the international community.

ethnography study of living cultures, using anthropological techniques like participant observation (where the anthropologist lives in the society being studied) and a reliance on informants. Ethnography has provided much data of use to archeologists as analogies.

ethnology the branch of anthropology that deals with the comparative study of contemporary cultures, acculturation, and human ecology.

ethology comparative study of animal behavior in its natural setting. Ethology is concerned with the causal mechanisms (both the stimuli that elicit behavior and the physiological mechanisms controlling it), as well as the development of behavior, its function, and its evolutionary history.

ethyl alcohol common name for ◊ethanol.

ethyne common name **acetylene** CHCH colorless inflammable gas produced by mixing calcium carbide and water. It is the simplest member of the ◊alkyne series of hydrocarbons. It is used in the manufacture of the synthetic rubber neoprene, and in oxyacetylene welding and cutting.

Etna volcano on the east coast of Sicily, 10,906 ft/3,323 m, the highest in Europe. About 90 eruptions have been recorded since 1800 BC , yet because of the rich soil, the cultivated zone on the lower slopes is densely populated, including the coastal town of Catania. The most recent eruption was in Dec 1985. Tours of this smoking volcano are conducted.

Etruscan member of an ancient people inhabiting Etruria, Italy (modern-day Tuscany and part of Umbria) from the 8th to 4th centuries BC. The Etruscan dynasty of the Tarquins ruled Rome 616–509 BC . At the height of their civilization, in the 6th century BC , the Etruscans achieved great wealth and power from their maritime strength. They were driven out of Rome 509 BC and eventually dominated by the Romans.

etymology study of the origin and history of words within and across languages. It has two major aspects: the study of the phonetic and written forms of words, and of the semantics or meanings of those words.

EU abbreviation for ◊European Union.

eucalyptus any tree of the genus Eucalyptus of the myrtle family Myrtaceae, native to Australia and Tasmania, where they are commonly known as gum trees. About 90% of Australian timber belongs to the eucalyptus genus, which comprises about 500 species. The trees have dark hardwood timber which is used principally for heavy construction as in railroad and bridge building. They are tall, aromatic, evergreen trees with pendant leaves and white, pink, or red flowers.

Eucharist chief Christian sacrament, in which bread is eaten and wine drunk in memory of the death of Jesus. Other names for it are the **Lord's Supper, Holy Communion**, and (among Roman Catholics, who believe that the bread and wine are transubstantiated, that is, converted to the body and blood of Christ) the **Mass**. The doctrine of transubstantiation was rejected by Protestant churches during the Reformation.

Euclid c.330–c.260 BC . Greek mathematician, who lived in Alexandria and wrote the *Stoicheia/Elements* in 13 books, of which nine deal with plane and solid geometry and four with number theory. His great achievement lay in the systematic arrangement of previous discoveries, based on axioms, definitions, and theorems.

Eugene city in W central Oregon, S of Portland, on the Willamette River; population (1990) 112,700. It is a processing and shipping center for agricultural products from the surrounding region; wood products are also manufactured.

The University of Oregon 1872 is here.

eugenics study of ways in which the physical and mental characteristics of the human race may be improved. The eugenic principle was abused by the Nazi Party in Germany during the 1930s and early 1940s to justify the attempted extermination of entire social and ethnic groups and the establishment of selective breeding programs.

Modern eugenics is concerned mainly with the elimination of genetic disease.

eukaryote in biology, one of the two major groupings into which all organisms are divided. Included are all organisms, except bacteria and cyanobacteria (◊blue-green algae), which belong to the ◊prokaryote grouping.

Eumenides in Greek mythology, appeasing name for the ◊Furies.

eunuch castrated man. Originally eunuchs were bed-chamber attendants in harems in the East, but as they were usually castrated to keep them from taking too great an interest in their charges, the term became applied more generally. In China, eunuchs were employed within the imperial harem from some 4,000 years ago and by medieval times wielded considerable political power. Eunuchs often filled high offices of state in India and Persia.

Euphrates (Arabic **Furat**) river, rising in E Turkey, flowing through Syria and Iraq and joining the river Tigris above Basra to form the river Shatt-al-Arab, at the head of the Persian/Arabian Gulf; 2,240 mi/3,600 km in length. The ancient cities of Babylon, Eridu, and Ur were situated along its course.

Euripides c.485–c.406 BC . Athenian tragic dramatist. He is ranked with ◊Aeschylus and ◊Sophocles as one of the three great tragedians. He wrote about 90 plays, of which 18 and some long fragments survive. These include *Alcestis* 438 BC , *Medea* 431, *Hippolytus* 428, the satyr-drama *Cyclops* about 424–423, *Electra* 417, *Trojan Women* 415, *Iphigenia in Tauris* 413, *Iphigenia in Aulis* about 414–412, and *The Bacchae* about 405 (the last two were produced shortly after his death).

Europa in Greek mythology, the daughter of the king of Tyre, carried off by Zeus (in the form of a bull); she personifies the continent of Europe.

Europe second-smallest continent, occupying 8% of the Earth's surface **area** 4,000,000 sq mi/10,400,000 sq km **largest cities** (population over 1.5 million) Athens, Barcelona, Berlin, Birmingham, Bucharest, Budapest, Hamburg, Istanbul, Kharkov, Kiev, Lisbon, London, Madrid, Manchester, Milan, Moscow, Paris, Rome, St Petersburg, Vienna, Warsaw **features** Mount Elbruz 18,517 ft/5,642 m in the Caucasus Mountains is the highest peak in Europe; Mont Blanc 15,772 ft/4,807 m is the highest peak in the Alps; lakes (over 2,000 sq mi/5,100 sq km) include Ladoga, Onega, Vänern; rivers (over 500 mi/800 km) include the Volga, Danube, Dnieper Ural, Don, Pechora, Dniester, Rhine, Loire, Tagus, Ebro, Oder, Prut, Rhône **physical** conventionally occupying that part of Eurasia to the W of the Ural Mountains, N of the Caucasus

Mountains and N of the Sea of Marmara; Europe lies entirely in the northern hemisphere between 36° N and the Arctic Ocean. About two-thirds of the continent is a great plain which covers the whole of European Russia and spreads westward through Poland to the Low Countries and the Bay of Biscay. To the N lie the Scandinavian highlands rising to 8,110 ft/2,472 m at Glittertind in the Jotenheim range of Norway. To the S, a series of mountain ranges stretch E–W (Caucasus, Balkans, Carpathians, Apennines, Alps, Pyrenees, and Sierra Nevada). The most westerly point of the mainland is Cape Roca in Portugal; the most southerly location is Tarifa Point in Spain; the most northerly point on the mainland is Nordkynn in Norway.

European Atomic Energy Commission (Euratom) organization established by the second Treaty of Rome 1957, which seeks the cooperation of member states of the European Union (formerly the European Community) in nuclear research and the rapid and large-scale development of nonmilitary nuclear energy.

European Community former name (to 1993) of the ◊European Union.

European Court of Justice the court of the European Union (EU), which is responsible for interpreting Community law and ruling on breaches by member states and others of such law. It sits in Luxembourg with judges from the member states.

European Economic Area agreement 1991 between the European Community (now the ◊European Union) and the ◊European Free Trade Association (EFTA) to create a zone of economic cooperation, allowing their 380 million citizens to transfer money, shares, and bonds across national borders and to live, study, or work in one another's countries. The pact, which took effect Jan 1994, was seen as a temporary arrangement since most EFTA members hoped, eventually, to join the EU.

European Monetary System (EMS) attempt by the European Community (now the European Union) to bring financial cooperation and monetary stability to Europe. It was established 1979 in the wake of the 1974 oil crisis, which brought growing economic disruption to European economies because of floating exchange rates. Central to the EMS is the ◊*Exchange Rate Mechanism* (ERM), a voluntary system of semifixed exchange rates based on the European Currency Unit (ECU).

European Parliament the parliament of the European Union, which meets in Strasbourg to comment on the legislative proposals of the European Commission. Members are elected for a five-year term. The European Parliament has 567 seats, apportioned on the basis of population, of which Germany has 99; the UK, France, and Italy have 87 each; Spain 64; the Netherlands 31; Belgium, Greece, and Portugal 25 each; Denmark 16; the Republic of Ireland 15; and Luxembourg 6.

European Space Agency (ESA) organization of European countries (Austria, Belgium, Denmark, France, Germany, Ireland, Italy, the Netherlands, Norway, Spain, Sweden, Switzerland, and the UK) that engages in space research and technology. It was founded 1975, with headquarters in Paris.

European Union (EU; formerly until 1993 *European Community*) political and economic alliance consisting of the European Coal and Steel Community (1952),

European Economic Community (EEC, popularly called the Common Market, 1957), and the European Atomic Energy Commission (Euratom, 1957). The original six members—Belgium, France, West Germany, Italy, Luxembourg, and the Netherlands—were joined by the UK, Denmark, and the Republic of Ireland 1973, Greece 1981, and Spain and Portugal 1986. East Germany was incorporated on German reunification 1990. Membership terms for Austria, Finland, Sweden, and Norway were agreed March 1994 (to take effect Jan 1995), and approved in national referendums in all but Norway, which rejected membership. Association agreements—providing for free trade within ten years and the possibility of full membership—were signed with Czechoslovakia, Hungary, and Poland 1991, subject to ratification, and with Romania 1992. In 1994 there were more than 340 million people in the EU countries.

europium soft, grayish, metallic element of the ◊lanthanide series, symbol Eu, atomic number 63, atomic weight 151.96. It is used in lasers and as the red phosphor in color televisions; its compounds are used to make control rods for nuclear reactors. It was named in 1901 by French chemist Eugène Demarçay (1852–1904) after the continent of Europe, where it was first found.

euthanasia in medicine, mercy killing of someone with a severe and incurable condition or illness. The Netherlands legalized voluntary euthanasia 1983, but is the only country to have done so. Approximately 2,700 patients there formally request euthanasia each year.

eutrophication excessive enrichment of rivers, lakes, and shallow sea areas, primarily by nitrate fertilizers washed from the soil by rain, by phosphates from fertilizers, and from nutrients in municipal sewage, and by sewage itself. These encourage the growth of algae and bacteria which use up the oxygen in the water, thereby making it uninhabitable for fishes and other animal life.

evangelicalism the beliefs of some Protestant Christian movements that stress biblical authority, faith, and the personal commitment of the "born again" experience.

Evangelical groups constituted the fastest-growing part of American Christianity during the 1970s and 1980s; their influence was spread through Bible colleges, Christian publishing houses and bookstores, television evangelism, and missionary efforts.

evangelist person traveling to spread the Christian gospel, in particular the authors of the four Gospels in the New Testament: Matthew, Mark, Luke, and John.

Evans Walker 1903–1975. US photographer. He is best known for his documentary photographs of people in the rural American South during the Great Depression. Many of his photographs appeared in James Agee's book *Let Us Now Praise Famous Men* 1941.

Born in St Louis, Evans was in 1938 the first photographer to have an exhibit at the Museum of Modern Art in New York City. From 1945 to 1965 he served as an associate editor of *Fortune* magazine, in which he published several photo essays. Throughout his career, he devoted much attention to photographing architecture. He also did a renowned series of photographs of people in the New York City subways.

Evansville industrial city in SW Indiana, on the Ohio River; population (1990) 126,300. Industries include pharmaceuticals and plastics. The University of Evansville is here.

The community, which dates to 1812, grew after the 1853 completion of the Wabash and Erie canal linking the Ohio at Evansville with Lake Erie.

evaporation process in which a liquid turns to a vapor without its temperature reaching boiling point. A liquid left to stand in a saucer eventually evaporates because, at any time, a proportion of its molecules will be fast enough (have enough kinetic energy) to escape through the attractive intermolecular forces at the liquid surface into the atmosphere. The temperature of the liquid tends to fall because the evaporating molecules remove energy from the liquid. The rate of evaporation rises with increased temperature because as the mean kinetic energy of the liquid's molecules rises, so will the number possessing enough energy to escape.

Eve in the Old Testament, the first woman, wife of ◊Adam. She was tempted by Satan (in the form of a snake) to eat the fruit of the Tree of Knowledge of Good and Evil, and then tempted Adam to eat of the fruit as well, thus bringing about their expulsion from the Garden of Eden.

evening primrose any plant of the genus *Oenothera*, family Onagraceae. Some 50 species are native to North America, several of which now also grow in Europe. Some are cultivated for their oil, which is rich in gamma-linoleic acid (GLA). The body converts GLA into substances which resemble hormones, and evening primrose oil is beneficial in alleviating the symptoms of ◊premenstrual tension. It is also used in treating eczema and chronic fatigue syndrome.

Everest, Mount (Nepalese *Sagarmatha* "head of the earth") the world's highest mountain above sea level, in the Himalayas, on the China–Nepal frontier; height 29,118 ft/8,872 m (recently measured by satellite to this new height from the former official height of 29,028 ft/8,848 m). It was first climbed by New Zealand mountaineer Edmund Hillary and Sherpa Tenzing Norgay 1953. More than 360 climbers have reached the summit; over 100 have died during the ascent.

Everglades area of swamps, marsh, and lakes in S ◊Florida; area 5,000 sq mi/12,950 sq km. A national park covers the southern tip.

evergreen in botany, a plant such as pine, spruce, or holly, that bears its leaves all year round. Most ◊conifers are evergreen. Plants that shed their leaves in autumn or during a dry season are described as ◊deciduous.

Evert Chris(tine) 1954– . US tennis player. She won her first Wimbledon title 1974, and has since won 21 Grand Slam titles. She became the first woman tennis player to win $1 million in prize money. She has an outstanding two-handed backhand and is a great exponent of baseline technique. Evert retired from competitive tennis 1989.

evolution slow process of change from one form to another, as in the evolution of the universe from its formation in the ◊Big Bang to its present state, or in the evolution of life on Earth. Some Christians and Muslims deny the theory of evolution as conflicting with the belief that God created all things (creationism). English naturalist Charles ◊Darwin, assigned the major role in evolutionary change to ◊natural selection acting on randomly occurring variations (now known to be produced by spontaneous

changes or ◊mutations in the genetic material of organisms).

exchange rate the price at which one currency is bought or sold in terms of other currencies, gold, or accounting units such as the special drawing right (SDR) of the ◊International Monetary Fund. Exchange rates may be fixed by international agreement or by government policy; or they may be wholly or partly allowed to "float" (that is, find their own level) in world currency markets.

Under the Reagan administration, the US dollar was allowed, even encouraged, to drop in relation to other currencies, especially the Japanese yen.

Exchange Rate Mechanism (ERM) voluntary system for controlling exchange rates within the European Union's ◊European Monetary System. The member currencies of the ERM are fixed against each other within a narrow band of fluctuation based on a central European Currency Unit (ECU) rate, but floating against nonmember countries. If a currency deviates significantly from the central ECU rate, the European Monetary Cooperation Fund and the central banks concerned intervene to stabilize the currency.

excise taxes imposed on goods, usually considered luxury items or those items quickly consumed. The taxes are paid prior to sale, the cost being passed on to the consumer.

exclamation point punctuation mark (!) used to indicate emphasis or strong emotion ("That's terrible!"). It is appropriate after interjections ("Rats!"), emphatic greetings ("Yo!"), and orders ("Shut up!"), as well as those sentences beginning *How* or *What* that are not questions ("How embarrassing!", "What a surprise!").

excommunication in religion, exclusion of an offender from the rights and privileges of the Roman Catholic Church; King John, Henry VIII, and Elizabeth I were all excommunicated.

excretion in biology, the removal of waste products from the cells of living organisms. In plants and simple animals, waste products are removed by diffusion, but in higher animals they are removed by specialized organs. In mammals the kidneys are the principle organs of excretion. Water and metabolic wastes are also excreted in the feces and, in humans, through the sweat glands; carbon dioxide and water are removed via the lungs.

executor in law, a person appointed in a will to carry out the instructions of the deceased. A person so named has the right to refuse to act. The executor also has a duty to bury the deceased, prove the will, and obtain a grant of probate (that is, establish that the will is genuine and obtain official approval of his or her actions).

The executor must also pay the liens, fees, and taxes on the estate before distributing the estate property to the heirs.

existentialism branch of philosophy based on the concept of an absurd universe where humans have free will. Existentialists argue that philosophy must begin from the concrete situation of the individual in such a world, and that humans are responsible for and the sole judge of their actions as they affect others, though no one else's existence is real to the individual. The origin of existentialism is usually traced back to the Danish philosopher ◊Kierkegaard; among its proponents were Martin Heidegger in Germany and Jean-Paul ◊Sartre in France.

Exodus second book of the Old Testament, which relates the departure of the Israelites from slavery in Egypt, under the leadership of ◊Moses, for the Promised Land of Canaan. The journey included the miraculous parting of the Red Sea, with the Pharaoh's pursuing forces being drowned as the waters returned.

The Exodus is also recorded in the *Hagadda*, which is read at the Seder (during the Jewish festival of Passover) to commemorate the deliverance. During the 40 years of wandering in the wilderness, Moses brought the Ten Commandments down from Mt. Sinai.

exorcism rite used in a number of religions for the expulsion of so-called evil spirits. In Christianity it is employed, for example, in the Roman Catholic and Pentecostal churches.

exosphere the uppermost layer of the ◊atmosphere. It is an ill-defined zone above the thermosphere, beginning at about 435 mi/700 km and fading off into the vacuum of space. The gases are extremely thin, with hydrogen as the main constituent.

expanded memory in computing, additional memory in an ◊MS-DOS-based computer, usually installed on an expanded-memory board. Expanded memory requires an expanded-memory manager, which gives access to a limited amount of memory at any one time, and is slower to use than extended memory. Software is available under both MS-DOS and ◊Windows to simulate expanded memory for those applications that require it.

expansion in physics, the increase in size of a constant mass of substance caused by, for example, increasing its temperature (thermal expansion) or its internal pressure. The *expansivity*, or coefficient of thermal expansion, of a material is its expansion (per unit volume, area, or length) per degree rise in temperature.

expansion board or *expansion card* printed circuit board that can be inserted into a computer in order to enhance its capabilities (for example, to increase its memory) or to add facilities (such as graphics).

export goods or service produced in one country and sold to another. Exports may be visible (goods such as automobiles physically exported) or invisible (services such as banking and tourism, that are provided in the exporting country but paid for by residents of another country).

export file in computing, a file stored by the computer in a standard format so that it can be accessed by other programs, possibly running on different makes of computer.

Expressionism style of painting, sculpture, and literature that expresses inner emotions; in particular, a movement in early 20th-century art in northern and central Europe. Expressionists tended to distort or exaggerate natural appearance in order to create a reflection of an inner world; the Norwegian painter Edvard Munch's *Skriket/The Scream* 1893 (National Gallery, Oslo) is perhaps the most celebrated example. Expressionist writers include August Strindberg and Frank Wedekind.

extinction in biology, the complete disappearance of a species. In the past, extinctions are believed to have occurred because species were unable to adapt quickly enough to a naturally changing environment. Today, most extinctions are due to human activity. Some species, such as the ◊dodo of Mauritius, the moas of New Zealand, and the passenger ◊pigeon of North America, were exterminated by hunting. Others

became extinct when their habitat was destroyed. See also ◊endangered species.

extradition surrender, by one state or country to another, of a person accused of a criminal offense in the state or country to which that person is extradited.

extrasensory perception (ESP) form of perception beyond and distinct from the known sensory processes. The main forms of ESP are clairvoyance (intuitive perception or vision of events and situations without using the senses); precognition (the ability to foresee events); and telepathy or thought transference (communication between people without using any known visible, tangible, or audible medium).

Verification by scientific study has yet to be achieved.

extroversion or *extraversion* personality dimension described by ◊Jung and later by Eysenck. The typical extrovert is sociable, impulsive, and carefree. The opposite of extroversion is introversion; the typical introvert is quiet and inward-looking.

Exxon Corporation the US's largest oil concern, founded 1888 as the Standard Oil Company (New Jersey), selling gasoline under the brand name Esso from 1926 and under the name Exxon in the US from 1972. The company was responsible for ◊oil spills in Alaska 1989 and New York harbor 1990.

Under a US government settlement 1991, Exxon was ordered to pay a fine of $100 million plus $900 million damages to repair environmental harm done to the Alaskan shoreline as a result of an oil spill from the *Exxon Valdez*. However, the settlement collapsed May 1991 and legal action against Exxon is likely to continue for several years.

Eyck Jan van *c.* 1390–1441. Flemish painter of the early northern Renaissance. He was one of the first to work in oils. His paintings are technically brilliant and sumptuously rich in detail and color. In his *Giovanni Arnolfini and his Wife* 1434 (National Gallery, London), the bride and groom appear in a domestic interior crammed with disguised symbols, a kind of pictorial marriage certificate.

eye the organ of vision. In the human eye, the light is focused by the combined action of the curved *cornea*, the internal fluids, and the *lens*. The insect eye is compound—made up of many separate facets—known as ommatidia, each of which collects light and directs it separately to a receptor to build up an image. Invertebrates have much simpler eyes, with no lenses. Among mollusks, cephalopods have complex eyes similar to those of vertebrates.

The mantis shrimp's eyes contain ten color pigments with which to perceive color; some flies and fishes have five, while the human eye has only three.

eyebright any flower of the genus *Euphrasia*, of the figwort family Scrophulariaceae. They are 1–12 in/2–30 cm high, bearing whitish flowers streaked with purple. The name indicates its traditional use as an eye-medicine. *E. americana* of the SE US, with pale lavender flowers in clusters, is an example.

eyeglasses pair of lenses fitted in a frame and worn in front of the eyes to correct or assist defective vision. Common defects of the eye corrected by such lenses are nearsightedness (myopia), corrected by using concave (spherical) lenses, farsightedness (hypermetropia), corrected by using convex (spherical) lenses, and astigmatism, corrected by using cylindrical lenses. Spherical and cylindrical lenses may be combined in

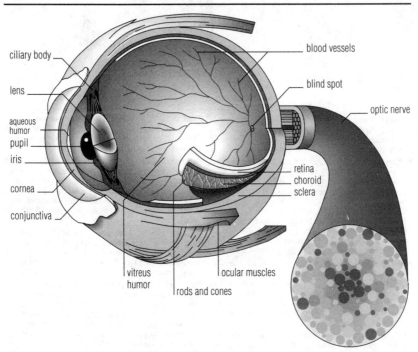

- ciliary body
- lens
- aqueous humor
- pupil
- iris
- cornea
- conjunctiva
- blood vessels
- blind spot
- optic nerve
- retina
- choroid
- sclera
- vitreus humor
- ocular muscles
- rods and cones

eye The human eye. The retina of the eye contains about 137 million light sensitive cells in an area of about 1 sq in/650 sq mm. There are 130 million rod cells for black and white vision and 7 million cone cells for color vision. The optic nerve contains about 1 million nerve fibers. The focusing muscles of the eye adjust about 100,000 times a day. To exercise the leg muscles to the same extent would need an 50 mi/80 km walk.

one lens. Bifocal glasses correct vision both at a distance and for reading by combining two lenses of different curvatures in one piece of glass. Today, lightweight plastic lenses are common instead of glass.

Eyre, Lake Australia's largest lake, in central South Australia, which frequently runs dry, becoming a salt marsh in dry seasons; area up to 3,500 sq mi/9,000 sq km. It is the continent's lowest point, 39 ft/12 m below sea level.

Fabergé Peter Carl 1846–1920. Russian goldsmith and jeweler. Among his masterpieces was a series of jeweled Easter eggs, the first of which was commissioned by Alexander III for the czarina 1884.

Fabian Society UK socialist organization for research, discussion, and publication, founded in London 1884. Its name is derived from the Roman commander Fabius Maximus, and refers to the evolutionary methods by which it hopes to attain socialism by a succession of gradual reforms. Early members included the playwright George Bernard Shaw and Beatrice and Sidney Webb. The society helped to found the Labour Representation Committee in 1900, which became the Labour Party in 1906.

fable story, in either verse or prose, in which animals or inanimate objects are given the mentality and speech of human beings to point out a moral. Fables are common in folklore and children's literature, and range from the short fables of the ancient Greek writer Aesop to the modern novel *Animal Farm* by George Orwell.

Fabricius Hieronymus (Italian *Geronimo Fabrici*) 1537–1619. Italian anatomist and embryologist. He made a detailed study of the veins and discovered the valves that direct the blood flow toward the heart. He also studied the development of chick embryos.

facsimile transmission full name for ◊*fax* or *telefax*.

factory farming intensive rearing of poultry or animals for food, usually on high-protein foodstuffs in confined quarters. Chickens for eggs and meat, and calves for veal are commonly factory farmed. Some countries restrict the use of antibiotics and growth hormones as aids to factory farming, because they can persist in the flesh of the animals after they are slaughtered. The emphasis is on productive yield rather than animal welfare so that conditions for the animals are often very poor. For this reason, many people object to factory farming on moral as well as health grounds.

Faeroe Islands or *Faroe Islands* or *Faeroes* (Danish *Faerøerne* "Sheep Islands") island group (18 out of 22 inhabited) in the N Atlantic, between the Shetland Islands and Iceland, forming an outlying part of ◊Denmark *area* 540 sq mi/1,399 sq km; largest islands are Strømø, østerø, Vagø, Suderø, Sandø, and Bordø *capital* Thorshavn on Strømø, population (1986) 15,287 *industries* fish, crafted goods *currency* Danish krone *population* (1986) 46,000 *languages* Faeroese, Danish *government* since 1948 the islands have had full self-government; they do not belong to the European Union *history* first settled by Norsemen in the 9th century, the Faeroes were a Norwegian province 1380–1709. Their parliament was restored 1852. They withdrew from the European Free Trade Association 1972.

Fagatogo capital of American ◊Samoa, situated on Pago Pago Harbour, Tutuila Island; population (1980) 30,124.

Fahd 1921– . King of Saudi Arabia from 1982, when he succeeded his half-brother Khalid. As head of government, he has been active in trying to bring about a solution to the Middle East conflicts.

Fahrenheit scale temperature scale invented 1714 by Gabriel Fahrenheit which was commonly used in English-speaking countries until the 1970s, after which the ◊Celsius scale was generally adopted, in line with the rest of the world. In the Fahrenheit scale, intervals are measured in degrees (°F); °F = (°C x $\frac{9}{5}$) + 32.

fainting sudden, temporary loss of consciousness caused by reduced blood supply to the brain. It may be due to emotional shock or physical factors, such as pooling of blood in the legs from standing still for long periods.

Fairbanks town in central Alaska, situated on the Chena Slough, a tributary of the Tanana River; population (1990) 30,800. Founded 1902, it became a gold-mining and fur-trading center and the terminus of the Alaska Railroad and the Pan-American Highway.

It functions as a service center for the mineral development of central and N Alaska. Fort Wainwright, Eielson Air Force Base, and the main campus of the University of Alaska are outside the city limits.

Fairbanks Douglas, Sr. Adopted name of Douglas Elton Ulman 1883–1939. US actor. He played acrobatic swashbuckling heroes in silent films such as *The Mark of Zorro* 1920, *The Three Musketeers* 1921, *Robin Hood* 1922, *The Thief of Bagdad* 1924, and *Don Quixote* 1925. He was married to film star Mary Pickford ("America's Sweetheart") 1920–35. In 1919 he founded United Artists with Charlie Chaplin and D W Griffith. He was the father of actor Douglas Fairbanks, Jr.

Fairfax Thomas, 3rd Baron Fairfax of Cameron 1612–1671. English general, commander in chief of the Parliamentary army in the English Civil War. With Oliver Cromwell he formed the New Model Army and defeated Charles I at Naseby. He opposed the king's execution, resigned in protest 1650 against the invasion of Scotland, and participated in the restoration of Charles II after Cromwell's death.

fairy tale magical story, usually a folk tale in origin. Typically in European fairy tales, a poor, brave, and resourceful hero or heroine goes through testing adventures to eventual good fortune.

Faisal Ibn Abd al-Aziz 1905–1975. King of Saudi Arabia from 1964. He was the younger brother of King Saud, on whose accession 1953 he was declared crown prince. He was prime minister 1953–60 and 1962–75. In 1964 he emerged victorious from a lengthy conflict with his brother and adopted a policy of steady modernization of his country. He was assassinated by his nephew.

falcon any bird of prey of the genus *Falco*, family Falconidae, order Falconiformes. Falcons are the smallest of the hawks (6–24 in/15–60 cm). They nest in high places and kill their prey by "stooping" (swooping down at high speed). They include the peregrine and kestrel.

Faldo Nick 1957– . English golfer who was the first Briton in 54 years to win three British Open titles, and the only person after Jack ◊Nicklaus to win two successive US Masters titles (1989 and 1990). He is one of only six golfers to win the Masters and British Open in the same year.

Falkland Islands (Argentine *Islas Malvinas*) British crown colony in the S Atlantic *area* 4,700 sq mi/ 12,173 sq km, made up of two main islands: East Falkland 2,610 sq mi/6,760 sq km, and West Falkland 2,090 sq mi/5,413 sq km *capital* Stanley; new port facilities opened 1984, Mount Pleasant airport 1985 *features* in addition to the two main islands, there are about 200 small islands, all with wild scenery and rich bird life *industries* wool, alginates (used as dyes and as a food additive) from seaweed beds *population* (1991) 2,100

Falklands War war between Argentina and Britain over disputed sovereignty of the Falkland Islands initiated when Argentina invaded and occupied the islands April 2, 1982. On the following day, the United Nations Security Council passed a resolution calling for Argentina to withdraw. A British task force was immediately dispatched and, after a fierce conflict in which more than 1,000 Argentine and British lives were lost, 12,000 Argentine troops surrendered and the islands were returned to British rule June 14–15, 1982.

Falla Manuel de (full name Manuel Maria de Falla y Matheu) 1876–1946. Spanish composer. His opera *La vida breve/Brief Life* 1905 (performed 1913) was followed by the ballets *El amor brujo/Love the Magician* 1915 and *El sombrero de tres picos/The Three-Cornered Hat* 1919, and his most ambitious concert work, *Noches en los jardines de España/Nights in the Gardens of Spain* 1916.

Fallopian tube or *oviduct* in mammals, one of two tubes that carry eggs from the ovary to the uterus. An egg is fertilized by sperm in the Fallopian tubes, which are lined with cells whose cilia move the egg toward the uterus.

fallout harmful radioactive material released into the atmosphere in the debris of a nuclear explosion (see ◊nuclear warfare) and descending to the surface of the Earth. Such material can enter the food chain, cause ◊radiation sickness, and last for hundreds of thousands of years (see ◊half-life).

family in biological classification, a group of related genera (see ◊genus). Family names are not printed in italic (unlike genus and species names), and by convention they all have the ending -idae (animals) or -aceae (plants and fungi). For example, the genera of hummingbirds are grouped in the hummingbird family, Trochilidae. Related families are grouped together in an ◊order.

family planning spacing or preventing the birth of children. Access to family-planning services (see ◊contraceptive) is a significant factor in women's health as well as in limiting population growth. If all those women who wished to avoid further childbirth were able to do so, the number of births would be reduced by 27% in Africa, 33% in Asia, and 35% in Latin America; and the number of women who die during pregnancy or childbirth would be reduced by about 50%.

famine severe shortage of food affecting a large number of people. Almost 750 million people (equivalent to double the population of Europe) worldwide suffer from hunger and malnutrition. The *food availability deficit* (FAD) theory explains famines as being caused by insufficient food supplies. A more recent theory is that famines arise when one group in a society loses its opportunity to exchange its labor or possessions for food.

fan-jet another name for ◊turbofan, the jet engine used by most airliners.

farad SI unit (symbol F) of electrical capacitance (how much electricity a ◊capacitor can store for a given voltage). One farad is a capacitance of one ◊coulomb per volt. For practical purposes the microfarad (one millionth of a farad) is more commonly used.

The farad is named for English scientist Michael Faraday, and replaced the now obsolete unit the jar (so called because it represented the charge stored in a Leiden jar, the earliest electrical circuit). One farad equals 9×10^8 jars.

Faraday Michael 1791–1867. English chemist and physicist. In 1821 he began experimenting with electromagnetism, and ten years later discovered the induction of electric currents and made the first dynamo. He subsequently found that a magnetic field will rotate the plane of polarization of light (see ◊polarized light). Faraday also investigated electrolysis.

farce broad popular comedy involving stereotyped characters in complex, often improbable situations frequently revolving around extramarital relationships (hence the term "bedroom farce").

Far East geographical term for all Asia east of the Indian subcontinent.

Farmer Frances 1913–1970. US actress. She starred in such films as *Come and Get It* 1936, *The Toast of New York* 1937, and *Son of Fury* 1942, before her career was ended by alcoholism and mental illness.

She published an autobiography, *Will There Really Be a Morning?*

Faroe Islands alternative spelling of the ◊Faeroe Islands, in the N Atlantic.

Farouk 1920–1965. King of Egypt 1936–52. He succeeded his father Fuad I. In 1952 a coup headed by General Muhammed Neguib and Colonel Gamal Nasser compelled him to abdicate, and his son Fuad II was temporarily proclaimed in his place.

Farsi or *Persian* language belonging to the Indo-Iranian branch of the Indo-European family, and the official language of Iran (formerly Persia). It is also spoken in Afghanistan, Iraq, and Tajikistan.

fascism political ideology that denies all rights to individuals in their relations with the state; specifically, the totalitarian nationalist movement founded in Italy 1919 by ◊Mussolini and followed by Hitler's Germany 1933.

Fascism was essentially a product of the economic and political crisis of the years after World War I. Units called *fasci di combattimento* (combat groups), from the Latin fasces, were originally established to oppose communism. The fascist party, the *Partitio Nazionale Fascista*, controlled Italy 1922–43. Fascism protected the existing social order by forcible suppression of the working-class movement and by providing scapegoats for popular anger such as outsiders who lived within the state: Jews, foreigners, or blacks; it also prepared the citizenry for the economic and psychological mobilization of war.

The atrocities committed by Nazi Germany and other fascist countries discredited fascism, but neofascist groups exist today in the US, Latin America, and many W European countries.

Fassbinder Rainer Werner 1946–1982. West German film director. He began as a fringe actor and founded his own "antitheater" before moving into films. His works are mainly stylized indictments of contemporary German society. He made more than 40 films, including *Die bitteren Tränen der Petra von Kant/The Bitter Tears of Petra von Kant* 1972, *Angst essen Seele auf/Fear Eats the Soul* 1974, and *Die Ehe von Maria Braun/The Marriage of Maria Braun* 1979.

fast breeder or *breeder reactor* alternative names for ◊fast reactor, a type of nuclear reactor.

fasting the practice of voluntarily going without food. It can be undertaken as a religious observance, a sign of mourning, a political protest (hunger strike), or for slimming purposes.

fast reactor or *fast breeder reactor* ◊nuclear reactor that makes use of fast neutrons to bring about fission. Unlike other reactors used by the nuclear-power industry, it has little or no moderator, to slow down neutrons. The reactor core is surrounded by a "blanket" of uranium carbide. During operation, some of this uranium is converted into plutonium, which can be extracted and later used as fuel.

fat in the broadest sense, a mixture of ◊lipids—chiefly triglycerides (lipids containing three ◊fatty acid molecules linked to a molecule of glycerol). More specifically, the term refers to a lipid mixture that is solid at room temperature (20°C); lipid mixtures that are liquid at room temperature are called *oils*. The higher the proportion of saturated fatty acids in a mixture, the harder the fat.

Fatah, al- Palestinian nationalist organization, founded 1958 to bring about an independent state of Palestine. It was the first Palestinian resistance group, based 1968–70 in Jordan, then in Lebanon, and from 1982 in Tunisia. Also called the Palestine National Liberation Movement, it is the main component of the ◊Palestine Liberation Organization. Its leader is Yassir ◊Arafat.

Fates in Greek mythology, the three female figures who determined the destiny of human lives. They were envisaged as spinners: Clotho spun the thread of life, Lachesis twisted the thread, and Atropos cut it off. They are analogous to the Roman Parcae and Norse Norns.

Fatimid dynasty of Muslim Shiite caliphs founded 909 by Obaidallah, who claimed to be a descendant of Fatima (the prophet Mohammed's daughter) and her husband Ali, in N Africa. In 969 the Fatimids conquered Egypt, and the dynasty continued until overthrown by Saladin 1171.

fatty acid or *carboxylic acid* organic compound consisting of a hydrocarbon chain, up to 24 carbon atoms long, with a carboxyl group (–COOH) at one end. The covalent bonds between the carbon atoms may be single or double; where a double bond occurs the carbon atoms concerned carry one instead of two hydrogen atoms. Chains with only single bonds have all the hydrogen they can carry, so they are said to be *saturated* with hydrogen. Chains with one or more double bonds are said to be *unsaturated* (see ◊polyunsaturate).

fatwa in Islamic law, an authoritative legal opinion on a point of doctrine. In 1989 a fatwa calling for the death of English novelist Salman ◊Rushdie was made by the Ayatollah ◊Khomeini of Iran, following publication of Rushdie's controversial and allegedly blasphemous book *The Satanic Verses*.

Faulkner William 1897–1962. US novelist who wrote in an experimental stream-of-consciousness style, often considered the finest 20th-century American writer. His works include *The Sound and the Fury* 1929, dealing with a favorite topic—the Southern family in decline; *As I Lay Dying* 1930; and *The Hamlet* 1940, *The Town* 1957, and *The Mansion* 1959, a trilogy covering the rise of the materialistic Snopes family. He was awarded the Nobel Prize for Literature in 1949.

fault in geology, a fracture in the Earth's crust along which the two sides have moved as a result of differing strains in the adjacent rock bodies. Displacement of rock masses horizontally or vertically along a fault may be microscopic, or it may be massive, causing major ◊earthquakes.

Faunus in Roman mythology, the god of fertility and prophecy, with goat's ears, horns, tail and hind legs, identified with the Greek ◊Pan.

Faust legendary magician who sold his soul to the Devil. The historical Georg Faust appears to have been a wandering scholar and conjurer in Germany at the start of the 16th century. Goethe, Heine, Thomas Mann, and Paul Valéry all used the legend, and it inspired musical works by Schumann, Berlioz, Gounod, Boito, and Busoni.

Fauvism style of painting characterized by a bold use of vivid colors inspired by the work of van Gogh, Cézanne, and Gaugin. A short-lived but influential art movement, Fauvism originated in Paris 1905 with the founding of the Salon d'Automne by Henri ◊Matisse and others, when the critic Louis Vauxcelles, on seeing a piece of conventional sculpture, said it was like "Donatello amid wild beasts" ("*Donatello chez les fauves*"). Rouault, Dufy, Marquet, Derain, and Signac were early Fauves.

Fawkes Guy 1570–1606. English conspirator in the ◊Gunpowder Plot to blow up King James I and the members of both Houses of Parliament. Fawkes, a Roman Catholic convert, was arrested in the cellar underneath the House Nov 5, 1605, tortured, and executed. The event is still commemorated in Britain and elsewhere every Nov 5 with bonfires, fireworks, and the burning of the "guy," an effigy.

fax (common name for *facsimile transmission* or *telefax*) the transmission of images over a ◊telecommunications link, usually the telephone network. When placed on a fax machine, the original image is scanned by a transmitting device and converted into coded signals, which travel via the telephone lines to the receiving fax machine, where an image is created that is a copy of the original. Photographs as well as printed text and drawings can be sent. The standard transmission takes place at 4,800 or 9,600 bits of information per second.

FBI abbreviation for ◊*Federal Bureau of Investigation*, agency of the US Department of Justice.

feather rigid outgrowth of the outer layer of the skin of birds, made of the protein keratin. Feathers provide insulation and facilitate flight. There are several types, including long quill feathers on the wings and tail, fluffy down feathers for retaining body heat, and contour feathers covering the body. The coloring of

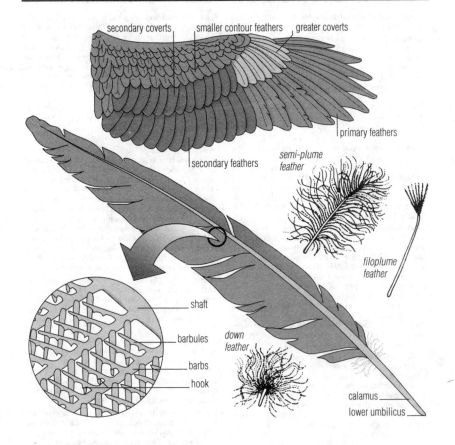

secondary coverts   smaller contour feathers   greater coverts

primary feathers

secondary feathers

semi-plume feather

filoplume feather

shaft

barbules

barbs

hook

down feather

calamus

lower umbilicus

feather *Types of feather. A bird's wing is made up of two types of feather: contour feathers and flight feathers. The primary and secondary feathers are flight feathers. The coverts are contour feathers, used to streamline the bird. Semiplume and down feathers insulate the bird's body and provide color.*

feathers is often important in camouflage or in courtship and other displays. Feathers are replaced at least once a year.

feces remains of food and other debris passed out of the digestive tract of animals. Feces consist of quantities of fibrous material, bacteria and other microorganisms, rubbed-off lining of the digestive tract, bile fluids, undigested food, minerals, and water.

Federal Bureau of Investigation (FBI) agency of the US Department of Justice that investigates violations of federal law not specifically assigned to other agencies, being particularly concerned with internal security. The FBI was established 1908 and built up a position of powerful autonomy during the autocratic directorship of J Edgar Hoover 1924–72. Louis Joseph Freeh, a former FBI agent and federal prosecutor, has been director since 1993.

federalism system of government in which two or more separate states unite into a ◊federation under a common central government. Many supporters of the

European Union see it as the forerunner of a federal Europe.

Federalist in US history, one who advocated the ratification of the US Constitution 1787–88 in place of the Articles of ◊Confederation. The Federalists became in effect the ruling political party during the presidencies of George Washington and John Adams 1789–1801, legislating to strengthen the authority of the newly created federal government.

The Federalists advocated reconciliation with Britain and were urban, educated, and vaguely antidemocratic.

federation political entity made up from a number of smaller units or states where the central government has powers over national issues such as foreign policy and defense, while the individual states retain a high degree of regional and local autonomy. A federation should be distinguished from a *confederation*, a looser union of states for mutual assistance. Contemporary examples of federated states established since 1750 include the US, Canada, Australia, India, and the Federal Republic of Germany.

feedback general principle whereby the results produced in an ongoing reaction become factors in modifying or changing the reaction; it is the principle used in self-regulating control systems, from a simple ◊thermostat and steam-engine governor to automatic computer-controlled machine tools. A fully computerized control system, in which there is no operator intervention, is called a *closed-loop feedback* system. A system that also responds to control signals from an operator is called an *open-loop feedback* system.

feldspar one of a group of rock-forming minerals; the chief constituents of ◊igneous rock. Feldspars all contain silicon, aluminum, and oxygen, linked together to form a framework; spaces within this structure are occupied by sodium, potassium, calcium, or occasionally barium, in various proportions. Feldspars form white, gray, or pink crystals and rank 6 on the ◊Mohs' scale of hardness.

Fellini Federico 1920–1993. Italian film director and screenwriter. His work has been a major influence on modern cinema. His films combine dream and fantasy sequences with satire and autobiographical detail. They include *I vitelloni/The Young and the Passionate* 1953, *La strada/The Street* 1954 (Academy Award), *Le notti di Cabiria/Nights of Cabiria* 1956 (Academy Award), *La dolce vita* 1960, *Otto e mezzo/8½* 1963 (Academy Award), *Satyricon* 1969, *Roma/Fellini's Rome* 1972, *Amarcord* 1974 (Academy Award), *La città delle donne/City of Women* 1980, and *Ginger e Fred/Ginger and Fred* 1986. He was presented with a Special Academy Award for his life's work 1993.

female circumcision or *female genital mutilation* operation on women analogous to male ◊circumcision. There are three types: *Sunna*, which involves cutting off the hood, and sometimes the tip, of the clitoris; *clitoridectomy*, the excision of the clitoris and removal of parts of the inner and outer labia; *infibulation* (most widely practiced in Sudan and Somalia), in which the labia are stitched, after excision, leaving a small hole.

feminism active belief in equal rights and opportunities for women; see ◊women's movement.

fencing sport of fighting with swords including the foil, derived from the light weapon used in practice duels; the épée, a heavier weapon derived from the duelling sword proper; and the *saber*, with a curved handle and narrow V-shaped blade. In saber fighting, cuts count as well as thrusts. Masks and protective jackets are worn, and hits are registered electronically in competitions. Men's fencing has been part of every Olympic program since 1896; women's fencing was included from 1924 but only using the foil.

Fenian movement Irish-American republican secret society, founded 1858 and named for the ancient Irish legendary warrior band of the Fianna. The collapse of the movement began when an attempt to establish an independent Irish republic by an uprising in Ireland 1867 failed, as did raids into Canada 1866 and 1870, and England 1867.

fennel any of several varieties of a perennial plant *Foeniculum vulgare* with feathery green leaves, of the carrot family Umbelliferae.

Fennels have an aniseed flavor, and the leaves and seeds are used in seasoning. The thickened leafstalks of sweet fennel *F. vulgare dulce* are eaten.

Fens, the level, low-lying tracts of land in E England, W and S of the Wash, about 70 mi/115 km N–S and 34 mi/55 km E–W. They fall within the counties of Lincolnshire, Cambridgeshire, and Norfolk, consisting of a huge area, formerly a bay of the North Sea, but now crossed by numerous drainage canals and forming some of the most productive agricultural land in Britain. The peat portion of the Fens is known as the *Bedford Level*.

Ferdinand (I) the Great *c.*1016–1065. King of Castile from 1035. He began the reconquest of Spain from the Moors and united all NW Spain under his and his brothers' rule.

Ferdinand V 1452–1516. King of Castile from 1474, *Ferdinand II* of Aragon from 1479, and *Ferdinand III* of Naples from 1504; first king of all Spain. In 1469 he married his cousin Isabella I, who succeeded to the throne of Castile 1474; they were known as the *Catholic Monarchs* because after 700 years of rule by the ◊Moors, they catholicized Spain. When Ferdinand inherited the throne of Aragon 1479, the two great Spanish kingdoms were brought under a single government for the first time. They introduced the Inquisition 1480; expelled the Jews, forced the final surrender of the Moors at Granada, and financed Columbus' expedition to the Americas, 1492.

Ferdinand II 1578–1637. Holy Roman emperor from 1619, when he succeeded his uncle Matthias; king of Bohemia from 1617 and of Hungary from 1618. A zealous Catholic, he provoked the Bohemian revolt that led to the Thirty Years' War. He was a grandson of Ferdinand I.

Fermanagh county of Northern Ireland *area* 648 sq mi/1,680 sq km *towns and cities* Enniskillen (county town), Lisnaskea, Irvinestown *features* in the center is a broad trough of low-lying land, in which lie Upper and Lower Lough Erne *industries* mainly agricultural; livestock, potatoes, tweeds, clothing, cotton thread *population* (1991) 50,000.

Fermat Pierre de 1601–1665. French mathematician, who with Blaise Pascal founded the theory of ◊probability and the modern theory of numbers and who made contributions to analytical geometry.

fermentation the breakdown of sugars by bacteria and yeasts using a method of respiration without oxygen (◊anaerobic). Fermentation processes have long been utilized in baking bread, making beer and wine, and producing cheese, yogurt, soy sauce, and many other foodstuffs.

Fermi Enrico 1901–1954. Italian-born US physicist who proved the existence of new radioactive elements produced by bombardment with neutrons, and discovered nuclear reactions produced by low-energy neutrons. His theoretical work included study of the weak nuclear force, one of the fundamental forces of nature, and (with Paul Dirac) of the quantum statistics of fermion particles. He was awarded a Nobel Prize 1938.

fermion in physics, a subatomic particle whose spin can only take values that are half-integers, such as $1/2$ or $3/2$. Fermions may be classified as leptons, such as the electron, and baryons, such as the proton and neutron. All elementary particles are either fermions or ◊bosons.

fermium synthesized, radioactive, metallic element of the ◊actinide series, symbol Fm, atomic number 100, relative atomic mass 257. Ten isotopes are known, the longest-lived of which, Fm-257, has a half-life of 80 days. Fermium has been produced only in minute quantities in particle accelerators.

fern plant of the class Filicineae, related to ◊gymnosperms and ◊angiosperms; however, ferns reproduce by spores and not seed. Most are perennial, spreading by low-growing roots. The leaves, known as fronds, vary widely in size and shape. Some taller types, such as tree-ferns, grow in the tropics. There are over 7,000 species.

Ferrari Enzo 1898–1988. Italian founder of the Ferrari automobile manufacturing company, which specializes in Grand Prix race cars and high-quality sports automobiles. He was a racing driver for Alfa Romeo in the 1920s, went on to become one of their designers, and in 1929 took over their racing division. In 1947 the first "true" Ferrari was seen. The Ferrari automobile has won more world championship Grands Prix than any other automobile.

ferret domesticated variety of the Old World ◊polecat. About 1.2 ft/35 cm long, it usually has yellowish-white fur and pink eyes, but may be the dark brown color of a wild polecat.

Ferrets may breed with wild polecats. They have been used since ancient times to hunt rabbits and rats.

fertilization in ◊sexual reproduction, the union of two ◊gametes (sex cells, often called egg and sperm) to produce a ◊zygote, which combines the genetic material contributed by each parent. In self-fertilization the male and female gametes come from the same plant; in cross-fertilization they come from different plants. Self-fertilization rarely occurs in animals; usually even ◊hermaphrodite animals cross-fertilize each other.

fertilizer substance containing some or all of a range of about 20 chemical elements necessary for healthy plant growth, used to compensate for the deficiencies of poor or depleted soil. Fertilizers may be *organic*, for example farmyard manure, composts, bonemeal, blood, and fishmeal; or *inorganic*, in the form of compounds, mainly of nitrogen, phosphate, and potash, which have been used on a very much increased scale since 1945.

Fès or *Fez* former capital of Morocco 808–1062, 1296–1548, and 1662–1912, in a valley N of the Great Atlas Mountains, 100 mi/160 km E of Rabat; population (1982) 563,000. Textiles, carpets, and leather are manufactured, and the *fez*, a brimless hat worn in S and E Mediterranean countries, is traditionally said to have originated here. Kairwan Islamic University dates from 859; a second university was founded 1961.

fetishism in anthropology, belief in the supernormal power of some inanimate object that is known as a fetish. Fetishism in some form is common to most cultures, and often has religio-magical significance.

fetishism in psychology, the transfer of erotic interest to an object, such as an item of clothing, whose real or fantasized presence is necessary for sexual gratification.

fetus stage in mammalian ◊embryo development. The human embryo is usually termed a fetus after the eighth week of development, when the limbs and external features of the head are recognizable.

feudalism main form of social organization in medieval Europe. A system based primarily on land, it involved a hierarchy of authority, rights, and power that extended from the monarch downward. An intricate network of duties and obligations linked royalty, nobility, lesser gentry, free tenants, villeins, and serfs. Feudalism was reinforced by a complex legal system and supported by the Christian church. With the growth of commerce and industry from the 13th century, feudalism gradually gave way to the class system as the dominant form of social ranking.

Fez alternative spelling of ◊Fès, a city in Morocco.

Fianna Fáil Republic of Ireland political party, founded by the Irish nationalist de Valera 1926. It has been the governing party in the Republic of Ireland 1932–48, 1951–54, 1957–73, 1977–81, 1982, and 1987– (from 1993 in coalition with Labour). It aims at the establishment of a united and completely independent all-Ireland republic.

fiber, dietary or *roughage* plant material that cannot be digested by human digestive enzymes; it consists largely of cellulose, a carbohydrate found in plant cell walls. Fiber adds bulk to the gut contents, assisting the muscular contractions that force food along the intestine. A diet low in fiber causes constipation and is believed to increase the risk of developing diverticulitis, diabetes, gall-bladder disease, and cancer of the large bowel—conditions that are rare in nonindustrialized countries, where the diet contains a high proportion of unrefined cereals.

fiberglass glass that has been formed into fine fibers, either as long continuous filaments or as a fluffy, short-fibered glass wool.

Fiberglass is heat-and fire-resistant and a good electrical insulator. It has applications in the field of fiber optics and as a strengthener for plastics in ◊GRP (glass-reinforced plastics).

fiber optics branch of physics dealing with the transmission of light and images through glass or plastic fibers known as ◊optical fibers.

Fibonacci Leonardo, also known as *Leonardo of Pisa* c.1175–c.1250. Italian mathematician. He published *Liber abaci* in Pisa 1202, which was instrumental in the introduction of Arabic notation into Europe. From 1960, interest increased in *Fibonacci numbers*, in their simplest form a sequence in which each number is the sum of its two predecessors (1, 1, 2, 3, 5, 8, 13, ...). They have unusual characteristics with possible applications in botany, psychology, and astronomy (for example, a more exact correspondence than is given by Bode's law to the distances between the planets and the Sun).

fiction in literature, any work in which the content is completely or largely invented. The term describes imaginative works of narrative prose (such as the novel or the short story), and is distinguished from *nonfiction* (such as history, biography, or works on practical subjects) and *poetry*.

field in physics, a region of space in which an object exerts a force on another separate object because of certain properties they both possess. For example, there is a force of attraction between any two objects that have mass when one is in the gravitational field of the other.

Field Sally 1946– . US film and television actress. She won an Academy Award for *Norma Rae* 1979 and again for *Places in the Heart* 1984. Her other films include *Hooper* 1978, *Absence of Malice* 1981, and *Murphy's Romance* 1985.

Prior to her movie career, she first became known as TV's *Flying Nun*, a role she played for several years.

fieldfare thrush *Turdus pilaris* of the family Muscicapidae; it has a pale-gray lower back and neck and a dark tail.

It breeds in Scandinavia and N Russia, and is a casual visitor to N North America.

Fielding Henry 1707–1754. English novelist. His greatest work, *The History of Tom Jones, a Foundling* 1749 (which he described as "a comic epic in prose"), realized for the first time in English the novel's potential for memorable characterization, coherent plotting, and perceptive analysis. In youth a prolific dramatist, he began writing novels with *An Apology for the Life of Mrs. Shamela Andrews* 1741, a merciless parody of Samuel ◊Richardson's *Pamela*.

Fields W C Adopted name of William Claude Dukenfield 1879–1946. US actor and screenwriter. His distinctive speech and professed attitudes such as hatred of children and dogs gained him enormous popularity in such films as *David Copperfield* 1935, *My Little Chickadee* (co-written with Mae West) and *The Bank Dick* both 1940, and *Never Give a Sucker an Even Break* 1941.

Fife region of E Scotland *area* 502 sq mi/1,300 sq km *towns and cities* administrative headquarters Glenrothes; Dunfermline, St Andrews, Kirkcaldy, Cupar *features* faces the North Sea and Firth of Forth; Lomond Hills in the NW (the only high land); rivers Eden and Leven; Rosyth naval base and dockyard (used for nuclear submarine refits) on northern shore of the Firth of Forth; Tentsmuir, possibly the earliest settled site in Scotland. The ancient palace of the Stuarts was at Falkland, and eight Scottish kings are buried at Dunfermline *industries* potatoes, cereals, sugar beet; electronics, petrochemicals (Mossmorran), light engineering, aluminum refining; coal mining has declined *population* (1991) 341,200.

fifth-generation computer anticipated new type of computer based on emerging microelectronic technologies with high computing speeds and ◊parallel processing. The development of very large-scale integration (◊VLSI) technology, which can put many more circuits on to an integrated circuit (chip) than is currently possible, and developments in computer hardware and software design may produce computers far more powerful than those in current use.

fig any tree of the genus *Ficus* of the mulberry family Moraceae, including the many cultivated varieties of *F. carica*, originally from W Asia. They produce two or three crops of fruit a year. Eaten fresh or dried, figs have a high sugar content and laxative properties.

fighting fish any of a SE Asian genus *Betta* of fishes of the gourami family, especially *B. splendens*, about 2 in/6 cm long and a popular aquarium fish. It can breathe air, using an accessory breathing organ above the gill, and can live in poorly oxygenated water. The male has large fins and various colors, including shining greens, reds, and blues. The female is yellowish brown with short fins.

figwort any Old World plant of the genus *Scrophularia* of the figwort family, which also includes foxgloves and snapdragons.

Members of the genus have square stems, opposite leaves, and open two-lipped flowers in a cluster at the top of the stem.

Fiji Republic of *area* 7,078 sq mi/18,333 sq km *capital* Suva *towns and cities* ports Lautoka and Levuka *physical* comprises 844 Melanesian and Polynesian islands and islets (about 110 inhabited), the largest being Viti Levu (4,028 sq mi/10,429 sq km) and Vanua Levu (2,146 sq mi/5,550 sq km); mountainous, volcanic, with tropical rainforest and grasslands *features* almost all islands surrounded by coral reefs; high volcanic peaks; crossroads of air and sea services between N America and Australia *head of state* Kamisese Mara from 1994 *head of government* Col Sitiveni Rabuka from 1992 *political system* democratic republic *political parties* National Federation Party (NFP), moderate left-of-center, Indian; Fijian Labour Party (FLP), left-of-center, Indian; United Front, Fijian; Fijian Political Party (FPP), Fijian centrist *exports* sugar, coconut oil, ginger, timber, canned fish, gold; tourism is important *currency* Fiji dollar *population* (1993) 758,300 (46% Fijian, holding 80% of the land communally, and 49% Indian, introduced in the 19th century to work the sugar crop); growth rate 2.1% p.a. *life expectancy* men 64, women 68 *languages* English (official), Fijian, Hindi *religions* Hindu 50%, Methodist 44% *literacy* 87% *GNP* $1,830 per head (1991) *chronology 1874* Fiji became a British crown colony. *1970* Independence achieved from Britain; Ratu Sir Kamisese Mara elected as first prime minister. *1987* April: general election brought to power an Indian-dominated coalition led by Dr Timoci Bavadra. May: military coup by Col Sitiveni Rabuka removed new government, who regained control within weeks. Sept: second military coup by Rabuka proclaimed Fiji a republic. Oct: Fiji ceased to be a member of the Commonwealth. Dec: civilian government restored with Rabuka retaining control of security as minister for home affairs. *1990* New constitution, favoring indigenous Fijians, introduced. *1992* General election produced coalition government; Col Rabuka (FPP) named as prime minister. *1993* President Ganilau died; Kamisese Mara became acting head of state. *1994* Mara sworn in as president. Rabuka and FPP reelected.

file in computing, a collection of data or a program stored in a computer's external memory (for example, on ◊disk). It might include anything from information on a company's employees to a program for an adventure game. *Serial files* hold information as a sequence of characters, so that, to read any particular item of data, the program must read all those that precede it. *Random-access files* allow the required data to be reached directly.

film, photographic strip of transparent material (usually cellulose acetate) coated with a light-sensitive emulsion, used in cameras to take pictures. The emulsion contains a mixture of light-sensitive silver halide salts (for example, bromide or iodide) in gelatin. When the emulsion is exposed to light, the silver salts are invisibly altered, giving a latent image, which is then made visible by the process of developing. Films differ in their sensitivities to light, this being indicated by their speeds. Color film consists of several layers of emulsion, each of which records a different color in the light falling on it.

filter in electronics, a circuit that transmits a signal of some frequencies better than others. A low-pass filter transmits signals of low frequency and direct current; a high-pass filter transmits high-frequency signals; a band-pass filter transmits signals in a band of frequencies.

filtration technique by which suspended solid particles in a fluid are removed by passing the mixture through a filter, usually porous paper, plastic, or cloth. The particles are retained by the filter to form a residue and the fluid passes through to make up the filtrate. For example, soot may be filtered from air, and suspended solids from water.

finch any of various songbirds of the family Fringillidae, in the order Passeriformes (perching birds).

They are seed-eaters with stout conical beaks and include goldfinches, crossbills, redpolls, and canaries.

fin de siècle (French "end of century") the art and literature of the 1890s; decadent.

fingerprint ridge pattern of the skin on a person's fingertips; this is constant through life and no two are exactly alike. Fingerprinting was first used as a means of identifying crime suspects in India, and was adopted by the English police 1901; it is now widely employed in police and security work.

Finland Republic of (*Suomen Tasavalta*) **area** 130,608 sq mi/338,145 sq km **capital** Helsinki **towns and cities** Tampere, Rovaniemi, Lahti; ports Turku, Oulu **physical** most of the country is forest, with low hills and about 60,000 lakes; one-third is within the Arctic Circle; archipelago in S; includes Åland Islands **features** Helsinki is the most northerly national capital on the European continent; at the 70th parallel there is constant daylight for 73 days in summer and 51 days of uninterrupted night in winter **head of state** Martti Ahtisaari from 1994 **head of government** Esko Aho from 1991 **political system** democratic republic **political parties** Social Democratic Party (SDP), moderate left of center; National Coalition Party (KOK), moderate right of center; Center Party (KP), centrist, rural-oriented; Finnish People's Democratic League (SKDL), left-wing; Swedish People's Party (SFP), independent Swedish-oriented; Finnish Rural Party (SMP), farmers and small businesses; Democratic Alternative, left-wing; Green Party **exports** metal, chemical, and engineering products (icebreakers and oil rigs), paper, sawn wood, clothing, fine ceramics, glass, furniture **currency** markka **population** (1993 est) 5,020,000; growth rate 0.5% p.a. **life expectancy** men 72, women 80 **languages** Finnish 93%, Swedish 6% (both official), small Saami-and Russian-speaking minorities **religions** Lutheran 97%, Eastern Orthodox 1.2% **literacy** 99% **GNP** $21,009 per head (1992) **chronology 1809** Finland annexed by Russia. **1917** Independence declared from Russia. **1920** Soviet regime acknowledged independence. **1939** Defeated by USSR in Winter War. **1941** Allowed Germany to station troops in Finland to attack USSR; USSR bombed Finland. **1944** Concluded separate armistice with USSR. **1948**

Finno-Soviet Pact of Friendship, Cooperation, and Mutual Assistance signed. **1955** Finland joined the United Nations and the Nordic Council. **1956** Urho Kekkonen elected president; reelected 1962, 1968, 1978. **1973** Trade treaty with European Economic Community signed. **1977** Trade agreement with USSR signed. **1982** Mauno Koivisto elected president. **1988** Koivisto reelected. **1991** Big swing to the center in general election. New coalition government formed. **1994** Martti Ahtisaari (SDP) elected president. National referendum gave positive support to European Union (formerly European Community) membership. **1995** Social Democrat Party defeated the Center Party.

Finland, Gulf of eastern arm of the ◊Baltic Sea, separating Finland from Estonia.

Finn Mac Cumhaill legendary Irish hero, identified with a general who organized an Irish regular army in the 3rd century. James Macpherson (1736–96) featured him (as Fingal) and his followers in the verse of his popular epics 1762–63, which were supposedly written by a 3rd-century bard, Ossian. Although challenged by the critic Dr Johnson, the poems were influential in the Romantic movement.

Finno-Ugric group or family of more than 20 languages spoken by some 22 million people in scattered communities from Norway in the west to Siberia in the east and to the Carpathian mountains in the south. The family includes Finnish, Lapp, and Hungarian.

fir any ◊conifer of the genus *Abies* in the pine family Pinaceae. The true firs include the balsam fir of N North America and the Eurasian silver fir *A. alba*. Douglas firs of the genus *Pseudotsuga* are native to W North America and the Far East.

firearm weapon from which projectiles are discharged by the combustion of an explosive. Firearms are generally divided into two main sections: ◊artillery (ordnance or cannon), with a bore greater than 1 in/2.54 cm, and ◊small arms, with a bore of less than 1 in/2.54 cm.

Although gunpowder was known in Europe 60 years previously, the invention of guns dates from 1300 to 1325, and is attributed to Berthold Schwartz, a German monk.

First World War another name for ◊World War I, 1914–18.

fiscal year a year as defined by a company or government for financial accounting purposes. A company can choose any 12-month period for its accounting year and in exceptional circumstances may determine a longer or shorter period as its fiscal year. It does not necessarily coincide with the calendar year.

For the US government, the budget year runs from Oct 1 to Sept 30. For businesses and financial institutions, it generally runs July 1 to June 30.

Fischer Bobby (Robert James) 1943– . US chess champion. In 1958, after proving himself in international competition, he became the youngest grand master in history. He was the author of *Games of Chess* 1959, and was also celebrated for his unorthodox psychological tactics. He won the world title from Boris Spassky in Reykjavik, Iceland, 1972 but retired the same year without defending his title. He returned to competitive chess 1992.

fish aquatic vertebrate that uses gills for obtaining oxygen from fresh or sea water. There are three main groups, not closely related: the bony fishes or Osteichthyes (goldfish, cod, tuna); the cartilaginous

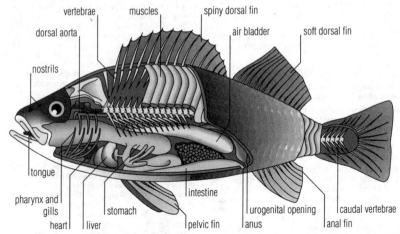

fish The anatomy of a fish. All fishes move through water using their fins for propulsion. The bony fishes, like the specimen shown here, constitute the largest group of fishes with about 20,000 species.

fishes or Chondrichthyes (sharks, rays); and the jawless fishes or Agnatha (hagfishes, lampreys).

fish farming or *aquaculture* raising fish (including mollusks and crustaceans) under controlled conditions in tanks and ponds, sometimes in offshore pens. It has been practiced for centuries in the Far East, where Japan today produces some 100,000 metric tons of fish a year; the US, Norway, and Canada are also big producers. In the 1980s 10% of the world's consumption of fish was farmed, notably carp, catfish, trout, Atlantic salmon, turbot, eel, mussels, clams, oysters, and shrimp.

fission in physics, the splitting of a heavy atomic nucleus into two or more major fragments. It is accompanied by the emission of two or three neutrons and the release of large amounts of ◊nuclear energy.

Fitzgerald Ella 1918– . US jazz singer. She is recognized as one of the finest, most lyrical voices in jazz, both in solo work and with big bands. She is celebrated for her smooth interpretations of George and Ira Gershwin and Cole Porter songs.

Fitzgerald F(rancis) Scott (Key) 1896–1940. US novelist and short-story writer. His early autobiographical novel *This Side of Paradise* 1920 made him known in the postwar society of the East Coast, and *The Great Gatsby* 1925 epitomizes the Jazz Age.

Fitzgerald was born in Minnesota. In 1920 he married Zelda Sayre (1900–1948). In 1924 the Fitzgeralds moved to the French Riviera, where they became members of a fashionable group of expatriates. Zelda, a schizophrenic, entered an asylum 1930. Her descent into mental illness forms the subject of *Tender is the Night* 1934. After her confinement Fitzgerald went to Hollywood to write screenplays and earn enough to pay Zelda's medical bills. He fell in love with Sheilah Graham but declined into alcoholism. His other works include numerous short stories and his novel *The Last Tycoon*, about the film business, which was unfinished at his death but was made into a major motion picture 1976.

fixed-point notation system in which numbers are represented using a set of digits with the decimal point always in its correct position. For very large and very small numbers this requires a lot of digits. In computing, the size of the numbers that can be handled in this way is limited by the capacity of the computer, and so the slower ◊floating-point notation is often preferred.

fjord or *fiord* narrow sea inlet enclosed by high cliffs. Fjords are found in Norway, New Zealand, and western parts of Scotland. They are formed when an overdeepened U-shaped glacial valley is drowned by a rise in sea-level. At the mouth of the fjord there is a characteristic lip causing a shallowing of the water. This is due to reduced glacial erosion and the deposition of moraine at this point.

flamenco music and dance of the Andalusian gypsies of S Spain, evolved from Andalusian and Arabic folk music. The *cante* (song) is sometimes performed as a solo but more often accompanied by guitar music and passionate improvised dance. Hand clapping, finger clicking (castanets are a more recent addition), and enthusiastic shouts are all features. Male flamenco dancers excel in powerful, rhythmic footwork while the female dancers place emphasis on the graceful and erotic movements of their hands and bodies.

flamethrower weapon emitting a stream of burning liquid which can be directed against troops or strongpoints.

flamingo long-legged and long-necked wading bird, family Phoenicopteridae, of the stork order Ciconiiformes. Largest of the family is the greater or roseate flamingo *Phoenicopterus ruber*, found in Africa, the Caribbean, and South America, with delicate pink plumage and 4 ft/1.25 m tall. They sift the mud for food with their downbent bills, and build colonies of high, conelike mud nests, with a little hollow for the eggs at the top.

Flanders region of the Low Countries that in the 8th and 9th centuries extended from Calais to the Scheldt and is now covered by the Belgian provinces of Oost

Vlaanderen and West Vlaanderen (East and West Flanders), the French *département* of Nord, and part of the Dutch province of Zeeland. The language is Flemish. East Flanders, capital Ghent, has an area of 1,158 sq mi/3,000 sq km and a population (1991) of 1,335,700. West Flanders, capital Bruges, has an area of 1,197 sq mi/3,100 sq km and a population (1991) of 1,106,800.

flatfish bony fishes of the order Pleuronectiformes, having a characteristically flat, asymmetrical body with both eyes (in adults) on the upper side. Species include flounders, turbots, halibuts, plaice, and the European soles.

flatworm invertebrate of the phylum Platyhelminthes. Some are free-living, but many are parasitic (for example, tapeworms and flukes). The body is simple and bilaterally symmetrical, with one opening to the intestine. Many are hermaphroditic (with both male and female sex organs) and practice self-fertilization.

Flaubert Gustave 1821–1880. French writer. One of the major novelists of the 19th century, he was the author of *Madame Bovary* 1857, *Salammbô* 1862, *L'Education sentimentale/Sentimental Education* 1869, and *La Tentation de Saint Antoine/The Temptation of St Anthony* 1874. Flaubert also wrote the short stories *Trois Contes/Three Tales* 1877. His dedication to art resulted in a meticulous prose style, realistic detail, and psychological depth, which is often revealed through interior monologue.

flax any plant of the genus *Linum*, family Linaceae. The species *L. usitatissimum* is the cultivated strain; **linen** is produced from the fiber in its stems. The seeds yield **linseed oil**, used in paints and varnishes. The plant, of almost worldwide distribution, has a stem up to 24 in/60 cm high, small leaves, and bright blue flowers.

flea wingless insect of the order Siphonaptera, with blood-sucking mouthparts. Fleas are parasitic on warm-blooded animals. Some fleas can jump 130 times their own height.

flamingo *The greater, or roseate, flamingo may seem strangely built but it is, in fact, perfectly adapted to its environment. Its long legs enable it to feed while standing in water; its beak is held horizontally beneath the water. Water flows into the beak and is expelled through a mesh of fine hairs which sieves out food particles.*

fleabane any of several plants of the genera *Erigeron* and *Pulicaria*, of the daisy or composite family. Poor Robin's plantain *E. pulchellus* has lavender-rayed flowers on tall, slender stalks and is native to E North America.

Fleming Alexander 1881–1955. Scottish bacteriologist who discovered the first antibiotic drug, ◊penicillin, in 1928. In 1922 he had discovered lysozyme, an antibacterial enzyme present in saliva, nasal secretions, and tears. While studying this, he found an unusual mold growing on a neglected culture dish, which he isolated and grew into a pure culture; this led to his discovery of penicillin. It came into use in 1941. In 1945 he won the Nobel Prize for Physiology and Medicine with Howard W. Florey and Ernst B. Chain, whose research had brought widespread realization of the value of penicillin.

Flevoland (formerly *IJsselmeerpolders*) low-lying province of the Netherlands, created 1986 **area** 544 sq mi/1,410 sq km **capital** Lelystad **towns and cities** Dronten, Almere **population** (1988) 194,000 **history** established 1986 out of land reclaimed from the IJsselmeer 1950–68.

flight or **aviation** people first took to the air in lighter-than-air craft such as balloons 1783 and began powered flight in 1852 in airships, but the history of aviation focuses on heavier-than-air craft called ◊airplanes. Developed from glider design, with wings, a tail, and a fuselage, the first successful flight of a powered, heavier-than-air craft was in 1896 by S P Langley's unmanned plane (*Model No 5*), for $3/4$ of a mile near the Potomac River; then, in 1903, the ◊Wright brothers flew the first piloted plane at Kitty Hawk. In 1903, Glenn Curtiss publicized flight in the US and began the first flying school in 1909. A competition for the development of airplanes was inspired by a series of flights and air races in the US and Europe, and planes came into their own during World War I, being used by both sides. Biplanes were generally succeeded by monoplanes in the 1920s and 1930s, and they used runways or water (seaplanes and flying boats) for takeoffs and landings at airfields that soon became airports. In these decades airlines were formed for international travel, airmail, and cargo. The first jet plane was produced in Germany in 1939, the Heinkel He-178, but conventional prop planes were used for most of the destruction and transport of World War II. The 1950s brought economical passenger air travel on turboprops and jet airliners, which by the 1970s flew transatlantic in about 6 hours. The Concorde, a supersonic jetliner, flies passengers over that route in about 3 hours.

flight simulator computer-controlled pilot-training device, consisting of an artificial cockpit mounted on hydraulic legs, that simulates the experience of flying a real aircraft. Inside the cockpit, the trainee pilot views a screen showing a computer-controlled projection of the view from a real aircraft, and makes appropriate adjustments to the controls. The computer monitors these adjustments, changes both the alignment of the cockpit on its hydraulic legs, and the projected view seen by the pilot. In this way a trainee pilot can progress to quite an advanced stage of training without leaving the ground.

flint compact, hard, brittle mineral (a variety of chert), brown, black, or gray in color, found in nodules in limestone or shale deposits. It consists of fine-grained silica, SiO_2 (usually ◊quartz), in cryptocrystalline form. Flint implements were widely used in prehistory.

floating-point notation system in which numbers are represented by means of a decimal fraction and an exponent. For example, in floating-point notation, 123,000,000,000 would be represented as 0.123 x 10^{12}, where 0.123 is the fraction, or mantissa, and 12 the exponent. The exponent is the power of 10 by which the fraction must be multiplied in order to obtain the true value of the number. In computing, floating-point notation enables programs to work with very large and very small numbers using only a few digits; however, it is slower than ◊fixed-point notation and suffers from small rounding errors.

floating point unit (FPU) in computing, a specially designed chip that performs floating-point calculations. Computers equipped with an FPU perform certain types of applications much faster than computers that lack one. In particular, graphics applications are faster with an FPU.

Flodden, Battle of the defeat of the Scots by the English under the Earl of Surrey Sept 9, 1513, on a site, 3 mi/5 km SE of Coldstream, in Northumberland, England; many Scots, including King James IV, were killed.

floppy disk in computing, a storage device consisting of a light, flexible disk enclosed in a cardboard or plastic jacket. The disk is placed in a disk drive, where it rotates at high speed. Data are recorded magnetically on one or both surfaces.

floptical disk or **erasable optical disk** in computing, a type of optical disk that can be erased and loaded with new data, just like a magnetic disk. By contrast, most optical disks are read-only. A single optical disk can hold as much as 1,000 megabytes of data, about 800 times more than a typical floppy disk. Floptical disks need a special disk drive, but some such drives are also capable of accepting standard 3.5 inch floppy disks.

Florence (Italian **Firenze**) capital of ◊Tuscany, N Italy, 55 mi/88 km from the mouth of the river Arno; population (1988) 421,000. It has printing, engineering, and optical industries; many crafts, including leather, gold and silver work, and embroidery; and its art and architecture attract large numbers of tourists. Notable medieval and Renaissance citizens included the writers Dante and Boccaccio, and the artists Giotto, Leonardo da Vinci, and Michelangelo.

Florida southeasternmost state of the US; mainly a peninsula jutting into the Atlantic, which it separates from the Gulf of Mexico; nickname Sunshine State **area** 58,672 sq mi/152,000 sq km **capital** Tallahassee **towns and cities** Miami, Tampa, Jacksonville **population** (1990) 12,937,900, one of the fastest-growing of the states; including 15% nonwhite; 10% Hispanic, (especially Cuban) **physical** 50% forested; lakes (including Okeechobee 695 sq mi/1,800 sq km); Everglades National Park (1,930 sq mi/5,000 sq km), with birdlife, cypresses, alligators **features** Palm Beach island resort, between the lagoon of Lake Worth and the Atlantic; Florida Keys; John F Kennedy Space Center at Cape Canaveral; Disney World theme park; beach resorts on Gulf and on Atlantic; Daytona International Speedway; barrier reef 200 mi/320km long is a national marine sanctuary, but the coral is dying at an increasing rate **industries** citrus fruits, melons, vegetables, fish, shellfish, phosphates, chemicals, electrical and electronic equipment, aircraft, fabricated metals **famous people** Chris Evert, Henry Flagler, James Weldon Johnson, Sidney Poitier, Philip Randolph, Joseph Stilwell **history** discovered by Ponce

de Leon and under Spanish rule from 1513 until its cession to England 1763; returned to Spain 1783 and purchased by the US 1819, becoming a state 1845.

It grew rapidly in the early 1920s, stimulated by feverish land speculation. Despite the 1926 collapse of the boom, migration continued, especially of retirees from the North. After World War II, resorts, agriculture, and industry grew in importance. The space center at Cape Canaveral also contributed to the state economy. More recently, Florida has become a banking center, a development often partially attributed to the sizable inflow of cash derived from the traffic in illegal drugs from Latin America. Because of its proximity to Caribbean nations, the state became a haven for refugees from such countries as Cuba and Haiti.

Hurricane Andrew ravaged South Florida and Louisiana August 1993, killing 13 and making 250,000 people homeless. It was the world's costliest insured loss as a result of a natural disaster.

flounder any of a number of ◊flatfishes of several genera. A common North American species is the southern flounder *Paralichthys lethostigma*, a valuable food fish about 20 in/50 cm long.

flow chart diagram, often used in computing, to show the possible paths that data can take through a system or program.

flower the reproductive unit of an ◊angiosperm or flowering ◊plant, typically consisting of four whorls of modified leaves: ◊sepals, ◊petals, ◊stamens, and ◊carpels. These are borne on a central axis or receptacle. The many variations in size, color, number, and arrangement of parts are closely related to the method of ◊pollination. Flowers adapted for wind pollination typically have reduced or absent petals and sepals and long, feathery ◊stigmas that hang outside the flower to trap airborne pollen. In contrast, the petals of insect-pollinated flowers are usually conspicuous and brightly colored.

flowering plant term generally used for ◊angiosperms, which bear flowers with various parts, including sepals, petals, stamens, and carpels.

Sometimes the term is used more broadly, to include both angiosperms and ◊gymnosperms, in which case the ◊cones of conifers and cycads are referred to as "flowers." Usually, however, the angiosperms and gymnosperms are referred to collectively as ◊seed plants, or spermatophytes.

flugelhorn alto valved brass band instrument of the bugle type. In B flat, it has a similar range to the cornet but is of mellower tone.

fluke any of various parasitic flatworms of the classes Monogenea and Digenea, that as adults live in and destroy the livers of sheep, cattle, horses, dogs, and humans. Monogenetic flukes can complete their life cycle in one host; digenetic flukes require two or more hosts, for example a snail and a human being, to complete their life cycle.

fluorescence in scientific usage, very short-lived ◊luminescence (a glow not caused by high temperature). Generally, the term is used for any luminescence regardless of the persistence. ◊Phosphorescence lasts a little longer.

fluoridation addition of small amounts of fluoride salts to drinking water by certain water authorities to help prevent tooth decay. Experiments in the US, Britain, and elsewhere have indicated that a concentration of fluoride of 1 part per million in tap water retards the decay of children's teeth by more than 50%.

fluoride negative ion (Fl⁻) formed when hydrogen fluoride dissolves in water; compound formed between fluorine and another element in which the fluorine is the more electronegative element (see ◊electronegativity, ◊halide).

fluorine pale yellow, gaseous, nonmetallic element, symbol F, atomic number 9, atomic weight 19. It is the first member of the halogen group of elements, and is pungent, poisonous, and highly reactive, uniting directly with nearly all the elements. It occurs naturally as the minerals fluorite (CaF_2) and cryolite (Na_3AlF_6). Hydrogen fluoride is used in etching glass, and the freons, which all contain fluorine, are widely used as refrigerants.

flute or *transverse flute* side-blown soprano woodwind instrument of considerable antiquity. The flute is difficult to master but capable of intricate melodies and expressive tonal shading. The player blows across an end hole, the air current being split by the opposite edge which causes pressure waves to form within the tube. The fingers are placed over holes in the tube to create different notes.

fly any insect of the order Diptera. A fly has a single pair of wings, antennae, and compound eyes; the hind wings have become modified into knoblike projections (halteres) used to maintain equilibrium in flight. There are over 90,000 species.

flying fish any of a family Exocoetidae of marine bony fishes of the order Beloniformes, best represented in tropical waters. They have winglike pectoral fins that can be spread to glide over the water.

flying fox fruit-eating ◊bat of the suborder Megachiroptera.

flying squirrel any of numerous species of squirrel, not closely related to the true squirrels. They are characterized by a membrane along the side of the body from forelimb to hindlimb (in some species running to neck and tail) which allows them to glide through the air. Several genera of flying squirrel are found in the Old World; the New World has the genus *Glaucomys*. Most species are E Asian.

Flynn Errol. Adopted name of Leslie Thompson 1909–1959. Australian-born US film actor. He is renowned for his portrayal of swashbuckling heroes in such films as *Captain Blood* 1935, *Robin Hood* 1938, *The Charge of the Light Brigade* 1938, *The Private Lives of Elizabeth and Essex* 1939, *The Sea Hawk* 1940, and *The Master of Ballantrae* 1953.

FM in physics, symbol for frequency ◊modulation, or the variation of the frequency of a carrier wave in accordance with the signal to be transmitted. Used in radio, FM is constant in amplitude and has much better signal-to-noise ratio than AM (amplitude modulation). It was invented by US electronic engineer Edwin Armstrong.

fog cloud that collects at the surface of the Earth, composed of water vapor that has condensed on particles of dust in the atmosphere. Cloud and fog are both caused by the air temperature falling below ◊dew point. The thickness of fog depends on the number of water particles it contains.

Fokker German military aircraft, extensively deployed in both world wars. The Fokker DR 1 triplane was famously used by Baron von Richthofen's Flying Circus during World War I; it was a highly maneuverable machine which caused great damage among Allied aircraft. The D VII, a powerful biplane which appeared early 1918, is generally considered to be one of the great combat aircraft of all time.

folic acid a ◊vitamin of the B complex. It is found in legumes, green leafy vegetables, and whole grains, and is also synthesized by intestinal bacteria. It is essential for growth, and plays many other roles in the body. Lack of folic acid causes anemia, diarrhea, and a red tongue.

folklore the oral traditions and culture of a people, expressed in legends, riddles, songs, tales, and proverbs. The term was coined 1846 by W J Thoms (1803–85), but the founder of the systematic study of the subject was Jakob ◊Grimm; see also ◊oral literature.

folk music body of traditional music, originally transmitted orally. Many folk songs originated as a rhythmic accompaniment to manual work or to mark a specific ritual. Folk song is usually melodic, not harmonic, and the modes used are distinctive of the country of origin; see ◊world music.

flying squirrel *Giant flying squirrels can glide over 440 yd/400 m between trees by stretching the broad, fur-covered membranes that extend from the sides of the body to the toes. They live in forested regions of Asia and are active at night.*

Fonda Henry 1905–1982. US actor. His engaging style made him ideal in the role of the American pioneer and honorable man. His many films include *The Grapes of Wrath* 1940, *My Darling Clementine* 1946, *12 Angry Men* 1957, and *On Golden Pond* 1981, for which he won the Academy Award for best actor. He was the father of actress Jane Fonda and actor and director Peter Fonda (1939–).

Fonda Jane 1937– . US actress. Her varied films roles include *Cat Ballou* 1965, *Barefoot in the Park* 1967, *Barbarella* 1968, *They Shoot Horses, Don't They?* 1969, *Julia*, 1977, *The China Syndrome* 1979, *On Golden Pond* 1981 (in which she appeared with her father, Henry Fonda). She won Academy Awards for *Klute* 1971 and *Coming Home* 1978.

She is active in promoting physical fitness and is married to businessman Ted Turner.

font or *fount* complete set of printed or display characters of the same typeface, size, and style (bold, italic, underlined, and so on).

Fonteyn Margot. Adopted name of Peggy (Margaret) Hookham 1919–1991. English ballet dancer. She made her debut with the Vic-Wells Ballet in *Nutcracker* 1934 and first appeared as Giselle 1937, eventually becoming prima ballerina of the Royal Ballet, London. Renowned for her perfect physique, clear line, musicality, and interpretive powers, she created many roles in Frederick ◊Ashton's ballets and formed a legendary partnership with Rudolf ◊Nureyev. She did not retire from dancing until 1979.

food anything eaten by human beings and other animals to sustain life and health. The building blocks of food are nutrients, and humans can utilize the following nutrients: *carbohydrates*, as starches found in bread, potatoes, and pasta; as simple sugars in sucrose and honey; as fibers in cereals, fruit, and vegetables; *proteins* as from nuts, fish, meat, eggs, milk, and some vegetables; *fats* as found in most animal products (meat, lard, dairy products, fish), also in margarine, nuts and seeds, olives, and edible oils; vitamins are found in a wide variety of foods, except for vitamin B_{12}, which is mainly found in animal foods; minerals are found in a wide variety of foods; good sources of calcium are milk and broccoli, for example; iodine from seafood; iron from liver and green vegetables; water is ubiquitous in nature; alcohol is found in fermented distilled beverages, from more than 40% in liquor to 0.01% in low-alcohol beers.

food chain in ecology, a sequence showing the feeding relationships between organisms in a particular ecosystem. Each organism depends on the next lowest member of the chain for its food.

food poisoning any acute illness characterized by vomiting and diarrhea and caused by eating food contaminated with harmful bacteria (for example, listeriosis), poisonous food (for example, certain mushrooms, puffer fish), or poisoned food (such as lead or arsenic introduced accidentally during processing). A frequent cause of food poisoning is ◊Salmonella bacteria. Salmonella comes in many forms, and strains are found in cattle, pigs, poultry, and eggs.

foot imperial unit of length (symbol ft), equivalent to 0.3048 m, in use in Britain since Anglo-Saxon times. It originally represented the length of a human foot. One foot contains 12 inches and is one-third of a yard.

foot-and-mouth disease contagious eruptive viral disease of cloven-hoofed mammals, characterized by blisters in the mouth and around the hooves. In cattle it causes deterioration of milk yield and abortions. It is an airborne virus which makes its eradication extremely difficult.

Inoculation with a vaccine is practiced in the US as a preventive measure.

football a contact sport played between two teams of 11 players with an inflated, pointed-oval ball. It is played on a field 100 yd/91 m long from goal line to goal line, with a goal posts on each of these lines, followed by a 10-yd/9-m end zone. The field is 53.3 yd/48.8 m wide. The team that scores the most points wins. Points are scored by running or passing the ball across the goal line (touchdown), by kicking it over the goal's crossbar after a touchdown (conversion or point after touchdown) or from the field during regular play (field goal), or by tackling an offensive player who has the ball in the end zone or blocking an offensive team's kick so it goes out of bounds from the end zone (safety). A touchdown counts 6 points, a field goal 3, a safety 2, and a conversion 1. Teams may attempt a 2-point conversion after a touchdown by running or passing the ball into the end zone. College and professional games consist of four 15-min quarters; high-school quarters are 12 min long. Players wear padded uniforms and helmets.

football: recent Super Bowl winners

1984	Los Angeles Raiders
1985	San Francisco 49ers
1986	Chicago Bears
1987	New York Giants
1988	Washington Redskins
1989	San Francisco 49ers
1990	San Francisco 49ers
1991	New York Giants
1992	Washington Redskins
1993	Dallas Cowboys
1994	San Francisco 49ers

football, association or *soccer* form of football originating in the UK, popular in Europe and Latin America. The modern game is played in the UK according to the rules laid down by the Football Association. Slight amendments to the rules take effect in certain competitions and overseas matches as laid down by the sport's world governing body, Fédération Internationale de Football Association (FIFA, 1904). FIFA organizes the competitions for the World Cup, held every four years since 1930.

force any influence that tends to change the state of rest or the uniform motion in a straight line of a body. The action of an unbalanced or resultant force results in the acceleration of a body in the direction of action of the force, or it may, if the body is unable to move freely, result in its deformation (see ◊Hooke's law). Force is a vector quantity, possessing both magnitude and direction; its SI unit is the newton.

forces, fundamental see ◊fundamental forces.

Ford Gerald R(udolph) 1913– . 38th president of the US 1974–77, a Republican. He was elected to the House of Representatives 1949, was nominated to the vice-presidency by Richard Nixon 1973 following the resignation of Spiro Agnew, and became president 1974, when Nixon was forced to resign following the ◊Watergate scandal. He pardoned Nixon and introduced an amnesty program for deserters and draft dodgers of the Vietnam War.

Ford Henry 1863–1947. US automobile manufacturer, who built his first automobile 1896 and founded the Ford Motor Company 1903. His Model T (1908–27) was the first automobile to be constructed solely by assembly-line methods and to be mass marketed; 15 million of these automobiles were made and sold.

Ford John. Adopted name of Sean O'Feeney 1895–1973. US film director. Active from the silent film era, he was one of the key creators of the "Western", directing *The Iron Horse* 1924; *Stagecoach* 1939 became his masterpiece. He won Academy Awards for *The Informer* 1935, *The Grapes of Wrath* 1940, *How Green Was My Valley* 1941, and *The Quiet Man* 1952.

foreclosure in law, the transfer of title of a mortgaged property from the mortgagor (borrower, usually a home owner) to the mortgagee (loaner, for example a bank) if the mortgagor is in breach of the mortgage agreement, usually by failing to make a number of payments on the mortgage (loan).

foreign aid see ◊aid, foreign

forensic science the use of scientific techniques to solve criminal cases. A multidisciplinary field embracing chemistry, physics, botany, zoology, and medicine, forensic science includes the identification of human bodies or traces. Traditional methods such as fingerprinting are still used, assisted by computers; in addition, blood analysis, forensic dentistry, voice and speech spectograms, and ◊genetic fingerprinting are increasingly applied. Chemicals, such as poisons and drugs, are analyzed by ◊chromatography. Ballistics (the study of projectiles, such as bullets), another traditional forensic field, makes use of tools such as the comparison microscope and the ◊electron microscope. ESDA (electrostatic document analysis) is a recent technique used for revealing indentations on paper, which helps determine if documents have been tampered with.

forestation planting of trees in areas that have not previously held forests. (*Reforestation* is the planting of trees in deforested areas.) Trees may be planted (1) to provide timber and wood pulp; (2) to provide firewood in countries where this is an energy source; (3) to bind soil together and prevent soil erosion; and (4) to act as windbreaks.

forestry the science of forest management. Recommended forestry practice aims at multipurpose crops, allowing the preservation of varied plant and animal species as well as human uses (lumbering, recreation). Forestry has often been confined to the planting of a single species, such as a rapid-growing conifer providing softwood for paper pulp and construction timber, for which world demand is greatest. In tropical countries, logging contributes to the destruction of ◊rainforests, causing global environmental problems. Small unplanned forests are woodland.

forget-me-not any marsh plant of the genus *Myosotis* of the borage family. These plants have hairy leaves; bear clusters of small blue, white, or red flowers; and are considered a symbol of fidelity and friendship. The European true forget-me-not *Myosotis scorpioides*, 12–28 in/30–70 cm in height, now grows widely in North America.

formaldehyde common name for ◊methanal.

formic acid common name for methanoic acid.

Formosa alternate name for ◊Taiwan.

formula in chemistry, a representation of a molecule, radical, or ion, in which the component chemical elements are represented by their symbols. An *empirical formula* indicates the simplest ratio of the elements in a compound, without indicating how many of them there are or how they are combined. A *molecular formula* gives the number of each type of element present in one molecule. A *structural formula* shows the relative positions of the atoms and the bonds between them. For example, for ethanoic acid, the empirical formula is CH_2O, the molecular formula is $C_2H_4O_2$, and the structural formula is CH_3COOH.

Formula is also another name for ◊chemical equation.

Forrestal James Vincent 1892–1949. US Democratic politician. As under secretary from 1940 and secretary of the navy from 1944, he organized its war effort, accompanying the US landings on the Japanese island Iwo Jima. He was the first secretary of the Department of Defense 1947–49, a post created to unify the three armed forces at the end of World War II.

He committed suicide after exhaustion and illness forced him to resign 1949. He wrote *The Forrestal Diaries*, which were published posthumously 1951.

Forster E(dward) M(organ) 1879–1970. English novelist. He was concerned with the interplay of personality and the conflict between convention and instinct. His novels include *A Room with a View* 1908, *Howards End* 1910, and *A Passage to India* 1924. He also wrote short stories, for example "The Eternal Omnibus" 1914; criticism, including *Aspects of the Novel* 1927; and essays, including Abinger Harvest 1936.

forsythia any temperate E Asian shrub of the genus *Forsythia* of the olive family Oleaceae, which bear yellow bell-shaped flowers in early spring before the leaves appear.

Fort-de-France capital, chief commercial center, and port of Martinique, West Indies, at the mouth of the Madame River; population (1990) 101,500. It trades in sugar, rum, and cacao.

Forth river in SE Scotland, with its headstreams rising on the northeast slopes of Ben Lomond. It flows approximately 45 mi/72 km to Kincardine where the *Firth of Forth* begins. The Firth is approximately 50 mii/80 km long, and is 16 mi/26 km wide where it joins the North Sea.

FORTRAN (acronym for *formula translation*) high-level computer-programming language suited to mathematical and scientific computations. Developed 1956, it is one of the earliest computer languages still in use. A recent version, Fortran 90, is now being used on advanced parallel computers. ◊BASIC was strongly influenced by FORTRAN and is similar in many ways.

Fort Sumter fort in Charleston Harbor, South Carolina, 4 mi/6.5 km SE of Charleston. The first shots of the US Civil War were fired here April 12, 1861, after its commander had refused the call to surrender made by the Confederate General Beauregard.

The attack was successful, with the South holding the fort until 1865; it had been prompted by President Lincoln's refusal to evacuate the fort and his decision instead to send reinforcements. Southern leaders felt they must attack to lend weight to their claims of independence.

fossil remains of an animal or plant preserved in rocks. Fossils may be formed by refrigeration (for example,

Arctic ◊mammoths in ice); carbonization (leaves in coal); formation of a cast (dinosaur or human footprints in mud); or mineralization of bones, teeth or shells. The study of fossils is called ◊paleontology.

fossil fuel fuel, such as coal, oil, and natural gas, formed from the fossilized remains of plants that lived hundreds of millions of years ago. Fossil fuels are a nonrenewable resource and will eventually run out. Extraction of coal and oil causes considerable environmental pollution, and burning coal contributes to problems of ◊acid rain and the ◊greenhouse effect.

Foster Jodie. Adopted name of Alicia Christian Foster 1962– . US film actress and director. She began acting as a child in a great variety of roles. She starred in *Taxi Driver* and *Bugsy Malone* both 1976, when only 14. Subsequent films include *The Accused* 1988 and *The Silence of the Lambs* 1991 (she won Academy Awards for both), and *Sommersby* 1993.

Foster Stephen Collins 1826–1864. US songwriter, composer of "The Old Folks at Home" 1851, "My Old Kentucky Home" 1853, and others, which mostly drew from the black minstrel style.

Foucault Jean Bernard Léon 1819–1868. French physicist who used a pendulum to demonstrate the rotation of the Earth on its axis, and invented the gyroscope.

Foucault Michel 1926–1984. French philosopher who rejected phenomenology and existentialism. He was concerned with how forms of knowledge and forms of human subjectivity are constructed by specific institutions and practices.

four-color process color ◊printing using four printing plates, based on the principle that any color is made up of differing proportions of the primary colors blue, red, and green. The first stage in preparing a color picture for printing is to produce separate films, one each for the blue, red, and green respectively in the picture (color separations). From these separations three printing plates are made, with a fourth plate for black (for shading or outlines). Ink colors complementary to those represented on the plates are used for printing—yellow for the blue plate, cyan for the red, and magenta for the green.

Four Freedoms, the four kinds of liberty essential to human dignity as defined in an address to the US Congress by President Franklin D ◊Roosevelt Jan 6, 1941: freedom of speech and expression, freedom of worship, freedom from want, and freedom from fear.

Before US entry into World War II, Roosevelt urged support of the democracies fighting to defend freedom, and two months later Congress passed the Lend-Lease Act. The Four Freedoms were the basis for the Atlantic Charter specifying Allied war aims 1941.

four-stroke cycle the engine-operating cycle of most gasoline and ◊diesel engines. The "stroke" is an upward or downward movement of a piston in a cylinder. In a gasoline engine the cycle begins with the induction of a fuel mixture as the piston goes down on its first stroke. On the second stroke (up) the piston compresses the mixture in the top of the cylinder. An electric spark then ignites the mixture, and the gases produced force the piston down on its third, power, stroke. On the fourth stroke (up) the piston expels the burned gases from the cylinder into the exhaust.

fourth-generation language in computing, a type of programming language designed for the rapid programming of ◊applications but often lacking the ability to control the individual parts of the computer. Such a language typically provides easy ways of designing screens and reports, and of using databases. Other "generations" (the term implies a class of language rather than a chronological sequence) are ◊machine code (first generation); ◊assembly languages, or low-level languages (second); and conventional high-level languages such as ◊BASIC and ◊PASCAL (third).

fowl chicken or chickenlike bird. Sometimes the term is also used for ducks and geese. The red jungle fowl *Gallus gallus* is the ancestor of all domestic chickens. It is a forest bird of Asia, without the size or egg-laying ability of many domestic strains. ◊Guinea fowl are of African origin.

fox The common or red fox is versatile and intelligent. It is a skillful hunter, preying on rodents, hares, birds, and insects. In urban areas, the red fox is a scavenger of garbage cans.

fox one of the smaller species of wild dog of the family Canidae, which live in Africa, Asia, Europe, North America, and South America. Foxes feed on a wide range of animals from worms to rabbits, scavenge for food, and also eat berries. They are very adaptable, maintaining high populations close to urban areas.

Fox Charles James 1749–1806. English Whig politician, son of the 1st Baron Holland. He entered Parliament 1769 as a supporter of the court, but went over to the opposition 1774. As secretary of state 1782, leader of the opposition to Pitt, and foreign secretary 1806, he welcomed the French Revolution and brought about the abolition of the slave trade.

foxglove any flowering plant of the genus *Digitalis*, family Scrophulariaceae, found in Europe and the Mediterranean region. It bears showy spikes of bell-like flowers, and grows up to 5 ft/1.5 m high.

fox-hunting the pursuit of a fox across country on horseback, aided by a pack of foxhounds, specially trained to track the fox's scent.

The aim is to catch and kill the fox. In draghunting, hounds pursue a prepared trail rather than a fox.

foxtrot ballroom dance originating in the US about 1914. It has alternating long and short steps, supposedly like the movements of the fox.

fractal an irregular shape or surface produced by a procedure of repeated subdivision. Generated on a computer screen, fractals are used in creating models for geographical or biological processes (for example, the creation of a coastline by erosion or accretion, or the growth of plants).

fraction in mathematics, a number that indicates one or more equal parts of a whole. Usually, the number of equal parts into which the unit is divided (denominator) is written below a horizontal line, and the number of parts comprising the fraction (numerator) is written above; thus ½ or ¾. Such fractions are called

Diesel four stroke cycle

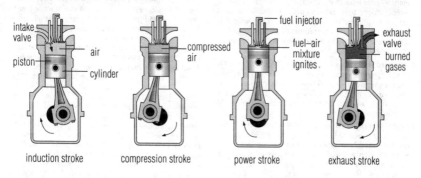

induction stroke   compression stroke   power stroke   exhaust stroke

Otto four stroke cycle

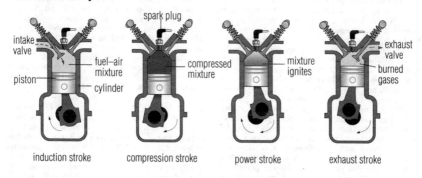

induction stroke   compression stroke   power stroke   exhaust stroke

Wankel engine

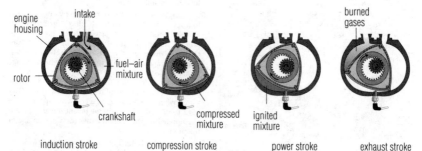

induction stroke   compression stroke   power stroke   exhaust stroke

four-stroke cycle

vulgar or *simple* fractions. The denominator can never be zero.

fracture break in the continuity of a bone, with or without displacement of any fragments. It may be pathological, the result of a relatively mild injury to an already diseased bone (as in osteomalacia and Paget's disease). Or, more often, it is the result of an injury to healthy bone.

fragile X syndrome the commonest inherited cause of mental retardation. It is inherited as an X-linked recessive condition and is so named because sufferers have a fragile site on one of their X chromosomes. Women carry two X chromosomes and are therefore more commonly affected than men, but less seriously. The gene was located 1991.

Fragonard Jean-Honoré 1732–1806. French painter. He was the leading exponent of the Rococo style (along with his master Boucher). His light-hearted subjects, often erotic, include *The Swing* about 1766 (Wallace Collection, London). Mme de Pompadour was one of his patrons.

France French Republic (*République Française*) *area* (including Corsica) 209,970 sq mi/543,965 sq km *capital* Paris *towns and cities* Lyons, Lille, Bordeaux, Toulouse, Nantes, Strasbourg; ports Marseille, Nice, Le Havre *physical* rivers Seine, Loire, Garonne, Rhône, Rhine; mountain ranges Alps, Massif Central, Pyrenees, Jura, Vosges, Cévennes; the island of Corsica *territories* Guadeloupe, French Guiana, Martinique, Réunion, St Pierre and Miquelon, Southern and Antarctic Territories, New Caledonia, French Polynesia, Wallis and Futuna *features* Ardennes forest, Auvergne mountain region, Riviera, Mont Blanc (15,781 ft/4,810 m), caves of Dordogne with relics of early humans; largest W European nation *head of state* Jacques Chirac from 1995 *head of government* Alain Juppé from 1995 *political system* liberal democracy *political parties* Socialist Party (PS), left of center; Rally for the Republic (RPR), neo-Gaullist conservative; Union for French Democracy (UDF), center-right; Republican Party (RP), center-right; French Communist Party (PCF), Marxist-Leninist; National Front, far right; Greens, environmentalist *exports* fruit (especially apples), wine, cheese, wheat, automobiles, aircraft, iron and steel, petroleum products, chemicals, jewelry, silk, lace; tourism is very important *currency* franc *population* (1994) 57,800,000 (including 4,500,000 immigrants, chiefly from Portugal, Algeria, Morocco, and Tunisia); growth rate 0.3% p.a. *life expectancy* men 73, women 81 *languages* French (regional languages include Basque, Breton, Catalan, and the Provençal dialect) *media* the use of foreign words in public announcements is prohibited *religions* Roman Catholic 90%, Protestant 2%,

Muslim 1% *literacy* 99% *GNP* $20,600 per head (1991) *chronology 1944–46* Provisional government headed by General Charles de Gaulle; start of Fourth Republic. *1954* Indochina achieved independence. *1956* Morocco and Tunisia achieved independence. *1957* Entry into European Economic Community. *1958* Recall of de Gaulle after Algerian crisis; start of Fifth Republic. *1959* De Gaulle became president. *1962* Algeria achieved independence. *1966* France withdrew from military wing of NATO. *1968* "May events" uprising of students and workers. *1969* De Gaulle resigned after referendum defeat; Georges Pompidou became president. *1974* Giscard d'Estaing elected president. *1981* François Mitterrand elected Fifth Republic's first socialist president. *1986* "Cohabitation" experiment, with the conservative Jacques Chirac as prime minister. *1988* Mitterrand reelected. Moderate socialist Michel Rocard became prime minister. Matignon Accord on future of New Caledonia approved by referendum. *1989* Greens gained 11% of vote in elections to European Parliament. *1991* French forces were part of the US-led coalition in the Gulf War. Edith Cresson became prime minister; Mitterrand's popularity rating fell rapidly. *1992* March: Socialist Party (PS) humiliated in regional and local elections; Greens and National Front polled strongly. April: Cresson replaced by Pierre Bérégovoy. Sept: referendum narrowly endorsed Maastricht Treaty. *1993* March: PS suffered heavy defeat in National Assembly elections. Edouard Balladur appointed prime minister; "cohabitation" government reestablished. May: Bérégovoy committed suicide. Michel Rocard appointed PS leader. *1994* Rocard resigned as PS leader; replaced by Emmanuelli Henri. *1995* Jacques Chirac elected president.

France Anatole. Pen name of Anatole François Thibault 1844–1924. French writer. He is renowned for the wit, urbanity, and style of his works. His earliest novel was *Le Crime de Sylvestre Bonnard/The Crime of Sylvester Bonnard* 1881; later books include the autobiographical series beginning with *Le Livre de mon ami/My Friend's Book* 1885, the satiric *L'Île des pingouins/Penguin Island* 1908, and *Les Dieux ont soif/The Gods Are Athirst* 1912. Nobel Prize for Literature 1921.

Francesca Piero della. See ◊Piero della Francesca, Italian painter.

franchise in politics, the eligibility, right, or privilege to vote at public elections.

franchise in business, the right given by one company to another to manufacture, distribute, or provide its branded products. It is usual for the franchiser to impose minimum quality conditions on its franchisees to make sure that customers receive a fair deal from the franchisee and ensure that the brand image is maintained.

Examples of franchise operations in the US include fast-food restaurants, auto-repair shops, and specialty stores, where the owner/managers have purchased the right to operate a brand-name business using materials supplied by the manufacturer for a percentage of the profits.

Francis I 1494–1547. King of France from 1515. He succeeded his cousin Louis XII, and from 1519 European politics turned on the rivalry between him and the Holy Roman emperor Charles V, which led to war 1521–29, 1536–38, and 1542–44. In 1525 Francis was captured at Pavia and released after signing a humiliating treaty. At home, he developed absolute monarchy.

Francis II 1544–1560. King of France from 1559 when he succeeded his father, Henri II. He married Mary Queen of Scots 1558. He was completely under the influence of his mother, ◊Catherine de' Medici.

Francis II 1768–1835. Holy Roman emperor 1792–1806. He became Francis I, Emperor of Austria 1804, and abandoned the title of Holy Roman emperor 1806. During his reign Austria was five times involved in war with France, 1792–97, 1798–1801, 1805, 1809, and 1813–14. He succeeded his father, Leopold II.

Francis Ferdinand Archduke of Austria, also known as ◊Franz Ferdinand.

Francis Joseph Emperor of Austria-Hungary, also known as ◊Franz Joseph.

Francis of Assisi, St 1182–1226. Italian founder of the Roman Catholic Franciscan order of friars 1209 and, with St Clare, of the Poor Clares 1212. In 1224 he is said to have undergone a mystical experience during which he received the *stigmata* (five wounds of Jesus). Many stories are told of his ability to charm wild animals, and he is the patron saint of ecologists. His feast day is Oct 4.

francium radioactive metallic element, symbol Fr, atomic number 87, relative atomic mass 223. It is one of the ◊alkali metals and occurs in nature in small amounts as a decay product of actinium. Its longest-lived isotope has a half-life of only 21 minutes. Francium was discovered and named in 1939 by Marguérite Perey to honor her country.

Franco Francisco (Paulino Hermenegildo Teódulo Bahamonde) 1892–1975. Spanish dictator from 1939. As a general, he led the insurgent Nationalists to victory in the Spanish ◊Civil War 1936–39, supported by Fascist Italy and Nazi Germany, and established a dictatorship. In 1942 Franco reinstated a Cortes (Spanish parliament), which in 1947 passed an act by which he became head of state for life.

Franco Itamar 1931– . Brazilian politician, president 1992–94. Replacing President Fernando Collor after his removal on charges of corruption, Franco came to the office with a clean record. He promised reform with stability but during his first months in office attracted widespread criticism, both from friends (for his working methods and lack of clear policies) and opponents (for his rapid privatization program). He was defeated by Fernando Henrique Cardoso in the Oct 1994 presidential election.

François French form of ◊Francis, two kings of France.

Franco-Prussian War 1870–71. The Prussian chancellor Bismarck put forward a German candidate for the vacant Spanish throne with the deliberate, and successful, intention of provoking the French emperor Napoleon III into declaring war. The Prussians defeated the French at ◊Sedan, then besieged Paris. The Treaty of Frankfurt May 1871 gave Alsace, Lorraine, and a large French indemnity to Prussia. The war established Prussia, at the head of a newly established German empire, as Europe's leading power.

frangipani any tropical American tree of the genus *Plumeria*, especially *P. rubra*, of the dogbane family Apocynaceae. Perfume is made from the strongly scented flowers.

Frank member of a group of Germanic peoples prominent in Europe in the 3rd to 9th centuries. Believed to have originated in Pomerania on the Baltic Sea, they had settled on the Rhine by the 3rd century, spread into the Roman Empire by the 4th century,

and gradually conquered most of Gaul, Italy, and Germany under the ◊Merovingian and Carolingian dynasties. The kingdom of the western Franks became France, the kingdom of the eastern Franks became Germany.

Frank Anne 1929–1945. German diarist. She fled to the Netherlands with her family 1933 to escape Nazi anti-Semitism (the ◊Holocaust).

During the German occupation of Amsterdam, they and two other families remained in a sealed-off room, protected by Dutch sympathizers 1942–44, when betrayal resulted in their deportation and Anne's death in Belsen concentration camp. Her diary of her time in hiding was published 1947.

Frankfurt-am-Main city in Hessen, Germany, 45 mi/72 km NE of Mannheim; population (1988) 592,000. It is a commercial and banking center, with electrical and machine industries, and an inland port on the river Main. An international book fair is held here annually.

Franklin Benjamin 1706–1790. US printer, publisher, author, scientist, and statesman. He proved that lightning is a form of electricity, distinguished between positive and negative electricity, and invented the lightning conductor. He was the first US ambassador to France 1776–85, and negotiated peace with Britain 1783. As a delegate to the ◊Continental Congress from Pennsylvania 1785–88, he helped to draft the ◊Declaration of Independence and the US ◊Constitution.

Franz Ferdinand or *Francis Ferdinand* 1863–1914. Archduke of Austria. He became heir to his uncle, Emperor Franz Joseph, in 1884 but while visiting Sarajevo June 28, 1914, he and his wife were assassinated by a Serbian nationalist. Austria used the episode to make unreasonable demands on Serbia that ultimately precipitated World War I.

Franz Joseph or *Francis Joseph* 1830–1916. Emperor of Austria-Hungary from 1848, when his uncle, Ferdinand I, abdicated. After the suppression of the 1848 revolution, Franz Joseph tried to establish an absolute monarchy but had to grant Austria a parliamentary constitution 1861 and Hungary equality with Austria 1867. He was defeated in the Italian War 1859 and the Prussian War 1866. In 1914 he made the assassination of his heir and nephew Franz Ferdinand the excuse for attacking Serbia, thus precipitating World War I.

fraud in law, an act of deception resulting in injury to another. To establish fraud it has to be demonstrated that (1) a false representation (for example, a factually untrue statement) has been made, with the intention that it should be acted upon; (2) the person making the representation knows it is false or does not attempt to find out whether it is true or not; and (3) the person to whom the representation is made acts upon it to his or her detriment.

Fraunhofer Joseph von 1787–1826. German physicist who did important work in optics. The dark lines in the solar spectrum (*Fraunhofer lines*), which reveal the chemical composition of the Sun's atmosphere, were accurately mapped by him.

Born in Bavaria, he was apprenticed to a glass cutter, and in 1807 founded an optical institute.

Frederick (I) Barbarossa ("red-beard") c.1123–1190. Holy Roman emperor from 1152. Originally duke of Swabia, he was elected emperor 1152, and was engaged in a struggle with Pope Alexander III

1159–77, which ended in his submission; the Lombard cities, headed by Milan, took advantage of this to establish their independence of imperial control. Frederick joined the Third Crusade, and was drowned while crossing a river in Anatolia.

Frederick II 1194–1250. Holy Roman emperor from 1212, called "the Wonder of the World". He led a crusade 1228–29 that recovered Jerusalem by treaty, without fighting. He quarrelled with the pope, who excommunicated him three times, and a feud began that lasted with intervals until the end of his reign. Frederick, who was a religious skeptic, is often considered the most cultured man of his age. He was the son of Henry VI.

Frederick (II) the Great 1712–1786. King of Prussia from 1740, when he succeeded his father Frederick William I. In that year he started the War of the ◊Austrian Succession by his attack on Austria. In the peace of 1745 he secured Silesia. The struggle was renewed in the Seven Years' War 1756–63. He acquired West Prussia in the first partition of Poland 1772 and left Prussia as Germany's foremost state. He was an efficient and just ruler in the spirit of the Enlightenment and a patron of the arts.

Frederick William I 1688–1740. King of Prussia from 1713, who developed Prussia's military might and commerce.

Frederick William III 1770–1840. King of Prussia from 1797. He was defeated by Napoleon 1806, but contributed to his final overthrow 1813–15 and profited by being allotted territory at the Congress of Vienna.

Free Church Protestant denominations in England and Wales that are not part of the Church of England; for example, the Methodist Church, Baptist Union, and United Reformed Church (Congregational and Presbyterian). These churches joined for common action in the Free Church Federal Council 1940.

Free Church of Scotland the body of Scottish Presbyterians who seceded from the Established Church of Scotland in the Disruption of 1843. In 1900 all but a small section that retains the old name, and is known as the *Wee Frees*, combined with the United Presbyterian Church to form the United Free Church, which reunited with the Church of Scotland 1929.

free enterprise or *free market* economic system where private capital is used in business with profits going to private companies and individuals. The term has much the same meaning as ◊capitalism.

freehold in England and Wales, ownership of land for an indefinite period. It is contrasted with a leasehold, which is always for a fixed period. In practical effect, a freehold is absolute ownership.

freemasonry the beliefs and practices of a group of linked national organizations open to men over the age of 21, united by a common code of morals and certain traditional "secrets". Modern freemasonry began in 18th-century Europe. Freemasons do much charitable work, but have been criticized in recent years for their secrecy, their male exclusivity, and their alleged use of influence within and between organizations (for example, the police or local government) to further each other's interests. There are approximately 6 million members.

free port port or sometimes a zone within a port, where cargo may be accepted for handling, processing, and reshipment without the imposition of tariffs or taxes. Duties and tax become payable only if the products are for consumption in the country to which the free port belongs.

free radical in chemistry, an atom or molecule that has an unpaired electron and is therefore highly reactive. Most free radicals are very short-lived. They are by-products of normal cell chemistry and rapidly oxidize other molecules they encounter. They are thought to do considerable damage. They are neutralized by protective enzymes.

freesia any plant of the South African genus *Freesia* of the iris family Iridaceae, commercially grown for their scented, funnel-shaped flowers.

Freetown capital of Sierra Leone, W Africa; population (1988) 470,000. It has a naval station and a harbor. Industries include cement, plastics, footwear, and oil refining. Platinum, chromite, diamonds, and gold are traded. It was founded as a settlement for freed slaves in the 1790s.

free trade economic system where governments do not interfere in the movement of goods between countries; there are thus no taxes on imports. In the modern economy, free trade tends to hold within economic groups such as the European Union (EU), but not generally, despite such treaties as the ◊General Agreement on Tariffs and Trade 1948 and subsequent agreements to reduce tariffs. The opposite of free trade is ◊protectionism.

free verse poetry without metrical form. At the beginning of the 20th century, many poets believed that the 19th century had accomplished most of what could be done with regular meter, and rejected it, in much the same spirit as John Milton in the 17th century had rejected rhyme, preferring irregular meters that made it possible to express thought clearly and without distortion.

free will the doctrine that human beings are free to control their own actions, and that these actions are not fixed in advance by God or fate. Some Jewish and Christian theologians assert that God gave humanity free will to choose between good and evil; others that God has decided in advance the outcome of all human choices (◊predestination), as in Calvinism.

freezing change from liquid to solid state, as when water becomes ice. For a given substance, freezing occurs at a definite temperature, known as the *freezing point*, that is invariable under similar conditions of pressure, and the temperature remains at this point until all the liquid is frozen. The amount of heat per unit mass that has to be removed to freeze a substance is a constant for any given substance, and is known as the latent heat of fusion.

Frémont John Charles 1813–1890. US soldier and politician who explored much of the Far West, was influential in the US acquisition of California, and ultimately saw his military career overshadowed by his political ambitions.

French native to or an inhabitant of France, as well as their descendents, culture, or primary language, which is one of the Romance languages (see ◊French language). There are also some sociolinguistic minorities within France who speak Catalan, Breton, Flemish, German, Corsican, or Basque.

French is also spoken in the former colonies, such as in Africa and Québec, Canada, and in overseas territories such as Martinique and French Guiana.

French Daniel Chester 1850–1931. US sculptor. He produced mainly public monuments. His most famous works include *The Minute Man* 1875 in Concord, Massachusetts, *John Harvard* 1884 at Harvard College, *Alma Mater* at Columbia University, and the imposing seated *Abraham Lincoln* 1922 in the Lincoln Memorial, Washington, DC.

Born in Exeter, New Hampshire, French briefly attended the Massachusetts Institute of Technology (MIT) before embarking on an artistic career. Trained in anatomy and sculpture in private studios in Boston, New York, and Europe, he was by far the most noted American sculptor of public monuments in the late 19th century.

French Community former association consisting of France and those overseas territories joined with it by the constitution of the Fifth Republic, following the 1958 referendum. Many of the constituent states withdrew during the 1960s, and it no longer formally exists, but in practice all former French colonies have close economic and cultural as well as linguistic links with France.

French Guiana (French *Guyane Française*) French overseas *département* from 1946, and administrative region from 1974, on the north coast of South America, bounded W by Surinam and E and S by Brazil *area* 32,230 sq mi/83,500 sq km *capital* Cayenne *towns and cities* St Laurent *features* Eurospace rocket launch pad at Kourou; Iles du Salut, which include Devil's Island *industries* timber, shrimps, gold *currency* franc *population* (1987) 89,000 *languages* 90% Creole, French, American Indian *famous people* Alfred ◊Dreyfus *history* first settled by France 1604, the territory became a French possession 1817; penal colonies, including Devil's Island, were established from 1852; by 1945 the shipments of convicts from France ceased.

French horn musical brass instrument, a descendant of the natural hunting horrn, valved and curved into a circular loop, with a funnel-shaped mouthpiece and wide bell.

French language member of the Romance branch of the Indo-European language family, spoken in France, Belgium, Luxembourg, Monaco, and Switzerland in Europe; also in Canada (principally in the province of Québec), various Caribbean and Pacific Islands (including overseas territories such as Martinique and French Guiana), and certain N and W African countries (for example, Mali and Senegal).

French Polynesia French Overseas Territory in the S Pacific, consisting of five archipelagos: Windward Islands, Leeward Islands (the two island groups comprising the ◊Society Islands), ◊Tuamotu Archipelago (including ◊Gambier Islands), ◊Tubuai Islands, and ◊Marquesas Islands *total area* 1,521 sq mi/3,940 sq km *capital* Papeete on Tahiti *industries* cultivated pearls, coconut oil, vanilla; tourism is important *population* (1990) 199,100 *languages* Tahitian (official), French *government* a high commissioner (Alain Ohrel) and Council of Government; two deputies are returned to the National Assembly in France *history* first visited by Europeans 1595; French Protectorate 1843; annexed to France 1880–82; became an Overseas Territory, changing its name from French Oceania 1958; self-governing 1977. Following demands for independence in ◊New Caledonia 1984–85, agitation increased also in Polynesia.

French Revolution the period 1789–1799 that saw the end of the French monarchy. Although the revolution began as an attempt to create a constitutional monarchy, by late 1792 demands for long-overdue reforms

resulted in the proclamation of the First Republic. The violence of the revolution, attacks by other nations, and bitter factional struggles, riots, and counterrevolutionary uprisings consumed the republic. This helped bring the extremists to power, and the bloody Reign of Terror followed. French armies then succeeded in holding off their foreign enemies and one of the generals, ◊Napoleon, seized power 1799.

frequency in physics, the number of periodic oscillations, vibrations, or waves occurring per unit of time. The unit of frequency is the hertz (Hz), one hertz being equivalent to one cycle per second.

frequency modulation see ◊FM.

fresco mural painting technique using water-based paint on wet plaster. Some of the earliest frescoes (about 1750–1400 BC) were found in Knossos, Crete (now preserved in the Heraklion Museum). Fresco reached its finest expression in Italy from the 13th to the 17th centuries. Giotto, Masaccio, Michelangelo, and many other artists worked in the medium. In the 20th century the Mexican muralists Orozco and Rivera used fresco.

Fresno city in central California, SE of San Jose, seat of Fresno County; population (1990) 354,200. It is the processing and marketing center for the fruits and vegetables of the San Joaquin Valley. Industries include glass, machinery, fertilizers, and vending machines.

Fresno was originally a stop on the Central Pacific Railroad.

Freud Sigmund 1865–1939. Austrian physician who pioneered the study of the unconscious mind. He developed the methods of free association and interpretation of dreams that are basic techniques of ◊psychoanalysis, and formulated the concepts of the ◊id, ◊ego, and ◊superego. His books include *Die Traumdeutung/The Interpretation of Dreams* 1900, *Totem and Taboo* 1913, and *Das Unbehagen in der Kultur/Civilization and its Discontents* 1930.

friction in physics, the force that opposes the relative motion of two bodies in contact. The *coefficient of friction* is the ratio of the force required to achieve this relative motion to the force pressing the two bodies together.

Friedan Betty 1921– . US liberal feminist. Her book *The Feminine Mystique* 1963 started the contemporary women's movement, both in the US and the UK. She was a founder of the National Organization for Women (NOW) 1966 (and its president 1966–70), the National Women's Political Caucus 1971, and the First Women's Bank 1973. Friedan also helped to organize the Women's Strike for Equality 1970 and called the First International Feminist Congress 1973.

Born in Peoria, Illinois, her other works include *It Changed My Life* 1976 and *The Second Stage* 1981, a call for a change of direction in the movement.

Friedman Milton 1912– . US economist. The foremost exponent of ◊monetarism, he argued that a country's economy, and hence inflation, can be controlled through its money supply, although most governments lack the "political will" to control inflation by cutting government spending and thereby increasing unemployment. He was awarded the Nobel Prize for Economics 1976.

Friedman argued for extending private choice among competing businesses into virtually all spheres of economic life. He suggested, for example, that the public school system be abolished and that parents pay to send their children to the school of their choosing. He was an influential adviser to presidents Nixon and Reagan and wrote several books.

Friendly Islands another name for ◊Tonga, a country in the Pacific.

Friends of the Earth (FoE or FOE) environmental pressure group, established in the UK 1971, that aims to protect the environment and to promote rational and sustainable use of the Earth's resources. It campaigns on issues such as acid rain; air, sea, river, and land pollution; recycling; disposal of toxic wastes; nuclear power and renewable energy; the destruction of rainforests; pesticides; and agriculture. FoE has branches in 30 countries.

Friends, Society of or *Quakers* Christian Protestant sect founded by George Fox in England in the 17th century. They were persecuted for their nonviolent activism, and many emigrated to form communities elsewhere, for example in Pennsylvania and New England. They now form a worldwide movement of about 200,000. Their worship stresses meditation and the freedom of all to take an active part in the service (called a meeting, held in a meeting house). They have no priests or ministers.

Friesland maritime province of the N Netherlands, which includes the Frisian Islands and land that is still being reclaimed from the former Zuyder Zee; the inhabitants of the province are called Frisians *area* 1,312 sq mi/3,400 sq km *capital* Leeuwarden *towns and cities* Drachten, Harlingen, Sneek, Heerenveen *features* sailing is popular; the *Elfstedentocht* (skating race on canals through 11 towns) is held in very cold winters *industries* livestock (Frisian cattle originated here; black Frisian horses), dairy products, small boats *population* (1990) 600,000 *history* ruled as a county of the Holy Roman Empire during the Middle Ages, Friesland passed to Saxony 1498 and, after a revolt, to Charles V of Spain. In 1579 it subscribed to the Treaty of Utrecht, opposing Spanish rule. In 1748 its stadholder, Prince William IV of Orange, became stadholder of all the United Provinces of the Netherlands

fritillary in botany, any plant of the genus *Fritillaria* of the lily family Liliaceae. The snake's head fritillary *F. meleagris* has bell-shaped flowers with purple-checkered markings.

fritillary in zoology, any of a large grouping of butterflies of the family Nymphalidae. Mostly medium-sized, fritillaries are usually orange and reddish with a black criss-cross pattern or spots above and with silvery spots on the underside of the hindwings.

frog any amphibian of the order Anura (Greek "tailless"). There are some 24 different families of frog, containing more than 3,800 species. There are no clear rules for distinguishing between frogs and toads. Frogs usually have squat bodies, hind legs specialized for jumping, and webbed feet for swimming. Many use their long, extensible tongues to capture insects. They vary in size from the tiny North American little grass frog *Limnaoedus ocularis*, 0.5 in/12 mm long, to the giant aquatic frog *Telmatobius culeus*, 20 in/50 cm long, of Lake Titicaca, South America. Frogs are widespread, inhabiting all continents except Antarctica, and they have adapted to a range of environments including deserts, forests, grasslands, and even high altitudes, with some species in the Andes and Himalayas existing above 19,600 ft/5,000 m.

frogman underwater warfare specialist; the name derives from their appearance when wearing wetsuits, flippers, and masks.

Fronde French revolts 1648–53 against the administration of the chief minister ◊Mazarin during Louis XIV's minority. In 1648–49 the Paris parlement attempted to limit the royal power, its leaders were arrested, Paris revolted, and the rising was suppressed by the royal army under Louis II Condé. In 1650 Condé led a new revolt of the nobility, but this was suppressed by 1653. The defeat of the Fronde enabled Louis to establish an absolutist monarchy in the later 17th century.

front in meteorology, the boundary between two air masses of different temperature or humidity. A *cold front* marks the line of advance of a cold air mass from below, as it displaces a warm air mass; a *warm front* marks the advance of a warm air mass as it rises up over a cold one. Frontal systems define the weather of the mid-latitudes, where warm tropical air is constantly meeting cold air from the poles.

front-end processor small computer used to coordinate and control the communications between a large mainframe computer and its input and output devices.

Frost Robert (Lee) 1874–1963. US poet. His accessible, colloquial blank verse, often flavored with New England speech patterns, is written with an individual voice and penetrating vision. His poems include "Mending Wall" ("Something there is that does not love a wall"), "The Road Not Taken," and "Stopping by Woods on a Snowy Evening" and are collected in *A Boy's Will* 1913, *North of Boston* 1914, *New Hampshire* 1924 (Pulitzer Prize), *Collected Poems* 1930 (Pulitzer Prize), *A Further Range* 1936 (Pulitzer Prize), and *A Witness Tree* 1942 (Pulitzer Prize).

frostbite the freezing of skin or flesh, with formation of ice crystals leading to tissue damage. The treatment is slow warming of the affected area; for example, by skin-to-skin contact or with lukewarm water. Frostbitten parts are extremely vulnerable to infection, with the risk of gangrene.

fructose $C_6H_{12}O_6$ a sugar that occurs naturally in honey, the nectar of flowers, and many sweet fruits; it is commercially prepared from glucose.

fruit in botany, the ripened ovary in flowering plants that develops from one or more seeds or carpels and encloses one or more seeds. Its function is to protect the seeds during their development and to aid in their dispersal. Fruits are often edible, sweet, juicy, and colorful. When eaten they provide vitamins, minerals, and enzymes, but little protein. Most fruits are borne by perennial plants. When fruits are eaten by animals the seeds pass through the alimentary canal unharmed, and are passed out with the feces.

f-stop in photography, one of a series of numbers on the lens barrel designating the size of the variable aperture; it stands for the focal length and follows an internationally accepted scale.

ft symbol for ◊*foot*, a measure of distance.

fuchsia any shrub or herbaceous plant of the genus *Fuchsia* of the evening-primrose family Onagraceae. Species are native to South and Central America and New Zealand, and bear red, purple, or pink bell-shaped flowers that hang downward.

fuel any source of heat or energy, embracing the entire range of materials that burn (combustibles). A *nuclear fuel* is any material that produces energy by nuclear fission in a nuclear reactor.

fuel cell cell converting chemical energy directly to electrical energy.

It works on the same principle as a battery but is continually fed with fuel, usually hydrogen. Fuel cells are silent and reliable (no moving parts) but expensive to produce.

fugue in music, a contrapuntal form with two or more subjects (principal melodies) for a number of parts, which enter in succession in direct imitation of each other or transposed to a higher or lower key, and may be combined in augmented form (larger note values). It represents the highest form of contrapuntal ingenuity in works such as J S Bach's *Das musikalische Opfer/The Musical Offering* 1747, on a theme of Frederick II of Prussia, and *Die Kunst der Fuge/The Art of the Fugue* published 1751, and Beethoven's *Grosse Fuge/Great Fugue* for string quartet 1825–26.

Fujairah or *Fujayrah* one of the seven constituent member states of the ◊United Arab Emirates; area 450 sq mi/1,150 sq km; population (1985) 54,000.

Fujian or *Fukien* province of SE China, bordering Taiwan Strait, opposite Taiwan *area* 47,517 sq mi/123,100 sq km *capital* Fuzhou *physical* dramatic mountainous coastline *features* being developed for tourists; designated as a pace-setting province for modernization 1980 *industries* sugar, rice, special aromatic teas, tobacco, timber, fruit *population* (1990) 30,048,000.

Fujimori Alberto 1939– . Peruvian politician, president from 1990. As leader of the newly formed Cambio 90 (Change 90) he campaigned on a reformist ticket and defeated his more experienced Democratic Front opponent. Lacking an assembly majority and faced with increasing opposition to his policies, he imposed military rule early 1992. In 1993 a plebiscite narrowly approved his constitutional reform proposals, allowing him to seek re-election 1995.

Fujiyama or *Mount Fuji* Japanese volcano and highest peak, on Honshu Island, near Tokyo; height 12,400 ft/ 3,778 m. Extinct since 1707, it has a ◊Shinto shrine and a weather station on its summit. Fuji has long been revered for its picturesque cone-shaped crater peak, and figures prominently in Japanese art, literature, and religion.

Fuller (Richard) Buckminster 1895–1983. US architect, engineer, and social philosopher. He embarked on an unorthodox career in an attempt to maximize energy resources through improved technology. In 1947 he invented the lightweight geodesic dome, a hemispherical space-frame of triangular components

linked by rods, independent of buttress or vault and capable of covering large-span areas. Within 30 years over 50,000 had been built.

fullerene form of carbon, discovered 1985, based on closed cages of carbon atoms. The molecules of the most symmetrical of the fullerenes are called ◊buckminsterfullerenes (or buckyballs). They are perfect spheres made up of 60 carbon atoms linked together in 12 pentagons and 20 hexagons fitted together like those of a spherical football. Other fullerenes with 28, 32, 50, 70, and 76 carbon atoms have also been identified.

fulmar any of several species of petrels of the family Procellariidae, which are similar in size and color to herring gulls. The northern fulmar *Fulmarus glacialis* is found in the N Atlantic and visits land only to nest, laying a single egg.

Fulton Robert 1745–1815. US gunsmith, artist, engineer, and inventor. He designed steamships based on those invented by James Rumsey 1787 and John Fitch 1790. With French support he built the first submarine, the *Nautilus* 1801. Combining the British-built steam engine with his own design of riverboat, a sidewheeler, he built and registered the *North River Steam Boat* 1807 (now erroneously known as the *Clermont*).

fumitory any plant of the genus *Fumeria*, family Fumariaceae, native to Europe and Asia. The common fumitory *F. officinalis* grows to 20 in/50 cm tall, and produces pink flowers tipped with blackish red; it has been used in medicine for stomach and liver complaints.

function in computing, a small part of a program that supplies a specific value—for example, the square root of a specified number, or the current date. Most programming languages incorporate a number of built-in functions; some allow programmers to write their own. A function may have one or more arguments (the values on which the function operates). A *function key* on a keyboard is one that, when pressed, performs a designated task, such as ending a program.

Functionalism in architecture and design, the principle of excluding everything that serves no practical purpose. Central to 20th-century ◊Modernism, the Functionalist ethic developed as a reaction against the 19th-century practice of imitating and combining earlier styles. Its finest achievements are in the realms of ◊Industrial architecture and office furnishings.

fundamental constant physical quantity that is constant in all circumstances throughout the whole universe. Examples are the electric charge of an electron, the speed of light, Planck's constant, and the gravitational constant.

fundamental forces in physics, the four fundamental interactions believed to be at work in the physical universe. There are two long-range forces: *gravity*, which keeps the planets in orbit around the Sun, and acts between all ◊particles that have mass; and the *electromagnetic force*, which stops solids from falling apart, and acts between all particles with ◊electric charge. There are two very short-range forces: the *weak force*, responsible for radioactive decay and for other subatomic reactions; and the *strong force*, which binds together the protons and neutrons in the nuclei of atoms.

fundamentalism in religion, an emphasis on basic principles or articles of faith. *Christian fundamentalism* emerged in the US just after World War I (as a

fuchsia Fuchsia flowers are bell-like and hang downward. The flowers attract honey bees and the fruits are eaten by birds.

reaction to theological modernism and the historical criticism of the Bible) and insisted on belief in the literal truth of everything in the Bible. *Islamic fundamentalism* insists on strict observance of Muslim Shari'a law.

In the 1950s a more moderate tendency broke off to form the evangelical movement, which claims to carry on the original intentions of Fundamentalism.

fungus (plural *fungi*) any of a group of organisms in the kingdom Fungi. Fungi are not considered plants. They lack leaves and roots; they contain no chlorophyll and reproduce by spores. Molds, yeasts, rusts, smuts, mildews, and mushrooms are all types of fungi.

fur the ◊hair of certain animals. Fur is an excellent insulating material and so has been used as clothing, although this is vociferously criticized by many groups on humane grounds. The methods of breeding or trapping animals are often cruel. Mink, chinchilla, and sable are among the most valuable, the wild furs being finer than the farmed. Fur such as mink is made up of a soft, thick, insulating layer called underfur and a top layer of longer, lustrous guard hairs.

Furies in Greek mythology, the Erinyes, appeasingly called the Eumenides ("kindly ones"). They were the daughters of Earth or of Night, represented as winged maidens with serpents twisted in their hair. They punished such crimes as filial disobedience, murder, inhospitality, and oath-breaking, but were also associated with fertility.

fusion in physics, the fusing of the nuclei of light elements, such as hydrogen, into those of a heavier element, such as helium. The resultant loss in their combined mass is converted into energy. Stars and thermonuclear weapons work on the principle of nuclear fusion.

So far no successful fusion reactor—one able to produce the required energy and contain the reaction— has been built. See ◊energy and ◊cold fusion.

futures trading buying and selling commodities (usually cereals and metals) at an agreed price for delivery several months ahead. The notional value of the futures contracts traded annually worldwide is $140,000 bn (1994). The volume of crude oil futures and options traded on the New York Mercantile Exchange amounts to 200 million barrels a day, almost four times the amount actually produced.

Futurism literary and artistic movement 1909–14, originating in Paris.

The Italian poet Marinetti published the *Futurist Manifesto* 1909 urging Italian artists to join him in Futurism. In their works the Futurists eulogized the modern world and the "beauty of speed and energy". Combining the shifting geometric planes of Cubism with vibrant colors, they aimed to capture the dynamism of a speeding automobile or train by the simultaneous repetition of forms. As a movement Futurism died out during World War I, but the Futurists' exultation in war and violence was seen as an early manifestation of ◊fascism.

Fuzhou or *Foochow* industrial port and capital of Fujian province, on Min River in SE China; population (1989) 1,270,000. It is a center for shipbuilding and steel production; rice, sugar, tea, and fruit pass through the port. There are joint foreign and Chinese factories.

fuzzy logic in mathematics and computing, a form of knowledge representation suitable for notions (such as "hot" or "loud") that cannot be defined precisely but depend on their context. For example, a jug of water may be described as too hot or too cold, depending on whether it is to be used to wash one's face or to make tea. The central idea of fuzzy logic is *probability of set membership*. For instance, referring to someone 5 ft 9 in/175 cm tall, the statement "this person is tall" (or "this person is a member of the set of tall people") might be about 70% true if that person is a man, and about 85% true if that person is a woman. Fuzzy logic enables computerized devices to reason more like humans, responding effectively to complex messages from their control panels and sensors.

G

g symbol for ◊*gram.*

G7 or *Group of Seven* the seven wealthiest nations in the world: the US, Japan, Germany, France, the UK, Italy, and Canada. Since 1975 their heads of government have met once a year to discuss economic and, increasingly, political matters. In 1994 Russia attended its fourth consecutive summit, raising expectations that it would eventually be asked to join the Group.

gabbro basic (low-silica) igneous rock formed deep in the Earth's crust. It contains pyroxene and calcium-rich feldspar, and may contain small amounts of olivine and amphibole. Its coarse crystals of dull minerals give it a speckled appearance.

Gable (William) Clark 1901–1960. US actor. A star for more than 30 years in 90 films, he played romantic roles such as Rhett Butler in *Gone with the Wind* 1939. His other films include *The Painted Desert* 1931 (his first), *It Happened One Night* 1934 (Academy Award), *Mutiny on the Bounty* 1935, and *The Misfits* 1961. He was nicknamed the "King of Hollywood".

Gabo Naum. Adopted name of Naum Neemia Pevsner 1890–1977. US abstract sculptor, born in Russia. One of the leading exponents of ◊Constructivism, he left the USSR for Germany 1922 and taught at the ◊Bauhaus in Berlin, a key center of design. He lived in Paris and England in the 1930s, then settled in the US 1946. He was one of the first artists to make kinetic sculpture and often used transparent colored plastics.

Gabon Gabonese Republic (*République Gabonaise*) *area* 103,319 sq mi/267,667 sq km *capital* Libreville *towns and cities* Port-Gentil and Owendo (ports); Masuku (Franceville) *physical* virtually the whole country is tropical rainforest; narrow coastal plain rising to hilly interior with savanna in E and S; Ogooué River flows N–W *features* Schweitzer hospital at Lambaréné; Trans-Gabonais railroad *head of state* Omar Bongo from 1964 *head of government* Casimir Oye-Mba from 1990 *political system* emergent democracy *political parties* Gabonese Democratic Party (PDG), nationalist; Morena Movement of National Recovery, left of center; Gabone Progress Party (PGP), left of center; National Rally of Woodcutters (RNB), centrist *exports* petroleum, manganese, uranium, timber *currency* CFA franc *population* (1993) 1,010,000 including 40 Bantu groups; growth rate 1.6% p.a. *life expectancy* men 52, women 55 *languages* French (official), Bantu *religions* Christian 96% (Roman Catholic 65%), small Muslim minority 1%, animist 3% *literacy* 61% *GNP* $3,780 per head (1991) *chronology* 1889 Gabon became part of the French Congo. *1960* Independence from France achieved; Léon M'ba became the first president. *1964* Attempted coup by rival party foiled with French help. M'ba died; he was succeeded by his protégé Albert-Bernard Bongo. *1968* One-party state established. *1973* Bongo reelected; converted to Islam, he changed his first name to Omar. *1986* Bongo reelected. *1989* Coup attempt against Bongo defeated. *1990* PDG won first multiparty elections since 1964 amid allegations of ballot rigging. *1993* Bongo reelected.

Gaborone capital of Botswana, mainly an administrative and government-service center; population (1990) 341,100. The University of Botswana and Swaziland (1976) is here. The city developed after it replaced Mafikeng as the country's capital 1965.

Gaddafi alternative form of ◊Quaddafi, Libyan leader.

gadolinium silvery-white metallic element of the lanthanide series, symbol Gd, atomic number 64, atomic weight 157.25. It is found in the products of nuclear fission and used in electronic components, alloys, and products needing to withstand high temperatures.

Gaelic language member of the Celtic branch of the Indo-European language family, spoken in Ireland, Scotland, and (until 1974) the Isle of Man.

Gaelic has been in decline for several centuries, discouraged until recently within the British state. There is a small Gaelic-speaking community in Nova Scotia, Canada.

Gagarin Yuri (Alexeyevich) 1934–1968. Soviet cosmonaut who in 1961 became the first human in space aboard the spacecraft *Vostok 1*.

Gaia or *Ge* in Greek mythology, the goddess of the Earth. She sprang from primordial Chaos and herself produced Uranus, by whom she was the mother of the Cyclopes and ◊Titans.

Gaia hypothesis theory that the Earth's living and nonliving systems form an inseparable whole that is regulated and kept adapted for life by living organisms themselves. The planet therefore functions as a single organism, or a giant cell. Since life and environment are so closely linked, there is a need for humans to understand and maintain the physical environment and living things around them. The hypothesis was elaborated by British scientist James (Ephraim) Lovelock (1919-) and first published in 1968.

gain in electronics, the ratio of the amplitude of the output signal produced by an amplifier to that of the input signal. In a voltage amplifier the voltage gain is the ratio of the output voltage to the input voltage; in an inverting operational amplifier (op-amp) it is equal to the ratio of the resistance of the feedback resistor to that of the input resistor.

Gainsborough Thomas 1727–1788. English landscape and portrait painter. In 1760 he settled in Bath and painted society portraits. In 1774 he went to London and became one of the original members of the Royal Academy. He was one of the first British artists to follow the Dutch example in painting realistic landscapes rather than imaginative Italianate scenery.

gal symbol for ◊*gallon*, ◊*galileo*.

Galahad in Arthurian legend, one of the knights of the Round Table. Galahad succeeded in the quest for the

◊Holy Grail because of his virtue. He was the son of Lancelot of the Lake.

Galápagos Islands (official name *Archipiélago de Colón*) group of 15 islands in the Pacific, belonging to Ecuador; area 3,000 sq mi/7,800 sq km; population (1982) 6,120. The capital is San Cristóbal on the island of the same name. The islands are a nature reserve. Their unique fauna (including giant tortoises, iguanas, penguins, flightless cormorants, and Darwin's finches, which inspired Charles ◊Darwin to formulate the principle of evolution by natural selection) is under threat from introduced species.

galaxy congregation of millions or billions of stars, held together by gravity. *Spiral galaxies*, such as the ◊Milky Way, are flattened in shape, with a central bulge of old stars surrounded by a disk of younger stars, arranged in spiral arms like a Catherine wheel. *Barred spirals* are spiral galaxies that have a straight bar of stars across their center, from the ends of which the spiral arms emerge. The arms of spiral galaxies contain gas and dust from which new stars are still forming. *Elliptical galaxies* contain old stars and very little gas. They include the most massive galaxies known, containing a trillion stars. At least some elliptical galaxies are thought to be formed by mergers between spiral galaxies. There are also irregular galaxies. Most galaxies occur in clusters, containing anything from a few to thousands of members.

Galbraith John Kenneth 1908– . Canadian-born US economist; he became a US citizen 1937. His major works include the *Affluent Society* 1958, in which he documents the tendency of the "invisible hand" of free-market capitalism to create private splendor and public squalor; *Economics and the Public Purpose* 1974; and *The Culture of Containment* 1992.

Galen *c.*130–*c.*200. Greek physician whose ideas dominated Western medicine for almost 1,500 years. Central to his thinking were the theories of humors and the threefold circulation of the blood. He remained the highest medical authority until Andreas Vesalius and William Harvey exposed the fundamental errors of his system.

Galilee, Sea of alternate name for Lake Tiberias in N Israel.

Galileo properly Galileo Galilei 1564–1642. Italian mathematician, astronomer, and physicist. He developed the astronomical telescope and was the first to see sunspots, the four main satellites of Jupiter, mountains and craters on the Moon, and the appearance of Venus going through "phases", thus proving it was orbiting the Sun. In mechanics, Galileo discovered that freely falling bodies, heavy or light, had the same, constant acceleration (although the story of his dropping cannonballs from the Leaning Tower of Pisa is questionable) and that a body moving on a perfectly smooth horizontal surface would neither speed up nor slow down.

gall bladder small muscular sac, part of the digestive system of most, but not all, vertebrates. In humans, it is situated on the underside of the liver and connected to the small intestine by the bile duct. It stores bile from the liver.

galley ship powered by oars, and usually also equipped with sails. Galleys typically had a crew of hundreds of oarsmen arranged in rows; they were used in warfare in the Mediterranean from antiquity until the 18th century.

gallium gray metallic element, symbol Ga, atomic number 31, atomic weight 69.75. It is liquid at room temperature. Gallium arsenide (GaAs) crystals are used in microelectronics, since electrons travel a thousand times faster through them than through silicon. The element was discovered in 1875 by Lecoq de Boisbaudran (1838–1912).

gallon unit of liquid measure, equal to 3.785 liters, and subdivided into four quarts or eight pints. The UK and Canadian imperial gallon is equivalent to 4.546 liters.

gallstone pebblelike, insoluble accretion formed in the human gall bladder or bile ducts from cholesterol or calcium salts present in bile. Gallstones may be symptomless or they may cause pain, indigestion, or jaundice. They can be dissolved with medication or removed, either by means of an endoscope, or, along with the gall bladder, in an operation known as cholecystectomy.

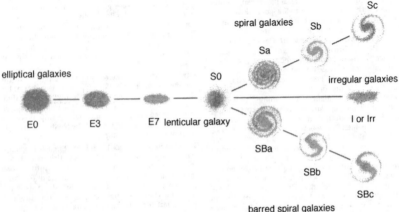

galaxy Galaxies were classified by US astronomer Edwin Hubble in 1925. He placed the galaxies in a "tuning-fork" pattern, in which the two prongs correspond to the barred and non-barred spiral galaxies.

Galsworthy John 1867–1933. English novelist and dramatist. His work examines the social issues of the Victorian period. He wrote *The Forsyte Saga* 1922 and its sequel *A Modern Comedy* 1929. His other novels include *The Country House* 1907 and *Fraternity* 1909; plays include *The Silver Box* 1906. Nobel Prize 1932.

Galway county on the W coast of the Republic of Ireland, in the province of Connacht; county town Galway; area 2,293 sq mi/5,940 sq km; population (1991) 180,300. Towns include Ballinasloe, Tuam, Clifden, and Loughrea (near which deposits of lead, zinc, and copper were found 1959).

Gama Vasco da *c*.1469–1524. Portuguese navigator who commanded an expedition in 1497 to discover the route to India around the Cape of Good Hope in modern South Africa. On Christmas Day 1497 he reached land, which he named Natal. He then crossed the Indian Ocean, arriving at Calicut May 1498, and returning to Portugal Sept 1499.

In 1502 he founded a Portuguese colony at Mozambique.

Gambia Republic of The *area* 4,018 sq mi/10,402 sq km *capital* Banjul *towns and cities* Serekunda, Bakau, Georgetown *physical* banks of the river Gambia flanked by low hills *features* smallest state in black Africa; stone circles; Karantaba obelisk marking spot where Mungo Park began his journey to the Niger River 1796 *head of state and government* (interim) Yahya Jammeh from 1994 *political system* interim military republic *political parties* Progressive People's Party (PPP), moderate centrist; National Convention Party (NCP), left of center *exports* groundnuts, palm oil, fish *currency* dalasi *population* (1993 est) 920,000; growth rate 1.9% p.a. *life expectancy* men 43, women 47 *languages* English (official), Mandinka, Fula and other native tongues *media* no daily newspaper; two official weeklies sell about 2,000 copies combined and none of the other independents more than 700 *religions* Muslim 90%, with animist and Christian minorities *literacy* men 39%, women 16% *GNP* $360 per head (1991) *chronology 1843* The Gambia became a crown colony. *1965* Independence achieved from Britain as a constitutional monarchy within the Commonwealth, with Dawda K. Jawara as prime minister. *1970* Declared itself a republic, with Jawara as president. *1972* Jawara reelected. *1981* Attempted coup foiled with the help of Senegal. *1982* Formed with Senegal the Confederation of Senegambia; Jawara reelected. *1987* Jawara reelected. *1989* Confederation of Senegambia dissolved. *1990* Gambian troops contributed to the stabilizing force in Liberia. *1994* Jawara ousted in military coup; Yahya Jammeh named as acting head of state.

gambling or *gaming* staking of money or anything else of value on the outcome of a competition. Forms of gambling include betting on sports results, casino games like blackjack and roulette, card games such as poker, and bridge, slot machines, or lotteries.

For many years certain forms of gambling were illegal in the US, but revenue needs in state and local governments led to the legalization of some gambling operations, such as casinos, state-wide lotteries, and off-track bookmakers.

Gambling is a multibillion-dollar operation worldwide and can be addictive. Gamblers Anonymous was set up in the US 1957 to help compulsive gamblers overcome their addiction.

gamete cell that functions in sexual reproduction by merging with another gamete to form a zygote.

Examples of gametes include sperm and egg cells. In most organisms, the gametes are haploid (they contain half the number of chromosomes of the parent), owing to reduction division or meiosis.

gamma radiation very high-frequency electromagnetic radiation, similar in nature to X-rays but of shorter wavelength, emitted by the nuclei of radioactive substances during decay or by the interactions of high-energy electrons with matter. Cosmic gamma rays have been identified as coming from pulsars, radio galaxies, and quasars, although they cannot penetrate the Earth's atmosphere.

gamma-ray astronomy the study of gamma rays from space. Much of the radiation detected comes from collisions between hydrogen gas and cosmic rays in our galaxy. Some sources have been identified, including the Crab nebula and the Vela pulsar (the most powerful gamma-ray source detected).

The US Gamma Ray Observatory was launched by US space shuttle *Atlantis* in April 1991 to study the gamma-ray sky for five years. The observatory cost $617 million and at 17 tons was the heaviest payload ever carried by space shuttle.

Gandhi (Mohandas Karamchand Gandhi, given the honorific name of *Mahatma* [Sanskrit "Great Soul"]) 1869–1948. Indian nationalist leader. A pacifist, he led the struggle for Indian independence from the UK by advocating nonviolent noncooperation (*satyagraha*, defense of and by truth) from 1915. He was imprisoned several times by the British authorities and was influential in the nationalist ◊Congress Party and in the independence negotiations 1947. He was assassinated by a Hindu nationalist in the violence that followed the partition of British India into India and Pakistan.

Gandhi Indira (born Nehru) 1917–1984. Indian politician, prime minister of India 1966–77 and 1980–84, and leader of the ◊Congress Party 1966–77 and subsequently of the Congress (I) party. She was assassinated 1984 by members of her Sikh bodyguard, resentful of her use of troops to clear malcontents from the Sikh temple at ◊Amritsar.

Gandhi Rajiv 1944–1991. Indian politician, prime minister from 1984 (following his mother Indira Gandhi's assassination) to Nov 1989. As prime minister, he faced growing discontent with his party's elitism and lack of concern for social issues. He was assassinated by a bomb at an election rally.

Ganges (Hindi *Ganga*) major river of India and Bangladesh; length 1,560 mi/2,510 km.

It is the most sacred river for Hindus.

Deforestation of the Ganges watershed has decreased the river's dry-season flow by 20%; the area regularly flooded in the wet season has increased about 40%; the annual cost of flood damage has risen from $120 million to $1 billion.

Gang of Four in Chinese history, the chief members of the radical faction that played a key role in directing the ◊Cultural Revolution and tried to seize power after the death of the communist leader Mao Zedong 1976. It included his widow, ◊Jiang Qing; the other members were three young Shanghai politicians: Zhang Chunqiao, Wang Hongwen, and Yao Wenyuan. The coup failed and the Gang of Four were arrested. Publicly tried in 1980, they were found guilty of treason.

gangrene death and decay of body tissue (often of a limb) due to bacterial action; the affected part gradually turns black and causes blood poisoning.

gannet N Atlantic seabird *Sula bassana* in the same family (Sulidae) as the boobies. When fully grown, it is white with black-tipped wings having a span of 5.6 ft/1.7 m. The young are speckled. It breeds on cliffs in nests made of grass and seaweed. Only one (white) egg is laid.

Gansu or *Kansu* province of NW China *area* 204,580 sq mi/530,000 sq km *capital* Lanzhou *features* subject to earthquakes; the "Silk Road" (now a motor road) passed through it in the Middle Ages, carrying trade to central Asia *industries* coal, oil, hydroelectric power from the Huang He (Yellow) River *population* (1990) 22,371,000, including many Muslims.

Ganymede in astronomy, the largest moon of the planet Jupiter, and the largest moon in the Solar System, 3,270 mi/5,260 km in diameter (larger than the planet Mercury). It orbits Jupiter every 7.2 days at a distance of 700,000 mi/1.1 million km. Its surface is a mixture of cratered and grooved terrain.

Garbo Greta. Adopted name of Greta Lovisa Gustafsson 1905–1990. Swedish-born US film actress. She went to the US 1925, and her captivating beauty and leading role in *Flesh and the Devil* 1927 made her one of Hollywood's greatest stars. Her later films include *Mata Hari* 1931, *Grand Hotel* 1932, *Queen Christina* 1933, *Anna Karenina* 1935, *Camille* 1936, and *Ninotchka* 1939. Her ethereal qualities and romantic mystery on the screen intermingled with her seclusion in private life. She retired 1941.

García Lorca Federico, Spanish poet. See ◊Lorca, Federico García.

García Márquez Gabriel 1928– . Colombian novelist. His sweeping novel *Cien años de soledad/One Hundred Years of Solitude* 1967 (which tells the story of a family over a period of six generations) is an example of magic realism, a technique used to heighten the intensity of realistic portrayal of social and political issues by introducing grotesque or fanciful material. Nobel Prize for Literature 1982.

gardenia subtropical and tropical trees and shrubs of Africa and Asia, genus *Gardenia*, of the madder family Rubiaceae, with evergreen foliage and flattened rosettes of fragrant waxen-looking blooms, often white in color.

Garibaldi Giuseppe 1807–1882. Italian soldier who played a central role in the unification of Italy by conquering Sicily and Naples 1860. From 1834 a member of the nationalist Mazzini's ◊Young Italy society, he was forced into exile until 1848 and again 1849–54. He fought against Austria 1848–49, 1859, and 1866, and led two unsuccessful expeditions to liberate Rome from papal rule in 1862 and 1867.

Garland Judy. Adopted name of Frances Gumm 1922–1969. US singer and actress. Her performances are marked by a compelling intensity. Her films include *The Wizard of Oz* 1939 (which featured the tune that was to become her theme song, "Over the Rainbow"), *Babes in Arms* 1939, *Strike Up the Band* 1940, *Meet Me in St Louis* 1944, *Easter Parade* 1948, *A Star is Born* 1954, and *Judgment at Nuremberg* 1961.

garlic perennial plant *Allium sativum* of the lily family Liliaceae, with white flowers. The bulb, made of small segments, or cloves, is used in cooking. Garlic has been used effectively as a fungicide in ◊sorghum. It also has antibacterial properties. Its effectiveness is probably due to allicin, a simple organic disulfide.

garnet group of silicate minerals with the formula $X_3Y_2(SiO_4)_3$, when X is calcium, magnesium, iron, or manganese, and Y is iron, aluminum, or chromium. Garnets are used as semiprecious gems (usually pink to deep red) and as abrasives.
They occur in metamorphic rocks such as gneiss and schist.

Garrick David 1717–1779. English actor and theater manager. From 1747 he became joint licensee of the Drury Lane Theatre with his own company, and instituted a number of significant theatrical conventions including concealed stage lighting and banishing spectators from the stage. He played Shakespearean characters such as Richard III, King Lear, Hamlet, and Benedick, and collaborated with George Colman (1732–1794) in writing the play *The Clandestine Marriage* 1766. He retired from the stage 1766, but continued as a manager.

Garrison William Lloyd 1805–1879. US editor and reformer who was an uncompromising opponent of slavery. He founded the abolitionist journal *The Liberator* 1831 and became a leader of the American Anti-Slavery Society. Although initially opposed to violence, he supported the Union cause in the Civil War. After the Emancipation Proclamation, he disbanded the Anti-Slavery Society and devoted his energies to prohibition, feminism, and Indian rights.
Born in Newburyport, Massachusetts, and trained as a printer, Garrison later worked as an editor of various publications in Boston, Vermont, and Baltimore.

Garrison, William Lloyd *Through his journal* The Liberator, *which he edited for over 30 years, US reformer William Lloyd Garrison denounced slavery, capital punishment, and war (though he supported the North in the American Civil War), and argued in favor of women's rights.*

Garvey Marcus (Moziah) 1887–1940. Jamaican political thinker and activist, an early advocate of black nationalism. He founded the UNIA (Universal Negro Improvement Association) in 1914, and moved to the US in 1916, where he established branches in New York and other northern cities. Aiming to achieve human rights and dignity for black people through black pride and economic self-sufficiency, he was considered one of the first militant black nationalists. He led a Back to Africa movement for black Americans to establish a black-governed country in Africa. The Jamaican cult of ◊Rastafarianism is based largely on his ideas.

gas in physics, a form of matter, such as air, in which the molecules move randomly in otherwise empty space, filling any size or shape of container into which the gas is put.

Gascony ancient province of SW France. With Guienne it formed the duchy of Aquitaine in the 12th century; Henry II of England gained possession of it through his marriage to Eleanor of Aquitaine in 1152, and it was often in English hands until 1451. It was then ruled by the king of France until it was united with the French royal domain 1607 under Henry IV.

gas exchange in biology, the exchange of gases between living organisms and the atmosphere, principally oxygen and carbon dioxide.

In animals, gas exchange is only respiratory (or using oxygen to convert food to energy). In plants, gas exchange is photosynthetic (or using carbon dioxide to make food) as well as respiratory.

Gaskell "Mrs" (Elizabeth Cleghorn, born Stevenson) 1810–1865. English novelist. Her most popular book, *Cranford* 1853, is the study of small, close-knit circle in a small town, modeled on Knutsford, Cheshire. Her other books, which often deal with social concerns, include *Mary Barton* 1848, *North and South* 1855, *Sylvia's Lovers* 1863–64, and the unfinished *Wives and Daughters* 1866. Also of note is her frank and sympathetic biography of her friend Charlotte ◊Brontë 1857.

gas mask face mask designed to filter out or neutralize chemical agents from the air inhaled by the wearer. The standard design consists of a molded face mask with goggles and a canister connected to the mask by a flexible pipe. The canister contains the protective chemicals and filters and they can easily be replaced by simply changing the canister.

gasoline mixture of hydrocarbons derived from petroleum, whose main use is as a fuel for internal combustion engines. It is colorless and highly volatile.

gasoline engine or *piston engine* the most commonly used source of power for motor vehicles, introduced by the German engineers Gottlieb Daimler and Karl Benz 1885. The gasoline engine is a complex piece of machinery made up of about 150 moving parts. It is a reciprocating piston engine (see ◊internal-combustion engine), in which a number of pistons move up and down in cylinders. The motion of the pistons rotates a crankshaft, at the end of which is a heavy flywheel. From the flywheel the power is transferred to the car's driving wheels via the transmission system of clutch, gearbox, and final drive.

gastroenteritis inflammation of the stomach and intestines, giving rise to abdominal pain, vomiting, and diarrhea. It may be caused by food or other poisoning, allergy, or infection. Dehydration may be severe and it is a particular risk in infants.

gastropod any member of a very large class (Gastropoda) of ◊mollusks. Gastropods are single-shelled (in a spiral or modified spiral form), have eyes on stalks, and move on a flattened, muscular foot. They have well-developed heads and rough, scraping tongues called radulae. Some are marine, some freshwater, and others land creatures, but all tend to inhabit damp places.

They include land snails, slugs, abalones, conches, coneshells, and cowries.

Gatling Richard Jordan 1818–1903. US inventor of a rapid-fire gun. Patented in 1862, the Gatling gun had ten barrels arranged as a cylinder rotated by a hand crank. Cartridges from an overhead hopper or drum dropped into the breech mechanism, which loaded, fired, and extracted them at a rate of 320 rounds per minute.

It was used in the Civil War and the Indian Wars that followed the settling of the American West. It was the precursor of the machine gun.

GATT acronym for ◊*General Agreement on Tariffs and Trade.*

Gaudí Antonio 1852–1926. Spanish architect. He is distinguished for his flamboyant ◊Art Nouveau style. Gaudí worked almost exclusively in Barcelona, designing both domestic and industrial buildings. He introduced color, unusual materials, and audacious technical innovations. His spectacular Church of the Holy Family, Barcelona, begun 1883, is still under construction.

gauge boson or *field particle* any of the particles that carry the four fundamental forces of nature (see ◊forces, fundamental). Gauge bosons are ◊elementary particles that cannot be subdivided, and include the photon, the graviton, the gluons, and the weakons.

Gauguin Paul 1848–1903. French Post-Impressionist painter. Going beyond the Impressionists' notion of reality, he sought a more direct experience of life in the rich colors of the South Sea islands and the magical rites of its people. His work, often heavily symbolic and decorative, is characterized by his sensuous use of pure colors. Among his paintings is *Le Christe jaune* 1889 (Albright-Knox Art Gallery, Buffalo, New York).

Gaul member of the Celtic-speaking peoples who inhabited France and Belgium in Roman times; also their territory. Certain Gauls invaded Italy around 400 BC, sacked Rome 387 BC, and settled between the Alps and the Apennines; this district, known as Cisalpine Gaul, was conquered by Rome in about 225 BC.

Gaulle Charles de. French politician, see Charles ◊de Gaulle.

Gaviria (Trujillo) Cesar 1947– . Colombian Liberal Party politician, president 1990–94; he was finance minister 1986–87 and minister of government 1987–89. He supported the extradition of drug traffickers wanted in the US and sought more US aid in return for stepping up the drug war.

Gawain in Arthurian legend, one of the knights of the Round Table who participated in the quest for the ◊Holy Grail. He is the hero of the 14th-century epic poem *Sir Gawayne and the Greene Knight.*

Gay John 1685–1732. English poet and dramatist. He wrote *Trivia* 1716, a verse picture of 18th-century London. His *The Beggar's Opera* 1728, a "Newgate pastoral" using traditional songs and telling of the love of Polly for highwayman Captain Macheath, was an extraordinarily popular success. Its satiric political touches led to the banning of *Polly*, a sequel.

gay politics political activity by homosexuals in pursuit of equal rights and an end to discrimination. A gay political movement first emerged in the late 1960s in New York with the founding of the Gay Liberation Front. It aimed to counter negative and critical attitudes to homosexuality and encouraged pride and solidarity among homosexuals.

Gazankulu ◊Black National State in Transvaal province, South Africa, with self-governing status from 1971; population (1985) 497,200.

Gaza Strip strip of land on the Mediterranean sea, under Israeli administration; capital Gaza; area 140 sq mi/363 sq km; population (1989) 645,000 of which 446,000 are refugees.

gazelle any of a number of species of lightly built, fast-running antelopes found on the open plains of Africa and S Asia, especially those of the genus *Gazella*.

Gdansk (German *Danzig*) Polish port; population (1990) 465,100. Oil is refined, and textiles, televisions, and fertilizers are produced. In the 1980s there were repeated antigovernment strikes at the Lenin shipyards.

GDP abbreviation for ◊*gross domestic product*.

gear toothed wheel that transmits the turning movement of one shaft to another shaft. Gear wheels may be used in pairs, or in threes if both shafts are to turn in the same direction. The gear ratio—the ratio of the number of teeth on the two wheels—determines the torque ratio, the turning force on the output shaft compared with the turning force on the input shaft. The ratio of the angular velocities of the shafts is the inverse of the gear ratio.

gecko any lizard of the family Gekkonidae. Geckos are common worldwide in warm climates, and have large heads and short, stout bodies. Many have no eyelids. Their adhesive toe pads enable them to climb vertically and walk upside down on smooth surfaces in their search for flies, spiders, and other prey.

The Texas banded gecko *Coleonyx brevis*, 4.5 in/12 cm long, is unusual in that it has no toe pads.

gazelle Thomson's gazelle from the open plains of Sudan, Kenya, and N Tanzania has a distinctive dark stripe along its sides. There are 15 races of Thomson's gazelle, varying only slightly in color and horn size.

Geiger counter any of a number of devices used for detecting nuclear radiation and/or measuring its intensity by counting the number of ionizing particles produced (see ◊radioactivity). It detects the momentary current that passes between ◊electrodes in a suitable gas when a nuclear particle or a radiation pulse causes the ionization of that gas. The electrodes are connected to electronic devices that enable the number of particles passing to be measured. The increased frequency of measured particles indicates the intensity of radiation. It is named for Hans Geiger.

German physicist Hans Geiger studied in Manchester, England, under Ernest ◊Rutherford, and was professor of physics at Kiel, Germany.

Geingob Hage Gottfried 1941– . Namibian politician, prime minister from 1990. Geingob was appointed founding director of the United Nations Institute for Namibia in Lusaka, 1975. He became the first prime minister of an independent Namibia March 1990.

Geisel Theodor Seuss, better known as *Dr Seuss* 1904–1991. US author. He wrote children's books including *And to Think That I Saw It on Mulberry Street* 1937 and the classic *Horton Hatches the Egg* 1940. After winning Academy Awards for documentary films 1946 and 1947, he returned to writing children's books, including *Horton Hears a Who* 1954 and *The Cat in the Hat* 1957.

gel solid produced by the formation of a three-dimensional cage structure, commonly of linked large-molecular-mass polymers, in which a liquid is trapped. It is a form of ◊colloid. A gel may be a jellylike mass (pectin, gelatin) or have a more rigid structure (silica gel).

gelatin water-soluble protein prepared from boiled hide and bone, used in cooking to set jellies, and in glues and photographic emulsions.

Gell-Mann Murray 1929– . US physicist. In 1964 he formulated the theory of the ◊quark as one of the fundamental constituents of matter. In 1969 he was awarded a Nobel Prize for his work on elementary particles and their interaction.

gem mineral valuable by virtue of its durability (hardness), rarity, and beauty, cut and polished for ornamental use, or engraved. Of 120 minerals known to have been used as gemstones, only about 25 are in common use in jewelry today; of these, the diamond, emerald, ruby, and sapphire are classified as precious, and all the others semiprecious, for example the topaz, amethyst, opal, and aquamarine.

Gemini prominent zodiacal constellation in the northern hemisphere represented as the twins Castor and Pollux. Its brightest star is Pollux; Castor is a system of six stars. The Sun passes through Gemini from late June to late July. Each Dec, the Geminid meteors radiate from Gemini. In astrology, the dates for Gemini are between about May 21 and June 21 (see ◊precession).

gen. in grammar, the abbreviation for *genitive*.

gender in grammar, one of the categories into which nouns are divided in many languages, such as masculine, feminine, and neuter (as in Latin, German, and Russian), masculine and feminine (as in French, Italian, and Spanish), or animate and inanimate (as in some North American Indian languages).

gene unit of inherited material, encoded by a strand of ◊DNA, and transcribed by ◊RNA. In higher organisms, genes are located on the ◊chromosomes. The term "gene", coined 1909 by the Danish geneticist Wilhelm Johannsen (1857–1927), refers to the inherited factor that consistently affects a particular character in an individual—for example, the gene for eye color. Also termed a Mendelian gene, after Austrian biologist Gregor Mendel, it occurs at a particular point or locus on a particular chromosome and may have several variants or ◊alleles, each specifying a particular form of that character—for example, the alleles for blue or brown eyes. Some alleles show dominance. These mask the effect of other alleles known as recessive.

genealogy the study and tracing of family histories.

In the US there are many genealogical societies that trace people's descent and some groups, such as the Daughters of the American Revolution, limit membership to those who can demonstrate a particular lineage.

gene bank collection of seeds or other forms of genetic material, such as tubers, spores, bacterial or yeast cultures, live animals and plants, frozen sperm and eggs, or frozen embryos. These are stored for possible future use in agriculture, plant and animal breeding, or in medicine, genetic engineering, or the restocking of wild habitats where species have become extinct. Gene banks will be increasingly used as the rate of extinction increases, depleting the Earth's genetic variety (biodiversity).

General Agreement on Tariffs and Trade (GATT) organization within the United Nations founded 1948 with the aim of encouraging ◊free trade between nations through low tariffs, abolitions of quotas, and curbs on subsidies.

General Motors the US's largest company, a vehicle manufacturer founded 1908 in Flint, Michigan, from a number of small carmakers; it went on to acquire many more companies, including those that produced the Oldsmobile, Pontiac, Cadillac, and Chevrolet. It has headquarters in Detroit and New York.

generation in computing, stage of development in computer electronics (see ◊computer generation) or a class of programming language (see ◊fourth-generation language).

gene replacement therapy (GRT) hypothetical treatment for hereditary diseases in which affected cells from a sufferer would be removed from the body, the ◊DNA repaired in the laboratory (◊genetic engineering), and the functioning cells reintroduced. Successful experiments have been carried out on animals.

genet small, nocturnal, meat-eating mammal, genus *Genetta*, in the mongoose and civet family (Viverridae). Most species live in Africa, but *G. genetta* is also found in Europe and the Middle East. It is about 1.6 ft/50 cm long with a 1.5 ft/45 cm tail, and grayish yellow with rows of black spots. It climbs well.

gene therapy proposed medical technique for curing or alleviating inherited diseases or defects; certain infections, and several kinds of cancer; see ◊gene replacement therapy. In 1990 a genetically engineered gene was used for the first time to treat a patient.

genetic code the way in which instructions for building proteins, the basic structural molecules of living matter, are "written" in the genetic material ◊DNA. This relationship between the sequence of bases (the subunits in a DNA molecule) and the sequence of ◊amino acids (the subunits of a protein molecule) is the basis of heredity. The code employs codons of three bases each; it is the same in almost all organisms, except for a few minor differences recently discovered in some protozoa.

genetic engineering deliberate manipulation of genetic material by biochemical techniques. It is often achieved by the introduction of new ◊DNA, usually by means of a virus or plasmid. This can be for pure research or to breed functionally specific plants, animals, or bacteria. These organisms with a foreign gene added are said to be transgenic.

genetic fingerprinting or *genetic profiling* technique used for determining the pattern of certain parts of the genetic material ◊DNA that is unique to each individual. Like conventional fingerprinting, it can accurately distinguish humans from one another, with the exception of identical siblings from multiple births. It can be applied to as little material as a single cell.

Genetic fingerprinting was developed in the UK by Alec Jeffreys (1950–), and was first allowed as a means of legal identification at a court in Britain 1987. In 1995 the UK opened the world's first national DNA database for those convicted of serious offenses.

In 1993 a positive identification was made of the remains of a US soldier who had died in Vietnam 29 years before. Subsequently the US Defense Department launched a screening program, tracking tissue samples from military personnel for possible use in identification.

genetics study of inheritance and of the units of inheritance (◊genes). The founder of genetics was Austrian biologist Gregor Mendel, whose experiments with plants, such as peas, showed that inheritance takes place by means of discrete "particles", which later came to be called genes.

Geneva (French *Genève*) Swiss city, capital of Geneva canton, on the shore of Lake Geneva; population (1990) city 167,200; canton 376,000. It is a point of convergence of natural routes and is a cultural and commercial center. Industries include the manufacture of watches, scientific and optical instruments, foodstuffs, jewelry, and musical boxes.

Geneva Convention international agreement 1864 regulating the treatment of those wounded in war, and later extended to cover the types of weapons allowed, the treatment of prisoners and the sick, and the protection of civilians in wartime. The rules were revised at conventions held 1906, 1929, and 1949, and by the 1977 Additional Protocols.

Geneva, Lake (French *Lac Léman*) largest of the central European lakes, between Switzerland and France; area 225 sq mi/580 sq km.

Genghis Khan *c.* ?1167–1227. Mongol conqueror, ruler of all Mongol peoples from 1206. He began the conquest of N China 1213, overran the empire of the shah of Khiva 1219–25, and invaded N India, while his lieutenants advanced as far as the Crimea. When he died, his empire ranged from the Yellow Sea to the Black Sea; it continued to expand after his death to extend from Hungary to Korea. Genghis Khan controlled probably a larger area than any other individual in history. He was not only a great military leader, but the creator of a stable political system.

genitive in the grammar of certain inflected languages, the form of a word used to indicate possession for nouns, pronouns, or adjectives.

Genoa (Italian *Genova*) historic city in NW Italy, capital of Liguria; population (1989) 706,700. It is Italy's largest port; industries include oil-refining, chemicals, engineering, and textiles.

genocide deliberate and systematic destruction of a national, racial, religious, or ethnic group defined by the exterminators as undesirable. The term is commonly applied to the policies of the Nazis during World War II (what they called the "final solution"—the extermination of all "undesirables" in occupied Europe, particularly the Jews). See ◊Holocaust.

genome the full complement of ◊genes carried by a single (haploid) set of ◊chromosomes. The term may be applied to the genetic information carried by an individual or to the range of genes found in a given species.

genotype the particular set of ◊alleles (variants of genes) possessed by a given organism. The term is usually used in conjunction with ◊phenotype, which is the product of the genotype and all environmental effects. See also ◊nature–nurture controversy.

genre a particular kind of work within an art form, differentiated by its structure, content, or style. For instance, the novel is a literary genre and the historical novel is a genre of the novel. The Western is a genre of film, and the symphonic poem is a musical genre.

Gentile da Fabriano *c*.1370–1427. Italian painter of frescoes and altarpieces. He was one of the most important exponents of the International Gothic style. Gentile was active in Venice, Florence, Siena, Orvieto, and Rome and collaborated with the artists Pisanello and Jacopo Bellini. His *Adoration of the Magi* 1423 (Uffizi, Florence) is typically rich in detail and color.

genus (plural *genera*) group of ◊species with many characteristics in common.

Thus all doglike species (including dogs, wolves, and jackals) belong to the genus *Canis* (Latin "dog"). Species of the same genus are thought to be descended from a common ancestor species. Related genera are grouped into ◊families.

Geoffrey of Monmouth *c*.1100–1154. Welsh writer and chronicler. While a canon at Oxford, he wrote *Historia Regum Britanniae/History of the Kings of Britain c*.1139, which included accounts of the semilegendary kings Lear, Cymbeline, and Arthur, and *Vita Merlini*, a life of the legendary wizard. He was bishop-elect of St Asaph, N Wales, 1151 and ordained a priest 1152.

geography the study of the Earth's surface; its topography, climate, and physical conditions, and how these factors affect people and society. It is usually divided into *physical geography*, dealing with landforms and climates, and *human geography*, dealing with the distribution and activities of peoples on Earth.

geological time time scale embracing the history of the Earth from its physical origin to the present day. Geological time is traditionally divided into eons (Phanerozoic, Proterozoic, and Archean), which in turn are divided into eras, periods, epochs, ages, and finally chrons.

geology science of the Earth, its origin, composition, structure, and history. It is divided into several branches: *mineralogy* (the minerals of Earth), *petrology* (rocks), *stratigraphy* (the deposition of successive beds of sedimentary rocks), *paleontology* (fossils), and *tectonics* (the deformation and movement of the Earth's crust).

geometry branch of mathematics concerned with the properties of space, usually in terms of plane (two-

dimensional) and solid (three-dimensional) figures. The subject is usually divided into **pure geometry**, which embraces roughly the plane and solid geometry dealt with in Euclid's *Elements*, and **analytical** or ◊**coordinate geometry**, in which problems are solved using algebraic methods. A third, quite distinct, type includes the non-Euclidean geometries.

George I 1660–1727. King of Great Britain and Ireland from 1714. He was the son of the first elector of Hanover, Ernest Augustus (1629–1698), and his wife Sophia, and a great-grandson of James I. He succeeded to the electorate 1698, and became king on the death of Queen Anne. He attached himself to the Whigs, and spent most of his reign in Hanover, never having learned English.

George II 1683–1760. King of Great Britain from 1727, when he succeeded his father, George I, whom he detested. He married Caroline of Anspach 1705. She supported Robert ◊Walpole's position as adviser, and Walpole rallied support for George during the ◊Jacobite rebellions against him.

George III 1738–1820. King of Great Britain and Ireland from 1760, when he succeeded his grandfather George II. His rule was marked by intransigence resulting in the loss of the American colonies, for which he shared the blame with his chief minister Lord North, and the emancipation of Catholics in England. Possibly suffering from porphyria, he had repeated attacks of insanity, permanent from 1811. He was succeeded by his son George IV.

George IV 1762–1830. King of Great Britain and Ireland from 1820, when he succeeded his father George III, for whom he had been regent during the king's period of insanity 1811–20. In 1785 he secretly married a Catholic widow, Maria Fitzherbert, but in 1795 also married Princess Caroline of Brunswick, in return for payment of his debts. He was a patron of the arts. His prestige was undermined by his treatment of Caroline (they separated 1796), his dissipation, and his extravagance. He was succeeded by his brother, the duke of Clarence, who became William IV.

George V 1865–1936. King of Great Britain from 1910, when he succeeded his father Edward VII. He was the second son, and became heir 1892 on the death of his elder brother Albert, Duke of Clarence. In 1893, he married Princess Victoria Mary of Teck (Queen Mary), formerly engaged to his brother. During World War I he made several visits to the front. In 1917, he abandoned all German titles for himself and his family. The name of the royal house was changed from Saxe-Coburg-Gotha (popularly known as Brunswick or Hanover) to Windsor.

George VI 1895–1952. King of Great Britain from 1936, when he succeeded after the abdication of his brother Edward VIII, who had succeeded their father George V. Created Duke of York 1920, he married in 1923 Lady Elizabeth Bowes-Lyon (1900–), and their children are Elizabeth II and Princess Margaret. During World War II, he visited the Normandy and Italian battlefields.

George, St patron saint of England. The story of St George rescuing a woman by slaying a dragon, evidently derived from the Perseus legend, first appears in the 6th century. The cult of St George was introduced into W Europe by the Crusaders. His feast day is April 23.

Georgetown capital and port of Guyana, situated at the mouth of the Demerara River on the Caribbean coast; population (1983) 188,000. There is food processing and shrimp fishing.

Georgetown or *Penang* chief port of the Federation of Malaysia, and capital of Penang, on the island of Penang; population (1980) 250,600. It produces textiles and toys.

Georgia state in SE US; nicknames Empire State of the South/Peach State *area* 152,600 sq km/58,904 sq mi *capital* Atlanta *towns and cities* Columbus, Savannah, Macon *features* Okefenokee National Wildlife Refuge (656 sq mi/1,700 sq km), Sea Islands, historic Savannah *industries* poultry, livestock, tobacco, corn, peanuts, cotton, soy beans, china clay, crushed granite, textiles, carpets, aircraft, paper products *population* (1990) 6,478,200 *famous people* Jim Bowie; Erskine Caldwell; Jimmy Carter; Ray Charles; Ty Cobb; Bobby Jones; Martin Luther King, Jr.; Margaret Mitchell; James Oglethorpe; Jackie Robinson *history* explored 1540 by Hernando de Soto; claimed by the British and named for George II of England; founded 1733 as a colony for the industrious poor by James Oglethorpe, a philanthropist; one of the original 13 states of the US. During the Civil War, it suffered from US General Sherman's fierce march to the sea.

Georgia Republic of *area* 26,911 sq mi/69,700 sq km *capital* Tbilisi *towns and cities* Kutaisi, Rustavi, Batumi, Sukhumi *physical* largely mountainous with a variety of landscape from the subtropical Black Sea shores to the ice and snow of the crest line of the Caucasus; chief rivers are Kura and Rioni *features* vacation resorts and spas on the Black Sea; good climate; two autonomous republics, Abkhazia and Adzharia; one autonomous region, South Ossetia *head of state* Eduard Shevardnadze from 1992 *head of government* Otar Patsatsia from 1993 *political system* emergent democracy *political parties* Georgian Popular Front, nationalist; National Democratic Party of Georgia, left of center; National Independence Party, nationalist; Georgian Social Democratic Party, centrist *products* tea, citrus and orchard fruits, tung oil, tobacco, vines, silk, hydroelectricity *currency* lari *population* (1993 est) 5,600,000 (Georgian 70%, Armenian 8%, Russian 8%, Azeri 6%, Ossetian 3%, Abkhazian 2%) *life expectancy* men 69, women 76 *language* Georgian *media* criticism of authorities banned on TV and radio 1993; restrictions on independent press *religion* Georgian Church, independent of the Russian Orthodox Church since 1917 *GNP* $1,640 per head (1991) *chronology 1918–21* Independent republic. *1921* Uprising quelled by Red Army and Soviet republic established. *1922–36* Linked with Armenia and Azerbaijan as the Transcaucasian Republic. *1936* Became separate republic within USSR. *1972* Drive against corruption by Georgian Communist Party (GCP) leader Eduard Shevardnadze. *1978* Outbreaks of violence by nationalists. *1981–88* Increasing demands for autonomy, spearheaded from 1988 by the Georgian Popular Front. *1989* March–April: Abkhazians demanded secession from Georgia, provoking interethnic clashes. April: GCP leadership purged. July: state of emergency imposed on Abkhazia; interethnic clashes in South Ossetia. Nov: sovereignty declared. *1990* Oct: nationalist coalition triumphed in supreme-soviet elections. Nov: Zviad Gamsakhurdia became president. Dec: GCP seceded from Communist Party of USSR; calls for Georgian independence. *1991* April: declared independence.

May: Gamsakhurdia popularly elected president. Aug: GCP outlawed and all relations with USSR severed. Sept: anti-Gamsakhurdia demonstrations; state of emergency declared. Dec: Georgia failed to join new Commonwealth of Independent States (CIS). *1992* Jan: Gamsakhurdia fled to Armenia; Tengiz Sigua appointed prime minister. Eduard Shevardnadze appointed interim president. July: admitted into United Nations (UN). Aug: fighting between Georgian troops and separatists in Abkhazia. Oct: Shevardnadze elected chair of new parliament. Clashes in South Ossetia and Abkhazia continued. *1993* Conflict with Abkhazi separatists intensified; Shevardnadze forced to seek Russian military help. Georgia joined CIS. Nov: pro-Gamsakhurdia revolt put down by government forces. Gamsakhurdia found dead. *1994* Feb: Abkhazi separatists agreed to UN peacekeeping force. Military cooperation pact signed with Russia.

geostationary orbit circular path 22,300 mi/35,900 km above the Earth's equator on which a ◊satellite takes 24 hours, moving from west to east, to complete an orbit, thus appearing to hang stationary over one place on the Earth's surface. Geostationary orbits are used particularly for communications satellites and weather satellites. They were first thought of by the author Arthur C Clarke. A *geosynchronous orbit* lies at the same distance from Earth but is inclined to the equator.

geothermal energy energy extracted for heating and electricity generation from natural steam, hot water, or hot dry rocks in the Earth's crust. Water is pumped down through an injection well where it passes through joints in the hot rocks. It rises to the surface through a recovery well and may be converted to steam or run through a heat exchanger. Dry steam may be directed through turbines to produce electricity. It is an important source of energy in volcanically active areas such as Iceland and New Zealand.

ger. in grammar, the abbreviation for ◊*gerund*.

geranium or cranesbill, plant of the genus *Geranium*, family Geraniaceae, which contains about 400 species. The plants are named after the long, beaklike process attached to the seed vessels.

When ripe, this splits into coiling spirals, which jerk the seeds out, assisting in their distribution.

gerbil any of numerous rodents of the family Cricetidae with elongated back legs and good hopping or jumping ability. Gerbils range from mouse-to rat-size, and have hairy tails. Many of the 13 genera live in dry, sandy, or sparsely vegetated areas of Africa and Asia.

Géricault Théodore (Jean Louis André) 1791–1824. French Romantic painter and graphic artist. *The Raft of the Medusa* 1819 (Louvre, Paris) was notorious in its day for exposing a relatively recent scandal in which shipwrecked sailors had been cut adrift and left to drown. His other works include *The Derby at Epsom* 1821 (Louvre, Paris) and pictures of cavalry. He also painted portraits, including remarkable studies of the insane, such as *A Kleptomaniac* 1822–23 (Musée des Beaux Arts, Ghent).

German native to or an inhabitant of Germany and their descendants, as well as their culture and language. In eastern Germany the Sorbs comprise a minority population who, in addition to German, speak a Slavic language. The Austrians and Swiss Germans speak German, although they are ethnically distinct. German-speaking minorities are found in France (Alsace-Lorraine), Romania (Transylvania), Czech Republic, Siberian Russia, Central Asia, Poland, Italy (Tyrol), and in areas that once belonged to the German Empire abroad.

Germanic languages branch of the Indo-European language family, divided into *East Germanic* (Gothic, now extinct), *North Germanic* (Danish, Faeroese, Icelandic, Norwegian, Swedish), and *West Germanic* (Afrikaans, Dutch, English, Flemish, Frisian, German, Yiddish).

germanium brittle, gray-white, weakly metallic (◊metalloid) element, symbol Ge, atomic number 32, relative atomic mass 72.6. It belongs to the silicon group, and has chemical and physical properties between those of silicon and tin. Germanium is a semiconductor material and is used in the manufacture of transistors and integrated circuits. The oxide is transparent to infrared radiation, and is used in military applications. It was discovered 1886 by German chemist Clemens Winkler (1838–1904).

German measles or *rubella* mild, communicable virus disease, usually caught by children. It is marked by a sore throat, pinkish rash, and slight fever, and has an incubation period of two to three weeks. If a woman contracts it in the first three months of pregnancy, it may cause serious damage to the unborn child.

For this reason immunization is recommended for girls.

Germany Federal Republic of (*Bundesrepublik Deutschland*) *area* 137,853 sq mi/357,041 sq km *capital* Berlin *towns and cities* Cologne, Munich, Essen, Frankfurt-am-Main, Dortmund, Stuttgart, Düsseldorf, Leipzig, Dresden, Chemnitz, Magdeburg; ports Hamburg, Kiel, Cuxhaven, Bremerhaven, Rostock *physical* flat in N, mountainous in S with Alps; rivers Rhine, Weser, Elbe flow N, Danube flows SE, Oder, Neisse flow N along Polish frontier; many lakes, including Müritz *environment* acid rain causing *Waldsterben* (tree death) affects more than half the country's forests; industrial E Germany has the highest sulfur-dioxide emissions in the world per head of population *features* Black Forest, Harz Mountains, Erzgebirge (Ore Mountains), Bavarian Alps, Fichtelgebirge, Thüringer Forest *head of state* Roman Herzog from 1994 *head of government* Helmut Kohl from 1982 *political system* liberal democratic federal republic *political parties* Christian Democratic Union (CDU), right of center; Christian Social Union (CSU), right of center; Social Democratic Party (SPD), left of center; Free Democratic Party (FDP), liberal; Greens, environmentalist; Republicans, far right; Party of Democratic Socialism (PDS), reform-communist (formerly Socialist Unity Party: SED) *exports* machine tools (world's leading exporter), automobiles, commercial vehicles, electronics, industrial goods, textiles, chemicals, iron, steel, wine, lignite (world's largest producer), uranium, coal, fertilizers, plastics *currency* Deutschmark *population* (1993 est) 80,800,000 (including nearly 5,000,000 "guest workers", *Gastarbeiter*, of whom 1,600,000 are Turks; the rest are Yugoslav, Italian, Greek, Spanish, and Portuguese); growth rate –0.7% p.a. *life expectancy* men 72, women 78 *languages* German, Sorbian *religions* Protestant 42%, Roman Catholic 35% *literacy* 99% *GNP* $23,650 per head (1991) *chronology 1945* Germany surrendered; country divided into four occupation zones (US, French, British, Soviet). *1948* Blockade of West Berlin. *1949* Establishment of

Federal Republic under the "Basic Law" Constitution with Konrad Adenauer as chancellor; establishment of the German Democratic Republic as an independent state. *1953* Uprising in East Berlin suppressed by Soviet troops. *1954* Grant of full sovereignty to both West Germany and East Germany. *1957* West Germany was a founder-member of the European Economic Community; recovery of Saarland from France. *1961* Construction of Berlin Wall. *1963* Retirement of Chancellor Adenauer. *1964* Treaty of Friendship and Mutual Assistance signed between East Germany and USSR. *1969* Willy Brandt became chancellor of West Germany. *1971* Erich Honecker elected SED leader in East Germany. *1972* Basic Treaty between West Germany and East Germany; treaty ratified 1973, normalizing relations between the two. *1974* Resignation of Brandt; Helmut Schmidt became chancellor. *1975* East German friendship treaty with USSR renewed for 25 years. *1982* Helmut Kohl became West German chancellor. *1987* Official visit of Honecker to the Federal Republic. *1988* Death of Franz-Josef Strauss, leader of the West German Bavarian CSU. *1989* West Germany: rising support for far right in local and European elections, declining support for Kohl. East Germany: mass exodus to West Germany began. Honecker replaced by Egon Krenz. National borders opened in Nov, including Berlin Wall. Reformist Hans Modrow appointed prime minister. Krenz replaced. *1990* March: East German multi-party elections won by coalition led by right-wing CDU. Oct 3: official reunification of East and West Germany. Dec 2: first all-German elections since 1932, resulting in a victory for Kohl. *1991* Kohl's popularity declined after tax increase. The CDU lost its Bundesrat majority to the SPD. Violent attacks on foreigners. *1992* Neo-Nazi riots against immigrants continued. *1993* Severe recession. Racist violence continued. Restrictions on refugee admission introduced. *1994* Kohl's nominee, Roman Herzog, elected president. CDU returned to power in general election, but with wafer-thin majority.

Germany, East (German Democratic Republic, GDR) country 1949–90, formed from the Soviet zone of occupation in the partition of Germany following World War II. East Germany became a sovereign state 1954, and was reunified with West Germany Oct 1990. For history before 1949, see ◊Germany: history;

for history after 1949, see ◊Germany, Federal Republic of.

Germany, West (Federal Republic of Germany) country 1949–90, formed from the British, US, and French occupation zones in the partition of Germany following World War II; reunified with East Germany Oct 1990. For history before 1949, see ◊Germany: history; for history after 1949, see ◊Germany, Federal Republic of.

germination in botany, the initial stages of growth in a seed, spore, or pollen grain. Seeds germinate when they are exposed to favorable external conditions of moisture, light, and temperature, and when any factors causing dormancy have been removed.

Geronimo 1829–1909. Chief of the Chiricahua Apache Indians and war leader. From 1875 to 1885, he fought US federal troops, as well as settlers encroaching on tribal reservations in the Southwest, especially in SE Arizona and New Mexico.

Geronimo fell from his horse following a drinking spree and lay on the cold ground overnight, resulting in his death from pneumonia.

Geronimo *Apache Indian chief Geronimo, who led his people against white settlers in Arizona for over ten years, shown here after his surrender 1886. He subsequently became a prosperous Christian farmer in Oklahoma and a national celebrity.*

Gershwin George 1898–1937. US composer. He wrote concert works including the tone poems *Rhapsody in Blue* 1924 and *An American in Paris* 1928, and popular

musicals and songs, many with lyrics by his brother *Ira Gershwin* (1896–1983), including "I Got Rhythm", "'S Wonderful", and "Embraceable You". His opera *Porgy and Bess* 1935 incorporated jazz rhythms and popular song styles in an operatic format.

gerund in the grammar of certain languages, such as Latin, a noun formed from a verb and functioning as a noun to express an action or state. In English, gerunds end in *-ing* and look identical to the present ◊participle.

Gesell Arnold Lucius 1880–1961. US psychologist and educator. He founded the Yale Clinic of Child Development which he directed 1911–48. Among the first to study the stages of normal development, he worked as a consultant to the Gesell Institute of Child Development, New Haven, Connecticut, which was founded 1950 to promote his educational ideas.

Gesell, born in Alma, Wisconsin, Gesell received his PhD from Clark University 1906. Appointed to the Yale University faculty, he received a medical degree from Yale 1915 and became a professor of child hygiene, publishing both scholarly and popular works on child psychology.

Gestapo (contraction of *Geheime Staatspolizei*) Nazi Germany's secret police, formed 1933, and under the direction of Heinrich ◊Himmler from 1934.

gestation in all mammals except the ◊monotremes (platypus and spiny anteaters), the period from the time of implantation of the embryo in the uterus to birth. This period varies among species; in humans it is about 266 days, in elephants 18–22 months, in cats about 60 days, and in some species of marsupial (such as opossum) as short as 12 days.

Getty J(ean) Paul 1892–1976. US oil billionaire, president of the Getty Oil Company from 1947, and founder of the Getty Museum (housing the world's highest-funded art collections) in Malibu, California.

Gettysburg site in Pennsylvania of a decisive battle won by the North in the ◊Civil War 1863. The site is now a national cemetery, at the dedication of which President Lincoln delivered the *Gettysburg Address* Nov 19, 1863, a speech in which he reiterated the principles of freedom, equality, and democracy embodied in the US Constitution.

geyser natural spring that intermittently discharges an explosive column of steam and hot water into the air due to the build-up of steam in underground chambers. One of the most remarkable geysers is Old Faithful, in Yellowstone National Park, Wyoming, US. Geysers also occur in New Zealand and Iceland.

g-force force that pilots and astronauts experience when their craft accelerate or decelerate rapidly. One *g* is the ordinary pull of gravity.

Early astronauts were subjected to launch and reentry forces of up to six *g* or more; in the space shuttle, more than three *g* is experienced on liftoff. Pilots and astronauts wear *g*-suits that prevent their blood pooling too much under severe *g*-forces, which can lead to unconsciousness.

Ghana Republic of *area* 91,986 sq mi/238,305 sq km *capital* Accra *towns and cities* Kumasi, and ports Sekondi-Takoradi, Tema *physical* mostly tropical lowland plains; bisected by river Volta *environment* forested areas shrank from 3.17 million sq mi/8.2 million sq km at the beginning of the 20th century to 730,000 sq mi/1.9 million sq km by 1990 *features* world's largest artificial lake, Lake Volta; relics of traditional kingdom of Ashanti: 32,000 chiefs and kings **head of state and government** Jerry Rawlings from 1981 **political system** emergent democracy **political parties** National Democratic Congress (NDC), left of center, progovernment; National Convention Party (NCP), centrist, progovernment **exports** cocoa, coffee, timber, gold, diamonds, manganese, bauxite **currency** cedi **population** (1993 est) 16,700,000; growth rate 3.2% p.a. **life expectancy** men 54, women 58 **languages** English (official) and African languages **media** all media are government-controlled and the two daily newspapers are government-owned **religions** animist 38%, Muslim 30%, Christian 24% **literacy** men 70%, women 51% **GNP** $400 per head (1992) **chronology 1957** Independence achieved from Britain, within the Commonwealth, with Kwame Nkrumah as prime minister. **1960** Ghana became a republic, with Nkrumah as president. **1964** Ghana became a one-party state. **1966** Nkrumah deposed and replaced by General Joseph Ankrah. **1969** Ankrah replaced by General Akwasi Afrifa, who initiated a return to civilian government. **1970** Edward Akufo-Addo elected president. **1972** Another coup placed Col. Acheampong at the head of a military government. **1978** Acheampong deposed in a bloodless coup led by Frederick Akuffo; another coup put Flight-Lt Jerry Rawlings in power. **1979** Return to civilian rule under Hilla Limann. **1981** Rawlings seized power again, citing the incompetence of previous governments. All political parties banned. **1989** Coup attempt against Rawlings foiled. **1992** New multiparty constitution approved. Partial lifting of ban on political parties. Nov: Rawlings won presidency in national elections. **1993** Fourth republic of Ghana formally inaugurated.

Ghent (Flemish **Gent**, French **Gand**) city and port in East Flanders, NW Belgium; population (1991) 230,200. Industries include textiles, chemicals, electronics, and metallurgy. The cathedral of St Bavon (12th–14th centuries) has paintings by van Eyck and Rubens.

ghetto any deprived area occupied by a minority group, whether voluntarily or not. Originally a ghetto was the area of a town where Jews were compelled to live, decreed by a law enforced by papal bull 1555. The term came into use 1516 when the Jews of Venice were expelled to an island within the city which contained an iron foundry. Ghettos were abolished, except in E Europe, in the 19th century, but the concept and practice were revived by the Germans and Italians 1940–45.

Ghiberti Lorenzo 1378–1455. Italian sculptor and goldsmith. In 1402 he won the commission for a pair of gilded bronze doors for Florence's Baptistry. He produced a second pair (1425–52), the *Gates of Paradise*, one of the masterpieces of the early Italian Renaissance. They show a sophisticated use of composition and perspective, and the influence of Classical models.

GI abbreviation for *government issue*; hence (in the US) a common soldier.

Giacometti Alberto 1901–1966. Swiss sculptor and painter. He trained in Italy and Paris. In the 1930s, in his Surrealist period, he began to develop his characteristic spindly constructions. His mature style of emaciated, rough-textured, single figures in bronze, based on wire frames, emerged in the 1940s.

gibbon any of several small S Asian apes of the genus *Hylobates*, including the subgenus *Symphalangus*. The common or lar gibbon *H. lar* is about 2 ft/60 cm tall, with a body that is hairy except for the buttocks, which distinguishes it from other types of apes. Gibbons have long arms and no tail. They are arboreal in habit, and very agile when swinging from branch to branch. On the ground they walk upright, and are more easily caught by predators.

Gibbon Edward 1737–1794. English historian. He wrote one major work, arranged in three parts, *The History of the Decline and Fall of the Roman Empire* 1776–88, a continuous narrative from the 2nd century AD to the fall of Constantinople 1453.

Gibbs Josiah Willard 1839–1903. US theoretical physicist and chemist who developed a mathematical approach to thermodynamics. His book *Vector Analysis* 1881 established vector methods in physics.

In 1863 he gained the first engineering doctorate awarded in the US, and in 1871 he became professor of mathematical physics at Yale University, where he remained until his death.

Gibraltar British dependency, situated on a narrow rocky promontory in S Spain **area** 2.5 sq mi/6.5 sq km **features** strategic naval and air base, with NATO underground headquarters and communications center; colony of Barbary apes; the frontier zone is adjoined by the Spanish port of La Línea **exports** mainly a trading center for the import and reexport of goods **population** (1988) 30,000 **history** captured from Spain 1704 by English admiral George Rooke (1650–1709), it was ceded to Britain under the Treaty of Utrecht 1713. A referendum 1967 confirmed the wish of the people to remain in association with the UK, but Spain continues to claim sovereignty and closed the border 1969–85. In 1989, the UK government announced it would reduce the military garrison by half. Ground troops were withdrawn 1991, but navy and airforce units remained.

Gibraltar, Strait of strait between N Africa and Spain, with the Rock of Gibraltar to the N north side and Jebel Musa to the S, the so-called Pillars of Hercules.

Gibson Charles Dana 1867–1944. US illustrator. He portrayed an idealized type of American young woman, known as the "Gibson Girl."

Gibson was born in Roxbury, Massachusetts. He worked for *Life* magazine, eventually becoming its editor. He also illustrated books and later painted in oils.

Gide André 1869–1951. French novelist, playwright, and critic. His work is largely autobiographical and concerned with the conflict between desire and conventional morality. It includes *L'Immoraliste/The Immoralist* 1902, *La Porte étroite/Strait Is the Gate* 1909, *Les Caves du Vatican/The Vatican Cellars* 1914, and *Les Faux-monnayeurs/The Counterfeiters* 1926. He was a cofounder of the influential literary periodical *Nouvelle Revue française* and kept an almost lifelong *Journal*. Nobel Prize for Literature 1947.

Gielgud John 1904– . English actor and director. He is renowned as one of the greatest Shakespearean actors of his time. He made his debut at the Old Vic 1921, and his numerous stage appearances ranged from roles in works by Chekhov and Sheridan to those of Alan Bennett, Harold Pinter, and David Storey. Gielgud's films include *Becket* 1964, *Oh! What a Lovely War* 1969, *Providence* 1977, *Chariots of Fire* 1980, and *Prospero's Books* 1991. He won an Academy Award for his role as a butler in *Arthur* 1981.

Gilbert W(illiam) S(chwenk) 1836–1911. English humorist and dramatist. He collaborated with composer Arthur ◊Sullivan, providing the libretti for their series of light comic operas from 1871 performed by the ◊D'Oyly Carte Opera Company; they include *HMS Pinafore* 1878, *The Pirates of Penzance* 1879, and *The Mikado* 1885.

Gilbert and Ellice Islands former British colony in the Pacific, known since independence 1978 as the countries of ◊Tuvalu and ◊Kiribati.

Gilgamesh hero of Sumerian, Hittite, Akkadian, and Assyrian legend, and lord of the Sumerian city of Uruk. The 12 verse books of the *Epic of Gilgamesh* were recorded in a standard version on 12 cuneiform tablets by the Assyrian king Ashurbanipal's scholars in the 7th century BC , and the epic itself is older than Homer's *Iliad* by at least 1,500 years.

gill in biology, the main respiratory organ of most fishes and immature amphibians, and of many aquatic invertebrates. In all types, water passes over the gills, and oxygen diffuses across the gill membranes into the circulatory system, while carbon dioxide passes from the system out into the water.

gill imperial unit of volume for liquid measure, equal to one-quarter of a pint or four fluid ounces (0.118 liter).

Gillespie Dizzy (John Birks) 1917–1993. US jazz trumpeter. With Charlie ◊Parker, he was the chief creator and exponent of the ◊bebop style (*Groovin' High* is a CD re-issue of their seminal 78-rpm recordings). Gillespie influenced many modern jazz trumpeters, including Miles Davis.

Gingrich Newt (Newton Leyroy) 1943– . US Republican politician, leader of the House of Representatives from 1995. A radical-right "Reaganite", he was the driving force behind his party's sensational victory in the congressional elections Nov 1994, when it gained a house majority for the first time since 1954. On taking office, he sought to implement a conservative, populist manifesto designed to reduce federal powers, balance the budget, tackle crime, and limit congressional terms.

ginkgo or *maidenhair tree* tree *Ginkgo biloba* of the gymnosperm (or naked-seed-bearing) division of plants. It may reach a height of 100 ft/30 m by the time it is 200 years old.

Ginsberg (Irwin) Allen 1926– . US poet and political activist. His reputation as a visionary, overtly political poet was established by ◊*Howl* 1956, which expressed and shaped the spirit of the ◊Beat Generation and criticized the materialism of contemporary US society. His poetry draws heavily on Oriental philosophies and utilizes mantric breath meditations.

Ginsburg Ruth Joan Bader 1933– . US judge. Appointed Supreme Court justice by President Clinton 1993, she is only the second woman to serve on the court.

Ginsburg made her reputation as a civil liberties lawyer in the 1960s and 1970s, particularly with the six cases on gender equality she argued before the Supreme Court 1973–76. She won five, establishing a legal framework for women's rights.

In the late 1960s and early 1970s, Ginsburg acted as director of the Women's Rights Project of the American Civil Liberties Union. She later gained a reputation as a moderate, precise judge on the US Court of Appeals of the District of Columbia 1980–93.

giraffe *The giraffe is a specialized offshoot of the deer family. The giraffe family is now restricted to two species: the okapi and the giraffe itself. The irregular coloration of the giraffe varies greatly, both geographically and between individuals. Some animals are almost white or black, or have few markings.*

ginseng plant *Panax ginseng*, family Araliaceae, with a thick, forked aromatic root used in alternative medicine as a tonic.

Giorgione da Castelfranco (Giorgio Barbarelli) *c.*1475–1510. Italian Renaissance painter. He was active in Venice, and was probably trained by Giovanni Bellini.

Giotto di Bondone 1267–1337. Italian painter and architect. His influence on the development of painting in Europe was profound. He broke away from the conventions of International Gothic and introduced a naturalistic style, painting saints as real people, lifelike and expressive; an enhanced sense of volume and space also characterizes his work. He painted cycles of frescoes in churches at Assisi, Florence, and Padua.

giraffe world's tallest mammal, *Giraffa camelopardalis*, belonging to the ruminant family Giraffidae. It stands over 18 ft/5.5 m tall, the neck accounting for nearly half this amount.The skin has a mottled appearance and is reddish brown and cream. Giraffes are found only in Africa, south of the Sahara Desert.

Girl Scout female member of a ◊Scout organization founded 1910 in the UK by Robert Baden-Powell and his sister Agnes. It was established in the US in 1912 by Juliette Low. The World Association of Girl Guides (as they are known in the UK) and Girl Scouts has over 6.5 million members.

Girondist member of the right-wing republican party in the French Revolution, so called because a number of their leaders came from the Gironde region. They were driven from power by the ◊Jacobins 1793.

Giscard d'Estaing Valéry 1926– . French conservative politician, president 1974–81. He was finance minister to de Gaulle 1962–66 and Pompidou 1969–74. As leader of the Union pour la Démocratie

Française, which he formed in 1978, Giscard sought to project himself as leader of a "new center".

Gish Lillian. Adopted name of Lillian de Guiche 1896–1993. US film and stage actress. She worked with the director D W Griffith, playing virtuous heroines in *Way Down East* and *Orphans of the Storm* both 1920. Deceptively fragile, she made a notable Hester in Victor Sjöström's *The Scarlet Letter* (based on the novel by Nathaniel Hawthorne). Her career continued well into the 1980s with movies such as *The Whales of August* 1987.

She was the sister of the actress *Dorothy Gish* (1898–1968).

Gîza, El or *al-Jizah* site of the Great Pyramids and Sphinx; a suburb of ◊Cairo, Egypt; population (1983) 1,500,000. It has textile and film industries.

glacier tongue of ice, originating in mountains in snowfields above the snowline, which moves slowly downhill and is constantly replenished from its source. The scenery produced by the erosive action of glaciers is characteristic and includes ◊glacial troughs (U-shaped valleys), corries, and arêtes. In lowlands, the laying down of moraine (rocky debris once carried by glaciers) produces a variety of landscape features.

gladiator in ancient Rome, a trained fighter, recruited mainly from slaves, criminals, and prisoners of war, who fought to the death in arenas for the entertainment of spectators. The custom was introduced into Rome from Etruria in 264 BC and continued until the 5th century AD .

gladiolus any plant of the genus *Gladiolus* of S European and African cultivated perennials of the iris family Iridaceae, with brightly colored, funnel-shaped flowers, borne in a spike; the swordlike leaves spring from a corm.

Gladstone William Ewart 1809–1898. British Liberal politician, repeatedly prime minister. He entered Parliament as a Tory in 1833 and held ministerial office, but left the party 1846 and after 1859 identified himself with the Liberals. He was chancellor of the Exchequer 1852–55 and 1859–66, and prime minister 1868–74, 1880–85, 1886, and 1892–94. He introduced elementary education 1870 and vote by secret ballot 1872 and many reforms in Ireland, although he failed in his efforts to get a Home Rule Bill passed.

Glamorgan (Welsh *Morgannwg*) three counties of S Wales—◊Mid Glamorgan, ◊South Glamorgan, and West Glamorgan—created 1974 from the former county of Glamorganshire. All are on the Bristol Channel.

gland specialized organ of the body that manufactures and secretes enzymes, hormones, or other chemicals. In animals, glands vary in size from small (for example, tear glands) to large (for example, the pancreas), but in plants they are always small, and may consist of a single cell. Some glands discharge their products internally, ◊endocrine glands, and others, exocrine glands, externally. Lymph nodes are sometimes wrongly called glands.

glandular fever or *infectious mononucleosis* viral disease characterized at onset by fever and painfully swollen lymph nodes; there may also be digestive upset, sore throat, and skin rashes. Lassitude persists for months and even years, and recovery can be slow. It is caused by the Epstein–Barr virus.

Glaser Donald Arthur 1926– . US physicist who invented the bubble chamber in 1952, for which he received the Nobel Prize for Physics in 1960.

Born in Cleveland, Ohio, he was educated at the Case Institute of Technology, did research at the University of Michigan, and in 1960 became professor at the University of California.

Glasgow city and administrative headquarters of Strathclyde, Scotland; population (1991) 662,900. Industries include engineering, chemicals, printing, whiskey distilling and blending, brewing, electronics, and textiles.

glasnost former Soviet leader Mikhail ◊Gorbachev's policy of liberalizing various aspects of Soviet life, such as introducing greater freedom of expression and information and opening up relations with Western countries. *Glasnost* was introduced and adopted by the Soviet government 1986.

glass transparent or translucent substance that is physically neither a solid nor a liquid. Although glass is easily shattered, it is one of the strongest substances known. It is made by fusing certain types of sand (silica); this fusion occurs naturally in volcanic glass (see ◊obsidian).

Glass Philip 1937– . US composer. As a student of Nadia Boulanger, he was strongly influenced by Indian music; his work is characterized by repeated rhythmic figures that are continually expanded and modified. His compositions include the operas *Einstein on the Beach* 1976, *Akhnaten* 1984, *The Making of the Representative for Planet 8* 1988, and the *"Low" Symphony* 1992 on themes from David Bowie's *Low* album.

glass snake or *glass lizard* any of a worldwide genus *Ophisaurus* of legless lizards of the family Anguidae. Their tails are up to three times the head–body length and are easily broken off.

The eastern glass lizard *O. ventralis* grows to 36 in/ 1.1 m and inhabits wet grasslands in the SE US.

glaucoma condition in which pressure inside the eye (intraocular pressure) is raised abnormally as excess fluid accumulates. It occurs when the normal outflow of fluid within the chamber of the eye (aqueous humor) is interrupted. As pressure rises, the optic nerve suffers irreversible damage, leading to a reduction in the field of vision and, ultimately, loss of eyesight.

Glendower Owen *c.*1359–*c.*1416. (Welsh *Owain Glyndwr*) Welsh nationalist leader of a successful revolt against the English in N Wales, who defeated Henry IV in three campaigns 1400–02, although Wales was reconquered 1405–13. Glendower disappeared 1416 after some years of guerrilla warfare.

gliding the art of using air currents to fly unpowered aircraft. Technically, gliding involves the gradual loss of altitude; gliders designed for soaring flight (utilizing air rising up a cliff face or hill, warm air rising as a "thermal" above sun-heated ground, and so on) are known as sailplanes. The sport of ◊hang gliding was developed in the 1970s.

global warming projected imminent climate change attributed to the ◊greenhouse effect.

Glorious Revolution in British history, the events surrounding the removal of James II from the throne and his replacement by Mary (daughter of Charles I) and William of Orange as joint sovereigns in 1689. James had become increasingly unpopular on account of his unconstitutional behavior and Catholicism. Various elements in England, including seven prominent politicians, plotted to invite the Protestant William to invade. Arriving at Torbay on Nov 5, 1688, William rapidly gained support and James was allowed to flee to France after the army deserted him. William and Mary then accepted a new constitutional settlement, the Bill of Rights 1689, which assured the ascendency of parliamentary power over sovereign rule.

Gloucestershire county of SW England *area* 1,019 sq mi/2,640 sq km *towns and cities* Gloucester (administrative headquarters), Stroud, Cheltenham, Tewkesbury, Cirencester *features* Cotswold Hills; river Severn and tributaries; Berkeley Castle, where Edward II was murdered; Prinknash Abbey, where pottery is made; Cotswold Farm Park, near Stow-on-the-Wold, which has rare and ancient breeds of farm animals; Tewkesbury Abbey, with early 12th-century nave *industries* cereals, fruit, dairy products; engineering; coal in the Forest of Dean; timber *population* (1991) 528,400

glow-worm wingless female of some luminous beetles (fireflies) in the family Lampyridae. The luminous organs situated under the abdomen serve to attract winged males for mating. There are about 2,000 species, distributed worldwide.

glucose or *dextrose* or *grape-sugar* $C_6H_{12}O_6$ sugar present in the blood, and found also in honey and fruit juices. It is a source of energy for the body, being produced from other sugars and starches to form the "energy currency" of many biochemical reactions also involving ◊ATP.

glue-sniffing or *solvent misuse* inhalation of the fumes from organic solvents of the type found in paints, lighter fuel, and glue, for their hallucinatory effects. As well as being addictive, solvents are dangerous for their effects on the user's liver, heart, and lungs. It is believed that solvents produce hallucinations by dissolving the cell membrane of brain cells, thus altering the way the cells conduct electrical impulses.

gluon in physics, a ◊gauge boson that carries the strong nuclear force, responsible for binding quarks together to form the strongly interacting subatomic particles known as ◊hadrons. There are eight kinds of gluon.

glycerine another name for ◊glycerol.

glycerol or *glycerine* or *propan-1,2,3-triol* $HOCH_2CH(OH)CH_2OH$ thick, colorless, odorless, sweetish liquid. It is obtained from vegetable and animal oils and fats (by treatment with acid, alkali, superheated steam, or an enzyme), or by fermentation of glucose, and is used in the manufacture of high explosives, in antifreeze solutions, to maintain moist conditions in fruits and tobacco, and in cosmetics.

glycine $CH_2(NH_2)COOH$ the simplest amino acid, and one of the main components of proteins. When purified, it is a sweet, colorless crystalline compound.

gnat any of various small flies of the order Diptera, that sometimes suck blood. In Britain, mosquitoes are often called gnats.

gneiss coarse-grained ◊metamorphic rock, formed under conditions of increasing temperature and pressure, and often occurring in association with schists and granites. It has a foliated, laminated structure, consisting of thin bands of micas and/or amphiboles alternating with granular bands of quartz and feldspar. Gneisses are formed during regional metamorphism;

paragneisses are derived from sedimentary rocks and *orthogneisses* from igneous rocks. Garnets are often found in gneiss.

Gnosticism esoteric cult of divine knowledge (a synthesis of Christianity, Greek philosophy, Hinduism, Buddhism, and the mystery cults of the Mediterranean), which flourished during the 2nd and 3rd centuries and was a rival to, and influence on, early Christianity. The medieval French Cathar heresy and the modern Mandean sect (in S Iraq) descend from Gnosticism.

GNP abbreviation for ◊*gross national product*.

gnu or *wildebeest* either of two species of African ◊antelope, genus *Connochaetes*, with a cowlike face, a beard and mane, and heavy curved horns in both sexes. The body is up to 4.2 ft/1.3 m at the shoulder and slopes away to the hindquarters.

Goa state of India *area* 1,428 sq mi/3,700 sq km *capital* Panaji *population* (1991) 1,168,600 *features* Portuguese colonial architecture; church with remains of St Francis Xavier. *history* captured by the Portuguese 1510; the inland area was added in the 18th century. Goa was incorporated into India as a union territory with Daman and Diu 1961 and became a state 1987.

goat ruminant mammal of the genus *Capra* in the family Bovidae, closely related to the sheep. Both males and females have horns and beards. They are sure-footed animals, and feed on shoots and leaves more than on grass.

Gobi Desert Asian desert divided between the Mongolian People's Republic and Inner Mongolia, China; 500 mi/800 km N–S, and 1,000 mi/1,600 km E–W. It is rich in fossil remains of extinct species.

Gobind Singh 1666–1708. Indian religious leader, the tenth and last guru (teacher) of Sikhism, 1675–1708, and founder of the Sikh brotherhood known as the Khalsa. On his death, the Sikh holy book, the *Guru Granth Sahib*, replaced the line of human gurus as the teacher and guide of the Sikh community.

God the concept of a supreme being, a unique creative entity, basic to several monotheistic religions (for example Judaism, Christianity, Islam); in many polytheistic cultures (for example Norse, Roman, Greek), the term "god" refers to a supernatural being who personifies the force behind an aspect of life (for example Neptune, Roman god of the sea).

Godard Jean-Luc 1930– . French film director. He was one of the leaders of New Wave cinema. His works are often characterized by experimental editing techniques and an unconventional dramatic form. His films include *A bout de souffle/Breathless* 1959, *Vivre sa Vie/It's My Life* 1962, *Weekend* 1968, *Sauve qui peut (la vie)/Slow Motion* 1980, and *Je vous salue, Marie/Hail Mary* 1985.

Godiva Lady *c.*1040–1080. Wife of Leofric, earl of Mercia (died 1057). Legend has it that her husband promised to reduce the heavy taxes on the people of Coventry if she rode naked through the streets at noon. The grateful citizens remained indoors as she did so, but "Peeping Tom" bored a hole in his shutters and was struck blind.

Godthaab (Greenlandic *Nuuk*) capital and largest town of Greenland; population (1982) 9,700. It is a storage center for oil and gas, and the chief industry is fish processing.

Godunov Boris 1552–1605. Czar of Russia from 1598, elected after the death of Fyodor I, son of Ivan the

Terrible. He was assassinated by a pretender to the throne who professed to be Dmitri, a brother of Fyodor and the rightful heir. The legend that has grown up around this forms the basis of Pushkin's play *Boris Godunov* 1831 and Mussorgsky's opera of the same name 1874.

Goebbels (Paul) Josef 1897–1945. German Nazi leader. As minister of propaganda from 1933, he brought all cultural and educational activities under Nazi control and built up sympathetic movements abroad to carry on the "war of nerves" against Hitler's intended victims. On the capture of Berlin by the Allies, he poisoned himself.

Goering Hermann Wilhelm 1893–1946. Nazi leader, German field marshal from 1938. He was part of Hitler's inner circle, and with Hitler's rise to power was appointed commissioner for aviation from 1933 and built up the Luftwaffe (airforce). He built a vast economic empire in occupied Europe, but later lost favor and was expelled from the party in 1945. Tried at Nuremberg for war crimes, he poisoned himself before he could be executed.

Goethe Johann Wolfgang von 1749–1832. German poet, novelist, and dramatist. He is generally considered the founder of modern German literature, and was the leader of the Romantic *Sturm und Drang* movement. His works include the autobiographical *Die Leiden des Jungen Werthers/The Sorrows of the Young Werther* 1774 and the poetic play ◊*Faust* 1808 and 1832, his masterpiece. A visit to Italy 1786–88 inspired the classical dramas *Iphigenie auf Tauris/Iphigenia in Tauris* 1787 and *Torquato Tasso* 1790.

Gogh Vincent van 1853–1890. Dutch Post-Impressionist painter. He tried various careers, including preaching, and began painting in thee 1880s, his early works often being somber depictions of peasant life, such as *The Potato Eaters* 1885 (Van Gogh Museum, Amsterdam). Influenced by both the Impressionists and Japanese prints, he developed a freer style characterized by intense color and expressive brushwork, as seen in his *Sunflowers* series 1888.

Gogol Nicolai Vasilyevich 1809–1852. Russian writer. His first success was a collection of stories, *Evenings on a Farm near Dikanka* 1831–32, followed by *Mirgorod* 1835. Later works include *Arabesques* 1835, the comedy play *The Inspector General* 1836, and the picaresque novel *Dead Souls* 1842, which satirizes Russian provincial society.

Goh Chok Tong 1941– . Singapore politician, prime minister from 1990. A trained economist, Goh became a Member of Parliament for the ruling People's Action Party 1976. Rising steadily through the party ranks, he was appointed deputy prime minister 1985, and subsequently chosen by the cabinet as Lee Kuan Yew's successor, first as prime minister and from 1992 also as party leader.

goiter enlargement of the thyroid gland seen as a swelling on the neck. It is most pronounced in simple goiter, which is caused by iodine deficiency. Much more common is toxic goiter or thyrotoxicosis, caused by overactivity of the thyroid gland.

Golan Heights (Arabic *Jawlan*) plateau on the Syrian border with Israel, bitterly contested in the ◊Arab-Israeli Wars and annexed by Israel Dec 14, 1981.

gold shiny, yellow, ductile and very malleable, metallic element, symbol Au (from Latin *aurum*, "gold"), atomic number 79, atomic weight 197. It occurs in nature frequently as a free metal and is highly resis-

Goebbels, (Paul) Josef *Josef Goebbels, German Nazi minister of propaganda under Hitler. Exempted from military service through a foot deformity, he attended eight universities before drifting into the Nazi party. There his ambition and ruthlessness and his skill in public relations made him second in power only to Hitler himself.*

tant to acids, tarnishing, and corrosion. Pure gold is the most malleable of all metals and is used as gold leaf or powder, where small amounts cover vast surfaces, such as gilded domes and statues.

Its purity is measured in ◊carats on a scale of 24 (24K = pure gold; 18K = 75% gold).

Goldberg Rube 1883–1970. US cartoonist whose most famous and widely read of his strips featured ridiculously complicated inventions. He produced several popular comic strips that were nationally syndicated from 1915. Goldberg also devoted time to political cartooning, winning a Pulitzer Prize 1948.

Born in San Francisco and trained in engineering at the University of California, he abandoned that profession and joined the staff of the *San Francisco Chronicle* 1904. He moved to New York City 1907.

Gold Coast former name for ◊Ghana, but historically the west coast of Africa from Cape Three Points to the Volta River, where alluvial gold is washed down. Portuguese and French navigators visited this coast in the 14th century, and a British trading settlement developed into the colony of the Gold Coast 1618. With its dependencies of Ashanti and Northern Territories plus the trusteeship territory of Togoland, it became Ghana 1957. The name is also used for many coastal resort areas—for example, in Florida, US.

Golden Fleece in Greek legend, the fleece of the winged ram Chrysomallus, which hung on an oak tree at Colchis and was guarded by a dragon. It was stolen by ◊Jason and the Argonauts.

Golden Horde the invading Mongol-Tatar army that first terrorized Europe from 1237 under the leadership of Batu Khan, a grandson of Genghis Khan. ◊Tamerlane broke their power 1395, and ◊Ivan III ended Russia's payment of tribute to them 1480.

goldfinch songbird of the genus *Carduelis*, found in Eurasia, N Africa, and North America.

The American goldfinch *C. tristis* is about 5 in/13 cm long and golden-brownish on top and underside, with white-barred wings and tail.

goldfish fish *Carassius auratus* of the ◊carp family, found in E Asia. Greenish-brown in its natural state, it has for centuries been bred by the Chinese, taking on highly colored and sometimes freakishly shaped forms. Goldfish can see a greater range of colors than any other animal tested.

Golding William 1911–1993. English novelist. His work is often principally concerned with the fundamental corruption and evil inherent in human nature. His first book, *Lord of the Flies* 1954, concerns the degeneration into savagery of a group of English schoolboys marooned on a Pacific island. *Pincher Martin* 1956 is a study of greed and self-delusion. Later novels include *The Spire* 1964 and *Darkness Visible* 1979. He was awarded the Nobel Prize for Literature 1983.

Goldsmith Oliver 1728–1774. Irish writer. His works include the novel *The Vicar of Wakefield* 1766; the poem "The Deserted Village" 1770; and the play *She Stoops to Conquer* 1773. In 1761 Goldsmith met Samuel Johnson, and became a member of his "club". *The Vicar of Wakefield* was sold (according to Johnson's account) to save him from imprisonment for debt.

gold standard system under which a country's currency is exchangeable for a fixed weight of gold on demand at the central bank. It was almost universally applied 1870–1914, but by 1937 no single country was on the full gold standard. Britain abandoned the gold standard 1931; the US abandoned it 1971. Holdings of gold are still retained because it is an internationally recognized commodity, which cannot be legislated upon or manipulated by interested countries.

Goldwater Barry 1909– . US Republican politician; presidential candidate in the 1964 election, when he was overwhelmingly defeated by Lyndon Johnson. As a US senator from Arizona 1953–86, he voiced the views of his party's right-wing faction. Many of Goldwater's conservative ideas were later adopted by the Republican right, especially the Reagan administration.

Born in Phoenix, Arizona, he attended military high school in Virginia and served in the Army Air Forces during World War II. He achieved the rank of major general 1962 in the Air Force Reserve. After a stint 1949 on the Phoenix city council, he ran successfully for the US Senate. He wrote *The Conscience of a Conservative* 1960 and *Why Not Victory?* 1962.

golf outdoor game in which a small rubber-cored ball is hit with a wooden-or iron-faced club into a series of holes using the least number of shots. On the first shot for each hole, the ball is hit from a tee, which elevates the ball slightly off the ground; subsequent strokes are played off the ground. Most courses have 18 holes and are approximately 6,000 yd/5,500 m in length.

The major golfing events are the British Open, first held in 1860; the US Open, first held in 1895; the US Masters, first held in 1934; and the US PGA, first held in 1916.

Goncourt, de the brothers Edmond 1822–1896 and Jules 1830–1870. French writers. They collaborated in producing a compendium, *L'Art du XVIIIème siècle/18th-Century Art* 1859–75, historical studies, and a *Journal* published 1887–96 that depicts French literary life of their day. Edmond de Goncourt founded the Académie Goncourt, opened 1903, which awards an annual prize, the Prix Goncourt, to the author of the best French novel of the year.

gonorrhea common sexually transmitted disease arising from infection with the bacterium *Neisseria gonorrhoeae*, which causes inflammation of the genitourinary tract. After an incubation period of two to ten days, infected men experience pain while urinating and a discharge from the penis; infected women often have no external symptoms.

González Márquez Felipe 1942– . Spanish socialist politician, leader of the Socialist Workers' Party (PSOE), prime minister from 1982. His party was reelected 1989 and 1993, but his popularity suffered from economic upheaval and allegations of corruption.

goose aquatic bird of several genera (especially *Anser*) in the family Anatidae, which also includes ducks and swans. Both genders are similar in appearance: they have short, webbed feet, placed nearer the front of the body than in other members of the order Anatidae, and the beak is slightly hooked. They feed entirely on grass and plants.

gooseberry several prickly shrubs of the genus *Ribes* in the saxifrage family, native to Eurasia and North America, and closely related to currants in the same genus. The fleshy, red, blackish or green fruits are edible. The pasture gooseberry *R. cyanosbati* is native to North America. The European gooseberry *R. Grossalaria* is cultivated in gardens.

gopher burrowing rodent of the genus *Citellus*, family Sciuridae. It is a kind of ground squirrel represented by some 20 species distributed across W North America and Eurasia. Length ranges from 6 in/15 cm to 16 in/90 cm, excluding the furry tail; coloring ranges from plain yellowish to striped and spotted species. The name *pocket gopher* is applied to the eight genera of the North American family Geomyidae.

Gopher (derived from *go for*) system for searching the ◊Internet for information. Gopher servers use a ◊menu system that allows the user to search the Internet for files based on keywords typed in by the user. In the course of its search it may use the software tools ftp, Archie, Veronica or WAIS without requiring any knowledge of these by the user.

Gorbachev Mikhail Sergeyevich 1931– . Soviet president, in power 1985–91. He was a member of the Politburo from 1980. As general secretary of the Communist Party (CPSU) 1985–91, and president of the Supreme Soviet 1988–91, he introduced liberal reforms at home (◊perestroika and ◊glasnost), proposed the introduction of multiparty democracy, and attempted to halt the arms race abroad. He became head of state 1989.

He was awarded the Nobel Peace Prize 1990 but his international reputation suffered in the light of harsh state repression of nationalist demonstrations in the Baltic states. Following an abortive coup attempt by hard-liners Aug 1991, international acceptance of independence for the Baltic states, and accelerated moves toward independence in other republics, Gorbachev's power base as Soviet president was greatly weakened and in Dec 1991 he resigned.

Gordimer Nadine 1923– . South African novelist, an opponent of apartheid and censorship. Her finest writing is characterized by beautiful evocations of the rural Transvaal, effective renderings of sexuality, and interacting characters from different racial backgrounds. Her first novel, *The Lying Days*, appeared 1953, her other works include *The Conservationist* 1974, the volume of short stories *A Soldier's Embrace* 1980, and *July's People* 1981. Nobel Prize for Literature 1991.

Gore Al (Albert Arnold, Jnr) 1948– . US vice president 1993– under President Bill Clinton. A Democrat, he served in the House of Representatives 1977–85 and the Senate 1985–93 and became noted for his concern for the environment.

Gorgon in Greek mythology, any of three sisters, Stheno, Euryale, and Medusa, who had wings, claws, enormous teeth, and snakes for hair. Medusa, the only one who was mortal, was killed by Perseus, but even in death her head was still so frightful that it turned the onlooker to stone.

gorilla largest of the apes, *Gorilla gorilla*, found in the dense forests of West Africa and mountains of central Africa. The male stands about 6 ft/1.8 m and weighs about 450 lb/200 kg. Females are about half the size. The body is covered with blackish hair, silvered on the back in older males. Gorillas live in family groups; they are vegetarian, highly intelligent, and will attack only in self-defense. They are dwindling in numbers, being shot for food by some local people, or by poachers taking young for zoos, but protective measures are having some effect.

gorilla *The gorilla is a gentle, intelligent, and sociable animal. On the ground it normally moves in a stooped posture, with knuckles of the hands resting on the ground. Females and young males climb trees, but adult males rarely do so because of their great weight.*

Göring Hermann. German spelling of ◊Goering, Nazi leader.

Gorky Maxim. Pen name of Alexei Peshkov 1868–1936. Russian writer. Born in Nizhni-Novgorod (named Gorky 1932–90 in his honor), he was exiled 1906–13 for his revolutionary principles. His works, which include the play *The Lower Depths* 1902 and the memoir *My Childhood* 1913–14, combine realism with optimistic faith in the potential of the industrial proletariat.

gorse or *furze* or **whin** Eurasian genus of plants *Ulex*, family Leguminosae, consisting of thorny shrubs with spine-shaped leaves densely clustered along the stems, and bright yellow, coconut-scented flowers.

Gospel in the New Testament generally, the message of Christian salvation; in particular the four written accounts of the life of Jesus by Matthew, Mark, Luke, and John. Although the first three give approximately the same account or synopsis (thus giving rise to the name "Synoptic Gospels"), their differences from John have raised problems for theologians.

gospel music vocal music developed in the 1920s in the black Baptist churches of the US South from spirituals. Outstanding among the early gospel singers was Mahalia Jackson, but from the 1930s to the mid-1950s male harmony groups predominated, among them the Dixie Hummingbirds, the Swan Silvertones, and the Five Blind Boys of Mississippi.

Göteborg (German *Gothenburg*) port and industrial city (ships, vehicles, chemicals) on the west coast of Sweden, at the mouth of the Göta River; population (1990) 433,000. It is Sweden's second largest city and is linked with Stockholm by the Göta Canal (built 1832).

Goth E Germanic people who settled near the Black Sea around AD 2nd century. There are two branches, the eastern Ostrogoths and the western Visigoths. The *Ostrogoths* were conquered by the Huns 372. They regained their independence 454 and under ◊Theodoric the Great conquered Italy 488–93; they disappeared as a nation after the Byzantine emperor ◊Justinian I reconquered Italy 535–55.

The *Visigoths* migrated to Thrace. Under ◊Alaric they raided Greece and Italy 395–410, sacked Rome, and established a kingdom in S France. Expelled from there by the Franks, they established a Spanish kingdom which lasted until the Moorish conquest of 711.

Gothic architecture style of architecture that flourished in Europe from the mid-12th century to the end of the 15th century. It is characterized by the vertical lines of tall pillars and spires, greater height in interior spaces, the pointed arch, rib vaulting, and the flying buttress.

Gounod Charles François 1818–1893. French composer and organist. His operas, notably *Faust* 1859 and *Roméo et Juliette* 1867, and church music, including *Messe solennelle/Solemn Mass* 1849, combine graceful melody and elegant harmonization. His *Méditation sur le prélude de Bach/Meditation on Bach's "Prelude"* 1889 for soprano and instruments, based on Prelude No 1 of Bach's *Well-Tempered Clavier*, achieved popularity as "Gounod's *Ave Maria*."

gourd names applied to various members of the family Cucurbitaceae, including melons, squashes, and pumpkins. In a narrower sense, the name is applied to an inedible, ornamental variety of pumpkin *Cucurbita pepa*.

gout hereditary form of ◊arthritis, marked by an excess of uric acid crystals in the tissues, causing pain and inflammation in one or more joints (usually of the feet or hands). Acute attacks are treated with anti-inflammatories.

government any system whereby political authority is exercised. Modern systems of government distinguish between liberal democracies, totalitarian (one-party) states, and autocracies (authoritarian, relying on force rather than ideology). The Greek philosopher Aristotle was the first to attempt a systematic classification of governments. His main distinctions were between government by one person, by few, and by many (monarchy, oligarchy, and democracy), although the characteristics of each may vary between states and each may degenerate into tyranny (rule by an oppressive elite in the case of oligarchy or by the mob in the case of democracy).

Goya Francisco José de Goya y Lucientes 1746–1828. Spanish painter and engraver. He painted portraits of four successive kings of Spain; his series of etchings include the famous *Caprichos* 1797–98 and *The Disasters of War* 1810–14, both depicting the horrors of the French invasion of Spain. Among his later works are the "Black Paintings" (Prado, Madrid), with such horrific images as *Saturn Devouring One of His Sons* about 1822.

Graces in Greek mythology, three goddesses (Aglaia, Euphrosyne, Thalia), daughters of Zeus and Hera, personifications of pleasure, charm, and beauty; the inspirers of the arts and the sciences.

Graf Steffi 1969– . German lawn-tennis player who brought Martina ◊Navratilova's long reign as the world's number-one female player to an end. Graf reached the semifinal of the US Open 1985 at the age of 16, and won five consecutive Grand Slam singles titles 1988–89. In 1994 she became the first defending Wimbledon ladies' singles champion to lose her title in the first round.

grafting in medicine, the operation by which an organ or other living tissue is removed from one organism and transplanted into the same or a different organism.

In horticulture, it is a technique widely used for propagating plants, especially woody species. A bud or shoot on one plant, termed the *scion*, is inserted into another, the *stock*, so that they continue growing together, the tissues combining at the point of union. In this way some of the advantages of both plants are obtained.

Graham Billy (William Franklin) 1918– . US Protestant evangelist, known for the dramatic staging and charismatic eloquence of his preaching. Graham has preached to millions during worldwide crusades and on television, bringing many thousands to a "decision for Christ".

Born in Charlotte, North Carolina, he graduated from Wheaton College (Illinois). His first evangelical crusade was Youth for Christ 1949. From then, under the auspices of the Billy Graham Evangelistic Association 1950, he conducted worldwide tours. Graham wrote *Peace with God* 1953, *World Aflame* 1965, and *The Challenge* 1969.

Graham Martha 1893–1991. US dancer, choreographer, teacher, and director. The greatest exponent of modern dance in the US, she developed a distinctive vocabulary of movement, the *Graham Technique*, now taught worldwide. Her pioneering technique, designed to express inner emotion and intention through dance forms, represented the first real alternative to classical ballet.

Grahame Kenneth 1859–1932. Scottish author. The early volumes of sketches of childhood, *The Golden Age* 1895 and *Dream Days* 1898, were followed by his masterpiece *The Wind in the Willows* 1908, an animal fantasy created for his young son, which was dramatized by A A Milne as *Toad of Toad Hall* 1929.

gram metric unit of mass; one-thousandth of a kilogram.

grammar Greek *grammatike tekhne* "art of letters" the principles of the correct use of language, dealing with the rules of structuring words into phrases, clauses, sentences, and paragraphs in an accepted way. Emphasis on the standardizing impact of print has meant that spoken or colloquial language is often perceived as less grammatical than written language, but all forms of a language, standard or otherwise, have their own grammatical systems of differing complexity. People often acquire several overlapping grammatical systems within one language; for example, one formal system for writing and standard communication and one less formal system for everyday and peer-group communication.

grammar school another name for a primary school, also called an elementary school. In the UK, a secondary school catering to children of high academic ability.

Grampian region of Scotland *area* 3,320 sq mi/8,600 sq km *towns and cities* Aberdeen (administrative headquarters) *features* part of the Grampian Mountains (the Cairngorm Mountains); valley of the river Spey, with its whiskey distilleries; Balmoral Castle (royal residence on the river Dee near Braemar, bought by Prince Albert 1852, and rebuilt in Scottish baronial style); Braemar Highland Games in Aug *industries* beef cattle (Aberdeen Angus and Beef Shorthorn), fishing, whiskey distilling, North Sea oil service industries, tourism (winter skiing) *population* (1991) 503,900 *famous people* John Barbour, Alexander Cruden, Ramsay MacDonald.

Granada city in the Sierra Nevada in Andalusia, S Spain; population (1986) 281,000. It produces textiles, soap, and paper. The *Alhambra*, a fortified hilltop palace, was built in the 13th and 14th centuries by the Moorish kings.

Grand Canal (Chinese *Da Yune*) the world's longest canal. It is 1,000 mi/1,600 km long and runs N from Hangzhou to Tianjin, China; it is 100–200 ft/30–61 m wide, and reaches depths of over 1 mi/1.5 km. The earliest section was completed 486 BC ; the central section linking the Chiang Jiang (Yangtse-Kiang) and Huang He (Yellow) rivers was built AD 605–610; and the northern section was built AD 1282–92, during the reign of Kublai Khan.

Grand Canyon gorge of multicolored rock strata cut by and containing the Colorado River, N Arizona. It is 217 mi/350 km long, and 4–18 mi/6–29 km wide, and reaches depths of over 1.1 mi/1.7 km. It was made a national park 1919. Millions of tourists visit the canyon each year.

John Wesley Powell and ten companions first traveled down the river through the gorge 1869.

Grand Forks city in E central North Dakota, US, on the Minnesota border, on the Red River, N of Fargo; seat of Grand Forks County; population (1990) 49,400. It serves the surrounding agricultural area; most of its industries, such as food-processing mills and fertilizer plants, are associated with agriculture.

The University of North Dakota 1883 is located here.

Grand Rapids city in W Michigan, US, on the Grand River; population (1990) 189,100. It produces furniture, motor bodies, plumbing fixtures, and electrical goods. A fur-trading post was founded here 1826, and the furniture industry developed in the 1840s. Gerald Ford, 38th president of the US, lived here.

grand slam in tennis, the four major tournaments: the Australian Open, the French Open, Wimbledon, and the US Open. In golf, it is also the four major tournaments: the US Open, the Masters, the British Open, and the PGA (Professional Golfers' Association). In baseball, a grand slam is a home run with runners on all the bases. A grand slam in bridge is when all 13 tricks are won by one team.

grand unified theory (GUT) in physics, a sought-for theory that would combine the theory of the strong nuclear force (called quantum chromodynamics) with the theory of the weak nuclear and electromagnetic forces. The search for the grand unified theory is part of a larger program seeking a ◊unified field theory, which would combine all the forces of nature (including gravity) within one framework.

Grange Red (Harold Edward). Nickname "the Galloping Ghost". 1903–1991. US American football player. He joined the Chicago Bears professional football team 1925, becoming one of the first superstars of the newly founded National Football League. In both the 1923 and 1924 seasons he was chosen All-American halfback and won his nickname for his extraordinary open-field running ability.

Born in Forksville, Pennsylvania, US and raised in Illinois, Grange attended the University of Illinois. He became a charter member of the Football Hall of Fame 1963.

granite coarse-grained ◊igneous rock, typically consisting of the minerals quartz, feldspar, and mica. It may be pink or gray, depending on the composition of the feldspar. Granites are chiefly used as building materials.

Grant Cary. Adopted name of Archibald Leach 1904–1986. British-born actor, a US citizen from 1942. His witty, debonair personality made him a screen favorite for more than three decades. He was directed by Alfred ◊Hitchcock in *Suspicion* 1941, *Notorious* 1946, *To Catch a Thief* 1955, and *North by Northwest* 1959. He received a 1970 Academy Award for general excellence.

Grant Ulysses S(impson) 1822–1885. US Civil War general in chief for the Union and 18th president of the US 1869–77. As a Republican president, he carried through a liberal ◊Reconstruction policy in the South. He failed to suppress extensive political corruption within his own party and cabinet, which tarnished the reputation of his second term.

Born Hiram Ulysses Grant in Point Pleasant, Ohio, he graduated from West Point 1843 and had an unsuccessful career in the army 1839–54 and in business. At the outbreak of the Civil War he received a commission on the Mississippi front. His military career nearly ended in failure when Confederate forces surprised him at the Battle of Shiloh 1862, but Abraham ◊Lincoln's support was unwavering and Grant quickly redeemed himself, showing an aggressive fighting spirit. By his capture of Vicksburg in 1863 he brought the whole Mississippi front under Northern control and slowly wore down the Confederate general Robert E Lee's resistance, receiving his surrender at Appomattox 1865. He was elected president 1868 and reelected 1872. As president, he reformed the civil service and ratified the Treaty of Washington with the UK 1871. His two volume *Memoirs* were very successful and restored his finances.

grape fruit of any vine of the genus *Vitis*, especially *V. vinifera*, of the Vitaceae family.

grapefruit round, yellow, juicy, sharp-tasting fruit of the evergreen tree *Citrus paradisi* of the Rutaceae family. The tree grows up to more than 30 ft/10 m and has dark shiny leaves and large white flowers. The large fruits grow in grapelike clusters (hence the name). Grapefruits were first established in the West Indies and subsequently cultivated in Florida by the 1880s; they are now also grown in Israel and South Africa. Some varieties have pink flesh.

graphic file format format in which computer graphics are stored and transmitted. There are two main types: ◊raster graphics in which the image is stored as a ◊bit map (arrangement of dots), and ◊vector graphics, in which the image is stored using geometric formulas. There are many different file formats, some of which are used by specific computers, operating systems or applications. Some formats use file compression, particularly those that are able to handle more than one color.

graphics used with computers, see ◊computer graphics.

graphics tablet or *bit pad* in computing, an input device in which a stylus or cursor is moved, by hand, over a flat surface. The computer can keep track of the position of the stylus, so enabling the operator to input drawings or diagrams into the computer.

Grant, Ulysses S(impson) *General Ulysses S Grant at City Point, near Hopewell, Virginia, June 1864. Respected as a war hero, Grant was nominated as the Republican Party's presidential candidate in 1868. He was elected and served two terms, marred by poor administration, financial scandals, and official corruption.*

graphite blackish gray, laminar, crystalline form of ◊carbon. It is used as a lubricant and as the active component of pencil lead.

graph plotter alternate name for a ◊plotter.

grass plant of the large family Gramineae of mono-cotyledons, with about 9,000 species distributed worldwide except in the Arctic regions. The majority are perennial, with long, narrow leaves and jointed, hollow stems; hermaphroditic flowers are borne in spikelets; the fruits are grainlike. Included are blue-grass, wheat, rye, corn, sugarcane, and bamboo.

Grass Günter 1927– . German writer. The grotesque humor and socialist feeling of his novels *Die Blechtrommel/The Tin Drum* 1959 and *Der Butt/The Flounder* 1977 are also characteristic of many of his poems.

grasshopper insect of the order Orthoptera, usually with strongly developed hind legs, enabling it to leap. The femur of each hind leg in the male usually has a row of protruding joints that produce the characteristic chirping when rubbed against the hard wing veins. Members of the order include ◊locusts, ◊crickets, and katydids.

The American grasshopper *Schistocera americana* is widespread in North America. The longhorned grasshoppers, or katydids, form the family Tettigoniidae, and have a similar life history, but differ from the Acrididae in having long antennae and in producing their chirping by the friction of the wing covers over one another (stridulation).

grass-of-Parnassus or *eastern parnassia* plant (*Parnassia glauca*), unrelated to grasses, found growing in moist grasslands and thickets of North America. It is low-growing, with a rosette of heart-shaped, stalked leaves, and has five-petaled, white flowers with conspicuous green veins.

gravel coarse ◊sediment consisting of pebbles or small fragments of rock, originating in the beds of lakes and streams or on beaches. Gravel is quarried for use in road building, railroad ballast, and for an aggregate in concrete. It is obtained from quarries known as gravel pits, where it is often found mixed with sand or clay.

Graves Robert (Ranke) 1895–1985. English poet and author. He was severely wounded on the Somme in World War I, and his frank autobiography *Goodbye to All That* 1929 is one of the outstanding war books. Other works include the poems *Over the Brazier* 1916; two historical novels of imperial Rome, *I Claudius* and *Claudius the God*, both 1934; and books on myth—for example, *The White Goddess* 1948.

gravity force of attraction that arises between objects by virtue of their masses. On Earth, gravity is the force of attraction between any object in the Earth's gravitational field and the Earth itself. It is regarded as one of the four ◊fundamental forces of nature, the other three being the ◊electromagnetic force, the strong nuclear force, and the weak nuclear force. The gravitational force is the weakest of the four forces, but it acts over great distances. The particle that is postulated as the carrier of the gravitational force is the graviton.

gravure one of the three main ◊printing methods, in which printing is done from a plate etched with a pattern of recessed cells in which the ink is held. The greater the depth of a cell, the greater the strength of the printed ink. Gravure plates are expensive to make, but the process is economical for high-volume printing and reproduces illustrations well.

gray SI unit (symbol Gy) of absorbed radiation dose. It replaces the rad (1 Gy equals 100 rad), and is defined as the dose absorbed when one kilogram of matter absorbs one joule of ionizing radiation. Different types of radiation cause different amounts of damage for the same absorbed dose; the SI unit of *dose equivalent* is the ◊sievert.

Gray Thomas 1716–1771. English poet. His "Elegy Written in a Country Churchyard" 1751 is one of the most quoted poems in English. Other poems include "Ode on a Distant Prospect of Eton College", "The Progress of Poesy", and "The Bard"; these poems are now seen as the precursors of Romanticism.

grayling freshwater fish *Thymallus arcticus* of the family Salmonidae. It has a long, multirayed dorsal fin and exhibits a coloration shading from silver to purple. It is found in N parts of North America, Europe, and Asia. It was once common in the Great Lakes.

Graz capital of Styria province, and second-largest city in Austria; population (1981) 243,400. Industries include engineering, chemicals, iron, and steel. It has a 15th-century cathedral and a university founded 1573. Lippizaner horses are bred near here.

Great Barrier Reef chain of coral reefs and islands about 1,250 mi/2,000 km long, off the E coast of Queensland, Australia, at a distance of 10–30 mi/15–45 km. It is believed to be the world's largest living organism and forms an immense natural breakwater, the coral rock forming a structure larger than all human-made structures on Earth combined. The formation of the reef is now thought to be a recent geological event.

Great Bear popular name for the constellation ◊Ursa Major.

Great Bear Lake lake on the Arctic Circle, in the Northwest Territories, Canada; area 12,275 sq mi/31,800 sq km.

Great Britain official name for ◊England, ◊Scotland, and ◊Wales, and the adjacent islands (except the Channel Islands and the Isle of Man) from 1603, when the English and Scottish crowns were united under James I of England (James VI of Scotland). With Northern ◊Ireland it forms the ◊United Kingdom.

Great Dividing Range E Australian mountain range, extending 2,300 mi/3,700 km N–S from Cape York Peninsula, Queensland, to Victoria. It includes the Carnarvon Range, Queensland, which has many Aboriginal cave paintings, the Blue Mountains in New South Wales, and the Australian Alps.

Great Lakes series of five freshwater lakes along the US–Canadian border: Lakes Superior, Michigan, Huron, Erie, and Ontario; total area 94,600 sq mi/245,000 sq km. Interconnecting canals make them navigable by large ships, and they are drained by the ◊St Lawrence River. The whole forms the St Lawrence Seaway. They are said to contain 20% of the world's surface fresh water.

The principal cargoes are iron ore and grain, both of which originate at Lake Superior ports. Iron ore is carried to other lake ports for transport to steel mills. Grain may be shipped to processing centers such as Buffalo, New York, or sent directly abroad.

Great Leap Forward change in the economic policy of the People's Republic of China introduced by ◊Mao Zedong under the second five-year plan of 1958–62. The aim was to achieve rapid and simultaneous agricultural and industrial growth through the creation of large new agro-industrial communes. The inefficient and poorly planned allocation of state resources led to the collapse of the strategy by 1960 and the launch of a "reactionary program", involving the use of rural markets and private subsidiary plots. More than 20 million people died in the Great Leap famines of 1959–61.

Great Plains semiarid region to the E of the Rocky Mountains, US, stretching as far as the 100th meridian of longitude through Oklahoma, Kansas, Nebraska, and the Dakotas. The plains, which cover one-fifth of the US, extend from Texas in the S over 1,500 mi/2,400 km N to Canada. Ranching and wheat farming have resulted in over-use of water resources to such an extent that available farmland has been reduced by erosion.

Great Rift Valley longest "split" in the Earth's surface; see ◊Rift Valley, Great.

Great Schism in European history, the period 1378–1417 in which rival popes had seats in Rome and in Avignon; it was ended by the election of Martin V during the Council of Constance 1414–17.

Great Slave Lake lake in the Northwest Territories, Canada; area 10,980 sq mi/28,450 sq km. It is the deepest lake (2,020 ft/615 m) in North America.

Great Wall of China continuous defensive wall stretching from W Gansu to the Gulf of Liaodong (1,450 mi/2,250 km). It was once even longer. It was built under the Qin dynasty from 214 BC to prevent incursions by the Turkish and Mongol peoples and extended westward by the Han dynasty. Some 25 ft/8 m high, it consists of a brick-faced wall of earth and stone, has a series of square watchtowers, and has been carefully restored. It is so large that it can be seen from space.

Great War another name for ◊World War I.

grebe any of 19 species of water birds belonging to the family Podicipedidae. The great crested grebe *Podiceps cristatus* is the largest of the Old World grebes. It lives in ponds and marshes in Eurasia, Africa, and Australia, feeding on fish. It grows to 20 in/50 cm long and has a white breast, with chestnut and black feathers on its back and head.

The head and neck feathers form a crest, especially prominent during the breeding season.

Greco, El (Doménikos Theotokopoulos) 1541–1614. painter called "the Greek" because he was born in Crete. He studied in Italy, worked in Rome from about 1570, and by 1577 had settled in Toledo, Spain. He painted elegant portraits and intensely emotional

Greece, ancient: chronology

c. 1600–1200 BC	The first Greek civilization, known as Mycenaean, owed much to the Minoan civilization of Crete and may have been produced by the intermarriage of Greek-speaking invaders with the original inhabitants.
c. 1300 BC	A new wave of invasions began. The Achaeans overran Greece and Crete, destroying the Minoan and Mycenaean civilizations and penetrating Asia Minor.
1000 BC	Aeolians, Ionians and Dorians had settled in the area that is now Greece. Many independent city-states, such as Sparta and Athens, had developed.
c. 800–500	During the Archaic Period, Ionian Greeks led the development of philosophy, science and lyric poetry. The Greeks became great sea traders, and founded colonies around the coasts of the Mediterranean and the Black Sea, from Asia Minor in the east to Spain in the west.
776	The first Olympic games held.
594	The laws of Solon took the first step toward a more democratic society.
c. 560–510	The so-called "tyranny" of the Pisistratids in Athens was typical of a pre-democratic stage that many Greek cities passed through after overturning aristocratic rule.
545	From this date the Ionian cities in Asia Minor fell under the dominion of the Persian Empire.
507	Cleisthenes, ruler of Athens, is credited with the establishment of democracy. Other cities followed this lead, but Sparta remained unique, a state in which a ruling race, organized on military lines, dominated the surrounding population.
500–338	The Classical Period in ancient Greece.
499–494	The Ionian cities, aided by Athens, revolted unsuccessfully against the Persians.
490	Darius of Persia invaded Greece only to be defeated by the Athenians at Marathon and forced to withdraw.
480	Another invasion by the Persian emperor Xerxes, after being delayed by the heroic defense of Thermopylae by 300 Spartans, was defeated at sea off Salamis.
479	The Persians defeated on land at Plataea.
478	The Ionian cities, now liberated, formed a naval alliance with Athens, the Delian League.
455–429	Under Pericles, the democratic leader of Athens, drama, sculpture, and architecture were at their peak.
433	The *Parthenon* in Athens was completed.
431–404	The Peloponnesian War destroyed the political power of Athens, but Athenian thought and culture remained influential. Sparta became the leading Greek power.
370	The philosopher Plato opened his Academy in Athens.
338	Phillip II of Macedon (359–336 BC) took advantage of the wars between the city-states and conquered Greece.
336–323	Rule of Phillip's son, Alexander the Great. Alexander overthrew the Persian Empire, conquered Syria and Egypt, and invaded the Punjab. After his death, his empire was divided among his generals, but his conquests had spread Greek culture across the known world.
280	Achaean League of 12 Greek city-states formed in an attempt to maintain their independence against Macedon, Egypt, and Rome.
146	Greece became part of the Roman Empire. Under Roman rule Greece remained a cultural center and Hellenistic culture remained influential.

religious scenes with increasingly distorted figures and flickering light; for example, *The Burial of Count Orgaz* 1586 (church of San Tomé, Toledo).

Greece Hellenic Republic (*Elliniki Dimokratia*) *area* 50,935 sq mi/131,957 sq km *capital* Athens *towns and cities* Larisa; ports Piraeus, Thessaloníki, Patras, Iráklion *physical* mountainous; a large number of islands, notably Crete, Corfu, and Rhodes *environment* acid rain and other airborne pollutants are destroying the Classical buildings and ancient monuments of Athens *features* Corinth canal; Mount Olympus; the Acropolis; many classical archeological sites; the Aegean and Ionian Islands *head of state* Constantine Karamanlis from 1990 *head of government* Andreas Papandreou from 1993 *political system* democratic republic *political parties* Panhellenic Socialist Movement (PASOK), democratic socialist; New Democracy Party (ND), center-right; Democratic Renewal (DIANA), centrist; Communist Party (KJKE), left-wing; Political Spring, moderate, left of center *exports* tobacco, fruit, vegetables, olives, olive oil, textiles, aluminum, iron and steel *currency* drachma *population* (1993 est) 10,300,000; growth rate 0.3% p.a. *life expectancy* men 74, women 79 *language* Greek *religion* Greek Orthodox 97% *literacy* men 98%, women 89% *GNP* $6,374 per head (1992) *chronology* **1829** Independence achieved from Turkish rule. **1912–13** Balkan Wars; Greece gained much land. **1941–44** German occupation of Greece. **1946** Civil war between royalists and communists; communists defeated. **1949** Monarchy reestablished with Paul as king. **1964** King Paul succeeded by his son Constantine. **1967** Army coup removed the king; Col George Papadopoulos became prime minister. Martial law imposed, all political activity banned. **1973** Republic proclaimed, with Papadopoulos as president. **1974** Former premier Constantine Karamanlis recalled from exile to lead government. Martial law and ban on political parties lifted; restoration of the monarchy rejected by a referendum. **1975** New constitution adopted, making Greece a democratic republic. **1980** Karamanlis resigned as prime minister and was elected president. **1981** Greece became full member of European Economic Community. Andreas Papandreou elected Greece's first socialist prime minister. **1983** Five-year military and economic cooperation agreement signed with US; ten-year economic cooperation agreement signed with USSR. **1985**

Papandreou reelected. **1988** Relations with Turkey improved. Mounting criticism of Papandreou. **1989** Papandreou defeated. Tzannis Tzannetakis became prime minister; his all-party government collapsed. Xenophon Zolotas formed new unity government. Papandreou charged with corruption. **1990** New Democracy Party (ND) won half of parliamentary seats in general election but no outright majority; Constantine Mitsotakis became premier; formed new all-party government. Karamanlis reelected president. **1992** Papandreou acquitted. Greece opposed recognition of independence of the Yugoslav breakaway republic of Macedonia. Parliament ratified Maastricht Treaty. **1993** PASOK won general election and Papandreou returned as prime minister. **1994** Trade embargo imposed against Former Yugoslav Republic of Macedonia.

Greek architecture the architecture of ancient Greece is the base for virtually all architectural developments in Europe. The Greeks invented the entablature, which allowed roofs to be hipped (inverted V-shape), and perfected the design of arcades with support columns. There were three styles, or orders, of columns: Doric (with no base), Ionic (with scrolled capitals), and Corinthian (with acanthus-leafed capitals).

Greek language member of the Indo-European language family, which has passed through at least five distinct phases since the 2nd millennium BC : *Ancient Greek* 14th–12th centuries BC ; *Archaic Greek*, including Homeric epic language, until 800 BC ; *Classical Greek* until 400 BC ; *Hellenistic Greek*, the common language of Greece, Asia Minor, W Asia, and Egypt to the 4th century AD , and *Byzantine Greek*, used until the 15th century and still the ecclesiastical language of the Greek Orthodox Church. *Modern Greek* is principally divided into the general vernacular (*Demotic Greek*) and the language of education and literature (*Katharevousa*).

Greek Orthodox Church see ◊Orthodox Church.

Greeley Horace 1811–1872. US editor, publisher, and politician. He founded the *New York Tribune* 1841 and, as a strong supporter of the Whig party, advocated many reform causes in his newspaper—among them, feminism and abolitionism. He was an advocate of American westward expansion, and is remembered for his advice "Go west, young man". One of the founders of the Republican party 1854, Greeley was the unsuccessful presidential candidate of the breakaway Liberal Republicans 1872.

Born in Amherst, New Hampshire, Greeley was trained as a printer and moved to New York City 1831. He worked on a variety of publications before founding the *New York Tribune*.

green audit inspection of a company to assess the total environmental impact of its activities or of a particular product or process.

Green Bay city in NE Wisconsin where the Little Fox River flows into Green Bay on Lake Michigan; seat of Brown County; population (1990) 96,400. It is a port of entry to the US through the St Lawrence Seaway and serves as a distribution center. Industries include paper and food products.

The Green Bay Packers team of the National Football League was organized here 1919.

green belt or *green way* area surrounding a large city, officially designated not to be built on but preserved as open space (for agricultural and recreational use or to be "forever wild").

Greene (Henry) Graham 1904–1991. English writer. His novels of guilt, despair, and penitence are set in a world of urban seediness or political corruption in many parts of the world. They include *Brighton Rock* 1938, *The Power and the Glory* 1940, *The Heart of the Matter* 1948, *The Third Man* 1949, *The Honorary Consul* 1973, and *Monsignor Quixote* 1982.

greenfinch songbird *Carduelis chloris*, common in Europe and N Africa. The male is green with a yellow breast, and the female is a greenish-brown.

greenfly plant-sucking insect, a type of ◊aphid.

greenhouse effect phenomenon of the Earth's atmosphere by which solar radiation, trapped by the Earth and re-emitted from the surface, is prevented from escaping by various gases in the air. The result is a rise in the Earth's temperature. The main greenhouse gases are carbon dioxide, methane, and ◊chlorofluorocarbons (CFCs). Fossil-fuel consumption and forest fires are the main causes of carbon-dioxide buildup; methane is a byproduct of agriculture (rice, cattle, sheep). Water vapor is another greenhouse gas.

Greenland (Greenlandic *Kalaalit Nunaat*) world's largest island, lying between the North Atlantic and

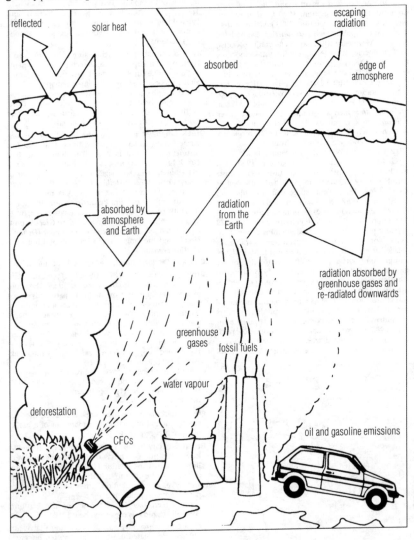

greenhouse effect

Arctic Oceans east of North America *area* 840,000 sq mi/2,175,600 sq km *capital* Godthaab (Greenlandic *Nuuk*) on the W coast *features* the whole of the interior is covered by a vast ice sheet (the remnant of the last glaciation, part of the N Polar icecap); the island has an important role strategically and in civil aviation, and shares military responsibilities with the US; there are lead and cryolite deposits, and offshore oil is being explored *economy* fishing and fish-processing *population* (1990) 55,500; Inuit (Ammassalik Eskimoan), Danish, and other European *language* Greenlandic (Ammassalik Eskimoan) *history* Greenland was discovered about 982 by Eric the Red, who founded colonies on the W coast soon after Eskimos from the North American Arctic had made their way to Greenland. Christianity was introduced to the Vikings about 1000. In 1261 the Viking colonies accepted Norwegian sovereignty, but early in the 15th century all communication with Europe ceased, and by the 16th century the colonies had died out, but the Eskimos had moved on to the east coast. It became a Danish colony in the 18th century, and following a referendum 1979 was granted full internal self-government 1981.

green movement collective term for the individuals and organizations involved in efforts to protect the environment. The movement encompasses political parties such as the ◊Green Party in Europe and international organizations like ◊Friends of the Earth and ◊Greenpeace.

Green Party political party aiming to "preserve the planet and its people", based on the premise that incessant economic growth is unsustainable. The leaderless party structure reflects a general commitment to decentralization. Green parties sprang up in W Europe in the 1970s and in E Europe from 1988. Parties in different countries are linked to one another but unaffiliated with any pressure group.

Greenpeace international environmental pressure group, founded 1971, with a policy of nonviolent direct action backed by scientific research. During a protest against French atmospheric nuclear testing in the S Pacific 1985, its ship *Rainbow Warrior* was sunk by French intelligence agents, killing a crew member. A protest against renewed French nuclear testing took place July 1995.

greenshank grayish shorebird *Tringa nebularia* of the sandpiper group. It has long olive-green legs and a slightly upturned bill. It breeds in N Europe and regularly migrates through the Aleutian Islands.

Greenwich Outer London borough of SE Greater London. Greenwich landmarks include the *Queen's House* 1637, designed by Inigo Jones, the first Palladian-style building in England; the *Royal Naval College*, designed by Christopher Wren 1694; the *Royal Observatory* (founded here 1675). The source of Greenwich Mean Time has been moved to Cambridge 1990, but the Greenwich meridian (0°) remains unchanged. The *Cutty Sark*, one of the great tea clippers, is preserved as a museum of sail.

Greenwich Mean Time (GMT) local time on the zero line of longitude (the *Greenwich meridian*), which passes through the Old Royal Observatory at Greenwich, London. It was replaced 1986 by coordinated universal time (UTC), but continued to be used to measure longitudes and the world's standard time zones; see ◊time.

Greer Germaine 1939– . Australian feminist who became widely known on the publication of her book *The Female Eunuch* 1970. Later works include *The Obstacle Race* 1979, a study of contemporary women artists; *Sex and Destiny: The Politics of Human Fertility* 1984; *Daddy, We Hardly Knew You* 1989; and *The Change* 1991, a positive view of the menopause. She is also a speaker and activist.

Gregorian chant any of a body of plainsong choral chants associated with Pope Gregory the Great (540–604), which became standard in the Roman Catholic Church.

Gregory (I) the Great (St Gregory) *c.*540–604. Pope from 590 who asserted Rome's supremacy and exercised almost imperial powers. In 596 he sent St ◊Augustine to England. He introduced the choral *Gregorian chant* into the liturgy. Feast day March 12.

Gregory VII (monastic name *Hildebrand*) *c.*1023–1085. Chief minister to several popes before his election to the papacy 1073. In 1077 he forced the Holy Roman emperor Henry IV to wait in the snow at Canossa for four days, dressed as a penitent, before receiving pardon. He was driven from Rome and died in exile. His feast day is May 25.

Gregory XIII 1502–1585. Pope from 1572 who introduced the reformed *Gregorian calendar*, still in use, in which a century year is not a leap year unless it is divisible by 400.

Grenada area (including the Grenadines, notably Carriacou) 131 sq mi/340 sq km *capital* St George's *towns and cities* Grenville, Hillsborough (Carriacou) *physical* southernmost of the Windward Islands; mountainous *features* Grand-Anse beach; Annandale Falls; the Great Pool volcanic crater *head of state* Elizabeth II from 1974, represented by governor-general Reginald Palmer from 1992 *head of government* Nicholas Braithwaite from 1990 *political system* emergent democracy *political parties* New National Party (NNP), centrist; Grenada United Labour Party (GULP), nationalist, left of center; National Democratic Congress (NDC), centrist; National Party (TNP), centrist *exports* cocoa, nutmeg, bananas, mace *currency* Eastern Caribbean dollar *population* (1993) 95,300 (84% of black African descent); growth rate –0.2% p.a. *life expectancy* 69 *languages* English (official); some French patois spoken *religion* Roman Catholic 60% *literacy* 96% *GNP* $2,180 per head (1991) *chronology 1974* Independence achieved from Britain; Eric Gairy elected prime minister. *1979* Gairy removed in bloodless coup led by Maurice Bishop; constitution suspended and a People's Revolutionary Government established. *1982* Relations with the US and Britain deteriorated as ties with Cuba and the USSR strengthened. *1983* After Bishop's attempt to improve relations with the US, he was overthrown by left-wing opponents. A coup established the Revolutionary Military Council (RMC), and Bishop and three colleagues were executed. The US invaded Grenada, accompanied by troops from other E Caribbean countries; RMC overthrown, 1974 constitution reinstated. *1984* The newly formed NNP won 14 of the 15 seats in the house of representatives and its leader, Herbert Blaize, became prime minister. *1989* Herbert Blaize lost leadership of NNP, remaining as head of government; he died and was succeeded by Ben Jones. *1990* Nicholas Braithwaite of the NDC became prime minister. *1991* Windward Islands confederation proposed.

Grenadines chain of about 600 small islands in the Caribbean Sea, part of the group known as the Windward Islands. They are divided between ◊St Vincent and ◊Grenada.

Grendel in the Old English epic poem *Beowulf*, the male monster that the hero has to kill.

He is a giant, human in shape, a descendent of Cain, living in a murky pond with his mother, among other strange and vicious sea-beasts.

Grenville George 1712–1770. British Whig politician, prime minister, and chancellor of the Exchequer, whose introduction of the ◊Stamp Act 1765 to raise revenue from the colonies was one of the causes of the American Revolution. His government was also responsible for prosecuting the radical John Wilkes.

Gretzky Wayne 1961– . Canadian ice-hockey player, probably the best in the history of the National Hockey League (NHL). Gretzky played with the Edmonton Oilers 1979–88 and with the Los Angeles Kings from 1988. He took just 11 years to break the NHL scoring record of 1,850 goals (accumulated by Gordie Howe over 26 years) and won the Hart Memorial Trophy as the NHL's most valuable player of the season a record nine times (1980–87, 1989). By the start of the 1990–91 season he had scored 1,979 goals.

Grey Charles, 2nd Earl Grey 1764–1845. British Whig politician. He entered Parliament 1786, and in 1806 became First Lord of the Admiralty, and foreign secretary soon afterwards. As prime minister 1830–34, he carried the Great Reform Bill to reshape the parliamentary representative system 1832 and the act abolishing slavery throughout the British Empire 1833.

Grey Lady Jane 1537–1554. Queen of England for nine days, July 10–19, 1553, the great-granddaughter of Henry VII. She was married 1553 to Lord Guildford Dudley (died 1554), son of the Duke of Northumberland. Edward VI was persuaded by Northumberland to set aside the claims to the throne of his sisters Mary and Elizabeth. When Edward died on July 6, 1553, Jane reluctantly accepted the crown and was proclaimed queen July 10. Mary, although a Roman Catholic, had popular support, and the Lord Mayor of London announced that she was queen July 19. Grey was executed on Tower Green.

Grieg Edvard Hagerup 1843–1907. Norwegian nationalist composer. Much of his music is small-scale, particularly his songs, dances, sonatas, and piano works, strongly identifying with Norwegian folk music. Among his orchestral works are the *Piano Concerto in A Minor* 1869 and the incidental music for Ibsen's *Peer Gynt* 1876, commissioned by Ibsen and the Norwegian government.

griffin mythical monster, the supposed guardian of hidden treasure, with the body, tail, and hind legs of a lion, and the head, forelegs, and wings of an eagle.

Griffith D(avid) W(ark) 1875–1948. US film director. He was an influential figure in the development of cinema as an art. He made hundreds of "one-reelers" 1908–13, in which he pioneered the techniques of masking, fade-out, flashback, crosscut, close-up, and long shot. After much experimentation with photography and new techniques he directed *The Birth of a Nation* 1915, about the aftermath of the Civil War, later criticized for its portrayal of African Americans.

Grimm brothers Jakob Ludwig Karl (1785–1863) and Wilhelm (1786–1859), philologists and collectors of German fairy tales such as "Hansel and Gretel" and "Rumpelstiltskin". Joint compilers of an exhaustive dictionary of German, they saw the study of language and the collecting of folk tales as strands in a single enterprise.

Gris Juan 1887–1927. Spanish painter, one of the earliest Cubists. He developed a distinctive geometrical style, often strongly colored. He experimented with paper collage and made designs for Diaghilev's *Ballets Russes* 1922–23.

Gromyko Andrei 1909–1989. President of the USSR 1985–88. As ambassador to the US from 1943, he took part in the Tehran, Yalta, and Potsdam conferences; as United Nations representative 1946–49, he exercised the Soviet veto 26 times. He was foreign minister 1957–85. It was Gromyko who formally nominated Mikhail Gorbachev as Communist Party leader 1985.

Gropius Walter Adolf 1883–1969. German architect. He lived in the US from 1937. He was an early exponent of the International Style defined by glass curtain walls, cubic blocks, and unsupported corners, for example, the model factory and office building at the 1914 Cologne Werkbund exhibition, designed with Adolph Meyer. A founder-director of the ◊Bauhaus school in Weimar 1919–28, he advocated teamwork in design and artistic standards in industrial production. He was responsible for the new Bauhaus premises at Dessau 1925–26, a hallmark of the International Style.

From 1937 he was professor of architecture at Harvard. He started the Architects Collaborative, a product of which was the Harvard Graduate Center 1949–50.

gross a particular figure or price, calculated before the deduction of specific items such as commission, discounts, interest, and taxes. The opposite is ◊net.

gross domestic product (GDP) value of the output of all goods and services produced within a nation's borders, normally given as a total for the year. It thus includes the production of foreign-owned firms within the country, but excludes the income from domestically owned firms located abroad. See also ◊gross national product.

gross national product (GNP) the most commonly used measurement of the wealth of a country.

GNP is defined as the total value of all goods and services produced by firms owned by the country concerned. It is measured as the ◊gross domestic product plus income from abroad, minus income earned during the same period by foreign investors within the country.

Grosz Georg 1893–1959. German Expressionist painter and graphic artist. He was a founder of the Berlin Dada group 1918. Grosz excelled in savage satirical drawings criticizing the government and the military establishment. After numerous prosecutions he fled his native Berlin 1932 and went to the US where he became a naturalized American 1938.

Grotius Hugo 1583–1645. Dutch jurist and politician, born in Delft. He became a lawyer, and later received political appointments. In 1618 he was arrested as a republican and sentenced to imprisonment for life. His wife contrived his escape 1620, and he settled in France, where he composed the *De Jure Belli et Pacis/On the Law of War and Peace* 1625, the foundation of international law. He was Swedish ambassador in Paris 1634–45.

ground an electrical connection between an appliance and the ground, which becomes part of the circuit. In the event of a fault in an electrical appliance (for example, involving connection between the live part of the circuit and the outer casing) the current flows to earth, causing no harm to the user.

groundnut another name for ◊peanut.

ground water water collected underground in porous rock strata and soils; it emerges at the surface as springs and streams. The groundwater's upper level is called the *water table*. Sandy or other kinds of beds that are filled with groundwater are called *aquifers*. Recent estimates are that usable ground water amounts to more than 90% of all the fresh water on Earth; however, keeping such supplies free of pollutants entering the recharge areas is a critical environmental concern.

Ground-water supplies vary from region to region depending on recharge rates and well use. Some areas such as W Texas and Oklahoma are in danger of depleting their groundwater supplies. In other areas, such as Long Island and New Jersey, overpumping has led to the encroachment of sea water into continental aquifers. Overall, however, the amount of usable fresh water in the ground is enormous.

grouper any of several species of large sea bass, especially the genera *Mycteroperca* and *Epinephelus*, found in warm waters.

grouse fowl-like game bird of the subfamily Tetraonidae, in the pheasant family, Phasianidae. The subfamily also includes quail, ptarmigan, and prairie chicken. Grouse are native to North America and N Europe. They are mostly ground-living. During the mating season the males undertake elaborate courtship displays in small individual territories (leks).

Among the most familiar are the ruffed grouse *Bonasa umbellus*, common in woods in N and E North America, and the blue grouse *Dendragapus obscurus* of W North America.

growth hormone (GH) or *somatotrophin* hormone from the anterior ◊pituitary gland that promotes growth of long bones and increases protein synthesis. If it is lacking in childhood, ◊dwarfism results; excess GH causes gigantism.

Grünewald (Mathias or Mathis Gothardt-Neithardt) *c.*1475–1528. German painter. He was active in Mainz, Frankfurt, and Halle. He was court painter, architect, and engineer to the archbishop of Mainz 1508–14. His few surviving paintings show an intense involvement with religious subjects. His *Isenheim Altarpiece* 1515 (Unterlinden Museum, Colmar, France), with its tortured figure of Jesus, recalls medieval traditions.

Guadalajara industrial city (textiles, glass, soap, pottery), capital of Jalisco state, W Mexico; population (1990) 2,847,000. It is a key communications center. It has a 16th–17th-century cathedral, the Governor's Palace, and an orphanage with murals by the Mexican painter José Orozco (1883–1949).

Guadalcanal largest of the ◊Solomon Islands; area 2,510 sq mi/6,500 sq km; population (1987) 71,000. Gold, copra, and rubber are produced. During World War II it was the scene of a major battle for control of the area that was won by US forces after six months of fighting.

Guadeloupe island group in the Leeward Islands, West Indies, an overseas *département* of France; area 658 sq mi/1,705 sq km; population (1990) 387,000. The main islands are Basse-Terre (on which is the chief

town of the same name) and Grande-Terre. Sugar refining and rum distilling are the main industries.

Guam largest of the ◊Mariana Islands in the W Pacific, an unincorporated territory of the US *area* 208 sq mi/540 sq km *capital* Agaña *towns and cities* Apra (port), Tamuning *features* major US air and naval base, much used in the Vietnam War; tropical, with much rain *industries* sweet potatoes, fish; tourism is important *currency* US dollar *population* (1990) 133,200 *languages* English, Chamorro (basically Malay-Polynesian) *religion* 96% Roman Catholic *government* popularly elected governor (Ricardo Bordallo from 1985) and single-chamber legislature. *recent history* ceded by Spain to the US 1898; occupied by Japan as an air and naval base 1941–44. Guam achieved full US citizenship and self-government from 1950. A referendum 1982 favored the status of a commonwealth, in association with the US.

guanaco hoofed ruminant *Lama guanacoe* of the camel family, found in South America on pampas and mountain plateaus. It grows to 4 ft/1.2 m at the shoulder, with head and body about 5 ft/1.5 m long. It is sandy brown in color, with a blackish face, and has fine wool. It lives in small herds and is the ancestor of the domestic ◊llama and ◊alpaca. It is also related to the other wild member of the camel family, the ◊vicuna.

Guangdong or *Kwantung* province of S China *area* 89,320 sq mi/231,400 sq km *capital* Guangzhou *features* tropical climate; Hainan, Leizhou peninsula, and the foreign enclaves of Hong Kong and Macao in the Pearl River delta *industries* rice, sugar, tobacco, minerals, fish *population* (1990) 62,829,000.

Guangzhou or *Kwangchow* or *Canton* capital of Guangdong province, S China; population (1989) 3,490,000. Industries include shipbuilding, engineering, chemicals, and textiles.

Guaraní member of a South American Indian people who formerly inhabited the area that is now Paraguay, S Brazil, and Bolivia. The Guaraní live mainly in reserves; few retain the traditional ways of hunting in the tropical forest, cultivation, and ritual warfare. About 1 million speak Guaraní, a member of the Tupian language group.

Guatemala Republic of (*República de Guatemala*) *area* 42,031 sq mi/108,889 sq km *capital* Guatemala City *towns and cities* Quezaltenango, Puerto Barrios (naval base) *physical* mountainous; narrow coastal plains; limestone tropical plateau in N; frequent earthquakes *environment* between 1960 and 1980 nearly 57% of the country's forest was cleared for farming *features* Mayan archeological remains, including site at Tikal *head of state and government* Ramiro de Leon Carpio from 1993 *political system* democratic republic *political parties* Guatemalan Republican Front (FRG), right-wing; National Advancement Party (PAN), centrist; Center Party (UCN), centrist; Christian Democratic Party (PDCG), right of center *exports* coffee, bananas, cotton, sugar, beef *currency* quetzal *population* (1993 est) 10,000,000 (Mayaquiche Indians 54%, mestizos (mixed race) 42%); growth rate 2.8% p.a. (87% of under-fives suffer from malnutrition) *life expectancy* men 62, women 67 *languages* Spanish (official); 40% speak 18 Indian languages *religions* Roman Catholic 80%, Protestant 20% *literacy* men 63%, women 47% *GNP* $930 per head (1991) *chronology* **1839** Independence achieved from Spain. **1954** Col. Carlos

Castillo became president in US-backed coup, halting land reform. *1963* Military coup made Col Enrique Peralta president. *1966* Cesar Méndez elected president. *1970* Carlos Araña elected president. *1974* General Kjell Laugerud became president. Widespread political violence precipitated by the discovery of falsified election returns in March. *1978* General Fernando Romeo became president. *1981* Growth of antigovernment guerrilla movement. *1982* General Angel Anibal became president. Army coup installed General Ríos Montt as head of junta and then as president; political violence continued. *1983* Montt removed in coup led by General Mejía Victores, who declared amnesty for the guerrillas. *1985* New constitution adopted; PDCG won congressional elections; Vinicio Cerezo elected president. *1989* Coup attempt against Cerezo foiled. Over 100,000 people killed and 40,000 reported missing since 1980. *1991* Jorge Serrano Elías of the Solidarity Action Movement elected president. Diplomatic relations with Belize established. *1993* President Serrano deposed; Ramiro de Leon Carpio elected president by assembly. *1994* Referendum supported constitutional reforms aimed at combating corruption. Peace talks held with rebels. Right-wing parties, led by FRG, won majority in congressional elections.

Guatemala City capital of Guatemala; population (1983) 1,300,000. It produces textiles, tires, footwear, and cement. It was founded 1776 when its predecessor (Antigua) was destroyed in an earthquake. It was severely damaged by another earthquake 1976.

guava tropical American tree *Psidium guajava* of the myrtle family Myrtaceae; the astringent yellow pear-shaped fruit is used to make guava jelly, or it can be stewed or canned. It has a high vitamin C content.

Guayaquil largest city and chief port of ◊Ecuador; population (1986) 1,509,100. The economic center of Ecuador, Guayaquil manufactures machinery and consumer goods, processes food, and refines petroleum. It was founded 1537 by the Spanish explorer Francisco de Orellana.

gudgeon any of an Old World genus *Gobio* of freshwater fishes of the carp family, especially *G. gobio* found in Europe and N Asia on the gravel bottoms of streams. It is olive-brown, spotted with black, and up to 20 cm/8 in long, with a distinctive barbel (a sensory fleshy filament) at each side of the mouth.

guelder rose or *snowball tree* cultivated shrub or small tree *Viburnum opulus*, native to Europe and N Africa, with spherical clusters of white flowers and shiny red berries.

It is closely related to high-bush cranberry *V. trilobum* of North America.

Guernsey second largest of the ◊Channel Islands; area 24.3 mi/63 sq km; population (1991) 58,900. The capital is St Peter Port. Products include electronics, tomatoes, flowers, and, more recently, butterflies; from 1975 it has been a major financial center. Guernsey cattle, which are a distinctive pale fawn color and give rich creamy milk, originated here.

guerrilla irregular soldier fighting in a small unofficial unit, typically against an established or occupying power, and engaging in sabotage, ambush, and the like, rather than pitched battles against an opposing army. Guerrilla tactics have been used both by resistance armies in wartime (for example, the Vietnam War) and in peacetime by national liberation groups

and militant political extremists (for example, the Tamil Tigers).

Guest Edgar Albert 1881–1959. US journalist and poet. From 1900 he wrote "Breakfast Table Chat" for the *Detroit Free Press*. The column combined light verse and folksy wisdom and was later nationally syndicated. Guest's best-selling collections of verse include *A Heap o' Livin'* 1916 and *Harbor Lights of Home* 1928.

Guevara Che (Ernesto) 1928–1967. Latin American revolutionary. He was born in Argentina and trained there as a doctor, but left his homeland 1953 because of his opposition to the right-wing president Perón. In effecting the Cuban revolution of 1959, he was second only to Castro and Castro's brother Raúl. In 1965 he went to the Congo to fight against white mercenaries, and then to Bolivia, where he was killed in an unsuccessful attempt to lead a peasant rising. He was an orthodox Marxist and renowned for his guerrilla techniques.

Guiana NE part of South America that includes ◊French Guiana, ◊Guyana, and ◊Suriname.

guild or *gild* medieval association, particularly of artisans or merchants, formed for mutual aid and protection and the pursuit of a common purpose, religious or economic. Guilds became politically powerful in Europe but after the 16th century their position was undermined by the growth of capitalism.

guillemot diving seabird of the auk family that breeds in large numbers on rocky N Atlantic and Pacific coasts. The common guillemot *Uria aalge* has a sharp bill and short tail, and sooty-brown and white plumage. The black guillemot *Cepphus grylle* of northern coasts is mostly black, with orange legs when breeding. Guillemots build no nest, but lay one large, almost conical egg.

Guinea Republic of (*République de Guinée*) **area** 94,901 sq mi/245,857 sq km **capital** Conakry **towns and cities** Labé, Nzérékoré, Kankan **physical** flat coastal plain with mountainous interior; sources of rivers Niger, Gambia, and Senegal; forest in SE **environment** large amounts of toxic waste from industrialized countries have been dumped in Guinea **features** Fouta Djallon, area of sandstone plateaus, cut by deep valleys **head of state and government** Lansana Conté from 1984 **political system** emergent democratic republic **political parties** Party of Unity and Progress (PUP), right of center; Rally of the Guinean People (RPG), left of center; Union for the New Republic (UNR), left of center; Party of Renewal and Progress (PRP), left of center **exports** coffee, rice, palm kernels, alumina, bauxite, diamonds **currency** syli or franc **population** (1993 est) 7,700,000; growth rate 2.3% p.a. **life expectancy** men 44, women 45 **languages** French (official), African languages **media** state-owned, but some criticism of the government tolerated; no daily newspaper **religions** Muslim 85%, Christian 10%, local 5% **literacy** men 35%, women 13% **GNP** $450 per head (1991) **chronology 1958** Full independence achieved from France; Sékou Touré elected president. *1977* Strong opposition to Touré's rigid Marxist policies forced him to accept return to mixed economy. *1980* Touré returned unopposed for fourth seven-year term. *1984* Touré died. Bloodless coup established a military committee for national recovery, led by Col Lansana Conté. *1985* Attempted coup against Conté while he was out of the country was foiled by loyal troops. *1990* Sent troops to join the multinational force that attempted to stabilize Liberia. New constitution approved. *1991* Antigovernment general strike by National Confederation of Guinea Workers (CNTG). *1993* Conté narrowly reelected.

Guinea-Bissau Republic of (*República da Guiné-Bissau*) *area* 13,944 sq mi/36,125 sq km *capital* Bissau *towns and cities* Mansôa, São Domingos *physical* flat coastal plain rising to savanna in E *features* the archipelago of Bijagós *head of state* João Bernardo Vieira from 1980 *head of government* Carlos Correia from 1991 *political system* emergent democracy *political parties* African Party for the Independence of Portuguese Guinea and Cape Verde (PAIGC), nationalist socialist; Party of Renovation and Development (PRD), left of center; Democratic Front: Guinea-Bissau Resistance–Bafata Movement (RGB-MB), left of center; Guinea-Bissau Resistance Movement (MRG), left of center *exports* rice, coconuts, peanuts, fish, timber *currency* peso *population* (1993 est) 1,050,000; growth rate 2.4% p.a. *life expectancy* men 42, women 45; 1990 infant mortality rate was 14.8% *languages* Portuguese (official), Crioulo (Cape Verdean dialect of Portuguese), African languages *religions* animism 54%, Muslim 38%, Christian 8% *literacy* men 50%, women 24% *GNP* $190 per head (1991) *chronology 1956* PAIGC formed to secure independence from Portugal. *1973* Two-thirds of the country declared independent, with Luiz Cabral as president of a state council. *1974* Independence achieved from Portugal. *1980* Cape Verde decided not to join a unified state. Cabral deposed, and João Vieira became chair of a council of revolution. *1981* PAIGC confirmed as the only legal party, with Vieira as its secretary-general. *1982* Normal relations with Cape Verde restored. *1984* New constitution adopted, making Vieira head of government as well as head of state. *1989* Vieira reelected. *1991* Other parties legalized. *1992* Multiparty electoral commission established. *1994* PAIGC and Vieira reelected in first multiparty elections.

Guinea Coast or *Gulf of Guinea* coast of W Africa between Cape Palmas, Liberia, and Cape Lopez, Gabon. The coastline features the Bight of Benin and the Bight of Bonny, and the rivers Volta, Niger, and Ogowé reach the sea here.

guinea fowl chickenlike African bird of the family Numididae. The group includes the helmet guinea fowl *Numida meleagris*, which has a horny growth on the head, white-spotted feathers, and fleshy cheek wattles. It is the ancestor of the domestic guinea fowl.

guinea pig species of ◊cavy, a type of rodent.

guitar six-stringed, or twelve-stringed, flat-bodied musical instrument, plucked or strummed with the fingers. The *Hawaiian guitar*, laid across the lap, uses a metal bar to produce a distinctive gliding tone; the solid-bodied *electric guitar*, developed in the 1950s by Les Paul and Leo Fender, mixes and amplifies vibrations from electromagnetic pickups at different points to produce a range of tone qualities.

Guizhou or *Kweichow* province of S China *area* 67,164 sq mi/174,000 sq km *capital* Guiyang *industries* rice, corn, nonferrous minerals *population* (1990) 32,392,000.

Gujarat or *Gujerat* state of W India *area* 75,656 sq mi/196,000 sq km *capital* Ahmedabad *features* heavily industrialized; includes most of the Rann of Kutch; the Gir Forest (the last home of the wild Asian lion) *industries* cotton, petrochemicals, oil, gas, rice, textiles *language* Gujarati (Gujerati), Hindi *population* (1991) 41,174,000.

Gujarati language member of the Indo-Iranian branch of the Indo-European language family, spoken in and around the state of Gujarat in W India. It is written in its own script, a variant of the Devanagari script used for Sanskrit and Hindi.

Gulf States those states bordering the Gulf of Mexico (Alabama, Florida, Louisiana, Mississippi, and Texas). The term also refers to oil-rich countries sharing the coastline of the ◊Persian Gulf (Bahrain, Iran, Iraq, Kuwait, Oman, Qatar, Saudi Arabia, and the United Arab Emirates).

Gulf Stream warm ocean ◊current that flows north from the warm waters of the Gulf of Mexico. Part of the current is diverted east across the Atlantic, where it is known as the *North Atlantic Drift*, and warms what would otherwise be a colder climate in the British Isles and NW Europe.

Gulf War war Jan 16–Feb 28, 1991, between Iraq and a coalition of 28 nations led by the US. (It is also another name for the Iran–Iraq War). The invasion and annexation of Kuwait by Iraq on Aug 2, 1990, provoked a buildup of US troops in Saudi Arabia, eventually totaling over 500,000. The UK subsequently deployed 42,000 troops, France 15,000, Egypt 20,000, and other nations smaller contingents. An air offensive lasting six weeks, in which "smart" weapons came of age, destroyed about one-third of Iraqi equipment and inflicted massive casualties. A 100-hour ground war followed, which effectively destroyed the remnants of the 500,000-strong Iraqi army in or near Kuwait.

gull seabird of the family Laridae, especially the genus *Larus*. Gulls are usually 10–30 in/25–75 cm long, white with gray or black on the back and wings, and have large beaks.

gum in botany, complex polysaccharides (carbohydrates) formed by many plants and trees, particularly by those from dry regions. They form four main groups: plant exudates (gum arabic); marine plant extracts (agar); seed extracts; and fruit and vegetable extracts. Some are made synthetically.

gun any kind of firearm or any instrument consisting of a metal tube from which a projectile is discharged; see also ◊artillery, and ◊small arms.

gunpowder or *black powder* the oldest known explosive, a mixture of 75% potassium nitrate (saltpeter), 15% charcoal, and 10% sulfur. Sulfur ignites at a low temperature, charcoal burns readily, and the potassium nitrate provides oxygen for the explosion. Although progressively replaced since the late 19th century by high explosives, gunpowder is still widely used for quarry blasting, fuses, and fireworks.

Gunpowder Plot in British history, the Catholic conspiracy to blow up James I and his parliament on Nov 5, 1605. It was discovered through an anonymous letter. Guy ◊Fawkes was found in the cellar beneath the Palace of Westminster, ready to fire a store of explosives. Several of the conspirators were killed, and Fawkes and seven others were executed.

Guomindang Chinese National People's Party, founded 1894 by ◊Sun Yat-sen, which overthrew the Manchu Empire 1912. From 1927 the right wing, led by ◊Chiang Kai-shek, was in conflict with the left, led by Mao Zedong until the Communist victory 1949 (except for the period of the Japanese invasion 1937–45). It survives as the dominant political party of Taiwan, where it is still spelled *Kuomintang*.

guru Hindi *gurū* Hindu or Sikh leader, or religious teacher.

Gustavus Adolphus (Gustavus or Gustaf II) 1594–1632. King of Sweden from 1611, when he succeeded his father Charles IX. He waged successful wars with Denmark, Russia, and Poland, and in the ◊Thirty Years' War became a champion of the Protestant cause. Landing in Germany 1630, he defeated the German general Wallenstein at Lützen, SW of Leipzig Nov 6, 1632, but was killed in the battle. He was known as the "Lion of the North".

Gustavus Vasa (Gustavus or Gustaf I) 1496–1560. King of Sweden from 1523, when he was elected after leading the Swedish revolt against Danish rule. He united and pacified the country and established Lutheranism as the state religion.

Gutenberg Johann *c.*1400–1468. German printer, the inventor of printing from movable metal type, based on the Chinese wood-block-type method (although Laurens Janszoon ◊Coster has a rival claim).

Guthrie Woody (Woodrow Wilson) 1912–1967. US folk singer and songwriter. His left-wing protest songs, "dustbowl ballads", and "talking blues" influenced, among others, Bob Dylan; they include "Deportees", "Hard Travelin'", and "This Land Is Your Land".

Guyana Cooperative Republic of *area* 82,978 sq mi/ 214,969 sq km *capital* (and port) Georgetown *towns and cities* New Amsterdam, Mabaruma *physical* coastal plain rises into rolling highlands with savanna in S; mostly tropical rainforest *features* Mount Roraima; Kaietur National Park, including Kaietur Fall on the Potaro (tributary of Essequibo) 821 ft/250 m *head of state* Cheddi Jagan from 1992 *head of government* Samuel Hinds from 1992 *political system* democratic republic *political parties* People's National Congress (PNC), Afro-Guyanan nationalist socialist; People's Progressive Party (PPP), Indian Marxist-Leninist *exports* sugar, rice, rum, timber, diamonds, bauxite, shrimps, molasses *currency* Guyanese dollar *population* (1993 est) 800,000 (51% descendants of workers introduced from India to work the sugar plantations after the abolition of slavery, 30% black, 5% American Indian; growth rate 2% p.a. *life expectancy* men 62, women 68 *languages* English (official), Hindi, American Indian *media* one government-owned daily newspaper; one independent paper published three times a week, on which the government puts pressure by withholding foreign exchange for newsprint; one weekly independent in the same position. There is also legislation that restricts exchange of information between public officials, government, and the press *religions* Christian 57%, Hindu 33%, Sunni Muslim 9% *literacy* men 98%, women 95% *GNP* $290 per head (1991) *chronology* *1831* Became British colony under name of British Guiana. *1953* Assembly elections won by left-wing PPP; Britain suspended constitution and installed interim administration, fearing communist takeover. *1961* Internal self-government granted; Cheddi Jagan became prime minister. *1964* PNC leader Forbes Burnham led PPP–PNC coalition. *1966* Independence achieved from Britain. *1970* Guyana became a republic within the Commonwealth. *1980* New constitution adopted. *1981* Forbes Burnham became first executive president under new constitution. *1985* Burnham died; succeeded by Desmond Hoyte. *1992* PPP had decisive victory in assembly elections; Cheddi Jagan became president.

Gwent county of S Wales, created 1974 *area* 533 sq mi/1,380 sq km *towns and cities* Cwmbran (administrative headquarters), Abergavenny, Newport, Tredegar *features* Wye Valley; Tintern Abbey; Legionary Museum at Caerleon, and Roman amphitheater; Chepstow and Raglan castles *industries* salmon and trout from the Wye and Usk rivers; iron and steel at Llanwern; sheep farming, market gardening; chemicals, aluminum, tin plate *population* (1991) 442,200 *languages* English; 2.4% Welsh-speaking.

Gwynedd county of NW Wales, created 1974 *area* 1,494 sq mi/3,870 sq km *towns and cities* Caernarvon (administrative headquarters), Bangor *features* Snowdonia National Park including Snowdon, the highest mountain in Wales 3,561 ft/1,085 m, and the largest Welsh lake, Llyn Tegid (Bala Lake); Caernarvon Castle.

gymnastics physical exercises, originally for health and training (so called from the way in which men of ancient Greece trained: *gymnos* "naked"). The *gymnasia* were schools for training competitors for public games.

Men's gymnastics includes high bar, parallel bars, horse vault, rings, pommel horse, and floor exercises. *Women's gymnastics* includes asymmetrical bars, side horse vault, balance beam, and floor exercises. Also popular are *sports acrobatics*, performed by gymnasts in pairs, trios, or fours to music, where the emphasis is on dance, balance, and timing, and *rhythmic gymnastics*, choreographed to music and performed by individuals or six-girl teams, with small hand apparatus such as a ribbon, ball, or hoop.

gymnosperm in botany, any plant whose seeds are exposed, as opposed to the structurally more advanced ◊angiosperms, where they are inside an ovary. The group includes conifers and related plants such as cycads and ginkgos, whose seeds develop in ◊cones. Fossil gymnosperms have been found in rocks about 350 million years old.

gynecology in medicine, a specialist branch concerned with disorders of the female reproductive system.

Haakon IV 1204–1263. King of Norway from 1217, the son of Haakon III. Under his rule, Norway flourished both militarily and culturally; he took control of the Faeroe Islands, Greenland 1261, and Iceland 1262–64. His court was famed throughout N Europe.

Haakon VII 1872–1957. King of Norway from 1905. Born Prince Charles, the second son of Frederick VIII of Denmark, he was elected king of Norway on separation from Sweden, and in 1906 he took the name Haakon. In World War II he carried on the resistance from Britain during the Nazi occupation of his country. He returned 1945.

Haarlem industrial city and capital of the province of North Holland, the Netherlands, 12 mi/20 km W of Amsterdam; population (1991) 149,500. At Velsea to the N a road-rail tunnel runs under the North Sea Canal, linking North and South Holland. Industries include chemicals, pharmaceuticals, textiles, and printing. Haarlem is renowned for flowering bulbs and has a 15th–16th-century cathedral and a Frans Hals museum.

habeas corpus in law, a writ directed to someone who has custody of a person, ordering him or her to bring the person before the court issuing the writ and to justify why the person is detained in custody.

Traditional rights to habeas corpus were embodied in law mainly owing to Lord Shaftesbury, in the English Habeas Corpus Act 1679. The main principles were adopted in the US Constitution.

Haber Fritz 1868–1934. German chemist whose conversion of atmospheric nitrogen to ammonia opened the way for the synthetic fertilizer industry. His study of the combustion of hydrocarbons led to the commercial "cracking" or fractional distillation of natural oil (petroleum) into its components (for example, diesel, gasoline, and paraffin). In electrochemistry, he was the first to demonstrate that oxidation and reduction take place at the electrodes; from this he developed a general electrochemical theory.

habitat in ecology, the localized ◊environment in which an organism lives. Habitats are often described by the dominant plant type or physical feature, such as a grassland habitat or rocky seashore habitat.

hacking unauthorized access to a computer, either for fun or for malicious or fraudulent purposes. Hackers generally use microcomputers and telephone lines to obtain access. In computing, the term is used in a wider sense to mean using software for enjoyment or self-education, not necessarily involving unauthorized access.

haddock marine fish *Melanogrammus aeglefinus* of the cod family found off the N Atlantic coast. It is brown with silvery underparts and black markings above the pectoral fins.

It can grow to a length of 3 ft/1 m. Haddock are important food fish; about 100 million lb/45 million kg are taken annually off the New England fishing banks alone.

Hades in Greek mythology, the underworld where spirits went after death, usually depicted as a cavern or pit underneath the Earth, the entrance of which was guarded by the three-headed dog Cerberus. It was presided over by the god Pluto or Hades (Roman Dis). Pluto was the brother of Zeus and married ◊Persephone, daughter of Demeter and Zeus.

Hadrian (Publius Aelius Hadrianus) AD 76–138. Roman emperor from 117. Born in Spain, he was adopted by his relative, the emperor Trajan, whom he succeeded. He abandoned Trajan's conquests in Mesopotamia and adopted a defensive policy, which included the building of Hadrian's Wall in Britain.

Hadrian's Wall Roman fortification built AD 122–126 to mark England's northern boundary and abandoned about 383; its ruins run 115 mi/185 km from Wallsend on the river Tyne to Maryport, W Cumbria. In some parts, the wall was covered with a glistening, white coat of mortar. The fort at South Shields, Arbeia, built to defend the eastern end, is being reconstructed.

hadron in physics, a subatomic particle that experiences the strong nuclear force. Each is made up of two or three indivisible particles called ◊quarks. The hadrons are grouped into the ◊baryons (protons, neutrons, and hyperons) and the ◊mesons (particles with masses between those of electrons and protons).

hemoglobin protein used by all vertebrates and some invertebrates for oxygen transport because the two substances combine reversibly. In vertebrates it occurs in red blood cells (erythrocytes), giving them their color.

hemophilia any of several inherited diseases in which normal blood clotting is impaired. The sufferer experiences prolonged bleeding from the slightest wound, as well as painful internal bleeding without apparent cause.

hafnium silvery, metallic element, symbol Hf, atomic number 72, atomic weight 178.49. It occurs in nature in ores of zirconium, the properties of which it resembles. Hafnium absorbs neutrons better than most metals, so it is used in the control rods of nuclear reactors; it is also used for light-bulb filaments.

Hague, The (Dutch *'s-Gravenhage* or *Den Haag*) capital of the province of South Holland and seat of the Netherlands government, linked by canal with Rotterdam and Amsterdam; population (1991) 444,200.

Hahn Otto 1879–1968. German physical chemist who discovered nuclear fission (see ◊nuclear energy). In 1938 with Fritz Strassmann (1902–1980), he discovered that uranium nuclei split when bombarded with neutrons, which led to the development of the atomic bomb. He was awarded the Nobel Prize for Chemistry 1944.

hahnium name proposed by US scientists for the element also known as ◊unnilpentium (atomic number

105), in honor of German nuclear physicist Otto Hahn. The symbol is Ha.

Haifa port in NE Israel, at the foot of Mount Carmel; population (1988) 222,600. Industries include oil refining and chemicals.

It is the capital of a district of the same name.

Haig Douglas, 1st Earl Haig 1861–1928. British army officer, commander in chief in World War I. His Somme offensive in France in the summer of 1916 made considerable advances only at enormous cost to human life, and his Passchendaele offensive in Belgium from July to Nov 1917 achieved little at a similar loss. He was created field marshal 1917 and, after retiring, became first president of the ◊British Legion 1921.

hail precipitation in the form of pellets of ice (hailstones). It is caused by the circulation of moisture in strong convection currents, usually within cumulonimbus ◊clouds.

Haile Selassie Ras (Prince) Tafari ("the Lion of Judah") 1892–1975. Emperor of Ethiopia 1930–74. He pleaded unsuccessfully to the League of Nations against the Italian conquest of his country 1935–36, and was then deposed and fled to the UK. He went to Egypt 1940 and raised an army which he led into Ethiopia Jan 1941 alongside British forces and was restored to the throne May 5. He was deposed by a military coup 1974 and died in captivity the following year. Followers of the Rastafarian religion (see ◊Rastafarianism) believe that he was the Messiah, the incarnation of God (Jah).

Hainan island in the South China Sea; area 13,124 sq mi/34,000 sq km; population (1990) 6,557,000. The capital is Haikou. In 1987 Hainan was designated a Special Economic Zone; in 1988 it was separated from Guangdong and made a new province. It is China's second-largest island.

Haiphong industrial port in N Vietnam; population (1989) 456,000. Among its industries are shipbuilding and the making of cement, plastics, phosphates, and textiles.

hair threadlike structure growing from mammalian skin. Each hair grows from a pit-shaped follicle in the outer skin layer (epidermal cells).

Hair consists of dead cells impregnated with the protein keratin.

Haiti Republic of (*République d'Haïti*) *area* 10,712 sq mi/ 27,750 sq km *capital* Port-au-Prince *towns and cities* Cap-Haïtien, Gonaïves, Les Cayes *physical* mainly mountainous and tropical; occupies W third of Hispaniola Island in Caribbean Sea; seriously deforested *features* oldest black republic in the world; only French-speaking republic in the Americas; island of La Tortuga off N coast was formerly a pirate lair *head of state* Jean-Bertrand Aristide from 1994 *head of government* Robert Malval from 1993 *political system* transitional *political parties* National Front for Change and Democracy (FNCD), left of center; National Alliance for Democracy and Progress (ANDP), right of center *exports* coffee, sugar, sisal, cotton, cocoa, bauxite *currency* gourde *population* (1993 est) 6,600,000; growth rate 1.7% p.a.; one of highest population densities in the world; about 1.5 million Haitians live outside Haiti (in US and Canada); about 400,000 live in virtual slavery in the Dominican Republic, where they went or were sent to cut sugar cane *life expectancy* men 55, women 58 *languages* French (official, spoken by literate 10% minority),

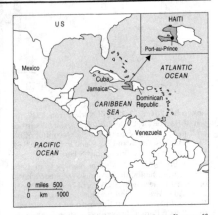

Creole (spoken by 90% black majority) *media* no official censorship, but journalists critical of the government have been beaten and killed. There are three daily papers, the largest of which has a circulation (1993) of 6,000, and four weekly newspapers (only one of these [*Libète*] is in Creole, the majority language, and its circulation (1993) is 12,000). Radio is more important than the press since most of the population are illiterate. There are many small radio stations and news is also circulated on cassette *religions* Christian 95% of which 80% Roman Catholic, voodoo 4% *literacy* men 59%, women 47% *GNP* $370 per head (1991) *chronology 1804* Independence achieved from France. *1915* Haiti invaded by US; remained under US control until 1934. *1957* Dr François Duvalier (Papa Doc) elected president. *1964* Duvalier pronounced himself president for life. *1971* Duvalier died, succeeded by his son, Jean-Claude (Baby Doc); thousands murdered during Duvalier era. *1986* Duvalier deposed; replaced by Lt Gen Henri Namphy as head of a governing council. *1988* Feb: Leslie Manigat became president. Namphy staged a military coup in June, but another coup in Sept led by Brig Gen Prosper Avril replaced him with a civilian government under military control. *1989* Coup attempt against Avril foiled; US aid resumed. *1990* Opposition elements expelled; Ertha Pascal-Trouillot acting president. *1991* Jean-Bertrand Aristide elected president but later overthrown in military coup led by Brig Gen Raoul Cedras. Efforts to reinstate Aristide failed. Joseph Nerette became interim head of state. Sanctions imposed by Organization of American States (OAS) and US. *1992* Economic sanctions eased by the US but increased by the OAS. Marc Bazin appointed premier. *1993* June: Bazin resigned; United Nations (UN) embargo imposed. July: Aristide's return agreed under UN-brokered accord. Aug: international sanctions lifted; Robert Malval nominated premier. Oct: Aristide's return blocked by military; UN embargo reimposed. Malval resigned but remained as caretaker prime minister. *1994* Cedras appointed Emile Jonassaint, a supporter of the military regime, to replace Nerette as president. Sept: threat of US invasion led to Cedras regime recognizing Aristide as president, under agreement brokered by former US president Jimmy Carter. Oct: Cedras relinquished power and withdrew to Panama; Aristide returned.

hajj pilgrimage to Mecca that should be undertaken by every Muslim at least once in a lifetime, unless he or she is prevented by financial or health difficulties. A Muslim who has been on hajj may take the additional name Hajji. Many of the pilgrims on hajj also visit Medina, where the prophet Mohammed is buried.

hake any of various marine fishes of the cod family, found in N European, African, and American waters. They have silvery, elongated bodies and attain a length of 3 ft/1 m. They have two dorsal fins and one long anal fin. The silver hake *Merluccius bilinearis* is an important food fish.

Halas George Stanley 1895–1983. US athlete and sports promoter. He was founder of the Chicago Bears of the National Football League and was an active player until 1929. He acted as coach until retirement 1967, introducing the T-formation and giving special emphasis to the passing offense.

Hale George Ellery 1868–1938. US astronomer who made pioneer studies of the Sun and founded three major observatories. In 1889 he invented the spectroheliograph, a device for photographing the Sun at particular wavelengths. In 1917 he established on Mount Wilson, California, a 100-in/2.5-m reflector, the world's largest telescope until superseded 1948 by the 200-in/5-m reflector on Mount Palomar, which Hale had planned just before he died.

Hale Nathan 1755–1776. American Revolution war hero, hanged by the British as a spy. He crossed British lines disguised as a teacher and told George ◊Washington that he wished "to be useful." He was sent behind enemy lines on Long Island to gather information about the British army. Captured, he was hanged. Reputedly his final words were "I only regret that I have but one life to lose for my country."

half-life during ◊radioactive decay, the time in which the strength of a radioactive source decays to half its original value. In theory, the decay process is never complete and there is always some residual radioactivity. For this reason, the half-life of a radioactive isotope is measured, rather than the total decay time. It may vary from millionths of a second to billions of years.

half note in music, a note value half the duration of a whole note. It is written as an empty white note-head with a stem. It is the basic unit of beat for the following meters: 2/2, 4/2, and cut time (alla breve).

halftone process technique used in printing to reproduce the full range of tones in a photograph or other illustration. The intensity of the printed color is varied from full strength to the lightest shades, even if one color of ink is used. The picture to be reproduced is photographed through a screen ruled with a rectangular mesh of fine lines, which breaks up the tones of the original into areas of dots that vary in frequency according to the intensity of the tone. In the darker areas the dots run together; in the lighter areas they have more space between them.

halibut any of several large flatfishes of the genus *Hippoglossus*, in the family Pleuronectidae, found in the Atlantic and Pacific oceans. The largest of the flatfishes, they may grow to 6 ft/2 m and weigh 200–300 lb/90–135 kg. They are very dark mottled brown or green above and pure white beneath. The Atlantic halibut *H. hippoglossus* is caught offshore at depths from 600 ft/180 m to 2,400 ft/730 m.

Halifax capital of Nova Scotia, E Canada's main port; population (1986) 296,000. Its industries include oil refining and food processing. There are six military bases in Halifax and it is a major center of oceanography. It was founded by British settlers 1749.

Hall Charles 1863–1914. US chemist who developed a process for the commercial production of aluminum 1886.

He found that when mixed with cryolite (sodium aluminum fluoride), the melting point of aluminum was lowered and electrolysis became commercially viable. It had previously been as costly as gold.

By 1890, Hall was in charge of the Aluminum Company of the US and aluminum utensils began to spread throughout the world.

Halley Edmond 1656–1742. English astronomer who not only identified 1705 the comet that was later to be known by his name, but also compiled a star catalog, detected the proper motion of stars using historical records, and began a line of research that—after his death—resulted in a reasonably accurate calculation of the astronomical unit.

Halley was also a pioneer geophysicist and meteorologist and worked in many other fields including mathematics. He was a friend of Isaac ◊Newton, whose *Principia* he financed.

Halley's comet comet that orbits the Sun about every 76 years, named for Edmond Halley who calculated its orbit. It is the brightest and most conspicuous of the periodic comets. Recorded sightings go back over 2,000 years. It travels around the Sun in the opposite direction to the planets. Its orbit is inclined at almost 20° to the main plane of the Solar System and ranges between the orbits of Venus and Neptune. It will next reappear 2061.

Halloween or Hallowe'en evening of Oct 31, immediately preceding the Christian feast of Allhallows or All Saints' Day. Customs associated with Halloween include children wearing masks or costumes, and "trick or treating"—from house to house collecting such treats as candy, fruit, and coins.

hallucinogen any substance that acts on the ◊central nervous system to produce changes in perception and mood and often hallucinations. Hallucinogens include ◊LSD, ◊peyote, and mescaline. Their effects are unpredictable and they are illegal in most countries.

halogen any of a group of five nonmetallic elements with similar chemical bonding properties: fluorine, chlorine, bromine, iodine, and astatine. They form a linked group in the ◊periodic table of the elements, descending from fluorine, the most reactive, to astatine, the least reactive. They combine directly with most metals to form salts, such as common salt (NaCl). Each halogen has seven electrons in its valence shell, which accounts for the chemical similarities displayed by the group.

halon organic chemical compound containing one or two carbon atoms, together with ◊bromine and other ◊halogens. The most commonly used are halon 1211 (bromochlorodifluoromethane) and halon 1301 (bromotrifluoromethane). The halons are gases and are widely used in fire extinguishers. As destroyers of the ozone layer, they are up to ten times more effective than ◊chlorofluorocarbons (CFCs), to which they are chemically related.

Hals Frans c.1581–1666. Flemish-born painter of lively portraits. His work includes the *Laughing Cavalier* 1624 (Wallace Collection, London), and large groups of military companies, governors of charities, and others (many examples in the Frans Hals Museum, Haarlem, the Netherlands). In the 1620s he experimented with genre scenes.

Halsey William Frederick 1882–1959. US admiral. A highly skilled naval air tactician, his handling of carrier fleets in World War II played a significant role in the eventual defeat of Japan. He was appointed commander of US Task Force 16 in the Pacific 1942 and almost immediately launched the Doolittle raid on Tokyo. He took part in operations throughout the Far East, including Santa Cruz, Guadalcanal, Bougainville, and the Battle of Leyte Gulf. He was promoted to fleet admiral 1945 and retired 1947.

He was appointed commander of the South Pacific Area Oct 1942 and from June 1943 alternated command of the US 3rd Fleet with Admiral Spruance. He led this fleet at the Battle of Leyte Gulf 1944; he almost fell into a Japanese trap but was saved by the timely appearance of Admiral Kincaid and the 7th Fleet.

Hamburg largest inland port of Europe, in Germany, on the river Elbe; population (1988) 1,571,000. Industries include oil, chemicals, electronics, and cosmetics.

Hamilton capital (since 1815) of Bermuda, on Bermuda Island; population about (1980) 1,617. It has a deep-sea harbor. Hamilton was founded 1612.

Hamilton Alexander 1757–1804. US politician who influenced the adoption of a constitution with a strong central government and was the first secretary of the Treasury 1789–95. He led the Federalist Party, and incurred the bitter hatred of Aaron Burr when he voted against Burr and in favor of Thomas Jefferson for the presidency 1801. Challenged to a duel by Burr, Hamilton was wounded and died the next day.

Hamilton Emma (born Amy Lyon), Lady Hamilton 1765–1815. wife of Sir William Hamilton (1730–1803) from 1791, envoy to the court of Naples, and mistress of Admiral Horatio ◊Nelson, whom she met in Naples in 1793. After his return from the Nile battle 1798, during the Napoleonic Wars, she became his mistress and their daughter, Horatia, was born 1801. After Nelson's death in battle 1805, Lady Hamilton spent her inheritance and died in poverty in Calais. She had been a great beauty and had posed for the great artists of her youth, especially George ◊Romney.

Hammarskjöld Dag 1905–1961. Swedish secretary-general of the United Nations 1953–61. He opposed Britain over the ◊Suez Crisis 1956. His attempts to solve the problem of the Congo (now Zaire), where he was killed in a plane crash, were criticized by the USSR. He was awarded the Nobel Peace Prize 1961.

hammer in track and field athletics, a throwing event in which only men compete. The hammer is a spherical weight attached to a chain with a handle. The competitor spins the hammer over his head to gain momentum, within the confines of a circle, and throws it as far as he can. The hammer weighs 16 lb/7.26 kg and may originally have been a blacksmith's hammer.

hammerhead any of several species of shark of the genus *Sphyrna*, found in tropical seas, characterized by having eyes at the ends of flattened extensions of the skull. Hammerheads can grow to 13 ft/4 m.

Hammerstein Oscar, II 1895–1960. US lyricist and librettist. He collaborated with Richard ◊Rodgers over a period of 16 years on some of the best-known American musicals, including *Oklahoma!* 1943 (Pulitzer Prize), *Carousel* 1945, *South Pacific* 1949 (Pulitzer Prize), *The King and I* 1951, and *The Sound of Music* 1959.

Hammett (Samuel) Dashiell 1894–1961. US crime novelist. He introduced the "hard-boiled" detective character into fiction and attracted a host of imitators, with works including *The Maltese Falcon* 1930 (filmed 1941), *The Glass Key* 1931 (filmed 1942), and his most successful novel, the light-hearted *The Thin Man* 1932 (filmed 1934). His Marxist politics were best expressed in *Red Harvest* 1929, which depicts the corruption of capitalism in "Poisonville".

Hammond city in the NW corner of Indiana, on the Calumet River, just S of Chicago; population (1990) 84,200. It is a major transportation center, connecting to Lake Michigan via the Calumet Canal. Industries include soap, cereal products, publishing, railroad equipment, and transportation facilities for the city's surrounding steel plants and oil refineries.

Hampshire county of S England *area* 1,455 sq mi/ 3,770 sq km *cities* Winchester (administrative headquarters), Southampton, Portsmouth, Gosport *features* New Forest, area 144 sq mi/373 sq km, a Saxon royal hunting ground *famous people* Jane Austen, Charles Dickens, Gilbert White.

Hampton Wade 1818–1902. US politician and Confederate military leader. During the Civil War 1861–65, he was appointed brigadier general in the cavalry 1862 and commander of the entire Confederate cavalry corps 1864. After the end of the war 1865 he returned to South Carolina, serving as governor 1876–79 and US senator 1879–91.

hamster rodent of the family Cricetidae with a thick-set body, short tail, and cheek pouches to carry food. Several genera are found across Asia and in SE Europe. Hamsters are often kept as pets.

Han member of the majority ethnic group in China, numbering about 990 million. The Hans speak a wide variety of dialects of the same monosyllabic language, a member of the Sino-Tibetan family. Their religion combines Buddhism, Taoism, Confucianism, and ancestor worship.

Hand Learned Billings 1872–1961. US jurist. He became federal district judge under President Taft 1909 and was appointed to the Second Circuit Court of Appeals by President Coolidge 1924. He served as chief judge of that court 1939–51, handing down opinions in landmark copyright, antitrust, and the constitutional First Amendment cases.

Handel Georg Friedrich 1685–1759. German composer, a British subject from 1726. His first opera, *Almira*, was performed in Hamburg 1705. In 1710 he was appointed kapellmeister to the elector of Hanover (the future George I of England). In 1712 he settled in England, where he established his popularity with such works as the *Water Music* 1717 (written for George I). His great choral works include the *Messiah* 1742 and the later oratorios *Samson* 1743, *Belshazzar* 1745, *Judas Maccabaeus* 1747, and *Jephtha* 1752.

handshake in computing, an exchange of signals between two devices that establishes the communications channels and protocols necessary for the devices to send and receive data.

Hangchow alternative transcription of ◊Hangzhou, a port in Zhejiang province, China.

hang gliding technique of unpowered flying using air currents, perfected by US engineer Francis Rogallo in the 1970s. The aeronaut is strapped into a carrier, attached to a sail wing of nylon stretched over an aluminum frame like a paper dart, and jumps into the air from a high place, where updrafts of warm air allow soaring on the "thermals". See ◊gliding.

Hangzhou or *Hangchow* port and capital of Zhejiang province, China; population (1989) 1,330,000. It has jute, steel, chemical, tea, and silk industries.

Hannibal 247–182 BC . Carthaginian general from 221 BC , son of Hamilcar Barca. His siege of Saguntum (now Sagunto, near Valencia) precipitated the Second ◊Punic War with Rome. Following a campaign in Italy (after crossing the Alps in 218), Hannibal was the victor at Trasimene in 217 and Cannae in 216, but he failed to take Rome. In 203 he returned to Carthage to meet a Roman invasion but was defeated at Zama in 202 and exiled in 196 at Rome's insistence.

Hanoi capital of Vietnam, on the Red River; population (1989) 1,088,900. Central Hanoi has one of the highest population densities in the world: 3,250 per acre/1,300 people per hectare. Industries include textiles, paper, and engineering.

Hanover industrial city, capital of Lower Saxony, Germany; population (1988) 506,000. Industries include machinery, vehicles, electrical goods, rubber, textiles, and oil refining.

Hanseatic League confederation of N European trading cities from the 12th century to 1669. At its height in the late 14th century the Hanseatic League included over 160 cities and towns, among them Lübeck, Hamburg, Cologne, Breslau, and Kraków. The basis of the league's power was its monopoly of the Baltic trade and its relations with Flanders and England. The decline of the Hanseatic League from the 15th century was caused by the closing and moving of trade routes and the development of nation states.

Hanukah or *Chanukah* Jewish festival of lights, which lasts eight days in December and celebrates the recapture of the Temple in Jerusalem by Judas Maccabaeus in 164 BC , and the "miracle" of one day's oil lasting for eight days when the Eternal Light was relit.

haploid having a single set of ◊chromosomes in each cell. Most higher organisms are ◊diploid—that is, they have two sets—but their gametes (sex cells) are haploid. Some plants, such as mosses, liverworts, and many seaweeds, are haploid, and male honey bees are haploid because they develop from eggs that have not been fertilized.

Hapsburg European royal family, former imperial house of Austria-Hungary. The name comes from the family castle in Switzerland. The Hapsburgs held the title Holy Roman emperor 1273–91,1298–1308, 1438–1740, and 1745–1806. They ruled Austria from 1278, under the title emperor 1806–1918.

hara-kiri ritual suicide of the Japanese samurai (military caste) since the 12th century. Today it is illegal. It was carried out to avoid dishonor or to demonstrate sincerity, either voluntarily or on the order of a feudal lord. The correct Japanese term is *seppuku*, and, traditionally, the ritual involved cutting open one's stomach with a dagger. It was then proper to have one's head struck off by another samurai's sword.

Harare capital of Zimbabwe, on the Mashonaland plateau, about 5,000 ft/1,525 m above sea level; population (1982) 656,000. It is the center of a rich farming area (tobacco and corn), with metallurgical and food processing industries.

Harbin or *Haerhpin* or *Pinkiang* port on the Songhua River, NE China, capital of Heilongjiang province;

population (1989) 2,800,000. Industries include metallurgy, machinery, paper, food processing, and sugar refining, and it is a major rail junction. Harbin was developed by Russian settlers after Russia was granted trading rights here 1896, and more Russians arrived as refugees after the October Revolution 1917. In World War II, it was the key objective of the Soviet invasion of Manchuria Aug 1945.

hard copy computer output printed on paper.

hard disk in computing, a storage device usually consisting of a rigid metal ◊disk coated with a magnetic material. Data are read from and written to the disk by means of a disk drive. The hard disk may be permanently fixed into the drive or in the form of a disk pack that can be removed and exchanged with a different pack. Hard disks vary from large units with capacities of more than 3,000 megabytes, intended for use with mainframe computers, to small units with capacities as low as 20 megabytes, intended for use with microcomputers.

Hardicanute c.1019–1042. King of Denmark from 1028, and of England from 1040; son of Canute. In England he was considered a harsh ruler.

Harding Warren G(amaliel) 1865–1923. 29th president of the US 1921–23, a Republican whose administration was known for its corruption. Harding entered the US Senate in 1914. As president he concluded the peace treaties with Germany, Austria, and Hungary, and in the same year called the Washington Conference. He opposed US membership in the ◊League of Nations, thus reinforcing the traditional US position of neutrality. There were charges of corruption among members of his cabinet (the ◊Teapot Dome Scandal), and Harding generally turned a benign eye to the activities of his close associates.

hardness physical property of materials that governs their use. Methods of heat treatment can increase the hardness of metals. A scale of hardness was devised by German–Austrian mineralogist Friedrich Mohs in the 1800s, based upon the hardness of certain minerals from soft talc (Mohs' hardness 1) to diamond (10), the hardest of all materials.

See also ◊Brinell hardness test. The *hardness of water* refers to the presence of dissolved minerals in it that prevent soap lathering, particularly compounds of calcium and magnesium. Treatment with a water softener may remove or neutralize them.

hardware the mechanical, electrical, and electronic components of a computer system, as opposed to the various programs, which constitute ◊software.

In a microcomputer, hardware might include the circuit boards, the power supply and housing of the processing unit, the VDT (screen), external memory devices such as disk drives, a printer, the keyboard, and so on.

Hardy Thomas 1840–1928. English novelist and poet. His novels, set in rural "Wessex" (his native West Country), portray intense human relationships played out in a harshly indifferent natural world. They include *Far From the Madding Crowd* 1874, *The Return of the Native* 1878, *The Mayor of Casterbridge* 1886, *The Woodlanders* 1887, *Tess of the d'Urbervilles* 1891, and *Jude the Obscure* 1895. His poetry includes the *Wessex Poems* 1898, the blank-verse epic of the Napoleonic Wars *The Dynasts* 1904–08, and several volumes of lyrics.

hare mammal of the genus *Lepus* of the family Leporidae (which also includes rabbits) in the order

Lagomorpha. Hares are larger than rabbits, with very long, black-tipped ears, long hind legs, and short, upturned tails.

Unlike rabbits, hares do not burrow. Their furred, open-eyed young (leverets) are cared for in a shallow depression rather than a specially prepared nest cavity. Jack rabbits and snowshoe rabbits are actually hares.

harebell perennial plant *Campanula rotundifolia* of the ◊bellflower family, with bell-shaped blue flowers, found on dry grassland and heaths. It is known in Scotland as the bluebell.

Hare Krishna popular name for a member of the ◊International Society for Krishna Consciousness, derived from their chant.

Hargreaves James English inventor who co-invented a carding machine for combing wool 1760. About 1764 he invented his "spinning jenny" (patented 1770), which enabled a number of threads to be spun simultaneously by one person.

Harlan John Marshall 1899–1971. US jurist and Supreme Court associate justice 1954–71. Chief counsel for the New York Crime Commission 1951–53, Harlan was appointed by President Eisenhower to the US Supreme Court 1954. As associate justice, he was a conservative, especially in the areas of free speech and civil and criminal rights.

Harlem commercial and residential district of Manhattan, New York City. The principal thoroughfare, 125th Street, runs E–W between the Hudson River and the East River. It was a Dutch settlement in 1658; it developed as a black population center from World War I. Harlem's heyday was the 1920s, when it established its reputation as the intellectual, cultural, and entertainment center of black America. Once noted for its music clubs and theaters, it retained the famed Apollo Theatre; the Dance Theater and Theater of Harlem are also here.

Harlingen city in the southeast corner of Texas, S of Corpus Christi and just N of the Mexican border; population (1990) 48,735. Connected to the Rio Grande by an intracoastal waterway, it serves as the processing and marketing area for the lower Rio Grande Valley. Industries include citrus-fruit processing and cotton products.

Harlow Jean. Adopted name of Harlean Carpenter 1911–1937. US film actress. She was the original "platinum blonde" and the wisecracking sex symbol of the 1930s. Her films include *Hell's Angels* 1930, *Red Dust* 1932, *Platinum Blonde* 1932, *Dinner at Eight* 1933, *China Seas* 1935, and *Saratoga* 1937, during the filming of which she died (her part was completed by a double).

harmonica or **mouth organ** pocket-sized reed organ blown directly from the mouth, invented by Charles Wheatstone 1829.

harmonium keyboard reed organ of the 19th century, powered by foot-operated bellows and incorporating lever-action knee swells to influence dynamics. It was invented by Alexandre Debain in Paris about 1842.

harmony in music, any simultaneous combination of sounds, as opposed to melody, which is a succession of sounds. Although the term suggests a pleasant or agreeable sound, it is applied to any combination of notes, whether consonant or dissonant. The theory of harmony deals with the formation of chords and their interrelation and logical progression.

Harold I King of England from 1035. The illegitimate son of Canute, known as *Harefoot*, he claimed the throne 1035 when the legitimate heir Hardicanute was in Denmark. He was elected king 1037.

Harold II *c.*1020–1066. King of England from Jan 1066. He succeeded his father Earl Godwin 1053 as earl of Wessex. In 1063 William of Normandy (◊William the Conqueror) tricked him into swearing to support his claim to the English throne, and when the Witan (a council of high-ranking religious and secular men) elected Harold to succeed Edward the Confessor, William prepared to invade. Meanwhile, Harold's treacherous brother Tostig (died 1066) joined the king of Norway, Harald Hardrada (1015–1066), in invading Northumbria. Harold routed and killed them at Stamford Bridge Sept 25. Three days later William landed at Pevensey, Sussex, and Harold was killed at the Battle of Hastings Oct 14, 1066.

harp plucked musical string instrument, with the strings stretched vertically within a wood and brass soundbox of triangular shape. The orchestral harp is the largest instrument of its type. It has up to 47 diatonically tuned strings, in a range of seven octaves, and seven double-action pedals to alter pitch. Composers for the harp include Mozart, Ravel, Salzedo, and Holliger.

Harper's Ferry village in W Virginia, where the Potomac and Shenandoah rivers meet. In 1859 antislavery leader John ◊Brown seized the federal government's arsenal here, an action that helped precipitate the Civil War.

During the war the strategically located settlement was the site of several engagements. In commemoration, Harper's Ferry National Historical Park is here.

harpsichord the largest and grandest of 18th-century keyboard string instruments, used in orchestras and as a solo instrument. The strings are plucked by "jacks" made of leather or quill, and multiple keyboards offering variation in tone are common. The revival of the harpsichord repertoire in the 20th century owes much to Wanda Landowska and Ralph Kirkpatrick (1911–1984).

Harpy in early Greek mythology, a wind spirit; in later legend the Harpies have horrific women's faces and the bodies of vultures.

harrier bird of prey of the genus *Circus*, family Accipitridae. Harriers have long wings and legs, short beaks and soft plumage. They are found throughout the world.

The northern harrier or marsh hawk *C. cyaneus* is native to North America.

Harrier the only truly successful vertical takeoff and landing fixed-wing aircraft, often called the *jump jet*. Built in Britain, it made its first flight 1966. It has a single jet engine and a set of swiveling nozzles. These deflect the jet exhaust vertically downward for takeoff and landing, and to the rear for normal flight. Designed to fly from confined spaces with minimal ground support, it refuels in midair.

Harriman (William) Averell 1891–1986. US diplomat. He was administrator of lend-lease in World War II and warned of the Soviet Union's aggressive intentions from his post as ambassador to the USSR 1943–46. He became Democratic secretary of commerce 1946–48 in Truman's administration, governor of New York 1955–58, and negotiator of the Nuclear Test Ban Treaty with the USSR 1963. He served the Lyndon Johnson administration 1968–69 in the opening rounds of the Vietnam War peace talks at which he was chief negotiator.

Harper's Ferry *A view of the town of Harper's Ferry, West Virginia, US, 1865. Of great strategic importance during the American Civil War, it changed hands several times. A stand by the Union army 1862 seriously delayed Robert E Lee's march north.*

Harris Louis 1921– . US pollster. He joined the Roper opinion polling organization 1947 and became a partner in that firm 1954. Developing his own research techniques, he founded Louis Harris and Associates 1956. Hired by the 1960 Kennedy presidential campaign, Harris gained a national reputation and later served as a consultant to the CBS television network and as a political columnist.

Harris Richard 1932– . Irish film actor. He is known for playing dominating characters in such films as *This Sporting Life* 1963. His other films include *Camelot* 1967, *A Man Called Horse* 1970, *Robin and Marian* 1976, *Tarzan the Ape Man* 1981, *The Field* 1990, and *Unforgiven* 1992.

Harrisburg capital city of Pennsylvania, located in the S central part of the state, on the Susquehanna River; seat of Dauphin County; population (1990) 52,400. Industries include steel, railroad equipment, food processing, printing and publishing, and clothing.

Harrison Benjamin 1833–1901. 23rd president of the US 1889–93, a Republican. He called the first Pan-American Conference, which led to the establishment of the Pan American Union, to improve inter-American cooperation, and develop commercial ties. In 1948 this became the ◊Organization of American States.

Harrison Rex (Reginald Carey) 1908–1990. English film and theater actor. He appeared in over 40 films and numerous plays, often portraying sophisticated and somewhat eccentric characters, such as the waspish Professor Higgins in *My Fair Lady* 1964 (Academy Award), the musical version of *Pygmalion*. His other films include *Blithe Spirit* 1945, *The Ghost and Mrs Muir* 1947, and *Dr Doolittle* 1967.

Harte (Francis) Bret 1839–1902. US writer and humorist of the American West. He founded *The*

Overland Monthly 1868, in which he wrote short stories of the pioneer West, such as "The Outcasts of Poker Flat" and "The Luck of Roaring Camp", and poetry. In 1871, with his popularity at its height, he went East and signed a contract with *The Atlantic Monthly* for $10,000 for 12 stories a year, the most money then offered to a US writer. He entered a creative slump, however, and from 1878 to 1885 served as US consul in Germany and Scotland, where he entertained the literary circles. He then settled permanently in England.

hartebeest large African antelope *Alcelaphus buselaphus* with lyre-shaped horns set close on top of the head in both sexes.

It may grow to 5 ft/1.5 m at the rather humped shoulders and up to 6 ft/2 m long. Although they are clumsy-looking runners, hartebeest can reach 40 mph/65 kph.

Hartford capital city of Connecticut, located in the N central part of the state, on the Connecticut River, NE of Waterbury; population (1990) 139,700. Industries include insurance, firearms, business office equipment, and tools. The Fundamental Orders of Connecticut, the first constitution that created a democratic government, was signed here 1639.

Harvey William 1578–1657. English physician who discovered the circulation of blood. In 1628 he published his book *De Motu Cordis/On the Motion of the Heart and the Blood in Animals*. He was court physician to James I and Charles I.

hashish drug made from the resin contained in the female flowering tops of hemp cannabis.

Hasidism or *Chasidism* religious sect of Orthodox Judaism, founded by Ba'al Shem Tov (c.1700–1760), based on study of ◊kabbala and popular piety.

It spread against strong opposition throughout E Europe during the 18th and 19th centuries, led by charismatic leaders, the *zaddikim*. They stressed piety and ecstatic prayer, denouncing the academic approach of Talmudic academies (see ◊Talmud). A later, more intellectual approach was instituted by the Lubavitch rabbi of Russia, now based in New York City. Hasidic men dress in the black suits and broad-brimmed hats of 18th-century European society, which they conservatively maintain.

Hassan II 1929– . King of Morocco from 1961. From 1976 he undertook the occupation of the part of Western Sahara ceded by Spain.

The result was a long and damaging guerrilla war against the Polisario fighters. Hassan is a moderate Arab leader, having met with Israeli leaders.

Hastings, Battle of battle Oct 14, 1066 at which William the Conqueror, Duke of Normandy, defeated Harold, King of England. The site is 6 mi/10 km inland from Hastings, at Senlac, Sussex; it is marked by Battle Abbey.

Hatteras cape on the coast of North Carolina, where the waters of the N Atlantic meet the Gulf Stream, causing great turbulence; it therefore is noted for ship-wrecks (more than 700 are said to have occurred here) and is nicknamed "the Graveyard of the Atlantic". Cape Hatteras National Seashore has both natural and historical interest, including a lighthouse and sea life typical of both the temperate and tropical zones.

Havana capital and port of Cuba, on the northwest coast of the island; population (1989) 2,096,100. Products include cigars and tobacco, sugar, coffee, and fruit. The palace of the Spanish governors and the stronghold of La Fuerza (1583) survive. Tourism, formerly a major source of revenue, ended when Fidel Castro came to power 1959.

Havel Václav 1936– . Czech dramatist and politician, president of Czechoslovakia 1989–92 and of the Czech Republic from 1993. His plays include *The Garden Party* 1963 and *Largo Desolato* 1985, about a dissident intellectual. Havel became widely known as a human-rights activist. He was imprisoned 1979–83 and again 1989 for support of Charter 77, a human-rights manifesto. As president of Czechoslovakia he sought to preserve a united republic, but resigned in recognition of the breakup of the federation 1992. In 1993 he became president of the newly independent Czech Republic.

Hawaii Pacific state of the US; nickname Aloha State *area* 6,485 sq mi/16,800 sq km *capital* Honolulu on Oahu *towns and cities* Hilo *physical* Hawaii consists of a chain of some 20 volcanic islands, of which the chief are (1) *Hawaii*, noted for Mauna Kea (13,788 ft/4,201 m), the world's highest island mountain and Mauna Loa (13,686 ft/4,170 m), the world's largest active volcanic crater; (2) *Maui*, the second largest of the islands; (3) *Oahu*, the third largest, with the greatest concentration of population and tourist attractions—for example, Waikiki beach and the Pearl Harbor naval base; (4) *Kauai*; and (5) *Molokai*, site of a historic leper colony *industries* sugar, coffee, pineapples, flowers, women's clothing *population* (1990) 1,108,200; 34% European, 25% Japanese, 14% Filipino, 12% Hawaiian, 6% Chinese *language* English *religions* Christianity; Buddhist minority *history* a Polynesian kingdom from the 6th century until 1893; Hawaii became a republic 1894; ceded itself to the US 1898, and became a US territory 1900. Japan's air attack on Pearl Harbor Dec 7, 1941, crippled the US Pacific fleet and turned the territory into an armed camp, under martial law, for the remainder of the war. Hawaii became a state 1959. Tourism is the chief source of income.

hawk any of various small to medium-sized birds of prey of the family Accipitridae, other than eagles, kites, ospreys, and vultures.

The name is used especially to describe the genera *Accipiter* and *Buteo*. Hawks have short, rounded wings compared with falcons, and keen eyesight.

Hawking Stephen 1942– . English physicist who has researched ◊black holes and gravitational field theory. His books include *A Brief History of Time* 1988, in which he argues that our universe is only one small part of a "super-universe" that has existed for ever and comprises an infinite number of universes like our own.

Hawkins Coleman (Randolph) 1904–1969. US virtuoso tenor saxophonist. He was, until 1934, a soloist in the swing band led by Fletcher Henderson (1898–1952), and was an influential figure in bringing the jazz saxophone to prominence as a solo instrument.

hawk moth or *sphinx moth* any of a family, Sphingidae, of moths with thick bodies and narrow wings. Some 1,000 species are distributed throughout the world, but they are mainly tropical. The large hawk-moth larva usually has a "horn" at the end of its body—for example, the bright-green tomato horn-worm *Protoparcequinquemaculata*.

Hawks Howard 1896–1977. US director, screenwriter, and producer of a wide range of classic films in virtually every American genre. Swift-moving and immensely accomplished, his films include the gangster movie *Scarface* 1932, screwball comedy *Bringing Up Baby* 1938, the *film noir* The Big Sleep 1946, and *Gentlemen Prefer Blondes* 1953.

hawthorn shrub or tree of the genus *Crataegus* of the rose family Rosaceae. Species are most abundant in E North America, but there are also many in Eurasia. All have alternate, toothed leaves and bear clusters of showy white, pink, or red flowers. Small applelike fruits can be red, orange, blue, or black. Hawthorns are popular as ornamentals.

Hawthorne Nathaniel 1804–1864. US author who wrote about Puritan New England and won fame with *The Scarlet Letter* 1850, a powerful novel set in Boston 200 years earlier. He wrote three other novels (*The House of the Seven Gables* 1851, *The Blithedale Romance* 1852, and *The Marble Faun* 1860), many volumes of short stories, and *Tanglewood Tales* 1853, classic Greek legends retold for children. His short stories, which include "My Kinsman", "Major Molineux" and "Young Goodman Brown", helped to establish the short story as an art form.

Haydn Franz Joseph 1732–1809. Austrian composer. A teacher of Mozart and Beethoven, he was a major exponent of the classical sonata form in his numerous chamber and orchestral works (he wrote more than 100 symphonies). He also composed choral music, including the oratorios *The Creation* 1798 and *The Seasons* 1801. He was the first great master of the string quartet.

Hayek Friedrich August von 1899–1992. Austrian economist. Born in Vienna, he taught at the London School of Economics 1931–50. His work *The Road to Serfdom* 1944 was a critical study of socialist trends in Britain. He won the 1974 Nobel Prize for Economics with Gunnar Myrdal.

He was professor of social and moral science at the University of Chicago 1950–62.

Hayes Rutherford Birchard 1822–1893. 19th president of the US 1877–81, a Republican. Born in Ohio, he was a major general on the Union side in the Civil War. During his presidency federal troops were withdrawn from the Southern states (after the ◊Reconstruction) and the Civil Service reformed.

hay fever allergic reaction to pollen, causing sneezing, with inflammation of the nasal membranes and conjunctiva of the eyes. Symptoms are due to the release of ◊histamine. Treatment is by antihistamine drugs.

Hayworth Rita. Adopted name of Margarita Carmen Cansino 1918–1987. US dancer and film actress. She gave vivacious performances in 1940s musicals and steamy, erotic roles in *Gilda* 1946 and *Affair in Trinidad* 1952. She was known as Hollywood's "goddess" during the height of her career. She was married to Orson Welles 1943–48 and appeared in his film *The Lady from Shanghai* 1948. She gave assured performances in *Pal Joey* 1957 and *Separate Tables* 1958.

Her later appearances were intermittent and she retired in 1972, a victim of Alzheimer's disease.

hazardous waste waste substance, usually generated by industry, which represents a hazard to the environment or to people living or working nearby. Examples include radioactive wastes, acidic resins, arsenic residues, residual hardening salts, lead, mercury, nonferrous sludges, organic solvents, and pesticides. Their economic disposal or recycling is the subject of research.

hazel shrub or tree of the genus *Corylus*, family Corylaceae, including the European common hazel or cob *C. avellana*, of which the filbert is the cultivated variety.

North American species include the American hazel *C. americana*.

H-bomb abbreviation for ◊*hydrogen bomb*.

HDTV abbreviation for ◊*high-definition television*.

health service government provision of medical care on a national scale.

State and local governments provide some public health services. The US provides care through private physicians and hospitals who are paid by the federally subsidized schemes *Medicare* and *Medicaid*. The Medicare health-insurance plan provides outpatient care for the elderly and disabled (toward which patients pay a share), and since 1985, fees for Medicare patients to join health-maintenance organizations (HMOs, covering visits to a group of doctors and hospital fees). The Medicaid state plan is paid to the state by the federal government for people unable to afford private care. US private health schemes include Blue Cross (established 1929) and Blue Shield (established 1917), as well as other insurance companies' plans.

health, world the health of people worldwide is monitored by the ◊World Health Organization (WHO). Outside the industrialized world in particular, poverty and degraded environmental conditions mean that easily preventable diseases are widespread: WHO estimated 1990 that 1 billion people, or 20% of the world's population, were diseased, in poor health, or malnourished. In North Africa and the Middle East, 25% of the population were ill.

Hearst Patty (Patricia) 1955– . US socialite. A granddaughter of the newspaper tycoon William Randolph Hearst, she was kidnapped 1974 by an urban guerrilla group, the Symbionese Liberation Army. She joined her captors in a bank robbery, was sought, tried, convicted, and imprisoned 1976–79.

She has since married and become active in charities and fundraising.

Hearst William Randolph 1863–1951. US newspaper publisher, celebrated for his introduction of banner headlines, lavish illustration, and the sensationalist approach known as "yellow journalism".

heart muscular organ that rhythmically contracts to force blood around the body of an animal with a circulatory system. Annelid worms and some other invertebrates have simple hearts consisting of thickened sections of main blood vessels that pulse regularly. An earthworm has ten such hearts. Vertebrates have one heart. A fish heart has two chambers—the thin-walled *atrium* (once called the auricle) that expands to receive blood, and the thick-walled *ventricle* that pumps it out. Amphibians and most reptiles have two atria and one ventricle; birds and mammals have two atria and two ventricles. The beating of the heart is controlled by the autonomic nervous system and an internal control center or pacemaker, the sinoatrial node.

heart attack or *myocardial infarction* sudden onset of gripping central chest pain, often accompanied by sweating and vomiting, caused by death of a portion of the heart muscle following obstruction of a coronary artery by thrombosis (formation of a blood clot). Half of all heart attacks result in death within the first two hours, but in the remainder survival has improved following the widespread use of thrombolytic (clot-buster) drugs.

heat form of internal energy possessed by a substance by virtue of the kinetic energy in the motion of its molecules or atoms. Heat energy is transferred by conduction, convection, and radiation. It always flows from a region of higher ◊temperature (heat intensity) to one of lower temperature. Its effect on a substance may be simply to raise its temperature, or to cause it to expand, melt (if a solid), vaporize (if a liquid), or increase its pressure (if a confined gas).

heat capacity in physics, the quantity of heat required to raise the temperature of an object by one degree. The *specific heat capacity* of a substance is the heat capacity per unit of mass, measured in joules per kilogram per kelvin ($J kg^{-1} K^{-1}$).

heath in botany, any woody, mostly evergreen shrub of the family Ericaceae, native to Europe, Africa, and North America. Many heaths have bell-shaped pendant flowers. In the Old World the genera *Erica* and *Calluna* are the most common heaths, and include ◊heather.

Included among the heaths are North American blueberries, rhododendrons, mountain laurel, and Labrador tea.

Heath Edward (Richard George) 1916– . British Conservative politician, party leader 1965–75. As prime minister 1970–74 he took the UK into the European Community (now the European Union) but was brought down by economic and industrial relations crises at home. He was replaced as party leader by Margaret Thatcher 1975, and became increasingly critical of her policies and her opposition to the UK's full participation in the EC. In 1993 he negotiated the release of three Britons held prisoner by Iraq.

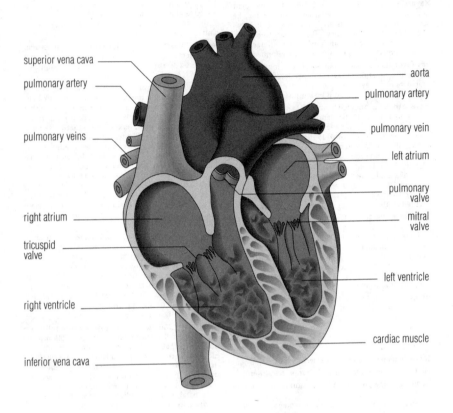

superior vena cava

pulmonary artery

pulmonary veins

right atrium

tricuspid valve

right ventricle

inferior vena cava

aorta

pulmonary artery

pulmonary vein

left atrium

pulmonary valve

mitral valve

left ventricle

cardiac muscle

heart The structure of the human heart. During an average lifetime, the human heart beats more than 2,000 million times and pumps 110 million gal/500 million l of blood. The average pulse rate is 70–72 beats per minute at rest for adult males, and 78–82 beats per minute for adult females.

heather low-growing evergreen shrub of the heath family, common on sandy or acid soil. The common heather *Calluna vulgaris* is a carpet-forming shrub, growing up to 24 in/60 cm high and bearing pale pink-purple flowers. It is found over much of Europe and has been introduced to North America.

heatstroke or *sunstroke* rise in body temperature caused by excessive exposure to heat.

Mild heatstroke is experienced as feverish lassitude, sometimes with simple fainting; recovery is prompt following rest and replenishment of salt lost in sweat. Severe heatstroke causes collapse akin to that seen in acute ◊shock, and is potentially lethal without prompt treatment, including cooling the body carefully and giving fluids to relieve dehydration.

heat treatment in industry, the subjection of metals and alloys to controlled heating and cooling after fabrication to relieve internal stresses and improve their physical properties. Methods include ◊annealing, quenching, and tempering.

heaven in Christianity and some other religions, the abode of God and the destination of the virtuous after death. Theologians now usually describe it as a place or state in which the soul experiences the full reality of God.

heavy metal in music, a style of rock characterized by histrionic guitar solos and a macho swagger. Heavy metal developed out of the hard rock of the late 1960s and early 1970s, was performed by such groups as Led Zeppelin and Deep Purple, and enjoyed a resurgence in the late 1980s. Bands include Van Halen (formed 1974), Def Leppard (formed 1977), and Guns 'n' Roses (formed 1987).

heavy metal in chemistry, a metallic element of high relative atomic mass, such as platinum, gold, and lead. Many heavy metals are poisonous and tend to accumulate and persist in living systems—for example, high levels of mercury (from industrial waste and toxic dumping) accumulate in shellfish and fish, which are in turn eaten by humans. Treatment of heavy-metal poisoning is difficult because available drugs are not able to distinguish between the heavy metals that are essential to living cells (zinc, copper) and those that are poisonous.

Various detoxification programs combining nutrition, herbs, fasts, and intestinal irrigation are often successful.

heavy water or *deuterium oxide* D_2O water containing the isotope deuterium instead of hydrogen (relative molecular mass 20 as opposed to 18 for ordinary water).

Hebei or *Hopei* or *Hupei* province of N China *area* 78,242 sq mi/202,700 sq km *capital* Shijiazhuang *features* includes special municipalities of Beijing and Tianjin *industries* cereals, textiles, iron, steel *population* (1990) 61,082,000.

Hebrew member of the Semitic people who lived in Palestine at the time of the Old Testament and who traced their ancestry to ◊Abraham.

Also the language of the Old Testament and Judaic literature, as well as the official language (since 1948) of the state of Israel, one of the Semitic languages of the Hamito-Semitic (Afro-Asiatic) family.

The Hebrew people were widely dispersed during the Roman Empire and learned the languages and cultures of those they lived among in Europe, the Near East, Asia, and (after 1492) the Americas, but continued using liturgical Hebrew in prayer, as well as the ancient Hebrew ◊alphabet to write both sacred works in Hebrew and secular works in ◊Yiddish, a 13th-century High German dialect. In the late 19th century, Hebrew was revived as a modern language, by the European Haskala movement, in both spoken and written forms.

Hebrew Bible the sacred writings of Judaism (some dating from as early as 1200 BC), called by Christians the ◊Old Testament. It includes the Torah (the first five books, ascribed to Moses), historical and prophetic books, and psalms, originally written in Hebrew and later translated into Greek (Pentateuch) and other languages.

Hebrew language member of the Hamito-Semitic language family spoken in SW Asia by the ancient Hebrews, sustained for many centuries in the Diaspora as the liturgical language of Judaism, revived by the late-19th-century Haskala movement, and developed in the 20th century as Israeli Hebrew, the national language of the state of Israel. It is the original language of the Old Testament of the Bible.

Hebrides group of more than 500 islands (fewer than 100 inhabited) off W Scotland; total area 1,120 sq mi/2,900 sq km. The Hebrides were settled by Scandinavians during the 6th to 9th centuries and passed under Norwegian rule from about 890 to 1266.

Hecate in Greek mythology, a goddess of the underworld and magic, sometimes identified with ◊Artemis and the Moon.

hectare metric unit of area equal to 2.47 acres (10,000 square meters), symbol ha.

Hector in Greek mythology, a Trojan prince, son of King Priam and husband of Andromache, who, in the siege of ◊Troy, was the foremost warrior on the Trojan side until he was killed by ◊Achilles.

hedgehog insectivorous mammal of the genus *Erinaceus*, native to Europe, Asia, and Africa. The body, including the tail, is 1 ft/30 cm long. It is grayish-brown in color, has a piglike snout, and is covered with sharp spines. When alarmed it can roll itself into a ball. Hedgehogs feed on insects, slugs, and carrion. Long-eared hedgehogs and desert hedgehogs are placed in different genera.

hedonism ethical theory that pleasure or happiness is, or should be, the main goal in life. Hedonist sects in ancient Greece were the Cyrenaics, who held that the pleasure of the moment is the only human good, and the ◊Epicureans, who advocated the pursuit of pleasure under the direction of reason. Modern hedonist philosophies, such as those of the British philosophers Jeremy Bentham and J S Mill, regard the happiness of society, rather than that of the individual, as the aim.

Hefner Hugh Marston 1926– . US publisher, founder of *Playboy* magazine 1953. With its distinctive rabbit logo, monthly "Playmate" centerfolds of nude women, and columns and interviews of opinion, fashion, and personal advice on sex and other topics, *Playboy* helped reshape the social attitudes of the postwar generation. In the early 1960s, the magazine's huge success led to the creation of a national chain of Playboy clubs and resorts.

Hegel Georg Wilhelm Friedrich 1770–1831. German philosopher who conceived of consciousness and the external object as forming a unity in which neither factor can exist independently, mind and nature being two abstractions of one indivisible whole. He believed development took place through dialectic: thesis and antithesis (contradiction) and synthesis, the resolution of contradiction. For Hegel, the task of philosophy was to comprehend the rationality of what already exists; leftist followers, including Karl Marx, used Hegel's dialectic to attempt to show the inevitability of radical change and to attack both religion and the social order of the European Industrial Revolution. He wrote *The Phenomenology of Spirit* 1807, *Encyclopedia of the Philosophical Sciences* 1817, and *Philosophy of Right* 1821.

hegemony political dominance of one power over others in a group in which all are supposedly equal. The term was first used for the dominance of Athens over the other Greek city-states, later applied to Prussia within Germany, and, in more recent times, to the US and the USSR with regard to the rest of the world.

Hegira or *Hijrah* flight from persecution of ◊Mohammed from Mecca to Medina in AD 622, marking the beginning of the Islamic era.

Heidegger Martin 1889–1976. German philosopher. In *Sein und Zeit/Being and Time* 1927 (translated 1962) he used the methods of Edmund ◊Husserl's phenomenology to explore the structures of human existence. His later writings meditated on the fate of a world dominated by science and technology.

Heifetz Jascha 1901–1987. Russian-born US violinist. He was one of the great virtuosos of the 20th century. He first performed at the age of five, and before he was 17 had played in most European capitals, and in the US, where he settled 1917. He popularized a clear, unemotional delivery suited to radio and recordings.

He appeared in several Hollywood movies, played in a trio with Artur Rubenstein and Grigor Piatigorsky, and after returning from the concert stage taught several violinists including Eugene Fodor.

Heilongjiang or *Heilungkiang* province of NE China, in ◊Manchuria *area* 178,950 sq mi/463,600 sq km *capital* Harbin *features* China's largest oil field, near Anda *industries* cereals, gold, coal, copper, zinc, lead, cobalt *population* (1990) 35,215,000.

Heilungkiang alternate name for ◊Heilongjiang, a Chinese province.

Heine Heinrich 1797–1856. German Romantic poet and journalist. He wrote *Reisebilder* 1826–31, blending travel writing and satire, and *Buch der Lieder/Book of Songs* 1827. From 1831 he lived mainly in Paris, working as a correspondent for German newspapers and publishing *Neue Gedichte/New Poems* 1844. He excelled in both the Romantic lyric and satire. Schubert and Schumann set many of his lyrics to music.

Heisenberg Werner Carl 1901–1976. German physicist who developed ◊quantum theory and formulated the ◊uncertainty principle, which concerns matter, radiation, and their reactions, and places absolute limits on the achievable accuracy of measurement. He was awarded a Nobel Prize 1932 for work he carried out when only 24.

Helen in Greek mythology, the daughter of Zeus and Leda, and the most beautiful of women. She married Menelaus, King of Sparta, but during his absence, was abducted by Paris, Prince of Troy. This precipitated the Trojan War. Afterwards she returned to Sparta with her husband.

Helena capital of Montana, located in the W central part of the state, near the Big Belt Mountains, S of the Missouri River; population (1990) 24,600. It was settled after gold was discovered 1864. Industries include agricultural products, machine parts, ceramics, paints, sheet metal, and chemicals.

Helicon mountain in central Greece, on which was situated a spring and a sanctuary sacred to the ◊Muses.

helicopter powered aircraft that achieves both lift and propulsion by means of a rotary wing, or rotor, on top of the fuselage. It can take off and land vertically, move in any direction, or remain stationary in the air. It can be powered by piston or jet engine. The ◊autogiro was a precursor.

Helios in Greek mythology, the sun god—thought to make his daily journey across the sky in a chariot—and father of Phaethon.

heliotrope decorative plant of the genus *Heliotropium* of the borage family Boraginaceae, with distinctive spikes of blue, lilac, or white flowers, including the Peruvian or cherry pie heliotrope *H. peruvianum*.

helium colorless, odorless, gaseous, nonmetallic element, symbol He, atomic number 2, atomic weight 4.0026. It is grouped with the ◊inert gases, is nonreactive, and forms no compounds. It is the second-most abundant element (after hydrogen) in the universe, and has the lowest boiling (−452°F/−268.9°C) and melting points (−458°F/−272.2°C) of all the elements. It is present in small quantities in the Earth's atmosphere from gases issuing from radioactive elements (from ◊alpha decay) in the Earth's crust; after hydrogen it is the second-lightest element.

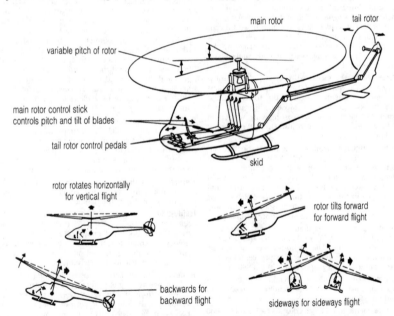

helicopter The helicopter is controlled by varying the rotor pitch (the angle of the rotor blade as it moves through the air). For backward flight, the blades in front of the machine have greater pitch than those behind the craft. This means that the front blades produce more lift and a backward thrust. For forward flight, the situation is reversed. In level flight, the blades have unchanging pitch.

hell in various religions, a place of posthumous punishment. In Hinduism, Buddhism, and Jainism, hell is a transitory stage in the progress of the soul, but in Christianity and Islam it is eternal (purgatory is transitory). Judaism does not postulate such punishment.

hellebore poisonous European herbaceous plant of the genus *Helleborus* of the buttercup family Ranunculaceae. The stinking hellebore *H. foetidus* has greenish flowers early in the spring.

The white, or false, hellebore *Veratrum viride* of North America is a poisonous member of the lily family Liliaceae.

helleborine temperate Old World orchid of the genera *Epipactis* and *Cephalanthera*, including the marsh helleborine *E. palustris* and the hellebore orchid *E. helleborine* introduced to North America.

The rattlesnake orchids (genus *Goodyera*) of North America are sometimes placed in the genus *Epipactis*.

Hellenic period (from *Hellas*, Greek name for Greece) classical period of ancient Greek civilization, from the first Olympic Games 776 BC until the death of Alexander the Great 323 BC .

Hellenistic period period in Greek civilization from the death of Alexander 323 BC until the accession of the Roman emperor Augustus 27 BC . Alexandria in Egypt was the center of culture and commerce during this period, and Greek culture spread throughout the Mediterranean region and the near East.

Hellespont former name of the ◊Dardanelles, the strait that separates Europe from Asia.

Helmholtz Hermann Ludwig Ferdinand von 1821–1894. German physiologist, physicist, and inventor of the ophthalmoscope for examining the inside of the eye. He was the first to explain how the cochlea of the inner ear works, and the first to measure the speed of nerve impulses. In physics he formulated the law of conservation of energy, and worked in thermodynamics.

The ophthalmoscope made possible the examination of the inside of the eye. This was a great advance in ophthalmic medicine, as was his ophthalmometer for measuring the curvature of the eye. He also studied magnetism, electricity, and the physiology of hearing.

Héloïse 1101–1164. Abbess of Paraclete in Champagne, France, correspondent and lover of ◊Abelard. She became deeply interested in intellectual study in her youth and was impressed by the brilliance of Abelard, her teacher, whom she secretly married.

After her affair with Abelard, and the birth of a son, Astrolabe, she became a nun 1129, and with Abelard's assistance, founded a nunnery at Paraclete. Her letters show her strong and pious character and her devotion to Abelard.

Helsinki (Swedish *Helsingfors*) capital and port of Finland; population (1990) 492,400, metropolitan area 978,000. Industries include shipbuilding, engineering, and textiles. The homes of the architect Eliel Saarinen and the composer Jean Sibelius outside the city are museums.

hematite principal ore of iron, consisting mainly of iron(III) oxide, Fe_2O_3. It occurs as *specular hematite* (dark, metallic luster), *kidney ore* (reddish radiating fibers terminating in smooth, rounded surfaces), and a red earthy deposit.

hematology branch of medicine concerned with disorders of the blood.

hematoma accumulation of blood in the tissues, causing a solid swelling. It may be due to injury, disease or a blood clotting disorder such as ◊hemophilia.

Hemingway Ernest (Miller) 1899–1961. US writer. War, bullfighting, and fishing are used symbolically in his work to represent honor, dignity, and primitivism—prominent themes in his short stories and novels, which include *A Farewell to Arms* 1929, *For Whom the Bell Tolls* 1941, and *The Old Man and the Sea* 1952 (Pulitzer Prize). His deceptively simple writing styles attracted many imitators. He received the Nobel Prize for Literature 1954.

hemlock plant *Conium maculatum* of the carrot family Umbelliferae, native to Europe, W Asia, and N Africa. Reaching up to 6 ft/2 m high, it bears umbels of small white flowers. The whole plant, especially the root and fruit, is poisonous, causing paralysis of the nervous system. The name hemlock is also applied to members of the genus *Tsuga* of North American and Asiatic conifers of the pine family.

hemoglobin protein that carries oxygen. In vertebrates it occurs in red blood cells, giving them their color. Oxygen attaches to hemoglobin in the lungs or gills where the amount dissolved in the blood is high. This process effectively increases the amount of oxygen that can be carried in the bloodstream. The oxygen is later released in the body tissues where it is at low concentration. Hemoglobin also works in carrying carbon dioxide away from tissues to the lungs or gills.

hemolysis destruction of red blood cells. Aged cells are constantly being lyzed (broken down), but increased wastage of red cells is seen in some infections and blood disorders. It may result in ◊jaundice (through the release of too much hemoglobin) and in ◊anemia.

hemolytic disease of the newborn or *erythroblastosis fetalis* rare form of hemolytic ◊anemia due to incompatibility of blood groups between mother and baby. It causes liver failure, brain damage, and sometimes death. It can be treated prenatally or immediately on delivery by exchange transfusion. See also ◊rhesus factor.

hemophilia any of several inherited diseases in which normal blood clotting is impaired. The sufferer usually experiences prolonged bleeding from the slightest wound, as well as painful internal bleeding without apparent cause.

hemorrhage loss of blood from the circulatory system. It is "manifest" when the blood can be seen, as when it flows from a wound, and "occult" when the bleeding is internal, as from an ulcer or internal injury.

hemorrhoids distended blood vessels (◊varicose veins) in the area of the anus, popularly called piles.

hemostasis natural or surgical stoppage of bleeding. In the natural mechanism, the damaged vessel contracts, restricting the flow, and blood platelets plug the opening, releasing chemicals essential to clotting.

hemp annual plant *Cannabis sativa*, family Cannabaceae. Originally from Asia, it is cultivated in most temperate countries for its fibers, produced in the outer layer of the stem, and used in ropes, twines, and, occasionally, in a type of linen or lace. Cannabis is obtained from certain varieties of hemp.

Henan or *Honan* province of E central China *area* 64,462 sq mi/167,000 sq km *capital* Zhengzhou *features* river plains of the Huang He (Yellow River); ruins of Xibo, the 16th-century BC capital of the Shang dynasty, were discovered here in the 1980s *industries* cereals, cotton *population* (1990) 85,510,000.

henbane poisonous plant *Hyoscyamus niger* of the nightshade family Solanaceae, found on waste ground throughout most of Europe and W Asia. A branching plant, up to 31 in/80 cm high, it has hairy leaves and a nauseous smell. The yellow flowers are bell-shaped. Henbane is used in medicine as a source of hyoscyamine and scopolamine.

Hench Philip Showalter 1896–1965. US physician who introduced cortisone treatment for rheumatoid arthritis for which he shared the 1950 Nobel Prize for Medicine with Edward Kendall and Tadeus Reichstein.

Hendrix Jimi (James Marshall) 1942–1970. US rock guitarist, songwriter, and singer. He was legendary for his virtuoso experimental technique and flamboyance. *Are You Experienced?* 1967 was his first album. His performance at the 1969 Woodstock festival included a memorable version of "The Star-Spangled Banner" and is recorded in the film *Woodstock* 1970. He greatly expanded the vocabulary of the electric guitar and influenced both rock and jazz musicians.

henna small shrub *Lawsonia inermis* of the loosestrife family Lythraceae, found in Iran, India, Egypt, and N Africa. The leaves and young twigs are ground to a powder, mixed to a paste with hot water, and applied to fingernails and hair, giving an orange-red hue. The color may then be changed to black by applying a preparation of indigo.

henry SI unit (symbol H) of ◊inductance (the reaction of an electric current against the magnetic field that surrounds it). One henry is the inductance of a circuit that produces an opposing voltage of one volt when the current changes at one ampere per second.

Henry Joseph 1797–1878. US physicist, inventor of the electromagnetic motor 1829 and of a telegraphic apparatus. He also discovered the principle of electromagnetic induction, roughly at the same time as Michael ◊Faraday, and the phenomenon of self-induction. A unit of inductance (henry) is named for him.

Henry I 1068–1135. King of England from 1100. Youngest son of William the Conqueror, he succeeded his brother William II. He won the support of the Saxons by granting them a charter and marrying a Saxon princess. An able administrator, he established a professional bureaucracy and a system of traveling judges. He was succeeded by Stephen.

Henry II 1133–1189. King of England from 1154, when he succeeded ◊Stephen. He was the son of Matilda and Geoffrey of Anjou (1113–1151). He curbed the power of the barons, but his attempt to bring the church courts under control had to be abandoned after the murder of Thomas à ◊Becket. During his reign the English conquest of Ireland began. He was succeeded by his son Richard I.

Henry III 1207–1272. King of England from 1216, when he succeeded John, but he did not rule until 1227. His financial commitments to the papacy and his foreign favorites led to de ◊Montfort's revolt 1264. Henry was defeated at Lewes, Sussex, and imprisoned. He was restored to the throne after the royalist victory at Evesham 1265. He was succeeded by his son Edward I.

Henry (III) the Black 1017–1056. King of Germany from 1028, Holy Roman emperor from 1039 (crowned 1046). He raised the empire to the height of its power, and extended its authority over Poland, Bohemia, and Hungary.

Henry IV (Bolingbroke) 1367–1413. King of England from 1399, the son of ◊John of Gaunt. In 1398 he was banished by ◊Richard II for political activity but returned 1399 to head a revolt and be accepted as king by Parliament. He was succeeded by his son Henry V.

He had difficulty in keeping the support of Parliament and the clergy. To win support he had to conciliate the church by a law for the burning of heretics and to make many concessions to Parliament.

Henry IV 1553–1610. King of France from 1589. Son of Antoine de Bourbon and Jeanne, Queen of Navarre, he was brought up as a Protestant and from 1576 led the ◊Huguenots. On his accession he settled the religious question by adopting Catholicism while tolerating Protestantism. He restored peace and strong government to France and brought back prosperity by measures for the promotion of industry and agriculture and the improvement of communications. He was assassinated by a Catholic extremist.

Henry V 1387–1422. King of England from 1413, son of Henry IV. Invading Normandy 1415 (during the Hundred Years' War), he captured Harfleur and defeated the French at ◊Agincourt. He invaded again 1417–19, capturing Rouen. His military victory forced the French into the Treaty of Troyes 1420, which gave Henry control of the French government. He married Catherine of Valois 1420 and gained recognition as heir to the French throne by his father-in-law Charles VI, but died before him. He was succeeded by his son Henry VI.

Henry VI 1421–1471. King of England from 1422, son of Henry V. He assumed royal power 1442 and sided with the party opposed to the continuation of the Hundred Years' War with France. After his marriage 1445, he was dominated by his wife, ◊Margaret of Anjou. The unpopularity of the government, especially after the loss of the English conquests in France, encouraged Richard, Duke of York, to claim the throne, and though York was killed 1460, his son Edward IV proclaimed himself king 1461 (see Wars of the ◊Roses). Henry was captured 1465, temporarily restored 1470, but again imprisoned 1471 and then murdered.

Henry VI 1165–1197. Holy Roman emperor from 1190. As part of his plan for making the empire universal, he captured and imprisoned Richard I of England and compelled him to do homage.

Henry VII 1457–1509. King of England from 1485, son of Edmund Tudor, Earl of Richmond (*c*.1430–1456), and a descendant of ◊John of Gaunt.

He spent his early life in Brittany until 1485, when he landed in Britain to lead the rebellion against Richard III which ended with Richard's defeat and death at Bosworth. By his marriage to Elizabeth of York 1486, he united the houses of York and Lancaster. Yorkist revolts continued until 1497, but Henry restored order after the Wars of the ◊Roses by the ◊Star Chamber and achieved independence from Parliament by amassing a private fortune through confiscations. He was succeeded by his son Henry VIII.

Henry VIII 1491–1547. King of England from 1509, when he succeeded his father Henry VII and married Catherine of Aragon, the widow of his brother.

During the period 1513–29 Henry pursued an active foreign policy, largely under the guidance of his Lord

Chancellor, Cardinal Wolsey who shared Henry's desire to make England stronger. Wolsey was replaced by Thomas More 1529 for failing to persuade the pope to grant Henry a divorce. After 1532 Henry broke with papal authority, proclaimed himself head of the church in England, dissolved the monasteries, and divorced Catherine. His subsequent wives were Anne Boleyn, Jane Seymour, Anne of Cleves, Catherine Howard, and Catherine Parr. He was succeeded by his son Edward VI.

Henry the Navigator 1394–1460. Portuguese prince, the fourth son of John I. He set up a school for navigators 1419 and under his patronage Portuguese sailors explored and colonized Madeira, the Cape Verde Islands, and the Azores; they sailed down the African coast almost to Sierra Leone.

Henson Jim (James Maury) 1936–1990. US puppeteer who created the television Muppet characters, including Kermit the Frog, Miss Piggy, and Fozzie Bear. The Muppets became popular on the children's educational TV series *Sesame Street*, which first appeared in 1969 and soon became regular viewing in over 80 countries. In 1976 Henson created *The Muppet Show*, which ran for five years and became one of the world's most widely seen TV programs, reaching 235 million viewers in 100 countries. Three Muppet movies followed.

hepatitis any inflammatory disease of the liver, usually caused by a virus. Other causes include alcohol, drugs, gallstones, ◊lupus erythematosus, and amebic ◊dysentery. Symptoms include weakness, nausea, and jaundice.

Hepburn Audrey (Audrey Hepburn-Rushton) 1929–1993. British actress of Anglo-Dutch descent. She often played innocent, childlike characters. Slender and doe-eyed, she set a different style from the more ample women stars of the 1950s. After playing minor parts in British films in the early 1950s, she became a Hollywood star in *Roman Holiday* 1951, such films as *Funny Face* 1957, *My Fair Lady* 1964, and *Wait Until Dark* 1968. Among her later films were *Robin and Marian* 1976.

Hepburn Katharine 1909– . US actress. She made feisty self-assurance her trademark. She appeared in such films as *Morning Glory* 1933 (Academy Award), *Little Women* 1933, *Bringing Up Baby* 1938, *The Philadelphia Story* 1940, *Woman of the Year* 1942, *The African Queen* 1951, *Pat and Mike* 1952 (with her frequent partner Spencer Tracy), *Guess Who's Coming to Dinner* 1967 (Academy Award), *Lion in Winter* 1968 (Academy Award), and *On Golden Pond* 1981 (Academy Award). She also had a distinguished stage career.

Hephaestus in Greek mythology, the god of fire and metalcraft (Roman Vulcan), son of Zeus and Hera, and husband of Aphrodite. He was lame.

Hepworth Barbara 1903–1975. English sculptor. She developed a distinctive abstract style, creating hollowed forms of stone or wood with spaces bridged by wires or strings; many later works are in bronze.

Hera in Greek mythology, the goddess of women and marriage (Roman Juno), sister-consort of Zeus, mother of Hephaestus, Hebe, and Ares.

Heracles in Greek mythology, a hero (Roman Hercules), son of Zeus and Alcmene, famed for strength. While serving Eurystheus, King of Argos, he performed 12 labors, including the cleansing of the Augean stables. Driven mad by the goddess Hera, he murdered his first wife Megara and their children, and was himself poisoned by mistake by his second wife Deianira.

Heraclitus *c.*544–483 BC . Greek philosopher who believed that the cosmos is in a ceaseless state of flux and motion, fire being the fundamental material that accounts for all change and motion in the world.

Nothing in the world ever stays the same, hence the dictum, "one cannot step in the same river twice".

Wisdom came from understanding this eternal dynamic, which unified the diversity of nature, as he wrote in *On Nature*. Heraclitus was born in Ephesus.

Herat capital of Herat province, and the largest city in W Afghanistan, on the N banks of the Hari Rud River; population (1980) 160,000. A principal road junction, it was a great city in ancient and medieval times.

Herbert George 1593–1633. English poet. His volume of religious poems, *The Temple*, appeared 1633, shortly before his death. His intense though quiet poems embody his religious struggles ("The Temper", "The Collar") or poignantly contrast mortality and eternal truth ("Vertue", "Life") in a deceptively simple language.

herbivore animal that feeds on green plants (or photosynthetic single-celled organisms) or their products, including seeds, fruit, and nectar. The most numerous type of herbivore is thought to be the zooplankton, tiny invertebrates in the surface waters of the oceans that feed on small photosynthetic algae. Herbivores are more numerous than other animals because their food is the most abundant. They form a vital link in the food chain between plants and carnivores.

Herculaneum ancient city of Italy between Naples and Pompeii. Along with Pompeii, it was buried when Vesuvius erupted AD 79. It was excavated from the 18th century onward.

Hercules Roman form of ◊Heracles.

heredity in biology, the transmission of traits from parent to offspring. See also ◊genetics.

Hereford and Worcester county in W central England *area* 1,517 sq mi/3,930 sq km *cities* Worcester (administrative headquarters), Hereford, Kidderminster, Evesham, Ross-on-Wye, Ledbury *features* rivers: Wye, Severn; Malvern Hills (high point Worcester Beacon 1,395 ft/425 m) and Black Mountains; fertile Vale of Evesham.

heresy (Greek *hairesis* "parties" of believers) doctrine opposed to orthodox belief, especially in religion. Those holding ideas considered heretical by the Christian church have included Gnostics, Arians, Pelagians, Montanists, Albigenses, Waldenses, Lollards, and Anabaptists.

hermaphrodite organism that has both male and female sex organs. Hermaphroditism is the norm in species such as earthworms and snails, and is common in flowering plants. Cross-fertilization is the rule among hermaphrodites, with the parents functioning as male and female simultaneously, or as one or the other sex at different stages in their development. Human hermaphrodites are extremely rare.

Hermes in Greek mythology, a god, son of Zeus and Maia; messenger of the gods. He wore winged sandals, a wide-brimmed hat, and carried a staff around which serpents coiled. Identified with the Roman Mercury and ancient Egyptian Thoth, he protected thieves, travelers, and merchants.

hernia or *rupture* protrusion of part of an internal organ through a weakness in the surrounding muscular wall, usually in the groin. The appearance is that of a rounded soft lump or swelling.

Herod Antipas 21 BC–AD 39. Tetrarch (governor) of the Roman province of Galilee, N Palestine, 4 BC –AD 39, son of Herod the Great. He divorced his wife to marry his niece Herodias, and was responsible for the death of John the Baptist. Jesus was brought before him on Pontius Pilate's discovery that he was a Galilean and hence of Herod's jurisdiction, but Herod returned him without giving any verdict. In AD 38 Herod Antipas went to Rome to try to persuade Emperor Caligula to give him the title of king, but was instead banished.

Herodotus *c.*484–424 BC . Greek historian. After four years in Athens, he traveled widely in Egypt, Asia, and the Black Sea region of E Europe, before settling at Thurii in S Italy 443 BC . He wrote a nine-book history of the Greek-Persian struggle that culminated in the defeat of the Persian invasion attempts 490 and 480 BC . Herodotus was the first historian to apply critical evaluation to his material, while also recording divergent opinions.

Herod the Great 74–4 BC . King of the Roman province of Judea, S Palestine, from 40 BC .

With the aid of Mark Antony, he established his government in Jerusalem 37 BC . He rebuilt the Temple in Jerusalem, but his Hellenizing tendencies made him suspect to orthodox Jewry. His last years were a reign of terror, and in the New Testament Matthew alleges that he ordered the slaughter of all the infants in Bethlehem to ensure the death of Jesus, whom he foresaw as a rival. He was the father of Herod Antipas.

heroin or *diamorphine* powerful opiate analgesic, an acetyl derivative of ◊morphine. It is more addictive than morphine but causes less nausea and is one of the most abused drugs in the US. Because of its powerful habit-forming qualities, its manufacture and import are forbidden in the US, even for medical use.

heron large to medium-sized wading bird of the family Ardeidae, which also includes bitterns, egrets, night herons, and boatbills. Herons have sharp bills, broad wings, long legs, and soft plumage. They are found mostly in tropical and subtropical regions, but also in temperate zones.

The great blue heron *Ardea herodias* is native to North America. Gray-blue overall, breeding adults have yellowish bills and ornate plumes on the head, neck, and back. A wader, it feeds mainly on fish and frogs.

herpes any of several infectious diseases caused by viruses of the herpes group. *Herpes simplex I* is the causative agent of a common inflammation, the cold sore. *Herpes simplex II* is responsible for genital herpes, a highly contagious, sexually transmitted disease characterized by painful blisters in the genital area. It can be transmitted in the birth canal from mother to newborn. *Herpes zoster* causes ◊shingles; another herpes virus causes chickenpox.

The Epstein–Barr virus of infectious ◊mononucleosis also belongs to this group.

Herrick Robert 1591–1674. English poet and cleric. He published *Hesperides* 1648, a collection of sacred and pastoral poetry admired for its lyric quality, including "Gather ye rosebuds" and "Cherry ripe".

herring any of various marine fishes of the herring family (Clupeidae), but especially the important food fish *Clupea harengus*. A silvered greenish-blue, it swims close to the surface, and may be 10–16 in/25–40 cm long. Herring travel in schools several miles long and wide. They are found in large quantities off the E coast of North America, and the shores of NE Europe. Overfishing and pollution have reduced their numbers.

Herschel William 1738–1822. German-born English astronomer. He was a skilled telescope maker, and pioneered the study of binary stars and nebulae. He discovered the planet Uranus 1781 and infrared solar rays 1801. He cataloged over 800 double stars, and found over 2,500 nebulae, cataloged by his sister Caroline Herschel; this work was continued by his son John Herschel. By studying the distribution of stars, William established the basic form of our Galaxy, the Milky Way.

Hertfordshire county in SE England *area* 629 sq mi/1,630 sq km *towns and cities* Hertford (administrative headquarters), St Albans, Watford, Hatfield, Hemel Hempstead, Bishop's Stortford, Letchworth (the first garden city, followed by Welwyn 1919 and Stevenage 1947) *features* rivers: Lea, Stort, Colne; part of the Chiltern Hills; Hatfield House; Knebworth House (home of Lord Lytton); Brocket Hall (home of Palmerston and Melbourne); home of G B ◊Shaw at Ayot St Lawrence; Berkhamsted Castle (Norman); Rothamsted agricultural experimental station *industries* engineering, aircraft, electrical goods, paper and printing; general agricultural goods *population* (1991) 951,500 *famous people* Graham Greene was born at Berkhamsted.

hertz SI unit (symbol Hz) of frequency (the number of repetitions of a regular occurrence in one second). Radio waves are often measured in megahertz (MHz), millions of hertz, and the ◊clock rate of a computer is usually measured in megahertz. The unit is named for Heinrich Hertz.

Herzegovina or *Hercegovina* part of ◊Bosnia-Herzegovina (which was formerly, until 1991, a republic of Yugoslavia).

Herzl Theodor 1860–1904. Austrian founder of the *Zionist* movement. He was born in Budapest and became a successful playwright and journalist, mainly in Vienna. The Dreyfus case convinced him that the only solution to the problem of anti-Semitism was the resettlement of the Jews in a state of their own. His book *Jewish State* 1896 launched political ◊Zionism, and he became the first president of the World Zionist Organization 1897.

Hess (Walter Richard) Rudolf 1894–1987. German Nazi leader. Imprisoned with Hitler 1924–25, he became his private secretary, taking down *Mein Kampf* from his dictation. In 1933 he was appointed deputy *Führer* to Hitler, a post he held until replaced by Goering Sept 1939. On May 10, 1941, he landed by air in the UK with his own compromise peace proposals and was held a prisoner of war until 1945, when he was tried at Nuremberg as a war criminal and sentenced to life imprisonment. He died in Spandau prison, Berlin.

Hess Victor 1883–1964. Austrian physicist who emigrated to the US shortly after sharing a Nobel Prize in 1936 for the discovery of cosmic radiation.

He was professor at Fordham University, New York, from 1938.

Hesse Hermann 1877–1962. German writer, a Swiss citizen from 1923. A conscientious objector in World War I and a pacifist opponent of Hitler, he published short stories, poetry, and novels, including *Peter*

Camenzind 1904, *Siddhartha* 1922, and *Steppenwolf* 1927. Later works, such as *Das Glasperlenspiel/The Glass Bead Game* 1943, show the influence of Indian mysticism and Jungian psychoanalysis. Nobel Prize for Literature 1946.

Hessen administrative region (German *Land*) of Germany *area* 8,145 sq mi/21,100 sq km *capital* Wiesbaden *towns and cities* Frankfurt-am-Main, Kassel, Darmstadt, Offenbach-am-Main *features* valleys of the rivers Rhine and Main; Taunus Mountains, rich in mineral springs, as at Homburg and Wiesbaden; see also ◊Swabia *industries* wine, timber, chemicals, automobiles, electrical engineering, optical instruments *population* (1988) 5,550,000 *religions* Protestant 61%, Roman Catholic 33% *history* until 1945, Hessen was divided in two by a strip of Prussian territory, the southern portion consisting of the valleys of the rivers Rhine and the Main, the northern being dominated by the Vogelsberg Mountains (2,442 ft/744 m). Its capital was Darmstadt.

heterosexuality sexual preference for, or attraction mainly to, persons of the opposite sex.

heterotroph any living organism that obtains its energy from organic substances produced by other organisms. All animals and fungi are heterotrophs, and they include herbivores, carnivores, and saprotrophs (those that feed on dead animal and plant material).

hexadecimal number system or *hex* number system to the base 16, used in computing. In hex the decimal numbers 0–15 are represented by the characters 0, 1, 2, 3, 4, 5, 6, 7, 8, 9, A, B, C, D, E, F.

Hexadecimal numbers are easy to convert to the computer's internal binary code and are more compact than binary numbers.

Hezbollah or *Hizbollah* (Party of God) extremist Muslim organization founded by the Iranian Revolutionary Guards who were sent to Lebanon after the 1979 Iranian revolution. Its aim is to spread the Islamic revolution of Iran among the Shiite population of Lebanon. Hezbollah is believed to be the umbrella movement of the groups that held many of the Western hostages taken from 1984. In 1993 Hezbollah guerrillas, opposed to the Middle East peace process, engaged in renewed hostilities with Israeli forces stationed in southern Lebanon.

Hialeah city in SE Florida just NW of Miami; population (1990) 188,000. Industries include clothing, furniture, plastics, and chemicals. Hialeah Park racetrack is a center for horse racing.

hibernation state of dormancy in which certain animals spend the winter. It is associated with a dramatic reduction in all metabolic processes, including body temperature, breathing, and heart rate. It is a fallacy that animals sleep throughout the winter.

hibiscus any plant of the genus *Hibiscus* of the mallow family.

Hibiscuses range from large herbaceous plants to trees. Popular as ornamental plants because of their brilliantly colored, red to white, bell-shaped flowers, they include *H. syriacus* and *H. rosa-sinensis* of Asia and the rose mallow *H. palustris* of North America.

Some tropical species provide fruit and timber: *H. tiliaceus* supplies timber and fibrous bark to South Pacific islanders; *H. sabdariffa* is cultivated in the West Indies and elsewhere for its fruit.

Hickok "Wild Bill" (James Butler) 1837–1876. US pioneer and law enforcer, a legendary figure in the West. In the Civil War he was a sharpshooter and scout for the Union army. He then served as marshal in Kansas, killing as many as 27 people. He was a prodigious gambler and was fatally shot from behind while playing poker in Deadwood, South Dakota.

He established his reputation as a gunfighter when he killed a fellow scout, turned traitor.

hickory tree of the genus *Carya* of the walnut family, native to North America and Asia. It provides a valuable timber, and all species produce nuts, although some are inedible. The pecan *C. illinoensis* is widely cultivated in the southern US, and the shagbark *C. ovata* in the northern US.

hidden file computer file in an ◊MS-DOS system that is not normally displayed when the directory listing command is given. Hidden files include certain system files, principally so that there is less chance of modifying or deleting them by accident, but any file can be made hidden if required.

hieroglyphic Egyptian writing system used from the mid-4th millennium BC to the 3rd century AD , which combines picture signs with those indicating letters. The direction of writing is normally from right to left, the signs facing the beginning of the line. It was deciphered 1822 by the French Egyptologist J F Champollion (1790–1832) with the aid of the ◊*Rosetta Stone*, which has the same inscription carved in hieroglyphic, demotic, and Greek.

High Church group in the Anglican Church that emphasizes aspects of Christianity usually associated with Catholics, such as ceremony and hierarchy. The term was first used in 1703 to describe those who opposed Dissenters, and later for groups such as the 19th-century ◊Oxford Movement.

high-definition television (HDTV) ◊television system offering a significantly greater number of scanning lines, and therefore a clearer picture, than that provided by conventional systems. The Japanese HDTV system, or Vision as it is trade-named in Japan, uses 1,125 scanning lines and an aspect ratio of 16:9 instead of the squarish 4:3 that conventional television uses. A European HDTV system, called HD-MAC, using 1,250 lines, is under development. In the US, a standard incorporating digital techniques is being discussed.

high jump field event in athletics in which competitors leap over a horizontal crossbar held between rigid uprights at least 12 ft/3.66 m apart. The bar is placed at increasingly higher levels. Elimination occurs after three consecutive failures to clear the bar.

Highland Region administrative region of Scotland *area* 10,077 sq mi/26,100 sq km *towns and cities* Inverness (administrative headquarters), Thurso, Wick *features* comprises almost half the country; Grampian Mountains; Ben Nevis (highest peak in the UK); Loch Ness, Caledonian Canal; Inner Hebrides; the Queen Mother's castle of Mey at Caithness; John O'Groats' House; Dounreay (with Atomic Energy Authority's prototype fast reactor, and a nuclear processing plant) *industries* oil services, winter sports, timber, livestock, grouse and deer hunting, salmon fishing *population* (1991) 209,400

Highlands one of the three geographical divisions of Scotland, lying to the N of a geological fault line that stretches from Stonehaven in the North Sea to Dumbarton on the Clyde. It is a mountainous region of hard rocks, shallow infertile soils, and high rainfall.

High Tech (abbreviation for *high technology*) in architecture, an approach to design, originating in the UK in the 1970s, which concentrates on technical innovation, often using exposed structure and services as a means of creating exciting forms and spaces. The Hong Kong and Shanghai Bank, Hong Kong, 1986, designed by Norman Foster, is a masterpiece of High Tech architecture.

hijacking illegal seizure or taking control of a vehicle and/or its passengers or goods. The term dates from 1923 and originally referred to the robbing of freight trucks. Subsequently it (and its derivative, "skyjacking") has been applied to the seizure of aircraft, usually in flight, by an individual or group, often with some political aim. International treaties (Tokyo 1963, The Hague 1970, and Montreal 1971) encourage cooperation against hijackers and make severe penalties compulsory.

Hijrah or *Hegira* the trip from Mecca to Medina of the prophet Mohammed, which took place AD 622 as a result of the persecution of the prophet and his followers. The Muslim calendar dates from this event, and the day of the Hijrah is celebrated as the Muslim New Year.

Hillary Edmund Percival 1919– . New Zealand mountaineer. In 1953, with Nepalese Sherpa mountaineer Tenzing Norgay, he reached the summit of Mount Everest, the first to climb the world's highest peak. As a member of the Commonwealth Transantarctic Expedition 1957–58, he was the first person since Scott to reach the South Pole overland, on Jan 3, 1958.

Hilliard Nicholas *c.*1547–1619. English miniaturist and goldsmith. He was court artist to Elizabeth I and James I. His sitters included the explorers Francis Drake and Walter Raleigh.

Hilton Conrad Nicholson 1887–1979. US entrepreneur, founder of the Hilton Hotel Corporation 1946.

During the 1930s he steadily expanded his chain of luxury hotels and resorts and reorganized it as the Hilton Hotel Corporation 1946. He based the firm's marketing appeal on its recognizable name and high-quality standardized service.

Born in San Antonio, New Mexico, Hilton attended the New Mexico School of Mines and joined his father in various business ventures after graduation 1909. Originally successful in banking, he entered the hotel business after World War I, retiring 1966. His autobiography, *Be My Guest*, was published 1957.

Himalayas vast mountain system of central Asia, extending from the Indian states of Kashmir in the W to Assam in the E, covering the S part of Tibet, Nepal, Sikkim, and Bhutan. It is the highest mountain range in the world. The two highest peaks are *Mount* ◊*Everest* and *Kangchenjunga*. Other major peaks include Makalu, Annapurna, and Nanga Parbat, all over 26,000 ft/8,000 m.

Himmler Heinrich 1900–1945. German Nazi leader, head of the ◊SS elite corps from 1929, the police and the ◊Gestapo secret police from 1936, and supervisor of the extermination of the Jews in E Europe. During World War II he replaced Goering as Hitler's second-in-command. He was captured May 1945 and committed suicide.

Hindenburg Paul Ludwig Hans von Beneckendorf und Hindenburg 1847–1934. German field marshal and right-wing politician. During World War I he was supreme commander and, with Ludendorff,

practically directed Germany's policy until the end of the war. He was president of Germany 1925–33.

Hindi language member of the Indo-Iranian branch of the Indo-European language family, the official language of the Republic of India, although resisted as such by the Dravidian-speaking states of the south. Hindi proper is used by some 30% of Indians, in such northern states as Uttar Pradesh and Madhya Pradesh.

Hinduism religion originating in N India about 4,000 years ago, which is superficially and in some of its forms polytheistic, but has a concept of the supreme spirit, ◊Brahman, above the many divine manifestations. These include the triad of chief gods (the Trimurti): Brahma, Vishnu, and Siva (creator, preserver, and destroyer). Central to Hinduism are the beliefs in reincarnation and ◊karma; the oldest scriptures are the *Vedas*. Temple worship is almost universally observed and there are many festivals. There are over 805 million Hindus worldwide. Women are not regarded as the equals of men but should be treated with kindness and respect. Muslim influence in N India led to the veiling of women and the restriction of their movements from about the end of the 12th century.

Hindu Kush mountain range in central Asia, length 500 m/800 km, greatest height Tirich Mir, 25,239 ft/7,690 in Pakistan. The narrow *Khyber Pass* (33 mi/53 km long) separates Pakistan from Afghanistan and was used by ◊Babur and other invaders of India. The present road was built by the British in the Afghan Wars.

Hindustan ("land of the Hindus") the whole of India, but more specifically the plain of the Ganges and Jumna rivers, or that part of India N of the Deccan.

Hindustani member of the Indo-Iranian branch of the Indo-European language family, closely related to Hindi and Urdu and originating in the bazaars of Delhi. It is a ◊lingua franca in many parts of the Republic of India.

Hine Lewis 1874–1940. US sociologist and photographer. His dramatic photographs of child labor conditions in US factories at the beginning of the 20th century led to changes in state and local labor laws.

Hipparchus *c.*190–*c.*120 BC . Greek astronomer who invented trigonometry, calculated the lengths of the solar year and the lunar month, discovered the precession of the equinoxes, made a catalog of 800 fixed stars, and advanced Eratosthenes' method of determining the situation of places on the Earth's surface by lines of latitude and longitude.

A native of Nicaea in Bithynia, he lived in Rhodes, and possibly in Alexandria.

hippie member of a youth movement of the late 1960s, also known as *flower power*, which originated in San Francisco, California, and was characterized by nonviolent anarchy, concern for the environment, and rejection of Western materialism. The hippies formed a politically outspoken, antiwar, artistically prolific counterculture in North America and Europe. Their colorful psychedelic style, inspired by drugs such as ◊LSD, emerged in fabric design, graphic art, and music by bands such as Love (1965–71), Jefferson Airplane (1965–74), and Pink Floyd.

Hippocrates *c.*460–*c.*370 BC . Greek physician, often called the father of medicine. Important Hippocratic ideas include cleanliness (for patients and physicians), moderation in eating and drinking, letting nature take its course, and living where the air is good. He believed that health was the result of the "humors" of the body being in balance; imbalance caused disease. These ideas were later adopted by ◊Galen.

hippopotamus large herbivorous, even-toed hoofed mammal of the family Hippopotamidae. The common hippopotamus *Hippopotamus amphibius* is found in Africa. It averages over 13 ft/4 m long, 5 ft/1.5 m high, weighs about 5 tons/4,500 kg, and has a brown or slate-gray skin. It is an endangered species.

hippopotamus *The common hippopotamus is adapted to life in the water, where it spends most of the day. It often lies submerged with only its eyes and nostrils above the surface. Its nostrils can be closed, and it has glands that give out an oily substance to protect its almost hairless skin.*

Hirabayashi v US US Supreme Court decision 1943 dealing with wartime legislation restricting the rights of citizens based on national origin. The case was brought in response to special curfews for Japanese-Americans on the US west coast. Hirabayashi charged that this and the forced relocation of Japanese-Americans during World War II was a violation of Fifth-Amendment rights.

The Court refused to rule on relocation measures (Korematsu v *US* 1944) but upheld Congress's curfew, judging that danger of internal sabotage in the war with Japan warranted this extraordinary measure.

Hirohito (regnal era name *Shōwa*) 1901–1989. Emperor of Japan from 1926, when he succeeded his father Taishō (Yoshihito). After the defeat of Japan in World War II 1945, he was made a figurehead monarch by the US-backed 1946 constitution. He is believed to have played a reluctant role in General Tōjō's prewar expansion plans. He was succeeded by his son ◊Akihito.

Hiroshige Andō 1797–1858. Japanese artist. He was one of the leading exponents of ukiyo-e prints, an art form whose flat, decorative style and choice of everyday subjects greatly influenced the development of Western art. His landscape prints, often employing snow or rain to create atmosphere, include *53 Stations on the Tokaido Highway* 1833. Whistler and van Gogh were among Western painters influenced by him.

Hiroshima industrial city and port on the south coast of Honshu Island, Japan, destroyed by the first wartime use of an atomic bomb Aug 6, 1945. The city has largely been rebuilt since the war; population (1990) 1,085,700.

Hispanic person of Latin American descent from the Spanish-speaking nations, either native-born or an immigrant.

Hispaniola (Spanish "little Spain") West Indian island, first landing place of Columbus in the New World,

Dec 6, 1492; it is now divided into ◊Haiti and the ◊Dominican Republic.

histamine inflammatory substance normally released in damaged tissues, which also accounts for many of the symptoms of ◊allergy. Substances that neutralize its activity are known as ◊antihistamines. Histamine was first described 1911 by British physiologist Henry Dale (1875–1968).

history record of the events of human societies. The earliest surviving historical records are the inscriptions denoting the achievements of Egyptian and Babylonian kings. As a literary form in the Western world, historical writing or ***historiography*** began with the Greek Herodotus in the 5th century BC , who was first to pass beyond the limits of a purely national outlook. Contemporary historians make extensive use of statistics, population figures, and primary records to justify historical arguments.

Hitchcock Alfred 1899–1980. English film director, a US citizen from 1955. A master of the suspense thriller, he was noted for his meticulously drawn storyboards that determined his camera angles and for his cameo "walk-ons" in his own films. His *Blackmail* 1929 was the first successful British talking film; *The Thirty-Nine Steps* 1935 and *The Lady Vanishes* 1939 are British suspense classics. He went to Hollywood 1940, where he made *Rebecca* 1940, *Notorious* 1946, *Strangers on a Train* 1951, *Rear Window* 1954, *Vertigo* 1958, *Psycho* 1960, and *The Birds* 1963. His last film was the comedy thriller *Family Plot* 1976.

Hitler Adolf 1889–1945. German Nazi dictator, born in Austria. He was *Führer* (leader) of the Nazi Party from 1921 and author of *Mein Kampf/My Struggle* 1925–27. As chancellor of Germany from 1933 and head of state from 1934, he created a dictatorship by playing

Hitchcock, Alfred *Suspense, melodrama, and fleeting personal appearances are the hallmarks of Alfred Hitchcock's films. A meticulous director, a supreme technician and visual artist, Hitchcock contributed significantly to the growth of cinema as an art form.*

party and state institutions against each other and continually creating new offices and appointments. His position was not seriously challenged until the "Bomb Plot" July 20, 1944, to assassinate him. In foreign affairs, he reoccupied the Rhineland and formed an alliance with the Italian Fascist Mussolini 1936, annexed Austria 1938, and occupied the Sudetenland under the ◊Munich Agreement. The rest of Czechoslovakia was annexed March 1939. The ◊Ribbentrop–Molotov pact was followed in Sept by the invasion of Poland and the declaration of war by Britain and France (see ◊World War II). He committed suicide as Berlin fell.

Hitler–Stalin pact another name for the ◊Ribbentrop–Molotov pact.

Hittite member of any of a succession of peoples who inhabited Anatolia and N Syria from the 3rd millennium to the 1st millennium BC . The city of Hattusas (now Bogazköy in central Turkey) became the capital of a strong kingdom which overthrew the Babylonian Empire. After a period of eclipse the Hittite New Empire became a great power (about 1400–1200 BC), which successfully waged war with Egypt. The Hittite language is an Indo-European language.

HIV (abbreviation for *human immunodeficiency virus*) The infectious agent that is believed to cause ◊AIDS.

Hobbes Thomas 1588–1679. English political philosopher and the first since Aristotle to attempt to develop a comprehensive theory of nature, including human behavior. In *Leviathan* 1651, he advocates absolutist government as the only means of ensuring order and security; he saw this as deriving from the social contract.

Ho Chi Minh adopted name of Nguyen Tat Thanh 1890–1969. North Vietnamese communist politician, premier and president 1954–69. Having trained in Moscow shortly after the Russian Revolution, he headed the communist Vietminh from 1941 and fought against the French during the ◊Indochina War 1946–54, becoming president and prime minister of the republic at the armistice. Aided by the communist bloc, he did much to develop industrial potential. He relinquished the premiership 1955, but continued as president. In the years before his death, Ho successfully led his country's fight against US-aided South Vietnam in the ◊Vietnam War 1954–75.

Ho Chi Minh City (until 1976 *Saigon*) chief port and industrial city of S Vietnam; population (1989) 3,169,100. Industries include shipbuilding, textiles, rubber, and food products. Saigon was the capital of the Republic of Vietnam (South Vietnam) from 1954 to 1976, when it was renamed.

Hockney David 1937– . English painter, printmaker, and designer, resident in California. He exhibited at the Young Contemporaries Show of 1961 and contributed to the Pop art movement. He developed an individual figurative style, as in his portrait *Mr and Mrs Clark and Percy* 1971 (Tate Gallery, London) and has experimented prolifically with technique. His views of swimming pools reflect a preoccupation with surface pattern and effects of light. He has also produced drawings, etchings (*Six Fairy Tales from the Brothers Grimm* 1970), photo collages, and sets for opera at La Scala, Milan, and the Metropolitan Opera House, New York.

Hoffa James Riddle "Jimmy" 1913–1975. notorious US labor union leader. A member of the Teamsters' (trucking) Union since 1931, he became its ruthless

president 1957. In 1964 he effected the first national contract for the truckers but was also convicted in two trials of fraud and jury tampering. He went to prison 1967 and retained his presidency until 1971, when President Nixon commuted his sentence on condition that he should not engage in union activity until 1980. Hoffa disappeared 1975, however, and is considered to have been murdered.

Hofmann Hans 1880–1966. German-born painter. He was active in Paris and Munich 1915–32, when he moved to the US. In addition to bold brushwork (he experimented with dribbling and dripping painting techniques in the 1940s), he used strong expressive colors. In the 1960s he moved toward a hard-edged abstract style.

He opened two art schools, in New York City and Provincetown, Massachusetts, and was influential among New York artists in the 1930s and 1940s. His teaching had a great impact on the Abstract Expressionists.

Hofstadter Robert 1915–1990. US nuclear physicist who made pioneering studies of nuclear structure and the elementary nuclear constituents, the proton and the neutron. He established that the proton and neutron were not pointlike, but had a definite volume and shape. He shared the 1961 Nobel Prize for Physics with Rudolf Mössbauer.

hog member of the ◊pig family.

Hogarth William 1697–1764. English painter and engraver. He produced portraits and moralizing genre scenes, such as the series of prints *A Rake's Progress* 1735. His portraits are remarkably direct and full of character, for example *Heads of Six of Hogarth's Servants* about 1750–55 (Tate Gallery, London).

hogweed any of various coarse weeds, such as ragweed *Ambrosia* and sow thistle *Sonchus*.

Hohenstaufen German family of princes, several members of which were Holy Roman emperors 1138–1208 and 1214–54. They were the first German emperors to make use of associations with Roman law and tradition to aggrandize their office, and included Conrad III; Frederick I (Barbarossa), the first to use the title Holy Roman emperor (previously the title Roman emperor was used); Henry VI; and Frederick II.

Hohenzollern German family, originating in Württemberg, the main branch of which held the titles of elector of Brandenburg from 1415, king of Prussia from 1701, and German emperor from 1871. The last emperor, Wilhelm II, was dethroned 1918 after the disastrous course of World War I. Another branch of the family were kings of Romania 1881–1947.

Hohhot or *Huhehot* city and capital of Inner Mongolia (Nei Mongol) autonomous region, China; population (1989) 870,000. Industries include textiles, electronics, and dairy products. There are Lamaist monasteries and temples here.

Hokkaido formerly (until 1868) *Yezo* or *Ezo* northernmost of the four main islands of Japan, separated from Honshu to the S by Tsugaru Strait and from Sakhalin to the N by Soy Strait; area 32,231 sq mi/83,500 sq km; population (1986) 5,678,000, including 16,000 Ainus. The capital is Sapporo. Natural resources include coal, mercury, manganese, oil and natural gas, timber, and fisheries. Coal mining and agriculture are the main industries.

Hokusai Katsushika 1760–1849. Japanese artist. He was the leading printmaker of his time and a major exponent of ukiyo-e. He published *36 Views of Mount Fuji* about 1823–29, and produced outstanding pictures of almost every kind of subject—birds, flowers, courtesans, and scenes from legend and everyday life.

Under the Wave at Kanagawa (British Museum, London) is typical.

Holbein Hans, *the Younger* 1497/98–1543. German painter and woodcut artist. The son and pupil of Hans Holbein the Elder, he was born in Augsburg. In 1515 he went to Basel, where he became friendly with the scholar and humanist Erasmus and illustrated his *Praise of Folly*; he painted three portraits of Erasmus 1523. He traveled widely in Europe and while in England as painter to Henry VIII he created a remarkable evocation of the English court in a series of graphic, perceptive portraits, the best-known being those of Henry VIII and of Thomas More. During his time at the English court, he also painted miniature portraits, inspiring Nicholas Hilliard. One of the finest graphic artists of his age, he executed a woodcut series *Dance of Death* about 152⁵, and designed title pages for Luther's New Testament and More's *Utopia*.

Holiday Billie. Adopted name of Eleanora Gough McKay 1915–1959. US jazz singer, also known as "Lady Day". She made her debut in Harlem clubs and became known for her emotionally charged delivery and idiosyncratic phrasing; she brought a blues feel to performances with swing bands. Songs she made her own include "Stormy Weather", "Strange Fruit", and "I Cover the Waterfront".

holism in philosophy, the concept that the whole is greater than the sum of its parts.

holistic medicine umbrella term for an approach that virtually all alternative therapies profess, which considers the overall health and lifestyle profile of a patient, and treats specific ailments not primarily as conditions to be alleviated but rather as symptoms of more fundamental disease.

Holland popular name for the ◊Netherlands; also two provinces of the Netherlands, North Holland and South Holland.

Hollerith Herman 1860–1929. US inventor of a mechanical tabulating machine, the first device for data processing. Hollerith's tabulator was widely publicized after being successfully used in the 1890 census. The firm he established, the Tabulating Machine Company, was later one of the founding companies of ◊IBM.

holly tree or shrub of the genus *Ilex*, family Aquifoliaceae, generally with glossy, sharp-pointed leaves and red berries. American holly *I. opaca* of the E US is used for Christmas decorations. Leaves of the Brazilian holly *I. paraguayensis* are used to make the tea yerba maté.

Holly Buddy. Adopted name of Charles Hardin Holley 1936–1959. US rock-and-roll singer, guitarist, and songwriter. He had a distinctive, hiccuping vocal style and was an early experimenter with recording techniques. Many of his hits with his band, the Crickets, such as "That'll Be the Day" 1957, "Peggy Sue" 1957, and "Maybe Baby" 1958, have become classics. He died in a plane crash.

hollyhock plant of the genus *Althaea* of the mallow family Malvaceae. *A. rosea*, originally a native of Asia, produces spikes of large white, yellow, or red flowers, 10 ft/3 m high when cultivated as a biennial.

Hollywood district in the city of Los Angeles, California; the center of the US movie industry from 1911. It is the home of film studios such as 20th Century Fox, MGM, Paramount, Columbia Pictures, United Artists, Disney, and Warner Brothers. Many film stars' homes are situated nearby in Beverly Hills and other communities adjacent to Hollywood.

Holmes Oliver Wendell 1841–1935. US jurist and Supreme Court justice 1902–32, noted for the elegance of his written opinions. He was appointed to the US Supreme Court by President Theodore Roosevelt, and during his office handed down landmark decisions in a number of antitrust, constitutional First Amendment, and labor law cases. He retired from the Court 1932.

holmium silvery, metallic element of the ◊lanthanide series, symbol Ho, atomic number 67, relative atomic mass 164.93. It occurs in combination with other rare-earth metals and in various minerals such as gadolinite. Its compounds are highly magnetic.

Holocaust, the the annihilation of an estimated 6 million Jews by the Hitler regime 1933–45 in the numerous extermination and ◊concentration camps, most notably Auschwitz, Sobibor, Treblinka, and Maidanek in Poland, and Belsen, Buchenwald, and Dachau in Germany. An additional 10 million people died during imprisonment or were exterminated, among them were Ukrainian, Polish, and Russian civilians and prisoners of war, Gypsies, socialists, homosexuals, and others (labeled "defectives"). Victims were variously starved, tortured, experimented on, and worked to death. Millions were executed in gas chambers, shot, or hanged. It was euphemistically termed the final solution (of the Jewish question).

Holocaust museums and memorial sites have been established in Israel and in other countries.

Holocene epoch of geological time that began 10,000 years ago, the second and current epoch of the Quaternary period. The glaciers retreated, the climate became warmer, and humans developed significantly.

holography method of producing three-dimensional (3-D) images by means of ◊laser light. Holography uses a photographic technique (involving the splitting of a laser beam into two beams) to produce a picture, or hologram, that contains 3-D information about the object photographed. Some holograms show meaningless patterns in ordinary light and produce a 3-D image only when laser light is projected through them, but reflection holograms produce images when ordinary light is reflected from them (as found on credit cards).

Holy Communion another name for the ◊Eucharist, a Christian sacrament.

Holy Grail in medieval Christian legend, the dish or cup used by Jesus at the Last Supper, supposed to have supernatural powers. Together with the spear with which he was wounded at the Crucifixion, it was an object of quest by King Arthur's knights in certain stories incorporated in the Arthurian legend.

Holy Roman Empire empire of ◊Charlemagne and his successors, and the German Empire 962–1806, both being regarded as the Christian (hence "holy") revival of the Roman Empire. At its height it comprised much of western and central Europe. See ◊Germany: history and ◊Hapsburg.

Holy Spirit third person of the Christian ◊Trinity, also known as the Holy Ghost or the Paraclete, usually depicted as a white dove.

Home Counties the counties in close proximity to London, England: Hertfordshire, Essex, Kent, Surrey, Buckinghamshire, Berkshire, and formerly Middlesex.

homeland or *Bantustan* before 1980, name for the ◊Black National States in the Republic of South Africa.

homeopathy or *homoeopathy* system of medicine based on the principle that symptoms of disease are part of the body's self-healing processes, and on the practice of administering extremely diluted doses of natural substances found to produce in a healthy person the symptoms manifest in the illness being treated.

Developed by German physician Samuel Hahnemann (1755–1843), the system is widely practiced today as an alternative to allopathic medicine, and many controlled tests and achieved cures testify its efficacy.

Homer according to ancient tradition, the author of the Greek narrative epics, the *Iliad* and the *Odyssey* (both derived from oral tradition). Little is known about the man, but modern research suggests that both poems should be assigned to the 8th century BC , with the *Odyssey* the later of the two. The predominant dialect in the poems indicates that Homer may have come from an Ionian Greek settlement, such as Smyrna or Chios, as was traditionally believed.

Homer Winslow 1836–1910. US painter and lithographer. He is known for his vivid seascapes, in both oil and watercolor, which date from the 1880s and 1890s.

He stayed in Britain for two years, then settled in Maine, but continued to travel to Canada, the West Indies, and elsewhere.

Home Rule, Irish movement to repeal the Act of ◊Union 1801 that joined Ireland to Britain and to establish an Irish parliament responsible for internal affairs. In 1870 Isaac Butt (1813–1879) formed the Home Rule Association and the movement was led in Parliament from 1880 by Charles ◊Parnell. After 1918 the demand for an independent Irish republic replaced that for home rule.

homicide in law, the killing of a human being. This may be unlawful, lawful, or excusable, depending on the circumstances. Unlawful homicides include ◊murder, ◊manslaughter, infanticide, and causing death by dangerous driving (vehicular homicide). Lawful homicide occurs where, for example, a police officer is justified in killing a criminal in the course of apprehension. Excusable homicide occurs when a person is killed in self-defense or by accident.

homosexuality sexual preference for, or attraction to, persons of one's own sex; in women it is referred to as ◊lesbianism.

Both sexes use the term "gay". Men and women who are attracted to both sexes are referred to as bisexual. The extent to which homosexual behavior is caused by biological or psychological factors is an area of disagreement among experts.

Honan alternate name for ◊*Henan*, a province of China.

Honda Japanese vehicle manufacturer, founded 1948. By the late 1980s the company was producing more than 1.5 million automobiles and 3 million motorcycles annually.

Honduras Republic of (*República de Honduras*) *area* 43,282 sq mi/112,100 sq km *capital* Tegucigalpa *towns and cities* San Pedro Sula; ports La Ceiba, Puerto Cortés *physical* narrow tropical coastal plain with mountainous interior, Bay Islands *features* archeological sites; Mayan ruins at Copán *head of state and government* Carlos Roberto Reina from 1993 *political system* democratic republic *political parties* Liberal Party of Honduras (PLH), center-left; National Party (PN), right-wing *exports* coffee, bananas, meat, sugar, timber (including mahogany, rosewood) *currency* lempira *population* (1993 est) 5,240,000 (mestizo, or mixed, 90%; Indians and Europeans 10%); growth rate 3.1% p.a. *life expectancy* men 64, women 68 *languages* Spanish (official), English, Indian languages *religion* Roman Catholic 97% *literacy* men 76%, women 71% *GNP* $570 per head (1991) *chronology 1838* Independence achieved from Spain. *1980* After more than a century of mostly military rule, a civilian government was elected, with Dr Roberto Suazo as president; the commander in chief of the army, General Gustavo Alvarez, retained considerable power. *1983* Close involvement with the US in providing naval and air bases and allowing Nicaraguan counter-revolutionaries ("Contras") to operate from Honduras. *1984* Alvarez ousted in coup led by junior officers, resulting in policy review toward US and Nicaragua. *1985* José Azcona elected president after electoral law changed, making Suazo ineligible for presidency. *1989* Government and opposition declared support for Central American peace plan to demobilize Nicaraguan Contras based in Honduras; Contras and their dependents in Honduras in 1989 thought to number about 55,000. *1990* Rafael Callejas (PN) inaugurated as president. *1992* Border dispute with El Salvador dating from 1861 finally resolved. *1993* PLH, under Carlos Roberto Reina, won assembly and presidential elections.

Honecker Erich 1912–1994. German communist politician, in power in East Germany 1973–89, elected chair of the council of state (head of state) 1976. He governed in an outwardly austere and efficient manner and, while favoring East–West détente, was a loyal ally of the USSR. In Oct 1989, following a wave of prodemocracy demonstrations, he was replaced as leader of the Socialist Unity Party (SED) and head of state by Egon Krenz, and in Dec expelled from the Communist Party.

honey sweet syrup produced by honey ◊bees from the nectar of flowers. It is stored in honeycombs and made in excess of their needs as food for the winter. Honey comprises various sugars, mainly levulose and dextrose, with enzymes, coloring matter, acids, and pollen grains. It has antibacterial properties and was widely used in ancient Egypt, Greece, and Rome as a wound salve. It is still popular for sore throats, in hot drinks or in lozenges.

honeysuckle vine or shrub of the genus *Lonicera*, family Caprifoliaceae. The common honeysuckle or woodbine *L. periclymenum* of Europe is a climbing plant with sweet-scented flowers, reddish and yellow-tinted outside and creamy white inside; it grows in the US.

Hong Kong British crown colony SE of China, in the South China Sea, comprising Hong Kong Island; the Kowloon Peninsula; many other islands, of which the largest is Lantau; and the mainland New Territories. It is due to revert to Chinese control 1997. *area* 413 sq mi/1,070 sq km *capital* Victoria (Hong Kong City) *towns and cities* Kowloon, Tsuen Wan (in the New Territories) *features* an enclave of

Kwantung province, China, it has one of the world's finest natural harbors; Hong Kong Island is connected with Kowloon by undersea railroad and ferries; a world financial center, its stock market has four exchanges; across the border of the New Territories in China itself is the Shenzhen special economic zone *exports* textiles, clothing, electronic goods, clocks, watches, cameras, plastic products; a large proportion of the exports and imports of S China are transshipped here; tourism is important *currency* Hong Kong dollar *population* (1986) 5,431,000; 57% Hong Kong Chinese, most of the remainder refugees from the mainland *languages* English, Chinese *media* Hong Kong has the most free press in Asia but its freedoms are not enshrined in law *religions* Confucianist, Buddhist, Taoist, with Muslim and Christian minorities *government* Hong Kong is a British dependency administered by a crown-appointed governor (Chris Patten from 1992) who presides over an unelected executive council, composed of 4 ex-officio and 11 nominated members, and a legislative council composed of 3 ex-officio members, 18 appointees, and 39 elected members (21 of these elected by constituencies each representing an occupational or professional group, and 18 directly elected by 9 geographical constituencies). In 1994 the Legislative Council, in defiance of China, passed the first stage of constitutional reforms which lowered the voting age to 18 and provided for elected local councils. *history* formerly part of China, Hong Kong Island was occupied by Britain 1841, during the first of the ◊Opium Wars, and ceded by China under the 1842 Treaty of Nanking. The colony, which developed into a major center for Sino-British trade was occupied by Japan 1941–45. Chinese refugees raised the colony's population from 1 million in 1946 to 5 million in 1980. Since 1975, 160,000 Vietnamese ◊boat people have fled to Hong Kong. Hong Kong's economy expanded rapidly during the corresponding period and the colony became one of Asia's major commercial, financial, and industrial centers, boasting the world's busiest container port from 1987. As the date (1997) for the termination of the New Territories' lease approached, negotiations on Hong Kong's future were opened between Britain and China 1982. These culminated in a unique agreement, signed in Beijing 1984, in which Britain agreed to transfer full sovereignty of the islands and New Territories to China 1997 in return for Chinese assurance that Hong Kong's social and economic freedom and capitalist lifestyle would be preserved for at least 50 years.

Honiara port and capital of the Solomon Islands, on the northwest coast of Guadalcanal Island, on the river Mataniko; population (1985) 26,000.

Honolulu capital city and port of Hawaii, on the south coast of Oahu; population (1990) 365,300. It is a vacation resort, noted for its beauty and tropical vegetation, with some industry.

The University of Hawaii's main campus is here, and there is an innovative state capitol building, dating from 1959. Pearl Harbor and Hickam Air Force Base are 7 mi/11 km to the NW. William Brown, a British sea captain, was the first European to see Honolulu, in 1794. It became the Hawaiian royal capital in the 19th century.

Honshu principal island of Japan. It lies between Hokkaido to the NE and Kyushu to the SW; area 89,205 sq mi/231,100 sq km, including 382 smaller islands; population (1990) 99,254,200. A chain of volcanic mountains runs along the island, which is subject to frequent earthquakes. The main cities are Tokyo, Yokohama, Osaka, Kobe, Nagoya, and Hiroshima.

Hooke Robert 1635–1703. English scientist and inventor, originator of ◊*Hooke's law*, and considered the foremost mechanic of his time. His inventions included a telegraph system, the spirit level, marine barometer, and sea gauge. He coined the term "cell" in biology.

Hooker John Lee 1917– . US blues guitarist, singer, and songwriter. He was one of the foremost blues musicians. His first record, "Boogie Chillen" 1948, was a blues hit and his percussive guitar style made him popular with a rock audience from the 1950s. His albums include *Urban Blues* 1968 and *Boom Boom* 1992 (also the title of his 1962 song).

Hooker Thomas 1586–1647. British colonial religious leader in America. A Puritan, he opposed the religious leadership of Cambridge colony, and led a group of his followers westward to the Connecticut Valley, founding Hartford 1636. He became the de facto leader of the colony and in 1639 helped to formulate Connecticut's first constitution, the Fundamental Orders.

Hooke's law law stating that the deformation of a body is proportional to the magnitude of the deforming force, provided that the body's elastic limit is not exceeded. If the elastic limit is not reached, the body will return to its original size once the force is removed. The law was discovered by Robert Hooke 1676.

hookworm parasitic roundworm (see ◊worm), of the genus *Necator*, with hooks around the mouth. It lives mainly in tropic and subtropic regions, but also in humid areas in temperate climates. The eggs are hatched in damp soil, and the larvae bore into the host's skin, usually through the soles of the feet. They make their way to the small intestine, where they live by sucking blood. The eggs are expelled with feces, and the cycle starts again. The human hookworm causes anemia, weakness, and abdominal pain. It is common in areas where defecation occurs outdoors.

hoopoe bird *Upupa epops* in the order Coraciiformes, slightly larger than a thrush, with a long, thin bill and a bright, buff-colored crest that expands into a fan shape. The wings are banded with black and white, and the rest of the plumage is black, white, and buff. This bird is the "lapwing" mentioned in the Old Testament.

Hoover Herbert Clark 1874–1964. 31st president of the US 1929–33, a Republican. He was secretary of commerce 1921–28. Hoover lost public confidence after the stock-market crash of 1929, when he opposed direct government aid for the unemployed in the Depression that followed.

Hoover was called upon to administer the European Food Program 1947, and in the late 1950s he headed two Hoover commissions that recommended reforms in government structure and operations.

Hoover J(ohn) Edgar 1895–1972. US lawyer and director of the Federal Bureau of Investigation (FBI) from its start 1924, where he built a powerful network for the detection of organized crime, including a national fingerprint collection.

Hoover Dam highest concrete dam in the US, 726 ft/221 m, on the Colorado River at the Arizona–Nevada border. It was begun during the Hoover administra-

Hoover, Herbert Clark *US Republican politician Herbert Hoover, whose term as president coincided with the financial collapse of 1929 and the ensuing Depression. Hoover, who believed in ultimate recovery through private enterprise, was criticized for the ineffectiveness of the measures he initiated.*

tion, built 1931–36. Known as Boulder Dam 1933–47, under the Roosevelt administration, its name was restored by President Truman since President Hoover was serving the Truman administration in postwar organization. The dam created Lake Meade, and has a hydroelectric power capacity of 1,300 megawatts.

Hope Bob. Adopted name of Leslie Townes Hope. 1903– . British-born US comedian, brought to the US in 1907. His earliest success was on Broadway and as a radio star in the 1930s. His film appearances include seven "Road" films made from 1940 with Bing Crosby and Dorothy Lamour. These include *The Road to Singapore* 1940, *The Road to Zanzibar* 1941, *The Road to Morocco* 1942, *The Road to Utopia* 1946, *The Road to Rio* 1946, *The Road to Bali* 1952, and *The Road to Hong Kong* 1953. He made other films, such as *Paleface* 1948, a comic western.

Hopei alternative transcription of ◊*Hebei*, a province of China.

Hopi member of a North American Indian people, presently numbering approximately 9,000, who live mainly in pueblos in the SW US, especially NE Arizona. They live in stone and adobe houses, forming small towns on rocky plateaus, farm, and herd sheep. Their language belongs to the Uto-Aztecan family.

Hopkins Anthony 1937– . Welsh actor. Among his stage appearances are *Equus, Macbeth, Pravda,* and the title role in *King Lear.* His films include *The Lion in Winter* 1968, *A Bridge Too Far* 1977, *The Elephant Man* 1980, *84 Charing Cross Road* 1986, *The Silence of the Lambs* (Academy Award) 1991, *Howards End* 1992, and *Shadowlands* and *The Remains of the Day*, both 1993.

Hopkins Gerard Manley 1844–1889. English poet and Jesuit priest. His work, which is marked by its originality of diction and rhythm and includes "The Wreck of the Deutschland" and "The Windhover", was published posthumously 1918 by Robert Bridges. His poetry is profoundly religious and records his struggle to gain faith and peace, but also shows freshness of feeling and delight in nature. His employment of "sprung rhythm" (combination of traditional regularity of stresses with varying numbers of syllables in each line) greatly influenced later 20th-century poetry.

Hopper Edward 1882–1967. US painter and etcher. He was one of the foremost American Realists. His views of life in New England and New York in the 1930s and 1940s, painted in rich, dark colors, convey a brooding sense of emptiness and solitude, as in *Nighthawks* 1942 (Art Institute, Chicago).

Hopper was a realist who never followed avant-garde trends.

Hopper Hedda 1890–1966. US actress and celebrity reporter. From 1915 she appeared in many silent films and after a brief retirement was hired as a radio gossip reporter in 1936. From 1938 Hopper wrote a syndicated newspaper column about the private lives of the Hollywood stars. She carried on a widely publicized feud with rival columnist Louella Parsons.

hops female fruit-heads of the hop plant *Humulus lupulus,* family Cannabiaceae; these are dried and used as a tonic and in flavoring beer. In designated areas in Europe, no male hops may be grown, since seedless hops produced by the unpollinated female plant contain a greater proportion of the alpha acid that gives beer its bitter taste.

Horace 65–8 BC . Roman lyric poet and satirist. He became a leading poet under the patronage of Emperor Augustus. His works include *Satires* 35–30 BC; the four books of *Odes*, about 25–24 BC ; *Epistles*, a series of verse letters; and an influential critical work, *Ars poetica.* They are distinguished by their style, wit, discretion, and patriotism.

horehound any plant of the genus *Marrubium* of the mint family Labiatae. The white horehound *M. vulgare,* found in Europe, N Africa, W Asia, and naturalized in North America, has a thick, hairy stem and clusters of dull white flowers; it has medicinal uses.

hormone product of the ◊endocrine glands, concerned with control of body functions. The major glands are the thyroid, parathyroid, pituitary, adrenal, pancreas, ovary, and testis. Hormones bring about changes in the functions of various organs according to the body's requirements. The hypothalamus, which adjoins the pituitary gland, at the base of the brain, is a control center for overall coordination of hormone secretion; the thyroid hormones determine the rate of general body chemistry; the adrenal hormones prepare the organism during stress for "fight or flight"; and the sexual hormones such as estrogen govern reproductive functions.

hormone-replacement therapy (HRT) use of ◊estrogen and progesterone to help limit the unpleasant effects of the menopause in women. The treatment was first used in the 1970s.

hornbeam any tree of the genus *Carpinus* of the birch family Betulaceae. They have oval, serrated leaves and bear pendant clusters of flowers, each with a nutlike seed attached to the base. The trunk is usually twisted, with smooth gray bark.

The American hornbeam *C. caroliniana* is native to the eastern US. The European hornbeam *C. betulus* is sometimes planted as an ornamental.

hornbill bird of the family of Bucerotidae, found in Africa, India, and Malaysia. Omnivorous, it is about 3 ft/1 m long, and has a powerful bill, usually surmounted by a bony growth or casque. During the breeding season, the female walls herself into a hole in a tree and does not emerge until the young are hatched.

hornet kind of ◊wasp.

Hornsby Rajah (Rogers) 1896–1963. US baseball player. He won the National League batting title in six consecutive seasons 1920–25. His .424 batting average 1924 is the highest achieved in the National League and he was voted the National League's most valuable player 1925. His lifetime batting average of .358 is the second-highest in history.

Hornsby was elected to the Baseball Hall of Fame 1942.

hornwort nonvascular plant of the class Anthocerotae; it is related to the ◊liverworts and ◊mosses, with which it forms the order Bryophyta. Hornworts are found in warm climates, growing on moist shaded soil. The name is also given to an aquatic flowering plant of the family Ceratophyllaceae. Found in slow-moving water, it has whorls of finely divided leaves and may grow up to 7 ft/2 m long.

Horowitz Vladimir 1904–1989. Russian-born US pianist. He made his US debut 1928 with the New York Philharmonic Orchestra. A leading interpreter of Liszt, Schumann, and Rachmaninov, he toured worldwide until the early 1950s, when he retired to devote more time to recording. His rare concert appearances 1965–86 displayed undiminished brilliance.

Horowitz married Arturo Toscanini's daughter, Wanda, 1933. In 1986 he made a pilgrimage to his homeland, giving a brilliant performance at the Moscow Conservatory of Music.

horse hoofed, odd-toed, grazing mammal *Equus caballus* of the family Equidae, which also includes zebras and asses. The many breeds of domestic horse of Euro-Asian origin range in color from white to gray, brown,

and black. The yellow-brown Mongolian wild horse or Przewalski's horse *E. przewalskii*, named for its Polish "discoverer" about 1880, is the only surviving species of wild horse.

horsefly any of over 2,500 species of fly, belonging to the family Tabanidae. The females suck blood from horses, cattle, and humans; males live on plants and suck nectar. The larvae are carnivorous.

horsepower imperial unit (abbreviation hp) of power, now replaced by the ◊watt. It was first used by the engineer James ◊Watt, who employed it to compare the power of steam engines with that of horses.

In the US one horsepower is equal to 746 watts, in the UK 745.7 watts, and in the metric system 735.5 watts.

horse racing sport of racing mounted or driven (hitched) horses. Two popular forms in the US are *flat racing*, in which thoroughbred horses are guided over a flat course by a rider called a jockey, and *harness racing*, in which a driver in a two-wheeled cart called a sulky drives a horse in one of two gaits: pacing (both legs on the same side are off the ground at the same time); trotting (diagonal legs are off the ground at the same time).

horseradish hardy perennial *Armouracia rusticana*, native to SE Europe but naturalized elsewhere, family Cruciferae. The thick, cream-colored root is strong-tasting and is often made into a condiment.

horseshoe crab marine arthropod of the order Xiphosura, class Merostomata, distantly related to spiders, which lives on the Atlantic coast of North America and the coasts of Asia. The upper side of the body is entirely covered with a rounded shell, and it has a long, spinelike tail. Horseshoe crabs grow up to 2 ft/60 cm long. They crawl along the bottom in coastal waters and lay their eggs in the sand at the high water mark.

horsetail plant of the genus *Equisetum*, related to ferns and club mosses; some species are also called *scouring rush*. There are about 35 living species, bearing their spores on cones at the stem tip. The upright stems are ribbed and often have spaced whorls of branches. Today they are of modest size, but hundreds of millions of years ago giant treelike forms existed.

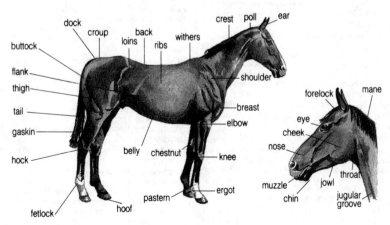

horse

horticulture art and science of growing flowers, fruit, and vegetables. Horticulture is practiced in gardens and orchards, along with millions of acres of land devoted to vegetable farming. Some areas, like California, have specialized in horticulture because they have the mild climate and light fertile soil most suited to these crops.

Horus in ancient Egyptian mythology, the hawkheaded sun god, son of Isis and Osiris, of whom the pharaohs were declared to be the incarnation.

hostage person taken prisoner as a means of exerting pressure on a third party, usually with threats of death or injury.

hot key in computing, a key stroke (or sequence of key strokes) that triggers a memory-resident program. Such programs are called terminate and stay resident. Hot keys should be chosen so that they do not conflict with key sequences in commonly used applications.

Houphouët-Boigny Félix 1905–1993. Ivory Coast right-wing politician, president 1960–93. He held posts in French ministries, and became president of the Republic of the Ivory Coast on independence 1960, maintaining close links with France, which helped to boost an already thriving economy and encourage political stability. Pro-Western and opposed to communist intervention in Africa, Houphouët-Boigny was strongly criticized for maintaining diplomatic relations with South Africa. He was reelected for a seventh term 1990 in multiparty elections, amid allegations of ballot rigging and political pressure.

Hours, Book of in medieval Europe, a collection of liturgical prayers for the use of the faithful.

Books of Hours contained short prayers and illustrations, with each prayer suitable for a different hour of the day, in honor of the Virgin Mary. The enormous demand for Books of Hours was a stimulus for the development of Gothic illumination. A celebrated example is the *Très Riches Heures du Duc de Berry*, illustrated in the early 15th century by the Limbourg brothers.

housefly fly of the genus *Musca*, found in and around dwellings, especially *M. domestica*, a common worldwide species. Houseflies are gray and have mouthparts adapted for drinking liquids and sucking moisture from food and manure.

house music dance music of the 1980s originating in the inner-city clubs of Chicago, combining funk with European high-tech pop, and using dub, digital sampling, and cross-fading. *Acid house* has minimal vocals and melody, instead surrounding the mechanically emphasized 4/4 beat with stripped-down synthesizer riffs and a wandering bass line. Other variants include *hip house*, with rap elements, and *acid jazz*.

House of Commons lower chamber of the UK ◊Parliament.

House of Lords upper chamber of the UK ◊Parliament.

House of Representatives, US lower chamber of the Congress. Revenue bills and impeachment charges must originate in the House, which also elects the president (as it did in 1800 and 1824) if there is no majority in the electoral college. Once bills are passed in the House, they are sent to the Senate for consideration.

Houston port in Texas; linked by canal to the Gulf of Mexico; population (1990) 1,630,600. It is a major center of the petroleum industry and of finance and commerce. It is also one of the busiest US ports.

Industrial products include refined petroleum, oilfield equipment, and petrochemicals, chief of which are synthetic rubber, plastics, insecticides, and fertilizers. Other products include iron and steel, electrical and electronic machinery, paper products, and milled rice. The Lyndon B Johnson Space Center, the University of Houston, and Rice University are here, as is the Astrodome, the world's first all-purpose, air-conditioned domed stadium. The Texas Medical Center is one of the world's finest, and there are major museums and performing-arts groups. Houston was first settled 1826. Its modern growth dates from the discovery of oil nearby 1901 and the completion of the Houston Ship Channel 1914.

hovercraft vehicle that rides on a cushion of high-pressure air, free from all contact with the surface beneath, invented by British engineer Christopher Cockerell 1959. Hovercraft need a smooth terrain when operating overland and are best adapted to use on waterways. They are useful in places where harbors have not been established.

Howard Catherine *c.*1520–1542. Queen consort of ◊Henry VIII of England from 1540. In 1541 the archbishop of Canterbury, Thomas Cranmer, accused her of being unchaste before marriage to Henry and she was beheaded 1542 after Cranmer made further charges of adultery.

Howard Leslie. Adopted name of Leslie Stainer 1893–1943. English actor. His films include *The Scarlet Pimpernel* 1935, *The Petrified Forest* 1936, *Pygmalion* 1938, and *Gone with the Wind* 1939.

He was killed during a secret wartime mission when the plane he was traveling in was shot down by the Germans, allegedly because Winston Churchill was thought to be aboard.

Howe Elias 1819–1867. US inventor, in 1846, of a ◊sewing machine using two threads, thus producing a lock stitch.

Born in Spencer, Massachusetts, Howe worked on several types of sewing machines before arriving at his invention that he marketed successfully in England. Eventually he manufactured the machine in Bridgeport, Connecticut, and marketed it successfully in the US.

Howe Julia Ward 1819–1910. US feminist and abolitionist who in 1862 wrote the poem "The Battle Hymn of the Republic"; sung to the tune of "John Brown's Body," it became associated with the Union side during the Civil War.

Hoxha Enver 1908–1985. Albanian Communist politician, the country's leader from 1954.

He founded the Albanian Communist Party 1941, and headed the liberation movement 1939–44. He was prime minister 1944–54, combining with foreign affairs 1946–53, and from 1954 was first secretary of the Albanian Party of Labor. In policy he was a Stalinist and independent of both Chinese and Soviet communism.

Hsuan Tung name adopted by Henry ◊P'u-i on becoming emperor of China 1908.

Hua Guofeng or *Hua Kuofeng* 1920– . Chinese politician, leader of the Chinese Communist Party (CCP) 1976–81, premier 1976–80. He dominated Chinese politics 1976–77, seeking economic modernization without major structural reform. From 1978 he was gradually eclipsed by Deng Xiaoping. Hua was ousted from the Politburo Sept 1982 but remained a member of the CCP Central Committee.

Huang He or *Hwang Ho* river in China; length 3,395 mi/ 5,464 km. It takes its name (meaning "yellow river") from its muddy waters. Formerly known as "China's sorrow" because of disastrous floods, it is now largely controlled through hydroelectric works and flood barriers.

Hubble Edwin Powell 1889–1953. US astronomer who discovered the existence of other ◊galaxies outside our own, and classified them according to their shape. His theory that the universe is expanding is now generally accepted.

Born in Marshfield, Missouri, Hubble originally studied law before joining Yerkes Observatory 1914, subsequently moving to Mount Wilson where in 1923 he discovered Cepheid variable stars outside our own Galaxy. In 1925 he introduced the classification of galaxies as spirals, barred spirals, and ellipticals. In 1929 he announced *Hubble's law*, which states that the galaxies are moving apart at a rate that increases with their distance.

Hubble's constant in astronomy, a measure of the rate at which the universe is expanding, named for Edwin Hubble. Observations suggest that galaxies are moving apart at a rate of 30–60 mps/50–100 kps for every million ◊parsecs of distance. This means that the universe, which began at one point according to the ◊Big Bang theory, is between 10 trillion and 20 trillion years old (probably closer to 20). UK astronomers argued 1993 for a lower value for the constant of between 24 and 54, indicating an older universe.

Hubble Space Telescope telescope placed into orbit around the Earth, at an altitude of 380 mi/610 km, by the space shuttle *Discovery* in April 1990. The telescope's position in space means that light from distant galaxies is not obscured by the atmosphere, and it therefore performs at least ten times better than any ground-based instrument.

Hubei or *Hupei* province of central China, through which flow the river Chang Jiang and its tributary the Han Shui *area* 72,375 sq mi/187,500 sq km *capital* Wuhan *features* high land in the W, the river Chang breaking through from Sichuan in the E; elsewhere low-lying, fertile land; many lakes *industries* beans, cereals, cotton, rice, vegetables, copper, gypsum, iron ore, phosphorous, salt *population* (1990) 53,969,000.

hubris in Greek thought, an act of transgression or overweening pride. In ancient Greek tragedy, hubris was believed to offend the gods, and to lead to retribution.

Hudson river of the NE US; length 300 mi/485 km. It rises in the Adirondack Mountains and flows S, emptying into a bay of the Atlantic Ocean at New York City.

It is navigable by small oceangoing vessels as far upstream as Albany and Troy, about 150 mi/240 km from its mouth. On its west shore are the Catskill Mountains, and near its mouth, the Palisades, a vertical rock face. The New York Barge Canal system links the Hudson to Lake Champlain, Lake Erie, and the St Lawrence River. The Hudson forms the boundary between New Jersey and New York, and the states are linked by bridges and tunnels. The Hudson River valley is known for scenery that inspired a school of landscape painters in the 19th century. First sighted at its mouth by the Italian navigator Giovanni da Verrazano in 1524, the river was explored upstream as far as modern Albany in 1609 by English navigator Henry Hudson, for whom it is named.

Hudson Henry *c.*1565–*c.*1611. English explorer. Under the auspices of the Muscovy Company 1607–08, he made two unsuccessful attempts to find the Northeast Passage to China. In Sept 1609, commissioned by the Dutch East India Company, he reached New York Bay and sailed 150 mi/240 km up the river that now bears his name, establishing Dutch claims to the area. In 1610, he sailed from London in the *Discovery* and entered what is now the Hudson Strait. After an icebound winter, he was turned adrift by a mutinous crew in what is now Hudson Bay.

Hudson had heard reports of two possible channels to the Pacific Ocean across North America. One of these had been described by English soldier and colonist John Smith. Since Hudson's search for the Northeast Passage proved unsuccessful, he chose to pursue Smith's suggestion.

Hudson Bay inland sea of NE Canada, linked with the Atlantic Ocean by *Hudson Strait* and with the Arctic Ocean by Foxe Channel; area 476,000 sq mi/ 1,233,000 sq km. It is named for Henry Hudson, who reached it 1610.

Hudson River School group of US landscape painters of the early 19th century. They were inspired by the dramatic scenery of the Hudson River Valley and the Catskill Mountains in New York State, and also by the Romantic landscapes of Turner and John Martin. The first artist to depict the region was Thomas Cole. The group also included Asher B Durand, Martin Joseph Heade, and Frederic Edwin Church.

Their works, often in a romantic vein, elevated landscape painting in importance in the US.

Hudson's Bay Company chartered company founded by Prince ◊Rupert 1670 to trade in furs with North American Indians. In 1783 the rival North West Company was formed, but in 1851 this became amalgamated with the Hudson's Bay Company. It is still Canada's biggest fur company, but today also sells general merchandise through department stores and has oil and natural gas interests.

Hughes Charles Evans 1862–1948. US jurist and public official, appointed to the US Supreme Court by President Taft 1910. He resigned 1916 to accept the Republican nomination for president, losing narrowly to the incumbent Wilson. He served as secretary of state 1921–25 under President Harding. As Supreme Court chief justice 1930–41, he presided over the constitutional tests of President Franklin D Roosevelt's New Deal legislation.

Hughes Howard R 1905–1976. US aviator, aircraft designer, film producer, and entrepreneur. He founded the Hughes Aircraft Company and broke the air speed record in a craft of his own design in 1935, reaching a speed of 352 mph/566 kph. His financial empire was based on his inheritance of the Hughes Tool Co., founded by his father. In the 1920s he formed the Hughes film studio and produced *Hell's Angels* 1930, *Scarface* 1932, and *The Outlaw* 1944 (which he also directed). A billionaire for most of his later years, he invested in Las Vegas real estate, airlines, and motion picture studios but lived like a hermit, protected by his staff.

Hughes (James) Langston 1902–1967. US poet and novelist. Known as "the poet laureate of Harlem", he became one of the foremost African American literary figures, writing such collections of poems as *The Weary Blues* 1926. In addition to his poetry he wrote a series of novels, short stories, and essays. His auto-biography *The Big Sea* appeared 1940.

Born in Joplin, Missouri, and raised in Cleveland, Ohio, Hughes had a poem published while still in high school. After briefly attending Columbia University, he traveled widely and continued to write. He published *The Weary Blues* shortly after graduating from Lincoln University.

Hughes Ted 1930– . English poet, poet laureate from 1984. His work includes *The Hawk in the Rain* 1957, *Lupercal* 1960, *Wodwo* 1967, and *River* 1983, and is characterized by its harsh portrayal of the crueler aspects of nature. In 1956 he married the poet Sylvia Plath.

Hugo Victor (Marie) 1802–1885. French poet, novelist, and dramatist. The *Odes et poésies diverses* appeared 1822, and his verse play *Hernani* 1830 established him as the leader of French Romanticism. More volumes of verse followed between his series of dramatic novels, which included *Notre-Dame de Paris* 1831, later filmed as *The Hunchback of Notre Dame* 1924, 1939, and *Les Misérables* 1862, adapted as a musical 1980.

Huguenot French Protestant in the 16th century; the term referred mainly to Calvinists. Severely perse-cuted under Francis I and Henry II, the Huguenots survived both an attempt to exterminate them (the **Massacre of ◊St Bartholomew** Aug 24, 1572) and the religious wars of the next 30 years. In 1598 Henry IV (himself formerly a Huguenot) granted them tolera-tion under the **Edict of Nantes**. Louis XIV revoked the edict 1685, attempting their forcible conversion, and 400,000 emigrated.

Provoked by Louis XIV they left, taking their indus-trial skills with them; many settled in North America, where they founded such towns as New Rochelle and New Paltz, New York. Only in 1802 was the Huguenot church again legalized in France.

Huhehot former name of ◊*Hohhot*, a city in Inner Mongolia.

Hui member of one of the largest minority ethnic groups in China, numbering about 25 million. Members of the Hui live all over China, but are con-centrated in the northern central region. They have been Muslims since the 10th century, for which they have suffered persecution both before and since the Communist revolution.

Hull Cordell 1871–1955. US Democratic politician. As Franklin D Roosevelt's secretary of state 1933–44, he opposed German and Japanese aggression. He sup-ported the Good Neighbor policy of nonintervention in Latin America. In his last months of office he paved the way for a system of collective security, for which he was called "father" of the United Nations. He was awarded the Nobel Peace Prize 1945.

Hull officially *Kingston upon Hull* city and port on the north bank of the Humber estuary, England, where the river Hull flows into it, England; population (1991) 254,100. It is linked with the south bank of the estuary by the Humber Bridge. Industries include fish processing, vegetable oils, flour milling, electrical goods, textiles, paint, pharmaceuticals, chemicals, car-avans, aircraft, and lumber milling.

Human Genome Project research scheme, begun 1988, to map the complete nucleotide sequence of human ◊DNA. There are approximately 80,000 differ-ent ◊genes in the human genome, and one gene may contain more than 2 million nucleotides. The knowl-edge gained is expected to help prevent or treat many crippling and lethal diseases, but there are potential ethical problems associated with knowledge of an individual's genetic makeup, and fears that it will lead to genetic engineering.

humanism belief in the high potential of human nature rather than in religious or transcendental val-ues. Humanism culminated as a cultural and literary force in 16th-century Renaissance Europe in line with the period's enthusiasm for classical literature and art, growing individualism, and the ideal of the all-round male who should be statesman and poet, scholar and warrior. ◊Erasmus is a great exemplar of Renaissance humanism.

Human Rights, Universal Declaration of charter of civil and political rights drawn up by the United Nations (UN) 1948. They include the right to life, lib-erty, education, and equality before the law; to free-dom of movement, religion, association, and information; and to a nationality.

human species, origins of evolution of humans from ancestral ◊primates. The African apes (gorilla and chimpanzee) are shown by anatomical and molecular comparisons to be the closest living relatives of humans. Humans are distinguished from apes by the size of their brain and jaw, their bipedalism, and their elaborate culture. Molecular studies put the date of the split between the human and African ape lines at 5–10 million years ago. There are only fragmentary remains of ape and *hominid* (of the human group) fossils from this period. Bones of the earliest known human ancestor, a hominid named *Australopithecus ramidus* 1994, were found in Ethiopia and dated as 4.4 million years old.

Australopithecus afarensis, hominids found in Ethiopia and Tanzania, date from 3.5 to 4 million years ago. These creatures walked upright and they were either direct ancestors or an offshoot of the line that led to modern humans.

Humber estuary in NE England formed by the Ouse and Trent rivers, which meet E of Goole and flow 38 mi/ 60 km to enter the North Sea below Spurn Head. The main ports are Hull on the north side, and Grimsby on the south side. The **Humber Bridge** (1981) is the longest single-span suspension bridge in the world.

Humberside county of NE England, created 1974 out of N Lincolnshire and parts of the East and West Ridings of Yorkshire *area* 1,355 sq mi/3,510 sq km *towns and cities* Beverley (administrative headquar-ters), Grimsby, Scunthorpe, Goole, Cleethorpes *fea-tures* Humber Bridge; fertile Holderness peninsula; Isle of Axholme, bounded by rivers Trent, Don, Idle, and Torne, where medieval open-field strip farming is still practiced *industries* petrochemicals, refined oil, processed fish, cereals, root crops, cattle *population* (1991) 858,000 *famous people* Andrew Marvell, John Wesley, Amy Johnson.

Humbert anglicized form of Umberto, two kings of Italy.

Hume David 1711–1776. Scottish philosopher. *A Treatise of Human Nature* 1739–40 is a central text of British empiricism. Hume denies the possibility of going beyond the subjective experiences of "ideas" and "impressions". The effect of this position is to invalidate metaphysics.

humidity the quantity of water vapor in a given volume of the atmosphere (absolute humidity), or the ratio of the amount of water vapor in the atmosphere to the saturation value at the same temperature (relative humidity). At ◊dew point the relative humidity is 100% and the air is said to be saturated. Condensation (the conversion of vapor to liquid) may then occur. Relative humidity is measured by various types of hygrometer.

hummingbird any of various birds of the family Trochilidae, found in the Americas. The name is derived from the sound produced by the rapid vibration of their wings. Hummingbirds are brilliantly colored, and have long, needlelike bills and tongues to obtain nectar from flowers and capture insects. They are the only birds able to fly backward. The Cuban bee hummingbird *Mellisuga helenae*, the world's smallest bird, is 2 in/5.5 cm long, and weighs less than 1 oz/2.5 g.

Humphrey Hubert (Horatio) 1911–1978. US political leader, vice president 1965–69. He was elected to the US Senate 1948, serving for three terms, distinguishing himself an eloquent and effective promoter of key legislation.

He was an unsuccessful presidential candidate 1960. Serving as vice president under Lyndon B Johnson, he made another unsuccessful run for the presidency 1968. He was reelected to the Senate in 1970 and 1976.

Hun member of any of a number of nomad Mongol peoples who were first recorded historically in the 2nd century BC , raiding across the Great Wall into China. They entered Europe about AD 372, settled in the area that is now Hungary, and imposed their supremacy on the Ostrogoths and other Germanic peoples. Under the leadership of Attila they attacked the Byzantine Empire, invaded Gaul, and threatened Rome. After Attila's death in 453 their power was broken by a revolt of their subject peoples. The *White Huns*, or Ephthalites, a kindred people, raided Persia and N India in the 5th and 6th centuries.

Hunan province of S central China *area* 81,253 sq mi / 210,500 sq km *capital* Changsha *features* Dongting Lake; farmhouse in Shaoshan village where Mao Zedong was born *industries* rice, tea, tobacco, cotton; nonferrous minerals *population* (1990) 60,660,000.

hundredweight unit (symbol cwt) of mass, equal to 100 lb (45.36 kg) in the US. In the UK and Canada, it equals 112 lb (50.8 kg), and is sometimes called the long hundredweight.

Hundred Years' War series of conflicts between England and France 1337–1453. Its origins lay with the English kings' possession of Gascony (SW France), which the French kings claimed as their fief, and with trade rivalries over ◊Flanders. The two kingdoms had a long history of strife before 1337, and the Hundred Years' War has sometimes been interpreted as merely an intensification of these struggles. It was caused by fears of French intervention in Scotland, which the English were trying to subdue, and by the claim of England's ◊Edward III (through his mother Isabel, daughter of Charles IV) to the crown of France.

Hungary Republic of (*Magyar Köztársaság*) *area* 35,910 sq mi/93,032 sq km *capital* Budapest *towns and cities* Miskolc, Debrecen, Szeged, Pécs *physical* Great Hungarian Plain covers E half of country; Bakony Forest, Lake Balaton, and Transdanubian Highlands in the W; rivers Danube, Tisza, and Raba *environment* an estimated 35%–40% of the population live in areas with officially "inadmissible" air and water pollution. In Budapest lead levels have reached 30 times the

maximum international standards *features* more than 500 thermal springs; Hortobágy National Park; Tokay wine area *head of state* Arpád Göncz from 1990 *head of government* Gyula Horn from 1994 *political system* emergent democratic republic *political parties* over 50, including Hungarian Socialist Party (HSP), left of center; Alliance of Free Democrats (AFD), centrist, radical free-market; Hungarian Democratic Forum (MDF), right of center; Independent Smallholders Party (ISP), centrist, agrarian; Christian Democratic People's Party (KDNP), right of center *exports* machinery, vehicles, iron and steel, chemicals, fruit and vegetables *currency* forint *population* (1993) 10,310,000 (Magyar 92%, Romany 3%, German 2.5%; Hungarian minority in Romania has caused some friction between the two countries); growth rate 0.2% p.a. *life expectancy* men 68, women 75 *language* Hungarian (or Magyar), one of the few languages of Europe with non-Indo-European origins; it is grouped with Finnish, Estonian, and others in the Finno-Ugric family *religion* Roman Catholic 67%, other Christian denominations 25% *literacy* 99% *GNP* $2,690 per head (1991) *chronology 1918* Independence achieved from Austro-Hungarian empire. *1919* A communist state formed for 133 days. *1920–44* Regency formed under Admiral Horthy, who joined Hitler's attack on the USSR. *1945* Liberated by USSR. *1946* Republic proclaimed; Stalinist regime imposed. *1949* Soviet-style constitution adopted. *1956* Hungarian national uprising; workers' demonstrations in Budapest; democratization reforms by Imre Nagy overturned by Soviet tanks; János Kádár installed as party leader. *1968* Economic decentralization reforms. *1983* Competition introduced into elections. *1987* VAT and income tax introduced. *1988* Kádár replaced by Károly Grosz. First free labor union recognized; rival political parties legalized. *1989* May: border with Austria opened. July: new four-person collective leadership of Hungarian Socialist Workers' Party (HSWP). Oct: new "transitional constitution" adopted, founded on multiparty democracy and new presidentialist executive. HSWP changed name to Hungarian Socialist Party, with Nyers as new leader. Kádár "retired". *1990* HSP reputation damaged by "Danubegate" bugging scandal. March–April: elections won by right-of-center coalition, headed by Hungarian Democratic Forum (MDF). May: József Antall, leader of the MDF, appointed premier. Aug:

Arpád Göncz elected president. *1991* Jan: devaluation of currency. June: legislation approved to compensate owners of land and property expropriated under communist government. Last Soviet troops departed. Dec: European Community (EC) association pact signed. *1993* June: formal invitation to apply for EC membership. Dec: József Antall died; succeeded by Peter Boross. *1994* Joined NATO "partnership for peace" program. HSP won clear majority in assembly elections; its leader, Gyula Horn, became prime minister. Coalition formed with centrist parties.

Hun Sen 1950– . Cambodian political leader, prime minister 1985–93, deputy prime minister from 1993. Originally a member of the Khmer Rouge army, he defected in 1977 to join Vietnam-based anti-Khmer Cambodian forces. His leadership was characterized by the promotion of economic liberalization and a thawing in relations with exiled non-Khmer opposition forces as a prelude to a compromise political settlement. After defeat of his Cambodian People's Party (CCP) in the 1993 elections, Hun Sen agreed to participate in a power-sharing arrangement as second premier.

Huntington city in W West Virginia, across the Ohio River from Ohio, NW of Charleston; seat of Cabell County; population (1990) 54,800. It is an important transportation center for coal mined to the S. Other industries include chemicals; metal, wood, and glass products; tobacco; and fruit processing.

Huntsville city in NE Alabama; population (1990) 159,800. Manufactured products include textiles, electrical and electronic goods, metal products, chemicals, machinery, and cosmetics. Just outside the city is the Redstone Arsenal, which includes an army missile center and the George C Marshall Space Flight Center. A branch of the University of Alabama and a space and rocket museum are here. Huntsville was settled 1805. During the Civil War, it was occupied and burned by Union troops. The University of Alabama is located at Tuscaloosa.

Hupei alternative transcription of ◊Hebei, a province of China.

Huron second largest of the Great Lakes of North America, on the US–Canadian border; area 23,160 sq mi/60,000 sq km. It includes Georgian Bay, Saginaw Bay, and Manitoulin Island.

hurricane revolving storm in tropical regions, called *typhoon* in the N Pacific. It originates at latitudes between 5° and 20° N or S of the equator, when the surface temperature of the ocean is above 27°C/80°F. A central calm area, called the eye, is surrounded by inwardly spiraling winds (counterclockwise in the

northern hemisphere) of up to 200 mph/320 kph. A hurricane is accompanied by lightning and torrential rain, and can cause extensive damage. In meteorology, a hurricane is a wind of force 12 or more on the ◊Beaufort scale. The most intense hurricane recorded in the Caribbean/Atlantic sector was Hurricane Gilbert in 1988, with sustained winds of 175 mph/280 kph and gusts of over 200 mph/320 kph.

Hussein Saddam 1937– . Iraqi politician, in power from 1968, president from 1979. He presided over the Iran-Iraq war 1980–88, and harshly repressed Kurdish rebels in N Iraq. He annexed Kuwait 1990 but was driven out by a US-dominated coalition army Feb 1991. Defeat in the ◊Gulf War led to unrest, and both the Kurds in the N and Shiites in the S rebelled. Savage repression of both revolts led to charges of genocide and the United Nations (UN) established "safe havens" in the N and "no-fly zones" in the S. Infringement of the latter led to US air strikes Jan 1993. Saddam has continued to defy UN resolutions.

Hussein ibn Talal 1935– . King of Jordan from 1952. By 1967 he had lost all his kingdom west of the river Jordan in the ◊Arab-Israeli Wars, and in 1970 suppressed the ◊Palestine Liberation Organization acting as a guerrilla force against his rule on the remaining East Bank territories. Subsequently, he became a moderating force in Middle Eastern politics, and in 1994 signed a peace agreement with Israel, ending a 46-year-old "state of war" between the two countries.

Husserl Edmund (Gustav Albrecht) 1859–1938. German philosopher, regarded as the founder of phenomenology, a philosophy concentrating on what is consciously experienced. His main works are *Logical Investigations* 1900, *Phenomenological Philosophy* 1913, and *The Crisis of the European Sciences* 1936.

Huston John 1906–1987. US film director, screenwriter, and actor. An impulsive and individualistic filmmaker, he often dealt with the themes of greed, treachery in human relationships, and the loner. His works as a director include *The Maltese Falcon* 1941 (his debut), *The Treasure of the Sierra Madre* 1948 (in which his father Walter Huston starred and for which both won Academy Awards), *The African Queen* 1951, and his last, *The Dead* 1987.

Hutchinson Anne Marbury 1591–1643. American colonial religious leader. In 1634, she and her family followed John Cotton from England to Massachusetts Bay Colony. Preaching a unique theology which emphasized the role of faith, she gained a wide following. The colony's leaders, including Cotton, felt threatened by Hutchinson and in 1637 she was banished and excommunicated. Settling in Long Island, she and her family were killed by Indians.

Born in England, Hutchinson was noted for her intellect and forceful personality.

Hutton James 1726–1797. Scottish geologist, known as the "founder of geology", who formulated the concept of uniformitarianism. In 1785 he developed a theory of the igneous origin of many rocks.

Hutu member of the majority ethnic group of both Burundi and Rwanda, numbering around 9,500,000. The Hutu tend to live as peasant farmers. Traditionally they have been dominated by the Tutsi minority; there is a long history of violent conflict between the two groups. The Hutu language belongs to the Bantu branch of the Niger-Congo family.

Huxley Aldous (Leonard) 1894–1963. English writer of novels, essays, and verse. From the disillusionment

---

hurricane: worst of the 20th century

date	location	deaths
1900 Aug–Sept	Galveston, Texas	6,000
1926 Oct 20	Cuba	600
1928 Sept 6–20	Southern Florida	1,836
1930 Sept 3	Dominican Republic	2,000
1938 Sept 21	Long Island, New York, New England	600
1942 Oct 15–16	Bengal, India	40,000
1963 Oct 4–8	(Flora) Caribbean	6,000
1974 Sept 19–20	(Fifi) Honduras	2,000
1979 Aug 30–Sept 7	(David) Caribbean, E US	1,100
1989 Sept 16–22	(Hugo) Caribbean, SE US	504

and satirical eloquence of *Crome Yellow* 1921, *Antic Hay* 1923, and *Point Counter Point* 1928, Huxley developed toward the Utopianism exemplified by *Island* 1962. The science fiction novel *Brave New World* 1932 shows human beings mass-produced in laboratories and rendered incapable of freedom by indoctrination and drugs. He was the grandson of Thomas Henry Huxley and brother of Julian Huxley.

Huxley Thomas Henry 1825–1895. English scientist and humanist. Following the publication of Charles Darwin's *On the Origin of Species* 1859, he became known as "Darwin's bulldog", and for many years was a prominent champion of evolution. He is considered the founder of scientific ◊humanism.

Hu Yaobang 1915–1989. Chinese politician, Communist Party (CCP) chair 1981–87. A protégé of the communist leader Deng Xiaoping, Hu presided over a radical overhaul of the party structure and personnel 1982–86. His death ignited the prodemocracy movement, which was eventually crushed in ◊Tiananmen Square in June 1989.

Huygens Christiaan 1629–1695. Dutch mathematical physicist and astronomer who proposed the wave theory of light. He developed the pendulum clock, discovered polarization, and observed Saturn's rings.

Hwang Ho alternative transcription of ◊Huang He, a river in China.

hyacinth any bulb-producing plant of the genus *Hyacinthus* of the lily family Liliaceae, native to the E Mediterranean and Africa. The cultivated hyacinth *H. orientalis* has large, scented, cylindrical heads of pink, white, or blue flowers. The ◊water hyacinth, genus *Eichhornia*, is unrelated, a floating plant from South America.

hybrid offspring from a cross between individuals of two different species, or two inbred lines within a species. In most cases, hybrids between species are infertile and unable to reproduce sexually. In plants, however, doubling of the chromosomes can restore the fertility of such hybrids.

Hybrids between different genera are extremely rare; an example is the *Cupressocyparis leylandii* cypress which, like some hybrids, shows exceptional vigor, or heterosis. In the wild, a "hybrid zone" may occur where the ranges of two related species meet.

Hyderabad capital city of the S central Indian state of Andhra Pradesh, on the river Musi; population (1981) 2,528,000. Products include carpets, silks, and metal inlay work. It was formerly the capital of the state of Hyderabad. Buildings include the Jama Masjid mosque and Golconda fort.

Hydra in Greek mythology, a huge monster with nine heads. If one were cut off, two would grow in its place. One of the 12 labors of ◊Heracles was to kill it.

hydra in zoology, any member of the family Hydridae, or freshwater polyps, of the phylum Cnidaria (coelenterates). The body is a double-layered tube (with six to ten hollow tentacles around the mouth), 0.5 in/1.25 cm long when extended, but capable of contracting to a small knob. Usually fixed to waterweed, hydras feed on minute animals that are caught and paralyzed by stinging cells on the tentacles.

hydrangea any flowering shrub of the genus *Hydrangea* of the saxifrage family Hydrangeaceae, native to Japan. Cultivated varieties of *H. macrophylla* normally produce round heads of pink flowers, but these may be blue if certain chemicals, such as alum or iron, are

in the soil. The name is from the Greek for "water vessel", after the cuplike seed capsules.

hydraulics field of study concerned with utilizing the properties of water and other liquids, in particular the way they flow and transmit pressure, and with the application of these properties in engineering. It applies the principles of hydrostatics and hydrodynamics. The oldest type of hydraulic machine is the *hydraulic press*, invented by Joseph Bramah in England 1795. The hydraulic principle of pressurized liquid increasing mechanical efficiency is commonly used on vehicle braking systems, the forging press, and the hydraulic systems of aircraft and excavators.

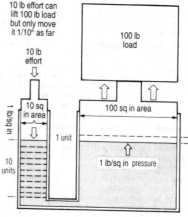

10 lb effort can lift 100 lb load but only move it 1/10" as far

10 lb effort

100 lb load

10 sq in area

100 sq in area

1 unit

1 lb/sq in

10 units

1 lb/sq in pressure

hydraulics

hydrocarbon any of a class of chemical compounds containing only hydrogen and carbon (for example, the alkanes and alkenes). Hydrocarbons are obtained industrially principally from petroleum and coal tar.

hydrochloric acid highly corrosive aqueous solution of hydrogen chloride (HCl, a colorless, corrosive gas). It has many industrial uses, including recovery of zinc from galvanized scrap iron and the production of chlorides and chlorine. It is also produced in the stomachs of animals for the purposes of digestion.

hydroelectric power (HEP) electricity generated by moving water. In a typical HEP scheme, water stored in a reservoir, often created by damming a river, is piped into water ◊turbines, coupled to electricity generators. In pumped storage plants, water flowing through the turbines is recycled. A tidal power station exploits the rise and fall of the tides. About one-fifth of the world's electricity comes from HEP.

hydrofoil wing that develops lift in the water in much the same way that an airplane wing develops lift in the air. A hydrofoil boat is one whose hull rises out of the water due to the lift, and the boat skims along on the hydrofoils. The first hydrofoil was fitted to a boat 1906. The first commercial hydrofoil went into operation 1956. One of the most advanced hydrofoil boats is the Boeing ◊jetfoil.

hydrogen colorless, odorless, gaseous, nonmetallic element, symbol H, atomic number 1, atomic weight 1.00797. It is the lightest of all the elements and occurs on Earth chiefly in combination with oxygen as water. Hydrogen is the most abundant element in the universe, where it accounts for 93% of the total number of atoms and 76% of the total mass. It is a component of most stars, including the Sun, whose heat and light are produced through the nuclear-fusion process that converts hydrogen into helium.

hydrogen bomb bomb that works on the principle of nuclear ◊fusion. Large-scale explosion results from the thermonuclear release of energy when hydrogen nuclei are fused to form helium nuclei. The first hydrogen bomb was exploded at Eniwetok Atoll in the Pacific Ocean by the US 1952.

The constant release of energy through nuclear fusion is the continuing reaction in the Sun and other stars; it can be duplicated by the triggering of tritium (hydrogen isotope of atomic weight 3.0170) by an ordinary atomic bomb.

hydrophyte plant adapted to live in water, or in water-logged soil.

hydroplane on a submarine, a moveable horizontal fin angled downward or upward when the vessel is descending or ascending. It is also a highly maneuverable motorboat with its bottom rising in steps to the stern, or a hydrofoil boat that skims over the surface of the water when driven at high speed.

hydroponics cultivation of plants without soil, using specially prepared solutions of mineral salts. Beginning in the 1930s, large crops were grown by hydroponic methods, at first in California but since then in many other parts of the world.

hyena any of three species of carnivorous mammals in the family Hyaenidae, living in Africa and Asia. Hyenas have extremely powerful jaws. They are scavengers, although they will also attack and kill live prey.

Hymen in Greek mythology, a god of the marriage ceremony. In painting, he is represented as a youth carrying a bridal torch.

Hypercard computer application developed for the Apple ◊Macintosh, in which data are stored as if on cards in a card-index system. A group of cards forms a stack. Additional features include the ability to link cards in different ways. Hypercard is very similar to ◊hypertext, although it does not conform to the rigorous definition of hypertext.

hypercharge in physics, a property of certain ◊elementary particles, analogous to electric charge, that accounts for the absence of some expected behavior (such as decay) in terms of the short-range strong nuclear force, which holds atomic nuclei together.

It is a number equal to twice the average charge of the particles concerned, divided by the elementary charge.

◊Protons and ◊neutrons, for example, have a hypercharge of +1, whereas a pion has a hypercharge of 0.

hypertension abnormally high ◊blood pressure due to a variety of causes, leading to excessive contraction of the smooth muscle cells of the walls of the arteries. It increases the risk of kidney disease, stroke, and heart attack.

hypertext system for viewing information (both text and pictures) on a computer screen in such a way that related items of information can easily be reached. For example, the program might display a map of a country; if the user clicks (with a ◊mouse) on a particular city, the program will display some information about that city.

hypnosis artificially induced state of relaxation in which suggestibility is heightened. The subject may carry out orders after being awakened, and may be made insensitive to pain. Hypnosis is sometimes used to treat addictions to tobacco or overeating, or to assist amnesia victims.

hypoglycemia condition of abnormally low level of sugar (glucose) in the blood, which starves the brain. It causes weakness, the shakes, and perspiration, sometimes fainting. Untreated victims have suffered paranoia and extreme anxiety. Treatment is by special diet.

hypotenuse the longest side of a right triangle, opposite the right angle. It is of particular application in Pythagoras's theorem (the square of the hypotenuse equals the sum of the squares of the other two sides), and in trigonometry where the ratios ◊sine and ◊cosine are defined as the ratios opposite/hypotenuse and adjacent/hypotenuse respectively.

hypothermia condition in which the deep (core) temperature of the body falls. If it is not discovered, coma and death ensue. Most at risk are the aged and babies (particularly if premature).

hyrax small mammal, forming the order Hyracoidea, that lives among rocks, in deserts, and in forests in Africa, Arabia, and Syria. It is about the size of a rabbit, with a plump body, short legs, short ears, brownish fur, and long, curved front teeth.

hyssop aromatic herb *Hyssopus officinalis* of the mint family Labiatae, found in Asia, S Europe, and around the Mediterranean. It has blue flowers, oblong leaves, and stems that are woody near the ground but herbaceous above.

hysterectomy surgical removal of all or part of the uterus (womb). The operation is performed to treat fibroids (benign tumors growing in the uterus) or cancer; also to relieve heavy menstrual bleeding. A woman who has had a hysterectomy will no longer menstruate and cannot bear children.

Ibadan city in SW Nigeria and capital of Oyo state; population (1981) 2,100,000. Industries include chemicals, electronics, plastics, and vehicles.

Iban recent replacement term for ◊Dyak.

Iberville Pierre Le Moyne, Sieur d' 1661–1706. French colonial administrator and explorer in America. With his brother, the Sieur de ◊Bienville, he led an expedition from France and established a colony at the mouth of the Mississippi River in America. In 1699–1700 they established settlements at the later sites of Biloxi, Mississippi, and New Orleans.

ibex any of various wild goats found in mountainous areas of Europe, NE Africa, and Central Asia. They grow to 3.5 ft/100 cm, and have brown or gray coats and heavy horns. They are herbivorous and live in small groups.

ibis any of various wading birds, about 2 ft/60 cm tall, in the same family, Threskiornidae, as spoonbills. Ibises have long legs and necks, and long, curved beaks. Various species occur in the warmer regions of the world.

The glossy ibis *Plegadis falcinellus* occurs in the SE US and in all continents except South America. The sacred ibis *Threskiornis aethiopica* of ancient Egypt is still found in the Nile basin. The Japanese ibis is in danger of extinction because of loss of its habitat; fewer than 25 birds remain.

Ibiza one of the ◊Balearic Islands, a popular tourist resort; area 230 sq mi/596 sq km; population (1986) 45,000. The capital and port, also called Ibiza, has a cathedral.

IBM (abbreviation for *International Business Machines*) multinational company, the largest manufacturer of computers in the world. The company is a descendant of the Tabulating Machine Company, formed 1896 by US inventor Herman ◊Hollerith to exploit his punched-card machines. It adopted its present name 1924. By 1991 it had an annual turnover of $64.8 billion and employed about 345,000 people. In 1992, however, it made a loss of $4.59 billion.

Ibn Saud 1880–1953. First king of Saudi Arabia from 1932. His father was the son of the sultan of Nejd, at whose capital, Riyadh, Ibn Saud was born. In 1891 a rival group seized Riyadh, and Ibn Saud went into exile with his father, who resigned his claim to the throne in his son's favor. In 1902 Ibn Saud recaptured Riyadh and recovered the kingdom, and by 1921 he had brought all central Arabia under his rule. In 1924 he invaded the Hejaz, of which he was proclaimed king in 1926.

Ibo or *Igbo* member of the W African Ibo culture group occupying SE Nigeria and numbering about 18,000,000. Primarily cultivators, they inhabit the richly forested tableland, bounded by the river Niger to the west and the river Cross to the east. They are divided into five main groups, and their languages belong to the Kwa branch of the Niger-Congo family.

Ibsen Henrik (Johan) 1828–1906. Norwegian dramatist and poet. His realistic and often controversial plays revolutionized European theater. Driven into exile 1864–91 by opposition to the satirical *Love's Comedy* 1862, he wrote the verse dramas *Brand* 1866 and *Peer Gynt* 1867, followed by realistic plays dealing with social issues, including *Pillars of Society* 1877, *A Doll's House* 1879, *Ghosts* 1881, *An Enemy of the People* 1882, and *Hedda Gabler* 1891. By the time he returned to Norway, he was recognized as the country's greatest living writer.

IC abbreviation for ◊*integrated circuit*.

Icarus in Greek mythology, the son of ◊Daedalus, who with his father escaped from the labyrinth in Crete by making wings of feathers fastened with wax. Icarus plunged to his death when he flew too near the Sun and the wax melted.

ice age any period of glaciation occurring in the Earth's history, but particularly that in the Pleistocene epoch, immediately preceding historic times. On the North American continent, ◊glaciers reached as far south as the Great Lakes, and an ice sheet spread over N Europe, leaving its remains as far south as Switzerland.

There were several glacial advances separated by interglacial stages during which the ice melted and temperatures were higher than today.

ice hockey a game played on ice between two teams of six, developed in Canada from field hockey or bandy. Players, who wear skates and protective clothing, use a curved stick to advance the puck (a rubber disk) and shoot it at the opponents' goal, a netted cage, guarded by the goalie. The other positions are the left and right defensemen and the left wing, center, and right wing. The latter three are offensive players. The team with the most goals scored at the end of the three 20-minute periods wins; an overtime period may be played if a game ends in a tie.

Iceland Republic of (*Lýdveldid Ísland*) *area* 39,758 sq mi/103,000 sq km *capital* Reykjavík *towns and cities* Akureyri, Akranes *physical* warmed by the Gulf Stream; glaciers and lava fields cover 75% of the country; active volcanoes (Hekla was once thought the gateway to Hell), geysers, hot springs, and new islands created offshore (Surtsey in 1963); subterranean hot water heats 85% of Iceland's homes *features* Thingvellir, where the oldest parliament in the world first met AD 930; shallow lake Mývatn (15 sq mi/38 sq km) in N *head of state* Vigdís Finnbogadóttir from 1980 *head of government* Davíd Oddsson from 1991 *political system* democratic republic *political parties* Independence Party (IP), right of center; Progressive Party (PP), radical socialist; People's Alliance (PA), socialist; Social Democratic Party (SDP), moderate, left of center; Citizens' Party, centrist; Women's Alliance, women-and family-oriented *exports* cod and other fish products, aluminum, diatomite *currency* krona *population* (1993 est) 270,000; growth rate 0.8% p.a.

life expectancy men 75, women 81 *language* Icelandic, the most archaic Scandinavian language *religion* Evangelical Lutheran 95% *literacy* 99% *GNP* $24,565 per head (1992) *chronology 1944* Independence achieved from Denmark. *1949* Joined NATO and Council of Europe. *1953* Joined Nordic Council. *1976* "Cod War" with UK. *1979* Iceland announced 200-mi/320-km exclusive fishing zone. *1983* Steingrímur Hermannsson appointed to lead a coalition government. *1985* Iceland declared itself a nuclear-free zone. *1987* New coalition government formed by Thorsteinn Pálsson after general election. *1988* Vigdís Finnbogadóttir re-elected president for a third term; Hermannsson led new coalition. *1991* Davíd Oddsson led new IP–SDP center-right coalition, becoming prime minister in the general election. *1992* Iceland defied world ban to resume whaling industry.

Iceni ancient people of E England, who revolted against occupying Romans under ◊Boudicca.

ice-skating see ◊skating.

ichneumon fly any parasitic wasp of the family Ichneumonidae. There are several thousand species in Europe, North America, and other regions. They have slender bodies, and females have unusually long, curved ovipositors (egg-laying instruments) that can pierce several inches of wood. The eggs are laid in the eggs, larvae, or pupae of other insects, usually butterflies or moths.

icon in the Greek or Eastern Orthodox church, a representation of Jesus, Mary, an angel, or a saint, in painting, low relief, or mosaic. The painted icons were traditionally done on wood. After the 17th century and mainly in Russia, a *riza*, or gold and silver covering that leaves only the face and hands visible (and may be adorned with jewels presented by the faithful in thanksgiving), was often added as protection.

icon in computing, a small picture on the computer screen, or ◊VDT, representing an object or function that the user may manipulate or otherwise use. It is a feature of graphical user interface (GUI) systems. Icons make computers easier to use by allowing the user to point to and click with a ◊mouse on pictures, rather than type commands.

iconography in art history, significance attached to symbols that can help to identify subject matter (for example, a saint holding keys usually represents St Peter) and place a work of art in its historical context. The pioneer of this approach was the German art historian Erwin Panofsky.

id in Freudian psychology, the instinctual element of the human mind, concerned with pleasure, which demands immediate satisfaction.

It is regarded as the ◊unconscious element of the human psyche, and is said to be in conflict with the ◊ego and the ◊superego.

Idaho state of northwestern US; nickname Gem State *area* 83,569 sq mi/216,500 sq km *capital* Boise *towns and cities* Pocatello, Idaho Falls *features* Rocky Mountains; Snake River, which runs through Hell's Canyon (7,647 ft/2,330 m), the deepest in North America, and has the National Reactor Testing Station on the plains of its upper reaches; Sun Valley ski and summer resort; Craters of the Moon National Monument; Nez Percé National Historic Park *industries* potatoes, wheat, livestock, timber, silver, lead, zinc, antimony *population* (1990) 1,006,700 *history* part of the Louisiana Purchase 1803; explored by Lewis and Clark 1805–06; first permanently settled by Mormons 1860, the same year gold was discovered. Settlement in the 1870s led to a series of battles between US forces and Indian tribes. Idaho became a state in 1890. The timber industry began 1906, and by World War I agriculture was a leading enterprise.

igneous rock rock formed from cooling magma or lava, and solidifying from a molten state. Igneous rocks are classified according to their crystal size, texture, chemical composition, or method of formation. They are largely composed of silica (SiO_2) and they are classified by their silica content into groups: acid (over 66% silica), intermediate (55%–66%), basic (45%–55%), and ultrabasic (under 45%).

Igneous rocks that crystallize below the Earth's surface are called plutonic or intrusive, depending on the depth of formation. They have large crystals produced by slow cooling; examples include diabase and granite. Those extruded at the surface are called extrusive or volcanic. Rapid cooling results in small crystals; basalt is an example.

Iguaçú Falls or *Iguassú Falls* waterfall in South America, on the border between Brazil and Argentina. The falls lie 12 mi/19 km above the junction of the river Iguaçú with the Paraná. The falls are divided by forested rocky islands and form a spectacular tourist attraction. The water plunges in 275 falls, many of which have separate names. They have a height of 269 ft/82 m and a width of about 2.5 mi/4 km.

iguana any lizard, especially the genus *Iguana*, of the family Iguanidae, which includes about 700 species and is chiefly confined to the Americas. The common iguana *I. iguana* of Central and South America is a vegetarian and may reach 6 ft/2 m in length.

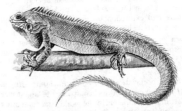

iguana *The common iguana lives mainly in trees but is an excellent swimmer. It has a characteristic crest of comblike spines running down the length of its back. Young animals are bright green, becoming darker with age.*

IJsselmeer lake in the Netherlands, area 470 sq mi/1,217 sq km. It was formed 1932 after the Zuider Zee was cut off from the North Sea by a dyke 20 mi/32 km long (the *Afsluitdijk*); it has been freshwater since 1944. The rivers Vecht, IJssel, and Zwatewater empty into the lake.

Ikhnaton or *Akhenaton*. King (pharaoh) of ancient Egypt of the 18th dynasty (*c.*1379–1362 BC), who may have ruled jointly for a time with his father Amenhotep III. He developed the cult of the Sun, ◊Aton, rather than the rival cult of Ammon, and removed his capital to ◊Akhetaton. Some historians believe that his attention to religious reforms rather than imperial defense led to the loss of most of Egypt's possessions in Asia.

Ile-de-France region of N France; area 4,632 sq mi/ 12,000 sq km; population (1986) 10,251,000. It includes the French capital, Paris, and the towns of Versailles, Sèvres, and St-Cloud and comprises the *départements* of Essonne, Val-de-Marne, Val d'Oise, Ville de Paris, Seine-et-Marne, Hauts-de-Seine, Seine-Saint-Denis, and Yvelines. From here the early French kings extended their authority over the whole country.

Iliad Greek epic poem, product of an oral tradition; it was possibly written down by 700 BC and is attributed to ◊Homer. The title is derived from Ilion, the Greek name for Troy. Its subject is the wrath of the Greek hero Achilles at the loss of his concubine Briseis, and at the death of his friend Patroclus, during the Greek siege of Troy.

The poems ends with the death of the Trojan hero Hector at the hands of Achilles.

Iliescu Ion 1930– . Romanian president from 1990. A former member of the Romanian Communist Party (PCR) and of Nicolae Ceausescu's government, Iliescu swept into power on Ceausescu's fall as head of the National Salvation Front.

Ilium in classical mythology, an alternate name for the city of ◊Troy, taken from its founder Ilus.

Illinois midwest state of the US; nickname Land of Lincoln/Prairie State *area* 56,395 sq mi/146,100 sq km *capital* Springfield *cities* Chicago, Rockford, Peoria, Decatur, Aurora *features* Lake Michigan; rivers: Mississippi, Illinois, Ohio, Rock; Cahokia Mounds, the largest group of prehistoric earthworks in the US; the Lincoln Home National Historic Site, Springfield; the University of Chicago; Mormon leader Joseph Smith's home, Nauvoo; the Art Institute and Field Museum, Chicago *industries* soy beans, cereals, meat and dairy products, machinery, electrical and electronic equipment *population* (1990) 11,430,600 *famous people* Jane Addams, Saul Bellow, Mother Cabrini, Clarence Darrow, Enrico Fermi, Ernest Hemingway, Jesse Jackson, Abraham Lincoln, Edgar Lee Masters, Ronald Reagan, Louis Sullivan, Frank Lloyd Wright *history* explored by Marquette and Joliet 1673; settled by the French in the 17th century; ceded to Britain by France 1763; passed to US control 1783; became a state 1818. Much settlement began 1825 following the opening of the Erie Canal. Spurred after the Civil War by the phenomenal growth of Chicago, Illinois became a major agricultural and industrial state, with heavy immigration. Labor unrest was reflected in the Haymarket Riot 1886 and Pullman strike 1894. The importance of heavy industry declined after 1950, but Chicago remained a major transport, trade, and finance center, and the state a leader in farm income; Illinois ranks first in agricultural exports and second in hog production. The enormous Fermi National Accelerator Laboratory is located at Batavia.

image compression in computing, one of a number of methods used to reduce the amount of information required to represent an image, so that it takes up less computer memory and can be transmitted more rapidly and economically via telecommunications systems. It plays a major role in fax transmission and in videophone and multimedia systems.

Imagism movement in Anglo-American poetry that flourished 1912–14 and affected much US and British poetry and critical thinking thereafter. A central figure was Ezra Pound, who asserted the principles of free verse, complex imagery, and poetic impersonality.

imago sexually mature stage of an ◊insect.

IMF abbreviation for ◊*International Monetary Fund*.

Imhotep Egyptian physician and architect, adviser to King Zoser (3rd dynasty). He is thought to have designed the step pyramid at Sakkara, and his tomb (believed to be in the N Sakkara cemetery) became a center of healing. He was deified as the son of Ptah and was identified with Aesculapius, the Greek god of medicine.

Immaculate Conception in the Roman Catholic Church, the belief that the Virgin Mary was, by a special act of grace, preserved free from ◊original sin from the moment she was conceived. This article of the Catholic faith was for centuries the subject of heated controversy, opposed by St Thomas Aquinas and other theologians, but generally accepted from about the 16th century. It became a dogma in 1854 under Pope Pius IX.

immunity the protection that organisms have against foreign microorganisms, such as bacteria and viruses, and against cancerous cells (see ◊cancer). The cells that provide this protection are called white blood cells, or leukocytes, and make up the immune system. They include neutrophils and macrophages, which can engulf invading organisms and other unwanted material, and natural killer cells that destroy cells infected by viruses and cancerous cells. Some of the most important immune cells are the B cells and T cells. Immune cells coordinate their activities by means of chemical messengers or lymphokines, including the antiviral messenger ◊interferon. The lymph nodes play a major role in organizing the immune response.

Immunity has been studied mostly in higher vertebrates, especially rodents, domestic animals, and primates.

immunization conferring immunity to infectious disease by artificial methods. The most widely used technique is ◊vaccination.

Immunization is an important public health measure. If most of the population has been immunized against a particular disease, it is impossible for an epidemic to take hold.

impact printer computer printer that creates characters by striking an inked ribbon against the paper beneath. Examples of impact printers are dot-matrix printers, daisywheel printers, and most types of line printer.

impala African antelope *Aepyceros melampus* found from Kenya to South Africa in savannas and open woodland. The body is sandy brown. Males have lyre-shaped horns up to 2.5 ft/75 cm ft long. Impala grow up to 5 ft/1.5 m long and 3 ft/90 cm tall. They live in herds and spring high in the air when alarmed.

impeachment judicial procedure by which government officials are accused of wrongdoing and brought to trial before a legislative body. In the US the House of Representatives may impeach offenders to be tried before the Senate, as in the case of President Andrew Johnson 1868. Richard ◊Nixon resigned the US presidency 1974 when threatened by impeachment.

imperial system traditional system of units developed in the UK, based largely on the foot, pound, and second (f.p.s.) system.

import product or service that one country purchases from another for domestic consumption, or for processing and reexporting (Hong Kong, for example, is heavily dependent on imports for its export business).

Imports may be visible (goods) or invisible (services). If an importing country does not have a counterbalancing value of exports, it may experience balance-of-payments difficulties and accordingly consider restricting imports by some form of protectionism (such as an import tariff or import quotas).

import file in computing, a file that can be read by a program even though it was produced as an ◊export file by a different program or make of computer.

impotence in medicine, a physical inability to perform sexual intercourse (the term is not usually applied to women). Impotent men fail to achieve an erection, and this may be due to illness, the effects of certain drugs, or psychological factors.

General fatigue or lack of interest may also cause impotence. Treatment for ongoing impotence includes counseling, behavioral therapy, and surgical implants.

Impressionism movement in painting that originated in France in the 1860s and dominated European and North American painting in the late 19th century. The Impressionists wanted to depict real life, to paint straight from nature, and to capture the changing effects of light. The term was first used abusively to describe Monet's painting *Impression: Sunrise* 1872 (Musée Marmottan, Paris); other Impressionists were Renoir and Sisley, and the style was adopted for periods by Cézanne, Manet, Degas, and others.

in abbreviation for ◊*inch*, a measure of distance.

Inca member of an ancient Peruvian civilization of Quechua-speaking Indians that began in the Andean highlands about 1200; by the time of the Spanish Conquest in the 1530s, the Inca ruled from Ecuador in the north to Chile in the south.

incarnation assumption of living form (plant, animal, human) by a deity, for example the gods of Greece and Rome, Hinduism, and Christianity (Jesus as the second person of the Trinity).

incendiary bomb bomb containing inflammable matter. Usually dropped by aircraft, incendiary bombs were used in World War I and incendiary shells were used against Zeppelin aircraft. Incendiary bombs were a major weapon in attacks on cities in World War II, causing widespread destruction. To hinder firefighters, delayed-action high-explosive bombs were usually dropped with them. In the Vietnam War, US forces used ◊napalm in incendiary bombs.

incest sexual intercourse between persons thought to be too closely related to marry; the exact relationships that fall under the incest taboo vary widely from society to society. A biological explanation for the incest taboo is based on the necessity to avoid inbreeding.

inch imperial unit of linear measure, a twelfth of a foot, equal to 2.54 centimeters.

Inchon formerly *Chemulpo* chief port of Seoul, South Korea; population (1990) 1,818,300. It produces steel and textiles.

incomes policy see ◊wage and price controls.

income tax a direct tax levied on corporate profits and on personal income, mainly wages and salaries, but which may include dividends, interests, rents, royalties, and the value of receipts other than in cash. It is one of the main instruments for achieving a government's income redistribution objectives.

indemnity in law, an undertaking to compensate another for damage, loss, trouble, or expenses, or the money paid by way of such compensation—for example, under fire insurance agreements.

In some laws, government officials are protected from paying indemnities and as such are "indemnified". Similarly directors of nonprofit corporations may be indemnified or corporations may indemnify their officers and directors by the purchase of insurance.

indentured labor work under a restrictive contract of employment for a fixed period in a foreign country in exchange for payment of passage, accommodation, and food. Indentured labor was the means by which many British people emigrated to North America during the colonial era, and in the 19th–early 20th centuries it was used to recruit Asian workers for employment elsewhere in European colonial empires.

Independence Day public holiday in the US, commemorating the adoption of the ◊Declaration of Independence July 4, 1776.

Ties with Britain were severed, and the "Fourth of July" has become one of America's most spirited celebrations.

index in economics, an indicator of a general movement in wages and prices over a specified period.

For example, the consumer price index (CPI) records charges in the ◊cost of living. The ◊Dow Jones index indicates the general movement of the New York stock exchange.

India Republic of (Hindi *Bharat*) *area* 1,222,396 sq mi/ 3,166,829 sq km *capital* Delhi *towns and cities* Bangalore, Hyderabad, Ahmedabad, Kanpur, Pune, Nagpur; ports Calcutta, Bombay, Madras *physical* Himalaya mountains on N border; plains around rivers Ganges, Indus, Brahmaputra; Deccan peninsula S of the Narmada River forms plateau between Western and Eastern Ghats mountain ranges; desert in W; Andaman and Nicobar Islands, Lakshadweep (Laccadive Islands) *environment* the controversial Narmada Valley Project is the world's largest combined hydroelectric irrigation scheme. In addition to displacing a million people, the damming of the holy Narmada River will submerge large areas of forest and farmland and create problems of waterlogging and salinization *features* Taj Mahal monument; Golden Temple, Amritsar; archeological sites and cave paintings (Ajanta); world's second most populous country *head of state* Shankar Dayal Sharma from 1992 *head*

318

of government P V Narasimha Rao from 1991 *political system* liberal democratic federal republic *political parties* All India Congress Committee (I), or Congress (I), cross-caste and cross-religion, left of center; Janata Dal, left of center; Bharatiya Janata Party (BJP), conservative Hindu-chauvinist; Communist Party of India (CPI), Marxist-Leninist; Communist Party of India–Marxist (CPI–M), West Bengal–based moderate socialist *exports* tea (world's largest producer), coffee, fish, iron and steel, leather, textiles, clothing, polished diamonds *currency* rupee *population* (1993 est) 903,000,000 (920 women to every 1,000 men); growth rate 2.0% p.a. *life expectancy* men 60, women 61 *language* Hindi (widely spoken in N India), English, and 14 other official languages: Assamese, Bengali, Gujarati, Kannada, Kashmiri, Malayalam, Marathi, Oriya, Punjabi, Sanskrit, Sindhi, Tamil, Telugu, Urdu *media* free press; government-owned broadcasting *religion* Hindu 80%, Sunni Muslim 10%, Christian 2.5%, Sikh 2% *literacy* men 62%, women 34% *GNP* $330 per head (1991). 315 million people subsist on less than $1 a day (1993) *chronology 1947* Independence achieved from Britain. *1950* Federal republic proclaimed. *1962* Border skirmishes with China. *1964* Death of Prime Minister Nehru. Border war with Pakistan over Kashmir. *1966* Indira Gandhi became prime minister. *1971* War with Pakistan leading to creation of Bangladesh. *1975–77* State of emergency proclaimed. *1977–79* Janata Party government in power. *1980* Indira Gandhi returned in landslide victory. *1984* Indira Gandhi assassinated; Rajiv Gandhi elected with record majority. *1987* Signing of "Tamil" Colombo peace accord with Sri Lanka; Indian Peacekeeping Force (IPKF) sent there. Public revelation of Bofors corruption scandal. *1988* New opposition party, Janata Dal, established by former finance minister V P Singh. Voting age lowered from 21 to 18. *1989* Congress (I) lost majority in general election, after Gandhi associates implicated in financial misconduct; Janata Dal minority government formed, with V P Singh prime minister. *1990* Central rule imposed in Jammu and Kashmir. P V Singh resigned; new minority Janata Dal government formed by Chandra Shekhar. Interethnic and religious violence in Punjab and elsewhere. *1991* Central rule imposed in Tamil Nadu. Shekhar resigned; elections called for May. May: Rajiv Gandhi assassinated. June: elections resumed, resulting in a Congress (I) minority government led by P V Narasimha Rao. Separatist violence continued. *1992* Congress (I) won control of state assembly and a majority in parliament in Punjab state elections. Split in Janata Dal opposition resulted in creation of National Front coalition party. Destruction of mosque in Ayodhya, N India, by Hindu extremists resulted in widespread communal violence. *1993* Sectarian violence in Bombay left 500 dead. Rao narrowly survived confidence vote in parliament. Earthquake in the Maharashtra state killed tens of thousands.

Indiana state of the midwest US; nickname Hoosier State *area* 36,168 sq mi/93,700 sq km *capital* Indianapolis *cities* Fort Wayne, Gary, Evansville, South Bend *features* Wabash River; Wyandotte Cavern; Indiana Dunes National Lakeshore; Indianapolis Motor Speedway and Museum; George Rogers National Historic Park, Vincennes; Robert Owen's utopian commune, New Harmony; Lincoln Boyhood National Memorial; the University of Notre Dame is located at South Bend *industries* corn, pigs, soy beans, limestone, machinery, electrical goods,

coal, steel, iron, chemicals *population* (1990) 5,544,200 *famous people* Hoagy Carmichael, Eugene V Debs, Theodore Dreiser, Michael Jackson, Cole Porter, J Dan Quayle, Wilbur Wright *history* explored for France by La Salle 1679–80; first colonial settlements established 1731–35 by French traders; ceded to Britain by France 1763; passed to US control 1783; became a state 1816. Indiana became an important industrial state in the early 20th century, with steel mills, oil refineries, and factories producing automobiles and auto parts. However, the state remained one-third rural in the mid-1980s, and agriculture retained much of its former importance.

Indianapolis capital and largest city of Indiana, on the White River; population (1990) 742,000. It is an industrial center and venue of the "Indianapolis 500" automobile race.

To end its heavy reliance on recession-prone auto manufacturing, the city has exploited its central location to become a warehouse, distribution, and convention center. Educational facilities include the Indiana University Medical Center, and there is a 60,000-seat domed stadium. Indianapolis was settled 1820. In 1967 surrounding Marion County was annexed to the city.

Indian languages traditionally, the languages of the subcontinent of India; since 1947, the languages of the Republic of India. These number some 200, depending on whether a variety is classified as a language or a dialect. They fall into five main groups, the two most widespread of which are the Indo-European languages (mainly in the north) and the Dravidian languages (mainly in the south).

Indian Ocean ocean between Africa and Australia, with India to the N, and the southern boundary being an arbitrary line from Cape Agulhas to S Tasmania; area 28,371,000 sq mi/73,500,000 sq km; average depth 12,708 ft/3,872 m. The greatest depth is the Java Trench 25,353 ft/7,725 m.

indie (short for *independent*) in music, a record label that is neither owned nor distributed by one of the large conglomerates ("majors") that dominate the industry. Without a corporate bureaucratic structure, the independent labels are often quicker to respond to new trends and more idealistic in their aims. What has become loosely known as *indie music* therefore tends to be experimental, amateurish, or at the cutting edge of street fashion.

indigenous the people, animals, and plants that are native to a region. Examples of indigenous peoples include Africans, Australian Aborigines, the Pacific Islanders, and American Indians. A World Council of Indigenous Peoples is based in Canada.

indigo violet-blue vegetable dye obtained from plants of the genus *Indigofera*, family Leguminosae, but now replaced by a synthetic product. It was once a major export crop of India.

indium soft, ductile, silver-white, metallic element, symbol In, atomic number 49, atomic weight 114.82. It occurs in nature in some zinc ores, is resistant to abrasion, and is used as a coating on metal parts. It was discovered 1863 by German metallurgists Ferdinand Reich (1799–1882) and Hieronymus Richter (1824–1898), who named it after the two indigo lines of its spectrum.

individualism in politics, a view in which the individual takes precedence over the collective: the opposite of collectivism. The term *possessive individualism* has been applied to the writings of John ◊Locke and Jeremy ◊Bentham, describing society as comprising individuals interacting through market relations.

Indo-Aryan languages another name for the ◊Indo-European languages.

Indochina French name given by the French to their colonies in SE Asia: ◊Cambodia, ◊Laos, and ◊Vietnam, which became independent after World War II.

Indochina War war of independence 1946–54 between the nationalist forces of what was to become Vietnam and France, the occupying colonial power.

Indo-European languages family of languages that includes some of the world's major classical languages (Sanskrit and Pali in India, Zend Avestan in Iran, Greek and Latin in Europe), as well as several of the most widely spoken languages (English worldwide; Spanish in Iberia, Latin America, and elsewhere; and the Hindi group of languages in N India). Indo-European languages were once located only along a geographical band from India through Iran into NW Asia, E Europe, the northern Mediterranean lands, N and W Europe and the British Isles.

Indo-Germanic languages former name for the ◊Indo-European languages.

Indonesia Republic of (*Republik Indonesia*) *area* 740,905 sq mi/1,919,443 sq km *capital* Jakarta *towns and cities* Bandung, Yogyakarta (Java), Medan, Banda Aceh, Palembang (Sumatra), Denpasar (Bali), Kupang (Timor); ports: Tanjung Priok, Surabaya, Semarang (Java), Ujung Pandang (Sulawesi) *physical* comprises 13,677 tropical islands: the Greater Sundas (including Java, Madura, Sumatra, Sulawesi, and Kalimantan [part of Borneo◊), the Lesser Sundas/Nusa Tenggara (including Bali, Lombok, Sumbawa, Flores, Sumba, Alor, Lomblen, Timor, Roti, and Savu), Maluku/Moluccas (over 1,000 islands including Ambon, Ternate, Tidore, Tanimbar, and Halmahera), and Irian Jaya (part of New Guinea) *environment* comparison of primary forest and 30— year-old secondary forest has shown that logging in Kalimantan has led to a 20% decline in tree species *head of state and government* T.N.J. Suharto from 1967 *political system* authoritarian nationalist republic *political parties* Sekber Golkar, ruling military-bureaucrat-farmers' party; United Development Party (PPP), moderate Islamic; Indonesian Democratic Party (PDI), nationalist Christian *exports* timber, oil, rubber, coffee, liquid natural gas, minerals, palm oil,

tea, tobacco *currency* rupiah *population* (1993) 187,800,000 (including 300 ethnic groups); growth rate 2% p.a. Indonesia is the world's fourth most populous country, surpassed only by China, India and US. It has the world's largest Muslim population; Java is one of the world's most densely populated areas *life expectancy* men 61, women 65 *languages* Bahasa Indonesia (official), closely related to Malay; there are 583 regional languages and dialects; Javanese is the most widely spoken local language *media* foreign investment in media is prohibited *religions* Muslim 88%, Christian 10%, Buddhist and Hindu 2% (the continued spread of Christianity, together with an Islamic revival, have led to greater religious tensions) *literacy* men 84%, women 68% *GNP* $620 per head (1992) *chronology 17th century* Dutch rule established. *1942* Occupied by Japan; nationalist puppet government established. *1945* Japanese surrender; nationalists declared independence under Achmed Sukarno. *1949* Formal transfer of Dutch sovereignty. *1950* Unitary constitution established. *1963* Western New Guinea (Irian Jaya) ceded by the Netherlands. *1965–66* Attempted communist coup; General T.N. J. Suharto imposed emergency administration, leading to deaths of hundreds of thousands of Indonesians. *1967* Sukarno replaced as president by Suharto. *1975* Guerrillas seeking independence for S Maluku seized train and Indonesian consulate in the Netherlands; Western hostages held. *1976* Forced annexation of former Portuguese colony of East Timor. *1984* Stepping up of transmigration program announced, to play crucial role in overall development strategy. *1986* Large numbers of Javanese settled on sparsely populated outer islands, particularly Irian Jaya, under transmigration program. *1989* Foreign debt reached $50 billion; Western creditors offered aid on condition that concessions were made to foreign companies and austerity measures introduced. *1991* Democracy forums launched to promote political dialogue. Massacre in East Timor. *1992* Ruling Golkar party reelected. East Timor rebel leader arrested; more than 1,000 rebels surrendered. *1993* President Suharto reelected for sixth consecutive five-year term; first civilian leader of Golkar installed. *1994* Sukarno's daughter, Magawati, elected head of PDI.

inductance in physics, a measure of the capability of an electronic circuit or circuit component to form a magnetic field or store magnetic energy when carrying a current. Its symbol is *L*, and its unit of measure is the ◊henry. The magnetic field produced induces voltages in the same circuit or a nearby circuit.

inductor device included in an electrical circuit because of its inductance.

indulgence in the Roman Catholic church, the total or partial remission of temporal punishment for sins which remain to be expiated after penitence and confession have secured exemption from eternal punishment. The doctrine of indulgence began as the commutation of church penances in exchange for suitable works of charity or money gifts to the church, and became a great source of church revenue. This trade in indulgences roused Luther in 1517 to initiate the Reformation. The Council of Trent 1563 recommended moderate retention of indulgences, and they continue, notably in "Holy Years".

Indus river in Asia, rising in Tibet and flowing 1,975 mi/ 3,180 km to the Arabian Sea. In 1960 the use of its waters, including those of its five tributaries, was divided between India (rivers Ravi, Beas, Sutlej) and Pakistan (rivers Indus, Jhelum, Chenab).

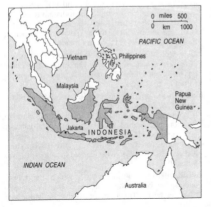

industrial design branch of artistic activity that came into being as a result of the need to design machine-made products, introduced by the Industrial Revolution in the 18th century. The purpose of industrial design is to ensure that goods satisfy the demands of fashion, style, function, materials, and cost.

industrial park area planned for industry, where space is available for large buildings and further expansion. Industrial parks often have good internal road layouts and occupy accessible sites near road or highway junctions but away from the central business district.

industrial relations relationship between employers and employees, and their dealings with each other. In most industries, wages and conditions are determined by *free collective bargaining* between employers and ◊labor unions. Some American and European countries have *worker participation* through profit-sharing and industrial democracy. Another solution is *co-ownership*, in which a company is entirely owned by its employees. The aim of good industrial relations is to achieve a motivated, capable work force that sees its work as creative and fulfilling. A breakdown in industrial relations can lead to an industrial dispute where one party takes industrial action.

When agreement cannot be reached by collective bargaining, outside arbitration is often sought. In the US, there is a highly developed system for private, third-party arbitration.

Industrial Revolution the sudden acceleration of technical and economic development that began in Britain in the second half of the 18th century. The traditional agrarian economy was replaced by one dominated by machinery and manufacturing, made possible through technical advances such as the steam engine. This transferred the balance of political power from the landowner to the industrial capitalist and created an urban working class. From 1830 to the early 20th century, the Industrial Revolution spread throughout Europe and the US and to Japan and the various colonial empires.

Industrial Workers of the World (IWW) labor movement founded in Chicago, US 1905, and in Australia 1907, the members of which were popularly known as the **Wobblies**. The IWW was dedicated to the overthrow of capitalism and the creation of a single union for workers, but divided on tactics.

At its peak, (1912–15), the organization claimed to have 100,000 members, mainly in western mining and lumber areas, and in the textile mills of New England. Demonstrations were violently suppressed by the authorities. It gradually declined in popularity after 1917. See also ◊syndicalism.

industry the extraction and conversion of raw materials, the manufacture of goods, and the provision of services. Industry can be either low technology, unspecialized, and labor-intensive, as in Third World countries, or highly automated, mechanized, and specialized, using advanced technology, as in the industrialized countries. Major trends in industrial activity 1960–90 were the growth of electronic, robotic, and microelectronic technologies, the expansion of the offshore oil industry, and the prominence of Japan and other Pacific-region countries in manufacturing and distributing electronics, computers, and motor vehicles.

Indus Valley civilization one of the four earliest ancient civilizations of the Old World (the other three

being the ◊Sumerian civilization 3500 BC ; ◊Egypt 3000 BC ; and ◊China 2200 BC), developing in the NW of the Indian subcontinent about 2500 BC .

inert gas or *noble gas* any of a group of six elements (helium, neon, argon, krypton, xenon, and radon), so named because they were originally thought not to enter into any chemical reactions. This is now known to be incorrect: in 1962, xenon was made to combine with fluorine, and since then, compounds of argon, krypton, and radon with fluorine and/or oxygen have been described.

inertia in physics, the tendency of an object to remain in a state of rest or uniform motion until an external force is applied, as stated by Isaac Newton's first law of motion (see ◊Newton's laws of motion).

infant mortality rate measure of the number of infants dying under one year of age, usually expressed as the number of deaths per 1,000 live births. Improved sanitation, nutrition, and medical care have considerably lowered figures throughout much of the world; for example in the 18th century in the US and UK infant mortality was about 500 per thousand, compared with under 10 per thousand in 1989. The lowest infant mortality rate is in Japan, at 4.5 per 1,000 live births. In much of the Third World, however, the infant mortality rate remains high.

infection invasion of the body by disease-causing organisms (pathogens, or germs) that become established, multiply, and produce symptoms. Bacteria and viruses cause most diseases, but diseases are also caused by other microorganisms, protozoans, and other parasites.

inferiority complex in psychology, a ◊complex described by Alfred ◊Adler based on physical inferiority; the term has been popularly used to describe general feelings of inferiority and the overcompensation that often ensues.

inferior planet a planet (Mercury or Venus) whose orbit lies between that of the Earth and the Sun.

infinity mathematical quantity that is larger than any fixed assignable quantity; symbol ∞. By convention, the result of dividing any number by zero is regarded as infinity.

inflation in economics, a rise in the general level of prices. The many causes include cost-push inflation, which results from rising production costs. *Demand-pull inflation* occurs when overall demand exceeds supply. *Suppressed inflation* occurs in controlled economies and is reflected in rationing, shortages, and black market prices. *Deflation*, a fall in the general level of prices, is the reverse of inflation. *Hyperinflation*, inflation of more than 50% in one month, has happened only 15 times this century.

influenza any of various viral infections primarily affecting the air passages, accompanied by systemic effects such as fever, chills, headache, joint and muscle pains, and lassitude. Treatment is with bed rest and analgesic drugs such as aspirin or paracetamol.

information superhighway popular collective name for the ◊Internet and other related large scale computer networks. The term was first used 1993 by US vice president Al Gore in a speech outlining plans to build a high-speed national data communications network.

information technology (IT) collective term for the various technologies involved in processing and transmitting information. They include computing, telecommunications, and microelectronics.

infrared radiation invisible electromagnetic radiation of wavelength between about 0.75 micrometers and 1 millimeter—that is, between the limit of the red end of the visible spectrum and the shortest microwaves. All bodies above the ◊absolute zero of temperature absorb and radiate infrared radiation. Infrared radiation is used in medical photography and treatment, and in industry, astronomy, and criminology.

infrastructure relatively permanent facilities that service an industrial economy. Infrastructure usually includes roads, railroads, other communication networks, energy and water supply, and education and training facilities. Some definitions also include sociocultural installations such as health-care and leisure facilities.

Ingres Jean-Auguste-Dominique 1780–1867. French painter. He was a student of David and a leading exponent of the Neo-Classical style. He studied and worked in Rome about 1807–20, where he began the *Odalisque* series of sensuous female nudes, then went to Florence, and returned to France 1824. His portraits painted in the 1840s–50s are meticulously detailed and highly polished.

injunction court order that forbids a person from doing something, or orders him or her to take certain action. Breach of an injunction is ◊contempt of court.

Inkatha Freedom Party (IFP) South African political party, representing the nationalist aspirations of the country's largest ethnic group, the Zulus. It was founded as a paramilitary organization 1975 by its present leader, Chief Gatsha ◊Buthelezi, with the avowed aim of creating a nonracial democratic political situation. Fighting between Inkatha and ◊African National Congress (ANC) supporters during the early 1990s cost thousands of lives. In April 1994, after an initial violent boycott, Buthelezi agreed to register the IFP in the country's first multiracial elections. The party emerged with 10% of the popular vote. Buthelezi was himself appointed home affairs minister in the new power-sharing administration.

ink-jet printer computer printer that creates characters and graphics by spraying very fine jets of quick-drying ink onto paper. Ink-jet printers range in size from small machines designed to work with microcomputers to very large machines designed for high-volume commercial printing.

Innocent III 1161–1216. Pope from 1198 who asserted papal power over secular princes, in particular over the succession of Holy Roman Emperors. He also made King ◊John of England his vassal, compelling him to accept Stephen Langton as archbishop of Canterbury. He promoted the fourth Crusade and crusades against the non-Christian Livonians and Letts, and the Albigensian heretics of S France.

Innsbruck capital of Tirol state, W Austria; population (1981) 117,000. It is a tourist and winter sports center and a route junction for the Brenner Pass. The 1964 and 1976 Winter Olympics were held here.

Inns of Court four private legal societies in London, England: Lincoln's Inn, Gray's Inn, Inner Temple, and Middle Temple. All lawyers (advocates in the English legal system) must belong to one of the Inns of Court. The main function of each Inn is the education, government, and protection of its members. Each is under the administration of a body of Benchers (judges and senior lawyers).

innuendo indirect, unpleasant comment; a sly hint. "I am sure you have brought up your child well—to the best of your ability, certainly." "I wouldn't take any books when you go to stay with Alan, if I were you. They have a habit of disappearing there." The second example is more blatant than the first, but the essence of an innuendo is that it must be capable of an innocent explanation. The speaker must be able to charge the listener with misinterpretation or oversensitivity, if the innuendo is challenged.

inoculation injection into the body of dead or weakened disease-carrying organisms or their toxins (◊vaccine) to produce immunity by inducing a mild form of a disease.

inorganic chemistry branch of chemistry dealing with the chemical properties of the elements and their compounds, excluding the more complex covalent compounds of carbon, which are considered in ◊organic chemistry.

input device device for entering information into a computer. Input devices include keyboards, joysticks, mice, light pens, touch-sensitive screens, graphics tablets, speech-recognition devices, and vision systems. Compare ◊output device.

inquest inquiry held by a ◊coroner into an unexplained death. At an inquest, evidence is on oath, and medical and other witnesses may be summoned.

insanity popular and legal term for mental disorder. In medicine the corresponding term is ◊psychosis.

insect any member of the class Insecta among the arthropods or jointed-legged animals. An insect's body is divided into head, thorax, and abdomen. The head bears a pair of feelers or antennae, and attached to the thorax are three pairs of legs and usually two pairs of wings.

The scientific study of insects is termed entomology. More than 1 million species are known, and several thousand new ones are discovered every year. Insects vary in size from 0.007 in/0.02 cm to 13.5 in/35 cm in length.

insecticide any chemical pesticide used to kill insects. Among the most effective insecticides are synthetic organic chemicals such as ◊DDT and dieldrin, which are chlorinated hydrocarbons. These chemicals, however, have proved persistent in the environment and are also poisonous to all animal life, including humans, and are consequently banned in many countries. Other synthetic insecticides include organic phosphorus compounds such as malathion. Insecticides prepared from plants, such as derris and pyrethrum, are safer to use but need to be applied frequently and carefully.

insectivore any animal whose diet is made up largely or exclusively of insects. In particular, the name is applied to mammals of the order Insectivora, which includes the shrews, hedgehogs, moles, and tenrecs.

insemination, artificial see ◊artificial insemination.

insider trading illegal use of privileged information in dealing on the stock exchanges—for example, when a company takeover bid is imminent. Insider trading is in theory detected by the Securities and Exchange Commission (SEC), and in 1988 the commission was authorized to offer bounties of up to 10% of the civil penalties to those who turned in inside traders. As one New York investment firm pleaded guilty to insider trading and paid more than $500 million in penalties, other stock markets, notably the French Bourse, suffered major inside-trading scandals.

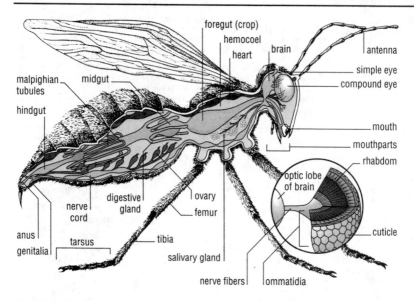

foregut (crop)
hemocoel
heart
brain
antenna
simple eye
compound eye
malpighian tubules
midgut
hindgut
mouth
mouthparts
rhabdom
optic lobe of brain
digestive gland
ovary
nerve cord
femur
anus
tibia
cuticle
genitalia
tarsus
salivary gland
nerve fibers
ommatidia

insect *Body plan of an insect. The general features of the insect body include a segmented body divided into head, thorax, and abdomen, jointed legs, feelers or antennas, and usually two pairs of wings. Insects often have compound eyes with a large field of vision.*

instinct in ◊ethology, behavior found in all equivalent members of a given species (for example, all the males, or all the females with young) that is presumed to be genetically determined.

insulin protein ◊hormone, produced by specialized cells in the islets of Langerhans in the pancreas, that regulates the metabolism (rate of activity) of glucose, fats, and proteins. Insulin was discovered by Canadian physician Frederick ◊Banting, who pioneered its use in treating ◊diabetes.

insurance contract guaranteeing compensation to the payer of periodic premiums against loss (under stipulated conditions) by fire, death, accident, and the like. Various consumer policies also insure legal or health services, paying bills or portions thereof, within the contracted conditions. Insurance is a major component of business activity, covering potential loss of property, inventory, or goods in transit.

integrated circuit (IC), popularly called *silicon chip*, a miniaturized electronic circuit produced on a single crystal, or chip, of a semiconducting material—usually silicon. It may contain many thousands of components and yet measure only 0.2 in/5 mm in square and 0.04 in/1 mm thick. The IC is encapsulated within a plastic or ceramic case, and linked via gold wires to metal pins with which it is connected to a printed circuit board and the other components that make up such electronic devices as computers and calculators.

Integrated Services Digital Network (ISDN) internationally developed telecommunications system for sending signals in ◊digital format along optical fibers and coaxial cable.

Intel manufacturer of the ◊microprocessors that form the basis of the IBM PC range and its clones. Recent

microprocessors are the 80386 and 80486 (the basis of machines referred to as 386 and 486 PCs), and the Pentium, released in 1993.

intelligence in military and political affairs, information, often secretly or illegally obtained, about other countries. *Counter-intelligence* is information on the activities of hostile agents. Much intelligence is gained by technical means, such as satellites and the electronic interception of data.

The Central Intelligence Agency is responsible for gathering foreign intelligence and for coordinating the reports of the several independent intelligence agencies. These include military intelligence branches within each armed service; the National Security Agency, responsible for technical intelligence gathering; and intelligence officers within the State Department and other executive agencies. Domestic intelligence is the responsibility of the ◊Federal Bureau of Investigation. Double agents are motivated by money, ideology, or dissatisfaction to provide information to the ostensible enemy, often doing great damage.

Moles are double agents who betray their own security services. Sleepers are agents who assume a normal life in the target country, often inactive for years until needed.

intelligence test test that attempts to measure innate intellectual ability, rather than acquired ability.

The French psychologist Alfred Binet (1857–1911) devised the first intelligence test in 1905. The concept of intelligence quotient (IQ) was adopted by US psychologist Lewis Terman in 1915. The IQ is calculated according to the formula: $IQ = MA/CA \times 100$ in which MA is "mental age" (the age at which an average child is able to perform given tasks) and CA is "chronological age", hence an average person has an IQ of 100 + 10. Intelligence tests were first used on a large scale in the US in 1917 during World War I for two million drafted men, and their subsequent widespread use for education and employment decisions has provoked protests from minority groups who contend the tests are culturally biased and discriminatory.

Intelsat (acronym for *International Telecommunications Satellite Organization*) organization established 1964 to operate a worldwide system of communications satellites. In 1994 it had 134 member nations and 22 satellites in orbit. Its headquarters are in Washington, DC. Intelsat satellites are stationed in geostationary orbit (maintaining their positions relative to the Earth) over the Atlantic, Pacific, and Indian Oceans. The first Intelsat satellite was *Early Bird*, launched 1965.

intensive care unit (ICU) or *intensive therapy unit (ITU)* high-technology medical facility concerned with the care of patients with acute life-threatening conditions. It is characterized by the use of the most advanced medical technology—electronic monitoring, mechanical ventilation, and other life-support measures—combined with skilled nursing and drugs.

interactive computing in computing, a system for processing data in which the operator is 'in direct communication with the computer, receiving immediate responses to input data. In ◊batch processing, by contrast, the necessary data and instructions are prepared in advance and processed by the computer with little or no intervention from the operator.

interactive video (IV) computer-mediated system that enables the user to interact with and control information (including text, recorded speech, or moving images) stored on video disk. IV is most commonly used for training purposes, using analog video disks, but has wider applications with digital video systems such as CD-I (Compact Disk Interactive, from Philips and Sony) which are based on the CD-ROM format derived from audio compact disks.

interest in finance, a sum of money paid by a borrower to a lender in return for the loan, usually expressed as a percentage per annum. *Simple interest* is interest calculated as a straight percentage of the amount loaned or invested. In *compound interest*, the interest earned over a period of time (for example, per annum) is added to the investment, so that at the end of the next period interest is paid on that total.

interface in computing, the point of contact between two programs or pieces of equipment. The term is most often used for the physical connection between the computer and a ◊peripheral device, which is used to compensate for differences in such operating characteristics as speed, data coding, voltage, and power consumption. For example, a *printer interface* is the cabling and circuitry used to transfer data from a computer to a printer, and to compensate for differences in speed and coding.

interference in physics, the phenomenon of two or more wave motions interacting and combining to produce a resultant wave of larger or smaller amplitude (depending on whether the combining waves are in or out of ◊phase with each other).

interferon naturally occurring cellular protein that makes up part of the body's defenses against viral disease. Three types (alpha, beta, and gamma) are produced by infected cells and enter the bloodstream and uninfected cells, making them immune to virus attack.

Intermediate Nuclear Forces Treaty agreement signed Dec 8, 1987, between the US and the USSR to eliminate all ground-based nuclear missiles in Europe that were capable of hitting only European targets (including European Russia). It reduced the countries' nuclear arsenals by some 2,000 (4% of the total). The treaty included provisions for each country to inspect the other's bases.

intermediate technology application of mechanics, electrical engineering, and other technologies, based on inventions and designs developed in scientifically sophisticated cultures, but utilizing materials, assembly, and maintenance methods found in technologically less advanced regions (known as the Third World).

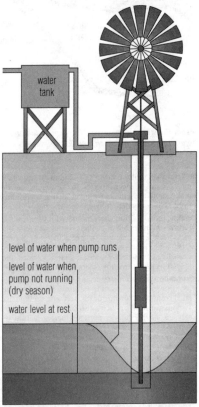

intermediate technology The simple windmill is an example of intermediate technology if it utilizes local materials and traditional design. In this way, there is no need for complex maintenance and repair, nor expensive spare parts.

internal-combustion engine heat engine in which fuel is burned inside the engine, contrasting with an external-combustion engine (such as the steam engine) in which fuel is burned in a separate unit. The ◊diesel engine and ◊gasoline engine are both internal-combustion engines. Gas ◊turbines and jet and ◊rocket engines are sometimes also considered to be internal-combustion engines because they burn their fuel inside their combustion chambers.

International, the coordinating body established by labor and socialist organizations, including:
First International or *International Working Men's Association* 1864–72, formed in London under Karl ◊Marx. *Second International* 1889–1940, founded in Paris. *Third (Socialist) International* or *Comintern* 1919–43, formed in Moscow by the Soviet leader Lenin, advocating from 1933 a popular front (communist, socialist, liberal) against the German dictator Hitler. *Fourth International* or *Trotskyist International* 1938, somewhat indeterminate, anti-Stalinist. *Revived Socialist International* 1951, formed in Frankfurt, Germany, a largely anticommunist association of social democrats.

International Bank for Reconstruction and Development specialized agency of the United Nations. Its popular name is the ◊World Bank.

International Court of Justice main judicial organ of the ◊United Nations, in The Hague, the Netherlands. It hears international law disputes as well as playing an advisory role to UN organs. It was set up by the UN charter 1945 and superseded the World Court. There are 15 judges, each from a different member state.

International Date Line (IDL) imaginary line that approximately follows the 180° line of longitude. The date is put forward a day when crossing the line going west, and back a day when going east. The IDL was chosen at the International Meridian Conference 1884.

International Labor Organization (ILO) agency of the United Nations, established 1919, which formulates standards for labor and social conditions. Its headquarters are in Geneva. It was awarded the Nobel Peace Prize 1969.

international law body of rules generally accepted as governing the relations between countries, pioneered by Hugo ◊Grotius, especially in matters of human rights, territory, and war.

International Monetary Fund (IMF) specialized agency of the ◊United Nations, headquarters Washington, DC, established under the 1944 ◊Bretton Woods agreement and operational since 1947. It seeks to promote international monetary cooperation and the growth of world trade, and to smooth multilateral payment arrangements among member states. IMF standby loans are available to members in balance-of-payments difficulties (the amount being governed by the member's quota), usually on the basis that the country must agree to take certain corrective measures.

International Organization for Standardization (ISO) international organization founded 1947 to standardize technical terms, specifications, units, and so on. Its headquarters are in Geneva.

International Society for Krishna Consciousness (ISKCON) or *Gaudiya Vaisnavism* Hindu sect based on the demonstration of intense love for Krishna (an incarnation of the god Vishnu), especially by chanting the mantra "Hare Krishna". Members wear distinctive yellow robes, and men often have their heads partly shaven. Their holy books are the Hindu scriptures and particularly the *Bhagavad-Gītā*, which they study daily.

International Style or *International Modern* architectural style, an early and influential phase of the ◊Modern Movement, originating in Western Europe in the 1920s, but finding its fullest expression in the 1930s, notably in the US. Although sometimes used to refer to the Modern Movement as a whole, it here describes an architectural output, centered around the 1920s and 1930s, with distinct stylistic qualities: a dominance of geometric, especially rectilinear, forms; emphasis on asymmetrical composition; large expanses of glazing; and white rendered walls.

Internet global, on-line computer network connecting governments, companies, universities, and many other networks and users. The service offers ◊electronic mail, conferencing and chat services, as well as the ability to access remote computers and send and retrieve files. It began in 1984 and by late 1994 was estimated to have over 40 million users on 11,000 networks in 70 countries, with an estimated one million new users joining each month.

Interpol (acronym for *International Criminal Police Organization*) agency founded following the Second International Judicial Police Conference 1923 with its headquarters in Vienna, and reconstituted after World War II with its headquarters in Paris. It has an international criminal register, fingerprint file, and methods index.

intestine in vertebrates, the digestive tract from the stomach outlet to the anus. The human *small intestine* is 20 ft/6 m long, 1.5 in/4 cm in diameter, and consists of the duodenum, jejunum, and ileum; the *large intestine* is 5 ft/1.5 m long, 2.5 in/6 cm in diameter, and includes the cecum, colon, and rectum. Both are muscular tubes comprising an inner lining that secretes alkaline digestive juice, a submucous coat containing fine blood vessels and nerves, a muscular coat, and a serous coat covering all, supported by a strong peritoneum, which carries the blood and lymph vessels, and the nerves. The contents are passed along slowly by peristalsis (waves of involuntary muscular action). The term intestine is also applied to the lower digestive tract of invertebrates.

Intifada Palestinian uprising; also the title of the involved *Liberation Army of Palestine*, a loosely organized group of adult and teenage Palestinians active 1987–93 in attacks on armed Israeli troops in the occupied territories of Palestine. Their campaign for self-determination included stone-throwing and gasoline bombing.

intrauterine device (IUD) or *coil*, a contraceptive device that is inserted into the womb (uterus). It is a tiny plastic object, sometimes containing copper. By causing a mild inflammation of the lining of the uterus it prevents fertilized eggs from becoming implanted.

intravenous method of delivery of a substance directly into a vein.

introversion personality dimension described by Carl ◊Jung. The typical introvert is preoccupied with himor herself and is generally not sociable. The opposite of introversion is ◊extroversion.

intrusion mass of ◊igneous rock that has formed by "injection" of molten rock, or magma, into existing cracks beneath the surface of the Earth, as distinct from a volcanic rock mass which has erupted from the surface. Intrusion features include vertical cylindrical structures such as stocks, pipes, and necks; sheet structures such as dykes that cut across the strata and sills that push between them; laccoliths, which are blisters that push up the overlying rock; and batholiths,

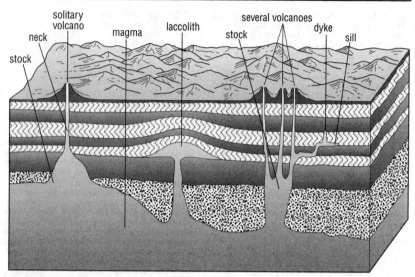

intrusion *Igneous intrusions can be a variety of shapes and sizes. Laccoliths are domed circular shapes, and can be many miles across. Sills are intrusions that flow between rock layers. Pipes or necks connect the underlying magma chamber to surface volcanoes.*

which represent chambers of solidified magma and contain vast volumes of rock.

Inuit people inhabiting the Arctic coasts of North America, the E islands of the Canadian Arctic, and the ice-free coasts of Greenland. Inuktitut, their language, has about 60,000 speakers; it belongs to the Eskimo-Aleut group. The Inuit object to the name Eskimos ("eaters of raw meat") given them by the Algonquin Indians.

Inverness town in Highland Region, Scotland, at the head of the Moray Firth, lying in a sheltered site at the mouth of the river Ness; population (1991) 62,200. It is a tourist center with tweed, tanning, engineering, distilling, iron-founding, boat-building, and electronics industries.

invertebrate an animal without a backbone. The invertebrates form all of the major divisions of the animal kingdom called phyla, with the exception of vertebrates. Invertebrates include the sponges, coelenterates, flatworms, nematodes, annelids, arthropods, mollusks, and echinoderms. Primitive aquatic chordates such as sea squirts and lancelets, which only have notochords and do not possess a vertebral column of cartilage or bone, are sometimes called invertebrate chordates, but this is misleading, since the notochord is the precursor of the backbone in advanced chordates.

inverted file in computing, a file that reorganizes the structure of an existing data file to enable a rapid search to be made for all records having one field falling within set limits.

investment in economics, the purchase of any asset with the potential to yield future financial benefit to the purchaser (such as a house, a work of art, stocks and shares, or even a private education).

investment trust public company that makes investments in other companies on behalf of its stockhold-ers. It may issue shares to raise capital and issue fixed interest securities.

in vitro fertilization (IVF) ("fertilization in glass") allowing eggs and sperm to unite in a laboratory to form embryos. The embryos produced are then implanted into the womb of the otherwise infertile mother (an extension of ◊artificial insemination). The first baby to be produced by this method was born 1978 in the UK. In cases where the Fallopian tubes are blocked, fertilization may be carried out by ***intra-vaginal culture***, in which egg and sperm are incubated (in a plastic tube) in the mother's vagina, then transferred surgically into the uterus.

Recent extensions of the in vitro technique have included the birth of a baby from a frozen embryo (Australia 1984) and from a frozen egg (Australia 1986). British doctors were pioneers in the field. The technique is now common in the US. As yet the success rate is relatively low; only 15%–20% of in vitro fertilizations result in live births.

iodine grayish-black nonmetallic element, symbol I, atomic number 53, atomic weight 126.9044. It is a member of the ◊halogen group. Its crystals give off, when heated, a violet vapor with an irritating odor resembling that of chlorine. It only occurs in combination with other elements. Its salts are known as iodides, which are found in sea water. As a mineral nutrient it is vital to the proper functioning of the thyroid gland, where it occurs in trace amounts as part of the hormone thyroxine. Absence of iodine from the diet leads to ◊goiter. Iodine is used in photography, in medicine as an antiseptic, and in making dyes.

IOM abbreviation for ◊*Isle of Man*, an island in the Irish Sea.

ion atom, or group of atoms, that is either positively charged (cation) or negatively charged (◊anion), as a result of the loss or gain of electrons during chemical reactions or exposure to certain forms of radiation.

Iona island in the Inner Hebrides; area 2,100 acres/850 hectares. A center of early Christianity, it is the site of a monastery founded 563 by St ◊Columba. It later became a burial ground for Irish, Scottish, and Norwegian kings. It has a 13th-century abbey.

Ionesco Eugène 1912–1994. Romanian-born French dramatist. He was a leading exponent of the Theatre of the Absurd. Most of his plays are in one act and concern the futility of language as a means of communication. These include *La Cantatrice chauve/The Bald Prima Donna* 1950, and *La Leçon/The Lesson* 1951. Later full-length plays include *Rhinocéros* 1958 and *Le Roi se meurt/Exit the King* 1961.

Ionian member of a Hellenic people from beyond the Black Sea who crossed the Balkans around 1980 BC and invaded Asia Minor. Driven back by the ◊Hittites, they settled all over mainland Greece, later being supplanted by the Achaeans.

ionic bond or *electrovalent bond* bond produced when atoms of one element donate electrons to atoms of another element, forming positively and negatively charged ◊ions respectively. The electrostatic attraction between the oppositely charged ions constitutes the bond. Sodium chloride (Na^+Cl^-) is a typical ionic compound.

ionosphere ionized layer of Earth's outer ◊atmosphere (38–620 mi/60–1,000 km) that contains sufficient free electrons to modify the way in which radio waves are propagated, for instance by reflecting them back to Earth. The ionosphere is thought to be produced by absorption of the Sun's ultraviolet radiation.

IOW abbreviation for ◊*Isle of Wight*, an island and county off the coast of S England.

Iowa state of the midwest US; nickname Hawkeye State *area* 56,279 sq mi/145,800 sq km *capital* Des Moines *towns and cities* Cedar Rapids, Davenport, Sioux City *features* Grant Wood Gallery, Davenport; Herbert Hoover birthplace, library, and museum near West Branch; "Little Switzerland" region in the NE, overlooking the Mississippi River; Effigy Mounds National Monument, near Marquette, a prehistoric Indian burial site *industries* cereals, soy beans, pigs and cattle, chemicals, farm machinery, electrical goods, hardwood lumber, minerals *population* (1990) 2,776,800 *famous people* "Bix" Beiderbecke, Buffalo Bill, Herbert Hoover, Glenn Miller, Lillian Russell, Grant Wood *history* Sauk and Fox Indians were forced to cede their lands 1832 in what is now E Iowa. Blessed with rich topsoil, Iowa quickly attracted settlers, and it became a state 1846. The economy remains based on agriculture; the state usually leads all others in the production of corn, soybeans, and hogs.

Iowa City city in E Iowa, on the Iowa River, S of Cedar Rapids, seat of Johnson County; population (1990) 59,700. It is a distribution center for the area's agricultural products. Other industries include printed matter and building materials. The University of Iowa (1847) is here.

IQ (abbreviation for *intelligence quotient*) the ratio between a subject's "mental" and chronological ages, multiplied by 100. A score of 100 ± 10 in an ◊intelligence test is considered average.

IRA abbreviation for ◊*Irish Republican Army*.

Iran Islamic Republic of (*Jomhori-e-Islami-e-Irân*; until 1935 *Persia*) *area* 636,128 sq mi/1,648,000 sq km

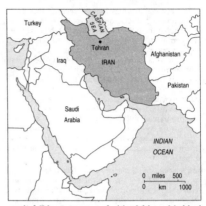

capital Tehran *towns and cities* Isfahan, Mashhad, Tabriz, Shiraz, Ahvaz; chief port Abadan *physical* plateau surrounded by mountains, including Elburz and Zagros; Lake Rezayeh; Dasht-Ekavir Desert; occupies islands of Abu Musa, Greater Tunb and Lesser Tunb in the Gulf *features* ruins of Persepolis; Mount Demavend 18,603 ft/5,670 m. *Leader of the Islamic Revolution* Seyed Ali Khamenei from 1989 *head of government* Ali Akbar Hashemi Rafsanjani from 1989 *political system* authoritarian Islamic republic *political party* Liberation Movement of Iran, Islamic human rights *exports* carpets, cotton textiles, metalwork, leather goods, oil, petrochemicals, fruit *currency* rial *population* (1993 est) 61,660,000 (including minorities in Azerbaijan, Baluchistan, Khuzestan/ Arabistan, and Kurdistan); growth rate 3.2% p.a. *life expectancy* men 67, women 68 *languages* Farsi (official), Kurdish, Turkish, Arabic, English, French *religions* Shiite Muslim (official) 92%, Sunni Muslim 5%, Zoroastrian 2%, Jewish, Baha'i, and Christian 1% *literacy* men 65%, women 43% *GNP* $2,320 per head (1991) *chronology* *1946* British, US, and Soviet forces left Iran. *1951* Oil fields nationalized by Prime Minister Mohammed Mossadegh. *1953* Mossadegh deposed and the US-backed shah, Mohammed Reza Shah Pahlavi, took full control of the government. *1975* The shah introduced single-party system. *1978* Opposition to the shah organized from France by Ayatollah Khomeini. *1979* Shah left the country; Khomeini returned to create Islamic state. Revolutionaries seized US hostages at embassy in Tehran; US economic boycott. *1980* Start of Iran–Iraq War. *1981* US hostages released. *1984* Egyptian peace proposals rejected. *1985* Fighting intensified in Iran–Iraq War. *1988* Cease-fire; talks with Iraq began. *1989* Khomeini called for the death of British writer Salman Rushdie. June: Khomeini died; Ali Khamenei elected interim Leader of the Revolution; speaker of Iranian parliament Hashemi Rafsanjani elected president. Secret oil deal with Israel revealed. *1990* Generous peace terms with Iraq accepted. *1991* Imprisoned British business executive released. Nearly one million Kurds arrived from Iraq, fleeing persecution by Saddam Hussein after the Gulf War. *1992* Pro-Rafsanjani moderates won assembly elections. *1993* President Rafsanjani reelected, but with a smaller margin.

Irangate US political scandal 1987 involving senior members of the Reagan administration (the name echoes the Nixon administration's ◊Watergate).

Congressional hearings 1986–87 revealed that the US government had secretly sold weapons to Iran in 1985 and traded them for hostages held in Lebanon by pro-Iranian militias, and used the profits to supply right-wing Contra guerrillas in Nicaragua with arms. The attempt to get around the law (Boland amendment) specifically prohibiting military assistance to the Contras also broke other laws in the process.

Congressional hearings 1986–87 revealed that the US government had secretly sold weapons to Iran in 1985 and traded them for hostages held in Lebanon by pro-Iranian militias, using the profits to supply right-wing contra guerrillas in Nicaragua with arms. The hearings were criticized for finding that the president was not responsible for the actions of his subordinates.

Iraq Republic of (*al Jumhouriya al `Iraqia*) *area* 167,881 sq mi/434,924 sq km *capital* Baghdad *towns and cities* Mosul and port of Basra *physical* mountains in N, desert in W; wide valley of rivers Tigris and Euphrates NW–SE *environment* a chemical-weapons plant covering an area of 25 sq mi/65 sq km, situated 50 mi/80 km NW of Baghdad, has been described by the UN as the largest toxic waste dump in the world *features* reed architecture of the marsh Arabs· ancient sites of Eridu, Babylon, Nineveh, Ur, Ctesiphon *head of state and government* Saddam Hussein al-Tikriti from 1979 *political system* one-party socialist republic *political party* Arab Ba'ath Socialist Party, nationalist socialist *exports* oil (prior to UN sanctions), wool, dates (80% of world supply) *currency* Iraqi dinar *population* (1993) 19,410,000 (Arabs 77%, Kurds 19%, Turks 2%); growth rate 3.6% p.a. *life expectancy* men 65, women 67 *languages* Arabic (official); Kurdish, Assyrian, Armenian *religions* Shiite Muslim 60%, Sunni Muslim 37%, Christian 3% *literacy* men 70%, women 49% *GNP* $2,140 per head (1986) *chronology* *1920* Iraq became a British League of Nations protectorate. *1921* Hashemite dynasty established, with Faisal I installed by Britain as king. *1932* Independence achieved from British protectorate status. *1958* Monarchy overthrown; Iraq became a republic. *1963* Joint Ba'athist-military coup headed by Col. Salem Aref and backed by US Central Intelligence Agency. *1968* Military coup put Maj Gen al-Bakr in power. *1979* Al-Bakr replaced by Saddam Hussein. *1980* War between Iraq and Iran broke out. *1985* Fighting intensified. *1988* Cease-fire; talks began with Iran. Iraq used chemical weapons against Kurdish

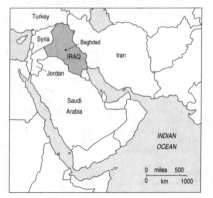

rebels seeking greater autonomy. *1989* Unsuccessful coup against President Hussein; Iraq launched ballistic missile in successful test. *1990* Peace treaty favoring Iran agreed. Aug: Iraq invaded and annexed Kuwait, precipitating another Gulf crisis.

US forces massed in Saudi Arabia at request of King Fahd. United Nations resolutions ordered Iraqi withdrawal from Kuwait and imposed total trade ban on Iraq; UN resolution sanctioning force approved. All foreign hostages released. *1991* Jan 16: US-led forces began aerial assault on Iraq; Iraq's infrastructure destroyed by bombing. Feb 23–28: land–sea–air offensive to free Kuwait successful. Uprisings of Kurds and Shiites brutally suppressed by surviving Iraqi troops. Allied troops withdrew after establishing "safe havens" for Kurds in the north, leaving a rapid-reaction force near the Turkish border. Allies threatened to bomb strategic targets in Iraq if full information about nuclear facilities denied to UN. *1992* UN imposed a "no-fly zone" over S Iraq to protect Shiites. *1993* Jan: Iraqi incursions into "no-fly zone" prompted US-led alliance aircraft to bomb "strategic" targets in Iraq. US also bombed a target in Baghdad in retaliation for an alleged plot against former president Bush, claiming "self-defense". Continued persecution of Shiites in S. *1994* Deployments of Iraqi troops along border with Kuwait prompted considerable US-led military response. *1995* UN sanctions extended. Turkish military force eliminates several PKK strongholds.

Ireland one of the British Isles, lying to the W of Great Britain, from which it is separated by the Irish Sea. It is divided into the Republic of ◊Ireland (which occupies the S, center, and NW of the island) and Northern ◊Ireland (which occupies the NE corner and forms part of the United Kingdom).

Ireland: history in prehistoric times Ireland underwent a number of invasions from Europe, the most important of which was that of the Gaels in the 3rd century BC . Christianity was introduced by St ◊Patrick about 432. From about 800 the Danes began to raid Ireland, and later founded Dublin and other coastal towns, until they were defeated by Brian Boru (king from 976) at Clontarf 1014. The Tudors adopted a policy of conquest, confiscation of Irish land, and plantation by English settlers, and further imposed the ◊Reformation and English law on Ireland. In 1641 the Irish began a revolt which was crushed by Oliver ◊Cromwell 1649. Another revolt 1689–91 was also defeated, and the Roman Catholic majority held down by penal laws. In 1739–41 a famine killed one-third of the population of 1.5 million.

William ◊Pitt induced the Irish parliament to vote itself out of existence by the Act of ◊Union, effective Jan 1, 1801, which brought Ireland under the aegis of the British crown. During another famine 1846–51, 1.5 million people emigrated, mostly to the US.

The *Easter Rising* took place April 1916, when nationalists seized the Dublin general post office and proclaimed a republic. After a week of fighting, the revolt was suppressed by the British army and most of its leaders executed. From 1918 to 1921 there was guerrilla warfare against the British army, especially by the Irish Republican Army (◊IRA), formed by Michael Collins 1919. In 1921 the Anglo-Irish Treaty resulted in partition and the creation of the Irish Free State in S Ireland. For history since that date, see ◊Ireland, Republic of; ◊Ireland, Northern.

Ireland, Northern constituent part of the United Kingdom *area* 5,196 sq mi/13,460 sq km *capital*

Belfast *towns and cities* Londonderry, Enniskillen, Omagh, Newry, Armagh, Coleraine *features* Mourne Mountains, Belfast Lough and Lough Neagh; Giant's Causeway; comprises the six counties (Antrim, Armagh, Down, Fermanagh, Derry, and Tyrone) that form part of Ireland's northernmost province of Ulster *exports* engineering, shipbuilding, textile machinery, aircraft components; linen and synthetic textiles; processed foods, especially dairy and poultry products; rubber products, chemicals *currency* pound sterling *population* (1991) 1,578,000 *languages* English; 5.3% Irish-speaking *religions* Protestant 51%, Roman Catholic 38% *famous people* Viscount Montgomery, Lord Alanbrooke *government* direct rule from the UK since 1972. Northern Ireland is entitled to send 12 members to the Westminster Parliament. The province costs the UK government £3 billion annually *history* for history pre-1921, see ↓Ireland: history The creation of Northern Ireland dates from 1921 when the Irish Free State (subsequently the Republic of Ireland) was established separately from the mainly Protestant counties of Ulster (six out of nine). In 1968–69 were there serious disturbances arising from Protestant political dominance and discrimination against the Roman Catholic minority in employment and housing. British troops were sent 1969 to restore peace and protect Catholics, but disturbances continued and in 1972 the parliament at Stormont was prorogued and superseded by direct rule from Westminster. Under the Anglo-Irish Agreement 1985, the Republic of Ireland was given a consultative role (via an Anglo-Irish conference) in the government of Northern Ireland. The agreement was approved by Parliament, but all 12 Ulster members gave up their seats, so that by-elections could be fought as a form of "referendum" on the views of the province itself. A similar boycotting of the Northern Ireland Assembly led to its dissolution 1986 by the UK government.

Talks held in Belfast April–Sept 1991—saw the first direct negotiations between the political parties for 16 years. In Sept 1993 it emerged that the Catholic nationalist Social Democratic Labour Party (SDLP) and Sinn Fein (political wing of the outlawed IRA) had held talks aimed at achieving a political settlement. This revelation prompted the British government to engage in bilateral talks with the main Northern Ireland parties, and in Dec 1993 London and Dublin issued a joint peace proposal, the Downing Street Declaration, for consideration by all parties. In August 1994 the Provisional IRA announced a unilateral cease-fire in an attempt to reach a non-violent solution.

Ireland, Republic of (*Eire*) *area* 27,146 sq mi/70,282 sq km *capital* Dublin *towns and cities* ports Cork, Dun Laoghaire, Limerick, Waterford *physical* central plateau surrounded by hills; rivers Shannon, Liffey, Boyne *features* Bog of Allen, source of domestic and national power; Macgillicuddy's Reeks, Wicklow Mountains; Lough Corrib, lakes of Killarney; Galway Bay and Aran Islands *head of state* Mary Robinson from 1990 *head of government* vacant *political system* democratic republic *political parties* Fianna Fáil (Soldiers of Destiny), moderate center-right; Fine Gael (Irish Tribe), moderate center-left; Labour Party, moderate, left of center; Progressive Democrats, radical free-enterprise *exports* livestock, dairy products, Irish whiskey, microelectronic components and assemblies, mining and engineering products, chemicals, clothing *currency* punt *population* (1993 est) 3,600,000; growth rate 0.1% p.a. *life expectancy* men 73, women

78 *languages* Irish Gaelic and English (both official) *religions* Roman Catholic 94% *literacy* 99% *GNP* $10,780 per head (1991) *chronology* *1916* Easter Rising: nationalists against British rule seized the Dublin general post office and proclaimed a republic; the revolt was suppressed by the British army and most of the leaders were executed. *1918–21* Guerrilla warfare against British army led to split in rebel forces. *1921* Anglo-Irish Treaty resulted in creation of the Irish Free State (Southern Ireland). *1937* Independence achieved from Britain. *1949* Eire left the Commonwealth and became the Republic of Ireland. *1973* Fianna Fáil defeated after 40 years in office; Liam Cosgrave formed a coalition government. *1977* Fianna Fáil returned to power, with Jack Lynch as prime minister. *1979* Lynch resigned, succeeded by Charles Haughey. *1981* Garret FitzGerald formed a coalition. *1983* New Ireland Forum formed, but rejected by the British government. *1985* Anglo-Irish Agreement signed. *1986* Protests by Ulster Unionists against the agreement. *1987* General election won by Charles Haughey. *1988* Relations with UK at low ebb because of disagreement over extradition decisions. *1989* Haughey failed to win majority in general election. Progressive Democrats given cabinet positions in coalition government. *1990* Mary Robinson elected president; John Bruton became Fine Gael leader. *1992* Jan: Haughey resigned. Feb: Albert Reynolds became Fianna Fáil leader and prime minister. June: National referendum approved ratification of Maastricht Treaty. Nov: Reynolds lost confidence vote; election result inconclusive. *1993* Fianna Fáil–Labour coalition formed; Reynolds reelected prime minister. Dec: Major and Reynolds issued joint Anglo-Irish peace proposal for Northern Ireland, the Downing Street Declaration. Six-year national development plan announced. *1994* Cease-fires announced by Catholic and Protestant paramilitaries in Northern Ireland. Nov: Reynolds resigned as premier and Fianna Fáil leader; Bertie Ahern elected new Fianna Fáil leader. John Bruton, Fine Gael, became prime minister.

Irian Jaya western portion of the island of New Guinea, part of Indonesia *area* 162,000 sq mi/420,000 sq km *capital* Jayapura *population* (1989) 1,555,700 *history* part of the Dutch East Indies 1828 as Western New Guinea; retained by the Netherlands after Indonesian independence 1949 but ceded to

Indonesia 1963 by the United Nations and remained part of Indonesia by an "Act of Free Choice" 1969. In the 1980s, 700,000 acres/283,500 hectares were given over to Indonesia's controversial transmigration program for the resettlement of farming families from overcrowded Java, causing destruction of rainforests and displacing indigenous people. In 1989 Indonesia began construction of a space launching pad on the island of Biak, near the equator, where the Earth's atmosphere is least thick.

iridium hard, brittle, silver-white, metallic element, symbol Ir, atomic number 77, atomic weight 192.2. It is twice as heavy as lead and is resistant to tarnish and corrosion. It is one of the so-called platinum group of metals; it occurs in platinum ores and as a free metal (native metal) with osmium in osmiridium, a natural alloy that includes platinum, ruthenium, and rhodium.

iris in anatomy, the colored muscular diaphragm that controls the size of the pupil in the vertebrate eye. It contains radial muscle that increases the pupil diameter and circular muscle that constricts the pupil diameter. Both types of muscle respond involuntarily to light intensity.

iris in botany, perennial northern temperate flowering plants of the genus *Iris*, family Iridaceae. The leaves are usually sword-shaped; the purple, white, or yellow flowers have three upright inner petals and three outward-and downward-curving sepals. The wild yellow iris is called flag.

iris The iris is a plant of northern temperate regions. Most have flattened leaves with large and showy flowers with an equal number of upright and pendulous petals, called standards and falls.

Irish Gaelic first official language of the Irish Republic, but much less widely used than the second official language, English. See ◊Gaelic language.

Irish Republican Army (IRA) militant Irish nationalist organization whose aim is to create a united Irish socialist republic including Ulster. The paramilitary wing of ◊Sinn Féin, it was founded 1919 by Michael Collins and fought a successful war against Britain 1919–21. It came to the fore again 1939 and its

activities intensified from 1968 onward. In 1970 a group in the north broke away to become the *Provisional IRA*, its objective being the expulsion of the British from Northern Ireland.

Committed to the use of force in trying to achieve its objectives, the IRA regularly carried out bombings and shootings. In 1979 it murdered Louis ◊Mountbatten, and its bomb attacks in Britain included an attempt to kill members of the UK cabinet during the Conservative Party conference in Brighton, Sussex, 1984. Several attacks were carried out against British military personnel serving outside the UK, especially in Germany.

In Sept 1994 the IRA announced a cessation of its military activities, responding to a joint UK-Irish peace initiative launched Dec 1993.

iron a hard, malleable and ductile, silver-gray metallic element, symbol Fe (from Latin *ferrum*), atomic number 26, atomic weight 55.847. It is the fourth-most abundant element (the second-most abundant metal after aluminum) in the Earth's crust. The central core of the Earth, the radius of which is believed to be 2,200 miles, is held to consist principally of iron with some nickel. When the amounts in the crust and core are combined, iron is probably the most abundant constituent element of the planet.

Iron Age developmental stage of human technology when weapons and tools were made from iron. Iron was produced in Thailand by about 1600 BC but was considered inferior in strength to bronze until about 1000 when metallurgical techniques improved and the alloy steel was produced by adding carbon during the smelting process.

ironclad wooden warship covered with armor plate. The first to be constructed was the French *Gloire* 1858, but the first to be launched was the British HMS *Warrior* 1859. The first battle between ironclads took place during the Civil War, when the Union *Monitor* fought the Confederate *Virginia* (formerly the *Merrimack*) March 9, 1862. The design was replaced by battleships of all-metal construction in the 1890s.

Iron Curtain in Europe after World War II, the symbolic boundary between capitalist West and communist East during the ◊Cold War. The term was popularized by the UK prime minister Winston Churchill from 1945.

Iroquois member of a confederation of NE North American Indians, the Six Nations (Cayuga, Mohawk, Oneida, Onondaga, and Seneca, with the Tuscarora after 1723), traditionally formed by Hiawatha (actually a priestly title) 1570.

The Iroquois lived in upstate New York, and their descendants live in New York, Ontario, Québec, and Oklahoma, on reservations and among the general public. The Mohawk steelworkers are famous for constructing the girders of skyscrapers such as the Empire State Building.

irradiation subjecting anything to radiation, including cancer tumors.

In optics, the term refers to the apparent enlargement of a brightly lit object when seen against a dark background.

Irrawaddy (Myanmar *Ayeryarwady*) chief river of Myanmar (Burma), flowing roughly N–S for 1,300 mi/2,090 km across the center of the country into the Bay of Bengal. Its sources are the Mali and N'mai rivers; its chief tributaries are the Chindwin and Shweli.

irrigation artificial water supply for dry agricultural areas by means of dams and channels. Drawbacks are that it tends to concentrate salts, ultimately causing soil infertility, and that rich river silt is retained at dams, to the impoverishment of the land and fisheries below them.

Isaiah In the Old Testament, the first major Hebrew prophet. The son of Amos, he was probably of high rank, and lived largely in Jerusalem.

He was influential in the court of ancient Judah until the Assyrian invasion of 701 BC .

ISBN (abbreviation for *International Standard Book Number*) code number used for ordering or classifying book titles. Every book printed now has a number on its back cover or jacket, preceded by the letters ISBN. It is a code to the country of origin and the publisher. The number is unique to the book, and will identify it anywhere in the world.

ischemic heart disease (IHD) disorder caused by reduced perfusion of the coronary arteries due to ◊atherosclerosis. It is the commonest cause of death in the Western world, leading to more than a million deaths each year in the US and about 160,000 in the UK. See also ◊coronary artery disease.

Early symptoms of IHD include ◊angina or palpitations, but sometimes a heart attack is the first indication that a person is affected.

Isfahan or *Esfahan* industrial city (steel, textiles, carpets) in central Iran; population (1986) 1,001,000. It was the ancient capital (1598–1722) of Abbas I, and its features include the Great Square, Grand Mosque, and Hall of Forty Pillars.

Isherwood Christopher (William Bradshaw) 1904–1986. British-born American novelist. He lived in Germany 1929–33 just before Hitler's rise to power, a period that inspired *Mr Norris Changes Trains* 1935 and *Goodbye to Berlin* 1939, creating the character of Sally Bowles (the basis of the musical *Cabaret* 1968). Returning to England, he collaborated with W H ◊Auden in three verse plays. He then moved to Hollywood.

Ishmael in the Old Testament, son of ◊Abraham and his wife Sarah's Egyptian maid Hagar; traditional ancestor of Mohammed and the Arab people. He and his mother were driven away by Sarah's jealousy. Muslims believe that it was Ishmael, not Isaac, whom God commanded Abraham to sacrifice, and that Ishmael helped Abraham build the Kaaba in Mecca.

Ishtar Mesopotamian goddess of love and war, worshiped by the Babylonians and Assyrians, and personified as the legendary queen Semiramis.

Isis the principal goddess of ancient Egypt. She was the daughter of Geb and Nut (Earth and Sky), and as the sister-wife of Osiris searched for his body after his death at the hands of his brother, Set. Her son Horus then defeated and captured Set, but cut off his mother's head because she would not allow Set to be killed. She was later identified with Hathor. The cult of Isis ultimately spread to Greece and Rome.

Islam religion founded in the Arabian peninsula in the early 7th century AD . It emphasizes the oneness of God, his omnipotence, benificence, and inscrutability. The sacred book is the *Koran* of the prophet ◊Mohammed, the Prophet or Messenger of Allah. There are two main Muslim sects: ◊*Sunni* and ◊*Shiite*. Other schools include *Sufism*, a mystical movement originating in the 8th century.

Islamabad capital of Pakistan from 1967, in the Potwar district, at the foot of the Margala Hills and immediately NW of Rawalpindi; population (1981) 201,000. The city was designed by Constantinos Doxiadis in the 1960s. The Federal Capital Territory of Islamabad has an area of 350 sq mi/907 sq km and a population (1985) of 379,000.

island area of land surrounded entirely by water. Australia is classed as a continent rather than an island, because of its size.

Isle of Man see ◊Man, Isle of.

Isle of Wight see ◊Wight, Isle of.

Ismail I 1486–1524. Shah of Persia from 1501, founder of the *Safavi dynasty*, who established the first national government since the Arab conquest and Shiite Islam as the national religion.

ISO abbreviation for ◊*International Organization for Standardization*.

isobar line drawn on maps and weather charts linking all places with the same atmospheric pressure (usually measured in millibars).

When used in weather forecasting, the distance between the isobars is an indication of the barometric gradient.

isogram or *isoline* on a map, a line that joins places of equal value. Examples are contour lines (joining places of equal height), ◊isobars (for equal pressure), isotherms (for equal temperature), and isohyets (for equal rainfall). Isograms are most effective when values change gradually and when there is plenty of data.

isolationism in politics, concentration on internal rather than foreign affairs; a foreign policy having no interest in international affairs that do not affect the country's own interests.

In the US, isolationism is as old as George Washington, who warned against "entangling alliances". Today it is usually associated with the Republican Party, especially politicians of the Midwest (for example, the Neutrality Acts 1935–39). Intervention by the US in both World Wars was initially resisted. In the 1960s some Republicans demanded the removal of the United Nations from American soil.

Isolde or *Iseult* in Celtic and medieval legend, the wife of King Mark of Cornwall who was brought from Ireland by his nephew ◊Tristan. She and Tristan accidentally drank the aphrodisiac given to her by her mother for her marriage, were separated as lovers, and finally died together.

isomer chemical compound having the same molecular composition and mass as another, but with different physical or chemical properties owing to the different structural arrangement of its constituent atoms. For example, the organic compounds butane $(CH_3(CH_2)_2CH_3)$ and methyl propane $(CH_3CH(CH_3)CH_3)$ are isomers, each possessing four carbon atoms and ten hydrogen atoms but differing in the way that these are arranged with respect to each other.

isotope one of two or more atoms that have the same atomic number (same number of protons), but which contain a different number of neutrons, thus differing in their atomic masses. They may be stable or radioactive, naturally occurring or synthesized. The term was coined by English chemist Frederick Soddy, pioneer researcher in atomic disintegration.

Israel State of (*Medinat Israel*) *area* 8,029 sq mi/20,800 sq km (as at 1949 armistice) *capital* Jerusalem (not recognized by the United Nations) *towns and cities* ports Tel Aviv/Jaffa, Haifa, 'Akko (formerly Acre), Eilat; Bat-Yam, Holon, Ramat Gan, Petach Tikva, Beersheba *physical* coastal plain of Sharon between Haifa and Tel Aviv noted since ancient times for fertility; central mountains of Galilee, Samariq, and Judea; Dead Sea, Lake Tiberias, and river Jordan Rift Valley along the E are below sea level; Negev Desert in the S; Israel occupies Golan Heights, West Bank, and Gaza *features* historic sites: Jerusalem, Bethlehem, Nazareth, Masada, Megiddo, Jericho; caves of the Dead Sea scrolls *head of state* Ezer Weizman from 1993 *head of government* Yitzhak Rabin from 1992 *political system* democratic republic *political parties* Israel Labour Party, moderate, left of center; Consolidation Party (Likud), right of center; Meretz (Vitality), left-of-center alliance *exports* citrus and other fruit, avocados, chinese leaves, fertilizers, diamonds, plastics, petrochemicals, textiles, electronics (military, medical, scientific, industrial), electro-optics, precision instruments, aircraft and missiles *currency* shekel *population* (1993) 5,300,000 (including 750,000 Arab Israeli citizens and over 1 million Arabs in the occupied territories); under the Law of Return 1950, "every Jew shall be entitled to come to Israel as an immigrant"; those from the East and E Europe are Ashkenazim, and those from Mediterranean Europe (Spain, Portugal, Italy, France, Greece) and Arab N Africa are Sephardim (over 50% of the population is now of Sephardic descent). Between Jan 1990 and April 1991, 250,000 Soviet Jews emigrated to Israel. An Israeli-born Jew is a Sabra. About 500,000 Israeli Jews are resident in the US. Growth rate 1.8% p.a. *life expectancy* men 74, women 78 *languages* Hebrew and Arabic (official); English, Yiddish, European, and W Asian languages *religions* Israel is a secular state, but the predominant faith is Judaism 83%; also Sunni Muslim, Christian, and Druse *literacy* 96% *GNP* $11,330 per head (1991) *chronology* **1948** Independent State of Israel proclaimed with David Ben-Gurion as prime minister; attacked by Arab nations, Israel won the War of Independence. Many displaced Arabs settled in refugee camps in the Gaza Strip and West Bank. **1952** Col Gamal Nasser of Egypt stepped up blockade of Israeli ports and support of Arab guerrillas in Gaza. **1956** Israel invaded Gaza and Sinai. **1957** Israel with-

drew from Gaza Strip under United Nations and US pressure. **1959** Egypt renewed blockade of Israeli trade through Suez Canal. **1963** Ben-Gurion resigned, succeeded by Levi Eshkol. **1964** Palestine Liberation Organization (PLO) founded with the aim of overthrowing the state of Israel. **1967** Nasser calls for destruction of Israel. Arab nations mobilize forces. Israel victorious in the Six-Day War. Gaza, West Bank, E Jerusalem, Sinai, and Golan Heights captured. **1968** Israel Labour Party formed, led by Golda Meir. **1969** Golda Meir became prime minister. **1973** Yom Kippur War: Israel attacked by Egypt and Syria. **1974** Golda Meir succeeded by Yitzhak Rabin. **1975** Suez Canal reopened. **1977** Menachem Begin elected prime minister. Egyptian president addressed the Knesset. **1978** Camp David talks. **1979** Egyptian-Israeli agreement signed. Israel agreed to withdraw from Sinai. **1980** Jerusalem declared capital of Israel. **1981** Golan Heights formally annexed. **1982** Israel pursued PLO fighters into Lebanon. **1983** Peace treaty between Israel and Lebanon signed but not ratified. **1985** Formation of government of national unity with Labour and Likud ministers. **1986** Yitzhak Shamir took over from Peres under power-sharing agreement. **1987** Outbreak of Palestinian uprising (Intifada) in West Bank and Gaza. **1988** Criticism of Israel's handling of Palestinian uprising in occupied territories; PLO acknowledged Israel's right to exist. **1989** New Likud–Labour coalition government formed under Shamir. Limited progress achieved on proposals for negotiations leading to elections in occupied territories. **1990** Coalition collapsed due to differences over peace process; international condemnation of Temple Mount killings. New Shamir right-wing coalition formed. **1991** Shamir gave cautious response to Middle East peace proposals. Some Palestinian prisoners released. Peace talks began in Madrid. **1992** Jan: Shamir lost majority in Knesset. June: Labour Party, led by Yitzhak Rabin, won elections; coalition formed under Rabin. Aug: US-Israeli loan agreement signed. Dec: 400 Hamas Islamic fundamentalists summarily expelled. **1993** Jan: Ban on contacts with PLO formally lifted. Feb: 100 of the expelled fundamentalists allowed to return. March: Ezer Weizman elected president; Binyamin "Bibi" Netanyahu elected leader of Likud party. July: Israel launched attacks against Hezbollah in S Lebanon. Sept: historic accord of mutual recognition signed by Israel and PLO, to result in partial autonomy for Palestinians and phased Israeli withdrawal from parts of occupied territories. Dec: last of Palestinian deportees in S Lebanon repatriated. **1994** Peace process threatened by extremist violence in occupied territories. May: first phase of 1993 peace accord (the Gaza–Jericho agreement) implemented: Israeli troops withdrawn, Palestinian police force drafted in. July: PLO leader, Yassir Arafat, returned to head interim governing body, the Palestinian National Authority (PNA). Peace agreement signed with Jordan. Violent attacks by Islamic extremists continued.

Istanbul city and chief seaport of Turkey; population (1990) 6,620,200. It produces textiles, tobacco, cement, glass, and leather. Founded as *Byzantium* about 660 BC, it was renamed *Constantinople* AD 330 and was the capital of the ◊Byzantine Empire until captured by the Turks 1453. As *Istamboul* it was capital of the Ottoman Empire until 1922.

IT abbreviation for ◊*information technology*.

Itaipu world's largest hydroelectric plant, situated on

the Paraná River, SW Brazil. A joint Brazilian-Paraguayan venture, it came into operation 1984; it supplies hydroelectricity to a wide area.

Italian native to or an inhabitant of Italy and their descendants, culture, and language. The language belongs to the Romance group of Indo-European languages.

Italian is spoken in S Switzerland and in areas of Italian settlement in the US, Argentina, the UK, Canada, and Australia.

Italian Somaliland former Italian trust territory on the Somali coast of Africa extending to 194,999 sq mi/502,300 sq km. Established 1892, it was extended 1925 with the acquisition of Jubaland from Kenya; administered from Mogadishu; under British rule 1941–50. Thereafter it reverted to Italian authority before uniting with British Somaliland 1960 to form the independent state of Somalia.

Italy Republic of (*Repubblica Italiana*) *area* 116,332 sq mi/301,300 sq km *capital* Rome *towns and cities* Milan, Turin; ports Naples, Genoa, Palermo, Bari, Catania, Trieste *physical* mountainous (Maritime Alps, Dolomites, Apennines) with narrow coastal lowlands; rivers Po, Adige, Arno, Tiber, Rubicon; islands of Sicily, Sardinia, Elba, Capri, Ischia, Lipari, Pantelleria; lakes Como, Maggiore, Garda *environment* Milan has the highest recorded level of sulfur-dioxide pollution of any city in the world. The Po River, with pollution ten times higher than officially recommended levels, is estimated to discharge around 250 metric tons of arsenic into the sea each year *features* continental Europe's only active volcanoes: Vesuvius, Etna, Stromboli; historic towns include Venice, Florence, Siena, Rome; Greek, Roman, Etruscan archeological sites *head of state* Oscar Luigi Scalfaro from 1992 *head of government* Lamberto Dini from 1995 *political system* democratic republic *political parties* Forza Italia, free-market, right of center; Northern League (LN), Milan-based, federalist, right of center; National Alliance (AN), neofascist (formerly the Italian Social Movement: MSI); Italian Popular Party (PPI), Catholic, centrist; Democratic Party of the Left (PDS), pro-European socialist (ex-communist); Italian Socialist Party (PSI), moderate socialist; Italian Republican Party (PRI), social democratic, left of center; Italian Social Democratic Party (PSDI), moderate, left of center; Liberals (PLI), right of center; Christian Democratic Center, Christian, centrist; Progressives, left-wing alliance; Democratic Monarchist Party, right of center *exports* wine (world's largest producer), fruit, vegetables, textiles (Europe's largest silk producer), clothing, leather goods, motor vehicles, electrical goods, chemicals, marble (Carrara), sulfur, mercury, iron, steel *currency* lira *population* (1993 est) 58,100,000; growth rate 0.1% p.a. *life expectancy* men 73, women 80 *languages* Italian; German, French, Slovene, and Albanian minorities *religion* Roman Catholic 100% (state religion) *literacy* men 98%, women 96% *GNP* $18,580 per head (1991) *chronology 1946* Monarchy replaced by a republic. *1948* New constitution adopted. *1954* Trieste (claimed by Yugoslavia after World War II) was divided between Italy and Yugoslavia. *1976* Communists proposed establishment of broad-based, left–right government, the "historic compromise"; rejected by Christian Democrats. *1978* Christian Democrat Aldo Moro, architect of the historic compromise, kidnapped and murdered by Red Brigade guerrillas infiltrated by Western intelligence agents. *1983* Bettino Craxi, a Socialist, became leader of broad coalition government. *1987* Craxi resigned; succeeding coalition fell within months. *1988* Christian Democrats' leader Ciriaco de Mita established five-party coalition including the Socialists. *1989* De Mita resigned after disagreements within his coalition government; succeeded by Giulio Andreotti. De Mita lost leadership of Christian Democrats; Communists formed "shadow government". *1991* Referendum approved electoral reform. *1992* Ruling coalition lost its majority in general election; President Cossiga resigned, replaced by Oscar Luigi Scalfaro. Giuliano Amato, deputy leader of PDS, accepted premiership. Lira devalued; Italy withdrew from Exchange Rate Mechanism. *1993* Investigation of corruption network exposed Mafia links with several notable politicians, including Craxi and Andreotti. Craxi resigned Socialist Party leadership; replaced by Giorgio Benvenutu and then Ottaviano del Turro. Amato resigned premiership; Carlo Ciampi, with no party allegiance, named as his successor. New electoral system adopted, based on 75% majority voting. *1994* Jan: Ciampi resigned pending general election. March: elections won by right-wing alliance led by Silvio Berlusconi. Coalition government formed with Berlusconi as premier. Members of neofascist AN given cabinet posts. *1995* Lamberto Dini became head of government.

iteration in computing, a method of solving a problem by performing the same steps repeatedly until a certain condition is satisfied. For example, in one method of ◊sorting, adjacent items are repeatedly exchanged until the data are in the required sequence.

iteration in mathematics, method of solving ◊equations by a series of approximations which approach the exact solution more and more closely. For example, to find the square root of N, start with a guess n_1; calculate $N/n_1 = x_1$; calculate $(n_1 + x_1)/2 = n_2$; calculate $N/n_1 = x_2$; calculate $(n_2 + x_2)/2 = n_3$. The sequence n_1, n_2, n_3 approaches the exact square root of N. Iterative methods are particularly suitable for work with computers and programmable calculators.

Itō Hirobumi, Prince 1841–1909. Japanese politician, prime minister 1887, 1892–96, 1898, 1900–01. He was a key figure in the modernization of Japan and was

involved in the Meiji restoration 1866–68 and in official missions to study forms of government in the US and Europe in the 1870s and 1880s. As minister for home affairs, he helped draft the Meiji constitution of 1889.

Ivan (III) the Great 1440–1505. Grand duke of Muscovy from 1462, who revolted against Tatar overlordship by refusing tribute to Grand Khan Ahmed 1480. He claimed the title of czar, and used the double-headed eagle as the Russian state emblem.

Ivan (IV) the Terrible 1530–1584. Grand duke of Muscovy from 1533; he assumed power 1544 and was crowned as first czar of Russia 1547. He conquered Kazan 1552, Astrakhan 1556, and Siberia 1581. He reformed the legal code and local administration 1555 and established trade relations with England. In his last years he alternated between debauchery and religious austerities, executing thousands and, in rage, his own son.

IVF abbreviation for ◊*in vitro fertilization.*

Iviza alternative spelling of ◊Ibiza, one of the ◊Balearic Islands.

ivory the hard white substance of which the teeth and tusks of certain mammals are composed. Among the most valuable are elephants' tusks, which are of unusual hardness and density. Ivory is used in carving and other decorative work, and is so valuable that poachers continue to illegally destroy the remaining wild elephant herds in Africa to obtain it.

Ivory Coast Republic of (*République de la Côte d'Ivoire*) *area* 124,471 sq mi/322,463 sq km *capital* Yamoussoukro *towns and cities* Bouaké, Daloa, Man; ports Abidjan, San-Pédro *physical* tropical rainforest (diminishing as exploited) in S; savanna and low mountains in N *environment* an estimated 85% of the country's forest has been destroyed by humans *features* Vridi canal, Kossou dam, Monts du Toura *head of state* Henri Konan Bedie from 1993 *head of government* Kablan Daniel Duncan from 1993 *political system* emergent democratic republic *political parties* Democratic Party of the Ivory Coast–African Democratic Rally (PDCI–RDA), nationalist, free-enterprise; Ivorian Popular Front (FPI), left of center *exports* coffee, cocoa, timber, petroleum products *currency* franc CFA *population* (1993 est) 13,500,000; growth rate 3.3% p.a. *life expectancy* men 53, women 56 *languages* French (official), over 60 native dialects

media the government has full control of the media *religions* animist 65%, Muslim 24%, Christian 11% *literacy* men 67%, women 40% *GNP* $690 per head (1991) *chronology 1904* Became part of French West Africa. *1958* Achieved internal self-government. *1960* Independence achieved from France, with Félix Houphouët-Boigny as president of a one-party state. *1985* Houphouët-Boigny reelected, unopposed. *1986* Name changed officially from Ivory Coast to Côte d'Ivoire. *1990* Houphouët-Boigny and PDCI reelected. *1993* Houphouët-Boigny died and was succeeded by parliamentary speaker, Henri Konan Bedie. Kablan Daniel Duncan appointed prime minister.

ivy any tree or shrub of the genus *Hedera* of the ginseng family Araliaceae. English or European ivy *H. helix* has shiny, evergreen, triangular or oval-shaped leaves, and clusters of small, yellowish-green flowers, followed by black berries. It climbs by means of rootlike suckers put out from its stem, and is injurious to trees.

Iwo Jima largest of the Japanese Volcano Islands in the W Pacific Ocean, 760 mi/1,222 km S of Tokyo; area 8 sq mi/21 sq km. Annexed by Japan 1891, it was captured by the US 1945 after fierce fighting. It was returned to Japan 1968.

Iwo Jima, Battle of intense fighting between Japanese and US forces Feb 19–March 17, 1945, during World War II. In Feb 1945, US marines landed on the island of Iwo Jima, a Japanese air base, intending to use it to prepare for a planned final assault on mainland Japan. The Japanese defenses were so strong that 5,000 US marines were killed before the island was captured from the Japanese.

Izetbegović Alija 1925– . Bosnia-Herzegovinan politician, president from 1990. A lifelong opponent of communism, he founded the Party of Democratic Action (PDA) 1990, ousting the communists in the multiparty elections that year. Adopting a moderate stance during the civil war in Bosnia-Herzegovina, he sought an honorable peace for his country in the face of ambitious demands from Serb and Croat political leaders.

Izmir formerly *Smyrna* port and naval base in Turkey; population (1990) 1,757,400. Products include steel, electronics, and plastics. The largest annual trade fair in the Middle East is held here. It is the headquarters of ◊North Atlantic Treaty Organization SE Command.

J in physics, the symbol for *joule*, the SI unit of energy.

jabiru stork *Jabiru mycteria* found in Central and South America. It is 5 ft/1.5 m high with white plumage. The head is black and red.

jacamar insect-eating bird of the family Galbulidae, in the same order as woodpeckers, found in Central and South America. It has a long, sharp-pointed bill, long tail, and paired toes. The plumage is brilliantly colored. The largest species grows up to 12 in/30 cm.

jacana one of seven species of wading birds, family Jacanidae, with very long toes and claws enabling it to walk on the flat leaves of river plants, hence the name "lily trotter". Jacanas are found in Mexico, Central America, South America, Africa, S Asia, and Australia. The female pheasant-tailed jacana *Hydrophasianus chirurgus* of Asia has a "harem" of two to four males.

jacaranda any tropical American tree of the genus *Jacaranda* of the bignonia family Bignoniaceae, with fragrant wood and showy blue or violet flowers, commonly cultivated in the southern US.

jackal any of several wild dogs of the genus *Canis*, found in S Asia, S Europe, and N Africa. Jackals can grow to 2.7 ft/80 cm long, and have grayish-brown fur and a bushy tail.

jackdaw Eurasian bird *Corvus monedula* of the crow family. It is mainly black, but grayish on sides and back of head, and about 1.1 ft/33 cm long. It nests in tree holes or on buildings.

Jackson largest city and capital of Mississippi, on the Pearl River; population (1990) 196,600. It produces furniture, cottonseed oil, and iron and steel castings, and owes its prosperity to the discovery of gas fields to the S in the 1930s. Named after Andrew Jackson, later president, it dates from 1821 and was virtually

jacana The American jacana, or lily trotter, is a common waterbird of lagoons and marshes in Mexico and Central America. Jacanas have extremely long toes and claws for walking on floating vegetation.

destroyed by Union troops 1863, during the Civil War.
Educational institutions include Jackson State University, Millsaps College, and the University of Mississippi Medical Center.

Jackson Andrew 1767–1845. 7th president of the US 1829–37, a Democrat. A major general in the War of 1812, he defeated a British force at New Orleans in 1815 (after the official end of the war in 1814) and was involved in the war that led to the purchase of Florida in 1819. The political organization he built as president, with Martin Van Buren (1782–1862), was the basis for the modern ◊Democratic Party.

Jackson Glenda 1936– . English actress and politician. She has made many stage appearances, including *Marat/Sade* 1966, and her films include the Oscar-winning *Women in Love* 1969, *Sunday Bloody Sunday* 1971, and *A Touch of Class* 1973. On television she played Queen Elizabeth I in *Elizabeth R* 1971. In 1992 she was elected to Parliament as a Labour Party member.

Jackson Jesse 1941– . US Democratic politician, a cleric and campaigner for minority rights. He contested his party's 1984 and 1988 presidential nominations in an effort to increase voter registration and to put black issues on the national agenda. He is an eloquent public speaker.

Jackson Michael 1958– . US rock singer and songwriter. His videos and live performances are meticulously choreographed. His first solo hit was "Got to Be There" 1971; his worldwide popularity peaked with the albums *Thriller* 1982 and *Bad* 1987. The follow-up was *Dangerous* 1991.

Jackson Stonewall (Thomas Jonathan) 1824–1863. US Confederate general in the Civil War. He acquired his nickname and his reputation at the Battle of Bull Run, from the firmness with which his brigade resisted the Northern attack.
In 1862 he organized the Shenandoah Valley campaign and assisted Robert E ◊Lee's invasion of Maryland. He helped to defeat General Joseph E Hooker's Union army at the Battle of Chancellorsville, Virginia, but was fatally wounded by one of his own soldiers in the confusion of battle.
A West Point graduate, after serving in the Mexican War 1846–48, he became professor of military tactics at the Virginia military institute.

Jacksonville port, resort, and commercial center in NE Florida, US; population (1990) 673,000. The port has naval installations and ship-repair yards. To the N the Cross-Florida Barge Canal links the Atlantic with the Gulf of Mexico. Manufactured goods include wood and paper products, chemicals, and processed food.

Jack the Ripper popular name for the unidentified mutilator and murderer of at least five women prostitutes in the Whitechapel area of London in 1888.
Several suspects have been suggested in extensive studies of the case, including members of the royal household.

Jacob in the Old Testament, Hebrew patriarch, son of Isaac and Rebecca, who obtained the rights of seniority from his twin brother Esau by trickery. He married his cousins Leah and Rachel, serving their father Laban seven years for each, and at the time of famine in Canaan joined his son Joseph in Egypt. His 12 sons were the traditional ancestors of the 12 tribes of Israel.

Jacobin member of an extremist republican club of the French Revolution founded at Versailles 1789, which later used a former Jacobin (Dominican) friary as its headquarters in Paris. Helped by ◊Danton's speeches, they proclaimed the French republic, had the king executed, and overthrew the moderate ◊Girondists 1792–93. Through the Committee of Public Safety, they began the Reign of Terror, led by ◊Robespierre. After its execution 1794, the club was abandoned and the name "Jacobin" passed into general use for any left-wing extremist.

Jacobite in Britain, a supporter of the royal house of Stuart after the deposition of James II in 1688. They include the Scottish Highlanders, who rose unsuccessfully under Claverhouse in 1689; and those who rose in Scotland and N England under the leadership of ◊James Edward Stuart, the Old Pretender, in 1715, and followed his son ◊Charles Edward Stuart in an invasion of England that reached Derby in 1745–46. After the defeat at ◊Culloden, Jacobitism disappeared as a political force.

jade semiprecious stone consisting of either jadeite, $NaAlSi_2O_6$ (a pyroxene), or nephrite, $Ca_2(Mg,Fe)_5$ $Si_8O_{22}(OH,F)_2$ (an amphibole), ranging from colorless through shades of green to black according to the iron content. Jade ranks 5.5–6.5 on the Mohs' scale of hardness.

Jaffa (biblical name *Joppa*) port in W Israel, part of ◊Tel Aviv from 1950.

jaguar largest species of ◊cat *Panthera onca* in the Americas, formerly ranging from the southwestern US to southern South America, but now extinct in most of North America. It can grow up to 8 ft/2.5 m long including the tail.

The background color of the fur varies from creamy white to brown or black, and is covered with black spots. The jaguar is usually solitary.

jaguarundi wild cat *Felis yaguoaroundi* found in forests in Central and South America. Up to 3.5 ft/1.1 m long, it is very slim with rather short legs and short rounded ears. It is uniformly colored dark brown or chestnut. A good climber, it feeds on birds and small mammals and, unusually for a cat, has been reported to eat fruit.

Jahangir "Holder of the World". Adopted name of Salim 1569–1627. Third Mogul emperor of India 1605–27, succeeding his father ◊Akbar the Great. The first part of his reign was marked by peace, prosperity and a flowering of the arts, but the latter half by rebellion and succession conflicts.

Jainism ancient Indian religion, sometimes regarded as an offshoot of Hinduism. Jains emphasize the importance of not injuring living beings, and their code of ethics is based on sympathy and compassion for all forms of life. They also believe in ◊karma but not in any deity. It is a monastic, ascetic religion. There are two main sects: the Digambaras and the Swetambaras. Jainism practises the most extreme form of nonviolence (*ahimsa⁻*) of all Indian sects, and influenced the philosophy of Mahatma Gandhi. Jains number

approximately 6 million; there are Jain communities throughout the world but the majority live in India.

Jaipur capital of Rajasthan, India; population (1981) 1,005,000. It was formerly the capital of the state of Jaipur, which was merged with Rajasthan 1949. Products include textiles and metal products.

Jakarta or *Djakarta* (formerly until 1949 *Batavia*) capital of Indonesia on the NW coast of Java; population (1980) 6,504,000. Industries include textiles, chemicals, and plastics; a canal links it with its port of Tanjung Priok where rubber, oil, tin, coffee, tea, and palm oil are among its exports; also a tourist center. Jakarta was founded by Dutch traders 1619.

Jamaica *area* 4,230 sq mi/10,957 sq km *capital* Kingston *towns and cities* Montego Bay, Spanish Town, St Andrew *physical* mountainous tropical island *features* Blue Mountains (so called because of the haze over them) renowned for their coffee; partly undersea ruins of pirate city of Port Royal, destroyed by an earthquake 1692 *head of state* Elizabeth II from 1962, represented by governor general Howard Felix Hanlan Cooke from 1991 *head of government* P.J. Patterson from 1992 *political system* constitutional monarchy *political parties* Jamaica Labour Party (JLP), moderate, centrist; People's National Party (PNP), left of center *exports* sugar, bananas, bauxite, rum, cocoa, coconuts, liqueurs, cigars, citrus *currency* Jamaican dollar *population* (1993 est) 2,523,000 (African 76%, mixed 15%, Chinese, Caucasian, East Indian); growth rate 2.2% p.a. *life expectancy* men 71, women 76 *languages* English, Jamaican creole *media* one daily newspaper 1834–1988 (except 1973–82), privately owned; sensational evening and weekly papers *religions* Protestant 70%, Rastafarian *literacy* men 98%, women 99% *GNP* $1,292 per head (1992) *chronology* *1494* Columbus reached Jamaica. *1509–1655* Occupied by Spanish. *1655* Captured by British. *1944* Internal self-government introduced. *1962* Independence achieved from Britain, with Alexander Bustamante of the JLP as prime minister. *1967* JLP reelected under Hugh Shearer. *1972* Michael Manley of the PNP became prime minister. *1980* JLP elected, with Edward Seaga as prime minister. *1983* JLP reelected, winning all 60 seats. *1988* Island badly damaged by Hurricane Gilbert. *1989* PNP won a decisive victory with Michael Manley returning as prime minister. *1992* Manley resigned, succeeded by P J Patterson. *1993* Landslide victory for PNP in general election.

James Henry 1843–1916. US novelist. He lived in Europe from 1875 and became a naturalized British subject 1915. His novels deal with the social, moral, and esthetic issues arising from the complex relationship of European to American culture. Initially a master of psychological realism, noted for the complex subtlety of his prose style, James became increasingly experimental, writing some of the essential works of early Modernism. His major novels include *The Portrait of a Lady* 1881, *The Bostonians* 1886, *What Maisie Knew* 1887, *The Ambassadors* 1903, and *The Golden Bowl* 1904. He also wrote more than a hundred shorter works of fiction, notably the novella *The Aspern Papers* 1888 and the supernatural/psychological riddle *The Turn of the Screw* 1898.

James Jesse 1847–1882. US bank and train robber, born in Missouri and a leader, with his brother Frank (1843–1915), of the Quantrill raiders, a Confederate guerrilla band in the Civil War. Frank later led his own gang.

Jesse was killed by Bob Ford, an accomplice; Frank remained unconvicted and became a farmer.

James P(hyllis) D(orothy), Baroness 1920– . English detective novelist. She created the characters Superintendent Adam Dalgliesh and private investigator Cordelia Gray. She was a tax official, hospital administrator, and civil servant before turning to writing. Her books include *Death of an Expert Witness* 1977, *The Skull Beneath the Skin* 1982, and *A Taste for Death* 1986.

James I 1566–1625. King of England from 1603 and Scotland (as *James VI*) from 1567. The son of Mary Queen of Scots and Lord Darnley, he succeeded on his mother's abdication from the Scottish throne, assumed power 1583, established a strong centralized authority, and in 1589 married Anne of Denmark (1574–1619).

As successor to Elizabeth I in England, he alienated the Puritans by his High Church views and Parliament by his assertion of ◊divine right, and was generally unpopular because of his favorites, such as Buckingham, and his schemes for an alliance with Spain. He was succeeded by his son Charles I.

James I 1394–1437. King of Scotland 1406–37, who assumed power 1424. He was a cultured and strong monarch whose improvements in the administration of justice brought him popularity among the common people. He was assassinated by a group of conspirators led by the Earl of Atholl.

James II 1633–1701. King of England and Scotland (as *James VII*) from 1685, second son of Charles I. He succeeded Charles II. James married Anne Hyde 1659 (1637–1671, mother of Mary II and Anne) and Mary of Modena 1673 (mother of James Edward Stuart). He became a Catholic 1671, which led first to attempts to exclude him from the succession, then to the rebellions of Monmouth and Argyll, and finally to the Whig and Tory leaders' invitation to William of Orange to take the throne in 1688. James fled to France, then led an uprising in Ireland 1689, but after defeat at the Battle of the ◊Boyne 1690 remained in exile in France.

James II 1430–1460. King of Scotland from 1437, who assumed power 1449. The only surviving son of James I, he was supported by most of the nobles and parliament. He sympathized with the Lancastrians during the Wars of the ◊Roses, and attacked English possessions in S Scotland. He was killed while besieging Roxburgh Castle.

James III 1451–1488. King of Scotland from 1460, who assumed power 1469. His reign was marked by rebellions by the nobles, including his brother Alexander, Duke of Albany. He was murdered during a rebellion supported by his son, who then ascended the throne as James IV.

James IV 1473–1513. King of Scotland from 1488, who married Margaret (1489–1541, daughter of Henry VII) in 1503. He came to the throne after his followers murdered his father, James III, at Sauchieburn. His reign was internally peaceful, but he allied himself with France against England, invaded 1513 and was defeated and killed at the Battle of ◊Flodden. James IV was a patron of poets and architects as well as a military leader.

James V 1512–1542. King of Scotland from 1513, who assumed power 1528. During the long period of his minority, he was caught in a struggle between pro-French and pro-English factions. When he assumed power, he allied himself with France and upheld Catholicism against the Protestants. Following an attack on Scottish territory by Henry VIII's forces, he was defeated near the border at Solway Moss 1542.

James VI of Scotland. See ◊James I of England.

James VII of Scotland. See ◊James II of England.

James Edward Stuart 1688–1766. British prince, known as the *Old Pretender* (for the ◊Jacobites, he was James III). Son of James II, he was born at St James's Palace and after the revolution of 1688 was taken to France. He landed in Scotland in 1715 to head a Jacobite rebellion but withdrew through lack of support. In his later years he settled in Rome.

Janáček Leoš 1854–1928. Czech composer. He became director of the Conservatoire at Brno 1919 and professor at the Prague Conservatoire 1920. His music, highly original and influenced by Moravian folk music, includes arrangements of folk songs, operas (*Jenufa* 1904, *The Cunning Little Vixen* 1924), and the choral *Glagolitic Mass* 1926.

Janus in Roman mythology, the god of doorways and passageways, patron of the beginning of the day, month, and year, after whom January is named; he is represented as having two faces, one looking forward and one back. In Roman ritual, the doors of Janus in the Forum were closed when peace was established.

Japan (*Nippon*) *area* 145,822 sq mi/377,535 sq km *capital* Tokyo *towns and cities* Fukuoka, Kitakyushu, Kyoto, Sapporo; ports Osaka, Nagoya, Yokohama, Kobe, Kawasaki *physical* mountainous, volcanic; comprises over 1,000 islands, the largest of which are Hokkaido, Honshu, Kyushu, and Shikoku *features* Mount Fuji, Mount Aso (volcanic), Japan Alps, Inland Sea archipelago *head of state* (figurehead) Emperor Akihito (Heisei) from 1989 *head of government* Tomiichi Murayama from 1994 *political system* liberal democracy *political parties* Liberal Democratic Party (LDP), right of center; Social Democratic Party of Japan (SDJP), former Socialist Party, left of center but moving toward center; Komeito (Clean Government Party), Buddhist, centrist; Democratic Socialist Party, centrist; Japanese Communist Party (JCP), socialist; Shinseito (Renewai Party), right-wing reformist; Japan New Party (JNP), centrist reformist *exports* televisions, cassette and video recorders, radios, cameras, computers, robots, other electronic and electrical equipment, motor vehicles, ships, iron, steel, chemicals, textiles *currency* yen *population* (1993 est) 124,900,000; growth rate 0.5% p.a. *life expectancy* men 76, women

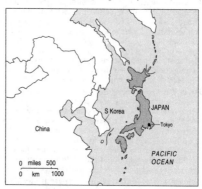

82 *languages* Japanese *religions* Shinto, Buddhist (often combined), Christian; 30% claim a personal religious faith *literacy* 99% *GNP* $29,794 per head (1992) *chronology 1867* End of shogun rule; executive power passed to emperor. Start of modernization of Japan. *1894–95* War with China; Formosa (Taiwan) and S Manchuria gained. *1902* Formed alliance with Britain. *1904–05* War with Russia; Russia ceded southern half of Sakhalin. *1910* Japan annexed Korea. *1914* Joined Allies in World War I. *1918* Received German Pacific islands as mandates. *1931–32* War with China; renewed 1937. *1941* Japan attacked US fleet at Pearl Harbor Dec 7 *1945* World War II ended with Japanese surrender. Allied control commission took power. Formosa and Manchuria returned to China. *1946* Framing of "peace constitution". Emperor Hirohito became figurehead ruler. *1952* Full sovereignty regained. *1958* Joined United Nations. *1968* Bonin and Volcano Islands regained. *1972* Ryukyu Islands regained. *1974* Prime Minister Tanaka resigned over Lockheed bribes scandal. *1982* Yasuhiro Nakasone elected prime minister. *1985* Yen revalued. *1987* Noboru Takeshita chosen to succeed Nakasone. *1988* Recruit scandal cast shadow over government and opposition parties. *1989* Emperor Hirohito (Sho¯wa) died; succeeded by his son Akihito. Many cabinet ministers implicated in Recruit scandal and Takeshita resigned; succeeded by Sosuke Uno. Aug: Uno resigned after sex scandal; succeeded by Toshiki Kaifu. *1990* Feb: new house of councillors' elections won by LDP. Public-works budget increased by 50% to encourage imports. *1991* Japan contributed billions of dollars to the Gulf War and its aftermath. Kaifu succeeded by Kiichi Miyazawa. *1992* Over 100 politicians implicated in new financial scandal. Emperor Akihito made first Japanese imperial visit to China. Trade surpluses reached record levels. *1993* Worst recession of postwar era but trade surpluses again reached record levels. Government lost no-confidence vote over electoral reform. LDP failed to win majority in general election, ending 38 years in power; Miyazawa resigned. New parties formed from LDP factions. Morihiro Hosokawa chosen as premier, heading non-LDP coalition. *1994* Feb: compromise political-reform package passed, after initial rejection by upper house. April: Hosokawa resigned, accused of corruption; Tsutomu Hata appointed prime minister, heading minority coalition government. June: Hata resigned; succeeded by SDJP leader, Tomiichi Murayama, leading an LDP-dominated coalition.

Jaruzelski Wojciech 1923– . Polish general, communist leader from 1981, president 1985–90. He imposed martial law for the first year of his rule, suppressed the opposition, and banned labor-union activity, but later released many political prisoners. In 1989, elections in favor of the free labor union Solidarity forced Jaruzelski to speed up democratic reforms, overseeing a transition to a new form of "socialist pluralist" democracy and stepping down as president 1990.

Jarvik 7 the first successful artificial heart intended for permanent implantation in a human being. Made from polyurethane plastic and aluminum, it is powered by compressed air. Barney Clark became the first person to receive a Jarvik 7, in Salt Lake City, Utah, Dec 1982; it kept him alive for 112 days.

The US Food and Drug Administration subsequently withdrew approval for artificial heart transplants because of evidence of adverse reactions.

jasmine any subtropical plant of the genus *Jasminum* of the olive family Oleaceae, with white or yellow flowers. The common jasmine *J. officinale* has fragrant pure white flowers yielding jasmine oil, used in perfumes; the Chinese winter jasmine *J. nudiflorum* has bright yellow flowers that appear before the leaves.

Jason in Greek mythology, the leader of the Argonauts who sailed in the *Argo* to Colchis in search of the ◊Golden Fleece. He eloped with ◊Medea, daughter of the king of Colchis, who had helped him achieve his goal, but later deserted her.

jaundice yellow discoloration of the skin and whites of the eyes caused by an excess of bile pigment in the bloodstream. Mild jaundice is common in newborns, but a serious form occurs in rhesus disease (see ◊rhesus factor)

Java or *Jawa* most important island of Indonesia, situated between Sumatra and Bali *area* (with the island of Madura) 51,000 sq mi/132,000 sq km *capital* Jakarta (also capital of Indonesia) *towns* ports include Surabaya and Semarang *physical* about half the island is under cultivation, the rest being thickly forested. Mountains and sea breezes keep temperatures down, but humidity is high, with heavy rainfall from Dec to March *features* a chain of mountains, some of which are volcanic, runs along the center, rising to 9,000 ft/2,750 m. The highest mountain, Semeru (12,060 ft/3,676 m), is in the E *industries* rice, coffee, cocoa, tea, sugar, rubber, quinine, teak, petroleum *population* (with Madura; 1989) 107,513,800, including people of Javanese, Sundanese, and Madurese origin, with differing languages *religion* predominantly Muslim *history* fossilized early human remains (*Homo erectus*) were discovered 1891–92. In central Java there are ruins of magnificent Buddhist monuments and of the Sivaite temple in Prambanan. The island's last Hindu kingdom, Majapahit, was destroyed about 1520 and followed by a number of short-lived Javanese kingdoms. The Dutch East India company founded a factory 1610. Britain took over during the Napoleonic period, 1811–16, and Java then reverted to Dutch control. Occupied by Japan 1942–45, Java then became part of the republic of ◊Indonesia.

javelin spear used in athletics events. The men's javelin is about 8.5 ft/260 cm long, weighing 28 oz/800 g; the women's 7.5 ft/230 cm long, weighing 21 oz/600 g. It is thrown from a scratch line at the end of a run-up. The center of gravity on the men's javelin was altered 1986 to reduce the vast distances (100 yd/90 m) that were being thrown.

jay any of several birds of the crow family Corvidae, generally brightly colored and native to Eurasia and the Americas, such as the blue jay. In the Eurasian common jay *Garrulus glandarius*, the body is fawn with patches of white, blue, and black on the wings and tail

jazz polyphonic syncopated music, characterized by solo virtuosic improvisation, which developed in the US at the turn of the 20th century. Initially music for dancing, often with a vocalist, it had its roots in black American and other popular music. Developing from ◊blues and spirituals (religious folk songs) in the southern states, it first came to prominence in the early 20th century in New Orleans, St Louis, and Chicago, with a distinctive flavor in each city. Traits common to all types of jazz are the modified rhythms of West Africa; the emphasis on improvisation; Western European harmony emphasizing the dominant seventh and the clash of major and minor thirds; characteristic textures and ◊timbres, first exemplified by a singer and rhythm section (consisting of a piano, bass, drums, and guitar or a combination of these instruments), and later by the addition of other instruments such as the saxophone and various brass instruments, and later still by the adoption of electrically amplified instruments.

Jedda alternative spelling for the Saudi Arabian port ◊Jiddah.

Jefferson Thomas 1743–1826. 3rd president of the US 1801–09, founder of the Democratic Republican Party. He published *A Summary View of the Rights of America* 1774 and as a member of the Continental Congresses of 1775–76 was largely responsible for the drafting of the ◊Declaration of Independence. He was governor of Virginia 1779–81, ambassador to Paris 1785–89, secretary of state 1789–93, and vice president 1797–1801.

He was supportive of the French Revolution and spent four years in France while dispatching advice through his ally James ◊Madison on the proposals for a Constitutional Convention. Upon his return to the political scene, he carried on his battle with Alexander ◊Hamilton, who held views of America directly opposed to his own agrarian, democratic inclinations.

Jefferson City capital of Missouri, located in the central part of the state, W of St Louis, on the Missouri River; population (1990) 35,500. Industries include agricultural products, shoes, electrical appliances, and cosmetics.

Jehovah's Witness member of a religious organization originating in the US 1872 under Charles Taze Russell (1852–1916). Jehovah's Witnesses attach great importance to Christ's second coming, which Russell predicted would occur 1914, and which Witnesses still believe is imminent. All Witnesses are expected to take part in house-to-house preaching; there are no clergy.

jellyfish marine invertebrate of the phylum Cnidaria (coelenterates) with an umbrella-shaped body composed of a semitransparent gelatinous substance, with a fringe of stinging tentacles. Most adult jellyfishes move freely, but during parts of their life cycle many are polyplike and attached. They feed on small animals that are paralyzed by stinging cells in the jellyfishes' tentacles.

Jenner Edward 1749–1823. English physician who pioneered vaccination. In Jenner's day, smallpox was a major killer. His discovery that inoculation with cowpox gives immunity to smallpox was a great medical breakthrough. He coined the word "vaccination" from the Latin word for cowpox, *vaccina*.

jerboa small, nocturnal, leaping rodent belonging to the family Dipodidae. There are about 25 species of jerboa, native to N Africa and SW Asia.

Jeremiah Old Testament Hebrew prophet, whose ministry continued 626–586 BC . He was imprisoned during ◊Nebuchadnezzar's siege of Jerusalem on suspicion of intending to desert to the enemy. On the city's fall, he retired to Egypt.

Jerome, St *c.*340–420. One of the early Christian leaders and scholars known as the Fathers of the Church. His Latin versions of the Old and New Testaments form the basis of the Roman Catholic Vulgate. He is usually depicted with a lion. Feast day Sept 30.

Jersey largest of the ◊Channel Islands; capital St Helier; area 45 sq mi/117 sq km; population (1991) 58,900. It is governed by a lieutenant-governor representing the English crown and an assembly. Jersey cattle were

originally bred here. Jersey gave its name to a woolen garment

Jerusalem ancient city of Palestine, divided 1948 between Jordan and the new republic of Israel; area (pre-1967) 14.5 sq mi/37.5 sq km, (post-1967) 42 sq mi/108 sq km, including areas of the West Bank; population (1989) 500,000, about 350,000 Israelis and 150,000 Palestinians. In 1950 the western New City was proclaimed as the Israeli capital, and, having captured from Jordan the eastern Old City 1967, Israel affirmed 1980 that the united city was the country's capital; the United Nations does not recognize the claim.

Jerusalem artichoke a variety of ◊artichoke.

Jesuit member of the largest and most influential Roman Catholic religious order (also known as the *Society of Jesus*) founded by Ignatius Loyola 1534, with the aims of protecting Catholicism against the Reformation and carrying out missionary work. During the 16th and 17th centuries Jesuits were missionaries in Japan, China, Paraguay, and among the North American Indians. The order had (1991) about 29,000 members (15,000 priests plus students and lay members). Jesuit schools and universities are renowned.

Jesus *c.*4 BC –AD 29 or 30. Hebrew preacher on whose teachings ◊Christianity was founded. According to the accounts of his life in the four Gospels, he was born in Bethlehem, Palestine, son of God and the Virgin Mary, and brought up by Mary and her husband Joseph as a carpenter in Nazareth. After adult baptism, he gathered 12 disciples, but his preaching antagonized the Roman authorities and he was executed by crucifixion. Three days later there came reports of his ◊resurrection and, later, his ascension to heaven.

jetfoil advanced type of ◊hydrofoil boat built by Boeing, propelled by water jets. It features horizontal, fully submerged hydrofoils fore and aft and has a sophisticated computerized control system to maintain its stability in all waters.

Jew follower of ◊Judaism, the Jewish religion. The term is also used to refer to those who claim descent from the ancient Hebrews, a Semitic people of the Middle East. Today, some may recognize their ethnic heritage but not practise the religious or cultural traditions. The term came into use in medieval Europe, based on the Latin name for Judeans, the people of Judah. Prejudice against Jews is termed ◊anti-Semitism.

jewelweed or *touch-me-not* any of various North American annual herbaceous plants of the genus *Impatiens* of the balsam family, usually growing in wet soil and having yellowish-orange, sometimes spotted flowers with short spurs. Their mature seed pods burst at the slightest touch.

Jiang Qing or *Chiang Ching* 1914–1991. Chinese communist politician, third wife of the party leader Mao Zedong. In 1960 she became minister for culture, and played a key role in the 1966–69 Cultural Revolution as the leading member of the Shanghai-based Gang of Four, who attempted to seize power 1976. Jiang was imprisoned 1981.

Jiangsu or *Kiangsu* province on the coast of E China *area* 39,449 sq mi/102,200 sq km *capital* Nanjing *features* the swampy mouth of the river Chang Jiang; the special municipality of Shanghai *industries* cereals, rice, tea, cotton, soy beans, fish, silk, ceramics, textiles, coal, iron, copper, cement *population* (1990) 67,057,000 *history* Jiangsu was originally part of the Wu kingdom, and Wu is still a traditional local name for the province. Jiangsu's capture by Japan in 1937 was an important step in that country's attempt to conquer China.

Jiangxi or *Kiangsi* province of SE China *area* 63,613 sq mi/164,800 sq km *capital* Nanchang *industries* rice, tea, cotton, tobacco, porcelain, coal, tungsten, uranium *population* (1990) 37,710,000 *history* the province was Mao Zedong's original base in the first phase of the Communist struggle against the Nationalists.

Jiang Zemin 1926– . Chinese political leader, state president from 1993. He succeeded ◊Zhao Ziyang as Communist Party leader after the Tiananmen Square massacre of 1989. Jiang is a cautious proponent of economic reform who has held with unswerving adherence to the party's "political line".

Jibuti variant spelling of ◊Djibouti, a republic of NE Africa.

Jiddah or *Jedda* port in Hejaz, Saudi Arabia, on the E shore of the Red Sea; population (1986) 1,000,000. Industries include cement, steel, and oil refining. Pilgrims pass through here on their way to Mecca.

Jilin or *Kirin* province of NE China in central ◊Manchuria *area* 72,182 sq mi/187,000 sq km *capital* Changchun *population* (1990) 24,659,000.

Jinan or *Tsinan* city and capital of Shandong province, China; population (1989) 2,290,000. It has food-processing and textile industries.

Jinnah Mohammed Ali 1876–1948. Indian politician, Pakistan's first governor-general from 1947. He was president of the Muslim League 1916, 1934–48, and by 1940 was advocating the need for a separate state of Pakistan; at the 1946 conferences in London he insisted on the partition of British India into Hindu and Muslim states.

Jinsha Jiang river that rises in SW China and forms the ◊Chang Jiang (Yangtze Kiang) at Yibin.

Joan of Arc, St 1412–1431. French military leader. In 1429 at Chinon, NW France, she persuaded Charles VII that she had a divine mission to expel the occupying English from N France (see ◊Hundred Years' War) and secure his coronation. She raised the siege of Orléans, defeated the English at Patay, north of Orléans, and Charles was crowned in Reims. However, she failed to take Paris and was captured May 1430 by the Burgundians, who sold her to the English. She was found guilty of witchcraft and heresy by a tribunal of French ecclesiastics who supported the English. She was burned to death at the stake in Rouen May 30, 1431. In 1920 she was canonized.

Jobs Steven Paul 1955– . US computer scientist. He co-founded ◊Apple Computer Inc with Steve Wozniak 1976, and founded NeXT Technology Inc.

Jodrell Bank site in Cheshire, England, of the Nuffield Radio Astronomy Laboratories of the University of Manchester. Its largest instrument is the 250 ft/76 m radio dish (the Lovell Telescope), completed 1957 and modified 1970. A 125 x 82 ft/38 x 25 m elliptical radio dish was introduced 1964, capable of working at shorter wave lengths.

Johannesburg largest city of South Africa, situated on the Witwatersrand River in Transvaal; population (1985) 1,609,000. It is the center of a large gold-mining industry; other industries include engineering works, meat-chilling plants, and clothing factories

John Augustus (Edwin) 1878–1961. Welsh painter. He is known for his portraits, including *The Smiling Woman* 1910 (Tate Gallery, London) of his second wife, Dorelia McNeill. His sitters included such literary and society figures as Thomas Hardy, Dylan Thomas, W B Yeats, and Cecil Beaton.

John Elton. Adopted name of Reginald Kenneth Dwight 1947– . English pop singer, pianist, and composer. His best-known album, *Goodbye Yellow Brick Road* 1973, includes the hit "Bennie and the Jets". His output is prolific and his hits have continued intermittently into the 1990s.

John (I) Lackland 1167–1216. King of England from 1199 and acting king from 1189 during his brother Richard the Lion-Hearted's absence on the third Crusade.

He lost Normandy and almost all the other English possessions in France to Philip II of France by 1205. His repressive policies and excessive taxation brought him into conflict with his barons, and he was forced to seal the ◊Magna Carta 1215. Later repudiation of it led to the first Barons' War 1215–17, during which he died.

John I 1357–1433. King of Portugal from 1385. An illegitimate son of Pedro I, he was elected by the Cortes (parliament). His claim was supported by an English army against the rival king of Castile, thus establishing the Anglo-Portuguese Alliance 1386.

He married Philippa of Lancaster, daughter of ◊John of Gaunt.

John Bull imaginary figure who is a personification of England, similar to the American Uncle Sam. He is represented in cartoons and caricatures as a prosperous farmer of the 18th century.

John of Gaunt 1340–1399. English nobleman and politician, born in Ghent, fourth son of Edward III, Duke of Lancaster from 1362. He distinguished himself during the Hundred Years' War. During Edward's last years, and the years before Richard II attained the age of majority, he acted as head of government, and Parliament protested against his corrupt rule

John Paul II (Karol Wojtyla) 1920– . Pope from 1978, the first non-Italian to be elected pope since 1522. He was born near Kraków, Poland. He has upheld the tradition of papal infallibility and has condemned artificial contraception, women priests, married priests, and modern dress for monks and nuns—views that have aroused criticism from liberalizing elements in the church.

Johns Jasper 1930– . US painter, sculptor, and printmaker. He was one of the foremost exponents of ◊Pop art. He rejected abstract art, favoring such mundane subjects as flags, maps, and numbers as a means of exploring the relationship between image and reality. His work employs pigments mixed with wax (encaustic) to create a rich surface with unexpected delicacies of color.

Born in Augusta, Georgia, he moved to New York City in 1952. In the 1960s his works became more abstract before veering toward Abstract Expressionism in the mid-1970s. He was also influenced by Marcel ◊Duchamp.

John, St New Testament apostle. Traditionally, he wrote the fourth Gospel and the Johannine Epistles (when he was bishop of Ephesus), and the Book of

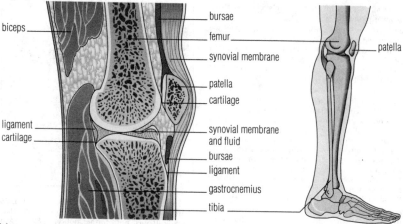

joint

Revelation (while exiled to the Greek island of Patmos). His emblem is an eagle; his feast day Dec 27.

Johnson Andrew 1808–1875. 17th president of the US 1865–69, a Democrat. He was a congressman from Tennessee 1843–53, governor of Tennessee 1853–57, senator 1857–62, and vice president 1865. He succeeded to the presidency on Lincoln's assassination (April 15, 1865). His conciliatory policy to the defeated South after the Civil War involved him in a feud with the Radical Republicans, culminating in his impeachment 1868 before the Senate, which failed to convict him by one vote.

Johnson Earvin ("Magic") 1959– . US basketball player. He played 1979–91 for the Los Angeles Lakers, winners of the National Basketball Association (NBA) championship 1980, 1982, 1985, 1987, and 1988. He was named the NBA's most valuable player 1980, 1982, and 1987. He played in the 1992 All-Star game and in the victorious 1992 US Olympic basketball team in Barcelona, Spain. He retired 1992 after discovering he was HIV positive.

Johnson Jack 1878–1968. US heavyweight boxer. He overcame severe racial prejudice to become the first black heavyweight champion of the world 1908 when he traveled to Australia to challenge Tommy Burns. The US authorities wanted Johnson "dethroned" because of his color but could not find suitable challengers until 1915, when he lost the title in a dubious fight decision to the giant Jess Willard.

Johnson Lyndon Baines 1908–1973. 36th president of the US 1963–69, a Democrat. He was elected to Congress 1937–49 and the Senate 1949–60. Born in Texas, he brought critical Southern support as John F Kennedy's vice-presidential running mate 1960, and became president on Kennedy's assassination.

Johnson Philip (Cortelyou) 1906– . US architect. He coined the term "International Style" 1932. Originally designing in the style of Mies van der Rohe, he later became an exponent of ◊Postmodernism. He designed the giant AT&T building in New York 1978, a pink skyscraper with a Chippendale-style cabinet top.

Johnson Samuel, known as "Dr Johnson", 1709–1784. English lexicographer, author, and critic. He was also

a brilliant conversationalist and the dominant figure in 18th-century London literary society. His *Dictionary*, published 1755, remained authoritative for over a century, and is still remarkable for the vigor of its definitions. In 1764 he founded the Literary Club.

Johnston Atoll coral island in the mid-Pacific, lying between the ◊Marshall Islands and Hawaii; area 1.1 sq mi/2.8 sq km. The island is only 8 ft/2.4 m above sea level and subject to hurricanes and tidal waves. It has the status of a National Wildlife Refuge but was contaminated by fallout from nuclear-weapons testing 1962, and has since 1971 been used as a repository for chemical weapons left over from the Korean and Vietnam wars. An unincorporated territory of the US, it is administered by the US Defense Nuclear Agency (DNA).

John the Baptist, St *c.*12 BC –*c.* AD 27. In the New Testament, an itinerant preacher. After preparation in the wilderness, he proclaimed the coming of the Messiah and baptized Jesus in the river Jordan. He was later executed by ◊Herod Antipas at the request of Salome, who demanded that his head be brought to her on a platter.

joint in any animal with a skeleton, a point of movement or articulation. In vertebrates, it is the point where two bones meet.

Joliet (or *Jolliet*) Louis 1645–1700. French-born Canadian explorer. He and Jesuit missionary Jacques ◊Marquette were the first to successfully chart the course of the Mississippi River down to its junction with the Arkansas River. They returned to Canada by way of the Illinois territory
The city of Joliet, Illinois, is named in his honor.

Joliot-Curie Irène (born Curie) 1897–1956 and Frédéric (born Joliot) 1900–1958. French physicists who made the discovery of artificial radioactivity, for which they were jointly awarded the 1935 Nobel Prize for Chemistry.

Jolson Al. Adopted name of Asa Yoelson 1886–1950. Russian-born US singer and entertainer. Popular in Broadway theater and vaudeville, he was chosen to star in the first talking picture, *The Jazz Singer* 1927.

Jolson, who got his start in vaudeville, was also a popular recording star.

Jonah Hebrew prophet whose name is given to a book in the Old Testament. According to this, he fled by ship to evade his mission to prophesy the destruction of Nineveh. The crew threw him overboard in a storm, as a bringer of ill fortune, and he spent three days and nights in the belly of a whale before coming to land.

Jones Inigo 1573–c.1652. English Classical architect. He introduced the Palladian style to England. Born in London, he studied in Italy where he encountered the works of Palladio. He was employed by James I to design scenery for Ben Jonson's masques and appointed Surveyor of the King's Works 1615–42. He designed the Queen's House, Greenwich, 1616–35, and his English Renaissance masterpiece, the Banqueting House in Whitehall, London, 1619–22. His work was to provide the inspiration for the Palladian Revival a century later.

jonquil species of small daffodil *Narcissus jonquilla*, family Amaryllidaceae, with yellow flowers. Native to Spain and Portugal, it is cultivated elsewhere.

Jonson Ben(jamin) 1572–1637. English dramatist, poet, and critic. *Every Man in his Humor* 1598 established the English "comedy of humors", in which each character embodies a "humor", or vice, such as greed, lust, or avarice. His first extant tragedy is *Sejanus* 1603, with Burbage and Shakespeare as members of the original cast. The great comedies of his middle years include *Volpone, or The Fox* 1606, *The Alchemist* 1610, and *Bartholomew Fair* 1614.

Joplin Janis 1943–1970. US blues and rock singer. She was lead singer with the San Francisco group Big Brother and the Holding Company 1966–68. Her biggest hit, Kris Kristofferson's "Me and Bobby McGee", was released on the posthumous *Pearl* album 1971. She died of a drug overdose.

Joplin Scott 1868–1917. US ragtime pianist and composer. He was active in Chicago. His "Maple Leaf Rag" 1899 was the first instrumental sheet music to sell a million copies, and "The Entertainer", as the theme tune of the film *The Sting* 1973, revived his popularity. He was an influence on Jelly Roll Morton and other early jazz musicians.

Jordan Hashemite Kingdom of (*Al Mamlaka al Urduniya al Hashemiyah*) *area* 34,434 sq mi/89,206 sq km (West Bank 2,269 sq mi/5,879 sq km) *capital* Amman *towns and cities* Zarqa, Irbid, Aqaba (the only port) *physical* desert plateau in E; rift valley separates E and W banks of the river Jordan *features* lowest point on Earth below sea level in the Dead Sea (–1,299 ft/–396 m); archaeological sites at Jerash and Petra. *head of state* King Hussein ibn Talai from 1952 *head of government* Abd al-Salam al-Mujali from 1993 *political system* constitutional monarchy *political parties* none *exports* potash, phosphates, citrus, vegetables *currency* Jordanian dinar *population* (1993 est) 4,100,000; growth rate 3.6% p.a. *life expectancy* men 66, women 70 *languages* Arabic (official), English *religions* Sunni Muslim 92%, Christian 8% *literacy* men 89%, women 70% *GNP* $1,120 per head (1991) *chronology* 1946 Independence achieved from Britain as Transjordan. *1949* New state of Jordan declared. *1950* Jordan annexed West Bank. *1953* Hussein ibn Talai officially became king of Jordan. *1958* Jordan and Iraq formed Arab Federation that ended when the Iraqi monarchy was deposed. *1967* Israel captured

and occupied West Bank. Martial law imposed. *1976* Lower house dissolved, political parties banned, elections postponed until further notice. *1982* Hussein tried to mediate in Arab-Israeli conflict. *1984* Women voted for the first time. *1985* Hussein and Yassir Arafat put forward framework for Middle East peace settlement. Secret meeting between Hussein and Israeli prime minister. *1988* Hussein announced decision to cease administering the West Bank as part of Jordan, passing responsibility to Palestine Liberation Organization (PLO), and the suspension of parliament. *1989* Prime Minister Zaid al-Rifai resigned; Hussein promised new parliamentary elections following criticism of economic policies. Riots over price increases of up to 50% following fall in oil revenues. First parliamentary elections for 22 years; Muslim Brotherhood won 25 of 80 seats but exiled from government; martial law lifted. *1990* Hussein unsuccessfully tried to mediate after Iraq's invasion of Kuwait. Massive refugee problems as thousands fled to Jordan from Kuwait and Iraq. *1991* 24 years of martial law ended; ban on political parties lifted. *1993* King Hussein publicly distanced himself from Iraqi leader Saddam Hussein. Candidates loyal to Hussein won majority in parliamentary elections; several leading Islamic fundamentalists lost their seats. *1994* Jan: economic cooperation pact singed with PLO. July: peace treaty signed with Israel, ending 46-year-old "state of war".

Jordan Michael 1963– . US basketball player. Playing for the Chicago Bulls 1984– , he led them to NBA championship 1991, 1992, and 1993. As a rookie he led the National Basketball Association (NBA) in points scored (2,313). During the 1986–87 season he scored 3,000 points, only the second player in NBA history to do so. He retired from professional basketball 1993 but returned in 1995.

In 1992 he became the world's highest paid sportsman, earning three times more in advertising endorsements than for playing basketball.

Joseph in the New Testament, the husband of the Virgin Mary, a descendant of King David of the Tribe of Judah, and a carpenter by trade.

Although Jesus was not the son of Joseph, Joseph was his legal father. According to Roman Catholic tradition, he had a family by a previous wife, and was an elderly man when he married Mary.

Joseph II 1741–1790. Holy Roman emperor from 1765, son of Francis I (1708–1765). The reforms he carried out after the death of his mother, ◊Maria Theresa, in 1780, provoked revolts from those who lost privileges.

Josephine Marie Josèphe Rose Tascher de la Pagerie 1763–1814. As wife of ◊Napoleon Bonaparte, she was empress of France 1804–1809. Born on Martinique, she married in 1779 Alexandre de ◊Beauharnais, who played a part in the French Revolution, and in 1796 Napoleon, who divorced her 1809 because she had not produced children.

Joseph of Arimathaea, St In the New Testament, a wealthy Hebrew, member of the Sanhedrin (supreme court), and secret supporter of Jesus. On the evening of the Crucifixion he asked the Roman procurator Pilate for Jesus' body and buried it in his own tomb. Feast day March 17.

joule SI unit (symbol J) of work and energy, replacing the ◊calorie (one joule equals 4.2 calories)

It is defined as the work done (energy transferred) by a force of one newton acting over one meter and equal to 10^7 ergs. It can also be expressed as the work done in one second by a current of one ampere at a potential difference of one volt. One ◊watt is equal to one joule per second.

Joule James Prescott 1818–1889. English physicist whose work on the relations between electrical, mechanical, and chemical effects led to the discovery of the first law of ◊thermodynamics.

journalism profession of reporting, photographing, or editing news events for the mass media—◊newspapers, magazines, radio, television, documentary films, and newsreels—and for news agencies. In 1992, at least 61 journalists were killed in the line of duty worldwide and 123 were in jail on Jan 1, 1993. The Pulitzer Award for outstanding journalism was founded by J ◊Pulitzer.

Joyce James (Augustine Aloysius) 1882–1941. Irish writer. He revolutionized the form of the English novel with his "stream of consciousness" technique. His works include *Dubliners* 1914 (short stories), *Portrait of the Artist as a Young Man* 1916, *Ulysses* 1922, and *Finnegans Wake* 1939.

joystick in computing, an input device that signals to a computer the direction and extent of displacement of a hand-held lever. It is similar to the joystick used to control the flight of an aircraft.

Juan Carlos 1938– . King of Spain. The son of Don Juan, pretender to the Spanish throne, he married Princess Sofia in 1962, eldest daughter of King Paul of Greece. In 1969 he was nominated by ◊Franco to succeed on the restoration of the monarchy intended to follow Franco's death; his father was excluded because of his known liberal views. Juan Carlos became king 1975.

Juárez Benito 1806–1872. Mexican politician, president 1861–65 and 1867–72. In 1861 he suspended repayments of Mexico's foreign debts, which prompted a joint French, British, and Spanish expedition to exert pressure. French forces invaded and created an empire for ◊Maximilian, brother of the Austrian emperor. After their withdrawal in 1867, Maximilian was executed, and Juárez returned to the presidency.

Judah or *Judea* district of S Palestine. After the death of King Solomon 937 BC , Judah adhered to his son Rehoboam and the Davidic line, whereas the rest of Israel elected Jeroboam as ruler of the northern kingdom. In New Testament times, Judah was the Roman province of Judea, and in current Israeli usage it refers to the southern area of the West Bank.

Judaism the religion of the ancient Hebrews and their descendants the Jews, based, according to the Old Testament, on a covenant between God and Abraham about 2000 BC , and the renewal of the covenant with Moses about 1200 BC . It rests on the concept of one eternal invisible God, whose will is revealed in the *Torah* and who has a special relationship with the Jewish people. The Torah comprises the first five books of the Bible (the Pentateuch), which contains the history, laws, and guide to life for correct behavior. Besides those living in Israel, there are large Jewish populations today in the US, the former USSR (mostly Russia, Ukraine, Belarus, and Moldova), the UK and Commonwealth nations, and in Jewish communities throughout the world. There are approximately 18 million Jews, with about 9 million in the Americas, 5 million in Europe, and 4 million in Asia, Africa, and the Pacific.

Judas Iscariot In the New Testament, the disciple who betrayed Jesus Christ. Judas was the treasurer of the group. At the last Passover supper, he arranged, for 30 pieces of silver, to point out Jesus to the chief priests so that they could arrest him. Afterward Judas was overcome with remorse and committed suicide.

judge person invested with power to hear and determine legal disputes.

In the US, the federal judiciary is chosen by executive appointments. It consists of Supreme Court justices, judges of the US district courts, magistrates, and administrative law judges. Similar offices exist at the state level with judges elected or appointed. There are also county and municipal judges elected to office.

judicial review in the US, the power of a court to decide whether legislative acts or executive actions are constitutional. The ultimate authority for judicial review is the Supreme Court.

judiciary in constitutional terms, the system of courts and body of judges in a country. The independence of the judiciary from other branches of the central authority is generally considered to be an essential feature of a democratic political system. This independence is often written into a nation's constitution and protected from abuse by politicians.

judo form of wrestling of Japanese origin. The two combatants wear loose-fitting, belted jackets and trousers to facilitate holds, and falls are broken by a square mat; when one has established a painful hold that the other cannot break, the latter signifies surrender by slapping the ground with a free hand. Degrees of proficiency are indicated by the color of the belt: for novices, white; after examination, brown (three degrees); and finally, black (nine degrees).

jujube tree of the genus *Zizyphus* of the buckthorn family Thamnaceae, with berrylike fruits.

Julian the Apostate *c.*331–363. Roman emperor. Born in Constantinople, the nephew of Constantine the Great, he was brought up as a Christian but early in life became a convert to paganism. Sent by Constantius to govern Gaul in 355, he was proclaimed emperor by his troops 360, and in 361 was marching on Constantinople when Constantius' death allowed a peaceful succession. He revived pagan worship and refused to persecute heretics. He was killed in battle against the Persians in the ◊Sassanian Empire.

Julius II 1443–1513. Pope 1503–13. A politician who wanted to make the Papal States the leading power in

Italy, he formed international alliances first against Venice and then against France. He began the building of St Peter's Church in Rome 1506 and was the patron of the artists Michelangelo and Raphael.

July Revolution revolution July 27–29, 1830, in France that overthrew the restored Bourbon monarchy of Charles X and substituted the constitutional monarchy of Louis Philippe, whose rule (1830–48) is sometimes referred to as the July Monarchy.

jumbo jet popular name for a generation of huge wide-bodied airliners including the Boeing 747, which is 232 ft/71 m long, has a wingspan of 196 ft/60 m, a maximum takeoff weight of nearly 400 metric tons, and can carry more than 400 passengers.

Juneau ice-free port and state capital of Alaska, on Gastineau Channel in the S Alaska panhandle; population (1980) 19,528. Juneau is the commercial and distribution center for the fur-trading and mining of the Panhandle region; also important are salmon fishing, fish processing, and lumbering.

A campus of the University of Alaska is here. Settled in 1880 by gold prospectors, Juneau was named the capital in 1900. In 1970 its boundaries were extended to cover 2,406 sq mi/6,232 sq km.

juneberry or *serviceberry* any tree or shrub of the genus *Amelanchier* of the rose family, having simple leaves, showy white flowers, and purple-black fruits. The Allegheny serviceberry *Amelanchier lavis*, native to the NE US, grows to a height of 40 ft/12 m and has edible fruit. Several species are grown as ornamentals.

Jung Carl Gustav 1875–1961. Swiss psychiatrist who collaborated with Sigmund ◊Freud until their disagreement in 1912 over the importance of sexuality in causing psychological problems.

Jung studied religion and dream symbolism, saw the unconscious as a source of spiritual insight, and distinguished between introversion and extroversion. His books include *Modern Man in Search of a Soul* 1933.

juniper aromatic evergreen tree or shrub of the genus *Juniperus* of the cypress family Cupressaceae, found throughout temperate regions. Its berries are used to flavor gin. Some junipers are erroneously called ◊cedars.

junk bond derogatory term for a security officially rated as "below investment grade". It is issued in order to raise capital quickly, typically to finance a takeover to be paid for by the sale of assets once the company is acquired. Junk bonds have a high yield, but are a high-risk investment

Juno in Roman mythology, the principal goddess, identified with the Greek ◊Hera. The wife of Jupiter and queen of heaven, she was concerned with all aspects of women's lives.

Jupiter or *Jove* in Roman mythology, the chief god, identified with the Greek ◊Zeus. He was god of the sky, associated with lightning and thunderbolts; protector in battle; and bestower of victory. The son of Saturn, he married his sister Juno, and reigned on Mount Olympus as lord of heaven. His most famous temple was on the Capitoline Hill in Rome.

Jupiter the fifth planet from the Sun, and the largest in the Solar System (equatorial diameter 88,700 mi/142,800 km), with a mass more than twice that of all the other planets combined, 318 times that of the Earth's. It takes 11.86 years to orbit the Sun, at an average distance of 484 million mi/778 million km,

and has at least 16 moons. It is largely composed of hydrogen and helium, liquefied by pressure in its interior, and probably with a rocky core larger than the Earth. Its main feature is the Great Red Spot, a cloud of rising gases, revolving counterclockwise, 8,500 mi/14,000 km wide and some 20,000 mi/30,000 km long.

Jura Mountains series of parallel mountain ranges running SW–NE along the French-Swiss frontier between the rivers Rhône and Rhine, a distance of 156 mi/250 km. The highest peak is *Crête de la Neige*, 5,650 ft/1,723 m.

Jurassic period of geological time 208–146 million years ago; the middle period of the Mesozoic era. Climates worldwide were equable, creating forests of conifers and ferns; dinosaurs were abundant, birds evolved, and limestones and iron ores were deposited.

In North America, the Nevadan orogeny marked the beginning of the Sierra Nevadas and other mountains.

jurisprudence the science of law in the abstract—that is, not the study of any particular laws or legal system, but of the principles upon which legal systems are founded.

jury body of lay people (usually 12, sometimes 6) sworn to decide the facts of a case and reach a verdict in a court of law. Juries, used mainly in English-speaking countries, are implemented primarily in criminal cases, but also sometimes in civil cases. The members of the jury are carefully selected by both prosecution and defense attorneys.

justice of the peace in some states, a public officer (magistrate), usually elected, with limited jurisdiction over a small district or part of a county. This includes the authority to try minor criminal cases, administer oaths, and officiate at marriages.

justification in printing and word processing, the arrangement of text so that it is aligned with either the left or right margin, or both.

Justinian I 483–565. Byzantine emperor from 527. He recovered N Africa from the Vandals, SE Spain from the Visigoths, and Italy from the Ostrogoths, largely owing to his great general Belisarius. He ordered the codification of Roman law, which has influenced European jurisprudence; he built the church of Sta Sophia in Constantinople, and closed the university in Athens 529.

Jute member of a Germanic people who originated in Jutland but later settled in Frankish territory. They occupied Kent, SE England, about 450, according to tradition under Hengist and Horsa, and conquered the Isle of Wight and the opposite coast of Hampshire in the early 6th century.

jute fiber obtained from two plants of the genus *Corchorus* of the linden family: *C. capsularis* and *C. olitorius*. Jute is used for sacks and sacking, upholstery, webbing, twine, and stage canvas.

Jutland (Danish *Jylland*) peninsula of N Europe; area 11,400 sq mi/29,500 sq km. It is separated from Norway by the Skagerrak and from Sweden by the Kattegat, with the North Sea to the W. The larger N part belongs to Denmark, the S part to Germany.

Juvenal c. AD 60–140. Roman satirical poet. His 16 surviving satires give an explicit and sometimes brutal picture of the corrupt Roman society of his time. He may have lived in exile under the emperor Domitian, and remained very poor.

K abbreviation for *thousand*, as in a salary of $50K.

K2 or *Chogori* second highest mountain above sea level, 28,261 ft/8,611 m, in the Karakoram range, in a disputed region of Pakistan. It was first climbed 1954 by an Italian expedition.

Kabardino-Balkar autonomous republic of Russia, in the N Caucasus Mountains; capital Nalchik; area 4,825 sq mi/12,500 sq km; population (1989) 760,000. Under Russian control from 1557, it was annexed 1827; it was an autonomous republic of the USSR 1936–91.

kabbala or *cabbala* (Hebrew "tradition") ancient esoteric Jewish mystical tradition of philosophy containing strong elements of pantheism yet akin to neoplatonism. Kabbalistic writing reached its peak between the 13th and 16th centuries. It is largely rejected by current Judaic thought as medieval superstition, but is basic to the Hasid sect.

Kabul capital of Afghanistan, 6,900 ft/2,100 m above sea level, on the river Kabul; population (1984) 1,179,300. Products include textiles, plastics, leather, and glass. It commands the strategic routes to Pakistan via the ◊Khyber Pass.

Kádár János 1912–1989. Hungarian communist leader, in power 1956–88, after suppressing the national uprising. As Hungarian Socialist Workers' Party (HSWP) leader and prime minister 1956–58 and 1961–65, Kádár introduced a series of market-socialist economic reforms, while retaining cordial political relations with the USSR.

He was ousted as party general secretary May 1988 and forced into retirement May 1989.

Kafka Franz 1883–1924. Czech novelist. He wrote in German. His three unfinished allegorical novels *Der Prozess/The Trial* 1925, *Der Schloss/The Castle* 1926, and *Amerika/America* 1927 were posthumously published despite his instructions that they should be destroyed. His short stories include "Die Verwandlung/ The Metamorphosis" 1915, in which a man turns into a huge insect. His vision of lonely individuals trapped in bureaucratic or legal labyrinths can be seen as a powerful metaphor for modern experience.

Kaifeng former capital of China, 907–1127, and of Honan province; population (1984) 619,200. It has lost its importance because of the silting-up of the nearby Huang He River.

Kaiser title formerly used by the Holy Roman emperors, Austrian emperors 1806–1918, and German emperors 1871–1918. The word, like the Russian "czar", is derived from the Latin *Caesar*.

Kalahari Desert semidesert area forming most of Botswana and extending into Namibia, Zimbabwe, and South Africa; area about 347,400 sq mi/900,000 sq km. The only permanent river, the Okavango, flows into a delta in the NW forming marshes rich in wildlife.

Its inhabitants are the nomadic Kung.

Kalamazoo city in SW Michigan, on the Kalamazoo River, SW of Lansing; seat of Kalamazoo County; population (1990) 80,300. Its industries include the processing of the area's agricultural products, automobile and transportation machinery parts, chemicals, and metal and paper products.

kale type of ◊cabbage.

Kali in Hindu mythology, the goddess of destruction and death. She is the wife of ◊Siva.

Kalmyk or *Kalmuck* autonomous republic in central Russia, on the Caspian Sea; area 29,300 sq mi/75,900 sq km; population (1989) 322,000; capital Elista. Industry is mainly agricultural. It was settled by migrants from China in the 17th century. The autonomous Soviet republic was abolished 1943–57 because of alleged collaboration of the people with the Germans during the siege of Stalingrad, but restored 1958.

Kamchatka mountainous peninsula separating the Bering Sea and Sea of Okhotsk, forming (together with the Chukchi and Koryak national districts) a region of E Siberian Russia. Its capital, Petropavlovsk, is the only town; agriculture is possible only in the S. Most of the inhabitants are fishers and hunters.

Kampala capital of Uganda, on Lake Victoria; population (1983) 455,000. It is linked by rail with Mombasa. Products include tea, coffee, textiles, fruit, and vegetables.

Kampuchea former name (1975–89) of ◊Cambodia.

Kandinsky Wassily 1866–1944. Russian painter. He was a pioneer of abstract art. Born in Moscow, he traveled widely, settling in Munich 1896. Between 1910 and 1914 he produced the series *Improvisations* and *Compositions*, the first known examples of purely abstract work in 20th-century art. He was an originator of the *Blaue Reiter* movement 1911–12. From 1921 he taught at the ◊Bauhaus school of design. He moved to Paris 1933, becoming a French citizen 1939.

kangaroo any marsupial of the family Macropodidae found in Australia, Tasmania, and New Guinea. Kangaroos are plant-eaters and most live in groups. They are adapted to hopping, the vast majority of species having very large back legs and feet compared with the small forelimbs. The larger types can jump 9 m/30 ft at a single bound. Most are nocturnal. Species vary from small rat kangaroos, only 1 ft/30 cm long, through the medium-sized wallabies, to the large red and great gray kangaroos, which are the largest living marsupials. These may be 5.9 ft/1.8 m long with 3.5 ft/ 1.1 m tails.

Ka Ngwane black homeland in Natal province, South Africa; population (1985) 392,800. It achieved self-governing status 1971.

Kanpur formerly *Cawnpore* capital of Kanpur district, Uttar Pradesh, India, SW of Lucknow, on the river Ganges; a commercial and industrial center (cotton,

kangaroo *The giant gray kangaroo may reach a weight of 200 lb/90 kg and a height of over 5 ft/1.5 m. Like the red kangaroo, the gray kangaroo lives in small herds, sheltering by rocky outcrops during the heat of the day and emerging during the night to feed and drink.*

wool, jute, chemicals, plastics, iron, steel); population (1981) 1,688,000.

Kansas state in central US; nickname Sunflower State *area* 82,296 sq mi/213,200 sq km *capital* Topeka *cities* Kansas City, Wichita, Overland Park *features* Dodge City, once "cowboy capital of the world"; Eisenhower Center, Abilene; Fort Larned and Fort Scott; Pony Express station, Hanover; Wichita Cowtown, a frontier-era reproduction *industries* wheat, cattle, coal, petroleum, natural gas, aircraft, minerals *population* (1990) 2,477,600 *famous people* Amelia Earhart; Dwight D Eisenhower; William Inge; Buster Keaton; Carry Nation; Charlie Parker *history* explored by Francisco de Coronado for Spain 1541 and La Salle for France 1682; ceded to the US 1803 as part of the Louisiana Purchase.

Kansas City city in Kansas, at the confluence of the Kansas and Missouri rivers, adjacent to Kansas City, Missouri; population (1990) 149,800. Food processing, electronics, and automobile-assembly plants are here, as well as the University of Kansas Medical Center. It was laid out in 1857 as Wyandotte and expanded in 1886.

Kansas City city in Missouri, at the confluence of the Kansas and Missouri rivers, adjacent to Kansas City, Kansas; population (1990) 435,100. Industries include steel and electronics manufactures, motor-vehicle assembly, and oil refining, and it is the financial, marketing, and distribution center of the region. The University of Missouri-Kansas City and the Kansas City Art Institute are among the schools here. The site was settled as a trading post by French fur trappers in 1821.

Kansu alternative spelling for the Chinese province ◊Gansu.

Kant Immanuel 1724–1804. German philosopher who believed that knowledge is not merely an aggregate of sense impressions but is dependent on the conceptual apparatus of the human understanding, which is itself not derived from experience. In ethics, Kant argued that right action cannot be based on feelings or inclinations but conforms to a law given by reason, the *categorical imperative*.

kaolinite or *kaolin* ◊clay mineral, hydrous aluminum silicate, $Al_2Si_2O_5(OH)_4$, formed mainly by the chemical weathering of ◊feldspar. It is important in the manufacture of porcelain and other ceramics, paper, rubber, paint, textiles, and medicines. It is mined in the US, the UK, France, Germany, and China.

kapok silky hairs that surround the seeds of certain trees, particularly the **kapok tree** *Bombax ceiba* of India and Malaysia, and the **silk-cotton tree** *Ceiba pentandra*, a native of tropical America. Kapok is used for stuffing cushions and mattresses and for sound insulation; oil obtained from the seeds is used in food and soap preparation.

Karachi largest city and chief seaport of Pakistan, and capital of Sind province, NW of the Indus delta; population (1981) 5,208,000. Industries include engineering, chemicals, plastics, and textiles. It was the capital of Pakistan 1947–59.

Karadžić Radovan 1945– . Montenegrin-born leader of the Bosnian Serbs, leader of the community's unofficial government from 1992. He cofounded the Serbian Democratic Party of Bosnia-Herzegovina (SDS-BH) 1990 and launched the siege of Sarajevo 1992, plunging the country into a prolonged and bloody civil war. Successive peace initiatives for the region failed due to his ambitious demands for Serbian territory.

Karajan Herbert von 1908–1989. Austrian conductor. He dominated European classical music performance after 1947. He was principal conductor of the Berlin Philharmonic Orchestra 1955–89, artistic director of the Vienna State Opera 1957–64, and of the Salzburg Festival 1956–60. A perfectionist, he cultivated an orchestral sound of notable smoothness and transparency; he also staged operas and directed his own video recordings. He recorded the complete Beethoven symphonies three times.

Kara-Kalpak autonomous republic of Uzbekistan *area* 61,000 sq mi/158,000 sq km *capital* Nukus *towns and cities* Munyak *industries* cotton, rice, wheat, fish *population* (1989) 1,214,000 *history* named for the Kara-Kalpak ("black hood") people who live S of the Sea of Aral and were conquered by Russia 1867. An autonomous Kara-Kalpak region was formed 1926 within Kazakhstan, transferred to the Soviet republic 1930, made a republic 1932, and attached to Uzbekistan 1936.

Karakoram mountain range in central Asia, divided among China, Pakistan, and India. Peaks include K2, Masharbrum, Gasharbrum, and Mustagh Tower. *Ladakh* subsidiary range is in NE Kashmir on the Tibetan border.

karaoke amateur singing in public to prerecorded backing tapes. Karaoke originated in Japan and spread to other parts of the world in the 1980s. Karaoke machines are jukeboxes of backing tracks to well-known popular songs, usually with a microphone attached and accompanying lyrics and video graphics displayed on a screen.

karat or *carat* the unit of purity in gold in the US. Pure gold is 24-karat; 22-karat (the purest used in jewelry) is 22 parts gold and two parts alloy (to give greater strength).

karate one of the ◊martial arts. Karate is a type of unarmed combat derived from *kempo*, a form of the Chinese Shaolin boxing. It became popular in the West in the 1930s.

Karelia autonomous republic of NW Russia *area* 66,550 sq mi/172,400 sq km *capital* Petrozavodsk *cities* Vyborg *physical* mainly forested *features* Lake Ladoga *industries* fishing, timber, chemicals, coal *population* (1991) 791,000 *history* Karelia was annexed to Russia by Peter the Great 1721 as part of the grand duchy of Finland. In 1917 part of Karelia was retained by Finland when it gained its independence from Russia. The remainder became an autonomous region 1920 and an autonomous republic 1923 of the USSR. Following the wars of 1939–40 and 1941–44, Finland ceded 18,000 sq mi/46,000 sq km of Karelia to the USSR. Part of this territory was incorporated in the Russian Soviet Republic and part in the Karelian autonomous republic. A movement for the reunification of Russian and Finnish Karelia emerged in the late 1980s.

Karloff Boris. Adopted name of William Henry Pratt 1887–1969. English-born US actor. He is best known for his work in the US. He achieved Hollywood stardom with his role as the monster in the film *Frankenstein* 1931. Several popular sequels followed as well as starring appearances in other horror films including *Scarface* 1932, *The Lost Patrol* 1934, and *The Body Snatcher* 1945.

karma (Sanskrit "fate") in Hinduism, the sum of a human being's actions, carried forward from one life to the next, resulting in an improved or worsened fate. Buddhism has a similar belief, except that no permanent personality is envisaged, the karma relating only to the physical and mental elements carried on from birth to birth, until the power holding them together disperses in the attainment of nirvana.

Karpov Anatoly 1951– . Russian chess player. He succeeded Bobby Fischer of the US as world champion 1975, and held the title until losing to Gary Kasparov 1985. He lost to Kasparov again in 1990.

Karroo two areas of semidesert in Cape Province, South Africa, divided into the *Great Karroo* and *Little Karroo* by the Swartberg Mountains. The two Karroos together have an area of about 100,000 sq mi/260,000 sq km.

Kashmir former part of Jammu state in the north of British India with a largely Muslim population, ruled by a Hindu maharajah, who joined it to the republic of India 1947. There was fighting between pro-India and pro-Pakistan factions, the former being the Hindu ruling class and the latter the Muslim majority, and open war between the two countries 1965–66 and 1971. It is today divided between the Pakistani area of Kashmir and the Indian state of Jammu and Kashmir. Since 1990 it has been riven by Muslim separatist violence, with more than 150,000 Indian troops deployed in Kashmir 1993. These were criticized by human-rights groups for torture, rape, and killing. Estimates of casualties 1990–93 range from 8,000 to 20,000.

Kashmir Pakistan-occupied area, 30,445 sq mi/78,900 sq km, in the NW of the former state of Kashmir, now ◊Jammu and Kashmir. Azad ("free") Kashmir in the W has its own legislative assembly based in Muzaffarabad while Gilgit and Baltistan regions to the N and E are governed directly by Pakistan. The ◊Northern Areas are claimed by India and Pakistan *population* 1,500,000 *towns and cities* Gilgit, Skardu *features* W Himalayan peak Nanga Parbat 26,660 ft/8,126 m, Karakoram Pass, Indus River, Baltoro Glacier.

Kasparov Gary 1963– . Russian chess player. When he beat his compatriot Anatoly Karpov to win the world title 1985, he was the youngest ever champion at 22 years 210 days.

Katmai active volcano in Alaska, US, 6,715 ft/2,046 m. Its major eruption 1912 created the "Valley of Ten Thousand Smokes". Katmai National Park, area 6,922 sq mi/17,928 sq km, was designated 1980.
The lake-filled crater formed from the eruption is lined with glaciers.

Katmandu or *Kathmandu* capital of Nepal; population (1981) 235,000. Founded in the 8th century on an ancient pilgrim and trade route from India to Tibet and China, it has a royal palace, Buddhist temples, and monasteries.

Kaunda Kenneth (David) 1924– . Zambian politician, president 1964–91. Imprisoned 1958–60 as founder of the Zambia African National Congress, he became in 1964 the first prime minister of Northern Rhodesia, then the first president of independent Zambia. In 1973 he introduced one-party rule. He supported the nationalist movement in Southern Rhodesia, now Zimbabwe, and survived a coup attempt 1980 thought to have been promoted by South Africa. He was elected chair of the Organization of African Unity 1970 and 1987. He lost the first multiparty elections, Nov 1991, to Frederick Chiluba.

Kawasaki industrial city (iron, steel, shipbuilding, chemicals, textiles) on Honshu Island, Japan; population (1990) 1,173,600.

Kazakh or *Kazak* member of a pastoral Kyrgyz people of Kazakhstan. Kazakhs also live in China (Xinjiang, Gansu, and Qinghai), Mongolia, and Afghanistan. There are 5–7 million speakers of Kazakh, a Turkic language belonging to the Altaic family. They are predominantly Sunni Muslim, although pre-Islamic customs have survived.

Kazakhstan Republic of *area* 1,049,150 sq mi/ 2,717,300 sq km *capital* Alma-Ata *towns and cities* Karaganda, Semipalatinsk, Petropavlovsk *physical* Caspian and Aral seas, Lake Balkhash; Steppe region *features* Baikonur Cosmodrome (space launch site at Tyuratam, near Baikonur) *head of state* Nursultan Nazarbayev from 1990 *head of government* Akezhan Kazhegeldin from 1994 *political system* emergent democracy *political parties* Congress of People's Unity of Kazakhstanis, moderate, centrist; People's Congress Party of Kazakhstan, moderate, ethnic; Independent Socialist Party of Kazakhstan (SPK), left-wing; Republican Party, right-of-center coalition *products* grain, copper, lead, zinc, manganese, coal, oil *currency* tenge *population* (1993 est) 17,200,000 (Kazakh 40%, Russian 38%, German 6%, Ukrainian 5%) *life expectancy* men 64, women 73 *language* Russian; Kazakh, related to Turkish *religion* Sunni Muslim *GNP* $2,470 per head (1991) *chronology* 1920 Autonomous republic in USSR. 1936 Joined the USSR and became a full union republic. 1950s Site of Nikita Khrushchev's ambitious "Virgin Lands" agricultural extension program. 1960s A large influx of Russian settlers turned the Kazakhs into a minority in their own republic. 1986 Riots in Alma-Alta after Gorbachev ousted local communist leader. 1989 Nursultan Nazarbayev became leader of the Kazakh Communist Party (KCP) and instituted economic and cultural reform programs. 1990 Nazarbayev became head of state. 1991 March: support pledged for continued union with USSR. Aug: Nazarbayev condemned attempted anti-Gorbachev coup; KCP abolished and replaced by Independent Socialist Party of Kazakhstan. Dec: joined new Commonwealth of Independent States; independence recognized by US. *1992* Admitted into United Nations. Trade agreement with US. *1993* New constitution increased authority of the president and made Kazakh the state language. Offer to dismantle nuclear arsenal in exchange for US aid. *1994* Agreement to form single economic zone with Uzbekistan. First parliamentary elections won by Nazarbayev's supporters, but without working majority.

Kazan capital of Tatarstan, central Russia, on the river Volga; population (1989) 1,094,000. It is a transport, commercial, and industrial center (engineering, oil refining, petrochemicals, textiles, large fur trade). Formerly the capital of a Tatar khanate, Kazan was captured by Ivan IV "the Terrible" 1552.

Kazan Elia 1909– . US stage and film director. He was a founder of the Actors Studio 1947. Plays he directed include *The Skin of Our Teeth* 1942, *A Streetcar Named Desire* 1947 (filmed 1951), *Death of a Salesman* 1949, and *Cat on a Hot Tin Roof* 1955; films include *Gentleman's Agreement* 1947 (Academy Award), *On the Waterfront* 1954, *East of Eden* 1955, and *The Visitors* 1972.

Kearny Stephen Watts 1794–1848. US military leader. As brigadier general he was given command of the Army of the West 1846. During the Mexican War 1846–48, he was the military governor of New Mexico and joined in the conquest of California 1847 becoming military governor.

Keaton Buster (Joseph Frank) 1896–1966. US comedian, actor, and film director. After being a star in vaudeville, he became one of the great comedians of the silent film era, with an inimitable deadpan expression (the "Great Stone Face") masking a sophisticated acting ability. His films include *One Week* 1920, *The Navigator* 1924, *The General* 1927, and *The Cameraman* 1928.

Keats John 1795–1821. English Romantic poet. He produced work of the highest quality and promise before dying at the age of 25. *Poems* 1817, *Endymion* 1818, the great odes (particularly "Ode to a Nightingale" and "Ode on a Grecian Urn" written 1819, published 1820), and the narratives "Lamia", "Isabella", and "The Eve of St Agnes" 1820, show his lyrical richness and talent for drawing on both classical mythology and medieval lore.

Kefauver (Carey) Estes 1903–1963. US Democratic politician. He was elected to the US House of Representatives 1939 and served in the US Senate 1948 until his death. He was an unsuccessful candidate for the Democratic presidential nomination 1952 and 1956.

Keillor Garrison 1942– . US writer and humorist. His hometown Anoka, Minnesota, in the American Midwest, inspired his popular, richly comic stories about Lake Wobegon, including *Lake Wobegon Days* 1985 and *Leaving Home* 1987, which often started as radio monologues about "the town that time forgot, that the decades cannot improve".

He first achieved prominence on National Public Radio's "Prairie Home Companion".

Kellogg Frank Billings 1856–1937. US political leader and diplomat. Elected to the US Senate 1916, he was appointed US ambassador to Great Britain by President Harding 1922 and secretary of state 1925.

He formulated the Kellogg–Briand Pact 1927, the international antiwar resolution, for which he was awarded the Nobel Peace Prize 1929.

Kelly Emmett 1898–1979. US clown and circus performer. He created his "Weary Willie" clown character while with the Hagenbeck-Wallace circus 1931. Joining the Ringling Brothers and Barnum and Bailey Circus 1942, he made "Weary Willie" into one of the most famous clowns in the world.

Kelly Gene (Eugene Curran) 1912– . US film actor, dancer, choreographer, and director. He was a major star of the 1940s and 1950s in a series of MGM musicals, including *On the Town* 1949, *Singin' in the Rain* 1952 (both of which he codirected), and *An American in Paris* 1951. He also directed *Hello Dolly* 1969.

He also acted in nonmusicals, such as *Marjorie Morningstar* 1958 and *Inherit the Wind* 1960.

Kelly Grace (Patricia) 1928–1982. US film actress. She starred in *High Noon* 1952, *The Country Girl* 1954, for which she received an Academy Award, and *High Society* 1955. She also starred in three Hitchcock films—*Dial M for Murder* 1954, *Rear Window* 1954, and *To Catch a Thief* 1955. She retired from acting after marrying Prince Rainier III of Monaco 1956.

After her marriage she devoted herself to the principality, raised three children, and was active in charities until she died in an automobile accident.

kelp collective name for large brown seaweeds, such as those of the Fucaceae and Laminariaceae families. Kelp is also a term for the powdery ash of burned seaweeds, a source of iodine.

Kelvin William Thomson, 1st Baron Kelvin 1824–1907. Irish physicist who introduced the *kelvin scale*, the absolute scale of temperature. His work on the conservation of energy 1851 led to the second law of ◊thermodynamics.

kelvin scale temperature scale used by scientists. It begins at ◊absolute zero (–273.15°C) and increases by the same degree intervals as the Celsius scale; that is, 0°C is the same as 273 K and 100°C is 373 K.

Kemal Atatürk Mustafa. Turkish politician; see ◊Atatürk.

Kempis Thomas à. Medieval German monk and religious writer; see ◊Thomas à Kempis.

Kennedy Edward (Moore) "Ted" 1932– . US Democratic politician. He aided his brothers John and Robert Kennedy in their presidential campaigns of 1960 and 1968 respectively, and entered politics as a senator from Massachusetts 1962. He failed to gain the presidential nomination 1980, largely because of questions about his delay in reporting an automobile crash at Chappaquiddick Island, near Cape Cod, Massachusetts, in 1969, in which his passenger, Mary Jo Kopechne, was drowned.

He is a spokesman for liberal causes including national health and gun control.

Kennedy John F(itzgerald) "Jack" 1917–1963. 35th president of the US 1961-63, a Democrat; the first Roman Catholic and the youngest person to be elected president. In foreign policy he carried through the unsuccessful ◊Bay of Pigs invasion of Cuba, and in 1963 secured the withdrawal of Soviet missiles from the island. His program for reforms at home, called the *New Frontier*, was posthumously executed by Lyndon Johnson. Kennedy was assassinated while on a visit to Dallas on Nov 22, 1963. Lee Harvey Oswald

(1939–1963), who was within a few days shot dead by Jack Ruby (1911–1967), was named as the assassin.

Kennedy Robert (Francis) 1925–1968. US Democratic politician and lawyer. He was presidential campaign manager for his brother John F ◊Kennedy 1960, and as attorney general 1961–64 pursued a racket-busting policy and promoted the Civil Rights Act of 1964. He was also a key aide to his brother. When John Kennedy's successor, Lyndon Johnson, preferred Hubert Humphrey for the 1964 vice-presidential nomination, Kennedy resigned and was elected senator from New York. In 1968 he campaigned for the Democratic Party's presidential nomination, but during a campaign stop in California was assassinated by Sirhan Bissara Sirhan (1944–   ), a Jordanian.

Kennedy Space Center ◊NASA launch site on Merritt Island, near Cape Canaveral, Florida, used for Apollo and space-shuttle launches. The first flight to land on the Moon (1969) and *Skylab*, the first orbiting laboratory (1973), were launched here.

The Center is dominated by the Vehicle Assembly Building, 525 ft/160 m tall, used for assembly of ◊Saturn rockets and space shuttles. It is named for Pres. John F. Kennedy.

Kennelly–Heaviside layer former term for the E layer of the ionosphere.

Kenneth I (called *MacAlpin*) King of Scotland from about 844. Traditionally, he is regarded as the founder of the Scottish kingdom (Alba) by virtue of his final defeat of the Picts about 844. He invaded Northumbria six times, and drove the Angles and the Britons over the river Tweed.

Kent county of SE England, known as the "garden of England" *area* 1,440 sq mi/3,730 sq km *towns and cities* Maidstone (administrative headquarters), Canterbury, Dover, Chatham, Rochester, Sheerness, Tunbridge Wells; resorts: Folkestone, Margate, Ramsgate *features* the North Downs; rivers: Thames, Darent, Medway, Stour (traditionally, a "man of Kent" comes from E of the Medway and a "Kentish man" from W Kent); New Ash Green, a new town; Romney Marsh; the Isles of Grain, Sheppey (on which is the resort of Sheerness, formerly a royal dockyard), and Thanet; Weald (agricultural area); Leeds Castle (converted to a palace by Henry VIII); Hever Castle (where Henry VIII courted Anne Boleyn); Chartwell (Churchill's country home), Knole, Sissinghurst Castle and gardens; the Brogdale Experimental Horticulture Station at Faversham has the world's finest collection of apple and other fruit trees; the former RAF Manston became Kent International Airport 1989. *industries* hops, apples, soft fruit, cement, paper, oil refining, shipbuilding. *population* (1991) 1,508,900 *famous people* Christopher Marlowe, Edward Heath.

Kentucky state in S central US; nickname Bluegrass State *area* 40,414 sq mi/104,700 sq km *capital* Frankfort *towns and cities* Louisville, Lexington, Owensboro, Covington, Bowling Green *features* bluegrass country; horse racing at Louisville (Kentucky Derby); Mammoth Cave National Park (main cave 4 mi/6.5 km long, up to 125 ft/38 m high, where Indian councils were once held); Abraham Lincoln's birthplace at Hodgenville; Fort Knox, US gold-bullion depository *industries* tobacco, cereals, textiles, coal, whiskey, horses, transport vehicles *population* (1990) 3,365,300 *famous people* Mohammed Ali, Daniel Boone, Louis D Brandeis, Kit Carson, Henry Clay, D W Griffith, Thomas Hunt Morgan, Harland "Colonel"

Sanders, Robert Penn Warren *history* Kentucky was the first region W of the Alleghenies settled by American pioneers. James Harrod founded Harrodsburg 1774; in 1775 Daniel Boone, who blazed his Wilderness Trail 1767, founded Boonesboro. Originally part of Virginia, Kentucky became a state 1792. Badly divided over the slavery question, the state was racked by guerrilla warfare and partisan feuds during the Civil War.

Kenya Republic of (*Jamhuri ya Kenya*) *area* 224,884 sq mi/582,600 sq km *capital* Nairobi *towns and cities* Kisumu, port Mombasa *physical* mountains and highlands in W and center; coastal plain in S; arid interior and tropical coast *environment* the elephant faces extinction as a result of poaching *features* Great Rift Valley, Mount Kenya, Lake Nakuru (salt lake with world's largest colony of flamingos), Lake Turkana (Rudolf), national parks with wildlife, Malindi Marine Reserve *head of state and government* Daniel arap Moi from 1978 *political system* emergent democratic republic *political parties* Kenya African National Union (KANU), nationalist, centrist; Forum for the Restoration of Democracy–Kenya (FORD–Kenya), left of center; Forum for the Restoration of Democracy–Asili (FORD–Asili), left of center; Democratic Party (DP), centrist *exports* coffee, tea, fruit and vegetables, petroleum products *currency* Kenya shilling *population* (1993 est) 27,900,000 (Kikuyu 21%, Luo 13%, Luhya 14%, Kelenjin 11%; Asian, Arab, European); growth rate 4.2% p.a. *life expectancy* men 59, women 63 *languages* Kiswahili (official), English; there are many local dialects *religions* Protestant 38%, Roman Catholic 28%, indigenous beliefs 26%, Muslim 6% *literacy* men 80%, women 59% *GNP* $340 per head (1991) *chronology 1895* British East African protectorate established. *1920* Kenya became a British colony. *1944* African participation in politics began. *1950* Mau Mau campaign began. *1953* Nationalist leader Jomo Kenyatta imprisoned by British authorities. *1956* Mau Mau campaign defeated, Kenyatta released. *1963* Achieved internal self-government, with Kenyatta as prime minister. *1964* Independence achieved from Britain as a republic within the Commonwealth, with Kenyatta as president. *1967* East African Community (EAC) formed with Tanzania and Uganda. *1977* Collapse of EAC. *1978* Death of Kenyatta. Succeeded by Daniel arap Moi. *1982* Attempted coup against Moi foiled. *1983* Moi reelected unopposed. *1984* Over 2,000 people massacred by government forces at Wajir. *1985–86* Thousands of forest villagers evicted and their homes

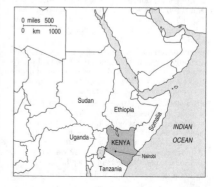

destroyed to make way for cash crops. *1988* Moi reelected. 150,000 evicted from state-owned forests. *1989* Moi announced release of all known political prisoners. Confiscated ivory burned in attempt to stop elephant poaching. *1990* Moi rejected requests for multiparty politics. *1991* Increased demands for political reform; multiparty system adopted. *1992* Constitutional amendment passed. Dec: Moi reelected in first multiparty elections amid allegations of fraud.

Kepler Johannes 1571–1630. German mathematician and astronomer. He formulated what are now called *Kepler's laws* of planetary motion: (1) the orbit of each planet is an ellipse with the Sun at one of the foci; (2) the radius vector of each planet sweeps out equal areas in equal times; (3) the squares of the periods of the planets are proportional to the cubes of their mean distances from the Sun.

keratin fibrous protein found in the ◊skin of vertebrates and also in hair, nails, claws, hooves, feathers, and the outer coating of horns.

Kérkyra Greek form of ◊Corfu, an island in the Ionian Sea.

kerosene thin oil obtained from the distillation of petroleum; a highly refined form is used in jet aircraft fuel. Kerosene is a mixture of hydrocarbons of the ◊paraffin series.

Kerouac Jack (Jean Louis) 1923–1969. US novelist. He named and epitomized the ◊Beat Generation of the 1950s. The first of his autobiographical, myth-making books, *The Town and the City* 1950, was followed by the rhapsodic *On the Road* 1957. His major contribution to poetry was *Mexico City Blues* 1959.

Kerry county of the Republic of Ireland, in the province of Munster; county town Tralee; area 1,814 sq mi/4,700 sq km; population (1991) 121,700. Low lying in the N, to the S are the highest mountains in Ireland, including Carrantuohill (part of ◊Macgillycuddy's Reeks), the highest peak in Ireland at 3,417 ft 1,041 m. The western coastline is deeply indented and there are many rivers and lakes, notable of which are the Lakes of Killarney.

Industries include engineering, woolens, shoes, cutlery, fishing, farming; tourism is important.

kestrel either of two small species of ◊falcon (genus *Falco*): the Eurasian kestrel *F. tinnunculus*, about 13.5 in/35 cm long, which occasionally visits E North America and the Aleutians; and the American kestrel or sparrowhawk *F. sparverius*, somewhat smaller, of most of North America. Both species are russet, gray, and tan in color, with the male American kestrel having more gray on its wings. They hunt mainly by hovering in mid-air while watching for grasshoppers and small mammals.

ketone member of the group of organic compounds containing the carbonyl group (C=O) bonded to two atoms of carbon (instead of one carbon and one hydrogen as in ◊aldehydes). Ketones are liquids or low-melting-point solids, slightly soluble in water.

kettle glacial geologic feature, formed when a block of stagnant ice from a receding glacier becomes isolated and buried in glacial outwash or drift before it finally melts. When the block disappears, it leaves a pit or depression called a kettle, in the drift. These depressions range from 15 ft/5 m to 8 mi/13 km in diameter, and some exceed 100 ft/33 m in depth.

key in music, the ◊diatonic scale around which a piece

of music is written; for example, a passage in the key of C major will mainly use the notes of the C major scale. The term is also used for the lever activated by a ◊keyboard player, such as a piano key, or the finger control on a woodwind instrument.

Key Francis Scott 1779–1843. US lawyer and poet. He wrote the song "The Star-Spangled Banner" while Fort McHenry, Baltimore, was besieged by British troops 1814; since 1931 it has been the national anthem of the US.

Key served as US attorney for the District of Columbia 1833–41.

keyboard in computing, an input device resembling a typewriter keyboard, used to enter instructions and data. There are many variations on the layout and labeling of keys. Extra numeric keys may be added, as may special-purpose function keys, whose effects can be defined by programs in the computer.

Keynes John Maynard, 1st Baron Keynes 1883–1946. English economist, whose *The General Theory of Employment, Interest, and Money* 1936 proposed the prevention of financial crises and unemployment by adjusting demand through government control of credit and currency. He is responsible for that part of economics now known as *macroeconomics*.

key-to-disk system or *key-to-tape system* in computing, a system that enables large amounts of data to be entered at a keyboard and transferred directly onto computer-readable disks or tapes.

kg symbol for ◊*kilogram*.

KGB secret police of the USSR, the *Komitet Gosudarstvennoy Bezopasnosti*/Committee of State Security, which was in control of frontier and general security and the forced-labor system. KGB officers held key appointments in all fields of daily life, reporting to administration offices in every major town. The KGB was superseded by the Russian Federal Security Agency on the demise of the Soviet Union 1991.

Khaddhafi alternate form for ◊Qaddafi, Libyan leader.

Khama Seretse 1921–1980. Botswanan politician, prime minister of Bechuanaland 1965, and first president of Botswana from 1966 until his death.

Kharkov capital of the Kharkov region, E Ukraine, 250 mi/400 km E of Kiev; population (1987) 1,587,000. It is a railroad junction and industrial city (engineering, tractors), close to the Donets Basin coalfield and Krivoy Rog iron mines. Kharkov was founded 1654 as a fortress town.

Khartoum capital and trading center of Sudan, at the junction of the Blue and White Nile; population (1983) 476,000, and of Khartoum North, across the Blue Nile, 341,000. Omdurman is also a suburb of Khartoum, giving the urban area a population of over 1.3 million.

Khmer or *Kmer* member of the largest ethnic group in Cambodia, numbering about 7 million. Khmer minorities also live in E Thailand and S Vietnam. The Khmer language belongs to the Mon-Khmer family of Austro-Asiatic languages.

Khmer Rouge communist movement in Cambodia (Kampuchea) formed in the 1960s. Controlling the country 1974–78, it was responsible for mass deportations and executions under the leadership of ◊Pol Pot. Since then it has conducted guerrilla warfare, and in 1991 gained representation in the governing body. The leader of the Khmer Rouge from 1985 is Khieu Samphan.

Khomeini Ayatollah Ruhollah 1900–1989. Iranian Shiite Muslim leader, born in Khomein, central Iran. Exiled for opposition to the Shah from 1964, he returned when the Shah left the country 1979, and established a fundamentalist Islamic republic. His rule was marked by a protracted war with Iraq, and suppression of opposition within Iran, executing thousands of opponents.

Khomeini was hostile toward both superpowers, held US embassy hostages 1979–81, and supported terrorist groups.

Khrushchev Nikita Sergeyevich 1894–1971. Soviet politician, secretary-general of the Communist Party 1953–64, premier 1958–64. He emerged as leader from the power struggle following Stalin's death and was the first official to denounce Stalin, in 1956. His de-Stalinization program gave rise to revolts in Poland and Hungary 1956. Because of problems with the economy and foreign affairs (a breach with China 1960; conflict with the US in the Cuban missile crisis 1962), he was ousted by Leonid Brezhnev and Alexei Kosygin.

Khwārizmī, al- Mohammed ibn-Mūsā *c.*780–*c.*850. Persian mathematician from Khwarizm (now Khiva, Uzbekistan), who lived and worked in Baghdad. He wrote a book on algebra, from part of whose title (*al-jabr*) comes the word "algebra", and a book in which he introduced to the West the Hindu-Arabic decimal number system.

The word "algorithm" is a corruption of his name.

Khyber Pass pass 33 mi/53 km long through the mountain range that separates Pakistan from Afghanistan. The Khyber Pass was used by invaders of India. The present road was constructed by the British during the Afghan Wars.

Kiangsi alternative spelling of ◊Jiangxi, a province of China.

Kiangsu alternative spelling of ◊Jiangsu, a province of China.

kibbutz Israeli communal collective settlement with collective ownership of all property and earnings, collective organization of work and decision-making, and communal housing for children. A modified version, the *Moshav Shitufi*, is similar to the collective farms that were typical of the former USSR. Other Israeli cooperative rural settlements include the *Moshav Ovdim*, which has equal opportunity, and the similar but less strict *Moshav* settlement.

kidnapping the abduction of a person against his or her will. It often involves holding persons for ransom. It may also take place in child-custody disputes or involve psychosexual motives.

kidney in vertebrates, one of a pair of organs responsible for fluid regulation, excretion of waste products, and maintaining the ionic composition of the blood. The kidneys are situated on the rear wall of the abdomen. Each one consists of a number of long tubules; the outer parts filter the aqueous components of blood, and the inner parts selectively reabsorb vital salts, leaving waste products in the remaining fluid (urine), which is passed through the ureter to the bladder.

kidney machine medical equipment used in ◊dialysis.

Kierkegaard Søren (Aabye) 1813–1855. Danish philosopher considered to be the founder of ◊existentialism. He argued that no system of thought could explain the unique experience of the individual.

He defended Christianity, suggesting that God cannot be known through reason, but only through a "leap of faith". His chief works are *Enten-Eller/Either-Or* 1843, *Begrebet Angest/Concept of Dread* 1844, and *Efterskrift/Postscript* 1846, which summed up much of his earlier writings.

Kiev capital of Ukraine, industrial center (chemicals, clothing, leatherwork), on the confluence of the Desna and Dnieper rivers; population (1987) 2,554,000. It was the capital of Russia in the Middle Ages.

Kigali capital of Rwanda, central Africa, 50 mi/80 km E of Lake Kivu; population (1981) 157,000. Products include coffee, hides, shoes, paints, and varnishes; there is tin mining.

Kikuyu member of Kenya's dominant ethnic group, numbering about three million. The Kikuyu are primarily cultivators, although many are highly educated and have entered the professions. Their language belongs to the Bantu branch of the Niger-Congo family.

Kildare county of the Republic of Ireland, in the province of Leinster; county town Naas; area 652 sq mi/1,690 sq km; population (1991) 122,516. It is wet and boggy in the N and includes part of the Bog of Allen; the village of Maynooth, with a training college for Roman Catholic priests; and the Curragh, a plain that is the site of the national stud and headquarters of Irish horse racing at Tully. Products include oats, barley, potatoes, and cattle.

Kilimanjaro volcano in ◊Tanzania, the highest mountain in Africa, 19,364 ft/5,900 m.

Kilkenny county of the Republic of Ireland, in the province of Leinster; county town Kilkenny; area 795 sq mi/2,060 sq km; population (1991) 73,600. It has the rivers Nore, Suir, and Barrow. Industries include coal mining, clothing, footwear, brewing, and agricultural activities such as cattle rearing and dairy farming.

killer whale or *orca* toothed whale *Orcinus orca* of the dolphin family, found in all seas of the world. It is black on top, white below, and grows up to 30 ft/9 m long. It is the only whale that has been observed to prey on other whales, as well as on seals and seabirds.

Killy Jean-Claude 1943– . French skier. He won all three gold medals (slalom, giant slalom, and downhill) at the 1968 Winter Olympics in Grenoble.

The first World Cup winner 1967, he retained the title 1968 and also won three world titles.

Kilmer Joyce 1886–1918. US poet. His first collection of poems *Summer of Love* was published 1911. He later gained an international reputation with the title work of *Trees and Other Poems* 1914.

kilobyte (K or KB) in computing, a unit of memory equal to 1,024 ◊bytes. It is sometimes used, less precisely, to mean 1,000 bytes.

kilogram SI unit (symbol kg) of mass equal to 1,000 grams (2.24 lb). It is defined as a mass equal to that of the international prototype, a platinum-iridium cylinder held at the International Bureau of Weights and Measures at Sèvres, France.

kilometer unit (symbol km) of length equal to 1,000 meters (3,280.89 ft).

kilowatt unit (symbol kW) of power equal to 1,000 watts or about 1.34 horsepower.

kilowatt-hour commercial unit of electrical energy (symbol kWh), defined as the work done by a power of 1,000 watts in one hour. It is used to calculate the cost of electrical energy taken from utility-company supplies.

Kim Il Sung 1912–1994. North Korean communist politician and marshal. He became prime minister 1948 and president 1972, retaining the presidency of the Communist Workers' party. He liked to be known as the "Great Leader" and campaigned constantly for the reunification of Korea. His son *Kim Jong Il* (1942–), known as the "Dear Leader", succeeded him.

Kim Young Sam 1927– . South Korean democratic politician, president from 1993. President of the New Democratic Party (NDP) from 1974, he lost his seat and was later placed under house arrest because of his opposition to President Park Chung Hee. In 1990 he merged the NDP with the ruling party to form the new Democratic Liberal Party (DLP). In the Dec 1992 presidential election he captured 42% of the national vote, assuming office Feb 1993.

kinesis (plural *kineses*) in biology, a nondirectional movement in response to a stimulus; for example, woodlice move faster in drier surroundings. *Taxis* is a similar pattern of behavior, but there the response is directional.

kinetic energy the energy of a body resulting from motion. It is contrasted with ◊potential energy.

kinetics alternate name for ◊dynamics. It is distinguished from *kinematics*, which deals with motion without reference to force or mass.

kinetic theory theory describing the physical properties of matter in terms of the behavior—principally movement—of its component atoms or molecules. The temperature of a substance is dependent on the velocity of movement of its constituent particles, increased temperature being accompanied by increased movement. A gas consists of rapidly moving atoms or molecules and, according to kinetic theory, it is their continual impact on the walls of the containing vessel that accounts for the pressure of the gas. The slowing of molecular motion as temperature falls, according to kinetic theory, accounts for the physical properties of liquids and solids, culminating in the concept of no molecular motion at ◊absolute zero (0K/–273°C).

King Billie Jean (born Moffitt) 1943– . US tennis player. She won a record 20 Wimbledon titles 1961–79 and 39 Grand Slam titles. She won the Wimbledon singles title six times, the US Open singles title four times, the French Open once, and the Australian Open once.

King Martin Luther Jr 1929–1968. US civil-rights campaigner, black leader, and Baptist minister. He first came to national attention as leader of the ◊Montgomery, Alabama, bus boycott 1955, and was one of the organizers of the massive (200,000 people) march on Washington, DC 1963 to demand racial equality. An advocate of nonviolence, he was awarded the Nobel Peace Prize 1964. He was assassinated in Memphis, Tennessee, by James Earl Ray (1928–).

king crab or *Alaskan king crab* large, edible crab *Paralithodescamtschatica*, of the N Pacific. The term "king crab" is sometimes used as another name for the ◊horseshoe crab.

kingdom the primary division in biological ◊classification. At one time, only two kingdoms were recognized: animals and plants. Today most biologists prefer a five-kingdom system, even though it still involves grouping together organisms that are probably unrelated. One widely accepted scheme is as follows: *Kingdom Animalia* (all multicellular animals); *Kingdom Plantae* (all plants, including seaweeds and other algae, except blue-green); *Kingdom Fungi* (all fungi, including the unicellular yeasts, but not slime molds); *Kingdom Protista* or *Protoctista* (protozoa, diatoms, dinoflagellates, slime molds, and various other lower organisms with eukaryotic cells); and *Kingdom Monera* (all prokaryotes—the bacteria and cyanobacteria, or ◊blue-green algae). The first four of these kingdoms make up the eukaryotes.

kingfisher heavy-billed bird of the worldwide family Alcedinidae, found near streams, ponds, and coastal areas. Kingfishers plunge-dive for fish and aquatic insects. The nest is usually a burrow in a riverbank.

The North American belted kingfisher *Ceryle alcyon* is about 13 in/33 cm long, slate gray and white (the female has a rust-colored band on the belly), and crested in both sexes.

kingfisher *The kingfisher, with its brilliantly colored plumage and daggerlike beak, is unmistakeable. It is found in Europe, N Africa to Asia, New Guinea, and the Solomon Islands. When hunting, it perches on a branch overhanging a stream or lake, watching for prey, or it flies low over the water, perhaps hovering for a few seconds before diving.*

Kingston capital and principal port of Jamaica, West Indies, the cultural and commercial center of the island; population (1983) 101,000, metropolitan area 525,000. Founded 1693, Kingston became the capital of Jamaica 1872.

Kingston upon Hull official name of ◊Hull, a city in NE England.

Kingstown capital and principal port of St Vincent and the Grenadines, West Indies, in the SW of the island of St Vincent; population (1989) 29,400.

Kinshasa formerly *Léopoldville* capital of Zaire on the river Zaïre, 250 mi/400 km inland from the port of Matadi; population (1984) 2,654,000. Industries include chemicals, textiles, engineering, food processing, and furniture. It was founded by the explorer Henry Stanley 1887.

kinship in anthropology, human relationship based on blood or marriage, and sanctified by law and custom. Kinship forms the basis for most human societies and for such social groupings as the family, clan, or tribe.

Kipling (Jcseph) Rudyard 1865–1936. English writer, born in India. *Plain Tales from the Hills* 1888, about Anglo-Indian society, contains the earliest of his masterly short stories. His books for children, including *The Jungle Book* 1894–95, *Just So Stories* 1902, *Puck of*

Pook's Hill 1906, and the novel *Kim* 1901, reveal his imaginative identification with the exotic. Poems such as "Danny Deever", "Gunga Din", and "If–" express an empathy with common experience, which contributed to his great popularity, together with a vivid sense of "Englishness" (sometimes denigrated as a kind of jingoist imperialism). His work is increasingly valued for its complex characterization and subtle moral viewpoints. Nobel Prize 1907.

Kirchner Ernst Ludwig 1880–1938. German Expressionist artist. He was a leading member of the *die Brücke* group in Dresden from 1905 and in Berlin from 1911. His Dresden work, which includes paintings and woodcuts, shows the influence of African and medieval art. In Berlin he turned to city scenes and portraits, using lurid colors and bold diagonal paint strokes recalling woodcut technique. He suffered a breakdown during World War I and settled in Switzerland, where he committed suicide.

Kirghizia alternative form of ◊Kyrgyzstan, a country in central Asia.

Kiribati Republic of *area* 277 sq mi/717 sq km *capital* (and port) Bairiki (on Tarawa Atoll) *physical* comprises 33 Pacific coral islands: the Kiribati (Gilbert), Rawaki (Phoenix), Banaba (Ocean Island), and three of the Line Islands including Kiritimati (Christmas Island) *environment* the islands are threatened by the possibility of a rise in sea level caused by global warming. A rise of approximately 1 ft/30 cm by the year 2040 will make existing fresh water brackish and undrinkable *features* island groups crossed by equator and International Date Line *head of state and government* Teburoro Tito from 1994 *political system* liberal democracy *political party* National Progressive Party, governing faction; opposition parties: Christian Democratic Party and the Kiribati United Party *exports* copra, fish *currency* Australian dollar *population* (1993 est) 77,000 (Micronesian); growth rate 1.7% p.a. *languages* English (official), Gilbertese *religions* Roman Catholic 48%, Protestant 45% *literacy* 90% (1985) *GNP* $750 per head (1991) *chronology 1892* Gilbert and Ellice Islands proclaimed a British protectorate. *1937* Phoenix Islands added to colony. *1950s* UK tested nuclear weapons on Kiritimati (formerly Christmas Island). *1962* US tested nuclear weapons on Kiritimati. *1975* Ellice Islands separated to become Tuvalu. *1977* Gilbert Islands granted internal self-government. *1979* Independence achieved from Britain, within the Commonwealth, as the Republic of Kiribati, with Ieremia Tabai as president. *1982 and 1985* Tabai reelected. *1985* Kiribati's first political party, the opposition Christian Democrats, formed. *1987* Tabai reelected. *1991* Tabai reelected but not allowed under constitution to serve further term; Teatao Teannaki won run-off presidential election. *1994* Government resigned, after losing vote of confidence. NPP defeated in general election. Teburoro Tito named head of state.

Kirin alternate name for ◊Jilin, a Chinese province.

Kirkland Gelsey 1952– . US ballerina. She danced with effortless technique and innate musicality. She joined the New York City Ballet 1968, where George Balanchine staged a new *Firebird* for her 1970 and Jerome Robbins chose her for his *Goldberg Variations* 1971 and other ballets. In 1974 Mikhail Baryshnikov sought her out and she joined the American Ballet Theater 1975, where they danced in partnership, for example in *Giselle*.

Kissinger Henry 1923– . German-born US diplomat. After a brilliant academic career at Harvard University, he was appointed national security adviser 1969 by President Nixon, and was secretary of state 1973–77. His missions to the USSR and China improved US relations with both countries, and he took part in negotiating US withdrawal from Vietnam 1973 and in Arab-Israeli peace negotiations 1973–75. Nobel Peace Prize 1973.

Kiswahili another name for the ◊Swahili language.

Kitchener Horatio Herbert, Earl Kitchener of Khartoum 1850–1916. British soldier and administrator. He defeated the Sudanese dervishes at Omdurman 1898 and reoccupied Khartoum. In South Africa, he was Chief of Staff 1900–02 during the Boer War, and commanded the forces in India 1902–09. He was appointed war minister on the outbreak of World War I, and drowned when his ship was sunk on the way to Russia.

kite one of about 20 birds of prey in the family Accipitridae, found in all parts of the world.

Kites have long, pointed wings and, usually, a forked tail. North America has five species, including the American swallow-tailed kite *Elanoides forficatus* of the SE US, which catches insects in flight as well as dropping down on snakes and lizards.

kiwi flightless bird *Apteryx australis* found only in New Zealand. It has long, hairlike brown plumage and a very long beak with nostrils at the tip. It is nocturnal and insectivorous. The egg is larger in relation to the bird's size (similar to a domestic chicken) than that of any other bird.

kiwi fruit or *Chinese gooseberry* fruit of a vinelike plant *Actinidithia chinensis*, family Actinidiaceae, commercially grown on a large scale in New Zealand. Kiwi fruits are egg-sized, oval, and of similar flavor to a gooseberry, with a fuzzy brown skin.

Bright-green fuzzless varieties are now available.

kiwi The little spotted kiwi is one of three species of kiwi found in New Zealand. Kiwis have a good sense of smell—rare among birds—which is used to locate worms for food. The nostrils are at the tip of the pointed bill.

Klammer Franz 1953– . Austrian skier who won a record 35 World Cup downhill races between 1974 and 1985. Olympic gold medallist 1976. He was the combined world champion 1974, and the World Cup downhill champion 1975–78 and 1983.

Klaus Václav 1941– . Czech politician and economist, prime minister of the Czech Republic from 1993. Prior to the breakup of Czechoslovakia, he served in the government of Václav Haval and was chair of Civic Form from 1990, breaking away to form the right-of-center Civic Democratic Party (CDP) 1991. The architect of Eastern Europe's most successful economic reform program, he has been a keen promoter of membership in the European Union (formerly the European Community).

Klee Paul 1879–1940. Swiss artist. He was one of the most original artists of the 20th century. He settled in Munich 1906, joined the *Blaue Reiter* group 1912, and worked at the Bauhaus school of design 1920–31, returning to Switzerland 1933. Endlessly inventive and playful, his many works are an exploration of the potential of line, plane, and color. Suggesting a childlike innocence, they are based on the belief in a reality beyond appearances. *Twittering Machine* 1922 (Museum of Modern Art, New York) is typical.

kleptomania behavioral disorder characterized by an overpowering desire to possess articles for which one has no need. In kleptomania, as opposed to ordinary theft, there is no obvious need or use for what is stolen and sometimes the sufferer has no memory of the theft.

Klimt Gustav 1862–1918. Austrian painter. He was influenced by Jugendstil (Art Nouveau) and Symbolism and was a founding member of the Vienna Sezession group 1897. His paintings have a jeweled effect similar to mosaics, for example *The Kiss* 1909 (Musée des Beaux-Arts, Strasbourg). His many portraits include *Judith I* 1901 (österreichische Galerie, Vienna).

Klondike former gold-mining area in ◊Yukon, Canada, named for the river valley where gold was found 1896. About 30,000 people moved to the area during the following 15 years. Silver is still mined here.

km symbol for ◊*kilometer.*

knapweed any of several weedy plants of the genus *Centaurea*, family Compositae. In the common knapweed *C. nigra*, also known as **hardhead**, the hard bract-covered buds break into purple composite heads. It is native to Europe and has been introduced to North America.

knighthood, order of fraternity carrying with it the rank of knight, admission to which is granted as a mark of royal favor or as a reward for public services. During the Middle Ages in Europe such fraternities fell into two classes, religious and secular. The first class, including the ◊*Templars* and the Knights of ◊*St John*, consisted of knights who had taken religious vows and devoted themselves to military service against the Saracens (Arabs) or other non-Christians.

Knossos chief city of Minoan Crete, near present-day Iráklion, 4 mi/6 km SE of Candia. The archeological site, excavated by Arthur Evans 1899–1935, dates from about 2000–1400 BC , and includes the palace throne room, the remains of frescoes, and construction on more than one level.

knot in navigation, unit by which a ship's speed is measured, equivalent to one ◊nautical mile per hour (one knot equals about 1.15 miles per hour). It is also sometimes used in aviation.

knotgrass annual plant *Polygonum aviculare* of the dock family. The small lance-shaped leaves have bases that sheathe the slender stems, giving a superficial resemblance to grass. Small pinkish flowers are followed by seeds that are a delicacy for birds. Knotgrass grows worldwide except in the polar regions.

The creeping grass *Paspalum distichum* of North America is sometimes also called knotgrass.

knowledge-based system (KBS) computer program that uses an encoding of human knowledge to help solve problems. It was discovered during research into ◊artificial intelligence that adding heuristics (rules of thumb) enabled programs to tackle problems that were otherwise difficult to solve by the usual techniques of computer science.

Knox John *c.*1505–1572. Scottish Protestant reformer, founder of the Church of Scotland. He spent several years in exile for his beliefs, including a period in Geneva where he met John ◊Calvin. He returned to Scotland 1559 to promote Presbyterianism. His books include *First Blast of the Trumpet Against the Monstrous Regiment of Women* 1558.

koala marsupial *Phascolarctos cinereus* of the family Phalangeridae, found only in E Australia. It feeds almost entirely on eucalyptus shoots. It is about 2 ft/60 cm long, and resembles a bear. The popularity of its grayish fur led to its almost complete extermination by hunters. Under protection since 1936, it has rapidly increased in numbers.

koala *The koala lives in eucalyptus trees, and comes down only to pass from one tree to another. Its diet is limited to a few species of eucalyptus, of which it will eat over 2 lb/1 kg each day.*

Kobe deep-water port in S Honshu, Japan; population (1990) 1,477,400. *Port Island*, an artificial island of 5 sq km/2 sq mi in Kobe harbor, was created 1960–68 from the rock of nearby mountains. It was one of the world's largest construction projects, and is now a residential and recreation area with a luxury hotel, amusement park, and conference centers. It is linked to the city by a driverless, computerized monorail. An earthquake Jan 1995 caused massive damage with an estimated 5,000 deaths, 25,000 people injured and over 45,000 homes destroyed.

København Danish name for ◊Copenhagen, the capital of Denmark.

Koch Robert 1843–1910. German bacteriologist. Koch and his assistants devised the techniques to culture bacteria outside the body, and formulated the rules for showing whether or not a bacterium is the cause of a disease. Nobel Prize for Medicine 1905.

Koestler Arthur 1905–1983. Hungarian-born English author. Imprisoned by the Nazis in France 1940, he escaped to England. His novel *Darkness at Noon* 1940, regarded as his masterpiece, is a fictional account of the Stalinist purges, and draws on his experiences as a prisoner under sentence of death during the Spanish Civil War.

Kohl Helmut 1930– . German conservative politician, leader of the Christian Democratic Union (CDU) from 1976, West German chancellor (prime minister) 1982–90. He oversaw the reunification of East and West Germany 1989–90 and in 1990 won a resounding victory to become the first chancellor of reunited Germany. His miscalculation of the true costs of reunification and their subsequent effects on the German economy led to a dramatic fall in his popularity, but as the economy recovered, so did his public esteem, enabling him to achieve a historic third electoral victory Oct 1994.

kohlrabi variety of kale *Brassica oleracea*. The leaves of kohlrabi shoot from a globular swelling on the main stem; it is used for food and resembles a turnip.

Kokoschka Oskar 1886–1980. Austrian Expressionist painter and writer who lived in England from 1938. Initially influenced by the Vienna ◊Sezession painters, he painted vivid seascapes and highly charged portraits. His writings include several plays.

Kollwitz Käthe 1867–1945. German sculptor and printmaker. Her early series of etchings depicting workers and their environment are bold, realistic, and harshly expressive. Later themes include war, death, and maternal love.

Köln German form of ◊Cologne, a city in Germany.

Komi autonomous republic in N central Russia; area 160,580 sq mi/717 sq km; population (1986) 1,200,000. Its capital is Syktyvkar.

Kommunizma, Pik or *Communism Peak* highest mountain in the ◊Pamirs, a mountain range in Tajikistan; 24,599 ft/7,495 m. As part of the former USSR, it was known as *Mount Garmo* until 1933 and *Mount Stalin* 1933–62.

kookaburra or *laughing jackass* largest of the world's ◊kingfishers *Dacelo novaeguineae*, found in Australia, with an extraordinary laughing call. It feeds on insects and other small creatures.

The body and tail measure 18 in/45 cm, the head is grayish with a dark eye stripe, and the back and wings are flecked brown with gray underparts. Its cry is one of the most familiar sounds of the bush of E Australia.

Koran (alternatively transliterated as *Quran*) sacred book of ◊Islam. Written in the purest Arabic, it contains 114 *suras* (chapters), and is stated to have been divinely revealed to the prophet Mohammed about 616.

Korbut Olga 1955– . Soviet gymnast who attracted world attention at the 1972 Olympic Games with her lively floor routine, winning three gold medals for the team, beam, and floor exercises.

Korea peninsula in E Asia, divided into north and south; see ◊Korea, North, and ◊Korea, South.

Korean native to or inhabitant of Korea; also the language and culture. There are approximately 33 million Koreans in South Korea, 15 million in North Korea, and 3 million elsewhere, principally in Japan, China (Manchuria), Russia, Kazakhstan, Uzbekistan, and the US.

Korean language language of Korea, written from the 5th century AD in Chinese characters until the invention of an alphabet by King Sejong 1443. The linguistic affiliations of Korean are unclear, but it may be distantly related to Japanese.

Korea, North Democratic People's Republic of (*Chosun Minchu-chui Inmin Konghwa-guk*) *area* 46,528 sq mi/120,538 sq km *capital* Pyongyang *towns and cities* Chongjin, Nampo, Wonsan *physical* wide coastal plain in W rising to mountains cut by deep valleys in interior *environment* the building of a hydroelectric dam at Kumgangsan on a tributary of the Han River has been opposed by South Korea as a potential flooding threat to central Korea *features* separated from South Korea by a military demarcation line; the richer of the two Koreas in mineral resources (copper, iron ore, graphite, tungsten, zinc, lead, magnesite, gold, phosphor, phosphates) *head of state* Kim Jong Il from 1994 *head of government* Kang Song San from 1992 *political system* communism *political parties* Korean Workers' Party (KWP), Marxist-Leninist (leads Democratic Front for the Reunification of the Fatherland, including North Korean Democratic Party and Religious Chungwoo Party) *exports* coal, iron, copper, textiles, chemicals *currency* won *population* (1993 est) 22,600,000; growth rate 2.5% p.a. *life expectancy* men 68, women 74 *language* Korean *media* state-controlled; only one radio station *religion* traditionally Buddhist, Confucian, but religious activity curtailed by the state *literacy* 99% *GNP* $1,038 per head (1991) *chronology 1910* Korea formally annexed by Japan. *1945* Russian and US troops entered Korea, forced surrender of Japanese, and divided the country in two. Soviet troops occupied North Korea. *1948* Democratic People's Republic of Korea declared. *1950* North Korea invaded South Korea to unite the nation, beginning the Korean War. *1953* Armistice agreed to end Korean War. *1961* Friendship and mutual assistance treaty signed with China. *1972* New constitution, with executive president, adopted. Talks with South Korea about possible reunification. *1980* Reunification talks broke down. *1983* Four South Korean cabinet ministers assassinated in Rangoon, Burma (Myanmar), by North Korean army officers. *1985* Improved relations with the USSR. *1989* Increasing evidence of nuclear-weapons development. *1990* Diplomatic contacts with South Korea and Japan suggested a thaw in North Korea's relations with rest of world. *1991* Became a member of the United Nations. Signed nonaggression agreement with South Korea; agreed to ban nuclear weapons. *1992* Signed Nuclear Safeguards Agreement, allowing international inspection of nuclear facilities. Also

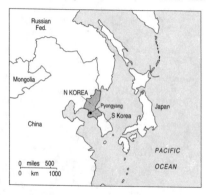

signed pact with South Korea for mutual inspection of nuclear facilities. Yon Hyong Muk replaced by Kang Song San. *1993* Threatened to withdraw from Nuclear Non-Proliferation Treaty. Resisted international inspection of nuclear-development sites; tension with US over nuclear capability. *1994* Kim Il Sung died; succeeded by his son, Kim Jong Il.

Korean War war 1950–53 between North Korea (supported by China) and South Korea, aided by the United Nations (the troops were mainly US). North Korean forces invaded the South June 25, 1950, and the Security Council of the United Nations, owing to a walk-out by the USSR, voted to oppose them. The North Koreans held most of the South when US reinforcements arrived Sept 1950 and forced their way through to the North Korean border with China. The Chinese retaliated, pushing them back to the original boundary Oct 1950; truce negotiations began 1951, although the war did not end until 1953.

Korea, South Republic of Korea (*Daehan Minguk*) *area* 38,161 sq mi/98,799 sq km *capital* Seoul *towns and cities* Taegu, ports Pusan, Inchon *physical* southern end of a mountainous peninsula separating the Sea of Japan from the Yellow Sea *features* Chomsongdae (world's earliest observatory); giant Popchusa Buddha; granite peaks of Soraksan National Park *head of state* Kim Young Sam from 1993 *head of government* Lee Young Tok from 1994 *political system* emergent democracy *political parties* Democratic Liberal Party (DLP), right of center; Democratic Party, left of center; Unification National Party (UNP), right of center *exports* steel, ships, chemicals, electronics, textiles and clothing, plywood, fish *currency* won *population* (1993 est) 44,200,000; growth rate 1.4% p.a. *life expectancy* men 68, women 74 *language* Korean *media* freedom of the press achieved 1987; large numbers of newspapers with large circulations. It is prohibited to say anything favorable about North Korea *religions* traditionally Buddhist, Confucian, and Chondokyo; Christian 28% *literacy* men 99%, women 94% *GNP* $6,749 per head (1992) *chronology* *1910* Korea formally annexed by Japan. *1945* Russian and US troops entered Korea, forced surrender of Japanese, and divided the country in two. US military government took control of South Korea. *1948* Republic proclaimed. *1950–53* War with North Korea. *1960* President Syngman Rhee resigned amid unrest. *1961* Military coup by General Park Chung-Hee. Industrial growth program. *1979* Assassination of President Park. *1980* Military takeover by General

Chun Doo Hwan. *1987* Adoption of more democratic constitution after student unrest. Roh Tae Woo elected president. *1988* Former president Chun, accused of corruption, publicly apologized and agreed to hand over his financial assets to the state. Seoul hosted Summer Olympic Games. *1989* Roh reshuffled cabinet, threatened crackdown on protesters. *1990* Two minor opposition parties united with Democratic Justice Party to form ruling Democratic Liberal Party. Diplomatic relations established with the USSR. *1991* Violent mass demonstrations against the government. New opposition grouping, the Democratic Party, formed. Entered United Nations. Nonaggression and nuclear pacts signed with North Korea. *1992* DLP lost absolute majority in March general election. Diplomatic relations with China established. Dec: Kim Young Sam, DLP candidate, won the presidential election. *1993* Feb: Kim Young Sam sworn in as president; Hwang In Sung appointed prime minister. Dec: Lee Hoi Chang succeeded Hwang as prime minister. *1994* US military presence stepped up after North Korea's refusal to allow full inspections of its nuclear-development sites. Lee Young Tok replaced Lee Hoi Chang as prime minister.

Kościusko highest mountain in Australia (7,316 ft/ 2,229 m), in New South Wales.

Kościuszko Tadeusz 1746–1817. Polish general and nationalist who served with George Washington in the American Revolution (1776–83). He returned to Poland 1784, fought against the Russian invasion that ended in the partition of Poland, and withdrew to Saxony. He returned 1794 to lead the revolt against the occupation, but was defeated by combined Russian and Prussian forces and imprisoned until 1796.

kosher conforming to religious law with regard to the preparation and consumption of food; in Judaism, conforming to the Mosaic law of the Book of Deuteronomy. For example, only animals that chew the cud and have cloven hooves (cows and sheep, but not pigs) may be eaten. There are rules governing their humane slaughter and their preparation (such as complete draining of blood) which also apply to fowl. Only fish with scales and fins may be eaten; shellfish may not. Milk products may not be cooked or eaten with meat or poultry, or until four hours after eating them. Utensils for meat must be kept separate from those for milk as well.

Kossuth Lajos 1802–1894. Hungarian nationalist and leader of the revolution of 1848. He proclaimed Hungary's independence of Hapsburg rule, became governor of a Hungarian republic 1849, and, when it was defeated by Austria and Russia, fled first to Turkey and then to exile in Britain and Italy.

Kosygin Alexei Nikolaievich 1904–1980. Soviet politician, prime minister 1964–80. He was elected to the Supreme Soviet 1938, became a member of the Politburo 1946, deputy prime minister 1960, and succeeded Khrushchev as premier (while Brezhnev succeeded him as party secretary). In the late 1960s Kosygin's influence declined.

Koussevitsky Serge 1874–1951. Russian musician and conductor. He is well known for his work in the US. He established his own orchestra in Moscow 1909, introducing works by Prokofiev, Rachmaninov, and Stravinsky. Although named director of the State Symphony after the Bolshevik Revolution 1917, Koussevitsky left the USSR for the US, becoming director of the Boston Symphony Orchestra 1924.

Kowloon peninsula on the Chinese coast forming part of the British crown colony of Hong Kong; the city of Kowloon is a residential area.

Krajina region on the frontier between Croatia and Bosnia-Herzegovina; the chief town is Knin. Dominated by Serbs, the region proclaimed itself an autonomous Serbian province after Croatia declared its independence from Yugoslavia 1991. Krajina was the scene of intense inter-ethnic fighting during the civil war in Croatia 1991–92 and, following the cease-fire Jan 1992, 10,000 UN troops were deployed here and in E and W Slavonia. In Jan 1993 Croatian forces launched a surprise offensive into Serbian-held territory in the region.

Kraków or *Cracow* city in Poland, on the river Vistula; population (1990) 750,500. It is an industrial center producing railroad wagons, paper, chemicals, and tobacco. It was capital of Poland about 1300–1595.

Krasnodar territory of SW Russia, in the N Caucasus Mountains, adjacent to the Black Sea; area 32,290 sq mi/83,600 sq km; population (1985) 4,992,000. The capital is Krasnodar. In addition to stock rearing and the production of grain, rice, fruit, and tobacco, oil is refined.

Krasnoyarsk territory of Russia in central Siberia stretching N to the Arctic Ocean; area 927,617 sq mi/ 2,401,600 sq km; population (1985) 3,430,000. The capital is Krasnoyarsk. It is drained by the Yenisei River. Mineral resources include gold, graphite, coal, iron ore, and uranium.

Kravchuk Leonid 1934– . Ukrainian politician, president 1990–94. Formerly a member of the Ukrainian Communist Party (UCP), he became its ideology chief in the 1980s. After the suspension of the UCP Aug 1991, Kravchuk became an advocate of independence and market-centered economic reform. He was defeated by former prime minister Leonid Kuchma in the July 1994 presidential elections.

Krebs Hans 1900–1981. German-born British biochemist who discovered the citric acid cycle, also known as the **Krebs cycle**, the final pathway by which food molecules are converted into energy in living tissues. For this work he shared with Fritz Lipmann the 1953 Nobel Prize for Medicine.

krill any of several Antarctic crustaceans of the order Euphausiacea, the most common species being *Euphausia superba*. Shrimplike, it is about 2.5 in/6 cm long, with two antennae, five pairs of legs, seven pairs of light organs along the body, and is colored orange above and green beneath.

Krishna incarnation of the Hindu god ◊Vishnu. The devotion of the bhakti movement is usually directed toward Krishna; an example of this is the ◊International Society for Krishna Consciousness. Many stories are told of Krishna's mischievous youth, and he is the charioteer of Arjuna in the *Bhagavad-Gi˜ta˜*.

Kruger Stephanus Johannes Paulus 1825–1904. President of the Transvaal 1883–1900. He refused to remedy the grievances of the uitlanders (English and other non-Boer white residents) and so precipitated the Second South African War.

krypton colorless, odorless, gaseous, nonmetallic element, symbol Kr, atomic number 36, atomic weight 83.80. It is grouped with the inert gases and was long believed not to enter into reactions, but it is now known to combine with fluorine under certain conditions; it remains inert to all other reagents. It is present in very small quantities in the air (about 114 parts per million). It is used chiefly in fluorescent lamps, lasers, and gas-filled electronic valves.

Kuala Lumpur capital of the Federation of Malaysia; area 93 sq mi/240 sq km; population (1990) 1,237,900. The city developed after 1873 with the expansion of tin and rubber trading; these are now its main industries. Formerly within the state of Selangor, of which it was also the capital, it was created a federal territory 1974.

Kublai Khan 1216–1294. Mongol emperor of China from 1259. He completed his grandfather ◊Genghis Khan's conquest of N China from 1240, and on his brother Mungo's death 1259 established himself as emperor of China. He moved the capital to Beijing and founded the Yuan dynasty, successfully expanding his empire into Indochina, but was defeated in an attempt to conquer Japan 1281.

Kubrick Stanley 1928– . US film director, producer, and screenwriter. His films include *Paths of Glory* 1957, *Dr Strangelove* 1964, *2001: A Space Odyssey* 1968, *A Clockwork Orange* 1971, and *The Shining* 1979.

kudu either of two species of African antelope of the genus *Tragelaphus*. The greater kudu *T. strepsiceros* is fawn-colored with thin white vertical stripes, and stands 4.2 ft/1.3 m at the shoulder, with head and body 8 ft/2.4 m long. Males have long spiral horns. The greater kudu is found in bush country from Angola to Ethiopia.

The similar lesser kudu *T. imberbis* lives in E Africa and is 3 ft/1 m at the shoulder.

Ku Klux Klan US secret society dedicated to white supremacy, founded 1866 in the southern states of the US to oppose ◊Reconstruction after the ◊Civil War and to deny political rights to the black population. Members wore hooded white robes to hide their identity, and burned crosses at their night-time meetings.

It was disbanded in 1869 under pressure from members who opposed violence. The group reemerged in 1915 as an antiblack, anti-Semitic, anti-Catholic, right-wing group that portrayed itself as fervently patriotic. Today the Klan has evolved into a paramilitary extremist group that has forged loose ties with other white supremacist groups.

kumquat small orange-yellow fruit of any of several evergreen trees of the genus *Fortunella*, family Rutaceae. Native to E Asia, kumquats are cultivated throughout the tropics. The tree grows 8–12 ft/2.4–3.6 m and has dark green shiny leaves and white scented flowers. The fruit is eaten fresh (the skin is edible), preserved, or candied. The oval or Nagami kumquat is the most common variety.

Kun Béla 1886–1938. Hungarian politician who created a Soviet republic in Hungary March 1919, which was overthrown Aug 1919 by a Western blockade and Romanian military actions. The succeeding regime under Admiral Horthy effectively liquidated both socialism and liberalism in Hungary.

kung fu Chinese art of unarmed combat (Mandarin *ch'üan fa*), one of the ◊martial arts. It is practiced in many forms, the most popular being *wing chun*, "beautiful springtime". The basic principle is to use attack as a form of defense.

Kunming formerly *Yunnan* capital of Yunnan province, China, on Lake Dian Chi, about 6,500 ft/ 2,000 m above sea level; population (1989) 1,500,000.

Industries include chemicals, textiles, and copper smelted with nearby hydroelectric power.

Kuomintang original spelling of the Chinese nationalist party, now known (outside Taiwan) as ◊Guomindang.

Kurd member of the Kurdish culture, living mostly in the Taurus and Sagros mountains of E Turkey, W Iran, and N Iraq in the region called ◊Kurdistan. Some 1 million Kurds were made homeless and 25,000 killed as a result of chemical-weapon attacks by Iraq 1984–89, and in 1991 more than 1 million were forced to flee their homes in N Iraq. They are predominantly Sunni Muslims, although there are some Shiites in Iran.

Kurdish language language belonging to the Indo-Iranian branch of the Indo-European family, closely related to Farsi (Persian). It is spoken by the Kurds, a geographically divided ethnic group. Its numerous dialects fall into two main groups: northern Kurmanji and southern Kurmanji (also known as Sorani). Around 60% of Kurds speak one of the northern Kurmanji dialects.

Kurdistan or *Kordestan* hilly region in SW Asia near Mount Ararat, where the borders of Iran, Iraq, Syria, Turkey, Armenia, and Azerbaijan meet; area 74,600 sq mi/193,000 sq km; total population around 18 million. It is the home of the ◊Kurds and is the area over which Kurdish nationalists have traditionally fought to win sovereignty. Also the name of a NW Iranian province, covering 9,650 sq mi/25,000 sq km.

Kuril Islands or *Kuriles* chain of about 50 small islands stretching from the NE of Hokkaido, Japan, to the S of Kamchatka, Russia; area 5,700 sq mi/14,765 sq km; population (1990) 25,000. Some of them are of volcanic origin. Two of the Kurils (Etorofu and Kunashiri) are claimed by Japan and Russia.

Kurosawa Akira 1929– . Japanese director. His film *Rashōmon* 1950 introduced Western audiences to Japanese cinema. Epics such as *Shichinin no samurai/Seven Samurai* 1954 combine spectacle with intimate human drama.

Kuwait State of (*Dowlat al Kuwait*) *area* 6,878 sq mi/ 17,819 sq km *capital* Kuwait (also chief port) *towns and cities* Jahra, Ahmadi, Fahaheel *physical* hot desert; islands of Failaka, Bubiyan, and Warba at NE corner of Arabian Peninsula *environment* during the Gulf War 1990–91, 650 oil wells were set alight and about 300,000 metric tons of oil were released into the waters of the Gulf leading to pollution haze, photochemical smog, acid rain, soil contamination, and water pollution *features* there are no rivers and rain is light; the world's largest desalination plants, built in the 1950s *head of state* Sheikh Jabir al-Ahmad al-Jabir as-Sabah from 1977 *head of government* Crown Prince Sheikh Saad al-Abdullah as-Salim as-Sabah from 1978 *political system* absolute monarchy *political parties* none *exports* oil *currency* Kuwaiti dinar *population* (1993 est) 1,600,000 (Kuwaitis 40%, Palestinians 30%); growth rate 5.5% p.a. *life expectancy* men 72, women 77 *languages* Arabic 78%, Kurdish 10%, Farsi 4% *religions* Sunni Muslim 45%, Shiite minority 30% *literacy* men 77%, women 67% *GNP* $16,380 per head (1989) *chronology 1914* Britain recognized Kuwait as an independent sovereign state. *1961* Full independence achieved from Britain, with Sheik Abdullah al-Salem al-Sabah as emir. *1965* Sheik Abdullah died; succeeded by his brother, Sheik Sabah. *1977* Sheik Sabah died;

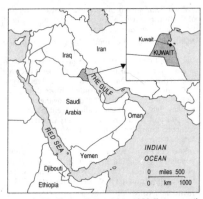

succeeded by Crown Prince Jabir. *1983* Shiite guerrillas bombed targets in Kuwait; 17 arrested. *1986* National assembly suspended. *1987* Kuwaiti oil tankers reflagged, received US Navy protection; missile attacks by Iran. *1988* Aircraft hijacked by pro-Iranian Shiites demanding release of convicted guerrillas; Kuwait refused. *1989* Two of the convicted guerrillas released. *1990* Prodemocracy demonstrations suppressed. Aug: Kuwait annexed by Iraq, causing extensive damage to property and environment. Emir set up government in exile in Saudi Arabia. *1991* Feb: Kuwait liberated by US-led coalition forces. New government omitted any opposition representatives. *1992* Reconstituted national assembly elected, with opposition nominees, including Islamic candidates, winning majority of seats. *1993* Jan: incursions by Iraq into Kuwait repelled by US-led air strikes on Iraqi military sites.

Kuwait City (Arabic *Al Kuwayt*) formerly *Qurein* chief port and capital of the state of Kuwait, on the southern shore of Kuwait Bay; population (1985) 44,300, plus the suburbs of Hawalli, population (1985) 145,100, Jahra, population (1985) 111,200, and as-Salimiya, population (1985) 153,400. Kuwait is a banking and investment center. It was heavily damaged during the Gulf War.

Kwajalien atoll in the Marshall Islands; held by the Japanese in World War II. When it was attacked and taken by US troops Feb 1944, its garrison of 8,000 men fought so fanatically that there were no survivors.

Kwa Ndebele black homeland in Transvaal province, South Africa; population (1985) 235,800. It achieved self-governing status 1981.

Kwangchow alternative transliteration of ◊Guangzhou, a city in China.

Kwangchu or *Kwangju* capital of South Cholla province, SW South Korea; population (1990) 1,144,700. It is at the center of a rice-growing region. A museum in the city houses a large collection of Chinese porcelain dredged up 1976 after lying for over 600 years on the ocean floor.

Kwangtung alternative transliteration of ◊Guangdong, a province of China.

kwashiorkor severe protein deficiency in children under five years, resulting in retarded growth, lethargy, ◊edema, diarrhea, and a swollen abdomen. It is common in Third World countries with a high incidence of malnutrition.

KwaZulu black homeland in Natal province, South Africa; population (1985) 3,747,000. It achieved self-governing status 1971. In 1994 it was placed under a state of emergency in the run-up to the first multiracial elections, after mounting violence by the Zulu-based ◊Inkatha party threatened to destabilize the election process.

Kweichow alternative transliteration of ◊Guizhou, a province of China.

Kyd Thomas *c.*1557–1595. English dramatist. He was the author of a bloody revenge tragedy, *The Spanish Tragedy* about 1588, which anticipated elements present in Shakespeare's *Hamlet*

Kyoto former capital of Japan 794–1868 (when the capital was changed to Tokyo) on Honshu Island, linked by canal with Biwa Lake; population (1989) 1,407,300. Industries include electrical, chemical, and machinery plants; silk weaving; and the manufacture of porcelain, bronze, and lacquerware.

Kyrgyzstan Republic of *area* 76,641 sq mi/198,500 sq km *capital* Bishkek (formerly Frunze) *towns and cities* Osh, Przhevalsk, Kyzyl-Kiya, Tormak *physical* mountainous, an extension of the Tian Shan range *head of state* Askar Akayev from 1990 *head of government* vacant *political system* emergent democracy *political parties* Democratic Kyrgyzstan, nationalist reformist; Asaba (Banner) Party and Free Kyrgyzstan Party, both opposition groupings; Social Democratic Party, nationalist *products* cereals, sugar, cotton, coal, oil, sheep, yaks, horses *currency* som *population* (1993 est) 4,600,000 (Kyrgyz 52%, Russian 22%, Uzbek 13%, Ukrainian 3%, German 2%) *life expectancy* men 65, women 73 *language* Kyrgyz, a Turkic language *religion* Sunni Muslim *GNP* $1,550 per head (1991) *chronology 1917–1924* Part of independent Turkestan republic. *1924* Became autonomous republic within USSR. *1936* Became full union republic within USSR. *1990* June: ethnic clashes resulted in state of emergency being imposed in Bishkek. Nov: Askar Akayev, a reform communist, chosen as state president. *1991* March: maintenance of Union endorsed by USSR referendum. Aug: President Akayev condemned attempted anti-Gorbachev coup in Moscow; Kyrgyz Communist Party, which supported the coup, suspended. Oct: Akayev directly elected president. Dec: joined new Commonwealth of Independent States; independence recognized by US. *1992* Joined the United Nations. *1993* New constitution adopted. *1994* Joined Central Asian Union. National referendum overwhelmingly supported Akayev's presidency.

Kyushu southernmost of the main islands of Japan, separated from Shikoku and Honshu islands by Bungo Channel and Suo Bay, but connected to Honshu by bridge and rail tunnel *area* 42,150 sq km/16,270 sq mi, including about 370 small islands *capital* Nagasaki *cities* Fukuoka, Kumamoto, Kagoshima *physical* mountainous, volcanic, with subtropical climate *features* the active volcano Aso-take (5,225 ft/ 1,592 m), with the world's largest crater *industries* coal, gold, silver, iron, tin, rice, tea, timber *population* (1986) 13,295,000.

l symbol for ◊*liter*, a measure of liquid volume.

Labor Day legal national holiday in honor of workers. In the US and Canada, Labor Day is celebrated on the first Monday in September. In many countries it coincides with ◊May Day.

labor-intensive production production where a large amount of labor is used relative to capital. For example, window-cleaning or brick-laying are labor-intensive jobs. Service industries tend to be far more labor-intensive than either primary or secondary industries.

labor union organization of employed workers formed to undertake collective bargaining with employers and to try to achieve improved working conditions for its members. Attitudes of government to unions and of unions to management vary greatly from country to country. Probably the most effective labor-union system is that of Sweden, and the most internationally known is the Polish ◊Solidarity.

Labour Party UK political party based on socialist principles, originally formed to represent workers. It was founded in 1900 and first held office in 1924. The first majority Labour government 1945–51 introduced ◊nationalization and the National Health Service, and expanded ◊social security. Labour was again in power 1964–70 and 1974–79. The party leader is elected by an electoral college, with a weighted representation of the Parliamentary Labour Party (30%), constituency parties (30%), and labor unions (40%).

Labrador area of NE Canada, part of the province of Newfoundland, lying between Ungava Bay on the NW, the Atlantic Ocean on the E, and the Strait of Belle Isle on the SE; area 102,699 sq mi/266,060 sq km; population (1986) 28,741. It consists primarily of a gently sloping plateau with an irregular coastline of numerous bays, fjords, inlets, and cliffs (60–120 m/ 200–400 ft high).

Industries include fisheries, timber and pulp, and many minerals. Hydroelectric resources include Churchill Falls on Churchill River, where one of the world's largest underground power houses is situated. There is a Canadian air force base at Goose Bay

laburnum any flowering tree or shrub of the genus *Laburnum* of the pea family Leguminosae. The seeds are poisonous. *L. anagyroides*, native to the mountainous parts of central Europe, is often grown as an ornamental tree. The flowers, in long drooping clusters, are bright yellow and appear in early spring; some varieties have purple or reddish flowers.

Labyrinth in Greek legend, the maze designed by the Athenian artisan Daedalus at Knossos in Crete for King Minos, as a home for the Minotaur—a monster, half man and half bull. After killing the Minotaur, Theseus, the prince of Athens, was guided out of the Labyrinth by a thread given to him by the king's daughter, Ariadne.

lace delicate, decorative, openwork textile fabric. Lace is a European craft with centers in Belgium, Italy,

France, Germany, and England.

lacewing insect of the families Hemerobiidae (the brown lacewings) and Chrysopidae (the green lacewings) of the order Neuroptera. Found throughout the world, lacewings are so called because of the intricate veining of their two pairs of semitransparent wings. They have narrow bodies and long thin antennae. The larvae (called aphid lions) are predators, especially on aphids.

lacquer waterproof resinous varnish obtained from Oriental trees *Toxicodendron verniciflua*, and used for decorating furniture and art objects. It can be applied to wood, fabric, leather, or other materials, with or without added colors. The technique of making and carving small lacquerwork objects was developed in China, probably as early as the 4th century BC , and was later adopted in Japan.

lacrosse ball game, adopted from the North American Indians, and named for a fancied resemblance of the lacrosse stick (crosse) to a bishop's crosier. Thongs across the curved end of the crosse form a pocket to carry the small rubber ball.

The field is approximately 110 yd/100 m long and a minimum of 60 yd/55 m wide in the men's game, which is played with 10 players per side; the women's field is larger, and there are 12 players per side. The goals are just under 6 ft/2 m square, with loose nets. The world championship was first held in 1967 for men, and in 1969 for women.

lactation secretion of milk in mammals, from the mammary glands. In late pregnancy, the cells lining the lobules inside the mammary glands begin extracting substances from the blood to produce milk. The supply of milk starts shortly after birth with the production of colostrum, a clear fluid consisting largely of water, protein, antibodies, and vitamins. The production of milk continues practically as long as the baby continues to suckle.

lactic acid or *2-hydroxypropanoic acid* CH_3CHOH-$COOH$ organic acid, a colorless, almost odorless liquid, produced by certain bacteria during fermentation and by active muscle cells when they are exercised hard and are experiencing oxygen debt. An accumulation of lactic acid in the muscles may cause cramp. It occurs in yogurt, buttermilk, sour cream, poor wine, and certain plant extracts, and is used in food preservation and in the preparation of pharmaceuticals.

lactose white sugar, found in solution in milk; it forms 5% of cow's milk. It is commercially prepared from the whey obtained in cheese-making. Like table sugar (sucrose), it is a disaccharide, consisting of two basic sugar units (monosaccharides), in this case, glucose and galactose. Unlike sucrose, it is tasteless.

Ladoga (Russian *Ladozhskoye*) largest lake on the continent of Europe, in Russia, just NE of St Petersburg; area 7,100 sq mi/18,400 sq km. It receives the waters of several rivers, including the Svir, which drains Lake Onega and runs to the Gulf of Finland by the river Neva.

Lady in the UK, the formal title of the daughter of an earl, marquis, or duke; and of any woman whose husband is above the rank of baronet or knight, as well as (by courtesy only) the wives of these latter ranks.

ladybug or **ladybird** beetle of the family Coccinellidae, generally red or yellow in color, with black spots. There are numerous species which, as larvae and adults, feed on aphids and scale-insect pests.

Lady Day British name for the Christian festival (March 25) of the Annunciation of the Virgin Mary; until 1752 it was the beginning of the legal year in England, and it is still a quarter day (date for the payment of quarterly rates or dues).

Lafayette city in W central Indiana, on the Wabash River, NW of Indianapolis, seat of Tippecanoe County; population (1990) 43,760. A distribution center for the area's agricultural products, its industries also include building materials, chemicals, wire, pharmaceuticals, and automobile parts.

Purdue University 1865 is nearby. The Battle of Tippecanoe was fought here 1811.

Lafayette Marie Joseph Gilbert de Motier, Marquis de Lafayette 1757–1834. French soldier and politician. He fought against Britain in the American Revolution 1777–79 and 1780–82. During the French Revolution he sat in the National Assembly as a constitutional royalist and in 1789 presented the Declaration of the Rights of Man. After the storming of the ◊Bastille, he was given command of the National Guard. In 1792 he fled the country after attempting to restore the monarchy and was imprisoned by the Austrians until 1797. He supported Napoleon Bonaparte in 1815, sat in the chamber of deputies as a Liberal from 1818, and played a leading part in the revolution of 1830.

La Fontaine Jean de 1621–1695. French poet. He was born at Château-Thierry, and from 1656 lived largely in Paris, the friend of the playwrights Molière and Racine, and the poet Boileau. His works include *Fables* 1668–94 and *Contes* 1665–74, a series of witty and bawdy tales in verse.

Lagos chief port and former capital of Nigeria, located at the western end of an island in a lagoon and linked by bridges with the mainland via Iddo Island; population (1983) 1,097,000. Industries include chemicals, metal products, and fish. One of the most important slaving ports, Lagos was bombarded and occupied by the British 1851, becoming the colony of Lagos 1862. Abuja was designated the new capital 1982 (officially recognized as such 1992).

Lahnda language spoken by 15–20 million people in Pakistan and N India. It is closely related to Punjabi and Romany, and belongs to the Indo-Iranian branch of the Indo-European language family.

Lahore capital of the province of Punjab and second city of Pakistan; population (1981) 2,920,000. Industries include engineering, textiles, carpets, and chemicals. It is associated with the Mogul rulers Akbar, Jahangir, and Aurangzeb, whose capital it was in the 16th and 17th centuries.

Laing R(onald) D(avid) 1927–1989. Scottish psychoanalyst, originator of the "social theory" of mental illness, for example that schizophrenia is promoted by family pressure for its members to conform to standards alien to themselves. His books include *The Divided Self* 1960 and *The Politics of the Family* 1971.

laissez faire theory that the state should not intervene in economic affairs, except to break up a monopoly.

The phrase originated with the Physiocrats, 18th-century French economists whose maxim was *laissez faire et laissez passer* (literally, "let go and let pass"—that is, leave the individual alone and let commodities circulate freely). The degree to which intervention should take place is still one of the chief problems of economics. The Scottish economist Adam ◊Smith justified the theory in *The Wealth of Nations*.

lake body of still water lying in depressed ground without direct communication with the sea. Lakes are common in formerly glaciated regions, along the courses of slow rivers, and in low land near the sea. The main classifications are by origin: *glacial lakes*, formed by glacial scouring; *barrier lakes*, formed by landslides and glacial moraines; *crater lakes*, found in volcanoes; and *tectonic lakes*, occurring in natural fissures.

Lake District region in Cumbria, England; area 700 sq mi/1,800 sq km. It contains the principal English lakes, which are separated by wild uplands rising to many peaks, including Scafell Pike (3,210 ft/978 m), the highest peak in England.

Lakshadweep group of 36 coral islands, 10 inhabited, in the Indian Ocean, 200 mi/320 km off the Malabar coast, forming a Union Territory of the Republic of India; area 12 sq mi/32 sq km; population (1991) 51,700. The administrative headquarters are on Kavaratti Island. Products include coir, copra, and fish. The religion is Muslim. The first Western visitor was Vasco da Gama 1499. The islands were British from 1877 until Indian independence and were created a Union Territory 1956. Formerly known as the Laccadive, Minicoy, and Amindivi Islands, they were renamed Lakshadweep 1973.

Lakshmi Hindu goddess of wealth and beauty, consort of Vishnu; her festival is Diwali.

Lamaism religion of Tibet and Mongolia, a form of Mahāyāna Buddhism. Buddhism was introduced into Tibet in AD 640, but the real founder of Lamaism was the Indian missionary Padma Sambhava who began his activity about 750. The head of the church is the ◊Dalai Lama, who is considered an incarnation of the Bodhisattva Avalokites´vara. On the death of the Dalai Lama great care is taken in finding the infant in whom he has been reincarnated.

Lamarck Jean Baptiste de 1744–1829. French naturalist whose now discredited theory of evolution, known as *Lamarckism*, was based on the idea that acquired characteristics (changes acquired in an individual's lifetime) are inherited, and that organisms have an intrinsic urge to evolve into better-adapted forms. His reputation was established through his *Philosophie Zoologique/Zoological Philosophy* 1809, which outlined his "transformist" (evolutionary) ideas.

Lamartine Alphonse de 1790–1869. French poet. He wrote romantic poems, including *Méditations poétiques* 1820, followed by *Nouvelles méditations/New Meditations* 1823, and *Harmonies* 1830. His *Histoire des Girondins/History of the Girondists* 1847 helped to inspire the revolution of 1848.

Lamb Charles 1775–1834. English essayist and critic. He collaborated with his sister **Mary Lamb** (1764–1847) on *Tales from Shakespeare* 1807, and his *Specimens of English Dramatic Poets* 1808 helped to revive interest in Elizabethan plays. As "Elia" he contributed essays to the *London Magazine* from 1820 (collected 1823 and 1833).

Lammas medieval festival of harvest, celebrated 1 Aug At one time it was an English quarter day (date for payment of quarterly rates or dues), and is still a quarter day in Scotland.

lammergeier Old World vulture *Gypaetus barbatus*, also known as the bearded vulture, with a wingspan of 9 ft/2.7 m. It ranges over S Europe, N Africa, and Asia, in wild mountainous areas. It feeds on offal and carrion and drops bones onto rocks to break them and so get at the marrow.

lamprey any of various eel-shaped jawless fishes belonging to the family Petromyzontidae. A lamprey feeds on other fish by fixing itself by its round mouth to its host and boring into the flesh with its toothed tongue. Lampreys breed in fresh water, and the young live as larvae for about five years before migrating to the sea.

Lancashire county of NW England *area* 1,173 sq mi/3,040 sq km *towns and cities* Preston (administrative headquarters), which forms part of Central Lancashire New Town from 1970 (together with Fulwood, Bamber Bridge, Leyland, and Chorley); Lancaster, Accrington, Blackburn, Burnley; ports Fleetwood and Heysham; seaside resorts Blackpool, Morecambe, and Southport *features* the river Ribble; the Pennines; the Forest of Bowland (moors and farming valleys); Pendle Hill *industries* formerly a world center of cotton manufacture, now replaced with high-technology aerospace and electronics industries. There is dairy farming and market gardening *population* (1991) 1,384,000

Lancaster Burt (Burton Stephen) 1913–1994. US film actor, formerly an acrobat. A star from his first film, *The Killers* 1946, he proved himself adept both at action roles and more complex character parts as in such films as *From Here to Eternity* 1953, *Elmer Gantry* 1960 (Academy Award), *The Leopard/Il Gattopardo* 1963, *The Swimmer* 1968, and *Atlantic City* 1980.

Lancaster, House of English royal house, a branch of the Plantagenets.

Lanchow alternative transcription of ◊Lanzhou, a city in China.

Land (plural *Länder*) federal state of Germany or Austria.

Land Edwin Herbert 1909–1991. US inventor of the ◊Polaroid Land camera 1947. The camera developed the film in one minute inside the camera and produced an "instant" photograph.

While a student at Harvard, Land became interested in polarized light and invented the sheet polarizer, which imbedded lined-up crystals in a clear plastic sheet. This tremendous advance had implications for camera filters, sunglasses and other optical equipment, and related products. Land set up a laboratory 1932, then established the Polaroid Corporation 1937–80. His research also led to a process for 3-D pictures, "instant" color film, "instant" motion pictures, and a new theory of color perception, the "retinex" theory 1977.

landfill site large holes in the ground used for dumping household and commercial waste. Landfill disposal has been the preferred option in the US and the UK for many years, with up to 85% of household waste being dumped in this fashion. However, the sites can be dangerous, releasing toxins and other leachates into the soil and the policy is itself wasteful both in terms of the materials dumped and land usage.

Landis Kenesaw Mountain 1866–1944. US judge and baseball commissioner. He was judge in the fraud trial of the infamous "Black Sox" who conspired with gamblers to deliberately lose the 1919 World Series. Appointed as the first commissioner of major-league baseball 1921 he established strict standards against players' involvement with betting.

Landsbergis Vytautas 1932– . President of Lithuania 1990–93. He became active in nationalist politics in the 1980s, founding and eventually chairing the anticommunist Sajudis independence movement 1988. When Sajudis swept to victory in the republic's elections March 1990, Landsbergis chaired the Supreme Council of Lithuania, becoming, in effect, president. He immediately drafted the republic's declaration of independence from the USSR which, after initial Soviet resistance, was recognized Sept 1991.

Landseer Edwin Henry 1802–1873. English painter, sculptor, and engraver of animal studies. Much of his work reflects the Victorian taste for sentimental and moralistic pictures, for example *Dignity and Impudence* 1839 (Tate Gallery, London). The *Monarch of the Glen* 1850 (John Dewar and Sons Ltd), depicting a highland stag, was painted for the House of Lords. His sculptures include the lions at the base of Nelson's Column in Trafalgar Square, London, 1857–67.

Land's End promontory of W Cornwall, 9 mi/15 km WSW of Penzance, the westernmost point of England.

Landsteiner Karl 1868–1943. Austrian-born US immunologist who discovered the ABO ◊blood group system 1900–02, and aided in the discovery of the Rhesus blood factors 1940. He also discovered the polio virus. He was awarded a Nobel Prize in 1930.

Lang Fritz 1890–1976. Austrian film director. His films are characterized by a strong sense of fatalism and alienation. His German films include *Metropolis* 1927, the sensational *M* 1931, in which Peter Lorre played a child-killer, and the series of Dr Mabuse films, after which he fled from the Nazis to Hollywood 1935. His US films include *Fury* 1936, *You Only Live Once* 1937, *Scarlet Street* 1945, *Rancho Notorious* 1952, and *The Big Heat* 1953. He returned to Germany and directed a third picture in the Dr Mabuse series 1960.

lang k d 1961– . Canadian singer. Her mellifluous voice and androgynous image gained her a wide following beyond the country-music field where she first established herself. Her albums are *Angel With a Lariat* 1987, the mainstream *Ingénue* 1992, and *Even Cowgirls get the Blues* 1993.

Lange Dorothea 1895–1965. US photographer. She was hired 1935 by the federal Farm Security Administration to document the westward migration of farm families from the Dust Bowl of the southern central US. Her photographs, characterized by a gritty realism, were widely exhibited and subsequently published as *An American Exodus: A Record of Human Erosion* 1939.

Langland William *c.*1332–*c.*1400. English poet. His alliterative *Vision Concerning Piers Plowman* appeared in three versions between about 1367 and 1386, but some critics believe he was only responsible for the first of these. The poem forms a series of allegorical visions, in which Piers develops from the typical poor peasant to a symbol of Jesus, and condemns the social and moral evils of 14th-century England.

Langobard another name for ◊Lombard, member of a Germanic people.

language human communication through speech, writing, or both. Different nationalities or ethnic groups typically have different languages or variations on particular languages; for example, Armenians speaking the Armenian language and the British and Americans speaking distinctive varieties of the English language. One language may have various dialects, which may be seen by those who use them as languages in their own right. The term is also used for systems of communication with languagelike qualities, such as *animal language* (the way animals communicate), *body language* (gestures and expressions used to communicate ideas), *sign language* (gestures for the deaf or for use as a ◊lingua franca, as among American Indians), and *computer languages* (such as BASIC and COBOL).

Languedoc-Roussillon region of S France, comprising the *départements* of Aude, Gard, Hérault, Lozère, and Pyrénées-Orientales; area 10,576 sq mi/27,400 sq km; population (1986) 2,012,000. Its capital is Montpellier, and products include fruit, vegetables, wine, and cheese.

langur any of various leaf-eating Old World monkeys of several genera, especially the genus *Presbytis*, that lives in trees in S Asia. There are about 20 species. Langurs are related to the colobus monkey of Africa.

Lanier Sidney 1842–1881. US poet and flutist. His *Poems* 1877 contain interesting metrical experiments, in accordance with the theories expounded in his *Science of English Verse* 1880, on the relation of verse to music.

Born in Georgia, he served in the Civil War, during which he contracted tuberculosis. He subsequently studied law, which he then abandoned for music, accepting the position of first flutist in the Peabody Orchestra, Baltimore. He wrote poetry and lectured extensively until his early death.

lanolin sticky, purified wax obtained from sheep's wool and used in cosmetics, soap, and leather preparation.

lanthanide any of a series of 15 metallic elements (also known as rare earths) with atomic numbers 57 (lanthanum) to 71 (lutetium). One of its members, promethium, is radioactive. All occur in nature. Lanthanides are grouped because of their chemical similarities (they are all bivalent), their properties differing only slightly with atomic number.

lanthanum soft, silvery, ductile and malleable, metallic element, symbol La, atomic number 57, atomic weight 138.91, the first of the lanthanide series. It is used in making alloys. It was named 1839 by Swedish chemist Carl Mosander (1797–1858).

Lanzhou or *Lanchow* capital of Gansu province, China, on the river Huang He, 120 mi/190 km S of the Great Wall; population (1989) 1,480,000. Industries include oil refining, chemicals, fertilizers, and synthetic rubber.

Laois or *Laoighis* county of the Republic of Ireland, in the province of Leinster; county town Port Laoise; area 664 sq mi/1,720 sq km; population (1991) 52,300. It was formerly known as *Queen's County*. It is flat, except for the Slieve Bloom Mountains in the NW, and there are many bogs. Industries include sugar beet, dairy products, woolens, and agricultural machinery.

Laos Lao People's Democratic Republic (*Saathiaranagr oat Prachhathippatay Prachhachhon Lao*) *area* 91,400 sq mi/236,790 sq km *capital* Vientiane *towns and cities* Luang Prabang (the former royal capital), Pakse, Savannakhet *physical* landlocked state with high mountains in E; Mekong River in W; jungle covers nearly 60% of land *features* Plain of Jars, where prehistoric people carved stone jars large enough to hold

a person *head of state* Nouhak Phoumsavan from 1992 *head of government* General Khamtay Siphandon from 1991 *political system* communism, one-party state *political party* Lao People's Revolutionary Party (LPRP, the only legal party) *exports* hydroelectric power from the Mekong is exported to Thailand, timber, teak, coffee, electricity *currency* new kip *population* (1993) 4,400,000 (Lao 48%, Thai 14%, Khmer 25%, Chinese 13%); growth rate 2.2% p.a. *life expectancy* men 50, women 53 (1989) *language* Lao (official), French *religions* Theravāda Buddhist 85%, animist beliefs among mountain dwellers *literacy* 84% *GNP* $230 per head (1991) *chronology 1893–1945* Laos was a French protectorate. *1945* Temporarily occupied by Japan. *1946* Retaken by France. *1950* Granted semiautonomy in French Union. *1954* Independence achieved from France. *1960* Right-wing government seized power. *1962* Coalition government established; civil war continued. *1973* Vientiane cease-fire agreement. Withdrawal of US, Thai, and North Vietnamese forces. *1975* Communist-dominated republic proclaimed with Prince Souphanouvong as head of state. *1986* Phoumi Vongvichit became acting president. *1988* Plans announced to withdraw 40% of Vietnamese forces stationed in the country. *1989* First assembly elections since communist takeover. *1991* New constitution approved. Kaysone Phomvihane elected president. General Khamtay Siphandon named as new premier. *1992* Nov: Phomvihane died; replaced by Nouhak Phoumsavan. Dec: new national assembly created, replacing supreme people's assembly. General election held, in which all candidates required LPRP approval.

Laotian member of an Indochinese people who live along the Mekong river system. There are approximately 9 million Laotians in Thailand and 2 million in Laos. The Laotian language is a Thai member of the Sino-Tibetan family.

Lao Zi or Lao Tzu *c.*604–531 BC . Chinese philosopher, commonly regarded as the founder of ◊Taoism, with its emphasis on the Tao, the inevitable and harmonious way of the universe. Nothing certain is known of his life. The *Tao Tê Ching*, the Taoist scripture, is attributed to him but apparently dates from the 3rd century BC .

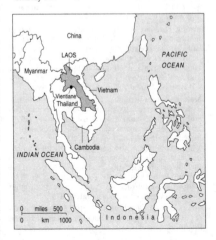

La Paz capital city of Bolivia, in Murillo province, 12,400 ft/3,800 m above sea level; population (1988) 1,049,800. Products include textiles and copper. Founded by the Spanish 1548 as Pueblo Nuevo de Nuestra Senõra de la Paz, it has been the seat of government since 1898.

lapis lazuli rock containing the blue mineral lazurite in a matrix of white calcite with small amounts of other minerals. It occurs in silica-poor igneous rocks and metamorphic limestones found in Afghanistan, Siberia, Iran, and Chile. Lapis lazuli was a valuable pigment of the Middle Ages, also used as a gemstone and in inlaying and ornamental work.

Laplace Pierre Simon, Marquis de Laplace 1749–1827. French astronomer and mathematician. In 1796, he theorized that the Solar System originated from a cloud of gas (the nebular hypothesis). He studied the motion of the Moon and planets, and published a five-volume survey of celestial mechanics, *Traité de méchanique céleste* 1799–1825. Among his mathematical achievements was the development of probability theory.

Lapland region of Europe within the Arctic Circle in Norway, Sweden, Finland, and the Kola Peninsula of NW Russia, without political definition. Its chief resources are chromium, copper, iron, timber, hydroelectric power, and tourism. The indigenous population are the Saami (formerly known as Lapps), a seminomadic herding people. Lapland has low temperatures, with three months' continuous daylight in summer and three months' continuous darkness in winter. There is summer agriculture.

La Plata capital of Buenos Aires province, Argentina; population (1980) 560,300. Industries include meat packing and petroleum refining. It was founded 1882.

la Plata, Río de estuary in South America; see ◊Plata, Río de la.

laptop computer portable microcomputer, small enough to be used on the operator's lap. It consists of a single unit, incorporating a keyboard, ◊floppy disk or ◊hard disk drives, and a screen. The screen often forms a lid that folds back in use. It uses a liquid-crystal or gas-plasma display, rather than the bulkier and heavier cathode-ray tubes found in most display terminals. A typical laptop computer measures about 8.3 x 11.7 in/210 x 297 mm (A4), is 2 in/5 cm thick, and weighs less than 6 lb 9 oz/3 kg.

lapwing Eurasian bird *Vanellus vanellus* of the plover family, also known as the **green plover** and, from its call, as the **peewit**. Bottle-green above and white below, with a long thin crest and rounded wings, it is about 1 ft/30 cm long. It inhabits moorland in Europe and Asia, making a nest scratched out of the ground. It is an occasional visitor to NE North America.

Laramie town in Wyoming, US, on the Laramie Plains, a plateau 7,500 ft/2,300 m above sea level, bounded N and E by the Laramie Mountains; population (1990) 26,680. The Laramie River, on which it stands, is linked with the Missouri via the Platte.

It is a commercial and transport center for a ranching and lumber-producing area; its manufactures include cement and wood products. On the overland trail and Pony Express route, Fort Laramie, built 1834, features in western legend. A rail line came through 1868, and Laramie was incorporated 1874.

larceny in the US, and formerly in the UK, theft, the taking of personal property without consent and with the intention of permanently depriving the owner of it.

In some US states, larceny in which the value of the property exceeds a specified amount is grand larceny; larceny involving lesser amounts is petty larceny.

larch any tree of the genus *Larix*, of the family Pinaceae. The common larch *L. decidua* grows to 130 ft/40 m. It is one of the few ◊conifer trees to shed its leaves annually. The small needlelike leaves are replaced every year by new bright-green foliage, which later darkens.

lark songbird of the family Alaudidae, found mainly in the Old World, but also in North America. Larks are brownish-tan in color and usually about 7 in/18 cm long; they nest on the ground in the open. The skylark *Alauda arvensis* is light-brown and sings as it rises almost vertically in the air.

The skylark has been introduced to Vancouver Island. The North American horned lark *Eremophila alpestris* has black "horns" and only a weak, twittering song.

Larkin Philip 1922–1985. English poet. His perfectionist, pessimistic verse includes *The North Ship* 1945, *The Whitsun Weddings* 1964, and *High Windows* 1974. He edited *The Oxford Book of 20th-Century English Verse* 1973. After his death, his letters and writings revealed an intolerance and misanthropy not found in his published material.

larkspur plant of the genus ◊delphinium.

La Rochefoucauld François, duc de La Rochefoucauld 1613–1680. French writer. His *Réflexions, ou sentences et maximes morales/Reflections, or Moral Maxims* 1665 is a collection of brief, epigrammatic, and cynical observations on life and society, with the epigraph "Our virtues are mostly our vices in disguise".

larva stage between hatching and adulthood in those species in which the young have a different appearance and way of life from the adults. Examples include tadpoles (frogs) and caterpillars (butterflies and moths). Larvae are typical of the invertebrates, some of which (for example, shrimps) have two or more distinct larval stages. Among vertebrates, it is only the amphibians and some fishes that have a larval stage.

laryngitis inflammation of the larynx, causing soreness of the throat, a dry cough, and hoarseness. The acute form is due to a virus or other infection, excessive use of the voice, or inhalation of irritating smoke, and may cause the voice to be completely lost. With rest, the inflammation usually subsides in a few days.

larynx in mammals, a cavity at the upper end of the trachea (windpipe) containing the vocal cords. It is stiffened with cartilage and lined with mucous membrane. Amphibians and reptiles have much simpler larynxes, with no vocal cords. Birds have a similar cavity, called the *syrinx*, found lower down the trachea, where it branches to form the bronchi. It is very complex, with well-developed vocal cords.

Lascaux cave system in SW France with prehistoric wall paintings. It is richly decorated with realistic and symbolic paintings of buffaloes, horses, and red deer of the Upper Paleolithic period, about 18,000 BC . The caves, near Montignac in the Dordogne, were discovered 1940. Similar paintings are found in Altamira, Spain. The opening of the Lascaux caves to tourists led to deterioration of the paintings; the caves were closed 1963 and a facsimile opened 1983.

laser (acronym for *light amplification by stimulated emission of radiation*) a device for producing a nar-

row beam of light, capable of traveling over vast distances without dispersion, and of being focused to
give enormous power densities (10^8 watts per cm^2 for
high-energy lasers). The laser operates on a principle
similar to that of the ◊maser (a high-frequency
microwave amplifier or oscillator). The uses of lasers
include communications (a laser beam can carry
much more information than can radio waves), cutting, drilling, welding, satellite tracking, medical and
biological research, and surgery.

laser printer computer printer in which the image to
be printed is formed by the action of a laser on a light-
sensitive drum, then transferred to paper by means of
an electrostatic charge. Laser printers are page printers, printing a complete page at a time. The printed
image, which can take the form of text or pictures, is
made up of tiny dots, or ink particles. The quality of
the image generated depends on the fineness of these
dots—most laser printers can print up to 300 dots per
in/120 dots per cm across the page.

Las Palmas or ***Las Palmas de Gran Canaria*** tourist
resort on the northeast coast of Gran Canaria, Canary
Islands; population (1991) 347,700. Products include
sugar and bananas.

Lassa fever acute disease caused by a virus, first
detected in 1969, and spread by a species of rat found
only in W Africa. It is classified as a hemorrhagic fever
and characterized by high fever, headache, muscle
pain, and internal bleeding. There is no known cure,
the survival rate being less than 50%.

Las Vegas city in Nevada known for its gambling casinos and nightclubs; population (1990) 258,300. Las
Vegas entertains millions of visitors each year and is
an important convention center. Founded 1855 in a
ranching area, the modern community developed
with the coming of the railroad 1905. The first casino-
hotel opened 1947.

The University of Nevada-Las Vegas is here, and
Nellis Air Force Base, Hoover Dam, and Lake Mead
National Recreation Area are nearby.

latent heat in physics, the heat absorbed or radiated
by a substance as it changes state (for example, from
solid to liquid) at constant temperature and pressure.

latex fluid of some plants (such as the rubber tree and
poppy), an emulsion of resins, proteins, and other
organic substances. It is used as the basis for making
rubber. The name is also applied to a suspension in
water of natural or synthetic rubber (or plastic) particles used in rubber goods, paints, and adhesives.

Latin Indo-European language of ancient Italy. Latin
has passed through four influential phases: as the language of (1) republican Rome, (2) the Roman Empire,
(3) the Roman Catholic Church, and (4) W European
culture, science, philosophy, and law during the
Middle Ages and the Renaissance. During the third
and fourth phases, much Latin vocabulary entered the
English language. It is the parent form of the
◊Romance languages, noted for its highly inflected
grammar and conciseness of expression.

Latin America large territory in the Western hemisphere south of the US, consisting of Mexico, Central
America, South America, and the West Indies. The
main languages spoken are Spanish, Portuguese, and
French.

latitude and longitude imaginary lines used to locate
position on the globe. Lines of latitude are drawn parallel to the equator, with 0° at the equator and 90° at
the north and south poles. Lines of longitude are

Point X lies on longitude 60°W

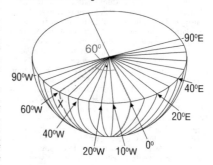

Point X lies on latitude 20°S

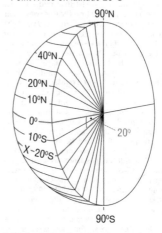

latitude and longitude *Locating a point on a globe
using latitude and longitude. Longitude is the angle
between the terrestrial meridian through a place and
the standard meridian 0° passing through Greenwich,
England. Latitude is the angular distance of a place
from the equator.*

drawn at right angles to these, with 0° (the Prime
Meridian) passing through Greenwich, England.

Latvia Republic of ***area*** 24,595 sq mi/63,700 sq km
capital Riga ***towns and cities*** Daugavpils, Liepāja,
Jurmala, Jelgava, Ventspils ***physical*** wooded lowland
(highest point 1,024 ft/312 m), marshes, lakes; 293
mi/472 km of coastline; mild climate ***environment***
coast littered with wrecks of Soviet vessels; ground
water around former Soviet bases contaminated;
cleanup cost of billions of dollars (1994) ***features***
Western Dvina River; Riga is largest port on the Baltic
after St Petersburg (formerly Leningrad) ***head of state***
Guntis Ulmanis from 1993 ***head of government*** Maris
Gailis from 1994 ***political system*** emergent democratic republic ***political parties*** Latvian Way, center-
right; Latvian Peasants' Union (LZS), center-left;

Union of Christian Democrats, right-of-center; Latvian National and Conservative Party (formerly National Independence Movement of Latvia: LNNK), far-right; Economic-Political Union (formerly known as Harmony for Latvia and Rebirth of the National Economy) *products* electronic and communications equipment, electric railroad carriages, motorcycles, consumer durables, timber, paper and woolen goods, meat and dairy products *currency* latis *population* (1993) 2,610,000 (Latvian 52%, Russian 34%, Byelorussian 5%, Ukrainian 3%) *life expectancy* men 64, women 75 *language* Latvian *religions* mostly Lutheran Protestant, with a Roman Catholic minority *GNP* $3,410 per head (1991) *chronology 1917* Soviets and Germans contested for control of Latvia. *1918* Feb: Soviet forces overthrown by Germany. Nov: Latvia declared independence. Dec: Soviet rule restored after German withdrawal. *1919* Soviet rule overthrown by British naval and German forces May–Dec; democracy established. *1934* Coup replaced established government. *1939* German-Soviet secret agreement placed Latvia under Russian influence. *1940* Incorporated into USSR as constituent republic. *1941–44* Occupied by Germany. *1944* USSR regained control. *1980* Nationalist dissent began to grow. *1988* Latvian Popular Front established to campaign for independence. Prewar flag readopted; official status given to Latvian language. Anatolijs Gorbunovs, ideological secretary of Communist Party (CP), elected president. *1989* Popular Front swept local elections. *1990* Jan: CP's monopoly of power abolished. March–April: Popular Front secured majority in elections. April: Latvian CP split into pro-independence and pro-Moscow wings. May: entered transitional period of independence from USSR. *1991* Jan: Soviet troops briefly seized key installations in Riga. March: overwhelming vote for independence in referendum. Aug: full independence declared at time of attempted anti-Gorbachev coup; CP outlawed. Sept: independence recognized by USSR and Western nations; joined United Nations (UN). *1992* Russia began pull-out of ex-Soviet troops. July: curbing of rights of noncitizens prompted Russia to request minority protection by UN. *1993* Latvian Way, led by acting president Gorbunovs, won most seats in general election. Guntis Ulmanis chosen as president, Gorbunovs as parliamentary speaker, and Valdis Birkavs as premier. *1994* July: Birkavs and his government resigned. Aug: last Russian troops departed. Maris Gailis appointed premier.

Latynina Larissa Semyonovna 1935– . Soviet gymnast, winner of more Olympic medals than any person in any sport. She won 18 between 1956 and 1964, including nine gold medals. She won a total of 12 individual Olympic and world championship gold medals.

Laud William 1573–1645. English priest; archbishop of Canterbury from 1633. Laud's High Church policy, support for Charles I's unparliamentary rule, censorship of the press, and persecution of the Puritans all aroused bitter opposition, while his strict enforcement of the statutes against enclosures and of laws regulating wages and prices alienated the propertied classes. His attempt to impose the use of the Prayer Book on the Scots precipitated the English ◊Civil War. Impeached by Parliament 1640, he was imprisoned in the Tower of London, summarily condemned to death, and beheaded.

laughing jackass another name for the ◊kookaburrer, an Australian kingfisher.

laurel any evergreen tree of the European genus *Laurus*, family Lauraceae, with glossy, aromatic leaves, yellowish flowers, and black berries. The leaves of sweet bay or poet's laurel *L. nobilis* are used in cooking. Several species are cultivated worldwide.

California laurel *Umbellularia californica* of the W US belongs to a different genus in the laurel family.

Laurel and Hardy British-born Stan Laurel (adopted name of Arthur Stanley Jefferson) 1890–1965 and Oliver Hardy 1892–1957. US film comedians. They were the most successful comedy team in Hollywood's history (Stan was slim, Oliver rotund). Their partnership began 1926, survived the transition from silent films to sound, and resulted in 104 short and feature-length films. Among these are the Oscar-winning *The Music Box* 1932, *Our Relations* 1936, and *A Chump at Oxford* 1940.

lava molten rock (usually 1500–2000°F/800–1100°C) that erupts from a ◊volcano and cools to form extrusive ◊igneous rock. It differs from magma in that it is molten rock on the surface; magma is molten rock below the surface. Lava that is high in silica is viscous and sticky and does not flow far; it forms a steep-sided conical volcano. Low-silica lava can flow for long distances and forms a broad flat volcano.

Laval Pierre 1883–1945. French right-wing politician. He was prime minister and foreign secretary 1931–32, and again 1935–36. In World War II he joined Pétain's ◊Vichy government as vice-premier in June 1940; dismissed in Dec 1940, he was reinstated by Hitler's orders as head of the government and foreign minister in 1942. After the war he was executed.

lavender sweet-smelling herb, genus *Lavandula*, of the mint family Labiatae, native to W Mediterranean countries. The bushy low-growing *L. angustifolia* has long, narrow, erect leaves of a silver-green color. The flowers, borne on a terminal spike, vary in color from lilac to deep purple and are covered with small fragrant oil glands. The oil is extensively used in pharmacy and the manufacture of perfumes.

Lavoisier Antoine Laurent 1743–1794. French chemist. He proved that combustion needed only a part of the air, which he called oxygen, thereby destroying the theory of phlogiston (an imaginary "fire element" released during combustion). With Pierre de Laplace, the astronomer and mathematician, he showed that water was a compound of oxygen and hydrogen. In this way he established the basic rules of chemical combination. He was guillotined during the French Revolution.

law body of rules and principles under which justice is administered or order enforced in a state or nation. In western Europe there are two main systems: Roman law and English law. US law is a modified form of English law.

law courts bodies that adjudicate in legal disputes. Civil and criminal cases are usually dealt with by separate courts. In many countries there is a hierarchy of courts that provide an appeal system.

Many counties and municipalities also have courts, usually limited to minor offenses. There are also a number of federal and state specialized judicial and quasi-judicial bodies dealing with administrative law. In the US, the head of the federal judiciary is the Supreme Court, which also hears appeals from the inferior federal courts and from the decisions of the highest state courts. The US Courts of Appeal—organized in circuits—deal with appeals from the US district courts in which civil and criminal cases are heard. State courts deal with civil and criminal cases involving state laws and usually consist of a Supreme Court or appeals court and courts in judicial districts.

law lords in England, the ten Lords of Appeal in Ordinary who, together with the Lord Chancellor and other peers, make up the House of Lords in its judicial capacity. The House of Lords is the final court of appeal in both criminal and civil cases. Law lords rank as life peers.

Lawrence D(avid) H(erbert) 1885–1930. English writer. His work expresses his belief in emotion and the sexual impulse as creative and true to human nature. The son of a miner, Lawrence studied at University College, Nottingham, and became a teacher. His writing first received attention after the publication of the semi-autobiographical *Sons and Lovers* 1913. Other novels include *The Rainbow* 1915, *Women in Love* 1921, and *Lady Chatterley's Lover* 1928. Lawrence also wrote short stories and poetry.

Lawrence T(homas) E(dward), known as *Lawrence of Arabia* 1888–1935. British soldier, scholar, and translator. Appointed to the military intelligence department in Cairo, Egypt, during World War I, he took part in negotiations for an Arab revolt against the Ottoman Turks, and in 1916 attached himself to the emir Faisal. He became a guerrilla leader of genius, combining raids on Turkish communications with the organization of a joint Arab revolt, described in *The Seven Pillars of Wisdom* 1926.

lawrencium synthesized, radioactive, metallic element, the last of the actinide series, symbol Lr, atomic number 103, atomic weight 262. Its only known isotope, Lr-257, has a half-life of 4.3 seconds and was originally synthesized at the University of California at Berkeley 1961 by bombarding californium with boron nuclei. The original symbol, Lw, was officially changed 1963.

laxative substance used to relieve constipation (infrequent bowel movement). Current medical opinion discourages regular or prolonged use. Regular exercise and a diet high in vegetable fiber is believed to be the best means of preventing and treating constipation.

lay reader in the Anglican Church, an unordained member of the church who is permitted under license from the bishop of the diocese to conduct some public services.

lb symbol for ◊pound (weight).

LCD abbreviation for ◊*liquid-crystal display*.

lead heavy, soft, malleable, gray, metallic element, symbol Pb (from Latin *plumbum*), atomic number 82, atomic weight 207.19. Usually found as an ore (most often in galena), it occasionally occurs as a free metal (native metal), and is the final stable product of the decay of uranium. Lead is the softest and weakest of the commonly used metals, with a low melting point; it is a poor conductor of electricity and resists acid corrosion. As a cumulative poison, lead enters the body from lead water pipes, lead-based paints, and leaded gasoline. (In humans, exposure to lead shortly after birth is associated with impaired mental health between the ages of two and four.) The metal is an effective shield against radiation and is used in batteries, glass, ceramics, and alloys such as pewter and solder.

lead–acid cell type of ◊battery.

Leadbelly nickname of Huddie ◊Ledbetter, US blues singer.

leaded gasoline gasoline containing the lead compound tetraethyllead, $(C_2H_5)_4Pb$, an antiknock agent. It improves the combustion of gasoline and the performance of an automobile engine. The lead from the exhaust fumes enters the atmosphere, mostly as simple lead compounds.

leaf lateral outgrowth on the stem of a plant, and in most species the primary organ of ◊photosynthesis. The chief leaf types are cotyledons (seed leaves), scale leaves (on underground stems), foliage leaves, and bracts (in the axil of which a flower is produced).

Leaves that fall in the autumn are termed deciduous, while evergreen leaves are persistent.

leaf insect insect of the order Phasmida, about 4 in/10 cm long, with a green, flattened body, remarkable for closely resembling the foliage on which it lives. It is most common in SE Asia.

Leaf insects are related to walking sticks and ◊mantises.

League of Arab States (Arab League) organization of Arab states established in Cairo 1945 to promote Arab unity, primarily in opposition to Israel. The original members were Egypt, Syria, Iraq, Lebanon, Transjordan (Jordan 1949), Saudi Arabia, and Yemen. They were later joined by Algeria, Bahrain, Djibouti, Kuwait, Libya, Mauritania, Morocco, Oman, Palestine, Qatar, Somalia, Sudan, Tunisia, and the United Arab Emirates. Despite the strains imposed on it by the 1990–91 Gulf War, the alliance survived.

League of Nations international organization formed after World War I to solve international disputes by arbitration. Established in Geneva, Switzerland, 1920, the league included representatives from states throughout the world, but was severely weakened by the US decision not to become a member, and had no power to enforce its decisions. It was dissolved 1946. Its subsidiaries included the *International Labour Organization* and the *Permanent Court of International Justice* in The Hague, Netherlands, both now under the auspices of the ◊United Nations.

The formation of the league was first suggested by President ◊Wilson in his Fourteen Points as part of the peace settlement for World War I. The US did not become a member since it did not ratify the the Treaty of ◊Versailles.

Leakey Louis (Seymour Bazett) 1903–1972. British archeologist, born in Kenya. In 1958, with his wife Mary Leakey, he discovered gigantic extinct-animal fossils in the ◊Olduvai Gorge in Tanzania, as well as many remains of an early human type.

Leakey Mary 1913– . British archeologist. In 1948 she discovered, on Rusinga Island, Lake Victoria, E Africa, the prehistoric ape skull known as *Proconsul*, about 20 million years old; and human remains at Laetoli, to the south, about 3,750,000 years old.

Lean David 1908–1991. English film director. His films, noted for their painstaking craftsmanship, include early work codirected with playwright Noël Coward. *Brief Encounter* 1946 established Lean as a leading talent. Among his later films are such accomplished epics as *The Bridge on the River Kwai* 1957 (Academy Award), *Lawrence of Arabia* 1962 (Academy Award), and *Dr Zhivago* 1965. The unfavorable reaction to *Ryan's Daughter* 1970 caused him to withdraw from filmmaking for over a decade, but *A Passage to India* 1984 represented a return to form.

Lear Edward 1812–1888. English artist and humorist. His *Book of Nonsense* 1846 popularized the limerick (a five-line humorous verse). He first attracted attention by his paintings of birds, and later turned to landscapes. He traveled to Italy, Greece, Egypt, and India, publishing books on his travels with his own illustrations, and spent most of his later life in Italy.

leasehold in law, land or property held by a tenant (lessee) for a specified period, (unlike ◊freehold, outright ownership) usually at a rent from the landlord (lessor).

leather material prepared from the hides and skins of animals, by tanning with vegetable tannins and chromium salts. Leather is a durable and water-resistant material, and is used for bags, shoes, clothing, and upholstery. There are three main stages in the process of converting animal skin into leather: cleaning, tanning, and dressing. Tanning is often a highly polluting process.

Lebanon Republic of (*al-Jumhouria al-Lubnaniya*) *area* 4,034 sq mi/10,452 sq km *capital* and port Beirut *towns and cities* ports Tripoli, Tyre, Sidon *physical* narrow coastal plain; Bekka valley N–S between Lebanon and Anti-Lebanon mountain ranges *environment* water table polluted; deforestation has left only 3% of the country forested; solid waste has been dumped in sea; fertilizers have caused soil salinity *features* Mount Hermon; Chouf Mountains; archeological sites at Baalbeck, Byblos, Tyre; until the civil war, the financial center of the Middle East *head of state* Elias Hrawi from 1989 *head of government* Rafik al-Hariri from 1992 *political system* emergent democratic republic *political parties* Phalangist Party, Christian, radical, right-wing; Progressive Socialist Party (PSP), Druse, moderate, socialist; National Liberal Party (NLP), Maronite, center-left; Parliamentary Democratic Front, Sunni Muslim, centrist; Lebanese Communist Party (PCL), nationalist, communist *exports* citrus and other fruit, vegetables; industrial products to Arab neighbors *currency* Lebanese pound *population* (1993 est) 2,900,000 (Lebanese 82%, Palestinian 9%, Armenian 5%); growth rate −0.1% p.a. *life expectancy* men 65, women 69 *languages* Arabic, French (both official), Armenian, English *media* independent media are barred from broadcasting news or discussing politics *religions* Muslim 57% (Shiite 33%, Sunni 24%), Christian (Maronite and Orthodox) 40%, Druse 3%

literacy men 88%, women 73% *GNP* $2,000 per head (1991) *chronology 1920–41* Administered under French mandate. *1944* Independence achieved. *1948–49* Lebanon joined first Arab war against Israel. Palestinian refugees settled in the south. *1964* Palestine Liberation Organization (PLO) founded in Beirut. *1967* More Palestinian refugees settled in Lebanon. *1971* PLO expelled from Jordan; established headquarters in Lebanon. *1975* Outbreak of civil war between Christians and Muslims. *1976* Cease-fire agreed; Syrian-dominated Arab deterrent force formed to keep the peace but considered by Christians as a occupying force. *1978* Israel invaded S Lebanon in search of PLO forces, shelling Israeli settlements on Lebanese border. International peacekeeping force established. Fighting broke out again. *1979* Part of S Lebanon declared an "independent free Lebanon". *1982* Bachir Gemayel became president but was assassinated before he could assume office; succeeded by his brother Amin Gemayel. Israel again invaded Lebanon. Palestinians withdrew from Beirut under supervision of international peacekeeping force. PLO moved its headquarters to Tunis. *1983* Agreement reached for the withdrawal of Syrian and Israeli troops but abrogated under Syrian pressure. *1984* Most of international peacekeeping force withdrawn. Muslim militia took control of W Beirut. *1985* Lebanon in chaos; many foreigners taken hostage. *1987* Syrian troops sent into Beirut. *1988* Agreement on a Christian successor to Gemayel failed; he established a military government; Selim al-Hoss set up rival government; threat of partition hung over the country. *1989* Christian leader General Michel Aoun declared "war of liberation" against Syrian occupation; Saudi Arabia and Arab League sponsored talks that resulted in new constitution recognizing Muslim majority; René Muhawad assassinated after 17 days as president; Elias Hrawi named successor; Aoun occupied presidential palace, rejected constitution. *1990* Release of Western hostages began. General Aoun surrendered and legitimate government restored, with Umar Karami as prime minister. *1991* Government extended control to the whole country. Treaty of cooperation with Syria signed. General Aoun pardoned. *1992* Karami resigned; succeeded by Rashid al-Solh. Remaining Western hostages released. General election boycotted by many Christians; pro-Syrian administration reelected with Rafik al-Hariri as prime minister. *1993* Israel launched attacks against Hezbollah strongholds in S Lebanon.

Lebowa black homeland in Transvaal province, South Africa; population (1985) 1,836,000. It achieved self-governing status 1972.

lecithin lipid (fat), containing nitrogen and phosphorus, that forms a vital part of the cell membranes of plant and animal cells. The name is from the Greek *lekithos* "egg yolk", eggs being a major source of lecithin.

Leconte de Lisle Charles Marie René 1818–1894. French poet. He was born on the Indian Ocean Island of Réunion, settled in Paris 1846, and headed the anti-Romantic group *Les Parnassiens* 1866–76. His work drew inspiration from the ancient world, as in *Poèmes antiques/Antique Poems* 1852, *Poèmes barbares/Barbaric Poems* 1862, and *Poèmes tragiques/Tragic Poems* 1884.

Le Corbusier assumed name of Charles-Edouard Jeanneret 1887–1965. Swiss-born French architect. He was an early and influential exponent of the Modern Movement and one of the most innovative of

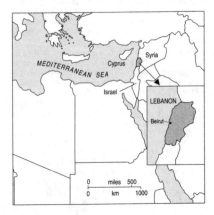

20th-century architects. His distinct brand of Functionalism first appears in his town-planning proposals of the early 1920s, which advocate "vertical garden cities" (multi-story villas, zoning of living and working areas, and traffic separation) as solutions to urban growth and chaos.

LED abbreviation for ◊*light-emitting diode*.

Leda in Greek mythology, the wife of Tyndareus and mother of ◊Clytemnestra. Zeus, who came to her as a swan, was the father of her other children: Helen of Troy and the twins Castor and Pollux.

Ledbetter Huddie, "Leadbelly" *c.*1888–1949. US musician. Better known by his nickname, he was born in Mooringsport, Louisiana, and spent his early years as a farmhand. Drawn to music at an early age, he traveled throughout the South and became well known for his blues guitar playing. In 1934 he was "discovered" by visiting folklorists John and Alan Lomax, who helped him begin a professional concert and recording career. Ledbetter was an important source of inspiration for the urban folk movement of the 1950s. His rendition of "Good Night, Irene" became a folk classic.

Lee Gypsy Rose 1914–1970. US entertainer. An "elegant lady" in striptease routines, she was popular in literary circles. Also a published author, she wrote two mystery novels, *The G-String Murders* 1941 and *Mother Finds a Body* 1942. Her autobiography *Gypsy: A Memoir* 1957 was adapted for stage 1959 and film 1962.

Lee Robert E(dward) 1807–1870. US military leader, Confederate commander in the ◊Civil War, and military strategist. In 1859 he suppressed John ◊Brown's raid on Harper's Ferry. Lee had freed his own slaves long before the war began, and he was opposed to secession, however his devotion to his native Virginia led him to join the Confederacy. At the outbreak of war he became military adviser to Jefferson ◊Davis, president of the Confederacy, and in 1862 commander of the Army of Northern Virginia. Lee actually had been offered command of the Union armies, but he resigned his commission to return to Virginia. During 1862–63 he made several raids into Northern territory but after his defeat at Gettysburg was compelled to take the defensive; he surrendered 1865 at Appomattox.

Lee and Yang Lee Tsung Dao (1926–) and Yang Chen Ning (1922–) Chinese physicists who studied how parity operates at the nuclear level. They found no proof for the claim, made by Wigner, that nuclear processes were indistinguishable from their mirror images, and that elementary particles made no distinction between left and right. In 1956 they predicted that parity was not conserved in weak interactions. They shared a Nobel Prize 1957.

leech annelid worm forming the class Hirudinea. Leeches inhabit fresh water, and in tropical countries infest damp forests. As bloodsucking animals they are injurious to people and animals, to whom they attach themselves by means of a strong mouth adapted to sucking. Their ancient use for medicinal purposes has recently been revived in some US hospitals to promote blood flow, as after an operation to reattach a severed finger.

Leeds industrial city in West Yorkshire, England, on the river Aire; population (1991 est) 680,700. Industries include engineering, printing, chemicals, glass, woolens, clothing, plastics, paper, metal goods, and leather goods. It is a center of communications where road, rail, and canal (to Liverpool and Goole) meet.

leek onionlike plant of the genus *Allium* of the lily family Liliaceae. The cultivated leek is a variety of the wild *A. ampeloprasum* of the Mediterranean area and Atlantic islands. The lower leaf parts form the bulb, which is eaten as a vegetable.

Lee Kuan Yew 1923– . Singapore politician, prime minister 1959–90. Lee founded the anticommunist Socialist People's Action Party 1954 and was elected the country's first prime minister 1959, and took Singapore out of the Malaysian federation 1965.

Lee Teng-hui 1923– . Taiwanese right-wing politician, vice president 1984–88, president and Kuomintang (see ◊Guomindang) party leader from 1988. Lee, the country's first island-born leader, is viewed as a reforming technocrat.

Lee Tsung-Dao 1926– . Chinese physicist whose research centered on the physics of weak nuclear forces. In 1956 Lee proposed that weak nuclear forces between elementary particles might disobey certain key assumptions for instance, the conservation of parity. He shared the 1957 Nobel Prize for Physics with his colleague Yang Chen Ning (1922–).

Lee originally trained in China; but a scholarship sent him to the US in 1946, working mostly on particle physics at the Princeton Institute of Advanced Study and at the University of California.

Leeuwenhoek Anton van 1632–1723. Dutch pioneer of microscopic research. He ground his own lenses, some of which magnified up to 200 times. With these he was able to see individual red blood cells, sperm, and bacteria, achievements not repeated for more than a century.

Leeward Islands (1) group of islands, part of the ◊Society Islands, in ◊French Polynesia, S Pacific; (2) general term for the northern half of the Lesser ◊Antilles in the West Indies; (3) former British colony in the West Indies (1871–1956) comprising Antigua, Montserrat, St Christopher (St Kitts)–Nevis, Anguilla, and the Virgin Islands.

left wing in politics, the socialist parties. The term originated in the French National Assembly of 1789, where the nobles sat in the place of honor to the right of the president, and the commons sat to the left. This arrangement has become customary in European parliaments, where the progressives sit on the left and the conservatives on the right.

legacy in law, a gift of personal property made by a testator in a will and transferred on the testator's death to the legatee. *Specific legacies* are definite named objects; a *general legacy* is a sum of money or item not specially identified; a *residuary legacy* is all the remainder of the deceased's personal estate after debts have been paid and the other legacies have been distributed.

Léger Fernand 1881–1955. French painter and designer. He was associated with ◊Cubism. From around 1909 he evolved a characteristic style of simplified forms, clear block outlines, and bold colors. Mechanical forms are constant themes in his work, which includes designs for the Swedish Ballet 1921–22, murals, and the abstract film *Ballet mécanique/Mechanical Ballet* 1924.

legislature lawmaking body or bodies in a political system. Some legislatures are unicameral (having one chamber), and some bicameral (with two).

legume plant of the family Leguminosae, which has a pod containing dry seeds. The family includes peas, beans, lentils, clover, and alfalfa (lucerne). Legumes are important in agriculture because of their specialized roots, which contain nodules containing bacteria capable of fixing nitrogen from the air and increasing the fertility of the soil. The edible seeds of legumes are called *pulses*.

Le Havre industrial port (engineering, chemicals, oil refining) in Normandy, NW France, on the river Seine; population (1990) 197,200. It is the largest port in Europe, and has transatlantic passenger links.

Leibniz Gottfried Wilhelm 1646–1716. German mathematician and philosopher. Independently of, but concurrently with, the British scientist Isaac Newton he developed the branch of mathematics known as ◊calculus. In his metaphysical works, such as *The Monadology* 1714, he argued that everything consisted of innumerable units, *monads*, the individual properties of which determined each thing's past, present, and future. Monads, although independent of each other, interacted predictably; this meant that Christian faith and scientific reason need not be in conflict and that "this is the best of all possible worlds". His optimism is satirized in Voltaire's *Candide*.

Leicester industrial city and administrative headquarters of Leicestershire, England, on the river Soar; population (1991) 270,500. Industries include food processing, hosiery, footwear, knitwear, engineering, electronics, printing, and plastics.

Leicester Robert Dudley, Earl of Leicester *c.* 1532–1588. English courtier. Son of the Duke of Northumberland, he was created Earl of Leicester 1564. Queen Elizabeth I gave him command of the army sent to the Netherlands 1585–87 and of the forces prepared to resist the threat of Spanish invasion 1588. His lack of military success led to his recall, but he retained Elizabeth's favor until his death.

Leicestershire county of central England *area* 984 sq mi/2,550 sq km *towns and cities* Leicester (administrative headquarters), Loughborough, Melton Mowbray, Market Harborough *features* river Soar; Rutland district (formerly England's smallest county, with Oakham as its county town); Rutland Water, one of Europe's largest reservoirs; Charnwood Forest; Vale of Belvoir (under which are large coal deposits) *industries* horses, cattle, sheep, dairy products, coal, Stilton cheese, hosiery, footwear, bell founding *population* (1991) 867,500 *famous people* Titus Oates, Thomas Babington Macaulay, C P Snow.

Leinster southeastern province of the Republic of Ireland, comprising the counties of Carlow, Dublin, Kildare, Kilkenny, Laois, Longford, Louth, Meath, Offaly, Westmeath, Wexford, and Wicklow; area 7,577 sq mi/19,630 sq km; capital Dublin; population (1991) 1,860,000.

Leipzig city in W Saxony, Germany, 90 mi/145 km SW of Berlin; population (1986) 552,000. Products include furs, leather goods, cloth, glass, automobiles, and musical instruments.

leishmaniasis any of several parasitic diseases caused by microscopic protozoans of the genus *Leishmania*, identified by William Leishman (1865–1926), and transmitted by sandflies. Leishmaniasis occurs in the Mediterranean region, Africa, Asia, and Central and S America. There are 12 million cases of leishmaniasis annually.

Leitrim county of the Republic of Ireland, in the province of Connacht, bounded NW by Donegal Bay; county town Carrick-on-Shannon; area 591 sq mi/1,530 sq km; population (1991) 25,300. The rivers Shannon, Bonet, Drowes, and Duff run through it. Industries include potatoes, cattle, linen, woolens, pottery, coal, iron, lead, sheep, and oats.

Lely Peter. Adopted name of Pieter van der Faes 1618–1680. Dutch painter. He was active in England from 1641, painting fashionable portraits in the style of van Dyck. His subjects included Charles I, Cromwell, and Charles II. He painted a series of admirals, *Flagmen* (National Maritime Museum, London), and one of *The Windsor Beauties* (Hampton Court, Richmond), fashionable women of Charles II's court.

Lemaître Georges Edouard 1894–1966. Belgian cosmologist who in 1927 proposed the ◊Big Bang theory of the origin of the universe. He predicted that the entire universe was expanding, which the US astronomer Edwin ◊Hubble confirmed. Lemaître suggested that the expansion had been started by an initial explosion, the Big Bang, a theory that is now generally accepted.

Le Mans industrial city in Sarthe *département*, W France; population (1990) 148,500, conurbation 191,000. It has a motor-racing circuit where the annual endurance 24-hour race (established 1923) for sports automobiles and their prototypes is held.

lemming small rodent of the family Cricetidae, especially the genus *Lemmus*, comprising four species worldwide in northern latitudes. It is about 5 in/12 cm long, with thick brownish fur, a small head, and a short tail. Periodically, when their population exceeds the available food supply, lemmings undertake mass migrations.

lemon sour fruit of the small, evergreen, semitropical lemon tree *Citrus limon*. It may have originated in NW India, and was introduced into Europe by the Spanish Moors in the 12th or 13th century. It is now grown in California, Florida, Italy, Spain, South Africa, and Australia.

lemon balm perennial herb *Melissa officinalis* of the mint family Labiatae, with lemon-scented leaves. It is widely used in teas, liqueurs, and medicines.

lemur prosimian ◊primate of the family Lemuridae, inhabiting Madagascar and the Comoro Islands. There are about 16 species, ranging from mouse-sized to dog-sized animals. Lemurs are arboreal, and some species are nocturnal. They have long, bushy tails, and feed on fruit, insects, and small animals. Many are threatened with extinction owing to loss of their forest habitat and, in some cases, from hunting.

Lena longest river in Asiatic Russia, 2,730 mi/4,400 km, with numerous tributaries. Its source is near Lake Baikal, and it empties into the Arctic Ocean through a delta 240 mi/400 km wide. It is ice-covered for half the year.

Lendl Ivan 1960– . Czech-born American lawn-tennis player. He has won eight Grand Slam singles titles, including the US and French titles three times each. He has won more than $15 million in prize money.

Lenin Vladimir Ilyich. Adopted name of Vladimir Ilyich Ulyanov 1870–1924. Russian revolutionary, first leader of the USSR, and communist theoretician. Active in the 1905 Revolution, Lenin had to leave Russia when it failed, settling in Switzerland in 1914. He returned to Russia after the February revolution of 1917 (see

◊Russian Revolution). He led the Bolshevik revolution in Nov 1917 and became leader of a Soviet government, concluded peace with Germany, and organized a successful resistance to White Russian (pro-czarist) uprisings and foreign intervention 1918–20. His modification of traditional Marxist doctrine to fit conditions prevailing in Russia became known as **Marxism-Leninism**, the basis of communist ideology.

Leningrad former name (1924–91) of the Russian city ◊St Petersburg.

Lennon John (Ono) 1940–1980. UK rock singer, songwriter, and guitarist; a founder member of the ◊Beatles. He lived in the US from 1971. Both before the band's breakup 1970 and in his solo career, he collaborated intermittently with his wife **Yoko Ono** (1933–   ). "Give Peace a Chance", a hit 1969, became an anthem of the peace movement. His solo work alternated between the confessional and the political, as on the album *Imagine* 1971. He was shot dead by a fan.

lens in optics, a piece of a transparent material, such as glass, with two polished surfaces—one concave or convex, and the other plane, concave, or convex—that modifies rays of light. A convex lens brings rays of light together; a concave lens makes the rays diverge. Lenses are essential to glasses, microscopes, telescopes, cameras, and almost all optical instruments.

Lent in the Christian church, the 40-day period of fasting that precedes Easter, beginning on Ash Wednesday, but omitting Sundays.

lentil annual Old World plant *Lens culinaris* of the pea family Leguminosae. The plant, which resembles vetch, grows 6–18 in/15–45 cm high and has white, blue, or purplish flowers. The seeds, contained in pods about 0.6 in/1.6 cm long, are widely used as food.

Leo zodiacal constellation in the northern hemisphere represented as a lion. The Sun passes through Leo from mid-Aug to mid-Sept Its brightest star is first-magnitude Regulus at the base of a pattern of stars called the Sickle. In astrology, the dates for Leo are between about July 23 and Aug 22 (see ◊precession).

lemur The fork-marked lemur is tree-dwelling, with large eyes that look forward over a small, pointed nose. The long, bushy tail is used for balance and, when held in different positions, as a signal to other lemurs.

Leo (I) the Great (St Leo) *c*.390–461. Pope from 440 who helped to establish the Christian liturgy. Leo summoned the Chalcedon Council where his Dogmatical Letter was accepted as the voice of St Peter. Acting as ambassador for the emperor Valentinian III (425–455), Leo saved Rome from devastation by the Huns by buying off their king, Attila.

Leo III *c*.750–816. Pope from 795. After the withdrawal of the Byzantine emperors, the popes had become the real rulers of Rome. Leo III was forced to flee because of a conspiracy in Rome and took refuge at the court of the Frankish king Charlemagne. He returned to Rome in 799 and crowned Charlemagne emperor on Christmas Day 800, establishing the secular sovereignty of the pope over Rome under the suzerainty of the emperor (who became the Holy Roman emperor).

Leo X Giovanni de' Medici 1475–1521. Pope from 1513. The son of Lorenzo the Magnificent of Florence, he was created a cardinal at 13. He bestowed on Henry VIII of England the title of Defender of the Faith. A patron of the arts, he sponsored the rebuilding of St Peter's Church, Rome. He raised funds for this by selling indulgences (remissions of punishment for sin), a sale that led the religious reformer Martin Luther to rebel against papal authority. Leo X condemned Luther in the bull *Exsurge domine* 1520 and excommunicated him in 1521.

León city in Castilla-León, Spain; population (1991) 146,300. It was the capital of the kingdom of León from the 10th century until 1230, when it was merged with Castile.

Leonard Elmore (John, Jr) 1925–   . US author of Westerns and thrillers. His writing is marked by vivid dialogue, as in *City Primeval* 1980, *Stick* 1983, *Freaky Deaky* 1988, and *Get Shorty* 1990.

Born in New Orleans, Leonard received a PhD in English from the University of Detroit and worked for an advertising agency while he churned out Westerns for pulp magazines. His *Hombre* 1961 became a motion picture 1967 starring Paul Newman. In the late 1960s Leonard changed genre, writing about city life and crime.

Leonardo da Vinci 1452–1519. Italian painter, sculptor, architect, engineer, and scientist.

One of the greatest figures of the Italian Renaissance, he was active in Florence, Milan, and, from 1516, France. As state engineer and court painter to the duke of Milan, he painted the *Last Supper* mural about 1495 (Sta Maria delle Grazie, Milan), and on his return to Florence painted the *Mona Lisa* (Louvre, Paris) about 1503–06. His notebooks and drawings show an immensely inventive and inquiring mind, studying aspects of the natural world from anatomy to aerodynamics.

León de los Aldamas industrial city (leather goods, footwear) in central Mexico; population (1986) 947,000.

leopard or *panther* cat *Panthera pardus*, found in Africa and Asia. The background color of the coat is golden, and the black spots form rosettes that differ according to the variety; black panthers are simply a color variation and retain the patterning as a "watered-silk" effect. The leopard is 5–8 ft/1.5–2.5 m long, including the tail, which may measure 3 ft/1 m.

Leopold I 1790–1865. King of the Belgians from 1831, having been elected to the throne on the creation of an independent Belgium. Through his marriage, when prince of Saxe-Coburg, to Princess Charlotte

leopard The leopard has exceptionally acute hearing, together with good sight and sense of smell. Leopards are agile and have been known to leap from trees onto prey. They climb well, often dragging prey high into trees for safety.

Augusta, he was the uncle of Queen Victoria of Great Britain and had considerable influence over her.

Leopold III 1901–1983. King of the Belgians 1934–51. He surrendered to the German army in World War II 1940. Postwar charges against his conduct led to a regency by his brother Charles and his eventual abdication 1951 in favor of his son Baudouin.

Lepanto, Battle of sea battle Oct 7, 1571, fought in the Mediterranean Gulf of Corinth off Lepanto (Italian name of the Greek port of *Naupaktos*), then in Turkish possession, between the Ottoman Empire and forces from Spain, Venice, Genoa, and the Papal States, jointly commanded by the Spanish soldier Don John of Austria. The combined western fleets overcame Muslim sea power. The Spanish writer Cervantes was wounded in the battle.

lepidoptera order of insects, including ◊butterflies and ◊moths, which have overlapping scales on their wings; the order consists of some 165,000 species.

leprosy or *Hansen's disease* chronic, progressive disease caused by a bacterium *Mycobacterium leprae* closely related to that of tuberculosis. The infection attacks the skin and nerves. Once common in many countries, leprosy is now confined almost entirely to the tropics. It is controlled with drugs.

lepton any of a class of light ◊elementary particles that are not affected by the strong nuclear force; they do not interact strongly with other particles or nuclei. The leptons are comprised of the ◊electron, ◊muon, and ◊tau, and their ◊neutrinos (the electron neutrino, muon neutrino, and tau neutrino), plus their six ◊antiparticles.

lesbianism homosexuality (sexual attraction to one's own sex) between women, so called from the Greek island of Lesbos (now Lesvos), the home of ◊Sappho the poet and her followers to whom the behavior was attributed.

Lesbos alternative spelling of ◊Lesvos, an island in the Aegean Sea.

Lesotho Kingdom of *area* 11,717 sq mi/30,355 sq km *capital* Maseru *towns and cities* Teyateyaneng, Mafeteng, Roma, Quthing *physical* mountainous with plateaus, forming part of South Africa's chief watershed *features* Lesotho is an enclave within South Africa *political system* constitutional monarchy *head of state* King Moshoeshoe II from 1995 *head of government* Ntsu Mokhehle from 1993 *political parties* Basotho National Party (BNP), traditionalist, nationalist; Basutoland Congress Party (BCP); Basotho Democratic Alliance (BDA) *exports* wool, mohair,

diamonds, cattle, wheat, vegetables *currency* maluti *population* (1993 est) 1,900,000; growth rate 2.7% p.a. *life expectancy* men 54, women 63 *languages* Sesotho, English (official), Zulu, Xhosa *religions* Protestant 42%, Roman Catholic 38% *literacy* 60% *GNP* $580 per head (1991) *chronology* *1868* Basutoland became a British protectorate. *1966* Independence achieved from Britain, within the Commonwealth, as the Kingdom of Lesotho, with Moshoeshoe II as king and Chief Leabua Jonathan as prime minister. *1970* State of emergency declared and constitution suspended. *1973* Progovernment interim assembly established; BNP won majority of seats. *1975* Members of the ruling party attacked by guerrillas backed by South Africa. *1985* Elections canceled because no candidates opposed BNP. *1986* South Africa imposed border blockade, forcing deportation of 60 African National Congress members. General Lekhanya ousted Chief Jonathan in coup. National assembly abolished. *1990* Moshoeshoe II dethroned by military council; replaced by his son Mohato as King Letsie III. *1991* Lekhanya ousted in military coup led by Col Elias Tutsoane Ramaema. Political parties permitted to operate. *1992* Ex-king Moshoeshoe returned from exile. *1993* Free elections ended military rule; Ntsu Mokhehle of BCP became prime minister. New constitution adopted. *1994* Fighting between rival army factions ended by peace deal, brokered by Organization of African Unity. Assembly dissolved by King Letsie; Prime Minister Mokhehle dismissed, but later reinstated.

Lesseps Ferdinand, Vicomte de Lesseps 1805–1894. French engineer, constructor of the ◊Suez Canal 1859–69; he began the ◊Panama Canal in 1879, but withdrew after failing to construct it without locks.

Lessing Doris (May) (née Taylor) 1919– . English novelist, brought up in Rhodesia. Concerned with social and political themes, particularly the place of women in society, her work includes *The Grass is Singing* 1950, the five-novel series *Children of Violence* 1952–69, *The Golden Notebook* 1962, *The Good Terrorist* 1985, and *The Fifth Child* 1988. She has also written an "inner space fiction" series *Canopus in Argus: Archives* 1979–83, and under the pen name "Jane Somers", *The Diary of a Good Neighbour* 1981.

Lesvos Greek island in the Aegean Sea, near the coast of Turkey *area* 831 sq mi/2,154 sq km *capital* Mytilene *industries* olives, wine, grain *population* (1981) 104,620 *history* ancient name Lesbos; an Aeolian settlement, the home of the poets Alcaeus and Sappho; conquered by the Turks from Genoa 1462; annexed to Greece 1913.

lettuce annual edible plant *Lactuca sativa*, family Compositae, believed to have been derived from the wild species *L. serriola*. There are many varieties, including the cabbage lettuce, with round or loose heads, and the Cos lettuce, with long, upright heads.

Iceberg and Romaine are the two salad varieties grown especially for US supermarkets, but Boston and Redleaf are sometimes shipped to markets.

leukemia any one of a group of cancers of the blood cells, with widespread involvement of the bone marrow and other blood-forming tissue. The central feature of leukemia is runaway production of white blood cells that are immature or in some way abnormal. These rogue cells, which lack the defensive capacity of healthy white cells, overwhelm the normal ones, leaving the victim vulnerable to infection. Treatment is with radiotherapy and cytotoxic drugs to suppress replication of abnormal cells, or by bone-marrow transplant.

leukocyte a white blood cell. Leukocytes are part of the body's defenses and give immunity against disease. There are several different types. Some (◊phagocytes and macrophages) engulf invading microorganisms, others kill infected cells, while ◊lymphocytes produce more specific immune responses. Human blood contains about 11,000 leukocytes to the cubic millimeter—about 1 to every 500 red cells.

Levellers democratic party in the English Civil War. The Levellers found wide support among Cromwell's New Model Army and the yeoman farmers, artisans, and small traders, and proved a powerful political force 1647–49. Their program included the establishment of a republic, government by a parliament of one house elected by male suffrage, religious toleration, and sweeping social reforms.

lever simple machine consisting of a rigid rod pivoted at a fixed point called the fulcrum, used for shifting or raising a heavy load or applying force in a similar way. Levers are classified into orders according to where the effort is applied, and the load-moving force developed, in relation to the position of the fulcrum.

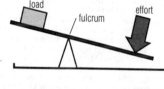

first-order lever

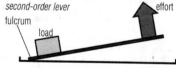

second-order lever

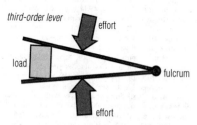

third-order lever

lever Types of lever. Practical applications of the first-order lever include the crowbar, seesaw, and scissors. The wheelbarrow and nutcrackers are second-order levers. A pair of tweezers, or tongs, is a third-order lever.

leveraged buyout in business, the purchase of a controlling proportion of the shares of a company by its own management, financed almost exclusively by borrowing. It is so called because the ratio of a company's long-term debt to its equity (capital assets) is known as its "leverage".

Lewis Carl (Frederick Carlton) 1961– . US track and field athlete who won eight gold medals and one silver in three successive Olympic Games. At the 1984 Olympic Games he equaled the performance of Jesse ◊Owens, winning gold medals in the 100 and 200 meters, 400-meter relay, and long jump.

Lewis Meriwether 1774–1809. US explorer. He was commissioned by president Thomas Jefferson to find a land route to the Pacific with William Clark (1770–1838). They followed the Missouri River to its source, crossed the Rocky Mountains (aided by an Indian woman, Sacajawea) and followed the Columbia River to the Pacific, then returned overland to St Louis 1804–06.

He was rewarded for his expedition with the governorship of the Louisiana Territory. His death, near Nashville, Tennessee, has been ascribed to suicide, but was more probably murder.

The detailed journals kept of the expedition added to an understanding of the region and facilitated westward expansion.

Lewis (Percy) Wyndham 1886–1957. US-born English writer and artist. He pioneered Vorticism, which with its feeling of movement sought to reflect the age of industry. He had a hard and aggressive style in both his writing and his painting. His literary works include the novels *Tarr* 1918 and *The Childermass* 1928, the essay "Time and Western Man" 1927, and autobiographies. Of his paintings, his portraits are memorable, such as those of the writers Edith Sitwell and T S Eliot.

Lhasa ("the Forbidden City") capital of the autonomous region of ◊Tibet, China, at 16,400 ft/5,000 m; population (1982) 105,000. Products include handicrafts and light industry. The holy city of ◊Lamaism, Lhasa was closed to Westerners until 1904, when members of a British expedition led by Col Francis E Younghusband visited the city. It was annexed with the rest of Tibet 1950–51 by China, and the spiritual and temporal head of state, the Dalai Lama, fled in 1959 after a popular uprising against Chinese rule. Monasteries have been destroyed and monks killed, and an influx of Chinese settlers has generated resentment. In 1988 and 1989 nationalist demonstrators were shot by Chinese soldiers.

liability in accounting, a financial obligation. Liabilities are placed alongside assets on a balance sheet to show the wealth of the individual or company concerned at a given date. Business organizations often distinguish between *current liabilities* such as overdrafts, trade credit and provisions, and *long-term liabilities* such as debentures, mortgages, and unsecured loans.

Liaoning province of NE China *area* 58,300 sq mi/151,000 sq km *capital* Shenyang *towns* Anshan, Fushun, Liaoyang *features* one of China's most heavily industrialized areas *industries* cereals, coal, iron, salt, oil *population* (1990) 39,460,000 *history* developed by Japan 1905–45, including the *Liaodong Peninsula*, whose ports had been conquered from the Russians.

libel in law, defamation published in a permanent form, such as in a newspaper, book, or broadcast.

A libel may be directed to a living or a dead person; either may be actionable. A person is defamed when publication of false and malicious statements hold the person up to public scorn, hatred, contempt, or ridicule, or impugn a person's capacity to perform a job. Truth of a published statement is a defense against an action for libel. With respect to public officials and public figures, the press has some protection against actions for libel in that malice and reckless disregard for the truth must be shown. See also ◊slander.

Liberal Democrats in UK politics, common name for the ◊Social and Liberal Democrats.

liberalism political and social theory that favors representative government, freedom of the press, speech, and worship, the abolition of class privileges, the use of state resources to protect the welfare of the individual, and international ◊free trade. It is historically associated with the Democratic Party in the US and the Liberal Party in the UK.

Liberal Party British political party, the successor to the ◊Whig Party, with an ideology of liberalism. In the 19th century, it represented the interests of commerce and industry. Its outstanding leaders were Palmerston, Gladstone, and Lloyd George. From 1914 it declined, and the rise of the Labour Party pushed the Liberals into the middle ground. The Liberals joined forces with the Social Democratic Party (SDP) as the Alliance for the 1983 and 1987 elections. In 1988, a majority of the SDP voted to merge with the Liberals to form the ◊Social and Liberal Democrats.

Liberia Republic of *area* 42,989 sq mi/111,370 sq km *capital* and port Monrovia *towns and cities* ports Buchanan, Greenville *physical* forested highlands; swampy tropical coast where six rivers enter the sea *features* nominally the world's largest merchant marine as minimal registration controls make Liberia's a flag of convenience; the world's largest rubber plantations *head of state and government* (interim) David Kpormakpor from 1994 *political system* emergent democratic republic *political parties* National Democratic Party of Liberia (NDLP), nationalist; Liberian Action Party (LAP); Liberian Unity Party (LUP); United People's Party (UPP); Unity Party (UP) *exports* iron ore, rubber (Africa's largest producer), timber, diamonds, coffee, cocoa, palm oil *currency* Liberian dollar *population* (1993 est) 2,700,000; growth rate 3% p.a. *life expectancy* men 54, women 57 *languages* English (official), over 20 Niger-Congo languages *media* two daily newspapers, one published under government auspices, the other independent and with the largest circulation (10,000 copies) *religions* animist 65%, Muslim 20%, Christian 15% *literacy* men 50%, women 29% *GNP* $440 per head (1987) *chronology* 1847 Founded as an independent republic. *1944* William Tubman elected president. *1971* Tubman died; succeeded by William Tolbert. *1980* Tolbert assassinated in coup led by Samuel Doe, who suspended the constitution and ruled through a People's Redemption Council. *1984* New constitution approved. NDPL founded by Doe. *1985* NDPL won decisive victory in allegedly rigged general election. Unsuccessful coup against Doe. *1990* Rebels under former government minister Charles Taylor controlled nearly entire country by July. Doe killed during a bloody civil war between rival rebel factions. Amos Sawyer became interim head of government. *1991* Sawyer reelected president. Taylor agreed to work with Sawyer. Peace agreement signed, but fighting continued; United Nations (UN) peacekeeping force drafted into republic. *1992* Monrovia under siege by Taylor's rebel forces. *1993* Peace agreement signed under OAU–UN auspices. Interim collective presidency

established prior to elections in 1994. *1994* Seven-month transitional government formed, under leadership of David Kpormakpor. Peace agreement signed by rival factions.

libido in Freudian psychology, the psychic energy, or life force, that is to be found even in a newborn child. The libido develops through a number of phases, identified by Freud as the *oral stage*, when a child tests everything by mouth, the *anal stage*, when the child gets satisfaction from control of its body, and the *genital stage*, when sexual instincts find pleasure in the outward show of love.

Libra faint zodiacal constellation in the southern hemisphere adjoining Scorpius, and represented as the scales of justice. The Sun passes through Libra during Nov. The constellation was once considered to be a part of Scorpius, seen as the scorpion's claws. In astrology, the dates for Libra are between about Sept 23 and Oct 23 (see ◊precession).

Libreville capital of Gabon, on the estuary of the river Gabon; population (1988) 352,000. Products include timber, oil, and minerals. It was founded 1849 as a refuge for slaves freed by the French. Since the 1970s the city has developed rapidly due to the oil trade.

Libya Great Socialist People's Libyan Arab Jamahiriya (*al-Jamahiriya al-Arabiya al-Libya al-Shabiya al-Ishtirakiya al-Uzma*) *area* 679,182 sq mi/1,759,540 sq km *capital* Tripoli *towns and cities* ports Benghazi, Misurata, Tobruk *physical* flat to undulating plains with plateaus and depressions stretch S from the Mediterranean coast to an extremely dry desert interior *environment* plan to pump water from below the Sahara to the coast risks rapid exhaustion of nonrenewable supply (Great Manmade River Project) *features* Gulf of Sirte; rock paintings of about 3000 BC in the Fezzan; Roman city sites include Leptis Magna, Sabratha *head of state and government* Col Moamer al-Qaddafi from 1969 *political system* one-party socialist state *political party* Arab Socialist Union (ASU), radical, left-wing *exports* oil, natural gas *currency* Libyan dinar *population* (1993 est) 4,700,000 (including 500,000 foreign workers); growth rate 3.1% p.a. *life expectancy* men 62, women 65 *language* Arabic *religion* Sunni Muslim 97% *literacy* men 75%, women 50% *GNP* $5,410 per head (1988) *chronology* 1911 Conquered by Italy. *1934* Colony named Libya. *1942* Divided into three provinces: Fezzan (under French control); Cyrenaica, Tripolitania (under British control). *1951* Achieved independence as the United Kingdom of Libya, under King Idris. *1969* King deposed in a coup led by Col. Moamer al-Qaddafi. Revolution Command Council set up and the Arab Socialist Union (ASU) proclaimed the only legal party. *1972* Proposed federation of Libya, Syria, and Egypt abandoned. *1980* Proposed merger with Syria abandoned. Libyan troops began fighting in Chad. *1981* Proposed merger with Chad abandoned. *1986* US bombing of Qaddafi's headquarters, following allegations of his complicity in terrorist activities. *1988* Diplomatic relations with Chad restored. *1989* US navy shot down two Libyan planes; reconciliation with Egypt. *1992* Qaddafi under international pressure to extradite suspected Lockerbie and UTA (Union de Transports Aeriens) bombers for trial outside Libya; several countries severed diplomatic and air links with Libya.

lichen any organism of the group Lichenes, which consists of a specific fungus and a specific alga existing in a mutually beneficial relationship. Found as colored patches or spongelike masses adhering to trees, rocks, and other substrates, lichens flourish under adverse conditions.

Lichtenstein Roy 1923– . US Pop artist. He uses advertising imagery and comic-strip techniques, often focusing on popular ideals of romance and heroism, as in *Whaam!* 1963 (Tate Gallery, London). He has also produced sculptures in brass, plastic, and enameled metal.

Lichtenstein's reputation was made with an exhibition in New York 1962. His controversial work is a commentary on American culture.

Liechtenstein Principality of (*Fürstentum Liechtenstein*) *area* 62 sq mi/160 sq km *capital* Vaduz *towns and cities* Balzers, Schaan, Ruggell *physical* landlocked Alpine; includes part of Rhine Valley in W *features* no airport or railroad station; easy tax laws make it an international haven for foreign companies and banks (some 50,000 companies are registered) *head of state* Prince Hans Adam II from 1989 *head of government* Mario Frick from 1993 *political system* constitutional monarchy *political parties* Fatherland Union (VU); Progressive Citizens' Party (FBP) *exports* microchips, dental products, small machinery, processed foods, postage stamps *currency* Swiss franc *population* (1993 est) 30,000 (33% foreign); growth rate 1.4% p.a. *life expectancy* men 78, women 83 (1989) *languages* German (official); an Alemannic dialect is also spoken *religions* Roman Catholic 87%, Protestant 8% *literacy* 99% *GNP* $33,000 per head (1991) *chronology 1342* Became a sovereign state. *1434* Present boundaries established. *1719* Former counties of Schellenberg and Vaduz constituted as the Principality of Liechtenstein. *1921* Adopted Swiss currency. *1923* United with Switzerland in a customs union. *1938* Prince Franz Josef II came to power. *1984* Prince Franz Joseph II handed over power to Crown Prince Hans Adam. Vote extended to women in national elections. *1989* Prince Franz Joseph II died; Hans Adam II succeeded him. *1990* Became a member of the United Nations. *1991* Became seventh member of European Free Trade Association. *1993* Mario Frick (28) became Europe's youngest head of government.

lied (German "song") musical dramatization of a poem, usually for solo voice and piano; referring to Romantic songs of Schubert, Schumann, Brahms, and Hugo Wolf.

lie detector instrument that records graphically body activities such as thoracic and abdominal respiration, blood pressure, pulse rate, and galvanic skin response (changes in electrical resistance of the skin). Marked changes in these activities when a person answers a question may indicate that the person is lying.

Liège (German *Luik*) industrial city (weapons, textiles, paper, chemicals), capital of Liège province in Belgium, SE of Brussels, on the river Meuse; population (1991) 194,600. The province of Liège has an area of 1,505 sq mi/3,900 sq km and a population (1991) of 999,600.

life the ability to grow, reproduce, and respond to such stimuli as light, heat, and sound. It is thought that life on Earth began about 4 trillion years ago. Over time, life has evolved from primitive single-celled organisms to complex multicellular ones. The earliest fossil evidence of life is threadlike chains of cells discovered in 1980 in deposits in NW Australia that have been dated as 3.5 trillion years old.

life cycle in biology, the sequence of developmental stages through which members of a given species

pass. Most vertebrates have a simple life cycle consisting of ◊fertilization of sex cells or ◊gametes, a period of development as an ◊embryo, a period of juvenile growth after hatching or birth, an adulthood including ◊sexual reproduction, and finally death. Invertebrate life cycles are generally more complex and may involve major reconstitution of the individual's appearance (◊metamorphosis) and completely different styles of life. Plants have a special type of life cycle with two distinct phases, known as ◊alternation of generations. Many insects such as cicadas, dragonflies, and mayflies have a long larvae or pupae phase and a short adult phase. Dragonflies live an aquatic life as larvae and an aerial life during the adult phase.

ligament strong flexible connective tissue, made of the protein ◊collagen, which joins bone to bone at moveable joints. Ligaments prevent bone dislocation (under normal circumstances) but permit joint flexion.

light electromagnetic waves in the visible range, having a wavelength from about 400 nanometers in the extreme violet to about 770 nanometers in the extreme red. Light is considered to exhibit particle and wave properties, and the fundamental particle, or quantum, of light is called the photon. The speed of light (and of all electromagnetic radiation) in a vacuum is approximately 186,000 mi/300,000 km per second, and is a universal constant denoted by c.

light-emitting diode (LED) means of displaying symbols in electronic instruments and devices. An LED is made of ◊semiconductor material, such as gallium arsenide phosphide, that glows when electricity is passed through it. The first digital watches and calculators had LED displays, but many later models use ◊liquid-crystal displays.

lighthouse structure carrying a powerful light to warn ships or airplanes that they are approaching a place (usually land) dangerous or important to navigation. The light is magnified and directed out to the horizon or up to the zenith by a series of mirrors or prisms. Increasingly lighthouses are powered by electricity and automated rather than staffed; the more recent models also emit radio signals. Only a minority of the remaining staffed lighthouses still use dissolved acetylene gas as a source of power.

lightning high-voltage electrical discharge between two charged rainclouds or between a cloud and the Earth, caused by the buildup of electrical charges. Air in the path of lightning ionizes (becomes conducting), and expands; the accompanying noise is heard as thunder. Currents of 20,000 amperes and temperatures of 54,000°F/30,000°C are common.

light pen in computing, a device resembling an ordinary pen, used to indicate locations on a computer screen. With certain computer-aided design (◊CAD) programs, the light pen can be used to instruct the computer to change the shape, size, position, and colors of sections of a screen image.

light-year in astronomy, the distance traveled by a beam of light in a vacuum in one year, approximately 5.88 trillion miles/9.46 trillion km.

Liguria coastal region of NW Italy, which includes the resorts of the Italian Riviera, lying between the western Alps and the Mediterranean Gulf of Genoa. The region comprises the provinces of Genova, La Spezia, Imperia, and Savona, with a population (1990) of 1,719,200 and an area of 2,093 sq mi/5,418 sq km. Genoa is the chief city and port.

lilac any flowering Old World shrub of the genus *Syringa* (such as *S. vulgaris*) of the olive family Oleaceae, bearing panicles (clusters) of small, sweetly scented, white or purplish flowers.

Lille (Flemish *Ryssel*) industrial city (textiles, chemicals, engineering, distilling), capital of Nord-Pas-de-Calais, France, on the river Deûle; population (1990) 178,300, metropolitan area 936,000. The world's first entirely automatic underground system was opened here 1982.

Lilongwe capital of Malawi since 1975, on the Lilongwe River; population (1987) 234,000. Products include tobacco and textiles. Capital Hill, 3 mi/5 km from the old city, is the site of government buildings and offices.

lily plant of the genus *Lilium*, family Liliaceae, of which there are some 80 species, most with showy, trumpet-shaped flowers growing from bulbs. The lily family includes hyacinths, tulips, asparagus, and plants of the onion genus. The term "lily" is also applied to many lilylike plants of allied genera and families.

lily of the valley plant *Convallaria majalis* of the lily family Liliaceae, growing in woods in North America, Europe, and N Asia. The small, pendant, white flowers are strongly scented. The plant is often cultivated.

Lima capital of Peru, an industrial city (textiles, chemicals, glass, cement) with its port at Callao; population (1988) 418,000, metropolitan area 4,605,000. Founded by the Spanish conquistador Francisco Pizarro 1535, it was rebuilt after destruction by an earthquake 1746.

limbo in Christian theology, a region for the souls of those who were not admitted to the divine vision. *Limbus infantum* was a place where unbaptized infants enjoyed inferior blessedness, and *limbus patrum* was where the prophets of the Old Testament dwelt. The word was first used in this sense in the 13th century by St Thomas Aquinas.

lime small thorny bush *Citrus aurantifolia* of the rue family Rutaceae, native to India. The white flowers are succeeded by light green or yellow fruits, limes, which resemble lemons but are more globular in shape.

lime another name for the ◊linden tree.

lime or *quicklime* CaO (technical name *calcium oxide*) white powdery substance used in making mortar and cement. It is made commercially by heating calcium carbonate ($CaCO_3$), obtained from limestone or chalk, in a lime kiln. Quicklime readily absorbs water to become calcium hydroxide (CaOH), known as slaked lime, which is used to reduce soil acidity.

limerick five-line humorous verse, often nonsensical, which first appeared in England about 1820 and was popularized by Edward ◊Lear. An example is: "There was a young lady of Riga, Who rode with a smile on a tiger; They returned from the ride With the lady inside, And the smile on the face of the tiger."

Limerick county of the Republic of Ireland, in the province of Munster; county town Limerick; area 1,038 sq mi/2,690 sq km; population (1991) 161,900. The land is fertile, with hills in the S. Industries include dairy products, lace, and hydroelectric power.

limestone sedimentary rock composed chiefly of calcium carbonate $CaCO_3$, either derived from the shells of marine organisms or precipitated from solution, mostly in the ocean. Various types of limestone are used as building stone.

limpet any of various marine ◊snails belonging to several families and genera, especially *Acmaea* and *Patella*. A limpet has a conical shell and adheres firmly to rocks by its disklike foot. Limpets leave their fixed positions only to graze on seaweeds, always returning to the same spot. They are found in the Atlantic and Pacific.

Limpopo river in SE Africa, rising in the Transvaal and reaching the Indian Ocean in Mozambique; length 1,000 mi/1,600 km.

Lincoln industrial city and capital of Nebraska; population (1990) 192,000. Industries include engineering, pharmaceuticals, electronic and electrical equipment, and food processing. It was known as *Lancaster* until 1867, when it was renamed for Abraham Lincoln and designated the state capital.

Educational institutions include the main campus of the University of Nebraska and Nebraska Wesleyan University.

Lincoln Abraham 1809–1865. 16th president of the US 1861–65, a Republican. In the ◊Civil War, his chief concern was the preservation of the Union from which the Confederate (Southern) slave states had seceded on his election. In 1863 he announced the freedom of the slaves with the Emancipation Proclamation. He was reelected in 1864 with victory for the North in sight, but was assassinated at the end of the war.

Lincoln was born in a log cabin in Kentucky. Self-educated, he practiced law from 1837 in Springfield, Illinois. Known as "Honest Abe", he was elected president in 1860 on a minority vote. His refusal to concede to Confederate demands for the evacuation of the federal garrison at Fort Sumter, Charleston, South Carliona, precipitated the first hostilities of the Civil War. In the Gettysburg Address 1863, he declared the aims of preserving a "nation conceived in liberty, and

Lincoln, Abraham *President of the US during the Civil War, Abraham Lincoln. His main aim was to preserve the union and prevent the secession of the Southern states.*

dedicated to the proposition that all men are created equal."

Lincolnshire county of E England *area* 2,274 sq mi/ 5,890 sq km *towns and cities* Lincoln (administrative headquarters), Skegness *features* Lincoln Wolds; marshy coastline; the Fens in the SE; rivers: Witham, Welland; 16th-century Burghley House; Belton House, a Restoration mansion *industries* cattle, sheep, horses, cereals, flower bulbs, oil *population* (1991) 584,500 *famous people* Isaac Newton, John Wesley, Alfred Tennyson, Margaret Thatcher.

Lindbergh Charles A(ugustus) 1902–1974. US aviator who made the first solo nonstop flight in 33.5 hours across the Atlantic (Roosevelt Field, Long Island, New York, to Le Bourget airport, Paris) 1927 in the *Spirit of St Louis*, a Ryan monoplane designed by him.

Born in Detroit, Michigan, Lindbergh was a barnstorming pilot before attending the US Army School in Texas 1924 and becoming an officer in the Army Air Service Reserve 1925. His son, Charles, Jr (1930–1932), was kidnapped and killed, a crime for which Bruno Hauptmann was convicted and executed. Ensuing legislation against kidnapping was called the Lindbergh Act. Although he championed US neutrality in the late 1930s, he flew 50 combat missions in the Pacific theater in World War II. He wrote *The Spirit of St Louis* 1953 (Pulitzer Prize).

linden or *lime* deciduous tree, genus *Tilia*, of the family Tiliaceae native to the northern hemisphere. The leaves are heart-shaped and coarsely toothed, and the flowers are cream-colored and fragrant.

linear accelerator or *linac* see ◊accelerator.

linen yarn spun and the textile woven from the fibers of the stem of the ◊flax plant. Used by the ancient Egyptians, linen was introduced by the Romans to northern Europe, where production became widespread. Religious refugees from the Low Countries in the 16th century helped to establish the linen industry in England, but here and elsewhere it began to decline in competition with cotton in the 18th century.

line printer computer ◊printer that prints a complete line of characters at a time. Line printers can achieve very high printing speeds of up to 2,500 lines a minute, but can print in only one typeface, cannot print graphics, and are very noisy. Until the late 1980s they were the obvious choice for high-volume printing, but high-speed ◊page printers, such as laser printers, are now preferred.

ling any of several deepwater long-bodied fishes of the cod family found in the N Atlantic.

ling another name for common ◊heather.

lingua franca any language that is used as a means of communication by groups who do not themselves normally speak that language; for example, English is a lingua franca used by Japanese doing business in Finland, or by Swedes in Saudi Arabia. The term comes from the mixture of French, Italian, Spanish, Greek, Turkish, and Arabic that was spoken around the Mediterranean from the time of the Crusades until the 18th century.

linguistics scientific study of language. Linguistics has many branches, such as origins (historical linguistics), the changing way language is pronounced (phonetics), derivation of words through various languages (etymology), development of meanings (semantics), and the arrangement and modifications of words to convey a message (grammar).

Linnaeus Carolus 1707–1778. Swedish naturalist and physician. His botanical work *Systema naturae* 1735 contained his system for classifying plants into groups depending on shared characteristics (such as the number of stamens in flowers), providing a much-needed framework for identification. He also devised the concise and precise system for naming plants and animals, using one Latin (or Latinized) word to represent the genus and a second to distinguish the species.

linnet Old World finch *Acanthis cannabina*. Mainly brown, the males, noted for their song, have a crimson crown and breast in summer.

linseed seeds of the flax plant *Linum usitatissimum*, from which linseed oil is expressed, the residue being used as cattle feed. The oil is used in paint, wood treatments and varnishes, and in the manufacture of linoleum.

lion cat *Panthera leo*, now found only in Africa and NW India. The coat is tawny, the young having darker spot markings that usually disappear in the adult. The male has a heavy mane and a tuft at the end of the tail. Head and body measure about 6 ft/2 m, plus 3 ft/ 1 m of tail, the lioness being slightly smaller. Lions produce litters of two to six cubs, and often live in prides of several adult males and females with several young.

Lipchitz Jacques 1891–1973. Lithuanian-born sculptor. He was active in Paris from 1909 and emigrated to the US 1941. He was one of the first Cubist sculptors, his best-known piece being *Man with a Guitar* 1916 (Museum of Modern Art, New York). In the 1920s he experimented with small open forms he called "transparents". His later works, often political allegories, were characterized by heavy, contorted forms.

Li Peng 1928– . Chinese communist politician, a member of the Politburo from 1985, and head of government from 1987. During the prodemocracy demonstrations of 1989 he supported the massacre of students by Chinese troops and the subsequent execution of others. He sought improved relations with the USSR before its demise, and has favored maintaining firm central and party control over the economy.

lipid any of a large number of esters of fatty acids, commonly formed by the reaction of a fatty acid with glycerol. They are soluble in alcohol but not in water. Lipids are the chief constituents of plant and animal waxes, fats, and oils.

Li Po 705–762. Chinese poet. He used traditional literary forms, but his exuberance, the boldness of his imagination, and the intensity of his feeling has won him recognition as perhaps the greatest of all Chinese poets. Although he was mostly concerned with higher themes, he is also remembered for his celebratory verses on drinking.

Lippi Filippino *c*.1457–1504. Italian painter of the Florentine school. He was trained by Botticelli. He produced altarpieces and several fresco cycles, full of detail and drama, elegantly and finely drawn. He was the son of Filippo Lippi.

Lippi Fra Filippo *c*.1406–1469. Italian painter. His works include frescoes depicting the lives of St Stephen and St John the Baptist in Prato Cathedral 1452–66. He also painted many altarpieces of Madonnas and groups of saints.

liquefaction the process of converting a gas to a liquid, normally associated with low temperatures and high pressures (see ◊condensation).

liquid state of matter between a ◊solid and a ◊gas. A liquid forms a level surface and assumes the shape of its container. Its atoms do not occupy fixed positions as in a crystalline solid, nor do they have freedom of movement as in a gas. Unlike a gas, a liquid is difficult to compress since pressure applied at one point is equally transmitted throughout (Pascal's principle). ◊Hydraulics makes use of this property.

liquidation in economics, the winding up of a company by converting all its assets into money to pay off its liabilities.

liquid-crystal display (LCD) display of numbers (for example, in a calculator) or pictures (such as on a pocket television screen) produced by molecules of a substance in a semiliquid state with some crystalline properties, so that clusters of molecules align in parallel formations. The display is a blank until the application of an electric field, which "twists" the molecules so that they reflect or transmit light falling on them.

liquorice perennial European herb *Glycyrrhiza glabra*, family Leguminosae. The long, sweet root yields an extract which is made into a hard black paste and used in confectionery and medicines.

Lisbon (Portuguese *Lisboa*) city and capital of Portugal, in the SW of the country, on the tidal lake and estuary formed by the river Tagus; population (1984) 808,000. Industries include steel, textiles, chemicals, pottery, shipbuilding, and fishing. It has been the capital since 1260 and reached its peak of prosperity in the period of Portugal's empire during the 16th century. In 1755 an earthquake killed 60,000 people and destroyed much of the city.

Lister Joseph, 1st Baron Lister 1827–1912. English surgeon and founder of antiseptic surgery, influenced by Louis ◊Pasteur's work on bacteria. He introduced dressings soaked in carbolic acid and strict rules of hygiene to combat wound sepsis in hospitals.

Liszt Franz 1811–1886. Hungarian pianist and composer. An outstanding virtuoso of the piano, he was an established concert artist by the age of 12. His expressive, romantic, and frequently chromatic works include piano music (*Transcendental Studies* 1851), masses and oratorios, songs, organ music, and a symphony. Much of his music is programmatic; he also originated the symphonic poem.

litchi or *lychee* evergreen tree *Litchi chinensis* of the soapberry family Sapindaceae. The delicately flavored ovate fruit is encased in a brownish rough outer skin and has a hard seed. The litchi is native to S China, where it has been cultivated for 2,000 years.

liter metric unit of volume (symbol l), equal since 1964 to one cubic decimeter (61.025 cu in, 1.057 liquid qt, or 0.91 dry qt). It was formerly defined as the volume occupied by one kilogram of pure water at 4°C at standard pressure, but this is slightly larger than one cubic decimeter.

literacy ability to read and write. The level at which functional literacy is set rises as society becomes more complex, and it becomes increasingly difficult for an illiterate person to find work and cope with the other demands of everyday life.

literature words set apart in some way from ordinary everyday communication. In the ancient oral traditions, before stories and poems were written down, literature had a mainly public function—mythic and religious. As literary works came to be preserved in

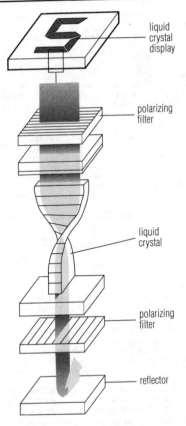

liquid crystal display

polarizing filter

liquid crystal

polarizing filter

reflector

liquid-crystal display, (LCD) *A liquid-crystal display consists of a liquid crystal sandwiched between polarizing filters similar to polaroid sunglasses. When a segment of the seven-segment display is electrified, the liquid crystal twists the polarized light from the front filter, allowing the light to bounce off the rear reflector and illuminate the segment.*

writing, and, eventually, printed, their role became more private, serving as a vehicle for the exploration and expression of emotion and the human situation.

lithium soft, ductile, silver-white, metallic element, symbol Li, atomic number 3, atomic weight 6.941. It is one of the ◊alkali metals, has a very low density (far less than most woods), and floats on water (specific gravity 0.57); it is the lightest of all metals. Lithium is used to harden alloys, and in batteries; its compounds are used in medicine to treat manic depression.

lithography printmaking technique invented in 1798 by Aloys Senefelder, based on the mutual repulsion of grease and water. A drawing is made with greasy crayon on an absorbent stone, which is then wetted. The wet stone repels ink (which is greasy) applied to the surface and the crayon absorbs it, so that the drawing can be printed. Lithographic printing is used in book production, posters, and prints, and this basic principle has developed into complex processes.

Lithuania Republic of *area* 25,174 sq mi/65,200 sq km *capital* Vilnius *towns and cities* Kaunas, Klaipeda, Siauliai, Panevezys *physical* central lowlands with gentle hills in W and higher terrain in SE; 25% forested; some 3,000 small lakes, marshes, and complex sandy coastline *features* river Nemen; white sand dunes on Kursiu Marios lagoon *head of state* Algirdas Brazauskas from 1993 *head of government* Adolfas Slezevicius from 1993 *political system* emergent democracy *political parties* Social Democratic Party, left of center; Democratic Labour Party (DLP), "reform communist"; Center Movement, centrist; Homeland Union–Lithuanian Conservatives (Tevynes Santara), right of center *products* heavy engineering, electrical goods, shipbuilding, cement, food processing, bacon, dairy products, cereals, potatoes *currency* litas *population* (1994) 3,740,000 (Lithuanian 80%, Russian 9%, Polish 7%, Byelorussian 2%) *life expectancy* men 67, women 76 *language* Lithuanian *religion* predominantly Roman Catholic *GNP* $2,710 per head (1991) *chronology 1918* Independence declared following withdrawal of German occupying troops at end of World War I; USSR attempted to regain power. *1919* Soviet forces overthrown by Germans, Poles, and nationalist Lithuanians; democratic republic established. *1920–39* Province and city of Vilnius occupied by Poles. *1926* Coup overthrew established government; Antanas Smetona became president. *1939* Secret German-Soviet agreement brought most of Lithuania under Soviet influence. *1940* Incorporated into USSR as constituent republic. *1941* Lithuania revolted against USSR and established own government. During World War II Germany again occupied the country. *1944* USSR resumed rule. *1944–52* Lithuanian guerrillas fought USSR. *1972* Demonstrations against Soviet government. *1980* Growth in nationalist dissent, influenced by Polish example. *1988* Popular front formed, the Sajudis, to campaign for increased autonomy. *1989* Lithuanian declared the state language; flag of independent interwar republic readopted. Communist Party (CP) split into pro-Moscow and nationalist wings. Communist local monopoly of power abolished. *1990* Feb: nationalist Sajudis won elections. March: Vytautas Landsbergis became president; unilateral declaration of independence rejected by USSR. *1991* Jan: Soviet paratroopers briefly occupied key buildings in Vilnius. Sept: independence recognized by USSR and Western nations; CP outlawed; admitted into United Nations. *1992* Nov: DLP, led by Algirdas Brazauskas, won majority vote in parliamentary elections. *1993* Brazauskas elected president. Last Russian troops departed. *1994* Application for NATO membership.

litmus dye obtained from various lichens and used in chemistry as an indicator to test the acidic or alkaline nature of aqueous solutions; it turns red in the presence of acid, and blue in the presence of alkali.

Little Bighorn, Battle of the engagement in Montana; Lieutenant Colonel George ◊Custer's defeat by the ◊Sioux Indians, June 25, 1876, under Chiefs Crazy Horse and ◊Sitting Bull, known as Custer's Last Stand. Custer ignored scouting reports of an overwhelming Indian force and led a column of 265 soldiers into a ravine where thousands of Indian warriors lay in wait. Custer and every one of his command were killed. US reprisals against the Indians followed, driving them from the area.

Little Dipper another name for the most distinctive part of the constellation ◊Ursa Minor, the Little Bear.

The name has also been applied to the stars in the ◊Pleiades open star cluster, the overall shape of the cluster being similar to that of the ◊Big Dipper.

Little Rock largest city and capital of Arkansas; population (1990) 175,800. Products include metal goods, oil-field and electronic equipment, chemicals, clothing, and processed food.

Educational institutions include the University of Arkansas at Little Rock. A French trading post was built here 1722, and in 1821 it became the territorial capital. Union forces captured the city 1863, during the Civil War. Federal troops were sent here 1957 to enforce the integration of all-white Central High School.

liver large organ of vertebrates, which has many regulatory and storage functions. The human liver is situated in the upper abdomen, and weighs about 4.5 lb/2 kg. It is divided into four lobes. The liver receives the products of digestion, converts glucose to glycogen (a long-chain carbohydrate used for storage), and breaks down fats. It removes excess amino acids from the blood, converting them to urea, which is excreted by the kidneys. The liver also synthesizes vitamins, produces bile and blood-clotting factors, and removes damaged red cells and toxins such as alcohol from the blood.

Liverpool city, seaport, and administrative headquarters of Merseyside, NW England; population (1991 est) 448,300. Liverpool is the UK's chief Atlantic port with miles of specialized, mechanized quays on the river Mersey. Present-day industries include flour-milling, sugar refining, electrical engineering, food processing, chemicals, soap, margarine, tanning, and motor vehicles. The Grand National steeplechase takes place at Aintree. The four members of the ◊Beatles pop group were born here.

Liverpool Robert Banks Jenkinson, 2nd Earl Liverpool 1770–1825. British Tory politician who was prime minister 1812–27. His government conducted the Napoleonic Wars to a successful conclusion, but its ruthless suppression of freedom of speech and of the press aroused such opposition that during 1815–20 revolution frequently seemed imminent.

liverwort plant of the class Hepaticae, of the bryophyte division of nonvascular plants, related to mosses, found growing in damp places.

Livingstone David 1813–1873. Scottish missionary explorer. In 1841 he went to Africa, reached Lake Ngami 1849, followed the Zambezi to its mouth, saw the Victoria Falls 1855, and went to East and Central Africa 1858–64, reaching Lakes Shirwa and Malawi. From 1866, he tried to find the source of the river Nile, and :eached Ujiji in Tanganyika in Nov 1871. British explorer Henry ◊Stanley joined Livingstone in Ujiji.

Livonia former region in Europe on the E coast of the Baltic Sea comprising most of present-day Latvia and Estonia. Livonia was independent until 1583, when it was divided between Poland and Sweden. In 1710 it was occupied by Russia, and in 1721 was ceded to Peter the Great, Czar of Russia.

Livy (Titus Livius) 59 BC–AD 17. Roman historian. He was the author of a *History of Rome* from the city's foundation to 9 BC, based partly on legend. It was composed of 142 books, of which 35 survive, covering the periods from the arrival of Aeneas in Italy to 293 BC and from 218 to 167 BC.

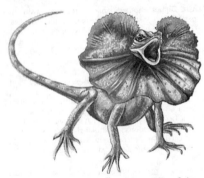

lizard The frilled lizard of N Australia and New Guinea has a rufflike collar of skin—up to 10 in/25 cm across—around its neck. The collar normally lies flat but, if alarmed, the lizard raises the brightly colored collar and opens its mouth to intimidate an enemy.

lizard reptile of the suborder Lacertilia, which together with snakes constitutes the order Squamata. Lizards are generally distinguishable from snakes by having four legs, moveable eyelids, eardrums, and a fleshy tongue, but some lizards are legless and snakelike in appearance. There are over 3,000 species of lizard worldwide.

Ljubljana (German *Laibach*) capital and industrial city (textiles, chemicals, paper, leather goods) of Slovenia, near the confluence of the rivers Ljubljanica and Sava; population (1991) 276,100. It has a nuclear research center and is linked with S Austria by the Karawanken road tunnel under the Alps (1979–83).

llama South American even-toed hoofed mammal *Lama glama* of the camel family, about 4 ft/1.2 m high at the shoulder. Llamas can be white, brown, or dark, sometimes with spots or patches. They are very hardy, and require little food or water. They spit profusely when annoyed.

Llewelyn I 1173–1240. Prince of Wales from 1194 who extended his rule to all Wales not in Norman hands, driving the English from N Wales 1212, and taking Shrewsbury 1215. During the early part of Henry III's reign, he was several times attacked by English armies. He was married to Joanna, illegitimate daughter of King John.

Llewelyn II ap Gruffydd *c.*1225–1282. Prince of Wales from 1246, grandson of Llewelyn I. In 1277 Edward I of England compelled Llewelyn to acknowledge him as overlord and to surrender S Wales. His death while leading a national uprising ended Welsh independence.

Lloyd George David 1863–1945. Welsh Liberal politician, prime minister of Britain 1916–22. A pioneer of social reform, as chancellor of the Exchequer 1908–15 he introduced old-age pensions 1908 and health and unemployment insurance 1911. The creation of the Irish Free State in 1921 and his pro-Greek policy against the Turks caused the collapse of his coalition government.

Lloyd Webber Andrew 1948– . English composer. His early musicals, with lyrics by Tim Rice, include *Joseph and the Amazing Technicolor Dreamcoat* 1968, *Jesus Christ Superstar* 1970, and *Evita* 1978, based on the life of the Argentine leader Eva Perón. He also wrote *Cats* 1981, based on T S Eliot's *Old Possum's Book of Practical Cats*, *Starlight Express* 1984, *The Phantom of the Opera* 1986, and *Aspects of Love* 1989.

loach carplike freshwater fish, family Cobitidae, with a long narrow body, and no teeth in the small, downward-pointing mouth, which is surrounded by barbels. Loaches are native to Asian and European waters.

loam type of fertile soil, a mixture of sand, silt, clay, and organic material. It is porous, which allows for good air circulation and retention of moisture.

lobby individual or pressure group that sets out to influence government action. The lobby is prevalent in the US, where the term originated in the 1830s from the practice of those wishing to influence state policy waiting for elected representatives in the lobby of the Capitol.

lobelia any temperate and tropical plant of the genus *Lobelia* of the bellflower family Lobeliaceae, with white to mauve flowers. Lobelias may grow to shrub size but are mostly small annual plants.
The cardinal lobelia *L. cardinalis* of E North America has large bright red flowers.

lobster large marine crustacean of the order Decapoda. Lobsters are grouped with freshwater ◊crayfish in the suborder Reptantia ("walking"), although both lobsters and crayfish can also swim, using their fanlike tails. Lobsters have eyes on stalks and long antennae, and are mainly nocturnal. They scavenge and eat dead or dying fish.
Species include the American lobster *Homarus americanus*; and the Norwegian lobster *Nephrops norvegicus*, a small orange species.

local government that part of government dealing mainly with matters concerning the inhabitants of a particular area or town, usually financed at least in part by local taxes. In the US and UK, local government has comparatively large powers and responsibilities.

Lochner Stephan *c.*1400–1451. German painter. Active in Cologne from 1442, he was a master of the International Gothic style. Most of his work is still in Cologne, notably the *Virgin in the Rose Garden* about 1440 (Wallraf-Richartz Museum) and *Adoration of the Magi* 1448 (Cologne Cathedral). His work combines the delicacy of the International Gothic style with the naturalism of Flemish painting.

Loch Ness Scottish lake; see ◊Ness, Loch.

lock construction installed in waterways to allow boats or ships to travel from one level to another. The earliest form, the *flash lock*, was first seen in the East in 1st-century AD China and in the West in 11th-century Holland. By this method barriers temporarily dammed a river and when removed allowed the flash flood to propel the waiting boat through any obstacle. This was followed in 12th-century China and 14th-century Holland by the *pound lock*. In this system the lock has gates at each end. Boats enter through one gate when the levels are the same both outside and inside. Water is then allowed in (or out of) the lock until the level rises (or falls) to the new level outside the other gate.

Locke John 1632–1704. English philosopher. His *Essay concerning Human Understanding* 1690 maintained that experience was the only source of knowledge (empiricism), and that "we can have knowlege no farther than we have ideas" prompted by such experience.

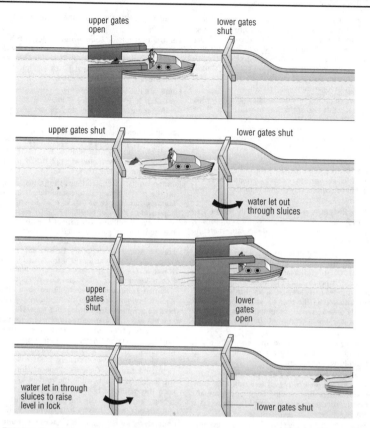

upper gates open

lower gates shut

upper gates shut

lower gates shut

water let out through sluices

upper gates shut

lower gates open

water let in through sluices to raise level in lock

lower gates shut

lock *Traveling downstream, a boat enters the lock with the lower gates closed. The upper gates are then shut and the water level lowered by draining through sluices. When the water level in the lock reaches the downstream level, the lower gates are opened.*

Two Treatises on Government 1690 helped to form contemporary ideas of liberal democracy.

locomotive engine for hauling railroad trains. In 1804 Richard Trevithick built the first steam engine to run on rails. Locomotive design did not radically improve until British engineer George Stephenson built the *Rocket* 1829, which featured a multitube boiler and blastpipe, standard in all following *steam locomotives*. Today most locomotives are diesel or electric: *diesel locomotives* have a powerful diesel engine, and *electric locomotives* draw their power from either an overhead cable or a third rail alongside the ordinary track.

locust swarming grasshopper, with short antennae and auditory organs on the abdomen, in the family Acrididae. As winged adults, flying in swarms, locusts may be carried by the wind hundreds of miles from their breeding grounds; on landing they devour all vegetation. Locusts occur in nearly every continent.

locust tree in botany, any of several trees of the genera *Robinia* and *Gleditsia* of the legume family, with primate compound leaves and many-seeded pods, of E US. The black locust *R. pseudoacacia* and the honey-locust *G. triacanthos* are examples. The name locust tree is also applied to the ◊carob, a small European tree.

lode geological deposit rich in certain minerals, generally consisting of a large vein or set of veins containing ore minerals. A system of veins that can be mined directly forms a lode, for example the mother lode of the California gold rush.

Lodge Henry Cabot, II 1902–1985. US diplomat. He was Eisenhower's presidential campaign manager and the US representative at the United Nations 1953–60. Ambassador to South Vietnam 1963–64 and 1965–67, he replaced W A Harriman as President Nixon's negotiator in the Vietnam peace talks 1969. He was a grandson of Henry Cabot Lodge.

Lódz´ industrial city (textiles, machinery, dyes) in central Poland, 75 mi/120 km SW of Warsaw; population (1990) 848,300.

loganberry hybrid between a ◊blackberry and a ◊raspberry with large, tart, dull-red fruit. It was developed by US judge James H Logan in 1881.

logarithm or *log* the exponent or index of a number to a specified base—usually 10. For example, the logarithm to the base 10 of 1,000 is 3 because $10^3 = 1,000$; the logarithm of 2 is 0.3010 because $2 = 10^{0.3010}$. Before the advent of cheap electronic calculators, multiplication and division could be simplified by being replaced with the addition and subtraction of logarithms.

logic branch of philosophy that studies valid reasoning and argument. It is also the way in which one thing may be said to follow from, or be a consequence of, another (deductive logic). Logic is generally divided into the traditional formal logic of Aristotle and the symbolic logic derived from Friedrich Frege and Bertrand Russell.

logical error in computing, an error in the program's design. A logical error may cause a program to fail to respond in the correct way to user requests or to crash completely.

logical positivism doctrine that the only meaningful propositions are those that can be verified empirically. Metaphysics, religion, and esthetics are therefore meaningless.

LOGO high-level computer programming language designed to teach mathematical concepts. Developed about 1970 at the Massachusetts Institute of Technology, it became popular in schools and with home computer users because of its "turtle graphics" feature. This allows the user to write programs that create line drawings on a computer screen, or drive a small mobile robot (a "turtle" or "buggy") around the floor.

log off or *log out* in computing, the process by which a user identifies himself or herself to a multi-user computer and leaves the system.

log on or *log in* in computing, the process by which a user identifies himself or herself to a multiuser computer and enters the system. Logging on usually requires the user to enter a password before access is allowed.

Loire longest river in France, rising in the Cévennes Mountains, at 4,430 ft/1,350 m and flowing for 650 mi/1,050 km first N then W until it reaches the Bay of Biscay at St Nazaire, passing Nevers, Orléans, Tours, and Nantes. It gives its name to the *départements* of Loire, Haute-Loire, Loire-Atlantique, Indre-et-Loire, Maine-et-Loire, and Saône-et-Loire. There are many châteaux and vineyards along its banks.

Lollard follower of the English religious reformer John ◊Wycliffe in the 14th century. The Lollards condemned the doctrine of the transubstantiation of the bread and wine of the Eucharist, advocated the diversion of ecclesiastical property to charitable uses, and denounced war and capital punishment. They were active from about 1377; after the passing of the statute *De heretico comburendo* ("The Necessity of Burning Heretics") 1401 many Lollards were burned, and in 1414 they raised an unsuccessful revolt in London, known as Oldcastle's rebellion.

Lombard or *Langobard* member of a Germanic people who invaded Italy in 568 and occupied Lombardy (named for them) and central Italy. Their capital was Monza. They were conquered by the Frankish ruler Charlemagne in 774.

Lombardi Vince(nt Thomas) 1913–1970. US football coach. As head coach of the Green Bay Packers 1959, he transformed a losing team into a major power, winning the first two Super Bowls 1967 and 1968. His last coaching position was with the Washington Redskins 1969–70.

Lombardy (Italian *Lombardia*) region of N Italy, including Lake Como; capital Milan; area 9,225 sq mi/23,900 sq km; population (1990) 8,939,400. It is the country's chief industrial area (chemicals, pharmaceuticals, engineering, textiles).

Lomé capital and port of Togo; population (1983) 366,000. It is a center for gold, silver, and marble crafts; industries include steel production and oil refining.

Lomond, Loch largest freshwater Scottish lake, 21 mi/37 km long, area 27 sq mi/70 sq km, divided between Strathclyde and Central regions. It is overlooked by the mountain *Ben Lomond* (192 ft/973 m) and is linked to the Clyde estuary.

London capital of England and the United Kingdom, on the river Thames; its metropolitan area, *Greater London*, has an area of 610 sq mi/1,580 sq km and population (1991) of 6,679,700 (larger metropolitan area about 9 million). The *City of London*, known as the "square mile", area 677 acres/274 hectares, is the financial and commercial center of the UK. Greater London from 1965 comprises the City of London and 32 boroughs. Popular tourist attractions include the Tower of London, St Paul's Cathedral, Buckingham Palace, Westminster Abbey, and Covent Garden.

Roman *Londinium* was established soon after the Roman invasion AD 43; in the 2nd century London became a walled city. Throughout the 19th century London was the largest city in the world (in population). *education and entertainment* Museums: British, Victoria and Albert, Natural History, Science museums; galleries: National Gallery, National Portrait Gallery, Hayward Gallery, Wallace Collection, Courtauld Institute Galleries. London University is the largest in Britain, while the Inns of Court have been the training school for lawyers since the 13th century. London has been the center of English drama since its first theater was built by James Burbage 1576.

Londonderry former name (to 1984) of the county and city of ◊Derry in Northern Ireland.

lone pair in chemistry, a pair of electrons in the outermost shell of an atom that are not used in bonding. In certain circumstances, they will allow the atom to bond with atoms, ions, or molecules (such as boron trifluoride, BF_3) that are deficient in electrons, forming coordinate covalent (dative) bonds in which they provide both of the bonding electrons.

Long Huey 1893–1935. US Democratic politician, nicknamed "the Kingfish", governor of Louisiana 1928–31, US senator from Louisiana 1930–35, legendary for his political rhetoric. He was popular with poor white voters for his program of social and economic reform, which he called the "Share Our Wealth" program. It represented a significant challenge to Franklin D Roosevelt's ◊New Deal economic program.

Born in Winnfield, Louisiana, he graduated from Tulane University with a law degree. He was fatally shot one month after announcing his intention to run for the presidency.

Longfellow Henry Wadsworth 1807–1882. US poet. He is remembered for his ballads ("Excelsior", "The Village Blacksmith", "The Wreck of the Hesperus") and the mythic narrative epics *Evangeline* 1847, *The Song of Hiawatha* 1855, and *The Courtship of Miles Standish* 1858.

Longford county of the Republic of Ireland, in the province of Leinster; county town Longford; area 401 sq mi/1,040 sq km; population (1991) 30,300. Low-lying with bogs it has the rivers Camlin, Inny, and Shannon (which forms its western boundary), and several lakes. Agricultural activities include stock rearing and the production of oats and potatoes.

Long Island island E of Manhattan and SE of Connecticut, separated from the mainland by Long Island Sound and the East River; 120 mi/193 km long by about 30 mi/48km wide; area 1,400 sq mi/3,627 sq km; population (1984) 6,818,480.

The two New York City boroughs of Queens and Brooklyn are the western eighth of the island with a combined population of 4,165,090 (1984). East of them are the counties of Nassau and Suffolk. On the S shore are the popular summer-resort communities of Coney Island, the Rockaways, Long Beach, Fire Island, and the Hamptons. Shea Stadium, and Belmont and Aqueduct raceways are here.

longitude see ◊latitude and longitude.

long jump field event in athletics in which competitors sprint up to and leap from a take-off board into a sandpit measuring 9 meters in length. The take-off board is 1 meter from the landing area. Each competitor usually has six attempts, and the winner is the one with the longest jump.

Long March in Chinese history, the 6,000 mi/10,000 km trek undertaken 1934–35 by ◊Mao Zedong and his communist forces from SE to NW China, under harassment from the Guomindang (nationalist) army.

Long Parliament English Parliament 1640–53 and 1659–60, which continued through the English Civil War. After the Royalists withdrew in 1642 and the Presbyterian right was excluded in 1648, the remaining ◊Rump ruled England until expelled by Oliver Cromwell in 1653. Reassembled 1659–60, the Long Parliament initiated the negotiations for the restoration of the monarchy.

loom any machine for weaving yarn or thread into cloth. The first looms were used to weave sheep's wool about 5000 BC . A loom is a frame on which a set of lengthwise threads (warp) is strung. A second set of threads (weft), carried in a shuttle, is inserted at right angles over and under the warp.

loon any of various birds of the genus *Gavia*, family Gavidae, found in N regions of the N hemisphere. Loons are specialized for swimming and diving. Their legs are set so far back that walking is almost impossible, and they come to land only to nest, but loons are powerful swimmers and good flyers.

They have straight bills and long bodies and feed on fish, crustaceans, and some water plants. There are just five species, the largest, the yellow-billed loon *G. adamsii*, being an Arctic species 2.5 ft/75 cm long.

loop in computing, short for ◊program loop.

loosestrife genus *Lysimachia* of plants of the primrose family (Primulaceae) including swampcandles *L. terrestris* of North America, with yellow and purple-streaked flowers on a spike. The name is also applied to members of the genus *Lythrum* of the loosestrife family, such as the European willow loosestrife *L. salicaria*, now a weed in NE US.

Lope de Vega (Carpio) Felix. Spanish poet and dramatist; see ◊Vega, Lope de.

Lorca Federico García 1898–1936. Spanish poet and playwright. His plays include *Bodas de sangre/Blood Wedding* 1933 and *La casa de Bernarda Alba/The House of Bernarda Alba* 1936. His poems include "Lament", written for the bullfighter Mejías. Lorca was shot by the Falangists during the Spanish Civil War.

Lord in the UK, prefix used informally as alternative to the full title of a marquess, earl, or viscount; normally also in speaking of a baron, and as a courtesy title before the forename and surname of younger sons of dukes and marquesses.

Lords, House of upper house of the UK parliament.

Lorenz Konrad 1903–1989. Austrian ethologist. Director of the Max Planck Institute for the Physiology of Behavior in Bavaria 1955–73, he wrote the studies of ethology (animal behavior) *King Solomon's Ring* 1952 and *On Aggression* 1966. In 1973 he shared the Nobel Prize for Medicine with Nikolaas Tinbergen and Karl von Frisch.

loris any of various small prosimian primates of the family Lorisidae. Lorises are slow-moving, arboreal, and nocturnal. They have very large eyes; true lorises have no tails. They climb without leaping, gripping branches tightly and moving on or hanging below them.

Lorrain Claude. French painter; see ◊Claude Lorrain.

Lorraine region of NE France in the upper reaches of the Meuse and Moselle rivers; bounded N by Belgium, Luxembourg, and Germany and E by Alsace; area 9,095 sq mi/23,600 sq km; population (1986) 2,313,000. It comprises the *départements* of Meurthe-et-Moselle, Meuse, Moselle, and Vosges, and its capital is Nancy. There are deposits of coal, iron ore, and salt; grain, fruit, and livestock are farmed. In 1871 the region was ceded to Germany as part of Alsace-Lorraine. The whole area saw heavy fighting in World War I.

Los Alamos town in New Mexico, which has had a center for atomic and space research since 1942. In World War II the first atom (nuclear fission) bomb was designed there (under Robert ◊Oppenheimer), based on data from other research stations; the ◊hydrogen bomb was also developed there.

The town has a population of 12,000.

Los Angeles city and port in SW California; population (1990) 3,485,400, metropolitan area of Los Angeles–Long Beach 14,531,530. Industries include aerospace, electronics, motor vehicles, chemicals, clothing, printing, and food processing.

Features include Hollywood, center of the movie industry since 1911; the Hollywood Bowl concert arena; and the Los Angeles County Museum of Art. Educational institutions include the University of California at Los Angeles and the University of Southern California.

Los Angeles was established as a Spanish settlement 1781, but it was a farming region with orange groves until the early 20th century. The aircraft industry, with its need for year-round flying weather, developed here. In 1992, racial disturbances resulted in 50 deaths and heavy damage.

Lothair I 795–855. Holy Roman emperor from 817 in association with his father Louis I. On Louis's death in 840, the empire was divided between Lothair and his brothers; Lothair took N Italy and the valleys of the rivers Rhône and Rhine.

Lothair II c. 1070–1137. Holy Roman emperor from 1133 and German king from 1125. His election as emperor, opposed by the ◊Hohenstaufen family of princes, was the start of the feud between the Guelph and Ghibelline factions, who supported the papal party and the Hohenstaufens' claim to the imperial throne respectively.

Lothian region of Scotland *area* 695 sq mi/1,800 sq km *towns and cities* Edinburgh (administrative headquarters), Livingston *features* fertile lowlands bordering on the Firth of Forth in N and rising gently in S; hills: Lammermuir, Moorfoot, Pentland; Bass Rock in the Firth of Forth, noted for seabirds *industries* bacon, vegetables, whiskey, dairy, engineering, electronics *population* (1991) 726,000 *famous people* Robert Louis Stevenson, Alexander Graham Bell, Arthur Conan Doyle.

lottery game of chance in which tickets sold may win a prize.

In the US, the players choose numbers that, if selected in a random drawing, can bring the winner millions of dollars. State-sponsored lotteries are a means of raising revenue, especially for education and other public needs. A national lottery began in the UK 1995.

Lotto Lorenzo c. 1480–1556. Italian painter. Born in Venice, he was active in Bergamo, Treviso, Venice, Ancona, and Rome. His early works were influenced by Giovanni Bellini; his mature style belongs to the High Renaissance. He painted religious works but is best known for his portraits, which often convey a sense of unease or air of melancholy.

lotus any of several different plants, especially the water lily *Nymphaea lotus*, frequent in Egyptian art, and *Nelumbo nucifera*, the pink Asiatic lotus, a sacred symbol in Hinduism and Buddhism, whose flower head floats erect above the water.

Lotus 1–2–3 ◊spreadsheet computer program, produced by Lotus Development Corporation. It first appeared in 1982 and its combination of spreadsheet, graphics display, and data management contributed to the rapid acceptance of the IBM Personal Computer in business.

loudspeaker electromechanical device that converts electrical signals into sound waves, which are radiated into the air. The most common type of loudspeaker is the *moving-coil speaker*. Electrical signals from, for example, a radio are fed to a coil of fine wire wound around the top of a cone. The coil is surrounded by a magnet. When signals pass through it, the coil becomes an electromagnet, which by moving causes the cone to vibrate, setting up sound waves.

Louis Joe. Assumed name of Joseph Louis Barrow 1914–1981. US boxer, nicknamed "the Brown Bomber". He was world heavyweight champion between 1937 and 1949 and made a record 25 successful defenses (a record for any weight).

Louis (I) the Pious 788–840. Holy Roman emperor from 814, when he succeeded his father Charlemagne.

Louis III 863–882. King of N France from 879, while his brother Carloman (866–884) ruled S France. He was the son of Louis II. Louis countered a revolt of the nobility at the beginning of his reign, and his resistance to the Normans made him a hero of epic poems.

Louis XI 1423–1483. King of France from 1461. He broke the power of the nobility (headed by ◊Charles the Bold) by intrigue and military power.

Louis XIV (called *the Sun King*) 1638–1715. King of France from 1643, when he succeeded his father Louis XIII; his mother was Anne of Austria. Until 1661 France was ruled by the chief minister, Jules Mazarin, but later Louis took absolute power, summed up in his saying *L'Etat c'est moi* ("I am the state"). Throughout his reign he was engaged in unsuccessful expansionist wars—1667–68, 1672–78, 1688–97, and 1701–13 (the War of the ◊Spanish Succession)—against various European alliances, always including Britain and the Netherlands. He was a patron of the arts.

Louis XV 1710–1774. King of France from 1715, with the Duke of Orléans as regent until 1723. He was the great-grandson of Louis XIV. Indolent and frivolous, Louis left government in the hands of his ministers, the Duke of Bourbon and Cardinal Fleury (1653–1743). On the latter's death he attempted to rule alone but became entirely dominated by his mistresses, Madame de Pompadour and Madame Du Barry. His foreign policy led to French possessions in Canada and India being lost to England.

Louis XVI 1754–1793. King of France from 1774, grandson of Louis XV, and son of Louis the Dauphin. He was dominated by his queen, ◊Marie Antoinette, and French finances fell into such confusion that in 1789 the ◊States General (parliament) had to be summoned, and the ◊French Revolution began. Louis lost his personal popularity in June 1791 when he attempted to flee the country, and in Aug 1792 the Parisians stormed the Tuileries palace and took the royal family prisoner. Deposed in Sept 1792, Louis was tried in Dec, sentenced for treason in Jan 1793, and guillotined.

Louis XVII 1785–1795. Nominal king of France, the son of Louis XVI. During the French Revolution he was imprisoned with his parents in 1792 and probably died in prison.

Louis XVIII 1755–1824. King of France 1814–24, the younger brother of Louis XVI. He assumed the title of king in 1795, having fled into exile in 1791 during the

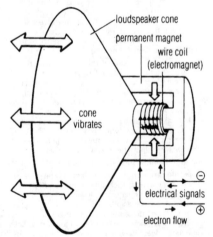

loudspeaker cone
permanent magnet
wire coil
(electromagnet)
cone vibrates
electrical signals
electron flow

loudspeaker A moving-coil loudspeaker. Electrical signals flowing through the wire coil turn it into an electromagnet, which moves as the signals vary. The attached cone vibrates, producing sound waves.

French Revolution, but became king only on the fall of Napoleon I in April 1814. Expelled during Napoleon's brief return (the "hundred days") in 1815, he resumed power after Napoleon's final defeat at Waterloo, pursuing a policy of calculated liberalism until ultra-royalist pressure became dominant after 1820.

Louisiana state in S US; nickname Pelican State *area* 52,457 sq mi/135,900 sq km *capital* Baton Rouge *towns and cities* New Orleans, Shreveport, Lafayette, Lake Charles, Monroe *features* New Orleans French Quarter: jazz, restaurants, Mardi Gras; Cajun country and the Mississippi River delta; Jean Lafitte National Park and Chalmette National Historical Park; plantation homes near Natchitoches *industries* rice, cotton, sugar, oil, natural gas, chemicals, sulfur, fish and shellfish, salt, processed foods, petroleum products, timber, paper *population* (1990) 4,220,000; including Cajuns, descendants of 18th-century religious exiles from Canada, who speak a French dialect *famous people* Louis Armstrong, P G T Beauregard, Huey Long *history* explored by the Spanish Piñeda 1519, Cabeza de Vaca 1528, and De Soto 1541 and by the French explorer La Salle 1862, who named it after Louis XIV and claimed it for France. It became Spanish 1762–1800, then French, then passed to the US 1803 under the ◊Louisiana Purchase; admitted to the Union as a state 1812.

Louisiana Purchase purchase by the US from France 1803 of an area covering about 828,000 sq mi/2,144,000 sq km, including the present-day states of Louisiana, Missouri, Arkansas, Iowa, Nebraska, North Dakota, South Dakota, and Oklahoma.

President Thomas ◊Jefferson, fearing that the French (having just acquired New Orleans from the Spanish) might restrict American access to the Mississippi, offered $10 million for the area to Napoleon, who initially refused. Faced with an impending war with Britain and reverses in his colonial campaigns, the French emperor then sold the entire territory for $15 million.

Louis Philippe 1773–1850. King of France 1830–48. Son of Louis Philippe Joseph, Duke of Orléans 1747–93; both were known as *Philippe Egalité* from their support of the 1792 Revolution. Louis Philippe fled into exile 1793–1814, but became king after the 1830 revolution with the backing of the rich bourgeoisie. Corruption discredited his regime, and after his overthrow, he escaped to the UK and died there.

Lourdes town in Midi-Pyrénées region, SW France, on the Gave de Pau River; population (1982) 18,000. Its Christian shrine to St Bernadette has a reputation for miraculous cures and Lourdes is an important Catholic pilgrimage center. The young peasant girl Bernadette Soubirous was shown the healing springs of the Grotte de Massabielle by a vision of the Virgin Mary 1858.

louse parasitic insect of the order Anoplura, which lives on mammals. It has a flat, segmented body without wings, and a tube attached to the head, used for sucking blood from its host.

Louth smallest county of the Republic of Ireland, in the province of Leinster; county town Dundalk; area 317 sq mi/820 sq km; population (1991) 90,700. It is low-lying. There is cattle-rearing, and oats and potatoes are grown.

Low Juliette Gordon 1860–1927. Founder of the Girl Scouts in the US. She formed a troop of 16 "Girl Guides" in Savannah 1912, based on UK scouting organizations founded by Robert Baden-Powell. Establishing national headquarters in Washington, DC 1913, she changed the name of the organization to the Girl Scouts of America (GSA).

Low Countries region of Europe that consists of ◊Belgium and the ◊Netherlands, and usually includes ◊Luxembourg.

Lowell Amy (Lawrence) 1874–1925. US poet. She began her career by publishing the conventional *A Dome of Many-Colored Glass* 1912 but eventually succeeded Ezra Pound as leader of the Imagists (see ◊Imagism). Her works, in free verse, include *Sword Blades and Poppy Seed* 1916.

She was a controversial figure who demonstrated her scorn for conventionality by, for example, openly smoking cigars.

Lowell Robert (Traill Spence, Jr) 1917–1977. US poet. His brutal yet tender verse stressed the importance of individualism, especially during times of war. His works include *Lord Weary's Castle* 1946 (Pulitzer Prize), *Life Studies* 1959, and *For the Union Dead* 1964.

Other works include *Land of Unlikeness* 1944, *The Mills of the Kaanaughs* 1951, *The Old Glory* 1965, *Near the Ocean* 1967, *The Dolphin* 1973 (Pulitzer Prize), and *Day by Day* 1977.

Lower Saxony (German *Niedersachsen*) administrative region (German *Land*) of N Germany *area* 18,296 sq mi/47,400 sq km *capital* Hanover *towns and cities* Brunswick, Osnabrück, Oldenburg, Göttingen, Wolfsburg, Salzgitter, Hildesheim *features* Lüneburg Heath *industries* cereals, automobiles, machinery, electrical engineering *population* (1988) 7,190,000 *religion* 75% Protestant, 20% Roman Catholic *history* formed 1946 from Hanover, Oldenburg, Brunswick, and Schaumburg-Lippe.

LSD abbreviation for *lysergic acid diethylamide*, a psychedelic drug and a hallucinogen, often producing states resembling those common in psychosis (for example, schizophrenia). It is derived from lysergic acid, originally extracted from poisonous ◊ergot alkaloids. Its use is illegal.

LSI (abbreviation for *large-scale integration*) the technology that enables whole electrical circuits to be etched into a piece of semiconducting material just a few millimeters square.

Luanda formerly *Loanda* capital and industrial port (cotton, sugar, tobacco, timber, textiles, paper, oil) of Angola; population (1988) 1,200,000. Founded 1575, it became a Portuguese colonial administrative center as well as an outlet for slaves transported to Brazil.

lubricant substance used between moving surfaces to reduce friction. Carbon-based (organic) lubricants, commonly called grease and oil, are recovered from petroleum distillation.

Lucas van Leyden 1494–1533. Dutch painter and engraver. Active in Leiden and Antwerp, he was a pioneer of Netherlandish genre scenes, for example *The Chess Players* (Staatliche Museen, Berlin). His woodcuts and engravings were inspired by Albrecht Dürer, whom he met in Antwerp 1521.

Lucas's work influenced ◊Rembrandt.

Luce Clare Boothe 1903–1987. US journalist, playwright, and politician. She was managing editor of *Vanity Fair* magazine 1933–34, and wrote several successful plays, including *The Women* 1936 and *Margin for Error* 1940, both of which were made into films.

She served as a Republican member of Congress 1943–47 and as ambassador to Italy 1953–57.

She was born in New York and married Henry Robinson ◊Luce in 1935.

Luce Henry Robinson 1898–1967. US publisher, founder of Time, Inc. It publishes several magazines, including the weekly news magazine *Time*, the weekly feature news magazine *People* , the weekly sports magazine *Sports Illustrated*, the monthly business magazine *Fortune*, and the monthly pictorial magazine *Life*. The company also owns Time-Life Books and the Home Box Office (HBO) cable television channel.

Born of missionary parents in Tengchow, China, Luce was educated at Yale and Oxford universities. He married Clare Boothe Luce in 1935.

Lucerne (German *Luzern*) capital and tourist center of Lucerne canton, Switzerland, on the river Reuss where it flows out of Lake Lucerne; population (1988) 60,600, canton (1990) 319,500. It developed around a Benedictine monastery, established about 750, and owes its prosperity to its position on the St Gotthard road and railroad.

Lucifer in Christian theology, another name for the ◊devil, the leader of the angels who rebelled against God. Lucifer is also another name for the morning star (the planet ◊Venus).

Lucknow capital and industrial city (engineering, chemicals, textiles, many handicrafts) of the state of Uttar Pradesh, India; population (1981) 1,007,000. During the Indian Mutiny against British rule, it was besieged July 2–Nov 16, 1857.

Lucretius (Titus Lucretius Carus) *c.* 99–55 BC. Roman poet and Epicurean philosopher whose *De Rerum natura/On the Nature of The Universe* envisaged the whole universe as a combination of atoms, and had some concept of evolutionary theory.

Lüda or *Lü-ta* or *Hüta* industrial port (engineering, chemicals, textiles, oil refining, shipbuilding, food processing) in Liaoning, China, on Liaodong Peninsula, facing the Yellow Sea; population (1986) 4,500,000. It comprises the naval base of Lüshun (known under 19th-century Russian occupation as Port Arthur) and the commercial port of Dalien (formerly Talien/Dairen).

Luddite one of a group of people involved in machine-wrecking riots in N England 1811–16. The organizer of the Luddites was referred to as General Ludd, but may not have existed. Many Luddites were hanged or transported to penal colonies, such as Australia.

Ludwig I 1786–1868. King of Bavaria 1825–48, succeeding his father Maximilian Joseph I. He made Munich an international cultural center, but his association with the dancer Lola Montez, who dictated his policies for a year, led to his abdication in 1848.

Ludwig II 1845–1886. King of Bavaria from 1864, when he succeeded his father Maximilian II. He supported Austria during the Austro-Prussian War 1866, but brought Bavaria into the Franco-Prussian War as Prussia's ally and in 1871 offered the German crown to the king of Prussia. He was the composer Richard Wagner's patron and built the Bayreuth theater for him. Declared insane 1886, he drowned himself soon after.

Luftwaffe German air force used both in World War I and (as reorganized by the Nazi leader Hermann Goering in 1933) in World War II. The Luftwaffe also covered antiaircraft defense and the launching of the flying bombs V1 and V2.

luge a one-or two-person racing sled, on which riders lie face up. Luges are raced by both men and women in the winter Olympics.

Lugosi Bela. Adopted name of Bela Ferenc Blasko 1882–1956. Hungarian-born US film actor. Acclaimed for his performance in *Dracula* on Broadway 1927, Lugosi began acting in feature films 1930. His appearance in the film version of *Dracula* 1931 marked the start of Lugosi's long career in horror films—among them, *Murders in the Rue Morgue* 1932, *The Raven* 1935, and *The Wolf Man* 1941.

Trained at the Academy of Theatrical Art in Budapest, Lugosi began his stage career with the Hungarian National Theater. After service in the Austro-Hungarian army in World War I, he immigrated to the US 1921.

lugworm any of a genus *Arenicola* of marine annelid worms that grow up to 10 in/25 cm long. They are common burrowers between tidemarks and are useful for their cleansing and powdering of the beach sand, of which they may annually bring to the surface about 2,000 tons per acre/5,000 metric tons per hectare.

Lukács Georg 1885–1971. Hungarian philosopher, one of the founders of "Western" or "Hegelian" Marxism, a philosophy opposed to the Marxism of the official communist movement.

Luke, St Traditionally the compiler of the third Gospel and of the Acts of the Apostles in the New Testament. He is the patron saint of painters; his emblem is a winged ox, and his feast day Oct 18.

lumbago pain in the lower region of the back, usually due to strain or faulty posture. If it occurs with ◊sciatica, it may be due to pressure on spinal nerves by a slipped disk. Treatment includes rest, application of heat, and skilled manipulation. Surgery may be needed in rare cases.

lumbar puncture another term for ◊spinal tap, a medical test.

lumen SI unit (symbol lm) of luminous flux (the amount of light passing through an area per second).

Lumière Auguste Marie 1862–1954 and Louis Jean 1864–1948. French brothers who pioneered cinematography. In 1895 they patented their cinematograph, a combined camera and projector operating at 16 frames per second, and opened the world's first cinema in Paris to show their films.

luminescence emission of light from a body when its atoms are excited by means other than raising its temperature. Short-lived luminescence is called fluorescence; longer-lived luminescence is called phosphorescence.

Lumumba Patrice 1926–1961. Congolese politician, prime minister of Zaire 1960. Imprisoned by the Belgians, but released in time to attend the conference giving the Congo independence in 1960, he led the National Congolese Movement to victory in the subsequent general election. He was deposed in a coup d'état, and murdered some months later.

lung large cavity of the body, used for ◊gas exchange. It is essentially a sheet of thin, moist membrane that is folded so as to occupy less space. Most tetrapod (four-limbed) vertebrates have a pair of lungs occupying the thorax. The lung tissue, consisting of multitudes of air

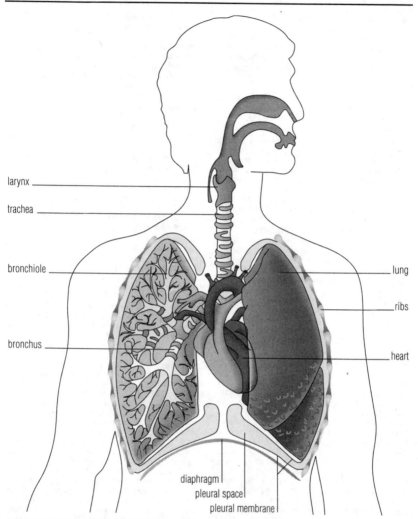

larynx

trachea

bronchiole

lung

ribs

bronchus

heart

diaphragm
pleural space
pleural membrane

lung *The human lungs contain 300,000 million tiny blood vessels which would stretch for 1,500 mi/2,400 km if laid end to end. A healthy adult at rest breathes 12 times a minute; a baby breathes at twice this rate. Each breath brings 350 milliliters of fresh air into the lungs, and expels 150 milliliters of stale air from the nose and throat.*

sacs and blood vessels, is very light and spongy, and functions by bringing inhaled air into close contact with the blood so that oxygen can pass into the organism and waste carbon dioxide can be passed out. The efficiency of lungs is enhanced by ◊breathing movements, by the thinness and moistness of their surfaces, and by a constant supply of circulating blood.

lungfish three genera of fleshy-finned bony fishes of the subclass Dipnoi, found in Africa, South America, and Australia. They have elongated bodies, and grow to about 6 ft/ 2 m, and in addition to gills have "lungs" with which they can breathe air during periods of drought conditions.

Luoyang or *Loyang* industrial city (machinery and tractors) in Henan province, China, S of the river Huang He; population 1,114,000. It was formerly the capital of China and an important Buddhist center in the 5th and 6th centuries.

lupin any plant of the genus *Lupinus*, of the pea family Leguminosae, including about 300 species. They are native to Mediterranean regions and parts of North and South America. Their spikes of pealike flowers may be white, yellow, blue, or pink.

The European lupin *L. albus* is cultivated in some places for cattle fodder and for manure.

lupus in medicine, any of various diseases characterized by lesions of the skin. One form (lupus vulgaris) is caused by the tubercle bacillus (see ◊tuberculosis). The organism produces ulcers that spread and eat away the underlying tissues. Treatment is primarily with standard antituberculous drugs, but ultraviolet light may also be used.

Lusaka capital of Zambia from 1964 (of Northern Rhodesia 1935–64), 230 mi/370 km NE of Livingstone; it is a commercial and agricultural center (flour mills, tobacco factories, vehicle assembly, plastics, printing); population (1988) 870,000.

lute member of a family of stringed musical instruments of the 14th–18th century, including the mandore, theorbo, and chitarrone. Lutes are pear-shaped with up to seven courses of strings (single or double), plucked with the fingers. Music for lutes is written in special notation called tablature and chords are played simultaneously, not arpeggiated as for guitar. Modern lutenists include Julian Bream and Anthony Rooley (1944–).

luteinizing hormone ◊hormone produced by the pituitary gland. In males, it stimulates the testes to produce androgens (male sex hormones). In females, it works together with follicle-stimulating hormone to initiate production of egg cells by the ovary. If fertilization occurs, it plays a part in maintaining the pregnancy by controlling the levels of the hormones estrogen and progesterone in the body.

lutetium silver-white, metallic element, the last of the ◊lanthanide series, symbol Lu, atomic number 71, relative atomic mass 174.97. It is used in the "cracking", or breakdown, of petroleum and in other chemical processes. It was named by its discoverer, French chemist Georges Urbain, (1872–1938) after his native city.

Luther Martin 1483–1546. German Christian church reformer, a founder of Protestantism. While he was a priest at the University of Wittenberg, he wrote an attack on the sale of indulgences (remissions of punishment for sin). The Holy Roman emperor Charles V summoned him to the Diet (meeting of dignitaries of the Holy Roman Empire) of Worms in Germany, in 1521, where he refused to retract his objections. Originally intending reform, his protest led to schism, with the emergence, following the Augsburg Confession 1530 (a statement of the Protestant faith), of a new Protestant church. Luther is regarded as the instigator of the Protestant revolution, and Lutheranism is now the major religion of many N European countries, including Germany, Sweden, and Denmark.

Formerly condemned by communism, Luther had by the 1980s been rehabilitated as a revolutionary socialist hero, and was claimed as patron saint in Germany.

Lutheranism form of Protestant Christianity derived from the life and teaching of Martin Luther; it is sometimes called Evangelical to distinguish it from the other main branch of European Protestantism, the Reformed. It is the largest Protestant body, including some 80 million persons, of whom 8.5 million are in the US and Canada.

Lutheranism in the US is divided into three main bodies: the Lutheran Church in America; the more conservative Lutheran Church, the Missouri Synod; and the American Lutheran Church (largely Norwegian and centered in the upper Midwest).

Lutyens Edwin Landseer 1869–1944. English architect. His designs ranged from the picturesque, such as Castle Drogo, Devon, 1910–30, to Renaissance-style country houses, and ultimately evolved into a Classical style as seen in the Cenotaph, London, 1919. His complex use of space, interest in tradition, and distorted Classical language have proved of great interest to a number of Postmodern architects, especially Robert Venturi.

lux SI unit (symbol lx) of illuminance or illumination (the light falling on an object). It is equivalent to one ◊lumen per square meter or to the illuminance of a surface one meter distant from a point source of one ◊candela.

Luxembourg capital of the country of Luxembourg, on the Alzette and Petrusse rivers; population (1985) 76,000. The 16th-century Grand Ducal Palace, European Court of Justice, and European Parliament secretariat are situated here, but plenary sessions of the parliament are now held only in Strasbourg, France. Industries include steel, chemicals, textiles, and processed food.

Luxembourg Grand Duchy of (*Grand-Duché de Luxembourg*) *area* 998 sq mi/2,586 sq km *capital* Luxembourg *towns and cities* Esch-sur-Alzette, Dudelange *physical* on the river Moselle; part of the Ardennes (Esling) forest in N *features* seat of the European Court of Justice, Secretariat of the European Parliament, international banking center; economically linked with Belgium *head of state* Grand Duke Jean from 1964 *head of government* Jacques Santer from 1984 *political system* liberal democracy *political parties* Christian Social Party (PCS), moderate, left of center; Luxembourg Socialist Workers' Party (POSL), moderate, socialist; Democratic Party (PD), center-left; Communist Party of Luxembourg, pro-European left-wing *exports* pharmaceuticals, synthetic textiles, steel *currency* Luxembourg franc *population* (1993) 395,200; growth rate 0% p.a. *life expectancy* men 72, women 79 *languages* French (official), local Letzeburgesch, German *religion* Roman Catholic 97% *literacy* 100% *GNP* $31,080 per head (1991) *chronology* *1354* Became a duchy. *1482* Under Hapsburg control. *1797* Ceded, with Belgium, to France. *1815* Treaty of Vienna created Luxembourg a grand duchy, ruled by the king of the Netherlands. *1830* With Belgium, revolted against Dutch rule. *1890* Link with Netherlands ended with accession of Grand Duke Adolphe of Nassau-Weilburg. *1948* With Belgium and the Netherlands, formed the Benelux customs union. *1960* Benelux became fully effective economic union. *1961* Prince Jean became acting head of state on behalf of his mother, Grand Duchess Charlotte. *1964* Grand Duchess Charlotte abdicated; Prince Jean became grand duke. *1974* Dominance of Christian Social Party challenged by socialists. *1979* Christian Social Party regained pre-eminence. *1991* Pact agreeing European free-trade area signed in Luxembourg. *1992* Vote in favor of ratification of Maastricht Treaty.

Luxemburg Rosa 1870–1919. Polish-born German communist. She helped found the Polish Social Democratic Party in the 1890s (which later became the Polish Communist Party). She was a leader of the left wing of the German Social Democratic Party from 1898 and collaborator with Karl Liebknecht in founding the communist Spartacus League 1918. She was murdered with him by army officers during the Jan 1919 Berlin workers' revolt.

Luxor (Arabic *al-Uqsur*) small town in Egypt on the E bank of the river Nile. The ancient city of Thebes is on the W bank, with the temple of Luxor built by Amenhotep III (*c.* 1411–1375 BC) and the tombs of the pharaohs in the Valley of the Kings.

Luzern German name of ◊Lucerne, a city in Switzerland.

Luzon largest island of the ◊Philippines; area 41,750 sq mi/108,130 sq km; capital Quezon City; population (1970) 18,001,270. The chief city is Manila, capital of the Philippines. Industries include rice, timber, and minerals. It has a US military bases.

LW abbreviation for *long wave*, a radio wave with a wavelength of over 3,300 ft/1,000 m; one of the main wavebands into which radio frequency transmissions are divided.

lychee alternative spelling of ◊litchi, a fruit-bearing tree.

Lycurgus Spartan lawgiver. He was believed to have been a member of the royal house of the ancient Greek city-state of Sparta, who, while acting as regent, gave the Spartans their constitution and system of education. Many modern scholars believe him to be purely mythical.

Lydia ancient kingdom in Anatolia (7th–6th centuries BC), with its capital at Sardis. The Lydians were the first Western people to use standard coinage. Their last king, Croesus, was defeated by the Persians in 546 BC.

lymph fluid found in the lymphatic system of vertebrates.

It returns excess, filtered tissue fluid and some protein to the bloodstream. Lymph vessels also transport fat from the digestive tract to the blood. Lymph moves in one direction only; flaplike valves prevent backflow.

lymph nodes small masses of lymphatic tissue in the body that occur at various points along the major lymphatic vessels. Tonsils and adenoids are large lymph nodes. As the lymph passes through them it is filtered, and bacteria and other microorganisms are engulfed by cells known as macrophages.

lymphocyte type of white blood cell with a large nucleus, produced in the bone marrow. Most occur in the ◊lymph and blood, and around sites of infection. *B lymphocytes* or B cells are responsible for producing ◊antibodies. *T lymphocytes* or T cells have several roles in the mechanism of ◊immunity.

lymphogranuloma venerum a sexually transmitted disease caused by the bacterium *Chlamydia trachomatis*, the same organism that causes the eye disease trachoma. The disease is characterized by genital ulcers, inflammation of the urinary tract, and swelling of the lymph nodes in the groin. Chronic pelvic inflammatory disease can result if left untreated.

lynching killing of an alleged offender by an individual or group having no legal authority. In the US it originated in 1780 with creation of a "committee of vigilance" in Virginia; it is named for a member of that committee, Captain William Lynch, to whom is attributed "Lynch's law". Later examples occurred mostly in the Southern states after the Civil War, and were racially motivated. During 1882–1900 the annual number of lynchings in the US varied between 96 and 231, but today it is an exceptional occurrence.

Similar behavior patterns exist in many societies, especially when access to regular courts is poor.

lynx cat *Felis lynx* found in rocky and forested regions of North America and Europe. About 3 ft/1 m in length, it has a short tail and tufted ears, and the long, silky fur is reddish brown or gray with dark spots. The North American bobcat or bay lynx *Felix rufus* looks

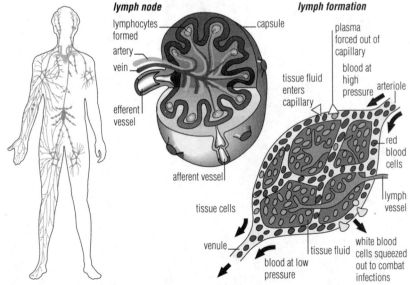

lymph node

lymphocytes formed
capsule
artery
vein
efferent vessel
afferent vessel

lymph formation

plasma forced out of capillary
blood at high pressure
arteriole
tissue fluid enters capillary
red blood cells
lymph vessel
tissue cells
white blood cells squeezed out to combat infections
venule
tissue fluid
blood at low pressure

lymph Lymph is the fluid that carries nutrients, and white blood cells to the tissues. Lymph enters the tissues from the capillaries (right) and is drained from the tissues by lymph vessels. The lymph vessels form a network (left) called the lymphatic system. At various points in the lymphatic system, lymph nodes (center) filter and clean the lymph.

similar but is smaller. Some zoologists place the lynx, the bobcat, and the caracal in a separate genus, *Lynx*.

Lyon (English *Lyons*) industrial city (textiles, chemicals, machinery, printing) and capital of Rhône *département*, Rhône-Alpes region, at the confluence of the rivers Rhône and Saône, 170 mi/275 km NNW of Marseille; population (1990) 422,400, conurbation 1,221,000. It is the third-largest city of France. Formerly a chief fortress of France, it was the ancient *Lugdunum*, taken by the Romans 43 BC.

lyre stringed instrument of great antiquity. It consists of a soundbox with two curved arms extended upward to a crosspiece to which four to ten strings are attached. It is played with a plectrum or the fingers. It originated in Asia, and was widespread in ancient Greece and Egypt.

lyrebird any bird of the order *Passeriformes*, forming the Australian family Menuridae. There are two species, both in the genus *Menura*. The male has a large lyre-shaped tail, brilliantly colored. Lyrebirds nest on the ground, and feed on insects, worms, and snails.

Lysander Spartan general, politician and admiral. He brought the ◊Peloponnesian War between Athens and Sparta to a successful conclusion by capturing the Athenian fleet at Aegospotami 405 BC, and by starving Athens into surrender in the following year. He set up puppet governments in Athens and its former allies, and tried to secure for himself the Spartan kingship, but was killed in battle with the Thebans 395 BC.

m symbol for ◊*meter*.

M Roman numeral for *1,000*.

MA abbreviation for *Master of Arts*, a degree of education.

Mabuse Jan Adopted name of Jan Gossaert *c.* 1478–*c.* 1533. Flemish painter. He was active chiefly in Antwerp. His common name derives from his birthplace, Maubeuge. His visit to Italy 1508 with Philip of Burgundy started a new vogue in Flanders for Italianate ornament and Classical detail in painting, including sculptural nude figures, as in his *Neptune and Amphitrite* about 1516 (Staatliche Museen, Berlin).

Macao Portuguese possession on the S coast of China, about 40 mi/65 km W of Hong Kong, from which it is separated by the estuary of the Canton River; it consists of a peninsula and the islands of Taipa and Colôane *area* 7 sq mi/17 sq km *capital* Macao, on the peninsula *features* the peninsula is linked to Taipa by a bridge and to Colôane by a causeway, both 1 mi/2 km long *currency* pataca *population* (1986) 426,000 *languages* Cantonese; Portuguese (official) *religions* Buddhist, with 6% Catholic minority.

macaque Old World monkey of the genus *Macaca*. Various species of these medium-sized monkeys live in forests from the Far East to N Africa. The ◊rhesus and the ◊Barbary ape are part of this group.

MacArthur Douglas 1880–1964. US general in World War II, commander of US forces in the Far East and, from March 1942, of the Allied forces in the SW Pacific. After the surrender of Japan he commanded the Allied occupation forces there. During 1950 he commanded the UN forces in Korea, but in April 1951, after expressing views contrary to US and UN policy, he was relieved of all his commands by President Truman.

He defended the Philippines against the Japanese 1941–42 and escaped to Australia when his small force was overwhelmed. He vowed at the time, "I shall return." He was responsible for the reconquest of New Guinea 1942–45 and of the Philippines 1944–45.

Macaulay Thomas Babington, Baron Macaulay 1800–1859. English historian, essayist, poet, and politician, secretary of war 1839–41. His *History of England* in five volumes 1849–61 celebrates the Glorious Revolution of 1688 as the crowning achievement of the Whig party.

macaw any of various large, brilliantly colored, long-tailed tropical American ◊parrots, especially the genus *Ara*.

Macbeth King of Scotland from 1040. The son of Findlaech, hereditary ruler of Moray, he was commander of the forces of Duncan I, King of Scotia, whom he killed in battle 1040. His reign was prosperous until

MacArthur, Douglas *US general Douglas MacArthur signing Japan's surrender documents on board USS Missouri in Tokyo Bay, Sept 2 1945. As Allied commander in the SW Pacific since 1942, he masterminded the defeat of Japan.*

Duncan's son Malcolm III led an invasion and killed him at Lumphanan.

McCarthy Joe (Joseph Raymond) 1908–1957. US right-wing Republican politician. His unsubstantiated claim 1950 that the State Department and US army had been infiltrated by communists started a wave of anti-communist hysteria, wild accusations, and blacklists, which continued until he was discredited 1954. He was censured by the US Senate for misconduct.

McCarthy Mary (Therese) 1912–1989. US novelist and critic. Much of her work looks probingly and scathingly at US society, including the satirical novel *The Groves of Academe* 1952, which describes the early anticommunist "witch hunts" of the era, and *The Group* 1963 (film 1966), her best-known novel, which follows the lives of eight Vassar graduates into their thirties.

McCartney Paul 1942– . UK rock singer, songwriter, and bass guitarist. He was a member of the ◊Beatles, and leader of the pop group Wings 1971–81. His subsequent solo hits have included collaborations with Michael Jackson and Elvis Costello. Together with composer Carl Davis, McCartney wrote the *Liverpool Oratorio* 1991, his first work of classical music.

McClellan George Brinton 1826–1885. Civil War general, the first general in chief of the Union forces 1861–62. He was dismissed twice by President Lincoln, for various delays in following up and attacking the Confederate army. After the rout at the Second Battle of ◊Bull Run, Lincoln asked McClellan to rebuild and reorganize the Union's Army of the Potomac. He saved Washington, DC, from the threatening Confederate forces but delayed his offense until the opportunity was lost. He was dismissed again at this point, ran unsuccessfully for the presidency against Lincoln on the Democratic ticket 1864, and became governor of New Jersey 1878–81.

McClintock Barbara 1902–1992. US geneticist who worked at the Carnegie Institute, Cold Spring Harbor, New York, in the early days of chromosome mapping, and made some important contributions. She was awarded a Nobel Prize 1983.

McCrea Joel 1905–1991. US film actor. He rapidly graduated to romantic leads in the 1930s and played in several major 1930s and 1940s productions, such as *Dead End* 1937 and *Sullivan's Travels* 1941. In later decades he was associated almost exclusively with the Western genre, notably *Ride the High Country* 1962, now recognized as a classic Western film.

Macdonald Flora 1722–1790. Scottish heroine who rescued Prince Charles Edward Stuart, the Young Pretender, after his defeat at Culloden 1746. Disguising him as her maid, she escorted him from her home in the Hebrides to France. She was arrested, but released 1747.

MacDonald (James) Ramsay 1866–1937. British politician, first Labour prime minister 1924 and 1929–31. Failing to deal with worsening economic conditions, he left the party to form a coalition government 1931, which was increasingly dominated by Conservatives, until he was replaced by Stanley Baldwin 1935.

Macedonia ancient region of Greece, forming parts of modern Greece, Bulgaria, and the Former Yugoslav Republic of Macedonia. Macedonia gained control of Greece after Philip II's victory at Chaeronea 338 BC. His son, ◊Alexander the Great, conquered a vast empire. Macedonia became a Roman province 146 BC.

Macedonia Former Yugoslav Republic of *area* 9,920 sq mi/25,700 sq km *capital* Skopje *towns and cities* Bitolj, Gostivar *physical* mountainous; rivers: Struma, Vardar; lakes: Ohrid, Prespa, Scutari; partly Mediterranean climate with hot summers *head of state* Kiro Gligorov from 1990 *head of government* Branko Crvenkovski from 1992 *political system* emergent democracy *political parties* Internal Macedonian Revolutionary Organization–Democratic Party for Macedonian National Unity (VMRO–DMPNE), centrist; League of Communists, left-wing *currency* Macedonian denar *population* (1992) 2,060,000 (Albanian 20%, Turkish 4.8%, Hungarian 2.7%, Serb 2.2%) *life expectancy* men 68, women 72 *language* Macedonian, closely allied to Bulgarian and written in Cyrillic *religions* Christian, mainly Orthodox; Muslim 2.5% *media* state controls major newspapers and broadcasting channels but independent papers and stations also exist *literacy* 90% *chronology* **1913** Ancient country of Macedonia divided between Serbia, Bulgaria, and Greece. **1918** Serbian part included in what was to become Yugoslavia. **1941–44** Occupied by Bulgaria. **1945** Created a republic within Yugoslav Socialist Federation. **1980** Rise of nationalism after death of Yugoslav leader Tito. **1990** Multiparty election produced inconclusive result. **1991** "Socialist' dropped from republic's name. Referendum supported independence. **1992** Independence declared, but international recognition withheld because of objections to name by Greece. **1993** April: Sovereignty recognized by UK and Albania; won United Nations membership under provisional name of Former Yugoslav Republic of Macedonia; Greece continued to block European Union (EU) recognition. Dec: formally recognized by six EU member states. **1994** Feb: recognized by US; trade embargo imposed by Greece. Oct: Gligorov reelected in first elections since independence.

Macedonia (Greek *Makedhonia*) mountainous region of N Greece, part of the ancient country of Macedonia which was divided between Serbia, Bulgaria, and Greece after the Balkan Wars of 1912–13. Greek Macedonia is bounded W and N by Albania and the Former Yugoslav Republic of Macedonia; area 13,200 sq mi/34,177 sq km; population (1991) 2,263,000. The chief city is Thessaloniki. Fertile valleys produce grain, olives, grapes, tobacco, and livestock. Mount Olympus rises to 9,570 ft/2,918 m on the border with Thessaly.

Macedonian person of Macedonian culture from the Former Yugoslav Republic of Macedonia and the surrounding area, especially Greece, Albania, and Bulgaria. Macedonian, a Slavic language belonging to the Indo-European family, has 1–1.5 million speakers. The Macedonians are predominantly members of the Greek Orthodox Church and write with a Cyrillic script. They are known for their folk arts.

McGraw John Joseph 1873–1934. US baseball manager. He became player-manager of the New York Giants 1902, and in this dual capacity led the team to two National League pennants and a World Series championship. After retiring as a player 1906, he managed the Giants to eight more pennants and two world championships.

He was elected to the Baseball Hall of Fame 1937.

Machiavelli Niccolò 1469–1527. Italian politician and author. His name is synonymous with cunning and cynical statecraft. In his most celebrated political writings, *Il principe/The Prince* 1513 and *Discorsi/Discourses*

1531, he discussed ways in which rulers can advance the interests of their states (and themselves) through an often amoral and opportunistic manipulation of other people.

machine device that allows a small force (the effort) to overcome a larger one (the load). There are three basic machines: the inclined plane (ramp), the lever, and the wheel and axle. All other machines are combinations of these three basic types. Simple machines derived from the inclined plane include the wedge, the gear, and the screw; the spanner is derived from the lever; the pulley from the wheel.

Mach number ratio of the speed of a body to the speed of sound in the undisturbed medium through which the body travels. Mach 1 is reached when a body (such as an aircraft) has a velocity greater than that of sound ("passes the sound barrier"), namely 1,087 ft/331 m per second at sea level. It is named for Austrian physicist Ernst Mach (1838–1916).

Machu Picchu ruined Inca city in Peru, built about ad 1500, NW of Cuzco, discovered 1911 by Hiram Bingham. It stands at the top of cliffs 1,000 ft/300 m high and contains the well-preserved remains of houses and temples.

Macintosh range of microcomputers produced by Apple Computers. The Apple Macintosh, introduced in 1984, was the first popular microcomputer with a graphical user interface.

Mack Connie. Adopted name of Cornelius McGillicuddy 1862–1956. US baseball manager. With the establishment of the American League 1901, he invested his own money in the Philadelphia Athletics ("A's") and became the team's first manager. In his record 50 years with the team 1901–51, he led them to nine American League pennants and five World Series championships.

He was elected to the Baseball Hall of Fame 1939.

Mackenzie Alexander 1764–1820. British explorer and fur trader. In 1789, he was the first European to see the river, now part of N Canada, named for him. In 1792–93 he crossed the Rocky Mountains to the Pacific coast of what is now British Columbia, making the first known crossing north of Mexico.

He was knighted in 1807.

Mackenzie River river in the Northwest Territories, Canada, flowing NW from Great Slave Lake to the Arctic Ocean; about 1,120 mi/1,800 km long. It is the main channel of the Finlay-Peace-Mackenzie system, 2,635 mi/4,241 km long.

mackerel any of various fishes of the mackerel family Scombroidia, especially the common mackerel *Scomber scombrus* found in the N Atlantic and Mediterranean. It weighs about 1.5 lb/0.7 kg, and is blue with irregular black bands down its sides, the latter and the under surface showing a metallic sheen. Like all mackerels, it has a deeply forked tail, and a sleek, streamlined body form.

McKinley William 1843–1901. 25th president of the US 1897–1901, a republican. His term as president was marked by the US's adoption of an imperialist policy, as exemplified by the Spanish-American War 1898 and the annexation of the Philippines. He was first elected to Congress 1876. He was assassinated in Buffalo, New York, and was succeeded by Theodore Roosevelt.

McKinley was born in Niles, Ohio, and became a lawyer. Throughout his political life, he was a trusted friend of business interests. He sat in the House of Representatives 1877–83 and 1885–91, and was governor of Ohio 1892–96. As president he presided over a period of prosperity and was drawn into foreign conflicts largely against his will.

McKinley, Mount peak in Alaska, US, the highest in North America, 20,320 ft/6,194 m; named for US president William McKinley.

The summit was first reached in 1913 by the Anglo-American explorer Hudson Stuck and three others. Mount McKinley, called Denali, "the high one", by the Indians, rises in the enlarged and renamed (1980) Denali National Park. See ◊Rocky Mountains.

MacLeish Archibald 1892–1982. US poet. He made his name with the long narrative poem *Conquistador* 1932, which describes Cortés' march to the Aztec capital, but his later plays in verse, *Panic* 1935 and *Air Raid* 1938, deal with contemporary problems.

Macmillan (Maurice) Harold, 1st Earl of Stockton 1894–1986. British Conservative politician, prime minister 1957–63; foreign secretary 1955 and chancellor of the Exchequer 1955–57. In 1963 he attempted to negotiate British entry into the European Economic Community, but was blocked by French president de Gaulle. Much of his career as prime minister was spent defending the retention of a UK nuclear weapon, and he was responsible for the purchase of US Polaris missiles 1962.

McPherson Aimee Semple 1890–1944. Canadian-born US religious leader. As a popular preacher, "Sister Aimee" reached millions through radio broadcasts of her weekly sermons, in which she emphasized the power of faith. She established the Church of the Four-Square Gospel in Los Angeles 1918.

Her brief but suspicious 1926 "disappearance" tarnished her reputation.

macro in computer programming, a new command created by combining a number of existing ones. For example, if a programming language has separate commands for obtaining data from the keyboard and for displaying data on the screen, the programmer might create a macro that performs both these tasks with one command. A *macro key* on the keyboard combines the effects of pressing several individual keys.

Madagascar Democratic Republic of (*Repoblika Demokratika n`i Madagaskar*) *area* 226,598 sq mi/587,041 sq km *capital* Antananarivo *towns and cities* chief port Toamasina, Antseranana, Fianarantsoa, Toliary *physical* temperate central highlands; humid valleys and tropical coastal plains; arid in S *environment* according to 1990 UN figures, 93% of the forest area has been destroyed and about 100,000 species have been made extinct *features* one of the last places to be inhabited, it evolved in isolation with unique animals (such as the lemur, now under threat from deforestation) *head of state* Albert Zafy from 1993 *head of government* Francisque Ravony from 1993 *political system* emergent democratic republic *political parties* National Front for the Defense of the Malagasy Socialist Revolution (FNDR); AKFM-Congress and AKFM-Renewal, both left of center; Social Democratic Party (PSD), center-left. Major parties operate in broad coalitions *exports* coffee, cloves, vanilla, sugar, chromite, shrimps *currency* Malagasy franc *population* (1993 est) 13,000,000, mostly of Malayo-Indonesian origin; growth rate 3.2% p.a. *life expectancy* men 54, women 57 *languages* Malagasy (official), French, English *religions* animist 50%,

Christian 40%, Muslim 10% *literacy* men 88%, women 73% *GNP* $254 per head (1992) *chronology* *1885* Became a French protectorate. *1896* Became a French colony. *1960* Independence achieved from France, with Philibert Tsiranana as president. *1972* Army took control of the government. *1975* Martial law imposed under a national military directorate. New Marxist constitution proclaimed the Democratic Republic of Madagascar, with Didier Ratsiraka as president. *1976* Front-Line Revolutionary Organization (AREMA) formed. *1977* National Front for the Defense of the Malagasy Socialist Revolution (FNDR) became the sole legal political organization. *1980* Ratsiraka abandoned Marxist experiment. *1983* Ratsiraka reelected, despite strong opposition from radical socialist National Movement for the Independence of Madagascar (MONIMA) under Monja Jaona. *1989* Ratsiraka reelected for third term after restricting opposition parties. *1990* Political opposition legalized; 36 new parties created. *1991* Antigovernment demonstrations. Ratsiraka formed new unity government. *1992* Constitutional reform approved by referendum. First multiparty elections won by Democrat coalition. *1993* Albert Zafy, leader of coalition, elected president. Pro-Zafy groups won majority in assembly elections.

Madagascar teal or *Bernier's teal* a small duck *Anas bernieri* apparently confined to a few small lakes and marshy areas in western Madagascar and now severely threatened with extinction. It is thought that there are at most a few hundred teal left alive and the opening of an airstrip nearby greatly increases the risk of sport shooting.

madder any plant of the genus *Rubia* of the family Rubiaceae, bearing small funnel-shaped flowers, especially the perennial vine *R. tinctorum*, the red root of which yields a red dye called alizarin (now made synthetically from coal tar).

Madeira group of islands forming an autonomous region of Portugal off the NW coast of Africa, about 260 mi/420 km N of the Canary Islands. Madeira, the largest, and Porto Santo are the only inhabited islands. The Desertas and Selvagens are uninhabited islets. Their mild climate makes them a year-round resort *area* 308 sq mi/796 sq km *capital* Funchal, on Madeira *physical* Pico Ruivo, on Madeira, is the highest mountain at 6,106 ft/1,861 m *industries* Madeira (a fortified wine), sugar cane, fruit, fish, handicrafts *population* (1986) 269,500 *history* Portuguese from the 15th century; occupied by Britain 1801 and 1807–14. In 1980 Madeira gained partial autonomy but remains a Portuguese overseas territory.

Madison capital of Wisconsin, 120 mi/193 km NW of Chicago, between lakes Mendota and Monona; population (1990) 191,300. Industries include agricultural machinery and medical equipment.

The main campus of the University of Wisconsin and the US Forest Products Laboratory are here. The city was founded 1836 as the territorial capital and named for James Madison, fourth president of the US.

Madison James 1751–1836. 4th president of the US 1809–17. Born in Port Conway, Virginia, Madison graduated from the College of New Jersey (now Princeton) 1771. In 1787 he became a member of the Philadelphia Constitutional Convention and took a leading part in drawing up the US Constitution and the Bill of Rights. He allied himself firmly with Thomas ◊Jefferson against Alexander ◊Hamilton in the struggle between the more democratic views of Jefferson and the aristocratic, upper-class sentiments of Hamilton. As secretary of state in Jefferson's government 1801–09, Madison completed the ◊Louisiana Purchase negotiated by James Monroe. During his period of office the War of 1812 with Britain took place.

Madonna Italian name for the Virgin ◊Mary, meaning "my lady".

Madonna Adopted name of Madonna Louise Veronica Ciccone 1958– . US pop singer and actress who presents herself on stage and in videos with an exaggerated sexuality. Her first hit was "Like a Virgin" 1984; others include "Material Girl" 1985 and "Like a Prayer" 1989. Her films include *Desperately Seeking Susan* 1985, *Dick Tracy* 1990, the documentary *In Bed with Madonna* 1991, and *A League of Their Own* 1992.

Madras industrial port (cotton, cement, chemicals, iron, and steel) and capital of Tamil Nadu, India, on the Bay of Bengal; population (1981) 4,277,000. Fort St George 1639 remains from the East India Company when Madras was the chief port on the E coast. Madras was occupied by the French 1746–48 and shelled by the German ship *Emden* 1914, the only place in India attacked in World War I.

Madrid industrial city (leather, chemicals, furniture, tobacco, paper) and capital of Spain and of Madrid province; population (1991) 2,984,600. Built on an elevated plateau in the center of the country, at 2,183 ft/655 m it is the highest capital city in Europe and has excesses of heat and cold. Madrid province has an area of 3,088 sq mi/8,000 sq km and a population of 4,855,000.

Madrid began as the Moorish city of Magerit. It was captured 1083 by King Alfonso VI of Castile and remained a small provincial town until Philip II made it his capital 1561.

Mafia secret society reputed to control organized crime such as gambling, loansharking, drug traffic, prostitution, and protection; connected with the Camorra of Naples. It originated in Sicily in the late Middle Ages and now operates chiefly there and in countries to which Italians have emigrated, such as the US. During the early 1990s it became increasingly evident that prominent Italian politicians had had dealings with the Mafia, and by 1993 many center and right-wing politicians had been discredited.

magazine a periodical publication, typically containing articles, essays, reviews, illustrations, and advertising. It is thought that the first magazine was *Le Journal des savants*, published in France 1665. Specialty magazines for various interests and hobbies appeared in the 20th century. In the US, subscriptions account for the majority of magazine sales.

Magellan Ferdinand 1480–1521. Portuguese navigator. In 1519 he set sail in the *Victoria* from Seville with the intention of reaching the East Indies by a westerly route. He sailed through the **Strait of Magellan** at the tip of South America, crossed an ocean he named the Pacific, and in 1521 reached the Philippines, where he was killed in a battle with the islanders. His companions returned to Seville 1522.

Magellan NASA space probe to ◊Venus, launched May 1989; it went into orbit around Venus Aug 1990 to make a detailed map of the planet by radar. It revealed volcanoes, meteorite craters, and fold mountains on the planet's surface. Magellan mapped 98% of Venus.

Magellanic Clouds in astronomy, the two galaxies nearest to our own galaxy. They are irregularly shaped, and appear as detached parts of the ◊Milky Way, in the southern constellations Dorado and Tucana.

maggot soft, plump, limbless larva of flies, a typical example being the larva of the blowfly which is deposited as an egg on flesh.

magi (singular *magus*) priests of the Zoroastrian religion of ancient Persia, noted for their knowledge of astrology. The term is used in the New Testament of the Latin Vulgate Bible where the King James Version gives "wise men". The magi who came to visit the infant Jesus with gifts of gold, frankincense, and myrrh (the *Adoration of the Magi*) were in later tradition described as "the three kings"—Caspar, Melchior, and Balthazar.

magic art of controlling the forces of nature by supernatural means such as charms and ritual. The central ideas are that like produces like (*sympathetic magic*) and that influence carries by contagion or association; for example, by the former principle an enemy could be destroyed through an effigy, by the latter principle through personal items such as hair or nail clippings.

magic realism in 20th-century literature, a fantastic situation realistically treated, as in the works of many Latin American writers such as Isabel Allende, Jorge Luis ◊Borges, and Gabriel ◊García Márquez.

Maginot Line French fortification system along the German frontier from Switzerland to Luxembourg built 1929–36 under the direction of the war minister, André Maginot. It consisted of semiunderground forts joined by underground passages, and was protected by antitank defenses; lighter fortifications continued the line to the sea. In 1940 German forces pierced the Belgian frontier line and outflanked the Maginot Line.

maglev (acronym for *magnetic levitation*) high-speed surface transport using the repellent force of superconductive magnets (see ◊superconductivity) to propel and support, for example, a train above a track.

magma molten rock material beneath the Earth's surface from which ◊igneous rocks are formed. ◊Lava is magma that has reached the surface and solidified, losing some of its components on the way.

Magna Carta in English history, the charter granted by King John 1215, traditionally seen as guaranteeing human rights against the excessive use of royal power. As a reply to the king's demands for excessive feudal dues and attacks on the privileges of the church, Archbishop Langton proposed to the barons the drawing-up of a binding document 1213. John was forced to accept this at Runnymede (now in Surrey) June 15, 1215.

magnesium lightweight, very ductile and malleable, silver-white, metallic element, symbol Mg, atomic number 12, relative atomic mass 24.305. It is one of the ◊alkaline-earth metals, and the lightest of the commonly used metals. Magnesium silicate, carbonate, and chloride are widely distributed in nature. The metal is used in alloys and flash photography. It is a necessary trace element in the human diet, and green plants cannot grow without it since it is an essential constituent of the photosynthetic pigment ◊chlorophyll ($C_{55}H_{72}MgN_4O_5$).

magnet any object that forms a magnetic field (displays ◊magnetism), either permanently or temporarily through induction, causing it to attract materials such

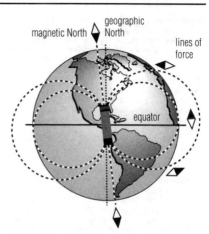

geographic
North

magnetic North

lines of force

equator

magnetic field The Earth's magnetic field is similar to that of a bar magnet with poles near, but not exactly at, the geographic poles. Compass needles align themselves with the magnetic field, which is horizontal near the equator and vertical at the magnetic poles.

as iron, cobalt, nickel, and alloys of these. It always has two magnetic poles, called north and south.

magnetic field region around a permanent magnet, or around a conductor carrying an electric current, in which a force acts on a moving charge or on a magnet placed in the field. The field can be represented by lines of force, which by convention link north and south poles and are parallel to the directions of a small compass needle placed on them. A magnetic field's magnitude and direction are given by the magnetic flux density, expressed in ◊teslas.

magnetic resonance imaging (MRI) diagnostic scanning system based on the principles of nuclear magnetic resonance. MRI yields finely detailed three-dimensional images of structures within the body without exposing the patient to harmful radiation. The technique is invaluable for imaging the soft tissues of the body, in particular the brain and the spinal cord.

magnetic storm in meteorology, a sudden disturbance affecting the Earth's magnetic field, causing anomalies in radio transmissions and magnetic compasses. It is probably caused by ◊sunspot activity.

magnetic strip or *magnetic stripe* thin strip of magnetic material attached to a plastic card (such as a credit card) and used for recording data.

magnetic tape narrow plastic ribbon coated with an easily magnetizable material on which data can be recorded. It is used in sound recording, audiovisual systems (videotape), and computing. For mass storage on commercial mainframe computers, large reel-to-reel tapes are still used, but cartridges are coming in. Various types of cartridge are now standard on minis and PCs, while audio cassettes are sometimes used with home computers.

magnetism phenomena associated with ◊magnetic fields. Magnetic fields are produced by moving charged particles: in electromagnets, electrons flow through a coil of wire connected to a battery; in permanent magnets, spinning electrons within the atoms generate the field.

magnification measure of the enlargement or reduction of an object in an imaging optical system. *Linear magnification* is the ratio of the size (height) of the image to that of the object. *Angular magnification* is the ratio of the angle subtended at the observer's eye by the image to the angle subtended by the object when viewed directly.

magnitude in astronomy, measure of the brightness of a star or other celestial object. The larger the number denoting the magnitude, the fainter the object. Zero or first magnitude indicates some of the brightest stars. Still brighter are those of negative magnitude, such as Sirius, whose magnitude is –1.46. *Apparent magnitude* is the brightness of an object as seen from Earth; *absolute magnitude* is the brightness at a standard distance of 10 parsecs (32.6 light-years).

magnolia tree or shrub of the genus *Magnolia*, family Magnoliaceae, native to North America and E Asia. Magnolias vary in height from 2 ft/60 cm to 150 ft/30 m. The large, fragrant single flowers are white, rose, or purple. The southern magnolia *M. grandiflora* of the US grows up to 80 ft/24 m tall and has white flowers 9 in/23 cm across.

magnolia In the magnolia's large flowers, the sepals are often indistinguishable from the petals and leaves. The earliest flowering plants must have looked like these some 160 million years ago.

magpie any bird of a genus *Pica* in the crow family. It feeds on insects, snails, young birds, and carrion, and is found in Europe, Asia, N Africa, and W North America.

The black-billed magpie *P. pica* of Eurasia and Western N America, about 18 in/45 cm long, has black and white plumage, the long tail having a metallic sheen.

Magritte René 1898–1967. Belgian Surrealist painter. His work focuses on visual paradoxes and everyday objects taken out of context. Recurring motifs include bowler hats, apples, and windows, for example *Golconda* 1953 (private collection), in which men in bowler hats are falling from the sky to a street below.

Magyar member of the largest ethnic group in Hungary, comprising 92% of the population. Magyars are of mixed Ugric and Turkic origin, and they arrived in Hungary toward the end of the 9th century. The Magyar language belongs to the Uralic group.

Mahathir bin Mohamed 1925– . Prime minister of Malaysia from 1981. Leader of the New United Malays' National Organization (UMNO Baru), his "look east" economic policy emulates Japanese industrialization.

Mahayana one of the two major forms of ♦Buddhism, common in China, Korea, Japan, and Tibet. Veneration of bodhisattvas (those who achieve enlightenment but remain on the human plane in order to help other living beings) is a fundamental belief in Mahayana, as is the idea that everyone has within them the seeds of Buddhahood.

Mahler Gustav 1860–1911. Austrian composer and conductor. His epic symphonies express a world-weary Romanticism in visionary tableaux incorporating folk music and pastoral imagery. He composed 14 symphonies (three unnumbered), many with voices, including *Symphony No 2 "Resurrection"* 1884–86, revised 1893–96, also orchestral lieder (songs) including *Das Lied von der Erde/The Song of the Earth* 1909 and *Kindertotenlieder/Dead Children's Songs* 1901–04.

Mahmud I 1696–1754. Ottoman sultan from 1730. After restoring order to the empire in Istanbul 1730, he suppressed the janissary rebellion 1731 and waged war against Persia 1731–46. He led successful wars against Austria and Russia, concluded by the Treaty of Belgrade 1739. He was a patron of the arts and also carried out reform of the army.

Mahmud II 1785–1839. Ottoman sultan from 1808 who attempted to westernize the declining empire, carrying out a series of far-reaching reforms in the civil service and army. The pressure for Greek independence after 1821 led to conflict with Britain, France, and Russia, and he was forced to recognize Greek independence 1830.

mahogany timber from any of several genera of trees found in the Americas and Africa. Mahogany is a tropical hardwood obtained chiefly by rainforest logging. It has a warm red color and takes a high polish.

maidenhair any fern of the genus *Adiantum*, especially *A. capillus-veneris*, with hairlike fronds terminating in small kidney-shaped, spore-bearing pinnules. It is widely distributed in the Americas, and is sometimes found in the British Isles.

Mailer Norman 1923– . US writer and journalist. One of the most prominent figures of postwar American literature, he gained wide attention with his first, best-selling book *The Naked and the Dead* 1948, a naturalistic war novel. His later works, which use sexual and scatological material, show his personal engagement with history, politics, and psychology.

mail merge in computing, a feature offered by some word-processing packages that enables a list of personal details, such as names and addresses, to be combined with a general document outline to produce individualized documents.

Maimonides Moses (Moses Ben Maimon) 1135–1204. Jewish rabbi and philosopher, born in Córdoba, Spain. Known as one of the greatest Hebrew scholars, he attempted to reconcile faith and reason.

Maine northeasternmost state of the US, largest of the New England states; nickname Pine Tree State *area* 33,273 sq mi/86,200 sq km *capital* Augusta *towns and cities* Portland, Lewiston, Bangor *physical* Appalachian Mountains; 80% of the state is forested *features* Acadia National Park, including Bar Harbor and most of Mount Desert Island; Baxter State Park, including Mount Katahadin; Roosevelt's Campobello International Park; canoeing along the Allagush Wilderness Waterway *industries* dairy and market garden produce, paper, pulp, timber, footwear, textiles, fish, lobster; tourism is important *population* (1990) 1,228,000 *famous people* Henry Wadsworth Longfellow, Kate Douglas Wiggin, Edward Arlington Robinson, Edna St Vincent Millay *history* permanently settled by the British from 1623; absorbed by Massachusetts 1691; became a state 1820.

In colonial days, white-pine masts were built for the Royal Navy at Falmouth (now Portland). Maine produces 98% of the nation's blueberries and has the largest papermaking capacity of any of the 50 states but is generally economically depressed.

mainframe large computer used for commercial data processing and other large-scale operations. Because of the general increase in computing power, the differences between the mainframe, ◊supercomputer, ◊minicomputer, and ◊microcomputer (personal computer) are becoming less marked.

Major John 1943– . British Conservative politician, prime minister from Nov 1990. He was foreign secretary 1989 and chancellor of the Exchequer 1989–90. His initial positive approach to European Community (now European Union) matters was hindered from 1991 by divisions within the Conservative Party. Major was returned to power in the April 1992 general election. His subsequent handling of a series of domestic crises called into question his ability to govern the country effectively, but he won support with his Back to Basics campaign and a joint UK-Irish peace initiative on Northern Ireland 1993. He convincingly won an early leadership election July 1995.

Majorca (Spanish *Mallorca*) largest of the ◊Balearic Islands, belonging to Spain, in the W Mediterranean *area* 1,405 sq mi/3,640 sq km *capital* Palma *features* the highest mountain is Puig Mayor, 4,741 ft/1,445 m *industries* olives, figs, oranges, wine, brandy, timber, sheep; tourism is the mainstay of the economy *population* (1981) 561,215 *history* captured 797 by the Moors, it became the kingdom of Majorca 1276, and was united with Aragon 1343.

Malabo port and capital of Equatorial Guinea, on the island of Bioko; population (1983) 15,253. It was founded in the 1820s by the British as *Port Clarence*. Under Spanish rule it was known as *Santa Isabel* (until 1973).

Málaga industrial seaport (sugar refining, distilling, brewing, olive-oil pressing, shipbuilding) and vacation resort in Andalusia, Spain; capital of Málaga province on the Mediterranean; population (1991) 524,800. Founded by the Phoenicians and taken by the Moors 711, Málaga was capital of the Moorish kingdom of Malaga from the 13th century until captured 1487 by the Catholic monarchs Ferdinand and Isabella.

Malagasy inhabitant of or native to Madagascar. The Malagasy language has about 9 million speakers; it belongs to the Austronesian family.

malapropism amusing slip of the tongue, arising from the confusion of similar-sounding words; for example, "the pineapple [pinnacle] of perfection". The term derives from the French *mal à propos* (inappropriate); historically, it is associated with Mrs Malaprop, a character in Richard Sheridan's play *The Rivals* 1775.

malaria infectious parasitic disease of the tropics transmitted by mosquitoes, marked by periodic fever and

an enlarged spleen. When a female mosquito of the *Anopheles* genus bites a human who has malaria, it takes in with the human blood one of four malaria protozoa of the genus *Plasmodium*. This matures within the insect and is then transferred when the mosquito bites a new victim.

Malawi Republic of (*Malawi*) *area* 45,560 sq mi/118,000 sq km *capital* Lilongwe *towns and cities* Blantyre (largest city and commercial center), Mzuzu, Zomba *physical* landlocked narrow plateau with rolling plains; mountainous W of Lake Malawi *features* one-third is water, including lakes Malawi, Chilara, and Malombe; Great Rift Valley; Nyika, Kasungu, and Lengare national parks; Mulanje Massif; Shire River *head of state and government* Bakili Muluzi from 1994 *political system* emergent democratic republic *political parties* Malawi Congress Party (MCP), multiracial, right-wing; United Democratic Front; Alliance for Democracy (Aford) *exports* tea, tobacco, cotton, peanuts, sugar *currency* kwacha *population* (1993 est) 9,700,000 (nearly 1 million refugees from Mozambique); growth rate 3.3% p.a. *life expectancy* men 48, women 50 *languages* English, Chichewa (both official) *media* foreign journalists who write negatively about the country are expelled or barred *religions* Christian 75%, Muslim 20% *literacy* 22% *GNP* $230 per head (1991) *chronology 1891* Became the British protectorate Nyasaland. *1964* Independence achieved from Britain, within the Commonwealth, as Malawi. *1966* Became a one-party republic, with Hastings Banda as president. *1971* Banda was made president for life. *1970s* Reports of human-rights violations and murder of Banda's opponents. *1986–89* Influx of nearly a million refugees from Mozambique. *1992* Calls for multiparty politics. Countrywide industrial riots caused many fatalities. Western aid suspended over human-rights violations. *1993* June: Referendum overwhelmingly supported ending of one-party rule; multiparty system introduced. Oct: Banda underwent brain surgery; presidential council appointed. Dec: Banda returned to office. *1994* Constitutional amendments approved. Bakili Muluzi elected president in first free elections for 30 years. Inconclusive assembly elections.

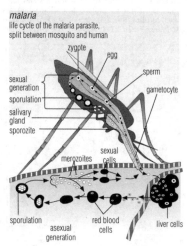

malaria
life cycle of the malaria parasite, split between mosquito and human

zygote
egg
sexual generation
sperm
sporulation
gametocyte
salivary gland
sporozite
sexual cells
merozoites
sporulation
red blood cells
asexual generation
liver cells

malaria

Malawi, Lake or *Lake Nyasa* African lake, bordered by Malawi, Tanzania, and Mozambique, formed in a section of the Great ◊Rift Valley. It is about 1,650 ft/ 500 m above sea level and 350 mi/560 km long, with an area of 14,280 sq mi/37,000 sq km, making it the 9th biggest lake in the world. It is intermittently drained to the S by the river Shiré into the Zambezi.

Malay language member of the Western or Indonesian branch of the Malayo-Polynesian language family, used in the Malay peninsula and many of the islands of Malaysia and Indonesia. The Malay language can be written in either Arabic or Roman scripts. The dialect of the S Malay peninsula is the basis of both Bahasa Malaysia and Bahasa Indonesia, the official languages of Malaysia and Indonesia. Bazaar Malay is a widespread pidgin variety used for trading and shopping.

Malaysia area 127,287 sq mi/329,759 sq km *capital* Kuala Lumpur *towns and cities* Johor Baharu, Ipoh, Georgetown (Penang), Kuching in Sarawak, Kota Kinabalu in Sabah *physical* comprises Peninsular Malaysia (the nine Malay states—Johore, Kedah, Kelantan, Negri Sembilan, Pahang, Perak, Perlis, Selangor, Trengganu—plus Malacca and Penang); and E Malaysia (Sabah and Sarawak); 75% tropical jungle; central mountain range; swamps in E *features* Mount Kinabalu (highest peak in SE Asia); Niah caves (Sarawak) *head of state* Jaafar bin Abd al-Rahman from 1994 *head of government* Mahathir bin Mohamed from 1981 *political system* liberal democracy *political parties* New United Malays' National Organization (UMNO Baru), Malay-oriented nationalist; Malaysian Chinese Association (MCA), Chinese-oriented conservative; Gerakan Party, Chinese-oriented, left of center; Malaysian Indian Congress (MIC), Indian-oriented; Democratic Action Party (DAP), left of center, multiracial but Chinese-dominated; Pan-Malayan Islamic Party (PAS), Islamic; Semangat '46 (Spirit of 1946), moderate, multiracial *exports* pineapples, palm oil, rubber, timber, petroleum (Sarawak), bauxite *currency* ringgit *population* (1993) 19,030,000 (Malaysian 47%, Chinese 32%, Indian 8%, others 13%); growth rate 2% p.a. *life expectancy* men 69, women 73 *languages* Malay (official), English, Chinese, Indian, and local languages *religions* Muslim (official), Buddhist, Hindu, local beliefs *literacy* men 87%, women 70% *GNP* $3,265

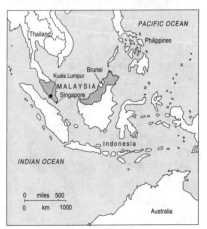

per head (1993) *chronology 1786* Britain established control. *1826* Became a British colony. *1963* Federation of Malaysia formed, including Malaya, Singapore, Sabah (N Borneo), and Sarawak (NW Borneo). *1965* Secession of Singapore from federation. *1969* Anti-Chinese riots in Kuala Lumpur. *1971* Launch of *bumiputra* ethnic-Malay-oriented economic policy. *1981* Election of Dr Mahathir bin Mohamed as prime minister. *1982 and 1986* Mahathir bin Mohamed re-elected. *1987* Arrest of over 100 opposition activists, including DAP leader, as Malay-Chinese relations deteriorated. *1988* Split in ruling UMNO party over Mahathir's leadership style; UMNO Baru (New UMNO) replaced UMNO. *1989* Semangat '46 set up by former members of UMNO, including ex-premier Tunku Abdul Rahman. *1990* Mahathir bin Mohamed reelected. *1991* New economic-growth program launched. *1993* Mahathir bin Mohamed reelected UMNO Baru president.

Malcolm III called *Canmore c.* 1031–1093. King of Scotland from 1058, the son of Duncan I (murdered by ◊Macbeth 1040). He fled to England when the throne was usurped by Macbeth, but recovered S Scotland and killed Macbeth in battle 1057. He was killed at Alnwick while invading Northumberland, England.

Malcolm X adopted name of Malcolm Little 1926–1965. US black nationalist leader born in Omaha, Nebraska. While serving a prison sentence for burglary 1946–53, he joined the ◊Black Muslims sect. On his release he campaigned for black separatism, condoning violence in self-defense, but 1964 modified his views to found the Islamic, socialist Organization of African-American Unity, preaching racial solidarity. He was assassinated.

The film *Malcolm X*, directed by Spike Lee, was released 1992.

Maldives Republic of (*Divehi Jumhuriya*) *area* 115 sq mi/ 298 sq km *capital* Malé *towns and cities* Seenu *physical* comprises 1,196 coral islands, grouped into 12 clusters of atolls, largely flat, none bigger than 5 sq mi/13 sq km, average elevation 6 ft/1.8 m; 203 are inhabited *environment* the threat of rising sea level has been heightened by the frequency of flooding in recent years *features* tourism developed since 1972 *head of state and government* Maumoon Abd al-Gayoom from 1978 *political system* authoritarian nationalism *political parties* none; candidates elected on the basis of personal influence and clan loyalties *exports* coconuts, copra, bonito (fish related to tuna), garments *currency* rufiya *population* (1993) 238,400; growth rate 3.7% p.a. *life expectancy* men 60, women 63 *languages* Divehi (Sinhalese dialect), English *religion* Sunni Muslim *literacy* 92% *GNP* $460 per head (1991) *chronology 1887* Became a British protectorate. *1953* Long a sultanate, the Maldive Islands became a republic within the Commonwealth. *1954* Sultan restored. *1965* Achieved full independence outside the Commonwealth. *1968* Sultan deposed; republic reinstated with Ibrahim Nasir as president. *1978* Nasir retired; replaced by Maumoon Abd al-Gayoom. *1982* Rejoined the Commonwealth. *1983* Al-Gayoom reelected. *1985* Became a founder member of South Asian Association for Regional Cooperation (SAARC). *1988* Al-Gayoom reelected. Coup attempt by mercenaries, thought to have the backing of former president Nasir, was foiled by Indian paratroops. *1993* Al-Gayoom reelected.

Malé capital and chief atoll of the Maldives in the Indian Ocean; population (1990) 55,100. It trades in copra, breadfruit, fish, and palm products; it is also a growing tourist center.

Mali Republic of (*République du Mali*) *area* 478,695 sq mi/1,240,142 sq km *capital* Bamako *towns and cities* Mopti, Kayes, Ségou, Timbuktu *physical* landlocked state with river Niger and savanna in S; part of the Sahara in N; hills in NE; Senegal River and its branches irrigate the SW *environment* a rising population coupled with recent droughts has affected marginal agriculture. Once in surplus, grain has had to be imported every year since 1965 *features* ancient town of Timbuktu; railroad to Dakar is the only outlet to the sea *head of state* Alpha Oumar Konare from 1992 *head of government* Ibrahim Boubaker Keita from 1994 *political system* emergent democratic republic *political parties* Alliance for Democracy in Mali (ADEMA), centrist; National Committee for Democratic Initiative (CNID), center-left; Sudanese Union–African Democratic Rally (US–RDA), Sudanese nationalist *exports* cotton, peanuts, livestock, fish *currency* franc CFA *population* (1993 est) 8,750,000; growth rate 2.9% p.a. *life expectancy* men 44, women 48 *languages* French (official), Bambara *religions* Sunni Muslim 90%, animist 9%, Christian 1% *literacy* men 41%, women 24% *GNP* $280 per head (1991) *chronology 1895* Came under French rule. *1959* With Senegal, formed the Federation of Mali. *1960* Became the independent Republic of Mali, with Modibo Keita as president. *1968* Keita replaced in an army coup by Moussa Traoré. *1974* New constitution made Mali a one-party state. *1976* New national party, the Malian People's Democratic Union, announced. *1983* Agreement between Mali and Guinea for eventual political and economic integration signed. *1985* Conflict with Burkina Faso lasted five days; mediated by International Court of Justice. *1991* Demonstrations against one-party rule. Moussa Traoré ousted in a coup led by Lt-Col Amadou Toumani Toure. New multiparty constitution agreed, subject to referendum. *1992* Referendum endorsed new democratic constitution. ADEMA won multiparty elections; Alpha Oumar Konare elected president. *1993* Antigovernment coup foiled.

mallard common wild duck *Anas platyrhynchos*, found almost worldwide, from which domestic ducks were bred. The male, which can grow to a length of 2 ft/60 cm, usually has a green head and brown breast, while the female is mottled brown. Mallards are omnivorous, dabbling ducks.

Mallarmé Stéphane 1842–1898. French poet. He founded the Symbolist school with Paul Verlaine. His belief that poetry should be evocative and suggestive was reflected in *L'Après-midi d'un faune/Afternoon of a Faun* 1876, which inspired the composer Debussy.

Malle Louis 1932– . French film director. After a period as assistant to director Robert Bresson, he directed *Les Amants/The Lovers* 1958, audacious for its time in its explicitness. His subsequent films, made in France and the US, include *Zazie dans le métro* 1961, *Viva Maria* 1965, *Pretty Baby* 1978, *Atlantic City* 1980, *Au Revoir les Enfants* 1988, *Milou en mai* 1989, and *Damage* 1993.

mallee small trees and shrubs of the genus *Eucalyptus* with many small stems and thick underground roots that retain water. Before irrigation farming began, dense thickets of mallee characterized most of NW Victoria, Australia, known as the mallee region.

Mallorca Spanish form of ◊Majorca, an island in the Mediterranean.

mallow any plant of the family Malvaceae, especially the genus *Malva*, including the North American rose mallow *Hibiscus palustris* and the European marsh mallow *Althaea officinalis*. Most have showy pink or purple flowers. See also ◊hollyhock, ◊cotton, ◊okra, ◊hibiscus.

Malmö industrial port (shipbuilding, engineering, textiles) in SW Sweden, situated across the öresund from Copenhagen, Denmark; population (1990) 233,900. Founded in the 12th century, Malmö is Sweden's third-largest city.

malnutrition the physical condition resulting from dietary deficiencies. These may be caused by lack of food resources (famine) or by lack of knowledge about ◊nutrition.

When essential nutrients are missing from the diet, opportunistic infection takes hold in weakened individuals, those with deficiency disease, and may kill before starvation occurs. A high global death rate linked to malnutrition has arisen from famine situations caused by global warming, droughts, and the ◊greenhouse effect as well as by sociopolitical factors, such as alcohol and drug abuse, poverty and war.

Malory Thomas English author. He is known for the prose romance *Le Morte d'Arthur* about 1470, a translation from the French, modified by material from other sources. It deals with the exploits of King Arthur's knights of the Round Table and the quest for the ◊Holy Grail.

Malraux André 1901–1976. French writer. An active antifascist, he gained international renown for his novel *La Condition humaine/Man's Estate* 1933, set during the Nationalist/Communist Revolution in China in the 1920s. *L'Espoir/Days of Hope* 1937 is set in Civil War Spain, where he was a bomber pilot in the International Brigade.

malt in brewing, grain (barley, oats, or wheat) artificially germinated and then dried in a kiln. Malts are fermented to make beers or lagers, or fermented and then distilled to produce spirits such as whiskey.

Malta Republic of (*Repubblika Ta'Malta*) *area* 124 sq mi/320 sq km *capital* and port Valletta *towns and cities* Rabat; port of Marsaxlokk *physical* includes islands of Gozo 26 sq mi/67 sq km and Comino 1 sq mi/ 2.5 sq km *features* occupies strategic location in central Mediterranean; large commercial dock facilities *head of state* Mifsud Bonnici from 1994 *head of government* Edward Fenech Adami from 1987 *political system* liberal democracy *political parties* Malta Labour Party (MLP), moderate, left of center; Nationalist Party, Christian, centrist, pro-European *exports* vegetables, knitwear, handmade lace, plastics, electronic equipment *currency* Maltese lira *population* (1993) 364,600; growth rate 0.7% p.a. *life expectancy* men 72, women 76 *languages* Maltese, English *religion* Roman Catholic 98% *literacy* 84% *GNP* $7,341 per head (1991) *chronology 1814* Annexed to Britain by the Treaty of Paris. *1947* Achieved self-government. *1955* Dom Mintoff of the Malta Labour Party (MLP) became prime minister. *1956* Referendum approved MLP's proposal for integration with the UK. Proposal opposed by the Nationalist Party. *1958* MLP rejected the British integration proposal. *1962* Nationalists elected, with Borg Olivier as prime minister. *1964* Independence achieved from Britain, within the Commonwealth. Ten-year defense and economic-aid treaty with UK signed. *1971* Mintoff reelected. 1964 treaty declared invalid and negotiations began for leasing the NATO base in Malta. *1972* Seven-year NATO agreement signed. *1974* Became a republic. *1979* British military base closed. *1984* Mintoff retired and was replaced by Mifsud Bonnici as prime minister and MLP leader. *1987* Edward Fenech Adami (Nationalist) elected prime minister. *1989* Vincent Tabone elected president. *1990* Formal application made for European Community membership. *1992* Nationalist Party returned to power in general election. *1994* Mifsud Bonnici elected president.

Malthus Thomas Robert 1766–1834. English economist and cleric. His "Essay on the Principle of Population" 1798 (revised 1803) argued for population control, since populations increase in geometric ratio and food supply only in arithmetic ratio, and influenced Charles ◊Darwin's thinking on natural selection as the driving force of evolution.

Maluku or *Moluccas* group of Indonesian islands *area* 28,764 sq mi/74,500 sq km *capital* Ambon, on Amboina *population* (1989 est) 1,814,000 *history* as the Spice Islands, they were formerly part of the Netherlands East Indies; the S Moluccas attempted secession from the newly created Indonesian republic from 1949; exiles continued agitation in the Netherlands.

mamba one of two venomous snakes, genus *Dendroaspis*, of the cobra family Elapidae, found in Africa S of the Sahara. Unlike cobras, they are not hooded.

Mameluke member of a powerful political class that dominated Egypt from the 13th century until their massacre 1811 by Mehmet Ali.

Mamet David 1947– . US dramatist, film screenwriter, and director. His plays, with their vivid, freewheeling language and urban settings, are often compared with those of Harold Pinter. His *American Buffalo* 1975, about a gang of hopeless robbers, was his first major success. It was followed by *Sexual Perversity in Chicago* 1978 and *Glengarry Glen Ross* 1983, a dark depiction of American business ethics, the film version of which he directed 1992. His other film work has included screenplays for *The Postman Always Rings Twice 1981*, *The Verdict* 1982, and *The Untouchables* 1987. He made his directorial debut with *House of Games* 1987, which used gambling as a metaphor for the bluff and double-bluff of relationships.

mammal animal characterized by having mammary glands in the female; these are used for suckling the young. Other features of mammals are ◊hair (very reduced in some species, such as whales); a middle ear formed of three small bones (ossicles); a lower jaw consisting of two bones only; seven vertebrae in the neck; and no nucleus in the red blood cells.
  Mammals include humans.

mammary gland in female mammals, a milk-producing gland derived from epithelial cells underlying the skin, active only after the production of young. In all but monotremes (egg-laying mammals), the mammary glands terminate in teats which aid infant suckling. The number of glands and their position vary between species.

Mammon evil personification of wealth and greed; originally a Syrian god of riches, cited in the New Testament as opposed to the Christian god.

mammoth extinct elephant of the genus *Mammuthus*, whose remains are found worldwide. Some were 50% taller than modern elephants.

Managua capital and chief industrial city of Nicaragua, on the lake of the same name; population (1985) 682,000. It has twice been destroyed by earthquake and rebuilt, 1931 and 1972; it was also badly damaged during the civil war in the late 1970s.

Manama (Arabic *Al Manamah*) capital and free trade port of Bahrain, on Bahrain Island; population (1988) 152,000. It handles oil and entrepôt trade.

manatee any plant-eating aquatic mammal of the genus *Trichechus* constituting the family Trichechidae in the order Sirenia (sea cows). Manatees occur in marine bays and sluggish rivers, usually in turbid water.

Manaus capital of Amazonas, Brazil, on the Rio Negro, near its confluence with the Amazon; population (1991) 996,700. It can be reached by sea-going vessels, although it is 1,000 mi/1,600 km from the Atlantic. Formerly a center of the rubber trade, it developed as a tourist center in the 1970s.

Manchester city in NW England, on the river Irwell, 31 mi/50 km E of Liverpool. It is a manufacturing (textile machinery, chemicals, rubber, engineering, electrical equipment, paper, printing, processed foods) and financial center; population (1991) 404,900. It is linked by the Manchester Ship Canal, opened 1894, to the river Mersey and the sea.

Manchu or *Qing* last ruling dynasty in China, from 1644 until its overthrow 1912; its last emperor was the infant ◊P'u-i. Originally a nomadic people from Manchuria, they established power through a series of successful invasions from the north, then granted trading rights to the US and Europeans, which eventually brought strife and the Boxer Rebellion.

Manchuria European name for the NE region of China, comprising the provinces of Heilongjiang, Jilin, and Liaoning. It was united with China by the Manchu dynasty 1644, but as the Chinese Empire declined, Japan and Russia were rivals for its control. The Russians were expelled after the ◊Russo-Japanese War 1904–05, and in 1932 Japan consolidated its position by creating a puppet state, *Manchukuo*, nominally led by the Chinese pretender to the throne Henry P'u-i. At the end of World War II the Soviets occupied Manchuria in a two-week operation Aug 1945. Japanese settlers were expelled when the region was returned to Chinese control.

Mandalay chief city of the Mandalay division of Myanmar (formerly Burma), on the river Irrawaddy, about 370 mi/495 km N of Yangon (Rangoon); population (1983) 533,000.

mandarin variety of the tangerine ◊orange *Citrus reticulata*.

Mandarin standard form of the ◊Chinese language. Historically it derives from the language spoken by *mandarins*, Chinese imperial officials, from the 7th century onward. It is used by 70% of the population and taught in schools of the People's Republic of China.

mandate in history, a territory whose administration was entrusted to Allied states by the League of Nations under the Treaty of Versailles after World War I. Mandated territories were former German and Turkish possessions (including Iraq, Syria, Lebanon, and Palestine). When the United Nations replaced the League of Nations 1945, mandates that had not achieved independence became known as trust territories.

Mandela Nelson (Rolihlahla) 1918– . South African politician and lawyer, president from 1994. He became president of the ◊African National Congress (ANC) 1991. Imprisoned from 1964, as organizer of the then banned ANC, he became a symbol of unity for the worldwide antiapartheid movement. In Feb 1990 he was released, the ban on the ANC having been lifted, and he entered into negotiations with the government about a multiracial future for South Africa. In May 1994 he was sworn in as South Africa's first post-apartheid president after the ANC won 62.65% of the popular vote in universal suffrage elections.

Mandela married the South African civil-rights activist Winnie Mandela 1955 (the couple separated 1992). In 1993 he was awarded the Nobel Prize for Peace jointly with South African president F W de Klerk.

mandolin plucked string instrument with four to six pairs of strings (courses), tuned like a violin, which flourished 1600–1800. It takes its name from its almond-shaped body (Italian *mandorla* "almond"). Vivaldi composed two concertos for the mandolin about 1736.

mandragora another name for the plant mandrake.

mandrake or *mandragora* plant of the Old World genus *Mandragora* of almost stemless plants with narcotic properties, of the nightshade family Solanaceae. They have large leaves, pale blue or violet flowers, and globose berries known as devil's apples.

mandrill large W African forest-living baboon *Mandrillus sphinx*, most active on the ground. It has large canine teeth like the drill *M. leucophaeus*, to which it is closely related. The nose is bright red and the cheeks striped with blue. There are red callosities on the buttocks; the fur is brown, apart from a yellow beard.

Manet Edouard 1832–1883. French painter. Active in Paris, he was one of the foremost French artists of the 19th century. Rebelling against the academic tradition, he developed a clear and unaffected realist style. His subjects were mainly contemporary, such as *A Bar at the Folies-Bergère* 1882 (Courtauld Art Gallery, London).

manganese hard, brittle, gray-white metallic element, symbol Mn, atomic number 25, atomic weight 54.9380. It resembles iron (and rusts), but it is not magnetic and is softer. It is used chiefly in making steel alloys, also alloys with aluminum and copper.

It is used in fertilizers, paints, and industrial chemicals. It is a necessary trace element in human nutrition.

mangelwurzel or *mangold* variety of the common beet *Beta vulgaris* used chiefly as feed for cattle and sheep, especially in Europe.

mango evergreen tree *Mangifera indica* of the cashew family Anacardiaceae, native to India but now widely cultivated for its oval fruits in other tropical and subtropical areas, such as the West Indies.

mangrove any of several shrubs and trees, especially of the mangrove family Rhizophoraceae, found in the muddy swamps of tropical and subtropical coasts and estuaries. By sending down aerial roots from their branches, they rapidly form close-growing mangrove thickets. Their timber is impervious to water and resists marine worms. Mangrove swamps are rich breeding grounds for fish and shellfish. These habitats are being destroyed in many countries.

Manhattan island 12.5 mi/20 km long and 2.5 mi/4 km wide, lying between the Hudson and East rivers and forming a borough of the city of ◊New York. It includes the Wall Street business center, Broadway and its theaters, Carnegie Hall (1891), the World Trade Center (1973), the Empire State Building (1931), the United Nations headquarters (1952), Madison Square Garden, and Central Park.

manic depression or *bipolar disorder* mental disorder characterized by recurring periods of ◊depression, which may or may not alternate with periods of inappropriate elation (mania) or overactivity.

Sufferers may be genetically predisposed to the condition. Some cases have been improved by taking prescribed doses of ◊lithium.

Manila industrial port (textiles, tobacco, distilling, chemicals, shipbuilding) and capital of the Philippines, on the island of Luzon; population (1990) 1,598,900, metropolitan area (including ◊Quezon City) 5,926,000.

manioc another name for the plant ◊cassava.

Man, Isle of island in the Irish Sea, a dependency of the British crown, but not part of the UK *area* 220 sq mi/570 sq km *capital* Douglas *towns and cities* Ramsey, Peel, Castletown *features* Snaefell 2,035 ft/620 m; annual TT (Tourist Trophy) motorcycle races, gambling casinos, Britain's first free port, tax haven; tailless Manx cat *industries* light engineering products; tourism, banking, and insurance are important *currency* the island produces its own coins and notes in UK currency denominations *population* (1991) 69,800 *language* English (Manx, nearer to Scottish than Irish Gaelic, has been almost extinct since the 1970s) *government* crown-appointed lieutenant-governor, a legislative council, and the representative House of Keys, which together make up the Court of Tynwald, passing laws subject to the royal assent. Laws passed at Westminster only affect the island if specifically so provided *history* Norwegian until 1266, when the island was ceded to Scotland; it came under UK administration 1765.

Manitoba prairie province of Canada *area* 250,900 sq mi/650,000 sq km *capital* Winnipeg *features* lakes Winnipeg, Winnipegosis, and Manitoba (area 1,814 sq mi/4,700 sq km); 50% forested *exports* grain, manufactured foods, beverages, machinery, furs, fish, nickel, zinc, copper, and the world's largest cesium deposits *population* (1991) 1,092,600 *history* trading posts and forts were built here by fur traders in the 18th century. The first settlers were dispossessed Scottish Highlanders 1812. Known as the Red River settlement, it was administered by the Hudson's Bay Company until purchased by the new dominion of Canada 1869. This prompted the Riel Rebellion 1869–70. It was given the name Manitoba when it became a province 1870. The area of the province was extended 1881 and 1912.

Mann Thomas 1875–1955. German novelist and critic. He was concerned with the theme of the artist's relation to society. His first novel was *Buddenbrooks* 1901, which, followed by *Der Zauberberg/The Magic Mountain* 1924, led to a Nobel Prize 1929. Notable among his works of short fiction is "Der Tod in Venedig/Death in Venice" 1913.

Mannerism in painting, sculpture, and architecture, a style characterized by a subtle but conscious breaking of the "rules" of classical composition—for example, displaying the human body in an off-center, distorted pose, and using harsh, non-blending colors. The term was coined by Giorgio Vasari and used to describe the 16th-century reaction to the peak of Renaissance Classicism. It includes the works of the painters Giovanni Rosso and Parmigianino, the architect Giulio Romano, and the sculptor Giambologna.

manor basic economic unit in ◊feudalism in Europe, established in England under the Norman conquest. It consisted of the lord's house and cultivated land, land rented by free tenants, land held by villagers, common land, woodland, and waste land.

Man Ray see Man ◊Ray.

Mansfield Katherine. Pen name of Kathleen Beauchamp 1888–1923. New Zealand writer. She lived most of her life in England. Her delicate artistry emerges not only in her volumes of short stories—such as *In a German Pension* 1911, *Bliss* 1920, and *The Garden Party* 1923—but also in her *Letters* and *Journal*.

manslaughter the unlawful killing of a human being in circumstances less culpable than ◊murder—for example, when the killer suffers extreme provocation, is in some way mentally ill (diminished responsibility), did not intend to kill but did so accidentally in the course of another crime or by behaving with criminal recklessness, or is the survivor of a genuine suicide pact that involved killing the other person.

manta or *manta ray* any of several large rays of the genera *Manta* and *Mobula*, fish in which two "horns" project forward from the sides of the huge mouth. These flaps of skin guide the plankton on which the fish feed into the mouth.   The largest of these rays can be 23 ft/7 m across and weigh 2,200 lb/1,000 kg.

Mantegna Andrea *c.* 1431–1506. Italian Renaissance painter and engraver, active chiefly in Padua and Mantua, where some of his frescoes remain. Paintings such as *The Agony in the Garden* about 1455 (National Gallery, London) reveal a dramatic, linear style, mastery of perspective, and strongly Classical architectural detail.

mantis any insect of the family Mantidae, related to cockroaches. Some species can reach a length of 8 in/20 cm. There are about 2,000 species of mantis, mainly tropical. The 4 in/10 cm-long Chinese praying mantis, proficient at garden pest control, is now naturalized in North America.

Mantle Mickey (Charles) 1931– . US baseball player, born in Spavinaw, Oklahoma. Signed by the New York

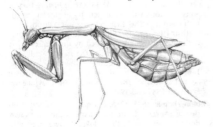

mantis *The praying mantis is a superbly designed predator. It waits motionless or slightly swaying as if in a breeze until prey appears. Many species are effectively camouflaged to look like dead leaves. The female mantis is notorious for eating its mate during copulation (although this behavior is relatively uncommon).*

Yankees, he broke into the major leagues 1951. A powerful switch-hitter (able to bat with either hand), he also excelled as a center-fielder. In 1956 he won baseball's Triple Crown, leading the American League in batting average, home runs, and runs batted in. He retired 1969 after 18 years with the Yankees and seven World Series championships.

He was elected to the Baseball Hall of Fame 1974.

Manx cat breed of domestic shorthaired cat originally bred in the Isle of Man, Britain. Its most distinctive feature is its nonexistent tail, the result of a natural mutation. In 1970 a long haired form of the Manx was bred in the US called the Cymric.

Maoism form of communism based on the ideas and teachings of the Chinese communist leader ◊Mao Zedong. It involves an adaptation of ◊Marxism to suit conditions in China and apportions a much greater role to agriculture and the peasantry in the building of socialism. Maoism stresses ideological, as well as economic, transformation, based on regular contact between party members and the general population.

Maori member of the Polynesian people of pre-European New Zealand, who numbered 294,200 in 1986, about 10% of the total population. Their language, Maori, belongs to the eastern branch of the Austronesian family.

Mao Zedong or *Mao Tse-tung* 1893–1976. Chinese political leader and Marxist theoretician. A founder of the Chinese Communist Party (CCP) 1921, Mao soon emerged as its leader. He organized the ◊Long March 1934–35 and the war of liberation 1937–49, following which he established a People's Republic and communist rule in China; he headed the CCP and government until his death. His influence diminished with the failure of his 1958–60 ◊Great Leap Forward, but he emerged dominant again during the 1966–69 ◊Cultural Revolution.

Mao adapted communism to Chinese conditions, as set out in the *Little Red Book*.

map diagrammatic representation of an area—for example, part of the Earth's surface or the distribution of the stars. Modern maps of the Earth are made using satellites in low orbit to take a series of overlapping stereoscopic photographs from which a three-dimensional image can be prepared. The earliest accurate large-scale maps appeared about 1580.

maple deciduous tree of the genus *Acer*, family Aceraceae, with lobed leaves and green flowers, followed by two-winged fruits, or samaras. There are over 200 species, chiefly in northern temperate regions. About 12 species are native to North America. The sugar maple *A. saccharum* is a source of maple syrup. *A. campestre* and *A. pseudoplatanus*, the ◊sycamore or great maple, are native to Europe.

map projection ways of depicting the spherical surface of the Earth on a flat piece of paper. Traditional projections include the *conic*, *azimuthal*, and *cylindrical*. The most famous cylindrical projection is the ◊Mercator projection, which dates from 1569. The weakness of these systems is that countries in different latitudes are disproportionately large, and lines of longitude and latitude appear distorted.

In 1973 German historian Arno Peters devised the *Peters projection* in which the countries of the world retain their relative areas. In 1992 the US physicist Mitchell Feigenbaum devised the *optimal conformal* projection, using a computer program to produce the minimum of inaccuracies.

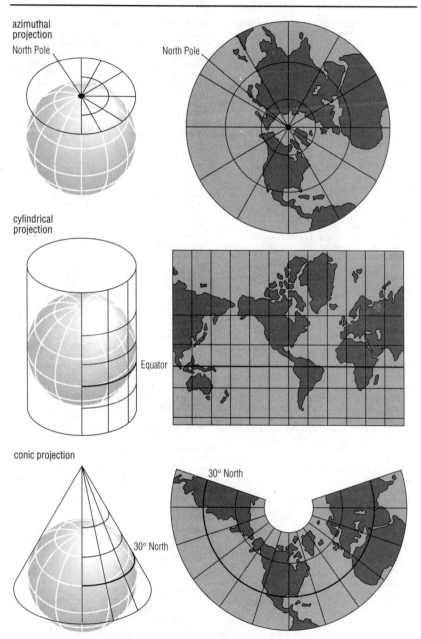

map projection Three widely used map projections. If a light were placed at the center of a transparent Earth, the shapes of the countries would be thrown as shadows on a sheet of paper. If the paper is flat, the azimuthal projection results; if it is wrapped around a cylinder or in the form of a cone, the cylindrical or conic projections result.

Maputo formerly (until 1975) *Lourenço Marques* capital of Mozambique, and Africa's second-largest port, on Delagoa Bay; population (1987) 1,006,800. Linked by rail with Zimbabwe and South Africa, it is a major outlet for minerals, steel, textiles, processed foods, and furniture.

marabou stork *Leptoptilos crumeniferus* found in Africa. It is about 4 ft/120 cm tall, has a bald head, and eats snakes, lizards, insects, and carrion. It is largely dark gray and white and has an inflatable throat pouch.

Maracaibo oil-exporting port in Venezuela, on the channel connecting Lake Maracaibo with the Gulf of Venezuela; population (1989) 1,365,308. It is the second-largest city in the country.

Maracaibo, Lake lake in NW Venezuela; area 5,400 sq mi/14,000 sq km. Oil was discovered here 1917.

Marat Jean Paul 1743–1793. French Revolutionary leader and journalist. He was elected to the National Convention 1792, where he carried on a long struggle with the right-wing ◊Girondists, ending in their overthrow May 1793. In July he was murdered by Charlotte Corday, a member of the Girondists.

Marat was a hero of the Paris revolutionary crowds. He was killed in his bath, where he generally worked, while treating a skin condition.

marathon athletics endurance race over 26 mi 385 yd/ 42,195 km. It was first included in the Olympic Games in Athens 1896. The distance varied until it was standardized 1924. More recently, races have been opened to wider participation, including social runners as well as those competing at senior level.

The current marathon distance was first used at the 1908 Olympic Games in London when the race was increased by an extra 385 yards to finish in front of the royal box. The best known US marathons are run annually in Boston, New York City, and Los Angeles.

Marathon, Battle of battle 490 BC in which the Athenians and their allies from Plateae defeated the invading Persians on the plain of Marathon, NE of Athens.

Marbella port and tourist resort on the Costa del Sol between Málaga and Algeciras in Andalucia, S Spain; population (1991) 80,645.

There are three bullrings, a Moorish castle, and the remains of a medieval defensive wall.

marble metamorphosed ◊limestone that takes and retains a good polish; it is used in building and sculpture. In its pure form it is white and consists almost entirely of calcite $CaCO_3$. Mineral impurities give it various colors and patterns. Carrara, Italy, is known for white marble.

Marceau Marcel 1923– . French mime artist. He is the creator of the clown-harlequin Bip and mime sequences such as "Youth, Maturity, Old Age, and Death".

Marches boundary areas of England with Wales, and England with Scotland. In the Middle Ages these troubled frontier regions were held by lords of the Marches, sometimes called *marchiones* and later earls of March.

Marconi Guglielmo 1874–1937. Italian electrical engineer and pioneer in the invention and development of radio. In 1895 he achieved radio communication over more than a mile, and in England 1896 he conducted successful experiments that led to the formation of the company that became Marconi's Wireless Telegraph Company Ltd. He shared the Nobel Prize for Physics 1909.

Marco Polo see ◊Polo, Marco.

Marcos Ferdinand 1917–1989. Filipino right-wing politician, president from 1965 to 1986, when he was forced into exile in Hawaii by a popular front led by Corazon ◊Aquino. He was backed by the US when in power, but in 1988 US authorities indicted him and his wife Imelda Marcos for racketeering and embezzlement.

Marcos Imelda 1930– . Filipino politician and socialite, wife of Ferdinand Marcos, in exile 1986–91. She was acquitted 1990 of defrauding US banks. Under indictment for misuse of Philippine state funds, she returned to Manila in Nov 1991 and was an unsuccessful candidate in the 1992 presidential elections. She was convicted of corruption and sentenced to 18–24 years imprisonment 1993, but remained free on bail.

Marcus Aurelius Antoninus adopted name of Marcus Annius Verus AD 121–180. Roman emperor from 161 and Stoic philosopher. He wrote the philosophical *Meditations*. Born in Rome, he was adopted by his uncle, the emperor Antoninus Pius, whom he succeeded in 161. He conceded an equal share in the rule to Lucius Verus (died 169).

Mardi Gras (French "fat Tuesday" from the custom of using up all the fat in the household before the beginning of ◊Lent) Shrove Tuesday. A festival was traditionally held on this day in Paris, and there are carnivals in many parts of the world, including New Orleans and Mobile, Alabama, in the US, and Brazil and Italy.

Margaret (Rose) 1930– . Princess of the UK, younger daughter of George VI and sister of Elizabeth II. In 1960 she married Anthony Armstrong-Jones, later created Lord Snowdon, but they were divorced 1978. Their children are *David, Viscount Linley* (1961–) and *Lady Sarah Armstrong-Jones* (1964–).

Margaret of Anjou 1430–1482. Queen of England from 1445, wife of ◊Henry VI of England. After the outbreak of the Wars of the ◊Roses 1455, she acted as the leader of the Lancastrians, but was defeated and captured at the battle of Tewkesbury 1471 by Edward IV.

margarine butter substitute made from animal fats and/or vegetable oils.

The French chemist Hippolyte Mège-Mouriès invented margarine 1889. Today, margarines are usually made with vegetable oils, such as soy, corn, or sunflower oil, giving a product low in saturated fats (see ◊polyunsaturate) and fortified with vitamins A and D.

Margrethe II 1940– . Queen of Denmark from 1972, when she succeeded her father Frederick IX. In 1967, she married the French diplomat Count Henri de Laborde de Monpezat, who took the title Prince Hendrik. Her heir is Crown Prince Frederick (1968–).

marguerite European plant *Leucanthemum vulgare* of the daisy family Compositae. It is a shrubby perennial and bears white daisylike flowers. Marguerite is also the name of a cultivated variety of ◊chrysanthemum.

Mariana Islands or *Marianas* archipelago in the NW Pacific E of the Philippines, divided politically into ◊Guam (an unincorporated territory of the US) and the ◊Northern Mariana Islands (a commonwealth of the US with its own internal government).

Mariana Trench lowest region on the Earth's surface; the deepest part of the sea floor. The trench is

1,500 mi/2,400 km long and is situated 200 mi/300 km E of the Mariana Islands, in the NW Pacific Ocean. Its deepest part is the gorge known as the Challenger Deep, which extends 36,210 ft/11,034 m below sea level.

Maria Theresa 1717–1780. Empress of Austria from 1740, when she succeeded her father, the Holy Roman emperor Charles VI; her claim to the throne was challenged and she became embroiled, first in the War of the ◊Austrian Succession 1740–48, then in the Seven Years' War 1756–63; she remained in possession of Austria but lost Silesia. The rest of her reign was peaceful and, with her son Joseph II, she introduced social reforms.

Marie Antoinette 1755–1793. Queen of France from 1774. She was the daughter of Empress Maria Theresa of Austria, and married ◊Louis XVI of France 1770. Her reputation for extravagance helped provoke the ◊French Revolution of 1789. She was tried for treason Oct 1793 and guillotined.

Marie de' Medici 1573–1642. Queen of France, wife of Henry IV from 1600, and regent (after his murder) for their son Louis XIII. She left the government to her favorites, the Concinis, until Louis XIII seized power and executed them 1617. She was banished but, after she led a revolt 1619, ◊Richelieu effected her reconciliation with her son. When she attempted to oust him again 1630, she was exiled.

marigold any of several plants of the family Compositae, especially the genus *Tagetes*, including pot marigold *Calendula officinalis* and the tropical American *T. patula*, commonly known as French marigold.

marijuana the dried leaves and flowers of the ◊hemp plant (*Cannabis sativa*), used as a recreational but illegal drug. It is eaten or inhaled and causes euphoria, distortion of time, and heightened sensations of sight and sound.

marimba bass ◊xylophone of Latin American origin with wooden rather than metal tubular resonators.

Mariner spacecraft series of US space probes that explored the planets Mercury, Venus, and Mars 1962–75.

Mariner 11 and 12 became *Voyager 1 and 2*, which reached Jupiter 1979, Saturn 1980–81, Uranus 1986, Neptune 1989, and continue to the present traveling beyond the Solar System.

maritime law that part of the law dealing with the sea: in particular, fishing rules, ships, and navigation. Seas are divided into *internal waters* governed by a state's internal laws (such as harbors, inlets); *territorial waters* (the area of sea adjoining the coast over which a state claims rights); the *continental shelf* (the seabed and subsoil that the coastal state is entitled to exploit beyond the territorial waters); and the *high seas*, where international law applies.

marjoram aromatic herb of the mint family Labiatae. Wild marjoram *Origanum vulgare* is found both in Europe and Asia and has become naturalized in the Americas; the culinary sweet marjoram *O. majorana* is widely cultivated.

Mark Antony (Marcus Antonius) 83–30 BC. Roman politician and soldier. He served under Julius ◊Caesar in Gaul, and was consul with him in 44, when he tried to secure for Caesar the title of king. After Caesar's assassination, he formed the Second Triumvirate with Octavian (later ◊Augustus) and Lepidus. In 42 he defeated Brutus and Cassius at Philippi. He took Egypt as his share of the empire and formed a liaison with ◊Cleopatra, but in 40 he returned to Rome to marry Octavia, the sister of Octavian. In 32 the Senate declared war on Cleopatra, and Antony, who had combined forces with Cleopatra, was defeated by Octavian at the battle of Actium 31 BC. He returned to Egypt and committed suicide.

marketing promoting goods and services to consumers. In the 20th century, marketing has played an increasingly larger role in determining company policy, influencing product development, pricing, methods of distribution, advertising, and promotion techniques.

Mark, St In the New Testament, Christian apostle and evangelist whose name is given to the second Gospel. It was probably written AD 65–70, and used by the authors of the first and third Gospels. He is the patron saint of Venice, and his emblem is a winged lion; feast day April 25.

marlin or *spearfish* any of several genera of open-sea fishes known as billfishes, of the family Istiophoridae, order Perciformes. Some 7 ft/2.5 m long, they are found in warmer waters, have elongated snouts, and high-standing dorsal fins. Members of the family include the sailfish *Istiophorus platypterus*, the fastest of all fishes over short distances—reaching speeds of 62 mph/100 kph—and the blue marlin *Makaira nigricans*, highly prized as a "game" fish.

Marlowe Christopher 1564–1593. English poet and dramatist. His work includes the blank-verse plays *Tamburlaine the Great c.* 1587, *The Jew of Malta c.* 1589, *Edward II* and *Dr Faustus*, both *c.* 1592, the poem *Hero and Leander* 1598, and a translation of Ovid's *Amores*.

marmoset small tree-dwelling monkey in the family Callithricidae, found in South and Central America. Most species have characteristic tufted ears, clawlike nails, and a handsome tail, and some only reach a body length of 7 in/18 cm. The tail is not prehensile. Some are known as tamarins.

marmot any of several large burrowing rodents of the genus *Marmota*, in the squirrel family Sciuridae. There are about 15 species. They eat plants and some insects. Marmots are found throughout the US and Canada, and from the Alps to the Himalayas. Marmots live in colonies, make burrows (one to each family), and hibernate. In North America *woodchucks* or *groundhogs* are types of marmots.

Marne, Battles of the in World War I, two unsuccessful German offensives. In the *First Battle* Sept 6–9, 1914, von Moltke attempted to encircle Paris but his advance was halted by the British Expeditionary Force and the French under Foch. The *Second Battle* July 15–Aug 4, 1918, formed the final thrust of the German Spring Offensive, eventually halted by a joint French, British, and US force under the French general Pétain.

Marquesas Islands (French *Iles Marquises*) island group in ◊French Polynesia, lying N of the Tuamotu Archipelago; area 490 sq mi/1,270 sq km; population (1988) 7,500. The administrative headquarters is Atuona on Hiva Oa. The islands were annexed by France 1842.

marquess or *marquis* title and rank of a nobleman who in the British peerage ranks below a duke and above an earl. The wife of a marquess is a marchioness.

Marquette Jacques 1637–1675. French Jesuit missionary and explorer. He went to Canada 1666, explored the upper lakes of the St Lawrence River, and in 1673 with Louis Jolliet (1645–1700), set out on a voyage down the Mississippi on which they made the first accurate record of its course.

In 1674 he and two companions camped near the site of present-day Chicago, making them the first Europeans to live there.

Márquez Gabriel García. See ◊García Márquez, Colombian novelist.

Marrakesh historic city in Morocco in the foothills of the Atlas Mountains, about 130 mi/210 km S of Casablanca; population (1982) 549,000. It is a tourist center, and has textile, leather, and food processing industries. Founded 1062, it has a medieval palace and mosques, and was formerly the capital of Morocco.

marriage legally or culturally sanctioned union of one man and one woman (monogamy); one man and two or more women (polygamy); one woman and two or more men (polyandry). The basis of marriage varies considerably in different societies (romantic love in the West; arranged marriages in some other societies), but most marriage ceremonies, contracts, or customs involve a set of rights and duties, such as care and protection, and there is generally an expectation that children will be born of the union to continue the family line, and maintain the family property.

Mars in Roman mythology, the god of war, depicted as a fearless warrior. The month of March is named for him. He is equivalent to the Greek Ares.

Mars fourth planet from the Sun, average distance 141.6 million mi/227.9 million km. It revolves around the Sun in 687 Earth days, and has a rotation period of 24 hr 37 min. It is much smaller than Venus or Earth, with a diameter 4,210 mi/6,780 km, and mass 0.11 that of Earth. Mars is slightly pearshaped, with a low, level northern hemisphere, which is comparatively uncratered and geologically "young", and a heavily cratered "ancient" southern hemisphere.

Marseille (English *Marseilles*) chief seaport of France, industrial center (chemicals, oil refining, metallurgy, shipbuilding, food processing), and capital of the *département* of Bouches-du-Rhône, on the Golfe du Lion, Mediterranean Sea; population (1990) 807,700.

marsh low-lying wetland. Freshwater marshes are common wherever groundwater, surface springs, streams, or run-off cause frequent flooding or more or less permanent shallow water. A marsh is alkaline whereas a ◊bog is acid. Marshes develop on inorganic silt or clay soils. Rushes are typical marsh plants. Large marshes dominated by papyrus, cattail, and reeds, with standing water throughout the year, are commonly called swamps.

Marshall George Catlett 1880–1959. US general and diplomat. He was army Chief of Staff in World War II, secretary of state 1947–49, and secretary of defense Sept 1950–Sept 1951. He foresaw the inevitability of US involvement in the war and prepared the army well for it. He initiated the ◊*Marshall Plan* 1947 and received the Nobel Peace Prize 1953.

Marshall John 1755–1835. US politician and jurist. He held office in the US House of Representatives 1799–1800 and was secretary of state 1800–01. As chief justice of the US Supreme Court 1801–35, he established the independence of the Court and the

supremacy of federal over state law, and his opinions became universally accepted interpretations of the US Constitution.

Marshall Islands area 69 sq mi/180 sq km *capital* Dalap-Uliga-Darrit (on Majuro atoll) *physical* comprises the Radak (13 islands) and Ralik (11 islands) chains in the W Pacific *features* coral reefs and shores; includes two atolls used for US atomic-bomb tests 1946–63, Eniwetok and Bikini, where radioactivity will last for 100 years; Kwajalein atoll (the largest) has a US intercontinental missile range *head of state and government* Amata Kabua from 1992 *political system* liberal democracy *political parties* no organized party system, but in 1991 an opposition grouping, the Ralik Ratak Democratic Party, was founded to oppose the ruling group *products* copra, phosphates, fish; tourism is important *currency* US dollar *population* (1990) 31,600 *language* English (official) *religions* Christian, mainly Roman Catholic, and local faiths *literacy* 93% *GNP* $16,516 per head (1990) *chronology* *1855* Occupied by Germany. *1914* Occupied by Japan. *1920–45* Administered by Japan under League of Nations mandate. *1946–63* Eniwetok and Bikini atolls used for US atomic-bomb tests; islanders later demanded rehabilitation and compensation for the damage. *1947* Became part of United Nations (UN) Pacific Islands Trust Territory, administered by the US. *1986* Compact of free association with US granted islands self-government, with US retaining military control and taking tribute. *1990* UN trust status terminated. *1991* Independence agreed; UN membership granted. *1992* Amata Kabua elected president.

Marshall Plan program of US economic aid to Europe, set up at the end of World War II, totaling $13,000 billion 1948–52. Officially known as the European Recovery Program, it was announced by Secretary of State George C. ◊Marshall in a speech at Harvard June 1947, but it was in fact the work of a State Department group led by Dean Acheson. The perceived danger of communist takeover in postwar Europe was the main reason for the aid effort.

marsh marigold plant *Caltha palustris* of the buttercup family Ranunculaceae, known as the kingcup in the UK and as the cowslip in the US. It grows in moist sheltered spots and has five-sepalled flowers of a brilliant yellow.

marsh rose a shrub 3–13 ft/1–4 m high *Orothamnus zeyheri*. It grows in South Africa and, although protected, is under threat, partly because of picking for its beautiful flowerheads.

Marston Moor, Battle of battle fought in the English Civil War July 2, 1644, on Marston Moor, 7 mi/11 km W of York. The Royalists were conclusively defeated by the Parliamentarians and Scots.

marsupial mammal in which the female has a pouch where she carries her young (born tiny and immature) for a considerable time after birth. Marsupials include omnivorous, herbivorous, and carnivorous species, among them the kangaroo, wombat, opossum, phalanger, bandicoot, dasyure, and wallaby.

The marsupial anteater *Myrmecobius* has no pouch.

marten small bushy-tailed carnivorous mammal of the genus *Martes* in the weasel family Mustelidae. Martens live in North America, Europe, and temperate regions of Asia, and are agile climbers of trees.

martial arts any of several styles of armed and unarmed combat developed in the East from ancient techniques and arts. Common martial arts include aikido, ◊judo, jujitsu, ◊karate, kendo, and ◊kung fu.

martial law replacement of civilian by military authorities in the maintenance of order.

In the US martial law is usually proclaimed by the president or the government of a state in areas of the country where the civil authorities have been rendered unable to act, or to act with safety.

martin any of several species of birds in the swallow family, Hirundinidae.

Only one species, the purple martin *Progne subis*, is native to North America. It is a dark, glossy purplish blue and about 8 in/20 cm long with a notched tail. It winters in South America.

Martinique French island in the West Indies (Lesser Antilles) *area* 417 sq mi/1,079 sq km *capital* Fort-de-France *features* several active volcanoes; Napoleon's empress Josephine was born in Martinique, and her childhood home is now a museum *industries* sugar, cocoa, rum, bananas, pineapples *population* (1990) 359,600 *history* Martinique was reached by Spanish navigators 1493, and became a French colony 1635; since 1972 it has been a French overseas region.

martyr one who voluntarily suffers death for refusing to renounce a religious faith. The first recorded Christian martyr was St Stephen, who was killed in Jerusalem shortly after Jesus' alleged ascension to heaven.

Marvell Andrew 1621–1678. English metaphysical poet and satirist. His poems include "To His Coy Mistress" and "Horatian Ode upon Cromwell's Return from Ireland". He was committed to the parliamentary cause, and was Member of Parliament for Hull from 1659. He devoted his last years mainly to verse satire and prose works attacking repressive aspects of government.

Marx Karl (Heinrich) 1818–1883. German philosopher, economist, and social theorist whose account of change through conflict is known as historical, or dialectical, materialism (see ◊Marxism). His *Das Kapital/Capital* 1867–95 is the fundamental text of Marxist economics, and his systematic theses on class struggle, history, and the importance of economic factors in politics have exercised an enormous influence on later thinkers and political activists.

Marx Brothers team of US film comedians: Leonard *Chico* (from the "chicks"—women—he chased) 1887–1961; Adolph, the silent *Harpo* (from the harp he played) 1888–1964; Julius *Groucho* (from his temper) 1890–1977; Milton *Gummo* (from his gumshoes, or galoshes) 1897–1977, who left the team before they began making films; and Herbert *Zeppo* (born at the time of the first zeppelins) 1901–1979, part of the team until 1935. They made a total of 13 zany films 1929–49 including *Animal Crackers* 1930, *Monkey Business* 1931, *Duck Soup* 1933, *A Day at the Races* 1937, *A Night at the Opera* 1935, and *Go West* 1940.

Marxism philosophical system, developed by the 19th-century German social theorists ◊Marx and ◊Engels, also known as *dialectical materialism*, under which matter gives rise to mind (materialism) and all is subject to change (from dialectic; see ◊Hegel). As applied to history, it supposes that the succession of feudalism, capitalism, socialism, and finally the classless society is inevitable. The stubborn resistance of any existing system to change necessitates its complete overthrow in the *class struggle*—in the case of capi-

Marx Brothers *US film and radio comedians; from left Zeppo, Groucho, Chico, and Harpo. Their inspired, anarchic clowning lifted their films far above the frail plot lines.*

talism, by the proletariat—rather than gradual modification.

Mary Queen of Scots 1542–1587. Queen of Scotland 1542–67. Also known as *Mary Stuart*, she was the daughter of James V. Mary's connection with the English royal line from Henry VII made her a threat to Elizabeth I's hold on the English throne, especially as she represented a champion of the Catholic cause. She was married three times. After her forced abdication she was imprisoned but escaped 1568 to England. Elizabeth I held her prisoner, while the Roman Catholics, who regarded Mary as rightful queen of England, formed many conspiracies to place her on the throne, and for complicity in one of these she was executed.

Mary in the New Testament, the mother of Jesus through divine intervention, wife of ◊Joseph. The Roman Catholic Church maintains belief in her ◊Immaculate Conception and bodily assumption into heaven, and venerates her as a mediator. Feast day of the Assumption is Aug 15.

Mary I (called *Bloody Mary*) 1516–1558. Queen of England from 1553. She was the eldest daughter of Henry VIII by Catherine of Aragon. When Edward VI died, Mary secured the crown without difficulty in spite of the conspiracy to substitute Lady Jane ◊Grey. In 1554 Mary married Philip II of Spain, and as a devout Roman Catholic obtained the restoration of papal supremacy and sanctioned the persecution of Protestants. She was succeeded by her half sister Elizabeth I.

Mary II 1662–1694. Queen of England, Scotland, and Ireland from 1688. She was the Protestant elder daughter of the Catholic ◊James II, and in 1677 was married to her cousin ◊William of Orange. After the 1688 revolution she accepted the crown jointly with William.

Maryland state of E US; nickname Old Line State/Free State *area* 12,198 sq mi/31,600 sq km *capital* Annapolis *cities* Baltimore, Silver Spring, Dundalk, Bethesda *features* Chesapeake Bay, an inlet of the Atlantic Ocean; horse racing (the Preakness Stakes at Baltimore); yacht racing and the US Naval Academy at Annapolis; historic Fort McHenry; Fort Meade, a government electronic-listening center; Baltimore harbor *industries* poultry, dairy products, machinery, steel, automobiles and parts, electric and electronic equipment, chemicals, fish and shellfish *population* (1990) 4,781,500 *famous people* Stephen Decatur, Francis Scott Key, Edgar Allan Poe, Frederick Douglass, Harriet Tubman, Upton Sinclair, H L Mencken, Babe Ruth, Billie Holiday *history* one of the original 13 states, first settled 1634; it became a state 1788.

In 1608 John Smith explored Chesapeake Bay, but the colony of Maryland, awarded by royal grant 1632 to Lord Baltimore for the settlement of English Catholics, dates from 1634. It ratified the federal Constitution 1788. During the British bombardment of Fort McHenry in the War of 1812, Francis Scott Key wrote the poem *The Star-Spangled Banner*, which later became the lyrics to the US national anthem. During the Civil War, the Confederate armies three times invaded Maryland. Between 1940 and 1980, Maryland's population more than tripled. Baltimore's port ranks second in handling foreign shipping.

Mary Magdalene, St In the New Testament, the woman whom Jesus cured of possession by evil spirits, was present at the Crucifixion and burial, and was the

first to meet the risen Jesus. She is often identified with the woman of St Luke's gospel who anointed Jesus' feet, and her symbol is a jar of ointment; feast day July 22.

Masaccio (Tommaso di Giovanni di Simone Guidi) 1401–1428. Florentine painter. He was a leader of the early Italian Renaissance. His frescoes in Sta Maria del Carmine, Florence, 1425–28, which he painted with Masolino da Panicale, show a decisive break with Gothic conventions. He was the first painter to apply the scientific laws of perspective, newly discovered by the architect Brunelleschi, and achieved a remarkable sense of space and volume.

Masai member of an E African people whose territory is divided between Tanzania and Kenya, and who number about 250,000. They were originally warriors and nomads, breeding humped zebu cattle, but some have adopted a more settled life. Their cooperation is being sought by the Kenyan authorities to help in wildlife conservation. They speak a Nilotic language belonging to the Nilo-Saharan family.

Masaryk Tomás (Garrigue) 1850–1937. Czechoslovak nationalist politician. He directed the revolutionary movement against the Austrian Empire, founding with Eduard Benes and Stefanik the Czechoslovak National Council, and in 1918 was elected first president of the newly formed Czechoslovak Republic. Three times re-elected, he resigned 1935 in favor of Benes.

maser (acronym for *microwave amplification by stimulated emission of radiation*) in physics, a high-frequency microwave amplifier or oscillator in which the signal to be amplified is used to stimulate unstable atoms into emitting energy at the same frequency. Atoms or molecules are raised to a higher energy level and then allowed to lose this energy by radiation emitted at a precise frequency. The principle has been extended to other parts of the electromagnetic spectrum as, for example, in the ◊laser.

Maseru capital of Lesotho, S Africa, on the Caledon River; population (1986) 289,000. Founded 1869, it is a center for diamond and cattle processing.

Masire Quett Ketumile Joni 1925– . President of Botswana from 1980. In 1962, with Seretse ◊Khama, he founded the Botswana Democratic Party (BDP) and in 1965 was made deputy prime minister. After independence 1966, he became vice president and, on Khama's death 1980, president, continuing a policy of nonalignment.

Mason James 1909–1984. English film actor. He portrayed romantic villains in British films of the 1940s. After *Odd Man Out* 1947 he worked in the US, often playing intelligent but troubled, vulnerable men, notably in *A Star Is Born* 1954. He returned to Europe 1960, where he made *Lolita* 1962, *Georgy Girl* 1966, and *Cross of Iron* 1977.

Other films include *Five Fingers* 1952 and *North by Northwest* 1959. His final role was in *The Shooting Party* 1984.

Mason–Dixon Line in the US, the boundary line between Maryland and Pennsylvania (latitude 39° 43′ 26.3″ N), named after Charles Mason (1730–1787) and Jeremiah Dixon (died 1777), English astronomers and surveyors who surveyed it 1763–67. It was popularly seen as dividing the North from the South.

mass in physics, the quantity of matter in a body as measured by its inertia. Mass determines the acceleration produced in a body by a given force acting on it, the acceleration being inversely proportional to the mass of the body. The mass also determines the force exerted on a body by ◊gravity on Earth, although this attraction varies slightly from place to place. In the SI system, the base unit of mass is the kilogram.

Mass in Christianity, the celebration of the ◊Eucharist.

Mass in music, the setting of the invariable parts of the Christian Mass, that is the *Kyrie, Gloria, Credo, Sanctus* with *Benedictus*, and *Agnus Dei*. A notable example is J S Bach's *Mass in B Minor*.

Massachusetts state of NE US; nickname Bay State/Old Colony State *area* 8,299 sq mi/21,500 sq km *capital* Boston *towns and cities* Worcester, Springfield, New Bedford, Brockton, Cambridge *population* (1990) 6,016,400 *features* Boston landmarks; Harvard University and the Massachusetts Institute of Technology, Cambridge; Cape Cod National Seashore; New Bedford and the islands of Nantucket and Martha's Vineyard; the battlefields of Lexington and Concord near Minute Man National Historical Park; Salem, site of witch trials; Plymouth Rock *industries* electronic, communications, and optical equipment; precision instruments; nonelectrical machinery; fish; cranberries; dairy products *famous people* Samuel Adams, Louis Brandeis, Emily Dickinson, Ralph Waldo Emerson, Robert Goddard, Nathaniel Hawthorne, Oliver Wendell Holmes, Winslow Homer, William James, John F Kennedy, Robert Kennedy, Robert Lowell, Paul Revere, Henry Thoreau, Daniel Webster *history* one of the original 13 states, it was first settled 1620 by the Pilgrims at Plymouth. After the ◊Boston Tea Party 1773, the American Revolution began at Lexington and Concord April 19, 1775, and the British evacuated Boston the following year. Massachusetts became a state 1788.

In the early 19th century the first large-scale factories were built here to turn out textiles. After World War II, high technology, sophisticated services, and tourism replaced textiles, footwear, and maritime activities as the mainspring of the economy.

mass spectrograph or *mass spectrometer* in physics, an apparatus for analyzing chemical composition. Positive ions (charged particles) of a substance are separated by an electromagnetic system, designed to focus particles of equal mass to a point where they can be detected. This permits accurate measurement of the relative concentrations of the various ionic masses present, particularly isotopes.

master file in computing, a file that is the main source of data for a particular application. Various methods of ◊file updating are used to ensure that the data in the master file is accurate and up to date.

Masters Edgar Lee 1869–1950. US poet. In *Spoon River Anthology* 1915, a collection of free-verse epitaphs, the people of a small town tell of their frustrated lives.

He published numerous other volumes of verse, novels, and biographies.

mastiff breed of powerful dog, usually fawn in color, that was originally bred in Britain for hunting purposes. It has a large head, wide-set eyes, and broad muzzle. It can grow up to 36 in/90 cm at the shoulder, and weigh 220 lb/100 kg.

mastodon any of an extinct family (Mastodontidae) of mammals of the elephant order (Proboscidea). They differed from elephants and mammoths in the structure of their grinding teeth. There were numerous species, among which the American mastodon *Mastodon americanum*, about 10 ft/3 m high, of the Pleistocene era, is well known. They were hunted by humans for food.

Mata Hari adopted name of Gertrud Margarete Zelle 1876–1917. Dutch courtesan, dancer, and probable spy. In World War I she had affairs with highly placed military and government officials on both sides and told Allied secrets to the Germans. She may have been a double agent, in the pay of both France and Germany. She was shot by the French on espionage charges.

materialism philosophical theory that there is nothing in existence over and above matter and matter in motion. Such a theory excludes the possibility of deities. It also sees mind as an attribute of the physical, denying idealist theories that see mind as something independent of body; for example, Descartes' theory of "thinking substance".

mathematics science of spatial and numerical relationships. The main divisions of *pure mathematics* include geometry, arithmetic, algebra, calculus, and trigonometry. Mechanics, statistics, numerical analysis, computing, the mathematical theories of astronomy, electricity, optics, thermodynamics, and atomic studies come under the heading of *applied mathematics*.

Mather Cotton 1663–1728. American theologian and writer. He was a Puritan minister in Boston, and wrote over 400 works of history, science, annals, and theology, including *Magnalia Christi Americana/The Great Works of Christ in America* 1702, a vast compendium of early New England history and experience. Mather appears to have supported the Salem witch-hunts. He wrote *Memorable Providences Relating to Witchcraft and Possession* 1689 and told of the witchcraft trials in *Wonders of the Invisible World* 1693.

Matisse Henri 1869–1954. French painter, sculptor, illustrator, and designer. He was one of the most original creative forces in early 20th-century art. Influenced by Impressionism, Post-Impressionism, and later Cubism, he developed a style characterized by surface pattern, strong, sinuous line, and brilliant color. Among his favored subjects were odalisques (women of the harem), bathers, and dancers; for example, *The Dance* 1910 (The Hermitage, St Petersburg). Later works include pure abstracts, as in his collages of colored paper shapes (*gouaches découpées*) and the designs 1949–51 for the decoration of a chapel for the Dominican convent in Vence, near Nice.

matriarchy form of social organization in which the mother is recognized as head of the family or group, with descent and kinship traced to the mother, and where women rule or dominate the group's organization.

matter in physics, anything that has mass and can be detected and measured. All matter is made up of ◊atoms, which in turn are made up of ◊elementary particles; it exists ordinarily as a solid, liquid, or gas. The history of science and philosophy is largely taken up with accounts of theories of matter, ranging from the hard "atoms" of Democritus to the "waves" of modern quantum theory.

Matterhorn (French *le Cervin*, Italian *il Cervino*) mountain peak in the Alps on the Swiss-Italian border; 14,690 ft/4,478 m.

Matthew, St Christian apostle and evangelist, the traditional author of the first Gospel. He is usually identified with Levi, who was a tax collector in the service of Herod Antipas, and was called by Jesus to be a disciple as he sat by the Lake of Galilee receiving customs dues. His emblem is a man with wings; feast day Sept 21.

Mauchly John William 1907–1980. US physicist and engineer who, in 1946, constructed the first general-purpose computer, the ENIAC, in collaboration with John Eckert. Their company was bought by Remington Rand 1950, and they built the UNIVAC 1 computer 1951 for the US census.

Maugham (William) Somerset 1874–1965. English writer. His work includes the novels *Of Human Bondage* 1915, *The Moon and Sixpence* 1919, and *Cakes and Ale* 1930; the short-story collections *The Trembling of a Leaf* 1921 and *Ashenden* 1928; and the plays *Lady Frederick* 1907 and *Our Betters* 1923.

Mau Mau Kenyan secret guerrilla movement 1952–60, an offshoot of the Kikuyu Central Association banned in World War II. Its aim was to end British colonial rule. This was achieved 1960 with the granting of Kenyan independence and the election of Jomo Kenyatta as Kenya's first prime minister.

Mauna Loa active volcano rising to a height of 13,678 ft/4,169 m in the Hawaii Volcanoes National Park on the island of Hawaii. It has numerous craters, including the second-largest active crater in the world.

Maundy Thursday in the Christian church, the Thursday before Easter. The ceremony of washing the feet of pilgrims on that day was instituted in commemoration of Jesus' washing of the apostles' feet and observed from the 4th century to 1754.

Maupassant Guy de 1850–1893. French author. He established a reputation with the short story "Boule de suif/Ball of Fat" 1880 and wrote some 300 short stories in all. His novels include *Une Vie/A Woman's Life* 1883 and *Bel-Ami* 1885. He was encouraged as a writer by Gustave ◊Flaubert.

Mauritania Islamic Republic of (*République Islamique de Mauritanie*) *area* 397,850 sq mi/1,030,700 sq km *capital* Nouakchott *towns and cities* port of Nouadhibou, Kaédi, Zouérate *physical* valley of river Senegal in S; remainder arid and flat *features* part of the Sahara Desert; dusty sirocco wind blows in March *head of state* Moaouia Ould Sidi Mohammed Taya from 1984 *head of government* Sidi Mohammed Ould Boubaker from 1993 *political system* emergent democratic republic *political parties* Democratic and Social Republican Party (DSRP), center-left, militarist; Union of Democratic Forces (UFD), center-left; Rally for Democracy and National Unity (RDNU), centrist; Mauritian Renewal Party (MPR), centrist; Umma, Islamic fundamentalist; Socialist and Democratic Popular Front Union (UDSP), left of center *exports* iron ore, fish, gypsum *currency* ouguiya *population* (1993 est) 2,200,000 (Arab-Berber 30%, black African 30%, Haratine—descendants of black slaves, who remained slaves until 1980—30%); growth rate 3% p.a. *life expectancy* men 46, women 50 *languages* French (official), Hasaniya Arabic, black African languages *religion* Sunni Muslim 99% *literacy* men 47%, women 21% *GNP* \$510 per head (1991) *chronology 1903* Became a French protectorate. *1960* Independence achieved from France, with Moktar Ould Daddah as president. *1975* Western Sahara ceded by Spain. Mauritania occupied the southern area and Morocco the north. Polisario Front formed in Sahara to resist

the occupation by Mauritania and Morocco. *1978* Daddah deposed in bloodless coup; replaced by Mohamed Khouna Ould Haidalla. Peace agreed with Polisario Front. *1981* Diplomatic relations with Morocco broken. *1984* Haidalla overthrown by Moaouia Ould Sidi Mohammed Taya. Polisario regime formally recognized. *1985* Relations with Morocco restored. *1989* Violent clashes between Mauritanians and Senegalese. *1991* Amnesty for political prisoners. Multiparty elections promised. Calls for resignation of President Taya. Political parties legalized; new multi-party constitution adopted. *1992* First multiparty elections won by ruling PRDS. Diplomatic relations with Senegal resumed.

Mauritius Republic of *area* 720 sq mi/1,865 sq km; the island of Rodrigues is part of Mauritius; there are several small island dependencies *capital* Port Louis *towns and cities* Beau Bassin-Rose Hill, Curepipe, Qatre Bornes *physical* mountainous, volcanic island surrounded by coral reefs *features* unusual wildlife includes flying fox and ostrich; it was the home of the dodo (extinct from about 1680) *head of state* Cassam Uteem from 1992 *head of government* Aneerood Jugnauth from 1982 *political system* liberal democratic republic *political parties* Mauritius Socialist Movement (MSM), moderate socialist-republican; Mauritius Labour Party (MLP), centrist, Hindu-oriented; Mauritius Social Democratic Party (PMSD), conservative, Francophile; Mauritius Militant Movement (MMM), Marxist-republican; Rodriguais People's Organization (OPR), left of center *exports* sugar, knitted goods, tea *currency* Mauritius rupee *population* (1993 est) 1,100,000, 68% of Indian origin; growth rate 1.5% p.a. *life expectancy* men 68, women 73 *languages* English (official), French, creole, Indian languages *religions* Hindu 51%, Christian 30%, Muslim 17% *literacy* 83% *GNP* \$3,000 per head (1992) *chronology 1814* Annexed to Britain by the Treaty of Paris. *1968* Independence achieved from Britain within the Commonwealth, with Seewoosagur Ramgoolam as prime minister. *1982* Aneerood Jugnauth became prime minister. *1983* Jugnauth formed the new MSM. Ramgoolam appointed governor-general. Jugnauth formed a new coalition government. *1985* Ramgoolam died; succeeded by Veersamy Ringadoo. *1987* Jugnauth's coalition reelected. *1990* Attempt to create a republic failed. *1991* Jugnauth's ruling MSM–MMM–OPR coalition won general election; pledge to secure republican status by 1992. *1992* Mauritius became a republic while remaining a member of the Commonwealth. Cassam Uteem elected president.

max. abbreviation for *maximum.*

maxim saying or proverb that gives moral guidance or a piece of advice on the way to live ("First come, first served"; "Better late than never").

Maximilian I 1459–1519. Holy Roman emperor from 1493, the son of Emperor Frederick III. He had acquired the Low Countries through his marriage to Mary of Burgundy 1477.

Maxwell (Ian) Robert (born Jan Ludvik Hoch) 1923–1991. Czech-born British publishing and newspaper proprietor who owned several UK national newspapers, including the *Daily Mirror*, the Macmillan Publishing Company, and the New York *Daily News*. At the time of his death by drowning the Maxwell domain carried debts of some \$3.9 billion.

Maxwell James Clerk 1831–1879. Scottish physicist. His main achievement was in the understanding of

◊electromagnetic waves: *Maxwell's equations* bring together electricity, magnetism, and light in one set of relations. He contributed to every branch of physical science—studying gases, optics, and the sensation of color. His theoretical work in magnetism prepared the way for wireless telegraphy and telephony.

Maya member of a group of Central American Indians who lived in agricultural villages in and around the Yucatán Peninsula and Guatemalan highlands from at least 3000 BC, and who developed a civilization of city-states that flourished from about AD 300 until about 900. Mayan sovereignty was maintained until late in the Spanish Conquest 1560s in some areas. Today they are Roman Catholic, live in farming and fishing villages, as well as the cities of Yucatán, Guatemala, Belize, and W Honduras. Many still speak Maya, a member of the Totonac-Mayan language family, as well as Spanish.

May Day first day of May. In many countries it is a national vacation in honor of labor; see also ◊Labor Day.

Mayflower the ship in which the ◊Pilgrims sailed 1620 from Plymouth, England, to found Plymouth plantation and Plymouth colony in present-day Massachusetts.

The *Mayflower* was one of two ships scheduled for departure in 1620. The second ship, the *Speedwell*, was deemed unseaworthy, so 102 people were crowded into the 90-foot *Mayflower*, which was bound for Virginia. The Mayflower Compact was drafted to establish self-rule for the Plymouth colony and to protect the rights of all the settlers.

mayfly any insect of the order Ephemerida (Greek *ephemeros* "lasting for a day", an allusion to the very brief life of the adult). The larval stage, which can last a year or more, is passed in water, the adult form developing gradually from the nymph through successive molts. The adult has transparent, net-veined wings.

Mayo county of the Republic of Ireland, in the province of Connacht; county town Castlebar; area 2,084 sq mi/5,400 sq km; population (1991) 110,700. It has wild Atlantic coast scenery. Features include Lough Conn; Achill Island; Croagh Patrick 2,510 ft/765 m, the mountain where St Patrick spent the 40 days of Lent in 441, climbed by pilgrims on the last Sunday of July each year; and the village of Knock, where two women claimed a vision of the Virgin with two saints 1879, now a site of pilgrimage. Industries include sheep and cattle farming, salmon fishing, potatoes, oats, and pigs.

mayor title of head of local administration for a town or city. Powers vary widely, although generally mayors oversee financial issues, local education, public safety, planning and zoning, taxation, and other aspects of municipal government.

Mays Willie (Howard Jr) 1931– . US baseball player who played with the New York (later San Francisco) Giants 1951–72 and the New York Mets 1973. He hit 660 career home runs, third best in baseball history, and was also an outstanding fielder and runner. He was the National League's Most Valuable Player 1954 and 1965.

Born in Westfield, Alabama, Mays was elected to the Baseball Hall of Fame 1979.

mayweed any of several species of the daisy family Compositae native to Europe and Asia, and naturalized elsewhere, including the European dog fennel or stinking daisy *Anthemis cotula*, naturalized in North America, and Eurasian pineapple mayweed *Matricaria matricarioides*. All have finely divided leaves.

Mazarin Jules 1602–1661. French politician who succeeded Richelieu as chief minister of France 1642. His attack on the power of the nobility led to the ◊Fronde and his temporary exile, but his diplomacy achieved a successful conclusion to the Thirty Years' War, and, in alliance with Oliver Cromwell during the British protectorate, he gained victory over Spain.

mazurka any of a family of traditional Polish dances from the 16th century, characterized by foot-stamping and heel-clicking, together with a turning movement. During the 18th and 19th centuries, it spread throughout Europe and in art music was made famous by Chopin's approximately 60 works in the genre.

Mazzini Giuseppe 1805–1872. Italian nationalist. He was a member of the revolutionary society, the Carbonari, and founded in exile the nationalist movement Giovane Italia (Young Italy) 1832. Returning to Italy on the outbreak of the 1848 revolution, he headed a republican government established in Rome, but was forced into exile again on its overthrow 1849. He acted as a focus for the movement for Italian unity (see ◊Risorgimento).

MBE abbreviation for *Member (of the Order) of the British Empire*, an honor first awarded 1917.

MD abbreviation for *Doctor of Medicine*.

ME abbreviation for *myalgic encephalitis*, a debilitating condition also known as ◊chronic fatigue syndrome.

mead alcoholic drink made from honey and water fermented with yeast, often with added spices. It was known in ancient times and was drunk by the Greeks, Britons, and Norse.

Mead Margaret 1901–1978. US anthropologist who popularized cultural relativity and challenged the conventions of Western society with *Coming of Age in Samoa* 1928 and subsequent works. Her fieldwork was later criticized. She was a popular speaker on civil liberties, ecological sanity, feminism, and population control.

Mead studied at Barnard College 1923 and Columbia University 1929. She also wrote *And Keep Your Powder Dry* 1942, about the US national character, and *Soviet Attitudes Toward Authority* 1951.

mean in mathematics, a measure of the average of a number of terms or quantities. The simple *arithmetic mean* is the average value of the quantities, that is, the sum of the quantities divided by their number. The *weighted mean* takes into account the frequency of the terms that are summed; it is calculated by multiplying each term by the number of times it occurs, summing the results and dividing this total by the total number of occurrences. The *geometric mean* of n quantities is the nth root of their product. In statistics, it is a measure of central tendency of a set of data.

measles acute virus disease (rubeola), spread by airborne infection.

Symptoms are fever, severe catarrh, small spots inside the mouth, and a raised, blotchy red rash appearing for about a week after two weeks' incubation. Prevention is by vaccination.

Meath county of the Republic of Ireland, in the province of Leinster; county town Trim; area 903 sq mi/2,340 sq km; population (1991) 105,600. Tara Hill, 509 ft/155 m high, was the site of a palace and coronation place of many kings of Ireland (abandoned in the 6th century) and St Patrick preached here. Sheep, cattle, oats, and potatoes are produced.

Mecca (Arabic *Makkah*) city in Saudi Arabia and, as birthplace of Mohammed, the holiest city of the Islamic world; population (1974) 367,000. In the center of Mecca is the Great Mosque, in the courtyard of which is the Kaaba, the sacred shrine containing the black stone believed to have been given to Abraham by the angel Gabriel.

mechanics branch of physics dealing with the motions of bodies and the forces causing these motions, and also with the forces acting on bodies in equilibrium. It is usually divided into ◊dynamics and ◊statics.

Meciar Vladimir 1942– . Slovak politician, prime minister of the Slovak Republic Jan 1993–March 1994 and again from Oct 1994. As leader of the Movement for a Democratic Slovakia (HZDS) from 1990, he sought an independent Slovak state. Under the federal system, Meciar became prime minister of the Slovak Republic 1990 and the new state's first prime minister Jan 1993. He resigned March 1994 after a no-confidence vote in parliament, but was returned as premier Oct 1994 following a general election victory.

Medawar Peter (Brian) 1915–1987. Brazilian-born British immunologist who, with Macfarlane Burnet, discovered that the body's resistance to grafted tissue is undeveloped in the newborn child, and studied the way it is acquired.

He shared the 1960 Nobel Prize for Medicine with Burnet (1899–1985), an Australian who also worked on acquired immunological tolerance.

Medea in Greek mythology, the sorceress daughter of the king of Colchis. When ◊Jason reached Colchis, she fell in love with him, helped him acquire the ◊Golden Fleece, and they fled together. When Jason later married Creusa, daughter of the king of Corinth, Medea killed his bride with the gift of a poisoned garment, and then killed her own two children by Jason.

Medellín industrial city (textiles, chemicals, engineering, coffee) in the Central Cordillera, Colombia, 5,048 ft/1,538 m above sea level; population (1985) 2,069,000. It is the second city of Colombia, and its drug capital, with 7,000 violent deaths in 1990.

median in mathematics and statistics, the middle number of an ordered group of numbers. If there is no middle number (because there is an even number of terms), the median is the ◊mean (average) of the two middle numbers. For example, the median of the group 2, 3, 7, 11, 12 is 7; that of 3, 4, 7, 9, 11, 13 is 8 (the average of 7 and 9).

In geometry, the term refers to a line from the vertex of a triangle to the midpoint of the opposite side.

Medici noble family of Florence, the city's rulers from 1434 until they died out 1737. Family members included ◊Catherine de' Medici, Pope ◊Leo X, Pope Clement VII, and ◊Marie de' Medici.

Medici Cosimo de' 1389–1464. Italian politician and banker. Regarded as the model for Machiavelli's *The Prince*, he dominated the government of Florence from 1434 and was a patron of the arts. He was succeeded by his inept son *Piero de' Medici* (1416–1469).

Medici Lorenzo de', *the Magnificent* 1449–1492. Italian politician, ruler of Florence from 1469. He was also a poet and a generous patron of the arts.

medicine the practice of preventing, diagnosing, and treating disease, both physical and mental; also any

substance used in the treatment of disease. The basis of medicine is anatomy (the structure and form of the body) and physiology (the study of the body's functions).

medicine, alternative forms of medical treatment that do not use synthetic drugs or surgery in response to the symptoms of a disease, but aim to treat the patient as a whole (◊holism). The emphasis is on maintaining health (with diet and exercise) and on dealing with the underlying causes rather than just the symptoms of illness. It may involve the use of herbal remedies and techniques like ◊acupuncture, ◊homeopathy, and ◊chiropractic.

Medina (Arabic *Madinah*) Saudi Arabian city, about 220 mi/355 km N of Mecca; population (1986 est) 500,000. It is the second holiest city in the Islamic world, and is believed to contain the tomb of Mohammed. It produces grain and fruit.

meditation act of spiritual contemplation, practiced by members of many religions or as a secular exercise. It is central practice in Buddhism. The Sanskrit term is *dhyana*. See also ◊transcendental meditation (TM).

Mediterranean Sea inland sea separating Europe from N Africa, with Asia to the E; extreme length 2,300 mi/ 3,700 km; area 1,145,000 sq mi/2,966,000 sq km. It is linked to the Atlantic Ocean (at the Strait of Gibraltar), Red Sea, and Indian Ocean (by the Suez Canal), Black Sea (at the Dardanelles and Sea of Marmara). The main subdivisions are the Adriatic, Aegean, Ionian, and Tyrrhenian seas. It is highly polluted.

Medusa in Greek mythology, a mortal woman who was transformed into a ◊Gorgon. Medusa was slain by Perseus; the winged horse ◊Pegasus was supposed to have sprung from her blood. Her head was so hideous—even in death—that any beholder was turned to stone.

mega- prefix denoting multiplication by a million. For example, a megawatt (MW) is equivalent to a million watts.

megabyte (Mb) in computing, a unit of memory equal to 1,024 ◊kilobytes. It is sometimes used, less precisely, to mean 1 million bytes.

megalith prehistoric stone monument of the late Neolithic or early Bronze Age. Megaliths include single, large uprights (menhirs); rows; circles, generally with a central "altar stone" (for example Stonehenge); and the remains of burial chambers with the covering earth removed, looking like a hut (dolmens).

Mehmet Ali 1769–1849. Pasha (governor) of Egypt from 1805, and founder of the dynasty that ruled until 1953. An Albanian in the Ottoman service, he had originally been sent to Egypt to fight the French. As pasha, he established a European-style army and navy, fought his Turkish overlord 1831 and 1839, and conquered Sudan.

Mehta Zubin 1936– . Indian-born US conductor. He has been music director of the New York Philharmonic from 1978. He specializes in robust, polished interpretations of 19th-and 20th-century repertoire, including contemporary US composers.

He was appointed music director of the Montreal Symphony 1961–67 and of the Los Angeles Philharmonic 1962–78, thus becoming the first person to direct two North American symphony orchestras simultaneously.

Meir Golda 1898–1978. Israeli Labour (*Mapai*) politician. Born in Russia, she emigrated to the US 1906, and in 1921 went to Palestine. She was foreign minister 1956–66 and prime minister 1969–74.

Criticism of the Israelis' lack of preparation for the 1973 Arab-Israeli War led to election losses for Labour and, unable to form a government, she resigned.

Mekong river rising as the Za Qu in Tibet and flowing to the South China Sea, through a vast delta (about 77,000 sq mi/200,000 sq km), through a vast delta (about km. It is being developed for irrigation and hydroelectricity by Cambodia, Laos, Thailand, and Vietnam.

Melanesia islands in the SW Pacific between Micronesia to the N and Polynesia to the E, embracing all the islands from the New Britain archipelago to Fiji.

melanoma highly malignant tumor of the melanin-forming cells (melanocytes) of the skin. It develops from an existing mole in up to two thirds of cases, but can also arise in the eye or mucous membranes.

Malignant melanoma is the most dangerous of the skin cancers; it is associated with brief but excessive exposure to sunlight. It is easily treated if caught early but deadly once it has spread. There is a genetic factor in some cases.

Melbourne capital of Victoria, Australia, near the mouth of the river Yarra; population (1990) 3,080,000. Industries include engineering, shipbuilding, electronics, chemicals, food processing, clothing, and textiles.

Mellon Andrew William 1855–1937. US financier born in Pittsburgh who donated his art collection to found the National Gallery of Art, Washington, DC, in 1937. His son, *Paul Mellon* (1907–) was its president 1963–79. He funded Yale University's Center for British Art, New Haven, Connecticut, and donated major works of art to both collections.

melodrama play or film with romantic and sensational plot elements, often concerned with crime, vice, or catastrophe. Originally a melodrama was a play with an accompaniment of music contributing to the dramatic effect. It became popular in the late 18th century, due to works like *Pygmalion* 1770, with pieces written by the French philosopher Jean-Jacques Rousseau. By the end of the 19th century, melodrama had become a popular genre of stage play.

melon any of several large, juicy (95% water), thick-skinned fruits of trailing plants of the gourd family Cucurbitaceae. The muskmelon *Cucumis melo* and the large red watermelon *Citrullus vulgaris* are two of the many edible varieties.

meltdown the melting of the core of a nuclear reactor, due to overheating.

To prevent such accidents all reactors have equipment intended to flood the core with water in an emergency. The reactor is housed in a strong containment vessel, designed to prevent radiation escaping into the atmosphere. The result of a meltdown is an area radioactively contaminated for 25,000 years or more.

melting point temperature at which a substance melts, or changes from solid to liquid form. A pure substance under standard conditions of pressure (usually one atmosphere) has a definite melting point. If heat is supplied to a solid at its melting point, the temperature does not change until the melting process is complete. The melting point of ice is 32°F or 0°C.

Melville Herman 1819–1891. US writer. His novel *Moby-Dick* 1851 was inspired by his whaling experiences in the South Seas and is considered to be one of the masterpieces of American literature. These experiences were also the basis for earlier fiction, such as the adventure narratives of *Typee* 1846 and *Omoo* 1847. *Billy Budd, Sailor* was completed just before his death and published 1924. He died in obscurity. *Moby-Dick* was filmed by John Huston in 1956. *Billy Budd* was the basis of an opera by Benjamin Britten 1951, which was made into a film 1962.

membrane in living things, a continuous layer, made up principally of fat molecules, that encloses a ◊cell or organelles within a cell. Certain small molecules can pass through the cell membrane, but most must enter or leave the cell via channels in the membrane made up of special proteins. The Golgi apparatus within the cell is thought to produce certain membranes.

Memling (or *Memlinc*) Hans *c.* 1430–1494. Flemish painter. He was born near Frankfurt-am-Main, Germany, but worked in Bruges. He painted religious subjects and portraits. *The Donne Triptych* about 1480 (National Gallery, London) is one of his best-known works.

memory in computing, the part of a system used to store data and programs either permanently or temporarily. There are two main types: immediate access memory and backing storage. Memory capacity is measured in ◊bytes or, more conveniently, in kilobytes (units of 1,024 bytes) or megabytes (units of 1,024 kilobytes).

Memphis ruined city beside the Nile, 12 mi/19 km S of Cairo, Egypt. Once the center of the worship of Ptah, it was the earliest capital of a united Egypt under King Menes about 3200 BC, but was superseded by Thebes under the new empire 1570 BC.

Memphis industrial port city (pharmaceuticals, food processing, cotton, timber, tobacco) on the Mississippi River, in Tennessee; population (1990) 610,300. The French built a fort here 1739, but Memphis was not founded until 1819. Its musical history includes Beale Street, home of the blues composer W C Handy, and Graceland, home of Elvis Presley; its recording studios and record companies (Sun 1953–68, Stax 1960–75) made it a focus of the music industry.

Mencken H(enry) L(ouis) 1880–1956. US essayist and critic. He was known as "the sage of Baltimore". His unconventionally phrased, satiric contributions to the periodicals *The Smart Set* and *American Mercury* (both of which he edited) aroused controversy. His critical reviews and essays were gathered in *Prejudices* 1919–27, comprising six volumes. His book, *The American Language* 1918, is often revised.

Mendeleyev Dmitri Ivanovich 1834–1907. Russian chemist who framed the periodic law in chemistry 1869, which states that the chemical properties of the elements depend on their atomic weights. This law is the basis of the ◊periodic table of the elements, in which the elements are arranged by atomic number and organized by their related groups.

Mendelism in genetics, the theory of inheritance originally outlined by Austrian biologist Gregor Mendel. He suggested that, in sexually reproducing species, all characteristics are inherited through indivisible "factors" (now identified with ◊genes) contributed by each parent to its offspring.

Mendelssohn (-Bartholdy) (Jakob Ludwig) Felix 1809–1847. German composer, also a pianist and conductor. His music has a lightness and charm of Classical music, applied to Romantic and descriptive subjects. Among his best-known works are *A Midsummer Night's Dream* 1827; the *Fingal's Cave* overture 1832; and five symphonies, which include the "Reformation" 1830, the "Italian" 1833, and the "Scottish" 1842. He was instrumental in promoting the revival of interest in J S Bach's music.

Menem Carlos (Saul) 1935– . Argentine politician, president from 1989; leader of the Peronist (Justicialist Party) movement. As president, he sent two warships to the Gulf to assist the US against Iraq in the 1992 Gulf War (the only Latin American country to offer support to the US).

menhir prehistoric standing stone; see ◊megalith.

meningitis inflammation of the meninges (membranes) surrounding the brain, caused by bacterial or viral infection. Bacterial meningitis, though treatable by antibiotics, is the more serious threat.

Mennonite member of a Protestant Christian sect, originating as part of the ◊Anabaptist movement in Zürich, Switzerland, 1523. Members refuse to hold civil office or do military service, and reject infant baptism. They were named Mennonites after Menno Simons (1496–1559), leader of a group in Holland.

Some Swiss and German Mennonites settled in Germantown, Pennsylvania, in 1683. From there they eventually spread to the Midwest and Canada. Additional groups went to the Great Plains. Of the 600,000 Mennonites in the world, some 250,000 are in the US.

menopause in women, the cessation of reproductive ability, characterized by menstruation (see ◊menstrual cycle) becoming irregular and eventually ceasing. The onset is at about the age of 50, but varies greatly. Menopause is usually uneventful, but some women suffer from complications such as flushing, excessive bleeding, and nervous disorders. Since the 1950s, ◊hormone-replacement therapy (HRT), using ◊estrogen alone or with progestogen, a synthetic form of ◊progesterone, has been developed to counteract such effects.

Menshevik member of the minority of the Russian Social Democratic Party, who split from the ◊Bolsheviks 1903. The Mensheviks believed in a large, loosely organized party and that, before socialist revolution could occur in Russia, capitalist society had to develop further. During the Russian Revolution they had limited power and set up a government in Georgia, but were suppressed 1922.

mens sana in corpore sano (Latin) a healthy mind in a healthy body.

menstrual cycle cycle that occurs in female mammals of reproductive age, in which the body is prepared for pregnancy. At the beginning of the cycle, a Graafian (egg) follicle develops in the ovary, and the inner wall of the uterus forms a soft spongy lining. The egg is released from the ovary, and the uterus lining (endometrium) becomes vascularized (filled with blood vessels). If fertilization does not occur, the corpus luteum (remains of the Graafian follicle) degenerates, and the uterine lining breaks down, and is shed. This is what causes the loss of blood that marks menstruation. The cycle then begins again. Human menstruation takes place from puberty to menopause, except during pregnancy, occurring about every 28 days.

mental disability arrested or incomplete development of mental capacities. It can be very mild, but in more severe cases is associated with social problems and difficulties in living independently. A person may be

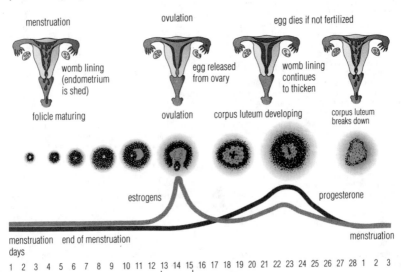

menstrual cycle From puberty to the menopause, most women produce a regular rhythm of hormones that stimulate the various stages of the menstrual cycle. The change in hormone levels may cause premenstrual tension.

born with a mental disability (for example, ◊Down's syndrome) or may acquire it through brain damage. There are between 90 and 130 million people in the world suffering such disabilities.

mental illness disordered functioning of the mind. Since normal working cannot easily be defined, the borderline between mild mental illness and normality is a matter of opinion (not to be confused with normative behavior). It is broadly divided into two categories: ◊neurosis, in which the patient remains in touch with reality; and ◊psychosis, in which perception, thought and belief are disordered.

menu in computing, a list of options, displayed on screen, from which the user may make a choice—for example, the choice of services offered to the customer by a bank cash dispenser: withdrawal, deposit, balance, or statement.

Menuhin Yehudi 1916– . US-born violinist and conductor. His solo repertoire extends from Vivaldi to Enescu. He recorded the Elgar *Violin Concerto* 1932 with the composer conducting, and commissioned the *Sonata* for violin solo 1944 from an ailing Bartók. He has appeared in concert with sitar virtuoso Ravi Shankar, and with jazz violinist Stephane Grappelli.

mercantilism economic theory, held in the 16th–18th centuries, that a nation's wealth (in the form of bullion or treasure) was the key to its prosperity. To this end, foreign trade should be regulated to create a surplus of exports over imports, and the state should intervene where necessary (for example, subsidizing exports and taxing imports). The bullion theory of wealth was demolished by Adam ◊Smith in Book IV of *The Wealth of Nations* 1776.

Mercator Gerardus 1512–1594. Latinized form of the name of the Flemish map-maker Gerhard Kremer. He devised the first modern atlas, showing *Mercator's projection* in which the parallels and meridians on maps are drawn uniformly at 90°. It is often used for navigational charts, because compass courses can be drawn as straight lines, but the true area of countries is increasingly distorted the further north or south they are from the equator. For other types, see ◊map projection.

mercenary soldier hired by the army of another country or by a private army. Mercenary military service originated in the 14th century, when cash payment on a regular basis was the only means of guaranteeing soldiers' loyalty. In the 20th century mercenaries have been common in wars and guerrilla activity in Asia, Africa, and Latin America.

merchant marine the passenger and cargo ships of a country. Most are owned by private companies. To avoid strict regulations on safety, union rules on crew wages, and so on, many ships are today registered under "flags of convenience", that is, flags of countries that do not have such rules.

mercury or *quicksilver* heavy, silver-gray, metallic element, symbol Hg (from Latin *hydrargyrum*), atomic number 80, atomic weight 200.59. It is a dense, mobile liquid with a low melting point (−37.96°F/−38.87°C). Its chief source is the mineral cinnabar, HgS, but it sometimes occurs in nature as a free metal.

Mercury in astronomy, the closest planet to the Sun, at an average distance of 36 million mi/58 million km. Its diameter is 3,030 mi/4,880 km, its mass 0.056 that of Earth. Mercury orbits the Sun every 88 days, and spins on its axis every 59 days. On its sunward side the surface temperature reaches over 752°F/400°C, but on the "night" side it falls to−274°F/−170°C. Mercury has an atmosphere with minute traces of argon and helium. In 1974 the US space probe *Mariner 10* discovered that its surface is cratered by meteorite impacts. Mercury has no moons.

Mercury in Roman mythology, a god, identified with the Greek ◊Hermes, and like him represented with winged sandals and a winged staff entwined with snakes. He was the messenger of the gods, and was associated particularly with commerce.

merganser any of several diving ducks of the genus *Mergus* with long, serrated bills for catching fish, including the common merganser or goosander *M. merganser* and the red-breasted merganser *M. serrator*. Most have crested heads. They are widely distributed in the northern hemisphere.

meridian half a great circle drawn on the Earth's surface passing through both poles and thus through all places with the same longitude. Terrestrial longitudes are usually measured from the Greenwich Meridian.

merino breed of sheep. Its close-set, silky wool is highly valued. The merino, originally from Spain, is now found all over the world, and is the breed on which the Australian wool industry is built.

Merit, Order of British order of chivalry, founded on the lines of an order of ◊knighthood.

merlin small ◊falcon *Falco columbarius* of Eurasia and North America, where it is also called *pigeon hawk*. The male, 10 in/26 cm long, has a gray-blue back and reddish brown barred front; the female, 13 in/32 cm long, is brown with streaks.

Merlin legendary magician and counselor to King ◊Arthur. Welsh bardic literature has a cycle of poems attributed to him, and he may have been a real person.

mermaid mythical sea creature (the male is a *merman*), having a human head and torso and a fish's tail. The dugong and seal are among suggested origins for the idea.

Merovingian dynasty Frankish dynasty, named for its founder, *Merovech* (5th century AD). His descendants ruled France from the time of Clovis (481–511) to 751.

Mersey river in NW England; length 70 mi/112 km. Formed by the confluence of the Goyt and Etherow rivers, it flows W to join the Irish Sea at Liverpool Bay. In 1990 the British government announced plans to build a 5,907 ft/1,800 m barrage across the Mersey estuary to generate electricity from tides.

Merseyside metropolitan county of NW England, created 1974; in 1986, most of the functions of the former county council were transferred to metropolitan district councils *area* 251 sq mi/650 sq km *towns and cities* Liverpool (administrative headquarters), Bootle, Birkenhead, St Helens, Wallasey, Southport *features* river Mersey; Merseyside Innovation Center (MIC), linked with Liverpool University and Polytechnic; Prescot Museum of clock-and watch-making; Speke Hall (Tudor), and Croxteth Hall and Country Park (a working country estate open to the public) *industries* chemicals, electrical goods, vehicles *population* (1991) 1,403,600 *famous people* George Stubbs, William Ewart Gladstone, the Beatles.

Mesolithic the Middle Stone Age developmental stage of human technology and of ◊prehistory.

meson in physics, an unstable subatomic particle made up of two indivisible elementary particles called ◊quarks. It has a mass intermediate between that of the electron and that of the proton, is found in cosmic radiation, and is emitted by nuclei under bombardment by very high-energy particles.

Mesopotamia the land between the Tigris and Euphrates rivers, now part of Iraq. The civilizations of Sumer and Babylon flourished here. Sumer (3500 BC) may have been the earliest urban civilization.

mesosphere layer in the Earth's ◊atmosphere above the stratosphere and below the thermosphere. It lies between about 31 mi/50 km and 50 mi/80 km above the ground.

Mesozoic era of geological time 245–65 million years ago, consisting of the Triassic, Jurassic, and Cretaceous periods. At the beginning of the era, the continents were joined together as Pangaea; dinosaurs and other giant reptiles dominated the sea and air; and ferns, horsetails, and cycads thrived in a warm climate worldwide. By the end of the Mesozoic era, the continents had begun to assume their present positions, flowering plants were dominant, and many of the large reptiles and marine fauna were becoming extinct.

Messiaen Olivier 1908–1992. French composer, organist, and teacher. His music is mystical in character, vividly colored, and incorporates transcriptions of birdsong. Among his works are the *Quartet for the End of Time* 1941, the large-scale *Turangalîla Symphony* 1949, and solo organ and piano pieces. As a teacher at the Paris Conservatoire from 1942, he influenced three generations of composers.

Messiah in Judaism and Christianity, the savior or deliverer. Jews from the time of the Old Testament exile in Babylon have looked forward to the coming of the Messiah. Christians believe that the Messiah came in the person of ◊Jesus, and hence called him the Christ.

Messina, Strait of channel in the central Mediterranean separating Sicily from mainland Italy; in Greek legend a monster (Charybdis), who devoured ships, lived in the whirlpool on the Sicilian side, and another (Scylla), who devoured sailors, in the rock on the Italian side. The classical hero Odysseus passed safely between them.

metabolism the chemical processes of living organisms enabling them to grow and to function. It involves a constant alternation of building up (*anabolism*) and breaking down (*catabolism*). For example, green plants build up complex organic substances from water, carbon dioxide, and mineral salts (photosynthesis); by digestion animals partially break down complex organic substances, ingested as food, and subsequently resynthesize them for use in their own bodies.

metal any of a class of chemical elements with certain chemical characteristics and physical properties: they are good conductors of heat and electricity; opaque but reflect light well; malleable, which enables them to be coldworked and rolled into sheets; and ductile, which permits them to be drawn into thin wires.

metal detector electronic device for detecting metal, usually below ground, developed from the wartime mine detector. In the head of the metal detector is a coil, which is part of an electronic circuit. The presence of metal causes the frequency of the signal in the circuit to change, setting up an audible note in the headphones worn by the user.

metallic bond the force of attraction operating in a metal that holds the atoms together. In the metal the ◊valence electrons are able to move within the crystal and these electrons are said to be delocalized. Their movement creates short-lived, positively charged ions. The electrostatic attraction between the delocalized electrons and the ceaselessly forming ions constitutes the metallic bond.

metallurgy the science and technology of producing metals, which includes extraction, alloying, and hardening. Extractive, or *process, metallurgy* is concerned with the extraction of metals from their ◊ores and refining and adapting them for use. *Physical metallurgy* is concerned with their properties and application. *Metallography* establishes the microscopic structures that contribute to hardness, ductility, and strength.

metamorphic rock rock altered in structure and composition by pressure, heat, or chemically active fluids after original formation. (If heat is sufficient to melt the original rock, technically it becomes an igneous rock upon cooling.) The term was coined in 1833 by Scottish geologist Charles Lyell (1797–1875).

metamorphosis period during the life cycle of many invertebrates, most amphibians, and some fish, during which the individual's body changes from one form to another through a major reconstitution of its tissues. For example, adult frogs are produced by metamorphosis from tadpoles, and butterflies are produced from caterpillars following metamorphosis within a pupa.

In classical thought and literature, metamorphosis is the transformation of a living being into another shape, either living or inanimate (for example Niobe). The Roman poet ◊Ovid wrote about this theme.

metaphor figure of speech using an analogy or close comparison between two things that are not normally treated as if they had anything in common. Metaphor is a common means of extending the uses and references of words. See also ◊simile.

metaphysical poets group of early 17th-century English poets whose work is characterized by ingenious, highly intricate wordplay and unlikely or paradoxical imagery. Among the exponents of this genre are John Donne, George Herbert, Andrew Marvell, Richard Crashaw, and Henry Vaughan.

metaphysics branch of philosophy that deals with first principles, in particular "being" (ontology) and "knowing" (◊epistemology), and that is concerned with the ultimate nature of reality. It has been maintained that no certain knowledge of metaphysical questions is possible.

meteor flash of light in the sky, popularly known as a *shooting* or *falling star*, caused by a particle of dust, a *meteoroid*, entering the atmosphere at speeds up to 45 mps/70 kps and burning up by friction at a height of around 60 mi/100 km. On any clear night, several *sporadic meteors* can be seen each hour.

meteorite piece of rock or metal from space that reaches the surface of the Earth, Moon, or other body. Most meteorites are thought to be fragments from asteroids, although some may be pieces from the heads of comets. Most are stony, although some are made of iron and a few have a mixed rock-iron composition.

Thousands of meteorites hit the Earth each year, but most fall in the sea or in remote areas and are never recovered. The largest known meteorite is one composed of iron, weighing 66 tons, which lies where it fell in prehistoric times at Grootfontein, Namibia. Meteor Crater in Arizona, about 4,000 ft/1,200 m in diameter and 650 ft/200 m deep, is the site of a meteorite impact about 50,000 years ago.

meteorology scientific observation and study of the ◊atmosphere, so that weather can be accurately forecast. Data from meteorological stations and weather satellites are collated by computer at central agencies, and forecast and weather maps based on current readings are issued at regular intervals. Modern analysis can give useful forecasts for up to six days ahead.

meter SI unit (symbol m) of length, equivalent to 1.093 yards or 39.37 inches. It is defined by scientists as the length of the path traveled by light in a vacuum during a time interval of 1/299,792,458 of a second.

meter in poetry, the recurring pattern of stressed and unstressed syllables in a line of verse. The unit of meter is a foot. Meter is classified by the number of feet to a line: a minimum of two and a maximum of eight. A line of two feet is a dimeter. They are then named, in order, trimeter, tetrameter, pentameter, hexameter, heptameter, and octameter.

meter in music, the timescale represented by the beat. Meter is regular, whereas rhythm is irregular.

methanal (common name *formaldehyde*) HCHO gas at ordinary temperatures, condensing to a liquid at –5.8°F/–21°C. It has a powerful, penetrating smell. Dissolved in water, it is used as a biological preservative. It is used in the manufacture of plastics, dyes, foam (for example urea-formaldehyde foam, used in insulation), and in medicine.

methane CH_4 the simplest hydrocarbon of the paraffin series. Colorless, odorless, and lighter than air, it burns with a bluish flame and explodes when mixed with air or oxygen. It is the chief constituent of natural gas and also occurs in the explosive firedamp of coal mines. Methane emitted by rotting vegetation forms marsh gas, which may ignite by spontaneous combustion to produce the pale flame seen over marshland and known as will-o'-the-wisp.

Methodism evangelical Protestant Christian movement that was founded by John ◊Wesley 1739 within the Church of England, but became a separate body 1795. The Methodist Episcopal Church was founded in the US 1784. There are over 50 million Methodists worldwide.

The itinerant, open-air preaching of John and Charles Wesley and George Whitefield drew immense crowds. The Methodist emphasis on emotion and the conversion experience proved equally popular in America, where the Wesleys went to preach in 1735. As the movement grew there during the Great Awakening, Wesley encouraged the formation of an independent American Methodist Church. There are now more than 20 separate Methodist groups in the US. The largest, the Methodist Church, was formed through the merger of various Methodist groups in 1938 and 1968.

methylated spirit alcohol that has been rendered undrinkable, and is used for industrial purposes, as a fuel for spirit burners or a solvent.

metric system system of weights and measures developed in France in the 18th century and recognized by other countries in the 19th century.

In 1960 an international conference on weights and measures recommended the universal adoption of a revised International System (Système International d'Unités, or SI), with seven prescribed "base units": the meter (m) for length, kilogram (kg) for mass, second (s) for time, ampere (A) for electric current, kelvin (K) for thermodynamic temperature, candela (cd) for luminous intensity, and mole (mol) for quantity of matter.

The metric system was made legal for most purposes in the US in the 19th century. A Metric Act was passed in the US in 1975 to promote the use, without compulsion, of the metric system.

metric ton or tonne unit of mass (symbol t or T) equal to 2,205 lb/1,000 kg.

metropolitan county in England, a group of six counties established under the Local Government Act 1972 in the largest urban areas outside London: Tyne and Wear, South Yorkshire, Merseyside, West Midlands, Greater Manchester, and West Yorkshire. Their elected assemblies (county councils) were abolished 1986 when most of their responsibilities reverted to the metropolitan district councils.

Metropolitan Opera Company foremost opera company in the US, founded 1883 in New York City. The Metropolitan Opera House (opened 1883) was demolished 1966, and the company moved to the new Metropolitan Opera House at the Lincoln Center.

Highlights of its history include: the "Golden Age" 1898–1903, when artists from all over the world appeared at the "Met"; the 1903 New York debut of Enrico Caruso; the 1955 appearance of Marian Anderson, and the first live telecast of a Metropolitan Opera production, Puccini's *La Bohème/Bohemian Life*, featuring Renata Scotto and Luciano Pavarotti, 1977.

Metternich Klemens (Wenzel Lothar), Prince von Metternich 1773–1859. Austrian politician, the leading figure in European diplomacy after the fall of Napoleon. As foreign minister 1809–48 (as well as chancellor from 1821), he tried to maintain the balance of power in Europe, supporting monarchy and repressing liberalism.

Mexican War war between the US and Mexico 1846–48, begun in territory disputed between Texas (annexed by the US 1845 but claimed by Mexico) and Mexico. It began when General Zachary Taylor invaded New Mexico after efforts to purchase what are now California and New Mexico failed. Mexico City was taken 1847, and under the Treaty of Guadaloupe Hidalgo that ended the war, the US acquired New Mexico and California, as well as clear title to Texas in exchange for $15 million.

Mexico United States of (*Estados Unidos Mexicanos*) *area* 756,198 sq mi/1,958,201 sq km *capital* Mexico City *towns and cities* Guadalajara, Monterrey; port Veracruz *physical* partly arid central highlands; Sierra Madre mountain ranges E and W; tropical coastal plains *environment* during the 1980s, smog levels in Mexico City exceeded World Health Organization standards on more than 300 days of the year. Air is polluted by 130,000 factories and 2.5 million vehicles *features* Rio Grande; 2,000 mi/3,218 km frontier with US; resorts Acapulco, Cancun, Mexicali, Tijuana; Baja California, Yucatán peninsula; volcanoes, including Popocatepetl; pre-Columbian archeological sites *head of state and government* Ernesto Zedillo Ponce de Leon from 1994 *political system* federal democratic republic *political parties* Institutional Revolutionary

US

ATLANTIC
OCEAN

MEXICO

Cuba

Mexico City

Belize

Guatemala

CARIBBEAN
SEA

PACIFIC
OCEAN

0 miles 500
0 km 1000

Party (PRI), moderate, left-wing; National Action Party (PAN), moderate Christian socialist *exports* silver, gold, lead, uranium, oil, natural gas, handicrafts, fish, shellfish, fruits and vegetables, cotton, machinery *currency* peso *population* (1993 est) 91,600,000 (mixed descent 60%, Indian 30%, Spanish descent 10%); 50% under 20 years of age; growth rate 2.6% p.a. *life expectancy* men 67, women 74 *languages* Spanish (official) 92%, Nahuatl, Maya, Zapoteco, Mixteco, Otomi *religion* Roman Catholic 97% *literacy* men 90%, women 85% *GNP* $2,870 per head (1991) *chronology 1821* Independence achieved from Spain. *1846–48* Mexico at war with US; loss of territory. *1848* Maya Indian revolt suppressed. *1864–67* Maximilian of Austria was emperor of Mexico. *1917* New constitution introduced, designed to establish permanent democracy. *1983–84* Financial crisis. *1985* Institutional Revolutionary Party (PRI) returned to power. Earthquake in Mexico City. *1986* International Monetary Fund (IMF) loan agreement signed to keep the country solvent until at least 1988. *1988* PRI candidate Carlos Salinas de Gortari elected president. Debt reduction accords negotiated with US. *1991* PRI won general election. *1992* Public outrage following Guadalajara gas-explosion disaster. *1993* Sept: electoral reforms passed. Donaldo Colosio Murrieta nominated PRI presidential candidate. *1994* Jan: attacks by rebel group, the Zapatista National Liberation Army (ZNLA), harshly put down by government troops. Government cease-fire announced; ZNLA awarded political recognition. March: peace accord signed. Colosio assassinated. Aug: Ernesto Zedillo Ponce de Leon (PRI) elected president.

Mexico City (Spanish *Ciudad de México*) capital, industrial (iron, steel, chemicals, textiles), and cultural center of Mexico, 7,400 ft/ 2,255 m above sea level on the S edge of the central plateau; population (1986) 18,748,000. It is thought to be one of the world's most polluted cities because of its position in a volcanic basin 7,400 ft/2,000 m above sea level. Pollutants gather in the basin causing a smog cloud.

mezzo-soprano female singing voice with an approximate range A4–F5, between contralto and soprano.

mg symbol for *milligram*.

mi symbol for ◊*mile*.

Miami industrial city (food processing, transportation and electronic equipment, clothing, and machinery) and port in Florida; population (1990) 358,500. It is the hub of finance, trade, and air transport for the US, Latin America, and the Caribbean. There has been an influx of immigrants from Cuba, Haiti, Mexico, and South America since 1959.

Michael 1921– . King of Romania 1927–30 and 1940–47. The son of Carol II, he succeeded his grandfather as king 1927 but was displaced when his father returned from exile 1930. In 1940 he was proclaimed king again on his father's abdication, overthrew 1944 the fascist dictatorship of Ion Antonescu (1882–1946), and enabled Romania to share in the victory of the Allies at the end of World War II. He abdicated and left Romania 1947.

Michaelmas Day in Christian church tradition, the festival of St Michael and all angels, observed Sept 29.

Michelangelo 1475–1564. properly Michelangelo Buonarroti. Italian sculptor, painter, architect, and poet. He was active in his native Florence and in Rome. His giant talent dominated the High Renaissance. The marble *David* 1501–04 (Accademia, Florence) set a new standard in nude sculpture. His massive figure style was translated into fresco in the Sistine Chapel 1508–12 and 1536–41 (Vatican). Other works in Rome include the dome of St Peter's basilica. His influence, particularly on the development of ◊Mannerism, was profound.

Michigan state in N central US; nickname Wolverine State/Great Lake State *area* 58,518 sq mi/151,600 sq km *capital* Lansing *cities* Detroit, Grand Rapids, Flint *features* Great Lakes: Superior, Michigan, Huron, Erie; Porcupine Mountains; Muskegon, Grand, St Joseph, and Kalamazoo rivers; over 50% forested; Isle Royale National Park; Pictured Rocks and Sleeping Bear national seashores; Henry Ford Museum and Greenfield Village, Dearborn *products* motor vehicles and equipment; nonelectrical machinery; iron and steel; chemicals; pharmaceuticals; dairy products *population* (1990) 9,295,300 *famous people* Edna Ferber, Gerald Ford, Henry Ford, Jimmy Hoffa, Diana Ross *history* temporary posts established in early 17th century by French explorers Brulé, Marquette, Joliet, and La Salle; first settled 1668 at Sault Sainte Marie; present-day Detroit settled 1701; passed to the British 1763 and to the US 1796; statehood achieved 1837.

Henry Ford's establishment of the moving assembly line in 1913–14 made Detroit the motor-vehicle-production capital of the world. Since then the state's fortunes have been closely tied to the fortunes of the motor industry, prospering in the 1920s, 1940s, and 1950s, but badly hurt by the Great Depression of the 1930s and competition from Japanese manufacturers since the 1970s.

Michigan, Lake lake in N central US, one of the Great Lakes; area 22,390 sq mi/58,000 sq km. Chicago and Milwaukee are its main ports.

micro- prefix (symbol µ) denoting a one-millionth part. For example, a micrometer (µm), or micron, is one-millionth of a meter.

microbiology the study of microorganisms, mostly viruses and single-celled organisms such as bacteria, protozoa, and yeasts. The practical applications of microbiology are in medicine (since many microorganisms cause disease); in brewing, baking, and other food and beverage processes, where the microorganisms carry out fermentation; and in genetic engineering, which is creating increasing interest in the field of microbiology.

microchip popular name for the silicon chip, or ◊integrated circuit.

microclimate the climate of a small area, such as a woodland or lake. Significant differences can exist between the climates of two neighboring areas—for example, a town is usually warmer than the surrounding countryside (forming a heat island), and a woodland cooler, darker, and less windy than an area of open land.

microcomputer or *micro* or *personal computer* small desktop or portable computer, typically designed to be used by one person at a time, although individual computers can be linked in a network so that users can share data and programs.

Its central processing unit is a ◊microprocessor, contained on a single integrated circuit.

microfiche sheet of film on which printed text is photographically reduced. See ◊microform.

microform generic name for media on which text or images are photographically reduced. The main examples are *microfilm* (similar to the film in an ordinary camera) and *microfiche* (flat sheets of film, generally 4 in/105 mm x 6 in/148 mm, holding the equivalent of 420 standard pages). Microform has the advantage of low reproduction and storage costs, but it requires special devices for reading the text. It is widely used for archiving and for storing large volumes of text, such as library catalogs.

micrometer or micron one-millionth of a meter.

Micronesia group of islands in the Pacific Ocean lying N of ◊Melanesia, including the Federated States of Micronesia, Belau, Kiribati, the Mariana and Marshall Islands, Nauru, and Tuvalu.

Micronesia Federated States of (FSM) *area* 270 sq mi/ 700 sq km *capital* Kolonia, in Pohnpei state *towns and cities* Moen, in Chuuk state; Lelu, in Kosrae state; Colonia, in Yap state *physical* an archipelago in the W Pacific *features* equatorial, volcanic island chain, with extensive coral, limestone, and lava shores *head of state and government* Bailey Olter from 1991 *political system* democratic federal state *political parties* no formally organized political parties *products* copra, fish products, tourism *currency* US dollar *population* (1990) 107,900 *languages* English (official) and local languages *religion* Christianity *literacy* 78% *GNP* $1,500 per head (1989) *chronology 16th century* Colonized by Spain. *1885* Purchased from Spain by Germany. *1914* Occupied by Japan. *1920* Administered by Japan under League of Nations mandate. *1944* Occupied by US. *1947* Administered by the US as part of the UN Pacific Islands Trust Territory, under the name of the Federated States of Micronesia (FSM). *1986* Compact of Free Association entered into with US. *1990* UN trust status terminated. Independent state established, with US responsible for defense and foreign affairs. *1991* First independent president elected. Entered into UN membership.

microorganism or *microbe* living organism invisible to the naked eye but visible under a microscope. Microorganisms include viruses and single-celled organisms such as bacteria, protozoa, yeasts, and some algae. The term has no taxonomic significance in biology. The study of microorganisms is known as microbiology.

microphone primary component in a sound-reproducing system, whereby the mechanical energy of sound waves is converted into electrical signals by means of a ◊transducer. One of the simplest is the telephone receiver mouthpiece, invented by Scottish–US inventor Alexander Graham Bell in 1876; other types of microphone are used with broadcasting and sound-film apparatus.

microprocessor complete computer ◊central processing unit contained on a single ◊integrated circuit, or chip. The appearance of the first microprocessor 1971 designed by Intel for a pocket calculator manufacturer heralded the introduction of the microcomputer. The microprocessor has led to a dramatic fall in the size and cost of computers which can now be found in washing machines, automobiles, and so on. Examples of microprocessors are the Intel 8086 family and the Motorola 68000 family.

microscope instrument for magnification with high resolution for detail. Optical and electron microscopes are the ones chiefly in use; other types include acoustic, ◊scanning tunneling, and atomic force microscopes. In 1988 a scanning tunneling microscope was used to photograph a single protein molecule for the first time.

Microsoft US software corporation, now the world's largest software supplier. Microsoft's first major product was ◊MS-DOS, written for IBM, but it has increased its hold on the personal computer market with the release of ◊Windows and related applications.

microwave ◊electromagnetic wave with a wavelength in the range 0.1 in to 12 in/0. 3 to 30 cm, or 300–300,000 megahertz (between radio waves and ◊infrared radiation). Microwaves are used in radar, in radio broadcasting, and in microwave heating and cooking.

Midas in Greek mythology, a king of Phrygia who was granted the gift of converting all he touched to gold. He soon regretted his gift, as his food and drink were also turned to gold. For preferring the music of Pan to that of Apollo, he was given ass's ears by the latter.

Middle Ages period of European history between the fall of the Roman Empire in the 5th century and the Renaissance in the 15th. Among the period's distinctive features were the unity of W Europe within the Roman Catholic Church, the feudal organization of political, social, and economic relations, and the use of art for largely religious purposes.

midge common name for many insects resembling ◊gnats, generally divided into biting midges (family Ceratopogonidae) that suck blood, and non-biting midges (family Chironomidae).

Mid Glamorgan (Welsh *Morgannwg Ganol*) county of S Wales, created 1974 *area* 394 sq mi/1,020 sq km *towns and cities* Cardiff (administrative center), Porthcawl, Aberdare, Merthyr Tydfil, Bridgend, Pontypridd *features* includes a small area of the former county of Monmouthshire to the E; mountains in the N; Caerphilly Castle, with its water defenses *products* the N was formerly a leading coal (Rhondda) and iron and steel area; Royal Mint at Llantrisant; agriculture in the S; Caerphilly mild cheese; sheep farming; light industry *population* (1991) 534,100 *languages* English, 8.5% Welsh-speaking *famous people* Geraint Evans.

Midi-Pyrénées region of SW France, comprising the *départements* of Ariège, Aveyron, Haute-Garonne, Gers, Lot, Hautes-Pyrénées, Tarn, and Tarn-et-Garonne *area* 17,486 sq mi/45,300 sq km *towns and cities* Toulouse (capital); Montauban, Cahors, Rodez,

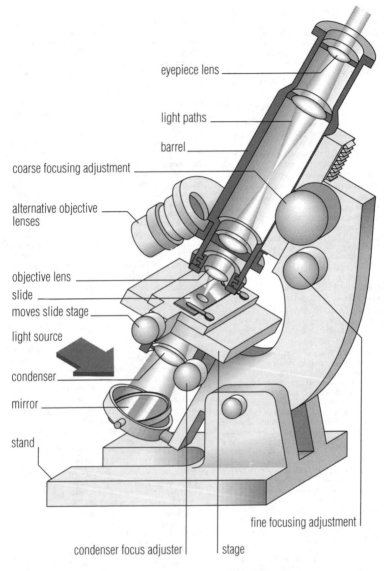

eyepiece lens

light paths

barrel

coarse focusing adjustment

alternative objective lenses

objective lens

slide

moves slide stage

light source

condenser

mirror

stand

fine focusing adjustment

condenser focus adjuster   stage

microscope *Terms used to describe an optical microscope. In essence, the optical microscope consists of an eyepiece lens and an objective lens, which are used to produce an enlarged image of a small object by focusing light from a light source. Optical microscopes can achieve magnifications of up to 1,500–2,000. Higher magnifications and resolutions are obtained by electron microscopes.*

Lourdes *features* several spa towns, winter resorts, and prehistoric caves *products* fruit, wine, livestock *population* (1986) 2,355,000 *history* occupied by the Basques since prehistoric times, this region once formed part of the prehistoric province of Gascony that was taken by the English 1154, recaptured by the French 1453, inherited by Henry of Navarre, and reunited with France 1607.

midshipman trainee naval officer. In the US, a midshipman is a student in training for the rank of ensign, in particular one at the US Naval Academy at Annapolis. In the British navy, a midshipman is a junior naval officer ranking just below sublieutenant.

Midway Islands two islands in the Pacific, 1,120 mi/ 1,800 km NW of Honolulu; area 2 sq mi/5 sq km; population (1980) 500. They were annexed by the US 1867, and are now administered by the US Navy. The naval *Battle of Midway* June 3–6, 1942, between the US and Japan, was a turning point in the Pacific in World War II; the US victory marked the end of Japanese expansion in the Pacific.

Midwest or *Middle West* large area of the N central US. It is loosely defined, but is generally taken to comprise the states of Illinois, Iowa, Wisconsin, Minnesota, Nebraska, Kansas, Missouri, North Dakota, and South Dakota and the portions of Montana, Wyoming, and Colorado E of the Rocky Mountains. Ohio, Michigan, and Indiana are often included. Traditionally its economy is divided between agriculture and heavy industry.

The majority of Midwesterners tend to be conservative socially and politically and less interested in international affairs than the general public in other parts of the country. The region is generally flat and well-watered, with good transportation links.

In its broadest sense, the Midwest has an area of 986,800 sq mi/2,556,000 sq km and a population of about 61.5 million.

migraine acute, sometimes incapacitating headache (generally only on one side), accompanied by nausea, that recurs, often with advance symptoms such as flashing lights. No cure has been discovered, but ergotamine normally relieves the symptoms. Some sufferers learn to avoid certain foods, such as chocolate, which suggests an allergic factor.

migrant labor people who move from place to place to work or harvest seasonal crops. Economic or political pressures often cause people to leave their homelands to earn wages in this way, but some families live this way for several generations. Since the Great Depression of the 1930s, many families lost land and homes and took to the road. Since the 1960s, unions for migrant farm workers have been formed, principally by Cesar ◊Chavez.

mildew any fungus that appears as a destructive growth on plants, paper, leather, or wood when exposed to damp; such fungi usually form a thin white coating.

mile imperial unit of linear measure. A statute mile is equal to 1,760 yards (1.60934 km), and an international nautical mile is equal to 2,026 yards (1,852 m).

militia body of civilian soldiers, usually with some military training, who are on call in emergencies, distinct from professional soldiers. In Switzerland, the militia is the national defense force, and every able-bodied man is liable for service in it. In the US the *National Guard* and in the UK the *Territorial Army* have supplanted earlier voluntary militias.

The US National Guard is trained and armed for deployment abroad as well as for disaster relief at home. In addition, at least 24 states by 1989 had paramilitary unpaid volunteer forces, generally known as state defense forces, chartered to suppress "civil disorders", fight "terrorists and saboteurs", and occupy "key facilities" in case of open dissent at home.

milk secretion of the ◊mammary glands of female mammals, with which they suckle their young (during ◊lactation). Over 85% is water, the remainder comprising protein, fat, lactose (a sugar), calcium, phosphorus, iron, and vitamins. The milk of cows, goats, and sheep is often consumed by humans, but regular drinking of milk after infancy is principally a Western practice.

Milky Way faint band of light crossing the night sky, consisting of stars in the plane of our Galaxy. The name Milky Way is often used for the Galaxy itself. It is a spiral ◊galaxy, about 100,000 light-years in diameter, containing at least 100 trillion ◊stars. The Sun is in one of its spiral arms, about 25,000 light-years from the center.

Mill John Stuart 1806–1873. English philosopher and economist who wrote *On Liberty* 1859, the classic philosophical defense of liberalism, and *Utilitarianism* 1863, a version of the "greatest happiness for the greatest number" principle in ethics. His progressive views inspired *On the Subjection of Women* 1869.

Millais John Everett 1829–1896. English painter. He was a founder member of the ◊Pre-Raphaelite *Brotherhood* (PRB) 1848. By the late 1850s he had left the PRB, and his style became more fluent and less detailed.

Millay Edna St Vincent 1892–1950. US poet. She wrote romantic, emotional verse, including *Renascence and Other Poems* 1917 and *The Harp-Weaver and Other Poems* 1923 (Pulitzer Prize 1924).

She was a favorite of the free-spirited youth of the 1920s. Born in Rockland, Maine, she moved to New York City's Greenwich Village and became a voice for political and social causes.

Miller Arthur 1915– . US dramatist. His plays deal with family relationships and contemporary American values, and include *Death of a Salesman* 1949 and *The Crucible* 1953, based on the Salem witch trials and reflecting the communist witch-hunts of Senator Joe ◊McCarthy. He was married 1956–61 to the film star Marilyn Monroe, for whom he wrote the film *The Misfits* 1960.

millet any of several grasses, family Gramineae, of which the grains are used as a cereal food and the stems as fodder.

milliliter one-thousandth of a liter (ml), equivalent to 1 cu cm (cc) or 0.0338 fluid ounce.

millimeter of mercury unit of pressure, used in barometers for measuring atmospheric pressure, defined as the pressure exerted by a column of mercury one millimeter high, at standard gravity and at a temperature of 32°F/0°C.

millipede any arthropod of the class Diplopoda. It has a segmented body, each segment usually bearing two pairs of legs, and the distinct head bears a pair of short clubbed antennae. Most millipedes are no more than 1 in/2.5 cm long; a few in the tropics are 12 in/30 cm.

Milosevic´ Slobodan 1941– . Serbian communist politician, party chief and president of Serbia from 1986; reelected Dec 1990 in multiparty elections and again Dec 1992. Milosevic wielded considerable influence over the Serb-dominated Yugoslav federal army during the 1991–92 civil war and continued to back Serbian militia in ◊Bosnia-Herzegovina 1992–94, although publicly disclaiming any intention to "carve up" the newly independent republic.

Milstar (acronym for *Military Strategic and Tactical Relay*) US communications satellite launched February 1994. It was designed to function in a nuclear war and broadcast orders to launch weapons. After the breakup of the Soviet Union the continuation of its development became controversial.

Milstein César 1927– . Argentine-born British molecular biologist who developed monoclonal antibodies, giving immunity against specific diseases. He shared the Nobel Prize for Medicine 1984.

Milton John 1608–1674. English poet. His epic *Paradise Lost* 1667 is one of the landmarks of English literature. Early poems including *Comus* (a masque performed 1634) and *Lycidas* (an elegy 1638) showed Milton's superlative lyric gift. Latin secretary to Oliver Cromwell during the Commonwealth period, he also wrote many pamphlets and prose works, including *Areopagitica* 1644, which opposed press censorship.

Milwaukee industrial port (meatpacking, brewing, engineering, machinery, electronic and electrical equipment, chemicals) in Wisconsin, on Lake Michigan; population (1990) 628,100. The site was settled 1818 and drew a large influx of German immigrants, beginning in the 1840s.

Educational institutions include Marquette University.

mimosa tree, shrub, or herb of the genus *Mimosa* of the family Mimosaceae, found in tropical and subtropical regions. All bear small, fluffy, golden, ball-like flowers.

min. abbreviation for *minute* (time); *minimum*.

mind, in philosophy, the presumed mental or physical being or faculty that enables a person to think, will, and feel; the seat of the intelligence and of memory; sometimes only the cognitive or intellectual powers, as distinguished from the will and the emotions.

mineral naturally formed inorganic substance with a particular chemical composition and a regularly repeating internal structure. Either in their perfect crystalline form or otherwise, minerals are the constituents of rocks. In more general usage, a mineral is any substance economically valuable for mining (including coal and oil, despite their organic origins).

Ice is also a mineral, the crystalline form of water, H_2O.

mineralogy study of minerals. The classification of minerals is based chiefly on their chemical composition and the kind of chemical bonding that holds these atoms together. The mineralogist also studies their crystallographic and physical characters, occurrence, and mode of formation.

Minerva in Roman mythology, the goddess of intelligence, and of handicrafts and the arts, equivalent to the Greek ◊Athena. From the earliest days of ancient Rome, there was a temple to her on the Capitoline Hill, near the Temple of Jupiter.

miniature painting painting on a very small scale, notably early manuscript paintings, and later miniature portraits, sometimes set in jeweled cases. The art of manuscript painting was developed in Classical times in the West and revived in the Middle Ages.

Several Islamic countries, for example Persia and India, developed strong traditions of manuscript art. Miniature portrait painting enjoyed a vogue in France and England in the 16th–19th centuries.

minicomputer multiuser computer with a size and processing power between those of a ◊mainframe and a ◊microcomputer. Nowadays almost all minicomputers are based on ◊microprocessors.

Minimalism movement in abstract art (mostly sculpture) and music toward severely simplified composition. Minimal art developed in the US in the 1950s in reaction to ◊Abstract Expressionism, shunning its emotive approach in favor of impersonality and elemental, usually geometric, shapes. It has found its fullest expression in sculpture, notably in the work of

Carl Andre, who employs industrial materials in modular compositions. In music, from the 1960s, it manifested itself in large-scale statements, usually tonal or even diatonic, and highly repetitive, based on a few "minimal" musical ideas. Major Minimalist composers are Steve Reich and Philip ◊Glass.

mining extraction of minerals from under the land or sea for industrial or domestic uses. Exhaustion of traditionally accessible resources has led to development of new mining techniques; for example, extraction of oil from offshore deposits and from land shale reserves. Technology is also under development for the exploitation of minerals from entirely new sources such as mud deposits and mineral nodules from the sea bed.

mink two species of carnivores of the weasel family, genus *Mustela*, usually found in or near water. They have rich, brown fur, and are up to 1.6 ft/50 cm long with bushy tails 8 in/20 cm long. They live in Eurasia (*M. lutreola*) and North America (*M. vison*).

Minnesota state in N midwest US; nickname Gopher State/North Star State *area* 84,418 sq mi/218,700 sq km *capital* St Paul *towns and cities* Minneapolis, Duluth, Bloomington, Rochester *features* sources of the Mississippi River and the Red River of the North; Voyageurs National Park near the Canadian border; Minnehaha Falls at Minneapolis; Mayo Clinic at Rochester; more than 15,000 lakes *products* cereals, soy beans, livestock, meat and dairy products, iron ore (about two-thirds of US output), nonelectrical machinery, electronic equipment *population* (1990) 4,375,100 *famous people* F Scott Fitzgerald, Hubert H Humphrey, Sinclair Lewis, Charles and William Mayo *history* first European exploration, by French fur traders, in the 17th century; region claimed for France by Daniel Greysolon, Sieur Duluth, 1679; part E of Mississippi River ceded to Britain 1763 and to the US 1783; part W of Mississippi passed to the US under the Louisiana Purchase 1803; became a territory 1849; statehood achieved 1858.

With the coming of the railroad in 1867, Minneapolis became the major US flour-milling center. Iron ore was discovered in the Mesabi, Cuyuna, and Vermilion ranges in the 1880s, and Duluth became a major Great Lakes port. In 1848 the value of manufactured products exceeded farm cash receipts for the first time as the state became increasingly urbanized and industrial.

minnow various small freshwater fishes of the carp family (Cyprinidae), found in streams and ponds worldwide. Most species are small and dully colored, but some are brightly colored. They feed on larvae and insects.

Red-bellied daces, genus *Chrosomus*, and cut-lipped minnows, genus *Exoglossum* are North American representatives.

minor legal term for those under the age of majority, which varies from country to country but is usually between 18 and 21. In the US (from 1971 for voting, and in some states for nearly all other purposes) and certain European countries (in Britain since 1970) the age of majority is 18.

Minorca (Spanish *Menorca*) second largest of the ◊Balearic Islands in the Mediterranean *area* 266 sq mi/689 sq km *towns and cities* Mahon, Ciudadela *products* copper, lead, iron; tourism is important *population* (1985) 55,500.

Minotaur in Greek mythology, a monster, half man and half bull, offspring of Pasiphaë, wife of King

Minos of Crete, and a bull. It lived in the Labyrinth at Knossos, and its victims were seven girls and seven youths, sent in annual tribute by Athens, until ◊Theseus killed it, with the aid of Ariadne, the daughter of Minos.

mint in botany, any aromatic plant, genus *Mentha*, of the family Labiatae, widely distributed in temperate regions. The plants have square stems, creeping rootstocks, and flowers, usually pink or purplish, that grow in a terminal spike. Mints include garden mint *M. spicata* and peppermint *M. piperita*.

mint in economics, a place where coins are stamped from metal under government authority.

In the US the official mint is the Bureau of the Mint, a division of the Treasury Department. The official Mint of the United States was established by the Coining Act 1792 in Philadelphia. The US Mint has general supervision of the four current coinage mints—in Denver, West Point, San Francisco, and Philadelphia—all of which are assay offices and bullion depositories. It directs the coinage of money, the manufacture of medals, and the custody of bullion.

minuet French country dance in three time adapted as a European courtly dance of the 17th century. The music was later used as the third movement of a classical four-movement symphony where its gentle rhythm provides a foil to the slow second movement and fast final movement.

minute unit of time consisting of 60 seconds; also a unit of angle equal to one sixtieth of a degree.

Miocene fourth epoch of the Tertiary period of geological time, 23.5–5.2 million years ago. At this time grasslands spread over the interior of continents, and hoofed mammals rapidly evolved.

Mir Soviet space station, the core of which was launched Feb 20, 1986. It is intended to be a permanently occupied space station.

Mir weighs almost 23 tons, is approximately 44 ft/13.5 m long, and has a maximum diameter of 13.6 ft/4.15 m. It carries a number of improvements over the earlier ◊Salyut series of space stations, including six docking ports; four of these can have scientific and technical modules attached to them.

Mira or *Omicron Ceti* brightest long-period pulsating ◊variable star, located in the constellation ◊Cetus. Mira was the first star discovered to vary periodically in brightness.

Mirabeau Honoré Gabriel Riqueti, Comte de 1749–1791. French politician, leader of the National Assembly in the French Revolution. He wanted to establish a parliamentary monarchy on the English model. From May 1790 he secretly acted as political adviser to the king.

Miranda Carmen. Adopted name of Maria de Carmo Miranda da Cunha 1909–1955. Portuguese dancer and singer. She lived in Brazil from childhood, moving to Hollywood 1939. Her Hollywood musicals include *Down Argentine Way* 1940 and *The Gang's All Here* 1943. Her hallmarks were extravagant costumes and headgear adorned with tropical fruits, a staccato singing voice, and fiery temperament.

Miró Joan 1893–1983. Spanish Surrealist painter. In the mid-1920s he developed an abstract style, lyrical and often witty, with ameba shapes, some linear, some highly colored, generally floating on a plain background.

miscarriage spontaneous expulsion of a fetus from the womb before it is capable of independent survival. Often, miscarriages are due to an abnormality in the developing fetus.

misdemeanor in US law, an offense less serious than a felony. A misdemeanor is an offense punishable by a relatively insevere penalty, such as a fine or short term in prison or a term of community service, while a felony carries more severe penalties, such as a term of imprisonment of a year or more up to the death penalty.

missile rocket-propelled weapon, which may be nuclear-armed (see ◊nuclear warfare). Modern missiles are often classified as surface-to-surface missiles (SSM), air-to-air missiles (AAM), surface-to-air missiles (SAM), or air-to-surface missiles (ASM). A *cruise missile* is in effect a pilotless, computer-guided aircraft; it can be sea-launched from submarines or surface ships, or launched from the air or the ground.

Mississippi river in the US, the main arm of the great river system draining the US between the Appalachian and the Rocky mountains. The length of the Mississippi is 2,350 mi/3,780 km; with its tributary the Missouri 3,740 mi/6,020 km.

Levees extend over more than 1,600 mi/2,575 km of its course because of the potentially dangerous spring flooding, as in 1993. St Louis is the chief central port on its banks.

Mississippi state in SE US; nickname Magnolia State/Bayou State *area* 47,710 sq mi/123,600 sq km *capital* Jackson *towns and cities* Biloxi, Meridian, Hattiesburg *features* rivers: Mississippi, Pearl, Big Black; Vicksburg National Military Park (Civil War site); Gulf Islands National Seashore; mansions and plantations, many in the Natchez area *products* cotton, rice, soy beans, chickens, fish and shellfish, lumber and wood products, petroleum and natural gas, transportation equipment, chemicals *population* (1990) 2,573,200 *famous people* Jefferson Davis, William Faulkner, Elvis Presley, Leontyne Price, Eudora Welty, Tennessee Williams, Richard Wright *history* first explored by Hernando de Soto for Spain 1540; settled by the French 1699, the English 1763; ceded to US 1798; statehood achieved 1817. After secession from the Union during the Civil War, it was readmitted 1870.

Mississippian US term for the Lower or Early ◊Carboniferous period of geological time, 363–323 million years ago. It is named for the state of Mississippi.

Missouri state in central US; nickname Show Me State/Bullion State *area* 69,712 sq mi/180,600 sq km *capital* Jefferson City *towns and cities* St Louis, Kansas City, Springfield, Independence *features* rivers: Mississippi, Missouri; Pony Express Museum at St Joseph; birthplace of Jesse James; Mark Twain and Ozark state parks; Harry S Truman Library at Independence *products* meat and other processed food, aerospace and transport equipment, lead, zinc *population* (1990) 5,117,100 *famous people* George Washington Carver, T S Eliot, Jesse James, Joseph Pulitzer, Harry S Truman, Mark Twain *history* explored by Hernando de Soto for Spain 1541; acquired by the US under the Louisiana Purchase 1803; achieved statehood 1821, following the Missouri Compromise of 1820.

Strong sympathy for both sides existed, but the state remained part of the Union during the Civil War;

many battles and skirmishes fostered a general lawlessness that continued in the postwar exploits of such bandits as Jesse and Frank James. While St Louis was eclipsed by Chicago as the commercial center of the Midwest, Kansas City benefited from the growth of the railroads. Missouri is second to Michigan in producing automobiles and ranks high in aerospace production.

Missouri major river in the central US, a tributary of the Mississippi, which it joins N of St Louis; length 2,683 mi/4,320 km.

It is formed by the confluence of the Jefferson, Gallatin, and Madison rivers in SW Montana and eventually forms the borders between Iowa and Nebraska and between Kansas and Missouri. Kansas City, Missouri, is the largest city on its banks. Since 1944 the muddy, turbulent river has been tamed by a series of locks and dams for irrigation and flood control.

mistletoe any of several parasitic evergreen shrubs of the genera *Viscum* and *Phoradendron* of the family Loranthaceae, especially American mistletoe *P. flavescens*, parasitic on broadleaved trees, and European mistletoe *V. album*. They grow on trees as branched bushes, with translucent white berries, and are used as Christmas decorations. See ◊Druidism.

mite minute ◊arachnid of the subclass Acari.

miter in the Christian church, the headdress worn by bishops, cardinals, and mitered abbots at solemn services. There are miters of many different shapes, but in the Western church they usually take the form of a tall cleft cap. The miter worn by the pope is called a tiara.

Mithras in Persian mythology, the god of light. Mithras represented the power of goodness, and promised his followers compensation for present evil after death. He was said to have captured and killed the sacred bull, from whose blood all life sprang. Mithraism was introduced into the Roman Empire 68 BC. By about AD 250, it rivaled Christianity in strength.

Mithridates VI Eupator (called *the Great*) 132–63 BC. King of Pontus (on the coast of modern Turkey, on the Black Sea), who became the greatest obstacle to Roman expansion in the E. He massacred 80,000 Romans in overrunning the rest of Asia Minor and went on to invade Greece. He was defeated by ◊Sulla in the First Mithridatic War 88–84; by Lucullus in the Second 83–81; and by ◊Pompey in the Third 74–64. He was killed by a soldier at his own order.

Mitsotakis Constantine 1918– . Greek politician, leader of the conservative New Democracy Party (ND) 1984–93, prime minister 1990–93. Minister for economic coordination 1965 (a post he held again 1978–80), he was arrested by the military junta 1967, but escaped from house arrest and lived in exile until 1974. In 1980–81 he was foreign minister. He resigned the leadership of the ND after its 1993 election defeat.

Mitterrand François 1916– . French socialist politician, president 1981–95. He held ministerial posts in 11 governments 1947–58, and founded the French Socialist Party (PS) 1971. In 1985 he introduced proportional representation, allegedly to weaken the growing opposition from left and right. Since 1982 his administrations combined economic orthodoxy with social reform.

Mix Tom (Thomas) 1880–1940. US film actor. He was the most colorful cowboy star of silent films. At their best, his films, such as *The Range Riders* 1910 and *King Cowboy* 1928, were fast-moving and full of impressive stunts. His talkies include *Destry Rides Again* 1932 and *The Miracle Rider* 1935.

After his death in an auto accident, his character lived on into the 1940s in a radio serial.

ml symbol for *milliliter*.

mm symbol for *millimeter*.

Mobutu Sese Seko Kuku Ngbeandu Wa Za Banga 1930– . Zairean president from 1965. He assumed the presidency in a coup. The harshness of some of his policies and charges of corruption attracted widespread international criticism. In 1991 opposition leaders forced Mobutu to agree formally to give up some of his powers, but the president continued to oppose constitutional reform initiated by his prime minister, Etienne Tshisekedi. Despite his opposition, a new transitional constitution was adopted 1994.

mockingbird North American songbird *Mimus polyglottos* of the mimic thrush family Mimidae, found in the US and Mexico. About 10 in/25 cm long, it is brownish gray, with white markings on the black wings and tail. It is remarkable for its ability to mimic the songs of other species.

mock orange or *syringa* deciduous shrub of the genus *Philadelphus*, family Philadelphaceae, including *P. coronarius*, which has white, strongly scented flowers, resembling those of the orange.

The common mock orange *P. inodorus* is native to the S US.

modem (acronym for *modulator/demodulator*) device for transmitting computer data over telephone lines. Such a device is necessary because the ◊digital signals produced by computers cannot, at present, be transmitted directly over the telephone network, which uses ◊analog signals. The modem converts the digital signals to analog, and back again. Modems are used for linking remote terminals to central computers and

Mitterrand, François *French socialist politician François Mitterrand.*

enable computers to communicate with each other anywhere in the world.

modern dance 20th-century dance idiom that evolved in opposition to traditional ballet by those seeking a freer and more immediate means of dance expression. Leading American exponents include Martha ◊Graham and Merce ◊Cunningham, and Isadora ◊Duncan.

Modernism in Protestantism, liberal thought which emerged early in the 20th century and attempted to reconsider Christian beliefs in the light of modern scientific theories and historical methods, without abandoning the essential doctrines. Modernism was condemned by Pope Pius X in 1907.

Modernism in the arts, a general term used to describe the 20th century's conscious attempt to break with the artistic traditions of the 19th century; it is based on a concern with form and the exploration of technique as opposed to content and narrative. In the visual arts, direct representationalism gave way to abstraction (see ◊abstract art); in literature, writers experimented with alternatives to orthodox sequential storytelling, such as stream of consciousness; in music, the traditional concept of key was challenged by atonality; and in architecture, Functionalism ousted decorativeness as a central objective.

Modigliani Amedeo 1884–1920. Italian artist. He was active in Paris from 1906. He painted and sculpted graceful nudes and portrait studies. His paintings—for example, the portrait of his mistress Jeanne Hébuterne, painted 1919 (Guggenheim Museum, New York)—have a distinctive style, the forms elongated and sensual.

modulation in radio transmission, the intermittent change of frequency, or amplitude, of a radio carrier wave, in accordance with the audio characteristics of the speaking voice, music, or other signal being transmitted. See ◊AM (amplitude modulation), and ◊FM (frequency modulation).

Mogadishu or *Mugdisho* capital and chief port of Somalia; population (1988) 1,000,000. It is a center for oil refining, food processing, and uranium mining. During the struggle to overthrow President Barre and the ensuing civil war 1991–92, much of the city was devastated and many thousands killed. From December 1992 UN peacekeeping troops (including a large contingent of US Marines) were stationed in the city to monitor a cease-fire and to protect relief operations.

However, mounting clashes between UN and Somali rebel forces 1993 resulted in the withdrawal of most US troops March 1994.

Mogul dynasty N Indian dynasty 1526–1858, established by ◊Babur, Muslim descendant of Tamerlane, the 14th-century Mongol leader. The Mogul emperors ruled until the last one, ◊Bahadur Shah II, was dethroned and exiled by the British; they included ◊Akbar, ◊Aurangzeb, and ◊Shah Jahan. The Moguls established a more extensive and centralized empire than their ◊Delhi sultanate forebears, and the Mogul era was one of great artistic achievement as well as urban and commercial development.

Mohács, Battle of Austro-Hungarian defeat of the Turks 1687, which effectively marked the end of Turkish expansion into Europe. Named after the river port of that name on the Danube in Hungary, which is also the site of a Turkish victory 1526.

Mohammed or *Muhammed, Mahomet c.* 570–632. Founder of Islam, born in Mecca on the Arabian peninsula. In about 616 he claimed to be a prophet and that the *Koran* was revealed to him by God (it was later written down by his followers). He fled from persecution to the town now known as Medina in 622: the flight, Hegira, marks the beginning of the Islamic era.

Mohave Desert arid region in S California, part of the Great Basin; area 15,000 sq mi/38,500 sq km.

Mohawk member of a North American Indian people, part of the ◊Iroquois confederation, who lived in the Mohawk Valley, New York, and now live on reservations in Ontario, Québec, and New York State, as well as among the general population. Their language belongs to the Macro-Siouan group. In 1990 Mohawks south of Montréal mounted a blockade in a dispute over land with the government of Québec province.

Mohican and Mahican or *Mohegan* two closely related North American Indian peoples, speaking an Algonquian language, who formerly occupied the Hudson Valley and parts of Connecticut, respectively. The novelist James Fenimore ◊Cooper confused the two peoples in his fictional account *The Last of the Mohicans* 1826.

Moholy-Nagy Laszlo 1895–1946. US photographer. Born in Hungary, he lived in Germany 1923–29, where he was a member of the Bauhaus school, and fled from the Nazis 1935. Through the publication of his illuminating theories and practical experiments, he had great influence on 20th-century photography and design.

Mohs' scale scale of hardness for minerals (in ascending order): 1 talc; 2 gypsum; 3 calcite; 4 fluorite; 5 apatite; 6 orthoclase; 7 quartz; 8 topaz; 9 corundum; 10 diamond.

Moi Daniel arap 1924– . Kenyan politician, president from 1978. Leader of Kenya African National Union (KANU), he became minister of home affairs 1964, vice president 1967, and succeeded Jomo Kenyatta as president. Since 1988 his rule has become increasingly authoritarian. In 1991, in the face of widespread criticism, he promised an eventual introduction of multiparty politics. In 1992 he was elected president in the first free elections amid widespread accusations of vote rigging.

molar one of the large teeth found toward the back of the mammalian mouth. The structure of the jaw, and the relation of the muscles, allows a massive force to be applied to molars. In herbivores the molars are flat with sharp ridges of enamel and are used for grinding, an adaptation to a diet of tough plant material. Carnivores have sharp powerful molars called carnassials, which are adapted for cutting meat.

molasses thick, usually dark, syrup obtained during the refining of sugar (either cane or beet) or made from varieties of sorghum.

Fermented sugar-cane molasses produces rum; fermented beet-sugar molasses yields ethyl alcohol.

Unsulfured raw molasses, called blackstrap, is a nutritious food, containing in 1 tablespoon 585 mg of potassium.

mold mainly saprophytic ◊fungi living on foodstuffs and other organic matter, a few being parasitic on plants, animals, or each other. Many are of medical or industrial importance; for example, penicillin.

molding the use of a pattern, hollow form, or matrix to give a specific shape to something in a plastic or molten state. Molds are commonly used for shaping plastics, clays, and glass. In injection molding, molten plastic, for example, is injected into a water-cooled mold and takes the shape of the mold when it solidifies. In blow molding, air is blown into a blob of molten plastic inside a hollow mold. In compression molding, synthetic resin powder is simultaneously heated and pressed into a mold.

When metals are used, the process is called casting.

Moldova Republic of *area* 13,012 sq mi/33,700 sq km *capital* Chisinau (Kishinev) *towns and cities* Tiraspol, Beltsy, Bendery *physical* hilly land lying largely between the rivers Prut and Dniester; N Moldova comprises the level plain of the Beltsy Steppe and uplands; the climate is warm and moderately continental *features* Black Earth region *head of state* Mircea Snegur from 1989 *head of government* Andrei Sangheli from 1994 *political system* emergent democracy *political parties* Gagauz-Khalky People's Movement (GKPM), Gagauz separatist; Christian Democratic Popular Front, Romanian nationalist; Agrarian Democratic Party (ADP), rural, moderate; Social Democratic Party of Moldova, left of center *products* wine, tobacco, canned goods *currency* leu *population* (1993 est) 4,500,000 (Moldavian 64%, Ukrainian 14%, Russian 13%, Gagauzi 4%, Bulgarian 2%) *life expectancy* men 65, women 72 *language* Moldavian, allied to Romanian *religion* Russian Orthodox *GNP* $2,170 per head (1991) *chronology* *1940* Bessarabia in the E became part of the Soviet Union whereas the W part remained in Romania. *1941* Bessarabia taken over by Romania–Germany. *1944* Red army reconquered Bessarabia. *1946–47* Widespread famine. *1988* A popular front, the Democratic Movement for Perestroika, campaigned for accelerated political reform. *1989* Jan–Feb: nationalist demonstrations in Chisinau. May: Moldavian Popular Front established. July: former Communist Party deputy leader Mircea Snegur became head of state. Aug: Moldavian language granted official status, triggering clashes between ethnic Russians and Moldavians. Nov: Gagauz region campaigned for autonomy. *1990* Feb: Popular Front polled strongly in supreme soviet elections. June: economic and political sovereignty declared; renamed Republic of Moldova. Oct: Gagauzi held unauthorized elections to independent parliament; state of emergency declared. Nov: state of emergency imposed in Trans-Dniester region when interethnic killings followed declaration of sovereignty in Oct. *1991* March: Moldova boycotted USSR's constitutional referendum. Aug: independence declared after abortive anti-Gorbachev coup; Communist Party outlawed. Dec: Moldova joined new Commonwealth of Independent States. *1992* Admitted into United Nations; diplomatic recognition granted by US. Union with Romania discussed. Trans-Dniester region fighting intensified. *1993* Cease-fire in Gagauz and Trans-Dniester regions. New constitution adopted. *1994* Parliamentary elections won by ADP, led by former communist Petro Luchinsky. Plebiscite rejected nationalist demands for merger with Romania. Andrei Sangheli became prime minister.

mole burrowing insectivore of the family Talpidae. Moles grow to 7 in/18 cm, and have acute senses of hearing, smell, and touch, but poor vision. They have shovel-like, clawed front feet for burrowing, and eat insects, grubs, and worms.

The eastern American mole *Scalopus aquaticus*, about 6 in/15 cm long, has blackish to coppery soft, dense fur and a long snout. Its eyes and ears are not visible externally. It excavates tunnels just under the surface, leaving raised ridges, in search of earthworms and insect larvae.

molecular weight the mass of a molecule, calculated relative to one-twelfth the mass of an atom of carbon-12. It is found by adding the molecular weights of the atoms that make up the molecule.

molecule group of two or more ◊atoms bonded together. A molecule of an element consists of one or more like ◊atoms; a molecule of a compound consists of two or more different atoms bonded together. Molecules vary in size and complexity from the hydrogen molecule (H_2) to the large macromolecules of proteins. They are held together by ionic bonds, in which the atoms gain or lose electrons to form ◊ions, or by covalent bonds, where electrons from each atom are shared in a new molecular orbital.

mole rat, naked small subterranean mammal *Heterocephalus glaber*, almost hairless, with a disproportionately large head. The mole rat is of importance to zoologists as one of the very few mammals that are eusocial, that is, living in colonies with sterile workers and one fertile female.

Molière pen name of Jean-Baptiste Poquelin 1622–1673. French satirical dramatist and actor. Modern French comedy developed from his work. In 1655 he wrote his first play, *L'Etourdi/The Blunderer*. His satires include *L'Ecole des femmes/The School for Wives* 1662, *Le Misanthrope* 1666, *Le Bourgeois Gentilhomme/The Would-Be Gentleman* 1670, *Le Malade imaginaire/The Imaginary Invalid* 1673, and *Tartuffe* 1664 (banned until 1697 for attacking the hypocrisy of the clergy).

mollusk any invertebrate of the phylum Molluska with a body divided into three parts, a head, a foot, and a visceral mass. The majority of mollusks are marine animals, but some inhabit fresh water, and a few are terrestrial. They include bivalves, mussels, octopuses, oysters, snails, slugs, and squids. The body is soft, limbless, and coldblooded. There is no internal skeleton, but many species have a hard shell covering the body.

Molotov Vyacheslav Mikhailovich. Assumed name of V M Skriabin 1890–1986. Soviet communist politician. He was chair of the Council of People's Commissars (prime minister) 1930–41 and foreign minister 1939–49 and 1953–56. He negotiated the 1939 nonaggression treaty with Germany (the ◊Ribbentrop–Molotov pact), and, after the German invasion 1941, the Soviet partnership with the Allies. His postwar stance prolonged the Cold War and in 1957 he was expelled from the government for Stalinist activities.

molybdenite molybdenum sulfide, MoS_2, the chief ore mineral of molybdenum. It possesses a hexagonal crystal structure similar to graphite, has a blue metallic luster, and is very soft (1–1.5 on Mohs' scale).

The largest source of molybdenite is a deposit in Colorado.

molybdenum heavy, hard, lustrous, silver-white, metallic element, symbol Mo, atomic number 42, atomic weight 95.94. The chief ore is the mineral molybdenite. The element is highly resistant to heat and conducts electricity easily. It is used in alloys, often to harden steels. It is a necessary trace element in human nutrition. It was named 1781 by Swedish chemist Karl

Scheele, after its isolation by P J Hjelm (1746–1813), for its resemblance to lead ore.

Mombasa industrial port (oil refining, cement) in Kenya (serving also Uganda and Tanzania), built on Mombasa Island and adjacent mainland; population (1984) 481,000. It was founded by Arab traders in the 11th century and was an important center for ivory and slave trading until the 16th century.

Monaco Principality of *area* 0.75 sq mi/1.95 sq km *capital* Monaco-Ville *towns and cities* Monte Carlo, La Condamine; heliport Fontvieille *physical* steep and rugged; surrounded landwards by French territory; being expanded by filling in the sea *features* aquarium and oceanographic center; Monte Carlo film festival, motor races, and casinos; world's second-smallest state *head of state* Prince Rainier III from 1949 *head of government* Jacques Dupont from 1991 *political system* constitutional monarchy under French protectorate *political parties* no formal parties, but lists of candidates: Liste Campora; Liste Medecin *exports* some light industry; economy dependent on tourism and gambling *currency* French franc *population* (1990) 30,000; growth rate –0.5% p.a. *languages* French (official), English, Italian *religion* Roman Catholic 95% *literacy* 99% (1985) *chronology 1861* Became an independent state under French protection. *1918* France given a veto over succession to the throne. *1949* Prince Rainier III ascended the throne. *1956* Prince Rainier married US actress Grace Kelly. *1958* Birth of male heir, Prince Albert. *1959* Constitution of 1911 suspended. *1962* New constitution adopted. *1993* Joined the United Nations.

Monaghan (Irish *Mhuineachain*) county of the Republic of Ireland, in the province of Ulster; county town Monaghan; area 498 sq mi/1,290 sq km; population (1991) 51,300. Products include cereals, linen, potatoes, and cattle. The county is low and rolling, and includes the rivers Finn and Blackwater.

Mondrian Piet (Pieter Mondriaan) 1872–1944. Dutch painter. A pioneer of abstract art, he lived in Paris 1919–38, then in London, and from 1940 in New York. He was a founder member of the De ◊Stijl movement and chief exponent of Neo-Plasticism, a rigorous abstract style based on the use of simple geometric forms and pure colors. He typically created a framework using vertical and horizontal lines, and filled the rectangles with primary colors, mid-gray, or black, others being left white. His *Composition in Red, Yellow and Blue* 1920 (Stedelijk, Amsterdam) is typical.

Monet Claude 1840–1926. French painter. He was a pioneer of Impressionism and a lifelong exponent of its ideals; his painting *Impression, Sunrise* 1872 gave the movement its name. In the 1870s he began painting the same subjects at different times of day to explore the ever-changing effects of light on color and form; the *Haystacks* and *Rouen Cathedral* series followed in the 1890s, and from 1899 he painted a series of *Water Lilies* in the garden of his house at Giverny, Normandy (now a museum).

monetarism economic policy, advocated by the economist Milton Friedman and the Chicago school of economists, that proposes control of a country's money supply to keep it in step with the country's ability to produce goods, with the aim of curbing inflation. Cutting government spending is advocated, and the long-term aim is to return as much of the economy as possible to the private sector, allegedly in the interests of efficiency.

money any common medium of exchange acceptable in payment for goods or services or for the settlement of debts; legal tender. Money is usually coinage (invented by the Chinese in the second millennium BC) and paper notes (used by the Chinese from about AD 800). Developments such as the check and credit card fulfill many of the traditional functions of money.

Mongol member of any of the various Mongol (or Mongolian) ethnic groups of Central Asia. Mongols live in Mongolia, Russia, Inner Mongolia (China), Tibet, and Nepal. The Mongol language belongs to the Altaic family; some groups of Mongol descent speak languages in the Sino-Tibetan family, however.

Mongol Empire empire established by ◊Genghis Khan, who extended his domains from Russia to N China and became khan of the Mongol tribes 1206. His grandson ◊Kublai Khan conquered China and used foreigners (such as the Venetian traveler Marco Polo) as well as subjects to administer his empire. The Mongols lost China 1367 and suffered defeats in the west 1380; the empire broke up soon afterwards.

Mongolia State of (*Outer Mongolia* until 1924; *People's Republic of Mongolia* until 1991) *area* 604,480 sq mi/1,565,000 sq km *capital* Ulaanbaatar *towns and cities* Darhan, Choybalsan *physical* high plateau with desert and steppe (grasslands) *features* Altai Mountains in SW; salt lakes; part of Gobi Desert in SE; contains both the world's southernmost permafrost and northernmost desert *head of state* Punsalmaagiyn Ochirbat from 1990 *head of government* Puntsagiyn Jasray from 1992 *political system* emergent democracy *political parties* Mongolian People's Revolutionary Party (MPRP), reform-communist; Mongolian Democratic Party (MDP), main opposition party; Mongolian Democratic Union *exports* meat and hides, minerals, wool, livestock, grain, cement, timber *currency* tugrik *population* (1993 est) 2,360,000; growth rate 2.8% p.a. *life expectancy* men 62, women 65 *languages* Khalkha Mongolian (official), Chinese, Russian, and Turkic languages *religion* officially none (Tibetan Buddhist Lamaism suppressed 1930s) *literacy* 90% *GNP* $112 per head (1990) *chronology 1911* Outer Mongolia gained autonomy from China. *1915* Chinese sovereignty reasserted. *1921* Chinese rule overthrown with Soviet help. *1924* People's Republic proclaimed. *1946* China recognized Mongolia's independence. *1966* 20-year friendship, cooperation, and mutual-assistance pact signed with USSR. Relations with China deteriorated. *1984* Yumjaagiyn Tsedenbal, effective leader, deposed and replaced by Jambyn Batmonh. *1987* Soviet troops reduced; Mongolia's external contacts broadened. *1989* Further Soviet troop reductions. *1990* Democratization campaign launched by Mongolian Democratic Union. Punsalmaagiyn Ochirbat's MPRP elected in free multiparty elections. Mongolian script readopted. *1991* Massive privatization program launched. The word "Republic" dropped from country's name. GDP declined by 10%. *1992* Jan: New constitution introduced. Economic situation worsened; GDP again declined by 10%. Puntsagiyn Jasray appointed new prime minister. *1993* Punsalmaagiyn Ochirbat won first direct presidential election.

Mongoloid referring to one of the three major varieties (see ◊races) of humans, *Homo sapiens sapiens*, including the indigenous peoples of Asia, the Indians of the Americas, Polynesians, and the Eskimos and Aleuts. General physical traits include dark eyes with epicanthic folds; straight to wavy dark hair; little beard or body hair; fair to tawny skin; low to medium-bridged noses; thin to medium lips. See also ◊Caucasoid, ◊Negroid.

mongoose any of various carnivorous mammals of the family Viverridae, especially the genus *Herpestes*. The Indian mongoose *H. mungo* is grayish in color and about 1.5 ft/50 cm long, with a long tail. It may be tamed and is often kept for its ability to kill snakes. The white-tailed mongoose *Ichneumia albicauda* of central Africa has a distinctive gray or white bushy tail.

monitor any of various lizards of the family Varanidae, found in Africa, S Asia, and Australasia. Monitors are generally large and carnivorous, with well-developed legs and claws and a long powerful tail that can be swung in defense.

monkey any of the various smaller, mainly tree-dwelling anthropoid primates, excluding humans and the ◊apes. The 125 species live in Africa, Asia, and tropical Central and South America. Monkeys eat mainly leaves and fruit, and also small animals. Several species are endangered due to loss of forest habitat, for example the woolly spider monkey and black saki of the Amazonian forest.

monkey puzzle or *Chilean pine* coniferous evergreen tree *Araucaria araucana* (see ◊araucaria), native to Chile; it has whorled branches covered in prickly leaves of a leathery texture.

monomer chemical compound composed of simple molecules from which ◊polymers can be made. Under certain conditions the simple molecules (of the monomer) join together (polymerize) to form a very long chain molecule (macromolecule) called a polymer. For example, the polymerization of ethene (ethylene) monomers produces the polymer polyethene (polyethylene).

$$2n\text{CH}_2 = \text{CH}_2 \ (\text{CH}_2\text{-CH}_2\text{-CH}_2\text{- CH}_2)_n$$

mononucleosis viral disease (also called "kissing disease", since it may be passed by body fluids, including saliva) characterized at onset by fever and painfully swollen lymph nodes (in the neck); there may also be digestive upset, sore throat, and skin rashes. Lassitude persists for months and even years, and recovery is often very slow. It is caused by the Epstein-Barr virus. A serious to fatal complication may be hepatitis.

monopoly in economics, the domination of a market for a particular product or service by a single company, which therefore has no competition and can keep prices high. In practice, a company can be said to have a monopoly when it controls a significant proportion of the market (technically an oligopoly).

Monopoly the world's biggest-selling copyrighted game, a board game of buying properties, building houses on them, and charging rent.

It was devised in the US 1934 by Charles B Darrow (1889–1967), with street names from Atlantic City, New Jersey, where he spent his vacations; he sold the game 1935 to Parker Brothers, US game manufacturers, for a royalty.

monorail railroad that runs on a single rail; the cars can be balanced on it or suspended from it. It was invented 1882 to carry light loads, and when run by electricity was called a *telpher*.

monotreme any member of the order Monotremata, the only living egg-laying mammals, found in Australasia. They include the echidnas and the platypus.

Monroe, James *James Monroe, remembered for the Monroe Doctrine, his warning to European nations not to interfere with the countries of the Americas.*

Monroe James 1758–1831. 5th president of the US 1817–25, a Democratic Republican. He served in the American Revolution, was minister to France 1794–96, and in 1803 negotiated the ◊Louisiana Purchase. He was secretary of state 1811–17. His name is associated with the ◊Monroe Doctrine.

Monroe was born in Westmoreland County, Virginia. He attended the College of William and Mary and studied law under his lifelong friend Thomas ◊Jefferson. During the Constitutional Convention he opposed ratification, fearing a central government with excessive power. As president, he presided over the so-called Era of Good Feeling, a period of domestic tranquility.

Monroe Marilyn. Adopted name of Norma Jean Mortenson or Baker 1926–1962. US film actress. The voluptuous blonde sex symbol of the 1950s, she made adroit comedies such as *Gentlemen Prefer Blondes* 1953, *How to Marry a Millionaire* 1953, *The Seven Year Itch* 1955, *Bus Stop* 1956, and *Some Like It Hot* 1959. Her second husband was baseball star Joe DiMaggio, and her third was playwright Arthur ◊Miller, who wrote *The Misfits* 1960 for her, a serious film that became her last. She committed suicide, taking an overdose of sleeping pills.

Monroe Doctrine declaration by US president James Monroe 1823 that any further European colonial ambitions in the western hemisphere would be threats to US peace and security, made in response to proposed European intervention against newly independent former Spanish colonies in South America. In return for the absence of such European ambitions the US would not interfere in European affairs. The doctrine, subsequently broadened, has been a recurrent theme in US foreign policy, although it has no basis in US or international law.

Monrovia capital and port of Liberia; population (1985) 500,000. Industries include rubber, cement, and gasoline processing.

monsoon wind pattern that brings seasonally heavy rain to S Asia; it blows toward the sea in winter and toward the land in summer. The monsoon may cause destructive flooding all over India and SE Asia from April to Sept, leaving thousands of people homeless each year.

monstera or *Swiss cheese plant* evergreen climbing plant, genus *Monstera*, of the arum family Araceae, native to tropical America. *M. deliciosa* is cultivated as a house plant. Areas between the veins of the leaves dry up, creating deep marginal notches and ultimately holes.

Montaigne Michel Eyquem de 1533–1592. French writer. He is regarded as the creator of the essay form. In 1580 he published the first two volumes of his *Essais*; the third volume appeared 1588. Montaigne deals with all aspects of life from an urbanely skeptical viewpoint. Through the translation by John Florio 1603, he influenced Shakespeare and other English writers.

Montana state in western US, on the Canadian border; nickname Treasure State *area* 147,143 sq mi/318,100 sq km *capital* Helena *towns and cities* Billings, Great Falls, Butte *physical* mountainous forests in the W, rolling grasslands in the E *features* rivers: Missouri, Yellowstone, Little Bighorn; Glacier National Park on the Continental Divide and Yellowstone National Park; Museum of the Plains Indian; Custer Battlefield National Monument; hunting and ski resorts *products* wheat (under irrigation), cattle, coal, copper, oil, natural gas, lumber, wood products *population* (1990) 799,100 *famous people* Gary Cooper, Myrna Loy *history* explored for France by Verendrye early 1740s; passed to the US 1803 in the Louisiana Purchase; first settled 1809; W Montana obtained from Britain in the Oregon Treaty 1846; influx of gold-seeking immigrants mid-19th century; fierce Indian wars 1867–77, which included "Custer's Last Stand" at the Little Bighorn with the Sioux; achieved statehood 1889.

Mont Blanc (Italian *Monte Bianco*) highest mountain in the ◊Alps, between France and Italy; height 15,772 ft/4,807 m. It was first climbed 1786 by Jacques Balmat and Michel Paccard of Chamonix.

Montcalm Louis-Joseph de Montcalm-Gozon, Marquis de 1712–1759. French general, appointed military commander in Canada 1756. He won a succession of victories over the British during the French and Indian War, but was defeated in 1759 by James ◊Wolfe at Québec on the Plains of Abraham, where both he and Wolfe were killed; this battle marked the end of French rule in Canada.

Monte Carlo town and luxury resort in the principality of ◊Monaco, situated on a rocky promontory NE of Monaco town; population (1982) 12,000. It is known for its Casino (1878) designed by architect Charles Garnier, and the Monte Carlo automobile rally and Monaco Grand Prix.

Monterrey industrial city (iron, steel, textiles, chemicals, food processing) in NE Mexico; population (1986) 2,335,000. It was founded 1597.

Monteverdi Claudio (Giovanni Antonio) 1567–1643. Italian composer. He contributed to the development of the opera with *La favola d'Orfeo/The Legend of Orpheus* 1607 and *L'incoronazione di Poppea/The Coronation of Poppea* 1642. He also wrote madrigals, motets, and sacred music, notably the *Vespers* 1610.

Montevideo capital and chief port (grain, meat products, hides) of Uruguay, on the Río de la Plata; population (1985) 1,250,000. Industries include meat packing, tanning, footwear, flour milling, and textiles.

Montezuma II 1466–1520. Aztec emperor 1502–20. When the Spanish conquistador Cortés invaded Mexico, Montezuma was imprisoned and killed during the Aztec attack on Cortés's force as it tried to leave Tenochtitlán, the Aztec capital city.

Montfort Simon de Montfort, Earl of Leicester *c.* 1208–1265. English politician and soldier. From 1258 he led the baronial opposition to Henry III's misrule during the second Barons' War and in 1264 defeated and captured the king at Lewes, Sussex. In 1265, as head of government, he summoned the first parliament in which the towns were represented; he was killed at the Battle of Evesham during the last of the Barons' Wars.

Montgomery state capital of Alabama, US; population (1990) 187,100.

The *Montgomery Bus Boycott* 1955 began here when a black passenger, Rosa Parks, refused to give up her seat to a white. Led by Martin Luther ◊King, Jr., the boycott was a landmark in the civil-rights campaign.

Montgomery was the first capital of the Confederacy in the first months of the Civil War before it was removed to Richmond, Virginia.

Montgomery Bernard Law, 1st Viscount Montgomery of Alamein 1887–1976. British field marshal. In World War II he commanded the 8th Army in N Africa in the Second Battle of El Alamein 1942. As commander of British troops in N Europe from 1944, he received the German surrender 1945.

Montréal inland port, industrial city (aircraft, chemicals, oil and petrochemicals, flour, sugar, brewing, meat packing) of Québec, Canada, on Montréal Island at the junction of the Ottawa and St Lawrence rivers; population (1986) 2,921,000.

mood in grammar, the form a verb takes to indicate the type of action the sentence expresses. The four moods a verb can take in English are indicative, interrogative, subjunctive, and imperative.

moon in astronomy, any natural ◊satellite that orbits a planet. Mercury and Venus are the only planets in the Solar System that do not have moons.

Moon natural satellite of Earth, 2,160 mi/3,476 km in diameter, with a mass 0.012 (approximately one-eightieth) that of Earth.

Its surface gravity is only 0.16 (one-sixth) that of Earth. Its average distance from Earth is 238,855 mi/384,400 km, and it orbits in a west-to-east direction every 27.32 days (the *sidereal month*). It spins on its axis with one side permanently turned toward Earth. The Moon has no atmosphere or water.

Moor any of the NW African Muslims, of mixed Arab and Berber origin, who conquered Spain and ruled its southern part from 711 to 1492, when they were forced to renounce their faith and became Christian (they were then known as *Moriscos*). The name (English form of Latin *Maurus*) was originally applied to an inhabitant of the Roman province of Mauritania, in NW Africa.

moor in earth science, a stretch of land, usually at a height, which is characterized by a vegetation of heather, coarse grass, and bracken. A moor may be poorly drained and contain boggy hollows.

Moore Henry 1898–1986. English sculptor. His subjects include the reclining nude, mother and child groups, the warrior, and interlocking abstract forms. Many of his post-1945 works are in bronze or marble, including monumental semiabstracts such as *Reclining Figure* 1957–58 (outside the UNESCO building, Paris), and often designed to be placed in landscape settings.

moorhen marsh bird *Gallinula chloropus* of the rail family, common in water of swamps, lakes, and ponds in Eurasia, Africa, and North and South America. It is about 13 in/33 cm long, and mainly brown and gray, but with a red bill and forehead, and a vivid white underside to the tail. The big feet are not webbed or lobed, but the moorhen can swim well.

moose large ◊deer *Alces alces* inhabiting N American and, where it is known as the elk, N Asia and N Europe. It is brown in color, stands about 6 ft/2 m at the shoulders, and has very large palmate antlers, a fleshy muzzle, a short neck, and long legs. It feeds on leaves and shoots.

Moravia (Czech *Morava*) area of central Europe, forming two regions of the Czech Republic: *South Moravia* (Czech *Jihomoravsky*) *area* 5,802 sq mi/15,030 sq km *capital* Brno *population* (1991) 2,048,900 *North Moravia* (Czech *Severomoravsky*) *area* 4,273 sq mi/11,070 sq km *capital* Ostrava *population* (1991) 1,961,500 *features* (N and S) river Morava; 25% forested *products* corn, grapes, wine in the S; wheat, barley, rye, flax, sugar beet in the N; coal and iron *history* part of the Avar territory since the 6th century; conquered by Charlemagne's Holy Roman Empire. In 874 the kingdom of Great Moravia was founded by the Slavic prince Sviatopluk, who ruled until 894. It was conquered by the Magyars 906, and became a fief of Bohemia 1029. It was passed to the Hapsburgs 1526, and became an Austrian crown land 1849. It was incorporated in the new republic of Czechoslovakia 1918, forming a province until 1949. From 1960 it was divided into two administrative regions, North and South Moravia; part of the Czech Republic from 1993.

Moravian member of a Christian Protestant sect, the *Moravian Brethren*. An episcopal church that grew out of the earlier Bohemian Brethren, it was established by the Lutheran Count Zinzendorf in Saxony 1722.

It is an unworldly practice, in doctrine close to Lutheranism, with a simplified church hierarchy and liturgy. There are about 63,000 Moravians in the US.

More (St) Thomas 1478–1535. English politician and author. From 1509 he was favored by ◊Henry VIII and employed on foreign embassies. He was a member of the privy council from 1518 and Lord Chancellor from 1529 but resigned over Henry's break with the pope. For refusing to accept the king as head of the church, he was executed. The title of his political book *Utopia* 1516 has come to mean any supposedly perfect society.

Before his execution More was imprisoned in the Tower of London for a year. He was canonized in 1935.

Mormon or *Latter-day Saint* member of a Christian sect, the Church of Jesus Christ of Latter-day Saints, founded at Fayette, New York, 1830 by Joseph ◊Smith. According to Smith, Mormon was an ancient prophet in North America; his *Book of Mormon* is accepted by Mormons as part of the Christian scriptures. Smith said he found the book, inscribed on golden tablets, with the help of the angel Moroni in 1827, and that he translated it from "reformed Egyptian" by using special glasses. Originally persecuted, the Mormons migrated West under Brigham ◊Young's leadership

and prospered. Today the worldwide membership in the Mormon church is about 6 million.

morning glory any twining or creeping plant of the genus *Ipomea*, especially *I. purpurea*, family Convolvulaceae, native to tropical America, with dazzling blue flowers. Small quantities of substances similar to the hallucinogenic drug ◊LSD are found in the seeds of some species.

Big-root morning glory *I. pandurata* is native to the E US.

Morocco Kingdom of (*al-Mamlaka al-Maghrebia*) *area* 177,070 sq mi/458,730 sq km (excluding Western Sahara) *capital* Rabat *towns and cities* Marrakesh, Fez, Meknès; ports Casablanca, Tangier, Agadir *physical* mountain ranges NE–SW; fertile coastal plains in W *features* Atlas Mountains; the towns Ceuta (from 1580) and Melilla (from 1492) are held by Spain; tunnel crossing the Strait of Gibraltar to Spain proposed 1985 *head of state* Hassan II from 1961 *head of government* Abd al-Latif Filali from 1994 *political system* constitutional monarchy *political parties* Constitutional Union (UC), right-wing; National Rally of Independents (RNI), royalist; Popular Movement (MP), moderate socialist; Istiqlal, nationalist, right of center; Socialist Union of Popular Forces (USFP), progressive socialist; National Democratic Party (PND), moderate, nationalist *exports* dates, figs, cork, wood pulp, canned fish, phosphates *currency* dirham (DH) *population* (1993 est) 27,000,000; growth rate 2.5% p.a. *life expectancy* men 62, women 65 *languages* Arabic (official) 75%, Berber 25%, French, Spanish *media* high tax on TV satellite dishes restricts their spread *religion* Sunni Muslim 99% *literacy* men 61%, women 38% *GNP* $1,030 per head (1991) *chronology 1912* Morocco divided into French and Spanish protectorates. *1956* Independence achieved as the Sultanate of Morocco. *1957* Sultan restyled king of Morocco. *1961* Hassan II came to the throne. *1969* Former Spanish province of Ifni returned to Morocco. *1972* Major revision of the constitution. *1975* Western Sahara ceded by Spain to Morocco and Mauritania. *1976* Guerrilla war in Western Sahara with the Polisario Front. Sahrawi Arab Democratic Republic (SADR) established in Algiers. Diplomatic relations between Morocco and Algeria broken. *1979* Mauritania signed a peace treaty with Polisario. *1983* Peace formula for Western Sahara, proposed by the Organization of African Unity (OAU), failed to uphold. *1984* Hassan signed an agreement for cooperation and mutual defense with Libya. *1987* Cease-fire agreed with

Polisario, but fighting continued. *1988* May: diplomatic relations with Algeria restored. Aug: United Nations peace plan accepted. *1989* Diplomatic relations with Syria restored. *1992* Mohammed Lamrani appointed prime minister; new constitution approved in referendum. *1993* Peace accord with Israel. June: opposition parties won first round of direct parliamentary elections. Sept: ruling coalition restored to power in second round of indirect elections. *1994* Abd-al Latif Filali became prime minister.

Moroni capital of the Comoros Republic, on Njazídja (Grand Comore); population (1980) 20,000. It has a small natural harbor from which coffee, cacao, and vanilla are exported.

morphine narcotic alkaloid $C_{17}H_{19}NO_3$ derived from ◊opium and prescribed only to alleviate severe pain. Its use produces serious side effects, including nausea, constipation, tolerance, and addiction, but it is highly valued for the relief of the terminally ill.

Morris William 1834–1896. English designer. A founder of the Arts and Crafts movement, also a socialist and writer, he shared the Pre-Raphaelite painters' fascination with medieval settings. In 1861 he cofounded a firm that designed and produced furniture, carpets, and a wide range of decorative wallpapers, many of which are still produced today. His Kelmscott Press, set up 1890 to print beautifully designed books, influenced printing and book design. The prose romances *A Dream of John Ball* 1888 and *News from Nowhere* 1891 reflect his socialist ideology. He also lectured on socialism.

Morse Samuel (Finley Breese) 1791–1872. US inventor. In 1835 he produced the first adequate electric telegraph (see ◊telegraphy), and in 1843 was granted $30,000 by Congress for an experimental line between Washington, DC and Baltimore. With his assistant Alexander Bain (1810–1877) he invented the Morse code.

Born in Charlestown, Massachusetts, Morse graduated from Yale 1810 and studied art in England. The first message 1844 transmitted between Washington and Baltimore was "What hath God wrought!"

Morse code international code for transmitting messages by wire or radio using signals of short (dots) and long (dashes) duration, originated by US inventor Samuel Morse for use on his invention, the telegraph (see ◊telegraphy).

mosaic design or picture, usually for a floor, wall or vault, produced by setting small pieces of marble, glass, or other materials in a cement ground. The ancient Greeks were the first to use a form of mosaic (for example, the Macedonian royal palace at Pella). Mosaic was commonly used by the Romans for their baths and villas (for example Hadrian's Villa at Tivoli) and reached its highest development in the early Byzantine period.

Moscow (Russian *Moskva*) industrial city, capital of Russia and of the Moskva region, and formerly (1922–91) of the USSR, on the Moskva River 400 mi/ 640 km SE of St Petersburg; population (1987) 8,815,000. Its industries include machinery, electrical equipment, textiles, chemicals, and many food products.

Moses Hebrew lawgiver and judge who led the Hebrews out of slavery in Egypt (Exodus) and, after wandering 40 years in the desert, brought them to the border (E of the Jordan) of the promised land of Canaan. On Mount Sinai he claimed to have received

from Jehovah the **Ten Commandments** engraved on tablets of stone. The first five books of the Old Testament—in Judaism, the ◊*Torah*—are called the *Five Books of Moses.*

Moslem alternative spelling of **Muslim,** a follower of ◊Islam.

mosque in Islam, a place of worship. Chief features are: the dome; the minaret, a balconied turret from which the faithful are called to prayer; the *mihrab,* or prayer niche, in one of the interior walls, showing the direction of the holy city of Mecca; and an open court surrounded by porticoes.

mosquito any fly of the family Culicidae. The female mosquito has needlelike mouthparts and sucks blood before laying eggs. Males feed on plant juices. Some mosquitoes carry diseases such as ◊malaria.

moss small nonflowering plant of the class Musci (10,000 species), forming with the ◊liverworts and the ◊hornworts the order Bryophyta. The stem of each plant bears rhizoids that anchor it; there are no true roots. Leaves spirally arranged on its lower portion have sexual organs at their tips. Most mosses flourish best in damp conditions where other vegetation is thin.

moth any of the various families of mainly night-flying insects of the order Lepidoptera, which also includes the butterflies. Their wings are covered with microscopic scales. The mouthparts are formed into a sucking proboscis, but certain moths have no functional mouthparts, and rely upon stores of fat and other reserves built up during the caterpillar stage. At least 100,000 different species of moth are known.

The corn earworm moth infests corn. The largest North American moths are the cecropia moth and polyphemus moth with wingspreads up to 5.5 in/ 14 cm.

mother-of-pearl or *nacre* the smooth lustrous lining in the shells of certain mollusks—for example pearl oysters, abalones, and mussels. When this layer is especially heavy it is used commercially for jewelry and decorations. Mother-of-pearl consists of calcium carbonate. See ◊pearl.

Mother's Day day set apart in the US, UK, and many European countries for honoring mothers. It is thought to have originated in Grafton, West Virginia, in 1908 when Anna Jarvis observed the anniversary of her mother's death.

In the US, Australia, and Canada, Mother's Day is observed on the second Sunday in May; in the UK it is known as Mothering Sunday and observed on the fourth Sunday of Lent.

Motherwell Robert 1915–1991. US painter, born in Aberdeen, Washington. He was associated with the New York school of ◊action painting. Borrowing from Picasso, Matisse, and the Surrealists, Motherwell's style of Abstract Expressionism retained some suggestion of the figurative. His works include the *Elegies to the Spanish Republic* 1949–76, a series of over 100 paintings devoted to the Spanish Civil War.

motion picture or *moving picture* see ◊cinema.

mot juste (French) the right word, just the word to suit the occasion.

motor anything that produces or imparts motion; a machine that provides mechanical power, particularly an electric motor. Machines that burn fuel (gasoline, diesel) are usually called engines, but the internal-combustion engine that propels vehicles has long been called a motor, hence "motoring" and "automobile" were used as early automotive terms. Actually the motor is a part of the ◊automobile engine.

motorcycle or *motorbike* two-wheeled vehicle propelled by a ◊gasoline engine. The motorbike is the lightweight version, with less power than the motorcycle, which may be equipped with a sidecar. The first successful motorized bicycle was built in France 1901, and US and British manufacturers first produced motorbikes 1903.

motorcycle racing speed contests on motorcycles. It has many different forms: *road racing* over open roads; *circuit racing* over purpose-built tracks; *speedway* over oval-shaped dirt tracks; *motocross* over natural terrain, incorporating hill climbs; and *trials*, also over natural terrain, but with the addition of artificial hazards.

motor neurone disease or *amyotrophic lateral sclerosis*, a chronic disease in which there is progressive degeneration of the nerve cells which instigate movement. It leads to weakness, wasting, and loss of muscle function and usually proves fatal within two to three years of onset. Motor neurone disease occurs in both hereditary and sporadic forms but its causes remain unclear. A gene believed to be implicated in familial cases was discovered 1993.

Motorola US semiconductor and electronics company which began by producing automobile radios and then television sets. In computing Motorola is best known for the 680x0 series of microprocessors used by the Apple ◊Macintosh range and other computers.

mountain natural upward projection of the Earth's surface, higher and steeper than a hill. The process of mountain building (orogeny) consists of volcanism, folding, faulting, and thrusting, resulting from the collision and welding together of two tectonic plates (see ◊plate tectonics). This process deforms the rock and compresses the sediment between the two plates into mountain chains.

mountain ash or *rowan* flowering tree of the genus *Sorbus*, family Rosaceae. It has pinnate leaves and large clusters of whitish flowers, followed by scarlet berries. The American mountain ash *S. americana* grows to 30 ft/9 m and is native to NE US. The European mountain ash or rowan tree *S. aucaparia* is planted widely as an ornamental.

mountain biking recreational sport that enjoyed increasing popularity in the 1990s. Mountain bikes first appeared on the mass market in the US in 1981, in the UK in 1984, and have been used in all aspects of cycling. However, it is also a competition sport, and the first world championship was held in France in 1987. The second world championship was held 1990 in Mexico. National mountain-bike championships have been held in the US since 1983 and in the UK since 1984. Mountain bikes have 10–15 gears, a toughened frame, and wider treads on the tires than ordinary bicycles.

mountaineering art and practice of mountain climbing. For major peaks of the Himalayas it was formerly thought necessary to have elaborate support from Sherpas (local people), fixed ropes, and oxygen at high altitudes (*siege-style* climbing). In the 1980s the *Alpine style* was introduced. This dispenses with these aids, and relies on human ability to adapt, Sherpa-style, to high altitude.

mountain gorilla highly endangered ape subspecies *Gorilla gorilla beringei* found in bamboo and rainforest on the Rwanda, Zaire, and Uganda borders in central Africa, with a total population of under 400. It is threatened by deforestation and illegal hunting for skins and the zoo trade.

Mountbatten Louis, 1st Earl Mountbatten of Burma 1900–1979. British admiral and administrator. In World War II he became chief of combined operations 1942 and commander in chief in SE Asia 1943. As last viceroy of India 1947 and first governor-general of India until 1948, he oversaw that country's transition to independence. He was killed by an Irish Republican Army bomb aboard his yacht in the Republic of Ireland.

He was a favorite relative of the royal family and counselor to Prince Charles.

mouse in computing, an input device used to control a pointer on a computer screen. It is a feature of graphical user interface (GUI) systems. The mouse is about the size of a pack of playing cards, is connected to the computer by a wire, and incorporates one or more buttons that can be pressed. Moving the mouse across a flat surface causes a corresponding movement of the pointer. In this way, the operator can manipulate objects on the screen and make menu selections.

mouse in zoology, one of a number of small rodents with small ears and a long, thin tail, belonging largely to the Old World family Muridae. The house mouse *Mus musculus* is distributed worldwide. It is 3 in/75 mm long, with a naked tail of equal length, and has a gray-brown body.

Native New World mice all belong to the family Cricetidae that is represented worldwide. American cricitids, sometimes called mice, include ◊voles and deer mice. *Jumping mice*, family Zapodidae, with enlarged back legs, live across the northern hemisphere.

movie camera or *motion picture camera* camera that takes a rapid sequence of still photographs—24 frames (pictures) each second. When the pictures are projected one after the other at the same speed onto a screen, they appear to show movement, because our eyes hold on to the image of one picture before the next one appears.

Mozambique People's Republic of (*República Popular de Moçambique*) *area* 308,561 sq mi/799,380 sq km *capital* and chief port Maputo *towns and cities* Beira, Nampula *physical* mostly flat tropical lowland; mountains in W *features* rivers Zambezi, Limpopo; "Beira Corridor" rail, road, and pipeline link with Zimbabwe *head of state* Joaquim Alberto Chissano from 1986 *head of government* Pascoal Mocumbi from 1994 *political system* emergent democratic republic *political parties* National Front for the Liberation of Mozambique (Frelimo), Marxist-Leninist; Renamo, or Mozambique National Resistance (MNR), former rebel movement *exports* prawns, cashews, sugar, cotton, tea, petroleum products, copra *currency* metical (replaced escudo 1980) *population* (1993 est) 16,600,000 (mainly indigenous Bantu peoples; Portuguese 50,000); growth rate 2.8% p.a.; nearly 1 million refugees in Malawi *life expectancy* men 47, women 50 *languages* Portuguese (official), 16 African languages *religions* animist 60%, Roman Catholic 18%, Muslim 16% *literacy* men 45%, women 21% *GNP* $70 per head (1991) *chronology* 1505 Mozambique became a Portuguese colony. *1962* Frelimo (liberation front) established. *1975* Independence achieved from

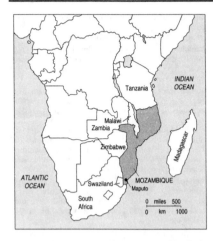

Portugal as a socialist republic, with Samora Machel as president and Frelimo as the sole legal party. *1977* Renamo resistance group formed. *1983* Reestablishment of good relations with Western powers. *1984* Nkomati accord of nonaggression signed with South Africa. *1986* Machel killed in airplane crash; succeeded by Joaquim Chissano. *1988* Tanzania announced withdrawal of its troops. South Africa provided training for Mozambican forces. *1989* Frelimo offered to abandon Marxism-Leninism; Chissano reelected. Renamo continued attacks on government facilities and civilians. *1990* One-party rule officially ended. Partial cease-fire agreed. *1991* Peace talks resumed in Rome, delaying democratic process. Attempted antigovernment coup thwarted. *1992* Peace accord signed, but fighting continued. *1994* Demobilization of contending armies completed; hostilities ceased. Chissano reelected in first multiparty elections.

Mozart Wolfgang Amadeus 1756–1791. Austrian composer and performer who showed astonishing precocity as a child and was an adult virtuoso. He was trained by his father, *Leopold Mozart* (1719–1787). From an early age he composed prolifically, his works including 27 piano concertos, 23 string quartets, 35 violin sonatas, and more than 50 symphonies including the E flat K543, G minor K550, and C major K551 ("Jupiter") symphonies, all composed 1788. His operas include *Idomeneo* 1780, *Entführung aus dem Serail/The Abduction from the Seraglio* 1782, *Le Nozze di Figaro/The Marriage of Figaro* 1786, *Don Giovanni* 1787, *Così fan tutte/Thus Do All Women* 1790, and *Die Zauberflöte/The Magic Flute* 1791. Together with Haydn, Mozart's music marks the height of the Classical age in its purity of melody and form.

MP abbreviation for *Member of Parliament.*

MS in education, abbreviation for *Master of Science* degree.

MS-DOS (abbreviation for *Microsoft Disk Operating System*) computer ◊operating system produced by Microsoft Corporation, widely used on ◊microcomputers with Intel x 86 family microprocessors. A version called PC-DOS is sold by IBM specifically for its personal computers. MS-DOS and PC-DOS are usually referred to as DOS. MS-DOS first appeared 1981, and was similar to an earlier system from Digital Research called CP/M.

Mubarak Hosni 1928– . Egyptian politician, president from 1981. Vice president to Anwar Sadat from 1975, Mubarak succeeded him on his assassination. He has continued to pursue Sadat's moderate policies, and has significantly increased the freedom of the press and of political association, while trying to repress the growing Islamic fundamentalist movement. He was reelected (uncontested) 1987 and 1993.

Muckrakers, the movement of US writers and journalists about 1880–1914 who aimed to expose political, commercial, and corporate corruption, and record frankly the age of industrialism, urban poverty, and conspicuous consumption. Novelists included Frank Norris, Theodore Dreiser, Jack London, and Upton Sinclair.

mucous membrane thin skin lining all animal body cavities and canals that come into contact with the air (for example, eyelids, breathing and digestive passages, genital tract). It secretes mucus, a moistening, lubricating, and protective fluid.

mudskipper fish of the goby family, genus *Periophthalmus*, found in brackish water and shores in the tropics, except for the Americas. It can walk or climb over mudflats, using its strong pectoral fins as legs, and has eyes set close together on top of the head. It grows up to 12 in/30 cm long.

muffler device in the exhaust system of automobiles and motorbikes. Gases leave the engine at supersonic speeds. The exhaust system and muffler are designed to slow them down, thereby silencing them.

Mugabe Robert (Gabriel) 1925– . Zimbabwean politician, prime minister from 1980 and president from 1987. He was in detention in Rhodesia for nationalist activities 1964–74, then carried on guerrilla warfare from Mozambique. As leader of ZANU he was in an uneasy alliance with Joshua ◊Nkomo of ZAPU (Zimbabwe African People's Union) from 1976.

Mujaheddin (Arabic *mujahid* "fighters", from *jihad* "holy war") Islamic fundamentalist guerrillas of contemporary Afghanistan and Iran.

Mukalla seaport capital of the Hadhramaut coastal region of S Yemen; on the Gulf of Aden 300 mi/480 km E of Aden; population (1984) 158,000.

mulberry any tree of the genus *Morus*, family Moraceae, consisting of a dozen species, including the black mulberry *M. nigra*.

It is native to W Asia and has heart-shaped, toothed leaves, and spikes of whitish flowers. It is widely cultivated for its fruit, which, made up of a cluster of small drupes, resembles a raspberry. The leaves of the Asiatic white mulberry *M. alba* are those used in feeding silkworms.

The red mulberry *M. rubra* of the E US also has large edible multiple fruit.

mule hybrid animal, usually the offspring of a male ass and a female horse.

mullah (Arabic "master") a teacher, scholar, or religious leader of Islam. It is also a title of respect given to various other dignitaries who perform duties connected with the sacred law.

mullet blunt-nosed warm-water fish of the family Mugilidae, found in the Atlantic and Pacific. The striped mullet *Mugil cephalus*, about 2 ft/60 cm long, is commonly netted and smoked. The name mullet is sometimes used for goatfishes, tropical reef fishes of the family Mullidae.

Mulliken Robert Sanderson 1896–1986. US chemist and physicist who received the 1966 Nobel Prize for Chemistry for his development of the molecular orbital theory.

He was professor at the University of Chicago 1931–61.

Mulroney Brian 1939– . Canadian politician. A former businessman, he replaced Joe Clark as Progressive Conservative Party leader 1983 and achieved a landslide in the 1984 election to become prime minister. He won the 1988 election on a platform of free trade with the US, and by the end of 1988 the Canada–US trade agreement was approved.

multimedia computer system that combines audio and video components to create an interactive application that uses text, sound, and graphics (still, animated, and video sequences). For example, a multimedia database of musical instruments may allow a user not only to search and retrieve text about a particular instrument but also to see pictures of it and hear it play a piece of music.

multiple sclerosis (MS) or *disseminated sclerosis* incurable chronic disease of the central nervous system, occurring in young or middle adulthood. Most prevalent in temperate zones, it affects more women than men. It is characterized by degeneration of the myelin sheath that surrounds nerves in the brain and spinal cord.

multiplexer in telecommunications, a device that allows a transmission medium to carry a number of separate signals at the same time—enabling, for example, several telephone conversations to be carried by one telephone line, and radio signals to be transmitted in stereo.

multiuser system or *multiaccess system* in computing, an operating system that enables several users to access the same computer at the same time. Each user has a terminal, which may be local (connected directly to the computer) or remote (connected to the computer via a modem and a telephone line). Multiaccess is usually achieved by *time-sharing*: the computer switches very rapidly between terminals and programs so that each user has sole use of the computer for only a fraction of a second but can work as if she or he had continuous access.

mummy any dead body, human or animal, that has been naturally or artificially preserved. Natural mummification can occur through freezing (for example, mammoths in glacial ice from 25,000 years ago), drying, or preservation in bogs or oil seeps. Artificial mummification may be achieved by embalming (for example, the mummies of ancient Egypt) or by freeze-drying.

mumps or *infectious parotitis* virus infection marked by fever, pain, and swelling of one or both parotid salivary glands (situated in front of the ears). It is usually shortlived in children, although meningitis is a possible complication. In adults the symptoms are more serious and it may cause sterility in men.

Munch Edvard 1863–1944. Norwegian painter and printmaker. He studied in Paris and Berlin, and his major works date from the period 1892–1908, when he lived mainly in Germany. His paintings often focus on neurotic emotional states. The *Frieze of Life* 1890s, a sequence of highly charged, symbolic paintings, includes some of his most characteristic images, such as *Skriket/The Scream* 1893. He later reused these in etchings, lithographs, and woodcuts.

Munich (German *München*) industrial city (brewing, printing, precision instruments, machinery, electrical goods, textiles), capital of Bavaria, Germany, on the river Isar; population (1986) 1,269,400.

Munich Pact or *Munich Agreement* pact signed on Sept 29, 1938, by the leaders of the UK (Neville ◊Chamberlain), France (Edouard Daladier), Germany (Hitler), and Italy (Mussolini), under which Czechoslovakia was compelled to surrender its Sudeten-German districts (the *Sudetenland*) to Germany. Chamberlain claimed it would guarantee "peace in our time", but it did not prevent Hitler from seizing the rest of Czechoslovakia in March 1939.

Munster southern province of the Republic of Ireland, comprising the counties of Clare, Cork, Kerry, Limerick, North and South Tipperary, and Waterford; area 9,318 sq mi/24,140 sq km; population (1991) 1,008,400.

muon an ◊elementary particle similar to the electron except for its mass which is 207 times greater than that of the electron. It has a half-life of 2 millionths of a second, decaying into electrons and neutrinos. The muon was originally thought to be a ◊meson and is thus sometimes called a mu meson, although current opinion is that it is a ◊lepton.

murder unlawful killing of one person by another. In the US, first-degree murder requires proof of premeditation; second-degree murder falls between first-degree murder and ◊manslaughter.

If the killer can show provocation by the victim (action or words that would make a reasonable person lose self-control) or diminished responsibility (an abnormal state of mind caused by illness, injury, or mental subnormality), the charge may be reduced to a less serious one. See also ◊assassination and ◊homicide.

Murdoch (Keith) Rupert 1931– . Australian-born US media magnate with worldwide interests. He became a US citizen in 1985. In the US, he has a 50% share of 20th Century Fox, six Metromedia TV stations, and newspaper and magazine publishing companies. His UK newspapers, generally right-wing, include the *Sun*, the *News of the World*, and *The Times*.

Murmansk seaport in NW Russia, on the Barents Sea; population (1987) 432,000. It is the largest city in the Arctic, Russia's most important fishing port, and the base of naval units and the icebreakers that keep the Northeast Passage open.

Murphy Audie 1924–1971. US actor and war hero. He starred mainly in low-budget Westerns. His more prestigious work includes *The Red Badge of Courage* 1951, *The Quiet American* 1958, and *The Unforgiven* 1960.

He was the most decorated soldier of World War II, and was promoted by Hollywood as such, in the film story of his war years *To Hell and Back* 1955, in which he starred.

Murray principal river of Australia, 1,600 mi/2,575 km long. It rises in the Australian Alps near Mount Kosciusko and flows W, forming the boundary between New South Wales and Victoria, and reaches the sea at Encounter Bay, South Australia. With its main tributary, the Darling, it is 2,330 mi /3,750 km.

Murrow Edward R(oscoe) 1908–1965. US broadcast journalist. Hired by the Columbia Broadcasting

System (CBS) 1935 to plan its educational programs, Murrow was named director of its European Bureau 1937. From London he covered the events of World War II. Murrow hosted the popular radio show *Hear It Now* 1948–51 and television shows *See It Now* 1951–58, *Person to Person* 1953–58, and *Small World* 1958–60. After leaving CBS, he served as director of the US Information Agency 1961–64.

Muscat or *Masqat* capital of Oman, E Arabia, adjoining the port of Matrah, which has a deep-water harbor; combined population (1982) 80,000. It produces natural gas and chemicals.

muscle contractile animal tissue that produces locomotion and power, and maintains the movement of body substances. Muscle is made of long cells that can contract to between one-half and one-third of their relaxed length.

muscular dystrophy any of a group of inherited chronic muscle disorders marked by weakening and wasting of muscle. Muscle fibers degenerate, to be replaced by fatty tissue, although the nerve supply remains unimpaired. Death occurs in early adult life.

Muse in Greek mythology, one of the nine daughters of Zeus and Mnemosyne (goddess of memory) and inspirers of creative arts: Calliope, epic poetry; Clio, history; Erato, love poetry; Euterpe, lyric poetry; Melpomene, tragedy; Polyhymnia, sacred song; Terpsichore, dance; Thalia, comedy; and Urania, astronomy.

Museveni Yoweri Kaguta 1945– . Ugandan general and politician, president from 1986. He led the opposition to Idi Amin's regime 1971–78 and was minister of defense 1979–80 but, unhappy with Milton Obote's autocratic leadership, formed the National Resistance Army (NRA). When Obote was ousted in a coup in 1985, Museveni entered into a brief power-sharing agreement with his successor, Tito Okello, before taking over as president. Museveni leads a broad-based coalition government.

mushroom fruiting body of certain fungi, consisting of an upright stem and a spore-producing cap with radiating gills on the undersurface. There are many edible species belonging to the genus *Agaricus*. See also ◊fungus and ◊toadstool.

Musial Stan(ley Frank). Nicknamed "Stan the Man". 1920– . US baseball player. During his playing career of 22 years, he led the National League 6 times in hits, 8 times in doubles, 5 times in triples, and 7 times in batting average. He played his last season 1963 and was hired by the Cardinals as an executive.
  Musial was elected to the Baseball Hall of Fame 1969.

music art of combining sounds into a coherent perceptual experience, typically in accordance with conventional patterns and for an esthetic purpose. Music is generally categorized as classical, ◊jazz, ◊pop music, ◊country and western, and so on.

musical 20th-century form of dramatic musical performance, combining elements of song, dance, and the spoken word, often characterized by lavish staging and large casts. It developed from the operettas and musical comedies of the 19th century.

musk in botany, perennial plant *Mimulus moschatus* of the family Scrophulariaceae; its small oblong leaves exude the musky scent from which it takes its name; it is also called *monkey flower*. Also any of several plants with a musky odor, including the musk mallow *Malva moschata* and the musk rose *Rosa moschata*.

musk deer any of three species of small deer of the genus *Moschus*, native to the mountains of central and NE Asia. A solitary animal, the musk deer is about 30–40 in/80–100 cm, sure-footed, and has large ears and no antlers. Males have long tusklike upper canine

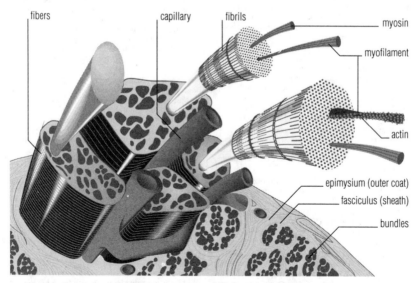

fibers   capillary   fibrils   myosin   myofilament   actin   epimysium (outer coat)   fasciculus (sheath)   bundles

muscle Muscles make up 35–45% of our body weight; there are over 650 skeletal muscles. Muscle cells may be up to 0.8 in/20 cm long. They are arranged in bundles, fibers, fibrils, and myofilaments.

teeth. They are hunted and farmed for their musk (a waxy substance secreted by the male from an abdominal gland), which is used as medicine or perfume.

musk ox ruminant *Ovibos moschatus* of the family Bovidae, native to the Arctic regions of North America. It displays characteristics of sheep and oxen, is about the size of a small domestic cow, and has long brown hair. At certain seasons it exhales a musky odor.

Muslim or *Moslem*, a follower of ◊Islam.

mussel one of a number of bivalve mollusks, some of them edible, such as *Mytilus edulis*, found in clusters attached to rocks around the N Atlantic and American coasts. It has a blue-black shell.

Mussolini Benito 1883–1945. Italian dictator 1925–43. As founder of the Fascist Movement (see ◊fascism) 1919 and prime minister from 1922, he became known as *Il Duce* ("the leader"). He invaded Ethiopia 1935–36, intervened in the Spanish Civil War 1936–39 in support of Franco, and conquered Albania 1939. In June 1940 Italy entered World War II supporting Hitler. Forced by military and domestic setbacks to resign 1943, Mussolini established a breakaway government in N Italy 1944–45, but was killed trying to flee the country.

Mussorgsky Modest Petrovich 1839–1881. Russian nationalist composer. He was a member of the group of five composers "The Five". His opera masterpiece *Boris Godunov* 1869, revised 1871–72, touched a political nerve and employed realistic transcriptions of speech patterns. Many of his works, including *Pictures at an Exhibition* 1874 for piano, were "revised" and orchestrated by others, including Rimsky-Korsakov, Ravel, and Shostakovich, and some have only recently been restored to their original harsh beauty.

mustard any of several annual plants of the family Cruciferae, with sweet-smelling yellow flowers. Brown and white mustard are cultivated as a condiment in Europe and North America. The seeds of brown mustard *Brassica juncea* and white mustard *Sinapis alba* are used in the preparation of table mustard.

mutation in biology, a change in the genes produced by a change in the ◊DNA that makes up the hereditary material of all living organisms. Mutations, the raw material of evolution, result from mistakes during replication (copying) of DNA molecules. Only a few improve the organism's performance and are therefore favored by ◊natural selection. Mutation rates are increased by certain chemicals and by radiation.

mutiny organized act of disobedience or defiance by two or more members of the armed services. In naval and military law, mutiny has always been regarded as one of the most serious of crimes, punishable in wartime by death.

mutualism an association between two organisms of different species whereby both profit from the relationship. See also ◊symbiosis.

Mwinyi Ali Hassan 1925– . Tanzanian socialist politician, president from 1985, when he succeeded Julius Nyerere. He began a revival of private enterprise and control of state involvement and spending.

Myanmar Union of (*Thammada Myanmar Naingngandaw*) (formerly *Burma*, until 1989) *area* 261,228 sq mi/676,577 sq km *capital* (and chief port) Yangon (formerly Rangoon) *towns and cities* Mandalay, Moulmein, Pegu *physical* over half is rainforest; rivers Irrawaddy and Chindwin in central lowlands ringed by mountains in N, W, and E *environment* landslides and flooding during the rainy season (June–Sept) are becoming more frequent as a result of deforestation *features* ruined cities of Pagan and Mingun *head of state and government* Than Shwe from 1992 *political system* military republic *political parties* National Unity Party (NUP), military-socialist ruling party; National League for Democracy (NLD), pluralist opposition grouping *exports* rice, rubber, jute, teak, jade, rubies, sapphires *currency* kyat *population* (1993) 42,330,000; growth rate 1.9% p.a. (includes Shan, Karen, Raljome, Chinese, and Indian minorities) *life expectancy* men 61, women 64 *language* Burmese *media* TV satellite dishes must be registered and are not legally on sale *religions* Hinayana Buddhist 85%, animist, Christian *literacy* men 89%, women 72% *GNP* $210 per head (1989) *chronology 1886* United as province of British India. *1937* Became crown colony in the British Commonwealth. *1942–45* Occupied by Japan. *1948* Independence achieved from Britain. Left the Commonwealth. *1962* General Ne Win assumed power in army coup. *1973–74* Adopted presidential-style "civilian" constitution. *1975* Opposition National Democratic Front formed. *1986* Several thousand supporters of opposition leader Suu Kyi arrested. *1988* Government resigned after violent demonstrations. Sept: General Saw Maung seized power in military coup; over 1,000 killed. *1989* Martial law declared; thousands arrested including advocates of democracy and human rights. Country renamed Myanmar and capital Yangon. *1990* Landslide victory for NLD in general election ignored by military junta; opposition leader Aung San Suu Kyi placed under house arrest. Breakaway opposition group formed "parallel government". *1991* Martial law and human rights abuses continued. Military offensives continued. Suu Kyi, still imprisoned, was awarded Nobel Prize for Peace. Pogrom against Muslim community in Arakan province, W Myanmar. *1992* Jan–Feb: further military crackdown on rebels. April: Saw Maung replaced by Than Shwe. Several political prisoners liberated. Sept: martial law lifted, but restrictions on political freedom remained. *1993* Constitutional convention agreed on a more liberal constitution. Suu Kyi arrest extended. Cease-fire agreed with northern-based rebels. *1995* Suu Kyi released.

Mycenaean civilization Bronze Age civilization that flourished in Crete, Cyprus, Greece, the Aegean Islands, and W Anatolia about 3000–1000 BC. During this period, magnificent architecture and sophisticated artifacts were produced.

My Lai massacre killing of 109 civilians in My Lai, a village in South Vietnam, by US troops in March 1968. An investigation in 1969 was followed by the conviction of Lt William Calley, commander of the platoon.

The incident also focused attention on the emotional pressures faced by US forces in Vietnam. Often unable to identify the enemy, soldiers adopted a policy of firing quickly.

myna or *mynah* any of various tropical starlings, family Sturnidae, of SE Asia. The glossy blackhill myna *Gracula religiosa* of India is a realistic mimic of sounds and human speech.

myopia or *nearsightedness* defect of the eye in which a person can see clearly only those objects that are close up. It is caused either by the eyeball being too long or by the cornea and lens system of the eye being too powerful, both of which cause the images of distant objects to be formed in front of the retina instead of on it. Nearby objects are sharply perceived. Myopia can be corrected by suitable glasses or contact lenses.

myrrh gum resin produced by small trees of the genus *Commiphora* of the bursera family, especially *C. myrrha*, found in Ethiopia and Arabia. In ancient times it was used for incense and perfume and in embalming.

myrtle evergreen shrub of the Old World genus *Myrtus*, family Myrtaceae. The commonly cultivated Mediterranean myrtle *M. communis* has oval opposite leaves and white flowers followed by purple berries, all of which are fragrant.

The Oregon myrtle or California laurel *Umbellularia california* belongs to the ◊laurel family. The wax myrtles (genus *Myrica*) of the US bear wax-covered nuts collected for candle making.

mystery religion any of various cults of the ancient world, open only to the initiated; for example, the cults of Demeter, Dionysus, Cybele, Isis, and Mithras. Underlying some of them is a fertility ritual, in which a deity undergoes death and resurrection and the initiates feed on the flesh and blood to attain communion with the divine and ensure their own life beyond the grave. The influence of mystery religions on early Christianity was considerable.

mysticism religious belief or spiritual experience based on direct, intuitive communion with the divine. It does not always involve an orthodox deity, though it is found in all the major religions—for example, kabbalism in Judaism, Sufism in Islam, and the bhakti movement in Hinduism.

The mystical experience is often rooted in ascetism and can involve visions, trances, and ecstasies; many religious traditions prescribe meditative and contemplative techniques for achieving mystical experience. Official churches fluctuate between acceptance of mysticism as a form of special grace, and suspicion of it as a dangerous deviation, verging on the heretical.

mythology body of traditional stories concerning the gods, supernatural beings, and heroes of a given culture, with whom humans may have relationships. Often a mythology may be intended to explain the workings of the universe, nature, or human history.

myxedema thyroid-deficiency disease developing in adult life, most commonly in middle-aged women. The symptoms are loss of energy and appetite, inability to keep warm, mental dullness, and dry, puffy skin. It is completely reversed by giving the thyroid hormone known as thyroxine.

n. abbreviation for ◊*noun* and *neuter*.

Nabokov Vladimir 1899–1977. US writer. He left his native Russia 1917 and began writing in English in the 1940s. His most widely known book is *Lolita* 1955, the story of the middle-aged Humbert Humbert's infatuation with a precocious girl of 12. His other books, remarkable for their word play and ingenious plots, include *Laughter in the Dark* 1938, *The Real Life of Sebastian Knight* 1945, *Pnin* 1957, and his memoirs *Speak, Memory* 1947.

Nader Ralph 1934– . US lawyer and consumer advocate. Called the "scourge of corporate morality", he led many major consumer campaigns. His book *Unsafe at Any Speed* 1965 led to US car-safety legislation.

Born in Winsted, Connecticut, he graduated from Princeton and Harvard universities and practiced law in Connecticut and Washington, DC. He investigated the lack of safety of color televisions, nuclear plants, and X-rays, as well as the procedures used by food and drug companies, overall job safety standards, and environmental pollution. The people who worked with and for him became known as "Nader's Raiders."

Nagasaki industrial port (coal, iron, shipbuilding) on Kyushu Island, Japan; population (1990) 444,600. Nagasaki was the only Japanese port open to European trade from the 16th century until 1859. An atomic bomb was dropped on it by the US Aug 9, 1945.

Nagorno-Karabakh autonomous region of ◊Azerbaijan *area* 1,700 sq mi/4,400 sq km *capital* Stepanakert *industries* cotton, grapes, wheat, silk *population* (1987) 180,000 (76% Armenian, 23% Azeri), the Christian Armenians forming an enclave within the predominantly Shiite Muslim Azerbaijan *history* An autonomous protectorate after the Russian Revolution 1917, Nagorno-Karabakh was annexed to Azerbaijan 1923 against the wishes of the largely Christian-Armenian population. From 1989, when the local council declared its intention to transfer control of the region to Armenia, the enclave was racked by fighting between local Armenian troops (reputedly backed by Armenia) and Azeri forces, both attempting to assert control. By Feb 1994, 18,000 people were reported to have been killed in the conflict and one million had become refugees.

Nagoya industrial seaport (automobiles, textiles, clocks) on Honshu Island, Japan; population (1990) 2,154,700. It has a shogun fortress 1610 and a notable Shinto shrine, Atsuta Jingu.

Nagpur industrial city (textiles, metals) in Maharashtra, India, on the river Pench; population (1981) 1,298,000. Pharmaceuticals, cotton goods, and hosiery are produced, and oranges are traded. Nagpur was founded in the 18th century, and was the former capital of Berar and Madhya Pradesh states.

Nagy Imre 1895–1958. Hungarian politician, prime minister 1953–55 and 1956. He led the Hungarian revolt against Soviet domination in 1956, for which he was executed.

Nahayan Sheik Sultan bin Zayed al-1918– . Emir of Abu Dhabi from 1969, when he deposed his brother, Sheik Shakhbut. He was elected president of the supreme council of the United Arab Emirates 1971. In 1991 he was implicated, through his majority ownership, in the international financial scandals associated with the Bank of Commerce and Credit International (BCCI).

Nairobi capital of Kenya, in the central highlands at 5,450 ft/1,660 m; population (1985) 1,100,000. It has light industry and food processing and is the headquarters of the United Nations Environment Program.

Naismith James 1861–1939. Canadian-born inventor of basketball. He invented basketball as a game to be played indoors during the winter, while attending the Young Men's Christian Association (YMCA) Training School in Springfield, Massachusetts, 1891. Among his books is *Basketball, Its Origin and Development*, published posthumously 1941.

Najibullah Ahmadzai 1947– . Afghan communist politician, leader of the People's Democratic Party of Afghanistan (PDPA) from 1986, and state president 1986–92. Although his government initially survived the withdrawal of Soviet troops Feb 1989, continuing pressure from the mujaheddin forces resulted in his eventual overthrow.

Nakasone Yasuhiro 1917– . Japanese conservative politician, leader of the Liberal Democratic Party (LDP) and prime minister 1982–87. He stepped up military spending and increased Japanese participation in international affairs, with closer ties to the US. He was forced to resign his party post May 1989 as a result of having profited from insider trading. After serving a two-year period of atonement, he rejoined the LDP April 1991.

Nakhichevan autonomous republic forming part of Azerbaijan, even though it is entirely outside the Azerbaijan boundary, being separated from it by Armenia; area 2,120 sq mi/5,500 sq km; population (1986) 272,000. Taken by Russia in 1828, it was annexed to Azerbaijan in 1924. Some 85% of the population are Muslim Azeris who maintain strong links with Iran to the south. Nakhichevan has been affected by the Armenia–Azerbaijan conflict; many Azeris have fled to Azerbaijan, and in Jan 1990 frontier posts and border fences with Iran were destroyed. In May 1992 Armenian forces made advances in the region, but Azeri forces had regained control by Aug. The republic has sought independence from Azerbaijan.

Namath Joe (Joseph William) 1943– . US football player. He played for the University of Alabama and in 1965 signed with the New York Jets of the newly established American Football League, leading them in 1969 to a historic upset victory over the Baltimore Colts in Super Bowl III. After leaving the Jets 1977, he briefly played with the Los Angeles Rams. He later became a sports broadcaster and actor.

Namib Desert coastal desert region in Namibia between the Kalahari Desert and the Atlantic Ocean. Its aridity is caused by the descent of dry air cooled by the cold Benguela current along the coast. The sand dunes of the Namib Desert are among the tallest in the world, reaching heights of 1,200 ft/370 m.

Namibia Republic of (formerly *South West Africa*) *area* 318,262 sq mi/824,300 sq km *capital* Windhoek *towns and cities* Swakopmund, Rehoboth, Rundu *physical* mainly desert *environment* 83% of rainfall evaporates as it hits the ground, making it the driest country in sub-Saharan Africa *features* Namib and Kalahari deserts; Orange River; Caprivi Strip links Namibia to Zambezi River; includes the enclave of Walvis Bay (area 432 sq mi/1,120 sq km) *head of state* Sam Nujoma from 1990 *head of government* Hage Geingob from 1990 *political system* democratic republic *political parties* South-West Africa People's Organization (SWAPO), socialist Ovambo-oriented; Democratic Turnhalle Alliance (DTA), moderate, multiracial coalition; United Democratic Front (UDF), disaffected ex-SWAPO members; National Christian Action (ACN), white conservative *exports* diamonds, uranium, copper, lead, zinc *currency* Namibian dollar *population* (1993 est) 1,550,000 (black African 85%, European 6%) *life expectancy* men 58, women 60 *languages* Afrikaans (spoken by 60% of white population), German, English (all official), several indigenous languages *religions* 51% Lutheran, 19% Roman Catholic, 6% Dutch Reformed Church, 6% Anglican *literacy* 38% *GNP* $1,120 per head (1991) *chronology 1884* German and British colonies established. *1915* German colony seized by South Africa. *1920* Administered by South Africa, under League of Nations mandate, as British South Africa. *1946* Full incorporation in South Africa refused by United Nations (UN). *1958* South-West Africa People's Organization (SWAPO) set up to seek racial equality and full independence. *1966* South Africa's apartheid laws extended to the country. *1968* Redesignated Namibia by UN. *1978* UN Security Council Resolution 435 for the granting of full sovereignty accepted by South Africa and then rescinded. *1988* Peace talks between South Africa, Angola, and Cuba led to agreement on full independence for Namibia. *1989* Unexpected incursion by SWAPO guerrillas from Angola into Namibia threatened agreed independence. Transitional constitution created by elected representatives; SWAPO dominant party. *1990* Liberal multiparty "independence" constitution adopted; independence achieved. Sam Nujoma elected president. *1991* Agreement on joint administration of disputed port of Walvis Bay reached with South Africa. *1993* South Africa relinquished claim to Walvis Bay sovereignty. Namibian dollar launched with South African rand parity.

Nanak 1469–*c.* 1539. Indian guru and founder of Sikhism, a religion based on the unity of God and the equality of all human beings. He was strongly opposed to caste divisions.

Nanchang industrial city (textiles, glass, porcelain, soap), capital of Jiangxi province, China, about 160 mi/260 km SE of Wuhan; population (1989) 1,330,000.

Nanjing or *Nanking* capital of Jiangsu province, China, 165 mi/270 km NW of Shanghai; center of industry (engineering, shipbuilding, oil refining), commerce, and communications; population (1989) 2,470,000. The bridge 1968 over the river Chang Jiang is the longest in China at 22,000 ft/6,705 m.

Nanking alternate name for ◊Nanjing, a city in China.

nanotechnology the building of devices on a molecular scale. Micromachines, such as gears smaller in diameter than a human hair, have been made at the AT&T Bell laboratories in New Jersey. Building large molecules with useful shapes has been accomplished by research groups in the US. A robot small enough to travel through the bloodstream and into organs of the body, inspecting or removing diseased tissue, was under development in Japan 1990.

Nansen Fridtjof 1861–1930. Norwegian explorer and scientist. In 1893, he sailed to the Arctic in the *Fram*, which was deliberately allowed to drift north with an iceflow. Nansen, accompanied by F Hjalmar Johansen (1867–1923), continued north on foot and reached 86° 14′ N, the highest latitude then attained. After World War I, Nansen became League of Nations high commissioner for refugees. Nobel Peace Prize 1923.

napalm fuel used in flamethrowers and incendiary bombs. Produced from jellied gasoline, it is a mixture of *na*phthenic and *palm*itic acids. Napalm causes extensive burns because it sticks to the skin even when aflame. It was widely used by the US Army during the Vietnam War.

naphtha the mixtures of hydrocarbons obtained by destructive distillation of petroleum, coal tar, and shale oil. It is a raw material for the petrochemical and plastics industries. The term was originally applied to naturally occurring liquid hydrocarbons.

Napier John 1550–1617. Scottish mathematician who invented ◊logarithms 1614 and "Napier's bones", an early mechanical calculating device for multiplication and division.

Naples (Italian *Napoli*) industrial port (shipbuilding, automobiles, textiles, paper, food processing) and capital of Campania, Italy, on the Tyrrhenian Sea; population (1988) 1,201,000. To the S is the Isle of Capri, and behind the city is Mount Vesuvius, with the ruins of Pompeii at its foot.

Naples, Kingdom of the southern part of Italy, alternately independent and united with ◊Sicily in the Kingdom of the Two Sicilies.

Napoleon I (Napoleon Bonaparte) 1769–1821. Emperor of the French 1804–14 and 1814–15. A general from 1796 in the ◊Revolutionary Wars, in 1799 he overthrew the ruling Directory (see ◊French Revolution) and made himself dictator. From 1803 he conquered most of Europe (the *Napoleonic Wars*) and installed his brothers as puppet kings (see ◊Bonaparte). After the Peninsular War and retreat from Moscow 1812, he was forced to abdicate 1814 and was banished to the island of Elba. In March 1815 he reassumed power but was defeated by British and Prussian forces at the Battle of ◊Waterloo and exiled to the island of St Helena. His internal administrative reforms and laws are still evident in France.

Napoleon II 1811–1832. Title given by the Bonapartists to the son of Napoleon I and Marie Louise; until 1814 he was known as the king of Rome and after 1818 as the duke of Reichstadt. After his father's abdication 1814 he was taken to the Austrian court, where he spent the rest of his life.

Napoleon III 1808–1873. Emperor of the French 1852–70, known as *Louis-Napoleon*. After two attempted coups (1836 and 1840) he was jailed, then went into exile, returning for the revolution of 1848, when he became president of the Second Republic but proclaimed himself emperor 1852. In 1870 he was maneuvered by the German chancellor Bismarck into war with Prussia (see ◊Franco-Prussian war); he was forced to surrender at Sedan, NE France, and the empire collapsed. He fled to England.

narcissus any bulbous plant of the genus *Narcissus*, family Amaryllidaceae. Species include the daffodil, jonquil, and narcissus. All have flowers with a cup projecting from the center.

Narcissus in Greek mythology, a beautiful youth who rejected the love of the nymph Echo and was condemned to fall in love with his own reflection in a pool. He pined away and in the place where he died a flower sprang up that was named for him.

narcotic pain-relieving and sleep-inducing drug. The term is usually applied to heroin, morphine, and other opium derivatives, but may also be used for other drugs which depress brain activity, including anesthetic agents and hypnotics.

Narmada River river that rises in the Maikala range in Madhya Pradesh state, central India, and flows 778 mi/1,245 km WSW to the Gulf of Khambat, an inlet of the Arabian Sea. Forming the traditional boundary between Hindustan and Deccan, the Narmada is a holy river of the Hindus.

narwhal toothed whale *Monodon monoceros*, found only in the Arctic Ocean. It grows to 16 ft/5 m long, has a gray and black body, a small head, and short flippers. The male has a single spirally fluted tusk that may be up to 9 ft/2.7 m long.

NASA (acronym for *National Aeronautics and Space Administration*) US government agency, founded 1958, for spaceflight and aeronautical research. Its headquarters are in Washington, DC, and its main installation is at the ◊Kennedy Space Center in Florida. NASA's early planetary and lunar programs included Pioneer spacecraft from 1958, which gathered data for the later crewed missions, the most famous of which took the first men to the Moon in *Apollo 11* on July 16–24, 1969.

The agency was founded 1958 by the National Aeronautics and Space Act.

Naseby, Battle of decisive battle of the English Civil War June 14, 1645, when the Royalists, led by Prince Rupert, were defeated by Oliver Cromwell and

General Fairfax. It is named for the nearby village of Naseby, 20 mi/32 km S of Leicester.

Nash (Frederic) Ogden 1902–1971. US poet and wit. He published numerous volumes of humorous, quietly satirical light verse, characterized by unorthodox rhymes and puns. They include *I'm a Stranger Here Myself* 1938, *Versus* 1949, and *Bed Riddance* 1970. Most of his poems first appeared in the *New Yorker* magazine, where he held an editorial post and did much to establish the magazine's tone.

Born in Rye, New York, Nash also wrote children's books and lyrics for such musicals as *A Touch of Venus* 1943.

Nashville port on the Cumberland River and capital of Tennessee, US; population (1990) 488,300. It is a banking and commercial center, and has large printing, music-publishing, and recording industries.

Most of the Bibles in the US are printed here, and it is the hub of the country-music business, being the home of the Grand Ole Opry and the Country Music Hall of Fame and Museum. Educational institutions include Vanderbilt and Fisk universities. The Southern Baptist Convention is headquartered here.

Nashville dates from 1778, and the Confederate army was defeated here 1864 in the Civil War.

Nassau capital and port of the Bahamas, on New Providence Island; population (1980) 135,000.

A tourist center, it is known for fine beaches and the resort community of Paradise Island across the harbor. The College of the Bahamas is here. English settlers founded it in the 17th century, and it was a supply base for Confederate blockade runners during the Civil War.

Nasser Gamal Abdel 1918–1970. Egyptian politician, prime minister 1954–56 and from 1956 president of Egypt (the United Arab Republic 1958–71). In 1952 he was the driving power behind the Neguib coup, which ended the monarchy. His nationalization of the Suez Canal 1956 led to an Anglo-French invasion and the ◊Suez Crisis, and his ambitions for an Egyptian-led union of Arab states led to disquiet in the Middle East (and in the West). Nasser was also an early and influential leader of the nonaligned movement.

Nast Thomas 1840–1902. German-born US illustrator and cartoonist. During the Civil War, Nast served as a staff artist for *Harper's Weekly* and later drew its editorial cartoons. His vivid caricatures established the donkey and the elephant as the symbols of Democrats and Republicans, respectively.

nastic movement plant movement that is caused by an external stimulus, such as light or temperature, but is directionally independent of its source, unlike ◊tropisms. Nastic movements occur as a result of changes in water pressure within specialized cells or differing rates of growth in parts of the plant.

nasturtium any plant of the genus *Nasturtium*, family Cruciferae, including watercress *N. officinale*, a perennial aquatic plant of Europe and Asia, grown as a salad crop. It also includes plants of the South American family Tropeolaceae, including the cultivated species *Tropeolum majus*, with orange or scarlet flowers, and *T. minus*, which has smaller flowers.

Natal province of South Africa, NE of Cape Province, bounded on the east by the Indian Ocean *area* 35,429 sq mi/91,785 sq km *capital* Pietermaritzburg *towns and cities* Durban *physical* slopes from the Drakensberg mountain range to a fertile subtropical coastal plain *features* Ndumu Game Reserve, Kosi Bay

narwhal The male narwhal, a toothed whale, has a spiral tusk up to 9 ft/2.7 m long. The tusk is actually an extended tooth which grows out of a hole in the upper lip. The tusk is not used as a weapon, although it may be used to dominate other males and to impress females.

Nature Reserve, Sodwana Bay National Park, Maple Lane Nature Reserve, and St Lucia National Park, which extends from coral reefs of the Indian Ocean north of Umfolozi River (whales, dolphins, turtles, crayfish), over forested sandhills to inland grasslands and swamps of Lake St Lucia, 125 sq mi/324 sq km (reedbuck, buffalo, crocodile, hippopotamus, black rhino, cheetah, pelican, flamingo, stork). It is under threat from titanium mining **industries** sugar cane, black wattle *Acacia mollissima*, corn, fruit, vegetables, tobacco, coal **population** (1985) 2,145,000

Nation Carrie Amelia Moore 1846–1911. US Temperance Movement crusader during the Prohibition 1920–33. Protesting against Kansas state's flagrant disregard for the prohibition law, she marched into illegal saloons with a hatchet, lecturing the patrons on the abuses of alcohol and smashing bottles and bar.

National Association for the Advancement of Colored People (NAACP) US civil-rights organization dedicated to ending inequality and segregation for African-Americans through nonviolent protest. Founded 1910, its first aim was to eradicate lynching. The NAACP campaigned to end segregation in state schools; it funded test cases that eventually led to the Supreme Court decision (Brown v Board of Education) 1954 outlawing school segregation, although it was only through the ◊civil-rights movement of the 1960s that desegregation was achieved. In 1987 the NAACP had about 500,000 members, black and white.

national debt debt incurred by the central government of a country to its own people and institutions and also to overseas creditors. A government can borrow from the public by means of selling interest-bearing bonds, for example, or from abroad. Traditionally, a major cause of national debt was the cost of war but in recent decades governments have borrowed heavily in order to finance development or nationalization, to support an ailing currency, or to avoid raising taxes.

In the US the net government debt as a proportion of gross national product rose steadily in the 1980s from only 19% in 1981 to 31% in 1988, as its borrowing increased to finance a huge influx of imported goods and to support increased defense spending.

National Health Service (NHS) UK government medical scheme; see ◊health service.

nationalism in politics, a movement that consciously aims to unify a nation, create a state, or liberate it from foreign or imperialistic rule. Nationalist movements became a potent factor in European politics during the 19th century; since 1900 nationalism has become a strong force in Asia and Africa and in the late 1980s revived strongly in E Europe.

nationalization policy of bringing a country's essential services and industries under public ownership. It was pursued, for example, by the UK Labour government 1945–51. In recent years the trend toward nationalization has slowed and in many countries (the UK, France, and Japan) reversed (◊privatization).

national park land set aside and conserved for public enjoyment. The first was Yellowstone National Park, established 1872. National parks include not only the most scenic places, but also places distinguished for their historic, prehistoric, or scientific interest, or for their superior recreational assets.

national security adviser an appointee of the executive branch, the head of the National Security Council, which, since the National Security Act 1947,

coordinates the defense and foreign policy of the US. Anthony Lake was appointed to the post 1993.

National Security Agency (NSA) largest and most secret of US intelligence agencies. Established 1952 to intercept foreign communications as well as to safeguard US transmissions, the NSA collects and analyzes computer communications, telephone signals, and other electronic data, and gathers intelligence. Known as the Puzzle Palace, its headquarters are at Fort Meade, Maryland (with a major facility at Menwith Hill, England).

National Socialism official name for the Nazi movement in Germany; see also ◊fascism.

Native American the modern, politically conscious term used by North ◊American Indians, ◊Eskimos, and Aleuts to describe themselves as a group, although each society maintains its autonomy and its own name.

NATO abbreviation for ◊*North Atlantic Treaty Organization*.

natural gas mixture of flammable gases found in the Earth's crust (often in association with petroleum). It is one of the world's three main fossil fuels (with coal and oil). Natural gas is a mixture of ◊hydrocarbons, chiefly methane, with ethane, butane, and propane. Natural gas is usually transported from its source by pipeline, although it may be liquefied for transport and storage and is, therefore, often used in remote areas where other fuels are scarce and expensive.

natural selection the process whereby gene frequencies in a population change through certain individuals producing more descendants than others because they are better able to survive and reproduce in their environment.

It was recognized by Charles Darwin and English naturalist Alfred Russel Wallace as the main process driving ◊evolution.

nature–nurture controversy or *environment–heredity controversy* long-standing dispute among philosophers and psychologists over the relative importance of environment, that is upbringing, experience and learning ("nurture"), and heredity, that is genetic inheritance ("nature"), in determining the makeup of an organism, as related to human personality and intelligence.

nature preserve area set aside to protect a habitat and the wildlife that lives within it, with only restricted admission for the public. A nature preserve often provides a sanctuary for rare species, and rare habitats, such as marshlands. The world's largest is Etosha Reserve, Namibia; area 38,415 sq mi/99,520 sq km.

Many state and local preserves have been established in the US since 1970. Some are called greenbelts and some are designated "forever wild", as well as those that are administered for limited or educational access.

Nauru island country in Polynesia, SW Pacific, W of Kiribati.

Nauru Republic of (*Naoero*) **area** 8 sq mi/21 sq km **capital** (seat of government) Yaren District **physical** tropical island country in SW Pacific; plateau encircled by coral cliffs and sandy beaches **features** lies just S of equator; one of three phosphate rock islands in the Pacific **head of state and government** Bernard Dowiyogo from 1989 **political system** liberal democracy **political party** Democratic Party of Nauru (DPN), opposition to government **exports** phosphates *currency* Australian dollar *population* (1993 est) 10,000 (mainly Polynesian; Chinese 8%, European 8%); growth rate 1.7% p.a. *languages* Nauruan (official), English *religions* Protestant 66%, Roman Catholic 33% *literacy* 99% (1988) *GNP* $160 million (1986); $9,091 per head (1985) *chronology 1888* Annexed by Germany. *1920* Administered by Australia, New Zealand, and UK until independence, except 1942–45, when it was occupied by Japan. *1968* Independence achieved, with "special member" British Commonwealth status. Hammer DeRoburt elected president. *1976* Bernard Dowiyogo elected president. *1978* DeRoburt reelected. *1986* DeRoburt briefly replaced as president by Kennan Adeang. *1987* DeRoburt reelected; Adeang established the Democratic Party of Nauru. *1989* DeRoburt replaced by Kensas Aroi, who was later succeeded by Dowiyogo. *1992* Dowiyogo reelected. *1993* Legal fight to recover lost trust fund and gain compensation from Australian government for environmental damage ended by an out-of-court settlement of A$120 million (£50 million) payable over 20 years.

nautical mile formerly various units of distance used in navigation; since 1959, an internationally agreed-on standard equaling the average length of one minute of arc on a great circle of the Earth, or 6,076.12 ft/1,852 m.

nautilus shelled ◊cephalopod, genus *Nautilus*, found in the Indian and Pacific oceans. The pearly nautilus *N. pompilius* has a chambered spiral shell about 8 in/20 cm in diameter. Its body occupies the outer chamber. The nautilus has a large number of short, grasping tentacles surrounding a sharp beak.

Navaho member of a peaceable agricultural North American Indian people; population about 200,000. They were attacked by Kit Carson and US troops 1864, and were rounded up and exiled. Their reservation, created 1868, is the largest in the US (25,000 sq mi/65,000 sq km), and is mainly in NE Arizona but extends into NW New Mexico and SE Utah. Many Navaho now herd sheep and earn an income from tourism, making and selling rugs, blankets, and silver and turquoise jewelry. Like the Apache, to whom they are related, the Navaho speak a Southern Athabaskan language.

Navarre, Kingdom of former kingdom comprising the Spanish province of Navarre and part of what is now the French *département* of Basses-Pyrénées. It resisted the conquest of the ◊Moors and was independent until it became French 1284 on the marriage of Philip IV to the heiress of Navarre. In 1479 Ferdinand of Aragon annexed Spanish Navarre, with French Navarre going to Catherine of Foix (1483–1512), who kept the royal title. Her grandson became Henry IV of France, and Navarre was absorbed in the French crown lands 1620.

navigation the science and technology of finding the position, course, and distance traveled by a ship, plane, or other craft. Traditional methods include the magnetic ◊compass and ◊sextant. Today the gyrocompass is usually used, together with highly sophisticated electronic methods, employing beacons of radio signals. Satellite navigation uses satellites that broadcast time and position signals.

Navratilova Martina 1956– . Czech tennis player who became a naturalized US citizen 1981. The most outstanding woman player of the 1980s, she had 55 Grand Slam victories by 1991, including 18 singles titles. She won the Wimbledon singles title a record nine times, including six in succession 1982–87. She was defeated by Conchita Martinez in the final of her last Wimbledon 1994.

Nazarbayev Nursultan 1940– . President of Kazakhstan from 1990. In the Soviet period he was prime minister of the republic 1984–89 and leader of the Kazakh Communist Party 1989–91, which established itself as the independent Socialist Party of Kazakhstan Sept 1991. He is an advocate of free-market policies, and yet also enjoys the support of the environmentalist lobby.

Nazareth town in Galilee, N Israel, SE of Haifa; population (1981) 64,000. According to the New Testament, it was the boyhood home of Jesus.

Nazism ideology based on racism, nationalism, and the supremacy of the state over the individual. The German Nazi party, the *Nationalsozialistische Deutsche Arbeiterpartei* (National Socialist German Workers' Party), was formed from the German Workers' Party (founded 1919) and led by Adolf ◊Hitler 1921–45.

Nazi–Soviet pact see ◊Hitler–Stalin pact.

nb abbreviation for *nota bene* (Latin "note well"), used in references and citations.

N'djamena capital of Chad, at the confluence of the Chari and Logone rivers, on the Cameroon border; population (1988) 594,000.

Neagh, Lough lake in Northern Ireland, 15 mi/25 km W of Belfast; area 153 sq mi/396 sq km. It is the largest lake in the British Isles.

Neanderthal hominid of the Mid-Late Paleolithic, named for the Neander Thal (valley) near Düsseldorf, Germany, where a skeleton was found 1856. *Homo sapiens neanderthalensis* lived from about 150,000 to 35,000 years ago and was similar in build to present-day people, but slightly smaller, stockier, and heavier-featured with a strong jaw and prominent brow ridges on a sloping forehead.

nearsightedness alternate name for ◊myopia.

Nebraska state in central US; nickname Cornhusker State/Blackwater State *area* 77,354 sq mi/200,400 sq km *capital* Lincoln *towns and cities* Omaha, Grand Island, North Platte *population* (1990) 1,578,400 *features* Rocky Mountain foothills; tributaries of the Missouri; Boys' Town for the homeless, near Omaha; the ranch of Buffalo Bill; the only unicameral legislature *industries* cereals, livestock, processed foods, fertilizers, oil, natural gas *famous people* Fred Astaire, William Jennings Bryan, Johnny Carson, Willa Cather, Henry Fonda, Harold Lloyd, Malcolm X *history* exploited by French fur traders in the early 1700s; ceded to Spain by France 1763; retroceded to France 1801; part of the Louisiana Purchase 1803; explored by Lewis and Clark 1804–06; first settlement at Bellevue 1823; became a territory 1854 and a state 1867 after the Union Pacific began its transcontinental railroad at Omaha 1865.

Nebuchadnezzar or *Nebuchadrezzar II*. king of Babylonia from 604 BC. Shortly before his accession he defeated the Egyptians at Carchemish and brought Palestine and Syria into his empire. Judah revolted, with Egyptian assistance, 596 and 587–586 BC; on both occasions he captured Jerusalem and took many Hebrews into captivity. He largely rebuilt Babylon and constructed the hanging gardens.

nebula cloud of gas and dust in space. Nebulae are the birthplaces of stars, but some nebulae are produced by gas thrown off from dying stars (see ◊supernova).

Nebulae are classified depending on whether they emit, reflect, or absorb light.

nectarine smooth, shiny-skinned variety of ◊peach, usually smaller than other peaches and with firmer flesh. It arose from a natural mutation.

Nefertiti or *Nofretete* queen of Egypt who ruled *c.* 1372–1350 BC ; wife of the pharaoh ◊Ikhnaton.

negative/positive in photography, a reverse image, which when printed is again reversed, restoring the original scene. It was invented by Fox Talbot about 1834.

Today the most common snapshots and photos are printed positives (on paper) made from film negatives.

Negev desert in S Israel that tapers to the port of Eilat. It is fertile under irrigation, and minerals include oil and copper.

Negroid referring to one of the three major varieties (see ◊races) of humans, *Homo sapiens sapiens,* mainly the indigenous peoples of Subsaharan Africa and some of the nearby islands in the Indian Ocean and the W Pacific. General physical traits include dark eyes, tightly curled dark hair, brown to very dark skin, little beard or body hair, low to medium-bridged wide noses, and wide or everted lips. See ◊Caucasoid, ◊Mongoloid.

Nehru Jawaharlal 1889–1964. Indian nationalist politician, prime minister from 1947. Before the partition (the division of British India into India and Pakistan), he led the socialist wing of the nationalist Congress Party, and was second in influence only to Mahatma Gandhi. He was imprisoned nine times by the British 1921–45 for political activities. As prime minister from the creation of the dominion (later republic) of India in Aug 1947, he originated the idea of non-alignment (neutrality toward major powers). His daughter was Prime Minister Indira Gandhi. His sister, Vijaya Lakshmi Pandit (1900–1990) was the UN General Assembly's first female president (1953–54).

Nelson Horatio, Viscount Nelson 1758–1805. English admiral. He joined the navy in 1770. In the Revolutionary Wars against France he lost the sight in his right eye 1794 and lost his right arm 1797. He became a national hero, and rear admiral, after the victory off Cape St Vincent, Portugal. In 1798 he tracked the French fleet to Aboukir Bay where he almost entirely destroyed it. In 1801 he won a decisive victory over Denmark at the Battle of ◊Copenhagen, and in 1805, after two years of blockading Toulon, another over the Franco-Spanish fleet at the Battle of ◊Trafalgar, near Gibraltar.

nematode unsegmented worm of the phylum Nematoda. Nematodes are pointed at both ends, with a tough, smooth outer skin. They include many free-living species found in soil and water, including the sea, but a large number are parasites, such as the roundworms and pinworms that live in humans, or the eelworms that attack plant roots. They differ from ◊flatworms in that they have two openings to the gut (a mouth and an anus).

Nemesis in Greek mythology, the goddess of retribution, who especially punished hubris (Greek *hybris*), violent acts carried through in defiance of the gods and human custom.

Neo-Classicism movement in art, architecture, and design in Europe and North America about 1750–1850, characterized by a revival of classical Greek and Roman styles. It superseded the Rococo style and was inspired both by the excavation of Pompeii and Herculaneum (which revived Roman styles) and by the theories of the cultural studies of the German art historian J J Winckelmann (which revived Greek styles). Leading figures of the movement were the architect Robert Adam; the painters David, Ingres, and Mengs; the sculptors Canova, Flaxman, and Thorvaldsen; and the designers Wedgwood, Hepplewhite, and Sheraton.

neo-Darwinism modern theory of ◊evolution, built up since the 1930s by integrating the 19th-century English scientist Charles ◊Darwin's theory of evolution through natural selection with the theory of genetic inheritance founded on the work of the Austrian biologist Gregor Mendel.

neodymium yellowish metallic element of the ◊lanthanide series, symbol Nd, atomic number 60, relative atomic mass 144.24. Its rose-colored salts are used in coloring glass, and neodymium is used in lasers.

Neo-Impressionism movement in French painting in the 1880s, an extension of Impressionist technique. It drew on contemporary theories on color and perception, building up form and color by painting dots side by side. ◊Seurat was the chief exponent; his minute technique became known as ◊*Pointillism*. Signac and Pissarro practiced the style for a few years.

Neolithic last period of the ◊Stone Age, characterized by settled communities based on agriculture and domesticated animals, and identified by sophisticated, finely honed stone tools, and ceramic wares. The earliest Neolithic communities appeared about 9000 BC in the Middle East, followed by Egypt, India, and China. In Europe farming began in about 6500 BC in the Balkans and Aegean, spreading north and east by 1000 BC.

neon colorless, odorless, nonmetallic, gaseous element, symbol Ne, atomic number 10, atomic weight 20.183. It is grouped with the ◊inert gases, is nonreactive, and forms no compounds. It occurs in small quantities in the Earth's atmosphere.

neo-Nazism the upsurge in racial and political intolerance in Western Europe of the early 1990s. In Austria, Belgium, France, Germany, and Italy, the growth of extreme right-wing political groupings, coupled with racial violence, particularly in Germany, has revived memories of the Nazi period in Hitler's Germany. Ironically, the liberalization of politics in the post-Cold War world has unleashed antiliberal forces hitherto checked by authoritarian regimes.

Neoplatonism school of philosophy that flourished during the declining centuries of the Roman Empire (3rd–6th centuries AD). NeoPlatonists argued that the highest stage of philosophy is attained not through reason and experience, but through a mystical ecstasy. Many later philosophers, including Nicholas of Cusa, were influenced by Neoplatonism.

neoteny in biology, the retention of some juvenile characteristics in an animal that seems otherwise mature. An example is provided by the axolotl, a salamander that can reproduce sexually although still in its larval form.

Nepal Kingdom of (*Nepal Adhirajya*) *area* 56,850 sq mi/147,181 sq km *capital* Katmandu *towns and cities* Pátan, Moráng, Bhádgáon *physical* descends from the Himalayan mountain range in N through foothills to the river Ganges plain in S *environment* described as

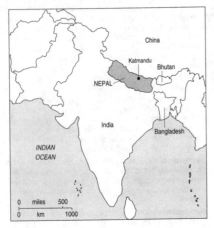

Neptune in Roman mythology, the god of the sea, equivalent of the Greek ◊Poseidon.

Neptune in astronomy, the eighth planet in average distance from the Sun. Neptune orbits the Sun every 164.8 years at an average distance of 2.794 billion mi/4.497 billion km. It is a giant gas (hydrogen, helium, methane) planet, with a diameter of 30,200 mi/48,600 km and a mass 17.2 times that of Earth. Its rotation period is 16 hours 7 minutes, and it has the highest winds in the Solar System. The methane in its atmosphere absorbs red light and gives the planet a blue coloring. It is believed to have a central rocky core covered by a layer of ice. Neptune has eight known moons.

neptunium silvery, radioactive metallic element of the ◊actinide series, symbol Np, atomic number 93, relative atomic mass 237.048. It occurs in nature in minute amounts in ◊pitchblende and other uranium ores, where it is produced from the decay of neutron-bombarded uranium in these ores. The longest-lived isotope, Np-237, has a half-life of 2.2 million years. The element can be produced by bombardment of U-238 with neutrons and is chemically highly reactive.

Nero adopted name of Lucius Domitius Ahenobarbus AD 37–68. Roman emperor from 54. In 59 he had his mother Agrippina and his wife Octavia put to death. The great fire at Rome 64 was blamed on the Christians, whom he subsequently persecuted. In 65 a plot against Nero was discovered. Further revolts followed 68, and he committed suicide.

Neruda Pablo. Pen name of Neftalí Ricardo Reyes y Basualto 1904–1973. Chilean poet and diplomat. His work includes lyrics and the epic poem of the American continent *Canto General* 1950. He was awarded the Nobel Prize for Literature 1971. He served as consul and ambassador to many countries.

nerve bundle of nerve cells enclosed in a sheath of connective tissue and transmitting nerve impulses to and from the brain and spinal cord. A single nerve may contain both motor and sensory nerve cells, but they function independently.

nerve cell or *neuron* elongated cell, the basic functional unit of the ◊nervous system that transmits information rapidly between different parts of the body. Each nerve cell has a cell body, containing the nucleus, from which trail processes called dendrites, responsible for receiving incoming signals. The unit of information is the *nerve impulse*, a traveling wave of chemical and electrical changes involving the membrane of the nerve cell. The cell's longest process, the axon, carries impulses away from the cell body.

nervous system the system of interconnected ◊nerve cells of most invertebrates and all vertebrates.

It is composed of the ◊central and ◊autonomic nervous systems. It may be as simple as the nerve net of coelenterates (for example, jellyfishes) or as complex as the mammalian nervous system, with a central nervous system comprising brain and spinal cord, and a peripheral nervous system connecting up with sensory organs, muscles, and glands.

Ness, Loch lake in Highland Region, Scotland, forming part of the Caledonian Canal; 22.5 mi/36 km long, 754 ft/229 m deep. There have been unconfirmed reports of a *Loch Ness monster* since the 15th century.

net of a particular figure or price, calculated after the deduction of specific items such as commission, discounts, interest, and taxes. The opposite is ◊gross.

the world's highest rubbish dump, Nepal attracts 270,000 tourists, trekkers, and mountaineers each year. An estimated 1,00 lb/500 kg of rubbish is left by each expedition trekking or climbing in the Himalayas. Since 1952 the foothills of the Himalayas have been stripped of 40% of their forest cover *features* Mount Everest, Mount Kangchenjunga; the only Hindu kingdom in the world; Lumbini, birthplace of the Buddha *head of state* King Birendra Bir Bikram Shah Dev from 1972 *head of government* Girija Prasad Koirala from 1991 *political system* constitutional monarchy *political parties* Nepali Congress Party (NCP), left of center; Communist Party of Nepal (Unified Marxist– Leninist–UML), left-wing *exports* jute, rice, timber, oilseed *currency* Nepalese rupee *population* (1993 est) 20,400,000 (mainly known by name of predominant clan, the Gurkhas; the Sherpas are a Buddhist minority of NE Nepal); growth rate 2.3% p.a. *life expectancy* men 54, women 53 *languages* Nepali (official); 20 dialects spoken *religions* Hindu 90%; Buddhist, Muslim, Christian *literacy* men 38%, women 13% *GDP* approximately £65 per person (1993–1994) *chronology* 1768 Nepal emerged as unified kingdom. *1815–16* Anglo-Nepali "Gurkha War"; Nepal became a British-dependent buffer state. *1846–1951* Ruled by the Rana family. *1923* Independence achieved from Britain. *1951* Monarchy restored. *1959* Constitution created elected legislature. *1960–61* Parliament dissolved by king; political parties banned. *1980* Constitutional referendum held following popular agitation. *1981* Direct elections held to national assembly. *1983* Overthrow of monarch-supported prime minister. *1986* New assembly elections returned a majority opposed to *panchayat* system of partyless government. *1988* Strict curbs placed on opposition activity; over 100 supporters of banned opposition party arrested; censorship imposed. *1989* Border blockade imposed by India in treaty dispute. *1990* Panchayat system collapsed after mass prodemocracy demonstrations; new constitution introduced; elections set for May 1991. *1991* Nepali Congress Party, led by Girija Prasad Koirala, won the general election. *1992* Communists led antigovernment demonstrations in Katmandu and Pátan. *1994* Koirala resigned, but remained as interim premier pending elections.

net assets either the total ◊assets of a company less its current liabilities (that is, the capital employed) or the total assets less current liabilities, debt capital, long-term loans and provisions, which would form the amount available to ordinary stockholders if the company were to be wound up.

Netherlands, the Kingdom of the (*Koninkrijk der Nederlanden*), popularly referred to as *Holland area* 41,863 sq km/16,169 sq mi *capital* Amsterdam *towns and cities* The Hague (seat of government), Utrecht, Eindhoven, Maastricht; chief port Rotterdam *physical* flat coastal lowland; rivers Rhine, Scheldt, Maas; Frisian Islands *territories* Aruba, Netherlands Antilles (Caribbean) *environment* the country lies at the mouths of three of Europe's most polluted rivers, the Maas, Rhine, and Scheldt. Dutch farmers contribute to this pollution by using the world's highest concentrations of nitrogen-based fertilizer per acre/hectare per year *features* polders (reclaimed land) make up over 40% of the land area; dyke (*Afsluitdijk*) 20 mi/32 km long 1932 has turned the former Zuider Zee inlet into the freshwater IJsselmeer; Delta Project series of dams 1986 forms sea defense in Zeeland delta of the Maas, Scheldt, and Rhine *head of state* Queen Beatrix

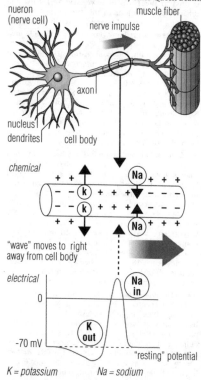

nueron (nerve cell)

muscle fiber

nerve impulse

axon

nucleus
dendrites   cell body

chemical

$+$ $+$ | Na | $+$ $+$ $+$
$-$ $-$ (k) $+$ $+$ $+$
$-$ $-$ (k) $+$ $+$ $+$
$+$ $+$ | Na | $+$ $+$ $+$

"wave" moves to right
away from cell body

electrical

Na
in

0

K
out

-70 mV

"resting" potential

$K = potassium$ $Na = sodium$

nerve cell *The anatomy and action of a nerve cell. The nerve cell or neuron consists of a cell body with the nucleus and projections called dendrites which pick up messages. An extension of the cell, the axon, connects one cell to the dendrites of the next. When a nerve cell is stimulated, waves of sodium (Na) and potassium (K) ions carry an electrical impulse down the axon.*

Wilhelmina Armgard from 1980 *head of government* Wim Kok from 1994 *political system* constitutional monarchy *political parties* Christian Democratic Appeal (CDA), Christian, right of center; Labour Party (PvDA), democratic socialist, left of center; People's Party for Freedom and Democracy (VVD), liberal, free-enterprise; Democrats 66 (D66), left of center *exports* dairy products, flower bulbs, vegetables, petrochemicals, electronics *currency* guilder *population* (1993) 15,240,000 (including 300,000 of Dutch-Indonesian origin absorbed 1949–64 from former colonial possessions); growth rate 0.4% p.a. *life expectancy* men 74, women 81 *language* Dutch *religions* Roman Catholic 40%, Protestant 31% *literacy* 99% *GNP* $21,030 per head (1992) *chronology 1940–45* Occupied by Germany during World War II. *1947* Joined Benelux customs union. *1948* Queen Juliana succeeded Queen Wilhelmina to the throne. *1949* Became a founding member of North Atlantic Treaty Organization (NATO). *1953* Dykes breached by storm; nearly 2,000 people and tens of thousands of cattle died in flood. *1958* Joined European Economic Community. *1980* Queen Juliana abdicated in favor of her daughter Beatrix. *1981* Opposition to cruise missiles averted their being sited on Dutch soil. *1989* Prime Minister Ruud Lubbers resigned; new Lubbers-led coalition elected. *1994* Government lost support in general election; new three-party coalition formed under PvDA leader, Wim Kok.

Netherlands Antilles two groups of Caribbean islands, part of the Netherlands with full internal autonomy, comprising ◊Curaçao and Bonaire off the coast of Venezuela (◊Aruba is considered separately), and St Eustatius, Saba, and the southern part of St Maarten in the Leeward Islands, 500 mi/800 km to the NE *area* 308 sq mi/797 sq km *capital* Willemstad on Curaçao *industries* oil from Venezuela refined here; tourism is important *languages* Dutch (official), Papiamento, English *population* (1983) 193,000.

Net, the abbreviation for *the ◊Internet.*

nettle any plant of the genus *Urtica*, family Urticaceae. Stinging hairs on the generally ovate leaves can penetrate the skin, causing inflammation. The common nettle *U. dioica* grows on waste ground in Europe and North America, where it was introduced.

network in computing, a method of connecting computers so that they can share data and ◊peripheral devices, such as printers. Internet is the computer network that connects major English-speaking institutions throughout the world, with around 12 million users.

neurology medical specialty concerned with the study and treatment of disorders of the brain, spinal cord, and peripheral nerves.

neuron another name for a ◊nerve cell.

neurosis in psychology, a general term referring to emotional disorders, such as anxiety, depression, and phobias. The main disturbance tends to be one of mood; contact with reality is relatively unaffected, in contrast to ◊psychosis.

neurotransmitter chemical that diffuses across a ◊synapse, and thus transmits impulses between ◊nerve cells, or between nerve cells and effector organs (for example, muscles). Common neurotransmitters are noradrenaline (which also acts as a hormone) and acetylcholine, the latter being most frequent at junctions between nerve and muscle. Nearly 50 different neurotransmitters have been identified.

neutrality the legal status of a country that decides not to choose sides in a war. Certain states, notably Switzerland and Austria, have opted for permanent neutrality. Neutrality always has a legal connotation. In peacetime, neutrality toward the big power alliances is called *nonalignment* (see ◊nonaligned movement).

neutralization in chemistry, a process occurring when the excess acid (or excess base) in a substance is reacted with added base (or added acid) so that the resulting substance is neither acidic nor basic.

neutrino in physics, any of three uncharged ◊elementary particles (and their antiparticles) of the ◊lepton class, having a mass too close to zero to be measured. The most familiar type, the antiparticle of the electron neutrino, is emitted in the beta decay of a nucleus. The other two are the muon and tau neutrinos.

neutron one of the three main subatomic particles, the others being the proton and the electron. The neutron is a composite particle, being made up of three ◊quarks, and therefore belongs to the ◊baryon group of the ◊hadrons. Neutrons have about the same mass as protons but no electric charge, and occur in the nuclei of all atoms except hydrogen. They contribute to the mass of atoms but do not affect their chemistry.

neutron star very small, "superdense" star composed mostly of ◊neutrons. They are thought to form when massive stars explode as ◊supernovae, during which the protons and electrons of the star's atoms merge, owing to intense gravitational collapse, to make neutrons. A neutron star may have the mass of up to three Suns, compressed into a globe only 12 mi/20 km in diameter.

Nevada state in western US; nickname Silver State/Sagebrush State *area* 110,550 sq mi/286,400 sq km *capital* Carson City *towns and cities* Las Vegas, Reno *population* (1990) 1,201,800 *physical* Mohave Desert; lakes: Tahoe, Pyramid, Mead; mountains and plateaus alternating with valleys *environment* decontamination project underway after the discovery that plutonium and other radioactive materials are leaking out through cracks in the rocks around an underground nuclear weapons testing site, ground water and wild animals near the site have been found to be contaminated

features legal gambling and prostitution (in some counties); entertainment at Las Vegas and Reno casinos; Lehman Caves National Monument *industries* mercury, barite, gold *history* explored by Kit Carson and John C Fremont 1843–45; ceded to the US after the Mexican War 1848; first permanent settlement a Mormon trading post 1848. Discovery of silver (the Comstock Lode) 1858 led to rapid population growth and statehood 1864.

New Age movement of the late 1980s characterized by an emphasis on the holistic view of body and mind, alternative (or complementary) medicines, personal growth therapies, and a loose mix of theosophy, ecology, oriental mysticism, and a belief in the dawning of an astrological age of peace and harmony.

Newark largest city (industrial and commercial) of New Jersey; population (1990) 275,200. Industries include electrical equipment, machinery, chemicals, paints, canned meats. The city dates from 1666, when a settlement called Milford was made on the site.

Since World War II, Newark has suffered from poverty and urban decay, and there was a major racial disturbance 1967. The airport was upgraded and modernized in the 1970s to serve New York City, and urban renewal projects in the 1980s have kept it a center for business and finance, especially insurance.

New Brunswick maritime province of E Canada *area* 28,332 sq mi/73,400 sq km *capital* Fredericton *towns and cities* St John, Moncton *features* Grand Lake, St John River; Bay of Fundy *industries* cereals, wood, paper, fish, lead, zinc, copper, oil, natural gas *population* (1991) 725,600; 37% French-speaking *history* first reached by Europeans (Cartier) 1534; explored by Champlain 1604; remained a French colony as part of Nova Scotia until ceded to England 1713. After the American Revolution many United Empire Loyalists settled here, and it became a province of the Dominion of Canada 1867.

New Caledonia island group in the S Pacific, a French overseas territory between Australia and the Fiji Islands *area* 7,170 sq mi/18,576 sq km *capital* Nouméa *physical* fertile, surrounded by a barrier reef *industries* nickel (the world's third-largest producer), chrome, iron *currency* CFP franc *population* (1983) 145,300 (43% Kanak (Melanesian), 37% European, 8% Wallisian, 5% Vietnamese and Indonesian, 4% Polynesian) *language* French (official) *religions* Roman Catholic 60%, Protestant 30% *history* New Caledonia was visited by Captain Cook 1774 and became French 1853. It has been a French Overseas Territory since 1958. A referendum on full independence is scheduled for 1998.

Newcastle-upon-Tyne industrial port and commercial and cultural center, in Tyne and Wear, NE England, on the river Tyne opposite Gateshead; administrative headquarters of Tyne and Wear and Northumberland; population (1991) 259,500. Industries include shipbuilding, marine and electrical engineering, chemicals, metals, flour-milling, soap, and paints. *history* Chiefly known as a coaling center, Newcastle first began to trade in coal in the 13th century.

New Deal in US history, the program introduced by President Franklin D. ◊Roosevelt 1933 to counter the Depression of 1929, including employment on public works, farm loans at low rates, and social reforms such as old-age and unemployment insurance, prevention of child labor, protection of employees against unfair practices by employers, and loans to local authorities for slum clearance. In the first 100 days of Roosevelt's administration, he introduced and pushed through Congress hundreds of programs and economic initiatives. The role of the federal government in the nation's economic life was strengthened to include policies that remain today.

New Delhi city adjacent to Old Delhi on the Yamuna River in the Union Territory of Delhi, N India; population (1991) 294,000. It is the administrative center of Delhi, and was designated capital of India by the British 1911. Largely designed by British architect Edwin Lutyens, New Delhi was officially inaugurated after its completion 1931. Chemicals, textiles, machine tools, electrical goods, and footwear are produced.

New England region of NE US, comprising the states of Maine, New Hampshire, Vermont, Massachusetts, Rhode Island, and Connecticut. It is a geographic region rather than a political entity, with an area of 66,672 sq mi/172,681 sq km. Boston is the principal urban center of the region, and Harvard and Yale are its major universities.

Its share of US income is larger than its share of population.

Newfoundland Canadian province on the Atlantic Ocean *area* 156,600 sq mi/405,700 sq km *capital* St John's *towns and cities* Corner Brook, Gander *physical* Newfoundland island and ◊Labrador on the mainland on the other side of the Straits of Belle Isle; rocky *features* Grand Banks section of the continental shelf rich in cod; home of the Newfoundland and Labrador dogs *industries* newsprint, fish products, hydroelectric power, iron, copper, zinc, uranium, offshore oil *population* (1991) 571,600 *history* colonized by Vikings about AD 1000; Newfoundland was reached by the English, under the Italian navigator Giovanni ◊Caboto, 1497. It was the first English colony, established 1583. French settlements were made and British sovereignty was not recognized until 1713. The province joined Canada 1949.

New Guinea island in the SW Pacific, N of Australia, comprising Papua New Guinea and the Indonesian province of Irian Jaya; total area about 342,000 sq mi/885,780 sq km. Part of the Dutch East Indies from 1828, West Irian was ceded by the United Nations to Indonesia 1963.

New Hampshire state in NE US; nickname Granite State *area* 9,264 sq mi/24,000 sq km *capital* Concord *towns and cities* Manchester, Nashua *population* (1990) 1,109,300 *features* White Mountains, including Mount Washington (with its cog railroad) and Mount Monadnock; the Connecticut River forms boundary with Vermont; earliest presidential-election party primaries every four years; no state income tax or sales tax; ski and tourist resorts *industries* dairy, poultry, fruits, and vegetables; electrical and other machinery; pulp and paper *famous people* Mary Baker Eddy, Robert Frost *history* settled as a fishing colony near Rye and Dover 1623; separated from Massachusetts colony 1679. As leaders in the Revolutionary cause, its leaders received the honor of being the first to declare independence from Britain July 4, 1776. It became a state 1788, one of the original 13 states.

New Jersey state in NE US; nickname Garden State *area* 7,797 sq mi/20,200 sq km *capital* Trenton *towns and cities* Newark, Jersey City, Paterson, Elizabeth *population* (1990) 7,730,200 *features* about 125 mi/200 km of seashore, including legalized gambling in Atlantic City and the Victorian beach resort of Cape May; Delaware Water Gap; Palisades along the west bank of the Hudson River; Princeton University; Morristown National Historic Park; Edison National Historic Site, Menlo Park; Walt Whitman House, Camden; Statue of Liberty National Monument (shared with New York); the Meadowlands stadium *industries* fruits and vegetables, fish and shellfish, chemicals, pharmaceuticals, soaps and cleansers, transport equipment, petroleum refining *famous people* Stephen Crane, Thomas Edison, Thomas Paine, Paul Robeson, Frank Sinatra, Bruce Springsteen, Woodrow Wilson *history* colonized in the 17th century by the Dutch (New Netherlands); ceded to England 1664; became a state 1787. It was one of the original 13 states.

New London port city in SE Connecticut, on Long Island Sound at the mouth of the Thames River; population (1990) 28,500.

It is a naval base and home of the US Coast Guard Academy and the US Submarine Officers School. Industries include submarine production, pharmaceuticals, and chemicals. Tourism is also important to the economy. Connecticut College is here. Settled 1646 as part of the Massachusetts Bay Colony, it served as a privateering base during the American Revolution, a whaling center during the 1800s, and an important base for ships during World War II.

Newman John Henry 1801–1890. English Roman Catholic theologian. While still an Anglican, he wrote a series of *Tracts for the Times*, which gave their name to the Tractarian Movement (subsequently called the ◊Oxford Movement) for the revival of Catholicism. He became a Catholic 1845 and was made a cardinal 1879. In 1864 his autobiography, *Apologia pro vita sua*, was published.

New Mexico state in southwestern US; nickname Land of Enchantment *area* 121,590 sq mi/315,000 sq km *capital* Santa Fe *towns and cities* Albuquerque, Las Cruces, Roswell *population* (1990) 1,515,100 *physical* more than 75% of the area lies over 3,900 ft/1,200 m above sea level; plains, mountains, caverns *features* Great Plains; Rocky Mountains; Rio Grande; Carlsbad Caverns, the largest known; Los Alamos atomic and space research center; White Sands Missile Range (also used by space shuttle); Kiowa Ranch, site of D H Lawrence's stay in the Sangre de Christos Mountains; Taos art colony; Santa Fe Opera Company; Navaho and Hopi Indian reservations; White Sands and Gila Cliff Dwellings national monuments *products* uranium, potash, copper, oil, natural gas, petroleum and coal products; sheep farming; cotton; pecans; vegetables *famous people* Billy the Kid, Kit Carson, Georgia O'Keeffe *history* explored by Francisco de Coronado for Spain 1540–42; Spanish settlement 1598 on the Rio Grande; Santa Fe founded 1610; most of New Mexico ceded to the US by Mexico 1848; became a state 1912. The first atomic bomb, a test device, was exploded in the desert near Alamogordo July 16, 1945. Oil and gas development and tourism now contribute to the state economy.

New Orleans city and Mississippi River port in Louisiana; population (1980) 557,500. With an outlet to the Gulf of Mexico, New Orleans has led all US ports in shipping tonnage handled. It is a commercial and manufacturing center, with the chief products refined petroleum and petrochemicals. Educational institutions include Tulane University. In the 18th century New Orleans was the capital of the Louisiana Territory. It passed to the US with the ◊Louisiana Purchase, and by 1852 it was the third-largest US city. It is the traditional birthplace of jazz and is famous for its ◊Mardi Gras.

Newport News industrial city (engineering, shipbuilding) and port of SE Virginia, US, at the mouth of the James River; population (1990) 170,000. With neighboring Chesapeake, Norfolk, and Portsmouth, it forms the Port of Hampton Roads, one of the chief US ports. It is the site of one of the world's largest shipyards.

The site was settled by the British around 1620. During the Civil War the first battle between ironclad ships (the *Monitor* and the *Merrimac*) 1862 took place off Newport News.

New South Wales state of SE Australia *area* 309,418 sq mi/801,600 sq km *capital* Sydney *towns and cities* Newcastle, Wollongong, Broken Hill *physical* Great Dividing Range (including Blue Mountains) and part of the Australian Alps (including Snowy Mountains and Mount Kosciusko); Riverina district, irrigated by the Murray-Darling-Murrumbidgee river system; other main rivers Lachlan, Macquarie-Bogan, Hawkesbury, Hunter, Macleay, and Clarence *features* a radio telescope at Parkes; Siding Spring Mountain 2,817 ft/859 m, NW of Sydney, with telescopes that can observe the central sector of the Galaxy. ◊Canberra forms an enclave within the state, and New South Wales administers the dependency of Lord Howe Island *products* cereals, fruit, sugar, tobacco, wool, meat, hides and skins, gold, silver, copper, tin, zinc, coal; hydroelectric power from the Snowy River *population* (1987) 5,570,000; 60% in Sydney *history* called New Wales by English explorer Capt. ◊Cook, who landed at Botany Bay 1770 and thought that the coastline resembled that of Wales. It was a convict settlement 1788–1850; opened to free settlement by 1819; achieved self-government 1856; and became a state of the Commonwealth of Australia 1901. During the first weeks of Jan 1994, bush fires ravaged the state's eastern coastline, burning 1.9 million acres/770,000 hectares and claiming four lives.

newspaper a daily or weekly publication in the form of folded sheets containing news, illustrations, timely comments, and advertising. Newsheets became commercial undertakings after the invention of printing and were introduced 1609 in Germany. The first newspaper in colonial America was *Publick Occurrences Both Forreign and Domestick*. It was planned as a monthly publication, but it was only published once, in Boston 1690. It was not until 1704 that another paper, the *News-Letter*, also published in Boston, appeared.

newt small salamander, of the family Salamandridae, found in Eurasia, NW Africa, and North America. The European newts, such as the smooth newt *Triturus vulgaris*, live on land for part of the year but enter a pond or lake to breed in the spring.

The red-spotted newt *Notophthalmus viridescens* of E North America, about 3.5 in/9 cm long, is olive green with red spots when adult. The young, called red efts, are bright orange and are terrestrial.

New Testament the second part of the ◊Bible, recognized by the Christian church from the 4th century as sacred doctrine. The New Testament includes the Gospels, which tell of the life and teachings of Jesus, the history of the early church, the teachings of St Paul, and mystical writings. It was written in Greek during the 1st and 2nd centuries AD, and the

individual sections have been ascribed to various authors by Biblical scholars.

newton SI unit (symbol N) of ◊force. One newton is the force needed to accelerate an object with mass of one kilogram by one meter per second per second. The weight of a medium size (3 oz/100 g) apple is one newton.

Newton Isaac 1642–1727. English physicist and mathematician who laid the foundations of physics as a modern discipline. He discovered the law of gravity, created calculus, discovered that white light is composed of many colors, and developed the three standard laws of motion still in use today. During 1665–66, he discovered the binomial theorem, and differential and integral calculus, and also began to investigate the phenomenon of gravitation. In 1685, he expounded his universal law of gravitation. His *Philosophiae naturalis principia mathematica*, usually referred to as *Principia*, was published in 1687, with the aid of Edmond ◊Halley.

Newton's laws of motion in physics, three laws that form the basis of Newtonian mechanics. (1) Unless acted upon by a net force, a body at rest stays at rest, and a moving body continues moving at the same speed in the same straight line. (2) A net force applied to a body gives it a rate of change of momentum proportional to the force and in the direction of the force. (3) When a body A exerts a force on a body B, B exerts an equal and opposite force on A; that is, to every action there is an equal and opposite reaction.

New World the Americas, so called by the first Europeans who reached them. The term also describes animals and plants of the western hemisphere.

New York largest city in the US, industrial port (printing, publishing, clothing), cultural, financial, and commercial center, in S New York State, at the junction of the Hudson and East rivers and including New York Bay. It comprises the boroughs of the Bronx, Brooklyn, Manhattan, Queens, and Staten Island; population (1990) 7,322,600, white 43.2%, African American 25.2%, Hispanic 24.4%. New York is also known as the Big Apple.

The two major airports are Kennedy International and La Guardia. The Port of New York is the nation's second-busiest harbor, although most active piers and harbors are now in New Jersey and Brooklyn. Tourism, conventions, and educational institutions are also important to the city's economy.

The Statue of Liberty stands on Liberty Island. Skyscrapers include the twin towers of the World Trade Center (1,350 ft/412 m) and the art deco Empire State Building (1,250 ft/381 m). St Patrick's Cathedral is 19th-century Gothic. Columbia University 1754 is the best known of a number of institutions of higher education. Other features include Central Park, Rockefeller Center, the United Nations complex, Carnegie Hall, Lincoln Center for the Performing Arts, the Broadway theater district, the New York Stock Exchange, Chinatown, and Greenwich Village.

The Italian navigator Giovanni da Verrazano (c1485–c1528) reached New York Bay 1524, and Henry Hudson explored it 1609. The Dutch established a settlement on Manhattan 1624, named New Amsterdam; this was captured by the English in 1664 and renamed New York. During the American Revolution, British troops occupied New York 1776–84. After the Revolution, New York was the capital of the US 1785–89. In the early 19th century, it passed

Philadelphia to become the nation's largest city, and for the next 100 years it swelled with immigrants.

New York state in NE US; nickname Empire State/Excelsior State *area* 49,099 sq mi/127,200 sq km *capital* Albany *towns and cities* New York, Buffalo, Rochester, Yonkers, Syracuse *population* (1990) 17,990,500 *physical* mountains: Adirondacks, Catskills; lakes: Champlain, Placid, Erie, Ontario; rivers: Mohawk, Hudson, St Lawrence (with Thousand Islands); Niagara Falls; Long Island; New York Bay *features* West Point, site of the US Military Academy 1801; horse racing at Belmont, Aqueduct, Saratoga Springs; colleges: Colgate, Cornell, Columbia, New York University, CUNY, SUNY, Juilliard, and Vassar; home of Franklin D Roosevelt at Hyde Park; home of Theodore Roosevelt, Oyster Bay; Erie Canal; United Nations headquarters; New York City *products* dairy products, apples, clothing, periodical and book printing and publishing, electronic components and accessories, office machines and computers, communications equipment, motor vehicles and equipment, pharmaceuticals, aircraft and parts *famous people* Aaron Burr, Grover Cleveland, James Fenimore Cooper, George Gershwin, Alexander Hamilton, Fiorello La Guardia, Washington Irving, Henry James, Herman Melville, Arthur Miller, Nelson Rockefeller, Franklin D Roosevelt, Theodore Roosevelt, Peter Stuyvesant, Walt Whitman *history* explored by the Italian navigator Giovanni da Verrazano for France 1524; explored by Henry Hudson for the Netherlands 1609; colonized by the Dutch from 1614; Manhattan Island purchased by Peter Minuit 1625; New Amsterdam annexed by the English 1664. The first constitution was adopted 1777, when New York became one of the original 13 states.

The Battle of Saratoga 1777, following which British troops surrendered, is considered the turning point of the American Revolution. By 1810 New York was the most populous of the states, a rank it maintained until the 1960s. The Erie Canal, completed 1825, provided a link between the Atlantic and the Great Lakes. By 1970, New York was suffering economic decline, particularly in manufacturing, but it remains an important industrial state.

New York Times v Sullivan US Supreme Court decision 1964 imposing limits on public officials to bring libel suits against journalists who criticize their actions as public servants. The case was brought by Police Commissioner Sullivan of Montgomery, Alabama, in response to a paid advertisement in the *Times* that accused Sullivan's police force of brutality and repression. The Court ruled public officials cannot recover damages in libel suits without proof that defamatory falsehoods have been published intentionally and with actual malice.

New Zealand Dominion of *area* 103,777 sq mi/ 268,680 sq km *capital* and port Wellington *towns and cities* Hamilton, Palmerston North, Christchurch, Dunedin; port Auckland *physical* comprises North Island, South Island, Stewart Island, Chatham Islands, and minor islands; mainly mountainous *overseas territories* Tokelau (three atolls transferred 1926 from former Gilbert and Ellice Islands colony); Niue Island (one of the Cook Islands, separately administered from 1903: chief town Alafi); Cook Islands are internally self-governing but share common citizenship with New

Zealand; Ross Dependency in Antarctica *features* Ruapehu in the North Island, 9,180 ft/2,797 m, highest of three active volcanoes; geysers and hot springs of the Rotorua district; Lake Taupo (238 sq mi/616 sq km), source of Waikato River; Kaingaroa state forest. In the South Island are the Southern Alps and Canterbury Plains *head of state* Elizabeth II from 1952 represented by governor general Catherine Tizard from 1990 *head of government* Jim Bolger from 1990 *political system* constitutional monarchy *political parties* Labour Party, moderate, left of center; New Zealand National Party, free-enterprise, center-right; Alliance Party, left of center, ecologists *exports* lamb, beef, wool, leather, dairy products, processed foods, kiwi fruit, seeds and breeding stock, timber, paper, pulp, light aircraft *currency* New Zealand dollar *population* (1993) 3,490,000 (European, mostly British, 87%; Polynesian, mostly Maori, 12%); growth rate 0.9% p.a. *life expectancy* men 73, women 79 *languages* English (official), Maori *religions* Protestant 50%, Roman Catholic 15% *literacy* 99% *GNP* $12,140 per head (1991) *chronology* *1840* New Zealand became a British colony. *1907* Created a dominion of the British Empire. *1931* Granted independence from Britain. *1947* Independence within the Commonwealth confirmed by the New Zealand parliament. *1972* National Party government replaced by Labour Party, with Norman Kirk as prime minister. *1974* Kirk died; replaced by Wallace Rowling. *1975* National Party returned, with Robert Muldoon as prime minister. *1984* Labour Party returned under David Lange. *1985* Non-nuclear military policy created disagreements with France and the US. *1987* National Party declared support for the Labour government's non-nuclear policy. Lange reelected. *1988* Free-trade agreement with Australia signed. *1989* Lange resigned over economic differences with finance minister (he cited health reasons); replaced by Geoffrey Palmer. *1990* Palmer replaced by Mike Moore. Labour Party defeated by National Party in general election; Jim Bolger became prime minister. *1991* Formation of amalgamated Alliance Party set to challenge two-party system. *1992* Ban on visits by US warships lifted. Referendum aproved change in voting system from 1996. *1993* National Party won general election with majority of one seat. *1994* Resignation of junior minister forced National Party into alliance with Labour.

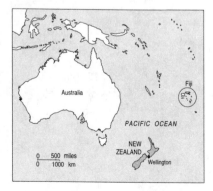

Ney Michael, Duke of Elchingen, Prince of Ney 1769–1815. Marshal of France under ◊Napoleon I, who commanded the rearguard of the French army during the retreat from Moscow, and for his personal courage was called "the bravest of the brave". When Napoleon returned from Elba, Ney was sent to arrest him, but instead deserted to him and fought at Waterloo. He was subsequently shot for treason.

Niagara Falls two waterfalls on the Niagara River, on the Canada–US border, between lakes Erie and Ontario and separated by Goat Island. The *American Falls* are 167 ft/51 m high, 1,080 ft/330 m wide; *Horseshoe Falls*, in Canada, are 160 ft/49 m high, 2,600 ft/790 m across.

The French explorer Samuel de Champlain may have seen Niagara Falls 1613, and Father Louis Hennepin viewed this natural wonder 1678. The use of hydroelectric power in North America was pioneered here 1881.

Niamey river port and capital of ◊Niger; population (1983) 399,000. It produces textiles, chemicals, pharmaceuticals, and foodstuffs.

Nicaragua Republic of (*República de Nicaragua*) *area* 49,363 sq mi/127,849 sq km *capital* Managua *towns and cities* León, Granada; chief ports Corinto, Puerto Cabezas, El Bluff *physical* narrow Pacific coastal plain separated from broad Atlantic coastal plain by volcanic mountains and lakes Managua and Nicaragua *features* largest state of Central America and most thinly populated; Mosquito Coast, Fonseca Bay, Corn Islands *head of state and government* Violeta Barrios de Chamorro from 1990 *political system* emergent democracy *political parties* Sandinista National Liberation Front (FSLN), Marxist-Leninist; Opposition Political Alliance (APO, formerly National Opposition Union: UNO), loose US-backed coalition *exports* coffee, cotton, sugar, bananas, meat *currency* cordoba *population* (1993 est) 4,200,000 (mestizo 70%, Spanish descent 15%, Indian or black 10%); growth rate 3.3% p.a. *life expectancy* men 65, women 68 *languages* Spanish (official), Indian, English *religion* Roman Catholic 95% *literacy* 81% *GNP* $340 per head (1991) *chronology 1838* Independence achieved from Spain. *1926–1933* Occupied by US marines. *1936* General Anastasio Somoza elected president; start of near-dictatorial rule by Somoza family. *1962* Sandinista National Liberation Front (FSLN) formed to fight Somoza regime. *1979* Somoza government

ousted by FSLN. *1982* Subversive activity against the government by right-wing Contra guerrillas promoted by the US. State of emergency declared. *1984* The US mined Nicaraguan harbors. Action condemned by World Court 1986 and $17 billion in reparations ordered. *1985* Denunciation of Sandinista government by US president Ronald Reagan. FSLN won assembly elections. *1987* Central American peace agreement cosigned by Nicaraguan leaders. *1988* Peace agreement failed. Nicaragua held talks with Contra rebel leaders. Hurricane left 180,000 people homeless. *1989* Demobilization of rebels and release of former Somozan supporters; cease-fire ended. *1990* FSLN defeated by UNO, a US-backed coalition; Violeta Barrios de Chamorro elected president. Anti-government riots. *1991* First presidential state visit to US for over fifty years. *1992* June: US aid suspended because of concern over role of Sandinista in Nicaraguan government. Sept: around 16,000 made homeless by earthquake. *1993* State of emergency declared in N Nicaragua following skirmishes between rival Contra and Sandinista rebel groups. *1994* Peace accord with remaining Contra rebels.

Nice city on the French Riviera; population (1990) 345,700. Founded in the 3rd century BC, it repeatedly changed hands between France and the Duchy of Savoy from the 14th to the 19th century. In 1860 it was finally transferred to France.

Nicene Creed one of the fundamental ◊creeds of Christianity, promulgated by the Council of Nicaea 325.

Nicholas I 1796–1855. Czar of Russia from 1825. His Balkan ambitions led to war with Turkey 1827–29 and the Crimean War 1853–56.

Nicholas II 1868–1918. Czar of Russia 1894–1917. He was dominated by his wife, Czarina Alexandra, who was under the influence of the religious charlatan ◊Rasputin. His mismanagement of the Russo-Japanese War and of internal affairs led to the revolution of 1905, which he suppressed, although he was forced to grant limited constitutional reforms. He took Russia into World War I in 1914, was forced to abdicate in 1917 after the ◊Russian Revolution, and was executed with his family.

Nicholas, St also known as *Santa Claus*, 4th Century AD. In the Christian church, patron saint of Russia, children, merchants, sailors, and pawnbrokers; bishop of Myra (now in Turkey). His legendary gifts of dowries to poor girls led to the custom of giving gifts to children on the eve of his feast day, Dec 6, still retained in some countries, such as the Netherlands; elsewhere the custom has been transferred to Christmas Day. His emblem is three balls.

Nicholson Jack 1937– . US film actor. In the late 1960s, he captured the mood of nonconformist, uncertain young Americans in such films as *Easy Rider* 1969 and *Five Easy Pieces* 1970. He subsequently became a mainstream Hollywood star, appearing in *Chinatown* 1974, *One Flew over the Cuckoo's Nest* (Academy Award) 1975, *The Shining* 1979, *Terms of Endearment* (Academy Award) 1983, *Batman* 1989, and *A Few Good Men* 1992.

nickel hard, malleable and ductile, silver-white metallic element, symbol Ni, atomic number 28, atomic weight 58.71. It occurs in igneous rocks and as a free metal (native metal), occasionally occurring in fragments of iron-nickel meteorites. It is a component of the Earth's core, which is held to consist principally of iron with some nickel. It has a high melting point, low electrical and thermal conductivity, and can be magnetized. It does not tarnish and therefore is much used for alloys, electroplating, and for coinage.

Nicosia capital of Cyprus, with leather, textile, and pottery industries; population (1987) 165,000. Nicosia was the residence of Lusignan kings of Cyprus 1192–1475. The Venetians, who took Cyprus 1489, surrounded Nicosia with a high wall, which still exists; the city fell to the Turks 1571. It was again partly taken by the Turks in the invasion 1974.

nicotine $C_{10}H_{14}N_2$ ¢alkaloid (nitrogenous compound) obtained from the dried leaves of the tobacco plant *Nicotiana tabacum* and used as an insecticide. A colorless oil, soluble in water, it turns brown on exposure to the air.

Niebuhr Reinhold 1892–1971. US Protestant theologian, a Lutheran minister. His *Moral Man and Immoral Society* 1932 denied the possibility of fulfilling religious and political utopian aspirations, a position that came to be known as Christian Realism. Niebuhr was a pacifist, activist, and socialist but advocated war to stop totalitarianism in the 1940s. From 1945 he founded Americans for Democratic Action and became an adviser to the State Department.

Nietzsche Friedrich Wilhelm 1844–1900. German philosopher who rejected the accepted absolute moral values and the "slave morality" of Christianity. He argued that "God is dead" and therefore people were free to create their own values. His ideal was the *übermensch*, or "Superman", who would impose his will on the weak and worthless. Nietzsche claimed that knowledge is never objective but always serves some interest or unconscious purpose.

Niger third-longest river in Africa, 2,600 mi/4,185 km. It rises in the highlands bordering Sierra Leone and Guinea, flows NE through Mali, then SE through Niger and Nigeria to an inland delta on the Gulf of Guinea. Its flow has been badly affected by the expansion of the Sahara Desert. It is sluggish and frequently floods its banks. It was explored by the Scotsman Mungo Park 1795–96.

Niger Republic of (*République du Niger*) *area* 457,953 sq mi/1,186,408 sq km *capital* Niamey *towns and cities* Zinder, Maradi, Tahoua *physical* desert plains between hills in N and savanna in S; river Niger in SW, Lake Chad in SE *features* part of the Sahara Desert and subject to Sahel droughts *head of state* Mahamane Ousmane from 1993 *head of government* Mahamadou Issoufou from 1993 *political system* emergent democratic republic *political parties* Alliance for the Forces of Change (AFC), moderate, left-of-center coalition; National Movement for a Development Society (MNSD), right of center *exports* peanuts, livestock, gum arabic, uranium *currency* franc CFA *population* (1993 est) 8,500,000; growth rate 2.8% p.a. *life expectancy* men 45, women 48 *languages* French (official), Hausa, Djerma, and other minority languages *religions* Sunni Muslim 85%, animist 15% *literacy* men 40%, women 17% *GNP* $300 per head (1991) *chronology 1960* Achieved full independence from France; Hamani Diori elected president. *1974* Diori ousted in army coup led by Seyni Kountché. *1977* Cooperation agreement signed with France. *1987* Kountché died; replaced by Col. Ali Saibu. *1989* Ali Saibu elected president without opposition. *1990* Multiparty politics promised. *1991* Saibu stripped of executive powers; transitional government formed. *1992* Transitional government collapsed.

Referendum endorsed the adoption of multiparty politics. Violent clashes with northern Tuareg seeking independence. *1993* AFC broad coalition won absolute majority in assembly elections. Mahamane Ousmane elected president in first free presidential election. *1994* Peace agreement reached with northern Tuareg.

Niger-Congo languages the largest group of languages in Africa. It includes about 1,000 languages and covers a vast area south of the Sahara desert, from the W coast to the E, and down the E coast as far as South Africa. It is divided into groups and subgroups; the most widely spoken Niger-Congo languages are Swahili (spoken on the E coast), the members of the Bantu group (southern Africa), and Yoruba (Nigeria).

Nigeria Federal Republic of *area* 356,576 sq mi/ 923,773 sq km *capital* Abuja *towns and cities* Ibadan, Ogbomosho, Kano; ports Lagos, Port Harcourt, Warri, Calabar *physical* arid savanna in N; tropical rainforest in S, with mangrove swamps along the coast; river Niger forms wide delta; mountains in SE *environment* toxic waste from northern industrialized countries has been dumped in Nigeria *features* harmattan (dry wind from the Sahara); rich artistic heritage, for example, Benin bronzes *head of state and government* General Sani Abacha from 1993 *political system* military republic *political parties* Social Democratic Party (SDP), left of center; National Republican Convention (NRC), right of center *exports* petroleum (largest oil resources in Africa), cocoa, peanuts, palm oil (Africa's largest producer), cotton, rubber, tin *currency* naira *population* (1993 est) 92,800,000 (Yoruba in W, Ibo in E, and Hausa-Fulani in N); growth rate 3.3% p.a. *life expectancy* men 51, women 54 *languages* English (official), Hausa, Ibo, Yoruba *media* all radio and television stations and almost 50% of all publishing owned by the federal government or the Nigerian states; many publications closed down after 1994 coup *religions* Sunni Muslim 50% (in N), Christian 40% (in S), local religions 10% *literacy* men 62%, women 40% *GNP* $290 per head (1991) *chronology 1914* N Nigeria and S Nigeria united to become Britain's largest African colony. *1954* Nigeria became a federation. *1960* Independence achieved from Britain within the Commonwealth. *1963* Became a republic, with Nnamdi Azikiwe as president. *1966* Military coup, followed by a counter-coup led by General Yakubu Gowon. Slaughter of many members of the Ibo tribe in north. *1967* Conflict over oil rev-

enues led to declaration of an independent Ibo state of Biafra and outbreak of civil war. *1970* Surrender of Biafra and end of civil war. *1975* Gowon ousted in military coup; second coup put General Olusegun Obasanjo in power. *1979* Shehu Shagari became civilian president. *1983* Shagari's government overthrown in coup led by Maj. Gen. Mohammedu Buhari. *1985* Buhari replaced in a bloodless coup led by Maj. Gen. Ibrahim Babangida. *1989* Two new political parties approved. *1991* Nine new states created. Babangida confirmed his commitment to democratic rule for 1992. *1992* Multiparty assembly elections won by Babangida's SDP. *1993* Moshood Abiola (SDP) won first free presidential elections; results suspended. Aug: Babangida resigned, nominating Ernest Shonekan as interim prime minister. General Sani Abacha took control; military rule restored and political parties dissolved. *1994* Abiola arrested and charged with treason.

nightingale songbird of the thrush family with a song of great beauty, heard at night as well as by day. About 6.5 in/16.5 cm long, it is dull brown, lighter below, with a reddish brown tail. It migrates to Europe and winters in Africa. It feeds on insects and small animals. It has a huge musical repertoire, built from about 900 melodic elements.

Nightingale Florence 1820–1910. English nurse, the founder of nursing as a profession. She took a team of nurses to Scutari (now üsküdar, Turkey) in 1854 and reduced the ◊Crimean War hospital death rate from 42% to 2%. In 1856 she founded the Nightingale School and Home for Nurses in London.

nightjar any of about 65 species of night-hunting birds forming the family Caprimulgidae. They have wide, bristly mouths for catching flying insects. Their distinctive calls have earned them such names as whippoorwill and church-will's-widow. Some are called nighthawks.

The whippoorwill of North America *Caprimulgus vociferus* measures about 10 in/25 cm in length, and is mottled gray-brown.

nightshade any of several plants in the family Solanaceae, which includes the black nightshade *Solanum nigrum*, bittersweet or woody nightshade *S. dulcamara*, and deadly nightshade or ◊belladonna.

Nihilist member of a group of Russian revolutionaries in the reign of Alexander II 1855–81. Despairing of reform, they saw change as possible only through the destruction of morality, justice, marriage, property, and the idea of God. In 1878 the Nihilists launched a guerrilla campaign leading to the murder of the czar 1881.

Nijinsky Vaslav 1890–1950. Russian dancer and choreographer. Noted for his powerful but graceful technique, he was a legendary member of ◊Diaghilev's Ballets Russes, for whom he choreographed Debussy's *Prélude à l'après-midi d'un faune* 1912 and *Jeux* 1913, and Stravinsky's *Le Sacre du printemps/The Rite of Spring* 1913.

Nile river in Africa, the world's longest, 4,160 mi/6,695 km. The **Blue Nile** rises in Lake Tana, Ethiopia, the **White Nile** at Lake Victoria, and they join at Khartoum, Sudan. The river enters the Mediterranean Sea at a vast delta in N Egypt.

Nineveh capital of the Assyrian Empire from the 8th century BC until its destruction by the Medes under King Cyaxares in 612 BC. It was situated on the river Tigris (opposite the present city of Mosul, Iraq) and was adorned with palaces.

Ningxia or *Ningxia Hui* autonomous region (formerly *Ninghsia-Hui*) of NW China **area** 65,620 sq mi/170,000 sq km *capital* Yinchuan *physical* desert plateau *products* cereals and rice under irrigation; coal *population* (1990) 4,655,000.

Nintendo Japanese games console and software manufacturer. Nintendo's most successful game is Super Mario Brothers.

niobium soft, gray-white, somewhat ductile and malleable, metallic element, symbol Nb, atomic number 41, atomic weight 92.906. It occurs in nature with tantalum, which it resembles in chemical properties. It is used in making stainless steel and other alloys for jet engines and rockets and for making superconductor magnets.

Nippon English transliteration of the Japanese name for ◊Japan.

nirvana (Sanskrit "a blowing out") in Buddhism, the attainment of perfect serenity by the eradication of all desires. To some Buddhists it means complete annihilation, to others it means the absorption of the self in the infinite.

niter or *saltpeter* potassium nitrate, KNO_3, a mineral found on and just under the ground in desert regions; used in explosives. Niter occurs in Bihar, India, Iran, and Cape Province, South Africa. The salt was formerly used for the manufacture of gunpowder, but the supply of niter for explosives is today largely met by making the salt from nitratine (also called Chile saltpeter, $NaNO_3$). Saltpeter is a preservative and is widely used for curing meats.

nitrate salt or ester of nitric acid, containing the NO_3^- ion. Nitrates are used in explosives, in the chemical and pharmaceutical industries, in curing meat (see ◊niter), and as fertilizers. They are the most water-soluble salts known and play a major part in the nitrogen cycle. Nitrates in the soil, whether naturally occurring or from inorganic or organic fertilizers, can be used by plants to make proteins and nucleic acids. However, runoff from fields can result in nitrate pollution.

nitric acid or *aqua fortis* HNO_3 fuming acid obtained by the oxidation of ammonia or the action of sulfuric acid on potassium nitrate. It is a highly corrosive acid, dissolving most metals, and a strong oxidizing agent. It is used in the nitration and esterification of organic substances, and in the making of sulfuric acid, nitrates, explosives, plastics, and dyes.

nitrite salt or ester of nitrous acid, containing the nitrite ion (NO_2^-). Nitrites are used as preservatives (for example, to prevent the growth of botulism spores) and as coloring agents in cured meats such as bacon and sausages.

nitrogen colorless, odorless, tasteless, gaseous, nonmetallic element, symbol N, atomic number 7, atomic weight 14.0067. It forms almost 80% of the Earth's atmosphere by volume and is a constituent of all plant and animal tissues (in proteins and nucleic acids). Nitrogen is obtained for industrial use by the liquefaction and fractional distillation of air. Its compounds are used in the manufacture of foods, drugs, fertilizers, dyes, and explosives.

nitrogen cycle the process of nitrogen passing through the ecosystem. Nitrogen, in the form of inorganic compounds (such as nitrates) in the soil, is absorbed by plants and turned into organic compounds (such as proteins) in plant tissue. A proportion of this nitrogen is eaten by ◊herbivores, with some of this in turn being passed on to the carnivores, which feed on the herbivores. The nitrogen is ultimately returned to the soil as excrement and when organisms die and are converted back to inorganic form by decomposers.

nitrogen fixation the process by which nitrogen in the atmosphere is converted into nitrogenous compounds by the action of microorganisms, such as cyanobacteria (see ◊blue-green algae) and bacteria, in conjunction with certain ◊legumes. Several chemical processes duplicate nitrogen fixation to produce fertilizers; see ◊nitrogen cycle.

nitroglycerine $C_3H_5(ONO_2)_3$ flammable, explosive oil produced by the action of nitric and sulfuric acids on glycerol. Although poisonous, it is used in cardiac medicine. It explodes with great violence if heated in a confined space and is used in the preparation of dynamite, cordite, and other high explosives.

nitrous oxide or **dinitrogen oxide** N_2O colorless, nonflammable gas that, used in conjunction with oxygen, reduces sensitivity to pain. In higher doses it is an anesthetic. Well tolerated, it is often combined with other anesthetic gases to enable them to be used in lower doses. It may be self-administered; for example, in childbirth. It is a greenhouse gas; about 10% of nitrous oxide released into the atmosphere comes from the manufacture of nylon. It used to be known as "laughing gas".

Niven David 1909–1983. Scottish-born US film actor. In Hollywood from the 1930s, his films include *Wuthering Heights* 1939, *Around the World in 80 Days* 1956, *Separate Tables* 1958 (Academy Award), *The Guns of Navarone* 1961, and *The Pink Panther* 1964. He published two best-selling volumes of autobiography, *The Moon's a Balloon* 1972 and *Bring on the Empty Horses* 1975.

Nixon Richard (Milhous) 1913–1994. 37th president of the US 1969–74, a Republican. He attracted attention as a member of the Un-American Activities Committee 1948, and was vice president to Eisenhower 1953–61. As president he was responsible for US withdrawal from Vietnam, and forged new links with China, but at home his culpability in the cover-up of the ◊Watergate scandal and the existence of a "slush fund" for political machinations during his reelection campaign 1972 led to his resignation 1974 when threatened with ◊impeachment.

Nkomo Joshua 1917– . Zimbabwean politician, vice president from 1988. As president of ZAPU (Zimbabwe African People's Union) from 1961, he was a leader of the black nationalist movement against the white Rhodesian regime. He was a member of Robert ◊Mugabe's cabinet 1980–82 and from 1987.

Nkrumah Kwame 1909–1972. Ghanaian nationalist politician, prime minister of the Gold Coast (Ghana's former name) 1952–57 and of newly independent Ghana 1957–60. He became Ghana's first president 1960 but was overthrown in a coup 1966. His policy of "African socialism" led to links with the communist bloc.

No or **Noh** classical, aristocratic Japanese drama which developed from the 14th to the 16th centuries and is still performed. There is a repertory of some 250 pieces, of which five, one from each of the several classes devoted to different subjects, may be put on in a performance lasting a whole day. Dance, mime, music, and chanting develop the mythical or historical themes. All the actors are men, some of whom wear masks and elaborate costumes; scenery is limited. No influenced kabuki drama.

Noah in the Old Testament, the son of Lamech and father of Shem, Ham, and Japheth, who, according to God's instructions, built a ship, the ark, so that he and his family and specimens of all existing animals might survive the Flood. There is also a Babylonian version of the tale, *The Epic of Gilgamesh*.

nobelium synthesized, radioactive, metallic element of the ◊actinide series, symbol No, atomic number 102, relative atomic mass 259. It is synthesized by bombarding curium with carbon nuclei.

Nobel Prize annual international prize, first awarded 1901 under the will of Alfred Nobel, Swedish chemist, who invented dynamite. The interest on the Nobel endowment fund is divided annually among the persons who have made the greatest contributions in the fields of physics, chemistry, medicine, literature, and world peace.

nonaligned movement countries adopting a strategic and political position of neutrality ("nonalignment") toward major powers, specifically the US and former USSR. Although originally used by poorer states, the nonaligned position was later adopted by oil-producing nations. The 1989 summit in Belgrade was attended by 108 member states. With the ending of the Cold War, the movement's survival was in doubt.

Nonconformist in religion, originally a member of the Puritan section of the Church of England clergy who, in the Elizabethan age, refused to conform to certain practices, for example the wearing of the surplice and kneeling to receive Holy Communion.

After 1662 the term was confined to members of independent Protestant churches in Great Britain.

nonmetal one of a set of elements (around 20 in total) with certain physical and chemical properties opposite to those of metals. Nonmetals accept electrons (see ◊electronegativity) and are sometimes called electronegative elements.

Nord-Pas-de-Calais region of N France; area 4,786 sq mi/12,400 sq km; population (1990) 3,965,100. Its capital is Lille, and it consists of the *départements* of Nord and Pas-de-Calais.

Norfolk county of E England *area* 2,069 sq mi/5,360 sq km *towns and cities* Norwich (administrative headquarters), King's Lynn; resorts: Great Yarmouth, Cromer, Hunstanton *features* low-lying with the Fens in the W and the Norfolk Broads in the E; rivers: Ouse, Yare, Bure, Waveney; Halvergate Marshes wildlife area; traditional reed thatching; Grime's Graves (Neolithic flint mines); shrine of Our Lady of Walsingham, a medieval and present-day center of pilgrimage; Blickling Hall (Jacobean); residence of Elizabeth II at Sandringham (built 1869–71) *products* cereals, turnips, sugar beets, turkeys, geese; offshore natural gas; fishing centered on Great Yarmouth *population* (1991) 745,600.

Norfolk seaport in SE Virginia, on the Atlantic Ocean at the mouth of the James and Elizabeth rivers; population (1990) 261,200. It is the headquarters of the US Navy's Atlantic fleet, and the home of 22 other Navy commands. Industries include shipbuilding, chemicals, and motor-vehicle assembly.

The Chesapeake Bay Bridge-Tunnel links it to the Delmarva peninsula. Old Dominion University is here. Norfolk was laid out in 1682. It suffered heavy damage during the American Revolution, was captured by Union forces in the Civil War, and grew rapidly during both world wars.

Noriega Manuel (Antonio Morena) 1940– . Panamanian soldier and politician, effective ruler of Panama from 1982, as head of the National Guard, until deposed by the US 1989. An informer for the US Central Intelligence Agency, he was known to be involved in drug trafficking as early as 1972. He enjoyed US support until 1987. In the 1989 US invasion of Panama, he was forcibly taken to the US. He was tried and convicted of trafficking 1992.

Norman any of the descendants of the Norsemen (to whose chief, Rollo, Normandy was granted by Charles III of France 911) who adopted French language and culture. During the 11th and 12th centuries they conquered England 1066 (under William the Conqueror), Scotland 1072, parts of Wales and Ireland, S Italy, Sicily, and Malta, and took a prominent part in the Crusades.

Normandy former duchy of NW France now divided into two regions: Haute-Normandie and ◊Basse-Normandie. Normandy was named for the Viking Norsemen (Normans), the people who conquered and settled in the area in the 9th century. As a French duchy it reached its peak under William the Conqueror and was renowned for its centers of learning established by Lanfranc and St Anselm. Normandy was united with England 1100–35. England and France fought over it during the Hundred Years' War, England finally losing it 1449 to Charles VII. In World War II the Normandy beaches were the site of the Allied invasion on D-day, June 6, 1944.

Norplant long-lasting hormonal contraceptive available in many countries 1983, consisting of six silicon-coated rods inserted beneath the skin in a woman's arm. The rods release the progestogen levonorgestrel in controlled doses, preventing pregnancy for five years. The main side effect is irregular and break-through bleeding.

In the US 1 million women had Norplant implants 1991–1994. Of these 20% requested early removal because of side effects.

Norse or *Norseman* a member of any of the ancient Scandinavian peoples, also called ◊Vikings when they traded, explored, and raided far afield from their homelands during the 8th–11th centuries, settling in Iceland, Greenland, Russia, the British Isles, and N France. The term is sometimes used to refer specifically to W Scandinavians or just to Norwegians.

Norseman early inhabitant of Norway. The term Norsemen is also applied to Scandinavian ◊Vikings who during the 8th–11th centuries raided and settled in Britain, Ireland, France, Russia, Iceland, and Greenland.

North Frederick, 8th Lord North 1732–1792. British Tory politician. He entered Parliament in 1754, became chancellor of the Exchequer in 1767, and was prime minister in a government of Tories and "king's friends" from 1770. His hard line against the American colonies was supported by George III, but in 1782 he was forced to resign by the failure of his policy. In 1783 he returned to office in a coalition with Charles ◊Fox. After its defeat, he retired from politics.

North Oliver 1943– . US Marine lieutenant colonel. In 1981 he joined the staff of the National Security Council (NSC), where he supervised the mining of Nicaraguan harbors 1983, an air-force bombing raid on Libya 1986, and an arms-for-hostages deal with Iran 1985, which, when uncovered 1985 (◊Irangate), forced his dismissal and trial.

North America third largest of the continents (when including Central America) *area* 9,500,000 sq mi/ 24,000,000 sq km *largest cities* (over 1 million) Mexico City, New York, Chicago, Toronto, Los Angeles, Montreal, Guadalajara, Monterrey, Philadelphia, Houston, Guatemala City, Vancouver, Detroit *population* (1990) 395 million; the aboriginal American Indian, Eskimo, and Aleut peoples are now a minority within a population predominantly of European immigrant origin. Many Africans were brought in as laborers by the slave trade. Asians were also brought in as laborers, and today immigration from Asia and Latin America is on the increase *physical* mountain belts to the E (Appalachians) and W, the latter including the Rocky Mountains and the Sierra Madre; coastal plain on the Gulf of Mexico, into which the Mississippi River system drains from the central Great Plains; the St Lawrence River and the Great Lakes form a rough crescent with the Great Bear and Great Slave lakes and Lakes Athabasca and Winnipeg around the exposed rock of the great Canadian/Laurentian Shield, into which Hudson Bay breaks from the N *features* wide climatic range, from arctic in Alaska and N Canada (only above freezing June–Sept) to the tropical in Central America, and arid in much of the W US; also, great extremes within the range, due to the vast size of the landmass *products* the immensity of the US home market makes it less dependent on imports; the industrial and technological strengths of the US automatically tend to exert a pull on Canada, Mexico, and Central America. The continent is unique in being dominated in this way by a single power, which also exerts great influence over the general world economy *languages* predominantly English, Spanish, French *religions* predominantly Christian.

North America: recent history

1903	The US leased the rights to the Panama Canal Zone.
1914	Panama Canal completed.
1948	Formation of OAS.
1949	Formation of NATO.
1961	The US backed the abortive invasion of Cuba by anti-Castro Cuban exiles.
1969	US space launch was the first to put a person on the Moon.
1960s–70s	Opposition to the Vietnam War caused domestic discord in the US.
1982	Canada gained its independence while remaining in the British Commonwealth.
1983	The US invaded Grenada to preserve the existing government.
1989	The US and Canada signed a free trade agreement. The US invaded Panama and took its leader, General Noriega, into custody.
1900	Collapse of Meech Lake accords, designed to resolve Canadian constitutional issues.
1990–91	Gulf War: US-led coalition, joined by Canada and other nations, drove the invader Iraq from Kuwait.
1992–93	The US, Canada, and Mexico reached accord on North American Free Trade Agreement (NAFTA), aimed at ending tariffs, and the treaty was signed.

Northamptonshire county of central England *area* 915 sq mi/2,370 sq km *towns and cities* Northampton (administrative headquarters), Kettering *features* rivers Welland and Nene; Canons Ashby, Tudor house, home of the Drydens for 400 years; churches with broached spires *products* cereals, cattle, sugar beet, shoemaking, food processing, printing, engineering *population* (1991) 578,500 *famous people* Richard III, Robert Browne, John Dryden.

North Atlantic Treaty Organization (NATO) association set up 1949 to provide for the collective defense of the major W European and North American states against the perceived threat from the USSR. The collapse of communism in eastern Europe from 1990 prompted the most radical review of its policy and defense strategy since its inception. After the E European Warsaw Pact was disbanded 1991, an adjunct to NATO, the *North Atlantic Cooperation Council*, was established, including all the former Soviet republics, with the aim of building greater security in Europe.

At the 1994 Brussels summit a "partnership for peace" program was formally launched, inviting former members of the Warsaw Pact and ex-Soviet republics to take part in military cooperation arrangements. By July 1994 the partnership included 12 of the 15 former Soviet republics, plus Hungary, the Slovak Republic, Bulgaria, Albania, the Czech Republic, Finland, and Sweden. At the same summit meeting leaders affirmed their readiness to use NATO air power to support UN forces in Bosnia-Herzegovina in protecting civilians from bombardment.

North Cape (Norwegian *Nordkapp*) cape in the Norwegian county of Finnmark; the most northerly point of Europe.

North Carolina state in E US; nickname Tar Heel State/Old North State area 52,650 sq mi/136,400 sq km *capital* Raleigh *towns and cities* Charlotte, Greensboro, Winston-Salem *features* Appalachian Mountains (including Blue Ridge and Great Smoky mountains), site of Fort Raleigh on Roanoke Island, Wright Brothers National Memorial at Kitty Hawk, the Research Triangle established 1956 (Duke University, University of North Carolina, and North Carolina State University) for high-tech industries, Cape Hatteras and Cape Lookout national seashores *industries* tobacco, corn, soybeans, livestock, poultry, textiles, clothing, cigarettes, furniture, chemicals, machinery *population* (1990) 6,628,600 *famous people* Billy Graham, O Henry, Jesse Jackson, Thomas Wolfe *history* Walter Raleigh sent out 108 colonists from Plymouth, England, 1585 under his cousin Richard Grenville, who established the first English settlement in the New World on Roanoke Island; Virginia Dare was born there 1587, the first child of English parentage born in America; the survivors were taken home by Drake 1586. Permanent settlement was made 1663; it was one of the original 13 states 1789.

In the Civil War, North Carolina was the last state to join the Confederacy but provided more troops than any other Southern state. After postwar recovery, textiles, tobacco products, and furniture came to dominate the economy. Tourism is now important to the state's economy.

North Dakota state in N US; nickname Flickertail State/Sioux State *area* 70,677 sq mi/183,100 sq km *capital* Bismarck *towns and cities* Fargo, Grand Forks, Minot *features* fertile Red River valley, Missouri Plateau; Garrison Dam on the Missouri River; Badlands, so called because the pioneers had great difficulty in crossing them (also site of Theodore Roosevelt's Elkhorn Ranch); International Peace Garden, on Canadian border; 90% of the land is cultivated *industries* cereals, meat products, farm equipment, oil, coal *population* (1990) 638,800 *famous people* Maxwell Anderson, Louis L'Amour *history* explored by La Verendrye's French Canadian expedition 1738–40; acquired by the US partly in the Louisiana Purchase 1803 and partly by treaty with Britain 1813. The earliest settlement was Pembina 1812, by Scottish and Irish families, and North Dakota became a state 1889, attracting many German and Norwegian settlers.

They and their descendants were hard hit by low prices in the 1920s and 1930s for the state's abundant wheat. Since 1950, North Dakota's oil, natural-gas, and lignite resources have contributed to a more diversified economic base, but it remains the most rural of all the states.

Northeast Passage sea route from the N Atlantic, around Asia, to the N Pacific, pioneered by Swedish explorer Nils Nordenskjöld 1878–79 and developed by the USSR in settling N Siberia from 1935. Russia owns offshore islands and claims it as an internal waterway; the US claims that it is international.

Northern Ireland see ◊Ireland, Northern.

Northern Mariana Islands archipelago in the NW Pacific, with ◊Guam known collectively as the Mariana Islands. The Northern Marianas are a commonwealth in union with the US. *area* 182 sq mi/471 sq km *capital* Garapan on Saipan *physical* 16 islands and atolls extending 350 mi/560 km N of Guam *political system* liberal democracy *political parties* Democratic Party, center-left; Republican Party, right of center; Territorial Party, nationalist *currency* US dollar *population* (1990) 43,300 *language* English *religion* mainly Roman Catholicism *history* came under Spanish control 1565; sold to Germany 1899; came under Japanese control 1914 and Japanese rule under a League of Nations mandate 1921. Taken by US marines in World War II, the islands became a UN Trust Territory administered by the US 1947 and a US commonwealth territory 1978. Granted internal self-government and full US citizenship 1986. UN Trusteeship status ended Dec 22, 1990.

Northern Rhodesia former name (to 1964) of ◊Zambia, a country in Africa.

Northern Territory territory of Australia *area* 519,633 sq mi/1,346,200 sq km *capital* Darwin (chief port) *towns and cities* Alice Springs *features* mainly within the tropics, although with wide range of temperature; very low rainfall, but artesian bores are used: Macdonald Ranges (Mount Zeil 4,956 ft/1,510 m); Cocos and Christmas Islands included in the territory 1984; 50,000–60,000-year-old rock paintings of animals, birds, and fish in Kakadu National Park *industries* beef cattle, prawns, bauxite (Gove), gold and copper (Tennant Creek), uranium (Ranger) *population* (1987) 157,000 *government* there is an administrator and a legislative assembly, and the territory is also represented in the federal parliament *history* originally part of New South Wales, it was annexed 1863 to South Australia but from 1911 until 1978 (when self-government was introduced) was under the control of the Commonwealth of Australia government. Mineral discoveries on land occupied by Aborigines led to a royalty agreement 1979.

North Korea see ◊Korea, North.

North Pole the northern point where an imaginary line penetrates the Earth's surface by the axis about which it revolves; see also ◊Poles and ◊Arctic.

North Sea sea to the E of Britain and bounded by the coasts of Belgium, the Netherlands, Germany, Denmark, and Norway; part of the Atlantic Ocean; area 202,000 sq mi/523,000 sq km; average depth 180 ft/55 m, greatest depth 2,165 ft/660 m. In the NE it joins the Norwegian Sea, and in the S it meets the Strait of Dover. It has fisheries (especially mackerel and herring), oil, and gas (discovered 1965).

Northumberland county of N England *area* 1,942 sq mi/5,030 sq km *towns and cities* Morpeth (administrative headquarters), Berwick-upon-Tweed, Hexham, Newcastle-upon-Tyne *features* Cheviot Hills; rivers: Tweed, upper Tyne; Northumberland National Park in the west; Holy Island; the Farne island group; part of Hadrian's Wall and Housestead's Fort; Alnwick and Bamburgh castles; Thomas Bewick museum; large moorland areas are used for military maneuvers; wild white cattle of Chillingham; Kielder Water (1982), the largest artificial lake in N Europe *industries* sheep *population* (1991) 304,700 *famous people* Thomas Bewick, Grace Darling, Jack Charlton.

Northumbria Anglo-Saxon kingdom that covered NE England and SE Scotland, comprising the 6th-century kingdoms of Bernicia (Forth–Tees) and Deira (Tees–Humber), united in the 7th century. It accepted the supremacy of Wessex 827 and was conquered by the Danes in the late 9th century.

Northwest Passage Atlantic–Pacific sea route around the north of Canada. Canada, which owns offshore islands, claims it as an internal waterway; the US insists that it is an international waterway and sent an icebreaker through without permission 1985.

Northwest Territories territory of Canada *area* 1,322,552 sq mi/3,426,300 sq km *capital* Yellowknife *physical* extends to the North Pole, to Hudson's Bay in the E, and in the W to the edge of the Canadian Shield *features* Mackenzie River; lakes: Great Slave, Great Bear; Miles Canyon *products* oil, natural gas, zinc, lead, gold, tungsten, silver *population* (1991) 54,000; over 50% native peoples (Indian, Inuit) *history* the area was the northern part of Rupert's Land, bought by the Canadian government from the Hudson's Bay Company 1869. An act of 1952 placed the Northwest Territories under a commissioner acting in Ottawa under the Ministry of Northern Affairs and Natural Resources. In 1990 territorial control of over 135,000 sq mi/350,000 sq km of the Northwest Territories was given to the ◊Inuit, and in 1992 the creation of an Inuit autonomous homeland, Nunavut, was agreed in a regional referendum.

North Yorkshire county of NE England, created 1974 from most of the North Riding and parts of East and West Ridings of Yorkshire *area* 3,212 sq mi/8,320 sq km *towns and cities* Northallerton (administrative headquarters), York; resorts: Harrogate, Scarborough, Whitby *features* England's largest county; including part of the Pennines, the Vale of York, and the Cleveland Hills and North Yorkshire Moors, which form a national park (within which is Fylingdales radar station to give early warning—4 minutes—of nuclear attack); Rievaulx Abbey; Yorkshire Dales National Park (including Swaledale, Wensleydale, and Bolton Abbey in Wharfedale); rivers: Derwent, Ouse; Fountains Abbey near Ripon, with Studley Royal Gardens; York Minster; Castle Howard, designed by

Vanbrugh, has Britain's largest collection of 18th–20th-century costume; largest accessible cavern in Britain, the Battlefield Chamber, Ingleton *industries* cereals, wool and meat from sheep, dairy products, coal, electrical goods, footwear, clothing, vehicles, plastics, foodstuffs *population* (1991) 702,200 *famous people* Alcuin, Guy Fawkes, W H Auden.

Norway Kingdom of (*Kongeriket Norge*) *area* 149,421 sq mi/387,000 sq km (includes Svalbard and Jan Mayen) *capital* Oslo *towns and cities* Bergen, Trondheim, Stavanger *physical* mountainous with fertile valleys and deeply indented coast; forests cover 25%; extends N of Arctic Circle *territories* dependencies in the Arctic (Svalbard and Jan Mayen) and in Antarctica (Bouvet and Peter I Island, and Queen Maud Land) *environment* an estimated 80% of the lakes and streams in the southern half of the country have been severely acidified by acid rain *features* fjords, including Hardanger and Sogne, longest 115 m/185 km, deepest 4,086 ft/1,245 m; glaciers in north; midnight sun and northern lights *head of state* Harald V from 1991 *head of government* Gro Harlem Brundtland from 1990 *political system* constitutional monarchy *political parties* Norwegian Labour Party (DNA), moderate left of center; Conservative Party, progressive, right of center; Christian People's Party (KrF), Christian, center-left; Center Party (SP), left of center, rural-oriented *exports* petrochemicals from North Sea oil and gas, paper, wood pulp, furniture, iron ore and other minerals, high-tech goods, sports goods, fish *currency* krone *population* (1993 est) 4,300,000; growth rate 0.3% p.a. *life expectancy* men 74, women 81 *languages* Norwegian (official); there are Saami-(Lapp) and Finnish-speaking minorities *religion* Evangelical Lutheran (endowed by state) 94% *literacy* 99% *GNP* $22,830 per head (1991) *chronology* *1814* Became independent from Denmark; ceded to Sweden. *1905* Links with Sweden ended; full independence achieved. *1940–45* Occupied by Germany. *1949* Joined North Atlantic Treaty Organization (NATO). *1952* Joined Nordic Council. *1957* King Haakon VII succeeded by his son Olaf V. *1960* Joined European Free Trade Association (EFTA). *1972* Application for membership in European Economic Community withdrawn after referendum. *1988* Gro Harlem Brundtland awarded Third World Prize. *1989* Jan P. Syse became prime minister. *1990* Brundtland returned to power. *1991* King Olaf V died; succeeded

by his son Harald V. *1992* Defied whaling ban to resume own whaling industry. Brundtland relinquished leadership of Labour Party. Formal application for European Community (EC) membership. *1993* Brundtland reelected. Growing opposition to EC membership. *1994* Terms of accession to European Union (formerly EC) agreed.

Norwich cathedral city in Norfolk, E England, on the river Wensum; administrative headquarters of Norfolk; population (1991) 120,900. Industries include financial services, shoes, clothing, chemicals, confectionery, engineering, printing, and insurance. It has a Norman castle, a 15th-century Guildhall, medieval churches, Tudor houses, and a Georgian Assembly House.

nose in humans, the upper entrance of the respiratory tract; the organ of the sense of smell. The external part is divided down the middle by a septum of ◊cartilage. The nostrils contain plates of cartilage that can be moved by muscles and have a growth of stiff hairs at the margin to prevent foreign objects from entering. The whole nasal cavity is lined with a ◊mucous membrane that warms and moistens the air as it enters and ejects dirt. In the upper parts of the cavity the membrane contains 50 million olfactory receptor cells (cells sensitive to smell).

notebook computer small ◊laptop computer. Notebook computers became available in the early 1990s and, even complete with screen and hard-disk drive, are no larger than a standard notebook.

Nottingham industrial city (engineering, coal mining, bicycles, textiles, knitwear, pharmaceuticals, tobacco, lace, electronics) and administrative headquarters of Nottinghamshire, England; population (1991) 263,500. Nottingham was founded by the Danes. The English Civil War began here 1642.

Nottinghamshire county of central England *area* 834 sq mi/2,160 sq km *towns and cities* Nottingham (administrative headquarters), Mansfield, Worksop, Newark *features* river Trent; the remaining areas of Sherwood Forest (home of ◊Robin Hood), formerly a royal hunting ground, are included in the "Dukeries"; Cresswell Crags (remains of prehistoric humans); D H Lawrence commemorative walk from Eastwood (where he lived) to Old Brinsley Colliery *industries* cereals, cattle, sheep, light engineering, footwear, limestone, ironstone, oil, cigarettes, tanning, furniture, pharmaceuticals, typewriters, gypsum, gravel. There are many orchards. *population* (1991) 980,600 *famous people* William Booth, D H Lawrence, Alan Sillitoe.

Nouakchott capital of Mauritania; population (1985) 500,000.

noun grammatical ◊part of speech that names a person, animal, object, quality, idea, or time. Nouns can refer to objects such as *house, tree* (*concrete nouns*); specific persons and places such as John Alden, the *White House* (*proper nouns*); ideas such as *love, anger* (*abstract nouns*). In English many simple words are both noun and verb (*jump, reign, rain*). Adjectives are sometimes used as nouns ("a *local* man", "one of the *locals*").

nova (plural *novae*) faint star that suddenly erupts in brightness by 10,000 times or more. Novae are believed to occur in close ◊binary star systems, where gas from one star flows to a companion ◊white dwarf. The gas ignites and is thrown off in an explosion at speeds of 930 mps/1,500 kps or more. Unlike a

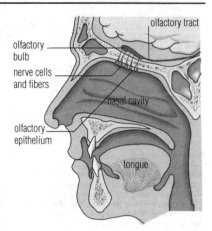

detail of olfactory epithelium

nose The structure of the nose. The organs of smell are confined to a small area in the roof of the nasal cavity. The olfactory cells are stimulated when certain molecules reach them. Smell is one of our most subtle senses: tens of thousands of smells can be distinguished. By comparison, taste, although closely related to smell, is a crude sensation. All the subtleties of taste depend upon smell.

◊supernova, the star is not completely disrupted by the outburst. After a few weeks or months it subsides to its previous state; it may erupt many more times.

Nova Scotia maritime province of E Canada *area* 21,423 sq mi/55,500 sq km *capital* Halifax (chief port) *towns and cities* Dartmouth, Sydney *features* Cabot Trail (Cape Breton Island); Alexander Graham Bell Museum; Fortress Louisbourg; Strait of Canso Superport, the largest deepwater harbor on the Atlantic coast of North America *industries* coal, gypsum, dairy products, poultry, fruit, forest products, fish products (including scallop and lobster) *physical* comprising a peninsula with a highly indented coastline extending SE from New Brunswick into the Atlantic Ocean, and Cape Breton Island which is linked to the mainland by the Canso Causeway *population* (1991) 897,500 *history* Nova Scotia was visited by the Italian navigator Giovanni ◊Caboto 1497. A French settlement was established 1604, but expelled 1613 by English colonists from Virginia. The name of the colony was changed from *Acadia* to Nova Scotia 1621. England and France contended for possession of the territory until Nova Scotia (which then included present-day New Brunswick and Prince Edward Island) was ceded to Britain 1713; Cape Breton Island remained French until 1763. Nova Scotia was one of the four original provinces of the Dominion of Canada.

Novgorod industrial city (chemicals, engineering, clothing, brewing) on the Volkhov River, NW Russia; a major trading city in medieval times; population (1987) 228,000.

Novosibirsk industrial city (engineering, textiles, chemicals, food processing) in W Siberian Russia, on the Ob River; population (1987) 1,423,000. Winter lasts eight months here.

Noyes John Humphrey 1811–1886. US religious and communal leader. He formulated the "doctrine of free love" 1837 and in 1848 founded the Oneida Community in central New York which served as a forum for his social experiments. In 1879 Noyes was forced to move to Canada to avoid legal action against him. The former community, which made silverware and steel traps, became a joint stock company 1881.

Nu U (Thakin) 1907– . Myanmar politician, prime minister of Burma (now Myanmar) for most of the period from 1948 to the military coup of 1962. Exiled from 1966, U Nu returned to the country 1980 and, in 1988, helped found the National League for Democracy opposition movement.

nuclear energy energy from the inner core or ◊nucleus of the atom, as opposed to energy released in chemical processes, which is derived from the electrons surrounding the nucleus.

Nuclear fusion is the release of thermonuclear energy by the conversion of hydrogen nuclei to helium nuclei, a continuing reaction in the Sun and other stars. Nuclear fusion is the principle behind thermonuclear weapons (the ◊hydrogen bomb). Attempts to harness fusion for commercial power production have so far not succeeded.

nuclear energy or *atomic energy* energy released from the inner core, or ◊nucleus, of the atom. Energy produced by *nuclear fission* (the splitting of uranium or plutonium nuclei) has been harnessed since the 1950s to generate electricity, and research continues into the possible controlled use of *nuclear fusion* (the fusing, or combining, of atomic nuclei).

nuclear physics study of the properties of the nucleus of the ◊atom, including the structure of nuclei; nuclear forces; the interactions between particles and nuclei; and the study of radioactive decay. The study of elementary particles is ◊particle physics.

nuclear reactor device for producing ◊nuclear energy in a controlled manner. There are various types of reactor in use, all using nuclear fission. In a gas-cooled reactor, a circulating gas under pressure (such as carbon dioxide) removes heat from the core of the reactor, which usually contains natural uranium. The reaction is controlled with neutron-absorbing rods made of boron. An advanced gas-cooled reactor (AGR) generally has enriched uranium as its fuel. A water-cooled reactor, such as the steam-generating heavy water (deuterium oxide) reactor, has water circulating through the hot core. The water is converted to steam, which drives turbo-alternators for generating electricity. The most widely used reactor is the pressurized-water reactor, which contains a sealed system of pressurized water that is heated to form steam in heat exchangers in an external circuit. The ◊breeder reactor has no moderator and uses fast neutrons to bring about fission; it produces more fuel than it consumes.

nuclear safety the use of nuclear energy has given rise to concern over safety. Anxiety has been heightened by accidents such as those at Windscale (UK), Three Mile Island (US), and Chernobyl (Ukraine).

There has also been mounting concern about the production and disposal of nuclear waste, the ◊radioactive and toxic by-products of the nuclear energy industry. Burial on land or at sea raises problems of safety, environmental pollution, and security. Nuclear waste has an active half-life of thousands of years and no guarantees exist for the safety of the various methods of disposal. Nuclear safety is still a controversial subject since governments will not recognize the hazards of ◊radiation and ◊radiation sickness.

nuclear warfare war involving the use of nuclear weapons. Nuclear-weapons research began in Britain 1940, but was transferred to the US after it entered World War II. The research program, known as the Manhattan Project, was directed by J Robert Oppenheimer. The worldwide total of nuclear weapons in 1990 was about 50,000, and the number of countries possessing nuclear weapons stood officially at five—US, USSR, UK, France, and China—although some other nations were thought either to have a usable stockpile of these weapons (Israel) or the ability to produce them quickly (Brazil, India, Pakistan, South Africa). *atomic bomb* The original weapon relied on use of a chemical explosion to trigger a chain reaction. The first test explosion was at Alamogordo, New Mexico, July 16, 1945; the first use in war was by the US against Japan Aug 6, 1945 over Hiroshima and three days later at Nagasaki. *hydrogen bomb* A much more powerful weapon than the atomic bomb, it relies on the release of thermonuclear energy by the condensation of hydrogen nuclei to helium nuclei (as happens in the Sun). The first detonation was at Eniwetok Atoll, Pacific Ocean, 1952 by the US. *neutron bomb* or enhanced radiation weapon (ERW) A very small hydrogen bomb that has relatively high radiation but relatively low blast, designed to kill (in up to six days) by a brief neutron radiation that leaves buildings and weaponry intact. *nuclear methods of attack* now include aircraft bombs, missiles (long-or short-range, surface to surface, air to surface, and surface to air), depth charges, and high-powered landmines ("atomic demolition munitions") to destroy bridges and roads.

nuclear waste the radioactive and toxic by-products of the nuclear-energy and nuclear-weapons industries. Nuclear waste may have an active life of several thousand years. Reactor waste is of three types: *high-level* spent fuel, or the residue when nuclear fuel has been removed from a reactor and reprocessed; *intermediate*, which may be long-or short-lived; and *low-level*, but bulky, waste from reactors, which has only short-lived radioactivity. Disposal, by burial on land or at sea, has raised problems of safety, environmental pollution, and security. In absolute terms, nuclear waste cannot be safely relocated or disposed of.

nucleon in particle physics, either a ◊proton or a ◊neutron, both particles present in the atomic nucleus. *Nucleon number* is an alternate name for the mass number of an atom.

nucleus in physics, the positively charged central part of an ◊atom, which constitutes almost all its mass. Except for hydrogen nuclei, which have only protons, nuclei are composed of both protons and neutrons. Surrounding the nuclei are electrons, of equal and opposite charge to that of the protons, thus giving the atom a neutral charge.

The nucleus was discovered by New Zealand physicist Ernest Rutherford in 1911 as a result of experiments in passing alpha particles through very thin gold foil.

nucleus in biology, the central, membrane-enclosed part of a eukaryotic cell, containing the chromosomes.

Nujoma Sam 1929– . Namibian left-wing politician, founder and leader of SWAPO (the South-West Africa People's Organization) from 1959, president from 1990. He was exiled in 1960 and controlled guerrillas from Angolan bases until the first free elections were held 1989, taking office early the following year.

Nukua'lofa capital and port of Tonga on Tongatapu Island; population (1986) 29,000.

number symbol used in counting or measuring. In mathematics, there are various kinds of numbers. The everyday number system is the decimal ("proceeding by tens") system, using the base ten. ◊*Real numbers* include all rational numbers (integers, or whole numbers, and fractions) and irrational numbers (those not expressible as fractions). ◊*Complex numbers* include the real and unreal numbers (real-number multiples of the square root of –1). The ◊binary number system, used in computers, has two as its base. The ordinary numerals, 0, 1, 2, 3, 4, 5, 6, 7, 8, and 9, give a counting system that, in the decimal system, continues to 10, 11, 12, 13, and so on. These are whole numbers (integers), with fractions represented as, for example, ¼, ½, ¾, or as decimal fractions (0.25, 0.5, 0.75).

Nuremberg (German *Nürnberg*) industrial city (electrical and other machinery, precision instruments, textiles, toys) in Bavaria, Germany; population (1988) 467,000. From 1933 the Nuremberg rallies were held here, and in 1945 the Nuremberg trials of war criminals.

Nuremberg trials after World War II, the trials of the 24 chief Nazi war criminals Nov 1945–Oct 1946 by an international military tribunal consisting of four judges and four prosecutors: one of each from the US, UK, USSR, and France. An appendix accused the German cabinet, general staff, high command, Nazi leadership corps, ◊SS, Sturmabteilung, and ◊Gestapo of criminal behavior.

Nureyev Rudolf 1938–1993. Russian dancer and choreographer. A soloist with the Kirov Ballet, he defected to the West during a visit to Paris 1961. Mainly associated with the Royal Ballet (London) and as Margot ◊Fonteyn's principal partner, he was one of the most brilliant dancers of the 1960s and 1970s. Nureyev danced in such roles as Prince Siegfried in *Swan Lake* and Armand in *Marguerite and Armand*, which was created especially for Fonteyn and Nureyev. He also danced and acted in films and on television and choreographed several ballets.

nursing care of the sick, the very young, the very old, and the disabled. Organized training originated 1836 in Germany, and was developed in Britain by the work of Florence ◊Nightingale, who, during the Crimean War, established standards of scientific, humanitarian care in military hospitals. Nurses give day-to-day care and carry out routine medical and surgical duties under the supervision of medical staff.

In the US, though registration (RN) is the responsi-

bility of individual states, an almost uniform standard has been established by the National League for Nursing (1952). There are a variety of degree programs.

nut any dry, single-seeded fruit that does not split open to release the seed, such as the chestnut. A nut is formed from more than one carpel, but only one seed becomes fully formed, the remainder aborting. The wall of the fruit, the pericarp, becomes hard and woody, forming the outer shell.

nutcracker either of two jaylike birds of the genus *Nucifraga*, in the crow family (Corvidae).

One, *N. caryocatactes*, is native to Eurasia; the other, Clark's nutcracker *N. columbiana*, 12 in/30 cm long, lives in W North America and has gray and black plumage and a powerful beak.

nuthatch small bird of the family Sittidae, with a short tail and pointed beak. Nuthatches climb head first up, down, and around tree trunks and branches, foraging for insects and their larvae.

The 5.5 in/14 cm long white-breasted nuthatch *Sitta carolinensis* of North America has a black cap, gray wings, and white underparts.

nutria or *coypu* South American water rodent *Myocastor coypus*, about 2 ft/60 cm long and weighing up to 20 lb/9 kg. It has a scaly, ratlike tail, webbed hind feet, a blunt, muzzled head, and large, orange incisors. The fur is reddish brown. It feeds on vegetation and lives in burrows in river and lake banks.

nutrition the strategy adopted by an organism to obtain the chemicals it needs to live, grow, and reproduce. Also, the science of food, and its effect on human and animal life, health, and disease. Nutrition involves the study of the basic nutrients required to sustain life, their bioavailability in foods and overall diet, and the effects upon them of cooking and storage. It is also concerned with dietary deficiency diseases.

Nuuk Greenlandic for ◊Godthaab, the capital of Greenland.

Nyasa former name for Lake ◊Malawi.

Nyasaland former name (to 1964) for ◊Malawi.

Nyerere Julius (Kambarage) 1922– . Tanzanian socialist politician, president 1964–85. He devoted himself from 1954 to the formation of the Tanganyika African National Union and subsequent campaigning for independence. He became chief minister 1960, was prime minister of Tanganyika 1961–62, president of the newly formed Tanganyika Republic 1962–64, and first president of Tanzania 1964–85.

nylon synthetic long-chain polymer similar in chemical structure to protein. Nylon was the first all-synthesized fiber, made from petroleum, natural gas, air, and water by the Du Pont firm in 1938. It is used in the manufacture of molded articles, textiles, and medical sutures. Nylon fibers are stronger and more elastic than silk and are relatively insensitive to moisture and mildew. Nylon is used for hosiery and woven goods, simulating other materials such as silks and furs; it is also used for carpets.

nymph in Greek mythology, a guardian spirit of nature. *Hamadryads* or *dryads* guarded trees; *naiads*, springs and pools; *oreads*, hills and rocks; and *Nereids*, the sea.

nymph in entomology, the immature form of insects that do not have a pupal stage; for example, grasshoppers and dragonflies. Nymphs generally resemble the adult (unlike larvae), but do not have fully formed reproductive organs or wings.

NZ abbreviation for ◊*New Zealand*.

oak any tree or shrub of the genus *Quercus* of the beech family Fagaceae, with over 300 known species widely distributed in temperate zones. Oaks are valuable for timber, the wood being durable and straight-grained. Their fruits are called acorns.

The 60 species of North American oaks are divided into two groups: white oaks and red oaks.

Oak Ridge town in Tennessee, on the Clinch River, noted for the Oak Ridge National Laboratory (1943), which manufactures plutonium for nuclear weapons; population (1990) 27,300. The community was founded 1942 as part of the Manhattan Project to develop an atomic bomb; by the end of World War II its population was more than 75,000. Ownership of the community passed to the residents in the late 1950s.

Electronic equipment and scientific instruments are also manufactured here. Oak Ridge Associated Universities is a research and educational center.

oarfish any of a family Regalecidae of deep-sea bony fishes, found in warm parts of the Atlantic, Pacific, and Indian oceans. Oarfish are large, up to 30 ft/9 m long, elongated, and compressed, with a fin along the back and a manelike crest behind the head. They have a small mouth, no teeth or scales, and large eyes. They are often reported as sea serpents.

OAS abbreviation for ◊*Organization of American States*.

oasis area of land made fertile by the presence of water near the surface in an otherwise arid region. The occurrence of oases affects the distribution of plants, animals, and people in the desert regions of the world.

oarfish The oarfish is a strange-looking deep-sea fish found in warm parts of the Atlantic, Pacific, and Indian oceans. It grows up to 30 ft/9 m long. Its silver body is compressed and the dorsal fin forms a manelike crest behind the head.

oat type of grass, genus *Avena*, a cereal food. The plant has long, narrow leaves and a stiff straw stem; the panicles of flowers, and later of grain, hang downward. The cultivated oat *Avena sativa* is produced for human and animal food.

Oates Titus 1649–1705. English conspirator. A priest, he entered the Jesuit colleges at Valladolid, Spain, and St Omer, France, as a spy 1677–78, and on his return to England announced he had discovered a "Popish Plot" to murder Charles II and re-establish Catholicism. Although this story was almost entirely false, many innocent Roman Catholics were executed during 1678–80 on Oates's evidence.

OAU abbreviation for ◊*Organization of African Unity*.

Ob river in Asian Russia, flowing 2,100 mi/3,380 km from the Altai Mountains through the W Siberian Plain to the Gulf of Ob in the Arctic Ocean. With its main tributary, the *Irtysh*, it is 3,480 mi/5,600 km long.

Oberösterreich German name for the federal state of ◊Upper Austria.

obesity condition of being overweight (generally, 20% or more above the desirable weight for one's sex, build, and height). Obesity increases susceptibility to disease, strains the vital organs, and reduces life expectancy; it is usually remedied by controlled weight loss, healthy diet and exercise.

One third of all people in the US were found to be obese in a 1994 study (an increase on the 1960–80 figure of one fourth).

oboe musical instrument of the woodwind family, a refined treble shawm of narrow tapering bore and exposed double reed. The oboe was developed by the Hotteterre family of makers about 1700 and was incorporated in the court ensemble of Louis XIV. In B flat, it has a rich tone of elegant finish. Oboe concertos have been composed by Vivaldi, Albinoni, Richard Strauss, and others. Heinz Holliger is a modern virtuoso oboist.

Obote (Apollo) Milton 1924– . Ugandan politician who led the independence movement from 1961. He became prime minister 1962 and was president 1966–71 and 1980–85, being overthrown by first Idi ◊Amin and then by Lt. Gen. Tito Okello.

observatory site or facility for observing astronomical or meteorological phenomena. The earliest recorded observatory was in Alexandria, N Africa, built by Ptolemy Soter in about 300 BC. The modern observatory dates from the invention of the telescope. Observatories may be ground-based, carried on aircraft, or sent into orbit as satellites, in space stations, and on the space shuttle.

obsidian black or dark-colored glassy volcanic rock, chemically similar to ◊granite, but formed by cooling rapidly on the Earth's surface at low pressure.

obstetrics medical specialty concerned with the management of pregnancy, childbirth, and the immediate postnatal period.

ocean great mass of salt water. Strictly speaking three oceans exist—the Atlantic, Indian, and Pacific—to which the Arctic is often added. They cover approximately 70% or 140,000,000 sq mi/363,000,000 sq km of the total surface area of the Earth. Water levels recorded in the world's oceans have shown an increase of 4–6 in/10–15 cm over the past 100 years.

Oceania general term for the islands of the central and S Pacific, including Australia, New Zealand, and the eastern half of New Guinea; although not strictly a continent, Oceania is often referred to as such to facilitate handling of global statistics *area* 3,300,000 sq mi/8,500,000 sq km (land area) *largest cities* (population over 500,000) Sydney, Melbourne, Brisbane, Perth, Adelaide, Auckland *features* the Challenger Deep in the Mariana Trench –36,201 ft/–11,034 m is the greatest known depth of sea in the world; Ayers Rock in Northern Territory, Australia, is the world's largest monolith; the Great Barrier Reef is the longest coral reef in the world; Mount Kosciusko 7,316 ft/2,229 m in New South Wales is the highest peak in Australia; Mount Cook 12,349 ft/3,764 m is the highest peak in New Zealand *physical* stretching from the Tropic of Cancer in the N to the southern tip of New Zealand, Oceania can be broadly divided into groups of volcanic and coral islands on the basis of the ethnic origins of their inhabitants: Micronesia (Guam, Kiribati, Mariana, Marshall, Caroline Islands), Melanesia (Papua New Guinea, Vanuatu, New Caledonia, Fiji, Solomon Islands) and Polynesia (Tonga, Samoa, Line Islands, Tuvalu, French Polynesia, Pitcairn); Australia (the largest island in the world) occupies more than 90% of the land surface; the highest point is Mount Wilhelm, Papua New Guinea 14,793 ft/4,509 m; the lowest point is Lake Eyre, South Australia –52 ft/–16 m; the longest river is the Murray in SE Australia 1,609 mi/2,590 km.

oceanography study of the oceans. Its subdivisions deal with each ocean's extent and depth, the water's evolution and composition, its physics and chemistry, the bottom topography, currents and wind effects, tidal ranges, the biology, and the various aspects of human use.

ocelot wild cat *Felis pardalis* of the southwestern US, Mexico, and Central and South America, up to 3 ft/1 m long with a 1.5 ft/45 cm tail. It weighs about 40 lb/18 kg and has a pale yellowish coat marked with longitudinal stripes and blotches. Hunted for its fur, it is close to extinction.

Ochs Adolph Simon 1858–1935. US newspaper publisher born in Cincinnati, Ohio, and raised in Tennessee. In 1896 he gained control of the then faltering *New York Times* and transformed it into a serious, authoritative publication. Among Ochs's innovations were a yearly index and a weekly book-review section.

O'Connell Daniel 1775–1847. Irish politician, called "the Liberator". Although ineligible, as a Roman Catholic, to take his seat, he was elected Member of Parliament for County Clare 1828 and so forced the government to grant Catholic emancipation. In Parliament he cooperated with the Whigs in the hope of obtaining concessions until 1841, when he launched his campaign for repeal of the union.

In 1823 he founded the Catholic Association to press Roman Catholic claims.

O'Connor Sandra Day 1930– . US jurist and the first female associate justice of the US Supreme Court 1981– . Considered a moderate conservative, she dissented in *Texas* v *Johnson* 1990, a decision that ruled that the legality of burning the US flag in protest was protected by the First Amendment.

Born in El Paso, Texas, O'Connor attended Stanford University and Stanford University Law School. She practiced law in California, in Germany with the US Quartermaster Corps, and in Arizona, where she also became active in the Republican Party. President Reagan appointed her to the US Supreme Court, where she generally espoused a conservative position.

OCR abbreviation for ◊*optical character recognition*.

octave in music, a span of eight notes as measured on the white notes of a piano keyboard. It corresponds to the consonance of first and second harmonics.

Octavian original name of ◊Augustus, the first Roman emperor.

October Revolution second stage of the ◊Russian Revolution 1917, when, on Oct 24 (Nov 6 in the Western calendar), the Bolshevik forces under Trotsky, and on orders from Lenin, seized the Winter Palace and arrested members of the Provisional Government. The following day the Second All-Russian Congress of Soviets handed over power to the Bolsheviks.

octopus any of an order (Octopoda) of ◊cephalopods, genus *Octopus*, having a round or oval body and eight arms with rows of suckers on each. They occur in all temperate and tropical seas, where they feed on crabs and other small animals.

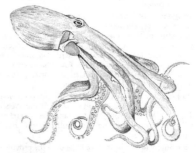

octopus *The octopus can swim by using its legs or by squirting water backward to create a kind of jet propulsion. More often, however, it uses its eight suckered tentacles to crawl across rocks on the seabed.*

Odessa seaport in Ukraine, on the Black Sea, capital of Odessa region; population (1989) 1,115,000. Products include chemicals, pharmaceuticals, and machinery.

Odets Clifford 1906–1963. US dramatist, famous for his play about a taxi drivers' strike, *Waiting for Lefty* 1935. The most renowned of the Depression-era social-protest dramatists, he also wrote such plays as *Awake and Sing* 1935, perhaps his finest, and *Golden Boy* 1937. In the late 1930s he went to Hollywood and became a successful film writer and director, but he continued to write plays, including *The Country Girl* 1950.

Odin chief god of Scandinavian mythology, the *Woden* or *Wotan* of the Germanic peoples. A sky god, he lives in Asgard, at the top of the world-tree, and from the Valkyries (the divine maidens) receives the souls of half of the heroic slain warriors, feasting with them in his great hall, Valhalla; the rest are feasted by Freya his wife. The son of Odin and Freya is Thor. Wednesday is named for Odin.

Odysseus chief character of Homer's *Odyssey*, king of the island of Ithaca; he is also mentioned in the *Iliad* as one of the leaders of the Greek forces at the siege of Troy. Odysseus was distinguished among Greek leaders for his cleverness and cunning. He appears in other later tragedies.

Odyssey Greek epic poem; the product of an oral tradition, it was probably written before 700 BC and is attributed to ◊Homer. It describes the voyage home of Odysseus after the fall of Troy, and the vengeance he takes with his son Telemachus on the suitors of his wife Penelope on his return. During his ten-year wanderings, he encounters the Cyclops, the enchantress Circe, Scylla and Charybdis, and the Sirens.

OECD abbreviation for ◊*Organization for Economic Cooperation and Development*.

Oedipus in Greek mythology, king of Thebes who unwittingly killed his father, Laius, and married his mother, Jocasta, in fulfillment of a prophecy. When he learned what he had done, he put out his eyes; Jocasta hanged herself. His story was dramatized by the Greek tragedian ◊Sophocles.

Oedipus complex in psychology, term coined by Sigmund ◊Freud for the unconscious antagonism of a son to his father, whom he sees as a rival for his mother's affection. For a girl antagonistic to her mother, as a rival for her father's affection, the term is *Electra complex*.

estrogen any of a group of hormones produced by the ◊ovaries of vertebrates; the term is also used for various synthetic hormones that mimic their effects. The principal estrogen in mammals is estradiol. Estrogens control female sexual development, promote the growth of female secondary sexual characteristics, stimulate egg production, and, in mammals, prepare the lining of the uterus for pregnancy.

Offa King of Mercia, England, from 757. He conquered Essex, Kent, Sussex, and Surrey; defeated the Welsh and the West Saxons; and established Mercian supremacy over all England south of the river Humber.

Offaly county of the Republic of Ireland, in the province of Leinster, between Galway on the W and Kildare on the E; county town Tullamore; area 772 sq mi/ 2,000 sq km; population (1991) 58,500. It is low-lying, with part of the Bog of Allen to the N.

Offa's Dyke defensive earthwork along the Welsh border, of which there are remains from the mouth of the river Dee to that of the river Severn. It represents the boundary secured by ◊Offa's wars with Wales.

Official Secrets Act UK act of Parliament 1889, prohibiting the disclosure of confidential material from government sources by employees. There is no public-interest defense, and disclosure of information already in the public domain is still a crime. Journalists who repeat disclosures may also be prosecuted. The act has seldom been enforced in recent years.

off line in computing, not connected, so that data cannot be transferred, for example, to a printer. The opposite of ◊on line.

offset printing the most common method of ◊printing, which uses smooth (often rubber) printing

plates. It works on the principle of ◊lithography: that grease and water repel one another.

O Henry pen name of US author William Sydney Porter.

Ohio state in N central US; nickname Buckeye State *area* 41,341 sq mi/107,100 sq km *capital* Columbus *towns and cities* Cleveland, Cincinnati, Dayton, Akron, Toledo, Youngstown, Canton *population* (1990) 10,847,100 *features* Ohio River; Lake Erie; Serpent Mound built by Hopewell Indians about 2nd–1st centuries BC) *industries* coal, cereals, livestock, dairy foods, machinery, chemicals, steel, motor vehicles, automotive and aircraft parts, rubber products, office equipment, refined petroleum *famous people* Sherwood Anderson, Neil Armstrong, Hart Crane, Thomas Edison, James Garfield, John Glenn, Ulysses S Grant, Zane Grey, Warren Harding, Benjamin Harrison, William H Harrison, Rutherford B Hayes, William McKinley, Paul Newman, Jesse Owens, John D Rockefeller, William T Sherman, William H Taft, James Thurber, Orville and Wilbur Wright *history* explored for France by René La Salle 1669; ceded to Britain by France 1763; first settled at Marietta (capital of the Northwest Territory) by Europeans 1788; statehood 1803.

ohm SI unit (symbol Ω) of electrical ◊resistance (the property of a substance that restricts the flow of electrons through it).

oil flammable substance, usually insoluble in water, and composed chiefly of carbon and hydrogen. Oils may be solids (fats and waxes) or liquids. The three main types are: *essential oils*, obtained from plants; *fixed oils*, obtained from animals and plants; and *mineral oils*, obtained chiefly from the refining of ◊petroleum.

oil crop plant from whose seeds vegetable oils are pressed. Cool temperate areas grow rapeseed and linseed; warm temperate regions produce sunflowers, olives, and soybeans; tropical regions produce groundnuts (peanuts); palm oil, and coconuts.

oil paint painting medium in which ground pigment is bound with oil, usually linseed.

oil palm African ◊palm tree *Elaeis guineensis*, the fruit of which yields valuable oils, used as food or processed into margarine, soaps, and livestock feeds.

oil spill leakage of oil from an oceangoing tanker, a pipeline, or other source. Oil spills are frequent and may cause enormous ecological harm. The annual spillage of oil is 8 million barrels a year. At any given time tankers are carrying 500 million barrels.

Oistrakh David Fyodorovich 1908–1974. Soviet violinist. He was celebrated for performances of both standard and contemporary Russian repertoire. Shostakovich wrote both his violin concertos for him. His son *Igor* (1931–) is equally renowned as a violinist. He was born in Odessa, S Ukraine.

okapi ruminant *Okapia johnstoni* of the giraffe family, although with much shorter legs and neck, found in the tropical rainforests of central Africa. Purplish brown with a creamy face and black and white stripes on the legs and hindquarters, it is excellently camouflaged. Okapis have remained virtually unchanged for millions of years.

Okeechobee lake in the N Everglades, Florida; 40 mi/65 km long and 25 mi/40 km wide. It is the largest lake in the southern US, about 700 sq mi/1,800 sq km.

Okeechobee has no single outlet but flows S through the Everglades.

O'Keeffe Georgia 1887–1986. US painter. She is known chiefly for her large, semiabstract studies of flowers and bones, such as *Black Iris* 1926 (Metropolitan Museum of Art, New York) and the *Pelvis Series* of the 1940s.

Okhotsk, Sea of arm of the N Pacific Ocean between the Kamchatka Peninsula and Sakhalin and bordered to the S by the Kuril Islands; area 361,700 sq mi/937,000 sq km. It is free of ice only in summer, and is often fogbound.

Okinawa group of islands, forming part of the Japanese ◊Ryukyu Islands in the W Pacific; the largest island is Okinawa *area* 869 sq mi/2,250 sq km *capital* Naha *features* Okinawa, the largest island of the group (area 453 sq mi/1,176 sq km; population (1990) 105,852), has a large US military base *population* (1990) 3,145,500 *history* virtually all buildings were destroyed in World War II. The principal island, Okinawa, was captured by the US in the *Battle of Okinawa* April 1–June 21, 1945, with 47,000 US casualties (12,000 dead) and 60,000 Japanese (only a few hundred survived as prisoners). During the invasion over 150,000 Okinawans, mainly civilians, died; many were massacred by Japanese forces. The island was returned to Japan 1972.

Oklahoma state in S central US; nickname Sooner State *area* 69,905 sq mi/181,100 sq km *capital* Oklahoma City *towns and cities* Tulsa, Lawton, Norman, Enid *features* Arkansas, Red, and Canadian rivers; Wichita and Ozark mountain ranges; the high plains have Indian reservations (Cherokee, Chickasaw, Choctaw, Creek, and Seminole); American Indian Hall of Fame; Chicasaw National Recreation Area *industries* cereals, peanuts, cotton, livestock, oil, natural gas, helium, machinery and other metal products *population* (1990) 3,145,600 *famous people* John Berryman, Ralph Ellison, Woody Guthrie, Mickey Mantle, Will Rogers, Jim Thorpe *history* explored for Spain by Francisco de Coronado 1541; most acquired by the US from France with the ◊Louisiana Purchase 1803.

The W Panhandle became US territory when Texas was annexed 1845. It was divided into Indian

okapi *The okapi has a prehensile tongue which is used to pick tasty leaves. The tongue is so long that the animal uses it to clean its eyes and eyelids. The okapi is found in the tropical forests of Zaire.*

Territory and Oklahoma Territory 1890, part of which was thrown open to settlers with lotteries and other hurried distribution of land. Together with what remained of Indian Territory, it became a state 1907.

Oklahoma City industrial city (oil refining, machinery, aircraft, electronic equipment), capital of Oklahoma, on the Canadian River; population (1990) 444,700. On April 22, 1889, a tent city of nearly 10,000 inhabitants was set up overnight as the area was opened to settlement. In 1910 Oklahoma City had 64,000 people and became the state capital. Oil was discovered in 1928, and derricks are situated even on the state capitol grounds. A General Motors auto plant was established here 1979.

On April 19, 1995, a terrorist bomb in a van left outside the Alfred Murrah Federal Building killed 167 people, the greatest death toll in a US terrorist bombing.

okra plant *Hibiscus esculentus* belonging to the Old World hibiscus family. Its red-and-yellow flowers are followed by long, sticky, green fruits known as *ladies' fingers* or *bhindi*. The fruits are cooked in soups and stews.

Old English general name for the range of dialects spoken by Germanic settlers in England between the 5th and 11th centuries AD, also known as ◊Anglo-Saxon. The literature of the period includes *Beowulf*, an epic in West Saxon dialect.

Old Pretender nickname of ◊James Edward Stuart, the son of James II of England.

Old Testament Christian term for the Hebrew ◊Bible, which is the first part of the Christian Bible. It contains 39 (according to Christianity) or 24 (according to Judaism) books, which include the origins of the world, the history of the ancient Hebrews and their covenant with God, prophetical writings, and religious poetry. The first five books (*The five books of Moses*) are traditionally ascribed to Moses and known as the Pentateuch (by Christians) or the ◊Torah (by Jews).

Olduvai Gorge deep cleft in the Serengeti steppe, Tanzania, where Louis and Mary ◊Leakey found prehistoric stone tools in the 1930s. They discovered Pleistocene remains of prehumans and gigantic animals 1958–59. The gorge has given its name to the *Olduvai culture*, a simple stone-tool culture of prehistoric hominids, dating from 2–0.5 million years ago.

Old World the continents of the eastern hemisphere, so called because they were familiar to Europeans before the Americas. The term is used as an adjective to describe animals and plants that live in the eastern hemisphere.

oleander or *rose bay* evergreen Mediterranean shrub *Nerium oleander* of the dogbane family Apocynaceae, with pink or white flowers and aromatic leaves that secrete the poison oleandrin.

oligarchy rule of the few, in their own interests. It was first identified as a form of government by the Greek philosopher Aristotle. In modern times there have been a number of oligarchies, sometimes posing as democracies; the paramilitary rule of the ◊Duvalier family in Haiti, 1957–86, is an example.

Oligocene third epoch of the Tertiary period of geological time, 35.5–3.25 million years ago. The name, from Greek, means "a little recent", referring to the presence of the remains of some modern types of animals existing at that time.

olive evergreen tree *Olea europaea* of the family Oleaceae. Native to Asia but widely cultivated in Mediterranean and subtropical areas, it grows up to 50 ft/15 m high, with twisted branches and opposite, lance-shaped silvery leaves. The white flowers are followed by green oval fruits that ripen a bluish black. They are preserved in brine or oil, dried, or pressed to make olive oil.

Olivier Laurence (Kerr), Baron Olivier 1907–1989. English actor and director. For many years associated with the Old Vic theater, he was director of the National Theatre company 1962–73. His stage roles include Henry V, Hamlet, Richard III, and Archie Rice in John Osborne's *The Entertainer* 1957 (filmed 1960). His acting and direction of filmed versions of Shakespeare's plays received critical acclaim for example, *Henry V* 1944 and *Hamlet* 1948 (Academy Award).

Olympic Games sporting contests originally held in Olympia, ancient Greece, every four years during a sacred truce; records were kept from 776 BC. Women were forbidden to be present, and the male contestants were naked. The ancient Games were abolished AD 394. The present-day games have been held every four years since 1896. Since 1924 there has been a separate winter Games program. From 1994 the winter and summer Games will be held two years apart.

Olympic games: venues

summer games/winter games

1896	Athens, Greece
1900	Paris, France
1904	St. Louis, Missouri
1908	London, England
1912	Stockholm, Sweden
1920	Antwerp, Belgium
1924	Paris, France/Chamonix, France
1928	Amsterdam, Holland/St. Moritz, Switzerland
1932	Los Angeles, California/Lake Placid, New York
1936	Berlin, Germany/Garmisch-Partenkirchen, Germany
1948	London, England/St. Moritz, Switzerland
1952	Helsinki, Finland/Oslo, Norway
1956	Melbourne, Australia*/Cortina d'Ampezzo, Italy
1960	Rome, Italy/Squaw Valley, Colorado
1964	Tokyo, Japan/Innsbruck, Austria
1968	Mexico City, Mexico/Grenoble, France
1972	Munich, West Germany/Sapporo, Japan
1976	Montréal, Québec, Canada/Innsbruck, Austria
1980	Moscow, USSR/Lake Placid, New York
1984	Los Angeles, California/Sarajevo, Yugoslavia
1988	Seoul, South Korea/Calgary, Alberta, Canada
1992	Barcelona, Spain/Albertville, France
1994	Lillehammer, Norway (winter games)
1996	Atlanta, Georgia (summer games)
2000	Sydney, Australia (summer games)

*because of quarantine restrictions, equestrian events were held in Stockholm, Sweden

Olympus (Greek *Olimbos*) any of several mountains in Greece and elsewhere, one of which is *Mount Olympus* in N Thessaly, Greece, 9,577 ft/2,918 m high. In ancient Greece it was considered the home of the gods.

Oman Sultanate of (*Saltanat `Uman*) *area* 105,000 sq mi/272,000 sq km *capital* Muscat *towns and cities* Salalah, Nizwa *physical* mountains to N and S of a high arid plateau; fertile coastal strip *features* Jebel Akhdar highlands; Kuria Muria islands; Masirah Island is used in aerial reconnaissance of the Arabian Sea and Indian Ocean; exclave on Musandam Peninsula controlling Strait of Hormuz *head of state and government* Qaboos bin Said from 1970 *political system* absolute monarchy *political parties* none *exports* oil, dates, silverware, copper *currency* rial Omani *population* (1993 est) 1,650,000; growth rate 3.0% p.a. *life expectancy* men 66, women 70 *languages* Arabic (official), English, Urdu, other Indian languages *religions* Ibadhi Muslim 75%, Sunni Muslim, Shiite Muslim, Hindu *literacy* 35% *GNP* $4,666 per head (1992) *chronology* *1951* The Sultanate of Muscat and Oman achieved full independence from Britain. Treaty of Friendship with Britain signed. *1970* After 38 years' rule, Sultan Said bin Taimur replaced in coup by his son Qaboos bin Said. Name changed to Sultanate of Oman. *1975* Left-wing rebels in south defeated. *1982* Memorandum of Understanding with UK signed, providing for regular consultation on international issues. *1985* Diplomatic ties established with USSR. *1991* Sent troops to Operation Desert Storm, as part of coalition opposing Iraq's occupation of Kuwait.

Omar alternative spelling of ◊Umar, 2nd caliph of Islam.

Omar Khayyám *c.* 1050–1123. Persian astronomer, mathematician, and poet. In the West, he is chiefly known as a poet through Edward Fitzgerald's version of *The Rubaiyat of Omar Khayyám* 1859.

Omayyad alternative spelling of ◊Umayyad dynasty.

ombudsman official who acts on behalf of the private citizen in investigating complaints against the government. The post is of Scandinavian origin; it was introduced in Sweden 1809, Denmark 1954, and Norway 1962, and spread to other countries from the 1960s.

Hawaii was the first state to appoint an ombudsman 1967.

omnivore animal that feeds on both plant and animal material. Omnivores have digestive adaptations intermediate between those of ◊herbivores and ◊carnivores, with relatively unspecialized digestive systems and gut microorganisms that can digest a variety of foodstuffs.

On occasion, when regular food supplies are low, most mammals become omnivores.

Omsk industrial city (agricultural and other machinery, food processing, lumber mills, oil refining) in Russia, capital of Omsk region, W Siberia; population (1987) 1,134,000. Its oil refineries are linked with Tuimazy in the Bashkir republic by a 1,000-mi/1,600-km pipeline.

onager wild ass *Equus hemionus* found in W Asia. Onagers are sandy brown, lighter underneath, and about the size of a small horse.

oncology medical specialty concerned with the diagnosis and treatment of neoplasms, especially cancer.

Onega, Lake second-largest lake in Europe, NE of St Petersburg, partly in Karelia, Russia; area 3,710 sq mi/9,600 sq km. The *Onega Canal*, along its S shore, is part of the Mariinsk system linking St Petersburg with the river Volga.

O'Neill Eugene (Gladstone) 1888–1953. US playwright. He is widely regarded as the greatest US dramatist. His plays, although tragic, are characterized by a down-to-earth quality and are often experimental in form, influenced by German Expressionism, Strindberg, and

Freud. They include the Pulitzer Prize-winning plays *Beyond the Horizon* 1920 and *Anna Christie* 1921, as well as *The Emperor Jones* 1920, *The Hairy Ape* 1922, *Desire Under the Elms* 1924, *The Iceman Cometh* 1946, and the posthumously produced autobiographical drama *A Long Day's Journey into Night* 1956 (written 1941), also a Pulitzer Prize winner. He was awarded the Nobel Prize for Literature 1936.

O'Neill was born in New York City, the son of stage actors James O'Neill and Ella Quinlan. His tumultuous family relationships would later provide much material for his plays.

onion bulbous plant *Allium cepa* of the lily family Liliaceae. Cultivated from ancient times, it may have originated in Asia. The edible part is the bulb, containing an acrid volatile oil and having a strong flavor.

on line in computing, connected, so that data can be transferred, for example, to a printer. The opposite of ◊off line.

onomatopoeia figure of speech that copies natural sounds. For example, the word "cuckoo" imitates the sound that the cuckoo makes.

Ontario province of central Canada *area* 412,480 sq mi/1,068,600 sq km *capital* Toronto *towns and cities* Hamilton, Ottawa (federal capital), London, Windsor, Kitchener, St Catharines, Oshawa, Thunder Bay, Sudbury *features* Black Creek Pioneer Village; ◊Niagara Falls; richest, chief manufacturing, most populated, and leading cultural province of English-speaking Canada *industries* nickel, iron, gold, forest products, motor vehicles, iron, steel, paper, chemicals, copper, uranium *population* (1986) 9,114,000 *history* first explored by the French in the 17th century, it came under British control 1763 (Treaty of Paris). An attempt 1841 to form a merged province with French-speaking Québec failed, and Ontario became a separate province of Canada 1867. Under the protectionist policies of the new federal government, Ontario gradually became industrialized and urban.

Since World War II, more than 2 million immigrants, chiefly from Europe, have settled in Ontario.

Ontario, Lake smallest and easternmost of the Great Lakes, on the US-Canadian border; area 7,400 sq mi/19,200 sq km. It is connected to Lake Erie by the Welland Canal and the Niagara River, and drains into the St Lawrence River. Its main port is Toronto.

onyx semiprecious variety of chalcedonic ◊silica (SiO_2) in which the crystals are too fine to be detected under a microscope, a state known as cryptocrystalline. It has straight parallel bands of different colors: milk-white, black, and red.

Oort Jan Hendrik 1900–1992. Dutch astronomer. In 1927, he calculated the mass and size of our Galaxy, the Milky Way, and the Sun's distance from its center, from the observed movements of stars around the Galaxy's center. In 1950 Oort proposed that comets exist in a vast swarm, now called the *Oort cloud*, at the edge of the Solar System.

opal form of ◊silica (SiO_2), often occurring as stalactites and found in many types of rock. The common opal is translucent, milk-white, yellow, red, blue, or green, and lustrous. Precious opal is opalescent, the characteristic play of colors being caused by close-packed silica spheres diffracting light rays within the stone.

Op art (abbreviation for *Optical art*) movement in abstract art during the late 1950s and 1960s, in which color and pattern were used to create optical effects, particularly the illusion of movement. Exponents include Victor Vasarély and Bridget Riley.

OPEC acronym for ◊*Organization of Petroleum-Exporting Countries.*

open-door policy economic philosophy of equal access by all nations to another nation's markets. The term was applied Sept 1899 by Secretary of State John Hay to the US policy toward China.

opera dramatic musical work in which singing takes the place of speech. In opera the music accompanying the action has paramount importance, although dancing and spectacular staging may also play their parts. Opera originated in late 16th-century Florence when the musical declamation, lyrical monologues, and choruses of Classical Greek drama were reproduced in current forms.

operating system (OS) in computing, a program that controls the basic operation of a computer. A typical OS controls the ◊peripheral devices, organizes the filing system, provides a means of communicating with the operator, and runs other programs.

operetta light form of opera, with music, dance, and spoken dialogue. The story line is romantic and sentimental, often employing farce and parody. Its origins lie in the 19th-century *opéra comique* and is intended to amuse. Examples of operetta are Jacques Offenbach's *Orphée aux enfers/Orpheus in the Underworld* 1858, Johann Strauss' *Die Fledermaus/The Flittermouse* 1874, and Gilbert and Sullivan's *The Pirates of Penzance* 1879 and *The Mikado* 1885.

ophthalmology medical specialty concerned with diseases of the eye and its surrounding tissues.

opium drug extracted from the unripe seeds of the opium poppy *Papaver somniferum* of SW Asia. An addictive ◊narcotic, it contains several alkaloids, including *morphine*, one of the most powerful natural painkillers and addictive narcotics known, and *codeine*, a milder painkiller.

Opium Wars two wars, the First Opium War 1839–42 and the Second Opium War 1856–60, waged by Britain against China to enforce the opening of Chinese ports to trade in opium. Opium from British India paid for Britain's imports from China, such as porcelain, silk, and, above all, tea.

opossum any of a family (Didelphidae) of marsupials native to North and South America. Most opossums are tree-living, nocturnal animals, with prehensile tails, and hands and feet well adapted for grasping. They range from 4 in/10 cm to 20 in/50 cm in length and are insectivorous, carnivorous, or, more commonly, omnivorous.

Most true opossums are confined to Central and South America, but the American opossum *Didelphis marsupialis*, with yellowish-gray fur, has spread its range into North America.

Oppenheimer J(ulius) Robert 1904–1967. US physicist. As director of the Los Alamos Science Laboratory 1943–45, he was in charge of the development of the atomic bomb (the Manhattan Project). When later he realized the dangers of radioactivity, he objected to the development of the hydrogen bomb, and was alleged to be a security risk 1953 by the US Atomic Energy Commission (AEC).

Oppenheimer was the son of a German immigrant. Before World War II he worked with the physicist Ernest Rutherford in Cambridge, England. In 1963 the

AEC, under G T Seaborg, granted him the Fermi award in physics.

optical character recognition (OCR) in computing, a technique for inputting text to a computer by means of a document reader. First, a ◊scanner produces a digital image of the text; then character-recognition software makes use of stored knowledge about the shapes of individual characters to convert the digital image to a set of internal codes that can be stored and processed by computer.

optical disk in computing, a storage medium in which laser technology is used to record and read large volumes of digital data. Types include ◊CD-ROM, WORM, and erasable optical disk.

optical fiber very fine, optically pure fiberglass through which light can be reflected to transmit images or data from one end to the other. Although expensive to produce and install, optical fibers can carry more data than traditional cables, and are less susceptible to interference.

optical illusion scene or picture that fools the eye. An example of a natural optical illusion is that the Moon appears bigger when it is on the horizon than when it is high in the sky, owing to the ◊refraction of light rays by the Earth's atmosphere.

optics branch of physics that deals with the study of ◊light and vision—for example, shadows and mirror images, lenses, microscopes, telescopes, and cameras. For all practical purposes light rays travel in straight lines, although Albert ◊Einstein demonstrated that they may be "bent" by a gravitational field. On striking a surface they are reflected or refracted with some absorption of energy, and the study of this is known as geometrical optics.

option in business, a contract giving the owner the right (as opposed to the obligation, as with futures contracts; see ◊futures trading) to buy or sell a specific quantity of a particular commodity or currency at a future date and at an agreed price, in return for a premium. The buyer or seller can decide not to exercise the option if it would prove disadvantageous.

optoelectronics branch of electronics concerned with the development of devices (based on the ◊semiconductor gallium arsenide) that respond not only to ◊electrons of electronic data transmission, but also to ◊photons.

oracle Greek sacred site where answers (also called oracles) were given by priests of a deity to inquirers about personal affairs or state policy. These were often ambivalent. The most celebrated was that of Apollo at ◊Delphi.

oral literature stories that are or have been transmitted in spoken form, such as public recitation, rather than through writing or printing. Most pre-literate societies have had a tradition of oral literature, including short folk tales, legends, myths, proverbs, and riddles as well as longer narrative works; and most of the ancient epics—such as the Greek *Odyssey* and the Mesopotamian *Gilgamesh*—seem to have been composed and added to over many centuries before they were committed to writing.

orange any of several evergreen trees of the genus *Citrus*, family Rutaceae, which bear blossom and fruit at the same time. Thought to have originated in SE Asia, orange trees are commercially cultivated in Spain, Israel, the US, Brazil, South Africa, and elsewhere. The sweet orange *C. sinensis* is the one commonly eaten fresh; the Jaffa, blood, and navel orange are varieties of this species.

Orange Free State province of the Republic of South Africa *area* 49,405 sq mi/127,993 sq km *capital* Bloemfontein *towns and cities* Springfontein, Kroonstad, Bethlehem, Harrismith, Koffiefontein *features* plain of the High Veld; Lesotho forms an enclave on the Natal–Cape Province border *industries* grain, wool, cattle, gold, oil from coal, cement, pharmaceuticals *population* (1987) 1,863,000; 82% ethnic Africans *history* original settlements were from 1810, and the state was recognized by Britain as independent 1854. Following the South African, or Boer, War 1899–1902, it was annexed by Britain until it entered the union as a province 1910.

orangutan ape *Pongo pygmaeus*, found solely in Borneo and Sumatra. Up to 5.5 ft/1.65 m in height, it is covered with long, red-brown hair and mainly lives a solitary, arboreal life, feeding chiefly on fruit. Now an endangered species, it is officially protected because its habitat is being systematically destroyed by ◊deforestation.

oratorio dramatic, non-scenic musical setting of religious texts, scored for orchestra, chorus, and solo voices. Its origins lie in the *Laude spirituali* performed by St Philip Neri's Oratory in Rome in the 16th century, followed by the first definitive oratorio in the 17th century by Cavalieri. The form reached perfection in such works as J S Bach's *Christmas Oratorio*, and Handel's *Messiah*.

orbit path of one body in space around another, such as the orbit of Earth around the Sun, or the Moon around Earth. When the two bodies are similar in mass, as in a ◊binary star, both bodies move around their common center of mass. The movement of objects in orbit follows Johann ◊Kepler's laws, which apply to artificial satellites as well as to natural bodies.

orchid any plant of the family Orchidaceae, which contains at least 15,000 species and 700 genera, distributed throughout the world except in the coldest areas, and most numerous in damp equatorial regions. The flowers are the most evolved of the plant kingdom, have three sepals and three petals and are sometimes solitary, but more usually borne in spikes, racemes, or panicles, either erect or drooping.

Such orchids include the showy orchis *Orchis spectabilis* and rattlesnake orchids (genus *Goodyera*) of North America.

orchid The orchid belongs to one of the largest flowering-plant families: there are possibly as many as 20,000 species. They have evolved complex mechanisms and structures to ensure successful pollination by insects.

order in biological classification, a group of related ◊families. For example, the horse, rhinoceros, and tapir families are grouped in the order Perissodactyla, the odd-toed ungulates, because they all have either one or three toes on each foot. The names of orders are not shown in italic (unlike genus and species names) and by convention they have the ending "-formes" in birds and fish; "-a" in mammals, amphibians, reptiles, and other animals; and "-ales" in fungi and plants. Related orders are grouped together in a ◊class.

ordinal number in mathematics, one of the series first, second, third, fourth,.... Ordinal numbers relate to order, whereas ◊cardinal numbers (1, 2, 3, 4,...) relate to quantity, or count.

ordination religious ceremony by which a person is accepted into the priesthood or monastic life in various religions. Within the Christian church, ordination authorizes a person to administer the sacraments.

Ordovician period of geological time 510–439 million years ago; the second period of the ◊Paleozoic era. Animal life was confined to the sea: reef-building algae and the first jawless fish are characteristic.

ore body of rock, a vein within it, or a deposit of sediment, worth mining for the economically valuable mineral it contains. The term is usually applied to sources of metals. Occasionally metals are found uncombined (native metals), but more often they occur as compounds such as carbonates, sulfides, or oxides. The ores often contain unwanted impurities that must be removed when the metal is extracted.

oregano any of several perennial herbs of the Labiatae family, especially the aromatic *Origanum vulgare*, also known as wild marjoram. It is native to the Mediterranean countries and W Asia and naturalized in the Americas. Oregano is extensively used to season Mediterranean cooking.

Oregon state in NW US, on the Pacific coast; nickname Beaver State *area* 97,079 sq mi/251,500 sq km *capital* Salem *towns and cities* Portland, Eugene *population* (1990) 2,842,300 *features* fertile Willamette river valley; rivers: Columbia, Snake; Crater Lake, deepest in the US (1,933 ft/589 m); mountains: Coast and Cascades; Oregon Dunes National Recreation Area, on Pacific coast *industries* wheat, livestock, timber, electronics *famous people* Chief Joseph, Ursula LeGuin, Linus Pauling, John Reed *history* coast sighted by Spanish and English sailors 16th–17th centuries; part of coastline charted by James Cook 1778 on his search for the Northwest Passage; claimed for the US 1792 by Robert Gray, whose ship *Columbia* sailed into the river now named for it; explored by Lewis and Clark 1805; Oregon Territory included Washington until 1853; Oregon achieved statehood 1859. Improved transportation helped make it the nation's leading lumber producer and a major exporter of food products. Development also was aided by hydroelectric projects, many of them undertaken by the federal government.

organ musical wind instrument of ancient origin. It produces sound from pipes of various sizes under applied pressure and has keyboard controls. Apart from its continued use in serious compositions and for church music, the organ has been adapted for light entertainment.

organ in biology, part of a living body, such as the liver or brain, that has a distinctive function or set of functions.

organic chemistry branch of chemistry that deals with carbon compounds. Organic compounds form the chemical basis of life and are more abundant than inorganic compounds. In a typical organic compound, each carbon atom forms bonds covalently with each of its neighboring carbon atoms in a chain or ring, and additionally with other atoms, commonly hydrogen, oxygen, nitrogen, or sulfur.

organic farming farming without the use of synthetic fertilizers (such as ◊nitrates and phosphates) or ◊pesticides (herbicides, insecticides, and fungicides) or other agrochemicals (such as hormones, growth stimulants, or fruit regulators).

Organization for Economic Cooperation and Development (OECD) international organization of 24 industrialized countries that provides a forum for discussion and coordination of member states' economic and social policies. Founded 1961, with its headquarters in Paris, the OECD superseded the Organization for European Economic Cooperation, which had been established 1948 to implement the ◊Marshall Plan.

Organization of African Unity (OAU) association established 1963 to eradicate colonialism and improve economic, cultural, and political cooperation in Africa. The secretary-general is Salim Ahmed Salim of Tanzania. Its headquarters are in Addis Ababa, Ethiopia.

Organization of American States (OAS) association founded 1948 by a charter signed by representatives of 30 North, Central, and South American states. It aims to maintain peace and solidarity within the hemisphere, and is also concerned with the social and economic development of Latin America.

Organization of Petroleum-Exporting Countries (OPEC) body established 1960 to coordinate price and supply policies of oil-producing states. Its concerted action in raising prices in the 1970s triggered worldwide recession but also lessened demand so that its influence was reduced by the mid-1980s. OPEC members in 1994 were: Algeria, Gabon, Indonesia, Iran, Iraq, Kuwait, Libya, Nigeria, Qatar, Saudi Arabia, the United Arab Emirates, and Venezuela.

orienteering sport of cross-country running and route-finding. Competitors set off at one-minute intervals and have to find their way, using map and compass, to various checkpoints (approximately 0.5 mi/0.8 km apart), where their control cards are marked. World championships have been held since 1966.

Orinoco river in N South America, flowing for about 1,500 mi/2,400 km through Venezuela and forming for about 200 mi/320 km the boundary with Colombia; tributaries include the Guaviare, Meta, Apure, Ventuari, Caura, and Caroni. It is navigable by large steamers for 700 mi/1,125 km from its Atlantic delta; rapids obstruct the upper river.

oriole any of two families of brightly colored songbirds. The Old World orioles of Africa and Eurasia belong to the family Oriolidae. New World orioles belong to the family Icteridae.

Icteridae also includes blackbirds, bobolinks, grackles, meadowlarks, cowbirds, and tanagers. The northern oriole *Icterus galbula* of North America has a black head and wings and bright orange underparts.

Orion in astronomy, a very prominent constellation in the equatorial region of the sky, identified with the hunter of Greek mythology.

It contains the bright stars Betelgeuse and Rigel, as well as a distinctive row of three stars that make up Orion's belt. Beneath the belt, marking the sword of Orion, is the Orion nebula; nearby is one of the most distinctive dark nebulae, the Horsehead.

Orkney Islands island group off the northeast coast of Scotland *area* 375 sq mi/970 sq km *towns and cities* Kirkwall (administrative headquarters), on Mainland (Pomona) *features* comprises about 90 islands and islets, low-lying and treeless; mild climate owing to the Gulf Stream; Skara Brae, a well-preserved Neolithic village on Mainland. On the island of Hoy is an isolated stack known as the Old Man of Hoy. The population, long falling, has in recent years risen as the islands' remoteness from the rest of the world attracts new settlers. Scapa Flow, between Mainland and Hoy, was a naval base in both world wars, and the German fleet scuttled itself here June 21, 1919 *industries* fishing and farming, beef cattle, poultry, fish curing, woolen weaving, wind power (Burgar Hill has the world's most productive wind-powered generator; a 300 KW wind turbine with blades 197 ft/60 m diameter, capable of producing 20% of the islands' energy needs) *population* (1989) 19,600 *famous people* Edwin Muir, John Rae *history* The population is of Scandinavian descent. Harald I (Fairhair) of Norway conquered the islands 876; they were pledged to James III of Scotland 1468 for the dowry of Margaret of Denmark and annexed by Scotland (the dowry unpaid) 1472.

Ormuzd another name for *Ahura Mazda*, the good god of ◊Zoroastrianism.

ornithology study of birds. It covers scientific aspects relating to their structure and classification, and their habits, song, flight, and value to agriculture as destroyers of insect pests. Worldwide scientific banding (or the fitting of coded rings to captured specimens) has resulted in accurate information on bird movements and distribution.

Interest in birds has led to the formation of societies for their protection, of which the Society for the Protection of Birds 1889 in Britain was the first. The Audubon Society 1905 in the US has similar aims.

Orpheus mythical Greek poet and musician. The son of Apollo and a muse, he married Eurydice, who died from the bite of a snake. Orpheus went down to Hades to bring her back and her return to life was granted on condition that he walk ahead of her without looking back. He did look back and Eurydice was irretrievably lost. In his grief, he offended the maenad women of Thrace, and was torn to pieces by them.

Ortega Saavedra Daniel 1945– . Nicaraguan socialist politician, head of state 1981–90. He was a member of the Sandinista Liberation Front (FSLN) which overthrew the regime of Anastasio Somoza 1979, later becoming its secretary-general. US-sponsored ◊Contra guerrillas opposed his government from 1982.

Orthodox Church or *Eastern Orthodox Church* or *Greek Orthodox Church* federation of self-governing Christian churches mainly found in E and SE Europe and parts of Asia. The center of worship is the Eucharist. There is a married clergy, except for bishops; the Immaculate Conception is not accepted. The highest rank in the church is that of ecumenical patriarch, or bishop of Istanbul.

There are approximately 130 million adherents.

orthopedics branch of medicine concerned with the surgery of bones and joints.

Orwell George. Pen name of Eric Arthur Blair 1903–1950. English author. His books include the satirical fable *Animal Farm* 1945, which included such slogans as "All animals are equal, but some are more equal than others", and the prophetic *Nineteen Eighty-Four* 1949, portraying the catastrophic excesses of state control over the individual. Other works include *Down and Out in Paris and London* 1933. A deep sense of social conscience and antipathy toward political dictatorship characterize his work.

oryx any of the genus *Oryx* of large antelopes native to Africa and Asia. The Arabian oryx *O. leucoryx*, at one time extinct in the wild, has been successfully reintroduced into its natural habitat using stocks bred in captivity.

Osaka industrial port (iron, steel, shipbuilding, chemicals, textiles) on Honshu Island, Japan; population (1990) 2,623,800, metropolitan area 8,000,000. It is the oldest city of Japan and was at times the seat of government in the 4th–8th centuries.

Osborn Henry Fairfield 1857–1935. US paleontologist. He made his first fossil-hunting expedition to the West 1877. He was staff paleontologist with the US Geological Survey 1900–24 and president of the American Museum of Natural History 1908–33.

Born in Fairfield, Connecticut, Osborn was educated at Princeton University. Appointed to the Princeton faculty 1881, he was named professor of biology at Columbia 1891. In the same year, he also began to serve as curator of vertebrate paleontology at the American Museum of Natural History.

Osborne John (James) 1929– . English dramatist. He became one of the first Angry Young Men (antiestablishment writers of the 1950s) of British theater with his debut play, *Look Back in Anger* 1956. Other plays include *The Entertainer* 1957, *Luther* 1960, *Inadmissible Evidence* 1964, and *A Patriot for Me* 1965.

osier any of several trees and shrubs of the willow genus *Salix*, cultivated for basket making; in particular, *S. viminalis*.

The name is also applied to several North American ◊dogwoods.

Osiris ancient Egyptian god, the embodiment of goodness, who ruled the underworld after being killed by ◊Set. The sister-wife of Osiris was ◊Isis or Hathor, and their son ◊Horus captured his father's murderer. The pharaohs were thought to be his incarnation.

Oslo capital and industrial port (textiles, engineering, timber) of Norway; population (1991) 461,600. The first recorded settlement was made in the 11th century by Harald III Hardrada, but after a fire 1624, it was entirely replanned by Christian IV and renamed *Christiania* 1624–1924.

Osman I or *Uthman I* 1259–1326. Turkish ruler from 1299. He began his career in the service of the Seljuk Turks, but in 1299 he set up a kingdom of his own in Bithynia, NW Asia, and assumed the title of sultan. He conquered a great part of Anatolia, so founding a Turkish empire. His successors were known as "sons of Osman", from which the term ◊Ottoman Empire is derived.

osmium hard, heavy, bluish white, metallic element, symbol Os, atomic number 76, atomic weight 190.2. It is the densest of the elements, and is resistant to tarnish and corrosion. It occurs in platinum ores and as a free metal with iridium in a natural alloy called osmiridium, containing traces of platinum, ruthenium, and rhodium. Its uses include pen points and light-bulb filaments; like platinum, it is a useful catalyst.

osmosis movement of solvent (liquid) through a semipermeable membrane separating solutions of different concentrations. The solvent passes from a less concentrated solution to a more concentrated solution until the two concentrations are equal. Applying external pressure to the solution on the more concentrated side arrests osmosis, and is a measure of the osmotic pressure of the solution.

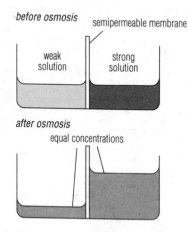

before osmosis
semipermeable membrane

weak solution

strong solution

after osmosis
equal concentrations

osmosis *Osmosis, the movement of liquid through a semipermeable membrane separating solutions of different concentrations, is essential for life. Osmosis transports water from the soil into the roots of plants, for example. It is applied in kidney dialysis to remove impurities from the blood.*

osprey bird of prey *Pandion haliaetus*, the single member of the family Pandionidae; sometimes erroneously called "fish hawk". To catch fish, it plunges feet first into the water. Dark brown above and a striking white below, the osprey measures 2 ft/60 cm with a 6 ft/2 m wingspan.

Ospreys occur on all continents except Antarctica and have faced extinction in several areas of habitation. Once on the verge of extinction in the US, it is now responding well to preservation programs.

osteopathy system of alternative medical practice that relies on physical manipulation to treat mechanical stress. It was developed over a century ago by US physician Andrew Taylor Still, who maintained that most ailments can be prevented or cured by techniques of spinal manipulation.

osteoporosis disease in which the bone substance becomes porous and brittle. It is common in older people, affecting more women than men. It may be treated with calcium supplements and etidronate. Approximately 1.7 million people worldwide, mostly women, suffer hip fractures, mainly due to osteoporosis. A single gene was discovered 1993 to have a major influence on bone thinning.

Ostia ancient Roman town near the mouth of the Tiber. Founded about 330 BC, it was the port of Rome

and had become a major commercial center by the 2nd century AD. It was abandoned in the 9th century. The present-day seaside resort *Ostia Mare* is situated nearby.

ostrich large flightless bird *Struthio camelus*, found in Africa. The male may be about 8 ft/2.5 m tall and weigh 300 lb/135 kg, and is the largest living bird. It has exceptionally strong legs and feet (two-toed) that enable it to run at high speed, and are also used in defense. It lives in family groups of one cock with several hens, each of which incubates about 14 eggs.

Ostrogoth member of a branch of the E Germanic people, the ◊Goths.

Othman alternative spelling of ◊Uthman, third caliph of Islam.

Otis Elisha Graves 1811–1861. US engineer who developed an elevator that incorporated a safety device, making it acceptable for passenger use in the first skyscrapers. The device, invented 1852, consisted of vertical ratchets on the sides of the elevator shaft into which spring-loaded catches engage and "lock" the elevator into position in the event of cable failure.

otitis inflammation of the ear. *Otitis externa*, occurring in the outer ear canal, is easily treated with antibiotics. Inflamed conditions of the middle ear (*otitis media*) or inner ear (*otitis interna*) are more serious, carrying the risk of deafness and infection of the brain. Treatment is with antibiotics or, more rarely, surgery.

Ottawa capital of Canada, in E Ontario, on the hills overlooking the Ottawa River and divided by the Rideau Canal into the Upper (western) and Lower (eastern) towns; population (1986) 301,000, metropolitan area (with adjoining Hull, Québec) 819,000. Industries include timber, pulp and paper, engineering, food processing, and publishing. It was founded 1826–32 as Bytown, in honor of John By (1781–1836), whose army engineers were building the Rideau Canal. It was renamed 1854 after the Outaouac Indians.

otter any of various aquatic carnivores of the weasel family, found on all continents except Australia. Otters have thick, brown fur, short limbs, webbed toes, and long, compressed tails. They are social, playful, and agile.

The genus *Lutra* includes the river otters of North America and Eurasia, about 3.5 ft/1 m long, including the tail. The sea otter *Enhydra lutris* of the N Pacific is the most aquatic. It sometimes lies on its back in the water, resting a stone on its chest, on which it breaks shellfish. The giant otter *Pteronura brasiliensis* of South America reaches 5 ft/1.5 m plus a 2.3 ft/70 cm tail.

Otto I 912–973. Holy Roman emperor from 962. He restored the power of the empire, asserted his authority over the pope and the nobles, ended the Magyar menace by his victory at the Lechfeld 955, and refounded the East Mark, or Austria, as a barrier against them.

Otto IV *c.* 1182–1218. Holy Roman emperor, elected 1198. He engaged in controversy with Pope Innocent III, and was defeated by the pope's ally, Philip of France, at Bouvines 1214.

Ottoman Empire Muslim empire of the Turks 1300–1920, the successor of the ◊Seljuk Empire. It was founded by ◊Osman I and reached its height with ◊Suleiman in the 16th century. Its capital was Istanbul (formerly Constantinople).

Ouagadougou capital and industrial center of Burkina Faso; population (1985) 442,000. Products include textiles, vegetable oil, and soap. The city has the palace of Moro Naba, emperor of the Mossi people, a neo-Romanesque cathedral, and a central avenue called the Champs Elysées. It was the capital of the Mossi empire from the 15th century.

Oughtred William 1575–1660. English mathematician, credited as the inventor of the slide rule 1622. His major work *Clavis mathematicae/The Key to Mathematics* 1631 was a survey of the entire body of mathematical knowledge of his day. It introduced the "x" symbol for multiplication, as well as the abbreviations "sin" for sine and "cos" for cosine.

ounce unit of mass, one-sixteenth of a pound ◊avoirdupois, equal to 437.5 grains (28.35 g); also one-twelfth of a pound troy, equal to 480 grains.

The *fluid ounce* is a measure of capacity, in the US equivalent to one-sixteenth of a pint, or eight fluid drams. In the UK and Canada, it equals one-twentieth of a pint.

ousel or *ouzel* ancient name of the blackbird. The ring ouzel *Turdus torquatus* is similar to a blackbird, but has a white band across the breast. It is found in Europe in mountainous and rocky country. Water ouzel is another name for the ◊dipper.

output device in computing, any device for displaying, in a form intelligible to the user, the results of processing carried out by a computer.

The most common output devices are the VDT (visual display terminal) and the printer.

Ovamboland region of N Namibia stretching along the Namibia–Angola frontier; the scene of conflict between SWAPO guerrillas and South African forces in the 1970s and 1980s.

ovary in female animals, the organ that generates the ◊ovum. In humans, the ovaries are two whitish rounded bodies about 1 in/25 mm by 1.5 in/35 mm, located in the lower abdomen to either side of the uterus. Every month, from puberty to the onset of the menopause, an ovum is released from the ovary. This is called ovulation, and forms part of the ◊menstrual cycle. In botany, an ovary is the expanded basal portion of the ◊carpel of flowering plants, containing one or more ovules. It is hollow with a thick wall to protect the ovules. Following fertilization of the ovum, it develops into the fruit wall or pericarp.

overpopulation too many people for the resources available in an area (such as food, land, and water). The consequences were first set out by English economist Thomas ◊Malthus at the start of the population explosion.

overture in music, the opening piece of a concert or opera, having the dual function of settling the audience and allowing the conductor and musicians to become acquainted with the ◊acoustics of a concert auditorium.

Ovid (Publius Ovidius Naso) 43 BC –AD 17. Latin poet. His poetry deals mainly with the themes of love (*Amores* 20 BC, *Ars amatoria/The Art of Love* 1 BC), mythology (*Metamorphoses* AD 2), and exile (*Tristia* AD 9–12).

ovovivipary method of animal reproduction in which fertilized eggs develop within the female (unlike ovipary), and the embryo gains no nutritional substances from the female (unlike vivipary). It occurs in some invertebrates, fishes, and reptiles.

ovulation in female animals, the process of releasing egg cells (ova) from the ◊ovary. In mammals it occurs as part of the ◊menstrual cycle.

ovum (plural *ova*) female gamete (sex cell) before fertilization. In animals it is called an egg, and is produced in the ovaries. In plants, where it is also known as an egg cell or oosphere, the ovum is produced in an ovule. The ovum is nonmotile. It must be fertilized by a male gamete before it can develop further, except in cases of ◊parthenogenesis.

Owen Wilfred 1893–1918. English poet. His verse, owing much to the encouragement of Siegfried Sassoon, expresses his hatred of war, for example *Anthem for Doomed Youth*, published 1921.

Owens Jesse (James Cleveland) 1913–1980. US track and field athlete who excelled in the sprints, hurdles, and the long jump. At the 1936 Berlin Olympics he won four gold medals.

owl any bird of the order Strigiformes, found worldwide. They are mainly nocturnal birds of prey, with mobile heads, soundless flight, acute hearing, and forward-facing immobile eyes, surrounded by "facial disks" of rayed feathers. All species lay white eggs, and begin incubation as soon as the first is laid. They regurgitate indigestible remains of their prey in pellets (castings).

The worldwide common barn owl *Tyto alba* is now diminished by pesticides and loss of habitat.

owl The barn-owl family can be distinguished from other owl groups by its heart-shaped face, relatively small eyes, and long slender legs. The long, hooked beak is usually concealed by feathers. All barn owls are hunters by night.

ox castrated male of domestic species of cattle, used in Third World countries for plowing and other agricultural purposes. Also the extinct wild ox or ◊aurochs of Europe, and extant wild species such as buffaloes and yaks.

oxalic acid $(COOH)_2.2H_2O$ white, poisonous solid, soluble in water, alcohol, and ether. Oxalic acid is found in rhubarb, and its salts (oxalates) occur in wood sorrel (genus *Oxalis*, family Oxalidaceae) and other plants. It also occurs naturally in human body cells. It is used in the leather and textile industries, in dyeing and bleaching, ink manufacture, metal polishes, and for removing rust and ink stains.

Oxford university city and administrative center of Oxfordshire in S central England, at the confluence of the rivers Thames (called the Isis around Oxford) and Cherwell; population (1991) 110,000. Oxford University has 36 colleges, the oldest being University

College (1249). Industries include motor vehicles at Cowley, steel products, electrical goods, paper, publishing, and English language schools. Tourism is important.

history The Royalist headquarters in the Civil War was here.

Oxford Movement also known as *Tractarian Movement* or *Catholic Revival* movement beginning 1833 that attempted to revive Catholic religion in the Church of England. The Oxford Movement by the turn of the century had transformed the Anglican communion, and survives today as Anglo-Catholicism.

Oxfordshire county of S central England *area* 1,007 sq mi/2,610 sq km *towns and cities* Oxford (administrative headquarters), Abingdon, Banbury, Henley-on-Thames, Witney, Woodstock *features* river Thames and tributaries; Cotswolds and Chiltern Hills; Vale of the White Horse (chalk hill figure at Uffington, 374 ft/114 m long); Oxford University; Blenheim Palace, Woodstock (started 1705 by Vanbrugh with help from Nicholas Hawksmoor, completed 1722), with landscaped grounds by Capability ◊Brown; Europe's major fusion project JET (Joint European Trust) at the UK Atomic Energy Authority's fusion laboratories at Culham *industries* cereals, automobiles, paper, bricks, cement *population* (1991) 553,800 *famous people* William Davenant, Flora Thompson, Winston Churchill, William Morris (founder of Morris Motors Ltd, and of Nuffield College, Oxford 1937)

oxidation in chemistry, the loss of ◊electrons, gain of oxygen, or loss of hydrogen by an atom, ion, or molecule during a chemical reaction.

oxide compound of oxygen and another element, frequently produced by burning the element or a compound of it in air or oxygen.

oxyacetylene torch gas torch that burns ethene (acetylene) in pure oxygen, producing a high-temperature (5,400°F/3,000°C) flame. It is widely used in welding to fuse metals. In the cutting torch, a jet of oxygen burns through metal already melted by the flame.

oxygen colorless, odorless, tasteless, nonmetallic, gaseous element, symbol O, atomic number 8, atomic weight 15.9994. It is the most abundant element in the Earth's crust (almost 50% by mass), forms about 21% by volume of the atmosphere, and is present in combined form in water and many other substances. Life on Earth evolved using oxygen, which is a by-product of ◊photosynthesis and the basis for ◊respiration in plants and animals.

oxyhemoglobin the oxygenated form of hemoglobin, the pigment found in the red blood cells. All vertebrates, and some invertebrates, use hemoglobin for oxygen transport because the two substances can combine reversibly. In mammals oxyhemoglobin forms in the lungs and is transported to the rest of the body, where the oxygen is released. The deoxygenated blood is then returned to the lungs.

oxymoron figure of speech, the combination of two or more words that are normally opposites, in order to startle. *Bittersweet* is an oxymoron, as are *cruel to be kind* and *beloved enemy.*

oyster bivalve ◊mollusk constituting the Ostreidae, or true oyster, family, having the upper valve flat, the lower concave, hinged by an elastic ligament. The mantle, lying against the shell, protects the inner body, which includes respiratory, digestive, and reproductive organs. Oysters commonly change their sex annually or more frequently; females may discharge up to a million eggs during a spawning period.

oyster catcher chunky shorebird of the family Haematopodidae, with a laterally flattened, heavy bill that can pry open mollusk shells.

The black and white American oyster catcher *Haematopus palliatus* is found on the Atlantic and S Pacific coasts.   ·

Özal Turgut 1927–1993. Turkish Islamic right-wing politician, prime minister 1983–89, president 1989–93. He was responsible for improving his country's relations with Greece, but his prime objective was to strengthen Turkey's alliance with the US.

Ozark Mountains area in the US (shared by Arkansas, Illinois, Kansas, Mississippi, Oklahoma) of ridges, valleys, and streams; highest point only 2,300 ft/700 m; area 50,000 sq mi/130,000 sq km. This heavily forested region between the Missouri and Arkansas rivers has agriculture and lead and zinc mines.

ozone O_3 highly reactive pale-blue gas with a penetrating odor. Ozone is an allotrope of oxygen (see ◊allotropy), made up of three atoms of oxygen. It is formed when the molecule of the stable form of oxygen (O_2) is split by ultraviolet radiation or electrical discharge. It forms a thin layer in the upper atmosphere, which protects life on Earth from ultraviolet rays, a cause of skin cancer.

ozone depleter any chemical that destroys the ozone in the stratosphere. Most ozone depleters are chemically stable compounds containing chlorine or bromine, which remain unchanged for long enough to drift up to the upper atmosphere. The best known are ◊chlorofluorocarbons (CFCs), but many other ozone depleters are known, including halons, used in some fire extinguishers; methyl chloroform and carbon tetrachloride, both solvents; some CFC substitutes; and the pesticide methyl bromide.

P

pacemaker medical device implanted under the skin of a patient whose heart beats inefficiently. It delivers minute electric shocks to stimulate the heart muscles at regular intervals and restores normal heartbeat.

Pacific Islands former (1947–1990) United Nations trust territory in the W Pacific captured from Japan during World War II. The territory comprised over 2,000 islands and atolls and was assigned to the US 1947. The islands were divided into four governmental units: the *Northern Mariana Islands* (except Guam) which became a self-governing commonwealth in union with the US 1975 (inhabitants granted US citizenship 1986); the ◊Marshall Islands, the Federated States of ◊Micronesia, and the Republic of ◊Belau (formerly Palau) became self-governing 1979–80, signing agreements of free association with the US 1986. In Dec 1990 the United Nations Security Council voted to dissolve its trusteeship over the islands with the exception of Belau. The Marshall Islands and the Federated States of Micronesia were granted UN membership 1991.

Pacific Ocean world's largest ocean, extending from Antarctica to the Bering Strait; area 64,170,000 sq mi/166,242,500 sq km; average depth 13,749 ft/4,188 m; greatest depth of any ocean 36,210 ft/11,034 m in the ◊Mariana Trench.

pacifism belief that violence, even in self-defense, is unjustifiable under any conditions and that arbitration is preferable to war as a means of solving disputes.

In the East, pacifism has roots in Buddhism, and nonviolent action was used by Mahatma ◊Gandhi in the struggle for Indian independence.

Padua (Italian *Padova*) city in N Italy, 28 mi/45 km W of Venice; population (1988) 224,000. The astronomer Galileo taught at the university, founded 1222.

page printer computer ◊printer that prints a complete page of text and graphics at a time. Page printers use electrostatic techniques, very similar to those used by photocopiers, to form images of pages, and range in size from small ◊laser printers designed to work with microcomputers to very large machines designed for high-volume commercial printing.

Pahlavi dynasty Iranian dynasty founded by Reza Khan (1877–1944), an army officer who seized control of the government 1921 and was proclaimed shah 1925. During World War II, Britain and the USSR were nervous about his German sympathies and occupied Iran 1941–46. They compelled him to abdicate 1941 in favor of his son Mohammed Reza Shah Pahlavi, who took office in 1956, with US support, and was deposed in the Islamic revolution of 1979.

Pahsien alternate name for ◊Chongqing, a port in SW China.

Paige Satchel (Leroy Robert) 1906–1982. US baseball player. As a pitcher, he established a near-legendary record, leading the Kansas City Monarchs of the Negro National League to the championship 1942. In 1948, with the end of racial segregation in the major leagues, Paige joined the Cleveland Indians. He later played with the St Louis Browns 1951–53.

He was elected to the Baseball Hall of Fame 1971.

Paine Thomas 1737–1809. English left-wing political writer. He was active in the American and French revolutions. His pamphlet *Common Sense* 1776 ignited passions in the American Revolution; others include *The Rights of Man* 1791 and *The Age of Reason* 1793. He advocated republicanism, deism, the abolition of slavery, and the emancipation of women.

paint any of various materials used to give a protective and decorative finish to surfaces or for making pictures. A paint consists of a pigment suspended in a vehicle, or binder, usually with added solvents. It is the vehicle that dries and hardens to form an adhesive film of paint. Among the most common kinds are cellulose paints (or lacquers), oil-based paints, emulsion paints, and special types such as enamels and primers.

painting the application of colored pigment to a surface. The chief methods of painting are: *tempera* emulsion painting, with a gelatinous (for example, egg yolk) rather than oil base; known in ancient Egypt *fresco* watercolor painting on plaster walls; the palace of Knossos, Crete, contains examples from about 2,000 BC *ink* developed in China for calligraphy in the Sung period and highly popular in Japan from the 15th century *oil* ground pigments in linseed, walnut, or other oil; spread from N to S Europe in the 15th century *watercolor* pigments combined with gum arabic and glycerol, which are diluted with water; the method was developed in the 15th–17th centuries for wash drawings *acrylic* synthetic pigments developed after World War II; the colors are very hard and brilliant.

Pakistan Islamic Republic of *area* 307,295 sq mi/796,100 sq km; one-third of Kashmir under Pakistani control *capital* Islamabad *towns and cities* Karachi, Lahore, Rawalpindi, Peshawar *physical* fertile Indus plain in E, Baluchistan plateau in W, mountains in N and NW *environment* about 68% of irrigated land is waterlogged or suffering from salinization *features* the "five rivers" (Indus, Jhelum, Chenab, Ravi, and Sutlej) feed the world's largest irrigation system; Tarbela (world's largest earthfill dam); K2 mountain; Khyber Pass; sites of the Indus Valley civilization *head of state* Farooq Leghari from 1993 *head of government* Benazir Bhutto from 1993 *political system* emergent democracy *political parties* Pakistan People's Party (PPP), moderate, Islamic, socialist; Islamic Democratic Alliance (IDA), including the Pakistan Muslim League (PML), Islamic conservative; Mohajir National Movement (MQM), Sind-based *mohajir* (Muslims previously living in India) settlers *exports* cotton textiles, rice, leather, carpets *currency* Pakistan rupee *population* (1993 est) 122,400,000 (Punjabi 66%, Sindhi 13%); growth rate 3.1% p.a. *life expectancy* men 59, women 59 *languages* Urdu and English (official); Punjabi, Sindhi, Pashto, Baluchi, other local dialects *religions* Sunni Muslim 75%, Shiite Muslim 20%,

472

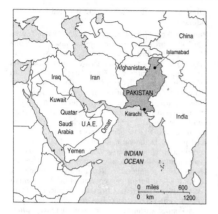

Hindu 4% *literacy* men 47%, women 21% *GNP* $400 per head (1991) *chronology 1947* Independence achieved from Britain, Pakistan formed following partition of British India. *1956* Proclaimed a republic. *1958* Military rule imposed by General Ayub Khan. *1969* Power transferred to General Yahya Khan. *1971* Secession of East Pakistan (Bangladesh). After civil war, power transferred to Zulfikar Ali Bhutto. *1977* Bhutto overthrown in military coup by General Zia ul-Haq; martial law imposed. *1979* Bhutto executed. *1981* Opposition Movement for the Restoration of Democracy formed. Islamization process pushed forward. *1985* Nonparty elections held, amended constitution adopted, martial law and ban on political parties lifted. *1986* Agitation for free elections launched by Benazir Bhutto. *1988* Zia introduced Islamic legal code, the Shari'a. He was killed in a military plane crash in Aug Benazir Bhutto elected prime minister Nov. *1989* Pakistan rejoined the Commonwealth. *1990* Army mobilized in support of Muslim separatists in Indian Kashmir. Bhutto dismissed on charges of incompetence and corruption. IDA, led by Nawaz Sharif, won Oct general election. *1991* Shari'a bill enacted; privatization and economic deregulation program launched. *1992* Sept: Floods devastated north of country. *1993* July: Khan and Sharif resigned, ending months of political stalemate; interim government formed. Oct: Benazir Bhutto reelected prime minister. Nov: Farooq Leghari elected president, pledging to restore full parliamentary system.

Palatinate (called the *Pfalz* in Germany) historic division of Germany, dating from before the 8th century. It was ruled by a *count palatine* (a count with royal prerogatives) and varied in size.

Palau former name (to 1981) of the Republic of ◊Belau.

Paleocene first epoch of the Tertiary period of geological time, 65–55 million years ago. Many types of mammals spread rapidly after the disappearance of the great reptiles of the Mesozoic.

Paleolithic earliest stage of human technology and development of the Stone Age; see ◊prehistory.

paleontology in geology, the study of ancient life that encompasses the structure of ancient organisms and their environment, evolution, and ecology, as revealed by their ◊fossils.

Paleozoic era of geological time 590–248 million years ago. It comprises the Cambrian, Ordovician, Silurian,

Devonian, Carboniferous, and Permian periods. The Cambrian, Ordovician, and Silurian constitute the Lower Paleozoic; the Devonian, Carboniferous, and Permian make up the Upper Paleozoic. The era includes the evolution of hard-shelled multicellular life forms in the sea; the invasion of land by plants and animals; and the evolution of fish, amphibians, and early reptiles. The earliest identifiable fossils date from this era. The climate was mostly warm with short ice ages. The continents were very different from the present ones but, toward the end of the era, all were joined together as a single world continent called Pangaea.

Palermo capital and seaport of Sicily; population (1988) 729,000. Industries include shipbuilding, steel, glass, and chemicals. It was founded by the Phoenicians in the 8th century BC.

Palestine historic geographical area at the E end of the Mediterranean sea, also known as the Holy Land because of its historic and symbolic importance for Jews, Christians, and Muslims. Early settlers included the Canaanites, Hebrews, and Philistines. Over the centuries it became part of the Egyptian, Assyrian, Babylonian, Macedonian, Ptolemaic, Seleucid, Roman, Byzantine, Arab, and Ottoman empires. Today, it comprises parts of modern Israel, and Jordan.

Palestine Liberation Organization (PLO) Arab organization founded 1964 to bring about an independent state in Palestine. It consists of several distinct groupings, the chief of which is al-◊Fatah, led by Yassir ◊Arafat, the president of the PLO from 1969. The PLO's original main aim was the destruction of the Israeli state, but over time it changed to establishing a Palestinian state alongside that of Israel, and in 1993 a peace agreement based on mutual recognition was reached with Israel. In 1994 Arafat returned to the newly liberated territories of Gaza and Jericho to head an interim civilian administration, the Palestinian National Authority. However, extremist groups, notably the militant wing of the Hamas fundamentalist group, opposed the accord and continued a campaign of violence within these territories.

Palladio Andrea 1518–1580. Italian Renaissance architect. He was noted for his harmonious and balanced classical structures. He designed numerous palaces and country houses in and around Vicenza, Italy, making use of Roman classical forms, symmetry, and proportion. The Villa Malcontenta and the Villa Rotonda are examples of houses designed from 1540 for patrician families of the Venetian Republic. He also designed churches in Venice and published his studies of classical form in several illustrated books.

His ideas were revived in England in the early 17th century by Inigo Jones and in the 18th century by Lord Burlington and Colen Campbell, and later by architects in Italy, Holland, Germany, Russia, and the US, where his ideas were introduced by Thomas Jefferson and had wide influence on Federal-period architecture.

palladium lightweight, ductile and malleable, silver-white, metallic element, symbol Pd, atomic number 46, atomic weight 106.4.

It is one of the so-called platinum group of metals, and is resistant to tarnish and corrosion. It often occurs in nature as a free metal in a natural alloy with platinum. Palladium is used as a catalyst, in alloys of gold (to make white gold) and silver, in electroplating, and in dentistry.

Pallas in Greek mythology, a title of the goddess ◊Athena.

palm plant of the family Palmae, characterized by a single tall stem bearing a thick cluster of large palmate or pinnate leaves at the top. The majority of the numerous species are tropical or subtropical. Some, such as the coconut, date, sago, and oil palms, are important economically.

Several palms are native to Florida.

Palma (Spanish *Palma de Mallorca*) industrial port (textiles, cement, paper, pottery), resort, and capital of the Balearic Islands, Spain, on Majorca; population (1991) 308,600. Palma was founded 276 BC as a Roman colony. It has a Gothic cathedral, begun 1229.

Palmas, Las port in the Canary Islands; see ◊Las Palmas.

Palm Beach luxurious winter resort in Florida, on an island between Lake Worth and the Atlantic; population (1990) 9,800.

Henry Flagler first developed the community as a resort in the 1890s, when he built the Royal Poinciana Hotel. It now has mansions, clubs, and large estates as well as resort hotels.

Palmer Samuel 1805–1881. English landscape painter and etcher. He lived in Shoreham, Kent, 1826–35 with a group of artists who were all followers of William Blake and referred to themselves as "the Ancients". Palmer's expressive landscapes have a visionary quality.

Palmerston Henry John Temple, 3rd Viscount 1781–1865. British politician. Initially a Tory. He broke with the Tories 1830 and sat in the Whig cabinets of 1830–34, 1835–41, and 1846–51 as foreign secretary. He was prime minister 1855–58 (when he rectified Aberdeen's mismanagement of the Crimean War, suppressed the Indian (Sepoy) Mutiny, and carried through the Second Opium War) and 1859–65 (when he almost involved Britain in the Civil War on the side of the South).

Palm Sunday in the Christian calendar, the Sunday before Easter and first day of Holy Week, commemorating Jesus' entry into Jerusalem, when the crowd strewed palm leaves in his path.

Pamirs central Asian plateau mainly in Tajikistan, but extending into China and Afghanistan, traversed by mountain ranges. Its highest peak is Kommunizma Pik (Communism Peak 24,600 ft/7,495 m) in the Akademiya Nauk range.

Pampas flat, treeless, Argentine plains, lying between the Andes Mountains and the Atlantic Ocean and rising gradually from the coast to the lower slopes of the mountains. The E Pampas contain large cattle ranches and the flax-and grain-growing area of Argentina; the W Pampas are arid and unproductive.

pampas grass any grass of the genus *Cortaderia*, native to South America, especially *C. argentea*, which is grown in gardens and has tall leaves and large panicles of white flowers.

Pan in Greek mythology, the god of flocks and herds (Roman Sylvanus), shown as a man with the horns, ears, and hoofed legs of a goat, and playing a shepherd's panpipe (or syrinx).

Pan-Africanist Congress (PAC) militant black South African nationalist group, which broke away from the African National Congress (ANC) 1959. More radical than the ANC, the Pan-Africanist Congress has a black-only policy for Africa. PAC was outlawed from 1960 to 1990. Its military wing is called Poqo ("we alone").

Panama Republic of (*República de Panamá*) *area* 29,768 sq mi/77,100 sq km *capital* Panamá (Panama City) *towns and cities* Cristóbal, Balboa, Colón, David *physical* coastal plains and mountainous interior; tropical rainforest in E and NW; Pearl Islands in Gulf of Panama *features* Panama Canal; Barro Colorado Island in Gatún Lake (reservoir supplying the canal), a tropical forest reserve since 1923; Smithsonian Tropical Research Institute *head of state and government* Ernesto Pérez Balladares from 1994 *political system* emergent democratic republic *political parties* Democratic Revolutionary Party (PRD), center-left; Labour Party (PALA), right of center; Panamanian Republican Party (PPR), right-wing; Nationalist Liberal Republican Movement (MOLIRENA), left of center; Authentic Panamanian Party (PPA), centrist; Christian Democratic Party (PDC), center-left *exports* bananas, petroleum products, copper, shrimps, sugar *currency* balboa *population* (1993 est) 2,510,000 (mestizo, or mixed race, 70%; West Indian 14%; European descent 10%; Indian (Cuna, Choco, Guayami) 6%); growth rate 2.2% p.a. *life expectancy* men 71, women 75 *languages* Spanish (official), English *religions* Roman Catholic 93%, Protestant 6% *literacy* men 88%, women 88% *GNP* $2,180 per head (1991) *chronology* *1821* Achieved independence from Spain; joined confederacy of Gran Colombia. *1903* Full independence achieved on separation from Colombia. *1974* Agreement to negotiate full transfer of the Panama Canal from the US to Panama. *1977* US–Panama treaties transferred the canal to Panama, effective from 1990, with the US guaranteeing its protection and an annual payment. *1984* Nicolás Ardito Barletta elected president. *1985* Barletta resigned; replaced by Eric Arturo del Valle. *1987* General Noriega (head of the National Guard and effective ruler) resisted calls for his removal, despite suspension of US military and economic aid. *1988* Del Valle replaced by Manuel Solis Palma. Noriega, charged with drug smuggling by the US, declared a state of emergency. *1989* Opposition won election; Noriega declared results invalid; Francisco Rodríguez sworn in as president. Coup attempt against Noriega failed; Noriega declared head of government by assembly. "State of war" with the US announced. US invasion deposed Noriega; Guillermo Endara installed as president. Noriega sought asylum in Vatican embassy; later surrendered and taken to US for trial. *1991* Attempted antigovernment coup foiled. Constitutional reforms approved by assembly, including abolition of a standing army. *1992* Noriega found guilty of drug offenses. Referendum rejected proposed constitutional reforms. *1994* Ernesto Pérez Balladares (PRD) elected president. Constitution amended; army formally abolished.

Panama Canal canal across the Panama isthmus in Central America, connecting the Pacific and Atlantic oceans; length 50 mi/80 km, with 12 locks. Built by the US 1904–14 after an unsuccessful attempt by the French, it was formally opened 1920. The *Panama Canal Zone* was acquired "in perpetuity" by the US 1903, comprising land extending about 3 mi/5 km on either side of the canal. The zone passed to Panama 1979, and control of the canal itself was ceded to Panama by the US Jan 1990 under the terms of the Panama Canal Treaty 1977. The Canal Zone has several US military bases.

Panama City capital of the Republic of Panama, near the Pacific end of the Panama Canal; population (1990) 584,800. Products include chemicals, plastics, and clothing. An earlier Panama, to the NE, founded 1519, was destroyed 1671, and the city was founded on the present site 1673.

pancreas in vertebrates, an accessory gland of the digestive system located close to the duodenum. When stimulated by the hormone secretin, it releases enzymes into the duodenum that digest starches, proteins, and fats. In humans, it is about 7 in/18 cm long, and lies behind and below the stomach. It contains groups of cells called the *islets of Langerhans*, which secrete the hormones insulin and glucagon that regulate the blood sugar level.

panda one of two carnivores of different families, native to NW China and Tibet. The *giant panda Ailuropoda melanoleuca* has black-and-white fur with black eye patches and feeds mainly on bamboo shoots, consuming about 17.5 lb/8 kg of bamboo per day. It can grow up to 4.5 ft/1.5 m long, and weigh up to 300 lb/140 kg. It is an endangered species. The *lesser*, or *red*, *panda Ailurus fulgens*, of the raccoon family, is about 1.5 ft/50 cm long, and is black and chestnut, with a long tail.

panda The lesser, or red, panda lives in the bamboo forests of Nepal, W Myanmar, and SW China. A quiet creature, it spends the day asleep, curled up on a branch with its head tucked into its chest and its tail over its head. It feeds on bamboo shoots, grass, roots, fruit, acorns, and the occasional bird's egg.

Pandora in Greek mythology, the first mortal woman. Zeus sent her to Earth with a box of evils (to counteract the blessings brought to mortals by ◊Prometheus' gift of fire); she opened the box, and the evils all flew out. Only hope was left inside as a consolation.

pangolin or *scaly anteater* any toothless mammal of the order Pholidota. There is only one genus (*Manis*), with seven species found in tropical Africa and SE Asia. They are long-tailed and covered with large, overlapping scales. The elongated skull contains a long, extensible tongue. Pangolins measure up to 3 ft/1 m in length; some are arboreal and others are terrestrial. All live on ants and termites.

Pankhurst Emmeline (born Goulden) 1858–1928. English suffragist. Founder of the Women's Social and Political Union 1903, she launched the militant suffragist campaign 1905. In 1926 she joined the Conservative Party and was a prospective Parliamentary candidate.

pansy cultivated violet derived from the European wild pansy *Viola tricolor*, and including many different varieties and strains. The flowers are usually purple, yellow, cream, or a mixture, and there are many highly developed varieties bred for size, color, or special markings. Several of the 400 different species are scented.

Pantanal large area of swampland in the Mato Grosso of SW Brazil, occupying 84,975 sq mi/220,000 sq km in the upper reaches of the Paraguay River; one of the world's great wildlife refuges of which 530 sq mi/1,370 sq km were designated a national park 1981.

pantheism doctrine that regards all of reality as divine, and God as present in all of nature and the universe. It is expressed in Egyptian religion and Brahmanism; stoicism, Neoplatonism, Judaism, Christianity, and Islam can be interpreted in pantheistic terms. Pantheistic philosophers include Bruno, Spinoza, Fichte, Schelling, and Hegel.

panther another name for the ◊leopard.

Papal States area of central Italy in which the pope was temporal ruler from 756 until the unification of Italy 1870.

Papandreou Andreas 1919– . Greek socialist politician, founder of the Pan-Hellenic Socialist Movement (PASOK), and prime minister 1981–89, when he became implicated in the alleged embezzlement and diversion of funds to the Greek government of $200 million from the Bank of Crete, headed by George Koskotas, and as a result lost the election. In Jan 1992 a trial cleared Papandreou of all corruption charges, and he was reelected prime minister Oct 1993.

papaya tropical tree *Carica papaya* of the family Caricaceae, native from Florida to South America. Varieties are grown throughout the tropics. The edible fruits resemble a melon, with orange-colored flesh and numerous blackish seeds in the central cavity; they may weigh up to 20 lb/9 kg.

Papeete capital and port of French Polynesia on the NW coast of Tahiti; population (1983) 79,000. Products include vanilla, copra, and mother-of-pearl.

paper thin, flexible material made in sheets from vegetable fibers (such as wood pulp) or rags and used for writing, drawing, printing, packaging, and various household needs. The name comes from papyrus, a form of writing material made from water reed, used in ancient Egypt. The invention of true paper, originally made of pulped fishing nets and rags, is credited to Tsai Lun, Chinese minister of agriculture, AD 105.

Papua New Guinea area 178,656 sq mi/462,840 sq km *capital* Port Moresby (on E New Guinea) *towns and cities* Lae, Rabaul, Madang *physical* mountainous; includes tropical islands of New Ireland, New Britain, and Bougainville; Admiralty Islands, D'Entrecasteaux Islands, and Louisiade Archipelago *features* world's largest swamps on SW coast; world's largest butterfly, orchids; Sepik River *head of state* Queen Elizabeth II of Britain, represented by governor-general Wiwa Korowi from 1991 *head of government* Julius Chan from 1994 *political system* liberal democracy *political parties* Papua New Guinea Party (Pangu Pati: PP), urban-and coastal-oriented nationalist; People's Democratic Movement (PDM), 1985 breakaway from the PP; National Party (NP), highlands-based; Melanesian Alliance (MA), Bougainville-based autonomy; People's Progress Party (PPP), conservative; People's Action Party (PAP), right of center *exports* copra, coconut oil, palm oil, tea, copper, gold, coffee *currency* kina *population* (1993 est) 3,900,000 (Papuans, Melanesians, Negritos, various minorities); growth rate 2.6% p.a. *life expectancy* men 55, women 57 *languages* English (official); pidgin English, 715 local languages *religions* Protestant 63%, Roman Catholic 31%, local faiths *literacy* men 65%, women 38% *GNP* \$820 per head (1991) *chronology 1883* Annexed by Queensland; became the Australian Territory of Papua. *1884* NE New Guinea annexed by Germany; SE claimed by Britain. *1914* NE New Guinea occupied by Australia. *1921–42* Held as a League of Nations mandate. *1942–45* Occupied by Japan. *1975* Independence achieved from Australia, within the Commonwealth, with Michael Somare as prime minister. *1980* Julius Chan became prime minister. *1982* Somare returned to power. *1985* Somare challenged by Paias Wingti, the deputy prime minister, who later formed a five-party coalition government. *1988* Wingti defeated on no-confidence vote and replaced by Rabbie Namaliu, who established a six-party coalition government. *1989* State of emergency imposed on Bougainville in response to separatist violence. *1990* Bougainville Revolutionary Army (BRA) issued unilateral declaration of independence. *1991* Economic boom as gold production doubled. Deputy Prime Minister Ted Diro found guilty of corruption. Wiwa Korowi replaced Vicent Serei Eri as governor-general. *1992* Wingti elected premier. *1994* Julius Chan (PPP) elected premier. Peace agreement with BRA.

papyrus type of paper made by the ancient Egyptians from the stem of the papyrus or paper reed *Cyperus papyrus,* family Cyperaceae.

paracetamol analgesic, particularly effective for musculoskeletal pain. It is as effective as aspirin in reducing fever, and less irritating to the stomach, but has little anti-inflammatory action. An overdose can cause severe, often irreversible or even fatal, liver and kidney damage.

Technically, it is acetaminophenol, a white crystalline powder $CH_3CONHC_6H_4OH$. It is sold under numerous trademarks (for example, Tylenol).

parachute any canopied fabric device strapped to a person or a package, used to slow down descent from a high altitude, or returning spent missiles or parts to a safe speed for landing, or sometimes to aid (through braking) the landing of a plane or missile. Modern designs enable the parachutist to exercise considerable control of direction, as in skydiving.

paradise in various religions, a place or state of happiness. Examples are the Garden of Eden and the Messianic kingdom; the Islamic paradise of the Koran is a place of sensual pleasure.

paraffin common name for ◊alkane, any member of the series of hydrocarbons with the general formula C_nH_{2n+2}. The lower members are gases, such as methane (marsh or natural gas). The middle ones (mainly liquid) form the basis of gasoline, kerosene, and lubricating oils, while the higher ones (paraffin waxes) are used in ointment and cosmetic bases.

Paraguay Republic of (*República del Paraguay*) *area* 157,006 sq mi/406,752 sq km *capital* Asunción *towns and cities* Puerto Presidente Stroessner, Pedro Juan Caballero; port Concepción *physical* low marshy plain and marshlands; divided by Paraguay River; Paraná River forms SE boundary *features* Itaipú dam on border with Brazil; Gran Chaco plain with huge

swamps *head of state and government* Juan Carlos Wasmosy from 1993 *political system* emergent democratic republic *political parties* National Republican Association (Colorado Party), right of center; Liberal Party (PL), right of center; Radical Liberal Party (PLR), centrist *exports* cotton, soybeans, timber, vegetable oil, maté *currency* guaraní *population* (1993) 4,500,000 (95% mixed Guarani Indian–Spanish descent); growth rate 3.0% p.a. *life expectancy* men 65, women 70 *languages* Spanish 6% (official), Guarani 90% *religion* Roman Catholic 97% *literacy* men 92%, women 88% *GNP* \$1,210 per head (1991) *chronology 1811* Independence achieved from Spain. *1865–70* War with Argentina, Brazil, and Uruguay; less than half the population survived and much territory lost. *1932–35* Territory won from Bolivia during the Chaco War. *1940–48* Presidency of General Higinio Morínigo. *1948–54* Political instability; six different presidents. *1954* General Alfredo Stroessner seized power. *1989* Stroessner ousted in coup led by General Andrés Rodríguez. Rodríguez elected president; Colorado Party won the congressional elections. *1991* Colorado Party successful in assembly elections. *1992* New constitution adopted. *1993* Free multiparty elections won by Colorado Party; Juan Carlos Wasmosy won first free presidential elections.

parakeet any of various small ◊parrots.

parallel lines and parallel planes in mathematics, straight lines or planes that always remain a constant distance from one another no matter how far they are extended. This is a principle of Euclidean geometry. Some non-Euclidean geometries, such as elliptical and hyperbolic geometry, however, reject Euclid's parallel axiom.

parallelogram in mathematics, a quadrilateral (four-sided plane figure) with opposite pairs of sides equal in length and parallel, and opposite angles equal. The diagonals of a parallelogram bisect each other. Its area is the product of the length of one side and the perpendicular distance between this and the opposite side. In the special case when all four sides are equal in length, the parallelogram is known as a rhombus, and when the internal angles are right angles, it is a rectangle or square.

paralysis loss of voluntary movement due to failure of nerve impulses to reach the muscles involved. It may result from almost any disorder of the nervous system, including brain or spinal cord injury, poliomyelitis, stroke, and progressive conditions such as a tumor or multiple sclerosis. Paralysis may also involve loss of sensation due to sensory nerve disturbance.

Paramaribo port and capital of Surinam, South America, 15 mi/24 km from the sea on the river Suriname; population (1980) 193,000. Products include coffee, fruit, timber, and bauxite. It was founded by the French on an Indian village 1540, made capital of British Surinam 1650, and placed under Dutch rule 1816–1975.

Paraná river in South America, formed by the confluence of the Río Grande and Paranaiba; the Paraguay joins it at Corrientes, and it flows into the Río de la Plata with the Uruguay; length 2,800 mi/4,500 km. It is used for hydroelectric power by Argentina, Brazil, and Paraguay.

paranoia mental disorder marked by delusions of grandeur or persecution. In popular usage, paranoia means baseless or exaggerated fear and suspicion.

parapsychology study of phenomena that are not within range of, or explicable by established science, for example, extrasensory perception. The faculty allegedly responsible for such phenomena, and common to humans and other animals, is known as *psi*.

parasite organism that lives on or in another organism (called the host) and depends on it for nutrition, often at the expense of the host's welfare. Parasites that live inside the host, such as liver flukes and tapeworms, are called *endoparasites*; those that live on the exterior, such as fleas and lice, are called *ectoparasites*.

parent–teacher association (PTA) group attached to a school consisting of parents and teachers who support the school by fund-raising and other activities. Throughout the US, PTAs are active as political pressure groups and as a way to involve parents in the public education process.

paresthesiae medical name for pins and needles. They indicate disturbance of a peripheral nerve—as, for example, by pressure.

Pareto Vilfredo 1848–1923. Italian economist and political philosopher. A vigorous opponent of socialism and liberalism, he justified inequality of income on the grounds of his empirical observation (*Pareto's law*) that income distribution remained constant whatever efforts were made to change it.

Paris port and capital of France, on the river Seine; *département* in the Île de France region; area 40.5 sq mi/105 sq km; population (1990) 2,175,200. Products include metal, leather, and luxury goods and chemicals, glass, and tobacco.

Paris Commune name given to two separate periods in the history of Paris:

The Paris municipal government 1789–94 was established after the storming of the ◊Bastille and remained powerful in the French Revolution until the fall of Robespierre 1794.

The provisional national government March 18–May 1871 was formed while Paris was besieged by the German troops during the Franco-Prussian War. It consisted of socialists and left-wing republicans, and is often considered the first socialist government in history. Elected after the right-wing National Assembly at Versailles tried to disarm the National Guard, it fell when the Versailles troops captured Paris and massacred 20,000–30,000 people May 21–28.

parish in the US, the ecclesiastical unit committed to one minister or priest. In Britain, a subdivision of a county often coinciding with an original territorial subdivision in Christian church administration, served by a parish church.

parity in economics, equality of price, rate of exchange, wages, and buying power. Parity ratios may be used in the setting of wages to establish similar status to different work groups. Parity in international exchange rates means that those on a par with each other share similar buying power. In the US, agricultural output prices are regulated by a parity system.

Park Mungo 1771–1806. Scottish explorer who traced the course of the Niger River 1795–97. He disappeared and probably drowned during a second African expedition 1805–06. He published *Travels in the Interior of Africa* 1799.

Park Chung Hee 1917–1979. President of South Korea 1963–79. Under his rule South Korea had one of the world's fastest-growing economies, but recession and his increasing authoritarianism led to his assassination 1979.

Parker Charlie (Charles Christopher "Bird", "Yardbird") 1920–1955. US alto saxophonist and jazz composer. He was associated with the trumpeter Dizzy Gillespie in developing the ◊bebop style. His skillful improvisations inspired performers on all jazz instruments.

Parkinson's disease or *parkinsonism* or *paralysis agitans* degenerative disease of the brain characterized by a progressive loss of mobility, muscular rigidity, tremor, and speech difficulties. The condition is mainly seen in people over the age of 50.

parliament legislative body of a country. The world's oldest parliament is the Icelandic Althing which dates from about 930. The UK Parliament is usually dated from 1265. The legislature of the US is called ◊Congress and comprises the ◊House of Representatives and the Senate.

Parliament, European governing body of the European Union (formerly the European Community); see ◊European Parliament.

Parnassus mountain in central Greece, height 8,064 ft/2,457 m, revered by the ancient Greeks as the abode of Apollo and the Muses. The sacred site of Delphi lies on its southern flank.

Parnell Charles Stewart 1846–1891. Irish nationalist politician. He supported a policy of obstruction and violence to attain ◊Home Rule, and became the president of the Nationalist Party 1877. His attitude led to his imprisonment 1881. His career was ruined 1890 when he was cited as corespondent in a divorce case.

parody in literature and the other arts, a work that imitates the style of another work, usually with mocking or comic intent; it is related to satire.

parrot any bird of the order Psittaciformes, abundant in the tropics, especially in Australia and South America. They are mainly vegetarian, and range in

parrot The gray parrot of the lowland forest and savanna of Kenya and Tanzania. Large flocks roost together in the trees at the forest edge, or on small river or lake islands. At sunrise, the birds fly off in pairs to search for food. They eat seeds, nuts, berries, and fruit, particularly the fruit of the oil palm.

size from the 3.5 in/8.5 cm in pygmy parrot to the 40 in/100 cm Amazon parrot. The smaller species are commonly referred to as parakeets. The plumage is often very colorful, and the call is usually a harsh screech. Several species are endangered.

parsec in astronomy, a unit (symbol pc) used for distances to stars and galaxies. One parsec is equal to 3.2616 ◊light years, 2.063 x 10^5 ◊astronomical units, and 3.086 x 10^{13} km.

parsley biennial herb *Petroselinum crispum* of the carrot family, Umbelliferae, cultivated for flavoring and its nutrient properties, being rich in vitamin C and minerals. Up to 1.5 ft/45 cm high, it has pinnate, aromatic leaves and yellow umbelliferous flowers.

parsnip temperate Eurasian biennial *Pastinaca sativa* of the carrot family Umbelliferae, with a fleshy edible root.

Parsons Louella 1893–1972. US newspaper columnist. Working for the ◊Hearst syndicate, she moved to Hollywood 1925 and began a gossip column and a popular radio program *Hollywood Hotel* 1934. For over 40 years she exerted great influence (some damaging) over the lives of stars and studios. She published her memoirs as *The Gay Illiterate* 1944 and *Tell It to Louella* 1961.

parthenogenesis development of an ovum (egg) without any genetic contribution from a male. Parthenogenesis is the normal means of reproduction in a few plants (for example, dandelions) and animals (for example, certain fish). Some sexually reproducing species, such as aphids, show parthenogenesis at some stage in their life cycle.

Parthia ancient country in W Asia in what is now NE Iran, capital Ctesiphon. Parthian ascendancy began with the Arsacid dynasty in 248 BC, and reached the peak of its power under Mithridates I in the 2nd century BC ; the region was annexed to Persia under the Sassanians AD 226.

participle in grammar, a form of the verb. English has two forms, a *present participle* ending in *-ing* (for example, "work*ing*" in "They were *working*", "*working* men", and "a hard-*working* team") and a *past participle* ending in *-ed* in regular verbs (for example, "train*ed*" in "They have been *trained* well", "*trained* soldiers", and "a well-*trained* team").

particle in grammar, a category that includes such words as *up, down, in, out*, which may be used either as ◊prepositions (also called *prepositional particles*), as in *up the street* and *down the stairs*, or as ◊adverbs (identified as *adverbial particles*), as in *pick up the book/pick the book up*. A verb with a particle (for example, *put up*) is a phrasal ◊verb.

particle physics the study of the properties of ◊elementary particles and of fundamental interactions (see ◊fundamental forces).

particle, subatomic see ◊subatomic particle.

partisan member of an armed group that operates behind enemy lines or in occupied territories during wars. The name "partisans" was first given to armed bands of Russians who operated against Napoleon's army in Russia during 1812, but has since been used to describe Russian, Yugoslav, Italian, Greek, and Polish Resistance groups against the Germans during World War II.

partnership two or more persons carrying on a common business for shared profit. The business can be of any kind—for instance, lawyers, shop owners, or window cleaners. A partnership differs from a corporation in that the individuals remain separate in identity and are not protected by limited liability, so that each partner is personally responsible for any debts of the partnership.

part of speech grammatical function of a word, described in the grammatical tradition of the Western world, based on Greek and Latin. The four major parts of speech are the noun, verb, adjective, and adverb; the minor parts of speech vary according to schools of grammatical theory, but include the article, conjunction, preposition, and pronoun.

partridge any of various medium-sized ground-dwelling fowl of the family Phasianidae, which also includes pheasants, quail, and chickens.

Partridges are Old World birds, some of which have become naturalized in North America, especially the European gray partridge *Perdix perdix*, with mottled brown back, gray speckled breast, and patches of chestnut on the sides.

Pasadena city in SW California, US, part of Greater ◊Los Angeles; population (1990) 131,600. Products include electronic equipment and precision instruments.

The California Institute of Technology and the Jet Propulsion Laboratory (administered jointly by the institute and the federal government) are here. Each New Year's Day, Pasadena is host to the Tournament of Roses parade and a major college football game at the Rose Bowl. Farmers from Indiana founded a settlement here 1874.

PASCAL (French acronym for *program appliqué à la selection et la compilation automatique de la littérature*) a high-level computer-programming language. Designed by Niklaus Wirth (1934–) in the 1960s as an aid to teaching programming, it is still widely used as such in universities, but is also recognized as a good general-purpose programming language. It was named for 17th-century French mathematician Blaise Pascal.

pascal SI unit (symbol Pa) of pressure, equal to one newton per square meter. It replaces bars and millibars (10^5 Pa equals one bar). It is named for the French mathematician Blaise Pascal.

Pascal Blaise 1623–1662. French philosopher and mathematician. He contributed to the development of hydraulics, calculus, and the mathematical theory of ◊probability.

pasqueflower plant *Anemone patens* of the buttercup family, native to the central US. It has a hairy stalk and hairy leaves near the base. The showy lavender-blue flowers are 2 in/5 cm across.

Passaic city in NW New Jersey, US, on the Passaic River, N of Jersey City; population (1990) 58,000. Products include television cables, chemicals, plastics, pharmaceuticals, and clothing.

passion flower climbing plant of the tropical American genus *Passiflora*, family Passifloraceae. It bears distinctive flower heads comprising a saucer-shaped petal base, a fringelike corona, and a central stalk bearing the stamens and ovary. Some species produce edible fruit.

Passover also called *Pesach* in Judaism, an eight-day spring festival which commemorates the exodus of the Israelites from Egypt and the passing over by the Angel of Death of the Jewish houses, so that only the

Egyptian firstborn sons were killed, in retribution for Pharaoh's murdering of all Jewish male infants.

pastel sticklike drawing or painting material consisting of ground pigment bound with gum; also works produced in this medium. Pastel is a form of painting in dry colors and produces a powdery surface, which is delicate and difficult to conserve. Exponents include Rosalba Carriere (1675–1785), La Tour, Chardin, Degas, and Mary Cassatt.

Pasternak Boris Leonidovich 1890–1960. Russian poet and novelist. His novel *Dr Zhivago* 1957 was banned in the USSR as a "hostile act", and was awarded a Nobel Prize (which Pasternak declined). *Dr Zhivago* has since been unbanned and Pasternak has been posthumously rehabilitated.

Pasteur Louis 1822–1895. French chemist and microbiologist who discovered that fermentation is caused by microorganisms. He also developed a vaccine for ◊rabies, which led to the foundation of the Institut Pasteur in Paris 1888.

pasteurization treatment of food to reduce the number of microorganisms it contains and so protect consumers from disease. Harmful bacteria are killed and the development of others is delayed. For milk, the method involves heating it to 161°F/72°C for 15 seconds followed by rapid cooling to 50°F/10°C or lower. The process also kills beneficial bacteria and reduces the nutritive property of milk.

Patagonia geographic area of South America, S of latitude 40° S, with sheep farming, and coal and oil resources. Sighted by Ferdinand Magellan 1520, it was claimed by both Argentina and Chile until divided between them 1881.

patent or *letters patent* documents conferring the exclusive right to make, use, and sell an invention for a limited period. Ideas are not eligible; neither is anything not new.

Pathan member of a people of NW Pakistan and Afghanistan, numbering about 14 million (1984). The majority are Sunni Muslims. The Pathans speak Pashto, a member of the Indo-Iranian branch of the Indo-European family.

pathogen in medicine, any microorganism that causes disease. Most pathogens are ◊parasites, and the diseases they cause are incidental to their search for food or shelter inside the host. Nonparasitic organisms, such as soil bacteria or those living in the human gut and feeding on waste foodstuffs, can also become pathogenic to a person whose immune system or liver is damaged. The larger parasites that can cause disease, such as nematode worms, are not usually described as pathogens.

pathology medical specialty concerned with the study of disease processes and how these provoke structural and functional changes in the body.

patriarch in the Old Testament, one of the ancestors of the human race, and especially those of the ancient Hebrews, from Adam to Abraham, Isaac, Jacob, and his sons (who became patriarchs of the Hebrew tribes). In the Eastern Orthodox Church, the term refers to the leader of a national church.

patriarchy form of social organization in which a man heads and controls the family unit. By extension, in a patriarchal society men also control larger social and working groups as well as government. The definition has been broadened by feminists to describe the dominance of male values throughout society.

Patrick, St 389–c. 461. Patron saint of Ireland. Born in Britain, probably in S Wales, he was carried off by pirates to six years' slavery in Antrim, Ireland, before escaping either to Britain or Gaul—his poor Latin suggests the former—to train as a missionary. He is variously said to have landed again in Ireland 432 or 456, and his work was a vital factor in the spread of Christian influence there. His symbols are snakes and shamrocks; feast day March 17.

patronage power to give a favored appointment to an office or position in politics, business, or the church; or sponsorship of the arts. Patronage was for centuries bestowed mainly by individuals (in Europe often royal or noble) or by the church.

In the 20th century, patrons have tended to be political parties, the state, and—in the arts—private industry and foundations.

Patton George (Smith) 1885–1945. US general in World War II, known as "Blood and Guts". During World War I, he formed the first US tank force and led it in action 1918. He became commanding general of the First Armoured Corps 1941. In 1942 he led the Western Task Force that landed at Casablanca, Morocco. After commanding the 7th Army, he led the 3rd Army across France and into Germany, and in 1945 took over the 15th Army.

Patton was an outspoken advocate of mobility and armor. He played a central role in stopping the German counteroffensive at the Battle of the Bulge Dec 1944–Jan 1945.

Pauli Wolfgang 1900–1958. Austrian physicist who originated the *exclusion principle*: in a given system no two fermions (electrons, protons, neutrons, or other elementary particles of half-integral spin) can be characterized by the same set of ◊quantum numbers. He also predicted the existence of neutrinos. He was awarded a Nobel Prize 1945 for his work on atomic structure.

Pauling Linus Carl 1901–1994. US chemist, author of *The Nature of the Chemical Bond*, 1939, and works describing the discovery of the helical structure of many proteins. His fundamental work on the nature of the chemical bond includes much new information about inter-atomic distances. Pauling also investigated the properties and uses of vitamin C as related to human health. He won the Nobel Prize for Chemistry 1954. In the 1950s Pauling became politically active and campaigned for a nuclear test-ban treaty; he received the Nobel Peace Prize in 1962.

Paul, St c. AD 3–c. AD 68. Christian missionary and martyr; in the New Testament, one of the apostles and author of 13 epistles. Originally opposed to Christianity, he took part in the stoning of St Stephen. He is said to have been converted by a vision on the road to Damascus. After his conversion he made great missionary journeys, for example to Philippi and Ephesus, becoming known as the Apostle of the Gentiles (non-Jews). His emblems are a sword and a book; feast day June 29.

Pavlov Ivan Petrovich 1849–1936. Russian physiologist who studied conditioned reflexes in animals. His work had a great impact on behavioral theory (see ◊behaviorism and learning theory). See also ◊conditioning. Nobel Prize for Medicine 1904.

Pavlova Anna 1881–1931. Russian dancer. Prima ballerina of the Imperial Ballet from 1906, she left Russia 1913, and went on to become one of the world's most celebrated exponents of classical ballet. With London as her home, she toured extensively with her own company, influencing dancers worldwide with roles such as *The Dying Swan* solo 1907. She was opposed to the modern reforms of Diaghilev's Ballets Russes, adhering strictly to conservative esthetics.

pawpaw or *papaw* small tree *Asimina triloba* of the custard-apple family Annonaceae, native to the eastern US. It bears oblong fruits 5 in/13 cm long with yellowish, edible flesh. The name pawpaw is also used for the ◊papaya.

Pawtucket city in NE Rhode Island, on the Blackstone River, NE of Providence; population (1990) 72,600. Industries include textiles, thread, machinery, and metal and glass products. It was the home of the first US water-powered cotton mill 1790.

Pays de la Loire agricultural region of W France, comprising the *départements* of Loire-Atlantique, Maine-et-Loire, Mayenne, Sarthe, and Vendée; capital Nantes; area 12,391 sq mi/32,100 sq km; population (1986) 3,018,000. Industries include shipbuilding and wine production.

Paz Octavio 1914– . Mexican poet and essayist. His works reflect many influences, including Marxism, Surrealism, and Aztec mythology. His long poem *Piedra del sol/Sun Stone* 1957 uses contrasting images, centering upon the Aztec Calendar Stone (representing the Aztec universe), to symbolize the loneliness of individuals and their search for union with others. Nobel Prize for Literature 1990.

PC abbreviation for ◊*personal computer*.

pea climbing plant *Pisum sativum*, family Leguminosae, with pods of edible seeds, grown since prehistoric times for food. The pea is a popular vegetable and is eaten fresh, canned, dried, or frozen. The sweet pea *Lathyrus odoratus* of the same family is grown for its scented, butterfly-shaped flowers.

peace movement collective opposition to war. The Western peace movements of the late 20th century can trace their origins to the pacifists of the 19th century and conscientious objectors during World War I.

In the US, opposition to the Vietnam War, which grew from the late 1960s, was the primary post-World War II peace movement. It greatly influenced US politics and society, although Ban the Bomb opposition was older, a post-World War II posture against nuclear weapons.

peach tree *Prunus persica*, family Rosaceae. It has ovate leaves and small, usually pink flowers. The yellowish edible fruits have thick velvety skins; the nectarine is a smooth-skinned variety.

peacock technically, the male of any of various large pheasants. The name is most often used for the common peacock *Pavo cristatus*, a bird of the pheasant family, native to S Asia. It is rather larger than a pheasant. The male has a large fan-shaped tail, brightly colored with blue, green, and purple "eyes" on a chestnut background. The female (peahen) is brown with a small tail.

Peale Norman Vincent 1898– . US Methodist leader born in Bowersville, Ohio. Through his radio program and book *The Art of Living* 1948, he became one of the best-known religious figures in the US. His *The Power of Positive Thinking* 1952 became a national bestseller. Peale was elected president of the Reformed Church in America in 1969.

peanut or *groundnut* or *monkey nut* South American vinelike annual plant *Arachis hypogaea*, family Leguminosae. After flowering, the flower stalks bend and force the pods into the earth to ripen underground. The nuts are a staple food in many tropical countries and are widely grown in the S US. They yield a valuable edible oil and are the basis for numerous processed foods.

pear tree *Pyrus communis*, family Rosaceae, native to temperate regions of Eurasia. It has a succulent edible fruit, less hardy than the apple.

pearl shiny, hard, rounded abnormal growth composed of nacre (or mother-of-pearl), a chalky substance. Nacre is secreted by many mollusks, and deposited in thin layers on the inside of the shell around a parasite, a grain of sand, or some other irritant body. After several years of the mantle (the layer of tissue between the shell and the body mass) secreting this nacre, a pearl is formed.

Pearl Harbor an inlet of the Pacific Ocean where the US naval base is situated in Hawaii on Oahu Island. It was the scene of a Japanese surprise air attack on Dec 7, 1941, which brought the US into World War II. It took place while Japanese envoys were holding so-called peace talks in Washington. About 3,300 US military personnel were killed, four battleships were lost, and a large part of the US Pacific fleet was destroyed or damaged. The Japanese, angered by US embargoes of oil and other war material and convinced that US entry into the war was inevitable, opted to strike a major blow in hopes of forcing US concessions. Instead, it galvanized public opinion and raised anti-Japanese sentiment to a fever pitch, with war declared thereafter.

Pearse Patrick Henry 1879–1916. Irish poet. He was prominent in the Gaelic revival, a leader of the ◊Easter Rising 1916. Proclaimed president of the provisional government, he was court-martialed and shot after its suppression.

Pearson Drew 1897–1969. US newspaper columnist. Although his frank, anonymously published exposé *Washington Merry-Go-Round* 1931 became a bestseller, he was fired from the *Baltimore Sun* when his authorship became known. In 1932, however, he began openly publishing a syndicated column of the same name, working in conjunction with Robert Allen until 1942. Pearson continued the column alone until his death, after which it was taken over by newspaper columnist and writer, Jack Anderson (1922–).

Pearson Lester Bowles 1897–1972. Canadian politician, leader of the Liberal Party from 1958, prime minister 1963–68. As foreign minister 1948–57, he represented Canada at the United Nations, playing a key role in settling the ◊Suez Crisis 1956. Nobel Peace Prize 1957.

Peary Robert Edwin 1856–1920. US polar explorer who, after several unsuccessful attempts, became the first person to reach the North Pole on April 6, 1909. In 1988 an astronomer claimed Peary's measurements were incorrect.

One of his companions on an 1891 voyage was Frederick A Cook who, in 1909, claimed he had reached the North Pole before Peary. Although Cook's claim is generally discredited, it continues to cast a shadow over Peary's achievement.

Peasants' Revolt the rising of the English peasantry in June 1381, the result of economic, social, and political disillusionment. It was sparked off by the imposition of a new poll tax, three times the rates of those imposed in 1377 and 1379. Led by Wat ◊Tyler and

Pearl Harbor *USS West Virginia after the surprise Japanese attack on the US naval base at Pearl Harbor in Hawaii Dec 7 1941. Despite its devastating impact, the attack was not the success it might have been since most of the US aircraft carriers, of vital importance in a Pacific war, were out of the harbor on maneuvers.*

John ◊Ball, rebels from SE England marched on London and demanded reforms. The authorities put down the revolt by deceit and force.

peat fibrous organic substance found in bogs and formed by the incomplete decomposition of plants such as sphagnum moss. N Asia, Canada, Finland, Ireland, and other places have large deposits, which have been dried and used as fuel from ancient times. Peat can also be used as a soil additive.

pecan nut-producing ◊hickory tree *Carya illinoensis* or *C. pecan*, native to central US and N Mexico and now widely cultivated. The tree grows to over 150 ft/45 m, and the edible nuts are smooth-shelled, the kernel resembling a smoothly ovate walnut.

peccary one of two species of the New World genus *Tayassu* of piglike hoofed mammals. A peccary has a gland in the middle of its back which secretes a strong-smelling substance. Peccaries are blackish in color, covered with bristles, and have tusks that point downward. Adults reach a height of 15 in/40 cm, and a weight of 60 lb/25 kg.

pediatrics medical specialty concerned with the care of children.

pedomorphosis in biology, an alternate term for ◊neoteny.

Peel Robert 1788–1850. British Conservative politician. As home secretary 1822–27 and 1828–30, he founded the modern police force (whose constables were called Bobbies in his honor) and in 1829 introduced Roman Catholic emancipation. He was prime minister 1834–35 and 1841–46, when his repeal of the ◊Corn Laws caused him and his followers to break with the party.

peerage in the UK, holders, in descending order, of the titles of duke, marquess, earl, viscount, and baron.

peer group in the social sciences, people who have a common identity based on such characteristics as similar social status, interests, age, or ethnic group. The concept has proved useful in analyzing the power and influence of coworkers, school friends, and ethnic and religious groups in socialization and social behavior.

Pegasus in Greek mythology, the winged horse that sprang from the blood of the Gorgon Medusa. He was transformed into a constellation.

Pei I(eoh) M(ing) 1917– . Chinese-born American architect, noted for innovative modern design and high-technology structures, particularly the use of glass walls. His buildings include the Mile High Center in Denver, the National Airlines terminal (now owned by TWA) at Kennedy Airport in New York City, the John Hancock tower in Boston, the National Gallery extension in Washington, DC, the Bank of China Tower, Hong Kong, and the glass pyramid in front of the Louvre, Paris.

Peirce Charles Sanders 1839–1914. US philosopher and logician born in Cambridge, Massachusetts. He was the founder of ◊pragmatism (which he later called pragmaticism), who argued that genuine conceptual distinctions must be correlated with some differences of practical effect. He wrote extensively on the logic of scientific inquiry, suggesting that truth could be conceived of as the object of an ultimate consensus.

Peking alternative transcription of ◊Beijing, the capital of China.

Peking man Chinese representative of an early species of human, found as fossils, 500,000–750,000 years old, in the cave of Choukoutien 1927 near Beijing (Peking). Peking man used chipped stone tools, hunted game, and used fire. Similar varieties of early human have been found in Java and E Africa. Their classification is disputed: some anthropologists classify them as *Homo erectus*, others as *Homo sapiens pithecanthropus*.

A skull found near Beijing 1927 was sent to the US 1941 but disappeared; others have since been found.

pelargonium flowering plant of the genus *Pelargonium* of the geranium family Geraniaceae, grown extensively in gardens, where it is familiarly known as the *geranium*. Ancestors of the garden hybrids came from southern Africa.

Pelé adopted name of Edson Arantes do Nascimento 1940– . Brazilian soccer player. A prolific goal scorer, he appeared in four World Cup competitions 1958–70 and led Brazil to three championships (1958, 1962, 1970).

pelican any of a family (Pelecanidae) of large, heavy water birds remarkable for the pouch beneath the bill which is used as a fishing net and temporary store for catches of fish. Some species grow up to 6 ft/1.8 m and have wingspans of 10 ft/3 m.

Peloponnese (Greek *Peloponnesos*) peninsula forming the S part of Greece; area 8,318 sq mi/21,549 sq km; population (1991) 1,077,000. It is joined to the mainland by the narrow isthmus of Corinth and is divided into the nomes (administrative areas) of Argolis, Arcadia, Achaea, Elis, Corinth, Lakonia, and Messenia, representing its seven ancient states.

Peloponnesian War conflict between Athens and Sparta, backed by their respective allies, 431–404 BC, originating in suspicions about the ambitions of the Athenian leader Pericles. It was ended by the Spartan general Lysander's capture of the Athenian fleet in 405, and his starving the Athenians into surrender in 404. Sparta's victory meant the destruction of the political power of Athens.

Peltier effect in physics, a change in temperature at the junction of two different metals produced when an electric current flows through them. The extent of the change depends on what the conducting metals are, and the nature of change (rise or fall in temperature) depends on the direction of current flow. It is named for the French physicist Jean Charles Peltier (1785–1845) who discovered it 1834.

pemmican preparation of dried lean bison or venison pounded into a paste with fat and dried berries and preserved as pressed cakes, once used as a food by Plains Indians. Similar preparations made from beef were used for high-energy rations by early Arctic explorers, and by mountaineers.

pen-based computer computer (usually portable), for which input is by means of a pen or stylus, rather than a keyboard.

Penda *c.* 577–654. King of Mercia, an Anglo-Saxon kingdom in England, from about 632.

He raised Mercia to a powerful kingdom, and defeated and killed two Northumbrian kings, Edwin 632 and Oswald 642. He was killed in battle by Oswy, king of Northumbria.

Penelope in Greek mythology, the wife of Odysseus, the king of Ithaca; their son was Telemachus. While Odysseus was absent at the siege of Troy she kept her many suitors at bay by asking them to wait until she had woven a shroud for her father-in-law, but unraveled her work each night. When Odysseus returned, after 20 years, he and Telemachus killed her suitors.

penguin any of an order (Sphenisciformes) of marine flightless birds, mostly black and white, found in the southern hemisphere. They range in size from 1.6 ft/40 cm to 4 ft/1.2 m tall, and have thick feathers to protect them from the intense cold. They are awkward on land, but their wings have evolved into flippers, making them excellent swimmers. Penguins congregate to breed in "rookeries", and often spend many months incubating their eggs while their mates are out at sea feeding.

penicillin any of a group of ◊antibiotic (bacteria killing) compounds obtained from filtrates of molds of the genus *Penicillium* (especially *P. notatum*) or produced synthetically. Penicillin was the first antibiotic to be discovered (by Alexander ◊Fleming); it kills a broad spectrum of bacteria, many of which cause disease in humans.

Peninsular War war 1808–14 caused by the French emperor Napoleon's invasion of Portugal and Spain. British expeditionary forces under Sir Arthur Wellesley (Duke of ◊Wellington), combined with Spanish and Portuguese resistance, succeeded in defeating the French at Vimeiro 1808, Talavera 1809, Salamanca 1812, and Vittoria 1813. The results were inconclusive, and the war was ended by Napoleon's abdication.

penis male reproductive organ containing the urethra, the channel through which urine and ◊semen are voided. It transfers sperm to the female reproductive tract to fertilize the ovum. In mammals, the penis is made erect by vessels that fill with blood, and in most mammals (but not humans) is stiffened by a bone.

Penn William 1644–1718. English Quaker and founder of Pennsylvania, born in London. He joined the Quakers 1667 and was imprisoned several times for his beliefs. In 1681 he obtained a grant of land in America, in settlement of a debt owed by Charles II to his father, on which he established the colony of Pennsylvania as a refuge for the persecuted Quakers. Penn made religious tolerance a cornerstone of his administration of the colony. He maintained good relations with neighboring colonies and with the Indians in the area, but his utopian ideals were not successful for the most part.

Pennines mountain system, "the backbone of England," broken by a gap through which the river Aire flows to the E and the Ribble to the W; length (Scottish border to the Peaks in Derbyshire) 250 mi/400 km. It is the watershed for the main rivers of NE England. The rocks are carboniferous limestone and millstone grit, the land high moorland and fell.

Pennsylvania state in NE US; nickname Keystone State *area* 45,316 sq mi/117,400 sq km *capital* Harrisburg *towns and cities* Philadelphia, Pittsburgh, Erie, Allentown, Scranton *features* Allegheny Mountains; rivers: Ohio, Susquehanna, Delaware; Independence National Historic Park, Philadelphia; Valley Forge National Historic Park; Gettysburg Civil War battlefield; Pennsylvania Dutch country; Poconos resort region *industries* hay, cereals, mushrooms, cattle, poultry, dairy products, cement, coal, steel, petroleum products, pharmaceuticals, motor vehicles and equipment, electronic components, textiles *population* (1990) 11,881,600 *famous people* Marian Anderson, Andrew Carnegie, Stephen Foster, Benjamin Franklin, Robert Fulton, Martha Graham, George C Marshall, Robert E Peary, Benjamin Rush, Gertrude Stein, John Updike *history* disputed by Sweden, the Netherlands, and England early 17th century; granted to Quaker William ◊Penn 1682 by English King Charles II, after the 1664 capture of New Netherlands. The Declaration of Independence was proclaimed in Philadelphia, and many important Revolutionary War battles were fought here 1777–78. One of the original 13 states, Pennsylvania was a leader in both agriculture and industry. The Battle of Gettysburg 1863 was a turning point in the Civil War for the Union cause. Until 1920, Pennsylvania was dominant in oil, coal, iron, steel, and textile production, but it already was losing its industrial lead when the Great Depression struck; the state now looks to agriculture, service-related industries, trade, and tourism for economic growth.

There was a breakdown at the Three Mile Island nuclear reactor plant in Harrisburg 1979.

pennyroyal European perennial plant *Mentha pulegium* of the mint family, with oblong leaves and whorls of purplish flowers. It is found growing in wet places on sandy soil.

A similar North American mint *Hedeoma pulegioides* that yields an aromatic oil is also called pennyroyal.

Pensacola port in NW Florida, on the Gulf of Mexico, with a large naval air-training station; population (1990) 58,200. Industries include chemicals, synthetic fibers, and paper.

The University of West Florida is here. Pensacola was founded by the Spanish 1696, passed to the British 1763, and returned to the Spanish again in the early 1780s. It was seized by US forces in 1814 and 1818 and was formally ceded with the rest of Florida in 1821. Union forces gained control of the city in 1862, during the Civil War.

pension a payment, not wages, made to a person (or his/her family) after fulfillment of certain conditions of service; an organized retirement plan. Pension plans vary widely, with some pensions calculated at a specified percentage of a worker's income, payable annually after retirement. Others provide lump-sum savings available for withdrawal at age 65. Employers sometimes match employee contributions; some plans are strictly employee contributions plus interest. Some plans are mandatory, others voluntary.

Pentagon the headquarters of the US Department of Defense, Arlington, Virginia. One of the world's largest office buildings (five-sided with a pentagonal central court), it houses the administrative and command headquarters for the US armed forces and has become synonymous with the military establishment bureaucracy.

Pentagon Papers Case US Supreme Court decision (*New York Times* v *US*; *US* v *Washington Post*) 1971 dealing with the right of the federal government to enjoin the publication of sensitive or classified material. The federal government filed the suit against the *Times* and the *Post* to discontinue publication of portions of "The Pentagon Papers," a set of classified documents about US involvement in Vietnam. The government argued that the threat to national security warranted the infringement on First Amendment rights. The Court ruled 6 to 3 to dismiss the government's suit, judging any suppression of the press, without proof of actual damage to national security, to be a violation of the First Amendment.

Pentecost in Judaism, the festival of *Shavuot*, celebrated on the 50th day after ◊Passover in commemoration of the giving of the Ten Commandments to Moses on Mount Sinai, and the end of the grain harvest; in the Christian church, Pentecost is the day on which the apostles experienced inspiration of the Holy Spirit, commemorated on Whit Sunday.

Pentecostal movement Christian revivalist movement originating in the US 1906. Spiritual renewal is sought through baptism by the Holy Spirit, as experienced by the apostles on the first Pentecost. It represented a reaction against the rigid theology and formal worship of the traditional churches. Glossolalia, or speaking in tongues, often occurs. Pentecostalists believe in the literal word of the Bible and faith healing. They disapprove of alcohol, tobacco, dancing, the theater, gambling, and so on. It is an intensely missionary faith, and recruitment in person and on television has been very rapid since the 1960s: worldwide membership is more than 20 million, and it is the world's fastest growing sector of Christianity.

peony any perennial plant of the genus *Paeonia*, family Paeoniaceae, remarkable for their brilliant flowers. Most popular are the common peony *P. officinalis*, the white peony *P. lactiflora*, and the taller tree peony *P. suffruticosa*.

Pepin the Short c. 714–c. 768. King of the Franks from 751. The son of Charles Martel, he acted as Mayor of the Palace to the last Merovingian king, Childeric III, deposed him and assumed the royal title himself, founding the Carolingian dynasty. He was ◊Charlemagne's father.

pepper climbing plant *Piper nigrum* native to the E Indies, of the Old World pepper family Piperaceae. When gathered green, the berries are crushed to release the seeds for the spice called black pepper. When the berries are ripe, the seeds are removed and their outer skin is discarded, to produce white pepper. Chili pepper, cayenne or red pepper, and the sweet peppers used as a vegetable come from ◊capsicums native to the New World.

peppermint perennial herb *Mentha piperita* of the mint family, native to Europe, with ovate, aromatic leaves and purple flowers. Oil of peppermint is used in medicine and confectionery.

peptide molecule comprising two or more ◊amino acid molecules (not necessarily different) joined by *peptide bonds*, whereby the acid group of one acid is linked to the amino group of the other (–CO.NH). The number of amino acid molecules in the peptide is indicated by referring to it as a di-, tri-, or polypeptide (two, three, or many amino acids).

Pepys Samuel 1633–1703. English diarist. His diary 1659–69 was a unique record of both the daily life of the period and his own intimate feelings. Written in shorthand, it was not deciphered until 1825. Pepys was imprisoned 1679 in the Tower of London on suspicion of being connected with the Popish Plot (see Titus ◊Oates).

percentage way of representing a number as a ◊fraction of 100. Thus 45 percent (45%) equals 45/100, and 45% of 20 is 45/100 x 20 = 9.

perch any of the largest order of spiny-finned bony fishes, the Perciformes, with some 8,000 species. This order includes the sea basses, cichlids, damselfishes, mullets, barracudas, wrasses, and gobies. Perches of the freshwater genus *Perca* are found in Europe, Asia, and North America. They have varied shapes and are usually a greenish color. They are very prolific, spawning when about three years old, and have voracious appetites.

The American yellow perch *P. flavescens*, to 12 in/30 cm, is abundant in lakes and streams, feeding on insects and other fishes.

percussion instrument musical instrument played by being struck with the hand or a beater. Percussion instruments can be divided into those that can be tuned to produce a sound of definite pitch, such as the timpani, tubular bells, glockenspiel, and xylophone, and those of indefinite pitch, including bass drum, tambourine, triangle, cymbals, and castanets.

Perelman S(idney) J(oseph) 1904–1979. US humorist. His work was often published in the *New Yorker* magazine, and he wrote film scripts for the Marx Brothers.

He shared an Academy Award for the script of *Around the World in 80 Days* 1956.

He was born in New York.

perennating organ in plants, that part of a biennial plant or herbaceous perennial that allows it to survive the winter; usually a root, tuber, rhizome, bulb, or corm.

perennial plant plant that lives for more than two years. Herbaceous perennials have aerial stems and leaves that die each autumn. They survive the winter by means of an underground storage (perennating) organ, such as a bulb or rhizome. Trees and shrubs or woody perennials have stems that persist above ground throughout the year, and may be either

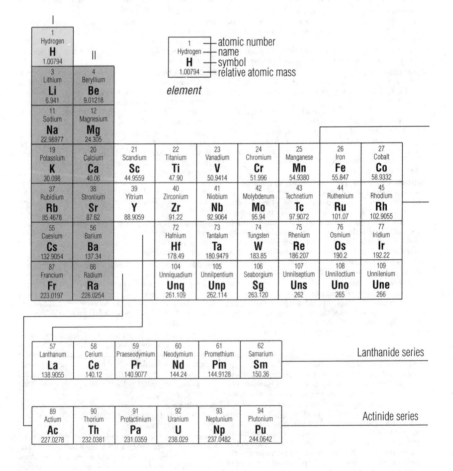

periodic table of the elements The periodic table of the elements arranges the elements into horizontal rows (called periods) and vertical columns (called groups) according to their atomic numbers. The elements in a group or column all

◊deciduous or ◊evergreen. See also ◊annual plant, ◊biennial plant.

Peres Shimon 1923– . Israeli socialist politician, prime minister 1984–86. As foreign minister in Yitzhak Rabin's Labour government from 1992, he negotiated the 1993 peace agreement with the Palestine Liberation Organization (PLO). He was awarded the 1994 Nobel Prize for Peace jointly with Israeli president, Rabin, and PLO leader, Yassir Arafat.

perestroika in Soviet politics, the wide-ranging economic and political reforms initiated from 1985 by Mikhail Gorbachev, finally leading to the demise of the Soviet Union. Originally, in the economic sphere, perestroika was conceived as involving "intensive development" concentrating on automation and improved labor efficiency. It evolved to attend increasingly to market indicators and incentives ("market socialism") and the gradual dismantling of the Stalinist central-planning system, with decision-taking being devolved to self-financing enterprises.

Pérez de Cuéllar Javier 1920– . Peruvian diplomat, secretary-general of the United Nations 1982–91. He raised the standing of the UN by his successful diplomacy in ending the Iran–Iraq War 1988 and securing the independence of Namibia 1989. In 1994 it was thought that he might seek the Peruvian presidency.

Pergamum ancient Greek city in W Asia Minor, which became the capital of an independent kingdom

have similar properties—for example, all the elements in the far right-hand column are inert gases. Nonmetals are shown in mid gray, metals in dark gray, and the metalloid (metal-like) elements in light gray. The elements in white are called transition elements.

283 BC under the Attalid dynasty. As the ally of Rome it achieved great political importance in the 2nd century BC, and became a center of art and culture. Close to its site is the modern Turkish town of Bergama.

pericarp wall of a ◊fruit. It encloses the seeds and is derived from the ovary wall.

Pericles *c.* 495–429 BC. Athenian politician who was effective leader of the city from 443 BC and under whom Athenian power reached its height. His policies helped to transform the Delian League into an Athenian empire, but the disasters of the ◊Peloponnesian War led to his removal from office 430 BC. Although quickly reinstated, he died soon after.

period punctuation mark (.). The term "period" is universally understood in English and is the preferred usage in North America; "full stop" is the preferred term in the UK. The period has two functions: to mark the end of a sentence and to indicate that a word has been abbreviated. It is also used in mathematics to indicate decimals and is then called a point.

periodic table of the elements classification of the elements to reflect the periodic law, namely that the properties of the chemical elements recur periodically when the elements are arranged in increasing order of their ◊atomic number and are shown in related groups.

Today's arrangement is by atomic numbers as devised by Moseley in 1913–14.

periodontal disease (formerly known as *pyorrhea*) disease of the gums and bone supporting the teeth, caused by the accumulation of plaque and microorganisms; the gums recede, and the teeth eventually become loose and may drop out unless treatment is sought. Bacteria can eventually erode the bone that supports the teeth, so that surgery becomes necessary.

peripheral device in computing, any item of equipment attached to and controlled by a computer. Peripherals are typically for input from and output to the user (for example, a keyboard or printer), storing data (for example, a disk drive), communications (such as a modem), or for performing physical tasks (such as a robot).

peritoneum transparent tissue lining the abdominal cavity and curving around all the visceral organs of vertebrates.

periwinkle in botany, any of several trailing blue-flowered evergreen plants of the genus *Vinca* of the dogbane family Apocynaceae. They range in length from 8 in/20 cm to 3 ft/1 m.

periwinkle in zoology, any marine snail of the family Littorinidae, found on the shores of Europe and E North America. Periwinkles have a conical spiral shell, and feed on algae.

Perkins Frances 1882–1965. US public official born in Boston. She became the first female cabinet officer when she served as secretary of labor under Franklin D. Roosevelt 1933–45. Under Truman she was a member of the federal civil service commission 1946–53.

Perm industrial city (shipbuilding, oil refining, aircraft, chemicals, lumber mills), and capital of Perm region, N Russia, on the Kama near the Ural Mountains; population (1987) 1,075,000. It was called Molotov 1940–57.

permafrost condition in which a deep layer of soil does not thaw out during the summer. Permafrost occurs under periglacial conditions. It is claimed that 26% of the world's land surface is permafrost.

Permian period of geological time 290–245 million years ago, the last period of the Paleozoic era. Its end was marked by a significant change in marine life, including the extinction of many corals and trilobites. Deserts were widespread, and terrestrial amphibians and mammal-like reptiles flourished. Cone-bearing plants (gymnosperms) came to prominence.

Perón (María Estela) Isabel (born Martínez) 1931– . President of Argentina 1974–76, and third wife of Juan Perón. She succeeded him after he died in office, but labor unrest, inflation, and political violence pushed the country to the brink of chaos. Accused of corruption, she was held under house arrest for five years. She went into exile in Spain.

Peron Juan Domingo 1895–1974. President of Argentina 1946–55 and 1973–74. A professional army officer, Perón took part in the right-wing military coup that toppled Argentina's government in 1943.

Perón María Eva (Evita) Duarte de 1919–1952. Argentinian populist leader, born in Buenos Aires. A successful film actress, she married Juan ◊Perón in 1945. When he became president the following year, she became his chief adviser and the unofficial minister of health and labor, devoting herself to helping the poor, improving education, and achieving women's suffrage. She was politically astute and sought the vice presidency in 1951 but was opposed by the army and withdrew. After her death from cancer in 1952, Juan's political strength began to decline.

perpendicular in mathematics, at a right angle; also, a line at right angles to another or to a plane. For a pair of skew lines (lines in three dimensions that do not meet), there is just one common perpendicular, which is at right angles to both lines; the nearest points on the two lines are the feet of this perpendicular.

perpetual motion the idea that a machine can be designed and constructed in such a way that, once started, it will continue in motion indefinitely without requiring any further input of energy (motive power). Such a device contradicts the two laws of thermodynamics that state that (1) energy can neither be created nor destroyed (the law of conservation of energy) and (2) heat cannot by itself flow from a cooler to a hotter object. As a result, all practical (real) machines require a continuous supply of energy, and no heat engine is able to convert all the heat into useful work.

Perry Matthew (Calbraith) 1794–1858. US naval officer, commander of the expedition of 1853 that reopened communication between Japan and the outside world after 250 years' isolation. Evident military superiority enabled him to negotiate the Treaty of Kanagawa 1854, giving the US trading rights with Japan.

In the 1830s and 1840s he developed an engineering corps for the US navy. He was the younger brother of Oliver Hazard ◊Perry.

Perry Oliver Hazard 1785–1819. US naval officer. During the Anglo-American War 1812–14 he played a decisive role in securing American control of Lake Erie. Ordered there in 1813, he was responsible for the decisive victory over the British at the Battle of Put-in-Bay and participated in the Battle of the Thames.

Persephone in Greek mythology, a goddess (Roman Proserpina), the daughter of Zeus and Demeter, and queen of the underworld. She was carried off to the underworld as the bride of Pluto, who later agreed that she should spend six months of the year above ground with her mother. The myth symbolizes the growth and decay of vegetation and the changing seasons.

Pershing John Joseph 1860–1948. US general, who commanded the American Expeditionary Force sent to France 1917–18 during World War I. He was responsible for more than 2 million men and fought successfully to keep them a separate unit.

Persia, ancient kingdom in SW Asia. The early Persians were a nomadic Aryan people who migrated through the Caucasus to the Iranian plateau.

7th century BC The Persians were established in the present region of Fars, which then belonged to the Assyrians. *550* BC Cyrus the Great overthrew the empire of the Medes, to whom the Persians had been subject, and founded the Persian Empire. *539* BC Having conquered all Anatolia, Cyrus added Babylonia (including Syria and Palestine) to his empire. *525* BC His son and successor Cambyses conquered Egypt. *521–485* BC Darius I organized an efficient centralized system of administration and extended Persian rule east into Afghanistan and NW India and as far north as the Danube, but the empire was weakened by internal dynastic struggles. *499–449* BC The Persian Wars with Greece ended Persian domination of the Aegean seaboard. *331* BC Alexander the Great drove the Persians under Darius III (died 330 BC) into retreat at Gaugamela on the Tigris, marking the end of the Persian Empire and the beginning of the Hellenistic period under the Seleucids. *250* BC –AD *230* The Arsacid dynasty established Parthia as the leading power in the region. *224* The Sassanian Empire was established in Persia and annexed Parthia. *637* Arabs took the capital, Ctesiphon, and introduced Islam in place of Zoroastrianism. For modern history see ◊Iran.

Persian Gulf or *Arabian Gulf* large shallow inlet of the Arabian Sea; area 90,000 sq mi/233,000 sq km. It divides the Arabian peninsula from Iran and is linked by the Strait of Hormuz and the Gulf of Oman to the Arabian Sea. Oil fields surround it in the Gulf States of Bahrain, Iran, Iraq, Kuwait, Oman, Qatar, Saudi Arabia, and the United Arab Emirates.

Persian language member of the Indo-Iranian branch of the Indo-European language family and the official language of the state once known as Persia but now called Iran. Persian is known to its own speakers as *Farsi*, the language of the province of Fars (Persia proper). It is written in a modified Arabic script, from right to left.

Persian Wars series of conflicts between Greece and Persia 499–449 BC. The eventual victory of Greece marked the end of Persian domination of the ancient world and the beginning of Greek supremacy.

persimmon any tree of the genus *Diospyros* of the ebony family Ebenaceae, especially the common persimmon *D. virginiana* of the SE US. Up to 60 ft/19 m high, the persimmon has alternate oval leaves and yellow-green unisexual flowers. The small, sweet, orange fruits are edible.

personal computer (PC) another name for ◊microcomputer. The term is also used, more specifically, to mean the IBM Personal Computer and computers compatible with it.

personal digital assistant (PDA) handheld computer designed to store names, addresses, and diary information. They aim to provide a more flexible and powerful alternative to the filofax or diary, but have met limited success.

personification figure of speech (poetic or imaginative expression) in which animals, plants, objects, and ideas are treated as if they were human or alive ("Clouds chased each other across the face of the Moon"; "Nature smiled on their work and gave it her blessing"; "The future beckoned eagerly to them").

Perth capital of Western Australia, with its port at nearby Fremantle on the Swan River; population (1990) 1,190,100. Products include textiles, cement, furniture, and vehicles. It was founded 1829 and is the commercial and cultural center of the state.

Peru Republic of (*República del Perú*) *area* 496,216 sq mi/1,285,200 sq km *capital* Lima, including port of Callao *towns and cities* Arequipa, Iquitos, Chiclayo, Trujillo *physical* Andes mountains NW–SE cover 27% of Peru, separating Amazon river-basin jungle in NE from coastal plain in W; desert along coast N–S *environment* an estimated 38% of the 3,100 sq mi/8,000 sq km of coastal lands under irrigation are either waterlogged or suffering from saline water. Only half the population has access to clean drinking water *features* Lake Titicaca; Atacama Desert; Nazca lines, monuments of Machu Picchu, Chan Chan, Charín de Huantar *head of state* Alberto Fujimori from 1990 *head of government* Efrain Goldenberg Schreiber from 1994 *political system* democratic republic *political parties* American Popular Revolutionary Alliance (APRA), moderate, left-wing; United Left (IU), left-wing; Change 90, centrist *exports* coca, coffee, alpaca, llama and vicuña wool, fish meal, lead (largest producer in South America), copper, iron, oil *currency* new sol *population* (1993) 22,130,000 (Indian, mainly Quechua and Aymara, 46%; mixed Spanish–Indian descent 43%); growth rate 2.6% p.a. *life expectancy* men 63, women 67 *languages* Spanish 68%, Quechua 27% (both official), Aymara 3% *religion* Roman Catholic 90% *literacy* men 92%, women 79% *GNP* $1,020 per head (1991) *chronology 1824* Independence achieved from Spain. *1849–74* Some 80,000–100,000 Chinese laborers arrived in Peru to fill menial jobs such as collecting guano. *1902* Boundary dispute with Bolivia settled. *1927* Boundary dispute with Colombia settled. *1942* Boundary dispute with Ecuador settled. *1948* Army

coup, led by General Manuel Odría, installed a military government. *1963* Return to civilian rule, with Fernando Belaúnde Terry as president. *1968* Return of military government in a bloodless coup by General Juan Velasco Alvarado. *1975* Velasco replaced, in a bloodless coup, by General Morales Bermúdez. *1979* New constitution approved. *1980* Return to civilian rule, with Fernando Belaúnde as president. Sendero Luminoso ("Shining Path") Maoist guerrilla group formed. *1981* Boundary dispute with Ecuador renewed. *1985* Belaúnde succeeded by Social Democrat Alan García Pérez. *1987* President García delayed the nationalization of Peru's banks after a vigorous campaign against the proposal. *1988* García pressured to seek help from the International Monetary Fund (IMF). Sendero Luminoso increased campaign of violence. *1989* Writer Mario Vargas Llosa entered presidential race; his Democratic Front won municipal elections. *1990* Alberto Fujimori defeated Vargas Llosa in presidential elections. Assassination attempt on president failed. *1992* April: Fujimori allied himself with army and suspended constitution, provoking international criticism. Sept–Oct: Sendero Luminoso leader Abimael Guzman Reynoso arrested and sentenced to life imprisonment after a show trial. Nov: new single-chamber legislature elected, replacing two-chamber system. *1993* Jan: constitution restored. Dec: new constitution adopted, enabling Fujimori to seek re-election.

pesticide any chemical used in farming, gardening, or indoors to combat pests. Pesticides are of three main types: *insecticides* (to kill insects), *fungicides* (to kill fungal diseases), and *herbicides* (to kill plants, mainly those considered weeds). Pesticides cause a number of pollution problems through spray drift onto surrounding areas, direct contamination of users or the public, and as residues on food.

The safest pesticides include those made from plants, such as the insecticides pyrethrum and derris.

Pétain Henri Philippe 1856–1951. French general and right-wing politician. His defense of Verdun 1916 during World War I made him a national hero. In World War II he became head of state June 1940 and signed an armistice with Germany. Removing the seat of government to Vichy, a health resort in central France, he established an authoritarian regime which collaborated with the Germans. He was imprisoned after the war.

With the Allied invasion he was taken to Germany, but returned 1945 and was sentenced to death for treason, the sentence being commuted to life imprisonment.

Peter (I) the Great 1672–1725. Czar of Russia from 1682 on the death of his brother Czar Feodor; he assumed control of the government 1689. He attempted to reorganize the country on Western lines; the army was modernized, a fleet was built, the administrative and legal systems were remodeled, education was encouraged, and the church was brought under state control. On the Baltic coast, where he had conquered territory from Sweden, Peter built his new capital, St Petersburg.

Peterborough city in Cambridgeshire, England, on the river Nene, noted for its 12th-century cathedral; population (1991) 153,200, one of the fastest growing cities in Europe. It has an advanced electronics industry. Nearby Flag Fen disclosed 1985 a well-preserved Bronze Age settlement of 660 BC.

Peterborough was designated a new town (planned to absorb overspill population) 1967.

Peter, St Christian martyr, the author of two epistles in the New Testament and leader of the apostles. He is regarded as the first bishop of Rome, whose mantle the pope inherits. His real name was Simon, but he was nicknamed Kephas ("Peter", from the Greek for "rock") by Jesus, as being the rock upon which he would build his church. His emblem is two keys; feast day June 29.

Petersburg city in SE Virginia, US, on the Appomattox River, S of Richmond; population (1990) 38,400. Industries include tobacco products, textiles, leather products, boat building, and chemicals. It was the site of Fort Henry 1646, as well as of American Revolution and Civil War battles.

Petipa Marius 1818–1910. French choreographer. He created some of the most important ballets in the classical repertory. For the Imperial Ballet in Russia he created masterpieces such as *Don Quixote* 1869, *La Bayadère* 1877, *The Sleeping Beauty* 1890, *Swan Lake* 1895 (with Ivanov), and *Raymonda* 1898.

Petra (Arabic *Wadi Musa*) ancient city carved out of the red rock at a site in Jordan, on the eastern slopes of the Wadi el Araba, 56 mi/90 km S of the Dead Sea. An Edomite stronghold and capital of the Nabataeans in the 2nd century, it was captured by the Roman emperor Trajan 106 and destroyed by the Arabs in the 7th century. It was forgotten in Europe until 1812 when the Swiss traveler Johann Ludwig Burckhardt (1784–1817) came across it.

Petrarch (Italian *Petrarca*) Francesco 1304–1374. Italian poet. He was a devotee of the Classical tradition. His *Il Canzoniere* is composed of sonnets in praise of his idealized love, "Laura", whom he first saw 1327 (she was a married woman and refused to become his mistress). The dialogue *Secretum meum/My Secret* is a spiritual biography.

petrel any of various families of seabirds, including the worldwide *storm petrels* (family Procellariidae), which include the smallest seabirds (some only 5 in/13 cm long), and the *diving petrels* (family Pelecanoididae) of the southern hemisphere, which feed by diving underwater and are characterized by having nostril tubes. They include ◊fulmars and ◊shearwaters.

petroleum or *crude oil* natural mineral oil, a thick greenish-brown flammable liquid found underground in permeable rocks. Petroleum consists of hydrocarbons mixed with oxygen, sulfur, nitrogen, and other elements in varying proportions. It is thought to be derived from ancient organic material that has been converted by, first, bacterial action, then heat and pressure (but its origin may be chemical also). From crude petroleum, various products are made by distillation and other processes; for example, fuel oil, gasoline, kerosene, diesel, lubricating oil, paraffin wax, and petroleum jelly.

Peugeot France's second-largest automobile manufacturer, founded 1885 when Armand Peugeot (1849–1915) began making bicycles; the company bought the rival firm Citroën 1974 and the European operations of the American Chrysler Company 1978.

pewter any of various alloys of mostly tin with varying amounts of lead, copper, or antimony. Pewter has been known for centuries and was once widely used for domestic utensils but is now used mainly for ornamental ware.

peyote spineless cactus *Lophopora williamsii* of N Mexico and the SW US. It has white or pink flowers.

Its buttonlike tops contain the hallucinogen *mescaline*, which is used by American Indians in religious ceremonies.

pH scale from 0 to 14 for measuring acidity or alkalinity. A pH of 7.0 indicates neutrality, below 7 is acid, while above 7 is alkaline. Strong acids, such as those used in automobile batteries, have a pH of about 2; strong alkalis such as sodium hydroxide are pH 13.

The pH value of a solution equals the negative logarithm of the concentration of hydrogen ions.

phagocyte type of ◊white blood cell, or leukocyte, that can engulf a bacterium or other invading microorganism. Phagocytes are found in blood, lymph, and other body tissues, where they also ingest foreign matter and dead tissue. A macrophage differs in size and life span.

Phalangist member of a Lebanese military organization (*Phalanges Libanaises*), since 1958 the political and military force of the Maronite Church in Lebanon.

phalarope any of a genus *Phalaropus* of small, elegant shorebirds in the sandpiper family (Scolopacidae). They have the habit of spinning in the water to stir up insect larvae. They are native to North America, the UK, and the polar regions of Europe.

The red-necked phalarope *P. lobatus*, gray *P. fulicarius*, and Wilson's phalarope *P. tricolor* can be found in North America.

Phanerozoic eon in Earth history, consisting of the most recent 570 million years. It comprises the Paleozoic, Mesozoic, and Cenozoic eras. The vast majority of fossils come from this eon, owing to the evolution of hard shells and internal skeletons. The name means "interval of well-displayed life".

Pharaoh Hebrew form of the Egyptian royal title Per-'o. This term, meaning "great house", was originally applied to the royal household, and after about 950 BC to the king.

Pharisee member of an ancient Hebrew political party and sect of Judaism that formed in Roman-occupied Palestine in the 2nd century BC in protest against all movements favoring Hellenization. The Pharisees were the party of the common man, standing for rabbi, prayer, and synagogue. They were opposed by the aristocratic Sadducees.

pharmacology study of the properties of drugs and their effects on the human body.

phase see ◊Moon.

pheasant any of various large, colorful Asiatic fowls of the family Phasianidae, which also includes grouse, quail, and turkey. The plumage of the male Eurasian ring-necked or common pheasant *Phasianus colchicus* is richly tinted with brownish-green, yellow, and red markings, but the female is a camouflaged brownish color. The nest is made on the ground. The male is polygamous.

phenol member of a group of aromatic chemical compounds with weakly acidic properties, which are characterized by a hydroxyl (OH) group attached directly to an aromatic ring. The simplest of the phenols, derived from benzene, is also known as phenol and has the formula C_6H_5OH. It is sometimes called *carbolic acid* and can be extracted from coal tar.

phenotype in genetics, visible traits, those actually displayed by an organism. The phenotype is not a direct reflection of the ◊genotype because some alleles are masked by the presence of other, dominant alleles.

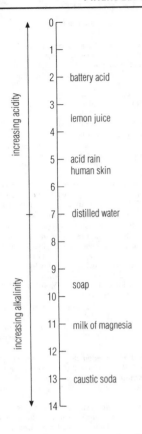

pH

The phenotype is further modified by the effects of the environment (for example, poor nutrition stunts growth).

pheromone chemical signal (such as an odor) that is emitted by one animal and affects the behavior of others. Pheromones are used by many animal species to attract mates.

Phidias or *Pheidias* Greek sculptor. He was active in Athens. He supervised the sculptural program for the Parthenon (most of it is preserved in the British Museum, London, and known as the Elgin marbles). He also executed the colossal statue of Zeus at Olympia, one of the ◊Seven Wonders of the World.

Philadelphia industrial city and the world's largest freshwater port, on the Delaware River at the junction of the Schuylkill River, in Pennsylvania; population (1990) 1,585,600, metropolitan area 5,899,300. Products include refined oil, chemicals, textiles, processed food, printing and publishing, and transportation equipment. It is also a major port of entry and a financial, corporate, and research center. The University of Pennsylvania, the Franklin Institute, and Temple University are here, and the Philadelphia Orchestra and Museum of Art are among the nation's finest. Independence National Historic Park contains Independence Hall (1732–59), where the Declaration of Independence was adopted 1776, and the Liberty Bell.

Philip "King". Name given to Metacomet by the English *c.* 1639–1676. American chief of the Wampanoag people. During the growing tension over Indian versus settlers' land rights, Philip was arrested and his people were disarmed 1671. Full-scale hostilities culminated in "King Philip's War" 1675, and Philip was defeated and murdered 1676. Although costly to the English, King Philip's War ended Indian resistance in New England.

Philip Duke of Edinburgh 1921– . Prince of the UK, husband of Elizabeth II, a grandson of George I of Greece and a great-great-grandson of Queen Victoria. He was born in Corfu, Greece, but brought up in England.

A naturalized British subject, taking the surname Mountbatten, he married Princess Elizabeth (from 1952 Queen Elizabeth II) in 1947, having the previous day received the title Duke of Edinburgh.

Philip II (Philip Augustus) 1165–1223. King of France from 1180. As part of his efforts to establish a strong monarchy and evict the English from their French possessions, he waged war in turn against the English kings Henry II, Richard I (with whom he also went on the Third Crusade), and John (whom he defeated, along with Emperor Otto IV, at the decisive battle of Bouvines in Flanders 1214).

Philip VI 1293–1350. King of France from 1328, first of the house of Valois, elected by the barons on the death of his cousin, Charles IV. His claim was challenged by Edward III of England, who defeated him at Crécy 1346.

Philip II of Macedon 382–336 BC. King of ◊Macedonia from 359 BC. He seized the throne from his nephew, for whom he was regent, defeated the Greek city-states at the battle of Chaeronea (in central Greece) 338 and formed them into a league whose forces could be united against Persia. He was assassinated while he was planning this expedition, and was succeeded by his son ◊Alexander the Great.

Philip II 1527–1598. King of Spain from 1556. He was born at Valladolid, the son of the Hapsburg emperor Charles V, and in 1554 married Queen Mary of England. On his father's abdication 1556 he inherited Spain, the Netherlands, and the Spanish possessions in Italy and the Americas, and in 1580 he annexed Portugal. His intolerance and lack of understanding of the Netherlanders drove them into revolt. Political and religious differences combined to involve him in war with England and, after 1589, with France. The defeat of the ◊Spanish Armada (the fleet sent to invade England in 1588) marked the beginning of the decline of Spanish power.

Philippines Republic of the (*Republika ng Pilipinas*) *area* 115,800 sq mi/300,000 sq km *capital* Manila (on Luzon) *towns and cities* Quezon City (Luzon), Zamboanga (Mindanao); ports Cebu, Davao (on Mindanao), and Iloilo *physical* comprises over 7,000 islands; volcanic mountain ranges traverse main chain N–S; 50% still forested. The largest islands are Luzon 41,754 sq mi/108,172 sq km and Mindanao 36,372 sq mi/94,227 sq km; others include Samar, Negros, Palawan, Panay, Mindoro, Leyte, Cebu, and the Sulu group *environment* cleared for timber, tannin, and the creation of fish ponds, the mangrove forest was reduced from 1,930 sq mi/5,000 sq km to 146 sq mi/380 sq km between 1920 and 1988 *features* Luzon,

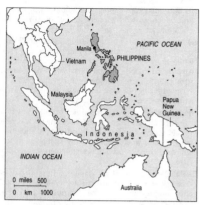

site of Clark Field, US air base used as a logistical base in Vietnam War; Subic Bay, former US naval base; Pinatubo volcano (5,770 ft/1,759 m); Mindanao has active volcano Apo (9,690 ft/2,954 m) and mountainous rainforest *head of state and government* Fidel Ramos from 1992 *political system* emergent democracy *political parties* People's Power, including the PDP–Laban Party and the Liberal Party, centrist pro-Aquino; Nationalist Party, Union for National Action (UNA), and Grand Alliance for Democracy (GAD), conservative opposition groupings; Mindanao Alliance, island-based decentralist body *exports* sugar, copra (world's largest producer) and coconut oil, timber, copper concentrates, electronics, clothing *currency* peso *population* (1993) 65,650,000 (93% Malaysian); growth rate 2.4% p.a. *life expectancy* men 63, women 67 *languages* Tagalog (Filipino, official); English and Spanish *religions* Roman Catholic 84%, Protestant 9%, Muslim 5% *literacy* men 90%, women 90% *GNP* $850 per head (1992) *chronology 1542* Named the Philippines (Filipinas) by Spanish explorers. *1565* Conquered by Spain. *1898* Ceded to the US after Spanish–American War. *1935* Granted internal self-government. *1942–45* Occupied by Japan. *1946* Independence achieved from US. *1965* Ferdinand Marcos elected president. *1983* Opposition leader Benigno Aquino murdered by military guard. *1986* Marcos overthrown by Corazon Aquino's People's Power movement. *1987* "Freedom constitution" adopted, giving Aquino mandate to rule until June 1992; People's Power won majority in congressional elections. Attempted right-wing coup suppressed. Communist guerrillas active. Government in rightward swing. *1988* Land Reform Act gave favorable compensation to holders of large estates. *1989* Referendum on southern autonomy failed; Marcos died in exile; Aquino refused his burial in Philippines. Sixth coup attempt suppressed with US aid; Aquino declared state of emergency. *1990* Seventh coup attempt survived by President Aquino. *1991* June: eruption of Mount Pinatubo, hundreds killed. Sept: Philippines Senate voted to urge withdrawal of all US forces. US renewal of Subic Bay lease rejected. Nov: Imelda Marcos returned. *1992* Fidel Ramos elected to replace Aquino. *1993* Police purged in government anticorruption move. Imelda Marcos sentenced to 18–24 years' imprisonment for corruption, later acquitted.

Philistine member of a seafaring people of non-Semitic origin who founded city-states on the Palestinian coastal plain in the 12th century BC, adopting a Semitic language and religion.

At war with the Israelites in the 11th–10th centuries BC, they were largely absorbed into the kingdom of Israel under King David, about 1000 BC, and later came under Assyrian rule.

philosophy branch of learning that includes metaphysics (the nature of being), epistemology (theory of knowledge), logic (study of valid inference), ethics, and esthetics. Philosophy is concerned with fundamental problems—including the nature of mind and matter, perception, self, free will, causation, time and space, and the existence of moral judgments—which cannot be resolved by a specific method.

phloem tissue found in vascular plants whose main function is to conduct sugars and other food materials from the leaves, where they are produced, to all other parts of the plant.

phlox any plant of the genus *Phlox*, native to North America and Siberia. Phloxes are small with alternate leaves and showy white, pink, red, or purple flowers.

Woodland phlox *P. divaricata* is native to central US.

Phnom Penh capital of Cambodia, on the Mekong River, 130 mi/210 km NW of Saigon; population (1989) 800,000. Industries include textiles and food-processing. It has been Cambodia's capital since the 15th century, and has royal palaces, museums, and pagodas.

On April 17 1975 the entire population (about 3 million) was forcibly evacuated by the Khmer Rouge communist movement; survivors later returned.

phobia excessive irrational fear of an object or situation—for example, agoraphobia (fear of open spaces and crowded places), acrophobia (fear of heights), and claustrophobia (fear of enclosed places). Behavior therapy is one form of treatment.

Phoenicia ancient Greek name for N ◊Canaan on the E coast of the Mediterranean. The Phoenician civilization flourished from about 1200 until the capture of Tyre by Alexander the Great in 332 BC. Seafaring traders and artisans, they are said to have circumnavigated Africa and established colonies in Cyprus, N Africa (for example, Carthage), Malta, Sicily, and Spain. Their cities (Tyre, Sidon, and Byblos were the main ones) were independent states ruled by hereditary kings but dominated by merchant ruling classes.

phoenix mythical Egyptian bird that burned itself to death on a pyre every 500 years and rose rejuvenated from the ashes.

Phoenix capital of Arizona; industrial city (steel, aluminum, electrical goods, food processing) and tourist center on the Salt River; population (1990) 983,400.

Settled 1868, Phoenix became the territorial capital 1889. The completion of a dam 1912 provided the water and power needed for economic development. Tremendous growth, beginning in the 1940s, has transformed Phoenix from what was largely a health resort and retirement community into a major economic center.

phonetics identification, description, and classification of sounds used in articulate speech. These sounds are codified in the International Phonetic Alphabet (a highly modified version of the English/Roman alphabet).

phonograph alternate name for ◊record player.

phosphate salt or ester of phosphoric acid. Incomplete neutralization of phosphoric acid gives rise to acid phosphates. Phosphates are used as fertilizers, and are required for the development of healthy root systems. They are involved in many biochemical processes, often as part of complex molecules, such as ◊ATP.

phosphor any substance that is phosphorescent, that is, gives out visible light when it is illuminated by a beam of electrons or ultraviolet light. The television screen is coated on the inside with phosphors that glow when beams of electrons strike them. Fluorescent lamp tubes are also phosphor-coated. Phosphors are also used in Day-Glo paints, and as optical brighteners in detergents.

phosphorescence in physics, the emission of light by certain substances after they have absorbed energy, whether from visible light, other electromagnetic radiation such as ultraviolet rays or X-rays, or cathode rays (a beam of electrons). When the stimulating energy is removed phosphorescence ceases, although it may persist for a short time after (unlike ◊fluorescence, which stops immediately).

phosphorus highly reactive, nonmetallic element, symbol P, atomic number 15, atomic weight 30.9738. It occurs in nature as phosphates (commonly in the form of the mineral apatite), and is essential to plant and animal life. Compounds of phosphorus are used in fertilizers, various organic chemicals, for matches and fireworks, and in glass and steel.

PhotoCD picture storage and viewing system developed by Kodak and Philips. The aim of Kodak's PhotoCD is to allow the user to put up to 100 photos onto compact disk: images are transferred from film to a PhotoCD disk and can then be viewed by means of Kodak's own PhotoCD player, which plugs into a television set, or by using suitable software on a multimedia PC.

photochemical reaction any chemical reaction in which light is produced or light initiates the reaction. Light can initiate reactions by exciting atoms or molecules and making them more reactive: the light energy becomes converted to chemical energy. Many photochemical reactions set up a ◊chain reaction and produce free radicals.

photocopier machine that uses some form of photographic process to reproduce copies of documents or illustrations. Most modern photocopiers, as pioneered by the Xerox Corporation, use electrostatic photocopying, or xerography ("dry writing").

photoelectric effect in physics, the emission of ◊electrons from a substance (usually a metallic surface) when it is struck by ◊photons (quanta of electromagnetic radiation), usually those of visible light or ultraviolet radiation.

photography process for reproducing images on sensitized materials by various forms of radiant energy, including visible light, ultraviolet, infrared, X-rays, atomic radiations, and electron beams.

photon in physics, the ◊elementary particle or "package" (quantum) of energy in which light and other forms of electromagnetic radiation are emitted. The photon has both particle and wave properties; it has no charge, is considered massless but possesses momentum and energy. It is one of the ◊gauge bosons, a particle that cannot be subdivided, and is the carrier of the ◊electromagnetic force, one of the fundamental forces of nature.

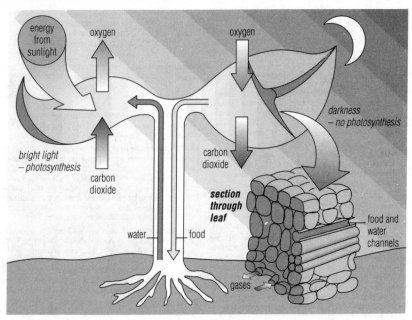

photosynthesis *Process by which green plants and some bacteria manufacture carbohydrates from water and atmospheric carbon dioxide, using the energy of sunlight. Photosynthesis depends on the ability of chlorophyll molecules within plant cells to trap the energy of light to split water molecules, giving off oxygen as a by-product. The hydrogen of the water molecules is then used to reduce carbon dioxide to simple carbohydrates.*

photosynthesis process by which green plants trap light energy and use it to drive a series of chemical reactions, leading to the formation of carbohydrates. All animals ultimately depend on photosynthesis because it is the method by which the basic food (sugar) is created. For photosynthesis to occur, the plant must possess ◊chlorophyll and must have a supply of carbon dioxide and water. Actively photosynthesizing green plants store excess sugar as starch (this can be tested for in the laboratory using iodine).

Phrygia former kingdom of W Asia covering the Anatolian plateau. It was inhabited in ancient times by an Indo-European people and achieved great prosperity in the 8th century BC under a line of kings bearing in turn the names Gordius and Midas, but then fell under Lydian rule. From Phrygia the cult of the Earth goddess Cybele was introduced into Greece and Rome.

Phyfe Duncan *c.* 1768–1854. Scottish-born US furnituremaker. Establishing his own workshop in New York City 1792, he gained a national reputation. Although derived from earlier English and Greco-Roman designs, the Phyfe style was distinctive in its simplicity of line with elaborate ornamentation and carving. In 1837 he reorganized his firm as Duncan Phyfe and Sons.

phylloxera any of a family (Phylloxeridae) of small, aphidlike, plant-sucking insects (order Homoptera) that attack the leaves and roots of some plants.

phylogeny historical sequence of changes that occurs in a given species during the course of its evolution. It

was once erroneously associated with ontogeny (the process of development of a living organism).

phylum (plural *phyla*) major grouping in biological classification. Mammals, birds, reptiles, amphibians, fishes, and tunicates belong to the phylum Chordata; the phylum Molluska consists of snails, slugs, mussels, clams, squid, and octopuses; the phylum Porifera contains sponges; and the phylum Echinodermata includes sea stars, sea urchins, and sea cucumbers. Among plants there are between four and nine phyla (or divisions) depending on the classification used. Related phyla are grouped together in a ◊kingdom; phyla are subdivided into ◊classes.

physical chemistry branch of chemistry concerned with examining the relationships between the chemical compositions of substances and the physical properties that they display. Most chemical reactions exhibit some physical phenomenon (change of state, temperature, pressure, or volume, or the use or production of electricity), and the measurement and study of such phenomena has led to many chemical theories and laws.

physics branch of science concerned with the laws that govern the structure of the universe, and the forms of matter and energy and their interactions. For convenience, physics is often divided into branches such as nuclear physics, particle physics, solid-and liquid-state physics, electricity, electronics, magnetism, optics, acoustics, heat, and thermodynamics. Before the 20th century, physics was known as *natural philosophy*.

physiology branch of biology that deals with the functioning of living organisms, as opposed to anatomy, which studies their structures.

physiotherapy treatment of injury and disease by physical means such as exercise, heat, manipulation, massage, and electrical stimulation.

pi symbol π, the ratio of the circumference of a circle to its diameter. The value of pi is 3.1415926, correct to seven decimal places. Common approximations to pi are 22/7 and 3.14, although the value 3 can be used as a rough estimation.

Piaget Jean 1896–1980. Swiss psychologist distinguished by his studies of child development in relation to thought processes, and concepts of space, time, causality, and objectivity.

Piaget believed this was a vital framework for studying human intelligence and he stressed the interaction of biological and environmental factors.

piano or **pianoforte** (originally **fortepiano**) stringed musical instrument played by felt-covered hammers activated from a keyboard. It is capable of dynamic gradation between soft (piano) and loud (forte) tones, hence its name. The first piano was constructed 1704 and introduced 1709 by Bartolommeo Cristofori, a harpsichord maker in Padua.

Picardy (French **Picardie**) region of N France, including Aisne, Oise, and Somme *départements* **area** 7,488 sq mi/19,400 sq km **population** (1986) 1,774,000 **industries** chemicals and metals **history** in the 13th century the name Picardy was used to describe the feudal smallholdings N of Paris added to the French crown by Philip II. During the Hundred Years' War the area was hotly contested by France and England, but it was eventually occupied by Louis XI 1477. Picardy once more became a major battlefield in World War I.

picaresque genre of novel that takes a rogue or villain for its central character, telling his or her story in episodic form. Daniel Defoe's *Moll Flanders*, Tobias Smollett's *Roderick Random*, Henry Fielding's *Tom Jones*, and Mark Twain's *Huckleberry Finn* are typical picaresque novels.

Picasso Pablo Ruiz y 1881–1973. Spanish artist. Active chiefly in France, he was one of the most inventive and prolific talents in 20th-century art. His Blue Period 1901–04 and Rose Period 1905–06 preceded the revolutionary *Les Demoiselles d'Avignon* 1907 (Museum of Modern Art, New York), which paved the way for Cubism. In the early 1920s he was considered a leader of the Surrealist movement. In the 1930s his work included metal sculpture, book illustration, and the mural *Guernica* 1937 (Prado, Madrid), a comment on the bombing of civilians in the Spanish Civil War. He continued to paint into his eighties.

Pickett George Edward 1825–1875. US military leader. At the outbreak of the Civil War 1861, he joined the Confederate army, rising to the rank of brigadier general 1862. Although he saw action in many battles, he is best remembered for leading the bloody, doomed "Pickett's Charge" at Gettysburg 1863.

Pickford Mary. Adopted name of Gladys Mary Smith. 1893–1979. Canadian-born US actress. The first star of the silent screen, she was known as "America's Sweetheart," and played innocent ingenue roles into her thirties. She and her second husband (from 1920), Douglas ◊Fairbanks, Sr, were known as "the world's sweethearts." With her husband and Charlie ◊Chaplin, she founded United Artists studio 1919. For many years she was the wealthiest and most influential woman in Hollywood.

Pict Roman term for a member of the peoples of N Scotland, possibly meaning "painted" (tattooed). Of pre-Celtic origin, and speaking a Celtic language which died out in about the 10th century, the Picts are thought to have inhabited much of England before the arrival of the Celtic Britons. They were united with the Celtic Scots under the rule of Kenneth MacAlpin 844.

pidgin language any of various trade jargons, contact languages, or ◊lingua francas arising in ports and markets where people of different linguistic backgrounds meet for commercial and other purposes.

Piedmont (Italian **Piemonte**) region of N Italy, bordering Switzerland to the N and France to the W, and surrounded, except to the E, by the Alps and the Apennines; area 9,804 sq mi/25,400 sq km; population (1990) 4,356,200. Its capital is Turin, and towns include Alessandria, Asti, Vercelli, and Novara. It also includes the fertile Po river valley. Products include fruit, grain, cattle, automobiles, and textiles.

Piero della Francesca c. 1420–1492. Italian painter. Active in Arezzo and Urbino, he was one of the major artists of the 15th century. His work has a solemn stillness and unusually solid figures, luminous color, and carefully calculated compositional harmonies. It includes a fresco series, *The Legend of the True Cross* (San Francesco, Arezzo), begun about 1452.

Pierre capital of South Dakota, located in the central part of the state, on the Missouri River, near the geographical center of North America; population (1990) 12,900. Industries include tourism and grain and dairy products. As Fort Pierre in the early 1800s, it served as a fur-trading post; in the late 1800s it was a supply center for gold miners.

Pietro da Cortona (Pietro Berrettini) 1596–1669. Italian painter and architect. He was a major influence in the development of the High Baroque. His enormous fresco *Allegory of Divine Providence* 1633–39 (Barberini Palace, Rome) glorifies his patron the pope and the Barberini family, and gives a convincing illusion of reality.

piezoelectric effect property of some crystals (for example, quartz) to develop an electromotive force or voltage across opposite faces when subjected to a mechanical strain, and, conversely, to expand or contract in size when subjected to an electromotive force. Piezoelectric crystal oscillators are used as frequency standards (for example, replacing balance wheels in watches), and for producing ◊ultrasound.

pig any even-toed hoofed mammal of the family Suidae. They are omnivorous, and have simple, nonruminating stomachs and thick hides. The Middle Eastern **wild boar** *Sus scrofa* is the ancestor of domesticated breeds; it is 4.5 ft/1.5 m long and 3 ft/1 m high, with formidable tusks, but not naturally aggressive.

pigeon any bird of the family Columbidae, sometimes also called doves, distinguished by their large crops, which, becoming glandular in the breeding season, secrete a milky fluid ("pigeon's milk") that aids digestion of food for the young. They are found worldwide.

pika or **mouse-hare** any small mammal of the family Ochotonidae, belonging to the order Lagomorpha (rabbits and hares). The single genus *Ochotona* contains about 15 species, most of which live in mountainous regions of Asia, although two species are native to North America.

pike any of a family Esocidae in the order Salmoniformes, of slender, freshwater bony fishes with narrow pointed heads and sharp, pointed teeth. The northern pike *Esox lucius*, of North America and Eurasia, may reach 7 ft/2.2 m and 20 lb/9 kg.

Pike Zebulon Montgomery 1779–1813. US explorer and military leader. In 1806 he was sent to explore the Arkansas River and to contest Spanish presence in the area. After crossing Colorado and failing to reach the summit of the peak later named for him, he was captured by the Spanish, who released him 1807. Promoted to brigadier general, he was killed in action in the War of Anglo-American War 1812–14.

Pilate Pontius Roman procurator of Judea AD 26–36. The New Testament Gospels describe his reluctant ordering of Jesus' crucifixion, but there has been considerable debate about his actual role in it.

pilchard any of various small, oily members of the herring family, Clupeidae, especially the commercial sardine of Europe *Sardina pilchardus*, and the California sardine *Sardinops sagax*.

pilgrimage journey to sacred places inspired by religious devotion. For Hindus, the holy places include Varanasi and the purifying river Ganges; for Buddhists, the places connected with the crises of Buddha's career; for the ancient Greeks, the shrines at Delphi and Ephesus among others; for Jews, the sanctuary at Jerusalem; and for Muslims, Mecca.

Pilgrims the emigrants who sailed from Plymouth, England, in the *Mayflower* on Sept 16, 1620, to found the first colony in New England at New Plymouth, Massachusetts. Of the 102 passengers, about a third were English Puritan refugees escaping religious persecution from Anglican England.

Pilgrim's Progress allegory by John ◊Bunyan, published 1678–84, that describes the journey through life to the Celestial City of a man called Christian. On his way through the Slough of Despond, the House Beautiful, Vanity Fair, Doubting Castle, and other landmarks, he meets a number of allegorical figures.

This work was often the only other book an American pioneer family owned and read, besides the Bible.

Pill, the commonly used term for the contraceptive pill, based on female hormones. The combined pill, which contains synthetic hormones similar to estrogen and progesterone, stops the production of eggs, and makes the mucus produced by the cervix hostile to sperm. It is the most effective form of contraception apart from sterilization, being more than 99% effective.

pillory former instrument of punishment consisting of a wooden frame set on a post, with holes in which the prisoner's head and hands were secured, similar to the stocks. Bystanders threw whatever was available at the miscreant.

Its use for punishing petty offenders ended in the US in Delaware 1905.

pimento or *allspice* tree found in tropical parts of the New World. The dried fruits of the species *Pimenta dioica* are used as a spice. Also, a sweet variety of ◊capsicum pepper (more correctly spelled *pimiento*).

pimpernel any plant of the genus *Anagallis* of the primrose family Primulaceae comprising about 30 species mostly native to W Europe. The European scarlet pimpernel *A. arvensis* grows in cornfields, the flowers opening only in full sunshine. It is naturalized in North America.

PIN (acronym for *personal identification number*) in banking, a unique number used as a password to establish the identity of a customer using an automatic cash dispenser. The PIN is normally encoded into the magnetic strip of the customer's bank card and is known only to the customer and to the bank's computer.

Pinatubo, Mount active volcano on Luzon Island, the Philippines, 55 mi/88 km N of Manila. Dormant for 600 years, it erupted June 1991, killing 343 people and leaving as many as 200,000 homeless. Surrounding rice fields were covered with 10 ft/3 m of volcanic ash.

Pindling Lynden (Oscar) 1930– . Bahamian politician, prime minister 1967–92. After studying law in London, he returned to the island to join the newly formed Progressive Liberal Party and then became the first black prime minister of the Bahamas.

pine any coniferous tree of the genus *Pinus*, family Pinaceae. There are 70–100 species, of which about 35 are native to North America. These are generally divided into two groupings: the soft pines and the hard pines. The oldest living species is probably the bristlecone pine *P. aristata*, native to California, of which some specimens are said to be 4,600 years old.

pineal body or *pineal gland* a cone-shaped outgrowth of the vertebrate brain. In some lower vertebrates, it develops a rudimentary lens and retina, which show it to be derived from an eye, or pair of eyes, situated on the top of the head in ancestral vertebrates. In fishes that can change color to match their background, the pineal perceives the light level and controls the color change. In birds, the pineal detects changes in daylight and stimulates breeding behavior as spring approaches. Mammals also have a pineal gland, but it is located deeper within the brain. In humans, it is a small piece of tissue attached by a stalk to the rear wall of the third ventricle of the brain.

pineapple plant *Ananas comosus* of the bromeliad family, native to South and Central America, but now cultivated in many other tropical areas, such as Hawaii and Queensland, Australia. The mauvish flowers are produced in the second year, and subsequently consolidate with their bracts into a fleshy fruit.

Pine Bluff city in SE Arkansas, on the Arkansas River, SE of Little Rock, seat of Jefferson County; population (1990) 57,100. Industries include paper, cotton, grain, and furniture.

Pinero Arthur Wing 1855–1934. English dramatist. A leading exponent of the "well-made" play, he enjoyed great contemporary success with his farces, beginning with *The Magistrate* 1885. More substantial social drama followed with *The Second Mrs Tanqueray* 1893, and comedies including *Trelawny of the "Wells"* 1898.

pink any annual or perennial plant of the genus *Dianthus* of the family Carophyllaceae. The stems have characteristically swollen nodes, and the flowers range in color from white through pink to purple. Members of the pink family include carnations, sweet williams, and baby's breath *Gypsophila paniculata*.

Pinochet (Ugarte) Augusto 1915– . Military ruler of Chile from 1973, when a coup backed by the US Central Intelligence Agency ousted and killed President Salvador Allende. Pinochet took over the presidency and governed ruthlessly, crushing all opposition. He was voted out of power when general elections were held Dec 1989 but remained head of the armed forces.

pint liquid or dry measure of volume or capacity. A liquid pint is equal to 16 fluid ounces or half a liquid quart (0.473 liter), while a dry pint is equal to half a dry quart (0.551 liter).

Pinter Harold 1930–　. English dramatist, originally an actor. He specializes in the tragicomedy of the breakdown of communication, broadly in the tradition of the Theatre of the Absurd—for example, *The Birthday Party* 1958 and *The Caretaker* 1960. Later plays include *The Homecoming* 1965, *Old Times* 1971, *Betrayal* 1978, and *Moonlight* 1993.

pinworm ◊nematode worm *Enterobius vermicularis*, an intestinal parasite of humans.

Pinyin Chinese phonetic alphabet approved 1956 by the People's Republic of China, and used since 1979 in transcribing all names of people and places from Chinese ideograms into other languages using the English/Roman alphabet. For example, the former transcription Chou En-lai becomes Zhou Enlai and Peking became Beijing.

pipit any of various sparrow-sized ground-dwelling songbirds of the genus *Anthus* of the family Motacillidae, which also includes wagtails.

The North American water pipit *A. spinoletta* lives near water in fields and on beaches. It is brown and tan with a slender bill.

piracy the taking of a ship, aircraft, or any of its contents, from lawful ownership, punishable under international law by the court of any country where the pirate may be found or taken. When the craft is taken over to alter its destination, or its passengers held to ransom, the term is ◊hijacking. Piracy is also used to describe infringement of ◊copyright.

Pirandello Luigi 1867–1936. Italian playwright, novelist, and short-story writer. His plays, which often deal with the themes of illusion and reality, and the tragicomic absurdity of life, include *Sei personaggi in cerca d'autore/Six Characters in Search of an Author* 1921, and *Enrico IV/Henry IV* 1922. The themes and innovative techniques of his plays anticipated the work of Brecht, O'Neill, Anouilh, and Genet. Nobel Prize 1934.

piranha any South American freshwater fish of the genus *Serrusalmus*, in the same order as cichlids. They can grow to 2 ft/60 cm long, and have razor-sharp teeth; some species may rapidly devour animals, especially if attracted by blood.

Pisa city in Tuscany, Italy; population (1988) 104,000. It has an 11th–12th-century cathedral. Its famous

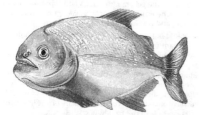

piranha *Red piranhas swim in shoals so large that they can devour even large animals quickly by their combined efforts. Their razor-sharp teeth and strong jaws can chop off pieces of flesh with great speed.*

campanile, the Leaning Tower of Pisa (repaired 1990), is 180 ft/55 m high and about 16.5 ft/5 m out of perpendicular. It has foundations only about 10 ft/3 m deep.

Pisces zodiac constellation, mainly in the northern hemisphere between Aries and Aquarius, near Pegasus. It is represented by two fish tied together by their tails. The constellation contains the *vernal equinox*, the point at which the Sun's path around the sky (the *ecliptic*) crosses the celestial equator. The Sun reaches this point around March 21 each year. In astrology, the dates for Pisces are between about Feb 19 and March 20 (see ◊precession).

pistachio deciduous Eurasian tree *Pistacia vera* of the cashew family Anacardiaceae, with green nuts, which are eaten salted or used to enhance and flavor foods.

pistil general term for the female part of a flower, either referring to one single ◊carpel or a group of several fused carpels.

piston barrel-shaped device used in reciprocating engines (steam, gasoline, diesel oil) to harness power. Pistons are driven up and down in cylinders by expanding steam or hot gases. They pass on their motion via a connecting rod and crank to a crankshaft, which turns the driving wheels. In a pump or compressor, the role of the piston is reversed, being used to move gases and liquids. See also ◊internal-combustion engine.

Piston Walter (Hamor) 1894–1976. US composer and teacher. His Neo-Classical works include eight symphonies, a number of concertos, chamber music, the orchestral suite *Three New England Sketches* 1959, and the ballet *The Incredible Flutist* 1938.

He was well regarded as a teacher; his pupils included Leonard Bernstein. He taught at Harvard University 1944–60.

Pitcairn Islands British colony in Polynesia, 3,300 mi/5,300 km NE of New Zealand *area* 10 sq mi/27 sq km *capital* Adamstown *features* the uninhabited Henderson Islands, an unspoiled coral atoll with a rare ecology, and tiny Ducie and Oeno islands, annexed by Britain 1902 *industries* fruit and souvenirs to passing ships *population* (1990) 52 *language* English *government* the governor is the British high commissioner in New Zealand *history* settled 1790 by nine mutineers from the British ship the *Bounty* together with some Tahitians; their occupation remained unknown until 1808.

pitch in chemistry, a black, sticky substance, hard when cold, but liquid when hot, used for waterproofing, roofing, and paving. It is made by the destructive distillation of wood or coal tar, and has been used since antiquity for caulking wooden ships.

pitch in music, the position of a note in the scale, dependent on the frequency of the predominant sound wave. In *concert pitch*, A above middle C is the reference tone to which instruments are tuned. *Perfect pitch* is an ability to name or reproduce any note heard or asked for; it does not necessarily imply high musical ability.

pitchblende or *uraninite* brownish-black mineral, the major constituent of uranium ore, consisting mainly of uranium oxide (UO_2). It also contains some lead (the final, stable product of uranium decay) and variable amounts of most of the naturally occurring radioactive elements, which are products of either the decay or the fissioning of uranium isotopes. The uranium yield is 50–80%; it is also a source of radium, polonium, and actinium. Pitchblende was first studied by Pierre and Marie ◊Curie, who found radium and polonium in its residues in 1898.

pitcher plant any of various insectivorous plants of the family Sarraceniaceae, especially the genera *Nepenthes* and *Sarracenia*, the leaves of which are shaped like a pitcher and filled with a fluid that traps and digests insects.

Pitt William, *the Elder*, 1st Earl of Chatham 1708–1778. British Whig politician, "the Great Commoner". As paymaster of the forces 1746–55, he broke with tradition by refusing to enrich himself; he was dismissed for attacking the Duke of Newcastle, the prime minister. He served effectively as prime minister in coalition governments 1756–61 (successfully conducting the Seven Years' War) and 1766–68.

He championed the Americans against the king, though rejecting independence, and collapsed during his last speech in the House of Lords—opposing the withdrawal of British troops—and died a month later.

Pitt William, *the Younger* 1759–1806. British Tory prime minister 1783–1801 and 1804–06. He raised the importance of the House of Commons, clamped down on corruption, carried out fiscal reforms, and effected the union with Ireland. He attempted to keep Britain at peace but underestimated the importance of the French Revolution and became embroiled in wars with France from 1793; he died on hearing of Napoleon's victory at Austerlitz.

Son of William Pitt the Elder, he became Britain's youngest prime minister 1783.

Pittsburgh industrial city (machinery, chemicals) in the NE US and the nation's largest inland port, where the Allegheny and Monongahela rivers join to form the Ohio River in Pennsylvania; population (1990) 369,900, metropolitan area 2,242,800.

Educational institutions include the University of Pittsburgh and Carnegie-Mellon University. Once a smoky, smoggy, steelmaking city, Pittsburgh was transformed by urban redevelopment from the 1960s and the demise of heavy industry into chiefly a corporate service center.

pituitary gland major ◊endocrine gland of vertebrates, situated in the center of the brain. It is attached to the hypothalamus by a stalk. The pituitary consists of two lobes. The posterior lobe is an extension of the hypothalamus, and is in effect nervous tissue. It stores two hormones synthesized in the hypothalamus. The anterior lobe secretes six hormones, some of which control the activities of other glands (thyroid, gonads, and adrenal cortex); others are direct-acting hormones affecting milk secretion and controlling growth.

Pius V 1504–1572. Pope from 1566. He excommunicated Elizabeth I of England, and organized the expedition against the Turks that won the victory of ◊Lepanto.

Pius IX 1792–1878. Pope from 1846. He never accepted the incorporation of the papal states and of Rome in the kingdom of Italy. He proclaimed the dogmas of the Immaculate Conception of the Virgin 1854 and papal infallibility 1870; his pontificate was the longest in history.

Pius XII (Eugenio Pacelli) 1876–1958. Pope from 1939. He was conservative in doctrine and politics, and condemned Modernism. He proclaimed the dogma of the bodily assumption of the Virgin Mary 1950 and in 1951 restated the doctrine (strongly criticized by many) that the life of an infant must not be sacrificed to save a mother in labor. He was criticized for failing to speak out against atrocities committed by the Germans during World War II and has been accused of collusion with the Nazis.

pixel (derived from *picture element*) single dot on a computer screen. All screen images are made up of a collection of pixels, with each pixel being either off (dark) or on (illuminated, possibly in color). The number of pixels available determines the screen's resolution.

Pizarro Francisco *c.* 1475–1541. Spanish conqueror of the Inca empire of Peru. Born in Spain, Pizarro traveled to the West Indies, where he met ◊Balboa and served as his lieutenant on the expedition that crossed Panama and resulted in their sighting of the Pacific Ocean 1513. While living in Panama, Pizarro heard of a wealthy Indian empire to the south, and beginning 1524 he explored the NW coast of South America, searching for gold and other riches. In 1531, with the permission of the king of Spain, he and 180 followers armed with cannon defeated the Inca king Atahualpa, later murdering him even though he gave them the large quantities of gold and silver they demanded. Pizarro founded Lima as the capital of Peru 1535. A feud then began among the Spanish leaders, and Pizarro was assassinated.

placebo any harmless substance, often called a "sugar pill", that has no active ingredient, but may nevertheless bring about improvement in the patient's condition.

placenta organ that attaches the developing ◊embryo or ◊fetus to the ◊uterus in placental mammals (mammals other than marsupials, platypuses, and echidnas). Composed of maternal and embryonic tissue, it links the blood supply of the embryo to the blood supply of the mother, allowing the exchange of oxygen, nutrients, and waste products. The two blood systems are not in direct contact, but are separated by thin membranes, with materials diffusing across from one system to the other. The placenta also produces hormones that maintain and regulate pregnancy. It is shed as part of the afterbirth.

plague term applied to any epidemic disease with a high mortality rate, but it usually refers to the bubonic plague. This is a disease transmitted by fleas (carried by the black rat) which infect the sufferer with the bacillus *Yersinia pestis*. An early symptom is swelling of lymph nodes, usually in the armpit and groin; such swellings are called "buboes". It causes virulent blood poisoning and the death rate is high.

plaice any of various flatfishes of the flounder group, especially the genera *Pleuronectes* and *Hippoglossoides*.

The American plaice *H. platessoides* grows to 2.5 ft/ 80 cm, and is valuable commercially.

Planck Max 1858–1947. German physicist who framed the quantum theory 1900. His research into the manner in which heated bodies radiate energy led him to report that energy is emitted only in indivisible amounts, called quanta, the magnitudes of which are proportional to the frequency of the radiation. His discovery ran counter to classical physics and is held to have marked the commencement of the modern science. Nobel Prize for Physics 1918.

plane in botany, any tree of the genus *Platanus*. Species include the oriental plane *P. orientalis*, a favorite plantation tree of the Greeks and Romans and the American plane or buttonwood *P. occidentalis*. A hybrid of these two is the London plane *P. x acerifolia*, with palmate, usually five-lobed leaves, which is widely planted in cities for its resistance to air pollution.

planet large celestial body in orbit around a star, composed of rock, metal, or gas. There are nine planets in the Solar System: Mercury, Venus, Earth, Mars, Jupiter, Saturn, Neptune, Uranus, and Pluto. The inner four, called the *terrestrial planets*, are small and rocky, and include the planet Earth. The outer planets, with the exception of Pluto, are called the giant planets, large balls of rock, liquid, and gas; the largest is Jupiter, which contains more than twice as much mass as all the other planets combined. Planets do not produce light, but reflect the light of their parent star.

planetarium optical projection device by means of which the motions of stars and planets are reproduced on a domed ceiling representing the sky.

Also, a building housing such a device, usually with auditoriums and scheduled lectures. About 60 such planetariums exist in the US.

planetesimal body of rock in space, smaller than a planet, attracted to other such bodies during planet formation. According to modern solar nebula theory, the Sun and the planets are thought to have formed from a rotating dust cloud generated by a supernova explosion.

plankton small, often microscopic, forms of plant and animal life that live in the upper layers of fresh and salt water, and are an important source of food for larger animals. Marine plankton is concentrated in areas where rising currents bring mineral salts to the surface.

plant organism that carries out ◊photosynthesis, has cellulose cell walls, complex cells, and is immobile. A few parasitic plants have lost the ability to photosynthesize but are still considered to be plants.

Plants are ◊autotrophs, that is, they make carbohydrates from water and carbon dioxide, and are the primary producers in all food chains, so that all animal life is dependent on them. They play a vital part in the carbon cycle, removing carbon dioxide from the atmosphere and generating oxygen. The study of plants is known as ◊botany.

Plantagenet English royal house, reigning 1154–1399, whose name comes from the nickname of Geoffrey, Count of Anjou (1113–1151), father of Henry II, who often wore in his hat a sprig of broom, *planta genista*. In the 1450s, Richard, Duke of York, took "Plantagenet" as a surname to emphasize his superior claim to the throne over Henry VI's.

plantain any plant of the genus *Plantago*, family Plantaginaceae. The great plantain *P. major* has oval leaves, grooved stalks, and spikes of green flowers with purple anthers followed by seeds, which are used in bird food.

plant classification taxonomy or classification of plants. Originally the plant kingdom included bacteria, diatoms, dinoflagellates, fungi, and slime molds, but these are not now thought of as plants. The groups that are always classified as plants are the bryophytes (mosses and liverworts), pteridophytes (ferns, horsetails, and club mosses), gymnosperms (conifers, yews, cycads, and ginkgos), and angiosperms (flowering plants). The angiosperms are split into monocotyledons (for example, orchids, grasses, lilies) and dicotyledons (for example, oak, buttercup, geranium, and daisy).

plasma in biology, the liquid component of the ◊blood.

plasma in physics, an ionized gas produced at extremely high temperatures, as in the Sun and other stars, which contains positive and negative charges in approximately equal numbers. It is a good electrical conductor. In thermonuclear reactions the plasma produced is confined through the use of magnetic fields.

plastic any of the stable synthetic materials that are fluid at some stage in their manufacture, when they can be shaped, and that later set to rigid or semirigid solids. Plastics today are chiefly derived from petroleum. Most are polymers, made up of long chains of identical molecules.

Plata, Río de la or *River Plate* estuary in South America into which the rivers Paraná and Uruguay flow; length 200 mi/320 km and width up to 150 mi/240 km. The basin drains much of Argentina, Bolivia, Brazil, Uruguay, and Paraguay, which all cooperate in its development.

plate tectonics theory formulated in the 1960s to explain the phenomena of ◊continental drift and seafloor spreading, and the formation of the major physical features of the Earth's surface. The Earth's outermost layer is regarded as a jigsaw of rigid major and minor plates up to 62 mi/100 km thick, which move relative to each other, probably under the influence of convection currents in the mantle beneath. Major landforms occur at the margins of the plates, where plates are colliding or moving apart—for example, volcanoes, fold mountains, ocean trenches, and ocean ridges.

Plath Sylvia 1932–1963. US poet and novelist. Her powerful, highly personal poems, often expressing a sense of desolation, are distinguished by their intensity and sharp imagery. Her *Collected Poems* 1981 was awarded a Pulitzer Prize. Her autobiographical novel *The Bell Jar* 1961 deals with the events surrounding a young woman's emotional breakdown.

platinum heavy, soft, silver-white, malleable and ductile, metallic element, symbol Pt, atomic number 78, atomic weight 195.09. It is the first of a group of six metallic elements (platinum, osmium, iridium, rhodium, ruthenium, and palladium) that possess similar traits, such as resistance to tarnish, corrosion, and attack by acid, and that often occur as free metals (native metals). They often occur in natural alloys with each other, the commonest of which is osmiridium. Both pure and as an alloy, platinum is used in dentistry, jewelry, and as a catalyst.

Plato c. 428–347 BC. Greek philosopher. He was a pupil of Socrates, teacher of Aristotle, and founder of the Academy school of philosophy. He was the author of philosophical dialogues on such topics as metaphysics, ethics, and politics. Central to his teachings is the notion of Forms, which are located outside the everyday world—timeless, motionless, and absolutely real.

platypus monotreme, or egg-laying, mammal *Ornithorhynchus anatinus*, found in Tasmania and E Australia. Semiaquatic, it has small eyes and no external ears, and jaws resembling a duck's beak. It lives in long burrows along river banks, where it lays two eggs in a rough nest. It feeds on water worms and insects, and when full-grown is 2 ft/60 cm long.

plebiscite referendum or direct vote by all the electors of a country or district on a specific question. Since the 18th century plebiscites have been employed on

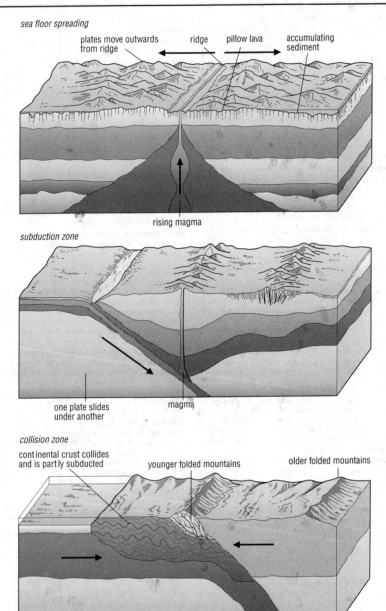

sea floor spreading

plates move outwards from ridge

ridge

pillow lava

accumulating sediment

rising magma

subduction zone

one plate slides under another

magma

collision zone

continental crust collides and is partly subducted

younger folded mountains

older folded mountains

plate tectonics *The three main types of action in plate tectonics. (top) Sea-floor spreading. The up-welling of magma forces apart the crust plates, producing new crust at the joint. Rapid extrusion of magma produces a domed ridge; more gentle spreading produces a central valley. (middle) The drawing downward of an oceanic plate beneath a continent produces a range of volcanic fold mountains parallel to the plate edge. (bottom) Collision of continental plates produces immense fold mountains, such as the Himalayas. Younger mountains are found near the coast with older ranges inland.*

platypus When the platypus was discovered 200 years ago, scientists thought the first specimens were fakes. It has some birdlike features, such as the duck's beak and webbed feet; it also lays eggs. The body has some reptilian characteristics, but is covered with hair like a mammal. Like a mammal, the platypus feeds its young with milk.

many occasions to decide to what country a particular area should belong; for example, in Upper Silesia and elsewhere after World War I, and in the Saar 1935.

Pleiades in astronomy, a star cluster about 400 light-years away in the constellation Taurus, representing the Seven Sisters of Greek mythology. Its brightest stars (highly luminous, blue-white giants only a few million years old) are visible to the naked eye, but there are many fainter ones.

Pleistocene first epoch of the Quaternary period of geological time, beginning 1.64 million years ago and ending 10,000 years ago. The polar ice caps were extensive and glaciers were abundant during the ice age of this period, and humans evolved into modern *Homo sapiens sapiens* about 100,000 years ago.

pleurisy inflammation of the pleura, the thin, secretory membrane that covers the lungs and lines the space in which they rest. Pleurisy is nearly always due to bacterial or viral infection, but may also be a complication of other diseases.

Plexiglas trademark for a clear, lightweight, tough plastic first produced in the US 1930. It is widely used for watch glasses, advertising signs, domestic baths, motorboat windshields, aircraft canopies, and protective shields. Its chemical name is polymethylmethacrylate (PMMA).

Plimsoll line loading mark painted on the hull of merchant ships, first suggested by English social reformer Samuel Plimsoll (1824–1898). It shows the depth to

TF	Tropical fresh water
F	Fresh water
T	Tropical salt water
S	Salt water in Summer
W	Salt water in Winter
WNA	Winter in North Atlantic
LR	Lloyd's Register

Plimsoll line The Plimsoll line on the hull of a ship indicates maximum safe loading levels for sea or fresh water, winter or summer, in tropical or northern waters.

which a vessel may be safely (and legally) loaded.

Pliny the Elder (Gaius Plinius Secundus) c. AD 23–79. Roman scientific encyclopedist and historian. Only his works on astronomy, geography, and natural history survive. He was killed in an eruption of Vesuvius, the volcano near Naples.

Pliocene fifth and last epoch of the Tertiary period of geological time, 5.2–1.64 million years ago. The earliest hominid, the humanlike ape *Australopithecines*, evolved in Africa.

PLO abbreviation for ◊*Palestine Liberation Organization*, founded 1964 to bring about an independent state of Palestine.

plotter or *graph plotter* device that draws pictures or diagrams under computer control.

Plotters are often used for producing business charts, architectural plans, and engineering drawings. *Flatbed plotters* move a pen up and down across a flat drawing surface, whereas *roller plotters* roll the drawing paper past the pen as it moves from side to side.

plover any shore bird of the family Charadriidae, found worldwide. Plovers are usually black or brown above, and white below, and have short bills. The largest of the ringed plovers is the killdeer *Charadrius vociferus*, called because of its cry.

plow the most important agricultural implement used for tilling the soil. The plow dates from about 3500 BC, when oxen were used to pull a simple wooden blade, or ard. In about 500 BC the iron share came into use.

plum tree *Prunus domestica*, bearing edible fruits that are smooth-skinned with a flat kernel. There are many varieties, including the Victoria, czar, egg-plum, greengage, and damson; the sloe *P. spinosa* is closely related. Dried plums are known as prunes.

Plutarch c. AD 46–120. Greek biographer and essayist. His *Parallel Lives* comprise paired biographies of famous Greek and Roman soldiers and politicians, followed by comparisons between the two. Thomas North's 1579 translation inspired Shakespeare's Roman plays.

Pluto in astronomy, the smallest and, usually, outermost planet of the Solar System. The existence of Pluto was predicted by calculation by Percival Lowell and the planet was located by Clyde Tombaugh in 1930. It orbits the Sun every 248.5 years at an average distance of 3.6 trillion mi/5.8 trillion km.

Its highly elliptical orbit occasionally takes it within the orbit of Neptune, as in 1979–99. Pluto has a diameter of about 1,400 mi/2,300 km, and a mass about 0.002 of that of Earth. It is of low density, composed of rock and ice, with frozen methane on its surface and a thin atmosphere.

Charon, Pluto's moon, was discovered 1978, revolving around Pluto with the same period as Pluto's rotation, remaining over the same point on Pluto's surface and showing the same face. It is composed mainly of ice and it is possible the pair may be a double planet system.

Pluto in Greek mythology, the lord of the underworld (Roman Dis), sometimes known as Hades. He was the brother of Zeus and Poseidon.

plutonium silvery-white, radioactive, metallic element of the ◊actinide series, symbol Pu, atomic number 94, relative atomic mass 239.13. It occurs in nature in minute quantities in ◊pitchblende and other ores, but is produced in quantity only synthetically. It has six allotropic forms (see ◊allotropy) and is one of three fissile elements (elements capable of splitting into other elements—the others are thorium and uranium). The element has awkward physical properties and is the most toxic substance known.

Plymouth city and seaport in Devon, England, at the mouth of the river Plym, with dockyard, barracks, and a naval base at Devonport; population (1981) 243,400. There are marine industries; clothing, radio equipment, and processed foods are produced. The city rises N of the Hoe headland where tradition has it that Francis ◊Drake played bowls as the Spanish Armada approached 1588. The *Mayflower* ◊Pilgrims sailed from here 1620.

PM10 (abbreviation for *particulate matter less than 10 micrometers across*) clusters of small particles, such as carbon particles, in the air that come mostly from vehicle exhausts. There is a link between increase in PM10 levels and a rise in death rate, increased hospital admissions, and asthma incidence. The elderly and those with chronic heart or lung disease are most at risk.

The US safety limit for PM10 levels is 150 micrograms per cubic meter. US studies suggest that there is no safe limit and an increase of 10 $\mu g/m^3$ causes a 1% rise in death rate. The Environmental Protection Agency estimates 60,000 deaths are caused annually by particulates.

pneumatic drill drill operated by compressed air, used in mining and tunneling, for drilling shot holes (for explosives), and in road repairs for breaking up pavements. It contains an air-operated piston that delivers hammer blows to the drill bit many times a second. The French engineer Germain Sommeiller (1815–1871) developed the pneumatic drill 1861 for tunneling in the Alps.

pneumectomy surgical removal of all or part of the lung.

pneumonia inflammation of the lungs, generally due to bacterial or viral infection but also to particulate matter or gases. It is characterized by a buildup of fluid in the alveoli, the clustered air sacs (at the ends of the air passages) where oxygen exchange takes place.

Pnom Penh alternative form of ◊Phnom Penh, the capital of Cambodia.

Po longest river in Italy, flowing from the Cottian Alps to the Adriatic Sea; length 415 mi/668 km. Its valley is fertile and contains natural gas. The river is heavily polluted with nitrates, phosphates, and arsenic.

Pocahontas *c.* 1595–1617. American Indian woman alleged to have saved the life of English colonist John Smith when he was captured by her father, Powhatan. Pocahontas was kidnapped 1613 by an Englishman, Samuel Argall, and she later married colonist John Rolfe (1585–1622) and was entertained as a princess at the English Court. Her marriage and conversion to Christianity brought about a period of peaceful relations between Indians and settlers, but she died of smallpox after her return to Virginia.

pochard any of various diving ducks found in Europe and North America, especially the genus *Aythya*.

In North America, the canvasback *A. valisineria*, the redhead *A. americana*, the ring-necked *A. collaris*, and two species of scaup, *A. marila* and *A. affinis*, are pochards.

podiatry the medical profession that deals with the specialized care of feet. Some podiatric treatments involve the use of orthopedic devices to correct fallen arches or improve improper positioning of feet during walking.

Poe Edgar Allan 1809–1849. US writer and poet born in Boston. His short stories are renowned for their horrific atmosphere, as in "The Fall of the House of Usher" 1839 and "The Masque of the Red Death" 1842, and for their acute reasoning (ratiocination), as in "The Gold Bug" 1843 and "The Murders in the Rue Morgue" 1841 (in which the investigators Legrand and Dupin anticipate Conan Doyle's Sherlock Holmes). His poems include "The Raven" 1845. He became an alcoholic and exhausted himself, dying at age 40. Poe was the first US poet to become internationally known and admired.

poet laureate poet of the British royal household, so called because of the laurel wreath awarded to eminent poets in the Graeco-Roman world. Early poets with unofficial status were Geoffrey Chaucer, John Skelton, Edmund Spenser, Samuel Daniel, and Ben Jonson. Ted ◊Hughes was appointed poet laureate 1984.

poetry the imaginative expression of emotion, thought, or narrative, frequently in metrical form and often using figurative language. Poetry has traditionally been distinguished from prose (ordinary written language) by rhyme or the rhythmical arrangement of words (◊meter).

pogrom unprovoked violent attack on an ethnic group, particularly Jews, carried out with official sanction. The Russian pogroms against Jews began 1881, after the assassination of Czar Alexander II, and again in 1903–06; persecution of the Jews remained constant until the Russian Revolution. Later there were pogroms in E Europe, especially in Poland after 1918, and in Germany under Hitler (see ◊Holocaust).

poikilothermy the condition in which an animal's body temperature is largely dependent on the temperature of the air or water in which it lives. It is characteristic of all animals except birds and mammals, which maintain their body temperatures by homeothermy (they are "warm-blooded").

poinsettia or *Christmas flower* winter-flowering shrub *Euphorbia pulcherrima*, with large red leaves encircling small greenish-yellow flowers. It is native to Mexico and tropical America and is a popular houseplant in North America and Europe.

Pointillism technique in oil painting developed in the 1880s by the Neo-Impressionist Georges Seurat. He used small dabs of pure color laid side by side to create form and an impression of shimmering light when viewed from a distance.

poison or *toxin* any chemical substance that, when introduced into or applied to the body, is capable of injuring health or destroying life. The liver removes some poisons from the blood. The majority of poisons may be divided into *corrosives*, such as sulfuric, nitric, and hydrochloric acids; *irritants*, including arsenic and copper sulfate; *narcotics* such as opium, and carbon monoxide; and *narcotico-irritants* from any substances of plant origin including carbolic acid and tobacco.

poison ivy North American plant *Rhus radicans* of the cashew family, having leaves composed of three leaflets, yellowish flowers, and ivory-colored, berrylike fruit. The leaves are variable and may be dull or shiny, leathery or thin, toothed or smooth-edged. It can grow as an erect shrub, trailing vine, or climber. All parts of the plant contain a heavy, nonvolatile oil that causes inflammation of the skin with itching rash, blisters, and/or swelling in susceptible persons. Numerous birds feed on the berries.

poison oak any of several North American subspecies of poison ivy *Rhus radicans*. Poison oak always grows as an erect shrub (to 10 in/25 cm tall) with three-parted leaves that are usually blunt-tipped and hairy on both sides. The irritating effects to humans are similar to those of poison ivy.

poison sumac shrub or small tree *Rhus vernix* of the cashew family that thrives in a swampy habitat. Its large leaves are composed of 7–13 pointed leaflets, and it bears clusters of white globular fruit. All its parts contain a dangerous skin irritant more virulent than that of poison ivy or poison oak.

Poitou-Charentes region of W central France, comprising the *départements* of Charente, Charente-Maritime, Deux-Sèvres, and Vienne *capital* Poitiers *area* 9,959 sq mi/25,800 sq km *industries* dairy products, wheat, chemicals, metal goods; brandy is made at Cognac *population* (1986) 1,584,000 *history* once part of the Roman province of Aquitaine, this region was captured by the Visigoths in the 5th century and taken by the Franks AD 507. The area was contested by the English and French until the end of the Hundred Years' War 1453, when it was incorporated into France by Charles II.

poker card game of US origin, in which two to eight people play (usually for stakes) and try to obtain a "hand" of five cards ranking higher than those of their opponents. The best scoring hand wins the "pot."

pokeweed tall North American herbaceous plant *Phytolacca americana* of the family Phytolaccaceae. It has pale greenish flowers and purple berries, the seeds of which are poisonous. North American Indians used the juice of the berries for staining.

Poland Republic of (*Polska Rzeczpospolita*) *area* 49,325 sq mi/127,886 sq km *capital* Warsaw *towns and cities* Lódz, Kraków, Wroclaw, Poznan, Katowice, Bydgoszcz, Lublin; ports Gdansk, Szczecin, Gdynia *physical* part of the great plain of Europe; Vistula, Oder, and Neisse rivers; Sudeten, Tatra, and Carpathian mountains on S frontier *environment* atmospheric pollution derived from coal (producing 90% of the country's electricity), toxic waste from industry, and lack of sewage treatment have resulted in the designation of 27 ecologically endangered areas. Half the country's lakes have been seriously contaminated and three-quarters of its drinking water does not meet official health standards *features* last wild European bison (only in protected herds) *head of state* Lech Walesa from 1990 *head of government* Waldemar Pawlak from 1993 *political system* emergent democratic republic *political parties* Freedom Union, moderate, centrist; Democratic Left Alliance, ex-communist; Catholic Action, coalition dominated by Christian National Union (CNU), right of center; Polish Peasant Party (PPP), moderate, agrarian; Confederation for an Independent Poland, center-right *exports* coal, softwood timber, chemicals, machinery, ships, vehicles, meat, copper (Europe's largest producer) *currency* zloty *population* (1993) 38,310,000; growth rate 0.6% p.a. *life expectancy* men 68, women 76 *languages* Polish (official), German *media* broadcasters required by law to "respect Christian values" *religion* Roman Catholic 95% *literacy* 99% *GNP* $1,830 per head (1991) *chronology* 1918 Poland revived as independent republic. *1939* German invasion and occupation. *1944* Germans driven out by Soviet forces. *1945* Polish boundaries redrawn at Potsdam Conference. *1947* Communist people's republic proclaimed. *1956* Poznan riots. Wladyslaw Gomulka installed as Polish United Workers' Party (PUWP) leader. *1970* Gomulka

replaced by Edward Gierek after Gdansk riots. *1980* Solidarity emerged as a free labor union following Gdansk disturbances. *1981* Martial law imposed by General Wojciech Jaruzelski. *1983* Martial law ended. *1984* Amnesty for political prisoners. *1985* Zbigniew Messner became prime minister. *1987* Referendum on economic reform rejected. *1988* Solidarity-led strikes and demonstrations called off after pay increases. Messner resigned; replaced by the reformist Mieczyslaw F Rakowski. *1989* Solidarity relegalized. April: new "socialist pluralist" constitution formed. June: widespread success for Solidarity in the first open elections for 40 years. July: Jaruzelski elected president. Sept: "Grand coalition", first non-Communist government since World War II formed; free-market restructuring began. *1990* Jan: PUWP dissolved. Lech Walesa elected president. *1991* Oct: Multiparty general election inconclusive. Five-party center-right coalition formed under Jan Olszewski. Treaty signed agreeing to complete withdrawal of Soviet troops. *1992* June: Olszewski ousted; succeeded by Waldemar Pawlak. July: Hanna Suchocka replaced Pawlak. *1993* April: Suchocka lost vote of confidence. May: privatization bill passed. June: formal invitation to apply for European Community (now European Union) membership. Oct: Pawlak appointed premier after inconclusive general election. *1994* Joined NATO "partnership for peace" program.

Polanski Roman 1933– . Polish film director. His films include *Repulsion* 1965, *Cul de Sac* 1966, *Rosemary's Baby* 1968, *Tess* 1979, *Frantic* 1988, and *Bitter Moon* 1992.

Polaris or *Pole Star* or *North Star* the bright star closest to the north celestial pole, and the brightest star in the constellation Ursa Minor. Its position is indicated by the "pointers" in Ursa Major. Polaris is a yellow ◊supergiant about 500 light-years away.

Polaroid camera instant-picture camera, invented by Edwin Land in the US 1947. The original camera produced black-and-white prints in about one minute. Modern cameras can produce black-and-white prints in a few seconds, and color prints in less than a minute. An advanced model has automatic focusing and exposure. It ejects a piece of film on paper immediately after the picture has been taken.

polar reversal changeover in polarity of the Earth's magnetic poles. Studies of the magnetism retained in rocks at the time of their formation have shown that in the past the Earth's north magnetic pole repeatedly became the south magnetic pole, and vice versa.

pole either of the geographic north and south points of the axis about which the Earth rotates. The geographic poles differ from the magnetic poles, which are the points toward which a freely suspended magnetic needle will point.

Pole person of Polish culture from Poland and the surrounding area.

There are 37–40 million speakers of Polish (including some in the US), a Slavic language belonging to the Indo-European family. The Poles are predominantly Roman Catholic, though there is an Orthodox Church minority. They are known for their distinctive cooking, folk festivals, and folk arts.

polecat Old World weasel *Mustela putorius* with a brown back and dark belly and two yellow face patches. The body is about 20 in/50 cm long and it has a strong smell from anal gland secretions. It is native to Asia, Europe, and N Africa. In North America, ◊skunks are sometimes called polecats. A ferret is a domesticated polecat.

Pole Star another name for ◊Polaris, the northern pole star. There is no bright star near the southern celestial pole.

police civil law-and-order force. In the US, law enforcement is the responsibility of municipal and state government except for violations of specific federal laws or cases in which state borders have been crossed. Unlike many countries, there is no national police force. The ◊Federal Bureau of Investigation assists state and local law-enforcement authorities.

polio (*poliomyelitis*) viral infection of the central nervous system affecting nerves that activate muscles. The disease used to be known as infantile paralysis. Two kinds of vaccine are available, one injected (see ◊Salk) and one given by mouth. The World Health Organization expects that polio will be eradicated by 2000.

Polish language member of the Slavonic branch of the Indo-European language family, spoken mainly in Poland. Polish is written in the Roman and not the Cyrillic alphabet and its standard form is based on the dialect of Poznan in W Poland.

Politburo contraction of "political bureau", the executive committee (known as the Presidium 1952–66) of the Supreme Soviet in the USSR, which laid down party policy. It consisted of about 12 voting and 6 candidate (nonvoting) members.

political party association of like-minded people organized with the purpose of seeking and exercising political power. A party can be distinguished from an interest or ◊pressure group which seeks to influence governments rather than aspire to office, although some pressure groups, such as the Green movement, have over time transformed themselves into political parties.

Polk James Knox 1795–1849. 11th president of the US 1845–49, a Democrat, born in North Carolina. He allowed Texas admission to the Union, and forced the war on Mexico that resulted in the annexation of California and New Mexico.

Polk was an associate of Andrew ◊Jackson, who influenced his strongly expansionist policies. A believer in manifest destiny, Polk pursued war with Mexico but avoided armed conflict with Britain over the Oregon–Canada boundary.

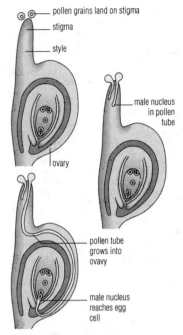

pollen Pollination, the process by which pollen grains transfer their male nuclei (gametes) to the ovary of a flower. (1) The pollen grains land on the stigma and (2) form a pollen tube that (3) grows down into the ovary. The male nuclei travel along the pollen tube.

pollack marine fish *Pollachius virens* of the cod family, growing to 2.5 ft/75 cm, and found close to the shore on both sides of the N Atlantic.

pollen the grains of ◊seed plants that contain the male gametes. In ◊angiosperms (flowering plants) pollen is produced within anthers; in most ◊gymnosperms (cone-bearing plants) it is produced in male cones. A pollen grain is typically yellow and, when mature, has a hard outer wall. Pollen of insect-pollinated plants (see ◊pollination) is often sticky and spiny and larger than the smooth, light grains produced by wind-pollinated species.

pollination the process by which pollen is transferred from one plant to another. The male ◊gametes are contained in pollen grains, which must be transferred from the anther to the stigma in ◊angiosperms (flowering plants), and from the male cone to the female cone in ◊gymnosperms (cone-bearing plants). Fertilization (not the same as pollination) occurs after the growth of the pollen tube to the ovary. Self-pollination occurs when pollen is transferred to a stigma of the same flower, or to another flower on the same plant; cross-pollination occurs when pollen is transferred to another plant.

polling in computing, a technique for transferring data from a terminal to the central computer of a ◊multiuser system. The computer automatically makes a connection with each terminal in turn, interrogates it to check whether it is holding data for transmission, and, if it is, collects the data.

Pollock Jackson 1912–1956. US painter. He was a pioneer of Abstract Expressionism and one of the foremost exponents of ◊action painting. His style is characterized by complex networks of swirling, interwoven lines of great delicacy and rhythmic subtlety.

pollution the harmful effect on the environment of by-products of human activity, principally industrial and agricultural processes—for example, noise, smoke, automobile emissions, chemical and radioactive effluents in air, seas, and rivers, pesticides, radiation, sewage (see ◊sewage disposal), and household waste. Pollution contributes to the ◊greenhouse effect.

polo stick-and-ball game played between two teams of four on horseback. It originated in Iran, spread to India and was first played in England 1869. Polo is played on the largest field of any game, measuring up to 300 yd/274 m by 200 yd/182 m. A small solid ball is struck with the side of a long-handled mallet through goals at each end of the field. A typical match lasts about an hour, and is divided into "chukkas" of 7½ minutes each. No pony is expected to play more than two chukkas in the course of a day.

Polo Marco 1254–1324. Venetian traveler and writer. He traveled overland to China 1271–75, and served the emperor Kublai Khan until he returned to Europe by sea 1292–95. He was captured while fighting for Venice against Genoa, and, while in prison 1296–98, dictated an account of his travels.

polonium radioactive, metallic element, symbol Po, atomic number 84, atomic weight 210. Polonium occurs in nature in small amounts and was isolated from ◊pitchblende. It is the element having the largest number of isotopes (27) and is 5,000 times as radioactive as radium, liberating considerable amounts of heat. It was the first element to have its radioactive properties recognized and investigated.

Pol Pot (also known as *Saloth Sar, Tol Saut,* and *Pol Porth*) 1925– . Cambodian politician and leader of the Khmer Rouge communist movement that overthrew the government 1975. After widespread atrocities against the civilian population, his regime was deposed by a Vietnamese invasion 1979. Pol Pot continued to help lead the Khmer Rouge despite officially resigning from all positions in 1989.

polyester synthetic resin formed by the ◊condensation of polyhydric alcohols (alcohols containing more than one hydroxyl group) with dibasic acids (acids containing two replaceable hydrogen atoms). Polyesters are thermosetting ◊plastics, used in making synthetic fibers, such as Dacron and Terylene, and constructional plastics. With fiberglass added as reinforcement, polyesters are used in automobile bodies and boat hulls.

polyethylene or *polyethene* polymer of the gas ethylene (technically called ethene, C_2H_4). It is a tough, white, translucent, waxy thermoplastic (which means it can be repeatedly softened by heating). It is used for packaging, bottles, toys, wood preservation, electric cable, pipes and tubing.

polygamy the practice of having more than one spouse at the same time. It is found among many peoples. Normally it has been confined to the wealthy and to chiefs and nobles who can support several women and their offspring, as among ancient Egyptians, Teutons, Irish, and Slavs. Islam limits the number of legal wives a man may have to four. Certain Christian sects—for example, the Anabaptists of Münster, Germany, and the Mormons—have practiced polygamy because it was the norm in the Old Testament.

polymer compound made up of a large long-chain or branching matrix composed of many repeated simple units (*monomers*). There are many polymers, both natural (cellulose, chitin, lignin) and synthetic (polyethylene and nylon, types of plastic). Synthetic polymers belong to two groups: thermosoftening and thermosetting (see ◊plastic).

Polynesia islands of Oceania E of 170° E latitude, including Hawaii, Kiribati, Tuvalu, Fiji, Tonga, Tokelau, Samoa, Cook Islands, and French Polynesia.

Polynesian a member of any of the seafaring peoples of Polynesia. They migrated by canoe from S Asia in about 2000 BC, peopling the islands of the S Pacific for about 2,000 years, and settling Hawaii last, from Tahiti. The Polynesian languages belong to the Oceanic branch of the Austronesian family.

polyunsaturate type of ◊fat or oil containing a high proportion of triglyceride molecules whose ◊fatty acid chains contain several double bonds. By contrast, the fatty-acid chains of the triglycerides in saturated fats (such as lard) contain only single bonds. Medical evidence suggests that polyunsaturated fats, used widely in margarines and cooking fats, are less likely to contribute to cardiovascular disease than saturated fats, but there is also some evidence that they may have adverse effects on health.

pomegranate deciduous shrub or small tree *Punica granatum*, family Punicaceae, native to SW Asia but cultivated widely in tropical and subtropical areas. The round, leathery, reddish yellow fruit contains numerous seeds that can be eaten fresh or made into wine.

Pomona in Roman mythology, goddess of fruit trees.

Pompeii ancient city in Italy, near the volcano ◊Vesuvius, 13 mi/21 km SE of Naples. In AD 63 an earthquake destroyed much of the city, which had been a Roman port and pleasure resort; it was completely buried beneath volcanic ash when Vesuvius erupted AD 79. Over 2,000 people were killed. Pompeii was rediscovered 1748 and the systematic excavation begun 1763 still continues.

Pompey the Great (Gnaeus Pompeius Magnus) 106–48 BC. Roman soldier and politician. From 60 BC to 53 BC, he was a member of the First Triumvirate with Julius ◊Caesar and Marcus Livius ◊Crassus.

Pompidou Georges 1911–1974. French conservative politician, president 1969–74. He negotiated a settlement with the Algerians 1961 and, as prime minister 1962–68, with the students in the revolt of May 1968.

Ponce de León Juan 1460–1521. Spanish explorer who discovered Florida. He sailed on Columbus's second voyage to the Americas 1493 and settled in the colony on Hispaniola, later conquering Puerto Rico 1508–09 and becoming its governor. In 1513, while searching for the legendary "fountain of youth" he discovered Florida, exploring much of its E coast and part of the W coast. Ponce de León returned to Florida in 1521 and was wounded in a battle with Indians. He died soon after in Cuba.

pondweed any aquatic plant of the genus *Potamogeton* that either floats on the water or is submerged. The leaves of floating pondweeds are broad and leathery, whereas leaves of the submerged forms are narrower and translucent; the flowers grow in green spikes.

Pontiac *c.* 1720–1769. North American Indian, chief of

Pony Express Though it has become an important part of the folk history of the Wild West, the Pony Express operated for little more than a year, soon being made redundant by the telegraph.

the Ottawa from 1755. Allied with the French during the French and Indian War, Pontiac was hunted by the British after the French withdrawal.

He led the "Conspiracy of Pontiac" 1763–64 in an attempt to resist British persecution. He achieved remarkable success against overwhelming odds but eventually signed a peace treaty 1766.

pony small horse under 4.5 ft/1.47 m (14.2 hands) shoulder height. Although of Celtic origin, all the pony breeds have been crossed with thoroughbred and Arab stock, except for the smallest—the hardy Shetland, which is less than 42 in/105 cm shoulder height.

Pony Express in the US, a system of mail-carrying by relays of horse riders that operated in the years 1860–61 between St Joseph, Missouri, and Sacramento, California, a distance of about 1,800 mi/2,900 km.

The Pony Express was a private venture by a company called Russell, Majors, and Waddell. 157 stations were set up along the route and the riders, who included William Cody, (Buffalo Bill), needed several changes of horses between each station.

Pop art movement of American and British artists in the mid-1950s and 1960s, reacting against the elitism of abstract art. Pop art imagery was drawn from advertising, comic strips, film, and television. Early exponents in the US were Jasper Johns, Jim Dine, Andy Warhol, Roy Lichtenstein, and Claes Oldenburg.

Pope Alexander 1688–1744. English poet and satirist. He established his reputation with the precocious *Pastorals* 1709 and Essay on Criticism 1711, which were followed by a parody of the heroic epic *The Rape of the Lock* 1712–14 and "Eloisa to Abelard" 1717. Other works include a highly Neo-Classical translation of Homer's *Iliad* and *Odyssey* 1715–26.

poplar deciduous tree of the genus *Populus*, or cottonwood trees of the willow family Salicaceae. When ripe, the feathery seeds borne on elongated clusters are blown far and wide by the wind. Balsam poplar *P. balsamifera* and eastern cottonwood *P. deltoides* are native to North America. Eurasian white poplar *P. alba* and Lombardy poplar *P. nigra* are grown widely as ornamentals. Aspens belong to the same genus.

pop music or *popular music* any contemporary music not categorizable as jazz or classical.

Characterized by strong rhythms of African origin, simple harmonic structures often repeated to strophic melodies, and the use of electrically amplified instruments, pop music generically includes the areas of jazz, rock, country and western, rhythm and blues, soul, and others. Pop became distinct from folk music with the advent of sound-recording techniques; electronic amplification and other technological innovations have played a large part in the creation of new styles. The traditional format is a song of roughly three minutes with verse, chorus, and middle eight bars.

Popocatépetl (Aztec "smoking mountain") volcano in central Mexico, 30 mi/50 km SE of Mexico City; 17,526 ft/5,340 m. It last erupted 1920.

poppy any plant of the genus *Papaver*, family Papaveraceae, that bears brightly colored, often dark-centered, flowers and yields a milky sap. Species include the crimson European field poppy *P. rheas* and the Asian ◊opium poppies. Closely related are the California poppy *Eschscholtzia californica* and the yellow horned or sea poppy *Glaucium flavum*.

population explosion the rapid and dramatic rise in world population that has occurred over the last few hundred years. Between 1959 and 1990, the world's population increased from 2.5 trillion to over 5 trillion people. It is estimated that it will be at least 6 trillion by the end of the century. Most of this growth is now taking place in the developing world.

porcelain (hardpaste) (hardpaste) translucent ceramic material with a shining finish, see ◊pottery and porcelain.

porcupine any ◊rodent with quills on its body, belonging to either of two families: Old World porcupines (family Hystricidae), terrestrial in habit and having long black-and-white quills; or New World porcupines (family Erethizontidae), tree-dwelling, with prehensile tails and much shorter quills.

porcupine A North American porcupine. The porcupine's appetite for vegetation can be so great that porcupines have been known to kill trees by stripping their bark.

porpoise any small whale of the family Delphinidae that, unlike dolphins, have blunt snouts without beaks. Common porpoises of the genus *Phocaena* can grow to 6 ft/1.8 m long; they feed on fish and crustaceans.

Porsche Ferdinand 1875–1951. German automotive engineer. The Volkswagen (German "people's automobile") was a Porsche product of the 1930s that became an international success (as the Beetle) in the 1950s–1970s. He also designed the original Porsche sports automobiles.

portable computer computer that can be carried from place to place. The term embraces a number of very different computers—from those that would be carried only with some reluctance to those, such as ◊laptop computers and ◊notebook computers, that can be comfortably carried and used in transit.

Port-au-Prince capital and industrial port (sugar, rum, textiles, plastics) of Haiti; population (1982) 763,000.

Porter Cole (Albert) 1891–1964. US composer and lyricist of witty musical comedies. His shows include *The Gay Divorce* 1932 (filmed 1934 as *The Gay Divorcee*), *Anything Goes* 1934, *Kiss Me, Kate* 1948, and *Silk Stockings* 1955. He also wrote movie musicals, such as *Born to Dance* 1936 and *High Society* 1956.

Porter Katherine Anne 1890–1980. US writer. She published three volumes of short stories (*Flowing Judas* 1930, *Pale Horse, Pale Rider* 1939, and *The Leaning Tower* 1944); a collection of essays, *The Days Before* 1952; and the allegorical novel *Ship of Fools* 1962 (filmed 1965). Her *Collected Short Stories* 1965 won a Pulitzer Prize.

Porter William Sydney. Pen name "O Henry". 1862–1910. US author. Born in Greensboro, North Carolina, Porter left home at an early age. Settling in Texas, he was convicted of embezzlement 1899 and served several years in prison. It was then that he began to write short stories, many with surprise endings, under the distinctive pen name " Henry." After his release 1902, he moved to New York City. Among the published collections are *The Four Million* (including "The Gift of the Magi") 1906, *The Voice of the City* 1908, and *Rolling Stones* 1913.

Portland industrial port and largest city of Maine, US, on Casco Bay, SE of Sebago Lake; population (1990) 64,400.

The University of Southern Maine is here. The home of the poet Henry Wadsworth Longfellow, who was born here, is now a museum.

Port Moresby capital and port of Papua New Guinea on the S coast of New Guinea; population (1987) 152,000.

Pôrto Alegre port and capital of Rio Grande do Sul state, S Brazil; population (1991) 1,254,600. It is a freshwater port for oceangoing vessels and is Brazil's major commercial center.

Port-of-Spain port and capital of Trinidad and Tobago, on the island of Trinidad; population (1988) 58,000. It has a cathedral (1813–28) and the San Andres Fort (1785).

Porto Novo capital of Benin, W Africa; population (1982) 208,258. It was a former Portuguese center for the slave and tobacco trade with Brazil and became a French protectorate 1863.

Port Said port in Egypt, on reclaimed land at the N end of the ◊Suez Canal; population (1983) 364,000. During the 1967 Arab-Israeli War the city was damaged and the canal blocked; Port Said was evacuated by 1969 but by 1975 had been largely reconstructed.

Portsmouth city and naval port in Hampshire, England, opposite the Isle of Wight; population (1991) 174,700. The naval dockyard was closed 1981 although some naval facilities remain. It is a continental ferry port. There are high-technology and manufacturing industries, including aircraft engineering, electronics, shipbuilding, and ship maintenance.

Portsmouth port and independent city in SE Virginia, US, on the Elizabeth River, seat of a US navy yard and training center; population (1990) 103,900. Manufactured goods include electronic equipment, chemicals, clothing, and processed food.

Portsmouth was a British naval base during the American Revolution. During the Civil War the Confederacy briefly held the naval shipyard here and converted the scuttled steamship USS *Merrimack* into the ironclad warship *Virginia*. It engaged the Union's *Monitor* March 9, 1862, in Hampton Roads in the first naval battle between ironclad vessels.

Portugal Republic of (*República Portuguesa*) *area* 35,521 sq mi/92,000 sq km (including the Azores and Madeira) *capital* Lisbon *towns and cities* Coimbra; ports Pôrto, Setúbal *physical* mountainous in N, plains in S *features* rivers Minho, Douro, Tagus (Tejo), Guadiana; Serra da Esterla mountains *head of state* Mario Alberto Nober Lopes Soares from 1986 *head of government* Aníbal Cavaco Silva from 1985 *political system* democratic republic *political parties* Social Democratic Party (PSD), moderate left of center; Socialist Party (PS), progressive socialist; Democratic Renewal Party (PRD), center-left; Democratic Social Center Party (CDS), moderate left of center *exports* wine, olive oil, resin, cork, sardines, textiles, clothing, pottery, pulpwood *currency* escudo *population* (1993 est) 10,450,000; growth rate 0.5% p.a. *life expectancy* men 71, women 78 *language* Portuguese *religion* Roman Catholic 97% *literacy* men 89%, women 82% *GNP* $5,620 per head (1991) *chronology 1928–68* Military dictatorship under António de Oliveira Salazar. *1968* Salazar succeeded by Marcello Caetano. *1974* Caetano removed in military coup led by General António Ribeiro de Spínola. Spínola replaced by General Francisco da Costa Gomes. *1975* African colonies became independent. *1976* New constitution, providing for return to civilian rule, adopted. Minority government appointed, led by Socialist Party leader Mario Soares. *1978* Soares resigned. *1980* Francisco Balsemão formed center-party coalition

505

after two years of political instability. *1982* Draft of new constitution approved, reducing powers of presidency. *1983* Center-left coalition government formed. *1985* Aníbal Cavaco Silva became prime minister. *1986* Mario Soares elected first civilian president in 60 years. Portugal joined European Community (now the European Union). *1988* Portugal joined Western European Union. *1989* Constitution amended to allow major state enterprises to be denationalized. *1991* Soares reelected president; PSD majority slightly reduced in assembly elections.

Portuguese language member of the Romance branch of the Indo-European language family; spoken by 120–135 million people worldwide, it is the national language of Portugal, closely related to Spanish and strongly influenced by Arabic. Portuguese is also spoken in Brazil, Angola, Mozambique, and other former Portuguese colonies.

Portuguese man-of-war any of a genus *Physalia* of phylum *Coelenterata* (see ◊coelenterate). They live in the sea, in colonies, and have a large air-filled bladder (or "float") on top and numerous hanging tentacles made up of feeding, stinging, and reproductive individuals. The float can be 1 ft/30 cm long.

Poseidon in Greek mythology, the chief god of the sea (Roman Neptune), brother of Zeus and Pluto. The brothers dethroned their father, Cronus, and divided his realm, Poseidon taking the sea; he was also worshiped as god of earthquakes. His sons were the merman sea god ◊Triton and the Cyclops Polyphemus.

positivism theory that confines genuine knowledge within the bounds of science and observation. The theory is associated with the French philosopher Auguste Comte and ◊empiricism. *Logical positivism* developed in the 1920s. It rejected any metaphysical world beyond everyday science and common sense, and confined statements to those of formal logic or mathematics.

positron in physics, the antiparticle of the electron; an ◊elementary particle having the same magnitude of mass and charge as an electron but exhibiting a positive charge. The positron was discovered in 1932 by US physicist Carl Anderson at Caltech, US, its existence having been predicted by the British physicist Paul Dirac 1928.

possum another name for the ◊opossum, a marsupial animal with a prehensile tail found in North, Central and South America. The name is also used for many of the smaller marsupials found in Australia.

poste restante (French) a system whereby mail is sent to a certain post office and kept there until collected by the person to whom it is addressed.

The US system of General Delivery is similar.

Post-Impressionism movement in painting that followed ◊Impressionism in the 1880s and 1890s, incorporating various styles. The term was first used by the English critic Roger Fry 1910 to describe the works of Cézanne, van Gogh, and Gauguin. Thought differing greatly in style and aims, these painters sought to go beyond Impressionism's concern with the ever-changing effects of light.

Postmodernism late 20th-century movement in the arts and architecture that rejects the preoccupation of ◊Modernism with purity of form and technique. Postmodern designers use an amalgam of style elements from the past, such as the Classical and the Baroque, and apply them to spare modern forms. Their slightly off-key familiarity creates a more immediate appeal than the austerities of Modernism.

post-mortem alternate name for ◊autopsy.

PostScript in computing, a page-description language developed by Adobe that has become a standard. PostScript is primarily a language for printing documents on laser printers, but it can be adapted to produce images on other types of devices.

potash general name for any potassium-containing mineral, most often applied to potassium carbonate (K_2CO_3) or potassium hydroxide (KOH). Potassium carbonate, originally made by roasting plants to ashes in earthenware pots, is commercially produced from the mineral sylvite (potassium chloride, KCl) and is used mainly in making artificial fertilizers, glass, and soap.

potassium soft, waxlike, silver-white, metallic element, symbol K (Latin *kalium*), atomic number 19, atomic weight 39.0983. It is one of the ◊alkali metals and has a very low density—it floats on water, and is the second lightest metal (after lithium). It oxidizes rapidly when exposed to air and reacts violently with water. Of great abundance in the Earth's crust, it is widely distributed with other elements and found in salt and mineral deposits in the form of potassium aluminum silicates.

potato perennial plant *Solanum tuberosum*, family Solanaceae, with edible tuberous roots that are rich in starch. Used by the Andean Indians for at least 2,000 years before the Spanish Conquest, the potato was introduced to Europe by the mid-16th century, and reputedly to England by the explorer Walter Raleigh.

See also *sweet potato* under ◊yam.

potential, electric in physics, the relative electrical state of an object. A charged conductor, for example, has a higher potential than the Earth, whose potential is taken by convention to be zero. An electric ◊cell (battery) has a potential in relation to emf (◊electromotive force), which can make current flow in an external circuit. The difference in potential between two points—the potential difference—is expressed in ◊volts; that is, a 12 V battery has a potential difference of 12 volts between its negative and positive terminals.

potential energy ◊energy possessed by an object by virtue of its relative position or state (for example, as in a compressed spring). It is contrasted with kinetic energy, the form of energy possessed by moving bodies.

potentiometer in physics, an electrical resistor that can be divided so as to compare, measure, or control voltages. In radio circuits, any rotary variable resistance (such as volume control) is referred to as a potentiometer.

Potomac river in West Virginia, Virginia, and Maryland states, US, rising in the Allegheny Mountains, and flowing SE through Washington DC, into Chesapeake Bay. It is formed by the junction of the N Potomac, about 95 mi/153 km long, and S Potomac, about 130 mi/209 km long, and is itself 285 mi/459 km long.

Large ships can sail upstream as far as Washington. The Potomac is of little economic importance, but historic sites such as Mount Vernon, the home of George Washington, are on its banks.

potpourri mixture of dried flowers and leaves—for example, rose petals, lavender, and verbena—and spices, used to scent the air.

Also a medley, anthology, or random mixture.

Potter Beatrix 1866–1943. English writer and illustrator of children's books. Her first little book was *The Tale of Peter Rabbit* 1900, followed by *The Tailor of Gloucester* 1902, based on her observation of family pets and wildlife around her home from 1905 in the English Lake District. Her tales are told with a childlike wonder, devoid of sentimentality, and accompanied by delicate illustrations.

pottery and porcelain ceramics in domestic and ornamental use, including earthenware, stoneware, and *bone china* (or softpaste porcelain). Made of 5% bone ash and china clay, bone china was first made in the West in imitation of Chinese porcelain. The standard British bone china was developed about 1800, with a body of clay mixed with ox bones; a harder version, called *parian*, was developed in the 19th century and was used for figurine ornaments.

Hardpaste *porcelain* is characterized by its hardness, ringing sound when struck, translucence, and shining finish, like that of a cowrie shell (Italian *porcellana*). It is made of kaolin and petuntse (fusible feldspar consisting chiefly of silicates reduced to a fine white powder); it is high-fired at 2,552°F/1,400°C. Porcelain first evolved from stoneware in China, about the 6th century AD. A formula for making porcelain was developed in the 18th century in Germany, also in France, Italy, and Britain. It was first produced in the US in the early 19th century.

potto arboreal, nocturnal, African prosimian primate *Perodicticus potto* belonging to the ◊loris family. It has a thick body, strong limbs, and grasping feet and hands, and grows to 16 in/40 cm long, with horny spines along its backbone, which it uses in self-defense. It climbs slowly, and eats insects, snails, fruit, and leaves.

Poughkeepsie city in SE New York, US, on the Hudson River, N of New York City; population (1990) 28,900. Products include chemicals, ball bearings, and cough drops. Vassar College is here. Settled by the Dutch 1687, it was the temporary capital of New York 1717.

pound British standard monetary unit, issued as a gold sovereign before 1914, as a note 1914–83, and as a circular yellow metal-alloy coin from 1983. The pound is also the name given to the unit of currency in Egypt, Lebanon, Malta, Sudan, and Syria.

pound imperial unit (symbol lb) of mass equal to 16 ounces (7,000 grains) avoirdupois, or 12 ounces (5,760 grains) troy; the metric equivalents are 0.45 kg and 0.37 kg respectively. It derives from the Roman *libra*, which weighed 0.327 kg.

Pound Ezra 1885–1972. US poet and cultural critic. He is regarded as one of the most important figures of 20th-century literature, and his work revolutionized modern poetry. His *Personae* and *Exultations* 1909 established and promoted the principles of ◊Imagism, and influenced numerous poets, including T S ◊Eliot. His largest work was his series of *Cantos* 1925–69 (intended to number 100), a highly complex, eclectic collage, which sought to create a unifying, modern cultural tradition.

Poussin Nicolas 1594–1665. French painter. Active chiefly in Rome, he was also court painter to Louis XIII 1640–43. He was the foremost exponent of 17th-century Baroque Classicism. He painted mythological and literary scenes in a strongly Classical style; for example, *Et in Arcadia Ego* 1638–39 (Louvre, Paris).

Powell Adam Clayton, Jr 1908–1972. US political leader. A leader of New York's African American community, he was appointed to the US Congress 1944, and later became chair of the House Education and Labor Committee. Following charges of corruption, he was denied his seat in Congress 1967. Reelected 1968, he won back his seniority by a 1969 decision of the US Supreme Court.

Powell Colin (Luther) 1937– . US general, chair of the Joint Chiefs of Staff from 1989–93 and, as such, responsible for the overall administration of the Allied forces in Saudi Arabia during the ◊Gulf War 1991. A Vietnam War veteran, he first worked in government 1972 and was national security adviser 1987–89.

power in mathematics, that which is represented by an exponent or index, denoted by a superior small numeral. A number or symbol raised to the power of 2—that is, multiplied by itself—is said to be squared (for example, 3^2, x^2), and when raised to the power of 3, it is said to be cubed (for example, 2^3, y^3).

power in physics, the rate of doing work or consuming energy. It is measured in watts (joules per second) or other units of work per unit time.

PowerPC ◊microprocessor produced by ◊Motorola as the successor to its 680X0 series of microprocessors. It uses RISC technology to provide great processing speed. The PowerPC chip was used in Apple's PowerMacintosh 1994.

Powys county of central Wales, created 1974 *area* 1,961 sq mi/5,080 sq km *towns* Llandrindod Wells (administrative headquarters) *features* Brecon Beacons National Park; Black Mountains; rivers: Wye, Severn, which both rise on Plynlimon in Dyfed; Lake Vyrnwy, artificial reservoir supplying Liverpool and Birmingham; alternative technology center near Machynlleth *industries* agriculture, dairy cattle, sheep *population* (1991) 117,500 *language* English, 20% Welsh-speaking

pragmatism philosophical tradition that interprets truth in terms of the practical effects of what is believed and, in particular, the usefulness of these effects. The US philosopher Charles ◊Peirce is often accounted the founder of pragmatism; it was further advanced by William James.

Prague (Czech *Praha*) city and capital of the Czech Republic on the river Vltava; population (1991) 1,212,000. Industries include automobiles, aircraft, chemicals, paper and printing, clothing, brewing, and food processing. It was the capital of Czechoslovakia 1918–93.

Prague Spring the 1968 program of liberalization, begun under a new Communist Party leader in Czechoslovakia. In Aug 1968 Soviet tanks invaded Czechoslovakia and entered the capital Prague to put down the liberalization movement initiated by the prime minister Alexander Dubcek, who had earlier sought to assure the Soviets that his planned reforms would not threaten socialism. Dubcek was arrested but released soon afterwards. Most of the Prague Spring reforms were reversed.

Praia port and capital of the Republic of Cape Verde, on the island of São Tiago (Santiago); population (1980) 37,500. Industries include fishing and shipping.

prairie the central North American plain, formerly grass-covered, extending over most of the region between the Rocky Mountains on the W and the Great Lakes and Ohio River on the E.

prairie dog any of the North American genus *Cynomys* of burrowing rodents in the squirrel family

(Sciuridae). They grow to 12 in/30 cm, plus a short 3 in/8 cm tail. Their "towns" can contain up to several thousand individuals. Their barking cry has given them their name. Persecution by ranchers has brought most of the five species close to extinction.

praseodymium silver-white, malleable, metallic element of the ◊lanthanide series, symbol Pr, atomic number 59, relative atomic mass 140.907. It occurs in nature in the minerals monzanite and bastnasite, and its green salts cause to color glass and ceramics. It was named in 1885 by Austrian chemist Carl von Welsbach (1858–1929).

prawn any of various ◊shrimps of the suborder Natantia ("swimming"), of the crustacean order Decapoda, as contrasted with lobsters and crayfishes, which are able to "walk". Species called prawns are generally larger than species called shrimps.

Praxiteles Greek sculptor. He was active in Athens. His *Aphrodite of Cnidus* about 350 BC (known through Roman copies) is thought to have initiated the tradition of life-size free-standing female nudes in Greek sculpture.

Precambrian in geology, the time from the formation of Earth (4.6 billion years ago) up to 570 million years ago. Its boundary with the succeeding Cambrian period marks the time when animals first developed hard outer parts (exoskeletons) and so left abundant fossil remains. It comprises about 85% of geological time and is divided into two periods: the Archean, in which no life existed, and the Proterozoic, in which there was life in some form.

precession slow wobble of the Earth on its axis, like that of a spinning top. The gravitational pulls of the Sun and Moon on the Earth's equatorial bulge cause the Earth's axis to trace out a circle on the sky every 25,800 years. The position of the celestial poles (see ◊celestial sphere) is constantly changing owing to precession, as are the positions of the equinoxes (the points at which the celestial equator intersects the Sun's path around the sky). The *precession of the equinoxes* means that there is a gradual westward drift in the ecliptic—the path that the Sun appears to follow—and in the coordinates of objects on the celestial sphere.

precipitation in chemistry, the formation of an insoluble solid in a liquid as a result of a reaction within the liquid between two or more soluble substances. If the solid settles, it forms a *precipitate*; if the particles of solid are very small, they will remain in suspension, forming a *colloidal precipitate* (see ◊colloid).

predestination in Christian theology, the doctrine asserting that God has determined all events beforehand, including the ultimate salvation or damnation of the individual human soul; see ◊free will.

pregnancy in humans, the period during which an embryo grows within the womb. It begins at conception and ends at birth, and the normal length is 40 weeks. Menstruation usually stops on conception. About one in five pregnancies fails, but most of these failures occur very early on, so the woman may notice only that her period is late. After the second month, the breasts become tense and tender, and the areas round the nipples become darker. Enlargement of the uterus can be felt at about the end of the third month, and thereafter the abdomen enlarges progressively. Pregnancy in animals is called ◊gestation.

prehistory human cultures before the use of writing. A classification system, the Three Age system, was devised 1816 by Danish archeologist Christian Thomsen, based on the predominant materials used by early humans for tools and weapons: ◊Stone Age, ◊Bronze Age, ◊Iron Age.

premenstrual syndrome (PMS) see ◊premenstrual tension.

premenstrual tension (PMT) or *premenstrual syndrome* medical condition caused by hormone changes and comprising a number of physical and emotional features that occur cyclically before menstruation and disappear with its onset. Symptoms include mood changes, breast tenderness, a feeling of bloatedness, and headache.

Preminger Otto (Ludwig) 1906–1986. Austrian-born US film producer, director, and actor. He directed *Margin for Error* 1942, *Laura* 1944, *The Moon Is Blue* 1953, *The Man with the Golden Arm* 1955, *Anatomy of a Murder* 1959, *Advise and Consent* 1962, and *Rosebud* 1974. His films are characterized by an intricate technique of storytelling and a masterly use of the wide screen and the traveling camera.

Born in Vienna, Preminger went to the US 1935.

preparatory school private high school that prepares students for entrance to a college or university.

preposition in grammar, a ◊part of speech coming before a noun or a pronoun to show a location (*in*, *on*), time (*during*), or some other relationship (for example, figurative relationships in phrases like "*by* heart" or "*on* time").

Pre-Raphaelite Brotherhood (PRB) group of British painters 1848–53; Dante Gabriel Rossetti, John Everett Millais, and Holman Hunt were founding members. They aimed to paint serious subjects, to study nature closely, and to shun the influence of the styles of painters after Raphael. Their subjects were mainly biblical and literary, painted with obsessive naturalism and attention to detail. Artists associated with the group include Edward Burne-Jones and William Morris.

presbyopia vision defect, an increasing inability with advancing age to focus on near objects.

Presbyterianism system of Christian Protestant church government, expounded during the Reformation by John Calvin in Geneva, which gives its name to the established church of Scotland and is also practiced in the US, England, the Netherlands, Switzerland, and elsewhere. There is no compulsory form of worship, and each congregation is governed by presbyters or elders (clerical or lay), who are of equal rank.

Congregations are grouped in presbyteries, synods, and general assemblies.

president in government, the usual title of the head of state in a republic; the power of the office may range from diplomatic figurehead to the actual head of the government. For presidents of the US, who head the executive branch and its agencies, see ◊United States and entries by name.

Presley Elvis (Aaron) 1935–1977. US singer and guitarist. He ˙vas the most influential performer of the rock-and-roll era. With his recordings for Sun Records in Memphis, Tennessee, 1954–55 and early hits such as "Heartbreak Hotel", "Hound Dog", and "Love Me Tender", all 1956, he created an individual vocal style,

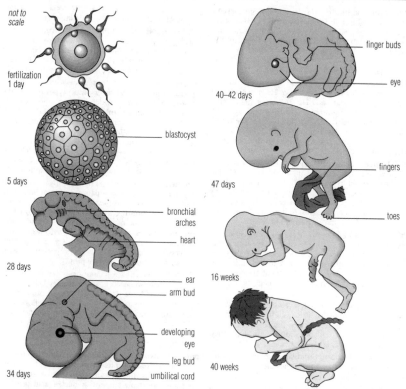

not to
scale

fertilization
1 day

blastocyst

5 days

bronchial
arches

heart

28 days

ear
arm bud

developing
eye

leg bud

34 days

umbilical cord

finger buds

eye

40–42 days

fingers

47 days

toes

16 weeks

40 weeks

pregnancy The development of a human embryo. Division of the fertilized egg, or ovum, begins within hours of conception. Within a week a ball of cells—a blastocyst—has developed. After the third week, the embryo has changed from a mass of cells into a recognizable shape. At four weeks, the embryo is 0.1 in/3 mm long, with a large bulge for the heart and small pits for the ears. At six weeks, the embryo is 0.6 in/1.5 cm with a pulsating heart and ear flaps. At the eighth week, the embryo is 1 in/2.5 cm long and recognizably human, with eyelids, small fingers, and toes. From the end of the second month, the embryo is almost fully formed and further development is mainly by growth. After this stage, the embryo is termed a fetus.

influenced by Southern blues, gospel music, country music, and rhythm and blues. His records continued to sell in their millions into the 1990s.

Presley was born in Tupelo, Mississippi. In addition to selling millions of records, Presley acted in 33 motion pictures. He died at Graceland, his mansion in Memphis, 1977, the victim of drug dependence.

pressure in physics, the force acting normally (at right angles) to a body per unit surface area. The SI unit of pressure is the pascal (newton per square meter), equal to 0.01 millibars. In a fluid (liquid or gas), pressure increases with depth. At the edge of Earth's atmosphere, pressure is zero, whereas at sea level atmospheric pressure due to the weight of the air above is about 100 kilopascals (1,013 millibars or 1 atmosphere). Pressure is commonly measured by means of a ◊barometer, manometer, or ◊Bourdon gauge.

pressure group or *interest group* or *lobby* association that puts pressure on governments, businesses, or parties to ensure laws and treatment favorable to its own interest. Pressure groups have played an increasingly

prominent role in contemporary Western democracies. In general they fall into two types: groups concerned with a single issue, such as nuclear disarmament, and groups attempting to promote their own interest, such as oil producers.

Pretoria administrative capital of the Union of South Africa from 1910 and capital of Transvaal province from 1860; population (1985) 741,300. Industries include engineering, chemicals, iron, and steel. Founded 1855, it was named for Boer leader Andries Pretorius (1799–1853).

Previn André (George) 1929– . German-born US conductor and composer. He was principal conductor of the London Symphony Orchestra 1968–79 and was appointed music director of Britain's Royal Philharmonic Orchestra 1985 (a post he relinquished the following year, staying on as principal conductor until 1991). He was also principal conductor of the Los Angeles Philharmonic 1986–89 and is now a guest conductor of many orchestras in Europe and the US.

Price Leontyne 1927– . US opera singer. She played a leading singing role in Ira Gershwin's revival of his musical *Porgy and Bess* 1952–54. Gaining a national reputation, she made her operatic debut in San Francisco 1957. She appeared at La Scala in Milan 1959 and became a regular member of the Metropolitan Opera in New York 1961.

Price Vincent 1911– . US actor who made his film debut in 1938 after a stage career. He is remembered for *Laura* 1944 and *Leave Her To Heaven* 1945 before becoming a star of horror films, including *Dragonwick* 1946, *House of Wax* 1953, the cult favorite *The Tingler* 1959, *The Fall of the House of Usher* 1960, and five more Roger Corman "campy" horrors through 1964. He is noted for hosting TV's *Mystery* series.

prickly pear cactus of the genus *Opuntia*, native to Central and South America, mainly Mexico and Chile, but naturalized in S Europe, N Africa, and Australia, where it is a pest. The common prickly pear *O. vulgaris* is low-growing, with flat, oval, stem joints, bright yellow flowers, and prickly, oval fruit; the flesh and seeds of the peeled fruit have a pleasant taste.

Priestley J(ohn) B(oynton) 1894–1984. English novelist, playwright, and critic. His first success was a novel about traveling theater, *The Good Companions* 1929. He followed it with a realist novel about London life, *Angel Pavement* 1930. As a playwright he was often preoccupied with theories of time, as in *An Inspector Calls* 1945.

primary in presidential election campaigns in the US, a statewide election to decide the candidates for the two main parties. Held in 35 states, primaries begin with New Hampshire in Feb and continue until June; they operate under varying complex rules.

primary sexual characteristic the endocrine gland producing maleness and femaleness. In males it is the testis and in females the ovary.

primate in zoology, any member of the order of mammals that includes monkeys, apes, and humans (together called **anthropoids**), as well as lemurs, bushbabies, lorises, and tarsiers (together called **prosimians**). Generally, they have forward-directed eyes, gripping hands and feet, opposable thumbs, and big toes. They tend to have nails rather than claws, with gripping pads on the ends of the digits, all adaptations to the arboreal, climbing mode of life.

prime number number that can be divided only by 1 or itself, that is, having no other factors. There is an infinite number of primes, the first ten of which are 2, 3, 5, 7, 11, 13, 17, 19, 23, and 29 (by definition, the number 1 is excluded from the set of prime numbers). The number 2 is the only even prime because all other even numbers have 2 as a factor.

primrose any plant of the genus *Primula*, family Primulaceae, with showy five-lobed flowers. The common primrose *P. vulgaris* is a woodland plant, native to Europe, bearing pale yellow flowers in spring. Related to it is the cowslip.

Prince Edward Island province of E Canada *area* 2,200 sq mi/5,700 sq km *capital* Charlottetown *features* Prince Edward Island National Park; Summerside Lobster Carnival *industries* potatoes, dairy products, lobsters, oysters, farm vehicles *population* (1991) 129,900 *history* first recorded visit by Cartier 1534, who called it Isle St-Jean; settled by French; taken by British 1758; annexed to Nova Scotia 1763; separate colony 1769; renamed for Prince Edward of Kent, father of Queen Victoria 1798; settled by Scottish 1803; joined Confederation 1873.

printed circuit board (PCB) electrical circuit created by laying (printing) "tracks" of a conductor such as copper on one or both sides of an insulating board. The PCB was invented in 1936 by Austrian scientist Paul Eisler, and was first used on a large scale in 1948.

printer in computing, an output device for producing printed copies of text or graphics. Types include the ◊*daisywheel printer*, which produces good-quality text but no graphics; the ◊*dot matrix printer*, which produces text and graphics by printing a pattern of small dots; the ◊*ink-jet printer*, which creates text and graphics by spraying a fine jet of quick-drying ink onto the paper; and the ◊*laser printer*, which uses electrostatic technology very similar to that used by a photocopier to produce high-quality text and graphics.

printing reproduction of text or illustrative material on paper, as in books or newspapers, or on an increasing variety of materials; for example, on plastic containers. The first printing used woodblocks, followed by carved wood type or molded metal type and hand-operated presses. Modern printing is effected by electronically controlled machinery. Current printing processes include electronic phototypesetting with ◊offset printing, and ◊gravure print.

printmaking creating a picture or design by printing from a plate (woodblock, stone, or metal sheet) that holds ink or color. The oldest form of print is the woodcut, common in medieval Europe, followed by line ◊engraving (from the 15th century), and ◊etching (from the 17th century); colored woodblock prints flourished in Japan from the 18th century.

◊Lithography was invented 1796.

prion (acronym for *proteinaceous infectious particle*) exceptionally small microorganism, a hundred times smaller than a virus. Composed of protein, and without any detectable amount of nucleic acid (genetic material), it is thought to cause diseases such as scrapie in sheep, and certain degenerative diseases of the nervous system in humans. How it can operate without nucleic acid is not yet known.

Researchers at the University of California 1982 first identified prions in living tissue.

prism in optics, a triangular block of transparent material (plastic, glass, silica) commonly used to "bend" a ray of light or split a beam into its spectral colors. Prisms are used as mirrors to define the optical path in binoculars, camera viewfinders, and periscopes. The dispersive property of prisms is used in the spectroscope.

prison place of confinement for those accused of and/or convicted of contravening the law; after conviction most jurisdictions claim to aim at rehabilitation and deterrence as well as punishment. For major crimes, life imprisonment or death may be the sentence. Parole and probation programs exist, and "work-release" furlough programs allow convicts to work outside the prison or make family visits during their sentences.

private enterprise sector of the economy in which economic activity is initiated through private capital and pursued for private profit. It is distinguished from ◊public spending, although public funds are often funneled into private enterprises, as with defense contractors or infrastructure development (public works contractors).

private sector the part of the economy that is owned and controlled by private individuals and business organizations such as private and public limited companies. In a free market economy, the private sector is responsible for allocating most of the resources within the economy. This contrasts with the ◊public sector where economic resources are owned and controlled by the state.

privatization policy or process of selling or transferring state-owned or public assets and services (notably nationalized industries) to private investors. Privatization of services involves the government contracting private firms to supply services previously supplied by public authorities.

The trend has grown worldwide, since inefficient state-run enterprises with little accountability required ever-larger subsidies. Governments in the US, the UK, France, Japan, and Italy have pursued the policy, as have a number of developing states that seek to stimulate economic activity. Poland and other East European states are moving away from the Communist system of state-run enterprises toward a free-market economy.

privet any evergreen shrub of the genus *Ligustrum* of the olive family Oleaceae, with dark green leaves, including the European common privet *L. vulgare*, with white flowers and black berries, naturalized in North America, and the native North American California privet *L. ovalifolium*, also known as hedge privet.

Privy Council council composed originally of the chief royal officials of the Norman kings in Britain; under the Tudors and early Stuarts it became the chief governing body. It was replaced from 1688 by the ◊cabinet, originally a committee of the council, and the council itself now retains only formal powers in issuing royal proclamations and orders in council. Cabinet ministers are automatically members, and it is presided over by the Lord President of the Council.

probability likelihood, or chance, that an event will occur, often expressed as odds, or in mathematics, numerically as a fraction or decimal.

In general, the probability that *n* particular events will happen out of a total of *m* possible events is n/m. A certainty has a probability of 1; an impossibility has a probability of 0. Empirical probability is defined as the number of successful events divided by the total possible number of events.

probate system for the administration of inheritance. Generally the function of probate (sometimes surrogate's) courts, probate determines the validity of wills, and the satisfaction of requirements of inheritance law. In the cases of persons dying without wills (intestacy), probate courts appoint administrators of estates.

probation in law, the placing of offenders under supervision of probation officers in the community, as an alternative to prison.

procedural programming programming in which programs are written as lists of instructions for the computer to obey in sequence. It closely matches the computer's own sequential operation.

procedure in computing, a small part of a computer program, which performs a specific task, such as clearing the screen or sorting a file. In some programming languages there is an overlap between procedures, ◊functions, and subroutines. Careful use of procedures is an element of ◊structured programming. A

procedural language, such as BASIC, is one in which the programmer describes a task in terms of how it is to be done, as opposed to a declarative language, such as PROLOG, in which it is described in terms of the required result. See ◊programming.

process control automatic computerized control of a manufacturing process, such as glassmaking. The computer receives ◊feedback information from sensors about the performance of the machines involved, and compares this with ideal performance data stored in its control program. It then outputs instructions to adjust automatically the machines' settings.

processing cycle in computing, the sequence of steps performed repeatedly by a computer in the execution of a program.

processor in computing, another name for the ◊central processing unit or ◊microprocessor of a computer.

Procyon or *Alpha Canis Minoris* brightest star in the constellation Canis Minor and the eighth brightest star in the sky. Procyon is a white star 11.4 light-years from Earth, with a mass of 1.7 Suns. It has a ◊white dwarf companion that orbits it every 40 years.

producer price index (PPI) measure of price changes. In 1978 the US government revised its reporting of wholesale price indexes to reflect separate price changes at three stages of the production process. Crude materials, intermediate goods, and finished goods were indexed separately, and each of these is a PPI. The finished goods index, the most cited PPI, and the consumer price index are the two most common measures of inflation and cost of living.

productivity in economics, the output produced by a given quantity of labor, usually measured as output per person employed in the firm, industry, sector, or economy concerned. Productivity is determined by the quality and quantity of the fixed ◊capital used by labor, and the effort of the workers concerned.

profit-sharing system whereby an employer pays workers a share of the company's profits, which is often a percentage based on annual salary and invested by the employer in a retirement plan operated or overseen by the employer. It may be paid as cash or shares of stock in the firm. It originated in France in the early 19th century and was widely practiced for a time within the cooperative movement.

progesterone ◊steroid hormone that occurs in vertebrates. In mammals, it regulates the menstrual cycle and pregnancy. Progesterone is secreted by the corpus luteum (the ruptured Graafian follicle of a discharged ovum).

program in computing, a set of instructions that controls the operation of a computer. There are two main kinds. applications programs, which carry out tasks for the benefit of the user—for example, word processing; and ◊systems programs, which control the internal workings of the computer. A ◊utility program is a systems program that carries out specific tasks for the user. Programs can be written in any of a number of ◊programming languages but are always translated into machine code before they can be executed by the computer.

program loop part of a computer program that is repeated several times. The loop may be repeated a fixed number of times (*counter-controlled loop*) or until a certain condition is satisfied (*condition-controlled loop*). For example, a counter-controlled loop might be used to repeat an input routine until exactly ten numbers have been input; a condition-controlled loop might be used to repeat an input routine until the data terminator "XXX" is entered.

programmer job classification for computer personnel. Programmers write the software needed for any new computer system or application.

programming writing instructions in a programming language for the control of a computer. *Applications programming* is for end-user programs, such as accounts programs or word-processing packages. *Systems programming* is for operating systems and the like, which are concerned more with the internal workings of the computer.

programming language in computing, a special notation in which instructions for controlling a computer are written. Programming languages may be classified as high-level languages or low-level languages. See also ◊source language.

program trading in finance, buying and selling a group of shares using a computer program to generate orders automatically whenever there is an appreciable movement in prices.

progression sequence of numbers each occurring in a specific relationship to its predecessor. An *arithmetic progression* has numbers that increase or decrease by a common sum or difference (for example, 2, 4, 6, 8); a *geometric progression* has numbers each bearing a fixed ratio to its predecessor (for example, 3, 6, 12, 24); and a *harmonic progression* has numbers whose reciprocals are in arithmetical progression, for example 1, ¾, ½, ¼.

Prohibition in US history, the period 1920–33 when the 18th Amendment to the US Constitution was in force, and the manufacture, transportation, and sale of intoxicating liquors were illegal. It represented the culmination of a long campaign by Populists, Progressives, temperance societies, and the Anti-Saloon League. This led to ◊bootlegging (the illegal distribution of liquor, often illicitly distilled), widespread disdain for the law, speakeasies, and greatly increased organized crime activity, especially in Chicago and towns near the Canadian border. Public opinion insisted on repeal 1933.

prokaryote in biology, an organism whose cells lack organelles (specialized segregated structures such as nuclei, mitochondria, and chloroplasts). Prokaryote DNA is not arranged in chromosomes but forms a coiled structure called a *nucleoid*. The prokaryotes comprise only the *bacteria* and *cyanobacteria* (see ◊blue-green algae); all other organisms are eukaryotes.

Prokofiev Sergey (Sergeyevich) 1891–1953. Soviet composer. His music includes operas such as *The Love for Three Oranges* 1921; ballets for Sergei Diaghilev, including *Romeo and Juliet* 1935; seven symphonies including the *Classical Symphony* 1916–17; music for film, including Eisenstein's *Alexander Nevsky* 1938; piano and violin concertos; songs and cantatas (for example, that composed for the 30th anniversary of the October Revolution); and *Peter and the Wolf* 1936 for children, to his own libretto after a Russian folk tale.

PROM (acronym for *programmable read-only memory*) in computing, a memory device in the form of an integrated circuit (chip) that can be programmed after manufacture to hold information permanently. PROM chips are empty of information when manufactured, unlike ROM (read-only memory) chips, which have information built into them. Other memory devices are EPROM (erasable programmable read-only memory) and ◊RAM (random-access memory).

Prohibition Detroit police inspecting illegal brewing equipment during Prohibition in the US. Despite a relentless campaign by the police and over 300,000 convictions, illegal drinking—and the organized crime that accompanied it—flourished during Prohibition. Some states and counties still maintain full or partial prohibition.

Prometheus in Greek mythology, a ◊Titan who stole fire from heaven for the human race. In revenge, Zeus had him chained to a rock where an eagle came each day to feast on his liver, which grew back each night, until he was rescued by the hero ◊Heracles.

promethium radioactive, metallic element of the ◊lanthanide series, symbol Pm, atomic number 61, relative atomic mass 145.

It occurs in nature only in minute amounts, produced as a fission product/by-product of uranium in ◊pitchblende and other uranium ores; for a long time it was considered not to occur in nature. The longest-lived isotope has a half-life of slightly more than 20 years.

It was named in 1949 after the Greek Titan Prometheus by G M Coryell for the element isolated by US physicists J A Marinsky and L E Glendenin.

prompt symbol displayed on a screen indicating that the computer is ready for input. The symbol used will vary from system to system and application to application. The current cursor position is normally next to the prompt. Generally prompts only appear in command line interfaces.

pronghorn ruminant mammal *Antilocapra americana* constituting the family Antilocapridae, native to the W US. It is light brown and about 3 ft/1 m high. It sheds its horns annually and can reach speeds of 60 mph/100 kph. The loss of prairies to agriculture, combined with excessive hunting, has brought this unique animal close to extinction.

pronghorn *The pronghorn is unique in that it sheds annually the sheaths that cover the horns. The sheath, more prominent in the male pronghorn, appears to form part of the horn itself.*

pronoun in grammar, a part of speech that is used in place of a noun, usually to save repetition of the noun. For example: "The people arrived around nine o'clock". "They" behaved as though we were expecting "them". Here, "they" and "them" are substitutes for repeating "the people".

proof spirit numerical scale used to indicate the alcohol content of an alcoholic drink. Proof spirit (or 100% proof spirit) acquired its name from a solution of alcohol in water which, when used to moisten gunpowder, contained just enough alcohol to permit it to burn.

In practice the proof scale is related to the alcohol content by a factor of two. Whiskey containing 40% alcohol, by volume, is 80 degrees proof. The UK uses a different scale; the same whiskey would be 70 degrees proof on the UK scale.

propaganda systematic spreading (propagation) of information or disinformation, usually to promote a religious or political doctrine with the intention of instilling particular attitudes or responses. As a system of disseminating information it was considered a legitimate instrument of government, but became notorious through the deliberate distortion of facts or the publication of falsehoods by totalitarian regimes, notably Nazi Germany.

propane C_3H_8 gaseous hydrocarbon of the ◊alkane series, found in petroleum and used as fuel.

propanone CH_3COCH_3 (common name *acetone*) colorless flammable liquid used extensively as a solvent, as in nail-varnish remover. It boils at 133.7°F/56.5°C, mixes with water in all proportions, and has a characteristic odor.

propellant substance burned in a rocket for propulsion. Two propellants are used: oxidizer and fuel are stored in separate tanks and pumped independently into the combustion chamber. Liquid oxygen (oxidizer) and liquid hydrogen (fuel) are common propellants, used, for example, in the space-shuttle main engines. The explosive charge that propels a projectile from a gun is also called a propellant.

propeller screwlike device used to propel some ships and airplanes. A propeller has a number of curved blades that describe a helical path as they rotate with the hub, and accelerate fluid (liquid or gas) backward during rotation. Reaction to this backward movement of fluid sets up a propulsive thrust forward. The marine screw propeller was developed by Francis Pettit Smith in the UK and Swedish-born John Ericson in the US and was first used 1839.

property the right to title and to control the use of a thing (such as land, a building, a work of art, or a computer program). In US law, a distinction is made between real property, which involves a degree of geographical fixity, and personal property, which does not.

Property is never absolute, since any society places limits on an individual's property (such as the right to transfer that property to another). Different societies have held widely varying interpretations of the nature of property and the extent of the rights of the owner to that property.

prophet person thought to speak from divine inspiration or one who foretells the future. In the Bible, the chief prophets were Elijah, Amos, Hosea, and Isaiah. In Islam, ◊Mohammed is believed to be the last and greatest of a long line of prophets beginning with Adam and including Moses and Jesus.

prophylaxis any measure taken to prevent disease, including exercise and vaccination. Prophylactic (preventive) medicine is an aspect of public-health provision that is receiving increasing attention.

prose spoken or written language without metrical regularity; in literature, prose corresponds more closely to the patterns of everyday speech than ◊poetry.

Proserpina in Roman mythology, the goddess of the underworld. Her Greek equivalent is ◊Persephone.

Prost Alain 1955– . French race-car driver who was world champion 1985, 1986, 1989, and 1993, and the first French world drivers' champion. To the end of the 1993 season he had won 51 Grand Prix from 199 starts. He retired 1993.

prostaglandin any of a group of complex fatty acids present in the body that act as messenger substances between cells. Effects include stimulating the contraction of smooth muscle (for example, of the womb during birth), regulating the production of stomach acid, and modifying hormonal activity. In excess, prostaglandins may produce inflammatory disorders such as arthritis. Synthetic prostaglandins are used to induce labor in humans and domestic animals.

prostatectomy surgical removal of the ◊prostate gland. In many men over the age of 60 the prostate gland enlarges, causing obstruction to the urethra. This causes the bladder to swell with retained urine, leaving the sufferer more prone to infection of the urinary tract.

prostate gland gland surrounding and opening into the urethra at the base of the bladder in male mammals.

prosthesis artificial device used to substitute for a body part which is defective or missing. Prostheses include artificial limbs, hearing aids, false teeth and eyes, heart ◊pacemakers and plastic heart valves and blood vessels.

prostitution receipt of money for sexual acts. Society's attitude toward prostitution varies according to place and period. In some countries, tolerance is combined with licensing of brothels and health checks of the prostitutes (both male and female).

protactinium silver–gray, radioactive, metallic element of the ◊actinide series, symbol Pa, atomic number 91, relative atomic mass 231.036. It occurs in nature in very small quantities, in ◊pitchblende and other uranium ores. It has 14 known isotopes; the longest-lived, Pa-231, has a half-life of 32,480 years.

protectionism in economics, the imposition of heavy duties. or import quotas by a government as a means of discouraging the import of foreign goods likely to compete with domestic products. Price controls, quota systems, and the reduction of surpluses are among the measures taken for agricultural products in the European Union. The opposite practice is ◊free trade.

protectorate formerly in international law, a small state under the direct or indirect control of a larger one. The 20th-century equivalent was a trust territory. In English history the rule of Oliver and Richard ◊Cromwell 1653–59 is referred to as *the Protectorate*.

pro tem abbreviation for *pro tempore* (Latin "for the time being").

Proterozoic eon of geological time, possible 3.5 trillion to 570 million years ago, the second division of the Precambrian. It is defined as the time of simple life, since many rocks dating from this eon show traces of biological activity, and some contain the fossils of bacteria and algae.

Protestantism one of the main divisions of Christianity, which emerged from Roman Catholicism at the ◊Reformation. The chief Protestant denominations are the Episcopalian (Anglican Communion in the UK), Baptists, Christian Scientists, Congregationalists (United Church of Christ), Lutherans, Methodists, Pentecostals, and Presbyterians, with a total membership in about 300 million.

protist in biology, a single-celled organism which has a eukaryotic cell, but which is not member of the plant, fungal, or animal kingdoms. The main protists are ◊protozoa.

proton positively charged ◊elementary particle, a constituent of the nucleus of all atoms. It belongs to the ◊baryon group of ◊hadrons and is composed of two up quarks and one down quark. A proton is extremely long-lived, with a life span of at least 10^{32} years. It carries a unit positive charge equal to the negative charge of an ◊electron. Its mass is almost 1,836 times that of an electron, or 1.673×10^{-24} g. The number of protons in the atom of an ◊element is equal to the atomic number of that element.

protoplasm contents of a living cell. Strictly speaking it includes all the discrete structures (organelles) in a cell, but it is often used simply to mean the jellylike material in which these float. The contents of a cell outside the nucleus are called ◊cytoplasm.

protozoan any of a group of single-celled, mainly heterotrophic organisms without rigid cell walls. Some, such as amebas, ingest other cells, but most are saprotrophs or parasites. They all require a fluid environment, and include ciliates, flagellates, rhizopods, and sporozoans.

Proust Marcel 1871–1922. French novelist and critic. His immense autobiographical work *A la Recherche du temps perdu/Remembrance of Things Past* 1913–27, consisting of a series of novels, is the expression of his childhood memories coaxed from his subconscious; it is also a precise reflection of life in France at the end of the 19th century.

Provence-Alpes-Côte d'Azur region of SE France, comprising the *départements* of Alpes-de-Haute-Provence, Hautes-Alpes, Alpes-Maritimes, Bouches-du-Rhône, Var, and Vaucluse; area 12,120 sq mi/31,400 sq km; capital Marseille; population (1986) 4,059,000. The *Côte d'Azur*, on the Mediterranean, is a tourist center. Provence was an independent kingdom in the 10th century, and the area still has its own language, Provençal.

Providence industrial seaport (jewelry, silverware, textiles and textile machinery, watches, chemicals, meat-packing) and capital of Rhode Island, on Narragansett Bay and the Providence River, 27 mi/43 km from the Atlantic Ocean; population (1990) 160,700.

Providence was founded 1636 by Roger Williams, who had been banished from Plymouth colony for his religious beliefs. By the early 18th century the community was thriving as a port for West Indian trade. It was an important base for American and French troops in the American Revolution.

Provo city in N central Utah, US, on the Provo River, SE of Salt Lake City; seat of Utah County; population (1990) 86,800. Industries include iron and steel, food processing, and electronics. Brigham Young University is here.

Prozac or *fluoxetine* antidepressant drug that functions mainly by boosting levels of the neurotransmitter serotonin in the brain. Side effects include nausea and loss of libido.

Prussia N German state 1618–1945 on the Baltic coast. It was an independent kingdom until 1867, when it became, under Otto von ◊Bismarck, the military power of the North German Confederation and part of the German Empire 1871 under the Prussian king Wilhelm I. West Prussia became part of Poland under the Treaty of ◊Versailles, and East Prussia was largely incorporated into the USSR after 1945.

Prut river that rises in the Carpathian Mountains of SW Ukraine, and flows 565 mi/900 km to meet the Danube at Reni. For part of its course it follows the eastern frontier of Romania.

pseudocarp in botany, a fruitlike structure that incorporates tissue that is not derived from the ovary wall. The additional tissues may be derived from floral parts such as the receptacle and ◊calyx. For example, the colored, fleshy part of a strawberry develops from the receptacle and the true fruits are small achenes—the "pips" embedded in its outer surface. Rose hips are a type of pseudocarp that consists of a hollow, fleshy receptacle containing a number of achenes within. Different types of pseudocarp include pineapples, figs, apples, and pears.

Psilocybe genus of mushroom with hallucinogenic properties, including the Mexican sacred mushroom *P. mexicana*, which contains compounds with effects similar to LSD (lysergic acid diethylamide, a hallucinogen). A related species *P. semilanceata* is found in N Europe.

psoriasis chronic, recurring skin disease characterized by raised, red, scaly patches, on the scalp, elbows, knees, and elsewhere. Tar preparations, steroid creams, and ultraviolet light are used to treat it, and sometimes it disappears spontaneously. Psoriasis may be accompanied by a form of arthritis (inflammation of the joints).

Psyche late Greek personification of the soul as a winged girl or young woman. The goddess Aphrodite was so jealous of Psyche's beauty that she ordered her son Eros, the god of love, to make Psyche fall in love with the worst of men. Instead, he fell in love with her himself.

psychedelic drug any drug that produces hallucinations or altered states of consciousness. Such sensory experiences may be in the auditory, visual, tactile, olfactory, or gustatory fields or in any combination. Among drugs known to have psychedelic effects are LSD (lysergic acid diethylamide), mescaline, and, to a mild degree, marijuana, along with a number of other plant-derived or synthetically prepared substances. Most of these drugs are known to cause temporary or recurring psychotic episodes.

psychiatry branch of medicine dealing with the diagnosis and treatment of mental disorder, normally divided into the areas of *neurotic conditions*, including anxiety, depression, and hysteria and *psychotic disorders* such as schizophrenia. Psychiatric treatment consists of drugs, analysis, or electroconvulsive therapy.

psychoanalysis theory and treatment method for neuroses, developed by Sigmund ◊Freud. The main treatment method involves the free association of ideas, and their interpretation by patient and analyst. It is typically prolonged.

psychology systematic study of human and animal behavior. The first psychology laboratory was founded 1879 by Wilhelm Wundt at Leipzig, Germany. The subject includes diverse areas of study and application, among them the roles of instinct, heredity, environment, and culture; the processes of sensation, perception, learning, and memory; the bases of motivation and emotion; and the functioning of thought, intelligence, and language. Significant psychologists have included Gustav Fechner, founder of psychophysics; Wolfgang Köhler, one of the gestalt or

"whole" psychologists; Sigmund Freud and his associates Carl Jung, Alfred Adler, and Hermann Rorschach (1884–1922); William James, Jean Piaget; Carl Rogers; Hans Eysenck; J B Watson; and B F Skinner.

psychosis or *psychotic disorder* general term for a serious mental disorder where the individual commonly loses contact with reality and may experience hallucinations (seeing or hearing things that do not exist) or delusions (fixed false beliefs). For example, in a paranoid psychosis, an individual may believe that others are plotting against him or her. A major type of psychosis is ◊schizophrenia.

psychosomatic of a physical symptom or disease thought to arise from emotional or mental factors.

psychotherapy psychological treatment for mental disorder, rather than physical treatments, such as ◊electroconvulsive therapy (ECT) or drugs. An example is ◊psychoanalysis.

pt symbol for ◊*pint*.

ptarmigan any of a genus *Lagopus* of hardy, northern ground-dwelling birds (family Phasianidae, which also includes ◊grouse), with feathered legs and feet.

pteridophyte simple type of vascular plant. The pteridophytes comprise four classes: the Psilosida, including the most primitive vascular plants, found mainly in the tropics; the Lycopsida, including the club mosses; the Sphenopsida, including the horsetails; and the Pteropsida, including the ferns. They do not produce seeds.

pterodactyl genus of ◊pterosaur.

pterosaur extinct flying reptile of the order Pterosauria, existing in the Mesozoic age. They ranged from starling size to a 40 ft/12 m wingspan. Some had horns on their heads that, when in flight, made a whistling to roaring sound.

Ptolemy (Claudius Ptolemaeus) *c.* 100–AD 170. Egyptian astronomer and geographer who worked in Alexandria. His *Almagest* developed the theory that Earth is the center of the universe, with the Sun, Moon, and stars revolving around it. In 1543 the Polish astronomer ◊Copernicus proposed an alternative to the *Ptolemaic system*. Ptolemy's *Geography* was a standard source of information until the 16th century.

ptomaine any of a group of toxic chemical substances (alkaloids) produced as a result of decomposition by bacterial action on proteins.

Ptomaine is not the relevant factor in "food poisoning", which is usually caused by bacteria of the genus *Salmonella*.

puberty stage in human development when the individual becomes sexually mature. It may occur from the age of ten upward. The sexual organs take on their adult form and pubic hair grows. In girls, menstruation begins, and the breasts develop; in boys, the voice breaks and becomes deeper, and facial hair develops.

public school in the US and many English-speaking countries, "public" schools are maintained by the state, and "private" schools are independent institutions, supported by fees. In England, the term "public school" denotes a private fee-paying school.

public sector part of the economy that is owned and controlled by the state, namely central government, local government, and government enterprises. In a command economy, the public sector allocates most of the resources in the economy. The opposite of the public sector is the ◊private sector, where resources are allocated by private individuals and business organizations.

public spending expenditure by government, covering the military, health, education, infrastructure, development projects, and the cost of servicing overseas borrowing.

Puccini Giacomo (Antonio Domenico Michele Secondo Maria) 1858–1924. Italian opera composer. His music shows a strong gift for melody and dramatic effect and his operas combine exotic plots with elements of *verismo* (realism). They include *Manon Lescaut* 1893, *La Bohème* 1896, *Tosca* 1900, *Madame Butterfly* 1904, and the unfinished *Turandot* 1926.

Puebla (de Zaragoza) industrial city (textiles, sugar refining, metallurgy, hand-crafted pottery and tiles) and capital of Puebla state, S central Mexico; population (1986) 1,218,000. Founded 1535 as *Pueblo de los Angeles*, it was later renamed for General de Zaragoza, who defeated the French here 1862.

Pueblo city in S central Colorado, US, on the Arkansas River, SE of Colorado Springs; population (1990) 98,600. Industries include steel, coal, lumber, and livestock and other agricultural products.

Pueblo Indian generic name for a member of any of the farming groups of the SW US and N Mexico, living in communal villages of flat-topped adobe or stone structures arranged in terraces. Surviving groups include the Hopi and the Zuni.

Puerto Rico the Commonwealth of, island of the West Indies (known as Porto Rico 1898–1932) *area* 3,475 sq mi/9,000 sq km *capital* San Juan *cities* ports: Mayagüez, Ponce *features* Old San Juan; nightclubs and casinos; rain forest of El Yunque; colonial-style San German; Arecibo Observatory *industries* apparel, textiles, pharmaceuticals, petroleum products, rum, refined sugar, coffee, computers, instruments, office machines, cattle, hogs, milk, cement *currency* US dollar *population* (1990) 3,522,000 *languages* Spanish and English (official) *religion* Roman Catholic *government* under the constitution of 1952, similar to that of the US, with a governor elected for four years and a legislative assembly with a senate and house of representatives *famous people* Roberto Clemente, José Ferrer, Eugenio María de Hostos, Raul Julia, Rita Moreno, Luís Muñoz Marín *history* visited 1493 by Columbus; annexed by Spain 1509; ceded to the US after the ◊Spanish-American War 1898; achieved commonwealth status with local self-government 1952.

Pulitzer Prize for Fiction (American)

1917	no award	1958	James Agee *A Death in the Family*
1918	Ernest Poole *His Family*	1959	Robert Lewis Taylor *The Travels of Jamie McPheeters*
1919	Booth Tarkington *The Magnificent Ambersons*		
1920	no award	1960	Allen Drury *Advise and Consent*
1921	Edith Wharton *The Age of Innocence*	1961	Harper Lee *To Kill a Mockingbird*
1922	Booth Tarkington *Alice Adams*	1962	Edwin O'Connor *The Edge of Sadness*
1923	Willa Cather *One of Ours*	1963	William Faulkner *The Reivers*
1924	Margaret Wilson *The Able McLaughlins*	1964	no award
1925	Edna Ferber *So Big*	1965	Shirley Ann Grau *The Keepers of the House*
1926	Sinclair Lewis *Arrowsmith*	1966	Katherine Anne Porter *The Collected Stories of Katherine Anne Porter*
1927	Louis Bromfield *Early Autumn*		
1928	Thornton Wilder *The Bridge at San Luis Rey*	1967	Bernard Malamud *The Fixer*
1929	Julia Peterkin *Scarlet Sister Mary*	1968	William Styron *The Confessions of Nat Turner*
1930	Oliver LaFarge *Laughing Boy*	1969	N Scott Momaday *House Made of Dawn*
1931	Margaret Ayer Barnes *Years of Grace*	1970	Jean Stafford *Collected Stories*
1932	Pearl S Buck *The Good Earth*	1971	no award
1933	T S Stribling *The Store*	1972	Wallace Stegner *Angle of Repose*
1934	Caroline Miller *Lamb in His Bosom*	1973	Eudora Welty *The Optimist's Daughter*
1935	Josephine Winslow Johnson *Now in November*	1974	no award
1936	Harold L Davis *Honey in the Horn*	1975	Michael Shaara *The Killer Angels*
1937	Margaret Mitchell *Gone With the Wind*	1976	Saul Bellow *Humboldt's Gift*
1938	John Phillips Marquand *The Late George Apley*	1977	no award
1939	Marjorie Kinnan Rawlings *The Yearling*	1978	James Alan McPherson *Elbow Room*
1940	John Steinbeck *The Grapes of Wrath*	1979	John Cheever *The Stories of John Cheever*
1941	no award	1980	Norman Mailer *The Executioner's Song*
1942	Ellen Glasgow *In This Our Life*	1981	John Kennedy Toole *A Confederacy of Dunces*
1943	Upton Sinclair *Dragon's Teeth*	1982	John Updike *Rabbit is Rich*
1944	Martin Flavin *Journey in the Dark*	1983	Alice Walker *The Color Purple*
1945	John Hersey *A Bell for Adano*	1984	William Kennedy *Ironweed*
1946	no award	1985	Alison Lurie *Foreign Affairs*
1947	Robert Penn Warren *All the King's Men*	1986	Larry McMurtry *Lonesome Dove*
1948	James A Michener *Tales of the South Pacific*	1987	Peter Taylor *A Summons to Memphis*
1949	James Gould Cozzens *Guard of Honor*	1988	Toni Morrison *Beloved*
1950	A B Guthrie Jr, *The Way West*	1989	Anne Tyler *Breathing Lessons*
1951	Conrad Richter *The Town*	1990	Oscar Hijuelos *The Mambo Kings Play Songs of Love*
1952	Herman Wouk *The Caine Mutiny*		
1953	Ernest Hemingway *The Old Man and the Sea*	1991	John Updike *Rabbit at Rest*
1954	no award	1992	Jane Simley *A Thousand Acres*
1955	William Faulkner *A Fable*	1993	Robert Olen Butler *A Good Scent from a Strange Mountain*
1956	Mackinlay Kantor *Andersonville*		
1957	no award	1994	E Annie Proulx *The Shipping News*

puffball globulous fruiting body of certain fungi (see ◊fungus) that cracks with maturity, releasing the enclosed spores in the form of a brown powder; for example, the common puffball *Lycoperdon perlatum*.

puffer fish fish of the family Tetraodontidae. As a means of defense it inflates its body with air or water until it becomes spherical and the skin spines become erect. Puffer fish are mainly found in warm waters, where they feed on mollusks, crustaceans, and coral.

puffin any of various sea birds of the genus *Fratercula* of the ◊auk family, found in the N Atlantic and Pacific. The puffin is about 14 in/35 cm long, with a white face and front, red legs, and a large deep bill, very brightly colored in summer. Having short wings and webbed feet, puffins are poor fliers but excellent swimmers. They nest in rock crevices, or make burrows, and lay a single egg.

Puget Sound inlet of the Pacific Ocean on the west coast of Washington State.

P'u-i (or *Pu-Yi*) Henry 1906–1967. Last emperor of China (as Hsuan Tung) from 1908 until his deposition 1912; he was restored for a week 1917. After his deposition he chose to be called Henry. He was president 1932–34 and emperor 1934–45 of the Japanese puppet state of Manchukuo (see ◊Manchuria).

Pulaski Casimir 1747–1779. Polish patriot and military leader. Hired by Silas ◊Deane and Benjamin Franklin in their campaign to recruit for the American Revolution 1775–83, he was placed in command of the Continental cavalry 1777. He saw action at Valley Forge 1777–78 and after a dispute with General Anthony Wayne, was given an independent cavalry command. He died in action in the siege of Savannah.

pull-down menu in computing, a list of options provided as part of a graphical user interface. The presence of pull-down menus is normally indicated by a row of single words at the top of the screen. When the user points at a word with a ◊mouse, a full menu appears (is pulled down) and the user can then select the required option.

pulley simple machine consisting of a fixed, grooved wheel, sometimes in a block, around which a rope or chain can be run. A simple pulley serves only to change the direction of the applied effort (as in a simple hoist for raising loads). The use of more than one pulley results in a mechanical advantage, so that a given effort can raise a heavier load.

pulsar celestial source that emits pulses of energy at regular intervals, ranging from a few seconds to a few thousandths of a second. Pulsars are thought to be rapidly rotating ◊neutron stars, which flash at radio and other wavelengths as they spin. They were discovered in 1967 by Jocelyn Bell (now Burnell) and Antony Hewish at the Mullard Radio Astronomy Observatory, Cambridge, England. Over 500 radio pulsars are now known in our Galaxy, although a million or so may exist.

pulse crop such as peas and beans. Pulses are grown primarily for their seeds, which provide a concentrated source of vegetable protein, and make a vital contribution to human diets in poor countries where meat is scarce, and among vegetarians. Soy beans are the major temperate protein crop in the West; most are used for oil production or for animal feed. In Asia, most are processed into soy milk and beancurd. Peanuts dominate pulse production in the tropical world and are generally consumed as human food.

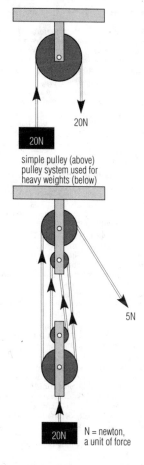

simple pulley (above)
pulley system used for
heavy weights (below)

20N

20N

20N

5N

N = newton,
a unit of force

pulley The mechanical advantage of a pulley increases with the number of rope strands. If a pulley system has four ropes supporting the load, the mechanical advantage is four, and a 5 Newton force will lift a 20 Newton load.

pulse impulse transmitted by the heartbeat throughout the arterial systems of vertebrates. When the heart muscle contracts, it forces blood into the aorta (the chief artery). Because the arteries are elastic, the sudden rise of pressure causes a throb or sudden swelling through them. The actual flow of the blood is about 2 ft/60 cm a second in humans. The average adult pulse rate is generally about 70 per minute. The pulse can be felt where an artery is near the surface, for example in the wrist or the neck.

puma also called *cougar* or *mountain lion* large wild cat *Felis concolor* found in North and South America. Tawny-coated, it is 4.5 ft/1.5 m long with a 3-ft/1-m tail. Cougars live alone, with each male occupying a distinct territory; they eat deer, rodents, and cattle. They have been hunted nearly to extinction.

pump any device for moving liquids and gases, or compressing gases.

Some pumps, such as the traditional *lift pump* used to raise water from wells, work by a reciprocating (up-and-down) action. Movement of a piston in a cylinder with a one-way valve creates a partial vacuum in the cylinder, thereby sucking water into it.

pumpkin gourd *Cucurbita pepo* of the family Cucurbitaceae. The large, spherical fruit has a thick, orange rind, pulpy flesh, and many seeds.

pun figure of speech, a play on words, or double meaning that is technically known as *paronomasia* (Greek "adapted meaning"). Double meaning can be accidental, often resulting from homonymy, or the multiple meaning of words; puns, however, are deliberate, intended as jokes or as clever and compact remarks.

punched card in computing, an early form of data storage and input, now almost obsolete. The 80-column card widely used in the 1960s and 1970s was a thin card, measuring 7.5 in x 3.33 in/190 mm x 84 mm, holding up to 80 characters of data encoded as small rectangular holes.

punctuation system of conventional signs (punctuation marks) and spaces employed to organize written and printed language in order to make it as readable, clear, and logical as possible.

The standard punctuation marks and conventions are the ◊period, comma, colon, semicolon, exclamation point, question mark, ◊apostrophe, asterisk, hyphen, and parenthesis (including dashes, brackets, and the use of parenthetical commas).

Pune formerly *Poona* city in Maharashtra, India; population (1985) 1,685,000. Products include chemicals, rice, sugar, cotton, paper, and jewelry.

Punic Wars three wars between ◊Rome and ◊Carthage: *First Punic War* 264–241 BC, resulted in the defeat of the Carthaginians under Hamilcar Barca and the cession of Sicily to Rome; *Second Punic War* 218–201 BC, Hannibal invaded Italy, defeated the Romans at Trebia, Trasimene, and at Cannae (under Fabius Maximus, but was finally defeated himself by ◊Scipio Africanus Major at Zama (now in Algeria); *Third Punic War* 149–146 BC, ended in the destruction of Carthage, and its possessions becoming the Roman province of Africa.

Punjab (Sanskrit "five rivers": the Indus tributaries Jhelum, Chenab, Ravi, Beas, and Sutlej) former state of British India, now divided between India and Pakistan. Punjab was annexed by Britain 1849 after the Sikh Wars (1845–46 and 1848–49), and formed into a province with its capital at Lahore. Under the British, W Punjab was extensively irrigated, and land was granted to Indians who had served in the British army.

Punjab state of NW India *area* 19,454 sq mi/50,400 sq km *capital* Chandigarh *towns and cities* Amritsar, Jalandhar, Faridkot, Ludhiana *features* mainly agricultural, crops chiefly under irrigation; longest life expectancy rates in India (59 for women, 64 for men); Harappa has ruins from the ◊Indus Valley civilization 2500 to 1600 BC *population* (1991) 20,190,800 *language* Punjabi *religions* 60% Sikh, 30% Hindu; there is friction between the two groups *history* in 1919 unrest led to the Punjab riots (see ◊Amritsar Massacre.

Punjab state of NE Pakistan *area* 79,263 sq mi/205,344 sq km *capital* Lahore *features* wheat cultivation (by irrigation) *population* (1981) 47,292,000 *languages* Punjabi, Urdu *religion* Muslim.

Punjab massacres in the violence occurring after the partition of India 1947, more than a million people died while relocating in the Punjab. The eastern section became an Indian state, while the western area, dominated by the Muslims, went to Pakistan. Violence occurred as Muslims fled from eastern Punjab, and Hindus and Sikhs moved from Pakistan to India.

punk movement of disaffected youth of the late 1970s, manifesting itself in fashions and music designed to shock or intimidate. *Punk rock* began in the UK and stressed aggressive performance within a three-chord, three-minute format, as exemplified by the Sex Pistols.

pupa nonfeeding, largely immobile stage of some insect life cycles, in which larval tissues are broken down, and adult tissues and structures are formed.

puppet figure manipulated on a small stage, usually by an unseen operator. The earliest known puppets are from 10th-century BC China. The types include *finger* or *glove puppets* (such as Punch); *string marionettes* (for which the composer Franz Joseph Haydn wrote his operetta *Dido* 1778); *shadow silhouettes* (operated by rods and seen on a lit screen, as in Java); and *bunraku* (devised in Osaka, Japan), in which three or four black-clad operators on stage may combine to work each puppet about 3 ft/1 m high.

In the US, Bill Baird has created more than 2,000 puppets, mainly for film and television.

Purcell Henry 1659–1695. English Baroque composer. His music balances high formality with melodic expression of controlled intensity, for example, the opera *Dido and Aeneas* 1689 and music for Dryden's *King Arthur* 1691 and for *The Fairy Queen* 1692. He wrote more than 500 works, ranging from secular operas and incidental music for plays to cantatas and church music.

purdah seclusion of women practiced by some Islamic and Hindu peoples. It had begun to disappear with the adoption of Western culture, but the fundamentalism of the 1980s revived it; for example, the wearing of the chador (an all-enveloping black mantle) in Iran.

The Koran actually requests only "modesty" in dress.

Purim Jewish festival celebrated in Feb or March (the 14th of Adar in the Jewish calendar), commemorating Esther, who saved the Jews from destruction in 473 BC during the Persian occupation.

Puritan from 1564, protestants in England and the American colonies who wished to eliminate Roman Catholic survivals in church ritual, or substitute a presbyterian for an episcopal form of church government. The term also covers the separatists who withdrew from the church altogether.

pus yellowish fluid that forms in the body as a result of bacterial infection; it includes white blood cells (leukocytes), living and dead bacteria, dead tissue, and serum. An enclosed collection of pus is called an abscess.

Pusan or *Busan* chief industrial port (textiles, rubber, salt, fishing) of South Korea; population (1985) 3,797,600. It was invaded by the Japanese 1592 and opened to foreign trade 1883.

Pushkin Aleksandr 1799–1837. Russian poet and writer. His works include the novel in verse *Eugene Onegin* 1823–31 and the tragic drama *Boris Godunov*

1825. Pushkin's range was wide, and his willingness to experiment freed later Russian writers from many of the archaic conventions of the literature of his time.

Puttnam David (Terence) 1941– . English film producer. He played a major role in reviving the British film industry internationally in the 1980s. Films include *Chariots of Fire* 1981 (Academy Award for best producer), *The Killing Fields* 1984, and *Memphis Belle* 1990. He was chairman and chief executive of Columbia Pictures 1986.

Pu-Yi alternative transliteration of the name of the last Chinese emperor, Henry ◊P'u-i.

Pygmy (sometimes *Negrillo*) member of any of several groups of small-statured, dark-skinned peoples of the rain forests of equatorial Africa. They were probably the aboriginal inhabitants of the region, before the arrival of farming peoples from elsewhere. They live nomadically in small groups, as hunter-gatherers; they also trade with other, settled people in the area.

pyramid four-sided building with triangular sides. Pyramids were used in ancient Egypt to enclose a royal tomb; for example, the Great Pyramid of Khufu/Cheops at El Gîza, near Cairo, 755 ft/230 m square and 481 ft/147 m high. The three pyramids at Gîza were considered one of the ◊Seven Wonders of the World.

Truncated pyramidal temple mounds were also built by the ancient Mexican and Peruvian civilizations, for example, at Teotihuacan and Cholula, near Mexico City, which is the world's largest in ground area (990 ft/300 m base, 195 ft/60 m high). Some New World pyramids were also used as royal tombs, for example, at the Mayan ceremonial center of Palenque.

Pyrenees (French *Pyrénées*; Spanish *Pirineos*) mountain range in SW Europe between France and Spain; length about 270 mi/435 km; highest peak Aneto (French Néthon) 11,172 ft/3,404 m. ◊Andorra is entirely within the range. Hydroelectric power has encouraged industrial development in the foothills.

pyrethrum popular name for some flowers of the genus *Chrysanthemum*, family Compositae. The ornamental species *C. coccineum*, and hybrids derived from it, are commonly grown in gardens. Pyrethrum powder, made from the dried flower heads of some species, is a powerful contact pesticide for aphids and mosquitoes.

pyridine C_5H_5N a heterocyclic compound. It is a liquid with a sickly smell and occurs in coal tar. It is soluble in water, acts as a strong ◊base, and is used as a solvent, mainly in the manufacture of plastics.

Pyrrhus *c.* 318–272 BC. King of Epirus, Greece, from 307, who invaded Italy 280, as an ally of the Tarentines against Rome. He twice defeated the Romans but with such heavy losses that a *Pyrrhic victory* has come to mean a victory not worth winning. He returned to Greece 275 after his defeat at Beneventum, and was killed in a riot in Argos.

Pythagoras *c.* 580–500 BC. Greek mathematician and philosopher who formulated the ◊Pythagorean theorem.

Pythagorean theorem in geometry, a theorem stating that in a right triangle, the square of the hypotenuse (the longest side) is equal to the sum of the squares of the other two sides (legs). If the hypotenuse is *c* units long and the lengths of the legs are *a* and *b*, then $c^2 = a^2 + b^2$.

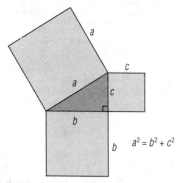

$$a^2 = b^2 + c^2$$

Pythagorean theorem *the Pythagorean theorem for right triangles is likely to have been known long before the time of Pythagoras. It was probably used by the ancient Egyptians to lay out the pyramids.*

python any constricting snake of the Old World subfamily Pythoninae of the family Boidae, which also includes ◊boas and the ◊anaconda. Pythons are found in the tropics of Africa, Asia, and Australia. Unlike boas, they lay eggs rather than produce living young. Some species are small, but the reticulated python *Python reticulatus* of SE Asia can grow to 33 ft/10 m.

Q

Qaboos bin Said 1940– . Sultan of Oman, the 14th descendant of the Albusaid family. Opposed to the conservative views of his father, he overthrew him 1970 in a bloodless coup and assumed the sultanship. Since then he has followed more liberal and expansionist policies, while maintaining his country's position of international nonalignment.

Qaddafi or *Khaddhafi* or *Gaddafi* Moamer al 1942– . Libyan revolutionary leader. Overthrowing King Idris 1969, he became virtual president of a republic, although he nominally gave up all except an ideological role 1974. He favors territorial expansion in N Africa reaching as far as Zaire, has supported rebels in Chad, and has proposed mergers with a number of countries. In 1986 US planes bombed his headquarters in a reprisal for alleged terrorist actions.

qat shrub *Catha edulis* of the staff-tree family Celastraceae. The leaves are chewed as a mild narcotic in some Arab countries. Its use was banned in Somalia 1983.

Qatar State of (*Dawlat Qatar*) *area* 4,402 sq mi/11,400 sq km *capital* and chief port Doha *towns* Dukhan, center of oil production *physical* mostly flat desert with salt flats in S *features* negligible rain and surface water; only 3% is fertile, but irrigation allows self-sufficiency in fruit and vegetables; extensive oil discoveries since World War II *head of state and government* Sheik Khalifa bin Hamad al-Thani from 1972 *political system* absolute monarchy *political parties* none *exports* oil, natural gas, petrochemicals, fertilizers, iron, steel *currency* riyal *population* (1993 est) 510,000 (half in Doha; Arab 40%, Indian 18%, Pakistani 18%); growth rate 3.7% p.a. *life expectancy* men 68, women 73 *languages* Arabic (official), English *religion* Sunni Muslim 95% *literacy* men 77%, women 73% *GNP* $15,870 per head (1990) *chronology* 1916 Qatar became a British protectorate. *1970* Constitution adopted, confirming the emirate as an absolute monarchy. *1971* Independence achieved from Britain. *1972* Emir Sheik Ahmad replaced in bloodless coup by his cousin, Crown Prince Sheik Khalifa. *1991* Forces joined United Nations coalition in Gulf War against Iraq.

Qinghai or *Tsinghai* province of NW China *area* 278,306 sq mi/721,000 sq km *capital* Xining *features* mainly desert, with nomadic herders *industries* oil, livestock, medical products *population* (1990) 4,457,000; minorities include 900,000 Tibetans (mostly nomadic herders); Tibetan nationalists regard the province as being under colonial rule.

Qld abbreviation for ◊*Queensland*, an Australian state.

Qom or *Qum* holy city of Shiite Muslims, in central Iran, 90 mi/145 km S of Tehran; population (1986) 551,000. The Islamic academy of Madresseh Faizieh 1920 became the headquarters of Ayatollah ◊Khomeini.

Quadruple Alliance in European history, three military alliances of four nations:

the Quadruple Alliance 1718 Austria, Britain, France, and the United Provinces (Netherlands) joined forces to prevent Spain from annexing Sardinia and Sicily; *the Quadruple Alliance 1813* Austria, Britain, Prussia, and Russia allied to defeat the French emperor Napoleon; renewed 1815 and 1818. *the Quadruple Alliance 1834* Britain, France, Portugal, and Spain guaranteed the constitutional monarchies of Spain and Portugal against rebels in the Carlist War.

quail any of several genera of small ground-dwelling birds of the family Phasianidae, which also includes grouse, pheasants, bobwhites, and prairie chickens.

The California quail *Callipepla californiensis* is one of five species of quail native to North America.

Quaker popular name, originally derogatory, for a member of the Society of ◊Friends.

Quant Mary 1934– . English fashion designer. She popularized the miniskirt in the UK and was one of the first designers to make clothes specifically for the teenage and early twenties market, producing bold, simple outfits which were in tune with the "swinging London" of the 1960s. In the 1970s she extended into cosmetics and textile design.

quantum theory or *quantum mechanics* in physics, the theory that ◊energy does not have a continuous range of values, but is, instead, absorbed or radiated discontinuously, in multiples of definite, indivisible units called quanta. Just as earlier theory showed how light, generally seen as a wave motion, could also in some ways be seen as composed of discrete particles (◊photons), quantum theory shows how atomic particles such as electrons may also be seen as having wavelike properties. Quantum theory is the basis of particle physics, modern theoretical chemistry, and the solid-state physics that describes the behavior of the silicon chips used in computers.

quark in physics, the ◊elementary particle that is the fundamental constituent of all ◊hadrons (baryons, such as neutrons and protons, and mesons). There are six types, or "flavors": up, down, top, bottom, strange, and charmed, each of which has three varieties, or "colors": red, yellow, and blue (visual color is not meant, although the analogy is useful in many ways). To each quark there is an antiparticle, called an antiquark.

quart a unit of liquid or dry measure of volume or capacity. One liquid quart is equal to one-quarter of a gallon, or two pints, or 32 fluid ounces (0.946 liter), while a dry quart is equal to one-eighth of a peck, or two dry pints (1.101 liter).

quartz crystalline form of ◊silica SiO_2, one of the most abundant minerals of the Earth's crust (12% by volume). Quartz occurs in many different kinds of rock, including sandstone and granite. It ranks 7 on the Mohs' scale of hardness and is resistant to chemical or mechanical breakdown. Quartzes vary according to the size and purity of their crystals. Quartz, which can also be made synthetically, is used in ornamental work and industry.

quasar (from *quasi*-stell*ar* object or QSO) one of the most distant extragalactic objects known, discovered 1963. Quasars appear starlike, but each emits more energy than 100 giant galaxies. They are thought to be at the center of galaxies, their brilliance emanating from the stars and gas falling toward an immense ◊black hole at their nucleus.

quassia any tropical American tree of the genus *Quassia*, family Simaroubaceae, with a bitter bark and wood. The heartwood of *Q. amara* is a source of quassiin, an infusion of which was formerly used as a tonic; it is now used in insecticides.

Quaternary period of geological time that began 1.64 million years ago and is still in process. It is divided into the ◊Pleistocene and ◊Holocene epochs.

Quayle (James) Dan(forth) 1947– . US Republican politician, vice president 1989–93. A congressman for Indiana 1977–81, he became a senator 1981.

Que. abbreviation for ◊*Québec*, a Canadian province.

Québec capital and industrial port (textiles, leather, timber. paper, printing, and publishing) of Québec province, on the St Lawrence River, Canada; population (1986) 165,000, metropolitan area 603,000.

Québec province of E Canada *area* 594,710 sq mi/ 1,540,700 sq km *capital* Quebec *towns and cities* Monteral, Laval, Sherbrooke, Verdun, Hull, Trois-Rivières *features* immense water-power resources (for example, the James Bay project) *industries* iron, copper, gold, zinc, cereals, potatoes, paper, textiles, fish, maple syrup (70% of world's output) *population* (1991) 6,811,800 *languages* French (the only official language since 1974, although 17% speak English). Language laws 1989 prohibit the use of English on street signs *history* known as New France 1534–1763; captured by the British and became province of Québec 1763–90, Lower Canada 1791–1846, Canada East 1846–67; one of the original provinces 1867. In the 1960s nationalist feelings (despite existing safeguards for Québec's French-derived civil law, customs, religion, and language) were encouraged by French president de Gaulle's exclamation *"Vive le Québec libre/*Long live free Québec" on a visit to the province, and led to the foundation of the Parti Québecois by René Lévesque 1968.

The Québec Liberation Front (FLQ) separatists had conducted a bombing campaign in the 1960s and fermented an uprising 1970; Parti Québécois won power 1976; a referendum on "sovereignty-association" (separation) was defeated 1980.

In 1982, when Canada severed its last legal ties with the UK, Québec opposed the new Constitution Act as denying the province's claim to an absolute veto over constitutional change. The right of veto was proposed for all provinces of Canada 1987, but the agreement was not ratified by its 1990 deadline and support for Quebec's independence grew. In 1989 the Parti Québécois was defeated by the Liberal Party. In a referendum 1992 Quebec's French-speaking population rejected constitutional reforms giving greater autonomy to the province.

quebracho any of several South American trees, genus *Schinopsis*, of the cashew family Anacardiaceae, with very hard wood, chiefly the red quebracho *S. lorentzii*, used in tanning.

Quechua or *Quichua* or *Kechua* member of the largest group of South American Indians. The

Quechua live in the Andean region. Their ancestors included the Inca, who established the Quechua language in the region. Quechua is the second official language of Peru and is widely spoken as a lingua franca in Ecuador, Bolivia, Columbia, Argentina, and Chile; it belongs to the Andean-Equatorial family.

Queen Maud Land region of Antarctica W of Enderby Land, claimed by Norway since 1939.

Queens mainly residential borough and county at the west end of Long Island, New York City; population (1980) 1,891,300.

It has sports arenas (Shea Stadium, Forest Hills Tennis Club, and the National Tennis Center at Flushing Meadows), a botanical garden, a museum, and several branches of the City University of New York. Both La Guardia and Kennedy airports are here.

Queensland state in NE Australia *area* 666,699 sq mi/ 1,727,200 sq km *capital* Brisbane *towns and cities* Townsville, Toowoomba, Cairns *features* Great Dividing Range, including Mount Bartle Frere 5,438 ft/1,657 m; Great Barrier Reef (collection of coral reefs and islands about 1,250 mi/2,000 km long, off the east coast); Gold Coast, 20 mi/32 km long, S of Brisbane; Mount Isa mining area; Sunshine Coast, a 60-mi/100-km stretch of coast N of Brisbane, between Rainbow Beach and Bribie Island, including the resorts of Noosa Heads, Coolum Beach, and Caloundra *industries* sugar, pineapples, beef, cotton, wool, tobacco, copper, gold, silver, lead, zinc, coal, nickel, bauxite, uranium, natural gas *population* (1987) 2,650,000 *history* part of New South Wales until 1859, when it became self-governing. In 1989 the ruling National Party was defeated after 32 years in power and replaced by the Labor Party.

quetzal long-tailed Central American bird *Pharomachus mocinno* of the trogon family. The male is brightly colored, with green, red, blue, and white feathers, and is about 4.3 ft/1.3 m long including tail. The female is smaller and lacks the tail and plumage.

Quetzalcoatl in pre-Columbian cultures of Central America, a feathered serpent god of air and water. In his human form, he was said to have been fair-skinned and bearded and to have reigned on Earth during a golden age. He disappeared across the eastern sea, with a promise to return.

Quezon City former capital of the Philippines 1948–76, northeastern part of metropolitan ◊Manila (the present capital), on Luzon Island; population (1990) 1,166,800. It was named for the Philippines' first president, Manuel Luis Quezon (1878–1944).

quicksilver another name for the element ◊mercury.

Quicktime multimedia utility developed by Apple, initially for the ◊Macintosh, but now also available for ◊Windows. Allows multimedia, such as sound and video, to be embedded in other documents.

quilt padded bed cover or the method used to make padded covers or clothing. The padded effect is achieved by sewing a layer of down, cotton, wool, or other stuffing between two outer pieces of material; patterned sewing is used (often diamond shapes or floral motifs).

In the US, group or family efforts resulted in quilting bees, where several people sewed and visited on certain days to finish the project (wedding, baby) and to have company in a vast, relatively unpopulated colonial farming region.

quince small tree *Cydonia oblonga*, family Rosaceae, native to W Asia. The bitter, yellow, pear-shaped fruit

quetzal *The long-tailed quetzal of Mexico and Central America was considered sacred by the ancient Maya and Aztecs. They associated the bird with the plumed serpent god Quetzalcoatl, and used its magnificent tail feathers in religious ceremonies.*

is used in preserves. Flowering quinces, genus *Chaenomeles*, are cultivated for their flowers.

quinine antimalarial drug extracted from the bark of the cinchona tree. Peruvian Indians taught French missionaries how to use the bark in 1630, but quinine was not isolated until 1820. It is a bitter alkaloid $C_{20}H_{24}N_2O_2$.

Quinn Anthony 1915– . Mexican-born US actor. In films from 1935, his roles frequently displayed volatile machismo and he often played larger-than-life characters. He is famous for the title role in *Zorba the Greek* 1964; other films include *Viva Zapata!* 1952 (Academy Award for best supporting actor) and Fellini's *La strada* 1954.

Quisling Vidkun 1887–1945. Norwegian politician. Leader from 1933 of the Norwegian Fascist Party, he aided the Nazi invasion of Norway 1940 by delaying mobilization and urging non-resistance. He was made premier by Hitler 1942, and was arrested and shot as a traitor by the Norwegians 1945. His name became a generic term for a traitor who aids an occupying force.

Quito capital and industrial city (textiles, chemicals, leather, gold, silver) of Ecuador, about 9,850 ft/ 3,000 m above sea level; population (1986) 1,093,300. It was an ancient settlement, taken by the Incas about 1470 and by the Spanish 1534. It has a temperate climate all year round.

Qum alternative spelling of ◊Qom, a city in Iran.

quotation marks or *quotes* punctuation marks (" ") used in pairs to mark off dialogue or quoted matter in a text.

In the US double quotes are commonly used, and single quotes within double; in the UK normal practice is the opposite. In some languages quotation marks are omitted around dialogue.

qv abbreviation for *quod vide* (Latin "which see").

QwaQwa black homeland of South Africa that achieved self-governing status 1974; population (1985) 181,600.

QWERTY standard arrangement of keys on a US or UK typewriter or computer keyboard. Q, W, E, R, T, and Y are the first six keys on the top alphabetic line. The arrangement was made to slow typists down in the days of mechanical keyboards in order that the keys would not jam together. Other European countries use different arrangements, such as AZERTY and QWERTZ, which are more appropriate to the language of the country.

Rabat capital of Morocco, industrial port (cotton textiles, carpets, leather goods) on the Atlantic coast, 110 mi/177 km W of Fez; population (1982) 519,000, Rabat-Salé 842,000. It is named for its original *ribat* or fortified monastery.

rabbit any of several genera of hopping mammals of the order Lagomorpha, which together with ◊hares constitute the family Leporidae. Rabbits differ from hares in bearing naked, helpless young and in occupying burrows.

Rabelais François 1495–1553. French satirist, monk, and physician. His name has become synonymous with bawdy humor. He was educated in the Renaissance humanist tradition and was the author of satirical allegories, including *La Vie inestimable de Gargantua/The Inestimable Life of Gargantua* 1535 and *Faits et dits héroïques du grand Pantagruel/Heroic Deeds and Sayings of the Great Pantagruel* 1533, about two giants (father and son).

rabies or *hydrophobia* viral disease of the central nervous system that can afflict all warm-blooded creatures. It is almost invariably fatal once symptoms have developed. Its transmission to humans is generally by a bite from an infected animal.

Rabin Yitzhak 1922– . Israeli Labour politician, prime minister 1974–77 and from 1992. His policy of favoring Palestinian self-government in the occupied territories contributed to the success of the center-left party in the 1992 elections. In Sept 1993 he signed a historic peace agreement with the Palestinian Liberation Organization (PLO), leading to a withdrawal of Israeli forces from Gaza and Jericho. He was awarded the 1994 Nobel Prize for Peace jointly with Israeli foreign minister, Shimon Peres, and PLO leader, Yassir Arafat.

raccoon any of several New World species of carnivorous mammals of the genus *Procyon*, in the family Procyonidae. The common raccoon *P. lotor* is about 2 ft/60 cm long, with a gray-brown body, a black-and-

raccoon Raccoons are good climbers and spend much of their time in trees, usually near water. Their varied diet includes small aquatic animals such as frogs, crayfish, and fish. The common raccoon, found in N America from S Canada to the Panama canal, was adopted as a pet by the early settlers.

white ringed tail, and a black "mask" around its eyes. The crab-eating raccoon *P. cancrivorus* of South America is slightly smaller and has shorter fur.

race in anthropology, the term applied to the varieties of modern humans, *Homo sapiens sapiens*, having clusters of distinctive physical traits in common. The three major varieties are ◊Caucasoid, ◊Mongoloid, and ◊Negroid. During the last 60,000 years, migrations and interbreeding have caused a range of variations to exist today, not distinct or "pure" races (which can exist only under conditions of isolation).

Rachmaninov Sergei (Vasilevich) 1873–1943. Russian composer, conductor, and pianist. After the 1917 Revolution he emigrated to the US. His music is melodious and emotional and includes operas, such as *Francesca da Rimini* 1906, three symphonies, four piano concertos, piano pieces, and songs. Among his other works are the *Prelude in C-Sharp Minor* 1882 and *Rhapsody on a Theme of Paganini* 1934 for piano and orchestra.

Racine Jean 1639–1699. French dramatist. He was an exponent of the classical tragedy in French drama, taking his subjects from Greek mythology and observing the rules of classical Greek drama. Most of his tragedies have women in the title role, for example *Andromaque* 1667, *Iphigénie* 1674, and *Phèdre* 1677.

racism belief in, or set of implicit assumptions about, the superiority of one's own ◊race or ethnic group, often accompanied by prejudice against members of an ethnic group different from one's own. Racism may be used to justify ◊discrimination, verbal or physical abuse, or even genocide, as in Nazi Germany, or as practiced by European settlers against American Indians in both North and South America.

rad unit of absorbed radiation dose, now replaced in the SI system by the ◊gray (one rad equals 0.01 gray), but still commonly used. It is defined as the dose when one kilogram of matter absorbs 0.01 joule of radiation energy (formerly, as the dose when one gram absorbs 100 ergs).

radar (acronym for *radio direction and ranging*) device for locating objects in space, direction finding, and navigation by means of transmitted and reflected high-frequency radio waves.

radar astronomy bouncing of radio waves off objects in the Solar System, with reception and analysis of the "echoes". Radar contact with the Moon was first made 1945 and with Venus 1961. The travel time for radio reflections allows the distances of objects to be determined accurately. Analysis of the reflected beam reveals the rotation period and allows the object's surface to be mapped. The rotation periods of Venus and Mercury were first determined by radar. Radar maps of Venus were obtained first by Earth-based radar and subsequently by orbiting space probes.

radian SI unit (symbol rad) of plane angles, an alternative unit to the ◊degree. It is the angle at the center of a circle when the center is joined to the two ends of an arc (part of the circumference) equal in length to the radius of the circle. There are 2π (approximately 6.284) radians in a full circle (360°).

radiation in physics, emission of radiant ◊energy as particles or waves—for example, heat, light, alpha particles, and beta particles (see ◊electromagnetic waves and ◊radioactivity). See also ◊atomic radiation.

radiation sickness sickness resulting from exposure to radiation, including X-rays, gamma rays, neutrons, and other nuclear radiation, as from weapons and fallout. Such radiation ionizes atoms in the body and causes nausea, vomiting, diarrhea, and other symptoms. The body cells themselves may be damaged even by very small doses, causing leukemia; genetic changes may be induced in the embryo, causing infants to be born damaged or mutated.

radical in chemistry, a group of atoms forming part of a molecule, which acts as a unit and takes part in chemical reactions without disintegration, yet often cannot exist alone; for example, the methyl radical $-CH_3$, or the carboxyl radical $-COOH$.

radio transmission and reception of radio waves. In radio transmission a microphone converts sound waves (pressure variations in the air) into ◊electromagnetic waves that are then picked up by a receiving aerial and fed to a loudspeaker, which converts them back into sound waves.

radioactive decay process of continuous disintegration undergone by the nuclei of radioactive elements, such as radium and various isotopes of uranium and the transuranic elements. This changes the element's atomic number, thus transmuting one element into another, and is accompanied by the emission of radiation. Alpha and beta decay are the most common forms.

radioactivity spontaneous alteration of the nuclei of radioactive atoms, accompanied by the emission of radiation. It is the property exhibited by the radioactive ◊isotopes of stable elements and all isotopes of radioactive elements, and can be either natural or induced. See ◊radioactive decay.

radio astronomy study of radio waves emitted naturally by objects in space, by means of a ◊radio telescope. Radio emission comes from hot gases (*thermal radiation*); electrons spiraling in magnetic fields (*synchrotron radiation*); and specific wavelengths (*lines*) emitted by atoms and molecules in space, such as the 8-in/21-cm line emitted by hydrogen gas.

radiocarbon dating or *carbon dating* method of dating organic materials (for example, bone or wood), used in archeology. Plants take up carbon dioxide gas from the atmosphere and incorporate it into their tissues, and some of that carbon dioxide contains the radioactive isotope of carbon, carbon-14. This decays at a known rate (half of it decays every 5,730 years); the time elapsed since the plant died can therefore be measured in a laboratory. Animals take carbon-14 into their bodies from eating plant tissues and their remains can be similarly dated. After 120,000 years so little carbon-14 is left that no measure is possible (see ◊half-life).

radio frequencies and wavelengths classification of, see ◊electromagnetic waves.

radio galaxy galaxy that is a strong source of electromagnetic waves of radio wavelengths. All galaxies, including our own, emit some radio waves, but radio galaxies are up to a million times more powerful.

radiography branch of science concerned with the use of radiation (particularly ◊X-rays) to produce images on photographic film or fluorescent screens. X-rays penetrate matter according to its nature, density, and thickness. In doing so they can cast shadows on photographic film, producing a radiograph. Radiography is widely used in medicine for examining bones and tissues and in industry for examining solid materials; for example, to check welded seams in pipelines

radioisotope (contraction of *radioactive isotope*) in physics, a naturally occurring or synthetic radioactive form of an element. Most radioisotopes are made by bombarding a stable element with neutrons in the core of a nuclear reactor. The radiations given off by radioisotopes are easy to detect and can in some instances penetrate substantial thicknesses of

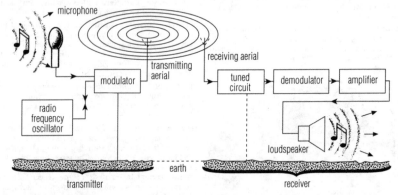

radio Radio transmission and reception. The radio frequency oscillator generates rapidly varying electrical signals, which are sent to the transmitting aerial. In the aerial, the signals produce radio waves (the carrier wave), which spread out at the speed of light. The sound signal is added to the carrier wave by the modulator. When the radio waves fall on the receiving aerial, they induce an electrical current in the aerial. The electrical current is sent to the tuning circuit, which picks out the signal from the particular transmitting station desired. The demodulator separates the sound signal from the carrier wave and sends it, after amplification, to the loudspeaker.

materials, and have profound effects (such as genetic ◊mutation) on living matter. Although dangerous, radioisotopes are used in the fields of medicine, industry, agriculture, and research.

Most natural isotopes of atomic mass below 208 are not radioactive. Those from 210 and up are all radioactive.

radio telescope instrument for detecting radio waves from the universe in ◊radio astronomy. Radio telescopes usually consist of a metal bowl that collects and focuses radio waves the way a concave mirror collects and focuses light waves. Radio telescopes are much larger than optical telescopes, because the wavelengths they are detecting are much longer than the wavelength of light. The largest single dish is 1,000 ft/305 m across, at Arecibo, Puerto Rico.

radiotherapy treatment of disease by ◊radiation from X-ray machines or radioactive sources. Radiation, which reduces the activity of dividing cells, is of special value for its effect on malignant tissues, certain nonmalignant tumors, and some diseases of the skin.

radio wave electromagnetic wave possessing a long wavelength (ranging from about 10^{-3} to 10^4 m) and a low frequency (from about 10^5 to 10^{11} Hz). Included in the radio-wave part of the spectrum are ◊microwaves, used for both communications and for cooking; ultra high-and very high-frequency waves, used for television and FM (◊frequency modulation) radio communications; and short, medium, and long waves, used for AM (amplitude modulation) radio communications. Radio waves that are used for communications have all been modulated (see ◊modulation) to carry information. Stars emit radio waves, which may be detected and studied using ◊radio telescopes.

radish annual herb *Raphanus sativus*, family Cruciferae. It is native to Europe and Asia, and cultivated for its fleshy, pungent, edible root, which is usually reddish but sometimes white or black.

radium white, radioactive, metallic element, symbol Ra, atomic number 88, atomic weight 226.02. It is one of the ◊alkaline-earth metals, found in nature in ◊pitchblende and other uranium ores. Of the 16 isotopes, the commonest, Ra-226, has a half-life of 1.622 years. The element was discovered and named in 1898 by Pierre and Marie ◊Curie, who were investigating the residues of pitchblende.

radon colorless, odorless, gaseous, radioactive, nonmetallic element, symbol Rn, atomic number 86, atomic weight 222. It is grouped with the ◊inert gases and was formerly considered non-reactive, but is now known to form some compounds with fluorine. Of the 20 known isotopes, only three occur in nature; the longest half-life is 3.82 days.

Rafsanjani Hojatoleslam Ali Akbar Hashemi 1934– . Iranian politician and cleric, president from 1989. When his former teacher Ayatollah ◊Khomeini returned after the revolution of 1979–80, Rafsanjani became the speaker of the Iranian parliament and, after Khomeini's death, state president and effective political leader.

ragwort any of several European perennial plants of the genus *Senecio*, family Compositae, usually with yellow-rayed flower heads; some are poisonous.

Golden ragwort or groundsel *S. aureus* is native to S US.

rail any wading bird of the family Rallidae, including the rails proper (genus *Rallus*), coots, moorhens, and gallinules. Rails have dark plumage, a short neck and wings, and long legs. They are 4–18 in/10–45 cm long.

railroad method of transport in which trains convey passengers and goods along a twin rail track (at first made of wood but later of iron or steel with ties wedging them apart and relatively parallel). Following the work of English steam pioneers such as James ◊Watt, George ◊Stephenson built the first public steam railroad, from Stockton to Darlington, 1825. This heralded extensive railroad building in Britain, continental Europe, and North America where trains contributed to western expansion. After World War II, steam engines were replaced by electric and diesel engines.

rainbow coalition or *rainbow alliance* in politics, from the mid-1980s, a loose, left-of-center alliance of people from several different sections of society that are traditionally politically underrepresented, such as nonwhite ethnic groups. Its aims include promoting minority rights and equal opportunities. A prime example was the Rev Jesse Jackson's political campaign in the 1980s seeking to represent an alliance of nonwhite political groupings.

rainforest dense forest usually found on or near the ◊equator where the climate is hot and wet. Heavy rainfall results as the moist air brought by the converging tradewinds rises because of the heat. Over half the tropical rainforests are in Central and South America, the rest in SE Asia and Africa. They provide the bulk of the oxygen needed for plant and animal respiration. Tropical rainforest once covered 14% of the Earth's land surface, but are now being destroyed at an increasing rate as their valuable timber is harvested and the land cleared for agriculture, causing problems of ◊deforestation. Although by 1991 over 50% of the world's rainforest had been removed, they still comprise about 50% of all growing wood on the planet, and harbor at least 40% of the Earth's species (plants and animals).

raku soft, freely hand-modeled earthenware pottery fired at low temperature and partly covered with lead glaze. *Raku* ware was first made in the late 16th century in Kyoto, Japan.

The name is also applied to a method of firing pots used extensively in Japan since the 18th century, and more recently in the US and Britain.

Raleigh or *Ralegh* Walter c. 1552–1618. English adventurer, writer, and courtier to Queen Elizabeth I. He organized expeditions to colonize North America 1584–87, all unsuccessful, and made exploratory voyages to South America 1595 and 1616. His aggressive actions against Spanish interests, including attacks on Spanish ports, brought him into conflict with the pacific James I. He was imprisoned for treason 1603–16 and executed on his return from an unsuccessful final expedition to South America. He is traditionally credited with introducing the potato to Europe and popularizing the use of tobacco.

RAM (acronym for *random-access memory*) in computing, a memory device in the form of a collection of integrated circuits (chips), frequently used in microcomputers. Unlike ◊ROM (read-only memory), RAM chips can be both read from and written to by the computer, but their contents are lost when the power is switched off. Microcomputers of the 1990s may have 16–32 megabytes of RAM.

Rama incarnation of ◊Vishnu, the supreme spirit of Hinduism. He is the hero of the epic poem the

Ramayana, and he is regarded as an example of morality and virtue.

Ramadan in the Muslim calendar, the ninth month of the year. Throughout Ramadan a strict fast is observed during the hours of daylight; Muslims are encouraged to read the whole Koran in commemoration of the Night of Power (which falls during the month) when, it is believed, Mohammed first received his revelations from the angel Gabriel.

Ramos Fidel (Eddie) 1928– . Philippine politician, president from 1992. He was Corazon ◊Aquino's staunchest ally as defense secretary, and was later nominated her successor. In 1993, as part of a government move to end corruption and human-rights abuses, Ramos purged the police force.

Ramsay William 1852–1916. Scottish chemist who, with Lord Rayleigh, discovered argon 1894. In 1895 Ramsay produced helium and in 1898, in cooperation with Morris Travers, identified neon, krypton, and xenon. In 1903, with Frederick Soddy, he noted the transmutation of radium into helium, which led to the discovery of the density and relative atomic mass of radium. Nobel Prize 1904.

Ramses II or *Rameses II* king (pharaoh) of ancient Egypt about 1304–1236 BC, the son of Seti I. He campaigned successfully against the Hittites, and built two rock temples at Abu Simbel in S Egypt.

Ramses III or *Rameses III* king (pharaoh) of ancient Egypt about 1200–1168 BC. He won victories over the Libyans and the Sea Peoples and asserted his control over Palestine.

Rand Sally (Helen Gould Beck) 1904–1979. US exotic dancer. During the 1930s she worked as a dancer in Chicago and developed her trademark nude dance routine to Chopin and Debussy, which featured the coy use of huge ostrich fans. Playing a role in the 1965 burlesque revival on Broadway, she continued to dance until 1978.

Her appearances at the 1933 Chicago Exposition and at later fairs and expositions across the country made her a popular favorite.

random access in computing, an alternative term for ◊direct access.

random number one of a series of numbers having no detectable pattern. Random numbers are used in ◊computer simulation and ◊computer games. It is impossible for an ordinary computer to generate true random numbers, but various techniques are available for obtaining pseudo-random numbers—close enough to true randomness for most purposes.

Rangers US Army special forces in World War II; specially trained and equipped highly mobile troops, modeled on the British ◊commandos.

The 1st Ranger Battalion was trained at the British commando training center in Scotland 1942, and four more battalions were then raised. They served in the landings in N Africa, Sicily, Italy, and Normandy with distinction. They were disbanded soon after the war.

Rangoon former name (to 1989) of ◊Yangon, the capital of Myanmar (Burma).

Rao P(amulaparti) V(enkata) Narasimha 1921– . Indian politician, prime minister of India from 1991 and Congress leader. He took over the party leadership after the assassination of Rajiv Gandhi. Elected prime minister the following month, he instituted a reform of the economy. He survived a vote of confidence 1993.

rape in botany, two plant species of the mustard family Cruciferae, *Brassica rapa* and *B. napus*, grown for their seeds, which yield a pungent edible oil. The common turnip is a variety of the former, and the rutabaga turnip of the latter.

rape in law, sexual intercourse without the consent of the subject.

Most cases of rape are of women by men. In Islamic law a rape accusation requires the support of four independent male witnesses.

Some jurisdictions allow charges of rape to be brought against husbands replacing older legal doctrine asserting a wife's duty to submit to sex with her spouse. Sexual intercourse with a minor, not necessarily involving penetration, is defined as statutory rape.

Raphael Sanzio (Raffaello Sanzio) 1483–1520. Italian painter. He was one of the greatest artists of the High Renaissance, active in Perugia, Florence, and Rome (from 1508), where he painted frescoes in the Vatican and for secular patrons. His religious and mythological scenes are harmoniously composed; his dignified portraits enhance the character of his sitters. Many of his designs were engraved, and much of his later work was the product of his studio.

rap music rapid, rhythmic chant over a prerecorded repetitive backing track. Rap emerged in New York 1979, and the macho, swaggering lyrics that initially predominated have roots in ritual boasts and insults. Different styles were flourishing by the 1990s, such as jazz rap, gangsta rap, and reggae rap.

rare-earth element alternate name for ◊lanthanide.

Ras el Khaimah or *Ra's al Khaymah* emirate on the Persian Gulf; area 652 sq mi/1,690 sq km; population (1980) 73,700. Products include oil, pharmaceuticals, and cement. It is one of the seven members of the ◊United Arab Emirates.

raspberry prickly cane plant of the genus *Rubus* of the Rosaceae family, native to Eurasia and North America, with white flowers followed by red fruits. These are eaten fresh and used for jam and wine.

Rasputin (Russian "dissolute") Grigory Efimovich 1871–1916. Siberian Eastern Orthodox mystic who acquired influence over the czarina Alexandra, wife of ◊Nicholas II, and was able to make political and ecclesiastical appointments. His abuse of power and notorious debauchery (reputedly including the czarina) led to his murder by a group of nobles.

Rastafarianism religion originating in the West Indies, based on the ideas of Marcus ◊Garvey, who called on black people to return to Africa and set up a black-governed country there. When Haile Selassie (*Ras Tafari*, "Lion of Judah") was crowned emperor of Ethiopia 1930, this was seen as a fulfillment of prophecy and some Rastafarians acknowledged him as an incarnation of God (*Jah*). There were about one million Rastafarians by 1990.

raster graphics computer graphics that are stored in the computer memory by using a map to record data (such as color and intensity) for every ◊pixel that makes up the image. When transformed (enlarged, rotated, stretched, and so on), raster graphics become ragged and suffer loss of picture resolution, unlike ◊vector graphics. Raster graphics are typically used for painting applications, which allow the user to create artwork on a computer screen much as if they were painting on paper or canvas.

rat any of numerous long-tailed ◊rodents (especially of the families Muridae and Cricetidae) larger than mice and usually with scaly, naked tails. The genus *Rattus* in the family Muridae includes the rats found in human housing.

ratio measure of the relative size of two quantities or of two measurements (in similar units), expressed as a proportion. For example, the ratio of vowels to consonants in the alphabet is 5:21; the ratio of 500 m to 2 km is 500:2,000, or 1:4.

rationalism in theology, the belief that human reason rather than divine revelation is the correct means of ascertaining truth and regulating behavior. In philosophy, rationalism takes the view that self-evident propositions deduced by reason are the sole basis of all knowledge (disregarding experience of the senses). It is usually contrasted with ◊empiricism, which argues that all knowledge must ultimately be derived from the senses.

rattlesnake any of various New World pit ◊vipers of the genera *Crotalus* and *Sistrurus* (the massasaugas and pygmy rattlers), distinguished by horny flat segments of the tail, which rattle when vibrated as a warning to attackers. They can grow to 8 ft/2.5 m long. The venom injected by some rattlesnakes can be fatal.

rattlesnake

Rauschenberg Robert 1925– . US Pop artist. He has created happenings and incongruous multimedia works, such as *Monogram* 1959 (Moderna Museet, Stockholm), a stuffed goat daubed with paint and wearing an automobile tire around its body. In the 1960s he returned to painting and used the silk-screen printing process to transfer images to canvas. He also made collages.

Ravel (Joseph) Maurice 1875–1937. French composer and pianist. His work is characterized by its sensuousness, exotic harmonics, and dazzling orchestral effects. Examples are the piano pieces *Pavane pour une infante défunte/Pavane for a Dead Infanta* 1899 and *Jeux d'eau/Waterfall* 1901, and the ballets *Daphnis et Chloë* 1912 and *Boléro* 1928.

raven any of several large ◊crows (genus *Corvus*). The common raven *C. corax* is about 2 ft/60 cm long, and has black, lustrous plumage. It is a scavenger, and is found only in the northern hemisphere.

ray any of several orders (especially Ragiformes) of cartilaginous fishes with a flattened body, winglike pectoral fins, and a whiplike tail.

Ray Man (adopted name of Emmanuel Rudnitsky) 1890–1976. US photographer, painter, and sculptor. He was active mainly in France and was associated with the Dada movement. His pictures often showed Surrealist images, for example the photograph *Le Violon d'Ingres* 1924.

Ray Satyajit 1921–1992. Indian film director. He was internationally known for his trilogy of life in his native Bengal: *Pather Panchali, Unvanquished,* and *The World of Apu* 1955–59.

Later films include *The Music Room* 1963, *Charulata* 1964, *The Chess Players* 1977, and *The Home and the World* 1984.

rayon any of various shiny textile fibers and fabrics made from ◊cellulose. It is produced by pressing whatever cellulose solution is used through very small holes and solidifying the resulting filaments. A common type is ◊viscose, which consists of regenerated filaments of pure cellulose. Acetate and triacetate are kinds of rayon consisting of filaments of cellulose acetate and triacetate.

Rayon was originally made in the 1930s from the Douglas fir tree.

reaction in chemistry, the coming together of two or more atoms, ions, or molecules with the result that a chemical change takes place. The nature of the reaction is portrayed by a chemical equation.

read-only storage in computing, a permanent means of storing data so that it can be read any number of times but cannot be modified. CD-ROM is a read-only storage medium; CD-ROMs come with the data already encoded on them.

Reagan Ronald (Wilson) 1911– . 40th president of the US 1981–89, a Republican. He was governor of California 1966–74, and a former Hollywood actor. Reagan was a hawkish and popular president. He adopted an aggressive policy in Central America, attempting to overthrow the government of Nicaragua, and invading Grenada 1983. In 1987, ◊Irangate was investigated by the Tower Commission; Reagan admitted that US–Iran negotiations had become an "arms for hostages deal", but denied knowledge of resultant funds being illegally sent to the Contras in Nicaragua. He increased military spending (sending the national budget deficit to

Reagan, Ronald (Wilson) *Ronald Reagan, US president 1981–89.*

record levels), cut social programs, introduced deregulation of domestic markets, and cut taxes. His ◊Strategic Defense Initiative, announced 1983, proved controversial owing to the cost and unfeasibility. He was succeeded by vice president George Bush.

realism in medieval philosophy, the theory that "universals" have existence, not simply as names for entities but as entities in their own right. In contemporary philosophy, the term stands for the doctrine that there is an intuitively appreciated reality apart from what is presented to the consciousness. It is opposed to idealism.

realism in the arts and literature generally, an unadorned, naturalistic approach to subject matter. More specifically, *Realism* refers to a movement in mid-19th-century European art and literature, a reaction against Romantic and Classical idealization and a rejection of conventional academic themes (such as mythology, history, and sublime landscapes) in favor of everyday life and carefully observed social settings.

real number in mathematics, any of the rational numbers (which include the integers) or irrational numbers. Real numbers exclude imaginary numbers, found in ◊complex numbers of the general form $a + bi$ where $i = \sqrt{-1}$, although these do include a real component a.

real-time system in computing, a program that responds to events in the world as they happen. For example, an automatic-pilot program in an aircraft must respond instantly in order to correct deviations from its course. Process control, robotics, games, and many military applications are examples of real-time systems.

receiver in law, a person appointed by a court to collect and manage the assets of an individual, company, or partnership in serious financial difficulties. In the case of bankruptcy, the assets may be sold and distributed by a receiver to creditors.

recession in economics, a fall in business activity lasting more than a few months, causing stagnation in a country's output.

The average decline has been about 10% although some recessions, such as 1981–82, can be longer and more severe.

recessive gene in genetics, an ◊allele (alternative form of a gene) that will show in the ◊phenotype (observed characteristics of an organism) only if its partner allele on the paired chromosome is similarly recessive. Alleles for blue eyes in humans, and for shortness in pea plants are recessive.

Recife industrial seaport (cotton textiles, sugar refining, fruit canning, flour milling) and naval base in Brazil; capital of Pernambuco state, at the mouth of the river Capibaribe; population (1991) 1,335,700. It was founded 1504.

recombination in genetics, any process that recombines, or "shuffles", the genetic material, thus increasing genetic variation in the offspring. The two main processes of recombination both occur during meiosis (reduction division of cells). One is *crossing over*, in which chromosome pairs exchange segments; the other is the random reassortment of chromosomes that occurs when each gamete (sperm or egg) receives only one of each chromosome pair.

Reconstruction in US history, the period 1865–77 after the Civil War during which the nation was reunited under the federal government after the defeat of the Confederacy. Southerners considered the handling of Reconstruction to be harsh and chaotic.

recorder any of a widespread range of woodwind instruments of the whistle type which flourished in consort ensembles in the Renaissance and Baroque eras, along with viol consorts, as an instrumental medium for polyphonic music. A modern consort may include a sopranino, soprano (descant), alto (treble), tenor, bass, and great bass.

record player device for reproducing recorded sound stored as a spiral groove on a vinyl disk. A motor-driven turntable rotates the record at a constant speed, and a stylus or needle on the head of a pick-up is made to vibrate by the undulations in the record groove. These vibrations are then converted to electrical signals by a ◊transducer in the head. After amplification, the signals pass to one or more loudspeakers, which convert them into sound. Alternative formats are ◊compact disk and ◊tape recording, magnetic.

rectifier in electrical engineering, a device used for obtaining one-directional current (DC) from an alternating source of supply (AC). (The process is necessary because almost all electrical power is generated, transmitted, and supplied as alternating current, but many devices, from television sets to electric motors, require direct current.) Types include plate rectifiers, thermionic ◊diodes, and ◊semiconductor diodes.

recursion in computing and mathematics, a technique whereby a ◊function or ◊procedure calls itself into use in order to enable a complex problem to be broken down into simpler steps. For example, a function that finds the factorial of a number n (calculates the product of all the whole numbers between 1 and n) would obtain its result by multiplying n by the factorial of $n-1$.

recycling processing of industrial and household waste (such as paper, glass, and some metals and plastics) so that it can be reused.

This saves expenditure on scarce raw materials, slows down the depletion of nonrenewable resources, and helps to reduce pollution.

red informal term for a leftist, revolutionary, or communist, which originated in the 19th century in the form "red republican", meaning a republican who favored a social as well as a political revolution, generally by armed violence. Red is the color adopted by socialist and communist parties.

To be soft on these political philosophies, one is thereby tainted "pink".

red blood cell or *erythrocyte* the most common type of blood cell, responsible for transporting oxygen around the body. It contains hemoglobin, which combines with oxygen from the lungs to form oxyhemoglobin. When transported to the tissues, these cells are able to release the oxygen because the oxyhemoglobin splits into its original constituents.

Red Cross international relief agency founded by the Geneva Convention 1864 at the instigation of the Swiss doctor Henri Dunant to assist the wounded and prisoners in war. Its symbol is a symmetrical red cross on a white ground. In addition to dealing with associated problems of war, such as refugees and the care of the disabled, the Red Cross is increasingly concerned with victims of natural disasters—floods, earthquakes, epidemics, and accidents.

The US National Red Cross was founded 1881.

red dwarf any star that is cool, faint, and small (about one-tenth the mass and diameter of the Sun). Red dwarfs burn slowly, and have estimated lifetimes of 100 trillion years. They may be the most abundant type of star, but are difficult to see because they are so faint. Two of the closest stars to the Sun, Proxima Centauri and Barnard's Star, are red dwarfs.

Redford (Charles) Robert 1937– . US actor and film director. His blond good looks and versatility earned him his first starring role in *Barefoot in the Park* 1967, followed by *Butch Cassidy and the Sundance Kid* 1969 and *The Sting* 1973 (both with Paul Newman).

His other films as an actor include *The Way We Were* 1973, *All the President's Men* 1976, *Out of Africa* 1985, *Havana* 1991, *Sneakers* 1992, and *Indecent Proposal* 1993. He won the Oscar for directing *Ordinary People* 1980, and followed with *The Milagro Beanfield War* 1988, and *A River Runs Through It* 1992. He established the Sundance Institute in Utah for the development of film talent.

red giant any large bright star with a cool surface. It is thought to represent a late stage in the evolution of a star like the Sun, as it runs out of hydrogen fuel at its center. Red giants have diameters between 10 and 100 times that of the Sun. They are very bright because they are so large, although their surface temperature is lower than that of the Sun, about 3,000°–5,000°F/ 2,000–3,000K (1,700–2,700°C).

Redgrave Michael 1908–1985. English actor. His stage roles included Hamlet and Lear (Shakespeare), Uncle Vanya (Chekhov), and the schoolmaster in Rattigan's *The Browning Version* (filmed 1951). On screen he appeared in *The Lady Vanishes* 1938, *The Importance of Being Earnest* 1952, and *Goodbye Mr Chips* 1959. He was the father of actresses Vanessa and Lynn Redgrave (1944–).

Redgrave Vanessa 1937– . English actress. She has played Shakespeare's Lady Macbeth and Cleopatra on the stage, Ellida in Ibsen's *Lady From the Sea* 1976 and 1979, and Olga in Chekhov's *Three Sisters* 1990. She won an Academy Award for best supporting actress for her title role in the film *Julia* 1976; other films include *Wetherby* 1985 and *Howards End* 1992. She is active in left-wing politics.

Redon Odilon 1840–1916. French Symbolist painter and graphic artist. He used fantastic symbols and images, sometimes mythological. From the 1890s he painted still lifes, flowers, and landscapes. His work was much admired by the Surrealists.

Redon made his reputation as a Symbolist in Paris around 1880.

Red Sea submerged section of the Great ◊Rift Valley (1,200 mi/2,000 km long and up to 200 mi/320 km mi wide). Egypt, Sudan, Ethiopia, and Eritrea (in Africa) and Saudi Arabia (Asia) are on its shores.

red shift in astronomy, the lengthening of the wavelengths of light from an object as a result of the object's motion away from us. It is an example of the ◊Doppler effect. The red shift in light from galaxies is evidence that the universe is expanding.

redstart any of several New World wood warblers (family Parulidae), especially the American redstart *Setophaga ruticulla*.

The male is black and orange with white underparts. Old World redstarts are small thrushes with a reddish tail, belonging to the genus *Phoenicurus*.

reduction in chemistry, the gain of electrons, loss of oxygen, or gain of hydrogen by an atom, ion, or molecule during a chemical reaction.

redwood giant coniferous tree, one of the two types of ◊sequoia.

reed any of various perennial tall, slender grasses of wet or marshy environments; in particular, species of the genera *Phragmites* and *Arundo*; also the stalk of any of these plants. The common reed *P. australis* attains a height of 10 ft/3 m, having stiff, erect leaves and straight stems bearing a plume of purplish flowers.

Reed John 1887–1920. US journalist and author born in Portland, Oregon, and educated at Harvard. As a supporter of the Bolsheviks, Reed published his account of the Russian Revolution in *Ten Days that Shook the World* 1919. Later indicted in the US for sedition, Reed fled to the Soviet Union, where he died in exile.

Reed Walter 1851–1902. US physician and medical researcher. His greatest work was carried out 1900–01 in Cuba, where a yellow-fever epidemic was ravaging US troops. His breakthrough isolation of the aedes mosquito as the sole carrier of yellow fever led to the eradication of the deadly disease.

referendum procedure whereby a decision on proposed legislation is referred to the electorate for settlement by direct vote of all the people.

refining any process that purifies or converts something into a more useful form. Metals usually need refining after they have been extracted from their ores by such processes as ◊smelting. Petroleum, or crude oil, needs refining before it can be used; the process involves fractional distillation, the separation of the substance into separate components or "fractions".

reflection the throwing back or deflection of waves, such as light or sound waves, when they hit a surface. The *law of reflection* states that the angle of incidence (the angle between the ray and a perpendicular line drawn to the surface) is equal to the angle of reflection (the angle between the reflected ray and a perpendicular to the surface).

reflex in animals, a very rapid involuntary response to a particular stimulus. It is controlled by the ◊nervous system. A reflex involves only a few nerve cells, unlike

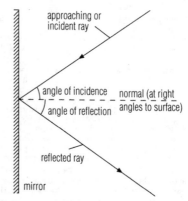

reflection *The law of reflection: the angle of incidence of a light beam equals the angle of reflection of the beam.*

the slower but more complex responses produced by the many processing nerve cells of the brain.

reflex camera camera that uses a mirror and prisms to reflect light passing through the lens into the viewfinder, showing the photographer the exact scene that is being shot. When the shutter button is released the mirror springs out of the way, allowing light to reach the film. The most common type is the single-lens reflex (◊SLR) camera. The twin-lens reflex (TLR) camera has two lenses: one has a mirror for viewing, the other is used for exposing the film.

Reformation religious and political movement in 16th-century Europe to reform the Roman Catholic church, which led to the establishment of Protestant churches. Anticipated from the 12th century by the Waldenses, Lollards, and Hussites, it was set off by German priest Martin ◊Luther 1517, and became effective when the absolute monarchies gave it support by challenging the political power of the papacy and confiscating church wealth.

refraction the bending of a wave of light, heat, or sound when it passes from one medium to another. Refraction occurs because waves travel at different velocities in different media.

refractory (of a material) able to resist high temperature, for example ◊ceramics made from clay, minerals, or other earthy materials. Furnaces are lined with refractory materials such as silica and dolomite.

refrigeration use of technology to transfer heat from cold to warm, against the normal temperature gradient, so that a body can remain substantially colder than its surroundings. Refrigeration equipment is used for the chilling and deep-freezing of food in food technology and in air conditioners and industrial processes.

refugee person fleeing from oppressive or dangerous conditions (such as political, religious, or military persecution) and seeking refuge in a foreign country. In 1993 there were an estimated 18 million refugees worldwide, whose resettlement and welfare were the responsibility of the United Nations High Commission for Refugees (UNHCR). An estimated average of 10,000 people a day become refugees.

Regency in Britain, the years 1811–20 during which ◊George IV (then Prince of Wales) acted as regent for his father ◊George III.

Regency style style of architecture and interior furnishings popular in England during the late 18th and early 19th centuries. It is characterized by restrained simplicity and the imitation of ancient classical elements, often Greek.

regeneration in biology, regrowth of a new organ or tissue after the loss or removal of the original. It is common in plants, where a new individual can often be produced from a "cutting" of the original. In animals, regeneration of major structures is limited to lower organisms; certain lizards can regrow their tails if these are lost, and new flatworms can grow from a tiny fragment of an old one. In mammals, regeneration is limited to the repair of tissue in wound healing and the regrowth of peripheral nerves following damage.

reggae predominant form of West Indian popular music of the 1970s and 1980s, characterized by a heavily accented offbeat and a thick bass line. The lyrics often refer to ◊Rastafarianism.

Musicians include Bob Marley, Lee "Scratch" Perry (1940– , performer and producer), and the group

Black Uhuru (1974–). Reggae is also played in the UK, South Africa, and elsewhere.

register in computing, a memory location that can be accessed rapidly; it is often built into the computer's central processing unit.

Some registers are reserved for special tasks—for example, an *instruction register* is used to hold the machine-code command that the computer is currently executing, while a *sequence-control register* keeps track of the next command to be executed. Other registers are used for holding frequently used data and for storing intermediate results.

Rehnquist William Hubbs 1924– . US jurist; associate justice 1971–86 and chief justice from 1986 of the US Supreme Court. As chief justice, he wrote the majority opinion for such cases as *Morrison* v *Olson* 1988, in which the court ruled that a special court can appoint special prosecutors to investigate crimes by high-ranking government officials, and *Hustler* v *Falwell* 1988, in which the Court ruled that public figures cannot be compensated for stress caused by parody that cannot possibly be taken seriously. In 1990 Rehnquist dissented on the Court's ruling that it is unconstitutional for states to have the right to require a teenager to notify her parents before having an abortion.

Reims (English *Reims*) capital of Champagne-Ardenne region, France; population (1990) 185,200. It is the center of the champagne industry and has textile industries. It was known in Roman times as *Durocorturum*. From 987 all but six French kings were crowned here. Ceded to England 1420 under the Treaty of Troyes, it was retaken by Joan of Arc, who had Charles VII consecrated in the 13th-century cathedral. In World War II, the German High Command formally surrendered here to US general Eisenhower May 7, 1945.

reincarnation belief that after death the human soul or the spirit of a plant or animal may live again in another human or animal. It is part of the teachings of many religions and philosophies, for example ancient Egyptian and Greek (the philosophies of Pythagoras and Plato), Buddhism, Hinduism, Jainism, certain Christian heresies (such as the Cathars), and theosophy. It is also referred to as *transmigration* or metempsychosis.

reindeer or *caribou* deer *Rangifer tarandus* of Arctic and subarctic regions, common to North America and Eurasia. About 4 ft/120 cm at the shoulder, it has a thick, brownish coat and broad hooves well adapted to travel over snow. It is the only deer in which both sexes have antlers; these can grow to 5 ft/150 cm long, and are shed in winter.

relativity in physics, the theory of the relative rather than absolute character of motion and mass, and the interdependence of matter, time, and space, as developed by German physicist Albert ◊Einstein in two phases: *special theory* (1905) Starting with the premises that (1) the laws of nature are the same for all observers in unaccelerated motion, and (2) the speed of light is independent of the motion of its source, Einstein postulated that the time interval between two events was longer for an observer in whose frame of reference the events occur in different places than for the observer for whom they occur at the same place. *general theory of relativity* (1915) The geometrical properties of space-time were to be conceived as modified locally by the presence of a body with mass. A planet's orbit around the Sun (as observed in three-dimensional space) arises from its natural trajectory in modified space-time; there is no need to invoke, as Isaac Newton did, a force of ◊gravity coming from the Sun and acting on the planet.

relay in electrical engineering, an electromagnetic switch. A small current passing through a coil of wire wound around an iron core attracts an ◊armature whose movement closes a pair of sprung contacts to complete a secondary circuit, which may carry a large current or activate other devices. The solid-state equivalent is a thyristor switching device.

relief in sculpture, particularly architectural sculpture, carved figures and other forms that project from the background. The Italian terms *basso-rilievo* (low relief), *mezzo-rilievo* (middle relief), and *alto-rilievo* (high relief) are used according to the extent to which the sculpture projects. The French term *bas-relief* is commonly used to mean low relief.

religion code of belief or philosophy that often involves the worship of a ◊God or gods. Belief in a supernatural power is not essential (absent in, for example, Buddhism and Confucianism), but faithful adherence is usually considered to be rewarded, for example, by escape from human existence (Buddhism), by a future existence (Christianity, Islam), or by worldly benefit (Soka Gakkai Buddhism).

rem acronym of *roentgen equivalent man* SI unit of radiation dose equivalent.

Some types of radiation do more damage than others for the same absorbed dose; the equivalent dose in rems is equal to the dose in rads multiplied by the relative biological effectiveness. One rem is approximately equivalent to the biological effect produced by one roentgen of X-ray or gamma-ray radiation. Humans can absorb up to 25 rems without immediate ill effects; 100 rems may produce radiation sickness; and more than 800 rems causes death.

Rembrandt Harmensz van Rijn 1606–1669. Dutch painter and etcher. He was one of the most prolific

reindeer *The reindeer ranges over the tundra of N Europe and Asia, Alaska, Canada, and Greenland. It is a social animal, living in large herds containing thousands of individuals. Some herds migrate hundreds of miles from their breeding grounds on the tundra to their winter feeding grounds farther south.*

and significant artists in Europe of the 17th century. Between 1629 and 1669 he painted some 60 penetrating self-portraits. He also painted religious subjects, and produced about 300 etchings and over 1,000 drawings. His major group portraits include *The Anatomy Lesson of Dr Tulp* 1632 (Mauritshuis, The Hague) and *The Night Watch* 1642 (Rijksmuseum, Amsterdam).

Remington Frederic 1861–1909. US artist and illustrator. He was known for his paintings, sculptures, and sketches of scenes of the American West, which he recorded during several trips to the region.

Born in Canton, New York, he trained at the Yale School of Fine Arts and at the Art Students League in New York City. He illustrated for Harper publications and other periodicals and for Theodore Roosevelt's *Ranch Life and the Hunting Trail* 1888.

Remington Philo 1816–1889. US inventor and businessman. He ran an arms business during the Civil War, when the firm had government contracts and later supplied several European armies with his new breech-loading rifles. In 1873 he became interested in the manufacture of typewriters, the first being demonstrated at the Centennial Exhibition in Philadelphia. By 1878, he produced the first typewriter with a shift key, which provided lower case as well as upper case letters. In 1879 his firm began making sewing machines.

remora any of a family of warm-water fishes that have an adhesive disk on the head, by which they attach themselves to whales, sharks, and turtles. These provide the remora with shelter and transport, as well as food in the form of parasites on the host's skin.

remote sensing gathering and recording information from a distance. Space probes have sent back photographs and data about planets as distant as Neptune. In archeology, surface survey techniques provide information without disturbing subsurface deposits.

REM sleep (acronym for *rapid-eye-movement* sleep) phase of sleep that recurs several times nightly in humans and is associated with dreaming. The eyes flicker quickly beneath closed lids.

Renaissance period and intellectual movement in European cultural history that is traditionally seen as ending the Middle Ages and beginning modern times. The Renaissance started in Italy in the 14th century and flourished in W Europe until about the 17th century.

The aim of Renaissance education was to produce the "complete human being" (*Renaissance man*), conversant in the humanities, mathematics and science (including their application in war), the arts and crafts, and athletics and sport; to enlarge the bounds of learning and geographical knowledge; to encourage the growth of skepticism and free thought, and the study and imitation of Greek and Latin literature and art. The revival of interest in classical Greek and Roman culture inspired artists, architects, and writers. Scientists and explorers proliferated as well.

Renaissance art movement in European art of the 15th and 16th centuries. It began in Florence, Italy, with the rise of a spirit of humanism and a new appreciation of the Classical Greek and Roman past. In painting and sculpture this led to greater naturalism and interest in anatomy and perspective. The 15th century is known as the *Classical Renaissance*. The *High Renaissance* (early 16th century) covers the careers of Leonardo da Vinci, Raphael, Michelangelo, and Titian in Italy and Dürer in Germany. *Mannerism* (roughly 1520s–90s) forms the final stage of the High Renaissance.

renewable energy power from any source that replenishes itself. Most renewable systems rely on ◊solar energy directly or through the weather cycle as ◊wave power, ◊hydroelectric power, or wind power via ◊wind turbines, or solar energy collected by plants (alcohol fuels, for example). In addition, the gravitational force of the Moon can be harnessed through tidal power stations, and the heat trapped in the center of the Earth is used via ◊geothermal energy systems.

renewable resource natural resource that is replaced by natural processes in a reasonable amount of time. Soil, water, forests, plants, and animals are all renewable resources as long as they are properly conserved. Solar, wind, wave, and geothermal energies are based on renewable resources.

rennet extract, traditionally obtained from a calf's stomach, that contains the enzyme rennin, used to coagulate milk in the cheesemaking process. The enzyme can now be chemically produced.

Renoir Jean 1894–1979. French film director. His films, characterized by their humanism and naturalistic technique, include *Boudu sauvé des eaux/Boudu Saved from Drowning* 1932, *La Grande Illusion* 1937, and *La Règle du jeu/The Rules of the Game* 1939. In 1975 he received an honorary Academy Award for his life's work. He was the son of the painter Pierre-Auguste Renoir.

Renoir Pierre-Auguste 1841–1919. French Impressionist painter. He met Monet and Sisley in the early 1860s, and together they formed the nucleus of the Impressionist movement. He developed a lively, colorful painting style with feathery brushwork (known as his "rainbow style") and painted many voluptuous female nudes, such as *The Bathers* about 1884–87 (Philadelphia Museum of Art, US). In his later years he turned to sculpture.

repetitive strain injury (RSI) inflammation of tendon sheaths, mainly in the hands and wrists, which may be disabling. It is found predominantly in factory workers involved in constant repetitive movements, and in high-speed typists. Some victims have successfully sued their employers for damages.

replication in biology, production of copies of the genetic material DNA; it occurs during cell division (◊mitosis and meiosis). Most mutations are caused by mistakes during replication.

repression in psychology, unconscious process said to protect a person from ideas, impulses, or memories that would threaten emotional stability were they to become conscious.

reproduction in biology, process by which a living organism produces other organisms similar to itself. There are two kinds: ◊asexual reproduction and ◊sexual reproduction.

reptile any member of a class (Reptilia) of vertebrates. Unlike amphibians, reptiles have hard-shelled, yolk-filled eggs that are laid on land and from which fully formed young are born. Some snakes and lizards retain their eggs and give birth to live young. Reptiles are coldblooded and produced from eggs, and the skin is usually covered with scales. The metabolism is slow, and in some cases (certain large snakes) intervals between meals may be months. Reptiles date back over 300 million years.

republic country where the head of state is not a monarch, either hereditary or elected, but usually a president whose role may or may not include political functions.

Republican Party one of the US's two main political parties, formed 1854. It is considered more conservative than the Democratic Party, favoring capital and big business and opposing state subvention and federal controls. In the late 20th century most presidents have come from the Republican Party, but in Congress Republicans have generally been outnumbered.

requiem in the Roman Catholic Church, a mass for the dead. Musical settings include those by Palestrina, Mozart, Berlioz, Verdi, Fauré, and Britten.

reserve currency in economics, a country's holding of internationally acceptable means of payment (major foreign currencies or gold); central banks also hold the ultimate reserve of money for their domestic banking sector. On the asset side of company balance sheets, undistributed profits are listed as reserves.

resin substance exuded from pines, firs, and other trees in gummy drops that harden in air. Varnishes are common products of the hard resins, and ointments come from the soft resins.

resistance in physics, that property of a substance that restricts the flow of electricity through it, associated with the conversion of electrical energy to heat; also the magnitude of this property. Resistance depends on many factors, such as the nature of the material, its temperature, dimensions, and thermal properties; degree of impurity; the nature and state of illumination of the surface; and the frequency and magnitude of the current. The SI unit of resistance is the ohm.

resistance movement opposition movement in a country occupied by an enemy or colonial power, especially in the 20th century; for example, the French resistance to Nazism in World War II.

After World War II resistance movements grew in Palestine, South America, and European colonial possessions in Africa and Asia, aimed at unsettling established regimes.

resolution in computing, the number of dots per unit length in which an image can be reproduced on a screen or printer. A typical screen resolution for color monitors is 75 dpi (dots per inch). A ◊laser printer will typically have a printing resolution of 300 dpi, and ◊dot matrix printers typically have resolutions from 60 dpi to 180 dpi. Photographs in books and magazines have a resolution of 1,200 dpi or 2,400 dpi.

resonance rapid and uncontrolled increase in the size of a vibration when the vibrating object is subject to a force varying at its natural frequency. In a trombone, for example, the length of the air column in the instrument is adjusted until it resonates with the note being sounded. Resonance effects are also produced by many electrical circuits. Tuning a radio, for example, is done by adjusting the natural frequency of the receiver circuit until it coincides with the frequency of the radio waves falling on the aerial.

respiration biochemical process whereby food molecules are progressively broken down (oxidized) to release energy in the form of ◊ATP. In most organisms this requires oxygen, but in some bacteria the oxidant is the nitrate or sulfate ion instead. In all higher

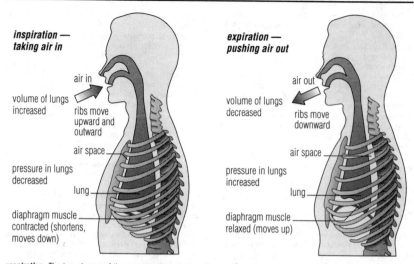

*inspiration —
taking air in*

air in

volume of lungs
increased

ribs move
upward and
outward

air space

pressure in lungs
decreased

lung

diaphragm muscle
contracted (shortens,
moves down)

*expiration —
pushing air out*

air out

volume of lungs
decreased

ribs move
downward

air space

pressure in lungs
increased

lung

diaphragm muscle
relaxed (moves up)

respiration *The two phases of the process of respiration. Gas exchange occurs in the alveoli, tiny air tubes in the lungs.*

organisms, respiration occurs in the mitochondria. Respiration is also used to mean breathing, in which oxygen is exchanged for carbon dioxide in the lung alveoli, though this is more accurately described as a form of ◊gas exchange.

Restoration in English history, the period when the monarchy, in the person of Charles II, was reestablished after the English Civil War and the fall of the ◊Protectorate 1660.

Restoration comedy style of English theater, dating from the Restoration (from 1660). It witnessed the first appearance of women on the English stage, most notably in the "breeches part", specially created in order to costume the actress in male attire, thus revealing her figure to its best advantage. The genre placed much emphasis on wit and sexual intrigues. Examples include Wycherley's *The Country Wife* 1675, Congreve's *The Way of the World* 1700, and Farquhar's *The Beaux' Stratagem* 1707.

restrictive trade practice any agreement between people in a particular trade or business that restricts free trade in a market. For example, several producers may join together to form a ◊cartel and fix prices; or a manufacturer may refuse to supply goods to a retailer if the retailer stocks the products of a rival company.

Often, these practices are illegal.

resurrection in Christian, Jewish, and Muslim belief, the rising from the dead that all souls will experience at the Last Judgment. The Resurrection also refers to Jesus rising from the dead on the third day after his crucifixion, a belief central to Christianity and celebrated at Easter.

resuscitation steps taken to revive anyone on the brink of death. The most successful technique for life-threatening emergencies, such as electrocution, near-drowning, or heart attack, is mouth-to-mouth resuscitation. Medical and paramedical staff are trained in cardiopulmonary resuscitation: the use of specialized equipment and techniques to attempt to restart the

breathing and/or heartbeat and stabilize the patient long enough for more definitive treatment.

retail-price index (RPI) indicator of variations in the cost of living, superseded in the US by the consumer price index.

retrovirus any of a family of ◊viruses (Retroviridae) containing the genetic material ◊RNA rather than the more usual ◊DNA.

revisionism political theory derived from Marxism that moderates one or more of the basic tenets of Marx, and is hence condemned by orthodox Marxists.

revolution any rapid, far-reaching, or violent change in the political, social, or economic structure of society. It is usually applied to political change: examples include the American Revolution, where the colonists broke free from their colonial ties and established a sovereign, independent, nation; the French Revolution, where an absolute monarchy was overthrown by opposition from inside the country and a popular uprising; and the Russian Revolution, where a repressive monarchy was overthrown by those seeking to institute widespread social and economic changes based on a socialist model. In 1989–90 the Eastern Bloc nations demonstrated against and voted out the Communist party, in many cases creating a prodemocracy revolution.

Revolutionary Wars series of wars 1791–1802 between France and the combined armies of England, Austria, Prussia, and others, during the period of the ◊French Revolution and ◊Napoleon's campaign to conquer Europe.

revolutions of 1848 series of revolts in various parts of Europe against monarchical rule. While some of the revolutionaries had republican ideas, many more were motivated by economic grievances. The revolution began in France with the overthrow of Louis Philippe and then spread to Italy, the Austrian Empire, and Germany, where the short-lived Frankfurt Parliament put forward ideas about political unity in Germany.

None of the revolutions enjoyed any lasting success, and most were violently suppressed within a few months.

revue stage presentation involving short satirical and topical items in the form of songs, sketches, and monologues; it originated in the late 19th century.

Turn-of-the-century revues were spectacular entertainments, notably those of Florenz Ziegfeld, but the "intimate revue" became increasingly popular, employing writers such as Noël Coward.

Reykjavik capital (from 1918) and chief port of Iceland, on the SW coast; population (1988) 93,000. Fish processing is the main industry. Reykjavik is heated by underground mains fed by volcanic springs. It was a seat of Danish administration 1801–1918.

Reynolds Albert 1933– . Irish politician, prime minister 1992–94. He joined Fianna Faíl 1977, and became prime minister when Charles Haughey was forced to resign Jan 1992. He fostered closer relations with Britain and in Dec 1993 he and UK prime minister John Major issued a joint peace initiative for Northern Ireland, the "Downing Street Declaration", which led to a general cease-fire the following year. He resigned as premier and Fianna Fáil leader Nov 1994.

Reynolds Burt 1936– . US film actor and director who excels in adventure films and comedies. He is known for doing his own stunts, since he started as a stuntman. His films include *Deliverance* 1972, the cult film *White Lightning* 1973, *Hustle* 1975, and *City Heat* 1984.

Reynolds Joshua 1723–1792. English portrait painter. He was active in London from 1752 and became the first president of the Royal Academy 1768. His portraits display a facility for striking and characterful compositions in a consciously grand manner. He often borrowed classical poses, for example *Mrs Siddons as the Tragic Muse* 1784 (San Marino, California).

rhea one of two flightless birds of the family Rheidae. The common rhea *Rhea americana* is 5 ft/1.5 m high and is distributed widely in South America. The smaller Darwin's rhea *Pterocnemia pennata* occurs only in the south of South America. They differ from the ostrich in their smaller size and in having a feathered neck and head, three-toed feet, and no plumelike tail feathers.

Rheims English version of ◊Reims, a city in France.

rhenium heavy, silver-white, metallic element, symbol Re, atomic number 75, atomic weight 186.2. It has chemical properties similar to those of manganese and a very high melting point (5,756°F/3,180°C), which makes it valuable as an ingredient in alloys.

It was identified and named in 1925 by German chemists W Noddack (1893–1960), I Tacke, and O Berg from the Latin name for the river Rhine.

rhesus factor group of ◊antigens on the surface of red blood cells of humans which characterize the rhesus blood group system. Most individuals possess the main rhesus factor (Rh+), but those without this factor (Rh–) produce ◊antibodies if they come into contact with it. The name comes from rhesus monkeys, in whose blood rhesus factors were first found.

rhesus monkey macaque monkey *Macaca mulatta* found in N India and SE Asia. It has a pinkish face, red buttocks, and long, straight, brown-gray hair. It can grow up to 2 ft/60 cm long, with a 8 in/20 cm tail.

rheumatic fever or *acute rheumatism* acute or chronic illness characterized by fever and painful swelling of joints. Some victims also experience involuntary movements of the limbs and head, a form of chorea. It is now rare in the developed world.

rheumatoid arthritis inflammation of the joints; a chronic progressive disease, it begins with pain and stiffness in the small joints of the hands and feet and spreads to involve other joints, often with severe disability and disfigurement. There may also be damage to the eyes, nervous system and other organs. The disease is treated with a range of drugs and with surgery, possibly including replacement of major joints.

Rhine (German *Rhein*, French *Rhin*) European river rising in Switzerland and reaching the North Sea via Germany and the Netherlands; length 820 mi/1,320 km. Tributaries include the Moselle and the Ruhr. The Rhine is linked with the Mediterranean by the Rhine–Rhône Waterway, and with the Black Sea by the Rhine–Main–Danube Waterway. It is the longest, and the dirtiest, river in Europe.

Rhineland-Palatinate (German *Rheinland-Pfalz*) administrative region (German *Land*) of Germany *area* 7,643 sq mi/19,800 sq km *capital* Mainz *towns and cities* Ludwigshafen, Koblenz, Trier, Worms *physical* wooded mountain country, river valleys of Rhine and Moselle *industries* wine (75% of German output), tobacco, chemicals, machinery, leather goods, pottery *population* (1992) 3,702,000

rhinoceros odd-toed hoofed mammal of the family Rhinocerotidae. The one-horned Indian rhinoceros *Rhinoceros unicornis* is up to 6 ft/2 m high at the shoulder, with a tubercled skin, folded into shieldlike pieces; the African rhinoceroses are smooth-skinned and two-horned. All are in danger of becoming extinct.

Rhode Island (officially Rhode Island and Providence Plantations) state in NE US; the smallest state of the US; nickname Ocean State *area* 1,197 sq mi/3,100 sq km *capital* Providence *cities* Cranston, Woonsocket *population* (1990) 1,003,464 *features* Narragansett Bay, with America's Cup yacht races; mansions of Newport; Block Island; Brown University; Rhode Island School of Design; University of Rhode Island *industries* poultry (Rhode Island Reds), jewelry, silverware, textiles, machinery, primary metals, rubber products, submarine assembly *famous people* George M Cohan, Anne Hutchinson, Matthew C Perry, Oliver Hazard Perry, Gilbert Stuart, Roger Williams *history* founded 1636 by Roger Williams, exiled from Massachusetts Bay colony for religious dissent; one of the original 13 states and still the smallest one in area. The principle trends in the 19th century were industrialization, immigration, and urbanization. Rhode Island is the most industrialized state, and it suffers from high unemployment, low-wage manufacturing industries, and susceptibility to recessions.

Rhodes (Greek *Ródhos*) Greek island, largest of the Dodecanese, in the E Aegean Sea *area* 545 sq mi/1,412 sq km *capital* Rhodes *industries* grapes, olives *population* (1981) 88,000 *history* settled by Greeks about 1000 BC ; the Colossus of Rhodes (fell 224 BC) was one of the ◊Seven Wonders of the World; held by the Knights Hospitallers of St John 1306–1522; taken from Turkish rule by the Italian occupation 1912; ceded to Greece 1947.

Rhodes Cecil (John) 1853–1902. South African politician, born in the UK, prime minister of Cape Colony 1890–96. He formed the British South Africa Company in 1889, which occupied Mashonaland and Matabeleland, thus forming *Rhodesia* (now Zambia and Zimbabwe).

The *Rhodes scholarships* were founded at Oxford University, UK, under his will, for students from the Commonwealth, the US, and Germany.

Rhodesia former name of ◊Zambia (Northern Rhodesia) and ◊Zimbabwe (Southern Rhodesia), in S Africa.

rhodium hard, silver-white, metallic element, symbol Rh, atomic number 45, atomic weight 102.905. It is one of the so-called platinum group of metals and is resistant to tarnish, corrosion, and acid. It occurs as a free metal in the natural alloy osmiridium and is used in jewelry, electroplating, and thermocouples.

rhododendron any of numerous shrubs of the genus *Rhododendron* of the heath family Ericaceae. Most species are evergreen. The leaves are usually dark and leathery, and the large racemes of flowers occur in all colors except blue. They thrive on acid soils. ◊Azaleas belong to the same genus.

Rhône river of S Europe; length 500 mi/810 km. It rises in Switzerland and flows through Lake Geneva to Lyon in France, where at its confluence with the Saône the upper limit of navigation is reached. The river turns due south, passes Vienne and Avignon, and takes in the Isère and other tributaries. Near Arles it divides into the *Grand* and *Petit Rhône*, flowing respectively SE and SW into the Mediterranean W of Marseille. Here it forms a two-armed delta; the area between the tributaries is the marshy region known as the Camargue.

Rhône-Alpes region of E France in the upper reaches of the Rhône; area 16,868 sq mi/43,700 sq km; population (1992) 5,344,000. It consists of the *départements* of Ain, Ardèche, Drôme, Isère, Loire, Rhône, Savoie, and Haute-Savoie. The chief city is Lyon. There are several wine-producing areas, including Chenas, Fleurie, and Beaujolais. Industrial products include chemicals, textiles, and motor vehicles.

rhubarb perennial plant *Rheum rhaponticum* of the buckwheat family Polygonaceae, grown for its pink, edible leaf stalks. The leaves contain ◊oxalic acid, and are poisonous. There are also wild rhubarbs native to Europe and Asia.

rhythm and blues (R & B) US popular music of the 1940s–60s, which drew on swing and jump-jazz rhythms and blues vocals, and was an important influence on rock and roll. It diversified into soul, funk, and other styles. R & B artists include Bo Diddley, Jackie Wilson (1934–84), and Etta James (*c.* 1938–).

Ribbentrop–Molotov pact nonaggression treaty signed by Germany and the USSR Aug 23, 1939. Under the terms of the treaty both countries agreed to remain neutral and to refrain from acts of aggression against each other if either went to war. Secret clauses allowed for the partition of Poland—German Nazi dictator Adolf Hitler was to acquire western Poland, Soviet dictator Joseph Stalin the eastern part. On Sept 1, 1939, Hitler invaded Poland. The pact ended when Hitler invaded Russia on June 22, 1941. See also ◊World War II.

riboflavin or *vitamin B₂* ◊vitamin of the B complex important in cell respiration. It is obtained from eggs, liver, and milk. A deficiency in the diet causes stunted growth.

ribonucleic acid full name of ◊RNA.

ribosome in biology, the protein-making machinery of the cell. Ribosomes are located on the endoplasmic

reticulum (ER) of eukaryotic cells, and are made of proteins and a special type of ◊RNA, ribosomal RNA. They receive messenger RNA (copied from the ◊DNA) and ◊amino acids, and "translate" the messenger RNA by using its chemically coded instructions to link amino acids in a specific order, to make a strand of a particular protein.

Ricardo David 1772–1823. English economist, author of *Principles of Political Economy* 1817. Among his discoveries were the principle of comparative advantage (that countries can benefit by specializing in goods they produce efficiently and trading internationally to buy others), and the law of diminishing returns (that continued increments of capital and labor applied to a given quantity of land will eventually show a declining rate of increase in output).

rice principal cereal of the wet regions of the tropics; derived from grass of the species *Oryza sativa*, probably native to India and SE Asia. It is unique among cereal crops in that it is grown standing in water. The yield is very large, and rice is said to be the staple food of one-third of the world population.

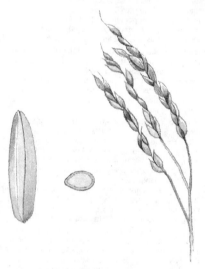

rice The rice plant is unique among cereal crops in that it is grown standing in water. The rice stem is adapted to allow oxygen to pass downward to the waterlogged roots. The grain is usually white, but there are red, brown, and black varieties. The thin skin of the grain is rich in oils, minerals, and vitamins.

Richard (I) the Lion-Hearted (French *Coeur-de-Lion*) 1157–1199. King of England from 1189, who spent all but six months of his reign abroad. He was the third son of Henry II, against whom he twice rebelled. In the third ◊Crusade 1191–92 he won victories at Cyprus, Acre, and Arsuf (against ◊Saladin), but failed to recover Jerusalem. While returning overland he was captured by the Duke of Austria, who handed him over to the emperor Henry VI, and he was held prisoner until a large ransom was raised. He then returned briefly to England, where his brother John I had been ruling in his stead. His later years were spent in warfare in France, where he was killed.

Richard II 1367–1400. King of England from 1377, effectively from 1389, son of Edward the Black Prince. He reigned in conflict with Parliament; they executed some of his associates 1388, and he executed some of the opposing barons 1397, whereupon he made himself absolute. Two years later, forced to abdicate in favor of ◊Henry IV, he was jailed and probably assassinated.

In 1399 his cousin Henry Bolingbroke, Duke of Hereford (later Henry IV), returned from exile to lead a revolt; Richard II was deposed by Parliament and imprisoned in Pontefract Castle, where he died mysteriously.

Richard III 1452–1485. King of England from 1483. The son of Richard, Duke of York, he was created Duke of Gloucester by his brother Edward IV, and distinguished himself in the Wars of the ◊Roses. On Edward's death 1483 he became protector to his nephew Edward V, and soon secured the crown for himself on the plea that Edward IV's sons were illegitimate. He proved a capable ruler, but the suspicion that he had murdered Edward V and his brother undermined his popularity. In 1485 Henry, Earl of Richmond (later ◊Henry VII), raised a rebellion, and Richard III was defeated and killed at ◊Bosworth.

Richardson Ralph (David) 1902–1983. English actor. He played many stage parts, including Falstaff (Shakespeare), Peer Gynt (Ibsen), and Cyrano de Bergerac (Rostand). He shared the management of the Old Vic theater with Laurence Olivier 1944–50. In later years he revealed himself as an accomplished deadpan comic.

Richelieu Armand Jean du Plessis de 1585–1642. French cardinal and politician, chief minister from 1624. He aimed to make the monarchy absolute; he ruthlessly crushed opposition by the nobility and destroyed the political power of the ◊Huguenots, while leaving them religious freedom. Abroad, he sought to establish French supremacy by breaking the power of the Hapsburgs; he therefore supported the Swedish king Gustavus Adolphus and the German Protestant princes against Austria and in 1635 brought France into the Thirty Years' War.

Richmond industrial city and port on the James River and capital of Virginia, US; population (1990) 219,000. It is a major tobacco market and distribution, commercial, and financial center of the surrounding region. Its diversified manufactures include tobacco products, chemicals, paper and printing, and textiles.

Educational institutions include the University of Richmond and Virginia Commonwealth University. The Museum of the Confederacy and Edgar Allan Poe Museum are here, as are the former homes of John Marshall and Robert E Lee and the graves of James Madison and Jefferson Davis. The first permanent colonial American settlement was established 1637. Richmond was the capital of the Confederacy 1861–65, and several Civil War battles were fought nearby.

Richter Burton 1931– . US high-energy physicist who, in the 1960s, designed the Stanford Positron Accelerating Ring (SPEAR). In 1974 Richter used SPEAR to produce a new particle, a hadeon, composed of a charmed quark and a charmed antiquark. The charmed quark had been first postulated by Sheldon Glashow in 1964. Richter shared the 1976 Nobel Physics Prize with Samuel Ting.

Richter scale scale based on measurement of seismic waves, used to determine the magnitude of an ◊earthquake at its epicenter. The magnitude of an earthquake differs from its intensity, measured by the Mercalli scale, which is subjective and varies from place to place for the same earthquake. The scale is named after US seismologist Charles Richter.

Rickenbacker Edward Vernon 1890–1973. US race-car driver, aviator, and airline executive. Born in Columbus, Ohil, he was a leading US fighter pilot during World War I and was later awarded the Conressional Medal of Honor for his wartime service. He purchased Eastern Airlines 1938 leaving briefly to serve as an adviser to the War Department during World War II. Taking on special missions, he ditched his plane in the Pacific Ocean, drifting for 23 days before being rescued. He was president of Eastern Airlines to 1959 and chairman of the board to 1963.

rickets defective growth of bone in children due to an insufficiency of calcium deposits. The bones, which do not harden adequately, are bent out of shape. It is usually caused by a lack of vitamin D and insufficient exposure to sunlight. Renal rickets, also a condition of malformed bone, is associated with kidney disease.

Riefenstahl Leni 1902– . German filmmaker. Her film of the Nazi rallies at Nuremberg, *Triumph des Willens/Triumph of the Will* 1934, vividly illustrated Hitler's charismatic appeal but tainted her career.

She trained as a dancer, appearing in films in the 1920s, but in the early 1930s formed her own production company, and directed and starred in *Das blaue Licht/The Blue Light* 1932. She also made a two-part documentary of the 1936 Berlin Olympics.

rifle ◊firearm that has spiral grooves (rifling) in its barrel. When a bullet is fired, the rifling makes it spin, thereby improving accuracy. Rifles were first introduced in the late 18th century.

Rift Valley, Great volcanic valley formed 10–20 million years ago by a crack in the Earth's crust and running about 5,000 mi/8,000 km from the Jordan Valley through the Red Sea to central Mozambique in SE Africa. It is marked by a series of lakes, including Lake Turkana (formerly Lake Rudolf), and volcanoes, such as Mount Kilimanjaro.

Riga capital and port of Latvia; population (1987) 900,000. A member of the ◊Hanseatic League from 1282, Riga has belonged in turn to Poland 1582, Sweden 1621, and Russia 1710. It was occupied by the Germans 1917 and then, after being seized by both Russian and German troops in the aftermath of World War I, became the capital of independent Latvia 1919–40. It was again occupied by Germany 1941–44, before being annexed by the USSR. It again became independent Latvia's capital 1991.

Rigel or *Beta Orionis* brightest star in the constellation Orion. It is a blue-white supergiant, with an estimated diameter 50 times that of the Sun. It is 900 light-years from Earth, and is about 100,000 times more luminous than our Sun. It is the seventh-brightest star in the sky.

Rights of Man and the Citizen, Declaration of the

historic French document. According to the statement of the French National Assembly 1789, these rights include representation in the legislature; equality before the law; equality of opportunity; freedom from arbitrary imprisonment; freedom of speech and religion; taxation in proportion to ability to pay; and security of property. In 1946 were added equal rights for women; right to work, join a union, and strike; leisure, social security, and support in old age; and free education.

right triangle triangle in which one of the angles is a right angle (90°). It is the basic form of triangle for defining trigonometrical ratios (for example, sine, cosine, and tangent) and for which the ◊Pythagorean theorem holds true. The longest side of a right triangle is called the hypotenuse.

right wing the more conservative or reactionary section of a political party or spectrum. It originated in the French national assembly 1789, where the nobles sat in the place of honor on the president's right, whereas the commons were on his left (hence ◊left wing).

Riley James Whitcomb 1849–1916. US poet. His first collection of poems, *The Old Swimmin' Hole*, was published 1883. His later collections include *Rhymes of Childhood* 1890 and *Home Folks* 1900. His use of the Midwestern vernacular and familiar themes earned him the unofficial title "The Hoosier Poet".

Rilke Rainer Maria 1875–1926. Austrian writer. His prose works include the semiautobiographical *Die Aufzeichnungen des Malte Laurids Brigge/The Notebook of Malte Laurids Brigge* 1910. His verse is characterized by a form of mystic pantheism that seeks to achieve a state of ecstasy in which existence can be apprehended as a whole.

Rimbaud (Jean Nicolas) Arthur 1854–1891. French Symbolist poet. His verse was chiefly written before the age of 20, notably *Les Illuminations* published 1886. From 1871 he lived with the poet Paul Verlaine.

Rimsky-Korsakov Nikolay Andreyevich 1844–1908. Russian nationalist composer. His operas include *The Maid of Pskov* 1873, *The Snow Maiden* 1882, *Mozart and Salieri* 1898, and *The Golden Cockerel* 1907, a satirical attack on despotism that was banned until 1909. He also wrote an influential text on orchestration.

rinderpest acute viral disease of cattle (sometimes also of sheep and goats) characterized by fever and bloody diarrhea, due to inflammation of the intestines. It can be fatal. Almost eliminated in the 1960s, it revived in Africa in the 1980s.

ringworm any of various contagious skin infections due to related kinds of fungus, usually resulting in circular, itchy, discolored patches covered with scales or blisters. The scalp and feet (athlete's foot) are generally involved. Treatment is with antifungal preparations.

Rio de Janeiro port and resort in E Brazil; population (1991) 5,487,300. Sugar Loaf Mountain stands at the entrance to the harbor. Rio was the capital of Brazil 1763–1960. The city is the capital of the state of Rio de Janeiro, which has a population of 13,267,100 (1987 est).

Rio Grande river rising in the Rocky Mountains in S Colorado, US, and flowing S to the Gulf of Mexico, where it is reduced to a trickle by irrigation demands on its upper reaches; length 1,900 mi/3,050 km. Its last 1,500 mi/2,400 km form the US–Mexican border (Mexican name *Río Bravo del Norte*).

Rio Grande do Norte state of NE Brazil; area 20,460 sq mi/53,000 sq km; population (1990) 2,522,700. Its capital is Natal. Industries include agriculture and textiles; there is offshore oil.

Rio Grande do Sul most southerly state of Brazil, on the frontier with Argentina and Uruguay; area 108,993 sq mi/282,184 sq km; population (1990) 9,348,300. Its capital is Pôrto Alegre. Industries include agriculture and cattle, food processing, and textiles.

Risorgimento 19th-century movement for Italian national unity and independence, begun 1815. Leading figures in the movement included Cavour, ◊Mazzini, and ◊Garibaldi. Uprisings 1848–49 failed, but with help from France in a war against Austria—to oust it from Italian provinces in the north—an Italian kingdom was founded 1861. Unification was finally completed with the addition of Venetia 1866 and the Papal States 1870.

river long water course that flows down a slope along a channel. It originates at a point called its *source*, and enters a sea or lake at its *mouth*. Along its length it may be joined by smaller rivers called *tributaries*. A river and its tributaries are contained within a drainage basin.

rivers, major

name and location	mi	km
Nile (NE Africa)	4,160	6,695
Amazon (South America)	4,080	6,570
Chang Jiang (China)	3,900	6,300
Mississippi–Missouri (US)	3,740	6,020
Ob–Irtysh (China/Kazakhstan/Russia)	3,480	5,600
Huang He (China)	3,395	5,464
Paraná (Brazil)	2,800	4,500
Zaïre (Africa)	2,800	4,500
Mekong (Asia)	2,750	4,425
Amur (Asia)	2,744	4,416
Lena (Russia)	2,730	4,400
Mackenzie (Canada)	2,635	4,241
Niger (Africa)	2,600	4,185
Yenisei (Russia)	2,550	4,100
Mississippi (US)	2,350	3,780
Murray–Darling (Australia)	2,330	3,750
Missouri (US)	2,328	3,725
Volga (Russia)	2,290	3,685

Rivera Diego 1886–1957. Mexican painter. He was active in Europe until 1921. An exponent of Social Realism, he received many public commissions for murals exalting the Mexican revolution. A vast cycle on historical themes (National Palace, Mexico City) was begun 1929. In the 1930s he visited the US and with Ben Shahn produced murals for the Rockefeller Center, New York (later overpainted because he included a portrait of Lenin).

Riviera the Mediterranean coast of France and Italy from Marseille to La Spezia. The most exclusive stretch of the Riviera, with the finest climate, is the Côte d'Azur, from Menton to St Tropez, which includes Monaco.

Riyadh (Arabic *Ar Riyad*) capital of Saudi Arabia and of the Central Province, formerly the sultanate of Nejd, in an oasis, connected by rail with Dammam on the Arabian Gulf; population (1986) 1,500,000.

RNA (abbreviation for *ribonucleic acid*) nucleic acid involved in the process of translating ◊DNA, the genetic material into proteins. It is usually single-stranded, unlike the double-stranded DNA, and consists of a large number of nucleotides strung together, each of which comprises the sugar ribose, a phosphate group, and one of four bases (uracil, cytosine, adenine, or guanine).

RNA is copied from DNA by the assemblage of free nucleotides against an unwound portion (a single strand) of the DNA, with DNA serving as the template.

roach any freshwater fish of the Eurasian genus *Rutilus*, of the carp family, especially *R. rutilus* of N Europe. It is dark green above, whitish below, with reddish lower fins; it grows to 1.2 ft/35 cm.

road specially constructed route for wheeled vehicles to travel on.

Reinforced tracks became necessary with the invention of wheeled vehicles in about 3000 BC and most ancient civilizations had some form of road network. The Romans developed engineering techniques that were not equaled for another 1,400 years.

In the US, the first roads were paved in colonial times, first with logs (corduroy roads), later with cobblestones and Belgian building blocks or brick, depending on the region.

robbery in law, a variety of theft: stealing from a person, using force, or the threat of force, to intimidate the victim.

Robbia, della Italian family of sculptors and architects. They were active in Florence. *Luca della Robbia* (1400–1482) created a number of major works in Florence, notably the marble *cantoria* (singing gallery) in the cathedral 1431–38 (Museo del Duomo), with lively groups of choristers. Luca also developed a characteristic style of glazed terracotta work.

Robbins Jerome 1918– . US dancer and choreographer. He was co-director of the New York City Ballet 1969–83 (with George Balanchine). His ballets are internationally renowned and he is considered the greatest US-born ballet choreographer. He also choreographed the musicals *The King and I* 1951, *West Side Story* 1957, and *Fiddler on the Roof* 1964.

Robert II *c.* 1054–1134. Eldest son of ◊William the Conqueror, succeeding him as Duke of Normandy (but not on the English throne) 1087. His brother ◊William II ascended the English throne, and they warred until 1096, after which Robert took part in the First Crusade. When his other brother ◊Henry I claimed the English throne 1100, Robert contested the claim and invaded England unsuccessfully 1101. Henry invaded Normandy 1106, and captured Robert, who remained a prisoner in England until his death.

Robert (I) the Bruce 1274–1329. King of Scotland from 1306. He shared in the national uprising led by William Wallace, and, after Wallace's execution 1305, rose once more against Edward I of England, and was crowned at Scone 1306. He defeated Edward II at ◊Bannockburn 1314. In 1328 the treaty of Northampton recognized Scotland's independence and Robert as king.

Robert II 1316–1390. King of Scotland from 1371. He was the son of Walter (1293–1326), steward of Scotland, who married Marjory, daughter of Robert the Bruce. He was the first king of the house of Stuart.

Robert III *c.* 1340–1406. King of Scotland from 1390, son of Robert II. He was unable to control the nobles, and the government fell largely into the hands of his brother, Robert, Duke of Albany (*c.* 1340–1420).

Robespierre Maximilien François Marie Isidore de 1758–1794. French politician in the ◊French Revolution. As leader of the ◊Jacobins in the National Convention, he supported the execution of Louis XVI and the overthrow of the right-wing republican Girondists, and in July 1793 was elected to the Committee of Public Safety. A year later he was guillotined; many believe that he was a scapegoat for the Reign of ◊Terror since he ordered only 72 executions personally.

robin one of two songbirds of the thrush family. (1) North American thrush, the robin *Turdus migratorius*, 10 in/25 cm long, gray brown with brick-red underparts. (2) Eurasian and African thrush *Erithacus rubecula*, 5 in/13 cm long, olive brown above with a red breast.

Robin Hood in English legend, an outlaw and champion of the poor against the rich, said to have lived in Sherwood Forest, Nottinghamshire, during the reign of Richard I (1189–99). He feuded with the sheriff of Nottingham, accompanied by Maid Marian and a band of followers known as his "merry men". He appears in ballads from the 13th century, but his first datable appearance is in Langland's *Piers Plowman* in the late 14th century.

Robinson Edward G. Adopted name of Emmanuel Goldenberg 1893–1973. US film actor. Born in Romania, he emigrated with his family to the US 1903. He was noted for his gangster roles, such as *Little Caesar* 1930, but also gave strong performances in psychological dramas such as *Scarlet Street* 1945.

His other films include *Dr Ehrlich's Magic Bullet* 1940, *Double Indemnity* 1944, *The Ten Commandments* 1956, and *Soylent Green* 1973.

Robinson Edwin Arlington 1869–1935. US poet. His verse, dealing mainly with psychological themes in a narrative style, is collected in volumes such as *The Children of the Night* 1897, which established his reputation. He was awarded three Pulitzer Prizes for poetry: *Collected Poems* 1922, *The Man Who Died Twice* 1925, and *Tristram* 1928.

Robinson Jackie (Jack Roosevelt) 1919–1972. US baseball player born in Cairo, Georgia. In 1947 he became the first African American in the major leagues, playing second base for the Brooklyn Dodgers and winning rookie of the year honors. In 1949 he was the National League's batting champion and was voted the league's most valuable player. He had a career batting average of .311. After retirement as a player 1956, Robinson served as the New York governor's special assistant for community affairs 1966–68.

He was elected to the Baseball Hall of Fame 1962.

Robinson Sugar Ray. Adopted name of Walker Smith 1920–1989. US boxer, world welterweight champion 1945–51; he defended his title five times. Defeating Jake LaMotta 1951, he took the middleweight title. He lost the title six times and won it seven times. He retired at the age of 45.

robot any computer-controlled machine that can be programmed to move or carry out work. Robots are often used in industry to transport materials or to perform repetitive tasks. For instance, robotic arms, fixed to a floor or workbench, may be used to paint machine parts or assemble electronic circuits. Other robots are designed to work in situations that would be dangerous to humans—for example, in defusing bombs or in space and deep-sea exploration. Some robots are equipped with sensors, such as touch sensors and video cameras, and can make be programmed to make simple decisions based on the sensory data received.

Rochester industrial city in New York, US, on the Genesee River, S of Lake Ontario; population (1990) 231,600. Its manufactured products include photographic equipment and optical and other precision instruments. It was the birthplace of the Xerox copier, and the world headquarters of the Eastman Kodak Company are here along with the famed Eastman School of Music.

Permanent settlement began 1812, and growth was spurred by the completion of the Erie Canal 1825. During the mid-19th century, Rochester was a focus for abolitionism and women's rights; Susan B Anthony and Frederick Douglass lived here.

Rochester commercial center with dairy and food-processing industries in Minnesota, US; population (1990) 70,745. Rochester is the home of the Mayo Clinic, part of a medical center established 1889.

The University of Minnesota medical school and the Mayo medical school are also here. The community was settled 1854 and named for Rochester, New York.

rock and roll pop music born of a fusion of rhythm and blues and country and western and based on electric guitar and drums. In the mid-1950s, with the advent of Elvis Presley, it became the heartbeat of teenage rebellion in the West and also had considerable impact on other parts of the world. It found perhaps its purest form in late-1950s rockabilly, the style of white Southerners in the US; the blanket term "rock" later came to comprise a multitude of styles.

The term rock and roll was popularized by US disk jockey Alan Freed (1922–1965) beginning in 1951 on radio and in stage shows hosted by him.

Rockefeller John D(avison) 1839–1937. US millionaire, founder of Standard Oil 1870 (which achieved control of 90% of US refineries by 1882). He founded the philanthropic *Rockefeller Foundation* 1913, to which his son *John D(avison) Rockefeller Jr* (1874–1960) devoted his life.

Born in Richford, New York, Rockefeller was brought up in Cleveland, Ohio, and after high school worked as a bookkeeper.

By 1867, after oil was discovered in the US (in Pennsylvania), he and his produce-market partners went into the business of refining kerosene. From this company grew Standard Oil, which by 1911 had ruthlessly created a monopoly on US oil refining and distribution. It was broken up by a US Supreme Court ruling into smaller companies.

rocket projectile driven by the reaction of gases produced by a fast-burning fuel. Unlike jet engines, which are also reaction engines, modern rockets carry their own oxygen supply to burn their fuel and do not require any surrounding atmosphere. For warfare, rocket heads carry an explosive device.

Rocky Mountains or *Rockies* largest North American mountain system. It extends from the junction with the Mexican plateau, N through the W central states of the US, through Canada to the Alaskan border, and then forms part of the Continental Divide, which separates rivers draining into the Atlantic or Arctic oceans from those flowing toward the Pacific Ocean. Mount Elbert is the highest peak, 14,433 ft/4,400 m. Some geographers consider the Yukon and Alaska ranges as part of the system, making the highest point Mount Mckinley (Denali) 20,320 ft/6,194 m.)

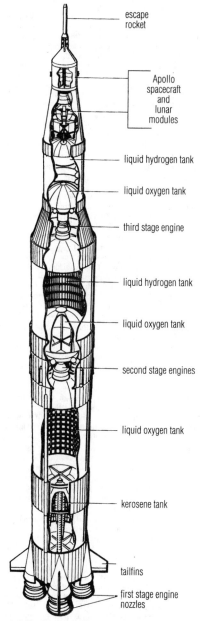

escape rocket

Apollo spacecraft and lunar modules

liquid hydrogen tank

liquid oxygen tank

third stage engine

liquid hydrogen tank

liquid oxygen tank

second stage engines

liquid oxygen tank

kerosene tank

tailfins

first stage engine nozzles

rocket The three-stage Saturn V rocket used in the Apollo moonshots of the 1960s and 1970s. It stood 365 ft/111 m high, as tall as a 30-story skyscraper, weighed 3,000 tons/2,700 metric tons when loaded with fuel, and developed a power equivalent to 50 Boeing 747 jumbo jets.

Rococo movement in the arts and architecture in 18th-century Europe, tending toward lightness, elegance, delicacy, and decorative charm. The term "Rococo" is derived from the French *rocaille* (rock- or shell-work), a style of interior decoration based on S-curves and scroll-like forms. Watteau's paintings and Sèvres porcelain belong to the French Rococo vogue. In the 1730s the movement became widespread in Europe, notably in the churches and palaces of S Germany and Austria. Chippendale furniture is an English example of the French Rococo style.

rodent any mammal of the worldwide order Rodentia, making up nearly half of all mammal species. Besides ordinary "cheek teeth", they have a single front pair of incisor teeth in both upper and lower jaw, which continue to grow as they are worn down.

Rodgers Richard (Charles) 1902–1979. US composer. He collaborated with librettist Lorenz Hart (1895–1943) on songs like "Blue Moon" 1934 and musicals like *On Your Toes* 1936. With Oscar Hammerstein II, he wrote many musicals, including *Oklahoma!* 1943, *South Pacific* 1949, *The King and I* 1951, and *The Sound of Music* 1959.

Rodin Auguste 1840–1917. French sculptor. He is considered the greatest of his day. He freed sculpture from the idealizing conventions of the time by his realistic treatment of the human figure, introducing a new boldness of style and expression. Examples are *Le Penseur/The Thinker* 1880 (Musée Rodin, Paris), *Le Baiser/The Kiss* 1886 (marble version in the Louvre, Paris), and *The Burghers of Calais* 1884–86 (copy in Embankment Gardens, Westminster, London).

roentgen or *röntgen* unit (symbol R) of radiation exposure, used for X-rays and gamma rays. It is defined in terms of the number of ions produced in one cubic centimeter of air by the radiation. Exposure to 1,000 roentgens gives rise to an absorbed dose of about 870 rads (8.7 grays), which is a dose equivalent of 870 rems (8.7 sieverts).

Rogers Richard 1933– . English High Tech architect. His works include the Pompidou Center in Paris 1977 (jointly with Renzo Piano), the Lloyd's of London building in London 1986, and the Reuters building at Blackwall Yard, London, 1992.

Rogers Roy. Adopted name of Leonard Slye 1912– . US actor who moved to Hollywood from radio. He was a singing cowboy of the 1930s and 1940s, one of the Sons of the Pioneers. His first Roy Rogers film *Under Western Stars* 1938, and he became "King of the Cowboys." He married his costar Dale Evans (who played in 20 of his films) in 1947.

Rogers Will (William Penn Adair) 1879–1935. US humorist and columnist for *The New York Times* from 1922, whose wry comments on current affairs won him national popularity. Born in Oologah Indian Territory (now Oklahoma), Rogers was first a cowboy and lariat-twirler before taking to the stage to specialize in aphorisms and homespun philosophy ("Everybody is ignorant, only on different subjects").

After beginning a Broadway career in 1915, which included Ziegfeld's Follies (1916–18, 1922, 1924–25), he moved to California to appear in motion pictures, including A Connecticut Yankee 1931 and *State Fair* 1933. He was killed in a plane crash in Alaska with famed pilot Wiley Post.

Roh Tae-woo 1932– . South Korean right-wing politician and general, president 1988–93. He held ministerial office from 1981 under President Chun, and

became chair of the ruling Democratic Justice Party 1985. He was elected president 1988, amid allegations of fraud and despite being connected with the massacre of about 2,000 antigovernment demonstrators 1980.

Roland died *c.* 778. French hero whose real and legendary deeds of valor and chivalry inspired many medieval and later romances, including the 11th-century *Chanson de Roland* and Ariosto's *Orlando furioso*. A knight of ◊Charlemagne, Roland was killed 778 with his friend Oliver and the 12 peers of France at Roncesvalles (in the Pyrenees) by Basques. He headed the rearguard during Charlemagne's retreat from his invasion of Spain.

role in the social sciences, the part(s) a person plays in society, either in helping the social system to work or in fulfilling social responsibilities toward others. *Role play* refers to the way in which children learn adult roles by acting them out in play (mothers and fathers, cops and robbers). Everyone has a number of roles to play in a society: for example, a woman may be an employee, mother, and wife at the same time.

roller any brightly colored bird of the Old World family Coraciidae, resembling crows but in the same order as kingfishers and hornbills. Rollers grow up to 13 in/32 cm long. The name is derived from the habit of some species of rolling over in flight.

Rolling Stones, the British band formed 1962, once notorious as the "bad boys" of rock. Original members were Mick Jagger (1943–), Keith Richards (1943–), Brian Jones (1942–1969), Bill Wyman (1936–), Charlie Watts (1941–), and the pianist Ian Stewart (1938–1985). A rock-and-roll institution, the Rolling Stones were still performing and recording in the 1990s.

Rollo First duke of Normandy *c.* 860–932. Viking leader. He left Norway about 875 and marauded, sailing up the Seine to Rouen. He besieged Paris 886, and in 912 was baptized and granted the province of Normandy by Charles III of France. He was its duke until his retirement to a monastery 927. He was an ancestor of William the Conqueror.

Rolls Charles Stewart 1877–1910. British engineer who joined with Henry Royce in 1905 to design and produce automobiles.

Rolls had trained as a mechanical engineer and worked in railroad production and as an automobile dealer before joining up with Royce. Before the business could flourish he died in a flying accident.

Rolls-Royce industrial company manufacturing automobiles and airplane engines, founded 1906 by Henry Royce and Charles ◊Rolls. The Silver Ghost automobile model was designed 1906, and produced until 1925, when the Phantom was introduced. In 1914, Royce designed the Eagle aircraft engine, used extensively in World War I. Royce also designed the Merlin engine, used in Spitfires and Hurricanes in World War II. Jet engines followed, and became an important part of the company.

ROM (acronym for *read-only memory*) in computing, a memory device in the form of a collection of integrated circuits (chips), frequently used in microcomputers. ROM chips are loaded with data and programs during manufacture and, unlike ◊RAM (random-access memory) chips, can subsequently only be read, not written to, by computer. However, the contents of the chips are not lost when the power is switched off, as happens in RAM.

Roman Catholicism one of the main divisions of the Christian religion, separate from the Eastern Orthodox Church from 1054, and headed by the pope. For history and beliefs, see ◊Christianity. Membership is about 585 million worldwide, concentrated in S Europe, Latin America, and the Philippines.

romance in literature, tales of love and adventure, in verse or prose, that became popular in France about 1200 and spread throughout Europe. There were Arthurian romances about the legendary King Arthur and his knights, and romances based on the adventures of Charlemagne and on classical themes. In the 20th century the term "romantic novel" is often used disparagingly, to imply a contrast with a realist novel.

Romance languages branch of Indo-European languages descended from the Latin of the Roman Empire ("popular" or "vulgar" as opposed to "classical" Latin). The present-day Romance languages with national status are French, Italian, Portuguese, Romanian, and Spanish.

Roman Empire from 27 BC to the 5th century AD ; see ◊Rome, ancient.

Romanesque architecture style of W European ◊architecture of the 10th to 12th centuries, marked by rounded arches, solid volumes, and emphasis on perpendicular elements. In England the style is also known as ◊Norman architecture.

Romania area 91,699 sq mi/237,500 sq km *capital* Bucharest *towns and cities* Brasov, Timisoara, Cluj-Napoca, Iasi; ports Galati, Constanta, Braila *physical* mountains surrounding a plateau, with river plains S and E *environment* although sulfur-dioxide levels are low, only 20% of the country's rivers can provide drinkable water *features* Carpathian Mountains, Transylvanian Alps; river Danube; Black Sea coast; mineral springs *head of state* Ion Iliescu from 1989 *head of government* Nicolai Vacaroiu from 1992 *political system* emergent democratic republic *political parties* Social Democracy Party of Romania (SDPR) (formerly the Democratic Party–National Salvation Front: DP–NSF), populist; Civic Alliance (CA), right of center; Convention for Democracy, umbrella organization for right-of-center National Liberal Party (NLP) and ethnic-Hungarian Magyar Democratic Union (UDM) *exports* petroleum products and oil field equipment, electrical goods, automobiles, cereals *currency* leu *population* (1993 est) 23,200,000 (Romanians 89%, Hungarians 7.9%, Germans 1.6%); growth rate 0.5% p.a. *life expectancy* men 69, women 74 *languages* Romanian (official), Hungarian, German *media* television is state-run; there are an estimated 900 newspapers and magazines, but only the progovernment papers have adequate distribution and printing facilities; denigrating the nation is a criminal offense *religion* Romanian Orthodox 80%, Roman Catholic 6% *literacy* 96% *GNP* $1,340 per head (1991) *chronology 1944* Pro-Nazi Antonescu government overthrown. *1945* Communist-dominated government appointed. *1947* Boundaries redrawn. King Michael abdicated and People's Republic proclaimed. *1949* New Soviet-style constitution adopted. Joined Comecon. *1952* Second new Soviet-style constitution. *1955* Romania joined Warsaw Pact. *1958* Soviet occupation forces removed. *1965* New constitution adopted. Ceausescu came to power (as Secretary General of Romanian Communist Party). *1974* Ceausescu created president. *1985–86* Winters of austerity and power cuts. *1987* Workers demonstrated against austerity program. *1988–89*

Relations with Hungary deteriorated over "systematization program". *1989* Bloody overthrow of Ceausescu regime in "Christmas Revolution"; Ceausescu and wife tried and executed; estimated 10,000 dead in civil warfare. Power assumed by new National Salvation Front, headed by Ion Iliescu. *1990* Securitate secret police replaced by new Romanian Intelligence Service; religious practices resumed; mounting strikes and protests against effects of market economy. *1991* Aug: privatization law passed. Sept: prime minister Peter Roman resigned following riots; succeeded by Theodor Stolojan heading a new cross-party coalition government. Dec: new constitution endorsed by referendum. *1992* Iliescu reelected president; Nicolai Vacaroiu appointed prime minister. *1993* Formal invitation to apply for European Community (now European Union) membership. *1994* Military cooperation pact signed with Bulgaria.

Romanian language member of the Romance branch of the Indo-European language family, spoken in Romania, Macedonia, Albania, and parts of N Greece. It has been strongly influenced by the Slavonic languages and by Greek. The Cyrillic alphabet was used until the 19th century, when a variant of the Roman alphabet was adopted.

Roman law legal system of ancient Rome that is now the basis of ◊civil law, one of the main European legal systems.

Roman numerals ancient European number system using symbols different from Arabic numerals (the ordinary numbers 1, 2, 3, 4, 5, and so on). The seven key symbols in Roman numerals, as represented today, are I (1), V (5), X (10), L (50), C (100), D (500), and M (1,000). There is no zero, and therefore no place-value as is fundamental to the Arabic system. The first ten Roman numerals are I, II, III, IV (or IIII), V, VI, VII, VIII, IX, and X. When a Roman symbol is preceded by a symbol of equal or greater value, the values of the symbols are added (XVI = 16).

When a symbol is preceded by a symbol of less value, the values are subtracted (XL = 40). A horizontal bar over a symbol indicates a multiple of 1,000 ($\bar{X}$ = 10,000).

Romanov dynasty rulers of Russia from 1613 to the ◊Russian Revolution 1917. Under the Romanovs, Russia developed into an absolutist empire.

Romanticism in literature, the visual arts, and music, a style that emphasizes the imagination, emotions, and creativity of the individual artist. Romanticism also refers specifically to late 18th-and early 19th-century European culture, as contrasted with 18th-century ◊Classicism.

Romanticism in music, a preoccupation with subjective emotion expressed primarily through melody, a use of folk idioms, and a cult of the artist-musician as visionary and hero (virtuoso). Often linked with nationalistic feelings, the Romantic movement reached its height in the late 19th century, as in the works of Schumann and Wagner.

Rome (Italian *Roma*) capital of Italy and of Lazio region, on the river Tiber, 17 mi/27 km from the Tyrrhenian Sea; population (1987) 2,817,000.

Rome has few industries but it is an important cultural, road, and rail center. A large section of the population finds employment in government offices. Remains of the ancient city include the Forum, Colosseum, and Pantheon.

Rome, ancient civilization based in Rome, which lasted for about 800 years. Traditionally founded 753 BC, Rome became a republic 510 BC. From then, its history is one of almost continual expansion until the murder of Julius ◊Caesar and foundation of the empire under ◊Augustus and his successors. At its peak under ◊Trajan, the Roman Empire stretched from Britain to Mesopotamia and the Caspian Sea. A long train of emperors ruling by virtue of military, rather than civil, power marked the beginning of Rome's long decline; under ◊Diocletian, the empire was divided into two parts—East and West—although temporarily reunited under ◊Constantine, the first emperor formally to adopt Christianity. The end of the Roman Empire is generally dated by the deposition of the last emperor in the west AD 476. The Eastern Empire continued until 1453 at ◊Constantinople.

Rome, Sack of invasion and capture of the city of Rome AD 140 by the Goths, generally accepted as marking the effective end of the Roman Empire.

Rome, Treaties of two international agreements signed March 25, 1957, by Belgium, France, West Germany, Italy, Luxembourg, and the Netherlands, which established the European Economic Community (now ◊European Union) and the European Atomic Energy Commission (EURATOM).

Rommel Erwin 1891–1944. German field marshal. He served in World War I, and in World War II he played an important part in the invasions of central Europe and France. He was commander of the N African offensive from 1941 (when he was nicknamed "Desert Fox") until defeated in the Battles of El Alamein and he was expelled from Africa March 1943.

Romney George 1734–1802. English portrait painter. He was active in London from 1762. He became, with Gainsborough and Reynolds, one of the most successful portrait painters of the late 18th century. He painted several portraits of Lady Hamilton, Admiral Nelson's mistress.

Romulus in Roman legend, founder and first king of Rome, the son of Mars and Rhea Silvia, daughter of Numitor, king of Alba Longa.

Romulus and his twin brother Remus were thrown into the Tiber by their great-uncle Amulius, who had deposed Numitor, but were suckled by a she-wolf and rescued by a shepherd. On reaching adulthood they killed Amulius and founded Rome.

Röntgen (or *Roentgen*) Wilhelm Konrad 1845–1923. German physicist who discovered X-rays 1895. While investigating the passage of electricity through gases, he noticed the ◊fluorescence of a barium platinocyanide screen. This radiation passed through some substances opaque to light, and affected photographic plates. Developments from this discovery have revolutionized medical diagnosis.

He received a Nobel Prize 1901. The unit of electromagnetic radiation (X-ray) is named roentgen or röntgen (r) after him.

rook gregarious European ◊crow *Corvus frugilegus*. The plumage is black and lustrous and the face bare; a rook can grow to 18 in/45 cm long. Rooks nest in colonies at the tops of trees.

Roosevelt Franklin D(elano) 1882–1945. 32nd president of the US 1933–45, a Democrat. He served as governor of New York 1929–33. Becoming president during the Great ◊Depression, he launched the ◊New *Deal* economic and social reform program, which made him popular with the people. After the outbreak of World War II he introduced lend-lease for the supply of war materials and services to the Allies and drew up the Atlantic Charter of solidarity. Once the US had entered the war 1941, he spent much time in meetings with Allied leaders. He was reelected for a fourth term 1944, but died 1945.

Roosevelt Theodore 1858–1919. 26th president of the US 1901–09, a Republican. After serving as governor of New York 1898–1900 he became vice president to ◊McKinley, whom he succeeded as president on McKinley's assassination 1901. He campaigned against the great trusts (associations of enterprises that reduce competition), while carrying on a jingoist foreign policy designed to enforce US supremacy over Latin America.

root the part of a plant that is usually underground, and whose primary functions are anchorage and the absorption of water and dissolved mineral salts. Roots usually grow downward and toward water (that is, they are positively geotropic and hydrotropic; see ◊tropism). Plants such as epiphytic orchids, which grow above ground, produce aerial roots that absorb moisture from the atmosphere. Others, such as ivy, have climbing roots arising from the stems, which serve to attach the plant to trees and walls.

root of an equation, a value that satisfies the equality. For example, $x = 0$ and $x = 5$ are roots of the equation $x^2 - 5x = 0$.

root crop plant cultivated for its swollen edible root (which may or may not be a true root). Potatoes are the major temperate root crop; the major tropical root crops are cassava, yams, and sweet potatoes. Root crops are second in importance only to cereals as human food. Roots have a high carbohydrate content, but their protein content rarely exceeds 2%. Consequently, communities relying almost exclusively upon roots may suffer from protein deficiency. Food production for a given area from roots is greater than from cereals.

roots music term originally denoting ◊reggae, later encompassing any music indigenous to a particular culture; see ◊world music.

Rosario industrial river port (sugar refining, meat packing, maté processing) in Argentina, 175 mi/280 km NW of Buenos Aires, on the river Paraná; population (1991) 1,078,400. It was founded 1725.

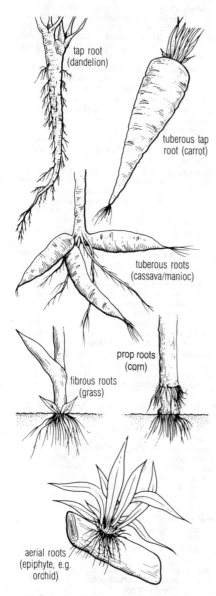

tap root
(dandelion)

tuberous tap
root (carrot)

tuberous roots
(cassava/manioc)

prop roots
(corn)

fibrous roots
(grass)

aerial roots
(epiphyte, e.g.
orchid)

root *Types of root. Many flowers (dandelion) and vegetables (carrot) have swollen tap roots with smaller lateral roots. The tuberous roots of the cassava are swollen parts of an underground stem modified to store food. The fibrous roots of the grasses are all of equal size. Prop roots grow out from the stem and then grow down into the ground to support a heavy plant. Aerial roots grow from stems but do not grow into the ground; many absorb moisture from the air.*

Roscommon (originally Ros-Comain, "wood around a monastery") county of the Republic of Ireland, in the province of Connacht; county town Roscommon; area 950 sq mi/2,460 sq km; population (1991) 51,900. It has rich pastures and is bounded on the E by the river Shannon, with lakes (Gara, Key, Allen) and bogs. There are the remains of a castle put up in the 13th century by English settlers. There is agriculture, especially cattle rearing.

rose any shrub or climber of the genus *Rosa*, family Rosaceae, with prickly stems and fragrant flowers in many different colors. Numerous cultivated forms have been derived from the Eurasian sweetbrier or eglantine *R. rubiginosa* and dogrose *R. canina*. There are many climbing varieties, but the forms more commonly cultivated are bush roses and standards (cultivated roses grafted on to a briar stem).

Roseau formerly *Charlotte Town* capital of ◊Dominica, West Indies, on the SW coast of the island; population (1981) 20,000.

rosemary evergreen shrub *Rosemarinus officinalis* of the mint family Labiatae, native to the Mediterranean and W Asia, with small, scented leaves. It is widely cultivated as a culinary herb and for the aromatic oil extracted from the clusters of pale blue or purple flowers.

Rosenberg Julius 1918–1953 and Ethel Greenglass 1915–1953. US married couple, convicted of being leaders of a nuclear-espionage ring passing information from Ethel's brother via courier to the USSR. The Rosenbergs were executed after much public controversy and demonstration. They were the only Americans executed for espionage during peacetime. The death penalty was ruled as justified because of the danger to the US from their actions. Recently published journals kept by ◊Khruschev further implicate the Rosenbergs.

Roses, Wars of the civil wars in England 1455–85 between the houses of ◊Lancaster (badge, red rose) and York (badge, white rose), both of whom claimed the throne through descent from the sons of Edward III. As a result of ◊Henry VI's lapse into insanity 1453, Richard, Duke of York, was installed as protector of the realm. Upon his recovery, Henry forced York to take up arms in self-defense.

Rosetta Stone slab of basalt with inscriptions from 197 BC, found near the town of Rosetta, Egypt, 1799. Giving the same text in three versions—Greek, hieroglyphic, and demotic script—it became the key to deciphering other Egyptian inscriptions.

Rosh Hashanah two-day vacation that marks the start of the Jewish New Year (first new moon after the autumn equinox), traditionally announced by blowing a ram's horn (a shofar).

Rosicrucians group of early 17th-century philosophers who claimed occult powers and employed the terminology of ◊alchemy to expound their mystical doc-, trines (said to derive from Paracelsus). Several societies have been founded in the US and Britain that claim to be their successors, such as the Rosicrucian Fraternity (1614 in Germany, 1861 in the US).

Ross James Clark 1800–1862. English explorer who discovered the north magnetic pole 1831. He also went to the Antarctic 1839; Ross Island, Ross Sea, and Ross Dependency are named for him.

Ross Dependency all the Antarctic islands and territories between 160° E and 150° W longitude and S of

60° S latitude; it includes Edward VII Land, Ross Sea and its islands, and parts of Victoria Land.

Rossellini Roberto 1906–1977. Italian film director. His World War II trilogy, *Roma città aperta/Rome, Open City* 1945, *Paisà/Paisan* 1946, and *Germania anno zero/Germany Year Zero* 1947, reflects his humanism, and is considered a landmark of European cinema.

In 1949 he made *Stromboli*, followed by other films in which his wife Ingrid Bergman appeared. After their divorce he made *General della Rovere* 1959 and embarked on television work.

Rossetti Christina (Georgina) 1830–1894. English poet. She was the sister of Dante Gabriel Rossetti and a devout High Anglican (see ◊Oxford movement). Her verse includes *Goblin Market and Other Poems* 1862 and expresses unfulfilled spiritual yearning and frustrated love. She was a skillful technician and made use of irregular rhyme and line length.

Rossetti Dante Gabriel 1828–1882. English painter and poet. He was a founding member of the ◊Pre-Raphaelite Brotherhood (PRB) 1848. As well as romantic medieval scenes, he produced many idealized portraits of women, including the spiritual *Beata Beatrix* 1864. His verse includes "The Blessed Damozel" 1850. His sister was the poet Christina Rossetti.

Rossini Gioacchino (Antonio) 1792–1868. Italian composer. His first success was the opera *Tancredi* 1813. In 1816 his "opera buffa" *Il barbiere di Siviglia/The Barber of Seville* was produced in Rome. During 1815–23 he produced 20 operas, and created (with Donizetti and Bellini) the 19th-century Italian operatic style.

Rostov-on-Don industrial port (shipbuilding, tobacco, automobiles, locomotives, textiles) in SW Russia, capital of Rostov region, on the river Don, 14 mi/23 km E of the Sea of Azov; population (1987) 1,004,000. Rostov dates from 1761 and is linked by river and canal with Volgograd on the river Volga.

Roth Philip 1933– . US novelist. His witty, sharply satirical, and increasingly fantastic novels depict the moral and sexual anxieties of 20th-century Jewish-American life, most notably in *Goodbye Columbus* 1959 and *Portnoy's Complaint* 1969.

Rothko Mark 1903–1970. Russian-born US painter. He was an Abstract Expressionist and a pioneer, toward the end of his life, of *Color Field* painting (an abstract style dominated by areas of unmodulated, strong color). Rothko produced several series of large-scale paintings in the 1950s and 1960s.

During the 1930s he painted for the Federal Arts Project and, with Adolph Gottlieb, founded the expressionist group The Ten. After his suicide 1970, his estate, consisting primarily of a huge number of his paintings, became the subject of a long legal battle.

rotifer any of the tiny invertebrates, also called "wheel animalcules", of the phylum Rotifera. Mainly freshwater, some marine, rotifers have a ring of cilia that carries food to the mouth and also provides propulsion. They are the smallest of multicellular animals—few reach 0.02 in/0.05 cm.

Rotterdam industrial port (brewing, distilling, shipbuilding, sugar and petroleum refining, margarine, tobacco) in the Netherlands and one of the foremost ocean cargo ports in the world, in the Rhine-Maas delta, linked by canal 1866–90 with the North Sea; population (1991) 582,266.

Rouault Georges 1871–1958. French painter, etcher, illustrator, and designer. He was one of the major religious artists of the 20th century. Early in his career he was associated with ◊Fauvism but created his own style using rich, dark colors and heavy outlines. His subjects include sad clowns, prostitutes, and evil lawyers. From about 1940 he painted mainly religious works.

Roundhead member of the Parliamentary party during the English Civil War 1640–60, opposing the royalist Cavaliers. The term referred to the short hair then worn only by men of the lower classes.

Rousseau Henri "Le Douanier" 1844–1910. French painter. A self-taught naive artist, his subjects include scenes of the Parisian suburbs and exotic junglescapes, painted with painstaking detail; for example, *Tropical Storm with a Tiger* 1891 (National Gallery, London).

Rousseau Jean-Jacques 1712–1778. French social philosopher and writer whose *Du Contrat social/Social Contract* 1762, emphasizing the rights of the people over those of the government, was a significant influence on the French Revolution. In the novel *Emile* 1762 he outlined a new theory of education.

rowan another name for the European ◊mountain ash tree.

rowing propulsion of a boat by oars, either by one rower with two oars (sculling) or by crews (two, four, or eight persons) with one oar each, often with a coxswain. Major events include the world championship, first held 1962 for men and 1974 for women, and the Boat Race (between England's Oxford and Cambridge universities), first held 1829.

In the US the Harvard–Yale boat race is held on the Thames at New London, Connecticut, and National Championships are held annually.

Rowlandson Thomas 1756–1827. English painter and illustrator, a caricaturist of Georgian social life. His series of drawings *Tour of Dr Syntax in Search of the Picturesque* was published 1809 and its two sequels followed 1812–21.

Royal Doulton British pottery firm. See Henry ◊Doulton.

Royal Greenwich Observatory the national astronomical observatory of the UK, founded 1675 at Greenwich, E London, England, to provide navigational information for sailors. After World War II it was moved to Herstmonceux Castle, Sussex; in 1990 it was transferred to Cambridge. It also operates telescopes on La Palma in the Canary Islands, including the 165-in/4.2-m William Herschel Telescope, commissioned 1987.

royalty in law, payment to the owner for rights to use or exploit literary or artistic copyrights and patent rights in new inventions of all kinds.

Oil, gas, and other mineral deposits are also subject to royalty payments.

Ruanda part of the former Belgian territory of Ruanda-Urundi until it achieved independence as ◊Rwanda, a country in central Africa.

rubber coagulated latex of a variety of plants, mainly from the New World. Most important is Para rubber, which derives from the tree *Hevea brasiliensis* of the spurge family. It was introduced from Brazil to SE Asia, where most of the world supply is now produced, the chief exporters being Peninsular Malaysia, Indonesia, Sri Lanka, Cambodia, Thailand, Sarawak, and Brunei. At about seven years the tree, which may grow to 60 ft/20 m, is ready for "tapping". Small incisions are made in the trunk and the latex drips into collecting cups. In pure form, rubber is white and has the formula $(C_5H_8)_n$.

rubber plant Asiatic tree *Ficus elastica* of the mulberry family Moraceae, native to Asia and N Africa, producing latex in its stem. It has shiny, leathery, oval leaves, and young specimens are grown as house plants.

rubella technical term for ◊German measles.

Rubens Peter Paul 1577–1640. Flemish painter. He brought the exuberance of Italian Baroque to N Europe, creating, with an army of assistants, innumerable religious and allegorical paintings for churches and palaces. These show mastery of drama in large compositions, and love of rich color. He also painted portraits and, in his last years, landscapes.

Rubicon ancient name of the small river flowing into the Adriatic that, under the Roman Republic, marked the boundary between Italy proper and Cisalpine Gaul. When ◊Caesar led his army across it 49 BC, he therefore declared war on the republic; hence to "cross the Rubicon" means to take an irrevocable step.

rubidium soft, silver-white, metallic element, symbol Rb, atomic number 37, atomic weight 85.47. It is one of the ◊alkali metals, ignites spontaneously in air, and reacts violently with water. It is used in photocells and vacuum-tube filaments.

Rubinstein Artur 1887–1982. Polish-born US pianist. His early encounters with Joseph Joachim and the Belgian violinist, conductor, and composer Eugène Ysaÿe (1858–1931) link his interpretations of Beethoven, Mozart, and Chopin with the virtuoso Romantic tradition. He was also a noted interpreter of de Falla.

He became a US citizen in 1946. Considered by many to be the greatest 20th-century piano virtuoso, he played with an intellectual and commanding tone, appeared in films, and made many distinctive recordings.

ruby the red transparent gem variety of the mineral ◊corundum Al_2O_3, aluminum oxide. Small amounts of chromium oxide, Cr_2O_3, substituting for aluminum oxide, give ruby its color. Natural rubies are found mainly in Myanmar (Burma), but rubies can also be produced artificially and such synthetic stones are used in ◊lasers.

rudd freshwater fish *Scardinius erythrophthalmus*, a type of minnow, belonging to the carp family Cypridae, common in lakes and slow rivers of Europe; now introduced in the US. Brownish green above and silvery below, with red fins and golden eyes, it can reach a length of 1.5 ft/45 cm and a weight of 2.2 lb/1 kg.

Rudolph I 1218–1291. Holy Roman emperor from 1273. Originally count of Hapsburg, he was the first Hapsburg emperor and expanded his dynasty by investing his sons with the duchies of Austria and Styria.

Rudolph II 1552–1612. Holy Roman emperor from 1576, when he succeeded his father Maximilian II. His policies led to unrest in Hungary and Bohemia, which led to the surrender of Hungary to his brother Matthias 1608 and religious freedom for Bohemia.

rue shrubby perennial herb *Ruta graveolens*, family Rutaceae, native to S Europe and temperate Asia. It bears clusters of yellow flowers. An oil extracted from the strongly scented, blue-green leaves is used in perfumery.

ruff bird *Philomachus pugnax* of the sandpiper family Scolopacidae. The name is taken from the frill of erectile feathers developed in the breeding season around the neck of the male. The ruff is found across N Europe and Asia, and migrates south in winter. It is a casual migrant throughout North America.

rugby contact sport that originated at the Rugby boys' school, England, 1823, when a boy picked up the ball and ran with it while playing soccer. Rugby is played with an oval ball.

Ruhr river in Germany; it rises in the Rothaargebirge Mountains and flows W to join the Rhine at Duisburg. The *Ruhr Valley* (142 mi/228 km), a metropolitan industrial area (petrochemicals, automobiles, iron and steel at Duisburg and Dortmund), was formerly a coal-mining center.

Ruisdael or *Ruysdael* Jacob van *c.* 1628–1682. Dutch landscape painter. He painted rural scenes near his native town of Haarlem and in Germany, and excelled in depicting gnarled and weatherbeaten trees. A notable example of his work is *The Jewish Cemetery* about 1660 (Gemäldegalerie, Dresden). The few figures in his pictures were painted by other artists.

ruminant any even-toed hoofed mammal with a rumen, the "first stomach" of its complex digestive system. Plant food is stored and fermented before being brought back to the mouth for chewing (chewing the cud) and then is swallowed to the next stomach. Ruminants include cattle, antelopes, goats, deer, and giraffes, all with a four-chambered stomach. Camels are also ruminants, but they have a three-chambered stomach.

Rump, the English parliament formed between Dec 1648 and Nov 1653 after Pride's purge of the ◊Long Parliament to ensure a majority in favor of trying Charles I. It was dismissed 1653 by Cromwell, who replaced it with the ◊Barebones Parliament.

rune character in the oldest Germanic script, chiefly adapted from the Latin alphabet, the earliest examples being from the 3rd century, and found in Denmark. Runes were scratched on wood, metal, stone, or bone.

run-time system in computing, programs that must be stored in memory while an application is executed.

Runyon (Alfred) Damon 1884–1946. US journalist, primarily a sports reporter, whose short stories in Guys and Dolls 1932 deal wryly with the seamier side of New York City life in his own invented jargon.

He reached the height of his popularity in the 1930s, writing a syndicated newspaper feature "As I See It".

Rupert Prince 1619–1682. English Royalist general and admiral, born in Prague, son of the Elector Palatine Frederick V and James I's daughter Elizabeth. Defeated by Cromwell at ◊Marston Moor and ◊Naseby in the Civil War, he commanded a privateering fleet 1649–52, until routed by Admiral Robert Blake, and, returning after the Restoration, was a distinguished admiral in the Dutch Wars. He founded the ◊Hudson's Bay Company.

rush any grasslike plant of the genus *Juncus*, family Juncaceae, found in wet places in cold and temperate regions. The round stems and flexible leaves of some species have been used for making mats and baskets since ancient times.

Rushdie (Ahmed) Salman 1947– . British writer. He was born in India of a Muslim family. His novel *The*

Satanic Verses 1988 (the title refers to verses deleted from the Koran) offended many Muslims with alleged blasphemy. In 1989 the Ayatollah Khomeini of Iran called for Rushdie and his publishers to be killed. Rushdie has been in hiding in the UK since with police protection.

Ruskin John 1819–1900. English art critic and social critic. He published five volumes of *Modern Painters* 1843–60 and *The Seven Lamps of Architecture* 1849, in which he stated his philosophy of art. His writings hastened the appreciation of painters considered unorthodox at the time, such as J M W ◊Turner and the ◊Pre-Raphaelite Brotherhood. His later writings were concerned with social and economic problems.

Russell Bertrand (Arthur William), 3rd Earl Russell 1872–1970. English philosopher and mathematician who contributed to the development of modern mathematical logic and wrote about social issues. His works include *Principia Mathematica* 1910–13 (with A N Whitehead), in which he attempted to show that mathematics could be reduced to a branch of logic; *The Problems of Philosophy* 1912; and *A History of Western Philosophy* 1946. He was an outspoken liberal pacifist.

Russell Charles Taze 1852–1916. US founder of the ◊Jehovah's Witness sect 1872. Born in Pittsburgh, Russell, a successful businessman, began studying the Bible after encountering some Adventists and becoming convinced that Christ's return was imminent. He came to believe that Christ's "invisible return" had taken place in 1874 and that in 1914 a series of apocalyptic events would culminate in Christ's thousand-year reign on Earth. In 1879 he founded the journal that became *The Watchtower*, which spread his ideas. The movement under his leadership survived the failure of his prophecies in 1914, and it continued to grow rapidly after his death.

Russell Jane 1921– . US actress. She was discovered by producer Howard Hughes. Her first film, *The Outlaw* 1943, was not properly released for several years because of censorship problems. Other films include *The Paleface* 1948, *Gentlemen Prefer Blondes* 1953, and *The Revolt of Mamie Stover* 1957.

She retired 1970.

Russia originally the prerevolutionary Russian Empire (until 1917), now accurately restricted to the ◊Russian Federation.

Russian Federation formerly (until 1991) *Russian Soviet Federal Socialist Republic (RSFSR) area* 6,591,100 sq mi/17,075,500 sq km *capital* Moscow *towns and cities* St Petersburg (Leningrad), Nizhni-Novgorod (Gorky), Rostov-on-Don, Samara (Kuibyshev), Tver (Kalinin), Volgograd, Vyatka (Kirov), Ekaterinburg (Sverdlovsk) *physical* fertile Black Earth district; extensive forests; the Ural Mountains with large mineral resources *features* the heavily industrialized area around Moscow; Siberia; includes 16 autonomous republics (capitals in parentheses): Bashkir (Ufa); Buryat (Ulan-Ude); Checheno-Ingush (Grozny); Chuvash (Cheboksary); Dagestan (Makhachkala); Kabardino-Balkar (Nalchik); Kalmyk (Elista); Karelia (Petrozavodsk); Komi (Syktyvkar); Mari (Yoshkar-Ola); Mordovia (Saransk); Vladikavkaz (formerly Ordzhonikidze); Tatarstan (Kazan); Tuva (Kizyl); Udmurt (Izhevsk); Yakut (Yakutsk) *head of state* Boris Yeltsin from 1990/91 *head of government* Viktor Chernomyrdin from 1992 *political system* emergent democracy *political parties* Russia's Choice, pro-Yeltsin reformist; Party of Russian Unity and

Accord, moderate reformist; Yabloko bloc, radical, free-market; Russian Communist Party, left-wing, conservative; Agrarian Party, centrist; Liberal Democratic Party, far-right, neofascist *products* iron ore, coal, oil, gold, platinum, and other minerals, agricultural produce *currency* ruble *population* (1993 est) 150,000,000 (82% Russian, Tatar 4%, Ukrainian 3%, Chuvash 1%) *life expectancy* men 64, women 74 *language* Great Russian *media* the two leading news agencies were brought under government control 1993; the publication of anything that aims to incite national, social, racial, or religious dissent is prohibited *religion* traditionally Russian Orthodox *GNP* $3,220 per head (1991) *chronology 1945* Became a founding member of United Nations (UN). *1988* Aug: Democratic Union formed in Moscow as political party opposed to totalitarianism. Oct: Russian-language demonstrations in Leningrad, czarist flag raised. *1989* March: Boris Yeltsin elected to USSR Congress of People's Deputies. Sept: conservative-nationalist Russian United Workers' Front established. *1990* May: anticommunist May Day protests in Red Square, Moscow; Yeltsin narrowly elected RSFSR president by Russian parliament. June: economic and political sovereignty declared; Ivan Silaev became Russian prime minister. Aug: Tatarstan declared sovereignty. Dec: rationing introduced in some cities; private land ownership allowed. *1991* June: Yeltsin directly elected president. July: Yeltsin abolished Communist Party cells from workplaces; sovereignty of the Baltic republics recognized by the republic. Aug: Yeltsin stood out against abortive anti-Gorbachev coup, emerging as key power-broker within Soviet Union; national guard established and pre-revolutionary flag restored. Sept: Silaev resigned as Russian premier. Nov: Yeltsin named prime minister; Soviet and Russian Communist Parties banned; Yeltsin's goverment gained control of Russia's economic assets and armed forces. Oct: Chechnya declared its independence. Dec: Yeltsin negotiated formation of new confederal Commonwealth of Independent States; Russia admitted into UN; independence recognized by US and European Community (now the European Union). *1992* Jan: assumed former USSR's permanent seat on UN Security Council; prices freed. Feb: demonstrations as living standards plummeted. March: 18 out of 20 republics signed treaty agreeing to remain within loose Russian Federation; Tatarstan and Chechnya refused to sign. Dec: Victor Chernomyrdin elected prime minister; new constitution agreed. START II arms-reduction agreement signed with US. *1993* March: power struggle between Yeltsin and Congress of People's Deputies. Sept: Yeltsin dissolved parliament. Sept–Oct: attempted coup, led by conservative opponents, foiled by troops loyal to Yeltsin. Dec: new parliament elected, with surprising successes for extremist Liberal Democratic Party. New constitution approved in plebiscite. *1994* Jan: prominent reformers quit cabinet. June: economic accord signed with European Union. Joined NATO "partnership for peace" program. Dec: Russian forces invaded breakaway republic of Chechnya. *1995* Conflict in Chechnya intensified; widespread criticism of Russian conduct as casualties mounted.

Russian Orthodox Church another name for the ◊Orthodox Church.

Russian Revolution two revolutions of Feb and Oct 1917 (Julian ◊calendar) that began with the overthrow of the Romanov dynasty and ended with the establishment of a communist soviet (council) state, the Union of Soviet Socialist Republics (USSR). In Oct Bolshevik workers and sailors under ◊Lenin seized government buildings and took over power.

Russo-Japanese War war between Russia and Japan 1904–05, which arose from conflicting ambitions in Korea and ◊Manchuria, specifically, the Russian occupation of Port Arthur (modern Dalian) 1896 and of the Amur province 1900. Japan successfully besieged Port Arthur May 1904–Jan 1905, took Mukden (modern Shenyang) on Feb 29–March 10, and on May 27 defeated the Russian Baltic fleet, which had sailed halfway around the world to Tsushima Strait. A peace was signed Aug 23, 1905. Russia surrendered its lease on Port Arthur, ceded S Sakhalin to Japan, evacuated Manchuria, and recognized Japan's interests in Korea.

russula any fungus of the genus *Russula*, comprising many species. They are medium to large mushrooms with flattened caps, and many are brightly colored.

rust reddish brown oxide of iron formed by the action of moisture and oxygen on the metal. It consists mainly of hydrated iron(III) oxide ($Fe_2O_3.H_2O$ and iron(III) hydroxide ($Fe(OH)_3$).

rust in botany, common name for the parasitic fungi of the order Uredinales, which appear on the leaves of their hosts as orange-red spots, later becoming darker. The commonest is the wheat rust *Puccinia graminis*.

rutabaga (or *rutabaga*) annual or biennial plant *Brassica napus*, widely cultivated for its edible root, which is yellow, purple, or white.

Ruthenia or *Carpathian Ukraine* region of central Europe, on the southern slopes of the Carpathian Mountains, home of the Ruthenes or Russniaks. Dominated by Hungary from the 10th century, it was part of Austria-Hungary until World War I. In 1918 it was divided between Czechoslovakia, Poland, and Romania; independent for a single day in 1938, it was immediately occupied by Hungary, captured by the USSR 1944 and incorporated 1945–47 (as the Transcarpathian Region) into Ukraine Republic, which became independent as Ukraine 1991.

ruthenium hard, brittle, silver-white, metallic element, symbol Ru, atomic number 44, atomic weight 101.07. It is one of the so-called platinum group of metals; it occurs in platinum ores as a free metal and in the natural alloy osmiridium. It is used as a hardener in alloys and as a catalyst; its compounds are used as coloring

agents in glass and ceramics.

Rutherford Ernest 1871–1937. New Zealand physicist, a pioneer of modern atomic science. His main research was in the field of radioactivity, and he discovered alpha, beta, and gamma rays. He named the nucleus, and was the first to recognize the nuclear nature of the atom.

Nobel Prize for Physics 1908.

rutherfordium synthesized radioactive element of the ◊transactinide series, symbol Sg, atomic number 106, atomic weight 263. It was first synthesized 1974 in the US and given the temporary name unnilhexium. The discovery was not confirmed until 1993. It was officially named 1994 after New Zealand physicist Ernest ◊Rutherford.

Ruysdael Jacob van. See ◊Ruisdael, Dutch painter.

Rwanda Republic of (*Republika y'u Rwanda*) *area* 10,173 sq mi/26,338 sq km *capital* Kigali *towns and cities* Butare, Ruhengeri *physical* high savanna and hills, with volcanic mountains in NW *features* part of lake Kivu; highest peak Mount Karisimbi 14,792 ft/4,507 m; Kagera River (whose headwaters are the source of the Nile) and National Park *head of state* Pasteur Bizimungu from 1994 *head of government* Faustin Twagiramungu from 1994 *political system* transitional *political parties* National Movement for Democracy and Development (MRND), moderate, centrist; Social Democratic Party (PSD), left of center; Christian Democratic Party (PDC), right of center; Republican Democratic Movement (MDR), Hutu nationalist; Rwanda Patriotic Front (FPR), Tutsi-led but claims to be multiethnic *exports* coffee, tea, pyrethrum *currency* franc *population* (1993 est) 7,700,000 (Hutu 90%, Tutsi 9%, Twa 1%); growth rate 3.3% p.a. During the 1993–94 civil war, hundreds of thousands were killed and many thousands more fled to neighboring countries *life expectancy* men 49, women 52 *languages* Kinyarwanda, French (official); Kiswahili *religions* Roman Catholic 54%, animist 23%, Protestant 12%, Muslim 9% *literacy* men 64%, women 37% *GNP* $260 per head (1991) *chronology 1916* Belgian troops occupied Rwanda; League of Nations mandated Rwanda and Burundi to Belgium as Territory of Ruanda-Urundi. *1959* Interethnic warfare between Hutu and Tutsi. *1962* Independence from Belgium achieved, with Grégoire Kayibanda as president. *1972* Renewal of interethnic fighting. *1973* Kayibanda ousted in a military coup led by Maj Gen Juvenal Habyarimana. *1978* New constitution approved; Rwanda remained a military-controlled

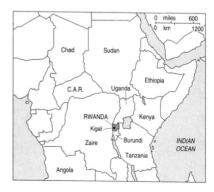

state. *1980* Civilian rule adopted. *1988* Refugees from Burundi massacres streamed into Rwanda. *1990* Government attacked by Rwandan Patriotic Front (FPR), a Tutsi military-political organization based in Uganda. *1992* Peace accord with FPR. *1993* Power-sharing agreement with government repudiated by FPR. Peace talks resumed. Aug: peace accord formally signed. United Nations mission sent to monitor peace agreement. *1994* President Habyarimana, with Burundian president Ntaryamira, killed in airplane crash, with fears that FPR responsible. Hundreds of thousands killed in ensuing civil war, with many Tutsis massacred by Hutu death squads; mass exodus of refugees to neighboring countries. June: interim government fled capital as FPR forces closed in. French peacekeeping troops drafted in; "safe zone" established in southwest. July: FPR installed transitional coalition government; moderate Hutu and FPR leader, Pasteur Bizimungu, appointed interim head of state.

Ryder Albert Pinkham 1847–1917. US painter born in New Bedford, Massachusetts. He developed one of the most original styles of his time. He painted with broad strokes that tended to simplify form and used yellowish colors that gave his works an eerie, haunted quality. His works are poetic, romantic, and filled with unreality; *Death on a Pale Horse* about 1910 (Cleveland Museum of Art) is typical.

rye cereal *Secale cereale* grown extensively in N Europe and other temperate regions. The flour is used to make dark-colored ("black") breads. Rye is grown mainly as a forage crop, but the grain is also used to make whiskey and breakfast cereals.

Ryle Martin 1918–1984. English radioastronomer. At the Mullard Radio Astronomy Observatory, Cambridge, he developed the technique of sky-mapping using "aperture synthesis", combining smaller dish aerials to give the characteristics of one large one. His work on the distribution of radio sources in the universe brought confirmation of the ◊Big Bang theory. He won, with Antony Hewish, the Nobel Prize for Physics 1974.

Ryukyu Islands southernmost island group of Japan, stretching toward Taiwan and including Okinawa, Miyako, and Ishigaki *area* 870 sq mi/2,254 sq km *capital* Naha, on Okinawa *features* 73 islands, some uninhabited; subject to typhoons *industries* sugar, pineapples, fish *population* (1985) 1,179,000 *history* originally an independent kingdom; ruled by China from the late 14th century until seized by Japan 1609 and controlled by the Satsuma feudal lords until 1868, when the Japanese government took over. Chinese claims to the islands were relinquished 1895. In World War II the islands were taken by US 1945 (see under ◊Okinawa); northernmost group, Oshima, restored to Japan 1953, the rest 1972.

S

S abbreviation for *south*.

Saarinen Eero 1910–1961. Finnish-born US architect. Son of Eliel ◊Saarinen. He is known for a wide range of innovative modern designs using a variety of creative shapes for buildings. His works include the TWA terminal at Kennedy Airport in New York City; Dulles Airport outside Washington, DC; the General Motors Technical Center in Warren, Michigan; Kresge Auditorium at the Massachusetts Institute of Technology; and US embassies in London and Oslo.

Saarinen Eliel 1873–1950. Finnish-born US architect and founder of the Finnish Romantic school. His most famous European work is the Helsinki railroad station. In the US he is particularly remembered for his designs for Cranbrook School in Bloomfield Hills, Michigan, and Christ Church in Minneapolis.

Saarland (French *Sarre*) *Land* (state) of Germany *area* 992 sq mi/2,570 sq km *capital* Saarbrücken *features* one-third forest; crossed NW–S by the river Saar *industries* cereals and other crops; cattle, pigs, poultry. Former flourishing coal and steel industries survive only by government subsidy *population* (1988) 1,034,000 *history* in 1919, the Saar district was administered by France under the auspices of the League of Nations; a plebiscite returned it to Germany 1935; Hitler gave it the name Saarbrücken. Part of the French zone of occupation 1945, it was included in the economic union with France 1947. It was returned to Germany 1957.

Sabah Sheik Jabir al Ahmadal Jabir al-1928– . Emir of Kuwait from 1977. He suspended the national assembly 1986, after mounting parliamentary criticism, ruling in a feudal, paternalistic manner. On the invasion of Kuwait by Iraq 1990 he fled to Saudi Arabia, returning to Kuwait March 1991. In 1992 a reconstituted national assembly was elected.

Sabatini Gabriela 1970– . Argentine tennis player who in 1986 became the youngest Wimbledon semifinalist for 99 years. She was ranked number three in the world behind Monica Seles and Steffi Graf in 1991.

Sabine member of an ancient people of central Italy, conquered by the Romans and amalgamated with them in the 3rd century BC. The so-called *rape of the Sabine women*—a mythical attempt by ◊Romulus in the early days of Rome to carry off the Sabine women to colonize the new city—is frequently depicted in art.

sable marten *Martes zibellina*, about 20 in/50 cm long and usually brown. It is native to N Eurasian forests, but now found mainly in E Siberia. The sable has diminished in numbers because of its valuable fur, which has long attracted hunters. Conservation measures and sable farming have been introduced to save it from extinction.

saccharide another name for a ◊sugar molecule.

saccharin or *ortho-sulfo benzimide* $C_7H_5NO_3S$ sweet, white, crystalline solid derived from coal tar and substituted for sugar. Since 1977 it has been regarded as potentially carcinogenic. Its use is not universally permitted and it has been largely replaced by other sweetening agents.

sacrament in Christian usage, observances forming the visible sign of inward grace. In the Roman Catholic Church there are seven sacraments: baptism, Holy Communion (Eucharist or mass), confirmation, rite of reconciliation (confession and penance), holy orders, matrimony, and the anointing of the sick.

Sacramento industrial port and capital (since 1854) of California, US, 80 mi/130 km NE of San Francisco; population (1990) 369,400, metropolitan area 1,481,100. It stands on the Sacramento River, which flows 382 mi/615 km through Sacramento Valley to San Francisco Bay. Industries include the manufacture of detergents and jet aircraft and food processing, including almonds, peaches, and pears.

Sadat Anwar 1918–1981. Egyptian politician. Succeeding ◊Nasser as president 1970, he restored morale by his handling of the Egyptian campaign in the 1973 war against Israel. In 1974 his plan for economic, social, and political reform to transform Egypt was unanimously adopted in a referendum. In 1977 he visited Israel to reconcile the two countries, and shared the Nobel Peace Prize with Israeli prime minister Menachem Begin 1978. He was assassinated by Islamic fundamentalists.

Sade Donatien Alphonse François, Comte de, known as the *Marquis de Sade* 1740–1814. French author. He was imprisoned for sexual offenses and finally committed to an asylum. He wrote plays and novels dealing explicitly with a variety of sexual practices, including sadism, deriving pleasure or sexual excitement from inflicting pain on others.

safflower Asian plant *Carthamus tinctorius*, family Compositae. It is thistlelike, and widely grown for the oil from its seeds, which is used in cooking, margarine, and paints and varnishes; the seed residue is used as cattle feed.

saffron plant *Crocus sativus* of the iris family, probably native to SW Asia, and formerly widely cultivated in Europe; also the dried orange-yellow stigmas of its purple flowers, used for coloring and flavoring.

saga prose narrative written down in the 11th–13th centuries in Norway and Iceland. The sagas range from family chronicles, such as the *Landnamabok* of Ari (1067–1148), to legendary and anonymous works such as the *Njala* saga.

sage perennial herb *Salvia officinalis* with gray-green aromatic leaves used for flavoring. It grows up to 20 in/ 50 cm high and has bluish lilac or pink flowers.

Sagittarius zodiac constellation in the southern hemisphere, represented as a centaur aiming a bow and arrow at neighboring Scorpius. The Sun passes through Sagittarius from mid-Dec to mid-Jan, including the winter solstice, when it is farthest south of the

sage Sage is a native of the arid areas of S Europe. The variety used in cooking is the nonflowering, broad-leafed sage. It has a very powerful flavor and can be used fresh or dried.

equator. The constellation contains many nebulae and globular clusters, and open star clusters. Kaus Australis and Nunki are its brightest stars. The center of our Galaxy, the Milky Way, is marked by the radio source Sagittarius A. In astrology, the dates for Sagittarius are between about Nov 22 and Dec 21 (see ◊precession).

sago starchy material obtained from the pith of the sago palm *Metroxylon sagu*. It forms a nutritious food and is used for manufacturing glucose and sizing textiles.

Sahara largest desert in the world, occupying 2,123,000 sq mi/5,500,000 sq km of N Africa from the Atlantic to the Nile, covering: W Egypt; part of W Sudan; large parts of Mauritania, Mali, Niger, and Chad; and southern parts of Morocco, Algeria, Tunisia, and Libya. Small areas in Algeria and Tunisia are below sea level, but it is mainly a plateau with a central mountain system, including the Ahaggar Mountains in Algeria, the Aïr Massif in Niger, and the Tibesti Massif in Chad, of which the highest peak is Emi Koussi, 11,208 ft/3,415 m. The area of the Sahara expanded by 251,000 sq mi/650,000 sq km 1940–90, but reforestation is being attempted in certain areas.

Saigon former name (to 1976) of ◊Ho Chi Minh City, Vietnam.

sailing pleasure cruising or racing a small and light vessel, whether sailing or power-driven. At the Olympic Games, seven categories exist: Soling, Flying Dutchman, Star, Finn, Tornado, 470, and Windglider or windsurfing (boardsailing), which was introduced at the 1984 Los Angeles games. All these Olympic categories are sail-driven. The Finn and Windglider are solos events; the Soling class is for three-person crews; all other classes are for crews of two.

saint holy man or woman respected for his or her wisdom, spirituality, and dedication to their faith. Within the Roman Catholic church a saint is officially recognized through canonization by the pope. Many saints are associated with miracles and canonization usually occurs after a thorough investigation of the lives and miracles attributed to them. In the Orthodox church saints are recognized by the patriarch and Holy Synod after recommendation by local

churches. The term is also used in Buddhism for individuals who have led a virtuous and holy life.

St Andrews town at the eastern tip of Fife, Scotland, 12 mi/19 km SE of Dundee; population (1987 est) 13,800. Its university (1411) is the oldest in Scotland, and the Royal and Ancient Club (1754) is the ruling body of golf.

St Bartholomew, Massacre of slaughter of ◊Huguenots (Protestants) in Paris, Aug 24–Sept 17, 1572, and until Oct 3 in the provinces. About 25,000 people are believed to have been killed. When ◊Catherine de' Medici's plot to have Admiral Coligny assassinated failed, she resolved to have all the Huguenot leaders killed, persuading her son Charles IX it was in the interest of public safety.

St Christopher (St Kitts)–Nevis Federation of *area* 104 sq mi/269 sq km (St Christopher 68 sq mi/176 sq km, Nevis 36 sq mi/93 sq km) *capital* Basseterre (on St Christopher) *towns and cities* Charlestown (largest on Nevis) *physical* both islands are volcanic *features* fertile plains on coast; black beaches *head of state* Queen Elizabeth II of Britain from 1983 represented by governor-general Clement Arrindell from 1983 *head of government* Kennedy Simmonds from 1980 *political system* federal constitutional monarchy *political parties* People's Action Movement (PAM), center-right; Nevis Reformation Party (NRP), Nevis-separatist; Labour Party, moderate left of center *exports* sugar, molasses, electronics, clothing *currency* Eastern Caribbean dollar *population* (1993 est) 44,000; growth rate 0.2% p.a. *life expectancy* men 69, women 72 *language* English *media* no daily newspaper; two weekly papers, published by the governing and opposition party respectively—both receive advertising support from the government *religion* Anglican 36%, Methodist 32%, other Protestant 8%, Roman Catholic 10% (1985 est) *literacy* 92% *GNP* $3,960 per head (1991) *chronology 1871–1956* Part of the Leeward Islands Federation. *1958–62* Part of the Federation of the West Indies. *1967* St Christopher, Nevis, and Anguilla achieved internal self-government, within the British Commonwealth, with Robert Bradshaw, Labour Party leader, as prime minister. *1971* Anguilla returned to being a British dependency. *1978* Bradshaw died; succeeded by Paul Southwell. *1979* Southwell died; succeeded by Lee L Moore. *1980* Coalition government led by Kennedy Simmonds. *1983* Full independence achieved within the Commonwealth. *1984* Coalition government reelected. *1989* Prime Minister Simmonds won a third successive term. *1993* Simmonds continued in office despite strong criticism of his leadership. Antigovernment demonstrations followed formation of minority coalition government after inconclusive elections.

Saint-Exupéry Antoine de 1900–1944. French author and pilot. He wrote the autobiographical *Vol de nuit/Night Flight* 1931 and *Terre des hommes/Wind, Sand, and Stars* 1939. His children's book *Le Petit Prince/The Little Prince* 1943 is also an adult allegory.

Saint-Gaudens Augustus 1848–1907. Irish-born US sculptor. He was one of the leading Neo-Classical sculptors of his time. His monuments include the *Admiral Farragut* 1878–81 in Madison Square Park, New York City, and the Adams Memorial 1891 in Rock Creek Cemetery, Washington, DC.

He also designed bronze medals, plaques, portrait tablets, and low reliefs. He was commissioned 1905 by President Theodore Roosevelt to redesign US gold coinage; the 1907 double eagle ($20) was the only design approved before his death.

St George's port and capital of Grenada, on the SW coast; population (1986) 7,500, urban area 29,000. It was founded 1650 by the French.

St Helens, Mount volcanic mountain in Washington State, US. When it erupted 1980 after being quiescent since 1857, it devastated an area of 230 sq mi/600 sq km and its height was reduced from 9,682 ft/2,950 m to 8,402 ft/2,560 m.

Saint John largest city of New Brunswick, Canada, on the Saint John River; population (1986) 121,000. It is a fishing port and has shipbuilding, timber, fish-processing, petroleum, refining, and textile industries. Founded by the French as *Saint-Jean* 1635, it was taken by the British 1758.

After the American Revolution, several thousand Loyalists from the US settled here 1783, and it was the first Canadian city to be incorporated 1785.

St John's port and capital of Antigua and Barbuda, on the NW coast of Antigua; population (1982) 30,000. It exports rum, cotton, and sugar.

Saint-Just Louis Antoine Léon Florelle de 1767–1794. French revolutionary. A close associate of ◊Robespierre, he became a member of the Committee of Public Safety 1793, and was guillotined with Robespierre.

Saint-Laurent Yves (Henri Donat Mathieu) 1936– . French fashion designer. He has had an exceptional influence on fashion in the second half of the 20th century. He began working for Christian ◊Dior 1955 and succeeded him as designer on Dior's death 1957. He established his own label 1962 and went on to create the first "power-dressing" looks for men and women: classic, stylish city clothes.

St Lawrence river in E North America. From ports on the ◊Great Lakes it forms, with linking canals (which also give great hydroelectric capacity to the river), the St Lawrence Seaway for oceangoing ships, ending in the Gulf of St Lawrence. It is 745 mi/1,200 km long and is icebound for four months each year.

St Louis city in Missouri, on the Mississippi River; population (1990) 396,700, metropolitan area 2,444,100. Its industries include aerospace equipment, aircraft, vehicles, chemicals, electrical goods, steel, food processing, and beer. Its central US location makes it a warehousing and distribution center and a hub of rail, truck, and airline transportation. St Louis and Washington universities are here, and the University of Missouri has a campus in the city.

St Lucia area 238 sq mi/617 sq km *capital* Castries *towns and cities* Vieux-Fort, Soufrière *physical* mountainous island with fertile valleys; mainly tropical forest *features* volcanic peaks; Gros and Petit Pitons *head of state* Queen Elizabeth II of Britain from 1979, represented by governor-general Stanislaus A James from 1992 *head of government* John Compton from 1982 *political system* constitutional monarchy *political parties* United Workers' Party (UWP), moderate left of center; St Lucia Labour Party (SLP), moderate left of center; Progressive Labour Party (PLP), moderate left of center *exports* coconut oil, bananas, cocoa, copra *currency* Eastern Caribbean dollar *population* (1993) 136,000; growth rate 2.8% p.a. *life expectancy* men 68, women 73 (1989) *languages* English; French patois *media* two independent biweekly newspapers *religion* Roman Catholic 90% *literacy* 93% *GNP*

$2,872 per head (1991) *chronology 1814* Became a British crown colony following Treaty of Paris. *1967* Acquired internal self-government as a West Indies associated state. *1979* Independence achieved from Britain within the Commonwealth. John Compton, leader of the United Workers' Party (UWP), became prime minister. Allan Louisy, leader of the St Lucia Labour Party (SLP), replaced Compton as prime minister. *1981* Louisy resigned; replaced by Winston Cenac. *1982* Compton returned to power at the head of a UWP government. *1987* Compton and UWP reelected with reduced majority. *1991* Integration with other Windward Islands proposed. *1992* Compton and UWP reelected.

St Paul capital and industrial city of Minnesota, adjacent to Minneapolis; population (1990) 272,200. Industries include electronics, publishing and printing, chemicals, refined petroleum, machinery, and processed food.

Educational institutions include Hamline University and Macalester College. The city is noted for its annual Winter Carnival and the St Paul Chamber Orchestra. French explorer Father Louis Hennepin visited the area 1680, but the first settlers did not arrive until 1838. St Paul became the territorial capital 1849. The first railroad reached here 1862.

St Petersburg capital of the St Petersburg region, Russia, at the head of the Gulf of Finland; population (1989 est) 5,023,500. Industries include shipbuilding, machinery, chemicals, and textiles. It was renamed *Petrograd* 1914 and was called *Leningrad* 1924–91, when its original name was restored. Built on a low and swampy site, St Petersburg is split up by the mouths of the river Neva, which connects it with Lake Ladoga. The climate is severe. The city became a seaport when it was linked with the Baltic by a ship canal built 1875–93. It is also linked by canal and river with the Caspian and Black seas, and in 1975 a seaway connection was completed via lakes Onega and Ladoga with the White Sea near Belomorsk.

St Petersburg seaside resort and industrial city (space technology) in W Florida; population (1990) 238,600. It is across Tampa Bay from ◊Tampa.

Besides aerospace and electronic equipment, the city produces boats and processed seafood. It is also a major tourist and retirement center. St Petersburg was plotted 1884 and grew as a resort with the arrival of the railroad in the late 1880s.

St Pierre and Miquelon territorial dependency of France, eight small islands off the S coast of Newfoundland, Canada

Saint-Saëns (Charles) Camille 1835–1921. French composer, pianist and organist. Among his many lyrical Romantic pieces are concertos, the symphonic poem *Danse macabre* 1875, the opera *Samson et Dalila* 1877, and the orchestral *Carnaval des animaux/ Carnival of the Animals* 1886.

St Vincent and the Grenadines area 150 sq mi/388 sq km, including islets of the Northern Grenadines 17 sq mi/43 sq km *capital* Kingstown *towns and cities* Georgetown, Chateaubelair *physical* volcanic mountains, thickly forested *features* Mustique, one of the Grenadines, a vacation resort; Soufrière volcano *head of state* Queen Elizabeth II of Britain from 1979, represented by governor-general David Jack from 1989 *head of government* James Mitchell from 1984 *political system* constitutional monarchy *political parties* New Democratic Party (NDP), moderate, left of center; St

Vincent Labour Party (SVLP), moderate, left of center *exports* bananas, taros, sweet potatoes, arrowroot, copra *currency* Eastern Caribbean dollar *population* (1993 est) 115,000; growth rate –4% p.a. *life expectancy* men 69, women 74 *languages* English; French patois *media* government-owned radio station; two privately owned weekly newspapers, subject to government pressure *religion* Anglican 47%, Methodist 28%, Roman Catholic 13% *literacy* 84% *GNP* $1,730 per head (1991) *chronology 1783* Became a British crown colony. *1958–62* Part of the West Indies Federation. *1969* Achieved internal self-government. *1979* Achieved full independence from Britain, within the Commonwealth, with Milton Cato as prime minister. *1984* James Mitchell replaced Cato as prime minister. *1989* Mitchell decisively reelected. *1991* Integration with other Windward Islands proposed. *1994* Mitchell reelected but with reduced majority.

Saipan island of the Marianas group about 1,200 mi/1,900 km N of New Guinea. It was occupied by the Japanese in World War II and when US troops recaptured it June 1944, several hundred Japanese civilians committed mass suicide rather than be captured.

It was invaded by US forces June 17, 1944, before the Japanese had completed their planned fortifications, but the clearing of the island was a slow and hard fight which lasted until July 17. Even then numbers of Japanese troops hid in the more remote areas until the war ended.

Sakhalin (Japanese *Karafuto*) island in the Pacific, N of Japan, that since 1947, with the Kurils, forms a region of Russia; capital Yuzhno-Sakhalinsk (Japanese *Toyohara*); area 28,564 sq mi/74,000 sq km; population (1981) 650,000, including aboriginal Ainu and Gilyaks. There are two parallel mountain ranges, rising to over 5,000 ft/1,525 m, which extend throughout its length, 600 mi/965 km.

Sakharov Andrei Dmitrievich 1921–1989. Soviet physicist, known both as the "father of the Soviet H-bomb" and as an outspoken human-rights campaigner. In 1948 he joined Igor Tamm in developing the hydrogen bomb; he later protested against Soviet nuclear tests and was a founder of the Soviet Human Rights Committee, winning the Nobel Peace Prize 1975. In 1980 he was sent to internal exile in Gorky (now Nizhni-Novgorod) for criticizing Soviet action in Afghanistan. At the end of 1986 he was allowed to return to Moscow and resume his place in the Soviet Academy of Sciences.

Saladin or *Sala-ud-din* 1138–1193. Born a Kurd, sultan of Egypt from 1175, in succession to the Atabeg of Mosul, on whose behalf he conquered Egypt 1164–74. He subsequently conquered Syria 1174–87 and precipitated the third ◊Crusade by his recovery of Jerusalem from the Christians 1187. Renowned for knightly courtesy, Saladin made peace with Richard I of England 1192.

salamander any tailed amphibian of the order *Urodela*. They are sometimes confused with lizards, but unlike lizards they have no scales or claws. Salamanders have smooth or warty moist skin. The order includes some 300 species, arranged in nine families, found mainly in the northern hemisphere. Salamanders include hellbenders, mudpuppies, waterdogs, sirens, mole salamanders, newts, and lungless salamanders (dusky, woodland, and spring salamanders).

Salamis, Battle of naval battle off the coast of the island of Salamis in which the Greeks defeated the Persians 480 BC.

Salazar Antonio de Oliveira 1889–1970. Portuguese prime minister 1932–68 who exercised a virtual dictatorship. During World War II he maintained Portuguese neutrality but fought long colonial wars in Africa (Angola and Mozambique) that impeded his country's economic development as well as that of the colonies.

Salem city and manufacturing center in Massachusetts, 15 mi/24 km NE of Boston; population (1990) 38,100.

Leather goods, electrical equipment, and machinery are manufactured here. Points of interest include Salem Maritime National Historic Site, the birthplace of Nathaniel Hawthorne, and the House of the Seven Gables 1668 that gave rise to his novel of the same name. Salem was settled 1626 and was the site of witchcraft trials 1692 that resulted in the execution of about 20 people.

Salem city in NW Oregon, settled about 1840 and made state capital 1859; population (1990) 107,800. It processes timber into wood products and has a prosperous fruit and vegetable canning industry.

Williamette University is here. Salem was established by Methodist missionaries 1840–41 and became the territorial capital 1851.

Salinas de Gortiari Carlos 1948– . Mexican politician, president 1988–94, a member of the dominant Institutional Revolutionary Party. During his presidency he was confronted with problems of drug trafficking and violent crime, including the murder of his nominated successor, Luis Donaldo Colosio, 1994.

Salinger J(erome) D(avid) 1919– . US writer. He wrote the classic novel of mid-20th-century adolescence *The Catcher in the Rye* 1951. He developed his lyrical Zen themes in *Franny and Zooey* 1961 and *Raise High the Roof Beams, Carpenters and Seymour: An Introduction*

Salinger, J(erome) D(avid) *J D Salinger's first and only novel* The Catcher in the Rye *1951, which describes an adolescent's rejection of the "phony" world of adults, soon became a cult classic. In the mid-1960s, by which time he had published three sets of closely related short stories, Salinger became a recluse and published nothing else.*

1963, short stories about a Jewish family named Glass, after which he stopped publishing.

Salisbury former name (to 1980) of ◊Harare, the capital of Zimbabwe.

Salk Jonas Edward 1914– . US physician and microbiologist. In 1954 he developed the original vaccine that led to virtual eradication of paralytic ◊polio in industrialized countries. He was director of the Salk Institute for Biological Studies, University of California, San Diego, 1963–75.

Sallust Gaius Sallustius Crispus 86–c. 34 BC. Roman historian, a supporter of Julius Caesar. He wrote vivid accounts of Catiline's conspiracy and the Jugurthine War.

salmon any of the various bony fishes of the family Salmonidae. More specifically the name is applied to several species of game fishes of the genera Salmo and Oncorhynchus of North America and Eurasia that mature in the ocean but, to spawn, return to the freshwater streams where they were born. Their normal color is silvery with a few dark spots, but the color changes at the spawning season.

Salmonella very varied group of bacteria that colonize the intestines of humans and some animals. Some strains cause typhoid and paratyphoid fevers, while others cause salmonella ◊food poisoning, which is characterized by stomach pains, vomiting, diarrhea, and headache. It can be fatal in elderly people, but others usually recover in a few days without antibiotics. Most cases are caused by contaminated animal products, especially poultry meat.

salsa Latin big-band dance music popularized by Puerto Ricans in New York City in the 1970s–80s and by, among others, the Panamanian singer Rubén Blades (1948–).

salt in chemistry, any compound formed from an acid and a base through the replacement of all or part of the hydrogen in the acid by a metal or electropositive radical. *Common salt* is sodium chloride (see ◊salt, common).

SALT abbreviation for *◊Strategic Arms Limitation Talks*, a series of US–Soviet negotiations 1969–79.

salt, common or *sodium chloride* NaCl white crystalline solid, found dissolved in sea water and as rock salt (halite) in large deposits and salt domes. Common salt is used extensively in the food industry as a preservative and for flavoring, and in the chemical industry in the making of chlorine and sodium.

Salt Lake City capital of Utah, on the river Jordan, 11 mi/18 km SE of the Great Salt Lake; population (1990) 159,900.

Founded 1847, it is the headquarters of the Church of Jesus Christ of Latter-Day Saints (Mormon Church). The Mormon Tabernacle, Mormon Temple, and University of Utah are here. Products include refined petroleum, metal goods, processed food, and textiles; nearby mining adds to the city's economy. Salt Lake City became the territorial capital 1856.

saltpeter former name for potassium nitrate (KNO₃), the compound used in making gunpowder (from about 1500). It occurs naturally, being deposited during dry periods in places with warm climates, such as India.

Salvador port and naval base in Bahia state, NE Brazil, on the inner side of a peninsula separating Todos Santos Bay from the Atlantic Ocean; population (1991) 2,075,400. Products include cocoa, tobacco,

and sugar. Founded 1510, it was the capital of Brazil 1549–1763.

Salvador, El republic in Central America; see ◊El Salvador.

Salvation Army Christian evangelical, social-service, and social-reform organization, originating 1865 in London, England, with the work of William Booth. Originally called the Christian Revival Association, it was renamed the East London Christian Mission in 1870 and from 1878 has been known as the Salvation Army, now a worldwide organization. It has military titles for its officials, is renowned for its brass bands, and its weekly journal is the *War Cry*.

It was established in the US 1880 and in Canada 1881 and has conducted missionary work throughout the world. It currently has about 300,000 US members.

Salween river rising in E Tibet and flowing 1,740 mi/ 2,800 km through Myanmar (Burma) to the Andaman Sea; it has many rapids.

Salyut series of seven space stations launched by the USSR 1971–82. Salyut was cylindrical in shape, 50 ft/ 15 m long, and weighed 21 tons/19 metric tons. It housed two or three cosmonauts at a time, for missions lasting up to eight months.

Salzburg capital of the state of Salzburg, W Austria, on the river Salzach; population (1981) 139,400. The city is dominated by the Hohensalzburg fortress. It is the seat of an archbishopric founded by St Boniface about 700 and has a 17th-century cathedral. Industries include stock rearing, dairy farming, forestry, and tourism. It is the birthplace of the composer Wolfgang Amadeus Mozart and an annual music festival has been held here since 1920.

Samara capital of Kuibyshev region, W central Russia, and port at the junction of the rivers Samara and Volga, situated in the center of the fertile middle Volga plain; population (1987) 1,280,000. Industries include aircraft, locomotives, cables, synthetic rubber, textiles, fertilizers, petroleum refining, and quarrying. It was called *Kuibyshev* from 1935, reverting to its former name Jan 1991.

Samaria region of ancient Israel. The town of Samaria (now *Sebastiyeh*) on the west bank of the river Jordan was the capital of Israel in the 10th–8th centuries BC. It was renamed *Sebarte* in the 1st century BC by the Roman administrator Herod the Great. Extensive remains have been excavated.

Samaritan member or descendant of the colonists forced to settle in Samaria (now N Israel) by the Assyrians after their occupation of the ancient kingdom of Israel 722 BC. Samaritans adopted a form of Judaism, but adopted only the Pentateuch, the five books of Moses of the Old Testament, and regarded their temple on Mount Gerizim as the true sanctuary.

samarium hard, brittle, gray-white, metallic element of the ◊lanthanide series, symbol Sm, atomic number 62, relative atomic mass 150.4. It is widely distributed in nature and is obtained commercially from the minerals monzanite and bastnasite. It is used only occasionally in industry, mainly as a catalyst in organic reactions. Samarium was discovered by spectroscopic analysis of the mineral samarskite and named in 1879 by French chemist Paul Lecoq de Boisbaudran (1838–1912) after its source.

Samoa volcanic island chain in the SW Pacific. It is divided into Western Samoa and American Samoa.

Samoa, American group of islands 2,610 mi/4,200 km S of Hawaii, administered by the US *area* 77 sq mi/200 sq km *capital* Fagatogo on Tutuila *features* five volcanic islands, including Tutuila, Tau, and Swain's Island, and two coral atolls. National park (1988) includes prehistoric village of Saua, virgin rainforest, flying foxes *exports* canned tuna, handicrafts *currency* US dollar *population* (1990) 46,800 *languages* Samoan and English *religion* Christian *government* as a non-self-governing territory of the US, under Governor A P Lutali, it is constitutionally an unincorporated territory of the US, administered by the Department of the Interior *history* the islands were acquired by the US Dec 1899 by agreement with Britain and Germany under the Treaty of Berlin. A constitution was adopted 1960 and revised 1967.

Samoa, Western Independent State of (*Samoa i Sisifo*) *area* 1,093 sq mi/2,830 sq km *capital* Apia (on Upolu island) *physical* comprises South Pacific islands of Savai'i and Upolu, with two smaller tropical islands and islets; mountain ranges on main islands *features* lava flows on Savai'i *head of state* King Malietoa Tanumafili II from 1962 *head of government* Tofilau Eti Alesana from 1988 *political system* liberal democracy *political parties* Human Rights Protection Party (HRPP), led by Tofilau Eti Alesana; Samoa Democratic Party (SDP), led by Sir Togiloa Peter; Samoa National Development Party (SNDP), led by Tupua Tamasese Efi and Va'ai Kolone. All "parties" are personality-based groupings *exports* coconut oil, copra, cocoa, fruit juice, cigarettes, timber *currency* talà *population* (1993 est) 200,000; growth rate 1.1% p.a. *life expectancy* men 64, women 69 *languages* English, Samoan (official) *religion* Protestant 70%, Roman Catholic 20% *literacy* 92% *GNP* $930 per head (1991) *chronology* **1899–1914** German protectorate. **1920–61** Administered by New Zealand. **1959** Local government elected. **1961** Referendum favored independence. **1962** Independence achieved within the Commonwealth, with Fiame Mata Afa Mulinu'u as prime minister. **1975** Mata Afa died. **1976** Tupuola Taisi Efi became first nonroyal prime minister. **1982** Va'ai Kolone became prime minister; replaced by Tupuola Efi. Assembly failed to approve budget; Tupuola Efi resigned; replaced by Tofilau Eti Alesana. **1985** Tofilau Eti Alesana resigned; head of state invited Va'ai Kolone to lead the government. **1988** Elections produced a hung parliament, with first Tupua Tamasese Efi (formerly Tupuola Taisi Efi) as prime minister and then Tofilau Eti Alesana. **1990** Universal adult suffrage introduced. **1991** Tofilau Eti Alesana reelected. Fiame Naome became first woman in cabinet.

Sampras Pete(r) 1971– . US tennis player, winner of Wimbledon 1993 and 1994. At the age of 19 years and 28 days, he became the youngest winner of the US Open 1990. A fine server and volleyer, Sampras also won the inaugural Grand Slam Cup in Munich 1990.

samurai member of the military caste in Japan from the mid-12th century until 1869, when the feudal system was abolished and all samurai pensioned off by the government. A samurai was an armed retainer of a *daimyo* (large landowner) with specific duties and privileges and a strict code of honor. A *ronin* was a samurai without feudal allegiance.

San'a capital of Yemen, SW Arabia, 200 mi/320 km N of Aden; population (1986) 427,000. A walled city, with fine mosques and traditional architecture, it is rapidly being modernized. Weaving and jewelry are local handicrafts.

San Andreas fault geological fault line stretching for 700 mi/1,125 km in a NW–SE direction through the state of California.

San Antonio city in S Texas; population (1990) 935,900. It is a commercial and financial center; industries include aircraft maintenance, oil refining, and meat packing.

Of great economic importance are Fort Sam Houston, four Air Force bases, South Texas Medical Center, and the Southwest Research Center. Educational institutions include Trinity University and the University of Texas at San Antonio. Points of interest include 18th-century Spanish missions and the Alamo, the Texan-occupied mission-fortress stormed in 1836 by Mexican troops who massacred the entire garrison.

San Bernardino city in California, 50 mi/80 km E of Los Angeles; population (1990) 164,200. Products include processed food, steel, and aerospace and electronic equipment.

Norton Air Force Base is just outside the city. San Bernardino was named by Spanish missionaries who arrived 1810. A group of Mormons platted the community in the 1850s.

sand loose grains of rock, sized 0.0025–0.08 in/0.0625–2.00 mm in diameter, consisting chiefly of ◊quartz, but owing their varying color to mixtures of other minerals. Sand is used in cement-making, as an abrasive, in glass-making, and for other purposes.

Sand George. Pen name of Amandine Aurore Lucie Dupin 1804–1876. French author. Her prolific literary output was often autobiographical. In 1831 she left her husband after nine years of marriage and, while living in Paris as a writer, had love affairs with Alfred de Musset, Chopin, and others. Her first novel *Indiana* 1832 was a plea for women's right to independence.

sandalwood fragrant heartwood of any of certain Asiatic and Australian trees of the genus *Santalum*, family Santalaceae, used for ornamental carving, in perfume, and burned as incense.

Sandburg Carl August 1878–1967. US poet born in Galesburg, Illinois. He worked as a farm laborer and a bricklayer, and his poetry celebrates ordinary life in the US, as in *Chicago Poems* 1916, *The People, Yes* 1936, and *Complete Poems* 1950 (Pulitzer Prize). In free verse, it is reminiscent of Walt Whitman's poetry. Sandburg also wrote a monumental biography of Abraham Lincoln, *Abraham Lincoln: The Prairie Years* 1926 (two volumes) and *Abraham Lincoln: The War Years* 1939 (four volumes; Pulitzer Prize).

Sanders George 1906–1972. Russian-born British actor. He was often cast as a smooth-talking cad. Most of his film career was spent in the US where he starred in such films as *Rebecca* 1940, *The Moon and Sixpence* 1942, *The Picture of Dorian Gray* 1944, and *All About Eve* 1950 (Academy Award for best supporting actor).

sandgrouse any bird of the family Pteroclidae. They look like long-tailed grouse, but are actually closely related to pigeons. They live in warm, dry areas of Europe, Asia, and Africa and have long wings, short legs, and thick skin.

sand hopper or **beachflea** any of various small crustaceans belonging to the order Amphipeda, with laterally compressed bodies, that live in beach sand and jump like fleas. The eastern sand hopper *Orchestia agilis* of North America is about 0.5 in/1.3 cm long.

San Diego city and military and naval base in California; population (1990) 1,110,500, metropolitan area 2,498,000. It is an important Pacific Ocean fishing port. Manufacturing includes aerospace and electronic equipment, metal fabrication, printing and publishing, seafood canning, and shipbuilding.

The US Navy's largest operational complex is here. Educational institutions include the Salk Institute of Biological Studies, San Diego State University, the University of San Diego, and the University of California at San Diego. Attractions include the San Diego Zoo and Sea World. A 16-mi/26-km transit line opened 1981 connects to Tijuana, Mexico.

Sandinista member of a Nicaraguan left-wing organization (Sandinist National Liberation Front, FSLN) named for Augusto César Sandino, a guerrilla leader killed in 1934.

sandpiper any of various shorebirds belonging to the family Scolopacidae, which includes godwits, ◊curlews, and ◊snipes.

Other members of the family include yellowlegs, tattlers, and dowitchers. The purple sandpiper *Calidris maritima* of E North America 9 in/23 cm long, has buff and brown plumage, orange-yellow legs, and a long, slender bill.

sandstone ◊sedimentary rocks formed from the consolidation of sand, with sand-sized grains (0.0025–0.08 in/0.0625–2 mm) in a matrix or cement. Their principal component is quartz. Sandstones are commonly permeable and porous, and may form freshwater ◊aquifers. They are mainly used as building materials.

San Francisco chief Pacific port of the US, in California; population (1990) 724,000, metropolitan area of San Francisco and Oakland 3,686,600. The city stands on a peninsula, on the south side of the Golden Gate Strait, spanned 1937 by the world's second-longest single-span bridge, 4,200 ft/1,280 m. The strait gives access to San Francisco Bay. Manufactured goods include textiles, fabricated metal products, electrical equipment, petroleum products, chemicals, and pharmaceuticals.

Sanger Frederick 1918– . English biochemist, the winner of two Nobel Prizes for Chemistry: one for his clarifying the structure of insulin, and the other, with two US scientists, for his work on the chemical structure of genes.

Sanger Margaret Higgins 1883–1966. US health reformer and crusader for birth control. In 1914 she founded the National Birth Control League. She founded and presided over the American Birth Control League 1921–28, the organization that later became the Planned Parenthood Federation of America, and the International Planned Parenthood Federation 1952.

San José capital of Costa Rica; population (1989) 284,600. Products include coffee, cocoa, and sugar cane. It was founded 1737 and has been the capital since 1823.

San José city in Santa Clara Valley, California; population (1990) 782,200. It is the center of "Silicon Valley", the site of many high-technology electronic firms turning out semiconductors and other computer components. There are also electrical, aerospace, missile, rubber, metal, and machine industries, and it is a commercial and transportation center for orchard crops and wines produced in the area.

San Jose State University is here, and the Lick Observatory is on nearby Mount Hamilton. San Jose was founded as California's first nonmilitary settlement in 1777 and served as the state capital 1849–51.

San Juan capital of Puerto Rico; population (1990) 437,750. It is a port and industrial city. Products include chemicals, pharmaceuticals, machine tools, electronic equipment, textiles, plastics, and rum.

The main campus of the University of Puerto Rico is here. San Juan was settled 1521 and remained under Spanish rule until 1898, when the island was ceded to the US.

San Marino Republic of (*Repubblica di San Marino*) **area** 24 sq mi/61 sq km **capital** San Marino **towns and cities** Serravalle (industrial center) **physical** on the slope of Mount Titano surrounded by Italian territory; one of the world's smallest states **head of state and government** two captains regent, elected for a six-month period **political system** direct democracy **political parties** San Marino Christian Democrat Party (PDCS), right of center; Progressive Democratic Party (PDP) (formerly the Communist Party: PCS), Socialist Unity Party (PSU), and Socialist Party (PSS), all three left of center **exports** wine, ceramics, paint, chemicals, building stone **currency** Italian lira **population** (1993) 24,000; growth rate 0.1% p.a. **life expectancy** men 70, women 77 **language** Italian **religion** Roman Catholic 95% **literacy** 96% **chronology 1862** Treaty with Italy signed; independence recognized under Italy's protection. **1947–86** Governed by a series of left-wing and center-left coalitions. **1986** Formation of Communist and PDCS "grand coalition". **1992** Joined the United Nations. PDCS withdrew from "grand coalition" to form alliance with PSS.

San Martín José de 1778–1850. South American revolutionary leader. He served in the Spanish army during the Peninsular War, but after 1812 he devoted himself to the South American struggle for independence, playing a large part in the liberation of Argentina, Chile, and Peru from Spanish rule.

San Pedro Sula main industrial and commercial city in NW Honduras, the second largest-city in the country; population (1989) 300,900. It trades in bananas, coffee, sugar, and timber and manufactures textiles, plastics, furniture, and cement.

San Salvador capital of El Salvador 30 mi/48 km from the Pacific Ocean, at the foot of San Salvador volcano (8,360 ft/2,548 m); population (1984) 453,000. Industries include food processing and textiles. Since its foundation 1525, it has suffered from several earthquakes.

Sanskrit the dominant classical language of the Indian subcontinent, a member of the Indo-Iranian group of the Indo-European language family, and the sacred language of Hinduism. The oldest form of Sanskrit is *Vedic*, the variety used in the *Vedas* and *Upanishads* (about 1500–700 BC).

Santa Anna Antonio López de 1795–1876. Mexican revolutionary who became general and dictator of Mexico for most of the years between 1824 and 1855. He led the attack on the ◊Alamo fort in Texas 1836.

Santa Barbara city in S California; population (1990) 85,571. It is the site of a campus of the University of California. The Santa Ynez Mountains are to the N. Vandenburg air force base is 50 mi/80 km to the NW.

Manufactures include aircraft and aerospace equipment, precision instruments, and electronic components, but the city is better known for its wealthy residents and as a resort. A Spanish presidio and a mission (still in use) were built here in the 1780s, and the first American settler arrived 1816.

Santa Claus the American name, derived from the Dutch, for St Nicholas. He is depicted as a fat, jolly old man with a long white beard, dressed in boots and a red hat and suit trimmed with white fur. He lives with Mrs Claus and his toy-making elves at the North Pole, and on Christmas Eve he travels in an airborne sleigh, drawn by eight reindeer, to deliver presents to good children, who are fast asleep when Santa arrives. The most popular legends claim that Santa lands his sleigh on rooftops, secretly entering homes through the chimney.

Santa Fe capital of New Mexico, on the Santa Fe River, 40 mi/65 km W of Las Vegas; population (1990) 55,900, many Spanish-speaking. A number of buildings date from the Spanish period, including a palace 1609–10; the cathedral 1869 is on the site of a monastery built 1622. Santa Fe produces American Indian jewelry and textiles; its chief industry is tourism.

It is home to many artists and is noted for theater and opera.

Santiago capital of Chile; population (1990) 4,385,500. Industries include textiles, chemicals, and food processing. It was founded 1541 and is famous for its broad avenues.

Santo Domingo capital and chief sea port of the Dominican Republic; population (1982) 1,600,000. Founded 1496 by Bartolomeo, brother of Christopher Columbus, it is the oldest colonial city in the Americas. Its cathedral was built 1515–40.

São Paulo city in Brazil, 45 mi/72 km NW of its port Santos; population (1991) 9,700,100, metropolitan area 15,280,000. It is 3,000 ft/900 m above sea level, and 2° S of the Tropic of Capricorn. It is South America's leading industrial city, producing electronics, steel, and chemicals; it has meat-packing plants and is the center of Brazil's coffee trade. It originated as a Jesuit mission 1554.

São Tomé port and capital of São Tomé e Príncipe, on the NE coast of São Tomé island, Gulf of Guinea; population (1984) 35,000. It exports cocoa and coffee.

São Tomé e Príncipe Democratic Republic of *area* 386 sq mi/1,000 sq km *capital* São Tomé *towns and cities* Santo Antonio, Santa Cruz *physical* comprises two main islands and several smaller ones, all volcanic; thickly forested and fertile *head of state* Miguel Trovoada from 1991 *head of government* Evaristo Carvalho from 1994 *political system* emergent democratic republic *political parties* Movement for the Liberation of São Tomé e Príncipe (MLSTP), nationalist socialist; Democratic Convergence Party–Reflection Group (PCD–EM), center-left *exports* cocoa, copra, coffee, palm oil and kernels *currency* dobra *population* (1993 est) 130,000; growth rate 2.5% p.a. *life expectancy* men 62, women 62 *languages* Portuguese (official), Fang (Bantu) *religions* Roman Catholic 80%, animist *literacy* 63% *GNP* $350 per head (1991) *chronology* *1471* Discovered by Portuguese. *1522–1973* A province of Portugal. *1973* Achieved internal self-government. *1975* Independence achieved from Portugal, with Manuel Pinto da Costa as president. *1978* New constitution adopted. *1984* Formally declared a nonaligned state. *1988* Unsuccessful coup attempt against da Costa. *1991* New constitution adopted. First multiparty elections held; Miguel Trovoada replaced Pinto da Costa. *1994*

Proposals for greater autonomy for Príncipe under consideration.

sapphire deep-blue, transparent gem variety of the mineral ◊corundum Al_2O_3, aluminum oxide. Small amounts of iron and titanium give it its color. A corundum gem of any color except red (which is a ruby) can be called a sapphire; for example, yellow sapphire.

Sappho *c.* 610–*c.* 580. Greek lyric poet. A native of Lesbos and contemporary of the poet Alcaeus, she was famed for her female eroticism (hence lesbianism). The surviving fragments of her poems express a keen sense of loss, and delight in the worship of the goddess ◊Aphrodite.

Sapporo capital of ◊Hokkaido prefecture, Japan; population (1990) 1,671,800. Industries include rubber and food processing. It is a winter sports center and was the site of the 1972 Winter Olympics. Giant figures are sculpted in ice at the annual snow festival.

Saracen ancient Greek and Roman term for an Arab, used in the Middle Ages by Europeans for all Muslims. The equivalent term used in Spain was ◊Moor.

Sarajevo capital of Bosnia-Herzegovina; population (1991) 526,000. Industries include engineering, brewing, chemicals, carpets, and ceramics. A Bosnian, Gavrilo Princip, assassinated Archduke ◊Franz Ferdinand here 1914, thereby precipitating World War I. From April 1992 the city was the target of a siege by Bosnian Serb forces in their fight to carve up the newly independent republic. A United Nations ultimatum and the threat of NATO bombing led to a cease-fire Feb 1994 and the effective end of the siege as Serbian heavy weaponry was withdrawn. Hostilities resumed later in the year.

Saratov industrial port (chemicals, oil refining) on the river Volga in W central Russia; population (1987) 918,000. It was established in the 1590s as a fortress to protect the Volga trade route.

Sarawak state of Malaysia, on the NW corner of the island of Borneo *area* 48,018 sq mi/124,400 sq km *capital* Kuching *physical* mountainous; the rainforest, which may be 10 million years old, contains several thousand tree species.

A third of all its plant species are endemic to Borneo. 30% of the forest was cut down 1963–89; timber is expected to run out 1995–2001 *industries* timber, oil, rice, pepper, rubber, and coconuts *population* (1991) 1,669,000; 24 ethnic groups make up almost half this number *history* Sarawak was granted by the Sultan of Brunei to English soldier James Brooke 1841, who became "Rajah of Sarawak". It was a British protectorate from 1888 until captured by the Japanese in World War II. It was a crown colony 1946–63, when it became part of Malaysia.

sarcoma malignant ◊tumor arising from the fat, muscles, bones, cartilage, or blood and lymph vessels and connective tissues. Sarcomas are much less common than ◊carcinomas.

sardine common name for various small fishes (◊pilchards) in the herring family.

Sardinia (Italian *Sardegna*) mountainous island, special autonomous region of Italy; area 9,303 sq mi/ 24,100 sq km; population (1990) 1,664,400. Its capital is Cagliari, and it exports cork and petrochemicals. It is the second-largest Mediterranean island and includes Costa Smeralda (Emerald Coast) tourist area in the NE and *nuraghi* (fortified Bronze Age dwellings).

After centuries of foreign rule, it became linked 1720 with Piedmont, and this dual kingdom became the basis of a united Italy 1861.

Sargasso Sea part of the N Atlantic Ocean (between 40° and 80°W and 25° and 30°N) left static by circling ocean currents, and covered with floating weed *Sargassum natans*.

Sarnoff David 1891–1971. Russian-born US broadcasting pioneer. He was named general manager of RCA 1921 and founded the first radio network, the National Broadcasting Co (NBC), as a broadcast subsidiary 1926. Named RCA president 1930 and board chairman 1947, Sarnoff was an early promoter of television broadcasting during the 1940s and the first to manufacture color sets and to transmit color programs in the 1950s.

Saroyan William 1908–1981. US author born in Fresno, California. He wrote short stories, such as "The Daring Young Man on the Flying Trapeze" 1934, idealizing the hopes and sentiments of the "little man". His plays, preaching a gospel of euphoric enjoyment, include *The Time of Your Life* (Pulitzer Prize; refused) 1939, about eccentricity; *My Heart's in the Highlands* 1939, about an uplifting bugle-player; *Love's Old Sweet Song* 1941, and *Talking to You* 1962.

Sartre Jean-Paul 1905–1980. French author and philosopher, a leading proponent of ◊existentialism. He published his first novel, *La Nausée/Nausea*, 1937, followed by the trilogy *Les Chemins de la Liberté/Roads to Freedom* 1944–45 and many plays, including *Huis Clos/In Camera* 1944. *L'Etre et le néant/Being and Nothingness* 1943, his first major philosophical work, sets out a radical doctrine of human freedom.

In the later work *Critique de la raison dialectique/ Critique of Dialectical Reason* 1960 he tried to produce a fusion of existentialism and Marxism.

SAS abbreviation for ◊*Special Air Service.*

Saskatchewan province of W Canada *area* 251,788 sq mi/652,300 sq km *capital* Regina *towns* Saskatoon, Moose Jaw, Prince Albert *physical* prairies in the S; to the N, forests, lakes, and subarctic tundra; Prince Albert National Park *industries* more than 60% of Canada's wheat; oil, natural gas, uranium, zinc, potash (world's largest reserves), copper, helium (the only western reserves outside the US) *population* (1991) 995,300 *history* once inhabited by Indians speaking Athabaskan, Algonquin, and Sioux languages, who depended on caribou and moose in the N and buffalo in the S. French trading posts established about 1750; owned by Hudson's Bay Company, first permanent settlement 1774; ceded to Canadian government 1870 as part of Northwest Territories; became a province 1905.

Sassanian Empire Persian empire founded AD 224 by Ardashir, a chieftain in the area of what is now Fars,

in Iran, who had taken over ◊Parthia; it was named for his grandfather, Sasan. The capital was Ctesiphon, near modern ◊Baghdad, Iraq. After a rapid period of expansion, when it contested supremacy with Rome, it was destroyed in 637 by Muslim Arabs at the Battle of Qadisiya.

Sassau-Nguesso Denis 1943– . Congolese socialist politician, president 1979–92. He progressively consolidated his position within the ruling left-wing Congolese Labour Party (PCT) and improving relations with France and the US. In 1990, in response to public pressure, he agreed that the PCT should abandon Marxism-Leninism and that a multiparty system should be introduced.

satellite any small body that orbits a larger one, either natural or artificial. Natural satellites that orbit planets are called moons. The first *artificial satellite*, *Sputnik 1*, was launched into orbit around the Earth by the USSR 1957. Artificial satellites are used for scientific purposes, communications, weather forecasting, and military applications. The largest artificial satellites can be seen by the naked eye.

satellite television transmission of broadcast signals through artificial communications satellites. Mainly positioned in ◊geostationary orbit, satellites have been used since the 1960s to relay television pictures around the world.

Higher-power satellites have more recently been developed to broadcast signals to cable systems or directly to people's homes.

Satie Erik (Alfred Leslie) 1866–1925. French composer. His piano pieces, such as the three *Gymnopédies* 1888, are precise and tinged with melancholy, and parody romantic expression with surreal commentary. His esthetic of ironic simplicity, as in the *Messe des pauvres/Poor People's Mass* 1895, acted as a nationalist antidote to the perceived excesses of German Romanticism.

Saturn in astronomy, the second-largest planet in the Solar System, sixth from the Sun, and encircled by bright and easily visible equatorial rings. Viewed through a telescope its color is ochre. Saturn orbits the Sun every 29.46 years at an average distance of 886,700,000 mi/1,427,000,000 km. Its equatorial diameter is 75,000 mi/ 20,000 km, but its polar diameter is 7,450 mi/12,000 k smaller, a result of its fast rotation and low density, the lowest of any planet.

The rings of Saturn could be the remains of a shattered moon, or they may always have existed in their present form.

Saturn in Roman mythology, the god of agriculture, identified by the Romans with the Greek god ◊Cronus. His period of rule was the ancient Golden Age. Saturn was dethroned by his sons Jupiter, Neptune, and Dis. At his festival, the Saturnalia in

---

satellite: largest natural planetary satellites

planet	satellite	diameter (mi/km)	mean distance from center of primary (km)	orbital period (days) (planet = 1)	reciprocal mass (planet = 1)
Jupiter	Ganymede	3,300/5,262	1,070,000	7.16	12,800
Saturn	Titan	3,200/5,150	1,221,800	15.95	4,200
Jupiter	Callisto	3,000/4,800	1,883,000	16.69	17,700
Jupiter	Io	2,240/3,630	421,600	1.77	21,400
Earth	Moon	2,160/3,476	384,400	27.32	81.3
Jupiter	Europa	1,900/3,138	670,900	3.55	39,700
Neptune	Triton	1,690/2,700	354,300	5.88	770

Dec, gifts were exchanged, and slaves were briefly treated as their masters' equals.

Saudi Arabia Kingdom of (*al-Mamlaka al-'Arabiya as-Sa'udiya*) *area* 849,400 sq mi/2,200,518 sq km *capital* Riyadh *towns and cities* Mecca, Medina, Taif; ports Jidda, Dammam *physical* desert, sloping to the Persian Gulf from a height of 9,000 ft/2,750 m the W *environment* oil pollution caused by the Gulf War 1990–91 has affected 285 mi/460 km of the Saudi coastline, threatening desalination plants and damaging the wildlife of saltmarshes, mangrove forest, and mudflats *features* Nafud Desert in N and the Rub'al Khali (Empty Quarter) in S, area 250,000 sq mi/650,000 sq km; with a ban on women drivers, there are an estimated 300,000 chauffeurs *head of state and government* King Fahd Ibn Abd al-Aziz from 1982 *political system* absolute monarchy *political parties* none *exports* oil, petroleum products *currency* rial *population* (1993 est) 17,500,000 (16% nomadic); growth rate 3.1% p.a. *life expectancy* men 64, women 68 *language* Arabic *media* TV satellite dishes were banned 1994 *religion* Sunni Muslim; there is a Shiite minority *literacy* men 73%, women 48% *GNP* $7,070 per head (1990) *chronology* *1926–32* Territories of Nejd and Hejaz united and kingdom established. *1953* King Ibn Saud died and was succeeded by his eldest son, Saud. *1964* King Saud forced to abdicate; succeeded by his brother, Faisal. *1975* King Faisal assassinated; succeeded by his half brother, Khalid. *1982* King Khalid died; succeeded by his brother, Crown Prince Fahd. *1987* Rioting by Iranian pilgrims caused 400 deaths in Mecca; diplomatic relations with Iran severed. *1990* Iraqi troops invaded and annexed Kuwait and massed on Saudi Arabian border. King Fahd called for help from US and UK forces. *1991* Allied with Western forces in Gulf War. Saudi Arabia attended Middle East peace conference. *1992* "Consultative council" formed. *1993* Introduction of regional assemblies countered by disbanding of human rights committee.

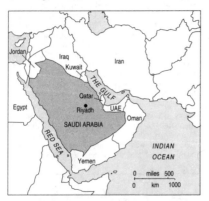

Saul in the Old Testament, the first king of Israel. He was anointed by Samuel and warred successfully against the neighboring Ammonites and Philistines, but fell from God's favor in his battle against the Amalekites. He became jealous and suspicious of ◊David and turned against him and Samuel. After being wounded in battle with the Philistines, in which his three sons died, he committed suicide.

savanna or *savannah* extensive open tropical grasslands, with scattered trees and shrubs. Savannas cover large areas of Africa, North and South America, and N Australia. The soil is acidic and sandy and generally considered suitable only as pasture for low-density grazing.

Savannah city and port of Georgia, US, 18 mi/29 km from the mouth of the Savannah River; population (1990) 137,600. Founded 1733, Savannah was the first city in the US to be laid out in geometrically regular blocks.

Manufactures include paper products, aircraft, transportation equipment, chemicals, and food products. The *Savannah*, the first steam-powered ship to cross the Atlantic, was built here. The first nuclear-powered merchant ship launched by the US 1959, was given the same name. Founded by James Oglethorpe in 1733, Savannah is the oldest settlement in Georgia and was its capital 1754–86. World cotton prices were set by the exchange here from the late 18th century until 1895.

Savimbi Jonas 1934–   . Angolan soldier and right-wing revolutionary, founder and leader of the National Union for the Total Independence of Angola (UNITA). From 1975 UNITA, under Savimbi's leadership, has tried to overthrow the government. An agreement between the two parties was reached May 1991, but fighting broke out again after elections Sept 1992. A peace agreement was reached 1994.

savings and loan association (S&L) a cooperative, mutual, savings organization that sells stock to its members. Created primarily to finance home mortgages, S&Ls at one time provided 40% of the funds for home purchases.

From 1986, an industry-wide crisis developed when, in some parts of the US, declining real estate values and rising unemployment reduced the value of investments and the ability of borrowers to repay loans. By 1989 the losses were enormous, and a federal bailout pledging more than $100 billion in taxpayer funds was negotiated.

Savonarola Girolamo 1452–1498. Italian reformer, a Dominican friar and an eloquent preacher. His crusade against political and religious corruption won him popular support, and in 1494 he led a revolt in Florence that expelled the ruling Medici family and established a democratic republic. His denunciations of Pope ◊Alexander VI led to his excommunication in 1497, and in 1498 he was arrested, tortured, hanged, and burned for heresy.

Savoy area of France between the Alps, Lake Geneva, and the river Rhône. A medieval duchy, it was made into the *départements* of Savoie and Haute-Savoie, in the Rhône-Alpes region.

sawfish any fish of the order Pristiformes of large, sharklike ◊rays, characterized by a flat, sawlike snout edged with teeth. The common sawfish *Pristis pectinatus*, also called the smalltooth, is more than 19 ft/6 m long. It has some 24 teeth along an elongated snout (6 ft/2 m) that can be used as a weapon.

sawfly any of several families of insects of the order Hymenoptera, related to bees, wasps, and ants, but lacking a "waist" on the body. The egg-laying tube (ovipositor) of the female is surrounded by a pair of sawlike organs, which it uses to make a slit in a plant stem to lay its eggs. Horntails are closely related.

Saxe-Coburg-Gotha Saxon duchy. Albert, the Prince Consort of Britain's Queen Victoria, was a son of the

1st Duke, Ernest I (1784–1844), who was succeeded by Albert's elder brother, Ernest II (1818–1893). It remained the name of the British royal house until 1917, when it was changed to Windsor.

saxifrage any plant of the genus *Saxifraga*, family Saxifragaceae, occurring in rocky, mountainous, and alpine situations in the northern hemisphere. They are low plants with groups of small white, pink, or yellow flowers.

Early saxifrage *S. virginiensis* is native to North America.

Saxon member of a Germanic tribe inhabiting the Danish peninsula and northern Germany. The Saxons migrated from their homelands, under pressure from the Franks, and spread into various parts of Europe, including Britain (see ◊Anglo-Saxon). They also undertook piracy in the North Sea and English Channel.

Saxony (German *Sachsen*) administrative *Land* (state) of Germany *area* 6,580 sq mi/17,036 sq km *capital* Dresden *towns* Leipzig, Chemnitz, Zwickau *physical* on the plain of the river Elbe north of the Erzgebirge mountain range *products* electronics, textiles, vehicles, machinery, chemicals, coal *population* (1990) 5,000,000 *history* conquered by Charlemagne 792, Saxony became a powerful medieval German duchy. The electors of Saxony were also kings of Poland 1697–1763. Saxony was part of East Germany 1946–90, forming a region with Anhalt.

Saxony-Anhalt administrative *Land* (state) of Germany *area* 10,000 sq mi/20,450 sq km *capital* Magdeburg *towns* Halle, Dessau *industries* chemicals, electronics, rolling stock, footwear, cereals, vegetables *population* (1990) 3,000,000 *history* Anhalt became a duchy 1863 and a member of the North German Confederation 1866. Between 1946 and 1990 it was joined to the former Prussian province of Saxony as a region of East Germany.

saxophone member of a hybrid brass instrument family of conical bore, with a single-reed woodwind mouthpiece and keyworks, invented about 1840 by Belgian instrument-maker Adolphe Sax (1814–1894).

sawfish *Sawfishes are related to skates and rays. They are large, flattened fishes averaging 16 ft in/5 m length but maximum weights of more than 5,000 lb/2,200 kg have been recorded. Sawfishes use their elongated, toothed snouts to grub for mollusks and crustaceans on muddy seabeds.*

Soprano, alto, tenor, and baritone forms remain current. The soprano saxophone is usually straight; the others are characteristically curved back at the mouthpiece and have an upturned bell. Initially a concert instrument of suave tone, the saxophone was incorporated into dance bands of the 1930s and 1940s, and assumed its modern guise as an abrasive solo jazz instrument after 1945. It has a voicelike ability to bend a note.

Say's law in economics, the "law of markets" formulated by Jean-Baptiste Say (1767–1832) to the effect that supply creates its own demand and that resources can never be underused.

scabies contagious infection of the skin caused by the parasitic itch mite *Sarcoptes scabiei*, which burrows under the skin to deposit eggs. Treatment is by antiparasitic creams and lotions.

scabious any plant of the Eurasian genus *Scabiosa* of the teasel family Dipsacaceae, with many small, usually blue, flowers borne in a single head on a tall stalk. The small scabious *S. columbaria* and the Mediterranean sweet scabious *S. atropurpurea* are often cultivated.

scalawag or *scallywag* in US history, a derogatory term for white Southerners who, during and after the ◊Civil War 1861–65, supported the Republican Party, and black emancipation and enfranchisement.

The reforms instituted by the scalawags were widely resented in the South, and their influence diminished with the rise of the Democratic party in the South.

scale in music, a sequence of pitches that establishes a key, and in some respects the character of a composition. A scale is defined by its starting note and may be *major* or *minor* depending on the order of intervals. A *chromatic scale* is the full range of 12 notes: it has no key because there is no fixed starting point.

scale insect any small plant-sucking insect (order *Homoptera*) of the superfamily Coccoidea. Some species are major pests—for example, the citrus mealy bug (genus *Pseudococcus*), which attacks citrus fruits in North America. The female is often wingless and legless, attached to a plant by the head and with the body covered with a waxy scale. The rare males are winged.

scallop any marine bivalve ◊mollusk of the family Pectinidae, with a fan-shaped shell. There are two "ears" extending from the socketlike hinge. Scallops use water-jet propulsion to move through the water to escape predators such as starfish. The giant Pacific scallop found from Alaska to California can reach 8 in/20 cm width.

Scandinavia peninsula in NW Europe, comprising Norway and Sweden; politically and culturally it also includes Denmark, Iceland, the Faeroe Islands, and Finland.

Scandinavian inhabitant of or native to Scandinavia (Denmark, Norway, Sweden, Iceland, and, often, Finland); also referring to the languages and cultures. The Scandinavian languages, including Faeroese, belong to the Indo-European family.

scandium silver-white, metallic element of the ◊lanthanide series, symbol Sc, atomic number 21, relative atomic mass 44.956.

Its compounds are found widely distributed in nature, but only in minute amounts. The metal has little industrial importance.

The element was discovered and named in 1879 by Swedish chemist Lars Nilson (1840–99), for Latin

Scandia, because it occurs in the Scandinavian mineral euxenite, on which he worked.

scanner in computing, a device that can produce a digital image of a document for input and storage in a computer. It uses technology similar to that of a photocopier. Small scanners can be passed over the document surface by hand; larger versions have a flat bed, like that of a photocopier, on which the input document is placed and scanned.

scanning in medicine, the noninvasive examination of body organs to detect abnormalities of structure or function. Detectable waves—for example, ◊ultrasound, gamma or ◊X-rays—are passed through the part to be scanned. Their absorption pattern is recorded, analyzed by computer, and displayed pictorially on a screen.

scarab any of a family Scarabaeidae of beetles, often brilliantly colored, and including ◊cockchafers, June beetles, and dung beetles. The *Scarabeus sacer* was revered by the ancient Egyptians as the symbol of resurrection.

Scarlatti (Giuseppe) Domenico 1685–1757. Italian composer. The eldest son of Alessandro ◊Scarlatti, he lived most of his life in Portugal and Spain in the service of the Queen of Spain. He wrote over 500 sonatas for harpsichord, short pieces in binary form demonstrating the new freedoms of keyboard composition and inspired by Spanish musical idioms.

Scarlatti (Pietro) Alessandro (Gaspare) 1660–1725. Italian Baroque composer. He was maestro di capella at the court of Naples and developed the opera form. He composed more than 100 operas, including *Tigrane* 1715, as well as church music and oratorios.

scarlet fever or *scarlatina* acute infectious disease, especially of children, caused by the bacteria in the *Streptococcus pyogenes* group. It is marked by fever, vomiting, sore throat and a bright red rash spreading from the upper to the lower part of the body. The rash is followed by the skin peeling in flakes. It is treated with antibiotics.

scarp and dip in geology, the two slopes formed when a sedimentary bed outcrops as a landscape feature. The scarp is the slope that cuts across the bedding plane; the dip is the opposite slope which follows the bedding plane. The scarp is usually steep, while the dip is a gentle slope.

Schiele Egon 1890–1918. Austrian Expressionist artist. Originally a landscape painter, he was strongly influenced by Art Nouveau, in particular Gustav Klimt, and developed a contorted linear style, employing strong colors.

His subject matter includes portraits and openly erotic nudes. In 1911 he was arrested for alleged obscenity.

Schiller Johann Christoph Friedrich von 1759–1805. German dramatist, poet, and historian. He wrote *Sturm und Drang* ("storm and stress") verse and plays, including the dramatic trilogy *Wallenstein* 1798–99. Much of his work concerns the aspirations for political freedom and the avoidance of mediocrity.

schist ◊metamorphic rock containing mica or another platy or elongate mineral, whose crystals are aligned to give a foliation (planar texture) known as schistosity. Schist may contain additional minerals such as ◊garnet.

schizophrenia mental disorder, a psychosis of unknown origin, which can lead to profound changes in personality, behavior, and perception, including delusions and hallucinations. It is more common in males and the early onset form is more severe than when the illness develops in later life. Modern treatment approaches include drugs, family therapy, stress reduction, and rehabilitation.

Schleswig-Holstein *Land* (state) of Germany *area* 6,060 sq mi/15,700 sq km *capital* Kiel *towns* Lübeck, Flensburg, Schleswig *features* river Elbe, Kiel Canal, Heligoland *industries* shipbuilding, mechanical and electrical engineering, food processing *population* (1988) 2,613,000 *religion* 87% Protestant; 6% Catholic *history* Schleswig (Danish *Slesvig*) and Holstein were two duchies held by the kings of Denmark from 1460, but were not part of the kingdom; a number of the inhabitants were German, and Holstein was a member of the Confederation of the Rhine formed 1815. Possession of the duchies had long been disputed by Prussia, and when Frederick VII of Denmark died without an heir 1863, Prussia, supported by Austria, fought and defeated the Danes 1864, and in 1866 annexed the two duchies. A plebiscite held 1920 gave the northern part of Schleswig to Denmark, which made it the province of Haderslev and Aabenraa; the rest, with Holstein, remained part of Germany.

Schliemann Heinrich 1822–1890. German archeologist. He earned a fortune in business, retiring in 1863 to pursue his lifelong ambition to discover a historical basis for Homer's *Iliad*. In 1871 he began excavating at Hissarlik, Turkey, a site which yielded the ruins of nine consecutive cities, and was indeed the site of Troy. His later excavations were at Mycenae 1874–76, where he discovered the ruins of the ◊Mycenaean civilization.

Schmidt Helmut 1918– . German socialist politician, member of the Social Democratic Party (SPD), chancellor of West Germany 1974–83. As chancellor, Schmidt introduced social reforms and continued Brandt's policy of ◊Ostpolitik. With the French president Giscard d'Estaing, he instigated annual world and European economic summits. He was a firm supporter of ◊NATO and of the deployment of US nuclear missiles in West Germany during the early 1980s.

Schoenberg Arnold (Franz Walter) 1874–1951. Austro-Hungarian composer. He was a US citizen from 1941. After Romantic early works such as *Verklärte Nacht/Transfigured Night* 1899 and the *Gurrelieder/Songs of Gurra* 1900–11, he experimented with atonality (absence of key), producing works such as *Pierrot lunaire/Moonstruck Pierrot* 1912 for chamber ensemble and voice, before developing the twelve-tone system of musical composition. This was further developed by his pupils Alban Berg and Anton ◊Webern.

scholasticism the theological and philosophical systems that were studied in both Christian and Judaic schools in Europe in the medieval period.

Scholasticism sought to integrate biblical teaching with Platonic and Aristotelian philosophy.

Schopenhauer Arthur 1788–1860. German philosopher whose *The World as Will and Idea* 1818 expounded an atheistic and pessimistic world view: an irrational will is considered as the inner principle of the world, producing an ever-frustrated cycle of desire, of which the only escape is esthetic contemplation or absorption into nothingness.

Schrödinger Erwin 1887–1961. Austrian physicist who advanced the study of wave mechanics (see ◊quantum theory). Born in Vienna, he became senior professor at the Dublin Institute for Advanced Studies 1940. He shared (with Paul Dirac) a Nobel Prize 1933.

Schubert Franz (Peter) 1797–1828. Austrian composer. His ten symphonies include the incomplete eighth in B minor (the "Unfinished") and the "Great" in C major. He wrote chamber and piano music, including the "Trout Quintet", and over 600 lieder (songs) combining the Romantic expression of emotion with pure melody. They include the cycles *Die schöne Müllerin/ The Beautiful Maid of the Mill* 1823 and *Die Winterreise/ The Winter Journey* 1827.

Schulz Charles Monroe 1922– . US cartoonist. His idea for the *Peanuts* cartoon strip was accepted by United Features Syndicate 1950. As the characters Snoopy, Charlie Brown, Lucy, and Linus became famous throughout the country, Schulz further promoted them through merchandise lines and television specials. In 1967 a musical based on the "Peanuts" characters, *You're a Good Man, Charlie Brown*, played on Broadway.

Schumann Robert Alexander 1810–1856. German composer and writer. His songs and short piano pieces portray states of emotion with great economy. Among his compositions are four symphonies, a violin concerto, a piano concerto, sonatas, and song cycles, such as *Dichterliebe/Poet's Love* 1840. Mendelssohn championed many of his works.

Schwarzkopf (H) Norman (nicknamed "Stormin' Norman") 1934– . US general who was supreme commander of the Allied forces in the ◊Gulf War 1991. He planned and executed a blitzkrieg campaign, "Desert Storm", sustaining remarkably few Allied casualties in the liberation of Kuwait. He was a battalion commander in the Vietnam War and deputy commander of the 1983 US invasion of Grenada.

Schwinger Julian 1918–1994. US quantum physicist. His research concerned the behavior of charged particles in electrical fields. This work, expressed entirely through mathematics, combines elements from quantum theory and relativity theory. Schwinger shared the Nobel Prize for Physics 1965 with Richard Feynman and Sin-Itiro Tomonaga (1906–1979).

sciatica persistent pain in the back and down the outside of one leg, along the sciatic nerve and its branches. Causes of sciatica include inflammation of the nerve or pressure of a displaced disk on a nerve root leading out of the lower spine.

science any systematic field of study or body of knowledge that aims, through experiment, observation, and deduction, to produce reliable explanation of phenomena, with reference to the material and physical world.

Scientology "applied religious philosophy" based on dianetics, founded in California in 1954 by L Ron Hubbard as the *Church of Scientology*. It claims to "increase man's spiritual awareness", but its methods of recruiting and retaining converts have been criticized. Its headquarters from 1959 have been in Sussex, England.

Scilly, Isles of or *Scilly Isles/Islands*, or *Scillies* group of 140 islands (five inhabited) and islets lying 25 mi/ 40 km SW of Land's End, England; administered by the Duchy of Cornwall; area 6.3 sq mi/16 sq km; population (1991) 2,050. They are known for subtropical gardens and produce many flowers for the UK.

Scipio Africanus Major 237–*c.* 183 BC. Roman general. He defeated the Carthaginians in Spain 210–206 BC, invaded Africa 204 BC, and defeated Hannibal at Zama 202 BC.

Scipio Africanus Minor *c.* 185–129 BC. Roman general, the adopted grandson of Scipio Africanus Major, also known as *Scipio Aemilianus*. He destroyed Carthage 146, and subdued Spain 133. He was opposed to his brothers-in-law, the Gracchi.

scorpion any arachnid of the order Scorpiones. Common in the tropics and subtropics, scorpions have large pincers and long tails ending in upcurved poisonous stings, though the venom is not usually fatal to a healthy adult human. Some species reach 10 in/25 cm. They produce live young rather than eggs, and hunt chiefly by night.

Scorpius zodiacal constellation in the southern hemisphere between Libra and Sagittarius, represented as a scorpion. The Sun passes briefly through Scorpius in the last week of Nov. The heart of the scorpion is marked by the red supergiant star Antares. Scorpius contains rich Milky Way star fields, plus the strongest ◊X-ray source in the sky, Scorpius X-1. In astrology, the dates for Scorpius are between about Oct 24 and Nov 21. (see ◊precession).

Scorsese Martin 1942– . US director, screenwriter, and producer. His films concentrate on complex characterization and the themes of alienation and guilt. Drawing from his Italian-American Catholic background, his work often deals with sin and redemption, as in his first major film *Boxcar Bertha* 1972. His influential, passionate, and forceful movies include *Mean Streets* 1973, *Taxi Driver* 1976, *Raging Bull* 1980, *The Last Temptation of Christ* 1988, *GoodFellas* 1990, and *Cape Fear* 1991.

Scot inhabitant of Scotland, part of Britain; or person of Scottish descent. Originally the Scots were a Celtic (Gaelic) people of N Ireland who migrated to Scotland in the 5th century.

Scotland the northernmost part of Britain, formerly an independent country, now part of the UK *area* 30,297 sq mi/78,470 sq km *capital* Edinburgh *towns* Glasgow, Dundee, Aberdeen *features* the Highlands in the N (with the Grampian Mountains); central Lowlands, including valleys of the Clyde and Forth, with most of the country's population and industries; Southern Uplands (including the Lammermuir Hills); and islands of the Orkneys, Shetlands, and Western Isles; the world's greatest concentration of nuclear weapons are at the UK and US bases on the Clyde, near Glasgow; 8,000-year-old pinewood forests once covered 3,706,500 acres/1,500,000 hectares, now reduced to 30,900 acres/12,500 hectares; remaining native woodlands remaining in the Highlands 1994 cover only 2% of the total area *industry* electronics, marine and aircraft engines, oil, natural gas, chemicals, textiles, clothing, printing, paper, food processing, tourism *currency* pound sterling *population* (1988 est) 5,094,000 *languages* English; Scots, a lowland dialect (derived from Northumbrian Anglo-Saxon); Gaelic spoken by 1.3%, mainly in the Highlands *religions* Presbyterian (Church of Scotland), Roman Catholic *famous people* Robert Bruce, Walter Scott, Robert Burns, Robert Louis Stevenson, Adam Smith *government* Scotland sends 72 members to the UK Parliament at Westminster. Local government is on similar lines to that of England, but there is a differing legal system There is a movement for an independent or devolved Scottish assembly.

Scots language the form of the English language as traditionally spoken and written in Scotland, regarded by some scholars as a distinct language. Scots derives from the Northumbrian dialect of Anglo-Saxon or Old English, and has been a literary language since the 14th century.

Scott Robert Falcon (known as *Scott of the Antarctic*) 1868–1912. English explorer who commanded two Antarctic expeditions, 1901–04 and 1910–12. On Jan 18, 1912, he reached the South Pole, shortly after Norwegian Roald ◊Amundsen, but on the return journey he and his companions died in a blizzard only a few miles from their base camp. His journal was recovered and published in 1913.

Scott Walter 1771–1832. Scottish novelist and poet. His first works were translations of German ballads, followed by poems such as *The Lady of the Lake* 1810 and *Lord of the Isles* 1815. He gained a European reputation for his historical novels such as *The Heart of Midlothian* 1818, *Ivanhoe* 1819, and *The Fair Maid of Perth* 1828. His last years were marked by frantic writing to pay off his debts, after the bankruptcy of his publishing company 1826.

Scottish Gaelic language see ◊Gaelic language.

Scout member of a worldwide youth organization that emphasizes character, citizenship, and outdoor life. It was founded (as the Boy Scouts) in England 1908 by Robert ◊Baden-Powell. His book *Scouting for Boys* 1908 led to the incorporation in the UK of the Boy Scout Association by royal charter in 1912.

The Boy Scouts of America was founded on the Baden-Powell model in 1910. There are about 3.5 million Boy Scouts in the US. Girl Scouts of the US was founded 1912, following the same model. There are about 2 million Girl Scouts, including Brownies (aged 6–8), Juniors (aged 9–11), Cadettes (12–14), and Seniors (14–17).

scrapie fatal disease of sheep and goats that attacks the central nervous system, causing deterioration of the brain cells. It is believed to be caused by a submicroscopic particle known as a prion and may be related to bovine spongiform encephalopathy, the disease of cattle known as "mad cow disease", and Creutzfeldt–Jakob disease in humans.

screen or *monitor* output device on which a computer displays information for the benefit of the operator. The commonest type is the ◊cathode-ray tube (CRT), which is similar to a television screen. Portable computers often use ◊liquid crystal display (LCD) screens. These are harder to read than CRTs, but require less power, making them suitable for battery operation.

scrolling in computing, the action by which data displayed on a VDT screen are automatically moved upward and out of sight as new lines of data are added at the bottom.

scuba (acronym for *self-contained underwater breathing apparatus*) another name for ◊aqualung.

sculpture artistic shaping of materials such as wood, stone, clay, metal, and, more recently, plastic and other synthetics. The earliest prehistoric human artifacts include sculpted stone figurines, and all ancient civilizations have left behind examples of sculpture. Many indigenous cultures have maintained rich traditions of sculpture. Those of Africa, South America, and the Caribbean in particular have been influential in the development of contemporary Western sculpture.

scurvy disease caused by deficiency of vitamin C (ascorbic acid), which is contained in fresh vegetables and fruit. The signs are weakness and aching joints and muscles, progressing to bleeding of the gums and other spontaneous hemorrhage, and drying-up of the skin and hair. It is reversed by giving the vitamin.

Scylla and Charybdis in Greek mythology, a sea monster and a whirlpool, between which Odysseus had to sail. Later writers located them in the Straits of Messina, between Sicily and Italy.

Scythia region north of the Black Sea between the Carpathian mountains and the river Don, inhabited by the Scythians 7th–1st centuries BC. From the middle of the 4th century, they were slowly superseded by the Sarmatians. The Scythians produced ornaments and vases in gold and electrum with animal decoration.

sea anemone invertebrate marine animal of the phylum Cnidaria with a tubelike body attached by the base to a rock or shell. The other end has an open "mouth" surrounded by stinging tentacles, which capture crustaceans and other small organisms. Many sea anemones are beautifully colored, especially those in tropical waters.

seabees World War II nickname for US Navy Construction Battalions (CBs).

Seaborg Glenn Theodore 1912– . US nuclear chemist associated with the preparation and synthesis of all the ◊transuranic elements with atomic numbers 94–105 at the Lawrence Radiation Laboratory, University of California at Berkeley. With Edwin M McMillan he produced plutonium in 1940, for which both shared the 1951 Nobel Prize for Chemistry. The element seaborgium was named for him 1994.

seaborgium name given briefly to element 106 1994. In October 1994 IUPAC changed the name to ◊rutherfordium following a new ruling that no element could be named for a living person.

sea cucumber any echinoderm of the class Holothuroidea with a cylindrical body that is tough-skinned, knobbed, or spiny. The body may be several feet in length. Sea cucumbers are sometimes called "cotton-spinners" from the sticky filaments they eject from the anus in self-defense.

sea gull see ◊gull.

sea horse any marine fish of several related genera, especially *Hippocampus*, of the family Syngnathidae, which includes the pipefishes. The body is small and compressed and covered with bony plates raised into tubercles or spines. The tail is prehensile, and the tubular mouth sucks in small shellfish and larvae as food.

The head and foreparts, usually carried upright, resemble those of a horse.

seakale perennial plant *Crambe maritima* of the family Cruciferae. In Europe the young shoots are cultivated as a vegetable.

seal aquatic carnivorous mammal of the families Otariidae and Phocidae (sometimes placed in a separate order, the Pinnipedia). The eared seals or sea lions (Otariidae) have small external ears, unlike the true seals (Phocidae). Seals have a streamlined body with thick blubber for insulation, and front and hind flippers. They feed on fish, squid, or crustaceans, and are commonly found in Arctic and Antarctic seas, but also in Mediterranean, Caribbean, and Hawaiian waters.

sea lily any ◊echinoderm of the class Crinoidea. In most, the rayed, cuplike body is borne on a sessile stalk (permanently attached to a rock) and has feathery arms in multiples of five encircling the mouth. However, some sea lilies are free-swimming and unattached.

sea lion any of several genera of ◊seals of the family Otariidae (eared seals), which also includes the fur seals. These streamlined animals have large fore flippers which they use to row themselves through the water. The hind flippers can be turned beneath the body to walk on land.

searching in computing, extracting a specific item from a large body of data, such as a file or table. The method used depends on how the data are organized. For example, a binary search, which requires the data to be in sequence, involves first deciding which half of the data contains the required item, then which quarter, then which eighth, and so on until the item is found.

sea slug any of an order (Nudibranchia) of marine gastropod mollusks in which the shell is reduced or absent. The order includes some very colorful forms, especially in the tropics. They are largely carnivorous, feeding on hydroids and ◊sponges.

seasonal affective disorder (SAD) form of depression which occurs in winter and is relieved by the coming of spring. Its incidence decreases closer to the equator. One type of SAD is associated with increased sleeping and appetite.

sea squirt or *tunicate* any solitary or colonial-dwelling saclike ◊chordate of the class Ascidiacea. A pouch-shaped animal attached to a rock or other base, it draws in food-carrying water through one siphon and expels it through another after straining it through numerous gill slits. The young are free-swimming tadpole-shaped organisms, which, unlike the adults, have a ◊notochord.

Seattle port (grain, timber, fruit, fish) of the state of Washington, situated between Puget Sound and Lake Washington; population (1990) 516,300, metropolitan area (with Everett) 2,559,200. It is a center for the manufacture of jet aircraft (Boeing), and also has shipbuilding, food processing, and paper industries.

There are two universities, Washington (1861) and Seattle (1891).

First settled 1852, as the nearest port for Alaska, Seattle grew in the late 19th century with the arrival of a transcontinental railroad 1884 and the Klondike gold rush of the 1890s. Since World War II the economy has been dominated by the aerospace industry. The 606-ft/185-m-high Space Needle was erected for the 1962 world's fair.

seal The Mediterranean monk seal breeds on remote rocky islets and cliffs of the E Atlantic. It has been found from the Canary Islands to the Mediterranean and along the Turkish coast to the Black Sea. The seals are easily upset by any disturbance, with pregnant females aborting, contributing to the decline of the species.

sea turtle any of various marine species of ◊turtles, some of which grow up to a length of up to 8 ft/2.5 m. They are excellent swimmers, having legs that are modified to oarlike flippers but make them awkward on land. The shell is more streamlined and lighter than that of other turtles. They often travel long distances to lay their eggs on the beaches where they were born.

sea urchin any of various orders of the class Echinoidea among the ◊echinoderms. They all have a globular body enclosed with plates of lime and covered with spines. Sometimes the spines are anchoring organs, and they also assist in locomotion. Sea urchins feed on seaweed and the animals frequenting them, and some are edible.

seaweed any of a vast collection of marine and freshwater, simple, multicellular plant forms belonging to the ◊algae and found growing from about high-water mark to depths of 300–600 ft/100–200 m. Some have holdfasts, stalks, and fronds, sometimes with air bladders to keep them afloat, and are green, blue-green, red, or brown.

Sebastiano del Piombo (Sebastiano Veneziano) *c.* 1485–1547. Italian painter of the High Renaissance. Born in Venice, he was a pupil of ◊Giorgione and developed a similar style of painting. In 1511 he moved to Rome, where his friendship with Michelangelo (and rivalry with Raphael) inspired him to his greatest works, such as *The Raising of Lazarus* 1517–19 (National Gallery, London). He also painted powerful portraits.

Sebastian, St Roman soldier, traditionally a member of Emperor Diocletian's bodyguard until his Christian faith was discovered. He was martyred by being shot with arrows. Feast day Jan 20.

second basic ◊SI unit (symbol sec or s) of time, one-sixtieth of a minute. It is defined as the duration of 9,192,631,770 cycles of regulation (periods of the radiation corresponding to the transition between two hyperfine levels of the ground state) of the cesium-133 isotope. In mathematics, the second is a unit (symbol ′) of angular measurement, equaling one-sixtieth of a minute, which in turn is one-sixtieth of a degree.

secondary education in the US, ◊education at a high school, coming after elementary school and before a college or university.

Second World War alternate name for ◊World War II, 1939–45.

secretary bird ground-hunting, long-legged, mainly gray-plumaged bird of prey *Sagittarius serpentarius,* about 4 ft/1.2 m tall, with an erectile head crest. It is protected in southern Africa because it eats poisonous snakes.

secretary of state the title of the cabinet official with responsibility for conducting the foreign affairs of the US. It is the senior cabinet post and is fourth in line of succession to the presidency in the event of death or incapacitation.

Secret Service any government ◊intelligence organization. The US Secret Service is a law-enforcement unit of the Treasury Department. It is charged with combating counterfeiters and has responsibility for protecting the president and other senior members of the government.

sect small ideological group, usually religious in nature, that may have moved away from a main group, often claiming a monopoly of access to truth or salvation. Sects are usually highly exclusive. They demand strict conformity, total commitment to their code of behavior, and complete personal involvement, sometimes to the point of rejecting mainstream society altogether in terms of attachments, names, possessions, and family.

Securities and Exchange Commission (*SEC*) official US agency created 1934, under Joseph P Kennedy, to ensure full disclosure to the investing public and protection against malpractice in the securities (stocks and bonds) and financial markets (such as ◊insider trading).

sedative any drug that has a calming effect, reducing anxiety and tension.

Sedatives will induce sleep in larger doses. Examples are ◊barbiturates, ◊narcotics, and ◊benzodiazepines.

sedge any perennial grasslike plant of the family Cyperaceae, especially the genus *Carex*, usually with three-cornered solid stems, common in low water or on wet and marshy ground.

sediment any loose material that has "settled"— deposited from suspension in water, ice, or air, generally as the water current or wind speed decreases. Typical sediments are, in order of increasing coarseness, clay, mud, silt, sand, gravel, pebbles, cobbles, and boulders.

sedimentary rock rock formed by the accumulation and cementation of deposits that have been laid down by water, wind, ice, or gravity. Sedimentary rocks cover more than two-thirds of the Earth's surface and comprise three major categories: clastic, chemically precipitated, and organic (or biogenic). Clastic sediments are the largest group and are composed of fragments of pre-existing rocks; they include clays, sands, and gravels.

sedition the stirring up of discontent, resistance, or rebellion against the government in power.

Seebeck effect in physics, the generation of a voltage in a circuit containing two different metals, or semiconductors, by keeping the junctions between them at different temperatures. Discovered by the German physicist Thomas Seebeck (1770–1831), it is also called the thermoelectric effect, and is the basis of the thermocouple. It is the opposite of the ◊Peltier effect (in which current flow causes a temperature difference between the junctions of different metals).

seed the reproductive structure of higher plants (◊angiosperms and ◊gymnosperms). It develops from a fertilized ovule and consists of an embryo and a food store, surrounded and protected by an outer seed coat, called the testa. The food store is contained either in a specialized nutritive tissue, the endosperm, or in the ◊cotyledons of the embryo itself. In angiosperms the seed is enclosed within a ◊fruit, whereas in gymnosperms it is usually naked and unprotected, once shed from the female cone. Following ◊germination the seed develops into a new plant.

seed plant any seed-bearing plant; also known as a *spermatophyte*.

The seed plants are subdivided into two classes: the ◊angiosperms, or flowering plants, and the ◊gymnosperms, principally the cycads and conifers. Together, they comprise the major types of vegetation found on land.

Sega Japanese games console and software manufacturer. Sega's most successful game is Sonic the Hedgehog.

Seine French river rising on the Langres plateau NW of Dijon, and flowing 472 mi/774 km NW to join the English Channel near Le Havre, passing through Paris and Rouen.

seismology study of earthquakes and how their shock waves travel through the Earth. By examining the global pattern of waves produced by an earthquake, seismologists can deduce the nature of the materials through which they have passed. This leads to an understanding of the Earth's internal structure.

Selene in Greek mythology, the goddess of the Moon. She was the daughter of a ◊Titan, and the sister of Helios and Eos. In later times she was identified with ◊Artemis.

selenium gray, nonmetallic element, symbol Se, atomic number 34, atomic weight 78.96. It belongs to the sulfur group and occurs in several allotropic forms that differ in their physical and chemical properties. It is an essential trace element in human nutrition.

Obtained from many sulfide ores and selenides, it is used as a red coloring for glass and enamel.

Seleucus I Nicator *c.* 358–280 BC. Macedonian general under Alexander the Great and founder of the *Seleucid Empire*. After Alexander's death 323 BC, Seleucus became governor and then (312 BC) ruler of Babylonia, founding the city of Seleucia on the river Tigris. He conquered Syria and had himself crowned king 306 BC, but his expansionist policies brought him into conflict with the Ptolemies of Egypt, and he was assassinated. He was succeeded by his son Antiochus I.

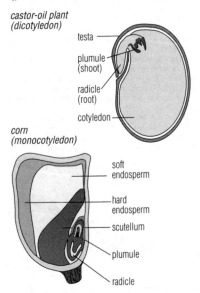

castor-oil plant (dicotyledon)

testa
plumule (shoot)
radicle (root)
cotyledon

corn (monocotyledon)

soft endosperm
hard endosperm
scutellum
plumule
radicle

seed The structure of seeds. The castor is a dicotyledon, a plant in which the developing plant has two leaves, developed from the cotyledon. In corn, a monocotyledon, there is a single leaf developed from the scutellum.

Seljuk Empire empire of the Turkish people (converted to Islam during the 7th century) under the leadership of the invading Tatars or Seljuk Turks. The Seljuk Empire 1055–1243 included Iran, Iraq and most of Anatolia and Syria. It was a loose confederation whose center was in Iran, jointly ruled by members of the family and led by a great sultan exercising varying degrees of effective power. It was succeeded by the ◊Ottoman Empire.

Sellafield site of a nuclear power station on the coast of Cumbria, NW England. It was known as *Windscale* until 1971, when the management of the site was transferred from the UK Atomic Energy Authority to British Nuclear Fuels Ltd. The plant is the world's greatest discharger of radioactive waste: between 1968 and 1979 180 kg of plutonium was discharged into the Irish Sea.

Sellers Peter 1925–1980. English comedian and film actor. He was noted for his skill at mimicry. He made his name in the madcap British radio program *The Goon Show* 1949–60. His films include *The Ladykillers* 1955, *I'm All Right Jack* 1960, *Dr Strangelove* 1964, five *Pink Panther* films 1964–78 (as the bumbling Inspector Clouseau), and *Being There* 1979.

Selznick David O(liver) 1902–1965. US film producer. His early work includes *King Kong, Dinner at Eight*, and *Little Women* all 1933. His independent company, Selznick International (1935–40), made such lavish films as *Gone with the Wind* 1939, *Rebecca* 1940, and *Duel in the Sun* 1946. His last film was *A Farewell to Arms* 1957.

semaphore visual signaling code in which the relative positions of two moveable pointers or hand-held flags stand for different letters or numbers. The system is used by ships at sea and for railroad signals.

Semarang port in N Java, Indonesia; population (1980) 1,027,000. There is a shipbuilding industry, and exports include coffee, teak, sugar, tobacco, kapok, and petroleum from nearby oil fields.

semen see ◊sperm.

semiconductor crystalline material with an electrical conductivity between that of metals (good) and insulators (poor). The conductivity of semiconductors can usually be improved by minute additions of different substances or by other factors. Silicon, for example, has poor conductivity at low temperatures, but this is improved by the application of light, heat, or voltage; hence silicon is used in ◊transistors, rectifiers, and ◊integrated circuits (silicon chips).

semiology or *semiotics* the study of the function of signs and symbols in human communication, both in language and by various nonlinguistic means. Beginning with the notion of the Swiss linguist Ferdinand de Saussure that no word or other sign (*signifier*) is intrinsically linked with its meaning (*signified*), it was developed as a scientific discipline, especially by Claude Lévi-Strauss and Roland Barthes.

semiotics synonym for ◊semiology.

Semite member of any of the peoples of the Middle East originally speaking a Semitic language, and traditionally said to be descended from Shem, a son of Noah in the Bible. Ancient Semitic peoples include the Hebrews, Ammonites, Moabites, Edomites, Babylonians, Assyrians, Chaldaeans, Phoenicians, and Canaanites. The Semitic peoples founded the monotheistic religions of Judaism, Christianity, and Islam.

They speak languages of the Hamito-Semitic branch of the Afro-Asiatic family.

Semitic languages branch of the Hamito-Semitic language.

Semmes Raphael 1809–1877. American naval officer. At the outbreak of the Civil War 1861, he joined the Confederate navy. He was placed in command of the British-built Confederate cruiser *Alabama* 1862 and drove Union ships from the Atlantic for nearly two years. His ship was lost in a battle with the disguised ironclad USS *Kearsarge* in the English Channel 1864.

Semtex plastic explosive, manufactured in the Czech Republic. It is safe to handle (it can only be ignited by a detonator) and difficult to trace, since it has no smell. It has been used by extremist groups in the Middle East and by the IRA in Northern Ireland.

Senate in ancient Rome, the "council of elders". Originally consisting of the heads of patrician families, it was recruited from ex-magistrates and persons who had rendered notable public service, but was periodically purged by the censors. Although nominally advisory, it controlled finance and foreign policy.

The US Senate consists of 100 members, two from each state, elected for a six-year term. The term also refers to the upper house of the Canadian parliament and to the upper chambers of Italy and France.

Sendak Maurice 1928– . US writer and book illustrator. His children's books with their deliberately arch illustrations include *Where the Wild Things Are* 1963, *In the Night Kitchen* 1970, and *Outside Over There* 1981.

Sendero Luminoso (Shining Path) Maoist guerrilla group active in Peru, formed 1980 to overthrow the government; until 1988 its activity was confined to rural areas. From 1992 its attacks intensified in response to a government crackdown.

Seneca Lucius Annaeus *c.* 4 BC–AD 65. Roman Stoic playwright, author of essays and nine tragedies. He was tutor to the future emperor Nero but lost favor after the latter's accession to the throne and was ordered to commit suicide. His tragedies were accepted as classical models by 16th-century dramatists.

Senegal Republic of (*République du Sénégal*) *area* 75,753 sq mi/196,200 sq km *capital* (and chief port) Dakar *towns and cities* Thiès, Kaolack *physical* plains rising to hills in SE; swamp and tropical forest in SW *features* river Senegal; the Gambia forms an enclave within Senegal *head of state* Abdou Diouf from 1981 *head of government* Habib Thiam from 1993 *political system* emergent socialist democratic republic *political parties* Senegalese Socialist Party (PS), democratic socialist; Senegalese Democratic Party (PDS), left of center *exports* peanuts, cotton, fish, phosphates *currency* franc CFA *population* (1993) 7,970,000; growth rate 3.1% p.a. *life expectancy* men 48, women 50 *languages* French (official); African dialects are spoken *religions* Muslim 80%, Roman Catholic 10%, animist *literacy* men 52%, women 25% *GNP* $720 per head (1991) *chronology* **1659** Became a French colony. **1854–65** Interior occupied by French. **1902** Became a territory of French West Africa. **1959** Formed the Federation of Mali with French Sudan. **1960** Independence achieved from France, but withdrew from the federation. Léopold Sédar Senghor, leader of the Senegalese Progressive Union (UPS), became president. **1966** UPS declared the only legal party. **1974** Pluralist system reestablished. **1976** UPS reconstituted as Senegalese Socialist Party (PS). Prime Minister Abdou Diouf nominated as Senghor's successor. **1980**

Senghor resigned; succeeded by Diouf. Troops sent to defend Gambia. *1981* Military help again sent to Gambia. *1982* Confederation of Senegambia came into effect. *1983* Diouf reelected. Post of prime minister abolished. *1988* Diouf decisively reelected. *1989* Diplomatic links with Mauritania severed after violent clashes left more than 450 people dead; over 50,000 people repatriated from both countries. Senegambia federation abandoned. *1991* Constitutional changes outlined; post of prime minister reinstated. *1992* Diplomatic links with Mauritania re-established. *1993* Diouf reelected. Assembly elections won by ruling PS.

Senghor Léopold (Sédar) 1906– . Senegalese politician and writer. He was the first president of independent Senegal 1960–80. Previously he was Senegalese deputy to the French National Assembly 1946–58, and founder of the Senegalese Progressive Union. He was also a well-known poet and a founder of *négritude*, a black literary and philosophical movement.

senile dementia ◊dementia associated with old age, often caused by ◊Alzheimer's disease.

Senna Ayrton 1960–1994. Brazilian race-car driver who was tragically killed at the 1994 San Marino Grand Prix at Imola. He won his first Grand Prix in Portugal 1985 and won 41 Grand Prix in 161 starts, including a record six wins at Monaco. Senna was world champion in 1988, 1990, and 1991.

Sennacherib King of Assyria from 705 BC. Son of Sargon II, he rebuilt the city of Nineveh on a grand scale, sacked Babylon 689, and defeated Hezekiah, king of Judah, but failed to take Jerusalem. He was assassinated by his sons, and one of them, Esarhaddon, succeeded him.

Sennett Mack. Adopted name of Michael Sinnott 1880–1960. Canadian-born US film director. After working as an actor in Biograph Studio films under D W Griffith 1908–11, he founded his own film production company, the Keystone Company 1911. As director, Sennett made hundreds of short slapstick comedies, cast Charlie ◊Chaplin in his first feature film (*Tillie's Punctured Romance* 1914), and started the career of Gloria Swanson. In the following years, Sennett developed the slapstick style of comedy, featuring the first flying custard pie and his Keystone Kops.

Seoul or *Soul* capital of South ◊Korea (Republic of Korea), near the Han River, and with its chief port at Inchon; population (1985) 10,627,800. Industries include engineering, textiles, food processing, electrical and electronic equipment, chemicals, and machinery.

sepal part of a flower, usually green, that surrounds and protects the flower in bud. The sepals are derived from modified leaves, and are collectively known as the ◊calyx.

Sephardi (plural *Sephardim*) Jew descended from those expelled from Spain and Portugal in the 15th century, or from those forcibly converted during the Inquisition to Christianity (Marranos). Many settled in N Africa and in the Mediterranean countries, as well as in the Netherlands, England, and Dutch colonies in the New World. Sephardim speak Ladino, a 15th-century Romance dialect, as well as the language of their nation.

septicemia technical term for blood poisoning.

sequencing in biochemistry, determining the sequence of chemical subunits within a large molecule. Techniques for sequencing amino acids in

proteins were established in the 1950s, insulin being the first for which the sequence was completed. Efforts are now being made to determine the sequence of base pairs within ◊DNA.

sequential file in computing, a file in which the records are arranged in order of a key field and the computer can use a searching technique, like a ◊binary search, to access a specific record.

sequoia two species of conifer in the redwood family Taxodiaceae, native to W US. The redwood *Sequoia sempervirens* is a long-lived timber tree, and one specimen, the Howard Libbey Redwood, is the world's tallest tree at 361 ft/110 m. The giant sequoia *Sequoiadendron giganteum* reaches up to 100 ft/30 m in circumference at the base, and grows almost as tall as the redwood. It is also (except for the bristlecone pine) the oldest living tree, some specimens being estimated at over 3,500 years of age.

sequoia The sequoia, or California redwood, is the tallest and largest tree. Twenty homes, a church, a mansion, and a bank have been built from the timber of one redwood.

Serb member of Yugoslavia's largest ethnic group, found mainly in Serbia, but also in the neighboring independent republics of Bosnia-Herzegovina and Croatia. Their language, generally recognized to be the same as Croat and hence known as Serbo-Croatian, belongs to the Slavic branch of the Indo-European family. It has more than 17 million speakers.

Serbia (Serbo-Croatian *Srbija*) constituent republic of Yugoslavia, which includes Kosovo and Vojvodina *area* 34,122 sq mi/88,400 sq km *capital* Belgrade *physical* fertile Danube plains in the N, mountainous in S (Dinaric Alps, Sar Mountains, N Albanian Alps, Balkan Mountains); rivers Sava, Tisza, Morava *features* includes the nominally autonomous provinces of *Kosovo*, capital Pristina, of which the predominantly Albanian population demands unification with Albania, and ◊*Vojvodina*, capital Novi Sad, largest town Subotica, with a predominantly Serbian population and a large Hungarian minority *population* (1991) 9,791,400 *language* the Serbian variant of Serbo-Croatian *religion* Serbian Orthodox *recent* *history* During World War II Serbia was under a puppet government set up by the Germans (94% of Serbian Jews were killed 1941–44); after the war it became a constituent republic of Yugoslavia.

From 1986 Slobodan ◊Milosevic as Serbian communist party chief and president waged a populist campaign to end the autonomous status of the provinces of Kosovo and Vojvodina. Serbia formally annexed Kosovo and Vojvodina Sept. 1990. Milosevic was reelected by a landslide majority Dec 1990, but in March 1991 there were anticommunist and anti-Milosevic riots in Belgrade.

The 1991 civil war in Yugoslavia arose from the Milosevic nationalist government attempting the forcible annexation of Serb-dominated regions in Croatia, making use of the largely Serbian federal army. In Oct 1991 Milosevic renounced territorial claims on Croatia pressured by threats of European Community (now European Union) and United Nations (UN) sanctions, but the fighting continued until a cease-fire was agreed Jan 1992. EC recognition of Slovenia's and Croatia's independence in Jan 1992 and Bosnia-Herzegovina's in April left Serbia dominating a greatly reduced "rump" Yugoslavia. A successor Yugoslavia, announced by Serbia and Montenegro April 1992, was rejected by the US and EC because of concerns over serious human rights violations in Kosovo and Serbia's continued backing of Bosnian Serbs in their fight to partition Bosnia-Herzegovina. In March 1992, and again in June, thousands of Serbs marched through Belgrade, demanding the ousting of Milosevic and an end to the war in Bosnia-Herzegovina. Milosevic was reelected Dec 1992.

Serbo-Croatian (or **Serbo-Croat**) the most widely spoken language in Yugoslavia. It is a member of the South Slavonic branch of the Indo-European family. The different dialects of Serbo-Croatian tend to be written by the Greek Orthodox Serbs in the Cyrillic script, and by the Roman Catholic Croats in the Latin script.

serial file in computing, a file in which the records are not stored in any particular order and therefore a specific record can be accessed only by reading through all the previous records.

Serpent Mound earthwork built by Hopewell Indians in the 2nd–1st centuries BC in Ohio. It is 1,330 ft/405 m long, 4 ft/1.3 m high, and about 19 ft/6 m across and may have been constructed in the shape of a snake for religious purposes.

Serpent Mound is in a state park in Adams County, Ohio.

Serra Junipero 1713–1784. Spanish missionary and explorer in America. A Franciscan friar, he pursued a missionary career and served in Querétaro 1750–58. He was transferred to Baja California with the expulsion of the Jesuits from Mexico 1767 and in 1769 led a missionary expedition to Alta California. He subsequently established several missions throughout the region.

serum clear fluid that separates out from clotted blood. It is blood plasma with the anticoagulant proteins removed, and contains ◊antibodies and other proteins, as well as the fats and sugars of the blood. It can be produced synthetically, and is used to protect against disease.

serval African wild cat *Felis serval*. It is a slender, long-limbed cat, about 3 ft/1 m long, with a yellowish-brown, black-spotted coat. It has large, sensitive ears, with which it locates its prey, mainly birds and rodents.

servomechanism automatic control system used in aircraft, motor automobiles, and other complex machines. A specific input, such as moving a lever or joystick, causes a specific output, such as feeding current to an electric motor that moves, for example, the rudder of the aircraft. At the same time, the position of the rudder is detected and fed back to the central control, so that small adjustments can continually be made to maintain the desired course.

sesame annual plant *Sesamum indicum* of the family Pedaliaceae, probably native to SE Asia. It produces oily seeds used for food and soap making.

set or *class* in mathematics, any collection of defined things (elements), provided the elements are distinct and that there is a rule to decide whether an element is a member of a set. It is usually denoted by a capital letter and indicated by curly brackets { }.

Set in Egyptian mythology, the god of night, the desert, and of all evils. Portrayed as a grotesque animal, Set was the murderer of ◊Osiris.

Seton St Elizabeth Ann Bayley 1774–1821. US religious leader and social benefactor. A convert to Roman Catholicism, she founded schools for the poor. Known as "Mother Seton," she was proclaimed the first American saint 1975.

In 1809, with her own funds, she established a Catholic elementary school in Baltimore. Soon afterward becoming a nun, she formed the Sisters of St Joseph and founded St Joseph's College for Women 1809.

Settlement, Act of in Britain, a law passed 1701 during the reign of King William III, designed to ensure a Protestant succession to the throne by excluding the Roman Catholic descendants of James II in favor of the Protestant House of Hanover. Elizabeth II still reigns under this act.

Seurat Georges 1859–1891. French artist. He originated, with Paul Signac, the Neo-Impressionist technique of ◊Pointillism (painting with small dabs rather than long brushstrokes). Examples of his work are *Bathers at Asnières* 1884 (National Gallery, London) and *Sunday on the Island of La Grande Jatte* 1886 (Art Institute of Chicago).

Seuss, Dr pseudonym of ◊Geisel, Theodore Seuss.

seven deadly sins in Christian theology, anger, avarice, envy, gluttony, lust, pride, and sloth.

Seven Weeks' War war 1866 between Austria and Prussia, engineered by the German chancellor ◊Bismarck. It was nominally over the possession of ◊Schleswig-Holstein, but it was actually to confirm Prussia's superseding Austria as the leading German state. The Prussian victory at the Battle of Sadowa was the culmination of General von Moltke's victories.

Seven Wonders of the World in antiquity, the pyramids of Egypt, the Hanging Gardens of Babylon, the temple of Artemis at Ephesus, the statue of Zeus at Olympia, the Mausoleum at Halicarnassus, the Colossus of Rhodes, and the Pharos (lighthouse) at Alexandria.

Severn river of Wales and England, rising on the NE side of Plynlimmon, N Wales, and flowing 210 mi/338 km through Shrewsbury, Worcester, and Gloucester to the Bristol Channel. It is the longest river in Great Britain. The *Severn bore* is a tidal wave up to 6 ft/2 m high.

Severus Lucius Septimius 146–211. Roman emperor. He held a command on the Danube when in 193 the emperor Pertinax was murdered. Proclaimed emperor by his troops, Severus proved an able administrator. He was born in N Africa, and was the only African to become emperor. He died at York while campaigning in Britain against the Caledonians.

Seville (Spanish *Sevilla*) city in Andalusia, Spain, on the Guadalquivir River, 60 mi/96 km N of Cadiz; population (1991) 683,500. Products include machinery, spirits, porcelain, pharmaceuticals, silk, and tobacco.

sewage disposal the disposal of human excreta and other waterborne waste products from houses, streets, and factories. Conveyed through sewers to sewage plants, sewage has to undergo a series of treatments to be acceptable for discharge into rivers or the sea, according to various local laws and ordinances. Raw sewage, or sewage that has not been treated adequately, is one serious source of water pollution and a cause of eutrophication.

sewing machine apparatus for the mechanical sewing of cloth, leather, and other materials by a needle, powered by hand, treadle, or belted electric motor. The popular lockstitch machine, using a double thread, was invented independently in the US by both Walter Hunt 1834 and Elias ◊Howe 1846. Howe's machine was the basis of the machine patented 1851 by US inventor Isaac ◊Singer.

sex determination process by which the sex of an organism is determined. In many species, the sex of an individual is dictated by the two sex chromosomes (X and Y) it receives from its parents. In mammals, some plants, and a few insects, males are XY, and females XX; in birds, reptiles, some amphibians, and butterflies the reverse is the case. In bees and wasps, males are produced from unfertilized eggs, females from fertilized eggs.

Environmental factors can affect some fish and reptiles, such as turtles, where sex is influenced by the temperature at which the eggs develop. In 1991 it was shown that maleness is caused by a single gene, 14 base pairs long, on the Y chromosome.

sexism belief in (or set of implicit assumptions about) the superiority of one's own sex, often accompanied by a ◊stereotype or preconceived idea about the opposite sex. Sexism may also be accompanied by ◊discrimination on the basis of sex, generally as practiced by men against women.

sextant navigational instrument for determining latitude by measuring the angle between some heavenly body and the horizon. It was invented by John Hadley (1682–1744) in 1730 and can be used only in clear weather.

sexually transmitted disease (STD) any disease transmitted by sexual contact, involving transfer of body fluids. STDs include not only traditional ◊venereal disease, but also a growing list of conditions, such as ◊AIDS and scabies, which are known to be spread primarily by sexual contact. Other diseases that are transmitted sexually include viral ◊hepatitis.

sexual reproduction reproductive process in organisms that requires the union, or ◊fertilization, of gametes (such as eggs and sperm). These are usually produced by two different individuals, although self-fertilization occurs in a few ◊hermaphrodites such as tapeworms. Most organisms other than bacteria and cyanobacteria (◊blue-green algae) show some sort of sexual process. Except in some lower organisms, the gametes are of two distinct types called eggs and sperm. The organisms producing the eggs are called females, and those producing the sperm, males. The fusion of a male and female gamete produces a *zygote*, from which a new individual develops. The alternatives to sexual reproduction are parthenogenesis and asexual reproduction by means of spores.

Seychelles Republic of *area* 175 sq mi/453 sq km *capital* Victoria (on Mahé island) *towns and cities* Cascade, Port Glaud, Misere *physical* comprises two distinct island groups, one concentrated, the other widely scattered, totaling over 100 islands and islets *features* Aldabra atoll, containing world's largest tropical lagoon; the unique "double coconut" (*coco de mer*); tourism is important *head of state and government* France-Albert René from 1977 *political system* emergent democracy *political parties* Seychelles People's Progressive Front (SPPF), nationalist socialist; Democratic Party (DP), centrist *exports* copra, cinna-

female reproductive system

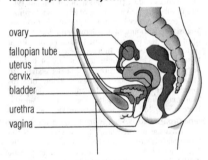

ovary
fallopian tube
uterus
cervix
bladder
urethra
vagina

male reproductive system

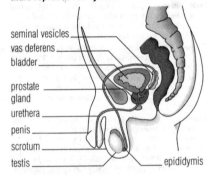

seminal vesicles
vas deferens
bladder
prostate gland
urethera
penis
scrotum
testis
epididymis

sexual reproduction The human reproductive organs. In the female, gametes called ova are produced regularly in the ovaries after puberty. The Fallopian tubes carry the ova to the uterus or womb, in which the baby will develop. In the male, sperm is produced inside the testes after puberty; about 10 million sperm cells are produced each day, enough to populate the world in six months. The sperm duct or vas deferens, a continuation of the epididymis, carries sperm to the urethra during ejaculation.

mon *currency* Seychelles rupee *population* (1993 est) 80,000; growth rate 2.2% p.a. *life expectancy* 66 years *languages* creole (Asian, African, European mixture) 95%, English, French (all official) *religion* Roman Catholic 90% *literacy* 89% *GNP* $5,430 per head (1991) *chronology* *1744* Became a French colony. *1794* Captured by British. *1814* Ceded by France to Britain; incorporated as a dependency of Mauritius. *1903* Became a separate British colony. *1975* Internal self-government agreed. *1976* Independence achieved from Britain as a republic within the Commonwealth, with James Mancham as president. *1977* France-Albert René ousted Mancham in an armed coup and took over presidency. *1979* New constitution adopted; Seychelles People's Progressive Front (SPPF) sole legal party. *1981* Attempted coup by South African mercenaries thwarted. *1984* René reelected. *1987* Coup attempt foiled. *1989* René reelected. *1991* Multiparty politics promised. *1992* Mancham returned from exile. Constitutional commission elected in multiparty elections. *1993* New constitution adopted. René defeated Mancham in first multiparty presidential elections.

Seyfert galaxy galaxy whose small, bright center is caused by hot gas moving at high speed around a massive central object, possibly a ◊black hole. Almost all Seyferts are spiral galaxies. They seem to be closely related to ◊quasars, but are about 100 times fainter. They are named for their discoverer Carl Seyfert (1911–1960).

Seymour Jane *c.* 1509–1537. Third wife of Henry VIII, whom she married in 1536. She died soon after the birth of her son Edward VI.

Shaanxi or *Shensi* province of NW China *area* 75,579 sq mi/195,800 sq km *capital* Xian *towns* Yan'an *physical* mountains; Huang He Valley, one of the earliest settled areas of China *industries* iron, steel, mining, textiles, fruit, tea, rice, wheat *population* (1990) 32,882,000.

shad any of several marine fishes, especially the genus *Alosa*, the largest (2 ft/60 cm long and 6 lb/ 2.7 kg in weight) of the herring family (Clupeidae). They migrate in shoals to breed in rivers.

The American shad *A. sapidissima*, once common along the Atlantic coast, was badly affected by stream pollution but is now making a comeback. It was successfully introduced along the Pacific in 1870. The gizzard shad *Dorosoma cepedianum* has been widely introduced into fresh waters of the US as food for other fishes.

shah (more formally, *shahanshah* "king of kings") traditional title of ancient Persian rulers, and also of those of the recent ◊Pahlavi dynasty in Iran.

Shah Jahan 1592–1666. Mogul emperor of India from 1628, under whom the dynasty reached its zenith. Succeeding his father ◊Jahangir, he extended Mogul authority into the Deccan plateau (E India), subjugating Ahmadnagar, Bijapur, and Golconda 1636, but lost Kandahar in the NW to the Persians 1653. His reign marked the high point of Indo-Muslim architecture, with Delhi being rebuilt as Shahjahanabad, while the Taj Mahal and Pearl Mosque were constructed at Agra. On falling seriously ill 1658 he was dethroned and imprisoned by his son ◊Aurangzeb.

Shaka or *Chaka* *c.* 1787–1828. Zulu chief who formed a Zulu empire in SE Africa. He seized power from his half brother 1816 and then embarked on a bloody military campaign to unite the Zulu clans. He was assassinated by his two half brothers.

Shaker popular name for a member of the Christian sect of the United Society of Believers in Christ's Second Appearing (and an offshoot of the ◊Quakers). This was founded by James and Jane Wardley in England about 1747 and taken to North America 1774 by Ann Lee (1736–84), the wife of a Manchester blacksmith, known as Mother Ann. She founded a colony in New York, and eventually 18 colonies existed in several states. Separation from the world in self-regulating farm communities, prescribed modes of simple dress and living conditions, celibacy, and faith healing characterized their way of life. The name was applied because of their ecstatic trembling and shaking during worship.

Shakespeare: the plays

title	performed/written (approximate)
early plays	
Henry VI Part I	1589–92
Henry VI Part II	1589–92
Henry VI Part III	1589–92
The Comedy of Errors	1592–93
The Taming of the Shrew	1593–94
Titus Andronicus	1593–94
The Two Gentlemen of Verona	1594–95
Love's Labours Lost	1594–95
Romeo and Juliet	1594–95
histories	
Richard III	1592–93
Richard II	1595–97
King John	1596–97
Henry IV Part I	1597–98
Henry IV Part II	1597–98
Henry V	1599
Roman plays	
Julius Caesar	1599–1600
Antony and Cleopatra	1607–08
Coriolanus	1607–08
the "great" or "middle" comedies	
A Midsummer Night's Dream	1595–96
The Merchant of Venice	1596–97
Much Ado About Nothing	1598–99
As You Like It	1599–1600
The Merry Wives of Windsor	1600–01
Twelfth Night	1601–02
the great tragedies	
Hamlet	1601–02
Othello	1604–05
King Lear	1605–06
Macbeth	1605–06
Timon of Athens	1607–08
the "dark" comedies	
Troilus and Cressida	1601–02
All's Well That Ends Well	1602–03
Measure for Measure	1604–05
late plays	
Pericles	1608–09
Cymbeline	1609–10
The Winter's Tale	1610–11
The Tempest	1611–12
Henry VIII	1612–13

Shakespeare William 1564–1616. English dramatist and poet. Established in London by 1589 as an actor and a dramatist, he was England's unrivaled dramatist until his death, and is considered the greatest English dramatist. His plays, written in blank verse with some prose, can be broadly divided into lyric plays, including *Romeo and Juliet* and *A Midsummer Night's Dream*; comedies, including *The Comedy of Errors*, *As You Like It*, *Much Ado About Nothing*, and *Measure For Measure*; historical plays, such as *Henry VI* (in three parts), *Richard III*, and *Henry IV* (in two parts), which often showed cynical political wisdom; and tragedies, such as *Hamlet*, *Macbeth*, and *King Lear*. He also wrote numerous sonnets.

shale fine-grained and finely layered ◊sedimentary rock composed of silt and clay. It is a weak rock, splitting easily along bedding planes to form thin, even slabs (by contrast, mudstone splits into irregular flakes). Oil shale contains kerogen, a solid bituminous material that yields ◊petroleum when heated.

shaman ritual leader who acts as intermediary between society and the supernatural world in many indigenous cultures of Asia, Africa, and the Americas. Also known as a *medicine man*, *seer*, or *sorcerer*, the shaman is expected to use special powers to cure illness and control good and evil spirits.

Shamir Yitzhak 1915– . Polish-born Israeli right-wing politician; prime minister 1983–84 and 1986–92; leader of the Likud (Consolidation Party) until 1993. He was foreign minister under Menachem Begin 1980–83, and again foreign minister in Shimon ◊Peres' unity government 1984–86.

shamrock several trifoliate plants of the family Leguminosae, including ◊clovers. St Patrick is said to have used one to illustrate the doctrine of the Holy Trinity, and it was made the national badge of Ireland.

Shandong or *Shantung* province of NE China *area* 59,174 sq mi/153,300 sq km *capital* Jinan *towns* ports: Yantai, Weihai, Qingdao, Shigiusuo *features* crossed by the Huang He River and the ◊Grand Canal; Shandong Peninsula *industries* cereals, cotton, wild silk, varied minerals *population* (1990) 84,393,000.

Shanghai port on the Huang-pu and Wusong rivers, Jiangsu province, China, 15 mi/24 km from the Chang Jiang estuary; population (1986) 6,980,000, the largest city in China. The municipality of Shanghai has an area of 2,239 sq mi/5,800 sq km and a population of 13,342,000. Industries include textiles, paper, chemicals, steel, agricultural machinery, precision instruments, shipbuilding, flour and vegetable-oil milling, and oil refining. It handles about 50% of China's imports and exports.

Shannon longest river in Ireland, rising in County Cavan and flowing 240 mi/386 km through loughs Allen and Ree and past Athlone, to reach the Atlantic Ocean through a wide estuary below Limerick. It is also the greatest source of electric power in the republic, with hydroelectric installations at and above Ardnacrusha, 3 mi/5 km N of Limerick.

Shansi alternative transliteration of the Chinese province of ◊Shanxi.

Shantung alternative transliteration of the Chinese province of ◊Shandong.

Shanxi or *Shansi* or *Shensi* province of NE China *area* 60,641 sq mi/157,100 sq km *capital* Taiyuan *towns* Datong *features* a drought-ridden plateau, partly surrounded by the ◊Great Wall *industries* coal, iron, fruit

population (1990) 28,759,000 *history* saw the outbreak of the Boxer Rebellion 1900.

Shapley Harlow 1885–1972. US astronomer, whose study of globular clusters showed that they were arranged in a halo around the Galaxy, and that the Galaxy was much larger than previously thought. He realized that the Sun was not at the center of the Galaxy as then assumed, but two-thirds of the way out to the rim.

Shapley joined the Mount Wilson Observatory, California, 1914.

Shari'a the law of ◊Islam believed by Muslims to be based on divine revelation, and drawn from a number of sources, including the Koran, the Hadith, and the consensus of the Muslim community. Under this law, *qisas*, or retribution, allows a family to exact equal punishment on an accused; *diyat*, or blood money, is payable to a dead person's family as compensation.

Sharif Omar. Adopted name of Michael Shalhoub 1932– . Egyptian-born actor (of Lebanese parents). He was Egypt's top male star before breaking into international films after his successful appearance in *Lawrence of Arabia* 1962.

His films include *Dr Zhivago* 1965, *Funny Girl* 1968, and *Funny Lady* 1975.

Sharjah or *Shariqah* third-largest of the seven member states of the ◊United Arab Emirates, situated on the Arabian Gulf NE of Dubai; area 1,004 sq mi/2,600 sq km; population (1985) 269,000. Since 1952 it has included the small state of Kalba. In 1974 oil was discovered offshore. Industries include ship repair, cement, paint, and metal products.

shark any member of various orders of cartilaginous fishes (class Chondrichthyes), found throughout the oceans of the world. There are about 400 known species of shark. They have tough, usually gray, skin covered in denticles (small toothlike scales). A shark's streamlined body has side pectoral fins, a high dorsal fin, and a forked tail with a large upper lobe. Five open gill slits are visible on each side of the generally pointed head. Most sharks are fish-eaters, and a few will attack humans. They range from several feet in length to the great *white shark* *Carcharodon carcharias*, 30 ft/9 m long, and the harmless plankton-feeding *whale shark* *Rhincodon typus*, over 50 ft/15 m in length.

shark *The great white shark of the Atlantic, Pacific, and Indian oceans is a large and aggressive fish. It has a reputation for eating humans. Like all sharks, the great white has a skeleton made of cartilage, not bone.*

Sharpeville black township in South Africa, 40 mi/65 km S of Johannesburg and N of Vereeniging; 69 people were killed here when police fired on a crowd of antiapartheid demonstrators March 21, 1960.

Shatt-al-Arab (Persian *Arvand*) waterway formed by the confluence of the rivers ◊Euphrates and ◊Tigris; length 120 mi/190 km to the Persian Gulf. Basra, Khorramshahr, and Abadan stand on it.

Shaw George Bernard 1856–1950. Irish dramatist. He was also a critic and novelist, and an early member of the socialist ◊Fabian Society. His plays combine comedy with political, philosophical, and polemic aspects, aiming to make an impact on his audience's social conscience as well as their emotions. They include *Arms and the Man* 1894, *Devil's Disciple* 1897, *Man and Superman* 1903, *Pygmalion* 1913, and *St Joan* 1923. Nobel Prize 1925.

Shays Daniel *c.* 1747–1825. American political agitator. In 1786 he led Shays Rebellion, an armed uprising of impoverished farmers. The riot was suppressed 1787 by a Massachusetts militia force, but it drew public attention to the plight of the western farmers and the need for a stronger central government. Shays was pardoned 1788.

Born in W Massachusetts, Shays served in the 5th Massachusetts Regiment during the American Revolution 1775–83, seeing action at the battles of Bunker Hill, Ticonderoga, and Saratoga.

shearwater any sea bird of the genus *Puffinus*, in the same family (Procellariidae) as the diving ◊petrels.

Sheba ancient name for S ◊Yemen (Sha'abijah). It was once renowned for gold and spices. According to the Old Testament, its queen visited Solomon; until 1975 the Ethiopian royal house traced its descent from their union.

sheep any of several ruminant, even-toed, hoofed mammals of the family Bovidae. Wild species survive in the uplands of central and E Asia, N Africa, S Europe and North America. The domesticated breeds are all classified as *Ovis aries*.

Sheffield industrial city on the river Don, South Yorkshire, England; population (1991) 501,200. From the 12th century, iron smelting was the chief industry, and by the 14th century, Sheffield cutlery, silverware, and plate were made. During the Industrial Revolution the iron and steel industries developed rapidly. It now produces alloys and special steels, cutlery of all kinds, permanent magnets, drills, and precision tools. Other industries include electroplating, type-founding, and the manufacture of optical glass.

sheik leader or chief of an Arab family or village; also Muslim title meaning "religious scholar".

shellac resin derived from secretions of the lac insect.

Shelley Mary Wollstonecraft 1797–1851. English writer. She was the daughter of Mary Wollstonecraft and William Godwin. In 1814 she eloped with the poet Percy Bysshe Shelley, whom she married 1816. Her novels include *Frankenstein* 1818, *The Last Man* 1826, and *Valperga* 1823.

Shelley Percy Bysshe 1792–1822. English lyric poet. He was a leading figure in the Romantic movement. Expelled from Oxford University for atheism, he fought all his life against religion and for political freedom. This is reflected in his early poems such as *Queen Mab* 1813. He later wrote tragedies including *The Cenci* 1818, lyric dramas such as *Prometheus Unbound* 1820, and lyrical poems such as "Ode to the West Wind". He drowned while sailing in Italy.

shellfish popular name for mollusks and crustaceans, including the whelk and periwinkle, mussel, oyster, lobster, crab, and shrimp.

Shensi alternative transcription of the Chinese province of ◊Shanxi.

Shenyang industrial city and capital of Liaoning province, China; population (1990) 4,500,000. It was the capital of the Manchu emperors 1625–44; their tombs are nearby.

Shepard Alan Bartlett, Jr 1923– . US astronaut. He undertook the first manned US space flight, the suborbital *Mercury-Redstone 3* mission on board the *Freedom 7* capsule May 1961, and commanded the *Apollo 14* lunar landing mission 1971. Born in East Derry, New Hampshire, he graduated 1944 from the US Naval Academy at Annapolis and served as a fighter pilot, test pilot, and aircraft readiness officer for the Atlantic fleet before becoming an astronaut.

Sheraton Thomas *c.* 1751–1806. English designer of elegant inlaid furniture. He was influenced by his predecessors Hepplewhite and ◊Chippendale.

Sheridan Philip Henry 1831–1888. Union general in the American ◊Civil War. Recognizing Sheridan's aggressive spirit, General Ulysses S ◊Grant gave him command of his cavalry in 1864, and soon after of the Army of the Shenandoah Valley, Virginia. In the final stage of the war, Sheridan forced General Robert E ◊Lee to retreat to Appomattox and surrender.

Sheridan Richard Brinsley 1751–1816. Irish dramatist and politician. His social comedies include *The Rivals* 1775, celebrated for the character of Mrs Malaprop, and *The School for Scandal* 1777. He also wrote a burlesque, *The Critic* 1779. In 1776 he became lessee of the Drury Lane Theatre. He became a member of Parliament 1780.

Sherman, William Tecumseh *US general William Tecumseh Sherman who as a leader of the Union forces in the American Civil War was second only to Ulysses Grant. Attempting to destroy Confederate supplies and morale, he waged an economic campaign against the civilian population of Georgia and the Carolinas, laying waste to the countryside.*

sheriff in the US, in all states but Rhode Island, the chief elected officer of a county law-enforcement agency, usually responsible for enforcement in unincorporated areas of the county and for the operation of the jail. The sheriff is also the officer of the local court who serves papers and enforces court orders.

Sherman US Medium Tank M4. It was used by all Allied armies in World War II, and although no match for the German Tiger or Panther until given a heavier gun, it proved reliable, easy to operate and maintain, and a suitable basis for several variations such as rocket-launchers, mine-clearers, swimming tanks, and self-propelled guns. In its basic form it weighed 32 tons, had a speed of 25 mph/40 kph, and a crew of five.

Sherman William Tecumseh 1820–1891. Union general in the ◊Civil War. In 1864 he captured and burned Atlanta; continued his march eastward, to the sea, laying Georgia waste; and then drove the Confederates northward. He was US Army chief of staff 1869–83.

Sherpa member of a people in NE Nepal related to the Tibetans and renowned for their mountaineering skill. They frequently work as support staff and guides for climbing expeditions. A Sherpa, Tensing Norgay, was one of the first two people to climb to the summit of Everest.

Shetland Islands islands off the N coast of Scotland, beyond the Orkney Islands *area* 541 sq mi/1,400 sq km *towns* Lerwick (administrative headquarters), on Mainland, largest of 19 inhabited islands *features* over 100 islands including Muckle Flugga (latitude 60° 51′ N) the northernmost of the British Isles *environment* In 1993 the *Braer* ran aground on Shetland spilling 85,000 metric tons of oil. In February 1994 50,000 birds, mostly guillemots and other fish-eating species, were washed up around the Islands. They appeared to have starved to death *industries* processed fish, handknits from Fair Isle and Unst, miniature Shetland ponies, herring fishing, salmon farming, cattle and sheep farming. Europe's largest oil port is Sullom Voe, Mainland *population* (1991) 22,500 *language* dialect derived from Norse, the islands having been a Norse dependency from the 9th century until 1472 when they were annexed by Scotland.

Shevardnadze Edvard 1928– . Georgian politician, Soviet foreign minister 1985–91, head of the state of Georgia from 1992. A supporter of ◊Gorbachev, he was first secretary of the Georgian Communist Party from 1972 and an advocate of economic reform. In 1985 he became a member of the Politburo, working for détente and disarmament. In July 1991, he resigned from the Communist Party (CPSU) and, along with other reformers and leading democrats, established the Democratic Reform Movement. In March 1992 he was chosen as chair of Georgia's ruling military council, and in Oct was elected speaker of parliament (equivalent to president).

Shihchiachuang alternative transliteration of the city of ◊Shijiazhuang in China.

Shi Huangdi or *Shih Huang Ti* 259–210 BC. Emperor of China who succeeded to the throne of the state of Qin in 246 BC and had reunited China as an empire by 228 BC. He burned almost all existing books in 213 BC to destroy ties with the past; rebuilt the ◊Great Wall of China; and was buried in Xian, Shaanxi province, in a tomb complex guarded by 10,000 life-size terracotta warriors (excavated in the 1980s).

Shiite or *Shiah* member of a sect of Islam that believes that ◊Ali was ◊Mohammed's first true successor. The Shiites are doctrinally opposed to the Sunni Muslims. They developed their own law differing only in minor directions, such as inheritance and the status of women. In Shi'ism, the clergy are empowered to intervene between God and humans, whereas among the Sunni, the relationship with God is direct and the clergy serve as advisers.

The Shiites are prominent in Iran, the Lebanon, and Indo-Pakistan, and are also found in Iraq and Bahrain.

Shijiazhuang or *Shihchiachuang* city and major railroad junction in Hebei province, China; population (1989) 1,300,000. Industries include textiles, chemicals, printing, and light engineering.

Shikoku smallest of the four main islands of Japan, S of Honshu, E of Kyushu; area 7,257 sq mi/18,800 sq km; population (1986) 4,226,000; chief town Matsuyama. Products include rice, wheat, soy beans, sugar cane, orchard fruits, salt, and copper.

shila or *sila* Buddhist term for ethical living. This includes the ethical component of the Eightfold Path: right speech, right action, and the right means of making a living. In addition, Buddhist monks have ten *shilas* or moral rules, including not killing and abstaining from alcohol.

shingles common name for ◊herpes zoster, a disease characterized by infection of sensory nerves, with pain and eruption of blisters along the course of the affected nerves.

Shinto the indigenous religion of Japan. It combines an empathetic oneness with natural forces and loyalty to the reigning dynasty as descendants of the Sun goddess, Amaterasu-Omikami. Traditional Shinto followers stressed obedience and devotion to the emperor, and an aggressive nationalistic aspect was developed by the Meiji rulers. Today Shinto has discarded these aspects.

ship large seagoing vessel. The Greeks, Phoenicians, Romans, and Vikings used ships extensively for trade, exploration, and warfare. The 14th century was the era of European exploration by sailing ship, largely aided by the invention of the compass. In the 15th century Britain's Royal Navy was first formed, but in the 16th–19th centuries Spanish and Dutch fleets dominated the shipping lanes of both the Atlantic and Pacific.

The ultimate sailing ships, the fast US and British tea clippers, were built in the 19th century. Also in the 19th century, iron was first used for some shipbuilding instead of wood. Steam-propelled ships of the late 19th century were followed by compound engine and turbine-propelled vessels from the early 20th century.

Shiva alternative spelling of ◊Siva, Hindu god.

shock in medicine, circulatory failure marked by a sudden fall of blood pressure and resulting in pallor, sweating, fast (but weak) pulse, and sometimes complete collapse. Causes include disease, injury, and psychological trauma.

Shoemaker Willie (William Lee) 1931– . US jockey 1949–90. He rode 8,833 winners from 40,351 mounts and his earnings exceeded $123 million. He retired Feb 1990 after finishing fourth on Patchy Groundfog at Santa Anita, California.

He was the leading US jockey 10 times. After his retirement he became a successful trainer before an automobile accident 1991 left him paralyzed. Standing 4 ft 11 in/1.5 m tall, he weighed about 95 lb/43 kg.

shogun in Japanese history, title of a series of military strongmen 1192–1868 who relegated the emperor's role to that of figurehead. Technically an imperial appointment, the office was treated as hereditary and was held by the Minamoto clan 1192–1219, by the ◊Ashikaga 1336–1573, and by the Tokugawa 1603–1868. The shogun held legislative, judicial, and executive power.

Shona member of a Bantu-speaking people of S Africa, comprising approximately 80% of the population of Zimbabwe. They also occupy the land between the Save and Pungure rivers in Mozambique, and smaller groups are found in South Africa, Botswana, and Zambia. The Shona are mainly farmers, living in scattered villages. The Shona language belongs to the Niger-Congo family.

short circuit direct connection between two points in an electrical circuit.

Its relatively low resistance means that a large current flows through it, bypassing the rest of the circuit, and this may cause the circuit to overheat dangerously.

shorthand any system of rapid writing, such as the abbreviations practiced by the Greeks and Romans. The first perfecter of an entirely phonetic system was Isaac Pitman, by which system speeds of about 300 words a minute are said to be attainable.

Short Parliament the English Parliament that was summoned by Charles I on April 13, 1640, to raise funds for his war against the Scots. It was succeeded later in the year by the ◊Long Parliament.

short story short work of prose fiction, which typically either sets up and resolves a single narrative point or depicts a mood or an atmosphere. The two seminal figures in the development of the modern short story are Guy de Maupassant and Anton Chekhov. Other outstanding short-story writers are Rudyard Kipling, Saki, Edgar Allan Poe, Ernest Hemingway, Isaac Babel, Katherine Mansfield, Jorge Luis Borges, and Sherwood Anderson.

Shostakovich Dmitry (Dmitriyevich) 1906–1975. Soviet composer. His music is tonal, expressive, and sometimes highly dramatic; it was not always to official Soviet taste. He wrote 15 symphonies, chamber and film music, ballets, and operas, the latter including *Lady Macbeth of Mtsensk* 1934, which was suppressed as "too divorced from the proletariat", but revived as *Katerina Izmaylova* 1963.

shot put in track and field, the sport of throwing (or putting) overhand from the shoulder a metal ball (or shot). Standard shot weights are 16 lb/7.26 kg for men and 8.8 lb/4 kg for women.

shrew insectivorous mammal of the family Soricidae, found in Eurasia and the Americas. It is mouselike, but with a long nose and pointed teeth. Its high metabolic rate means that it must eat almost constantly.

The common shrew *Sorex araneus* is about 3 in/7.5 cm long.

shrike "butcher-bird" of the family Laniidae, of which there are over 70 species, living mostly in Africa, but also in Eurasia and North America. They often impale insects and small vertebrates on thorns. They can grow to 14 in/35 cm long, and have gray, black, or brown plumage.

shrimp crustacean related to the ◊prawn. It has a cylindrical, semitransparent body, with ten jointed legs. Some shrimps grow as large as 10 in/25 cm long.

Shropshire county of W England. Sometimes abbreviated to *Salop*, it was officially known as Salop from 1974 until local protest reversed the decision 1980 *area* 1,347 sq mi/3,490 sq km *towns* Shrewsbury (administrative headquarters), Telford, Oswestry, Ludlow *features* bisected, on the Welsh border, NW–SE by the river Severn; Ellesmere, the largest of several lakes; the Clee Hills rise to about 1,800 ft/610 m in the SW; Ironbridge Gorge open-air museum of industrial archeology, with the Iron Bridge (1779), the world's first cast-iron bridge *industries* chiefly agricultural: sheep and cattle, cereals, sugar beet. It is the main iron-producing county in England *population* (1991) 406,400 *famous people* Charles Darwin, A E Housman, Wilfred Owen, Gordon Richards

SI abbreviation for *Système International [d'Unités]* (French "International System [of Metric Units]"); see ◊SI units.

Sibelius Jean (Christian) 1865–1957. Finnish composer. His works include nationalistic symphonic poems such as *En saga* 1893 and *Finlandia* 1900, a violin concerto 1904, and seven symphonies.

Siberia Asian region of Russia, extending from the Ural Mountains to the Pacific Ocean *area* 4,650,000 sq mi/12,050,000 sq km *towns* Novosibirsk, Omsk, Krasnoyarsk, Irkutsk *features* long and extremely cold winters; forests covering about 1,930,000 sq mi/ ·5,000,000 sq km; the Siberian tiger, the world's largest cat, is an endangered species *industries* hydroelectric power from rivers Lena, Ob, and Yenisei; forestry; mineral resources, including gold, diamonds, oil, natural gas, iron, copper, nickel, cobalt.

Sibyl in Roman mythology, one of many prophetic priestesses, notably one from Cumae near Naples. She offered to sell to the legendary king of Rome, Tarquinius Superbus, nine collections of prophecies, the *Sibylline Books*, but the price was too high. When she had destroyed all but three, he bought those for the identical price, and they were kept for consultation in emergency at Rome.

Sichuan or *Szechwan* province of central China *area* 219,634 sq mi/569,000 sq km *capital* Chengdu *towns* Chongqing *features* surrounded by mountains, it was the headquarters of the Nationalist government 1937–45, and China's nuclear research centers are here. It is China's most populous administrative area *industries* rice, coal, oil, natural gas *population* (1990) 107,218,000.

Sicily (Italian *Sicilia*) the largest Mediterranean island, an autonomous region of Italy; area 9,920 sq mi/25,700 sq km; population (1990) 5,196,800. Its capital is Palermo, and towns include the ports of Catania, Messina, Syracuse, and Marsala. It exports Marsala wine, olives, citrus, refined oil and petrochemicals, pharmaceuticals, potash, asphalt, and marble. The region also includes the islands of Lipari, Egadi, Ustica, and Pantelleria. Etna, 10,906 ft/3,323 m high, is the highest volcano in Europe; its last major eruption was in 1971.

Sickert Walter (Richard) 1860–1942. English artist. His Impressionist cityscapes of London and Venice, portraits, and domestic and music-hall interiors capture subtleties of tone and light, often with a melancholic atmosphere.

sickle-cell disease hereditary chronic blood disorder common among people of black African descent; also found in the E Mediterranean, parts of the Persian Gulf, and in NE India. It is characterized by distortion and fragility of the red blood cells, which are lost too rapidly from the circulation. This often results in ◊anemia.

Siegfried legendary Germanic and Norse hero. His story, which may contain some historical elements, occurs in the German *Nibelungenlied/Song of the Nibelung* and in the Norse *Elder* or *Poetic Edda* and the prose *Völsunga Saga* (in the last two works, the hero is known as Sigurd).

siemens SI unit (symbol S) of electrical conductance, the reciprocal of the impedance of an electrical circuit. One siemens equals one ampere per volt. It was formerly called the mho or reciprocal ohm.

Sierra Leone Republic of *area* 27,710 sq mi/71,740 sq km *capital* Freetown *towns and cities* Koidu, Bo, Kenema, Makeni *physical* mountains in E; hills and forest; coastal mangrove swamps *features* hot and humid climate (138 in/3,500 mm rainfall p.a.) *head of state and government* military council headed by Capt. Valentine Strasser from 1992 *political system* transitional *political parties* All People's Congress (APC), moderate socialist; United Front of Political Movements (UNIFORM), center-left. Party political activity suspended from 1992 *exports* palm kernels, cocoa, coffee, ginger, diamonds, bauxite, rutile *currency* leone *population* (1993 est) 4,400,000; growth rate 2.5% p.a. *life expectancy* men 41, women 45 *languages* English (official), local languages *media* no daily newspapers; 13 weekly papers, of which 11 are independent but only one achieves sales of over 5,000 copies. Press regulations introduced Feb 1993 threatened half the country's newspapers with closure *religions* animist 52%, Muslim 39%, Protestant 6%, Roman Catholic 2% (1980 est) *literacy* men 30%, women 11% *GNP* $210 per head (1991) *chronology 1808* Became a British colony. *1896* Hinterland declared a British protectorate. *1961* Independence achieved from Britain within the Commonwealth, with Milton Margai, leader of Sierra Leone People's Party (SLPP), as prime minister. *1964* Milton succeeded by his half brother, Albert Margai. *1967* Election results disputed by army, who set up a National Reformation Council and forced the governor-general to leave. *1968* Army revolt made Siaka Stevens, leader of the All People's Congress (APC), prime minister. *1971* New constitution adopted, making Sierra Leone a republic, with Stevens as president. *1978* APC declared only legal party. Stevens sworn in for another seven-year term. *1985* Stevens retired; succeeded by Maj Gen Joseph Momoh. *1989* Attempted coup against President Momoh foiled. *1991* Referendum endorsed multiparty politics. *1992* Military take-over; President Momoh fled. Party politics suspended. National Provisional Ruling Council established under Capt Valentine Strasser.

Sierra Madre chief mountain system of Mexico, consisting of three ranges, enclosing the central plateau of the country; highest point Pico de Orizaba 18,700 ft/5,700 m. The Sierra Madre del Sur ("of the south") runs along the SW Pacific coast.

sievert SI unit (symbol Sv) of radiation dose equivalent. It replaces the rem (1 Sv equals 100 rem). Humans can absorb up to 0.25 Sv without immediate ill effects; 1 Sv may produce radiation sickness; and more than 8 Sv causes death.

Sigismund 1368–1437. Holy Roman emperor from 1411. He convened and presided over the Council of Constance 1414–18, where he promised protection to the religious reformer Huss, but imprisoned him after his condemnation for heresy and acquiesced in his burning. King of Bohemia from 1419, he led the military campaign against the Hussites.

Sihanouk Norodom 1922– . Cambodian politician, king 1941–55 and from 1993. He was prime minister 1955–70, when his government was overthrown in a military coup led by Lon Nol. With Pol Pot's resistance front, he overthrew Lon Nol 1975 and again became prime minister 1975–76, when he was forced to resign by the ◊Khmer Rouge. He returned from exile Nov 1991 under the auspices of a United Nations–brokered peace settlement to head a coalition intended to comprise all Cambodia's warring factions (the Khmer Rouge, however, continued fighting). He was reelected king after the 1993 elections, in which the royalist party won a majority.

Sikhism religion professed by 14 million Indians, living mainly in the Punjab. Sikhism was founded by Nanak (1469–c. 1539). Sikhs believe in a single God who is the immortal creator of the universe and who has never been incarnate in any form, and in the equality of all human beings; Sikhism is strongly opposed to caste divisions.

Their holy book is the *Guru Granth Sahib*. Guru Gobind Singh (1666–1708) instituted the *Khanda-di-Pahul*, the baptism of the sword, and established the Khalsa ("pure"), the company of the faithful. The Khalsa wear the five Ks: *kes*, long hair; *kangha*, a comb; *kirpan*, a sword; *kachh*, short trousers; and *kara*, a steel bracelet. Sikh men take the last name "Singh" ("lion") and women "Kaur" ("princess").

Sikh Wars two wars in India between the Sikhs and the British: The *First Sikh War 1845–46* followed an invasion of British India by Punjabi Sikhs. The Sikhs were defeated and part of their territory annexed. The *Second Sikh War 1848–49* arose from a Sikh revolt in Multan. They were defeated, and the British annexed the Punjab.

Sikorsky Igor 1889–1972. Ukrainian-born US engineer who built the first successful helicopter. He designed a series of aircraft for the Russian aviation service in World War I, but following the revolution emigrated to the US 1918, where he first constructed multiengined flying boats. His first helicopter (the VS300) flew 1939 and a commercial version (the R3) went into production 1943.

Silesia region of Europe that has long been disputed because of its geographical position, mineral resources, and industrial potential; now in Poland and the Czech Republic with metallurgical industries and a coalfield in Polish Silesia. Dispute began in the 17th century with claims on the area by both Austria and Prussia. It was seized by Prussia's Frederick the Great, which started the War of the ◊Austrian Succession; this was finally recognized by Austria 1763, after the Seven Years' War. After World War I, it was divided in 1919 among newly formed Czechoslovakia, revived Poland, and Germany, which retained the largest part. In 1945, after World War II, all German Silesia east of the Oder-Neisse line was transferred to Polish administration; about 10 million inhabitants of German origin, both there and in Czechoslovak Silesia, were expelled.

silica silicon dioxide, SiO_2, the composition of the most common mineral group, of which the most familiar form is quartz. Other silica forms are ◊chalcedony, chert, opal, tridymite, and cristobalite.

Common sand consists largely of silica in the form of quartz.

silicon brittle, nonmetallic element, symbol Si, atomic number 14, atomic weight 28.086. It is the second-most abundant element (after oxygen) in the Earth's crust and occurs in amorphous and crystalline forms. In nature it is found only in combination with other elements, chiefly with oxygen in silica (silicon dioxide, SiO_2) and the silicates. These form the mineral ◊quartz, which makes up most sands, gravels, and beaches.

silicon chip ◊integrated circuit with microscopically small electrical components on a piece of silicon crystal only a few millimeters square.

Silicon Valley nickname given to Santa Clara County, California, since the 1950s the site of many high-technology electronic firms, whose prosperity is based on the silicon chip.

silk fine soft thread produced by the larva of the ◊silkworm moth when making its cocoon. It is soaked, carefully unwrapped, and used in the manufacture of textiles. The introduction of synthetics originally harmed the silk industry, but rising standards of living have produced an increased demand for real silk. It is manufactured in China, India, Japan, and Thailand.

silk-screen printing or *serigraphy* method of ◊printing based on stencilling. It can be used to print on most surfaces, including paper, plastic, cloth, and wood. An impermeable stencil (either paper or photosensitized gelatin plate) is attached to a finely meshed silk screen that has been stretched on a wooden frame, so that the ink passes through to the area beneath only where an image is required. The design can also be painted directly on the screen with varnish. A series of screens can be used to add successive layers of color to the design.

silkworm usually the larva of the *common silkworm moth Bombyx mori*. After hatching from the egg and maturing on the leaves of white mulberry trees (or a synthetic substitute), it spins a protective cocoon of fine silk thread 900 ft/275 m long. To keep the thread intact, the moth is killed before emerging from the cocoon, and several threads are combined to form the commercial silk thread woven into textiles.

Sills Beverly. Adopted name of Belle Silverman 1929– . US operatic soprano. Her high-ranging coloratura is allied to a subtle emotional control in French and Italian roles, notably as principal in Donizetti's *Lucia di Lammermoor* and Puccini's *Manon Lescaut*.

She joined the New York City Opera 1955. Her Metropolitan Opera debut was in 1975; in 1979 she became director of the New York City Opera, announcing her retirement 1988.

Silurian period of geological time 439–409 million years ago, the third period of the Paleozoic era. Silurian sediments are mostly marine and consist of shales and limestone. Luxuriant reefs were built by coral-like organisms. The first land plants began to evolve during this period, and there were many ostracoderms (armored jawless fishes). The first jawed fishes (called acanthodians) also appeared.

silver white, lustrous, extremely malleable and ductile, metallic element, symbol Ag (from Latin *argentum*), atomic number 47, atomic weight 107.868. It occurs in nature in ores and as a free metal; the chief ores are sulfides, from which the metal is extracted by smelting with lead. It is one of the best metallic conductors of both heat and electricity; its most useful compounds are the chloride and bromide, which darken on exposure to light and are the basis of photographic emulsions.

silverfish wingless insect, a type of ◊bristletail.

Simenon Georges 1903–1989. Belgian crime writer. Initially a pulp fiction writer, in 1931 he created Inspector Maigret of the Paris Sûreté who appeared in a series of detective novels.

simile figure of speech that in English uses the conjunctions *like* and *as* to express comparisons ("run like the devil"; "as deaf as a post"). It is sometimes confused with ◊metaphor.

Simon (Marvin) Neil 1927– . US dramatist and screenwriter. His stage plays (which were made into films) include the wryly comic *Barefoot in the Park* 1963 (filmed 1967), *The Odd Couple* 1965 (filmed 1968), and *The Sunshine Boys* 1972 (filmed 1975), and the more serious, autobiographical trilogy *Brighton Beach Memoirs* 1983 (filmed 1986), *Biloxi Blues* 1985 (filmed 1988), and *Broadway Bound* 1986 (filmed 1991). He has also written screenplays and co-written musicals.

Simon Herbert 1916– . US social scientist. He researched decisionmaking in business corporations, and argued that maximum profit was seldom the chief motive. He was awarded the Nobel Prize for Economics 1978.

Simon Paul 1942– . US pop singer and songwriter. In a folk-rock duo with Art Garfunkel (1942–), he had such hits as "Mrs Robinson" 1968 and "Bridge Over Troubled Water" 1970. Simon's solo work includes the critically acclaimed album *Graceland* 1986, for which he drew on Cajun and African music.

Sinai Egyptian peninsula, at the head of the Red Sea; area 25,000 sq mi/65,000 sq km. Resources include oil, natural gas, manganese, and coal; irrigation water from the river Nile is carried under the Suez Canal.

Sinan 1489–1588. Ottoman architect. He was chief architect to Suleiman the Magnificent from 1538. Among the hundreds of buildings he designed are the Suleimaniye mosque complex in Istanbul 1551–58 and the Selimiye mosque in Adrinople (now Edirne) 1569–74.

Sinatra Frank (Francis Albert) 1915– . US singer and film actor. Celebrated for his phrasing and emotion, especially on love ballads, he is particularly associated with the song "My Way". His films from 1941 include *From Here to Eternity* 1953 (Academy Award) and *Guys and Dolls* 1955.

From 1943 to 1945, he was a soloist on the radio program *Your Hit Parade*, earning even wider popularity.

Sinclair Upton (Beall) 1878–1968. US novelist. His polemical concern for social reform was reflected in his prolific output of documentary novels. His most famous novel, *The Jungle* 1906, is an important example of naturalistic writing, which exposed the horrors of the Chicago meatpacking industry and led to a change in food-processing laws. His later novels include *King Coal* 1917, *Oil!* 1927, and his 11-volume Lanny Budd series 1940–53, including *Dragon's Teeth* 1942, which won a Pulitzer Prize.

He was a committed Socialist who was actively involved in politics.

sine in trigonometry, a function of an angle in a right-angled triangle which is defined as the ratio of the length of the side opposite the angle to the length of the hypotenuse (the longest side).

Singapore Republic of *area* 240 sq mi/622 sq km *capital* Singapore City *towns and cities* Jurong, Changi

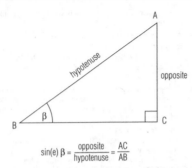

$$\sin(e)\,\beta = \frac{\text{opposite}}{\text{hypotenuse}} = \frac{AC}{AB}$$

sine *The sine is a function of an angle in a right triangle found by dividing the length of the side opposite the angle by the length of the hypotenuse (the longest side). Sine (usually abbreviated sin) is one of the fundamental trigonometric ratios.*

physical comprises Singapore Island, low and flat, and 57 small islands *features* Singapore Island is joined to the mainland by causeway across Strait of Johore; temperature range 69°–93°F/21°–34°C *head of state* Ong Teng Cheong from 1993 *head of government* Goh Chok Tong from 1990 *political system* liberal democracy with strict limits on dissent *political parties* People's Action Party (PAP), conservative; Workers' Party (WP), socialist; Singapore Democratic Party (SDP), liberal pluralist *exports* electronics, petroleum products, rubber, machinery, vehicles *currency* Singapore dollar *population* (1993 est) 2,800,000 (Chinese 75%, Malay 14%, Tamil 7%); growth rate 1.2% p.a. *life expectancy* men 72, women 77 *languages* Malay (national tongue), Chinese, Tamil, English (all official) *media* TV satellite dishes are not allowed for households, only for business. Foreign broadcasts may be banned *religions* Buddhist, Taoist, Muslim, Hindu, Christian *literacy* 88% *GNP* $13,058 per head (1992) *chronology 1819* Singapore leased to British East India Company. *1858* Placed under crown rule. *1942* Invaded and occupied by Japan. *1945* Japanese removed by British forces. *1959* Independence achieved from Britain; Lee Kuan Yew became prime minister. *1963* Joined new Federation of Malaysia. *1965* Left federation to become an independent republic. *1984* Opposition made advances in parliamentary elections. *1986* Opposition leader convicted of perjury and prohibited from standing for election. *1988* Ruling conservative party elected to all but one of available assembly seats; increasingly authoritarian rule. *1990* Lee Kuan Yew resigned as prime minister; replaced by Goh Chok Tong. *1991* PAP and Goh Chok Tong reelected. *1992* Lee Kuan Yew surrendered PAP leadership to Goh Chok Tong. *1993* Ong Teng Cheong elected president, with increased powers.

Singapore City capital of Singapore, on the SE coast of the island of Singapore; population (1980) 2,413,945. It is an oil refining center and port.

Singer Isaac Bashevis 1904–1991. Polish-born US novelist and short-story writer. He lived in the US from 1935. His works, written in Yiddish, often portray traditional Jewish life in Poland and the US, and the loneliness of old age. They include *The Family Moskat* 1950 and *Gimpel the Fool and Other Stories* 1957. Nobel Prize 1978.

He fled Nazi-dominated Europe and became a US citizen 1942.

Singer Isaac Merit 1811–1875. US inventor of domestic and industrial sewing machines. Within a few years of opening his first factory 1851, he became the world's largest manufacturer (despite charges of patent infringement by Elias ◊Howe), and by the late 1860s more than 100,000 Singer sewing machines were in use in the US alone.

singularity in astrophysics, the point in ◊space–time at which the known laws of physics break down. Singularity is predicted to exist at the center of a black hole, where infinite gravitational forces compress the infalling mass of a collapsing star to infinite density. It is also thought, according to the Big Bang model of the origin of the universe, to be the point from which the expansion of the universe began.

Sinhalese member of the majority ethnic group of Sri Lanka (70% of the population). Sinhalese is the official language of Sri Lanka; it belongs to the Indo-Iranian branch of the Indo-European family, and is written in a script derived from the Indian Pali form. The Sinhalese are Buddhists. Since 1971 they have been involved in a violent struggle with the Tamil minority, who are seeking independence.

Sinkiang-Uighur alternative transliteration of ◊Xinjiang Uygur, an autonomous region of NW China.

Sinn Féin Irish nationalist party founded by Arthur Griffith (1872–1922) in 1905; in 1917 Eamon ◊de Valera became its president. It is the political wing of the Irish Republican Army (IRA), and is similarly split between comparative moderates and extremists. In 1985 it gained representation in 17 out of 26 district councils in Northern Ireland. Its president from 1978 is Gerry Adams. In 1994, following the declaration of a cessation of military activities by the IRA, Sin Féin was poised to enter the political process aimed at securing lasting peace in Northern Ireland.

Sino-Japanese Wars two wars waged by Japan against China 1894–95 and 1931–45 to expand to the mainland. Territory gained in the First Sino-Japanese War (Korea) and in the 1930s (Manchuria, Shanghai) was returned at the end of World War II.

Sino-Tibetan languages group of languages spoken in SE Asia. This group covers a large area, and includes Chinese and Burmese, both of which have numerous dialects. Some classifications include the Tai group of languages (including Thai and Lao) in the Sino-Tibetan family.

sinusitis painful inflammation of one of the sinuses, or air spaces, that surround the nasal passages. Most cases clear with antibiotics and nasal decongestants, but some require surgical drainage.

siren in Greek mythology, a sea ◊nymph who lured sailors to their deaths along rocky coasts by her singing. ◊Odysseus, in order to hear the sirens safely, tied himself to the mast of his ship and stuffed his crew's ears with wax.

Sirius or *Dog Star* or *Alpha Canis Majoris* the brightest star in the sky, 8.6 light-years from Earth in the constellation Canis Major. Sirius is a white star with a mass 2.3 times that of the Sun, a diameter 1.8 times that of the Sun, and a luminosity of 23 Suns. It is orbited every 50 years by a white dwarf, Sirius B, also known as the Pup.

sisal strong fiber made from various species of ◊agave, such as *Agave sisalina*.

siskin North American finch *Spinus pinus* with yellow markings, or greenish-yellow bird *Carduelis spinus* in the finch family Fringillidae, about 5 in/12 cm long, found in Eurasia.

Sisyphus in Greek mythology, a king of Corinth who, as punishment for his evil life, was condemned in the underworld to roll a huge stone uphill; it always fell back before he could reach the top.

sitar Indian stringed instrument, of the lute family. It has a pear-shaped body and long neck supported by an additional gourd resonator at the opposite end. A principal solo instrument, it has seven metal strings extending over movable frets and two concealed strings that provide a continuous drone. It is played with a plectrum, producing a luminous and supple melody responsive to nuances of pressure. Its most celebrated exponent in the West has been Ravi Shankar.

Sitting Bull *c.* 1834–1893. North American Indian chief who agreed to Sioux resettlement 1868. When the treaty was broken by the US, he led the Sioux against Lieutenant Colonel ◊Custer at the Battle of the ◊Little Bighorn 1876.

situationism in ethics, the doctrine that any action may be good or bad depending on its context or situation. Situationists argue that no moral rule can apply in all situations and that what may be wrong in most cases may be right if the end is sufficiently good. In general, situationists believe moral attitudes are more important than moral rules.

SI units (French *Système International d'Unités*) standard system of scientific units used by scientists worldwide.

Originally proposed in 1960, it replaces the m.k.s., ◊c.g.s., and f.p.s. systems. It is based on seven basic units: the meter (m) for length, kilogram (kg) for mass, second (s) for time, ampere (A) for electrical current, kelvin (K) for temperature, mole (mol) for amount of substance, and candela (cd) for luminosity.

Siva or *Shiva* in Hinduism, the third chief god (with Brahma and Vishnu). As Mahadeva (great lord), he is the creator, symbolized by the phallic *lingam*, who restores what as Mahakala he destroys. He is often sculpted as Nataraja, performing his fruitful cosmic dance.

Six-Day War another name for the third ◊Arab-Israeli War.

skate, any of several species of flatfish of the ray group. The common skate *Raja batis* is up to 6 ft/1.8 m long and grayish, with black specks. Its egg cases ("mermaids' purses") are often washed ashore by the tide.

skateboard single flexible board mounted on wheels and steerable by weight positioning. As a land alternative to surfing, skateboards developed in California in the 1960s and became a worldwide craze in the 1970s. Skateboarding is practiced in urban environments and has enjoyed a revival since the late 1980s.

skating self-propulsion on ice by means of bladed skates, or on other surfaces by skates with small rollers (wheels of wood, metal, or plastic).

The chief competitive ice-skating events are figure skating, for singles or pairs, ice-dancing, and simple speed skating. The first world ice-skating championships were held in 1896.

skeleton the rigid or semirigid framework that supports and gives form to an animal's body, protects its internal organs, and provides anchorage points for its muscles. The skeleton may be composed of bone and cartilage (vertebrates), chitin (arthropods), calcium carbonate (mollusks and other invertebrates), or silica (many protists). The human skeleton is composed of 206 bones.

skepticism ancient philosophical view that absolute knowledge of things is ultimately unobtainable, hence the only proper attitude is to suspend judgment. Its origins lay in the teachings of the Greek philosopher Pyrrho, who maintained that peace of mind lay in renouncing all claims to knowledge.

skiing self-propulsion on snow by means of elongated runners (skis) for the feet, slightly bent upward at the tip. It is a popular recreational sport, as cross-country ski touring or as downhill runs on mountain trails; events include downhill; slalom, in which a series of turns between flags have to be negotiated; cross-country racing; and ski jumping, when jumps of over 490 ft/150 m are achieved from ramps up to 295 ft/ 90 m high. Speed-skiing uses skis approximately one-third longer and wider than normal with which speeds of up to 125 mph/200 kph have been recorded.

skin the covering of the body of a vertebrate. In mammals, the outer layer (epidermis) is dead and its cells are constantly being rubbed away and replaced from below; it helps to protect the body from infection and to prevent dehydration. The lower layer (dermis)

Sitting Bull Sioux Indian chief Sitting Bull fought a rearguard action against white incursions into Indian lands. He defeated General Custer at the Battle of Little Bighorn, June 25 1876.

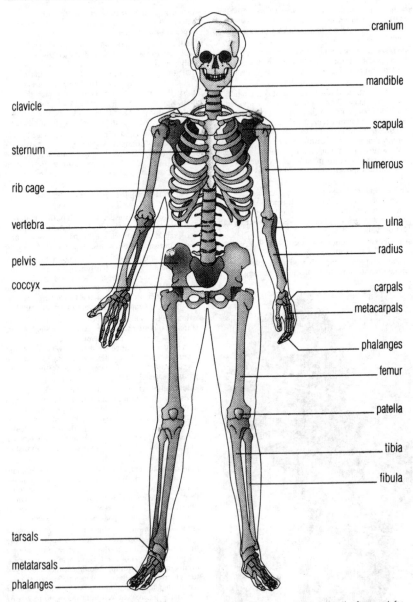

skeleton The human skeleton is made up of 206 bones and provides a strong but flexible supportive framework for the body.

contains blood vessels, nerves, hair roots, and sweat and sebaceous glands, and is supported by a network of fibrous and elastic cells.

skink lizard of the family Scincidae, a large family of about 700 species found throughout the tropics and subtropics. The body is usually long and the legs are reduced. Some skinks are legless and rather snakelike. Many are good burrowers, or can "swim" through sand, like the *sandfish* genus *Scincus* of N Africa. Some skinks lay eggs, others bear live young.

Skinner B(urrhus) F(rederic) 1903–1990. US psychologist, a radical behaviorist who rejected mental

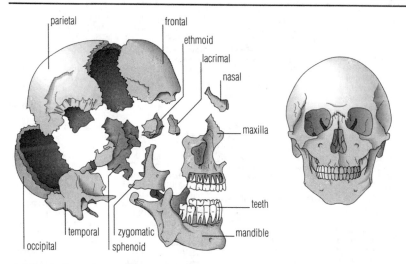

skull The skull is a protective box for the brain, eyes, and hearing organs. It is also a framework for the teeth and flesh of the face. The cranium has eight bones: occipital, two temporal, two parietal, frontal, sphenoid, ethmoid. The face has 14 bones, the main ones being two maxillae, two nasal, two zygoma, two lacrimal, and the mandible.

concepts, seeing the organism as a "black box" where internal processes are not significant in predicting behavior. He studied operant conditioning and maintained that behavior is shaped and maintained by its consequences.

skua dark-colored gull-like seabird, family Stercorariidae, living in Arctic and Antarctic waters. Skuas can grow up to 2 ft/60 cm long and are good fliers. They are aggressive scavengers, and seldom fish for themselves but force gulls to disgorge their catch, and also eat chicks of other birds.

skull in vertebrates, the collection of flat and irregularly shaped bones (or cartilage) that enclose the brain and the organs of sight, hearing, and smell, and provide support for the jaws. In mammals, the skull consists of 22 bones joined by sutures. The floor of the skull is pierced by a large hole (foramen magnum) for the spinal cord and a number of smaller apertures through which other nerves and blood vessels pass.

skunk North American mammal of the weasel family. The common skunk *Mephitis mephitis* has a long, arched body, short legs, a bushy tail, and black fur with white streaks on the back. In self-defense, it discharges a foul-smelling fluid.

Skye largest island of the Inner Hebrides, off the W coast of Scotland; area 672 sq mi/1,740 sq km; population (1987) 8,100. It is separated from the mainland by the Sound of Sleat. The chief port is Portree. The economy is based on crofting, tourism, and livestock. A privately financed toll bridge to the island is due to be completed 1995.

Skylab US space station, launched May 14, 1973, made from the adapted upper stage of a Saturn V rocket. At 82.5 tons/75 metric tons, it was the heaviest object ever put into space, and was 84 ft/25.6 m long. *Skylab* contained a workshop for carrying out experiments in weightlessness, an observatory for monitoring the Sun, and cameras for photographing the Earth's surface.

skylark a type of ◊lark.

slander spoken defamatory statement; if written, or broadcast on radio or television, it constitutes ◊libel.
A slander must involve making false statements and be shown to damage the person defamed.

slash and burn simple agricultural method whereby natural vegetation is cut and burned, and the clearing then farmed for a few years until the soil loses its fertility, whereupon farmers move on and leave the area to regrow. Although this is possible with a small, widely dispersed population, it becomes unsustainable with more people and is now a form of ◊deforestation.

slate fine-grained, usually gray metamorphic rock that splits readily into thin slabs along its cleavage planes. It is the metamorphic equivalent of ◊shale.

Slav member of an Indo-European people in central and E Europe, the Balkans, and parts of N Asia, speaking closely related ◊Slavonic languages. The ancestors of the Slavs are believed to have included the Sarmatians and Scythians. Moving west from Central Asia, they settled in E and SE Europe during the 2nd and 3rd millennia BC.

slavery the enforced servitude of one person (a slave) to another or one group to another. A slave has no personal rights and is the property of another person through birth, purchase, or capture. Slavery goes back to prehistoric times but declined in Europe after the fall of the Roman Empire. During the imperialism of Spain, Portugal, and Britain in the 16th–18th centuries and in the American South in the 17th–19th centuries, slavery became a mainstay of an agricultural factory economy, with millions of Africans sold to work on plantations in North and South America. Millions more died in the process, but the profits from this trade were enormous. Slavery was abolished in the British Empire 1833 and in the US at the end of the Civil War 1863–65, but continues illegally in some countries.

Slavonia region of E Croatia bounded by the Sava, Drava, and Danube rivers; Osijek is the largest town. E and W Slavonia declared themselves autonomous provinces of Serbia following Croatia's declaration of independence from Yugoslavia 1991, and the region was the scene of fierce fighting between Croatian forces and Serb-dominated Yugoslav federal troops 1991–92. After the cease-fire 1992, 10,000 UN troops were deployed in E and W Slavonia and contested Krajina.

Slavonic languages or *Slavic languages* branch of the Indo-European language family spoken in central and E Europe, the Balkans, and parts of N Asia. The family comprises the *southern group* (Slovene, Serbo-Croatian, Macedonian, and Bulgarian); the *western group* (Czech and Slovak, Sorbian in Germany, and Polish and its related dialects); and the *eastern group* (Russian, Ukrainian, and Belarusian).

SLD abbreviation for ◊*Social and Liberal Democrats*, British political party.

sleep state of natural unconsciousness and activity that occurs at regular intervals in most mammals and birds, though there is considerable variation in the amount of time spent sleeping. Sleep differs from hibernation in that it occurs daily rather tha:. seasonally, and involves less drastic reductions in metabolism. The function of sleep is unclear. People deprived of sleep become irritable, uncoordinated, forgetful, hallucinatory, and even psychotic.

sleeping sickness or *trypanosomiasis* infectious disease of tropical Africa, a form of trypanosomiasis. Early symptoms include fever, headache, and chills, followed by ◊anemia and joint pains. Later, the disease attacks the central nervous system, causing drowsiness, lethargy, and, if left untreated, death. Sleeping sickness is caused by either of two ◊trypanosomes, *Trypanosoma gambiense* or *T. rhodesiense*. Control is by eradication of the tsetse fly, which transmits the disease to humans.

Sligo county of the Republic of Ireland, in the province of Connacht, situated on the Atlantic coast of NW Ireland; area 695 sq mi/1,800 sq km; population (1991) 54,700. It is hilly. There is livestock and dairy farming.

slime mold an extraordinary organism that shows some features of ◊fungus and some of ◊protozoa. Slime molds are not closely related to any other group, although they are often classed, for convenience, with the fungi.

sloe fruit of the ◊blackthorn.

sloth South American mammal, about 2.5 ft/70 cm long, of the order Edentata. Sloths are grayish brown and have small rounded heads, rudimentary tails, and prolonged forelimbs. Each foot has long curved claws adapted to clinging upside down from trees. They are vegetarian.

Species include the *three-toed sloth* or *ai Bradypus tridactylus*, and the *two-toed sloth Choloepus didactylus* of northern South America.

Slovakia one of the two republics that formed the Federative Republic of Czechoslovakia. Settled in the 5th–6th centuries by Slavs; it was occupied by the Magyars in the 10th century, and was part of the kingdom of Hungary until 1918, when it became a province of Czechoslovakia. Slovakia was a puppet state under German domination 1939-45, and was abolished as an administrative division in 1949. Its

capital and chief town was Bratislava. It was reestablished as a sovereign state, the ◊Slovak Republic, after the breakup of Czechoslovakia 1993.

Slovak Republic Slovak Republic (*Slovenská Republika*) *area* 18,940 sq mi/49,035 sq km *capital* Bratislava *towns and cities* Kosice, Nitra, Presov, Banská Bystrica *physical* W range of the Carpathian Mountains including Tatra and Beskids in N; Danube plain in S; numerous lakes and mineral springs *features* fine beech and oak forests with bears and wild boar *head of state* Michal Kovak from 1993 *head of government* Vladimir Meciar from 1994 *political system* emergent democracy *political parties* Civic Democratic Union–People against Violence (PAV), center-left; Movement for a Democratic Slovakia (HZDS), center-left, nationalist; Christian Democratic Movement (KSDH), right of center; Slovak National Party, nationalist; Party of the Democratic Left, left-wing, ex-communist; Coexistence, representing Hungarian minority *exports* iron ore, copper, mercury, magnesite, armaments, chemicals, textiles, machinery *currency* koruna (based on Czechoslovak koruna) *population* (1992) 5,300,000 (including 600,000 Hungarians and other minorities); growth rate 0.4% p.a. *life expectancy* men 68, women 75 *language* Slovak (official) *media* some government interference *religion* Roman Catholic (over 50%), Lutheran, Reformist, Orthodox *literacy* 100% *GDP* $10,000 million (1990); $1,887 per head *chronology 906–1918* Under Magyar domination. *1918* Independence achieved from Austro-Hungarian Empire; Slovaks joined Czechs in forming Czechoslovakia as independent nation. *1948* Communists assumed power in Czechoslovakia. *1968* Slovak Socialist Republic created under new federal constitution. *1989* Prodemocracy demonstrations in Bratislava; new political parties formed, including PAV, and later legalized; Communist Party stripped of powers. Dec: new government formed with Václav Havel as president. *1991* Increasing Slovak separatism. March: PAV splinter group, the HZDS, formed under Slovak premier Vladimir Meciar, pledging greater autonomy for Slovakia. April: Meciar dismissed, replaced by Jan Carnogursky; pro-Meciar rallies in Bratislava. *1992* March: PAV became CDU. June: HZDS dominant in assembly elections; Havel resigned. Aug: agreement on separate Czech and Slovak states. New constitution

adopted. *1993* Jan: Slovak Republic became sovereign state, with Meciar, leader of HZDS, as prime minister. Feb: Michal Kovak became president. June: gained membership in United Nations and Council of Europe; formal invitation to apply for European Community membership. *1994* Jan: Joined NATO's "partnership for peace" program. March: Meciar ousted on vote of no-confidence; replaced by Jozef Moravcik, heading a non-HZDS coalition. Oct: HZDS won most seats in general election; Meciar returned to power.

Slovene member of the Slavic people of Slovenia and parts of the Austrian Alpine provinces of Styria and Carinthia. There are 1.5–2 million speakers of Slovene, a language belonging to the South Slavonic branch of the Indo-European family. The Slovenes use the Roman alphabet and the majority belong to the Roman Catholic Church.

Slovenia Republic of *area* 7,817 sq mi/20,251 sq km *capital towns and cities* Maribor, Kranj, Celji; chief port: Koper *physical* mountainous; Sava and Drava rivers *head of state* Milan Kucan from 1990 *head of government* Janez Drnovsek from 1992 *political system* emergent democracy *political parties* Slovenian Christian Democrats, right of center; Slovenian People's Party (SPP), right of center; Liberal Democratic Party (LDS), left of center; Democratic Party of Slovenia (LDP), left of center *products* grain, sugarbeet, livestock, timber, cotton and woolen textiles, steel, vehicles *currency* tolar *population* (1993 est) 2,000,000 (Slovene 91%, Croat 3%, Serb 2%) *life expectancy* men 67, women 75 *language* Slovene, resembling Serbo-Croat, written in Roman characters *religion* Roman Catholic *literacy* 99% *GNP* $7,150 per head (1991) *chronology 1918* United with Serbia and Croatia. *1929* The kingdom of Serbs, Croats, and Slovenes took the name of Yugoslavia. *1945* Became a constituent republic of Yugoslav Socialist Federal Republic. *mid-1980s* The Slovenian Communist Party liberalized itself and agreed to free elections. Yugoslav counterintelligence (KOV) began repression. *1989* Jan: Social Democratic Alliance of Slovenia launched as first political organization independent of Communist Party. Sept: constitution changed to allow secession from federation. *1990* April: nationalist DEMOS coalition secured victory in first multiparty parliamentary elections; Milan Kucan became president. July: sovereignty declared. Dec: independence overwhelmingly approved in referendum. *1991* June: independence declared; 100 killed after federal army intervened; cease-fire brokered by European Community (now European Union). July: cease-fire agreed. Oct: withdrawal of Yugoslav army completed. Dec: DEMOS coalition dissolved. *1992* Jan: EC recognized Slovenia's independence. April: Janez Drnovsek appointed prime minister; independence recognized by US. May: admitted into United Nations. Dec: Liberal Democrats and Christian Democrats won assembly elections; Kucan reelected president. *1993* Drnovsek reelected prime minister.

slow-worm harmless species of lizard *Anguis fragilis*, once common in Europe, now a protected species in Britain. Superficially resembling a snake, it is distinguished by its small mouth and movable eyelids. It is about 1 ft/30 cm long, and eats worms and slugs.

SLR abbreviation for *single-lens reflex*, a type of ◊camera in which the image can be seen through the lens before a picture is taken.

slug air-breathing gastropod related to the snails, but with absent or much reduced shell.

small arms guns that can be carried by hand. The first small arms were portable handguns in use in the late 14th century, supported on the ground and ignited by hand. Today's small arms range from breech-loading single-shot rifles and shotguns to sophisticated automatic and semiautomatic weapons. In 1990, 10,567 people were killed by handguns in the US, compared with 91 in Switzerland, 87 in Japan, 68 in Canada,and 13 in Sweden. From 1988 guns accounted for more deaths among teenage US males than all other causes put together.

smallpox acute, highly contagious viral disease, marked by aches, fever, vomiting, and skin eruptions leaving pitted scars. Widespread vaccination programs have eradicated this often fatal disease.

smart card plastic card with an embedded microprocessor and memory. It can store, for example, personal data, identification, and bank-account details, to enable it to be used as a credit or debit card. The card can be loaded with credits, which are then spent electronically, and reloaded as needed. Possible other uses range from hotel door "keys" to passports.

smart drug any drug or combination of nutrients (vitamins, amino acids, minerals, and sometimes herbs) said to enhance the functioning of the brain, increase mental energy, lengthen the span of attention, and improve the memory. As yet there is no scientific evidence to suggest that these drugs have any significant effect on healthy people.

smart weapon programmable bomb or missile that can be guided to its target by laser technology, TV homing technology, or terrain-contour matching (TERCOM). A smart weapon relies on its pinpoint accuracy to destroy a target rather than on the size of its warhead.

smelt small fish, usually marine, although some species are freshwater.
They occur in Europe and North America. The most common European smelt is the sparling *Osmerus eperlanus*.

smelting processing a metallic ore in a furnace to produce the metal. Oxide ores such as iron ore are smelted with coke (carbon), which reduces the ore into metal and also provides fuel for the process.

Smetana Bedrich 1824–1884. Bohemian composer. He established a Czech nationalist style in, for example, the operas *Prodaná Nevesta/The Bartered Bride* 1866 and *Dalibor* 1868, and the symphonic suite *Má Vlast/My Country* 1875–80. He conducted the National Theatre of Prague 1866–74.

Smith Adam 1723–1790. Scottish economist, often regarded as the founder of political economy. His *The Wealth of Nations* 1776 defined national wealth in terms of labor. The cause of wealth is explained by the division of labor—dividing a production process into several repetitive operations, each carried out by different workers. Smith advocated the free working of individual enterprise, and the necessity of "free trade".

Smith Bessie 1894–1937. US jazz and blues singer. Known as the "Empress of the Blues", she established herself in the 1920s after she was discovered by Columbia Records. She made over 150 recordings accompanied by such greats as Louis Armstrong and Benny Goodman.

Her popularity waned in the Depression and she died after an auto accident.

Smith John 1580–1631. English colonist. After an adventurous early life he took part in the colonization of Virginia, acting as president of the North American colony 1608–09. He explored New England in 1614, which he named, and published pamphlets on America and an autobiography. His trade with the Indians may have kept the colonists alive in the early years.

Smith Joseph 1805–1844. US founder of the ◊Mormon religious sect.

Born in Vermont, he received his first religious call in 1820, and in 1827 claimed to have been granted the revelation of the *Book of Mormon* (an ancient American prophet). He founded the Church of Jesus Christ of Latter-day Saints in Fayette, New York, 1830. The headquarters of the church was moved to Kirkland, Ohio, 1831; to Missouri 1838; and to Nauvoo, Illinois, 1840. Hostility to Smith intensified when rumors that he had taken several wives began to circulate; Smith publicly opposed polygamy and acknowledged only one wife. He was jailed after some of his followers destroyed the printing press of a newspaper that had attacked him, and a mob stormed the jail and killed him. Smith's chief works are *Doctrines and Covenants* and *Pearl of Great Price.*

Smithsonian Institution established 1846 in Washington, DC, following a bequest of $100,000 from James Smithson for this purpose.

Branches of the institution include research laboratories, collections, and exhibits in a wide range of fields in the arts and sciences. It sponsors scientific expeditions and publishes the results.

smokeless fuel fuel that does not give off any smoke when burned, because all the carbon is fully oxidized to carbon dioxide (CO_2). Natural gas, oil, and coke are smokeless fuels.

smoking inhaling the fumes from burning substances, generally ◊tobacco in the form of ◊cigarettes. The practice can be habit-forming and is dangerous to health, since carbon monoxide and other toxic materials result from the combustion process. A direct link between lung cancer and tobacco smoking was established 1950; the habit is also linked to respiratory and coronary heart diseases. In the West, smoking is now forbidden in many public places because even *passive smoking*—breathing in fumes from other people's cigarettes—can be harmful.

Some illegal drugs, such as crack and ◊opium, are also smoked.

Smollett Tobias George 1721–1771. Scottish novelist. He wrote the picaresque novels *Roderick Random* 1748, *Peregrine Pickle* 1751, *Ferdinand Count Fathom* 1753, *Sir Launcelot Greaves* 1760–62, and *Humphrey Clinker* 1771. His novels are full of gusto and vivid characterization.

smuggling illegal import or export of prohibited goods or the evasion of customs duties on dutiable goods. Smuggling has a long tradition in most border and coastal regions; goods smuggled include tobacco, spirits, diamonds, gold, and illegal drugs.

The smuggling of illegal substances such as cocaine and marijuana into the US from Mexico and various South American countries is a serious problem today.

Smuts Jan Christian 1870–1950. South African politician and soldier; prime minister 1919–24 and 1939–48. He supported the Allies in both world wars

and was a member of the British imperial war cabinet 1917–18.

snail air-breathing gastropod mollusk with a spiral shell. There are thousands of species, on land and in water. The typical snails of the genus *Helix* have two species in Europe. The common garden snail *H. aspersa* is very destructive to plants.

The Roman snail *Helix pomatia* is "corralled" for the gourmet food market. Overcollection has depleted the population. The French eat as much as 11 lb/ 5 kg of snails per capita each year.

snake reptile of the suborder Serpentes of the order Squamata, which also includes lizards. Snakes are characterized by an elongated limbless body, possibly evolved because of subterranean ancestors. One of the striking internal modifications is the absence or greatly reduced size of the left lung. The skin is covered in scales, which are markedly wider underneath where they form. There are 3,000 species found in the tropical and temperate zones, but none in New Zealand, Ireland, Iceland, and near the poles. Only three species are found in Britain: the adder, smooth snake, and grass snake.

Snake tributary of the Columbia River, in NW US; length 1,038 mi/1,670 km. It flows 40 mi/65 km through Hell's Canyon, one of the deepest gorges in the world.

Extensive irrigation in S Idaho makes possible the farmland that grows Idaho potatoes and other crops.

snapdragon perennial herbaceous plant of the genus *Antirrhinum*, family Scrophulariaceae, with spikes of brightly colored two-lipped flowers.

snipe European marsh bird of the family Scolopacidae, order Charadriiformes; species include common snipe *Gallinago gallinago* and the rare great snipe *G. media*, of which the males hold spring gatherings to show their prowess. It is closely related to the ◊woodcock.

snooker indoor game derived from ◊billiards (via pool). It is played with 22 balls: 15 red, one each of yellow, green, brown, blue, pink, and black, and one white cueball. Red balls are worth one point when sunk, while the colored balls have ascending values from two points for the yellow to seven points for the black. The world professional championship was first held in 1927. The world amateur championship was first held 1963.

snowdrop bulbous plant *Galanthus nivalis*, family Amaryllidaceae, native to Europe, with white, bell-shaped flowers, tinged with green, in early spring.

snow leopard a type of ◊leopard.

soap mixture of the sodium salts of various ◊fatty acids: palmitic, stearic, and oleic acid. It is made by the action of sodium hydroxide (caustic soda) or potassium hydroxide (caustic potash) on fats of animal or vegetable origin. Soap makes grease and dirt disperse in water in a similar manner to a ◊detergent.

soap opera television or radio serial melodrama. It originated in the US as a series of daytime programs sponsored by soap-powder and detergent manufacturers.

The popularity of the genre has led to soap operas being shown at peak viewing times in many languages and countries.

Sobchak Anatoly 1937– . Soviet centrist politician, mayor of St Petersburg from 1990, cofounder of the Democratic Reform Movement (with former foreign minister ◊Shevardnadze), and member of the Soviet parliament 1989–91. He prominently resisted the abortive anti-Gorbachev attempted coup of Aug 1991.

soccer or *football* ball game originating in the UK, popular in Europe, the Middle East, and North and South America. It is played between two teams each of 11 players, on a field 100–130 yd/90–120 m long and 50–100 yd/45–90 m wide, with a spherical, inflated (traditionally leather) ball, circumference 27 in/0.69 m. The object of the game is to send the ball with the feet or head into the opponents' goal, an area 8 yd/7.31 m wide and 8 ft/2.44 m high.

Social and Liberal Democrats official name for the British political party formed 1988 from the former Liberal Party and most of the Social Democratic Party. The common name for the party is the *Liberal Democrats*.

social costs and benefits in economics, the costs and benefits to society as a whole that result from economic decisions. These include private costs (the financial cost of production incurred by firms) and benefits (the profits made by firms and the value to people of consuming goods and services) and external costs and benefits (affecting those not directly involved in production or consumption); pollution is one of the external costs.

social democracy political ideology or belief in the gradual evolution of a democratic ◊socialism within existing political structures. The earliest was the German Sozialdemokratische Partei (SPD) 1891 (today one of the two main German parties), which had been created 1875 by the amalgamation of other groups including August Bebel's earlier German Social Democratic Workers' Party, founded 1869. Parties along the lines of the German model were founded in the last two decades of the 19th century in a number of countries, including Austria, Belgium, the Netherlands, Hungary, Poland, and Russia. The British Labour Party is in the social democratic tradition.

Social Democratic Labour Party (SDLP) Northern Irish left-wing political party, formed 1970. It aims ultimately at Irish unification, but distances itself from violent tactics, for example, those used by the Irish Republican Army (IRA), adopting a constitutional, conciliatory role. The SDLP, led by John Hume (1937–), was responsible for initiating talks with the leader of Sinn Féin, Gerry Adams, 1993, which prompted a joint UK-Irish peace initiative and set in motion a Northern Ireland cease-fire 1994.

Social Democratic Party (SDP) British centrist political party 1981–90, formed by members of Parliament who resigned from the Labour Party. The 1983 and 1987 general elections were fought in alliance with the Liberal Party as the *Liberal/SDP Alliance*. A merger of the two parties was voted for by the SDP 1987, and the new party became the ◊Social and Liberal Democrats, leaving a rump SDP that folded 1990.

socialism movement aiming to establish a classless society by substituting public for private ownership of the means of production, distribution, and exchange. The term has been used to describe positions as widely apart as anarchism and social democracy. Socialist ideas appeared in classical times; in early Christianity; among later Christian sects such as the ◊Anabaptists and ◊Diggers; and, in the 18th and early 19th centuries, were put forward as systematic political aims by Jean-Jacques Rousseau, Claude Saint-Simon, François Fourier, and Robert Owen, among others. See also Karl ◊Marx and Friedrich ◊Engels.

Social Realism in painting, art that realistically depicts subjects of social concern, such as poverty and deprivation. Those described as Social Realists include: in the US, members of the Ashcan School and Ben Shahn; in the UK, the "kitchen sink group", for example John Bratby; and in Mexico, the muralists Orozco and Rivera.

social science the group of academic disciplines that investigate how and why people behave the way they do, as individuals and in groups. The term originated with the 19th-century French thinker Auguste ◊Comte. The academic social sciences are generally listed as sociology, economics, anthropology, political science, and psychology.

social security state provision of financial aid to alleviate poverty and to provide income to retired persons and disabled workers. The term "social security" was first applied officially in the US, in the Social Security Act 1935. The term usually refers specifically to old-age pensions, which have a contributory element, unlike "welfare." The federal government is responsible for social security (medicare, retirement, survivors', and disability insurance); unemployment insurance is covered by a joint federal-state system for industrial workers, but few in agriculture are covered; and welfare benefits are the responsibility of individual states, with some federal assistance. The program is an important source of income for the growing population of retired Americans. Politically sacrosanct, the benefits pose a growing burden for the working-age population.

Society Islands (French *Archipel de la Société*) archipelago in ◊French Polynesia, divided into the Windward Islands and the Leeward Islands; area 650 sq mi/1,685 sq km; population (1983) 142,000. The administrative headquarters is Papeete on ◊Tahiti. The *Windward Islands* (French *Iles du Vent*) have an area of 460 sq mi/1,200 sq km and a population (1983) of 123,000. They comprise Tahiti, Moorea (area 51 sq mi/132 sq km; population 7,000), Maio (or Tubuai Manu; 3.5 sq mi/9 sq km; population 200), and the smaller Tetiaroa and Mehetia. The *Leeward Islands* (French *Iles sous le Vent*) have an area of 156 sq mi/404 sq km and a population of 19,000. They comprise the volcanic islands of Raiatea (including the main town of Uturoa), Huahine, Bora-Bora, Maupiti, Tahaa, and four small atolls. Claimed by France 1768, the group became a French protectorate 1843 and a colony 1880.

sociobiology study of the biological basis of all social behavior, including the application of population genetics to the evolution of behavior. It builds on the concept of inclusive fitness, contained in the notion of the "selfish gene". Contrary to some popular interpretations, it does not assume that all behavior is genetically determined.

sociology systematic study of society, in particular of social order and social change, social conflict and social problems. It studies institutions such as the family, law, and the church, as well as concepts such as norm, role, and culture. Sociology attempts to study people in their social environment according to certain underlying moral, philosophical, and political codes of behavior.

Socrates *c.* 469–399 BC. Athenian philosopher. He wrote nothing but was immortalized in the dialogues of his pupil Plato. In his desire to combat the skepticism of the ◊sophists, Socrates asserted the possibility of genuine knowledge. In ethics, he put forward the view that the good person never knowingly does wrong. True knowledge emerges through dialogue and systematic questioning and an abandoning of uncritical claims to knowledge.

Socratic method method of teaching used by Socrates, in which he aimed to guide pupils to clear thinking on ethics and politics by asking questions and then exposing their inconsistencies in cross-examination. This method was effective against the ◊sophists.

sodium soft, waxlike, silver-white, metallic element, symbol Na (from Latin *natrium*), atomic number 11, atomic weight 22.898. It is one of the ◊alkali metals and has a very low density, being light enough to float on water. It is the sixth-most abundant element (the fourth-most abundant metal) in the Earth's crust. Sodium is highly reactive, oxidizing rapidly when exposed to air and reacting violently with water. Its most familiar compound is sodium chloride (common salt), which occurs naturally in the oceans and in salt deposits left by dried-up ancient seas.

sodium chloride or *common salt* or *table salt* NaCl white, crystalline compound found widely in nature. It is a a typical ionic solid with a high melting point (801°C/1,474°F); it is soluble in water, insoluble in organic solvents, and is a strong electrolyte when molten or in aqueous solution. Found in concentrated deposits, it is widely used in the food industry as a flavoring and preservative, and in the chemical industry in the manufacture of sodium, chlorine, and sodium carbonate.

Sofia or *Sofiya* capital of Bulgaria since 1878; population (1990) 1,220,900. Industries include textiles, rubber, machinery, and electrical equipment. It lies at the foot of the Vitosha Mountains.

softball bat-and-ball game similar to ◊baseball. Among the differences between the two sports are playing-field dimensions and equipment specifications; softball diamonds are smaller overall. The distance between bases is 60 ft/18.3 m; pitchers stand 46 ft/14 m from home plate; and the softball itself (which is about as hard as a baseball) is approximately 12 in/30.5 cm in circumference (a baseball is about 9 in/23 cm). In proportional terms of weight to size, a softball is lighter than a baseball and therefore, when pitched or batted, generally will not attain the speed and distance of a well-hit baseball. Softball bats can be no longer than 34 in/86.4 cm.

A regulation softball game is seven innings (for baseball it is nine). A legally delivered softball must be thrown underhand. Nearly 175,000 teams are registered with the US Amateur Softball Association.

soft-sectored disk another name for an unformatted blank disk; see ◊disk formatting.

software a computer program needed to make computer ◊hardware function. A word-processing program or a ◊spreadsheet are examples of software packages.

soil loose covering of broken rocky material and decaying organic matter overlying the bedrock of the Earth's surface. Various types of soil develop under different conditions: deep soils form in warm wet climates and in valleys; shallow soils form in cool dry areas and on slopes. *Pedology*, the study of soil, is significant because of the relative importance of different soil types to agriculture.

soil erosion the wearing away and redistribution of the Earth's soil layer.

It is caused by the action of water, wind, and ice,

and also by improper methods of ◊agriculture. If unchecked, soil erosion results in the formation of deserts (desertification). It has been estimated that 20% of the world's cultivated topsoil was lost between 1950 and 1990.

solar energy energy derived from the Sun's radiation. The amount of energy falling on just 0.3861 sq mi/1 sq km is about 4,000 megawatts, enough to heat and light a small town. In one second the Sun gives off 13 million times more energy than all the electricity used in the US in one year. *Solar heaters* have industrial or domestic uses. They usually consist of a black (heat-absorbing) panel containing pipes through which air or water, heated by the Sun, is circulated, either by thermal ◊convection or by a pump.

solar pond natural or artificial "pond", such as the Dead Sea, in which salt becomes more soluble in the Sun's heat. Water at the bottom becomes saltier and hotter, and is insulated by the less salty water layer at the top. Temperatures at the bottom reach about 212°F/100°C and can be used to generate electricity.

solar radiation radiation given off by the Sun, consisting mainly of visible light, ◊ultraviolet radiation, and ◊infrared radiation, although the whole spectrum of ◊electromagnetic waves is present, from radio waves to X-rays. High-energy charged particles such as electrons are also emitted, especially from solar flares. When these reach the Earth, they cause magnetic storms (disruptions of the Earth's magnetic field), which interfere with radio communications.

solar system the Sun (a star) and all the bodies orbiting it: the nine ◊planets (Mercury, Venus, Earth, Mars, Jupiter, Saturn, Uranus, Neptune, and Pluto), their moons, the asteroids, and the comets. It is thought to have formed from a cloud of gas and dust in space about 4.6 billion years ago. The Sun contains 99% of the mass of the Solar System.

solar wind stream of atomic particles, mostly protons and electrons, from the Sun's corona, flowing outward at speeds of between 200 mps/300 kps and 600 mps/1,000 kps.

solder any of various alloys used when melted for joining metals such as copper, its common alloys (brass and bronze), and tin-plated steel, as used for making food cans.

sole flatfish found in temperate and tropical waters. The *common sole Solea solea*, also called *Dover sole*, is found in the southern seas of NW Europe. Up to 20 in/50 cm long, it is a prized food fish, as is the *sand* or *French sole Pegusa lascaris* further south.

solenoid coil of wire, usually cylindrical, in which a magnetic field is created by passing an electric current through it (see ◊electromagnetic field). This field can be used to move an iron rod placed on its axis.

Mechanical valves attached to the rod can be operated by switching the current on or off, so converting electrical energy into mechanical energy. Solenoids are used to relay energy from the battery of an automobile to the starter motor by means of the ignition switch.

solid in physics, a state of matter that holds its own shape (as opposed to a liquid, which takes up the shape of its container, or a gas, which totally fills its container). According to ◊kinetic theory, the atoms or molecules in a solid are not free to move but merely vibrate about fixed positions, such as those in crystal lattices.

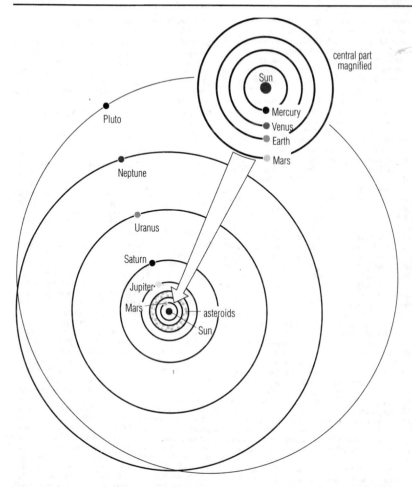

Solar System Most of the objects in the Solar System lie close to the plane of the ecliptic. The planets are tiny compared to the Sun. If the Sun were the size of a basketball, the planet closest to the Sun, Mercury, would be the size of a mustard seed 48 ft/15 m from the Sun. The most distant planet, Pluto, would be a pinhead 1 mi/1.6 km away from the Sun. The Earth, which is the third planet out from the Sun, would be the size of a pea 100 ft/32 m from the Sun.

Solidarity (Polish *Solidarnosc*) national confederation of independent labor unions in Poland, formed under the leadership of Lech ◊Walesa Sept 1980. An illegal organization from 1981 to 1989, it was then elected to head the Polish government. Divisions soon emerged in the leadership and in 1990 its political wing began to fragment (Walesa resigned as chairman in Dec of that year). In the Sept 1993 elections Solidarity gained less than 5% of the popular vote.

solid-state circuit electronic circuit where all the components (resistors, capacitors, transistors, and diodes) and interconnections are made at the same time, and by the same processes, in or on one piece of single-crystal silicon. The small size of this construction accounts for its use in electronics for space vehicles

and aircraft.

solipsism in philosophy, a view that maintains that the self is the only thing that can be known to exist. It is an extreme form of ◊skepticism. The solipsist sees himself or herself as the only individual in existence, assuming other people to be a reflection of his or her own consciousness.

soliton solitary wave that maintains its shape and velocity, and does not widen and disperse in the normal way. The mathematical equations that sum up the behavior of solitons are being used to further research in nuclear fusion and superconductivity.

It is so named from a solitary wave seen on a canal by Scottish engineer John Scott Russell (1808–1882), who raced after it on his horse.

Solomon c. 974–c. 937 BC. In the Old Testament, third king of Israel, son of David by Bathsheba. During a peaceful reign, he was famed for his wisdom and his alliances with Egypt and Phoenicia. The much later biblical Proverbs, Ecclesiastes, and Song of Songs are attributed to him. He built the temple in Jerusalem with the aid of heavy taxation and forced labor, resulting in the revolt of N Israel.

Solomon Islands area 10,656 sq mi/27,600 sq km *capital* Honiara (on Guadalcanal) *towns and cities* Gizo, Yandina *physical* comprises all but the northernmost islands (which belong to Papua New Guinea) of a Melanesian archipelago stretching nearly 900 mi/1,500 km. The largest is Guadalcanal (area 2,510 sq mi/6,500 sq km); others are Malaita, San Cristobal, New Georgia, Santa Isabel, Choiseul; mainly mountainous and forested *features* rivers ideal for hydroelectric power *head of state* Elizabeth II represented by governor-general George Gerea Dennis Lepping from 1988 *head of government* Francis Billy Hilly from 1993 *political system* constitutional monarchy *political parties* People's Alliance Party (PAP), center-left; United Party (UP), right of center; Group for National Unity and Reconciliation, centrist *exports* fish products, palm oil, copra, cocoa, timber *currency* Solomon Island dollar *population* (1993) 349,500 (Melanesian 95%, Polynesian 4%); growth rate 3.9% p.a. *life expectancy* men 66, women 71 *languages* English (official); there are some 120 Melanesian dialects *religions* Anglican 34%, Roman Catholic 19%, South Sea Evangelical 17% *literacy* 24% *GNP* $560 per head (1991) *chronology* **1893** Solomon Islands placed under British protection. **1978** Independence achieved from Britain within the Commonwealth, with Peter Kenilorea as prime minister. **1981** Solomon Mamaloni of the People's Progressive Party (PPP) replaced Kenilorea as prime minister. **1984** Kenilorea returned to power, heading a coalition government. **1986** Kenilorea resigned after allegations of corruption; replaced by his deputy, Ezekiel Alebua. **1988** Kenilorea elected deputy prime minister. Joined Vanuatu and Papua New Guinea to form the Spearhead Group, aiming to preserve Melanesian cultural traditions. **1989** Solomon Mamaloni, now leader of the People's Action Party (PAP), elected prime minister; formed PAP-dominated coalition. **1990** Mamaloni resigned as PAP party leader, but continued as head of a government of national unity. **1993** Francis Billy Hilly, an independent politician, elected prime minister.

Solomon's seal any perennial plant of the genus *Polygonatum* of the lily family Liliaceae, native to Europe and found growing in moist, shady woodland areas. They have bell-like white or greenish-white flowers drooping from the leaf axils of arching stems, followed by blue or black berries.

Great Solomon's seal *P. commutatum* is native to E North America.

Solon c. 638–558 BC. Athenian statesman. As one of the chief magistrates about 594 BC, he carried out the cancellation of all debts from which land or liberty was the security and the revision of the constitution that laid the foundations of Athenian democracy.

solstice either of the days on which the Sun is farthest north or south of the celestial equator each year. The *summer solstice*, when the Sun is farthest north, occurs around June 21; the *winter solstice* around Dec 22.

solution two or more substances mixed to form a single, homogenous phase. One of the substances is the ◊*solvent* and the others (*solutes*) are said to be dissolved in it.

solvent substance, usually a liquid, that will dissolve another substance (see ◊solution). Although the commonest solvent is water, in popular use the term refers to low-boiling-point organic liquids, which are harmful if used in a confined space. They can give rise to respiratory problems, liver damage, and neurological complaints.

Solyman I alternative spelling of ◊Suleiman, Ottoman sultan.

Solzhenitsyn Alexander (Isayevich) 1918– . Soviet novelist. He became a US citizen 1974. He was in prison and exile 1945–57 for anti-Stalinist comments. Much of his writing is semiautobiographical and highly critical of the system, including *One Day in the Life of Ivan Denisovich* 1962, which deals with the labor camps under Stalin, and *The Gulag Archipelago* 1973, an exposé of the whole Soviet labor-camp network. This led to his expulsion from the USSR 1974. He was awarded a Nobel Prize 1970. He returned to live in the USSR 1994.

Somalia Somali Democratic Republic (*Jamhuriyadda Dimugradiga Somaliya*) *area* 246,220 sq mi/637,700 sq km *capital* Mogadishu *towns and cities* Hargeisa, Kismayu, port Berbera *physical* mainly flat, with hills in N *environment* destruction of trees for fuel and by grazing livestock has led to an increase in desert area *features* occupies a strategic location on the Horn of Africa *head of state and government* Ali Mahdi Mohammed from 1991 *political system* transitional *political parties* Somali Revolutionary Socialist Party (SRSP), nationalist, socialist. Other parties, mainly clan-based: United Somali Congress (USC), Hawiye clan; Somali Patriotic Movement (SPM), Darod clan; Somali Salvation Patriotic Front (SSDF), Majertein clan; Somali Democratic Alliance (SDA), Gadabursi clan; United Somali Front (USF), Issa clan *exports* livestock, skins, hides, bananas, fruit *currency* Somali shilling *population* (1993 est) 8,000,000 (including 350,000 refugees in Ethiopia and 50,000 in Djibouti); growth rate 3.1% p.a. *life expectancy* men 45, women 49 *languages* Somali, Arabic (both official), Italian, English *religion* Sunni Muslim 99% *literacy* men 36%, women 14% *GNP* $170 per head (1989) *chronology* **1884–87** British protectorate of Somaliland established. **1889** Italian protectorate of Somalia established. **1960** Independence achieved from Italy and Britain. **1963** Border dispute with Kenya; diplomatic relations broken with Britain. **1968** Diplomatic relations with Britain restored. **1969** Army coup led by Maj Gen Mohamed Siad Barre; constitution suspended, Supreme Revolutionary Council set up; name changed to Somali Democratic Republic. **1978** Defeated in eight-month war with Ethiopia. Armed insurrection began in north. **1979** New constitution for socialist one-party state adopted. **1982** Antigovernment Somali National Movement formed. Oppressive countermeasures by government. **1987** Barre reelected president. **1989** Dissatisfaction with government and increased guerrilla activity in north. **1990** Civil war intensified. Constitutional reforms promised. **1991** Mogadishu captured by rebels; Barre fled; Ali Mahdi Mohammed named president; free elections promised. Secession of NE Somalia, as the Somaliland Republic, announced. Cease-fire signed, but later collapsed. Thousands of casualties as a result of heavy fighting in capital. **1992** Western food-aid convoys hijacked by "warlords". Dec: United Nations

(UN) peacekeeping troops, led by US Marines, sent in to protect relief operations; dominant warlords agreed truce. *1993* March: leaders of armed factions agreed to federal system of government, based on 18 autonomous regions. June: US-led UN forces destroyed headquarters of warlord General Mohammed Farah Aidid after killing of Pakistani peacekeeping troops. Incidents involving UN and Somali forces increased. Oct: US announced March 1994 as date for withdrawal of most of its troops. *1994* March: Ali Mahdi Mohammed and Aidid signed truce. Majority of Western peacekeeping troops withdrawn. Clan-based fighting continued.

Somaliland region of Somali-speaking peoples in E Africa including the former British Somaliland Protectorate (established 1887) and Italian Somaliland (made a colony 1927, conquered by Britain 1941 and administered by Britain until 1950)—which both became independent 1960 as the Somali Democratic Republic, the official name for ◊Somalia—and former French Somaliland, which was established 1892, became known as the Territory of the Afars and Issas 1967, and became independent as ◊Djibouti 1977.

Somerset county of SW England *area* 1,336 sq mi/ 3,460 sq km *towns* Taunton (administrative headquarters); Wells, Bridgwater, Glastonbury, Yeovil *features* rivers Avon, Parret, and Exe; marshy coastline on the Bristol Channel; Mendip Hills (including Cheddar Gorge and Wookey Hole, a series of limestone caves where Stone Age flint implements and bones of extinct animals have been found); Quantock Hills; Exmoor; Blackdown Hills *industries* engineering, dairy products, cider, food processing, textiles *population* (1991) 460,400 *famous people* John Pym, Henry Fielding, Ernest Bevin.

Somme, Battle of the Allied offensive in World War I July–Nov 1916 at Beaumont-Hamel-Chaulnes, on the river Somme in N France, during which severe losses were suffered by both sides. It was planned by the Marshal of France, Joseph Joffre, and UK commander in chief Douglas Haig; the Allies lost over 600,000 soldiers and advanced 8 mi/13 km. It was the first battle in which tanks were used. The German offensive around St Quentin March–April 1918 is sometimes called the Second Battle of the Somme.

Somoza Anastasio 1896–1956. Nicaraguan soldier and politician. As head of the Nicaraguan army, he deposed President Juan Bautista Sacasa, his uncle, 1936 and assumed the presidency the following year, ruling as a dictator until his assassination 1956. During his rule, Somoza exiled most of his political foes and amassed a fortune. He was succeeded by his sons Luis Somoza Debayle (1922–67), who was president 1957–63, and Anastasio Somoza Debayle (1925–80), who ruled 1963–79, when he was overthrown by the leftist Sandinista rebels (he, too, was later assassinated).

sonar (acronym for *sound navigation and ranging*) method of locating underwater objects by the reflection of ultrasonic waves. The time taken for an acoustic beam to travel to the object and back to the source enables the distance to be found since the velocity of sound in water is known. Sonar devices, or *echo sounders*, were developed 1920.

sonata in music, an essay in instrumental composition for a solo player or a small ensemble and consisting of a single movement or series of movements. The name signifies that the work is not beholden to a text or existing dance form, but is self-sufficient.

Sondheim Stephen (Joshua) 1930–   . US composer and lyricist. He wrote the lyrics of Leonard Bernstein's *West Side Story* 1957 and composed witty and sophisticated musicals, including *A Little Night Music* 1973, *Pacific Overtures* 1976, *Sweeney Todd* 1979, *Into the Woods* 1987, and *Sunday in the Park with George* 1989.

song a setting of words to music for one or more singers, with or without instrumental accompaniment. Song may be sacred, for example a psalm, motet, or cantata, or secular, for example a folk song or ballad. In verse song, the text changes in mood while the music remains the same; in ◊lied and other forms of art song, the music changes in response to the emotional development of the text.

Songhai Empire former kingdom of NW Africa, founded in the 8th century, which developed into a powerful Muslim empire under the rule of Sonni Ali (reigned 1464–92). It superseded the ◊Mali Empire and extended its territory, occupying an area that included parts of present-day Guinea, Burkina Faso, Senegal, Gambia, Mali, Mauritania, Niger, and Nigeria. In 1591 it was invaded and overthrown by Morocco.

sonic boom noise like a thunderclap that occurs when an aircraft passes through the ◊sound barrier, or begins to travel faster than the speed of sound. It happens when the cone-shaped shock wave caused by the plane touches the ground.

sonnet fourteen-line poem of Italian origin introduced to England by Thomas Wyatt in the form used by Petrarch (rhyming *abba abba cdcdcd* or *cdecde*) and followed by Milton and Wordsworth; Shakespeare used the form *abab cdcd efef gg*.

sophist one of a group of 5th-century BC itinerant lecturers on culture, rhetoric, and politics. Skeptical about the possibility of achieving genuine knowledge, they applied bogus reasoning and were concerned with winning arguments rather than establishing the truth. ◊Plato regarded them as dishonest and *sophistry* came to mean fallacious reasoning.

Sophocles *c.* 496–406 BC. Athenian dramatist. He is attributed with having developed tragedy by introducing a third actor and scene-painting, and ranked with ◊Aeschylus and ◊Euripides as one of the three great tragedians. He wrote some 120 plays, of which seven tragedies survive. These are *Antigone* 443 BC, *Oedipus the King* 429, *Electra* 410, *Ajax, Trachiniae, Philoctetes* 409 BC, and *Oedipus at Colonus* 401 (produced after his death). A large fragment of his satyric play *Ichneutae* also survives.

soprano in music, the highest range of the female voice. Some operatic roles require the extended upper range of a *coloratura* soprano, for example Kiri ◊Te Kanawa.

sorghum or *great millet* or *Guinea corn* any cereal grass of the genus *Sorghum*, native to Africa but cultivated widely in India, China, the US, and S Europe. The seeds are used for making bread. Durra is a member of the genus.

sorrel any of several plants of the genus *Rumex* of the buckwheat family Polygonaceae. *R. acetosa* is grown for its bitter salad leaves. ◊Dock plants are of the same genus.

sorting in computing, arranging data in sequence. When sorting a collection, or file, of data made up of several different fields, one must be chosen as the *key field* used to establish the correct sequence. For example, the data in a company's mailing list might include fields for each customer's first names, surname, address, and telephone number. For most purposes the company would wish the records to be sorted alphabetically by surname; therefore, the surname field would be chosen as the key field.

SOS internationally recognized distress signal, using letters of the ◊Morse code (... –...).

soul music emotionally intense style of ◊rhythm and blues sung by, among others, Sam Cooke, Aretha Franklin, and Al Green (1946–). A synthesis of blues, gospel music, and jazz, it emerged in the 1950s. Sometimes all popular music made by African-Americans is labeled soul music.

sound physiological sensation received by the ear, originating in a vibration that communicates itself as a pressure variation in the air and travels in every direction, spreading out as an expanding sphere. All sound waves in air travel with a speed dependent on the temperature; under ordinary conditions, this is about 1,070 ft/330 m per second. The pitch of the sound depends on the number of vibrations imposed on the air per second, but the speed is unaffected. The loudness of a sound is dependent primarily on the amplitude of the vibration of the air.

sound barrier concept that the speed of sound, or sonic speed (about 760 mph/1,220 kph at sea level), constitutes a speed limit to flight through the atmosphere, since a badly designed aircraft suffers severe buffeting at near sonic speed owing to the formation of shock waves. US test pilot Chuck Yeager first flew through the "barrier" in 1947 in a Bell X-1 rocket plane. Now, by careful design, such aircraft as Concorde can fly at supersonic speed with ease, though they create in their wake a ◊sonic boom.

soundcard printed circuit board that, coupled with a set of speakers, enables a computer to reproduce music and sound effects. 16-bit soundcards give better reproduction than 8-bit soundcards, and usually offer stereo sound.

sound synthesis the generation of sound (usually music) by electronic ◊synthesizer.

soundtrack band at one side of a motion picture film on which the accompanying sound is recorded. Usually it takes the form of an optical track (a pattern of light and shade). The pattern is produced on the film when signals from the recording microphone are made to vary the intensity of a light beam. During playback, a light is shone through the track on to a photocell, which converts the pattern of light falling on it into appropriate electrical signals. These signals are then fed to loudspeakers to recreate the original sounds.

source language in computing, the language in which a program is written, as opposed to machine code, which is the form in which the program's instructions are carried out by the computer. Source languages are classified as either high-level languages or low-level languages, according to whether each notation in the source language stands for many or only one instruction in machine code.

Sousa John Philip 1854–1932. US bandmaster and composer of marches. He wrote "The Stars and Stripes Forever!" 1897.

He became known as a brilliant bandmaster during his tenure as leader of the Marine Band 1880–92. He went on to form the Sousa Band 1892 and toured internationally with this group until his death. In addition to about 140 stirring marches, he composed operettas, symphonic poems, suites, waltzes, and songs.

South Africa Republic of (*Republiek van Suid-Afrika*) *area* 471,723 sq mi/1,222,081 sq km *capital* and port Cape Town (legislative), Pretoria (administrative), Bloemfontein (judicial) *towns and cities* Johannesburg; ports Durban, Port Elizabeth, East London *physical* southern end of large plateau, fringed by mountains and lowland coastal margin *territories* Marion Island and Prince Edward Island in the Antarctic *features* Drakensberg Mountains, Table Mountain; Limpopo and Orange rivers; the Veld and the Karoo; part of Kalahari Desert; Kruger National Park *environment* poor farming practices have lead to the loss of 400 million metric tons of topsoil annually 1984–1994. *head of state and government* Nelson Mandela from 1994 *political system* liberal democracy *political parties* African National Congress (ANC), left of center; National Party (NP), right of center; Inkatha Freedom Party (IFP), Zulu nationalist; Freedom Front, far-right; Democratic Party (DP), moderate, center-left; Pan-Africanist Congress (PAC), black, left-wing *exports* corn, sugar, fruit, wool, gold (world's largest producer), platinum, diamonds, uranium, iron and steel, copper; mining and minerals are largest export industry, followed by arms manufacturing *currency* rand *population* (1993) 32,590,000 (73% black: Zulu, Xhosa, Sotho, Tswana; 18% white: 3% mixed, 3% Asian); growth rate 2.5% p.a. *life expectancy* men 60, women 66 *languages* English and Afrikaans; main African languages: Xhosa, Zulu, and Sesotho (all official) *religions* Dutch Reformed Church 40%, Anglican 11%, Roman Catholic 8%, other Christian 25%, Hindu, Muslim *literacy* 70% *GNP* $2,530 per head (1991) *chronology* 1910 Union of South Africa formed from two British colonies and two Boer republics. *1912* African National Congress (ANC) formed. *1948* Apartheid system of racial discrimination initiated by Daniel Malan, leader of National Party (NP). *1955* Freedom Charter adopted by ANC. *1958* Malan succeeded as prime minister by Hendrik Verwoerd. *1960* ANC banned. *1961* South Africa withdrew from Commonwealth and became a republic. *1962* ANC leader Nelson Mandela jailed. *1964* Mandela, Walter Sisulu, Govan Mbeki, and five other ANC leaders sentenced to life imprisonment.

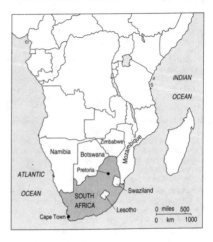

1966 Verwoerd assassinated; succeeded by B J Vorster. *1976* Soweto uprising. *1977* Death in custody of Pan African Congress activist Steve Biko. *1978* Vorster resigned and was replaced by Pieter W Botha. *1984* New constitution adopted, giving segregated representation to Coloreds and Asians and making Botha president. Nonaggression pact with Mozambique signed but not observed. *1985* Growth of violence in black townships. *1986* Commonwealth agreed on limited sanctions. US Congress voted to impose sanctions. Some major multinational companies closed down their South African operations. *1987* Government formally acknowledged the presence of its military forces in Angola. *1988* Botha announced "limited constitutional reforms". South Africa agreed to withdraw from Angola and recognize Namibia's independence as part of regional peace accord. *1989* Botha gave up NP leadership and state presidency. F W de Klerk became president. ANC activists released; beaches and public facilities desegregated. Elections held in Namibia to create independence government. *1990* ANC ban lifted; Nelson Mandela released from prison. NP membership opened to all races. ANC leader Oliver Tambo returned. Daily average of 35 murders and homicides recorded. *1991* Mandela and Zulu leader Mangosuthu Buthelezi urged end to fighting between ANC and Inkatha. Mandela elected ANC president. Revelations of government support for Inkatha threatened ANC cooperation. De Klerk announced repeal of remaining apartheid laws. South Africa readmitted to international sport; US lifted sanctions. PAC and Buthelezi withdrew from negotiations over new constitution. *1992* Constitution leading to all-races majority rule approved by whites-only referendum. Massacre of

civilians at black township of Boipatong near Johannesburg by Inkatha, aided and abetted by police, threatened constitutional talks. *1993* Feb: de Klerk and Nelson Mandela agreed to formation of government of national unity after free elections. April: ANC leader Chris Hani assassinated by white extremist. Sept: agreement on transitional multiracial council to administer country in run-up to elections. Oct: on-going constitutional talks boycotted by new Freedom Alliance (Inkatha, white right-wing groups, and leaders of Bophuthatswana and Ciskei). Dec: interim majority-rule constitution adopted. *1994* Jan: invitation to rejoin the Commonwealth. March: Bophuthatswana annexed after popular uprising and attempted takeover by white right-wing extremists. Inkatha supporters massacred in Johannesburg; state of emergency declared in Natal/KwaZulu. April: Buthelezi persuaded to enter elections; Inkatha campaign of violence called off. Ultraright bombings in Johannesburg and Pretoria. ANC won landslide victory in first non-racial elections. May: Mandela inaugurated as president. Buthelezi appointed home affairs minister.

South America fourth largest of the continents, nearly twice as large as Europe, extending S from ◊Central America. *area* 6,893,429 sq mi/17,854,000 sq km *largest cities* (over 3.5 million inhabitants) Buenos Aires, São Paulo, Rio de Janeiro, Bogotá, Santiago, Lima, Caracas *features* Andes in the W; Brazilian and Guiana highlands; central plains from the Orinoco basin to Patagonia; Parana-Paraguay-Uruguay system flowing to form the La Plata estuary; Amazon river basin, with its remaining great forests and their rich fauna and flora *industries* coffee; cocoa; sugar; bananas; oranges; wine; meat and fish products;

South America: history

20,000 BC	Humans began to populate the continent.
c. 1000–300 BC	Chavín civilization flourished in Peru.
1494	Treaty of Tordesillas assigned what is now Brazil to Portugal, the rest of South America to Spain.
15th century	The Inca civilization developed in Peru.
16th century	Spain and Portugal invaded and conquered South America, killing and enslaving the people.
1513	The Spanish explorer Balboa discovered the Pacific Ocean.
1532–35	Francisco Pizarro conquered Peru and the Incas for Spain.
1780	Peruvian Túpac Amaru (José Condorcanqui), who claimed descent from Inca chieftains, led a revolt against Spanish rule and was executed.
19th century	Simon Bolívar and José de San Martín liberated South America's Spanish colonies. Brazil gained independence without struggle. Massive European immigration.
1818	Chile declared independence.
1822	Bolívar and San Martín met but failed to agree on plans for South American independence.
1865–70	President F S Lopez involved Paraguay in a war with Brazil, Argentina, and Uruguay. Paraguay was defeated and over half its population killed, including Lopez.
1879–83	Pacific War, between Chile and the forces of Bolivia and Peru, ended with Chile's acquisition of all of Bolivia's coastal territory and part of Peru's southern coast. Bolivia still seeks access to the coast.
1889	Brazilian monarchy overthrown and republic established.
1932–35	Chaco war, between Paraguay and Bolivia; the territorial dispute which caused it was settled by arbitration 1938.
1930s	US Marines intervened in Nicaragua.
1952	Bolivian revolution, with nationalization of the tin mines.
1970–73	CIA-backed military coup ended the rule of Salvador Allende's elected socialist government in Chile.
1977	Panama and the US signed a treaty to give Panama control of the Panama Canal in 1999.
20th century	Rapid industrialization and population growth.
1980s	Widespread inability to meet interest payments on loans incurred from economically powerful countries to finance rapid industrialization and capture export markets.
1982	Argentina's invasion of the Falkland Islands triggered war with the UK; the UK regained the Islands.
1992	The first Earth Summit convened in Rio de Janeiro, Brazil, in an effort to cooperate in solving global environmental problems. Celebration in the US of Columbus' first voyage to the New World; Native American representatives protested.

cotton; wool; handicrafts; minerals incuding oil, silver, iron ore, copper **population** (1985) 263,300,000: originally ◊American Indians, who survive chiefly in Bolivia, Peru, and Ecuador and are increasing in number. In addition there are many mestizo (people of mixed Spanish or Portuguese and Indian ancestry) elsewhere; many people originally from Europe, largely Spanish, Italian, and Portuguese; and many of African descent, originally imported as slaves **languages** Spanish, Portuguese (chief language in Brazil), many American Indian languages **religions** Roman Catholic, Indian beliefs

Southampton seaport in Hampshire, S England, on Southampton Water; population (1991) 196,800. Industries include marine engineering, chemicals, plastics, flour-milling, cables, electrical goods, and tobacco. It is a major passenger and container port. There is an oil refinery at Fawley.

South Australia state of the Commonwealth of Australia **area** 379,824 sq mi/984,000 sq km **capital** Adelaide (chief port) **towns** Whyalla, Mount Gambier **features** Murray Valley irrigated area, including winegrowing Barossa Valley; lakes: Eyre, Torrens; mountains: Mount Lofty, Musgrave, Flinders; parts of the Nullarbor Plain, and Great Victoria and Simpson deserts; experimental rocket range in the arid N at Woomera **industries** meat and wool (80% of area cattle and sheep grazing), wines and spirits, dried and canned fruit, iron (Middleback Range), coal (Leigh Creek), copper, uranium (Roxby Downs), oil and natural gas in the NE, lead, zinc, iron, opals, household and electrical goods, vehicles **population** (1987) 1,388,000; 1% Aborigines **history** possibly known to the Dutch in the 16th century; surveyed by Dutch navigator Abel Tasman 1644; first European settlement 1834; province 1836; became a state 1901. In 1963 British nuclear tests were made at Maralinga, in which Aborigines were said to have died.

South Bend city on the St Joseph River, N Indiana, US; population (1990) 105,500. Industries include the manufacture of agricultural machinery, automobiles, and aircraft equipment.

The University of Notre Dame is on the outskirts. The community developed around a fur-trading post established 1823.

South Carolina state in SE; nickname Palmetto State **area** 31,112 sq mi/80,600 sq km **capital** Columbia **towns** Charleston, Greenville-Spartanburg **population** (1990) 3,486,700 **features** large areas of woodland; subtropical climate in coastal areas; antebellum Charleston; Myrtle Beach and Hilton Head Island ocean resorts **industries** tobacco, soy beans, lumber, textiles, clothing, paper, wood pulp, chemicals, nonelectrical machinery, primary and fabricated metals **famous people** John C Calhoun, "Dizzy" Gillespie, DuBose Heyward, Francis Marion, John B Watson **history** explored first by De Gordillo for Spain 1521; Charles I gave the area (known as Carolina) to Robert Heath (1575–1649) in 1629.

South Dakota state in W US; nickname Coyote or Sunshine State **area** 77,123 sq mi/199,800 sq km **capital** Pierre **cities** Sioux Falls, Rapid City, Aberdeen **physical** Great Plains; Black Hills (which include granite Mount Rushmore, on whose face giant relief portrait heads of former presidents Washington, Jefferson, Lincoln, and T Roosevelt are carved); Badlands **industries** cereals, hay, livestock, gold (second-largest US producer), meat products **population** (1990) 696,000 **famous people** Crazy Horse, Sitting

Bull, Ernest O Lawrence **history** first explored 1743 by Verendrye for France; claimed by France 18th century; passed to the US as part of the Louisiana Purchase 1803; explored by Lewis and Clark 1804–06; first permanent settlement, Fort Pierre 1817, reached by first Missouri River steamboat 1831. A gold rush brought thousands of prospectors and settlers to the Black Hills by railroad 1873–74, and South Dakota became a state 1889.

South Georgia island in the S Atlantic, a British crown colony administered with the South Sandwich Islands; area 1,450 sq mi/3,757 sq km. There has been no permanent population since the whaling station was abandoned 1966. South Georgia lies 800 mi/1,300 km SE of the Falkland Islands, of which it was a dependency until 1985. The British Antarctic Survey has a station on nearby Bird Island.

South Glamorgan (Welsh **De Morgannwg**) county of S Wales, created 1974 **area** 161 sq mi/416 sq km **towns** Cardiff (administrative headquarters), Barry, Penarth **features** mixed farming in the fertile Vale of Glamorgan; Welsh Folk Museum at St Fagans, near Cardiff **industries** dairy farming, industry (steel, plastics, engineering) in the Cardiff area **population** (1991) 392,800 **languages** English, 6.5% Welsh-speaking **famous people** Sarah Siddons, Shirley Bassey, R S Thomas.

South Korea see ◊Korea, South.

South Sandwich Islands actively volcanic uninhabited British Dependent Territory; area 130 sq mi/337 sq km Along with ◊South Georgia, 470 mi/750 km to the NW, it is administered from the Falkland Islands. They were claimed by Capt Cook 1775 and named for his patron John Montagu, the 4th Earl of Sandwich. The islands were annexed by the UK 1908 and 1917. In Dec 1976, 50 Argentine "scientists" landed on Southern Thule and were removed June 1982. There is an ice-free port off Cumberland Bay. Over 21 million penguins breed on Zavadovski Island.

South Sea Bubble financial crisis in Britain in 1720. The South Sea Company, founded 1711, which had a monopoly of trade with South America, offered in 1719 to take over more than half the national debt in return for further concessions. Its 100 shares rapidly rose to 1,000, and an orgy of speculation followed. When the "bubble" burst, thousands were ruined.

The discovery that cabinet ministers had been guilty of corruption led to a political crisis.

South, the historically, the states of the US bounded on the N by the ◊Mason–Dixon Line, the Ohio River, and the E and N borders of Missouri, with an agrarian economy based on plantations worked by slaves, and which seceded from the Union 1861, beginning the Civil War, as the ◊Confederacy. The term is now loosely applied in a geographical and cultural sense, with Texas often regarded as part of the Southwest rather than the South.

By its broadest definition, the South consists of 16 states (including Texas and Oklahoma) and the District of Columbia, with an area of 898,575 sq mi/ 2,327,309 sq km.

South West Africa former name (to 1968) of ◊Namibia.

South Yorkshire metropolitan county of NE England, created 1974; in 1986, most of the functions of the former county council were transferred to the metropolitan district councils **area** 602 sq mi/1,560 sq km **towns** Barnsley, Sheffield, Doncaster **features** river

Don; part of Peak District National Park *industries* metal work, coal, dairy, sheep, arable farming *population* (1991) 1,262,600 *famous people* Ian Botham, Arthur Scargill.

sovereignty absolute authority within a given territory. The possession of sovereignty is taken to be the distinguishing feature of the state, as against other forms of community. The term has an internal aspect, in that it refers to the ultimate source of authority within a state, such as a parliament or monarch, and an external aspect, where it denotes the independence of the state from any outside authority.

soviet originally a strike committee elected by Russian workers in the 1905 revolution; in 1917 these were set up by peasants, soldiers, and factory workers. The soviets sent delegates to the All-Russian Congress of Soviets to represent their opinions to a future government. They were later taken over by the ◊Bolsheviks.

Soviet Union alternate name for the former Union of Soviet Socialist Republics (◊USSR).

Soweto (acronym for *South West Township*) racially segregated urban settlement in South Africa, SW of Johannesburg; population (1983) 915,872. It has experienced civil unrest because of the ◊apartheid regime.

soybean leguminous plant *Glycine max*, native to E Asia, in particular Japan and China. Originally grown as a forage crop, it is increasingly used for human consumption in cooking oils and margarine, as a flour, soy milk, soy sauce, or processed into tofu, miso, or textured vegetable protein.

---

space flight: chronology

1903	Russian scientist Konstantin Tsiolkovsky published the first practical paper on aeronautics.
1926	US engineer Robert Goddard launched the first liquid-fuel rocket.
1937–45	In Germany, Wernher von Braun developed the V2 rocket.
1957	Oct 4 : The first space satellite, *Sputnik 1* (USSR, Russian "fellow-traveler"), orbited the Earth at a height of 142–558 mi/229–898 km in 96.2 min.
	Nov 3: *Sputnik 2* was launched carrying a dog, "Laika"; it died on board seven days later.
1958	Jan 31: *Explorer 1*, the first US satellite, discovered the Van Allen radiation belts.
1961	April 12: the first crewed spaceship, *Vostok 1* (USSR), with Yuri Gagarin on board, was recovered after a single orbit of 89.1 min at a height of 88–109 mi/142–175 km.
1962	Feb 20: John Glenn in *Friendship 7* (US) became the first American to orbit the Earth. *Telstar* (US), a communications satellite, sent the first live television transmission between the US and Europe.
1963	June 16–19: Valentina Tereshkova in *Vostok 1* (USSR) became the first woman in space.
1967	April 24: Vladimir Komarov was the first person to be killed in space research, when his ship, *Soyuz 1* (USSR), crash-landed on the Earth.
1969	July 20: Neil Armstrong of *Apollo 11* (US) was the first person to walk on the Moon.
1970	Nov 10: *Luna 17* (USSR) was launched; its space probe, *Lunokhod*, took photographs and made soil analyses of the Moon's surface.
1971	April 19: *Salyut 1* (USSR), the first orbital space station, was established; it was later visited by the *Soyuz 11* crewed spacecraft.
1973	*Skylab 2*, the first US orbital space station, was established.
1975	July 15–24: *Apollo 18* (US) and *Soyuz 19* (USSR) made a joint flight and linked up in space.
1979	The European Space Agency's satellite launcher, *Ariane 1*, was launched.
1981	April 12: The first reusable crewed spacecraft, the space shuttle *Columbia* (US), was launched.
1986	Space shuttle *Challenger* (US) exploded shortly after take-off, killing all seven crew members.
1988	US shuttle program resumed with launch of *Discovery*. Soviet shuttle *Buran* was launched from the rocket *Energiya*. Soviet cosmonauts Musa Manarov and Vladimir Titov in space station *Mir* spent a record 365 days 59 min in space.
1990	April: Hubble Space Telescope (US) was launched from Cape Canaveral.
	June 1: X-ray and ultraviolet astronomy satellite *ROSAT* (US/Germany/UK) was launched from Cape Canaveral.
	Dec 2: *Astro-1* ultraviolet observatory and the Broad Band X-ray Telescope were launched from the space shuttle *Columbia*.
	Japanese television journalist Toyohiro Akiyama was launched with Viktor Afanasyev and Musa Manarov to the space station *Mir*.
1991	April 5: The Gamma Ray Observatory was launched from the space shuttle *Atlantis* to survey the sky at gamma-ray wavelengths.
	May 18: Astronaut Helen Sharman, the first Briton in space, was launched with Anatoli Artsebarsky and Sergei Krikalek to *Mir* space station, returning to Earth May 26 in *Soyuz TM-11* with Viktor Afanasyev and Musa Manarov. Manarov set a record for the longest time spent in space, 541 days, having also spent a year aboard *Mir* 1988.
1992	European satellite *Hipparcos*, launched 1989 to measure the position of 120,000 stars, failed to reach geostationary orbit and went into a highly elliptical orbit, swooping to within 308 mi/500 km of the Earth every ten hours. The mission was later retrieved.
	May 16: Space shuttle *Endeavor* returned to Earth after its maiden voyage. During its mission, it circled the Earth 141 times and traveled 2.5 million mi/4 million km
	Oct 23: *LAGEOS II* (Laser Geodynamics Satellite) was released from the space shuttle *Columbia* into an orbit so stable that it will still be circling the Earth in billions of years.
	Dec: Space shuttle *Endeavor* successfully carried out mission to replace the Hubble Space Telescope's solar panels and repair its mirror.
1994	Feb 4 Japan's heavy-lifting *H-2* rocket was launched successfully, carrying an uncrewed shuttle craft.

Soyinka Wole 1934– . Nigerian author. He was a political prisoner in Nigeria 1967–69. His works include the play *The Lion and the Jewel* 1963; his prison memoirs *The Man Died* 1972; *Aké, The Years of Childhood* 1982, an autobiography, and *Isara*, a fictionalized memoir 1989. He was the first African to receive the Nobel Prize for Literature, in 1986.

Soyuz Soviet series of spacecraft, capable of carrying up to three cosmonauts. Soyuz spacecraft consist of three parts: a rear section containing engines; the central crew compartment; and a forward compartment that gives additional room for working and living space. They are now used for ferrying crews up to space stations, though they were originally used for independent space flight.

space or *outer space* the void that exists beyond Earth's atmosphere. Above 75 mi/120 km, very little atmosphere remains, so objects can continue to move quickly without extra energy. The space between the planets is not entirely empty, but filled with the tenuous gas of the ◊solar wind as well as dust specks.

Spacelab small space station built by the European Space Agency, carried in the cargo bay of the US space shuttle, in which it remains throughout each flight, returning to Earth with the shuttle. Spacelab consists of a pressurized module in which astronauts can work, and a series of pallets, open to the vacuum of space, on which equipment is mounted.

space probe any instrumented object sent beyond Earth to collect data from other parts of the Solar System and from deep space. The first probe was the Soviet *Lunik 1*, which flew past the Moon 1959. The first successful planetary probe was the US *Mariner 2*, which flew past Venus 1962, using transfer orbit. The first space probe to leave the Solar System was *Pioneer 10* 1983. Space probes include *Galileo, Giotto, Magellan, Mars Observer, Ulysses*, the ◊Moon probes, and the Mariner, Pioneer, Viking, and Voyager series. Japan launched its first space probe 1990.

space shuttle reusable crewed spacecraft. The first was launched April 12, 1981, by the US. It was developed by NASA to reduce the cost of using space for commercial, scientific, and military purposes. After leaving its payload in space, the space-shuttle orbiter can be flown back to Earth to land on a runway, and is then available for reuse.

The space-shuttle orbiter, the part that goes into space, is 122 ft/37.2 m long and weighs 75 tons. Although most of its cargoes will be unmanned, two to eight crew members may occupy the orbiter's nose section for up to 30 days. In its cargo bay the orbiter can carry up to 32 tons of satellites, scientific equipment, ◊Spacelab, or military payloads.

space station any large structure designed for human occupation in space for extended periods of time. Space stations are used for carrying out astronomical observations and surveys of Earth, as well as for biological studies and the processing of materials in weightlessness. The first space station was ◊*Salyut 1*, and the US has launched ◊*Skylab*.

space–time in physics, combination of space and time used in the theory of ◊relativity. When developing relativity, Albert Einstein showed that time was in many respects like an extra dimension (or direction) to space. Space and time can thus be considered as entwined into a single entity, rather than two separate things.

Spain (*España*) *area* 194,960 sq mi/504,750 sq km *capital* Madrid *towns and cities* Zaragoza, Seville, Murcia,

Córdoba; ports Barcelona, Valencia, Cartagena, Málaga, Cádiz, Vigo, Santander, Bilbao *physical* central plateau with mountain ranges; lowlands in S *territories* Balearic and Canary Islands; in N Africa: Ceuta, Melilla, Alhucemas, Chafarinas Is, Peñón de Vélez *features* rivers Ebro, Douro, Tagus, Guadiana, Guadalquivir; Iberian Plateau (Meseta); Pyrenees, Cantabrian Mountains, Andalusian Mountains, Sierra Nevada *head of state* King Juan Carlos I from 1975 *head of government* Felipe González Márquez from 1982 *political system* constitutional monarchy *political parties* Socialist Workers' Party (PSOE), democratic socialist; Popular Party (PP), center-right *exports* citrus fruits, grapes, pomegranates, vegetables, wine, sherry, olive oil, canned fruit and fish, iron ore, cork, vehicles, textiles, petroleum products, leather goods, ceramics *currency* peseta *population* (1993 est) 39,200,000; growth rate 0.2% p.a. *life expectancy* men 74, women 80 *languages* Spanish (Castilian, official), Basque, Catalan, Galician, Valencian, Majorcan *religion* Roman Catholic 99% *literacy* men 97%, women 93% *GNP* \$14,290 per head (1992) *chronology 1936–39* Civil war; General Francisco Franco became head of state and government; fascist party Falange declared only legal political organization. *1947* General Franco announced restoration of the monarchy after his death, with Prince Juan Carlos as his successor. *1975* Franco died; succeeded as head of state by King Juan Carlos I. *1978* New constitution adopted with Adolfo Suárez, leader of the Democratic Center Party, as prime minister. *1981* Suárez resigned; succeeded by Leopoldo Calvo Sotelo. Attempted military coup thwarted. *1982* Socialist Workers' Party (PSOE), led by Felipe González, won a sweeping electoral victory. Basque separatist organization (ETA) stepped up its guerrilla campaign. *1985* ETA's campaign spread to vacation resorts. *1986* Referendum confirmed NATO membership. Spain joined the European Economic Community. *1988* Spain joined the Western European Union. *1989* PSOE lost seats to hold only parity after general election; González formed "tactical alliance" with Catalan and Basque parties. Talks between government and ETA collapsed and truce ended. *1992* ETA's "armed struggle" resumed. *1993* Allegations of corruption within PSOE. González narrowly won general election and formed new minority government.

Spanish an inhabitant of Spain or a person of Spanish descent, as well as the culture and Romance language of such persons. The standard Spanish language,

Castilian, originated in the kingdoms of Castile and Aragon (Catalan and Basque languages are also spoken in Spain).

Spanish-American War brief war 1898 between Spain and the US over Spanish rule in Cuba and the Philippines; the complete defeat of Spain made the US a colonial power. The Treaty of Paris ceded the Philippines, Guam, and Puerto Rico to the US; Cuba became independent. The US paid $20 million to Spain. Thus ended Spain's colonial presence in the Americas.

Spanish Armada fleet sent by Philip II of Spain against England in 1588. Consisting of 130 ships, it sailed from Lisbon and carried on a running fight up the Channel with the English fleet of 197 small ships under Howard of Effingham and Francis ◊Drake. The Armada anchored off Calais but fireships forced it to put to sea, and a general action followed off Gravelines. What remained of the Armada escaped around the N of Scotland and W of Ireland, suffering many losses by storm and shipwreck on the way. Only about half the original fleet returned to Spain.

Spanish Civil War 1936–39. See ◊Civil War, Spanish.

Spanish language member of the Romance branch of the Indo-European language family, traditionally known as Castilian and originally spoken only in NE Spain. As the language of the court, it has been the standard and literary language of the Spanish state since the 13th century. It is now a world language, spoken in Mexico and all South and Central American countries (except Brazil, Guyana, Surinam, and French Guiana) as well as in the Philippines, Cuba, Puerto Rico, and much of the US.

Spanish Main common term for the Caribbean Sea in the 16th–17th centuries, but more properly the South American mainland between the river Orinoco and Panama.

Spanish Sahara former name for ◊Western Sahara.

Spanish Succession, War of the war 1701–14 of Britain, Austria, the Netherlands, Portugal, and Denmark (the Allies) against France, Spain, and Bavaria. It was caused by Louis XIV's acceptance of the Spanish throne on behalf of his grandson, Philip, in defiance of the Partition Treaty of 1700, under which it would have passed to Archduke Charles of Austria (later Holy Roman emperor Charles VI).

spark plug plug that produces an electric spark in the cylinder of a gasoline engine to ignite the fuel mixture. It consists essentially of two electrodes insulated from one another. High-voltage (18,000 V) electricity is fed to a central electrode via the distributor. At the base of the electrode, inside the cylinder, the electricity jumps to another electrode earthed to the engine body, creating a spark.

sparrow any of a family (Passeridae) of small Old World birds of the order Passeriformes with short, thick bills, including the now worldwide house or English sparrow *Passer domesticus*.

Many numbers of the New World family Emberizidae, which includes ◊warblers, orioles, and buntings are also called sparrows; for example, the North American song sparrow *Melospize melodia*.

sparrow hawk alternate (but no longer correct) name for the American ◊kestrel. The name now only refers to a small woodland ◊hawk *Accipiter nisus* found in Eurasia and N Africa. It has a long tail and short wings. The male grows to 11 in/28 cm long, and the female 15 in/38 cm. It hunts small birds.

Sparta ancient Greek city-state in the S Peloponnese (near Sparte), developed from Dorian settlements in the 10th century BC. The Spartans, known for their military discipline and austerity, took part in the ◊Persian and ◊Peloponnesian Wars.

Spartacus Thracian gladiator who in 73 BC led a revolt of gladiators and slaves in Capua, near Naples, and swept through southern Italy and Cisalpine Gaul. He was eventually caught by Roman general ◊Crassus 71 BC and Spartacus and his followers were crucified.

Special Air Service (SAS) specialist British regiment recruited from regiments throughout the army. It has served in Malaysia, Oman, Yemen, the Falklands, Northern Ireland, and during the 1991 Gulf War, as well as against international urban guerrillas, as in the siege of the Iranian embassy in London 1980.

special education education, often in separate "special schools", for children with specific physical or mental problems or disabilities.

In the US, the federal department of education has been leading the recent movement toward "mainstreaming", which calls for the integration of students with special needs into the normal school system whenever practical.

species in biology, a distinguishable group of organisms that resemble each other or consist of a few distinctive types (as in polymorphism), and that can all interbreed to produce fertile offspring. Species are the lowest level in the system of biological classification.

specific heat capacity in physics, quantity of heat required to raise unit mass (1 kg) of a substance by one kelvin (1°C). The unit of specific heat capacity in the SI system is the ◊joule per kilogram kelvin (J kg^{-1} K^{-1}).

spectroscopy the study of spectra (obtained by the use of an optical instrument called a spectroscope) associated with atoms or molecules in solid, liquid, or gaseous phase. Spectroscopy can be used to identify unknown compounds and is an invaluable tool to scientists, industry (for example, pharmaceuticals for purity checks), and medical workers.

spectrum (plural *spectra*) in physics, an arrangement of frequencies or wavelengths when electromagnetic radiations are separated into their constituent parts. Visible light is part of the electromagnetic spectrum and most sources emit waves over a range of wavelengths that can be broken up or "dispersed"; white light can be separated into red, orange, yellow, green, blue, indigo, and violet. The visible spectrum was first studied by Isaac ◊Newton, who showed in 1672 how white light could be broken up into different colors.

speech synthesis or *voice output* computer-based technology for generating speech. A speech synthesizer is controlled by a computer, which supplies strings of codes representing basic speech sounds (phonemes); together these make up words. Speech-synthesis applications include children's toys, automobile and aircraft warning systems, and talking books for the blind.

speech writing system computing system that enables data to be input by voice. It includes a microphone, and ◊soundcard that plugs into the computer and converts the analog signals of the voice to digital signals. Examples include DragonDictate, and IBM's Personal Dictation System released 1994.

speed of light speed at which light and other ◊electromagnetic waves travel through empty space.

Its value is 186,281 mi/299,792,458 m per second. The speed of light is the highest speed possible, according to the theory of ◊relativity, and its value is independent of the motion of its source and of the observer. It is impossible to accelerate any material body to this speed because it would require an infinite amount of energy.

speed of sound speed at which sound travels through a medium, such as air or water. In air at a temperature of 32°F/0°C, the speed of sound is 1,087 ft/331 m per second. At higher temperatures, the speed of sound is greater; at 64°F/18°C it is 1,123 ft/342 m per second.

It is greater in liquids and solids; for example, in water it is around 4,724 ft/1,440 m per second, depending on the temperature.

speedwell any flowering plant of the genus *Veronica* of the snapdragon family Scrophulariaceae. Of the many wild species, most are low-growing with small, bluish flowers.

Brookline speedwell *V. americana* grows in marshes all across North America.

Speer Albert 1905–1981. German architect and minister in the Nazi government during World War II. He was appointed Hitler's architect and, like his counterparts in Fascist Italy, chose an overblown Classicism to glorify the state, for example, his plan for the Berlin and Nuremberg Party Congress Grounds 1934. He built the New Reich Chancellery, Berlin, 1938–39 (now demolished) but his designs for an increasingly megolomaniac series of buildings in a stark Classical style were never realized, notably the Great Assembly Hall for Berlin.

speleology scientific study of caves, their origin, development, physical structure, flora, fauna, folklore, exploration, mapping, photography, cave-diving, and rescue work. *Potholing*, which involves following the course of underground rivers or streams, has become a popular sport.

Spender Stephen (Harold) 1909– . English poet and critic. His earlier poetry has a left-wing political content, as in *Twenty Poems* 1930, *Vienna* 1934, *The Still Centre* 1939, and *Poems of Dedication* 1946. Other works include the verse drama *Trial of a Judge* 1938, the autobiography *World within World* 1951, and translations. His *Journals 1939–83* were published 1985.

Spenser Edmund *c.* 1552–1599. English poet. He has been called the "poet's poet" because of his rich imagery and command of versification. His major work is the moral allegory *The Faerie Queene*, of which six books survive (three published 1590 and three 1596). Other books include *The Shepheard's Calendar* 1579, *Astrophel* 1586, the love sonnets *Amoretti* and the *Epithalamion* 1595.

sperm or *spermatozoon* in biology, the male ◊gamete of animals. Each sperm cell has a head capsule containing a nucleus, a middle portion containing mitochondria (which provide energy), and a long tail (flagellum). See ◊sexual reproduction.

spermatophyte in botany, another name for a ◊seed plant.

spermicide any cream, jelly, pessary, or other preparation that kills the ◊sperm cells in semen. Spermicides are used for contraceptive purposes, usually in combination with a ◊condom or ◊diaphragm. Sponges impregnated with spermicide have been developed but are not yet in widespread use. Spermicide used alone is only 75% effective in preventing pregnancy.

Sphinx mythological creature, represented in Egyptian, Assyrian, and Greek art as a lion with a human head. In Greek myth the Sphinx killed all those who came to her and failed to answer her riddle about what animal went firstly on four legs, then on two, and lastly on three: the answer is humanity (baby, adult, and old person with stick). She committed suicide when ◊Oedipus gave the right answer.

Spica or *Alpha Virginis* the brightest star in the constellation Virgo and the 16th brightest star in the sky. Spica has a true luminosity of over 1,500 times that of the Sun, and is 140 light years from Earth. It is also a spectroscopic ◊binary star, the components of which orbit each other every four days.

spice any aromatic vegetable substance used as a condiment and for flavoring food. Spices are mostly obtained from tropical plants, and include pepper, nutmeg, ginger, and cinnamon. They have little food value but increase the appetite and may facilitate digestion.

spider any arachnid (eight-legged animal) of the order Araneae. There are about 30,000 known species. Unlike insects, the head and breast are merged to form the cephalothorax, connected to the abdomen by a characteristic narrow waist. There are eight legs, and usually eight simple eyes. On the undersurface of the abdomen are spinnerets, usually six, which exude a viscid fluid. This hardens on exposure to the air to form silky threads, used to make silken egg cases, silk-lined tunnels, or various kinds of webs and snares for catching prey that is then wrapped. The fangs of spiders inject substances to subdue and digest prey, the juices of which are then sucked into the stomach by the spider.

spider plant African plant of the genus *Chlorophytum* of the lily family. Two species, *C. comosum* and *C. elatum*, are popular house plants. They have long narrow variegated leaves and produce flowering shoots

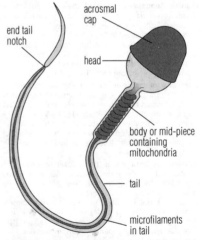

acrosmal cap

end tail notch

head

body or mid-piece containing mitochondria

tail

microfilaments in tail

sperm, or spermatozoon *Only a single sperm is needed to fertilize a female egg, or ovum. Yet up to 500 million may start the journey toward the egg. Once a sperm has fertilized an egg, the egg's wall cannot be penetrated by other sperm. The unsuccessful sperm die after about three days.*

from which the new plants grow. The flowers are small and white. Spider plants absorb toxins from the air and therefore have a purifying action on the local atmosphere.

Spielberg Steven 1947–   . US film director, writer, and producer. His highly successful films, including *Jaws* 1975, *Close Encounters of the Third Kind* 1977, *Raiders of the Lost Ark* 1981, and *ET* 1982 gave popular cinema a new "respectable" appeal. He also directed *Indiana Jones and the Temple of Doom* 1984, *The Color Purple* 1985, *Indiana Jones and the Last Crusade* 1989, and *Schindler's List* 1993, based on Thomas Keneally's novel, which won 7 Academy Awards, including those for Best Picture and Best Director.

Spillane Mickey (Frank Morrison) 1918–   . US crime novelist. He began by writing for pulp magazines and became an internationally best-selling author with books featuring private investigator Mike Hammer, a violent vigilante who wages an amoral war on crime. His most popular novels include *I, the Jury* 1947 and *Kiss Me Deadly* 1953 (both made into films in the *noir* style in the 1950s).

A TV series was based on Mike Hammer.

spin in physics, the intrinsic angular momentum of a subatomic particle, nucleus, atom, or molecule, which continues to exist even when the particle comes to rest. A particle in a specific energy state has a particular spin, just as it has a particular electric charge and mass. According to ◊quantum theory, this is restricted to discrete and indivisible values, specified by a spin quantum number. Because of its spin, a charged particle acts as a small magnet and is affected by magnetic fields.

spina bifida congenital defect in which part of the spinal cord and its membranes are exposed, due to incomplete development of the spine (vertebral column). It is a neural tube defect.

spinach annual plant *Spinacia oleracea* of the goosefoot family Chenopodiaceae. It is native to Asia and widely cultivated for its leaves, which are eaten as a vegetable.

spinal cord major component of the ◊central nervous system in vertebrates, encased in the spinal column. It consists of bundles of nerves enveloped in three layers of membrane (the meninges).

It is a thick cord of nerve tissue enclosed by dorsal extensions from each vertebra along the spinal column. It runs from the medulla oblongata of the brain all the way down the back.

spinal tap or *lumbar puncture* insertion of a hollow needle between two lumbar (lower back) vertebrae to

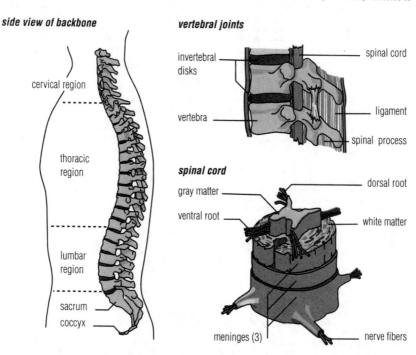

side view of backbone

cervical region

thoracic region

lumbar region

sacrum

coccyx

vertebral joints

invertebral disks

vertebra

spinal cord

ligament

spinal process

spinal cord

gray matter

ventral root

dorsal root

white matter

meninges (3)

nerve fibers

spine The human spine extends every night during sleep. During the day, the cartilage disks between the vertebra are squeezed when the body is in a vertical position, standing or sitting, but at night, with pressure released, the disks swell and the spine lengthens by about 0.3 in/8 mm.

withdraw a sample of cerebrospinal fluid (CSF) for testing. Normally clear and colorless, the CSF acts as a fluid buffer around the brain and spinal cord. Changes in its quantity, color, or composition may indicate neurological damage or disease.

spine the backbone of vertebrates. It consists of separate disk-shaped bony units (vertebrae), processes that enclose and protect the spinal cord. The spine connects with the skull, ribs, back muscles, and pelvis.

spinning art of drawing out and twisting fibers (originally wool or flax) into a long thread, or yarn, by hand or machine. Synthetic fibers are extruded as a liquid through the holes of a spinneret.

Spinning was originally done by hand, then with the spinning wheel, and in about 1767 in England James ◊Hargreaves built the *spinning jenny*, a machine that could spin 8, then 16, bobbins at once. Later, Samuel Crompton's *spinning mule* 1779 had a moving carriage carrying the spindles and is still in use today.

Spinoza Benedict or Baruch 1632–1677. Dutch philosopher who believed in a rationalistic pantheism that owed much to Descartes' mathematical appreciation of the universe. Mind and matter are two modes of an infinite substance that he called God or Nature, good and evil being relative. He was a determinist, believing that human action was motivated by self-preservation.

spiny anteater alternate name for ◊echidna.

spirea any herbaceous plant or shrub of the genus *Spiraea*, family Rosaceae, which includes many cultivated species with ornamental panicles of flowers.

spiritualism belief in the survival of the human personality and in communication between the living and those who have "passed on". The spiritualist movement originated in the US in 1848. Adherents to this religious denomination practise *mediumship*, which claims to allow clairvoyant knowledge of distant events and spirit healing. The writer Arthur Conan Doyle and the Victorian prime minister Gladstone were converts.

Spitsbergen mountainous island with a deeply indented coastline in the Arctic Ocean, the main island in the Norwegian archipelago of ◊Svalbard, 408 mi/657 km N of Norway; area 15,075 sq mi/39,043 sq km. Fishing, hunting, and coal mining are the chief economic activities. The Norwegian Polar Research Institute operates an all-year scientific station on the west coast. Mount Newton rises to 5,620 ft/1,713 m.

Spitz Mark Andrew 1950– . US swimmer. He won a record seven gold medals at the 1972 Olympic Games, all in world record times. He won 11 Olympic medals in total (four in 1968) and set 26 world records between 1967 and 1972. His attempt to qualify for the 1992 Olympics failed.

spleen organ in vertebrates, part of the reticulo-endothelial system, which helps to process ◊lymphocytes. It also regulates the number of red blood cells in circulation by destroying old cells, and stores iron. It is situated on the left side of the body, behind the stomach.

Split (Italian *Spalato*) port in Croatia, on the Adriatic coast; population (1991) 189,400. Industries include engineering, cement, and textiles. Split was bombed during 1991 as part of Yugoslavia's blockade of the Croatian coast.

Spode Josiah 1754–1827. English potter. Around 1800, he developed bone porcelain (made from bone ash,

china stone, and china clay), which was produced at all English factories in the 19th century. Spode became potter to King George III 1806.

Spokane city on the Spokane River, E Washington, US; population (1990) 177,200. It is situated in a mining, timber, and rich agricultural area, and is the seat of Gonzaga University (1887).

Spokane was incorporated 1881 and was the site of Expo '74 (International Exposition of Environment).

sponge any saclike simple invertebrate of the phylum Porifera, usually marine. A sponge has a hollow body, its cavity lined by cells bearing flagellae, whose whiplike movements keep water circulating, bringing in a stream of food particles. The body walls are strengthened with protein (as in the bath sponge) or small spikes of silica, or a framework of calcium carbonate.

spoonbill any of several large wading birds of the Ibis family (Threskiornithidae), characterized by a long, flat bill, dilated at the tip in the shape of a spoon. Spoonbills are white or pink, and up to 3 ft/90 cm tall.

The roseate spoonbill *Ajaia ajaja* of North and South America is found in shallow open water, which it sifts for food.

spore small reproductive or resting body, usually consisting of just one cell. Unlike a ◊gamete, it does not need to fuse with another cell in order to develop into a new organism. Spores are produced by the lower plants, most fungi, some bacteria, and certain protozoa. They are generally light and easily dispersed by wind movements.

spreadsheet software package which enables the user to analyze data because it will perform calculations and routine mathematical operations. A ◊cash flow forecast could be prepared on a spreadsheet.

spring in geology, a natural flow of water from the ground, formed at the point of intersection of the water table and the ground's surface. The source of water is rain that has percolated through the overlying rocks. During its underground passage, the water may have dissolved mineral substances that may then be precipitated at the spring (hence, a mineral spring).

springbok South African antelope *Antidorcas marsupialis* about 30 in/80 cm at the shoulder, with head and body 4 ft/1.3 m long. It may leap 10 ft/3 m or more in the air when startled or playing, and has a fold of skin along the middle of the back which is raised to a crest in alarm. Springboks once migrated in herds of over a million, but are now found only in small numbers where protected.

Springfield capital and agricultural and mining center of Illinois, US; population (1990) 105,200. President Abraham Lincoln was born and is buried here.

Lincoln lived and practiced law in Springfield from 1837 until he became president 1861. His home and tomb are historic sites. Sangamon State University is here. Springfield was settled 1818 and became the state capital 1837.

Springfield city in Massachusetts, US; population (1990) 157,000. It was the site (1794–1968) of the US arsenal and armory, known for the Springfield rifle.

Basketball originated here 1891, and points of interest include the National Basketball Hall of Fame. The community dates from 1636.

Springfield city and agricultural center in Missouri, US; population (1990) 140,500. Industries include electronic equipment and processed food.

The city is also a tourist center for the Ozark

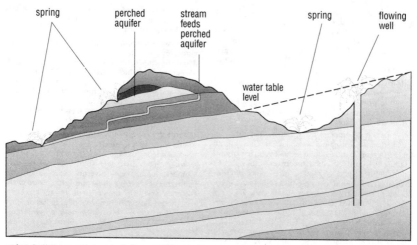

spring *Springs occur where water-laden rock layers (aquifers) reach the surface. Water will flow from a well whose head is below the water table.*

Mountains and the home of Southwest Missouri State University. Springfield was settled 1829.

Springsteen Bruce 1949– . US rock singer, songwriter, and guitarist. His music combines melodies in traditional rock idiom and reflective lyrics about working-class life and the pursuit of the American dream on such albums as *Born to Run* 1975, *Born in the US* 1984, and *Human Touch* 1992.

spruce coniferous tree of the genus *Picea* of the pine family, found over much of the northern hemisphere. Pyramidal in shape, spruces have rigid, prickly needles and drooping, leathery cones.

Some are important forestry trees, such as sitka spruce *P. sitchensis*, native to W North America, and the Norway spruce *P. abies*, now planted widely in North America.

spruce *Spruces are evergreen trees of the pine family. They have hard sharp needles and soft leathery cones hanging from the branches. Perhaps the most familiar is the traditional Christmas tree, the Norway spruce.*

Sputnik series of ten Soviet Earth-orbiting satellites. *Sputnik 1* was the first artificial satellite, launched Oct 4, 1957. It weighed 185 lb/84 kg, with a 23 in/58 cm diameter, and carried only a simple radio transmitter which allowed scientists to track it as it orbited Earth. It burned up in the atmosphere 92 days later. Sputniks were superseded in the early 1960s by the Cosmos series.

sq abbreviation for *square* (measure).

square root in mathematics, a number that when squared (multiplied by itself) equals a given number. For example, the square root of 25 (written $\sqrt{25}$) is ± 5, because $5 \times 5 = 25$, and $(-5) \times (-5) = 25$. As an exponent, a square root is represented by $\frac{1}{2}$, for example, $16^{1/2} = 4$.

squash or *squash rackets* racket-and-ball game usually played by two people on an enclosed court, derived from rackets. Squash became a popular sport in the 1970s and later gained competitive status. There are two forms of squash: the American form, which is played in North and some South American countries, and the English, which is played mainly in Europe and Commonwealth countries such as Pakistan, Australia, and New Zealand.

squill bulb-forming perennial plant of the genus *Scilla*, family Liliaceae, found growing in dry places near the sea in W Europe. Cultivated species usually bear blue flowers either singly or in clusters at the top of the stem.

squint or *strabismus* common condition in which one eye deviates in any direction. A squint may be convergent (with the bad eye turned inward), divergent (outward), or, in rare cases, vertical. A convergent squint is also called *cross-eye*.

squirrel rodent of the family Sciuridae. Squirrels are found worldwide except for Australia, Madagascar, and polar regions. Some are tree dwellers; these generally have bushy tails, and some, with membranes between their legs, are called ◊flying squirrels. Others are terrestrial, generally burrowing forms called ground squirrels; these include chipmunks, gophers, marmots, and prairie dogs.

The small red squirrel *Tamia sciurus* of Alaska, Canada, the Rocky Mountains, and NE US, grows to 14 in/35 cm including the tail. The larger eastern gray squirrel *Sciurus carolinensis* of E North America grows to 20 in/50 cm including tail.

SRAM (acronym for *static random-access memory*) computer memory device in the form of a silicon chip used to provide immediate access memory. SRAM is faster but more expensive than DRAM (dynamic random-access memory).

Sri Lanka Democratic Socialist Republic of (*Prajathanrika Samajawadi Janarajaya Sri Lanka*) (until 1972 *Ceylon*) *area* 25,328 sq mi/65,600 sq km *capital* (and chief port) Colombo *towns and cities* Kandy; ports Jaffna, Galle, Negombo, Trincomalee *physical* flat in N and around the coast; hills and mountains in S and central interior *features* Adam's Peak (7,538 ft / 2,243 m); ruined cities of Anuradhapura, Polonnaruwa *head of state* Dingiri Banda Wijetunge from 1993 *head of government* Chandrika Kumaratunga from 1994 *political system* liberal democratic republic *political parties* United National Party (UNP), right of center; Sri Lanka Freedom Party (SLFP), left of center; Democratic United National Front (DUNF), center-left; Tamil United Liberation Front (TULF), Tamil autonomy; Eelam People's Revolutionary Liberation Front (EPLRF), Indian-backed Tamil-secessionist "Tamil Tigers" *exports* tea, rubber, coconut products, graphite, sapphires, rubies, other gemstones *currency* Sri Lanka rupee *population* (1993 est) 17,800,000 (Sinhalese 74%, Tamils 17%, Moors 7%); growth rate 1.8% p.a. *life expectancy* men 70, women 74 *languages* Sinhala, Tamil, English *religions* Buddhist 69%, Hindu 15%, Muslim 8%, Christian 7% *literacy* men 93%, women 84% *GNP* $539 per head (1992) *chronology* 1802. Ceylon became a British colony. *1948* Ceylon achieved independence from Britain within the Commonwealth. *1956* Sinhala established as the official language. *1959* Prime Minister Solomon Bandaranaike assassinated. *1972* Socialist Republic of Sri Lanka proclaimed. *1978* Presidential constitution adopted by new government headed by Junius Jayawardene of the UNP. *1983* Tamil guerrilla violence escalated; state of emergency imposed. *1987* President Jayawardene and Indian prime minister Rajiv Gandhi signed Colombo Accord. Violence continued despite cease-fire policed by Indian troops. *1988* Left-wing guerrillas campaigned against Indo-Sri Lankan peace pact. Prime Minister Ranasinghe Premadasa elected president. *1989* Premadasa became president; Dingiri Banda Wijetunga, prime minister. Leaders of the TULF and the banned Sinhala extremist People's Liberation Front (JVP) assassinated. *1990* Indian peacekeeping force withdrawn. Violence continued. *1991* March: defense minister Ranjan Wijeratne assassinated; Sri Lankan army killed 2,552 Tamil Tigers at Elephant Pass. Oct: impeachment motion against President Premadasa failed. Dec: new party, the Democratic United National Front (DUNF), formed by former members of the UNP. *1992* Several hundred Tamil Tiger rebels killed in army offensive, code-named "Strike Force Two". *1993* DUNF leader assassinated; government responsibility suspected. President Premadasa assassinated; succeeded by Dingiri Banda Wijetunge. Tamil hostility to government forces continued. *1994* UNP narrowly defeated in general

election; Chandrika Kumaratunga became prime minister, leading SLFP-led left-of-center coalition. UNP presidential candidate assassinated.

SS German *Schutz-Staffel* "protective squadron" Nazi elite corps established 1925. Under ◊Himmler its 500,000 membership included the full-time *Waffen-SS* (armed SS), which fought in World War II, and spare-time members. The SS performed state police duties and was brutal in its treatment of the Jews and others in the concentration camps and occupied territories. It was condemned as an illegal organization at the Nuremberg Trials of war criminals.

Staffordshire county of W central England *area* 1,050 sq mi/2,720 sq km *towns* Stafford (administrative headquarters), Stoke-on-Trent, Newcastle-under-Lyme *features* largely flat; river Trent and its tributaries; Cannock Chase; Keele University 1962; Staffordshire bull terriers *industries* china and earthenware in the Potteries and the upper Trent basin, especially Wedgwood; dairy farming. Coal mining has declined *population* (1991) 1,031,100 *famous people* Arnold Bennett, Peter de Wint, Robert Peel, Josiah Wedgwood.

stagflation economic condition (experienced in the US in the 1970s) in which rapid inflation is accompanied by stagnating, even declining, output and by increasing unemployment. It is a recently coined term to explain a condition that violates many of the suppositions of classical economics. Under the Carter administration, interest rates skyrocketed, prices rose dramatically, and a deep recession occurred. The increase in ◊OPEC petroleum prices was a major contributing factor.

stainless steel widely used ◊alloy of iron, chromium, and nickel that resists rusting. Its chromium content also gives it a high tensile strength. It is used for cutlery and kitchen fittings. Stainless steel was first produced in the UK 1913 and in Germany 1914.

stalactite and stalagmite cave structures formed by the deposition of calcite dissolved in ground water. *Stalactites* grow downward from the roofs or walls and can be icicle-shaped, straw-shaped, curtain-shaped, or formed as terraces. *Stalagmites* grow upward from the cave floor and can be conical, fir-cone-shaped, or resemble a stack of saucers. Growing stalactites and stalagmites may meet to form a continuous column from floor to ceiling.

Stalin Joseph. Adopted name (Russian "steel") of Joseph Vissarionovich Djugashvili 1879–1953. Soviet politician. A member of the October Revolution Committee 1917, Stalin became general secretary of the Communist Party 1922. After ◊Lenin's death 1924, Stalin sought to create "socialism in one country" and clashed with ◊Trotsky, who denied the possibility of socialism inside Russia until revolution had occurred in W Europe. Stalin won this ideological struggle by 1927, and a series of five-year plans was launched to collectivize industry and agriculture from 1928. All opposition was eliminated in the Great Purge 1936–38. During World War II, Stalin intervened in the military direction of the campaigns against Nazi Germany. He managed to not only bring the USSR through the war but helped it emerge as a superpower, although only at an immense cost in human suffering to his own people. After the war, Stalin quickly turned E Europe into a series of Soviet satellites and maintained an autocratic rule domestically. His role was denounced after his death by Khrushchev and other members of the Soviet regime.

Stalingrad former name (1925–61) of the Russian city of ◊Volgograd.

stamen male reproductive organ of a flower. The stamens are collectively referred to as the androecium. A typical stamen consists of a stalk, or filament, with an anther, the pollen-bearing organ, at its apex, but in some primitive plants, such as *Magnolia*, the stamen may not be markedly differentiated.

Stamp Act UK act of Parliament in 1765 that sought to raise enough money from the American colonies to cover the cost of their defense.

Refusal to use the required tax stamps and a blockade of British merchant shipping in the colonies forced repeal of the act the following year. It helped to precipitate the ◊American Revolution.

standard deviation in statistics, a measure (symbol ø or *s*) of the spread of data. The deviation (difference) of each of the data items from the mean is found, and their values squared. The mean value of these squares is then calculated. The standard deviation is the square root of this mean.

standard form method of writing numbers often used by scientists, particularly for very large or very small numbers. The numbers are written with one digit before the decimal point and multiplied by a power of 10. The number of digits given after the decimal point depends on the accuracy required. For example, the ◊speed of light is 1.8628×10^5 mi/2.9979×10^8 m per second.

standard temperature and pressure (STP) in chemistry, a standard set of conditions for experimental measurements, to enable comparisons to be made between sets of results. Standard temperature is 0°C and standard pressure 1 atmosphere (101,325 Pa).

standard time alternate name for ◊zone standard time.

Standish Miles *c.* 1584–1656. American colonial military leader. As military adviser to the Pilgrims, he arrived in New England 1621 and obtained a charter for Plymouth colony from England 1925. Although one of the most influential figures in colonial New England, he is best remembered through US poet Henry Longfellow's *The Courtship of Miles Standish* 1863.

He later established the nearby town of Duxbury and settled there 1637.

Stanislavsky Konstantin Sergeivich 1863–1938. Russian actor, director, and teacher of acting. He rejected the declamatory style of acting in favor of a more realistic approach, concentrating on the psychological basis for the development of character. The Actors Studio is based on his methods. As a director, he is acclaimed for his productions of the great plays of ◊Chekhov.

Stanley Henry Morton. Adopted name of John Rowlands 1841–1904. Welsh-born US explorer and journalist who made four expeditions to Africa. He and David ◊Livingstone met at Ujiji 1871 and explored Lake Tanganyika. He traced the course of the river Zaïre (Congo) to the sea 1874–77, established the Congo Free State (Zaire) 1879–84, and charted much of the interior 1887–89.

Stanton Edwin McMasters 1814–1869. US public official, secretary of war 1862–68. A lawyer and a Democrat, he was appointed US attorney general by President Buchanan 1860 and then secretary of war by Republican president Lincoln 1862.

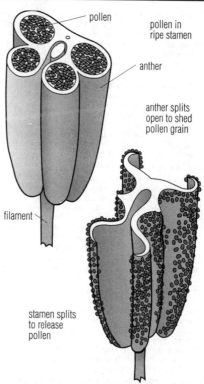

stamen *The stamen is the male reproductive organ of a flower. It has a thin stalk called a filament with an anther at the tip. The anther contains pollen sacs, which split to release tiny grains of pollen.*

Although retained in office by President Andrew Johnson, Stanton eventually broke with him over Reconstruction policies and was forced to resign 1868. He was named to the US Supreme Court 1869 by President Grant, but died before taking office.

Stanton Elizabeth Cady 1815–1902. US feminist who, with Susan B Anthony, founded the National Woman Suffrage Association 1869, the first women's movement in the US, and was its first president. She and Anthony wrote and compiled the *History of Women's Suffrage* 1881–86. Stanton also worked for the abolition of slavery.

star luminous globe of gas, mainly hydrogen and helium, which produces its own heat and light by nuclear reactions. Although stars shine for a very long time—many billions of years—they are not eternal, and have been found to change in appearance at different stages in their lives.

starch widely distributed, high-molecular-mass ◊carbohydrate, produced by plants as a food store; main dietary sources are cereals, legumes, and tubers, including potatoes. It consists of varying proportions of two ◊glucose polymers (polysaccharides): straight-chain (amylose) and branched (amylopectin) molecules.

Star Chamber in English history, a civil and criminal court, named for the star-shaped ceiling decoration of the room in the Palace of Westminster, London, where its first meetings were held. Created in 1487 by Henry VII, the Star Chamber comprised some 20 or 30 judges. It was abolished 1641 by the ◊Long Parliament.

starfish or *seastar* any ◊echinoderm of the subclass Asteroidea with arms radiating from a central body. Usually there are five arms, but some species have more. They are covered with spines and small pincer-like organs. There are also a number of small tubular processes on the skin surface that assist in locomotion and respiration. Starfish are predators, and vary in size from 0.5 in/1.2 cm to 3 ft/90 cm.

star fruit fruit of the carambola tree.

starling any member of a large widespread Old World family (Sturnidae) of chunky, dark, generally gregarious birds of the order Passeriformes. The European starling *Sturnus vulgaris*, common in N Eurasia, has been naturalized in North America from the late 19th century. The black, speckled plumage is glossed with green and purple. Its own call is a bright whistle, but it is a mimic of the songs of other birds.
It is about 8 in/20 cm long.

Star Wars popular term for the ◊Strategic Defense Initiative announced by US president Reagan in 1983.

States General former French parliament that consisted of three estates: nobility, clergy, and commons. First summoned 1302, it declined in importance as the power of the crown grew. It was not called at all 1614–1789 when the crown needed to institute fiscal reforms to avoid financial collapse. Once called, the demands made by the States General formed the first phase in the ◊French Revolution. States General is also the name of the Dutch parliament.

static electricity ◊electric charge that is stationary, usually acquired by a body by means of electrostatic induction or friction. Rubbing different materials can produce static electricity, as seen in the sparks produced on combing one's hair or removing a nylon shirt. In some processes static electricity is useful, as in paint spraying where the parts to be sprayed are charged with electricity of opposite polarity to that on the paint droplets, and in xerography.

statics branch of mechanics concerned with the behavior of bodies at rest and forces in equilibrium, and distinguished from ◊dynamics.

statistics branch of mathematics concerned with the collection and interpretation of data. For example, to determine the ◊mean age of the children in a school, a statistically acceptable answer might be obtained by calculating an average based on the ages of a representative sample, consisting, for example, of a random tenth of the pupils from each class. ◊Probability is the branch of statistics dealing with predictions of events.

status quo (Latin "the state in which") the current situation, without change.

Stavropol territory of the Russian Federation, lying N of the Caucasus Mountains; area 31,128 sq mi/80,600 sq km; population (1985) 2,715,000. The capital is Stavropol. Irrigated land produces grain and sheep are also reared. There are natural gas deposits.

steady-state theory in astronomy, a rival theory to that of the ◊Big Bang, which claims that the universe has no origin but is expanding because new matter is being created continuously throughout the universe. The theory was proposed 1948 by Hermann Bondi, Thomas Gold (1920–), and Fred Hoyle, but was dealt a severe blow in 1965 by the discovery of ◊cosmic background radiation (radiation left over from the formation of the universe) and is now largely rejected.

stealth technology methods used to make an aircraft as invisible as possible, primarily to radar detection but also to detection by visual means and heat sensors. This is achieved by a combination of aircraft-design elements: smoothing off all radar-reflecting sharp edges; covering the aircraft with radar-absorbent materials; fitting engine coverings that hide the exhaust and heat signatures of the aircraft; and other, secret technologies.

steam in chemistry, a dry, invisible gas formed by vaporizing water.
The visible cloud that normally forms in the air when water is vaporized is due to minute suspended water particles. Steam is widely used in chemical and other industrial processes and for the generation of power.

steam engine engine that uses the power of steam to produce useful work. It was the principal power source during the British Industrial Revolution in the 18th century. The first successful steam engine was built 1712 by English inventor Thomas Newcomen at Dudley, West Midlands, and it was developed further by Scottish mining engineer James Watt from 1769 and by English mining engineer Richard Trevithick, whose high-pressure steam engine 1802 led to the development of the steam locomotive.

steel alloy or mixture of iron and up to 1.7% carbon, sometimes with other elements, such as manganese, phosphorus, sulfur, and silicon. The US, Russia, Ukraine, and Japan are the main steel producers. Steel has innumerable uses, including ship and automobile manufacture, skyscraper frames, and machinery of all kinds.

steel band musical ensemble common in the West Indies, consisting mostly of percussion instruments made from oil drums that give a sweet, metallic ringing tone.

Stefan–Boltzmann constant in physics, a constant relating the energy emitted by a black body (a hypothetical body that absorbs or emits all the energy falling on it) to its temperature. Its value is 5.6697 x 10^{-8} W m^{-2} K^{-4}.

Steffens Lincoln 1866–1936. US journalist. Born in San Francisco, Steffens joined the *New York Evening Post* 1892, served as editor of the *New York Commercial Advertiser* 1897–1901 and joined the staff of *McClure's Magazine*. Intent on exposing corruption and fraud in high places, he joined forces with writers Ida Tarbell and Ray Stannard Baker and initiated the style of investigative journalism since known as "muckraking." Steffens later covered the Mexican Revolution and befriended Lenin.

Steichen Edward 1897–1973. Luxembourg-born US photographer, who with Alfred ◊Stieglitz helped to establish photography as an art form. His style evolved during his career from painterly impressionism to realism.
During World War I he helped to develop aerial photography, and in World War II he directed US naval-combat photography. He turned to fashion and advertising 1923–38, working mainly for *Vogue* and

Vanity Fair magazines. He was in charge of the Museum of Modern Art's photography collection 1947–62, where in 1955 he organized the renowned "Family of Man" exhibition.

Stein Gertrude 1874–1946. US writer. She influenced authors Ernest ◊Hemingway, Sherwood Anderson, and F Scott ◊Fitzgerald with her radical prose style. Drawing on the stream-of-consciousness psychology of William James and on the geometry of Cezanne and the Cubist painters in Paris, she evolved a "continuous present" style made up of constant repetition and variation of simple phrases. Her work includes the self-portrait *The Autobiography of Alice B. Toklas* 1933.

Steinbeck John (Ernst) 1902–1968. US novelist. His realist novels, such as *In Dubious Battle* 1936, *Of Mice and Men* 1937, and *The Grapes of Wrath* 1939 (Pulitzer Prize) (filmed 1940), portray agricultural life in his native California, where migrant farm laborers from the Oklahoma dust bowl struggled to survive. Nobel Prize 1962.

Steinem Gloria 1934– . US journalist and liberal feminist who emerged as a leading figure in the US women's movement in the late 1960s. She was also involved in radical protest campaigns against racism and the Vietnam War. She cofounded the Women's Action Alliance 1970 and *Ms* magazine. In 1983 a collection of her articles was published as *Outrageous Acts and Everyday Rebellions*.

Steiner Rudolf 1861–1925. Austrian philosopher, originally a theosophist, who developed his own mystic and spiritual teaching, anthroposophy, designed to develop the whole human being. A number of Steiner schools follow a curriculum laid down by him with a strong emphasis on the arts.

Steinmetz Charles 1865–1923. German-born US engineer who formulated the **Steinmetz hysteresis law** in 1891, which describes the dissipation of energy that occurs when a system is subject to an alternating magnetic force.

He worked on the design of alternating current transmission and from 1894 to his death served as consulting engineer to General Electric.

Stella Frank 1936– . US painter. He was a pioneer of the hard-edged geometric trend in abstract art that followed Abstract Expressionism. From around 1960 he also experimented with shaped canvases.

Stendhal pen name of Marie Henri Beyle 1783–1842. French novelist. His novels *Le Rouge et le noir/The Red and the Black* 1830 and *La Chartreuse de Parme/The Charterhouse of Parma* 1839 were pioneering works in their treatment of disguise and hypocrisy; a review of the latter by fellow novelist ◊Balzac in 1840 furthered Stendhal's reputation.

Stephen *c.* 1097–1154. King of England from 1135. A grandson of William the Conqueror, he was elected king 1135, although he had previously recognized Henry I's daughter Matilda as heiress to the throne. Matilda landed in England 1139, and civil war disrupted the country until 1153, when Stephen acknowledged Matilda's son, Henry II, as his own heir.

Stephen, St The first Christian martyr; he was stoned to death. Feast day Dec 26.

Stephenson George 1781–1848. English engineer who built the first successful steam locomotive, and who also invented a safety lamp in 1815. He was appointed engineer of the Stockton and Darlington Railroad, the world's first public railroad, in 1821, and of the Liverpool and Manchester Railroad in 1826.

steppe the temperate grasslands of Europe and Asia. Sometimes the term refers to other temperate grasslands and semiarid desert edges.

stepper motor electric motor that can be precisely controlled by signals from a computer. The motor turns through a precise angle each time it receives a signal pulse from the computer. By varying the rate at which signal pulses are produced, the motor can be run at different speeds or turned through an exact angle and then stopped. Switching circuits can be constructed to allow the computer to reverse the direction of the motor.

steradian SI unit (symbol sr) of measure of solid (three-dimensional) angles, the three-dimensional equivalent of the ◊radian. One steradian is the angle at the center of a sphere when an area on the surface of the sphere equal to the square of the sphere's radius is joined to the center.

stereophonic sound system of sound reproduction using two complementary channels leading to two loudspeakers, which gives a more natural depth to the sound. Stereo recording began with the introduction of two-track magnetic tape in the 1950s.

sterilization any surgical operation to terminate the possibility of reproduction. In women, this is normally achieved by sealing or tying off the ◊Fallopian tubes (tubal ligation) so that fertilization can no longer take place. In men, the transmission of sperm is blocked by ◊vasectomy.

Sterne Laurence 1713–1768. Irish writer. He created the comic antihero Tristram Shandy in *The Life and Opinions of Tristram Shandy, Gent* 1759–67, an eccentrically whimsical and bawdy novel which foreshadowed many of the techniques and devices of 20th-century novelists, including James Joyce. His other works include *A Sentimental Journey through France and Italy* 1768.

steroid in biology, any of a group of cyclic, unsaturated alcohols (lipids without fatty acid components), which, like sterols, have a complex molecular structure consisting of four carbon rings. Steroids include the sex hormones, such as ◊testosterone, the corticosteroid hormones produced by the ◊adrenal gland, bile acids, and ◊cholesterol. The term is commonly used to refer to ◊anabolic steroid. In medicine, synthetic steroids are used to treat a wide range of conditions.

Stevens John Paul 1920– . US jurist and associate justice of the US Supreme Court from 1975, appointed by President Ford. A moderate whose opinions and dissents were wide-ranging, he opined that the death penalty is not by definition cruel and unusual punishment in *Jurek v Texas* 1976, and that the burning of the US flag in protest is unconstitutional in *Texas v Johnson*.

Stevenson Adlai 1900–1965. US Democratic politician. He is best known as the losing Democratic nominee in two presidential elections against Dwight ◊Eisenhower 1952 and 1956. He served in the Franklin D ◊Roosevelt administration in the 1930s and 1940s and became a successful reform-minded governor of Illinois 1949–52. He was named ambassador to the UN by John F ◊Kennedy 1961.

Stevenson Robert Louis 1850–1894. Scottish novelist and poet. He wrote the adventure novel *Treasure Island* 1883. Later works included the novels

Kidnapped 1886, *The Master of Ballantrae* 1889, *The Strange Case of Dr Jekyll and Mr Hyde* 1886, and the anthology *A Child's Garden of Verses* 1885.

Stewart James 1908–1993. US actor. He made his Broadway debut 1932 and soon after worked in Hollywood. Speaking with a soft, slow drawl, he specialized in the role of the stubbornly honest, ordinary American in such films as *Mr Smith Goes to Washington* 1939, *The Philadelphia Story* 1940 (Academy Award), *It's a Wonderful Life* 1946, *Harvey* 1950, *The Man from Laramie* 1955, and *Anatomy of a Murder* 1959. His films with director Alfred Hitchcock include *Rope* 1948, *Rear Window* 1954, *The Man Who Knew Too Much* 1956, and *Vertigo* 1958.

Born in Indiana, Pennsylvania, he was an air force pilot in World War II.

Stewart Potter 1915–1985. US jurist, appointed associate justice of the US Supreme Court 1958–81 by President Eisenhower. Seen as a moderate, he is known for upholding civil rights for minorities and for opinions on criminal procedure.

stick insect insect of the order Phasmida, closely resembling a stick or twig.

Many species are wingless. The longest reach a length of 1 ft/30 cm.

stickleback any fish of the family Gasterosteidae, found in marine and fresh waters of the northern hemisphere. It has a long body that can grow to 7 in/ 18 cm. The spines along a stickleback's back take the place of the first dorsal fin, and can be raised to make the fish difficult to eat for predators. After the eggs have been laid the female takes no part in rearing the young: the male builds a nest for the eggs, which he then guards and rears for the first two weeks.

Stieglitz Alfred 1864–1946. US photographer who was mainly responsible for the recognition of photography as an art form. After forming the multimedia Photo-Secession Group at 291 Fifth Avenue, New York, with Edward ◊Steichen, he began the magazine *Camera Work* 1902–17. Through exhibitions, competitions, and publication at his galleries, he helped establish a photographic esthetic.

Stijl, De group of 20th-century Dutch artists and architects led by Piet ◊Mondrian from 1917. The group promoted Mondrian's "Neo-Plasticism", an abstract style that sought to establish universal principles of design based on horizontal and vertical lines, the three primary colors, and black, white, and gray. They had a strong influence on the ◊Bauhaus school.

stimulant any substance that acts on the brain to increase alertness and activity; for example, ◊amphetamine. When given to children, stimulants may have a paradoxical, calming effect. Stimulants cause liver damage, are habit-forming, have limited therapeutic value, and are now prescribed only to treat narcolepsy and severe obesity.

stipule outgrowth arising from the base of a leaf or leaf stalk in certain plants. Stipules usually occur in pairs or fused into a single semicircular structure.

They may have a leaflike appearance, as in rose plants *Rosa*; be spiny, as in black locust *Robinia pseudoacacia*; or look like small scales. In some species they are large and contribute significantly to the photosynthetic area, as in the garden pea *Pisum sativum*.

stoat another name for the ◊ermine or short-tailed weasel *Mustela erminea*, used for Old World members of this northern hemisphere species.

stock in finance, proportional ownership in a corporation. Once offered by a corporation going public, stock can be bought and sold on a ◊stock exchange, but the corporation has no obligation to buy it back. Sold to raise capital, stock gives the holder specified rights, including the right to examine the books and the right to vote for the directors. Dividends can be paid, in cash or in stock, when the corporation declares a profit.

stock in botany, any of several herbaceous plants of the genus *Matthiola* of the Crucifer family, commonly grown as garden ornamentals. Many cultivated varieties, including simple-stemmed, queen's, and ten-week, have been derived from the wild stock *M. incana*; *M. bicornis* becomes aromatic at night and is known as night-scented (or evening) stock.

stock-car racing sport popular in the US. Stock cars are high-powered sports automobiles that race on specially built tracks at distances up to 400–500 mi/640–800 km. The sport is governed in the US by the National Associaton for Stock-Car Auto Racing (NASCAR) founded 1947.

stock exchange institution for the buying and selling of stock in publicly held corporations. An exchange trades in stocks that are already issued. Trading is done only by members who have purchased or inherited a "seat" on the exchange. They can act as brokers for nonmembers, on a commission basis, or as floor brokers, acting for other members. Registered traders have no contact with the public but trade only their private accounts. The world's largest exchanges are in New York, London, and Tokyo, and stock prices are watched carefully as indicators of confidence in the economy.

Stockhausen Karlheinz 1928– . German composer of avant-garde music. He has continued to explore new musical sounds and compositional techniques since the 1950s. His major works include *Gesang der Jünglinge* 1956, *Kontakte* 1960 (electronic music), and *Sirius* 1977.

Stockholm capital and industrial port of Sweden; population (1990) 674,500. It is built on a number of islands linked by a network of bridges. Industries include engineering, brewing, electrical goods, paper, textiles, and pottery.

Stock Market Crash a 1929 panic in the US following an artificial stock market boom 1927–29 fed by speculation of shares bought on 10% margin. On Oct 24, 1929, 13 million shares changed hands, with further heavy selling on Oct 28, and the disposal of 16 million shares on Oct 29. Many stockholders were ruined, banks and businesses failed, and unemployment rose to approximately 17 million during the Great Depression 1929–40 that ensued.

stock rights issue in finance, new shares offered to existing stockholders to raise new capital. Stockholders receive a discount on the market price while the company benefits from not having the costs of a relaunch of the new issue.

stoicism Greek school of philosophy, founded about 300 BC by Zeno of Citium. The stoics were pantheistic materialists who believed that happiness lay in accepting the law of the universe. They emphasized human brotherhood, denounced slavery, and were internationalist. The name is derived from the porch on which Zeno taught.

Stokowski Leopold 1882–1977. US conductor. An outstanding innovator, he promoted contemporary music with enthusiasm, was an ardent popularist, and introduced changes in orchestral seating. He cooperated with Bell Telephone Laboratories in early stereophonic recording experiments in the mid-1930s. He was also a major collaborator with Walt Disney in the programming and development of "Fantasound" optical surround-sound recording technology for the animated film *Fantasia* 1940.

He led the Philadelphia Orchestra 1912–38, established the All-American Youth Orchestra, and gave low-priced concerts at the New York City Center.

stoma (plural *stomata*) in botany, a pore in the epidermis of a plant. Each stoma is surrounded by a pair of guard cells that are crescent-shaped when the stoma is open but can collapse to an oval shape, thus closing off the opening between them. Stomata allow the exchange of carbon dioxide and oxygen (needed for ◊photosynthesis and ◊respiration) between the internal tissues of the plant and the outside atmosphere.

stomach the first cavity in the digestive system of animals. In mammals it is a bag of muscle situated just

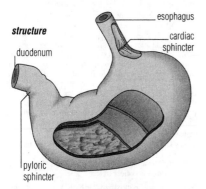

structure

esophagus

cardiac
sphincter

duodenum

pyloric
sphincter

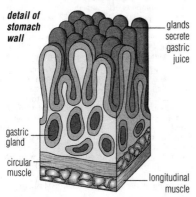

*detail of
stomach
wall*

glands
secrete
gastric
juice

gastric
gland

circular
muscle

longitudinal
muscle

stomach *The human stomach can hold about 2.6 pt/ 1.5 l of liquid. The digestive juices are acidic enough to dissolve metal. To avoid damage, the cells of the stomach lining are replaced quickly—500,000 cells are replaced every minute, and the whole stomach lining every three days.*

below the diaphragm. Food enters it from the esophagus, is digested by the acid and ◊enzymes secreted by the stomach lining, and then passes into the duodenum. Some plant-eating mammals have multichambered stomachs that harbor bacteria in one of the chambers to assist in the digestion of ◊cellulose.

The gizzard is part of the stomach in birds.

Stone Harlan Fiske 1872–1946. US jurist. He was associate justice to the US Supreme Court 1925–41 and chief justice 1941–46 under President Roosevelt.

During World War II he authored opinions favoring federal war powers and regulation of aliens.

stone plural *stone* British unit (symbol st) of mass (chiefly used to express body mass) equal to 14 pounds avoirdupois (6.35 kg).

Stone Age the developmental stage of humans in ◊prehistory before the use of metals, when tools and weapons were made chiefly of stone, especially flint. The Stone Age is subdivided into the Old or Paleolithic, the Middle or Mesolithic, and the New or Neolithic. The people of the Old Stone Age were hunters and gatherers, whereas the Neolithic people took the first steps in agriculture, the domestication of animals, weaving, and pottery.

stonecrop any of several plants of the genus *Sedum* of the orpine family Crassulaceae, a succulent herb with fleshy leaves and clusters of starlike flowers. Stonecrops are characteristic of dry, rocky places and some grow on walls.

Stonehenge megalithic monument dating from about 2000 BC on Salisbury Plain, Wiltshire, England. It consisted originally of a circle of 30 upright stones, their tops linked by lintel stones to form a continuous circle about 100 ft/30 m across. Within the circle was a horseshoe arrangement of five trilithons (two uprights plus a lintel, set as five separate entities), and a so-called "altar stone"—an upright pillar—on the axis of the horseshoe at the open, NE end, which faces in the direction of the rising sun.

It has been suggested that it served as an observatory.

stork any of a family (Ciconiidea) of long-legged, long-necked wading birds with long, powerful wings, and long bills used for spearing prey. Some species grow up to 5 ft/1.5 m tall.

Stowe Harriet Beecher 1811–1896. US suffragist, abolitionist, and author. Her antislavery novel *Uncle Tom's Cabin* was first published serially 1851–52. The inspiration came to her in a vision 1848, and the book brought immediate success.

She also published other works from 1856, including the New England novels *The Minister's Wooing* 1859 and *Old-Town Folks* 1869, as well as essays and religious poems.

Strachey (Giles) Lytton 1880–1932. English critic and biographer. He was a member of the ◊Bloomsbury Group of writers and artists. His *Landmarks in French Literature* was written 1912. The mocking and witty treatment of Cardinal Manning, Florence Nightingale, Thomas Arnold, and General Gordon in *Eminent Victorians* 1918 won him recognition. His biography of *Queen Victoria* 1921 was more affectionate.

Stradivari Antonio (Latin form *Stradivarius*) 1644–1737. Italian stringed instrumentmaker, generally considered the greatest of all violinmakers. He was born in Cremona and studied there with Niccolò Amati. He produced more than 1,100 instruments from his family workshops, over 600 of which survive.

Stowe, Harriet Beecher *Harriet Beecher Stowe, author of Uncle Tom's Cabin 1851–52. With its vivid depiction of the suffering of families torn apart by slavery, the novel greatly influenced the abolitionist cause.*

The secret of his skill is said to be in the varnish but is probably a combination of fine proportioning and aging.

Strasberg Lee 1902–1982. US actor and artistic director of the Actors Studio from 1948. He developed Method acting from ◊Stanislavsky's system; pupils have included Marlon Brando, Paul Newman, Julie Harris, Kim Hunter, Geraldine Page, Al Pacino, and Robert De Niro.

Strasbourg city on the river Ill, in Bas-Rhin *département*, capital of Alsace, France; population (1990) 255,900. Industries include automobile manufacture, tobacco, printing and publishing, and preserves. The ◊Council of Europe meets here, and sessions of the European Parliament alternate between Strasbourg and Luxembourg.

Strategic Arms Limitation Talks (SALT) series of US-Soviet discussions aimed at reducing the rate of nuclear-arms buildup. (See also ◊disarmament.) The talks, delayed by the Soviet invasion of Czechoslovakia 1968, began in 1969 between US president Lyndon Johnson and Soviet leader Brezhnev. Neither the SALT I accord (effective 1972–77) nor SALT II called for reductions in nuclear weaponry, merely a limit on the expansion of these forces. SALT II was mainly negotiated by US president Ford before 1976 and signed by Soviet leader Brezhnev and President Carter in Vienna in 1979. It was never fully ratified because of the Soviet occupation of Afghanistan, although the terms of the accord were respected by both sides until President ◊Reagan exceeded its limitations during his second term 1985–89.

Strategic Arms Reduction Talks (START) a phase in US-Soviet peace discussions. START began with talks in Geneva 1983, leading to the signing of the ◊Intermediate Nuclear Forces Treaty (INF) 1987. In 1989 proposals for reductions in conventional weapons were added to the agenda. As the Cold War drew to a close from 1989, the two nations moved rapidly toward total agreement, and in July 1991 the START treaty was signed in Moscow. See also ◊disarmament.

Strategic Defense Initiative (SDI) also called *Star Wars*, attempt by the US to develop a defense system against incoming nuclear missiles, based in part outside the Earth's atmosphere. It was announced by President Reagan in March 1983, and the research had by 1990 cost over $16.5 billion. In 1988, the Joint Chiefs of Staff announced that they expected to be able to intercept no more than 30% of incoming missiles.

Stratford-upon-Avon market town on the river Avon, in Warwickshire, England; population (1986 est) 20,900. It is the birthplace of William ◊Shakespeare and has the Royal Shakespeare Theatre 1932.

Strathclyde region of Scotland *area* 5,367 sq mi/ 13,900 sq km *towns* Glasgow (administrative headquarters), Paisley, Greenock, Kilmarnock, Clydebank, Hamilton, Coatbridge, Prestwick *features* includes some of Inner ◊Hebrides; river Clyde; part of Loch Lomond; Glencoe, site of the massacre of the Macdonald clan; Breadalbane; islands: Arran, Bute, Mull *industries* dairy, pig, and poultry products; shipbuilding; engineering; coal from Ayr and Lanark; oil-related services *population* (1991) 2,248,700, half the population of Scotland *famous people* William Burrell, David Livingstone, James Keir Hardie.

stratosphere that part of the atmosphere 6–25 mi/ 10–40 km from the Earth's surface, where the temperature slowly rises from a low of –67°F/–55°C to around 32°F/0°C. The air is rarefied and at around 15 mi/25 km much ◊ozone is concentrated.

Strauss Johann (Baptist) 1825–1899. Austrian conductor and composer. He was the son of composer Johann Strauss (1804–1849). In 1872 he gave up conducting and wrote operettas, such as *Die Fledermaus/ The Flittermouse* 1874, and numerous waltzes, such as *The Blue Danube* and *Tales from the Vienna Woods*, which gained him the title "the Waltz King".

Strauss Richard (Georg) 1864–1949. German composer and conductor. He followed the German Romantic tradition but had a strongly personal style, characterized by his bold, colorful orchestration. He first wrote tone poems such as *Don Juan* 1889, *Till Eulenspiegel's Merry Pranks* 1895, and *Also sprach Zarathustra/Thus Spake Zarathustra* 1896. He then moved on to opera with *Salome* 1905 and *Elektra* 1909, both of which have elements of polytonality. He reverted to a more traditional style with *Der Rosenkavalier/The Knight of the Rose* 1909–10.

He spent his final years in the US, teaching and composing at the Eastman School of Music in New York.

Stravinsky Igor 1882–1971. Russian composer. He later adopted French (1934) and US (1945) nationalities. He studied under ◊Rimsky-Korsakov and wrote the music for the Diaghilev ballets *The Firebird* 1910, *Petrushka* 1911, and *The Rite of Spring* 1913 (controversial at the time for their unorthodox rhythms and harmonies). His versatile work ranges from his

Neo-Classical ballet *Pulcinella* 1920 to the choral-orchestral *Symphony of Psalms* 1930. He later made use of serial techniques in such works as the *Canticum Sacrum* 1955 and the ballet *Agon* 1953–57.

strawberry low-growing perennial plant of the genus *Fragaria*, family Rosaceae, widely cultivated for its red, fleshy fruits, which are rich in vitamin C. Wild strawberry *F. virginiana* has small aromatic fruits and grows over much of the eastern half of North America. Cultivated strawberries are hybrids between North American wild species and European species.

streetcar or *trolley* transport system, widespread in the US and Europe from the late 19th to the mid-20th century, where wheeled vehicles ran on parallel rails.

stress in psychology, any event or situation that makes heightened demands on a person's mental or emotional resources. Stress can be caused by overwork, anxiety about exams, money, or job security, unemployment, bereavement, poor relationships, marriage breakdown, sexual difficulties, poor living or working conditions, and constant exposure to loud noise.

stridulatory organs in insects, organs that produce sound when rubbed together. Crickets rub their wings together, but grasshoppers rub a hind leg against a wing. Stridulation is thought to be used for attracting mates, but may also serve to mark territory.

Temperatures can be determined from the stridulations of crickets: adding 40 to the number of chirps counted in 15 seconds gives the approximate temperature in Fahrenheit.

strike stoppage of work by employees (with picketing), often as members of a labor union, to obtain or resist change in wages, hours, or conditions. A "lockout" is a weapon of an employer to thwart or enforce such change by preventing employees from working. Another measure is "work to rule," when production is virtually brought to a halt by strict observance of union rules.

Strindberg August 1849–1912. Swedish dramatist and novelist. His plays are in a variety of styles including historical dramas, symbolic dramas (the two-part *Dödsdansen/The Dance of Death* 1901) and "chamber plays" such as *Spöksonaten/The Ghost [Spook] Sonata* 1907. *Fadren/The Father* 1887 and *Fröken Julie/Miss Julie* 1888 are among his best-known works.

string in computing, a group of characters manipulated as a single object by the computer. In its simplest form a string may consist of a single letter or word—for example, the single word SMITH might be established as a string for processing by a computer. A string can also consist of a combination of words, spaces, and numbers—for example, 33 MAIN STREET ANYTOWN ANYSTATE could be established as a single string.

strip mining or *open-pit mining* mining from the surface rather than by tunneling underground. Coal, iron ore, and phosphates are often extracted by strip mining. Often the mineral deposit is covered by soil, which must first be stripped off, usually by large machines such as walking draglines and bucket-wheel excavators. The ore deposit is then broken up by explosives and collected from the surface.

Stroheim Erich von. Assumed name of Erich Oswald Stroheim 1885–1957. Austrian actor and director. In Hollywood from 1914, he was successful as an actor in villainous roles. His career as a director, which produced films such as *Foolish Wives* 1922, was wrecked by his extravagance (*Greed* 1923) and he returned to

acting in such films as *La Grande Illusion* 1937 and *Sunset Boulevard* 1950.

He also directed *Queen Kelly* 1928 (unfinished).

stroke or *cerebrovascular accident* or *apoplexy* interruption of the blood supply to part of the brain due to a sudden bleed in the brain (cerebral hemorrhage) or embolism or ◊thrombosis. Strokes vary in severity from producing almost no symptoms to proving rapidly fatal. In between are those (often recurring) that leave a wide range of impaired function, depending on the size and location of the event.

strong force one of the four ◊fundamental forces of nature, the other three being the electromagnetic force, gravity, and the weak force. The strong force was first described by Japanese physicist Hideki Yukawa 1935. It is the strongest of all the forces, acts only over very small distances within the nucleus of the atom (10^{-13} cm), and is responsible for binding together ◊quarks to form ◊hadrons, and for binding together protons and neutrons in the atomic nucleus. The particle that is the carrier of the strong force is the ◊gluon, of which there are eight kinds, each with zero mass and zero charge.

strontium soft, ductile, pale-yellow, metallic element, symbol Sr, atomic number 38, atomic weight 87.62. It is one of the ◊alkaline-earth metals, widely distributed in small quantities only as a sulfate or carbonate. Strontium salts burn with a red flame and are used in fireworks and signal flares.

structuralism 20th-century philosophical movement that has influenced such areas as linguistics, anthropology, and literary criticism. Inspired by the work of the Swiss linguist Ferdinand de Saussure, structuralists believe that objects should be analyzed as systems of relations, rather than as positive entities.

structured programming in computing, the process of writing a program in small, independent parts. This makes it easier to control a program's development and to design and test its individual component parts. Structured programs are built up from units called *modules*, which normally correspond to single ◊procedures or ◊functions. Some programming languages, such as PASCAL and Modula-2, are better suited to structured programming than others.

strychnine $C_{21}H_{22}O_2N_2$ bitter-tasting, poisonous alkaloid. It is a poison that causes violent muscular spasms, and is usually obtained by powdering the seeds of plants of the genus *Strychnos* (for example *S. nux vomica*). Curare is a related drug.

Stuart or *Stewart* royal family who inherited the Scottish throne in 1371 and the English throne in 1603, holding it until 1714, when Queen Anne died without heirs and the house of Stuart was replaced by the house of Hanover.

Stubbs George 1724–1806. English artist. He is renowned for his paintings of horses. After the publication of his book of engravings *The Anatomy of the Horse* 1766, he was widely commissioned as an animal painter. The dramatic *Lion Attacking a Horse* 1770 (Yale University Art Gallery, New Haven, Connecticut) and the peaceful *Reapers* 1786 (Tate Gallery, London) show the variety of mood in his painting.

sturgeon any of a family (Acipenseridae) of large, primitive, bony fishes with five rows of bony plates, small sucking mouths, and chin barbels used for exploring the bottom of the water for prey.

North American species include the Atlantic sturgeon *Acipenser oxyrhynchus*, over 10 ft/3 m long.

Stuttgart capital of Baden-Württemberg, on the river Neckar, Germany; population (1988) 565,000. Industries include the manufacture of vehicles and electrical goods, foodstuffs, textiles, papermaking and publishing; it is a fruit-growing and wine-producing center.

There are two universities. Stuttgart was founded in the 10th century.

Styx in Greek mythology, the river surrounding the underworld.

subatomic particle any of the subdivisions of the atom, including those ◊elementary particles that combine to form all ◊matter. See also ◊particle physics.

sublimation in chemistry, the conversion of a solid to vapor without passing through the liquid phase.

subliminal message any message delivered beneath the human conscious threshold of perception. It may be visual (words or images flashed between the frames of a cinema or TV film), or aural (a radio message broadcast constantly at very low volume).

Attempts to use subliminal perception in advertising have raised public fears of manipulation; there is little evidence to show that such messages are effective.

submarine vessel capable of traveling and functioning under water, used in research and military operations. The first underwater boat was constructed for James I of England by the Dutch scientist Cornelius van Drebbel (1572–1633) in 1620. In the 1760s, the American David Bushnell (1742–1824) designed a submarine called *Turtle* for attacking British ships, and in 1800, Robert Fulton designed a submarine called *Nautilus* for Napoleon for the same purpose. Submarines, from the oceangoing to the midget type, played a vital role in both world wars. In particular, German U-boats caused great difficulty to Allied merchant shipping. The first nuclear-powered submarine, the *Nautilus*, was launched by the US 1954.

submersible vessel designed to operate under water, especially a small submarine used by engineers and research scientists as a ferry craft to support diving operations. The most advanced submersibles are the so-called lock-out type, which have two compartments: one for the pilot, the other to carry divers. The diving compartment is pressurized and provides access to the sea.

subpoena in law, an order requiring someone who might not otherwise come forward of his or her own volition to give evidence before a court or judicial official at a specific time and place. A witness who fails to comply with a subpoena is in ◊contempt of court.

substitution reaction in chemistry, the replacement of one atom or functional group in an organic molecule by another.

subway or, in UK, *underground* rail service that runs underground. The first underground line in the world was in London. Opened 1863, it was essentially a roofed-in trench. The London Underground is still the longest, with over 250 mi/400 km of routes. Many major cities throughout the world have extensive systems; New York's subway system and Moscow's each handle millions of passengers a day.

succession in ecology, a series of changes that occur in the structure and composition of the vegetation in a given area from the time it is first colonized by plants (*primary succession*), or after it has been disturbed by fire, flood, or clearing (*secondary succession*).

Sucre legal capital and judicial seat of Bolivia; population (1988) 95,600. It stands on the central plateau at an altitude of 9,320 ft/2,840 m.

sucrose or *cane sugar* or *beet sugar* $C_{12}H_{22}O_{10}$ a sugar found in the pith of sugar cane and in sugar beets. It is popularly known as ◊sugar.

Sudan Democratic Republic of (*Jamhuryat es-Sudan*) *area* 967,489 sq mi/2,505,800 sq km *capital* Khartoum *towns and cities* Omdurman, Juba, Wadi Medani, al-Obeid, Kassala, Atbara, al-Qadarif, Kosti; chief port Port Sudan *physical* fertile valley of river Nile separates Libyan Desert in W from high rocky Nubian Desert in E *environment* the building of the Jonglei Canal to supply water to N Sudan and Egypt threatens the grasslands of S Sudan *features* Sudd swamp; largest country in Africa *head of state* General Omar Hassan Ahmed al-Bashir from 1989 *head of government* Sadiq al-Mahdi from 1993 *political system* military republic *political parties* New National Umma Party (NNUP), Islamic, nationalist; Democratic Unionist Party (DUP), moderate, nationalist; National Islamic Front, Islamic, nationalist (banned since 1989) *exports* cotton, gum arabic, sesame seed, peanuts, sorghum *currency* Sudanese pound, being replaced by Sudanese dinar (1 dinar = 10 Sudanese pounds) *population* (1993) 30,830,000; growth rate 2.9% p.a. *life expectancy* men 51, women 53 *languages* Arabic 51% (official), local languages *religions* Sunni Muslim 73%, animist 18%, Christian 9% (in south) *literacy* men 43%, women 12% *GNP* $400 per head (1990) *chronology 1820* Sudan ruled by Egypt. *1885* Revolt led to capture of Khartoum by self-

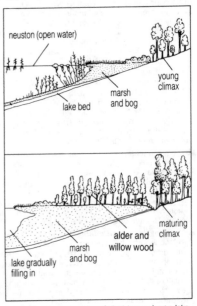

succession *The succession of plant types along a lake. As the lake gradually fills in, a mature climax community of trees forms inland from the shore. Extending out from the shore, a series of plant communities can be discerned with small, rapidly growing species closest to the shore.*

proclaimed Mahdi. *1896–98* Anglo-Egyptian offensive led by Lord Kitchener subdued revolt. *1899* Sudan administered as an Anglo-Egyptian condominium. *1955* Civil war between Muslim north and non-Muslim south broke out. *1956* Sudan achieved independence from Britain and Egypt as a republic. *1958* Military coup replaced civilian government with Supreme Council of the Armed Forces. *1964* Civilian rule reinstated. *1969* Coup led by Col Gaafar Mohammed Nimeri established Revolutionary Command Council (RCC); name changed to Democratic Republic of Sudan. *1970* Union with Egypt agreed in principle. *1971* New constitution adopted; Nimeri confirmed as president; Sudanese Socialist Union (SSU) declared only legal party. *1972* Proposed Federation of Arab Republics, comprising Sudan, Egypt, and Syria, abandoned. Addis Ababa conference proposed autonomy for southern provinces. *1974* National assembly established. *1983* Nimeri reelected. Shari'a (Islamic law) imposed. *1985* Nimeri deposed in a bloodless coup led by General Swar al-Dahab; transitional military council set up. State of emergency declared. *1986* More than 40 political parties fought general election; coalition government formed. *1987* Virtual civil war with Sudan People's Liberation Army (SPLA). *1988* Sadiq al-Mahdi formed a new coalition. Another flare-up of civil war between N and S created tens of thousands of refugees. Floods made 1.5 million people homeless. Peace pact signed with SPLA. *1989* Sadiq al-Mahdi overthrown in coup led by General Omar Hassan Ahmed el-Bashir. *1990* Civil war continued with new SPLA offensive. *1991* Federal system introduced, with division of country into nine states. *1993* March: SPLA leaders announced unilateral cease-fire. April: peace talks began. Oct: civilian government, headed by Sadiq al-Mahdi, replaced military council; army retained ultimate control. *1994* Feb: government renewed attacks on SPLA strongholds in south.

Sudetenland mountainous region in NE Bohemia, Czech Republic, extending eastward along the border with Poland. Sudetenland was annexed by Germany under the ◊Munich Agreement 1938; it was returned to Czechoslovakia 1945.

Suetonius (Gaius Suetonius Tranquillus) c. AD 69–140. Roman historian. He was the author of *Lives of the Caesars* (Julius Caesar to Domitian).

Suez Canal artificial waterway, 100 mi/160 km long, from Port Said to Suez, linking the Mediterranean and Red seas, separating Africa from Asia, and providing the shortest eastward sea route from Europe.

It was opened 1869, nationalized 1956, blocked by Egypt during the Arab-Israeli War 1967, and not reopened until 1975.

Suez Crisis military confrontation Oct–Dec 1956 following the nationalization of the Suez Canal by President Nasser of Egypt. In an attempt to reassert international control of the canal, Israel launched an attack, after which British and French troops landed. Widespread international censure forced the withdrawal of the British and French. The crisis resulted in the resignation of British prime minister Eden.

Suffolk county of E England *area* 1,467 sq mi/3,800 sq km *towns* Ipswich (administrative headquarters), Bury St Edmunds, Lowestoft, Felixstowe *features* undulating lowlands and flat coastline; rivers: Waveney, Alde, Deben, Orwell, Stour, Little Ouse; part of the Norfolk Broads; Minsmere marshland bird reserve, near

Aldeburgh; site of Sutton Hoo (7th-century ship-burial); site of Sizewell B, Britain's first pressurized-water nuclear reactor plant, scheduled to start operating 1994 (application to build a second reactor, Sizewell C, was made 1993) *industries* cereals, sugar beet, working horses (Suffolk punches), fertilizers, agricultural machinery, fishing *population* (1991) 636,300

suffragist or *suffragette* a woman fighting for the right to vote. In the US, the suffragist movement officially began at the Seneca Falls Convention 1848. Elizabeth Cady ◊Stanton and Susan B Anthony founded the National Woman Suffrage Association 1869. At about the same time, Lucy Stone formed the American Woman Suffrage Association. The two groups merged 1890 as the National American Woman Suffrage Association. The perseverance of this group and others led to the ratification of the 19th Amendment 1920, which gave US women the right to vote.

sugar any sweet, soluble crystalline carbohydrate, either a monosaccharide or disaccharide. The major sources are tropical sugar cane *Saccharum officinarum*, which accounts for about two-thirds of production, and temperate sugar beet *Beta vulgaris*. ◊Honey also contains sugars.

Suharto Raden 1921– . Indonesian politician and general, president from 1967. Formerly Chief of Staff under ◊Sukarno, he dealt harshly with a left-wing attempt to unseat his predecessor and then assumed power himself. He ended confrontation with Malaysia, invaded East Timor 1975, and reached a cooperation agreement with Papua New Guinea 1979. His authoritarian rule has met with domestic opposition from the left. He was reelected 1973, 1978, 1983, 1988, and 1993.

Sukarno Achmed 1901–1970. Indonesian nationalist, president 1945–67. During World War II he cooperated in the local administration set up by the Japanese, replacing Dutch rule. After the war he became the first president of the new Indonesian republic, becoming president-for-life in 1966; he was ousted by ◊Suharto.

Sulawesi formerly *Celebes* island in E Indonesia, one of the Sunda Islands; area (with dependent islands) 73,000 sq mi/190,000 sq km; population (1980) 10,410,000. It is mountainous and forested and produces copra and nickel.

Suleiman or *Solyman* 1494–1566. Ottoman sultan from 1520, known as **the Magnificent** and **the Lawgiver**. Under his rule, the Ottoman Empire flourished and reached its largest extent. He made conquests in the Balkans, the Mediterranean, Persia, and N Africa, but was defeated at Vienna in 1529 and Valletta (on Malta) in 1565. He was a patron of the arts, a poet, and an administrator.

sulfate SO_4^{2-} salt or ester derived from sulfuric acid. Most sulfates are water soluble (the exceptions are lead, calcium, strontium, and barium sulfates), and require a very high temperature to decompose them.

sulfide compound of sulfur and another element in which sulfur is the more electronegative element. Sulfides occur in a number of minerals. Some of the more volatile sulfides have extremely unpleasant odors (hydrogen sulfide smells of bad eggs).

sulfite SO_3^{2-} salt or ester derived from sulfurous acid.

sulfonamide any of a group of compounds containing the chemical group sulfonamide (SO_2NH_2) or its derivatives, which were, and still are in some cases, used to treat bacterial diseases. Sulfadiazine ($C_{10}H_{10}N_4O_2S$) is an example.

sulfur brittle, pale-yellow, nonmetallic element, symbol S, atomic number 16, atomic weight 32.064. It occurs in three allotropic forms: two crystalline (rhombic and monoclinic) and one amorphous. It burns in air with a blue flame and a stifling odor; it is insoluble in water but soluble in carbon disulfide. It is found abundantly in volcanic regions and occurs in nature in combination with metals and other substances, as well as a free, brittle, crystalline solid.

sulfur dioxide SO_2 a pungent gas, produced by burning sulfur in air or oxygen.

sulfuric acid H_2SO_4 (also called oil of vitriol) dense, oily, colorless liquid that gives out heat when added to water. It is used extensively in the chemical industry, gasoline refining, and in manufacturing fertilizers, detergents, explosives, and dyes.

sulfurous acid H_2SO_3 solution of sulfur dioxide (SO_2) in water. It is a weak acid.

Sulla Lucius Cornelius 138–78 BC. Roman general and politician, a leader of the senatorial party. Forcibly suppressing the democrats by marching on Rome in 88 BC, he departed for a successful campaign against ◊Mithridates VI of Pontus. The democrats seized power in his absence, but on his return in 82 Sulla captured Rome and massacred all opponents. The reforms he introduced as dictator, which strengthened the Senate, were conservative and short-lived. He retired 79 BC.

Sullivan Arthur (Seymour) 1842–1900. English composer. He wrote operettas in collaboration with William Gilbert, including *HMS Pinafore* 1878, *The Pirates of Penzance* 1879, and *The Mikado* 1885. Their partnership broke down 1896. Sullivan also composed serious instrumental, choral, and operatic works—for example, the opera *Ivanhoe* 1890—which he valued more highly than the operettas.

Sullivan Louis Henry 1856–1924. US architect. He was a leader of the Chicago School and an early developer of the skyscraper. His skyscrapers include the Wainwright Building, St Louis, 1890, the Guaranty Building, Buffalo, 1894, and the Carson, Pirie and Scott Store, Chicago, 1899. He was the teacher of Frank Lloyd ◊Wright.

Sumatra or *Sumatera* second-largest island of Indonesia, one of the Sunda Islands; area 182,800 sq mi/473,600 sq km; population (1989) 36,882,000. East of a longitudinal volcanic mountain range is a wide plain; both are heavily forested. Products include rubber, rice, tobacco, tea, timber, tin, and petroleum.

Sumerian civilization the world's earliest civilization, dated about 3500 BC, and located at the confluence of the Tigris and Euphrates rivers in lower Mesopotamia (present-day Iraq). It was a city-state with priests as secular rulers. Sumerian culture was based on the taxation of the surplus produced by agricultural villagers to support the urban ruling class.

Sun the ◊star at the center of the Solar System. Its diameter is 865,000 mi/1,392,000 km; its temperature at the surface is about 5,800K (9,980°F/5,530°C), and at the center 15,000,000K (27,000,000°F/15,000,000°C). It is composed of about 70% hydrogen and 30% helium, with other elements making up less than 1%. The Sun's energy is generated by nuclear fusion reactions that turn hydrogen into helium at its center. The

gas core is far denser than mercury or lead on Earth. The Sun is about 4.7 trillion years old, with a predicted lifetime of 10 quadrillion years.

Sunbelt popular name for the southern and southwestern continental US because of the warm climate. The Sunbelt is growing much faster in population than the northern US, with a steady migration of retirees and high-tech and service industries. The 20 states that, roughly, comprise the Sunbelt have a population of more than 110 million. The largest city in the Sunbelt is Los Angeles.

Sundanese member of the second-largest ethnic group in the Republic of Indonesia. There are more than 20 million speakers of Sundanese, a member of the western branch of the Austronesian family. Like their neighbors, the Javanese, the Sundanese are predominantly Muslim.

They are known for their performing arts, especially *jaipongan* dance traditions, and distinctive batik fabrics.

sundew any insectivorous plant of the genus *Drosera*, family Droseraceae, with viscid hairs on the leaves for catching prey.

sunfish any of various small members of the North American family (Centrarchidae) of freshwater bony fishes with compressed, almost circular bodies ranging from 6 in/15 cm to 12 in/30 cm and including bluegills, pumpkinseeds, rock bass, and crappies. The considerably larger basses also belong to this family. Ocean sunfishes of the family Molidae have disk-shaped, abruptly truncated bodies. The 10 ft/3 m species *Mola mola* is found worldwide.

sunflower tall plant of the genus *Helianthus*, family Compositae. The common sunflower *H. annuus*, probably native to Mexico, grows to 15 ft/ 4.5 m in

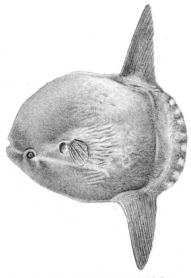

sunfish Shaped like an ancient stone axhead, the extraordinary sunfish inhabits the temperate to tropical waters of the Indian, Pacific, and Atlantic oceans. Although they may reach 13 ft /4 m in length, sunfishes feed mainly on plankton.

favorable conditions. It is commercially cultivated in the US, central Europe, Russia, Ukraine, and Australia for the oil-bearing seeds that follow the yellow-petalled flowers.

Sunni member of the larger of the two main sects of ◊Islam, with about 680 million adherents. Sunni Muslims believe that the first three caliphs were all legitimate successors of the prophet Mohammed, and that guidance on belief and life should come from the Koran and the Hadith, and from the Shari'a, not from a human authority or spiritual leader. Imams in Sunni Islam are educated lay teachers of the faith and prayer leaders. The name derives from the *Sunna*, Arabic "code of behavior", the body of traditional law evolved from the teaching and acts of Mohammed.

sunspot dark patch on the surface of the Sun, actually an area of cooler gas, thought to be caused by strong magnetic fields that block the outward flow of heat to the Sun's surface. Sunspots consist of a dark central *umbra*, about 4,000K (6,700°F/3,700°C), and a lighter surrounding *penumbra*, about 5,500K (9,400°F/5,200°C). They last from several days to over a month, ranging in size from 1,250 mi/2000 km to groups stretching for over 62,000 mi/100,000 km.

Sun Yat-sen or *Sun Zhong Shan* 1867–1925. Chinese revolutionary leader, founder of the ◊Guomindang (nationalist party) 1894, and provisional president of the Republic of China 1912 after playing a vital part in deposing the emperor. He was president of a break-away government from 1921.

Super Bowl US professional football championship, inaugurated 1966. It is the annual end-of-season contest between the American Football Conference (AFC) and the National Football Conference (NFC) champions.

See ◊football.

supercomputer the fastest, most powerful type of computer, capable of performing its basic operations in picoseconds (quadrillionths of a second), rather than nanoseconds (trillionths of a second), like most other computers.

superconductivity in physics, increase in electrical conductivity at low temperatures. The resistance of some metals and metallic compounds decreases uniformly with decreasing temperature until at a critical temperature (the superconducting point), within a few degrees of absolute zero (0 K/−459.67°F/−273.16°C), the resistance suddenly falls to zero. The phenomenon was discovered by Dutch scientist Heike Kamerlingh-Onnes (1853–1926) in 1911.

supercooling in physics, the lowering in temperature of a saturated solution without crystallization taking place, forming a supersaturated solution. Usually crystallization rapidly follows the introduction of a small (seed) crystal or agitation of the supercooled solution.

superego in Freudian psychology, the element of the human mind concerned with the ideal, responsible for ethics and self-imposed standards of behavior. It is characterized as a form of conscience, restraining the ◊ego, and responsible for feelings of guilt when the moral code is broken.

supergiant the largest and most luminous type of star known, with a diameter of up to 1,000 times that of the Sun and absolute magnitudes of between −5 and −9. Supergiants are likely to become ◊supernovae.

Superior, Lake largest and deepest of the Great Lakes and the largest freshwater lake in the world; area about 31,700 sq mi/82,100 sq km. It is bordered by the Canadian province of Ontario and the US states of Minnesota, Wisconsin, and Michigan. As the western-most of the Great Lakes, Superior is at the western end of the St Lawrence Seaway.

supernova the explosive death of a star, which temporarily attains a brightness of 100 million Suns or more, so that it can shine as brilliantly as a small galaxy for a few days or weeks. Very approximately, it is thought that a supernova explodes in a large galaxy about once every 100 years. Many supernovae remain undetected because of obscuring by interstellar dust—astronomers estimate some 50%.

supersonic speed speed greater than that at which sound travels, measured in ◊Mach numbers. In dry air at 32°F/0°C, sound travels at about 727 mph/ 1,170 kph, but decreases its speed with altitude until, at 39,000 ft/12,000 m, it is only 658 mph/1,060 kph.

Superstring Theory in physics and astronomy, the theory that attempts to link the four ◊fundamental forces. It postulates that each force emerged separately during the expansion of the very early universe from the ◊Big Bang. It also postulates viewing matter as tiny vibrating strings instead of particles within a universe of more than the currently known four dimensions. Continuing research pursues a model based on a ten-dimensional universe, present at ◊singularity. At the Big Bang, the ten dimensions split into two components, with four dimensions expanded into the current observable universe while the other six dimensions contracted to a point in space.

supply-side economics school of economic thought advocating government policies that allow market forces to operate freely, by such as privatization and cuts in public spending and income tax, reductions in trade-union power, and cuts in the ratio of unemployment benefits to wages. Supply-side economics developed as part of the monetarist (see ◊monetarism) critique of Keynesian economics.

Supreme Court highest US judicial tribunal, composed since 1869 of a chief justice (William Rehnquist from 1986) and eight associate justices. Appointments are made for life by the president, with the advice and consent of the Senate, and justices can be removed only by impeachment.

The US Supreme Court hears appeals from decisions of the US Court of Appeals and from the state supreme courts. It also adjudicates questions of constitutional propriety and conflicts between the executive and legislative branches of the federal government.

Surabaya port on the island of Java, Indonesia; population (1980) 2,028,000. It has oil refineries and shipyards and is a naval base.

surface tension in physics, the property that causes the surface of a liquid to behave as if it were covered with a weak elastic skin; this is why a needle can float on water. It is caused by the exposed surface's tendency to contract to the smallest possible area because of unequal cohesive forces between ◊molecules at the surface. Allied phenomena include the formation of droplets, the concave profile of a meniscus, and the capillary action by which water soaks into a sponge.

surfing sport of riding on the crest of large waves while standing on a narrow, keeled surfboard, usually of light synthetic material such as fiberglass, about 6 ft/1.8 m long (or about 8–9 ft/2.4–7 m known as the Malibu), as first developed in Hawaii and Australia. Windsurfing is a recent development.

surgery branch of medicine concerned with the treatment of disease, abnormality or injury by operation. Traditionally it has been performed by means of cutting instruments, but today a number of technologies are used to treat or remove lesions, including ultrasonic waves and laser surgery.

Suriname Republic of (*Republiek Suriname*) *area* 63,243 sq mi/163,820 sq km *capital* Paramaribo *towns and cities* Nieuw Nickerie, Brokopondo, Nieuw Amsterdam *physical* hilly and forested, with flat and narrow coastal plain *features* Suriname River *head of state and government* Ronald Venetiaan from 1991 *political system* emergent democratic republic *political parties* Party for National Unity and Solidarity (KTPI)*, Indonesian, left-of-center; Suriname National Party (NPS)*, Creole, left-of-center; Progressive Reform Party (VHP)*, Indian, left-of-center; New Front For Democracy (NF) *members of Front for Democracy and Development (FDD) *exports* alumina, aluminum, bauxite, rice, timber *currency* Suriname guilder *population* (1990 est) 408,000 (Hindu 37%, Creole 31%, Javanese 15%); growth rate 1.1% p.a. *life expectancy* men 66, women 71 (1989) *languages* Dutch (official), Sranan (creole), English, others *religions* Christian 30%, Hindu 27%, Muslim 20% *literacy* 65% (1989) *GNP* $1.1 bn (1987); $2,920 per head (1985) *chronology 1667* Became a Dutch colony. *1954* Achieved internal self-government as Dutch Guiana. *1975* Independence achieved from the Netherlands, with Dr Johan Ferrier as president and Henck Arron as prime minister; 40% of the population emigrated to the Netherlands. *1980* Arron's government overthrown in army coup; Ferrier refused to recognize military regime; appointed Dr Henk Chin A Sen to lead civilian administration. Army replaced Ferrier with Dr Chin A Sen. *1982* Army, led by Lt Col Desi Bouterse, seized power, setting up a Revolutionary People's Front. *1985* Ban on political activities lifted. *1986* Antigovernment rebels brought economic chaos to Suriname. *1987* New constitution approved. *1988* Ramsewak Shankar elected president. *1989* Bouterse rejected peace accord reached by President Shankar with guerrilla insurgents, vowed to continue fighting. *1990* Shankar deposed in army coup. *1991* Johan Kraag became interim president. New Front for Democracy won assembly majority. Ronald Venetiaan elected president. *1992* Peace accord with guerrilla groups.

Surrealism movement in art, literature, and film that developed out of ◊Dada around 1922. Led by André ◊Breton, who produced the *Surrealist Manifesto* 1924, the Surrealists were inspired by the thoughts and visions of the subconscious mind. They explored varied styles and techniques, and the movement became the dominant force in Western art between world wars I and II.

Surrey county of S England *area* 641 sq mi/1,660 sq km *towns* Kingston upon Thames (administrative headquarters), Guildford, Woking, Reigate, Leatherhead *features* rivers: Thames, Mole, Wey; hills: Box and Leith; North Downs; Runnymede, Thameside site of the signing of Magna Carta; Yehudi Menuhin School; Kew Palace and Royal Botanic Gardens; in 1989 it was the most affluent county in Britain—average income 40% above national average *industries* vegetables, agricultural products, service industries *population* (1991) 1,018,000 *famous people* John Galsworthy, Aldous Huxley, Laurence Olivier, Eric Clapton.

surveying the accurate measuring of the Earth's crust, or of land features or buildings. It is used to establish boundaries, and to evaluate the topography for engineering work. The measurements used are both linear and angular, and geometry and trigonometry are applied in the calculations.

Sūrya in Hindu mythology, the Sun god, son of the sky god Indra. His daughter, also named Sūrya, is a female impersonation of the Sun.

suspension mixture consisting of small solid particles dispersed in a liquid or gas, which will settle on standing. An example is milk of magnesia, which is a suspension of magnesium hydroxide in water.

Sussex former county of England, on the south coast, now divided into East Sussex and West Sussex.

Sutherland Joan 1926– . Australian soprano. She is noted for her commanding range and impeccable technique. She made her debut England 1952, in *The Magic Flute*; later roles included *Lucia di Lammermoor*, Donna Anna in *Don Giovanni*, and Desdemona in *Otello*. She retired from the stage 1990.

She usually performed under the baton of her husband, conductor Richard Bonynge.

Suu Kyi Aung San 1945– . Myanmar (Burmese) politician and human rights campaigner, leader of the National League for Democracy (NLD), the main opposition to the military junta. When the NLD won the 1990 elections, the junta refused to surrender power, and placed Suu Kyi under house arrest. She was awarded the Nobel Prize for Peace 1991 in recognition of her "nonviolent struggle for democracy and human rights" in Myanmar. She is the daughter of former Burmese premier ◊Aung San.

Suva capital and industrial port of Fiji, on Viti Levu; population (1981) 68,000. It produces soap and coconut oil.

Svalbard Norwegian archipelago in the Arctic Ocean. The main island is Spitsbergen; other islands include North East Land, Edge Island, Barents Island, and Prince Charles Foreland.

Swabia (German *Schwaben*) historic region of SW Germany, an independent duchy in the Middle Ages. It includes Augsburg and Ulm and forms part of the *Länder* (states) of Baden-Württemberg, Bavaria, and Hessen.

Swahili language belonging to the Bantu branch of the Niger-Congo family, widely used in east and central Africa. Swahili originated on the E African coast as a *lingua franca* used among traders, and contains many Arabic loan words. It is an official language in Kenya and Tanzania.

swallow any bird of the family Hirundinidae of small, insect-eating birds in the order Passeriformes, with long, narrow wings and deeply forked tails. Swallows feed while flying.

Species include the barn swallow *Hirundo rustica* and the purple martin *Progne subis*.

swan any of several large, long-necked, aquatic, web-footed birds of the family Anatidae, which also includes ducks and geese.

Species include the Old World mute swan *Cygnus olor*, with all-white plumage, now introduced in parks worldwide, and the *black swan* of Australia, *C. atratus*. The North American *trumpeter swan C. buccinator* is the largest, with a wingspan of 8 ft/ 2.4 m. This species was nearly extinct by 1900, and although numbers have recovered, it is still endangered. Pairing is generally for life, and the young are called cygnets.

Swaziland Kingdom of (*Umbuso weSwatini*) *area* 6,716 sq mi/17,400 sq km *capital* Mbabane *towns and cities* Manzini, Big Bend *physical* central valley; mountains in W (Highveld); plateau in E (Lowveld and Lubombo plateau) *features* landlocked enclave between South Africa and Mozambique *head of state* King Mswati III from 1986 *head of government* Prince Jameson Mbilini Dlamini from 1993 *political system* transitional absolute monarchy *political parties* Imbokodvo National Movement (INM), nationalist monarchist; Swaziland United Front (SUF), left of center; Swaziland Progresssive Party (SPP), left of center; People's United Democratic Movement, left of center *exports* sugar, canned fruit, wood pulp, asbestos *currency* lilangeni *population* (1993 est) 835,000; growth rate 3% p.a. *life expectancy* men 53, women 60 *languages* Swazi 90%, English (both official) *religions* Christian 57%, animist *literacy* 72% *GNP* \$1,060 per head (1991) *chronology 1903* Swaziland became a special High Commission territory. *1967* Achieved internal self-government. *1968* Independence achieved from Britain, within the Commonwealth, as the Kingdom of Swaziland, with King Sobhuza II as head of state. *1973* The king suspended the constitution and assumed absolute powers. *1978* New constitution adopted. *1982* King Sobhuza died; his place was taken by one of his wives, Dzeliwe, until his son, Prince Makhosetive, reached the age of 21. *1983* Queen Dzeliwe ousted by another wife, Ntombi. *1984* After royal power struggle, it was announced that the crown prince would become king at 18. *1986* Crown prince formally invested as King Mswati III. *1987* Power struggle developed between advisory council Liqoqo and Queen Ntombi over accession of king. Mswati dissolved parliament; new government elected with Sotsha Dlamini as prime minister. *1991* Calls for democratic reform. *1992* Revised constitution adopted. Mswati dissolved parliament, assuming interim "executive powers". Multiparty assembly elections held.

Sweden Kingdom of (*Konungariket Sverige*) *area* 173,745 sq mi/450,000 sq km *capital* Stockholm *towns and cities* Göteborg, Malmö, Uppsala, Norrköping, Västerås *physical* mountains in W; plains in S; thickly forested; more than 20,000 islands off the Stockholm coast *environment* of the country's 90,000 lakes, 20,000 are affected by acid rain; 4,000 are so severely acidified that no fish are thought to survive in them *features* lakes, including Vänern, Vättern, Mälaren, Hjälmaren; islands of öland and Gotland; wild elk *head of state* King Carl XVI Gustaf from 1973 *head of government* Ingvar Carlsson from 1994 *political system* constitutional monarchy *political parties* Christian Democratic Party (KdS), Christian, centrist; Left Party (VP), European, Marxist; Social Democratic Labour Party (SDAP), moderate, left of center; Moderate Party (MS), right of center; Liberal Party (FP), center-left; Center Party (CP), centrist; Green (MpG), ecological; New Democracy (NG), right-wing, populist *exports* aircraft, vehicles, ballbearings, drills, missiles, electronics, petrochemicals, textiles, furnishings, ornamental glass, paper, iron and steel *currency* krona *population* (1993 est) 8,700,000 (including 17,000 Saami [Lapps] and 1.2 million immigrants from Turkey, Yugoslavia, Greece, Iran, Finland and other Nordic countries); growth rate 0.1% p.a. *life expectancy* men 75, women 81 *languages* Swedish; there are Finnish-and Saami-speaking minorities *media* press freedom law dating from 1766 gives every citizen free access to all public documents except civil

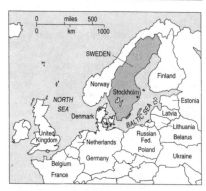

servants' papers, and these can legally be leaked to journalists. An exception is made for cases that would constitute a grave threat to national security. *religion* Lutheran (official) 95% *literacy* 99% *GNP* \$25,490 per head (1991) *chronology 12th century* United as an independent nation. *1397–1520* Under Danish rule. *1914–45* Neutral in both world wars. *1951–76* Social Democratic Labour Party (SAP) in power. *1969* Olof Palme became SAP leader and prime minister. *1971* Constitution amended, creating a single-chamber Riksdag, the governing body. *1975* Monarch's last constitutional powers removed. *1976* Thorbjörn Fälldin, leader of the Center Party, became prime minister, heading center-right coalition. *1982* SAP, led by Palme, returned to power. *1985* SAP formed minority government, with communist support. *1986* Olof Palme murdered. Ingvar Carlsson became prime minister and SAP party leader. *1988* SAP reelected with reduced majority; Green Party gained representation in Riksdag. *1990* SAP government resigned. *1991* Formal application for European Community (EC) membership. Election defeat for SAP; Carlsson resigned. Center-right coalition formed; Carl Bildt became new prime minister. *1992* Agreement between Bildt's center-right coalition and right-wing New Democracy party to collaborate in solving country's economic problems. *1994* Carlsson formed minority government after SAP won most seats in general election. National referendum narrowly supported application for European Union (formerly EC) membership.

sweet cicely plant *Myrrhis odorata* of the carrot family Umbelliferae, native to S Europe; the root is eaten as a vegetable, and the aniseed-flavored leaves are used in salads.

Also, one of several North American plants (genus *Osmorhiza*) of the same family with clusters of small white flowers.

sweet potato tropical American plant *Ipomea batatas* of the morning-glory family Convolvulaceae; the white-orange tuberous root is used as a source of starch and alcohol and eaten as a vegetable.

swift any fast-flying, short-legged bird of the family Apodidae, of which there are about 75 species, found largely in the tropics. They are 4–11 in/9–23 cm long, with brown or gray plumage, long, pointed wings, and usually a forked tail. They are capable of flying 70 mph/110 kph.

The chimney swift *Chaetura pelagica*, which breeds in North America, is 5.5 in/13 cm long, with a cigar-shaped body and a short, stubby, superficially unforked tail.

Swift Jonathan 1667–1745. Irish satirist and Anglican cleric. He wrote *Gulliver's Travels* 1726, an allegory describing travel to lands inhabited by giants, miniature people, and intelligent horses. Other works include *The Tale of a Tub* 1704, attacking corruption in religion and learning; contributions to the Tory paper *The Examiner*, of which he was editor 1710–11; the satirical *A Modest Proposal* 1729, which suggested that children of the poor should be eaten; and many essays and pamphlets.

swimming self-propulsion of the body through water. As a competitive sport there are four strokes: crawl, breaststroke, backstroke, and butterfly. (In freestyle events, the crawl is usually used, since it is the "fastest" stroke for most swimmers; but any stroke may be used.) Distances of races vary from 25 yards up to the mile or more. Swimming meets are held in pools and at beach clubs (for the events longer than the mile).

swing music jazz style popular in the 1930s–40s, a big-band dance music with a simple harmonic base of varying tempo from the rhythm section (percussion, guitar, piano), harmonic brass and woodwind sections (sometimes strings), and superimposed solo melodic line from, for example, trumpet, clarinet, or saxophone. Exponents included Benny Goodman, Duke Ellington, and Glenn Miller, who introduced jazz to a mass white audience.

Switzerland Swiss Confederation (German *Schweiz*, French *Suisse*, Romansch *Svizra*) *area* 15,946 sq mi/41,300 sq km *capital* Bern *towns and cities* Zürich, Geneva, Lausanne; river port Basel (on the Rhine) *physical* most mountainous country in Europe (Alps and Jura mountains); highest peak Dufourspitze 15,203 ft/4,634 m in Apennines *environment* an estimated 43% of coniferous trees, particularly in the central Alpine region, have been killed by acid rain, 90% of which comes from other countries. Over 50% of bird species are classified as threatened *features* winter sports area of the upper valley of the river Inn (Engadine); lakes Maggiore, Lucerne, Geneva, Constance *head of state and government* Otto Stich from 1994 *government* federal democratic republic *political parties* Radical Democratic Party (FDP),

radical, center-left; Social Democratic Party (SPS), moderate, left of center; Christian Democratic People's Party (PDC), Christian, moderate, centrist; Swiss People's Party (SVP), center-left; Liberal Party (PLS), federalist, center-left; Green Party, ecological *exports* electrical goods, chemicals, pharmaceuticals, watches, precision instruments, confectionery *currency* Swiss franc *population* (1993) 6,900,000; growth rate 0.2% p.a. *life expectancy* men 75, women 81 *languages* German 65%, French 18%, Italian 12%, Romansch 1% (all official) *religions* Roman Catholic 50%, Protestant 48% *literacy* 99% *GNP* $32,250 per head (1991) *chronology 1648* Became independent of the Holy Roman Empire. *1798–1815* Helvetic Republic established by French revolutionary armies. *1847* Civil war resulted in greater centralization. *1874* Principle of the referendum introduced. *1971* Women given the vote in federal elections. *1984* First female cabinet minister appointed. *1986* Referendum rejected proposal for membership in United Nations. *1989* Referendum supported abolition of citizen army and military service requirements. *1991* 18-year-olds allowed to vote for first time in national elections. Four-party coalition remained in power. *1992* Closer ties with European Community (now European Union) rejected in national referendum. *1994* Otto Stich appointed president, with Kaspar Villiger as vice president.

swordfish marine bony fish *Xiphias gladius*, the only member of its family (Xiphiidae), characterized by a long swordlike beak protruding from the upper jaw. It may reach 15 ft/4.5 m in length and weigh 1000 lb/450 kg.

sycamore or *plane tree* any of several Eurasian trees of the genus *Platanus* of the family Plantanaceae. Species include the oriental plane tree *P. orientalis*, a favorite of the Greeks and Romans; the American sycamore *P. occidentalis* of the eastern US; and the Arizona sycamore *P. wrightii*.

All species have pendulous burrlike fruits and some grow to 100 ft/30 m high.

Sydney capital and port of New South Wales, Australia; population (1990) 3,656,900. Industries include engineering, oil refining, electronics, scientific equipment, chemicals, clothing, and furniture. It is a financial center, and has three universities. The 19th-century Museum of Applied Arts and Sciences is the most popular museum in Australia.

syllogism set of philosophical statements devised by Aristotle in his work on logic. It establishes the conditions under which a valid conclusion follows or does not follow by deduction from given premises. The following is an example of a valid syllogism: "All men are mortal, Socrates is a man, therefore Socrates is mortal."

symbiosis any close relationship between two organisms of different species, and one where both partners benefit from the association. A well-known example is the pollination relationship between insects and flowers, where the insects feed on nectar and carry pollen from one flower to another. This is sometimes known as ◊mutualism.

Strictly speaking, symbiosis refers to continuous, intimate contact between mutually benefiting species, such as the fungus and alga in ◊lichen.

symbolism in the arts, the use of symbols as a device for concentrating or intensifying meaning. In particular, the term is used for a late 19th-century movement in

French poetry, associated with Paul Verlaine, Stéphane Mallarmé, and Arthur Rimbaud, who used words for their symbolic rather than concrete meaning.

Symbolism late 19th-century movement in French poetry, which inspired a similar trend in French painting. The Symbolist painters rejected Realism and Impressionism, seeking to express moods and psychological states through color, line, and form. Their subjects were often mythological, mystical, or fantastic. Statuesque female figures were often used to embody qualities or emotions. Gustave Moreau was a leading Symbolist painter. Other Symbolist painters include Puvis de Chavannes and Odilon Redon in France, and Edward Burne-Jones in the UK.

symmetry exact likeness in shape about a given line (axis), point, or plane. A figure has symmetry if one half can be rotated and/or reflected onto the other. (Symmetry preserves length, angle, but not necessarily orientation.) In a wider sense, symmetry exits if a change in the system leaves the essential features of the system unchanged; for example, reversing the sign of electric charges does not change the electrical behavior of an arrangement of charges.

symphony abstract musical composition for orchestra, traditionally in four separate but closely related movements. It developed from the smaller ◊sonata form, the Italian ◊overture, and the concerto grosso.

synagogue Jewish place of worship, also called a temple by the non-Orthodox. As an institution it dates from the destruction of the Temple in Jerusalem AD 70, although it had been developing from the time of the Babylonian Exile as a substitute for the Temple. In antiquity it was a public meeting hall where the Torah was also read, but today it is used primarily for prayer and services. A service requires a quorum (*minyan*) of ten adult Jewish men.

synapse junction between two ◊nerve cells, or between a nerve cell and a muscle (a neuromuscular junction), across which a nerve impulse is transmitted. The two cells are separated by a narrow gap called the *synaptic cleft*. The gap is bridged by a chemical ◊neurotransmitter, released by the nerve impulse.

syndicalism political movement in 19th-century Europe that rejected parliamentary activity in favor of direct action, culminating in a revolutionary general strike to secure worker ownership and control of industry. After 1918 syndicalism was absorbed in communism, although it continued to have an independent existence in Spain until the late 1930s.

synesthesia the experience of one sense as a result of the stimulation of a different sense; for example, an experience of color may result from hearing a sound. This experience is sometimes imitated in the arts. The poet Baudelaire used the phrase "scarlet fanfare", while composers, such as Skryabin and Schoenberg, asked for colors to be projected to accompany their works, for example, Skryabin's *Poem of Fire* 1913.

Synge J(ohn) M(illington) 1871–1909. Irish dramatist. He was a leading figure in the Irish dramatic revival of the early 20th century. His six plays reflect the speech patterns of the Aran Islands and W Ireland. They include *In the Shadow of the Glen* 1903, *Riders to the Sea* 1904, and *The Playboy of the Western World* 1907, which caused riots at the Abbey Theatre, Dublin, when first performed.

synthesis in chemistry, the formation of a substance or compound from more elementary compounds. The synthesis of a drug can involve several stages from the initial material to the final product; the complexity of these stages is a major factor in the cost of production.

synthesizer device that uses electrical components to produce sounds. In *preset synthesizers*, the sound of various instruments is produced by a built-in computer-type memory. In *programmable synthesizers* any number of new instrumental or other sounds may be produced at the will of the performer. *Speech synthesizers* can break down speech into 128 basic elements (allophones), which are then combined into words and sentences, as in the voices of electronic teaching aids.

synthetic any material made from chemicals. Since the 1900s, more and more of the materials used in everyday life are synthetics, including plastics (polythene, polystyrene), synthetic fibers (nylon, acrylics, polyesters), synthetic resins, and synthetic rubber. Most naturally occurring organic substances are now made synthetically, especially pharmaceuticals.

syphilis sexually transmitted disease caused by the spiral-shaped bacterium (spirochete) *Treponema pallidum*. Untreated, it runs its course in three stages over many years, often starting with a painless hard sore, or chancre, developing within a month on the area of infection (usually the genitals). The second stage, months later, is a rash with arthritis, hepatitis, and/or meningitis. The third stage, years later, leads eventually to paralysis, blindness, insanity, and death. The Wassermann test is a diagnostic blood test for syphilis.

Syracuse industrial city on Lake Onondaga, in New York State; population (1990) 163,900. Industries include the manufacture of electrical and other machinery, paper, and food processing.

There are canal links with the ◊Great Lakes, and the Hudson and St Lawrence rivers.

Syracuse University is here. Syracuse was settled in the 1780s on the site of a former Iroquois capital and developed as a salt-mining center.

Syria Syrian Arab Republic (*al-Jamhuriya al-Arabya as-Suriya*) *area* 71,506 sq mi/185,200 sq km *capital* Damascus *towns and cities* Aleppo, Homs, Hama; chief port Latakia *physical* mountains alternate with fertile plains and desert areas; Euphrates River *features* Mount Hermon, Golan Heights; crusader castles (including Krak des Chevaliers); Phoenician city sites (Ugarit), ruins of ancient Palmyra *head of state and*

government Hafez al-Assad from 1971 *political system* socialist republic *political parties* National Progressive Front (NPF), pro-Arab, socialist; Communist Action Party, socialist *exports* cotton, cereals, oil, phosphates, tobacco *currency* Syrian pound *population* (1993) 13,400,000; growth rate 3.5% p.a. *life expectancy* men 65, women 69 *languages* Arabic 89% (official), Kurdish 6%, Armenian 3% *religions* Sunni Muslim 74%; ruling minority Alawite, and other Islamic sects 16%; Christian 10% *literacy* men 78%, women 51% *GNP* $1,110 per head (1991) *chronology 1946* Achieved full independence from France. *1958* Merged with Egypt to form the United Arab Republic (UAR). *1961* UAR disintegrated. *1967* Six-Day War resulted in the loss of territory to Israel. *1970–71* Syria supported Palestinian guerrillas against Jordanian troops. *1971* Following a bloodless coup, Hafez al-Assad became president. *1973* Israel consolidated its control of the Golan Heights after the Yom Kippur War. *1976* Substantial numbers of troops committed to the civil war in Lebanon. *1978* Assad reelected. *1981–82* Further military engagements in Lebanon. *1982* Islamic militant uprising suppressed; 5,000 dead. *1984* Presidents Assad and Gemayel approved plans for government of national unity in Lebanon. *1985* Assad secured the release of 39 US hostages held in an aircraft hijacked by extremist Shiite group, Hezbollah. Assad reelected. *1987* Improved relations with US and attempts to secure the release of Western hostages in Lebanon. *1989* Diplomatic relations with Morocco restored.

Continued fighting in Lebanon; Syrian forces reinforced in Lebanon; diplomatic relations with Egypt restored. *1990* Diplomatic relations with Britain restored. *1991* Syria fought against Iraq in Gulf War. President Assad agreed to US Middle East peace plan. Assad re-elected president. *1993* Syria joined Iraq and other Arab countries in boycotting United Nations treaty outlawing production and use of chemical weapons. *1994* Israeli offer of partial withdrawal from Golan Heights.

system flow chart type of ◊flow chart used to describe the flow of data through a particular computer system.

system implementation in computing, the process of installing a new computer system.

systems design in computing, the detailed design of an application package. The designer breaks the system down into component programs and designs the required input forms, screen layouts, and printouts. Systems design forms a link between systems analysis and ◊programming.

systems program in computing, a program that performs a task related to the operation and performance of the computer system itself. For example, a systems program might control the operation of the display screen, or control and organize backing storage. In contrast, an ◊applications program is designed to carry out tasks for the benefit of the computer user.

Szechwan alternative spelling for the central Chinese province of ◊Sichuan.

Table Bay wide bay on the north coast of the Cape of Good Hope, South Africa, on which Cape Town stands. It is overlooked by *Table Mountain* (highest point Maclear's Beacon 3,568 ft/1,087 m), the cloud that often hangs above it being known as the "table-cloth".

table tennis or *ping pong* indoor game played on a rectangular table by two or four players. It was developed in Britain about 1880 and derived from lawn tennis. World championships were first held 1926.

Tacitus Publius Cornelius c. AD 55–c. 120. Roman historian. A public orator in Rome, he was consul under Nerva 97–98 and proconsul of Asia 112–113. He wrote histories of the Roman Empire, *Annales* and *Historiae*, covering the years AD 14–68 and 69–97 respectively. He also wrote a *Life of Agricola* 97 (he married Agricola's daughter 77) and a description of the Germanic tribes, *Germania* 98.

Taegu third-largest city in South Korea, situated between Seoul and Pusan; population (1990) 2,228,800. Nearby is the Haeinsa Temple, one of the country's largest monasteries and repository of the *Triptaka Koreana*, a collection of 80,000 wood blocks on which the Buddhist scriptures are carved. Grain, fruit, textiles, and tobacco are produced.

tae kwon do Korean ◊martial art similar to ◊karate, which includes punching and kicking. It was included in the 1988 Olympic Games as a demonstration sport.

Taft Robert Alphonso 1889–1953. US right-wing Republican senator from 1939, and a candidate for the presidential nomination 1940, 1944, 1948, and 1952. He sponsored the Taft–Hartley Labor Act 1947, restricting union power. He was the son of President William Taft.

Taft William Howard 1857–1930. 27th president of the US 1909–13, a Republican. He was secretary of war 1904–08 in Theodore Roosevelt's administration, but as president his conservatism provoked Roosevelt to stand against him in the 1912 election. Taft served as chief justice of the Supreme Court 1921–30.

Tagalog member of the majority ethnic group living around Manila on the island of Luzon, in the Philippines, who number about 10 million (1988). The Tagalog live by fishing and trading. In its standardized form, known as Pilipino, Tagalog is the official language of the Philippines, and belongs to the Western branch of the Austronesian family. The Tagalog religion is a mixture of animism, Christianity, and Islam.

tagging, electronic long-distance monitoring of the movements of people charged with or convicted of a crime, thus enabling them to be detained in their homes rather than in prison.

Tagore Rabindranath 1861–1941. Bengali Indian writer. He translated into English his own verse *Gitanjali* ("song offerings") 1912 and his verse play *Chitra* 1896. Nobel Prize for Literature 1913.

Taft, William Howard William Taft, 27th US president and later chief justice, the only person to have headed both the executive and the judicial branches of the US government. As chief justice of the US Supreme Court, Taft improved the efficiency of the judicial machinery by securing the passage of the Judiciary Act 1925.

Tahiti largest of the Society Islands, in ◊French Polynesia; area 402 sq mi/1,042 sq km; population (1983) 116,000. Its capital is Papeete. Tahiti was visited by Capt James ◊Cook 1769 and by Admiral ◊Bligh of the *Bounty* 1788. It came under French control 1843 and became a colony 1880.

Tai member of any of the groups of SE Asian peoples who speak Tai languages, all of which belong to the Sino-Tibetan language family. There are over 60 million speakers, the majority of whom live in Thailand. Tai peoples are also found in SW China, NW Myanmar (Burma), Laos, and N Vietnam.

T'ai Chi series of 108 complex, slow-motion movements, each named (for example, the White Crane Spreads Its Wings) and designed to ensure effective circulation of the *chi*, or intrinsic energy of the universe, through the mind and body. It derives partly from the Shaolin ◊martial arts of China and partly from ◊Taoism.

Taipei or *Taibei* capital and commercial center of Taiwan; population (1990) 2,719,700. Industries include electronics, plastics, textiles, and machinery. The National Palace Museum 1965 houses the world's greatest collection of Chinese art, brought here from the mainland 1948.

Taiping Rebellion popular revolt 1850–64 that undermined China's Qing dynasty. By 1853 the rebels had secured control over much of the central and lower Chang Jiang valley region, instituting radical, populist land reforms. Civil war continued until 1864, when the Taipings, weakened by internal dissension, were overcome by the provincial Hunan army of Zeng Guofan and the Ever-Victorious Army, led by American F T Ward and British soldier Charles Gordon.

Taiwan Republic of China (*Chung Hua Min Kuo*) *area* 13,965 sq mi/36,179 sq km *capital* Taipei *towns and cities* ports Kaohsiung, Keelung *physical* island (formerly Formosa) off People's Republic of China; mountainous, with lowlands in W *environment* industrialization has taken its toll: an estimated 30% of the annual rice crop is dangerously contaminated with mercury, cadmium, and other heavy metals *features* Penghu (Pescadores), Jinmen (Quemoy), Mazu (Matsu) islands *head of state* Lee Teng-hui from 1988 *head of government* Lien Chan from 1993 *political system* emergent democracy *political parties* Nationalist Party of China (Kuomintang: KMT), anticommunist, Chinese nationalist; Democratic Progressive Party (DPP), centrist-pluralist, pro-self-determination grouping; Workers' Party (kuntang), left of center *exports* textiles, steel, plastics, electronics, foodstuffs *currency* New Taiwan dollar *population* (1993 est) 21,000,000 (Taiwanese 84%, mainlanders 14%); growth rate 1.4% p.a. *life expectancy* 70 men, 75 women *languages* Mandarin Chinese (official); Taiwan, Hakka dialects *religions* officially atheist; Taoist, Confucian, Buddhist, Christian *literacy* 91% GNP \$8,815 per head (1991) *chronology 1683* Taiwan (Formosa) annexed by China. *1895* Ceded to Japan. *1945* Recovered by China. *1949* Flight of Nationalist government to Taiwan after Chinese communist revolution. *1954* US–Taiwanese mutual defense treaty. *1971* Expulsion from United Nations. *1972* Commencement of legislature elections. *1975* President Chiang Kai-shek died; replaced as Kuomintang leader by his son, Chiang Ching-kuo. *1979* US severed diplomatic relations and annulled 1954 security pact. *1986* DPP formed as opposition to the nationalist Kuomintang. *1987* Martial law lifted; opposition parties legalized; press restrictions lifted. *1988* President Chiang Ching-kuo died; replaced by Taiwanese-born Lee Teng-hui. *1989* Kuomintang won assembly elections. *1990* Formal move toward normalization of relations with China. Hau Pei-tsun became prime minister. *1991* President Lee Teng-hui declared end to civil war with China. Constitution amended. Kuomintang won landslide victory in assembly elections. *1992* Diplomatic relations with South Korea severed. Dec: Kuomintang lost support to DPP in first fully democratic elections but still secured majority of seats. *1993* Lien Chan appointed prime minister. Cooperation pact with China signed. *1995* Cabinet approved easing ban on transportation links with China.

Tajikistan Republic of *area* 55,251 sq mi/143,100 sq km *capital* Dushanbe *towns and cities* Khodzhent (formerly Leninabad), Kurgan-Tyube, Kulyab *physical* mountainous, more than half of its territory lying above 10,000 ft/3,000 m; huge mountain glaciers, which are the source of many rapid rivers *features* Pik Kommunizma (Communism Peak); health resorts and mineral springs *head of state* Imamali Rakhmanov from 1992 *head of government* Abduljalil Samadov from 1993 *political system* emergent democracy *political parties* Socialist (formerly Communist) Party of Tajikistan (SPT); Democratic Party; Islamic Revival Party *products* fruit, cereals, cotton, cattle, sheep, silks, carpets, coal, lead, zinc, chemicals, oil, gas *currency* Russian ruble *population* (1993 est) 5,700,000 (Tajik 63%, Uzbek 24%, Russian 8%, Tatar 1%, Kyrgyz 1%, Ukrainian 1%) *life expectancy* men 67, women 72 *language* Tajik, similar to Farsi (Persian) *religion* Sunni Muslim *GNP* \$1,050 per head (1991) *chronology 1921* Part of Turkestan Soviet Socialist Autonomous Republic. *1929* Became a constituent republic of USSR. *1990* Ethnic Tajik-Armenian conflict in Dushanbe resulted in rioting against Communist Party of Tajikistan (CPT); state of emergency and curfew imposed. *1991* Jan: curfew lifted in Dushanbe. March: maintenance of Soviet Union endorsed in referendum; President Makhkamov forced to resign after failed anti-Gorbachev coup; CPT broke links with Moscow. Sept: declared independence; Rakhman Nabiyev, former CPT leader, elected president; CPT renamed Socialist Party of Tajikistan; state of emergency declared. Dec: joined new Commonwealth of Independent States (CIS). *1992* Feb: joined the Muslim Economic Cooperation Organization. March: admitted into United Nations; US diplomatic recognition achieved. Violent anti-Nabiyev demonstrations by Islamic and prodemocracy groups. Sept: Nabiyev forced to resign; chairman of the Supreme Soviet, Akbasho Iskandrov, took over as interim head of state. Civil war between pro-and anti-Nabiyev forces. Nov: Iskandrov resigned; office of president abolished; Imamali Rakhmanov took over as chairman of the Supreme Soviet (effective head of state). Human rights violations alleged. *1993* Jan: government forces regained control of most of country. March: CIS peacekeeping forces drafted in. Aug: amnesty offered to rebels. Sept: cease-fire announced.

Taj Mahal white marble mausoleum built 1630–53 on the river Jumna near Agra, India. Erected by Shah Jahan to the memory of his favorite wife, it is a celebrated example of Indo-Islamic architecture, the fusion of Muslim and Hindu styles.

takahe flightless bird *Porphyrio mantelli* of the rail family, native to New Zealand. It is about 2 ft/60 cm tall, with blue and green plumage and a red beak. The takahe was thought to have become extinct at the end of the 19th century, but in 1948 small numbers were rediscovered in the tussock grass of a mountain valley on South Island.

takeover in business, the acquisition by one company of a sufficient number of shares in another company to have effective control of that company—usually 51%, although it may be as little as 30%.

talc $Mg_3Si_4O_{10}(OH)_2$, mineral, hydrous magnesium silicate. It occurs in tabular crystals, but the massive impure form, known as *steatite* or *soapstone*, is more common. It is formed by the alteration of magnesium compounds and usually found in metamorphic rocks. Talc is very soft, ranked 1 on the Mohs' scale of hardness. It is used as talcum powder in cosmetics, lubricants, and as an additive in paper manufacture.

Taligent joint ◊IBM/◊Apple project to develop an object-oriented operating system. Taligent's rivals are NeXTStep and Cairo.

Tallahassee capital of Florida; an agricultural and lumbering center; population (1990) 124,800. The Spanish explorer Hernando ◊de Soto founded an Indian settlement here 1539, and the site was chosen as the Florida territorial capital 1821.

Florida State University and Florida Agricultural and Mechanical University are here.

Talleyrand Charles Maurice de Talleyrand-Périgord 1754–1838. French politician and diplomat. As bishop of Autun 1789–91 he supported moderate reform during the ◊French Revolution, was excommunicated by the pope, and fled to the US during the Reign of Terror (persecution of antirevolutionaries). He returned and became foreign minister under the Directory 1797–99 and under Napoleon 1799–1807. He represented France at the Congress of Vienna 1814–15.

Tallinn (German *Reval*) naval port and capital of Estonia; population (1987) 478,000. Industries include electrical and oil-drilling machinery, textiles, and paper. Founded 1219, it was a member of the ◊Hanseatic League; it passed to Sweden 1561 and to Russia 1750. Vyshgorod castle (13th century) and other medieval buildings remain. It is a yachting center.

Tallis Thomas *c.* 1505–1585. English composer. He was a master of ◊counterpoint. His works include *Tallis's Canon* ("Glory to thee my God this night") 1567, the antiphonal *Spem in alium non habui* (about 1573) for 40 voices in various groupings, and a collection of 34 motets, *Cantiones sacrae*, 1575 (of which 16 are by Tallis and 18 by Byrd).

Talmud the two most important works of post-Biblical Jewish literature. The Babylonian and the Palestinian (or Jerusalem) Talmud provide a compilation of ancient Jewish law and tradition. The Babylonian Talmud was edited at the end of the 5th century AD and is the more authoritative version for later Judaism; both Talmuds are written in a mix of Hebrew and Aramaic. They contain the commentary (*gemara*) on the *Mishna* (early rabbinical commentaries compiled about AD 200), and the material can be generally divided into *halakhah*, consisting of legal and ritual matters, and *haggadah*, concerned with ethical, theological, and folklorist matters.

tamarind evergreen tropical tree *Tamarindus indica*, family Leguminosae, native to the Old World, with pinnate leaves and reddish yellow flowers, followed by pods. The pulp surrounding the seeds is used medicinally and as a flavoring.

tamarisk any small tree or shrub of the genus *Tamarix*, flourishing in warm, salty, desert regions of Europe and Asia where no other vegetation is found. The common tamarisk *T. gallica* has scalelike leaves and spikes of very small, pink flowers.

tambourine musical percussion instrument of ancient origin, almost unchanged since Roman times, consisting of a shallow drum with a single skin and loosely set jingles in the rim that accentuate the beat.

Tamerlane or *Tamburlaine* or *Timur i Leng* ("Timur the Lame") 1336–1405. Mongol ruler of Samarkand, in Uzbekistan, from 1369 who conquered Persia, Azerbaijan, Armenia, and Georgia. He defeated the ◊Golden Horde 1395, sacked Delhi 1398, invaded Syria and Anatolia, and captured the Ottoman sultan in Ankara 1402; he died invading China. He was a descendant of the Mongol leader Genghis Khan and the great-grandfather of Babur, founder of the Mogul Empire.

Tamil member of the majority ethnic group living in the Indian state of Tamil Nadu (formerly Madras). Tamils also live in S India, N Sri Lanka, Malaysia, Singapore, and South Africa, totaling 35–55 million worldwide. Tamil belongs to the Dravidian family of languages; written records in Tamil date from the 3rd century BC. The 3 million Tamils in Sri Lanka are predominantly Hindu, unlike the Sinhalese, the majority group in Sri Lanka, who are mainly Buddhist. The *Tamil Tigers*, most prominent of the various Tamil groupings, are attempting to create a separate homeland in N Sri Lanka through both political and military means.

tamoxifen ◊estrogen-blocking drug used to treat breast cancer and also infertility. It kills cancer cells by preventing formation of the tiny blood vessels that supply the tumor. Without a blood supply the tumor shrinks as its cells die. Side effects include hot flushes, skin rashes, vaginal discharge, and more rarely, endometrial cancer. Trials are underway to investigate its potential for preventing breast cancer in healthy women with a family history of the disease.

Tampa port and resort on Tampa Bay in W Florida; population (1990) 280,000. Industries include fruit and vegetable canning, shipbuilding, and the manufacture of fertilizers, clothing, beer, and cigars.

The University of South Florida and Busch Gardens are here. Economic growth was spurred in the 1880s by the discovery of phosphates in the area, the arrival of the railroad, and the establishment of a cigar-making industry.

Tampere (Swedish *Tammerfors*) city in SW Finland; population (1990) 172,600, metropolitan area 258,000. Industries include textiles, paper, footwear, and turbines. It is the second-largest city in Finland.

tanager any of various New World passerine birds, of the family Emberizidae, which also includes ◊blackbirds, ◊orioles, and grackles. Tanagers that breed in N America all belong to the genus *Piranga* and include the scarlet tanager *P. olivacea*, about 7 in/18 cm long. There are about 230 species in forests of Central and South America; all males are brilliantly colored.

Tanganyika, Lake lake 2,534 ft/772 m above sea level in the Great Rift Valley, E Africa, with Zaire to the W, Zambia to the S, and Tanzania and Burundi to the E. It is about 400 mi/645 km long, with an area of about

tanager *The male scarlet tanager is distinguished by its bright red plumage and black wings and tail. It lives in the canopy of deciduous woodland in central and eastern US.*

12,000 sq mi/31,000 sq km, and is the deepest lake (4,710 ft/1,435 m) in Africa. The mountains around its shores rise to about 8,860 ft/2,700 m. The chief ports on the lake are Bujumbura (Burundi), Kigoma (Tanzania), and Kalémié (Zaire).

Tang dynasty the greatest of China's imperial dynasties, which ruled 618–907. Founded by the sui official Li Yuan (566–635), it extended Chinese authority into central Asia, Tibet, Korea, and Annam, establishing what was then the world's largest empire. The dynasty's peak was reached during the reign (712–56) of Emperor Minghuang (Hsuan-tsung).

tangent in geometry, a straight line that touches a curve and gives the gradient of the curve at the point of contact. At a maximum, minimum, or point of inflection, the tangent to a curve has zero gradient. Also, in trigonometry, a function of an acute angle in a right triangle, defined as the ratio of the length of the side opposite the angle to the length of the side adjacent to it; a way of expressing the gradient of a line.

tangerine small ◊orange *Citrus reticulata*.

Tangier or *Tangiers* or *Tanger* port in N Morocco, on the Strait of Gibraltar; population (1982) 436,227. It was a Phoenician trading center in the 15th century BC. Captured by the Portuguese 1471, it passed to England 1662 as part of the dowry of Catherine of Braganza, but was abandoned 1684, and later became a lair of ◊Barbary Coast pirates. From 1923 Tangier and a small surrounding enclave became an international zone, administered by Spain 1940–45. In 1956 it was transferred to independent Morocco and became a free port 1962.

tango dance for couples, developed in Argentina during the early 20th century, or the music for it. The dance consists of two long sliding steps followed by three short steps and stylized body positions. The music is in moderately slow duple time (2/4) and employs syncopated rhythms.

tank armored fighting vehicle that runs on tracks and is fitted with weapons systems capable of defeating other tanks and destroying life and property. The term was originally a code name for the first effective tracked and armored fighting vehicle, invented by the British soldier and scholar Ernest Swinton, and first used in the Battle of the Somme 1916.

tansy perennial herb *Tanacetum vulgare*, family Compositae, native to Europe. The yellow flower heads grow in clusters on stalks up to 4 ft tall/120 cm and the aromatic leaves are used in cooking.

tantalum hard, ductile, lustrous, gray-white, metallic element, symbol Ta, atomic number 73, atomic weight 180.948. It occurs with niobium in tantalite and other minerals. It can be drawn into wire with a very high melting point and great tenacity, useful for lamp filaments subject to vibration. It is also used in alloys, for corrosion-resistant laboratory apparatus and chemical equipment, as a catalyst in manufacturing synthetic rubber, in tools and instruments, and in rectifiers and capacitors.

Tantalus in Greek mythology, a king who deceived the gods by serving them human flesh at a banquet. His crimes were punished in Tartarus (a part of the underworld) by the provision of food and drink he could not reach. He was the father of Pelops.

Tantrism forms of Hinduism and Buddhism that emphasize the division of the universe into male and female forces that maintain its unity by their interaction. Tantric Hinduism is associated with magical and sexual yoga practices that imitate the union of Siva and Sakti, as described in scriptures known as the *Tantras*. In Buddhism, the *Tantras* are texts attributed to the Buddha, describing methods of attaining enlightenment.

Tanzania United Republic of (*Jamhuri ya Muungano wa Tanzania*) *area* 364,865 sq mi/945,000 sq km *capital* Dodoma (since 1983) *towns and cities* Zanzibar Town, Mwanza; chief port and former capital Dar es Salaam *physical* central plateau; lakes in N and W; coastal plains; lakes Victoria, Tanganyika, and Nyasa *environment* the black rhino faces extinction as a result of poaching *features* comprises islands of Zanzibar and Pemba; Mount Kilimanjaro, 19,340 ft/ 5,895 m, the highest peak in Africa; Serengeti National Park, Olduvai Gorge; Ngorongoro Crater, 9 mi/ 14.5 km across, 2,500 ft/762 m deep *head of state and government* Ali Hassan Mwinyi from 1985 *political system* transitional *political parties* Revolutionary Party of Tanzania (CCM), African, socialist, the only legal party until 1992. Opposition groups have since been formed *exports* coffee, cotton, sisal, cloves, tea, tobacco, cashew nuts, diamonds *currency* Tanzanian shilling *population* (1993 est) 28,200,000; growth rate 3.5% p.a. *life expectancy* men 49, women 54 *languages* Kiswahili, English (both official) *religions* Muslim 35%, Christian 35%, traditional 30% *literacy* 65% *GNP* $2,424 million (1991). GNP per capita $100. *chronology 16th–17th centuries* Zanzibar under Portuguese control. *1890–1963* Zanzibar a British protectorate. *1920–46* Tanganyika administered as a British League of Nations mandate. *1946–62* Tanganyika under United Nations (UN) trusteeship. *1961* Tanganyika achieved independence from Britain, within the Commonwealth, with Julius Nyerere as prime minister. *1962* Tanganyika became a republic with Nyerere as president. *1964* Tanganyika and Zanzibar became the United Republic of Tanzania with Nyerere as president. *1967* East African Community (EAC) formed. Nyerere committed himself to building a socialist state (the Arusha Declaration). *1977* Revolutionary Party of Tanzania (CCM) proclaimed the only legal party. EAC dissolved. *1978* Ugandan forces repulsed after crossing into Tanzania. *1979* Tanzanian troops sent to Uganda to help overthrow the president, Idi Amin. *1985* Nyerere retired from presidency but stayed on as CCM leader; Ali Hassan Mwinyi became president. *1990* Nyerere surrendered CCM leadership; replaced by President Mwinyi. *1992* CCM agreed to abolish one-party rule; multiparty system approved. *1993* Referendum promised on issue of separate governments for the mainland and Zanzibar.

Taoism Chinese philosophical system, traditionally founded by the Chinese philosopher Lao Zi 6th century BC. He is also attributed authorship of the scriptures, *Tao Te Ching*, although these were apparently compiled 3rd century BC. The "tao" or "way" denotes the hidden principle of the universe, and less stress is laid on good deeds than on harmonious interaction with the environment, which automatically ensures right behavior. The magical side of Taoism is illustrated by the *I Ching* or *Book of Changes*, a book of divination.

tap dancing rapid step dance, derived from clog dancing. Its main characteristic is the tapping of toes and heels accentuated by steel taps affixed to the shoes. It was popularized in vaudeville and in 1930s films by such dancers as Fred Astaire and Bill "Bojangles" Robinson (1878–1949).

tape recording, magnetic method of recording electric signals on a layer of iron oxide, or other magnetic material, coating a thin plastic tape. The electrical signals from the microphone are fed to the electromagnetic recording head, which magnetizes the tape in accordance with the frequency and amplitude of the original signal. The impulses may be audio (for sound recording), video (for television), or data (for computer). For playback, the tape is passed over the same, or another, head to convert magnetic into electrical signals, which are then amplified for reproduction. Tapes are easily demagnetized (erased) for reuse, and come in cassette, cartridge, or reel form.

tapeworm any of various parasitic flatworms of the class Cestoda. They lack digestive and sense organs, can reach 50 ft/15 m in length, and attach themselves to the host's intestines by means of hooks and suckers. Tapeworms are made up of hundreds of individual segments, each of which develops into a functional hermaphroditic reproductive unit capable of producing numerous eggs. The larvae of tapeworms usually reach humans in imperfectly cooked meat or fish, causing anemia and intestinal disorders.

tapioca granular starch used in cooking, produced from the ◊cassava root.

tapir any of the odd-toed hoofed mammals (perissodactyls) of the single genus *Tapirus*, now constituting the family Tapiridae. There are four species living in the American and Malaysian tropics. They reach 3 ft/1 m at the shoulder and weigh up to 770 lb/350 kg. Their survival is in danger because of destruction of the forests.

Tapirs have thick, hairy, black skin, short tails, and short trunks. They are vegetarian, harmless, and shy. They are related to the ◊rhinoceros, and slightly more distantly to the horse.

Their general body form is rounded in back and tapering up front, with a short tail and a short trunk.

taproot in botany, a single, robust, main ◊root that is derived from the embryonic root, or radicle, and grows vertically downward, often to considerable depth. Taproots are often modified for food storage and are common in biennial plants such as the carrot *Daucus carota*, where they act as ◊perennating organs.

tar dark brown or black viscous liquid obtained by the destructive distillation of coal, shale, and wood. Tars consist of a mixture of hydrocarbons, acids, and bases. Creosote and ◊paraffin are produced from wood tar.

tarantella S Italian dance in very fast compound time (6/8); also a piece of music composed for, or in the rhythm of, this dance. Although commonly believed to be named for the tarantula spider, it is more likely named for the S Italian town of Taranto. It became popular during the 19th century, several composers writing tarantellas employing a perpetuum mobile in order to generate intense energy. Examples include those by Chopin, Liszt, and Weber.

Taranto naval base and port in Puglia region, SE Italy; population (1988) 245,000. It is an important commercial center, and its steelworks are part of the new industrial complex of S Italy. It was the site of the ancient Greek *Tarentum*, founded in the 8th century BC by ◊Sparta, and was captured by the Romans 272 BC.

tarantula Any of the numerous large, hairy spiders of the family *Theraphosidae*, with large poison fangs, native to the SW US and tropical America. The name is also used for the wolf spider *Lycosa tarantula* with a 1 in/2.5 cm body. It spins no web, relying on its speed in hunting to catch its prey.

tariff tax or duty placed on goods when they are imported into a country or trading bloc (such as the European Union) from outside. The aim of tariffs is to reduce imports by making them more expensive.

taro or *eddo* plant *Colocasia esculenta* of the arum family Araceae, native to tropical Asia; the tubers are edible and are the source of Polynesian poi (a fermented food).

tarot cards fortune-telling aid consisting of 78 cards: the *minor arcana* in four suits (resembling playing cards) and the *major arcana*, 22 cards with densely symbolic illustrations that have links with astrology and the ◊kabbala.

Tarquinius Superbus (Tarquin the Proud) Last king of Rome 534–510 BC. He abolished certain rights of Romans, and made the city powerful. According to legend, he was deposed when his son Sextus raped Lucretia.

tarragon perennial bushy herb *Artemisia dracunculus* of the daisy family Compositae, native to the Old World, growing to 5 ft/1.5 m, with narrow leaves and small green-white flower heads arranged in groups. Tarragon contains an aromatic oil; its leaves are used to flavor salads, pickles, and tartar sauce. It is closely related to wormwood.

tarsier any of three species of the prosimian primates, genus *Tarsius*, of the East Indies and the Philippines. These survivors of early primates are about the size of a rat with thick, light-brown fur, very large eyes, and long feet and hands. They are nocturnal, arboreal, and eat insects and lizards.

tartan woolen cloth woven in specific checkered patterns individual to Scottish clans, with stripes of different widths and colors crisscrossing on a colored background; it is used in making skirts, kilts, trousers, and other articles of clothing.

Tarzan fictitious hero inhabiting the African rainforest, created by US writer Edgar Rice ◊Burroughs in *Tarzan of the Apes* 1914, with numerous sequels. He and his partner Jane have featured in films, comic strips, and television series.

Tashkent capital of Uzbekistan; population (1990) 2,100,000. Industries include the manufacture of mining machinery, chemicals, textiles, and leather goods. Founded in the 7th century, it was taken by the Turks in the 12th century and captured by Tamerlane 1361. In 1865 it was taken by the Russians. It was severely damaged by an earthquake 1966.

Tasman Abel Janszoon 1603–1659. Dutch navigator. In 1642, he was the first European to see Tasmania. He also made the first European sightings of New Zealand, Tonga, and Fiji.

Tasmania formerly (1642–1856) *Van Diemen's Land* island off the south coast of Australia; a state of the Commonwealth of Australia *area* 26,171 sq mi/67,800 sq km *capital* Hobart *towns and cities* Launceston (chief port) *features* an island state (including small islands in the Bass Strait, and Macquarie Island); Franklin River, a wilderness area saved from a hydroelectric scheme 1983, which also has a prehistoric site; unique fauna including the

Tasmanian devil *industries* wool, dairy products, apples and other fruit, timber, iron, tin, coal, copper, silver *population* (1987) 448,000 *history* the first European to visit here was Abel Tasman 1642; the last of the Tasmanian Aboriginals died 1876. Tasmania joined the Australian Commonwealth as a state 1901.

Tasmanian devil carnivorous marsupial *Sarcophilus harrisii*, in the same family (Dasyuridae) as native "cats". It is about 2.1 ft/65 cm long with a 10 in/25 cm bushy tail. It has a large head, strong teeth, and is blackish with white patches on the chest and hind parts. It is nocturnal, carnivorous, and can be ferocious when cornered. It has recently become extinct in Australia and survives only in remote parts of Tasmania.

Tasmanian devil *The Tasmanian devil, despite its name, is not particularly aggressive—it is more likely to scavenge for dead animals than to attack living ones. Nevertheless, its powerful jaws, capable of crushing large bones, are to be respected.*

Tasmanian wolf or *thylacine* carnivorous marsupial *Thylacinus cynocephalus*, in the family Dasyuridae. It is doglike in appearance and can be nearly 6 ft/2 m from nose to tail tip. It was hunted to probable extinction in the 1930s, but there are still occasional unconfirmed reports of sightings.

taste sense that detects some of the chemical constituents of food. The human ◊tongue can distinguish only four basic tastes (sweet, sour, bitter, and salty) but it is supplemented by the sense of smell. What we refer to as taste is really a composite sense made up of both taste and smell.

Tatar or *Tartar* member of a Turkic people, the descendants of the mixed Mongol and Turkic followers of ◊Genghis Khan, called the Golden Horde because of the wealth they gained by plunder.

The vast Tatar state was conquered by Russia 1552. The Tatars now live mainly in the Russian autonomous republic of Tatarstan, W Siberia, Turkmenistan, and Uzbekistan (where they were deported from the Crimea 1944). There are over 5 million speakers of the Tatar language, which belongs to the Turkic branch of the Altaic family. The Tatar people are mainly Muslim, although some have converted to the Orthodox Church.

Tatarstan formerly *Tatar Autonomous Republic* autonomous republic of E Russia *area* 26,250 sq mi/68,000 sq km *capital* Kazan *industries* oil, chemicals, textiles, timber *population* (1986) 3,537,000 (48% Tatar, 43% Russian) *history* a territory of Volga-Kama Bulgar state from the 10th century when Islam was introduced; conquered by the Mongols 1236; the capital of the powerful Khanate of Kazan until conquered by Russia 1552; an autonomous republic from 1920. In recent years the republic (mainly Muslim and

an important industrial and oil-producing area) has seen moves toward increased autonomy.

tau ◊elementary particle with the same electric charge as the electron but a mass nearly double that of a proton. It has a lifetime of around 3 x 10⁻¹³ seconds and belongs to the ◊lepton family of particles—those that interact via the electromagnetic, weak nuclear, and gravitational forces, but not the strong nuclear force.

Taurus zodiacal constellation in the northern hemisphere near Orion, represented as a bull. The Sun passes through Taurus from mid-May to late June. Its brightest star is Aldebaran, seen as the bull's red eye. Taurus contains the Hyades and Pleiades open ◊star clusters, and the Crab nebula. In astrology, the dates for Taurus are between about April 20 and May 20 (see ◊precession).

tautology repetition of the same thing in different words. For example, it is tautologous to say that something is *most unique*, since something unique cannot, by definition, be comparative.

taxation the raising of money from individuals and organizations by state and local governments, to pay for the goods and services they provide. Taxation can be direct (a deduction from income) or indirect (added to the purchase price of goods or services—that is, a tax on consumption).

Taxodium tree genus of the redwood family (Taxodiaceae). Also called ◊wormwood.

taxonomy another name for the ◊classification of living organisms.

Tay longest river in Scotland; length 118 mi/189 km. Rising in NW Central region, it flows NE through Loch Tay, then E and SE past Perth to the Firth of Tay, crossed at Dundee by the Tay Bridge, before joining the North Sea. The Tay has salmon fisheries; its main tributaries are the Tummel, Isla, and Earn.

Taylor Elizabeth 1932– . English-born US actress. Noted for both her beauty and acting skill, her films include *Lassie Come Home* 1942, *National Velvet* 1944, *Father of the Bride* 1950, *Giant* 1956, *Raintree County* 1957, *Cat on a Hot Tin Roof* 1958, *Butterfield 8* 1960 (Academy Award), *Cleopatra* 1963, and *Who's Afraid of Virginia Woolf?* 1966 (Academy Award). She appeared on Broadway in *The Little Foxes* 1981.

Taylor Zachary 1784–1850. 12th president of the US 1849–50. A veteran of the War of 1812 and a hero of the Mexican War (1846–48), he was nominated for the presidency by the Whigs in 1848 and was elected, but died less than one and a half years into his term. He was succeeded by Vice President Millard Fillmore.

Taylor was born in Virginia but grew up in frontier Kentucky. Known by his nickname "Old Rough and Ready," Taylor won his greatest fame in the Mexican War. His short term in office was dominated by controversies over the slavery issue, with him supporting the antislavery elements that were pushing for the admission to the Union of more free states.

Tayside region of Scotland *area* 2,973 sq mi/7,700 sq km *towns and cities* Dundee (administrative headquarters), Perth, Arbroath, Forfar *features* river Tay; ◊Grampian Mountains; Lochs Tay and Rannoch; hills: Ochil and Sidlaw; vales of the North and South Esk *industries* beef and dairy products, soft fruit from the fertile Carse of Gowrie (SW of Dundee); wool products; hydroelectric power stations *population* (1991) 383,800 *famous people* J M Barrie, John Buchan, Princess Margaret.

TB abbreviation for the infectious disease ◊*tuberculosis.*

Tbilisi formerly *Tiflis* capital of the independent republic of Georgia; industries include textiles, machinery, ceramics, and tobacco; population (1987) 1,194,000. Dating from the 5th century, it is a center of Georgian culture, with fine medieval churches. Anti-Russian demonstrations were quashed here by troops 1981 and 1989; the latter clash followed rejected demands for autonomy from the Abkhazia enclave, and resulted in 19 or more deaths from poison gas (containing chloroacetophenone) and 100 injured. In Dec 1991 at least 50 people were killed as well-armed opposition forces attempted to overthrow President Gamsakhurdia, eventually forcing him to flee.

Tchaikovsky Pyotr Il'yich 1840–1893. Russian composer. His strong sense of melody, personal expression, and brilliant orchestration are clear throughout his many Romantic works, which include six symphonies, three piano concertos, a violin concerto, operas (for example, *Eugene Onegin* 1879), ballets (for example, *The Nutcracker* 1891–92), orchestral fantasies (for example, *Romeo and Juliet* 1870), and chamber and vocal music.

He was invited to conduct the opening night program at Carnegie Hall, in New York City, 1891.

TCP/IP (abbreviation for *transport control protocol/Internet protocol*) in computing, set of network protocols, developed principally by the US Department of Defense. TCP/IP is widely used, particularly in ◊Unix and on the ◊Internet.

tea evergreen shrub *Camellia sinensis*, family Theaceae, of which the fermented, dried leaves are infused to make a beverage of the same name. Known in China as early as 2737 BC, tea was first brought to Europe AD 1610 and rapidly became a popular drink. In 1823 it was found growing wild in N India, and plantations were later established in Assam and Sri Lanka; producers today include Africa, South America, Georgia, Azerbaijan, Indonesia, and Iran.

In the US, tea with lemon and honey is a cold remedy, but iced tea has become a year-round soft drink, sold in cans like colas. After the American Revolution, the new US citizens turned away from tea (as being British) and imported ◊coffee instead. Only after 200 years did tea revive its popularity in the US.

teak tropical Asian timber tree *Tectona grandis*, family Verbenaceae, with yellowish wood used in furniture and shipbuilding.

teal any of various small, short-necked dabbling ducks of the genus *Anas*. The drakes generally have a bright head and wing markings. The green-winged teal *A. crecca* is about 14 in/35 cm long.

Teapot Dome Scandal US political scandal that revealed the corruption of President ◊Harding's administration. It centered on the leasing of naval oil reserves 1921 at Teapot Dome, Wyoming, without competitive bidding, as a result of bribing the secretary of the interior, Albert B. Fall (1861–1944). Fall was tried and imprisoned 1929.

tear gas any of various volatile gases that produce irritation and watering of the eyes, used by police against crowds and used in chemical warfare. The gas is delivered in pressurized, liquid-filled canisters or grenades, thrown by hand or launched from a specially adapted rifle. Gases (such as Mace) cause violent coughing and blinding tears, which pass when the victim breathes fresh air, and there are no lasting effects.

teasel erect, prickly, biennial herb *Dipsacus fullonum*, family Dipsacaceae, native to Eurasia. The dry, spiny seed heads were once used industrially to tease, or raise the nap of, cloth.

technetium silver-gray, radioactive, metallic element, symbol Tc, atomic number 43, atomic weight 98.906. It occurs in nature only in extremely minute amounts, produced as a fission product from uranium in ◊pitchblende and other uranium ores. Its longest-lived isotope, Tc-99, has a half-life of 216,000 years. It is a superconductor and is used as a hardener in steel alloys and as a medical tracer.

technology the use of tools, power, and materials, generally for the purposes of production. Almost every human process for getting food and shelter depends on complex technological systems, which have been developed over a 3-million-year period. Significant milestones include the advent of the ◊steam engine 1712, the introduction of ◊electricity and the ◊internal combustion engine in the mid-1870s, and recent developments in communications, ◊electronics, and the nuclear and space industries. The *advanced technology* (highly automated and specialized) on which modern industrialized society depends is frequently contrasted with the *low technology* (labor-intensive and unspecialized) that characterizes some developing countries. ◊*Intermediate technology* is an attempt to adapt scientifically advanced inventions to less developed areas by using local materials and methods of manufacture.

Tecumseh 1768–1813. North American Indian chief of the Shawnee. He attempted to unite the Indian peoples from Canada to Florida against the encroachment of white settlers, but the defeat of his brother *Tenskwatawa*, "the Prophet", at the battle of Tippecanoe in Nov 1811 by W H Harrison, governor of the Indiana Territory, largely destroyed the confederacy built up by Tecumseh.

He allied himself with the British in the War of 1812, during which he helped take Detroit, fomented the Creek War 1813 in the South, and led an invasion of Ohio. He was killed in Canada at the Battle of the Thames 1813, a battle won by Harrison, who would campaign for the presidency 1840 largely on the strength of his military exploits against Tecumseh.

Teflon trade name for polytetrafluoroethene (PTFE), a tough, waxlike, heat-resistant plastic used for coating nonstick cookware and in gaskets and bearings.

Tegucigalpa capital of Honduras; population (1989) 608,000. Industries include textiles and food-processing. It was founded 1524 as a gold-and silver-mining center.

Tehran capital of Iran; population (1986) 6,043,000. Industries include textiles, chemicals, engineering, and tobacco. It was founded in the 12th century and made the capital 1788 by Mohammed Shah. Much of the city was rebuilt in the 1920s and 1930s. Tehran is the site of the Gulistan Palace (the former royal residence). There are three universities; the Shahyad Tower is a symbol of modern Iran.

Te Kanawa Kiri 1944– . New Zealand soprano. Te Kanawa's first major role was the Countess in Mozart's *The Marriage of Figaro* at Covent Garden, London, 1971. Her voice combines the purity and intensity of the upper range with an extended lower range of great richness and resonance. Apart from classical roles, she has also featured popular music in her repertoire, such as the 1984 recording of Leonard Bernstein's *West Side Story*.

tektite small, rounded glassy stone, found in certain regions of the Earth, such as Australasia. Tektites are probably the scattered drops of molten rock thrown out by the impact of a large ◊meteorite.

Tel Aviv officially *Tel Aviv-Jaffa* city in Israel, on the Mediterranean coast; population (1987) 320,000. Industries include textiles, chemicals, sugar, printing, and publishing. Tel Aviv was founded 1909 as a Jewish residential area in the Arab town of Jaffa, with which it was combined 1949; their ports were superseded 1965 by Ashdod to the south. During the ◊Gulf War 1991, Tel Aviv became a target for Iraqi missiles as part of Saddam Hussein's strategy to break up the Arab alliance against him.

telecommunications communications over a distance, generally by electronic means. Long-distance voice communication was pioneered 1876 by Scottish-born US scientist Alexander Graham Bell when he invented the telephone. Today it is possible to communicate with most countries by telephone cable, or by satellite or microwave link, with over 100,000 simultaneous conversations and several television channels being carried by the latest satellites. ◊Integrated-Services Digital Network (ISDN) makes videophones and high-quality fax possible; the world's first large-scale center of ISDN began operating in Japan 1988. ISDN is a system that transmits voice and image data on a single transmission line by changing them into digital signals. The chief method of relaying long-distance calls on land is microwave radio transmission.

telecommuting working from home with a fax and a ◊modem linked to the office of the employing company.

telegraphy transmission of coded messages along wires by means of electrical signals. The first modern form of telecommunication, it now uses printers for the transmission and receipt of messages. Telex is an international telegraphy network.

Telemann Georg Philipp 1681–1767. German Baroque composer, organist, and conductor. He conducted at the Johanneum, Hamburg, from 1721. His prolific output of concertos for both new and old instruments, including violin, viola da gamba, recorder, flute, oboe, trumpet, horn, and bassoon, represent a methodical and fastidious investigation into the tonal resonances and structure of the new Baroque orchestra, research noted by J S Bach. Other works include 25 operas, numerous sacred cantatas, and instrumental fantasias.

telepathy "the communication of impressions of any kind from one mind to another, independently of the recognized channels of sense", as defined by F W H Myers (1843–1901), cofounder 1882 of the Psychical Research Society, who coined the term.

telephone instrument for communicating by voice over long distances, invented by Scottish-born US inventor Alexander Graham ◊Bell 1876. The transmitter (mouthpiece) consists of a carbon microphone, with a diaphragm that vibrates when a person speaks into it. The diaphragm vibrations compress grains of carbon to a greater or lesser extent, altering their resistance to an electric current passing through them. This sets up variable electrical signals, which travel along the telephone lines to the receiver of the person being called. There they cause the magnetism of an electromagnet to vary, making a diaphragm above the electromagnet vibrate and give out sound waves, which mirror those that entered the mouthpiece originally.

teleprinter or *teletypewriter* transmitting and receiving device used in telecommunications to handle coded messages. Teleprinters are automatic typewriters keyed telegraphically to convert typed words into electrical signals (using a 5-unit Baudot code, see ◊baud) at the transmitting end, and signals into typed words at the receiving end.

telescope optical instrument that magnifies images of faint and distant objects; any device for collecting and focusing light and other forms of electromagnetic radiation. It is a major research tool in astronomy and is used to sight over land and sea; small telescopes can be attached to cameras and rifles. A telescope with a large aperture, or opening, can distinguish finer detail and fainter objects than one with a small aperture. The *refracting telescope* uses lenses, and the *reflecting telescope* uses mirrors. A third type, the *catadioptric telescope*, is a combination of lenses and mirrors. See also ◊radio telescope.

teletext broadcast system of displaying information on a television screen. The information—typically about news items, entertainment, sport, and finance—is constantly updated. Teletext is a form of ◊videotext, pioneered in Britain.

television (TV) reproduction at a distance by radio waves of visual images. For transmission, a television camera converts the pattern of light it takes in into a pattern of electrical charges. This is scanned line by line by a beam of electrons from an electron gun, resulting in variable electrical signals that represent the visual picture. These vision signals are combined with a radio carrier wave and broadcast as magnetic waves. The TV aerial picks up the wave and feeds it to the receiver (TV set). This separates out the vision signals, which pass to a cathode-ray tube. The vision signals control the strength of a beam of electrons from an electron gun, aimed at the screen and making it glow more or less brightly. At the same time the beam is made to scan across the screen line by line, mirroring the action of the gun in the TV camera. The result is a recreation of the pattern of light that entered the camera. Thirty pictures are built up each second with interlaced scanning in North America (25 in Europe), with a total of 525 lines in North America and Japan (625 lines in Europe).

telex (acronym for *tel*eprinter *ex*change) international telecommunications network that handles telegraph messages in the form of coded signals. It uses ◊teleprinters for transmitting and receiving, and makes use of land lines (cables) and radio and satellite links to make connections between subscribers.

Teller Edward 1908– . Hungarian-born US physicist. A member of the Manhattan Project 1941–45, he was involved in developing the first atomic bombs. and played a central role in the development and testing of the first hydrogen bomb 1952.

tellurium silver-white, semimetallic (metalloid) element, symbol Te, atomic number 52, relative atomic mass 127.60. Chemically it is similar to sulfur and selenium, and it is considered one of the sulfur group. It occurs naturally in telluride minerals, and is used in coloring glass blue-brown, in the electrolytic refining of zinc, in electronics, and as a catalyst in refining petroleum.

Telugu language spoken in SE India. It is the official language of Andhra Pradesh, and is also spoken in Malaysia, giving a total number of speakers of around 50 million. Written records in Telugu date

television transmitter (essentials)

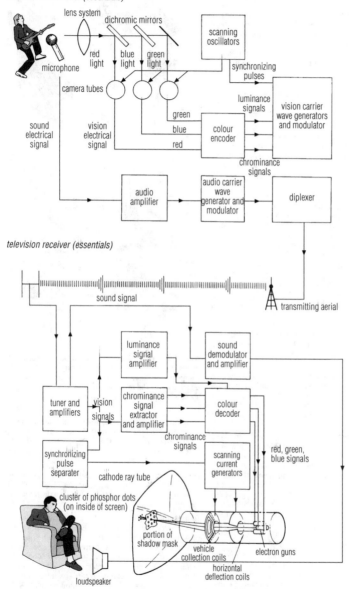

television receiver (essentials)

television *Simplified block diagram of a complete color television system— transmitting and receiving. The camera separates the picture into three colors—red, blue, green—by using filters and different camera tubes for each color. The audio signal is produced separately from the video signal. Both signals are transmitted from the same aerial using a special coupling device called a diplexer. There are four sections in the receiver: the aerial, the tuners, the decoders, and the display. As in the transmitter, the audio and video signals are processed separately. The signals are amplified at various points.*

from the 7th century AD. Telugu belongs to the Dravidian family.

temperance movement societies dedicated to curtailing the consumption of alcohol by total prohibition, local restriction, or encouragement of declarations of personal abstinence ("the pledge"). Temperance movements were first set up in the US, Ireland, and Scotland, then in the N of England in the 1830s.

temperature degree or intensity of heat of a body, and the condition that determines whether or not it will transfer heat to, or receive heat from, another body according to the laws of ◊thermodynamics. It is measured in degrees Celsius (also called centigrade) or Fahrenheit.

Templars or *Knights Templar* or *Order of Poor Knights of Christ and of the Temple of Solomon* military religious order founded in Jerusalem 1119–20 to protect pilgrims traveling to the Holy Land. They played an important part in the ◊Crusades of the 12th and 13th centuries.

Temple Shirley 1928– . US actress who became the most successful child star of the 1930s. The charming, curly-haired, dimpled tot's films include *Bright Eyes* 1934, in which she sang "On the Good Ship Lollipop"; *Little Miss Marker* 1934; *The Little Colonel* 1935; *Captain January* 1936; *Heidi* 1937; and *The Little Princess* 1939.

Temple of Jerusalem the center of Jewish national worship in both ancient and modern days. The Western or Wailing Wall is the surviving part of the western wall of the platform of the enclosure of the Temple. Solomon built the Temple *c.* 950 BC but it was destroyed by Nebuchadnezzar in 586 BC. It was rebuilt in the late 6th century BC, restored by the Maccabees and later by Herod the Great, but destroyed by the Romans in AD 70. Since then, Jews have come here to pray, to mourn their dispersion and the loss of their homeland.

tench European freshwater bony fish *Tinca tinca,* a member of the carp family, now established in North America. It is about 18 in/45 cm long, weighing 4.5 lb/2 kg, colored olive green above and gray beneath. The scales are small and there is a barbel at each side of the mouth.

Ten Commandments in the Old Testament, the laws given by God to the Hebrew leader Moses on Mount Sinai, engraved on two tablets of stone.

They are: to have no other gods besides Jehovah; to make no idols; not to misuse the name of God; to keep the sabbath holy; to honor one's parents; not to commit murder, adultery, or theft; not to give false evidence; not to be covetous. They form the basis of Jewish and Christian moral codes; the "tablets of the Law" given to Moses are also mentioned in the Koran. The giving of the Ten Commandments is celebrated in the Jewish festival of *Shavuot* (see ◊Pentecost).

tendon or *sinew* cord of tough, fibrous connective tissue that joins muscle to bone in vertebrates. Tendons are largely composed of the protein collagen, and because of their inelasticity are very efficient at transforming muscle power into movement.

tendril in botany, a slender, threadlike structure that supports a climbing plant by coiling around suitable supports, such as the stems and branches of other plants. It may be a modified stem, leaf, leaflet, flower, leaf stalk, or stipule (a small appendage on either side of the leaf stalk), and may be simple or branched. The tendrils of Virginia creeper *Parthenocissus quinquefolia*

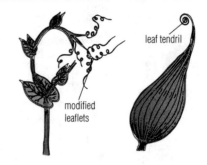

leaf tendril

modified leaflets

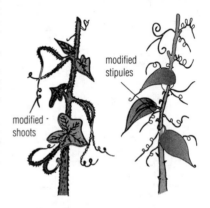

modified stipules

modified shoots

tendril *Tendrils are specially modifed leaves, shoots, or stems. They support the plant by twining around the stems of other plants nearby, as in the pea, or they may attach themselves to suitable surfaces by means of suckers, as in the virginia creeper.*

are modified flower heads with suckerlike pads at the end that stick to walls, while those of the grapevine *Vitis* grow away from the light and thus enter dark crevices where they expand to anchor the plant firmly.

Tenerife largest of the ◊Canary Islands, Spain; area 795 sq mi/2,060 sq km; population (1981) 557,000. *Santa Cruz* is the main town, and *Pico de Teide* is an active volcano.

Tennessee state in E central US; nickname Volunteer State *area* 42,151 sq mi/109,200 sq km *capital* Nashville *towns and cities* Memphis, Knoxville, Chattanooga, Clarksville *features* Tennessee Valley Authority; Great Smoky Mountains National Park; Grand Old Opry, Nashville; Beale Street Historic District and Graceland, estate of Elvis Presley, Memphis; research centers, including Oak Ridge National Laboratory *industries* cereals, cotton, tobacco, soybeans, livestock, timber, coal, zinc, copper, chemicals *population* (1990) 4,877,200 *famous people* Davy Crockett, David Farragut, W C Handy, Cordell Hull, Andrew Jackson, Andrew Johnson, Dolly Parton, John Crowe Ransom, Bessie Smith *history* settled by Europeans 1757; became a state 1796. Tennessee was deeply divided in the Civil War; the battles of Shiloh, Murfreesboro, Chattanooga, and Nashville were fought here.

Tennessee Valley Authority (TVA) US government corporation founded 1933 to develop the Tennessee River basin (an area of some 40,000 sq mi/104,000 sq km) by building hydroelectric power stations, producing and distributing fertilizers, and similar activities. The TVA was associated with President Franklin D. Roosevelt's ◊New Deal, promoting economic growth by government investment.

tennis racket and ball game invented toward the end of the 19th century. It was introduced by Major Clopton Wingfield at a Christmas party at Nantclwyn, Wales, in 1873. His game was then called "Sphairistike". It derived from court tennis. Although played on different surfaces (grass, wood, shale, clay, concrete), it is sometimes still called "lawn tennis".

The aim of the two or four players is to strike the ball into the prescribed area of the court, with oval-headed rackets (strung with gut or nylon), in such a way that it cannot be returned. Major events include the *Davis Cup*, first contested in 1900 for international men's competition; Wimbledon, a UK open event for players of both sexes; and the US, French, and Australian Opens.

Tennyson Alfred, 1st Baron Tennyson 1809–1892. English poet. He was poet laureate 1850–92. His verse has a majestic, musical quality. His works include "The Lady of Shalott", "The Lotus Eaters", "Ulysses", "Break, Break, Break", "The Charge of the Light Brigade"; the longer narratives *Locksley Hall* 1832 and *Maud* 1855; the elegy *In Memoriam* 1850; and a long series of poems on the Arthurian legends *The Idylls of the King* 1857–85.

tenpins or *tenpin bowling* indoor sport popular in North America. The object is to bowl a ball down an alley at ten pins. The game is usually between two players or teams. A game of tenpins is made up of ten "frames". The frame is the bowler's turn to play and in each frame he or she may bowl twice. One point is scored for each pin knocked down, with bonus points for knocking all ten pins down in either one ball or two. The player or team making the greater score wins.

tequila Mexican alcoholic drink distilled from the ◊agave plant. It is named for the place, near Guadalajara, where the conquistadors first developed it from Aztec *pulque*, which would keep for only a day.

terbium soft, silver-gray, metallic element of the ◊lanthanide series, symbol Tb, atomic number 81, relative atomic mass 158.925. It occurs in gadolinite and other ores, with yttrium and ytterbium, and is used in lasers, semiconductors, and television tubes. It was named in 1843 by Swedish chemist Carl Mosander (1797–1858) for the town of Ytterby, Sweden, where it was first found.

Terence (Publius Terentius Afer) 190–159 BC. Roman dramatist. Born in Carthage, he was taken as a slave to Rome where he was freed and came under the patronage of the Roman general Scipio Africanus Minor. His surviving six comedies (including *The Eunuch* 161 BC) are subtly characterized and based on Greek models. They were widely read and performed during the Middle Ages and the Renaissance.

Teresa Mother. Born Agnes Bojaxhiu 1910– . Roman Catholic nun. She was born in Skopje, Macedonia, and at 18 entered a Calcutta convent and became a teacher. In 1948 she became an Indian citizen and founded the Missionaries of Charity, an order for men and women based in Calcutta that helps abandoned children and the dying. She was awarded the Nobel Peace Prize 1979.

terminal in computing, a device consisting of a keyboard and display screen (◊VDT)—or, in older systems, a teleprinter—to enable the operator to communicate with the computer. The terminal may be physically attached to the computer or linked to it by a telephone line (remote terminal). A "dumb" terminal has no processor of its own, whereas an "intelligent" terminal has its own processor and takes some of the processing load away from the main computer.

termite any member of the insect order Isoptera. Termites are soft-bodied social insects living in large colonies which include one or more queens (of relatively enormous size and producing an egg every two seconds), much smaller kings, and still smaller soldiers, workers, and immature forms. Termites build galleried nests of soil particles that may be 20 ft/6 m high.

tern any of various lightly built seabirds placed in the same family (Laridae) as gulls and characterized by pointed wings and bill and usually a forked tail. Terns plunge-dive after aquatic prey. They are 8–20 in/20–50 cm long, and usually colored in combinations of white and black.

terracotta brownish-red baked clay, usually unglazed, used in building, sculpture, and pottery. The term is specifically applied to small figures or figurines, such as those found at Tanagra in central Greece. Excavations at Xian, China, have revealed life-size terracotta figures of the army of the Emperor Shi Huangdi dating from the 3rd century BC.

terra firma (Latin) dry land; solid ground.

terrapin general name for any turtle that frequents fresh or brackish water. The name is sometimes specifically used for the tidewater diamondback terrapins (genus *Malaclemys*) of E North America.

Terre Haute city in W Indiana, US, on the Wabash River; population (1990) 57,500. Industries include plastics, chemicals, and glass. Terre Haute was laid out 1816.

Points of interest include the birthplace of author Theodore Dreiser and the home of labor leader Eugene V Debs. Indiana State University is here.

terrier any of various breeds of highly intelligent, active dogs. They are usually small. Types include the bull, cairn, West Highland white, fox, Irish, Scottish, Sealyham, Skye, and Yorkshire terriers. They were originally bred for hunting rabbits and following quarry such as foxes down into burrows.

Terror, Reign of period of the ◊French Revolution when the Jacobins were in power (Oct 1793–July 1794) under ◊Robespierre and instituted mass persecution of their opponents. About 1,400 were executed, mainly by guillotine, until public indignation rose and Robespierre was overthrown in July 1794.

Tertiary period of geological time 65–1.64 million years ago, divided into five epochs: Paleocene, Eocene, Oligocene, Miocene, and Pliocene. During the Tertiary, mammals took over all the ecological niches left vacant by the extinction of the dinosaurs, and became the prevalent land animals. The continents took on their present positions, and climatic and vegetation zones as we know them became established. Within the geological time column the Tertiary follows the Cretaceous period and is succeeded by the Quaternary period.

tesla SI unit (symbol T) of magnetic flux density. One tesla represents a flux density of one ◊weber per square meter, or 10^4 gauss. It is named for the Croatian engineer Nikola Tesla.

testis (plural *testes*) the organ that produces ◊sperm in male (and hermaphrodite) animals. In vertebrates it is one of a pair of oval structures that are usually internal, but in mammals (other than elephants and marine mammals), the paired testes (or testicles) descend from the body cavity during development, to hang outside the abdomen in a scrotal sac. The testes also secrete the male sex hormone androgen.

testosterone in vertebrates, hormone secreted chiefly by the testes, but also by the ovaries and the cortex of the adrenal glands. It promotes the development of secondary sexual characteristics in males. In animals with a breeding season, the onset of breeding behavior is accompanied by a rise in the level of testosterone in the blood.

tetanus or *lockjaw* acute disease caused by the toxin of the bacillus *Clostridium tetani*, which usually enters the body through a wound. The bacterium is chiefly found in richly manured soil. Untreated, in seven to ten days tetanus produces muscular spasm and rigidity of the jaw spreading to other parts of the body, convulsions, and death. There is a vaccine, and the disease may be treatable with tetanus antitoxin and antibiotics.

tête-à-tête (French "head-to-head") private meeting between two people.

tetrachloromethane CCl_4 or *carbon tetrachloride* chlorinated organic compound that is a very efficient solvent for fats and greases, and was at one time the main constituent of household dry-cleaning fluids and of fire extinguishers used with electrical and gasoline fires. Its use became restricted after it was discovered to be carcinogenic and it has now been largely removed from educational and industrial laboratories.

tetracycline one of a group of antibiotic compounds having in common the four-ring structure of chlortetracycline, the first member of the group to be isolated. They are prepared synthetically or obtained from certain bacteria of the genus *Streptomyces*. They are broad-spectrum antibiotics, effective against a wide range of disease-causing bacteria.

tetrahedron (plural *tetrahedra*) in geometry, a solid figure (polyhedron) with four triangular faces; that is, a ◊pyramid on a triangular base. A regular tetrahedron has equilateral triangles as its faces.

Teutonic Knight member of a German Christian military order, the *Knights of the Teutonic Order*, founded 1190 by Hermann of Salza in Palestine. They crusaded against the pagan Prussians and Lithuanians from 1228 and controlled Prussia until the 16th century. Their capital was Marienburg (now Malbork, Poland).

Texas state in southwestern US; nickname Lone Star State *area* 266,803 sq mi/691,200 sq km *capital* Austin *towns and cities* Houston, Dallas-Fort Worth, San Antonio, El Paso, Corpus Christi, Lubbock *features* Rio Grande River, Red River; arid Staked Plains, reclaimed by irrigation; the Great Plains; Gulf Coast resorts; Lyndon B Johnson Space Center, Houston; Alamo, San Antonio; Big Bend and Guadalupe Mountains national parks *industries* rice, cotton,

sorghum, wheat, hay, livestock, shrimps, meat products, lumber, wood and paper products, petroleum (nearly one-third of US production), natural gas, sulfur, salt, uranium, chemicals, petrochemicals, nonelectrical machinery, fabricated metal products, transportation equipment, electric and electronic equipment *population* (1990) 16,986,500 *famous people* James Bowie, George Bush, Buddy Holly, Sam Houston, Howard Hughes, Lyndon B Johnson, Janis Joplin, Katherine Anne Porter, Patrick Swayze, Tina Turner *history* settled by the Spanish 1682; part of Mexico 1821–36; Santa Anna massacred the Alamo garrison 1836, but was defeated by Sam Houston at San Jacinto the same year; Texas became an independent republic 1836–45, with Houston as president; in 1845 it became a state of the US. Texas is the only state in the US to have previously been an independent republic.

text editor in computing, a program that allows the user to edit text on the screen and to store it in a file. Text editors are similar to ◊word processors, except that they lack the ability to format text into paragraphs and pages and to apply different typefaces and styles.

TGV (abbreviation for *train à grande vitesse*) (French "high-speed train") French electrically powered train that provides the world's fastest rail service. Since it began operating 1981, it has carried more than 100 million passengers between Paris and Lyon, at average speeds of 167 mph/268 kph. In 1990, a TGV broke the world speed record, reaching a speed of 320.2 mph/515.3 kph (about half that of a passenger jet aircraft) on a stretch of line near Tours.

In its regular service, the TGV covers the 264 mi/425 km distance between Paris and Lyon in two hours.

Thackeray William Makepeace 1811–1863. English novelist and essayist. He was a regular contributor to *Fraser's Magazine* and *Punch*. His first novel was *Vanity Fair* 1847–48, followed by *Pendennis* 1848, *Henry Esmond* 1852 (and its sequel *The Virginians* 1857–59), and *The Newcomes* 1853–55, in which Thackeray's tendency to sentimentality is most marked.

Thai member of the majority ethnic group living in Thailand and N Myanmar (Burma). Thai peoples also live in SW China, Laos, and N Vietnam. They speak Tai languages, all of which belong to the Sino-Tibetan language family. There are over 60 million speakers, the majority of whom live in Thailand. Most Thais are Buddhists, but the traditional belief in spirits, *phi*, remains.

Thailand Kingdom of (*Prathet Thai* or *Muang Thai*) *area* 198,108 sq mi/513,115 sq km *capital* and chief port Bangkok *towns and cities* Chiangmai, Nakhon Sawan river port *physical* mountainous, semiarid plateau in NE, fertile central region, tropical isthmus in S *environment* tropical rainforest was reduced to 18% of the land area 1988 (from 93% in 1961); logging was banned by the government 1988 *features* rivers Chao Phraya, Mekong, Salween; ancient ruins of Sukhothai and Ayurrhaya *head of state* King Bhumibol Adulyadej from 1946 *head of government* Chuan Leekpai from 1992 *political system* military-controlled emergent democracy *political parties* New Aspiration Party (NAP), centrist; Democratic Party (DP), center-left; Palang Dharma (PD), anticorruption; Social Action Party (Kij Sangkhom), right of center; Thai Nation (Chart Thai), conservative, pro-business; Chart Pattana (National Development), conservative

exports rice, textiles, rubber, tin, rubies, sapphires, corn, tapioca *currency* baht *population* (1993) 57,800,000 (Thai 75%, Chinese 14%); growth rate 2% p.a. *media* about 20 daily papers, the largest (*Thai Rath*) having a circulation of 1 million (1992). Self-censorship and some state interference. Six TV channels (two owned by the army and three state-controlled); 496 radio stations (1992), none privately owned *life expectancy* men 65, women 69 *languages* Thai and Chinese (both official); regional dialects *religions* Buddhist 95%, Muslim 4% *literacy* men 96%, women 90% *GNP* $1,580 per head (1991) *chronology* *1782* Siam absolutist dynasty commenced. *1896* Anglo-French agreement recognized Siam as independent buffer state. *1932* Constitutional monarchy established. *1939* Name of Thailand adopted. *1941–44* Japanese occupation. *1947* Military seized power in coup. *1972* Withdrawal of Thai troops from South Vietnam. *1973* Military government overthrown. *1976* Military reassumed control. *1980* General Prem Tinsulanonda assumed power. *1983* Civilian government formed; martial law maintained. *1988* Prime Minister Prem resigned; replaced by Chatichai Choonhavan. *1989* Thai pirates continued to murder, pillage, and kidnap Vietnamese "boat people" at sea. *1991* Military seized power in coup. Interim civilian government formed under Anand Panyarachun. Mass demonstrations against new military-oriented constitution. *1992* General election produced five-party coalition; appointment of General Suchinda Kraprayoon as premier provoked widespread riots; Suchinda forced to flee. New coalition government led by Chuan Leekpai.

thalassemia or *Cooley's anemia* any of a group of chronic hereditary blood disorders that are widespread in the Mediterranean countries, Africa, the Far East, and the Middle East. They are characterized by an abnormality of the red blood cells and bone marrow, with enlargement of the spleen. The genes responsible are carried by about 100 million people worldwide.

Thalberg Irving Grant 1899–1936. US film-production executive born in Brooklyn, New York. At the age of 20 "the boy genius," was head of production at Universal Pictures, and in 1924 he became production supervisor of the newly formed Metro-Goldwyn-Mayer (MGM). He was responsible for such prestige films as *Ben-Hur* 1926 and *Mutiny on the Bounty* 1935. With Louis B. Mayer, he built up MGM into one of the biggest Hollywood studios of the 1930s.

Among his most memorable productions were *Grand Hotel* 1932 and *A Night at the Opera* 1935.

thallium soft, bluish white, malleable, metallic element, symbol Tl, atomic number 81, atomic weight 204.37. It is a poor conductor of electricity. Its compounds are poisonous and are used as insecticides and rodent poisons; some are used in the optical-glass and infrared-glass industries and in photocells.

Thames river in S England; length 210 mi/338 km. The longest river in England, it rises in the Cotswold Hills above Cirencester and is tidal as far as Teddington. Below London there is protection from flooding by means of the Thames Barrier (1982). The headstreams unite at Lechlade.

Thanksgiving (Day) national holiday in the US (fourth Thursday in Nov) and Canada (second Monday in Oct), first celebrated by the Pilgrim settlers in Massachusetts after their first harvest 1621.

In the US it was proclaimed a national holiday 1863. Since 1942 it has been celebrated, by act of Congress, on the fourth Thursday in November. The original day of thanksgiving was proclaimed by Massachusetts governor William Bradford after the Pilgrims had survived their first winter, owing largely to help from their Indian ally Massasoit.

Thatcher Margaret Hilda (born Roberts), Baroness Thatcher of Kesteven 1925– . British Conservative politician, prime minister 1979–90. She was education minister 1970–74 and Conservative Party leader 1975–90. In 1982 she sent British troops to recapture

Thatcher, Margaret Hilda (born Roberts), Baroness Thatcher of Kesteven Conservative politician and former prime minister Margaret Thatcher, whose brand of Conservatism and European policy eventually provoked a crisis in her party and the government. The 1990 leadership challenge led to her resignation as prime minister, an office she had held since 1979, and her replacement as leader of the Conservative Party, a post she had held for nearly 16 years.

the Falkland Islands from Argentina. She confronted labor-union power, sold off public utilities to the private sector, and reduced the influence of local government. In 1990 splits in the cabinet over the issues of Europe and consensus government forced her resignation. An astute Parliamentary tactician, she tolerated little disagreement, either from the opposition or from within her own party.

Thatcherism political outlook comprising a belief in the efficacy of market forces, the need for strong central government, and a conviction that self-help is preferable to reliance on the state, combined with a strong element of ◊nationalism. The ideology is associated with Margaret Thatcher but stems from an individualist view found in Britain's 19th-century Liberal and 20th-century Conservative parties, and is no longer confined to Britain.

theater performance by actors for an audience; it may include ◊drama, dancing, music, mime, and ◊puppets. The term is also used for the place or building in which dramatic performances take place. Theater history can be traced to Egyptian religious ritualistic drama as long ago as 3200 BC. The first known European theaters were in Greece from about 600 BC.

theater, alternative theater which, since the 1960s, has functioned outside the commercial mainstream, usually in an experimental style and in untraditional venues. In New York this is synonymous with off-off-Broadway, in London with fringe and alternative comedy.

Thebes capital of Boeotia in ancient Greece. In the Peloponnesian War it was allied with Sparta against Athens. For a short time after 371 BC when Thebes defeated Sparta at Leuctra, it was the most powerful state in Greece. Alexander the Great destroyed it 336 BC and although it was restored, it never regained its former power.

Thebes Greek name of an ancient city (*Niut-Ammon*) in Upper Egypt, on the Nile. Probably founded under the first dynasty, it was the center of the worship of Ammon, and the Egyptian capital under the New Kingdom from about 1600 BC. Temple ruins survive near the villages of Karnak and Luxor, and in the nearby *Valley of the Kings* are buried the 18th–20th dynasty kings, including Tutankhamen and Amenhotep III.

Themistocles c. 525–c. 460 BC. Athenian soldier and politician. Largely through his success in persuading the Athenians to build a navy, Greece was saved from Persian conquest. He fought with distinction in the Battle of ◊Salamis 480 BC during the Persian War. About 470 he was accused of embezzlement and conspiracy against Athens, banished and fled to Asia, where Artaxerxes, the Persian king, received him with favor.

Theodora 508–548. Byzantine empress from 527. She was originally the mistress of Emperor Justinian before marrying him in 525. She earned a reputation for charity, courage, and championing the rights of women.

Theodoric the Great c. 455–526. King of the Ostrogoths from 474 in succession to his father. He invaded Italy 488, overthrew King Odoacer (whom he murdered) and established his own Ostrogothic kingdom there, with its capital in Ravenna. He had no strong successor, and his kingdom eventually became part of the Byzantine Empire of Justinian.

theology study of God or gods, either by reasoned deduction from the natural world or through revelation, as in the scriptures of Christianity, Islam, or other religions.

theorem mathematical proposition that can be deduced by logic from a set of axioms (basic facts that are taken to be true without proof). Advanced mathematics consists almost entirely of theorems and proofs, but even at a simple level theorems are important.

theory in science, a set of ideas, concepts, principles, or methods used to explain a wide set of observed facts. Among the major theories of science are ◊relativity, ◊quantum theory, ◊evolution, and ◊plate tectonics.

thermal conductivity in physics, the ability of a substance to conduct heat. Good thermal conductors, like good electrical conductors, are generally materials with many free electrons (such as metals).

thermodynamics branch of physics dealing with the transformation of heat into and from other forms of energy. It is the basis of the study of the efficient working of engines, such as the steam and internal-combustion engines. The three laws of thermodynamics are (1) energy can be neither created nor destroyed, heat and mechanical work being mutually convertible; (2) it is impossible for an unaided self-acting machine to convey heat from one body to another at a higher temperature; and (3) it is impossible by any procedure, no matter how idealized, to reduce any system to the ◊absolute zero of temperature in a finite number of operations. Put into mathematical form, these laws have widespread applications in physics and chemistry.

thermometer instrument for measuring temperature. There are many types, designed to measure different temperature ranges to varying degrees of accuracy. Each makes use of a different physical effect of temperature.

Thermopylae, Battle of battle during the ◊Persian Wars 480 BC when Leonidas, king of Sparta, and 300 men defended the pass of Thermopylae to the death against a much greater force of Persians. The pass led from Thessaly to Phocis in central Greece.

Thermos originally a trademarked name for a container for keeping things either hot or cold for several hours. It has two silvered glass walls enclosing a vacuum, filled into a metal or plastic outer case. This design reduces the three forms of heat transfer: radiation (prevented by the silvering) and conduction and convection (prevented by the vacuum). A vacuum flask is therefore equally efficient at keeping cold liquids cold, or hot liquids hot. It was invented by the Scottish chemist James Dewar (1842–1923) about 1872 to store liquefied gases.

thermosphere layer in the Earth's ◊atmosphere above the mesosphere and below the exosphere. Its lower level is about 50 mi/80 km above the ground, but its upper level is undefined. The ionosphere is located in the thermosphere. In the thermosphere the temperature rises with increasing height to several thousand degrees Celsius. However, because of the thinness of the air, very little heat is actually present.

thermostat temperature-controlling device that makes use of feedback. It employs a temperature sensor (often a bimetallic strip) to operate a switch or valve to control electricity or fuel supply. Thermostats are used in central heating, ovens, and automobile engines.

Theseus in Greek mythology, a hero of ◊Attica, supposed to have united the states of the area under a constitutional government in Athens. Ariadne, whom he later abandoned on Naxos, helped him find his way through the Labyrinth to kill the ◊Minotaur. He also fought the Amazons and was one of the ◊Argonauts.

Thessaloníki (English *Salonika*) port in Macedonia, NE Greece, at the head of the Gulf of Thessaloníki; the second-largest city in Greece; population (1981) 706,200. Industries include textiles, shipbuilding, chemicals, brewing, and tanning. It was founded from Corinth by the Romans 315 BC as *Thessalonica* (to whose inhabitants St Paul addressed two epistles), captured by the Saracens AD 904 and by the Turks 1430, and restored to Greece 1912.

thiamine or *vitamin B₁* a water-soluble vitamin of the B complex. It is found in seeds and grain. Its absence from the diet causes the disease beriberi.

Thimbu or *Thimphu* capital since 1962 of the Himalayan state of Bhutan; population (1987) 15,000. There is a 13th-century fortified monastery, Tashichoedzong, and the Memorial Charter to the Third King (1974).

Third World or *developing world* those countries that are less developed than the industrialized free-market countries of the West (First World) and the industrialized former Communist countries (Second World). Third World countries are the poorest, as measured by their income per head of population, and are concentrated in Asia, Africa, and Latin America.

Thirteen Colonies 13 American colonies that signed the ◊Declaration of Independence from Britain 1776. Led by George Washington, the Continental Army defeated the British army in the ◊American Revolution 1776–81 to become the original 13 United States of America: Connecticut, Delaware, Georgia, Maryland, Massachusetts, New Hampshire, New Jersey, New York, North Carolina, Pennsylvania, Rhode Island, South Carolina, and Virginia. They were united first under the Articles of ◊Confederation and from 1789, the US ◊Constitution.

38th parallel demarcation line between North (People's Democratic Republic of) and South (Republic of) Korea, agreed at the Yalta Conference 1945 and largely unaltered by the Korean War 1950–53.

32nd note in music, a note value 1/32nd the duration of a whole note. It is written as a filled, black notehead with a stem and three flags (tails).

Thirty Years' War major war 1618–48 in central Europe. Beginning as a German conflict between Protestants and Catholics, it was gradually transformed into a struggle to determine whether the ruling Austrian Hapsburg family could gain control of all Germany. The war caused serious economic and demographic problems in central Europe. Under the *Peace of Westphalia* the German states were granted their sovereignty and the emperor retained only nominal control.

thistle prickly plant of several genera, such as *Carduus*, *Carlina*, *Onopordum*, and *Cirsium*, in the family Compositae. The stems are spiny, the flower heads purple, white, or yellow and cottony, and the leaves deeply indented with prickly margins. The thistle is the Scottish national emblem.

Thomas Lowell (Jackson) 1892–1981. US journalist, a radio commentator for the Columbia Broadcasting System (CBS) 1930–76. Traveling to all World War II theaters of combat and to remote areas of the world, he became one of America's best-known journalists.

He helped create the romantic image of T E Lawrence. Thomas' first-person account of the Arab Revolt was published as *With Lawrence in Arabia* 1924.

Thomas Norman Mattoon 1884–1968. US political leader, six times Socialist candidate for president 1928–48. One of the founders of the American Civil Liberties Union 1920, he also served as a director of the League for Industrial Democracy 1922–37. He was a brilliant speaker and published *A Socialist's Faith* 1951.

By 1950, he noted, most of his so-called radical platform had been adopted by the US, such as Social Security and public-health programs.

Thomas à Kempis 1380–1471. German Augustinian monk who lived at the monastery of Zwolle. He took his name from his birthplace Kempen; his real surname was Hammerken. His *De Imitatio Christi/Imitation of Christ* is probably the most widely known devotional work ever written.

Thomas Aquinas medieval philosopher; see ◊Aquinas, St Thomas.

Thomson George Paget 1892–1975. English physicist whose work on ◊interference phenomena in the scattering of electrons by crystals helped to confirm the wavelike nature of particles. He shared a Nobel Prize with C J ◊Davisson 1937.

Thomson J(oseph) J(ohn) 1856–1940. English physicist who discovered the ◊electron. He was responsible for organizing the Cavendish atomic research laboratory at Cambridge University, UK. His work inaugurated the electrical theory of the atom and piloted English physicist Francis Aston's discovery of ◊isotopes. He was awarded the Nobel Prize for Physics 1906 for his research into the electrical conductivity of gases.

Thor in Norse mythology, the god of thunder (his hammer), and represented as a man of enormous strength defending humanity against demons. He was the son of Odin and Freya, and Thursday is named for him.

thorax in tetrapod vertebrates, the part of the body containing the heart and lungs, and protected by the rib cage; in arthropods, the middle part of the body, between the head and abdomen.

Thoreau Henry David 1817–1862. US author. One of the most influential figures of 19th-century US literature, he is best known for his vigorous defense of individualism and the simple life. His work *Walden, or Life in the Woods* 1854 stimulated the back-to-nature movement, and he completed some 30 volumes based on his daily nature walks. His essay "Civil Disobedience" 1849, prompted by his refusal to pay taxes, advocated peaceful resistance to unjust laws and had a wide impact, even in the 20th century.

Born in Concord, Massachusetts, Thoreau graduated from Harvard University. His friend, transcendentalist Ralph Waldo ◊Emerson, encouraged him to write and offered him land near Walden Pond on which to set up his experiment 1845–47 in living a life close to nature, requiring little manual labor and allowing him time to write.

thorium dark-gray, radioactive, metallic element of the ◊actinide series, symbol Th, atomic number 90, relative atomic mass 232.038. It is one of three fissile elements (the others are uranium and plutonium), and its longest-lived isotope has a half-life of 1.39×10^{10} years. Thorium is used to strengthen alloys. It was discovered by Jöns Berzelius 1828.

thorn apple or **jimson weed** annual plant *Datura stramonium* of the nightshade family, growing to 6 ft/2 m in northern temperate and subtropical areas; native to America and naturalized worldwide. It bears white or violet trumpet-shaped flowers and capsulelike fruit that split to release black seeds. All parts of the plant are poisonous.

The fruit of the ◊hawthorn is also called thorn apple.

Thorpe Jim (James Francis) 1888–1953. US athlete. A member of the 1912 US Olympic Team in Stockholm, he won gold medals for the decathlon and pentathlon but was forced to return when he admitted that he had played semiprofessional baseball. He played major-league baseball 1913–19 and was an outstanding player of professional football 1917–29. His Olympic medals were restored to him by the Amateur Athletic Union 1973.

He was named All-American in 1911 and 1912 and was posthumously elected to the Football Hall of Fame 1963.

Thoth in Egyptian mythology, the god of wisdom and learning. He was represented as a scribe with the head of an ibis, the bird sacred to him.

Thrace (Greek *Thráki*) ancient region of the Balkans, SE Europe, formed by parts of modern Greece and Bulgaria. It was held successively by the Greeks, Persians, Macedonians, and Romans.

Three Mile Island island in the Shenandoah River near Harrisburg, Pennsylvania, US, site of a nuclear power station which was put out of action following a major accident March 1979. Opposition to nuclear power in the US was reinforced after this accident and safety standards reassessed.

thrips any of a number of tiny insects of the order Thysanoptera, usually with feathery wings. Many of the 3,000 species live in flowers and suck their juices, causing damage and spreading disease. Others eat fungi, decaying matter, or smaller insects.

throat in human anatomy, the passage that leads from the back of the nose and mouth to the ◊trachea and ◊esophagus. It includes the pharynx and the ◊larynx, the latter being at the top of the trachea. The word "throat" is also used to mean the front part of the neck, both in humans and other vertebrates.

thrombosis condition in which a blood clot forms in a vein or artery, causing loss of circulation to the area served by the vessel. If it breaks away, it often travels to the lungs, causing pulmonary embolism.

thrush any bird of the large family Turdidae, order Passeriformes, found worldwide and known for their song. Thrushes are usually brown with speckles of other colors. They are 5–12 in/12–30 cm long.

North American species include the hermit thrush *Catharus guttatus*, a beautiful songster; the wood thrush *Hylocichla mustelina*; and the American robin *Turdus migratorius*.

Thucydides *c.* 455–400 BC. Athenian historian. He exercised military command in the ◊Peloponnesian War with Sparta, but was banished from Athens in 424. In his *History of the Peloponnesian War*, he gave a detailed account of the conflict down to 411.

thulium soft, silver-white, malleable and ductile, metallic element, of the ◊lanthanide series, symbol Tm, atomic number 69, atomic weight 168.94. It is the least abundant of the rare-earth metals, and was first found in gadolinite and various other minerals. It is used in arc lighting.

Thurber James (Grover) 1894–1961. US humorist. His short stories, written mainly for the *New Yorker* magazine, include "The Secret Life of Walter Mitty" 1932. His doodle drawings include fanciful impressions of dogs.

Born in Columbus, Ohio, Thurber was partially blind as a result of an accident in childhood; he became totally blind in the last ten years of his life but continued to work. His stories and sketches are collected in *Is Sex Necessary?* (with E B White) 1929, *The Middle-Aged Man on the Flying Trapeze* 1935, *The Last Flower* 1939, and *My World and Welcome to It* 1942.

thyme herb, genus *Thymus*, of the mint family Labiatae. Garden thyme *T. vulgaris*, native to the Mediterranean, grows to 1 ft/30 cm high, and has pinkish flowers. Its aromatic leaves are used for seasoning.

thymus organ in vertebrates, situated in the upper chest cavity in humans. The thymus processes ◊lymphocyte cells to produce T lymphocytes (T denotes "thymus-derived"), which are responsible for binding to specific invading organisms and killing them or rendering them harmless.

thyroid ◊endocrine gland of vertebrates, situated in the neck in front of the trachea. It secretes several hormones, principally thyroxine, an iodine-containing hormone that stimulates growth, metabolism, and other functions of the body. The thyroid gland may be thought of as the regulator gland of the body's metabolic rate. If it is overactive, as in hyperthyroidism, the sufferer feels hot and sweaty, has an increased heart rate, diarrhea, and weight loss. Conversely, an underactive thyroid leads to *myxedema*, a condition characterized by sensitivity to the cold, constipation, and weight gain. In infants, an underactive thyroid leads to *cretinism*, a form of mental retardation.

Tiananmen Square paved open space in central Beijing (Peking), China, the largest public square in the world (area 0.14 sq mi/0.4 sq km). On June 3–4, 1989, more than 1,000 unarmed protesters were killed by government troops in a massacre that crushed China's emerging prodemocracy movement.

Tian Shan (Chinese *Tien Shan*) mountain system in central Asia. *Pik Pobedy* on the Xinjiang-Kyrgyz border is the highest peak at 24,415 ft/7,440 m.

Tiberius (Tiberius Claudius Nero) 42 BC –AD 37. Roman emperor, the stepson, adopted son, and successor of Augustus from AD 14. He was a cautious ruler whose reign was marred by the heavy incident of trials for treason or conspiracy. Tiberius fell under the influence of Sejanus who encouraged the emperor's fear of assassination and was instrumental in Tiberius's departure from Rome to Caprae (Capri). He never returned to Rome.

Tibet autonomous region of SW China (Pinyin form *Xizang*); *area* 471,538 sq mi/1,221,600 sq km *capital* Lhasa *features* Tibet occupies a barren plateau bounded S and SW by the Himalayas and N by the Kunlun Mountains, traversed W to E by the Bukamanga, Karakoram, and other mountain ranges, and having an average elevation of 13,000–15,000 ft/4,000–4,500 m. The Sutlej, Brahmaputra, and Indus rivers rise in Tibet, which has numerous lakes, many of which are salty. The ◊yak is the main domestic animal *government* Tibet is an autonomous region of China, with its own People's Government and People's Congress. The controlling force in Tibet is the Communist Party of China, represented locally by First Secretary Wu Jinghua from 1985. Tibetan nationalists regard the province as being under colonial rule *industries* wool, borax, salt, horn, musk, herbs, furs, gold, iron pyrites, lapis lazuli, mercury, textiles, chemicals, agricultural machinery *population* (1991) 2,190,000 including 2,090,000 Tibetan nationalists (95.4%); many Chinese have settled in Tibet; 2 million Tibetans live in China outside Tibet *religion* traditionally Lamaist (a form of Mahayana Buddhism) *history* Tibet was an independent kingdom from the 5th century AD. It came under nominal Chinese rule about 1700. From 1910–13 the capital, Lhasa, was occupied by Chinese troops, after which independence was reestablished. China regained control 1951 when the historic ruler and religious leader, the ◊Dalai Lama, was driven from the country and the monks (who formed 25% of the population) were forced out of the monasteries. Between 1951 and 1959 the Chinese People's Liberation Army (PLA) controlled Tibet, although the Dalai Lama returned as nominal spiritual and temporal head of state. In 1959 a Tibetan uprising spread from bordering regions to Lhasa and was supported by Tibet's local government. The rebellion was suppressed by the PLA, prompting the Dalai Lama and 9,000 Tibetans to flee to India. The Chinese proceeded to dissolve the Tibet local government, abolish serfdom, collectivize agriculture, and suppress ◊Lamaism. In 1965 Tibet became an autonomous region of China. Chinese rule continued to be resented, however, and the economy languished.

tibia the anterior of the pair of bones found between the ankle and the knee. In humans, the tibia is the shinbone.

tick any of an arachnid group (Ixodoidea) of large bloodsucking mites. Many carry and transmit diseases to mammals (including humans) and birds.

tidal wave misleading name for a tsunami.

tide rise and fall of sea level due to the gravitational forces of the Moon and Sun. High tide occurs at an average interval of 12 hr 24 min 30 sec. The highest or *spring tides* are at or near new and full Moon; the lowest or *neap tides* when the Moon is in its first or third quarter. Some seas, such as the Mediterranean, have very small tides.

Tiepolo Giovanni Battista (Giambattista) 1696–1770. Italian painter. He was one of the first exponents of Italian Rococo and created monumental Rococo decorative schemes in palaces and churches in NE Italy, SW Germany, and Madrid 1762–70. His style is lighthearted, his colors light and warm, and he made great play with illusion.

Tierra del Fuego island group divided between Chile and Argentina. It is separated from the mainland of South America by the Strait of Magellan, and Cape Horn is at the southernmost point. The chief town, Ushuaia, Argentina, is the world's most southerly town. Industries include oil and sheep farming.

Tiffany Louis Comfort 1848–1933. US artist and glassmaker. He was the son of Charles Louis Tiffany, who founded Tiffany and Company, the New York City jewelers. He produced stained-glass windows, iridescent Favrile (from Latin *faber* "craftsman") glass, and lampshades in the Art Nouveau style. He used glass that contained oxides of iron and other elements to produce rich colors.

In 1881 he founded his own decorating firm. By 1893, he began producing his glass art objects, which remained popular through the 1920s and enjoyed a resurgence of popularity from the 1950s on.

tiger largest of the great cats *Panthera tigris*, formerly found in much of central and S Asia but nearing extinction because of hunting and the destruction of its natural habitat.

The tiger can grow to 12 ft/3.6 m long and weigh 660 lbs/ 300 kg; it has a yellow-orange coat with black stripes. It is solitary, and feeds on large ruminants. It is a good swimmer.

Tigré or *Tigray* region in the northern highlands of Ethiopia; area 25,444 sq mi/65,900 sq km. The chief town is Mekele. The region had an estimated population of 2.4 million in 1984, at a time when drought and famine were driving large numbers of people to fertile land in the S or into neighboring Sudan. Since 1978 a guerrilla group known as the Tigré People's Liberation Front (TPLF) has been fighting for regional autonomy. In 1989 government troops were forced from the province, and the TPLF advanced toward Addis Ababa, playing a key role in the fall of the Ethiopian government May 1991.

Tigris (Arabic *Shatt Dijla*) river flowing through Turkey and Iraq (see also ◊Mesopotamia), joining the ◊Euphrates above Basra, where it forms the ◊Shatt-al-Arab; length 1,000 mi/1,600 km.

Tijuana city and resort in NW Mexico; population (1990) 742,700. It is known for horse races and casinos. ◊San Diego adjoins it across the US border.

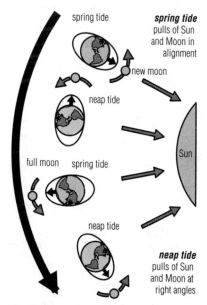

spring tide

spring tide
pulls of Sun and Moon in alignment

new moon

neap tide

full moon   spring tide

Sun

neap tide

neap tide
pulls of Sun and Moon at right angles

tide *The gravitational pull of the Moon is the main cause of the tides. Water on the side of the Earth nearest the Moon feels the Moon's pull and accumulates directly under the Moon. When the Sun and the Moon are in line, at new and full moon, the gravitational pull of Sun and Moon are in line and produce a high spring tide. When the Sun and Moon are at right angles, lower neap tides occur.*

Tilden Samuel Jones 1814–1886. US politician. A Democrat, he was governor of New York 1874–76, elected on a reform ticket. He received the Democratic presidential nomination 1876, and although he received a plurality of popular votes, the 1877 electoral college awarded the majority of electoral votes to Rutherford B Hayes.

timber wood used in construction, furniture, and paper pulp. Hardwoods include tropical mahogany, teak, ebony, rosewood, temperate oak, elm, beech, and eucalyptus. All except eucalyptus are slow-growing, and world supplies are near exhaustion. Softwoods comprise the conifers (pine, fir, spruce, and larch), which are quick to grow and easy to work but inferior in quality of grain. White woods include ash, birch, and cottonwood; all have light-colored timber, are fast-growing, and can be used through modern methods as veneers on cheaper timber.

Timbuktu or **Tombouctou** town in Mali; population (1976) 20,500. A camel caravan center from the 11th century on the fringe of the Sahara, since 1960 it has been surrounded by the southward movement of the desert, and the former canal link with the river Niger is dry.

Products include salt.

time continuous passage of existence, recorded by division into hours, minutes, and seconds. Formerly the measurement of time was based on the Earth's rotation on its axis, but this was found to be irregular. Therefore the second, the standard ◊SI unit of time, was redefined 1956 in terms of the Earth's annual orbit of the Sun, and 1967 in terms of a radiation pattern of the element cesium.

Universal time (UT), based on the Earth's actual rotation, was replaced by coordinated universal time (UTC) 1972, the difference between the two involving the addition (or subtraction) of leap seconds on the last day of June or Dec. From 1986 the term Greenwich Mean Time was replaced by UTC.

time-sharing in computing, a way of enabling several users to access the same computer at the same time. The computer rapidly switches between user ◊terminals and programs, allowing each user to work as if he or she had sole use of the system.

Timor largest and most easterly of the Lesser Sunda Islands, part of Indonesia; area 12,973 sq mi/33,610 sq km. Its indigenous people were the Atoni; successive migrants have included the Malay, Melanesian, Chinese, Arab, and Gujerati. Portugal established a colonial administration in Timor 1702, but the claim was disputed by the Dutch as well as by the Timorese, who frequently rebelled. In 1913, Timor was divided into **West Timor** and ◊**East Timor** and subjected to Dutch and Portuguese control respectively; during the Second World War both parts were occupied by Japan. West Timor (capital Kupang) became part of Indonesia on independence. East Timor (capital Dili), comprising the enclave on the NW coast, and the islands of Atauro and Jaco, was seized by Indonesia 1975 (it became an Indonesian province 1976). The annexation is not recognized by the United Nations, and guerrilla warfare by local people seeking independence continues. Since 1975 over 500,000 Timorese have been killed by Indonesian troops or have resettled in West Timor. Products include coffee, corn, rice, and coconuts.

tin soft, silver-white, malleable and somewhat ductile, metallic element, symbol Sn (from Latin *stannum*), atomic number 50, atomic weight 118.69. Tin exhibits ◊allotropy, having three forms: the familiar lustrous metallic form above 55.8°F/13.2°C; a brittle form above 321.8°F/161°C; and a gray powder form below 55.8°F/13.2°C (commonly called tin pest or tin disease). The metal is quite soft (slightly harder than lead) and can be rolled, pressed, or hammered into extremely thin sheets; it has a low melting point. In nature it occurs rarely as a free metal. It resists corrosion and is therefore used for coating and plating other metals.

tinamou any fowl-like bird of the South American order Tinamiformes, of which there are some 45 species. They are up to 16 in/40 cm long, and their drab color provides good camouflage. They are excellent runners but poor flyers and are thought to be related to the ratites (flightless birds). Tinamous are mainly vegetarian, but sometimes eat insects. They escape predators by remaining still or by burrowing through dense cover.

Tinbergen Niko(laas) 1907–1988. Dutch zoologist. He was one of the founders of ◊ethology, the scientific study of animal behavior in natural surroundings. Specializing in the study of instinctive behavior, he shared a Nobel Prize with Konrad ◊Lorenz and Karl von Frisch 1973. He is the brother of Jan Tinbergen.

tinnitus in medicine, constant buzzing or ringing in the ears. The phenomenon may originate from prolonged exposure to noisy conditions (drilling, machinery, or loud music) or from damage to or disease of the middle or inner ear. The victim may become overwhelmed by the relentless noise in the head.

Tintoretto adopted name of Jacopo Robusti 1518–1594. Italian painter. He was active in Venice. His dramatic religious paintings are spectacularly lit and full of movement, such as his huge canvases of the lives of Christ and the Virgin in the Scuola di San Rocco, Venice, 1564–88.

Tipperary county of the Republic of Ireland, in the province of Munster, divided into North and South Ridings; county town Clonmel; area 1,643 sq mi/4,255 sq km; population (1991) 132,600. It includes part of the Golden Vale, a dairy-farming region. There is horse and greyhound breeding.

Tirana or **Tiranë** capital (since 1920) of Albania; population (1990) 210,000. Industries include metallurgy, cotton textiles, soap, and cigarettes. It was founded in the early 17th century by Turks when part of the Ottoman Empire. Although the city is now largely composed of recent buildings, some older districts and mosques have been preserved.

Tirol federal province of Austria; area 4,864 sq mi/12,600 sq km; population (1989) 619,600. Its capital is Innsbruck, and it produces diesel engines, optical instruments, and hydroelectric power. Tirol was formerly a province (from 1363) of the Austrian Empire, divided 1919 between Austria and Italy.

tissue in biology, any kind of cellular fabric that occurs in an organism's body. Several kinds of tissue can usually be distinguished, each consisting of cells of a particular kind bound together by cell walls (in plants) or extracellular matrix (in animals). Thus, nerve and muscle are different kinds of tissue in animals, as are parenchyma and sclerenchyma in plants.

Titan in astronomy, largest moon of the planet Saturn, with a diameter of 3,200 mi/5,150 km and a mean distance from Saturn of 759,000 mi/1,222,000 km. It was discovered 1655 by Dutch mathematician and astronomer Christiaan ◊Huygens, and is the second largest moon in the Solar System (Ganymede, of Jupiter, is larger).

Titan in Greek mythology, any of the giant children of Uranus and Gaia, who included Cronus, Rhea, Themis, and Oceanus. Cronus and Rhea were in turn the parents of Zeus, who ousted Cronus as the ruler of the world.

Titanic British passenger liner, supposedly unsinkable, that struck an iceberg and sank off the Grand Banks of Newfoundland on its first voyage April 14–15, 1912; 1,513 lives were lost. In 1985 it was located by robot submarine 2.5 mi/4 km down in an ocean canyon, preserved by the cold environment. In 1987 salvage operations began.

titanium strong, lightweight, silver-gray, metallic element, symbol Ti, atomic number 22, atomic weight 47.90. The ninth-most abundant element in the Earth's crust, its compounds occur in practically all igneous rocks and their sedimentary deposits. It is very strong and resistant to corrosion, so it is used in building high-speed aircraft and spacecraft; it is also widely used in making alloys, as it unites with almost every metal except copper and aluminum. Titanium oxide is used in high-grade white pigments.

Titian anglicized form of Tiziano Vecellio c. 1487–1576. Italian painter. Active in Venice, he was one of the greatest artists of the High Renaissance. In 1533 he became court painter to Charles V, Holy Roman emperor, whose son Philip II of Spain later became his patron. Titian's work is richly colored, with inventive composition. He produced a vast number of portraits, religious paintings, and mythological scenes, including *Bacchus and Ariadne* 1520–23 (National Gallery, London), *Venus and Adonis* 1554 (Prado, Madrid), and the *Pietà* about 1575 (Accademia, Venice).

Titicaca lake in the Andes, 12,500 ft/3,810 m above sea level and 4,000 ft/1,220 m above the tree line; area 3,200 sq mi/8,300 sq km, the largest lake in South America. It is divided between Bolivia (port at Guaqui) and Peru (ports at Puno and Huancane). It has enormous edible frogs, and is one of the few places in the world where reed boats are still made (Lake Tana in Ethiopia is another).

titmouse any of a family (Paridae) of small birds of the order Passeriformes, found worldwide except in South America and Australia. There are 65 species, all agile and hardy, and often seen hanging upside down from twigs to feed. In North America many of the species are called chickadees.

Tlingit member of a North American Indian people of the NW coast, living in S Alaska and N British Columbia. They used to carve wooden poles representing their family crests, showing such animals as the raven, whale, octopus, beaver, bear, wolf, and the mythical "thunderbird". Their language is related to the Athabaskan languages.

TM abbreviation for ◊transcendental meditation.

TNT (abbreviation for *trinitrotoluene*) $CH_3C_6H_2(NO_2)_3$, a powerful high explosive. It is a yellow solid, prepared in several isomeric forms from toluene by using sulfuric and nitric acids.

toad any of the more terrestrial warty-skinned members of the tailless amphibians (order Anura). The name commonly refers to members of the genus *Bufo*, family Bufonidae, which are found worldwide, except for the Australian and polar regions.

The American toad *B. americanus* reaches 3.5 in/9 cm and is found from suburban backyards to mountain wildernesses throughout the NE US.

toadstool common name for many umbrella-shaped fruiting bodies of fungi.

The term is normally applied to those that are inedible or poisonous.

tobacco any large-leaved plant of the genus *Nicotiana* of the nightshade family Solanaceae, native to tropical parts of the Americas. *N. tabacum* is widely cultivated in warm, dry climates for use in cigars and cigarettes, and in powdered form as snuff.

Tobago island in the West Indies; part of the republic of ◊Trinidad and Tobago.

Tobin James 1918– . US Keynesian economist. He was awarded a Nobel Prize 1981 for his "general equilibrium" theory, which states that other criteria than monetary considerations are applied by households and firms when making decisions on consumption and investment. He is critical of monetarists for putting too much emphasis on a single asset—money—and he has analyzed the impact of changes in fiscal or monetary policy on the economy as a whole. He also has examined the process of portfolio selection, considering the trade-off between risk and yield across a broad range of assets.

Tocqueville Alexis de 1805–1859. French politician and political scientist, author of the first analytical study of the US Constitution, *De la Démocratie en Amérique/ Democracy in America* 1835, and of a penetrating description of France before the Revolution, *L'Ancien Régime et la Révolution/The Old Regime and the Revolution* 1856.

Togo Republic of (*République Togolaise*) *area* 21,930 sq mi/56,800 sq km *capital* Lomé *towns and cities* Sokodé, Kpalimé *physical* two savanna plains, divided by range of hills NE–SW; coastal lagoons and marsh *environment* the homes of thousands of people in Keto were destroyed by coastal erosion as a result of the building of the Volta dam *features* Mono Tableland, Oti Plateau, Oti River *head of state* Etienne Gnassingbé Eyadéma from 1967 *head of government* Edem Kodjo from 1994 *political system* emergent democracy *political parties* Rally of the Togolese People (RPT) (formerly Assembly of the Togolese People: RPT), centrist, nationalist; Action Committee for Renewal (CAR), left of center; Togolese Union for Democracy (UTD), left of center; Union for Justice and Democracy (UJD), nationalist, socialist; New Force Coordination (CFN), left of center *exports* phosphates, cocoa, coffee, coconuts *currency* franc CFA *population* (1993 est) 4,100,000; growth rate 3% p.a. *life expectancy* men 53, women 57 *languages* French (official), Ewe, Kaber *religions* animist 46%, Catholic 28%, Muslim 17%, Protestant 9% *literacy* men 56%, women 31% *GNP* $1,530 million (1991). GNP per capita $410. *chronology 1885–1914* Togoland was a German protectorate until captured by Anglo-French forces. *1922* Divided between Britain and France under League of Nations mandate. *1946* Continued under United Nations trusteeship. *1956* British Togoland integrated with Ghana. *1960* French Togoland achieved independence from France as the Republic of Togo with Sylvanus Olympio as head of state. *1963* Olympio killed in a military coup. Nicolas Grunitzky became president. *1967* Grunitzky replaced by Lt. Gen. Etienne Gnassingbé Eyadéma in bloodless *coup.* **1969** Assembly of the Togolese People (RPT) formed as sole legal political party. **1975** EEC Lomé convention signed in Lomé, establishing trade links with developing countries. **1979** Eyadéma returned in election. Further EEC Lomé convention signed. **1986** Attempted coup failed. **1991** Eyadéma legalized opposition parties. National conference elected Joseph Kokou Koffigoh head of interim government. Three antigovernment coups foiled. **1992** Overwhelming referendum support for multiparty politics; new constitution adopted. **1993** President Eyadéma won first multiparty elections. **1994** Antigovernment coup foiled. Opposition coalition won assembly elections. Eyadéma appointed Edem Kodjo prime minister, rejecting opposition nominee.

Tokugawa military family that controlled Japan as ◊shoguns 1603–1868. *Tokugawa Ieyasu* (1542–1616) was the Japanese general and politician who established the Tokugawa shogunate. The Tokugawa were feudal lords who ruled about one-fourth of Japan. Undermined by increasing foreign incursions, they were overthrown by an attack of provincial forces from Choshu, Satsuma, and Tosa, who restored the Meiji emperor to power.

Tokyo capital of Japan, on Honshu Island; population (1990) 8,163,100, metropolitan area over 12 million. The Sumida River delta separates the city from its suburb of Honjo. It is Japan's main cultural and industrial center (engineering, chemicals, textiles, electrical goods). Founded in the 16th century as *Yedo* (or *Edo*), it was renamed when the emperor moved his court here from Kyoto 1868. An earthquake 1923 killed 58,000 people and destroyed much of the city, which was again severely damaged by Allied bombing in World War II when 60% of Tokyo's housing was destroyed; US firebomb raids of 1945 were particularly destructive with over 100,000 people killed in just one night of bombing 9 March. The subsequent rebuilding has made it into one of the world's most modern cities.

Toledo city on the river Tagus, Castilla–La Mancha, central Spain; population (1982) 62,000. It was the capital of the Visigoth kingdom 534–711 (see ◊Goth), then became a Moorish city, and was the Castilian capital 1085–1560.

Toledo port on Lake Erie, Ohio, at the mouth of the Maumee River; population (1990) 332,900. Industries include food processing and the manufacture of vehicles, electrical goods, and glass. A French fort was built 1700, but permanent settlement did not begin until after the War of 1812.

The University of Toledo is here.

Tolstoy Leo Nikolaievich 1828–1910. Russian novelist. He wrote *War and Peace* 1863–69 and *Anna Karenina* 1873–77. From 1880 Tolstoy underwent a profound spiritual crisis and took up various moral positions, including passive resistance to evil, rejection of authority (religious or civil) and private ownership, and a return to basic mystical Christianity. He was excommunicated by the Orthodox Church, and his later works were banned.

Toltec member of an ancient American Indian people who ruled much of Mexico in the 10th–12th centuries, with their capital and religious center at Tula, NE of Mexico City. They also constructed a similar city at Chichén Itzá in Yucatán. After the Toltecs' fall the Aztecs took over much of their former territory, except for the regions regained by the Maya.

tomato annual plant *Lycopersicon esculentum* of the nightshade family Solanaceae, native to South America. It is widely cultivated for the many-seeded red fruit (technically a berry), used in salads and cooking.

tomography the technique of using X-rays or ultrasound waves to procure images of structures deep within the body for diagnostic purposes. In modern medical imaging there are several techniques, such as the ◊CAT scan (computerized axial tomography).

ton unit (symbol t) of mass. The *short ton*, used in the US and Canada, is 2,000 lb/907 kg. The *long ton*, used in the UK, is 2,240 lb/1,016 kg. The *metric ton* or *tonne* is 1,000 kg/2,205 lb.

Tonga Kingdom of (*Pule'anga Fakatu'i 'o Tonga*) or *Friendly Islands area* 290 sq mi/750 sq km *capital* Nuku'alofa (on Tongatapu island) *towns and cities* Pangai, Neiafu *physical* three groups of islands in SW Pacific, mostly coral formations, but actively volcanic in W *features* of 170 islands in the Tonga group, 36 are inhabited *head of state* King Taufa'ahau Tupou IV from 1965 *head of government* Baron Vaea from 1991 *political system* constitutional monarchy *political parties* none, but one opposition group calling for constitutional reform, Pro-Democracy Movement *currency* Tongan dollar or pa'anga *population* (1993 est) 105,000; growth rate 2.4% p.a. *life expectancy* men 69, women 74 *languages* Tongan (official), English *religions* Wesleyan 47%, Roman Catholic 14%, Free Church of Tonga 14%, Mormon 9%, Church of Tonga 9% *literacy* 99% *GNP* $1,100 per head (1991) *chronology 1831* Tongan dynasty founded by Prince Taufa'ahau Tupou. *1900* Became a British protectorate. *1965* Queen Salote died; succeeded by her son, King Taufa'ahau Tupou IV. *1970* Independence from Britain, but remained within the Commonwealth. *1993* Six prodemocracy candidates elected. Calls for reform of absolutist power.

tongue in tetrapod vertebrates, a muscular organ usually attached to the floor of the mouth. It has a thick root attached to a U-shaped bone (hyoid), and is covered with a ◊mucous membrane containing nerves and taste buds. It is the main organ of taste. The tongue directs food to the teeth and into the throat for chewing and swallowing. In humans, it is crucial for speech; in other animals, for lapping up water and for grooming, among other functions. In some animals, such as frogs, it can be flipped forward to catch insects; in others, such as anteaters, it serves to reach for food found in deep holes.

tonne the metric ton of 1,000 kg/2,204.6 lb; equivalent to 0.9842 of an imperial ◊ton.

tonsillitis inflammation of the ◊tonsils.

tonsils in higher vertebrates, masses of lymphoid tissue situated at the back of the mouth and throat (palatine tonsils), and on the rear surface of the tongue (lingual tonsils). The tonsils contain many ◊lymphocytes and are part of the body's defense system against infection.

tooth in vertebrates, one of a set of hard, bonelike structures in the mouth, used for biting and chewing food, and in defense and aggression. In humans, the first set (20 milk teeth) appear from age six months to two and a half years. The permanent ◊dentition replaces these from the sixth year onward, the wisdom teeth (third molars) sometimes not appearing until the age of 25 or 30. Adults have 32 teeth.

topaz mineral, aluminum fluosilicate, $Al_2(F_2SiO_4)$. It is usually yellow, but pink if it has been heated, and is used as a gemstone when transparent. It ranks 8 on the Mohs' scale of hardness.

Topeka capital of Kansas, US; population (1990) 119,900. It is a center for agricultural trade, and its products include processed food, printed materials, and rubber and metal products.

The Menninger Foundation, a noted psychiatric center, is here.

The community was platted 1854 and developed as a railroad center. It was made the state capital 1861.

topography the surface shape and composition of the landscape, comprising both natural and artificial features, and its study. Topographical features include the relief and contours of the land; the distribution of mountains, valleys, and human settlements; and the patterns of rivers, roads, and railroads.

topology branch of geometry that deals with those properties of a figure that remain unchanged even when the figure is transformed (bent, stretched)—for example, when a square painted on a rubber sheet is deformed by distorting the sheet.

Topology has scientific applications, as in the study of turbulence in flowing fluids.

The map of a subway system is an example of the topological representation of a network; connectivity (the way the lines join together) is preserved, but shape and size are not.

Torah in ◊Judaism, the first five books of the Hebrew Bible (Christian Old Testament). It contains a traditional history of the world from the Creation to the death of Moses; it also includes the Hebrew people's covenant with their one God, rules for religious observance, and guidelines for social conduct, including the Ten Commandments.

tornado extremely violent revolving storm with swirling, funnel-shaped clouds, caused by a rising column of warm air propelled by strong wind. A tornado can rise to a great height, but with a diameter of only a few hundred yards or less. Tornadoes move with wind speeds of 100–300 mph/160–480 kph, destroying everything in their path. They are common in the central US and Australia.

Toronto (North American Indian "place of meeting") known until 1834 as *York*. port and capital of Ontario, Canada, on Lake Ontario; metropolitan population (1985) 3,427,000. It is Canada's main industrial and commercial center (banking, shipbuilding, automobiles, farm machinery, food processing, publishing) and also a cultural center, with theaters and a film industry. A French fort was established 1749, and the site became the provincial capital 1793.

torpedo self-propelled underwater missile, invented 1866 by British engineer Robert Whitehead. Modern torpedoes are homing missiles; some resemble mines in that they lie on the seabed until activated by the acoustic signal of a passing ship. A television camera enables them to be remotely controlled, and in the final stage of attack they lock on to the radar or sonar signals of the target ship.

torpedo or *electric ray* any species of the order Torpediniformes of mainly tropical rays (cartilaginous fishes), whose electric organs between the pectoral fin and the head can give a powerful shock. They can grow to 6 ft in/180 cm length.

torque the turning effect of force on an object. A turbine produces a torque that turns an electricity generator in a power station. Torque is measured by multiplying the force by its perpendicular distance from the turning point.

torsion in physics, the state of strain set up in a twisted material; for example, when a thread, wire, or rod is twisted, the torsion set up in the material tends to return the material to its original state. The *torsion balance*, a sensitive device for measuring small gravitational or magnetic forces, or electric charges, balances these against the restoring force set up in them in a torsion suspension.

tortoise any member of the family Testudinidae, the land-living members of the order Chelonia, which includes all ◊turtles, terrestrial or aquatic. The shell of tortoises is generally more domed than that of aquatic

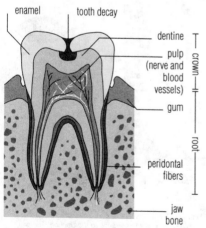
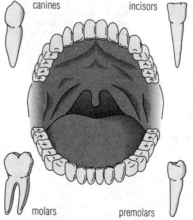

tooth Adults have 32 teeth: two incisors, one canine, two premolars, and three molars on each side of each jaw. Each tooth has three parts: crown, neck, and root. The crown consists of a dense layer of mineral, the enamel, surrounding hard dentine with a soft center, the pulp.

turtles; their hind legs are stumpy and columnar; the front legs are often shovel-shaped for digging. Tortoises are herbivorous and occur in the warmer regions of all continents except Australia. Tortoises range in size from 4 in/10 cm to 5 ft/150 cm, and some are known to live for 150 years.

totalitarianism government control of all activities within a country, overtly political or otherwise, as in fascist or communist dictatorships. Examples of totalitarian regimes are Italy under Benito ◊Mussolini 1922–45; Germany under Adolph ◊Hitler 1933–45; the USSR under Joseph ◊Stalin from the 1930s until his death in 1953; and more recently Romania under Nicolae ◊Ceausescu 1974–89.

totemism the belief in individual or clan kinship with an animal, plant, or object. This totem is sacred to those concerned, and they are forbidden to eat or desecrate it; marriage within the clan is usually forbidden. Totemism occurs among Pacific Islanders and Australian Aborigines, and was formerly prevalent throughout Europe, Africa, and Asia. Most North and South American Indian societies had totems as well.

toucan any South and Central American forest-dwelling bird of the family Ramphastidae. Toucans have very large, brilliantly colored beaks and often handsome plumage. They live in small flocks and eat fruits, seeds, and insects. They nest in holes in trees, where the female lays 2–4 eggs; both parents care for the eggs and young. There are 37 species, ranging from 1 ft/30 cm to 2 ft/60cm in size.

touch screen in computing, an input device allowing the user to communicate with the computer by touching a display screen with a finger. In this way, the user can point to a required ◊menu option or item of data. Touch screens are used less widely than other pointing devices such as the ◊mouse or ◊joystick.

Toulouse capital of Haute-Garonne *département*, SW France, on the river Garonne, SE of Bordeaux; population (1990) 365,900. The chief industries are textiles and aircraft construction (Concorde was built here). It was the capital of the Visigoths (see ◊Goth) and later of Aquitaine 781–843.

Toulouse-Lautrec Henri Marie Raymond de 1864–1901. French artist. Associated with the Impressionists, he was active in Paris where he painted entertainers and prostitutes in a style characterized by strong colors, bold design, and brilliant draftsmanship. From 1891 his lithographic posters were a great success, skillfully . executed and yet retaining the spontaneous character of sketches. His later work was to prove vital to the development of poster art.

touraco any fruit-eating African bird of the family Musophagidae. They have long tails, erectile crests, and short, rounded wings. The largest are 28 in/70 cm in long.

Tour de France French road race for professional cyclists held annually over approximately 3,000 mi/4,800 km of primarily French roads. The race takes about three weeks to complete and the route varies each year, often taking in adjoining countries, but always ending in Paris. A separate stage is held every day, and the overall leader at the end of each stage wears the coveted "yellow jersey" (French *maillot jaune*).

Tower of London fortress on the bank of the river Thames to the east of the City of London, England. The keep, or White Tower, was built about 1078 by Bishop Gundulf on the site of Roman and British fortifications.

It is surrounded by two strong walls and a moat (now dry), and was for centuries a royal residence and the principal state prison.

toxemia condition in which poisons are spread throughout the body by the bloodstream, such as those produced by ◊pathogens or by localized cells in the body.

toxic poisonous or harmful. Radioactivity, air and water pollutants, and poisons ingested or inhaled—for example, lead from automobile exhausts, asbestos, and chlorinated solvents are some toxic substances that occur in the environment; generally the effects take some time to become apparent (anything from a few hours to many years). The cumulative effects of toxic waste pose a serious threat to the ecological stability of the planet.

toxin any poison produced by another living organism (usually a bacterium) that can damage the living body. In vertebrates, toxins are broken down by ◊enzyme action, mainly in the liver.

trace element chemical element necessary in minute quantities for the health of a plant or animal. For example, magnesium, which occurs in chlorophyll, is essential to photosynthesis, and iodine is needed by the thyroid gland of mammals for making hormones that control growth and body chemistry.

trachea tube that forms an airway in air-breathing animals. In land-living ◊vertebrates, including humans, it is also known as the *windpipe* and runs from the

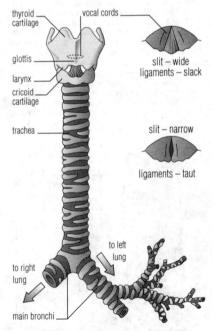

trachea *The human trachea, or windpipe. The larynx, or voice box, lies at the entrance to the trachea. The two vocal cords are membranes that normally remain open and still. When they are drawn together, the passage of air makes them vibrate and produce sounds.*

larynx to the upper part of the chest. Its diameter is about 1.5 cm/0.6 in and its length 4 in/10 cm.

tracheotomy or *tracheostomy* surgical opening in the windpipe (trachea), usually created for the insertion of a tube to enable the patient to breathe. It is done either to bypass an airway impaired by disease or injury, or to safeguard it during surgery or a prolonged period of mechanical ventilation.

trachoma chronic eye infection, resembling severe ◊conjunctivitis. The conjunctiva becomes inflamed, with scarring and formation of pus, and there may be damage to the cornea. It is caused by a viruslike organism (◊chlamydia), and is a disease of dry tropical regions. Although it responds well to antibiotics, numerically it remains the biggest single cause of blindness worldwide.

Tracy Spencer 1900–1967. US actor. He was distinguished for his understated, seemingly effortless, natural performances. His films include *Captains Courageous* 1937 and *Boys' Town* 1938 (for both of which he won Academy Awards), and he starred with Katharine Hepburn in nine films, including *Adam's Rib* 1949 and *Guess Who's Coming to Dinner* 1967, his final appearance.

He was one of Hollywood's most versatile performers.

tradescantia any plant of the genus *Tradescantia* of the family Commelinaceae, native to North and Central America. The spiderwort *T. virginiana* is a cultivated garden plant; the wandering jew *T. albiflora* is a common house plant, with green oval leaves tinged with pink or purple or silver-striped.

trade wind prevailing wind that blows toward the equator from the northeast and southeast. Trade winds are caused by hot air rising at the equator and the consequent movement of air from north and south to take its place. The winds are deflected toward the west because of the Earth's west-to-east rotation.

The unpredictable calms known as the ◊doldrums lie at their convergence.

Trafalgar, Battle of battle Oct 21, 1805, in the Napoleonic Wars. The British fleet under Admiral Nelson defeated a Franco-Spanish fleet; Nelson was mortally wounded. The victory laid the foundation for British naval supremacy throughout the 19th century. It is named for Cape Trafalgar, a low headland in SW Spain, near the western entrance to the Straits of Gibraltar.

tragedy in the ◊theater, a play dealing with a serious theme, traditionally one in which a character meets disaster as a result either of personal failings or circumstances beyond his or her control. Historically the classical view of tragedy, as expressed by the Greek tragedians Aeschylus, Euripides, and Sophocles, and the Roman tragedian Seneca, has been predominant in the Western tradition.

Trajan (Marcus Ulpius Trajanus) AD 52–117. Roman emperor and soldier, born in Seville. He was adopted as heir by Nerva, whom he succeeded AD 98.

tramway transport system for use in cities, where wheeled vehicles run along parallel rails. Streetcars are powered either by electric conductor rails below ground or by conductor arms connected to overhead wires. Greater maneuverability is achieved with the trolley bus, similarly powered by conductor arms overhead but without tracks.

tranquilizer common name for any drug for reducing anxiety or tension (anxiolytic), such as ◊benzo-

diazepines, barbiturates, antidepressants, and beta-blockers. The use of drugs to control anxiety is becoming much less popular, because most of the drugs used are capable of inducing dependence.

transactinide element any of a series of nine radioactive, metallic elements with atomic numbers that extend beyond the ◊actinide series, those from 104 (rutherfordium) to 112 (unnamed). They are grouped because of their expected chemical similarities (they are all bivalent), the properties differing only slightly with atomic number. All have ◊half-lives that measure less than two minutes.

transaction file in computing, a file that contains all the additions, deletions, and amendments required during ◊file updating to produce a new version of a ◊master file.

Trans-Alaskan Pipeline one of the world's greatest civil engineering projects, the construction of a pipeline to carry petroleum (crude oil) 800 mi/1,285 km from N Alaska to the ice-free port of Valdez. It was completed 1977 after three years' work and much criticism by ecologists.

transcendental meditation (TM) technique of focusing the mind, based in part on Hindu meditation. Meditators are given a mantra (a special word or phrase) to repeat over and over to themselves; such meditation is believed to benefit the practitioner by relieving stress and inducing a feeling of well-being and relaxation. It was introduced to the West by Maharishi Mahesh Yogi and popularized by the Beatles pop group in the late 1960s.

transducer device that converts one form of energy into another. For example, a thermistor is a transducer that converts heat into an electrical voltage, and an electric motor is a transducer that converts an electrical voltage into mechanical energy. Transducers are important components in many types of sensor, converting the physical quantity to be measured into a proportional voltage signal.

transformer device in which, by electromagnetic induction, an alternating current (AC) of one voltage is transformed to another voltage, without change of ◊frequency. Transformers are widely used in electrical apparatus of all kinds, and in particular in power transmission where high voltages and low currents are utilized.

transistor solid-state electronic component, made of ◊semiconductor material, with three or more ◊electrodes, that can regulate a current passing through it. A transistor can act as an amplifier, oscillator, photocell, or switch, and (unlike earlier electron tubes) usually operates on a very small amount of power. Transistors commonly consist of a tiny sandwich of ◊germanium or ◊silicon, alternate layers having different electrical properties because they are impregnated with minute amounts of different impurities. A crystal of pure germanium or silicon would act as an insulator (nonconductor).

transparency in photography, a picture on slide film. This captures the original in a positive image (direct reversal) and can be used for projection or printing on positive-to-positive print material, for example by the Cibachrome or Kodak R-type process.

transpiration the loss of water from a plant by evaporation. Most water is lost from the leaves through pores known as ◊stomata, whose primary function is to allow ◊gas exchange between the plant's internal tissues and the atmosphere. Transpiration from the

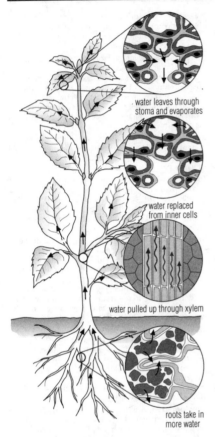

water leaves through stoma and evaporates

water replaced from inner cells

water pulled up through xylem

roots take in more water

transpiration The loss of water from a plant by evaporation is known as transpiration. Most of the water is lost through the surface openings, or stomata, on the leaves. The evaporation produces what is known as the transpiration stream, a tension that draws water up from the roots through the xylem, water-carrying vessels in the stem.

leaf surfaces causes a continuous upward flow of water from the roots via the ◊xylem, which is known as the transpiration stream.

transplant in medicine, the transfer of a tissue or organ from one human being to another or from one part of the body to another (skin grafting). In most organ transplants, the operation is for life-saving purposes, though the immune system tends to reject foreign tissue. Careful matching and immunosuppressive drugs must be used, but these are not always successful.

transsexual person who identifies himself or herself completely with the opposite sex, believing that the wrong sex was assigned at birth. Unlike *transvestites*, who desire to dress in clothes traditionally worn by the opposite sex; transsexuals think and feel emotionally in a way typically considered appropriate to

members of the opposite sex, and may undergo surgery to modify external sexual characteristics.

Trans-Siberian Railroad railroad line connecting the cities of European Russia with Omsk, Novosibirsk, Irkutsk, and Khabarovsk, and terminating at Vladivostok on the Pacific coast. It was built 1891–1905; from St Petersburg to Vladivostok is about 5,400 mi/8,700 km. A northern line, 1,928 mi/3,102 km long, was completed 1984 after ten years' work.

transubstantiation in Christian theology, the doctrine that the whole substance of the bread and wine changes into the substance of the body and blood of Jesus when consecrated in the ◊Eucharist.

transuranic element or *transuranium element* chemical element with an atomic number of 93 or more—that is, with a greater number of protons in the nucleus than has uranium. All transuranic elements are radioactive. Neptunium and plutonium are found in nature; the others are synthesized in nuclear reactions.

Transylvania mountainous area of central and NW Romania, bounded to the S by the Transylvanian Alps (an extension of the ◊Carpathian Mountains). Formerly a principality, with its capital at Cluj, it was part of Hungary from about 1000 until its people voted to unite with Romania 1918. It is the home of the vampire legends.

trapezoid in geometry, a four-sided plane figure (quadrilateral) with only two sides parallel. If the parallel sides have lengths a and b and the perpendicular distance between them is h (the height of the trapezoid), its area $A = 1/2h(a + b)$.

tree perennial plant with a woody stem, usually a single stem or "trunk", made up of ◊wood and protected by an outer layer of ◊bark. It absorbs water through a ◊root system. There is no clear dividing line between shrubs and trees, but sometimes a minimum achievable height of 20 ft/6 m is used to define a tree.

tree-and-branch filing system in computing, a filing system where all files are stored within directories, like folders in a filing cabinet. These directories may in turn be stored within further directories. The root directory contains all the other directories and may be thought of as equivalent to the filing cabinet. Another way of picturing the system is as a tree with branches from which grow smaller branches, ending in leaves (individual files).

trefoil any of several ◊clover plants of the genus *Trifolium* of the pea family Leguminosae, the leaves of which are divided into three leaflets. The name is also used for other plants with leaves divided into three lobes.

trematode parasitic flatworm with an oval non-segmented body, of the class Trematoda, including the ◊fluke.

Trent, Council of conference held 1545–63 by the Roman Catholic Church at Trento, N Italy, initiating the ◊Counter-Reformation; see also ◊Reformation.

Trevino Lee Buck 1939– . US golfer who won his first major title, the 1968 US Open, as a virtual unknown, and won it again in 1971. He has also won the British Open and US PGA titles twice, and is one of only five players to have won the US Open and British Open in the same year. He played in six Ryder Cup matches and was non-playing captain in 1985.

triangle in geometry, a three-sided plane figure, the sum of whose interior angles is 180°. Triangles can be classified by the relative lengths of their sides. A *scalene triangle* has three sides of unequal length; an *isosceles triangle* has at least two equal sides; an *equilateral triangle* has three equal sides (and three equal angles of 60°).

Triassic period of geological time 245–208 million years ago, the first period of the Mesozoic era. The continents were fused together to form the world continent Pangaea. Triassic sediments contain remains of early dinosaurs and other reptiles now extinct. By late Triassic times, the first mammals had evolved.

triathlon test of stamina involving three sports: swimming 2.4 mi/3.8 km, cycling 112 mi/180 km, and running a marathon 26 mi 385 yd/42.195 km, each one immediately following the last.

tribune Roman magistrate of plebeian family, elected annually to defend the interests of the common people; only two were originally chosen in the early 5th century BC, but there were later ten. They could veto the decisions of any other magistrate.

triceratops any of a genus *Triceratops* of massive, horned dinosaurs of the order Ornithischia. They had three horns and a neck frill and were up to 25 ft/8 m long; they lived in the Cretaceous period.

Trident nuclear missile deployed on certain US nuclear-powered submarines in the 1990s also being installed on four UK submarines. Each missile has eight warheads (MIRVs) and each of the four submarines will have 16 Trident D-5 missiles. The Trident replaced the earlier Polaris and Poseidon missiles.

triggerfish any marine bony fish of the family Balistidae, with a laterally compressed body, up to 2 ft/60 cm long, and deep belly. They have small mouths but strong jaws and teeth. The first spine on the dorsal fin locks into an erect position, allowing them to fasten themselves securely in crevices for protection; it can only be moved by depressing the smaller third ("trigger") spine.

triglyceride chemical name for ◊fat.

trigonometry branch of mathematics that solves problems relating to plane and spherical triangles. Its principles are based on the fixed proportions of sides for a particular angle in a right-angled triangle, the simplest of which are known as the ◊sine, ◊cosine, and ◊tangent (so-called trigonometrical ratios). It is of practical importance in navigation, surveying, and simple harmonic motion in physics.

trilobite any of a large class (Trilobita) of extinct, marine, invertebrate arthropods of the Paleozoic era, with a flattened, oval body, 0.4–26 in/1–65 cm long. The hard-shelled body was divided by two deep furrows into three lobes.

Trinidad and Tobago Republic of *area* Trinidad 1,864 sq mi/4,828 sq km and Tobago 116 sq mi/300 sq km *capital* Port-of-Spain *towns and cities* San Fernando, Arima, Scarborough (Tobago) *physical* comprises two main islands and some smaller ones; coastal swamps and hills E–W *features* Pitch Lake, a self-renewing source of asphalt used by 16th-century explorer Walter Raleigh to repair his ships *head of state* Noor Hassanali from 1987 *head of government* Patrick Manning from 1991 *political system* democratic republic *political parties* National Alliance for Reconstruction (NAR), nationalist, left of center; People's National Movement (PNM), nationalist, moderate, centrist; National Development Party (NDP), center-left ; United National Congress (UNC),

left of center *exports* oil, petroleum products, chemicals, sugar, cocoa *currency* Trinidad and Tobago dollar *population* (1993 est) 1,300,000 (African descent 40%, Indian 40%, European 16%, Chinese and others 2%), 1.2 million on Trinidad; growth rate 1.6% p.a. *life expectancy* men 68, women 72 *languages* English (official), Hindi, French, Spanish *media* freedom of press guaranteed by constitution and upheld by government; there are two independent morning newspapers and several weekly tabloids *religions* Roman Catholic 32%, Protestant 29%, Hindu 25%, Muslim 6% *literacy* 96% *GNP* $2,878 per head (1991) *chronology 1888* Trinidad and Tobago united as a British colony. *1956* People's National Movement (PNM) founded. *1959* Achieved internal self-government, with PNM leader Eric Williams as chief minister. *1962* Independence achieved from Britain, within the Commonwealth, with Williams as prime minister. *1976* Became a republic, with Ellis Clarke as president and Williams as prime minister. *1981* Williams died and was succeeded by George Chambers, with Arthur Robinson as opposition leader. *1986* National Alliance for Reconstruction (NAR), headed by Arthur Robinson, won general election. *1987* Noor Hassanali became president. *1990* Attempted antigovernment coup foiled. *1991* General election saw victory for PNM, with Patrick Manning as prime minister.

Trinity in Christianity, the union of three persons—Father, Son, and Holy Ghost/Spirit—in one godhead. The precise meaning of the doctrine has been the cause of unending dispute, and was the chief cause of the split between the Eastern Orthodox and Roman Catholic churches. *Trinity Sunday* occurs on the Sunday after Pentecost (Whitsun).

triode three-electrode thermionic tube containing an anode and a cathode (as does a ◊diode) with an additional negatively biased control grid. Small variations in voltage on the grid bias result in large variations in the current. The triode was commonly used in amplifiers until largely superseded by the ◊transistor. The tube was invented by the US radio engineer Lee De Forest.

Triple Alliance pact from 1882 between Germany, Austria-Hungary, and Italy to offset the power of Russia and France. It was last renewed 1912, but during World War I Italy's initial neutrality gradually changed and it denounced the alliance 1915. The term also refers to other alliances: 1668—England, Holland, and Sweden; 1717—Britain, Holland, and France (joined 1718 by Austria); 1788—Britain, Prussia, and Holland; 1795—Britain, Russia, and Austria.

Triple Entente alliance of Britain, France, and Russia 1907–17. In 1911 this became a military alliance and formed the basis of the Allied powers in World War I against the Central Powers, Germany and Austria-Hungary.

The failure of the alliance system to create a stable balance of power, coupled with widespread horror of the carnage created by World War I, led to attempts to create international cooperation with the League of Nations.

triple nose-leaf bat one of many threatened bats in Africa, *Triaenops persicus* is found scattered along much of the coastal regions of east Africa and faces threats from disturbance of the caves in which it breeds. Tourism development, resulting in disturbance to coral caves which the bats inhabit, is a particular problem.

trireme ancient Greek warship with three banks of oars as well as sails, 115 ft/38 m long. They were used at the Battle of ◊Salamis and by the Romans until the 4th century AD.

Tristan legendary Celtic hero who fell in love with Isolde, the bride he was sent to win for his uncle King Mark of Cornwall. The story became part of the Arthurian cycle and is the subject of Wagner's opera *Tristan und Isolde* 1865.

tritium radioactive isotope of hydrogen, three times as heavy as ordinary hydrogen, consisting of one proton and two neutrons. It has a half-life of 12.5 years.

Triton in Greek mythology, a merman sea god, the son of ◊Poseidon and the sea goddess Amphitrite. Traditionally, he is shown blowing on a conch shell.

trogon any species of the order Trogoniformes of tropical birds, up to 1.7 ft/50 cm long, with resplendent plumage, living in the Americas and Afro-Asia. Most striking is the ◊quetzal.

Trojan horse seemingly innocuous but treacherous gift from an enemy. In Greek mythology, during the siege of Troy, an enormous wooden horse left by the Greek army outside the gates of the city. When the Greeks had retreated, the Trojans, believing it to be a religious offering, brought the horse in. Greek soldiers then emerged from within the hollow horse and opened the city gates to enable Troy to be captured.

trombone brass wind instrument of mainly cylindrical bore, incorporating a movable slide which allows a continuous glissando (slide) in pitch over a span of half an octave. A descendant of the Renaissance sackbut, the Baroque trombone has a shallow cup mouthpiece and modestly flared bell giving a firm, noble tone, to which the modern wide bell adds a brassy sheen. The tenor and bass trombones are staple instruments of the orchestra and brass band, also of Dixieland and jazz bands, either separately or as a tenor-bass hybrid.

trompe l'oeil painting that gives a convincing illusion of three-dimensional reality. As an artistic technique, it has been in common use in most stylistic periods in the West, originating in Classical Greek art.

Trondheim fishing port in Norway; population (1990) 137,800. It has canning, textile, margarine, and soap industries. It was the medieval capital of Norway, and Norwegian kings are crowned in the cathedral (1066–93). Trondheim was occupied by the Germans 1940–45.

tropics the area between the tropics of Cancer and Capricorn, defined by the parallels of latitude approximately 23°30′ N and S of the equator. They are the limits of the area of Earth's surface in which the Sun can be directly overhead. The mean monthly temperature is over 68°F/20°C.

tropism or *tropic movement* the directional growth of a plant, or part of a plant, in response to an external stimulus such as gravity or light. If the movement is directed toward the stimulus it is described as positive; if away from it, it is negative. *Geotropism* for example, the response of plants to gravity, causes the root (positively geotropic) to grow downward, and the stem (negatively geotropic) to grow upward.

troposphere lower part of the Earth's ◊atmosphere extending about 6.5 mi/10.5 km from the Earth's surface, in which temperature decreases with height to about –76°F/–60°C except in local layers of temperature inversion. The *tropopause* is the upper boundary of the troposphere, above which the temperature increases slowly with height within the atmosphere. All of the Earth's weather takes place within the troposphere.

Trotsky Leon. Adopted name of Lev Davidovitch Bronstein 1879–1940. Russian revolutionary. He joined the Bolshevik party and took a leading part in the seizure of power 1917 and raising the Red Army that fought the Civil War 1918–20. In the struggle for power that followed ◊Lenin's death 1924, ◊Stalin defeated Trotsky, and this and other differences with the Communist Party led to his exile 1929. He settled in Mexico, where he was assassinated with an ice pick at Stalin's instigation. Trotsky believed in world revolution and in permanent revolution (see ◊Trotskyism), and was an uncompromising, if liberal, idealist.

Trotskyism form of Marxism advocated by Leon Trotsky. Its central concept is that of *permanent revolution*. In his view a proletarian revolution, leading to a socialist society, could not be achieved in isolation, so it would be necessary to spark off further revolutions throughout Europe and ultimately worldwide. This was in direct opposition to the Stalinist view that socialism should be built and consolidated within individual countries.

trotting another name for the sport of harness racing.

Troy (Latin *Ilium*) ancient city (now Hissarlik in Turkey) of Asia Minor, just S of the Dardanelles, besieged in the legendary ten-year Trojan War (mid-13th century BC), as described in Homer's *Iliad*. According to the legend, the city fell to the Greeks, who first used the stratagem of leaving behind, in a feigned retreat, a large wooden horse containing armed infiltrators to open the city's gates. Believing it to be a religious offering, the Trojans took it within the walls.

troy system system of units used for precious metals and gems. The pound troy (0.37 kg) consists of 12 ounces (each of 120 carats) or 5,760 grains (each equal to 65 mg).

Truffaut François 1932–1984. French New Wave film director and actor. He was formerly a critic. A popular, romantic, and intensely humane filmmaker, he wrote and directed a series of semiautobiographical films starring Jean-Pierre Léaud, beginning with *Les Qatre Cent Coups/The 400 Blows* 1959. His other films include *Jules et Jim* 1961, *Fahrenheit 451* 1966, *L'Enfant sauvage/The Wild Child* 1970, and *La Nuit américaine/ Day for Night* 1973 (Academy Award).

He was influenced by Alfred Hitchcock, and also drew on Surrealist and comic traditions.

truffle subterranean fungus of the order Tuberales. Certain species are valued as edible delicacies; in particular, *Tuber melanosporum*, generally found growing under oak trees. It is native to the Périgord region of France but cultivated in other areas as well. It is rounded, blackish brown, externally covered with warts, and with blackish flesh.

Truman Harry S 1884–1972. 33rd president of the US 1945–53, a Democrat. In Jan 1945 he became vice-president to Franklin D Roosevelt, and president when Roosevelt died in April that year. He played an important role at the Potsdam Conference, used ◊atomic bombs against Japan to end World War II, launched the ◊Marshall Plan to restore Western Europe's postwar economy, and nurtured the European Community (now the European Union) and NATO (including the rearmament of West

Germany). He believed in the ◊United Nations (UN) and when South Korea was invaded by North Korea 1950, had US forces join the UN forces, with General ◊MacArthur at their head. He fired MacArthur 1951 when the general's war policy conflicted with UN aims.

Trumbull John 1756–1843. American artist. He was known for his series of historical paintings of war scenes from the American revolution (1775–83), the most famous of which was his depiction of the signing of the Declaration of Independence 1776.

Born in Lebanon, Connecticut, the son of Governor Jonathan Trumbull, he was educated at Harvard University and saw action during the American Revolution. In 1780 he traveled to England to study art with Benjamin ◊West and was briefly imprisoned for espionage, returning to the US 1789.

trumpet member of an ancient family of lip-reed instruments existing worldwide in a variety of forms and materials, and forming part of the brass section in a modern orchestra. Its distinguishing features are a generally cylindrical bore and straight or coiled shape, producing a penetrating tone of stable pitch for signaling and ceremonial use. Valve trumpets were introduced around 1820, giving access to the full range of chromatic pitches.

trust arrangement whereby a person or group of people (the trustee or trustees) hold property for others (the beneficiaries) entitled to the beneficial interest. A trust can be a legal arrangement under which A is empowered to administer property belonging to B for the benefit of C. A and B may be the same person; B and C may not.

A unit trust holds and manages a number of marketable securities; by buying a "unit" in such a trust, the purchaser has a proportionate interest in each of the securities so that his or her risk is spread.

A business trust is formed by linking several companies by transferring shares in them to trustees; or by the creation of a holding company, whose shares are exchanged for those of the separate companies.

trypanosome any parasitic flagellate protozoan of the genus *Trypanosoma* that lives in the blood of vertebrates, including humans. They often cause serious diseases, called trypanosomiases, such as sleeping sickness or Chagas' disease, and are transmitted by the bite of such insects as tsetse flies or assassin bugs.

Tsavo national park in SE Kenya, established 1948. One of the world's largest, it occupies 8,036 sq mi/20,821 sq km.

tsetse fly any of a number of blood-feeding African flies of the genus *Glossina*, some of which transmit the disease nagana to cattle and sleeping sickness to human beings. Tsetse flies may grow up to 0.6 in/1.5 cm long.

tuba member of a family of valved lip-reed brass instruments of conical bore and deep, mellow tone, introduced around 1830 as bass members of the orchestra brass section and the brass band. The tuba is surprisingly agile and delicate for its size and pitch, qualities exploited by Berlioz, Ravel, and Vaughan Williams.

tube or *electron tube* in electronics, a glass tube containing gas at low pressure, which is used to control the flow of electricity in a circuit. Three or more metal electrodes are inset into the tube. By varying the voltage on one of them, called the grid electrode, the current through the tube can be controlled, and the tube can act as an amplifier. Tubes have been replaced for

most applications by ◊transistors. However, they are still used in high-power transmitters and amplifiers, and in some hi-fi systems.

tuber swollen region of an underground stem or root, usually modified for storing food. The potato is a *stem tuber*, as shown by the presence of terminal and lateral buds, the "eyes" of the potato. *Root tubers*, for example dahlias, developed from adventitious roots (growing from the stem, not from other roots) lack these. Both types of tuber can give rise to new individuals and so provide a means of vegetative reproduction.

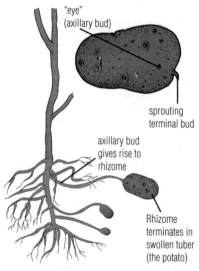

tuber Tubers are produced underground from stems, as in the potato, or from roots, as in the dahlia. Tubers can grow into new plants.

tuberculosis (TB) formerly known as *consumption* or *phthisis* infectious disease caused by the bacillus *Mycobacterium tuberculosis*. It takes several forms, of which pulmonary tuberculosis is by far the most common. A vaccine, BCG, was developed around 1920 and the first antituberculosis drug, streptomycin, in 1944. The bacterium is mostly kept in check by the body's immune system; about 5% of those infected develop the disease.

Tucson resort city in the Sonora Desert in SE Arizona, US; population (1990) 405,400. It stands 2,500 ft/760 m above sea level, and the Santa Catalina Mountains to the NE rise to about 9,000 ft/2,750 m. Industries include aircraft, electronics, and copper smelting. Tucson passed from Mexico to the US 1853 and was the territorial capital 1867–77.

The University of Arizona is here, and Kitt Peak National Observatory is in the area.

Tudjman Franjo 1922– . Croatian nationalist leader and historian, president from 1990. As leader of the center-right Croatian Democratic Union (HDZ), he led the fight for Croatian independence. During the 1991–92 civil war, his troops were hampered by lack of arms and the military superiority of the

Serb-dominated federal army, but Croatia's independence was recognized following a successful United Nations-negotiated cease-fire Jan 1992. Tudjman was reelected Aug 1992.

Tudor dynasty English dynasty 1485–1603, descended from the Welsh Owen Tudor (*c.* 1400–1461), second husband of Catherine of Valois (widow of Henry V of England). Their son Edmund married Margaret Beaufort (1443–1509), the great-granddaughter of ◊John of Gaunt, and was the father of Henry VII, who became king by overthrowing Richard III 1485. The dynasty ended with the death of Elizabeth I 1603.

tufa or *travertine* soft, porous, ◊limestone rock, white in color, deposited from solution from carbonate-saturated ground water around hot springs and in caves.

tulip plant of the genus *Tulipa*, family Liliaceae, usually with single goblet-shaped flowers on the end of an upright stem and leaves of a narrow oval shape with pointed ends. It is widely cultivated as a garden flower.

tumor overproduction of cells in a specific area of the body, often leading to a swelling or lump. Tumors are classified as benign or malignant (see ◊cancer).

tuna any of various large marine bony fishes of the mackerel family, especially the genus *Thunnus*, popular as food and game. Albacore *T. alalunga*, bluefin tuna *T. thynnus*, and yellowfin tuna *T. albacares* are commercially important.

tundra region of high latitude almost devoid of trees, resulting from the presence of ◊permafrost. The vegetation consists mostly of grasses, sedges, heather, mosses, and lichens. Tundra stretches in a continuous belt across N North America and Eurasia.

tungsten hard, heavy, gray-white, metallic element, symbol W (from German *Wolfram*), atomic number 74, atomic weight 183.85. It occurs in the minerals wolframite, scheelite, and hubnerite. It has the highest melting point of any metal (6,170°F/3,410°C) and is added to steel to make it harder, stronger, and more elastic; its other uses include high-speed cutting tools, electrical elements, and thermionic couplings. Its salts are used in the paint and tanning industries.

tunicate alternate name for ◊sea squirt.

Tunis capital and chief port of Tunisia; population (1984) 597,000. Industries include chemicals and textiles. Founded by the Arabs, it was captured by the Turks 1533, then occupied by the French 1881 and by the Axis powers 1942–43. The ruins of ancient ◊Carthage are to the NE.

Tunisia Tunisian Republic (*al-Jumhuriya at-Tunisiya*) *area* 63,378 sq mi/164,150 sq km *capital* and chief port Tunis *towns and cities* ports Sfax, Sousse, Bizerta *physical* arable and forested land in N graduates toward desert in S *features* fertile island of Jerba, linked to mainland by causeway (identified with island of lotus-eaters); Shott el Jerid salt lakes; holy city of Kairouan, ruins of Carthage *head of state* Zine el-Abidine Ben Ali from 1987 *head of government* Hamed Karoui from 1989 *political system* emergent democratic republic *political parties* Constitutional Democratic Rally (RCD), nationalist, moderate, socialist; Popular Unity Movement (MUP), radical, left of center; Democratic Socialists Movement (MDS), left of center; Renovation Movement (MR), reformed communists *exports* oil, phosphates, chemicals, textiles, food, olive oil *currency* dinar *population* (1993 est) 8,600,000; growth rate 2% p.a. *life expectancy*

men 68, women 71 *languages* Arabic (official), French *media* publications must be authorized; the offense of defamation is used to protect members of the government from criticism *religions* Sunni Muslim 95%; Jewish, Christian *literacy* men 74%, women 56% *GNP* $1,450 per head (1991) *chronology 1883* Became a French protectorate. *1955* Granted internal self-government. *1956* Independence achieved from France as a monarchy, with Habib Bourguiba as prime minister. *1957* Became a republic with Bourguiba as president. *1975* Bourguiba made president for life. *1985* Diplomatic relations with Libya severed. *1987* Bourguiba removed Prime Minister Rashed Sfar and appointed Zine el-Abidine Ben Ali. Ben Ali declared Bourguiba incompetent and seized power. *1988* Constitutional changes toward democracy announced. Diplomatic relations with Libya restored. *1989* Government party, RCD, won all assembly seats in general election. *1991* Opposition to US actions during the Gulf War. Crackdown on religious fundamentalists. *1992* Western criticism of human rights transgressions. *1994* Ben Ali and RCD reelected.

turbine engine in which steam, water, gas, or air is made to spin a rotating shaft by pushing on angled blades, like a fan. Turbines are among the most powerful machines. Steam turbines are used to drive generators in power stations and ships' propellers; water turbines spin the generators in hydroelectric power plants; and gas turbines (as jet engines; see ◊jet propulsion) power most aircraft and drive machines in industry.

turbocharger turbine-driven device fitted to engines to force more air into the cylinders, producing extra power. The turbocharger consists of a "blower", or ◊compressor, driven by a turbine, which in most units is driven by the exhaust gases leaving the engine.

turbofan jet engine of the type used by most airliners, so called because of its huge front fan. The fan sends air not only into the engine for combustion but also around the engine for additional thrust. This results in a faster and more fuel-efficient propulsive jet.

turboprop jet engine that derives its thrust partly from a jet of exhaust gases, but mainly from a propeller powered by a turbine in the jet exhaust. Turboprops are more economical than turbojets but can be used only at relatively low speeds.

turbot any of various flatfishes of the flounder group prized as food, especially *Scophthalmus maximus* found in European waters. It grows up to 3 ft/1 m long and weighs up to 30 lb/14 kg. It is brownish above and whitish underneath.

Turin (Italian *Torino*) capital of Piedmont, NW Italy, on the river Po; population (1988) 1,025,000. Industries include iron, steel, automobiles, silk and other textiles, fashion goods, chocolate, and wine. There is a university, established 1404, and a 15th-century cathedral. Features include the Palazzo Reale (Royal Palace) 1646–58 and several gates to the city. It was the first capital of united Italy 1861–64.

Turing Alan Mathison 1912–1954. English mathematician and logician. In 1936 he described a "universal computing machine" that could theoretically be programmed to solve any problem capable of solution by a specially designed machine. This concept, now called the *Turing machine*, foreshadowed the digital computer.

Turin shroud ancient piece of linen bearing the image of a body, claimed to be that of Jesus. Independent tests carried out 1988 by scientists in Switzerland, the US, and the UK showed that the cloth of the shroud dated from between 1260 and 1390. The shroud, property of the pope, is kept in Turin Cathedral, Italy.

Turk member of any of the Turkic-speaking peoples of Asia and Europe, especially the principal ethnic group of Turkey. Turkic languages belong to the Altaic family and include Uzbek, Ottoman, Turkish, Azeri, Turkoman, Tatar, Kirghiz, and Yakut.

turkey any of several large game birds of the pheasant family, native to the Americas. The wild turkey *Meleagris gallopavo* reaches a length of 4.3 ft/1.3 m, and is native to North and Central American woodlands. The domesticated turkey derives from the wild species. The ocellated turkey *Agriocharis ocellata* is found in Central America; it has eyespots on the tail.

Turkey Republic of (*Türkiye Cumhuriyeti*) *area* 300,965 sq mi/779,500 sq km *capital* Ankara *towns and cities* ports Istanbul and Izmir *physical* central plateau surrounded by mountains *environment* only 0.3% of the country is protected by national parks and reserves compared with a global average of 7% per country *features* Bosporus and Dardanelles; Mount Ararat (highest peak Great Ararat, 16,854 ft/5,137 m); Taurus Mountains in SW (highest peak Kaldi Dag, 12,255 ft/3,734 m); sources of rivers Euphrates and Tigris in E; archeological sites include çatal Hüyük, Ephesus, and Troy; rock villages of Cappadocia; historic towns (Antioch, Iskenderun, Tarsus) *head of state* Suleiman Demirel from 1993 *head of government* Tansu Ciller from 1993 *political system* democratic republic *political parties* Motherland Party (ANAP), Islamic, nationalist, right of center; Social Democratic Populist Party (SHP), moderate, left of center; True Path Party (DYP), center-right; Welfare Party (RP), Islamic fundamentalist *exports* cotton, yarn, hazelnuts, citrus, tobacco, dried fruit, chromium ores *currency* Turkish lira *population* (1993) 58,870,000 (Turkish 85%, Kurdish 12%); growth rate 2.1% p.a. *life expectancy* men 65, women 68 *languages* Turkish (official), Kurdish, Arabic *religion* Sunni Muslim 98% *literacy* men 90%, women 71% *GNP* $1,820 per head (1991) *chronology 1919–22* Turkish War of Independence provoked by Greek occupation of Izmir. Mustafa Kemal (Atatürk), leader of nationalist congress, defeated Italian, British, French, and Greek forces. *1923* Treaty of Lausanne established Turkey as independent republic under Kemal. Westernization began. *1950* First free elections; Adnan Menderes became prime minister. *1960* Menderes executed after military coup by General Cemal Gürsel. *1965* Suleiman Demirel became prime minister. *1971* Army forced Demirel to resign. *1973* Civilian rule returned under Bulent Ecevit. *1974* Turkish troops sent to protect Turkish community in Cyprus. *1975* Demirel returned to head of a right-wing coalition. *1978* Ecevit returned, as head of coalition, in the face of economic difficulties and factional violence. *1979* Demeril returned. Violence grew. *1980* Army took over, and Bulent Ulusu became prime minister. Harsh repression of political activists attracted international criticism. *1982* New constitution adopted. *1983* Ban on political activity lifted. Turgut Özal became prime minister. *1987* Özal maintained majority in general election. *1988* Improved relations and talks with Greece. *1989* Turgut Özal elected president; Yildirim Akbulut became prime minister. Application to join

European Community rejected. *1991* Mesut Yilmaz became prime minister. Turkey sided with United Nations coalition against Iraq in Gulf War. Conflict with Kurdish minority continued. Coalition government formed under Suleiman Demirel. *1992* Earthquake claimed thousands of lives. *1993* Özal died and was succeeded by Demirel. Tansu Ciller became prime minister. Kurdish separatist activity escalated, with attacks on Turkish premises in European cities. Government crackdown on separatists. *1994* Islamicists made gains in municipal elections. *1995* Government offensive launched against PKK bases in N. Iraq; condemned by international community.

Turkish language language of central and W Asia, the national language of Turkey. It belongs to the Altaic language family. Varieties of Turkish are spoken in NW Iran and several of the Central Asian Republics, and all have been influenced by Arabic and Persian.

Turkmenistan Republic of *area* 188,406 sq mi/488,100 sq km *capital* Ashkhabad *towns and cities* Chardzhov, Mary (Merv), Nebit-Dag, Krasnovodsk *physical* some 90% of land is desert including the Kara Kum "Black Sands" desert (area 120,000 sq mi/310,800 sq km) *features* on the edge of the Kara Kum desert is the Altyn Depe, "golden hill", site of a ruined city with a ziggurat, or stepped pyramid; river Amu Darya; rich deposits of petroleum, natural gas, sulfur, and other industrial raw materials *head of state* Saparmurad Niyazov from 1991 *head of government* Sakhat Muradov from 1992 *political system* socialist pluralist *political parties* Democratic Party of Turkmenistan, ex-communist, pro-Niyazov; Turkmen Popular Front (Agzybirlik), nationalist; Party of Islamic Resistance, Islamic fundamentalist *products* silk, karakul, sheep, astrakhan fur, carpets, chemicals, rich deposits of petroleum, natural gas, sulfur, and other industrial raw materials *currency* manat *population* (1993 est) 4,000,000 (Turkmen 72%, Russian 10%, Uzbek 9%, Kazakh 3%, Ukrainian 1%) *life expectancy* men 63, women 70 *language* West Turkic, closely related to Turkish *religion* Sunni Muslim *GNP* $1,700 per head (1991) *chronology 1921* Part of Turkestan Soviet Socialist Autonomous Republic. *1925* Became a constituent republic of USSR. *1990* Aug: economic and political sovereignty declared. Oct: Communist Party leader Saparmurad Niyazov elected state president. *1991* Niyazov sworn in as president. March: maintenance of the Union endorsed in

USSR referendum. Aug: Niyazov initially supported attempted anti-Gorbachev coup. Oct: independence declared. Dec: joined new Commonwealth of Independent States. *1992* Feb: joined the Muslim Economic Cooperation Organization. March: admitted into United Nations; US diplomatic recognition achieved. May: new constitution adopted. June: Niyazov reelected, uncontested. Nov–Dec: Sakhat Muradov popularly elected as prime minister. *1994* Nationwide referendum overwhelmingly backed Niyazov's presidency.

Turks and Caicos Islands British crown colony in the West Indies, the southeastern archipelago of the Bahamas *area* 166 sq mi/430 sq km *capital* Cockburn Town on Grand Turk *features* a group of some 30 islands, of which six are inhabited. The largest is the uninhabited *Grand Caicos*; others include *Grand Turk* (population 3,100), *South Caicos* (1,400), *Middle Caicos* (400), *North Caicos* (1,300), *Providenciales* (1,000), and *Salt Cay* (300); since 1982 the Turks and Caicos have developed as a tax haven *government* governor, with executive and legislative councils (chief minister from 1987 Michael John Bradley, Progressive National Party) *exports* crayfish and conch (flesh and shell) *currency* US dollar *population* (1980) 7,500, 90% of African descent *languages* English, French Creole *religion* Christian *history* secured by Britain 1766 against French and Spanish claims, the islands were a Jamaican dependency 1873–1962, and in 1976 attained internal self-government.

turmeric perennial plant *Curcuma longa* of the ginger family, native to India and the East Indies; also the ground powder from its tuberous rhizomes, used in curries to give a yellow color, and as a dyestuff.

Turner Joseph Mallord William 1775–1851. English landscape painter. He was one of the most original artists of his day. He traveled widely in Europe, and his landscapes became increasingly Romantic, with the subject often transformed in scale and flooded with brilliant, hazy light. Many later works anticipate Impressionism; for example, *Rain, Steam and Speed* 1844 (National Gallery, London).

Turner Lana (Julia Jean Mildred Frances) 1920– . US actress. She was known as the "Sweater Girl" during World War II and appeared in melodramatic films of the 1940s and 1950s such as *Peyton Place* 1957. Her other films include *The Postman Always Rings Twice* 1946, *The Three Musketeers* 1948, and *Imitation of Life* 1959.

Her debut was in *They Won't Forget* 1937, after her legendary "discovery" at a Hollywood soda fountain at the age of 16.

Turner Nat 1800–1831. US slave and Baptist preacher. Believing himself divinely appointed, he led 60 slaves in a revolt—the *Southampton Insurrection* of 1831—in Southampton County, Virginia. Before he and 16 of the others were hanged, at least 55 slave-owners had been killed.

He eluded capture for 6 weeks following the uprising, which so alarmed slave owners that repressive measures forbidding the educating of any blacks were swiftly enacted. Widespread torture and execution followed as owners exacted retribution, and the abolition movement in the south was abandoned.

Turner Richmond Kelly 1885–1961. US admiral. A specialist in amphibious warfare, Turner was Commander South Pacific Amphibious Force July 1942 and conducted the US landings at Guadalcanal Aug 1942. He then directed the landings in New Georgia and the Gilbert Islands. Transferred to the Central Pacific Theatre 1944, he was responsible for operations in the Marshall Islands and the Marianas, and in 1945 for the landings on Iwo Jima and Okinawa.

turnip biennial plant *Brassica rapa* cultivated in temperate regions for its edible white-or yellow-fleshed root and the young leaves, which are used as a green vegetable. Closely allied to it is the ◊rutabaga *Brassica napus*.

turnpike road road with a gate or barrier preventing access until a toll had been paid, common from the mid-16th–19th centuries.

turpentine solution of resins distilled from the sap of conifers, used in varnish and as a paint solvent but now largely replaced by white spirit.

Turpin Dick 1706–1739. English highwayman. The son of an innkeeper, he turned to highway robbery, cattle-thieving, and smuggling, and was hanged at York, England.

turquoise mineral, hydrous basic copper aluminum phosphate. Blue-green, blue, or green, it is a gemstone. Turquoise is found in the southwestern US, Australia, Egypt, Ethiopia, France, Germany, Iran, Turkestan, and Mexico. It was originally introduced into Europe through Turkey, from which its name is derived.

turtle any member of the reptilian order Chelonia, characterized by a horn-covered bony shell consisting of an upper and lower portion joined along the sides. The main divisions are the hidden-necked turtles (Cryptodira) that withdraw their heads in an S-shaped vertical curve and the side-necked turtles (Pleurodira) that withdraw their heads in a horizontal, sideways curve. See also ◊terrapin, ◊tortoise, and ◊sea turtle.

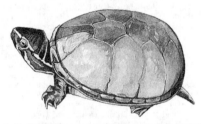

turtle *The common musk turtle lives in the slow, shallow, muddy streams of the US. Also known as the stinkpot, this turtle gives off an offensive-smelling fluid when disturbed.*

Tuscany (Italian *Toscana*) region of N central Italy, on the west coast; area 8,878 sq mi/23,000 sq km; population (1990) 3,562,500. Its capital is Florence, and cities include Pisa, Livorno, and Siena. The area is mainly agricultural, with many vineyards, such as in the Chianti hills; it also has lignite and iron mines and marble quarries (Carrara marble is from here). The Tuscan dialect has been adopted as the standard form of Italian. Tuscany was formerly the Roman *Etruria*, and inhabited by Etruscans around 500 BC. In medieval times the area was divided into small states, united under Florentine rule during the 15th–16th centuries. It became part of united Italy 1861.

Tussaud Madame (Anne Marie Grosholtz) 1761–1850. French wax-modeler. In 1802 she established an exhibition of wax models of celebrities in London. It was destroyed by fire 1925, but reopened 1928.

Tutankhamen king (pharaoh) of ancient Egypt of the 18th dynasty, about 1360–1350 BC. A son of Ikhnaton (also called Amenhotep IV), he was about 11 at his accession. In 1922 his tomb was discovered by the British archeologists Lord Carnarvon and Howard Carter in the Valley of the Kings at Luxor, almost untouched by tomb robbers. The contents included many works of art and his solid-gold coffin, which are now displayed in a city of Cairo museum.

Tutsi minority ethnic group living in Rwanda and Burundi. Although fewer in number, they have traditionally been politically dominant over the Hutu majority and the Twa (or Pygmies). In Burundi, positions of power were monopolized by the Tutsis, who carried out massacres in response to Hutu rebellions, notably in 1972 and 1988. In Rwanda, where the balance of power is more even, Tutsis were massacred in their thousands by Hutu militia during the 1994 civil war.

Tutu Desmond (Mpilo) 1931– . South African priest, Anglican archbishop of Cape Town and general secretary of the South African Council of Churches 1979–84. One of the leading figures in the struggle against apartheid in the Republic of South Africa, he was awarded the 1984 Nobel Peace Prize.

Tuvalu South West Pacific State of (formerly *Ellice Islands*) *area* 9.5 sq mi/25 sq km *capital* Funafuti *physical* nine low coral atolls forming a chain of 650 mi/579 km in the SW Pacific *features* maximum height above sea level 20 ft/6 m; coconut palms are main vegetation *head of state* Elizabeth II from 1978, represented by governor general Tomu Malaefono Sione from 1993 *head of government* Kamuta Laatasi from 1993 *political system* liberal democracy *political parties* none; members are elected to parliament as independents *exports* copra, handicrafts, stamps *currency* Australian dollar *population* (1993 est) 10,000 (Polynesian 96%); growth rate 3.4% p.a. *life expectancy* 60 men, 63 women *languages* Tuvaluan, English *religion* Christian (Protestant) *literacy* 95% *GDP* $711 per head (1983) *chronology 1892* Became a British protectorate forming part of the Gilbert and Ellice Islands group. *1916* The islands gained colonial status. *1975* The Ellice Islands were separated from the Gilbert Islands. *1978* Independence achieved from Britain, within the Commonwealth, with Toaripi Lauti as prime minister; reverted to former name Tuvalu. *1981* Dr Tomasi Puapua replaced Lauti as premier. *1986* Islanders rejected proposal for republican status. *1989* Bikenibeu Paeniu became prime minister. *1993* Kamuta Laatasi became prime minister.

Twain Mark. Pen name of Samuel Langhorne Clemens 1835–1910. US writer. He established his reputation with the comic masterpiece *The Innocents Abroad* 1869 and two classic American novels, in dialect, *The Adventures of Tom Sawyer* 1876 and *The Adventures of Huckleberry Finn* 1885. He also wrote satire, as in *A Connecticut Yankee at King Arthur's Court* 1889.

twin one of two young produced from a single pregnancy. Human twins may be genetically identical (monozygotic), having been formed from a single fertilized egg that splits into two cells, both of which became implanted. Nonidentical (fraternal or dizygotic) twins are formed when two eggs are fertilized at the same time.

two-stroke cycle operating cycle for internal combustion piston engines. The engine cycle is completed after just two strokes (movement up or down) of the piston, which distinguishes it from the more common ◊four-stroke cycle. Power mowers and lightweight motorcycles use two-stroke gasoline engines, which are cheaper and simpler than four-strokes.

Tyler John 1790–1862. 10th president of the US 1841–45, succeeding William H Harrison, who died after only one month in office. Tyler was the first US vice president to succeed to the presidency. Because he was not in favor of many of the Whig Party's policies, he was constantly at odds with the cabinet and Congress, until elections forced the Whigs from power and enabled Tyler to reorganize his cabinet. His government negotiated the Webster–Ashburton Treaty, which settled the Maine–New Brunswick boundary dispute in Canada 1842 and annexed Texas 1845.

Tyler, John *10th US president John Tyler was the first vice-president to succeed to the presidency. His administration was marked by the end of the Second Seminole War in Florida 1842, the Ashburton treaty (which settled a dispute with Britain over the border between Maine and Canada) 1842, and the admittance of Texas and Florida to the Union 1845.*

Tyler Wat English leader of the ◊Peasants' Revolt of 1381. He was probably born in Kent or Essex, and may have served in the French wars. After taking Canterbury, he led the peasant army to Blackheath, outside London, and went on to invade the city. At Mile End King Richard II met the rebels and promised to redress their grievances, which included the imposition of a poll tax. At a further conference at Smithfield, London, Tyler was murdered.

Tyndale William 1492–1536. English translator of the Bible. The printing of his New Testament (the basis of the King James Version) was begun in Cologne 1525 and, after he had been forced to flee, completed in Worms. He was strangled and burned as a heretic at Vilvorde in Belgium.

typewriter keyboard machine that produces characters on paper. The earliest known typewriter design was patented by Henry Mills in England 1714. However, the first practical typewriter was built 1867 in Milwaukee, Wisconsin, by Christopher Sholes, Carlos Glidden, and Samuel Soulé. By 1873 Remington and Sons, US gunmakers, produced under contract the first typing machines for sale and 1878 patented the first with lower-case as well as upper-case (capital) letters.

typhoid fever acute infectious disease of the digestive tract, caused by the bacterium *Salmonella typhi*, and usually contracted through a contaminated water supply. It is characterized by bowel hemorrhage and damage to the spleen. Treatment is with antibiotics.

typhoon violent revolving storm, a ◊hurricane in the W Pacific Ocean.

typhus any one of a group of infectious diseases caused by bacteria transmitted by lice, fleas, mites, and ticks. Symptoms include fever, headache, and rash. The most serious form is epidemic typhus, which also affects the brain heart, lungs, and kidneys and is associated with insanitary overcrowded conditions. Treatment is by antibiotics.

typography design and layout of the printed word. Typography began with the invention of writing and developed as printing spread throughout Europe after the invention of metal moveable type by Johann ◊Gutenberg about 1440. Hundreds of variations have followed since, but the basic design of the Frenchman Nicholas Jensen (about 1420–1480), with a few modifications, is still the ordinary ("roman") type used in printing.

Ease of reading is sought in text typefaces; ornament is sought in display typefaces.

tyrannosaurus any of a genus *Tyrannosaurus* of gigantic flesh-eating ◊dinosaurs, order Saurischia, that lived in North America and Asia about 70 million years ago. They had two feet, were up to 50 ft/15 m long, 20 ft/6.5 m tall, weighed 10 metric tons, and had teeth 6 in/15 cm long.

tire (North American *tire*) inflatable rubber hoop fitted round the rims of bicycle, automobile, and other road-vehicle wheels. The first pneumatic rubber tire was patented in 1845 by the Scottish engineer Robert William Thomson (1822–73), but it was Scottish inventor John Boyd Dunlop of Belfast who independently reinvented pneumatic tires for use with bicycles 1888–89. The rubber for automobile tires is hardened by vulcanization.

Tyrone county of Northern Ireland *area* 1,220 sq mi/ 3,160 sq km *towns and cities* Omagh (county town), Dungannon, Strabane, Cookstown *features* rivers: Derg, Blackwater, Foyle; Lough Neagh; Sperrin Mountains *industries* mainly agricultural: barley, flax, potatoes, turnips, cattle, sheep *population* (1991) 158,500.

Tyrrhenian Sea arm of the Mediterranean Sea surrounded by mainland Italy, Sicily, Sardinia, Corsica, and the Ligurian Sea. It is connected to the Ionian Sea through the Straits of Messina. Islands include Elba, Ustica, Capri, Stromboli, and the Lipari Islands.

Ubangi-Shari former name (to 1958) of the ◊Central African Republic.

Uccello Paolo. Adopted name of Paolo di Dono 1397–1475. Italian painter. Active in Florence, he was one of the first to experiment with perspective. His surviving paintings date from the 1430s onward. Decorative color and detail dominate his later pictures. His works include *St George and the Dragon* about 1460 (National Gallery, London).

Udmurt (Russian *Udmurtskaya*) autonomous republic in the W Ural foothills, central Russia *area* 16,200 sq mi/42,100 sq km *capital* Izhevsk *industries* timber, flax, potatoes, peat, quartz *population* (1985) 1,559,000 (58% Russian, 33% Udmurt, 7% Tatar) *history* conquered in the 15th–16th centuries; constituted the Votyak Autonomous Region 1920; name changed to Udmurt 1932; Autonomous Republic 1934; part of the independent republic of Russia from 1991.

Ufa industrial city (engineering, oil refining, petrochemicals, distilling, timber) and capital of the Bashkir autonomous republic, central Russia, on the river Bielaia, in the W Urals; population (1987) 1,092,000. It was founded by Russia 1574 as a fortress.

UFO abbreviation for ◊*unidentified flying object.*

Uganda Republic of *area* 91,351 sq mi/236,600 sq km *capital* Kampala *towns and cities* Jinja, M'Bale, Entebbe, Masaka *physical* plateau with mountains in W; forest and grassland; arid in NE *features* Ruwenzori Range (Mount Margherita, 16,765 ft/,110 m); national parks with wildlife (chimpanzees, crocodiles; Owen Falls on White Nile where it leaves Lake Victoria; Lake Albert in W *head of state and government* Yoweri Museveni from 1986 *political system* emergent democratic republic *political parties* National Resistance Movement (NRM), left of center; Democratic Party (DP), center-left; Conservative Party (CP), center-right; Uganda People's Congress (UPC), left of center; Uganda Freedom Movement (UFM), left of center. From 1986, political parties were forced to suspend activities *exports* coffee, cotton, tea, copper *currency* Uganda new shilling *population* (1993 est) 19,000,000 (largely the Baganda, after whom the country is named; also Langi and Acholi, some surviving Pygmies); growth rate 3.3% p.a. *life expectancy* men 51, women 55 *languages* English (official), Kiswahili, Luganda, and other African languages *religions* Roman Catholic 33%, Protestant 33%, Muslim 16%, animist *literacy* men 62%, women 35% *GNP* $170 per head (1990) *chronology 1962* Independence achieved from Britain, within the Commonwealth, with Milton Obote as prime minister. *1963* Proclaimed a federal republic with King Mutesa II (of Baganda) as president. *1966* King Mutesa ousted in coup led by Obote, who ended the federal status and became executive president. *1969* All opposition parties banned after assassination attempt on Obote. King Mutesa deposed. *1971* Obote overthrown in army coup led by Maj. Gen. Idi Amin Dada; ruthlessly dictatorial regime established; nearly 49,000 Ugandan Asians expelled; over 300,000 opponents of regime killed. *1978* Amin forced to leave country by opponents backed by Tanzanian troops. Provisional government set up with Yusuf Lule as president. Lule replaced by Godfrey Binaisa. *1978–79* Fighting broke out against Tanzanian troops. *1980* Binaisa overthrown by army. Elections held and Milton Obote returned to power. *1985* After opposition by National Resistance Army (NRA), and indiscipline in army, Obote ousted by Brig. Tito Okello; constitution suspended; power-sharing agreement entered into with NRA leader Yoweri Museveni. *1986* Power-sharing agreement ended; Museveni became president, heading broad-based coalition government. *1993* King of Baganda reinstated as formal monarch, in the person of Ronald Muwenda Mutebi II. *1994* Museveni's supporters won majority of seats in constituent assembly, elected to study proposed new constitution.

UHF (abbreviation for *ultra high frequency*) referring to radio waves of very short wavelength, used, for example, for television broadcasting.

UK abbreviation for the ◊*United Kingdom.*

Ukraine *area* 233,089 sq mi/603,700 sq km *capital* Kiev *towns and cities* Kharkov, Donetsk, Odessa, Dnepropetrovsk, Lugansk (Voroshilovgrad), Lviv (Lvov), Mariupol (Zhdanov), Krivoi Rog, Zaporozhye *physical* Russian plain; Carpathian and Crimean Mountains; rivers: Dnieper (with the Dnieper dam 1932), Donetz, Bug *features* Askaniya-Nova Nature Reserve (established 1921); health spas with mineral springs *head of state* Leonid Kuchma from 1994 *head of government* Vitaly Masol from 1994 *political system* emergent democracy *political parties* Ukrainian People's Movement (Rukh), moderate nationalist; Communist Party of the Ukraine (CPU), left-wing, antinationalist (banned 1991; re-legalized 1993); Peasants' Party of the Ukraine (PPU), conservative

agrarian; Socialist Party of the Ukraine (SPU), left-wing, antinationalist *products* grain, coal, oil, various minerals *currency* grivna *population* (1993 est) 52,000,000 (Ukrainian 73%, Russian 22%, Byelorussian 1%, Russian-speaking Jews 1%—some 1.5 million have emigrated to the US, 750,000 to Canada) *life expectancy* men 66, women 75 *language* Ukrainian (Slavonic) *religions* traditionally Ukrainian Orthodox; also Ukrainian Catholic *GNP* $2,340 per head (1991) *chronology 1918* Independent People's Republic proclaimed. *1920* Conquered by Soviet Red Army. *1921* Poland allotted charge of W Ukraine. *1932–33* Famine caused the deaths of more than 7.5 million people. *1939* W Ukraine occupied by Red Army. *1941–44* Under Nazi control; Jews massacred at Babi Yar; more than 5 million Ukrainians and Ukrainian Jews deported and exterminated. *1944* Soviet control reestablished. *1945* Became a founder member of the United Nations. *1946* Ukrainian Uniate Church proscribed and forcibly merged with Russian Orthodox Church. *1986* April: Chernobyl nuclear disaster. *1989* Rukh established as a political party. Ban on Ukrainian Uniate Church lifted. *1990* July: voted to proclaim sovereignty; former Communist Party (CP) leader Leonid Kravchuk indirectly elected president; sovereignty declared. *1991* Aug: demonstrations during the abortive anti-Gorbachev coup; independence declared, pending referendum; CP activities suspended. Oct: voted to create independent army. Dec: Kravchuk popularly elected president; independence endorsed in referendum; joined new Commonwealth of Independent States; independence acknowledged by US and European Community. *1992* Jan: prices freed. Feb: prices "temporarily" re-regulated. May: Crimean sovereignty declared, then rescinded. Aug: joint control of Black Sea fleet agreed with Russia. *1993* July: agreement to dismantle nuclear arsenal with US funding. Sept: President Kravchuk took direct rule, eliminating post of prime minister. Nov: START-I nuclear arms reduction treaty ratified. *1994* April: election gains for radical nationalists in W and Russian unionists in E and Crimea. July: former premier Leonid Kuchma elected president. Oct: large-scale privatization and decentralization program announced.

Ukrainian member of the majority ethnic group living in Ukraine; there are minorities in Siberian Russia, Kazakhstan, Poland, Slovakia, and Romania. There are 40–45 million speakers of Ukrainian, a member of the East Slavonic branch of the Indo-European family, closely related to Russian. Ukrainian-speaking communities are also found in Canada and the US.

Ulaanbaatar or *Ulan Bator* (formerly until 1924 *Urga*) capital of the Mongolian Republic; a trading center producing carpets, textiles, vodka; population (1991) 575,000.

ulcer any persistent breach in a body surface (skin or mucous membrane). It may be caused by infection, irritation, or tumor and is often inflamed. Common ulcers include aphthous (mouth), gastric (stomach), duodenal, decubitus ulcers (pressure sores), and those complicating varicose veins.

Ulster former kingdom in Northern Ireland, annexed by England 1461, from Jacobean times a center of English, and later Scottish, settlement on land confiscated from its owners; divided 1921 into Northern Ireland (counties Antrim, Armagh, Down, Fermanagh, Londonderry [now Derry], and Tyrone) and the Republic of Ireland (counties Cavan, Donegal, and Monaghan).

Ulster Defense Association (UDA) Northern Ireland Protestant paramilitary organization responsible for a number of sectarian killings. Fanatically loyalist, it established a paramilitary wing (the Ulster Freedom Fighters) to combat the ◊Irish Republican Army (IRA) on its own terms and by its own methods. No political party has acknowledged any links with the UDA. In 1994, following a cessation of military activities by the IRA, the UDA, along with other Protestant paramilitary organisations, declared a cease-fire.

Ulster Freedom Fighters (UFF) paramilitary wing of the ◊Ulster Defense Association.

ultrasonics study and application of the sound and vibrations produced by ultrasonic pressure waves (see ◊ultrasound).

ultrasound pressure waves similar in nature to sound waves but occurring at frequencies above 20,000 Hz (cycles per second), the approximate upper limit of human hearing (15–16 Hz is the lower limit).

ultrasound scanning or *ultrasonography* in medicine, the use of ultrasonic pressure waves to create a diagnostic image. It is a safe, noninvasive technique that often eliminates the need for exploratory surgery.

Ultrasound scanning is especially valuable in obstetrics, where it has revolutionized fetal evaluation and diagnosis.

ultraviolet radiation light rays invisible to the human eye, of wavelengths from about 4×10^{-4} to 5×10^{-6} millimeters (where the ◊X-ray range begins). Physiologically, they are important but also dangerous, causing the formation of vitamin D in the skin and producing sunburn in excess. They are strongly germicidal and may be produced artificially by mercury vapor and arc lamps for therapeutic use.

Ulysses Roman name for ◊Odysseus, the Greek mythological hero.

Umar 581–644. Adviser of the prophet Mohammed. In 634 he succeeded Abu Bakr as caliph (civic and religious leader of Islam), and conquered Syria, Palestine, Egypt, and Persia. He was assassinated by a slave. The Mosque of Omar in Jerusalem is attributed to him.

Umayyad dynasty Arabian dynasty of the Islamic empire who reigned as caliphs (civic and religious leaders of Islam) 661–750, when they were overthrown by Abbasids. A member of the family, Abd al-Rahmam, escaped to Spain and in 756 assumed the title of emir of Córdoba. His dynasty, which took the title of caliph in 929, ruled in Córdoba until the early 11th century.

umbrella bird bird of tropical South and Central America, family Contingidae. The Amazonian species *Cephalopterus ornatus* has an inflatable wattle at the neck to amplify its humming call, and in display elevates a long crest (4 in/12 cm) lying above the bill so that it rises umbrellalike above the head. These features are less noticeable in the female, which is brownish, whereas the male is blue-black.

Umbria· mountainous region of Italy in the central Apennines, including the provinces of Perugia and Terni; area 3,281 sq mi/8,500 sq km; population (1990) 822,700. Its capital is Perugia, and the river Tiber rises in the region. Industries include wine, grain, olives, tobacco, textiles, chemicals, and metalworking. This is the home of the Umbrian school of artists, including Raphael.

Umm al Qaiwain one of the ◊United Arab Emirates.

UN abbreviation for the ◊*United Nations*.

unbundling in computing, marketing or selling products, usually hardware and software, separately rather than as a single package.

uncertainty principle or *indeterminacy principle* in quantum mechanics, the principle that it is meaningless to speak of a particle's position, momentum, or other parameters, except as results of measurements; measuring, however, involves an interaction (such as a ◊photon of light bouncing off the particle under scrutiny), which must disturb the particle, though the disturbance is noticeable only at an atomic scale. The principle implies that one cannot, even in theory, predict the moment-to-moment behavior of such a system.

unconscious in psychoanalysis, part of the personality of which the individual is unaware, and which contains impulses or urges that are held back, or repressed, from conscious awareness.

underground economy unofficial economy of a country, which includes undeclared earnings from a second job ("moonlighting") and enjoyment of undervalued goods and services (such as company "perks"), designed for tax evasion purposes. In industrialized countries, it has been estimated to equal about 10% of ◊gross domestic product.

Underground Railroad in US history, a network established in the North before the ◊Civil War to provide sanctuary and assistance for escaped black slaves. Safe houses, transport facilities, and "conductors" existed to lead the slaves to safety in the North and Canada, although the number of fugitives who secured their freedom by these means may have been exaggerated.

unemployment lack of paid employment. The unemployed are usually defined as those out of work who are available for and actively seeking work. Unemployment is measured either as a total or as a percentage of those who are available for work, known as the working population or labor force. Periods of widespread unemployment in the US and Europe in the 20th century include 1929–1930s, and the years since the mid-1970s.

UNESCO (acronym for *United Nations Educational, Scientific, and Cultural Organization*) agency of the UN, established 1946, with its headquarters in Paris. The US, contributor of 25% of its budget, withdrew 1984 on grounds of its "overpoliticization and mismanagement", and Britain followed 1985.

ungulate general name for any hoofed mammal. Included are the odd-toed ungulates (perissodactyls) and the even-toed ungulates (artiodactyls), along with subungulates such as elephants.

Uniate Church any of the ◊Orthodox Churches that accept the Catholic faith and the supremacy of the pope and are in full communion with the Roman Catholic Church, but retain their own liturgy and separate organization.

unicellular organism animal or plant consisting of a single cell. Most are invisible without a microscope but a few, such as the giant ◊ameba, may be visible to the naked eye. The main groups of unicellular organisms are bacteria, protozoa, unicellular algae, and unicellular fungi or yeasts. Some become disease-causing agents, ◊pathogens.

Unicode in computing, proposed 16-bit character encoding system, intended to cover all characters in all languages (including Chinese and similar languages) and to be backward compatible with ◊ASCII.

unicorn mythical animal referred to by classical writers, said to live in India and resembling a horse, but with one spiraled horn growing from the forehead.

It was especially important in medieval Christian symbolism and lore.

unidentified flying object or *UFO* any light or object seen in the sky whose immediate identity is not apparent. Despite unsubstantiated claims, there is no evidence that UFOs are alien spacecraft. On investigation, the vast majority of sightings turn out to have been of natural or identifiable objects, notably bright stars and planets, meteors, aircraft, and satellites, or to have been perpetrated by pranksters. The term *flying saucer* was coined in 1947 and has been in use since.

Unification Church or *Moonies* church founded in Korea 1954 by the Reverend Sun Myung Moon. The number of members (often called "moonies") is about 200,000 worldwide. The theology unites Christian and Taoist ideas and is based on Moon's book *Divine Principle*, which teaches that the original purpose of creation was to set up a perfect family, in a perfect relationship with God.

unified field theory in physics, the theory that attempts to explain the four fundamental forces (strong nuclear, weak nuclear, electromagnetic, and gravity) in terms of a single unified force (see ◊particle physics).

Union, Act of 1707 act of Parliament that brought about the union of England and Scotland; that of 1801 united England and Ireland. The latter was revoked when the Irish Free State was constituted 1922.

UNITA (acronym for *Uniao Nacional para a Independencia Total de Angola*/National Union for the Total Independence of Angola) Angolan nationalist movement founded by Jonas ◊Savimbi 1966. Backed by South Africa, UNITA continued to wage guerrilla warfare against the ruling MPLA regime after the latter gained control of the country in 1976. A peace agreement was signed May 1991, but fighting recommenced Sept 1992 after Savimbi disputed an election victory for the ruling party, and escalated into a bloody civil war 1993. A peace agreement was signed 1994.

Unitarianism a Christian denomination that rejects the orthodox doctrine of the Trinity, asserts the fatherhood of God and the brotherhood of humanity, and gives a preeminent position to Jesus as a religious teacher, while denying his divinity.

Unitarianism arose independently in the 16th century in Poland, where its chief exponent was Faustus Socinus (1539–1604), and in the Transylvanian region of Hungary and Romania. During the 17th century a number of English writers began to accept Jesus' humanity while denying the doctrine of the Trinity. American Unitarianism emerged as a secession movement from the Congregational Church in New England. The transcendentalism of ◊Emerson and ◊Thoreau was a major influence on American Unitarianism. The chief Unitarian body in the US is the Unitarian Universalist Association, formed 1961 by the merger of the American Unitarian Association and the Universalist Church.

Unitas John Constantine 1933–   . US football player. He was signed by the Baltimore Colts 1956 and as Colt quarterback for 17 seasons, Unitas led the team to five NFL championship titles in the years 1958–71. Following his release from the Colts, Unitas played for the San Diego Chargers 1973. He was one of the greatest passers in the history of the game.

He was elected to the Football Hall of Fame 1979.

United Arab Emirates (UAE) (*Ittihad al-Imarat al-Arabiyah*) federation of the emirates of Abu Dhabi, Ajman, Dubai, Fujairah, Ras al Khaimah, Sharjah, Umm al Qaiwain **total area** 32,292 sq mi/83,657 sq km **capital** Abu Dhabi **towns and cities** (chief port) Dubai **physical** desert and flat coastal plain; mountains in E **features** linked by dependence on oil revenues **head of state and government** Sheik Zayed bin Sultan al-Nahayan of Abu Dhabi from 1971 **supreme council of rulers** *Abu Dhabi* Sheik Sultan Zayed bin al-Nahayan, president (1966); *Ajman* Sheik Humaid bin Rashid al-Nuami (1981); *Dubai* Sheik Maktoum bin Rashid al-Maktoum (1990); *Fujairah* Sheik Hamad bin Mohammed al-Sharqi (1974); *Ras al Khaimah* Sheik Saqr bin Mohammed al-Quasimi (1948); *Sharjah* Sheik Sultan bin Mohammed al-Quasimi (1972); *Umm al Qaiwain* Sheik Rashid bin Ahmad al-Mu'alla (1981) **political system** absolutism **political parties** none **exports** oil, natural gas, fish, dates **currency** UAE dirham **population** (1993) 2,100,000 (10% nomadic); growth rate 6.1% p.a. **life expectancy** men 70, women 74 **languages** Arabic (official), Farsi, Hindi, Urdu, English **religions** Muslim 96%, Christian, Hindu **literacy** 55% **GNP** $19,870 per head (1990) **chronology** *1952* Trucial Council established. *1971* Federation of Arab Emirates formed; later dissolved. Six Trucial States formed United Arab Emirates, with ruler of Abu Dhabi, Sheik Zayed, as president. Provisional constitution adopted. *1972* The seventh state, Ras al Khaimah, joined the federation. *1976* Sheik Zayed threatened to relinquish presidency unless progress toward centralization became more rapid. *1985* Diplomatic and economic links with USSR and China established. *1987* Diplomatic relations with Egypt restored. *1990–91* Iraqi invasion of Kuwait opposed; UAE fights with UN coalition. *1991* Bank of Commerce and Credit International, controlled by Abu Dhabi's ruler, collapsed. *1992* Border dispute with Iran.

United Arab Republic union formed 1958, broken 1961, between ◊Egypt and ◊Syria. Egypt continued to use the name after the breach up until 1971.

United Kingdom of Great Britain and Northern Ireland (UK) **area** 94,247 sq mi/244,100 sq km **capital** London **towns and cities** Birmingham, Glasgow, Leeds, Sheffield, Liverpool, Manchester, Edinburgh, Bradford, Bristol, Belfast, Newcastle-upon-Tyne, Cardiff **physical** became separated from European continent about 6000 BC ; rolling landscape, increasingly mountainous toward the N, with Grampian Mountains in Scotland, Pennines in N England, Cambrian Mountains in Wales; rivers include Thames, Severn, and Spey **territories** Anguilla, Bermuda, British Antarctic Territory, British Indian Ocean Territory, British Virgin Islands, Cayman Islands, Falkland Islands, Gibraltar, Hong Kong (until 1997), Montserrat, Pitcairn Islands, St Helena and Dependencies (Ascension, Tristan da Cunha), Turks and Caicos Islands **environment** an estimated 67% (the highest percentage in Europe) of forests have been damaged by acid rain **features** milder climate than N Europe because of Gulf Stream; considerable rainfall. Nowhere more than 74.5 mi/120 km from sea; indented coastline, various small islands **head of state** Queen Elizabeth II from 1952 **head of government** John Major from 1990 **political system** liberal

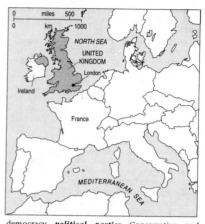

democracy **political parties** Conservative and Unionist Party, right of center; Labour Party, moderate left of center; Social and Liberal Democrats, center-left; Scottish National Party (SNP), Scottish nationalist; Plaid Cymru (Welsh Nationalist Party), Welsh nationalist; Official Ulster Unionist Party (OUP), Democratic Unionist Party (DUP), Ulster People's Unionist Party (UPUP), all Northern Ireland right of center, in favor of remaining part of United Kingdom; Social Democratic Labour Party (SDLP), Northern Ireland, moderate left of center; Sinn Féin, Northern Ireland, socialist, pro-united Ireland; Green Party, ecological **exports** cereals, rape, sugar beet, potatoes, meat and meat products, poultry, dairy products, electronic and telecommunications equipment, engineering equipment and scientific instruments, oil and gas, petrochemicals, pharmaceuticals, fertilizers, film and television programs, aircraft **currency** pound sterling (£) **population** (1993 est) 58,000,000 (81.5% English, 9.6% Scottish, 1.9% Welsh, 2.4% Irish, 1.8% Ulster); growth rate 0.1% p.a. **religions** Christian (55% Protestant, 10% Roman Catholic); Muslim, Jewish, Hindu, Sikh **life expectancy** men 73, women 79 **languages** English, Welsh, Gaelic **media** four conglomerates control 85% of daily and Sunday newspaper circulation as well as most TV advertising revenue (1994) **literacy** 99% **GNP** $16,080 per head (1991) **chronology** *1707* Act of Union between England and Scotland under Queen Anne. *1721* Robert Walpole unofficially first prime minister, under George I. *1783* Loss of North American colonies that form US; Canada retained. *1801* Act of Ireland united Britain and Ireland. *1819* Peterloo massacre: cavalry charged a meeting of supporters of parliamentary reform. *1832* Great Reform Bill became law, shifting political power from upper to middle class. *1838* Chartist working-class movement formed. *1846* Corn Laws repealed by Robert Peel. *1851* Great Exhibition in London. *1867* Second Reform Bill, extending the franchise, introduced by Disraeli and passed. *1906* Liberal victory; program of social reform. *1911* Powers of House of Lords curbed. *1914* Irish Home Rule Bill introduced. *1914–18* World War I. *1916* Lloyd George became prime minister. *1920* Home Rule Act incorporated NE of Ireland (Ulster) into the United Kingdom of Great Britain and Northern Ireland. *1921* Ireland, except for Ulster, became a dominion (Irish Free State, later Eire, 1937). *1924* First Labour government led by

Ramsay MacDonald. *1926* General Strike. *1931* Coalition government; unemployment reached 3 million. *1939* World War II began. *1940* Winston Churchill became head of coalition government. *1945* Labour government under Clement Attlee; welfare state established. *1951* Conservatives under Winston Churchill defeated Labour. *1956* Suez Crisis. *1964* Labour victory under Harold Wilson. *1970* Conservatives under Edward Heath defeated Labour. *1972* Parliament prorogued in Northern Ireland; direct rule from Westminster began. *1973* UK joined European Economic Community. *1974* Three-day week, coal strike; Wilson replaced Heath. *1976* James Callaghan replaced Wilson as prime minister. *1977* Liberal–Labour pact. *1979* Victory for Conservatives under Margaret Thatcher. *1981* Formation of Social Democratic Party (SDP). Riots occurred in inner cities. *1982* Unemployment over 3 million. Falklands War. *1983* Thatcher reelected. *1984–85* Coal strike, the longest in British history. *1986* Abolition of metropolitan counties. *1987* Thatcher reelected for third term. *1988* Liberals and most of SDP merged into the Social and Liberal Democrats, leaving a splinter SDP. Inflation and interest rates rose. *1989* The Green Party polled 2 million votes in the European elections. *1990* Riots as poll tax introduced in England. Troops sent to the Persian Gulf following Iraq's invasion of Kuwait. British hostages held in Iraq, later released. Britain joined European exchange rate mechanism (ERM). Thatcher replaced by John Major as Conservative leader and prime minister. *1991* British troops took part in US-led war against Iraq under United Nations umbrella. Severe economic recession and rising unemployment. *1992* Recession continued. April: Conservative Party won fourth consecutive general election, but with reduced majority. John Smith replaced Neil Kinnock as Labour leader. Sept: sterling devalued and UK withdrawn from ERM. Oct: drastic coal mine closure program encountered massive public opposition; later implemented. Major's popularity at unprecedentedly low rating. Nov: government motion in favor of ratification of Maastricht Treaty narrowly passed. Revelations of past arms sales to Iraq implicated senior government figures, including the prime minister. *1993* Recession continued. Chancellor of the Exchequer replaced. July: Maastricht Treaty ratified by parliament. Dec: peace proposal for Northern Ireland, the Downing Street Declaration, issued jointly with Irish government. *1994* Criticism of government's handling of European Union issues. Major under increasing pressure to step down. May: Liberal Democrats made substantial gains in local elections. Sudden death of Labour leader, John Smith. June: Conservatives suffered defeats in European elections. July: Tony Blair elected new Labour leader. Aug: Irish Republican Army declared unilateral cease-fire in Northern Ireland. Oct: Protestant paramilitary cease-fire announced. Mounting allegations of corruption within Conservative Party. *1995* July: early leadership election won by John Major. Michael Heseltine appointed deputy prime minister.

United Nations (UN) association of states for international peace, security, and cooperation, with its headquarters in New York. The UN was established 1945 as a successor to the ◊League of Nations, and has played a role in many areas, such as refugees, development assistance, disaster relief, and cultural cooperation. Its membership in 1994 stood at 184 states, and the total proposed budget for 1994–95 was $2,468 million.

Boutros ◊Boutros-Ghali became secretary-general 1992.

United Nations Security Council the most powerful body of the UN. It has five permanent members—the US, Russia, the UK, France, and China—which exercise a veto in that their support is requisite for all decisions, plus ten others, five of which are elected each year by the General Assembly for a two-year term; retiring members are not eligible for reelection. At any one time the ten rotating members must comprise five countries from Africa and Asia, two from Latin America, one from E Europe, and two from W Europe.

United States (US) officially *United States of America* (US) country in North America, extending from the Atlantic Ocean in the east to the Pacific Ocean in the west, bounded north by Canada and south by Mexico, and including the outlying states of Alaska and Hawaii.

United States (US) area 3,618,770 sq mi /9,368,900 sq km *capital* Washington, D.C. *cities* New York, Los Angeles, Chicago, Philadelphia, Detroit, San Francisco, Washington, Dallas, San Diego, San Antonio, Houston, Boston, Baltimore, Phoenix, Indianapolis, Memphis, Honolulu, San José *physical* topography and vegetation from tropical (Hawaii) to arctic (Alaska); mountain ranges parallel with E and W coasts; the Rocky Mountains separate rivers emptying into the Pacific from those flowing into the Gulf of Mexico; Great Lakes in N; rivers include Hudson, Mississippi, Missouri, Colorado, Columbia, Snake, Rio Grande, Ohio *environment* the US produces the world's largest quantity of municipal waste per person (1,900 lb/850 kg) annually *features* see individual states *territories* the commonwealths of Puerto Rico and Northern Marianas; the federated states of Micronesia; Guam, the US Virgin Islands, American Samoa, Wake Island, Midway Islands, Marshall Islands, Belau, and Johnston and Sand Islands *head of state and government* Bill Clinton from 1993 *political system* liberal democracy *political parties* Democratic Party, liberal, center; Republican Party, center-right *currency* US dollar *population* (1990 est) 250,372,000 (white 80%, black 12%, Asian/Pacific islander 3%,

United States: presidents and elections

year elected/ took office	president	party	losing candidate(s)	party
1789	1. George Washington	Federalist	no opponent	
1792	reelected		no opponent	
1796	2. John Adams	Federalist	Thomas Jefferson	Democrat–Republican
1800	3. Thomas Jefferson	Democrat–Republican	Aaron Burr	Democrat–Republican
1804	reelected		Charles Pinckney	Federalist
1808	4. James Madison	Democrat–Republican	Charles Pinckney	Federalist
1812	reelected		DeWitt Clinton	Federalist
1816	5. James Monroe	Democrat–Republican	Rufus King	Federalist
1820	reelected		John Quincy Adams	Democrat–Republican
1824	6. John Quincy Adams	Democrat–Republican	Andrew Jackson	Democrat–Republican
			Henry Clay	Democrat–Republican
			William H Crawford	Democrat–Republican
1828	7. Andrew Jackson	Democrat	John Quincy Adams	National Republican
1832	reelected		Henry Clay	National Republican
1836	8. Martin Van Buren	Democrat	William Henry Harrison	Whig
1840	9. William Henry Harrison	Whig	Martin Van Buren	Democrat
1841	10. John Tyler[1]	Whig		
1844	11. James K Polk	Democrat	Henry Clay	Whig
1848	12. Zachary Taylor	Whig	Lewis Cass	Democrat
1850	13. Millard Fillmore[2]	Whig		
1852	14. Franklin Pierce	Democrat	Winfield Scott	Whig
1856	15. James Buchanan	Democrat	John C Fremont	Republican
1860	16. Abraham Lincoln	Republican	Stephen Douglas	Democrat
			John Breckinridge	Democrat
			John Bell	Constitutional Union
1864	reelected		George McClellan	Democrat
1865	17. Andrew Johnson[3]	Democrat		
1868	18. Ulysses S Grant	Republican	Horatio Seymour	Democrat
1872	reelected		Horace Greeley	Democrat–Liberal
1876	19. Rutherford B Hayes	Republican	Samuel Tilden	Democrat
1880	20. James A Garfield	Republican	Winfield Hancock	Democrat
1881	21. Chester A Arthur[4]	Republican		
1884	22. Grover Cleveland	Democrat	James Blaine	Republican
1888	23. Benjamin Harrison	Republican	Grover Cleveland	Democrat
1892	24. Grover Cleveland	Democrat	Benjamin Harrison	Republican
			James Weaver	People's
1896	25. William McKinley	Republican	William J Bryan	Democrat–People's
1900	reelected		William J Bryan	Democrat
1901	26. Theodore Roosevelt[5]	Republican		
1904	reelected		Alton B Parker	Democrat
1908	27. William H Taft	Republican	William Jennings Bryan	Democrat
1912	28. Woodrow Wilson	Democrat	Theodore Roosevelt	Progressive
			William H Taft	Republican
1916	reelected		Charles E Hughes	Republican
1920	29. Warren G Harding	Republican	James M Cox	Democrat
1923	30. Calvin Coolidge[6]	Republican		
1924	reelected		John W Davis	Democrat
			Robert M LaFollette	Progressive
1928	31. Herbert Hoover	Republican	Alfred E Smith	Democrat
1932	32. Franklin D Roosevelt	Democrat	Herbert Hoover	Republican
			Norman Thomas	Socialist
1936	reelected		Alfred Landon	Republican
1940	reelected		Wendell Willkie	Republican
1944	reelected		Thomas E Dewey	Republican
1945	33. Harry S Truman[7]	Democrat		
1948	reelected		Thomas E Dewey	Republican
			J Strom Thurmond	States' Rights
			Henry A Wallace	Progressive
1952	34. Dwight D Eisenhower	Republican	Adlai E Stevenson	Democrat
1956	reelected		Adlai E Stevenson	Democrat
1960	35. John F Kennedy	Democrat	Richard M Nixon	Republican
1963	36. Lyndon B Johnson[8]	Democrat		
1964	reelected		Barry M Goldwater	Republican
1968	37. Richard M Nixon	Republican	Hubert H Humphrey	Democrat
			George C Wallace	American Independent
1972	reelected		George S McGovern	Democrat
1974	38. Gerald R Ford[9]	Republican		
1976	39. Jimmy Carter	Democrat	Gerald R Ford	Republican
1980	40. Ronald Reagan	Republican	Jimmy Carter	Democrat
			John B Anderson	Independent
1984	reelected		Walter Mondale	Democrat
1988	41. George Bush	Republican	Michael Dukakis	Democrat
1992	42. William Clinton	Democrat	George Bush	Republican

[1] became president on death of Harrison
[2] became president on death of Taylor
[3] became president on assassination of Lincoln
[4] became president on assassination of Garfield
[5] became president on assassination of McKinley
[6] became president on death of Harding
[7] became president on death of Franklin D Roosevelt
[8] became president on assassination of Kennedy
[9] became president on resignation of Nixon

American Indian, Inuit, and Aleut 1%, Hispanic [included in above percentages] 9%); growth rate 0.9% p.a. *life expectancy* men 72, women 79 (1989) *languages* English, Spanish *religions* Christian 86.5% (Roman Catholic 26%, Baptist 19%, Methodist 8%, Lutheran 5%), Jewish 1.8%, Muslim 0.5%, Buddhist and Hindu less than 0.5% *literacy* 99% (1989) *GNP* $3,855 bn (1983); $13,451 per head *chronology 1776* Declaration of Independence. *1787* US Constitution drawn up. *1789* Washington elected as first president. *1803* Louisiana Purchase. *1812–14* War with England, arising from commercial disputes caused by Britain's struggle with Napoleon. *1819* Florida purchased from Spain. *1836* The battle of the Alamo, Texas, won by Mexico. *1841* First wagon train left Missouri for California. *1846* Mormons, under Brigham Young, founded Salt Lake City, Utah. *1846–48* Mexican War resulted in cession to US of Arizona, California, part of Colorado and Wyoming, Nevada, New Mexico, Texas, and Utah. *1848–49* California gold rush. *1860* Lincoln elected president. *1861–65* Civil War between North and South. *1865* Slavery abolished. Lincoln assassinated. *1867* Alaska bought from Russia. *1890* Battle of Wounded Knee, the last major battle between American Indians and US troops. *1898* War with Spain ended with the Spanish cession of Philippines, Puerto Rico, and Guam; it was agreed that Cuba be independent. Hawaii annexed. *1917–18* US entered World War I. *1919–21* Wilson's 14 Points became base for League of Nations. *1920* Women achieved the vote. *1924* American Indians made citizens by Congress. *1929* Wall Street stock-market crash. *1933* Franklin D Roosevelt's New Deal to alleviate thevDepression put into force. *1941–45* The Japanese attack on Pearl Harbor Dec 1941 precipitated US entry into World War II. *1945* US ended war in the Pacific by dropping A-bombs on Hiroshima and Nagasaki, Japan. *1950–53* US involvement in Korean War. McCarthy anticommunist investigations (HUAC) became a "witch hunt". *1954* Civil Rights legislation began with segregation ended in public schools. *1957* Civil Rights bill on voting. *1958* First US satellite in orbit. *1961* Bay of Pigs abortive CIA-backed invasion of Cuba. *1963* President Kennedy assassinated; Lyndon B Johnson assumed the presidency. *1964–68* "Great Society" civil-rights and welfare measures in the Omnibus Civil Rights bill. *1964–75* US involvement in Vietnam War. *1965* US intervention in Dominican Republic. *1969* US astronaut Neil Armstrong was the first human on the Moon. *1973* OPEC oil embargo almost crippled US industry and consumers. Inflation began. *1972–74* Watergate scandal began in effort to reelect Nixon and ended just before impeachment; Nixon resigned as president; replaced by Ford, who pardoned Nixon. *1975* Final US withdrawal from Vietnam. *1979* US–Chinese diplomatic relations normalized. *1979–80* Iranian hostage crisis; relieved by Reagan concessions and released on his inauguration day Jan 1981. *1981* Space shuttle mission was successful. *1983* US invasion of Grenada. *1986* "Irangate" scandal over secret US government arms sales to Iran, with proceeds to antigovernment Contra guerrillas in Nicaragua. *1987* Reagan and Gorbachev (for USSR) signed intermediate-range nuclear forces treaty. Wall Street stock-market crash. *1988* US became world's largest debtor nation, owing $532 billion. George Bush elected president. *1989* Bush met Gorbachev at Malta, end to Cold War declared; large cuts announced for US military; US invaded Panama; Noriega taken into custody. *1990*

Bush and Gorbachev met again. US troops sent to Middle East following Iraq's invasion of Kuwait. *1991* Jan–Feb: US-led assault drove Iraq from Kuwait in Gulf War. US support was given to the USSR during the dissolution of communism and the recognition of independence of the Baltic republics. July: Strategic Arms Reduction Treaty (START) signed at US–Soviet summit held in Moscow. Nov: Bush co-hosted Middle East peace conference in Spain. *1992* Bush's popularity slumped as economic recession continued. Widespread riots in Los Angeles. Nov: Democrats, led by Bill Clinton, won presidential elections for first time since 1980; independent candidate Ross Perot captured nearly 20% of votes. *1993* Jan: Clinton inaugurated. Feb: medium-term economic plan proposed by Clinton to Congress to cut federal budget deficit. Sep: Clinton pushed to pass his program of reforms of medical insurance and government bueaucracy. Nov: North American Free Trade Agreement (NAFTA) between US, Canada, and Mexico approved by Congress; wide-ranging anti-crime bill passed. *1994* Jan: signs of economic recovery. Whitewater affair, alleging Clinton's involvement in dubious financial dealings in the 1980s. Trade embargo against Vietnam lifted after 19 years. March: US backed NATO action against Serbia in Bosnia-Herzegovina. Most US troops withdrawn from Somalia. *1995* Republicans sought passage of 10-point populist manifesto, "Contract with America".

United States literature early US literature falls into two distinct periods: *colonial writing* of the 1600s–1770s, largely dominated by the Puritans, and *post-Revolutionary literature* from the 1780s, when the ideal of US literature developed, and poetry, fiction, and drama began to evolve on national principles. Early 19th-century *Romanticism* contrasted sharply with the social realism of subsequent *post-Civil War writing*. 20th-century US writers have continued the trend toward realism, as well as developing various forms of modernist experimentation.

Best-selling authors of popular fiction now include Judith Kravitz, Sidney Sheldon, Anne Rice, Stephen King, and John Grisham.

universal indicator in chemistry, a mixture of ◊pH indicators, used to gauge the acidity or alkalinity of a solution. Each component changes color at a different pH value, and so the indicator is capable of displaying a range of colors, according to the pH of the test solution, from red (at pH 1) to purple (at pH 13).

The pH of a substance may be found by adding a few drops of universal indicator and noting the color, or by dipping in an absorbent paper strip that has been impregnated with the indicator.

universe all of space and its contents, the study of which is called cosmology. The universe is thought to be between 10 billion and 20 billion years old, and is mostly empty space, dotted with ◊galaxies for as far as telescopes can see. The most distant detected galaxies and ◊quasars lie 10 billion light years or more from Earth, and are moving farther apart as the universe expands. Several theories attempt to explain how the universe came into being and evolved, for example, the ◊Big Bang theory of an expanding universe originating in a single explosive event, and the contradictory ◊steady-state theory.

Unix multiuser ◊operating system designed for minicomputers but becoming increasingly popular on large microcomputers, workstations, mainframes, and supercomputers. It was developed by AT&T's Bell Laboratories in the US during the late 1960s, using the programming language ◊C.

Unknown Soldier unidentified dead soldier, for whom a tomb is erected as a memorial to other unidentified soldiers killed in war.

The Tomb of the Unknown Soldier is in Arlington, Virginia. Belgium, France, the UK, and other countries also have Unknown Soldier tombs.

unleaded gasoline gasoline manufactured without the addition of antiknock. It has a slightly lower octane rating than leaded gasoline, but has the advantage of not polluting the atmosphere with lead compounds. Many automobiles can be converted to running on unleaded gasoline by altering the timing of the engine, and most new automobiles are designed to do so.

Automobiles fitted with a ◊catalytic converter must use unleaded fuel.

unnilennium synthesized radioactive element of the ◊transactinide series, symbol Une, atomic number 109, atomic weight 266. It was first produced in 1982 at the Laboratory for Heavy Ion Research in Darmstadt, Germany, by fusing bismuth and iron nuclei; it took a week to obtain a single new, fused nucleus.

unnilhexium temporary identification assigned to the element seaborgium 1974–1994.

unniloctium synthesized, radioactive element of the ◊transactinide series, symbol Uno, atomic number 108, atomic weight 265. It was first synthesized in 1984 by the Laboratory for Heavy Ion Research in Darmstadt, Germany.

unnilpentium synthesized, radioactive, metallic element of the ◊transactinide series, symbol Unp, atomic number 105, atomic weight 262. Six isotopes have been synthesized, each with very short (fractions of a second) half-lives. Two institutions claim to have been the first to produce it: the Joint Institute for Nuclear Research in Dubna, Russia, in 1967 (proposed name **nielsbohrium**); and the University of California at Berkeley, who disputed the Soviet claim, in 1970 (proposed name **hahnium**).

unnilquadium synthesized, radioactive, metallic element, the first of the ◊transactinide series, symbol Unq, atomic number 104, atomic weight 262. It is produced by bombarding californium with carbon nuclei and has ten isotopes, the longest-lived of which, Unq-262, has a half-life of 70 seconds.

Two institutions claim to be the first to have synthesized it: the Joint Institute for Nuclear Research in Dubna, Russia, in 1964 (proposed name **kurchatovium**); and the University of California at Berkeley, in 1969 (proposed name **rutherfordium**).

unnilseptium synthesized, radioactive element of the ◊transactinide series, symbol Uns, atomic number 107, atomic weight 262. It was first synthesized by the Joint Institute for Nuclear Research in Dubna, Russia, in 1976; in 1981 the Laboratory for Heavy Ion Research in Darmstadt, Germany, confirmed its existence.

unsaturated compound chemical compound in which two adjacent atoms are bonded by a double or triple covalent bond.

unshielded twisted pair (UTP) form of cabling used for ◊local area networks, now commonly used as an alternative to ◊coaxial cable.

Unzen active volcano on the Shimbara peninsula, Kyushu Island, Japan, opposite the city of Kumamoto. Its eruption June 1991 led to the evacuation of 10,000 people.

Upanishad one of a collection of Hindu sacred treatises, written in Sanskrit, connected with the ◊Vedas but composed later, about 800–200 BC. Metaphysical and ethical, their doctrine equated the atman (self) with the Brahman (supreme spirit)—"*Tat tvam asi*" ("Thou art that")—and developed the theory of the transmigration of souls.

Updike John (Hoyer) 1932– . US writer. Associated with the *New Yorker* magazine from 1955, he soon established a reputation for polished prose, poetry, and criticism. His novels include *The Poorhouse Fair* 1959, *The Centaur* 1963, *Couples* 1968, *The Witches of Eastwick* 1984, *Roger's Version* 1986, and *S.* 1988, and deal with the tensions and frustrations of contemporary US middle-class life and their effects on love and marriage.

Upper Austria (German *Oberösterreich*) mountainous federal province of Austria, drained by the river Danube; area 4,632 sq mi/12,000 sq km; population (1987) 1,294,000. Its capital is Linz. In addition to wine, sugar beet and grain, there are reserves of oil. Manufactured products include textiles, chemicals, and metal goods.

Upper Volta former name (to 1984) of ◊Burkina Faso.

Ur ancient city of the ◊Sumerian civilization, in modern Iraq. Excavations by the British archeologist Leonard Woolley show that it was inhabited from about 3500 BC. He discovered evidence of a flood that may have inspired the *Epic of ◊Gilgamesh* as well as the biblical account, and remains of ziggurats, or step pyramids.

Ural Mountains (Russian *Ural'skiy Khrebet*) mountain system running from the Arctic Ocean to the Caspian Sea, traditionally separating Europe from Asia. The highest peak is Naradnaya, 6,214 ft/1,894 m. It has vast mineral wealth.

uranium hard, lustrous, silver-white, malleable and ductile, radioactive, metallic element of the ◊actinide series, symbol U, atomic number 92, atomic weight 238.029. It is the most abundant radioactive element in the Earth's crust, its decay giving rise to essentially all radioactive elements in nature; its final decay product is the stable element lead. Uranium combines readily with most elements to form compounds that are extremely poisonous. The chief ore is ◊pitchblende, in which the element was discovered by German chemist Martin Klaproth 1789; he named it after the planet Uranus, which had been discovered 1781.

Uranus in Greek mythology, the primeval sky god, whose name means "Heaven". He was responsible for both the sunshine and the rain, and was the son and husband of ◊Gaia, the goddess of the Earth. Uranus and Gaia were the parents of ◊Cronus and the ◊Titans.

Uranus the seventh planet from the Sun, discovered by William ◊Herschel 1781. It is twice as far out as the sixth planet, Saturn. Uranus has a diameter of 31,600 mi/50,800 km and a mass 14.5 times that of Earth. It orbits the Sun in 84 years at an average distance of 1.8 billion mi/2.9 billion km. The spin axis of Uranus is tilted at 98°, so that one pole points toward the Sun, giving extreme seasons. It has 15 moons, and in 1977 was discovered to have thin rings around its equator.

Data derived from the space probe *Voyager 1* in 1986

revealed that Uranus is covered with a cloud layer under which a hot ocean of superheated water exists.

Urdu language member of the Indo-Iranian branch of the Indo-European language family, related to Hindi and written not in Devanagari but in Arabic script. Urdu is strongly influenced by Farsi (Persian) and Arabic. It is the official language of Pakistan and is used by Muslims in India.

urea $CO(NH_2)_2$ waste product formed in the mammalian liver when nitrogen compounds are broken down. It is excreted in urine. When purified, it is a white, crystalline solid. In industry it is used to make urea-formaldehyde plastics (or resins), pharmaceuticals, and fertilizers.

uremia excess of urea (a nitrogenous waste product) in the blood, caused by kidney damage.

uric acid $C_5H_4N_4O_3$ nitrogen-containing waste substance, formed from the breakdown of food and body protein.

It is only slightly soluble in water. Uric acid is the normal means by which most land animals that develop in a shell (birds, reptiles, insects, and land gastropods) deposit their waste products. The young are unable to get rid of their excretory products while in the shell and therefore store them in this insoluble form.

urinary system system of organs that removes nitrogenous waste products and excess water from the bodies of animals. In vertebrates, it consists of a pair of kidneys, which produce urine; ureters, which drain the kidneys; and (in bony fishes, amphibians, some reptiles, and mammals) a bladder that stores the urine

before its discharge. In mammals, the urine is expelled through the urethra; in other vertebrates, the urine drains into a common excretory chamber called a cloaca, and the urine is not discharged separately.

Ursa Major the third largest constellation in the sky, in the north polar region. Its seven brightest stars make up the familiar shape of the **Big Dipper** or **Plow**. The second star of the "handle" of the dipper, called Mizar, has a companion star, Alcor. Two stars forming the far side of the "bowl" (one of them, Dubhe, being the constellation's brightest star) act as pointers to the north pole star, Polaris.

Ursa Minor constellation in the northern sky. It is shaped like a dipper, with the north pole star Polaris at the end of the handle.

It contains the orange subgiant Kochab, about 95 light-years from Earth.

Uruguay Oriental Republic of (*República Oriental del Uruguay*) *area* 68,031 sq mi/176,200 sq km *capital* Montevideo *towns and cities* Salto, Paysandú *physical* grassy plains (pampas) and low hills *features* rivers Negro, Uruguay, Río de la Plata *head of state and government* Luis Alberto Lacalle Herrera from 1989 *political system* democratic republic *political parties* Colorado Party (PC), progressive, center-left; National (Blanco) Party (PN), traditionalist, right of center; Amplio Front (FA), moderate, left-wing *exports* meat and meat products, leather, wool, textiles *currency* nuevo peso *population* (1993 est) 3,200,000 (Spanish, Italian; mestizo, mulatto, black); growth rate 0.7% p.a. *life expectancy* men 69, women 76 *language* Spanish *media* the Ministry of Defense controls

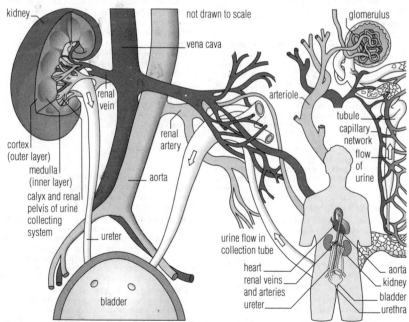

urinary system *The human urinary system. At the bottom right, the complete system in outline; on the left, the arrangement of blood vessels connected to the kidney; at the top right, a detail of the network of vessels within a kidney.*

broadcasting licenses; press heavily dependent on official advertising. Four national and two Montevideo daily papers, combined circulation 500,000 copies per week (1993); all proprietors associated with political parties *religion* Roman Catholic 66% *literacy* men 97%, women 96% *GNP* $2,860 per head (1991) *chronology 1825* Independence declared from Brazil. *1836* Civil war. *1930* First constitution adopted. *1966* Blanco party in power, with Jorge Pacheco Areco as president. *1972* Colorado Party returned, with Juan Maria Bordaberry Arocena as president. *1976* Bordaberry deposed by army; Dr Méndez Manfredini became president. *1984* Violent antigovernment protests after ten years of repressive rule. *1985* Agreement reached between the army and political leaders for return to constitutional government. Colorado Party won general election; Dr Julio Maria Sanguinetti became president. *1986* Government of national accord established under President Sanguinetti's leadership. *1989* Luis Alberto Lacalle Herrera elected president. *1992* Criticisms of government's "market-orientated" economic policies.

Urumqi or *Urumchi* industrial city and capital of Xinjiang Uygur autonomous region, China, at the northern foot of the Tian Shan Mountains; population (1989) 1,110,000. It produces cotton textiles, cement, chemicals, iron, and steel.

US abbreviation for the *United States* (popular and most frequent name used by speakers of American English for the nation).

USA abbreviation (official) for the ◊*United States of America*; *US Army*.

USDA abbreviation for the *US Department of Agriculture*.

USENET (acronym for *users' network*) the world's largest ◊bulletin board system: a part of the ◊Internet. It consists of ◊e-mail messages and articles organized into newsgroups. It functions by bringing together people with common interests to exchange views and information. USENET is uncensored.

user-friendly term used to describe the ease of use of a computer system, particularly for those with little understanding or familiarity with computers. Even for experienced users, user-friendly programs are quicker to learn.

user interface in computing, the procedures and methods through which the user operates a program. These might include ◊menus, input forms, error messages, and keyboard procedures. A graphical user interface (GUI or WIMP) is one that makes use of icons (small pictures) and allows the user to make menu selections with a mouse.

USGS abbreviation for the *US Geological Survey*, part of the department of the interior.

Ushuaia southernmost town in the world, at the tip of Tierra del Fuego, Argentina, less than 620 mi/1,000 km from Antarctica; population (1991) 29,700. It is a free port and naval base.

USIA abbreviation for *US Information Agency*, the government's information and public relations arm.

USO abbreviation for *United Service Organizations*; sent concert parties and entertainers to all parts of the world where US troops were serving.

USSR abbreviation for the former *Union of Soviet Socialist Republics*.

Ustase Croatian nationalist terrorist organization founded 1929 and led by Ante Pavelic against the Yugoslav state. During World War II, it collaborated with the Nazis and killed thousands of Serbs, Romanies, and Jews. It also carried out deportations and forced conversions to Roman Catholicism in its attempt to create a "unified" Croatian state.

Utah state in western US; nickname Beehive State/Mormon State *area* 84,881 sq mi/219,900 sq km *capital* Salt Lake City *towns and cities* Provo, Ogden *physical* Colorado Plateau to the E, mountains in center, Great Basin to the W, Great Salt Lake *features* Great American Desert; Colorado river system; Dinosaur and Rainbow Bridge national monuments; five national parks: the Arches, Bryce Canyon, Canyonlands, Capitol Reef, Zion; auto racing at Bonneville Salt Flats; Mormon temple and tabernacle, Salt Lake City *industries* wool, gold, silver, copper, coal, salt, steel *population* (1990) 1,722,850 *famous people* Brigham Young *history* explored first by Franciscan friars for Spain 1776; Great Salt Lake discovered by US frontier scout Jim Bridger 1824; part of the area ceded by Mexico 1848; developed by Mormons, still by far the largest religious group in the state; territory 1850, but not admitted to statehood until 1896 because of Mormon reluctance to relinquish plural marriage.

uterus hollow muscular organ of female mammals, located between the bladder and rectum, and connected to the Fallopian tubes above and the vagina below. The embryo develops within the uterus, and in placental mammals is attached to it after implantation via the ◊placenta and umbilical cord. The lining of the uterus changes during the ◊menstrual cycle. In humans and other higher primates, it is a single structure, but in other mammals it is paired.

Uthman c. 574–656. Third caliph (leader of the Islamic empire) from 644, a son-in-law of the prophet Mohammed. Under his rule the Arabs became a naval power and extended their rule to N Africa and Cyprus, but Uthman's personal weaknesses led to his assassination. He was responsible for the compilation of the authoritative version of the Koran, the sacred book of Islam.

Uthman I another name for the Turkish sultan ◊Osman I.

utilitarianism philosophical theory of ethics outlined by the philosopher Jeremy ◊Bentham and developed by John Stuart Mill. According to utilitarianism, an action is morally right if it has consequences that lead to happiness, and wrong if it brings about the reverse. Thus society should aim for the greatest happiness of the greatest number.

utility program in computing, a systems program designed to perform a specific task related to the operation of the computer when requested to do so by the computer user. For example, a utility program might be used to complete a screen dump, format a disk, or convert the format of a data file so that it can be accessed by a different applications program.

Utopia any ideal state in literature, named for philosopher Thomas More's ideal commonwealth in his book *Utopia* 1516. Other versions include Plato's *Republic*, Francis Bacon's *New Atlantis*, and *City of the Sun* by the Italian Tommaso Campanella (1568–1639). Utopias are a common subject in science fiction.

UTP abbreviation for ◊*unshielded twisted pair*.

Utrecht province of the Netherlands lying SE of Amsterdam, on the Kromme Rijn (Crooked Rhine) *area* 513 sq mi/1,330 sq km *capital* Utrecht *towns and cities* Amersfoort, Zeist, Nieuwegeun, Veenendaal *industries* chemicals, livestock, textiles, electrical goods *population* (1991) 1,026,800 *history* ruled by the bishops of Utrecht in the Middle Ages, the province was sold to the emperor Charles V of Spain 1527. It became a center of Protestant resistance to Spanish rule and, with the signing of the Treaty of Utrecht, became one of the seven United Provinces of the Netherlands 1579.

Utrecht, Union of in 1579, the union of seven provinces of the N Netherlands—Holland, Zeeland, Friesland, Groningen, Utrecht, Gelderland, and Overijssel—that, as the United Provinces, became the basis of opposition to the Spanish crown and the foundation of the present-day Dutch state.

Utrillo Maurice 1883–1955. French artist. He painted townscapes of his native Paris, many depicting Montmartre, often from postcard photographs. His almost naive style (he was self-taught) is characterized by his subtle use of pale tones and muted colors.

Utrillo was the son of Suzanne Valadon, a trapeze-performer who was encouraged to become an artist herself after posing as a model for many painters of the day. His work from 1909–14 (his "white period") is considered his best.

Uzbek member of certain Turkic-speaking peoples of Uzbekistan (where they form 70% of the population) and neighboring regions.

Uzbekistan Republic of *area* 172,741 sq mi/447,400 sq km *capital* Tashkent *towns and cities* Samarkand, Bukhara, Namangan *physical* oases in the deserts; rivers: Amu Darya, Syr Darya; Fergana Valley; rich in mineral deposits *environment* in 1993 around 75% of the population living round the Aral Sea were suffering from illness, with alarming increases in typhoid

and hepatitis A. Local fruit and vegetables contained dangerous levels of pesticides and nitrates, and infant mortality was three times the national average. In the former fishing town of Muynak 70% of the population of 2,000 had precancerous conditions *features* more than 20 hydroelectric plants; three natural gas pipelines *head of state* Islam Karimov from 1990 *head of government* Abd al-Hashim Mutalov from 1991 *political system* socialist pluralist *political parties* National Democratic (formerly Communist) Party, reform-socialist; Democratic Party, tolerated opposition *products* rice, dried fruit, vines (all grown by irrigation); cotton, silk *currency* som *population* (1993 est) 21,700,000 (Uzbek 71%, Russian 8%, Tajik 5%, Kazakh 4%) *life expectancy* men 66, women 73 *language* Uzbek, a Turkic language *religion* Sunni Muslim *GNP* $1,350 per head (1991) *chronology 1921* Part of Turkestan Soviet Socialist Autonomous Republic. *1925* Became constituent republic of the USSR. *1944* Some 160,000 Meskhetian Turks forcibly transported from their native Georgia to Uzbekistan by Stalin. *1989* Tashlak, Yaipan, and Ferghana were the scenes of riots in which Meskhetian Turks were attacked; 70 killed and 850 wounded. *1990* June: economic and political sovereignty declared; former Uzbek Communist Party (UCP) leader Islam Karimov became president. *1991* March: supported "renewed federation" in USSR referendum. Aug: attempted anti-Gorbachev coup in Moscow initially supported by President Karimov, who later resigned from Soviet Communist Party (CPSU) Politburo; UCP broke with CPSU; independence declared. Dec: joined new Commonwealth of Independent States. *1992* Jan: violent food riots in Tashkent. March: joined the United Nations; US diplomatic recognition achieved. New constitution adopted. *1993* Crackdown on Islamic fundamentalists. *1994* Agreement to form single economic zone with Kazakhstan.

V Roman numeral for *five*; in physics, symbol for *volt*.

v in physics, symbol for *velocity*.

vaccine any preparation of modified pathogens (viruses or bacteria) that is introduced into the body, usually either orally or by a hypodermic syringe, to induce the specific ◊antibody reaction that produces ◊immunity against a particular disease.

vacuole in biology, a fluid-filled, membrane-bound cavity inside a cell. It may be a reservoir for fluids that the cell will secrete to the outside, or may be filled with excretory products or essential nutrients that the cell needs to store.

In amebas (single-cell animals), vacuoles are sites for digestion of engulfed food particles. A plant cell usually has a large central vacuole to increase its surface area for food absorption.

vacuum in general, a region completely empty of matter; in physics, any enclosure in which the gas pressure is considerably less than atmospheric pressure (101,325 pascals).

Vaduz capital of the European principality of Liechtenstein; industries include engineering and agricultural trade; population (1984) 5,000.

vagina the lower part of the reproductive tract in female mammals, linking the uterus to the exterior. It admits the penis during sexual intercourse, and is the birth canal down which the baby passes during delivery.

valence the combining capacity of an ◊atom or ◊radical, determined by the number of electrons that an atom will add, lose, or share when it reacts with another atom. Elements that lose electrons (such as hydrogen and the ◊metals) have a positive valence; those that add electrons (such as oxygen and other nonmetals) have a negative valence.

valence shell in chemistry, outermost shell of electrons in an ◊atom. It contains the ◊valence electrons. Elements with four or more electrons in their outermost shell can show variable valence. Chlorine can show valencies of 1, 3, 5, and 7 in different compounds.

Valencia industrial city (wine, fruit, chemicals, textiles, ship repair) in Valencia region, E Spain; population (1991) 777,400. The Community of Valencia, consisting of Alicante, Castellón, and Valencia, has an area of 8,994 sq mi/23,300 sq km and a population of 3,772,000.

Valentine, St according to tradition a bishop of Terni martyred at Rome, now omitted from the calendar of saints' days as probably nonexistent. His festival was Feb 14, but the custom of sending "valentines" to a loved one on that day seems to have arisen because the day accidentally coincided with the Roman mid-February festival of Lupercalia.

Valentino Rudolph. Adopted name of Rodolfo Alfonso Guglielmi di Valentina d'Antonguolla 1895–1926. Italian-born US film actor and dancer. He was the archetypal romantic lover of the Hollywood silent era.

His screen debut was 1919, but his first starring role was in *The Four Horsemen of the Apocalypse* 1921. His subsequent films include *The Sheik* 1921 and *Blood and Sand* 1922.

His fans never forgot him after a premature death from peritonitis.

Valhalla in Norse mythology, the hall in ◊Odin's palace where he feasted with the souls of those heroes killed in battle that went to join him after death.

validation in computing, the process of checking input data to ensure that it is complete, accurate, and reasonable. Although it would be impossible to guarantee that only valid data are entered into a computer, a suitable combination of validation checks should ensure that most errors are detected.

Valkyrie in Norse mythology, any of the female attendants of ◊Odin. They selected the most valiant warriors to die in battle and escorted them either to Valhalla or to the abode of Freya.

Valletta capital and port of Malta; population (1987) 9,000, urban area 101,000.

Valley Forge site in Pennsylvania 20 mi/32 km NW of Philadelphia, where George Washington's army spent the winter of 1777–78 in great hardship during the ◊American Revolution.

Of the 10,000 men there, 2,500 died of disease and the rest suffered from lack of rations and other supplies; many deserted.

During that winter, Washington introduced Prussian officers who trained the irregulars. The Franco-American alliance 1778 boosted morale and brought new recruits to the army, which emerged from the ordeal to inflict heavy losses on the British.

Valley of the Kings burial place of ancient kings opposite ◊Thebes, Egypt, on the left bank of the Nile.

Valparaíso industrial port (sugar, refining, textiles, chemicals) in Chile, on the Pacific Ocean; capital of Valparaíso province; population (1990) 276,800. Founded 1536, it was occupied by the English naval adventurers Francis ◊Drake 1578 and John Hawkins 1595, pillaged by the Dutch 1600, and bombarded by Spain 1866; it has also suffered from earthquakes.

value-added tax (VAT) tax on goods and services. VAT is imposed by the European Community on member states. The tax varies from state to state. An agreed proportion of the tax money is used to fund the EC.

valve in animals, a structure for controlling the direction of the blood flow. In humans and other vertebrates, the contractions of the beating heart cause the correct blood flow into the arteries because a series of valves prevent back flow. Diseased valves, detected as "heart murmurs," have decreased efficiency.

vampire bat any South and Central American bat of the family Desmodontidae, of which there are three species. The *common vampire Desmodus rotundus* is found from N Mexico to central Argentina; its head and body grow to 3.5 in/9 cm. Vampires feed on the blood of birds and mammals; they slice a piece of skin from a sleeping animal with their sharp incisor teeth and lap up the flowing blood.

vanadium silver-white, malleable and ductile, metallic element, symbol V, atomic number 23, atomic weight 50.942. It occurs in certain iron, lead, and uranium ores and is widely distributed in small quantities in igneous and sedimentary rocks. It is used to make steel alloys, to which it adds tensile strength.

Van Allen James (Alfred) 1914– . US physicist whose instruments aboard the first US satellite *Explorer 1* 1958 led to the discovery of the Van Allen belts, two zones of intense radiation around the Earth. He pioneered high-altitude research with rockets after World War II.

Van Allen radiation belts two zones of charged particles around the Earth's magnetosphere, discovered 1958 by US physicist James Van Allen. The atomic particles come from the Earth's upper atmosphere and the ◊solar wind, and are trapped by the Earth's magnetic field. The inner belt lies 620–3,100 mi/ 1,000–5,000 km above the equator, and contains ◊protons and ◊electrons. The outer belt lies 9,300–15,500 mi/15,000–25,000 km above the equator, but is lower around the magnetic poles. It contains mostly electrons from the solar wind.

Van Buren Martin 1782–1862. Eighth president of the US 1837–41, a Democrat, who had helped establish the ◊Democratic Party. He was secretary of state 1829–31, minister to Britain 1831–33, vice president 1833–37, and president during the Panic of 1837, the worst US economic crisis until that time, caused by land speculation in the West. Refusing to intervene, he advocated the establishment of an independent treasury, one not linked to the federal government, worsening the depression and losing the 1840 election.

Born of Dutch ancestry in Kinderhook, New York, Van Buren as president attempted to hold the Southern states in the Union by advocating a strict states' rights position on slavery, but his refusal to annex Texas alienated many Southerners.

Vancouver industrial city (oil refining, engineering, shipbuilding, aircraft, timber, pulp and paper, textiles, fisheries) in Canada, its chief Pacific seaport, on the mainland of British Columbia; population (1986) 1,381,000.

Vandal member of a Germanic people related to the ◊Goths. In the 5th century AD the Vandals invaded Roman ◊Gaul and Spain, many settling in Andalusia (formerly Vandalitia) and others reaching N Africa 429. They sacked Rome 455 but were defeated by Belisarius, general of the emperor ◊Justinian, in the 6th century.

Vanderbilt Cornelius 1794–1877. US industrialist who made a fortune in steamships and (from the age of 70) by financing railroads. He defeated stock raids and takeover attempts by other financiers in the process of amassing a fortune of more than $100 million. Despite his wealth, he did not engage in any philanthropic activities until near his death, when he gave $1 million to what would become Vanderbilt University.

van der Waals' law modified form of the ◊gas laws that includes corrections for the non-ideal behavior of real gases (the molecules of ideal gases occupy no space and exert no forces on each other). It is named for Dutch physicist J D van der Waals (1837–1923).

van Dyck Anthony. Flemish painter; see ◊Dyck, Anthony van.

van Eyck Jan Flemish painter; see ◊Eyck, Jan van.

van Gogh Vincent. Dutch painter; see ◊Gogh, Vincent van.

vanilla any climbing orchid of the genus *Vanilla*, native to tropical America but cultivated elsewhere, with fragrant, large, white or yellow flowers. The dried and fermented fruit, or podlike capsules, of *V. planifolia* are the source of the vanilla flavoring used in cooking and baking.

Van Rensselaer Stephen 1764–1839. American public official and soldier. A commander during the Anglo-American War of 1812–14 he suffered a serious defeat

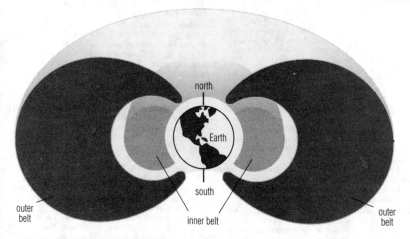

Van Allen radiation belts The Van Allen belts of trapped charged particles are a hazard to spacecraft, affecting on-board electronics and computer systems. Similar belts have been discovered around the planets Mercury, Jupiter, Saturn, Uranus, and Neptune.

at Queenstown, Canada. He was a US congressman 1822–29. As president of the New York Canal Commission 1825–39 he oversaw the construction of the Erie Canal.

He founded the Rensselaer Polytechnic Institute 1824.

Vanuatu Republic of (*Ripablik Blong Vanuatu*) *area* 5,714 sq mi/14,800 sq km *capital* Vila (on Efate) *towns and cities* Luganville (on Espíritu Santo) *physical* comprises around 70 islands, including Espíritu Santo, Malekula, and Efate; densely forested, mountainous *features* three active volcanoes *head of state* Jean Marie Leye from 1994 *head of government* Maxime Carlot from 1991 *political system* democratic republic *political parties* Union of Moderate Parties (UMP), Francophone centrist; National United Party (NUP), formed by Walter Lini; Vanua'aku Pati (VP), Anglophone centrist; Melanesian Progressive Party (MPP), Melanesian centrist; Fren Melanesian Party *exports* copra, fish, coffee, cocoa *currency* vatu *population* (1993 est) 200,000 (90% Melanesian); growth rate 3.3% p.a. *life expectancy* men 67, women 71 *languages* Bislama 82%, English, French (all official) *literacy* 67% *religions* Presbyterian 40%, Roman Catholic 16%, Anglican 14%, animist 15% *GNP* $1,120 per head (1991) *chronology 1906* Islands jointly administered by France and Britain. *1975* Representative assembly established. *1978* Government of national unity formed, with Father Gerard Leymang as chief minister. *1980* Revolt on the island of Espíritu Santo delayed independence but it was achieved within the Commonwealth, with George Kalkoa (adopted name Sokomanu) as president and Father Walter Lini as prime minister. *1988* Dismissal of Lini by Sokomanu led to Sokomanu's arrest for treason. Lini reinstated. *1989* Sokomanu sentenced to six years' imprisonment; succeeded as president by Fred Timakata. *1991* Lini voted out by party members; replaced by Donald Kalpokas. General election produced UMP–NUP coalition under Maxime Carlot. *1994* Timakata succeeded as president by Jean Marie Leye.

vapor one of the three states of matter (see also ◊solid and ◊liquid). The molecules in a vapor move randomly and are far apart, the distance between them, and therefore the volume of the vapor, being limited only by the walls of any vessel in which they might be contained. A vapor differs from a ◊gas only in that a vapor can be liquefied by increased pressure, whereas a gas cannot unless its temperature is lowered below its critical temperature; it then becomes a vapor and may be liquefied.

vapor density density of a gas, expressed as the ◊mass of a given volume of the gas divided by the mass of an equal volume of a reference gas (such as hydrogen or air) at the same temperature and pressure. It is equal approximately to half the molecular weight of the gas.

Varanasi or *Benares* holy city of the Hindus in Uttar Pradesh, India, on the river Ganges; population (1981) 794,000. There are 1,500 golden shrines, and a 3 mi/5 km frontage to the Ganges with sacred stairways (ghats) for purification by bathing.

variable in mathematics, a changing quantity (one that can take various values), as opposed to a ◊constant. For example, in the algebraic expression $y = 4x^3 + 2$, the variables are x and y, whereas 4 and 2 are constants.

variable star in astronomy, a star whose brightness changes, either regularly or irregularly, over a period

ranging from a few hours to months or even years. The Cepheid variables regularly expand and contract in size every few days or weeks.

varicose veins or *varicosis* condition where the veins become swollen and twisted. The veins of the legs are most often affected; other vulnerable sites include the rectum (◊hemorrhoids) and testes.

vas deferens in male vertebrates, a tube conducting sperm from the testis to the urethra. The sperm is carried in a fluid secreted by various glands, and can be transported very rapidly when the smooth muscle in the wall of the vas deferens undergoes rhythmic contraction, as in sexual intercourse.

vasectomy male sterilization; an operation to cut and tie the ducts (see ◊vas deferens) that carry sperm from the testes to the penis. Vasectomy does not affect sexual performance, but the semen produced at ejaculation no longer contains sperm.

Vatican City State (*Stato della Città del Vaticano*) *area* 109 acres/0.4 sq km *physical* forms an enclave in the heart of Rome, Italy *features* Vatican Palace, official residence of the pope; basilica and square of St Peter's; churches in and near Rome, the pope's summer villa at Castel Gandolfo; the world's smallest state *head of state* John Paul II from 1978 *head of government* Cardinal Rosalio Jose Castillo Lara (President of Pontifical Commission) *political system* absolute Catholicism *currency* Vatican City lira; Italian lira *population* (1985) 1,000 *languages* Latin (official), Italian *religion* Roman Catholic *chronology 1929* Lateran Treaty recognized sovereignty of the pope. *1947* New Italian constitution confirmed the sovereignty of the Vatican City State. *1978* John Paul II became the first non-Italian pope for more than 400 years. *1985* New concordat signed under which Roman Catholicism ceased to be Italy's state religion. *1992* Relations with East European states restored.

Vatican Council either of two Roman Catholic ecumenical councils called by Pope Pius IX 1869 (which met 1870) and by Pope John XXIII 1959 (which met 1962). These councils deliberated over elements of church policy.

Vaughan Williams Ralph 1872–1958. English composer. His style was tonal and often evocative of the English countryside through the use of folk themes. Among his works are the orchestral *Fantasia on a Theme by Thomas Tallis* 1910; the opera *Sir John in Love* 1929, featuring the Elizabethan song "Greensleeves"; and nine symphonies 1909–57.

VDT abbreviation for ◊visual display terminal.

vector graphics computer graphics that are stored in the computer memory by using geometric formulas. Vector graphics can be transformed (enlarged, rotated, stretched, and so on) without loss of picture resolution. Vector graphics are typically used for drawing applications, allowing the user to create and modify technical diagrams such as designs for houses or automobiles.

Veda the most sacred of the Hindu scriptures, hymns written in an old form of Sanskrit; the oldest may date from 1500 or 2000 BC. The four main collections are: the *Rig-veda* (hymns and praises); *Yajur-Veda* (prayers and sacrificial formulae); *Sâma-Veda* (tunes and chants); and *Atharva-Veda*, or Veda of the Atharvans, the officiating priests at the sacrifices.

Vega or *Alpha Lyrae* brightest star in the constellation Lyra and the fifth-brightest star in the sky. It is a blue-white star, 25 light-years from Earth, with a luminosity 50 times that of the Sun.

Vega Lope Felix de (Carpio) 1562–1635. Spanish poet and dramatist. He was one of the founders of modern Spanish drama. He wrote epics, pastorals, odes, sonnets, novels, and, reputedly, over 1,500 plays (of which 426 are still in existence), mostly tragicomedies. He set out his views on drama in *Arte nuevo de hacer comedias/The New Art of Writing Plays* 1609, in which he defended his innovations while reaffirming the classical forms. *Fuenteovejuna* about 1614 has been acclaimed as the first proletarian drama.

vein in animals with a circulatory system, any vessel that carries blood from the body to the heart. Veins contain valves that prevent the blood from running back when moving against gravity. They always carry deoxygenated blood, with the exception of the veins leading from the lungs to the heart in birds and mammals, which carry newly oxygenated blood.

Vela constellation of the southern hemisphere near Carina, represented as the sails of a ship. It contains large wisps of gas—called the Gum nebula after its discoverer, the Australian astronomer Colin Gum (1924–1960)—believed to be the remains of one or more ◊supernovae. Vela also contains the second optical ◊pulsar (a pulsar that flashes at a visible wavelength) to be discovered.

Its four brightest stars are second-magnitude, one of them being Suhail, about 490 light-years from Earth.

Velázquez Diego Rodríguez de Silva y 1599–1660. Spanish painter. He was the outstanding Spanish artist of the 17th century. In 1623 he became court painter to Philip IV in Madrid, where he produced many portraits of the royal family as well as occasional religious paintings, genre scenes, and other subjects. Notable among his portraits is *Las Meninas/The Maids of Honor* 1656 (Prado, Madrid), while *Women Frying Eggs* 1618 (National Gallery of Scotland, Edinburgh) is a typical genre scene.

veldt subtropical grassland in South Africa, equivalent to the ◊Pampas of South America.

vena cava either of the two great veins of the trunk, returning deoxygenated blood to the right atrium of the ◊heart. The *superior vena cava*, beginning where the arches of the two innominate veins join high in the chest, receives blood from the head, neck, chest, and arms; the *inferior vena cava*, arising from the junction of the right and left common iliac veins, receives blood from all parts of the body below the diaphragm.

venereal disease (VD) any disease mainly transmitted by sexual contact, although commonly the term is used specifically for gonorrhea and syphilis, both occurring worldwide, and chancroid ("soft sore") and lymphogranuloma venerum, seen mostly in the tropics. The term *sexually transmitted disease* (STD) is more often used to encompass a growing list of conditions passed on primarily, but not exclusively, by sexual contact.

Veneto region of NE Italy, comprising the provinces of Belluno, Padova (Padua), Treviso, Rovigo, Venezia (Venice), and Vicenza; area 7,102 sq mi/18,400 sq km; population (1990) 4,398,100. Its capital is Venice, and towns include Padua, Verona, and Vicenza. The Veneto forms part of the N Italian plain, with the delta of the river Po; it includes part of the Alps and Dolomites, and Lake Garda. Products include cereals, fruit, vegetables, wine, chemicals, ships, and textiles.

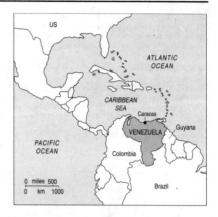

Venezuela Republic of (*República de Venezuela*) *area* 352,162 sq mi/912,100 sq km *capital* Caracas *towns and cities* Barquisimeto, Valencia; port Maracaibo *physical* Andes Mountains and Lake Maracaibo in NW; central plains (llanos); delta of river Orinoco in E; Guiana Highlands in SE *features* Angel Falls, world's highest waterfall *head of state and government* Rafael Caldera from 1994 *government* federal democratic republic *political parties* Democratic Action Party (AD), moderate left of center; Social Christian Party (COPEI), Christian center-right; Movement toward Socialism (MAS), left of center *exports* coffee, timber, oil, aluminum, iron ore, petrochemicals *currency* bolívar *population* (1993) 20,410,000 (mestizos 70%, white (Spanish, Portuguese, Italian) 20%, black 9%, American Indian 2%); growth rate 2.8% p.a. *life expectancy* men 67, women 74 *languages* Spanish (official), Indian languages 2% *religions* Roman Catholic 96%, Protestant 2% *literacy* men 87%, women 90% *GNP* $2,610 per head (1991) *chronology* **1961** New constitution adopted, with Rómulo Betancourt as president. **1964** Dr Raúl Leoni became president. **1969** Dr Rafael Caldera became president. **1974** Carlos Andrés Pérez became president. **1979** Dr Luis Herrera became president. **1984** Dr Jaime Lusinchi became president; social pact established between government, labor unions, and business; national debt rescheduled. **1987** Widespread social unrest triggered by inflation; student demonstrators shot by police. **1988** Carlos Andrés Pérez elected president. Payments suspended on foreign debts. **1989** Economic austerity program enforced by $4.3 billion loan from International Monetary Fund. Price increases triggered riots; 300 people killed. Feb: martial law declared. May: General strike. Elections boycotted by opposition groups. **1992** Attempted antigovernment coups failed. **1993** Pérez resigned, accused of corruption; Ramon José Velasquez succeeded him as interim head of state. Dec: former president Dr Rafael Caldera reelected. **1994** Feb: Caldera sworn in as president. May: Pérez arrested.

Venice (Italian *Venezia*) city, port, and naval base on the NE coast of Italy; population (1990) 79,000. It is the capital of Veneto region. The old city is built on piles on low-lying islands in a salt-water lagoon, sheltered from the Adriatic Sea by the Lido and other small strips of land. There are about 150 canals crossed by some 400 bridges. Apart from tourism (it draws 8 million tourists a year), industries include glass, jewelry, textiles, and lace. Venice was an independent trading republic from the 10th century, ruled by a doge, or chief magistrate, and was one of the centers of the Italian Renaissance.

Venn diagram in mathematics, a diagram representing a ◊set or sets and the logical relationships between them. The sets are drawn as circles. An area of overlap between two circles (sets) contains elements that are common to both sets, and thus represents a third set. Circles that do not overlap represent sets with no elements in common (disjoint sets). The method is named for the British logician John Venn (1834–1923).

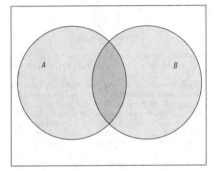

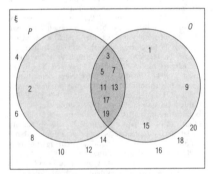

ξ = set of whole numbers from 1 to 20
O = set of odd numbers
P = set of prime numbers

Venn diagram Venn diagram. (a) a Venn diagram of two intersecting sets; (b) a Venn diagram showing the set of whole numbers from 1 to 20 and the subsets P and O of prime and odd numbers, respectively. The intersection of P and O contains all the prime numbers that are also odd.

ventral surface the front of an animal. In vertebrates, the side furthest from the backbone; in invertebrates, the side closest to the ground. The positioning of the main nerve pathways on the ventral side is a characteristic of invertebrates.

ventricle in zoology, either of the two lower chambers of the heart that force blood into the circulation by contraction of their muscular walls. The term also refers to any of four cavities within the brain in which cerebrospinal fluid is produced.

venture capital or *risk capital* financing provided by venture capital companies, individuals, and merchant banks for medium-or long-term business ventures that are not their own and in which there is a strong element of risk.

Venus in Roman mythology, the goddess of love and beauty, equivalent to the Greek ◊Aphrodite. The patrician Romans believed that they were descended from Aeneas, who was the son of the goddess and Anchises, a Trojan noble. She was venerated as the goddess of military victory and patroness of spring.

Venus second planet from the Sun. It orbits the Sun every 225 days at an average distance of 67.2 million mi/108.2 million km and can approach the Earth to within 24 million mi/38 million km, closer than any other planet. Its diameter is 7,500 mi/12,100 km and its mass is 0.82 that of Earth. Venus rotates on its axis more slowly than any other planet, once every 243 days and from east to west, the opposite direction to the other planets (except Uranus and possibly Pluto). Venus is shrouded by clouds of sulfuric acid droplets that sweep across the planet from east to west every four days. The atmosphere is almost entirely carbon dioxide, which traps the Sun's heat by the ◊greenhouse effect and raises the planet's surface temperature to 900°F/480°C, with an atmospheric pressure of 90 times that at the surface of the Earth.

Venus flytrap insectivorous plant *Dionaea muscipula* of the sundew family, native to the SE US; its leaves have two hinged blades that close and entrap insects.

verb grammatical part of speech for what someone or something does (*to go*), experiences (*to live*), or is (*to be*). Verbs involve the grammatical categories known as number (singular or plural: "He *runs*; they *run*"), voice (active or passive: "She *writes* books; it *is written*"), mood (statements, questions, orders, emphasis, necessity, condition), aspect (completed or continuing action: "She *danced*; she *was dancing*"), and tense (variation according to time: simple present tense, present progressive tense, simple past tense, and so on).

verbena any plant of the genus *Verbena*, family Verbenaceae, of about 100 species, mostly found in the American tropics. The leaves are fragrant and the tubular flowers arranged in close spikes in colors ranging from white to rose, violet, and purple. The garden verbena is a hybrid annual.

Verdi Giuseppe (Fortunino Francesco) 1813–1901. Italian opera composer of the Romantic period. He who took his native operatic style to new heights of dramatic expression. In 1842 he wrote the opera *Nabucco*, followed by *Ernani* 1844 and *Rigoletto* 1851. Other works include *Il trovatore* and *La traviata* both 1853, *Aïda* 1871, and the masterpieces of his old age, *Otello* 1887 and *Falstaff* 1893. His *Requiem* 1874 commemorates Alessandro Manzoni.

verification in computing, the process of checking that data being input to a computer have been accurately copied from a source document.

This may be done visually, by checking the original copy of the data against the copy shown on the VDT screen. A more thorough method is to enter the data twice, using two different keyboard operators, and then to check the two sets of input copies against each other. The checking is normally carried out by the computer itself.

Vermeer Jan 1632–1675. Dutch painter. He was active in Delft. Most of his pictures are ◊genre scenes, characterized by a limpid clarity, a distinct air of stillness, and color harmonies often based on yellow and blue. He frequently depicted solitary women in domestic settings, as in *The Lacemaker* about 1655 (Louvre, Paris).

Vermont state in NE US; nickname Green Mountain State *area* 9,611 sq mi/24,900 sq km *capital* Montpelier *towns and cities* Burlington, Rutland, Barre *features* brilliant autumn foliage and winter sports; Green Mountains; Lake Champlain *industries* apples, maple syrup, dairy products, china clay, granite, marble, slate, business machines, paper and allied products; tourism is important *population* (1990) 562,800 *famous people* Chester A Arthur, Calvin Coolidge, John Dewey *history* explored by the Frenchman Samuel de Champlain from 1609; settled by French 1666 and English 1724; became a state 1791.

Verne Jules 1828–1905. French author. He wrote tales of adventure that anticipated future scientific developments: *Five Weeks in a Balloon* 1862, *Journey to the Center of the Earth* 1864, *Twenty Thousand Leagues under the Sea* 1870, and *Around the World in Eighty Days* 1873.

Verona industrial city (printing, paper, plastics, furniture, pasta) in Veneto, Italy, on the Adige River; population (1988) 259,000. It also trades in fruit and vegetables.

Veronese Paolo (Paolo Caliari) *c.* 1528–1588. Italian painter. He was active mainly in Venice (from about 1553). He specialized in grand decorative schemes, such as his ceilings in the Doge's Palace in Venice, with their *trompe l'oeil* effects and inventive detail. Whether religious, mythological, historical, or allegorical, his paintings celebrate the power and splendor of Venice.

Versailles, Treaty of peace treaty after World War I between the Allies and Germany, signed June 28, 1919. It established the League of Nations. Germany surrendered Alsace-Lorraine to France, and large areas in the east to Poland, and made smaller cessions to Czechoslovakia, Lithuania, Belgium, and Denmark. The Rhineland was demilitarized, German rearmament was restricted, and Germany agreed to pay reparations for war damage. The treaty was never ratified by the US, which made a separate peace with Germany and Austria 1921.

vertebral column the backbone, giving support to an animal and protecting the spinal cord. It is made up of a series of bones or vertebrae running from the skull to the tail with a central canal containing the nerve fibers of the spinal cord. In tetrapods the vertebrae show some specialization with the shape of the bones varying according to position. In the chest region the upper or thoracic vertebrae are shaped to form connections to the ribs. The backbone is only slightly flexible to give adequate rigidity to the animal structure.

vertebrate any animal with a backbone. The 41,000 species of vertebrates include mammals, birds, reptiles, amphibians, and fishes. They include most of the larger animals, but in terms of numbers of species are only a tiny proportion of the world's animals. The zoological taxonomic group Vertebrata is a subgroup of the ◊phylum Chordata.

vertigo dizziness; a whirling sensation accompanied by a loss of any feeling of contact with the ground. It may be due to temporary disturbance of the sense of balance (as in spinning for too long on one spot), psychological reasons, disease such as labyrinthitis, or intoxication.

Vesalius Andreas 1514–1564. Belgian physician who revolutionized anatomy. His great innovations were to perform postmortem dissections and to make use of illustrations in teaching anatomy.

Vespasian (Titus Flavius Vespasianus) AD 9–79. Roman emperor from AD 69. Proclaimed emperor by his soldiers while he was campaigning in Palestine, he reorganized the eastern provinces, and was a capable administrator. He was responsible for the construction of the Colosseum in Rome, which was completed by his son Titus.

Vesta in Roman mythology, the goddess of the hearth, equivalent to the Greek Hestia. In Rome, the sacred flame in her shrine in the Forum represented the spirit of the community, and was kept constantly lit by the six *Vestal Virgins*.

Vesuvius (Italian *Vesuvio*) active volcano SE of Naples, Italy; height 4,190 ft/1,277 m. In 79 BC it destroyed the cities of Pompeii, Herculaneum, and Stabiae.

Veterans Day the name adopted 1954 for ◊Armistice Day and from 1971 observed by most states on the fourth monday in Oct.

veterinary science the study, prevention, and cure of disease in animals. More generally, it covers animal anatomy, breeding, and relations to humans.

The American Veterinary Medical Association was formed 1883.

veto (Latin "I forbid") exercise by a sovereign, branch of legislature, or other political power, of the right to prevent the enactment or operation of a law, or the taking of some course of action.

Under the US Constitution, the president may veto legislation, although that veto may, in turn, be overruled by a two-thirds majority in Congress. At the United Nations, members of the Security Council can exercise a veto on resolutions.

VGA (abbreviation for *video graphics array*) in computing, a color display system that provides either 16 colors on screen and a resolution of 640 x 480, or 256 colors with a resolution of 320 x 200. SVGA (Super VGA) provides even higher resolution and more colors.

VHF (abbreviation for *very high frequency*) referring to radio waves that have very short wavelengths (10 m–1 m). They are used for interference-free FM transmissions (see ◊frequency modulation). VHF transmitters have a relatively short range because the waves cannot be reflected over the horizon like longer radio waves.

vibraphone electrically amplified musical percussion instrument resembling a ◊xylophone but with metal keys. Spinning disks within resonating tubes under each key add a tremulant effect that can be controlled in speed with a foot pedal.

viburnum any small tree or shrub of the genus *Viburnum* of the honeysuckle family Caprifoliaceae, found in temperate and subtropical regions, including the ◊wayfaring tree, the laurustinus, and the guelder rose of Europe and Asia, and the North American blackhaws and arrowwoods.

vice versa (Latin) the other way around.

Vichy government in World War II, the right-wing government of unoccupied France after the country's defeat by the Germans June 1940, named for the spa town of Vichy, France, where the national assembly was based under Prime Minister Pétain until the liberation 1944. *Vichy France* was that part of France not occupied by German troops until Nov 1942. Authoritarian and collaborationist, the Vichy regime cooperated with the Germans even after they had moved to the unoccupied zone Nov 1942. It imprisoned some 135,000 people, interned another 70,000, deported some 76,000 Jews, and sent 650,000 French workers to Germany.

Victoria state of SE Australia *area* 87,854 sq mi/ 227,600 sq km *capital* Melbourne *towns and cities* Geelong, Ballarat, Bendigo *physical* part of the Great Dividing Range, running E–W and including the larger part of the Australian Alps; Gippsland lakes; shallow lagoons on the coast; the ◊mallee shrub region *industries* sheep, beef cattle, dairy products, tobacco, wheat, vines for wine and dried fruit, orchard fruits, vegetables, gold, brown coal (Latrobe Valley), oil and natural gas (Bass Strait) *population* (1987) 4,184,000; 70% in the Melbourne area *history* annexed for Britain by Capt. Cook 1770; settled in the 1830s; after being part of New South Wales became a separate colony 1851, named for the queen; became a state 1901.

Victoria 1819–1901. Queen of the UK from 1837, when she succeeded her uncle William IV, and empress of India from 1876. In 1840 she married Prince ◊Albert of Saxe-Coburg and Gotha. Her relations with her prime ministers ranged from the affectionate (Melbourne and Disraeli) to the stormy (Peel, Palmerston, and Gladstone). Her golden jubilee 1887 and diamond jubilee 1897 marked a waning of republican sentiment, which had developed with her withdrawal from public life on Albert's death 1861.

Only child of Edward, duke of Kent, fourth son of George III, she was born in London. She and Albert had four sons and five daughters. After Albert's death 1861 she lived mainly in retirement. Nevertheless, she kept control of affairs, refusing the prince of Wales (Edward VII) any active role.

Victoria Cross British decoration for conspicuous bravery in wartime, instituted by Queen Victoria 1856.

Victoria, Lake or *Victoria Nyanza* largest lake in Africa; area over 26,800 sq mi/69,400 sq km; length 255 mi/410 km. It lies on the equator at an altitude of 3,728 ft/1,136 m, bounded by Uganda, Kenya, and Tanzania. It is a source of the river Nile.

vicuna ◊ruminant mammal *Lama vicugna* of the camel family that lives in herds on the Andean plateau. It can run at speeds of 30 mph/50 kph. It has good eyesight, fair hearing, and a poor sense of smell. It was hunted close to extinction for its meat and soft brown fur, which was used in textile manufacture, but the vicuna is now a protected species; populations are increasing thanks to strict conservation measures. It is related to the ◊alpaca, the ◊guanaco, and the ◊llama.

video adapter in computing, an ◊expansion board that allows display of graphics and color. Commonly used video adapters for IBM PC-based systems are Hercules, CGA, EGA, VGA, XGA, and SVGA.

video camera or *camcorder* portable television camera that takes moving pictures electronically on magnetic tape. It produces an electrical output signal corresponding to rapid line-by-line scanning of the field of view. The output is recorded on videocassette and is played back on a television screen via a videocassette recorder.

videocassette recorder VCR device for recording pictures and sound on cassettes or spools of magnetic tape. The first commercial VCR was launched 1956 for the television broadcasting industry, but from the late 1970s cheaper models developed for home use, to record broadcast programs for future viewing and to view rented or owned videocassettes of commercial films.

video disk disk with pictures and sounds recorded on it, played back by laser. The video disk is a type of ◊compact disk.

video tape recorder (VTR) device for recording visuals and sound on spools of magnetic tape. It is used in television broadcasting.

videotext system in which information (text and simple pictures) is displayed on a television (video) screen. There are two basic systems, known as ◊teletext and ◊viewdata. In the teletext system information is broadcast with the ordinary television signals, whereas in the viewdata system information is relayed to the screen from a central data bank via the telephone network. Both systems require the use of a television receiver (or a connected VTR) with special decoder.

Vienna (German *Wien*) capital of Austria, on the river Danube at the foot of the Wiener Wald (Vienna Woods); population (1986) 1,481,000. Industries include engineering and the production of electrical goods and precision instruments.

Vientiane (Lao *Vieng Chan*) capital and chief port of Laos on the Mekong River; population (1985) 377,000. Noted for its pagodas, canals, and houses on stilts, it is a trading center for forest products and textiles. The Temple of the Heavy Buddha, the Pratuxai triumphal arch, and the Black Stupa are here. The

vicuna *The vicuna is a species of llama found in the high Andes. It lives in small herds of 6–12 females with a lone male. The male keeps watch, uttering a shrill whistle at the least sign of danger, and acts to protect the retreating herd.*

Great Sacred Stupa to the NE of the city is the most important national monument in Laos.

Vietnam Socialist Republic of (*Công Hòa Xa Hôi Chu Nghia Viêt Nam*) *area* 127,259 sq mi/329,600 sq km *capital* Hanoi *towns and cities* ports Ho Chi Minh City (formerly Saigon), Da Nang, Haiphong *physical* Red River and Mekong deltas, center of cultivation and population; tropical rainforest; mountainous in N and NW *environment* during the Vietnam War an estimated 5.4 million acres/2.2 million hectares of forest were destroyed. The country's National Conservation Strategy is trying to replant 500 million trees each year *features* Karst hills of Halong Bay, Cham Towers *head of state* Le Duc Anh from 1992 *head of government* Vo Van Kiet from 1991 *political system* communism *political party* Communist Party *exports* rice, rubber, coal, iron, apatite *currency* dong *population* (1993 est) 70,400,000 (750,000 refugees, majority ethnic Chinese left 1975–79, some settled in SW China, others fled by sea—the "boat people"—to Hong Kong and elsewhere); growth rate 2.4% p.a. *life expectancy* men 62, women 66 *languages* Vietnamese (official), French, English, Khmer, Chinese, local languages *media* independent newspapers prohibited by law 1989; central government approval is required for appointment of editors *religions* Buddhist, Taoist, Confucian, Christian *literacy* men 90%, women 84% *GNP* $200 per head (1990) *chronology 1945* Japanese removed from Vietnam at end of World War II. *1946* Vietminh war against French began. *1954* France defeated at Dien Bien Phu. Vietnam divided along 17th parallel. *1964* US troops entered Vietnam War. *1973* Paris cease-fire agreement. *1975* Saigon captured by North Vietnam. *1976* Socialist Republic of Vietnam proclaimed. *1978* Admission into Comecon. Vietnamese invasion of Cambodia. *1979* Sino-Vietnamese border war. *1986* Retirement of "old guard" leaders. *1987–88* Over 10,000 political prisoners released. *1988–89* Troop withdrawals from Cambodia continued. *1989* "Boat people" leaving Vietnam murdered and robbed at sea

by Thai pirates. Troop withdrawal from Cambodia completed. Hong Kong forcibly repatriated some Vietnamese refugees. *1991* Vo Van Kiet replaced Do Muoi as prime minister. Cambodia peace agreement signed. Relations with China normalized. *1992* Sept: Le Duc Anh elected president. Dec: relations with South Korea normalized. *1994* US 30-year-old trade embargo removed.

Vietnamese member of the majority group (90%) of peoples inhabiting Vietnam and referring to their language and culture, which is also called Annamese. Although Annamese is an independent language, it has been influenced by Chinese and there are Khmer loan words.

Vietnam War 1954–1975 war between communist North Vietnam and US-backed South Vietnam.

Vietnam War: chronology 1957–75

1957	Insurgent communist Vietcong began an offensive against the south. US provided limited amounts of indirect aid to South Vietnamese government.
1963	Military coup overthrew and killed Diem.
1964	Tonkin Gulf incident, when US destroyers were reportedly attacked by North Vietnamese, triggered US entry into the war.
1965 Jan	Major defeat of government forces at Binh-Gia, E of Saigon, by communists.
March	US began regular bombing of North Vietnam.
July	US began to send in combat troops.
1966	President Johnson increased numbers of US ground forces.
1967	US troops invaded the Demilitarized Zone (DMZ).
1968 Jan	Vietcong began Tet Offensive with attacks around Saigon, Hue, and Khe Sanh.
March	My Lai massacre by US troops.
May	Peace talks between US and North Vietnam began in Paris.
Nov	US bombing of North Vietnam halted.
1969 Jan	Paris peace talks included Vietcong and South Vietnam.
Sept	President Nixon announced phased withdrawal of 550,000 American troops in an attempt to "Vietnamize" the war. Death of Ho Chi Minh, succeeded by Ton Duc Thang.
Nov–Dec	Widespread anti-Vietnam War demonstrations in US.
1970	Fighting extended to Cambodia in an attempt to eliminate communist bases. Government of Prince Sihanouk overthrown and a republic proclaimed.
1971	South Vietnamese forces moved into Laos with US air support, in a further bid to cut off communist supply lines. US broke off peace talks in Paris.
1972 March	Major North Vietnamese offensive only halted by US bombing campaign and shelling of North Vietnam. US ground forces did not participate.
1973 Jan	Cease-fire agreement and withdrawal of remaining US forces.
1973–74	South Vietnamese forces gradually overwhelmed.
1975	North Vietnamese captured Saigon (renamed Ho Chi Minh City).

Following the division of French Indochina into North and South Vietnam and the Vietnamese defeat of the French 1954, US involvement in Southeast Asia grew through the SEATO pact. Noncommunist South Vietnam was viewed, in the context of the 1950s and the ◊cold war, as a bulwark against the spread of communism throughout SE Asia. Advisers and military aid were dispatched to the region at increasing levels because of the so-called domino theory, which contended that the fall of South Vietnam would precipitate the collapse of neighboring states. The US spent $141 bn in aid to the South Vietnamese government. Corruption and inefficiency within the South Vietnamese government led the US to assume ever greater responsibility for the war effort, until 1 million US combat troops were engaged.

viewdata system of displaying information on a television screen in which the information is extracted from a computer data bank and transmitted via the telephone lines. It is one form of ◊videotext. The British Post Office (now British Telecom) developed the first viewdata system, Prestel, 1975. Similar systems are now in widespread use in other countries. Users have access to a large store of information, presented on the screen in the form of "pages".

Viking or *Norseman* medieval Scandinavian sea warrior. They traded with and raided Europe in the 8th–11th centuries, and often settled there. In France the Vikings were given ◊Normandy. Under Sweyn I they conquered England 1013, and his son Canute was king of England as well as Denmark and Norway. In the east they established the first Russian state and founded ◊Novgorod. They reached the Byzantine Empire in the south, and in the west sailed the seas to Ireland, Iceland, Greenland, and North America; see ◊Eric the Red, Leif ◊Ericsson.

Villard Oswald Garrison 1872–1949. US editor and civil rights leader. A founder of the National Association for the Advancement of Colored People (NAACP), he was active in antiwar movements. He was president of the *New York Evening Post* 1900–18 and editor of the magazine *The Nation* 1918–32.

His autobiography, *Fighting Years*, appeared 1939.

villeinage system of serfdom that prevailed in Europe in the Middle Ages.

A villein was a peasant who gave dues and services to his lord in exchange for land. In France until the 13th century, "villeins" could refer to rural or urban non-nobles, but after this, it came to mean exclusively rural non-noble freemen. In Norman England, it referred to free peasants of relatively high status. At the time of the Domesday Book, the villeins were the most numerous element in the English population, providing the labor force for the manors.

villus plural *villi* small fingerlike projection extending into the interior of the small intestine and increasing the absorptive area of the intestinal wall. Digested nutrients, including sugars and amino acids, pass into the villi and are carried away by the circulating blood.

Vilnius capital of Lithuania; population (1987) 566,000. Industries include engineering and the manufacture of textiles, chemicals, and foodstuffs.

vincristine ◊alkaloid extracted from the blue periwinkle plant (*Vinca rosea*). Developed as an anticancer agent, it has revolutionized the treatment of childhood acute leukemias; it is also included in ◊chemotherapy regimens for some lymphomas (cancers arising in the lymph tissues) and lung and breast

cancers. Side effects, such as nerve damage and loss of hair, are severe but usually reversible.

vine or *grapevine* any of various climbing woody plants of the genus *Vitis*, family Vitaceae, especially *V. vinifera*, native to Asia Minor and cultivated from antiquity. Its fruit is eaten or made into wine or other fermented drinks; dried fruits of certain varieties are known as raisins and currants. Many other species of climbing plant are also termed vines.

Vinson Frederick Moore 1890–1953. US jurist. He held office in the US House of Representatives 1924–28 and 1930–38 and was appointed chief justice of the US Supreme Court 1946–53 by President Truman. He defended federal intervention in social and economic matters.

He supported civil rights, writing the majority opinion in *Shelly* v *Kraemer* 1948, ruling that state courts may not enforce discrimination by private landlords, and *McLaurin* v *Oklahoma State Regents* 1950, attacking the "separate but equal" doctrine.

viol member of a Renaissance family of bowed six-stringed musical instruments with flat backs and narrow shoulders that flourished particularly in England about 1540–1700, before their role was taken by the violins. Normally performing as an ensemble or consort, their repertoire is a development of madrigal style with idiomatic decoration.

viola bowed, stringed musical instrument, the alto member of the ◊violin family. With its dark, vibrant tone, it is suitable for music of reflective character, as in Stravinsky's *Elegy* 1944. Its principal function is supportive in string quartets and orchestras.

violet plant of the genus *Viola*, family Violaceae, with toothed leaves and mauve, blue, or white flowers, such as the Canada violet *V. canadensis* and primrose violet *V. primulifolia* of North America and the sweet violet *V. odorata* of Europe. The pansy is also a kind of violet.

violin bowed, four-stringed musical instrument, the smallest and highest pitched (treble) of the ◊violin family.

The strings are tuned in fifths (G3, D4, A4, and E5).

viper any front-fanged venomous snake of the family Viperidae. Vipers range in size from 1 ft/30 cm to 10 ft/3 m and often have diamond or jagged markings. Most give birth to live young.

Virgil (Publius Vergilius Maro) 70–19 BC. Roman poet. He wrote the *Eclogues* 37 BC, a series of pastoral poems; the *Georgics* 30 BC, four books on the art of farming; and his epic masterpiece, the *Aeneid* 30–19 BC. He was patronized by Maecenas on behalf of Octavian (later the emperor Augustus).

virginal in music, a small type of ◊harpsichord.

Virginia state in E US; nickname Old Dominion *area* 40,762 sq mi/105,600 sq km *capital* Richmond *towns and cities* Norfolk, Virginia Beach, Newport News, Hampton, Chesapeake, Portsmouth *features* Blue Ridge Mountains, which include the Shenandoah National Park; Arlington National Cemetery; Mount Vernon (home of George Washington 1752–99); Monticello (Thomas Jefferson's home near Charlottesville); Stratford Hall (Robert E Lee's birthplace at Lexington); Williamsburg restoration; Jamestown and Yorktown historic sites *industries* sweet potatoes, corn, tobacco, apples, peanuts, coal, ships, trucks, paper, chemicals, processed food, textiles *population* (1990) 6,187,400.

Virgin Islands group of about 100 small islands, northernmost of the Leeward Islands in the Antilles, West Indies. Tourism is the main industry.

They comprise the *US Virgin Islands* St Thomas (with the capital, Charlotte Amalie), St Croix, St John, and about 50 small islets; area 135 sq mi/350 sq km; population (1990) 101,800; and the *British Virgin Islands* Tortola (with the capital, Road Town), Virgin Gorda, Anegada, and Jost van Dykes, and about 40 islets; area 58 sq mi/150 sq km; population (1987) 13,250.

Christopher Columbus reached these islands 1493. They were divided between Britain and Denmark 1666. Denmark sold its islands to the US 1917; they form an unincorporated territory, with residents electing a governor and legislature.

Virgo zodiacal constellation, the second largest in the sky. It is represented as a maiden holding an ear of wheat. The Sun passes through Virgo from late Sept to the end of Oct Virgo's brightest star is the first-magnitude ◊Spica. Virgo contains the nearest large cluster of galaxies to us, 50 million light-years away, consisting of about 3,000 galaxies centered on the giant elliptical galaxy M87. Also in Virgo is the nearest ◊quasar, 3C 273, an estimated 3 billion light-years distant. In astrology, the dates for Virgo are between about Aug 23 and Sept 22 (see ◊precession).

virtual memory in computing, a technique whereby a portion of the computer backing storage, or external, ◊memory is used as an extension of its immediate-access, or internal, memory. The contents of an area of the immediate-access memory are stored on, say, a hard disk while they are not needed, and brought back into main memory when required.

virtual reality advanced form of computer simulation, in which a participant has the illusion of being part of an artificial environment. The participant views the environment through two tiny television screens (one for each eye) built into a visor. Sensors detect movements of the participant's head or body, causing the apparent viewing position to change. Gloves (datagloves) fitted with sensors may be worn, which allow the participant seemingly to pick up and move objects in the environment.

virus infectious particle consisting of a core of nucleic acid (DNA or RNA) enclosed in a protein shell. Viruses are acellular and able to function and reproduce only if they can invade a living cell to use the cell's system to replicate themselves. In the process they may disrupt or alter the host cell's own DNA. The healthy human body reacts by producing an antiviral protein, ◊interferon, which prevents the infection spreading to adjacent cells.

virus in computing, a piece of ◊software that can replicate and transfer itself from one computer to another, without the user being aware of it. Some viruses are relatively harmless, but others can damage or destroy data. They are written by anonymous programmers, often maliciously, and are spread along telephone lines or on ◊floppy disks. Antivirus software can be used to detect and destroy well-known viruses, but new viruses continually appear and these may bypass existing antivirus programs.

Visconti Luchino 1906–1976. Italian film, opera, and theater director. The film *Ossessione* 1942 pioneered Neo-Realist cinema despite being subject to censorship problems from the fascist government. His later works include *Rocco and His Brothers* 1960, *The Leopard* 1963, *The Damned* 1969, and *Death in Venice* 1971. His powerful social commentary led to clashes with the Italian government and Roman Catholic Church.

viscose yellowish, syrupy solution made by treating cellulose with sodium hydroxide and carbon disulfide. The solution is then regenerated as continuous filament for the making of ◊rayon and as cellophane.

viscosity in physics, the resistance of a fluid to flow, caused by its internal friction, which makes it resist flowing past a solid surface or other layers of the fluid. It applies to the motion of an object moving through a fluid as well as the motion of a fluid passing by an object.

Vishnu in Hinduism, the second in the triad of gods (with Brahma and Siva) representing three aspects of the supreme spirit. He is the *Preserver*, and is believed to have assumed human appearance in nine *avataras*, or incarnations, in such forms as Rama and Krishna. His worshipers are the Vaishnavas.

Visigoth member of the western branch of the ◊Goths, an E Germanic people.

vision defect any abnormality of the eye that causes less-than-perfect sight. In a *nearsighted* eye, the lens is fatter than normal, causing light from distant objects to be focused in front and not on the retina. A person with this complaint, called ◊myopia, cannot see clearly for distances over a few yards, and needs glasses with diverging lenses. *Farsightedness*, also called hypermetropia, is caused by an eye lens thinner than normal that focuses light from distant objects behind the retina. The sufferer cannot see close objects clearly, and needs converging-lens glasses. There are other vision defects, such as ◊color blindness and ◊astigmatism.

Visual Basic computer language based on ◊BASIC.

visual display terminal (VDT) computer terminal consisting of a keyboard for input data and a screen for displaying output. The oldest and the most popular type of VDT screen is the ◊cathode-ray tube (CRT), which uses essentially the same technology as a television screen. Other types use plasma display technology and ◊liquid-crystal displays.

vitamin any of various chemically unrelated organic compounds that are necessary in small quantities for the normal functioning of the human body. Many act as coenzymes, small molecules that enable ◊enzymes to function effectively. They are normally present in adequate amounts in a balanced diet. Deficiency of a vitamin may lead to a metabolic disorder ("deficiency disease"), which can be remedied by sufficient intake of the vitamin. They are generally classified as *water-soluble* (B and C) or *fat-soluble* (A, D, E, and K).

vitreous humor transparent jellylike substance behind the lens of the vertebrate ◊eye. It gives rigidity to the spherical form of the eye and allows light to pass through to the retina.

vitriol any of a number of sulfate salts. Blue, green, and white vitriols are copper, ferrous, and zinc sulfate, respectively.

Oil of vitriol is sulfuric acid.

Vivaldi Antonio (Lucio) 1678–1741. Italian Baroque composer, violinist, and conductor. He wrote 23 symphonies; 75 sonatas; over 400 concertos, including *The Four Seasons* 1725 for violin and orchestra; over 40 operas; and much sacred music. His work was largely neglected until the 1930s.

Known as the "Red Priest", because of his flaming

hair color, Vivaldi spent much of his church career teaching music at a girl's orphanage. He wrote for them and for himself.

vivisection literally, cutting into a living animal. Used originally to mean experimental surgery or dissection practiced on a live subject, the term is often used by antivivisection campaigners to include any experiment on animals, surgical or otherwise.

Vladivostok port (naval and commercial) in E Siberian Russia, at the Amur Bay on the Pacific coast; population (1987) 615,000. It is kept open by icebreakers during winter. Industries include shipbuilding and the manufacture of precision instruments.

VLSI (abbreviation for *very large-scale integration*) in electronics, the early-1990s level of advanced technology in the microminiaturization of ◊integrated circuits, and an order of magnitude smaller than ◊LSI (large-scale integration).

vocal cords the paired folds, ridges, or cords of tissue within a mammal's larynx, and a bird's syrinx. Air constricted between the folds or membranes makes them vibrate, producing sounds. Muscles in the larynx change the pitch of the sounds produced, by adjusting the tension of the vocal cords.

vocational education education relevant to a specific job or career.

Community colleges provide two-year training in the trades as well as secretarial, business, accounting, and other business and job-related studies. Technical colleges may be two-year, four-year, or prestigious advanced degree institutions, such as the Massachusetts Institute of Technology or Rensselaer Polytechnical Institute.

vodka strong colorless alcoholic beverage distilled from rye, potatoes, or barley.

voice mail in computing, ◊electronic mail including spoken messages and audio. Messages can also be generated electronically using ◊speech synthesis.

Vojvodina autonomous province in N Serbia, Yugoslavia, 1945–1990; area 8,299 sq mi/21,500 sq km; population (1991) 2,012,500, including 1,110,000 Serbs and 390,000 Hungarians, as well as Croat, Slovak, Romanian, and Ukrainian minorities. Its capital is Novi Sad. In Sept 1990 Serbia effectively stripped Vojvodina of its autonomous status, causing antigovernment and anticommunist riots in early 1991.

volatile in chemistry, term describing a substance that readily passes from the liquid to the vapor phase. Volatile substances have a high ◊vapor pressure.

volatile memory in computing, ◊memory that loses its contents when the power supply to the computer is disconnected.

volcano crack in the Earth's crust through which hot magma (molten rock) and gases well up. The magma is termed lava when it reaches the surface. A volcanic mountain, usually cone shaped with a crater on top, is formed around the opening, or vent, by the buildup of solidified lava and ashes (rock fragments). Most volcanoes arise on plate margins (see ◊plate tectonics), where the movements of plates generate magma or allow it to rise from the mantle beneath. However, a number are found far from plate-margin activity, on "hot spots" where the Earth's crust is thin.

vole any of various rodents of the family Cricetidae, subfamily Microtinae, distributed over Europe, Asia, and North America, and related to hamsters and lemmings. They are characterized by stout bodies and short tails. They have brown or gray fur, and blunt noses, and some species reach a length of 12 in/30 cm. They feed on grasses, seeds, aquatic plants, and insects. Many show remarkable fluctuations in numbers over 3–4 year cycles.

Volga longest river in Europe; 2,290 mi/3,685 km, 2,200 mi/3,540 km of which are navigable. It drains most of the central and eastern parts of European Russia, rises in the Valdai plateau, and flows into the Caspian Sea 55 mi/88 km below the city of Astrakhan.

Volgograd formerly (until 1925) *Czaritsyn* and (1925–61) *Stalingrad* industrial city (metal goods, machinery, lumber mills, oil refining) in SW Russia, on the river Volga; population (1987) 988,000.

volleyball indoor and outdoor team game played on a court between two teams of six players each. A net is placed across the center of the court, and players hit the ball with their hands over it, the aim being to ground it in the opponents' court.

volt SI unit (symbol V) of electromotive force or electric potential. A small battery usually has a potential of one or two volts; the domestic electricity supply in the US is 110 volts. A high-tension transmission line may carry up to 765,000 volts.

Voltaire Pen name of François-Marie Arouet 1694–1778. French writer. He was the embodiment of the 18th-century ◊Enlightenment. He wrote histories, books of political analysis and philosophy, essays on science and literature, plays, poetry, and satirical fables. A trenchant satirist of social and political evils, he was often forced to flee from his enemies and was twice imprisoned. His many works include *Lettres philosophiques sur les Anglais/Philosophical Letters on the English* 1733 (essays in favor of English ways, thought, and political practice); *Le Siècle de Louis XIV/The Age of Louis XIV* 1751; the satirical fable *Candide* 1759, his best-known work; and *Dictionnaire philosophique* 1764.

Vonnegut Kurt, Jr. 1922– . US writer whose work generally has surrealistic elements, satire, and fantasy and depicts the flaws of contemporary society. His novel *Slaughterhouse Five* 1969 mixes his World War II experience of the fire-bombing of Dresden, Germany, with a fantasy world on the planet Tralfamadore with the science-fiction element dominated by absurdism and earthly black humor.

Von Neumann John 1903–1957. Hungarian-born US scientist and mathematician, known for his pioneering work on computer design. He invented his "rings of operators" (called Von Neumann algebras) in the late 1930s, and also contributed to set theory, games theory, cybernetics (with his theory of self-reproducing automata, called *Von Neumann machines*), and the development of the atomic and hydrogen bombs.

voodoo set of magical beliefs and practices, followed in some parts of Africa, South America, and the West Indies, especially Haiti. It arose in the 17th century on slave plantations as a combination of Roman Catholicism and W African religious traditions; believers retain membership in the Roman Catholic church.

vote expression of opinion by ballot, show of hands, or other means. For direct vote, see ◊plebiscite and ◊referendum. In parliamentary elections the results can be calculated in a number of ways.

***Voyager* probes** two US space probes, originally ◊Mariners. *Voyager 1*, launched Sept 5, 1977, passed

Jupiter March 1979, and reached Saturn Nov 1980. *Voyager 2* was launched earlier, Aug 20, 1977, on a slower trajectory that took it past Jupiter July 1979, Saturn Aug 1981, Uranus Jan 1986, and Neptune Aug 1989. Like the Pioneer probes, the *Voyagers* are on their way out of the Solar System. Their tasks now include helping scientists to locate the position of the heliopause, the boundary at which the influence of the Sun gives way to the forces exerted by other stars.

Voyager 2 was not intended to visit Uranus and Neptune, but scientists were able to reprogram its computer to take it past those planets. *Voyager 2* passed by Neptune at an altitude of 3,000 mi/4,800 km; its radio signals took 4 hours 6 minutes to reach Earth.

VRAM (acronym for *video random-access memory*) in computing, form of ◊RAM that allows simultaneous access by two different devices, so that graphics can be handled at the same time as data is updated. VRAM improves graphic display performance.

Vulcan in Roman mythology, the god of fire and destruction, later identified with the Greek god ◊Hephaestus.

Vulgate the Latin translation of the Bible produced by St Jerome in the 4th century.

It is the oldest surviving version of the entire Bible and differs from earlier Latin translations in working from the Hebrew rather than the Greek. In 1546 it was adopted by the Council of Trent as the official Roman Catholic Bible and was later used for official English versions like the Douai.

vulture *the vulture is a heavily built bird. There are 15 species in Africa, Asia and Europe, with a further seven species in the US. Most have dark plumage, bare head and neck, strongly curved beak, and powerful talons.*

vulture any of various carrion-eating birds of prey with naked heads and necks and with keen senses of sight and smell. Vultures are up to 3.3 ft/1 m long, with wingspans of up to 11.5 ft/3.5 m. The plumage is usually dark, and the head brightly colored.

W abbreviation for *west*; in physics, symbol for *watt*.

Waco city in E central Texas, US, on the Brazos River, S of Fort Worth; population (1990) 103,600. It is an agricultural shipping center for cotton, grain, and livestock; industries include aircraft parts, glass, cement, tires, and textiles.

Baylor University (1845) is here. On Aug 19, 1993, more than 70 members of the Branch Davidian religious cult were killed during a seige by the FBI and Bureau of Alcohol, Tobacco and Firearms (ATF).

wadi in arid regions of the Middle East, a steep-sided valley containing an intermittent stream that flows in the wet season.

wage and price controls government directives freezing or limiting wages and prices, usually in time of emergency, such as wars or in the event of severe ◊inflation.

Wagner Honus (John Peter) 1874–1955. US baseball player. He had an impressive lifetime batting average of.329. In addition to his fielding skills, he was a great runner; his career record of 722 stolen bases won him the nickname "the Flying Dutchman".

Wagner was elected to the Baseball Hall of Fame 1936.

Wagner Richard 1813–1883. German opera composer. He revolutionized the 19th-century conception of opera, envisaging it as a wholly new art form in which musical, poetic, and scenic elements should be unified through such devices as the leitmotif. His operas include *Tannhäuser* 1845, *Lohengrin* 1848, and *Tristan und Isolde* 1865. In 1872 he founded the Festival Theatre in Bayreuth; his masterpiece *Der Ring des Nibelungen/The Ring of the Nibelung*, a sequence of four operas, was first performed there 1876. His last work, *Parsifal*, was produced 1882.

wagtail any slim narrow-billed bird of the genus *Motacilla*, about 7 in/18 cm long, with a characteristic flicking movement of the tail. There are about 30 species, found mostly in Eurasia and Africa.

Wahabi puritanical Saudi Islamic sect founded by Mohammed ibn-Abd-al-Wahab (1703–1792), which regards all other sects as heretical. By the late 20th century it had spread throughout the Arabian peninsula; it still remains the official ideology of the Saudi Arabian kingdom.

Wailing Wall or (in Judaism) *Western Wall* the remaining part of the ◊Temple in Jerusalem, a sacred site of pilgrimage and prayer for Jews. There they offer prayers either aloud ("wailing") or on pieces of paper placed between the stones of the wall.

Wainwright Jonathan 1883–1953. US general. He served in the Philippines 1940 as commander of the North Luzon Force. Under the command of ◊MacArthur he fell back into the Bataan peninsula when the Japanese invaded 1941. He was unable to withstand the Japanese invasion, and surrendered May 5, 1942. He took part in the Bataan Death March,

survived to be imprisoned in Manchuria for the remainder of the war, and was present to see the Japanese surrender signed on board USS *Missouri* Sept 2, 1945.

Wajda Andrzej 1926– . Polish film and theater director. He was one of the major figures in postwar European cinema. His films have great intensity and are frequently concerned with the predicament and disillusion of individuals caught up in political events. His works include *Ashes and Diamonds* 1958, *Man of Marble* 1977, *Man of Iron* 1981, *Danton* 1982, and *Korczak* 1990.

He was also mentor to filmmaker Roman Polanski.

Waldsterben (German "forest death") tree decline related to air pollution, common throughout the industrialized world. It appears to be caused by a mixture of pollutants; the precise chemical mix varies between locations, but it includes acid rain, ozone, sulfur dioxide, and nitrogen oxides.

Wales (Welsh *Cymru*) Principality of; constituent part of the UK, in the W between the British Channel and the Irish Sea *area* 8,021 sq mi/20,780 sq km *capital* Cardiff *towns and cities* Swansea, Wrexham, Newport, Carmarthen *features* Snowdonia Mountains (Snowdon 3,561 ft/1,085 m, the highest point in England and Wales) in the NW and in the SE the Black Mountains, Brecon Beacons, and Black Forest ranges; rivers Severn, Wye, Usk, and Dee *exports* traditional industries, such as coal (there are no functioning pits left in Wales) and steel, have declined, but varied modern and high-technology ventures are being developed. There are oil refineries. Wales has the largest concentration of Japanese-owned plants in the UK. It also has the highest density of sheep in the world and a dairy industry; tourism is important *currency* pound sterling *population* (1991) 2,835,100 *languages* English, 19% Welsh-speaking *religions* Nonconformist Protestant denominations; Roman Catholic minority *government* returns 38 members to the UK Parliament. *chronology* for ancient history, see also ◊Britain, ancient *c. 400 BC* Wales occupied by Celts from central Europe. *AD 50–60* Wales became part of the Roman Empire. *c. 200* Christianity adopted. *c. 450–600* Wales became the chief Celtic stronghold in the west since the Saxons invaded and settled in S Britain. The Celtic tribes united against England. *8th century* Frontier pushed back to ◊Offa's Dyke. *9th–11th centuries* Vikings raided the coasts. At this time Wales was divided into small states organized on a clan basis, although princes such as Rhodri (844–878), Howel the Good (*c.* 904–949), and Griffith ap Llewelyn (1039–1063) temporarily united the country. *11th–12th centuries* Continual pressure on Wales from the Normans across the English border was resisted, notably by ◊Llewelyn I and II. *1277* Edward I of England accepted as overlord by the Welsh. *1284* Edward I completed the conquest of Wales that had been begun by the Normans. *1294*

Revolt against English rule put down by Edward I. *1350–1500* Welsh nationalist uprisings against the English; the most notable was that led by Owen Glendower. *1485* Henry Tudor, a Welshman, became Henry VII of England. *1536–43* Acts of Union united England and Wales after conquest under Henry VIII. Wales sent representatives to the English Parliament; English law was established in Wales; English became the official language. *18th century* Evangelical revival made Nonconformism a powerful factor in Welsh life. A strong coal and iron industry developed in the south. *19th century* The miners and ironworkers were militant supporters of Chartism, and Wales became a stronghold of labor unionism and socialism. *1893* University of Wales founded. *1920s–30s* Wales suffered from industrial depression; unemployment reached 21% 1937, and a considerable exodus of population took place. *post-1945* Growing nationalist movement and a revival of the language, earlier suppressed or discouraged. *1966* Plaid Cymru, the Welsh National Party, returned its first member to Westminster. *1979* Referendum rejected a proposal for limited home rule. *1988* Bombing campaign against estate agents selling Welsh properties to English buyers. For other history, see also ◊England: history; ◊United Kingdom.

Walesa Lech 1943– . Polish labor-union leader, president of Poland from 1990. He founded ◊Solidarity (Solidarnosc) in 1980, an organization, independent of the Communist Party, which forced substantial political and economic concessions from the Polish government 1980–81 until being outlawed. He was awarded the Nobel Prize for Peace 1983.

Wales, Prince of title conferred on the eldest son of the UK's sovereign. Prince ◊Charles was invested as 21st prince of Wales at Caernarvon 1969 by his mother, Elizabeth II.

Walker Alice 1944– . US poet, novelist, critic, and essay writer. She has been active in the US civil-rights movement since the 1960s and, as an African American woman, wrote about the double burden of racist and sexist oppression, about colonialism, and the quest for political and spiritual recovery. Her novel *The Color Purple* 1982 (filmed 1985), told in the form of letters, won the Pulitzer Prize. Her other works include *Possessing the Secret of Joy* 1992, which deals passionately with female circumcision.

wallaby any of various small and medium-sized members of the ◊kangaroo family.

Wallace George Corley 1919– . US politician who was opposed to integration; he was governor of Alabama 1963–67, 1971–79, and 1983–87. He contested the presidency in 1968 as an independent (the American Independent Party) and in 1972 campaigned for the Democratic nomination but was shot at a rally and became partly paralyzed.

wallflower European perennial garden plant *Cheiranthus cheiri*, family Cruciferae, with fragrant red or yellow flowers in spring.

Walloon member of a French-speaking people of SE Belgium and adjacent areas of France. The name "Walloon" is etymologically linked to "Welsh".

Wall Street the financial center of the US on lower Manhattan Island in New York City. It is often synonymous with the New York Stock Exchange, which is housed there. The street was so named because of a stockade erected by the Dutch 1653.

Wall Street crash 1929 panic selling on the New York Stock Exchange following an artificial boom 1927–29 fed by speculation. On Oct 24, 1929, 13 million shares changed hands, with further heavy selling on Oct 28 and the disposal of 16 million shares on Oct 29. Many stockholders were ruined, banks and businesses failed, and in the ◊Depression that followed, unemployment rose to approximately 17 million.

walnut genus *Juglans* of trees of the family Juglandaceae, closely related to hickories. Walnuts have pinnately compound leaves and nuts enclosed in a thick leathery husk. Six species, including the black walnut *J. nigra* and the butternut *J. cinerea*, are native to the US. About 15 other species occur in South America and Eurasia. The English walnut *J. regia*, originally from SE Europe and Asia, is cultivated widely for its nut crop.

Walpole Robert, 1st Earl of Orford 1676–1745. British Whig politician, the first "prime minister" as First Lord of the Treasury and chancellor of the Exchequer 1715–17 and 1721–42. He encouraged trade and tried to avoid foreign disputes (until forced into the War of Jenkins's Ear with Spain 1739).

walrus Arctic marine carnivorous mammal *Odobenus rosmarus* of the same family (Otaridae) as the eared ◊seals. It can reach 13 ft/4 m in length, and weigh up to 3,000 lb/1,400 kg. It has webbed flippers, a bristly moustache, and large tusks. It is gregarious except at breeding time and feeds mainly on mollusks. It has been hunted close to extinction for its ivory tusks, hide, and blubber. The Alaskan walrus is close to extinction.

walrus The walrus is a member of the Odobenidae family. Like the sea lion, it can bring its hind flippers forward under the body to help it move on land. Both sexes have tusks, and male tusks sometimes reach a length of 3 ft/1 m.

Walsh Raoul 1887–1981. US film director. He was originally an actor. A specialist in tough action stories, he made a number of outstanding films, including *The Thief of Bagdad* 1924, *The Roaring Twenties* 1939, *Objective Burma!* 1945, and *White Heat* 1949.
He retired 1964.

waltz ballroom dance in moderate triple time (3/4) that developed in Germany and Austria during the late 18th century from the Austrian *Ländler* (traditional peasants' country dance). Associated particularly with Vienna and the ◊Strauss family, the waltz has remained popular up to the present day and has inspired composers including Chopin, Brahms, and Ravel.

Wanamaker John 1838–1922. US retailer who developed the modern department store. He established his own firm, John Wanamaker and Company, 1869. Renting an abandoned railroad depot 1876, he merchandised goods in distinct departments; he publicized his stores through extensive advertising.

A staunch Republican, Wanamaker served as postmaster general in the Benjamin Harrison administration 1889–93.

Wang An 1920–1990. Chinese-born US engineer, founder of Wang Laboratories 1951, one of the world's largest computer companies in the 1970s. He emigrated to the US 1945 and three years later invented the computer memory core, the most common device used for storing computer data before the invention of the integrated circuit (chip).

Wankel engine rotary gasoline engine developed by the German engineer Felix Wankel (1902–1988) in the 1950s. It operates according to the same stages as the ◊four-stroke gasoline engine cycle, but these stages take place in different sectors of a figure-eight chamber in the space between the chamber walls and a triangular rotor. Power is produced once on every turn of the rotor. The Wankel engine is simpler in construction than the four-stroke piston gasoline engine, and produces rotary power directly (instead of via a crankshaft). Problems with rotor seals have prevented its widespread use.

wapiti alternate name for ◊elk.

Warbeck Perkin *c.* 1474–1499. Flemish pretender to the English throne. Claiming to be Richard, brother of Edward V, he led a rising against Henry VII in 1497, and was hanged after attempting to escape from the Tower of London.

warbler any of two families of songbirds, order Passeriformes.

warfarin poison that induces fatal internal bleeding in rats; neutralized with sodium hydroxide, it is used in medicine as an anticoagulant in the treatment of ◊thrombosis: it prevents blood clotting by inhibiting the action of vitamin K. It can be taken orally and begins to act several days after the initial dose.

Warhol Andy. Adopted name of Andrew Warhola 1928–1987. US Pop artist and filmmaker. He made his name in 1962 with paintings of Campbell's soup cans, Coca-Cola bottles, and film stars. In his New York studio, the Factory, he and his assistants produced series of garish silk-screen prints. His films include the semi-documentary *Chelsea Girls* 1966 and *Trash* 1970.

War of 1812 a war between the US and Britain caused by British interference with American trade (shipping) as part of Britain's economic warfare against Napoleonic France. US sailors were impressed from American ships, and a blockade was imposed on US shipping by Britain. Also, British assistance was extended to Indians harassing the NW settlements (see ◊Tecumseh). President Madison authorized the beginning of hostilities against the British on the high seas and in Canada. US forces failed twice in attempts to invade British-held Canada but achieved important naval victories, while in 1814 British forces occupied Washington, DC and burned the White House and the Capitol. A treaty signed at Ghent, Belgium, in Dec 1814 ended the conflict. Before news of the treaty reached the US, American troops under Andrew ◊Jackson defeated the British at New Orleans 1815.

War Powers Act US Congressional legislation passed 1973, over President Nixon's veto, aimed at restricting the president's introduction of US forces into potentially hostile situations without Congressional

declaration of war. The act has been considered unconstitutional by each president since its passage, and its provisions generally have been ignored by both Congress and presidents.

Warren Earl 1891–1974. US jurist and chief justice of the US Supreme Court 1953–69. He served as governor of California 1943–53. As chief justice, he presided over a moderately liberal court, taking a stand against racial discrimination and ruling that segregation in schools was unconstitutional. He headed the commission that investigated 1963–64 President Kennedy's assassination.

Warren Robert Penn 1905–1989. US poet and novelist born in Guthrie, Kentucky. He is the only author to have received a Pulitzer Prize for both prose and poetry. His work explored the moral problems of the South. His most important novel, *All the King's Men* 1946 (Pulitzer Prize 1947), depicts the rise and fall of a back-country demagogue modeled on the career of Huey ◊Long. He also won Pulitzer Prizes for *Promises* 1968 and *Now and Then: Poems* 1976–78. He was a senior figure of the New Criticism, and the first official US poet laureate 1986–88.

Warsaw (Polish *Warszawa*) capital of Poland, on the river Vistula; population (1990) 1,655,700. Industries include engineering, food processing, printing, clothing, and pharmaceuticals.

wart protuberance composed of a local overgrowth of skin. The common wart (*verruca vulgaris*) is due to a virus infection. It usually disappears spontaneously within two years, but can be treated with peeling applications, burning away (cautery), or freezing (cryosurgery).

wart hog African wild ◊pig *Phacochoerus aethiopicus*, which has a large head with a bristly mane, fleshy pads beneath the eyes, and four large tusks. It has short legs and can grow to 2.5 ft/80 cm at the shoulder.

Warwick Richard Neville, Earl of Warwick 1428–1471. English politician, called *the Kingmaker*. During the Wars of the ◊Roses he fought at first on the Yorkist side against the Lancastrians, and was largely responsible for placing Edward IV on the throne. Having quarreled with him, he restored Henry VI in 1470, but was defeated and killed by Edward at Barnet, Hertfordshire.

Warwickshire county of central England *area* 764 sq mi/1,980 sq km *towns and cities* Warwick (administrative headquarters), Royal Leamington Spa, Nuneaton, Rugby, Stratford-upon-Avon *features* river Avon; Kenilworth and Warwick castles; remains of the "Forest of Arden" (portrayed by Shakespeare in *As You Like It*); site of the Battle of Edgehill; annual Royal Agricultural Show held at Stoneleigh *industries* mainly agricultural, engineering, textiles *population* (1991) 484,200 *famous people* William Shakespeare, George Eliot, Rupert Brooke.

Wash, the bay of the North Sea between Norfolk and Lincolnshire, England. The rivers Nene, Ouse, Welland, and Witham drain into the Wash.

Washington state in northwestern; nickname Evergreen State/Chinook State *area* 68,206 sq mi/ 176,700 sq km *capital* Olympia *towns and cities* Seattle, Spokane, Tacoma *features* Columbia River; national parks: Olympic (Olympic Mountains), Mount Rainier (Cascade Range), North Cascades; 90 dams *industries* apples and other fruits, potatoes, livestock, fish, timber, processed food, wood products, paper and allied products, aircraft and aerospace equipment, aluminum *pop-*

ulation (1990) 4,866,700 (including 1.4% Indians, mainly of the Yakima people) *famous people* Bing Crosby, Jimi Hendrix, Mary McCarthy, Theodore Roethke *history* explored by Spanish, British, and Americans in the 18th century; settled from 1811; became a territory 1853 and a state 1889.

Rival American and British territorial claims threatened war in the early 1840s that was settled by the Oregon Treaty 1846.

The transcontinental railroad arrived 1883. Radical labor activity repressed 1919. The New Deal era brought many public-works projects, and Boeing became the largest employer in World War II. Mount St Helens erupted here 1980, and many in the state are now fighting to close the antiquated and dangerous nuclear plant at Hanford.

Washington George 1732–1799. Commander of the American forces during the Revolutionary War and 1st president of the US 1789–97, known as "the father of his country". An experienced soldier, he had fought in campaigns against the French during the French and Indian War. He was elected to the Virginia House of Burgesses 1759 and was a leader of the Virginia militia, gaining valuable exposure to wilderness fighting. As a strong opponent of the British government's policy, he sat in the Continental Congresses of 1774 and 1775, and on the outbreak of the ◊American Revolution was chosen commander in chief of the Continental army. After many setbacks, he accepted the surrender of British general Cornwallis at Yorktown 1781.

After the war Washington retired to his Virginia estate, Mount Vernon, but in 1787 he reentered politics as president of the Constitutional Convention in Philadelphia and was elected US president 1789. Although he attempted to draw his ministers from all factions, his aristocratic outlook alienated his secretary of state, Thomas Jefferson, with whose resignation in 1793 the two-party system originated. Washington accepted the fiscal policy championed by Alexander ◊Hamilton and oversaw the payment of the foreign and domestic debt incurred by the new nation. He also shaped the powers of the presidency, assuming some implied powers not specified in the Constitution–among them, the power to create a national bank.

Washington, DC (District of Columbia) national capital of the US, on the Potomac River *area*69 sq mi/ 180 sq km *features* designed by French engineer Pierre L'Enfant (1754–1825) and completed by Andrew Ellicott and Benjamin Banneker. Among buildings of architectural note are the Capitol, the Pentagon, the White House, the Washington Monument, and the Jefferson and Lincoln memorials. The National Gallery has an outstanding collection of paintings; libraries include the Library of Congress, the National Archives, and the Folger Shakespeare Library. The Smithsonian Institution and its several museums are on the National Mall. *population* (1983) 606,900 (metropolitan area, extending outside the District of Columbia, 3 million) *history* the District of Columbia, initially land ceded from Maryland 1788 and Virginia 1789, was established by an act of Congress 1790–91 and was first used as the seat of Congress Dec 1, 1800. The Virginia portion was returned 1846. The right to vote in national elections was not granted to residents until 1961. Local self-rule began 1975. In 1988 Washington had the highest murder rate of any large city in the US.

wasp any of several families of winged stinging insects of the order Hymenoptera, characterized by a thin stalk between the thorax and the abdomen. Wasps can be social or solitary. Among social wasps, the queens devote themselves to egg laying, the fertilized eggs producing female workers; the males come from unfertilized eggs and have no sting. The larvae are fed on insects, but the mature wasps feed mainly on fruit and sugar. In winter, the fertilized queens hibernate, but the other wasps die.

waste materials that are no longer needed and are discarded. Examples are household waste, industrial waste (which often contains toxic chemicals), medical waste (which may contain organisms that cause disease), and ◊nuclear waste (which is radioactive). By ◊recycling, some materials in waste can be reclaimed for further use. In 1990 the industrialized nations generated 2 billion metric tons of waste. In the US, 40 metric tons of solid waste are generated annually per person, roughly twice as much as in Europe or Japan.

water H_2O liquid without color, taste, or odor. It is an oxide of hydrogen. Water begins to freeze at 32°F/0°C, and to boil at 212°F/100°C. When liquid, it is virtually incompressible; frozen, it expands by 1/11 of its volume. At 39.2°F/4°C, one cubic centimeter of water has a mass of one gram; this is its maximum density, forming the unit of specific gravity. It has the highest known specific heat, and acts as an efficient solvent, particularly when hot. Most of the world's water is in the sea; less than 0.01% is fresh water.

water boatman any water ◊bug of the family Corixidae that feeds on plant debris and algae. It has a flattened body 0.6 in/1.5 cm long, with oarlike legs.

waterbuck any of several African ◊antelopes of the genus *Kobus* which usually inhabit swampy tracts and reedbeds. They vary in size from 6 ft/1.4 m to 7.25 ft/ 2.1 m long, are up to 4.5 ft/1.4 m tall at the shoulder, and have long brown fur. The large curved horns, normally carried only by the males, have corrugated surfaces. Some species have white patches on the buttocks. Lechwe, kor, and defassa are alternative names for some of the species.

watercolor painting method of painting with pigments mixed with water, known in China as early as the 3rd century. The art as practiced today began in England in the 18th century with the work of Paul Sandby and was developed by Thomas Girtin, John Sell Cotman, and J M W Turner. Other outstanding watercolorists were Raoul Dufy, Paul Cézanne, and John Marin. The technique of watercolor painting requires great skill since its transparency rules out overpainting.

watercress perennial aquatic plant *Nasturtium officinale* of the crucifer family, found in Europe and Asia, and cultivated as a salad crop.

water flea any aquatic crustacean in the order Cladocera, of which there are over 400 species. The commonest species is *Daphnia pulex*, used in the pet trade to feed tropical fish.

waterfowl any water bird, but especially any member of the family Anatidae, which consists of ducks, geese, and swans.

Watergate US political scandal, named for the building in Washington, DC that housed the Democrats' campaign headquarters in the 1972 presidential election. Five men, hired by the Republican Committee to Reelect the President (CREEP), were caught after breaking into the Watergate with complex electronic surveillance equipment. Investigations revealed that the White House was implicated in the break-in, and that there was a "slush fund", used to finance unethical activities, including using the CIA and the Internal Revenue Service for political ends, setting up paramilitary operations against opponents, altering and destroying evidence, and bribing defendants to lie or remain silent. In Aug 1974, President ◊Nixon was forced by the Supreme Court to surrender to Congress tape recordings of conversations he had held with administration officials, which indicated his complicity in a cover-up. Nixon resigned rather than face impeachment for obstruction of justice and other crimes.

water glass common name for sodium metasilicate (Na_2SiO_3). It is a colorless, jellylike substance that dissolves readily in water to give a solution used for preserving eggs and fireproofing porous materials such as cloth, paper, and wood. It is also used as an adhesive for paper and cardboard and in the manufacture of soap and silica gel, a substance that absorbs moisture.

water hyacinth tropical aquatic plant *Eichhornia crassipes* of the pickerelweed family Pontederiaceae. In one growing season 25 plants can produce 2 million new plants. It is liable to choke waterways, depleting the water of nutrients and blocking the sunlight, but can be used as a purifier of sewage-polluted water as well as in making methane gas, compost, concentrated protein, paper, and baskets. Originating in South America, it now grows in more than 50 countries.

water lily aquatic plant of the family Nymphaeaceae. The fleshy roots are embedded in mud and the large round leaves float on the water. The cup-shaped flowers may be white, pink, yellow, or blue.

The white water lily *Nymphaea odorata* is common in E North America as is the yellow-flowered spatterdock *Nuphar advena*. *Victoria regia*, with leaves about 6 ft/2 m in diameter, occurs in South America.

Waterloo, Battle of battle on June 18, 1815, in which British forces commanded by Wellington defeated the French army of Emperor Napoleon near the village of Waterloo, 8 mi/13 km S of Brussels, Belgium. Napoleon found Wellington's army isolated from his allies and began a direct offensive to smash them, but the British held on until joined by the Prussians under General Blücher. Four days later Napoleon abdicated for the second and final time.

watermelon large ◊melon *Citrullus vulgaris* of the gourd family, native to tropical Africa, with pink, white, or yellow flesh studded with black seeds and a green rind. It is widely cultivated in subtropical regions such as the southern US.

water pollution any addition to fresh or sea water that disrupts biological processes or causes a health hazard. Common pollutants include nitrate, pesticides, and sewage (see ◊sewage disposal), though a huge range of industrial contaminants, such as chemical byproducts and residues created in the manufacture of various goods, also enter water—legally, accidentally, and through illegal dumping.

water polo water sport developed in England 1869, originally called "soccer-in-water". The aim is to score goals, as in soccer, at each end of a swimming pool. It is played by teams of seven on each side (from squads of 13).

water skiing water sport in which a person is towed across water on a ski or skis, wider than those used for

skiing on snow, by means of a rope (75 ft/23 m long) attached to a speedboat. Competitions are held for overall performances, slalom, tricks, and jumping.

water strider any of various insect-eating aquatic ◊bugs of the family Gerridae that use their long legs to skate along the water surface without breaking through.

water table the upper level of ground water (water collected underground in porous rocks). Water that is above the water table will drain downward; a spring forms where the water table cuts the surface of the ground. The water table rises and falls in response to rainfall and the rate at which water is extracted, for example, for irrigation and industry.

Watson James Dewey 1928– . US biologist whose research on the molecular structure of DNA and the genetic code, in collaboration with Francis ◊Crick, earned him a shared Nobel Prize in 1962. Based on earlier works, they were able to show that DNA formed a double helix of two spiral strands held together by base pairs. Watson resigned as head of the US government's ◊human genome project in April 1992.

Watson Tom (Thomas Sturgess) 1949– . US golfer who won the British Open five times (1975, 1977, 1980, 1982, 1983) and by 1990 was ranked third in career earnings in professional golf.

Watson, born in Kansas City, Missouri, joined the professional golfer's tour before his graduation from Stanford University 1971. He won the US Open 1982 and the Masters 1977 and 1981, and led the Professional Golfers Association (PGA) in money earnings 1977–80 and 1984.

watt SI unit (symbol W) of power (the rate of expenditure or consumption of energy). A light bulb, for example, may use 40, 100, or 150 watts of power; an electric heater will use several kilowatts (thousands of watts). The watt is named for the Scottish engineer James Watt.

One watt equals 0.00134 horsepower.

Watt James 1736–1819. Scottish engineer who developed the steam engine. He made Thomas Newcomen's steam engine vastly more efficient by cooling the used steam in a condenser separate from the main cylinder.

wattle certain species of ◊acacia in Australia, where their fluffy golden flowers are the national emblem. The leathery leaves, adapted to drought conditions, further avoid loss of water through transpiration by turning their edges to the direct rays of the sun. Wattles are used for tanning and in fencing.

Waugh Evelyn (Arthur St John) 1903–1966. English novelist. His social satires include *Decline and Fall* 1928, *Vile Bodies* 1930, and *The Loved One* 1948. A Roman Catholic convert from 1930, he developed a serious concern with religious issues in *Brideshead Revisited* 1945. *The Ordeal of Gilbert Pinfold* 1957 is largely autobiographical.

wave in physics, a disturbance traveling through a medium (or space). There are two types: in a *longitudinal wave* (such as a sound wave) the disturbance is parallel to the wave's direction of travel; in a *transverse wave* (such as an ◊electromagnetic wave) it is perpendicular. The medium (for example the Earth, for seismic waves) is not permanently displaced by the passage of a wave.

wave in the oceans, a ridge or swell formed by wind or other causes. The power of a wave is determined by

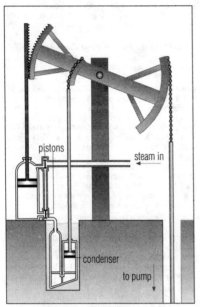

pistons

steam in

condenser

to pump

Watt, James *James Watt's steam engines, dating from 1769, were an improvement on that of Thomas Newcomen in that they had a separate condenser and permitted steam to be admitted alternately on either side of the piston.*

the strength of the wind and the distance of open water over which the wind blows (the fetch). Waves are the main agents of ◊coastal erosion and deposition: sweeping away or building up beaches, creating spits and berms, and wearing down cliffs by their hydraulic action and by the corrasion of the sand and shingle that they carry. A ◊tsunami (misleadingly called a "tidal wave") is formed after a submarine earthquake.

wavelength the distance between successive crests of a ◊wave. The wavelength of a light wave determines its color; red light has a wavelength of about 700 nanometers, for example. The complete range of wavelengths of electromagnetic waves is called the electromagnetic ◊spectrum.

wave power power obtained by harnessing the energy of water waves. Various schemes have been advanced since 1973, when oil prices rose dramatically and an energy shortage threatened. In 1974 the British engineer Stephen Salter developed the duck—a floating boom whose segments nod up and down with the waves. The nodding motion can be used to drive pumps and spin generators. Another device, developed in Japan, uses an oscillating water column to harness wave power.

wax solid fatty substance of animal, vegetable, or mineral origin.
Waxes are composed variously of ◊esters, ◊fatty acids, free ◊alcohols, and solid hydrocarbons.

waxbill any of a group of small mainly African seed-eating birds in the family Estrildidae, order

Passeriformes, which also includes the grass finches of Australia. Waxbills grow to 6 in/15 cm long, are brown and gray with yellow, red, or brown markings, and have waxy-looking red or pink beaks.

waxwing any of several fruit-eating birds of the order Passeriformes, family Bombycillidae. They are found in the northern hemisphere. The Bohemian waxwing *Bombycilla garrulus* of North America and Eurasia is about 7 in/18 cm long, and is grayish brown above with a reddish chestnut crest, black streak at the eye, and variegated wings. It undertakes mass migrations in some years.

wayfaring tree European shrub *Viburnum lantana* of the honeysuckle family, with clusters of fragrant white flowers, found on limy soils; naturalized in the NE US.

Wayne Anthony ("Mad Anthony") 1745–1796. American Revolutionary War officer and Indian fighter. He secured a treaty 1795 that made possible the settlement of Ohio and Indiana. He built Fort Wayne, Indiana.
A surveyor and farmer, he assisted Benedict ◊Arnold in his retreat from Québec, was with George Washington at Valley Forge 1777–78, took Stony Point, New York, and was then trapped by Cornwallis' superior force at Green Spring, Virginia, but escaped and served under General Greene in Georgia before retiring to farming and business interests. President Washington recalled him 1792 as a major general to command the Army of the West against the Indians.

Wayne John ("Duke"). Adopted name of Marion Morrison 1907–1979. US actor. He played the archetypal Western hero: plain-speaking, brave, and solitary. His films include *Stagecoach* 1939, *Red River* 1948, *She Wore a Yellow Ribbon* 1949, *The Searchers* 1956, *Rio Bravo* 1959, *The Man Who Shot Liberty Valance* 1962, and *True Grit* 1969 (Academy Award). He was active in conservative politics.

weakon or *intermediate vector boson* in physics, a ◊gauge boson that carries the weak nuclear force, one of the fundamental forces of nature. There are three types of weakon, the positive and negative W particle and the neutral Z particle.

weasel any of various small, short-legged, lithe carnivorous mammals with bushy tails, especially the genus *Mustela*, found worldwide except Australia. They feed mainly on small rodents although some, like the mink *M. vison*, hunt aquatic prey. Most are 5–10 in/12–25 cm long, excluding tail.

weaver any small bird of the family Ploceidae, order Passeriformes, mostly about 6 in long/15 cm, which includes the house ◊sparrow. The majority of weavers are African, a few Asian. The males use grasses to weave elaborate globular nests in bushes and trees. Males are often more brightly colored than females.

weaving the production of textile fabric by means of a loom. The basic process is the interlacing at right angles of longitudinal threads (the warp) and horizontal threads (the weft), the latter being carried across from one side of the loom to the other by a type of bobbin called a shuttle.

Webb (Martha) Beatrice (born Potter) 1858–1943 and Sidney (James), Baron Passfield 1859–1947. English social reformers, writers, and founders of the London School of Economics (LSE) 1895. They were early members of the socialist ◊Fabian Society, and were married in 1892.

weber SI unit (symbol Wb) of magnetic flux (the magnetic field strength multiplied by the area through which the field passes). It is named for German chemist Wilhelm Weber. One weber equals 10^8 ◊maxwells.

Weber Carl Maria Friedrich Ernst von 1786–1826. German composer. He established the Romantic school of opera with *Der Freischütz/The Marksman* 1821 and *Euryanthe* 1823. He was kapellmeister (chief conductor) at Breslau 1804–06, Prague 1813–16, and Dresden 1816. He died during a visit to London where he produced his opera *Oberon* 1826, written for the Covent Garden Theatre.

Webern Anton (Friedrich Wilhelm von) 1883–1945. Austrian composer. He wrote spare, enigmatic miniatures combining a pastoral poetic with severe structural rigor. A Renaissance musical scholar, he became a pupil of Arnold ◊Schoenberg, whose twelve-tone system he reinterpreted as abstract design in works such as the *Concerto for Nine Instruments* 1931–34 and the *Second Cantata* 1941–43. His constructivist esthetic influenced the postwar generation of advanced composers.

Webster John *c*. 1580–1634. English dramatist. He ranks after Shakespeare as the greatest tragedian of his time, and is the Jacobean whose plays are most frequently performed today. His two great plays *The White Devil* 1612 and *The Duchess of Malfi* 1614 are dark, violent tragedies obsessed with death and decay.

Webster Noah 1758–1843. US lexicographer whose books on grammar and spelling and *American Dictionary of the English Language* 1828 standardized US English.

Webster learned 26 languages and began the scientific study of ◊etymology. Following the American Revolution, he was prompted by patriotic sentiment to create schoolbooks that would impart that sentiment to young students. His *Blue-Backed Speller* sold nearly 100 million copies in a century.

Wedgwood Josiah 1730–1795. English pottery manufacturer. He set up business in Staffordshire in the early 1760s to produce his agateware as well as unglazed blue or green stoneware (jasper) decorated with white Neo-Classical designs, using pigments of his own invention.

Weems Mason Locke 1759–1825. American writer and cleric. His biography *The Life and Memorable Actions of George Washington*, published around 1800, contained the first published version of the "cherry-tree" legend which was responsible for much of the Washington myth. He also wrote lives of Francis Marion 1809 and Benjamin Franklin 1815.

weever fish any of a family (Trachinidae) of marine bony fishes of the perch family, especially the genus *Trachinus*, with poison glands on dorsal fin and gill cover that can give a painful sting. It grows up to 2 in/5 cm long, has eyes near the top of the head, and lives on sandy seabeds.

weevil any of a superfamily (Curculionoidea) of ◊beetles, usually less than 0.25 in/6 mm long, and with a head prolonged into a downward beak, which is used for boring into plant stems and trees for feeding.

weight the force exerted on an object by ◊gravity. The weight of an object depends on its mass—the amount of material in it—and the strength of the Earth's gravitational pull, which decreases with height. Consequently, an object weighs less at the top of a mountain than at sea level. On the Moon, an object has only one-sixth of its weight on Earth, because the pull of the Moon's gravity is one-sixth that of the Earth.

weight lifting the sport of lifting the heaviest possible weight above one's head to the satisfaction of judges. In international competitions there are two standard lifts: *snatch* and *jerk*.

Weill Kurt (Julian) 1900–1950. German composer. He was a US citizen from 1943. He wrote chamber and orchestral music and collaborated with Bertolt ◊Brecht on operas such as *Die Dreigroschenoper/The Threepenny Opera* 1928 and *Aufstieg und Fall der Stadt Mahagonny/The Rise and Fall of the City of Mahagonny* 1930, all attacking social corruption (*Mahagonny* caused a riot at its premiere in Leipzig). In 1935 he left Germany for the US where he wrote a number of successful scores for Broadway, among them the antiwar musical *Johnny Johnson* 1936 (including the often covered "September Song") and *Street Scene* 1947 based on an Elmer Rice play set in the Depression.

Weimar Republic the constitutional republic in Germany 1919–33, which was crippled by the election of antidemocratic parties to the Reichstag (parliament), and then subverted by the Nazi leader Hitler after his appointment as chancellor 1933. It took its name from the city where in Feb 1919 a constituent assembly met to draw up a democratic constitution.

Weizmann Chaim 1874–1952. Zionist leader, the first president of Israel (1948–52), and chemist. Born in Russia, he became a naturalized British subject, and as director of the navy's laboratories 1916–19 discovered a process for manufacturing acetone, a solvent. He conducted the negotiations leading up to the Balfour Declaration, which favored a Jewish state. He became head of the Hebrew University in Jerusalem, then in 1948 became the first president of the new republic of Israel.

Weizsäcker Richard, Baron von 1920– . German Christian Democrat politician, president 1984–94. He began his career as a lawyer and was also active in the German Protestant church and in Christian Democratic Union party politics. He was elected to the West German Bundestag (parliament) 1969 and served as mayor of West Berlin from 1981, before being elected federal president 1984.

Welch Robert H W, Jr 1899–1985. US anticommunist crusader and business executive. He founded the extreme right-wing John Birch Society 1958 in memory of the American Baptist missionary. A supporter of the losing Republican presidential candidate Barry Goldwater 1964, Welch later became increasingly venomous in his accusations against supposed communist agents and sympathizers.

He founded the magazine *American Opinion* 1956.

welding joining pieces of metal (or nonmetal) at faces rendered plastic or liquid by heat or pressure (or both). The principal processes today are gas and arc welding, in which the heat from a gas flame or an electric arc melts the faces to be joined. Additional "filler metal" is usually added to the joint.

welfare state political system under which the state (rather than the individual or the private sector) has responsibility for the welfare of its citizens. Services such as unemployment and sickness benefits, family allowances and income supplements, pensions, medical care, and education may be provided and financed through state insurance schemes and taxation.

Welles (George) Orson 1915–1985. US actor and film and theater director. His first film was *Citizen Kane* 1941, which he produced, directed, and starred in. Using innovative lighting, camera angles and movements, it is a landmark in the history of cinema, yet he subsequently directed very few films in Hollywood. His performances as an actor include the character of Harry Lime in *The Third Man* 1949.

A child prodigy, Welles made his acting debut at 16 in Dublin and toured with Katherine Cornell's company in the US. As his career declined he became a familiar voice and face in US television commercials, and made guest appearances on TV shows.

Wellington capital and industrial port (woollen textiles, chemicals, soap, footwear, bricks) of New Zealand on North Island on the Cook Strait; population (1991) 149,600, urban area 324,800. The harbor was sighted by Capt James Cook 1773.

Wellington Arthur Wellesley, 1st Duke of Wellington 1769–1852. British soldier and Tory politician. As commander in the ◊Peninsular War, he expelled the French from Spain 1814. He defeated Napoleon Bonaparte at Qatre-Bras and Waterloo 1815, and was a member of the Congress of Vienna. As prime minister 1828–30, he was forced to concede Roman Catholic emancipation.

Wells H(erbert) G(eorge) 1866–1946. English writer. He is best remembered for his "scientific romances" such as *The Time Machine* 1895 and *The War of the Worlds* 1898. His later novels had an antiestablishment, anticonventional humor remarkable in its day, for example *Kipps* 1905 and *Tono-Bungay* 1909. His many other books include *Outline of History* 1920 and *The Shape of Things to Come* 1933, a number of his prophecies from which have since been fulfilled. He also wrote many short stories.

Welles, US actor and director Orson Welles had an enormous influence on American and European film makers.

Welsh people of ◊Wales; see also ◊Celts. The term is thought to be derived from an old Germanic term for "foreigner", and so linked to Walloon (Belgium) and Wallachian (Romania). It may also derive from the Latin *Volcae*, the name of a Celtic people of France.

Welsh corgi breed of dog with a foxlike head and pricked ears, originally bred for cattle herding. The coat is dense, with several varieties of coloring. Corgis are about 12 in/30 cm at the shoulder, and weigh up to 27 lb/12 kg.

Welsh language in Welsh *Cymraeg* member of the Celtic branch of the Indo-European language family, spoken chiefly in the rural north and west of Wales; it is the strongest of the surviving Celtic languages, and in 1991 was spoken by 18.7% of the Welsh population.

Welty Eudora 1909– . US novelist and short-story writer. Her works reflect life in the American South and are notable for their creation of character and accurate rendition of local dialect. Her novels include *Delta Wedding* 1946, *Losing Battles* 1970, and *The Optimist's Daughter* 1972.

The Collected Stories of Eudora Welty appeared in 1980. The autobiographical work *One Writer's Beginnings* 1984 is a warm recounting of the people, places, and incidents that influenced Welty's work.

Wenceslas, St 907–929. Duke of Bohemia who attempted to Christianize his people and was murdered by his brother. He is patron saint of the Czech Republic and the "good King Wenceslas" of a popular carol. Feast day Sept 28.

Wesley John 1703–1791. English founder of ◊Methodism. When the pulpits of the Church of England were closed to him and his followers, he took the gospel to the people. For 50 years he rode about the country on horseback, preaching daily, largely in the open air. His sermons became the doctrinal standard of the Wesleyan Methodist Church.

West Benjamin 1738–1820. American Neo-Classical painter born in Pennsylvania. He was active in London from 1763. He enjoyed the patronage of George III for many years and was a noted history painter. His *The Death of General Wolfe* 1770 (National Gallery, Ottawa) began a vogue for painting recent historical events in contemporary costume.

West Bank area (2,270 sq mi/5,879 sq km) on the west bank of the river Jordan; population (1988) 866,000. The West Bank was taken by the Jordanian army 1948 at the end of the Arab–Israeli war that followed the creation of the state of Israel, and was captured by Israel during the Six-Day War June 5–10 1967. The continuing Israeli occupation and settlement of the area created tensions with the Arab population and after 1987, as the Intifada (uprising) gained strength in the occupied territories, Israeli-military presence increased signficantly. In 1993 an Israeli-PLO preliminary accord was signed, promising partial autonomy for Palestinians and phased withdrawal of Israeli troops from occupied territories.

West Bengal state of NE India *area* 33,929 sq mi/87,900 sq km *capital* Calcutta *towns and cities* Asansol, Durgarpur *physical* occupies the west part of the vast alluvial plain created by the rivers Ganges and Brahmaputra, with the Hooghly River; annual rainfall in excess of 100 in/250 cm *industries* rice, jute, tea, coal, iron, steel, automobiles, locomotives, aluminum, fertilizers *population* (1991) 67,982,700

West, American: chronology

1250	An unidentified epidemic weakened the American Indian civilization.
1550	Horses were introduced by the Spanish. Francisco Coronado made his expedition into the southwest.
1804	Meriwether Lewis and William Clark explored the Louisiana Purchase lands for President Jefferson.
1805	Zebulon Pike explorations.
1819	Major Stephen Long, a US government topographical engineer, explored the Great Plains.
1822	The Santa Fe Trail was established.
1824	The Great Salt Lake was discovered by Jim Bridger, "mountain man", trapper, and guide.
1836	Davy Crockett and other Texans were defeated by Mexicans at the Battle of the Alamo.
1840–60	The Oregon Trail was in use.
1846	The Mormon trek was made to Utah under Brigham Young.
1846–48	The Mexican War.
1849–56	The California gold rush.
1860	The Pony Express (St Joseph, Missouri–San Francisco, California) was in operation April 3–Oct 22; it was superseded by the telegraph.
1863	On Jan 1 the first homestead was filed; this was followed by the settlement of the Western Prairies and Great Plains.
1865–90	Wars were fought against the Indians, accompanied by the rapid extermination of the buffalo, upon which much of Great Plains and Indian life depended.
1867–80s	Period of the "cattle kingdom", and cow trails such as the Chisholm Trail from Texas to the railheads at Abilene, Wichita, and Dodge City.
1869	The first transcontinental railroad was completed.
1876	The Battle of Little Bighorn.
1890	The Battle of Wounded Knee; official census declaration that the West no longer had a frontier line.

Western genre of popular fiction and film based on the landscape and settlement of the American West, with emphasis on the conquest of Indian territory. It developed in American dime novels and frontier literature. The Western became established in written form with such novels as Owen Wister's *The Virginian* 1902 and Zane Grey's *Riders of the Purple Sage* 1912. From the earliest silent films, movies extended the Western mythology and, with Italian "spaghetti" Westerns and Japanese Westerns, established it as an international form.

Western Australia state of Australia *area* 974,843 sq mi/2,525,500 sq km *capital* Perth *towns and cities* main port Fremantle, Bunbury, Geraldton, Kalgoorlie-Boulder, Albany *features* largest state in Australia; Monte Bello Islands; rivers Fitzroy, Fortescue, Gascoyne, Murchison, Swan; NW coast subject to hurricanes (willy-willies); Lasseter's Reef *industries* wheat, fresh and dried fruit, meat and dairy products, natural gas (northwest shelf) and oil (Canning Basin), iron (the Pilbara), copper, nickel, uranium, gold, diamonds *population* (1987) 1,478,000 *history* a short-lived convict settlement at King George Sound 1826; first non-convict settlement founded at Perth 1829 by Capt James Stirling (1791–1865); self-government 1890; became a state 1901.

Western Isles island area of Scotland, comprising the Outer Hebrides (Lewis, Harris, North and South Uist, and Barra) *area* 1,120 sq mi/2,900 sq km *towns and cities* Stornoway on Lewis (administrative headquarters) *features* divided from the mainland by the Minch channel; Callanish monolithic circles of the Stone Age on Lewis *industries* Harris tweed, sheep, fish, cattle *population* (1991) 29,100 *famous people* Flora MacDonald.

Western Sahara formerly *Spanish Sahara* disputed territory in NW Africa bounded to the N by Morocco, to the E and S by Mauritania, and to the W by the Atlantic Ocean *area* 103,011 sq mi/266,800 sq km *capital* Laâyoune (Arabic *El Aaiún*) *towns and cities* Dhakla *features* electrically monitored fortified wall enclosing the phosphate area *exports* phosphates *currency* dirham *population* (1988) 181,400; another estimated 165,000 live in refugee camps near Tindouf, SW Algeria. Ethnic composition: Sawrawis (traditionally nomadic herders) *language* Arabic *religion* Sunni Muslim *government* administered by Morocco

West Germany see ◊Germany, West.

West Indian inhabitant of or native to the West Indies, or person of West Indian descent. The West Indies are culturally heterogeneous; in addition to the indigenous Carib and Arawak Indians, there are peoples of African, European, and Asian descent, as well as peoples of mixed descent.

West Indies archipelago of about 1,200 islands, dividing the Atlantic Ocean from the Gulf of Mexico and the Caribbean Sea. The islands are divided into: *Bahamas*; *Greater Antilles* Cuba, Hispaniola (Haiti, Dominican Republic), Jamaica, and Puerto Rico; *Lesser Antilles* Aruba, Netherlands Antilles, Trinidad and Tobago, the Windward Islands (Grenada, Barbados, St Vincent, St Lucia, Martinique, Dominica, Guadeloupe), the Leeward Islands (Montserrat, Antigua, St Christopher (St Kitts)–Nevis, Barbuda, Anguilla, St Martin, British and US Virgin Islands), and many smaller islands.

Westinghouse George 1846–1914. US inventor and manufacturer. The most profitable of his designs was an air brake for railroad automobiles, perfected 1869. Westinghouse later devised a system of railroad signals and an efficient means of distributing natural gas. His greatest success came with the establishment of the Westinghouse Electric Co. 1886, through which he adapted alternating current for domestic and industrial use.

Weston Edward 1886–1958. US photographer. A founding member of the "f/64" group (after the smallest lens opening), a school of photography advocating sharp definition. He is noted for the technical mastery, composition, and clarity in his California landscapes, clouds, gourds, cacti, and nude studies.

Westphalia, Treaty of agreement 1648 ending the ◊Thirty Years' War. The peace marked the end of the supremacy of the Holy Roman Empire and the emergence of France as a dominant power. It recognized the sovereignty of the German states, Switzerland, and the Netherlands; Lutherans, Calvinists, and Roman Catholics were given equal rights.

West Sussex county on the south coast of England *area* 780 sq mi/2,020 sq km *towns and cities* Chichester (administrative headquarters), Crawley, Horsham, Haywards Heath, Shoreham (port); resorts: Worthing, Littlehampton, Bognor Regis *physical* the Weald, South Downs; rivers: Arun, West Rother, Adur *population* (1991) 692,800.

West Virginia state in E central; nickname Mountain State *area* 24,279 sq mi/62,900 sq km *capital* Charleston *towns and cities* Huntington, Wheeling *physical* Allegheny Mountains; Ohio River *features* port of Harper's Ferry, restored as when John Brown seized the US armory 1859 *industries* apples, corn, poultry, dairy and meat products, coal, natural gas, oil, chemicals, synthetic fibers, plastics, steel, glass, pottery *population* (1990) 1,793,500 *famous people* Pearl S Buck, Thomas "Stonewall" Jackson, Walter Reuther, Cyrus Vance

West Virginia State Board of Education v Barnette one of the "flag salute" Supreme Court cases 1943 dealing with mandatory recitation of the pledge of allegiance in public school. Barnette issued a legal challenge to a West Virginia statute requiring all public-school children to salute the flag. A Jehovah's Witness, he argued that his child's First-Amendment freedom of religion was being denied, since reciting the pledge was against his religious principles. The Court invalidated the law because it violated First-Amendment rights to freedom of religion, speech, and thought.

wetland permanently wet land area or habitat. Wetlands include areas of marsh, fen, bog, flood plain, and shallow coastal areas. Wetlands are extremely fertile. They provide warm, sheltered waters for fisheries, lush vegetation for grazing livestock, and an abundance of wildlife. Estuaries and seaweed beds are more than 16 times as productive as the open ocean.

Wexford county of the Republic of Ireland, in the province of Leinster; county town Wexford; 907 sq mi/2,350 sq km; population (1991) 102,000. The port of Rosslare has ferry links to England. Industries include fish, livestock, oats, barley, potatoes, cattle, agricultural machinery, and food processing. It was the first Irish county to be colonized from England 1169.

whale any marine mammal of the order Cetacea, with front limbs modified into flippers and with internal vestiges of hind limbs. The order is divided into the toothed whales (Odontoceti) and the baleen whales (Mysticeti). The toothed whales include ◊dolphins and ◊porpoises, along with large forms such as sperm whales. The baleen whales, with plates of modified mucous membrane called baleen in the mouth, are all large in size and include finback and right whales. There were hundreds of thousands of whales at the beginning of the 20th century, but they have been hunted close to extinction.

whaling the hunting of whales, largely discontinued 1986. Whales are killed for whale oil (made from the thick layer of fat under the skin called "blubber"), used for food and cosmetics; for the large reserve of oil in the head of the sperm whale, used in the leather industry; and for *ambergris*, a waxlike substance from the intestines, used in making perfumes. There are synthetic substitutes for all these products. Whales are also killed for their meat, which is eaten by the Japanese and was used as pet food in the US and Europe.

wheat cereal plant derived from the wild *Triticum*, a grass native to the Middle East. It is the chief cereal used in breadmaking and is widely cultivated in temperate climates suited to its growth. Wheat is killed by frost, and damp renders the grain soft, so warm, dry regions produce the most valuable grain.

wheatear small (6 in/15 cm long) migratory bird *Oenanthe oenanthe* of the family Muscicapidae, in the order Passeriformes. The family also includes the thrushes. Wheatears are found throughout the Old World and also breed in far northern parts of North America. The plumage is light gray above and white below, with a white patch on the back, a black face-patch, and black and white wings and tail.

whelk any of various families of large marine snails with a thick spiral shell, especially the family Buccinidae. Whelks are scavengers, and also eat other shellfish. The largest grow to 16 in/40 cm long. Tropical species, such as the conches, can be very colorful.

The common northern whelk *Buccinum undatum* is widely distributed around the North Sea and the Atlantic.

Whig Party in the UK, predecessor of the Liberal Party. The name was first used of rebel ◊Covenanters and then of those who wished to exclude James II from the English succession (as a Roman Catholic). They were in power continuously 1714–60 and pressed for industrial and commercial development, a vigorous foreign policy, and religious toleration. During the French Revolution, the Whigs demanded parliamentary reform in Britain, and from the passing of the Reform Bill in 1832 became known as Liberals.

whippet breed of dog resembling a small greyhound. It grows to 22 in/56 cm at the shoulder, and 20 lb/9 kg in weight.

The whippet was developed in England for racing. It was probably produced by crossing a terrier and a greyhound.

whip snake or *coachwhip* any of the various species of nonpoisonous slender-bodied tree-dwelling snakes of the New World genus *Masticophis*, family Colubridae. They are closely allied to members of the genus *Coluber* of SW North America, Eurasia, Australasia, and N Africa, some of which are called whip snakes in the Old World, but racers in North America.

whiskey or whisky a strong alcoholic beverage made from a fermented mash of various cereals: Scotch whisky from malted barley; Irish whiskey usually from barley, and North American whiskey and bourbon from rye and corn. Scotch and other whiskeys are usually blended; pure malt whiskeys are more expensive. Whiskey is generally aged in wooden casks for 4–12 years.

whist card game for four, predecessor of ◊bridge, in which the partners try to win a majority of the 13 tricks (the highest card played being the winner of the trick).

Whistler James Abbott McNeill 1834–1903. US painter and etcher. He was active in London from 1859. Influenced by Japanese prints, he painted riverscapes and portraits that show subtle composition and color harmonies: for example, *Arrangement in Grey and*

Black: Portrait of the Painter's Mother 1871 (Louvre, Paris).

Whistler was born in Lowell, Massachusetts. He originally attended West Point, left after failing a course, and worked as a draftsman. In 1855 he went to Paris where he was associated with the Impressionists.

White Byron Raymond 1917– . US jurist. He worked to elect John F Kennedy to the presidency 1960 and was appointed by him as associate justice of the Supreme Court, serving 1962–93. He was a moderate conservative, usually dissenting on the rights of criminals, but upholding the right of accused citizens to trial by jury.

He also played professional football, with the Pittsburgh Pirates (now Steelers) 1938 and for the Detroit Lions 1940–41. He was elected to the Football Hall of Fame 1954.

White E(lwyn) B(rooks) 1899–1985. US writer. He was long associated with the *New Yorker* magazine and renowned for his satire, such as *Is Sex Necessary?* 1929 (with the humorist James Thurber).

With William Strunk, Jr, he published *The Elements of Style* 1935, considered a definitive style manual for the English language. White also wrote children's classics: *Stuart Little* 1945, *Charlotte's Web* 1952, and *The Trumpet of the Swan* 1970.

whitebait any of the fry (young) of various silvery fishes, especially ◊herring. It is also the name for a Pacific smelt *Osmerus mordax*.

whitebeam tree *Sorbus aria*, native to S Europe, usually found growing on chalk or limestone. It can reach 60 ft/20 m. It takes its name from the pinnately compound leaves, which have a dense coat of short white hairs on the underside.

It is a type of ◊mountain ash.

white blood cell or *leukocyte* one of a number of different cells that play a part in the body's defenses and give immunity against disease. Some (phagocytes and macrophages) engulf invading microorganisms, others kill infected cells, while lymphocytes produce more specific immune responses. White blood cells are colorless, with clear or granulated cytoplasm, and are capable of independent ameboid movement. They occur in the blood, ◊lymph and elsewhere in the body's tissues.

white dwarf small, hot ◊star, the last stage in the life of a star such as the Sun. White dwarfs have a mass similar to that of the Sun, but only 1% of the Sun's diameter, similar in size to the Earth. Most have surface temperatures of 14,400°F/8,000°C or more, hotter than the Sun. Yet, being so small, their overall luminosities may be less than 1% of that of the Sun. The Milky Way contains an estimated 50 billion white dwarfs.

Whitefield George 1714–1770. British Methodist evangelist. He was a student at Oxford University and took orders in 1738, but was suspended for his unorthodox doctrines and methods. For many years he traveled through Britain and America, and by his preaching contributed greatly to the Great Awakening. He died while visiting New England.

whitefish any of various freshwater fishes, genera *Coregonus* and *Prosopium* of the salmon family, found in lakes and rivers of North America and Eurasia. They include the whitefish *C. clupeaformis* and cisco *C. artedi*.

White House official residence of the president of the US, in Washington, DC. It is a plain edifice of sandstone, built in Italian Renaissance style 1792–99 to the designs of James Hoban, who also restored it after it was burned by the British 1814; it was then painted white to hide the scars.

The structure was completely restored by the Truman administration; the interior was redecorated 1960–63 by First Lady Jacqueline Kennedy. The offices of the president's staff in the White House and nearby buildings are often collectively referred to as "The White House." The president's study and ceremonial office is known from its shape as the Oval Office. The building includes living quarters for the president, the presidential family, and staff and public rooms for dinners, concerts, and receptions. The presidential apartment is separate from the rest of the mansion, which is open to visitors and public tours as a museum. The name White House, first recorded in 1811, is often adapted to refer to other residences of the president; for example, Little White House, at Warm Springs, Georgia, where Franklin D Roosevelt died; Western White House, at San Clemente, California, where Nixon had a home.

whitethroat any of several Old World warblers of the genus *Sylvia*, found in scrub, hedges, and wood clearings of Eurasia in summer, migrating to Africa in winter. They are about 5.5 in/14 cm long.

whiting any of various edible marine bony fishes, especially the silver hake and various kingfishes, genus *Menticirrhus*.

Whitman Walt(er) 1819–1892. US poet. He published ◊*Leaves of Grass* 1855, which contains the symbolic ◊"Song of Myself". It used unconventional free verse

Whitman, Walt *US poet Walt Whitman, whose breaking away from conventional form made him one of the most influential writers of his generation. The main themes in his poetry include the sacredness of the self, the beauty of death, the equality of all people, brotherly love, and the immortality of the soul.*

(with no rhyme or regular rhythm) and scandalized the public by its frank celebration of sexuality.

Whitney Eli 1765–1825. US inventor who in 1794 patented the cotton gin, a device for separating cotton fiber from its seeds. Also a manufacturer of firearms, he created a standardization system that was the precursor of the assembly line.

Born in Westborough, Massachusetts, Whitney graduated from Yale 1792. His invention of the cotton gin revolutionized the cotton industry in the South. In a shop in New Haven, Connecticut, he manufactured muskets under a contract from the US government, using power-driven tools to produce interchangeable parts.

Whit Sunday Christian church festival held seven weeks after Easter, commemorating the descent of the Holy Spirit on the Apostles. The name is probably derived from the white garments worn by candidates for baptism at the festival. Whit Sunday corresponds to the Jewish festival of Shavuot (Pentecost).

Whittier John Greenleaf 1807–1892. US poet. He was a powerful opponent of slavery, as shown in the verse *Voices of Freedom* 1846. Among his other works are *Legends of New England in Prose and Verse, Songs of Labor* 1850, and the New England nature poem "Snow-Bound" 1866.

He was also a journalist and humanitarian. Many of his poems have been set to music, and are sung as church hymns.

Whittle Frank 1907– . British engineer who patented the basic design for the turbojet engine 1930. In the Royal Air Force he worked on jet propulsion 1937–46. In May 1941 the Gloster E 28/39 aircraft first flew with the Whittle jet engine. Both the German (first operational jet planes) and the US jet aircraft were built using his principles.

WHO acronym for ◊*World Health Organization*.

whooping cough or *pertussis* acute infectious disease, seen mainly in children, caused by colonization of the air passages by the bacterium *Bordetella pertussis*. There may be catarrh, mild fever, and loss of appetite, but the main symptom is violent coughing, associated with the sharp intake of breath that is the characteristic "whoop", and often followed by vomiting and severe nose bleeds. The cough may persist for weeks.

whydah any of various African birds of the genus *Vidua*, order Passeriformes, of the weaver family. They lay their eggs in the nests of waxbills, which rear the young. Young birds resemble young waxbills, but the adults do not resemble adult waxbills. Males have long tail feathers used in courtship displays.

WI abbreviation for ◊*West Indies*, an archipelago of islands between the Gulf of Mexico and the Caribbean Sea, and the Atlantic Ocean.

Wichita industrial city (oil refining, aircraft, motor vehicles) in S Kansas; population (1990) 304,000. Wichita was founded about 1867.

It became a stopover on the Chisholm cattle-driving trail; when the railroad arrived 1872, the city became a major cattle-shipping point. Petroleum was discovered nearby 1915, and aircraft manufacture began 1920. Wichita State University is here.

Wicklow county of the Republic of Ireland, in the province of Leinster; county town Wicklow; area 784 sq mi/2,030 sq km; population (1991) 97,300. It has the Wicklow Mountains, the rivers Slane and Liffey, and the coastal resort Bray. The village of Shillelagh

gave its name to rough cudgels of oak or blackthorn made there. The main occupation is agriculture.

wide area network in computing, a ◊network that connects computers distributed over a wide geographical area.

Wiener Norbert 1894–1964. US mathematician, credited with the establishment of the science of cybernetics in his book *Cybernetics* 1948. In mathematics, he laid the foundation of the study of stochastic processes (those dependent on random events).

Wiesel Elie 1928– . US academic and human-rights campaigner, born in Romania. He was held in Buchenwald concentration camp during World War II, and has assiduously documented wartime atrocities against the Jews in an effort to alert the world to the

whydah During the breeding season the male paradise whydah has elongated black tail feathers 11 in/28 cm long. The paradise whydah lives in dry bush country in central Africa.

dangers of racism and violence. Nobel Peace Prize 1986.

Wiesel sought to remind new generations of the Nazi atrocities so that they might never be repeated. He is considered the most eloquent spokesman of the death-camp survivors.

wigeon either of two species of dabbling duck of genus *Anas*.

The American wigeon *A. americana*, about 19 in/ 48 cm long, is found along both coasts in winter and breeds inland. Males have a white-capped head and a green eye stripe.

The Eurasian wigeon *A. penelope* has a dark head without eye stripe. It is a regular winter visitor along both North American coasts.

Wight, Isle of island and county of S England *area* 147 sq mi/380 sq km *towns and cities* Newport (administrative headquarters); resorts: Ryde, Sandown, Shanklin, Ventnor *features* the *Needles*, a group of pointed chalk rocks up to 100 ft/30 m high in the sea to the W; the *Solent*, the sea channel between Hampshire and the island (including the anchorage of *Spithead* opposite Portsmouth, used for naval reviews); *Cowes*, venue of Regatta Week and headquarters of the Royal Yacht Squadron; Osborne House, near Cowes, a home of Queen Victoria, for whom it was built 1845; Farringford, home of the poet Alfred Tennyson, near Freshwater *industries* chiefly agricultural; shipbuilding; tourism *population* (1991) 124,600 *famous people* Robert Hooke, Thomas Arnold.

Wilberforce William 1759–1833. English reformer who was instrumental in abolishing slavery in the British Empire. He entered Parliament 1780; in 1807 his bill for the abolition of the slave trade was passed, and in 1833, largely through his efforts, slavery was abolished throughout the empire.

Wilde Cornel(ius Louis) 1915–1989. Austrian-born US actor and film director. He worked in the US from 1932. He starred as the composer and pianist Chopin in *A Song to Remember* 1945, and directed *The Naked Prey* 1966, *Beach Red* 1967, and *No Blade of Grass* 1970.

Wilde Oscar (Fingal O'Flahertie Wills) 1854–1900. Irish writer. With his flamboyant style and quotable conversation, he dazzled London society and, on his lecture tour 1882, the US. He published his only novel, *The Picture of Dorian Gray*, 1891, followed by a series of sharp comedies, including *A Woman of No Importance* 1893 and *The Importance of Being Earnest* 1895. In 1895 he was imprisoned for two years for homosexual offenses; he died in exile in France.

wildebeest another name for ◊gnu.

Wilder Billy 1906– . Austrian-born accomplished US screenwriter and film director. He worked in the US from 1934. He directed and coscripted the cynical *Double Indemnity* 1944, *The Lost Weekend* (Academy Award for best director) 1945, *Sunset Boulevard* 1950, *Some Like It Hot* 1959, and *The Apartment* (Academy Award) 1960.

Wilder Thornton (Niven) 1897–1975. US dramatist and novelist. He won Pulitzer prizes for the novel *The Bridge of San Luis Rey* 1927, and for the plays *Our Town* 1938 and *The Skin of Our Teeth* 1942. His farce *The Matchmaker* 1954 was filmed 1958. In 1964 it was adapted into the hit stage musical *Hello, Dolly!*, also made into a film.

wilderness area of uninhabited land which has never been disturbed by humans, which is usually located

some distance from towns and cities. According to estimates by US group Conservation International, 52% (90 million sq km) of the Earth's total land area was still undisturbed 1994.

In the US wilderness areas are specially designated by Congress and protected by federal agencies; some are "forever wild".

Wilkins Maurice Hugh Frederick 1916– . New Zealand-born British scientist. In 1962 he shared the Nobel Prize for Medicine with Francis ◊Crick and James ◊Watson for his work on the molecular structure of nucleic acids, particularly ◊DNA, using X-ray diffraction.

William (I) the Conqueror *c.* 1027–1087. King of England from 1066. He was the illegitimate son of Duke Robert the Devil and succeeded his father as duke of Normandy 1035. Claiming that his relative King Edward the Confessor had bequeathed him the English throne, William invaded the country 1066, defeating ◊Harold II at Hastings, Sussex, and was crowned king of England.

William (II) Rufus ("the Red") *c.* 1056–1100. King of England from 1087, the third son of William the Conqueror. He spent most of his reign attempting to capture Normandy from his brother ◊Robert II, duke of Normandy. His extortion of money led his barons to revolt and caused confrontation with Bishop Anselm. He was killed while hunting in the New Forest, Hampshire, and was succeeded by his brother Henry I.

William (III) of Orange 1650–1702. King of Great Britain and Ireland from 1688, the son of William II of Orange and Mary, daughter of Charles I. He was offered the English crown by the parliamentary opposition to James II. He invaded England 1688 and in 1689 became joint sovereign with his wife, ◊Mary II. He spent much of his reign campaigning, first in Ireland, where he defeated James II at the battle of the Boyne 1690, and later against the French in Flanders. He was succeeded by Mary's sister, Anne.

William IV 1765–1837. King of Great Britain and Ireland from 1830, when he succeeded his brother George IV; third son of George III. He was created duke of Clarence 1789, and married Adelaide of Saxe-Meiningen (1792–1849) 1818. During the Reform Bill crisis he secured its passage by agreeing to create new peers to overcome the hostile majority in the House of Lords. He was succeeded by Victoria.

William I 1797–1888. King of Prussia from 1861 and emperor of Germany from 1871; the son of Friedrich Wilhelm III. He served in the Napoleonic Wars 1814–15 and helped to crush the 1848 revolution. After he succeeded his brother Friedrich Wilhelm IV to the throne of Prussia, his policy was largely dictated by his chancellor ◊Bismarck, who secured his proclamation as emperor.

William II 1859–1941. Emperor of Germany from 1888, the son of Frederick III and Victoria, daughter of Queen Victoria of Britain. In 1890 he forced Chancellor Bismarck to resign and began to direct foreign policy himself, which proved disastrous. He encouraged warlike policies and built up the German navy. In 1914 he first approved Austria's ultimatum to Serbia and then, when he realized war was inevitable, tried in vain to prevent it. In 1918 he fled to Holland, after Germany's defeat and his abdication.

William the Lion 1143–1214. King of Scotland from 1165. He was captured by Henry II while invading

England 1174, and forced to do homage, but Richard I abandoned the English claim to suzerainty for a money payment 1189. In 1209 William was forced by King John to renounce his claim to Northumberland.

William the Silent 1533–1584. Prince of Orange from 1544. Leading a revolt against Spanish rule in the Netherlands from 1573, he briefly succeeded in uniting the Catholic south and Protestant northern provinces, but the former provinces submitted to Spain while the latter formed a federation 1579 (Union of Utrecht) which repudiated Spanish suzerainty 1581.

Williams Tennessee (Thomas Lanier) 1911–1983. US dramatist. His work is characterized by fluent dialogue and searching analysis of the psychological deficiencies of his characters. His plays, usually set in the Deep South against a background of decadence and degradation, include *The Glass Menagerie* 1945, *A Streetcar Named Desire* 1947, and *Cat on a Hot Tin Roof* 1955, the last two of which earned Pulitzer Prizes.

His other plays include *Suddenly Last Summer* 1958 and *Sweet Bird of Youth* 1959. After writing *The Night of the Iguana* 1961, also awarded the Pulitzer Prize, he entered a period of ill health, and none of his subsequent plays succeeded. However, his earlier work earned him a reputation as one of America's preeminent dramatists.

Williams Roger c. 1603–1683. American colonist, founder of the Rhode Island colony 1636, based on democracy and complete religious freedom. He tried to maintain good relations with the Indians of the region, although he fought against them in the Pequot War and King Philip's War.

He came to America as a Puritan minister in Massachusetts 1631 but was banished from the colony 1635 for his "dangerous opinions"; he deplored theocracy and advocated separation of church and state. He then founded Providence 1636, disavowed Puritanism 1639, and returned to England to secure a patent with full religious freedom for his colony in the face of threats from the Puritans. He subsequently returned to Rhode Island and was the colony's president 1654–57; there he founded the first Baptist Church in America.

Williams Ted (Theodore Samuel) 1918– . US baseball player. Establishing a lifetime batting average of .344, he was six times the American League batting champion and twice won the most valuable player award. In 1947 he became the second player ever to twice win the Triple Crown (leading the league in batting, home runs, and runs batted in for a season).

Williams retired as a player 1960 and served as manager of the Washington Senators 1969–71 and the Texas Rangers 1972. He was elected to the Baseball Hall of Fame 1966.

willow any tree or shrub of the genus *Salix*, family Salicaceae. There are over 350 species, mostly in the northern hemisphere, and they flourish in damp places. The leaves are often lance-shaped, and the male and female catkins are found on separate trees.

North American species include black willow *S. nigra* and Pacific willow *S. lasiandra*. The weeping willow *S. babylonica* is a native of China, cultivated worldwide.

willowherb plant of the genus *Epilobium*, a perennial weed. Fireweed *E. angustifolium* is common in woods and waste places, especially after forest fires in areas

bordering the Arctic. It grows to 4 ft/1.2 m with long terminal racemes of red or purplish flowers.

Wilson Edmund 1895–1972. US critic and writer. Perhaps the foremost American social and literary critic of the 20th century, he was an editor of *Vanity Fair* 1920–21, the *New Republic* 1926–31, and *The New Yorker* 1944–48. Among his most influential works are *Axel's Castle* 1931, a survey of symbolism, and *The Wound and the Bow* 1941, a study of the relationship of neurosis to creativity.

Wilson (James) Harold, Baron Wilson of Rievaulx 1916–95. British Labour politician, party leader from 1963, prime minister 1964–70 and 1974–76. His premiership was dominated by the issue of UK admission to membership in the European Community (now the European Union), the social contract (unofficial agreement with the labor unions), and economic difficulties.

Wilson (Thomas) Woodrow 1856–1924. 28th president of the US 1913–21, a Democrat. He kept the US out of World War I until 1917, and in Jan 1918 issued his "Fourteen Points" as a basis for a just peace settlement.

At the peace conference in Paris he secured the inclusion of the ◊League of Nations in individual peace treaties, but these were not ratified by Congress, so the US did not join the League. Nobel Peace Prize 1919.

Wilson, born in Staunton, Virginia, was educated at Princeton University, of which he became president 1902–10. In 1910 he became governor of New Jersey. Elected US president 1912, he initiated antitrust legislation and secured valuable economic and social reforms in his progressive "New Freedom" program. Wilson also instituted a federal income tax, the first since the Civil War.

Wilson, Woodrow *US president Woodrow Wilson, who took the US into World War I. He created the basis for a peace settlement and the League of Nations. An idealist, Wilson could not overturn the traditional isolationism of the US, and he failed to obtain the Senate's acceptance of the treaty that set up the League of Nations.*

Wiltshire county of SW England *area* 1,343 sq mi/ 3,480 sq km *towns and cities* Trowbridge (administrative headquarters), Salisbury, Swindon, Wilton *features* Marlborough Downs; Savernake Forest; rivers: Kennet, Wylye, Salisbury and Bristol Avons; Salisbury Plain, a military training area used since Napoleonic times; Longleat House (Marquess of Bath); Wilton House (Earl of Pembroke); Stourhead, with 18th-century gardens; Neolithic Stonehenge, Avebury stone circle, Silbury Hill, West Kennet Long Barrow, finest example of a long barrow in Wiltshire, dating from the 3rd millennium BC. *industries* wheat, cattle, pig and sheep farming, rubber, engineering, clothing, brewing *population* (1991) 564,500 *famous people* Christopher Wren, William Talbot, Isaac Pitman.

WIMP (acronym for *windows, icons, menus, pointing device*) in computing, another name for graphical user interface (GUI).

Winchester drive in computing, a small hard-disk drive commonly used with microcomputers; *Winchester disk* has become synonymous with ◊hard disk.

wind the lateral movement of the Earth's atmosphere from high-pressure areas (anticyclones) to low-pressure areas (depression). Its speed is measured using an anemometer or by studying its effects on, for example, trees by using the ◊Beaufort Scale. Although modified by features such as land and water, there is a basic worldwide system of trade winds, westerlies, and polar easterlies.

Windhoek capital of Namibia; population (1988) 115,000. It is just N of the Tropic of Capricorn, 180 mi/290 km from the W coast.

window in computing, a rectangular area on the screen of a graphical user interface. A window is used to display data and can be manipulated in various ways by the computer user.

Windows graphical user interface (GUI) from Microsoft that has become the standard for IBM PCs and clones using the ◊MS-DOS operating system.

wind turbine windmill of advanced aerodynamic design connected to an electricity generator and used in wind-power installations. Wind turbines can be either large propeller-type rotors mounted on a tall tower, or flexible metal strips fixed to a vertical axle at top and bottom. In 1990, over 20,000 wind turbines were in use throughout the world, generating 1,600 megawatts of power.

wing in biology, the modified forelimb of birds and bats, or the membranous outgrowths of the exoskeleton of insects, which give the power of flight. Birds and bats have two wings. Bird wings have feathers attached to the fused digits ("fingers") and forearm bones, while bat wings consist of skin stretched between the digits. Most insects have four wings, which are strengthened by wing veins.

Winnipeg capital and industrial city (processed foods, textiles, transportation, and transportation equipment) in Manitoba, Canada, on the Red River, S of Lake Winnipeg; population (1986) 623,000. Established as Winnipeg 1870 on the site of earlier forts, the city expanded with the arrival of the Canadian Pacific Railroad 1881.

The city annexed several adjacent communities 1972 to become the largest Canadian city W of Toronto. The University of Manitoba and University of Winnipeg are here.

wintergreen any of several plants of the genus *Gaultheria* of the heath family Ericaceae, especially *G. procumbens* of NE North America, creeping underground and sending up tiny shoots. Oil of wintergreen, used in treating rheumatism, is extracted from its leaves. Wintergreen is also the name for various plants of the family Pyrolaceae, including the genus *Pyrola* and the green pipsissewa *Chimaphila maculata* of N North America and Eurasia.

Wisconsin state in N central US; nickname Badger State *area* 56,163 sq mi/145,500 sq km *capital* Madison *cities* Milwaukee, Green Bay, Racine *features* lakes: Superior, Michigan; Mississippi River; Door peninsula *industries* leading US dairy state; corn, hay, industrial and agricultural machinery, engines and turbines, precision instruments, paper products, automobiles and trucks, plumbing equipment *population* (1990) 4,891,800 *famous people* Edna Ferber, Harry Houdini, Joseph McCarthy, Spencer Tracy, Orson Welles, Thornton Wilder, Frank Lloyd Wright *history* explored by Jean Nicolet for France 1634; originally settled near Ashland by the French; passed to Britain 1763; included in US 1783. Wisconsin became a territory 1836 and a state 1848.

Wise Stephen Samuel 1874–1949. Hungarian-born US religious leader. Ordained as a reform rabbi 1893, he served congregations in New York City 1893–1900 and Portland, Oregon, 1900–07, after which he became rabbi of the Free Synagogue in New York. He was president of the American Jewish Congress 1924–49.

His autobiography, *Challenging Years*, appeared 1949.

wisent another name for the European ◊bison.

wisteria any climbing shrub of the genus *Wisteria*, including *W. sinensis*, of the family Leguminosae, native to eastern US and east Asia. Wisterias have racemes of bluish, white, or pale mauve flowers, and pinnate leaves (leaves on either side of the stem).

witch doctor alternate name for a ◊shaman.

witch hazel any flowering shrub or small tree of the genus *Hamamelis* of the witch-hazel family, native to North America and E Asia, especially *H. virginiana*. An astringent extract prepared from the bark or leaves is used in medicine as an eye lotion and a liniment.

Wittgenstein Ludwig 1889–1951. Austrian philosopher. His *Tractatus Logico-Philosophicus* 1922 postulated the "picture theory" of language: that words represent things according to social agreement. He subsequently rejected this idea, and developed the idea that usage was more important than convention.

Witwatersrand or *the Rand* economic heartland of S Transvaal, South Africa. Its reef, which stretches nearly 60 mi/100 km, produces over half the world's gold. Gold was first found here 1854. The chief city of the region is Johannesburg.

Wodehouse P(elham) G(renville) 1881–1975. English novelist. He became a US citizen 1955. His humorous novels portray the accident-prone world of such characters as the socialite Bertie Wooster and his invaluable and impeccable manservant Jeeves, and Lord Emsworth of Blandings Castle with his prize pig, the Empress of Blandings.

Woden or *Wodan* the foremost Anglo-Saxon god, whose Norse counterpart is ◊Odin.

wolf any of two species of large wild dogs of the genus *Canis*. The gray or timber wolf *C. lupus*, of North

America and Eurasia, is highly social, measures up to 3 ft/90 cm at the shoulder, and weighs up to 100 lb/45 kg. It has been greatly reduced in numbers except for isolated wilderness regions.

Wolfe James 1727–1759. British soldier who served in Canada and commanded a victorious expedition against the French general Montcalm in Québec on the Plains of Abraham, during which both commanders were killed. The British victory established their supremacy over Canada.

Wolfe Thomas (Clayton) 1900–1938. US novelist born in Asheville, North Carolina. He is noted for the unrestrained rhetoric and emotion of his prose style. He wrote four long and hauntingly powerful autobiographical novels, mostly of the South: *Look Homeward, Angel* 1929, *Of Time and the River* 1935, *The Web and the Rock* 1939, and *You Can't Go Home Again* 1940 (the last two published posthumously).

Wollstonecraft Mary 1759–1797. British feminist, member of a group of radical intellectuals called the English Jacobins, whose book *A Vindication of the Rights of Women* 1792 demanded equal educational opportunities for women. She married William Godwin and died giving birth to a daughter, Mary (later Mary ◊Shelley).

Wolsey Thomas c. 1475–1530. English cleric and politician. In Henry VIII's service from 1509, he became archbishop of York 1514, cardinal and lord chancellor 1515, and began the dissolution of the monasteries.

His reluctance to further Henry's divorce from Catherine of Aragon, partly because of his ambition to be pope, led to his downfall 1529. He was charged with high treason 1530 but died before being tried.

wolverine largest land member *Gulo gulo* of the weasel family (Mustelidae), found in Europe, Asia, and North America. It is stocky in build, about 3.3 ft/1 m long. Its long, thick fur is dark brown on the back and belly and lighter on the sides. It covers food that it cannot eat with an unpleasant secretion. Destruction of habitat and trapping for its fur have greatly reduced its numbers.

wombat any of a family (Vombatidae) of burrowing, herbivorous marsupials, native to Tasmania and S Australia. They are about 3.3 ft/1 m long, heavy, with a big head, short legs and tail, and coarse fur.

women's movement the campaign for the rights of women, including social, political, and economic equality with men. Early European campaigners of the 17th–19th centuries fought for women's right to own property, to have access to higher education, and to vote (see ◊suffragist). Once women's suffrage was achieved in the 20th century, the emphasis of the movement shifted to the goals of equal social and economic opportunities for women, including employment.

In the US 1991, only 8% of senior executives were women; some 40% of women's jobs were part-time and 80% of these were low-paid. But 32% of all small US businesses were run by women 1993, compared with 5% in 1970.

women's services the organized military use of women on a large scale, a 20th-century development. First, women replaced men in factories, on farms, and in noncombat tasks during wartime; they are now found in combat units in many countries, including the US, Cuba, the UK, and Israel.

The US has a separate Women's Army Corps (WAC), established 1948, which developed from the Women's

Army Auxiliary Corps (WAAC); but in the navy and air force women are integrated into the general structure. There are separate nurse corps for the three services.

wood the hard tissue beneath the bark of many perennial plants; it is composed of water-conducting cells, or secondary xylem, and gains its hardness and strength from deposits of lignin. *Hardwoods*, such as oak, and *softwoods*, such as pine, have commercial value as structural material and for furniture.

Wood Grant 1892–1942. US painter. He was based mainly in his native Iowa. Though his work is highly stylized, he struck a note of hard realism in his studies of farmers, notably in *American Gothic* 1930 (Art Institute, Chicago).

He also painted landscapes and somewhat humorous scenes: for example, *Daughters of Revolution* 1932 (Cincinnati Art Museum), which satirized membership in patriotic societies.

Wood Natalie. Adopted name of Natasha Gurdin 1938–1981. US film actress. She started out as a child star. Her films include *Miracle on 34th Street* 1947, *Rebel Without a Cause* 1955, *The Searchers* 1956, and *Bob and Carol and Ted and Alice* 1969.

Other films include *Splendor in the Grass* 1961 and *Gypsy* 1962. She was married to actor Robert Wagner and died by drowning.

woodcarving art form practiced in many parts of the world since prehistoric times: for example, the NW Pacific coast of North America, in the form of totem poles, and W Africa, where there is a long tradition of woodcarving, notably in Nigeria. Woodcarvings survive less often than sculpture in stone or metal because of the comparative fragility of the material.

woodcock either of two species of wading birds, genus *Scolopax*, of the family Scolopacidae, which have barred plumage, long bills, and live in wet woodland areas.

The American woodcock *S. minor*, about 11 in/28 cm long, is shortlegged and short-necked, with a long, straight bill. It nests in moist woodlands and thickets throughout E North America. The Eurasian woodcock *S. rusticola*, somewhat larger, is similar in appearance and habits.

woodlouse any of the several families of mostly terrestrial crustaceans of the order Isopoda (especially the sow bugs, genera *Onisais* and *Porcellio*) that live in damp places under rocks or fallen timber. They have rounded oval, evenly segmented bodies and flat undersides. Some species of sow bugs can roll up when threatened. The pillbugs (family Arma-dillidiidae) typically roll up. Rock slaters (family Ligiidae) are amphibious on ocean beaches.

woodpecker bird of the family Picidae, which drills holes in trees to obtain insects. There are about 200 species worldwide. The largest of these, the imperial woodpecker *Campephilus imperialis* of Mexico, is very rare and may already be extinct.

North American woodpeckers include four species of sapsuckers (genus *Sphyrapicus*), which drill and then tap holes in trees for sap and the attracted insects. The pileated woodpecker *Dryocopus pileatus* is the largest, about 17 in/43 cm in long, with a red crest.

Woodward Robert 1917–1979. US chemist who worked on synthesizing a large number of complex molecules. These included quinine 1944, cholesterol 1951, chlorophyll 1960, and vitamin B_{12} 1971. Nobel Prize 1965.

Woodward worked throughout his career at Harvard University, Boston.

Woolf Virginia (born Virginia Stephen) 1882–1941. English novelist and critic. In novels such as *Mrs Dalloway*, *To the Lighthouse* 1927, and *The Waves* 1931, she used a "stream of consciousness" technique to render inner experience. In *A Room of One's Own* 1929, *Orlando* 1928, and *The Years* 1937, she examines the importance of economic independence for women and other feminist principles.

Woollcott Alexander 1887–1943. US theater critic and literary figure. He was *The New York Times'* theater critic 1914–22, a regular contributor to *The New Yorker* from its inception 1925, and hosted the radio interview program *Town Crier* 1929–42. He appeared on stage in *The Man Who Came to Dinner* 1939 as a character based on himself. Woollcott was a member of the Algonquin Hotel Round Table of wits in New York City, together with Robert Benchley and Dorothy Parker.

Worcester industrial port (textiles, engineering, printing) in central Massachusetts, US, on the Blackstone River; population (1990) 169,800. It was permanently settled 1713.

Educational institutions include Clark University and Worcester Polytechnic Institute.

word in computing, a group of bits (binary digits) that a computer's central processing unit treats as a single working unit. The size of a word varies from one computer to another and, in general, increasing the word length leads to a faster and more powerful computer. In the late 1970s and early 1980s, most microcomputers were 8-bit machines. During the 1980s 16-bit microcomputers were introduced and 32-bit microcomputers are now available. Mainframe computers may be 32-bit or 64-bit machines.

WordPerfect word processing program for various computers produced by WordPerfect Corp. It was first released 1982 and by 1987 was the dominant ◊MS-DOS word processor, rapidly eclipsing the previous leader, WordStar, by offering many more features, despite having the reputation of being difficult to learn.

word processor in computing, a program that allows the input, amendment, manipulation, storage, and retrieval of text; or a computer system that runs such software. Since word-processing programs became available to microcomputers, the method has been gradually replacing the typewriter for producing letters or other text.

Wordsworth William 1770–1850. English Romantic poet. In 1797 he moved with his sister Dorothy to Somerset to be near ◊Coleridge, collaborating with him on *Lyrical Ballads* 1798 (which included "Tintern Abbey"). From 1799 he lived in the Lake District, and later works include *Poems* 1807 (including "Intimations of Immortality") and *The Prelude* (written by 1805, published 1850). He was appointed poet laureate 1843.

workstation high-performance desktop computer with strong graphics capabilities, traditionally used for engineering (◊CAD and ◊CAM), scientific research, and desktop publishing.

World Bank popular name for the *International Bank for Reconstruction and Development* specialized agency of the United Nations that borrows in the commercial market and lends on commercial terms. It was established 1945 under the 1944 Bretton Woods agreement, which also created the International Monetary Fund. The *International Development Association* is an arm of the World Bank.

World Cup the most prestigious competition in international soccer, held every four years; the 1994 competition was held in the US. World Cup events are also held in rugby union, cricket, and other sports.

World Health Organization (WHO) agency of the United Nations established 1946 to prevent the spread of diseases and to eradicate them. It has a staff of about 4,500. Its headquarters are in Geneva, Switzerland.

world music or *roots music* any music whose regional character has not been lost in the melting pot of the pop industry. Examples are W African mbalax, E African soukous, S African mbaqanga, French Antillean zouk, Javanese gamelan, Latin American salsa and lambada, Cajun music, European folk music, and rural blues.

World Trade Organization (WTO) world trade monitoring body established Jan 1995, following approval of the Final Act of the Uruguay Round of the General Agreement on Tariffs and Trade (GATT). Under the Final Act, the WTO, a permanent trading body with a status commensurate with that of the International Monetary Fund or the World Bank, effectively replaced GATT. The WTO monitors agreements to reduce barriers to trade, such as tariffs, subsidies, quotas, and regulations which discriminate against imported products.

World War I 1914–1918. War between the Central European Powers (Germany, Austria–Hungary, and allies) on one side and the Triple Entente (Britain and the British Empire, France, and Russia) and their allies, including the US (which entered 1917), on the other side. An estimated 10 million lives were lost and twice that number were wounded. It was fought on the eastern and western fronts, in the Middle East, in Africa, and at sea. Towards the end of the war Russia withdrew because of the Russian Revolution 1917. The peace treaty of Versailles 1919 was the formal end to the war.

World War II 1939–1945. War between Germany, Italy, and Japan (the Axis powers) on one side, and Britain, the Commonwealth, France, the US, the USSR, and China (the Allied powers) on the other. An estimated 55 million lives were lost, 20 million of them citizens of the USSR. The war was fought in the Atlantic and Pacific theaters.

World Wide Fund for Nature (WWF, formerly the *World Wildlife Fund*) international organization established 1961 to raise funds for conservation by public appeal. Projects include conservation of particular species, for example, the tiger and giant panda, and special areas, such as the Simen Mountains, Ethiopia.

In 1990, it had 3.7 million members in 28 countries. Its headquarters are in Gland, Switzerland.

World-Wide Web hypertext system for publishing information over the ◊Internet. The ease of use of the Web has led to a rapid expansion of the Internet.

worm any of various elongated limbless invertebrates belonging to several phyla. Worms include the flatworms, such as flukes and tapeworms; the roundworms or ◊nematodes, such as the eelworm and the hookworm; the marine ribbon worms or nemerteans; and the segmented worms or ◊annelids.

Wounded Knee *Chief Big Foot, one of the leaders of the Sioux Indians, died at Wounded Knee, South Dakota, 1890. Throughout the 19th century, but especially from the 1850s onward, the American Indians were subjected to a systematic policy of dispossession, resettlement, and suppression. The massacre at Wounded Knee in the winter of 1890 marked the final defeat of the Sioux and the end of the Indian Wars.*

wormwood any plant of the genus *Artemisia*, family Compositae, especially the aromatic herb *A. absinthium*, the leaves of which are used in absinthe. Tarragon is a member of this genus.

Wounded Knee site on the Oglala Sioux Reservation, South Dakota, US, of a confrontation between the US Army and American Indians. Chief Sitting Bull was killed, supposedly resisting arrest, on Dec 15, 1890, and on Dec 29 a group of Indians involved in the Ghost Dance Movement (aimed at resumption of Indian control of North America with the aid of the spirits of dead braves) were surrounded and 153 killed.

W particle in physics, an ⟡elementary particle, one of the weakons responsible for transmiting the weak nuclear force).

wrack any of the large brown ⟡seaweeds characteristic of rocky shores. The bladder wrack *Fucus vesiculosus* has narrow, branched fronds up to 3.3 ft/1 m long, with oval air bladders, usually in pairs on either side of the midrib or central vein.

wrasse any bony fish of the family Labridae, found in temperate and tropical seas. They are slender and often brightly colored, with a single long dorsal fin. They have elaborate courtship rituals, and some species can change their coloring and sex. Species vary in size from 2 in/5 cm to 6.5 ft/2 m.

The hogfish *Labrus maximus*, found along S Atlantic shores of North America, is a fine food fish up to 2 ft/0.6 m long, with rapidly changing reddish colors.

wren any of a family (Troglodytidae) of small birds of order Passeriformes, with slender, slightly curved bills, and uptilted tails.

The house wren of North America *Troglodytes aedon* is common in brush, farmyard, and park.

Wren Christopher 1632–1723. English architect. His ingenious use of a refined and sober Baroque style can be seen in his best-known work, St Paul's Cathedral, London, 1675–1710, and in the many churches he built in London including St Mary-le-Bow, Cheapside, 1670–77 and St Bride's, Fleet Street, 1671–78. Other works include the Sheldonian Theatre, Oxford, 1664–69; Greenwich Hospital, London, begun 1694; and Marlborough House, London, 1709–10 (now much altered).

wrestling sport popular in ancient Egypt, Greece, and Rome, and included in the Olympics from 704 BC. The two main modern international styles are *Greco-Roman*, concentrating on above-waist holds, and *freestyle*, which allows the legs to be used to hold or trip; in both the aim is to throw the opponent to the ground.

Wright Frank Lloyd 1869–1959. US architect. He is known for "organic architecture", in which buildings reflect their natural surroundings. From the 1890s, he developed his celebrated *prairie house* style, a series of low, spreading houses with projecting roofs. He later diversified, employing reinforced concrete to explore a variety of geometric forms. Among his buildings are his Wisconsin home, Taliesin East, 1925, in prairie-house style; Falling Water, near Pittsburgh, Pennsylvania, 1936, a house of cantilevered terraces straddling a waterfall; and the Guggenheim Museum, New York, 1959, a spiral ramp rising from a circular plan.

Wright Orville 1871–1948 and Wilbur 1867–1912. US inventors; brothers who pioneered piloted, powered flight. Inspired by Otto Lilienthal's gliding, they perfected their piloted glider 1902. In 1903 they built a powered machine, a 12-hp 750-lb/341-kg plane, and became the first to make a successful powered flight, near Kitty Hawk, North Carolina. Orville flew 120 ft/ 36.6 m in 12 sec; Wilbur, 852 ft/260 m in 59 sec.

Both brothers were born in Dayton, Ohio, and became interested in flight at early ages. By 1903 they had built and flown a power-driven plane; they received a patent in 1906 and in 1909 set up the American Wright Corp to produce planes for the War Department.

writ in law, a document issued by a court requiring performance of certain actions.

Examples include a writ of habeas corpus, a writ of certiorari by which the US Supreme Court calls up cases from inferior courts for review, or writ of attachment of property in civil litigation.

writing any written form of communication using a set of symbols: see ◊alphabet, ◊cuneiform, ◊hieroglyphic. The last two used ideographs (picture writing) and phonetic word symbols side by side, as does modern Chinese. Syllabic writing, as in Japanese, develops from the continued use of a symbol to represent the sound of a short word. Some 8,0000 year-old inscriptions, thought to be pictographs, were found on animal bones and tortoise shells in Henan province, China, at a Neolithic site at Jiahu. They are thought to predate by 2,500 years the oldest known writing (Mesopotamian cuneiform of 3,500 BC).

Wroclaw formerly *Breslau* industrial river port in Poland, on the river Oder; population (1990) 643,200. Industries include shipbuilding, engineering, textiles, and electronics. It was the capital of the German province of Lower Silesia until 1945.

Wuhan river port and capital of Hubei province, China, at the confluence of the Han and Chang Jiang rivers, formed 1950 as one of China's greatest industrial areas by the amalgamation of Hankou, Hanyang, and Wuchang; population (1989) 3,710,000. It produces iron, steel, machine tools, textiles, and fertilizer.

Wycliffe John *c.* 1320–1384. English religious reformer. He attacked abuses in the church, maintaining that the Bible rather than the church was the supreme authority. He criticized such fundamental doctrines as priestly absolution, confession, and indulgences, and set disciples to work on translating the Bible into English. He sent out bands of traveling preachers, was denounced as a heretic, but died peacefully at Lutterworth.

Wyeth Andrew (Newell) 1917– . US painter. His portraits and landscapes, usually in watercolor or tempera, are naturalistic, minutely detailed, and often convey a strong sense of the isolation of the countryside; for example, *Christina's World* 1948 (Museum of Modern Art, New York).

Born in Chadds Ford, Pennsylvania, the son of artist-illustrator N C Wyeth, he is among the most popular of contemporary US artists. His paintings depict people of the land, especially Wyeth's own surroundings in Chadds Ford and Maine, where his summer home is located. His son James Browning Wyeth (1946–) is also an artist.

Wyoming state in western US: nickname Equality State *area* 97,812 sq mi/253,400 sq km *capital* Cheyenne *cities* Casper, Laramie *features* Rocky Mountains; national parks: Yellowstone (including the geyser Old Faithful), Grand Teton *industries* oil, natural gas, sodium salts, coal, uranium, sheep, beef *population* (1990) 453,600 *famous people* Buffalo Bill, Jackson Pollock *history* acquired by US from France as part of the ◊Louisiana Purchase 1803; Fort Laramie, a trading post, settled 1834; women acheived the vote 1869; became a state 1890.

WYSIWYG (acronym for *what you see is what you get*) in computing, a program that attempts to display on the screen a faithful representation of the final printed output. For example, a WYSIWYG ◊word processor would show actual page layout—line widths, page breaks, and the sizes and styles of type.

X

Xavier, St Francis 1506–1552. Spanish Jesuit missionary. He went to the Portuguese colonies in the East Indies, arriving at Goa 1542. He was in Japan 1549–51, establishing a Christian mission that lasted for 100 years. He returned to Goa in 1552, and sailed for China, but died of fever there. He was canonized 1622.

X chromosome larger of the two sex chromosomes, the smaller being the ◊Y chromosome. These two chromosomes are involved in sex determination. Females have two X chromosomes, males have an X and a Y. Genes carried on the X chromosome produce the phenomenon of sex linkage.

xenon colorless, odorless, gaseous, nonmetallic element, symbol Xe, atomic number 54, atomic weight 131.30. It is grouped with the ◊inert gases and was long believed not to enter into reactions, but is now known to form some compounds, mostly with fluorine. It is a heavy gas present in very small quantities in the air (about one part in 20 million).

Xenophon c. 430–354 BC. Greek historian, philosopher, and soldier. He was a disciple of ◊Socrates (described in Xenophon's *Symposium*). In 401 he joined a Greek mercenary army aiding the Persian prince Cyrus, and on the latter's death took command. His *Anabasis* describes how he led 10,000 Greeks on a 1,000-mile/1,600-km march home across enemy territory. His other works include *Memorabilia*, *Apology*, and *Hellenica/A History of My Times*.

xerophyte plant adapted to live in dry conditions. Common adaptations to reduce the rate of ◊transpiration include a reduction of leaf size, sometimes to

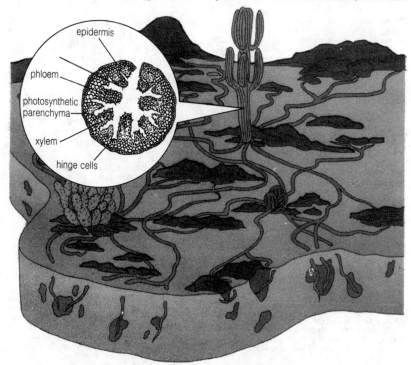

epidermis
phloem
photosynthetic parenchyma
xylem
hinge cells

xerophyte *Xerophytes are plants that can survive long periods without water. Features that ensure survival during drought include a reduction in leaf size (or leaves reduced to spines), sunken stomata, water storage cells, and permanently rolled leaves. The rolled leaf of a xerophyte is shown in the inset. Many xerophytes have extensive root systems to take full advantage of occasional rains. Creosote bushes, for example, have roots in excess of 400 ft/ 120 m long.*

spines or scales; a dense covering of hairs over the leaf to trap a layer of moist air (as in edelweiss); and permanently rolled leaves or leaves that roll up in dry weather (as in vinemesquite grass). Many desert cacti are xerophytes.

Xerxes *c.* 519–465 BC. King of Persia from 485 BC when he succeeded his father Darius. In 480, at the head of a great army which was supported by the Phoenician navy, he crossed the Dardanelles over a bridge of boats. He captured and burned Athens, but the Persian fleet was defeated at Salamis and Xerxes was forced to retreat. His general Mardonius remained behind in Greece, but was defeated by the Greeks at Plataea 479. Xerxes was eventually murdered in a court intrigue.

XGA (abbreviation for *extended graphics array*) color display system which is better than ◊VGA, providing either 256 colors on screen and a resolution of 1,024 x 768 or 25,536 colors with a resolution of 640 x 480.

Xhosa member of a Bantu people of southern Africa, living mainly in the Black National State of Transkei. Traditionally, the Xhosa were farmers and pastoralists, with a social structure based on a monarchy. Many are now town-dwellers, and provide much of the unskilled labor in South African mines and factories. Their Bantu language belongs to the Niger-Congo family.

Xia dynasty or *Hsia dynasty* China's first legendary ruling family, *c.* 2200–*c.* 1500 BC, reputedly founded by the model emperor Yu the Great. He is believed to have controlled floods by constructing dykes. Archeological evidence suggests that the Xia dynasty really did exist, as a Bronze Age civilization where writing was being developed, with its capital at Erlidou (Erh-li-t'ou) in Henan (Honan).

Xian industrial city and capital of Shaanxi province, China; population (1989) 2,710,000. It produces chemicals, electrical equipment, and fertilizers.

Xingú region in Pará, Brazil, crossed by branches of the Xingú River which flows for 1,200 mi/1,900 km to the Amazon Delta. In 1989 Xingú Indians protested at the creation of a vast, intrusive lake for the Babaquara and Kararao dams of the Altamira complex.

Xinjiang Uygur or *Sinkiang Uighur* autonomous region of NW China *area* 635,665 sq mi/1,646,800 sq km *capital* Urumqi *features* largest of Chinese administrative areas; Junggar Pendi (Dzungarian Basin) and Tarim Pendi (Tarim Basin, which includes ◊Lop Nor, China's nuclear testing ground, although the research centers were moved to the central province of Sichuan 1972) separated by the Tian Shan Mountains *industries* cereals, cotton, fruit in valleys and oases; uranium, coal, iron, copper, tin, oil *population* (1990) 15,156,000; the region has 13 recognized ethnic minorities, the largest being 6 million Uigurs (Muslim descendants of Turks) *religion* 50% Muslim *history* under Manchu rule from the 18th century. Large sections were ceded to Russia 1864 and 1881; China has raised the question of their return and regards the frontier between Xinjiang Uygur and Tajikistan, which runs for 300 mi/480 km, as undemarcated.

Xiongnu or *Hsiung-nu* Turkish-speaking nomad horseriding peoples from central Asia, who founded an extensive Chinese steppe empire and harried N Chinese states in the 3rd century BC. The Great Wall of China was then extended to strengthen defenses against them. The Xiongnu later became vassals of China, being employed as frontier troops.

X-ray band of electromagnetic radiation in the wavelength range 10^{-11} to 10^{-9} m (between gamma rays and ultraviolet radiation; see ◊electromagnetic waves). Applications of X-rays make use of their short wavelength (as in X-ray diffraction) or their penetrating power (as in medical X-rays of internal body tissues). X-rays are dangerous and can cause cancer.

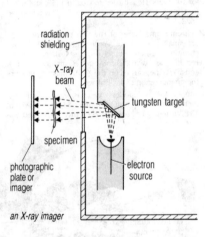

an X-ray imager

X-ray An X-ray image. The X-rays are generated by high-speed electrons impinging on a tungsten target. The rays pass through the specimen and on to a photographic plate or imager.

X-Windows graphical user interface for Unix. X-Windows was developed at the Massachusetts Institute of Technology, and is ultimately intended to be a standard for windowing systems. X-Windows is now controlled by X-OPEN as part of the drive toward open systems in the Unix world.

xylem tissue found in vascular plants, whose main function is to conduct water and dissolved mineral nutrients from the roots to other parts of the plant. Xylem is composed of a number of different types of cell, and may include long, thin, usually dead cells known as tracheids; fibers (schlerenchyma); thin-walled parenchyma cells; and conducting vessels.

xylophone musical ◊percussion instrument of African and Indonesian origin, consisting of a series of resonant hardwood bars of varying lengths, each with its own distinct pitch, arranged in sequence and played with hard sticks. It first appeared as an orchestral instrument in Saint-Saëns' *Danse macabre* 1874, illustrating dancing skeletons.

yachting pleasure cruising or racing a small and light vessel, whether sailing or power-driven. At the Olympic Games, seven sail-driven categories exist: Soling, Flying Dutchman, Star, Finn, Tornado, 470, and Windglider or windsurfing (boardsailing). The Finn and Windglider are solo events; the Soling class is for three-person crews; all other classes are for crews of two.

yak species of cattle *Bos grunniens*, family Bovidae, which lives in wild herds at high altitudes in Tibet. It stands about 6 ft/2 m at the shoulder and has long shaggy hair on the underparts. It has large, upward-curving horns and humped shoulders. It is in danger of becoming extinct.

Yakut (Russian *Yakutskaya*) autonomous republic in Siberian Russia *area* 1,197,760 sq mi/3,103,000 sq km *capital* Yakutsk *features* one of world's coldest inhabited places; river Lena *industries* furs, gold, natural gas, some agriculture in the S *population* (1986) 1,009,000 (50% Russians, 37% Yakuts) *history* the nomadic Yakuts were conquered by Russia in the 17th century; Yakut was a Soviet republic 1922–91. It remained an autonomous republic within the Russian Federation after the collapse of the Soviet Union 1991, since when it has agitated for greater independence.

yakuza Japanese gangster. Organized crime in Japan is highly structured, and the various syndicates between them employed some 110,000 people 1989, with a turnover of an estimated 1.5 trillion yen. The *yakuza* have been unofficially tolerated and are very powerful.

Yale University US university, founded 1701 in New Haven, Connecticut. It was named for Elihu Yale (1648–1721), born in Boston, Massachusetts, one-time governor of Fort St George, Madras, India.

Yale, an Ivy League school, is considered one of the preeminent US universities, attracting great numbers of foreign students as well as superior US high school graduates. Presidents George Bush and Gerald Ford, among many prominent Americans, attended Yale.

yam any climbing plant of the genus *Dioscorea*, family Dioscoreaceae, cultivated in tropical regions; its starchy tubers are eaten as a vegetable. The Mexican yam *D. composita* contains a chemical used in the manufacture of the contraceptive pill.

Yamoussoukro capital of ◊Ivory Coast; population (1986) 120,000. The economy is based on tourism and agricultural trade.

Yangon formerly (until 1989) *Rangoon* capital and chief port of Myanmar (Burma) on the Yangon River, 20 mi/32 km from the Indian Ocean; population (1983) 2,459,000. Products include timber, oil, and rice. The city *Dagon* was founded on the site AD 746; it was given the name Rangoon (meaning "end of conflict") by King Alaungpaya 1755.

Yangtze-Kiang alternative transcription of ◊Chang Jiang, the longest river in China.

Yankee initially, a disparaging term for a Dutch free-booter, later applied to English settlers by colonial Dutch in New York. Now it may be a colloquial term for a New Englander, any US northerner (used in the South), or any American (used outside the US).

Yao member of a people living in S China, N Vietnam, N Laos, Thailand, and Myanmar (Burma), and numbering about 4 million (1984). The Yao language may belong to either the Sino-Tibetan or the Thai language family. The Yao incorporate elements of ancestor worship in their animist religion.

Yaoundé capital of Cameroon, 130 mi/210 km E of the port of Douala; population (1984) 552,000. Industries include tourism, oil refining, and cigarette manufacturing.

yard unit (symbol yd) of length, equivalent to three feet (0.9144 m).

yarrow or *milfoil* perennial herb *Achillea millefolium* of the family Compositae, with feathery, scented leaves and flat-topped clusters of white or pink flowers.

Y chromosome smaller of the two sex chromosomes. In male mammals it occurs paired with the other type of sex chromosome (X), which carries far more genes. The Y chromosome is the smallest of all the mammalian chromosomes and is considered to be largely inert (that is, without direct effect on the physical body). See also ◊sex determination.

yd abbreviation for *yard*.

yeast one of various single-celled fungi (especially the genus *Saccharomyces*) that form masses of minute

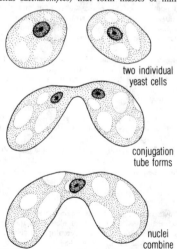

two individual
yeast cells

conjugation
tube forms

nuclei
combine

yeast *Yeast cells can join together or conjugate. Later the cell contents divide into four individual spores, each with a thick wall. When the original cell wall breaks open, the spores can germinate to form normal yeast cells.*

circular or oval cells by budding. When placed in a sugar solution the cells multiply and convert the sugar into alcohol and carbon dioxide. Yeasts are used as fermenting agents in baking, brewing, and the making of wine and spirits. Brewer's yeast *S. cerevisiae* is a rich source of vitamin B.

yeast artificial chromosome (YAC) fragment of ◊DNA from the human genome inserted into a yeast cell. The yeast replicates the fragment along with its own DNA. In this way the fragments are copied to be preserved in a gene library. YACs are characteristically between 250,000 and 1 million base pairs in length. A ◊cosmid works in the same way.

Yeats W(illiam) B(utler) 1865–1939. Irish poet. He was a leader of the Celtic revival and a founder of the ◊Abbey Theatre in Dublin. His early work was romantic and lyrical, as in the poem "The Lake Isle of Innisfree" and the plays *The Countess Cathleen* 1892 and *The Land of Heart's Desire* 1894. His later books of poetry include *The Wild Swans at Coole* 1917 and *The Winding Stair* 1929. He was a senator of the Irish Free State 1922–28. Nobel Prize for Literature 1923.

Yedo or **Edo** former name of ◊Tokyo, Japan, until 1868.

yeheb nut a small tree *Cordeauxia adulis* found in Ethiopia and Somalia and formerly much valued as a food source for its nuts. Although cultivated as a food crop in Kenya and Sudan, it is now critically endangered in the wild and has at most three known sites remaining.

yellow archangel flowering plant *Lamiastrum galeobdolon* of the mint family Labiatae, found over much of Europe. It grows up to 2 ft/60 cm tall and has nettle-like leaves and whorls of yellow flowers, the lower lips streaked with red in early summer.

yellow fever or **yellow jack** acute tropical viral disease, prevalent in the Caribbean area, Brazil, and on the west coast of Africa. The yellow fever virus is an arbovirus transmitted by mosquitoes. Its symptoms include a high fever, headache, joint and muscle pains, vomiting and yellowish skin (jaundice, possibly leading to liver failure); the heart and kidneys may also be affected. Mortality is high in serious cases.

yellowhammer Eurasian bird *Emberiza citrinella* of the bunting family Emberizidae. About 6.5 in/16.5 cm long, the male has a yellow head and underside, a chestnut rump, and a brown-streaked back. The female is duller.

The name is sometimes also used for a subspecies of the northern flicker *Colaptes auratus*, a North American woodpecker with a spotted belly and yellow underwings.

Yellow River English name for the ◊Huang He River, China.

Yellow Sea gulf of the Pacific Ocean between China and Korea; area 180,000 sq mi/466,200 sq km. It receives the Huang He (Yellow River) and Chang Jiang.

Yellowstone National Park largest US nature reserve, established 1872, on a broad plateau in the Rocky Mountains, chiefly in NW Wyoming, but also in SW Montana and E Idaho; area 3,469 sq mi/8,983 sq km. The park contains more than 3,000 geysers and hot springs, including periodically erupting Old Faithful. It is one of the world's greatest wildlife refuges. Much of the park was ravaged by forest fires 1988.

John Colter, a trapper, explored the area in 1807.

Yeltsin Boris Nikolayevich 1931– . Russian politician, president of the Russian Soviet Federative Socialist Republic (RSFSR) 1990–91, and president of the newly independent Russian Federation from 1991. He directed the Federation's secession from the USSR and the formation of a new, decentralized confederation, the ◊Commonwealth of Independent States (CIS), with himself as the most powerful leader.

In the abortive Aug 1991 coup, Yeltsin supported President Gorbachev. As the economic situation deteriorated within Russia, his leadership came under increasing challenge, but in April 1992 he persuaded 18 of the 20 autonomous republics in the Russian Federation to sign a federative treaty. In Jan 1993 Yeltsin and US president Bush signed the START II treaty in Moscow.

An attempted coup by parliamentary leaders Sept–Oct 1993 was successfully thwarted, but unexpected far-right gains in Dec assembly elections forced him to compromise his economic policies and rely increasingly on the support of the military.

Yemen Republic of (*al Jamhuriya al Yamaniya*) *area* 205,367 sq mi/531,900 sq km *capital* San'a *towns and cities* Ta'iz; and chief port Aden *physical* hot moist coastal plain, rising to plateau and desert *features* once known as *Arabia felix* because of its fertility, includes islands of Perim (in strait of Bab-el-Mandeb, at S entrance to Red Sea), Socotra, and Kamaran *head of state* Ali Abdullah Saleh from 1990 *head of government* (interim) Mohammed Said al-Attar *political system* emergent democratic republic *political parties* Yemen Socialist Party (YSP), left of center; General People's Congress (GPC), centrist; Yemeni Islah Party (YIP), Islamic; National Opposition Front, left of center *exports* cotton, coffee, grapes, vegetables *currency* rial in the north, dinar in the south *population* (1993) 13,000,000; growth rate 2.7% p.a. *life expectancy* men 52, women 52 *language* Arabic *religion* Sunni Muslim 63%, Shiite Muslim 37% *literacy* men 53%, women 26% *GNP* $540 per head (1991) *chronology 1918* Yemen became independent. *1962* North Yemen declared the Yemen Arab Republic (YAR), with Abdullah al-Sallal as president. Civil war broke out between royalists and republicans. *1967* Civil war ended with the republicans victorious. Sallal deposed and replaced by Republican Council. The People's Republic of South Yemen was formed. *1970* People's Republic of South Yemen renamed People's Democratic Republic of Yemen. *1971–72* War between South Yemen and the YAR;

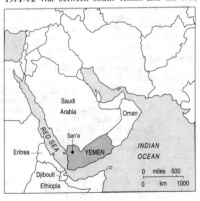

union agreement signed but not kept. *1974* Ibrahim al-Hamadi seized power in North Yemen and Military Command Council set up. *1977* Hamadi assassinated and replaced by Ahmed ibn Hussein al-Ghashmi. *1978* Constituent people's assembly appointed in North Yemen and Military Command Council dissolved. Ghashmi killed by envoy from South Yemen; succeeded by Ali Abdullah Saleh. War broke out again between the two Yemens. South Yemen president deposed and YSP formed. *1979* Cease-fire agreed with commitment to future union. *1983* Saleh elected president of North Yemen for a further five-year term. *1984* Joint committee on foreign policy for the two Yemens met in Aden. *1985* Ali Nasser reelected secretary-general of the YSP in South Yemen; removed his opponents. Three bureau members killed. *1986* Civil war in South Yemen; Ali Nasser dismissed. New administration under Haydar Abu Bakr al-Attas. *1988* President Saleh reelected in North Yemen. *1989* Draft constitution for single Yemen state published. *1990* Border between two Yemens opened; countries formally united May 22 as Republic of Yemen. *1991* New constitution approved. *1992* Antigovernment riots. *1993* General People's Congress won most seats in general elections but no overall majority; five-member presidential council elected, including Ali Abdullah Saleh as president and YSP leader, Ali Salim al-Baidh, as vice president. *1994* Fighting erupted between northern forces, led by President Saleh, and southern forces, led by Vice President al-Baidh. May: southern Yemen announced its secession. July: Saleh inflicted crushing defeat on al-Baidh, effectively ending civil war.

Yemen, North former country in SW Asia. It was united with South Yemen 1990 as the Republic of Yemen.

Yemen, South former country in SW Asia. It was united with North Yemen 1990 as the Republic of Yemen.

Yenisei river in Asian Russia, rising in the Tuva region and flowing across the Siberian plain into the Arctic Ocean; length 2,550 mi/4,100 km.

Yerevan industrial city (tractor parts, machine tools, chemicals, bricks, bicycles, wine, fruit canning) and capital of Armenia, a few miles N of the Turkish border; population (1987) 1,168,000. It was founded in the 7th century and was alternately Turkish and Persian from the 15th century until ceded to Russia 1828. Armenia became an independent republic 1991.

yeti Tibetan for the abominable snowman.

Yevtushenko Yevgeny Aleksandrovich 1933– . Soviet poet. He aroused controversy with his anti-Stalinist "Stalin's Heirs" 1956, published with Khrushchev's support, and "Babi Yar" 1961, which attacked Russian as well as Nazi anti-Semitism. His other works include the long poem *Zima Junction* 1956, the novel *Berries* 1981, and *Precocious Autobiography* 1963.

yew any evergreen coniferous tree of the genus *Taxus* of the family Taxaceae, native to the northern hemisphere. The leaves and bright red berrylike seeds are poisonous; the wood is hard and close-grained.

Yi member of a people living in S China; there are also Yi populations in Laos, Thailand, and Vietnam, totaling about 5.5 million (1987). The Yi are farmers, producing both crops and livestock. Their language belongs to the Sino-Tibetan family; their religion is animist.

Yiddish language member of the west Germanic

branch of the Indo-European language family, deriving from 13th–14th-century Rhineland German and spoken by northern, central, and eastern European Jews, who have carried it to Israel, the US, and many other parts of the world. It is written in the Hebrew alphabet and has many dialects reflecting European areas of residence, as well as many borrowed words from Polish, Russian, Lithuanian, and other languages encountered.

yin and yang the passive (characterized as feminine, negative, intuitive) and active (characterized as masculine, positive, intellectual) principles of nature. Their interaction is believed to maintain equilibrium and harmony in the universe and to be present in all things. In Taoism and Confucianism they are represented by two interlocked curved shapes within a circle, one white, one black, with a spot of the contrasting color within the head of each.

yoga Hindu philosophical system attributed to Patanjali, who lived about 150 BC at Gonda, Uttar Pradesh, India. He preached mystical union with a personal deity through the practice of self-hypnosis and a rising above the senses by abstract meditation, adoption of special postures, and ascetic practices. As practiced in the West, yoga is more a system of mental and physical exercise, and of induced relaxation as a means of relieving stress.

yogurt also called *yogurt* or *yoghourt* semisolid curdlike dairy product made from milk fermented with bacteria. It was originally made by nomadic tribes of Central Asia, from mare's milk in leather pounches attached to their saddles. It spread to the Asian and Mediterranean regions, where it is drunk plain, but honey, sugar, and fruit were added in Europe and the US, and the product was made solid and creamy, to be eaten by spoon.

Yokohama Japanese port on Tokyo Bay; population (1990) 3,220,350. Industries include shipbuilding, oil refining, engineering, textiles, glass, and clothing.

Yom Kippur the Jewish Day of ◊Atonement.

Yom Kippur War the surprise attack on Israel October 1973 by Egypt and Syria; see ◊Arab–Israeli Wars. It is named for the Jewish national holiday on which it began, the holiest day of the Jewish year.

Yonkers city in Westchester County, New York, on the Hudson River, just N of the Bronx, New York City; population (1990) 188,100.

Products include machinery, processed foods, chemicals, clothing, and electric and electronic equipment. Yonkers was a Dutch settlement from about 1650.

Sarah Lawrence College is here.

York cathedral and industrial city (railroad rolling stock, scientific instruments, sugar, chocolate, and glass) in North Yorkshire, N England *population* (1991) 100,600 *features* The Gothic York Minster, containing medieval stained glass. Much of the 14th-century city wall survives. Jorvik Viking Center, opened 1984 after excavation of a site at Coppergate, contains wooden remains of Viking houses. The National Railroad Museum and the 19th-century railroad station; and the university 1963.

Yoruba member of the majority ethnic group living in SW Nigeria; there is a Yoruba minority in E Benin. They number approximately 20 million in all, and their language belongs to the Kwa branch of the Niger-Congo family. The Yoruba established powerful city-states in the 15th century, known for their advanced culture which includes sculpture, art, and music.

Young Brigham 1801–1877. US ◊Mormon religious leader, born in Vermont. He joined the Mormon Church, or Church of Jesus Christ of Latter-day Saints, 1832, and three years later was appointed an apostle. After a successful recruiting mission in Liverpool, England, he returned to the US and, as successor of Joseph Smith (who had been murdered), led the Mormon migration to the Great Salt Lake in Utah 1846, founded Salt Lake City, and headed the colony until his death.

He was appointed governor of Utah territory 1850 and defied federal pressure to repudiate the Mormon practice of polygamy. Young himself had 27 wives and fathered 56 children.

Young Cy (Denton True) 1867–1955. US baseball player. As a pitcher of unequaled skill and stamina, he established a lifetime record of 511 victories. In 16 seasons, he finished with 20 or more wins, 5 times exceeding 30. He was nicknamed "Cy" for his "cyclone" pitch.

The Cy Young Award, given annually to the outstanding pitcher in both the American and National leagues, is named for him.

He was elected to the Baseball Hall of Fame 1937.

Young John Watts 1930– . US astronaut, the first person to make six space flights. His first flight was on *Gemini 3* 1965, followed by *Gemini 10* 1966. In 1969 he flew on *Apollo 10* and landed on the Moon with *Apollo 16* 1972. He was commander of the first flight of the space shuttle *Columbia* 1981.

Young Men's Christian Association (YMCA) international organization founded 1844 by George Williams (1821–1905) in London and 1851 in the US. It aims at self-improvement—spiritual, intellectual, and physical.

There are about 12 million members in the US in 2,200 groups.

YMCAs provide dormitories and rooms for both transients and residents; educational, sports, and civic programs; and recreation facilities for members and for military troops in wartime.

Young Pretender nickname of ◊Charles Edward Stuart, claimant to the Scottish and English thrones.

Young Women's Christian Association YWCA organization for the welfare of women and girls, founded London 1855. The first YWCA in the US was formally established 1858 in New York City; another followed in Boston, Massachusetts, 1866. Both were in response to the effects of the Industrial Revolution on women. Its facilities and activities are similar to those of the YMCA.

Youth Hostels Association (YHA) registered charity founded in Britain 1930 to promote knowledge and care of the countryside by providing cheap overnight accommodation for young people on active vacations (such as walking or cycling). Types of accommodation range from castles to log cabins.

In the US, the American Youth Hostels provide information, equipment, trips, and accommodation for hiking, biking, skiing, canoeing, and horseback riding for people of all ages.

Ypres (Flemish *Ieper*) Belgian town in W Flanders, 25 mi/40 km S of Ostend, a site of three major battles 1914–17 fought in World War I. The Menin Gate 1927 is a memorial to British soldiers lost in these battles.

yucca plant of the genus *Yucca*, family Liliaceae, with over 40 species found in Latin America and southwest

US. The leaves are stiff and sword-shaped and the flowers white and bell-shaped.

Yugoslavia area 22,503 sq mi/58,300 sq km *capital* Belgrade *towns and cities* Kraljevo, Leskovac, Pristina, Novi Sad, Titograd *head of state* Zoran Lilic from 1993 *head of government* Radoje Kontic from 1993 *political system* socialist pluralist republic *political parties* Socialist Party of Serbia, ex-communist; Serbian Renaissance Movement, pro-monarchist; Democratic Party, Serbia-based, liberal, free-market; Montenegro League of Communists; Democratic Coalition of Muslims; Alliance of Reform Forces, Montenegro-based *exports* machinery, electrical goods, chemicals, clothing, tobacco *currency* dinar *population* (1992) 10,460,000 *life expectancy* men 70, women 76 *language* Serbian variant of Serbo-Croatian, Slovenian *religion* Eastern Orthodox 41% (Serbs), Roman Catholic 12% (Croats), Muslim 3% *literacy* 93% *GNP* $154.1 bn; $6,540 per head (1988) *chronology 1918* Creation of Kingdom of the Serbs, Croats, and Slovenes. *1929* Name of Yugoslavia adopted. *1941* Invaded by Germany. *1945* Yugoslav Federal Republic formed under leadership of Tito; communist constitution introduced. *1948* Split with USSR. *1953* Self-management principle enshrined in constitution. *1961* Nonaligned movement formed under Yugoslavia's leadership. *1974* New constitution adopted. *1980* Tito died; collective leadership assumed power. *1988* Economic difficulties: 1,800 strikes, 250% inflation, 20% unemployment. Ethnic unrest in Montenegro and Vojvodina; party reshuffled and government resigned. *1989* Reformist Croatian Ante Markovic became prime minister. Ethnic riots in Kosovo province against Serbian attempt to end autonomous status of Kosovo and Vojvodina; state of emergency imposed. May: inflation rose to 490%; tensions with ethnic Albanians rose. *1990* Multiparty systems established in Serbia and Croatia. *1991* June: Slovenia and Croatia declared independence, resulting in clashes between federal and republican armies; Slovenia accepted European Community (EC)-sponsored peace pact. Dec: President Stipe Mesic and Prime Minister Ante Markovic resigned. *1992* Jan: EC-brokered cease-fire in Croatia; EC and US recognized Slovenia's and Croatia's independence. Bosnia-Herzegovina and Macedonia declared independence. April: Bosnia-Herzegovina recognized as independent by EC and US.

New Federal Republic of Yugoslavia (FRY) proclaimed by Serbia and Montenegro but not recognized externally. May: Western ambassadors left Belgrade. International sanctions imposed against Serbia and Montenegro. June: Dobrica Cosic became president. July: Milan Panic became prime minister. Sept: UN membership suspended. Oct: Panic lost vote of confidence and removed from office. *1993* June: Cosic removed from office; replaced by Zoran Lilic. Antigovernment rioting in Belgrade. Radoje Kontic became prime minister. Macedonia recognized as independent under name of Former Yugoslav Republic of Macedonia. Economy severely damaged by international sanctions. *1994* Border blockade imposed against Bosnian Serbs; sanctions eased as a result.

Yukon territory of NW Canada *area* 186,631 sq mi/ 483,500 sq km *capital* Whitehorse *towns and cities* Dawson, Mayo *features* named for its chief river, the Yukon; includes the highest point in Canada, Mount Logan, 19,850 ft/ 6,050 m; Klondike Gold Rush International Historical Park, which extends into Alaska *industries* gold, silver, lead, zinc, oil, natural gas, coal *population* (1991) 26,500 *history* settlement dates from the gold rush 1896–1910, when 30,000 people moved to the ◊Klondike river valley (silver is now worked there). It became separate from the Northwest Territories 1898, with Dawson as the capital 1898–1951. Construction of the Alcan Highway during World War II helped provide the basis for further development.

Yukon River river in North America, 1,979 mi/3,185 km long, flowing from Lake Tagish in Yukon Territory into Alaska, where it empties into the Bering Sea.

Yunnan province of SW China, adjoining Myanmar (Burma), Laos, and Vietnam *area* 168,373 sq mi/ 436,200 sq km *capital* Kunming *physical* rivers: Chang Jiang, Salween, Mekong; crossed by the Burma Road; mountainous and well forested *industries* rice, tea, timber, wheat, cotton, rubber, tin, copper, lead, zinc, coal, salt *population* (1990) 36,973,000.

Z

Zagreb industrial city (leather, linen, carpets, paper, and electrical goods) and capital of Croatia, on the Sava River; population (1991) 706,800. Zagreb was a Roman city (*Aemona*) and has a Gothic cathedral. Its university was founded 1874. The city was damaged by bombing Oct 1991 during the Croatian civil war.

Zahir Shah Mohammed 1914– . King of Afghanistan 1933–73. Zahir, educated in Kabul and Paris, served in the government 1932–33 before being crowned king. He was overthrown 1973 by a republican coup and went into exile. He became a symbol of national unity for the ◊Mujaheddin Islamic fundamentalist resistance groups.

Zahir ud-Din Mohammed first Mogul emperor of India; see ◊Babur.

Zaire Republic of (*République du Zaïre*) (formerly *Congo*) *area* 905,366 sq mi/2,344,900 sq km *capital* Kinshasa *towns and cities* Lubumbashi, Kananga, Kisangani; ports Matadi, Boma *physical* Zaïre River basin has tropical rainforest and savanna; mountains in E and W *features* lakes Tanganyika, Mobutu Sese Seko, Edward; Ruwenzori mountains *head of state* Mobutu Sese Seko Kuku Ngbendu wa Zabanga from 1965 *head of government* Leon Kengo Wa Dondo from 1994 *political system* transitional *political parties* Popular Movement of the Revolution (MPR), African socialist; Democratic Forces of Congo-Kinshasa (formerly Sacred Union, an alliance of some 130 opposition groups), moderate, centrist *exports* coffee, copper, cobalt (80% of world output), industrial diamonds, palm oil *currency* zaïre *population* (1993 est) 40,256,000; growth rate 2.9% p.a. *life expectancy* men 52, women 56 *language* French (official), Swahili, Lingala, other African languages; over 300 dialects *religion* Christian 70%, Muslim 10% *literacy* men 84%, women 61% *GNP* \$220 per head (1990) *chronology* **1908** Congo Free State annexed to Belgium. **1960** Independence achieved from Belgium as Republic of the Congo. Civil war broke out between central government and Katanga province. **1963** Katanga war ended. **1965** Col Mobutu seized power in coup. **1967** New constitution adopted. **1970** Mobutu elected president. **1971** Country became the Republic of Zaire. **1972** The Popular Movement of the Revolution (MPR) became the only legal political party. Katanga province renamed Shaba. **1974** Foreign-owned businesses and plantations seized by Mobutu and given in political patronage. **1977** Original owners of confiscated properties invited back. Mobutu reelected; Zairians invaded Shaba province from Angola, repulsed by Belgian paratroopers. **1978** Second unsuccessful invasion from Angola. **1990** Mobutu announced end of ban on multiparty politics, following internal dissent. **1991** Sept: after antigovernment riots, Mobutu agreed to share power with opposition; Etienne Tshisekedi appointed premier. Oct: Tshisekedi dismissed; opposition government formed. **1992** Aug: Tshisekedi reinstated against Mobutu's wishes. Oct: renewed rioting. Dec: interim parliament, the High Council of the Republic (HCR), formed, with Tshisekedi as premier. **1993** Jan: army mutiny. March: Tshisekedi dismissed by Mobutu and replaced by Faustin Birindwa, but Tshisekedi disputed decision. **1994** Reconstituted interim parliament installed, the Parliament of Transition, incorporating HCR. April: interim constitution adopted. Kengo Wa Dondo elected prime minister, with Mobutu's agreement.

Zaïre River formerly (until 1971) *Congo* second-longest river in Africa, rising near the Zambia–Zaire border (and known as the *Lualaba River* in the upper reaches) and flowing 2,800 mi/4,500 km to the Atlantic Ocean, running in a great curve that crosses the equator twice, and discharging a volume of water second only to the Amazon. The chief tributaries are the Ubangi, Sangha, and Kasai.

Zambezi river in central and SE Africa; length 1,650 mi/2,650 km from NW Zambia through Mozambique to the Indian Ocean, with a wide delta near Chinde. Major tributaries include the Kafue in Zambia. It is interrupted by rapids, and includes on the Zimbabwe–Zambia border the Victoria Falls (Mosi-oa-tunya) and Kariba Dam, which forms the reservoir of Lake Kariba with large fisheries.

Zambia Republic of *area* 290,579 sq mi/752,600 sq km *capital* Lusaka *towns and cities* Kitwe, Ndola, Kabwe, Chipata, Livingstone *physical* forested plateau cut through by rivers *features* Zambezi River, Victoria Falls, Kariba Dam *head of state and government* Frederick Chiluba from 1991 *political system* emergent democratic republic *political parties* United National Independence Party (UNIP), African socialist; Movement for Multiparty Democracy (MMD), moderate, left of center; National Democratic Alliance (Nada), moderate, centrist *exports* copper, cobalt, zinc, emeralds, tobacco *currency* kwacha *population* (1993 est) 9,000,000; growth rate 3.3% p.a. *life expectancy* men 54, women 57 *language* English (official); Bantu dialects *religion* Christian 66%, animist, Hindu, Muslim *media* defamation of the president is prohibited *literacy* men 81%, women 65% *GNP* \$420 per head (1990) *chronology* **1899–1924** As Northern Rhodesia, under administration of the British South Africa Company. **1924** Became a British protectorate. **1964** Independence achieved from Britain, within the Commonwealth, as the Republic of Zambia with Kenneth Kaunda as president. **1972** UNIP declared the only legal party. **1976** Support for the Patriotic Front in Rhodesia declared. **1980** Unsuccessful coup against President Kaunda. **1985** Kaunda elected chair of the African Front Line States. **1987** Kaunda elected chair of the Organization of African Unity. **1988** Kaunda reelected unopposed for sixth term. **1991** New multiparty constitution adopted. MMD won landslide election victory; Frederick Chiluba became president. **1992** Food and water shortages caused by severe drought. **1993** State of emergency declared after rumors of planned antigovernment coup.

Zanzibar island region of Tanzania *area* 640 sq mi/ 1,658 sq km/ (50 mi/80 km long) *towns and cities* Zanzibar *industries* cloves, copra *population* (1985) 571,000 *history* settled by Arab traders in the 7th century; occupied by the Portuguese in the 16th century; became a sultanate in the 17th century; under British protection 1890–1963. Together with the island of Pemba, some nearby islets, and a strip of mainland territory, it became a republic 1963. It merged with Tanganyika as Tanzania 1964.

Zapata Emiliano 1879–1919. Mexican Indian revolutionary leader. He led a revolt against dictator Porfirio Díaz (1830–1915) from 1911 under the slogan "Land and Liberty", to repossess for the indigenous Mexicans the land taken by the Spanish. By 1915 he was driven into retreat, and was assassinated.

Zapotec member of a North American Indian people of S Mexico, now numbering approximately 250,000, living mainly in Oaxaca. The Zapotec language, which belongs to the Oto-Mangean family, has nine dialects. The ancient Zapotec built the ceremonial center of Monte Albán 1000–500 BC. They developed one of the classic Mesoamerican civilizations by AD 300, but declined under pressure from the Mixtecs from 900 until the Spanish Conquest 1530s.

Zappa Frank (Francis Vincent) 1940–1993. US rock musician, bandleader, and composer. His crudely satirical songs (*Joe's Garage* 1980), deliberately bad taste, and complex orchestral and electronic compositions (*Hot Rats* 1969, *Jazz from Hell* 1986) make his work hard to categorize. His group the Mothers of Invention 1965–73, was part of the 1960s avant-garde, and the Mothers' hippie parody *We're Only in It for the Money* 1967 was popular with its target.

zebra black and white striped member of the horse genus *Equus* found in Africa; the stripes serve as camouflage or dazzle and confuse predators. It is about 5 ft/1.5 m high at the shoulder, with a stout body and a short, thick mane. Zebras live in family groups and herds on mountains and plains, and can run up to 40 mph/60 kph. Males are usually solitary.

zebra *Burchell's zebras show great variation in stripe pattern, both between individuals and over the geographical range. In southern Africa, the stripes on the hind parts of the body tend to be lighter. The base color may be white or yellowish, and the stripes may be light to dark brown or black.*

zebu any of a species of ◊cattle *Bos indicus* found domesticated in E Asia, India, and Africa. It is usually light-colored, with large horns and a large fatty hump near the shoulders. It is used for pulling loads, and is held by some Hindus to be sacred. There are about 30 breeds.

Zedekiah last king of Judah 597–586 BC. Placed on the throne by Nebuchadnezzar, he rebelled, was forced to witness his sons' execution, then was blinded and sent to Babylon. The witness to these events was the prophet Jeremiah, who describes them in the Old Testament.

Zeeland province of the SW Netherlands *area* 691 sq mi/1,790 sq km *capital* Middelburg *towns and cities* Vlissingen, Terneuzen, Goes *features* mostly below sea level, Zeeland is protected by a system of dykes *industries* cereals, potatoes *population* (1991) 357,000 *history* disputed by the counts of Flanders and Holland during the Middle Ages, Zeeland was annexed to Holland 1323 by Count William III.

Zen form of ◊Buddhism introduced from India to Japan via China in the 12th century. *Koan* (paradoxical questions), tea-drinking, and sudden enlightenment are elements of Zen practice. Soto Zen was spread by the priest Dogen (1200–1253), who emphasized work, practice, discipline, and philosophical questions to discover one's Buddha-nature in the "realization of self".

zenith uppermost point of the celestial horizon, immediately above the observer; the nadir is below, diametrically opposite. See ◊celestial sphere.

Zeno of Elea *c.* 490–430 BC. Greek philosopher who pointed out several paradoxes that raised "modern" problems of space and time. For example, motion is an illusion, since an arrow in flight must occupy a determinate space at each instant, and therefore must be at rest.

Zeppelin Ferdinand, Count von Zeppelin 1838–1917. German airship pioneer. On retiring from the army 1891, he devoted himself to the study of aeronautics, and his first airship was built and tested 1900. During World War I a number of Zeppelin airships bombed England. They were also used for luxury passenger transport but the construction of hydrogen-filled airships with rigid keels was abandoned after several disasters in the 1920s and 1930s. Zeppelin also helped to pioneer large multi-engine bomber planes.

Zeus in Greek mythology, the chief of the gods (Roman Jupiter). He was the son of Cronus, whom he overthrew; his brothers included Pluto and Poseidon, his sisters Demeter and Hera. As the supreme god he dispensed good and evil and was the father and ruler of all humankind. His emblems are the thunderbolt and aegis (shield), representing the thundercloud. The colossal ivory and gold statue of the seated god, made by Phidias for the temple of Zeus in the Peloponnese, was one of the ◊Seven Wonders of the World.

Zhao Ziyang 1918– . Chinese politician, prime minister 1980–87 and secretary of the Chinese Communist Party 1987–89. His reforms included self-management and incentives for workers and factories. He lost his secretaryship and other posts after the Tiananmen Square massacre in Beijing June 1989.

Zhejiang or *Chekiang* province of SE China *area* 39,295 sq mi/101,800 sq km *capital* Hangzhou *features* smallest of the Chinese provinces; the base of the Song dynasty 12th–13th centuries; densely populated industries rice, cotton, sugar, jute, corn; timber on the uplands *population* (1990) 41,446,000.

Zhelev Zhelyu 1935– . Bulgarian politician, president from 1990. In 1989 he became head of the opposition Democratic Forces coalition. He is a proponent of market-centered economic reform and social peace.

Zhengzhou or *Chengchow* industrial city (light engineering, cotton textiles, foods) and capital (from 1954) of Henan province, China, on the Huang Ho River; population (1989) 1,660,000.

Zhou dynasty or *Chou dynasty* Chinese succession of rulers *c.* 1066–256 BC, during which cities emerged and philosophy flourished. The dynasty was established by the Zhou, a seminomadic people from the Wei Valley region, W of the great bend in the Huang He (Yellow River). Zhou influence waned from 403 BC, as the Warring States era began.

Zhou Enlai or *Chou En-lai* 1898–1976. Chinese politician. Zhou, a member of the Chinese Communist Party (CCP) from the 1920s, was prime minister 1949–76 and foreign minister 1949–58. He was a moderate Maoist and weathered the Cultural Revolution. He played a key role in foreign affairs.

zidovudine (formerly *AZT*) antiviral drug used in the treatment of ◊AIDS. It is not a cure for AIDS but is effective in prolonging life; it does not, however, delay the onset of AIDS in people carrying the virus.

ziggurat in ancient Babylonia and Assyria, a step pyramid of sun-baked brick faced with glazed bricks or tiles on which stood a shrine. The Tower of Babel as described in the Bible may have been a ziggurat.

Zimbabwe Republic of *area* 150,695 sq mi/390,300 sq km *capital* Harare *towns and cities* Bulawayo, Gweru, Kwekwe, Mutare, Hwange *physical* high plateau with central high veld and mountains in E; rivers Zambezi, Limpopo *features* Hwange National Park, part of Kalahari Desert; ruins of Great Zimbabwe *head of state and government* Robert Mugabe from 1987 *political system* emergent democratic republic *political parties* Zimbabwe African National Union–Patriotic Front (ZANU–PF), African socialist; Forum Party, moderate, centrist *exports* tobacco, asbestos, cotton, coffee, gold, silver, copper *currency* Zimbabwe dollar *population* (1993 est) 10,700,000 (Shona 80%, Ndbele 19%; about 100,000 whites); growth rate 3.5%

p.a. *life expectancy* men 59, women 63 *language* English (official), Shona, Sindebele *religion* Christian, Muslim, Hindu, animist *literacy* men 74%, women 60% *GNP* $620 per head (1991) *chronology* *1889–1923* As Southern Rhodesia, under administration of British South Africa Company. *1923* Became a self-governing British colony. *1961* Zimbabwe African People's Union (ZAPU) formed, with Joshua Nkomo as leader. *1962* ZAPU declared illegal. *1963* Zimbabwe African National Union (ZANU) formed, with Robert Mugabe as secretary-general. *1964* Ian Smith became prime minister. ZANU banned. Nkomo and Mugabe imprisoned. *1965* Smith declared unilateral independence. *1966–68* Abortive talks between Smith and UK prime minister Harold Wilson. *1974* Nkomo and Mugabe released. *1975* Geneva conference set date for constitutional independence. *1979* Smith produced new constitution and established a government with Bishop Abel Muzorewa as prime minister. New government denounced by Nkomo and Mugabe. Conference in London agreed independence arrangements (Lancaster House Agreement). *1980* Independence achieved from Britain, with Robert Mugabe as prime minister and Rev. Canaan Banana as president. *1981* Rift between Mugabe and Nkomo. *1982* Nkomo dismissed from the cabinet, leaving the country temporarily. *1984* ZANU-PF party congress agreed to create a one-party state in future. *1985* Relations between Mugabe and Nkomo improved. Troops sent to Matabeleland to suppress rumored insurrection; 5,000 civilians killed. *1987* White-roll seats in the assembly were abolished. President Banana retired; Mugabe combined posts of head of state and prime minister as executive president. *1988* Nkomo returned to the cabinet and was appointed vice president. *1989* Opposition party, the Zimbabwe Unity Movement, formed by Edgar Tekere; draft constitution drawn up, renouncing Marxism–Leninism; ZANU and ZAPU formally merged. *1990* ZANU–PF reelected. State of emergency ended. Opposition to creation of one-party state. *1992* United Front formed to oppose ZANU–PF. March: Mugabe declared dire effects of drought and famine a national disaster. *1993* Moderate, business-orientated Forum Party formed.

zinc hard, brittle, bluish white, metallic element, symbol Zn, atomic number 30, atomic weight 65.37. The principal ore is sphalerite or zinc blende (zinc sulfide, ZnS). Zinc is little affected by air or moisture at ordinary temperatures; its chief uses are in alloys such as brass and in coating metals (for example, galvanized iron). Its compounds include zinc oxide, used in ointments (as an astringent) and cosmetics, paints, glass, and printing ink.

zinnia any annual plant of the genus *Zinnia*, family Compositae, native to Mexico and South America, notably the cultivated hybrids of *Z. elegans*, with brightly colored, daisylike flowers.

Zion Jebusite (Amorites of Canaan) stronghold in Jerusalem captured by King David, and the hill on which he built the Temple, symbol of Jerusalem and of Jewish national life.

Zionism political movement advocating the reestablishment of a Jewish homeland in Palestine, the "promised land" of the Bible, with its capital Jerusalem, the "city of Zion".

zipper fastening device used in clothing, invented in the US by Whitcomb Judson 1891, originally for doing up shoes. It has two sets of interlocking teeth,

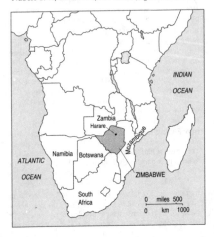

INDIAN

OCEAN

Zambia
Harare

Mozambique

ATLANTIC

Namibia   Botswana

OCEAN   ZIMBABWE

South
Africa

0   miles 500
0   km   1000

meshed by means of a slide that moves up and down. It did not become widely used in the clothing industry till the 1930s.

zirconium lustrous, grayish-white, strong, ductile, metallic element, symbol Zr, atomic number 40, atomic weight 91.22. It occurs in nature as the mineral zircon (zirconium silicate), from which it is obtained commercially. It is used in some ceramics, alloys for wire and filaments, steel manufacture, and nuclear reactors, where its low neutron absorption is advantageous.

zither a member of a family of musical instruments that have strings attached across a flat sound-board and are plucked, bowed, or struck with a beater, to play a note. Examples are the dulcimer, the Japanese koto, and a 45-stringed folk instrument from Austria and Germany.

Zi Xi or *Tz'u-hsi* c. 1834–1908. Empress dowager of China. She was presented as a concubine to the emperor Xianfeng. On his death 1861 she became regent for her young son Tongzhi (1856–1875) until 1873 and, after his death, for her nephew Guangxu (1871–1908) until 1889. A ruthless conservative, she blocked the Hundred Days' Reform launched in 1898 and assumed power again, having Guangxu imprisoned. Her policies helped deny China a peaceful transition to political and economic reform.

zodiac zone of the heavens containing the paths of the Sun, Moon, and planets. When this was devised by the ancient Greeks, only five planets were known, making the zodiac about 16° wide. In astrology, the zodiac is divided into 12 signs, each 30° in extent: Aries, Taurus, Gemini, Cancer, Leo, Virgo, Libra, Scorpio, Sagittarius, Capricorn, Aquarius, and Pisces. These do not cover the same areas of sky as the astronomical constellations.

Zoë c. 978–1050. Byzantine empress who ruled from 1028 until 1050. She gained the title by marriage to the heir apparent Romanus III Argyrus, but was reputed to have poisoned him (1034) in order to marry her lover Michael. He died 1041 and Zoë and her sister Theodora were proclaimed joint empresses. Rivalry led to Zoë marrying Constantine IX Monomachus with whom she reigned until her death.

Zola Émile Edouard Charles Antoine 1840–1902. French novelist and social reformer. With *La Fortune des Rougon/The Fortune of the Rougons* 1867 he began a series of some 20 naturalistic novels, portraying the fortunes of a French family under the Second Empire. They include *Le Venter de Paris/The Underbelly of Paris* 1873, *Nana* 1880, and *La Débâcle/The Debacle* 1892. In 1898 he published *J'accuse/I Accuse*, a pamphlet indicting the persecutors of ◊Dreyfus, for which he was prosecuted for libel but later pardoned.

zone standard time or *standard time* the time in any of the 24 time zones, each an hour apart, into which the Earth is divided. The respective times depend on their distances, east or west of Greenwich, England. In North America the eight zones (Atlantic, Eastern, Central, Mountain, Pacific, Alaska, Hawaii-Aleutian, and Samoa) use the mean solar times of meridians 15° apart, starting with 60° longitude. (See also ◊time.)

zoo (abbreviation for *zoological gardens*) place where animals are kept in captivity. Originally created purely for visitor entertainment and education, zoos have become major centers for the breeding of endangered species of animals; a 1984 report identified 2,000 vertebrate species in need of such maintenance. The Arabian oryx has already been preserved in this way; it was captured 1962, bred in captivity, and released again in the desert 1972, where it has flourished.

zoology branch of biology concerned with the study of animals. It includes description of present-day animals, the study of evolution of animal forms, anatomy, physiology, embryology, behavior, and geographical distribution.

Zoroastrianism pre-Islamic Persian religion founded by the Persian prophet Zoroaster in the 6th century BC, and still practiced by the Parsees in India. The ◊*Zend-Avesta* are the sacred scriptures of the faith. The theology is dualistic, **Ahura Mazda** or *Ormuzd* (the good God) being perpetually in conflict with **Ahriman** (the evil God), but the former is assured of eventual victory. There are approximately 100,000 (1991) Zoroastrians worldwide; membership is restricted to those with both parents belonging to the faith.

Z particle in physics, an ◊elementary particle, one of the weakons responsible for carrying the weak nuclear force.

zucchini small variety of marrow, *Cucurbita pepo*, of the Cucurbitaceae family. It is cultivated as a vegetable and harvested before it is fully mature, at 6–8 in/15–20 cm. In the UK it is known as a courgette.

Zuider Zee former sea inlet in the NW Netherlands, closed off from the North Sea by a 20-mi/32-km dyke 1932; much of it has been reclaimed as land. The remaining lake is called the IJsselmeer.

Zulu member of a group of southern African peoples mainly from Natal, South Africa. Their present homeland, KwaZulu, represents the nucleus of the once extensive and militaristic Zulu kingdom. Today many Zulus work in the industrial centers around Johannesburg and Durban. The Zulu language, closely related to Xhosa, belongs to the Bantu branch of the Niger-Congo family. Many Zulus, as supporters of the political organization ◊Inkatha, violently opposed the nonracial constitution adopted in South Africa 1993, threatening to boycott the 1994 elections unless their demands for greater autonomy were met.

Zürich financial center and industrial city (machinery, electrical goods, textiles) on Lake Zürich; population (1990) 341,300. Situated at the foot of the Alps, it is the capital of Zürich canton and the largest city in Switzerland.

Zwingli Ulrich 1484–1531. Swiss Protestant, born in St Gallen. He was ordained a Roman Catholic priest 1506, but by 1519 was a Reformer and led the Reformation in Switzerland with his insistence on the sole authority of the Scriptures. He was killed in a skirmish at Kappel during a war against the cantons that had not accepted the Reformation.

APPENDICES

Conversion tables

to convert from imperial to metric	multiply by	multiply by	to convert from metric to imperial
length			
inches	25.4	0.03937	millimeters
feet	0.3048	3.2808	meters
yards	0.9144	1.0936	meters
furlongs	0.201	4.971	kilometers
miles	1.6093	0.6214	kilometers
area			
square inches	6.4516	0.1550	square centimeters
square feet	0.0929	10.7639	square meters
square yards	0.8361	1.1960	square meters
square miles	2.5900	0.3861	square kilometers
acres	4046.86	0.000247	square meters
acres	0.4047	2.47105	hectares
hectares	0.001	1.000	square kilometers
volume, capacity			
cubic inches	16.3871	0.0610	cubic centimeters
cubic feet	0.02832	35.3134	cubic meters
cubic yards	0.7646	1.3079	cubic meters
fluid ounces	28.4131	0.0352	milliliters
pints	0.5683	1.760	liters
quarts	1.1365	0.88	liters
imperial gallons	4.54609	0.21997	liters
US gallons	3.7854	0.2642	liters
mass/weight			
ounces	28.3495	0.03527	grams
pounds	0.4536	2.2046	kilograms
stone (14 lb)	6.3503	0.1575	kilograms
tons (imperial)	1016.05	0.00098	kilograms
tons (US)	907.2	0.001	kilograms
tons (imperial)	0.9842	1.0161	metric tons
tons (US)	0.9072	1.102	metric tons
speed			
miles per hour	1.6093	0.6214	kilometers per hour
feet per second	0.3048	3.2808	meters per second
force			
pound force	4.448	0.2248	newton
kilogram force	9.8096	0.1019	newton
pressure			
pounds per square inch	6.89476	0.1450	kilopascals
tons per square inch	15.4443	0.0647	megapascals
atmospheres	101.325	0.00000986	newtons per square meter
atmospheres	14.69	0.068	pounds per square inch
energy			
calorie	4.186	0.238	joule
kilowatt hour	3.600000	0.000000277	joule
power			
horsepower	0.7457	1.341	kilowatts
fuel consumption			
miles per gallon	0.3540	2.825	kilometers per liter
miles per US gallon	0.4251	2.3521	kilometers per liter
gallons per mile	2.8248	0.3540	liters per kilometer
US gallons per mile	2.3521	0.4251	liters per kilometer

Temperature scales

The freezing point and boiling point of water are 0°C and 100°C on the Celsius (centigrade) scale (100 degrees), and 32°F and 212°F on the Fahrenheit scale (180 degrees). So Celsius and Fahrenheit temperatures can be converted as follows:

$$C = (F - 32) \times {}^{100}\!/_{180}$$
$$F = (C \times {}^{180}\!/_{100}) + 32$$

Is there a temperature that is the same on both scales? The answer is yes: −40° (F and C).

Table of equivalent temperatures

°F	°C		°F	°C		°F	°C
212.0	100		140.0	60		68.0	20
210.2	99		138.2	59		66.2	19
208.4	98		136.4	58		64.4	18
206.6	97		134.6	57		62.6	17
204.8	96		132.8	56		60.8	16
203.0	95		131.0	55		59.0	15
201.2	94		129.2	54		57.2	14
199.4	93		127.4	53		55.4	13
197.6	92		125.6	52		53.6	12
195.8	91		123.8	51		51.8	11
194.0	90		122.0	50		50.0	10
192.2	89		120.2	49		48.2	9
190.4	88		118.4	48		46.4	8
188.6	87		116.6	47		44.6	7
186.8	86		114.8	46		42.8	6
185.0	85		113.0	45		41.0	5
183.2	84		111.2	44		39.2	4
181.4	83		109.4	43		37.4	3
179.6	82		107.6	42		35.6	2
177.8	81		105.8	41		33.8	1
176.0	80		104.0	40		32.0	0
174.2	79		102.2	39		30.2	−1
172.4	78		100.4	38		28.4	−2
170.6	77		98.6	37		26.6	−3
168.8	76		96.8	36		24.8	−4
167.0	75		95.0	35		23.0	−5
165.2	74		93.2	34		21.2	−6
163.4	73		91.4	33		19.4	−7
161.6	72		89.6	32		17.6	−8
159.8	71		87.8	31		15.8	−9
158.0	70		86.0	30		14.0	−10
156.2	69		84.2	29		12.2	−11
154.4	68		82.4	28		10.4	−12
152.6	67		80.6	27		8.6	−13
150.8	66		78.8	26		6.8	−14
149.0	65		77.0	25		5.0	−15
147.2	64		75.2	24		3.2	−16
145.4	63		73.4	23		1.4	−17
143.6	62		71.6	22		−0.4	−18
141.8	61		69.8	21		−2.2	−19

Money: world currencies

country	currency	country	currency
Afghanistan	afghâni	French Guiana	French franc
Albania	lek	French Pacific Islands	CFP franc
Algeria	dinar	Gabon	CFA franc
Andorra	French franc	Gambia	dalasi
	Spanish peseta	Germany	Deutschmark
Angola	kwanza	Ghana	cedi
Antigua	East Caribbean dollar	Gibraltar	Gibraltar pound
Argentina	peso	Greece	drachma
Aruba	florin	Greenland	Danish kroner
Australia	Australian dollar	Grenada	East Caribbean dollar
Austria	schilling	Guadaloupe	local franc
Azores	port escudo	Guam	US dollar
Bahamas	Bahamian dollar	Guatemala	quetzal
Bahrain	dinar	Guinea	Guinea franc
Balearic Islands	Spanish peseta	Guinea-Bissau	Guinea-Bissau peso
Bangladesh	taka	Guyana	Guyanese dollar
Barbados	Barbados dollar	Haiti	goude
Belgium	Belgian franc	Honduras	lempira
Belize	Belize dollar	Hong Kong	Hong Kong dollar
Benin	CFA franc	Hungary	forint
Bermuda	Bermudian dollar	Iceland	Icelandic krona
Bhutan	ngultrum	India	Indian rupee
Bolivia	boliviano	Indonesia	rupiah
Botswana	pula	Iran	Iranian rial
Bouvet Island	Norwegian krone	Iraq	Iraqi dinar
Brazil	real	Irish Republic	punt
Brunei	Brunei dollar	Israel	shekel
Bulgaria	lev	Italy	Italian lira
Burkina Faso	CFA franc	Jamaica	Jamaican dollar
Burundi	Burundi franc	Japan	yen
Cambodia	riel	Jordan	Jordanian dinar
Cameroon	CFA franc	Kenya	Kenyan shilling
Canada	Canadian dollar	Kiribati	Australian dollar
Canary Islands	Spanish peseta	Korea, North	won
Cape Verde	Cape Verde escudo	Korea, South	won
Cayman Islands	Cayman Island dollar	Kuwait	Kuwaiti dinar
Central African Republic	CFA franc	Laos	new kip
Chad	CFA franc	Latvia	latis
Chile	Chilean peso	Lebanon	Lebanese pound
China	Renminbi yuan	Lesotho	maluti
Colombia	Colombian peso	Liberia	Liberian dollar
Commonwealth		Libya	Libyan dinar
of Ind States	ruble	Liechtenstein	Swiss franc
Comoros	CFA franc	Lithuania	Lita
Congo	CFA franc	Luxembourg	Luxembourg franc
Costa Rica	colón	Macao	pataca
Cote d'Ivoire	CFA franc	Madagascar	Malagasy franc
Cuba	Cuban peso	Madeira	Portuguese escudo
Cyprus	Cyprus pound	Malawi	kwacha
Czech Republic	koruna	Malaysia	ringgit
Denmark	Danish kroner	Maldive Islands	rufiya
Djibouti Republic	Djibouti franc	Mali Republic	CFA franc
Dominica	East Caribbean dollar	Malta	Maltese lira
Dominican Republic	Dominican peso	Martinique	local franc
Ecuador	sucre	Mauritania	ouguiya
Egypt	Egyptian pound	Mauritius	Mauritian rupee
El Salvador	colón	Mexico	Mexican peso
Equatorial Guinea	CFA franc	Monaco	French franc
Estonia	kroon	Mongolia	tugrik
Ethiopia	birr	Montserrat	East Caribbean dollar
Falkland Islands	Falkland pound	Morocco	dirham
Faroe Islands	Danish kroner	Mozambique	metical
Fiji Islands	Fiji dollar	Myanmar	kyat
Finland	markka	Namibia	South African Rand
France	French franc	Nauru Island	Australian dollar

country	currency	country	currency
Nepal	Nepalese rupee	Somali Republic	Somali shilling
Netherlands	guilder	South Africa	rand(c)
Netherlands Antilles	Antillian guilder	Spain	peseta
New Zealand	New Zealand dollar	Sri Lanka	Sri Lankan rupee
Nicaragua	gold cordoba	Sudan Republic	Sudanese dinar
Niger Republic	CFA franc	Surinam	Surinam guilder
Nigeria	naira	Swaziland	lilangeni
Norway	Norwegian krone	Sweden	krona
Oman	Omani rial	Switzerland	Swiss franc
Pakistan	Pakistani rupee	Syria	Syrian pound
Panama	balboa	Taiwan	New Taiwan dollar
Papua New Guinea	kina	Tanzania	Tanzanian shilling
Paraguay	guarani	Thailand	baht
Peru	new sol	Togo Republic	CFA franc
Philippines	peso	Tonga Islands	pa'anga
Pitcairn Islands	New Zealand dollar	Trinidad and Tobago	Trinidad and Tobago dollar
Poland	zloty	Tunisia	Tunisian dinar
Portugal	escudo	Turkey	Turkish lira
Puerto Rico	US dollar	Turks and Caicos Islands	US dollar
Qatar	riyal	Tuvalu	Australian dollar
Réunion Islands	French franc	Uganda	new shilling
Romania	leu	Ukraine	karbovanets
Rwanda	Rwandan franc	United Arab Emirates	UAE dirham
St Christopher	East Caribbean dollar	United Kingdom	pound sterling
St Helena	pound sterling	United States	US dollar
St Lucia	East Caribbean dollar	Uruguay	nuevo peso
St Pierre	French franc	Vanuatu	vatu
St Vincent	East Caribbean dollar	Vatican City State	lira
San Marino	Italian lira	Venezuela	bolivar
São Tomé e Principe	dobra	Vietnam	dong
Saudi Arabia	riyal	Virgin Islands, British	US dollar
Senegal	CFA franc	Virgin Islands, US	US dollar
Seychelles	Seychelles rupee	Western Samoa	taia
Sierra Leone	leone	Yemen, Republic of	rial
Singapore	Singapore dollar	Yugoslavia	New Yugoslav dinar
Slovak Republic	koruna	Zaire Republic	zaire
Slovenia	tolar	Zambia	kwacha
Solomon Islands	Solomon Island dollar	Zimbabwe	Zimbabwe dollar

SI units

Base units

quantity	unit name	unit symbol	definition
length	meter	m	length of the path traveled by light in vacuum during a time interval of 1/299,792,458 of a second
mass	kilogram	kg	mass of the international prototype of the kilogram, in the Bureau International des Poids et Mésures at Sèvres, near Paris, France
time	second	s	duration of 9,129,631,770 periods of the radiation corresponding to the transition between the two hyperfine levels of the ground state of the cesium-133 atom
electric current	ampere	A	that constant current which, if maintained in two straight parallel conductors of negligible circular cross-section, and placed 1 meter apart in vacuum, would produce between these conductors a force equal to 2×10^{-7} newton per meter of length
thermodynamic temperature	kelvin	K	the fraction 1/273.15 of the thermodynamic temperature of the triple point of water, where water, ice and water vapor are in equilibrium
luminous intensity	candela	cd	the luminous intensity, in a given direction, of a source that emits monochromatic radiation of frequency 540×10^{12} Hz and has a radiant intensity in that direction of 1/683 watts per steradian
amount of substance	mole	mol	the amount of substance of a system which contains as many elementary entities as there are atoms in 0.012 kilograms of carbon–12

supplementary and derived units

quantity	unit name	unit symbol
plane angle	radian	rad
solid angle	steradian	sr
area	square meter	m^2
volume	cubic meter	m^3
velocity, speed	meter per second	$m\ s^{-1}$
angular velocity	radian per second	$rad\ s^{-1}$
acceleration	meter per second squared	$m\ s^{-2}$
angular acceleration	radian per second squared	$rad\ s^{-2}$
frequency	hertz (= cycle per second)	Hz
rotational frequency	reciprocal second	s^{-1}
density, mass density	kilogram per cubic meter	$kg\ m^3$
momentum	kilogram meter per second	$kg\ m\ s^{-1}$
angular momentum	kilogram meter squared per second	$kg\ m^2\ s^{-1}$
moment of inertia	kilogram meter squared	$kg\ m^2$
force	newton	$N\ (kg\ m\ s^{-2})$
moment of force (torque)	newton meter	N m
pressure, stress	pascal	$Pa\ (N\ m^{-2})$
viscosity (kinematic)	meter squared per second	$m^2\ s^{-1}$
viscosity (dynamic)	pascal second	$Pa\ s\ (N\ s\ m^{-2})$
surface tension	newton per meter	$N\ m^{-1}$
energy, work, quantity of heat	joule	J (N m)
power, radiant flux	watt	$W\ (J\ s^{-1})$
temperature	degree Celsius	°C
thermal coefficient of linear expansion	reciprocal kelvin	K^{-1}
heat flux density, irradiance	watt per square meter	$W\ m^{-2}$
thermal conductivity	watt per meter Kelvin	$W\ m^{-1}\ K^{-1}$
coefficient of heat transfer	watt per square meter kelvin	$W\ m^{-2}\ K^{-1}$
heat capacity	joule per kelvin	$J\ K^{-1}$
specific heat capacity	joule per kilogram kelvin	$J\ kg^{-1}\ K^{-1}$
entropy	joule per kelvin	$J\ K^{-1}$
specific entropy	joule per kilogram kelvin	$J\ kg^{-1}\ K^{-1}$
specific energy, specific latent heat	joule per kilogram	$J\ kg^{-1}$
quantity of electricity, electric charge	coulomb	(A s)
electric potential, potential difference, electromotive force	volt	$V\ (W\ A^{-1})$
electric field strength	volt per meter	$V\ m^{-1}$
electric resistance	ohm	$\Omega\ (V\ A^{-1})$
electric conductance	siemens	$S\ (A\ V^{-1})$
electric capacitance	farad	$F\ (A\ s\ V^{-1})$

SI units (*continued*)

Supplementary and derived units

quantity	unit name	unit symbol
magnetic flux	weber	Wb (V s)
inductance	henry	H (V s A^{-1})
magnetic flux density	tesla	T (Wb m^{-2})
magnetic field strength	ampere per meter	A m^{-1}
luminous flux	lumen	lm (cd sr)
luminance	candela per square meter	(cd m^{-2})
illuminance	lux	lx (lm m^{-2})
radiation activity	becquerel	Bq (s^{-1})
radiation absorbed dose	gray	Gy (J kg^{-1})

SI multiplying prefixes

multiple	prefix	symbol	example
1000000000000000000 (10^{18})	exa-	E	Eg (exagram)
1000000000000000 (10^{15})	peta-	P	PJ (petajoule)
1000000000000 (10^{12})	tera-	T	TV (teravolt)
1000000000 (10^{9})	giga-	G	GW (gigawatt)
1000000 (10^{6})	mega-	M	MHz (megahertz)
1000 (10^{3})	kilo-	k	kg (kilogram)
100 (10^{2})	hecto-	h	hm (hectometer)
10	deca-	da-	daN (decanewton)
0.1 (10^{-1})	deci-	d	dC (decicoulomb)
0.01 (10^{-2})	centi-	c	cm (centimeter)
0.001 (10^{-3})	milli-	m	mA (milliampere)
0.000001 (10^{-6})	micro-	μ	μF (microfarad)
0.000000001 (10^{-9})	nano-	n	nm (nanometer)
0.000000000001 (10^{-12})	pico-	p	ps (picosecond)
0.000000000000001 (10^{-15})	femto-	f	frad (femtoradian)
0.000000000000000001 (10^{-18})	atto-	a	aT (attotesla)

Large numbers

Nomenclature for large numbers varies in different countries. In the US and France, numbers advance by increments of a thousand:

billion	1,000,000,000	1×10^9
trillion	1,000,000,000,000	1×10^{12}
quadrillion	1,000,000,000,000,000	1×10^{15}

However, in the UK and Germany numbers have traditionally advanced by increments of a million:

million	1,000,000	1×10^6
billion	1,000,000,000,000	1×10^{12}
trillion	1,000,000,000,000,000,000	1×10^{18}
quadrillion	1,000,000,000,000,000,000,000,000	1×10^{24}

This has a certain amount of logic on its side, particularly for classical scholars:

billion = million^2 (bi-)
trillion = million^3 (tri-)
quadrillion = million^4 (quadr-)

US usage is starting to prevail in the UK as well, particularly as it is now universally used by economists and statisticians. The higher numbers, in both styles, are as follows:

number	US	UK
quintillion	1×10^{18}	1×10^{30}
sextillion	1×10^{21}	1×10^{36}
septillion	1×10^{24}	1×10^{42}
octillion	1×10^{27}	1×10^{48}
nonillion	1×10^{30}	1×10^{54}
decillion	1×10^{33}	1×10^{60}
vigintillion	1×10^{63}	1×10^{120}
centillion	1×10^{303}	1×10^{600}

Decibels

Decibels (dB) measure the relative intensity or loudness of sound. A difference of 10 dB between two sounds means that the intensity of one sound is ten times louder than that of the other. Because of the way the ear responds to such differences in sound intensity, this tenfold difference results in one sound being perceived to be twice as loud as the other. So, for example, a 20 dB sound is twice as loud as a 10 dB sound; 30 dB is four times louder; 40 dB is eight times louder; and so on. One decibel is the smallest difference that the ear can detect between sounds. Sounds of 120 dB and upward cause physical pain.

decibels	typical sound
0	threshold of hearing
10	rustle of leaves in gentle breeze
10	quiet whisper
20	average whisper
20–50	quiet conversation
30	house in country (average situation)
40	house in city (average situation)
40–45	hotel; theater (between performances)
50–65	loud conversation
50–55	small retail establishment
55	commercial garage
55–60	medium-size office; residential street
60–65	restaurant; factory or warehouse office
65	large office
65–70	traffic on busy street
65–90	train
75–80	factory (light/medium work)
95–100	riveter
90	heavy traffic
90–100	thunder
110–140	jet aircraft on take-off
130	threshold of pain
140–190	space rocket at take-off

Roman numerals

The basic Roman numerals are:

I	1
V	5
X	10
L	50
C	100
D	500
M	1,000

Other numbers are formed from these by adding or subtracting. The value of a symbol following another of the same or greater value is added: II = 2; III = 3; CC = 200. The value of a symbol preceding one of greater value is subtracted: IX = 9; CM = 900. The value of a symbol standing between two of greater value is subtracted from that of the second, the remainder being added to the first: XIX = 19.

The first twelve numbers are best known from the clock face:

I	1	II	2	III	3	IV	4
V	5	VI	6	VII	7	VIII	8
IX	9	X	10	XI	11	XII	12

Roman numerals are usually written in capital letters, but may be written in lower case, as in numbering subdivisions (Act I scene iv), or the preliminary pages of a book.

A bar over a symbol indicates multiplication by 1,000:
L̄ 50,000

Time zones and relative times

The surface of the Earth is divided into 24 time zones. Each zone represents 15° of longitude or 1 hour of time. Countries to the east of London, England, and the Greenwich meridian are ahead of Greenwich Mean Time (GMT) and countries to the west are behind. The time indicated in the table below is fixed by law and is called standard time. Use of daylight saving time varies widely. At 12.00 noon, Greenwich Mean Time, the standard time elsewhere around the world is as follows:

Abu Dhabi	16.00	Dublin	12.00	Oslo	13.00
Accra	12.00	Florence	13.00	Ottawa	07.00
Addis Ababa	15.00	Frankfurt	13.00	Panama City	07.00
Adelaide	21.30	Gdansk	13.00	Paris	13.00
Alexandria	14.00	Geneva	13.00	Perth	20.00
Algiers	13.00	Gibraltar	13.00	Port Said	14.00
Amman	14.00	Hague, The	13.00	Prague	13.00
Amsterdam	13.00	Harare	14.00	Quebec	07.00
Anchorage	02.00	Havana	07.00	Rangoon	18.30
Ankara	14.00	Helsinki	14.00	Rawalpindi	17.00
Athens	14.00	Ho Chi Minh City	19.00	Reykjavik	12.00
Auckland	24.00	Hobart	22.00	Rio de Janeiro	09.00
Baghdad	15.00	Hong Kong	20.00	Riyadh	15.00
Bahrain	15.00	Istanbul	14.00	Rome	13.00
Bangkok	19.00	Jakarta	19.00	San Francisco	04.00
Barcelona	13.00	Jerusalem	14.00	Santiago	08.00
Beijing	20.00	Johannesburg	14.00	Seoul	21.00
Beirut	14.00	Karachi	17.00	Shanghai	20.00
Belgrade	13.00	Kiev	15.00	Singapore	20.00
Berlin	13.00	Kuala Lumpur	20.00	Sofia	14.00
Berne	13.00	Kuwait	15.00	St Petersburg	15.00
Bogota	07.00	Kyoto	21.00	Stockholm	13.00
Bombay	17.30	Lagos	13.00	Sydney	22.00
Bonn	13.00	Le Havre	13.00	Taipei	20.00
Brazzaville	13.00	Lima	07.00	Tashkent	18.00
Brisbane	22.00	Lisbon	12.00	Tehran	15.30
Brussels	13.00	Los Angeles	04.00	Tel Aviv	14.00
Bucharest	14.00	Luanda	13.00	Tenerife	12.00
Budapest	13.00	Luxembourg	13.00	Tokyo	21.00
Buenos Aires	09.00	Lyon	13.00	Toronto	07.00
Cairo	14.00	Madras	17.30	Tripoli	13.00
Calcutta	17.30	Madrid	13.00	Tunis	13.00
Canberra	22.00	Manila	20.00	Valparaiso	08.00
Cape Town	14.00	Marseille	13.00	Vancouver	04.00
Caracas	08.00	Mecca	15.00	Vatican City	13.00
Casablanca	12.00	Melbourne	22.00	Venice	13.00
Chicago	06.00	Mexico City	06.00	Vienna	13.00
Cologne	13.00	Milan	13.00	Vladivostok	22.00
Colombo	17.30	Minsk	15.00	Volgograd	16.00
Copenhagen	13.00	Monrovia	11.00	Warsaw	13.00
Dacca	18.00	Montevideo	09.00	Washington	07.00
Damascus	14.00	Montreal	07.00	Wellington	24.00
Dar es Salaam	15.00	Moscow	15.00	Winnipeg	06.00
Darwin	21.30	Munich	13.00	Yokohama	21.00
Delhi	17.30	Nairobi	15.00	Zagreb	13.00
Denver	05.00	New Orleans	06.00	Zurich	13.00
Djakarta	20.00	New York	07.00		
Dubai	16.00	Nicosia	14.00		

Calendars

The calendar is the division of the year into months, weeks and days, and the method of ordering the years. All early calendars except the ancient Egyptian were lunar. The word "calendar" comes from the Latin *Kalendae* or *calendae*, the first day of the month on which, in Ancient Rome, solemn proclamation was made of the appearance of the new moon. The Western or Gregorian calendar derives from the Julian calendar instituted by Julius Caesar 46 BC. From year one, an assumed date of the birth of Jesus, dates are calculated backward (BC "before Christ" or BCE "before common era" and forward (AD Latin *anno Domini* "in the year of the Lord" or CE "common era"). The lunar month (period between one new moon and the next) naturally averages 29.5 days, but the Western calendar uses for convenience a calendar month with a complete number of days, 30 or 31 (Feb has 28). For adjustments, since there are slightly fewer than six extra hours a year left over, they are added to Feb as a 29th day every fourth year (leap year), century years being excepted unless they are divisible by 400. For example, 1896 was a leap year; 1900 was not, but 2000 will be. The next leap year is 1996.

The Gregorian calendar

The Julian calendar was adjusted by Pope Gregory XIII 1582, who eliminated the accumulated error caused by the faulty calculation of the length of a year and avoided its recurrence by restricting century leap years to those divisible by 400. Other states only gradually changed from Old Style to New Style; Britain and its colonies adopted the Gregorian calendar 1752, when the error amounted to 11 days, and Sept 3 1752 became Sept 14 (at the same time the beginning of the year was put back from March 25 to Jan 1). Russia did not adopt it until the October Revolution of 1917, so that the event (then Oct 25) is currently celebrated Nov 7.

Months

The month names in most English and European languages were probably derived as follows:

January	Janus, Roman god
February	Februar, Roman festival of purification
March	Mars, Roman god
April	Latin *aperire*, "to open"
May	Maia, Roman goddess
June	Juno, Roman goddess
July	Julius Caesar, Roman general
August	Augustus, Roman emperor
September	Latin *septem*, "seven"
October	Latin *octo*, "eight"
November	Latin *novem*, "nine"
December	Latin *decem*, "ten"

September, October, November, December were originally the seventh, eighth, ninth and tenth months of the Roman year.

Days of the week

The names of the days are derived as follows:

English	Latin	Saxon
Sunday	Dies Solis	Sun's Day
Monday	Dies Lunae	Moon's Day
Tuesday	Dies Martis	Tiu's Day
Wednesday	Dies Mercurii	Woden's Day
Thursday	Dies Jovis	Thor's Day
Friday	Dies Veneris	Frigg's Day
Saturday	Dies Saturni	Saeternes' Day

Tiu: Anglo-Saxon counterpart of Nordic Tyr, son of Odin, God of War, closest to Mars (Greek Ares), son of Roman God Jupiter (Greek Zeus) *Woden:* Anglo-Saxon counterpart of Odin, Nordic dispenser of victory, closest to Mercury (Greek Hermes), Roman messenger of victory *Thor:* Nordic God of Thunder, eldest son of Odin, closest to Roman Jupiter (Greek Zeus) *Frigg* (or Freyja): wife of Odin, the Nordic Goddess of Love, equivalent to Venus (Greek Aphrodite)

Chinese calendar

The Chinese calendar is lunar, with a cycle of 60 years. Both the traditional and, from 1911, the Western calendar are in use in China.

Islamic calendar

The Islamic calendar is reckoned from the year of the *hejirah*, or flight of Mohammed from Mecca to Medina. The corresponding date in the Julian calendar is July 16 AD 622. The years are purely lunar, and consist of 12 months with alternately 29 or 30 days, plus one extra day at the end of the 12th month (Dhul-Hijjah) in leap years, which occur at stated intervals in each cycle of 30 years.

Islamic calendar 1416–1417 AH

The beginning of the month in the Islamic calendar depends on the visibility of the new moon; therefore dates may differ from those stated here

Hijrah month	1416 AH			1417 AH		
Muharram	May	31	1995	May	20	1996
Safar	June	30	1995	June	19	1996
Rabi'a I	July	28	1995	July	17	1996
Rabi'a II	July	28	1995	July	17	1996
Jumada I	Sept	25	1995	Sept	14	1996
Jumada II	Oct	25	1995	Oct	14	1996
Rajab	Nov	24	1995	Nov	13	1996
Sha'ban	Dec	23	1995	Dec	12	1996
Ramadan	Jan	21	1996	Jan	10	1997
Shawwal	Feb	20	1996	Feb	9	1997
Dhul-Qi'da	March	21	1996	March	10	1997
Dhul-Hijja	April	20	1996	April	9	1997

Important days	1416 AH			1417 AH		
Hijrah New Year	June	20	1995	June	9	1996
Ashura'	June	29	1995	June	18	1996
Birthday of the prophet Mohammed	Aug	29	1995	Aug	18	1996
Lailat-Ul-Isra'walmi'raj	Dec	29	1995	Jan	8	1996
Lailat-ul-Bara'ah	Jan	26	1996	Jan	15	1997
Ramadan	Feb	11	1996	Jan	31	1997
Lailat-ul-Qadr	March	8	1996	Feb	25	1997
Eid-ul-Fitr	March	13	1996	March	2	1997
Arafat	May	19	1996	May	8	1997
Eid-ul-Adha	May	20	1996	May	9	1997

AH—anno Hegirae, *the Muslim era*

Jewish calendar

The Jewish calendar is a complex combination of lunar and solar cycles, varied by considerations of religious observance. A year may have 12 or 13 months, each of which normally alternates between 29 and 30 days; the New Year (Rosh Hashanah) falls between Sept 5 and Oct 5. The calendar dates from the hypothetical creation of the world (taken as Oct 7 3761 BC). Some say that the Jewish calendar as used today was formalized in AD 358 by Rabbi Hillel II; others that this occurred later. A Jewish year is one of the following six types:

Minimal Common	353 days
Regular Common	354 days
Full Common	355 days
Minimal Leap	383 days
Regular Leap	384 days
Full Leap	385 days

Jewish calendar AM 5755–5756

Jewish month	AM 5755			AM 5756		
Tishri 1	Sept	6–7	1994	Sept	25–26	1995
Marcheshvan 1	Oct	5–6	1994	Oct	24	1995
Kislev 1	Nov	4	1994	Nov	23	1995
Tebet 1	Dec	3–4	1994	Dec	23	1995
Shebat 1	Jan	2	1995	Jan	22	1996
Adar** 1	Feb	1/Mar 3	1995	Feb	20	1996
Nisan 1	Apr	1	1995	Mar	21	1996
Iyar 1	May	1	1995	Apr	19	1996
Sivan 1	May	30	1995	May	19	1996
Tammuz 1	June	10	1995	June	17	1996
Ab 1	July	28	1995	July	17	1996
Elul 1	Aug	27	1995	Aug	15	1996

Jewish fasts and festivals

date in Jewish calendar		fast/festival	date 1996–1997	
Tishri	1–2	Rosh Hashanah (New Year)	Sept	14–15
Tishri	3	Fast of Gedaliah*	Sept	16
Tishri	10	Yom Kippur (Day of Atonement)	Sept	23
Tishri	15–21	Succoth (Feast of Tabernacles)	Sept	28–Oct 5
Kislev	25	Chanukah (Dedication of the Temple) begins	Dec	6–13
Tebet	10	Fast of Tebet	Dec	20
Adar**	13	Fast of Esther†	Feb	20 1997
Adar**	14	Purim	Feb	21
Adar**	15	Shushan Purim	Feb	22
Nisan	14	Taanit Behorim (Fast of the Firstborn)	April	21
Nisan	15–22	Pesach (Passover)	April	22–29
Nisan	27	Yom Ha-Shoah (Holocaust Day)	May	4
Iyar	4	Yom Ha'Zikharon (Remembrance Day)	May	11
Iyar	5	Yom Ha'Atzmaut (Independence Day)	May	12
Iyar 33rd	18	Day of Counting the Omer	May	25
Iyar	28	Yom Yerushalayim (Jerusalem Day)	June	4
Sivan	6–7	Shavuot (Festival of Weeks)	May	11–12
Tammuz	17	Fast of Tammuz 17*	July	22
Ab	9	Fast of Ab 9*	Aug	12

*If these dates fall on the sabbath the fast is kept on the following day.
**Ve-Adar in leap years.
†This fast is observed on Adar 11 (or Ve-Adar 11 in leap years) if Adar 13 falls on a sabbath.
AM anno mundi, in the year of the world

Christian festivals and holy days

| Jan | 1 | The naming of Jesus. The Circumcision of Christ. The Solemnity of Mary Mother of God | July | 25 | St James the Apostle |
| Aug | 6 | | | | The Transfiguration of our Lord |

Jan	1	The naming of Jesus. The Circumcision of Christ. The Solemnity of Mary Mother of God	July	25	St James the Apostle
			Aug	6	The Transfiguration of our Lord
			Aug	24	St Bartholomew the Apostle
Jan	6	Epiphany	Sept	1	New Year (Eastern Orthodox Church)
Jan	25	The Conversion of St Paul	Sept	8	The Nativity of the Blessed Virgin Mary
Feb	2	The Presentation of Christ in the Temple	Sept	14	The Exaltation of the Holy Cross
			Sept	21	St Matthew the Apostle
March	19	St Joseph of Nazareth, Husband of the Blessed Virgin Mary	Sept	29	St Michael and All Angels (Michaelmas)
			Oct	18	St Luke the Evangelist
March	25	The Annunciation of Our Lord to the Blessed Virgin Mary	Oct	28	St Simon and St Jude, Apostles
			Nov	1	All Saints
April	25	St Mark the Evangelist	Nov	21	Presentation of the Blessed Virgin Mary in the Temple
May	1	St Philip and St James, Apostles			
May	14	St Matthias the Apostle	Nov	30	St Andrew the Apostle
May	31	The Visitation of the Blessed Virgin Mary	Dec	8	The Immaculate Conception of the Blessed Virgin Mary
June	11	St Barnabas the Apostle	Dec	25	Christmas
June	24	The Birth of St John the Baptist	Dec	26	St Stephen the first Martyr
June	29	St Peter the Apostle	Dec	27	St John the Evangelist
July	3	St Thomas the Apostle	Dec	28	The Holy Innocents
July	22	St Mary Magdalen			

Movable Christian feasts 1994–2025

	Ash Wednesday	Easter Day	Ascension Day	Pentecost (Whit Sunday)	Advent Sunday
1994	Feb 16	Apr 3	May 12	May 22	Nov 27
1995	Mar 1	Apr 16	May 25	Jun 4	Dec 3
1996	Feb 21	Apr 7	May 16	May 26	Dec 1
1997	Feb 12	Mar 30	May 8	May 18	Nov 30
1998	Feb 25	Apr 12	May 21	May 31	Nov 29
1999	Feb 17	Apr 4	May 13	May 23	Nov 28
2000	Mar 8	Apr 23	Jun 1	Jun 11	Dec 3
2001	Feb 28	Apr 15	May 24	Jun 3	Dec 2
2002	Feb 13	Mar 31	May 9	May 19	Dec 1
2003	Mar 5	Apr 20	May 29	Jun 8	Nov 30
2004	Feb 25	Apr 11	May 20	May 30	Nov 28
2005	Feb 29	Mar 7	May 5	May 15	Nov 27
2006	Mar 1	Apr 16	May 25	Jun 4	Dec 3
2007	Feb 21	Apr 8	May 17	May 27	Dec 2
2008	Feb 6	Mar 23	May 1	May 11	Nov 30
2009	Feb 25	Apr 12	May 21	May 31	Nov 29
2010	Feb 17	Apr 4	May 13	May 23	Nov 28
2011	Mar 9	Apr 24	Jun 2	Jun 12	Nov 27
2012	Feb 22	Apr 8	May 17	May 27	Dec 2
2013	Feb 13	Mar 31	May 9	May 19	Dec 1
2014	Mar 5	Apr 20	May 29	Jun 8	Nov 30
2015	Feb 18	Apr 5	May 14	May 24	Nov 29
2016	Mar 10	Mar 27	May 5	May 15	Nov 27
2017	Mar 1	Apr 16	May 25	Jun 4	Dec 3
2018	Feb 14	Apr 1	May 10	May 20	Dec 2
2019	Mar 6	Apr 21	May 30	Jun 9	Dec 1
2020	Feb 26	Apr 12	May 21	May 31	Nov 29
2021	Feb 17	Apr 4	May 13	May 23	Nov 28
2022	Mar 2	Apr 17	May 26	Jun 5	Nov 27
2023	Feb 22	Apr 9	May 18	May 28	Dec 3
2024	Feb 14	Mar 31	May 9	May 19	Dec 1
2025	Mar 5	Apr 20	May 29	Jun 8	Nov 30

Advent Sunday is the fourth Sunday before Christmas Day; Ash Wednesday is the first day of Lent, and falls in the seventh week before Easter. Holy Week is the week before Easter Day, and includes Palm Sunday, Maundy Thursday, Good Friday, and Easter Eve. Ascension Day is 40 days after Easter Day. Pentecost (Whit Sunday) is seven weeks after Easter Day. Trinity Sunday is eight weeks after Easter Day.

Hindu festivals

Jan	Makar Sankranti/Til Sankranti/Lohri, Pongal, Kumbha Mela at Prayag (every 12 years)
Jan–Feb	Vasanta Panchami/Shri Panchami/Saraswati Puja, Bhogali Bihu, Mahashivratri
Feb 20	Ramakrishna Utsav
Feb–March	Holi
March–April	Ugadi, Basora, Rama Navami, Hanuman Jayanti
April	Vaisakhi
April–May	Akshaya Tritiya, Chittrai
May–June	Ganga Dasa-hara, Nirjala Ekadashi, Snan-yatra
June–July	Ratha-yatra/Jagannatha, Ashadhi Ekadashi/Toli Ekadashi
July–Aug	Teej, Naga Panchami, Raksha Bandhan/Shravana Purnima/Salono/Rakhi Purnima
Aug–Sept	Onam, Ganesha Chaturthi, Janamashtami/Krishna Jayanti
Sept–Oct	Mahalaya/Shraddha/Pitri Paksha/Kanagat, Navaratri/Durga Puja/Dassehra, Lakshmi Puja
Oct 2	Gandhi Jayanti
Oct–Nov	Divali/Deepavali Chhath, Karttika Ekadashi/Devuthna Ekadashi/Tulsi Ekadashi, Karttika Purnima/Tripuri Purnima, Hoi, Skanda Shasti
Nov–Dec	Vaikuntha Ekadashi, Lakshmi Puja (Orissa)

Buddhist festivals

Burma

April 16–17	New Year
May–June	The Buddha's Birth, Enlightenment and Death
July	The Buddha's First Sermon. Beginning of the Rains Retreat
Oct	End of the Rains Retreat
Nov	Kathina Ceremony

China

June–August	Summer Retreat
Aug	Festival of Hungry Ghosts
Aug	Gautama Buddha's Birth
Aug	Kuan-Yin

Sri Lanka

April 13	New Year
May–June	The Buddha's Birth, Enlightenment and Death
June–July	Establishment of Buddhism in Sri Lanka
July	The Buddha's First Sermon
July–Aug	Procession of the Month of Asala
Sept	The Buddha's First Visit to Sri Lanka
Dec–Jan	Arrival of Sanghamitta

Thailand

April 13–16	New Year
May	The Buddha's Enlightenment
May–June	The Buddha's Cremation
July–Oct	Rains Retreat
Oct	End of the Rains Retreat
Nov	Kathina Ceremony
Nov	Festival of Lights
Feb	All Saints' Day

Tibet

Feb	New Year
May	The Buddha's Birth, Enlightenment and Death
June	Dzamling Chisang
June–July	The Buddha's First Sermon
Oct	The Buddha's Descent from Tushita
Nov	Death of Tsongkhapa
Jan	The Conjunction of Nine Evils and the Conjunction of Ten Virtues

Patron saints

saint	occupation	saint	occupation
Adam	gardeners	Honoratus	bakers
Albert the Great	scientists	Isidore	farmers
Alphonsus Liguori	theologians	Ivo	lawyers
Amand	brewers, hotelkeepers	James	laborers
Andrew	fishermen	Jean-Baptiste Vianney	priests
Angelico	artists	Jerome	librarians
Anne	miners	Joan of Arc	soldiers
Apollonia	dentists	John Baptist de la Salle	teachers
Augustine	theologians	John Bosco	laborers
Barbara	builders, miners	John of God	book trade, nurses, printers
Bernadino (Felter)	bankers	Joseph	carpenters
Bernadino of Siena	advertisers	Joseph (Arimathea)	gravediggers, undertakers
Camillus de Lellis	nurses	Joseph (Cupertino)	astronauts
Catherine of Alexandria	librarians, philosophers	Julian the Hospitaler	hotelkeepers
Cecilia	musicians, poets, singers	Lawrence	cooks
Christopher	motorists, sailors	Leonard	prisoners
Cosmas and Damian	barbers, chemists, doctors, surgeons	Louis	sculptors
Crispin	shoemakers	Lucy	glassworkers, writers
Crispinian	shoemakers	Luke	artists, butchers, doctors, glassworkers, sculptors, surgeons
David	poets		
Dismas	undertakers	Martha	cooks, housewives, servants, waiters
Dominic	astronomers		
Dorothy	florists	Martin of Tours	soldiers
Eligius	blacksmiths, jewelers, metalworkers	Matthew	accountants, bookkeepers, tax collectors
Erasmus	sailors	Michael	grocers, policemen
Fiacre	gardeners, taxi drivers	Our Lady of Loreto	aviators
Florian	firemen	Peter	fishermen
Francis de Sales	authors, editors, journalists	Raymond Nonnatus	midwives
Francis of Assisi	merchants	Sebastian	athletes, soldiers
Francis of Paola	sailors	Thérèse of Lisieux	florists
Gabriel	messengers, postal workers, radio workers, television workers	Thomas (Apostle)	architects, builders
		Thomas Aquinas	philosophers, scholars, students, theologians
Genesius	actors, secretaries	Thomas More	lawyers
George	soldiers	Vitus	actors, comedians, dancers
Gregory	singers	Wenceslaus	brewers
Gregory the Great	musicians, teachers	Zita	servants
Homobonus	tailors		

The Seven Wonders of the World

Ancient works of art and architecture, considered by the Greek and Roman world to be awe-inspiring in size or splendor. Usually considered to include the following:

The Pyramids of Egypt

These monumental masonry structures are located on the west bank of the Nile, over a 60 mile distance southward from Gizeh, near Cairo. They were built from 3000 to 1800 BC as royal tombs. The oldest pyramid is that of Zoser at Saqqara, built c. 2650 BC. The Great Pyramid of Cheops is a solid mass of limestone covering more than 13 acres/5 ha.

The Hanging Gardens of Babylon

These gardens are said to have been built by King Nebuchadnezzar II around 600 BC, supposedly to please one of his Persian concubines, who was pining for the mountains of her homeland. The gardens were laid out on a brick terrace about 400 ft/120 m square, and rising nearly 82 ft/25 m above the ground, watered from storage tanks on the highest terrace.

The Statue of Zeus at Olympia

This statue was made of marble, inlaid with ivory and gold. Constructed by the sculptor Phidias about 430 BC, it is said to have been 400 ft/12 m high.

The Colossus of Rhodes

This bronze statue of Apollo was erected about 280 BC by the sculptor Chares, who worked on it for 12 years. It stood at the harbor entrance of the seaport of Rhodes.

The Temple of Artemis

This temple, one of the greatest of ancient times, was erected at Ephesus about 350 BC. It was burned by the Goths in AD 262.

The Tomb of Mausolus

This marble tomb was built by Queen Artemisia for her husband Mausolus who died in 353 BC. It stood at Halicarnassus in Asia Minor (now part of southeastern Turkey). Adorned with the work of four sculptors, it stood about 135 ft/40 m high. It is the source of the term mausoleum.

The Pharos of Alexandria

This marble watchtower and lighthouse stood on the island of Pharos in the harbor of Alexandria. It was built about 270 BC, during the reign of King Ptolemy II, by the Greek architect Sostratos. Estimates of its height range from 200 to 600 ft/60 to 180 m.

Playing cards and dice chances

Poker hands

hand	number possible	odds against
royal flush	4	649,739 to 1
other straight flush	36	72,192 to 1
four of a kind	624	4,164 to 1
full house	3,744	693 to 1
flush	5,108	508 to 1
straight	10,200	254 to 1
three of a kind	54,912	46 to 1
two pairs	123,552	20 to 1
one pair	1,098,240	4 to 3
nothing	1,302,540	1 to 1
total	2,598,960	

dice (probabilities on two dice with a single toss)

total count	odds against
2	35 to 1
3	17 to 1
4	11 to 1
5	8 to 1
6	31 to 5
7	5 to 1
8	31 to 5
9	8 to 1
10	11 to 1
11	17 to 1
12	35 to 1

dice (probabilities of consecutive winning plays)

number of consecutive wins	by 7, 11 or point
1	244 in 495
2	6 in 25
3	3 in 25
4	1 in 17
5	1 in 34
6	1 in 70
7	1 in 141
8	1 in 287
9	1 in 582

bridge (odds against suit distribution in a hand)

suit distribution in a hand	odds against
4-4-3-2	4 to 1
5-4-2-2	8 to 1
6-4-2-1	20 to 1
7-4-1-1	254 to 1
8-4-1-0	2,211 to 1
13-0-0-0	158,753,389,899 to 1

Wedding anniversaries

In many Western countries, different wedding anniversaries have become associated with gifts of different materials. There is variation between countries.

anniversary	material
1st	paper
2nd	cotton
3rd	leather
4th	linen
5th	wood
6th	iron
7th	copper, wool
8th	bronze
9th	pottery, china
10th	tin, aluminum
11th	steel
12th	silk, linen
13th	lace
14th	ivory
15th	crystal
20th	china
25th	silver
30th	pearl
35th	coral
40th	ruby
45th	sapphire
50th	gold
55th	emerald
60th	diamond
70th	platinum

Birthstones

month	stone	quality
January	garnet	constancy
February	amethyst	sincerity
March	bloodstone	courage
April	diamond	innocence and lasting love
May	emerald	success and hope
June	pearl	health and purity
July	ruby	love and contentment
August	agate	married happiness
September	sapphire	wisdom
October	opal	hope
November	topaz	fidelity
December	turquoise	harmony

Signs of the zodiac

spring

Aries	The Ram	March 21– April 20
Taurus	The Bull	April 21 – May 21
Gemini	The Twins	May 22 – June 21

summer

Cancer	The Crab	June 22 – July 23
Leo	The Lion	July 24 – Aug 23
Virgo	The Virgin	Aug 24 – Sept 23

autumn

Libra	The Balance	Sept 24 – Oct 23
Scorpio	The Scorpion	Oct 24 – Nov 22
Sagittarius	The Archer	Nov 23 – Dec 21

winter

Capricorn	The Goat	Dec 22 – Jan 20
Aquarius	The Water Bearer	Jan 21 – Feb 19
Pisces	The Fishes	Feb 20 – March 20

Abbreviations

A in physics, symbol for *ampere*, a unit of electrical current.

A1 *first class* (of ships).

AA *Alcoholics Anonymous*, a voluntary self-help organization established to combat alcoholism.

AAA the *American Automobile Association*.

ABC *American Broadcasting Company*.

ab init. *ab initio* (Latin *from the beginning*).

ABM *anti ballistic missile*.

a/c *account*.

AC in Physics, *alternating current*

AC/DC Attachment to either *alternating or direct current*. Bisexual.

ACLU *American Civil Liberties Union*.

ACV *air-cushion vehicle*.

AD in the Christian calender, *Anno Domini* (Latin *in the year of the Lord*); used with dates.

ADA *Americans for Democratic Action*, an organization set up to examine legal cases involving the US Bill of Rights.

ADB *Asian Development Bank*.

ADC in electronics, *analog-to-digital converter*.

ADH *antidiuretic hormone*, part of the system maintaining a correct salt/water balance in vertebrates.

adj. in grammar, *adjective*.

ADP *adenosine diphosphate*, a raw material in the manufacture of ATP, the molecule used by all cells to drive their chemical reactions.

adv. *adverb*.

AEW *airborne early warning*, a military surveillance system.

AF *Air Force*.

AFB *Air Force Base*.

AFD *accelerated freeze drying*, a common method of food preservation.

AFL-CIO *American Federation of Labor and Congress of Industrial Organizations*.

AFT *American Federation of Teachers*.

AFV *armored fighting vehicle*.

AG *Aktiengesellschaft* (German *limited company*).

AH with reference to the Islamic calendar, *anno hegirae* (Latin *year of the flight*—of Mohammed, from Mecca to Medina).

AIDS *acquired immune deficiency syndrome*, the newest and gravest of sexually transmitted diseases or STDs.

AK postcode for *Alaska*.

a.k.a. *also known as*.

AL postcode for *Alabama*.

AL *American League*.

ALADI *Associacion Latino-Americana de Integration* or *Latin American Integration Association*, organization promoting trade in the region.

AM in physics, *amplitude modulation*, one way in which radio waves are altered for the transmission of broadcasting signals.

AMA *American Medical Association*.

a.m. or *A.M.* *antemeridiem* (Latin *before noon*).

AMF *Arab Monetary Fund*.

amp in physics, *ampere*, a unit of electrical current.

ANC *African National Congress*; South African nationalist organization.

AMVETS *American Veterans of World War II and Korea*.

ANSI *American National Standards Institution*, the body which sets official procedures, in computing and electronics for example.

ANZUS acronym for *Australia, New Zealand, and the United States* (Pacific Security Treaty), a military alliance established 1951. It was replaced 1954 by the *Southeast Asia Treaty Organization*, (SEATO).

a.p. in physics, *atmospheric pressure*.

APC *armored personnel carrier*, a battlefield vehicle.

API *Applications Program Interface*, a standard environment in which computer programs are written.

approx. *approximately*.

AR postcode for *Arkansas*.

ARC *American Red Cross*.

ARV *American Revised Version* of the Bible.

ASA In photography a numbering system for rating the speed of films, devised by the *American Standards Association*, superseded by ISO.

a.s.a.p. *as soon as possible*.

ASAT acronym for *antisatellite weapon*.

ASCAP *American Society of Composers, Authors and Publishers*.

ASCII *American Standard Code for Information Interchange*, in computing a coding system in which numbers are assigned to letters, digits and punctuation symbols.

ASEAN *Association of South East Asian Nations*, formed in 1967. The members are Indonesia, Malaysia, the Philippines, Singapore, Thailand and Brunei.

ASH *Action on Smoking and Health*.

ASL *American Sign Language*.

ASPAC *Asian and Pacific Council*.

ASPCA *American Society for Prevention of Cruelty to Animals*.

ASSR *Autonomous Soviet Socialist Republic*.

AT & T *American Telephone and Telegraph*.

AUS *Army of the United States*.

AWACS acronym for *Airborne Warning and Control System*.

AZ postcode for *Arizona*.

AWOL acronym for *absent without leave*

BA in education, *Bachelor of Arts* degree.

BAFTA *British Academy of Film and Television Arts*.

BASIC acronym for *Beginner's All-purpose Symbolic Instruction Code*, a computer language used by many small and personal computer systems.

B & B *bed and breakfast*.

BC in the Christian calendar, *before Christ*; used with dates.

BCE *before the Common Era*; used with dates (instead of BC) particularly by non-Christians, and some theologians in recognition of the multiplicity of belief worldwide.

BCG *bacillus of Calmette and Guérin*, used as a vaccine to confer active immunity to tuberculosis (TB).

bhp *brake horsepower*.

biog. *biography*.

BIS *Bank for International Settlements* based in Basel, Switzerland

BMI *Broadcast Music Incorporated*.

BMR *basal metabolic rate*, the amount of energy needed just to stay alive.

BS *Bachelor of Science* degree.

BTO *big time operator*.

Btu symbol for *British thermal unit*.

Abbreviations (continued)

BYO	*bring your own*—usually a bottle to a party.	**COIN**	acronym for *coounter insurgency,* the suppression by a state's armed forces of uprisings against the state.
c.	*circa* (Latin *about*); used with dates that are uncertain.		
c	*centum* (Latin *hundred*); *century; centigrade; Celsius.*	**COLA**	acronym for *cost-of-living adjustment.*
		Comintern	*Communist International.*
CA	postal code for *California.*	**Conrail**	or ConRail *Consolidated Rail Corporation.*
CACM	*Central American Common Market.*	**CORE**	*Congress of Racial Equality,* a nonviolent civil rights organization.
CAD	*computer-aided design,* used in architecture, electronics and engineering to test designs or give three-dimensional views.		
		CPA	*certified public accountant.*
		CPP	*current purchasing power.*
cal	symbol for *calorie.*	**CRC**	*Civil Rights Commission.*
CAM	*computer-aided manufacture.*	**CRT**	*cathode-ray tube.*
Cantab	*Cantabrigiensis* (Latin *of Cambridge*).	**CSCE**	*Conference on Security and Cooperation in Europe,* popularly known as the Helsinki Conference.
CAP	*Common Agricultural Policy.*		
CARICOM	*Caribbean Community and Common Market.*		
CB	*citizens band* (radio).	**CT**	postcode for *Connecticut.*
CBS	*Columbia Broadcasting System.*	**cu**	*cubic* (measure).
CC	*county council; cricket club.*	**cwo**	*cash with order.*
cc	symbol for *cubic centimeter, carbon copy/copies.*	**cwt**	symbol for *hundredweight,* a unit of weight equal to 100 lb (45.36 kg) in the US and 112 lb (50.8 kg) in the UK and Canada.
CCASG	*Cooperative Council for the Arab States of the Gulf.*		
		d.	*day; diameter; died.*
CCIT	*Comité Consultatif International Téléphonique et Télégraphique,* an organization that sets international communications standards.	**D**	*500* in the Roman numeral system.
		DA	*district attorney;* also *Department of Agriculture*
		dc	in music, the *da capo* (Italian *from the beginning)*
CD	*compact disk;* certificate of deposit; *Corps Diplomatique* (French *Diplomatic Corps*).	**DC**	in physics, the *direct current* (electricity); the *District of Columbia; Detective Constable.*
CD-I	*Compact Disc-Interactive*		
CD-ROM	*Compact Disc-Read-Only Memory*	**DCM**	*Distinguished Conduct Medal.*
CDT	*Central Daylight Time.*	**DD**	*Doctor of Divinity.*
CE	*Common Era; Church of England* (often *C of E*).	**DE**	postcode for *Delaware.*
		DFC	*Distinguished Flying Cross.*
CentCom	*Central Command,* a military strikeforce.	**DFM**	*Distinguished Flying Medal.*
CENTO	*Central Treaty Organization.*	**DI**	*Department of the Interior; Detective Inspector; donor insemination; drill instructor.*
CEO	*chief executive officer.*		
cf.	*confer* (Latin *compare*).		
CFC	*chlorofluorocarbon.*	**diag.**	*diagram.*
CFE	*conventional forces in Europe.*	**DJ**	*District Judge.*
CIA	*Central Intelligence Agency.*	**DJI**	*Dow Jones Index,* the New York Stock Exchange index.
CID	the UK *Criminal Investigation Department.*		
cif	*cost, insurance, and freight* or *charged in full.* Many countries value their imports on this basis,whereas exports are usually valued *fob.*	**DJIA**	*Dow Jones Industrial Average,* an index based on the prices of 30 major companies.
		DM	*Deutschmark,* the unit of currency in Germany.
CIO	*Congress of Industrial Organizations.*	**DMus**	*Doctor of Music.*
CIP	*Cataloging in Publication.*	**DNA**	*deoxyribonucleic acid.*
CIS	*Commonwealth of Independant States,* the successor body to the USSR, established in 1992.	**do.**	*ditto.*
		DOD	*Department of Defense.*
		DOE	*Department of Energy.*
CISC	*complex instruction set computer,* a microprocessor that offers a large number of instructions.	**DOS**	in computing, *disk operating system.*
		DPhil	*Doctor of Philosophy.*
		DSC	*Distinguished Service Cross.*
CITES	*Convention on International Trade in Endangered Species,* an international agreement that prohibits the trade in endangered species.	**DSM**	*Distinguished Service Medal.*
		DST	*Daylight Saving Time.*
		E	*east.*
		EC	*European Community.*
CLU	*Civil Liberties Union.*	**ECG**	*electrocardiogram.*
cm	symbol for *centimeter.*	**ECM**	*electronic counter measures,* military jargon for disrupting telecommunications.
CND	*Campaign for Nuclear Disarmament.*		
c/o	*care of.*		
co.	*company.*	**ECOWAS**	acronym for *Economic Community of West African States.*
CO	*Commanding Officer;* postcode for *Colorado.*		
COBOL	acronym for *Common Business Orientated Language;* widely used programming language.	**ECT**	*electroconvulsive therapy.*
		ECU	*European Currency Unit.*
		EDT	*Eastern daylight time.*
COD	*cash on delivery.*	**EEC**	*European Economic Community.*
COI	*Central Office of Information.*	**EFTA**	acronym for *European Free Trade Association.*

Abbreviations (continued)

EFTPOS	acronym of *electronic funds transfer at point of sale*.	**G24**	*Group of Twenty Four* (industrialized nations).
e.g.	*exempli gratia* (Latin *for the sake of example*).	**G77**	*Group of Seventy Seven* (developing countries).
emf	in physics, *electromotive force*.	**GA**	postcode for *Georgia; General of the Army*.
EMS	*European Monetary System*.	**gal**	symbol for *gallon*.
ENT	in medicine, *ear, nose, and throat*. It is usually applied to a specialist clinic or hospital department.	**GAO**	*General Accounting Office*.
		GAW	*guaranteed annual wage*.
		GATT	acronym for *General Agreement on Tariffs and Trade*.
E & O E	*errors and omissions excepted*.		
EPA	*Environmental Protection Agency*, an agency set up to control water and air quality, industrial and commercial wastes, pesticides, noise and traffic.	**GCC**	*Gulf Cooperation Council*.
		GDP	*Gross Domestic Product*.
		GDR	*German Democratic Republic* (East Germany).
EPNS	*electroplated nickel silver*.	**gen.**	in grammar, *genitive*.
ERA	*Equal Rights Amendment*, referring to sexual and other equality under the US constitution.	**ger.**	in grammar, *gerund*.
		GHQ	*general headquarters*.
ERM	*Exchange Rate Mechanism*.	**GI**	*government issue*; hence a common soldier.
ESA	*European Space Agency*.	**GmbH**	*Gesellshaft mit beschrankter Haftung* (German *limited liability company*).
est.	*estimate(d)*.		
EST	*Eastern standard time; electric shock treatment; electroshock therapy*.	**GNP**	*Gross National Product*.
		GOP	*Grand Old Party* (the Republican Party).
et al.	*et alii* (Latin *and others*); used in bibliography.	**GRP**	*glass-reinforced plastic*, a plastic material strengthened by fiberglass.
etc.	*et cetera* (Latin *and the rest*).	**GU**	postcode for *Guam*.
ETV	*educational television*.	**ha**	symbol for *hectare*.
EU	*European Union*.	**HF**	in physics, *high frequency*.
ex lib.	*ex libris* (Latin *from the library of*).	**HGV**	*heavy goods vehicle*.
°F	symbol for degrees *Fahrenheit*.	**HI**	postcode for *Hawaii*.
FAA	*Federal Aviation Agency*.	**HIV**	*human immunodeficiency virus*.
f.a.o.	*for the attention of*.	**Hon.**	*Honorable*.
FBI	*Federal Bureau of Investigation*.	**hp**	symbol for *horsepower*.
FDN	*Nicaraguan Democratic Front*.	**HQ**	*headquarters*.
fem.	in grammar, *feminine*.	**HR**	*House of Representatives*.
ff	*folios*; and *the following*; used in reference citation and bibliography.	**HRH**	*His/Her Royal Highness*.
		HRT	*hormone replacement therapy*.
fig.	*figure*.	**ht**	*height*.
fl.	*floruit* (Latin *he/she flourished*).	**HUD**	*Department of Housing and Urban Development*.
FL	postcode for *Florida*.		
FM	in physics, *frequency modulation*. Used in radio, FM is constant in amplitude and varies the frequency of the carrier wave.	**HUGO**	*Human Genome Organization*.
		h.v.	*high velocity*.
		HWM	*high water mark*.
FAO	*Food and Agriculture Organization*, a United Nations agency concerned with improving nutrition and food and timber production throughout the world.	**Hz**	in physics, the symbol for *hertz*.
		IA	postcode for *Iowa*.
		IADB	*Inter-American Development Bank*.
		IAEA	*International Atomic Energy Agency*.
FDA	*Food and Drug Administration*.	**ibid.**	*ibidem* (Latin *in the same place*); used in reference citation.
FEPC	*Fair Employment Practices Committee*.		
FET	*Federal Excise Tax*.	**IBRD**	*International Bank for Reconstruction and Development*, also known as the World Bank.
FHA	*Federal Housing Administration*.		
fob	*free on board*, used to describe a valuation of goods at point of embarkation.		
FOIA	*Freedom of Information Act*.	**ICAO**	*International Civil Aviation Organization*, a United Nations agency which regulates safety and efficiency and air law.
FORTRAN	*formula translation*, in computing a programming language used especially in science.		
		ICBM	*intercontinental ballistic missile*.
		ICC	*Interstate Commerce Commission*.
FRS	*Federal Reserve System*.	**ICCPR**	*International Covenant on Civil and Political Rights* (of the UN).
F.R.S.	*Fellow of the Royal Society*.		
FSLIC	*Federal Savings and Loan Insurance Corporation*.	**ICES**	*International Council for the Exploration of the Sea*.
ft	*foot*, a measure of distance.	**ICW**	*International Congress of Women*.
FTC	*Federal Trade Commission*, antimonopoly organization.	**id.**	*idem* (Latin *the same*); used in reference citation.
FYI	*for your information*.	**ID**	postcode for *Idaho; identification*.
g	symbol for *gram*.	**IDA**	*International Development Association*, a United Nations agency affiliated to the World Bank.
G7	*Group of Seven*, the seven wealthiest nations in the world: the US, Japan, Germany, France, the UK, Italy and Canada.		
		IDL	*International Date Line*, a modification of the

Abbreviations (continued)

	180th meridian that marks the difference in time between east and west.
IDP	**International Driving Permit.**
i.e.	**id est** (Latin *that is*).
IEA	**International Energy Agency.**
IEEE	**Institute of Electrical and Electronic Engineers**, which sets technical standards for electrical equipment and computer data exchange.
IFAD	**International Fund for Agricultural Development**, a United Nations agency.
IFALPA	**International Federation of Air Line Pilots' Association.**
IFAW	**International Fund for Animal Welfare.**
IFIP	**International Federation for Information Processing.**
IFL	**International Friendship League.**
IKBS	**intelligent knowledge-based system**, in computing.
IL	postcode for **Illinois.**
ILA	**International Law Association.**
ILC	**International Law Commission**, a United Nations body.
ILO	**International Labour Organization**, part of the United Nations, which formulates standards for labor and social conditions.
IMF	**International Monetary Fund.**
in	**inch**, a measure of distance.
IN	postcode for **Indiana.**
Inc.	**Incorporated.**
INCB	**International Narcotics Control Board**, a United Nations agency.
INF	**intermediate nuclear forces.**
IQ	**intelligence quotient.**
ir	in physics, **infrared.**
IRA	**Irish Republican Army.**
IRCAM	the French **Institut de Recherche et de Coordination Acoustique-Musique** organization in Paris for research into electronic music, using computers, and synthesizers, founded 1976.
IRS	**Internal Revenue Service.**
ISBN	**International Standard Book Number**, used for ordering or classifying book titles.
ISD	**international subscriber dialling.**
ISDN	**Integrated Services Digital Network**, an internationally developed telecommunications system for sending signals in digital format along optical fibers and coaxial cable.
ITU	**intensive therapy unit**, a high-technology facility for treating the critically ill or injured.
IUCN	**International Union for the Conservation of Nature.**
IUD	**intrauterine device.**
IUPAC	**International Union of Pure and Applied Chemistry.**
IVF	**in vitro fertilization.**
IWW	**Industrial Workers of the World.**
J	**joule**, SI unit of energy.
JA	**Judge Advocate.**
jnr, jr	**junior.**
J.D.	**Juris Doctor** (Doctor of Laws).
JD	**Justice Department.**
JDL	**Jewish Defense League.**
JFK	**John Fitzgerald Kennedy**, US president 1961–63.
JIT	**just-in-time**, a production management practice that can reduce expenses and improve efficiency.
JP	**justice of the peace.**
J.S.D.	**Doctor of the Science of Law.**
k.	**karat.**
K	symbol for **kelvin**, a unit of temperature; **kilobyte** (computing); chemical symbol for **potassium**; 1000.
KBE	**Knight(Commander of the Order) of the British Empire.**
kcal	symbol for **kilocalorie.**
kg	symbol for **kilogram.**
KG	**Knight of the Order of the Garter.**
KGB	**Komitet Gosudarstvennoye Bezhopaznosti** (Russian *Committee of State Security*). Succeeded by the Russian Federal Security Agency.
KJV	**King James Version**, of the Bible.
KKK	**Ku Klux Klan.**
km	symbol for **kilometer.**
KMT	**Kuomintang**, Chinese Nationalist Party, also known as Guomindang.
kph	or **km/h** symbol for **kilometers per hour.**
KS	postcode for **Kansas.**
kW	**kilowatt.**
KY	postcode for **Kentucky.**
L	Roman numeral for 50.
l	symbol for **liter**, a measure of liquid volume.
LA	postcode for **Louisiana**; Los Angeles.
LAES	**Latin American Economic System**, organization for cooperation in the region.
LAIA	**Latin American Integration Association**, an organization aiming to create a common market in Latin America.
lat.	**latitude.**
lb	symbol for **pound** (weight).
LBJ	**Lyndon Baines Johnson**, US president 1963–69.
lbw	**leg before wicket** (cricket).
lc	in typography, **lower case**, or *small* letters, as opposed to capitals.
LC	**Library of Congress.**
LF	in physics, **low frequency.**
Lib.	**Liberal.**
loc. cit.	**loco citato** (Latin *at the place cited*); used in reference citation.
log	in mathematics, **logarithm.**
long.	**longitude.**
LPN	**Licensed Practical Nurse.**
LRV	**lunar roving vehicle.**
Ltd	**Limited.**
LW	**low wave**, a radio wave with a wavelength of over 3,300ft/1,000; one of the main wavebands into which radio frequency transmissions are divided.
LWM	**low water mark.**
m	symbol for **meter**, a unit of length; **male; married; mile.**
M	Roman numeral for **1,000.**
MA	**Master of Arts** degree of education; postcode for the state of **Massachusetts.**
MAD	**mutual assured destruction**; the basis of the theory of deterrence by possession of nuclear weapons.
Man.	**Manitoba**, Canadian province.
masc.	in grammar, **masculine.**
MASH	**mobile army surgical hospital.**
max.	**maximum.**

Abbreviations (continued)

mb, Mb or MB *megabyte.*

MBE *Member (of the Order) of the British Empire.*

MC *Member of Congress.*

MCC *Marylebone Cricket Club.*

MD *Doctor of Medicine*; postcode for *Maryland.*

MDMA *methylenedioxymethamphetamine*, a psychedelic drug, also known as *ecstasy.*

MDR *minimum daily requirement.*

MDT *Mountain Daylight Time.*

ME postcode for *Maine*; *myalgic encephalomyelitis*, a debilitating condition also known as postviral fatigue syndrome.

MEP *Member of the European Parliament.*

Messrs *messieurs* (French *sirs* or *gentlemen*) used in formal writing to address an organization or group of people.

MFA *Multi-Fiber Arrangement.*

mg symbol for *milligram.*

Mgr in the Roman Catholic Church, *Monsignor.*

MH *Medal of Honor*, the highest award given in the US for the navy and army for gallantry in action.

MHR (US and Australia) *Member of the House of Representatives.*

mi symbol for *mile.*

MI postcode for *Michigan.*

MICV *mechanized infantry combat vehicle.*

MIDAS *missile defense alarm system.*

MIDI *Musical Instrument Digital Interface*, a manufacturer's standard allowing different pieces of digital music equipment used in composing and recording to be freely connected.

min. *minute* (time); *minimum.*

MIRV *multiple independently targeted reentry vehicle*, used in nuclear warfare.

MMR *measles, mumps, rubella (vaccine).*

ml symbol for *milliliter.*

MLR *minimum lending rate.*

mm symbol for *millimeter.*

mmHg symbol for *millimeter of mercury.*

MN postcode for *Minnesota.*

MO postcode for *Missouri.*

MOBS *multiple-orbit bombardment system, a nuclear weapon system.*

modem *modulator/demodulator*, a device for transmitting computer data over telephone lines.

m.o.m. *middle of month.*

mp in chemistry, the *melting point.*

MP *military policeman*; *Member of Parliament* (UK).

mpg *miles per gallon.*

mph *miles per hour.*

Mr *mister*, title used before a name to show that the person is male.

MRA *Moral Rearmament*, an international movement calling for *moral and spiritual renewal.*

MRBM *medium-range ballistic missile.*

MRG *Minority Rights Group.*

Mrs title used before a name to show that the person is married and female originally *mistress.*

Ms title used before a woman's name; pronounced *miz.*

MS postcode for *Mississippi.*

M.S. in education, *Master of Science* degree.

MSG *monosodium glutamate.*

MS(S) or ms(s) *manuscript(s).*

MST *Mountain Standard Time.*

MT postcode for *Montana.*

MU in economics, the *monetary unit.*

n. *noun.*

N *north, newton*, and the chemical symbol for *nitrogen.*

NAACP *National Association for the Advancement of Colored People*, a civil rights organization dedicated to ending inequality and segregation through nonviolent protest.

NAFTA *North American Free Trade Agreement.*

NAMS *national air-monitoring sites.*

NASA *National Aeronautics and Space Administration.*

NATO *North Atlantic Treaty Organization.*

NB postcode for *New Brunswick*; *nota bene* (Latin *note well*), used in references and citations.

NBC *National Broadcasting Company*, television and radio network.

NBS *National Bureau of Standards*, the US federal standards organization, on whose technical standards all US weights and measures are based.

NC postcode for *North Carolina.*

ND postcode for *North Dakota.*

NDE *near-death experience.*

NE postcode for *Nebraska.*

nem. con. *nemine contradicente* (Latin *with no one opposing*).

nem. diss. *nemine dissentiente* (Latin *with no one dissenting*).

NET *National Educational Television.*

NF postcode for *Newfoundland.*

NFC *National Football Conference.*

NFL *National Football League.*

NG *National Guard*, a militia force recruited by each state of the US.

NH postcode for *New Hampshire.*

NHS *National Health Service*, the UK state-financed health service.

NIEO *New International Economic Order.*

NJ postcode for *New Jersey.*

NL *National League* (baseball) .

NM postcode for *New Mexico.*

n.o. *not out* (cricket).

no. *number.*

nom. in grammar, *nominative.*

NOW *National Organization for Women.*

NPA *New People's Army* (Philippines).

NRA *National Rifle Association of America.*

NRC *Nuclear Regulatory Commission.*

NS *Nova Scotia.*

NSA *National Security Agency*, the largest and most secret of US intelligence agencies, which intercepts foreign communications as well as safeguards US transmissions.

NSAID *nonsteroidal anti-inflammatory drug.*

NSC *National Security Council.*

NSF *National Science Foundation.*

NSPCA *National Society for the Prevention of Cruelty to Animals.*

NSW *New South Wales.*

Abbreviations (continued)

NT	*Northern Territory*, Australia.		cards.
NTP	*normal temperature and pressure, former name for STP (standard temperature and pressure).*	**P/L**	*profit and loss.*
		p & p	*postage and packing.*
		plc	*public limited company.*
NV	postcode for *Nevada*.	**PLO**	*Palestine Liberation Organization.*
NY	postcode for *New York*.	**plur.**	in grammar, *plural.*
NZ	*New Zealand.*	**PM**	*prime minister.*
o/a	*on account.*	**p.m.**	*postmeridiem* (Latin *after noon*).
OAPEC	*Organization of Arab Petroleum Exporting Countries.*	**PO**	*Post Office.*
		POW	*prisoner of war.*
OAS	*Organization of American States.*	**pp**	*per procurationem* (Latin *by proxy*).
OAU	*Organization of African Unity.*	**ppm**	*parts per million.* An alternative (but numerically equivalent) unit used in chemistry is milligrams per liter (mg l⁻¹).
ob.	*obiit* (Latin *he/she died*).		
OBE	*Officer of the Order of the British Empire.*		
OCAM	acronym from *Organisation Commune Africaine et Mauricienne*, body for economic cooperation in Africa.	**PR**	*public relations; proportional representation.*
		PR	*Puerto Rico.*
OCAS	*Organization of Central American States.*	**pref.**	in grammar, *prefix.*
OCD	*obsessive compulsive disorder; Office of Civil Defense.*	**pro tem**	*pro tempore* (Latin *for the time being*).
		PS	*post scriptum* (Latin *after writing*).
OD	*officer of the day; olive drab, the color and material of US army uniforms; overdose; overdrawn.*	**PST**	*Pacific Standard Time.*
		pt	*pint.*
		PTO	*please turn over.*
OE	*Old English.*	**PX**	*Post Exchange*, an organization that provides shopping and canteen facilities for armed forces at home and abroad.
OH	postcode for *Ohio*.		
OIC	*Organization of the Islamic Conference*, international Muslim solidarity association.		
		QED	*quod erat demonstrandum* (Latin *which was to be proved*).
OK	postcode for *Oklahoma*.		
o.n.o.	*or near(est) offer.*	**Qld**	*Queensland.*
Ont.	postcode for *Ontario*.	**quant. suff.**	*quantum sufficit* (Latin *as much as suffices*).
op. cit.	*opere citato* (Latin *in the work cited*), used in reference citation.	**Que.**	*Québec.*
		qv	*quod vide* (Latin *which see*).
OPEC	*Organization of Petroleum-Exporting Countries.*	**RA**	*Royal Academy* of Art, London, founded 1768; *Regular Army.*
OR	postcode for *Oregon*.	**R & B**	*rhythm and blues.*
OST	*Office of Science and Technology.*	**RC**	*Red Cross; Roman Catholic.*
OT	*Old Testament.*	**R & D**	*research and development.*
OXFAM	*Oxford Committee for Famine Relief.*	**re**	Latin *with regard to.*
Oxon.	*Oxoniensis* (Latin *of Oxford*).	**Rev**	*Reverend.*
oz	symbol for *ounce.*	**RI**	postcode for *Rhode Island*.
p	in music, *piano* (Italian *softly*).	**RIP**	*requiescat in pace* (Latin *may he/she rest in peace*).
p(p).	*page(s).*		
p.a.	*per annum* (Latin *yearly*).	**RN**	*Registered Nurse.*
PA	postcode for *Pennsylvania.*	**rpm**	*revolutions per minute.*
PAC	*political action committee*, any organization that raises funds for political candidates.	**RPV**	*remotely piloted vehicle*, a flying TV camera for military use.
part.	in grammar, *participle.*	**RSFSR**	*Russian Soviet Federal Socialist Republic*, the largest constituent republic of the former USSR.
PBS	*Public Broadcasting Service.*		
PC	*personal computer; political correctness.*		
PC	*Peace Corps*, organization that provides skilled people to work in developing countries.	**RSI**	*repetitive strain injury.*
		RSPB	*Royal Society for the Protection of Birds.*
		RSV	*Revised Standard Version* of the Bible.
PCB	*polychlorinated biphenyl; printed circuit board.*	**RSVP**	*répondez s'il vous plaît* (French *please reply*).
PCM	*pulse-code modulation.*	**Rt Hon**	*Right Honorable*, the title of British members of Parliament.
PCP	*phencyclohexyl-piperidine*, a powerful hallucinogenic drug, also known as angel dust.		
		r.v.	*recreational vehicle.*
		S	*south.*
PDT	*Pacific Daylight Time.*	**SA**	*South Africa; South Australia.*
PEN	*Poets, Playwrights, Editors, Essayists, Novelists*, literary association established 1921.	**SAARC**	*South Asian Association for Regional Cooperation.*
		SAC	*Strategic Air Command*, the headquarters commanding all US land-based strategic missile and bomber forces, located in Colorado.
per pro	*per procurationem* (Latin *by the agency of*).		
PFC	*Private First Class.*		
PhD	*Doctor of Philosophy* degree.		
Phil.	*Philadelphia.*	**SACEUR**	*Supreme Allied Commander Europe*, part of NATO's military command.
PIN	*personal identification number.* Used to make transactions using cash or credit	**SACLANT**	*Supreme Allied Commander Atlantic*, part of

Abbreviations (continued)

NATO's military command.

SACSEA *Supreme Allied Command, SE Asia*, part of NATO's military command.

SAD *seasonal affective disorder.*

SADCC *Southern African Development Coordination Conference*, economic organization of countries in the region.

SAG *Screen Actors' Guild*, a labor union for television and film actors.

SAGE *semiautomatic ground environment* (military).

SALT *Strategic Arms Limitation Talks*, a series of US-Soviet negotiations 1969–79.

SAS *Special Air Service*, a specialist British regiment recruited from regiments throughout the army.

SASE *self-addressed stamped envelope.*

Sask. *Saskatchewan.*

SAT *Scholastic Aptitude Test.*

sc. *scilicet* (Latin *let it be understood*).

SC postcode for *South Carolina.*

SCLC *Southern Christian Leadership Conference*, a civil-rights organization founded in 1957 by Martin Luther King.

SD postcode for *South Dakota.*

SDI *Strategic Defense Initiative*, a defense system against incoming nuclear missiles, based in part outside the Earth's atmosphere. It is popularly known as Star Wars.

SEATO *Southeast Asia Treaty Organization.*

sec *second*, a unit of time.

SEC *Securities and Exchange Commission*, the official agency created to ensure full disclosure to the investing public and protection against malpractice in the securities and financial markets.

SELA *Sistema Economico Latino-Americana* or Latin American Economic System.

seq. *sequentes* (Latin *the following*).

SFSR *Soviet Federal Socialist Republic.*

SHAPE *Supreme Headquarters Allied Powers Europe.*

SHF *superhigh frequency.*

SI *Système International [d'Unités]* (French *International System [of Metric Units]*).

sing. *singular.*

SIS *Special Intelligence Service.*

SJC *Supreme Judicial Court.*

SLBM *submarine-launched ballistic missile.*

SLR *single-lens reflex*, a type of camera in which the image can be seen through the lens before a picture is taken.

SMSA *Standard Metropolitan Statistical Area*, a city area chosen for gathering demographic data.

SOS internationally recognized distress signal, using letters of the Morse code (...—...).

SPC *South Pacific Commission*, economic organization of countries in the region.

SPCA *Society for the Prevention of Cruelty to Animals.*

SPCC *Society for the Prevention of Cruelty to Children.*

SPF *South Pacific Forum*, organization of countries in the region.

SPQR *Senatus Populusque Romanus* (Latin *the Senate and the Roman People*).

sq *square* (measure).

Sr *senior; señor.*

SSBN *strategic submarine, ballistic nuclear.*

SSI *Supplemental Security Income*, for the aged, blind and disabled.

SSR *Soviet Socialist Republic.*

START *Strategic Arms Reduction Talks.*

STD *sexually transmitted disease.*

suff. in grammar, *suffix.*

SWAT *Special Weapons and Tactics.*

t symbol for *ton* or *tonne.*

tal. qual. *talis qualis* (Latin *just as they come*).

Tas. *Tasmania.*

TASM *tactical air-to-surface missile.*

Tass acronym for the Soviet news agency *Telegrafnoye Agentstvo Sovyetskovo Soyuza.*

TB the infectious disease *tuberculosis.*

TD *Teachta Dála* (Irish *a member of the Irish parliament*).

TEFL *teaching of English as a foreign language.*

temp. *temperature; temporary.*

TESL *teaching of English as a second language.*

TIR *Transports Internationaux Routiers* (French *International Road Transport*).

TM *transcendental meditation.*

T-man *a special investigator of the Treasury Department* (informal) .

TN postcode for *Tennessee.*

TT *Tourist Trophy; teetotal; tuberculin tested.*

TTL *transistor-transistor logic*, a family of integrated circuits with fast switching speeds commonly used in building electronic devices.

TUC *Trades Union Congress.*

TX postcode for *Texas.*

U postcode for *Utah.*

UAW *United Automobile Workers.*

UFO *unidentified flying object.*

UHT *ultra heat treated.*

UK *United Kingdom.*

UMT *universal military training.*

UMW *United Mine Workers.*

UN *United Nations.*

UNCTAD *United Nations Commission on Trade and Development.*

UNEP *United Nations Environmental Program.*

UNHCR *United Nations High Commission for Refugees.*

UNICEF *United Nations International Children's Emergency Fund.*

UNITA *National Union for the Total Independence of Angola*, Angolan nationalist movement backed by South Africa.

UPC *universal product code.*

US the *United States of America* (popular and most frequent name used by speakers of American English for the nation).

USA *United States of America*; (official) *US Army.*

USAF *United States Air Force.*

USAID *United States Agency for International Development.*

USDA *US Department of Agriculture.*

USGS *US Geological Survey*, part of the department of the interior.

USIA *US Information Agency.*

USMC *United States Marine Corps.*

USN *United States Navy.*

Abbreviations (continued)

USO	*United Service Organizations.*
USS	*United States Ship.*
USSR	*Union of Soviet Socialist Republics.*
UV	*ultraviolet.*
V	Roman numeral for *five*; in physics, symbol for *volt.*
v	in physics, symbol for *velocity.*
VA	postcode for *Virginia*; *Veterans' Administration.*
VAT	*value-added tax.*
vb	in grammar, *verb.*
VDT	*visual display terminal* an electronic output device for displaying the data processed by a computer on a screen.
VFW	*Veterans of Foreign Wars.*
VHF	*very high frequency.*
v.i.	in grammar, *verb intransitive.*
VI	*Virgin Islands*; *Vancouver Island.*
VIP	*very important person.*
viz	*videlicet* (Latin *that is to say, namely*).
VLF	in physics, *very low frequency.*
voc.	in grammar, *vocative.*
vol	*volume.*
VR	*velocity ratio.*
VSTOL	*vertical/short takeoff and landing* aircraft capable of taking off and landing either vertically or using a very short length of runway.
v.t.	in grammar, *verb transitive.*
VT	postcode for *Vermont.*
W	*west*; in physics, symbol for *watt.*
WA	postcode for *Washington* (state); *Western Australia.*
WAC	*Women's Army Corps.*
WACC	*World Association for Christian Communications.*

WAF	*Women in the Air Force.*
WASP	*Women Airforce Service Pilots.*
Waves or WAVES	*Women Accepted for Volunteer Emergency Service.*
w.c.	*water closet*, or toilet.
WCC	*World Council of Churches*, international Christian body.
WHO	acronym for *World Health Organization.*
WI	*West Indies*; postcode for *Wisconsin.*
wpm	*words per minute.*
wt	*weight.*
WTO	*Warsaw Treaty Organization.*
WV	postcode for *West Virginia.*
WWF	*World Wide Fund for Nature* (formerly World Wildlife Fund).
WY	postcode for *Wyoming.*
WYSIWYG	in computing *what you see is what you get*, a program that attempts to display on the screen a faithful representation of the final printed output.
X	Roman numeral *ten*; a person or thing unknown.
x	in mathematics, an unknown quantity.
yd	*yard.*
YHA	*Youth Hostels Association.*
YMCA	*Young Men's Christian Association.* Also known as the *Y.*
YWCA	*Young Women's Christian Association.* Also known as the *Y.*
Z	in physics, the symbol for *impedance* (electricity and magnetism).
zB	*zum Beispiel* (German *for example*).
zip, Zip or ZIP	*zone improvement program* (US postcodes).
ZST	*zone standard time.*